D1178717

This Bible belongs to

_____

NEW WORLD TRANSLATION

— OF THE —

HOLY
SCRIPTURES

Rendered From the Original Languages
by the NEW WORLD BIBLE TRANSLATION COMMITTEE
—Revised 2013—

"THIS IS WHAT THE SOVEREIGN LORD JEHOVAH
[יהוה, *YHWH*] SAYS: ' . . . LOOK! I AM CREATING NEW
HEAVENS AND A NEW EARTH; AND THE FORMER
THINGS WILL NOT BE CALLED TO MIND, NOR WILL
THEY COME UP INTO THE HEART.'"

—Isaiah 65:13, 17; also see 2 Peter 3:13.

Available in whole or in part
in over 120 languages. For
a complete list of languages,
see www.jw.org.

Total Printed of All Editions
of the *New World Translation:*

201,324,734 Copies

November 2013 Printing

This publication is not
for sale. It is provided as
part of the worldwide Bible
educational work of
Jehovah's Witnesses.

*New World Translation of the
Holy Scriptures*

English (*nwt*-E)

Made in the United States
of America

900 Red Mills Road
Wallkill, NY 12589-3223
U.S.A.

An Introduction to God's Word

The Bible contains God's message, or word, for us today. It shows us how to live our lives successfully and how to gain God's approval. It also answers the following questions:

1. Who is God?

2. How can you learn about God?

3. Who wrote the Bible?

4. Is the Bible scientifically accurate?

5. What is the Bible's message?

6. What did the Bible foretell about the Messiah?

7. What does the Bible foretell about our day?

8. Is God to blame for human suffering?

9. Why do humans suffer?

10. What does the Bible promise for the future?

11. What happens when someone dies?

12. What hope can we have for the dead?

13. What does the Bible say about work?

14. How can you manage your assets?

15. How can you find happiness?

16. How can you cope with anxiety?

17. How can the Bible help your family?

18. How can you draw close to God?

19. What is contained in the various books of the Bible?

20. How can you get the most out of your Bible reading?

HOW TO FIND BIBLE VERSES

The Bible is a collection of 66 smaller books. It is divided into two sections: the Hebrew-Aramaic Scriptures ("Old Testament") and the Greek Scriptures ("New Testament"). Each Bible book is divided into chapters and verses. When scriptures are cited, the first number after the name of the book indicates the chapter, and the next number or numbers refer to the verse or verses. For example, Genesis 1:1 refers to Genesis chapter 1, verse 1.

Who is God?

"May people know that you, whose name is Jehovah,
you alone are the Most High over all the earth."

Psalm 83:18 [Page 819]

"Know that Jehovah is God. He is the one who made us,
and we belong to him."

Psalm 100:3 [Page 831]

"I am Jehovah. That is my name; I give my glory to
no one else, nor my praise to graven images."

Isaiah 42:8 [Page 993]

"Everyone who calls on the name of Jehovah
will be saved."

Romans 10:13 [Page 1518]

"Of course, every house is constructed by someone,
but the one who constructed all things is God."

Hebrews 3:4 [Page 1602]

"Lift up your eyes to heaven and see. Who has created these things? It is the One who brings out their army by number; he calls them all by name. Because of his vast dynamic energy and his awe-inspiring power, not one of them is missing."

Isaiah 40:26 [Page 990]

Question 2

How can you learn about God?

"This book of the Law should not depart from your mouth, and you must read it in an undertone day and night, in order to observe carefully all that is written in it; for then your way will be successful and then you will act wisely."

Joshua 1:8 [Page 325]

"They continued reading aloud from the book, from the Law of the true God, clearly explaining it and putting meaning into it; so they helped the people to understand what was being read."

Nehemiah 8:8 [Page 677]

"Happy is the man who does not walk according to the advice of the wicked . . . , but his delight is in the law of Jehovah, and he reads His law in an undertone day and night. . . . Everything he does will succeed."

Psalm 1:1-3 [Page 753]

"Philip ran alongside and heard him reading aloud Isaiah the prophet, and he said: 'Do you actually know what you are reading?' He said: 'Really, how could I ever do so unless someone guided me?'"

Acts 8:30, 31 [Page 1473]

"His invisible qualities are clearly seen from the world's creation onward, because they are perceived by the things made, even his eternal power and Godship, so that they are inexcusable."

Romans 1:20 [Page 1507]

"Ponder over these things; be absorbed in them, so that your advancement may be plainly seen by all people."

1 Timothy 4:15 [Page 1590]

"Let us consider one another so as to incite to love and fine works, not forsaking our meeting together."

Hebrews 10:24, 25 [Page 1610]

"If any one of you is lacking in wisdom, let him keep asking God, for he gives generously to all and without reproaching, and it will be given him."

James 1:5 [Page 1616]

Question 3

Who wrote the Bible?

"Moses wrote down all the words of Jehovah."
Exodus 24:4 [Page 145]

"Daniel saw a dream and visions of his head as he lay
on his bed. Then he wrote down the dream;
he recorded a complete account of the matters."
Daniel 7:1 [Page 1217]

"When you received God's word, which you heard
from us, you accepted it not as the word of men
but, just as it truthfully is, as the word of God."
1 Thessalonians 2:13 [Page 1581]

"All Scripture is inspired of God and beneficial for
teaching."
2 Timothy 3:16 [Page 1595]

"Prophecy was at no time brought by man's will,
but men spoke from God as they were moved by
holy spirit."
2 Peter 1:21 [Page 1627]

Is the Bible scientifically accurate?

"He stretches out the northern sky over empty space, suspending the earth upon nothing."

Job 26:7 [Page 727]

"All the streams flow into the sea, yet the sea is not full. To the place from which the streams flow, there they return so as to flow again."

Ecclesiastes 1:7 [Page 916]

"There is One who dwells above the circle of the earth."

Isaiah 40:22 [Page 989]

What is the Bible's message?

"I will put enmity between you and the woman and between your offspring and her offspring. He will crush your head, and you will strike him in the heel."

Genesis 3:15 [Page 46]

"By means of your offspring all nations of the earth will obtain a blessing for themselves because you have listened to my voice."

Genesis 22:18 [Page 68]

"Let your Kingdom come. Let your will take place, as in heaven, also on earth."

Matthew 6:10 [Page 1312]

"For his part, the God who gives peace will crush Satan under your feet shortly."

Romans 16:20 [Page 1524]

"When all things will have been subjected to him, then the Son himself will also subject himself to the One who subjected all things to him, that God may be all things to everyone."

1 Corinthians 15:28 [Page 1541]

"Now the promises were spoken to Abraham and to his offspring . . . , who is Christ. Moreover, if you belong to Christ, you are really Abraham's offspring."
Galatians 3:16, 29 [Pages 1559, 1560]

"The kingdom of the world has become the Kingdom of our Lord and of his Christ, and he will rule as king forever and ever."
Revelation 11:15 [Page 1650]

"So down the great dragon was hurled, the original serpent, the one called Devil and Satan, who is misleading the entire inhabited earth; he was hurled down to the earth, and his angels were hurled down with him."
Revelation 12:9 [Page 1650]

"He seized the dragon, the original serpent, who is the Devil and Satan, and bound him for 1,000 years."
Revelation 20:2 [Page 1658]

What did the Bible foretell about the Messiah?

PROPHECY	FULFILLMENT
"You, O Bethlehem Ephrathah, . . . from you will come out for me the one to be ruler in Israel." Micah 5:2 [Page 1267]	"After Jesus had been born in Bethlehem of Judea in the days of Herod the king, look! astrologers from the East came to Jerusalem." Matthew 2:1 [Page 1307]
"They divide my garments among themselves, and they cast lots for my clothing." Psalm 22:18 [Page 767]	"Now when the soldiers had nailed Jesus to the stake, they took his outer garments and divided them into four parts . . . But the inner garment was without a seam, being woven from top to bottom. So they said to one another: 'Let us not tear it, but let us cast lots over it to decide whose it will be.'" John 19:23, 24 [Page 1455]

PROPHECY	FULFILLMENT
"He is guarding all his bones; not one of them has been broken." Psalm 34:20 [Page 777]	"On coming to Jesus, they saw that he was already dead, so they did not break his legs." John 19:33 [Page 1456]
"He was pierced for our transgression." Isaiah 53:5 [Page 1011]	"One of the soldiers jabbed his side with a spear, and immediately blood and water came out." John 19:34 [Page 1456]
"They paid my wages, 30 pieces of silver." Zechariah 11:12, 13 [Page 1296]	"Then one of the Twelve, the one called Judas Iscariot, went to the chief priests and said: 'What will you give me to betray him to you?' They stipulated to him 30 silver pieces." Matthew 26:14, 15; 27:5 [Pages 1342, 1345]

What does the Bible foretell about our day?

"Nation will rise against nation and kingdom against kingdom . . . All these things are a beginning of pangs of distress."

Matthew 24:7, 8 [Page 1338]

"Many false prophets will arise and mislead many; and because of the increasing of lawlessness, the love of the greater number will grow cold."

Matthew 24:11, 12 [Page 1339]

"When you hear of wars and reports of wars, do not be alarmed; these things must take place, but the end is not yet."

Mark 13:7 [Page 1369]

"There will be great earthquakes, and in one place after another food shortages and pestilences; and there will be fearful sights and from heaven great signs."

Luke 21:11 [Page 1416]

"In the last days critical times hard to deal with will be here. For men will be lovers of themselves, lovers of money, boastful, haughty, blasphemers, disobedient to parents, unthankful, disloyal, having no natural affection, not open to any agreement, slanderers, without self-control, fierce, without love of goodness, betrayers, headstrong, puffed up with pride, lovers of pleasures rather than lovers of God, having an appearance of godliness but proving false to its power."

2 Timothy 3:1-5 [Page 1595]

Is God to blame for human suffering?

"It is unthinkable for the true God to act wickedly, for the Almighty to do wrong!"

Job 34:10 [Page 736]

"When under trial, let no one say: 'I am being tried by God.' For with evil things God cannot be tried, nor does he himself try anyone."

James 1:13 [Page 1616]

"Throw all your anxiety on him, because he cares for you."

1 Peter 5:7 [Page 1625]

"Jehovah is not slow concerning his promise, as some people consider slowness, but he is patient with you because he does not desire anyone to be destroyed but desires all to attain to repentance."

2 Peter 3:9 [Page 1629]

Why do humans suffer?

"The swift do not always win the race, nor do the mighty win the battle, nor do the wise always have the food, nor do the intelligent always have the riches, nor do those with knowledge always have success, because time and unexpected events overtake them all."

Ecclesiastes 9:11 [Page 924]

"Through one man sin entered into the world and death through sin, and so death spread to all men because they had all sinned—."

Romans 5:12 [Page 1512]

"For this purpose the Son of God was made manifest, to break up the works of the Devil."

1 John 3:8 [Page 1632]

"The whole world is lying in the power of the wicked one."

1 John 5:19 [Page 1635]

What does the Bible promise for the future?

"The righteous will possess the earth, and they will live forever on it."

Psalm 37:29 [Page 781]

"The earth remains forever."

Ecclesiastes 1:4 [Page 915]

"He will swallow up death forever, and the Sovereign Lord Jehovah will wipe away the tears from all faces."

Isaiah 25:8 [Page 968]

"At that time the eyes of the blind will be opened, and the ears of the deaf will be unstopped. At that time the lame will leap like the deer, and the tongue of the speechless will shout for joy. For waters will burst forth in the wilderness, and streams in the desert plain."

Isaiah 35:5, 6 [Page 982]

"He will wipe out every tear from their eyes, and death will be no more, neither will mourning nor outcry nor pain be anymore. The former things have passed away."

Revelation 21:4 [Page 1659]

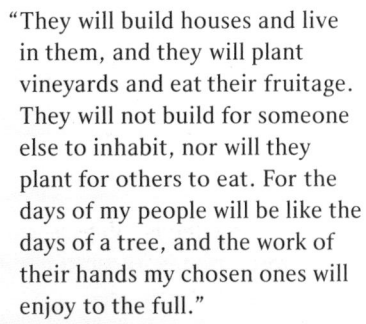

"They will build houses and live in them, and they will plant vineyards and eat their fruitage. They will not build for someone else to inhabit, nor will they plant for others to eat. For the days of my people will be like the days of a tree, and the work of their hands my chosen ones will enjoy to the full."

Isaiah 65:21, 22 [Page 1027]

What happens when someone dies?

"His spirit goes out, he returns to the ground; on that very day his thoughts perish."

Psalm 146:4 [Page 869]

"The living know that they will die, but the dead know nothing at all . . . Whatever your hand finds to do, do with all your might, for there is no work nor planning nor knowledge nor wisdom in the Grave, where you are going."

Ecclesiastes 9:5, 10 [Page 923]

"[Jesus] added: 'Lazarus our friend has fallen asleep, but I am traveling there to awaken him.' Jesus, however, had spoken about his death. But they imagined he was speaking about taking rest in sleep. Then Jesus said to them plainly: 'Lazarus has died.'"

John 11:11, 13, 14 [Pages 1442, 1443]

Question 12

What hope can we have for the dead?

"Do not be amazed at this, for the hour is coming in which all those in the memorial tombs will hear his voice and come out."

John 5:28, 29 [Page 1432]

"There is going to be a resurrection of both the righteous and the unrighteous."

Acts 24:15 [Page 1499]

"I saw the dead, the great and the small, standing before the throne, and scrolls were opened. But another scroll was opened; it is the scroll of life. The dead were judged out of those things written in the scrolls according to their deeds. And the sea gave up the dead in it, and death and the Grave gave up the dead in them, and they were judged individually according to their deeds."

Revelation 20:12, 13 [Page 1659]

What does the Bible say about work?

"Have you seen a man skillful at his work? He will stand before kings; he will not stand before common men."
Proverbs 22:29 [Page 902]

"Let the one who steals steal no more; rather, let him do hard work, doing good work with his hands, so that he may have something to share with someone in need."
Ephesians 4:28 [Page 1567]

"Everyone should eat and drink and find enjoyment for all his hard work. It is the gift of God."
Ecclesiastes 3:13 [Page 918]

Question 14

How can you manage your assets?

"The one who loves having a good time will come to poverty; the one who loves wine and oil will not grow rich."

Proverbs 21:17 [Page 900]

"The borrower is a slave to the lender."

Proverbs 22:7 [Page 901]

"Who of you wanting to build a tower does not first sit down and calculate the expense to see if he has enough to complete it? Otherwise, he might lay its foundation but not be able to finish it, and all the onlookers would start to ridicule him, saying: 'This man started to build but was not able to finish.'"

Luke 14:28-30 [Page 1406]

"When they had eaten their fill, he said to his disciples: 'Gather together the fragments left over, so that nothing is wasted.'"

John 6:12 [Page 1433]

How can you find happiness?

"Better is a dish of vegetables where there is love than a fattened bull where there is hatred."

Proverbs 15:17 [Page 892]

"I, Jehovah, am your God, the One teaching you to benefit yourself, the One guiding you in the way you should walk."

Isaiah 48:17 [Page 1004]

"Happy are those conscious of their spiritual need, since the Kingdom of the heavens belongs to them."

Matthew 5:3 [Page 1310]

"You must love your neighbor as yourself."

Matthew 22:39 [Page 1336]

"Just as you want men to do to you, do the same way to them."

Luke 6:31 [Page 1389]

"Happy are those hearing the word of God and keeping it!"

Luke 11:28 [Page 1400]

"When a person has an abundance, his life does not result from the things he possesses."

Luke 12:15 [Page 1402]

"So, having food and clothing, we will be content with these things."

1 Timothy 6:8 [Page 1591]

"There is more happiness in giving than there is in receiving."

Acts 20:35 [Page 1493]

Question 16

How can you cope with anxiety?

"Throw your burden on Jehovah, and he will sustain you. Never will he allow the righteous one to fall."
Psalm 55:22 [Page 795]

"The plans of the diligent surely lead to success, but all who are hasty surely head for poverty."
Proverbs 21:5 [Page 899]

"Do not be afraid, for I am with you. Do not be anxious, for I am your God. I will fortify you, yes, I will help you, I will really hold on to you with my right hand of righteousness."
Isaiah 41:10 [Page 991]

"Who of you by being anxious can add one cubit to his life span?"
Matthew 6:27 [Page 1313]

"So never be anxious about the next day, for the next day will have its own anxieties. Each day has enough of its own troubles."
Matthew 6:34 [Page 1313]

"Make sure of the more important things."

Philippians 1:10 [Page 1571]

"Do not be anxious over anything, but in everything
by prayer and supplication along with thanksgiving,
let your petitions be made known to God; and the peace
of God that surpasses all understanding will guard your
hearts and your mental powers by means
of Christ Jesus."

Philippians 4:6, 7 [Page 1574]

How can the Bible help your family?

HUSBANDS/FATHERS

"In the same way husbands should love their wives as their own bodies. A man who loves his wife loves himself, for no man ever hated his own body, but he feeds and cherishes it . . . Each one of you must love his wife as he does himself."
Ephesians 5:28, 29, 33 [Page 1569]

"Fathers, do not be irritating your children, but go on bringing them up in the discipline and admonition of Jehovah."
Ephesians 6:4 [Page 1569]

WIVES

"The wife should have deep respect for her husband."
Ephesians 5:33 [Page 1569]

"You wives, be in subjection to your husbands, as it is becoming in the Lord."
Colossians 3:18 [Page 1579]

CHILDREN

"Children, be obedient to your parents in union with
the Lord, for this is righteous. 'Honor your father
and your mother' is the first command with a promise:
'That it may go well with you and you may remain
a long time on the earth.'"

Ephesians 6:1-3 [Page 1569]

"You children, be obedient to your parents in
everything, for this is well-pleasing to the Lord."

Colossians 3:20 [Page 1579]

How can you draw close to God?

"O Hearer of prayer, to you people of all sorts will come."

Psalm 65:2 [Page 800]

"Trust in Jehovah with all your heart, and do not rely on your own understanding. In all your ways take notice of him, and he will make your paths straight."

Proverbs 3:5, 6 [Page 876]

"This means everlasting life, their coming to know you, the only true God, and the one whom you sent, Jesus Christ."

John 17:3 [Page 1451]

"In fact, [God] is not far off from each one of us."

Acts 17:27 [Page 1488]

"This is what I continue praying, that your love may abound still more and more with accurate knowledge and full discernment."

Philippians 1:9 [Page 1571]

"If any one of you is lacking in wisdom, let him keep asking God, for he gives generously to all and without reproaching, and it will be given him."

James 1:5 [Page 1616]

"Draw close to God, and he will draw close to you. Cleanse your hands, you sinners, and purify your hearts, you indecisive ones."

James 4:8 [Page 1619]

"This is what the love of God means, that we observe his commandments; and yet his commandments are not burdensome."

1 John 5:3 [Page 1634]

Question 19

What is contained in the various books of the Bible?

HEBREW SCRIPTURES ("OLD TESTAMENT")

PENTATEUCH (5 BOOKS):

Genesis, Exodus, Leviticus, Numbers, Deuteronomy
From creation to the founding of the ancient nation of Israel

HISTORICAL BOOKS (12 BOOKS):

Joshua, Judges, Ruth
Israel's entry into the Promised Land and events thereafter

1 and 2 Samuel, 1 and 2 Kings, 1 and 2 Chronicles
History of the nation of Israel down to the destruction
of Jerusalem

Ezra, Nehemiah, Esther
History of the Jews after returning from exile in Babylon

POETIC BOOKS (5 BOOKS):

Job, Psalms, Proverbs, Ecclesiastes, Song of Solomon
Collections of wise sayings and songs

PROPHETIC BOOKS (17 BOOKS):

Isaiah, Jeremiah, Lamentations, Ezekiel, Daniel, Hosea,
Joel, Amos, Obadiah, Jonah, Micah, Nahum, Habakkuk,
Zephaniah, Haggai, Zechariah, Malachi
Prophecies, or predictions, concerning God's people

CHRISTIAN GREEK SCRIPTURES ("NEW TESTAMENT")

THE FOUR GOSPELS (4 BOOKS):

Matthew, Mark, Luke, John
History of Jesus' life and ministry

ACTS OF APOSTLES (1 BOOK):

History of the start of the Christian congregation and missionary activity

LETTERS (21 BOOKS):

Romans, 1 and 2 Corinthians, Galatians, Ephesians, Philippians, Colossians, 1 and 2 Thessalonians
Letters to various Christian congregations

1 and 2 Timothy, Titus, Philemon
Letters to individual Christians

Hebrews, James, 1 and 2 Peter, 1, 2, and 3 John, Jude
General letters to Christians

REVELATION (1 BOOK):

Series of prophetic visions given to the apostle John

How can you get the most out of your Bible reading?

ANSWER THESE QUESTIONS AS YOU READ YOUR BIBLE:

What does this tell me about Jehovah God?

How does this section of the Scriptures contribute to the Bible's message?

How can I apply this in my life?

How can I use these verses to help others?

"Your word is a lamp to my foot, and a light for my path."

Psalm 119:105

[Page 853]

FOREWORD

The Holy Bible is God's written communication to all of us. We must study it to get to know its Author. (John 17:3; 2 Timothy 3:16) Within its pages, Jehovah God reveals his purpose for humans and for their earthly home. —Genesis 3:15; Revelation 21:3, 4.

No other book has such an impact on people's lives. The Bible inspires us to reflect Jehovah's qualities of love, mercy, and compassion. It gives hope, helping people to endure even the worst suffering. And it continues to expose the elements of this world that are out of harmony with the perfect will of God.—Psalm 119:105; Hebrews 4:12; 1 John 2:15-17.

Originally composed in Hebrew, Aramaic, and Greek, the Bible has been translated, in whole or in part, into about 2,600 languages. It is by far the most widely translated and distributed book in history. We should expect nothing less. Bible prophecy states: "This good news of the Kingdom [the key message contained in the Bible] will be preached in all the inhabited earth for a witness to all the nations, and then the end will come." —Matthew 24:14.

Recognizing the importance of the Bible's message, we have undertaken the revision of this text with a profound respect for the content of the Bible. We feel the full weight of our responsibility to convey its message accurately. This revised edition has built on the fine foundation laid in previous editions of the *New World Translation of the Holy Scriptures,* a Bible that was first released more than 60 years ago. However, the English language has changed during the past half century. Such change prompted current members of the New World Bible Translation Committee to initiate this comprehensive revision. Our goal has been to produce a translation that is not only faithful to the original texts but also clear and easy to read. The Appendix articles "Principles of Bible Translation," "Features of This Revision," and "How the Bible Came to Us" discuss some of the linguistic refinements that were made in this edition.

Those who love Jehovah God and worship him desire an accurate, understandable translation of God's Word. (1 Timothy 2:4) To that end, we have made this revision available in English, with the intention of translating it into as many languages as possible. It is our hope and prayer that you, dear reader, will find this edition of the Holy Scriptures beneficial as you endeavor to "seek God . . . and really find him."—Acts 17:27.

New World Bible Translation Committee
August 2013

NAMES AND ORDER OF THE BOOKS

OF THE HEBREW-ARAMAIC SCRIPTURES

OF THE CHRISTIAN GREEK SCRIPTURES

GENESIS

1 In the beginning God created the heavens and the earth.[a]

2 Now the earth was formless and desolate,* and there was darkness upon the surface of the watery deep,#[b] and God's active force△[c] was moving about over the surface of the waters.[d]

3 And God said: "Let there be light." Then there was light.[e]

4 After that God saw that the light was good, and God began to divide the light from the darkness. **5** God called the light Day, but the darkness he called Night.[f] And there was evening and there was morning, a first day.

6 Then God said: "Let there be an expanse[g] between the waters, and let there be a division between the waters and the waters."[h] **7** Then God went on to make the expanse and divided the waters beneath the expanse from the waters above the expanse.[i] And it was so. **8** God called the expanse Heaven.* And there was evening and there was morning, a second day.

9 Then God said: "Let the waters under the heavens be collected together into one place, and let the dry land appear."[j] And it was so. **10** God called the dry land Earth,[k] but the collecting of the waters, he called

Seas.[a] And God saw that it was good.[b] **11** Then God said: "Let the earth cause grass to sprout, seed-bearing plants and fruit trees according to their kinds, yielding fruit along with seed on the earth." And it was so. **12** And the earth began to produce grass, seed-bearing plants[c] and trees yielding fruit along with seed, according to their kinds. Then God saw that it was good. **13** And there was evening and there was morning, a third day.

14 Then God said: "Let there be luminaries*[d] in the expanse of the heavens to make a division between the day and the night,[e] and they will serve as signs for seasons and for days and years.[f] **15** They will serve as luminaries in the expanse of the heavens to shine upon the earth." And it was so. **16** And God went on to make the two great luminaries, the greater luminary for dominating the day[g] and the lesser luminary for dominating the night, and also the stars.[h] **17** Thus God put them in the expanse of the heavens to shine upon the earth **18** and to dominate by day and by night and to make a division between the light and the darkness.[i] Then God saw that it was good. **19** And there was evening and there was morning, a fourth day.

CHAP. 1
a Ps 102:25
  Isa 42:5
  Isa 45:18
  Ro 1:20
  Heb 1:10
  Re 4:11
  Re 10:6
b Pr 8:27, 28
c Ps 33:6
  Isa 40:26
d Ps 104:5, 6
e Isa 45:7
  2Co 4:6
f Ge 8:22
g Ge 1:20
h 2Pe 3:5
i Ge 7:11
  Pr 8:27, 28
j Job 38:8, 11
  Ps 104:6-9
  Ps 136:6
k Ps 95:5

Second Col.
a Pr 8:29
b De 32:4
c Ps 104:14
d De 4:19
e Ps 104:19
f Ge 8:22
g Ps 136:7, 8
h Ps 8:3
  Jer 31:35
i Ps 74:16

1:2 *Or "empty." #Or "the surging waters." △Or "God's spirit." 1:8 *Or "Sky."

1:14 *Or "lights."

20 Then God said: "Let the waters swarm with living creatures,* and let flying creatures fly above the earth across the expanse of the heavens."#a **21** And God created the great sea creatures# and all living creatures* that move and swarm in the waters according to their kinds and every winged flying creature according to its kind. And God saw that it was good. **22** With that God blessed them, saying: "Be fruitful and become many and fill the waters of the sea,b and let the flying creatures become many in the earth." **23** And there was evening and there was morning, a fifth day.

24 Then God said: "Let the earth bring forth living creatures* according to their kinds, domestic animals and creeping animals# and wild animals of the earth according to their kinds."c And it was so. **25** And God went on to make the wild animals of the earth according to their kinds and the domestic animals according to their kinds and all the creeping animals of the ground according to their kinds. And God saw that it was good.

26 Then God said: "Let usd make man in our image,e according to our likeness,f and let them have in subjection the fish of the sea and the flying creatures of the heavens and the domestic animals and all the earth and every creeping animal that is moving on the earth."g **27** And God went on to create the man in his image, in God's image he created him; male and female he created them.h **28** Further, God blessed them, and God said to them: "Be fruitful and become many, fill the eartha and subdue it,b and have in subjectionc the fish of the sea and the flying creatures of the heavens and every living creature that is moving on the earth."

29 Then God said: "Here I have given to you every seed-bearing plant that is on the entire earth and every tree with seed-bearing fruit. Let them serve as food for you.d **30** And to every wild animal of the earth and to every flying creature of the heavens and to everything moving on the earth in which there is life,* I have given all green vegetation for food."e And it was so.

31 After that God saw everything he had made, and look! it was very good.f And there was evening and there was morning, a sixth day.

2 Thus the heavens and the earth and everything in them* were completed.g **2** And by the seventh day, God had completed the work that he had been doing,* and he began to rest on the seventh day from all his work that he had been doing.*h **3** And God went on to bless the seventh day and to declare it sacred, for on it God has been resting from all the work that he has created, all that he purposed to make.

4 This is a history of the heavens and the earth in the time they were created, in the day that Jehovah* God made earth and heaven.i

5 No bush of the field was yet on the earth and no vegetation of the field had begun sprouting, because Jehovah God had

CHAP. 1
a Ge 2:19
b Ne 9:6
Ps 104:25
c Ge 2:19
d Pr 8:30
Joh 1:3
Col 1:16
e 1Co 11:7
f Ge 5:1
Jas 3:9
g Ge 9:2
h Ps 139:14
Mt 19:4
Mr 10:6
1Co 11:7, 9

Second Col.
a Ge 9:1
b Ge 2:15
c Ps 8:4, 6
d Ge 9:3
Ps 104:14
Ac 14:17
e Ps 147:9
Mt 6:26
f De 32:4
Ps 104:24
1Ti 4:4
CHAP. 2
g Ne 9:6
Ps 146:6
h Ex 31:17
Heb 4:4
i Isa 45:18

1:20, 21, 24 *Or "souls." **1:20** #Or "sky." **1:21** #Or "monsters." **1:24** #Or "moving animals," apparently including reptiles and forms of animal life different from the other categories.

1:30 *Or "life as a soul; a living soul." **2:1** *Lit., "and all their army." **2:2** *Or "making." **2:4** *The first occurrence of God's distinctive personal name, יהוה (YHWH). See App. A4.

not made it rain on the earth and there was no man to cultivate the ground. **6** But a mist would go up from the earth, and it watered the entire surface of the ground.

7 And Jehovah God went on to form the man out of dust[a] from the ground and to blow into his nostrils the breath of life,[b] and the man became a living person.*[c] **8** Further, Jehovah God planted a garden in E′den,[d] toward the east; and there he put the man whom he had formed.[e] **9** Thus Jehovah God made to grow out of the ground every tree that was pleasing to look at and good for food and also the tree of life[f] in the middle of the garden and the tree of the knowledge of good and bad.[g]

10 Now there was a river flowing out of E′den to water the garden, and from there it divided into four rivers.* **11** The name of the first is Pi′shon; it is the one encircling the entire land of Hav′i·lah, where there is gold. **12** The gold of that land is good. Bdellium gum and onyx stone are also there. **13** The name of the second river is Gi′hon; it is the one encircling the entire land of Cush. **14** The name of the third river is Hid′de·kel;*[h] it is the one going to the east of As·syr′i·a.[i] And the fourth river is the Eu·phra′tes.[j]

15 Jehovah God took the man and settled him in the garden of E′den to cultivate it and to take care of it.[k] **16** Jehovah God also gave this command to the man: "From every tree of the garden you may eat to satisfaction.[l] **17** But as for the tree of the knowledge of good and bad, you must not eat from it, for in

the day you eat from it you will certainly die."*[a]

18 Then Jehovah God said: "It is not good for the man to continue to be alone. I am going to make a helper for him, as a complement of him."[b] **19** Now Jehovah God had been forming from the ground every wild animal of the field and every flying creature of the heavens, and he began bringing them to the man to see what he would call each one; and whatever the man would call each living creature,* that became its name.[c] **20** So the man named all the domestic animals and the flying creatures of the heavens and every wild animal of the field, but for man there was no helper as a complement of him. **21** So Jehovah God caused the man to fall into a deep sleep, and while he was sleeping, he took one of his ribs and then closed up the flesh over its place. **22** And Jehovah God built the rib that he had taken from the man into a woman, and he brought her to the man.[d]

23 Then the man said:

"This is at last bone of my
　bones
And flesh of my flesh.
This one will be called
　Woman,
Because from man she was
　taken."[e]

24 That is why a man will leave his father and his mother and he will stick to* his wife, and they will become one flesh.[f] **25** And both of them continued to be naked,[g] the man and his wife; yet they were not ashamed.

3 Now the serpent[h] was the most cautious* of all the wild animals of the field that Jehovah God had made. So it said to the woman: "Did God really say that

---

CHAP. 2

a　Ge 3:19
　　Ps 103:14
　　Ec 3:20

b　Ge 7:22
　　Isa 42:5
　　Ac 17:25

c　1Co 15:45, 47

d　Ge 2:15
　　Ge 3:23

e　Ge 1:26

f　Ge 3:22, 24
　　Re 2:7

g　Ge 2:17

h　Da 10:4

i　Ge 10:8, 11

j　Ge 15:18
　　De 11:24

k　Ge 1:28
　　Ge 2:8
　　Ps 115:16

l　Ge 2:8, 9
　　Ge 3:2

Second Col.

a　Ge 3:19
　　Ps 146:4
　　Ec 9:5, 10
　　Eze 18:4
　　Ro 5:12
　　1Co 15:22

b　1Co 11:8, 9
　　1Ti 2:13

c　Ge 1:26

d　Mt 10:9
　　1Ti 2:13

e　1Co 11:8

f　Mal 2:16
　　Mt 19:5
　　Mr 10:7, 8
　　Ro 7:2
　　1Co 6:16
　　Eph 5:31
　　Heb 13:4

g　Ge 3:7

CHAP. 3

h　2Co 11:3
　　Re 12:9
　　Re 20:2

2:7 *Or "soul." Hebrew, *ne′phesh,* which literally means "a breathing creature." See Glossary. 2:10 *Lit., "it became four heads." 2:14 *Or "Tigris."

2:19 *Or "soul." 2:24 *Or "remain with." 3:1 *Or "shrewdest; craftiest."

you must not eat from every tree of the garden?"[a] **2** At this the woman said to the serpent: "We may eat of the fruit of the trees of the garden.[b] **3** But God has said about the fruit of the tree that is in the middle of the garden:[c] 'You must not eat from it, no, you must not touch it; otherwise you will die.'" **4** At this the serpent said to the woman: "You certainly will not die.[d] **5** For God knows that in the very day you eat from it, your eyes will be opened and you will be like God, knowing good and bad."[e]

6 Consequently, the woman saw that the tree was good for food and that it was something desirable to the eyes, yes, the tree was pleasing to look at. So she began taking of its fruit and eating it.[f] Afterward, she also gave some to her husband when he was with her, and he began eating it.[g] **7** Then the eyes of both of them were opened, and they realized that they were naked. So they sewed fig leaves together and made loin coverings for themselves.[h]

8 Later they heard the voice of Jehovah God as he was walking in the garden about the breezy part of the day, and the man and his wife hid from the face of Jehovah God among the trees of the garden. **9** And Jehovah God kept calling to the man and saying to him: "Where are you?" **10** Finally he said: "I heard your voice in the garden, but I was afraid because I was naked, so I hid myself." **11** At that he said: "Who told you that you were naked?[i] Have you eaten from the tree from which I commanded you not to eat?"[j] **12** The man said: "The woman whom you gave to be with me, she gave me fruit from the tree, so I ate." **13** Jehovah God then said to the woman: "What is this you have done?" The woman re-

plied: "The serpent deceived me, so I ate."[a]

14 Then Jehovah God said to the serpent:[b] "Because you have done this, you are the cursed one out of all the domestic animals and out of all the wild animals of the field. On your belly you will go, and you will eat dust all the days of your life. **15** And I will put enmity*[c] between you[d] and the woman[e] and between your offspring#[f] and her offspring.#[g] He will crush△ your head,[h] and you will strike▨ him in the heel."[i]

16 To the woman he said: "I will greatly increase the pain of your pregnancy; in pain you will give birth to children, and your longing will be for your husband, and he will dominate you."

17 And to Adam* he said: "Because you listened to your wife's voice and ate from the tree concerning which I gave you this command,[j] 'You must not eat from it,' cursed is the ground on your account.[k] In pain you will eat its produce all the days of your life.[l] **18** It will grow thorns and thistles for you, and you must eat the vegetation of the field. **19** In the sweat of your face you will eat bread* until you return to the ground, for out of it you were taken.[m] For dust you are and to dust you will return."[n]

20 After this Adam named his wife Eve,* because she was to become the mother of everyone living.[o] **21** And Jehovah God made long garments from skins for Adam and for his wife, to clothe them.[p] **22** Jehovah God then said: "Here the man has become like one of us in know-

CHAP. 3
a Ge 2:17
b Ge 2:16
c Ge 2:8, 9
d Joh 8:44
  1Jo 3:8
e Ge 3:22
f 2Co 11:3
  1Ti 2:14
  Jas 1:14, 15
g Ro 5:12
h Ge 3:21
i Ge 2:25
j Ge 2:17

Second Col.
a 2Co 11:3
  1Ti 2:14
b Ge 3:1
c Re 12:7, 17
d Re 12:9
e Re 12:1
f Joh 8:44
  1Jo 3:10
g Ge 22:18
  Ge 49:10
  Ga 3:16, 29
h Re 20:2, 10
i Mt 27:50
  Ac 3:15
j Ge 2:17
k Ge 5:29
l Ro 8:20
m Ge 2:7
n Ps 104:29
  Ec 3:20
  Ec 12:7
o Ac 17:26
p Ge 3:7

3:15 *Or "hostility." #Lit., "seed." △Or "bruise; strike." ▨Or "bruise; crush." 3:17 *Meaning "Earthling Man; Mankind; Humankind." 3:19 *Or "food." 3:20 *Meaning "Living One."

ing good and bad.ᵃ Now in order that he may not put his hand out and take fruit also from the tree of life,ᵇ and eat and live forever,*—" **23** With that Jehovah God expelled him from the garden of E'denᶜ to cultivate the ground from which he had been taken.ᵈ **24** So he drove the man out, and he posted at the east of the garden of E'den the cherubsᵉ and the flaming blade of a sword that was turning continuously to guard the way to the tree of life.

4 Now Adam had sexual relations with his wife Eve, and she became pregnant.ᶠ When she gave birth to Cain,ᵍ she said: "I have produced* a male child with the help of Jehovah." **2** Later she again gave birth, to his brother Abel.ʰ

Abel became a shepherd of the flock, but Cain became a cultivator of the ground. **3** After some time, Cain brought some fruits of the land as an offering to Jehovah. **4** But Abel brought some firstlings of his flock,ⁱ including their fat. While Jehovah looked with favor on Abel and on his offering,ʲ he did not look with any favor on Cain and on his offering. So Cain grew hot with anger and was dejected.* **6** Then Jehovah said to Cain: "Why are you so angry and dejected? **7** If you turn to doing good, will you not be restored to favor?* But if you do not turn to doing good, sin is crouching at the door, and its craving is to dominate you; but will you get the mastery over it?"

8 After that Cain said to his brother Abel: "Let us go over into the field." So while they were in the field, Cain assaulted his brother Abel and killed

him.ᵃ **9** Later on, Jehovah said to Cain: "Where is your brother Abel?" and he said: "I do not know. Am I my brother's guardian?" **10** At this He said: "What have you done? Listen! Your brother's blood is crying out to me from the ground.ᵇ **11** And now you are cursed in banishment from the ground that has opened its mouth to receive your brother's blood from your hand.ᶜ **12** When you cultivate the ground, it will not give you back its produce.* You will become a wanderer and a fugitive in the earth." **13** At this Cain said to Jehovah: "The punishment for my error is too great to bear. **14** Today you are driving me from the land,* and I will be hidden from your face; and I will become a wanderer and a fugitive on the earth, and anyone who finds me will certainly kill me." **15** So Jehovah said to him: "For that reason, anyone who kills Cain will suffer vengeance seven times."

So Jehovah set up* a sign for Cain in order that no one finding him would strike him. **16** Then Cain went away from before Jehovah and took up residence in the land of Exile,* to the east of E'den.ᵈ

17 Afterward Cain had sexual relations with his wife,ᵉ and she became pregnant and gave birth to E'noch. Then he engaged in building a city and named the city after his son E'noch. **18** Later I'rad was born to E'noch. And I'rad became father to Me·hu'ja·el, and Me·hu'ja·el became father to Me·thu'sha·el, and Me·thu'sha·el became father to La'mech.

19 La'mech took two wives for himself. The name of the first

CHAP. 3
a Ge 3:5

b Ge 2:9

c Ge 2:8

d Ge 3:19

e Ps 80:1
Isa 37:16
Eze 10:4

CHAP. 4
f Ge 1:28

g 1Jo 3:10-12
Jude 11

h Mt 23:35

i Ex 13:12

j Heb 11:4

Second Col.
a Mt 23:35
1Jo 3:10-12
Jude 11

b Heb 12:24

c Ge 9:5

d Ge 2:8

e Ge 5:4

3:22 *Or "to time indefinite." 4:1 *Or "given birth to." 4:5 *Lit., "and his face fell." 4:7 *Or "will there not be an exaltation?"

4:12 *Lit., "power." 4:14 *Lit., "from the face of the ground." 4:15 *Or "established." 4:16 *Or "the land of Nod."

was A'dah, and the name of the second was Zil'lah. **20** A'dah gave birth to Ja'bal. He was the founder of those who dwell in tents and have livestock. **21** His brother's name was Ju'bal. He was the founder of all those who play the harp and the pipe.* **22** Also, Zil'lah gave birth to Tu'bal-cain, who forged every sort of tool of copper and iron. And the sister of Tu'bal-cain was Na'a·mah. **23** Then La'mech composed these words for his wives A'dah and Zil'lah:

"Hear my voice, you wives of La'mech;
Give ear to my saying:
A man I have killed for wounding me,
Yes, a young man for striking me.
24 If 7 times Cain is to be avenged,ª
Then La'mech 77 times."

25 Adam again had sexual relations with his wife, and she gave birth to a son. She named him Seth*ᵇ because, as she said, "God has appointed for me another offspring# in place of Abel, because Cain killed him."ᶜ **26** There was also born to Seth a son, and he named him E'nosh.ᵈ At that time people began calling on the name of Jehovah.

5 This is the book of Adam's history. In the day that God created Adam, he made him in the likeness of God.ᵉ **2** Male and female he created them.ᶠ On the day they were created,ᵍ he blessed them and named them Man.*

3 Adam lived for 130 years and then became father to a son in his likeness, in his image, and

---

4:21 *Or "flute." 4:25 *Meaning "Appointed; Put; Set." #Lit., "seed." 5:2 *Or "Adam; Mankind."

CHAP. 4
a Ge 4:15

b Ge 5:3
1Ch 1:1

c Ge 4:8
Mt 23:35
Heb 11:4

d Ge 5:6
Lu 3:23, 38

CHAP. 5
e Ge 1:26
Jas 3:9

f Ge 1:27
Mr 10:6

g Ge 2:23
Isa 45:12
Mt 19:4

Second Col.
a Ge 4:25

b Ge 2:17
Ge 3:19
Ro 6:23
1Co 15:22

c Ge 4:26
Lu 3:23, 38

d Lu 3:23, 37

e Lu 3:23, 37

f Jude 14

g Lu 3:23, 37

---

he named him Seth.ª **4** After becoming father to Seth, Adam lived for 800 years. And he became father to sons and daughters. **5** So all the days of Adam's life amounted to 930 years, and then he died.ᵇ

6 Seth lived for 105 years and then became father to E'nosh.ᶜ **7** After becoming father to E'nosh, Seth lived for 807 years. And he became father to sons and daughters. **8** So all the days of Seth amounted to 912 years, and then he died.

9 E'nosh lived for 90 years and then became father to Ke'nan. **10** After becoming father to Ke'nan, E'nosh lived for 815 years. And he became father to sons and daughters. **11** So all the days of E'nosh amounted to 905 years, and then he died.

12 Ke'nan lived for 70 years and then became father to Ma·hal'a·lel.ᵈ **13** After becoming father to Ma·hal'a·lel, Ke'nan lived for 840 years. And he became father to sons and daughters. **14** So all the days of Ke'nan amounted to 910 years, and then he died.

15 Ma·hal'a·lel lived for 65 years and then became father to Ja'red.ᵉ **16** After becoming father to Ja'red, Ma·hal'a·lel lived for 830 years. And he became father to sons and daughters. **17** So all the days of Ma·hal'a·lel amounted to 895 years, and then he died.

18 Ja'red lived for 162 years and then became father to E'noch.ᶠ **19** After becoming father to E'noch, Ja'red lived for 800 years. And he became father to sons and daughters. **20** So all the days of Ja'red amounted to 962 years, and then he died.

21 E'noch lived for 65 years and then became father to Me·thu'se·lah.ᵍ **22** After becoming father to Me·thu'se·lah, E'noch continued to walk with the true God* for 300 years. And he became father to sons and daughters. **23** So all the days of E'noch amounted to 365 years. **24** E'noch kept walking with the true God.ª Then he was no more, for God took him.ᵇ

25 Me·thu'se·lah lived for 187 years and then became father to La'mech.ᶜ **26** After becoming father to La'mech, Me·thu'se·lah lived for 782 years. And he became father to sons and daughters. **27** So all the days of Me·thu'se·lah amounted to 969 years, and then he died.

28 La'mech lived for 182 years and then became father to a son. **29** He named him Noah,*ᵈ saying: "This one will bring us comfort# from our labor and from the painful toil of our hands because of the ground that Jehovah has cursed."ᵉ **30** After becoming father to Noah, La'mech lived for 595 years. And he became father to sons and daughters. **31** So all the days of La'mech amounted to 777 years, and then he died.

32 After Noah reached 500 years of age, he became father to Shem,ᶠ Ham,ᵍ and Ja'pheth.ʰ

6 Now when men started to grow in number on the surface of the ground and daughters were born to them, **2** the sons of the true God*ⁱ began to notice that the daughters of men were beautiful. So they began taking as wives all whom they chose. **3** Then Jehovah said: "My spirit will not tolerate man indefinitely,ʲ because he is only flesh.* Accordingly, his days will amount to 120 years."ᵏ

4 The Neph'i·lim* were on the earth in those days and afterward. During that time the sons of the true God continued to have relations with the daughters of men, and these bore sons to them. They were the mighty ones of old times, the men of fame.

5 Consequently, Jehovah saw that man's wickedness was great on the earth and that every inclination of the thoughts of his heart was only bad all the time.ª **6** Jehovah regretted* that he had made men on the earth, and his heart was saddened.#ᵇ **7** So Jehovah said: "I am going to wipe men whom I have created off the surface of the ground, man together with domestic animals, creeping animals, and flying creatures of the heavens, for I regret that I have made them." **8** But Noah found favor in the eyes of Jehovah.

9 This is the history of Noah.

Noah was a righteous man.ᶜ He proved himself faultless* among his contemporaries.# Noah walked with the true God.ᵈ **10** In time Noah became father to three sons, Shem, Ham, and Ja'pheth.ᵉ **11** But the earth had become ruined in the sight of the true God, and the earth was filled with violence. **12** Yes, God looked upon the earth, and it was ruined;ᶠ all flesh* had ruined its way on the earth.ᵍ

13 After that God said to Noah: "I have decided to put an end to all flesh, because the earth is full of violence on account of them, so I am bringing them to ruin together with the earth.ʰ **14** Make for yourself an

CHAP. 5
a Ge 6:9
   De 8:6
   De 13:4
   3Jo 4
   Jude 14, 15

b Joh 3:13
   Heb 11:5

c Lu 3:23, 36

d Ge 7:1
   Eze 14:14
   Mt 24:37
   Heb 11:7
   1Pe 3:20
   2Pe 2:5

e Ge 3:17

f Ge 10:21
   Ge 11:10
   Lu 3:23, 36

g Ge 6:10
   Ge 10:6

h Ge 10:2

CHAP. 6
i Job 1:6
   Job 38:7
   2Pe 2:4
   Jude 6

j Ge 7:4
   1Pe 3:20

k 2Pe 3:9

Second Col.
a Ge 8:21
   Jer 17:9
   Mt 15:19

b Ps 78:40, 41

c Ge 7:1
   Eze 14:14
   Heb 11:7

d 2Pe 2:5

e Ge 5:32

f Re 11:18

g Mt 24:37-39
   2Pe 2:5

h Ge 7:4

5:22 *Lit., "the God." See Glossary. **5:29** *Probably meaning "Rest; Consolation." #Or "relief." **6:2** *A Hebrew idiom that refers to angelic sons of God. **6:3** *Or possibly, "because he acts according to the flesh."

6:4 *Possibly meaning "The Fellers," that is, those who cause others to fall down. See Glossary. **6:6** *Or "was grieved." #Or "and he felt hurt at his heart." **6:9** *Or "blameless." #Lit., "his generations." **6:12** *Or "people."

ark* from resinous wood.ᵃ You will make compartments in the ark and cover it with tar#ᵇ inside and outside. **15** This is how you will make it: The ark should be 300 cubits* long, 50 cubits wide, and 30 cubits high. **16** You will make a window for light* for the ark, one cubit from the top. You should put the entrance of the ark in its sideᶜ and make it with a lower deck, a second deck, and a third deck.

17 "As for me, I am going to bring floodwatersᵈ upon the earth to destroy from under the heavens all flesh that has the breath of life.* Everything on the earth will perish.ᵉ **18** And I am establishing my covenant with you, and you must go into the ark, you, your sons, your wife, and your sons' wives with you.ᶠ **19** And bring into the ark two of every sort of living creatureᵍ in order to preserve them alive with you, a male and a female;ʰ **20** of the flying creatures according to their kinds, the domestic animals according to their kinds, and all creeping animals of the ground according to their kinds, two of each will go in there to you to preserve them alive.ⁱ **21** For your part, you are to collect and take with you every kind of food to eat,ʲ to serve as food for you and for the animals."

22 And Noah did according to all that God had commanded him. He did just so.ᵏ

7 After that Jehovah said to Noah: "Go into the ark, you and all your household, because you are the one I have found to

be righteous before me among this generation.ᵃ **2** You must take with you every kind of clean animal by sevens,*ᵇ the male and its mate; and of every animal that is not clean just two, the male and its mate; **3** also of the flying creatures of the sky by sevens,* male and female, to preserve their offspring alive over all the earth.ᶜ **4** For in just seven days, I will make it rainᵈ on the earth for 40 days and 40 nights,ᵉ and I will wipe from the surface of the ground every living thing that I have made."ᶠ **5** Then Noah did everything that Jehovah had commanded him.

6 Noah was 600 years old when the floodwaters came upon the earth.ᵍ **7** So Noah, along with his sons, his wife, and his sons' wives, went into the ark ahead of the floodwaters.ʰ **8** Of every clean animal and of every animal that is not clean and of the flying creatures and of everything that moves on the ground,ⁱ **9** they went inside the ark to Noah by twos, male and female, just as God had commanded Noah. **10** And seven days later the floodwaters came upon the earth.

11 In the 600th year of Noah's life, in the second month, on the 17th day of the month, on that day all the springs of the vast watery deep burst open and the floodgates of the heavens were opened.ʲ **12** And the rain poured down on the earth for 40 days and 40 nights. **13** On that very day, Noah went into the ark along with his sons, Shem, Ham, and Ja′pheth,ᵏ and his wife and the three wives of his sons.ˡ **14** They went in with every wild animal accord-

---

CHAP. 6

a Heb 11:7

b Ge 14:10
  Ex 2:3

c Ge 7:16

d Ge 1:7
  Ge 7:6, 11

e Ge 7:21
  Ps 104:29
  Mt 24:39
  2Pe 2:5

f Ge 7:13

g Ge 8:17

h Ge 7:2

i Ge 7:14, 15

j Ge 1:29, 30

k Ex 40:16
  Heb 11:7

Second Col.

CHAP. 7

a Ge 6:9
  Heb 10:38
  Heb 11:7
  1Pe 3:12
  2Pe 2:5, 9

b Ge 8:20

c Ge 7:23
  Ge 8:19

d Ge 2:5

e Ge 7:11, 12

f Ge 6:7, 17

g Ge 8:13

h Lu 17:27
  Heb 11:7

i Ge 6:19, 20

j Ge 1:7
  Ge 8:2

k Ge 9:18
  1Ch 1:4

l Ge 6:18
  1Pe 3:20
  2Pe 2:5

6:14 *Lit., "a chest"; a large vessel. #Or "pitch." **6:15** *A cubit equaled 44.5 cm (17.5 in.). See App. B14. **6:16** *Hebrew, tso′har. Another view is that the tso′har refers to a roof with a one-cubit pitch, or incline, rather than an opening for light or a window. **6:17** *Or "the spirit of life."

7:2 *Or possibly, "seven pairs of every clean animal." **7:3** *Or possibly, "seven pairs of the flying creatures of the sky."

ing to its kind, and every domestic animal according to its kind, and every creeping animal of the earth according to its kind, and every flying creature according to its kind, every bird, every winged creature. **15** They kept going to Noah inside the ark, two by two, of every sort of flesh that has the breath of life.* **16** So they went in, male and female of every sort of flesh, just as God had commanded him. After that Jehovah shut the door behind him.

17 The flooding continued* for 40 days on the earth, and the waters kept increasing and began carrying the ark, and it was floating high above the earth. **18** The waters became overwhelming and kept increasing greatly upon the earth, but the ark floated on the surface of the waters. **19** The waters overwhelmed the earth so greatly that all the tall mountains under the whole heavens were covered.ᵃ **20** The waters rose up to 15 cubits* above the mountains.

21 So all living creatures* that were moving on the earth perishedᵇ—the flying creatures, the domestic animals, the wild animals, the swarming creatures, and all mankind.ᶜ **22** Everything on dry land that had the breath of life* in its nostrils died.ᵈ **23** So He wiped every living thing from the surface of the earth, including man, animals, creeping animals, and the flying creatures of the sky. They were all wiped off the earth;ᵉ only Noah and those with him in the ark survived.ᶠ **24** And the wa-

ters continued overwhelming the earth for 150 days.ᵃ

8 But God gave attention to* Noah and to all the wild animals and domestic animals that were with him in the ark,ᵇ and God caused a wind to blow over the earth, and the waters began to subside. **2** The springs of the watery deep and the floodgates of the heavens were stopped up, so that the rain from the heavens stopped falling.*ᶜ **3** Then the waters began to recede progressively from the earth. By the end of 150 days, the waters had subsided. **4** In the seventh month, on the 17th day of the month, the ark came to rest on the mountains of Arʹa·rat. **5** And the waters were steadily decreasing until the tenth month. In the tenth month, on the first of the month, the tops of the mountains appeared.ᵈ

6 So at the end of 40 days, Noah opened the window that he had made in the ark **7** and sent out a raven; it continued flying outside and returning, until the waters dried off the earth.

8 Later he sent out a dove to see whether the waters had receded from the surface of the ground. **9** The dove did not find any resting-place to perch,* so it returned to him into the ark because the waters were still covering the surface of the whole earth.ᶠ So he reached his hand out and brought it inside the ark. **10** He waited seven more days, and once again he sent out the dove from the ark. **11** When the dove came to him toward evening, he saw that there was a freshly plucked olive leaf in its bill! So Noah knew that the waters had receded

---

CHAP. 7

a 2Pe 3:5, 6

b Ge 6:7, 17

c Lu 17:27

d Ge 2:7
Ge 7:15
Ec 3:19
Isa 42:5

e Ge 6:7
2Pe 3:5, 6

f Mt 24:37-39
1Pe 3:20
2Pe 2:5, 9

Second Col.
a Ge 8:3

CHAP. 8

b Ge 6:19, 20
Heb 11:7

c Ge 7:11, 12

d Ge 7:20

e Ge 6:16

f Ge 7:19

7:15 *Or "the spirit of life." 7:17 *Or "kept coming." 7:20 *A cubit equaled 44.5 cm (17.5 in.). See App. B14. 7:21 *Lit., "all flesh." 7:22 *Or "the breath of the spirit of life."

8:1 *Lit., "remembered." 8:2 *Or "was restrained." 8:9 *Or "for the sole of its foot."

from the earth.[a] **12** He waited still another seven days. Then he sent out the dove, but it did not return to him anymore.

13 Now in the 601st year,[b] in the first month, on the first day of the month, the waters had drained from the earth; and Noah removed the covering of the ark and saw that the surface of the ground was drying. **14** In the second month, on the 27th day of the month, the earth had dried off.

15 God now said to Noah: **16** "Go out of the ark, you, your wife, your sons, and your sons' wives.[c] **17** Bring out with you all the living creatures of every sort of flesh,[d] of the flying creatures and of the animals and of all the creeping animals of the earth, that they may multiply* on the earth and be fruitful and become many on the earth."[e]

18 So Noah went out, together with his sons,[f] his wife, and his sons' wives. **19** Every living creature, every creeping animal and every flying creature, everything that moves on the earth, went out of the ark by families.[g] **20** Then Noah built an altar[h] to Jehovah and took some of all the clean animals and of all the clean flying creatures[i] and offered burnt offerings on the altar.[j] **21** And Jehovah began to smell a pleasing* aroma. So Jehovah said in his heart: "Never again will I curse* the ground[k] on man's account, for the inclination of the heart of man is bad from his youth up;[l] and never again will I strike down every living thing as I have done.[m] **22** From now on, the earth will never cease to have seed-sowing and harvest, cold and heat, summer and winter, and day and night."[n]

9 God went on to bless Noah and his sons and to say to them: "Be fruitful and become many and fill the earth.[a] **2** A fear of you and a terror of you will continue upon every living creature of the earth and upon every flying creature of the heavens, upon everything that moves on the ground and upon all the fish of the sea. They are now given into your hand.*[b] **3** Every moving animal that is alive may serve as food for you.[c] Just as I gave you the green vegetation, I give them all to you.[d] **4** Only flesh with its life*—its blood[e]—you must not eat.[f] **5** Besides that, I will demand an accounting for your lifeblood.* I will demand an accounting from every living creature; and from each man I will demand an accounting for the life of his brother.[g] **6** Anyone shedding man's blood, by man will his own blood be shed,[h] for in God's image He made man.[i] **7** As for you, be fruitful and become many, and increase abundantly on the earth and multiply."[j]

8 Then God said to Noah and to his sons with him: **9** "I am now establishing my covenant with you[k] and with your offspring after you, **10** and with every living creature* that is with you, the birds, the animals, and all the living creatures of the earth with you, all those that came out of the ark—every living creature of the earth.[l] **11** Yes, I establish my covenant with you: Never again will all flesh* be destroyed by the waters of a flood, and never again will a flood bring the earth to ruin."[m]

12 And God added: "This is the sign of the covenant that I

CHAP. 8
a Ge 7:20
  Ge 8:3
b Ge 7:6, 11
c Ge 7:7
  1Pe 3:20
  2Pe 2:5
d Ge 6:19, 20
  Ge 7:14, 15
e Ge 1:22
f Ge 6:10
g Ge 7:13, 14
h Ge 12:7
i Ge 7:2
  Le 20:25
j De 27:6
k Ge 3:17
  Ge 5:29
l Ge 6:5
  Ec 7:20
  Mt 15:19
m Ge 6:7, 17
  Ge 9:11
  Isa 54:9
n Ge 1:14
  Ps 74:17
  Ec 1:4

Second Col.

CHAP. 9
a Ge 1:28
b Ge 1:26
  Jas 3:7
c 1Ti 4:3
d Ge 1:29
e Le 17:11, 14
f Le 3:17
  Le 7:26
  Le 17:10, 13
  De 12:16, 23
  Ac 15:20, 29
  Ac 21:25
g Ge 4:8, 10
  Ex 21:12
h Ex 20:13
  Nu 35:30
  Mt 26:52
i Ge 1:27
j Ge 1:28
  Ge 10:32
k Ge 9:15
  Isa 54:9
l Ge 8:17
m Ge 8:21

---

am making between me and you and every living creature* that is with you, for all future generations. **13** I put my rainbow in the cloud, and it will serve as a sign of the covenant between me and the earth. **14** Whenever I bring a cloud over the earth, then the rainbow will certainly appear in the cloud. **15** And I will certainly remember my covenant that I made between me and you and every living creature of every kind;* and never again will the waters become a flood to destroy all flesh.ᵃ **16** And the rainbow will occur in the cloud, and I will certainly see it and remember the everlasting covenant between God and every living creature* of every kind* on the earth."

17 God repeated to Noah: "This is the sign of the covenant that I establish between me and all flesh that is on the earth."ᵇ

18 Noah's sons who came out of the ark were Shem, Ham, and Ja'pheth.ᶜ Ham later became the father of Ca'naan.ᵈ **19** These three were Noah's sons, and all the earth's population came from them and spread abroad.ᵉ

20 Now Noah started off as a farmer, and he planted a vineyard. **21** When he drank of the wine, he became intoxicated, and he uncovered himself inside his tent. **22** Ham, the father of Ca'naan, saw his father's nakedness, and he told his two brothers outside. **23** So Shem and Ja'pheth took a garment and put it upon both their shoulders and walked in backward. Thus they covered their father's nakedness while their faces were turned away, and they did not see their father's nakedness.

24 When Noah woke up from his wine and learned what his youngest son had done to him, **25** he said:

"Cursed be Ca'naan.ᵃ
Let him become the lowest slave to his brothers."ᵇ

26 And he added:

"Praised be Jehovah, the God of Shem,
And let Ca'naan become a slave to him.ᶜ
27 Let God grant ample space to Ja'pheth,
And let him reside in the tents of Shem.
Let Ca'naan become a slave to him also."

28 Noah continued to live for 350 years after the Flood.ᵈ **29** So all the days of Noah amounted to 950 years, and he died.

10 This is the history of Noah's sons, Shem,ᵉ Ham, and Ja'pheth.

Sons were born to them after the Flood.ᶠ **2** The sons of Ja'pheth were Go'mer,ᵍ Ma'gog,ʰ Ma'da·i, Ja'van, Tu'bal,ⁱ Me'shech,ʲ and Ti'ras.ᵏ

3 The sons of Go'mer were Ash'ke·naz,ˡ Ri'phath, and To·gar'mah.ᵐ

4 The sons of Ja'van were E·li'shah,ⁿ Tar'shish,ᵒ Kit'tim,ᵖ and Do'da·nim.

5 From these the inhabitants of the islands spread into their lands, according to their languages and their families and by their nations.

6 The sons of Ham were Cush, Miz'ra·im,ᑫ Put,ʳ and Ca'naan.ˢ

7 The sons of Cush were Se'ba,ᵗ Hav'i·lah, Sab'tah, Ra'a·mah,ᵘ and Sab'te·ca.

The sons of Ra'a·mah were She'ba and De'dan.

8 Cush became father to Nim'rod. He was the first to become a mighty one on the

---

CHAP. 9
a Ge 8:21

b Ge 9:12, 13

c Ge 5:32
Ge 7:7
Ge 10:1

d Ge 10:6

e Ge 10:32

Second Col.
a De 7:1

b Jos 17:13

c Jg 1:28

d Ge 7:6

CHAP. 10
e Lu 3:23, 36

f Ge 9:18, 19

g Eze 38:6

h Eze 38:2

i Isa 66:19
Eze 27:13

j Ps 120:5
Eze 32:26

k 1Ch 1:5-7

l Jer 51:27

m Eze 27:14
Eze 38:6

n Eze 27:7

o Jon 1:3

p Isa 23:1

q Ge 50:11

r Jer 46:9
Na 3:9

s Nu 34:2
1Ch 1:8-10

t Ps 72:10

u Eze 27:22

9:12 *Or "soul." 9:15, 16 *Or "every living soul of all flesh."

earth. **9** He became a mighty hunter in opposition to Jehovah. That is why there is a saying: "Just like Nim′rod, a mighty hunter in opposition to Jehovah." **10** The beginning of his kingdom was* Ba′bel,ᵃ E′rech,ᵇ Ac′cad, and Cal′neh, in the land of Shi′nar.ᶜ **11** From that land he went into As·syr′i·aᵈ and built Nin′e·veh,ᵉ Re·ho′both-Ir, Ca′lah, **12** and Re′sen, between Nin′e·veh and Ca′lah: This is the great city.*

13 Miz′ra·im became father to Lu′dim,ᶠ An′a·mim, Le·ha′bim, Naph·tu′him,ᵍ **14** Path·ru′sim,ʰ Cas·lu′him (from whom the Phi·lis′tines ̕ came), and Caph′to·rim.ʲ

15 Ca′naan became father to Si′don,ᵏ his firstborn, and Heth,ˡ **16** as well as the Jeb′u·site,ᵐ the Am′or·ite,ⁿ the Gir′ga·shite, **17** the Hi′vite,ᵒ the Ark′ite, the Si′nite, **18** the Ar′vad·ite,ᵖ the Zem′a·rite, and the Ha′math·ite.ᑫ Afterward, the families of the Ca′naan·ites were scattered. **19** So the boundary of the Ca′naan·ites was from Si′don as far as Ge′rar,ʳ near Gaz′a,ˢ as far as Sod′om, Go·mor′rah,ᵗ Ad′mah, and Ze·boi′im,ᵘ near La′sha. **20** These were the sons of Ham according to their families and their languages, by their lands and their nations.

21 Children were also born to Shem, the forefather of all the sons of E′berᵛ and the brother of Ja′pheth the oldest.* **22** The sons of Shem were E′lam,ʷ As′shur,ˣ Ar·pach′shad,ʸ Lud, and A′ram.ᶻ

23 The sons of A′ram were Uz, Hul, Ge′ther, and Mash.

24 Ar·pach′shad became father to She′lah,ᵃ and She′lah became father to E′ber.

25 Two sons were born to E′ber. The name of the one was Pe′leg,*ᵇ because in his lifetime the earthᵍ was divided. The name of his brother was Jok′tan.

26 Jok′tan became father to Al·mo′dad, She′leph, Ha·zar·ma′veth, Je′rah,ᵈ **27** Ha·do′ram, U′zal, Dik′lah, **28** O′bal, A·bim′a·el, She′ba, **29** O′phir,ᵉ Hav′i·lah, and Jo′bab; all of these were the sons of Jok′tan.

30 Their place of dwelling extended from Me′sha as far as Se′phar, the mountainous region of the East.

31 These were the sons of Shem according to their families and their languages, by their lands and their nations.ᶠ

32 These were the families of the sons of Noah according to their family lines and by their nations. From these the nations were spread abroad in the earth after the Flood.ᵍ

11 Now all the earth continued to be of one language and of one set of words.* **2** As they traveled eastward, they discovered a valley plain in the land of Shi′nar,ʰ and they began dwelling there. **3** Then they said to one another: "Come! Let us make bricks and bake them with fire." So they used bricks instead of stone, and bitumen as mortar. **4** They now said: "Come! Let us build a city for ourselves and a tower with its top in the heavens, and let us make a celebrated name for ourselves, so that we will not be scattered over the entire face of the earth." ̕

CHAP. 10

a Ge 11:9
b Ezr 4:9
c Da 1:2
d Mic 5:6
e Jon 3:3
  Mt 12:41
f Jer 46:9
g 1Ch 1:11, 12
h Eze 29:14
i Jos 13:2, 3
  Jer 47:4
j De 2:23
k Jos 13:6
  Mr 7:24
l Ge 25:10
  Ge 27:46
  1Ch 1:13-16
m Jg 1:21
n Ge 15:16
  De 3:8
o Jos 11:3
p Eze 27:11
q 1Ki 8:65
r Ge 20:1
s Jos 15:20, 47
  Ac 8:26
t Ge 13:10
  Ge 19:24
  Jude 7
u De 29:23
v Ge 11:17
w Ezr 4:9
  Ac 2:8, 9
x Eze 27:23
y Ge 11:10
z 1Ch 1:17

Second Col.

a Ge 11:12
  Lu 3:23, 35
b Ge 11:16
c 1Ch 1:19
d 1Ch 1:20-23
e 1Ki 9:28
  1Ki 10:11
f Ge 10:5
g Ge 9:7
  Ge 9:19
  Ac 17:26

CHAP. 11

h Ge 10:9, 10
  Da 1:2
i Ge 9:1

10:10 *Or "The first cities of his kingdom were." **10:12** *Or possibly, "They form the great city." **10:21** *Or possibly, "and the older brother of Japheth."

10:25 *Meaning "Division." ᵍOr "earth's population." **11:1** *Or "of one vocabulary."

5 Then Jehovah went down to see the city and the tower that the sons of men had built. **6** Jehovah then said: "Look! They are one people with one language,[a] and this is what they have started to do. Now there is nothing that they may have in mind to do that will be impossible for them. **7** Come! Let us[b] go down there and confuse their language in order that they may not understand one another's language." **8** So Jehovah scattered them from there over the entire face of the earth,[c] and they gradually left off building the city. **9** That is why it was named Ba′bel,*[d] because there Jehovah confused the language of all the earth, and Jehovah scattered them from there over the entire face of the earth.

10 This is the history of Shem.[e]

Shem was 100 years old when he became father to Ar·pach′shad[f] two years after the Flood. **11** After becoming father to Ar′pach′shad, Shem continued to live 500 years. And he became father to sons and daughters.[g]

12 Ar·pach′shad lived for 35 years and then became father to She′lah.[h] **13** After becoming father to She′lah, Ar·pach′shad continued to live 403 years. And he became father to sons and daughters.

14 She′lah lived for 30 years and then became father to E′ber.[i] **15** After becoming father to E′ber, She′lah continued to live 403 years. And he became father to sons and daughters.

16 E′ber lived for 34 years and then became father to Pe′leg.[j] **17** After becoming father to Pe′leg, E′ber continued to live 430 years. And he became father to sons and daughters.

18 Pe′leg lived for 30 years and then became father to Re′u.[k]

19 After becoming father to Re′u, Pe′leg continued to live 209 years. And he became father to sons and daughters.

20 Re′u lived for 32 years and then became father to Se′rug. **21** After becoming father to Se′rug, Re′u continued to live 207 years. And he became father to sons and daughters.

22 Se′rug lived for 30 years and then became father to Na′hor. **23** After becoming father to Na′hor, Se′rug continued to live 200 years. And he became father to sons and daughters.

24 Na′hor lived for 29 years and then became father to Te′rah.[a] **25** After becoming father to Te′rah, Na′hor continued to live 119 years. And he became father to sons and daughters.

26 Te′rah lived for 70 years, after which he became father to A′bram,[b] Na′hor,[c] and Ha′ran.

27 This is the history of Te′rah.

Te′rah became father to A′bram, Na′hor, and Ha′ran; and Ha′ran became father to Lot.[d] **28** While his father Te′rah was still alive, Ha′ran died in the land of his birth, in Ur[e] of the Chal·de′ans.[f] **29** A′bram and Na′hor took wives for themselves. The name of A′bram's wife was Sar′ai,[g] and the name of Na′hor's wife was Mil′cah,[h] the daughter of Ha′ran, the father of Mil′cah and Is′cah. **30** Now Sar′ai was barren;[i] she had no child.

31 Te′rah then took A′bram his son and Lot his grandson,[j] the son of Ha′ran, and Sar′ai his daughter-in-law, the wife of A′bram his son, and they went with him out of Ur of the Chal·de′ans to go to the land of Ca′naan.[k] In time they came to Ha′ran[l] and began dwelling there. **32** The days of Te′rah were 205 years. Then Te′rah died in Ha′ran.

CHAP. 11
a Ge 11:1
b Ge 1:26
c De 32:8
d Jer 50:1
e Ge 6:10
  Lu 3:23, 36
f Ge 10:22
  1Ch 1:17
g Ge 10:21
h Ge 10:24
  1Ch 1:18
  Lu 3:23, 35
i Ge 10:21
  1Ch 1:18
j Ge 10:25
  1Ch 1:19
k Lu 3:23, 35

Second Col.
a Ge 11:32
  Lu 3:23, 34
b Ge 12:7
  Ge 15:1, 6
  Ge 17:5
  Jas 2:23
c Jos 24:2
d Ge 12:4
  Ge 19:1
  2Pe 2:7
e Ge 15:7
  Ne 9:7
f Ac 7:4
g Ge 12:11
  Ge 17:15
  Ge 20:12, 13
  1Pe 3:6
h Ge 22:20
  Ge 24:15
i Ge 16:1, 2
  Ro 4:19
  Heb 11:11
j Ge 11:27, 28
k Ge 10:19
l Ge 12:4
  Ge 27:42, 43
  Ac 7:2, 4

11:9 *Meaning "Confusion."

12 And Jehovah said to A'bram: "Go out from your land and away from your relatives and from the house of your father to the land that I will show you.[a] **2** I will make you a great nation, and I will bless you, and I will make your name great, and you will become a blessing.[b] **3** I will bless those who bless you, and I will curse him who calls down evil on you,[c] and all the families of the ground will certainly be blessed* by means of you."[d]

4 So A'bram went just as Jehovah had told him, and Lot went with him. A'bram was 75 years old when he left Ha'ran.[e] **5** A'bram took his wife Sar'ai[f] and Lot the son of his brother[g] and all the goods that they had accumulated[h] and the people* whom they had acquired in Ha'ran, and they set out for the land of Ca'naan.[i] When they reached the land of Ca'naan, **6** A'bram traveled through the land as far as the site of She'chem,[j] near the big trees of Mo'reh.[k] At that time the Ca'naan·ites were in the land. **7** Jehovah then appeared to A'bram and said: "To your offspring*[l] I am going to give this land."[m] So he built an altar there to Jehovah, who had appeared to him. **8** Later he moved from there to the mountainous region east of Beth'el[n] and pitched his tent with Beth'el on the west and A'i[o] on the east. There he built an altar to Jehovah[p] and began to call on the name of Jehovah.[q] **9** Afterward, A'bram broke camp and journeyed toward the Neg'eb,[r] moving his camp from one place to another.

10 Now a famine arose in the land, and A'bram went down toward Egypt to reside there for a while,*[a] because the famine in the land was severe.[b] **11** As he was about to enter Egypt, he said to his wife Sar'ai: "Please listen! I know what a beautiful woman you are.[c] **12** So when the Egyptians see you, they will surely say, 'This is his wife.' Then they will kill me but keep you alive. **13** Please say you are my sister, so that it may go well with me because of you, and my life will be spared."*[d]

14 As soon as A'bram entered Egypt, the Egyptians noticed that the woman was very beautiful. **15** And the princes of Phar'aoh also saw her, and they began praising her to Phar'aoh, so that the woman was taken to the house of Phar'aoh. **16** He treated A'bram well because of her, and he acquired sheep, cattle, male and female donkeys, male and female servants, and camels.[e] **17** Then Jehovah struck Phar'aoh and his household with severe plagues because of Sar'ai, A'bram's wife.[f] **18** So Phar'aoh called A'bram and said: "What is this you have done to me? Why did you not tell me that she was your wife? **19** Why did you say, 'She is my sister,'[g] so that I was about to take her as my wife? Here is your wife. Take her and go!" **20** So Phar'aoh gave his men orders concerning him, and they sent him away with his wife and all that he had.[h]

13 A'bram then went up out of Egypt to the Neg'eb,[i] he and his wife and all that he had, together with Lot. **2** A'bram was very rich in livestock, silver, and gold.[j] **3** He camped in one place after another as he traveled from the Neg'eb to Beth'el, until he arrived at the place where his tent had been between

---

12:3 *Or "will obtain a blessing for themselves." 12:5 *Or "souls." 12:7 *Lit., "seed."

12:10 *Or "to live there as a foreigner." 12:13 *Or "my soul will stay alive."

Beth'el and A'i,[a] **4** to the place where he had previously built an altar. There A'bram called on the name of Jehovah.

5 Now Lot, who was traveling with A'bram, also owned sheep, cattle, and tents. **6** So the land did not allow for all of them to stay in the same place; their goods had become so many that they could no longer dwell together. **7** As a result, a quarrel arose between the herders of A'bram's livestock and the herders of Lot's livestock. (At that time the Ca'naan·ites and the Per'iz·zites were dwelling in the land.)[b] **8** So A'bram said to Lot:[c] "Please, there should be no quarreling between me and you and between my herdsmen and your herdsmen, for we are brothers. **9** Is not the whole land available to you? Please, separate from me. If you go to the left, then I will go to the right; but if you go to the right, then I will go to the left." **10** So Lot raised his eyes and saw that the whole district of the Jordan[d] was a well-watered region (before Jehovah destroyed Sod'om and Go·mor'rah), like the garden of Jehovah,[e] like the land of Egypt, as far as Zo'ar.[f] **11** Then Lot chose for himself the whole district of the Jordan, and Lot moved his camp to the east. So they separated from each other. **12** A'bram lived in the land of Ca'naan, but Lot lived among the cities of the district.[g] Finally he set up his tent near Sod'om. **13** Now the men of Sod'om were wicked, gross sinners against Jehovah.[h]

14 Jehovah said to A'bram, after Lot had separated from him: "Raise your eyes, please, and look from the place where you are, to the north and south, east and west, **15** because all the land that you see, I will give

to you and your offspring* as a lasting possession.[a] **16** And I will make your offspring* like the dust particles of the earth, so that if anyone could count the dust particles of the earth, then your offspring* could be counted.[b] **17** Get up, travel through the length and breadth of the land, for to you I am going to give it." **18** So A'bram continued to live in tents. Later he came and dwelled among the big trees of Mam're,[c] which are in Heb'ron,[d] and there he built an altar to Jehovah.[e]

14 Now in the days of Am'ra·phel king of Shi'nar,[f] Ar'i·och king of El·la'sar, Ched·or·la·o'mer[g] king of E'lam,[h] and Ti'dal king of Goi'im, **2** these made war with Be'ra king of Sod'om,[i] Bir'sha king of Go·mor'rah,[j] Shi'nab king of Ad'mah, Shem·e'ber king of Ze·boi'im,[k] and the king of Be'la, that is, Zo'ar. **3** All of these joined forces at the Valley* of Sid'dim,[l] that is, the Salt Sea.[#m]

4 They had served Ched·or·la·o'mer for 12 years, but they rebelled in the 13th year. **5** So in the 14th year, Ched·or·la·o'mer and the kings who were with him came and defeated the Reph'a·im in Ash'te·roth-kar·na'im, the Zu'zim in Ham, the E'mim[n] in Sha'veh-kir·i·a·tha'im, **6** and the Hor'ites[o] in their mountain of Se'ir[p] down to El-pa'ran, which is at the wilderness. **7** Then they turned back and came to En-mish'pat, that is, Ka'desh,[q] and conquered the whole territory of the A·mal'ek·ites[r] and also the Am'or·ites[s] who were dwelling in Haz'a·zon-ta'mar.[t]

8 At this point, the king of Sod'om went on the march, and also the king of Go·mor'rah,

CHAP. 13
a Ge 12:8, 9
  Jos 7:2
b Ge 10:19
c Ge 11:27
d Ge 19:28
e Ge 2:8, 9
f Ge 19:20-22
g Ge 19:28, 29
h Ge 18:20
  Ge 19:5
  2Pe 2:6-8
  Jude 7

Second Col.
a Ge 12:7
  Ge 15:18
  Ge 24:7
  Ex 33:1
b Ge 12:2
  Ge 15:1, 5
  Ex 1:7
  Heb 11:12
c Ge 18:1
  Ge 23:19
  Ge 25:9, 10
  Ge 35:27
d Ge 23:2
e Ge 12:7

CHAP. 14
f Ge 10:9, 10
g Ge 14:17
h Ge 10:22
i Ge 10:19
  Ge 13:12
j Ge 13:10, 12
k De 29:23
l Ge 14:10
m Nu 34:2, 12
n De 2:10, 11
o De 2:12
p Ge 36:8
q Nu 20:1
r Ge 36:12
  1Sa 15:2
s Ge 10:15, 16
t 2Ch 20:2

13:15, 16 *Lit., "seed." 14:3 *Or "Low Plain." #That is, the Dead Sea.

the king of Ad′mah, the king of Ze·boi′im, and the king of Be′la, that is, Zo′ar, and they drew up in battle formation against them in the Valley* of Sid′dim, 9 against Ched·or·la·o′mer king of E′lam, Ti′dal king of Goi′im, Am′ra·phel king of Shi′nar, and Ar′i·och king of El·la′sar^a—four kings against the five. 10 Now the Valley* of Sid′-dim was full of bitumen pits, and the kings of Sod′om and Go·mor′rah tried to escape and fell into them, and those who remained fled to the mountainous region. 11 Then the victors took all the goods of Sod′-om and Go·mor′rah and all their food and went on their way.^b 12 They also took Lot, the son of A′bram's brother who was dwelling in Sod′om,^c as well as his goods, and they continued on their way.

13 After that a man who had escaped came and told A′bram the Hebrew. He was then dwelling* among the big trees of Mam′re the Am′or·ite,^d the brother of Esh′col and A′ner.^e These men were allies of A′bram. 14 Thus A′bram heard that his relative*^f had been taken captive. With that he mobilized his trained men, 318 servants born in his household, and went in pursuit up to Dan.^g 15 During the night, he divided his forces, and he and his servants attacked and defeated them. And he pursued them up to Ho′bah, which is north of Damascus. 16 He recovered all the goods, and he also recovered Lot his relative, his goods, the women, and the other people.

17 After A′bram returned from defeating Ched·or·la·o′mer and the kings who were with him, the king of Sod′om went out to meet A′bram at the Valley* of Sha′veh, that is, the Valley of the King.^a 18 And Mel·chiz′e-dek^b king of Sa′lem^c brought out bread and wine; he was priest of the Most High God.^d

19 Then he blessed him and said:

"Blessed be A′bram by the Most High God,
Maker of heaven and earth;
20 And praised be the Most High God,
Who has handed your oppressors over to you!"

And A′bram gave him a tenth of everything.^e

21 After that the king of Sod′-om said to A′bram: "Give me the people,* but take the goods for yourself." 22 But A′bram said to the king of Sod′om: "I raise my hand in an oath to Jehovah the Most High God, Maker of heaven and earth, 23 that I will not take anything that is yours, from a thread to a sandal lace, so that you may not say, 'I made A′bram rich.' 24 I will take nothing except what the young men have already eaten. As for the share of the men who went with me, A′ner, Esh′col, and Mam′re^f—let them take their share."

15 After this the word of Jehovah came to A′bram in a vision, saying: "Do not fear,^g A′bram. I am a shield for you.^h Your reward will be very great."^i 2 A′bram replied: "Sovereign Lord Jehovah, what will you give me, seeing that I continue childless and the one who will inherit my house is a man of Damascus, E·li·e′zer?"^j 3 A′bram added: "You have given me no offspring,*^k and a member^# of my household is succeeding me as heir. 4 But look! Jehovah's

---

CHAP. 14
a Ge 14:1, 2
b Ge 14:16
c Ge 19:1
d Ge 13:18
e Ge 14:24
f Ge 11:27
g Jg 18:29

Second Col.
a 2Sa 18:18
b Ps 110:4
   Heb 6:20
c Heb 7:1, 2
d Ps 83:18
   Heb 5:5, 10
e Heb 7:4
f Ge 14:13

CHAP. 15
g Ps 27:1
   Isa 41:10
   Ro 8:31
   Heb 13:6
h De 33:29
   Pr 30:5
i Ge 17:5, 6
j Ge 24:2, 3
k Ge 12:7
   Ac 7:5

14:8, 10, 17 * Or "Low Plain." 14:13 * Or "dwelling in tents." 14:14 * Lit., "brother." 14:21 * Or "souls." 15:3 * Lit., "seed." # Lit., "son."

word in reply to him was, "This man will not succeed you as heir, but your own son* will succeed you as heir."[a]

5 He now brought him outside and said: "Look up, please, to the heavens and count the stars, if you are able to do so." Then he said to him: "So your offspring* will become."[b] **6** And he put faith in Jehovah,[c] and He counted* it to him as righteousness.[d] **7** Then he added: "I am Jehovah, who brought you out of Ur of the Chal·de′ans to give you this land as your possession."[e] **8** To this he said: "Sovereign Lord Jehovah, how will I know that I will take possession of it?" **9** He replied to him: "Take for me a three-year-old heifer, a three-year-old female goat, a three-year-old ram, a turtledove, and a young pigeon." **10** So he took all of these and cut them in two and put each part opposite the other,* but he did not cut up the birds. **11** Then the birds of prey began to descend on the carcasses, but A′bram kept driving them away.

12 When the sun was about to set, a deep sleep fell upon A′bram and a great and frightening darkness descended on him. **13** Then He said to A′bram: "Know for certain that your offspring* will be foreigners in a land not theirs and that the people there will enslave them and afflict them for 400 years.[f] **14** But I will judge the nation they will serve,[g] and after that they will go out with many goods.[h] **15** As for you, you will go to your forefathers in peace; you will be buried at a good old age.[a] **16** But they will return here[b] in the fourth generation, because the error of the Am′orites has not yet reached its full measure."[c]

17 When the sun had set and it had become very dark, a smoking furnace appeared, and a fiery torch passed between the pieces. **18** On that day Jehovah made with A′bram a covenant,[d] saying: "To your offspring* I will give this land,[e] from the river of Egypt to the great river, the river Eu·phra′tes:[f] **19** the land of the Ken′ites,[g] the Ken′iz·zites, the Kad′mon·ites, **20** the Hit′tites,[h] the Per′iz·zites,[i] the Reph′a·im,[j] **21** the Am′or·ites, the Ca′naan·ites, the Gir′ga·shites, and the Jeb′u·sites."[k]

16 Now A′bram's wife Sar′ai had borne him no children,[l] but she had an Egyptian servant whose name was Ha′gar.[m] **2** So Sar′ai said to A′bram: "Please now! Jehovah has prevented me from bearing children. Please, have relations with my servant. Perhaps I can have children by means of her."[n] So A′bram listened to what Sar′ai said. **3** After A′bram had lived for ten years in the land of Ca′naan, A′bram's wife Sar′ai took her Egyptian servant Ha′gar and gave her to her husband A′bram as his wife. **4** So he had relations with Ha′gar, and she became pregnant. When she realized that she was pregnant, she began to despise her mistress.

5 At this Sar′ai said to A′bram: "The injury done to me is your fault. I was the one who put my servant in your arms,* but when she realized that she was pregnant, she began to despise me. May Jehovah judge between me and you." **6** So A′bram said to Sar′ai: "Look! Your servant is under

CHAP. 15
a Ge 17:15, 16
Ge 21:12
b Ge 22:17
De 1:10
Ro 4:18
Heb 11:12
c Heb 11:8
d Ro 4:13, 22
Ga 3:6
Jas 2:23
e Ge 11:31
Ne 9:7
f Ge 21:9
Ex 1:13, 14
Ex 3:7
Ac 7:6, 7
g Ex 7:4
Nu 33:4
h Ex 3:22
Ps 105:37
Second Col.
a Ge 25:8
b Jos 14:1
Ac 7:7
c 1Ki 21:26
2Ki 21:11
d Ge 17:19
Ge 22:17
e Ex 3:8
f 1Ki 4:21
g 1Sa 15:6
h Jos 1:4
i Ex 3:17
j Jos 17:15
k De 7:1
CHAP. 16
l Ge 15:2, 3
m Ga 4:25
n Ge 30:1, 3

15:4 *Lit., "one who comes out of your inward parts." 15:5, 13, 18 *Lit., "seed." 15:6 *Or "credited." 15:10 *Or "put each part of them so as to match the other." 16:5 *Lit., "in your bosom."

your authority. Do to her whatever you think is best." Then Sar'ai humiliated her, and she ran away from her.

7 Later Jehovah's angel found her at a spring of waters in the wilderness, the spring on the way to Shur.[a] **8** And he said: "Ha'gar, servant of Sar'ai, where have you come from and where are you going?" To this she said: "I am running away from my mistress Sar'ai." **9** Jehovah's angel then said to her: "Return to your mistress and humble yourself under her hand." **10** Then Jehovah's angel said: "I will greatly multiply your offspring,* so that they will be too numerous to count."[b] **11** Jehovah's angel added: "Here you are pregnant, and you will give birth to a son, and you must name him Ish'ma·el,* for Jehovah has heard your affliction. **12** He will be a wild donkey* of a man. His hand will be against everyone, and everyone's hand will be against him, and he will dwell opposite all his brothers."[#]

13 Then she called on the name of Jehovah, who was speaking to her: "You are a God of sight,"[c] for she said: "Have I here actually looked upon the one who sees me?" **14** That is why the well was called Be'er-la'hai-ro'i.* (It is between Ka'desh and Be'red.) **15** So Ha'gar bore to A'bram a son, and A'bram named his son, whom Ha'gar bore, Ish'ma·el.[d] **16** A'bram was 86 years old when Ha'gar bore Ish'ma·el to him.

17 When A'bram was 99 years old, Jehovah appeared to A'bram and said to him: "I am God Almighty. Walk before me and prove yourself faultless.* **2** I will establish my covenant between me and you,[a] and I will multiply you very, very much."[b]

3 At this A'bram fell facedown, and God continued to speak with him, saying: **4** "As for me, look! my covenant is with you,[c] and you will certainly become a father of many nations.[d] **5** Your name will no longer be A'bram;* your name will become Abraham,[#] for I will make you a father of many nations. **6** I will make you very, very fruitful and will make you become nations, and kings will come from you.[e]

7 "And I will keep my covenant between me and you[f] and your offspring* after you throughout their generations for an everlasting covenant, to be God to you and to your offspring* after you. **8** And I will give to you and to your offspring* after you the land in which you lived as a foreigner[g]—the entire land of Ca'naan—for a lasting possession, and I will be their God."[h]

9 God said further to Abraham: "As for you, you are to keep my covenant, you and your offspring* after you throughout their generations. **10** This is my covenant between me and you, that you and your offspring* after you will keep: Every male among you must get circumcised.[i] **11** You must circumcise the flesh of your foreskins, and it will serve as a sign of the covenant between me and you.[j] **12** Throughout your generations, every male among you

---

CHAP. 16
a Ge 25:17, 18
  Ex 15:22

b Ge 17:20
  Ge 25:13-16
  1Ch 1:29-31

c Pr 15:3

d Ge 21:9
  Ga 4:22, 24

Second Col.

CHAP. 17
a Ge 15:18
  Ps 105:8-11

b Ge 22:17
  De 1:10
  Heb 11:11, 12

c Ps 105:9-11

d Ge 13:16
  Ro 4:17

e Ge 35:10, 11

f Lu 1:72, 73

g Ex 6:4
  Heb 11:8, 9

h De 14:2

i Ge 21:4
  Ro 2:29

j Ac 7:8
  Ro 4:11

16:10; 17:7-10 *Lit., "seed." **16:11** *Meaning "God Hears." **16:12** *Or "an onager," a kind of wild donkey, though some think that it refers to a zebra. Likely a reference to an independent disposition. #Or possibly, "and he will live in hostility to all his brothers." **16:14** *Meaning "Well of the Living One Who Sees Me."

17:1 *Or "blameless." **17:5** *Meaning "Father Is High (Exalted)." #Meaning "Father of a Crowd (Multitude); Father of Many."

eight days old must be circumcised,[a] anyone who is born in the house and anyone who is not one of your offspring* and who was purchased with money from a foreigner. 13 Every man born in your house and every man purchased with your money must be circumcised,[b] and my covenant in your flesh must serve as a lasting covenant. 14 If any uncircumcised male will not circumcise the flesh of his foreskin, that person* must be cut off# from his people. He has broken my covenant."

15 Then God said to Abraham: "As for your wife Sar'ai,*[c] you must not call her Sar'ai, because Sarah# will become her name. 16 I will bless her and also give you a son by her;[d] I will bless her and she will become nations; kings of peoples will come from her." 17 At this Abraham fell facedown and began to laugh and to say in his heart:[e] "Will a man 100 years old have a child born to him, and will Sarah, a woman 90 years old, give birth?"[f]

18 So Abraham said to the true God: "O that Ish'ma·el might live before you!"[g] 19 To this God said: "Your wife Sarah will definitely bear you a son, and you must name him Isaac.#[h] And I will establish my covenant with him for an everlasting covenant to his offspring* after him.[i] 20 But as regards Ish'ma·el, I have heard you. Look! I will bless him and will make him fruitful and will multiply him very, very much. He will produce 12 chieftains, and I will make him become a great nation.[j] 21 However, I will estab-

CHAP. 17
a Lu 2:21

b Ex 12:44

c Ge 11:29

d Ge 18:10

e Ge 18:12

f Ro 4:19
  Heb 11:11

g Ge 16:11

h Mt 1:2

i Ge 26:24

j Ge 16:10
  Ge 21:13, 18
  Ge 25:13-16
  1Ch 1:29-31

Second Col.
a Ge 26:3
  Heb 11:8, 9

b Ge 18:10, 14
  Ge 21:1

c Ge 17:13

d Ac 7:8
  Ro 4:11

e Ge 16:16

CHAP. 18
f Ge 16:7
  Jg 13:21

g Ge 13:18
  Ge 14:13

h Ge 19:1

i Ge 19:2
  Ge 24:32

lish my covenant with Isaac,[a] whom Sarah will bear to you at this appointed time next year."[b]

22 When God finished speaking with him, he went up from Abraham. 23 Abraham then took Ish'ma·el his son and all the men born in his house and everyone he had purchased with money, every male in the household of Abraham, and he circumcised the flesh of their foreskins on that very day, just as God had spoken with him.[c] 24 Abraham was 99 years old when he had the flesh of his foreskin circumcised.[d] 25 And Ish'ma·el his son was 13 years old when he had the flesh of his foreskin circumcised.[e] 26 On that very day, Abraham was circumcised and also his son Ish'ma·el. 27 All the men of his household, anyone born in the house and anyone purchased with money from a foreigner, were also circumcised with him.

18 Afterward, Jehovah[f] appeared to him among the big trees of Mam're[g] while he was sitting at the entrance of the tent during the hottest part of the day. 2 He looked up and saw three men standing some distance from him.[h] When he saw them, he ran from the entrance of the tent to meet them, and he bowed down to the ground. 3 Then he said: "Jehovah, if I have found favor in your eyes, please do not pass by your servant. 4 Please, let a little water be brought and have your feet washed;[i] then recline under the tree. 5 Seeing that you have come here to your servant, let me bring a piece of bread so that you may refresh yourselves.* Then you may go on your way." At this they said: "All right. You may do as you have spoken."

17:12, 19 *Lit., "seed." 17:14 *Or "soul." #Or "put to death." 17:15 *Possibly meaning "Contentious." #Meaning "Princess." 17:19 #Meaning "Laughter."

18:5 *Lit., "strengthen your heart."

6 So Abraham hurried to the tent to Sarah and said: "Quick! Get three measures* of fine flour, knead the dough, and make loaves of bread." **7** Next Abraham ran to the herd and chose a tender and good young bull. He gave it to the attendant, who hurried to prepare it. **8** He then took butter and milk and the young bull that he had prepared and set the food before them. Then he stood by them under the tree as they were eating.ª

9 They said to him: "Where is your wife Sarah?"ᵇ He replied: "Here in the tent." **10** So one of them continued: "I will surely return to you next year at this time, and look! your wife Sarah will have a son."ᶜ Now Sarah was listening at the tent entrance, which was behind the man. **11** Abraham and Sarah were old, being advanced in years.ᵈ Sarah was past the age of childbearing.*ᵉ **12** So Sarah began to laugh to herself, saying: "After I am worn out and my lord is old, will I really have this pleasure?"ᶠ **13** Then Jehovah said to Abraham: "Why did Sarah laugh and say, 'Am I really going to give birth even though I am old?' **14** Is anything too extraordinary for Jehovah?ᵍ I will return to you next year at this appointed time, and Sarah will have a son." **15** But Sarah denied it, saying, "I did not laugh!" for she was afraid. At this he said: "Yes! You did laugh."

16 When the men got up to leave and looked down toward Sod'om,ʰ Abraham was walking with them to escort them. **17** Jehovah said: "Am I keeping hidden from Abraham what I am going to do?ⁱ **18** Why, Abra-

---

ham is surely going to become a great and mighty nation, and all the nations of the earth will be blessed* by means of him.ª **19** For I have come to know him in order that he may command his sons and his household after him to keep Jehovah's way by doing what is right and just,ᵇ so that Jehovah may bring about what he has promised concerning Abraham."

20 Then Jehovah said: "The outcry against Sod'om and Gomor'rah is indeed great,ᶜ and their sin is very heavy.ᵈ **21** I will go down to see whether they are acting according to the outcry that has reached me. And if not, I can get to know it."ᵉ

22 Then the men left from there and went toward Sod'om, but Jehovahᶠ remained with Abraham. **23** Then Abraham approached and said: "Will you really sweep away the righteous with the wicked?ᵍ **24** Suppose there are 50 righteous men within the city. Will you, then, sweep them away and not pardon the place for the sake of the 50 righteous who are inside it? **25** It is unthinkable that you would act in this manner by putting the righteous man to death with the wicked one so that the outcome for the righteous man and the wicked is the same!ʰ It is unthinkable of you.ⁱ Will the Judge of all the earth not do what is right?"ʲ **26** Then Jehovah said: "If I find in Sod'om 50 righteous men in the city, I will pardon the whole place for their sake." **27** But Abraham again responded: "Please, here I have presumed to speak to Jehovah, whereas I am dust and ashes. **28** Suppose the 50 righteous should lack five. Because of the five will you destroy the whole

---

18:6 *Lit., "seah measures." A seah equaled 7.33 L (6.66 dry qt). See App. B14. 18:11 *Lit., "The way according to women had ceased for Sarah."

18:18 *Or "will obtain a blessing for themselves."

CHAP. 18

a Heb 13:2

b Ge 17:15

c Ge 17:21
Ge 21:2
Ro 9:9

d Ge 17:17

e Ro 4:19

f Heb 11:11
1Pe 3:6

g Isa 40:29
Mt 19:26
Lu 1:36, 37

h Ge 13:12

i Ps 25:14
Am 3:7

Second Col.

a Ge 12:1-3
Ga 3:14

b De 4:9

c 2Pe 2:7, 8

d Ge 13:13
Jude 7

e Ge 11:5
Ex 3:7, 8
Ps 14:2

f Ge 31:11
Ge 32:30

g Nu 16:22

h Ps 37:10, 11
Pr 29:16
Mal 3:18
Mt 13:49

i De 32:4

j Job 34:12
Isa 33:22

city?" To this he said: "I will not destroy it if I find there 45."[a]

29 But yet again he spoke to him and said: "Suppose 40 are found there." He answered: "I will not do it for the sake of the 40." **30** But he continued: "Jehovah, please, do not become hot with anger,[b] but let me go on speaking: Suppose only 30 are found there." He answered: "I will not do it if I find 30 there." **31** But he continued: "Please, here I have presumed to speak to Jehovah: Suppose only 20 are found there." He answered: "I will not destroy it for the sake of the 20." **32** Finally he said: "Jehovah, please, do not become hot with anger, but let me speak just once more: Suppose only ten are found there." He answered: "I will not destroy it for the sake of the ten." **33** When Jehovah finished speaking to Abraham, he went his way[c] and Abraham returned to his place.

19 The two angels arrived at Sod'om by evening, and Lot was sitting in the gate of Sod'om. When Lot saw them, he got up to meet them and bowed down with his face to the earth.[d] **2** And he said: "Please, my lords, turn aside, please, into the house of your servant and stay overnight and have your feet washed. Then you may get up early and travel on your way." To this they said: "No, we will stay overnight in the public square." **3** But he was so insistent with them that they went with him to his house. Then he made a feast for them, and he baked unleavened bread, and they ate.

4 Before they could lie down to sleep, the men of the city—the men of Sod'om from boy to old man, all of them—surrounded the house in one mob. **5** And they kept calling out to Lot and saying to him: "Where are the men who came in to you tonight?

Bring them out to us so that we may have sex with them."[a]

6 Then Lot went out to them to the doorway, and he shut the door behind him. **7** He said: "Please, my brothers, do not act wickedly. **8** Please, here I have two daughters who have never had sexual relations with a man. Please, let me bring them out to you for you to do to them whatever seems good to you. But do not do anything to these men, for they have come under the shelter* of my roof."[b] **9** At this they said: "Stand back!" And they added: "This lone foreigner came to live here, and yet he dares to judge us! Now we are going to do worse to you than to them." And they crowded in* on Lot and moved forward to break down the door. **10** So the men reached out their hands and brought Lot into the house with them, and they shut the door. **11** But they struck the men who were at the entrance of the house with blindness, from the least to the greatest, so that they wore themselves out trying to find the doorway.

12 Then the men said to Lot: "Do you have anyone else here? Sons-in-law, your sons, your daughters, and all your people in the city, bring out of this place! **13** For we are going to destroy this place, because the outcry against them has indeed grown great* before Jehovah,[c] so that Jehovah sent us to destroy the city." **14** So Lot went out and began to speak to his sons-in-law who were to marry his daughters, and he kept saying: "Get up! Get out of this place, because Jehovah will destroy the city!" But to his sons-in-law, he seemed to be joking.[d]

CHAP. 18
a Nu 14:18
Ps 86:15

b Ex 34:6

c Ge 18:2, 22

CHAP. 19
d Ge 18:2, 22

Second Col.
a Jude 7

b Jg 19:23, 24

c Ge 13:13
Ge 18:20

d Lu 17:28

19:8 *Or "protection." Lit., "shadow." 19:9 *Or "pressed heavily." 19:13 *Or "loud."

15 As dawn was breaking, the angels became urgent with Lot, saying: "Get up! Take your wife and your two daughters who are here with you, so that you will not be swept away in the error of the city!"[a] **16** When he kept lingering, then because of Jehovah's compassion for him,[b] the men seized hold of his hand and the hand of his wife and the hands of his two daughters, and they brought him out and stationed him outside the city.[c] **17** As soon as they had brought them to the outskirts, he said: "Escape for your life!* Do not look behind you[d] and do not stand still in any part of the district![e] Escape to the mountainous region so that you may not be swept away!"

18 Then Lot said to them: "Not there, please, Jehovah! **19** Please, now, your servant has found favor in your eyes and you are showing great kindness* to me by preserving me# alive,[f] but I am not able to flee to the mountainous region because I am afraid that disaster may overtake me and I will die.[g] **20** Please, now, this town is nearby and I can flee there; it is only a small place. May I, please, escape there? It is only a small place. Then I will survive."* **21** So he said to him: "Very well, I will also show you consideration[h] by not overthrowing the town you speak of.[i] **22** Hurry! Escape there, because I cannot do anything until you arrive there!"[j] That is why he named the town Zo'ar.*[k]

23 The sun had risen over the land when Lot arrived at Zo'ar. **24** Then Jehovah made it rain sulfur and fire on Sod'om and Go·mor'rah—it came from Jehovah,

vah, from the heavens.[a] **25** So he overthrew these cities, yes, the entire district, including all the inhabitants of the cities and the plants of the ground.[b] **26** But Lot's wife, who was behind him, began to look back, and she became a pillar of salt.[c]

27 Now Abraham got up early in the morning and went to the place where he had stood before Jehovah.[d] **28** When he looked down toward Sod'om and Go·mor'rah and all the land of the district, he saw quite a sight. There was dense smoke rising from the land like the dense smoke of a kiln![e] **29** So when God destroyed the cities of the district, God kept Abraham in mind by sending Lot out from the cities he overthrew, the cities where Lot had been dwelling.[f]

30 Later Lot went up from Zo'ar with his two daughters and began living in the mountainous region,[g] because he was afraid to live in Zo'ar.[h] So he began living in a cave with his two daughters. **31** And the firstborn said to the younger: "Our father is old, and there is not a man in the land to have relations with us according to the custom of the whole earth. **32** Come, let us give our father wine to drink, and let us lie down with him and preserve offspring from our father."

33 So that night they kept giving their father wine to drink; then the firstborn went in and lay down with her father, but he did not know when she lay down and when she got up. **34** Then on the next day, the firstborn said to the younger: "Here I lay down with my father last night. Let us give him wine to drink tonight also. Then you go in and lie down with him, and let us preserve offspring from our father." **35** So that night also, they repeatedly gave their father wine

---

CHAP. 19
a Lu 17:29-31
b Ex 33:19
c 2Pe 2:7-9
d Lu 9:62
e Ge 13:10
f Ps 143:11
g Ps 6:4
h Ps 34:15
i Ge 19:30
  Ps 68:20
j 2Pe 3:9
k Ge 14:2

Second Col.
a De 29:23
  Lu 17:29
  2Pe 2:6
b Ge 13:10
c Lu 17:32
  Heb 10:38
d Ge 18:2, 22
e Jude 7
f 2Pe 2:7, 8
g Ge 19:17
h Ge 19:20, 22

19:17 *Or "soul." 19:19 *Or "loyal love." #Or "my soul." 19:20 *Or "my soul will live on." 19:22 *Meaning "Smallness."

to drink; then the younger went and lay down with him, but he did not know when she lay down and when she got up. **36** So both daughters of Lot became pregnant by their father. **37** The firstborn gave birth to a son and named him Mo′ab.ᵃ He is the father of the Mo′ab·ites of today.ᵇ **38** The younger also gave birth to a son, and she named him Ben-am′mi. He is the father of the Am′mon·itesᶜ of today.

20 Now Abraham moved his camp from thereᵈ to the land of the Neg′eb and began dwelling between Ka′deshᵉ and Shur.ᶠ While he was residing* at Ge′rar,ᵍ **2** Abraham repeated concerning his wife Sarah: "She is my sister."ʰ So A·bim′e·lech king of Ge′rar sent for Sarah and took her.ⁱ **3** Afterward, God came by night to A·bim′e·lech in a dream and said to him: "Here you are as good as dead because of the woman whom you have taken,ʲ since she is married and belongs to another man."ᵏ **4** However, A·bim′e·lech had not gone near her.* So he said: "Jehovah, will you kill a nation that is really innocent?ᵏ **5** Did he not say to me, 'She is my sister,' and did she too not say, 'He is my brother'? I did this with an honest heart and innocent hands." **6** Then the true God said to him in the dream: "I know that you did this with an honest heart, so I held you back from sinning against me. That is why I did not allow you to touch her. **7** Now return the man's wife, for he is a prophet,ˡ and he will make supplication for youᵐ and you will keep living. But if you are not returning her, know that you will surely die, you and all who are yours."

8 A·bim′e·lech got up early in the morning and called all his servants and told them all these things, and they became very frightened. **9** Then A·bim′e·lech called Abraham and said to him: "What have you done to us? What sin have I committed against you that you would bring upon me and my kingdom such a great sin? What you have done to me was not right." **10** And A·bim′e·lech went on to say to Abraham: "What were your intentions when you did this thing?"ᵃ **11** Abraham said: "It was because I said to myself, 'Surely there is no fear of God in this place, and they will kill me because of my wife.'ᵇ **12** And besides, she really is my sister, the daughter of my father but not the daughter of my mother, and she became my wife.ᶜ **13** So when God caused me to wander from the house of my father,ᵈ I said to her: 'Let this be how you show loyal love to me: Everywhere we go, say of me, "He is my brother."'"ᵉ

14 A·bim′e·lech then took sheep and cattle and male and female servants and gave them to Abraham, and he returned his wife Sarah to him. **15** A·bim′e·lech also said: "Here my land is available to you. Dwell wherever you please." **16** And to Sarah he said: "Here I give 1,000 pieces of silver to your brother.ᶠ It is a sign of your innocence* to all who are with you and before everybody, and you are cleared of reproach." **17** And Abraham began to make supplication to the true God, and God healed A·bim′e·lech and his wife and his slave girls, and they began having children; **18** for Jehovah had made all the women of the house of A·bim′e·lech

---

CHAP. 19
a De 2:9

b 1Ch 18:2

c De 2:19
Jg 11:4
Ne 13:1
Zep 2:9

CHAP. 20
d Ge 13:18

e Nu 13:26

f Ge 25:17, 18

g Ge 10:19
Ge 26:6

h Ge 12:11-13
Ge 20:11, 12

i Ge 12:15

j Ge 12:17
Ps 105:14

k De 22:22

l Ps 105:14, 15

m Job 42:8

Second Col.
a Ge 12:18, 19
Ge 26:9, 10

b Ge 12:11, 12
Ge 26:7

c Ge 11:29

d Ge 12:1

e Ge 12:13

f Ge 20:2, 12

20:1 *Or "living as a foreigner." 20:4 *That is, he had not had sexual relations with her. #Or "righteous."

20:16 *Lit., "Look, it is for you a covering of the eyes."

barren* because of Sarah, Abraham's wife.[a]

21 Jehovah turned his attention to Sarah just as he had said, and Jehovah did for Sarah what he had promised.[b] 2 So Sarah became pregnant[c] and then bore a son to Abraham in his old age at the appointed time God had promised him.[d] 3 Abraham named his newborn son, whom Sarah bore to him, Isaac.[e] 4 And Abraham circumcised his son Isaac when he was eight days old, just as God had commanded him.[f] 5 Abraham was 100 years old when his son Isaac was born to him. 6 Then Sarah said: "God has brought me laughter; everybody hearing of it will laugh with me."* 7 And she added: "Who would have said to Abraham, 'Sarah will certainly nurse children'? Yet, I have given birth to a son for him in his old age."

8 Now the child grew and was weaned, and Abraham prepared a big feast on the day that Isaac was weaned. 9 But Sarah kept noticing that the son of Ha′gar[g] the Egyptian, whom she had borne to Abraham, was mocking Isaac.[h] 10 So she said to Abraham: "Drive out this slave girl and her son, for the son of this slave girl is not going to be an heir along with my son, with Isaac!"[i] 11 But what she said about his son was very displeasing to Abraham.[j] 12 Then God said to Abraham: "Do not be displeased by what Sarah is saying to you about the boy and about your slave girl. Listen to her,* for what will be called your offspring* will be through Isaac.[k] 13 As for the son of the slave girl,[l] I will also make a nation out

of him,[a] because he is your offspring."#

14 So Abraham got up early in the morning and took bread and a skin bottle of water and gave it to Ha′gar. He set these on her shoulder and then sent her away along with the boy.[b] So she departed and wandered about in the wilderness of Be′er-she′ba.[c] 15 Finally the water in the skin bottle was used up, and she pushed the boy under one of the bushes. 16 Then she went on and sat down by herself, about the distance of a bowshot away, because she said: "I do not want to watch the boy die." So she sat down at a distance and began to cry aloud and to weep.

17 At that God heard the voice of the boy,[d] and God's angel called to Ha′gar from the heavens and said to her:[e] "What is the matter with you, Ha′gar? Do not be afraid, for God has heard the voice of the boy there where he is. 18 Get up, lift the boy and take hold of him with your hand, for I will make him a great nation."[f] 19 Then God opened her eyes and she saw a well of water, and she went and filled the skin bottle with water and gave the boy a drink. 20 And God was with the boy[g] as he grew up. He lived in the wilderness and became an archer. 21 He took up dwelling in the wilderness of Pa′ran,[h] and his mother took a wife for him from the land of Egypt.

22 At that time A·bim′e·lech together with Phi′col the chief of his army said to Abraham: "God is with you in everything you are doing.[i] 23 So now swear to me here by God that you will not deal falsely with me and with my offspring and with my descendants, and that you will deal with me and with the land where you have been residing with the same loyal love that I

CHAP. 20
a Ge 12:17

CHAP. 21
b Ge 18:10

c Heb 11:11

d Ge 17:21
  Ge 18:10, 14
  Ro 9:9

e Ge 17:19
  Jos 24:3
  Ro 9:7

f Ge 17:12
  Le 12:3
  Ac 7:8

g Ge 16:4, 15

h Ge 15:13
  Ga 4:22, 29

i Ge 15:2, 4
  Ga 4:30

j Ge 17:18

k Ge 17:19
  Ro 9:7
  Heb 11:18

l Ga 4:22

Second Col.
a Ge 16:9, 10
  Ge 17:20
  Ge 25:12, 16

b Ge 25:5, 6

c Ge 22:19

d Ge 16:11

e Ge 16:7, 8

f 1Ch 1:29-31

g Ge 16:16

h Nu 10:12

i Ge 20:17, 18
  Ge 26:26, 28

20:18 * Or "had completely closed every womb of the house of Abimelech." 21:6 *Or possibly, "laugh at me." 21:12 *Lit., "to her voice." 21:12, 13 #Lit., "seed."

have shown you."[a] **24** So Abraham said: "I swear to this."

25 However, Abraham complained to A·bim′e·lech about the well of water that the servants of A·bim′e·lech had violently seized.[b] **26** A·bim′e·lech replied: "I do not know who did this; you did not tell me about it, and I heard nothing about it until today." **27** At that Abraham took sheep and cattle and gave them to A·bim′e·lech, and the two of them made a covenant. **28** When Abraham set seven female lambs apart from the flock by themselves, **29** A·bim′e·lech said to Abraham: "Why have you set these seven female lambs here by themselves?" **30** Then he said: "You are to accept the seven female lambs from my hand as a witness that I dug this well." **31** That is why he called that place Be′er-she′ba,*[c] because there both of them had taken an oath. **32** So they made a covenant[d] at Be′er-she′ba, after which A·bim′e·lech got up together with Phi′col the chief of his army, and they returned to the land of the Phi·lis′tines.[e] **33** After that he planted a tamarisk tree at Be′er-she′ba, and there he called on the name of Jehovah,[f] the everlasting God.[g] **34** And Abraham stayed* in the land of the Phi·lis′tines for a long time.*[h]

22 Now after this the true God put Abraham to the test,[i] and he said to him: "Abraham!" to which he replied: "Here I am!" **2** Then he said: "Take, please, your son, your only son whom you so love,[j] Isaac,[k] and travel to the land of Mo·ri′ah[l] and offer him up there as a burnt offering on one of the mountains that I will designate to you."

3 So Abraham got up early in the morning and saddled his donkey and took two of his servants along with him and his son Isaac. He split the wood for the burnt offering, and then he rose and traveled to the place that the true God indicated to him. **4** On the third day, Abraham looked up and saw the place from a distance. **5** Abraham now said to his servants: "You stay here with the donkey, but the boy and I will go over there and worship and return to you."

6 So Abraham took the wood for the burnt offering and put it on his son Isaac. Then he took in his hands the fire and the knife,* and the two of them walked on together. **7** Then Isaac said to his father Abraham: "My father!" He replied: "Yes, my son!" So he continued: "Here are the fire and the wood, but where is the sheep for the burnt offering?" **8** To this Abraham said: "God himself will provide the sheep for the burnt offering,[a] my son." And both of them walked on together.

9 Finally they reached the place that the true God had indicated to him, and Abraham built an altar there and arranged the wood on it. He bound his son Isaac hand and foot and put him on the altar on top of the wood.[b] **10** Then Abraham reached out his hand and took the knife* to kill his son.[c] **11** But Jehovah's angel called to him from the heavens and said: "Abraham, Abraham!" to which he answered: "Here I am!" **12** Then he said: "Do not harm the boy, and do not do anything at all to him, for now I do know that you are God-fearing because you have not withheld your

---

CHAP. 21
a Ge 20:14, 15

b Ge 26:15, 20

c Ge 26:32, 33

d Ge 26:26, 28

e Ge 10:13, 14
  Ge 26:1

f Ge 12:8, 9
  Ge 26:25

g Ps 90:2
  Isa 40:28
  1Ti 1:17

h Heb 11:8, 9

CHAP. 22
i Heb 11:17

j Joh 3:16

k Ge 17:19
  Jos 24:3
  Ro 9:7

l 2Ch 3:1

Second Col.
a Joh 1:29
  1Pe 1:18, 19

b Joh 10:17, 18

c Heb 11:17

21:31 *Meaning "Well of the Oath; Well of Seven." **21:34** *Or "resided as a foreigner." #Lit., "many days."

22:6, 10 *Or "slaughtering knife."

son, your only one, from me."ᵉ
13 At that Abraham looked up, and there just beyond him was a ram caught by its horns in a thicket. So Abraham went and took the ram and offered it up as a burnt offering in place of his son. **14** And Abraham named that place Je·ho'vah-ji'reh.* This is why it is still said today: "In the mountain of Jehovah it will be provided."ᵇ

15 And Jehovah's angel called to Abraham a second time from the heavens, **16** saying: "'By myself I swear,' declares Jehovah,ᶜ 'that because you have done this and you have not withheld your son, your only one,ᵈ **17** I will surely bless you and I will surely multiply your offspring* like the stars of the heavens and like the grains of sand on the seashore,ᵉ and your offspring* will take possession of the gate* of his enemies.ᶠ **18** And by means of your offspring*ᵍ all nations of the earth will obtain a blessing for themselves because you have listened to my voice.'"ʰ

19 After that Abraham returned to his servants, and they got up and went back together to Be'er·she'ba;ⁱ and Abraham continued to dwell at Be'er·she'ba.

20 After this it was reported to Abraham: "Here Mil'cah has also borne sons to Na'hor your brother:ʲ **21** Uz his firstborn, Buz his brother, Kem·u'el the father of A'ram, **22** Che'sed, Ha'zo, Pil'dash, Jid'laph, and Be·thu'el.ᵏ **23** Be·thu'el became the father of Re·bek'ah.ˡ Mil'cah bore these eight to Na'hor the brother of Abraham. **24** His concubine, whose name was Reu'mah, also bore sons: Te'bah, Ga'ham, Ta'hash, and Ma'a·cah.

23 And Sarah lived for 127 years; these were the years of Sarah's life.ᵃ **2** So Sarah died in Kir'i·ath-ar'ba,ᵇ that is, Heb'ron,ᶜ in the land of Ca'naan,ᵈ and Abraham began to mourn and to weep over Sarah. **3** Then Abraham got up from before his dead wife and he said to the sons of Heth:ᵉ **4** "I am a foreigner and settler among you.ᶠ Give me a property to serve as a burial place in your midst so that I may remove my dead for burial." **5** At this the sons of Heth answered Abraham: **6** "Hear us, my lord. You are a chieftain of God* among us.ᵍ You may bury your dead in the choicest of our burial places. None of us will hold back his burial place from you to prevent you from burying your dead."

7 So Abraham got up and bowed down to the people of the land, to the sons of Heth,ʰ **8** and said to them: "If you* agree to let me remove my dead for burial, then listen to me and urge E'phron the son of Zo'har **9** to sell me the cave of Mach·pe'lah, which belongs to him; it is at the edge of his field. Let him sell it to me in your presence for the full amount of silverⁱ so that I may have a property for a burial place."ʲ

10 Now E'phron was sitting among the sons of Heth. So E'phron the Hit'tite answered Abraham in the hearing of the sons of Heth, and before all who entered the gate of his city,ᵏ saying: **11** "No, my lord! Listen to me. I give you both the field and the cave that is in it. In the presence of the sons of my people, I give it to you. Bury your dead." **12** At that Abraham bowed down before the people of the land **13** and spoke to

---

CHAP. 22
a Heb 11:17-19
Jas 2:21

b Ge 22:2
2Ch 3:1

c Heb 6:13,14

d Joh 3:16
Ro 8:32
Heb 11:17

e Ge 13:14, 16
Ge 15:1, 5
Ac 3:25

f Ps 2:8
Da 2:44

g Ge 3:15
Ro 9:7
Ga 3:16

h Ga 3:8

i Ge 21:31

j Ge 11:26, 29

k Ge 25:20

l Ge 24:15
Ro 9:10

Second Col.

CHAP. 23
a Ge 17:17

b Jos 14:15

c Ge 35:27
Nu 13:22

d Ge 12:5

e Ge 10:15

f Ge 17:1, 8
Heb 11:9, 13

g Ge 21:22

h 1Ch 1:13

i Ge 23:15

j Ge 25:9, 10
Ge 49:29-33
Ge 50:13, 14

k Ru 4:1

22:14 *Meaning "Jehovah Will Provide; Jehovah Will See to It." 22:17, 18 *Lit., "seed." 22:17 *Or "the cities."

23:6 *Or possibly, "a great chieftain." 23:8 *Or "your souls."

E'phron in the hearing of the people, saying: "Listen to me, if you will! I will give you the full amount of silver for the field. Take it from me, in order that I may bury my dead there."

14 Then E'phron answered Abraham: **15** "My lord, listen to me. This land is worth 400 silver shekels,* but what is that between me and you? So bury your dead." **16** Abraham listened to E'phron, and Abraham weighed out to E'phron the amount of silver that he had mentioned in the hearing of the sons of Heth, 400 silver shekels* according to the weight accepted by the merchants.[a] **17** Thus the field of E'phron in Mach·pe'lah, which was in front of Mam're—the field and the cave in it and all the trees within the boundaries of the field—became confirmed as **18** Abraham's purchased property in the presence of the sons of Heth, before all those entering the gate of his city. **19** After that Abraham buried his wife Sarah in the cave of the field of Mach·pe'lah in front of Mam're, that is, Heb'ron, in the land of Ca'naan. **20** Thus the field and the cave that was in it were transferred by the sons of Heth to Abraham as property for a burial place.[b]

24 Abraham was now old, advanced in years, and Jehovah had blessed Abraham in everything.[c] **2** Abraham said to his servant, the oldest one of his household, who was managing all he had:[d] "Please put your hand under my thigh, **3** and I will make you swear by Jehovah, the God of the heavens and the God of the earth, that you will not take a wife for my son from the daughters of the Ca'naanites, among whom I am dwell-

ing.[a] **4** You must go instead to my country and to my relatives[b] and take a wife for my son, for Isaac."

5 However, the servant said to him: "What if the woman is not willing to come with me to this land? Must I then return your son to the land from which you came?"[c] **6** At this Abraham said to him: "See that you do not take my son there.[d] **7** Jehovah the God of the heavens, who took me from my father's house and from the land of my relatives[e] and who spoke with me and swore to me:[f] 'To your offspring*[g] I am going to give this land,'[h] he will send his angel ahead of you,[i] and you will certainly take a wife for my son from there.[j] **8** But if the woman is unwilling to come with you, you will be free from this oath. But you must not take my son there." **9** With that the servant put his hand under the thigh of Abraham his master and swore to him concerning this matter.[k]

10 So the servant took ten of his master's camels and departed, taking along all sorts of good things from his master. Then he went on his way to Mes·o·po·ta'mi·a, to the city of Na'hor. **11** He had the camels kneel down at a well of water outside the city. It was about evening, the time when the women would go out to draw water. **12** Then he said: "Jehovah the God of my master Abraham, please grant me success this day, and show your loyal love to my master Abraham. **13** Here I am standing at a spring of water, and the daughters of the men of the city are coming out to draw water. **14** May it happen that the young woman to whom I say, 'Please let down your water jar so that I may take a drink,' and who

---

CHAP. 23
a Ac 7:15, 16

b Ge 25:9, 10
Ge 49:29-33
Ge 50:13, 14

CHAP. 24
c Ge 13:2

d Ge 15:2, 3

Second Col.
a Ge 28:1
De 7:1, 3
2Co 6:14

b Ge 22:20-23

c Ge 11:27, 28
Ge 15:7

d Heb 11:15

e Ge 12:1
Heb 11:8

f Mic 7:20
Lu 1:72, 73
Heb 6:13, 14

g Heb 11:18

h Ge 13:14, 15
Ge 26:3, 4
De 34:4
Ac 7:4, 5

i Heb 1:7, 14

j Ge 12:5

k Ge 24:2, 3

23:15, 16 *A shekel equaled 11.4 g (0.367 oz t). See App. B14.

24:7 *Lit., "seed."

replies, 'Take a drink, and I will also water your camels,' let this be the one you choose for your servant Isaac; and by this let me know that you have shown your loyal love to my master."

15 Even before he finished speaking, Re·bek'ah, who was the daughter of Be·thu'el[a] the son of Mil'cah[b] the wife of Na'hor,[c] Abraham's brother, came out with her water jar on her shoulder. **16** Now the young woman was very beautiful, a virgin; no man had had sexual relations with her. She went down to the spring, filled her water jar, and then came back up. **17** At once the servant ran to meet her and said: "Please give me a little sip of water from your jar." **18** In turn she said: "Drink, my lord." With that she quickly lowered her jar upon her hand and gave him a drink. **19** When she finished giving him a drink, she said: "I will also draw water for your camels until they are done drinking." **20** So she quickly emptied her jar into the drinking trough and ran again and again to the well to draw water, and she kept drawing water for all his camels. **21** The whole time the man silently stared at her in amazement, wondering whether Jehovah had made his trip successful or not.

22 When the camels had finished drinking, the man took out for her a gold nose ring weighing a half shekel* and two bracelets of gold weighing ten shekels,* **23** and he said: "Please tell me, whose daughter are you? Is there any room at your father's house for us to spend the night?" **24** At that she said to him: "I am the daughter of Be·thu'el[d] the son of Mil'cah, whom she bore to Na'hor."[e] **25** And she added: "We have both straw and

much fodder and also a place to spend the night." **26** Then the man bowed down and prostrated himself before Jehovah **27** and said: "May Jehovah be praised, the God of my master Abraham, for he has not abandoned his loyal love and his faithfulness toward my master. Jehovah has guided me to the house of the brothers of my master."

28 And the young woman ran to tell her mother's household about these things. **29** Now Re·bek'ah had a brother whose name was La'ban.[a] So La'ban ran to the man who was outside at the spring. **30** When he saw the nose ring and the bracelets on the hands of his sister and heard the words of his sister Re·bek'ah, who was saying, "This is the way the man spoke to me," he came to meet the man, who was still there standing by the camels at the spring. **31** At once he said: "Come, you who are blessed by Jehovah. Why do you keep standing out here? I have made the house ready and a place for the camels." **32** With that the man came into the house, and he* unharnessed the camels and gave straw and fodder to the camels and water to wash his feet and the feet of the men who were with him. **33** However, when something to eat was set before him, he said: "I will not eat until I have told you what I have to say." So La'ban said: "Speak!"

34 Then he said: "I am Abraham's servant.[b] **35** And Jehovah has blessed my master very much, and he has made him very wealthy by giving him sheep and cattle, silver and gold, male and female servants, and camels and donkeys.[c] **36** Further, Sarah the wife of my master bore a son to my master after she grew old,[d] and he will give him

---

CHAP. 24
a Ge 22:23

b Ge 11:29

c Ge 11:26

d Ge 22:23

e Ge 11:29

Second Col.
a Ge 25:20
　Ge 29:10

b Ge 15:2, 3

c Ge 12:15, 16
　Ge 13:2
　Ge 24:1

d Ge 21:1, 2
　Ro 4:19
　Heb 11:11

24:22 *A shekel equaled 11.4 g (0.367 oz t). See App. B14.

24:32 *Probably referring to Laban.

everything he has.[a] **37** So my master made me swear, saying: 'You must not take a wife for my son from the daughters of the Ca'naan·ites, in whose land I am dwelling.[b] **38** No, but you will go to the house of my father and to my family,[c] and you must take a wife for my son.'[d] **39** But I said to my master: 'What if the woman is unwilling to come with me?'[e] **40** He said to me: 'Jehovah, before whom I have walked,[f] will send his angel[g] with you and will certainly give success to your journey, and you must take a wife for my son from my family and from the house of my father.[h] **41** You will be released from your oath to me if you go to my family and they will not give her to you. This will release you from your oath.'[i]

42 "When I got to the spring today, I said: 'Jehovah the God of my master Abraham, if you will make my journey successful, **43** here I am standing at a spring. What must take place is that when a young woman comes out to draw water, I will say, "Please, let me drink a little water from your jar," **44** and she will say to me, "You take a drink, and I will also draw water for your camels." Let that woman be the one whom Jehovah has chosen for the son of my master.'[k]

45 "Before I was finished speaking in my heart, there was Re·bek'ah coming out with her jar on her shoulder, and she made her way down to the spring and began to draw water. Then I said to her: 'Give me a drink, please.'[l] **46** So she quickly lowered her jar from her shoulder and said: 'Take a drink,[m] and I will also water your camels.' Then I took a drink, and she also watered the camels. **47** After that I asked her, 'Whose daughter are you?' to which she re-

plied, 'The daughter of Be·thu'el the son of Na'hor, whom Mil'cah bore to him.' So I put the ring on her nose and the bracelets on her hands.[a] **48** And I bowed down and prostrated myself before Jehovah and praised Jehovah the God of my master Abraham,[b] who had led me on the right path to take the daughter of the brother of my master for his son. **49** And now tell me if you wish to show loyal love and faithfulness toward my master; but if not, tell me, so that I may proceed one way or the other."*[c]

50 Then La'ban and Be·thu'el answered: "This is from Jehovah. We are not able to say yes or no to you.* **51** Here is Re·bek'ah before you. Take her and go, and let her become a wife to the son of your master, just as Jehovah has spoken." **52** When Abraham's servant heard their words, he at once bowed down on the ground before Jehovah. **53** And the servant began to bring out articles of silver and of gold and garments and to give them to Re·bek'ah, and he gave valuable things to her brother and to her mother. **54** After that he and the men with him ate and drank, and they spent the night there.

When he got up in the morning, he said: "Send me off to my master." **55** To this her brother and her mother said: "Let the young woman stay with us at least ten days. Then she can go." **56** But he said to them: "Do not detain me, seeing that Jehovah has made my journey successful. Send me off, in order that I may go to my master." **57** So they said: "Let us call the young woman and inquire of her." **58** They called Re·bek'ah and said to her:

CHAP. 24

a Ge 25:5

b Ge 24:2, 3
Ge 28:1

c Ge 22:20-23

d Ge 24:4

e Ge 24:5

f Ge 48:15

g Heb 1:7, 14

h Ge 11:25

i Ge 24:9

j Ge 24:16

k Ge 24:14

l Ge 24:15, 17

m Ge 24:18

Second Col.

a Ge 24:22, 23

b Ge 24:27

c Ge 24:8

24:49 *Lit., "turn to the right hand or to the left." 24:50 *Or "We are unable to speak bad or good to you."

"Will you go with this man?" She replied: "I am willing to go."

59 So they sent off their sister Re·bek'ah[a] and her nurse*[b] and Abraham's servant and his men. 60 And they blessed Rebek'ah and said to her: "Our sister, may you become thousands times ten thousand,* and let your offspring# take possession of the gate△ of those who hate them."[c] 61 Then Re·bek'ah and her female attendants rose, got on the camels, and followed the man. So the servant took Re·bek'ah and went on his way.

62 Now Isaac had come from the direction of Be'er-la'hai-roi,[d] for he was dwelling in the land of the Neg'eb.[e] 63 And Isaac was out walking in the field about nightfall to meditate.[f] When he looked up, why, he saw that camels were coming! 64 When Re·bek'ah looked up, she caught sight of Isaac, and she quickly got down from the camel. 65 Then she asked the servant: "Who is that man there walking in the field to meet us?" And the servant said: "It is my master." So she took her veil to cover herself. 66 And the servant told Isaac all the things he had done. 67 After that Isaac brought her into the tent of Sarah his mother.[g] Thus he took Re·bek'ah as his wife; and he fell in love with her,[h] and Isaac found comfort after the loss of his mother.[i]

25 Now Abraham again took a wife, and her name was Ke·tu'rah. 2 In time she bore him Zim'ran, Jok'shan, Me'dan, Mid'i·an,[j] Ish'bak, and Shu'ah.[k]

3 Jok'shan became father to She'ba and De'dan.

The sons of De'dan were As·shu'rim, Le·tu'shim, and Le·um'mim.

4 The sons of Mid'i·an were E'phah, E'pher, Ha'noch, A·bi'da, and El·da'ah.

All of these were the sons of Ke·tu'rah.

5 Later on Abraham gave everything he had to Isaac,[a] 6 but Abraham gave gifts to his sons by his concubines. Then while he was still alive, he sent them eastward, away from Isaac his son,[b] to the land of the East.

7 The years of Abraham's life were 175 years. 8 Then Abraham breathed his last and died at a good old age, old and satisfied, and was gathered to his people.* 9 His sons Isaac and Ish'ma·el buried him in the cave of Mach·pe'lah in the field of E'phron the son of Zo'har the Hit'tite that is in front of Mam're,[c] 10 the field that Abraham had purchased from the sons of Heth. There Abraham was buried, with his wife Sarah.[d] 11 After Abraham's death, God continued to bless his son Isaac,[e] and Isaac was dwelling near Be'er-la'hai-roi.[f]

12 This is the history of Ish'ma·el[g] the son of Abraham whom Ha'gar[h] the Egyptian, the servant of Sarah, bore to Abraham.

13 Now these are the names of the sons of Ish'ma·el by their names according to their family origins: Ish'ma·el's firstborn Neba'ioth,[i] then Ke'dar,[j] Ad'be·el, Mib'sam,[k] 14 Mish'ma, Du'mah, Mas'sa, 15 Ha'dad, Te'ma, Je'tur, Na'phish, and Ked'e·mah. 16 These are the sons of Ish'ma·el, and these are their names by their settlements and by their encampments,* 12 chieftains according to their clans.[l] 17 And Ish'ma·el lived for 137 years.

CHAP. 24
a Ge 28:5
b Ge 35:8
c Ge 22:15, 17
d Ge 16:14
  Ge 25:11
e Ge 12:9
  Ge 20:1
  Nu 13:22
  Jg 1:9
f Ps 77:12
  Ps 143:5
g Heb 11:9
h Ge 26:8
i Ge 23:2, 19

CHAP. 25
j Ge 37:28
  Ex 2:15
  Nu 31:2
  Jg 6:2
k 1Ch 1:32, 33

Second Col.
a Ge 24:36
b Ge 21:14
c Ge 23:8, 9
  Ge 49:29, 30
d Ge 23:2, 19
e Ge 17:19
  Ge 26:12-14
f Ge 16:14
g Ge 16:10, 11
h Ga 4:24
i Ge 36:2, 3
  Isa 60:7
j Ps 120:5
  Jer 49:28
  Eze 27:21
k 1Ch 1:29-31
l Ge 17:20

24:59 *That is, her nurse who now served as an attendant. 24:60 *Or "become the mother of thousands of myriads." #Lit., "seed." △Or "the cities."

25:8 *This is a poetic expression for death. 25:16 *Or "walled camps."

Then he breathed his last and died and was gathered to his people.* 18 And they took up dwelling from Hav'i·lah[a] near Shur,[b] which is close to Egypt, as far as As·syr'i·a. He settled near all his brothers.*[c]

19 And this is the history of Isaac the son of Abraham.[d]

Abraham became father to Isaac. 20 Isaac was 40 years old when he married Re·bek'ah, the daughter of Be·thu'el[e] the A·ra·mae'an of Pad'dan-a'ram, the sister of La'ban the A·ra·mae'an. 21 And Isaac kept pleading with Jehovah regarding his wife, because she was barren; so Jehovah responded to his plea, and his wife Re·bek'ah became pregnant. 22 And the sons within her began to struggle with each other,[f] so that she said: "If this is the way it is, why should I go on living?" So she inquired of Jehovah. 23 And Jehovah said to her: "Two nations are in your womb,[g] and two peoples will be separated from within you;[h] and the one nation will be stronger than the other nation,[i] and the older will serve the younger."[j]

24 When the time came for her to give birth, look! twins were in her womb. 25 Then the first came out red all over and was like a garment of hair,[k] so they named him E'sau.*[l] 26 After that his brother came out and his hand was holding onto the heel of E'sau,[m] so he named him Jacob.*[n] Isaac was 60 years old when she gave birth to them.

27 As the boys got bigger, E'sau became a skilled hunter,[o] a man of the field, but Jacob was a blameless man, dwell-

ing in tents.[a] 28 And Isaac loved E'sau because it meant game in his mouth, whereas Re·bek'ah loved Jacob.[b] 29 On one occasion Jacob was boiling some stew when E'sau returned from the field exhausted. 30 So E'sau said to Jacob: "Quick, please, give me some* of the red stew that you have there,* for I am exhausted!"[a] That is why his name was E'dom.*[c] 31 To this Jacob said: "First sell me your right as firstborn!" 32 And E'sau continued: "Here I am about to die! What use is a birth-right to me?" 33 And Jacob added: "Swear to me first!" So he swore to him and sold his right as firstborn to Jacob.[e] 34 Then Jacob gave E'sau bread and lentil stew, and he ate and drank, and he got up and went away. Thus E'sau despised the birthright.

26 Now there was a famine in the land, in addition to the first famine that occurred in the days of Abraham,[f] so that Isaac went to A·bim'e·lech king of the Phi·lis'tines, in Ge'rar. 2 Then Jehovah appeared to him and said: "Do not go down to Egypt. Dwell in the land that I designate to you. 3 Reside as a foreigner in this land,[g] and I will continue with you and bless you because to you and to your offspring* I will give all these lands,[h] and I will carry out the oath that I swore to your father Abraham:[i] 4 'I will multiply your offspring* like the stars of the heavens;[j] and I will give to your offspring* all these lands;[k] and by means of your offspring,* all nations of the earth will obtain a blessing for themselves,'[l] 5 on account of the fact that Abraham listened to my voice and continued

---

CHAP. 25
a 1Sa 15:7
b Ge 16:7, 8
c Ge 16:11, 12
d Ge 22:2
  Mt 1:1, 2
e Ge 22:23
f Ro 9:10
g Ps 139:15
h Ge 36:31
  Nu 20:14
i Ge 27:29, 30
  De 2:4
j 2Sa 8:14
  Mal 1:2, 3
  Ro 9:10-13
k Ge 27:11
l Ge 27:32
  Ge 36:9
  Mal 1:3
m Ho 12:3
n Ge 27:36
o Ge 27:3, 5

Second Col.
a Heb 11:9
b Ge 27:6, 7, 46
c Ge 36:1
d Ge 21:16, 17
e Heb 12:16

CHAP. 26
f Ge 12:10
g Ge 20:1
  Heb 11:8, 9
h Ge 12:7
  Ge 15:18
i Ge 22:16-18
  Ps 105:9-11
  Heb 6:13, 14
j Ge 15:1, 5
  Heb 11:12
k Ge 34:4
l Ge 12:1-3
  Ac 3:25
  Ga 3:8

25:17 *This is a poetic expression for death. 25:18 *Or possibly, "He lived in hostility to all his brothers." 25:25 *Meaning "Hairy." 25:26 *Meaning "One Seizing the Heel; Supplanter."

25:30 *Or "give me a swallow." #Lit., "the red, this the red." △Or "famished." ⊠Meaning "Red." 26:3, 4 *Lit., "seed."

to keep my requirements, my commands, my statutes, and my laws."[a] **6** So Isaac continued to dwell in Ge′rar.[b]

7 When the men of the place kept asking about his wife, he would say: "She is my sister."[c] He was afraid to say, "She is my wife," for he said, "The men of the place might kill me because of Re·bek′ah," for she was beautiful in appearance.[d] **8** After some time had passed, A·bim′e·lech king of the Phi·lis′tines was looking out of the window, and he saw Isaac displaying affection for* Re·bek′ah his wife.[e] **9** At once A·bim′e·lech called Isaac and said: "She is actually your wife! Why did you say, 'She is my sister'?" At this Isaac said to him: "I said it for fear I should die because of her."[f] **10** But A·bim′e·lech continued: "What have you done to us? One of the people could easily have lain down with your wife, and you would have brought guilt upon us!"[h] **11** Then A·bim′e·lech commanded all the people, saying: "Anybody touching this man and his wife will surely be put to death!"

12 And Isaac began to sow seed in that land, and in that year he reaped 100 times what he sowed, for Jehovah was blessing him.[i] **13** The man became wealthy, and he continued to prosper until he became very wealthy. **14** He acquired flocks of sheep and herds of cattle and a large body of servants,[j] and the Phi·lis′tines began to envy him.

15 So the Phi·lis′tines took soil and stopped up all the wells that his father's servants had dug in the days of Abraham.[k] **16** A·bim′e·lech then said to Isaac: "Move from our neighborhood, for you have grown far stronger than we are." **17** So Isaac moved from there and en-

camped in the valley* of Ge′rar[a] and began dwelling there. **18** And Isaac again dug the wells that had been dug in the days of his father Abraham but that the Phi·lis′tines had stopped up after Abraham's death,[b] and he called them by the names that his father had given them.[c]

19 When the servants of Isaac were digging in the valley,* they found a well of fresh water. **20** And the shepherds of Ge′rar began quarreling with the shepherds of Isaac, saying: "The water is ours!" So he named the well E′sek,* because they had quarreled with him. **21** And they started digging another well, and they began quarreling over it also. So he named it Sit′nah.* **22** Later he moved away from there and dug another well, but they did not quarrel over it. So he named it Re·ho′both* and said: "It is because now Jehovah has given us ample room and has made us fruitful in the land."[d]

23 Then he went up from there to Be′er-she′ba.[e] **24** That night Jehovah appeared to him and said: "I am the God of your father Abraham.[f] Do not be afraid,[g] for I am with you, and I will bless you and multiply your offspring* on account of Abraham my servant."[h] **25** So he built an altar there and called on the name of Jehovah.[i] And Isaac pitched his tent there,[j] and his servants dug a well there.

26 Later A·bim′e·lech came to him from Ge′rar with A·huz′zath his personal adviser and Phi′col the chief of his army.[k] **27** At this Isaac said to them: "Why have you come to me, seeing that you hated me and sent me

CHAP. 26
a Ge 17:10, 23
  Ge 22:3, 12
  Heb 11:8
  Jas 2:21

b Ge 26:17

c Ge 12:11-13

d Ge 24:16

e Ge 24:67

f Ge 20:11

g Ge 12:18

h Ge 20:9

i Ge 24:34, 35

j Ge 12:16

k Ge 21:27, 30

Second Col.
a Ge 10:19
  Ge 20:1

b Ge 21:25

c Ge 21:31

d Ge 17:5, 6
  Ge 28:1, 3

e Ge 21:31

f Ge 17:1
  Ge 28:13

g Ge 15:1

h Ge 17:19
  Ps 105:9-11

i Ge 12:8, 9

j Heb 11:9

k Ge 21:32

26:8 *Or "embracing."

26:17, 19 *Or "wadi." 26:20 *Meaning "Contention." 26:21 *Meaning "Accusation." 26:22 *Meaning "Broad Places." 26:24 *Lit., "seed."

away from your neighborhood?" **28** To this they said: "We have clearly seen that Jehovah has been with you.[a] So we said, 'Let there, please, be an oath of obligation between us and you, and let us make a covenant with you[b] **29** that you will do nothing bad to us just as we have not harmed you, seeing that we have done only good to you in that we sent you away in peace. You now are the blessed of Jehovah.'" **30** Then he made a feast for them, and they ate and drank. **31** In the morning they got up early and swore an oath to each other.[c] After that Isaac sent them away, and they went from him in peace.

32 On that day the servants of Isaac came and reported to him about the well that they had dug,[d] and they told him: "We have found water!" **33** So he named it Shi'bah. That is why the name of the city is Be'er-she'ba[e] to this day.

34 When E'sau was 40 years old, he took as wife Ju'dith the daughter of Be·e'ri the Hit'tite and also Bas'e·math the daughter of E'lon the Hit'tite.[f] **35** They were a source of great grief* to Isaac and Re·bek'ah.[g]

27 Now when Isaac was old and his eyes were too weak to see, he called E'sau[h] his older son and said: "My son!" He replied: "Here I am!" **2** And he went on to say: "I have now grown old. I do not know the day of my death. **3** So at this time take, please, your weapons, your quiver and your bow, and go out to the field and hunt some wild game for me.[i] **4** Then make the kind of tasty dish that I am fond of and bring it to me. Then I will eat it so that I* may bless you before I die."

26:35 *Lit., "bitterness of spirit." 27:4 *Or "my soul."

5 However, Re·bek'ah was listening while Isaac spoke to E'sau his son. And E'sau went out into the field to hunt game and to bring it in.[a] **6** And Re·bek'ah said to Jacob her son:[b] "I just heard your father speaking to your brother E'sau, saying, **7** 'Bring me some game and make me a tasty dish. Then let me eat so that I may bless you before Jehovah before my death.'[c] **8** And now, my son, listen carefully and do what I am instructing you.[d] **9** Go, please, to the herd and get me two of the best young goats from there so that I may prepare from them a tasty dish for your father, just the way he likes it. **10** Then take it to your father to eat, in order that he may bless you before his death."

11 Jacob said to his mother Re·bek'ah: "But E'sau my brother is a hairy man,[e] and my skin is smooth. **12** What if my father feels me?[f] Then I will certainly appear to be mocking him, and I will bring upon myself a curse rather than a blessing." **13** At this his mother said to him: "Upon me be the curse meant for you, my son. Just do as I say and go, get them for me."[g] **14** So he went and got them and brought them to his mother, and his mother made a tasty dish, just the way his father liked it. **15** After that Re·bek'ah took her older son E'sau's finest garments, which she had in the house, and put them on her younger son Jacob.[h] **16** She also put the skins of the young goats on his hands and on the hairless part of his neck.[i] **17** Then she handed the tasty dish and the bread that she had made to her son Jacob.[j]

18 So he went in to his father and said: "My father!" to which he said: "Here I am! Who are you, my son?" **19** Jacob said to

---

CHAP. 26
a Ge 21:22
b Ge 21:27
c Ge 21:22-24
d Ge 26:18
e Jg 20:1
f Ge 36:2, 3
g Ge 27:46
Ge 28:8

CHAP. 27
h Ge 25:28
i Ge 25:27

Second Col.
a Ge 27:30
b Ge 25:28
c Ge 27:30, 31
d Ge 27:13, 43
e Ge 25:25
Ge 27:23
f Ge 27:21
g Ge 27:8, 43
h Ge 25:23, 26
i Ge 25:25
Ge 27:11
j Ge 27:9

his father: "I am E'sau your first-born.[a] I have done just as you told me. Sit up, please, and eat some of my game, so that you* may bless me."[b] **20** At that Isaac said to his son: "How were you so quick in finding it, my son?" He replied: "Because Jehovah your God brought it to me." **21** Then Isaac said to Jacob: "Come near, please, that I may feel you, my son, to know whether you are really my son E'sau or not."[c] **22** So Jacob came near to his father Isaac, and he felt him, after which he said: "The voice is the voice of Jacob, but the hands are the hands of E'sau."[d] **23** He did not recognize him because his hands were hairy like the hands of his brother E'sau. So he blessed him.[e]

24 After that he asked: "Are you really my son E'sau?" to which he replied: "I am." **25** Then he said: "Bring me some of the wild game for me to eat, my son, then I* will bless you." With that he brought it to him and he ate, and he brought him wine and he drank. **26** Then Isaac his father said to him: "Come near, please, and kiss me, my son."[f] **27** So he came near and kissed him, and he could smell the scent of his garments.[g] Then he blessed him and said:

"See, the scent of my son is like the scent of the field that Jehovah has blessed. **28** May the true God give you the dews of the heavens[h] and the fertile soils of the earth[i] and an abundance of grain and new wine.[j] **29** Let peoples serve you, and let nations bow low to you. Be master over your brothers, and let the sons of your mother bow low to you.[k] Cursed be everyone

who curses you, and blessed be everyone who blesses you."[a]

30 Now Isaac had just finished blessing Jacob, and Jacob had barely left the presence of his father Isaac when his brother E'sau came back from his hunting.[b] **31** He too prepared a tasty dish and brought it to his father, and he said to his father: "Let my father get up and eat some of his son's game, in order that you* may bless me." **32** At this his father Isaac said to him: "Who are you?" to which he said: "I am your son, your firstborn, E'sau."[c] **33** And Isaac began to tremble violently, so he said: "Who was it, then, who hunted for game and brought it to me? I already ate it before you arrived, and I blessed him—and he will surely be blessed!"

34 On hearing his father's words, E'sau began to cry out in an extremely loud and bitter manner and to say to his father: "Bless me, yes, me too, my father!"[d] **35** But he said: "Your brother came deceitfully so that he might get the blessing meant for you." **36** At this he said: "Is he not rightly named Jacob,* that he might supplant me these two times?[e] My birthright he has already taken,[f] and now he has taken my blessing!"[g] Then he added: "Have you not reserved a blessing for me?" **37** But Isaac answered E'sau: "Here I have appointed him master over you,[h] and I have given him all his brothers as servants, and I have bestowed grain and new wine for his support.[i] What is left that I can do for you, my son?"

38 E'sau said to his father: "Is there just one blessing that you have, my father? Bless me, yes, me too, my father!" With that

CHAP. 27
a Ge 25:31-33
Ro 9:10-12

b Ge 27:4

c Ge 27:11, 12

d Ge 27:16

e Heb 11:20

f Ge 48:10

g Ge 25:27
Ge 27:15

h De 11:11

i Nu 13:26, 27

j Ge 27:37
De 7:13

k Ge 25:23

_____
Second Col.
a Ge 12:1, 3
Ge 28:1, 3
Ge 31:42
Eze 25:12, 13

b Ge 27:3

c Ge 25:25, 31
Heb 12:16

d Heb 12:16, 17

e Ge 25:26
Ge 32:28
Ho 12:3

f Ge 25:32-34

g Ge 27:28

h Ge 25:23
Ge 27:29
Ro 9:10, 12

i De 33:28

27:19, 31 *Or "your soul." 27:25 *Or "my soul."

27:36 *Meaning "One Seizing the Heel; Supplanter."

E'sau cried loudly and burst into tears.[a] **39** So his father Isaac answered him:

"See, away from the fertile soils of the earth your dwelling will be, and away from the dew of the heavens above.[b] **40** And by your sword you will live,[c] and you will serve your brother.[d] But when you grow restless, you will indeed break his yoke off your neck."[e]

41 However, E'sau harbored animosity against Jacob because of the blessing his father had given him,[f] and E'sau kept saying in his heart: "The days of mourning for my father are getting closer.[g] After that I am going to kill Jacob my brother." **42** When the words of her older son E'sau were told to Re·bek'ah, she at once sent for her younger son Jacob and said to him: "Look! Your brother E'sau is planning to take revenge by killing you.* **43** Now, my son, do as I say. Get up and run away to my brother La'ban at Ha'ran.[h] **44** Dwell with him for a while until your brother's rage calms down, **45** until your brother's anger toward you subsides and he forgets what you have done to him. Then I will send for you from there. Why should I lose both of you in one day?"

46 After that Re·bek'ah kept saying to Isaac: "I am disgusted with my life because of the daughters of Heth.[i] If Jacob ever takes a wife from the daughters of Heth, like these daughters of the land, what good is my life?"[j]

28 So Isaac called Jacob and blessed him and commanded him, saying: "You must not take a wife from the daughters of Ca'naan.[k] **2** Go away to Pad'dan-a'ram to the house of Be·thu'el, your mother's father, and from there take for yourself a wife from the daughters of La'ban,[a] your mother's brother. **3** God Almighty will bless you and make you fruitful and multiply you, and you will certainly become a congregation of peoples.[b] **4** And he will give to you the blessing of Abraham,[c] to you and to your offspring* with you, so that you may take possession of the land where you have been living as a foreigner, which God has given to Abraham."[d]

5 So Isaac sent Jacob away, and he departed for Pad'dan-a'ram, to La'ban the son of Be·thu'el the A·ra·mae'an,[e] the brother of Re·bek'ah,[f] the mother of Jacob and E'sau.

6 E'sau saw that Isaac had blessed Jacob and had sent him away to Pad'dan-a'ram to take a wife from there and that when he blessed him, he commanded him, "Do not take a wife from the daughters of Ca'naan,"[g] **7** and that Jacob obeyed his father and his mother and departed for Pad'dan-a'ram.[h] **8** E'sau then realized that the daughters of Ca'naan were displeasing to his father Isaac,[i] **9** so E'sau went to Ish'ma·el and took as wife Ma'ha·lath the daughter of Abraham's son Ish'ma·el, the sister of Ne·ba'ioth, in addition to the other wives he already had.[j]

10 Jacob departed from Be'er-she'ba and kept going toward Ha'ran.[k] **11** In time he came to a place and prepared to spend the night there because the sun had set. So he took one of the stones of that place and set it to rest his head on and lay down there.[l] **12** Then he had a dream, and look! there was a stairway* set on the earth, and its top reached up to the heavens; and there were God's angels

---

CHAP. 27
a Heb 12:16, 17

b Jos 24:4
Heb 11:20

c Ge 32:6
Nu 20:18

d Ge 25:23
2Sa 8:14
Mal 1:2, 3

e 2Ki 8:20
2Ch 28:17

f Am 1:11

g Ge 35:28, 29

h Ge 28:5

i Ge 26:34, 35
Ge 28:8

j Ge 24:2, 3

CHAP. 28
k Ge 24:34, 37
Ex 34:15, 16
1Ki 11:1-3
2Co 6:14

Second Col.
a Ge 29:16

b Ge 17:5
Ge 46:15, 19
1Ch 2:1, 2

c Ge 12:2, 3

d Ge 12:7
Ge 15:13
Ge 17:1, 8
Heb 11:9

e Ge 25:20

f Ge 24:29

g Ge 28:1
2Co 6:14

h Ge 27:43

i Ge 27:46

j Ge 36:2, 3

k Ge 11:31
Ge 27:43

l Ge 28:18, 19

27:42 *Or "comforting himself with thoughts of killing you."

28:4 *Lit., "seed." 28:12 *Or "ladder."

ascending and descending on it.[a]
13 And look! there was Jehovah stationed above it, and he said: "I am Jehovah the God of Abraham your father and the God of Isaac.[b] The land on which you are lying, to you I am going to give it and to your offspring.[*c] 14 And your offspring[*] will certainly become like the dust particles of the earth,[d] and you will spread abroad to the west and to the east and to the north and to the south, and by means of you and by means of your offspring[*] all the families of the ground will certainly be blessed."[#e] 15 I am with you, and I will safeguard you wherever you go, and I will return you to this land.[f] I will not leave you until I have done what I have promised you."[g]

16 Then Jacob awoke from his sleep and said: "Truly Jehovah is in this place, and I did not know it." 17 And he grew fearful and added: "How awe-inspiring this place is! This can only be the house of God,[h] and this is the gate of the heavens."[i] 18 So Jacob got up early in the morning and took the stone on which he had rested his head and set it up as a pillar and poured oil on top of it.[j] 19 So he named that place Beth'el,[*] but previously the city's name was Luz.[k]

20 Jacob then made a vow, saying: "If God will continue with me and will protect me on my journey and will give me bread to eat and garments to wear 21 and I return in peace to the house of my father, then Jehovah will certainly have proved to be my God. 22 And this stone that I have set up as a pillar will become a house of God,[l] and without fail I will give

you a tenth of everything you give to me."

29 After that Jacob resumed his journey and traveled on to the land of the people of the East. 2 Now he saw a well in the field and three droves of sheep lying down next to it, because they usually watered the droves from that well. There was a large stone over the mouth of the well. 3 When all the droves had been gathered there, they rolled away the stone from the mouth of the well, and they watered the flocks, after which they returned the stone to its place over the mouth of the well.

4 So Jacob said to them: "My brothers, what place are you from?" to which they said: "We are from Ha'ran."[a] 5 He said to them: "Do you know La'ban[b] the grandson of Na'hor?"[c] to which they said: "We know him." 6 At this he said to them: "Is he well?" They replied: "He is well. And here is his daughter Rachel[d] coming with the sheep!" 7 Then he said: "It is still the middle of the day. It is not the time for gathering the herds. Water the sheep, and then go feed them." 8 To this they said: "We are not allowed to do so until all the droves are gathered and they roll the stone away from the mouth of the well. Then we water the sheep."

9 While he was yet speaking with them, Rachel came with her father's sheep, for she was a shepherdess. 10 When Jacob saw Rachel, the daughter of La'ban his mother's brother, and the sheep of La'ban his mother's brother, Jacob immediately approached and rolled the stone away from the mouth of the well and watered the sheep of La'ban his mother's brother. 11 Then Jacob kissed Rachel and raised his voice and burst into tears. 12 And Jacob began to tell Rachel that he was

CHAP. 28
a Joh 1:51
  Heb 1:7, 14

b Ge 26:24, 25

c Ge 12:7
  Ge 28:4
  Ps 105:9-11

d Ge 13:14, 16
  1Ki 4:20

e Ge 18:18
  Ge 22:15, 18

f Ge 35:6

g Ge 31:3
  Nu 23:19
  Jos 23:14
  Heb 6:18

h Ps 47:2

i Ge 35:1

j Ge 31:13

k Ge 35:6
  Jos 16:1, 2

l Ge 35:1

Second Col.

CHAP. 29
a Ge 27:42, 43
  Ac 7:2

b Ge 24:29

c Ge 24:24
  Ge 31:53

d Ge 46:19
  Ru 4:11

the relative* of her father and that he was the son of Re·bek′ah. And she ran off and told her father.

13 As soon as La′ban[a] heard the report about Jacob the son of his sister, he ran to meet him. He embraced him and kissed him and brought him into his house. And he began to tell La′ban all these things. 14 La′ban said to him: "You are indeed my bone and my flesh."* So he stayed with him a full month.

15 La′ban then said to Jacob: "Just because you are my relative,*[b] should you serve me for nothing? Tell me, what are your wages to be?"[c] 16 Now La′ban had two daughters. The name of the older was Le′ah, and the name of the younger, Rachel.[d] 17 But the eyes of Le′ah had no luster, whereas Rachel had become a very attractive and beautiful woman. 18 Jacob had fallen in love with Rachel, so he said: "I am willing to serve you seven years for your younger daughter Rachel."[e] 19 To this La′ban said: "It is better for me to give her to you than to give her to another man. Keep dwelling with me." 20 And Jacob served seven years for Rachel,[f] but in his eyes they were like just a few days because of his love for her.

21 Then Jacob said to La′ban: "Give over my wife because my days are up, and let me have relations with her." 22 With that La′ban gathered all the men of the place and made a feast. 23 But during the evening, he resorted to taking his daughter Le′ah and bringing her to him that he might have relations with her. 24 La′ban also gave his female servant Zil′pah to his daughter Le′ah as a ser-

vant.[a] 25 In the morning Jacob saw that it was Le′ah! So he said to La′ban: "What have you done to me? Was it not for Rachel that I served you? Why have you tricked me?"[b] 26 To this La′ban said: "It is not our custom here to give the younger woman before the firstborn. 27 Celebrate the week of this woman. After that you will also be given this other woman in exchange for serving me seven more years."[c] 28 Jacob did so and celebrated the week of this woman, after which he gave him his daughter Rachel as a wife. 29 Besides, La′ban gave his female servant Bil′hah[d] to his daughter Rachel as her servant.[e]

30 Then Jacob had relations also with Rachel, and he loved Rachel more than Le′ah, and he served him for another seven years.[f] 31 When Jehovah saw that Le′ah was unloved,* he then enabled her to become pregnant,*[g] but Rachel was barren.[h] 32 So Le′ah became pregnant and gave birth to a son and named him Reu′ben,*[i] for she said: "It is because Jehovah has looked upon my affliction,[j] for now my husband will begin to love me." 33 And she again became pregnant and gave birth to a son and then said: "It is because Jehovah has listened, in that I was unloved, so he gave me this one also." Then she named him Sim′e·on.*[k] 34 And she became pregnant yet again and gave birth to a son and said: "Now this time my husband will join himself to me, because I have borne him three sons." Therefore, he was named Le′vi.*[l] 35 And she became pregnant once more and gave birth to

---

CHAP. 29
a Ge 24:29

b Ge 28:5

c Ge 30:27, 28
  Ge 31:7

d Ru 4:11

e Ge 31:41

f Ge 30:26
  Ho 12:12

Second Col.
a Ge 16:1, 2
  Ge 30:9
  Ge 46:18

b Ge 31:7, 42

c Ge 31:41

d Ge 35:22

e Ge 30:1, 3

f Ho 12:12

g Ge 46:15
  Ru 4:11

h Ge 30:22

i Ge 35:22
  Ge 37:22
  Ge 49:3, 4
  Ex 6:14
  1Ch 5:1

j Ge 30:20
  1Sa 1:5, 6
  Lu 1:24, 25

k Ge 34:25
  Ge 49:5
  1Ch 4:24

l Ge 34:25
  Ge 49:5
  Ex 6:16
  Nu 3:12
  1Ch 6:1

29:12, 15 *Lit., "brother." 29:14 *Or "my blood relative."

29:31 *Lit., "hated." #Lit., "he opened her womb." 29:32 *Meaning "See, a Son!" 29:33 *Meaning "Hearing." 29:34 *Meaning "Adherence; Joined."

a son and then said: "This time I will praise Jehovah." She therefore named him Judah.*ᵃ After that she stopped giving birth.

30 When Rachel saw that she had borne no children to Jacob, she became jealous of her sister and began to say to Jacob: "Give me children or else I will die." **2** At this Jacob's anger flared up against Rachel, and he said: "Am I in the place of God, who has prevented you from having children?"* **3** So she said: "Here is my slave girl Bil'hah.ᵇ Have relations with her in order that she may bear children for me* and that through her, I too may have children." **4** With that she gave him her servant Bil'hah as a wife, and Jacob had relations with her.ᶜ **5** Bil'hah became pregnant and in time bore Jacob a son. **6** Then Rachel said: "God has acted as my judge and has also listened to my voice, so that he gave me a son." That is why she named him Dan.*ᵈ **7** Bil'hah, Rachel's servant, became pregnant once more and in time bore Jacob a second son. **8** Then Rachel said: "With strenuous wrestlings I have wrestled with my sister. I have also come off the winner!" So she named him Naph'ta·li.*ᵉ

9 When Le'ah saw that she had stopped having children, she took her servant Zil'pah and gave her to Jacob as a wife.ᶠ **10** And Le'ah's servant Zil'pah bore a son to Jacob. **11** Then Le'ah said: "With good fortune!" So she named him Gad.*ᵍ **12** After that Zil'pah, Le'ah's servant, bore a second son to Jacob. **13** Then Le'ah said: "With my happiness! For the daughters will certainly pronounce me happy."ᵃ So she named him Ash'er.*ᵇ

14 Now Reu'benᶜ was walking in the days of the wheat harvest, and he found mandrakes in the field. So he brought them to his mother Le'ah. Then Rachel said to Le'ah: "Give me, please, some of your son's mandrakes." **15** At this she said to her: "Is it a small matter that you took my husband?ᵈ Would you now take my son's mandrakes also?" So Rachel said: "Very well. He will lie down with you tonight in exchange for your son's mandrakes."

16 When Jacob was coming from the field in the evening, Le'ah went out to meet him and said: "It is with me you are going to have relations, because I have hired you outright with my son's mandrakes." So he lay down with her that night. **17** And God heard and answered Le'ah, and she became pregnant and in time bore to Jacob a fifth son. **18** Then Le'ah said: "God has given me my wages* because I have given my servant to my husband." So she named him Is'sa·char.*ᵉ **19** And Le'ah became pregnant once more and in time bore a sixth son to Jacob.ᶠ **20** Then Le'ah said: "God has endowed me, yes, me, with a good endowment. At last, my husband will tolerate me,ᵍ for I have borne him six sons."ʰ So she named him Zeb'u·lun.*ⁱ **21** Afterward she bore a daughter and named her Di'nah.ʲ

22 Finally God remembered Rachel, and God heard and

CHAP. 29
a Ge 35:23
Ge 37:26
Ge 44:18
Ge 49:8
1Ch 2:3
Re 5:5

CHAP. 30
b Ge 29:29

c Ge 35:22

d Ge 35:25
Ge 46:23
Ge 49:16

e Ge 35:25
Ge 46:24
Ge 49:21
De 33:23

f Ge 35:26

g Ge 49:19
Nu 32:33

Second Col.
a Lu 1:46, 48

b Ge 35:26
Ge 46:17
Ge 49:20
De 33:24

c Ge 29:32

d Ge 29:30

e Ge 35:23
Ge 46:13
Ge 49:14
De 33:18

f Ru 4:11

g Ge 29:32

h Ge 35:23
Ge 46:15
Ps 127:3

i Ge 46:14
Ge 49:13
De 33:18

j Ge 34:1

29:35 *Meaning "Praised; Object of Praise." 30:2 *Or "has withheld the fruit of the womb from you?" 30:3 *Lit., "give birth upon my knees." 30:6 *Meaning "Judge." 30:8 *Meaning "My Wrestlings." 30:11 *Meaning "Good Fortune."

30:13 *Meaning "Happy; Happiness." 30:18 *Or "a hireling's wages." *Meaning "He Is Wages." 30:20 *Meaning "Toleration."

answered her by enabling her to become pregnant.*ᵃ **23** And she became pregnant and gave birth to a son. Then she said: "God has taken away my reproach!"ᵇ **24** So she named him Joseph,*ᶜ saying: "Jehovah is adding another son to me."

25 After Rachel had given birth to Joseph, Jacob immediately said to La'ban: "Send me away so that I may go to my place and to my land.ᵈ **26** Give over my wives and my children, for whom I have served with you, that I may go, for you well know how I have served you."ᵉ **27** Then La'ban said to him: "If I have found favor in your eyes,—I have understood by the omens* that Jehovah is blessing me because of you." **28** And he added: "Stipulate your wages to me, and I will give them."ᶠ **29** So Jacob said to him: "You know how I have served you and how your herd has fared with me;ᵍ **30** you had little before my coming, but your herd has increased and multiplied, and Jehovah has blessed you since I arrived. So when will I do something for my own house?"ʰ

31 Then he said: "What should I give you?" And Jacob said: "You will give me nothing whatsoever! If you will do this one thing for me, I will resume shepherding your flock and guarding it.ⁱ **32** I will pass through your whole flock today. You set aside from there every sheep speckled and with color patches and every dark-brown sheep among the young rams and any color-patched and speckled one among the she-goats. From now on, these must

become my wages.ᵃ **33** And my righteousness* must speak for me on a future day when you come to look over my wages; every one that is not speckled and color-patched among the she-goats and dark brown among the young rams will be considered stolen if it is with me."

34 To this La'ban said: "That is fine! Let it be according to your word."ᵇ **35** Then on that day, he set aside the he-goats striped and color-patched and all the she-goats speckled and color-patched, every one in which there was any white and every one dark brown among the young rams, and gave them into the care of his sons. **36** After that he set a distance of three days' journey between himself and Jacob, and Jacob was shepherding the flocks of La'ban that remained over.

37 Jacob then took freshly cut staffs of the storax, almond, and plane trees, and he peeled white spots in them by exposing the white wood of the staffs. **38** Then he placed the staffs that he had peeled in front of the flock, in the gutters, in the drinking troughs, where the flocks would come to drink, that they might get into heat in front of them when they came to drink.

39 So the flocks would get into heat in front of the staffs, and the flocks would produce striped, speckled, and color-patched offspring. **40** Then Jacob separated the young rams and turned the flocks to face the striped ones and all the dark-brown ones among the flocks of La'ban. Then he separated his own flocks and did not mix them with La'ban's flocks. **41** And whenever the robust animals would get into heat, Jacob would place the staffs in

---

CHAP. 30
a Ge 29:31

b Lu 1:24, 25

c Ge 35:24
Ge 45:4
De 33:13
Ac 7:9

d Ge 28:15
Ge 31:13

e Ge 31:41
Ho 12:12

f Ge 31:7

g Ge 31:38

h Ge 32:9, 10

i Ho 12:12

Second Col.
a Ge 31:7

b Ge 31:8

30:22 *Lit., "and God listened to her and opened her womb." 30:24 *A shortened form of Josiphiah, which means "May Jah Add (Increase)." 30:27 *Or "from the evidence."

30:33 *Or "honesty."

the gutters before the eyes of the flocks, that they might get into heat by the staffs. **42** But when the animals were weak, he would not place the staffs there. So the weak ones always came to be La′ban's, but the robust ones became Jacob's.[a]

43 And the man grew very prosperous, and he acquired great flocks and male and female servants and camels and donkeys.[b]

31 In time he heard what the sons of La′ban were saying: "Jacob has taken everything that belonged to our father, and from what belonged to our father, he has amassed all this wealth."[c] **2** When Jacob would look at the face of La′ban, he saw that his attitude toward him was not what it used to be.[d] **3** Finally Jehovah said to Jacob: "Return to the land of your fathers and to your relatives,[e] and I will continue with you." **4** Then Jacob sent a message to Rachel and Le′ah to come out to the field to his flock, **5** and he said to them:

"I have seen that your father's attitude toward me has changed,[f] but the God of my father has been with me.[g] **6** You yourselves certainly know that I have served your father with all my power.[h] **7** And your father has tried to cheat me and has changed my wages ten times; but God has not allowed him to do me harm. **8** If on the one hand he would say, 'The speckled ones will be your wages,' then the whole flock produced speckled ones; but if on the other hand he would say, 'The striped ones will be your wages,' then the whole flock produced striped ones.[i] **9** So God kept taking your father's livestock away from him and giving it to me. **10** Once when the flock got into heat, I raised

my eyes and saw in a dream that the he-goats mating with the flock were striped, speckled, and spotty.[a] **11** Then the angel of the true God said to me in the dream, 'Jacob!' to which I said, 'Here I am.' **12** And he continued, 'Raise your eyes, please, and see that all the he-goats mating with the flock are striped, speckled, and spotty, for I have seen all that La′ban is doing to you.[b] **13** I am the true God of Beth′el,[c] where you anointed a pillar and where you made a vow to me.[d] Now get up, go out of this land, and return to the land of your birth.'"[e]

14 At this Rachel and Le′ah answered him: "Is there any share left for us to inherit in our father's house? **15** Does he not consider us as foreigners, since he has sold us and has been using up the money given for us?[f] **16** All the riches that God has taken away from our father are ours and our children's.[g] So, then, do everything that God has told you to do."[h]

17 Then Jacob got up and lifted his children and his wives on the camels,[i] **18** and he began driving all his herd and all the goods that he had accumulated,[j] the livestock in his possession that he had accumulated in Pad′dan-a′ram, to go to Isaac his father in the land of Ca′naan.[k]

19 Now La′ban had gone to shear his sheep, and Rachel stole the teraphim statues*[l] that belonged to her father.[m] **20** Moreover, Jacob outwitted La′ban the A·ra·mae′an, for he had not told him that he was running away. **21** And he ran away and crossed the River,*[n] he and all he had. Then he headed toward the mountainous region of Gil′e·ad.[o] **22** On the third day, La′ban was

---

CHAP. 30
a Ge 31:9

b Ge 32:5
  Ge 36:6, 7

CHAP. 31
c Ge 30:33

d Ge 30:27

e Ge 28:15
  Ge 32:9
  Ge 35:27

f Ge 30:27

g Ge 48:15

h Ge 30:29, 30

i Ge 30:32

Second Col.
a Ge 30:39

b Ge 29:25
  Ge 31:39

c Ge 12:8, 9
  Ge 35:15

d Ge 28:18, 22

e Ge 35:14
  Ge 37:1

f Ge 31:41
  Ho 12:12

g Ge 31:1

h Ge 31:3

i Ge 33:13

j Ge 30:42, 43

k Ge 35:27

l Ge 35:2
  Jos 24:2

m Ge 31:14

n Ge 15:18

o Nu 32:1

31:19 *Or "household gods; idols."
31:21 *That is, the Euphrates.

told that Jacob had run away. **23** So he took his brothers* with him and pursued him for a journey of seven days and caught up with him in the mountainous region of Gil′e·ad. **24** Then God came to La′ban the A·ra·mae′an[a] in a dream by night[b] and said to him: "Be careful about what you say to Jacob, either good or bad."*[c]

25 So La′ban approached Jacob, as Jacob had pitched his tent in the mountain and La′ban had encamped with his brothers in the mountainous region of Gil′e·ad. **26** Then La′ban said to Jacob: "What have you done? Why have you resorted to outwitting me and carrying my daughters off like captives taken by the sword? **27** Why did you run away secretly and outwit me and not tell me? If you had told me, I could have sent you away with rejoicing and with songs, with tambourine and with harp. **28** But you did not give me a chance to kiss my grandchildren* and my daughters. You have acted foolishly. **29** It is in my power to do harm to you, but the God of your father spoke to me last night, saying, 'Be careful about what you say to Jacob, either good or bad.'[d] **30** Now you have gone because you have been longing to return to the house of your father, but why have you stolen my gods?"[e]

31 Jacob answered La′ban: "It was because I was afraid, for I said to myself, 'You might take your daughters away from me by force.' **32** Anyone with whom you find your gods will not live. Before our brothers, examine what I have, and take what is yours." But Jacob did not know

---

31:23 *Or, "relatives." 31:24 *Lit., "Watch yourself that you do not speak with Jacob from good to bad." 31:28 *Lit., "sons."

CHAP. 31
a Ge 25:20
Ho 12:12

b Ge 20:3

c Ps 105:15

d Ge 31:24

e Ge 31:19
Ge 35:2

Second Col.
a Ge 46:18, 25

b Le 15:19

c Ge 31:19

d Ge 30:27

e 1Sa 17:34

f Ge 47:9

g Ge 31:7

h Ge 28:13
Ge 31:29

---

that Rachel had stolen them. **33** So La′ban went into the tent of Jacob and into the tent of Le′ah and into the tent of the two slave girls,[a] but did not find them. Then he came out of Le′ah's tent and went into Rachel's tent. **34** Meanwhile, Rachel had taken the teraphim statues and put them in the woman's saddle basket of the camel, and she was sitting on them. So La′ban searched through the whole tent but did not find them. **35** Then she said to her father: "Do not be angry, my lord, because I am not able to get up before you, for the customary thing with women is upon me."[b] So he searched on carefully but did not find the teraphim statues.[c]

36 At that Jacob became angry and began to criticize La′ban. Jacob then said to La′ban: "What is my offense, and for what sin are you hotly pursuing me? **37** Now that you have searched through all my goods, what have you found that belongs to your house? Put it here in front of my brothers and your brothers, and let them decide between the two of us. **38** During these 20 years that I have been with you, your sheep and your goats never miscarried,[d] and I never ate the rams of your flock. **39** I did not bring you any animal torn by wild beasts.[e] I would stand the loss of it myself. Whether the animal was stolen by day or was stolen by night, you would demand compensation from me. **40** By day the heat consumed me, and the cold by night, and sleep would flee from my eyes.[f] **41** This makes 20 years for me in your house. I have served you 14 years for your two daughters and 6 years for your flock, and you kept changing my wages ten times.[g] **42** If the God of my father,[h] the God of Abraham and the One whom Isaac fears,*[a] had not been on my side, you would now have sent me away empty-handed. God has seen my affliction and the toil of my hands, and that is why he reproved you last night."[b]

43 Then La′ban answered Jacob: "The daughters are my daughters and the children my children, and the flock my flock, and everything you are looking at is mine and my daughters'. What can I do today against these or against their children whom they have borne? **44** Now come, let us make a covenant, you and I, and it will serve as a witness between us." **45** So Jacob took a stone and set it up as a pillar.[c] **46** Then Jacob said to his brothers: "Pick up stones!" And they took stones and made a pile. After that they ate there on the pile of stones. **47** And La′ban began calling it Je′gar-sa·ha·du′tha,* but Jacob called it Gal′e·ed.*

48 La′ban then said: "This pile of stones is a witness between me and you today." That is why he named it Gal′e·ed,[d] **49** and the Watchtower, for he said: "Let Jehovah keep watch between you and me when we are out of each other's sight. **50** If you mistreat my daughters and if you start taking wives in addition to my daughters, though there is no man with us, remember that God will be a witness between you and me." **51** La′ban went on to say to Jacob: "Here is this pile of stones, and here is the pillar that I have erected between you and me. **52** This pile of stones is a witness, and the pillar is something that bears witness,[e] that I

will not pass beyond this pile of stones to bring harm to you and you will not pass beyond this pile of stones and this pillar to bring harm to me. **53** Let the God of Abraham[a] and the God of Na′hor, the God of their father, judge between us." And Jacob swore by the One whom his father Isaac fears.*[b]

54 After that Jacob offered a sacrifice in the mountain and invited his brothers to eat bread. So they ate and spent the night in the mountain. **55** However, La′ban got up early in the morning and kissed his grandchildren*[c] and his daughters and blessed them.[d] Then La′ban departed and returned home.[e]

32 Jacob then went on his way, and the angels of God met up with him. **2** As soon as he saw them, Jacob said: "This is the camp of God!" So he named that place Ma·ha·na′im.*

3 Then Jacob sent messengers ahead of him to his brother E′sau in the land of Se′ir,[f] the territory* of E′dom,[g] **4** and he commanded them: "This is what you will say to my lord, to E′sau, 'This is what your servant Jacob says: "I have resided* with La′ban for a long time until now.[h] **5** And I have acquired bulls, donkeys, sheep, and male and female servants,[i] and I send this message to inform my lord, in order to find favor in your eyes."'"

6 In time the messengers returned to Jacob, saying: "We met your brother E′sau, and he is now on his way to meet you, and there are 400 men with him."[j] **7** And Jacob became very frightened and anxious.[k] So he divided the peo-

---

CHAP. 31
a Ge 31:53
b Ge 31:24
c Ge 28:18
d Ge 31:22, 23
e Ge 31:44, 45

Second Col.
a Ge 17:1, 7
b Ge 31:42
c Ge 31:28
d Ge 24:59, 60
e Ge 27:43
  Ge 28:2

CHAP. 32
f Ge 27:39
  Ge 36:8
  De 2:5
  Jos 24:4
g Ge 25:30
h Ge 31:41
i Ge 30:43
  Ge 33:11
j Ge 33:1, 2
k Ge 27:41
  Ge 32:11

31:42 *Lit., "the fear of Isaac." **31:47** *An Aramaic expression meaning "Witness Pile." *A Hebrew expression meaning "Witness Pile." **31:53** *Lit., "by the fear of his father Isaac." **31:55** *Lit., "sons." **32:2** *Meaning "Two Camps." **32:3** *Lit., "field." **32:4** *Or "resided as a foreigner."

ple who were with him, as well as the flocks, the cattle, and the camels, into two camps. **8** He said: "If E'sau attacks the one camp, then the other camp will be able to escape."

9 After that Jacob said: "O God of my father Abraham and God of my father Isaac, O Jehovah, you who are saying to me, 'Return to your land and to your relatives, and I will deal well with you,'ᵃ **10** I am unworthy of all the loyal love and of all the faithfulness that you have shown toward your servant,ᵇ for with only my staff I crossed this Jordan and now I have become two camps.ᶜ **11** Save me, I pray you,ᵈ from the hand of my brother E'sau, for I am afraid of him that he may come and attack me,ᵉ as well as the mothers and their children. **12** And you have said: 'I will certainly deal well with you, and I will make your offspring* like the grains of sand of the sea, which are too numerous to count.'"ᶠ

13 And he spent the night there. Then he took some of his possessions as a gift for E'sau his brother:ᵍ **14** 200 female goats, 20 male goats, 200 female sheep, 20 rams, **15** 30 camels nursing their young, 40 cows, 10 bulls, 20 female donkeys and 10 full-grown male donkeys.ʰ

16 He handed them over to his servants, one drove after another, and he said to his servants: "Cross over ahead of me, and you are to set a space between one drove and the next." **17** He also commanded the first one: "In case E'sau my brother should meet you and ask, 'To whom do you belong, and where are you going, and to whom do these ahead of you belong?' **18** then you should say, 'To your servant Jacob. It is a

gift sent to my lord, to E'sau,ᵃ and look! he himself is also behind us.'" **19** And he commanded also the second, the third, and all those following the droves: "According to this word, you are to speak to E'sau when you meet him. **20** And you should also say, 'Here is your servant Jacob behind us.'" For he said to himself: 'If I appease him by sending a gift ahead of me,ᵇ then afterward when I see him, he may give me a kindly reception.' **21** So the gift crossed over ahead of him, but he himself spent the night in the camp.

22 Later during that night, he rose and took his two wivesᶜ and his two female servantsᵈ and his 11 young sons and crossed over the ford of Jab'bok.ᵉ **23** So he took them and brought them across the stream,* and he brought over everything else he had.

24 Finally Jacob was left by himself. Then a man began to wrestle with him until the dawn broke.ᶠ **25** When he saw that he had not prevailed over him, he touched the socket of his hip; and the socket of Jacob's hip was dislocated during his wrestling with him.ᵍ **26** After that he said: "Let me go, for the dawn is breaking." To this he said: "I am not going to let you go until you bless me."ʰ **27** So he said to him: "What is your name?" to which he said: "Jacob." **28** Then he said: "Your name will no longer be Jacob but Israel,*ⁱ for you have contended with Godʲ and with men and you have at last prevailed." **29** In turn Jacob inquired: "Tell me, please, your name." However, he said: "Why is it that you ask my name?"ᵏ With that he blessed

---

CHAP. 32
a Ge 31:3, 13

b Ge 28:15
  Ps 100:5

c Ge 28:10
  Ge 30:43
  Ge 32:7

d Ps 34:4

e Ge 27:41

f Ge 28:14
  Ge 46:2, 3
  Ex 1:7
  Ex 32:13
  Ac 7:17

g Ge 33:10

h Ge 30:43

Second Col.
a Ge 33:8

b Ge 43:11
  1Sa 25:18

c Ge 29:30
  Ru 4:11

d Ge 30:3, 9

e De 3:16
  Jos 12:2
  Jg 11:13

f Ho 12:3

g Ge 32:31, 32

h Ho 12:4

i Ge 35:10

j Ho 12:3

k Jg 13:17, 18

32:12 *Lit., "seed."

32:23 *Or "torrent valley; wadi." **32:28** *Meaning "Contender (Perseverer) With God" or "God Contends."

him there. **30** So Jacob named the place Pe·ni′el,*[a] for he said, "I have seen God face-to-face, yet my life# was preserved."[b]

31 And the sun rose upon him as soon as he passed by Pe·nu′el,* but he was limping because of his hip.[c] **32** That is why to this day the sons of Israel are not accustomed to eat the thigh sinew,* which is on the socket of the hip joint, because he touched the socket of Jacob's hip joint by the thigh sinew.

33 Now Jacob raised his eyes and saw E′sau coming, and 400 men were with him.[d] So he divided the children among Le′ah, Rachel, and the two female servants.[e] **2** He put the female servants and their children in front,[f] Le′ah and her children after them,[g] and Rachel[h] and Joseph behind them. **3** Then he himself went ahead of them and bowed down to the earth seven times as he came near to his brother.

4 But E′sau ran to meet him, and he embraced him and kissed him, and they burst into tears. **5** When he raised his eyes and saw the women and the children, he said: "Who are these with you?" to which he said: "The children with whom God has favored your servant."[i] **6** At that the female servants came forward with their children and bowed down, **7** and Le′ah too came forward with her children, and they bowed down. Then Joseph came forward with Rachel, and they bowed down.[j]

8 E′sau said: "What is the purpose of all this camp of travelers that I have met?"[k] He replied: "In order to find favor in the eyes of my lord."[l] **9** Then E′sau said: "I have a great

many possessions, my brother.[a] Keep what is yours." **10** However, Jacob said: "No, please. If I have found favor in your eyes, you must take my gift from my hand, because I brought it so that I could see your face. And I have seen your face as though seeing God's face, in that you received me with pleasure.[b] **11** Take, please, the gift conveying my blessing that was brought to you,[c] for God has favored me and I have everything I need."[d] And he continued to urge him, so that he took it.

12 Later E′sau said: "Let us move out and go, and let me go in advance of you." **13** But he said to him: "My lord is aware that the children are delicate[e] and that in my care are sheep and cattle nursing their young. If they are driven too quickly for one day, then the whole flock will die. **14** Let my lord, please, go on ahead of his servant, but I will continue the journey more slowly at the pace of my livestock and of the children until I come to my lord at Se′ir."[f] **15** Then E′sau said: "Please, let me leave some of my people with you." To this he said: "Why do this? Just let me find favor in the eyes of my lord." **16** So that day E′sau went on his way back to Se′ir.

17 And Jacob journeyed to Suc′coth,[g] and he built a house for himself and he made shelters for his herd. That was why he named the place Suc′coth.*

18 After journeying from Pad′dan-a′ram,[h] Jacob arrived safely at the city of She′chem[i] in the land of Ca′naan,[j] and he set up his camp near the city. **19** Then he acquired a portion of the field where he pitched his tent from the sons of Ha′mor, the father of She′chem, for 100

CHAP. 32
a 1Ki 12:25

b Ge 16:7, 13
  Jg 6:22
  Joh 1:18

c Ge 32:25

CHAP. 33
d Ge 32:6

e Ge 32:22

f Ge 30:7, 12

g Ge 30:19

h Ge 30:22-24

i Ge 32:22
  Ps 127:3

j Ge 33:2

k Ge 32:16

l Ge 32:4, 5

Second Col.
a Ge 36:6, 7

b Ge 32:11, 20

c Ge 32:13-15

d Ge 30:43

e Ge 31:17

f Ge 32:3

g Jos 13:24, 27
  1Ki 7:46

h Ge 25:20
  Ge 28:6

i Jos 24:1

j Ge 10:19
  Ge 12:6

32:30 *Meaning "Face of God." # Or "soul." **32:31** *Or "Peniel." **32:32** *Lit., "the sinew of the thigh nerve."

33:17 *Meaning "Booths; Shelters."

pieces of money.[a] **20** There he set up an altar and called it God, the God of Israel.[b]

34 Now Di′nah, Jacob's daughter by Le′ah,[c] used to go out to spend time with* the young women of the land.[d] **2** When She′chem, the son of Ha′mor the Hi′vite,[e] a chieftain of the land, saw her, he took her and lay down with her and violated her. **3** And he* became very attached to Di′nah, the daughter of Jacob, and he fell in love with the young woman and spoke persuasively to her.[#] **4** Finally She′chem said to Ha′mor[f] his father: "Get me this young woman to be my wife."

5 When Jacob heard that he had defiled Di′nah his daughter, his sons were with his herd in the field. So Jacob kept silent until they returned. **6** Later Ha′mor, She′chem's father, went out to speak with Jacob. **7** But the sons of Jacob heard about it and returned from the field right away. They were offended and very angry because he had disgraced Israel by lying down with Jacob's daughter,[g] something that should not be done.[h]

8 Ha′mor spoke with them, saying: "My son She′chem longs for* your daughter. Please give her to him as his wife, **9** and form marriage alliances* with us. Give us your daughters, and take our daughters for yourselves.[i] **10** You may dwell with us, and the land will become available for you. Dwell and carry on trade in it and settle in it." **11** Then She′chem said to her father and to her brothers: "Let me find favor in your eyes, and I will give you whatever you ask

me. **12** You can demand from me a very high bride price and gift.[a] I am willing to give whatever you may say to me. Just give me the young woman as a wife."

13 And Jacob's sons answered She′chem and Ha′mor his father deceitfully because he had defiled Di′nah their sister. **14** They said to them: "We cannot possibly do such a thing, to give our sister to a man who is not circumcised,*[b] for that is a disgrace to us. **15** We can only consent on this condition: that you become like us and circumcise all your males.[c] **16** Then we will give our daughters to you, and we will take your daughters for ourselves, and we will dwell with you and become one people. **17** But if you do not listen to us and get circumcised, then we will take our daughter and go."

18 Their words pleased Ha′mor[d] and She′chem, Ha′mor's son.[e] **19** The young man did not delay in doing what they asked,[f] because he found delight in Jacob's daughter, and he was the most honorable of the whole house of his father.

20 So Ha′mor and his son She′chem went to the city gate and spoke to the men of their city,[g] saying: **21** "These men wish to be at peace with us. Let them dwell in the land and carry on trade in it, for the land is large enough to accommodate them. We can take their daughters as wives, and our daughters we can give to them.[h] **22** Only on this one condition will the men consent to dwell with us in order to become one people: that every male among us be circumcised just the way they are circumcised.[i] **23** Then, will not

---

CHAP. 33

a Jos 24:32
Ac 7:15, 16

b Ge 35:1, 7

CHAP. 34

c Ge 30:19, 21
Ge 46:15

d Ge 26:34, 35
Ge 27:46

e De 7:1
1Ch 1:13-15

f Ge 33:18, 19

g 2Sa 13:22

h Heb 13:4

i Ge 24:2, 3

Second Col.

a Ge 24:53
Ho 3:2

b Ge 17:9, 12

c Ge 17:10

d Ge 33:18, 19

e Ge 34:2

f Ge 34:15

g Zec 8:16

h Ge 34:8, 9

i Ge 17:11

34:1 *Or "to see." **34:3** *Or "his soul." #Lit., "spoke to the heart of the young woman." **34:8** *Or "The soul of my son Shechem is attached to." **34:9** *Or "and intermarry."

34:14 *Lit., "who has a foreskin."

their possessions, their wealth, and all their livestock be ours? So let us give them our consent that they may dwell with us." **24** All those going out by the gate of his city listened to Ha′mor and to his son She′chem, and all the males got circumcised, all those going out of the city gate.

25 However, on the third day, when they were still in pain, two sons of Jacob, Sim′e·on and Le′vi, Di′nah's brothers,[a] each took his sword and went into the unsuspecting city and killed every male.[b] **26** They killed Ha′mor and his son She′chem with the sword and then took Di′nah from She′chem's house and left. **27** Jacob's other sons came upon the slain men and plundered the city because they had defiled their sister.[c] **28** They took their flocks, their herds, their donkeys, and whatever was in the city and in the field. **29** They also took all their possessions, captured all their little children and their wives, and plundered everything in the houses.

30 At this Jacob said to Sim′e·on and to Le′vi:[d] "You have brought great trouble* on me in making me a stench to the inhabitants of the land, to the Ca′naan·ites and the Per′iz·zites. I am few in number, and they will certainly gather together to attack me and I will be annihilated, I and my house." **31** But they said: "Should anyone treat our sister like a prostitute?"

35 After that God said to Jacob: "Rise, go up to Beth′el[e] and dwell there, and make an altar there to the true God, who appeared to you when you were running away from E′sau your brother."[f]

2 Then Jacob said to his

34:30 *Or "brought ostracism."

CHAP. 34
a Ge 46:15

b Ge 49:5-7

c Ge 34:2

d Ge 49:5

CHAP. 35
e Ge 28:19
  Ge 31:13

f Ge 27:42-44

Second Col.
a Ge 31:19
  De 5:7
  Jos 23:7
  1Co 10:14

b Ge 28:13, 15
  Ge 31:42

c Ge 28:19

d Ge 28:20-22

e Ge 24:59

f Ge 25:26
  Ge 27:36

g Ge 32:28

h Ge 17:1
  Ex 6:3
  Re 15:3

i Ge 48:3, 4

j Ge 17:5, 6
  Joh 12:13

---

household and to all who were with him: "Get rid of the foreign gods that are in your midst,[a] and cleanse yourselves and change your garments, **3** and let us rise and go up to Beth′el. There I will make an altar to the true God, who answered me in the day of my distress and who has been with me wherever* I have gone."[b] **4** So they gave Jacob all the foreign gods they had and the earrings that were in their ears, and Jacob buried* them under the big tree that was close to She′chem.

5 When they traveled on, the terror of God struck the cities around them, so they did not chase after the sons of Jacob. **6** Jacob eventually came to Luz,[c] that is, Beth′el, in the land of Ca′naan, he and all the people with him. **7** There he built an altar and called the place El-beth′el,* because there the true God had revealed himself to him when he had run away from his brother.[d] **8** Later Deb′o·rah,[e] Re·bek′ah's nurse, died and was buried at the foot of Beth′el under an oak. So he named it Al′lon-bac′uth.*

9 God appeared to Jacob once again while he was coming from Pad′dan-a′ram and blessed him. **10** God said to him: "Your name is Jacob.[f] Your name will no longer be Jacob, but Israel will be your name." And he began to call him Israel.[g] **11** God further said to him: "I am God Almighty.[h] Be fruitful and become many. Nations and a congregation of nations will come from you,[i] and kings will descend from you.*[j] **12** As for the land that I have given to Abraham and to Isaac, to you I will

---

35:3 *Or "in the way." 35:4 *Or "hid."
35:7 *Meaning "God of Bethel." 35:8
*Meaning "Oak of Weeping." 35:11
*Lit., "come out of your loins."

give it, and to your offspring* after you I will give the land."[a] **13** Then God went up from him at the place where he had spoken with him.

14 So Jacob set up a pillar in the place where he had spoken with him, a pillar of stone, and he poured a drink offering on it and poured oil on it.[b] **15** And Jacob continued to call the place where God had spoken with him Beth'el.[c]

16 Then they pulled away from Beth'el. And while they were still some distance from Eph'rath, Rachel began to give birth, and her labor was very difficult. **17** But while she was struggling to deliver the child, the midwife said to her: "Do not be afraid, for you will have this son also."[d] **18** Just as her life was slipping away* (for she was dying), she named him Ben-o'ni,# but his father called him Benjamin.△e **19** So Rachel died and was buried on the way to Eph'rath, that is, Beth'le·hem.[f] **20** Jacob set up a pillar over her grave; it is the pillar of Rachel's grave to this day.

21 After that Israel pulled away and pitched his tent a distance beyond the tower of E'der. **22** Once while Israel was dwelling in that land, Reu'ben went and lay down with Bil'hah his father's concubine, and Israel heard about it.[g]

So there were 12 sons of Jacob. **23** The sons by Le'ah were Jacob's firstborn Reu'ben,[h] then Sim'e·on, Le'vi, Judah, Is'sa·char, and Zeb'u·lun. **24** The sons by Rachel were Joseph and Benjamin. **25** And the sons by Bil'hah, Rachel's servant, were Dan and Naph'ta·li. **26** And the sons by Zil'pah, Le'ah's servant, were Gad and Ash'er. These are Jacob's sons, who were born to him in Pad'dan-a'ram.

27 Jacob eventually came to where his father Isaac was at Mam're,[a] to Kir'i·ath-ar'ba, that is, Heb'ron, where Abraham and also Isaac had resided as foreigners.[b] **28** Isaac lived to be 180 years old.[c] **29** Then Isaac breathed his last and died and was gathered to his people,* after a long and satisfying life;# and his sons E'sau and Jacob buried him.[d]

36 This is the history of E'sau, that is, E'dom.[e] **2** E'sau took his wives from the daughters of Ca'naan: A'dah[f] the daughter of E'lon the Hit'tite;[g] and O·hol·i·ba'mah[h] the daughter of A'nah, the granddaughter of Zib'e·on the Hi'vite; **3** and Bas'e·math,[i] Ish'ma·el's daughter, the sister of Ne·ba'ioth.[j]

4 And A'dah bore El'i·phaz to E'sau, and Bas'e·math bore Reu'el, **5** and O·hol·i·ba'mah bore Je'ush, Ja'lam, and Kor'ah.[k]

These are the sons of E'sau, who were born to him in the land of Ca'naan. **6** After that E'sau took his wives, his sons, his daughters, all the members* of his household, his herd and all his other beasts, and all the wealth he had accumulated[l] in the land of Ca'naan and he went to another land some distance away from Jacob his brother.[m] **7** For their goods had become too many for them to dwell together, and the land where they were residing* was not able to sustain them because of their herds. **8** So E'sau took up

---

CHAP. 35
a Ge 15:18
De 34:4

b Ge 28:18

c Ge 28:19

d Ge 30:22-24

e Ge 46:21
Ge 49:27
De 33:12

f Ge 48:7
Mic 5:2
Mt 2:6

g Ge 49:3, 4
1Ch 5:1

h Ge 49:3

Second Col.
a Ge 31:17, 18

b Ge 15:13
Heb 11:9

c Ge 25:20, 26

d Ge 49:30, 31

CHAP. 36
e Ge 25:30
Eze 25:12, 13
Ro 9:13

f Ge 36:10

g Ge 26:34

h Ge 36:18

i Ge 36:17

j Ge 25:13
Ge 28:9

k 1Ch 1:35

l Ge 33:9

m Ge 27:39
Ge 32:3

35:12 *Lit., "seed." **35:18** *Or "her soul was going out." #Meaning "Son of My Mourning." △Meaning "Son of the Right Hand."

35:29 *This is a poetic expression for death. #Lit., "old and full of days." **36:6** *Or "souls." **36:7** *Or "living as foreigners."

dwelling in the mountainous region of Se'ir.[a] E'sau is E'dom.[b]

9 And this is the history of E'sau the father of E'dom in the mountainous region of Se'ir.[c]

10 These are the names of the sons of E'sau: El'i·phaz the son of A'dah, E'sau's wife; Reu'el the son of Bas'e·math, E'sau's wife.[d]

11 The sons of El'i·phaz were Te'man,[e] O'mar, Ze'pho, Ga'tam, and Ke'naz.[f] **12** Tim'na became the concubine of El'i·phaz, E'sau's son. In time she bore to El'i·phaz, Am'a·lek.[g] These are the sons of A'dah, E'sau's wife.

13 These are the sons of Reu'el: Na'hath, Ze'rah, Sham'mah, and Miz'zah. These were the sons of Bas'e·math,[h] E'sau's wife.

14 These were the sons of O·hol·i·ba'mah the daughter of A'nah, the granddaughter of Zib'e·on, E'sau's wife, whom she bore to E'sau: Je'ush, Ja'lam, and Kor'ah.

15 These are the sheikhs* of the sons of E'sau:[i] The sons of El'i·phaz, E'sau's firstborn: Sheikh Te'man, Sheikh O'mar, Sheikh Ze'pho, Sheikh Ke'naz,[j] **16** Sheikh Kor'ah, Sheikh Ga'tam, and Sheikh Am'a·lek. These are the sheikhs of El'i·phaz[k] in the land of E'dom. These are the sons by A'dah.

17 These are the sons of Reu'el, E'sau's son: Sheikh Na'hath, Sheikh Ze'rah, Sheikh Sham'mah, and Sheikh Miz'zah. These are the sheikhs of Reu'el in the land of E'dom.[l] These are the sons by Bas'e·math, E'sau's wife.

18 Finally these are the sons of O·hol·i·ba'mah, E'sau's wife: Sheikh Je'ush, Sheikh Ja'lam, and Sheikh Kor'ah. These are the sheikhs of O·hol·i·ba'mah the daughter of A'nah, E'sau's wife.

19 These are the sons of E'sau, and these are their sheikhs. He is E'dom.[a]

20 These are the sons of Se'ir the Hor'ite, the inhabitants of the land:[b] Lo'tan, Sho'bal, Zib'e·on, A'nah,[c] **21** Di'shon, E'zer, and Di'shan.[d] These are the sheikhs of the Hor'ites, the sons of Se'ir, in the land of E'dom.

22 The sons of Lo'tan were Ho'ri and He'mam, and Lo'tan's sister was Tim'na.[e]

23 These are the sons of Sho'bal: Al'van, Man'a·hath, E'bal, She'pho, and O'nam.

24 These are the sons of Zib'e·on:[f] A'iah and A'nah. This is the A'nah who found the hot springs in the wilderness while he was tending the donkeys for Zib'e·on his father.

25 These are the children of A'nah: Di'shon and O·hol·i·ba'mah the daughter of A'nah.

26 These are the sons of Di'shon: Hem'dan, Esh'ban, Ith'ran, and Che'ran.[g]

27 These are the sons of E'zer: Bil'han, Za'a·van, and A'kan.

28 These are the sons of Di'shan: Uz and A'ran.[h]

29 These are the sheikhs of the Hor'ites: Sheikh Lo'tan, Sheikh Sho'bal, Sheikh Zib'e·on, Sheikh A'nah, **30** Sheikh Di'shon, Sheikh E'zer, and Sheikh Di'shan.[i] These are the sheikhs of the Hor'ites according to their sheikhs in the land of Se'ir.

31 Now these are the kings who reigned in the land of E'dom[j] before any king reigned over the Israelites.*[k] **32** Be'la son of Be'or reigned in E'dom, and the name of his city was Din'ha·bah. **33** When Be'la died, Jo'bab son of Ze'rah from Boz'rah began to reign

---

CHAP. 36

a Ge 14:6
  De 2:5

b Ge 25:30

c De 2:12

d 1Ch 1:35

e Ge 36:34

f Ge 36:40, 42
  1Ch 1:36

g Ex 17:8
  Nu 13:29
  Nu 24:20
  De 25:19
  1Sa 15:8
  1Sa 30:1

h Ge 26:34

i Ex 15:15

j 1Ch 1:53, 54

k 1Ch 1:36

l Nu 20:23
  1Ki 9:26

Second Col.

a Ge 25:30
  Ge 32:3

b Ge 14:6
  De 2:12, 22

c 1Ch 1:40

d 1Ch 1:38

e 1Ch 1:39

f Ge 36:2

g 1Ch 1:41

h 1Ch 1:42

i 1Ch 1:38

j Nu 20:14

k De 17:14, 15
  1Sa 10:19
  1Ch 1:43-50

36:15 *A sheikh was a tribal chief.

36:31 *Lit., "the sons of Israel."

in his place. **34** When Jo'bab died, Hu'sham from the land of the Te'man·ites began to reign in his place. **35** When Hu'sham died, Ha'dad son of Be'dad, who defeated the Mid'i·an·ites[a] in the territory* of Mo'ab, began to reign in his place, and the name of his city was A'vith. **36** When Ha'dad died, Sam'lah from Mas·re'kah began to reign in his place. **37** When Sam'lah died, Sha'ul from Re·ho'both by the River began to reign in his place. **38** When Sha'ul died, Ba'al-ha'nan the son of Ach'-bor began to reign in his place. **39** When Ba'al-ha'nan the son of Ach'bor died, Ha'dar began to reign in his place. The name of his city was Pa'u, and the name of his wife was Me·het'a·bel the daughter of Ma'tred the daughter of Me'za·hab.

40 So these are the names of the sheikhs of E'sau according to their families, according to their places, by their names: Sheikh Tim'na, Sheikh Al'vah, Sheikh Je'-theth,[b] **41** Sheikh O·hol·i-ba'mah, Sheikh E'lah, Sheikh Pi'non, **42** Sheikh Ke'naz, Sheikh Te'man, Sheikh Mib'-zar, **43** Sheikh Mag'di·el, and Sheikh I'ram. These are the sheikhs of E'dom according to their settlements in the land of their possession.[c] This is E'sau the father of E'dom.[d]

37 Jacob continued to dwell in the land of Ca'naan, where his father had lived as a foreigner.[e]

2 This is the history of Jacob. When Joseph[f] was 17 years old, the young man was tending the flock[g] with the sons of Bil'hah[h] and the sons of Zil'pah,[i] the wives of his father. And Joseph brought a bad report about them to their father. **3** Now Is-rael loved Joseph more than all his other sons[a] because he was the son of his old age, and he had a special robe* made for him. **4** When his brothers saw that their father loved him more than all his brothers, they began to hate him, and they could not speak peaceably to him.

5 Later Joseph had a dream and told it to his brothers,[b] and they found further reason to hate him. **6** He said to them: "Please listen to this dream that I had. **7** There we were binding sheaves in the middle of the field when my sheaf got up and stood erect and your sheaves encircled and bowed down to my sheaf."[c] **8** His brothers said to him: "Are you really going to make yourself king over us and dominate us?"[d] So they found another reason to hate him, because of his dreams and what he said.

9 After that he had still another dream, and he related it to his brothers: "I have had another dream. This time the sun and the moon and 11 stars were bowing down to me."[e] **10** Then he related it to his father as well as his brothers, and his father rebuked him and said to him: "What is the meaning of this dream of yours? Am I as well as your mother and your brothers really going to come and bow down to the earth to you?" **11** And his brothers grew jealous of him,[f] but his father kept the saying in mind.

12 His brothers now went to pasture their father's flock near She'chem.[g] **13** Israel later said to Joseph: "Your brothers are tending flocks near She'chem, are they not? Come, and let me send you to them." At this he said to him: "I am ready!" **14** So he said to him: "Go, please, and see whether your brothers are well. See how the flock is, and bring word back to me." With that

---

CHAP. 36
a Ge 25:1, 2
  Ex 2:15
  Nu 31:2

b 1Ch 1:51-54

c De 2:5

d Ge 25:30
  Ge 36:8

CHAP. 37
e Ge 23:3, 4
  Ge 28:1, 4
  Heb 11:8, 9

f Ge 30:25
  Ge 46:19

g Ge 47:3

h Ge 35:25

i Ge 35:26

Second Col.
a 1Ch 2:1, 2

b Ge 37:19

c Ge 42:6, 9

d Ge 45:8
  Ge 49:26

e Ge 44:14
  Ge 45:9

f Ac 7:9

g Ge 33:18

36:35 *Lit., "field."   37:3 *Or "a beautiful long garment."

he sent him away from the valley* of Heb'ron,[a] and he went on toward She'chem. 15 Later a man found him as he was wandering in a field. The man asked him: "What are you looking for?" 16 To this he said: "I am looking for my brothers. Please tell me, where are they tending flocks?" 17 The man continued: "They have pulled away from here, for I heard them saying, 'Let us go to Do'than.'" So Joseph went after his brothers and found them at Do'than.

18 Now they caught sight of him from a distance, and before he reached them, they began plotting against him to put him to death. 19 So they said to one another: "Look! Here comes that dreamer.[b] 20 Come, now, let us kill him and pitch him into one of the waterpits, and we will say that a vicious wild animal devoured him. Then let us see what will become of his dreams." 21 When Reu'ben[c] heard this, he tried to rescue him from them. So he said: "Let us not take his life."*[d] 22 Reu'ben said to them: "Do not shed blood.[e] Throw him into this waterpit in the wilderness, but do not harm* him."[f] His purpose was to rescue him from them in order to return him to his father.

23 So as soon as Joseph came to his brothers, they stripped Joseph of his robe, the special robe that he wore,[g] 24 and they took him and threw him into the waterpit. At the time the pit was empty; there was no water in it.

25 Then they sat down to eat. When they looked up, there was a caravan of Ish'ma·el·ites[h] coming from Gil'e·ad. Their camels were carrying labdanum gum, balsam, and resinous bark,[i] and

they were on their way down to Egypt. 26 At this Judah said to his brothers: "What profit would there be if we killed our brother and covered over his blood?[a] 27 Come, now, let us sell him[b] to the Ish'ma·el·ites, and do not let our hand be upon him. After all, he is our brother, our flesh." So they listened to their brother. 28 And when the Mid'i·an·ite[c] merchants were passing by, they lifted Joseph up out of the waterpit and sold him to the Ish'-ma·el·ites for 20 pieces of silver.[d] These men took Joseph into Egypt.

29 Later when Reu'ben returned to the waterpit and saw that Joseph was not in the waterpit, he ripped his garments apart. 30 When he returned to his brothers, he exclaimed: "The child is gone! And I—what am I going to do?"

31 So they took Joseph's robe and slaughtered a male goat and dipped the robe in the blood. 32 After that they sent the special robe to their father and said: "This is what we found. Please examine whether this is your son's robe or not."[e] 33 Then he examined it and exclaimed: "It is my son's robe! A vicious wild animal must have devoured him! Joseph is surely torn to pieces!" 34 With that Jacob ripped his garments apart and put sackcloth around his waist and mourned his son for many days. 35 And all his sons and all his daughters kept trying to comfort him, but he kept refusing to take comfort, saying: "I will go down into the Grave*[f] mourning my son!" And his father continued weeping for him.

36 Now the Mid'i·an·ites sold him in Egypt to Pot'i·phar, a court official of Phar'aoh[g] and the chief of the guard.[h]

CHAP. 37
a Ge 23:19
  Ge 35:27

b Ge 37:5

c Ge 49:3

d Ge 9:5
  Ex 20:13

e Ge 4:8, 10
  Ge 42:22

f Ge 42:21

g Ge 37:3

h Ge 25:12

i Ge 43:11

Second Col.
a Ge 4:8, 10

b Ac 7:9

c Ge 25:1, 2

d Ge 40:15
  Ge 45:4
  Ps 105:17

e Ge 37:3

f Ge 42:38
  Ge 44:29
  Ps 89:48
  Ec 9:10
  Ho 13:14
  Ac 2:27
  Re 20:13

g Ge 39:1

h Ge 40:2, 3

37:14 *Or "low plain." 37:21 *Or "strike his soul." 37:22 *Or "lay a hand on."

37:35 *Or "Sheol," that is, the common grave of mankind. See Glossary.

38 About that time Judah left his brothers and pitched his tent near an A·dul′lam·ite man named Hi′rah. 2 There Judah saw the daughter of a certain Ca′naan·ite[a] named Shu′a. So he took her and had relations with her, 3 and she became pregnant. Later she bore a son, and he named him Er.[b] 4 Again she became pregnant and bore a son and named him O′nan. 5 Yet again she bore a son and named him She′lah. He* was in Ach′zib[c] when she bore him.

6 In time Judah took a wife for Er his firstborn, and her name was Ta′mar.[d] 7 But Er, Judah's firstborn, was displeasing to Jehovah; so Jehovah put him to death. 8 In view of that, Judah said to O′nan: "Have relations with your brother's wife and perform brother-in-law marriage with her and raise up offspring for your brother."[e] 9 But O′nan knew that the offspring would not be considered his.[f] So when he did have relations with his brother's wife, he wasted his semen on the ground so as not to give offspring to his brother.[g] 10 What he did was bad in the eyes of Jehovah, so he also put him to death.[h] 11 Judah said to Ta′mar his daughter-in-law: "Dwell as a widow in the house of your father until my son She′lah grows up," for he said to himself: 'He too may die like his brothers.'[i] So Ta′mar went and stayed in her own father's house.

12 Some time passed, and Judah's wife, the daughter of Shu′a,[j] died. Judah kept the mourning period, and then he went to his sheepshearers in Tim′nah[k] with his companion Hi′rah the A·dul′lam·ite.[l] 13 Ta′mar was told: "Here your father-in-law is going up to Tim′nah to shear his sheep." 14 With that

she removed her widow's clothing and veiled herself and covered herself with a shawl and sat down at the entrance of E·na′im, which is on the road to Tim′nah, for she saw that She′lah had grown up and yet she had not been given to him as a wife.[a]

15 When Judah caught sight of her, he at once took her for a prostitute, because she had covered her face. 16 So he turned aside to her by the road and said: "Allow me, please, to have relations with you," for he did not know that she was his daughter-in-law.[b] However, she said: "What will you give me that you may have relations with me?" 17 To this he said: "I will send a young goat from my herd." But she said: "Will you give a security until you send it?" 18 He continued: "What security should I give you?" to which she said: "Your seal ring[c] and your cord and your rod that is in your hand." Then he gave them to her and had relations with her, and she became pregnant by him. 19 After that she got up and went away and removed her shawl and clothed herself with her widow's clothing.

20 And Judah sent the young goat by the hand of his companion the A·dul′lam·ite,[d] to get back the security from the hand of the woman, but he never found her. 21 He inquired of the men of her place, saying: "Where is that temple prostitute in E·na′im along the road?" But they said: "No temple prostitute has ever been in this place." 22 Finally he returned to Judah and said: "I never found her, and besides, the men of the place said, 'No temple prostitute has ever been in this place.'" 23 So Judah said: "Let her take them for herself, in order that we may not fall into contempt. At any rate,

---

CHAP. 38
a Ge 24:2, 3
　Ge 28:1

b Nu 26:19

c Jos 19:29, 31

d Mt 1:3

e De 25:5, 6
　Mt 22:24

f Ru 4:6

g De 25:7, 9

h 1Ch 2:3

i Nu 26:19

j Ge 38:2

k Jos 15:10, 12
　Jg 14:1

l Ge 38:1

Second Col.
a De 25:5

b Ge 38:11

c Ge 41:42
　1Ki 21:8

d Ge 38:1

38:5 *That is, Judah.

I have sent this young goat, but you never found her."

24 However, about three months later, Judah was told: "Ta′mar your daughter-in-law has acted as a prostitute, and she is also pregnant by her prostitution." At that Judah said: "Bring her out and let her be burned."[a] **25** As she was being brought out, she sent word to her father-in-law: "I am pregnant by the man to whom these belong." Then she added: "Please examine to whom these belong, the seal ring and the cord and the rod."[b] **26** Then Judah examined them and said: "She is more righteous than I am, because I did not give her to She′-lah my son."[c] And he had no further sexual relations with her after that.

27 When the time came for her to give birth, there were twins in her womb. **28** As she was giving birth, one put out his hand, and the midwife immediately took a scarlet thread and tied it around his hand, saying: "This one came out first." **29** But as soon as he drew back his hand, his brother came out, and she exclaimed: "What a breach you have made for yourself!" So he was named Pe′rez.*[d] **30** Afterward his brother came out, around whose hand the scarlet thread was tied, and he was named Ze′rah.[e]

39 Now Joseph was taken down to Egypt,[f] and an Egyptian named Pot′i·phar,[g] a court official of Phar′aoh and chief of the guard, bought him from the Ish′ma·el·ites[h] who had taken him down there. **2** But Jehovah was with Joseph.[i] As a result, he became successful and was put over the house of his master, the Egyptian. **3** And

his master saw that Jehovah was with him and that Jehovah was making everything that he did successful.

4 Joseph kept finding favor in his eyes, and he became his personal attendant. So he appointed him over his house, and he put him in charge of all that was his. **5** From the time he appointed him over his house and in charge of all that was his, Jehovah kept blessing the house of the Egyptian because of Joseph, and Jehovah's blessing came to be on all that he had in the house and in the field.[a] **6** He eventually left everything that was his in Joseph's care, and he gave no thought to anything except the food he was eating. Moreover, Joseph grew to be well-built and handsome.

7 Now after these things, the wife of his master began to cast her eyes on Joseph and say: "Lie down with me." **8** But he refused and said to his master's wife: "Here my master does not know what is with me in the house, and he has entrusted everything he has into my care. **9** There is no one greater in this house than I am, and he has not withheld from me anything at all except you, because you are his wife. So how could I commit this great badness and actually sin against God?"[b]

10 So day after day she spoke to Joseph, but he never consented to lie with her or to remain with her. **11** But on one of the days when he went into the house to do his work, none of the household servants were in the house. **12** Then she grabbed hold of him by his garment and said: "Lie down with me!" But he left his garment in her hand and fled outside. **13** As soon as she saw that he had left his garment in her hand and had fled outside,

---

38:29 * Meaning "Rupture," probably referring to a perineal rupture.

14 she began to cry out to the men of her house and to say to them: "Look! He brought to us this Hebrew man to make us a laughingstock. He came to me to lie down with me, but I began to cry out at the top of my voice. **15** Then as soon as he heard me raising my voice and screaming, he left his garment beside me and fled outside." **16** After that she laid his garment beside her until his master came to his house.

17 Then she told him the same thing, saying: "The Hebrew servant whom you brought to us came to me to make me a laughingstock. **18** But as soon as I raised my voice and began to scream, he left his garment beside me and fled outside." **19** As soon as his master heard the words his wife spoke to him, saying: "These are the things your servant did to me," his anger blazed. **20** So Joseph's master took him and gave him over to the prison, the place where the prisoners of the king were kept under arrest, and he remained there in the prison.[a]

21 But Jehovah continued with Joseph and kept showing loyal love to him and granting him favor in the eyes of the chief officer of the prison.[b] **22** So the chief officer of the prison put Joseph in charge of all the prisoners in the prison, and everything that they were doing there, he was the one having it done.[c] **23** The chief officer of the prison was looking after absolutely nothing that was in Joseph's care, for Jehovah was with Joseph and Jehovah made whatever he did successful.[d]

40 After these things, the chief cupbearer[e] of the king of Egypt and the chief baker sinned against their lord, the king of Egypt. **2** So Pharaoh grew indignant at his two of-

ficers, the chief cupbearer and the chief baker,[a] **3** and he committed them to the jail of the house of the chief of the guard,[b] to the place where Joseph was a prisoner.[c] **4** Then the chief of the guard assigned Joseph to be with them and to take care of them,[d] and they remained in jail for some time.*

5 The cupbearer and the baker of the king of Egypt, who were confined in the prison, each had a dream on the same night, and each dream had its own interpretation. **6** The next morning, when Joseph came in and saw them, they looked dejected. **7** So he asked the officers of Pharaoh who were in custody with him in his master's house: "Why are your faces gloomy today?" **8** At this they said to him: "We each had a dream, but there is no interpreter with us." Joseph said to them: "Do not interpretations belong to God?[e] Relate it to me, please."

9 So the chief cupbearer related his dream to Joseph, saying to him: "In my dream, there was a vine before me. **10** And on the vine, there were three twigs, and as it was sprouting shoots, it blossomed, and its clusters ripened into grapes. **11** And Pharaoh's cup was in my hand, and I took the grapes and squeezed them out into Pharaoh's cup. After that I put the cup in Pharaoh's hand." **12** Then Joseph said to him: "This is its interpretation: The three twigs are three days. **13** Three days from now, Pharaoh will bring you out,* restoring you to your office,[f] and you will put Pharaoh's cup into his hand as you did before when you were his cupbearer.[g] **14** Nevertheless, you must remember me

CHAP. 39
a Ps 105:17, 18

b Ge 40:2, 3
Ps 105:19
Ac 7:9

c Ge 39:6

d Ge 49:22, 25
Ac 7:9, 10

CHAP. 40
e Ge 40:11

Second Col.
a Ge 40:20-22

b Ge 37:36

c Ge 39:20
Ps 105:17, 18

d Ge 39:22

e Ge 41:15, 16
Da 2:28, 45

f Ge 41:12, 13

g Ge 40:20, 21

40:4 *Lit., "days." **40:13** *Lit., "lift up your head."

when things go well with you. Please show me loyal love and mention me to Phar'aoh, in order to get me out of this place. **15** I was, in fact, kidnapped from the land of the Hebrews,[a] and I have not done anything here for which they should put me in prison."*[b]

16 When the chief baker saw that Joseph had interpreted something good, he said to him: "I too was in my dream, and there were three baskets of white bread on my head, **17** and in the top basket, there were all sorts of baked goods for Phar'aoh, and there were birds eating them out of the basket on top of my head." **18** Then Joseph answered, "This is its interpretation: The three baskets are three days. **19** Three days from now, Phar'aoh will behead you* and will hang you on a stake, and the birds will eat your flesh from you."[c]

20 Now the third day was Phar'aoh's birthday,[d] and he made a feast for all his servants, and he brought out* both the chief cupbearer and the chief baker in the presence of his servants. **21** And he returned the chief cupbearer to his post of cupbearer, and he continued to hand the cup to Phar'aoh. **22** But he hanged the chief baker, just as Joseph had interpreted to them,[e] **23** However, the chief cupbearer did not remember Joseph; he kept forgetting him.[f]

41 At the end of two full years, Phar'aoh dreamed[g] that he was standing by the Nile River. **2** And there, coming up from the river, were seven fine-looking, fat cows, and they were feeding on the Nile grass.[h]

3 There were seven other cows that looked ugly and thin coming up after them from the Nile, and they stood alongside the fat cows by the bank of the Nile. **4** Then the ugly, thin cows began to eat up the seven fine-looking, fat cows. At this Phar'aoh woke up.

5 Then he went back to sleep and had a second dream. There were seven ears of grain coming up on one stalk, full and choice.[a] **6** And growing up after them were seven ears of grain that were thin and scorched by the east wind. **7** And the thin ears of grain began to swallow up the seven full and choice ears of grain. At this Phar'aoh woke up and realized that it was a dream.

8 But in the morning, his spirit became agitated. So he sent for all the magic-practicing priests of Egypt and all her wise men. Phar'aoh related his dreams to them, but there was no one who could interpret them for Phar'aoh.

9 At that the chief cupbearer spoke with Phar'aoh, saying: "I am confessing my sins today. **10** Phar'aoh was indignant at his servants. So he committed me to the jail of the house of the chief of the guard, both me and the chief baker.[b] **11** After that we each had a dream on the same night. He and I each had a dream with its own interpretation.[c] **12** And there with us was a young Hebrew man, a servant of the chief of the guard.[d] When we related them to him,[e] he interpreted for us the meaning of each dream. **13** It happened exactly as he had interpreted to us. I was restored to my office, but the other man was hanged."[f]

14 So Phar'aoh sent for Joseph,[g] and they brought him quickly from the prison.*[h] He shaved and changed his clothes and went in to Phar'aoh.

CHAP. 40
a Ge 37:28

b Ge 39:7, 8

c Ge 40:20, 22

d Mr 6:21

e Ge 40:8

f Ge 40:14

CHAP. 41
g Da 2:1

h Ge 41:18-21

Second Col.
a Ge 41:22-24

b Ge 40:2, 3

c Ge 40:5

d Ge 39:1

e Ge 40:8

f Ge 40:21, 22

g Ps 105:20

h Ge 40:15

40:15; 41:14 *Lit., "the cistern; the pit."
40:19 *Lit., "lift up your head from you."
40:20 *Lit., "he lifted up the head of."

15 Then Phar'aoh said to Joseph: "I had a dream, but there is no one to interpret it. Now I have heard it said about you that you can hear a dream and interpret it."[a] **16** At this Joseph answered Phar'aoh: "I need not be considered! God will speak concerning Phar'aoh's welfare."[b]

17 Phar'aoh went on to say to Joseph: "In my dream I was standing on the bank of the Nile River. **18** And there, coming up from the Nile, were seven fine-looking, fat cows, and they began to feed on the Nile grass.[c] **19** And there were seven other cows coming up after them, poor and very bad-looking and thin. I have never seen such bad-looking cows in all the land of Egypt. **20** And the skinny, bad cows began to eat up the first seven fat cows. **21** But when they had consumed them, no one could have known that they had done so, since their appearance was just as bad as at the start. At that I woke up.

22 "After that I saw in my dream seven ears of grain coming up on one stalk, full and choice.[d] **23** Growing up after them were seven ears of shriveled grain, thin and scorched by the east wind. **24** Then the thin ears of grain began to swallow up the seven choice ears of grain. So I told it to the magic-practicing priests,[e] but there was no one who could explain it to me."[f]

25 Then Joseph said to Phar'aoh: "The dreams of Phar'aoh are one and the same. The true God has told to Phar'aoh what He will do.[g] **26** The seven good cows are seven years. Likewise, the seven good ears of grain are seven years. The dreams are one and the same. **27** The seven skinny and bad cows that came up after them are seven years, and the seven empty ears of grain, scorched by the east wind, will prove to be seven years of famine. **28** This is just as I told to Phar'aoh: The true God has caused Phar'aoh to see what He will do.

29 "There are to be seven years of great abundance in all the land of Egypt. **30** But seven years of famine will certainly arise after them, and all the abundance in the land of Egypt will certainly be forgotten, and the famine will exhaust the land.[a] **31** And the previous abundance in the land will not be remembered because of the famine afterward, for it will be very severe. **32** The dream was given twice to Phar'aoh because the matter has been firmly established by the true God, and the true God will soon carry it out.

33 "So now let Phar'aoh look for a man who is discreet and wise and place him over the land of Egypt. **34** Let Phar'aoh take action and appoint overseers in the land, and he should collect one fifth of the produce of Egypt during the seven years of abundance.[b] **35** And let them collect all the food during these coming good years, and let them stockpile grain under Phar'aoh's authority as food to be stored in the cities and safeguarded there.[c] **36** The food should serve as a supply for the land for the seven years of famine that will occur in the land of Egypt, so that the land may not perish in the famine."[d]

37 This proposal seemed good to Phar'aoh and all his servants. **38** So Phar'aoh said to his servants: "Can another man be found like this one in whom there is the spirit of God?" **39** Phar'aoh then said to Joseph: "Since God has caused you to know all of this, there is no one as discreet and wise as you. **40** You will personally be over

CHAP. 41
a Da 5:12
Ac 7:9, 10

b Ge 40:8
Da 2:23, 28

c Ge 41:2-4

d Ge 41:5-7

e Ge 41:8
Da 2:2

f Da 2:27
Da 4:7

g Da 2:28
Am 3:7

Second Col.
a Ac 7:11

b Ge 41:26, 47

c Ge 41:48, 49
Ac 7:12

d Ge 45:9, 11
Ge 47:13, 19

my house, and all my people will obey you implicitly.[a] Only in my role as king* will I be greater than you." 41 And Phar'aoh added to Joseph: "See, I am putting you over all the land of Egypt."[b] 42 Then Phar'aoh removed his signet ring from his own hand and put it on Joseph's hand and clothed him with garments of fine linen and placed a necklace of gold around his neck. 43 Moreover, he had him ride in the second chariot of honor that he had, and they would call out ahead of him, "A·vrékh!"* Thus he put him over all the land of Egypt.

44 Phar'aoh further said to Joseph: "I am Phar'aoh, but without your authorization, no man may do a single thing* in all the land of Egypt."[c] 45 After that Phar'aoh gave Joseph the name Zaph'e·nath·pa·ne'ah and gave him As'e·nath[d] the daughter of Pot·i'phe·ra the priest of On* as a wife. And Joseph began to oversee* the land of Egypt.[e] 46 Joseph was 30 years old[f] when he stood before* Phar'aoh king of Egypt.

Then Joseph went out from before Phar'aoh and traveled throughout all the land of Egypt. 47 And during the seven years of abundance, the land went on producing plentifully.* 48 And he kept collecting all the food of the seven years from the land of Egypt, and he would stockpile the food in the cities. In each city he would store the food from the fields around it. 49 Joseph continued stockpiling grain in very great quantity, like

the sand of the sea, until finally they gave up measuring it because it could not be measured.

50 Before the year of the famine arrived, two sons were born to Joseph,[a] whom As'e·nath the daughter of Pot·i'phe·ra the priest of On* bore to him. 51 Joseph named the firstborn Ma·nas'seh,*[b] for he said, "God has made me forget all my trouble and all the house of my father." 52 And he named the second one E'phra·im,*[c] for he said, "God has made me fruitful in the land of my affliction."[d]

53 Then the seven years of abundance in the land of Egypt ended,[e] 54 and the seven years of famine began, just as Joseph had said.[f] The famine developed in all the lands, but in all the land of Egypt there was bread.*[g] 55 Eventually, all the land of Egypt suffered from the famine, and the people began to cry to Phar'aoh for bread.[h] Then Phar'aoh said to all the Egyptians: "Go to Joseph, and do whatever he tells you."[i] 56 The famine continued over all the surface of the earth.[j] Then Joseph began to open up all the granaries that were among them and to sell to the Egyptians,[k] as the famine had a strong grip on the land of Egypt. 57 Moreover, people of all the earth came to Egypt to buy from Joseph, because the famine had a strong grip on all the earth.[l]

42 When Jacob learned that there was grain in Egypt,[m] he said to his sons: "Why do you just keep looking at one another?" 2 He added: "I have heard that there is grain in Egypt. Go down there and buy some for us, so that we may stay alive and

---

CHAP. 41
a Ge 39:6
   Ps 105:21
   Ac 7:9, 10

b Da 5:7

c Ge 44:18
   Ge 45:8
   Ac 7:9, 10

d Ge 46:20

e Ps 105:21

f Nu 4:3
   2Sa 5:4
   Lu 3:23

Second Col.
a Ge 48:5

b Ge 50:23
   Nu 1:34, 35

c Ge 48:17
   Nu 1:32, 33
   De 33:17
   Jos 14:4

d Ps 105:17, 18
   Ac 7:9, 10

e Ge 41:26

f Ge 41:30
   Ac 7:11

g Ge 45:9, 11
   Ge 47:17

h Ge 47:13

i Ps 105:21

j Ge 43:1

k Ge 41:48, 49
   Ge 47:16

l Ge 47:4

CHAP. 42
m Ge 41:48, 49

41:40 *Or "Only with regard to the throne." 41:43 *Apparently a term calling for honor and dignity to be shown. 41:44 *Lit., "lift up his hand or his foot." 41:45 *That is, Heliopolis. #Or "travel through." 41:46 *Or "when he entered the service of." 41:47 *Lit., "by handfuls."

41:50 *That is, Heliopolis. 41:51 *Meaning "One Making Forgetful; One Who Makes Forget." 41:52 *Meaning "Doubly Fruitful." 41:54 *Or "food."

not die."[a] **3** So ten of Joseph's brothers[b] went down to buy grain from Egypt. **4** But Jacob did not send Benjamin,[c] Joseph's brother, with his other brothers, for he said: "Perhaps a fatal accident may befall him."[d]

5 So Israel's sons came along with the others who were coming to buy, because the famine had extended to the land of Ca'naan.[e] **6** Joseph was the man in authority over the land,[f] and he was the one who sold grain to all the people of the earth.[g] So Joseph's brothers came and bowed low to him with their faces to the ground.[h] **7** When Joseph saw his brothers, he immediately recognized them, but he concealed his identity from them.[i] So he spoke harshly with them and said: "Where have you come from?" to which they said: "From the land of Ca'naan to buy food."[j]

8 Thus Joseph recognized his brothers, but they did not recognize him. **9** Joseph immediately remembered the dreams that he had dreamed about them,[k] and he said to them: "You are spies! You have come to see the vulnerable areas* of the land!" **10** Then they said to him: "No, my lord, but your servants have come to buy food. **11** We are all sons of but one man. We are upright men. Your servants do not act as spies." **12** But he said to them: "Not so! You have come to see the vulnerable areas of the land!" **13** At this they said: "Your servants are 12 brothers.[l] We are the sons of but one man[m] in the land of Ca'naan, and the youngest is now with our father,[n] whereas the other one is no more."[o]

14 However, Joseph said to them: "It is just as I said to you—'You are spies!' **15** By this you will be tested: As surely as

CHAP. 42
a Ac 7:12

b 1Ch 2:1, 2

c Ge 35:18, 19
  Ge 42:38
  Ge 44:20

d Ge 43:14

e Ge 41:57
  Ac 7:11

f Ge 41:44
  Ge 45:8
  Ps 105:21
  Ac 7:9, 10

g Ge 47:14

h Ge 37:7, 9

i Ge 42:23

j Ge 37:1
  Ac 7:11, 12

k Ge 37:7-9

l 1Ch 2:1, 2

m Ex 1:1-4

n Ge 35:18, 19
  Ge 42:38
  Ge 43:7

o Ge 37:27, 35
  Ge 44:20

Second Col.
a Ge 42:34
  Ge 43:29

b Ge 45:21, 23

c Ge 37:18, 28
  Ge 50:17
  Ac 7:9

d Ge 37:21

e Ge 9:5

f Ge 43:30

g Ge 42:19

h Ge 43:23

Phar'aoh lives, you will not leave this place until your youngest brother comes here.[a] **16** Send one of you to bring your brother while you remain in bondage. In this way, your words may be tested out to see if you are telling the truth. And if not, then, as surely as Phar'aoh lives, you are spies." **17** With that he put them together in custody for three days.

18 Joseph said to them on the third day: "Do this and live, for I fear God. **19** If you are upright, let one of your brothers remain in bondage in your house of custody, but the rest of you may go and take grain to alleviate the famine in your households.[b] **20** Then bring your youngest brother to me, so that your words will be found trustworthy and you will not die." And they did so.

21 And they said to one another: "We are surely being punished on account of our brother,[c] because we saw his distress* when he begged us to show compassion, but we did not listen. That is why this distress has come upon us." **22** Then Reu'ben answered them: "Did I not say to you, 'Do not sin against the child,' but you would not listen?[d] Now his blood is certainly being asked back."[e] **23** But they did not know that Joseph understood, for there was an interpreter between them. **24** So he turned away from them and began to weep.[f] When he returned and spoke to them again, he took Sim'e·on[g] from them and bound him before their eyes.[h] **25** Joseph then gave the command to fill up their bags* with grain and to return each man's money to his own sack and to give them

---

42:21 *Or "the distress of his soul."
42:25 *Or "receptacles."

42:9 *Or "weakened condition."

provisions for the journey. This was done for them.

26 So they loaded their grain on their donkeys and left from there. 27 When one of them opened his sack to give fodder to his donkey at the lodging place, he saw his money there in the mouth of his bag. 28 At that he said to his brothers: "My money has been returned, and now here it is in my bag!" Then their hearts sank, and trembling, they turned to one another and said: "What is this that God has done to us?"

29 When they came to Jacob their father in the land of Ca′naan, they told him all the things that had befallen them, saying: 30 "The man who is the lord of the country spoke harshly with us[a] and accused us of spying on the country. 31 But we said to him, 'We are upright men. We are not spies.[b] 32 We are 12 brothers,[c] the sons of our father. One is no more,[d] and the youngest is now with our father in the land of Ca′naan.'[e] 33 But the man who is the lord of the country said to us, 'By this I will know that you are upright: Leave one of your brothers with me.[f] Then take something to alleviate the famine in your households and go.[g] 34 And bring your youngest brother to me, so that I may know that you are not spies but upright men. I will then give your brother back to you, and you may carry on trade in the land.'"

35 As they were emptying their sacks, here was each one's bag of money in his sack. When they and their father saw their bags of money, they became afraid. 36 Jacob their father exclaimed to them: "It is I you have bereaved![h] Joseph is no more,[i] and Sim′e·on is no more,[j] and you are going to take Benjamin! It is upon me

that all these things have come!" 37 But Reu′ben said to his father: "You may put to death my own two sons if I do not bring him back to you.[a] Give him over to my care, and I will return him to you."[b] 38 However, he said: "My son will not go down with you, because his brother is dead and he alone is left.[c] If a fatal accident should befall him on the journey you would make, then you would certainly bring down my gray hairs to the Grave*[d] in grief."[e]

43 Now the famine was severe in the land.[f] 2 So when they had finished eating the grain they had brought from Egypt,[g] their father said to them: "Return and buy a little food for us." 3 Then Judah said to him: "The man clearly warned us, 'You must not see my face again unless your brother is with you.'[h] 4 If you send our brother with us, we will go down and buy food for you. 5 But if you do not send him, we will not go down, for the man said to us, 'You must not see my face again unless your brother is with you.'"[i] 6 And Israel[j] asked: "Why did you have to bring this trouble on me by telling the man that you had another brother?" 7 They replied: "The man directly inquired concerning us and our relatives, saying, 'Is your father still alive? Do you have another brother?' and we told him these facts.[k] How could we possibly know that he would say, 'Bring your brother down'?"[l]

8 Judah then urged Israel his father: "Send the boy with me,[m] and let us go on our way so that we may live and not die[n]—we and you and our children.[o] 9 I will be a guarantee for his safety.*[p]

CHAP. 42
a Ge 42:7, 9
b Ge 42:11
c Ge 42:13
d Ge 37:28, 35
e Ge 35:18, 19
　 Ge 42:4
f Ge 42:19
g Ge 42:2
h Ge 43:14
i Ge 37:28, 35
j Ge 42:24

Second Col.
a Ge 37:22
　 Ge 46:9
b Ge 43:8, 9
　 Ge 44:32
c Ge 37:31-34
　 Ge 44:20
d Ps 89:48
　 Ec 9:10
　 Ho 13:14
　 Ac 2:27
　 Re 20:13
e Ge 37:34, 35
　 Ge 44:29

CHAP. 43
f Ge 41:30
　 Ac 7:11
g Ge 42:1, 2
h Ge 42:15
i Ge 42:15
j Ge 32:28
k Ge 42:13
l Ge 42:16
m Ge 37:26
　 Ge 42:38
n Ge 42:1, 2
o Ac 7:14
p Ge 44:32

42:38 *Or "Sheol," that is, the common grave of mankind. See Glossary. 43:9 *Or "be surety for him."

You may hold me responsible. If I fail to return him to you and present him to you, I will have sinned against you for all time. **10** But if we had not delayed, we could have been there and back twice by now."

11 So Israel their father said to them: "If it must be so, then do this: Take the finest products of the land in your bags* and carry them down to the man as a gift:[a] a little balsam,[b] a little honey, labdanum, resinous bark,[c] pistachio nuts, and almonds. **12** Take double the money with you; and also take back the money that was returned in the mouth of your bags.[d] Maybe it was a mistake. **13** Take your brother and go, return to the man. **14** May God Almighty grant you pity from the man, so that he may release to you your other brother and Benjamin. But as for me, if I must be bereaved, I will be bereaved!"[e]

15 So the men took this gift, and they took double the money in their hand and Benjamin. Then they rose and went on their way down to Egypt and again stood before Joseph.[f] **16** When Joseph saw Benjamin with them, he at once said to the man who was over his house: "Take the men to the house and slaughter animals and prepare the meal, for the men are to eat with me at noon." **17** Immediately the man did just as Joseph had said,[g] and he took them to Joseph's house. **18** But the men became afraid when they were taken to Joseph's house, and they began to say: "It is because of the money that was returned in our bags the last time that we are being brought here. Now they will attack us and make us slaves and take our donkeys!"[h]

19 So they approached the man who was over Joseph's house and spoke to him at the entrance of the house. **20** They said: "Pardon us, my lord! We did come down the first time to buy food.[a] **21** But when we arrived at our lodging place and began opening our bags, why, here was the money of each one in the mouth of his bag, our money in full weight.[b] So we would like to return it personally. **22** And we have brought more money to buy food. We do not know who placed our money in our bags."[c] **23** Then he said: "It is all right. Do not be afraid. Your God and the God of your father put treasure in your bags. Your money came first to me." After that he brought out Sim′e·on to them.[d]

24 Then the man brought them into Joseph's house and gave them water for washing their feet, and he gave fodder for their donkeys. **25** And they prepared the gift[e] for Joseph's coming at noon, for they had heard that they were going to eat a meal there.[f] **26** When Joseph went into the house, they brought their gift to him into the house and prostrated themselves to him to the ground.[g] **27** After this he inquired about their welfare and said: "How is your aged father of whom you have spoken? Is he still alive?"[h] **28** To this they said: "Your servant our father is well. He is still alive." Then they bowed down and prostrated themselves.[i]

29 When he looked up and saw Benjamin his brother, the son of his mother,[j] he said: "Is this your brother, the youngest one of whom you have spoken to me?"[k] He added: "May God show you his favor, my son." **30** Joseph then hurried out, because he was overcome with emotion for his brother, and he looked for a place to weep. So he went

---

CHAP. 43
a Ge 32:20

b Jer 8:22
Eze 27:17

c Ge 37:25

d Ge 42:25, 35

e Ge 42:36

f Ge 37:7, 9

g Ge 41:39, 40

h Ge 42:25, 35

Second Col.
a Ge 42:3

b Ge 42:27

c Ge 43:12

d Ge 42:23, 24

e Ge 43:11

f Ge 43:16

g Ge 37:7, 9
Ge 42:6

h Ge 43:7

i Ge 37:7, 9

j Ge 35:24

k Ge 42:13

43:11 *Or "receptacles."

into a private room and gave way to tears there.[a] **31** After that he washed his face and went out, now in control of himself, and he said: "Serve the meal." **32** They served him by himself and them by themselves, and the Egyptians with him ate by themselves, for the Egyptians could not eat a meal with the Hebrews, because that is a detestable thing to the Egyptians.[b]

33 The brothers* were seated before him, the firstborn according to his right as firstborn[c] and the youngest according to his youth, and they kept looking at one another in amazement. **34** He kept sending portions of food from his table to theirs, but he increased Benjamin's portion five times the size of the portions of all the others.[d] So they continued banqueting and drinking with him to the full.

44 Later he commanded the man who was over his house: "Fill the bags of the men with as much food as they can carry, and place the money of each one in the mouth of his bag.[e] **2** But you must place my cup, the silver cup, in the mouth of the bag of the youngest, along with the money for his grain." So he did as Joseph had instructed.

3 In the morning when it had become light, the men were sent away with their donkeys. **4** They had not gone far from the city when Joseph said to the man who was over his house: "Get up! Chase after the men! When you overtake them, say to them, 'Why have you repaid bad for good? **5** Is not this what my master drinks from and uses to read omens expertly? It is a wicked thing you have done.'"

6 So he overtook them and spoke these words to them.

7 But they said to him: "Why does my lord say such a thing? It is unthinkable that your servants would do anything like this. **8** Why, the money that we found in the mouth of our bags we brought back to you from the land of Ca′naan.[a] How, then, could we steal silver or gold from the house of your master? **9** If it is found with one of your slaves, let him die, and the rest of us will also become slaves to my master." **10** So he said: "Let it be as you say: The one with whom it is found will become my slave, but the rest of you will be innocent." **11** With that each one quickly lowered his bag to the ground and opened it. **12** He searched carefully, starting with the oldest and finishing with the youngest. Finally the cup was found in Benjamin's bag.[b]

13 Then they ripped their garments apart, and each of them lifted his load back onto his donkey and returned to the city. **14** When Judah[c] and his brothers went into Joseph's house, he was still there; and they fell to the ground before him.[d] **15** Joseph said to them: "What is this deed that you have done? Did you not know that a man like me can expertly read omens?"[e] **16** At this Judah replied: "What can we say to my master? What can we speak? And how can we prove ourselves righteous? The true God has found out the error of your slaves.[f] We are now slaves to my master, both we and the one in whose hand the cup was found!" **17** However, he said: "It is unthinkable for me to do this! The man in whose hand the cup was found is the one who will become a slave to me.[g] As for the rest of you, go up in peace to your father."

CHAP. 43
a Ge 42:23, 24

b Ge 46:33, 34
  Ex 8:26

c Ge 49:3
  De 21:17

d Ge 45:22

CHAP. 44
e Ge 42:25

Second Col.
a Ge 43:12

b Ge 44:2

c Ge 43:8
  Ge 44:32

d Ge 37:7, 9

e Ge 44:5

f Ge 37:18, 28
  Ge 42:21, 22

g Ge 44:9

43:33 *Lit., "They."

18 Judah now approached him and said: "I beg you, my master, please let your slave speak a word in my master's ears, and do not become angry with your slave, for you are like Phar'aoh himself.[a] **19** My master asked his slaves, 'Do you have a father or a brother?' **20** So we said to my master, 'We do have an aged father and a child of his old age, the youngest.[b] But his brother is dead,[c] so he is the only remaining son of his mother,[d] and his father loves him.' **21** After that you said to your slaves, 'Bring him down to me so that I may see him.'[e] **22** But we said to my master, 'The boy is not able to leave his father. If he did leave him, his father would certainly die.'[f] **23** Then you said to your slaves, 'Unless your youngest brother comes down with you, you may not see my face anymore.'[g]

24 "So we went up to your slave my father and told him the words of my master. **25** Later our father said, 'Return and buy a little food for us.'[h] **26** But we said, 'We are not able to go down. If our youngest brother is with us we will go down, for we cannot see the man's face unless our youngest brother is with us.'[i] **27** Then your slave my father said to us, 'You well know that my wife bore but two sons to me.[j] **28** But one of them left me and I said: "He must surely have been torn to pieces!"[k] and I have not seen him until now. **29** If you were to take this one also out of my sight and a fatal accident were to befall him, you would certainly bring down my gray hairs to the Grave[*][l] with calamity.'[m]

30 "And now if I return to your slave my father without the boy along with us, since his own life[*] is bound up with this one's life,[*] **31** then as soon as he sees that the boy is not there, he will die, and your slaves will indeed bring down the gray hairs of your slave our father to the Grave[*] in grief. **32** Your slave gave a guarantee to my father for the boy, saying, 'If I fail to bring him back to you, then I will have sinned against my father forever.'[a] **33** So now, please, let your slave stay instead of the boy as my master's slave, in order that the boy may return with his brothers. **34** How can I return to my father without the boy along with me? I could not bear looking on when this calamity befalls my father!"

45 At this Joseph could no longer control himself before all his attendants.[b] So he cried out: "Have everyone leave me!" No one else stayed with him while Joseph made himself known to his brothers.[c]

2 Then he began to weep so loudly that the Egyptians heard it and Phar'aoh's house heard it. **3** Finally Joseph said to his brothers: "I am Joseph. Is my father still alive?" But his brothers were unable to answer him at all, because they were astonished on account of him. **4** So Joseph said to his brothers: "Come close to me, please." With that they came close to him.

Then he said: "I am Joseph your brother, whom you sold into Egypt.[d] **5** But now do not be upset and do not reproach one another because you sold me here; because God has sent me ahead of you for the preservation of life.[e] **6** This is the second year of the famine in the land,[f] and there are yet five years in which there will be no plowing or harvest. **7** But God sent

---

CHAP. 44
a Ge 41:44
  Ge 45:8

b Ge 42:13
  Ge 43:7

c Ge 37:31-34

d Ge 35:18, 19

e Ge 42:15
  Ge 43:29

f Ge 42:38

g Ge 42:20

h Ge 43:2

i Ge 43:5

j Ge 29:18
  Ge 30:22-24
  Ge 35:18, 19
  Ge 46:19

k Ge 37:33

l Ps 16:10
  Ec 9:10
  Ho 13:14
  Ac 2:27
  Re 20:13

m Ge 37:34, 35
  Ge 42:38
  Ps 88:3

Second Col.
a Ge 43:9

CHAP. 45
b Ge 43:30

c Ac 7:13

d Ge 37:28
  Ac 7:9

e Ge 47:23, 25
  Ge 50:20
  Ps 105:17

f Ge 41:30
  Ge 47:18

44:29, 31 *Or "Sheol," that is, the common grave of mankind. See Glossary.

44:30 *Or "soul."

me ahead of you in order to preserve for you a remnant[a] on the earth* and to keep you alive by a great deliverance. **8** So, then, it was not you who sent me here, but it was the true God, in order to appoint me as chief adviser* to Phar'aoh and lord for all his house and ruler over all the land of Egypt.[b]

9 "Return quickly to my father, and you must say to him, 'This is what your son Joseph has said: "God has appointed me lord over all Egypt.[c] Come down to me. Do not delay.[d] **10** You must dwell in the land of Go'shen,[e] where you will be near me—you, your sons, your grandsons, your flocks, your herds, and everything you have. **11** I will supply you with food there, for there are yet five years of famine.[f] Otherwise, you and your house and everything you have will come to poverty.'" **12** You and my brother Benjamin can now see with your own eyes that I am really the one speaking to you.[g] **13** So you must tell my father about all my glory in Egypt and everything you have seen. Now hurry and bring my father down here."

14 Then he embraced* his brother Benjamin and gave way to weeping, and Benjamin wept with his arms around his neck.[h] **15** And he kissed all his brothers and wept over them, and after that his brothers spoke with him.

16 The news reached the house of Phar'aoh: "Joseph's brothers have come!" It was good in the eyes of Phar'aoh and his servants. **17** So Phar'aoh said to Joseph: "Tell your brothers, 'Do this: Load your beasts of burden and go to the land of Ca'-

naan, **18** and take your father and your households and come here to me. I will give you the good things of the land of Egypt, and you will eat* the richest# part of the land.[a] **19** And you are commanded to tell them:[b] "Do this: Take wagons[c] from the land of Egypt for your children and your wives, and you must bring your father on one of them and come here.[d] **20** Do not worry about your belongings,[e] for the best of all the land of Egypt is yours."'"

21 And the sons of Israel did so, and Joseph gave them wagons according to Phar'aoh's orders, and he gave them provisions for the journey. **22** To each of them he gave individual changes of clothing, but to Benjamin he gave 300 silver pieces and five changes of clothing.[f] **23** And to his father he sent the following: ten donkeys carrying good things of Egypt and ten female donkeys carrying grain and bread and sustenance for his father for the journey. **24** So he sent his brothers off, and as they departed, he said to them: "Do not become upset with one another on the way."[g]

25 Then they went up from Egypt and came into the land of Ca'naan to their father Jacob. **26** Then they reported to him: "Joseph is still alive, and he is the ruler over all the land of Egypt!"[h] But his heart grew numb because he did not believe them.[i] **27** When they went on telling him all the words that Joseph had spoken to them and when he saw the wagons that Joseph had sent to carry him, the spirit of their father Jacob began to revive. **28** Israel exclaimed: "It is enough! My son Joseph is still alive! I must go and see him before I die!"[j]

CHAP. 45
a Ge 46:26

b Ps 105:21
  Ac 7:9, 10

c Ge 45:26

d Ac 7:14

e Ge 46:33, 34
  Ge 47:1
  Ex 8:22
  Ex 9:26

f Ge 47:12

g Ge 42:23

h Ge 46:29

Second Col.
a Ge 47:6

b Ge 41:39, 40

c Ge 45:27
  Ge 46:5

d Ge 47:9

e Ge 46:6

f Ge 43:34

g Ge 42:21, 22

h Ps 105:21

i Ge 42:38
  Ge 44:27, 28

j Ge 46:30

45:7 *Or "in the land." **45:8** *Lit., "as father." **45:14** *Lit., "fell upon the neck of."

45:18 *Or "live off." #Or "fat."

46 So Israel took all that he had* and departed. When he arrived at Be'er-she'ba,[a] he offered sacrifices to the God of his father Isaac.[b] **2** Then God spoke to Israel in a vision by night and said: "Jacob, Jacob!" to which he said: "Here I am!" **3** He said: "I am the true God, the God of your father.[c] Do not be afraid to go down to Egypt, for there I will make you into a great nation.[d] **4** I myself will go down with you to Egypt, and I myself will also bring you back from there,[e] and Joseph will lay his hand on your eyes."*[f]

5 After that Jacob departed from Be'er-she'ba, and the sons of Israel transported Jacob their father and their children and their wives in the wagons that Phar'aoh had sent to transport him. **6** They took along their herds and their goods, which they had accumulated in the land of Ca'naan. And so they came into Egypt, Jacob and all his offspring with him. **7** He brought with him into Egypt his sons and his grandsons, his daughters and his granddaughters—all his offspring.

8 Now these are the names of Israel's sons who came into Egypt,[g] Jacob and his sons: Jacob's firstborn was Reu'ben.[h]

9 The sons of Reu'ben were Ha'noch, Pal'lu, Hez'ron, and Car'mi.[i]

10 The sons of Sim'e·on were Jem·u'el, Ja'min, O'had, Ja'chin, Zo'har, and Sha'ul[k] the son of a Ca'naan·ite woman.

11 The sons of Le'vi were Ger'shon, Ko'hath, and Me·rar'i.[m]

12 The sons of Judah[n] were Er, O'nan, She'lah,[o] Pe'rez,[p] and Ze'rah.[q] However, Er and O'nan died in the land of Ca'naan.[a]

The sons of Pe'rez came to be Hez'ron and Ha'mul.[b]

13 The sons of Is'sa·char were To'la, Pu'vah, Iob, and Shim'ron.[c]

14 The sons of Zeb'u·lun[d] were Se'red, E'lon, and Jah'le·el.[e]

15 These are the sons of Le'ah, whom she bore to Jacob in Pad'dan-a'ram, together with his daughter Di'nah.[f] All his sons and his daughters* numbered 33.

16 The sons of Gad[g] were Ziph'i·on, Hag'gi, Shu'ni, Ez'bon, E'ri, Ar·o'di, and A·re'li.[h]

17 The sons of Ash'er[i] were Im'nah, Ish'vah, Ish'vi, and Be·ri'ah, and their sister was Se'rah.

The sons of Be·ri'ah were He'ber and Mal'chi·el.[j]

18 These are the sons of Zil'pah,[k] whom La'ban gave to his daughter Le'ah. She bore these to Jacob: 16 persons* in all.

19 The sons of Jacob's wife Rachel were Joseph[l] and Benjamin.[m]

20 There were born to Joseph in the land of Egypt Manas'seh[n] and E'phra·im,[o] whom As'e·nath[p] the daughter of Pot·i'phe·ra the priest of On* bore to him.

21 The sons of Benjamin[q] were Be'la, Be'cher, Ash'bel, Ge'ra,[r] Na'a·man, E'hi, Rosh, Mup'pim, Hup'pim,[s] and Ard.[t]

22 These are the sons of Rachel who were born to Jacob: 14 persons* in all.

23 The son* of Dan[u] was Hu'shim.[v]

CHAP. 46
a Ge 21:31
b Ge 31:42
   Ex 3:6
c Ge 28:13
d Ge 12:1, 2
   Ex 1:7
   De 26:5
e Ge 15:16
   Ge 28:15
   Ge 47:29, 30
   Ge 50:13
f Ge 50:1
g Ex 1:1-4
h Ge 35:23
   1Ch 5:1
i Nu 26:5, 6
j Ge 29:33
k Nu 26:12, 13
   1Ch 4:24
l Ge 29:34
m 1Ch 6:16
n Ge 29:35
   Re 5:5
o Ge 38:2-5
p Lu 3:23, 33
q Ge 38:30

Second Col.
a Ge 38:7, 9, 10
b Nu 26:21
   1Ch 2:5
c Nu 26:23, 24
   1Ch 7:1
d Ge 30:20
e Nu 26:26
f Ge 30:21
g Ge 30:11
h Nu 26:15-17
i Ge 30:13
j Nu 26:44, 45
k Ge 29:24
l Ge 30:24
m Ge 35:18
n Ge 41:51
o Ge 41:52
p Ge 41:50
q 1Ch 7:6
r 1Ch 8:1, 3
s 1Ch 7:12
t Nu 26:38-40
u Ge 30:6
v Nu 26:42

46:1 *Or "all who were his." **46:4** *That is, to close them at Jacob's death. **46:15** *Or "All the souls of his sons and daughters." **46:18** *Or "16 souls." **46:20** *That is, Heliopolis. **46:22** *Or "14 souls." **46:23** *Lit., "sons."

24 The sons of Naph′ta·li[a] were Jah′ze·el, Gu′ni, Je′zer, and Shil′lem.[b]

25 These are the sons of Bil′hah, whom La′ban gave to his daughter Rachel. She bore these to Jacob: seven persons* in all.

26 All those* who descended from Jacob and went into Egypt with him, aside from the wives of Jacob's sons, were 66.[c] **27** Joseph's sons who were born to him in Egypt were two.* All the people* of the house of Jacob who came into Egypt were 70.[d]

28 Jacob sent Judah[e] ahead to tell Joseph that he was on the way to Go′shen. When they came into the land of Go′shen,[f] **29** Joseph had his chariot prepared and went up to meet Israel his father at Go′shen. When he presented himself to him, he at once embraced him* and wept for some time.* **30** Then Israel said to Joseph: "Now I am ready to die; I have seen your face and know that you are still alive."

31 Joseph then said to his brothers and to his father's household: "Let me go up and report to Phar′aoh[g] and tell him, 'My brothers and my father's household who were in the land of Ca′naan have come here to me.[h] **32** The men are shepherds,[i] and they raise livestock,[j] and they have brought their flocks and their herds and all that they have.'[k] **33** When Phar′aoh calls you and asks, 'What is your occupation?' **34** you must say, 'Your servants have raised livestock from our youth until now, both we and our forefathers,'[l] so that you may dwell in the land of Go′shen,[m] for every herder of sheep is detestable to the Egyptians."[n]

46:25 *Or "seven souls." **46:26** *Or "All the souls." **46:27** *Or "two souls." #Or "souls." **46:29** *Lit., "fell upon his neck." #Or "wept on his neck again and again."

CHAP. 46
a Ge 30:8

b Nu 26:48, 49

c Ge 35:10, 11

d Ex 1:5
   De 10:22
   Ac 7:14

e Ge 43:8
   Ge 44:18

f Ge 45:10
   Ge 47:1

g Ge 41:39, 40

h Ge 45:19
   Ac 7:13

i Ge 31:17, 18
   Ge 47:3

j Ge 31:38

k Ge 46:6

l Ge 30:35, 36

m Ge 45:17, 18
   Ge 47:27

n Ge 43:32

Second Col.

CHAP. 47
a Ge 46:31

b Ge 45:10
   Ex 8:22

c Ac 7:13

d Ge 12:16
   Ge 26:12, 14
   Ge 31:17, 18
   Ge 46:33, 34

e Ge 15:13
   De 26:5
   Ps 105:23
   Ac 7:6

f Ac 7:11

g Ge 45:10

h Ge 45:17, 18

i Job 14:1, 2

j Ge 25:7
   Ge 35:28

---

47 So Joseph went and reported to Phar′aoh:[a] "My father and my brothers and their flocks and their herds and all that they possess have come from the land of Ca′naan, and they are in the land of Go′shen."[b] **2** He took five of his brothers and presented them to Phar′aoh.[c]

3 Phar′aoh said to his brothers: "What is your occupation?" They replied to Phar′aoh: "Your servants are herders of sheep, both we and our forefathers."[d] **4** Then they said to Phar′aoh: "We have come to reside as foreigners in the land[e] because there are no pastures for the flock of your servants, for the famine is severe in the land of Ca′naan.[f] So please let your servants dwell in the land of Go′shen."[g] **5** At that Phar′aoh said to Joseph: "Your father and your brothers have come here to you. **6** The land of Egypt is at your disposal. Have your father and your brothers dwell in the very best part of the land.[h] Let them dwell in the land of Go′shen, and if you know of any capable men among them, put them in charge of my livestock."

7 Then Joseph brought in Jacob his father and presented him to Phar′aoh, and Jacob blessed Phar′aoh. **8** Phar′aoh asked Jacob: "How old are you?" **9** Jacob said to Phar′aoh: "The years of my wanderings* are 130. Few and distressing the years of my life have been,[i] and they are not as long as the years of the lives of my forefathers during their wanderings."*[j] **10** After that Jacob blessed Phar′aoh and went out from before him.

11 So Joseph settled his father and his brothers, and he gave them a possession in the

---

47:9 *Or "sojourning; residing as a foreigner." #Or "sojourning; residing as foreigners."

land of Egypt, in the very best part of the land, in the land of Ram′e·ses,[a] just as Phar′aoh had commanded. **12** And Joseph kept supplying his father and his brothers and the entire household of his father with food* according to the number of their children.

13 Now there was no food* in all the land, because the famine was very severe, and the land of Egypt and the land of Ca′naan became exhausted as a result of the famine.[b] **14** Joseph was collecting all the money that was to be found in the land of Egypt and in the land of Ca′naan for the grain that people were buying,[c] and Joseph kept bringing the money into Phar′aoh's house. **15** In time the money from the land of Egypt and the land of Ca′naan was spent, and all the Egyptians began coming to Joseph, saying: "Give us food! Why should we die before your very eyes because our money has run out?" **16** Then Joseph said: "If your money has run out, hand over your livestock, and I will give you food in exchange for your livestock." **17** So they began bringing their livestock to Joseph, and Joseph kept giving them food in exchange for their horses, the livestock of the flock and of the herd, and the donkeys, and he kept providing them with food in exchange for all their livestock during that year.

18 When that year came to its close, they began coming to him the next year and saying: "We will not hide from my lord that the money and the stock of domestic animals have already been given to my lord. We have nothing left for my lord but our bodies and our land. **19** Why should we die before your eyes, both we and our land? Buy us and our land in exchange for

47:12, 13 *Lit., "bread."

food, and we together with our land will become slaves to Phar′aoh. Give us seed so that we may live and not die and that our land may not become desolate." **20** Joseph then bought all the land of the Egyptians for Phar′aoh because every Egyptian sold his field, for the famine was very severe; and the land became Phar′aoh's.

21 Then he moved the people into cities, from one end of the territory of Egypt to its other end.[a] **22** Only the land of the priests he did not buy,[b] because the rations for the priests were from Phar′aoh and they lived on their rations that Phar′aoh gave them. That is why they did not sell their land. **23** Then Joseph said to the people: "See, I have today bought you and your land for Phar′aoh. Here is seed for you, and you must sow the land with it. **24** When it produces, give a fifth to Phar′aoh,[c] but four parts will be yours as seed for the field and as food for you and for those in your houses and for your children to eat." **25** So they said: "You have preserved our lives.[d] Let us find favor in the eyes of my lord, and we will become slaves to Phar′aoh."[e] **26** Then Joseph made it a decree, which is valid until today over the land of Egypt, that a fifth belongs to Phar′aoh. It was only the land of the priests that did not become Phar′aoh's.[f]

27 Israel continued to dwell in the land of Egypt, in the land of Go′shen,[g] and they settled in it and were fruitful and increased greatly.[h] **28** And Jacob lived on in the land of Egypt for 17 years, so that the days of Jacob's life came to be 147 years.[i]

29 The time was approaching for Israel to die,[j] so he called his son Joseph and said: "If, now, I have found favor in your eyes, place your hand, please,

---

CHAP. 47
a Ge 45:10
  Ex 1:8, 11
  Ex 12:37
  Nu 33:3

b Ge 41:30, 31

c Ge 41:56
  Ge 44:25

Second Col.
a Ge 41:48, 49

b Ge 41:45

c Ge 41:34

d Ge 45:5
  Ac 7:11

e Ge 47:19

f Ge 47:22

g Ge 47:4

h Ex 1:7
  De 10:22
  Ps 105:24
  Ac 7:17

i Ge 47:9

j Ge 49:33

under my thigh, and show loyal love and faithfulness to me. Please, do not bury me in Egypt.[a] **30** When I die,* you must carry me out of Egypt and bury me in the grave of my forefathers."[b] Accordingly, he said: "I will do just as you say." **31** Then he said: "Swear to me." So he swore to him.[c] At that Israel bowed down at the head of his bed.[d]

48 After these things, Joseph was told: "Look, your father is getting weak." At that he took his two sons Ma·nas′seh and E′phra·im with him.[e] **2** Then Jacob was told: "Here your son Joseph has come to you." So Israel gathered his strength and sat up on his bed. **3** And Jacob said to Joseph:

"God Almighty appeared to me at Luz in the land of Ca′naan and blessed me.[f] **4** And he said to me, 'I am making you fruitful, and I will make you many, and I will transform you into a congregation of peoples,[g] and I will give this land to your offspring* after you as a lasting possession.'[h] **5** Now your two sons who were born to you in the land of Egypt before I came to you in Egypt are mine.[i] E′phra·im and Ma·nas′seh will become mine just as Reu′ben and Sim′e·on are mine.[j] **6** But the children born to you after them will become yours. They will be called by the name of their brothers in their inheritance.[k] **7** As for me, when I was coming from Pad′dan, Rachel died[l] alongside me in the land of Ca′naan, while there was yet a good stretch of land before coming to Eph′rath.[m] So I buried her there on the way to Eph′rath, that is, Beth′le·hem."[n]

8 Then Israel saw Joseph's sons and asked: "Who are these?" **9** So Joseph said to his

father: "They are my sons whom God has given me in this place."[a] At this he said: "Bring them to me, please, so that I may bless them."[b] **10** Now the eyes of Israel were failing from age, and he was unable to see. So Joseph brought them close to him, and he kissed them and embraced them. **11** Israel said to Joseph: "I never imagined I would see your face,[c] but here God has also let me see your offspring.* **12** Joseph then removed them from Israel's knees, and he bowed down with his face to the ground.

13 Joseph now took the two of them, E′phra·im[d] with his right hand to Israel's left and Ma·nas′seh[e] with his left hand to Israel's right, and brought them close to him. **14** However, Israel put out his right hand and placed it on E′phra·im's head, although he was the younger, and he placed his left hand on Ma·nas′seh's head. He purposely laid his hands this way, since Ma·nas′seh was the firstborn.[f] **15** Then he blessed Joseph and said:[g]

"The true God before whom
    my fathers Abraham and
    Isaac walked,[h]
The true God who has been
    shepherding me during all
    my life until this day,[i]
16 The angel who has been recovering me from all calamity,[j] bless the boys.[k]
Let my name be called
    upon them and the name of
    my fathers, Abraham and
    Isaac,
Let them increase to a multitude in the earth."[l]

17 When Joseph saw that his father kept his right hand placed on E′phra·im's head, it was displeasing to him, so he tried to take hold of his father's hand to move it from E′phra·im's head to Ma·nas′seh's head. **18** Joseph said to his father: "Not

---

CHAP. 47
a Ge 46:4
  Ge 50:13
  Ac 7:15, 16
b Ge 25:9, 10
  Ge 49:29, 30
c Ge 50:5
d Heb 11:21

CHAP. 48
e Ge 41:50
  Jos 14:4
f Ge 28:13, 19
  Ho 12:4
g Ge 35:10, 11
h Ge 28:13, 14
i Jos 14:4
  1Ch 5:1
j Ge 35:23
k Jos 13:29
  Jos 16:5
l Ge 35:19
m Mic 5:2
n 1Sa 17:12
  Mt 2:6

Second Col.
a Ge 41:50
b Heb 11:21
c Ge 37:34, 35
  Ge 42:36
  Ge 46:30
d Ge 41:52
e Ge 41:51
f Ge 41:51
  Ge 46:20
g 1Ch 5:2
h Ge 17:1
  Ge 24:40
i Ge 28:13
  Ps 23:1
j Ge 28:15
  Ge 31:11
  Ps 34:7
k Ge 32:26
l Ex 1:7
  Nu 26:34, 37

47:30 *Lit., "lie down with my fathers."
48:4, 11 *Lit., "seed."

so, my father, because this is the firstborn.[a] Put your right hand on his head." **19** But his father kept refusing and said: "I know it, my son, I know it. He too will become a people, and he too will become great. Nevertheless, his younger brother will become greater than he will,[b] and his offspring* will become the full equivalent of nations."[c] **20** So he continued to bless them on that day,[d] saying:

"Let Israel mention you when they pronounce blessings, saying,

'May God make you like E'phra·im and like Ma·nas'-seh.'"

Thus he kept putting E'phra·im before Ma·nas'seh.

21 Then Israel said to Joseph: "Look, I am dying,[e] but God will certainly continue with you and return you to the land of your forefathers.[f] **22** As for me, I do give you one portion of land* more than to your brothers, which I took from the hand of the Am'or·ites with my sword and my bow."

49 And Jacob called his sons and said: "Gather yourselves together that I may tell you what will happen to you in the final part of the days. **2** Assemble yourselves and listen, you sons of Jacob, yes, listen to Israel your father.

3 "Reu'ben,[g] you are my firstborn,[h] my vigor and the beginning of my procreative power, the excellence of dignity and the excellence of strength. **4** With recklessness like turbulent waters, you will not excel, because you have gone up to your father's bed.[i] At that time you defiled* my bed. He actually went on to it!

5 "Sim'e·on and Le'vi are brothers.[a] Instruments of violence are their slaughter weapons.[b] **6** Into their company do not come, O my soul.* With their assembly do not join, O my honor,# because in their anger they killed men,[c] and for their pleasure they hamstrung bulls. **7** Cursed be their anger, because it is cruel, and their fury, because it is harsh.[d] Let me disperse them in Jacob, and let me scatter them in Israel.[e]

8 "As for you, Judah,[f] your brothers will praise you.[g] Your hand will be on the neck of your enemies.[h] The sons of your father will bow down before you.[i] **9** Judah is a lion cub.[j] From the prey, my son, you will certainly go up. He has crouched down and stretched himself out like a lion, and like a lion, who dares rouse him? **10** The scepter will not depart from Judah,[k] neither the commander's staff from between his feet, until Shi'loh* comes,[l] and to him the obedience of the peoples will belong.[m] **11** Tying his donkey to a vine and his donkey's colt to a choice vine, he will wash his clothing in wine and his garment in the blood of grapes. **12** Dark red are his eyes from wine, and his teeth are white from milk.

13 "Zeb'u·lun[n] will reside by the seashore, by the shore where the ships lie anchored,[o] and his remote border will be toward Si'-don.[p]

14 "Is'sa·char[q] is a strong-boned donkey, lying down between the two saddlebags. **15** And he will see that the resting-place is good and that the land is pleasant. He will bend his shoulder to bear the burden and will submit to forced labor.

CHAP. 48
a Ge 41:51
b Nu 2:18-21
c Nu 1:32, 33
d Heb 11:21
e Ge 50:24
f Ge 15:14
  Ge 26:3
  De 31:8

CHAP. 49
g De 33:6
h Ge 29:32
  Ex 6:14
  1Ch 5:1
i Ge 35:22

Second Col.
a Ge 29:33, 34
  Ge 35:23
b Ge 34:25
c Ge 34:7
d Ge 34:25
e Jos 19:1
  Jos 21:41
f Ge 29:35
  De 33:7
g Ge 43:8, 9
  Ge 46:28
  1Ch 5:2
h Jg 1:2
i Nu 10:14
  2Sa 5:3
j Re 5:5
k Nu 24:17
  2Sa 2:4
  2Sa 7:16, 17
l Isa 9:6
  Lu 1:32
  Heb 7:14
m Ps 2:8
  Isa 11:10
  Mt 2:6
n De 33:18, 19
o Mt 4:13
p Jos 19:10
q De 33:18
  1Ch 7:5

48:19 *Lit., "seed." 48:22 *Or "one slope of land." Lit., "one shoulder." 49:4 *Or "profaned."

49:6 *See Glossary. #Or possibly, "disposition." 49:10 *Meaning "He Whose It Is; He to Whom It Belongs."

16 "Dan[a] will judge his people as one of the tribes of Israel.[b] **17** Let Dan be a serpent by the roadside, a horned snake beside the path, that bites the heels of the horse so that its rider falls backward.[c] **18** I will wait for salvation from you, O Jehovah.

19 "As for Gad,[d] a marauder band will raid him, but he will raid at their heels.[e]

20 "Ash′er's[f] bread* will be abundant,[#] and he will provide food fit for a king.[g]

21 "Naph′ta·li[h] is a slender doe. He is speaking words of elegance.[i]

22 "Joseph[j] is the offshoot of a fruitful tree, a fruitful tree by a spring, whose branches extend over the wall. **23** But the archers kept harassing him and shot at him and kept harboring animosity against him.[k] **24** And yet his bow remained in place,[l] and his hands stayed strong and agile.[m] This was from the hands of the powerful one of Jacob, from the shepherd, the stone of Israel. **25** He* is from the God of your father, and he will help you, and he is with the Almighty, and he will bless you with the blessings of the heavens above, with the blessings of the deep below,[n] with the blessings of the breasts and womb. **26** The blessings of your father will be superior to the blessings of the eternal mountains, to the desirable things of the enduring hills.[o] They will continue upon the head of Joseph, upon the crown of the head of the one singled out from his brothers.[p]

27 "Benjamin[q] will keep on tearing like a wolf.[r] In the morning he will eat the prey, and in the evening he will divide spoil."[s]

28 All of these are the 12 tribes of Israel, and this is what

their father said to them when he was blessing them. He gave each of them an appropriate blessing.[a]

29 After that he gave these commands to them: "I am being gathered to my people.*[b] Bury me with my fathers in the cave that is in the field of E′phron the Hit′tite,[c] **30** the cave in the field of Mach·pe′lah in front of Mam′re in the land of Ca′naan, the field that Abraham purchased from E′phron the Hit′tite as a property for a burial place. **31** There they buried Abraham and his wife Sarah.[d] There they buried Isaac[e] and his wife Re·bek′ah, and there I buried Le′ah. **32** The field and the cave that is in it were purchased from the sons of Heth."[f]

33 Thus Jacob finished giving these instructions to his sons. Then he drew his feet up onto the bed and breathed his last and was gathered to his people.*[g]

50 Joseph then threw himself on his father[h] and wept over him and kissed him. **2** After that Joseph commanded his servants, the physicians, to embalm[i] his father. So the physicians embalmed Israel, **3** and they took the full 40 days for him, for this is the full period for the embalming, and the Egyptians continued to shed tears for him 70 days.

4 When the days of mourning for him passed, Joseph spoke to Phar′aoh's court,* saying: "If I have found favor in your eyes, give this message to Phar′aoh: **5** 'My father made me swear,[j] saying: "Look! I am dying.[k] You are to bury me in my burial place,[l] which I have excavated in the land of Ca′naan."[m] Please, let me go up and bury

---

CHAP. 49
a De 33:22
b Jg 13:2, 24
Jg 15:20
c Jg 14:19
Jg 15:15
d De 33:20
e Jos 13:8
f De 33:24
g 1Ki 4:7, 16
h De 33:23
i Mt 4:13, 15
j De 33:13-17
k Ge 37:5, 8
Ge 40:15
l Ge 50:20
m Jos 1:1, 6
Jg 11:32
n De 33:13
o Jos 17:14
p De 33:16
q De 33:12
r Jg 20:15, 16
1Sa 9:16
s Es 2:5
Es 8:7

Second Col.
a Heb 11:21
b Ge 35:29
Ge 49:33
c Ge 23:17, 18
d Ge 23:2, 19
Ge 25:9, 10
e Ge 35:29
f Ge 23:17, 18
g Ac 7:15

CHAP. 50
h Ge 46:4
i Ge 50:26
j Ge 47:29-31
k Ge 48:21
l Ge 46:4
Ge 47:29
m Ge 23:17, 18
Ge 49:29, 30

49:20 *Or "food." #Lit., "fat." 49:25 *That is, Joseph.

49:29, 33 *This is a poetic expression for death. 50:4 *Or "household."

my father, after which I will return.'" **6** Phar'aoh replied: "Go and bury your father just as he made you swear."[a]

7 So Joseph went up to bury his father, and all of Phar'aoh's servants went with him, the elders[b] of his court and all the elders of the land of Egypt **8** and all of Joseph's household and his brothers and the household of his father.[c] Only their little children and their flocks and their herds they left in the land of Go'shen. **9** Chariots[d] and horsemen also went up with him, and the camp was very numerous. **10** Then they came to the threshing floor of A'tad, which is in the region of the Jordan, and there they carried on a very great and bitter mourning, and he kept mourning for his father seven days. **11** The inhabitants of the land, the Ca'naanites, saw them mourning at the threshing floor of A'tad, and they exclaimed: "This is a great mourning for the Egyptians!" That is why it was named A'bel-miz'ra·im,* which is in the region of the Jordan.

12 So his sons did for him exactly as he had instructed them.[e] **13** His sons carried him into the land of Ca'naan and buried him in the cave of the field of Mach·pe'lah, the field in front of Mam're that Abraham had purchased from E'phron the Hit'tite as property for a burial place.[f] **14** After he buried his father, Joseph returned to Egypt with his brothers and all those who had gone with him to bury his father.

15 When Joseph's brothers saw that their father was dead, they said: "It may be that Joseph is harboring animosity against us and that he will repay us for

all the evil that we did to him."[a] **16** So they sent a message to Joseph in these words: "Your father gave this command before his death: **17** 'This is what you are to say to Joseph: "I beg you, please pardon the transgression of your brothers and the sin they committed in bringing such harm to you."' Now, please, pardon the transgression of the servants of your father's God." And Joseph wept when they spoke to him. **18** Then his brothers also came and fell down before him and said: "Here we are as slaves to you!"[b] **19** Joseph said to them: "Do not be afraid. Am I in the place of God? **20** Although you meant to harm me,[c] God intended it to turn out well and to preserve many people alive, as he is doing today.[d] **21** So now do not be afraid. I will keep supplying you and your little children with food."[e] Thus he comforted them and spoke reassuringly to them.

22 And Joseph continued to dwell in Egypt, he and the household of his father, and Joseph lived for 110 years. **23** Joseph saw the third generation of E'phra·im's sons,[f] also the sons of Ma'chir,[g] Ma·nas'seh's son. They were born upon Joseph's knees.* **24** At length Joseph said to his brothers: "I am dying, but God will without fail turn his attention to you,[h] and he will certainly bring you up out of this land to the land about which he swore to Abraham, to Isaac, and to Jacob."[i] **25** So Joseph made the sons of Israel swear, saying: "God will without fail turn his attention to you. You must take my bones up out of here."[j] **26** And Joseph died at the age of 110, and they had him embalmed,[k] and he was put in a coffin in Egypt.

CHAP. 50
a Ge 47:31

b Ps 105:21, 22

c Ge 46:27

d Ge 41:43
  Ge 46:29

e Ge 47:29

f Ge 23:17, 18
  Ge 25:9, 10
  Ge 35:27
  Ge 49:29, 30

Second Col.
a Ge 37:18, 28
  Ge 42:21
  Ps 105:17

b Ge 37:7, 9

c Ge 37:18

d Ge 45:5
  Ps 105:17

e Ge 47:12

f 1Ch 7:20

g Jos 17:1
  1Ch 7:14

h Ex 4:31

i Ge 12:7
  Ge 17:8
  Ge 26:3
  Ge 28:13

j Ex 13:19
  Jos 24:32
  Heb 11:22

k Ge 50:2

50:11 *Meaning "Mourning of the Egyptians."

50:23 *That is, treated as sons and given special favor.

EXODUS

OUTLINE OF CONTENTS

---

1 Now these are the names of Israel's sons who came into Egypt with Jacob, each man who came with his household:[a] **2** Reu′ben, Sim′e·on, Le′vi, and Judah;[b] **3** Is′sa·char, Zeb′u·lun, and Benjamin; **4** Dan and Naph′ta·li; Gad and Ash′er.[a] **5** And all those* who were born to Jacob[#] were 70 people,[△] but Joseph was already

CHAP. 1
a Ge 46:8

b 1Ch 2:3, 4

Second Col.
a Ge 46:17

1:5 *Or "the souls." #Lit., "who came out from the thigh of Jacob." △Or "souls."

in Egypt.[a] **6** Joseph eventually died,[b] and also all his brothers and all that generation. **7** And the Israelites* became fruitful and began to increase greatly, and they kept on multiplying and growing mightier at an extraordinary rate, so that the land became filled with them.[c]

8 In time there arose over Egypt a new king, one who did not know Joseph. **9** So he said to his people: "Look! The people of Israel are more numerous and mightier than we are.[d] **10** Let us deal shrewdly with them. Otherwise, they will continue to multiply, and if a war breaks out, they will join our enemies and fight against us and leave the country."

11 So they appointed chiefs of forced labor* over them to oppress them with hard labor,[e] and they built storage cities for Phar'aoh, namely, Pi'thom and Ra·am'ses.[f] **12** But the more they would oppress them, the more they would multiply and the more they kept spreading out, so they felt sick with fear because of the Israelites.[g] **13** Consequently, the Egyptians forced the Israelites into harsh slavery.[h] **14** They made their life bitter with hard labor, as they worked with clay mortar and bricks and in every form of slavery in the field. Yes, they made them toil in harsh conditions in every form of slavery.[i]

15 Later the king of Egypt spoke to the Hebrew midwives whose names were Shiph'rah and Pu'ah, **16** and he told them: "When you help the Hebrew women to give birth[j] and you see them on the stool for childbirth,* you must put the child to death if it is a son;

but if it is a daughter, she must live." **17** However, the midwives feared the true God, and they did not do what the king of Egypt told them. Instead, they would keep the male children alive.[a] **18** In time the king of Egypt called the midwives and said to them: "Why have you kept the male children alive?" **19** The midwives said to Phar'aoh: "The Hebrew women are not like the Egyptian women. They are lively and have already given birth before the midwife can come in to them."

20 So God dealt well with the midwives, and the people kept increasing and becoming very mighty. **21** And because the midwives had feared the true God, he later gave them families. **22** Finally Phar'aoh commanded all his people: "You are to throw every newborn son of the Hebrews into the Nile River, but you are to keep every daughter alive."[b]

2 About that time, a certain man of the house of Le'vi married a daughter of Le'vi.[c] **2** And the woman became pregnant and gave birth to a son. When she saw how beautiful he was, she kept him concealed for three months.[d] **3** When she was no longer able to conceal him,[e] she took a papyrus basket* and coated it with bitumen and pitch and put the child in it and placed it among the reeds by the bank of the Nile River. **4** But his sister* stood at a distance to see what would happen to him.

5 When Phar'aoh's daughter came down to bathe in the Nile, her female attendants were walking by the side of the Nile. And she caught sight of the basket in the middle of the reeds. She immediately sent her slave girl to get it.[g] **6** When she

---

CHAP. 1
a Ge 46:26
  De 10:22
  Ac 7:14

b Ge 50:26

c Ge 46:3
  De 26:5
  Ac 7:17-19

d Ps 105:24, 25

e Ge 15:13
  Ex 3:7
  Nu 20:15
  De 26:6

f Ge 47:11

g Ex 1:7
  Ps 105:24, 25

h Ex 2:23
  Ac 7:6

i Le 26:13

j Eze 16:4

Second Col.
a Ge 9:5, 6

b Ac 7:18, 19

CHAP. 2
c Ex 6:20
  Nu 26:59

d Ac 7:20
  Heb 11:23

e Ac 7:18, 19

f Ex 15:20
  1Ch 6:3
  Mic 6:4

g Ac 7:21

1:7 *Lit., "sons of Israel." 1:11 *Or "appointed taskmasters." 1:16 *Or "the birth stool."

2:3 *Or "ark; chest."

opened it, she saw the child, and the boy was crying. She felt compassion for him, but she said: "This is one of the children of the Hebrews." **7** Then his sister said to Phar′aoh's daughter: "Shall I go and call a nursing woman from the Hebrews to nurse the child for you?" **8** Phar′aoh's daughter said to her: "Go!" At once the girl went and called the child's mother.ᵃ **9** Phar′aoh's daughter then said to her: "Take this child with you and nurse him for me, and I will pay you." So the woman took the child and nursed him. **10** When the child grew older, she brought him to Phar′aoh's daughter, and he became a son to her.ᵇ She named him Moses* and said: "It is because I have drawn him out of the water."ᶜ

11 Now in those days, after Moses had become an adult,* he went out to his brothers to look at the burdens they were bearing,ᵈ and he caught sight of an Egyptian beating a Hebrew, one of his brothers. **12** So he looked this way and that, and seeing no one, he killed the Egyptian and hid him in the sand.ᵉ

13 But he went out on the following day, and there were two Hebrew men fighting with each other. So he said to the one in the wrong: "Why do you strike your companion?"ᶠ **14** At this he said: "Who appointed you as a prince and a judge over us? Are you planning to kill me just as you killed the Egyptian?"ᵍ Moses now was afraid and said: "Surely the matter has become known!"

15 Then Phar′aoh heard about it, and he attempted to kill Moses; but Moses ran away from Phar′aoh and went to dwell

in the land of Mid′i·an,ᵃ and he sat down by a well. **16** Now the priest of Mid′i·anᵇ had seven daughters, and these came to draw water and to fill the troughs to water their father's flock. **17** But as usual, the shepherds came and drove them away. At this Moses got up and helped* the women and watered their flock. **18** When they came home to their father Reu′el,*ᶜ he exclaimed: "How is it that you have come home so quickly today?" **19** They replied: "A certain Egyptianᵈ rescued us from the shepherds, and he even drew water for us and watered the flock." **20** He said to his daughters: "But where is he? Why did you leave the man behind? Call him, so that he may eat with us." **21** After that Moses consented to stay with the man, and he gave his daughter Zip·po′rahᵉ to Moses in marriage. **22** Later she bore a son, and he named him Ger′shom,*ᶠ for he said, "I have become a foreign resident in a foreign land."ᵍ

23 After a long time,* the king of Egypt died,ʰ but the Israelites continued to groan because of the slavery and to cry out in complaint, and their cry for help because of the slavery kept going up to the true God.ⁱ **24** In time God heard their groaning,ʲ and God remembered his covenant with Abraham, Isaac, and Jacob.ᵏ **25** So God looked on the Israelites; and God took notice.

3 Moses became a shepherd of the flock of his father-in-law Jeth′ro,ⁱ the priest of Mid′i·an. While he was leading the flock to the west side of the wilderness, he eventually came to the mountain of the true God, to

---

CHAP. 2

a Ex 6:20

b Heb 11:24, 25

c Ac 7:21

d Ex 1:11
 Ex 3:7
 Ac 7:23

e Ac 7:24

f Ac 7:26

g Ac 7:27, 28

Second Col.

a Ge 25:1, 2
 Ex 3:1
 Ex 4:19

b Ex 18:12

c Ex 4:18
 Ex 18:1
 Nu 10:29

d Ac 7:22

e Ex 18:2-4
 Nu 12:1

f 1Ch 23:15

g Ac 7:29

h Ex 7:7
 Ac 7:30

i Ex 3:7
 1Ki 8:51

j Ac 7:34

k Ge 15:13, 14
 Ex 6:5
 Nu 20:15, 16

CHAP. 3

l Ex 2:16
 Ex 18:1

2:10 *Meaning "Drawn Out," that is, saved out of the water. 2:11 *Or "as Moses was becoming strong."

2:17 *Or "defended." 2:18 *That is, Jethro. 2:22 *Meaning "A Foreign Resident There." 2:23 *Lit., "many days."

Ho'reb.[a] **2** Then Jehovah's angel appeared to him in a flame of fire in the midst of a thornbush.[b] As he kept looking, he saw that the thornbush was on fire, and yet the thornbush was not consumed. **3** So Moses said: "I will go over to inspect this unusual sight to see why the thornbush does not burn up." **4** When Jehovah saw that he went over to look, God called to him out of the thornbush and said: "Moses! Moses!" to which he said: "Here I am." **5** Then he said: "Do not come any nearer. Remove your sandals from your feet, because the place where you are standing is holy ground."

6 He went on to say: "I am the God of your father, the God of Abraham,[c] the God of Isaac,[d] and the God of Jacob."[e] Then Moses hid his face, because he was afraid to look at the true God. **7** Jehovah added: "I have certainly seen the affliction of my people who are in Egypt, and I have heard their outcry because of those who force them to work; I well know the pains they suffer.[f] **8** I will go down to rescue them out of the hand of the Egyptians[g] and to bring them up out of that land to a land good and spacious, a land flowing with milk and honey,[h] the territory of the Ca'naan·ites, the Hit'tites, the Am'or·ites, the Per'iz·zites, the Hi'vites, and the Jeb'u·sites.[i] **9** Now look! The outcry of the people of Israel has reached me, and I have seen also the harsh way that the Egyptians are oppressing them.[j] **10** Now come, I will send you to Phar'aoh, and you will bring my people the Israelites out of Egypt."[k]

11 However, Moses said to the true God: "Who am I that I should go to Phar'aoh and bring the Israelites out of Egypt?" **12** To this he said: "I will prove to be with you,[l] and this is the

sign for you that it was I who sent you: After you have brought the people out of Egypt, you people will serve* the true God on this mountain."[a]

13 But Moses said to the true God: "Suppose I go to the Israelites and say to them, 'The God of your forefathers has sent me to you,' and they say to me, 'What is his name?'[b] What should I say to them?" **14** So God said to Moses: "I Will Become What I Choose* to Become."#[c] And he added: "This is what you are to say to the Israelites, 'I Will Become has sent me to you.'"[d] **15** Then God said once more to Moses:

"This is what you are to say to the Israelites, 'Jehovah the God of your forefathers, the God of Abraham,[e] the God of Isaac,[f] and the God of Jacob,[g] has sent me to you.' This is my name forever,[h] and this is how I am to be remembered from generation to generation. **16** Now go, and gather the elders of Israel and say to them, 'Jehovah the God of your forefathers has appeared to me, the God of Abraham, Isaac, and Jacob, and he said: "I have certainly taken notice of you[i] and of what is being done to you in Egypt. **17** So I say, I will take you away from affliction[j] at the hands of the Egyptians to the land of the Ca'naan·ites, the Hit'-tites, the Am'or·ites,[k] the Per'iz-zites, the Hi'vites, and the Jeb'u-sites,[l] to a land flowing with milk and honey."'[m] **18** "They will certainly listen to your voice,[n] and you will go, you and the elders of Israel, to the king of Egypt, and you men should say to him: 'Jehovah the God of the Hebrews[o] has communicated with us. So,

CHAP. 3	
a	Ex 24:12, 13
	1Ki 19:8, 9
b	Ac 7:30-34
c	Ge 17:1, 7
d	Ge 26:24
e	Ge 28:13
	Ge 32:9
	Mt 22:32
	Ac 7:32
f	Ex 1:11
	Isa 63:9
	Ac 7:34
g	Ex 12:51
h	Nu 13:26, 27
	De 27:3
i	Ge 10:15-17
	Ex 33:1, 2
	De 7:1
	Jos 3:10
	Ne 9:7, 8
j	Ex 1:11
k	Ps 105:26, 38
	Ac 7:34
l	De 31:23
	Jos 1:5
	Isa 41:10
	Ro 8:31
	Php 4:13

Second Col.

a	Ex 19:2
	De 4:11, 12
b	Ex 15:3
	Ps 96:8
	Ps 135:13
	Ho 12:5
	Joh 17:26
	Ro 10:13
c	Job 23:13
	Isa 14:27
	Joh 12:28
d	Ex 6:3, 7
	Ro 9:17
e	Ge 17:1, 7
f	Ge 26:24
g	Ge 28:13
	Mt 22:32
h	Ps 135:13
i	Ge 50:24
	Ex 13:19
j	Ge 15:13, 14
	Le 26:13
k	Ge 15:16
l	Ex 23:23
m	Nu 13:27
	De 8:7-9
n	Ex 4:31
o	Ge 14:13

please, let us make a three-day journey into the wilderness so that we may sacrifice to Jehovah our God.'[a] **19** But I myself well know that the king of Egypt will not give you permission to go unless a mighty hand compels him.[b] **20** So I will have to stretch out my hand and strike Egypt with all my extraordinary acts that I will do in it, and after that he will send you out.[c] **21** And I will give this people favor in the eyes of the Egyptians, and when you go, you will by no means go empty-handed.[d] **22** Each woman must ask her neighbor and the woman lodging in her house for articles of silver and of gold as well as clothing, and you will put them on your sons and your daughters; and you will plunder the Egyptians."[e]

4 However, Moses answered: "But suppose they do not believe me and do not listen to my voice,[f] for they will say, 'Jehovah did not appear to you.'" **2** Then Jehovah said to him: "What is that in your hand?" He answered: "A rod." **3** He said: "Throw it on the ground." So he threw it on the ground, and it became a serpent;[g] and Moses fled from it. **4** Jehovah now said to Moses: "Reach out your hand and seize it by the tail." So he reached out and seized it, and it became a rod in his hand. **5** God then said: "This is so that they may believe that Jehovah the God of their forefathers, the God of Abraham, the God of Isaac, and the God of Jacob,[h] has appeared to you."[i]

6 Jehovah said to him once more: "Put your hand, please, into the upper fold of your garment." So he put his hand into the fold of his garment. When he drew it out, why, his hand was stricken with leprosy like snow![j] **7** Then he said: "Return your

hand into the upper fold of your garment." So he returned his hand into his garment. When he drew it out of the garment, it was restored like the rest of his flesh! **8** He said: "If they will not believe you or pay attention to the first sign, then they will certainly heed the next sign.[a] **9** Still, even if they will not believe these two signs and refuse to listen to your voice, you will take some water from the Nile River and pour it out on the dry land, and the water that you take from the Nile will become blood on the dry land."[b]

10 Moses now said to Jehovah: "Pardon me, Jehovah, but I have never been a fluent speaker, neither in the past nor since you have spoken to your servant, for I am slow of speech* and slow of tongue."[c] **11** Jehovah said to him: "Who made a mouth for man, or who makes them speechless, deaf, clearsighted, or blind? Is it not I, Jehovah? **12** So go now, and I will be with you as you speak,* and I will teach you what you should say."[d] **13** But he said: "Pardon me, Jehovah, please send anyone whom you want to send." **14** Then Jehovah's anger blazed against Moses, and he said: "What about your brother Aaron[e] the Levite? I know that he can speak very well. And he is now on his way here to meet you. When he sees you, his heart will rejoice.[f] **15** So you must speak to him and put the words in his mouth,[g] and I will be with you and him as you speak,[h] and I will teach you men what to do. **16** He will speak for you to the people, and he will be your spokesman, and you will serve as God to him.*[i] **17** And you

---

CHAP. 3
a Ex 5:3
  Ex 10:25, 26

b Ex 5:2
  Ex 14:8
  Ro 9:17

c Ex 7:3
  Ex 12:33
  De 6:22

d Ex 11:2
  Ex 12:35, 36

e Ge 15:13, 14
  Ex 12:36

CHAP. 4
f Ex 2:13, 14

g Ex 7:9

h Lu 20:37

i Ex 3:16
  Ex 4:31

j Nu 12:10

Second Col.
a Ac 7:36

b Ex 4:30

c Ex 6:12
  Nu 12:3
  Jer 1:6
  Ac 7:22

d Isa 50:4
  Mr 13:11

e Nu 26:59

f Ex 4:27

g Ex 4:28

h Jer 1:9

i Ex 7:1, 2

4:10 *Lit., "heavy of mouth." 4:12 *Lit., "with your mouth." 4:16 *Or "will be representing God to him."

will take this rod in your hand and perform the signs with it."ᵃ

18 So Moses went back to Jeth'ro his father-in-lawᵇ and said to him: "I want to go, please, and return to my brothers who are in Egypt to see whether they are still alive." Jeth'ro said to Moses: "Go in peace." **19** After that Jehovah said to Moses in Mid'i·an: "Go, return to Egypt, because all the men who were seeking to kill you* are dead."ᶜ

20 Then Moses took his wife and his sons and lifted them onto a donkey, and he started back to the land of Egypt. Moreover, Moses took the rod of the true God in his hand. **21** Then Jehovah said to Moses: "After you have returned to Egypt, see that you perform before Phar'aoh all the miracles that I have empowered you to do.ᵈ But I will allow his heart to become obstinate,ᵉ and he will not send the people away.ᶠ **22** You must say to Phar'aoh, 'This is what Jehovah says: "Israel is my son, my firstborn.ᵍ **23** I say to you, Send my son away so that he may serve me. But if you refuse to send him away, I am going to kill your son, your firstborn."'"ʰ

24 Now on the road at the lodging place, Jehovahⁱ met him and was seeking to put him to death.ʲ **25** Finally Zip·po'rahᵏ took a flint* and circumcised her son and caused his foreskin to touch his feet and said: "It is because you are a bridegroom of blood to me." **26** So He let him go. At that time she said, "a bridegroom of blood," because of the circumcision.

27 Then Jehovah said to Aaron: "Go into the wilderness to meet Moses."ˡ So he went and met him at the mountain of the true Godᵐ and greeted him with

a kiss. **28** And Moses told Aaron all the words of Jehovah, who had sent him,ᵃ and all the signs that He had commanded him to do.ᵇ **29** After that Moses and Aaron went and gathered all the elders of the Israelites.ᶜ **30** Aaron told them all the words that Jehovah had spoken to Moses, and he performed the signsᵈ before the eyes of the people. **31** At this the people believed.ᵉ When they heard that Jehovah had turned his attention to the Israelitesᶠ and that he had seen their affliction,ᵍ they bowed down and prostrated themselves.

5 Afterward, Moses and Aaron went in and said to Phar'aoh: "This is what Jehovah the God of Israel says, 'Send my people away so that they may celebrate a festival to me in the wilderness.'" **2** But Phar'aoh said: "Who is Jehovah,ʰ that I should obey his voice to send Israel away?ⁱ I do not know Jehovah at all, and what is more, I will not send Israel away."ʲ **3** But they said: "The God of the Hebrews has communicated with us. Please, we want to make a three-day journey into the wilderness and sacrifice to Jehovah our God;ᵏ otherwise, he will strike us with disease or with the sword." **4** The king of Egypt replied to them: "Why is it, Moses and Aaron, that you are taking the people away from their work? Return to your labor!"*ˡ **5** And Phar'aoh continued: "Look at how many people of the land there are, and you would have them rest from their labor."

6 That same day, Phar'aoh commanded the taskmasters and their foremen: **7** "You must no longer give straw to the people to make bricks.ᵐ Let them go

---

CHAP. 4
a Ex 8:5
　Ex 17:5, 6
　Nu 20:11

b Ex 2:18, 21
　Ex 18:1
　Nu 10:29

c Ex 2:15

d Ex 7:9

e Ex 7:3
　Ex 8:15
　Ex 9:12
　Ex 11:10
　Ro 9:17, 18

f Ex 7:22

g De 7:6
　De 14:2
　Ho 11:1
　Ro 9:4

h Ex 12:29

i Nu 22:22
　1Ch 21:16

j Ge 17:14

k Ex 2:16, 21

l Ex 4:14

m Ex 3:1
　Ex 20:18
　Ex 24:16

Second Col.
a Ex 4:15

b Ex 4:8

c Ex 3:16
　Ex 24:1

d Ex 4:3, 6, 9

e Ex 3:18

f Ge 50:25

g Ex 1:14
　Ex 3:7
　De 26:6

CHAP. 5
h Ex 7:5
　Ex 9:15, 16

i 2Ki 18:28, 35

j Ex 3:19

k Ex 3:18

l Ex 1:11

m Ex 1:14

4:19 *Or "seeking your soul." 4:25 *Or "flint knife."

5:4 *Or "burdens."

and gather straw for themselves. **8** But you must still impose on them the same quota of bricks as they made in the past. Do not reduce it for them, for they are relaxing.* That is why they are crying out, 'We want to go, we want to sacrifice to our God!' **9** Make them work harder, and keep them busy so that they will not pay attention to lies."

10 So the taskmasters[a] and their foremen went out and said to the people: "Here is what Phar'aoh has said, 'I am giving you no more straw. **11** Go and get your own straw for yourselves wherever you can find it, but your work will not be reduced at all.'" **12** Then the people scattered throughout all the land of Egypt to gather stubble for straw. **13** And the taskmasters kept urging them: "You must each finish your work every day, just as when straw was provided." **14** Also the foremen of the Israelites, whom Phar'-aoh's taskmasters had appointed over them, were beaten.[b] They asked them: "Why did you not reach the quota of bricks that you used to make? It happened both yesterday and today."

15 So the foremen of the Israelites went in and complained to Phar'aoh: "Why are you treating your servants this way? **16** No straw is given to your servants, yet they are saying to us, 'Make bricks!' Your servants are beaten, but your own people are at fault." **17** But he said: "You are relaxing,* you are relaxing!*[c] That is why you are saying, 'We want to go, we want to sacrifice to Jehovah.'[d] **18** So now go, get back to work! No straw will be given to you, but you must still produce your quota of bricks."

19 Then the foremen of the Israelites saw that they were in

serious trouble because of the order: "You must not reduce your daily quota of bricks at all." **20** After that they met up with Moses and Aaron, who were standing there to meet them as they came out from Phar'aoh. **21** At once they said to them: "May Jehovah look upon you and judge, since you have made Phar'aoh and his servants despise us* and you have put a sword in their hand to kill us."[a] **22** Then Moses turned to Jehovah and said: "Jehovah, why have you afflicted this people? Why have you sent me? **23** From the time that I went in before Phar'aoh to speak in your name,[b] he has dealt worse with this people,[c] and you have certainly not rescued your people."[d]

6 So Jehovah said to Moses: "Now you will see what I will do to Phar'aoh.[e] A mighty hand will force him to send them away, and a mighty hand will force him to drive them out of his land."[f]

2 Then God said to Moses: "I am Jehovah. **3** And I used to appear to Abraham, Isaac, and Jacob as God Almighty,[g] but with regard to my name Jehovah[h] I did not make myself known to them.[i] **4** I also established my covenant with them to give them the land of Ca'naan, the land in which they lived as foreigners.[j] **5** Now I myself have heard the groaning of the people of Israel, whom the Egyptians are enslaving, and I remember my covenant.[k]

6 "Therefore, say to the Israelites: 'I am Jehovah, and I will bring you out from under the burdens of the Egyptians and rescue you from their slavery,[l] and I will reclaim you with an outstretched* arm and with

---

CHAP. 5
a Ex 1:11

b Ex 2:11

c Ex 5:7, 8

d Ex 5:3

Second Col.
a Ex 6:9

b Ex 5:1

c Ex 5:6, 9

d Ex 3:8

CHAP. 6
e Ex 14:13

f Ex 9:3
Ex 11:1
Ex 12:29, 31

g Ge 17:1
Ge 35:10, 11

h Ps 83:18
Lu 11:2
Joh 12:28
Ac 15:14
Re 15:3

i Ge 12:8
Ge 28:16
Jer 32:20

j Ge 15:18
Ge 28:4

k Ge 17:1, 7
Ex 2:24

l De 4:20

5:8, 17 *Or "are lazy."

5:21 *Or "have made us smell offensive to Pharaoh and to his servants." **6:6** *Or "a powerful."

great judgments.[a] **7** And I will take you in as my people, and I will be your God,[b] and you will certainly know that I am Jehovah your God who is bringing you out from under the burdens of Egypt. **8** And I will bring you into the land that I swore with an oath* to give to Abraham, Isaac, and Jacob; and I will give it to you as something to possess.[c] I am Jehovah.'"[d]

9 Moses later gave this message to the Israelites, but they did not listen to Moses because of their discouragement and because of the harsh slavery.[e]

10 Then Jehovah spoke to Moses, saying: **11** "Go in and tell Phar'aoh, Egypt's king, that he should send the Israelites away out of his land." **12** However, Moses replied to Jehovah: "Look! The Israelites have not listened to me;[f] how will Phar'aoh ever listen to me, as I speak with difficulty?"*[g] **13** But Jehovah again told Moses and Aaron what commands to give to the Israelites and to Phar'aoh, Egypt's king, in order to bring the Israelites out of the land of Egypt.

14 These are the heads of the house of their fathers: The sons of Reu'ben, Israel's firstborn,[h] were Ha'noch, Pal'lu, Hez'ron, and Car'mi.[i] These are the families of Reu'ben.

15 The sons of Sim'e·on were Jem·u'el, Ja'min, O'had, Ja'chin, Zo'har, and Sha'ul, the son of a Ca'naan·ite woman.[j] These are the families of Sim'e·on.

16 These are the names of the sons of Le'vi,[k] according to their family descents: Ger'shon, Ko'hath, and Me·rar'i.[l] The length of Le'vi's life was 137 years.

17 The sons of Ger'shon were Lib'ni and Shim'e·i, according to their families.[m]

18 The sons of Ko'hath were Am'ram, Iz'har, Heb'ron, and Uz'zi·el.[a] The length of Ko'hath's life was 133 years.

19 The sons of Me·rar'i were Mah'li and Mu'shi.

These were the families of the Levites, according to their family descents.[b]

20 Now Am'ram took Joch'e·bed, his father's sister, as his wife.[c] She bore him Aaron and Moses.[d] The length of Am'ram's life was 137 years.

21 The sons of Iz'har were Kor'ah,[e] Ne'pheg, and Zich'ri.

22 The sons of Uz'zi·el were Mish'a·el, El·za'phan,[f] and Sith'ri.

23 Now Aaron took E·li'she·ba, Am·min'a·dab's daughter, the sister of Nah'shon,[g] as his wife. She bore him Na'dab, A·bi'hu, El·e·a'zar, and Ith'a·mar.[h]

24 The sons of Kor'ah were As'sir, El·ka'nah, and A·bi'a·saph.[i] These were the families of the Kor'ah·ites.[j]

25 El·e·a'zar,[k] Aaron's son, took one of the daughters of Pu'ti·el as his wife. She bore him Phin'e·has.[l]

These are the heads of the paternal houses of the Levites, according to their families.[m]

26 This is the Aaron and Moses to whom Jehovah said: "Bring the people of Israel out of the land of Egypt, company by company."*[n] **27** It was they who spoke to Phar'aoh, Egypt's king, to bring the people of Israel out of Egypt. It was this Moses and Aaron.[o]

28 On that day when Jehovah spoke to Moses in the land of Egypt, **29** Jehovah told Moses: "I am Jehovah. Speak to Phar'aoh, king of Egypt, everything I am speaking to you." **30** Then Moses said before Jehovah:

CHAP. 6

a De 26:8
  1Ch 17:21
  Ac 13:17

b Ex 29:45
  De 7:6
  2Sa 7:24
  Ps 33:12

c Ge 15:18
  Ge 26:3
  Ge 35:12
  Ex 32:13

d Ex 20:2
  Isa 42:8

e Ex 5:21

f Ex 5:21
  Ex 6:9

g Ex 4:10
  Ac 7:22

h Ge 49:3

i Ge 46:9

j 1Ch 4:24

k Ge 29:34

l Ge 46:11
  Nu 26:57

m Nu 3:18

Second Row

a Nu 3:19

b Nu 3:20

c Ex 2:1
  Nu 26:59

d 1Ch 23:13

e Nu 16:1, 32
  Nu 26:10

f Le 10:4
  Nu 3:30

g Ru 4:19-21
  Mt 1:4

h Nu 3:2

i Nu 26:10, 11

j Nu 26:58
  1Ch 9:19

k Nu 3:32

l Nu 25:7
  Nu 31:6
  Jos 22:31
  Jg 20:28

m Ex 6:19

n Ex 7:2, 4
  Ex 12:41
  Ac 7:35

o Ps 77:20

6:8 *Lit., "I raised my hand." 6:12 *Lit., "I am uncircumcised in lips."

6:26 *Lit., "according to their armies."

"Look! I speak with difficulty,* so how will Phar'aoh ever listen to me?"[a]

7 Jehovah then said to Moses: "See, I have made you like God* to Phar'aoh, and Aaron your own brother will become your prophet.[b] **2** You are to repeat everything that I will command you, and Aaron your brother will speak to Phar'aoh, and he will send the Israelites away from his land. **3** As for me, I will allow Phar'aoh's heart to become obstinate,[c] and I will multiply my signs and my miracles in the land of Egypt.[d] **4** But Phar'aoh will not listen to you, and I will lay my hand upon Egypt and bring my multitudes,* my people, the Israelites, out of the land of Egypt with great judgments.[e] **5** And the Egyptians will certainly know that I am Jehovah[f] when I stretch out my hand against Egypt and bring the Israelites out from among them." **6** Moses and Aaron did what Jehovah had commanded them; they did just so. **7** Moses was 80 years old and Aaron was 83 years old when they spoke to Phar'aoh.[g]

8 Jehovah now said to Moses and Aaron: **9** "If Phar'aoh says to you, 'Perform a miracle,' then tell Aaron, 'Take your rod and throw it down before Phar'aoh.' It will become a big snake."[h] **10** So Moses and Aaron went in to Phar'aoh and did exactly as Jehovah had commanded. Aaron threw his rod down before Phar'aoh and his servants, and it became a big snake. **11** However, Phar'aoh summoned the wise men and the sorcerers, and the magic-practicing priests of Egypt[i] also did the same thing with their magic.*[j] **12** Each one

threw down his rod, and they became big snakes; but Aaron's rod swallowed up their rods. **13** Still, Phar'aoh's heart became obstinate,[a] and he did not listen to them, just as Jehovah had said.

14 Then Jehovah said to Moses: "Phar'aoh's heart is unresponsive.[b] He has refused to send the people away. **15** Go to Phar'aoh in the morning. Look! He is going out to the water! And you should station yourself to meet him by the edge of the Nile River; and take with you in your hand the rod that turned into a serpent.[c] **16** And you must say to him, 'Jehovah the God of the Hebrews has sent me to you,[d] and he says: "Send my people away so that they may serve me in the wilderness," but you have not obeyed until now. **17** This is what Jehovah says: "By this you will know that I am Jehovah.[e] Here I am striking the water that is in the Nile River with the rod that is in my hand, and it will turn into blood. **18** And the fish that are in the Nile will die, and the Nile will stink, and the Egyptians will find it impossible to drink water from the Nile."'"

19 Then Jehovah said to Moses: "Say to Aaron, 'Take your rod and stretch out your hand over the waters of Egypt,[f] over its rivers, over its canals,* over its marshes,[g] and over all its reservoirs, that they may become blood.' There will be blood in all the land of Egypt, even in the wooden and stone containers." **20** Immediately Moses and Aaron did just as Jehovah had commanded. He lifted up the rod and struck the water that was in the Nile River before the eyes of Phar'aoh and his servants, and all the water that was in

---

6:30 *Lit., "I am uncircumcised in lips." 7:1 *Lit., "made you God." 7:4 *Lit., "my armies." 7:11 *Or "their magic arts."

7:19 *That is, canals from the Nile.

CHAP. 6
a Ex 4:10
Ex 6:12

CHAP. 7
b Ex 4:14-16
Ex 4:30

c Ex 4:21
Ex 7:13, 22
Ex 8:15, 19
Ex 9:12, 35
Ex 10:20, 27
Ex 11:10
Ex 14:8
Ro 9:17, 18

d Ex 3:19, 20
Ps 105:26, 27
Ac 7:36

e Ex 12:12, 51

f Ex 7:17
Ex 8:9, 10
Ex 8:22
Ex 9:29
Ex 14:4

g De 34:7
Ac 7:22, 23

h Ex 4:2, 3

i Ge 41:8
2Ti 3:8

j Ex 7:20, 22
Ex 8:7, 18
Ex 9:11

Second Col.
a Ex 7:3

b Ex 10:1

c Ex 4:2, 3

d Ex 3:18

e Ex 7:5
Ex 8:9, 10
Ex 8:22
Ex 9:29
Ex 14:4

f Ex 9:22
Ex 10:12
Ex 14:21

g Ex 8:5

the river was turned into blood.[a] **21** And the fish that were in the river died,[b] and the river began to stink, and the Egyptians were unable to drink water from the Nile,[c] and there was blood throughout the land of Egypt.

22 Nevertheless, the magic-practicing priests of Egypt did the same thing with their secret arts,[d] so that Phar'aoh's heart continued to be obstinate, and he did not listen to them, just as Jehovah had said.[e] **23** Then Phar'aoh returned to his house, and he did not take this to heart either. **24** So all the Egyptians were digging all around the Nile for water to drink, because they could not drink any water of the Nile. **25** And seven full days passed after Jehovah struck the Nile.

8 Then Jehovah said to Moses: "Go in to Phar'aoh and say to him, 'This is what Jehovah says: "Send my people away so that they may serve me.[f] **2** If you keep refusing to send them away, I will plague all your territory with frogs.[g] **3** And the Nile River will swarm with frogs, and they will come up and enter into your house, into your bedroom, on your bed, into the houses of your servants and on your people, into your ovens, and into your kneading troughs.*[h] **4** On you, on your people, and on all your servants, the frogs will come up."'"

5 Jehovah later said to Moses: "Say to Aaron, 'Stretch out your hand with your rod over the rivers, the Nile canals, and the marshes, and make the frogs come up over the land of Egypt.'" **6** So Aaron stretched out his hand over the waters of Egypt, and the frogs began to come up and to cover

8:3 *Or "bowls."

CHAP. 7
a Ps 78:44

b Ps 105:29

c Ex 7:18, 24

d Ex 7:11, 12
Ex 8:7, 18
Ex 9:11
2Ti 3:8

e Ex 3:19

CHAP. 8
f Ex 3:12

g Ps 78:45

h Ps 105:30

Second Col.
a Ex 7:11, 12
Ex 7:20, 22
Ex 8:17, 18
Ex 9:11
2Ti 3:8

b Ex 10:16-19

c Ex 9:14
Ex 15:11
Ps 83:18
Ps 86:8
Isa 46:9
Jer 10:6, 7
Ro 9:17

d Ex 8:3

e Ex 8:30, 31
Ex 9:33

f Ex 4:21
Ex 7:3

g Ps 105:31

the land of Egypt. **7** However, the magic-practicing priests did the same thing by their secret arts, and they too made the frogs come up over the land of Egypt.[a] **8** Phar'aoh then called Moses and Aaron and said: "Plead with Jehovah to remove the frogs from me and my people,[b] as I want to send the people away so that they may sacrifice to Jehovah." **9** Then Moses said to Phar'aoh: "I leave to you the honor of telling me when I should plead to have the frogs removed from you, your servants, your people, and your houses. Only in the Nile River will they be left." **10** To this he said: "Tomorrow." So he said: "It will be according to your word so that you may know that there is no one else like Jehovah our God.[c] **11** The frogs will depart from you, your houses, your servants, and your people. They will be left only in the Nile."[d]

12 So Moses and Aaron went out from Phar'aoh, and Moses pleaded with Jehovah about the frogs that He had brought upon Phar'aoh.[e] **13** Then Jehovah did as Moses asked, and the frogs began to die in the houses, the courtyards, and the fields. **14** They were piling them up in countless heaps, and the land began to stink. **15** When Phar'aoh saw that there was relief, he hardened his heart[f] and he refused to listen to them, just as Jehovah had said.

16 Jehovah now said to Moses: "Say to Aaron, 'Stretch out your rod and strike the dust of the earth, and it must become gnats in all the land of Egypt.'" **17** And they did this. Aaron stretched out his hand with his rod and struck the dust of the earth, and the gnats came on man and beast. All the dust of the earth became gnats in all the land of Egypt.[g] **18** The magic-practicing priests tried to do the same and produce gnats by their secret arts,[a] but they could not. And the gnats came on man and beast. **19** So the magic-practicing priests said to Phar'-aoh: "It is the finger of God!"[b] But Phar'aoh's heart continued to be obstinate, and he did not listen to them, just as Jehovah had said.

20 Then Jehovah said to Moses: "Get up early in the morning and station yourself in front of Phar'aoh. Look! He is coming out to the water! And you must say to him, 'This is what Jehovah has said: "Send my people away so that they may serve me. **21** But if you do not send my people away, I will send on you, your servants, and your people and into your houses the gadfly;* and the houses of Egypt will be full of gadflies, and they will even cover the ground they* stand on. **22** On that day I will certainly set apart the land of Go'shen, where my people are dwelling. No gadflies will exist there,[c] and by this you will know that I, Jehovah, am here in the land.[d] **23** And I will make a distinction between my people and your people. Tomorrow this sign will take place."'"

24 And Jehovah did so, and heavy swarms of gadflies began to invade the house of Phar'aoh and the houses of his servants and all the land of Egypt.[e] The land was ruined by the gadflies.[f] **25** Finally, Phar'aoh called Moses and Aaron and said: "Go, sacrifice to your God in the land." **26** But Moses said: "It is not proper to do so, because what we would sacrifice to Jehovah our God would be detestable to the Egyptians.[g] If we would make a sacrifice that was detest-

able to the Egyptians right before their eyes, would they not stone us? **27** We will make a three-day journey into the wilderness, and there we will sacrifice to Jehovah our God, just as he has said to us."[a]

28 Phar'aoh now said: "I will send you away to sacrifice to Jehovah your God in the wilderness. Only, you must not go so far away. Plead in my behalf."[b] **29** Then Moses said: "Now I am going away from you, and I will plead with Jehovah, and the gadflies will depart from Phar'aoh, his servants, and his people tomorrow. But Phar'aoh must stop trifling* with us by refusing to send the people away to sacrifice to Jehovah."[c] **30** Moses then went out from Phar'aoh and pleaded with Jehovah.[d] **31** So Jehovah did according to Moses' word, and the gadflies departed from Phar'aoh, his servants, and his people. Not one was left. **32** However, Phar'aoh again hardened his heart and did not send the people away.

9 So Jehovah said to Moses: "Go in to Phar'aoh and say to him, 'This is what Jehovah the God of the Hebrews has said: "Send my people away so that they may serve me.[e] **2** But if you refuse to send them away and you keep holding them, **3** look! Jehovah's hand[f] will come against your livestock in the field. On the horses, the donkeys, the camels, the herd, and the flock, there will be a devastating plague.[g] **4** And Jehovah will certainly make a distinction between the livestock of Israel and the livestock of Egypt, and nothing that belongs to the Israelites will die."'"[h] **5** Moreover, Jehovah set an appointed time, saying: "Tomorrow Jehovah will do this in the land."

CHAP. 8
a Ex 7:11, 12
Ex 7:20, 22
Ex 8:7
Ex 9:11

b Ex 31:18
Lu 11:20

c Ex 9:4, 26
Ex 10:23
Ex 12:13

d 1Sa 17:46
1Ki 20:28
2Ki 19:17, 19

e Ex 8:3

f Ps 78:45
Ps 105:31

g Ge 46:33, 34
Ex 10:25, 26

Second Col.
a Ex 3:18

b Ex 8:8
Ex 9:28

c Ex 8:15

d Ex 9:33

CHAP. 9
e Ex 5:1
Ex 8:1

f Ex 7:4

g Ex 9:15

h Ex 8:22
Ex 10:23
Ex 11:7
Ex 12:13

8:21 *A type of fly that bites.   #That is, the Egyptians.

8:29 *Or "playing games."

6 And Jehovah did this on the very next day, and all sorts of livestock of Egypt began to die,[a] but not one of Israel's livestock died. **7** When Phar'aoh inquired, look! not so much as one of Israel's livestock had died. Nevertheless, Phar'aoh's heart continued to be unresponsive, and he did not send the people away.[b]

8 Jehovah then said to Moses and Aaron: "Fill both of your hands with soot from a kiln, and Moses must throw it into the air in front of Phar'aoh. **9** And it will become a fine dust on all the land of Egypt, and it will become festering boils on man and beast in all the land of Egypt."

10 So they took soot from a kiln and stood before Phar'aoh, and Moses tossed it into the air, and it became festering boils breaking out on man and beast. **11** The magic-practicing priests were unable to stand before Moses because of the boils, for they had developed on the magic-practicing priests and on all the Egyptians.[c] **12** But Jehovah allowed Phar'aoh's heart to become obstinate, and he did not listen to them, just as Jehovah had told Moses.[d]

13 Then Jehovah said to Moses: "Get up early in the morning and station yourself in front of Phar'aoh, and say to him, 'This is what Jehovah the God of the Hebrews has said: "Send my people away so that they may serve me. **14** For now I am directing all my blows to strike your heart, your servants, and your people, so that you may know that there is no one like me in all the earth.[e] **15** For by now I could have thrust my hand out to strike you and your people with a devastating plague, and you would have been wiped out*

from the earth. **16** But for this very reason I have kept you in existence: to show you my power and to have my name declared in all the earth.[a] **17** Are you still behaving arrogantly against my people by not sending them away? **18** Here I will cause a very great hail to rain down tomorrow about this time, such as has never occurred in Egypt from the day it was founded until now. **19** Therefore, send word to bring all your livestock and all that is yours in the field under shelter. Every man and beast caught in the field and not brought into the house will die when the hail comes down on them."'"

20 Anyone among Phar'aoh's servants who feared Jehovah's word quickly brought his own servants and his livestock into the houses, **21** but whoever did not take Jehovah's word to heart left his servants and his livestock in the field.

22 Jehovah now said to Moses: "Stretch out your hand toward the heavens, so that hail may come down on all the land of Egypt,[b] on man and beast and all the vegetation of the field in the land of Egypt."[c] **23** So Moses stretched out his rod toward the heavens, and Jehovah sent thunder and hail, and fire* fell down to the earth, and Jehovah kept making it rain down hail on the land of Egypt. **24** There was hail, and there was fire flashing in the midst of the hail. It was very heavy; there had never been any like it in the land since Egypt had become a nation.[d] **25** The hail struck everything in the field throughout the land of Egypt, from man to beast, and it struck down all the vegetation and shattered all the trees of the field.[e] **26** Only in

---

CHAP. 9
a Ps 78:48

b Ex 4:21

c Ex 7:11, 12
Ex 7:20, 22
Ex 8:7, 18
2Ti 3:8

d Ex 4:21
Ex 8:31, 32
Ex 14:17

e Ex 8:9, 10
2Sa 7:22
Ps 83:18

Second Col.
a Ex 14:17
Jos 2:9, 10
1Ch 16:24
Pr 16:4
Isa 63:12
Ro 9:17

b Ps 78:47
Ps 105:32

c Ex 10:4, 5

d Ex 9:18

e Ps 105:33

9:15 *Or "effaced."

9:23 *Perhaps describing powerful lightning.

the land of Go'shen, where the Israelites were, there was no hail.[a]

27 So Phar'aoh sent for Moses and Aaron and said to them: "I have sinned this time. Jehovah is righteous, and I and my people are in the wrong. 28 Plead with Jehovah that there may be an end to God's thunder and hail. Then I will be willing to send you away, and you will not stay any longer." 29 So Moses said to him: "As soon as I go out of the city, I will spread out my hands before Jehovah. The thunder will stop and the hail will not continue any longer, so that you may know that the earth belongs to Jehovah.[b] 30 But as for you and your servants, I know already that even then, you will not fear Jehovah God."

31 Now the flax and the barley had been struck down, because the barley was in the ear and the flax had flower buds. 32 But the wheat and the spelt had not been struck down, because they were later crops.* 33 Moses now went out of the city from Phar'aoh and spread out his hands before Jehovah, and the thunder and the hail stopped and the rain quit pouring down on the earth.[c] 34 When Phar'aoh saw that the rain, the hail, and the thunder had stopped, he sinned again and hardened his heart,[d] he as well as his servants. 35 And Phar'aoh's heart continued obstinate, and he did not send the Israelites away, just as Jehovah had stated through Moses.[e]

10 Then Jehovah said to Moses: "Go in to Phar'aoh, for I have allowed his heart and the hearts of his servants to become unresponsive,[f] so that I may display these signs of mine

right before him,[a] 2 and in order that you may declare to your sons and your grandsons how severely I have dealt with Egypt and what signs I have performed among them;[b] and you will certainly know that I am Jehovah."

3 So Moses and Aaron went in to Phar'aoh and said to him: "This is what Jehovah the God of the Hebrews has said, 'How long will you refuse to submit to me?[c] Send my people away so that they may serve me. 4 For if you keep refusing to send my people away, here I am bringing locusts within your boundaries tomorrow. 5 And they will cover the surface of the earth, and it will not be possible to see the ground. They will eat up what escaped the hail and was left for you, and they will eat all your trees that are growing in the field.[d] 6 They will fill your houses, the houses of all your servants, and the houses of all Egypt to an extent that your fathers and your grandfathers never saw from the time they have been in this land until today.'"[e] With that he turned and went out from Phar'aoh.

7 Then Phar'aoh's servants said to him: "How long will this man continue to menace* us? Send the men away so that they may serve Jehovah their God. Do you not yet realize that Egypt has been ruined?" 8 So Moses and Aaron were brought back to Phar'aoh, and he said to them: "Go, serve Jehovah your God. But just who will be going?" 9 Then Moses said: "We will go with our young people, our old people, our sons, our daughters, our sheep, and our cattle,[f] because we will hold a festival to Jehovah."[g] 10 He said to them: "If I ever send you and your children away, then Jehovah is

---

CHAP. 9
a Ex 8:22
Ex 9:3, 4
Ex 10:23
Ex 11:7
Ex 12:13

b Ex 7:5, 17
Ex 8:9, 10
Ex 8:22
Ex 14:4
De 10:14
Ps 24:1

c Ex 10:17-19

d Ex 4:21
Ex 8:13, 15

e Ex 7:4

CHAP. 10
f Ex 4:21
Ex 9:34

Second Col.
a Ex 9:15, 16
Ps 78:12
Ro 9:17

b Ex 13:3, 8
De 4:9
De 6:20-22
Ps 44:1

c Ex 9:17

d Ex 9:31, 32

e Ex 9:24

f Ex 10:25, 26

g Ex 3:18
Ex 5:1

9:32 * Or "were seasonally late."

10:7 * Lit., "be a snare to."

indeed with you!ᵃ It is clear that you intend to do something evil. **11** No! Only your men may go and serve Jehovah, for that is what you requested." With that they were driven out from before Phar′aoh.

12 Jehovah now said to Moses: "Stretch out your hand over the land of Egypt for the locusts, so that they may come up over the land of Egypt and eat up all the vegetation of the land, everything that the hail has let remain." **13** At once Moses stretched out his rod over the land of Egypt, and Jehovah caused an east wind to blow on the land all that day and all night. The morning came, and the east wind brought the locusts. **14** And the locusts came up over all the land of Egypt and settled down on the whole territory of Egypt.ᵇ It was extremely severe;ᶜ never before had there been so many locusts, nor would there ever be so many again. **15** They covered the surface of the entire land, and the land grew dark with them; they devoured all the vegetation of the land and all the fruit of the trees that the hail had left; nothing green was left on the trees or on the vegetation of the field in all the land of Egypt.

16 So Phar′aoh quickly called Moses and Aaron and said: "I have sinned against Jehovah your God and against you. **17** Now, please, pardon my sin just this once, and plead with Jehovah your God that he just remove this deadly plague from upon me." **18** So he* went out from Phar′aoh and pleaded with Jehovah.ᵈ **19** Then Jehovah caused the wind to shift, and it became a very stiff west wind, and it carried the locusts away and drove them into the Red Sea. Not a single lo-

cust remained in all the territory of Egypt. **20** However, Jehovah allowed Phar′aoh's heart to become obstinate,ᵃ and he did not send the Israelites away.

21 Jehovah then said to Moses: "Stretch out your hand toward the heavens so that there may be darkness over the land of Egypt, a darkness so thick that it can be felt." **22** Moses immediately stretched out his hand toward the heavens, and there was a dense darkness in all the land of Egypt for three days.ᵇ **23** They did not see one another, and none of them got up from where they were for three days; but all the Israelites had light in their dwellings.ᶜ **24** Phar′aoh then called Moses and said: "Go, serve Jehovah.ᵈ Only your sheep and your cattle will remain behind. Even your children may go with you." **25** But Moses said: "You yourself will also provide us with* sacrifices and burnt offerings, and we will offer them to Jehovah our God.ᵉ **26** Our livestock will also go with us. Not an animal* will be allowed to remain, because we will be using some of them to worship Jehovah our God, and we do not know what we will offer in worship to Jehovah until we arrive there." **27** So Jehovah allowed Phar′aoh's heart to become obstinate, and he did not consent to send them away.ᶠ **28** Phar′aoh said to him: "Get out of my sight! Make sure that you do not try to see my face again, for on the day you see my face, you will die." **29** To this Moses said: "Just as you have spoken, I will not try to see your face again."

11 Then Jehovah said to Moses: "One more plague I am going to bring upon Phar′aoh and Egypt. After that he will

---

CHAP. 10
a Ex 12:31, 32

b Ps 78:46

c Ex 10:5
Ps 105:34, 35

d Ex 8:30, 31

Second Col.
a Ex 7:3
Ex 11:10
Ro 9:17, 18

b Ps 105:28

c Ex 8:21, 22
Ex 9:3, 6
Ex 9:26
Ex 11:7
Ex 12:13

d Ex 8:28
Ex 9:28

e Ex 3:18
Ex 5:3

f Ex 4:21
Ex 14:4

10:18 *Apparently Moses.   **10:25** *Or "allow us to have."   **10:26** *Lit., "a hoof."

send you away from here.[a] When he does send you away, he will literally drive you out of here.[b] **2** Now tell the people that all the men and women should ask their neighbor for articles of silver and of gold."[c] **3** And Jehovah gave the people favor in the eyes of the Egyptians. Moreover, Moses himself had become highly esteemed in the land of Egypt among Phar′aoh's servants and among the people.

4 Moses then said: "This is what Jehovah has said, 'About midnight I am going out into the midst of Egypt,[d] **5** and every firstborn in the land of Egypt will die,[e] from the firstborn of Phar′aoh who is sitting on his throne to the firstborn of the slave girl who is working at the hand mill, and every firstborn of the livestock.[f] **6** Throughout all the land of Egypt, there will be a great outcry such as has never occurred nor will ever occur again.[g] **7** But not even a dog will bark* at the Israelites, at the men or their livestock, so that you may know that Jehovah can make a distinction between the Egyptians and the Israelites.'[h] **8** And all your servants will certainly come down to me and prostrate themselves to me, saying, 'Go, you and all the people who follow you.'[i] And after that I will go out." With that he went out from Phar′aoh in the heat of anger.

9 Jehovah then said to Moses: "Phar′aoh will not listen to you,[j] in order for my miracles to be multiplied in the land of Egypt."[k] **10** Moses and Aaron performed all these miracles before Phar′aoh,[l] but Jehovah allowed Phar′aoh's heart to become obstinate, so that he did not send the Israelites away from his land.[m]

11:7 *Lit., "sharpen its tongue."

12 Jehovah now said to Moses and Aaron in the land of Egypt: **2** "This month will be the beginning of the months for you. It will be the first of the months of the year for you.[a] **3** Speak to the entire assembly of Israel, saying, 'On the tenth day of this month, they should each take for themselves a sheep[b] for their father's house, a sheep to a house. **4** But if the household is too small for the sheep, they* and their nearest neighbor should share it between themselves in their house according to the number of people.# When making the calculation, determine how much of the sheep each one will eat. **5** Your sheep should be a sound,[c] one-year-old male. You may choose from the young rams or from the goats. **6** You must care for it until the 14th day of this month,[d] and the whole congregation of the assembly of Israel must slaughter it at twilight.*[e] **7** They must take some of the blood and splash it on the two doorposts and the upper part of the doorway of the houses in which they eat it.[f]

8 "'They must eat the meat on this night.[g] They should roast it over the fire and eat it along with unleavened bread[h] and bitter greens.[i] **9** Do not eat any of it raw or boiled, cooked in water, but roast it over the fire, its head together with its shanks and its inner parts. **10** You must not save any of it until morning, but any of it left over until morning you should burn with fire.[j] **11** And this is how you should eat it, with your belt fastened,* sandals on your feet, and your staff in your hand; and you should eat it in a hurry. It is Jehovah's Passover. **12** For I

12:4 *Lit., "he." #Or "souls." 12:6 *Lit., "between the two evenings." 12:11 *Lit., "with your hips girded."

CHAP. 11
a De 4:34

b Ex 12:31, 32

c Ex 3:21, 22
Ex 12:35, 36
Ps 105:37

d Ex 12:29

e Ex 4:22, 23
Ps 78:51
Ps 105:36
Ps 136:10
Heb 11:28

f Ex 12:12

g Ex 12:30

h Ex 8:22
Ex 9:3, 4
Ex 10:23
Ex 12:13

i Ex 12:33

j Ex 3:19
Ex 7:4
Ro 9:17, 18

k Ex 7:3

l Ps 135:9

m Ex 4:21
Ex 9:15, 16
Ex 10:20

Second Col.

CHAP. 12
a Ex 13:4
Ex 23:15
Nu 28:16
De 16:1

b Joh 1:29
1Co 5:7
Re 5:6

c Le 22:18-20
De 17:1
1Pe 1:19

d Nu 28:16

e Ex 12:18
Le 23:5
De 16:6

f 1Co 5:7
Heb 11:28

g De 16:6, 7

h Ex 13:3
Ex 34:25
De 16:3
1Co 5:8

i Nu 9:11

j Le 7:15
Le 22:29, 30
De 16:4

will pass through the land of Egypt on this night and strike every firstborn in the land of Egypt, from man to beast;[a] and I will execute judgment on all the gods of Egypt.[b] I am Jehovah. 13 The blood will serve as your sign on the houses where you are; and I will see the blood and pass over you, and the plague will not come on you to destroy you when I strike the land of Egypt.[c]

14 "'This day will serve as a memorial for you, and you must celebrate it as a festival to Jehovah throughout your generations. As a lasting statute, you should celebrate it. 15 Seven days you are to eat unleavened bread.[d] Yes, on the first day you are to remove the sourdough from your houses, because anyone eating what is leavened from the first day down to the seventh, that person* must be cut off# from Israel. 16 On the first day you will hold a holy convention, and on the seventh day, another holy convention. No work is to be done on these days.[e] Only what every person* needs to eat, that alone may be prepared for you.

17 "'You must keep the Festival of Unleavened Bread,[f] for on this very day, I will bring your multitudes* out of the land of Egypt. And you must keep this day throughout your generations as a lasting statute. 18 In the first month, on the 14th day of the month, in the evening, you are to eat unleavened bread until the 21st day of the month, in the evening.[g] 19 No sourdough is to be found in your houses for seven days, because if anyone eats what is leavened, whether he is a foreigner or a native of the land,[h] that person* must be

cut off# from the assembly of Israel.[a] 20 You should not eat anything leavened. In all your homes, you are to eat unleavened bread.'"

21 Moses promptly called all the elders of Israel[b] and said to them: "Go and select young animals* for each of your families, and slaughter the Passover sacrifice. 22 Then you must dip a bunch of hyssop into the blood that is in a basin and strike the upper part of the doorway and the two doorposts with the blood; and none of you should go out of the entrance of his house until morning. 23 Then when Jehovah passes through to plague the Egyptians and sees the blood on the upper part of the doorway and on the two doorposts, Jehovah will certainly pass over the entrance, and he will not allow the plague of death* to enter into your houses.[c]

24 "You must observe this event as a lasting regulation for you and your sons.[d] 25 And when you come into the land that Jehovah will give you just as he has stated, you must keep this observance.[e] 26 And when your sons ask you, 'What does this observance mean to you?'[f] 27 you must say, 'It is the sacrifice of the Passover to Jehovah, who passed over the houses of the Israelites in Egypt when he plagued the Egyptians, but he spared our houses.'"

Then the people bowed low and prostrated themselves. 28 So the Israelites went and did just as Jehovah had commanded Moses and Aaron.[g] They did just so.

29 Then at midnight, Jehovah struck down every firstborn in the land of Egypt,[h] from the

---

CHAP. 12
a Ex 11:4, 5
  Ex 12:29

b Nu 33:4

c Ex 8:22
  Ex 9:4, 26
  Ex 10:23
  Ex 11:7

d Ex 23:15
  Le 23:6

e Le 23:8

f Le 23:6
  Lu 22:1
  1Co 5:8

g Le 23:5, 6

h Nu 9:14

_____

Second Col.
a De 16:3
  1Co 5:7

b Ex 3:16
  Nu 11:16

c Heb 11:28

d De 16:3

e Jos 5:10

f Ex 13:3, 8
  De 6:6, 7

g Heb 11:28

h Nu 33:4
  Ps 78:51
  Ps 105:36

12:15, 16, 19 *Or "soul." 12:15, 19 #Or "put to death." 12:17 *Lit., "armies." 12:21 *That is, young sheep or goats. 12:23 *Lit., "the ruination."

firstborn of Phar'aoh who was sitting on his throne to the firstborn of the captive who was in the prison,* and every firstborn of the animals.ᵃ 30 Phar'aoh got up that night along with all his servants and all the other Egyptians, and there was a great outcry among the Egyptians, because there was not a house where someone was not dead.ᵇ 31 At once he called Moses and Aaronᶜ by night and said: "Get up, get out from among my people, both you and the other Israelites. Go and serve Jehovah, just as you have said.ᵈ 32 Take also your flocks and your herds and go, just as you have said.ᵉ But you must also bless me."

33 And the Egyptians began to urge the people to depart quicklyᶠ out of the land "because," as they said, "we are all as good as dead!"ᵍ 34 So the people carried their flour dough before it was leavened, with their kneading troughs* wrapped up in their clothing on their shoulder. 35 The Israelites did what Moses had told them and asked the Egyptians for articles of silver and of gold as well as clothing.ʰ 36 Jehovah gave the people favor in the eyes of the Egyptians, so that they gave them what they asked for, and they plundered the Egyptians.ⁱ

37 Then the Israelites departed from Ram'e·ses'ʲ for Suc'coth,ᵏ about 600,000 men on foot, besides children.ˡ 38 And a vast mixed company*ᵐ also went with them, as well as flocks and herds, a great number of livestock. 39 They began to bake the dough that they brought from Egypt into round loaves of unleavened bread. It was not leavened, because they had been driven out of Egypt so suddenly that they had not prepared any provisions for themselves.ᵃ

40 The dwelling of the Israelites, who had dwelled in Egypt,ᵇ was 430 years.ᶜ 41 At the end of the 430 years, on this very day, all the multitudes* of Jehovah went out of the land of Egypt. 42 It is a night on which they will celebrate Jehovah's bringing them out of the land of Egypt. This night is to be observed to Jehovah by all the people of Israel throughout their generations.ᵈ

43 Then Jehovah said to Moses and Aaron, "This is the statute of the Passover: No foreigner may eat of it.ᵉ 44 But if someone has a slave man who was purchased with money, you should circumcise him.ᶠ Only then may he share in eating it. 45 A settler and a hired worker may not eat of it. 46 In one house it is to be eaten. You must not take any of the meat outside of the house, and you must not break any of its bones.ᵍ 47 All the assembly of Israel are to celebrate it. 48 If a foreigner resides with you and he wants to celebrate the Passover to Jehovah, every male of his must be circumcised. Then he may come near to celebrate it, and he will become like a native of the land. But no uncircumcised man may eat of it.ʰ 49 One law will apply for the native and for the foreigner who is residing among you."ⁱ

50 So all the Israelites did just as Jehovah had commanded Moses and Aaron. They did just so. 51 On this very day, Jehovah brought the Israelites along with their multitudes* out of the land of Egypt.

CHAP. 12
a Ge 15:14
  Ex 11:4, 5
  Nu 3:13
  Ps 135:8

b Ex 11:6

c Ex 10:28, 29

d Ex 3:19, 20
  Ex 6:1
  Ex 10:8-11
  Ps 105:38

e Ex 10:26

f Ex 12:11

g Ex 10:7

h Ge 15:14
  Ex 3:21
  Ex 11:2
  Ps 105:37

i Ex 3:22

j Ge 47:11
  Ex 1:11

k Nu 33:5

l Ge 12:1, 2
  Ge 15:1, 5
  Ge 46:2, 3
  Ex 1:7
  Nu 2:32

m Nu 11:4

Second Col.
a Ex 12:31

b Ge 46:2, 3
  Ge 47:27
  Ac 13:17

c Ga 3:17

d De 16:1

e Le 22:10

f Ge 17:12, 23

g Nu 9:12
  Ps 34:19, 20
  Joh 19:33, 36

h Nu 9:14

i Le 24:22
  Nu 15:16

12:29 *Lit., "the house of the cistern."
12:34 *Or "bowls." 12:38 *That is, a mixed company of non-Israelites, including Egyptians.

12:41, 51 *Lit., "armies."

13 Jehovah spoke further to Moses, saying: **2** "Sanctify* to me every firstborn male[a] among the Israelites. The first male to be born, of both human and animal, belongs to me."[a]

3 Then Moses said to the people: "Remember this day on which you went out of Egypt,[b] from the house of slavery, because with a mighty hand Jehovah brought you out of here.[c] So nothing leavened may be eaten. **4** You are going out on this day, in the month of A'bib.*[d] **5** When Jehovah has brought you into the land of the Ca'naanites, the Hit'tites, the Am'orites, the Hi'vites, and the Jeb'usites,[e] which he swore to your forefathers to give you,[f] a land flowing with milk and honey,[g] then you must keep this observance in this month. **6** Seven days you are to eat unleavened bread,[h] and on the seventh day, there will be a festival to Jehovah. **7** Unleavened bread is to be eaten for the seven days;[i] and nothing leavened is to be found with you,[j] and no sourdough is to be found with you within all your territory.* **8** And you must tell your son on that day, 'It is because of what Jehovah did for me when I came out of Egypt.'[k] **9** And this will serve for you as a sign on your hand and as a memorial* on your forehead,*[l] so that Jehovah's law may be in your mouth, for with a mighty hand Jehovah brought you out of Egypt. **10** You must keep this statute at its appointed time from year to year.[m]

11 "When Jehovah brings you into the land of the Ca'naanites, which he has sworn to give

to you and to your forefathers,[a] **12** you must devote to Jehovah every firstborn male,* as well as every male firstling of the livestock that you acquire. The males belong to Jehovah.[b] **13** Every firstling donkey you are to redeem with a sheep, and if you do not redeem it, then you must break its neck. And every firstborn male of your sons you are to redeem.[c]

14 "In case your son should ask you later on, 'What does this mean?' then you should say to him, 'With a mighty hand Jehovah brought us out of Egypt, from the house of slavery.[d] **15** When Phar'aoh stubbornly refused to send us away,[e] Jehovah killed every firstborn in the land of Egypt, from the firstborn of man to the firstborn of beast.[f] That is why I am sacrificing to Jehovah all the firstborn males,* and I redeem every firstborn of my sons.' **16** This must serve as a sign on your hand and as a headband on your forehead,*[g] for with a mighty hand Jehovah brought us out of Egypt."

17 Now when Phar'aoh sent the people away, God did not lead them by the way of the land of the Phi·lis'tines, although it was near. For God said: "The people may change their minds when they are confronted by war and will return to Egypt." **18** So God made the people go around by the way of the wilderness of the Red Sea.[h] But it was in battle formation that the Israelites went up out of the land of Egypt. **19** Moses also took Joseph's bones with him, because Joseph had made the sons of Israel solemnly swear: "God will not fail to turn his attention to you, and you must take my

---

CHAP. 13
a Nu 3:13
Nu 18:15
De 15:19
Lu 2:22, 23

b Ex 12:42
De 16:3

c De 4:34
Ne 9:10

d De 16:1

e Ex 3:8
Ex 34:11

f Ge 15:18
Ex 6:5, 8

g Ex 3:17
De 8:7-9

h Ex 12:15
Ex 34:18

i Ex 23:15

j De 16:3

k Ex 12:26, 27

l Ex 12:14
De 11:18

m Ex 12:24, 25

Second Col.
a Ge 15:18

b Ex 22:29
Ex 34:19, 20
Le 27:26
Nu 3:13
Lu 2:22, 23

c Nu 18:15

d De 7:7, 8

e Ex 5:2

f Ex 12:29
Ps 78:51

g De 11:18

h Ex 14:2, 3
Nu 33:5

13:2 *Or "Set apart." #Lit., "every firstborn that opens each womb." 13:4 *See App. B15. 13:7 *Lit., "boundaries." 13:9 *Or "reminder." 13:9, 16 #Lit., "between your eyes."

13:12 *Lit., "everyone that opens the womb." 13:15 *Lit., "everything that opens the womb."

bones up out of here with you."[a]
20 They departed from Suc'coth and encamped at E'tham, at the edge of the wilderness.

21 Now Jehovah was going ahead of them by day in a pillar of cloud to lead them along the way,[b] and by night in a pillar of fire to give them light, so that they could travel by day and by night.[c] **22** The pillar of cloud would not move away from before the people during the day, nor the pillar of fire at night.[d]

14 Jehovah now said to Moses: **2** "Tell the Israelites that they should turn back and encamp before Pi·ha·hi'roth, between Mig'dol and the sea, within view of Ba'al·ze'phon.[e] You are to encamp facing it by the sea. **3** Then Phar'aoh will say about the Israelites, 'They are wandering in confusion in the land. The wilderness has closed in on them.' **4** I will allow Phar'aoh's heart to become obstinate,[f] and he will chase after them, and I will glorify myself by means of Phar'aoh and all his army;[g] and the Egyptians will certainly know that I am Jehovah."[h] So that is what they did.

5 Later it was reported to the king of Egypt that the people had run away. Immediately, Phar'aoh and his servants had a change of heart regarding the people,[i] and they said: "Why did we do this and release Israel from serving as slaves for us?" **6** So he made his war chariots ready, and he took his people with him.[j] **7** He took 600 chosen chariots and all the other chariots of Egypt, with warriors on every one of them. **8** Thus Jehovah allowed the heart of Phar'aoh king of Egypt to become obstinate, and he chased after the Israelites, while the Israelites were going out with confidence.*[k] **9** The

---

14:8 *Lit., "with uplifted hand."

CHAP. 13
a Ge 50:24, 25
  Jos 24:32
  Heb 11:22

b Ex 14:19

c Nu 9:15
  Ps 78:14

d Ps 105:39
  1Co 10:1

CHAP. 14
e Ex 13:17, 18

f Ex 7:13
  Ro 9:17, 18

g Ex 9:15, 16
  Ex 15:11
  Ex 18:10, 11
  Jos 2:9, 10

h Ex 7:5
  Ex 8:22

i Ex 12:33

j Ex 14:23

k Nu 33:3

Second Col.
a Ex 15:9

b Jos 24:6, 7
  Ne 9:9

c Ex 16:3
  Ex 17:3
  Nu 14:2-4
  Ps 106:7

d Ex 5:21
  Ex 6:6, 9

e Nu 14:9
  De 20:3
  2Ch 20:15, 17
  Ps 27:1
  Ps 46:1
  Isa 41:10

f 2Ch 20:17

g Ex 14:30
  Ex 15:5
  Ps 136:15

h De 1:30
  De 20:4
  2Ch 20:29

i Ex 9:15, 16

j Ex 14:4
  Ro 9:17, 18

Egyptians chased after them,[a] and all the chariot horses of Phar'aoh and his cavalrymen and his army were catching up with them while they were camping by the sea, by Pi·ha·hi'roth, facing Ba'al·ze'phon.

10 When Phar'aoh got closer, the Israelites raised their eyes and saw the Egyptians pursuing them. The Israelites became terrified and began to cry out to Jehovah.[b] **11** They said to Moses: "Is it because there are no burial places in Egypt that you have brought us here to die in the wilderness?[c] What have you done to us by leading us out of Egypt? **12** Is this not the very thing we told you in Egypt when we said, 'Let us alone, so that we may serve the Egyptians'? For it is better for us to serve the Egyptians than to die in the wilderness."[d] **13** Then Moses said to the people: "Do not be afraid.[e] Stand firm and see the salvation of Jehovah that he will perform for you today.[f] For the Egyptians whom you see today, you will never ever see again.[g] **14** Jehovah himself will fight for you,[h] and you will keep silent."

15 Jehovah now said to Moses: "Why do you keep crying out to me? Tell the Israelites that they should break camp. **16** As for you, lift up your rod and stretch out your hand over the sea and divide it, so that the Israelites may go through the midst of the sea on dry ground. **17** As for me, I am allowing the hearts of the Egyptians to become obstinate, so that they will go in after them; thus I will glorify myself by means of Phar'aoh and all his army, his war chariots, and his cavalrymen.[i] **18** And the Egyptians will certainly know that I am Jehovah when I glorify myself by means of Phar'aoh, his war chariots, and his cavalrymen."[j]

19 Then the angel of the true God[a] who was going ahead of the camp of Israel departed and went to their rear, and the pillar of cloud that was in front of them moved to the rear and stood behind them.[b] **20** So it came between the camp of the Egyptians and the camp of Israel.[c] On the one side, it was a dark cloud. On the other side, it was lighting up the night.[d] So the one camp did not come near the other camp all night long.

21 Moses now stretched out his hand over the sea;[e] and Jehovah drove the sea back with a strong east wind all night long, turning the sea basin into dry ground,[f] and the waters divided.[g] **22** So the Israelites went through the midst of the sea on dry ground,[h] while the waters formed a wall on their right hand and on their left.[i] **23** The Egyptians pursued them, and all Phar′aoh's horses, his war chariots, and his cavalrymen began going after them into the midst of the sea.[j] **24** During the morning watch,* Jehovah looked at the camp of the Egyptians from within the pillar of fire and cloud,[k] and he threw the camp of the Egyptians into confusion. **25** He kept taking wheels off their chariots so that they were driving them with difficulty, and the Egyptians were saying: "Let us flee from any contact with Israel, because Jehovah is fighting for them against the Egyptians."[l]

26 Then Jehovah said to Moses: "Stretch out your hand over the sea so that the waters may come back over the Egyptians, their war chariots, and their cavalrymen." **27** Moses at once stretched out his hand over the sea, and as morning approached,

the sea returned to its normal condition. As the Egyptians fled from it, Jehovah shook the Egyptians off into the midst of the sea.[a] **28** The returning waters covered the war chariots and the cavalrymen and all of Phar′aoh's army who had gone into the sea after them.[b] Not so much as one among them was allowed to survive.[c]

29 But the Israelites walked on dry ground in the midst of the seabed,[d] and the waters formed a wall on their right hand and on their left.[e] **30** Thus Jehovah saved Israel on that day from the hand of the Egyptians,[f] and Israel saw the Egyptians dead on the seashore. **31** Israel also saw the great power* that Jehovah wielded against the Egyptians, and the people began to fear Jehovah and to put faith in Jehovah and in his servant Moses.[g]

15 At that time Moses and the Israelites sang this song to Jehovah:[h]

"Let me sing to Jehovah, for he has become highly exalted.[i]
The horse and its rider he has hurled into the sea.[j]

2 My strength and my might is Jah,* since he has become my salvation.[k]
This is my God, and I will praise him;[l] my father's God,[m] and I will exalt him.[n]

3 Jehovah is a powerful warrior.[o] Jehovah is his name.[p]

4 Phar′aoh's chariots and his army He has cast into the sea,[q]
And his finest warriors have sunk into the Red Sea.[r]

5 The surging waters covered them; down into the depths they sank like a stone.[s]

CHAP. 14

a Ge 48:16
  Ex 32:34
  Nu 20:16
  Jude 9
b Ex 13:21
c Jos 24:6, 7
d Ps 105:39
e Ex 14:16
  Ac 7:36
f Jos 2:9, 10
  Ps 66:6
  Ps 106:9
  Ps 114:3
g Ne 9:10, 11
  Ps 78:13
  Ps 136:13
  Isa 63:12
h 1Co 10:1
  Heb 11:29
i Ex 15:8
j Ex 14:17
k Ex 13:21
l Ex 14:4

Second Col.

a Ex 15:1, 4
b Ex 15:5, 10
  De 11:3, 4
  Jos 24:6, 7
  Ne 9:10, 11
  Ps 78:53
  Heb 11:29
c Ex 14:13
  Ps 106:11
  Ps 136:15
d Ps 77:19
e Ex 15:8
f De 4:20
  Ps 106:8-11
g Ex 4:31
  Ex 19:9
  Ps 106:12

CHAP. 15

h Jg 5:1
  2Sa 22:1
  Re 15:3
i Ex 9:16
  Ex 18:10, 11
  Ps 106:11, 12
j Ex 15:21
  Ps 136:15
k Isa 12:2
l 2Sa 22:47
  Isa 25:1
m Ps 3:15
n Ps 83:18
  Ps 148:13
o Ps 24:8
p Ex 6:3
  Isa 42:8
q Ex 14:27
r Ex 14:6, 7
s Ne 9:10, 11

14:24 *That is, about 2:00 a.m. until 6:00 a.m.

14:31 *Lit., "hand." 15:2 *"Jah" is a shortened form of the name Jehovah.

6 Your right hand, O Jehovah,
　　is great in power;[a]
Your right hand, O Jehovah,
　　can shatter an enemy.
7 In your great majesty you
　　can throw down those who
　　rise up against you;[b]
You send out your burning
　　anger, it eats them up like
　　stubble.
8 By a breath from your
　　nostrils waters massed
　　together;
They stood still, holding
　　back the floods;
The surging waters con-
　　gealed in the heart of the
　　sea.
9 The enemy said: 'I will
　　pursue! I will overtake!
I will divide spoil until I am*
　　satisfied!
I will draw my sword! My
　　hand will subdue them!'[c]
10 You blew with your breath,
　　the sea covered them;[d]
They sank like lead in majes-
　　tic waters.
11 Who among the gods is like
　　you, O Jehovah?[e]
Who is like you, showing
　　yourself mighty in holi-
　　ness?[f]
The One to be feared with
　　songs of praise, the One
　　doing wonders.[g]
12 You stretched out your right
　　hand, and the earth swal-
　　lowed them up.[h]
13 In your loyal love you have
　　led the people whom you
　　have redeemed;[i]
In your strength you will
　　guide them to your holy
　　place of dwelling.
14 Peoples must hear;[j] they will
　　shudder;
Anguish* will seize the
　　inhabitants of Phi·lis'ti·a.

CHAP. 15

a Ps 60:5
　Ps 89:13

b Isa 37:23

c Ex 14:5, 9

d Ex 14:21, 28

e De 3:24
　2Sa 7:22

f Isa 6:3

g Ex 11:9

h Ps 78:53
　Heb 11:29

i Ps 106:10

j Nu 14:13, 14

__Second Col.__

a Nu 22:1, 3

b Jos 2:9-11
　Jos 5:1

c De 11:25

d 2Sa 7:23
　Isa 43:1

e Nu 20:14, 17
　Nu 21:21, 22

f Ps 80:8

g Ps 10:16

h Ex 14:23

i Ex 14:28

j Ex 14:22

k Ex 9:16
　Ex 18:11

l Ex 14:27, 28
　Ps 106:11, 12

15 At that time the sheikhs* of
　　E'dom will be terrified,
And trembling will take hold
　　of the mighty rulers# of
　　Mo'ab.[a]
All the inhabitants of Ca'-
　　naan will be disheartened.[b]
16 Fear and dread will fall upon
　　them.[c]
Because of the greatness of
　　your arm they will be as
　　motionless as a stone
Until your people pass by,
　　O Jehovah,
Until the people whom you
　　produced[d] pass by.[e]
17 You will bring them and plant
　　them in the mountain of
　　your inheritance,[f]
The established place that
　　you have prepared for
　　yourself to inhabit,
　　O Jehovah,
A sanctuary, O Jehovah, that
　　your hands have estab-
　　lished.
18 Jehovah will rule as king
　　forever and ever.[g]
19 When Phar'aoh's horses with
　　his war chariots and his
　　cavalrymen went into the
　　sea,[h]
Then Jehovah brought back
　　the waters of the sea upon
　　them,[i]
But the people of Israel
　　walked on dry ground
　　through the midst of the
　　sea."[j]

20 Then Mir'i·am the prophetess, Aaron's sister, took a tambourine in her hand, and all
the women followed her with
tambourines and with dances.
21 Mir'i·am sang in response to
the men:

　　"Sing to Jehovah, for he has
　　　become highly exalted.[k]
　　The horse and its rider he
　　　has hurled into the sea."[l]

15:9 *Or "my soul is." **15:14** *Lit.,
"Birth pangs." **15:15** *A sheikh was a tribal chief. #Or
"the despots."

22 Moses later led Israel away from the Red Sea, and they went out to the wilderness of Shur and marched on for three days in the wilderness, but they did not find water. **23** They came to Ma′rah,* ᵃ but they were not able to drink the water from Ma′rah because it was bitter. That is why he named it Ma′rah. **24** So the people began to murmur against Moses,ᵇ saying: "What are we to drink?" **25** He cried out to Jehovah,ᶜ and Jehovah directed him to a tree. When he threw it into the water, the water became sweet.

There He established for them a regulation and a case for judgment, and there He put them to the test.ᵈ **26** He said: "If you will strictly listen to the voice of Jehovah your God and will do what is right in his eyes and will pay attention to his commandments and keep all his regulations,ᵉ I will not bring upon you any of the diseases that I brought upon the Egyptians,ᶠ for I, Jehovah, am healing you."ᵍ

27 After that they came to E′lim, where there were 12 springs of water and 70 palm trees. So they camped there by the water.

16 After they departed from E′lim, the entire assembly of the Israelites eventually came to the wilderness of Sin,ʰ which is between E′lim and Si′nai, on the 15th day of the second month after their departure from the land of Egypt. **2** Then the entire assembly of the Israelites began to murmur against Moses and Aaron in the wilderness.ⁱ **3** The Israelites kept saying to them: "If only we had died by Jehovah's hand in the land of Egypt while we were sitting by the pots of meat,ʲ while we were eat-ing bread to satisfaction. Now you have brought us out into this wilderness to put this whole congregation to death by famine."ᵃ

4 Then Jehovah said to Moses: "Here I am raining down bread for you from the heavens,ᵇ and each of the people should go out to gather his amount day by day,ᶜ so that I may put them to the test to see whether they will walk in my law or not.ᵈ **5** But on the sixth dayᵉ when they prepare what they have gathered, it is to be double the amount that they pick up on each of the other days."ᶠ

6 So Moses and Aaron said to all the Israelites: "In the evening you will certainly know that it is Jehovah who brought you out of the land of Egypt.ᵍ **7** In the morning you will see Jehovah's glory, for he has heard your murmurings against Jehovah. Who are we that you should murmur against us?" **8** Moses continued: "When Jehovah gives you meat to eat in the evening and in the morning bread to satisfaction, you will see that Jehovah has heard your murmurings that you are murmuring against him. But who are we? Your murmurings are not against us, but against Jehovah."ʰ

9 Then Moses said to Aaron: "Tell the entire assembly of the Israelites, 'Come near before Jehovah, for he has heard your murmurings.'"ⁱ **10** As soon as Aaron had spoken to the entire assembly of the Israelites, they turned and faced toward the wilderness, and look! Jehovah's glory appeared in the cloud.ʲ

11 Jehovah spoke further to Moses, saying: **12** "I have heard the murmurings of the Israelites.ᵏ Tell them, 'At twilight* you will eat meat, and in the morning you will be satisfied

---

CHAP. 15
a Nu 33:8

b Ex 16:2, 3
  Ex 17:3
  1Co 10:6, 10

c Ex 17:4

d Ex 16:4
  De 8:2

e De 28:1

f De 7:12, 15

g Ex 23:25
  Ps 103:3

CHAP. 16
h Nu 33:10, 11

i Ex 15:24
  1Co 10:6, 10

j Nu 11:4
  Nu 14:2, 3

Second Col.
a Ex 17:3
  Nu 16:13

b Ps 78:24, 25
  Ps 105:40
  Joh 6:31, 32
  Joh 6:58
  1Co 10:1, 3

c Mt 6:11

d De 8:2

e Ex 35:2

f Ex 16:22

g Ex 6:7
  Nu 16:28, 29

h Nu 21:7
  1Sa 8:7

i Ex 16:2
  Nu 11:1

j Ex 13:21
  Nu 16:19
  Mt 17:5

k Nu 14:27

15:23 *Meaning "Bitterness."

16:12 *Lit., "Between the two evenings."

with bread,[a] and you will certainly know that I am Jehovah your God.'"[b]

13 So that evening quail came and covered the camp,[c] and in the morning a layer of dew was all around the camp. **14** When the layer of dew evaporated, there was a fine, flaky substance on the surface of the wilderness,[d] as fine as frost on the ground. **15** When the Israelites saw it, they began to say to one another, "What is it?" for they did not know what it was. Moses said to them: "It is the bread that Jehovah has given you for food.[e] **16** This is what Jehovah has commanded, 'Each one should gather it according to how much he can eat. You are to take an omer measure[*][f] for each individual according to the number of the people[#] that each of you has in his tent.'" **17** The Israelites began to do so; they gathered it, some gathering much and some gathering little. **18** When they would measure it by the omer, the one who had gathered much had no surplus and the one who had gathered little had no shortage.[g] They each gathered it according to what they could eat.

19 Then Moses said to them: "Nobody should leave any of it until the morning."[h] **20** But they did not listen to Moses. When some men left some of it until the morning, it bred worms and stank, and Moses became indignant at them. **21** They would pick it up up morning by morning, each one according to what he could eat. When the sun got hot, it melted.

22 On the sixth day, they picked up twice as much bread,[i] two omer measures for each person. So all the chieftains of the assembly came and reported it

to Moses. **23** At that he said to them: "It is what Jehovah has said. Tomorrow there will be a complete rest,[*][a] a holy sabbath to Jehovah.[a] Bake what you need to bake, and boil what you need to boil;[b] then save whatever is left over and keep it until the morning." **24** So they saved it until the morning, just as Moses had commanded, and it did not stink nor were there maggots in it. **25** Then Moses said: "Eat it today, because today is a sabbath to Jehovah. Today you will not find it on the ground. **26** You will pick it up for six days, but on the seventh day, the Sabbath,[c] there will be none." **27** However, some of the people did go out to pick it up on the seventh day, but they found nothing.

28 So Jehovah said to Moses: "How long will you refuse to keep my commandments and my laws?[d] **29** Take notice of the fact that Jehovah has given you the Sabbath.[e] That is why he is giving you the bread for two days on the sixth day. Everyone must stay where he is; nobody is to leave his locality on the seventh day." **30** So the people observed the Sabbath[*] on the seventh day.[f]

31 The house of Israel named the bread "manna."[*] It was white like coriander seed, and its taste was like that of flat cakes with honey.[g] **32** Then Moses said: "This is what Jehovah has commanded, 'Fill an omer measure of it as something to be kept throughout your generations,[h] so that they may see the bread that I gave you to eat in the wilderness when I was bringing you out of the land of Egypt.'" **33** So Moses said to Aaron:

CHAP. 16
a Ps 105:40

b Ex 4:5
  Ex 6:7

c Nu 11:31, 34
  Ps 78:27-29

d Nu 11:7
  De 8:3
  Ne 9:15

e Nu 21:5
  De 8:14, 16
  Jos 5:11, 12
  Joh 6:31, 32
  Joh 6:58
  1Co 10:1, 3

f Ex 16:36

g 2Co 8:15

h Mt 6:11, 34

i Ex 16:5

Second Col.
a Ex 20:8
  Ex 31:15
  Ex 35:2
  Le 23:3

b Nu 11:7, 8

c Ex 20:9, 10
  Ex 31:13
  De 5:15

d Nu 14:11
  Ps 78:10
  Ps 106:13

e Ex 31:13

f Le 23:3
  De 5:13, 14

g Ex 16:15
  Nu 11:7

h Ps 105:5, 40

16:16 *About 2.2 L (2 dry qt). See App. B14. #Or "souls."

16:23 *Or "a sabbath observance." 16:30 *Or "rested." 16:31 *Probably from the Hebrew expression "What is it?"

"Take a jar and put in it an omer measure of manna and deposit it before Jehovah as something to be kept throughout your generations."[a] 34 Just as Jehovah commanded Moses, Aaron placed it before the Testimony[b] so that it might be preserved. 35 The Israelites ate the manna for 40 years,[c] until they came to a land that was inhabited.[d] They ate the manna until they came to the frontier of the land of Ca′naan.[e] 36 Now an omer is a tenth of an e′phah measure.*

17 The entire assembly of the Israelites departed from the wilderness of Sin[f] by stages according to the order of Jehovah,[g] and they camped at Reph′i-dim.[h] But there was no water for the people to drink.

2 So the people began quarreling with Moses[i] and saying: "Give us water to drink." But Moses said to them: "Why are you quarreling with me? Why do you keep putting Jehovah to the test?"[j] 3 But the people were very thirsty for water there, and they kept murmuring against Moses[k] and saying: "Why have you brought us up out of Egypt to kill us and our sons and our livestock with thirst?" 4 Finally Moses cried out to Jehovah: "What should I do with this people? A little longer and they will stone me!"

5 Then Jehovah said to Moses: "Go ahead of the people, and take with you some of the elders of Israel and your rod with which you struck the Nile River.[l] Take it in your hand and walk on. 6 Look! I will be standing before you there on the rock in Ho′reb. You must strike the rock, and water will come out of it, and the people will drink it."[m] Moses did so before the eyes of the elders

of Israel. 7 So he named the place Mas′sah*[a] and Mer′i·bah*[b] because of the quarreling of the Israelites and because they put Jehovah to the test[c] by saying: "Is Jehovah in our midst or not?"

8 Then the A·mal′ek·ites[d] came and fought against Israel in Reph′i·dim.[e] 9 At this Moses said to Joshua:[f] "Choose men for us and go out to fight against the A·mal′ek·ites. Tomorrow I will stand on top of the hill, with the rod of the true God in my hand." 10 Then Joshua did just as Moses told him,[g] and he fought against the A·mal′ek·ites. And Moses, Aaron, and Hur[h] went up to the top of the hill.

11 As long as Moses kept his hands lifted up, the Israelites prevailed, but as soon as he would let down his hands, the A·mal′ek·ites prevailed. 12 When the hands of Moses were heavy, they took a stone and put it under him, and he sat on it. Then Aaron and Hur, one on each side, supported his hands, so that his hands remained steady until the sun set. 13 Thus Joshua defeated Am′a·lek and his people with the sword.[i]

14 Jehovah now said to Moses: "Write this as a memorial* in the book and repeat it to Joshua, 'I will completely wipe out the memory of Am′a·lek from under the heavens.'"[j] 15 Then Moses built an altar and named it Je·ho′vah-nis′si,* 16 saying: "Because his hand is against the throne of Jah,[k] Jehovah will have war with Am′a·lek from generation to generation."[l]

18 Now Jeth′ro the priest of Mid′i·an, Moses' father-in-law,[m] heard about all that God had done for Moses and

---

CHAP. 16
a Heb 9:4

b Ex 27:21

c De 8:2
Ne 9:21
Ps 78:24

d Jos 5:11, 12

e Nu 33:48
De 34:1

CHAP. 17
f Nu 33:12

g Nu 33:2

h Nu 33:14

i Ex 5:19, 21
Nu 14:2, 3
Nu 20:3

j Nu 14:22
Ps 78:18, 22
Ps 106:14

k Ex 16:2, 3

l Ex 7:20

m Nu 20:8
De 8:14, 15
Ne 9:15
Ps 78:15
Ps 105:41
1Co 10:1, 4

Second Col.
a De 9:22

b Ps 81:7

c De 6:16
Ps 95:8, 9
Heb 3:8, 9

d Ge 36:12

e De 25:17
1Sa 15:2

f Nu 11:28

g Jos 11:15

h Ex 24:13, 14
Jos 11:12

i Nu 14:20
De 25:19
1Ch 4:42, 43

k Re 19:1

l 1Sa 15:20
Es 9:24

CHAP. 18
m Ex 2:16, 21
Ex 3:1

16:36 *An ephah equaled 22 L (20 dry qt). See App. B14.

17:7 *Meaning "Testing; Trial." #Meaning "Quarreling." 17:14 *Or "reminder." 17:15 *Meaning "Jehovah Is My Signal Pole."

for his people Israel, how Jehovah had brought Israel out of Egypt.[a] **2** Jeth'ro, Moses' father-in-law, had taken in Zip-po'rah, Moses' wife, when she was sent back to him, **3** along with her two sons.[b] One son was named Ger'shom,*[c] because Moses said, "I have become a foreign resident in a foreign land," **4** and the other was named E-li-e'zer,* because he said, "The God of my father is my helper, who rescued me from Phar'aoh's sword."[d]

5 So Jeth'ro, Moses' father-in-law, along with Moses' sons and his wife, came to Moses into the wilderness where he was camping at the mountain of the true God.[e] **6** Then he sent word to Moses: "I, your father-in-law Jeth'ro,[f] am coming to you with your wife and her two sons." **7** At once Moses went out to meet his father-in-law, and he bowed down and kissed him. Each of them asked about the other's welfare, and then they went into the tent.

8 Moses related to his father-in-law all that Jehovah had done to Phar'aoh and Egypt in behalf of Israel,[g] all the hardships that had befallen them along the way,[h] and how Jehovah had delivered them. **9** Jeth'ro rejoiced over all the good that Jehovah had done for Israel by rescuing them from Egypt.* **10** Then Jeth'ro said: "Praised be Jehovah, who rescued you from Egypt and from Phar'-aoh, and who rescued the people from under Egypt's control. **11** Now I know that Jehovah is greater than all the other gods,[i] because of what he did to those who acted arrogantly against his people." **12** Then Jeth'ro, Mo-

ses' father-in-law, brought a burnt offering and sacrifices for God, and Aaron and all the elders of Israel came to eat a meal with Moses' father-in-law before the true God.

13 On the next day, Moses sat down as usual to serve as judge for the people, and the people kept standing before Moses from morning until evening. **14** When Moses' father-in-law saw all that he was doing for the people, he said: "What is this that you are doing for the people? Why do you sit here alone with all the people standing before you from morning until evening?" **15** Moses said to his father-in-law: "Because the people keep coming to me to inquire of God. **16** When a case arises, it comes to me and I must judge between one person and the other, and I have made known the decisions of the true God and his laws."[a]

17 Moses' father-in-law said to him: "What you are doing is not good. **18** You will surely wear out, both you and this people who are with you, because this is too big a load for you and you cannot carry it by yourself. **19** Now listen to me. I will give you advice, and God will be with you.[b] You serve as representative for the people before the true God,[c] and you must bring the cases to the true God.[d] **20** You should warn them about what the regulations and the laws are[e] and make known to them the way in which they should walk and the work that they should do. **21** But you should select from the people capable men[f] fearing God, trustworthy men hating dishonest profit,[g] and appoint these over them as chiefs over thousands, chiefs over hundreds, chiefs over fifties, and chiefs over tens.[h] **22** They should judge the people when

---

18:3 *Meaning "A Foreign Resident There." 18:4 *Meaning "My God Is Helper." 18:9 *Lit., "from the hand of Egypt."

CHAP. 18
a Jos 2:9, 10
Jos 9:3, 9

b Ac 7:29

c Ex 2:22

d Ex 2:15

e Ex 19:2
1Ki 19:8, 9

f Ex 4:18
Nu 10:29

g Ex 7:3
Ex 14:27, 28
De 4:34

h Ex 15:22
Ex 16:3

i Ex 15:11
Ps 95:3
Ps 97:9

Second Col.
a De 4:5
De 5:1

b Jos 1:5, 17

c Ex 20:19

d Nu 27:1-5

e De 7:11

f Nu 11:16, 17
De 1:13
Ac 6:3

g Ex 23:8
1Ti 3:2, 3
Tit 1:7
1Pe 5:2

h De 1:15
Ac 14:23

cases arise,* and they will bring every difficult case to you,[a] but every minor case they will decide. Make it easier for yourself by letting them share the load along with you.[b] **23** If you do this, and God so commands you, you will be able to stand the strain, and everyone will go home satisfied."

24 Moses immediately listened to his father-in-law and did all that he had said. **25** Moses chose capable men out of all Israel and appointed them heads over the people, as chiefs of thousands, chiefs of hundreds, chiefs of fifties, and chiefs of tens. **26** So they judged the people when cases arose. A difficult case they would bring to Moses,[c] but every minor case they would judge. **27** After that Moses saw his father-in-law off,[d] and he went his way to his land.

19 In the third month after the Israelites went out of the land of Egypt, on the same day, they came to the wilderness of Si′nai. **2** They pulled away from Reph′i·dim[e] and came to the wilderness of Si′nai and camped in the wilderness. Israel camped there in front of the mountain.[f]

3 Then Moses went up to the true God, and Jehovah called to him from the mountain,[g] saying: "This is what you are to say to the house of Jacob and to tell the Israelites, **4** 'You have seen for yourselves what I did to the Egyptians,[h] in order to carry you on wings of eagles and bring you to myself.[i] **5** Now if you will strictly obey my voice and keep my covenant, you will certainly become my special property* out of all peoples,[j] for the whole earth belongs to me.[k] **6** You will become to me a kingdom of priests and a holy nation.'[l] These

are the words that you are to say to the Israelites."

7 So Moses went and summoned the elders of the people and declared to them all these words that Jehovah had commanded him.[a] **8** After that all the people answered unanimously: "All that Jehovah has spoken, we are willing to do."[b] Moses immediately took the people's response to Jehovah. **9** And Jehovah said to Moses: "Look! I am coming to you in a dark cloud, so that the people may hear when I speak with you and so that they may always put faith in you as well." Then Moses reported the words of the people to Jehovah.

10 Then Jehovah said to Moses: "Go to the people and sanctify them today and tomorrow, and they must wash their clothing. **11** And they must be ready for the third day, because on the third day Jehovah will come down upon Mount Si′nai before the eyes of all the people. **12** You must set boundaries for the people all around it and tell them, 'Beware of going up to the mountain or touching its border. Anybody touching the mountain will surely be put to death. **13** No hand is to touch him, but he will either be stoned or be shot through.* Whether beast or man, he will not live.'[c] But at the sound of the ram's horn[d] they may come up to the mountain."

14 Then Moses went down from the mountain to the people, and he began to sanctify the people, and they washed their clothing.[e] **15** He said to the people: "Get ready for the third day. Abstain from sexual relations."*

16 On the morning of the third day, there was thunder and

CHAP. 18
a Le 24:10, 11
  Nu 15:32, 33
  De 1:17

b Nu 11:17

c Ac 15:2

d Nu 10:29

CHAP. 19
e Ex 17:1

f Ex 3:1, 12

g Ac 7:38

h De 4:34

i De 32:11, 12
  Isa 63:9

j 1Ki 8:53
  Ps 135:4

k De 10:14

l Le 11:44
  De 7:6
  1Pe 2:9
  Re 5:9, 10

Second Col.
a Ex 24:3

b Ex 24:7
  Jos 24:24

c Heb 12:20

d Ex 20:18

e Ex 19:10

18:22 *Lit., "in every time." **19:5** *Or "treasured possession."

19:13 *Perhaps shot with an arrow. **19:15** *Lit., "Do not approach a woman."

lightning, and there was a heavy cloud[a] on the mountain and a very loud sound of a horn, and all the people in the camp began to tremble.[b] **17** Moses now brought the people out of the camp to meet the true God, and they took their place at the base of the mountain. **18** Mount Si'nai smoked all over, because Jehovah came down upon it in fire;[c] and its smoke was rising like the smoke of a kiln, and the whole mountain was trembling violently.[d] **19** As the sound of the horn grew louder and louder, Moses spoke, and the voice of the true God answered him.

20 So Jehovah came down upon Mount Si'nai to the top of the mountain. Then Jehovah called Moses to the top of the mountain, and Moses went up.[e] **21** Jehovah now said to Moses: "Go down and warn the people not to try to force their way through to look at Jehovah, or many of them will perish. **22** And let the priests who regularly come near to Jehovah sanctify themselves, so that Jehovah may not strike* them.[f] **23** Moses then said to Jehovah: "The people are not able to come up to Mount Si'nai because you already warned us, saying, 'Set boundaries around the mountain, and make it sacred.'"[g] **24** However, Jehovah said to him: "Go, descend, and come back up, you and Aaron with you, but do not let the priests and the people force their way through to come up to Jehovah, so that he may not strike them."[h] **25** So Moses descended to the people and told them.

20 Then God spoke all these words:[i]

2 "I am Jehovah your God, who brought you out of the land

of Egypt, out of the house of slavery.[a] **3** You must not have any other gods besides me.*[b]

4 "You must not make for yourself a carved image or a form* like anything that is in the heavens above or on the earth below or in the waters under the earth.[c] **5** You must not bow down to them nor be enticed to serve them,[d] for I, Jehovah your God, am a God who requires exclusive devotion,[e] bringing punishment for the error of fathers upon sons, upon the third generation and upon the fourth generation of those who hate me, **6** but showing loyal love to the thousandth generation of those who love me and keep my commandments.[f]

7 "You must not take up the name of Jehovah your God in a worthless way,[g] for Jehovah will not leave unpunished the one who takes up His name in a worthless way.[h]

8 "Remember the Sabbath day to keep it sacred.[i] **9** You are to labor and do all your work for six days,[j] **10** but the seventh day is a sabbath to Jehovah your God. You must not do any work, neither you nor your son nor your daughter nor your slave man nor your slave girl nor your domestic animal nor your foreign resident who is inside your settlements.*[k] **11** For in six days Jehovah made the heavens and the earth, the sea, and all that is in them, and he began to rest on the seventh day.[l] That is why Jehovah blessed the Sabbath day and made it sacred.

12 "Honor your father and your mother,[m] so that you may live a long time in the land that Jehovah your God is giving you.[n]

13 "You must not murder.[o]

CHAP. 19
a De 4:11
  1Ki 8:12
  9P 97:2
b Heb 12:18-21
c Ex 24:17
  De 4:11, 12
  2Ch 7:1-3
d Ps 68:8
e Ex 24:12
f Le 10:1, 2
  1Ch 13:10
g Ex 19:12
h Nu 16:19, 35

CHAP. 20
i De 5:22
  Ac 7:38

Second Col.
a De 5:6
  Ho 13:4
b De 5:7-10
c Le 26:1
  De 4:15, 16
  Isa 40:25
  Ac 17:29
d Ex 23:24
  1Co 10:20
  1Jo 5:21
e Ex 34:14
  Mt 4:10
  Lu 10:27
f Ec 12:13
g Le 19:12
h Le 24:15, 16
  De 5:11
i Ex 16:23
  Ex 31:13, 14
  De 5:12-14
j Ex 23:12
k Ex 16:29
  Ex 34:21
l Ge 2:2
m Ex 21:15
  Le 19:3
  Pr 1:8
n De 5:16
  Mt 15:4
  Eph 6:2, 3
o Ge 9:6
  De 5:17
  Jas 2:11
  1Jo 3:15
  Re 21:8

19:22 *Lit., "break through on."

20:3 *Or "in defiance of me." Lit., "against my face." **20:4** *Or "representation." **20:10** *Lit., "gates."

14 "You must not commit adultery.[a]

15 "You must not steal.[b]

16 "You must not testify falsely when you are a witness against your fellow man.[c]

17 "You must not desire your fellow man's house. You must not desire your fellow man's wife[d] nor his slave man nor his slave girl nor his bull nor his donkey nor anything that belongs to your fellow man."[e]

18 Now all the people were witnessing the thunder and lightning, the sound of the horn, and the mountain smoking; and seeing this made them tremble and stand at a distance.[f] **19** So they said to Moses: "You speak with us, and we will listen, but do not let God speak with us, for fear that we will die."[g] **20** So Moses said to the people: "Do not be afraid, for the true God has come to put you to the test,[h] in order that the fear of him may continue with you so that you may not sin."[i] **21** So the people kept standing at a distance, but Moses went near to the dark cloud where the true God was.[j]

22 Then Jehovah said to Moses: "This is what you are to say to the Israelites, 'You have seen for yourselves that I spoke with you from heaven.[k] **23** You must not make gods of silver alongside me, and you must not make gods of gold for yourselves.[l] **24** An altar of earth you are to make for me, and you will sacrifice on it your burnt offerings, your communion sacrifices,* your flock, and your herd. In every place where I cause my name to be remembered[m] I will come to you and I will bless you. **25** If you make an altar of stones for me, you must not build it using stones cut with tools.*[n] For if you do use your

chisel on it, you will profane it. **26** And you must not go up by steps to my altar, that your private parts* may not be exposed upon it.'

21

"These are the judicial decisions that you are to convey to them:[a]

2 "If you buy a Hebrew slave,[b] he will serve as a slave for six years, but in the seventh year, he will be set free without paying anything.[c] **3** If he came by himself, he will go out by himself. If he is the husband of a wife, then his wife must go out with him. **4** If his master gives him a wife and she bears him sons or daughters, the wife and her children will become her master's, and he will go out by himself.[d] **5** But if the slave should insist and say, 'I love my master, my wife, and my sons; I do not want to be set free,'[e] **6** his master must bring him before the true God. Then he will bring him up against the door or the doorpost, and his master will pierce his ear through with an awl, and he will be his slave for life.

7 "If a man sells his daughter as a slave, she will not go free the same way that a slave man does. **8** If her master is not pleased with her and he does not designate her as a concubine but causes her to be purchased by someone else,* he will not be entitled to sell her to foreigners, for he has betrayed her. **9** If he selects her for his son, he is to grant her the rights of a daughter. **10** If he takes another wife for himself, the sustenance, the clothing, and the marriage due[f] of the first wife are not to be diminished. **11** If he will not render these three things to her, then she is to go free without paying any money.

CHAP. 20

a Ge 39:7-9
  De 5:18
  Pr 6:32
  Mt 5:27, 28
  Ro 13:9
  1Co 6:18
  Heb 13:4

b Le 19:11
  De 5:19
  Mr 10:19
  1Co 6:9, 10
  Eph 4:28

c Le 19:16
  De 5:20
  De 19:16-19

d Mt 5:28

e De 5:21
  Ro 7:7

f Ex 19:16
  Heb 12:18, 19

g Ac 7:38
  Ga 3:19

h De 8:2

i Jos 24:14
  Job 28:28
  Pr 1:7

j De 5:5
  Ps 97:2

k De 4:36
  Ne 9:13

l Ac 17:29

m De 12:5, 6
  2Ch 6:6

n De 27:5
  Jos 8:30, 31

Second Col.

CHAP. 21

a Ex 24:3
  De 4:14

b Le 25:39, 40

c De 15:12

d De 15:12

e De 15:16, 17

f 1Co 7:3

20:24 *Or "your peace offerings."
20:25 *Or "using hewn stones."

20:26 *Lit., "your nakedness." 21:8 *Lit., "to be redeemed."

12 "Anyone who strikes a man so that he dies must be put to death.[a] **13** But if he does it unintentionally and the true God lets it happen, I will designate for you a place where he can flee.[b] **14** If a man becomes very angry with his fellow man and he deliberately kills him,[c] the man must die even if you have to take him from my altar.[d] **15** One who strikes his father or his mother must be put to death.[e]

16 "If anyone kidnaps a man[f] and sells him or is caught holding him,[g] he must be put to death.[h]

17 "Anyone who curses* his father or his mother must be put to death.[i]

18 "This is what should happen if men quarrel and one strikes his fellow man with a stone or a fist* and he does not die but is confined to his bed: **19** If he is able to get up and walk around outdoors with the aid of a staff, then the one who struck him must be free from punishment. He will only make compensation for the time the injured man lost from his work until he is completely healed.

20 "If a man strikes his slave man or his slave girl with a stick and that one dies by his hand, that one must be avenged.[j] **21** However, if he survives for one or two days, he is not to be avenged, because he is someone bought with his owner's money.

22 "If men should struggle with each other and they hurt a pregnant woman and she gives birth prematurely*[k] but no fatality* results, the offender must pay the damages imposed on him by the husband of the woman; and he must pay it through

CHAP. 21
a Ge 9:6
  Nu 35:30
  Mt 5:21

b Nu 35:11
  Nu 35:22-25
  De 4:42
  De 19:3-5
  Jos 20:7-9

c Nu 15:30

d De 19:11, 12
  1Ki 1:50
  1Ki 2:29
  1Jo 3:15

e Ex 20:12

f Ge 40:15

g Ge 37:28

h De 24:7

i Le 20:9
  Pr 20:20
  Pr 30:11, 17
  Mt 15:4

j Ge 9:5, 6
  Le 24:17

k Ps 139:16
  Jer 1:5

Second Col.

a Ex 18:25, 26
  De 16:18
  De 17:8

b Ge 9:6
  Le 24:17
  Nu 35:31
  Re 21:8

c Le 24:20
  Mt 5:38

d Eph 6:9
  Col 4:1

e Ge 9:5
  Nu 35:33

f Ex 22:6
  Ex 22:14
  De 22:8

the judges.[a] **23** But if a fatality does occur, then you must give life for life,*[b] **24** eye for eye, tooth for tooth, hand for hand, foot for foot,[c] **25** burn for burn, wound for wound, blow for blow.

26 "If a man strikes the eye of his slave man or the eye of his slave girl and he destroys it, he is to let the slave go free in compensation for his eye.[d] **27** And if he knocks out the tooth of his slave man or of his slave girl, he is to let the slave go free in compensation for his tooth.

28 "If a bull gores a man or a woman and that one dies, the bull must be stoned to death[e] and its meat is not to be eaten; but the owner of the bull is free from punishment. **29** But if a bull was in the habit of goring and its owner had been warned but he would not keep it under guard and it killed a man or a woman, the bull is to be stoned and its owner is also to be put to death. **30** If a ransom* is imposed on him, he must give as the redemption price for his life* all that may be imposed on him. **31** Whether it gored a son or a daughter, it is to be done to the bull's owner according to this judicial decision. **32** If the bull gored a slave man or a slave girl, he will give the price of 30 shekels* to that one's master, and the bull will be stoned to death.

33 "If a man uncovers or digs a pit and does not cover it and a bull or a donkey falls into it, **34** the owner of the pit is to make compensation.[f] He is to pay the price to its owner, and the dead animal will become his. **35** If a man's bull hurts another's bull and it dies, then they

---

21:17 *Or "calls down evil upon." 21:18 *Or possibly, "a tool." 21:22 *Lit., "and her children come out." #Or "serious injury."

21:23 *Or "soul for soul." 21:30 *Or "reparation." #Or "soul." 21:32 *A shekel equaled 11.4 g (0.367 oz t). See App. B14.

must sell the live bull and divide the price paid for it; they should also divide the dead animal. **36** Or if it was known that a bull had been in the habit of goring but its owner would not keep it under guard, he must make compensation with bull for bull, and the dead one will become his own.

22 "If a man steals a bull or a sheep and he slaughters or sells it, he is to compensate with five bulls for the bull and four sheep for the sheep.[a]

2 ("If a thief[b] is found in the act of breaking in and he gets struck and dies, there is no bloodguilt for him. **3** But if it happens after sunrise, there is bloodguilt for him.)

"He must make compensation. If he has nothing, then he must be sold for the things he stole. **4** If what he stole is found alive in his possession, whether it is a bull or a donkey or a sheep, he is to make double compensation.

5 "If anyone puts his animals out to graze in a field or a vineyard and lets them graze in someone else's field, he is to make compensation with the best of his own field or with the best of his own vineyard.

6 "If a fire starts and spreads to thornbushes and it causes sheaves or standing grain or a field to be consumed, the one who started the fire must make compensation for what was burned.

7 "If a man gives his fellow man money or articles to keep and these are stolen from the fellow man's house, if the thief is found, he must make double compensation.[c] **8** If the thief is not found, the owner of the house must be brought before the true God[d] in order to determine whether he put his hand on the goods of his fellow man. **9** In all cases of illegal posses-

sion of goods, concerning a bull, a donkey, a sheep, a garment, or anything lost of which he may say, 'This is mine!' both parties will present their case before the true God.[a] The one whom God pronounces guilty is to make double compensation to his fellow man.[b]

10 "If a man gives his fellow man a donkey or a bull or a sheep or any domestic animal to keep and it dies or gets maimed or gets led away while nobody is looking, **11** there should be an oath made between them before Jehovah, that he did not lay his hand on the goods of his fellow man; and the owner must accept it. The other man is not to make compensation.[c] **12** But if the animal has been stolen from him, he is to make compensation to its owner. **13** If it was torn by a wild animal, he is to bring it as evidence. He is not to make compensation for something torn by a wild animal.

14 "But if anybody asks to borrow an animal from his fellow man and it gets maimed or it dies while its owner is not with it, the man who borrowed it must make compensation. **15** If its owner is with it, he is not to make compensation. If it was hired, the money paid for the hire is the compensation.

16 "Now if a man seduces a virgin who is not engaged and he lies down with her, he must pay the bride-price for her to become his wife.[d] **17** If her father absolutely refuses to give her to him, he is to pay the money at the rate of the bride-price.

18 "You must not allow a sorceress to live.[e]

19 "Anyone lying down with an animal must surely be put to death.[f]

20 "Whoever sacrifices to any gods but Jehovah alone is to be devoted to destruction.[g]

CHAP. 22
a 2Sa 12:6
  Lu 19:8

b Ex 20:15

c Ex 22:4

d De 16:18
  De 19:17
_____
Second Col.
a De 16:18
  De 25:1

b Ex 22:4

c Le 6:2-5

d De 22:28, 29

e Le 19:26
  Le 20:6
  De 18:10-12
  1Sa 28:3
  Ga 5:20
  Re 22:15

f Le 18:23
  Le 20:15
  De 27:21

g Nu 25:3
  1Ki 18:40
  1Co 10:20

21 "You must not mistreat a foreign resident or oppress him,[a] for you were foreign residents in the land of Egypt.[b]

22 "You must not afflict any widow or fatherless child.*[c] **23** If you afflict him at all, so that he cries out to me, I will unfailingly hear his outcry;[d] **24** and my anger will blaze, and I will kill you with the sword, and your wives will become widows, and your children will be fatherless.

25 "If you lend money to anyone poor* of my people, someone who is dwelling with you, you must not become like a moneylender# to him. You must not charge him interest.[e]

26 "If you seize the garment of your fellow man as security for a loan,*[f] you are to return it to him by sunset. **27** For it is his only covering, his clothing to cover his body;* in what will he lie down to sleep?[g] When he cries out to me, I will certainly hear, for I am compassionate.*[h]

28 "You must not curse* God[i] nor curse a chieftain# among your people.[j]

29 "You must not hesitate to make offerings from your abundant produce and the overflow of your presses.*[k] The firstborn of your sons you are to give to me.[l] **30** This is what you should do with your bull and your sheep:[m] Seven days it will continue with its mother. On the eighth day, you are to give it to me.[n]

31 "You should prove yourselves holy people to me,[o] and you must not eat the flesh of anything in the field that has been torn by a wild animal.[p] You should throw it to the dogs.

	CHAP. 22
a	Le 25:35
b	Le 19:33, 34
	De 10:19
c	De 27:19
	Jas 1:27
d	Ps 10:18
	Jas 5:4
e	Le 25:35, 36
	De 23:19
	Lu 6:34, 35
f	De 24:6
g	De 24:13
h	De 10:18
	Ps 34:6
i	Le 24:11, 14
j	Ec 10:20
	Ac 23:5
	Jude 8
k	Pr 3:9
	2Co 9:7
l	Ex 13:2
m	De 15:19
n	Le 22:27
o	Le 19:2
	Nu 15:40
	1Pe 1:15
p	Le 22:3, 8

Second Col.

	CHAP. 23
a	Le 19:16
	Pr 6:16, 19
b	De 19:18, 19
	Pr 19:5
c	Le 19:15
d	Pr 25:21
	1Th 5:15
e	De 22:4
	Lu 6:27
	Ro 12:21
f	De 16:19
	2Ch 19:7
g	Pr 17:15
	Ro 1:18
	Ro 2:6
h	Ec 7:7
i	Le 19:34
j	Le 25:3, 4

23 "You must not spread* a report that is not true.[a] Do not cooperate with a wicked one by becoming a malicious witness.[b] **2** You must not follow after the crowd to do evil, and you must not pervert justice by giving testimony to go along with the crowd.* **3** You must show impartiality in the dispute of a poor person.[c]

4 "If you come upon your enemy's bull or his donkey straying, you must return it to him.[d] **5** If you see that the donkey of someone who hates you has fallen under its load, you must not ignore it and leave. You must help him release the animal.[e]

6 "You are not to pervert the judgment of the poor one among you in his legal case.[f]

7 "Have nothing to do with a false accusation,* and do not kill the innocent and the righteous, for I will not declare the wicked one righteous.#[g]

8 "You must not accept a bribe, for the bribe blinds clearsighted men and can distort the words of righteous men.[h]

9 "You must not oppress a foreign resident. You know how it feels to be a foreigner,* because you were foreign residents in the land of Egypt.[i]

10 "You are to sow your land with seed and gather its produce for six years.[j] **11** But the seventh year you should leave it uncultivated and let it lie fallow, and the poor among your people will eat of it, and what they leave, the wild animals of the field will eat. That is what you should do with your vineyard and your olive grove.

12 "Six days you are to do

22:22 *Or "orphan." **22:25** *Or "afflicted." #Or "usurer." **22:26** *Or "as a pledge." **22:27** *Lit., "skin." #Or "gracious." **22:28** *Or "revile." #Or "ruler." **22:29** *That is, oil presses and winepresses.

23:1 *Lit., "take up." **23:2** *Or "testimony that is popular." **23:7** *Lit., "word." #Or "acquit the wicked one." **23:9** *Or "know the life (soul) of a foreigner."

your work; but on the seventh day, you are to cease from your labor, in order that your bull and your donkey may rest and the son of your slave girl and the foreign resident may refresh themselves.[a]

13 "You must be careful to do all that I have said to you,[b] and you must not mention the names of other gods; they should not be heard on your lips.*[c]

14 "Three times a year you are to celebrate a festival to me.[d] **15** You will observe the Festival of Unleavened Bread.[e] You will eat unleavened bread for seven days, just as I have commanded you, at the appointed time in the month of A'bib,*[f] for at that time you came out of Egypt. No one is to appear before me empty-handed.[g] **16** Also, you are to observe the Festival of Harvest* of the first ripe fruits of your labors, of what you sow in the field;[h] and the Festival of Ingathering* at the end of the year, when you gather in from the field the results of your labors.[i] **17** Three times a year all your men* are to appear before the true Lord, Jehovah.[j]

18 "You must not offer the blood of my sacrifice with anything leavened. And the sacrifices of fat offered at my festivals should not stay overnight until the morning.

19 "You are to bring the best of the first ripe fruits of your ground to the house of Jehovah your God.[k]

"You must not boil a young goat in its mother's milk.[l]

20 "I am sending an angel ahead of you[m] to guard you on the way and to bring you into

the place that I have prepared.[a] **21** Pay attention to him, and obey his voice. Do not rebel against him, for he will not pardon your transgressions,[b] because my name is in him. **22** However, if you strictly obey his voice and do all that I say, I will show hostility to your enemies and oppose those who oppose you. **23** For my angel will go ahead of you and will bring you to the Am'or·ites, the Hit'tites, the Per'iz·zites, the Ca'naan·ites, the Hi'vites, and the Jeb'u·sites, and I will annihilate them.[c] **24** You must not bow down to their gods or be persuaded to serve them, and you must not imitate their practices.[d] Instead, you must demolish them and smash their sacred pillars.[e] **25** You must serve Jehovah your God,[f] and he will bless your bread and your water.[g] I will remove sickness from among you.[h] **26** The women in your land will not suffer a miscarriage or be barren,[i] and I will give you a full life span.*

27 "I will send the fear of me ahead of you,[j] and I will throw into confusion all the people you encounter, and I will cause all your enemies to flee from you in defeat.*[k] **28** I will send the feeling of dejection* ahead of you,[l] and it will drive the Hi'vites, the Ca'naan·ites, and the Hit'tites out from before you.[m] **29** I will not drive them out from before you in one year, so that the land does not become desolate and the wild animals of the field multiply against you.[n] **30** Little by little I will drive them out from before you, until you become fruitful and take possession of the land.[o]

CHAP. 23

a Ex 20:9, 10
  De 5:14

b De 4:9

c De 12:3
  Jos 23:6, 7

d De 16:16

e Le 23:6
  Lu 22:7

f Ex 12:18

g De 16:17

h Nu 28:26
  De 16:9, 10
  Ac 2:1

i De 16:13
  Ne 8:14
  Joh 7:2

j De 12:5, 6

k Nu 18:8, 12
  1Co 15:20

l De 14:21
  Pr 12:10

m Ex 14:19

___

Second Col.

a Nu 20:16

b Nu 14:35
  Jos 24:11

c Ex 34:11
  Jos 5:13, 14
  Jos 24:8

d Ex 20:5
  Le 18:3
  De 12:30
  2Ch 33:2

e Ex 20:5
  Nu 33:52

f De 6:13
  De 10:12
  Jos 22:5
  Mt 4:10

g De 7:13

h De 7:15

i De 7:14
  De 28:4

j De 2:25
  Jos 2:9

k De 7:23, 24

l De 7:20
  Jos 2:11

m Nu 24:11

n De 7:22

o De 9:4

___

23:13 *Lit., "mouth." 23:15 *See App. B15. 23:16 *Also known as the Festival of Weeks, or Pentecost. #Also known as the Festival of Booths (Tabernacles). 23:17 *Or "males."

23:26 *Or "I will make the number of your days full." 23:27 *Or "I will make all your enemies turn their back to you." 23:28 *Or possibly, "panic; terror."

31 "I will set your boundary from the Red Sea to the sea of the Phi·lis'tines to the wilderness to the River;*[a] for I will give the inhabitants of the land into your hand, and you will drive them out from before you.[b] **32** You must not make a covenant with them or their gods.[c] **33** They should not dwell in your land, so that they may not cause you to sin against me. If you should serve their gods, it would surely become a snare to you.[d]

24 Then he said to Moses: "Go up to Jehovah, you and Aaron, Na'dab and A·bi'hu,[e] and 70 of the elders of Israel, and bow down from a distance. **2** Moses should approach Jehovah by himself; but the others should not approach, and the people should not go up with him."[f]

3 Then Moses came and related to the people all the words of Jehovah and all the judicial decisions,[g] and all the people answered with one voice: "All the words that Jehovah has spoken, we are willing to do."[h] **4** So Moses wrote down all the words of Jehovah.[i] Then he got up early in the morning and built at the foot of the mountain an altar and 12 pillars corresponding to the 12 tribes of Israel. **5** After that he sent young Israelite men, and they offered up burnt offerings and sacrificed bulls as communion sacrifices[j] to Jehovah. **6** Then Moses took half of the blood and put it in bowls, and half the blood he sprinkled on the altar. **7** Then he took the book of the covenant and read it aloud to the people.[k] And they said: "All that Jehovah has spoken we are willing to do, and we will be obedient."[l] **8** So Moses took the blood and sprinkled

23:31 * That is, the Euphrates.

it on the people[a] and said: "This is the blood of the covenant that Jehovah has made with you in harmony with all these words."[b]

9 Moses and Aaron, Na'dab and A·bi'hu, and 70 of the elders of Israel went up, **10** and they saw the God of Israel.[c] Under his feet was what seemed like a sapphire pavement, and it was as pure as the heavens themselves.[d] **11** He did not harm the distinguished men of Israel,[e] and they saw a vision of the true God and ate and drank.

12 Jehovah now said to Moses: "Come up to me on the mountain and stay there. I will give you the stone tablets with the law and the commandment that I will write for their instruction."[f] **13** So Moses got up with his attendant Joshua,[g] and Moses went up the mountain of the true God.[h] **14** But to the elders he had said: "Wait here for us until we return to you.[i] You have Aaron and Hur[j] with you. Whoever has a legal case may go to them."[k] **15** Then Moses went up the mountain while the cloud was covering it.[l]

16 Jehovah's glory[m] remained on Mount Si'nai,[n] and the cloud covered it for six days. On the seventh day he called to Moses from the midst of the cloud. **17** To the Israelites who were watching, the appearance of Jehovah's glory was like a consuming fire on the mountaintop. **18** Moses then entered into the cloud and went up the mountain.[o] And Moses stayed on the mountain 40 days and 40 nights.[p]

25 Jehovah then said to Moses: **2** "Tell the people of Israel to take up a contribution for me; from every person whose heart moves him, you are to take up my contribution.[q] **3** This is the contribution that you are to accept from them: gold,[r] silver,[s] copper,[t] **4** blue

CHAP. 23
a Ge 15:18
  De 1:7
  Jos 1:4
  1Ki 4:21
b Jg 1:4
  Jg 11:21
c Ex 34:12
  Nu 25:1, 2
  De 7:2
  2Co 6:14
d Jos 23:12, 13
  Jg 1:28
  Ps 106:36

CHAP. 24
e Le 10:1
f Ex 20:21
  Nu 12:8
g Ex 21:1
  De 4:1
h De 5:27
  Jos 24:22
i Ex 34:27
  De 31:9
j Le 3:1
  Le 7:11
k De 31:11
  Ac 13:15
l Ex 19:8

Second Col.
a Heb 12:24
b Heb 9:18-20
c Joh 1:18
d Eze 1:26
  Re 4:3
e Ex 24:1
f De 5:22
g Nu 11:28
h Ex 24:2
i Ex 32:1
j Ex 17:10
k Ex 18:25, 26
l Ex 19:9
m Ex 16:10
  Le 9:23
  Nu 16:42
n Ex 19:11
o Ex 19:20
p Ex 34:28
  De 9:9

CHAP. 25
q Ex 35:4-9
  1Ch 29:9
  2Co 9:7
r Ex 38:24
s Ex 38:25
t Ex 38:3
  Ex 38:29

thread, purple wool,* scarlet material," fine linen, goat hair, 5 ram skins dyed red, sealskins, acacia wood,ᵃ 6 oil for the lamps,ᵇ balsam for the anointing oilᶜ and the perfumed incense,ᵈ 7 and onyx stones and other stones to be set in the eph'odᵉ and the breastpiece.ᶠ 8 They are to make a sanctuary for me, and I will reside* among them.ᵍ 9 You are to make it, the tabernacle and all its furnishings, following exactly the pattern* that I am showing you.ʰ

10 "They are to make an ark* of acacia wood, two and a half cubits* long and a cubit and a half wide and a cubit and a half high.ⁱ 11 Then you will overlay it with pure gold.ʲ Inside and outside you are to overlay it, and you will make a border* of gold all around it.ᵏ 12 And you will cast four rings of gold for it and attach them above its four feet, with two rings on one side and two rings on the other side. 13 And you will make poles of acacia wood and overlay them with gold.ˡ 14 You will put the poles through the rings on the sides of the Ark in order to carry the Ark with them. 15 The poles will stay in the rings of the Ark; they are not to be removed from it.ᵐ 16 You will place in the Ark the Testimony that I will give you.ⁿ

17 "You will make a cover of pure gold, two and a half cubits long and a cubit and a half wide.ᵒ 18 You are to make two cherubs of gold; you will make them of hammered work on the two ends of the cover.ᵖ 19 Make the cherubs on the two ends,

one cherub on each end of the cover. 20 The cherubs are to spread out their two wings upward, overshadowing the cover with their wings,ᵃ and they will face each other. The faces of the cherubs will be turned toward the cover. 21 You will put the coverᵇ on the Ark, and in the Ark you will place the Testimony that I will give you. 22 I will present myself to you there and speak with you from above the cover.ᶜ From between the two cherubs that are on the ark of the Testimony, I will make known to you all that I will command you for the Israelites.

23 "You will also make a tableᵈ of acacia wood, two cubits long and a cubit wide and a cubit and a half high.ᵉ 24 You will overlay it with pure gold and make a golden border* around it. 25 You will make a rim around it a handbreadth" wide and a border* of gold to go around the rim. 26 You will make for it four rings of gold and place the rings on the four corners, where the four legs are attached. 27 The rings are to be close to the rim as holders for the poles for carrying the table. 28 You will make the poles of acacia wood and overlay them with gold and carry the table with them.

29 "You will also make its dishes, its cups, its pitchers, and its bowls from which they will pour drink offerings. You are to make them out of pure gold.ᶠ 30 And you will put the showbread on the table before me constantly.ᵍ

31 "You will make a lampstandʰ of pure gold. The lampstand is to be made of hammered work. Its base, its stem, its branches, its cups, its knobs, and its blossoms will be one

---

CHAP. 25
a Ex 36:20
b Ex 27:20
c Ex 30:23-25
d Ex 30:34, 35
e Ex 28:6
f Ex 28:15
g Ex 29:45
  1Ki 6:13
  Heb 9:11
h 1Ch 28:12
  Ac 7:44
  Heb 8:5
  Heb 9:9
i Ex 37:1-5
j Heb 9:4
k Ex 30:1, 3
l Ex 30:1, 5
  1Ch 15:15
m 1Ki 8:8
n Ex 31:18
  Ex 40:20
  1Ki 8:9
  Heb 9:4
o Ex 37:6-9
p 1Sa 4:4
  Heb 9:5

Second Col.
a 1Ki 8:7
  1Ch 28:18
b Ex 40:20
  Heb 9:4, 5
c Ex 30:6
  Le 16:2
  Nu 7:89
  Jg 20:27
  Ps 80:1
d Ex 40:22
  Le 24:6
  Nu 3:30, 31
  Heb 9:2
e Ex 37:10-15
f Ex 37:16
  Nu 4:7
  1Ki 7:48, 50
g Le 24:5, 6
  1Sa 21:6
  1Ch 9:32
  2Ch 13:11
  Mt 12:4
h Ex 40:24
  1Ki 7:48, 49
  Heb 9:2

25:4 *Or "wool dyed reddish-purple." "Or "coccus scarlet material." 25:8 *Or "tabernacle." 25:9 *Or "design." 25:10 *Or "chest." "A cubit equaled 44.5 cm (17.5 in.). See App. B14. 25:11, 24, 25 *Or "molding."

25:25 "About 7.4 cm (2.9 in.). See App. B14.

piece.[a] **32** And six branches will extend out from the sides of the lampstand, three branches from one side and three branches from the other side. **33** Three cups shaped like almond flowers will be on the one set of branches, with knobs and blossoms alternating, and three cups shaped like almond flowers on the other set of branches, with knobs and blossoms alternating. This is how the six branches will extend out from the stem of the lampstand. **34** On the stem of the lampstand are four cups shaped like almond flowers, with its knobs and its blossoms alternating. **35** A knob will be under the first two branches that extend out of the stem and a knob under the next two branches and a knob under the next two branches, for the six branches extending out from the stem. **36** The knobs and the branches and the whole lampstand are to be one piece of pure, hammered gold.[b] **37** You will make seven lamps for it, and when the lamps are lit, they will shine on the area in front of it.[c] **38** Its snuffers* and its fire holders are to be of pure gold.[d] **39** It should be made, along with these utensils, from a talent* of pure gold. **40** See that you make them after their pattern* that was shown to you on the mountain.[e]

26 "You are to make the tabernacle[f] with ten tent cloths of fine twisted linen, blue thread, purple wool, and scarlet material. You are to make them with embroidered cherub[g] designs.[h] **2** Each tent cloth will be 28 cubits* long and 4 cubits wide. All the tent cloths are to

be the same size.[a] **3** Five tent cloths are to be joined one to another to form a series, and the other five tent cloths will be joined in a series. **4** You will make loops of blue thread on the edge of the one tent cloth at the end of the series, and you are to do the same on the outermost edge of the other set where it will join. **5** You will make 50 loops on the one tent cloth and 50 loops on the edge of the other tent cloth so that they will be opposite each other where they join. **6** You are to make 50 gold clasps and join the tent cloths together with the clasps, and the tabernacle will form one unit.[b]

7 "You will also make cloths of goat hair[c] for the tent over the tabernacle. You will make 11 tent cloths.[d] **8** Each tent cloth will be 30 cubits long and 4 cubits wide. All 11 tent cloths are to be the same size. **9** You are to join five of the tent cloths together and join the other six tent cloths together, and you are to fold over the sixth tent cloth at the front of the tent. **10** And you are to make 50 loops on the edge of the one tent cloth, the outermost one in the series, and 50 loops on the edge of the tent cloth at the other place where they join. **11** You are to make 50 copper clasps and put the clasps in the loops and join the tent together, and it will become one unit. **12** The remaining part of the tent cloths will serve as an overhanging. Half of the tent cloth that remains will hang over the back of the tabernacle. **13** The remaining length of the cloths of the tent will serve as an overhanging for the tabernacle by one cubit on each side, in order to cover it.

14 "You will also make a covering for the tent of ram skins dyed red and over that a covering of sealskins.[e]

25:38 *Or "tongs." **25:39** *A talent equaled 34.2 kg (1,101 oz t). See App. B14. **25:40** *Or "design." **26:2** *A cubit equaled 44.5 cm (17.5 in.). See App. B14.

CHAP. 25
a Ex 37:17-24

b Nu 8:4

c Ex 30:8
Le 24:2, 3
Nu 8:2
2Ch 13:11

d Nu 4:9

e Ex 39:42
Nu 8:4
Ac 7:44
Heb 8:5

CHAP. 26
f Heb 8:5
Heb 9:9, 11

g Ge 3:24
Ps 99:1

h Ex 36:8-13

Second Col.
a Nu 4:25

b Ex 39:33, 34

c Ex 35:26

d Ex 36:14-18

e Ex 36:19

15 "You will make the panel frames[a] for the tabernacle out of acacia wood standing upright.[b] **16** Each panel frame is to be ten cubits high and a cubit and a half wide. **17** Each panel frame has two tenons* joined to each other. That is how you should make all the panel frames of the tabernacle. **18** You are to make 20 panel frames for the south side of the tabernacle, facing south.

19 "You will make 40 silver socket pedestals[c] under the 20 panel frames: two socket pedestals under the one panel frame for its two tenons and two socket pedestals under each following panel frame for its two tenons.[d] **20** For the other side of the tabernacle, the northern side, make 20 panel frames **21** and their 40 silver socket pedestals, two socket pedestals under one panel frame and two socket pedestals under each following panel frame. **22** For the rear section of the tabernacle to the west, you will make six panel frames.[e] **23** You will make two panel frames to serve as the two rear corner posts of the tabernacle. **24** They should be doubled from the bottom to the top, up to the first ring. This should be done for both of them, and they will form the two corner posts. **25** And there will be eight panel frames and their 16 silver socket pedestals, two socket pedestals under the one panel frame and two socket pedestals under each following panel frame.

26 "You will make bars of acacia wood, five for the panel frames of the one side of the tabernacle,[f] **27** and five bars for the panel frames of the other side of the tabernacle, and five bars for the panel frames of the side of the tabernacle to

the west, for the rear section. **28** The middle bar that runs along the center of the panel frames should extend from end to end.

29 "You will overlay the panel frames with gold,[a] and you will make their rings of gold as holders for the bars, and you will overlay the bars with gold. **30** You must set up the tabernacle according to its plan that you were shown in the mountain.[b]

31 "You are to make a curtain[c] of blue thread, purple wool, scarlet material, and fine twisted linen. It will be made with cherubs embroidered on it. **32** You will hang it on four pillars of acacia overlaid with gold. Their hooks are to be of gold. The pillars are set on four socket pedestals of silver. **33** You will hang the curtain under the clasps and bring the ark of the Testimony[d] there within the curtain. The curtain will make a division for you between the Holy[e] and the Most Holy.[f] **34** You must put the cover on the ark of the Testimony in the Most Holy.

35 "You will place the table outside the curtain, with the lampstand[g] opposite the table on the south side of the tabernacle; and the table you will put on the north side. **36** You will make a screen* for the entrance of the tent out of blue thread, purple wool, scarlet material, and fine twisted linen woven together.[h] **37** You will make five pillars of acacia for the screen* and overlay them with gold. Their hooks are to be of gold, and you will cast five socket pedestals of copper for them.

27 "You will make the altar of acacia wood;[i] it will be five cubits* long and five cubits wide. The altar should be square

CHAP. 26	
a	Nu 4:29, 31
b	Ex 36:20-23
c	Nu 3:36
d	Ex 36:24-26
e	Ex 36:27-30
f	Ex 36:31-33

Second Col.

a	Ex 12:35, 36 Ex 36:34
b	Ex 19:3 Ex 25:9 Ac 7:44 Heb 8:5
c	Ex 36:35, 36 Lu 23:45 Heb 6:19 Heb 9:3 Heb 10:19, 20
d	1Ki 8:6
e	Ex 40:22, 26
f	Ex 40:21 Le 16:2 1Ki 8:6 Heb 9:2-4 Heb 9:12, 24
g	Le 24:2, 3 1Ki 7:48, 49
h	Ex 36:37, 38

CHAP. 27	
i	Ex 40:29 2Ch 4:1 Heb 13:10

26:17 *Or "upright posts."

26:36, 37 *Or "curtain." 27:1 *A cubit equaled 44.5 cm (17.5 in.). See App. B14.

and three cubits high.[a] **2** You will make horns[b] on its four corners; the horns will be part of the altar, and you will overlay the altar with copper.[c] **3** You will make buckets for clearing away its ashes,* along with shovels, bowls, forks, and fire holders, and you will make all its utensils of copper.[d] **4** You will make a grating for the altar, a network of copper, and on the network four rings of copper at its four corners. **5** You will set it down below the rim of the altar, and the network will extend partway down into the altar. **6** You will make poles of acacia wood for the altar and overlay them with copper. **7** The poles will be inserted into the rings so that the poles are on the two sides of the altar when it is carried.[e] **8** You will make the altar in the form of a hollow chest of planks. It should be made just as He showed you on the mountain.[f]

9 "You will make the courtyard[g] of the tabernacle. For the south side, facing south, the courtyard will have hanging curtains of fine twisted linen, 100 cubits long for the one side.[h] **10** It will have 20 pillars with 20 copper socket pedestals. The hooks of the pillars and their connectors* are of silver. **11** The hanging curtains for the north side will also be 100 cubits long, along with its 20 pillars and their 20 copper socket pedestals, with silver hooks and connectors* for the pillars. **12** There are to be hanging curtains on the west side for 50 cubits across the width of the courtyard, with ten pillars and ten socket pedestals. **13** The width of the courtyard

on the east side toward the sunrise is 50 cubits. **14** There will be 15 cubits of hanging curtains on the one side, with three pillars and three socket pedestals.[a] **15** And for the other side, there will be 15 cubits of hanging curtains, with three pillars and three socket pedestals.

16 "The entrance of the courtyard should have a screen* 20 cubits long made of blue thread, purple wool, scarlet material, and fine twisted linen woven together,[b] with four pillars and their four socket pedestals.[c] **17** All the pillars surrounding the courtyard will have silver fasteners and silver hooks, but their socket pedestals will be of copper.[d] **18** The courtyard is to be 100 cubits long,[e] 50 cubits wide, and 5 cubits high, made from fine twisted linen, and it should have copper socket pedestals. **19** All the utensils and the items used in the service of the tabernacle, as well as its tent pins and all the pins of the courtyard, are to be of copper.[f]

20 "You are to command the Israelites to bring you pure, beaten olive oil for the lighting, in order to keep the lamps burning constantly.[g] **21** In the tent of meeting, outside the curtain that is near the Testimony,[h] Aaron and his sons will arrange to keep the lamps lit from evening until morning before Jehovah.[i] It is a lasting statute for all their generations to be carried out by the Israelites.[j]

28 "You are to summon from the Israelites your brother Aaron, along with his sons, so that he may serve as priest to me[k]—Aaron,[l] along with Na'dab and A·bi'hu,[m] El·e·a'zar and Ith'a·mar,[n] the sons of Aaron.[o] **2** You are to make holy garments for Aaron your brother, for glory

---

27:3 *Or "fatty ashes," that is, ashes soaked with the fat of the sacrifices.
27:10, 11 *Or "rings; hoops; bands" for attachments.
27:16 *Or "curtain."

CHAP. 27

a Ex 38:1-7

b Le 4:25

c 1Ki 8:64

d 1Ki 7:45

e Nu 4:14, 15

f Ex 25:40
  1Ch 28:12
  Ac 7:44
  Heb 8:5

g Ex 40:8
  1Ki 6:36

h Ex 38:9-15

Second Col.

a Ex 39:33, 40

b Ex 35:25

c Ex 38:18, 19

d Ex 38:17

e Ex 27:9

f Ex 38:20
  Nu 3:36, 37

g Ex 39:33, 37
  Le 24:1-3

h Ex 26:33
  Ex 40:3
  Heb 9:2, 3

i Ex 30:8

j Nu 18:23

CHAP. 28

k Le 8:2
  Heb 5:1

l Heb 5:4

m Le 10:1
  Nu 26:61

n Ex 38:21
  Le 10:16
  1Ch 24:2

o Ex 6:23
  1Ch 6:3

and beauty.[a] 3 You are to speak to all those who are skillful,[*] those whom I have filled with the spirit of wisdom,[b] and they will make Aaron's garments for his sanctification, so that he may serve as priest to me.

4 "These are the garments that they will make: a breastpiece,[c] an eph'od,[d] a sleeveless coat,[e] a checkered robe, a turban,[f] and a sash;[g] they will make these holy garments for your brother Aaron and his sons, so that he may serve as priest to me. 5 The skilled workers will use the gold, the blue thread, the purple wool, the scarlet material, and the fine linen.

6 "They are to make the eph'od of gold, blue thread, purple wool, scarlet material, and fine twisted linen, and it should be embroidered.[h] 7 It is to have two attached shoulder pieces that join it at its two edges. 8 The woven belt,[*i] which is attached to the eph'od for tying it securely in position, should be of the same materials: gold, blue thread, purple wool, scarlet material, and fine twisted linen.

9 "You are to take two onyx stones[j] and engrave on them the names of the sons of Israel,[k] 10 six names on the one stone and the six remaining names on the other stone, in the order of their births. 11 A stone engraver will engrave the names of the sons of Israel on the two stones as he would engrave them as a seal.[l] Then you are to have them mounted in gold settings. 12 You are to put the two stones on the shoulder pieces of the eph'od as memorial stones for the sons of Israel,[m] and Aaron must carry their names before Jehovah on his two shoulder pieces as a memorial. 13 You are to make set-

tings of gold 14 and two chains of pure gold twisted like a cord,[a] and you must attach the corded chains to the settings.[b]

15 "You are to have an embroiderer make the breastpiece of judgment.[c] It should be made like the eph'od, out of gold, blue thread, purple wool, scarlet material, and fine twisted linen.[d] 16 It should be square when doubled, a span* long and a span wide. 17 You should set in it mounted stones, four rows of stones. The first row is ruby, topaz, and emerald. 18 The second row is turquoise, sapphire, and jasper. 19 The third row is *lesh'em* stone,* agate, and amethyst. 20 The fourth row is chrys'o·lite, onyx, and jade. They should be mounted in settings of gold. 21 The stones will correspond to the names of the 12 sons of Israel. Each one should be engraved like a seal, each name representing one of the 12 tribes.

22 "You are to make wreathed chains on the breastpiece, like cords of pure gold.[e] 23 You are to make two rings of gold for the breastpiece and attach the two rings to the two ends of the breastpiece. 24 You are to put the two cords of gold through the two rings at the ends of the breastpiece. 25 You will put the two ends of the two cords through the two settings, and you must attach them to the shoulder pieces of the eph'od, at the front. 26 You are to make two rings of gold and set them at the two ends on the inside edge of the breastpiece, facing the eph'od.[f] 27 You should make two more rings of gold on the front of the eph'od, below

---

CHAP. 28

a Ex 29:5
Le 8:7

b Ex 31:6
Ex 36:1

c Ex 39:8, 15
Le 8:8

d Ex 39:2

e Ex 39:22

f Ex 39:27, 28
Ex 39:30, 31
Le 8:9

g Ex 39:27, 29
Le 8:7

h Ex 39:2-5

i Ex 29:5

j Ex 35:5, 9
Ex 35:27

k Ex 1:1-4

l Ex 39:6, 14

m Ex 39:7

Second Col.

a Ex 39:15

b Ex 39:18

c Ex 28:30
Le 8:8
Nu 27:21

d Ex 39:8-14

e Ex 39:15-18

f Ex 39:19-21

28:3 *Lit., "wise of heart." 28:8 *Or "waistband."

28:16 *That is, the span of the hand, about 22.2 cm (8.75 in.). See App. B14.
28:19 *An unidentified precious stone, possibly referring to amber, hyacinth, opal, or tourmaline.

the two shoulder pieces, close to where it is joined, above the woven belt* of the eph'od.[a] 28 The breastpiece should be held in place by a blue cord, tying its rings to the rings of the eph'od. This will keep the breastpiece in place on the eph'od, above the woven belt.*

29 "Aaron must carry the names of the sons of Israel on the breastpiece of judgment over his heart when he comes into the Holy as a constant memorial before Jehovah. 30 You will put the U'rim and the Thum'mim*[b] into the breastpiece of judgment, and they must be over Aaron's heart when he comes in before Jehovah, and Aaron must carry the means for making judgments of the Israelites over his heart before Jehovah constantly.

31 "You are to make the sleeveless coat of the eph'od entirely of blue thread.[c] 32 There will be an opening at the top* in the middle of it. Its opening should have a border woven all around it by a loom worker. It should be like the opening of a coat of mail, so that it will not be torn. 33 You should make pomegranates of blue thread, purple wool, and scarlet material all around its hem, along with bells of gold in between them. 34 You should alternate a bell of gold and a pomegranate, a bell of gold and a pomegranate, all around the hem of the sleeveless coat. 35 It must be worn by Aaron so that he may minister, and the sound from it must be heard when he goes into the sanctuary before Jehovah and when he comes out, so that he will not die.[d]

36 "You are to make a shining plate of pure gold and engrave on it as one would en-

grave a seal: 'Holiness belongs to Jehovah.'[a] 37 You must fasten it to the turban[b] with a blue cord; it is to remain on the front of the turban. 38 It will be on Aaron's forehead, and Aaron will bear responsibility when someone commits an error against the holy things,[c] which the Israelites sanctify when they offer them as holy gifts. It must always remain on his forehead, so that they may gain approval before Jehovah.

39 "You are to weave the checkered robe of fine linen, make a turban of fine linen, and make a woven sash.[d]

40 "You will also make robes, sashes, and headgear for Aaron's sons,[e] for glory and beauty.[f] 41 You will clothe your brother Aaron and his sons with him, and you are to anoint them[g] and install them*[h] and sanctify them, and they will serve as priests to me. 42 Also make linen shorts* for them to cover their naked flesh.[i] These are to extend from the hips to the thighs. 43 These must be worn by Aaron and his sons when they come into the tent of meeting or when they approach the altar to minister in the holy place, so that they may not incur guilt and die. It is a permanent statute for him and his offspring* after him.

29 "This is what you are to do to sanctify them to serve as priests to me: Take a young bull, two unblemished rams,[j] 2 unleavened bread, unleavened ring-shaped loaves mixed with oil, and unleavened wafers spread with oil.[k] You are to make them with fine wheat flour 3 and put them in a basket and present them in the basket,[l] along with the bull and the two rams.

CHAP. 28
a Ex 28:8
  Le 8:7

b Le 8:8
  Nu 27:21
  De 33:8
  1Sa 28:6
  Ezr 2:62, 63

c Ex 39:22-26
  Le 8:7

d Le 16:2
  Nu 18:7

Second Col.
a Ex 39:30, 31
  Le 8:9
  1Ch 16:29
  Ps 93:5
  1Pe 1:16

b Ex 29:6

c Ex 22:9
  Nu 18:1

d Ex 28:4
  Ex 39:27-29

e Le 8:13

f Ex 28:2

g Ex 29:4, 7
  Ex 30:30
  Ac 10:38
  2Co 1:21

h Ex 29:8, 9
  Le 8:33
  Nu 3:2, 3

i Le 6:10

CHAP. 29
j Le 8:2
  De 17:1

k Le 6:20

l Le 8:26

28:27, 28 *Or "waistband." 28:30 *See Glossary. 28:32 *Or "for the head."

28:41 *Lit., "and fill their hand." 28:42 *Or "undergarments." 28:43 *Lit., "seed."

4 "You will present Aaron and his sons at the entrance of the tent of meeting[a] and wash them with water.[b] **5** Then you are to take the garments[c] and clothe Aaron with the robe, the sleeveless coat of the eph'od, the eph'od, and the breastpiece, and you are to tie the woven belt* of the eph'od securely around his waist.[d] **6** You will put the turban on his head and put the holy sign of dedication* on the turban;[e] **7** and take the anointing oil[f] and pour it on his head and anoint him.[g]

8 "Then bring his sons forward and clothe them with the robes[h] **9** and wrap the sashes around them, Aaron as well as his sons, and put on their headgear; and the priesthood will become theirs as a permanent statute.[i] This is how you should install Aaron and his sons to serve as priests.*[j]

10 "You are now to present the bull before the tent of meeting, and Aaron and his sons will lay their hands on the bull's head.[k] **11** Slaughter the bull before Jehovah, at the entrance of the tent of meeting.[l] **12** Take some of the bull's blood on your finger and put it on the horns of the altar,[m] and pour out all the rest of the blood at the base of the altar.[n] **13** Then take all the fat[o] that covers the intestines, the appendage on the liver, and the two kidneys and the fat that is on them, and burn them so that they smoke on the altar.[p] **14** But the bull's flesh and its skin and its dung, you will burn with fire outside the camp. It is a sin offering.

15 "Then take the one ram, and Aaron and his sons are to lay their hands on the ram's head.[a] **16** Slaughter the ram and take its blood and sprinkle it on all sides of the altar.[b] **17** Cut the ram into its pieces, and wash its intestines[c] and its shanks, and arrange the pieces together with its head. **18** You must burn the entire ram, making it smoke on the altar. It is a burnt offering to Jehovah, a pleasing* aroma.[d] It is an offering made by fire to Jehovah.

19 "Next you are to take the other ram, and Aaron and his sons are to lay their hands on the ram's head.[e] **20** Slaughter the ram and take some of its blood and put it on Aaron's right earlobe and on his sons' right earlobe and on the thumb of their right hand and the big toe of their right foot, and sprinkle the blood on all sides of the altar. **21** Then take some of the blood that is on the altar and some of the anointing oil[f] and spatter it on Aaron and his garments and on his sons and his sons' garments, so that he and his garments and his sons and their garments may be holy.[g]

22 "Then take from the ram the fat, the fat tail, the fat that covers the intestines, the appendage of the liver, the two kidneys and the fat that is on them,[h] and the right leg, for it is a ram of installation.[i] **23** Take also a round loaf of bread and a ring-shaped loaf of oiled bread and a wafer out of the basket of unleavened bread that is before Jehovah. **24** You must place them all in the hands of Aaron and in the hands of his sons, and you are to wave them back and forth as a wave offering before Jehovah. **25** Then you will take them out of their hands and burn them on the altar, on top of the burnt offering, as a pleas-

CHAP. 29

a Ex 26:36
  Ex 40:28
  Le 8:2; 3

b Le 8:6
  Heb 10:22

c Ex 28:4
  Le 8:7
  Le 16:4

d Ex 28:8

e Ex 28:36
  Ex 39:30
  Le 8:9

f Ex 30:23-25

g Le 8:12
  Ps 133:2
  Isa 61:1
  Ac 10:38

h Ex 28:40
  Le 8:13

i Ex 28:1-3
  Ex 28:40, 43
  Ex 40:15

j Ex 28:41

k Le 8:14-17

l Le 4:3

m Ex 27:2

n Le 4:7

o Le 3:17

p Le 4:8-10

Second Col.

a Le 1:4
  Le 8:18-21

b Heb 9:22

c Le 1:13

d Ge 8:21

e Le 8:22-24

f Ex 30:23-25

g Le 8:30

h Le 3:9, 10

i Le 8:22
  Le 8:25-28

29:5 *Or "waistband." 29:6 *Or "the holy diadem." 29:9 *Lit., "fill the hand of Aaron and the hand of his sons."

29:18 *Or "appeasing; soothing." Lit., "restful."

ing aroma before Jehovah. It is an offering made by fire to Jehovah.

26 "Then take the breast of the ram of installation,[a] which is offered in behalf of Aaron, and wave it back and forth as a wave offering before Jehovah, and it will become your portion. **27** You are to sanctify the breast of the wave offering and the leg of the sacred portion that was waved and that was taken from the ram of installation,[b] from what was offered for Aaron and for his sons. **28** It is to become Aaron's and his sons' by a permanent regulation to be carried out by the Israelites, for it is a sacred portion, and it will become a sacred portion to be given by the Israelites. It is their sacred portion for Jehovah from their communion sacrifices.[d]

29 "The holy garments[e] that belong to Aaron will be used by his sons[f] after him when they are anointed and installed as priests. **30** The priest from among his sons who succeeds him and who comes into the tent of meeting to minister in the holy place will wear them for seven days.[g]

31 "You will take the ram of installation and boil its flesh in a holy place.[h] **32** Aaron and his sons will eat[i] the flesh of the ram and the bread that is in the basket at the entrance of the tent of meeting. **33** They are to eat the things with which atonement was made to install them as priests* and to sanctify them. But an unauthorized person may not eat them, for they are something holy.[j] **34** If any of the flesh of the installation sacrifice and of the bread is left over until the morning, then you must

burn what is left with fire.[a] It must not be eaten, for it is something holy.

35 "You are to do this way to Aaron and his sons, according to all that I have commanded you. You will take seven days to install them as priests.*[b] **36** You will offer the bull of the sin offering daily for an atonement, and you are to purify the altar from sin by making atonement for it, and you must anoint it to sanctify it.[c] **37** You will take seven days to make atonement for the altar, and you must sanctify it so that it may become a most holy altar.[d] Anyone who touches the altar is to be holy.

38 "This is what you will offer on the altar: two one-year-old rams each day, continually.[e] **39** Offer the one young ram in the morning and the other ram at twilight.*[f] **40** A tenth part of an e'phah measure* of fine flour mixed with a fourth of a hin of beaten oil, and a drink offering of a fourth of a hin of wine, will go for the first young ram. **41** You will offer the second young ram at twilight,* along with the same grain and drink offerings as in the morning. You will render it as a pleasing aroma, an offering made by fire to Jehovah. **42** It is to be a regular burnt offering throughout your generations at the entrance of the tent of meeting before Jehovah, where I will present myself to you to speak to you there.[g]

43 "I will present myself there to the Israelites, and it will be sanctified by my glory.[h] **44** I will sanctify the tent of meeting and the altar, and I will sanctify Aaron and his sons[i] so

---

CHAP. 29

a Le 8:29
Ps 99:6

b Ex 29:22

c Le 7:34
Le 10:14

d Le 7:11, 14

e Le 28:4

f Nu 20:26

g Le 8:35

h Le 8:31

i 1Co 9:13

j Le 22:10
Nu 3:10

Second Col.

a Le 8:32

b Le 8:4, 33

c Ex 30:26, 28
Le 8:11
Nu 7:1

d Ex 40:10

e 2Ch 2:4
Heb 7:27
Heb 10:11

f Nu 28:4-6

g Ex 25:22
Le 1:1
Nu 17:4

h Ex 40:34
Nu 12:5
1Ki 8:11

i Le 22:9

29:25, 41 *Or "appeasing; soothing." Lit., "restful." **29:33, 35** *Lit., "to fill their hand." **29:33** *Lit., "a stranger," that is, a man not of Aaron's family.

29:39, 41 *Lit., "between the two evenings." **29:40** *An ephah equaled 22 L (20 dry qt). See App. B14. A hin equaled 3.67 L (7.75 pt). See App. B14.

that they may serve as priests to me. **45** I will reside* among the people of Israel, and I will be their God.ª **46** And they will certainly know that I am Jehovah their God, who brought them out of the land of Egypt so that I may reside among them.ᵇ I am Jehovah their God.

30 "You are to make an altar as a place for burning incense;ᶜ you will make it of acacia wood.ᵈ **2** It should be square, one cubit* long, one cubit wide, and two cubits high. Its horns will be one piece with it.ᵉ **3** You are to overlay it with pure gold: its top surface, its sides all around, and its horns; and you are to make a gold border* around it. **4** You will also make two rings of gold for it below its border* on two opposite sides, and these will hold the poles to carry it. **5** Make the poles of acacia wood and overlay them with gold. **6** You are to put it before the curtain that is near the ark of the Testimony,ᶠ before the cover that is over the Testimony, where I will present myself to you.ᵍ

7 "Aaronʰ will burn perfumed incenseⁱ on it,ʲ making it smoke on the altar when he maintains the lampsᵏ each morning. **8** Also, when Aaron lights the lamps at twilight,* he will burn the incense. It is a regular incense offering before Jehovah throughout your generations. **9** You must not offer on it unauthorized incenseˡ or a burnt offering or a grain offering, and you must not pour a drink offering on it. **10** Aaron must make atonement on its horns once a year.ᵐ With some of the blood of the sin offering of the atonement,ⁿ he will make atonement

for it once a year throughout your generations. It is most holy to Jehovah."

11 Then Jehovah said to Moses: **12** "Whenever you take a census and count the sons of Israel,ª each one must give a ransom for his life* to Jehovah at the time of the census. This is so that no plague may be brought upon them when they are registered. **13** This is what all those who are registered will give: a half shekel* by the standard shekel of the holy place.*ᵇ Twenty geʹrahsᐃ equal a shekel. A half shekel is the contribution to Jehovah.ᶜ **14** Everyone registered who is 20 years old and up will give Jehovah's contribution.ᵈ **15** The rich should not give more and the poor should not give less than the half shekel* as a contribution to Jehovah to make atonement for your lives.* **16** You are to take the silver money of the atonement from the Israelites and give it in behalf of the service of the tent of meeting, that it may serve as a remembrance before Jehovah for the Israelites, to make atonement for your lives."*

17 Jehovah spoke further to Moses, saying: **18** "Make a copper basin and its stand for washing;ᵉ then place it between the tent of meeting and the altar and put water into it.ᶠ **19** Aaron and his sons will wash their hands and their feet there.ᵍ **20** When they go into the tent of meeting or when they approach the altar to minister and to make offerings of fire and smoke to Jehovah, they will wash with water so that they do not die. **21** They must wash their hands

---

CHAP. 29
a Ex 25:8
  Le 26:12
  Zec 2:11
  2Co 6:16

b Ex 20:2

CHAP. 30
c Ex 40:5

d Ex 37:25-28

e Ex 27:1, 2
  Le 4:7

f Ex 26:33
  Heb 9:3

g Ex 25:22

h 1Ch 23:13

i Ex 30:34, 35

j Nu 16:39, 40
  1Sa 2:27, 28
  Lu 1:9

k Ex 27:20

l Le 10:1
  2Ch 26:18
  Eze 8:11, 12

m Le 23:27
  Heb 9:7

n Le 16:5, 6
  Le 16:18, 19

Second Col.
a Ex 38:25
  Nu 1:2
  2Sa 24:10, 15

b Le 27:25

c 2Ch 24:9
  Mt 17:24

d Ex 38:26
  Nu 1:3
  Nu 26:1, 2

e Ex 38:8
  Le 8:11
  1Ki 7:38

f Ex 40:7

g Ex 40:30, 31
  Heb 10:22

29:45 *Or "tabernacle." 30:2 *About 44.5 cm (17.5 in.). See App. B14. 30:3, 4 *Or "molding." 30:8 *Lit., "between the two evenings."

30:12 *Or "soul." 30:13, 15 *A shekel equaled 11.4 g (0.367 oz t). See App. B14. 30:13 *Or "by the holy shekel." ᐃA gerah equaled 0.57 g (0.01835 oz t). See App. B14. 30:15, 16 *Or "souls."

and their feet so that they may not die, and it must serve as a permanent regulation for them, for him and his offspring, throughout their generations."[a]

22 Jehovah continued to speak to Moses: **23** "Next, take the choicest perfumes: 500 units of solidified myrrh, and half that amount, 250 units, of sweet cinnamon, 250 units of sweet calamus, **24** and 500 units of cassia, measured by the standard shekel of the holy place,*[b] along with a hin# of olive oil. **25** Then make out of it a holy anointing oil; it should be skillfully blended together.*[c] It is to be a holy anointing oil.

26 "You are to anoint the tent of meeting[d] and the ark of the Testimony with it, **27** as well as the table and all its utensils, the lampstand and its utensils, the altar of incense, **28** the altar of burnt offering and all its utensils, and the basin and its stand. **29** You must sanctify them that they may become most holy.[e] Anyone touching them is to be holy.[f] **30** And you will anoint Aaron[g] and his sons[h] and sanctify them to serve as priests to me.[i]

31 "You will speak to the Israelites, saying, 'This is to continue as a holy anointing oil to me during your generations.[j] **32** It is not to be applied to the flesh of mankind, and you must not make anything with a composition like it. It is something holy. It is to continue as something holy for you. **33** Anyone who makes an ointment like it and who puts some of it on an unauthorized person* must be cut off# from his people.'"[k]

34 Then Jehovah said to Moses: "Take equal portions of these perfumes:[a] stacte drops, onycha, perfumed galbanum, and pure frankincense. **35** Make it into an incense;[b] the spice mixture should be skillfully blended,* salted,[c] pure, and holy. **36** You are to pound some of it into fine powder and put some of it before the Testimony in the tent of meeting, where I will present myself to you. It should be most holy to you. **37** You must not make for your own use the incense that you make with this composition.[d] You are to regard it as something holy to Jehovah. **38** Whoever makes any like it to enjoy its smell must be cut off# from his people."

31 Jehovah continued to speak to Moses, saying: **2** "See, I have chosen* Bezalel[e] the son of U'ri the son of Hur of the tribe of Judah.[f] **3** I will fill him with the spirit of God, giving him wisdom, understanding, and knowledge of every kind of craftsmanship, **4** for making artistic designs, for working with gold, silver, and copper, **5** for cutting and setting stones,[g] and for making every kind of wood product.[h] **6** Moreover, to assist him I have appointed O·ho'li·ab[i] the son of A·his'a·mach of the tribe of Dan, and I am putting wisdom into the heart of all those who are skillful,* so that they may make everything I have commanded you:[j] **7** the tent of meeting,[k] the ark of the Testimony[l] and the cover[m] that is on it, all the utensils of the tent, **8** the table[n] and its utensils, the lampstand of pure gold and all its utensils,[o] the altar of incense,[p] **9** the altar of burnt offering[q] and all its

---

CHAP. 30
a 2Ch 4:6

b Nu 3:47

c Ex 37:29

d Ex 40:9
Nu 7:1

e Le 8:10

f Ex 29:37

g Le 8:12

h Nu 3:2, 3

i Ex 40:15

j Ex 37:29
1Ki 1:39
Ps 89:20

k Ex 30:37, 38

Second Col.
a Ex 25:3, 6

b Ex 37:29
Ps 141:2
Re 5:8

c Le 2:13

d Ex 30:31, 32

CHAP. 31
e Ex 37:1

f Ex 35:30-34
1Ch 2:20

g Ex 28:9-11

h 2Ch 2:13, 14

i Ex 38:23

j Ex 36:1

k Ex 36:8

l Ex 37:1

m Ex 37:6

n Ex 37:10

o Ex 37:17, 24

p Ex 37:25

q Ex 38:1
Ex 40:6

30:24 *Or "by the holy shekel." # A hin equaled 3.67 L (7.75 pt). See App. B14. 30:25, 35 *Or "like the work of an ointment maker." 30:33 *Lit., "a stranger," that is, a man not of Aaron's family. 30:33, 38 #Or "put to death."

31:2 *Lit., "called by name." 31:6 *Lit., "wise of heart."

utensils, the basin and its stand,[a] **10** the finely woven garments, the holy garments for Aaron the priest, the garments of his sons to serve as priests,[b] **11** the anointing oil, and the perfumed incense for the sanctuary.[c] They will do everything I have commanded you."

12 Jehovah said further to Moses: **13** "Speak to the Israelites and tell them, 'Especially, you are to keep my sabbaths,[d] for it is a sign between me and you during your generations in order that you may know that I, Jehovah, am sanctifying you. **14** You must keep the Sabbath, for it is something holy to you.[e] Whoever profanes it must be put to death. If anyone does any work on it, then that person* must be cut off[g] from among his people.[f] **15** Six days work may be done, but on the seventh day is a sabbath of complete rest.[g] It is something holy to Jehovah. Anyone doing work on the Sabbath day must be put to death. **16** The Israelites must keep the Sabbath; they must observe the Sabbath during all their generations. It is a lasting covenant. **17** It is an enduring sign between me and the people of Israel,[h] for in six days Jehovah made the heavens and the earth and on the seventh day he rested and refreshed himself.'"[i]

18 Now as soon as he had finished speaking with him on Mount Si′nai, he gave Moses two tablets of the Testimony,[j] tablets of stone written on by God's finger.[k]

32 Meanwhile, the people saw that Moses was taking a long time coming down from the mountain.[l] So the people gathered around Aaron and said to him: "Get up, make for us a god who will go ahead of us,[m] be-

cause we do not know what has happened to this Moses, the man who led us up out of the land of Egypt." **2** At this Aaron said to them: "Take the gold earrings[a] from the ears of your wives, your sons, and your daughters and bring them to me." **3** So all the people began taking off the gold earrings that were in their ears and bringing them to Aaron. **4** Then he took the gold from them, and he formed it with an engraving tool and made it into a statue* of a calf.[b] They began to say: "This is your God, O Israel, who led you up out of the land of Egypt."[c]

5 When Aaron saw this, he built an altar before it. Then Aaron called out: "There is a festival to Jehovah tomorrow." **6** So they got up early on the next day and began offering up burnt offerings and presenting communion sacrifices. After that the people sat down to eat and drink. Then they got up to have a good time.[d]

7 Jehovah now said to Moses: "Go, descend, because your people, whom you led up out of the land of Egypt, have corrupted themselves.[e] **8** They have quickly deviated from the way I commanded them to go.[f] They have made for themselves a statue* of a calf, and they keep bowing down to it and sacrificing to it and saying, 'This is your God, O Israel, who led you up out of the land of Egypt.'" **9** Jehovah went on to say to Moses: "I have seen that this is an obstinate* people.[g] **10** So now let me be, and I will exterminate them in my burning anger, and let me make a great nation from you instead."[h]

11 Then Moses appealed to* Jehovah his God[i] and said: "Why,

---

CHAP. 31

a Ex 30:18
  Ex 38:8

b Ex 28:2, 15
  Ex 39:1, 27
  Le 8:7

c Ex 30:25, 35
  Ex 37:29

d Ex 20:8
  Le 19:30
  Col 2:16, 17

e De 5:12

f Ex 35:2
  Nu 15:32, 36

g Ex 16:23
  Ex 20:10

h Ex 31:13

i Ge 2:2

j Ex 24:12
  Ex 32:15
  De 4:13
  De 9:15

k Mt 12:28
  Lu 11:20
  2Co 3:3

CHAP. 32

l Ex 24:18
  De 9:9

m Ac 7:40

Second Col.

a Ex 12:35, 36

b De 9:16
  Isa 46:6
  Ac 7:41

c Ex 20:4
  Ne 9:18
  Ps 106:19, 20

d 1Co 10:7

e De 4:15-18

f Ex 18:20
  Ex 20:3

g Ex 34:9
  De 9:6
  Ac 7:51

h Nu 14:12
  De 9:14

i Ps 106:23

31:14 *Or "soul." #Or "put to death."

32:4, 8 *Or "molten statue." **32:9** *Lit., "stiff-necked." **32:11** *Or "softened the face of."

O Jehovah, should you turn your burning anger against your people after bringing them out of the land of Egypt with great power and with a mighty hand?[a] **12** Why should the Egyptians say, 'He had evil intentions when he led them out. He wanted to kill them in the mountains and exterminate them from the surface of the earth'?[b] Turn from your burning anger and reconsider* your decision to bring this calamity on your people. **13** Remember your servants Abraham, Isaac, and Israel, to whom you swore by yourself and said: 'I will multiply your offspring* like the stars of the heavens,[c] and I will give all this land that I have designated to your offspring,* so that they may take it as a permanent possession.'"[d]

14 So Jehovah began to reconsider* the calamity that he had spoken of bringing on his people.[e]

15 Moses then turned and went down from the mountain with the two tablets of the Testimony[f] in his hand.[g] The tablets were inscribed on both sides; they were written on the front and on the back. **16** The tablets were the workmanship of God, and the writing was the writing of God engraved on the tablets.[h] **17** When Joshua began to hear the noise of the people because of their shouting, he said to Moses: "There is the sound of battle in the camp." **18** But Moses said:

"It is not the sound of singing
    over a victory,*
And it is not the sound of
    wailing over a defeat;
I hear the sound of another
    kind of singing."

19 As soon as Moses got near the camp and saw the calf[a] and the dances, his anger began to blaze, and he threw the tablets from his hands and shattered them at the foot of the mountain.[b] **20** He took the calf that they had made and he burned it with fire and crushed it into powder;[c] then he scattered it on the water and made the Israelites drink it.[d] **21** And Moses said to Aaron: "What did this people do to you that you have brought a great sin upon them?" **22** Aaron replied: "Do not be enraged, my lord. You well know that the people are inclined to do evil.[e] **23** So they said to me, 'Make for us a god who will go ahead of us, for we do not know what has happened to this Moses, the man who led us up out of the land of Egypt.'[f] **24** So I said to them, 'Whoever has any gold must take it off and give it to me.' Then I threw it into the fire and out came this calf."

25 Moses saw that the people were unrestrained, for Aaron had let them go unrestrained, so that they were a disgrace before their opposers. **26** Then Moses took his position in the gate of the camp and said: "Who is on Jehovah's side? Come to me!"[g] And all the Levites gathered around him. **27** He now said to them: "This is what Jehovah the God of Israel has said, 'Each of you must fasten on his sword and pass through all the camp from gate to gate, killing his brother, his neighbor, and his close companion.'"[h] **28** The Levites did what Moses said. So about 3,000 men were killed on that day. **29** Then Moses said: "Set yourselves apart* for Jehovah today, for each of you has gone against his own son and his own brother;[i] today he will give you a blessing."[j]

CHAP. 32
a De 9:18, 19

b De 9:28

c Ge 22:15-17
  Ge 35:10, 11
  Heb 6:13, 14

d Ge 13:14, 15
  Ge 26:3, 4

e Ps 106:45

f Ex 40:20
  De 5:22

g De 9:15

h Ex 31:18
  De 9:10

Second Col.
a Ne 9:18
  Ps 106:19, 20
  Ac 7:41

b De 9:16, 17

c De 7:25

d De 9:21

e Ex 15:24
  Ex 16:2
  Ex 17:2
  De 9:7
  De 31:27

f Ex 32:1
  Ac 7:40

g Jos 24:15
  2Ki 10:15

h Nu 25:5

i Nu 25:11
  De 13:6-9

j De 33:8, 9

32:12 *Or "feel regret over." **32:13** *Lit., "seed." **32:14** *Or "felt regret over." **32:18** *Or "a mighty act."

32:29 *Lit., "Fill your hand."

30 On the very next day, Moses said to the people: "You committed a very great sin, and now I will go up to Jehovah to see if I can make amends for your sin."[a] **31** So Moses returned to Jehovah and said: "What a great sin this people has committed! They made themselves a god of gold;[b] **32** But now if you are willing, pardon their sin;[c] if not, please wipe me out from your book that you have written."[d] **33** However, Jehovah said to Moses: "Whoever has sinned against me, I will wipe him out of my book. **34** Go now, lead the people to the place about which I have spoken to you. Look! My angel will go ahead of you,[e] and on the day when I make an accounting, I will bring punishment on them for their sin." **35** Then Jehovah began plaguing the people because they had made the calf, the one that Aaron had made.

33 Jehovah said further to Moses: "Go on your way from here with the people whom you led up out of the land of Egypt. Journey to the land about which I swore to Abraham, Isaac, and Jacob, saying, 'To your offspring* I will give it.'[f] **2** I will send an angel ahead of you[g] and drive out the Ca·naan·ites, the Am'or·ites, the Hit'tites, the Per'iz·zites, the Hi'vites, and the Jeb'u·sites.[h] **3** Go up to a land flowing with milk and honey.[i] But I will not go in the midst of you, for you are an obstinate* people,[j] and I might exterminate you on the way."[k]

4 When the people heard this harsh word, they began to mourn, and not one of them put on his ornaments. **5** Jehovah said to Moses: "Say to the Israelites, 'You are an obstinate* people.'[l] In one moment I could go through the midst of you and exterminate you.[a] So now keep your ornaments off while I consider what to do to you.'" **6** So from Mount Ho'reb onward, the Israelites refrained from wearing* their ornaments.

7 Now Moses took his tent and pitched it outside the camp, at some distance from the camp, and he called it a tent of meeting. Everyone inquiring of Jehovah[b] would go out to the tent of meeting, which was outside the camp. **8** As soon as Moses went out to the tent, all the people would rise and stand at the entrance of their own tents, and they would gaze after Moses until he entered into the tent. **9** As soon as Moses would go into the tent, the pillar of cloud[c] would come down and stand at the entrance of the tent while God spoke with Moses.[d] **10** When all the people saw the pillar of cloud standing at the entrance of the tent, each of them rose and bowed down at the entrance of his own tent. **11** Jehovah spoke to Moses face-to-face,[e] just as one man would speak to another man. When he returned to the camp, Joshua[f] the son of Nun, his minister and attendant,[g] would not depart from the tent.

12 Now Moses said to Jehovah: "See, you are saying to me, 'Lead this people up,' but you have not let me know whom you will send with me. Moreover, you have said, 'I know you by name,* and you have also found favor in my eyes.' **13** Please, if I have found favor in your eyes, make me know your ways,[h] so that I may know you and continue to find favor in your eyes. Consider, too, that this nation is your people."[i] **14** So he said: "I my-

CHAP. 32
a Nu 16:47
Nu 21:7
De 9:18
b Ex 20:23
c Nu 14:19
d Php 4:3
Re 3:5
e Ex 23:20
Ex 33:2
CHAP. 33
f Ge 12:7
Ge 26:3
g Ex 23:20
Ex 32:34
h De 7:1, 22
Nu 24:11
i Ex 3:8
De 8:7-9
j Ex 32:9
De 9:6
Ac 7:51
k Ex 32:10
Nu 16:21
l Ex 34:9
De 9:6
Ac 7:51

Second Col.
a Nu 16:45
b Ex 18:25, 26
Nu 27:1-5
c Ex 13:21
Ps 99:7
d Nu 11:16, 17
Nu 12:5
e Ex 33:22, 23
Nu 12:8
De 34:10
Joh 1:18
Joh 6:46
Ac 7:38
f Nu 11:28
De 1:38
Jos 1:1
g Ex 17:9
Ex 24:13
h Ps 25:4
Ps 27:11
Ps 86:11
Ps 119:33
Isa 30:21
i De 9:26

33:1 *Lit., "seed." **33:3, 5** *Lit., "stiffnecked." **33:6** *Lit., "stripped off." **33:12** *Or "I have chosen you."

self* will go with you,[a] and I will
give you rest."[b] **15** Then Moses
said to him: "If you yourself are*
not going along, do not lead us
up from here. **16** How will it be
known that I have found favor in
your eyes, I and your people? Is
it not by your going along with
us,[c] so that I and your people
will be distinguished from every
other people on the face of the
earth?"[d]

17 Jehovah went on to say to
Moses: "I will also do this thing
that you request, because you
have found favor in my eyes and
I know you by name." **18** Then
he said: "Please show me your
glory." **19** But he said: "I will
make all my goodness pass before your face, and I will declare before you the name of
Jehovah;[e] and I will favor the
one whom I favor, and I will show
mercy to the one to whom I show
mercy."[f] **20** But he added: "You
cannot see my face, for no man
can see me and live."

21 Jehovah said further:
"Here is a place near me. Station
yourself on the rock. **22** When
my glory is passing by, I will
place you in a crevice of the
rock, and I will shield you with
my hand until I have passed by.
23 After that I will take my hand
away, and you will see my back.
But my face may not be seen."[g]

34 Then Jehovah said to Moses: "Carve out for your-
self two tablets of stone like the
first ones,[h] and I will write on the
tablets the words that appeared
on the first tablets,[i] which you
shattered.[j] **2** Get ready for the
morning, as you will go up in the
morning to Mount Si'nai and station yourself before me there on
the top of the mountain.[k] **3** But
nobody may go up with you, and
nobody else should be seen anywhere on the mountain. Not even
the flocks or herds should graze
in front of that mountain."[a]

4 So Moses carved out two
tablets of stone like the first
ones and got up early in the
morning and went up Mount Si'-
nai, just as Jehovah had commanded him, and he took the
two tablets of stone in his hand.
5 Then Jehovah came down[b] in
the cloud and stationed himself with him there and declared
the name of Jehovah.[c] **6** Jehovah was passing before him
and declaring: "Jehovah, Jehovah, a God merciful[d] and compassionate,*[e] slow to anger[f] and
abundant in loyal love#[g] and
truth,△[h] **7** showing loyal love to
thousands,[i] pardoning error and
transgression and sin,[j] but he
will by no means leave the guilty
unpunished,[k] bringing punishment for the error of fathers
upon sons and upon grandsons,
upon the third generation and
upon the fourth generation."[l]

8 Moses hurried to bow low
to the earth and prostrate himself. **9** Then he said: "If, now,
I have found favor in your eyes,
O Jehovah, then please, Jehovah, go along with us in our
midst,[m] although we are an obstinate* people,[n] and forgive our
error and our sin,[o] and take us
as your own possession." **10** In
turn he said: "Here I am making
a covenant: Before all your people, I will do wonderful things
that have never been done* in all
the earth or among all the nations,[p] and all the people among
whom you live will see the work
of Jehovah, for it is an awe-
inspiring thing that I am doing
with you.[q]

11 "Pay attention to what I am
commanding you today.[r] Here I

33:14 *Lit., "My face." **33:15** *Lit., "If your face is."

34:6 *Or "gracious." #Or "loving-kindness." △Or "faithfulness." **34:9** *Lit., "stiff-necked." **34:10** *Or "created."

CHAP. 33

a Ex 13:21, Ex 40:34, Jos 1:5, 17, Isa 63:9
b Jos 21:44, Jos 23:1
c Nu 14:13, 14
d De 4:34, 2Sa 7:23, Ps 147:20
e Ex 3:13, Ex 6:3, Ex 34:6
f Ro 9:15
g Joh 1:18

CHAP. 34

h De 10:1
i De 9:10
j Ex 32:19, De 9:17
k Ex 19:20, Ex 24:12

Second Col.

a Ex 19:12, 13
b Ac 7:38
c Ex 6:3, Ex 33:19
d Lu 6:36
e Ex 22:27, 2Ch 30:9, Ne 9:17, Ps 86:15, Joe 2:13
f Nu 14:18, 2Pe 3:9
g Jer 31:3, La 3:22, Mic 7:18
h Ps 31:5, Ro 2:2
i Da 9:4
j Ps 103:12, Isa 55:7, Eph 4:32, 1Jo 1:9
k De 32:35, Jos 24:19, Ro 2:5, 2Pe 2:4, Jude 14, 15
l Ex 20:5, De 30:19, 1Sa 15:2
m Ex 33:14
n Ex 32:9, Ex 33:3
o Nu 14:19
p 2Sa 7:23, Ps 147:19, 20
q Ex 33:16, De 10:21
r Ex 19:5, 6, De 12:28

am driving out from before you the Am′or·ites, the Ca′naan-ites, the Hit′tites, the Per′iz-zites, the Hi′vites, and the Jeb′-u·sites.ᵃ 12 Be careful that you do not make a covenant with the inhabitants of the land to which you are going,ᵇ or it may prove to be a snare among you.ᶜ 13 But you are to pull down their altars, you are to shatter their sacred pillars, and their sacred poles* you are to cut down.ᵈ 14 You must not bow down to another god,ᵉ for Jehovah is known for* requir-ing exclusive devotion.# Yes, he is a God who requires exclusive devotion.ᶠ 15 Be careful not to make a covenant with the inhab-itants of the land, because when they prostitute themselves to their gods and sacrifice to their gods,ᵍ someone will invite you and you will eat from his sac-rifice.ʰ 16 Then you will sure-ly take some of their daughters for your sons,ⁱ and their daugh-ters will prostitute themselves to their gods and cause your sons to prostitute themselves to their gods.ʲ

17 "You must not make gods of cast metal.ᵏ

18 "You are to observe the Festival of Unleavened Bread.ˡ You will eat unleavened bread, just as I have commanded you; do this for seven days at the appointed time in the month of A′bib,*ᵐ because it was in the month of A′bib that you came out of Egypt.

19 "Every firstborn male* is mine,ⁿ including all your live-stock, whether the first male bull or sheep.ᵒ 20 The firstling of a donkey you are to redeem with a

sheep. But if you do not redeem it, then you must break its neck. You are to redeem every first-born of your sons.ᵃ No one may appear before me empty-handed.

21 "Six days you are to work, but on the seventh day you will rest.*ᵇ Even during plowing time and in harvest, you will rest.

22 "And you will celebrate your Festival of Weeks with the first ripe fruits of the wheat har-vest, and the Festival of Ingath-ering* at the turn of the year.ᶜ

23 "Three times a year, all your men* are to appear be-fore the true Lord, Jehovah, the God of Israel.ᵈ 24 For I will drive the nations away from be-fore you,ᵉ and I will enlarge your territory, and nobody will desire your land while you are going up to see the face of Jehovah your God three times a year.

25 "You must not offer the blood of my sacrifice along with anything leavened.ᶠ The sacrifice of the festival of the Passover should not be kept overnight un-til the morning.ᵍ

26 "The best of the first ripe fruits of your soil you are to bring to the house of Jehovah your God.ʰ

"You must not boil a young goat in its mother's milk."ⁱ

27 Jehovah went on to say to Moses: "You are to write down these words,ʲ because in accor-dance with these words, I am making a covenant with you and with Israel."ᵏ 28 And he re-mained there with Jehovah 40 days and 40 nights. He ate no bread and drank no water.ˡ And He wrote on the tablets the words of the covenant, the Ten Commandments.*ᵐ

CHAP. 34
ᵃ Ex 3:8
 Ex 33:2
 De 7:1
ᵇ De 7:2
ᶜ Ex 23:32, 33
ᵈ Ex 23:24
 De 12:3
ᵉ Ex 20:3
 1Co 10:14
 1Jo 5:21
ᶠ Jos 24:19
ᵍ 1Co 10:20
ʰ Nu 25:2
 2Co 6:14
ⁱ Ezr 9:2
ʲ De 7:4
 De 31:16
 Jg 2:17
 Jg 8:33
 1Ki 11:2
 Ne 13:26
 Ps 106:28
ᵏ Ex 32:8
 Le 19:4
ˡ Le 23:6
ᵐ Ex 23:15
ⁿ Ex 13:2
 Lu 2:23
ᵒ Ex 22:30

Second Col.
ᵃ Ex 13:15
 Nu 18:15, 16
ᵇ De 5:12
ᶜ Ex 23:16
 Le 23:34
ᵈ De 16:16
ᵉ Ex 34:11
ᶠ Ex 23:18
ᵍ Ex 12:10
 Nu 9:12
ʰ Nu 18:8, 12
 De 26:2
 Pr 3:9
ⁱ Ex 23:19
 De 14:21
ʲ Ex 24:4
 De 31:9, 11
ᵏ Ex 24:8
 De 4:13
ˡ De 9:18
ᵐ Ex 31:18
 De 10:2

34:13 *See Glossary. 34:14 *Lit., "Je-hovah, his name is." #Or "not toler-ating rivals." 34:18 *See App. B15. 34:19 *Lit., "Everything that opens the womb."

34:21 *Or "keep sabbath." 34:22 *Also known as the Festival of Booths (Tabernacles). 34:23 *Or "males." 34:28 *Lit., "the Ten Words." Also known as the Decalogue.

29 Moses then came down from Mount Si'nai, and the two tablets of the Testimony were in his hand.[a] When he came down from the mountain, Moses did not know that the skin of his face was emitting rays because he had been speaking with God. **30** When Aaron and all the Israelites saw Moses, they noticed that the skin of his face emitted rays and they were afraid to go near him.[b]

31 But Moses called to them, so Aaron and all the chieftains of the assembly came to him, and Moses spoke with them. **32** After that all the Israelites came near to him, and he gave them all the commands that Jehovah had given him on Mount Si'nai.[c] **33** When Moses would finish speaking with them, he would put a veil over his face.[d] **34** But when Moses would go in before Jehovah to speak with him, he would take off the veil until he went out.[e] Then he went out and revealed to the Israelites the commands he had received.[f] **35** And the Israelites saw that the skin of Moses' face emitted rays; then Moses put the veil back over his face until he went in to speak with God.*[g]

35 Moses later gathered the entire assembly of the Israelites together and said to them: "These are the things that Jehovah has commanded to be done:[h] **2** Work may be done for six days, but the seventh day will become something holy to you, a sabbath of complete rest to Jehovah.[i] Anybody doing work on it will be put to death.[j] **3** You must not light a fire in any of your dwelling places on the Sabbath day."

4 Moses then said to the entire assembly of the Israelites:

"This is what Jehovah has commanded, **5** 'Take up a contribution for Jehovah from among yourselves.[a] Let everyone with a willing heart[b] bring a contribution for Jehovah: gold, silver, copper, **6** blue thread, purple wool, scarlet material, fine linen, goat hair,[c] **7** ram skins dyed red, sealskins, acacia wood, **8** oil for the lamps, balsam for the anointing oil and for the perfumed incense,[d] **9** onyx stones, and other stones for setting in the eph'od[e] and the breastpiece.[f]

10 "'Let all who are skilled*[g] among you come and make everything that Jehovah has commanded, **11** namely, the tabernacle with its tent and its covering, its clasps and its panel frames, its bars, its pillars, and its socket pedestals; **12** the Ark[h] and its poles,[i] the cover,[j] and the curtain[k] for the screen; **13** the table[l] and its poles and all its utensils and the showbread;[m] **14** the lampstand[n] for light and its utensils and its lamps and the oil for lighting;[o] **15** the altar of incense[p] and its poles; the anointing oil and the perfumed incense;[q] the screen* for the tabernacle's entrance; **16** the altar of burnt offering[r] and its copper grating, its poles and all its utensils; the basin and its stand;[s] **17** the hanging curtains of the courtyard,[t] its pillars and its socket pedestals; the screen* of the entrance to the courtyard; **18** the tent pins of the tabernacle and the tent pins of the courtyard and their cords;[u] **19** the finely woven garments[v] for ministering in the sanctuary, the holy garments for Aaron[w] the priest, and the garments of his sons for serving as priests.'"

20 So all the assembly of the Israelites went out from

CHAP. 34	
a	Ex 32:15
b	2Co 3:7
c	Ex 24:3
	De 1:3
d	2Co 3:13
e	2Co 3:16
f	De 27:10
g	2Co 3:7, 13
CHAP. 35	
h	Ex 34:32
i	Ex 20:9, 10
	Le 23:3
j	Ex 31:14, 15
	Nu 15:32, 35
Second Col.	
a	Ex 25:2-7
	Ex 35:29
b	2Co 8:12
	2Co 9:7
c	Ex 26:7
	Ex 36:8
d	Ex 25:3, 6
e	Ex 28:9
	Ex 39:14
f	Ex 28:15
g	Ex 31:6
	Ex 36:1
h	Ex 25:10
i	Ex 25:13
j	Ex 25:17
k	Ex 26:31
l	Ex 25:23
m	Ex 25:30
	Le 24:5, 6
n	Ex 25:31
o	Ex 27:20
p	Ex 30:1
	Ex 37:25
	Ex 40:5
q	Ex 30:34, 35
r	Ex 27:1
s	Ex 30:18
	Ex 38:8
t	Ex 27:9
u	Ex 27:19
v	Ex 31:6, 10
	Ex 39:33, 41
w	Ex 39:1

34:35 *Lit., "him."

35:10 *Lit., "wise of heart." 35:15, 17 *Or "curtain."

before Moses. 21 Then everyone whose heart impelled him[a] and everyone whose spirit incited him came and brought their contribution for Jehovah to be used for the tent of meeting, for all its service, and for the holy garments. 22 They kept coming, the men along with the women, each with a willing heart, bringing brooches, earrings, rings, and all other jewelry, as well as all sorts of articles of gold. They all presented their offerings* of gold to Jehovah.[b] 23 And all who had blue thread, purple wool, scarlet material, fine linen, goat hair, ram skins dyed red, and sealskins brought them. 24 All those contributing silver and copper brought Jehovah's contribution, and all who had acacia wood for any part of the work brought it.

25 All the skilled women[c] spun with their hands, and they brought what they had spun: blue thread, purple wool, scarlet material, and fine linen. 26 And all the skilled women whose hearts impelled them spun the goat hair.

27 And the chieftains brought onyx stones and other stones to be set in the eph′od and the breastpiece,[d] 28 and the balsam and the oil for lighting and for the anointing oil[e] and for the perfumed incense.[f] 29 All the men and women whose hearts incited them brought something for the work that Jehovah, through Moses, had commanded to be done; the Israelites brought it as a voluntary offering to Jehovah.[g]

30 Then Moses said to the Israelites: "See, Jehovah has chosen Bez′al·el the son of U′ri the son of Hur of the tribe of Judah.[h] 31 He has filled him with the spirit of God, giving him wisdom,

understanding, and knowledge of every sort of craftsmanship 32 for making artistic designs, for working with gold, silver, and copper, 33 for cutting and setting stones, and for making all kinds of artistic wood products. 34 And he has put it into his heart to teach, he and O·ho′li·ab[a] the son of A·his′a·mach of the tribe of Dan. 35 He has filled them with skill*[b] to do all the work of a craftsman, an embroiderer, and a weaver using blue thread, purple wool, scarlet material, and fine linen, and of a loom worker. These men will do every sort of work and prepare every sort of design.

36 "Bez′al·el will work along with O·ho′li·ab and every skilled man* to whom Jehovah has given wisdom and understanding so as to know how to do all the work of the holy service just as Jehovah has commanded."[c]

2 Moses then called Bez′al·el and O·ho′li·ab and every skilled man into whose heart Jehovah had put wisdom,[d] everyone whose heart impelled him to volunteer to do the work.[e] 3 Then they took from Moses all the contribution[f] that the Israelites had brought for the work of the holy service. However, these continued to bring him voluntary offerings, morning after morning.

4 Then after they started the holy work, all the skilled workers were coming, one after another, 5 and they were telling Moses: "The people are bringing much more than what is required for the work that Jehovah has commanded to be done." 6 So Moses commanded that an announcement be made throughout the camp, saying: "Men and

---

CHAP. 35
a Ex 25:2
  Ex 36:2
  2Co 8:12
  2Co 9:7

b Ex 38:24

c Ex 28:3
  Ex 31:6
  Ex 36:8

d Ex 28:15, 28
  Ex 39:15, 21

e Ex 30:23-25

f Ex 30:34, 35

g Ex 36:5
  2Co 9:7

h Ex 31:2-6

Second Col.
a Ex 36:1

b Ex 31:3

CHAP. 36
c Ex 25:9
  Ex 31:6

d Ex 28:3
  Ex 35:10

e Ex 35:21, 26

f Ex 35:5-9
  Pr 3:9
  2Co 9:7

35:22 *Or "wave offerings."   35:35 *Lit., "wisdom of heart."   36:1 *Lit., "every man wise of heart."

women, do not bring any more goods for the holy contribution." With that the people were restrained from bringing in anything else. 7 The goods were enough for all the work to be done, and more than enough.

8 So all the skilled workers[a] made the tabernacle[b] of ten tent cloths of fine twisted linen, blue thread, purple wool, and scarlet material; he* made them with cherubs embroidered on them.[c] 9 Each tent cloth was 28 cubits* long and 4 cubits wide. All the tent cloths were the same size. 10 Then he joined five of the tent cloths together, and the other five tent cloths he joined together. 11 After that he made loops of blue thread on the edge of the one tent cloth where it would join. He did the same on the edge of the outermost tent cloth at the corresponding place where it would join. 12 He made 50 loops on the one tent cloth and 50 loops on the other edge of the tent cloth at the place where it would join so that the loops would be opposite one another. 13 Finally, he made 50 gold clasps and joined the tent cloths together with the clasps, so that the tabernacle became one unit.

14 Then he made tent cloths of goat hair for the tent over the tabernacle. He made 11 tent cloths.[d] 15 Each tent cloth was 30 cubits long and 4 cubits wide. The 11 tent cloths were the same size. 16 Then he joined five of the tent cloths together, and he joined the other six tent cloths together. 17 Next he made 50 loops along the edge of the outermost tent cloth where it joined, and he made 50 loops along the edge of the oth-

er tent cloth that joined with it. 18 And he made 50 copper clasps for joining the tent together to become one unit.

19 He made a covering for the tent out of ram skins dyed red and a covering out of sealskins to go over that.[a]

20 Then he made out of acacia wood[b] the tabernacle's panel frames, which stood upright.[c] 21 Each panel frame was ten cubits high and one and a half cubits wide. 22 Each panel frame had two tenons* joined to each other. That is how he made all the panel frames of the tabernacle. 23 Thus he made the panel frames for the south side of the tabernacle, 20 panel frames, facing south. 24 Then he made 40 socket pedestals of silver to go under the 20 panel frames, two socket pedestals beneath one panel frame for its two tenons and two socket pedestals under each following panel frame for its two tenons.[d] 25 For the other side of the tabernacle, the northern side, he made 20 panel frames 26 and their 40 socket pedestals of silver, two socket pedestals beneath the one panel frame and two socket pedestals beneath each of the other panel frames.

27 For the rear section of the tabernacle to the west, he made six panel frames.[e] 28 He made two panel frames as corner posts of the tabernacle at the two rear corners. 29 The posts were doubled from the bottom to the top, up to the first ring. That is what he did with the two corner posts. 30 So they amounted to eight panel frames along with their 16 socket pedestals of silver, two socket pedestals under each panel frame.

31 Then he made bars of acacia wood, five bars for the panel

CHAP. 36
a Ex 31:6

b Ex 25:9
Ex 39:32
Heb 9:9

c Ex 26:1-6

d Ex 26:7-11

Second Col.
a Ex 26:14

b Ex 25:10, 23
Ex 27:1
Ex 30:5
Ex 36:36

c Ex 26:15-18

d Ex 26:19-21

e Ex 26:22-25

36:8 *Evidently referring to Bezalel. 36:9 *A cubit equaled 44.5 cm (17.5 in.). See App. B14.

36:22 *Or "upright posts."

frames of the one side of the tabernacle[a] **32** and five bars for the panel frames of the other side of the tabernacle and five for the panel frames of the tabernacle for the rear section to the west. **33** Then he made the middle bar to extend along the middle of the panel frames from one end to the other. **34** He overlaid the panel frames with gold, and he made their rings of gold as holders for the bars, and he overlaid the bars with gold.[b]

35 Then he made a curtain[c] of blue thread, purple wool, scarlet material, and fine twisted linen. He made it with cherubs[d] embroidered on it.[e] **36** Then he made for it four acacia pillars and overlaid them with gold, along with hooks of gold, and cast four socket pedestals of silver for them. **37** Next he made a screen* for the entrance of the tent out of blue thread, purple wool, scarlet material, and fine twisted linen woven together,[f] **38** as well as its five pillars and their hooks. He overlaid their tops and their connectors* with gold, but their five socket pedestals were of copper.

37 Bez·al′el[g] then made the Ark[h] of acacia wood. It was two and a half cubits* long and a cubit and a half wide and a cubit and a half high.[i] **2** He overlaid it with pure gold inside and outside and made a border* of gold around it.[j] **3** After that he cast four rings of gold for it, for above its four feet, with two rings on its one side and two rings on its other side. **4** He next made poles of acacia wood and overlaid them with gold.[k] **5** Then he put the poles through

the rings on the sides of the Ark for carrying the Ark.[a]

6 He made the cover of pure gold.[b] It was two and a half cubits long and a cubit and a half wide.[c] **7** He then made two cherubs[d] of hammered gold on both ends of the cover.[e] **8** One cherub was on one end, and the other cherub on the other end. He made the cherubs on both ends of the cover. **9** The two cherubs spread out their wings upward, overshadowing the cover with their wings.[f] They were facing each other, and their faces were turned toward the cover.[g]

10 He then made the table of acacia wood.[h] It was two cubits long, a cubit wide, and a cubit and a half high.[i] **11** And he overlaid it with pure gold and made a border* of gold around it. **12** Next he made a rim the width of a handbreadth# to go around it and a border* of gold to go around the rim. **13** Further, he cast four rings of gold for it and placed the rings on the four corners where the four legs were attached. **14** The rings were near the rim, as holders for the poles used for carrying the table. **15** Then he made the poles of acacia wood and overlaid them with gold for carrying the table. **16** After that he made out of pure gold the utensils that went on the table—its dishes, its cups, its bowls, and its pitchers from which drink offerings would be poured.[j]

17 Then he made the lampstand[k] of pure gold. He made the lampstand of hammered work. Its base, its stem, its cups, its knobs, and its blossoms were one piece.[l] **18** Six branches were extending out from its stem, three branches of the

CHAP. 36

a Ex 26:26-28

b Ex 26:29

c Ex 40:21
Heb 10:19, 20

d Ge 3:24

e Ex 26:31, 32

f Ex 26:36, 37

CHAP. 37

g Ex 31:2-5
Ex 38:22

h Ex 40:3
Nu 10:33

i Ex 25:10-15

j Heb 9:4

k 2Ch 5:9

Second Col.

a Jos 3:8

b Le 16:2, 14
1Ch 28:11

c Ex 25:17-20

d Ge 3:24

e Ex 40:20

f Heb 9:5

g 1Sa 4:4
Ps 80:1

h Ex 40:4

i Ex 25:23-28

j Ex 25:29

k Ex 40:24
Le 24:4
2Ch 13:11

l Ex 25:31-39

36:37 *Or "curtain." 36:38 *Or "rings; hoops; bands" for attachments. 37:1 *A cubit equaled 44.5 cm (17.5 in.). See App. B14. 37:2, 11, 12 *Or "molding."

37:12 #About 7.4 cm (2.9 in.). See App. B14.

lampstand from its one side and three branches from its other side. **19** Three cups shaped like almond flowers were on the one set of branches, with knobs and blossoms alternating, and three cups shaped like almond flowers were on the other set of branches, with knobs and blossoms alternating. This was done for the six branches extending out from the stem of the lampstand. **20** And on the stem of the lampstand were four cups shaped like almond flowers, with knobs and blossoms alternating. **21** There was a knob under the first two branches that extended out of the stem and a knob under the next two branches and a knob under the next two branches, for the six branches extending out from the stem of the lampstand. **22** The knobs and the branches and the whole lampstand were made to be one piece of pure, hammered gold. **23** Then he made its seven lamps[a] and its snuffers* and its fire holders out of pure gold. **24** He made it, along with all its utensils, from a talent* of pure gold.

25 He now made the altar of incense[b] out of acacia wood. It was square, a cubit long, a cubit wide, and two cubits high. Its horns were one piece with it.[c] **26** He overlaid it with pure gold, its top surface and its sides all around and its horns, and he made a border* of gold around it. **27** He made two rings of gold for it below its border* on two opposite sides to hold the poles used for carrying it. **28** After that he made the poles of acacia wood and overlaid them with gold. **29** He also made the holy anointing

oil[a] and the pure, perfumed incense,[b] skillfully blended.*

38 He made the altar of burnt offering out of acacia wood. It was square, five cubits* long, five cubits wide, and three cubits high.[c] **2** Then he made its horns on its four corners. Its horns were one piece with it. Next he overlaid it with copper.[d] **3** After that he made all the utensils of the altar, the cans, the shovels, the bowls, the forks, and the fire holders. All its utensils he made of copper. **4** He also made a grating for the altar, a network of copper, under its rim, down toward its center. **5** He cast four rings on the four corners near the grating of copper, as holders for the poles. **6** After that he made the poles of acacia wood and overlaid them with copper. **7** He inserted the poles into the rings on the sides of the altar for carrying it. He made the altar in the form of a hollow chest of planks.

8 Then he made the basin of copper[e] and its copper stand; he used the mirrors* of the women who were organized to serve at the entrance of the tent of meeting.

9 Then he made the courtyard.[f] For the south side of the courtyard, facing south, he made the hanging curtains of fine twisted linen, for 100 cubits.[g] **10** There were 20 pillars and 20 socket pedestals of copper, and the hooks of the pillars and their connectors* were of silver. **11** Also, for the north side, there were 100 cubits of hanging curtains. Their 20 pillars and their

---

CHAP. 37
a Nu 8:2

b Ex 30:7
Ex 40:5
Ps 141:2
Re 8:3

c Ex 30:1-5

Second Col.
a Ex 30:25, 33
Ex 40:9

b Ex 30:34, 35
Ps 141:2

CHAP. 38
c Ex 27:1-8
Ex 40:10

d 2Ch 1:5

e Ex 30:18
Le 8:11
1Ki 7:23

f Ex 40:8

g Ex 27:9-15

37:23 *Or "tongs." 37:24 *A talent equaled 34.2 kg (1,101 oz t). See App. B14. 37:26, 27 *Or "molding."

37:29 *Or "like the work of an ointment maker." 38:1 *A cubit equaled 44.5 cm (17.5 in.). See App. B14. 38:8 *That is, highly polished metal mirrors. 38:10 *Or "rings; hoops; bands" for attachments.

20 socket pedestals were of copper. The hooks of the pillars and their connectors* were of silver. **12** But for the west side, the hanging curtains were for 50 cubits. There were ten pillars and ten socket pedestals, and the hooks of the pillars and their connectors* were of silver. **13** The width of the east side, toward the sunrising, was 50 cubits. **14** There were 15 cubits of hanging curtains on the one wing, with three pillars and three socket pedestals. **15** And for the other wing on the other side of the entrance of the courtyard, there were hanging curtains for 15 cubits, with three pillars and three socket pedestals. **16** All the hanging curtains around the courtyard were of fine twisted linen. **17** The socket pedestals for the pillars were of copper, the hooks of the pillars and their connectors* were of silver, the tops were overlaid with silver, and there were silver fasteners for all the pillars of the courtyard.[a]

18 The screen* of the entrance of the courtyard was woven of blue thread, purple wool, scarlet material, and fine twisted linen. It was 20 cubits long and 5 cubits high, the same height as the hanging curtains of the courtyard.[b] **19** Their four pillars and their four socket pedestals were made of copper. Their hooks were of silver, and their tops and connectors* were overlaid with silver. **20** All the tent pins for the tabernacle and around the courtyard were of copper.[c]

21 The following is the inventory of the tabernacle, the tabernacle of the Testimony,[d] which was inventoried at the command of Moses, as the responsibility of the Levites[a] under the direction of Ith′a·mar[b] the son of Aaron the priest. **22** Bez′al·el[c] the son of U′ri the son of Hur of the tribe of Judah did all that Jehovah had commanded Moses. **23** With him was O·ho′li·ab[d] the son of A·his′a·mach of the tribe of Dan, a craftsman and an embroiderer and a weaver of the blue thread, the purple wool, the scarlet material, and the fine linen.

24 All the gold that was used for all the work of the holy place equaled the amount of the gold of the wave offering,[e] 29 talents* and 730 shekels[g] by the standard shekel of the holy place.[Δ] **25** And the silver of the ones registered of the assembly was 100 talents and 1,775 shekels by the standard shekel of the holy place.[Δ] **26** The half shekel for each individual was half a shekel by the standard shekel of the holy place[Δ] for every man who was among those registered from 20 years of age and up,[f] amounting to 603,550.[g] **27** The casting of the socket pedestals of the holy place and the socket pedestals of the curtain amounted to 100 talents; 100 socket pedestals equaled 100 talents, one talent for each socket pedestal.[h] **28** From the 1,775 shekels, he made hooks for the pillars and overlaid their tops and joined them together.

29 The copper of the offering* was 70 talents and 2,400 shekels. **30** With this he made the socket pedestals of the entrance of the tent of meeting, the copper altar and its copper grating, all the utensils of the altar, **31** the socket ped-

---

CHAP. 38	
a	Ex 27:17
b	Ex 27:16
c	Ex 27:19
d	Ex 25:16 Ex 31:18 Nu 17:7
Second Col.	
a	Nu 3:6 Nu 4:46, 47
b	Ex 6:23 Nu 4:28 1Ch 6:3
c	Ex 31:2-5 Ex 35:30 Ex 36:1 Ex 37:1 2Ch 1:5
d	Ex 31:6 Ex 35:34 Ex 36:2
e	Ex 35:22
f	Ex 30:15
g	Ex 12:37 Nu 1:45, 46
h	Ex 26:19-21 Ex 26:25, 32

38:11, 12, 17, 19 *Or "rings; hoops; bands" for attachments. **38:18** *Or "curtain." **38:24** *A talent equaled 34.2 kg (1,101 oz t). See App. B14. #A shekel equaled 11.4 g (0.367 oz t). See App. B14. **38:24-26** ΔOr "by the holy shekel." **38:29** *Or "wave offering."

estals around the courtyard, the socket pedestals of the entrance of the courtyard, and all the tent pins of the tabernacle and all the tent pins[a] around the courtyard.

39 From the blue thread, the purple wool, and the scarlet material,[b] they made finely woven garments for ministering in the holy place. They made the holy garments that were for Aaron,[c] just as Jehovah had commanded Moses.

2 He made the eph′od[d] of gold, blue thread, purple wool, scarlet material, and fine twisted linen. 3 They hammered plates of gold into thin sheets, and he cut it into threads to work in with the blue thread, the purple wool, the scarlet material, and the fine linen, and it was embroidered. 4 They made shoulder pieces for it that were attached, and it was joined to them at its two edges. 5 And the woven belt,* which was attached to the eph′od for tying it securely in position,[e] was made of the same material, of gold, blue thread, purple wool, scarlet material, and fine twisted linen, just as Jehovah had commanded Moses.

6 Then they mounted the onyx stones in gold settings, and they engraved them with the names of the sons of Israel, as they would engrave a seal.[f] 7 He placed them on the shoulder pieces of the eph′od as memorial stones for the sons of Israel,[g] just as Jehovah had commanded Moses. 8 Then he made the breastpiece[h] with the workmanship of an embroiderer, like the workmanship of the eph′od, out of gold, blue thread, purple wool, scarlet material, and fine twisted linen.[i] 9 It was square when doubled. They made the breast-

piece, which, when doubled, was as long and as wide as the span of the hand.* 10 They set four rows of stones in it. The first row was ruby, topaz, and emerald. 11 The second row was turquoise, sapphire, and jasper. 12 The third row was lesh′em stone,* agate, and amethyst. 13 And the fourth row was chrys′o·lite, onyx, and jade. They were mounted in settings of gold. 14 The stones corresponded to the names of the 12 sons of Israel, and the names were engraved like a seal, each name representing one of the 12 tribes.

15 Then they made wreathed chains on the breastpiece, like cords of pure gold.[a] 16 And they made two settings of gold and two rings of gold and attached the two rings to the two corners of the breastpiece. 17 After that they put the two cords of gold through the two rings at the corners of the breastpiece. 18 Then they put the two ends of the two cords through the two settings and attached them to the shoulder pieces on the front of the eph′od. 19 Next they made two rings of gold and set them at the two ends on the inside edge of the breastpiece, facing the eph′od.[b] 20 Then they made two more rings of gold and put them on the front of the eph′od, below the shoulder pieces and above the place where the woven belt* joined the eph′od. 21 Finally, they tied the breastpiece with a blue cord from its rings to the rings of the eph′od, in order to keep the breastpiece in its place on the eph′od, above the woven belt,* just as Jehovah had commanded Moses.

39:5, 20, 21 *Or "waistband."

39:9 *About 22.2 cm (8.75 in.). See App. B14. **39:12** *An unidentified precious stone, possibly referring to amber, hyacinth, opal, or tourmaline.

CHAP. 38
a Ex 27:19

CHAP. 39
b Ex 35:23

c Ex 28:4, 5
Ex 29:5
Ex 35:10, 19

d Ex 28:6-8
Le 8:7

e Ex 29:5

f Ex 28:9, 10

g Ex 28:12

h Le 8:8

i Ex 28:15-21

Second Col.
a Ex 28:22-25

b Ex 28:26-28

22 Then he made the sleeveless coat of the eph'od, woven by a loom worker, all of blue thread.[a] 23 The opening of the sleeveless coat was in the middle of it, like the opening of a coat of mail. Its opening had a border around it, so that it would not be torn. 24 Next they made on the hem of the sleeveless coat pomegranates of blue thread, purple wool, and scarlet material, twisted together. 25 And they made bells of pure gold and put the bells in between the pomegranates all around the hem of the sleeveless coat, in between the pomegranates; 26 they alternated a bell and a pomegranate, a bell and a pomegranate, all around the hem of the sleeveless coat, which was used for ministering, just as Jehovah had commanded Moses.

27 And they made the robes of fine linen, woven by a loom worker, for Aaron and his sons,[b] 28 and the turban[c] of fine linen, the ornamental headgear[d] of fine linen, the linen shorts*[e] of fine twisted linen, 29 and the sash of fine twisted linen, blue thread, purple wool, and scarlet material woven together, just as Jehovah had commanded Moses.

30 Finally, they made the shining plate, the holy sign of dedication,* out of pure gold and inscribed on it an inscription as one would engrave a seal: "Holiness belongs to Jehovah."[f] 31 They attached to it a cord made from blue thread in order to put it on the turban, just as Jehovah had commanded Moses.

32 So all the work for the tabernacle, the tent of meeting, was completed, and the Israelites did everything that Jehovah had commanded Moses.[g] They did just so.

33 Then they brought the tabernacle[a] to Moses, the tent[b] and all its utensils: its clasps,[c] its panel frames,[d] its bars[e] and its pillars and its socket pedestals;[f] 34 its covering of ram skins dyed red,[g] its covering of sealskins, the curtain for the screen;[h] 35 the ark of the Testimony and its poles[i] and the cover;[j] 36 the table, all its utensils[k] and the showbread; 37 the lampstand of pure gold, its lamps,[l] the row of lamps, and all its utensils[m] and the oil for lighting;[n] 38 the altar[o] of gold, the anointing oil,[p] the perfumed incense,[q] the screen*[r] for the entrance of the tent; 39 the altar of copper[s] and its grating of copper, its poles,[t] all its utensils,[u] the basin and its stand;[v] 40 the hanging curtains of the courtyard, its pillars and its socket pedestals,[w] the screen*[x] for the entrance of the courtyard, its tent cords and its tent pins[y] and all the utensils for the service of the tabernacle, for the tent of meeting; 41 the finely woven garments for ministering in the sanctuary, the holy garments for Aaron the priest,[z] and the garments of his sons for serving as priests.

42 According to all that Jehovah had commanded Moses, that was how the Israelites did all the work.[a] 43 When Moses inspected all their work, he saw that they had done it just as Jehovah had commanded; and Moses blessed them.

40 Then Jehovah said to Moses: 2 "On the first day of the first month, you are to set up the tabernacle, the tent of meeting.[b] 3 Place the ark of the Testimony in it,[c] and screen off the Ark with the curtain.[d] 4 You are to bring the table[e] in and arrange the things that be-

CHAP. 39	
a	Ex 28:31-35
b	Ex 28:39, 40
c	Ex 28:4
d	Ex 29:8, 9
e	Ex 28:42
f	Ex 28:36, 37
	Le 8:9
g	Ex 25:40
	Heb 8:5

Second Col.	
a	Ex 36:8
b	Ex 36:14
c	Ex 36:18
d	Ex 36:20
e	Ex 36:31
f	Ex 36:24
g	Ex 36:19
h	Ex 36:35
i	Ex 37:1, 4
j	Ex 37:6
k	Ex 37:10, 16
l	Ex 37:17, 23
m	Ex 25:38
n	Ex 35:27, 28
o	Ex 37:25
p	Ex 37:29
q	Ex 30:34, 35
r	Ex 36:37
s	Ex 38:1, 4
t	Ex 38:6
u	Ex 38:30
v	Ex 30:18
	Ex 38:8
w	Ex 38:9-11
x	Ex 38:18
y	Ex 38:20
z	Ex 28:3
a	Ex 35:10
	Ex 36:1

CHAP. 40	
b	Nu 7:1
c	Ex 25:21
d	Nu 4:5
	Heb 9:3
e	Ex 26:35

39:28 *Or "undergarments." 39:30 *Or "the holy diadem."

39:38, 40 *Or "curtain."

long on it and bring in the lampstand[a] and light its lamps.[b] **5** Then put the golden altar for incense[c] before the ark of the Testimony and put the screen* for the entrance of the tabernacle in place.[d]

6 "You are to put the altar of burnt offering[e] before the entrance of the tabernacle, the tent of meeting, **7** and place the basin between the tent of meeting and the altar and put water in it.[f] **8** Then set up the courtyard[g] around it and put up the screen*[h] for the entrance of the courtyard. **9** Next you are to take the anointing oil[i] and anoint the tabernacle and all that is in it,[j] and sanctify it and all its utensils, so that it will become something holy. **10** You are to anoint the altar of burnt offering and all its utensils and sanctify the altar, so that it will become a most holy altar.[k] **11** And anoint the basin and its stand and sanctify it.

12 "Then bring Aaron and his sons near to the entrance of the tent of meeting, and wash them with water.[l] **13** And you are to clothe Aaron with the holy garments[m] and anoint him[n] and sanctify him, and he will serve as priest to me. **14** After that bring his sons near, and clothe them with robes.[o] **15** You are to anoint them just as you anointed their father,[p] so that they will serve as priests to me, and their anointing will serve continually for them as a lasting priesthood during their generations."[q]

16 Moses did according to all that Jehovah had commanded him.[r] He did just so.

17 In the first month, in the second year, on the first day of the month, the tabernacle was set up.[s] **18** When Moses set up

the tabernacle, he put its socket pedestals[a] down, set up the panel frames,[b] put its bars[c] in, and set up its pillars. **19** He spread out the tent[d] over the tabernacle and placed the covering[e] of the tent over it, just as Jehovah had commanded Moses.

20 After that he took the Testimony[f] and put it into the Ark[g] and placed the poles[h] on the Ark and put the cover[i] on the Ark.[j] **21** He brought the Ark into the tabernacle and put the curtain[k] of the screen in place and screened off the ark of the Testimony,[l] just as Jehovah had commanded Moses.

22 Next he put the table[m] in the tent of meeting on the north side of the tabernacle outside the curtain, **23** and he arranged the row of bread[n] on it before Jehovah, just as Jehovah had commanded Moses.

24 He placed the lampstand[o] in the tent of meeting in front of the table, on the south side of the tabernacle. **25** He lit the lamps[p] before Jehovah, just as Jehovah had commanded Moses.

26 He next placed the golden altar[q] in the tent of meeting before the curtain, **27** in order to make perfumed incense[r] smoke on it,[s] just as Jehovah had commanded Moses.

28 Then he put the screen*[t] for the entrance of the tabernacle in place.

29 He placed the altar of burnt offering[u] at the entrance of the tabernacle, the tent of meeting, so that he might offer up the burnt offering[v] and the grain offering on it, just as Jehovah had commanded Moses.

30 He then placed the basin between the tent of meeting and the altar and put water in it for washing.[w] **31** Moses and Aaron and his sons washed their hands and their feet at it.

CHAP. 40

a Ex 25:31
  Heb 9:2
b Ex 25:37
c Ex 30:1
d Ex 26:36
e Ex 38:1
f Ex 30:18
g Ex 27:9
h Ex 27:16
  Ex 38:18
i Ex 30:23-25
j Le 8:10
  Nu 7:1
k Ex 29:36, 37
  Le 8:11
l Le 8:6
m Ex 29:5
  Le 8:7
n Le 8:12
  Ps 133:2
o Le 8:13
p Le 8:30
q Heb 7:11
r Ex 39:43
  De 4:2
s Nu 7:1
  Nu 9:15

Second Col.

a Ex 36:24
b Ex 26:15
c Ex 36:31
d Ex 26:7
e Ex 26:14
f Ex 31:18
g Ex 25:22
  Ex 37:1
h Ex 37:4
  1Ki 8:8
i Ex 37:6
  1Ch 28:11
j Le 16:2
k Ex 36:35
  Heb 10:19, 20
l Heb 9:3
m Ex 37:10
  Heb 9:2
n Ex 25:30
  Mt 12:4
o Ex 37:17
p Ex 25:37
  Ex 37:23
q Ex 30:1
  Ex 37:25
r Ex 30:34, 35
s Ex 30:7
t Ex 26:36
  Ex 36:37
u Ex 38:1
v Ex 29:38
w Ex 30:18

40:5, 8, 28 *Or "curtain."

32 Whenever they went into the tent of meeting or approached the altar, they would wash,[a] just as Jehovah had commanded Moses.

33 Finally he set up the courtyard[b] around the tabernacle and the altar and put up the screen* for the entrance of the courtyard.[c]

So Moses finished the work. **34** And the cloud began to cover the tent of meeting, and Jehovah's glory filled the tabernacle.[d] **35** Moses was not able to go into the tent of meeting because the cloud remained over it, and Jehovah's glory filled the tabernacle.[a]

36 And when the cloud lifted from the tabernacle, the Israelites would break camp during all stages of their journey.[b] **37** However, if the cloud did not lift up, then they would not break camp until the day it lifted.[c] **38** For Jehovah's cloud was over the tabernacle by day, and a fire remained over it by night in the sight of all the house of Israel during all stages of their journey.[d]

40:33 * Or "curtain."

CHAP. 40
a Ex 30:18, 19
b Ex 27:9
  Ex 38:9
c Ex 38:18
d Nu 9:15
  Re 15:8

Second Col.
a 2Ch 5:14
b Nu 10:11
  Ne 9:19
c Nu 9:17, 22
d Ex 13:21
  Nu 9:16
  Ps 78:14

LEVITICUS

OUTLINE OF CONTENTS

1 And Jehovah called Moses and spoke to him from the tent of meeting,[a] saying: **2** "Speak to the Israelites* and tell them, 'If any one of you would present an offering to Jehovah from the domestic animals, you should present your offering from the herd or from the flock.[b]

3 "'If his offering is a burnt offering from the herd, he should present a sound male animal.[c] He should present it of his own free will[d] before Jehovah at the entrance of the tent of meeting. **4** He is to lay his hand on the head of the burnt offering,

and it will be accepted in his behalf to make atonement for him.

5 "'Then the young bull must be slaughtered before Jehovah, and the sons of Aaron, the priests,[a] will present the blood and sprinkle the blood on all sides of the altar,[b] which is at the entrance of the tent of meeting. **6** The burnt offering should be skinned and cut into pieces.[c] **7** The sons of Aaron, the priests, are to put fire on the altar[d] and arrange wood on the fire. **8** The sons of Aaron, the priests, will arrange the pieces of the offering[e] with the head and the suet* over the

CHAP. 1
a Ex 40:34

b Le 22:18-20

c De 15:19, 21
Mal 1:14

d 2Co 9:7

Second Col.
a Heb 10:11

b Heb 9:13, 14

c Le 7:8

d Le 6:12

e 1Ki 18:23

1:2 *Lit., "sons of Israel."

1:8 *Or "the fat around the kidneys."

wood that is on the fire on the altar. **9** Its intestines and its shanks will be washed with water, and the priest is to make all of it smoke on the altar as a burnt offering, an offering made by fire of a pleasing* aroma to Jehovah.[a]

10 "'If his offering for a burnt offering is from the flock,[b] from the young rams or the goats, he should present a sound male.[c] **11** It is to be slaughtered at the north side of the altar before Jehovah, and the sons of Aaron, the priests, will sprinkle its blood on all sides of the altar.[d] **12** He will cut it up into pieces, and with its head and its suet,* the priest will arrange them over the wood on the fire on the altar. **13** He will wash the intestines and the shanks with water, and the priest will present all of it and make it smoke on the altar. It is a burnt offering, an offering made by fire of a pleasing* aroma to Jehovah.

14 "'However, if he offers birds as a burnt offering to Jehovah, he will present his offering from the turtledoves or the young pigeons.[e] **15** The priest will present it at the altar and make it smoke on the altar, but its blood should be drained out on the side of the altar. **16** He should remove its crop and its feathers and throw them beside the altar, to the east, to the place for the ashes.*[f] **17** He will split it at its wings without dividing it into two parts. Then the priest will make it smoke on the altar over the wood that is on the fire. It is a burnt offering, an offering made by fire of a pleasing* aroma to Jehovah.

1:9, 13, 17; 2:2, 9 *Or "appeasing; soothing." Lit., "restful." **1:12** *Or "the fat around the kidneys." **1:16** *Or "fatty ashes," that is, ashes soaked with the fat of the sacrifices.

CHAP. 1

a   Ge 8:20, 21
   Nu 15:2, 3

b   Ge 4:4

c   Le 12:6
   Le 22:18-20

d   Ex 29:16-18
   Le 8:18-21
   Le 9:12-14

e   Le 5:7
   Le 12:8
   Lu 2:24

f   Ex 27:3
   Le 4:11, 12
   Le 6:10

Second Col.

CHAP. 2

a   Le 9:17
   Nu 15:2-4

b   Ex 29:1-3
   Le 6:14, 15
   Nu 7:13

c   Nu 5:25, 26

d   Le 7:9, 10

e   Le 10:12
   Nu 18:9

f   Le 8:26, 28
   Nu 6:13, 19

g   Le 6:20, 21

h   Nu 28:9

i   Le 2:2
   Le 5:11, 12

j   Ex 29:38-41
   Nu 28:4-6

k   Nu 18:9

l   Le 6:14, 17

---

2 "'Now if someone* presents a grain offering[a] to Jehovah, his offering must be fine flour, and he should pour oil on it and put frankincense on it.[b] **2** Then he will bring it to the sons of Aaron, the priests, and the priest will take a handful of the fine flour and oil and all its frankincense, and he will make it smoke as a token offering[c] on the altar, an offering made by fire of a pleasing* aroma to Jehovah. **3** Whatever is left of the grain offering belongs to Aaron and his sons[d] as something most holy[e] from Jehovah's offerings made by fire.

4 "'If you present a grain offering that has been baked in the oven, it should be of fine flour, unleavened ring-shaped loaves mixed with oil or unleavened wafers spread with oil.[f]

5 "'If your offering is a grain offering from the griddle,[g] it should be of fine, unleavened flour mixed with oil. **6** It should be broken into pieces, and you are to pour oil on it.[h] It is a grain offering.

7 "'If your offering is a grain offering prepared in a pan, it should be made of fine flour with oil. **8** You should bring the grain offering that was made of these to Jehovah, and it will be presented to the priest, who will bring it near to the altar. **9** And the priest will lift off some of the grain offering as a token offering[i] and make it smoke on the altar as an offering made by fire of a pleasing* aroma to Jehovah.[j] **10** What is left of the grain offering belongs to Aaron and his sons as something most holy of Jehovah's offerings by fire.[k]

11 "'No grain offering that you present to Jehovah should be leavened,[l] for you must not

---

2:1 *Or "a soul." **2:2, 9** *Or "as a memorial (representative) portion of it."

make any sourdough or honey smoke as an offering made by fire to Jehovah.

12 "'You may present them to Jehovah as an offering of the firstfruits,[a] but they must not be brought to the altar as a pleasing* aroma.

13 "'Every grain offering you make is to be seasoned with salt; and you must not allow the salt of the covenant of your God to be missing from your grain offering. Along with every offering of yours, you will present salt.[b]

14 "'If you present the grain offering of the first ripe fruits to Jehovah, you should present new grain* roasted with fire, coarsely crushed new kernels, as the grain offering of your first ripe fruits.[c] **15** You are to put oil on it and place frankincense on it. It is a grain offering. **16** The priest will make it smoke as a token offering,*[d] that is, some of the coarse grain and oil along with all its frankincense, as an offering made by fire to Jehovah.

3 "'If his offering is a communion sacrifice*[e] and if he is presenting it from the herd, whether a male or a female, he should present a sound animal before Jehovah. **2** He is to lay his hand on the head of his offering, and it will be slaughtered at the entrance of the tent of meeting; and Aaron's sons, the priests, will sprinkle the blood on all sides of the altar. **3** He will present part of the communion sacrifice as an offering made by fire to Jehovah:[f] the fat[g] that covers the intestines, all the fat that surrounds the intestines, **4** and the two kidneys

with the fat on them that is near the loins. He will also remove the appendage of the liver along with the kidneys.[a] **5** Aaron's sons will make it smoke on the altar on top of the burnt offering that is placed on the wood that is over the fire;[b] it is an offering made by fire as a pleasing* aroma to Jehovah.[c]

6 "'If his offering is from the flock for a communion sacrifice to Jehovah, he will present a sound male or a female animal.[d] **7** If he is presenting a young ram as his offering, then he will present it before Jehovah. **8** He will lay his hand on the head of his offering, and it will be slaughtered in front of the tent of meeting. Aaron's sons will sprinkle its blood on all sides of the altar. **9** He will present the fat from the communion sacrifice as an offering made by fire to Jehovah.[e] He will remove the entire fat tail near the backbone, the fat that covers the intestines, all the fat that surrounds the intestines, **10** and the two kidneys with the fat on them that is near the loins. He will also remove the appendage of the liver along with the kidneys.[f] **11** And the priest will make it smoke on the altar as food,* an offering made by fire to Jehovah.[g]

12 "'If his offering is a goat, then he will present it before Jehovah. **13** He will lay his hand on its head, and it will be slaughtered before the tent of meeting, and Aaron's sons must sprinkle its blood on all sides of the altar. **14** The part he will present as his offering made by fire to Jehovah is the fat that covers the intestines, all the fat that surrounds the intestines,[h] **15** and the two kidneys with the fat on

---

CHAP. 2
a Ex 23:19
  Nu 15:20
  2Ch 31:5
  Pr 3:9

b Eze 43:23, 24

c Ex 23:16
  Ex 34:22
  Nu 28:26

d Le 5:11, 12
  Le 6:14, 15

CHAP. 3
e Le 22:21
  Nu 6:13, 14

f Le 7:29-31

g Ex 29:13
  Le 7:23-25
  1Ki 8:64

Second Col.
a Le 7:1-4

b Le 6:12

c Le 4:29, 31

d Nu 6:13, 14

e Ex 29:22
  Le 9:18-20
  2Ch 7:7

f Le 4:8, 9
  Le 9:10

g Le 4:31

h Le 4:24, 26

2:12; 3:5 *Or "appeasing; soothing." Lit., "restful." 2:14 *Or "present green ears." 2:16 *Or "as a memorial (representative) portion of it." 3:1 *Or "a sacrifice of peace offerings."

3:11 *Lit., "bread," that is, as God's share of the communion sacrifice.

them that is near the loins. He will also remove the appendage of the liver along with the kidneys. **16** The priest will make them smoke on the altar as food,* an offering made by fire for a pleasing# aroma. All the fat belongs to Jehovah.ª

17 "'It is a lasting statute for your generations, in all your dwelling places: You must not eat any fat or any bloodᵇ at all.'"

4 Jehovah went on to say to Moses: **2** "Tell the Israelites, 'If someone* sins unintentionallyᶜ by doing any of the things that Jehovah commanded should not be done:

3 "'If the anointed priestᵈ sinsᵉ and brings guilt on the people, then he must present a sound young bull to Jehovah as a sin offering for the sin he committed.ᶠ **4** He will bring the bull to the entrance of the tent of meetingᵍ before Jehovah and lay his hand on the bull's head, and he is to slaughter the bull before Jehovah.ʰ **5** Then the anointed priestⁱ will take some of the bull's blood and bring it into the tent of meeting; **6** and the priest will dip his finger in the bloodʲ and spatter some of the blood seven timesᵏ before Jehovah in front of the curtain of the holy place. **7** The priest will also put some of the blood on the horns of the altar of perfumed incense,ˡ which is before Jehovah in the tent of meeting; and he will pour all the rest of the bull's blood at the base of the altar of burnt offering,ᵐ which is at the entrance of the tent of meeting.

8 "'He will then remove all the fat of the bull of the sin offering, including the fat that cov-

ers the intestines and the fat that surrounds the intestines, **9** and the two kidneys with the fat on them that is near the loins. And he will remove the appendage of the liver along with the kidneys.ª **10** It will be the same as what is removed from a bull of the communion sacrifice.ᵇ And the priest will make them smoke on the altar of burnt offering.

11 "'But as for the skin of the bull and all its flesh along with its head, its shanks, its intestines, and its dungᶜ— **12** all the rest of the bull—he will have it taken to the outskirts of the camp to a clean place where the ashes* are discarded, and he will burn it on wood in the fire.ᵈ It should be burned where the ashes are discarded.

13 "'Now if the entire assembly of Israel has become guilty by committing a sin unintentionally,ᵉ but the congregation was unaware that they had done something that Jehovah commanded them not to do,ᶠ **14** and then the sin becomes known, the congregation must present a young bull for a sin offering and bring it before the tent of meeting. **15** The elders of the assembly will lay their hands on the bull's head before Jehovah, and the bull will be slaughtered before Jehovah.

16 "'Then the anointed priest will bring some of the bull's blood into the tent of meeting. **17** The priest is to dip his finger into the blood and spatter some of it seven times before Jehovah in front of the curtain.ᵍ **18** He will then put some of the blood on the horns of the altarʰ that is before Jehovah, which is in the tent of meeting; and he will pour all the rest of the blood at the base of the altar of burnt offer-

---

CHAP. 3
a Le 7:23
  1Sa 2:15-17

b Ge 9:4
  Le 17:10, 13
  De 12:23
  Ac 15:20, 29

CHAP. 4
c Le 5:17
  Nu 15:27, 28

d Le 8:12
  Le 21:10

e Nu 12:1, 11

f Heb 5:1-3
  Heb 7:27

g Le 6:25

h Ex 29:10, 11

i Ex 30:30

j Le 8:15, 16

k Le 16:14, 19

l Ex 30:10

m Le 5:9

Second Col.
a Le 9:8, 10

b Le 3:3, 4

c Ex 29:14

d Le 8:14, 17
  Heb 13:11

e Jos 7:11

f Nu 15:22-24

g Ex 26:31
  Ex 40:21
  Heb 10:19, 20

h Ex 30:1, 6

3:16 *Lit., "bread," that is, as God's share of the communion sacrifice. #Or "appeasing; soothing." Lit., "restful."
4:2 *Or "a soul."

4:12 *Or "fatty ashes," that is, ashes soaked with the fat of the sacrifices.

ing, which is at the entrance of the tent of meeting.[a] **19** He will remove all its fat and make it smoke on the altar.[b] **20** He is to do to the bull just as he did to the other bull of the sin offering. That is how he will do it, and the priest will make atonement for them,[c] and they will be forgiven. **21** He will have the bull taken to the outskirts of the camp and will burn it, just as he burned the first bull.[d] It is a sin offering for the congregation.[e]

22 "'When a chieftain[f] unintentionally sins by doing one of all the things that Jehovah his God commands should not be done and has become guilty, **23** or if he becomes aware of a sin that he has committed against the commandment, then he must bring a sound young male goat as his offering. **24** He will lay his hand on the head of the young goat and slaughter it in the place where the burnt offering is slaughtered before Jehovah.[g] It is a sin offering. **25** The priest will take some of the blood of the sin offering with his finger and put it on the horns[h] of the altar of burnt offering, and he will pour the rest of its blood at the base of the altar of burnt offering.[i] **26** He will make all its fat smoke on the altar like the fat of the communion sacrifice;[j] and the priest will make atonement for him for his sin, and it will be forgiven him.

27 "'If any one* of the people of the land sins unintentionally and becomes guilty by doing one of the things that Jehovah commands should not be done,[k] **28** or if he becomes aware of a sin that he has committed, then he should bring a sound young female goat as his offering for the sin he has com-

mitted. **29** He will lay his hand on the head of the sin offering and slaughter the sin offering in the same place as the burnt offering.[a] **30** The priest will take some of its blood with his finger and put it on the horns of the altar of burnt offering, and he will pour all the rest of its blood at the base of the altar.[b] **31** He will remove all its fat,[c] just as the fat is removed from the communion sacrifice,[d] and the priest will make it smoke on the altar as a pleasing* aroma to Jehovah; and the priest will make atonement for him, and it will be forgiven him.

32 "'But if he offers a lamb as his sin offering, he should bring a sound female lamb. **33** He will lay his hand on the head of the sin offering and slaughter it as a sin offering in the place where the burnt offering is slaughtered.[e] **34** The priest will take some of the blood of the sin offering with his finger and put it on the horns of the altar of burnt offering,[f] and he will pour all the rest of its blood at the base of the altar. **35** He will remove all its fat the same way that the fat of the young ram of the communion sacrifice is removed, and the priest will make them smoke on the altar on top of Jehovah's offerings made by fire;[g] and the priest will make atonement for him for the sin that he has committed, and it will be forgiven him.[h]

5 "'If someone* sins because he has heard a public call to testify*[i] and he is a witness or has seen or learned about it and

---

CHAP. 4
a Ex 27:1
  Ex 40:6

b Le 3:16

c Ex 32:30
  Le 16:17
  Nu 15:25
  Eph 1:7
  Heb 2:17

d Le 4:11, 12

e Le 16:15
  1Jo 2:1, 2

f Ex 18:21

g Le 1:10, 11
  Le 6:25
  Le 7:2

h Le 9:8, 9
  Le 16:18
  Heb 9:22

i Le 8:15

j Le 3:3-5

k Nu 15:27-29

Second Col.
a Le 1:10, 11
  Le 6:25

b Le 4:25
  Le 8:15
  Le 9:8, 9
  Heb 9:22

c Le 3:16

d Le 3:3, 4

e Le 1:10, 11

f Le 4:25
  Le 16:18

g Ex 29:13, 14
  Le 3:3, 4
  Le 6:12
  Le 9:8, 10

h Nu 15:28
  Le 1:7
  1Jo 1:7
  1Jo 2:1, 2

CHAP. 5
i Pr 29:24

4:27 *Or "any soul."

4:31 *Or "appeasing; soothing." Lit., "restful." **5:1** *Or "a soul." *Lit., "a voice of a curse (oath)." Probably an announcement regarding a wrongdoing that included a curse pronounced against the wrongdoer or against the witness in case he failed to testify.

he does not report it, then he will answer for his error.

2 "'Or when a person* touches anything unclean, whether the dead body of an unclean wild animal, an unclean domestic animal, or an unclean swarming creature,ᵃ he is unclean and has become guilty even if he does not realize it. **3** Or in case someone without being aware of it touches human uncleannessᵇ—anything unclean that may make him unclean—and he comes to know it, then he becomes guilty.

4 "'Or if someone* rashly swears to do something—whether it is to do good or to do evil, no matter what it may be—and he was unaware of it, but then he realizes that he has sworn rashly, he becomes guilty.*ᶜ

5 "'If he becomes guilty as respects one of these things, then he must confessᵈ in what way he has sinned. **6** He will also bring his guilt offering to Jehovah for the sin that he committed,ᵉ namely, a female from the flock, either a female lamb or a young female goat, for a sin offering. Then the priest will make atonement for him for his sin.

7 "'If, though, he cannot afford a sheep, he must bring to Jehovah two turtledoves or two young pigeonsᶠ as his guilt offering for the sin, one for a sin offering and one for a burnt offering.ᵍ **8** He is to bring them to the priest, who will present first the one for the sin offering and nip off its head at the front of its neck, without severing it. **9** He will spatter some of the blood of the sin offering on the side of the altar, but the remainder of the blood will be drained out at the base of the altar.ʰ It is a sin offering. **10** He will han-

dle the other one as a burnt offering according to the regular procedure;ᵃ and the priest will make atonement for him for the sin that he has committed, and it will be forgiven him.ᵇ

11 "'Now if he cannot afford two turtledoves or two young pigeons, he must bring as his offering for his sin a tenth of an eʹphah*ᶜ of fine flour for a sin offering. He should not add oil to it or place frankincense on it, for it is a sin offering. **12** He will bring it to the priest, and the priest will take from it his handful as a token offering* and make it smoke on the altar on top of Jehovah's offerings made by fire. It is a sin offering. **13** The priest will make atonement for him for the sin that he has committed, any one of these sins, and it will be forgiven him.ᵈ The remainder of the offering will become the priest's,ᵉ just like the grain offering.'"ᶠ

14 Jehovah continued to speak to Moses, saying: **15** "If someone* behaves unfaithfully by unintentionally sinning against the holy things of Jehovah,ᵍ he is to bring to Jehovah a sound ram from the flock as a guilt offering;ʰ its value in silver shekels# is set according to the standard shekel of the holy place.ᐞⁱ **16** And he will make compensation for the sin he has committed against the holy place and he will also add a fifth of its value.ʲ He will give it to the priest, so that the priest may make atonementᵏ for him with the ram of the guilt offering, and it will be forgiven him.ˡ

17 "If someone* sins by doing any of the things that Jehovah

CHAP. 5

a Le 11:21-24
Le 17:15
De 14:8

b Le 12:2
Le 13:3
Le 15:3
Nu 19:11

c Mt 5:33

d Nu 5:7
Ps 32:5
Pr 28:13
1Jo 1:9

e Le 7:1
Le 14:2, 12
Le 19:20, 21
Nu 6:12

f Lu 2:24

g Le 12:7, 8
Le 14:21, 22
Le 15:13-15

h Le 1:4, 5
Le 7:2
Heb 9:22

Second Col.

a Le 1:15-17

b Le 6:7

c Ex 16:36

d Le 4:26

e Le 2:10
Le 7:1, 6

f Le 6:14-16
1Co 9:13

g Le 10:17, 18

h Le 6:6

i Ex 30:13
Le 27:25

j Le 6:4, 5
Le 22:14
Nu 5:6, 7

k Ex 32:30

l Le 6:7
Le 19:22

5:2 *Or "soul." **5:4, 15, 17** *Or "a soul." **5:4** #The implication seems to be that he does not fulfill his vow.

5:11 *A tenth of an eʹphah equaled 2.2 L (2 dry qt). See App. B14. **5:12** *Or "as a memorial (representative) portion of it." **5:15** #A shekel equaled 11.4 g (0.367 oz t). See App. B14. ᐞOr "by the holy shekel."

commands should not be done, even if he is not aware of it, he is still guilty and will answer for his error.[a] **18** He should bring to the priest a sound ram from the flock according to the estimated value, for a guilt offering.[b] Then the priest will make atonement for him for the unintentional mistake that he unknowingly committed, and it will be forgiven him. **19** It is a guilt offering. He has certainly become guilty of sinning against Jehovah."

6 Jehovah went on to say to Moses: **2** "If someone* sins and behaves unfaithfully toward Jehovah[c] by deceiving his neighbor in connection with something entrusted to him,[d] or something deposited with him, or he robs or defrauds his neighbor, **3** or he finds something lost and is deceptive about it, and if he swears falsely over any such sin he may commit,[e] this is what he should do: **4** If he has sinned and is guilty, he must return what he stole, what he extorted, what he took by fraud, what was entrusted to him, or the lost thing that he found, **5** or anything about which he swore falsely, and he must make full compensation for it,[f] and he will add to it a fifth of its value. He will give it to the owner on the day his guilt is proved. **6** And he will bring to the priest as his guilt offering to Jehovah a sound ram from the flock according to the assessed value, for a guilt offering.[g] **7** The priest will make atonement for him before Jehovah, and he will be forgiven for anything he may have done resulting in his guilt."[h]

8 Jehovah continued to speak to Moses, saying: **9** "Command Aaron and his sons and say, 'This is the law of the burnt offering:[i] The burnt offering will remain on the hearth on the altar all night long until the morning, and the fire will be kept burning on the altar. **10** The priest will clothe himself with his official dress of linen,[a] and he will put the linen shorts*[b] on over his flesh. Then he will remove the ashes*[c] of the burnt offering that the fire had consumed on the altar and place them beside the altar. **11** Then he will take off his garments[d] and put on other garments and take the ashes to a clean place outside the camp.[e] **12** The fire will be kept burning on the altar. It must not go out. The priest must burn wood[f] on it each morning and arrange the burnt offering over it, and he will make the fat of the communion sacrifices smoke over it.[g] **13** Fire will be kept constantly burning on the altar. It must not go out.

14 "'Now this is the law of the grain offering:[h] You sons of Aaron are to present it before Jehovah in front of the altar. **15** One of them will take a handful from the fine flour of the grain offering and some of its oil and all the frankincense that is on the grain offering, and he will make it smoke on the altar as a pleasing* aroma for a token offering# to Jehovah.[i] **16** Aaron and his sons will eat what is left of it.[j] It will be eaten as unleavened bread in a holy place. They will eat it in the courtyard of the tent of meeting.[k] **17** It should not be baked with anything leavened.[l] I have given it as their share out of my offerings made by fire.[m] It is something most holy,[n] like the sin offering and like the guilt offering. **18** Every

---

CHAP. 5
a Le 5:2

b Le 6:6

CHAP. 6
c Nu 5:6

d Ex 22:7
Le 19:11

e Ex 22:10, 11
Le 19:12
Eph 4:25
Col 3:9

f Le 5:15, 16
Nu 5:6, 7

g Le 5:15
Le 7:1
Isa 53:10

h Le 5:18

i Ex 29:38-42
Nu 28:3
Heb 10:11

Second Col.
a Ex 28:39
Le 16:32
Eze 44:17

b Ex 28:42
Ex 39:27, 28

c Ex 27:3
Le 1:16

d Le 16:23
Eze 44:19

e Le 4:3, 12

f Le 1:7
Ne 13:30, 31

g Le 3:5, 16

h Le 2:1
Nu 15:3, 4

i Le 2:2, 9
Le 5:11, 12

j Le 2:3
Le 5:13
Eze 44:29
1Co 9:13

k Le 10:12

l Le 2:11

m Nu 18:9

n Le 2:3, 10

6:2 *Or "a soul."

6:10 *Or "undergarments." #Or "fatty ashes," that is, ashes soaked with the fat of the sacrifices. **6:15** *Or "appeasing; soothing." Lit., "restful." #Or "as a memorial (representative) portion of it."

male among the sons of Aaron will eat it.[a] It is their permanent allowance throughout your generations from Jehovah's offerings made by fire.[b] Everything that touches them* will become holy.'"

19 Jehovah spoke again to Moses: **20** "This is the offering that Aaron and his sons will present to Jehovah on the day he is anointed:[c] the tenth of an e′phah*[d] of fine flour as a regular grain offering,[e] half of it in the morning and half of it in the evening. **21** It will be made with oil on a griddle.[f] You will bring it well-mixed with oil and present it in pieces as a baked product of the grain offering as a pleasing* aroma to Jehovah. **22** The anointed priest who succeeds him from among his sons[g] will make it. It is a lasting regulation: As a whole offering it will be made to smoke to Jehovah. **23** Every grain offering of a priest should be a whole offering. It must not be eaten."

24 Jehovah spoke again to Moses and said: **25** "Tell Aaron and his sons, 'This is the law of the sin offering:[h] In the place where the burnt offering is slaughtered,[i] the sin offering will also be slaughtered before Jehovah. It is a most holy thing. **26** The priest who offers it for sin will eat it.[j] It will be eaten in a holy place, in the courtyard of the tent of meeting.[k]

27 "'Everything that touches its flesh will become holy, and when anyone spatters some of its blood on his garment, you should wash what was spattered with blood in a holy place. **28** The earthenware vessel in which it was boiled is to

be shattered. But if it was boiled in a copper vessel, then the vessel must be scoured and washed with water.

29 "'Every male among the priests will eat it.[a] It is something most holy.[b] **30** However, no sin offering is to be eaten if some of its blood is brought into the tent of meeting to make atonement in the holy place.[c] It is to be burned with fire.

7 "'This is the law of the guilt offering:[d] It is something most holy. **2** They will slaughter the guilt offering in the place where they slaughter the burnt offerings, and its blood[e] should be sprinkled on all sides of the altar.[f] **3** He will present all its fat,[g] including the fat tail, the fat that covers the intestines, **4** and the two kidneys with their fat that is near the loins. He will also remove the appendage of the liver along with the kidneys.[h] **5** The priest will make them smoke on the altar as an offering made by fire to Jehovah.[i] It is a guilt offering. **6** Every male among the priests will eat it,[j] and it should be eaten in a holy place. It is something most holy.[k] **7** The law regarding the sin offering applies to the guilt offering; it belongs to the priest who makes atonement with it.[l]

8 "'When the priest presents the burnt offering for someone, the skin[m] of the burnt offering that was presented to the priest will become his.

9 "'Every grain offering that is baked in the oven or prepared in the pan or on the griddle[n] belongs to the priest who presents it. It will become his.[o] **10** But every grain offering that is mixed with oil[p] or that is dry[q] will be for all of Aaron's sons; each will have an equal share.

11 "'Now this is the law of the communion sacrifice[r] that one

---

CHAP. 6
a Nu 18:10
b Le 24:8, 9
c Ex 30:30
  Heb 5:1
d Ex 16:36
e Ex 29:1, 2
  Ex 29:40, 41
  Le 2:1
  Le 9:17
  Nu 28:4, 5
f Le 2:5
  Le 7:9
  1Ch 23:29
g De 10:6
h Le 4:3
i Le 1:3, 11
j Le 10:17
  Nu 18:9
  Eze 44:29
k Ex 27:9
  Le 6:14, 16
  Eze 42:13

Second Col.
a Le 6:14, 18
  Le 21:21, 22
  Nu 18:10
b Le 6:25
c Le 4:5
  Le 10:18
  Le 16:27
  Heb 13:11

CHAP. 7
d Le 5:6
  Le 6:6
  Le 14:2, 12
  Le 19:20, 21
  Nu 6:12
e Heb 9:22
f Le 3:1, 2
  Le 5:9
g Ex 29:13, 14
  Le 3:9, 17
  Le 4:8, 9
  Le 8:18, 20
h Le 3:3, 4
i Le 3:14-16
j Le 5:13
  Le 6:14, 16
  Nu 18:9
k Le 2:3
l Le 6:25, 26
  Le 14:13
m Ex 29:14
  Le 1:6
n Le 6:20, 21
  1Ch 23:29
o Le 2:3-7
  Nu 18:9
  1Co 9:13
p Le 14:21
  Le 5:11
  Nu 5:15
r Le 3:1
  Le 7:20
  Le 22:21
  1Co 10:16

6:18 *Or "the offerings." 6:20 *A tenth of an ephah equaled 2.2 L (2 dry qt). See App. B14. 6:21 *Or "appeasing; soothing." Lit., "restful."

may present to Jehovah: **12** If he presents it as an expression of thanksgiving,ᵃ he will present along with the thanksgiving sacrifice unleavened ring-shaped loaves mixed with oil, unleavened wafers spread with oil, and ring-shaped loaves made with fine flour, well-mixed and blended with oil. **13** He will present his offering along with ring-shaped loaves of leavened bread and the thanksgiving sacrifice of his communion sacrifices. **14** He is to present from it one of each offering as a sacred portion to Jehovah; it will belong to the priest who sprinkles the blood of the communion sacrifices.ᵇ **15** The flesh of the thanksgiving sacrifice of his communion sacrifices is to be eaten on the day he offers it. He must not save any of it until morning.ᶜ

16 "'If the sacrifice of his offering is a vowᵈ or a voluntary offering,ᵉ it is to be eaten on the day he presents his sacrifice, and what is left of it may also be eaten on the next day. **17** But whatever is left of the flesh of the sacrifice on the third day is to be burned with fire.ᶠ **18** However, if any of the flesh of his communion sacrifice is eaten on the third day, the one presenting it will not be accepted with approval. It will not be credited to him; it is an offensive thing, and the person* who eats some of it will answer for his error.ᵍ **19** Flesh that touches anything unclean is not to be eaten. It is to be burned with fire. Everyone who is clean may eat the clean flesh.

20 "'But any person* who is unclean and eats the flesh of the communion sacrifice, which is for Jehovah, that person* must

be cut off△ from his people.ᵃ **21** If someone* touches anything unclean, whether the uncleanness of a manᵇ or an unclean animalᶜ or any unclean disgusting thing,ᵈ and eats some of the flesh of the communion sacrifice, which is for Jehovah, that person* must be cut off△ from his people.'"

22 Jehovah continued to speak to Moses, saying: **23** "Tell the Israelites, 'You must not eat any fatᵉ of a bull or a young ram or a goat. **24** The fat of an animal found dead and the fat of an animal killed by another animal may be used for any other purpose, but you must never eat it.ᶠ **25** For whoever eats fat from an animal that he presents as an offering made by fire to Jehovah must be cut off△ from his people. **26** "'You must not eat any bloodᵍ in any of your dwelling places, whether that of birds or that of animals. **27** Anyone* who eats any blood must be cut off△ʰ from his people.'"

28 Jehovah went on to speak to Moses, saying: **29** "Tell the Israelites, 'Whoever presents his communion sacrifice to Jehovah will bring part of the offering from his communion sacrifice to Jehovah.ⁱ **30** He will bring in his own hands the fatʲ along with the breast as an offering made by fire to Jehovah, and he will wave it back and forth as a wave offeringᵏ before Jehovah. **31** The priest will make the fat smoke on the altar,ˡ but the breast will belong to Aaron and his sons.ᵐ

32 "'You will give the right leg as a sacred portion to the priest from your communion sacrifices.ⁿ **33** The son of Aaron who presents the blood

---

CHAP. 7
a Le 22:29
2Ch 29:31

b Le 6:25, 26
Le 10:14
Nu 18:8

c Le 22:29, 30

d Le 22:21

e Le 22:23
De 12:5, 6

f Le 19:5, 6

g Le 19:7, 8

Second Col.
a Nu 19:20

b Le 12:2, 4

c Le 11:21-24
De 14:7

d Le 11:10
De 14:10

e Le 3:16, 17
Le 4:8-10
1Sa 2:16, 17

f Ex 22:31
Le 17:15

g Ge 9:4
Le 3:17
Le 17:10
De 12:16
1Sa 14:33
Ac 15:20, 29

h Le 17:14

i Le 3:1

j Le 3:3

k Ex 29:24
Le 8:25-27
Le 9:21

l Le 3:3-5

m Le 8:29

n Ex 29:27, 28
Le 10:14
Nu 6:20

7:18, 20, 21 *Or "soul." 7:20 *Or "the soul."

7:20, 21, 25, 27 △Or "put to death." 7:21 *Or "a soul." 7:27 *Or "Any soul."

of the communion sacrifices and the fat will have the right leg as his portion.[a] **34** For I take the breast of the wave offering and the leg of the sacred portion from the communion sacrifices of the Israelites, and I give them to Aaron the priest and his sons as a lasting regulation for the Israelites.[b]

35 "'This was the portion from Jehovah's offerings made by fire to be set aside for the priests, for Aaron and his sons, on the day he presented them to serve as priests to Jehovah.[c] **36** Jehovah commanded to give them this portion from the Israelites on the day he anointed them.[d] It is a permanent statute for their generations.'"

37 This is the law concerning the burnt offering,[e] the grain offering,[f] the sin offering,[g] the guilt offering,[h] the installation sacrifice,[i] and the communion sacrifice,[j] **38** just as Jehovah commanded Moses on Mount Si'nai[k] in the day he commanded the Israelites to present their offerings to Jehovah in the wilderness of Si'nai.[l]

8 Jehovah continued to speak to Moses, saying: **2** "Take Aaron and his sons with him,[m] the garments,[n] the anointing oil,[o] the bull of the sin offering, the two rams, and the basket of unleavened bread,[p] **3** and make all the assembly gather together at the entrance of the tent of meeting."

4 Then Moses did just as Jehovah had commanded him, and the assembly gathered together at the entrance of the tent of meeting. **5** Moses now said to the assembly: "This is what Jehovah has commanded us to do." **6** So Moses brought Aaron and his sons near and washed them with water.[q] **7** After that he put the robe[r] on him, wrapped him with the sash,[s] clothed him

with the sleeveless coat,[a] and put the eph'od[b] on him and tied it with the woven belt*[c] of the eph'od, binding it securely on him. **8** Next he placed the breastpiece[d] on him and put the U'rim and the Thum'mim[e] in the breastpiece. **9** Then he placed the turban[f] on his head, and he put on the front of the turban the shining plate of gold, the holy sign of dedication,*[g] just as Jehovah had commanded Moses.

10 Moses then took the anointing oil and anointed the tabernacle and all that was in it[h] and sanctified them. **11** After that he spattered some of it seven times on the altar and anointed the altar and all its utensils and the basin and its stand in order to sanctify them. **12** Finally he poured some of the anointing oil on Aaron's head and anointed him in order to sanctify him.[i]

13 Moses then brought Aaron's sons near and clothed them with robes and wrapped them with sashes and put* headgear on them,[j] just as Jehovah had commanded Moses.

14 Then he brought the bull of the sin offering, and Aaron and his sons laid their hands on the head of the bull of the sin offering.[k] **15** Moses slaughtered it and took the blood[l] with his finger and put it on the horns of the altar on all sides, and he purified the altar from sin, but the rest of the blood he poured at the base of the altar, in order to sanctify it to make atonement on it. **16** After that he took all the fat that was on the intestines, the appendage of the liver, and the two kidneys and their fat, and Moses made them smoke on the altar.[m] **17** Then he had the rest of the bull, its skin, its flesh, and its dung, burned with fire

---

CHAP. 7
a De 18:3
b Le 10:14
c Ex 28:1
  Ex 29:4, 7
  Ex 40:13
d Ex 40:15
  Le 8:12
e Le 6:9
f Le 2:1
  Le 6:14
g Le 6:25
h Le 5:6
  Le 7:1
i Ex 29:1
  Le 6:20
j Le 3:1
k Ex 34:27
l Le 1:2

CHAP. 8
m Ex 28:1
n Ex 28:4
  Ex 39:33, 41
o Ex 30:23-25
  Ex 40:15
p Ex 29:1, 2
q Ex 29:4
  Ex 40:12
r Ex 28:39
s Ex 39:27, 29

Second Col.
a Ex 39:22
b Ex 28:6
  Ex 39:2
c Ex 28:8
  Ex 29:5
  Ex 39:20
d Ex 28:15
  Ex 39:9
e Ex 28:30
f Ex 29:6
  Ex 39:27, 28
g Ex 28:36
  Ex 39:30
h Ex 30:26-28
i Ex 29:4, 7
  Ex 30:30
  Ex 40:13
  Le 21:10
  Ps 133:2
j Ex 28:40
  Ex 29:8, 9
k Ex 29:10-14
  Le 4:3, 4
  Le 16:6
l Heb 9:21, 22
m Le 4:8, 9

8:7 *Or "waistband." 8:9 *Or "the holy diadem." 8:13 *Or "wrapped."

outside the camp,[a] just as Jehovah had commanded Moses.

18 He now brought the ram of the burnt offering near, and Aaron and his sons laid their hands on the head of the ram.[b] **19** Moses then slaughtered it and sprinkled the blood on all sides of the altar. **20** He cut the ram into its pieces, and Moses made the head, the pieces, and the suet* smoke. **21** He washed the intestines and the shanks with water, and Moses made the entire ram smoke on the altar. It was a burnt offering as a pleasing* aroma. It was an offering made by fire to Jehovah, just as Jehovah had commanded Moses.

22 Then he brought the second ram, the ram of the installation,[c] and Aaron and his sons laid their hands on the ram's head.[d] **23** Moses slaughtered it and took some of its blood and put it on Aaron's right earlobe and on the thumb of his right hand and on the big toe of his right foot. **24** Next Moses brought Aaron's sons forward and put some of the blood on their right earlobe and on the thumb of their right hand and on the big toe of their right foot; but Moses sprinkled the rest of the blood on all sides of the altar.[e]

25 Then he took the fat, the fat tail, all the fat that was on the intestines, the appendage of the liver, the two kidneys and their fat, and the right leg.[f] **26** He took out of the basket of unleavened bread that was before Jehovah one unleavened ring-shaped loaf,[g] one ring-shaped loaf of oiled bread,[h] and one wafer. He then placed them on the pieces of fat and the right leg. **27** After that he put all of

them on the palms of Aaron and the palms of his sons and began to wave them back and forth as a wave offering before Jehovah. **28** Then Moses took them from their hands and made them smoke on the altar on top of the burnt offering. They were an installation sacrifice as a pleasing* aroma. It was an offering made by fire to Jehovah.

29 Moses then took the breast and waved it back and forth as a wave offering before Jehovah.[a] From the installation ram it became the portion for Moses, just as Jehovah had commanded Moses.[b]

30 And Moses took some of the anointing oil[c] and some of the blood that was on the altar and spattered it on Aaron and his garments and on his sons and the garments of his sons who were with him. Thus he sanctified Aaron and his garments and his sons[d] and their garments.[e]

31 Then Moses said to Aaron and his sons: "Boil[f] the flesh at the entrance of the tent of meeting, and you will eat it there with the bread that is in the installation basket, just as I was commanded, 'Aaron and his sons will eat it.'[g] **32** What is left over of the flesh and the bread you will burn with fire.[h] **33** You must not go out from the entrance of the tent of meeting for seven days, until the days for completing your installation are over, because it will take seven days to install you as priests.*[i] **34** Jehovah commanded that we do what we have done today in order to make atonement for you.[j] **35** You will stay at the entrance of the tent of meeting day and night for seven days[k] and carry out your obligation to Jehovah,[l] so that you may not die; for so I have been commanded."

CHAP. 8
a Le 4:11, 12
  Le 16:27

b Ex 29:15-18
  Le 1:4

c Le 8:33

d Ex 29:19, 20

e Ex 24:6

f Ex 29:22-25

g Le 2:4

h Ex 29:1, 2

Second Col.
a Le 7:29, 30

b Ex 29:26, 27
  Le 7:34, 35

c Ex 30:30

d Nu 3:2, 3

e Ex 29:21

f Le 6:28

g Ex 29:31, 32
  1Co 9:13

h Ex 29:34

i Ex 29:30, 35
  Nu 3:2, 3

j Ex 29:36
  Le 17:11

k Ex 29:37

l Nu 1:53

8:20 *Or "the fat around the kidneys."
8:21, 28 *Or "appeasing; soothing." Lit., "restful."

8:33 *Lit., "fill your hand."

36 And Aaron and his sons did all the things that Jehovah had commanded by means of Moses.

9 On the eighth day,[a] Moses called Aaron and his sons and the elders of Israel. **2** He said to Aaron: "Take for yourself a young calf for a sin offering[b] and a ram for a burnt offering, sound ones, and present them before Jehovah. **3** But you will say to the Israelites, 'Take a male goat for a sin offering and a calf and a young ram, each a year old, sound ones, for a burnt offering, **4** and a bull and a ram for communion sacrifices,[c] to sacrifice them before Jehovah, and a grain offering[d] mixed with oil, for today Jehovah will appear to you.'"[e]

5 So they took what Moses had commanded before the tent of meeting. Then the whole assembly came forward and stood before Jehovah. **6** And Moses said: "This is what Jehovah has commanded you to do, so that the glory of Jehovah may appear to you."[f] **7** Then Moses said to Aaron: "Approach the altar and present your sin offering[g] and your burnt offering, and make atonement in your own behalf[h] and in behalf of your house; and present the offering of the people,[i] and make atonement in their behalf,[j] just as Jehovah has commanded."

8 Aaron immediately approached the altar and slaughtered the calf of the sin offering that was for him.[k] **9** Then Aaron's sons presented the blood[l] to him, and he dipped his finger in the blood and put it on the horns of the altar, and he poured the rest of the blood at the base of the altar.[m] **10** He made the fat and the kidneys and the appendage of the liver from the sin offering smoke on the altar, just as Jehovah had commanded

Moses.[a] **11** And he burned the flesh and the skin with fire outside the camp.[b]

12 Then he slaughtered the burnt offering, and Aaron's sons handed him the blood, and he sprinkled it on all sides of the altar.[c] **13** They handed him the pieces of the burnt offering along with the head, and he made them smoke on the altar. **14** Further, he washed the intestines and the shanks and made them smoke on the burnt offering on the altar.

15 He then presented the offering of the people and took the goat of the sin offering that was for the people and slaughtered it and made a sin offering with it like the first one. **16** And he presented the burnt offering and handled it according to the regular procedure.[d]

17 He next presented the grain offering,[e] filling his hand with some of it and making it smoke on the altar, in addition to the burnt offering of the morning.[f]

18 After that he slaughtered the bull and the ram of the communion sacrifice that was for the people. Then Aaron's sons handed him the blood, and he sprinkled it around on all sides of the altar.[g] **19** As for the pieces of fat of the bull,[h] the fat tail of the ram, the fat covering the internal organs, the kidneys, and the appendage of the liver,[i] **20** they placed all those pieces of fat on the breasts, after which he made the pieces of fat smoke on the altar.[j] **21** But the breasts and the right leg Aaron waved back and forth as a wave offering before Jehovah, just as Moses had commanded.[k]

22 Then Aaron raised his hands toward the people and blessed them[l] and came down from making the sin offering and the burnt offering and the com-

---

CHAP. 9
a Le 8:35

b Le 4:3

c Le 3:1

d Le 2:4
Le 6:14

e Ex 29:43

f Ex 16:10
Ex 24:16
Ex 40:34

g Le 4:3

h Heb 7:27

i Heb 5:1-3

j Le 16:33

k Le 4:3, 4

l Heb 9:22

m Le 4:7
Le 8:14, 15

Second Col.
a Le 4:8-10

b Le 4:11, 12
Heb 13:11

c Le 1:5

d Le 1:3
Le 6:9

e Le 2:1, 11, 13

f Ex 29:39

g Le 3:1, 2

h Le 3:3, 4

i Le 3:9, 10

j Le 7:29-31

k Ex 29:27, 28

l Nu 6:23-27
De 10:8
De 21:5
1Ch 23:13

munion sacrifices. **23** Finally Moses and Aaron went into the tent of meeting and came out and blessed the people.[a]

Jehovah's glory now appeared to all the people,[b] **24** and fire came out from Jehovah[c] and began consuming the burnt offering and the pieces of fat on the altar. When all the people saw it, they started shouting and they fell with their faces to the ground.[d]

10 Later Aaron's sons Na′dab and A·bi′hu[e] each took his fire holder and put fire in it and placed incense[f] on it. Then they began offering before Jehovah unauthorized fire,[g] which he had not commanded them to do. **2** At this a fire came out from before Jehovah and consumed them,[h] so that they died before Jehovah.[i] **3** Then Moses said to Aaron: "This is what Jehovah has said, 'I will be made holy among those near to me,[j] and I will be glorified before all the people.'" And Aaron kept silent.

4 So Moses called Mish′a·el and El·za′phan, the sons of Uz′zi·el,[k] Aaron's uncle, and said to them: "Come here, carry your brothers from in front of the holy place to a place outside the camp." **5** So they came forward and carried the men away in their robes to a place outside the camp, just as Moses had told them.

6 Moses then said to Aaron and his other sons El·e·a′zar and Ith′a·mar: "Do not let your heads go ungroomed or tear your garments,[l] so that you may not die and that God may not become indignant against all the assembly. Your brothers of the whole house of Israel will weep over those whom Jehovah has killed by the fire. **7** You must not go out from the entrance of the tent of meeting or you will die, for Je-

hovah's anointing oil is upon you."[a] So they did according to Moses' word.

8 Then Jehovah said to Aaron: **9** "Do not drink wine or other alcoholic beverages, you and your sons with you, when you come into the tent of meeting,[b] so that you will not die. It is a permanent statute for your generations. **10** This is to distinguish between the holy thing and the profane and between the unclean thing and the clean,[c] **11** and to teach the Israelites all the regulations that Jehovah has spoken to them through Moses."[d]

12 Then Moses spoke to Aaron and to El·e·a′zar and Ith′a·mar, his sons who were left: "Take what was left of the grain offering from Jehovah's offerings made by fire and eat it as unleavened bread near the altar,[e] because it is something most holy.[f] **13** You must eat it in a holy place,[g] because it is your allowance and the allowance of your sons from Jehovah's offerings made by fire, for this is what I have been commanded. **14** You will also eat the breast of the wave offering and the leg of the sacred portion[h] in a clean place, you and your sons and your daughters with you,[i] because these things have been given as your allowance and the allowance of your sons from the communion sacrifices of the Israelites. **15** They will bring the leg of the sacred portion and the breast of the wave offering along with the offerings of fat made by fire, in order to wave the wave offering back and forth before Jehovah; and it will serve as a permanent allowance for you and your sons with you,[j] just as Jehovah has commanded."

16 And Moses diligently searched for the goat of the sin offering,[k] and he discovered that

---

CHAP. 9

a 2Sa 6:18
  2Ch 6:3

b Le 9:6

c Jg 6:21
  1Ch 21:26

d 1Ki 18:38, 39
  2Ch 7:1, 3

CHAP. 10

e Ex 6:23
  1Ch 24:2

f Ex 30:34, 35
  Le 16:12

g Ex 30:9
  Le 10:9
  Le 16:1, 2

h Nu 16:35

i Nu 26:61

j Ex 19:22

k Ex 6:18

l Le 21:10

Second Col.

a Ex 28:41
  Le 8:12
  Le 21:11, 12

b Eze 44:21

c Eze 44:23

d De 33:10
  2Ch 17:8, 9
  Ne 8:7, 8
  Mal 2:7

e Le 6:14, 16

f Le 21:22

g Le 6:26
  Nu 18:10

h Ex 29:26-28
  Le 7:31, 34
  Le 9:21

i Le 22:13
  Nu 18:11

j 1Co 9:13

k Le 9:3, 15

it had been burned up. So he grew indignant at El·e·a′zar and Ith′a·mar, Aaron's sons who were left, and he said: 17 "Why did you not eat the sin offering in the holy place,[a] since it is something most holy and he has given it to you so that you may answer for the error of the assembly and make atonement for them before Jehovah? 18 Look! Its blood has not been brought inside the holy place.[b] You certainly should have eaten it in the holy place, just as I was commanded." 19 Aaron replied to Moses: "Look! Today they presented their sin offering and their burnt offering before Jehovah,[c] and yet these things happened to me. If I had eaten the sin offering today, would that have been pleasing to Jehovah?" 20 When Moses heard that, he was satisfied.

11 Then Jehovah said to Moses and Aaron: 2 "Tell the Israelites, 'These are the living creatures of the earth* that you may eat:[d] 3 Every animal that has a split hoof and a cleft in its hooves and that chews the cud may be eaten.

4 "'But you must not eat these animals that chew the cud or have a split hoof: the camel, which chews the cud but does not have a split hoof. It is unclean for you.[e] 5 Also the rock badger,[f] because it chews the cud but does not have a split hoof. It is unclean for you. 6 Also the hare, because it chews the cud but does not have a split hoof. It is unclean for you. 7 Also the pig,[g] because it has a split hoof and a cleft in the hoof but does not chew the cud. It is unclean for you. 8 You must not eat any of their flesh or touch their dead body. They are unclean for you.[h]

9 "'This is what you may eat of everything in the waters: Anything in the waters that has fins and scales, whether in the seas or in the rivers, it you may eat.[a] 10 But anything in the seas and in the rivers that has no fins and scales, among all the swarming creatures and of every other living creature* that is in the waters, it is a loathsome thing for you. 11 Yes, they should be loathsome to you, and you must not eat any of their flesh[b] and you must loathe their carcasses. 12 Everything in the waters that has no fins and scales is a loathsome thing to you.

13 "'These are the flying creatures that you are to loathe; they should not be eaten, for they are loathsome: the eagle,[c] the osprey, the black vulture,[d] 14 the red kite and every kind of black kite, 15 every kind of raven, 16 the ostrich, the owl, the gull, every kind of falcon, 17 the little owl, the cormorant, the long-eared owl, 18 the swan, the pelican, the vulture, 19 the stork, every kind of heron, the hoopoe, and the bat. 20 Every winged swarming creature* that goes on all fours is something loathsome to you.

21 "'Of the winged swarming creatures that move on all fours, you may eat only those that have jointed legs above their feet for leaping on the ground. 22 Of these you may eat: various kinds of migratory locusts, other edible locusts,[e] crickets, and grasshoppers. 23 All other winged swarming creatures with four legs are something loathsome to you. 24 By these you would make yourselves unclean. Everyone touching their dead bodies will be unclean until the evening.[f] 25 Anyone carrying any

---

CHAP. 10
a Le 6:25, 26
  Eze 44:29

b Le 6:29, 30

c Le 9:8, 12

CHAP. 11
d De 14:4-6
  Eze 4:14

e De 14:7, 8

f Pr 30:26

g Isa 65:4
  Isa 66:3, 17

h Ac 10:14

Second Col.
a De 14:9, 10

b De 14:3

c Job 39:27, 30

d De 14:12-19

e Mt 3:4
  Mr 1:6

f Le 14:46, 47
  Le 15:8
  Le 17:15
  Le 22:4-6

11:2 *Or "the land animals."   11:10 *Or "soul."   11:20 *Or "Every insect."

of their dead bodies should wash his garments;[a] he will be unclean until the evening.

26 "'Any animal that has a split hoof but does not have a cleft and does not chew its cud is unclean to you. Everyone touching them will be unclean.[b] **27** Every living creature that walks on paws among the creatures that walk on all fours is unclean to you. Everyone touching their dead bodies will be unclean until the evening. **28** The one who carries their dead bodies should wash his garments,[c] and he will be unclean until the evening.[d] They are unclean to you.

29 "'These are the swarming creatures of the earth that are unclean to you: the mole rat, the mouse,[e] every kind of lizard, **30** the gecko, the large lizard, the newt, the sand lizard, and the chameleon. **31** These swarming creatures are unclean to you.[f] Everyone touching their dead bodies will be unclean until the evening.[g]

32 "'Now anything they fall on when they die will be unclean, whether a wooden utensil, a garment, a skin, or a piece of sackcloth. Any utensil that is used should be immersed in water, and it will be unclean until the evening; then it will be clean. **33** If they fall into an earthenware vessel, you are to smash it, and anything that was in it will be unclean.[h] **34** Any kind of food that comes in contact with water from such a vessel will be unclean, and any drinkable liquid in such a vessel will be unclean. **35** Anything their dead bodies fall on will be unclean. Whether oven or small stove, it should be broken into pieces. They are unclean, and they will remain unclean to you. **36** Only a spring and a cistern for storing water will continue clean, but anyone touching their dead bod-

ies will be unclean. **37** If their dead bodies fall on a plant seed that is to be sown, it is clean. **38** But if water is put on a seed and part of their dead body falls on it, the seed is unclean to you.

39 "'Now if an animal that you use for food dies, whoever touches its dead body will be unclean until the evening.[a] **40** Whoever eats any of its dead body should wash his garments, and he will be unclean until the evening.[b] Whoever carries off its dead body should wash his garments, and he will be unclean until the evening. **41** Every swarming creature of the earth is something loathsome.[c] It must not be eaten. **42** You must not eat any creature that crawls on its belly, any creature that goes on all fours, or any of earth's swarming creatures with a great number of legs, for they are something loathsome.[d] **43** Do not make yourselves* loathsome by means of any swarming creature, and do not defile yourselves and become unclean by them.[e] **44** For I am Jehovah your God,[f] and you must sanctify yourselves and become holy,[g] because I am holy.[h] So you must not make yourselves* unclean by any swarming creature that moves on the earth. **45** For I am Jehovah, who is leading you up out of the land of Egypt to prove myself God to you,[i] and you must be holy,[j] because I am holy.[k]

46 "'This is the law about the animals, the flying creatures, every living creature* that moves through the waters, and concerning every creature* that swarms on the earth, **47** in order to make a distinction between the unclean and the clean and between the living creatures

CHAP. 11
a Le 14:2, 8
  Le 15:2, 5
  Nu 19:10

b De 14:7, 8

c Le 17:15, 16

d Le 5:2

e Isa 66:17

f De 14:19

g Le 11:24
  Le 22:4, 5

h Le 15:12

Second Col.
a Le 11:23, 24
  Nu 19:11, 16

b Le 17:15
  Le 22:3, 8
  De 14:21
  Eze 4:14
  Eze 44:31

c Le 11:21

d De 14:3

e Le 20:25

f Ex 20:2

g Ex 19:6
  Le 19:2
  De 14:2
  1Th 4:7

h 1Pe 1:15, 16
  Re 4:8

i Ex 6:7
  Ex 29:46
  Ho 11:1

j Ex 22:31
  Nu 15:40
  De 7:6

k Le 20:7, 26
  Jos 24:19
  1Sa 2:2

11:43, 44 *Or "your souls." 11:46 *Or "soul."

that may be eaten and those that may not be eaten.'"[a]

12 Jehovah went on to say to Moses: **2** "Tell the Israelites, 'If a woman becomes pregnant* and gives birth to a male, she will be unclean for seven days, just as she is in the days of the impurity when she is menstruating.[b] **3** On the eighth day, the flesh of his foreskin will be circumcised.[c] **4** She will continue cleansing herself from the blood for the next 33 days. She should not touch any holy thing, and she should not come into the holy place until she fulfills the days of her purification.

5 "'If she should give birth to a female, she will then be unclean for 14 days, just as she would be during her menstruation. She will continue cleansing herself from the blood for the next 66 days. **6** When the days of her purification for a son or a daughter are completed, she will bring a young ram in its first year for a burnt offering[d] and a young pigeon or a turtledove for a sin offering to the entrance of the tent of meeting, to the priest. **7** He will present it before Jehovah and make atonement for her, and she will be clean from her flow of blood. This is the law about the woman who gives birth to either a male or a female. **8** But if she cannot afford a sheep, she must then take two turtledoves or two young pigeons,[e] one for a burnt offering and one for a sin offering, and the priest will make atonement for her, and she will be clean.'"

13 Jehovah continued to speak to Moses and Aaron, saying: **2** "If a man develops on his skin* a swelling, a scab, or a blotch and it could become the disease of lepro-

sy*[a] on his skin, he must then be brought to Aaron the priest or to one of his sons, the priests.[b] **3** The priest will examine the infection on his skin. When the hair in the infection has turned white and the appearance of the infection is deeper than the skin, it is the disease of leprosy. The priest will examine it and declare him unclean. **4** But if the blotch on his skin is white and its appearance is not deeper than the skin and the hair has not turned white, the priest will then quarantine the infected person for seven days.[c] **5** The priest will then examine him on the seventh day, and if it appears that the infection has stopped and has not spread on the skin, the priest will quarantine him for another seven days.

6 "The priest should examine him again on the seventh day, and if the infection has faded and has not spread in the skin, the priest will declare him clean;[d] it was only a scab. The man will then wash his garments and be clean. **7** But if the scab* has definitely spread on the skin after he appears before the priest to establish his purification, he will then appear again* before the priest. **8** The priest will examine it, and if the scab has spread in the skin, the priest will then declare him unclean. It is leprosy.[e]

9 "If the disease of leprosy develops in a man, he must then be brought to the priest, **10** and the priest will examine him.[f] If there is a white swelling on the skin and it has turned the

---

CHAP. 11
a Le 20:25
　Eze 44:23

CHAP. 12
b Le 15:19

c Ge 17:12
　Ge 21:4
　Lu 1:59
　Lu 2:21, 22
　Joh 7:22

d Le 1:10

e Le 1:14
　Le 5:7
　Le 14:21, 22
　Lu 2:24

Second Col.

CHAP. 13
a Nu 12:10, 12
　2Ch 26:19
　Mt 8:3

b De 24:8
　Eze 44:23
　Mal 2:7
　Lu 17:14

c Le 13:50
　Le 14:38
　Nu 12:15

d Mt 8:4
　Mr 1:44
　Lu 5:14
　Lu 17:14

e Le 13:15, 25, 30, 42
　Nu 12:10, 12

f Le 13:3

12:2 *Or "conceives seed."　**13:2** *Lit., "in the skin of his flesh."

13:2 *The Hebrew word rendered "leprosy" is broad in meaning and can include various contagious skin diseases. It may also include certain infections found on clothing and in houses.　**13:7** *Or "the infection."　#Or "a second time."

hair white and there is an open sore[a] in the swelling, **11** it is chronic leprosy on his skin, and the priest will declare him unclean. He should not quarantine him,[b] for he is unclean. **12** Now if the leprosy breaks out all over the skin and the leprosy covers the person with the disease from head to foot, as far as the priest can see, **13** and the priest has examined him and sees that the leprosy has covered all his skin, he will then declare the infected person clean.* All of it has turned white, and he is clean. **14** But whenever an open sore appears in it, he will be unclean. **15** When the priest sees the open sore, he will declare him unclean.[c] The open sore is unclean. It is leprosy.[d] **16** But if the open sore again turns white, he will then come to the priest. **17** The priest will examine him,[e] and if the infection has turned white, the priest will then declare the infected person clean. He is clean.

18 "If a person develops a boil on his skin and it heals, **19** but in the place of the boil a white swelling or a reddish-white blotch has developed, he must then show himself to the priest. **20** The priest will examine it,[f] and if it appears to be deeper than the skin and its hair has turned white, the priest will then declare him unclean. It is the disease of leprosy that has broken out in the boil. **21** But if the priest examines it and sees that there is no white hair in it and it is not deeper than the skin and appears faded, the priest will then quarantine him for seven days.[g] **22** And if it has clearly spread on the skin, the priest will then declare him unclean. It is a disease. **23** But if the blotch stays in one place and has

not spread, it is only the inflammation from the boil, and the priest will declare him clean.[a]

24 "Or if someone has a scar from the fire and the raw flesh of the scar becomes a reddish-white blotch or a white one, **25** the priest will then examine it. If the hair in the blotch has turned white and it appears to be deeper than the skin, it is leprosy that has broken out in the scar, and the priest will declare him unclean. It is the disease of leprosy. **26** But if the priest examines it and sees that there is no white hair in the blotch and it is not deeper than the skin and it is faded, the priest will then quarantine him for seven days.[b] **27** The priest will examine him on the seventh day, and if it has clearly spread on the skin, the priest will then declare him unclean. It is the disease of leprosy. **28** But if the blotch stays in one place and has not spread over the skin and it is faded, it is only a swelling of the scar, and the priest will declare him clean, because it is an inflammation of the scar.

29 "When a man or a woman develops an infection on the head or on the chin, **30** the priest will then examine the infection.[c] If it appears to be deeper than the skin and the hair is yellow and thin, the priest will then declare such one unclean; it is an infection of the scalp or the beard. It is leprosy of the head or of the chin. **31** But if the priest sees that the infection does not appear to be deeper than the skin and there is no black hair in it, the priest should quarantine the infected person for seven days.[d] **32** The priest will examine the infection on the seventh day, and if the infected area has not spread and no yellow hair has developed in it and the appearance of the infected

---

CHAP. 13
a Le 13:24, 25

b Le 13:4

c De 24:8

d Le 13:8

e Lu 5:14
  Lu 17:14

f Eze 44:23

g Le 13:4, 50
  Le 14:38
  Nu 12:15

Second Col.
a Mt 8:4
  Mr 1:44
  Lu 5:14
  Lu 17:14

b Le 13:4, 50
  Le 14:38
  Nu 12:15

c De 24:8
  Mal 2:7

d Le 13:4, 50
  Le 14:38
  Nu 12:15

13:13 *Or "not contagious."

area is not deeper than the skin, **33** the person should have himself shaved, but he will not have the infected area shaved. Then the priest will quarantine the infected person for seven days.

34 "The priest will again examine the infected area on the seventh day, and if the infection of the scalp and beard has not spread on the skin and it does not appear deeper than the skin, the priest must then declare him clean, and he should wash his garments and be clean. **35** But if the infection clearly spreads on the skin after his purification, **36** the priest will examine him, and if the infection has spread on the skin, the priest does not need to look for yellow hair; that person is unclean. **37** But if the examination shows that the infection has not spread and black hair has grown on it, the infection has been healed. He is clean, and the priest will declare him clean.[a]

38 "If a man or a woman develops blotches on the skin* and the blotches are white, **39** the priest will examine them.[b] If the skin blotches are faded white, it is a harmless rash that has broken out on the skin. That person is clean.

40 "If a man loses the hair of his head and becomes bald, he is clean. **41** If he loses the hair on the front of his head and becomes bald there, he is clean. **42** But if a reddish-white sore develops on the bald part of his scalp or on his forehead, it is leprosy breaking out on his scalp or on his forehead. **43** The priest will examine him, and if the swelling from the infection is reddish-white on the bald spot on top of his head or on his forehead and it looks like leprosy on his skin, **44** he is a lep-

er. He is unclean, and the priest should declare him unclean because of the disease on his head. **45** As for the leper who has the disease, his garments should be torn and his head should be left ungroomed and he should cover over his mustache and call out, 'Unclean, unclean!' **46** He will be unclean the whole time that he has the disease. Since he is unclean, he should live in isolation. His dwelling place will be outside the camp.[a]

47 "If the disease of leprosy contaminates a garment, whether a woolen or a linen garment, **48** either in the warp or in the woof of the linen or of the wool, or in a skin or in anything made of skin, **49** and the yellowish-green or reddish stain from the disease contaminates the garment, a skin, the warp, the woof, or any article of skin, it is a contamination from leprosy, and it should be shown to the priest. **50** The priest will examine the disease, and he must quarantine the disease for seven days.[b] **51** When he examines the disease on the seventh day and sees that it has spread in the garment, in the warp, in the woof, or in the skin (regardless of what the skin is used for), the disease is malignant leprosy, and it is unclean.[c] **52** He should burn the garment or the warp or the woof in the wool or in the linen or any article of skin in which the disease has developed, for it is malignant leprosy. It should be burned in the fire.

53 "But if the priest examines it and the disease has not spread in the garment or in the warp or in the woof or in any article of skin, **54** the priest will then command that they should wash the contaminated item, and he will quarantine it for another seven days. **55** The priest will then examine the contaminated

---

CHAP. 13
a Mt 8:4
  Mr 1:44
  Lu 5:14
  Lu 17:14

b Le 13:2

Second Col.
a Nu 5:2
  Nu 12:14
  2Ki 7:3
  2Ch 26:20, 21

b Le 13:4
  Le 14:38
  Nu 12:15

c Le 14:44, 45

13:38 *Lit., "in the skin of their flesh."

item after it has been thoroughly washed. If the appearance of the contamination has not changed, even if the disease has not spread, it is unclean. You should burn it in the fire because it has been eaten away, either from its underside or from its outside.

56 "But if the priest has examined it and the contaminated part is faded after it has been thoroughly washed, he will then tear it out of the garment or the skin or the warp or the woof. **57** However, if it still appears in another part of the garment or in the warp or in the woof or in any article of skin, it is spreading, and you should burn any contaminated item in the fire.[a] **58** But when the contamination disappears from the garment or the warp or the woof or any article of skin that you wash, it should be washed a second time, and it will be clean.

59 "This is the law of the disease of leprosy in a garment of wool or of linen, or in the warp or in the woof, or in any article of skin, for declaring it clean or unclean."

14 Jehovah continued to speak to Moses, saying: **2** "This is to be the law of the leper on the day his purification is established, when he is to be brought to the priest.[b] **3** The priest will go outside the camp and examine him. If the leper has been cured of the leprosy, **4** the priest will command him to bring two live clean birds, cedarwood, scarlet material, and hyssop for his cleansing.[c] **5** The priest will command that the one bird be killed in an earthenware vessel over running water. **6** But he should take the living bird along with the cedarwood, the scarlet material, and the hyssop, and dip them together in the blood of the bird that was killed over the

running water. **7** Then he will spatter it seven times on the one cleansing himself from the leprosy and declare him clean, and he will set the living bird free in the open field.[a]

8 "The one cleansing himself must wash his garments and shave off all his hair and bathe in water, and he will be clean. Afterward, he may come into the camp, but he will dwell outside his tent for seven days. **9** On the seventh day, he should shave off all the hair on his head and his chin and his eyebrows. After he shaves off all his hair, he will wash his garments and bathe himself in water, and he will be clean.

10 "On the eighth day, he will take two sound young rams, one sound female lamb[b] in its first year, three tenths of an eʹphah* of fine flour mixed with oil as a grain offering,[c] and one log measure* of oil;[d] **11** and the priest who declares him clean will present the man who is cleansing himself, along with the offerings, before Jehovah at the entrance of the tent of meeting. **12** The priest will take the one young ram and offer it as a guilt offering[e] together with the log measure of oil, and he will wave them back and forth as a wave offering before Jehovah.[f] **13** Then he will slaughter the young ram in the place where the sin offering and the burnt offering are usually slaughtered,[g] in a holy place, because, like the sin offering, the guilt offering belongs to the priest.[h] It is something most holy.[i]

14 "Then the priest will take some of the blood of the guilt offering, and the priest will put

CHAP. 13
a Le 13:52

CHAP. 14
b Le 13:2
Mt 8:4
Mr 1:44
Lu 5:14
Lu 17:14

| c Le 14:49-53 |
| Nu 19:6, 9 |
| Ps 51:7 |

Second Col.
a Le 16:22

| b Le 4:32 |

| c Le 2:1 |

| d Mr 1:44 |

| e Le 6:6 |

| f Le 14:21, 24 |

| g Le 1:10, 11 |
| Le 4:3, 4 |

| h Le 2:3 |
| Le 7:7 |
| 1Co 9:13 |
| 1Co 10:18 |

| i Le 6:25 |

14:10 *Three tenths of an ephah equaled 6.6 L (6 dry qt). See App. B14. *A log equaled 0.31 L (0.66 pt). See App. B14.

it on the right earlobe of the one cleansing himself and on the thumb of his right hand and on the big toe of his right foot. **15** And the priest will take some of the log measure of oil[a] and pour it into his own left palm. **16** The priest will then dip his right finger into the oil that is in his left palm and spatter some of the oil with his finger seven times before Jehovah. **17** Then the priest will put some of the remaining oil in his palm on the right earlobe of the one cleansing himself and on the thumb of his right hand and on the big toe of his right foot over the blood of the guilt offering. **18** The priest will put what is left over of the oil in his palm on the head of the one cleansing himself, and the priest will make atonement for him before Jehovah.[b]

19 The priest will sacrifice the sin offering[c] and make atonement for the one cleansing himself from his impurity, and afterward he will slaughter the burnt offering. **20** And the priest will offer up the burnt offering and the grain offering[d] on the altar, and the priest will make atonement for him,[e] and he will be clean.[f]

21 "However, if he is poor and does not have enough means, he will then take one young ram as a guilt offering for a wave offering, in order to make atonement for himself, along with one tenth of an e'phah* of fine flour mixed with oil as a grain offering, a log measure of oil, **22** and two turtledoves or two young pigeons, according to his means. The one will serve as a sin offering, and the other as a burnt offering.[g] **23** On the eighth day,[h] he will bring them for establishing his purification

to the priest at the entrance of the tent of meeting before Jehovah.[a]

24 "The priest will take the young ram of the guilt offering[b] and the log measure of oil, and the priest will wave them back and forth as a wave offering before Jehovah.[c] **25** He will then slaughter the young ram of the guilt offering, and the priest will take some of the blood of the guilt offering and put it on the right earlobe of the one cleansing himself and on the thumb of his right hand and on the big toe of his right foot.[d] **26** The priest will pour some of the oil into his own left palm,[e] **27** and he will then spatter with his right finger some of the oil that is in his left palm seven times before Jehovah. **28** And the priest will put some of the oil that is in his palm on the right earlobe of the one cleansing himself and on the thumb of his right hand and on the big toe of his right foot on the same places that he put the blood of the guilt offering. **29** The priest will then put what is left over of the oil in his palm on the head of the one cleansing himself, in order to make atonement for him before Jehovah.

30 "He will offer up one of the turtledoves or one of the young pigeons, according to his means,[f] **31** the one he can afford, as a sin offering and the other as a burnt offering[g] along with the grain offering; and the priest will make atonement for the one cleansing himself before Jehovah.[h]

32 "This is the law for the one in whom the disease of leprosy was but who does not have the means when establishing his purification."

33 Then Jehovah said to Moses and Aaron: **34** "When you come into the land of Ca'naan,[i] which I am giving you

---

CHAP. 14
a Le 14:10

b Le 6:7
1Jo 1:7
1Jo 2:1, 2

c Le 5:6

d Le 2:1
Le 14:10
Nu 15:4

e Mt 8:4

f Le 14:9
Mr 1:44
Lu 5:14
Lu 17:14

g Le 1:14
Le 5:7
Le 12:8

h Le 15:13, 14

Second Col.
a Le 14:10, 11

b Le 6:6

c Le 14:12

d Le 14:14

e Le 14:15-18

f Le 12:8
Le 14:22

g Le 5:7

h Le 14:20

i Nu 35:10

14:21 *A tenth of an ephah equaled 2.2 L (2 dry qt). See App. B14.

as a possession,[a] and I contaminate a house in your land with the disease of leprosy,[b] 35 the one to whom the house belongs should then come and tell the priest, 'Some kind of contamination has appeared in my house.' 36 The priest will give orders to clear out the house before he comes to examine the contamination, in order that he may not declare everything that is in the house unclean; and after that the priest will come in to inspect the house. 37 He will examine the affected area, and if the walls of the house are contaminated with yellowish-green or reddish depressions and they appear to be deeper than the wall surface, 38 the priest will then go out of the house to the entryway of the house and quarantine the house for seven days.[c]

39 "Then the priest will return on the seventh day and make an inspection. If the contamination has spread in the walls of the house, 40 the priest will then give orders, and the contaminated stones must be torn out and thrown outside the city into an unclean place. 41 Then he is to have the inside of the house thoroughly scraped, and the plaster and mortar that is removed should be discarded outside the city in an unclean place. 42 They will then insert other stones in the place of the stones they removed, and he should use different mortar and have the house plastered.

43 "If, though, the contamination returns and breaks out in the house after the stones were torn out and the house was scraped and replastered, 44 the priest will then go in and inspect it. If the contamination has spread in the house, it is malignant leprosy[d] in the house. The house is unclean. 45 He will then have the house pulled down—its stones, its timbers, and all the plaster and mortar of the house—and carried outside the city to an unclean place.[a] 46 But whoever enters the house any of the days it is quarantined[b] will be unclean until the evening;[c] 47 and whoever lies down in the house should wash his garments, and whoever eats in the house should wash his garments.

48 "However, if the priest comes and sees that the contamination has not spread in the house after the house was replastered, the priest will then declare the house clean, because the contamination has been healed. 49 In order to purify the house from uncleanness,* he will take two birds, cedarwood, scarlet material, and hyssop.[d] 50 He is to kill the one bird in an earthenware vessel over running water. 51 Then he will take the cedarwood, the hyssop, the scarlet material, and the live bird and dip them in the blood of the bird that was killed and in the running water, and he must spatter it toward the house seven times.[e] 52 And he will purify the house from uncleanness* with the blood of the bird, the running water, the live bird, the cedarwood, the hyssop, and the scarlet material. 53 He will then set the live bird free outside the city in the open field and make atonement for the house, and it will be clean.

54 "This is the law respecting any case of leprosy, infection of the scalp or the beard,[f] 55 leprosy of the garment[g] or the house,[h] 56 and respecting swellings, scabs, and blotches,[i] 57 in order to determine when something is unclean and when something is clean.[j] This is the law about leprosy."[k]

CHAP. 14

a Ge 17:8

b De 7:12, 15

c Le 13:4, 50
Nu 12:15

d Le 13:51

_____
Second Col.
a Le 14:41

b Le 14:38

c Le 11:23-25
Le 15:8
Le 17:15
Le 22:4-6

d Le 14:3, 4
Nu 19:6, 7

e Le 14:6, 7

f Le 13:30

g Le 13:47

h Le 14:34

i Le 13:2

j Le 10:10
Eze 44:23

k De 24:8

_____
14:49, 52 *Lit., "sin."

15 Jehovah continued to speak to Moses and Aaron, saying: **2** "Speak to the Israelites and tell them, 'If a man has a discharge from his genital organ,* this discharge makes him unclean.ᵃ **3** He is unclean from the discharge, whether the discharge continues to flow from his genitals or is obstructed, he is still unclean.

4 "'Any bed that the one with the discharge lies on will be unclean, and anything he sits on will be unclean. **5** A man who touches his bed must wash his garments, and he should bathe in water and be unclean until the evening.ᵇ **6** Anyone who sits on an article that the one having a discharge sat on should wash his garments, bathe in water, and be unclean until the evening. **7** Whoever touches the flesh of the one having a discharge should wash his garments, bathe in water, and be unclean until the evening. **8** If the one who has a discharge spits on someone clean, that person must wash his garments, bathe in water, and be unclean until the evening. **9** Any saddle that the one with the discharge rides on will be unclean. **10** Anyone touching anything that was under him will be unclean until the evening, and anyone who carries those items will wash his garments, bathe in water, and be unclean until the evening. **11** If the one with the dischargeᶜ has not washed his hands in water and he touches someone, that person must then wash his garments, bathe in water, and be unclean until the evening. **12** An earthenware vessel that the one having a discharge touches should be smashed, and any wooden vessel should be washed with water.ᵈ

13 "'When the discharge stops and the person becomes clean from it, he will then count seven days for his purification, and he must wash his garments, bathe himself in running water, and he will be clean.ᵃ **14** On the eighth day, he should take two turtledoves or two young pigeonsᵇ and come before Jehovah at the entrance of the tent of meeting and give them to the priest. **15** And the priest will offer them, the one as a sin offering and the other as a burnt offering, and the priest will make atonement for him before Jehovah concerning his discharge.

16 "'Now if a man has an emission of semen, he should bathe his whole body in water and be unclean until the evening.ᶜ **17** He must wash with water any garment and any skin with semen on it, and it will be unclean until the evening.

18 "'When a man lies with a woman and has an emission of semen, they should bathe in water and be unclean until the evening.ᵈ

19 "'If a woman has a discharge of blood from her body, she will continue in her menstrual impurity for seven days.ᵉ Anyone touching her will be unclean until the evening.ᶠ **20** Anything she lies down on in her menstrual impurity will be unclean, and everything she sits on will be unclean.ᵍ **21** Anyone touching her bed should wash his garments, bathe in water, and be unclean until the evening. **22** Anyone touching any article she sat on should wash his garments, bathe in water, and be unclean until the evening. **23** If she sat on the bed or on another article, his touching it will make him unclean until the evening.ʰ **24** And if a man lies down with her and her menstrual impurity comes

---

15:2 *Lit., "his flesh."

CHAP. 15
a Le 22:4
Nu 5:2

b Le 11:24, 25
Le 14:46, 47
Le 17:15
Le 22:6

c Le 15:2

d Le 11:32, 33

Second Col.
a Le 14:8

b Le 1:14

c Le 22:4
De 23:10, 11

d Ex 19:15
1Sa 21:5

e Le 12:2, 5

f Le 20:18

g Le 15:4-6

h Le 15:10

on him,[a] he will then be unclean for seven days, and any bed on which he lies down will be unclean.

25 "'When a woman's discharge of blood flows for many days[b] when it is not the regular time of her menstruation,[c] or if she should have a flow longer than her usual menstruation, she will be unclean during all the days of her discharge, as in the days of her menstrual impurity. **26** Any bed she lies on during the days of her discharge will become like the bed of her menstrual impurity,[d] and any article she sits on will become unclean like the uncleanness of her menstrual impurity. **27** Anyone touching them will be unclean, and he must wash his garments, bathe in water, and be unclean until the evening.[e]

28 "'However, when she is clean from her discharge, she will count for herself seven days, and afterward she will be clean.[f] **29** On the eighth day, she should take two turtledoves or two young pigeons,[g] and she will bring them to the priest at the entrance of the tent of meeting.[h] **30** The priest will make the one a sin offering and the other a burnt offering, and the priest will make atonement for her before Jehovah concerning her unclean discharge.[i]

31 "'Thus you must keep the Israelites separate from their uncleanness, so that they do not die in their uncleanness by defiling my tabernacle, which is in their midst.[j]

32 "'This is the law about the man having a discharge, the man who is unclean because of an emission of semen,[k] **33** the woman during her menstrual impurity,[l] any male or female who has a discharge flowing from the body,[m] and a man who lies down with an unclean woman.'"

16 Jehovah spoke to Moses after the death of Aaron's two sons who died for approaching Jehovah.[a] **2** Jehovah said to Moses: "Tell Aaron your brother that he may not come at just any time into the holy place[b] inside the curtain,[c] in front of the cover on the Ark, so that he may not die,[d] for I will appear over the cover[e] in a cloud.[f]

3 "This is what Aaron should bring when he comes into the holy place: a young bull for a sin offering[g] and a ram for a burnt offering.[h] **4** He should put on the holy linen robe,[i] and the linen shorts*[j] should cover his body,# and he should wrap himself with the linen sash[k] and his head with the linen turban.[l] They are holy garments.[m] He will bathe himself in water[n] and put them on.

5 "He should take from the assembly of the Israelites[o] two young male goats for a sin offering and one ram for a burnt offering.

6 "Aaron must then present the bull of the sin offering, which is for himself, and he will make atonement in behalf of himself[p] and his house.

7 "He will then take the two goats and make them stand before Jehovah at the entrance of the tent of meeting. **8** Aaron will draw lots over the two goats, the one lot for Jehovah and the other lot for A·za′zel.* **9** Aaron will present the goat that was designated by lot[q] for Jehovah and make it a sin offering. **10** But the goat designated by lot for A·za′zel should be brought alive to stand before Jehovah in order to perform the atonement upon it, so that it may be sent away to A·za′zel into the wilderness.[r]

CHAP. 15
a Le 18:19 Le 20:18
b Mt 9:20 Lu 8:43
c Le 15:19
d Le 15:21
e Le 15:22
f Le 15:13
g Le 1:14
h Le 15:14, 15
i Le 12:7
j Le 19:30 Nu 5:3 Nu 19:20
k Le 15:16
l Le 15:19
m Le 15:2, 25
Second Col.
CHAP. 16
a Le 10:1, 2
b Le 23:27
c Ex 40:21 Heb 6:19 Heb 9:3, 7
d Nu 4:19, 20
e Ex 25:22
f Ex 40:34
g Le 4:3
h Le 1:3
i Ex 28:39
j Ex 28:42
k Ex 39:27, 29
l Ex 28:4
m Ex 28:2
n Ex 30:20 Heb 10:22
o Heb 7:27
p Heb 5:1-3
q Pr 16:33
r Le 14:7, 53 Le 16:21, 22 Isa 53:4 Ro 15:3

16:4 *Or "undergarments." # Or "his exposed flesh." **16:8** *Possibly meaning "Goat That Disappears."

11 "Aaron will present the bull of the sin offering, which is for himself, and make atonement in behalf of himself and his house; afterward he will slaughter the bull of the sin offering, which is for himself.[a]

12 "He will then take the fire holder[b] full of burning coals from the altar[c] before Jehovah and two handfuls of fine perfumed incense,[d] and he will bring them inside the curtain.[e] **13** He will also put the incense on the fire before Jehovah,[f] and the cloud of the incense will envelop the Ark cover,[g] which is on the Testimony,[h] so that he may not die.

14 "He will take some of the bull's blood[i] and spatter it with his finger in front of the cover on the east side, and he will spatter some of the blood with his finger seven times before the cover.[j]

15 "He will then slaughter the goat of the sin offering, which is for the people,[k] and bring its blood inside the curtain[l] and do with its blood[m] the same as he did with the bull's blood; he is to spatter it toward the cover and before the cover.

16 "He must make atonement for the holy place concerning the acts of uncleanness of the Israelites and concerning their transgressions and their sins,[n] and that is what he should do for the tent of meeting, which is located among them in the midst of their acts of uncleanness.

17 "No other man should be in the tent of meeting from the time he goes in to make atonement in the holy place until he comes out. He will make atonement in behalf of himself and his house[o] and in behalf of the entire congregation of Israel.[p]

18 "He will then come out to the altar,[q] which is before Jehovah, and make atonement for it, and he will take some of the bull's blood and some of the goat's blood and put it on the horns of the altar on all sides. **19** He will also spatter some of the blood on it with his finger seven times and cleanse it and sanctify it from the acts of uncleanness of the Israelites.

20 "When he has finished making atonement[a] for the holy place and the tent of meeting and the altar,[b] he will also present the live goat.[c] **21** Aaron will lay both his hands on the head of the live goat and confess over it all the errors of the Israelites and all their transgressions and all their sins, and he will put them on the head of the goat[d] and send it away into the wilderness by the hand of a man designated to do this.* **22** The goat will carry upon itself all their errors[e] into a desert land,[f] and he will send the goat away into the wilderness.[g]

23 "Aaron will then enter into the tent of meeting and take off the linen garments that he put on when he went into the holy place, and he will lay them down there. **24** He must bathe himself* in water[h] in a holy place and put on his garments;[i] then he will come out and offer up his burnt offering[j] and the people's burnt offering[k] and make atonement in his own behalf and in behalf of the people.[l] **25** He will make the fat of the sin offering smoke on the altar.

26 "The man who sent away the goat for A·za'zel[m] should wash his garments and bathe himself in water, and after that he may come into the camp.

27 "And the bull of the sin offering and the goat of the sin offering, whose blood was brought into the holy place to make

---

CHAP. 16

a Le 16:6
b Heb 9:4
c Ex 40:29
  Le 6:13
  Nu 16:46
d Ex 30:34-36
  Re 5:8
  Re 8:3-5
e Le 16:2
  Heb 6:19
  Heb 10:19, 20
f Ex 25:22
  2Ki 19:15
g Ex 25:18, 21
  1Ch 28:11
h Ex 34:29
i Heb 9:22
j Ro 3:25
  Heb 9:12
  Heb 9:24, 25
  Heb 10:4, 12
k Le 16:5
  Heb 2:17
  Heb 5:1-3
  Heb 9:26
  1Jo 3:1, 2
l Heb 6:19
  Heb 9:3, 7
  Heb 10:19, 20
m Le 17:11
n Ec 7:20
o Le 16:6
p Mr 10:45
  Heb 2:9
  Heb 7:27
  Heb 9:7, 12
  Re 1:5
q Ex 38:1

Second Col.

a Heb 9:23
b Le 16:16
c Le 16:8, 10
d Isa 53:5, 6
  2Co 5:21
e Isa 53:12
  Eph 1:7
  Heb 9:28
  1Pe 2:24
  1Jo 3:5
f Ps 103:12
  Heb 13:12
g Le 16:10
h Ex 30:20
i Ex 28:4
  Le 8:7
j Le 16:3
k Le 16:5
l Eph 1:7
m Le 16:8, 21

16:21 *Or "a man standing ready."
16:24 *Lit., "his flesh."

atonement, will be taken outside the camp, and their skins and their flesh and their dung will be burned in the fire.[a] **28** The one who burns them should wash his garments and bathe himself in water, and after that he may come into the camp.

29 "It will serve as a lasting statute for you: In the seventh month, on the tenth of the month, you should afflict yourselves,* and you must not do any work,[b] whether a native or a foreigner who is residing among you. **30** On this day atonement[c] will be made for you, to declare you clean. You will be clean from all your sins before Jehovah.[d] **31** It is a sabbath of complete rest for you, and you should afflict yourselves."[e] It is a lasting statute.

32 "The priest who is anointed[f] and installed* to serve as priest[g] in place of his father[h] will make atonement and put on the linen garments,[i] the holy garments.[j] **33** He will make atonement for the holy sanctuary,[k] the tent of meeting,[l] and the altar;[m] and he will make atonement for the priests and for all the people of the congregation.[n] **34** This will serve as a lasting statute for you,[o] to make atonement for the Israelites concerning all their sins once each year."[p]

So he did just as Jehovah had commanded Moses.

17 Jehovah went on to say to Moses: **2** "Speak to Aaron and his sons and all the Israelites and say to them, 'This is what Jehovah has commanded: **3** "'If any man of the house of Israel slaughters a bull or a young ram or a goat in the camp or if he slaughters it outside the camp, **4** instead of bringing it to the entrance of the tent of meeting to present it as an offering to Jehovah before the tabernacle of Jehovah, bloodguilt will be counted to that man. He has shed blood, and that man must be cut off* from among his people. **5** This is so that the Israelites will bring the sacrifices, which they now sacrifice in the open field, to Jehovah, to the entrance of the tent of meeting, to the priest. They are to sacrifice these as communion sacrifices to Jehovah.[a] **6** And the priest will sprinkle the blood on Jehovah's altar at the entrance of the tent of meeting and make the fat smoke as a pleasing* aroma to Jehovah.[b] **7** So they should no longer offer sacrifices to the goatlike demons,*[c] with which they are prostituting themselves.[d] This will serve as a lasting statute for you throughout your generations.'"

8 "You should say to them, 'Any man of the house of Israel or any foreigner who is residing in your midst who offers up a burnt offering or a sacrifice **9** and does not bring it to the entrance of the tent of meeting to offer it to Jehovah must be cut off* from his people.[e]

10 "'If any man of the house of Israel or any foreigner who is residing in your midst eats any sort of blood,[f] I will certainly set my face against the one* who is eating the blood, and I will cut him off[g] from among his people. **11** For the life* of the flesh is in the blood,[g] and I myself have given it on the altar[h] for you to make atonement for yourselves,* because it is the

---

CHAP. 16
a Le 4:11, 12
  Heb 13:11, 12
b Le 23:27, 28
  Nu 29:7
c Joh 3:16
  Ro 8:32
  Tit 2:13, 14
  1Jo 1:7
  1Jo 3:16
d Jer 33:8
  Heb 9:13, 14
  Heb 10:2
e Le 23:32
f Ex 29:4, 7
  Le 8:12
g Le 8:33
h Nu 20:26
i Ex 28:39
  Ex 39:27, 28
j Ex 28:2
  Ex 29:29
  Le 16:4
k Le 16:16
l Le 16:20
m Le 16:18
n Le 16:24
  1Jo 2:1, 2
o Le 23:31
  Nu 29:7
p Ex 30:10
  Heb 9:7

Second Col.

CHAP. 17
a Le 3:1, 2
  Le 7:11
b Le 3:3-5
  Le 7:29-31
c De 32:17
  Jos 24:14
d Ex 34:15
  De 31:16
e Le 1:3
  De 12:5, 6
  De 12:13, 14
f Ge 9:4
  Le 3:17
  Le 7:26
  Le 19:26
  1Sa 14:33
  Ac 15:20, 29
g Le 17:14
  De 12:23
h Le 8:15
  Le 16:18

16:29 *Or "your souls." To "afflict oneself" is generally understood to mean various forms of self-denial, including fasting. 16:31; 17:11 *Or "your souls." 16:32 *Lit., "whose hand will be filled."

17:4, 9 *Or "put to death." 17:6 *Or "appeasing; soothing." Lit., "restful." 17:7 *Lit., "the goats." 17:10, 11 *Or "soul." 17:10 *Or "put him to death."

blood that makes atonement[a] by means of the life* in it. 12 That is why I have said to the Israelites: "None* of you should eat blood, and no foreigner who is residing in your midst[b] should eat blood."[c]

13 "If one of the Israelites or some foreigner who is residing in your midst is hunting and catches a wild animal or a bird that may be eaten, he must pour its blood out[d] and cover it with dust. 14 For the life* of every sort of flesh is its blood, because the life* is in it. Consequently, I said to the Israelites: "You must not eat the blood of any sort of flesh because the life* of every sort of flesh is its blood. Anyone eating it will be cut off."*[e] 15 If anyone,* whether a native or a foreigner, eats an animal found dead or one torn by a wild animal,[f] he must then wash his garments and bathe in water and be unclean until the evening;[g] then he will be clean. 16 But if he does not wash them and does not bathe himself,* he will answer for his error."[h]

18 Jehovah continued to speak to Moses, saying: 2 "Speak to the Israelites and say to them, 'I am Jehovah your God.[i] 3 You must not behave as they do in the land of Egypt, where you were dwelling, and you must not do what they do in the land of Ca'naan, where I am bringing you.[j] And you must not walk in their statutes. 4 You should carry out my judicial decisions, and you should keep my statutes and walk in them.[k] I am Jehovah your God. 5 You must keep my statutes and my judicial decisions; anyone who does so will live by means of them.[l] I am Jehovah.

6 "'No man among you should approach any of his close relatives to have sexual relations.*[a] I am Jehovah. 7 You must not have sexual relations with your father, and you must not have sexual relations with your mother. She is your mother, and you must not have sexual relations with her.

8 "'You must not have sexual relations with your father's wife.[b] It is exposing your father to shame.*

9 "'You must not have sexual relations with your sister, either the daughter of your father or the daughter of your mother, whether she is born in the same household or born outside of it.[c]

10 "'You must not have sexual relations with the daughter of your son or the daughter of your daughter, because they are your own nakedness.

11 "'You must not have sexual relations with the daughter of your father's wife, the offspring of your father, because she is your sister.

12 "'You must not have sexual relations with your father's sister. She is your father's blood relative.[d]

13 "'You must not have sexual relations with your mother's sister, because she is your mother's blood relative.

14 "'You must not expose your father's brother to shame* by having sexual relations with his wife. She is your aunt.[e]

15 "'You must not have sexual relations with your daughter-in-law.[f] She is your son's wife, and you must not have relations with her.

CHAP. 17
a Mt 26:28
  Ro 3:25
  Ro 5:9
  Eph 1:7
  Heb 9:22
  Heb 13:12
  1Pe 1:2
  1Jo 1:7
  Re 1:5

b Ex 12:49

c De 12:23

d De 12:16
  De 15:23

e Le 17:10, 11

f Ex 22:31
  De 14:21

g Le 11:40

h Nu 19:20

CHAP. 18
i Ge 17:7
  Ex 6:7

j Ex 23:24
  Le 20:23

k Le 20:22
  De 4:1

l Lu 10:27, 28
  Ro 10:5
  Ga 3:12

Second Col.
a Le 20:17

b Ge 35:22
  Ge 49:4
  Le 20:11
  2Sa 16:21
  1Co 5:1

c Le 20:17
  De 27:22
  2Sa 13:10-12

d Le 20:19

e Le 20:20

f Le 20:12

17:11, 14 *Or "soul." 17:12 *Or "No soul." 17:14 *Or "put to death." 17:15 *Or "any soul." 17:16 *Lit., "his flesh."

18:6 *Lit., "to uncover nakedness," here and in subsequent occurrences. 18:8 *Lit., "It is your father's nakedness." 18:14 *Lit., "expose the nakedness of your father's brother."

16 "'You must not have sexual relations with your brother's wife,ᵃ because it is exposing your brother to shame.*

17 "'You must not have sexual relations with a woman and her daughter.ᵇ You must not take the daughter of her son and the daughter of her daughter in order to have relations. They are her close relatives; it is an obscene act.*

18 "'You must not take a woman in addition to her sister as a rival wifeᶜ and have sexual relations with her while her sister is alive.

19 "'You must not approach a woman during her menstrual impurity to have sexual relations with her.ᵈ

20 "'You must not have sexual intercourse with the wife of your fellow man,* making yourself unclean.ᵉ

21 "'You must not allow any of your offspring to be offered* to Mo'lech.ᶠ You must not profane the name of your God in that way.ᵍ I am Jehovah.

22 "'You must not lie down with a male in the same way that you lie down with a woman.ʰ It is a detestable act.

23 "'A man must not have sexual intercourse with an animal to become unclean by it; nor should a woman offer herself to an animal to have intercourse with it.ⁱ It is a violation of what is natural.

24 "'Do not make yourselves unclean by any of these things, for it is by all these things that the nations that I am driving out from before you have made themselves unclean.ʲ **25** Therefore, the land is unclean, and I

will bring punishment on it for its error, and the land will vomit its inhabitants out.ᵃ **26** But you yourselves must keep my statutes and my judicial decisions,ᵇ and you must not do any of these detestable things, whether a native or a foreigner who is residing among you.ᶜ **27** For all these detestable things were done by the men who lived in the land before you,ᵈ and now the land is unclean. **28** Then the land will not have to vomit you out for defiling it in the same way that it will vomit out the nations that were before you. **29** If anyone does any of these detestable things, all those* doing them must be cut off# from among their people. **30** You must keep your obligation to me by not practicing any of the detestable customs that were carried on before you,ᵉ so that you do not make yourselves unclean by them. I am Jehovah your God.'"

19 Jehovah spoke further to Moses, saying: **2** "Speak to the entire assembly of the Israelites and tell them, 'You should be holy, because I, Jehovah your God, am holy.ᶠ

3 "'Each of you should respect* his mother and his father,ᵍ and you should keep my sabbaths.ʰ I am Jehovah your God. **4** Do not turn to worthless godsⁱ or make for yourselves gods of cast metal.ʲ I am Jehovah your God.

5 "'Now if you offer a communion sacrifice to Jehovah,ᵏ you should sacrifice it in such a way that you gain approval for yourselves.ˡ **6** It should be eaten on the day of your sacrifice and on the next day, but what is left over until the third day should be burned in the fire.ᵐ **7** If,

---

CHAP. 18
a Le 20:21
  De 25:5
  Mr 6:17, 18
b Le 20:14
  De 27:23
c Ge 30:15
d Le 15:19, 24
  Le 20:18
e Ex 20:14
  Le 20:10
  De 22:22
  Pr 6:29
  Mt 5:27, 28
  1Co 6:9, 10
  Heb 13:4
f Le 20:2
  De 18:10
  1Ki 11:7
  2Ki 23:10
g Le 20:3
h Ge 19:5
  Le 20:13
  Jg 19:22
  Ro 1:26, 27
  1Co 6:9, 10
  Jude 7
i Ex 22:19
  Le 20:15, 16
j Le 20:23
  De 18:12

Second Col.
a Ge 15:16
b Le 20:22
  De 4:1, 40
c Ex 12:49
d De 20:17, 18
  2Ki 16:2, 3
  2Ki 21:1, 2
e Le 18:3
  Le 20:23
  De 18:9

CHAP. 19
f Le 11:44
  Isa 6:3
  1Pe 1:15, 16
  Re 4:8
g Ex 20:12
  Eph 6:2
  Heb 12:9
h Ex 20:8, 11
  Ex 31:13
  Lu 6:5
i Le 26:1
  Ps 96:5
  Hab 2:18
  1Co 10:14
j Ex 20:4, 23
  De 27:15
k Le 3:1
l Le 7:11, 12
m Le 7:17, 18

18:16 *Lit., "it is your brother's nakedness." **18:17** *Or "shameful conduct; lewdness." **18:20** *Or "your neighbor; your associate." **18:21** *Or "devoted; sacrificed."

18:29 *Or "the souls." #Or "put to death." **19:3** *Lit., "fear."

though, any of it is eaten on the third day, it is an offensive thing that will not be accepted with approval. **8** The one eating it will answer for his error because he has profaned a holy thing of Jehovah, and that person* must be cut off# from his people.

9 "'When you reap the harvest of your land, you must not reap the edge of your field completely and you must not pick up the gleaning* of your harvest.f **10** Also, you must not gather the leftovers of your vineyard or pick up the scattered grapes of your vineyard. You should leave them for the poor*b and the foreign resident. I am Jehovah your God.

11 "'You must not steal,c you must not deceive,d and you must not deal falsely with one another. **12** You must not swear to a lie in my namee and thus profane the name of your God. I am Jehovah. **13** You must not defraud your fellow man,f and you must not rob.g You should not withhold the wages of a hired worker all night until morning.h

14 "'You must not curse* a deaf man or put an obstacle before a blind man,i and you must be in fear of your God.j I am Jehovah.

15 "'You must not be unjust in your judgment. You must not show partiality to the poor or show preference to the rich.k With justice you should judge your fellow man.

16 "'You must not go around spreading slander among your people.l You must not stand up against the life* of your fellow man.#m I am Jehovah.

CHAP. 19
a Le 23:22
  De 24:19
b De 15:7
c Ex 20:15
  Eph 4:28
d Le 6:2
  Pr 12:22
  Eph 4:25
e Ex 20:7
  Mt 5:33, 37
  Jas 5:12
f Pr 22:16
  Mr 10:19
g Pr 22:22
h De 24:15
  Jer 22:13
  Jas 5:4
i De 27:18
j Le 25:17
  Ne 5:15
  Pr 1:7
  Pr 8:13
  1Pe 2:17
k Ex 23:3
  De 1:16, 17
  De 16:19
  2Ch 19:6
  Ro 2:11
  Jas 2:9
l Ps 15:1, 3
m Ex 20:16
  1Ki 21:13

Second Col.
a Pr 10:18
  1Jo 2:9
  1Jo 3:15
b Ps 141:5
  Pr 9:8
  Mt 18:15
c Pr 20:22
  Ro 12:19
d Mt 5:43, 44
  Mt 22:39
  Ro 13:9
  Ga 5:14
  Jas 2:8
e De 22:9
f De 22:11
g Le 6:6, 7
h De 26:1, 2
  Pr 3:9
i Le 3:17
  Le 17:13
  De 12:23
  Ac 15:20, 29

---

17 "'You must not hate your brother in your heart.a You should by all means reprove your fellow man,b so that you will not bear sin along with him.

18 "'You must not take vengeancec nor hold a grudge against the sons of your people, and you must love your fellow man as yourself.d I am Jehovah.

19 "'You should keep my statutes: You must not interbreed two sorts of your domestic animals. You must not sow your field with two sorts of seed,e and you must not wear a garment made with two sorts of thread mixed together.f

20 "'Now if a man lies down with a woman and has intercourse with her and she is a servant who is designated for another man, but she has not been redeemed or given her freedom, there should be a punishment. However, they should not be put to death, for she was not yet set free. **21** He should bring his guilt offering to Jehovah to the entrance of the tent of meeting, a ram of guilt offering.g **22** The priest will make atonement for him with the ram of the guilt offering before Jehovah for the sin that he committed, and he will be forgiven for the sin that he committed.

23 "'When you come into the land and you plant any tree for food, you must consider its fruitage impure and forbidden.* For three years it will be forbidden# to you. It must not be eaten. **24** But in the fourth year, all its fruit will be holy for rejoicing before Jehovah.h **25** Then in the fifth year, you may eat its fruit in order to add its produce to your harvest. I am Jehovah your God.

26 "'You must eat nothing containing blood.i

19:8 *Or "soul." #Or "put to death." **19:9** *Or "what is left." **19:10** *Or "afflicted." **19:14** *Or "call down evil upon." **19:16** *Lit., "blood." #Or possibly, "You must not stand by when your fellow man's life is endangered."

19:23 *Lit., "as its foreskin." #Lit., "uncircumcised."

"'You must not look for omens or practice magic.*a

27 "'You must not shave* the hair on the side of your head* or disfigure the edges of your beard.*b

28 "'You must not make cuts in your flesh for a dead person,*c and you must not make tattoo markings on yourselves. I am Jehovah.

29 "'Do not dishonor your daughter by making her a prostitute,*d so that the land may not commit prostitution and be filled with loose morals.*e

30 "'You must keep my sabbaths,*f and you must show reverence* for my sanctuary. I am Jehovah.

31 "'Do not turn to the spirit mediums,*g and do not consult fortune-tellers*h so as to become unclean by them. I am Jehovah your God.

32 "'Before gray hair you should rise up,*i and you must show honor to an older man,*j and you must be in fear of your God.*k I am Jehovah.

33 "'If a foreigner resides with you in your land, you must not mistreat him.*l 34 The foreigner who resides with you should become to you like a native among you;*m and you must love him as yourself, for you were foreign residents in the land of Egypt.*n I am Jehovah your God.

35 "'You must not use dishonest standards in measuring length, weight, or volume.*o 36 You should use accurate scales, accurate weights, an accurate dry measure,* and an accurate liquid measure.*#p I am Je-

CHAP. 19
a Ex 8:7
De 18:10-12
Ga 5:19, 20
Re 21:8
b Le 21:1, 5
c De 14:1
d De 23:17
e Heb 13:4
1Pe 4:3
f Le 20:10
Ex 31:13
g Le 20:6
De 18:10-12
1Ch 10:13
Isa 8:19
h Le 20:27
Ac 16:16
i Pr 16:31
Pr 20:29
j Job 32:6
Pr 23:22
1Ti 5:1
k Job 28:28
Pr 1:7
Pr 8:13
1Pe 2:17
l Ex 23:9
m Le 12:49
n Ex 22:21
o De 25:13, 15
Pr 20:10
p Pr 11:1

Second Col.
a Le 18:5
De 4:6

CHAP. 20
b Le 18:21
De 18:10
c Eze 5:11
d Le 13:6-9
e Ex 20:5
f Le 19:31
De 18:10-12
Ga 5:19, 20
Re 21:8
g Le 20:27
Ac 16:16
h 1Ch 10:13
i Le 11:44
1Pe 1:15, 16
j Le 18:4
Ec 12:13
k Ex 31:13
Le 21:8
1Th 5:23
2Th 2:13

hovah your God, who brought you out of the land of Egypt. 37 So you must keep all my statutes and all my judicial decisions, and you must follow them.*a I am Jehovah.'"

20 Jehovah went on speaking to Moses, saying: 2 "You are to say to the Israelites, 'Any man of Israel and any foreigner who resides in Israel who gives any of his offspring to Mo′lech should be put to death without fail.*b The people of the land should stone him to death. 3 I myself will set my face against that man, and I will cut him off* from among my people, because he has given some of his offspring to Mo′lech and has defiled my holy place*c and has profaned my holy name. 4 If the people of the land should deliberately close their eyes to what that man does when he gives his offspring to Mo′lech and they do not put him to death,*d 5 then I myself will certainly set my face against that man and his family.*e I will cut off* that man from his people along with all who join him in prostituting themselves to Mo′lech.

6 "'As for the person* who turns to the spirit mediums*f and the fortune-tellers*g so as to commit spiritual prostitution with them, I will certainly turn against that person* and cut him off# from his people.*h

7 "'You must sanctify yourselves and become holy,*i because I am Jehovah your God. 8 And you must keep my statutes and carry them out.*j I am Jehovah, who is sanctifying you.*k

9 "'If there is any man who curses* his father or his mother, he should be put to death

---

19:27 *Or "trim; cut." #Or "cut your sidelocks." 19:28 *Or "for a soul." The Hebrew word ne′phesh here refers to a dead person. 19:30 *Or "stand in awe of." Lit., "fear." 19:36 *Lit., "an accurate ephah." See App. B14. #Lit., "an accurate hin." See App. B14.

20:3, 6 #Or "put him to death." 20:5 *Or "put to death." 20:6 *Or "soul." 20:9 *Or "calls down evil upon."

without fail.[a] Since he has cursed his father or his mother, his own blood is upon him.

10 "'Now regarding a man who commits adultery with another man's wife: The one who commits adultery with the wife of his fellow man should be put to death without fail, the adulterer and the adulteress.[b] **11** A man who lies down with his father's wife has exposed his father to shame.*[c] Both of them should be put to death without fail. Their own blood is upon them. **12** If a man lies down with his daughter-in-law, both of them should be put to death without fail. They have violated what is natural. Their own blood is upon them.[d]

13 "'If a man lies down with a male the same as one lies down with a woman, both of them have done a detestable thing.[e] They should be put to death without fail. Their own blood is upon them.

14 "'If a man takes a woman and her mother, it is an obscene act.*[f] They should burn him and them in the fire,[g] so that obscene conduct may not continue among you.

15 "'If a man has intercourse with a beast, he should be put to death without fail, and you should kill the beast.[h] **16** If a woman approaches any beast to have intercourse with it,[i] you must kill the woman and the beast. They should be put to death without fail. Their own blood is upon them.

17 "'If a man has sexual relations with his sister, the daughter of his father or the daughter of his mother, and he sees her nakedness and she sees his nakedness, it is a disgrace.[j] They

must be cut off* before the eyes of the sons of their people. He has exposed his sister to shame.# He should answer for his error.

18 "'If a man lies down with a menstruating woman and has sexual relations with her, both he and she have exposed her flow of blood.[a] Both of them must be cut off* from among their people.

19 "'You must not have sexual relations with your mother's sister or your father's sister, because that would be exposing a blood relative to shame.[b] They should answer for their error. **20** A man who lies down with his uncle's wife has exposed his uncle to shame.*[c] They should die childless. **21** If a man takes his brother's wife, it is something abhorrent.[d] He has exposed his brother to shame.* They should become childless.

22 "'You must keep all my statutes and all my judicial decisions[e] and carry them out,[f] so that the land where I am bringing you to dwell will not vomit you out.[g] **23** You must not walk in the statutes of the nations that I am driving out from before you;[h] for they have done all these things and I abhor them.[i] **24** That is why I said to you: "You will take possession of their land, and I will give it to you as your possession, a land flowing with milk and honey.[j] Jehovah your God I am, who has set you apart from the peoples."[k] **25** You must make a distinction between the clean animal and the unclean and between the unclean bird and the

---

CHAP. 20

a Ex 21:17
De 27:16
Pr 20:20
Mt 15:4

b De 5:18
De 22:22
Ro 7:3
1Co 6:9, 10

c Le 18:8
De 27:20

d Le 18:15, 29

e Ge 19:5
Le 18:22
Jg 19:22
Ro 1:26, 27
1Co 6:9, 10
Jude 7

f Le 18:17
De 27:23

g Le 21:9

h Ex 22:19
De 27:21

i Le 18:23

j Le 18:9
De 27:22

Second Col.

a Le 18:19

b Le 18:12, 13

c Le 18:14

d Le 18:16
De 25:5

e Ex 21:1
De 5:1

f Ec 12:13

g Le 18:26, 28

h Le 18:3, 24
De 12:30

i Le 18:27
De 9:5

j Ex 3:17
Ex 6:8
De 8:7-9
Eze 20:6

k Ex 19:5
Ex 33:16
1Ki 8:53
1Pe 2:9

20:11 *Lit., "his father's nakedness." 20:14 *Or "shameful conduct; lewdness."

20:17, 18 *Or "put to death." 20:17 #Lit., "his sister's nakedness." 20:20 *Lit., "his uncle's nakedness." 20:21 *Lit., "his brother's nakedness."

clean;[a] you must not make yourselves* loathsome by means of an animal or a bird or anything that creeps on the ground that I set apart for you to regard as unclean.[b] **26** You must be holy to me, because I, Jehovah, am holy,[c] and I am setting you apart from the peoples to become mine.[d]

27 "'Any man or woman who acts as a spirit medium or is a fortune-teller* should be put to death without fail.[e] The people should stone them to death. Their own blood is upon them.'"

21 Jehovah went on to say to Moses: "Talk to the priests, Aaron's sons, and say to them, 'No one should defile himself for a dead person* among his people.[f] **2** But he may do so for a close blood relative, for his mother, his father, his son, his daughter, his brother, **3** and he may defile himself for his sister if she is a virgin who is near to him and has not yet married. **4** He may not defile himself and make himself profane for a woman who belongs to a husband of his people. **5** They should not make their heads bald[g] or shave off the fringe of their beard or make cuts on their body.[h] **6** They should be holy to their God,[i] and they should not profane the name of their God,[j] for they are presenting Jehovah's offerings made by fire, the bread* of their God, and they must be holy.[k] **7** They should not marry a prostitute,[l] a woman who has been defiled, or a woman divorced from her husband,[m] because the priest is holy to his God.[n] **8** You must sanctify him,[n] because he is one presenting the bread of your God. He should be holy to you, because I, Jehovah, the one sanctifying you, am holy.[a]

9 "'Now if the daughter of a priest should profane herself by committing prostitution, she is profaning her father. She should be burned in the fire.[b]

10 "'The high priest of his brothers, on whose head the anointing oil is poured[c] and who has been installed* to wear the priestly garments,[d] should not let his head go ungroomed or tear his garments.[e] **11** He should not approach any dead person;** he may not defile himself even for his father or his mother. **12** He should not go out from the sanctuary and should not profane the sanctuary of his God,[g] for the sign of dedication, the anointing oil of his God,[h] is upon him. I am Jehovah.

13 "'He must take as a wife a woman who is a virgin.[i] **14** He may not marry a widow, a divorced woman, one who has been defiled, or a prostitute; but he should take a virgin from his people as a wife. **15** He should not profane his offspring* among his people,[j] for I am Jehovah, who is sanctifying him.'"

16 Jehovah continued to speak to Moses, saying: **17** "Tell Aaron, 'No man of your offspring* throughout their generations who has a defect may approach to present the bread of his God. **18** If there is any man who has a defect, he may not approach: a man who is blind or lame or has a disfigured face* or one limb too long, **19** a man with a

CHAP. 20
a Le 11:46, 47
De 14:4-20

b Le 11:43

c Le 19:2
Ps 99:5
1Pe 1:15, 16
Re 4:8

d De 7:6

e Ex 22:18
Le 19:31
Le 20:6
De 18:10-12
Re 21:8

CHAP. 21
f Nu 19:14

g De 14:1

h Le 19:27, 28

i Ex 29:44

j Le 18:21
Le 19:12
Le 22:32

k Isa 52:11
1Pe 1:15, 16

l Le 19:29

m De 24:1
Eze 44:22

n Ex 28:41

Second Col.
a Ex 28:36
Le 11:45
Le 20:7, 8

b Le 20:14

c Le 8:12

d Ex 28:2
Ex 29:29
Le 16:32

e Ge 37:34
Le 10:6

f Nu 6:7
Nu 19:11, 14

g Le 10:7

h Le 8:12

i Eze 44:22

j Ezr 9:2

20:25 *Or "your souls." 20:27 *Or "has a spirit of prediction." 21:1 *Or "for a soul." 21:6 *Or "food," referring to sacrifices.

21:10 *Lit., "whose hand was filled." 21:11 *Or "any dead soul." The Hebrew word *ne′phesh* is here connected to a Hebrew word meaning "dead." 21:15, 17 *Lit., "seed." 21:18 *Lit., "or with his nose slit."

fractured foot or a fractured hand, **20** a hunchback or a dwarf,* or a man with an eye defect or eczema or ringworm or damaged testicles.ᵃ **21** No man of the offspring* of Aaron the priest who has a defect may approach to present Jehovah's offerings made by fire. Because he has a defect, he may not approach to present the bread of his God. **22** He may eat the bread of his God from the most holy thingsᵇ and from the holy things.ᶜ **23** However, he may not come near the curtain,ᵈ and he may not approach the altar,ᵉ because there is a defect in him; and he should not profane my sanctuary,ᶠ for I am Jehovah, who is sanctifying them.'"ᵍ

24 So Moses spoke to Aaron and his sons and all the Israelites.

22 Jehovah spoke further to Moses, saying: **2** "Tell Aaron and his sons that they should be careful how they handle* the holy things of the Israelites and not profane my holy nameʰ regarding the things they are sanctifying to me.ⁱ I am Jehovah. **3** Say to them, 'Throughout your generations, any of your offspring who, while he is unclean, comes near to the holy things that the Israelites sanctify to Jehovah, that person* will be cut off* from before me.ʲ I am Jehovah. **4** No man of Aaron's offspring who has leprosyᵏ or a dischargeˡ may eat of the holy things until he becomes clean,ᵐ neither the man who touches someone who became unclean by a dead person,*ⁿ nor a man who has a seminal emission,ᵒ **5** nor a man who touches an un-

clean swarming creatureᵃ or who touches a man who is unclean for any reason and who can make him unclean.ᵇ **6** The person* who touches any of these will be unclean until the evening and may not eat any of the holy things, but he should bathe himself in water.ᶜ **7** When the sun has set, he will be clean, and afterward he may eat some of the holy things because it is his food.ᵈ **8** Also, he should not eat any animal found dead or anything torn by wild animals and become unclean by it.ᵉ I am Jehovah.

9 "'They must keep their obligation to me, so that they may not incur sin because of it and have to die for it because they were profaning it. I am Jehovah, who is sanctifying them.

10 "'No unauthorized person* may eat anything holy.ᶠ No foreign guest of a priest or hired worker may eat anything holy. **11** But if a priest should purchase someone* with his own money, that person may share in eating it. Slaves born in his house may also share in eating his food.ᵍ **12** If the daughter of a priest should marry someone who is not a priest,* she may not eat of the contribution of the holy things. **13** But if the daughter of a priest should become a widow or is divorced and she has no offspring and she returns to her father's house as in her youth, she may eat some of her father's food;ʰ but no unauthorized person* may eat it.

14 "'Now if a man eats a holy thing by mistake, he must add a fifth of its value and give the holy offering to the priest.ⁱ **15** So they should not profane

---

CHAP. 21
a De 23:1

b Le 2:10
Le 6:14, 16
Le 24:8, 9
Nu 18:9

c Le 22:10
Nu 18:19

d Ex 30:6

e Ex 38:1

f Ex 25:8

g Ex 28:41

CHAP. 22
h Le 21:6

i Ex 28:38
Nu 18:32

j Le 7:20

k Le 13:2

l Le 15:2

m Le 14:2
Le 15:13

n Le 21:1
Nu 19:11, 22

o Le 15:16

Second Col.
a Le 11:24, 43

b Le 15:7, 19

c Nu 19:6, 7

d Nu 18:11

e Ex 22:31
Le 17:15
De 14:21

f Ex 29:33

g Nu 18:11

h Le 10:14
Nu 18:19

i Le 5:15, 16

21:20 *Or possibly, "emaciated."
21:21 *Lit., "seed." 22:2 *Lit., "they should separate themselves from."
22:3, 6 *Or "soul." 22:3 #Or "put to death." 22:4 *Or "by a soul."

22:10 *Lit., "No stranger," that is, a man not of Aaron's family. 22:11 *Or "a soul." 22:12 *Or "marry a stranger." 22:13 *Lit., "stranger," that is, a man not of Aaron's family.

the holy things of the Israelites that they contribute to Jehovah[a] **16** and cause themselves to incur punishment for their guilt because of eating their holy things; for I am Jehovah, who is sanctifying them.'"

17 Jehovah continued speaking to Moses, saying: **18** "Speak to Aaron and his sons and all the Israelites and say to them, 'When an Israelite man or a foreign resident in Israel presents a burnt offering[b] to Jehovah to fulfill his vows or to make a voluntary offering,[c] **19** he should present a sound male[d] from the herd, the young rams, or the goats, in order to gain approval. **20** You must not present anything with a defect,[e] for it will not serve to gain approval for you.

21 "'If a man presents a communion sacrifice[f] to Jehovah to pay a vow or as a voluntary offering, it should be a sound animal from the herd or the flock, in order to gain approval. No defect at all should be in it. **22** No offering should be blind, have a fracture, a cut, a wart, scabbiness, or ringworm; you must not present any of these to Jehovah or make such an offering on the altar for Jehovah. **23** You may present a bull or a sheep with a limb that is too long or too short as a voluntary offering, but it will not be accepted with approval as a vow offering. **24** You must not present to Jehovah one having the testicles damaged or crushed or pulled off or cut off, and you should not offer such animals in your land. **25** And you must not present any of these from the bread of a foreigner as the bread of your God, for they are corrupted and defective. They will not be accepted with approval for you.'"

26 Jehovah spoke further to Moses, saying: **27** "When a bull

or a young ram or a goat is born, it will continue with its mother for seven days,[a] but from the eighth day forward it will be accepted with approval as an offering, an offering made by fire to Jehovah. **28** As for a bull or a sheep, you must not slaughter it and its young on the same day.[b]

29 "If you sacrifice a thanksgiving sacrifice to Jehovah,[c] you should sacrifice it to gain approval for yourselves. **30** It should be eaten on that day. You must not leave any of it until morning.[d] I am Jehovah.

31 "You must keep my commandments and carry them out.[e] I am Jehovah. **32** You must not profane my holy name,[f] and I must be sanctified in the midst of the Israelites.[g] I am Jehovah, who is sanctifying you,[h] **33** the one bringing you out of the land of Egypt to prove myself God to you.[i] I am Jehovah."

23 Jehovah continued speaking to Moses, saying: **2** "Speak to the Israelites and tell them, 'The seasonal festivals[j] of Jehovah that you should proclaim[k] are holy conventions. These are my seasonal festivals:

3 "'Six days work may be done, but on the seventh day is a sabbath of complete rest,[l] a holy convention. You may not do any sort of work. It is to be a sabbath to Jehovah wherever you dwell.[m]

4 "'These are the seasonal festivals of Jehovah, holy conventions that you should proclaim at the times appointed for them: **5** In the first month, on the 14th day of the month,[n] at twilight* is the Passover[o] to Jehovah.

6 "'On the 15th day of this month is the Festival of Unleavened Bread to Jehovah.[p] Seven days you should eat unleavened bread.[q] **7** On the first day,

---

CHAP. 22
a Nu 18:32
b Nu 15:14, 16
c Le 7:16
   Nu 15:3
   De 12:5, 6
d Le 1:3
   Le 22:22
e De 15:19, 21
   De 17:1
   Mal 1:8
   Heb 9:14
   1Pe 1:19
f Le 3:1

Second Col.
a Ex 22:30
b Ex 23:19
   De 22:6
c Le 7:12
d Le 7:15
e Le 19:37
   Nu 15:40
   De 4:40
f Le 18:21
   Le 19:12
g Le 10:3
h Le 19:5
   Le 20:8
   Le 21:8
i Le 6:7
   Le 11:45

CHAP. 23
j Ex 23:14
   Le 23:37
k Nu 10:10
l Ex 16:30
   Ex 20:10
   Ac 15:21
m Ne 13:22
n Nu 9:2, 3
   Nu 28:16
o Ex 12:3, 6
   De 16:1
   1Co 5:7
p Nu 28:17
   1Co 5:8
q Ex 12:15
   Ex 13:6
   Ex 34:18

23:5 *Lit., "between the two evenings."

you will observe a holy convention.[a] You should not do any hard work. **8** But you are to present an offering made by fire to Jehovah for seven days. There will be a holy convention on the seventh day. You should not do any hard work.'"

9 Jehovah continued to speak to Moses, saying: **10** "Speak to the Israelites and tell them, 'When you eventually come into the land that I am giving you and you have reaped its harvest, you must bring a sheaf of the firstfruits[b] of your harvest to the priest.[c] **11** And he will wave the sheaf back and forth before Jehovah to gain approval for you. The priest should wave it on the day after the Sabbath. **12** On the day you have the sheaf waved, you must offer a sound young ram in its first year, as a burnt offering to Jehovah. **13** Its grain offering will be two tenths of an e'phah* of fine flour mixed with oil, as an offering made by fire to Jehovah, a pleasing" aroma. Its drink offering will be a fourth of a hin△ of wine. **14** You must not eat any bread, roasted grain, or new grain until this day, until you bring the offering of your God. It is a lasting statute for all your generations wherever you dwell.

15 "'You are to count seven sabbaths from the day after the Sabbath, from the day that you bring the sheaf of the wave offering.[d] They should be complete weeks. **16** You will count off 50 days[e] until the day after the seventh Sabbath, and then you should present a new grain offering to Jehovah.[f] **17** You should bring from your dwelling places

two loaves as a wave offering. These should be made of two tenths of an e'phah* of fine flour. They should be baked with leaven,[a] as first ripe fruits to Jehovah.[b] **18** And you should present along with the loaves seven sound male lambs, each a year old, and one young bull and two rams.[c] They will serve as a burnt offering to Jehovah along with the corresponding grain offering and drink offerings, as an offering made by fire, of a pleasing" aroma to Jehovah. **19** And you must offer one young goat as a sin offering[d] and two male lambs, each a year old, as a communion sacrifice.[e] **20** The priest will wave them back and forth along with the loaves of the first ripe fruits, as a wave offering before Jehovah, together with the two male lambs. They should serve as something holy to Jehovah for the priest.[f] **21** On this day you will make a proclamation[g] for a holy convention for yourselves. You may not do any hard work. It is a lasting statute in all your dwelling places for all your generations.

22 "'When you reap the harvest of your land, you must not reap the edge of your field completely and you should not pick up what is left from your harvest.[h] You should leave it for the poor*[i] and for the foreign resident.[j] I am Jehovah your God.'"

23 Jehovah went on speaking to Moses, saying: **24** "Tell the Israelites, 'In the seventh month, on the first of the month, you should observe a complete rest, a memorial signaled by a trumpet blast,[k] a holy convention. **25** You may not do any hard work, and you will present an offering made by fire to Jehovah.'"

26 Jehovah spoke further to Moses, saying: **27** "However,

CHAP. 23
a Ex 12:16

b 1Co 15:20, 23

c Nu 18:8, 12
Pr 3:9
Eze 44:30

d Ex 34:22
De 16:9, 10

e Ac 2:1

f Nu 28:26-31
De 16:16

Second Col.
a Le 7:11, 13

b Ex 23:16
Ex 34:22

c Nu 28:26, 27

d Le 4:23

e Le 3:1

f Le 7:34
Le 10:14
Nu 18:9
De 18:4
1Co 9:13

g Nu 10:10

h Le 19:9
De 24:19
Ru 2:2, 3

i Isa 58:7

j Le 19:33

k Nu 10:10
Nu 29:1

23:13, 17 *Two tenths of an ephah equaled 4.4 L (4 dry qt). See App. B14. **23:13, 18** "Or "appeasing; soothing." Lit., "restful." **23:13** △A hin equaled 3.67 L (7.75 pt). See App. B14.

23:22 *Or "afflicted."

on the tenth of this seventh month is the Day of Atonement.[a] You should observe a holy convention, and you must afflict yourselves*[b] and present an offering made by fire to Jehovah. **28** You are not to do any sort of work on this particular day because it is a day of atonement to make atonement[c] for you before Jehovah your God. **29** Anyone* who will not afflict himself*[#] on this day will be cut off[△] from his people.[d] **30** And I will destroy from among his people every person* who does any sort of work on this day. **31** You must not do any sort of work. It is a lasting statute for all your generations wherever you dwell. **32** It is a sabbath of complete rest for you, and you will afflict yourselves*[e] on the ninth of the month in the evening. You should observe your sabbath from evening to evening."

33 Jehovah continued speaking to Moses, saying: **34** "Tell the Israelites, 'On the 15th day of this seventh month is the Festival of Booths* for seven days to Jehovah.[f] **35** There is to be a holy convention on the first day, and you should not do any hard work. **36** Seven days you must present an offering made by fire to Jehovah. On the eighth day, you should observe a holy convention,[g] and you should present an offering made by fire to Jehovah. It is a solemn assembly. You may not do any hard work.

37 "'These are the seasonal festivals[h] of Jehovah that you

should proclaim as holy conventions[a] for presenting an offering made by fire to Jehovah: the burnt offering[b] and the grain offering[c] of the sacrifice and the drink offerings[d] according to the daily schedule. **38** These are in addition to what is offered on Jehovah's sabbaths,[e] and your gifts,[f] your vow offerings,[g] and your voluntary offerings,[h] which you should give to Jehovah. **39** However, on the 15th day of the seventh month, when you have gathered the produce of the land, you should celebrate the festival of Jehovah for seven days.[i] On the first day is a complete rest and on the eighth day is a complete rest.[j] **40** On the first day, you will take the fruit of majestic trees, the fronds of palm trees,[k] the branches of leafy trees and poplars of the valley,* and you will rejoice[l] before Jehovah your God for seven days.[m] **41** You will celebrate it as a festival to Jehovah for seven days in the year.[n] As a lasting statute during all your generations, you should celebrate it in the seventh month. **42** You should dwell in the booths for seven days.[o] All the natives in Israel should dwell in the booths, **43** so that your future generations may know[p] that it was in the booths that I made the Israelites dwell when I was bringing them out of the land of Egypt.[q] I am Jehovah your God.'"

44 So Moses spoke of the seasonal festivals of Jehovah to the Israelites.

24 Jehovah continued to speak to Moses, saying: **2** "Command the Israelites to bring to you pure, beaten olive oil for the lights, to keep the lamps lit constantly.[r] **3** Outside the curtain of the Testimony in the tent of meeting, Aaron

---

CHAP. 23
a Ex 30:10
  Le 25:9
b Le 16:29, 30
  Nu 29:7
c Le 16:34
  Heb 9:12,
  24-26
  Heb 10:10
  1Jo 2:1, 2
d Nu 9:13
  Nu 15:30
e Le 16:29-31
  Le 23:27
  Nu 29:7
f Ex 23:16
  Nu 29:12
  De 16:13
  Ezr 3:4
  Ne 8:14-18
  Joh 7:2
g Ne 8:18
h Le 23:14
  De 16:16

Second Col.
a Nu 28:26
  Nu 29:7
b Le 1:3
c Le 2:1, 11
d Nu 15:5
  Nu 28:6, 7
e Le 16:23
  Le 20:8
  Ex 31:13
f Ex 28:38
  Nu 18:29
g De 12:11
h Nu 29:39
  De 12:6
  1Ch 29:9
  2Ch 35:8
  Ezr 2:68
i De 16:13
j Nu 29:12
k Ne 8:15
  Re 7:9
l Ne 8:10
m De 16:15
n Nu 29:12
o De 31:10, 11
p De 31:13
  Ps 78:6
q Ex 12:37, 38
  Nu 24:5

CHAP. 24
r Ex 27:20, 21
  Nu 8:2

23:27 *Or "your souls." To "afflict oneself" is generally understood to mean various forms of self-denial, including fasting. **23:29** *Or "Any soul." #Or possibly, "not fast." △Or "put to death." **23:30** *Or "soul." **23:32** *Or "your souls." **23:34** *Or "Temporary Shelters."

23:40 *Or "wadi."

should arrange to keep the lamps lit from evening to morning before Jehovah constantly. It is a permanent statute for all your generations. **4** He should set the lamps in order on the lampstand[a] of pure gold before Jehovah constantly.

5 "You will take fine flour and bake it into 12 ring-shaped loaves. Two tenths of an e′phah* should go into each loaf. **6** You will place them in two sets of layers, six to the layer set,[b] on the table of pure gold before Jehovah.[c] **7** You should put pure frankincense on each layer set, and it will serve as the bread for a token offering*[d] made by fire to Jehovah. **8** On each Sabbath day, he should regularly arrange it before Jehovah.[e] It is a lasting covenant with the Israelites. **9** It will become Aaron's and his sons',[f] and they will eat it in a holy place,[g] because it is something most holy for him from Jehovah's offerings made by fire, as a lasting regulation."

10 Now among the Israelites was a son of an Israelite woman and an Egyptian man,[h] and a fight broke out between him and an Israelite man in the camp. **11** The son of the Israelite woman began to abuse the Name* and to curse# it.[i] So they brought him to Moses.[j] Incidentally, his mother was She′lo′mith, the daughter of Dib′ri of the tribe of Dan. **12** They placed him in custody until Jehovah's decision was made clear to them.[k]

13 Then Jehovah said to Moses: **14** "Bring the one who cursed to the outside of the camp, and all those who heard

him must lay their hands on his head, and then the entire assembly must stone him.[a] **15** And you should tell the Israelites, 'If any man curses his God, he will answer for his sin. **16** So the abuser of Jehovah's name should be put to death without fail.[b] The entire assembly should stone him without fail. The foreign resident should be put to death the same as the native for his abusing the Name.

17 "'If a man takes a human life,* he should be put to death without fail.[c] **18** Anyone who strikes and kills a domestic animal* should make compensation for it, life for life.# **19** If a man injures his fellow man, then what he has done should be done to him.[d] **20** Fracture for fracture, eye for eye, tooth for tooth, the same sort of injury he inflicted should be inflicted on him.[e] **21** The man who strikes and kills an animal should make compensation for it,[f] but the one who strikes and kills a man should be put to death.[g]

22 "'One judicial decision will apply for you, whether a foreign resident or a native,[h] because I am Jehovah your God.'"

23 Moses then spoke to the Israelites, and they brought the one who uttered the curse to the outside of the camp, and they stoned him.[i] Thus the Israelites did just as Jehovah had commanded Moses.

25 Jehovah spoke further to Moses on Mount Si′nai, saying: **2** "Speak to the Israelites and tell them, 'When you eventually come into the land that I am giving you,[j] then the land will observe a sabbath to Jehovah.[k] **3** Six years you

---

CHAP. 24

a Ex 25:31
  Ex 39:33, 37
  Heb 9:2

b Ex 40:22, 23
  1Sa 21:4
  Mr 2:25, 26

c Ex 25:23, 24
  1Ki 7:48

d Le 2:2
  Le 6:15

e Nu 4:7
  1Ch 9:32
  2Ch 2:4

f Le 21:22
  Le 22:10
  1Sa 21:4, 6
  Mt 12:3, 4
  Lu 6:3, 4

g Le 6:14, 16

h Ex 12:38
  Nu 11:4

i Ex 20:7
  Ex 22:28
  Le 19:12

j Ex 18:22

k Ex 18:15, 16
  Nu 15:32, 34

Second Col.

a Nu 15:32, 35
  De 17:7

b De 5:11

c Ge 9:6
  Ex 21:12
  Nu 35:31
  De 19:11-13

d Ex 21:23, 24

e De 19:21
  Mt 5:38

f Ex 22:1

g Ge 9:6
  Ex 21:12

h Ex 12:49
  Le 17:10
  Le 19:34
  Nu 9:14
  Nu 15:16

i Nu 15:33, 36
  De 17:7

CHAP. 25

j Ge 15:16

k Le 26:34
  2Ch 36:20, 21

24:5 *Two tenths of an ephah equaled 4.4 L (4 dry qt). See App. B14. 24:7 *Or "as a memorial (representative) portion of it." 24:11 *That is, the name Jehovah, as indicated by vss. 15 and 16. #Or "call down evil upon."

24:17 *Or "fatally strikes any human soul." 24:18 *Or "And one who fatally strikes the soul of an animal." #Or "soul for soul."

should sow your field with seed, and six years you should prune your vineyard, and you will gather the land's produce.[a] **4** But in the seventh year, there should be a sabbath of complete rest for the land, a sabbath to Jehovah. You should not sow your field with seed or prune your vineyard. **5** You must not reap what grows on its own from the grain left after the harvest, and the grapes of your unpruned vine you must not gather. There should be a year of complete rest for the land. **6** However, you may eat the food that grows in the land during its sabbath; you, your male and female slaves, your hired worker, and the foreign settlers who are residing with you may eat it, **7** as well as the domestic and the wild animals in your land. Everything the land produces may be eaten.

8 "'You will count off seven sabbath years, seven times seven years, and the days of the seven sabbath years will amount to 49 years. **9** You will then sound the horn loudly in the seventh month, on the tenth of the month; on the Day of Atonement,[b] you should cause the sound of the horn to be heard in all your land. **10** You must sanctify the 50th year and proclaim liberty in the land to all its inhabitants.[c] It will become a Jubilee for you, and each of you will return to his property and each of you should return to his family.[d] **11** A Jubilee is what that 50th year will become for you. You will not sow seed or reap what grew on its own from leftover grain nor gather the grapes of unpruned vines.[e] **12** For it is a Jubilee. It is to be holy to you. You may eat only what the land produces by itself.[f]

13 "'In this year of the Jubilee, each of you should re-

turn to his property.[a] **14** If you sell anything to your fellow man or if you buy from him, do not exploit one another.[b] **15** You should buy from your fellow man, taking into account the number of the years after the Jubilee, and he should sell to you according to the remaining years for crops.[c] **16** If there are many years remaining, he may increase its purchase price, and when there are few years left, he should reduce its purchase price, because he is selling you the number of crops to be produced. **17** No one among you should exploit his fellow man,[d] and you must be in fear of your God,[e] for I am Jehovah your God.[f] **18** By your carrying out my statutes and keeping my judicial decisions, you will dwell in security in the land.[g] **19** The land will give its fruitage,[h] and you will eat to satisfaction and dwell there in security.[i]

20 "'But if you should say: "What will we eat in the seventh year if we may not sow seed or gather our crops?"[j] **21** I will command my blessing for you in the sixth year, and the land will yield a crop sufficient for three years.[k] **22** Then you will sow seed in the eighth year and eat from the old crop until the ninth year. Until its crop arrives, you will eat from the old.

23 "'The land should not be sold on a permanent basis,[l] because the land is mine.[m] For you are foreign residents and settlers from my standpoint,[n] **24** Throughout the land of your possession, you should grant the right of buying back the land.

25 "'If your brother becomes poor and has to sell some of his property, a repurchaser who is closely related to him must come and buy back what his brother sold.[o] **26** If anyone has

---

CHAP. 25

a Ex 23:10, 11

b Le 16:30
  Le 23:27, 28

c Isa 61:1, 2
  Lu 4:18, 19
  Ro 8:20, 21

d Le 27:24
  Nu 36:4
  De 15:1

e Le 25:5

f Ex 23:11
  Le 25:6

Second Col.

a Le 25:29, 30
  Le 27:24

b 1Sa 12:3
  Pr 14:31

c Le 27:18

d Le 19:13
  Pr 22:22

e Le 25:43
  Pr 1:7
  Pr 8:13

f Isa 33:22

g De 12:10
  Ps 4:8
  Pr 1:33

h Ps 67:6

i Le 26:3-5

j Le 25:4, 5
  Mt 6:25

k Ge 26:12
  De 28:8
  Mal 3:10

l 1Ki 21:3

m Ps 24:1

n 1Ch 29:15

o Ru 2:20
  Ru 4:4-6

no repurchaser but he becomes prosperous and finds the means to repurchase it, **27** he should calculate its value for the years since he sold it and refund the difference to the man whom he sold it to. Then he may return to his property.[a]

28 "'But if he does not find the means to get it back from him, what he sold will remain with the purchaser until the Jubilee year;[b] and it will revert to him in the Jubilee, and he will return to his property.[c]

29 "'Now if a man should sell a home in a walled city, his right of repurchase will also continue until the end of the year from the time of his completing the sale; his right of repurchase[d] will be valid a whole year. **30** But if it is not bought back by the end of one full year, the house within the walled city will become the permanent property of its purchaser throughout his generations. It should not be released in the Jubilee. **31** However, the houses of settlements with no surrounding wall should be considered to be part of the field of the countryside. The right of repurchase should continue for it, and it should be released in the Jubilee.

32 "'As for the houses of the Levites within their cities,[e] the Levites will have the permanent right to repurchase them. **33** When the property of the Levites is not bought back, the house sold in the city belonging to them will also be released in the Jubilee,[f] because the houses of the cities of the Levites are their property among the Israelites.[g] **34** Moreover, the field of pasture ground[h] surrounding their cities may not be sold, for it is their permanent possession.

35 "'If your brother who is nearby becomes poor and cannot support himself, you must

sustain him[a] as you would a foreign resident and a settler,[b] so that he may keep alive with you. **36** Do not take interest or make a profit* from him.[c] You must be in fear of your God,[d] and your brother will keep alive with you. **37** You must not lend him your money on interest[e] or give out your food for profit. **38** I am Jehovah your God, who brought you out of the land of Egypt[f] to give you the land of Ca′naan, to prove myself your God.[g]

39 "'If your brother who lives nearby becomes poor and he has to sell himself to you,[h] you must not force him to do slave labor.[i] **40** He should be treated like a hired worker,[j] like a settler. He should serve with you until the Jubilee year. **41** Then he will leave you, he and his children* with him, and return to his family. He should return to the property of his forefathers.[k] **42** For they are my slaves whom I brought out of the land of Egypt.[l] They should not sell themselves the way a slave is sold. **43** You must not treat him cruelly,[m] and you must be in fear of your God.[n] **44** Your male and female slaves are to come from the nations around you, from them you may buy a male or a female slave. **45** Also from the sons of the foreign settlers who are residing with you,[o] from them and from their families that are born to them in your land you may buy slaves, and they will become your possession. **46** You may pass them on as an inheritance to your sons after you to inherit as a permanent possession. You may use them as workers, but you must not subject your Israelite brothers to cruel treatment.[p]

47 "'But if a foreign resident or a settler among you be-

25:36 *Or "take usury." 25:41 *Lit., "sons."

comes wealthy and your brother has become poor alongside him and must sell himself to the foreign resident or the settler who lives among you, or to a member of the family of the foreign resident, **48** he will continue to have the right of repurchase after he has sold himself. One of his brothers may buy him back,[a] **49** or his uncle or the son of his uncle may buy him back, or any close relative,* one of his family, may buy him back.

"'Or if he himself has become wealthy, he may also buy himself back.[b] **50** He should calculate with his purchaser the time from the year he sold himself to him until the Jubilee year,[c] and the money of his sale will correspond to the number of years.[d] His workdays during that time will be assessed at the rate of a hired worker.[e] **51** If there are many years remaining, he should pay his repurchase price in proportion to the years that are left. **52** But if only a few years remain until the Jubilee year, he should then calculate for himself and pay his repurchase price in proportion to the years remaining. **53** He should continue to serve him year by year as a hired worker; and you should see to it that he does not treat him cruelly.[f] **54** However, if he cannot buy himself back on these terms, he will then go free in the year of Jubilee,[g] he and his children* with him.

55 "'For the Israelites are my own slaves. They are my slaves whom I brought out of the land of Egypt.[h] I am Jehovah your God.

26 "'You must not make worthless gods for yourselves,[i] and you must not set up a carved image[j] or a sacred pillar for yourselves, and you must not put a stone figure[a] in your land in order to bow down toward it;[b] for I am Jehovah your God. **2** You should keep my sabbaths and show reverence for* my sanctuary. I am Jehovah.

3 "'If you continue walking in my statutes and keeping my commandments and you carry them out,[c] **4** I will give you showers of rain at their proper time,[d] and the land will yield its produce,[e] and the trees of the field will give their fruit. **5** Your threshing season will extend until your grape harvest, and the grape harvest will extend until the sowing season; and you will eat your bread to satisfaction and dwell in security in your land.[f] **6** I will put peace in the land,[g] and you will lie down with no one making you afraid;[h] and I will rid the land of vicious wild animals, and a sword of war will not pass through your land. **7** You will certainly pursue your enemies, and they will fall before you by the sword. **8** Five of you will pursue 100, and 100 of you will pursue 10,000, and your enemies will fall before you by the sword.[i]

9 "'I will direct my favor to* you and make you fruitful and multiply you,[j] and I will keep my covenant with you.[k] **10** While you are still eating the old produce of the preceding year, you will need to clear out the old to make way for the new. **11** And I will place my tabernacle in your midst,[l] and I* will not reject you. **12** I will walk among you and be your God,[m] and you for your part will be my people.[n] **13** I am Jehovah your God, who brought you out of the land of Egypt to

---

CHAP. 25
a Le 25:25
b Le 25:26, 27
c Le 25:10
d Le 25:15, 16
e De 15:18
f Le 25:40, 43
  Col 4:1
g Ex 21:3
h Ex 20:2
  Le 25:42

CHAP. 26
i Ex 20:4
  Le 19:4
  Ac 17:29
  1Co 8:4
j De 5:8

Second Col.
a Nu 33:52
b Da 3:18
  1Co 10:14
c De 11:13-15
  Ec 12:13
d De 28:12
  Isa 30:23
  Eze 34:26
  Joe 2:23
e Ps 67:6
  Ps 85:12
f Le 25:18
g 1Ch 22:9
  Ps 29:11
  Hag 2:9
h Mic 4:4
i De 28:7
  Jos 23:10
  Jg 7:15, 16
  Jg 15:15, 16
  1Ch 11:20
j De 28:4
k Ex 6:4
l Ex 25:8
  Eze 37:26
  Re 21:3
m De 23:14
n Ex 6:7
  2Co 6:16

25:49 *Or "any blood relative." 25:54 *Lit., "sons." 26:2 *Or "stand in awe of." Lit., "fear." 26:9 *Lit., "will turn to." 26:11 *Or "my soul."

be their slaves no longer, and I broke the bars of your yoke and made you walk with heads held high.*

14 "However, if you will not listen to me or keep all these commandments,[a] and if you reject my statutes,[b] and if you* abhor my judicial decisions so that you do not keep all my commandments, and you violate my covenant,[c] 16 I, for my part, will do the following to you: I will punish you with distress, with tuberculosis and burning fever, making your eyes fail and your life* waste away. You will sow your seed simply for nothing, for your enemies will eat it.[d] 17 I will set my face against you, and you will be defeated by your enemies;[e] and those who hate you will tread on you,[f] and you will flee when no one is pursuing you.[g]

18 "If even this does not make you listen to me, I will have to chastise you seven times as much for your sins. 19 I will break your stubborn pride and make your heavens like iron[h] and your earth like copper. 20 You will exhaust your strength for nothing, as your land will not yield its produce,[i] and the trees of the land will not produce fruit.

21 "But if you keep walking in opposition to me and refuse to listen to me, I will then have to strike you seven times as much, according to your sins. 22 I will send the wild animals of the field among you,[j] and they will bereave you of children[k] and annihilate your domestic animals and reduce your numbers, and your roads will be deserted.[l]

23 "If in spite of these things you do not accept my correction[m] and you insist on walking

in opposition to me, 24 then I too will walk in opposition to you, and I myself will strike you seven times for your sins. 25 I will bring an avenging sword upon you for breaking the covenant.[a] If you gather yourselves into your cities, I will send disease into your midst,[b] and you will be given into the hand of an enemy.[c] 26 When I destroy your supply* of bread,*[d] ten women will be able to bake your bread in only one oven and then ration your bread by weight;[e] and you will eat but you will not be satisfied.[f]

27 "If in spite of this you will not listen to me and you insist on walking in opposition to me, 28 I will intensify my opposition to you,[g] and I myself will have to chastise you seven times for your sins. 29 So you will have to eat the flesh of your sons, and you will eat the flesh of your daughters.[h] 30 I will annihilate your sacred high places[i] and cut down your incense stands and pile your carcasses on the carcasses of your disgusting idols,*[j] and I* will turn away from you in disgust.[k] 31 I will give your cities to the sword[l] and make your sanctuaries desolate, and I will not smell the pleasing* aromas of your sacrifices. 32 I myself will make the land desolate,[m] and your enemies who are dwelling in it will stare in amazement over it.[n] 33 And I will scatter you among the nations,[o] and I will unsheathe a sword after you;[p] and your land will be made desolate,[q] and your cities will be devastated.

CHAP. 26
a De 28:15
b 2Ki 17:15
c Ex 24:7
De 31:16
Heb 8:9
d De 28:22, 33
Jg 6:3
e De 28:15, 25
Jg 2:14
1Sa 4:10
f Ps 106:41
La 1:5
g Le 26:36
h De 11:17
1Ki 17:1
i Jer 12:13
Hag 1:6, 10
j De 32:24
Jer 15:3
k Eze 5:17
l Jg 5:6
Isa 33:8
Zec 7:14
m Isa 1:16
Jer 2:30
Jer 5:3

Second Col.
a Ex 24:7
b De 28:21
Jer 24:10
Am 4:10
c Jg 2:14
1Sa 4:10
d Eze 5:16
e Eze 4:16
f Isa 9:20
Mic 6:14
Hag 1:6
g Jer 21:5
h De 28:53
2Ki 6:29
Jer 19:9
La 4:10
Eze 5:10
i 2Ch 34:3
Isa 27:9
j 1Ki 13:2
2Ki 23:8, 20
Eze 6:5
k Ps 78:58, 59
l Jer 25:9, 10
2Ch 36:17
Ne 2:3
Isa 1:7
Jer 4:7
m Jer 9:11
n Jer 28:37
De 29:22-24
Jer 18:16
La 2:15
Eze 5:15
o Ps 44:11
p Jer 9:16
Eze 12:14
q Zec 7:14

26:13 *Lit., "walk erect." 26:15 *Or "your souls." 26:16 *Or "soul." 26:26 *Lit., "rod." Possibly referring to rods used for storing bread. *Or "food." 26:30 *The Hebrew term may be related to a word for "dung" and is used as an expression of contempt. *Or "my soul." 26:31 *Or "appeasing; soothing." Lit., "restful."

34 "'At that time the land will pay off its sabbaths all the days it lies desolate, while you are in the land of your enemies. At that time the land will rest,* as it must repay its sabbaths.ª **35** All the days it lies desolate it will rest, because it did not rest during your sabbaths when you were dwelling on it.

36 "'As for those who survive,ᵇ I will fill their hearts with despair in the lands of their enemies; and the sound of a blowing leaf will cause them to flee, and they will flee like someone running from the sword and fall without anyone pursuing them.ᶜ **37** They will stumble over one another like those running from a sword, though no one is pursuing them. You will not be able to resist your enemies.ᵈ **38** You will perish among the nations,ᵉ and the land of your enemies will consume you. **39** Those of you who remain will be left to rot in the lands of your enemiesᶠ because of your error. Yes, they will rot away because of the errors of their fathers.ᵍ **40** Then they will confess their own errorʰ and the error and unfaithfulness of their fathers and admit that they behaved unfaithfully by walking in opposition to me.ⁱ **41** Then I also walked in opposition to themʲ by bringing them into the land of their enemies.ᵏ

"'Perhaps then their uncircumcised* heart will be humbled,ˡ and then they will pay off their error. **42** And I will remember my covenant with Jacob,ᵐ and my covenant with Isaac,ⁿ and I will remember my covenant with Abraham,º and I will remember the land. **43** While the land was abandoned by them, it was paying

off its sabbathsª and lying desolate without them, and they were paying for their error, because they rejected my judicial decisions and they* abhorred my statutes.ᵇ **44** But despite all of this, while they are in the land of their enemies, I will never completely reject themᶜ nor cast them away to the point of exterminating them, which would violate my covenantᵈ with them, for I am Jehovah their God. **45** For their sakes I will remember the covenant with their ancestorsᵉ whom I brought out of the land of Egypt under the eyes of the nations,ᶠ in order to prove myself their God. I am Jehovah.'"

46 These are the regulations, the judicial decisions, and the laws that Jehovah established between himself and the Israelites on Mount Si′nai through Moses.ᵍ

27 Jehovah continued to speak to Moses, saying: **2** "Speak to the Israelites and tell them, 'If a man makes a special vowʰ to offer the estimated value of a person* to Jehovah, **3** the estimated value of a male from 20 to 60 years old will be 50 shekels* of silver by the standard shekel of the holy place.ᵈ **4** But if it is a female, the estimated value will be 30 shekels. **5** If the age is from 5 to 20 years old, the estimated value of the male will be 20 shekels and 10 shekels for the female. **6** If the age is from one month up to five years old, the estimated value of the male will be five shekels of silver and three shekels of silver for the female.

7 "'If the age is 60 years and over, the estimated value will be 15 shekels for the male and

---

CHAP. 26
a 2Ch 36:20, 21
b Isa 24:6
c Le 26:17
  Isa 30:17
d Jos 7:12
  Jg 2:14
  Jer 37:10
e De 4:27
  De 28:48
  Jer 42:17
f De 28:65
g Ex 20:5
  Nu 14:18
h 1Ki 8:33
  Ne 9:2
  Eze 6:9
  Da 9:5
i Eze 36:31
j Le 26:24
k 1Ki 8:47
  2Ch 36:20
l De 30:6
  Jer 4:4
  Ac 7:51
m Ge 28:13
n Ge 26:3
o Ge 12:7
  De 4:31
  Ps 106:45

Second Col.
a Le 26:34
  2Ch 36:20, 21
b 2Ki 17:15
c De 4:31
  2Ki 13:23
  Ne 9:31
d De 4:13
  Jer 14:21
e Ex 24:3, 8
  De 9:9
f Le 20:9
g Le 27:34
  De 6:1

CHAP. 27
h De 23:21
  Jg 11:30, 31
  1Sa 1:11

26:34 *Or "keep sabbath." 26:41 *Or "stubborn." 26:43 *Or "their souls." 27:2 *Or "soul." 27:3 *A shekel equaled 11.4 g (0.367 oz t). See App. B14. ᵈOr "by the holy shekel."

10 shekels for the female. **8** But if he is too poor to pay the estimated value,[a] the person will stand before the priest, and the priest will set a value on him. The priest will make the valuation according to what the one making the vow can afford.[b]

9 "'If the vow involves an animal that is suitable for offering to Jehovah, whatever may be given to Jehovah will become something holy. **10** He may not replace it or exchange it with good for bad or with bad for good. But if he should exchange it with one animal for another animal, the original and what is exchanged for it will both become holy. **11** If it is an unclean animal[c] that may not be presented as an offering to Jehovah, he will then stand the animal before the priest. **12** The priest will then set its value, as to whether it is good or bad. The value estimated by the priest will stand. **13** But if he ever wants to buy it back, he must then give a fifth of it in addition to the estimated value.[d]

14 "'Now if a man should sanctify his house as something holy to Jehovah, the priest will then set its value, whether it is good or bad. According to the value that the priest sets, that is what it will cost.[e] **15** But if the one who sanctifies his house wants to buy it back, he must then give a fifth of the money of the estimated value in addition to it, and it will become his.

16 "'If a man sanctifies to Jehovah some of the field that he possesses, the value will be estimated in proportion to the seed needed to sow it: a ho′mer* of barley seed will be 50 shekels of silver. **17** If he sanctifies his field from the year of Jubi-

lee,[a] the estimated value stands. **18** If he sanctifies his field after the Jubilee, the priest will calculate for him the price in proportion to the years that are left until the next year of Jubilee, and a deduction should be made from the estimated value.[b] **19** But if the one who sanctified it should ever buy the field back, he must then give a fifth of the money of the estimated value in addition to it, and it will remain his. **20** Now if he should not buy the field back and the field is sold to another man, it may not be bought back again. **21** When the field is released in the Jubilee, it will become something holy to Jehovah, as a field that is devoted to him. It will become the property of the priests.[c]

22 "'If a man sanctifies to Jehovah a field he purchased that is not part of his hereditary property,[d] **23** the priest will calculate for him the amount of the valuation up until the year of Jubilee, and he will give the estimated value on that day.[e] It is something holy to Jehovah. **24** In the year of Jubilee, the field will return to the one he bought it from, to the one land belongs to.[f]

25 "'Every value should be estimated by the standard shekel of the holy place. The shekel should amount to 20 ge′rahs.*

26 "'However, no one should sanctify the firstborn of the animals, since it is born as the firstborn for Jehovah.[g] Whether bull or sheep, it already belongs to Jehovah.[h] **27** If it is among the unclean animals and he redeems it according to the estimated value, he should give a fifth of it in addition to it.[i] But if it is not bought back, it will be sold according to the estimated value.

CHAP. 27

a Le 5:7, 11
Le 12:8
Le 14:21

b Lu 21:2-4
2Co 8:12

c Le 20:25
De 14:7, 8

d Le 27:19

e Le 27:11, 12

Second Col.

a Le 25:10

b Le 25:15, 16

c Nu 18:8, 14

d Le 25:25

e Le 27:11, 12
Le 27:18

f Le 25:10, 28

g Ex 13:2
Nu 18:17

h Ex 22:30
De 15:19

i Le 27:11-13

27:16 *A homer equaled 220 L (200 dry qt). See App. B14.

27:25 *A gerah equaled 0.57 g (0.01835 oz t). See App. B14.

28 "'But no devoted thing that a man devotes unconditionally* to Jehovah from his belongings be sold or bought back, whether from mankind or animals or the field he possesses. Every devoted thing is something most holy to Jehovah.ᵃ **29** Furthermore, no condemned* person who is set apart for destruction may be redeemed.ᵇ He should be put to death without fail.ᶜ

30 "'Every tenth part*ᵈ of the land, whether from the produce of the field or the fruit of the trees, belongs to Jehovah. It is something holy to Jehovah. **31** If a man ever wants to buy any of his tenth part back, he should give a fifth of it in addition to it. **32** As for every tenth part of the herd and flock, everything that passes under the shepherd's staff, the tenth animal* should become something holy to Jehovah. **33** He should not examine whether it is good or bad, neither should he exchange it. But if he would ever try to exchange it, both the original and what is exchanged for it should become something holy.ᵃ It may not be bought back.'"

34 These are the commandments that Jehovah gave to Moses for the Israelites on Mount Siʹnai.ᵇ

27:28 *Or "devotes to destruction."
27:29 *Or "devoted." 27:30 *Or "Every tithe."
27:32 *Lit., "head."

CHAP. 27
a Nu 18:8, 14

b Nu 21:2

c Jos 6:17
1Sa 15:3, 18

d Ge 14:20
Ge 28:22
Nu 18:21, 26
De 14:22
2Ch 31:5
Ne 13:12
Mal 3:10
Lu 11:42
Heb 7:5

Second Col.
a Le 27:9, 10

b Ex 3:1
Nu 1:1

NUMBERS

OUTLINE OF CONTENTS

1 And Jehovah spoke to Moses in the wilderness of Si'nai,[a] in the tent of meeting,[b] on the first day of the second month, in the second year of their coming out of the land of Egypt.[c] He said: **2** "Take a census[d] of the whole assembly of the Israelites* individually[#] according to their families, according to their paternal houses, according to the count of the names of all the males. **3** You and Aaron are to register by their companies* all those from 20 years old and up[e] who can serve in the army in Israel.

4 "Take with you one man from each tribe; each one is to be a head of his paternal house.[f] **5** These are the names of the men who will stand with you: of Reu'ben, E·li'zur[g] the son of Shed'e·ur; **6** of Sim'e·on, She·lu'mi·el[h] the son of Zu·ri·shad'dai; **7** of Judah, Nah'shon[i] the son of Am·min'a·dab; **8** of Is'sa·char, Ne·than'el[j] the son of Zu'ar; **9** of Zeb'u·lun, E·li'ab[k] the son of He'lon; **10** of the sons of Joseph: from E'phra·im,[l] E·lish'a·ma the son of Am·mi'hud; from Ma·nas'seh, Ga·ma'li·el the son of Pe·dah'zur; **11** of Benjamin, Ab'i·dan[m] the son of Gid·e·o'ni; **12** of Dan, A·hi·e'zer[n] the son of Am·mi·shad'dai; **13** of Ash'er, Pa'gi·el[o] the son of Och'ran; **14** of Gad, E·li'a·saph[p] the son of Deu'el; **15** of Naph'ta·li, A·hi'ra[q] the son of E'nan. **16** These are the ones summoned from the assembly. They are the chieftains[r] of the tribes of their fathers, the heads of the thousands of Israel."[s]

17 So Moses and Aaron took these men who had been designated by name. **18** They gathered all the assembly on the first day of the second month, so that they might be registered individually by name, by family, and by their paternal houses, from 20 years old and up,[a] **19** just as Jehovah had commanded Moses. So he registered them in the wilderness of Si'nai.[b]

20 The sons of Reu'ben, the descendants of Israel's firstborn,[c] were listed by name, by family, and by their paternal houses. All the males from 20 years old and up who could serve in the army were counted individually, **21** and the number registered of the tribe of Reu'ben was 46,500.

22 The descendants of Sim'e·on[d] were listed by name, by family, and by their paternal houses. All the males from 20 years old and up who could serve in the army were counted individually, **23** and the number registered of the tribe of Sim'e·on was 59,300.

24 The descendants of Gad[e] were listed by name, by family, and by their paternal houses. All the males from 20 years old and up who could serve in the army were counted, **25** and the number registered of the tribe of Gad was 45,650.

26 The descendants of Ju'dah[f] were listed by name, by family, and by their paternal houses. All the males from 20 years old and up who could serve in the army were counted, **27** and the number registered of the tribe of Judah was 74,600.

28 The descendants of Is'sa·char[g] were listed by name, by family, and by their paternal houses. All the males from 20 years old and up who could serve in the army were counted, **29** and the number registered of the tribe of Is'sa·char was 54,400.

30 The descendants of Zeb'u·lun[h] were listed by name, by

CHAP. 1

a Ex 19:1
  Ac 7:38

b Ex 25:22

c Ex 40:17

d Ex 30:12

e Ex 30:14

f Ex 18:25
  Nu 1:16
  Jos 22:13, 14
  Jos 23:2
  1Ch 27:1

g Nu 2:10

h Nu 7:11, 36

i Ru 4:20
  Lu 3:23, 32

j Nu 10:15

k Nu 7:11, 24

l Ge 48:20

m Nu 2:22

n Nu 7:11, 66

o Nu 7:11, 72

p Nu 2:14
  Nu 7:11, 42
  Nu 10:20

q Nu 2:29
  Nu 10:27

r Ex 18:21
  Nu 7:2

s De 1:15

Second Col.

a Ex 30:14

b Nu 26:1, 2

c Ge 29:32
  Nu 2:10, 11

d Ge 29:33
  Ge 46:10
  Nu 2:12, 13

e Ge 30:10, 11
  Ge 46:16
  Nu 2:14, 15

f Ge 29:35
  Ge 46:12
  Nu 2:3, 4
  1Ch 5:2
  Mt 1:2
  Heb 7:14

g Ge 30:17, 18
  Ge 46:13
  Nu 2:5, 6

h Ge 30:20
  Nu 2:7, 8

1:2 *Lit., "sons of Israel." # Or "head by head of them." 1:3 *Lit., "according to their armies."

family, and by their paternal houses. All the males from 20 years old and up who could serve in the army were counted, **31** and the number registered of the tribe of Zeb'u·lun was 57,400.

32 The descendants of Joseph through E'phra·im[a] were listed by name, by family, and by their paternal houses. All the males from 20 years old and up who could serve in the army were counted, **33** and the number registered of the tribe of E'phra·im was 40,500.

34 The descendants of Ma·nas'seh[b] were listed by name, by family, and by their paternal houses. All the males from 20 years old and up who could serve in the army were counted, **35** and the number registered of the tribe of Ma·nas'seh was 32,200.

36 The descendants of Benjamin[c] were listed by name, by family, and by their paternal houses. All the males from 20 years old and up who could serve in the army were counted, **37** and the number registered of the tribe of Benjamin was 35,400.

38 The descendants of Dan[d] were listed by name, by family, and by their paternal houses. All the males from 20 years old and up who could serve in the army were counted, **39** and the number registered of the tribe of Dan was 62,700.

40 The descendants of Ash'er[e] were listed by name, by family, and by their paternal houses. All the males from 20 years old and up who could serve in the army were counted, **41** and the number registered of the tribe of Ash'er was 41,500.

42 The descendants of Naph'ta·li[f] were listed by name, by family, and by their paternal houses. All the males from

CHAP. 1
a Ge 41:51, 52
Ge 46:20
Ge 48:17-19
Nu 2:18, 19

b Nu 2:20, 21

c Ge 43:29
Ge 46:21
Nu 2:22, 23

d Ge 30:4-6
Ge 46:23
Nu 2:25, 26
Nu 10:25

e Ge 35:26
Nu 2:27, 28

f Ge 30:7, 8
Ge 46:24
Nu 2:29, 30
Nu 26:48

Second Col.
a Ge 13:16
Ge 22:17
Ge 46:3
Ex 38:26
Nu 2:32

b Ge 29:34
Ge 46:11
Nu 3:12

c Nu 2:33
Nu 26:63, 64

d Nu 26:62, 63

e Ex 31:18

f Ex 38:21
Nu 3:6, 8

g Nu 4:15
Nu 4:24-26
Nu 4:31-33

h Nu 3:30, 31
Nu 4:12

i Nu 2:17
Nu 3:23, 29
Nu 3:35, 38

j Nu 10:17, 21

k Nu 3:10
Nu 18:22

l Nu 2:2, 34

m Nu 8:19
Nu 18:5

20 years old and up who could serve in the army were counted, **43** and the number registered of the tribe of Naph'ta·li was 53,400.

44 These were registered by Moses together with Aaron and the 12 chieftains of Israel, each representing his paternal house. **45** All the Israelites from 20 years old and up who could serve in the army in Israel were registered by their paternal house, **46** and the total number registered was 603,550.[a]

47 But the Levites[b] were not registered in among them by the tribe of their fathers.[c] **48** So Jehovah told Moses: **49** "Only the tribe of Le'vi you are not to register, and you should not include the number of them along with the other Israelites.[d] **50** You should appoint the Levites over the tabernacle of the Testimony[e] and over all its utensils and over everything that belongs to it.[f] They will carry the tabernacle and all its utensils,[g] and they will minister at it,[h] and they are to camp around the tabernacle.[i] **51** Whenever the tabernacle is to be moved, the Levites should take it down;[j] and when the tabernacle is to be reassembled, the Levites should set it up; and any unauthorized person* who comes near should be put to death.[k]

52 "Each Israelite should set up his tent in his assigned camp, each man according to his three-tribe division*[l] by their companies." **53** And the Levites should encamp around the tabernacle of the Testimony, so that no indignation may arise against the assembly of the Israelites;[m] and the Levites must be

1:51 *Lit., "any stranger," that is, a non-Levite. 1:52 *Or "by his standard (banner)." #Lit., "according to their armies."

responsible for the care of° the tabernacle of the Testimony."ª

54 The people of Israel did all that Jehovah had commanded Moses. They did just so.

2 Jehovah now spoke to Moses and Aaron, saying: **2** "The Israelites should encamp where their three-tribe divisionᵇ is assigned, each man near the banner* of his paternal house. They should camp facing the tent of meeting, all around it.

3 "Those camping on the east side, toward the sunrise, will be the three-tribe division of the encampment of Judah by their companies;* the chieftain for the sons of Judah is Nah′shonᶜ the son of Am·min′a·dab. **4** Those registered in his army are 74,-600.ᵈ **5** Camping alongside him will be the tribe of Is′sa·char; the chieftain for the sons of Is′sa·char is Ne·than′elᵉ the son of Zu′ar. **6** Those registered in his army are 54,400.ᶠ **7** Next is the tribe of Zeb′u·lun; the chieftain for the sons of Zeb′u·lun is E·li′abᵍ the son of He′lon. **8** Those registered in his army are 57,-400.ʰ

9 "All those registered in the armies of the camp of Judah are 186,400. They should break camp first.ⁱ

10 "The three-tribe division of the encampment of Reu′benʲ by their companies* will be toward the south; the chieftain for the sons of Reu′ben is E·li′zurᵏ the son of Shed′e·ur. **11** Those registered in his army are 46,500.ˡ **12** Camping alongside him will be the tribe of Sim′e·on; the chieftain for the sons of Sim′e·on is She·lu′mi·elᵐ the son of Zu·ri·shad′dai. **13** Those registered in his army are 59,-300.ⁿ **14** Next is the tribe of

Gad; the chieftain for the sons of Gad is E·li′a·saphª the son of Reu′el. **15** Those registered in his army are 45,650.ᵇ

16 "All those registered in the armies of the camp of Reu′ben are 151,450, and they should break camp second.ᶜ

17 "When the tent of meeting is moved,ᵈ the camp of the Levites should be in the middle of the other camps.

"They should travel in the same order as they encamp,ᵉ with each in his place, according to their three-tribe divisions.

18 "The three-tribe division of the encampment of E′phra·im by their companies* will be toward the west; the chieftain for the sons of E′phra·im is E·lish′a·maᶠ the son of Am·mi′-hud. **19** Those registered in his army are 40,500.ᵍ **20** Next to him will be the tribe of Ma·nas′-seh;ʰ the chieftain for the sons of Ma·nas′seh is Ga·ma′li·elⁱ the son of Pe·dah′zur. **21** Those registered in his army are 32,-200.ʲ **22** Next is the tribe of Benjamin; the chieftain for the sons of Benjamin is Ab′i·danᵏ the son of Gid·e·o′ni. **23** Those registered in his army are 35,400.ˡ

24 "All those registered in the armies of the camp of E′phra·im are 108,100, and they should break camp third.ᵐ

25 "The three-tribe division of the encampment of Dan by their companies* will be toward the north; the chieftain for the sons of Dan is A·hi·e′-zerⁿ the son of Am·mi·shad′dai. **26** Those registered in his army are 62,700.º **27** Camping alongside him will be the tribe of Ash′er; the chieftain for the sons of Ash′er is Pa′gi·elᵖ the son of Och′ran. **28** Those registered in his army are 41,500.ᑫ **29** Next is the tribe of Naph′ta·li; the chieftain for the sons of Naph′ta·li is A·hi′raʳ the son of

---

CHAP. 1
a Nu 8:24
  Nu 18:2, 3
  1Ch 23:32

CHAP. 2
b Nu 1:52
c Nu 7:12
  Nu 10:14
  Ru 4:20
  Mt 1:4
d Nu 1:27
e Nu 7:11, 18
  Nu 10:15
f Nu 1:29
g Nu 7:11, 24
  Nu 10:16
h Nu 1:31
i Nu 10:14
j Nu 1:20
k Nu 7:11, 30
  Nu 10:18
l Nu 1:21
m Nu 7:11, 36
  Nu 10:19
n Nu 1:23

Second Col.
a Nu 7:11, 42
  Nu 10:20
b Nu 1:25
c Nu 10:18
d Nu 1:51
e 1Co 14:33, 40
f Nu 7:11, 48
  Nu 10:22
g Nu 1:33
h Ge 48:20
i Nu 7:11, 54
  Nu 10:23
j Nu 1:35
k Nu 7:11, 60
  Nu 10:24
l Nu 1:37
m Nu 10:22
n Nu 7:11, 66
  Nu 10:25
o Nu 1:39
p Nu 7:11, 72
  Nu 10:26
q Nu 1:41
r Nu 7:11, 78
  Nu 10:27

1:53 *Or "for guarding; for carrying out their service at." 2:2 *Or "sign." 2:3, 10, 18, 25 *Lit., "according to their armies."

E'nan. **30** Those registered in his army are 53,400.[a]

31 "All those registered in the camp of Dan are 157,600. They should break camp last,[b] according to their three-tribe divisions."

32 These were the Israelites who were registered according to their paternal houses; the total of those in the camps registered for the army was 603,550.[c] **33** But the Levites did not get registered[d] along with the other Israelites,[e] just as Jehovah had commanded Moses. **34** The Israelites did everything that Jehovah had commanded Moses. This is how they encamped by their three-tribe divisions[f] and how they broke camp,[g] each by family and according to their paternal houses.

3 Now these were the family lines* of Aaron and Moses in the day that Jehovah spoke with Moses on Mount Si'nai.[h] **2** These were the names of Aaron's sons: the firstborn Na'dab, and A·bi'hu,[i] El·e·a'zar,[j] and Ith'a·mar.[k] **3** These were the names of Aaron's sons, the anointed priests who had been installed* to serve as priests.[l] **4** However, Na'dab and A·bi'hu died before Jehovah when they offered unauthorized fire before Jehovah[m] in the wilderness of Si'nai, and they did not have any sons. But El·e·a'zar[n] and Ith'a·mar[o] continued to serve as priests along with Aaron their father.

5 Jehovah then said to Moses: **6** "Bring the tribe of Le'vi[p] forward, and stand them before Aaron the priest, and they will minister[q] to him. **7** They are to fulfill their responsibilities toward him and toward all the assembly before the tent of meeting by carrying out their service

in connection with the tabernacle. **8** They are to take care of all the utensils[a] of the tent of meeting and to carry out their responsibilities toward the Israelites by taking care of the services related to the tabernacle.[b] **9** You are to give the Levites to Aaron and his sons. They are given ones, given to him from the Israelites.[c] **10** You should appoint Aaron and his sons, and they are to carry out their priestly duties,[d] and any unauthorized person* who comes near should be put to death."[e]

11 Jehovah continued to speak to Moses, saying: **12** "As for me, look! I take the Levites from among the Israelites in place of all the firstborn* of the Israelites,[f] and the Levites will become mine. **13** For every firstborn is mine.[g] In the day that I struck every firstborn in the land of Egypt,[h] I sanctified to myself every firstborn in Israel from man to beast.[i] They are to become mine. I am Jehovah."

14 Jehovah spoke further to Moses in the wilderness of Si'nai,[j] saying: **15** "Register the sons of Le'vi by their paternal houses and by their families. You should register every male from a month old and up."[k] **16** So Moses registered them at the order of Jehovah, just as he had been commanded. **17** These were the names of the sons of Le'vi: Ger'shon, Ko'hath, and Me·rar'i.[l]

18 Now these were the names of the sons of Ger'shon by their families: Lib'ni and Shim'e·i.[m]

19 The sons of Ko'hath by their families were Am'ram, Iz'har, Heb'ron, and Uz'zi·el.[n]

20 The sons of Me·rar'i by their families were Mah'li[o] and Mu'shi.[p]

CHAP. 2

a Nu 1:43
b Nu 10:25
c Ge 15:5
　Ex 38:26
　Nu 1:46
　Nu 14:29
　Nu 26:51, 64
d Nu 1:47
　Nu 26:62, 63
e Nu 3:15
f Nu 2:2
g Nu 10:28

CHAP. 3

h Ex 19:2
i Le 10:1
　1Ch 24:2
j Ex 6:25
　De 10:6
k Ex 6:23
　Ex 38:21
　1Ch 6:3
l Ex 28:1
　Le 8:2, 3
m Le 10:1, 2
n Nu 3:32
　Nu 20:26
o Nu 4:28
　Nu 7:8
p Nu 8:6
　Nu 18:2
q Nu 1:50
　Nu 8:11

Second Col.

a Nu 4:12
b Nu 1:51
c Nu 8:15, 16
　Nu 18:6
d Ex 40:15
　Nu 18:7
e Nu 16:39, 40
　1Sa 6:19
　2Ch 26:16, 18
f Nu 3:41, 45
g Ex 13:2
　Ex 34:19
　Nu 18:15
　Lu 2:23
h Ex 13:15
i Le 27:26
j Ex 19:1
k Nu 3:39
l Ex 6:16
　Nu 26:57
　1Ch 23:6
m Ex 6:17
n Ex 6:18
o 1Ch 6:29
p Ex 6:19

3:1 *Lit., "the generations." **3:3** *Lit., "whose hands had been filled."

3:10 *Lit., "any stranger," that is, a man not of Aaron's family. **3:12** *Lit., "of every firstborn opening the womb."

These were the families of the Levites by their paternal houses.

21 From Ger'shon came the family of the Lib'nites[a] and the family of the Shim'e·ites. These were the families of the Ger'-shon·ites. **22** The number of all their males a month old and up who were registered was 7,500.[b] **23** The families of the Ger'-shon·ites were encamped behind the tabernacle[c] toward the west. **24** The chieftain of the paternal house of the Ger'shon·ites was E·li'a·saph the son of La'-el. **25** The responsibility of the sons of Ger'shon[d] in the tent of meeting was to care for the tabernacle and the tent,[e] its covering,[f] the screen*[g] of the entrance of the tent of meeting, **26** the hanging curtains[h] of the courtyard, the screen*[i] of the entrance of the courtyard that surrounds the tabernacle and the altar, its tent cords, and all the service connected with these.

27 From Ko'hath came the family of the Am'ram·ites, the family of the Iz'har·ites, the family of the Heb'ron·ites, and the family of the Uz'zi·el·ites. These were the families of the Ko'hath-ites.[j] **28** The number of all the males from a month old and up was 8,600; they were responsible for taking care of the holy place.[k] **29** The families of the sons of Ko'hath camped on the south side of the tabernacle.[l] **30** The chieftain of the paternal house of the families of the Ko'-hath·ites was E·li·za'phan the son of Uz'zi·el.[m] **31** Their responsibility was to care for the Ark,[n] the table,[o] the lampstand,[p] the altars,[q] the utensils[r] used to minister in the holy place, the screen,*[s] and all the service connected with these.[t] **32** The head chieftain of the Levites was El·e·a'zar[u] the son of

Aaron the priest, who had the oversight of those taking care of the responsibilities of the holy place.

33 From Me·rar'i came the family of the Mah'lites and the family of the Mu'shites. These were the families of the Me-rar'i.[a] **34** The number of all the males from a month old and up who were registered was 6,200.[b] **35** The chieftain of the paternal house of the families of Me-rar'i was Zu'ri·el the son of Ab'-i·ha·il. They were encamped on the north side of the tabernacle.[c] **36** The sons of Me·rar'i were responsible for overseeing the panel frames[d] of the tabernacle, its bars,[e] its pillars,[f] its socket pedestals, all its utensils,[g] and all the service connected with these,[h] **37** as well as the pillars that were all around the courtyard and their socket pedestals,[i] their tent pins, and their tent cords.

38 Those camping in front of the tabernacle toward the east, before the tent of meeting toward the sunrise, were Moses and Aaron and his sons. They were responsible for taking care of the sanctuary as their obligation in behalf of the Israelites. Any unauthorized person* coming near would be put to death.[j]

39 All the Levite males from a month old and up, whom Moses and Aaron registered by their families at the order of Jehovah, were 22,000.

40 Then Jehovah said to Moses: "Register all the firstborn males of the Israelites from a month old and up,[k] count them, and make a list of their names. **41** You must take the Levites for me—I am Jehovah—in place of all the firstborn of the Israelites,[l] and take the domestic animals

---

CHAP. 3
a 1Ch 6:20
b Nu 4:38-40
c Nu 1:53
d Nu 4:24-26
e Ex 26:7
f Ex 26:14
g Ex 26:36
h Ex 27:9
i Ex 27:16
j Nu 3:19
k Ex 4:34-36
l Nu 1:53
m Ex 6:22
  1Ch 6:18
n Ex 25:10
o Ex 25:23
p Ex 25:31
q Ex 27:1, 2
  Ex 30:1-3
r Ex 38:3
s Ex 26:31
t Nu 4:15
u Nu 4:16
  Nu 20:28

Second Col.
a Nu 3:20
  Nu 26:58
b Nu 4:42-44
c Nu 1:53
d Ex 36:20
e Ex 36:31
f Ex 26:32, 37
  Ex 36:37, 38
g Ex 27:19
h Nu 4:31, 32
i Ex 27:10, 11
j Nu 3:10
k Nu 3:15
l Nu 3:12

3:25, 26, 31 *Or "curtain."

3:38 *Lit., "Any stranger," that is, a non-Levite.

of the Levites in place of all the firstborn of the domestic animals of the Israelites."[a] **42** Moses then registered all the firstborn among the Israelites, just as Jehovah had commanded him. **43** The number of all the firstborn males who were registered by name from a month old and up was 22,273.

44 Jehovah continued to speak to Moses, saying: **45** "Take the Levites in place of all the firstborn among the Israelites, and take the domestic animals of the Levites in place of their domestic animals, and the Levites must become mine. I am Jehovah. **46** As the ransom price[b] of the 273 of the firstborn of the Israelites who are in excess of the Levites,[c] **47** you are to take five shekels* for each individual,[d] according to the standard shekel of the holy place.* A shekel is 20 ge′rahs.*[e] **48** You are to give the money to Aaron and his sons as the ransom price of those who are in excess of them." **49** So Moses took the money of the redemption price from those who were in excess of the ransom price of the Levites. **50** He took the money from the firstborn of the Israelites, 1,365 shekels, according to the standard shekel of the holy place. **51** Then Moses gave the money of the ransom price to Aaron and his sons according to the word* of Jehovah, just as Jehovah had commanded Moses.

4 Jehovah now spoke to Moses and Aaron, saying: **2** "A census should be taken of the sons of Ko′hath[f] from among the sons of Le′vi, by their families and by their paternal hous-

es, **3** all those from 30[a] to 50 years old[b] who are in the group assigned to work in the tent of meeting.[c]

4 "This is the service of the sons of Ko′hath in the tent of meeting.[d] It is something most holy: **5** Aaron and his sons will come in when the camp is departing and take down the screening curtain[e] and cover the ark[f] of the Testimony with it. **6** They will put a sealskin covering over it and spread out a solid blue cloth over it and put its carrying poles[g] in place.

7 "They will also spread out a blue cloth over the table of showbread,[h] and they will put on it the dishes, the cups, the bowls, and the pitchers of the drink offering;[i] the regular offering of bread[j] should remain on it. **8** They will spread out a scarlet cloth over them and cover it with a sealskin covering and put its carrying poles[k] in place. **9** Then they will take a blue cloth and cover the lampstand[l] for the light, along with its lamps,[m] its snuffers,* its fire holders,[n] and all its containers for oil that are used to maintain it. **10** They will wrap it and all its utensils in a sealskin covering and put it on a carrying bar. **11** And they will spread out a blue cloth over the golden altar,[o] cover it with a sealskin covering, and put its carrying poles[p] in place. **12** They will then take all the utensils[q] of the ministry with which they regularly minister in the holy place and put them in a blue cloth and cover them with a sealskin covering and put them on a carrying bar.

13 "They should remove the ashes* from the altar[r] and spread out a cloth of purple

---

CHAP. 3
a Ex 13:2
  Nu 18:15

b Nu 18:15

c Nu 3:39, 43

d Nu 18:15, 16

e Le 27:25

CHAP. 4
f Nu 3:19, 27

Second Col.
a 1Ch 23:3
  Lu 3:23

b Nu 8:25, 26

c Nu 4:30
  1Ch 6:48

d Nu 3:30, 31
  Nu 4:15

e Ex 26:31
  Ex 40:3
  Le 16:2

f Ex 25:10

g Ex 25:13

h Ex 25:23, 24

i Ex 25:29

j Le 24:5, 6

k Ex 25:28

l Ex 25:31

m Ex 25:37

n Ex 25:38

o Ex 30:1
  Ex 37:25, 26

p Ex 30:5

q Nu 3:30, 31

r Le 6:12

3:47 *A shekel equaled 11.4 g (0.367 oz t). See App. B14. *Or "by the holy shekel." ^A gerah equaled 0.57 g (0.01835 oz t). See App. B14. **3:51** *Lit., "mouth."

4:9 *Or "tongs." **4:13** *Or "fatty ashes," that is, ashes soaked with the fat of the sacrifices.

wool over it. **14** They will put on it all its utensils that are used when they minister at the altar: the fire holders, the forks, the shovels, and the bowls, all the utensils of the altar;[a] and they are to spread a sealskin covering over it and put its carrying poles[b] in place.

15 "Aaron and his sons must finish covering the holy place[c] and all the utensils of the holy place when the camp is departing. Then the sons of Ko′hath will come in to carry them,[d] but they must not touch the holy place or they will die.[e] These things are the responsibility* of the sons of Ko′hath in connection with the tent of meeting.

16 "El·e·a′zar[f] the son of Aaron the priest is responsible for overseeing the oil of the lighting,[g] the perfumed incense,[h] the regular grain offering, and the anointing oil.[i] He has oversight of the entire tabernacle and all that is in it, including the holy place and its utensils."

17 Jehovah spoke further to Moses and Aaron, saying: **18** "Do not let the tribe of the families of the Ko′hath·ites[j] be cut off from among the Levites. **19** But do this for them that they may remain alive and not die because of approaching the most holy things.[k] Aaron and his sons will go in and assign each of them to his service and what he is to carry. **20** They must not come in and see the holy things even for an instant, or they will die."[l]

21 Then Jehovah spoke to Moses, saying: **22** "A census should be taken of the sons of Ger′shon[m] by their paternal houses and their families. **23** You are to register all those from 30 to 50 years old who are in the group assigned to serve

in the tent of meeting. **24** This is what the families of the Ger′shon·ites are assigned to care for and to carry:[a] **25** They will carry the tent cloths of the tabernacle,[b] the tent of meeting, its covering and the sealskin covering that is on top over it,[c] the screen* of the entrance of the tent of meeting,[d] **26** the hanging curtains of the courtyard,[e] the screen* of the entrance of the courtyard[f] that surrounds the tabernacle and the altar, their tent cords and all their utensils and everything used in its service. This is their assignment. **27** All the service and the loads of the Ger′shonites[g] should be overseen by Aaron and his sons; you will assign all these loads as their responsibility. **28** This is the service that the families of the Ger′shonites are to carry out in the tent of meeting,[h] and their responsibilities are under the direction of Ith′a·mar[i] the son of Aaron the priest.

29 "As for the sons of Me·rar′i,[j] you will register them by family and by their paternal house. **30** From 30 to 50 years old you will register them, all who are in the group assigned to the service of the tent of meeting. **31** This is what they are responsible for carrying[k] in connection with their service at the tent of meeting: the panel frames[l] of the tabernacle, its bars,[m] its pillars,[n] its socket pedestals;[o] **32** the pillars[p] of the surrounding courtyard, their socket pedestals,[q] their tent pins,[r] and their tent cords together with all their equipment and all the service connected with these. You will assign to them by name the equipment they are responsible for carrying. **33** This is how the families

CHAP. 4	
a	Ex 27:3
b	Ex 27:6
c	Nu 4:5
d	Nu 7:6-9
	1Ch 15:2
e	2Sa 6:6, 7
f	Nu 3:32
g	Ex 27:20
h	Ex 30:34, 35
i	Ex 30:23-25
j	Nu 3:27
k	Nu 4:4
l	Ex 19:21
	1Sa 6:19
m	Nu 3:21

Second Col.	
a	Nu 3:25, 26
b	Ex 26:1
c	Ex 26:7, 14
d	Ex 26:36
e	Ex 27:9
f	Ex 27:16
g	Nu 3:21, 23
h	Nu 3:25, 26
i	Ex 6:23
	Nu 4:33
	Nu 7:8
j	Ex 6:19
	Nu 3:33
k	Nu 3:36, 37
l	Ex 26:15
m	Ex 26:26
n	Ex 26:37
	Ex 36:38
o	Ex 26:19
	Ex 38:27
p	Ex 27:10
q	Ex 27:11
r	Ex 27:19

4:15 *Lit., "load."   4:25, 26 *Or "curtain."

of the sons of Me·rar′i[a] are to serve at the tent of meeting, under the direction of Ith′a·mar the son of Aaron the priest."[b]

34 Moses and Aaron and the chieftains[c] of the assembly then registered the sons of the Ko′hath·ites[d] by their families and by their paternal house, **35** all those from 30 to 50 years old who were in the group assigned to the service of the tent of meeting.[e] **36** The total of those registered by their families was 2,750.[f] **37** These were registered from the families of the Ko′hath·ites, all those who were serving at the tent of meeting. Moses and Aaron registered them at the order of Jehovah through Moses.[g]

38 The sons of Ger′shon[h] were registered by their families and by their paternal house, **39** all those from 30 to 50 years old who were in the group assigned to the service at the tent of meeting. **40** The total of those registered by their families and by their paternal house was 2,630.[i] **41** This was the registration of the families of the sons of Ger′shon, all those who were serving at the tent of meeting. Moses and Aaron had them registered at the order of Jehovah.[j]

42 The sons of Me·rar′i were registered by their families and by their paternal house, **43** all those from 30 to 50 years old who were in the group assigned to the service at the tent of meeting.[k] **44** The total of those registered of them by their families was 3,200.[l] **45** This was the registration of the families of the sons of Me·rar′i, whom Moses and Aaron registered at the order of Jehovah through Moses.[m]

46 Moses and Aaron and the chieftains of Israel registered all these Levites by their fami-

lies and by their paternal houses; **47** they were from 30 to 50 years old, and all were assigned to serve and carry loads in connection with the tent of meeting.[a] **48** The total of those registered was 8,580.[b] **49** They were registered at the order of Jehovah through Moses, each according to his assigned service and his load; they were registered just as Jehovah had commanded Moses.

5 Jehovah spoke further to Moses, saying: **2** "Command the Israelites to send out of the camp every leprous person[c] and everyone having a discharge[d] and everyone unclean by a dead person.*[e] **3** Whether a male or a female, you should send them out. You should send them outside the camp, so that they may not contaminate[f] the camps of those in whose midst I am dwelling."*[g] **4** Therefore, the Israelites did so and sent them outside the camp. Just as Jehovah told Moses, so the Israelites did.

5 Jehovah continued speaking to Moses, saying: **6** "Tell the Israelites, 'If a man or a woman commits any of the sins of mankind and acts unfaithfully toward Jehovah, that person* has become guilty.[h] **7** He* must confess[i] the sin that he has# committed and return the full amount as compensation for his guilt and also add a fifth of its value;[j] he is to give it to the one he wronged. **8** But if the victim does not have a close relative to receive the compensation, it should be returned to Jehovah and will belong to the priest, apart from the ram of atonement with which he will make atonement for him.[k]

CHAP. 4
a Nu 3:33
b Nu 4:28
c Nu 1:16
d Nu 3:19, 27
e Nu 4:47
Nu 8:25, 26
f Nu 3:27, 28
g Nu 3:15
h Nu 3:21
i Nu 3:21, 22
j Nu 4:22, 23
k Nu 8:25, 26
l Nu 3:33, 34
m Nu 4:29

Second Col.
a Nu 4:15
Nu 4:24-26
Nu 4:31-33
b Nu 3:39

CHAP. 5
c Le 13:45, 46
d Le 15:2
e Le 22:4
Nu 19:11
f Nu 19:22
g Ex 25:8
Le 26:11
h Le 5:1, 17
i Le 5:5
Jos 7:19
Jas 5:16
j Le 6:4, 5
k Le 5:16
Le 6:6, 7
Le 7:7

5:2 *Or "by a soul." See Glossary. **5:3** *Or "tabernacling." **5:6** *Or "soul." **5:7** *Lit., "They." #Lit., "they have."

9 "'Every holy contribution[a] from the Israelites that is presented to the priest should become his.[b] **10** The holy things of each person will remain his own. Whatever each one gives to the priest, that will belong to the priest.'"

11 Jehovah went on to speak to Moses, saying: **12** "Speak to the Israelites and tell them, 'This is what should be done if a man's wife goes astray and is unfaithful to him **13** and another man has sexual relations with her,[c] but it was unknown to her husband and remains undiscovered, so that she has defiled herself but there is no witness against her and she has not been caught; **14** Whether the husband becomes jealous and suspicious of his wife's faithfulness when she has defiled herself, or whether he is jealous and suspicious of his wife's faithfulness when she has not defiled herself, **15** the man must bring his wife to the priest, along with an offering for her, a tenth of an e'phah* of barley flour. He must not pour oil on it nor put frankincense on it, because it is a grain offering of jealousy, a grain offering bringing guilt to mind.

16 "'The priest will bring her forward and make her stand before Jehovah.[d] **17** The priest will take holy water in an earthenware vessel, and the priest will take some of the dust from the floor of the tabernacle and put it in the water. **18** And the priest will make the woman stand before Jehovah and unbind the woman's hair and put in her palms the grain offering for a reminder, that is, the grain offering of jealousy,[e] and the priest will have in his hand the bitter water that brings a curse.[f]

19 "'The priest will then make her swear, saying to the woman: "If no other man had sexual relations with you while you were under your husband's authority[a] and you have not gone astray and become defiled, may you be free of the effect of this bitter water that brings a curse. **20** But if you have gone astray while under your husband's authority by defiling yourself, and you have had sexual relations with another man[b] besides your husband—" **21** The priest will then make the woman swear an oath that includes a curse, and the priest will say to the woman: "May Jehovah make you an object for cursing and for an oath among your people, as Jehovah makes your thigh* fall away[#] and causes your abdomen to swell. **22** This water that brings a curse will enter into your intestines to cause your abdomen to swell and make your thigh* fall away."[#] To this the woman should say: "Amen! Amen!"[△]

23 "'Then the priest should write these curses in the book and wash them off into the bitter water. **24** He will then make the woman drink the bitter water that brings a curse, and the water that brings a curse will enter into her and produce bitterness. **25** And the priest should take the grain offering of jealousy[c] from the woman's hand and wave the grain offering back and forth before Jehovah, and he will bring it near the altar. **26** The priest will take a handful of the grain offering as a token offering and make it smoke on the altar,[d] and afterward he will make the woman drink the water. **27** When he makes her

---

CHAP. 5
a Le 6:14, 17
  Le 7:1, 6
  Le 10:12, 13

b Ex 29:27, 28
  Nu 18:8
  De 18:3
  Eze 44:29
  1Co 9:13

c Le 18:20
  De 5:18

d Jer 17:10
  Heb 13:4

e Nu 5:15, 25

f Nu 5:22, 24

Second Col.
a Ro 7:2

b Le 18:20
  1Co 6:9, 10

c Nu 5:15

d Le 2:9

5:15 *A tenth of an ephah equaled 2.2 L (2 dry qt). See App. B14.

5:21, 22 *Evidently referring to the reproductive organs. 5:21, 22 #Or "waste away." This may suggest loss of fertility. 5:22 △Or "So be it! So be it!"

drink the water, if she has defiled herself and committed an act of unfaithfulness toward her husband, the water that brings a curse will then enter into her and become something bitter, and her abdomen will swell, and her thigh* will fall away,[a] and the woman will become an object of cursing among her people. **28** However, if the woman has not defiled herself and is clean, she will then be free from such punishment, and she will be able to conceive and produce offspring.

29 "'This is the law about jealousy,[a] when a woman may go astray and defile herself while under her husband's authority, **30** or in the case of a man who becomes jealous and suspects his wife of unfaithfulness; he should make his wife stand before Jehovah, and the priest must carry out toward her all this law. **31** The man will be free from guilt, but his wife will answer for her guilt.'"

6 Jehovah spoke further to Moses and said: **2** "Speak to the Israelites and tell them, 'If a man or a woman takes a special vow to live as a Naz'i·rite*[b] to Jehovah, **3** he should keep away from wine and other alcoholic beverages. He should not drink the vinegar of wine or the vinegar of anything alcoholic.[c] He should not drink any liquid made from grapes, nor eat grapes, whether fresh or dried. **4** All the days of his Naziriteship he should not eat anything made from the grapevine, from the unripe grapes to the skins.

5 "'All the days of the vow of his Naziriteship no razor should

pass over his head.[a] He is to remain holy by letting the hair of his head grow until the days of his being set apart to Jehovah are completed. **6** He should not approach* a dead person* during all the days he remains separated to Jehovah. **7** Even if his father or his mother or his brother or his sister should die, he may not defile himself,[b] because the sign of his Naziriteship to his God is upon his head.

8 "'He is holy to Jehovah all the days of his Naziriteship. **9** But if someone should suddenly die alongside him[c] and he defiles the hair symbolizing his separation to God,* he must shave his head[d] on the day he establishes his purification. He should shave it on the seventh day. **10** And on the eighth day, he should bring two turtledoves or two young pigeons to the priest at the entrance of the tent of meeting. **11** The priest will prepare one as a sin offering and the other as a burnt offering and make atonement for him for his sin[e] in connection with the dead person.* Then he must sanctify his head on that day. **12** And he must separate himself again to Jehovah for the days of his Naziriteship, and he will bring a young ram in its first year as a guilt offering. However, the former days will go uncounted because he defiled his Naziriteship.

13 "'Now this is the law about the Naz'i·rite: When he completes the days of his Naziriteship,[f] he will be brought to the entrance of the tent of meeting. **14** There he must present his offering to Jehovah: one sound young ram in its

---

CHAP. 5
a Nu 5:14, 15

CHAP. 6
b Jg 13:5

c Le 10:9
Am 2:11, 12
Lu 1:15

Second Col.
a Jg 13:5
Jg 16:17
1Sa 1:11

b Le 21:1, 11

c Nu 19:14

d Nu 6:13, 18

e Le 5:8, 10

f Nu 30:2
Ec 5:4

5:27 *Evidently referring to the reproductive organs. #Or "waste away." This may suggest loss of fertility. 6:2 *Hebrew, *na·zir*, meaning "One Singled Out; Dedicated One; Separated One." 6:6 *Or "come anywhere near." #Or "soul." See Glossary. 6:9 *Or "defiles the head of his Naziriteship." 6:11 *Or "with a soul." See Glossary.

first year as a burnt offering,[a] one sound female lamb in its first year as a sin offering,[b] one sound ram as a communion sacrifice,[c] **15** a basket of unleavened ring-shaped loaves of fine flour mixed with oil, unleavened wafers smeared with oil, and their grain offering[d] and their drink offerings.[e] **16** The priest will present them before Jehovah and will offer up his sin offering and his burnt offering. **17** He will offer the ram as a communion sacrifice to Jehovah along with the basket of unleavened loaves, and the priest will present its grain offering[f] and its drink offering.

18 "'The Naz'i·rite must then shave the uncut hair of his head*[g] at the entrance of the tent of meeting, and he will take the hair of his head grown during his Naziriteship and put it on the fire that is under the communion sacrifice. **19** And the priest must take a boiled[h] shoulder from the ram, one unleavened ring-shaped loaf from the basket, and one unleavened wafer, and put them on the palms of the Naz'i·rite after he has had the sign of his Naziriteship shaved off. **20** And the priest must wave them back and forth as a wave offering before Jehovah.[i] It is something holy for the priest, along with the breast of the wave offering and the leg of the contribution.[j] Afterward, the Naz'i·rite may drink wine.

21 "'This is the law about the Naz'i·rite[k] who makes a vow: If he vows and can afford to make an offering to Jehovah that is beyond the requirements of his Naziriteship, he must then carry out his vow out of regard for the law of his Naziriteship.'"

6:18 *Or "the head of his Naziriteship."

22 Then Jehovah said to Moses: **23** "Tell Aaron and his sons, 'This is the way you should bless[a] the people of Israel. Say to them:

24 "May Jehovah bless you[b] and safeguard you.

25 May Jehovah make his face shine upon you,[c] and may he favor you.

26 May Jehovah lift up his face toward you and grant you peace."'[d]

27 And they must place my name upon the people of Israel,[e] that I may bless them."[f]

7 On the day that Moses finished setting up the tabernacle,[g] he anointed it[h] and sanctified it, together with all its furnishings, the altar, and all its utensils.[i] When he had anointed and sanctified these things,[j] **2** the chieftains of Israel,[k] the heads of their paternal houses, made an offering. These chieftains of the tribes who presided over the registration **3** brought before Jehovah their offering of six covered wagons and 12 oxen, a wagon for two chieftains and a bull* for each one; and they presented them before the tabernacle. **4** Jehovah said to Moses: **5** "Accept these things from them, as they will be used for the service of the tent of meeting, and you should give them to the Levites, to each one as needed for his duties."

6 So Moses accepted the wagons and the cattle and gave them to the Levites. **7** He gave two wagons and four oxen to the sons of Ger'shon, according to what was needed for their duties;[l] **8** and he gave four wagons and eight oxen to the sons of Me·rar'i, according to what was needed for their duties, under the direction of Ith'a·mar the son

7:3 *Or "an ox."

CHAP. 6
[a] Le 1:10
[b] Le 4:32
[c] Le 3:1
[d] Le 2:1
Le 6:14
[e] Nu 15:8, 10
[f] Le 2:9
[g] Nu 6:5
[h] Le 8:31
[i] Ex 29:23, 24
[j] Le 7:34
[k] Jg 13:5

Second Col.
[a] Le 9:22
De 10:8
[b] Ru 2:4
Ps 134:3
[c] Nu 31:16
Ps 67:1
[d] Ps 29:11
Lu 2:14
[e] De 28:10
Isa 43:7, 10
[f] Ps 5:12
Ps 67:7

CHAP. 7
[g] Ex 40:17
[h] Ex 30:26
[i] Le 8:10
[j] Ex 40:10
[k] Ex 18:21
Nu 1:4, 16
[l] Nu 3:25, 21
Nu 4:24-26

of Aaron the priest.[a] 9 But he did not give any to the sons of Ko'hath because their duties involved the service of the holy place,[b] and they carried the holy things on their shoulders.[c]

10 Now the chieftains made their presentation at the inauguration*[d] of the altar on the day it was anointed. When the chieftains presented their offering before the altar, 11 Jehovah said to Moses: "One chieftain each day, on successive days, will present his offering for the inauguration of the altar."

12 The one who presented his offering on the first day was Nah'shon[e] the son of Am·min'a·dab of the tribe of Judah. 13 His offering was one silver dish weighing 130 shekels* and one silver bowl weighing 70 shekels by the standard shekel of the holy place,*[f] both of them full of fine flour mixed with oil for a grain offering;[g] 14 one gold cup* weighing 10 shekels, full of incense; 15 one young bull, one ram, and one male lamb in its first year for a burnt offering;[h] 16 one young goat for a sin offering;[i] 17 and for a communion sacrifice,[j] two cattle, five rams, five male goats, and five male lambs each a year old. This was the offering of Nah'shon the son of Am·min'a·dab.[k]

18 On the second day, Nethan'el[l] the son of Zu'ar, the chieftain of Is'sa·char, made a presentation. 19 He presented as his offering one silver dish weighing 130 shekels and one silver bowl weighing 70 shekels by the standard shekel of the holy place,[m] both of them full of fine flour mixed with oil for a

grain offering;[a] 20 one gold cup weighing 10 shekels, full of incense; 21 one young bull, one ram, and one male lamb in its first year for a burnt offering;[b] 22 one young goat for a sin offering;[c] 23 and for a communion sacrifice,[d] two cattle, five rams, five male goats, and five male lambs each a year old. This was the offering of Nethan'el the son of Zu'ar.

24 On the third day, the chieftain for the sons of Zeb'u·lun, E·li'ab[e] the son of He'lon, 25 made his offering of one silver dish weighing 130 shekels and one silver bowl weighing 70 shekels by the standard shekel of the holy place,[f] both of them full of fine flour mixed with oil for a grain offering;[g] 26 one gold cup weighing 10 shekels, full of incense; 27 one young bull, one ram, and one male lamb in its first year for a burnt offering;[h] 28 one young goat for a sin offering;[i] 29 and for a communion sacrifice,[j] two cattle, five rams, five male goats, and five male lambs each a year old. This was the offering of E·li'ab[k] the son of He'lon.

30 On the fourth day, the chieftain for the sons of Reu'ben, E·li'zur[l] the son of Shed'e·ur, 31 made his offering of one silver dish weighing 130 shekels and one silver bowl weighing 70 shekels by the standard shekel of the holy place,[m] both of them full of fine flour mixed with oil for a grain offering;[n] 32 one gold cup weighing 10 shekels, full of incense; 33 one young bull, one ram, and one male lamb in its first year for a burnt offering;[o] 34 one young goat for a sin offering;[p] 35 and for a communion sacrifice,[q] two cattle, five rams, five male goats, and five male lambs each a year old. This was the offering of E·li'zur[r] the son of Shed'e·ur.

CHAP. 7

a Nu 3:36, 37
  Nu 4:31-33

b Nu 3:30, 31
  Nu 4:15

c 2Sa 6:13
  1Ch 15:15

d 1Ki 8:63
  2Ch 7:5

e Nu 1:4, 7
  Nu 2:3
  Ru 4:20
  Mt 1:4

f Le 27:25

g Le 2:1

h Le 1:3

i Le 4:22, 23

j Le 3:1

k Ex 6:23
  Lu 3:23, 33

l Nu 1:4, 8
  Nu 2:5
  Nu 10:15

m Le 27:25

Second Col.

a Le 2:1

b Le 1:3

c Le 4:22, 23

d Le 3:1

e Nu 2:7
  Nu 10:16

f Le 27:25

g Le 2:1

h Le 1:3

i Le 4:22, 23

j Le 3:1

k Nu 1:4, 9

l Nu 2:10
  Nu 10:18

m Le 27:25

n Le 2:1

o Le 1:3

p Le 4:22, 23

q Le 3:1

r Nu 1:4, 5

7:10 *Or "dedication." 7:13 *A shekel equaled 11.4 g (0.367 oz t). See App. B14. #Or "by the holy shekel." 7:14 *Or "small bowl."

36 On the fifth day, the chieftain for the sons of Sim'e·on, She·lu'mi·el[a] the son of Zu·ri·shad'dai, **37** made his offering of one silver dish weighing 130 shekels and one silver bowl weighing 70 shekels by the standard shekel of the holy place,[b] both of them full of fine flour mixed with oil for a grain offering;[c] **38** one gold cup weighing 10 shekels, full of incense; **39** one young bull, one ram, and one male lamb in its first year for a burnt offering;[d] **40** one young goat for a sin offering;[e] **41** and for a communion sacrifice,[f] two cattle, five rams, five male goats, and five male lambs each a year old. This was the offering of She·lu'mi·el[g] the son of Zu·ri·shad'dai.

42 On the sixth day, the chieftain for the sons of Gad, E·li'a·saph[h] the son of Deu'el, **43** made his offering of one silver dish weighing 130 shekels and one silver bowl weighing 70 shekels by the standard shekel of the holy place,[i] both of them full of fine flour mixed with oil for a grain offering;[j] **44** one gold cup weighing 10 shekels, full of incense; **45** one young bull, one ram, and one male lamb in its first year for a burnt offering;[k] **46** one young goat for a sin offering;[l] **47** and for a communion sacrifice,[m] two cattle, five rams, five male goats, and five male lambs each a year old. This was the offering of E·li'a·saph[n] the son of Deu'el.

48 On the seventh day, the chieftain for the sons of E'phra·im, E·lish'a·ma[o] the son of Am·mi'hud, **49** made his offering of one silver dish weighing 130 shekels and one silver bowl weighing 70 shekels by the standard shekel of the holy place,[p] both of them full of fine flour mixed with oil for a grain offering;[q] **50** one gold cup weigh-ing 10 shekels, full of incense; **51** one young bull, one ram, and one male lamb in its first year for a burnt offering;[a] **52** one young goat for a sin offering;[b] **53** and for a communion sacrifice,[c] two cattle, five rams, five male goats, and five male lambs each a year old. This was the offering of E·lish'a·ma[d] the son of Am·mi'hud.

54 On the eighth day, the chieftain for the sons of Ma·nas'seh, Ga·ma'li·el[e] the son of Pe·dah'zur, **55** made his offering of one silver dish weighing 130 shekels and one silver bowl weighing 70 shekels by the standard shekel of the holy place,[f] both of them full of fine flour mixed with oil for a grain offering;[g] **56** one gold cup weighing 10 shekels, full of incense; **57** one young bull, one ram, and one male lamb in its first year, for a burnt offering;[h] **58** one young goat for a sin offering;[i] **59** and for a communion sacrifice,[j] two cattle, five rams, five male goats, and five male lambs each a year old. This was the offering of Ga·ma'li·el[k] the son of Pe·dah'zur.

60 On the ninth day, the chieftain[l] for the sons of Ben·jamin, Ab'i·dan[m] the son of Gid·e·o'ni, **61** made his offering of one silver dish weighing 130 shekels and one silver bowl weighing 70 shekels by the standard shekel of the holy place,[n] both of them full of fine flour mixed with oil for a grain offering;[o] **62** one gold cup weighing 10 shekels, full of incense; **63** one young bull, one ram, and one male lamb in its first year for a burnt offering;[p] **64** one young goat for a sin offering;[q] **65** and for a communion sacrifice,[r] two cattle, five rams, five male goats, and five male lambs each a year old. This was the

CHAP. 7
a Nu 2:12
b Le 27:25
c Le 2:1
d Le 1:3
e Le 4:22, 23
f Le 3:1
g Nu 1:4, 6
h Nu 2:14
  Nu 10:20
i Le 27:25
j Le 2:1
k Le 1:3
l Le 4:22, 23
m Le 3:1
n Nu 1:4, 14
o Nu 2:18
  Nu 10:22
p Le 27:25
q Le 2:1

Second Col.
a Le 1:3
b Le 4:22, 23
c Le 3:1
d Nu 1:4, 10
e Nu 2:20
  Nu 10:23
f Le 27:25
g Le 2:1
h Le 1:3
i Le 4:22, 23
j Le 3:1
k Nu 1:4, 10
l Nu 1:16
m Nu 2:22
  Nu 10:24
n Le 27:25
o Le 2:1
p Le 1:3
q Le 4:22, 23
r Le 3:1

offering of Ab·i·dan° the son of Gid·e·o′ni.

66 On the tenth day, the chieftain for the sons of Dan, A·hi·e′zer[b] the son of Am·mi·shad′dai, **67** made his offering of one silver dish weighing 130 shekels and one silver bowl weighing 70 shekels by the standard shekel of the holy place,[c] both of them full of fine flour mixed with oil for a grain offering;[d] **68** one gold cup weighing 10 shekels, full of incense; **69** one young bull, one ram, and one male lamb in its first year for a burnt offering;[e] **70** one young goat for a sin offering;[f] **71** and for a communion sacrifice,[g] two cattle, five rams, five male goats, and five male lambs each a year old. This was the offering of A·hi·e′zer[h] the son of Am·mi·shad′dai.

72 On the 11th day, the chieftain for the sons of Ash′er, Pa′gi·el[i] the son of Och′ran, **73** made his offering of one silver dish weighing 130 shekels and one silver bowl weighing 70 shekels by the standard shekel of the holy place,[j] both of them full of fine flour mixed with oil for a grain offering;[k] **74** one gold cup weighing 10 shekels, full of incense; **75** one young bull, one ram, and one male lamb in its first year for a burnt offering;[l] **76** one young goat for a sin offering;[m] **77** and for a communion sacrifice,[n] two cattle, five rams, five male goats, and five male lambs each a year old. This was the offering of Pa′gi·el[o] the son of Och′ran.

78 On the 12th day, the chieftain for the sons of Naph′ta·li, A·hi′ra[p] the son of E′nan, **79** made his offering of one silver dish weighing 130 shekels and one silver bowl weighing 70 shekels by the standard shekel of the holy place,[q] both of them full of fine flour mixed with

---

CHAP. 7
a Nu 1:4, 11

b Nu 2:25
Nu 10:25

c Le 27:25

d Le 2:1

e Le 1:3

f Le 4:22, 23

g Le 3:1

h Nu 1:4, 12

i Nu 2:27
Nu 10:26

j Le 27:25

k Le 2:1

l Le 1:3

m Le 4:22, 23

n Le 3:1

o Nu 1:4, 13

p Nu 2:29
Nu 10:27

q Le 27:25

Second Col.
a Le 2:1

b Le 1:3

c Le 4:22, 23

d Le 3:1

e Nu 1:4, 15

f Nu 7:10
Ezr 2:68

g Nu 7:13-17

h Le 27:25

i Nu 7:10

j Nu 7:1

k Ex 33:9
Nu 11:17
Nu 12:8

l Ex 25:22
Ex 37:6

m Ex 25:18
1Sa 4:4
Ps 80:1

---

oil for a grain offering;[a] **80** one gold cup weighing 10 shekels, full of incense; **81** one young bull, one ram, and one male lamb in its first year for a burnt offering;[b] **82** one young goat for a sin offering;[c] **83** and for a communion sacrifice,[d] two cattle, five rams, five male goats, and five male lambs each a year old. This was the offering of A·hi′ra[e] the son of E′nan.

84 This was the inauguration offering[f] of the altar from the chieftains of Israel when it was anointed: 12 silver dishes, 12 silver bowls, 12 gold cups;[g] **85** each silver dish weighing 130 shekels and each bowl weighing 70 shekels, all the silver of the vessels amounting to 2,400 shekels by the standard shekel of the holy place;[h] **86** the 12 gold cups full of incense each weighed 10 shekels by the standard shekel of the holy place, all the gold of the cups amounting to 120 shekels. **87** All the cattle for the burnt offering were 12 bulls, 12 rams, 12 male lambs each a year old and their grain offerings, and 12 young goats for a sin offering; **88** and all the cattle of the communion sacrifice amounted to 24 bulls, 60 rams, 60 male goats, and 60 male lambs each a year old. This was the inauguration offering[i] of the altar after it was anointed.[j]

89 Whenever Moses went into the tent of meeting to speak with God,*[k] he would hear the voice conversing with him from above the cover[l] of the ark of the Testimony, from between the two cherubs;[m] and God would speak to him.

8 Jehovah spoke to Moses, saying: **2** "Speak to Aaron and tell him, 'When you light up the lamps, the seven lamps

---

7:89 *Lit., "him."

should shine on the area in front of the lampstand.'"[a] **3** So Aaron did this: He lit up its lamps for the area in front of the lampstand,[b] just as Jehovah had commanded Moses. **4** This is how the lampstand was made: It was hammered work of gold; from its stem to its blossoms, it was hammered work.[c] The lampstand was made according to the vision[d] that Jehovah had shown Moses.

5 Jehovah spoke again to Moses, saying: **6** "Take the Levites from among the Israelites, and cleanse them.[e] **7** This is how you should cleanse them: Sprinkle sin-cleansing water on them, and they must shave their whole body with a razor, wash their garments, and cleanse themselves.[f] **8** Then they will take a young bull[g] and its grain offering[h] of fine flour mixed with oil, and you will take another young bull for a sin offering.[i] **9** And you are to present the Levites before the tent of meeting and gather all the assembly of the Israelites.[j] **10** When you present the Levites before Jehovah, the Israelites are to lay their hands on the Levites.[k] **11** And Aaron must offer* the Levites before Jehovah as a wave offering[l] from the Israelites, and they will carry out the service of Jehovah.[m]

12 "Then the Levites will lay their hands on the heads of the bulls[n] and offer the one as a sin offering and the other as a burnt offering to Jehovah to make atonement[o] for the Levites. **13** And you will have the Levites stand before Aaron and his sons and offer* them as a wave offering to Jehovah. **14** You must separate the Levites from among the Israelites, and the Levites will become mine.[p] **15** Afterward, the

Levites will come in to serve at the tent of meeting. This is how you should cleanse them and offer* them as a wave offering. **16** For they are given ones, given to me from among the Israelites. In place of all those who are firstborn* of the Israelites,[a] I will take them for myself. **17** For every firstborn among the Israelites is mine, both man and animal.[b] I sanctified them to myself on the day I struck down every firstborn in the land of Egypt.[c] **18** I will take the Levites in place of all the firstborn among the Israelites. **19** I will give the Levites as given ones to Aaron and his sons from among the Israelites, to carry out the service in behalf of the Israelites at the tent of meeting[d] and to make atonement for the Israelites, so that no plague may occur among the Israelites[e] because the people of Israel come near the holy place."

20 Moses and Aaron and all the assembly of the Israelites did this with the Levites. In accord with all that Jehovah had commanded Moses regarding the Levites, that is what the Israelites did with them. **21** So the Levites purified themselves and washed their garments,[f] after which Aaron offered* them as a wave offering before Jehovah.[g] Then Aaron made atonement for them to cleanse them.[h] **22** Thereafter, the Levites went in to carry out their service at the tent of meeting before Aaron and his sons. Just as Jehovah had commanded Moses respecting the Levites, so they did with them.

23 Jehovah now spoke to Moses, saying: **24** "This applies to the Levites: From 25 years old

---

CHAP. 8
a Ex 25:37
  Ex 40:24, 25
  Le 24:2

b Heb 9:2

c Ex 37:17

d Ex 25:9, 40
  1Ch 28:12, 19

e Ex 29:4
  Isa 52:11

f Ex 30:18, 19
  Le 16:28
  Nu 19:7

g Le 1:3

h Le 2:1

i Le 4:3

j Le 8:2, 3

k Nu 3:9, 41

l Le 7:30
  Nu 8:21

m Nu 1:50
  Nu 3:6
  2Ch 31:2

n Ex 29:10

o Le 1:4

p Nu 3:45
  Nu 16:9

Second Col.
a Nu 3:12

b Ex 13:2, 12
  Le 27:26

c Ex 12:29
  Ex 13:15

d Nu 3:9
  Nu 18:6
  1Ch 23:32
  Eze 44:11

e Nu 1:53
  Nu 18:5
  1Sa 6:19

f Nu 8:7

g Nu 8:11

h Nu 8:12

8:11, 13, 15 *Lit., "wave," that is, cause to move back and forth.

8:16 *Or "all the firstborn opening the wombs." 8:21 *Lit., "waved," that is, caused to move back and forth.

and up, a man will join the company of those in the service of the tent of meeting. **25** But after the age of 50 years, he will retire from the service company and not serve any longer. **26** He may minister to his brothers who are taking care of the responsibilities at the tent of meeting, but he must not perform the service there. This is what you are to do regarding the Levites and their responsibilities."[a]

9 Jehovah spoke to Moses in the wilderness of Si'nai in the first month[b] of the second year after they had come out of the land of Egypt, saying: **2** "The Israelites should prepare the Passover sacrifice[c] at its appointed time.[d] **3** On the 14th day of this month at twilight,* you should prepare it at its appointed time. According to all its statutes and all its set procedures, you should prepare it."[e]

4 So Moses told the Israelites to prepare the Passover sacrifice. **5** Then they prepared the Passover sacrifice in the first month, on the 14th day of the month at twilight,* in the wilderness of Si'nai. According to all that Jehovah had commanded Moses, so the Israelites did.

6 Now there were men who had become unclean by touching a dead body,*[f] so that they were not able to prepare the Passover sacrifice on that day. So those men presented themselves before Moses and Aaron on that day[g] **7** and said to him: "We are unclean because of touching a dead body.* Why should we be kept from presenting the offering to Jehovah at its appointed time among the Israelites?"[h] **8** At this Moses said to them:

"Wait there, and let me hear what Jehovah may command regarding you."[a]

9 Then Jehovah said to Moses: **10** "Tell the Israelites, 'Although any man among you or of your future generations should become unclean by touching a dead body*[b] or should be off on a distant journey, he must still prepare the Passover sacrifice to Jehovah. **11** They should prepare it in the second month,[c] on the 14th day at twilight.* They should eat it together with unleavened bread and bitter greens.[d] **12** They must not let any of it remain until morning,[e] and they should not break any bone in it.[f] They should prepare it according to every statute regarding the Passover. **13** But if a man was clean or was not off on a journey and neglected to prepare the Passover sacrifice, that person* must then be cut off[#] from his people,[g] because he did not present the offering of Jehovah at its appointed time. That man will answer for his sin.

14 "'And if a foreign resident is residing with you, he should also prepare the Passover sacrifice to Jehovah.[h] He should do so according to the statute of the Passover and its set procedure.[i] There should exist one statute for you, both for the foreign resident and for the native of the land.'"[j]

15 Now on the day the tabernacle was set up,[k] the cloud covered the tabernacle, the tent of the Testimony, but in the evening what appeared to be fire remained over the tabernacle until morning.[l] **16** That is what continued to take place: The cloud would cover it by day, and the appearance of fire by

---

CHAP. 8
a Nu 1:53
Nu 3:32
Nu 18:4

CHAP. 9
b Ex 40:2
Nu 1:1

c Ex 12:27

d Ex 12:3, 6
Le 23:5
De 16:1
1Co 5:7

e Ex 12:8

f Nu 5:2
Nu 19:14, 16

g Ex 18:15
Nu 15:33
Nu 27:1, 2

h Le 7:21
De 16:2

Second Col.
a Ex 25:22
Le 16:2
Ps 99:6

b Nu 5:2

c 2Ch 30:2, 15

d Ex 12:8

e Ex 12:10

f Ex 12:46
Ps 34:20
Joh 19:36

g Ex 12:15

h Ex 12:19, 48

i Ex 12:8

j Le 24:22
De 31:12

k Ex 40:2, 17

l Ex 40:34, 38

9:3, 5, 11 *Lit., "between the two evenings." 9:6 *Or "by a human soul." 9:7 *Or "because of a human soul."

9:10 *Or "by a soul." 9:13 *Or "soul." #Or "put to death."

night.ᵃ **17** Whenever the cloud lifted from the tent, the Israelites would promptly depart,ᵇ and in the place where the cloud would remain, there is where the Israelites would encamp.ᶜ **18** At the order of Jehovah the Israelites would depart, and at the order of Jehovah they would encamp.ᵈ As long as the cloud remained over the tabernacle, they would remain encamped. **19** When the cloud would stay over the tabernacle for many days, the Israelites would obey Jehovah and not depart.ᵉ **20** Sometimes the cloud would remain for a few days over the tabernacle. At the order of Jehovah they would remain encamped, and at the order of Jehovah they would depart. **21** Sometimes the cloud would remain only from evening until morning, and when the cloud lifted in the morning, they would depart. Whether it was day or night when the cloud lifted, they would depart.ᶠ **22** Whether it was two days, a month, or longer, as long as the cloud stayed over the tabernacle, the Israelites remained encamped and would not depart. But when it lifted, they would depart. **23** At the order of Jehovah they would encamp, and at the order of Jehovah they would depart. They kept their obligation to Jehovah at the order of Jehovah through Moses.

10 Jehovah then said to Moses: **2** "Make two trumpetsᵍ for yourself; make them of hammered silver, and use them to summon the assembly and to break up the camps. **3** When both of them are blown, the whole assembly must be summoned to you at the entrance of the tent of meeting.ʰ **4** If just one is blown, only the chieftains, the heads of the thousands of Israel, will be summoned to you.ⁱ

CHAP. 9
a Ex 13:22
Ne 9:19
b Nu 10:11, 34
c Ex 40:36, 37
d Ex 17:1
Nu 10:11-13
e Ex 40:37
f Ex 40:36
Ps 78:14

CHAP. 10
g Le 23:24
h Nu 1:18
De 29:10, 11
i Ex 18:21
Nu 1:16
Nu 7:2
De 1:15
De 5:23

Second Col.
a Nu 2:3
b Nu 2:10
c Nu 10:3
d Nu 31:6
1Ch 15:24
1Ch 16:6
2Ch 29:26
Ne 12:35, 41
e 2Ch 13:12
f 1Ch 15:28
2Ch 5:12
2Ch 7:6
Ezr 3:10
g Le 23:24
Nu 29:1
h Nu 28:11
i Le 3:1
j Ex 6:7
Le 11:45
k Nu 1:1
l Nu 9:17
Ps 78:14
m Ex 40:36
Nu 2:9, 16,
17, 24, 31
n Nu 12:16
Nu 13:26
De 1:1, 2
o Nu 2:34
Nu 9:23
p Nu 1:4, 7
Nu 2:3

5 "When you sound a fluctuating trumpet blast, the camps of those to the eastᵃ should depart. **6** When you sound a fluctuating trumpet blast a second time, the camps of those to the southᵇ should depart. They should sound the trumpet blasts in this way each time one of them departs.

7 "Now when calling the congregation together, you should blow the trumpets,ᶜ but not with fluctuating blasts. **8** Aaron's sons, the priests, should blow the trumpets,ᵈ and the use of them will serve as a lasting statute for you throughout your generations.

9 "If you should go to war in your land against an oppressor who is harassing you, you should sound a war call on the trumpets,ᵉ and you will be remembered by Jehovah your God and be saved from your enemies.

10 "Also, on your joyous occasionsᶠ—your festivalsᵍ and at the beginning of your months—you are to sound the trumpets over your burnt offeringsʰ and your communion sacrifices;ⁱ they will serve as a reminder for you before your God. I am Jehovah your God."ʲ

11 Now in the second year, in the second month, on the 20th day of the month,ᵏ the cloud lifted from over the tabernacleˡ of the Testimony. **12** So the Israelites began to pull away from the wilderness of Siʹnai in the order established for their departure,ᵐ and the cloud settled in the wilderness of Paʹran.ⁿ **13** This was the first time they departed following the order of Jehovah through Moses.ᵒ

14 So the three-tribe division of the camp of the sons of Judah departed first by their companies,* and Nahʹshonᵖ the son of

---
10:14 * Lit., "according to their armies."

Am·min′a·dab was over its company. **15** Over the company of the tribe of the sons of Is′sa·char was Ne·than′el[a] the son of Zu′ar. **16** Over the company of the tribe of the sons of Zeb′u·lun was E·li′ab[b] the son of He′lon.

17 When the tabernacle was taken down,[c] the sons of Ger′shon[d] and the sons of Me·rar′i,[e] who carried the tabernacle, departed.

18 Then the three-tribe division of the camp of Reu′ben departed by their companies,* and E·li′zur[f] the son of Shed′e·ur was over its company. **19** Over the company of the tribe of the sons of Sim′e·on was She·lu′mi·el[g] the son of Zu·ri·shad′dai. **20** Over the company of the tribe of the sons of Gad was E·li′a·saph[h] the son of Deu′el.

21 Then the Ko′hath·ites, who carried the sanctuary items,[i] departed. The tabernacle was to be set up by the time they arrived.

22 Then the three-tribe division of the camp of the sons of E′phra·im departed by their companies,* and E·lish′a·ma[j] the son of Am·mi′hud was over its company. **23** Over the company of the tribe of the sons of Ma·nas′seh was Ga·ma′li·el[k] the son of Pe·dah′zur. **24** Over the company of the tribe of the sons of Benjamin was Ab′i·dan[l] the son of Gid·e·o′ni.

25 Then the three-tribe division of the camp of the sons of Dan departed by their companies,* forming the rear guard for all the camps, and A·hi·e′zer[m] the son of Am·mi·shad′dai was over its company. **26** Over the company of the tribe of the sons of Ash′er was Pa′gi·el[n] the son of Och′ran. **27** Over the company of the tribe of the sons of Naph′ta·li was A·hi′ra[o] the son of

E′nan. **28** This was the order of departure that the Israelites and their companies* followed when they would depart.[a]

29 Then Moses said to Ho′bab the son of Reu′el*[b] the Mid′i·an·ite, the father-in-law of Moses: "We are setting out for the place about which Jehovah said, 'I will give it to you.'[c] Do come with us,[d] and we will treat you well, because Jehovah has promised good things for Israel."[e] **30** But he said to him: "I will not go. I will return to my own country and to my relatives." **31** At this he said: "Please do not leave us, for you know where we should camp in the wilderness, and you can serve as our guide.* **32** And if you do come with us,[f] whatever goodness Jehovah shows to us, we will surely show to you."

33 So they began marching from the mountain of Jehovah[g] for a journey of three days, and the ark[h] of Jehovah's covenant traveled before them for the three-day journey to search out a resting-place for them.[i] **34** And Jehovah's cloud[j] was over them by day when they set out from the encampment.

35 Whenever the Ark was moved, Moses would say: "Rise up, O Jehovah,[k] and let your enemies be scattered, and let those who hate you flee from before you." **36** And when it would rest, he would say: "Do return, O Jehovah, to the countless* thousands of Israel."[l]

11 Now the people began to complain bitterly before Jehovah. When Jehovah heard it, his anger flared, and a fire from Jehovah began to blaze against them and to consume some on the outskirts of the camp. **2** When the people

---

CHAP. 10
a Nu 1:4, 8
  Nu 2:5
b Nu 2:7
c Nu 1:51
d Nu 3:25, 26
e Nu 3:36, 37
f Nu 1:4, 5
  Nu 2:10
g Nu 1:5, 6
  Nu 2:12
h Nu 1:4, 14
  Nu 2:14
i Nu 3:30, 31
  Nu 4:15
  Nu 7:9
j Nu 1:4, 10
  Nu 2:18, 24
k Nu 1:4, 10
  Nu 2:20
l Nu 1:4, 11
  Nu 2:22
m Nu 1:4, 12
  Nu 2:25, 31
n Nu 1:4, 13
  Nu 2:27
o Nu 1:4, 15
  Nu 2:29

Second Col.
a Nu 2:34
b Ex 2:16, 18
  Ex 3:1
  Ex 18:1, 5
c Ge 12:7
  Ge 13:14, 15
  Ge 15:18
d Jg 1:16
  Jg 4:11
  1Sa 15:6
e Ex 3:8
  Ex 6:7
f Jg 1:16
  Jg 4:11
g Ex 3:1
  Ex 19:3
  Ex 24:16
  De 5:2
h Ex 25:10, 17
i De 1:32, 33
  Jos 3:3, 4
j Ex 13:21
  Ne 9:12
  Ps 78:14
k Ps 132:8
l De 1:10

10:18, 22, 25, 28 *Lit., "according to their armies."

10:29 *That is, Jethro. 10:31 *Or "eyes." 10:36 *Or "myriads of."

began to cry out to Moses, he made supplication to Jehovah,[a] and the fire died out. **3** So that place was given the name Tab'e-rah,* because a fire from Jehovah had blazed against them.[b]

4 The mixed crowd*[c] who were in their midst then expressed selfish longing,[d] and the Israelites too began to weep again and say: "Who will give us meat to eat?[e] **5** How fondly we remember the fish that we used to eat without cost in Egypt, also the cucumbers, the watermelons, the leeks, the onions, and the garlic![f] **6** But now we* are withering away. We see nothing at all except this manna."[g]

7 Incidentally, the manna[h] was like coriander seed,[i] and it looked like bdellium gum. **8** The people would spread out and pick it up and grind it in hand mills or pound it in a mortar. Then they would boil it in cooking pots or make it into round loaves,[j] and it tasted like an oiled sweet cake. **9** When the dew descended on the camp by night, the manna would also descend on it.[k]

10 Moses heard the people weeping, family after family, each man at the entrance of his tent. And Jehovah became very angry,[l] and Moses was also very displeased. **11** Then Moses said to Jehovah: "Why have you afflicted your servant? Why have I not found favor in your eyes, so that you put the burden of all this people on me?[m] **12** Did I conceive all this people? Did I give birth to them, so that you should tell me, 'Carry them in your bosom, just as an attendant* carries the nursing child,' to the land that you swore

to give to their forefathers?[a] **13** From where will I get meat to give to all this people? For they keep weeping before me, saying, 'Give us meat to eat!' **14** I am not able to bear all this people by myself; it is too much for me.[b] **15** If this is how you are going to treat me, please kill me right now.[c] If I have found favor in your eyes, do not make me see any more calamity."

16 Jehovah replied to Moses: "Gather for me 70 men from the elders of Israel, men whom you recognize as* elders and officials of the people,[d] and take them to the tent of meeting, and have them stand there with you. **17** I will come down[e] and speak with you there,[f] and I will take away some of the spirit[g] that is on you and place it on them, and they will help you in bearing the burden of the people so that you may not have to bear it alone.[h] **18** You should say to the people, 'Sanctify yourselves for tomorrow,[i] for you will certainly eat meat, because you have wept in Jehovah's hearing[j] and have said: "Who will give us meat to eat? It was better for us in Egypt."[k] Jehovah will certainly give you meat, and you will eat.[l] **19** You will eat, not one day nor 2 days nor 5 days nor 10 days nor 20 days, **20** but for a whole month of days, until it comes out of your nostrils and it has become loathsome to you,[m] for you rejected Jehovah, who is in your midst, and you were weeping before him, saying: "Why is it that we have come out of Egypt?"'"[n]

21 Then Moses said: "The people I am among number 600,-000 men[o] on foot, and yet you yourself have said, 'Meat I will give them, and they will eat

---

CHAP. 11

a Ex 32:11
De 9:19
Ps 106:23
Jas 5:16

b De 9:22

c Ex 12:37, 38
Le 24:10

d 1Co 10:6, 10

e Ps 78:18, 22
Ps 106:14

f Ex 16:3

g Ex 16:35
Nu 21:5

h Ex 16:14
Ne 9:20
Joh 6:31

i Ex 16:31

j Ex 16:16, 23

k Ps 78:24

l Nu 11:1

m Ex 17:4
De 1:12

Second Col.

a Ge 13:14, 15
Ge 26:3

b Ex 18:17, 18
De 1:9

c 1Ki 19:2, 4
Job 6:8, 9

d De 16:18

e Ex 19:11
Ex 25:22
Ex 34:5
Nu 12:5

f Nu 11:25
Nu 12:8

g 1Sa 10:6
2Ki 2:15
Ne 9:20
Ac 2:17

h Ex 18:21, 22

i Ex 19:10

j Ex 16:7

k Nu 11:4, 5

l Ex 16:8

m Ps 78:29

n Nu 21:5

o Ex 12:37
Ex 38:26
Nu 1:45, 46

11:3 *Meaning "Burning," that is, a conflagration; blaze. **11:4** *Apparently the non-Israelites among them. **11:6** *Or "our souls." **11:12** *Or "a male nurse."

11:16 *Or "who you know are; who are known to you as."

enough for a whole month of days'! 22 If whole flocks and herds were slaughtered, would it be enough for them? Or if all the fish of the sea were caught, would it be enough for them?"

23 Jehovah then said to Moses: "Is the hand of Jehovah too short?ᵃ Now you will see whether what I say will happen to you or not."

24 So Moses went out and spoke the words of Jehovah to the people. And he gathered 70 men from the elders of the people and had them stand around the tent.ᵇ 25 Then Jehovah came down in a cloudᵈ and spoke to himᵈ and took away some of the spiritᵉ that was on him and put it on each of the 70 elders. And as soon as the spirit settled down on them, they began to behave as prophets,*ᶠ but they did not do it again.

26 There were two of the men still in the camp. Their names were El′dad and Me′dad. And the spirit began to settle down on them, as they were among those whose names had been written down, but they had not gone out to the tent. So they began to behave as prophets in the camp. 27 And a young man ran and reported to Moses: "El′dad and Me′dad are behaving as prophets in the camp!" 28 Then Joshuaᵍ the son of Nun, the minister of Moses from his youth, responded and said: "My lord Moses, restrain them!"ʰ 29 But Moses said to him: "Are you jealous for me? No, I wish that all of Jehovah's people were prophets and that Jehovah would put his spirit on them!" 30 Later Moses returned to the camp along with the elders of Israel.

31 Then a wind from Jehovah sprang up and began driving quail from the sea and causing

---

CHAP. 11

a Ge 18:14
  Isa 59:1
  Mr 10:27
  Lu 1:37

b Nu 11:16

c Ex 33:9
  Nu 12:5
  De 31:15

d Ps 99:7

e Nu 11:17
  2Ki 2:9, 15

f 1Sa 10:6
  1Sa 19:20

g Ex 17:9
  Ex 24:13
  Ex 33:11
  Nu 27:18-20
  De 31:3

h Mr 9:38

Second Col.

a Ex 16:13
  Ps 78:26, 27

b Ps 78:30, 31
  1Co 10:10

c Nu 33:16
  De 9:22

d 1Co 10:6

e Nu 33:17

CHAP. 12

f Ex 2:16, 21

g Ex 4:14-16
  Ex 4:30
  Ex 15:20
  Ex 28:30
  Mic 6:4

h Nu 11:1

i Mt 11:29

j Ex 34:5
  Nu 11:25

---

them to fall around the camp,ᵃ about a day's journey on this side and a day's journey on the other side, all around the camp, and they were about two cubits* deep on the ground. 32 So all that day and all night and all the next day, the people stayed up and gathered the quail. No one gathered less than ten ho′mers,* and they kept spreading them all around the camp for themselves. 33 But while the meat was still between their teeth, before it could be chewed, Jehovah's anger blazed against the people, and Jehovah began striking the people with a very great slaughter.ᵇ

34 So they gave that place the name Kib′roth-hat·ta′a·vah,*ᶜ because there they buried the people who showed selfish craving.ᵈ 35 From Kib′roth-hat·ta′a·vah the people departed for Ha·ze′roth, and they remained at Ha·ze′roth.ᵉ

12 Now Mir′i·am and Aaron began to speak against Moses because of the Cush′ite wife he had married, for he had taken a Cush′ite wife.ᶠ 2 They were saying: "Is it only by Moses that Jehovah has spoken? Has he not also spoken through us?"ᵍ And Jehovah was listening.ʰ 3 Now the man Moses was by far the meekest of all the men*ⁱ on the face of the earth.

4 Jehovah suddenly said to Moses and Aaron and Mir′i·am: "Go out, the three of you, to the tent of meeting." So the three of them went out. 5 And Jehovah came down in the pillar of cloudʲ and stood at the entrance of the

---

11:31 *A cubit equaled 44.5 cm (17.5 in.). See App. B14. 11:32 *A homer equaled 220 L (200 dry qt). See App. B14. 11:34 *Meaning "Burial Places of the Craving." 12:3 *Or "was very humble (mild-tempered), more so than any other man."

tent and called Aaron and Mir′i-am. Both of them went forward. **6** He then said: "Hear my words, please. If there was a prophet of Jehovah among you, I would make myself known to him in a vision,[a] and I would speak to him in a dream.[b] **7** But it is not that way with my servant Moses! He is being entrusted with all my house.[c] **8** Face-to-face* I speak to him,[d] openly, not by riddles; and the appearance of Jehovah is what he sees. Why, then, did you not fear to speak against my servant, against Moses?"

9 So Jehovah's anger burned against them, and he departed from them. **10** The cloud moved away from over the tent, and look! Mir′i·am was struck with leprosy as white as snow.[e] Then Aaron turned toward Mir′i·am, and he saw that she was struck with leprosy.[f] **11** Immediately Aaron said to Moses: "I beg you, my lord! Please do not hold this sin against us! We have acted foolishly in what we have done. **12** Please, do not let her continue like someone dead, whose flesh is half eaten away at birth!" **13** And Moses began to cry out to Jehovah, saying: "O God, please heal her! Please!"[g]

14 Jehovah replied to Moses: "If her father would spit directly in her face, would she not be humiliated for seven days? Let her be quarantined for seven days outside the camp,[h] and afterward she may be brought back in." **15** So Mir′i·am was quarantined outside the camp for seven days,[i] and the people did not break camp until Mir′i·am was brought back in. **16** Then the people departed from Ha·ze′roth[j]

and began camping in the wilderness of Pa′ran.[a]

13 Jehovah now spoke to Moses, saying: **2** "Send out men to spy* the land of Ca′naan, which I am giving to the Israelites. You are to send out one man from each ancestral tribe, each one a chieftain[b] among them."[c]

3 So Moses sent them out from the wilderness of Pa′ran[d] at the order of Jehovah. All the men were heads of the Israelites. **4** These are their names: of the tribe of Reu′ben, Sham·mu′a the son of Zac′cur; **5** of the tribe of Sim′e·on, Sha′phat the son of Ho′ri; **6** of the tribe of Judah, Ca′leb[e] the son of Je·phun′neh; **7** of the tribe of Is′sa·char, I′gal the son of Joseph; **8** of the tribe of E′phra·im, Ho·she′a[f] the son of Nun; **9** of the tribe of Benjamin, Pal′ti the son of Ra′phu; **10** of the tribe of Zeb′u·lun, Gad′di·el the son of So′di; **11** of the tribe of Joseph,[g] for the tribe of Ma·nas′seh,[h] Gad′di the son of Su′si; **12** of the tribe of Dan, Am′mi·el the son of Ge·mal′li; **13** of the tribe of Ash′er, Se′thur the son of Mi′cha·el; **14** of the tribe of Naph′ta·li, Nah′bi the son of Voph′si; **15** of the tribe of Gad, Geu′el the son of Ma′chi. **16** These are the names of the men whom Moses sent to spy out the land. And Moses gave the name Joshua*[i] to Ho·she′a the son of Nun.

17 When Moses was sending them to spy out the land of Ca′naan, he said to them: "Go up there into the Neg′eb, and then go up into the mountainous region.[j] **18** You must see what kind of land it is[k] and whether the people who are dwelling in it are strong or weak, few or many,

CHAP. 12
a Ge 15:1
  Ge 46:2
  Ex 24:9-11

b Ge 31:10, 11

c Heb 3:2, 5

d Ex 33:11
  De 34:10

e De 24:9

f 2Ch 26:19

g Ex 32:11
  Jas 5:16

h Le 13:45, 46
  Nu 5:2

i De 24:9

j Nu 11:35
  Nu 33:18

Second Col.
a Nu 10:12

CHAP. 13
b Ex 18:25
  De 1:15

c Nu 1:22, 23

d Nu 12:16
  De 1:19

e Nu 13:30
  Nu 14:30, 38
  Nu 34:18, 19
  1Ch 4:15

f Nu 11:28
  Nu 13:16
  Nu 14:30
  Nu 34:17

g Ge 48:5

h Ge 48:17, 19

i Ex 17:9

j De 1:7

k Ex 3:8
  De 8:7

12:7 *Lit., "In all my house, he is proving himself faithful." 12:8 *Lit., "Mouth to mouth."

13:2 *Or "to scout." 13:16 *Or "Jehoshua," meaning "Jehovah Is Salvation."

19 and whether the land is good or bad and whether the cities they are dwelling in are encampments or fortifications. **20** And find out whether the land is rich* or poor*[a] and whether there are trees in it or not. You must be courageous[b] and take some of the fruitage of the land." Now it was the season of the first ripe grapes.[c]

21 So they went up and spied out the land from the wilderness of Zin[d] to Re'hob[e] to Le'bo-ha'math.*[f] **22** When they went up into the Neg'eb, they came to Heb'ron,[g] where A-hi'man, She'shai, and Tal'mai,[h] the An'a-kim,[i] were living. Incidentally, Heb'ron had been built seven years before Zo'an of Egypt. **23** When they came to the Valley* of Esh'col,[j] there they cut down a branch with one cluster of grapes, which two of the men had to carry on a bar, as well as some of the pomegranates and figs.[k] **24** They called that place the Valley* of Esh'col*[j] because of the cluster that the Israelites cut down from there.

25 At the end of 40 days,[m] they returned from spying out the land. **26** So they came back to Moses and Aaron and all the assembly of the Israelites in the wilderness of Pa'ran, at Ka'desh.[n] They brought back a report to all the assembly and showed them the fruitage of the land. **27** This is what they reported to Moses: "We entered the land into which you sent us, and it is indeed flowing with milk and honey,[o] and this is its fruitage.[p] **28** Nevertheless, the people who dwell in the land are strong, and the fortified cities are very great. We also saw the

An'a-kim there.[a] **29** The A-mal'-ek-ites[b] are dwelling in the land of the Neg'eb,[c] and the Hit'tites, the Jeb'u-sites,[d] and the Am'or-ites[e] are dwelling in the mountainous region, and the Ca'naan-ites[f] are dwelling by the sea[g] and along the Jordan."

30 Then Ca'leb tried to calm the people as they stood before Moses by saying: "Let us go up immediately, and we are sure to take possession of it, because we can surely conquer it."[h] **31** But the men who went up with him said: "We are not able to go up against the people, because they are stronger than we are."[i] **32** And they kept on giving the Israelites a bad report[j] about the land that they had spied out, saying: "The land that we passed through to spy out is a land that devours its inhabitants, and all the people whom we saw in it are men of extraordinary size.[k] **33** And there we saw the Neph'i-lim, the sons of A'nak,[l] who are from* the Neph'i-lim, and in comparison we seemed like grasshoppers, both to us and to them."

14 Then all the assembly raised their voice, and the people continued crying out and weeping all through that night.[m] **2** All the Israelites began to murmur against Moses and Aaron,[n] and the whole assembly spoke against them, saying: "If only we had died in the land of Egypt, or if only we had died in this wilderness! **3** Why is Jehovah bringing us to this land to fall by the sword?[o] Our wives and children will become plunder.[p] Is it not better for us to return to Egypt?"[q] **4** They were even saying to one another: "Let us appoint a leader and return to Egypt!"[r]

CHAP. 13
a Ne 9:25
  Eze 20:6
b De 31:6
  Jos 1:6, 9
c Nu 13:23
d Nu 34:2, 3
  Jos 15:1
e 2Sa 10:6, 8
f Nu 34:8
g Ge 13:18
  Jos 15:13
  Jos 21:11, 12
h Jg 1:10
i De 9:1, 2
  Jos 11:21
j Nu 32:9
k De 1:25
  De 8:7-9
l De 1:24
m Nu 14:33, 34
n De 1:19
o Ex 3:8
  Le 20:24
p De 1:25

Second Col.
a Nu 13:22, 33
  De 1:27, 28
b Ge 36:12
  Ex 17:8
  1Sa 15:3
c Nu 13:17
d Jg 1:21
  2Sa 5:6, 7
e Ge 10:15, 16
f Ex 23:23
  De 7:1
  De 20:17
g Ge 10:19
h Jos 14:7, 8
i Nu 32:9
j Nu 14:36
k Am 2:9
l De 1:28
  De 9:1, 2

CHAP. 14
m De 1:32, 33
n De 1:27
  Ps 106:25
o Ps 78:40
p Nu 14:31
  De 1:39
q Nu 11:5
r Ne 9:17

13:20 *Lit., "fat." #Lit., "lean." **13:21** *Or "the entrance of Hamath." **13:23, 24** *Or "Wadi." **13:24** #Meaning "Cluster of Grapes."

13:33 *Or "descendants of."

5 At this Moses and Aaron fell with their faces to the ground before the whole assembled congregation of the Israelites. **6** Joshua[a] the son of Nun and Ca'leb[b] the son of Je·phun'neh, who were among those who spied out the land, ripped their garments apart, **7** and they said this to all the assembly of the Israelites: "The land that we passed through to spy out is a very, very good land.[c] **8** If Jehovah is pleased with us, he will certainly bring us into this land and give it to us, a land that is flowing with milk and honey.[d] **9** But you must not rebel against Jehovah, and you must not fear the people of the land,[e] for we will devour them.* Their protection has been removed from them, and Jehovah is with us.[f] Do not fear them."

10 However, all the assembly talked about stoning them.[g] But Jehovah's glory appeared on the tent of meeting to all the people of Israel.[h]

11 Then Jehovah said to Moses: "How much longer will this people treat me without respect,[i] and how much longer will they not put faith in me in spite of all the signs that I performed among them?[j] **12** Let me strike them with pestilence and drive them away, and let me make you into a nation greater and mightier than they are."[k]

13 But Moses said to Jehovah: "Then the Egyptians, from whose midst you brought this people out by your power, will hear,[l] **14** and they will speak about it to the inhabitants of this land. These also have heard that you, Jehovah, are among this people[m] and have appeared to them face-to-face.[n] You are Jehovah, and your cloud is standing over them, and you are going before them in the pillar of cloud by day and in the pillar of fire by night.[a] **15** If you put this people to death all at once,* the nations who have heard of your fame would say this: **16** 'Jehovah was not able to bring this people into the land he swore to give them, so he slaughtered them in the wilderness.'[b] **17** Please, now, Jehovah, let your power be great, as you promised when you said: **18** 'Jehovah, slow to anger and abundant in loyal love,*[c] pardoning error and transgression, but he will by no means leave the guilty unpunished, bringing punishment for the error of fathers upon sons, upon the third generation and upon the fourth generation.'[d] **19** Forgive, please, the error of this people according to your great loyal love, just as you have pardoned this people from Egypt until now."[e]

20 Then Jehovah said: "I forgive them according to your word.[f] **21** But on the other hand, as surely as I live, all the earth will be filled with the glory of Jehovah.[g] **22** However, not one of the men who have seen my glory and my signs[h] that I performed in Egypt and in the wilderness and yet have kept testing me[i] these ten times and have not listened to my voice[j] **23** will ever see the land about which I swore to their fathers. No, not one of those treating me without respect will see it.[k] **24** But because my servant Ca'leb[l] had a different spirit and kept following after me wholeheartedly, I will certainly bring him into the land where he went, and his offspring will take possession of it.[m] **25** Since the A·mal'ek·ites and

---

CHAP. 14
a Nu 13:8, 16
b Nu 13:6, 16
  Nu 14:30
c Nu 13:26, 27
  De 1:25
  De 8:7, 8
d Ex 3:8
e De 7:17, 18
  De 20:3
f Ex 33:16
  De 20:1
g Ex 17:4
h Ex 16:10
i Ex 16:28
  Nu 14:22, 23
j De 9:23
  Heb 3:19
k Ex 32:10
l Ex 32:12
  Eze 20:9
m Ex 15:13, 14
  Jos 2:10
  Jos 5:1
n De 4:12
  De 5:4

Second Col.
a Ex 13:21
  Ps 78:14
b De 9:28
c Ps 103:8
  Mic 7:18
d Ex 34:6, 7
e Ex 34:9
  Ps 78:38
f Jas 5:16
g Ps 72:19
  Hab 2:14
h Ne 9:17
i Ex 17:2
  Ps 95:9
  Ps 106:14
  Heb 3:16
j Ps 81:11
k Nu 26:63, 64
  Nu 32:11
  De 1:35
  Ps 95:11
  Ps 106:26
  Heb 3:18
  Heb 4:3
l Nu 13:30
  Nu 26:65
m Jos 14:9, 14

14:9 *Lit., "for they are bread to us." 14:15 *Lit., "as one man." 14:18 *Or "loving-kindness."

the Ca'naan·ites[a] are dwelling in the valley,* you should turn back tomorrow and set off for the wilderness by the way of the Red Sea."[b]

26 Jehovah then said to Moses and Aaron: 27 "How much longer will this evil assembly keep up this murmuring against me?[c] I have heard what the Israelites are murmuring against me.[d] 28 Say to them, '"As surely as I live," declares Jehovah, "I will do to you just what I have heard you speak![e] 29 In this wilderness your corpses will fall,[f] yes, the whole number of you from 20 years old and up who were registered, all of you who have murmured against me.[g] 30 None of you will enter into the land that I swore* to have you reside in[h] except Ca'leb the son of Je·phun'neh and Joshua the son of Nun.[i]

31 "'And I will bring in your children, who you said would become plunder,[j] and they will get to know the land that you have rejected.[k] 32 But your own corpses will fall in this wilderness. 33 Now your sons will become shepherds in the wilderness 40 years,[l] and they will have to answer for your acts of unfaithfulness* until the last one of your corpses falls in the wilderness.[m] 34 According to the number of the days that you spied out the land, 40 days,[n] a day for a year, a day for a year, you will answer for your errors 40 years,[o] for you will know what it means to oppose me.*

35 "'I, Jehovah, have spoken. This is what I will do to all this evil assembly, those who have gathered together against me: In this wilderness they will

14:25 *Or "low plain." 14:30 *Lit., "I lifted my hand." 14:33 *Lit., "prostitution." 14:34 *Or "to have me as an enemy."

come to their end, and here they will die.[a] 36 The men whom Moses sent to spy out the land and who caused the whole assembly to murmur against him when they returned with a bad report about the land,[b] 37 yes, the men who brought back the bad report about the land will be struck down and die before Jehovah.[c] 38 But Joshua the son of Nun and Ca'leb the son of Je·phun'neh, who were among those who went to spy out the land, will certainly keep living."'"[d]

39 When Moses spoke these words to all the Israelites, the people began to mourn a great deal. 40 Moreover, they got up early in the morning and tried to go up to the top of the mountain, saying: "Here we are ready to go up to the place that Jehovah spoke about, for we have sinned."[e] 41 But Moses said: "Why are you going beyond the order of Jehovah? This will not succeed. 42 Do not go up, for Jehovah is not with you; and you will be defeated by your enemies.[f] 43 For the A·mal'ek·ites and the Ca'naan·ites are there to face you,[g] and you will fall by the sword. Because you turned away from following Jehovah, Jehovah will not be with you."[h]

44 However, they presumptuously went toward the top of the mountain,[i] but the ark of Jehovah's covenant and Moses did not move away from the middle of the camp.[j] 45 Then the A·mal'ek·ites and the Ca'naanites who were dwelling in that mountain came down and struck them, scattering them as far as Hor'mah.[k]

15 Jehovah spoke further to Moses, saying: 2 "Speak to the Israelites and say to them, 'When you eventually come into the land that I am giving you to dwell in[l] 3 and you make

an offering by fire to Jehovah from the herd or from the flock—whether a burnt offering[a] or a sacrifice to perform a special vow or a voluntary offering[b] or an offering during your seasonal festivals,[c] in order to make a pleasing* aroma to Jehovah[d]— 4 the one presenting his offering must also present to Jehovah a grain offering of fine flour,[e] a tenth of an e′phah,* mixed with a fourth of a hin# of oil. 5 You should also offer wine as a drink offering, a fourth of a hin, together with the burnt offering[f] or for the sacrifice of each male lamb. 6 Or for a ram, you should make a grain offering of two tenths of an e′phah measure of fine flour mixed with a third of a hin of oil. 7 And you should present wine as a drink offering, a third of a hin, as a pleasing* aroma to Jehovah.

8 "'But if you should offer a male of the herd as a burnt offering[g] or a sacrifice to perform a special vow[h] or communion sacrifices to Jehovah,[i] 9 you should also present together with the male of the herd a grain offering[j] of three tenths of an e′phah measure of fine flour mixed with half a hin of oil. 10 You should also present wine as a drink offering,[k] half a hin, as an offering made by fire, as a pleasing* aroma to Jehovah. 11 This is what should be done for each bull or for each ram or for each of the male lambs or of the goats. 12 Whatever may be the number that you offer, that is what you should do for each one, according to their number. 13 This is how every native-born Israelite should present an

offering made by fire, as a pleasing* aroma to Jehovah.

14 "'If a foreigner who is residing with you or one who has been in your midst for many of your generations should also make an offering by fire, as a pleasing* aroma to Jehovah, he should do just as you do.[a] 15 You who are of the congregation and the foreigner who is residing with you will have one statute. It will be a lasting statute for all your generations. The foreign resident should be the same as you before Jehovah.[b] 16 There should be one law and one judicial decision for you and for the foreigner who is residing with you.'"

17 Jehovah went on to say to Moses: 18 "Speak to the Israelites and tell them, 'When you come into the land where I am bringing you 19 and you eat any of the bread* of the land,[c] you should make a contribution to Jehovah. 20 You should make a contribution of the first-fruits[d] of your coarse meal as ring-shaped loaves. Like the contribution of a threshing floor is the way you should contribute it. 21 Some of the first-fruits of your coarse meal you should give as a contribution to Jehovah throughout your generations.

22 "'Now if you make a mistake and fail to observe all these commandments that Jehovah has spoken to Moses, 23 all that Jehovah has commanded you through Moses from the day that Jehovah commanded and onward for your generations, 24 and if it was done by mistake and without the knowledge of the assembly, the whole assembly must offer one young bull as a burnt offering for a pleasing* aroma to Jehovah, together with

---

CHAP. 15
a Le 1:2, 3

b Le 7:16
  Le 22:18, 19
  Le 22:21

c Le 23:4
  Nu 28:16
  Nu 29:1
  De 16:13, 16

d Le 1:9

e Ex 29:40
  Le 2:1, 11

f Nu 28:6, 7
  Nu 28:11, 14

g Le 1:3

h Le 7:16

i Le 3:1, 3
  Le 7:11

j Le 6:14
  Nu 28:11, 12
  Nu 29:6

k Nu 28:11, 14

Second Col.
a Ex 12:49
  Le 24:22
  Nu 9:14

b Le 19:34

c Jos 5:11, 12

d Ex 23:19
  Le 2:14
  Nu 18:8, 12
  De 26:1, 2
  Pr 3:9

15:3, 7, 10, 13, 14, 24 *Or "appeasing; soothing." Lit., "restful." 15:4 *A tenth of an ephah equaled 2.2 L (2 dry qt). See App. B14. #A hin equaled 3.67 L (7.75 pt). See App. B14.

15:19 *Or "food."

its grain offering and its drink offering according to the regular procedure,[a] and one young goat as a sin offering.[b] 25 The priest will make atonement for the whole assembly of the Israelites, and it will be forgiven them,[c] because it was a mistake, and they brought as their offering an offering made by fire to Jehovah and their sin offering before Jehovah for their mistake. 26 It will be forgiven the whole assembly of the Israelites and the foreigner who is residing in their midst, because it was by mistake on the part of all the people.

27 "'If any person* should sin by mistake, then he must present a female goat in its first year for a sin offering.[d] 28 And the priest will make atonement for the person* who made a mistake by an unintentional sin before Jehovah, so as to make atonement for it, and it will be forgiven him.[e] 29 As for the native-born among the Israelites and the foreigner who is residing in their midst, there should be one law for you in the matter of doing something unintentionally.[f]

30 "'But the person* who does something deliberately,[g] whether he is native-born or a foreign resident, is blaspheming Jehovah and must be cut off* from among his people. 31 Because he has despised Jehovah's word and broken his commandment, that person* should be cut off without fail.[h] His own error is upon him.'"[i]

32 While the Israelites were in the wilderness, they found a man collecting pieces of wood on the Sabbath day.[j] 33 Those who found him collecting wood brought him up to Moses and

Aaron and the whole assembly. 34 They committed him into custody[a] because it had not been specified what should be done to him.

35 And Jehovah said to Moses: "The man should be put to death without fail,[b] and the whole assembly should stone him outside the camp."[c] 36 So the whole assembly brought him outside the camp and stoned him so that he died, just as Jehovah had commanded Moses.

37 Jehovah went on to say this to Moses: 38 "Speak to the Israelites and tell them that they must make for themselves fringed edges on the skirts of their garments throughout their generations, and they are to put a blue string above the fringed edge of the skirt.[d] 39 'You must have this fringed edge so that you will see it and remember all the commandments of Jehovah and observe them.[e] You must not follow your own hearts and eyes, which are leading you to spiritual prostitution.[f] 40 This will help you remember, and you will observe all my commandments and be holy to your God.[g] 41 I am Jehovah your God, who brought you out of the land of Egypt in order to prove myself your God.[h] I am Jehovah your God.'"[i]

16 Then Kor'ah[j] the son of Iz'har,[k] the son of Ko'hath,[l] the son of Le'vi,[m] got up together with Da'than and A·bi'ram the sons of E·li'ab,[n] and On the son of Pe'leth, of the sons of Reu'ben.[o] 2 They rose up against Moses along with 250 Israelite men, chieftains of the assembly, chosen ones of the congregation, prominent men. 3 So they gathered together against[p] Moses and Aaron and said to them: "We have had enough of you! The whole assembly is holy,[q] all of them, and Jehovah is in their

---

CHAP. 15
a Nu 15:8-10
b Nu 28:15
c Le 4:20
  Heb 2:17
  1Jo 2:1, 2
d Le 4:27, 28
e Le 4:32, 35
f Ex 12:49
  Le 24:22
  Nu 9:14
  Nu 15:15
g Ex 21:14
  De 17:12
  Heb 10:26, 27
h Heb 10:28
i Eze 18:20
j Ex 20:9, 10
  Ex 35:2
  De 5:13, 14

Second Col.
a Le 24:11, 12
b Ex 31:14
c Le 24:14
d De 22:12
  Mt 23:5
e De 11:18
f Ex 34:15
g Le 11:44
  Ro 12:1
  1Pe 1:15
h Ge 17:8
  Ex 29:45
  Le 25:38
i Ex 3:15
  Ex 6:2, 3

CHAP. 16
j Jude 11
k Ex 6:21
l Ex 6:18
m Ex 6:16
n Nu 26:7-9
o Ge 46:8
p Nu 12:1, 2
  Nu 14:2
  Ps 106:16
q Ex 19:6

15:27, 28, 30, 31 *Or "soul." 15:30 #Or "put to death."

midst.[a] Why, then, should you exalt yourselves above the congregation of Jehovah?"

4 When Moses heard this, he at once fell facedown. **5** Then he said to Kor′ah and to all his supporters: "In the morning Jehovah will make known who belongs to him[b] and who is holy and who should approach him,[c] and whomever he may choose[d] will approach him. **6** Do this: Take fire holders,[e] Kor′ah and all your supporters,[f] **7** and put fire in them and place incense on them before Jehovah tomorrow, and the man whom Jehovah will choose,[g] he is the holy one. You sons of Le′vi[h] have gone far enough!"

8 Moses then said to Kor′ah: "Listen, please, you sons of Le′vi. **9** Does it seem to you such a little thing that the God of Israel has separated you from the assembly of Israel[i] and allowed you to approach him in order to perform the service of Jehovah's tabernacle and to stand before the assembly to minister to them,[j] **10** and that he brought you near to him along with all your brothers, the sons of Le′vi? Must you also try to secure the priesthood?[k] **11** For this reason, you and all your supporters who are gathering together are against Jehovah. As for Aaron, who is he that you should murmur against him?"[l]

12 Moses later sent for Da′than and A·bi′ram[m] the sons of E·li′ab, but they said: "We are not going to come! **13** Is it so little a thing that you have brought us up out of a land flowing with milk and honey to put us to death in the wilderness?[n] Now do you also want to make yourself an absolute ruler over us?* **14** As it is, you have not brought us into any land flow-

ing with milk and honey[a] or given us an inheritance of field and vineyard. Would you bore out the eyes of those men? We are not going to come!"

15 So Moses became very angry and said to Jehovah: "Do not turn to look at their grain offering. Not one donkey have I taken away from them, nor have I harmed one of them."[b]

16 Then Moses said to Kor′ah: "Present yourself with all your supporters before Jehovah tomorrow, you and they and Aaron. **17** Each one should take his fire holder and put incense on it, and each will present his fire holder before Jehovah, 250 fire holders, together with you and Aaron, each with his fire holder." **18** So each of them took his fire holder, and they put fire and incense on them and stood at the entrance of the tent of meeting together with Moses and Aaron. **19** When Kor′ah had gathered his supporters[c] against them at the entrance of the tent of meeting, Jehovah's glory appeared to all the assembly.[d]

20 Jehovah now told Moses and Aaron: **21** "Separate yourselves from among this group, so that I may exterminate them in an instant."[e] **22** At this, they fell with their faces to the ground and said: "O God, the God of the spirit of all people,*[f] will one man's sin cause you to become indignant against the entire assembly?"[g]

23 Jehovah then said to Moses: **24** "Speak to the assembly and tell them, 'Get away from around the tents of Kor′ah, Da′than, and A·bi′ram!'"[h]

25 Then Moses got up and went to Da′than and A·bi′ram, and the elders[i] of Israel went with him. **26** He told the

---

16:13 *Or "to lord it over us?"

16:22 *Lit., "the spirits of all flesh."

CHAP. 16

a Ex 29:45

b 2Ti 2:19

c Ex 28:43
　Le 21:6

d Ex 28:1
　Nu 17:5
　Ps 105:26

e Le 10:1

f Nu 16:2

g Nu 3:10

h Nu 16:1

i Nu 3:9, 41

j Nu 1:53
　Nu 3:6
　Nu 4:4
　De 10:8

k Php 2:3

l Ex 16:8
　Ps 106:16

m Nu 16:1

n Ex 16:3
　Nu 14:28, 29

Second Col.

a Ex 3:8
　Le 20:24

b 1Sa 12:1, 3
　Ac 20:33
　2Co 7:2

c Nu 16:2

d Nu 12:5
　Nu 14:10

e Nu 3:10, 38
　Nu 16:45

f Job 12:10
　Ec 3:19
　Ec 12:7

g Ge 18:23

h Nu 16:1, 2

i Nu 11:16

assembly: "Move away, please, from the tents of these wicked men and do not touch anything that belongs to them, so that you may not be swept away in all their sin." 27 They immediately moved away from the tents of Korʹah, Daʹthan, and A·biʹram, from every side, and Daʹthan and A·biʹram came out, taking their stand at the entrance of their tents, together with their wives, their sons, and their little children.

28 Then Moses said: "By this you will know that Jehovah has sent me to do all these things, that it is not of my own heart:* 29 If these people die a natural death as all men do and if their punishment is the same as that of all mankind, then Jehovah has not sent me.ᵃ 30 But if Jehovah does something extraordinary with them and the ground opens* and swallows them and everything that belongs to them and they go down alive into the Grave,ᵇ you will certainly know that these men have treated Jehovah disrespectfully."

31 As soon as he finished speaking all these words, the ground beneath them split apart.ᵇ 32 And the earth opened* and swallowed them up, along with their households and everyone who belonged to Korʹahᶜ and all their goods. 33 So they and all who belonged to them went down alive into the Grave,# and the earth covered them over, so that they perished from the midst of the congregation.ᵈ 34 All the Israelites who were around them fled at their screaming, for they said:

"We are afraid that the earth may swallow us up!" 35 Then a fire came out from Jehovahᵃ and consumed the 250 men offering the incense.ᵇ

36 Jehovah now said to Moses: 37 "Tell El·e·aʹzar the son of Aaron the priest to take the fire holdersᶜ out of the fire, for they are holy. Also tell him to scatter the fire some distance away. 38 The fire holders of the men who sinned at the cost of their lives* should be made into thin metal plates to overlay the altar,ᵈ because they presented them before Jehovah, and they became holy. They should serve as a sign to the Israelites."ᵉ 39 So El·e·aʹzar the priest took the copper fire holders that had been presented by those who were burned up, and beat them to overlay the altar, 40 just as Jehovah had told him through Moses. It was a reminder for the Israelites that no unauthorized person* who is not of the offspring of Aaron should approach to burn incense before Jehovahᶠ and that no one should become like Korʹah and his supporters.ᵍ

41 On the very next day, the whole assembly of the Israelites began to murmur against Moses and Aaron,ʰ saying: "You two have put Jehovah's people to death." 42 When the assembly had gathered together against Moses and Aaron, they then turned toward the tent of meeting, and look! the cloud covered it, and Jehovah's glory began to appear.ⁱ

43 Moses and Aaron went before the tent of meeting,ʲ 44 and Jehovah said to Moses: 45 "You men, remove yourselves from among this assembly, so that I may exterminate them in an instant."ᵏ At this

---

CHAP. 16
a De 18:21, 22

b Nu 26:10
De 11:6
Ps 106:17

c Ex 6:24
Nu 26:11
1Ch 6:31, 37

d Jude 11

Second Col.
a Le 10:1, 2
Nu 11:1

b Nu 16:17
Nu 26:10
Ps 106:18

c Nu 16:6, 7

d Ex 38:1

e Nu 16:5
Nu 17:10

f Nu 3:10
Nu 18:7
2Ch 26:16-18

g Ps 106:17
Jude 11

h Nu 14:2

i Ex 16:7
Nu 14:10
Nu 16:19

j Nu 20:2, 6

k Ex 23:20, 21
1Co 10:6, 10

16:28 *Or "my own accord." 16:30 *Lit., "opens its mouth." 16:30, 33 #Or "Sheol," that is, the common grave of mankind. See Glossary. 16:32 *Lit., "opened its mouth."

16:38 *Or "sinned against their own souls." 16:40 *Lit., "no stranger."

they fell with their faces to the ground.[a] **46** Moses then said to Aaron: "Take the fire holder and put fire from the altar[b] in it and put incense on it and go quickly to the assembly and make atonement for them,[c] because indignation has gone out from Jehovah. The plague has started!" **47** Aaron at once took it, just as Moses had said, and ran into the midst of the congregation, and look! the plague had started among the people. So he put the incense on the fire holder and began making atonement for the people. **48** He kept standing between the dead and the living, and the scourge eventually stopped. **49** Those who died from the scourge amounted to 14,700, besides those dead on account of Kor′ah. **50** When at last Aaron returned to Moses at the entrance of the tent of meeting, the scourge had been stopped.

17 Jehovah now said to Moses: **2** "Speak to the Israelites and take from them one rod for each paternal house, from the chieftains of each paternal house,[d] 12 rods in all. Write the name of each one on his rod. **3** You should write Aaron's name on Le′vi's rod, because there is one rod for the head of each paternal house. **4** Deposit the rods in the tent of meeting before the Testimony,[e] where I regularly present myself to you.[f] **5** And the rod of the man whom I choose[g] will bud, and I will put a stop to the murmuring of the Israelites against me,[h] which they are also murmuring against you."[i]

6 So Moses spoke to the Israelites, and all their chieftains gave him rods—a rod for each chieftain of a paternal house, 12 rods—and Aaron's rod was among their rods. **7** Then

Moses deposited the rods before Jehovah in the tent of the Testimony.

8 On the next day, when Moses went into the tent of the Testimony, look! Aaron's rod for the house of Le′vi had budded and was bringing forth buds and blossoming flowers and bearing ripe almonds. **9** Moses then brought out all the rods from before Jehovah to all the people of Israel. They looked at them, and each man took his own rod.

10 Jehovah then said to Moses: "Put Aaron's rod[a] back before the Testimony as something to be kept for a sign[b] to the sons of rebelliousness,[c] so that their murmurings against me may cease and so that they may not die." **11** Moses immediately did just as Jehovah had commanded him. He did just so.

12 The Israelites then said to Moses: "Now we will die, we will surely perish, we are all going to perish! **13** Anyone who even comes close to Jehovah's tabernacle will die![d] Must we end up dying that way?"[e]

18 Jehovah then said to Aaron: "You and your sons and your paternal house with you will be answerable for any error against the sanctuary,[f] and you and your sons with you will be answerable for any error against your priesthood.[g] **2** Also bring near your brothers of the tribe of Le′vi, your ancestral tribe, so that they may join you and minister to you[h] and your sons before the tent of the Testimony.[i] **3** They are to fulfill their responsibilities to you and to the entire tent.[j] However, they must not come near the utensils of the holy place and the altar, so that neither they nor you may die.[k] **4** They will join you and carry out their responsibilities regarding the tent of meeting and all the service of the tent,

---

CHAP. 16
a Nu 16:21, 22

b Le 6:12

c Ex 34:9
Nu 8:19

CHAP. 17
d Nu 1:4, 16

e Ex 34:29

f Ex 25:22
Ex 30:36
Le 16:2

g Nu 16:5

h Nu 11:1
Nu 14:27
Nu 16:11
1Co 10:6, 10

i Nu 14:2
Nu 16:13, 41

Second Col.
a Heb 9:4

b Nu 16:38

c De 9:7
De 31:27

d Nu 1:51
Nu 18:4, 7

e Nu 16:49

CHAP. 18
f Ex 25:8
Le 21:10-12

g Ex 28:38
Le 22:9
Nu 18:23

h Nu 3:6
Nu 8:22
Nu 16:9

i Nu 1:53

j Nu 3:25, 26
Nu 3:30, 31
Nu 3:36, 37

k Nu 4:15, 20
Nu 16:39, 40

and no unauthorized person*
may come near to you.[a] **5** You
must carry out your responsibility toward the holy place[b] and
the altar,[c] so that no further indignation[d] may come against
the people of Israel. **6** I myself
have taken your brothers, the
Levites, from among the Israelites as a gift for you.[e] They
are given to Jehovah to care
for the service of the tent of
meeting.[f] **7** You and your sons
are responsible for your priestly duties pertaining to the altar
and what is inside the curtain,[g]
and you are to render this service.[h] I have given the service
of the priesthood as a gift to
you, and any unauthorized person* who approaches should be
put to death."[i]

8 Jehovah spoke further to
Aaron: "I myself put you in
charge of the contributions
made to me.[j] I have given to you
and to your sons a portion of all
the holy things contributed by
the Israelites as a permanent allowance.[k] **9** This will be yours
out of the most holy offerings
made by fire: every offering they
make, including their grain offerings[l] and their sin offerings[m] and
their guilt offerings[n] that they
bring to me. It is something most
holy for you and for your sons.
10 In a most holy place you
should eat it.[o] Every male may
eat it. It will be something holy
to you.[p] **11** This also belongs to
you: the gifts they contribute[q]
together with all the wave offerings[r] of the Israelites. I have giv-
en them to you and your sons
and your daughters with you as a
permanent allowance.[s] Everyone
clean in your house may eat it.[t]

12 "All the best of the oil and
all the best of the new wine
and the grain, their firstfruits,[a]
which they give to Jehovah,
I give them to you.[b] **13** The
first ripe fruits of everything
from their land, which they will
bring to Jehovah, will become
yours.[c] Everyone clean in your
house may eat it.

14 "Every devoted thing* in
Israel should become yours.[d]

15 "Every firstborn of all living things,*[e] which they will present to Jehovah, whether man
or animal, should become yours.
However, you should without fail
redeem the firstborn of mankind,[f] and the firstborn of the
unclean animals you should redeem.[g] **16** You should redeem
it with the redemption price
when it is a month old and
up, by the estimated value
of five silver shekels,*[h] according to the standard shekel of
the holy place.# It is 20 ge′-
rahs.△ **17** Only the firstborn
bull or firstborn male lamb or
firstborn goat you should not
redeem.[i] They are something
holy. You should sprinkle their
blood on the altar,[j] and their
fat you should make smoke as
an offering made by fire for
a pleasing* aroma to Jehovah.[k]
18 And their flesh should become yours. Like the breast
of the wave offering and like
the right leg, it should become
yours.[l] **19** All the holy contributions that the Israelites will
contribute to Jehovah,[m] I have
given to you and your sons
and your daughters with you as
a permanent allowance.[n] It is a

18:4, 7 *Lit., "stranger," that is, a non-Levite.

18:14 *That is, everything made sacred to God by being irrevocably and irredeemably devoted to God. **18:15** *Lit., "of all flesh." **18:16** *A shekel equaled 11.4 g (0.367 oz t). See App. B14. #Or "the holy shekel." △A gerah equaled 0.57 g (0.01835 oz t). See App. B14. **18:17** *Or "appeasing; soothing." Lit., "restful."

CHAP. 18
a Nu 1:51; Nu 3:10
b Le 24:2, 3; Nu 3:32
c Ex 30:7
d Nu 16:46
e Nu 3:9, 12; Nu 8:15, 16
f Nu 8:19
g Le 16:2, 12; Heb 9:3, 7
h 1Sa 2:28; Heb 5:4
i Nu 3:10; Nu 16:39, 40
j Ex 23:19; Le 27:28, 30; Nu 18:11, 26
k Le 7:34; Nu 5:9
l Le 2:3
m Le 5:11, 12; Le 6:25, 26
n Le 7:1, 7
o Ex 29:32; Le 6:14, 16; Le 10:12, 13
p Le 6:18; Le 7:1, 6; Le 14:13; Le 21:22
q Nu 15:20; Eze 44:30
r Ex 29:27; Le 7:34
s Le 10:14; De 18:3
t Le 22:4-6

Second Col.
a Pr 3:9
b Le 2:14; De 18:4
c Ex 23:19
d Le 27:21, 28
e Ex 13:2; Le 27:26; Nu 3:13
f Ex 13:13
g Ex 34:20; Le 27:27
h Le 27:6
i Ex 22:30; De 15:19
j Le 17:11
k Le 3:16
l Ex 29:26; Le 7:31, 34
m Ex 23:19; Nu 15:18, 19; Nu 18:11, 26; Nu 31:28, 29
n 2Ch 31:4

lasting covenant of salt* before Jehovah for you and your offspring with you."

20 Jehovah went on to say to Aaron: "In their land you will not have an inheritance, and no portion of land among them will become yours.ᵃ I am your portion and your inheritance in the midst of the Israelites.ᵇ

21 "Now see that I have given to the sons of Leʹvi every tenth partᶜ in Israel as an inheritance in return for the service they are carrying out, the service of the tent of meeting. 22 No longer may the people of Israel approach the tent of meeting, or else they will incur sin and die. 23 The Levites themselves are to carry out the service of the tent of meeting, and they are the ones who will answer for their error.ᵈ It is a lasting statute during all your generations that they should not take possession of an inheritance among the Israelites.ᵉ 24 For I have given to the Levites as an inheritance the tenth part contributed by the people of Israel, which they will contribute to Jehovah. That is why I have said to them, 'In the midst of the Israelites, they should not take possession of an inheritance.'ᶠ

25 Then Jehovah said to Moses: 26 "You should tell the Levites, 'You will receive from the Israelites the tenth part that I have given to you from them for your inheritance,ᵍ and you should contribute from it a tenth part of the tenth part as a contribution to Jehovah.ʰ 27 And it will be considered your contribution, as though it were the grain of the threshing floorⁱ or the full production of the winepress or oil press. 28 In this way you will also give a con-

tribution to Jehovah from all the tenth parts that you receive from the Israelites, and from them you are to give the contribution for Jehovah to Aaron the priest. 29 You will make every sort of contribution to Jehovah from the very best of all the gifts given to youᵃ as something holy.'

30 "And you must say to them, 'When you contribute the best of them, then it will be considered for the Levites as the produce of the threshing floor and as the produce of the winepress or oil press. 31 You and your household may eat it in any place, because it is your wages in return for your service at the tent of meeting.ᵇ 32 You will not incur sin in this as long as you contribute the best from them, and you must not profane the holy things of the Israelites, or you will die.'"ᶜ

19 Jehovah spoke again to Moses and Aaron, saying: 2 "This is a statute of the law that Jehovah has commanded, 'Tell the Israelites that they should take for you a sound red cow in which there is no defectᵈ and upon which no yoke has come. 3 You are to give it to El·e·aʹzar the priest, and he will lead it outside the camp, and it will be slaughtered before him. 4 Then El·e·aʹzar the priest will take some of its blood with his finger and spatter its blood seven times straight toward the front of the tent of meeting.ᵉ 5 The cow will then be burned before his eyes. Its skin and its flesh and its blood together with its dung will be burned.ᶠ 6 And the priest will take cedarwood, hyssop,ᵍ and scarlet material and throw them into the fire where the cow is being burned. 7 The priest will then wash his garments and bathe himself* in

---

CHAP. 18
a Nu 26:62, 63
   De 10:9
   De 14:27
   Jos 14:3

b De 18:1, 2
   Jos 18:7
   Eze 44:28

c Le 27:30
   Ne 10:37
   Ne 12:44
   Heb 7:5

d Nu 3:6, 7
   Nu 18:1

e Jos 13:33

f De 10:9

g Nu 18:21
   De 12:19

h Ne 10:38

i Nu 15:20

Second Col.
a Nu 18:8, 12

b 1Co 9:13

c Le 22:2, 15

CHAP. 19
d Le 22:20
   Mal 1:14

e Heb 9:13, 14

f Le 4:11, 12

g Ps 51:7

18:19 *That is, a permanent and unchanging covenant.

19:7 *Lit., "his flesh."

water, and afterward he may come into the camp; but the priest will be unclean until the evening.

8 "'The one who burned the cow will wash his garments in water and bathe himself* in water, and he will be unclean until the evening.

9 "'A clean man will gather up the ashes of the cow[a] and deposit them outside the camp in a clean place, and they should be kept by the assembly of the Israelites to prepare water that will be used for cleansing.[b] It is a sin offering. **10** The one gathering the ashes of the cow will wash his garments and be unclean until the evening.

"'This will serve the Israelites and the foreigner who is residing in their midst as a lasting statute.[c] **11** Anyone touching any dead person* will be unclean for seven days.[d] **12** Such one should purify himself with the water* on the third day, and on the seventh day he will be clean. But if he does not purify himself on the third day, on the seventh day he will not be clean. **13** Everyone who touches the corpse of any dead person* and does not purify himself has defiled Jehovah's tabernacle,[e] and that person* must be cut off[△] from Israel.[f] Because the water for cleansing[g] has not been sprinkled on him, he continues unclean. His uncleanness remains upon him.

14 "'This is the law that applies when a man dies in a tent: Everyone who enters the tent and everyone who already in the tent will be unclean for sev-

en days. **15** Every opened container with no lid tied on it is unclean.[a] **16** Everyone in the open field who touches someone killed with the sword or a corpse or the bone of a man or a burial place will be unclean for seven days.[b] **17** They should take for the unclean one some of the ashes of the sin offering that was burned and pour running water on them in a container. **18** Then a clean man[c] will take hyssop[d] and dip it into the water and spatter it on the tent and on all the containers and on the people* who were there and on the one who touched the bone or the slain one or the corpse or the burial place. **19** The clean person will spatter it on the unclean one on the third day and on the seventh day, and he will purify him from sin on the seventh day;[e] then he should wash his garments and bathe in water, and he will become clean in the evening.

20 "'But the man who is unclean and who will not purify himself, that person* must be cut off[△] from the congregation,[f] because he has defiled Jehovah's sanctuary. The water for cleansing was not sprinkled on him, so he is unclean.

21 "'This will serve as a lasting statute for them: The one spattering the water for cleansing[g] should wash his garments, and the one touching the water for cleansing will be unclean until the evening. **22** Anything the unclean one touches will be unclean, and the person* who touches it will be unclean until the evening.'"[h]

20 In the first month, the entire assembly of the Israelites came into the wilderness of Zin, and the people began dwell-

---

CHAP. 19
a Heb 9:13, 14

b Nu 19:13, 21

c Ex 12:49
Le 24:22
Nu 15:15

d Le 21:1, 11
Nu 5:2
Nu 6:9
Nu 9:6
Nu 31:19

e Le 15:31

f Le 22:3
Heb 10:28

g Nu 9:9

Second Col.
a Le 11:31, 32

b Nu 19:11
Nu 31:19

c Nu 19:9

d Ps 51:7

e Le 14:9
Nu 19:12
Nu 31:19

f Nu 19:13

g Nu 19:18
Heb 9:9, 10
Heb 9:13, 14

h Le 15:4, 5

19:8 *Lit., "his flesh." 19:11 *Or "the corpse of any human soul." See Glossary. 19:12 *Lit., "it." 19:13 *Or "a corpse, the soul of any human who has died." See Glossary. 19:13, 20, 22 *Or "soul." 19:13, 20 △Or "put to death."

19:18 *Or "souls."

ing in Ka′desh.[a] It was there that Mir′i·am[b] died and was buried.

2 Now there was no water for the assembly,[c] and they gathered together against Moses and Aaron. **3** The people were quarreling with Moses,[d] saying: "If only we had died when our brothers died before Jehovah! **4** Why have you brought Jehovah's congregation into this wilderness for us and our livestock to die here?[e] **5** And why have you led us up out of Egypt to bring us into this evil place?[f] It is no place for seed and figs and vines and pomegranates, and there is no water to drink."[g] **6** Then Moses and Aaron came from before the congregation to the entrance of the tent of meeting and fell with their faces to the ground, and Jehovah's glory began to appear to them.[h]

7 Then Jehovah said to Moses: **8** "Take the rod and call the assembly together, you and Aaron your brother, and speak to the crag before their eyes that it may give its water, and you will bring out water for them from the crag and give the assembly and their livestock something to drink."[i]

9 So Moses took the rod from before Jehovah,[j] just as He had commanded him. **10** Then Moses and Aaron called the congregation together before the crag, and he said to them: "Hear, now, you rebels! Must we bring out water for you from this crag?"[k] **11** With that Moses lifted his hand up and struck the crag twice with his rod, and much water began to pour out, and the assembly and their livestock began to drink.[l]

12 Jehovah later said to Moses and Aaron: "Because you did not show faith in me and sanctify me before the eyes of the people of Israel, you will not bring this congregation into

the land that I will give them."[a] **13** These are the waters of Mer′i·bah,*[b] where the Israelites quarreled with Jehovah, so that he was sanctified among them.

14 Then Moses sent messengers from Ka′desh to the king of E′dom:[c] "This is what your brother Israel[d] says, 'You well know all the hardship that we have experienced. **15** Our fathers went to Egypt,[e] and we dwelled in Egypt many years,*[f] and the Egyptians mistreated us and our fathers.[g] **16** Finally we cried out to Jehovah,[h] and he heard us and sent an angel[i] and brought us out of Egypt, and here we are in Ka′desh, a city on the border of your territory. **17** Please let us pass through your land. We will not pass through any field or vineyard, and we will not drink the water of any well. We will march on the King's Road without turning to the right or the left until we pass through your territory.'"[j]

18 However, E′dom said to him: "You may not pass through our territory. If you do, I will come out with the sword to meet you." **19** In turn the Israelites said to him: "By the highway we will go up, and if we and our livestock drink your water, we will pay for it.[k] We want nothing more than to pass through on foot."[l] **20** Still he said: "You may not pass through."[m] With that E′dom came out to encounter him with many people and a strong army.* **21** So E′dom refused to allow Israel to pass through his territory; therefore, Israel turned away from him.[n]

22 The people of Israel, the entire assembly, departed from Ka′desh and came to Mount Hor.[o] **23** Then Jehovah said to Moses and Aaron in Mount Hor by

---

CHAP. 20

a Nu 13:26
  Nu 20:22
  Nu 33:36
  De 2:14

b Ex 15:20
  Nu 26:59
  Mic 6:4

c Ex 17:1

d Ex 17:2

e Ex 14:11
  Nu 16:13, 14
  Nu 21:5

f De 8:14, 15

g De 8:7, 8

h Ex 16:10
  Nu 14:10

i Ex 17:5, 6
  Ps 78:15
  Ps 105:41
  Ps 114:8
  Isa 48:21

j Ex 7:12, 19
  Nu 17:10

k Ps 106:32, 33

l 1Co 10:1, 4

Second Col.

a Nu 27:12-14
  De 1:37
  De 3:26
  De 32:51, 52
  De 34:4
  Jos 1:2

b Ps 106:32, 33

c Jg 11:17

d Ge 36:8
  De 2:4
  De 2:22

e Ge 46:6

f Ge 15:13
  Ex 12:40

g Ex 1:11, 14

h Ex 2:23
  Ex 3:7

i Ex 14:19
  Ex 23:20
  Ex 33:2

j Nu 21:21, 22
  De 2:26, 27

k De 2:5, 6

l De 2:26, 28

m Jg 11:17

n De 2:8
  Jg 11:18

o Nu 21:4
  Nu 33:37
  Nu 34:2, 7

20:13 *Meaning "Quarreling." 20:15 *Lit., "days." 20:20 *Lit., "hand."

the border of the land of E'dom: 24 "Aaron will be gathered to his people.*ᵃ He will not enter the land that I will give to the Israelites, because you both rebelled against my order regarding the waters of Mer'i·bah.ᵇ 25 Take Aaron and his son El·e·a'zar and bring them up into Mount Hor. 26 Remove Aaron's garmentsᶜ and clothe El·e·a'zarᵈ his son with them, and Aaron will die there."*

27 So Moses did just as Jehovah had commanded, and they climbed Mount Hor before the eyes of all the assembly. 28 Then Moses removed Aaron's garments and clothed El·e·a'zar his son with them. After that Aaron died there on the top of the mountain.ᵉ And Moses and El·e·a'zar came down from the mountain. 29 When all the assembly saw that Aaron had died, the entire house of Israel wept for Aaron for 30 days.ᶠ

21 When the Ca'naan·ite king of A'rad,ᵍ who dwelled in the Neg'eb, heard that Israel had come by the way of Ath'a·rim, he attacked Israel and carried away some of them as captives. 2 So Israel made this vow to Jehovah: "If you give this people into my hand, I will without fail devote their cities to destruction. 3 So Jehovah listened to Israel's voice and gave the Ca'naan·ites over to them, and they devoted them and their cities to destruction. Therefore, they named the place Hor'mah.*ʰ

4 As they continued their journey from Mount Horⁱ by the way of the Red Sea in order to go around the land of E'dom,ʲ the people* became wea-

ry of the journey. 5 And the people kept speaking against God and Moses,ᵃ saying: "Why have you brought us up out of Egypt to die in the wilderness? There is no food and no water,ᵇ and we* have come to hate* this contemptible bread."ᶜ 6 So Jehovah sent poisonous* serpents among the people, and they kept biting the people, so that many Israelites died.ᵈ

7 So the people came to Moses and said: "We have sinned by speaking against Jehovah and against you.ᵉ Intercede with Jehovah so that he may remove the serpents from us." And Moses interceded on behalf of the people.ᶠ 8 Then Jehovah said to Moses: "Make a replica of a poisonous* snake and put it on a pole. Then when anyone has been bitten, he will have to look at it in order to keep alive." 9 Moses at once made a serpent of copperᵍ and put it on the pole,ʰ and whenever a serpent had bitten a man and he looked at the copper serpent, he survived.ⁱ

10 After that the Israelites departed and camped in O'both.ʲ 11 Then they departed from O'both and camped in I'ye·ab'a·rim,ᵏ in the wilderness that faces Mo'ab, toward the east. 12 From there they departed and camped by the Valley* of Ze'red.ˡ 13 From there they departed and camped in the region of the Ar'non,ᵐ which is in the wilderness that extends from the border of the Am'or·ites, for the Ar'non is the boundary of Mo'ab, between Mo'ab and the Am'or·ites. 14 That is why the book of the Wars of Jehovah speaks of "Va'heb in Su'phah and the valleys* of Ar'non, 15 and the de-

CHAP. 20
a Nu 33:38 De 32:50
b Nu 20:12 De 32:51, 52
c Ex 28:2 Ex 29:29
d Ex 6:23 Nu 4:16
e Nu 33:39 De 10:6 De 32:50
f De 34:8

CHAP. 21
g Nu 33:40 Jos 12:7, 14
h Nu 14:45
i Nu 33:41
j Nu 20:21 De 2:8 Jg 11:18

Second Col.
a Ex 14:11 Ex 15:24 Nu 16:13
b Nu 20:5
c Ex 16:15 Nu 11:6 Ps 78:24, 25
d 1Co 10:6, 9
e Ps 78:34
f Ex 32:11
g 2Ki 18:1, 4
h Joh 3:14, 15
i Joh 6:40
j Nu 33:43
k Nu 33:44
l De 2:13
m Nu 22:36 Jg 11:18

20:24 *This is a poetic expression for death. 20:26 *Lit., "will be gathered and die there." 21:3 *Meaning "A Devoting to Destruction." 21:4 *Or "the soul of the people."

21:5 *Or "our souls." *Or "abhor." 21:6, 8 *Or "fiery." 21:12 *Or "Wadi." 21:14 *Or "wadis."

scent* of the valleys,# which extends toward the settlement of Ar and adjoins the border of Mo'ab."

16 Next they went on to Be'er. This is the well about which Jehovah said to Moses: "Gather the people, and let me give them water."

17 At that time, Israel sang this song:

"Spring up, O well!
  —Respond* to it!
18 The well that princes dug,
  that nobles of the people excavated,
  With a commander's staff
  and with their own staffs."

Then they went from the wilderness on to Mat'ta·nah, **19** from Mat'ta·nah on to Na·hal'i·el, and from Na·hal'i·el on to Ba'moth.ᵃ **20** They went from Ba'moth on to the valley that is in the territory* of Mo'ab,ᵇ on top of Pis'gah,ᶜ which overlooks Je·shi'mon.#ᵈ

21 Israel now sent messengers to Si'hon, the king of the Am'or·ites, saying:ᵉ **22** "Let us pass through your land. We will not turn aside into a field or a vineyard. We will not drink water from any well. We will march on the King's Road until we pass through your territory."ᶠ **23** But Si'hon did not allow Israel to pass through his territory. Instead, Si'hon gathered all his people and went out against Israel in the wilderness and came to Ja'haz and began fighting with Israel.ᵍ **24** But Israel defeated him with the swordʰ and took possession of his landⁱ from the Ar'nonʲ to the Jab'bok,ᵏ near the Am'mon·ites, because Ja'zerˡ borders the territory of the Am'mon·ites.ᵐ

25 So Israel took all these cities, and they began dwelling in all the cities of the Am'or·ites,ᵃ in Hesh'bon and all its dependent* towns. **26** For Hesh'bon was the city of Si'hon, the king of the Am'or·ites, who had fought with the king of Mo'ab and taken all his land from him as far as the Ar'non. **27** That is what gave rise to the taunting proverbial saying:

"Come to Hesh'bon.
  Let the city of Si'hon be built
  and firmly established.
28 For a fire came out of Hesh'bon, a flame from the town of Si'hon.
  It has consumed Ar of Mo'ab, the lords of the high places of the Ar'non.
29 Woe to you, Mo'ab! You will be destroyed, O people of Che'mosh!ᵇ
  He makes his sons fugitives and his daughters captives of Si'hon, the king of the Am'or·ites.
30 Let us shoot at them;
  Hesh'bon will be destroyed as far as Di'bon;ᶜ
  Let us desolate it as far as No'phah;
  Fire will spread as far as Med'e·ba."ᵈ

31 So Israel began to dwell in the land of the Am'or·ites. **32** Moses then sent some men to spy on Ja'zer.ᵉ They captured its dependent* towns and drove out the Am'or·ites who were there. **33** After that they turned and went up by way of Ba'shan. And Ogᶠ the king of Ba'shan came out with all his people to meet them in battle at Ed're·i.ᵍ **34** Jehovah said to Moses: "Do not be afraid of him,ʰ for I will give him and all his people and his land into your hand,ⁱ and you will do to him just as you did to Si'hon the

---

CHAP. 21
a Jos 13:15, 17
b Nu 33:49
c De 3:27
  De 34:1
d Nu 23:28
e De 2:26-28
f Nu 20:14, 17
g De 2:30-35
  De 29:7
  Jg 11:19, 20
h Ps 135:10, 11
i Nu 32:33
  Ne 9:22
j Nu 21:13
  De 3:16
k Jg 11:21, 22
l Nu 32:1
  1Ch 6:77, 81
m Jos 12:1, 2

_____

Second Col.
a Ge 10:15, 16
  Ge 15:16
  Ex 3:8
  De 7:1
b Nu 11:23, 24
  1Ki 11:7
  2Ki 23:13
c Jos 13:15, 17
d Jos 13:8, 9
e Nu 32:1
f De 3:11
  De 4:47
  Jos 13:8, 12
g De 3:1
  De 3:8, 10
h De 20:3
i Ex 23:27
  De 7:24

21:15 *Lit., "mouth." #Or "wadis."
21:17 *Or "Sing." 21:20 *Lit., "field."
#Or possibly, "the desert; the wilderness."

21:25, 32 *Or "surrounding."

king of the Am′or·ites, who lived in Hesh′bon."ᵃ **35** So they kept striking him down, along with his sons and all his people, until none of his people survived,ᵇ and they took possession of his land.ᶜ

22 Then the Israelites departed and camped on the desert plains of Mo′ab across the Jordan from Jer′i·cho.ᵈ **2** Now Ba′lakᵉ the son of Zip′por saw all that Israel had done to the Am′or·ites, **3** and Mo′ab became very frightened of the people, because they were so many; indeed, Mo′ab felt sick with fear because of the Israelites.ᶠ **4** So Mo′ab said to the elders of Mid′i·an:ᵍ "Now this congregation will devour all our surroundings, just as a bull devours the grass in the field."

Ba′lak the son of Zip′por was king of Mo′ab at that time. **5** He sent messengers to Ba′laam the son of Be′or at Pe′thor,ʰ which is by the River* in his native land. He summoned him, saying: "Look! A people has come out of Egypt. Look! They have covered the face# of the earth,△ⁱ and they are dwelling right in front of me. **6** Now, please, come and curse this people for me,ʲ for they are mightier than I am. Perhaps I can defeat them and drive them out of the land, for I well know that the one whom you bless is blessed and the one whom you curse is cursed."

7 So the elders of Mo′ab and the elders of Mid′i·an traveled with the fee for divination in their hands and went to Ba′laamᵏ and conveyed to him Ba′lak's message. **8** At that he said to them: "Spend the night here, and I will bring back to you whatever word Jehovah speaks to me." So

---

22:5 *Evidently, the Euphrates. **22:5, 11** #Lit., "eye." **22:5, 11** △Or "land."

CHAP. 21
a De 3:2
  Ps 135:10, 11

b De 3:3

c Jos 12:4-6

CHAP. 22
d Nu 33:48

e Jos 24:9
  Jg 11:25

f Ex 15:15
  De 2:25

g Nu 31:7, 8
  Jos 13:15, 21

h De 23:3, 4
  Jos 13:22
  2Pe 2:15

i Ge 13:14, 16

j Nu 23:7
  Jos 24:9
  Ne 13:1, 2

k 2Pe 2:15
  Jude 11

Second Col.
a Nu 22:20

b Nu 22:5, 6
  Nu 23:7, 11
  Nu 24:10

c Ge 12:1-3
  Ge 22:15, 17
  De 33:29

d Nu 24:13

e Nu 22:8

f Nu 22:35
  Nu 23:11, 12

---

the princes of Mo′ab stayed with Ba′laam.

9 Then God came to Ba′laam and said:ᵃ "Who are these men with you?" **10** Ba′laam said to the true God: "Ba′lak the son of Zip′por, the king of Mo′ab, has sent me a message, saying, **11** 'Look! The people who are coming out of Egypt are covering the face# of the earth.△ Now come and put a curse on them for me.ᵇ Perhaps I may be able to fight against them and drive them out.'" **12** But God said to Ba′laam: "You must not go with them. You must not curse the people, for they are blessed."ᶜ

13 Ba′laam got up in the morning and said to the princes of Ba′lak: "Go to your land, for Jehovah has refused to let me go with you." **14** So the princes of Mo′ab departed and returned to Ba′lak and said: "Ba′laam has refused to come with us."

15 However, Ba′lak again sent princes, more numerous and more distinguished than the first group. **16** They came to Ba′laam and said to him: "This is what Ba′lak the son of Zip′por has said, 'Please do not let anything hinder you from coming to me, **17** for I will honor you greatly and I will do anything you tell me to do. So come, please, and curse this people for me.'" **18** But Ba′laam answered the servants of Ba′lak: "If Ba′lak were to give me his own house full of silver and gold, I could not do anything beyond the order of Jehovah my God, whether small or great.ᵈ **19** But please stay here tonight also, so that I may learn what else Jehovah will tell me."ᵉ

20 Then God came to Ba′laam by night and said to him: "If these men have come to summon you, go along with them. But you may speak only the words that I tell you to say."ᶠ

21 So Ba'laam got up in the morning and saddled his donkey* and went with the princes of Mo'ab.[a]

22 But God's anger blazed because he was going, and Jehovah's angel stationed himself in the road to resist him. Now Ba'laam was riding on his donkey, and two of his attendants were with him. **23** And when the donkey saw Jehovah's angel standing in the road with a drawn sword in his hand, it tried to turn off the road into the field. But Ba'laam began to beat the donkey to make it return to the road. **24** Then Jehovah's angel stood in a narrow path between two vineyards, with stone walls on both sides. **25** When the donkey saw Jehovah's angel, it began to squeeze itself against the wall and it jammed Ba'laam's foot against the wall, and Ba'laam began beating it again.

26 Jehovah's angel now passed by again and stood in a narrow place where there was no way to turn to the right or to the left. **27** When the donkey saw Jehovah's angel, it lay down under Ba'laam, so Ba'laam became furious and kept beating the donkey with his staff. **28** Finally Jehovah caused the donkey to speak,*[b] and it said to Ba'laam: "What have I done to you to make you beat me these three times?"[c] **29** Ba'laam replied to the donkey: "It is because you have made a fool of me. If only I had a sword in my hand, I would kill you!" **30** Then the donkey said to Ba'laam: "Am I not your donkey that you have ridden on all your life until today? Have I ever treated you this way before?" He replied: "No!" **31** Then Jehovah

uncovered Ba'laam's eyes,[a] and he saw Jehovah's angel standing in the road with a drawn sword in his hand. At once he bowed low and prostrated himself on his face.

32 Then Jehovah's angel said to him: "Why have you beaten your donkey these three times? Look! I myself came out to offer resistance, because your way is in defiance of my will.[b] **33** The donkey saw me and tried to turn away from me these three times.[c] Supposing it had not turned away from me! By now I would have killed you and let the donkey live." **34** Ba'laam said to Jehovah's angel: "I have sinned, because I did not know that it was you standing in the road to meet me. And now if it is bad in your eyes, I will go back." **35** But Jehovah's angel said to Ba'laam: "Go with the men, but you may speak only the words that I tell you." So Ba'laam continued going with the princes of Ba'lak.

36 When Ba'lak heard that Ba'laam had come, he immediately went out to meet him at the city of Mo'ab, which is on the bank of the Ar'non on the border of the territory. **37** Ba'lak said to Ba'laam: "Did I not send for you? Why did you not come to me? Did you think I am not able to honor you greatly?"[d] **38** Ba'laam replied to Ba'lak: "Well, I have come to you now. But will I be allowed to say anything? I can only speak words that God puts in my mouth."[e]

39 So Ba'laam went with Ba'lak, and they came to Kir'i·ath-hu'zoth. **40** Ba'lak sacrificed cattle and sheep and sent some to Ba'laam and the princes who were with him. **41** In the morning Ba'lak took Ba'laam and brought him up to Ba'moth-ba'al; from there he could see all the people.[f]

CHAP. 22
a 2Pe 2:15
  Jude 11

b 2Pe 2:15, 16

c Nu 22:32

Second Col.
a 2Ki 6:17

b Nu 22:12
  2Pe 2:15, 16

c Nu 22:23
  Nu 22:25
  Nu 22:27

d Nu 22:16, 17
  Nu 24:10, 11

e Nu 23:26
  Nu 24:13

f Nu 23:13, 14

22:21 *Lit., "female donkey." 22:28 *Lit., "opened the mouth of the female donkey."

23 Then Ba′laam said to Ba′lak: "Build on this spot seven altars,[a] and prepare seven bulls and seven rams for me." **2** Ba′lak immediately did just as Ba′laam had said. And Ba′lak and Ba′laam offered up a bull and a ram on each altar.[b] **3** Ba′laam then said to Ba′lak: "Stay here by your burnt offering, and I will go. Perhaps Jehovah will get in touch with me. Whatever he reveals to me, I will tell you." So he went to a barren hill.

4 Then God got in touch with Ba′laam,[c] who said to Him: "I set the seven altars in rows, and I offered up a bull and a ram on each altar." **5** Jehovah put this word in the mouth of Ba′laam:[d] "Return to Ba′lak, and this is what you are to say." **6** So he returned and saw that Ba′lak and all the princes of Mo′ab were standing by his burnt offering. **7** Then he spoke this proverbial saying:[e]

"Ba′lak the king of Mo′ab has brought me from A′ram,[f]
From the mountains of the east:
'Do come to curse Jacob for me.
Yes, come to denounce Israel.'[g]

8 How could I put a curse on those whom God has not cursed?
And how could I denounce those whom Jehovah has not denounced?[h]

9 From the top of the rocks I see them,
And from the hills I see them.
As a people they dwell there alone;[i]
They do not count themselves among the nations.[j]

10 Who can number the dust particles of Jacob[k]
Or count even the fourth part of Israel?

Let me* die the death of the upright,
And let my end be like theirs."

11 Ba′lak then said to Ba′laam: "What have you done to me? I brought you to put a curse on my enemies, and here you have done nothing but bless them."[a] **12** He answered: "Must I not speak whatever Jehovah puts in my mouth?"[b]

13 Ba′lak said to him: "Please come with me to another place from which you can see them. You will see only a part of them; you will not see them all. Put a curse on them for me from there."[c] **14** So he took him to the field of Zo′phim, to the top of Pis′gah,[d] and built seven altars and offered up a bull and a ram on each altar.[e] **15** So Ba′laam said to Ba′lak: "Stay here by your burnt offering while I get in touch with Him over there." **16** And Jehovah got in touch with Ba′laam and put this word in his mouth:[f] "Return to Ba′lak, and this is what you are to say." **17** So he came to him and saw that he was waiting by his burnt offering, and the princes of Mo′ab were with him. Ba′lak asked him: "What has Jehovah said?" **18** Then he spoke this proverbial saying:[g]

"Get up, Ba′lak, and listen.
Hear me, O son of Zip′por.

19 God is not a mere man who tells lies,[h]
Nor a son of man who changes his mind.*[i]
When he says something, will he not do it?
When he speaks, will he not carry it out?[j]

20 Look! I have been taken to bless;

23:10 *Or "my soul." **23:19** *Or "who feels regret."

CHAP. 23
a Nu 22:41

b Nu 23:13, 14
  Nu 23:28-30

c Nu 22:20

d Nu 22:35

e Nu 23:18
  Nu 24:3

f Ge 10:22
  Nu 22:5
  De 23:3, 4

g Nu 22:6

h Nu 22:12

i 1Ki 8:53

j Ex 33:16

k Ge 13:14, 16
  Ge 22:17
  Ex 1:7

Second Col.
a Nu 24:10
  Jos 24:10
  Ne 13:1, 2

b Nu 22:38
  Nu 24:13

c Nu 22:11

d De 34:1

e Nu 22:41
  Nu 23:1
  Nu 23:28, 29

f Nu 22:35
  Nu 23:5

g Nu 23:7
  Nu 24:3

h Ps 89:35
  Tit 1:2

i 1Sa 15:29

j Isa 14:24
  Isa 46:10
  Mic 7:20

Now He has blessed,[a] and I cannot reverse it.[b]

21 He does not tolerate any magical power against Jacob,
And he does not allow any trouble against Israel.
Jehovah his God is with them,[c]
And he is loudly hailed as king among them.

22 God is bringing them out of Egypt.[d]
He is like the horns of a wild bull for them.[e]

23 For there are no omens of doom against Jacob,[f]
Nor any divination against Israel.[g]
At this time it may be said about Jacob and Israel:
'Look at what God has done!'

24 Here is a people who will rise up like a lion,
And like the lion, it will raise itself up.[h]
It will not lie down until it eats prey
And drinks the blood of the slain ones."

25 Ba′lak then said to Ba′-laam: "If on the one hand you cannot put any curse on him, then on the other hand you should not bless him either." 26 Ba′laam answered Ba′lak: "Did I not say to you, 'I will do all that Jehovah says'?"[i]

27 Ba′lak said to Ba′laam: "Please come and let me take you to yet another place. Perhaps it will be right in the eyes of the true God for you to put a curse on him for me from there."[j] 28 So Ba′lak took Ba′laam to the top of Pe′-or, which looks toward Je·shi′-mon.*[k] 29 Then Ba′laam said to Ba′lak: "Build seven altars on this spot, and prepare seven

23:28 *Or possibly, "the desert; the wilderness."

CHAP. 23
a Ge 12:1, 2
  Ge 22:15, 17
  Nu 22:12

b Nu 22:18

c Ex 13:21
  Ex 23:20
  Ex 29:45
  Isa 8:10

d Ex 20:2

e Nu 24:8

f Ge 12:1, 3

g Nu 22:7

h Nu 24:9

i Nu 22:38
  Nu 23:12

j Nu 23:13

k Nu 21:20

Second Col.
a Nu 22:41
  Nu 23:1, 14

CHAP. 24
b Nu 23:3, 15
  Nu 23:23

c Nu 2:2
  Nu 23:9

d 1Sa 19:20

e Nu 23:7, 18

f Nu 24:16

g Nu 1:52
  Nu 2:2

h Nu 22:11

i De 8:7

j Ge 49:10
  Ps 2:6
  Joh 1:49

k Nu 24:20

l 1Ch 14:2
  Da 2:44
  Re 11:15

---

bulls and seven rams for me."[a] 30 So Ba′lak did just as Ba′laam had said, and he offered up a bull and a ram on each altar.

24 When Ba′laam saw that it pleased* Jehovah to bless Israel, he did not go away again to search for omens of doom,[b] but he turned his face to the wilderness. 2 When Ba′-laam raised his eyes and saw Israel encamped by his tribes,[c] then the spirit of God came upon him.[d] 3 He then spoke this proverbial saying:[e]

"The saying of Ba′laam the son of Be′or,
And the saying of a man whose eyes have been opened,
4 The saying of the one hearing the word of God,
Who saw a vision of the Almighty,
Who has bowed down with his eyes uncovered:[f]
5 How beautiful are your tents, O Jacob,
Your tabernacles, O Israel![g]
6 Like the valleys* they have extended a long way,[h]
Like gardens by the river,
Like aloes that Jehovah has planted,
Like cedars by the waters.
7 Water keeps trickling from his two leather buckets,
And his seed* is sown by many waters.[i]
His king[j] also will be greater than A′gag,[k]
And his kingdom will be exalted.[l]
8 God is bringing him out of Egypt;
He is like the horns of a wild bull for them.

24:1 *Lit., "was good in the eyes of." 24:6 *Or "wadis." 24:7 *Or "offspring."

He will consume the nations,
his oppressors,[a]
And their bones he will
gnaw, and he will shatter
them with his arrows.

9 He has crouched down, he
has lain down like the lion,
And like a lion, who dares
rouse him?
Those blessing you are
blessed,
And those cursing you are
cursed."[b]

10 Then Ba′lak became furious with Ba′laam. Ba′lak scornfully clapped his hands together and said to Ba′laam: "It was to put a curse on my enemies that I called you,[c] but now you have done nothing but bless them these three times. 11 Now go home immediately. I intended to honor you greatly,[d] but look! Jehovah has deprived you of honor."

12 Ba′laam replied to Ba′lak: "Did I not say to the messengers you sent, 13 'If Ba′lak were to give me his house full of silver and gold, I could not of my own will* do anything beyond the order of Jehovah, whether good or bad. I will only speak what Jehovah will tell me'?[e] 14 And now I am going away to my people. Come and let me advise you what this people will do to your people in the future."* 15 So he spoke this proverbial saying:[f]

"The saying of Ba′laam
the son of Be′or,
And the saying of a man
whose eyes have been
opened,[g]
16 The saying of the one hearing the word of God,
And the one having the
knowledge of the Most
High,

A vision of the Almighty
he saw
While bowing down with his
eyes uncovered:
17 I will see him, but not now;
I will behold him, but not
soon.
A star[a] will come out of
Jacob,
And a scepter[b] will rise out
of Israel.[c]
And he will certainly break
apart the forehead of
Mo′ab*[d]
And the skull of all the sons
of tumult.
18 And E′dom will become
a possession,[e]
Yes, Se′ir[f] the possession
of his enemies,[g]
While Israel is displaying
his courage.
19 And out of Jacob one will
be subduing,[h]
And he will destroy any
survivor from the city."

20 When he saw Am′a·lek, he continued his proverbial saying:

"Am′a·lek was the first of the
nations,[i]
But in the end he will
perish."[j]

21 When he saw the Ken′ites,[k] he continued his proverbial saying:

"Secure is your dwelling,
and set on the crag is
your abode.
22 But someone will burn Ka′in
down.
How long before As·syr′i·a
carries you away captive?"

23 And he continued his proverbial saying:

"Woe! Who will survive when
God does this?
24 Ships will come from the
coast of Kit′tim,[l]
And they will afflict
As·syr′i·a,[m]

CHAP. 24	
a	Ex 23:27 De 9:5
b	Ge 12:1-3 Ge 27:29
c	Nu 22:10, 11 Nu 23:11 Ne 13:1, 2
d	Nu 22:16, 17
e	Nu 22:18, 38
f	Nu 23:7
g	Nu 24:3, 4
Second Col.	
a	Re 22:16
b	Ps 110:2 Heb 1:8
c	2Sa 7:16, 17 Isa 9:7
d	2Sa 8:2 1Ch 18:2 Ps 108:9
e	Ge 27:37 2Sa 8:14 Am 9:11, 12
f	Ge 36:8 Jos 24:4
g	1Ch 4:42, 43 Eze 25:14
h	Ge 49:10 Ps 2:9 Ps 72:11 Re 6:2 Re 19:15
i	Ex 17:8, 14
j	De 25:19 1Sa 15:3 1Ch 4:43
k	Ge 15:18, 19 Jg 1:16
l	Ge 10:2, 4 Eze 27:6
m	Na 3:18

24:13 *Lit., "from my heart." 24:14
*Or "in the end of the days."

24:17 *Or "the temples of Moab's head."

And they will afflict E'ber.
But he too will utterly perish."

25 Then Ba'laam[a] got up and went and returned to his place. Ba'lak also went his own way.

25 When Israel was dwelling in Shit'tim,[b] the people started to commit sexu-
al immorality with the daughters of Mo'ab.[c] **2** The women invited the people to the sacrifices of their gods,[d] and the people be-
gan to eat and to bow down to their gods.[e] **3** So Israel joined in worship of* the Ba'al of Pe'or,[f] and Jehovah became enraged with Israel. **4** Jehovah said to Moses: "Take all the leaders* of these people and hang them up before Jehovah in broad daylight,# that the burning anger of Jehovah may turn back from Is-
rael." **5** Then Moses said to the judges of Israel:[g] "Each one of you should kill his men who joined in worship of* the Ba'al of Pe'or."[h]

6 But just then, there came one of the Israelites bringing near to his brothers a Mid'-
i·an·ite woman[i] before the eyes of Moses and of all the assembly of the Israelites, while they were weeping at the entrance of the tent of meeting. **7** When Phin'-
e·has[j] the son of El·e·a'zar the son of Aaron the priest saw it, he immediately rose up from the midst of the assembly and took a spear* in his hand. **8** Then he went after the man of Israel into the tent and pierced both of them through, the man of Is-
rael and the woman through her genital parts. At that the scourge on the Israelites was halted.[k] **9** Those who died from the scourge amounted to 24,000.[l]

10 Then Jehovah said to Mo-
ses: **11** "Phin'e·has[a] the son of El·e·a'zar the son of Aaron the priest has turned my wrath away from the people of Israel because he tolerated no rivalry at all toward me among them.[b] So I have not exterminated the Isra-
elites in my insistence on exclu-
sive devotion.[c] **12** Therefore, say, 'I am giving him my covenant of peace. **13** And it will serve as the covenant of a last-
ing priesthood for him and his offspring after him,[d] because he tolerated no rivalry toward his God[e] and he made atonement for the people of Israel.'"

14 Incidentally, the name of the Israelite man who was put to death along with the Mid'i·an·i-
tess was Zim'ri the son of Sa'lu, a chieftain of a paternal house of the Sim'e·on·ites. **15** The name of the Mid'i·an·ite woman who was put to death was Coz'-
bi the daughter of Zur;[f] he was a leader of the clans of a paternal house in Mid'i·an.[g]

16 Jehovah later said to Moses: **17** "Harass the Mid'i·an-
ites and strike them down,[h] **18** because they have been harassing you with their cunning dealings against you in the affair of Pe'or[i] and of Coz'bi the daughter of a chieftain of Mid'i-
an, their sister who was put to death[j] in the day of the scourge over the affair of Pe'or."[k]

26 After the scourge,[l] Jeho-
vah said to Moses and El·e·a'zar the son of Aaron the priest: **2** "Take a census of the whole assembly of the Israelites from 20 years of age and up, by their paternal houses, counting all those who can serve in the army in Israel."[m] **3** So Moses and El·e·a'zar[n] the priest spoke with them in the desert plains of Mo'ab[o] by the Jordan at Jer'-
i·cho,[p] saying: **4** "Take a census of them from the age of 20 years

---

CHAP. 24
a Nu 31:7, 8

CHAP. 25
b Jos 2:1
  Mic 6:5
c Nu 31:16
  1Co 10:8
  Re 2:14
d Ex 34:15
  1Co 10:20
e Nu 20:5
f De 4:3
  Jos 22:17
  Ps 106:28, 29
  Ho 9:10
g Ex 18:21
h Ex 22:20
  Ex 32:25, 27
  De 13:6-9
i Nu 25:14, 15
j Nu 6:25
  Jos 22:30
k Ps 106:30
l Nu 25:4
  De 4:3
  1Co 10:8

Second Col.
a Nu 25:7
b Ps 106:30, 31
c Ex 20:5
  Ex 34:14
  De 4:24
d 1Ch 6:4
  Ezr 7:1, 5
  Ezr 8:1, 2
e 1Ki 19:10
f Nu 31:7, 8
  Jos 13:21
g 1Ch 1:32, 33
h Nu 31:1, 2
i Nu 25:3
  Nu 31:16
j Nu 25:8, 15
k Nu 25:9

CHAP. 26
l Nu 25:7, 8
m Ex 30:12
  Ex 38:26
  Nu 1:2
n Nu 20:26
o Nu 22:1
  Nu 33:48
p Jos 6:1

25:3 *Or "attached itself to." 25:4 *Lit., "heads." #Lit., "in front of the sun." 25:5 *Or "attached themselves to." 25:7 *Or "lance."

and up, just as Jehovah commanded Moses."[a]

Now the sons of Israel who went out of the land of Egypt were: **5** Reu'ben,[b] Israel's firstborn; Reu'ben's sons[c] were: of Ha'noch, the family of the Ha'noch·ites; of Pal'lu, the family of the Pal'lu·ites; **6** of Hez'ron, the family of the Hez'ron·ites; of Car'mi, the family of the Car'mites. **7** These were the families of the Reu'ben·ites, and their registered ones amounted to 43,730.[d]

8 The son of Pal'lu was E·li'ab. **9** And the sons of E·li'ab were Nem'u·el, Da'than, and A·bi'ram. This Da'than and A·bi'ram were chosen ones of the assembly who fought against Moses[e] and Aaron along with Kor'ah's group[f] when they fought against Jehovah.[g] **10** Then the earth opened* and swallowed them up. As for Kor'ah, he died with his supporters when the fire consumed 250 men.[h] And they became a warning example.[i] **11** However, the sons of Kor'ah did not die.[j]

12 The sons of Sim'e·on[k] by their families were: of Nem'u·el, the family of the Nem'u·el·ites; of Ja'min, the family of the Ja'min·ites; of Ja'chin, the family of the Ja'chin·ites; **13** of Ze'rah, the family of the Ze'rah·ites; of Sha'ul, the family of the Sha·u'lites. **14** These were the families of the Sim'e·on·ites: 22,200.[l]

15 The sons of Gad[m] by their families were: of Ze'phon, the family of the Ze'phon·ites; of Hag'gi, the family of the Hag'gites; of Shu'ni, the family of the Shu'nites; **16** of Oz'ni, the family of the Oz'nites; of E'ri, the family of the E'rites; **17** of Ar'od, the family of the Ar'od·ites; of A·re'li, the family of the A·re'lites. **18** These were the fami-

lies of the sons of Gad, and their registered ones were 40,500.[a]

19 The sons of Judah[b] were Er and O'nan.[c] However, Er and O'nan died in the land of Ca'naan.[d] **20** And the sons of Judah by their families were: of She'lah,[e] the family of the She·la'nites; of Pe'rez,[f] the family of the Per'e·zites; of Ze'rah,[g] the family of the Ze'rah·ites. **21** And the sons of Pe'rez were: of Hez'ron,[h] the family of the Hez'ron·ites; of Ha'mul,[i] the family of the Ha·mu'lites. **22** These were the families of Judah, and their registered ones were 76,500.[j]

23 The sons of Is'sa·char[k] by their families were: of To'la,[l] the family of the To'la·ites; of Pu'vah, the family of the Pu'nites; **24** of Ja'shub, the family of the Jash'u·bites; of Shim'ron, the family of the Shim'ron·ites. **25** These were the families of Is'sa·char, and their registered ones were 64,300.[m]

26 The sons of Zeb'u·lun[n] by their families were: of Se'red, the family of the Ser'e·dites; of E'lon, the family of the E'lon·ites; of Jah'le·el, the family of the Jah'le·el·ites. **27** These were the families of the Ze·bu'lu·nites, and their registered ones were 60,500.[o]

28 The sons of Joseph[p] by their families were: Ma·nas'seh and E'phra·im.[q] **29** The sons of Ma·nas'seh[r] were: of Ma'chir,[s] the family of the Ma'chir·ites; and Ma'chir became father to Gil'e·ad;[t] of Gil'e·ad, the family of the Gil'e·ad·ites. **30** These were the sons of Gil'e·ad: of Ie'zer, the family of the Ie'zer·ites; of He'lek, the family of the He'lek·ites; **31** of As'ri·el, the family of the As'ri·el·ites; of She'chem, the family of the She'chem·ites; **32** of She·mi'da, the family of the She·mi'da·ites; of He'pher, the family of the

CHAP. 26
a Nu 1:3
b Ge 29:32
c Ge 46:8, 9
  Ex 6:14
d Nu 1:21
e Nu 16:12
f Nu 16:1
g Nu 16:5, 19
  De 11:6
  Ps 106:17
h Nu 16:32, 35
  Ps 106:18
i Nu 16:38
  1Co 10:10, 11
j Ex 6:24
  Nu 26:58
  Ps 42:Sup
k Ge 35:23
  Ge 46:10
  Ex 6:15
  1Ch 4:24
l Nu 1:23
m Ge 35:26
  Ge 46:16

Second Col.
a Nu 1:25
b Ge 29:35
  Ge 46:12
c Ge 38:2-4
d Ge 38:7-10
e Ge 38:2, 5
  Ge 38:26
  1Ch 4:21
f Ge 38:29
  Ru 4:18
  Mt 1:3
g Ge 38:30
  1Ch 2:4
h Ru 4:19
i 1Ch 2:5
j Nu 1:27
k Ge 30:18
  Ge 35:23
  Ge 46:13
  1Ch 7:1
l 1Ch 7:2
m Nu 1:29
n Ge 30:20
  Ge 46:14
o Nu 1:31
p Ge 30:24
  Ge 35:24
  Ge 46:20
q Ge 41:52
r Ge 41:51
s Ge 50:23
  De 3:15
  1Ch 7:14
t Jos 17:1

He'pher·ites. **33** Now Ze·lo'phe·had the son of He'pher had no sons, only daughters,[a] and the names of the daughters of Ze·lo'phe·had[b] were Mah'lah, Noah, Hog'lah, Mil'cah, and Tir'zah. **34** These were the families of Ma·nas'seh, and their registered ones were 52,700.[c]

35 These were the sons of E'phra·im[d] by their families: of Shu'the·lah,[e] the family of the Shu'thel·a'hites; of Be'cher, the family of the Be'cher·ites; of Ta'han, the family of the Ta'han·ites. **36** And these were the sons of Shu'the·lah: of E'ran, the family of the E'ran·ites. **37** These were the families of the sons of E'phra·im, and their registered ones were 32,500.[f] These were the sons of Joseph by their families.

38 The sons of Benjamin[g] by their families were: of Be'la,[h] the family of the Be'la·ites; of Ash'bel, the family of the Ash'bel·ites; of A·hi'ram, the family of the A·hi'ram·ites; **39** of Shephu'pham, the family of the Shu'pham·ites; of Hu'pham, the family of the Hu'pham·ites. **40** The sons of Be'la were Ard and Na'a·man:[i] of Ard, the family of the Ard'ites; of Na'a·man, the family of the Na'a·mites. **41** These were the sons of Benjamin by their families, and their registered ones were 45,600.[j]

42 These were the sons of Dan[k] by their families: of Shu'ham, the family of the Shu'ham·ites. These were the families of Dan by their families. **43** All the families of the Shu'ham·ites, of their registered ones, were 64,400.[l]

44 The sons of Ash'er[m] by their families were: of Im'nah, the family of the Im'nites; of Ish'vi, the family of the Ish'vites; of Be·ri'ah, the family of the Be·ri'ites; **45** of the sons of Be·ri'ah: of He'ber, the fami-

ly of the He'ber·ites; of Mal'chi·el, the family of the Mal'chi·el·ites. **46** The name of Ash'er's daughter was Se'rah. **47** These were the families of the sons of Ash'er, and their registered ones were 53,400.[a]

48 The sons of Naph'ta·li[b] by their families were: of Jah'ze·el, the family of the Jah'ze·el·ites; of Gu'ni, the family of the Gu'nites; **49** of Je'zer, the family of the Je'zer·ites; of Shil'lem, the family of the Shil'lem·ites. **50** These were the families of Naph'ta·li by their families, and their registered ones were 45,400.[c]

51 This is the total of those registered of the Israelites: 601,730.[d]

52 After that Jehovah said to Moses: **53** "Among these the land should be divided as an inheritance according to the list of the names.*[e] **54** For the larger groups, you should increase the inheritance, and for the smaller groups, you should reduce the inheritance.[f] Each group's inheritance should be given in proportion to the number of those registered. **55** However, the land should be apportioned by lot.[g] They should receive their inheritance according to the names of the tribes of their fathers. **56** Each inheritance will be determined by lot and apportioned among the larger and the smaller groups."

57 Now these were the registered ones of the Levites[h] by their families: of Ger'shon, the family of the Ger'shon·ites; of Ko'hath,[i] the family of the Ko'hath·ites; of Me·rar'i, the family of the Me·rar'ites. **58** These were the families of the Levites: the family of the Lib'nites,[j] the family of the Heb'ron·ites,[k] the

---

CHAP. 26

a Nu 27:7
  1Ch 7:15

b Nu 36:11

c Nu 1:35

d Ge 41:52

e 1Ch 7:20

f Nu 1:33
  Jos 17:17

g Ge 35:24
  Ge 46:21
  1Ch 8:1

h 1Ch 7:6

i 1Ch 8:3, 4

j Nu 1:37

k Ge 30:6

l Nu 1:39

m Ge 30:13
  Ge 35:26
  Ge 46:17
  1Ch 7:30

Second Col.

a Nu 1:41

b Ge 30:8
  Ge 35:25
  Ge 46:24
  1Ch 7:13

c Nu 1:43

d Ex 38:26
  Nu 1:46, 49
  Nu 14:29

e Jos 11:23
  Jos 14:1

f Nu 33:54

g Nu 34:13
  Jos 14:2
  Jos 17:4
  Jos 18:6
  Pr 16:33

h Ge 46:11
  Ex 6:16

i Nu 3:19

j Ex 6:17
  Nu 3:18

k Nu 3:27

26:53 *Or "proportionate to the number of names listed."

family of the Mah′lites,[a] the family of the Mu′shites,[b] the family of the Kor′ah·ites.[c]

Ko′hath became father to Am′ram.[d] **59** And the name of Am′ram's wife was Joch′e·bed,[e] Le′vi's daughter, whom his wife bore to Le′vi in Egypt. And to Am′ram she bore Aaron and Moses and their sister Mir′i·am.[f] **60** Then to Aaron there were born Na′dab, A·bi′hu, El·e·a′zar, and Ith′a·mar.[g] **61** But Na′dab and A·bi′hu died for presenting unauthorized fire before Jehovah.[h]

62 The total of those registered was 23,000, all males from a month old and up.[i] For they were not registered among the Israelites,[j] because no inheritance was to be given to them among the Israelites.[k]

63 These were the ones registered by Moses and El·e·a′zar the priest when they registered the Israelites in the desert plains of Mo′ab by the Jordan at Jer′i·cho. **64** But among them there was no one who had been registered by Moses and Aaron the priest in the census of the Israelites taken in the wilderness of Si′nai.[l] **65** For Jehovah had said concerning them: "They will die without fail in the wilderness."[m] So there was not a man left of them except Ca′leb the son of Je·phun′neh and Joshua the son of Nun.[n]

27 Then the daughters of Ze·lo′phe·had,[o] the son of He′pher, the son of Gil′e·ad, the son of Ma′chir, the son of Ma·nas′seh, of the families of Ma·nas′seh the son of Joseph, approached. The names of his daughters were Mah′lah, Noah, Hog′lah, Mil′cah, and Tir′zah. **2** They stood before Moses, El·e·a′zar the priest, the chieftains,[p] and all the assembly at the entrance of the tent of meeting and said: **3** "Our father died in the wil-

derness, but he was not among the group who banded together against Jehovah, the supporters of Kor′ah,[a] but he died for his own sin and he did not have any sons. **4** Why should the name of our father be lost from his family because he had no son? Give us a possession among our father's brothers." **5** So Moses presented their case before Jehovah.[b]

6 Jehovah then said this to Moses: **7** "The daughters of Ze·lo′phe·had are correct. You should by all means give them the possession as an inheritance among their father's brothers and transfer their father's inheritance to them.[c] **8** And tell the Israelites, 'If a man dies without having a son, you must then cause his inheritance to pass to his daughter. **9** And if he has no daughter, you will give his inheritance to his brothers. **10** And if he has no brothers, you will give his inheritance to his father's brothers. **11** And if his father has no brothers, you will give his inheritance to the closest blood relative in his family, and he will take possession of it. This will serve as a statute by judicial decision for the Israelites, just as Jehovah has commanded Moses.'"

12 Then Jehovah said to Moses: "Go up into this mountain of Ab′a·rim,[d] and view the land that I will give the Israelites.[e] **13** When you have seen it, you will also be gathered to your people,*[f] just as Aaron your brother was,[g] **14** because when the assembly was quarreling with me in the wilderness of Zin, you rebelled against my order to sanctify me before them by means of the waters.[h] These are the waters of Mer′i·bah[i] at

---

27:13 *This is a poetic expression for death.

CHAP. 26
a Ex 6:19
  Nu 3:33
b Nu 3:20
  1Ch 23:23
c Ex 6:24
d Ex 6:18
  Nu 3:19
e Ex 2:1
  Ex 6:20
f Ex 15:20
  Mic 6:4
g Ex 6:23
  Ex 24:9
h Le 10:1, 2
  Nu 3:2, 4
  1Ch 24:2
i Nu 3:39
j Nu 1:49
k Nu 18:24
  De 10:9
  De 14:27
  Jos 14:3
l Nu 1:2
  De 2:14
  1Co 10:5
m Heb 3:17
n Nu 14:29, 30
  Jos 14:14
  Jos 19:49

CHAP. 27
o Nu 26:33
p Ex 18:25, 26

Second Col.
a Nu 14:35
  Nu 16:1, 2
  Nu 16:19, 35
b Ex 18:15, 16
  Ex 33:11
  Le 24:11, 12
c Nu 36:2
  Jos 17:3, 4
d Nu 33:47
  De 32:48, 49
e Ge 13:14, 15
  De 3:27
  De 32:52
  De 34:1
f Nu 31:2
  De 34:7
g Nu 20:24, 28
  Nu 33:38
  De 10:6
  De 32:50
h Nu 20:10, 12
  De 1:37
i Ps 106:32, 33

Ka'desh[a] in the wilderness of Zin."[b]

15 Then Moses said to Jehovah: **16** "Let Jehovah, the God of the spirit of all people,* appoint over the assembly a man **17** who will go out and come in before them and who will lead them out and bring them in, so that Jehovah's assembly may not become like sheep that have no shepherd." **18** So Jehovah said to Moses: "Take Joshua the son of Nun, a man in whom there is spirit, and lay your hand on him.[c] **19** Then stand him before El·e·a'zar the priest and before all the assembly, and you must commission him before their eyes.[d] **20** You are to confer some of your authority* on him,[e] so that all the assembly of the Israelites may listen to him.[f] **21** He will stand before El·e·a'zar the priest, who will inquire in his behalf by the judgment of the U'rim[g] before Jehovah. At his order they will go out and at his order they will come in, he and all the Israelites with him and all the assembly."

22 So Moses did just as Jehovah had commanded him. He took Joshua and stood him before El·e·a'zar the priest and before all the assembly, **23** and he laid his hands on him and commissioned him,[h] just as Jehovah had spoken through Moses.[i]

28 Jehovah next said to Moses: **2** "Command the Israelites and tell them, 'You should take care that you present to me my offering, my bread. My offerings by fire as a pleasing* aroma to me must be made at their appointed times.'[j]

3 "And say to them, 'This is the offering made by fire that

you will present to Jehovah: two sound year-old male lambs a day as a burnt offering regularly.[a] **4** The one male lamb you will offer in the morning, and the other male lamb you will offer at twilight,*[b] **5** together with a tenth of an e'phah* of fine flour mixed with a fourth of a hin# of beaten oil as a grain offering.[c] **6** It is a regular burnt offering,[d] which was established at Mount Si'nai as a pleasing# aroma, an offering made by fire to Jehovah, **7** along with its drink offering, a fourth of a hin for each male lamb.[e] Pour out the alcoholic drink in the holy place as a drink offering to Jehovah. **8** And you will offer the other male lamb at twilight.* With the same grain offering as that made in the morning and with its same drink offering, you will present it as an offering made by fire as a pleasing# aroma to Jehovah.[f]

9 "'However, on the Sabbath day,[g] the offering should be two sound year-old male lambs and two tenths of an e'phah measure of fine flour mixed with oil as a grain offering, together with its drink offering. **10** This is the burnt offering for the Sabbath, along with the regular burnt offering and its drink offering.[h]

11 "'At the start of each month* you will present as a burnt offering to Jehovah two young bulls, one ram, and seven sound male lambs each a year old,[i] **12** and three tenth measures of fine flour mixed with oil as a grain offering[j] for each bull and two tenth measures of fine flour mixed with oil as a grain offering for the one ram,[k]

CHAP. 27

a De 1:2

b Jos 15:1

c De 34:9
Ac 6:5, 6

d De 31:7

e De 1:38
De 31:3
De 34:10

f Jos 1:17

g Ex 28:30
1Sa 23:9
1Sa 28:6
Ne 7:65

h Nu 27:18

i De 3:28
De 31:14, 23

CHAP. 28

j 2Ch 8:13
Ne 10:32, 33

Second Col.

a Ex 29:38
Le 6:9
Eze 46:15

b Ex 29:39

c Ex 29:40
Nu 15:4

d Ex 29:38, 40
2Ch 2:4
Ezr 3:3

e Ex 29:39, 40

f Ex 29:41

g Ex 16:29
Ex 20:10
Eze 20:12

h Nu 28:3, 7

i Nu 10:10
1Ch 23:31
2Ch 2:4
Ne 10:32, 33

j Le 2:11

k Le 1:10

27:16 *Lit., "the spirits of all flesh." 27:20 *Or "dignity." 28:2, 6, 8 #Or "appeasing; soothing." Lit., "restful."

28:4, 8 *Lit., "between the two evenings." 28:5 *A tenth of an ephah equaled 2.2 L (2 dry qt). See App. B14. #A hin equaled 3.67 L (7.75 pt). See App. B14. 28:11 *Lit., "of your months."

13 and a tenth measure of fine flour mixed with oil as a grain offering for each male lamb, as a burnt offering, a pleasing* aroma,[a] an offering made by fire to Jehovah. 14 And their drink offerings should be half a hin of wine for a bull[b] and a third of a hin for the ram[c] and a fourth of a hin for a male lamb.[d] This is the monthly burnt offering each month throughout the year. 15 Also, one young goat should be offered as a sin offering to Jehovah in addition to the regular burnt offering together with its drink offering.

16 "'In the first month, on the 14th day of the month, will be Jehovah's Passover.[e] 17 And on the 15th day of this month, there will be a festival. Unleavened bread will be eaten for seven days.[f] 18 On the first day there will be a holy convention. You must not do any hard work. 19 And you will present as a burnt offering made by fire to Jehovah two young bulls, one ram, and seven male lambs each a year old. You should offer sound animals.[g] 20 You should offer them with their grain offerings of fine flour mixed with oil,[h] three tenth measures for a bull and two tenth measures for the ram. 21 You will offer a tenth measure respectively for each male lamb of the seven male lambs, 22 as well as one goat as a sin offering to make atonement for you. 23 Aside from the morning burnt offering, which is for the regular burnt offering, you will offer these. 24 You will offer these in the same manner each day for seven days as food,[#] an offering made by fire as a pleasing* aroma to Jehovah. It should be offered along with the regular

burnt offering and its drink offering. 25 On the seventh day you should hold a holy convention.[a] You must not do any hard work.[b]

26 "'On the day of the first ripe fruits,[c] when you present a new grain offering to Jehovah,[d] you should hold a holy convention in your feast of weeks.[e] You must not do any hard work.[f] 27 You will present as a burnt offering for a pleasing* aroma to Jehovah two young bulls, one ram, and seven male lambs each a year old,[g] 28 and as their grain offering of fine flour mixed with oil, three tenth measures for each bull, two tenth measures for the one ram, 29 a tenth measure respectively for each male lamb of the seven male lambs, 30 as well as one young goat to make atonement for you.[h] 31 You will offer them in addition to the regular burnt offering and its grain offering. They should be sound animals,[i] along with their drink offerings.

29 "'And in the seventh month, on the first of the month, you should hold a holy convention. You must not do any hard work.[j] It is a day on which you should sound the trumpet.[k] 2 You will offer as a burnt offering for a pleasing* aroma to Jehovah one young bull, one ram, and seven male lambs each a year old, all of them sound, 3 and their grain offering of fine flour mixed with oil, three tenths of an e'phah measure for the bull, two tenth measures for the ram, 4 and one tenth measure for each male lamb of the seven male lambs, 5 and one young male goat as a sin offering to make atonement for you. 6 This is in addition to the monthly burnt offering and its grain offering[l] and the regular burnt offering and its grain offering,[m] together with their

---

CHAP. 28

a Le 1:10, 13

b Nu 15:8, 10

c Nu 15:6, 7

d Nu 15:5

e Ex 12:14
Le 23:5
De 16:1
Eze 45:21
1Co 5:7

f Ex 12:15
Le 23:6
1Co 5:8

g Le 22:20, 22
De 15:21

h Le 2:1

Second Col.

a Ex 13:6

b Ex 12:16
Le 23:8
De 16:8

c Ex 23:16

d Le 23:15, 16

e Ex 34:22
De 16:10
Ac 2:1

f Le 23:16, 21

g Le 23:16, 18

h Le 23:16, 19

i Le 1:3

CHAP. 29

j Le 23:24, 25

k Nu 10:2
Ps 81:3

l Nu 28:11-13

m Nu 28:3, 5

28:13, 24, 27; 29:2 *Or "appeasing; soothing." Lit., "restful." 28:24 #Lit., "bread."

drink offerings,[a] according to the regular procedure for them, as a pleasing* aroma, an offering made by fire to Jehovah.

7 "'And on the tenth of this seventh month, you should hold a holy convention,[b] and you must afflict yourselves.* You must not do any work.[c] **8** And you will present as a burnt offering to Jehovah, as a pleasing* aroma, one young bull, one ram, and seven male lambs each a year old, all of them sound.[d] **9** And as their grain offering of fine flour mixed with oil, three tenth measures for the bull, two tenth measures for the one ram, **10** a tenth measure respectively for each male lamb of the seven male lambs, **11** as well as one young goat as a sin offering, aside from the sin offering of atonement[e] and the regular burnt offering and its grain offering, together with their drink offerings.

12 "'And on the 15th day of the seventh month, you should hold a holy convention. You must not do any hard work, and you must celebrate a festival to Jehovah seven days.[f] **13** And you will present as a burnt offering,[g] an offering made by fire as a pleasing* aroma to Jehovah, 13 young bulls, 2 rams, and 14 male lambs each a year old, all of them sound.[h] **14** And as their grain offering of fine flour mixed with oil, three tenth measures for each bull of the 13 bulls, two tenth measures for each ram of the 2 rams, **15** and a tenth measure for each male lamb of the 14 male lambs, **16** as well as one young goat as a sin offering, aside from the regular burnt offering, its grain offering, and its drink offering.[i]

17 "'And on the second day, 12 young bulls, 2 rams, and 14 male lambs each a year old, all of them sound,[a] **18** and their grain offering and their drink offerings for the bulls, the rams, and the male lambs by their number according to the regular procedure, **19** as well as one young goat as a sin offering, aside from the regular burnt offering and its grain offering, together with their drink offerings.[b]

20 "'And on the third day, 11 bulls, 2 rams, and 14 male lambs each a year old, all of them sound,[c] **21** and their grain offering and their drink offerings for the bulls, the rams, and the male lambs by their number according to the regular procedure, **22** as well as one goat as a sin offering, aside from the regular burnt offering and its grain offering and its drink offering.[d]

23 "'And on the fourth day, 10 bulls, 2 rams, and 14 male lambs each a year old, all of them sound,[e] **24** their grain offering and their drink offerings for the bulls, the rams, and the male lambs by their number according to the regular procedure, **25** as well as one young goat as a sin offering, aside from the regular burnt offering, its grain offering, and its drink offering.[f]

26 "'And on the fifth day, 9 bulls, 2 rams, and 14 male lambs each a year old, all of them sound,[g] **27** and their grain offering and their drink offerings for the bulls, the rams, and the male lambs by their number according to the regular procedure, **28** as well as one goat as a sin offering, aside from the regular burnt offering and its grain offering and its drink offering.[h]

29 "'And on the sixth day, 8 bulls, 2 rams, and 14 male

CHAP. 29

a Nu 28:6, 7

b Le 16:29

c Le 23:27-31

d Le 1:3
Le 22:22
De 15:21
De 17:1

e Le 16:3

f Ex 23:16
Le 23:34-36
De 16:13-15
Ne 8:14-18

g Ezr 3:4

h Le 22:22
De 17:1

i Nu 28:3-8

Second Col.

a Le 22:22
De 17:1

b Nu 28:3-8

c Le 22:22
De 17:1

d Nu 28:3-8

e Le 22:22
De 17:1

f Nu 28:3-8

g De 15:21
De 17:1

h Nu 28:3-8

29:6, 8, 13 * Or "appeasing; soothing." Lit., "restful." **29:7** * Or "your souls." To "afflict oneself" is generally understood to mean various forms of self-denial, including fasting.

lambs each a year old, all of them sound,[a] **30** and their grain offering and their drink offerings for the bulls, the rams, and the male lambs by their number according to the regular procedure, **31** as well as one goat as a sin offering, aside from the regular burnt offering, its grain offering, and its drink offerings.[b]

32 "'And on the seventh day, 7 bulls, 2 rams, and 14 male lambs each a year old, all of them sound,[c] **33** and their grain offering and their drink offerings for the bulls, the rams, and the male lambs by their number according to the regular procedure for them, **34** as well as one goat as a sin offering, aside from the regular burnt offering, its grain offering, and its drink offering.[d]

35 "'On the eighth day, you should hold a solemn assembly. You should not do any hard work.[e] **36** You will present as a burnt offering, an offering made by fire as a pleasing* aroma to Jehovah, one bull, one ram, and seven male lambs each a year old, all of them sound,[f] **37** and their grain offering and their drink offerings for the bull, the ram, and the male lambs by their number according to the regular procedure, **38** as well as one goat as a sin offering, aside from the regular burnt offering and its grain offering and its drink offering.[g]

39 "'These you will offer to Jehovah at your seasonal festivals,[h] in addition to your vow offerings[i] and your voluntary offerings[j] as your burnt offerings[k] and your grain offerings[j] and your drink offerings[m] and your communion sacrifices.'"[n] **40** Moses told the Is-

raelites everything that Jehovah had commanded him.

30 Then Moses spoke to the heads[a] of the tribes of Israel, saying: "This is the word that Jehovah has commanded: **2** If a man makes a vow[b] to Jehovah or swears an oath[c] to impose on himself* a vow of abstinence, he must not violate his word.[d] He should do everything he vowed he would do.[e]

3 "And if a woman makes a vow to Jehovah or she imposes a vow of abstinence on herself when she is young and living in the house of her father **4** and her father hears her vow or her abstinence vow that she has imposed on herself* and her father offers no objection, all her vows will stand, and every abstinence vow that she has imposed on herself will stand. **5** But if her father forbids her when he hears that she has imposed vows or abstinence vows on herself, it will not stand. Jehovah will forgive her because her father forbade her.[f]

6 "However, if she should marry a husband while under her vow or the rash promise that she has imposed on herself **7** and her husband hears of it and offers no objection on the day he hears of it, her vows or her abstinence vows that she has imposed on herself will stand. **8** But if her husband forbids her on the day he hears of it, he may annul the vow or the rash promise that she imposed on herself,[g] and Jehovah will forgive her.

9 "But if a widow or a divorced woman makes a vow, everything that she has imposed on herself will be binding on her.

10 "However, if a woman imposed the vow or the abstinence vow on herself while in the

---

CHAP. 29

a Le 22:22
　De 17:1

b Nu 28:3-8

c Le 22:22
　De 17:1

d Nu 28:3-8

e Le 23:36, 39

f Le 22:22
　De 17:1

g Nu 28:3-8

h Le 23:2
　De 16:16

i De 12:5, 6

j Le 7:16
　Le 22:21

k Le 1:3

l Le 2:1

m Nu 15:5

n Le 3:1

Second Col.

CHAP. 30

a Ex 18:25

b Ge 28:20-22
　Jg 11:30, 31

c Ps 132:1-5

d De 23:21
　Ps 116:14
　Ps 119:106
　Ec 5:4
　Mt 5:33

e Ps 50:14
　Ps 66:13

f Ex 20:12

g Ro 7:2
　1Co 11:3
　Eph 5:22

29:36 *Or "appeasing; soothing." Lit., "restful."

30:2 *Or "to bind an obligation upon his soul." 30:4 *Or "her soul."

house of her husband **11** and her husband heard it and has not objected or disapproved, all her vows or any abstinence vow that she imposed on herself will stand. **12** But if on the day he heard them her husband completely annulled whatever vows or abstinence vow she swore to, they will not stand.[a] Her husband annulled them, and Jehovah will forgive her. **13** Regarding any vow or any oath involving an abstinence vow to practice self-denial,* her husband should establish it or her husband should annul it. **14** But if her husband offers no objection at all from day to day, he also establishes all her vows or all her abstinence vows that are upon her. He establishes them because he did not object on the day he heard her make them. **15** But if he annuls them later, sometime after the day he heard them, he will bear the consequences of her guilt.[b]

16 "These are the regulations that Jehovah commanded Moses relating to a husband and his wife, and relating to a father and his young daughter living in his house."

31 Jehovah then told Moses: **2** "Take vengeance[c] for the Israelites on the Mid′i·an·ites.[d] Afterward you will be gathered to your people."*[e]

3 So Moses spoke to the people, saying: "Equip men from among you for battle* against Mid′i·an and to execute Jehovah's vengeance on Mid′i·an. **4** You should send 1,000 of each tribe of all the tribes of Israel into the army." **5** So from the thousands of Israel,[f] 1,000 were assigned from each tribe, 12,000 equipped for battle.*

6 Then Moses sent them out, 1,000 from each tribe to the army, along with Phin′e·has[a] the son of El·e·a′zar the priest for the army, who had the holy utensils and the signal trumpets[b] in his hand. **7** They waged war against Mid′i·an, just as Jehovah had commanded Moses, and they killed every male. **8** Along with the others slain, they killed the kings of Mid′i·an, namely, E′vi, Re′kem, Zur, Hur, and Re′ba, the five kings of Mid′i·an. They also killed Ba′laam[c] the son of Be′or with the sword. **9** But the Israelites carried off captive the women and children of Mid′i·an. They also plundered all their domestic animals, all their livestock, and all their possessions. **10** And all their cities in which they had settled and all their encampments* they burned with fire. **11** And they took all the spoil and all the plunder, both humans and animals. **12** Then they brought the captives, the plunder, and the spoil to Moses and El·e·a′zar the priest and to the assembly of the Israelites, to the camp in the desert plains of Mo′ab[d] near the Jordan at Jer′i·cho.

13 Then Moses and El·e·a′zar the priest and all the chieftains of the assembly went out to meet them outside the camp. **14** But Moses grew indignant at the appointed men of the combat forces, the chiefs of the thousands and the chiefs of the hundreds who were coming in from the military expedition. **15** Moses said to them: "Have you preserved all the females alive? **16** Look! They are the ones who by Ba′laam's word induced the Israelites to commit unfaithfulness[e] toward Jehovah over the affair of Pe′or,[f] so that the scourge came upon the

---

CHAP. 30
a 1Co 11:3
  1Pe 3:1

b De 23:21

CHAP. 31
c Ps 94:1
  Isa 1:24
  Na 1:2

d Nu 22:7
  Nu 25:1-3
  Nu 25:17, 18
  1Co 10:8
  Re 2:14

e Nu 27:12, 13
  De 32:48-50

f Nu 26:51

Second Col.
a Nu 25:7, 8

b Nu 10:2, 9

c Nu 22:12
  2Pe 2:15
  Re 2:14

d Nu 22:1

e Nu 25:1, 2
  Re 2:14

f Nu 25:17, 18
  De 4:3
  Jos 22:17

30:13 *Or "a vow to afflict the soul."
31:2 *This is a poetic expression for death. 31:3, 5 *Or "for the army."
31:10 *Or "walled camps."

assembly of Jehovah.[a] **17** Now you should kill every male among the children and kill every woman who has had sexual relations with a man. **18** But you may keep alive all the young girls who have not had sexual relations with a man.[b] **19** And you should camp outside the camp seven days. Every one of you who has killed someone* and every one of you who has touched someone slain[c] should purify himself[d] on the third day and on the seventh day, you and your captives. **20** And you should purify from sin every garment, every article of skin, everything made of goat hair, and every article of wood."

21 El·e·a′zar the priest then said to the men of the army who had gone into the battle: "This is the statute of the law that Jehovah commanded Moses, **22** 'Only the gold, the silver, the copper, the iron, the tin, and the lead, **23** everything that can be processed with fire, you should pass through the fire, and it will be clean. However, it should also be purified by the water for cleansing.[e] Everything that cannot be processed with fire, you should pass through the water. **24** And you should wash your garments on the seventh day and be clean, and then you may come into the camp.'"[f]

25 Jehovah then said this to Moses: **26** "Take an inventory of the plunder, counting the captives both of humans and animals; do this together with El·e·a′zar the priest and the heads of the paternal houses of the assembly. **27** Divide what was plundered into two parts to be shared between those in the army who took part in the battle and all the rest of the assembly.[g] **28** As a tax for Jehovah, you should take from the soldiers who went out into the battle one soul* out of every 500, of the people, the herd, the donkeys, and the flock. **29** You should take it from their half and give it to El·e·a′zar the priest as Jehovah's contribution.[a] **30** From the half given to the Israelites, you should take one out of 50, of the people, the herd, the donkeys, the flock, and every sort of domestic animal, and give them to the Levites,[b] who care for the responsibilities connected with Jehovah's tabernacle."[c]

31 So Moses and El·e·a′zar the priest did just as Jehovah had commanded Moses. **32** The spoils, the rest of the plunder that the people of the expedition had taken, amounted to 675,000 of the flock, **33** 72,000 of the herd, **34** and 61,000 donkeys. **35** The women who had not had sexual relations with a man[d] amounted to 32,000 women.* **36** The half that was the share of those who went out into the battle amounted to 337,500 of the flock. **37** The tax for Jehovah from the flock amounted to 675. **38** And there were 36,000 of the herd, and the tax on them for Jehovah was 72. **39** And there were 30,500 donkeys, and the tax on them for Jehovah was 61. **40** And there were 16,000 humans,* and the tax on them for Jehovah was 32 persons.* **41** Then Moses gave the tax as Jehovah's contribution to El·e·a′zar the priest,[e] just as Jehovah had commanded Moses.

42 From the half belonging to the Israelites, which Moses had divided off from the portion that belonged to the men who waged war, **43** that half of the flock amounted to 337,500, **44** and of

---

CHAP. 31
a Nu 25:9
1Co 10:8

b Nu 31:35

c Nu 5:2
Nu 19:11, 16

d Nu 19:20

e Nu 19:9

f Nu 19:19, 20

g Jos 22:7, 8
1Sa 30:24

Second Col.
a Nu 18:20, 29

b De 12:19

c Nu 3:6, 7
Nu 18:2, 3
1Ch 23:32

d Nu 31:18

e Nu 18:8, 19

31:19 *Or "a soul."   **31:28** *See Glossary.   **31:35, 40** *Or "souls."   **31:40** *Or "human souls."

the herd, 36,000, **45** and of the donkeys, 30,500, **46** and of the people,* 16,000. **47** Then Moses took from the half belonging to the Israelites one out of 50, of the people and of the animals, and gave them to the Levites,ᵃ who cared for the responsibility of Jehovah's tabernacle,ᵇ just as Jehovah had commanded Moses.

48 Then the appointed men who were of the thousands of the army,ᶜ the chiefs of the thousands and the chiefs of the hundreds, approached Moses, **49** and they said to Moses: "Your servants have taken the count of the men of war who are under our command, and not one has been reported missing from us.ᵈ **50** So let us each present what he has found as Jehovah's offering, articles of gold, ankle chains, bracelets, signet rings, earrings, and other jewelry, in order to make atonement for ourselves* before Jehovah."

51 So Moses and El·e·a′zar the priest accepted the gold from them, all the jewelry. **52** All the gold of the contribution that they made to Jehovah amounted to 16,750 shekels,* from the chiefs of the thousands and the chiefs of the hundreds. **53** The men of the army had each taken plunder for himself. **54** Moses and El·e·a′zar the priest accepted the gold from the chiefs of the thousands and of the hundreds and brought it into the tent of meeting as a reminder* for the people of Israel before Jehovah.

32 Now the sons of Reu′benᵉ and the sons of Gadᶠ had very large quantities of livestock, and they saw that the lands of Ja′zerᵍ and Gil′e·ad were a good region for livestock. **2** So the sons of Gad and the sons of Reu′ben approached Moses, El·e·a′zar the priest, and the chieftains of the assembly and said: **3** "At′a·roth, Di′bon, Ja′zer, Nim′rah, Hesh′bon,ᵃ E·le·a′leh, Se′bam, Ne′bo,ᵇ and Be′on,ᶜ **4** the land that Jehovah defeated before the assembly of Israel,ᵈ is a good land for livestock, and your servants have much livestock."ᵉ **5** They continued: "If we have found favor in your eyes, let this be the land given to your servants as a possession. Do not make us cross the Jordan."

6 Then Moses said to the sons of Gad and the sons of Reu′ben: "Are your brothers to go to war while you yourselves keep dwelling here? **7** Why should you discourage the people of Israel from crossing into the land that Jehovah is certain to give them? **8** That is what your fathers did when I sent them from Ka′desh-bar′ne·a to see the land.ᶠ **9** When they went up to the Valley* of Esh′colᵍ and saw the land, they discouraged the people of Israel from going into the land that Jehovah was to give them.ʰ **10** Jehovah's anger blazed on that day so that he swore:ⁱ **11** 'The men who came up out of Egypt from 20 years old and up will not see the landʲ of which I have sworn to Abraham, Isaac, and Jacob,ᵏ because they have not followed me wholeheartedly— **12** except Ca′lebˡ the son of Je·phun′neh the Ken′iz·zite and Joshuaᵐ the son of Nun, because they have followed Jehovah wholeheartedly.'ⁿ **13** So Jehovah's anger blazed against Israel and he made them wander about in the wilderness for 40 years,ᵒ until all the generation that was

---

CHAP. 31
a De 12:19

b Nu 3:6, 7
Nu 18:2, 3
1Ch 23:32

c Nu 31:4

d Ex 23:27
Le 26:7, 8

CHAP. 32
e Nu 26:7

f Nu 26:18

g Nu 21:32

Second Col.
a Nu 21:26

b Nu 33:47

c Nu 32:37, 38

d Nu 21:23, 24
De 2:24

e De 2:35

f Nu 13:31
Jos 14:7, 8

g Nu 13:23
De 1:24

h Nu 13:32
De 1:26-28

i Ps 95:11
Eze 20:15
Heb 3:18

j Nu 14:29, 30
De 2:14

k Ge 13:14, 15
Ge 26:3
Ge 28:13

l Nu 13:30

m Jos 19:49

n Nu 14:24
De 1:34-38
Jos 14:8

o Nu 14:33
De 29:5
Jos 5:6
Ps 95:10
Ac 13:18

31:46 *Or "the human souls." 31:50 *Or "our souls." 31:52 *A shekel equaled 11.4 g (0.367 oz t). See App. B14. 31:54 *Or "memorial."

32:9 *Or "Wadi."

doing evil in the eyes of Jehovah came to its end.[a] **14** Now here you have risen in the place of your fathers as a brood of sinful men who increase the burning anger of Jehovah against Israel. **15** If you turn back from following him, he will certainly leave them again in the wilderness, and you will bring ruin to all this people."

16 They later approached him and said: "Let us build here stone pens for our livestock and cities for our children. **17** But we will continue ready for battle[b] and will go before the Israelites until we have brought them to their place, while our children will dwell in the fortified cities, safe from the inhabitants of the land. **18** We will not return to our houses until each of the Israelites has received his land as an inheritance.[c] **19** For we will not receive an inheritance with them on the other side of the Jordan and beyond, because we have received our inheritance on the east side of the Jordan."[d]

20 Moses replied to them: "If you will do this: Take up arms before Jehovah for the war;[e] **21** and if every one of you takes up arms and crosses the Jordan before Jehovah as he drives away his enemies from before him[f] **22** until the land is subdued before Jehovah,[g] afterward you may return[h] and be free from guilt before Jehovah and Israel. Then this land will become your possession before Jehovah.[i] **23** But if you do not do this, you will have sinned against Jehovah. In that case, know that your sin will catch up with you. **24** So you may build cities for your children and pens for your flocks,[j] but you must do what you have promised."

25 The sons of Gad and the sons of Reu'ben said this to Moses: "Your servants will do just as my lord is commanding. **26** Our children, our wives, our livestock, and all our domestic animals will stay there in the cities of Gil'e·ad,[a] **27** but your servants will cross over, every man armed for battle to wage war before Jehovah,[b] just as my lord is speaking."

28 So Moses gave a command concerning them to El·e·a'zar the priest, to Joshua the son of Nun, and to the heads of the paternal houses of the tribes of Israel. **29** Moses said to them: "If the sons of Gad and the sons of Reu'ben cross over the Jordan with you, every man armed for the war before Jehovah, and the land is subdued before you, you will then give them the land of Gil'e·ad as a possession.[c] **30** But if they do not take up arms and cross over with you, they will then settle among you in the land of Ca'naan."

31 To this the sons of Gad and the sons of Reu'ben answered: "What Jehovah has spoken to your servants is what we will do. **32** We will take up arms and cross over before Jehovah to the land of Ca'naan,[d] but the possession we are to inherit will be on this side of the Jordan." **33** So Moses gave to them—to the sons of Gad, the sons of Reu'ben,[e] and to the half tribe of Ma·nas'seh[f] the son of Joseph—the kingdom of Si'hon[g] the king of the Am'or·ites and the kingdom of Og[h] the king of Ba'shan, the land belonging to its cities in those territories, and the cities of the surrounding land.

34 And the sons of Gad built* Di'bon,[i] At'a·roth,[j] A·ro'er,[k] **35** At'roth-sho'phan, Ja'zer,[l] Jog'be·hah,[m] **36** Beth-nim'rah,[n] and Beth-ha'ran,[o] fortified cities, and they built stone pens for

32:34 *Or "rebuilt."

CHAP. 32

a Nu 26:63, 64
  De 2:14
  1Co 10:5
  Heb 3:17

b De 3:18
  Jos 4:12

c Jos 22:1, 4

d Nu 32:33
  Jos 12:1
  Jos 13:8

e Jos 4:13

f Ps 78:55

g Jos 11:23
  Jos 18:1
  Ps 44:2

h Jos 22:4, 9

i De 3:19, 20
  Jos 1:14, 15
  Jos 13:8

j Nu 32:16
  Nu 32:34-38

Second Col.

a Jos 1:12-14

b Jos 4:12

c Jos 13:15, 24

d Jos 4:13

e De 3:12

f Jos 22:7

g Nu 21:23, 24
  De 2:31

h De 3:4

i Nu 33:45
  Jos 13:15, 17

j Nu 32:3, 4

k De 2:36
  Jos 12:1, 2

l Nu 21:32

m Jg 8:11

n Nu 32:3, 4

o Jos 13:27, 28

the flocks. **37** And the sons of Reu'ben built Hesh'bon,[a] E·le·a'leh,[b] Kir·i·a·tha'im,[c] **38** Ne'bo,[d] and Ba'al·me'on[e]—their names being changed—and Sib'mah; and they began to rename the cities that they rebuilt.

39 The sons of Ma'chir[f] the son of Ma·nas'seh marched against Gil'e·ad and captured it and drove away the Am'orites who were in it. **40** So Moses gave Gil'e·ad to Ma'chir the son of Ma·nas'seh, and he began dwelling in it.[g] **41** And Ja'ir the son of Ma·nas'seh marched against them and captured their tent villages, and he began to call them Hav'voth-ja'ir.*[h] **42** And No'bah marched against and captured Ke'nath and its dependent* towns, and he began to call it No'bah by his own name.

33 These were the stages of the journey of the people of Israel when they went out of the land of Egypt[i] by their companies*[j] under the direction of Moses and Aaron.[k] **2** Moses kept recording the departure places by the stages of their journey at the order of Jehovah, and these were their stages from one departure place to another:[l] **3** They departed from Ram'e·ses[m] in the first month, on the 15th day of the month.[n] On the very day after the Passover,[o] the Israelites went out with confidence* before the eyes of all the Egyptians. **4** Meanwhile, the Egyptians were burying all the firstborn whom Jehovah had struck down among them,[p] for Jehovah had executed judgments on their gods.[q]

5 So the Israelites departed from Ram'e·ses and camped at

Suc'coth.[a] **6** Then they departed from Suc'coth and camped at E'tham,[b] which is on the edge of the wilderness. **7** Next they departed from E'tham and turned back toward Pi·ha·hi'roth, which is in view of Ba'al-ze'phon,[c] and they camped before Mig'dol.[d] **8** After that they departed from Pi·ha·hi'roth and passed through the midst of the sea[e] to the wilderness[f] and kept marching a three-day journey in the wilderness of E'tham[g] and camped at Ma'rah.[h]

9 Then they departed from Ma'rah and came to E'lim. Now in E'lim there were 12 springs of water and 70 palm trees, so they camped there.[i] **10** Next they departed from E'lim and camped by the Red Sea. **11** After that they departed from the Red Sea and camped in the wilderness of Sin.[j] **12** Then they departed from the wilderness of Sin and camped at Doph'kah. **13** Later they departed from Doph'kah and camped at A'lush. **14** They next departed from A'lush and camped at Reph'i·dim,[k] where there was no water for the people to drink. **15** After that they departed from Reph'i·dim and camped in the wilderness of Si'nai.[l]

16 They departed from the wilderness of Si'nai and camped at Kib'roth-hat·ta'a·vah.[m] **17** Then they departed from Kib'roth-hat·ta'a·vah and camped at Ha·ze'roth.[n] **18** After that they departed from Ha·ze'roth and camped at Rith'mah. **19** Next they departed from Rith'mah and camped at Rim'mon-pe'rez. **20** Then they departed from Rim'mon-pe'rez and camped at Lib'nah. **21** They departed from Lib'nah and camped at Ris'sah. **22** Next they departed from Ris'sah and camped at Ke·he·la'thah.

CHAP. 32
a Nu 21:26
b Nu 32:3, 4
c Jos 13:15, 19
d Nu 32:3, 4
e Jos 13:15, 17
f Nu 26:29
g De 3:13
    Jos 13:31
    Jos 17:1
h De 3:14
    Jos 13:29, 30

CHAP. 33
i Ex 12:51
j Ex 13:18
k Jos 24:5
    1Sa 12:8
l Nu 9:17
m Ge 47:11
    Ex 12:37
n Ex 12:2
    Ex 13:4
o Ex 12:3, 6
    De 16:1
p Ex 12:29
    Ps 78:51
q Ex 12:12
    Ex 18:11

Second Col.
a Ex 12:37
b Ex 13:20
c Ex 14:9
d Ex 14:2
e Ex 14:22
f Ex 15:22
g Ex 13:20
h Ex 15:23
i Ex 15:27
j Ex 16:1
k Ex 17:1, 8
l Ex 18:5
    Ex 19:1, 2
    Nu 1:1
    Nu 3:4
    Nu 9:1
m Nu 11:34
    De 9:22
n Nu 11:35
    Nu 12:16

32:41 *Meaning "Tent Villages of Jair."
32:42 *Or "surrounding." 33:1 *Lit., "according to their armies." 33:3 *Lit., "with uplifted hand."

23 Then they departed from Ke·he·la'thah and camped at Mount She'pher.

24 After that they departed from Mount She'pher and camped at Har·a'dah. 25 Then they departed from Har·a'dah and camped at Mak·he'loth. 26 Next they departed[a] from Mak·he'loth and camped at Ta'hath. 27 After that they departed from Ta'hath and camped at Te'rah. 28 Then they departed from Te'rah and camped at Mith'kah. 29 Later they departed from Mith'kah and camped at Hash·mo'nah. 30 Next they departed from Hash·mo'nah and camped at Mo·se'roth. 31 Then they departed from Mo·se'roth and camped at Ben'e·ja'a·kan.[b] 32 And they departed from Ben'e·ja'a·kan and camped at Hor-hag·gid'gad. 33 Next they departed from Hor-hag·gid'gad and camped at Jot'ba·thah.[c] 34 Later they departed from Jot'ba·thah and camped at A·bro'nah. 35 Then they departed from A·bro'nah and camped at E'zi·on·ge'ber.[d] 36 After that they departed from E'zi·on·ge'ber and camped in the wilderness of Zin,[e] that is, Ka'desh.

37 Later they departed from Ka'desh and camped at Mount Hor,[f] on the frontier of the land of E'dom. 38 And Aaron the priest went up into Mount Hor at the order of Jehovah and died there in the 40th year after the Israelites left the land of Egypt, in the fifth month, on the first of the month.[g] 39 Aaron was 123 years old at his death on Mount Hor.

40 Now the king of A'rad,[h] the Ca'naan·ite who was dwelling in the Neg'eb in the land of Ca'naan, heard about the coming of the Israelites.

41 In time they departed from Mount Hor[i] and camped at Zal·mo'nah. 42 After that they departed from Zal·mo'nah and camped at Pu'non. 43 Next they departed from Pu'non and camped at O'both.[a] 44 Then they departed from O'both and camped at I'ye-ab'a·rim, on the border of Mo'ab.[b] 45 Later they departed from I'yim and camped at Di'bon-gad.[c] 46 After that they departed from Di'bon-gad and camped at Al'mon-dib·la·tha'im. 47 Then they departed from Al'mon-dib·la·tha'im and camped in the mountains of Ab'a·rim[d] before Ne'bo.[e] 48 Finally they departed from the mountains of Ab'a·rim and camped on the desert plains of Mo'ab by the Jordan at Jer'i·cho.[f] 49 They continued camping along the Jordan, from Beth-jesh'i·moth as far as A'bel-shit'tim,[g] on the desert plains of Mo'ab.

50 Jehovah spoke to Moses on the desert plains of Mo'ab by the Jordan at Jer'i·cho, saying: 51 "Speak to the Israelites and tell them, 'You are crossing the Jordan into the land of Ca'naan.[h] 52 You must drive away all the inhabitants of the land from before you and destroy all their carvings of stone[i] and all their metal statues,*[j] and you should demolish all their sacred high places.[k] 53 And you will take possession of the land and dwell in it, because I will certainly give you the land as a possession.[l] 54 You must apportion the land by lot[m] as a possession among your families. To the larger group you should increase his inheritance, and to the smaller group you should reduce his inheritance.[n] Everyone's inheritance will be where his lot falls. You will receive your property as an inheritance by the tribes of your fathers.[o]

33:52 *Or "molten statues."

CHAP. 33
a Nu 9:17

b De 10:6

c De 10:7

d De 2:8
  1Ki 9:26

e Nu 20:1
  Nu 27:14
  De 32:51
  Jos 15:1

f Nu 20:22

g De 10:6

h Nu 21:1

i Nu 21:4

Second Col.
a Nu 21:10

b Ge 19:36, 37
  Nu 21:11, 13

c Nu 32:34

d Nu 27:12
  De 32:48, 49

e Nu 34:1

f Nu 22:1

g Nu 25:1
  Jos 2:1

h Jos 3:17

i Le 26:1

j Le 19:4
  De 27:15

k Ex 23:24
  Ex 34:13, 17
  De 7:5
  De 12:3

l De 32:8

m Pr 16:33

n Nu 26:53, 54

o Jos 15:1
  Jos 16:1
  Jos 18:11

55 "'If, though, you do not drive the inhabitants of the land away from before you,[a] those whom you allow to remain will be as irritants in your eyes and thorns in your sides, and they will harass you in the land where you will dwell.[b] **56** And I will do to you what I intended to do to them.'"[c]

34 And Jehovah spoke further to Moses, saying: **2** "Give these instructions to the Israelites: 'When you go into the land of Ca'naan,[d] this is the land that will fall to you as an inheritance, the land of Ca'naan according to its boundaries.[e]

3 "'Your southern border will extend from the wilderness of Zin alongside E'dom, and your south boundary on the east will be from the extremity of the Salt Sea.[*][f] **4** Your boundary will change direction to pass south of the ascent of A·krab'bim[g] and continue to Zin, and its end will be south of Ka'desh-bar'ne·a.[h] Then it will extend to Ha'zar-ad'dar[i] and continue to Az'mon. **5** The boundary will change direction at Az'mon to the Wadi* of Egypt, and its end will be at the Sea.[*][j]

6 "'Your western boundary will be the Great Sea* and the coast. This will become your western boundary.[k]

7 "'Now this will be your northern boundary: From the Great Sea you will mark your boundary out to Mount Hor.[l] **8** From Mount Hor you will mark out the boundary to Le'bo-ha'math,[*][m] and the end of the boundary will be at Ze'dad.[n] **9** And the boundary will extend to Ziph'ron, and its end will be

Ha'zar-e'nan.[a] This will become your northern boundary.

10 "'Then you should mark as your boundary on the east from Ha'zar-e'nan to She'pham. **11** The boundary will extend from She'pham to Rib'lah to the east of A'in, and the border will go down and cross the eastern slope of the Sea of Chin'ne·reth.[*][b] **12** The border will extend to the Jordan, and its end will be the Salt Sea.[c] This will be your land[d] and the boundaries surrounding it.'"

13 So Moses instructed the Israelites, saying: "This is the land that you will apportion as your possession by lot,[e] just as Jehovah has commanded to give to the nine and a half tribes. **14** For the tribe of the Reu'ben·ites by their paternal house, the tribe of the Gad'ites by their paternal house, and the half tribe of Ma·nas'seh have already taken their inheritance.[f] **15** The two and a half tribes have already taken their inheritance east of the region of the Jordan by Jer'i·cho, toward the sunrising."[g]

16 Jehovah spoke further to Moses, saying: **17** "These are the names of the men who will divide the land for you to possess: El·e·a'zar[h] the priest and Joshua[i] the son of Nun. **18** And you will take one chieftain out of each tribe to divide the land as your inheritance.[j] **19** These are the names of the men: of the tribe of Judah,[k] Ca'leb[l] the son of Je·phun'neh; **20** of the tribe of the sons of Sim'e·on,[m] She·mu'el the son of Am·mi'hud; **21** of the tribe of Benja·min,[n] E·li'dad the son of Chis'lon; **22** of the tribe of the sons of Dan,[o] a chieftain, Buk'ki the son of Jog'li; **23** of the sons of

---

34:3 * That is, the Dead Sea. **34:5** * See Glossary. # That is, the Great Sea, the Mediterranean. **34:6** * That is, the Mediterranean. **34:8** * Or "the entrance of Hamath."

34:11 * That is, the lake of Gennesaret, or the Sea of Galilee.

Joseph[a] from the tribe of the sons of Ma·nas'seh,[b] a chieftain, Han'ni·el the son of E'phod; **24** from the tribe of the sons of E'phra·im,[c] a chieftain, Kem·u'el the son of Shiph'tan; **25** of the tribe of the sons of Zeb'u·lun,[d] a chieftain, E·li·za'phan the son of Par'nach; **26** of the tribe of the sons of Is'sa·char,[e] a chieftain, Pal'ti·el the son of Az'zan; **27** of the tribe of the sons of Ash'er,[f] a chieftain, A·hi'hud the son of She·lo'mi; **28** of the tribe of the sons of Naph'ta·li,[g] a chieftain, Ped·ah'el the son of Am·mi'hud. **29** These are the ones whom Jehovah commanded to distribute the land to the Israelites in the land of Ca'naan.[h]

35 Jehovah went on to speak to Moses on the desert plains of Mo'ab by the Jordan[i] at Jer'i·cho, saying: **2** "Instruct the Israelites that they are to give the Levites cities to inhabit out of the inheritance they will possess,[j] and they should give the Levites the pastures around the cities.[k] **3** They will inhabit the cities, and the pastures will be for their livestock, their goods, and all their other animals. **4** The pastures of the cities that you will give the Levites will extend for 1,000 cubits* from the wall all around the city. **5** You should measure outside the city 2,000 cubits on the east side, 2,000 cubits on the south side, 2,000 cubits on the west side, and 2,000 cubits on the north side, with the city in the middle. These will be the pastures of their cities.

6 "The cities that you will give to the Levites will be 6 cities of refuge,[l] which you will give for the manslayer to flee to,[m] as well as 42 other cities. **7** You are to give to the Levites a total

of 48 cities, together with their pastures.[a] **8** The cities you give them will be from the possession of the Israelites.[b] From the larger group you will take many, and from the smaller group you will take few.[c] Each group will give some of its cities to the Levites in proportion to the inheritance that it receives."

9 Jehovah continued to speak to Moses, saying: **10** "Speak to the Israelites and tell them, 'You are crossing the Jordan to the land of Ca'naan.[d] **11** You should choose cities convenient for yourselves to serve as cities of refuge, where the manslayer who unintentionally kills someone* should flee.[e] **12** These cities will serve as a refuge for you from the blood avenger,[f] so that the manslayer will not die until he stands trial before the assembly.[g] **13** The six cities of refuge that you provide will serve this purpose. **14** You will provide three cities on this side of the Jordan[h] and three cities in the land of Ca'naan[i] to serve as cities of refuge. **15** These six cities will serve as a refuge for the Israelites, for the foreign resident,[j] and for the settler among them, for anyone to flee there who unintentionally kills someone.*[k]

16 "'But if he struck him with an iron instrument and he dies, he is a murderer. The murderer should be put to death without fail.[l] **17** And if he struck him with a stone that could cause death and he dies, he is a murderer. The murderer should be put to death without fail. **18** And if he struck him with a wooden instrument that could cause death and he dies, he is a murderer. The murderer should be put to death without fail.

CHAP. 34
a Ge 46:20
　Ge 48:5
　Jos 16:1
b Jos 17:1
c Jos 16:5
d Jos 19:10
e Jos 19:17
f Jos 19:24
g Jos 19:32
h Nu 34:18
　De 32:8
　Jos 19:51
　Ac 17:26

CHAP. 35
i Nu 22:1
　Nu 36:13
j De 18:1
　Jos 14:4
k Le 25:32-34
　Jos 21:3
　2Ch 11:14
l Jos 20:2,
　3, 7, 8
　Jos 21:13, 21,
　27, 32, 36, 38
m De 4:42

Second Col.
a Jos 21:3
b Ge 49:7
c Nu 26:54
　Nu 33:54
d Ex 3:8
　Ex 23:23
　Nu 34:2
e Ex 21:12, 13
　De 4:42
　De 19:4, 5
f Nu 35:19
　De 19:6
g De 19:11, 12
　Jos 20:5, 9
h De 4:41-43
i De 19:8, 9
　Jos 20:7
j Ex 12:49
　Le 19:34
　Nu 15:16
k Jos 20:2, 3
l Ge 9:5
　Ex 21:12
　Le 24:17
　De 19:11, 12

35:4 *A cubit equaled 44.5 cm (17.5 in.). See App. B14.

35:11, 15 *Or "strikes a soul."

19 "'The avenger of blood is the one who will put the murderer to death. When he encounters him, he himself will put him to death. **20** If death resulted because he pushed him out of hatred or threw something at him with malicious intent,*[a] **21** or out of hatred he struck him with his hand, and he died, the one who struck him will be put to death without fail. He is a murderer. The avenger of blood will put the murderer to death when he encounters him.

22 "'But if it was unexpectedly and not out of hatred that he pushed him or threw any article at him without malicious intent,*[b] **23** or if he did not see him and caused a stone to fall on him and he was not an enemy or seeking his injury, and the person died, **24** the assembly should then judge between the one who struck him and the avenger of blood, in harmony with these judgments.[c] **25** The assembly should then save the manslayer from the hand of the avenger of blood and return him to his city of refuge to which he had fled, and he must dwell in it until the death of the high priest who was anointed with the holy oil.[d]

26 "'But if the manslayer goes out of the boundary of his city of refuge to which he fled **27** and the avenger of blood finds him outside the boundary of his city of refuge and slays the manslayer, he has no bloodguilt. **28** For he must dwell in his city of refuge until the high priest's death. But after the high priest's death, the manslayer may return to the land that he owns.[e] **29** These things will serve for you as a statute for judgment throughout your generations in all your dwelling places.

30 "'Whoever kills a person* should be put to death as a murderer[a] on the testimony[#] of witnesses;[b] but no one* will be put to death on the testimony of just one witness. **31** You must take no ransom for the life* of a murderer who is deserving to die, for he should be put to death without fail.[c] **32** And you must not take a ransom for one who has fled to his city of refuge, allowing him to resume dwelling in his land before the death of the high priest.

33 "'You must not pollute the land in which you live, for blood pollutes the land,[d] and there may be no atonement for the blood that has been spilled on the land except by the blood of the one who spilled it.[e] **34** You must not defile the land in which you dwell, in which I am residing; for I, Jehovah, am residing in the midst of the people of Israel.'"[f]

36 The family heads of the descendants of Gil'e·ad the son of Ma'chir[g] the son of Ma·nas'seh of the families of the sons of Joseph approached and spoke before Moses and the chieftains, the family heads of the Israelites. **2** They said: "Jehovah commanded my lord to distribute the land by lot[h] as an inheritance to the Israelites; and my lord was commanded by Jehovah to give the inheritance of our brother Ze·lo'phe·had to his daughters.[i] **3** If they marry men from another Israelite tribe, the women's inheritance will also be withdrawn from the inheritance of our fathers and be added to the inheritance of the tribe to which they would then belong, so that it would be withdrawn from the lot of our inheritance. **4** Now when the Jubilee[j]

CHAP. 35
[a] Ex 21:14
    De 19:11, 12

[b] Ex 21:12, 13
    De 19:4, 5
    Jos 20:2, 3

[c] Nu 35:12
    Jos 20:4, 5

[d] Ex 29:4, 7

[e] Jos 20:6

Second Col.
[a] Ge 9:6
    Ex 20:13

[b] De 17:6
    De 19:15
    Heb 10:28

[c] Ge 9:5
    Ex 21:14
    De 19:13

[d] Ge 4:8, 10
    Ps 106:38
    Lu 11:50

[e] Ge 9:6

[f] Ex 25:8
    Le 26:12

CHAP. 36
[g] Nu 26:29

[h] Nu 26:55
    Nu 33:54

[i] Nu 27:1-7

[j] Le 25:10

35:20 *Lit., "while lying in wait." **35:22** *Lit., "without lying in wait."

35:30, 31 *Or "soul." **35:30** #Lit., "mouth."

takes place for the people of Israel, the women's inheritance will also be added to the inheritance of the tribe to which they then belong, so that their inheritance would be withdrawn from the inheritance of the tribe of our fathers."

5 Then Moses commanded the Israelites at the order of Jehovah: "What the tribe of the sons of Joseph is saying is correct. **6** This is the word that Jehovah has commanded for the daughters of Ze·lo′phe·had: 'They may marry whomever they wish. However, they should marry someone from a family of the tribe of their father. **7** No inheritance of the Israelites should circulate from tribe to tribe, for the Israelites should hold on to the inheritance of the tribe of their forefathers. **8** And every daughter who possesses an inheritance among the tribes of Israel should become a wife of a descendant of her father's tribe,[a] so that the Israelites may keep possession of the inheritance of their forefathers. **9** No inheritance should circulate from one tribe to another tribe, for the tribes of Israel should hold on to their own inheritance.'"

10 The daughters of Ze·lo′phe·had did just as Jehovah had commanded Moses.[b] **11** So Mah′lah, Tir′zah, Hog′lah, Mil′cah, and Noah, the daughters of Ze·lo′phe·had,[c] married the sons of their father's brothers. **12** They became wives of men from the families of Ma·nas′seh the son of Joseph so that their inheritance would remain in the tribe of their father's family.

13 These are the commandments and the judicial decisions that Jehovah gave to the Israelites through Moses on the desert plains of Mo′ab by the Jordan at Jer′i·cho.[d]

Second Col.

CHAP. 36
a 1Ch 23:22

b Nu 36:6

c Nu 27:1

d Nu 26:3
  Nu 33:50
  Nu 35:1

DEUTERONOMY

OUTLINE OF CONTENTS

1 These are the words that Moses spoke to all Israel in the region of the Jordan in the wilderness, on the desert plains in front of Suph, between Pa'ran, To'phel, La'ban, Ha·ze'roth, and Di'za·hab. **2** It is 11 days from Ho'reb to Ka'desh-bar'ne·a[a] by way of Mount Se'ir. **3** In the 40th year,[b] in the 11th month, on the first of the month, Moses spoke to the Israelites[*] according to all that Jehovah had instructed him to tell them. **4** This was after he defeated Si'hon[c] the king of the Am'or·ites, who was dwelling in Hesh'bon, and Og[d] the king of Ba'shan, who was dwelling in Ash'ta·roth, in Ed're·i.[e] **5** In the region of the Jordan in the land of Mo'ab, Moses undertook to explain this Law,[f] saying:

6 "Jehovah our God told us in Ho'reb, 'You have stayed long enough in this mountainous region.[g] **7** Turn and set out for the mountainous region of the Am'or·ites[h] and toward all their neighbors in the Ar'a·bah,[i] the mountainous region, the Sheph'e·lah, the Neg'eb, and the seacoast,[j] the land of the Ca'naan-

ites, and Leb'a·non,[*a] up to the great river, the river Eu·phra'tes.[b] **8** See, I have set the land before you. Go in and take possession of the land about which Jehovah swore to your fathers, to Abraham, Isaac,[c] and Jacob,[d] to give it to them and their offspring[*] after them.'[e]

9 "And I told you at that time, 'I am not able to carry you by myself.[f] **10** Jehovah your God has multiplied you, and here you are today as numerous as the stars of the heavens.[g] **11** May Jehovah, the God of your forefathers, multiply you[h] a thousand times as many as you are, and may he bless you just as he has promised you.[i] **12** How can I bear by myself the burden of you and the load of you and your quarreling?[j] **13** Select wise, discreet, and experienced men of your tribes, and I will appoint them as heads over you.'[k] **14** You answered me, 'What you have told us to do is good.' **15** So I took the heads of your tribes, wise and experienced men, and appointed them as heads over you, chiefs of thou-

CHAP. 1
a De 9:23
b Nu 32:13
  Nu 33:38
c Nu 21:23, 24
  Jos 12:1, 2
d Nu 21:33-35
e Jos 13:8, 12
f De 4:8
  De 17:18
g Ex 19:1
  Nu 10:11, 12
h Ge 15:16
i Jos 12:2, 3
j Jos 9:1, 2

Second Col.
a Jos 13:1, 5
  1Ki 9:19
b Ge 15:18
c Ge 26:3
d Ge 28:13
e Ge 12:7
  Ge 13:14, 15
  Ge 17:1, 7
f Ge 15:1, 5
  Ex 32:13
  Nu 26:51
  De 10:22
h 1Ki 3:8
i Ge 12:1-3
  Ge 22:15, 17
  Ge 26:3, 4
  Ex 23:25
j Ex 18:17, 18
  Nu 11:11
  Nu 20:3
k Ex 18:21

1:3 *Lit., "sons of Israel."

1:7 *Evidently, the Lebanon mountain range. 1:8 *Lit., "seed."

sands, chiefs of hundreds, chiefs of fifties, chiefs of tens, and officers of your tribes.[a]

16 "At that time I instructed your judges, 'When you hear a case between your brothers, you are to judge with righteousness[b] between a man and his brother or a foreign resident.[c] **17** You must not be partial in judgment.[d] You should hear the small one the same as the great one.[e] You must not become intimidated by men,[f] for the judgment belongs to God;[g] and if a case is too difficult for you, you should present it to me, and I will hear it.'[h] **18** At that time I instructed you regarding all the things that you should do.

19 "Then we departed from Ho'reb and marched through all that great and fearsome wilderness[i] that you saw on the way to the mountainous region of the Am'or·ites,[j] just as Jehovah our God had commanded us, and we eventually came to Ka'desh-bar'ne·a.[k] **20** I then said to you, 'You have come to the mountainous region of the Am'or·ites, which Jehovah our God is giving to us. **21** See, Jehovah your God has given the land over to you. Go up, take possession of it, just as Jehovah, the God of your forefathers, has told you.[l] Do not be afraid or terrified.'

22 "However, all of you approached me and said, 'Let us send men ahead of us to search out the land for us and bring word back to us as to what route we should take and what kind of cities we will encounter.'[m] **23** The suggestion seemed good to me, so I selected 12 of your men, one for each tribe.[n] **24** They left and went up into the mountainous region[o] and reached the Valley* of Esh'col and spied it out. **25** They took

some of the fruitage of the land and carried it back to us, and they brought word back to us, 'The land that Jehovah our God is giving us is good.'[a] **26** But you refused to go up, and you rebelled against the order of Jehovah your God.[b] **27** You kept grumbling in your tents and were saying, 'It was because Jehovah hated us that he brought us out of the land of Egypt to hand us over to the Am'or·ites to annihilate us. **28** What kind of place are we going to? Our brothers made us lose heart*[c] by saying, "They are a people greater and taller than we are, and their cities are great and fortified to the heavens,#[d] and we saw the sons of the An'a·kim[e] there."'

29 "So I said to you, 'Do not be struck with terror or be afraid because of them.[f] **30** Jehovah your God will go before you and will fight for you,[g] just as he did in Egypt before your very eyes.[h] **31** And you saw in the wilderness how Jehovah your God carried you just as a man carries his son, everywhere you went until you came to this place.' **32** But despite all of this, you did not put faith in Jehovah your God,[i] **33** who was going ahead of you on the way, to spy out a place for you to camp. He appeared by fire at night and by a cloud in the daytime to show you the way you should walk.[j]

34 "All the while Jehovah heard what you were saying, and he became indignant and solemnly swore,[k] **35** 'Not one of these men of this evil generation will see the good land that I swore to give to your fathers,[l] **36** except Ca'leb the son of Je·phun'neh. He will see it,

CHAP. 1
a Ex 18:25

b Ex 23:8
De 16:18
Joh 7:24

c Ex 22:21
Le 19:34
Le 24:22

d Le 19:15
Ro 2:11

e Ex 23:3

f Pr 29:25

g 2Ch 19:6

h Ex 18:25, 26

i Nu 10:12
De 8:14, 15
Jer 2:6

j Nu 13:29

k Nu 13:26

l Ex 23:27
De 1:8

m Nu 13:1, 2

n Nu 13:3

o Nu 13:17

Second Col.
a Nu 13:23-27

b Nu 14:1-4

c Nu 32:9
Jos 14:7, 8

d Nu 13:28, 33

e Nu 13:22
Jos 11:21

f Nu 14:9

g Ex 14:14
Jos 10:42

h Nu 14:22

i Ps 78:22
Ps 106:24
Heb 3:16, 19
Jude 5

j Ex 13:21
Ex 40:36
Nu 10:33, 34
Ps 78:14

k Nu 14:28, 35
Nu 32:10-12
De 2:14
Ps 95:11
Heb 3:11

l Nu 14:29, 35
1Co 10:1, 5
Heb 3:17

1:24 *Or "Wadi."

1:28 *Lit., "caused our heart to melt."
#That is, with towering walls.

and I will give the land on which he walked to him and to his sons, because he has followed Jehovah wholeheartedly.*[a] 37 (Jehovah even became angry with me because of you, and he said, "You too will not go in there.[b] 38 Joshua the son of Nun, who stands before you,[c] is the one who will enter into the land.[d] Make him strong,*[e] for he will cause Israel to inherit it.") 39 Moreover, your children whom you said would become plunder[f] and your sons who today do not know good or bad, these will enter, and I will give it to them to possess.[g] 40 But as for you, turn back and depart for the wilderness by the way of the Red Sea.'[h]

41 "At this you said to me, 'We have sinned against Jehovah. We will now go up and fight, just as Jehovah our God has commanded us!' So each of you put on his weapons of war, and you thought it would be an easy thing to go up the mountain.[i] 42 But Jehovah said to me, 'Tell them: "You must not go up and fight, for I will not be with you.[j] If you do, you will be defeated by your enemies."' 43 So I spoke to you, but you did not listen. Instead, you rebelled against Jehovah's order and presumptuously tried to go up the mountain. 44 Then the Am'or·ites who were dwelling in that mountain came out to meet you and chased you away like bees do, and they scattered you in Se'ir as far as Hor'mah. 45 So you returned and began to weep before Jehovah, but Jehovah did not listen to you or pay attention to you. 46 That is why you kept dwelling in Ka'desh for as long as you did.

1:36 *Lit., "fully; completely." 1:38 *Or possibly, "God has made him strong."

CHAP. 1
a Nu 14:24
Jos 14:9

b Nu 20:12
Nu 27:13, 14
De 3:26
Ps 106:32

c Ex 33:11
Nu 11:28

d Nu 14:38

e Nu 27:18
De 31:7
Jos 1:6, 9

f Nu 14:3

g Nu 14:30, 31

h Nu 14:25

i Nu 14:39-45

j Le 26:14, 17

Second Col.

CHAP. 2
a Nu 14:25

b Nu 20:14
De 23:7

c Ge 27:39, 40
Ge 36:8, 9

d Ex 15:15
Ex 23:27

e De 32:8
Jos 24:4
Ac 17:26

f Nu 20:18, 19

g De 29:5
Ne 9:21
Ps 23:1
Ps 34:9, 10

h Nu 20:20, 21

i 2Ch 8:17

j Nu 21:13
Jg 11:17, 18
2Ch 20:10

k Ge 19:36, 37

l Ge 14:5

m De 3:11
1Ch 20:6

2 "Then we turned and departed for the wilderness by the way of the Red Sea, just as Jehovah had told me,[a] and we traveled for many days around Mount Se'ir. 2 Finally Jehovah said to me, 3 'You have gone around this mountain long enough. Now turn north. 4 And give this command to the people: "You will pass by the border of your brothers, the descendants of E'sau,[b] who are dwelling in Se'ir,[c] and they will be afraid of you,[d] and you must be very careful. 5 Do not engage in hostilities with* them, for I will not give you any of their land, not even the space of a footprint, because I have given Mount Se'ir to E'sau as his possession.[e] 6 You should give them money for the food you will eat, and you should pay for the water you will drink.[f] 7 For Jehovah your God has blessed you in all that you have done. He is fully aware of your walking through this great wilderness. These 40 years Jehovah your God has been with you, and you have lacked nothing."'[g] 8 So we passed by our brothers, the descendants of E'sau,[h] who are dwelling in Se'ir, keeping away from the way of the Ar'a·bah, from E'lath and from E'zi·on·ge'ber.[i]

"Next we turned and traveled by the way of the wilderness of Mo'ab.[j] 9 Jehovah then said to me, 'Do not engage in hostilities or in war with Mo'ab, for I will not give you any of his land as a possession because I have given Ar as a possession to the descendants of Lot.[k] 10 (The E'mim[l] formerly lived there, a people great and numerous and tall like the An'a·kim. 11 The Reph'a·im[m] were also considered like the An'a-

---

2:5 *Or "Do not provoke."

kim,[a] and the Mo'ab·ites used to call them E'mim. **12** Previously, the Hor'ites[b] were living in Se'ir, but the descendants of E'sau dispossessed and annihilated them and settled in their place,[c] just as Israel will do to the land that is their possession, which Jehovah will certainly give to them.) **13** Now go and cross over the Valley* of Ze'red.' So we crossed over the Valley* of Ze'red.[d] **14** The time it took us to walk from Ka'desh-bar'ne·a until we crossed the Valley* of Ze'red was 38 years, until the entire generation of the men of war had perished from the camp, just as Jehovah had sworn to them.[e] **15** Jehovah's hand was against them to eliminate them from the camp until they had perished.[f]

16 "As soon as all the men of war had died off from among the people,[g] **17** Jehovah spoke to me again, saying, **18** 'Today you are to pass by the territory of Mo'ab, that is, Ar. **19** When you come near to the Am'mon·ites, do not harass or provoke them, for I will not give you any of the land of the Am'monites as a possession, because I have given it to the descendants of Lot as their possession.[h] **20** This too used to be considered the land of the Reph'a·im.[i] (The Reph'a·im formerly lived there, and the Am'mon·ites used to call them Zam·zum'mim. **21** They were a great and numerous and tall people like the An'a·kim;[j] but Jehovah annihilated them before the Am'monites, and these drove them out and settled in their place. **22** That is what he did for the descendants of E'sau, who now dwell in Se'ir,[k] when he annihilated the Hor'ites[l] from before them, so that they could dispossess them and dwell in their place to this

2:13, 14 * Or "Wadi."

CHAP. 2	
a	Nu 13:22, 33
b	Ge 14:6
	Ge 36:20
c	Ge 27:39, 40
d	Nu 21:12
e	Nu 14:33
	Nu 32:11
	De 1:35
	Ps 95:11
	Heb 3:18
	Jude 5
f	1Co 10:1, 5
g	Nu 26:63, 64
h	Ge 19:36, 38
	De 2:9
	Jg 11:15
	2Ch 20:10
	Ac 17:26
i	Ge 15:18-20
	De 3:11
j	Nu 13:33
	De 9:1, 2
k	Ge 36:8
l	Ge 14:6
	De 2:12

Second Col.	
a	Ge 10:19
b	Ge 10:13, 14
c	Nu 21:13
d	Nu 21:23
e	Ex 15:14
	Ex 23:27
	De 11:25
	Jos 2:9, 10
f	Jos 13:15, 18
	Jos 21:8, 37
g	De 20:10
h	Nu 21:21, 22
i	Ro 9:18
j	Nu 21:25
k	Nu 32:33
	Ps 135:10-12

very day. **23** As for the Av'vim, they had dwelled in settlements as far as Gaz'a[a] until the Caph'to·rim,[b] who came out from Caph'tor,* annihilated them and settled in their place.)

24 "'Get up, and make your way across the Ar'non Valley.*[c] See, I have given into your hand Si'hon[d] the Am'or·ite, king of Hesh'bon. So begin taking possession of his land, and engage him in war. **25** This day I will start to put the dread and the fear of you upon all the people under the heavens who hear the report about you. They will be disturbed and will tremble* because of you.'[e]

26 "Then I sent messengers from the wilderness of Ked'e·moth[f] to King Si'hon of Hesh'bon, with these peaceful words,[g] **27** 'Let me pass through your land. I will remain on the road and not turn to the right or to the left.[h] **28** I will eat only the food and drink only the water that you will sell to me. Just allow me to pass through on foot **29** —that is what the descendants of E'sau dwelling in Se'ir and the Mo'ab·ites dwelling in Ar did for me—until I pass over the Jordan into the land that Jehovah our God is giving to us.' **30** But King Si'hon of Hesh'bon did not let us pass through, because Jehovah your God allowed his spirit to become obstinate[i] and his heart to become hard, in order to give him into your hand as is now the case.[j]

31 "Then Jehovah said to me, 'See, I have already begun to give Si'hon and his land over to you. Start to take possession of his land.'[k] **32** When Si'hon came out along with all his people to meet us in battle

2:23 *That is, Crete. 2:24 *Or "Wadi Arnon." 2:25 *Or "have pains like those of childbirth."

at Ja'haz,[a] 33 Jehovah our God handed him over to us, so that we defeated him, his sons, and all his people. 34 We captured all his cities at that time and devoted every city to destruction, including men, women, and children.[b] 35 We plundered only the livestock for ourselves along with the spoils from the cities that we had captured. 36 From A·ro'er,[c] which is on the rim of the Ar'non Valley* (including the city that is in the valley), as far as Gil'e·ad, no town was beyond our reach. Jehovah our God handed them all over to us.[d] 37 However, you did not approach the land of the Am'mon·ites,[e] the whole bank of the Valley* of Jab'bok[f] and the cities of the mountainous region, or any other place forbidden by Jehovah our God.

3 "Then we turned and went up by way of Ba'shan. And Og, the king of Ba'shan, came out with all his people to meet us in battle at Ed're·i.[g] 2 So Jehovah said to me, 'Do not be afraid of him, for I will give him and all his people and his land into your hand, and you will do to him just as you did to Si'hon the king of the Am'or·ites, who lived in Hesh'bon.' 3 So Jehovah our God also gave King Og of Ba'shan and all his people into our hand, and we kept striking him down until none of his people survived. 4 We then captured all his cities. There was no town that we did not take from them —60 cities, all the region of Ar'gob, the kingdom of Og in Ba'shan.[h] 5 All these cities were fortified with high walls, gates, and bars, along with a great number of rural towns. 6 However, we devoted them to de-

struction,[a] just as we had done to King Si'hon of Hesh'bon, in devoting every city to destruction, including men, women, and children.[b] 7 And we took all the livestock and the spoil of the cities for ourselves.

8 "At that time we seized the land of the two Am'or·ite kings[c] who were in the region of the Jordan, from the Ar'non Valley* as far as Mount Her'mon[d] 9 (the mountain that the Si·do'ni·ans used to call Sir'i·on and the Am'or·ites used to call Se'nir), 10 all the cities of the tableland,* all Gil'e·ad, and all Ba'shan as far as Sal'e·cah and Ed're·i,[e] the cities of the kingdom that belonged to Og in Ba'shan. 11 For King Og of Ba'shan was the last remaining one of the Reph'a·im. His bier* was made of iron,[g] and it is still in Rab'bah of the Am'mon·ites. It is nine cubits[Δ] long and four cubits wide, by the standard cubit. 12 At that time we took possession of this land: from A·ro'er,[f] which is by the Ar'non Valley,* and half of the mountainous region of Gil'e·ad, and I have given its cities to the Reu'ben·ites and the Gad'ites.[g] 13 And the rest of Gil'e·ad and all Ba'shan of the kingdom of Og I have given to the half tribe of Ma·nas'seh.[h] All the region of Ar'gob, which belongs to Ba'shan, was known as the land of the Reph'a·im.

14 "Ja'ir[i] the son of Ma·nas'seh took all the region of Ar'gob[j] as far as the boundary of the Gesh'ur·ites and the Ma·ac'a·thites[k] and named those villages of Bashan after himself, Hav'voth-ja'ir,*[l] to this day. 15 And I have given Gil'e·ad to Ma'chir.[m] 16 And to the

---

CHAP. 2
a Nu 21:23, 24
　Jg 11:20

b De 20:16, 17

c De 3:12
　De 4:47, 48
　Jos 13:8, 9

d Ps 44:3

e De 3:16
　Jg 11:15

f Nu 21:23, 24

CHAP. 3
g Nu 21:33-35

h Nu 32:33
　De 29:7, 8
　Jos 13:29, 30

Second Col.
a Le 27:29

b Le 18:25

c Nu 32:33

d Jos 12:1, 2

e Nu 21:33

f Nu 32:34

g Nu 32:33

h Nu 32:39
　Jos 13:29-31
　1Ch 5:23

i 1Ch 2:22

j De 3:4

k Jos 13:13

l Nu 32:40, 41

m Nu 32:39
　Jos 17:1

2:36; 3:8, 12 *Or "Wadi Arnon." 2:37 *Or "Wadi."

3:10 *Or "plateau." 3:11 *Or "sarcophagus; coffin." #Or possibly, "black basalt." Δ A cubit equaled 44.5 cm (17.5 in.). See App. B14. 3:14 *Meaning "Tent Villages of Jair."

Reu'ben·ites and the Gad'ites,[a] I have given from Gil'e·ad to the Ar'non Valley,* with the middle of the valley as a boundary, and as far as Jab'bok, the valley that is the boundary of the Am'mon·ites, **17** and the Ar'a·bah and the Jordan and the border, from Chin'ne·reth to the Sea of the Ar'a·bah, the Salt Sea,* at the base of the slopes of Pis'gah toward the east.[b]

18 "I then gave you this command: 'Jehovah your God has given you this land to take possession of it. All your valiant men will take up arms and cross over before your brothers, the Israelites.[c] **19** Only your wives, your children, and your livestock (I well know that you have a great deal of livestock) will continue dwelling in the cities that I have given you, **20** until Jehovah gives your brothers rest, as he does for you, and they also have taken possession of the land that Jehovah your God will give them across the Jordan. Then you will come back, each one to his possession that I have given you.'[d]

21 "At that time I gave this command to Joshua:[e] 'You have seen with your own eyes what Jehovah your God has done to these two kings. Jehovah will do the same thing to all the kingdoms into which you will cross over.[f] **22** You must not be afraid of them, for Jehovah your God is the one fighting for you.'[g]

23 "At that time I pleaded with Jehovah, saying, **24** 'O Sovereign Lord Jehovah, you have begun to show your servant your greatness and your mighty arm,[h] for what god in the heavens or on the earth performs such mighty deeds as

you?[a] **25** Please let me pass over and see the good land that is across the Jordan, this good mountainous region and Leb'anon.'[b] **26** But Jehovah was still furious with me because of you,[c] and he would not listen to me. Rather, Jehovah said to me, 'Enough from you! Never speak to me again about this matter. **27** Go up to the top of Pis'gah,[d] and look to the west and north and south and east and view the land with your eyes, for you will not cross over this Jordan.[e] **28** Commission Joshua[f] and encourage him and strengthen him, because he is the one who will cross over[g] before this people and he is the one who will cause them to inherit the land that you will see.' **29** All this happened while we were dwelling in the valley in front of Beth-pe'or.[h]

4 "Now, O Israel, listen to the regulations and the judicial decisions that I am teaching you to observe, so that you may live[i] and go in and take possession of the land that Jehovah, the God of your forefathers, is giving you. **2** You must not add to the word that I am commanding you, neither must you take away from it,[j] so as to keep the commandments of Jehovah your God that I am commanding you.

3 "Your own eyes have seen what Jehovah did in the case of the Ba'al of Pe'or; Jehovah your God annihilated from your midst every man who walked after the Ba'al of Pe'or.[k] **4** But you who are holding fast to Jehovah your God are all alive today. **5** See, I have taught you regulations and judicial decisions,[l] just as Jehovah my God has commanded me, so that you may observe them in the land you will take possession of. **6** You must carefully follow them,[m] because this will show wisdom[n] and understanding[o] on your part before

---

CHAP. 3
a Nu 32:33
  Jos 22:9
b Nu 34:11, 12
c Nu 32:20-22
d Jos 1:14, 15
  Jos 22:4, 8
e Nu 11:28
  Nu 14:30
  Nu 27:18
  Jos 10:25
g Ex 14:14
  Ex 15:3
  De 1:30
  De 20:4
  Jos 10:42
h Ex 15:16
  De 11:2

Second Col.
a Ex 15:11
  2Sa 7:22
  1Ki 8:23
  Ps 86:8
  Jer 10:6, 7
b Ex 3:8
  De 1:7
  De 11:11, 12
c Nu 20:12
  Nu 27:13, 14
  De 4:21
  Ps 106:32
d Nu 27:12
e De 34:1, 4
f Nu 27:18-20
  De 1:38
  De 31:7
g Jos 1:1, 2
h De 4:45, 46
  De 34:5, 6

CHAP. 4
i Le 18:5
j De 12:32
  Pr 30:5, 6
  Re 22:18, 19
k Nu 25:5, 9
  Ps 106:28
  Ho 9:10
  1Co 10:7, 8
l Le 26:46
  Nu 30:16
  Nu 36:13
  De 6:1
m 1Ki 2:3
n Ps 111:10
o Ps 119:98,
  100

the peoples who will hear about all these regulations, and they will say, 'This great nation is undoubtedly a wise and understanding people.'[a] **7** For what great nation has gods as near to it as Jehovah our God is to us whenever we call on him?[b] **8** And what great nation has righteous regulations and judicial decisions like this entire Law that I am putting before you today?[c]

9 "Just be careful and watch yourself closely,* so that you may not forget the things that your eyes have seen and so that they may not depart from your heart all the days of your life. You must also make them known to your sons and to your grandsons.[d] **10** On the day that you stood before Jehovah your God in Ho′reb, Jehovah said to me, 'Congregate the people together to me so that I may let them hear my words,[e] in order that they may learn to fear me[f] all the days that they are alive on the ground and that they may teach their sons.'[g]

11 "So you came near and stood at the base of the mountain, and the mountain was burning with fire up to the very heavens;* there was darkness, cloud, and thick gloom.[h] **12** And Jehovah began to speak to you out of the fire.[i] You heard the sound of words, but you saw no form—there was only a voice.[k] **13** And he declared his covenant to you,[l] which he commanded you to observe—the Ten Commandments.*[m] Afterward, he wrote them on two tablets of stone.[n] **14** At that time Jehovah commanded me to teach you regulations and judicial decisions, which you are to observe in the

CHAP. 4
a 1Ki 4:34
　1Ki 10:4-7
　Da 1:19, 20

b Ex 25:8
　Le 26:12
　De 5:26
　2Sa 7:23

c Ps 147:19, 20

d Ge 18:19
　De 6:6, 7

e Ex 19:9

f Ex 20:20
　De 5:29

g Pr 22:6
　Eph 6:4

h Ex 19:18
　Heb 12:18, 19

i De 9:10

j Isa 40:18
　Joh 1:18
　Joh 4:24

k Ex 20:22

l Ex 19:5
　De 5:2
　De 9:9
　Heb 9:19, 20

m Ex 20:1
　Ex 34:28
　De 10:4

n Ex 24:12
　Ex 31:18
　Ex 32:19
　Ex 34:1

Second Col.
a Ex 20:4
　De 27:15
　Isa 40:18
　Ac 17:29
　1Co 10:14

b De 5:8
　Ro 1:22, 23

c 1Sa 5:4

d De 17:2, 3
　2Ki 17:16
　Eze 8:16

e Ex 19:5

f Ps 106:32

g Nu 20:12
　De 31:1, 2

h De 3:27

i Ex 24:3

j Ex 20:4

land you will enter to take possession of.

15 "Therefore, watch yourselves closely*—since you did not see any form on the day Jehovah spoke to you in Ho′reb out of the middle of the fire— **16** that you may not act corruptly by making for yourselves any carved image having the form of any symbol, the representation of male or female,[a] **17** the representation of any animal on the earth or the representation of any bird that flies in the sky,[b] **18** the representation of anything creeping on the ground or the representation of any fish in the waters under the earth.[c] **19** And when you raise your eyes to the heavens and see the sun and the moon and the stars—all the army of the heavens—do not get seduced and bow down to them and serve them.[d] Jehovah your God has given them to all the peoples under the whole heavens. **20** But you are the ones Jehovah took and brought out of the iron-smelting furnace, out of Egypt, to become the people of his personal possession,*[e] as you are today.

21 "Jehovah became angry with me because of you,[f] and he swore that I should not cross the Jordan or go into the good land that Jehovah your God is giving you as an inheritance.[g] **22** For I am to die in this land; I will not cross the Jordan,[h] but you will cross over and take possession of this good land. **23** Be careful that you do not forget the covenant of Jehovah your God that he made with you,[i] and do not make for yourselves a carved image, the form of anything forbidden to you by Jehovah your God.[j] **24** For Jehovah your God is a consuming fire,[a] a God who requires exclusive devotion.[b]

25 "If you become father to sons and grandsons and you have lived a long time in the land and you act ruinously and make a carved image[c] of any kind and you do what is evil in the eyes of Jehovah your God so as to offend him,[d] 26 I do take the heavens and the earth as witnesses against you today that you will surely and quickly perish from the land that you are crossing the Jordan to take possession of. You will not last long on it, but you will be utterly annihilated.[e] 27 Jehovah will scatter you among the peoples,[f] and just a few of you will survive[g] among the nations to which Jehovah will have driven you. 28 There you will have to serve gods of wood and stone made by human hands,[h] gods that cannot see or hear or eat or smell.

29 "If you search for Jehovah your God from there, you will certainly find him,[i] if you inquire for him with all your heart and with all your soul.*[j] 30 When you are in great distress and all these things have happened to you in later times, then you will return to Jehovah your God and listen to his voice.[k] 31 For Jehovah your God is a merciful God.[l] He will not desert you or bring you to ruin or forget the covenant that he swore to your forefathers.[m]

32 "Ask, now, about the former days before your time, from the day when God created man on the earth; search from one end of the heavens to the other end of the heavens. Has anything so great ever happened or has anything like it ever been heard of?[n] 33 Have any other people heard the voice of God speaking

out of the fire the way you have heard it and kept on living?[a] 34 Or has God ever attempted to take for himself a nation out of the midst of another nation along with judgments,* with signs, with miracles,[b] with war,[c] with a mighty hand,[d] with an outstretched arm, and with terrifying deeds,[e] as Jehovah your God did for you in Egypt before your very eyes? 35 You yourselves have been shown these things so you will know that Jehovah is the true God;[f] there is no other besides him.[g] 36 He made you hear his voice from the heavens to correct you, and on the earth he made you see his great fire, and his words you heard from out of the fire.[h]

37 "Because he loved your forefathers and has chosen their offspring* after them,[i] you were brought out of Egypt in his presence by his great power. 38 From before you he drove away nations greater and mightier than you, to bring you in and give you their land as an inheritance, as it is today.[j] 39 Know, therefore, on this day, and take it to heart that Jehovah is the true God in the heavens above and on the earth beneath.[k] There is no other.[l] 40 You must keep his regulations and his commandments that I am commanding you today, in order that it may go well with you and your sons after you, so that you may long remain in the land that Jehovah your God is giving you."[m]

41 At that time Moses set apart three cities on the eastern side of the Jordan.[n] 42 If any manslayer unintentionally kills his fellow man and he did not previously hate him,[o] he must flee to one of these cities and live.[p] 43 The cities are Be'zer[q] in the wilderness on the

CHAP. 4	
a	Ex 24:17
	De 9:3
	Heb 12:29
b	Ex 20:5
	Ex 34:14
	Nu 25:11
	Lu 10:27
c	Jg 18:30
	2Ki 21:1, 7
d	2Ki 17:16, 17
e	Le 18:24, 28
	Le 26:27, 32
f	De 28:64
	Ne 1:8
g	De 28:62
h	De 28:15, 36
	Jer 16:13
	Eze 20:39
i	2Ch 15:4, 15
j	De 30:1-3
	De 30:8-10
	1Ki 8:48, 49
	Jer 29:13
	Joe 2:12
k	2Ch 33:13
	Ne 1:9
l	Ex 34:6
	De 30:3
	2Ch 30:9
	Ne 9:31
	Isa 54:7
	Isa 55:7
m	Le 26:42
n	Ps 44:1

Second Col.	
a	De 5:26
b	Ex 7:3
c	Ex 15:3
d	Ex 13:3
e	De 26:8
	Ps 78:43-51
f	Ex 6:7
g	Ex 15:11
	De 32:39
	1Sa 2:2
	Isa 45:18
	Mr 12:32
h	Ex 19:18
	Ex 20:22
i	De 10:15
	Ps 105:6
j	Ex 23:28
	De 7:1
	De 9:1
	Jos 3:10
k	2Ch 20:6
	Isa 44:6
m	Ge 48:3, 4
n	Nu 35:14
o	Nu 35:22-24
p	Nu 35:11, 25
	De 19:4, 5
q	Jos 21:8, 36

4:29 *See Glossary.   4:34 *Or "trials." 4:37 *Lit., "seed."

tableland* for the Reu'ben·ites, Ra'moth[a] in Gil'e·ad for the Gad'-ites, and Go'lan[b] in Ba'shan for the Ma·nas'sites.[c]

44 Now this is the Law[d] that Moses set before the people of Israel. **45** These are the reminders, the regulations, and the judicial decisions that Moses gave to the Israelites after they came out of Egypt,[e] **46** in the region of the Jordan, in the valley opposite Beth-pe'or,[f] in the land of King Si'hon of the Am'or-ites, who was dwelling in Hesh'-bon,[g] whom Moses and the Israelites defeated after coming out of Egypt.[h] **47** And they took possession of his land and of the land of King Og[i] of Ba'shan, the two kings of the Am'or·ites who were in the region east of the Jordan, **48** from A·ro'er,[j] which is on the rim of the Ar'non Valley,* up to Mount Si'on, that is, Her'mon,[k] **49** and all the Ar'a-bah in the region east of the Jordan, and as far as the Sea of the Ar'a·bah,* at the base of the slopes of Pis'gah.[l]

5 Moses then summoned all Israel and said to them: "Hear, O Israel, the regulations and the judicial decisions that I am announcing to you today, and you must learn them and carefully observe them. **2** Jehovah our God made a covenant with us in Ho'reb.[m] **3** It was not with our forefathers that Jehovah made this covenant, but with us, all of us alive here today. **4** Jehovah spoke face-to-face with you in the mountain, out of the fire.[n] **5** I was standing between Jehovah and you at that time[o] to convey to you the word of Jehovah, for you were afraid because of the fire and did not go up the mountain.[p] He said:

6 "'I am Jehovah your God, who brought you out of the land of Egypt, out of the house of slavery.[a] **7** You must never have any other gods besides me.*[b]

8 "'You must not make for yourself a carved image[c] or a form* like anything that is in the heavens above or on the earth below or in the waters under the earth. **9** You must not bow down to them nor be led to serve them,[d] for I, Jehovah your God, am a God who requires exclusive devotion,[e] bringing punishment for the error of fathers upon sons, upon the third generation and upon the fourth generation of those who hate me,[f] **10** but showing loyal love* to the thousandth generation of those who love me and keep my commandments.

11 "'You must not take up the name of Jehovah your God in a worthless way,[g] for Jehovah will not leave anyone unpunished who takes up his name in a worthless way.[h]

12 "'Observe the Sabbath day to keep it sacred, just as Jehovah your God commanded you.[i] **13** You are to labor and do all your work in six days,[j] **14** but the seventh day is a sabbath to Jehovah your God.[k] You must not do any work,[l] neither you nor your son nor your daughter nor your slave man nor your slave girl nor your bull nor your donkey nor any of your domestic animals nor your foreign resident who is inside your cities,*[m] in order that your slave man and your slave girl may rest the same as you.[n] **15** Remember that you became a slave in the land of Egypt and that Jehovah your God brought you out of there

---

CHAP. 4
a Jos 21:8, 38
b Jos 21:27
c Jos 20:8, 9
d De 17:18
  De 27:2, 3
  Ga 3:24
e Le 26:46
  De 4:1
f De 1:5
  De 3:29
g Nu 21:26
h Nu 21:23, 24
i Nu 21:33
  De 3:4
j De 2:36
  De 3:12
k De 3:8, 9
l De 3:16, 17
  De 34:1

CHAP. 5
m Ex 19:5
  Heb 9:19, 20
n Ex 19:9, 18
  Ac 7:38
o Ex 20:19
  Ga 3:19
p Ex 19:16

Second Col.
a Ex 13:3
  Ex 20:2
b Ex 20:3-6
  2Ki 17:35
c Le 26:1
  De 4:15, 16
  De 4:23
  De 27:15
  Ac 17:29
d Ex 23:24
  1Co 10:14
e Ex 34:14
  De 4:24
  Isa 42:8
  Mt 4:10
f Ex 34:6, 7
  Le 19:12
h Ex 20:7
  Le 24:16
i Ex 16:23
  Ex 20:8-10
  Ex 31:13
j Ex 34:21
k Ex 16:29
l Ne 13:15
m Ex 23:12
n De 10:17
  Eph 6:9

4:43 *Or "plateau." 4:48 *Or "Wadi Arnon." 4:49 *That is, the Salt Sea, or the Dead Sea.

5:7 *Or "in defiance of me." Lit., "against my face." 5:8 *Or "representation." 5:10 *Or "loving-kindness." 5:14 *Lit., "gates."

with a mighty hand and an out-stretched arm.[a] That is why Jehovah your God commanded you to observe the Sabbath day.

16 "'Honor your father and your mother,[b] just as Jehovah your God has commanded you, so that you may live a long time and you may prosper* in the land that Jehovah your God is giving you.[c]

17 "'You must not murder.[d]

18 "'Neither must you commit adultery.[e]

19 "'Neither must you steal.[f]

20 "'Neither must you testify to a falsehood against your fellow man.[g]

21 "'Neither must you desire your fellow man's wife.[h] Neither must you selfishly desire your fellow man's house nor his field nor his slave man nor his slave girl nor his bull nor his donkey nor anything that belongs to your fellow man.'[i]

22 "These commandments* Jehovah spoke to all your congregation on the mountain, out of the fire, the cloud, and the thick gloom,[j] with a loud voice, and he added nothing further; then he wrote them on two tablets of stone and gave them to me.[k]

23 "But as soon as you had heard the voice out of the darkness, while the mountain was burning with fire,[l] all the heads of your tribes and the elders approached me. **24** Then you said, 'Here Jehovah our God has shown us his glory and his greatness, and we have heard his voice out of the fire.[m] Today we have seen that God can speak with man and he can keep living.[n] **25** Now, why should we die? For this great fire may consume us. If we continue hearing the voice of Jehovah our God,

we are sure to die. **26** For who is there of all flesh* who has heard the voice of the living God speaking out of the fire as we did and yet goes on living? **27** You yourself must go near to hear all that Jehovah our God will say, and you will be the one to tell us all that Jehovah our God says to you, and we will listen and do it.'[a]

28 "So Jehovah heard the words you spoke to me, and Jehovah said to me, 'I have heard the words that this people have spoken to you. All they have said is good.[b] **29** If only they would always have a heart inclined to fear me[c] and to keep all my commandments;[d] then it would go well with them and their sons forever![e] **30** Go say to them: "Return to your tents." **31** But you should stay here with me, and let me tell you all the commandments, the regulations, and the judicial decisions that you should teach to them and that they are to observe in the land that I am giving them to take possession of.' **32** Now you people should be careful to do just as Jehovah your God has commanded you.[f] You must not turn to the right or to the left.[g] **33** You should walk in all the way that Jehovah your God has commanded you,[h] in order that you may live and prosper and prolong your days in the land that you will take possession of.[i]

6 "Now these are the commandments, the regulations, and the judicial decisions that Jehovah your God has given to teach you, so that you may observe them when you cross over into the land that you are to take possession of, **2** in order that you may fear Jehovah your God and keep all his statutes and his commandments that I

CHAP. 5

a Ex 6:6
  De 4:34
b Ex 21:15
  Le 19:3
  De 27:16
  Pr 1:8
  Mr 7:10
c Ex 20:12
  Eph 6:2, 3
d Ge 9:6
  Ex 20:13
  Nu 35:20, 21
  Mt 5:21
  Ro 13:9
e Ex 20:14
  1Co 6:18
  Heb 13:4
f Ex 20:15
  Le 19:11
  Pr 30:8, 9
  1Co 6:10
  Eph 4:28
g Ex 20:16
  Ex 23:1
  Le 19:16
  De 19:16-19
  Pr 6:16, 19
  Pr 19:5
h Mt 5:28
i Ex 20:17
  Lu 12:15
  Ro 7:7
j Ex 19:9, 18
k Ex 24:12
  Ex 31:18
  De 4:12, 13
l Ex 20:18
  Heb 12:18, 19
m Ex 24:17
n De 4:33, 36

Second Col.

a Ex 20:19
  Heb 12:18, 19
b De 18:16, 17
c De 10:12
  Job 28:28
  Pr 1:7
  Mt 10:28
  1Pe 2:17
d Pr 4:4
  Pr 7:2
  Ec 12:13
  Isa 48:18
  1Jo 5:3
e Ps 19:8, 11
  Jas 1:25
f De 6:3, 25
  De 8:1
g De 12:32
  Jos 1:7, 8
h De 10:12
i De 4:40
  De 12:28
  Ro 10:5

5:16 *Or "and it may go well with you."
5:22 *Lit., "words."

5:26 *Or "all mankind."

am commanding you—you and your son and your grandson[a]—all the days of your life, so that you may live a long time.[b] 3 And you must listen, O Israel, and carefully observe them, so that you may prosper and become very many in the land flowing with milk and honey, just as Jehovah, the God of your forefathers, has promised you.

4 "Listen, O Israel: Jehovah our God is one Jehovah.[c] 5 You must love Jehovah your God with all your heart and all your soul*[d] and all your strength."[e] 6 These words that I am commanding you today must be on your heart, 7 and you must inculcate them in* your sons[f] and speak of them when you sit in your house and when you walk on the road and when you lie down and when you get up.[g] 8 Tie them as a reminder on your hand, and they must be like a headband on your forehead.*[h] 9 Write them on the doorposts of your house and on your gates.

10 "When Jehovah your God brings you into the land that he swore to your forefathers Abraham, Isaac, and Jacob to give you[i]—great and fine cities that you did not build,[j] 11 houses full of all sorts of good things that you did not work for, hewn cisterns that you did not dig, and vineyards and olive trees that you did not plant—and you have eaten and become satisfied,[k] 12 be careful not to forget Jehovah,[l] who brought you out of the land of Egypt, out of the house of slavery. 13 Jehovah your God you should fear,[m] and him you should serve,[n] and by his name you should swear.[o] 14 You must not follow after other gods, any gods of

the peoples who are all around you,[a] 15 for Jehovah your God who is in your midst is a God who requires exclusive devotion.[b] Otherwise, the anger of Jehovah your God will blaze against you[c] and he will annihilate you from the face of the earth.[d]

16 "You must not put Jehovah your God to the test[e] the way you put him to the test at Mas'sah.[f] 17 You should diligently observe the commandments of Jehovah your God and his reminders and his regulations that he has commanded you to observe. 18 You must do what is right and good in Jehovah's eyes, in order that you may prosper and that you may enter and take possession of the good land about which Jehovah has sworn to your forefathers,[g] 19 by driving out all your enemies from before you, just as Jehovah has promised.[h]

20 "In the future, when your son asks you, 'What is the meaning of the reminders, the regulations, and the judicial decisions that Jehovah our God has commanded you?' 21 then you will say to your son, 'We became slaves to Phar'aoh in Egypt, but Jehovah brought us out of Egypt with a mighty hand. 22 So before our eyes Jehovah kept sending signs and miracles, great and devastating, upon Egypt,[i] upon Phar'aoh, and upon all his household.[j] 23 And he brought us out from there in order to bring us here to give us the land about which he had sworn to our forefathers.[k] 24 Then Jehovah commanded us to carry out all these regulations and to fear Jehovah our God for our lasting good,[l] so that we could keep alive,[m] as we are today. 25 And it will mean righteousness for us if we are careful to observe all these com-

CHAP. 6
a Ge 18:19
  De 4:9
b Pr 3:1, 2
c De 5:7
  Isa 42:8
  Zec 14:9
  Mr 12:29, 32
  1Co 8:6
d De 10:12
  De 11:13
  De 30:6
  Mt 22:37
e Mr 12:30, 33
  Lu 10:27
f Ge 18:19
  De 4:9
  Pr 22:6
  Eph 6:4
g De 11:19
h De 11:18
i Ge 15:18
j Jos 24:13
  Ps 105:44
k De 8:10
l Jg 3:7
m De 10:12
  De 13:4
n Lu 4:8
o Jer 12:16

Second Col.
a Ex 34:14
b Ex 20:5
  De 4:24
c Ex 32:9, 10
  Nu 25:3
  De 11:16, 17
  Jg 2:14
d 2Ki 17:18
e Mt 4:7
  Lu 4:12
  1Co 10:9
f Ex 17:2, 7
  Ps 95:8, 9
  Heb 3:8, 9
g Ge 15:18
h Ex 23:30
i Ex 7:3
j De 4:34
k Ex 13:5
  De 1:8
l Ps 111:10
  Pr 14:27
m Le 18:5
  De 4:1
  Ga 3:12

6:5 *See Glossary. #Or "vital force; resources." 6:7 *Or "repeat them to; impress them upon." 6:8 *Lit., "between your eyes."

mandments in obedience to* Jehovah our God, just as he has commanded us.'[a]

7 "When Jehovah your God brings you into the land you are about to enter and take possession of,[b] he will also clear away populous nations from before you:[c] the Hit′tites, the Gir′ga·shites, the Am′or·ites,[d] the Ca′naan·ites, the Per′iz·zites, the Hi′vites, and the Jeb′u·sites,[e] seven nations more populous and mightier than you are.[f] **2** Jehovah your God will give them over to you, and you will defeat them.[g] You should without fail devote them to destruction.[h] You must not make any covenant with them nor show them any favor.[i] **3** You must not form any marriage alliances* with them. Do not give your daughters to their sons or take their daughters for your sons.[j] **4** For they will turn your sons away from following me to serve other gods;[k] then Jehovah's anger will blaze against you, and he will swiftly annihilate you.[l]

5 "Instead, this is what you should do to them: Tear down their altars, break up their sacred pillars,[m] cut down their sacred poles,*[n] and burn up their graven images.[o] **6** For you are a holy people to Jehovah your God, and Jehovah your God has chosen you to become his people, his special property,* out of all the peoples who are on the face of the earth.[p]

7 "It was not because you were the most numerous of all the peoples that Jehovah showed affection for you and chose you,[q] for you were the smallest of all the peoples.[r] **8** Rather, it was because of Jehovah's love for you and because he kept the oath that he had sworn to your forefathers[a] that Jehovah brought you out with a mighty hand, to redeem you from the house of slavery,[b] from the power* of Phar′aoh king of Egypt. **9** You well know that Jehovah your God is the true God, the faithful God, keeping his covenant and loyal love to a thousand generations of those who love him and keep his commandments.[c] **10** But those who hate him he will repay to their face with destruction.[d] He will not be slow to deal with those who hate him; he will repay them to their face. **11** Therefore, take care to keep the commandments and the regulations and the judicial decisions that I am commanding you today, by observing them.

12 "If you continue listening to these judicial decisions and you observe them and carry them out, Jehovah your God will keep the covenant and the loyal love about which he swore to your forefathers. **13** He will love you and bless you and multiply you. Yes, he will bless you with many children*[e] and with the produce of your soil, your grain, your new wine, your oil,[f] the calves of your herds and the lambs of your flocks, in the land that he swore to your forefathers to give to you.[g] **14** You will become the most blessed of all the peoples;[h] no man or woman among you will be childless, nor will your livestock be without young.[i] **15** Jehovah will take away from you all sickness, and he will not bring upon you any of the terrible diseases that you have known in Egypt.[j] Instead, he will bring them upon all those who hate you. **16** You are to destroy* all the peoples whom Jehovah your God gives

CHAP. 6
a Ec 12:13; Ro 10:5

CHAP. 7
b De 31:3
c Ex 33:2; Jos 3:10
d Ge 15:16
e Ge 10:15-17
f De 20:1
g Nu 33:52
h Le 27:29; Jos 6:17; Jos 10:28
i Ex 23:32; Ex 34:15; De 20:16, 17
j Jos 23:12, 13; 1Ki 11:1, 2; Ezr 9:2
k Ex 34:16; 1Ki 11:4
l De 6:14, 15
m Ex 23:24; Ex 34:13
n De 16:21, 22
o De 7:25; De 12:2, 3
p Ex 19:5, 6; De 14:2; Am 3:2
q De 10:15
r De 10:22

Second Col.
a Ge 22:16, 17
b Ex 6:6; Ex 13:3, 14
c Ex 34:6, 7
d Pr 2:22; 2Pe 3:7
e Le 26:9
f Le 26:4
g Ge 13:14, 15
h De 33:29; Ps 147:20
i Ex 23:26; De 28:11; Ps 127:3
j De 28:15, 27

6:25 *Lit., "before." **7:3** *Or "not intermarry." **7:5** *See Glossary. **7:6** *Or "treasured possession."

7:8 *Lit., "hand." **7:13** *Lit., "bless the fruit of your womb." **7:16** *Lit., "devour."

over to you.[a] You* must not feel sorry for them,[b] and you must not serve their gods,[c] because that would be a snare to you.[d]

17 "If you should say in your heart, 'These nations outnumber us. How can I drive them away?'[e] you must not be afraid of them.[f] You should remind yourself of what Jehovah your God did to Phar′aoh and all Egypt,[g] 19 the great judgments* that your eyes saw and the signs and the miracles[h] and the mighty hand and the outstretched arm with which Jehovah your God brought you out.[i] That is what Jehovah your God will do to all the peoples you fear.[j] 20 Jehovah your God will send the feeling of dejection* upon them until those who were left remaining[k] and who were concealing themselves from before you perish. 21 Do not be struck with terror because of them, for Jehovah your God is with you,[l] a great and awe-inspiring God.[m]

22 "Jehovah your God will certainly drive these nations away from before you little by little.[n] You will not be allowed to put an end to them quickly, so that the wild animals of the field will not multiply against you. 23 Jehovah your God will give them over to you and utterly defeat them until they are annihilated.[o] 24 He will give their kings into your hand,[p] and you will wipe out their names from under the heavens.[q] Nobody will stand up to you,[r] until you have exterminated them.[s] 25 You should burn the graven images of their gods in the fire.[t] Do not desire the silver and the gold on them or take it for yourself,[u] so that you are not ensnared by it, for it is some-

thing detestable to Jehovah your God.[a] 26 You must not bring a detestable thing into your house and thereby become something devoted to destruction like it. You should utterly loathe it and absolutely detest it, because it is something devoted to destruction.

8 "You should be careful to observe every commandment that I am giving you today, so that you may continue living[b] and multiply and go in and take possession of the land about which Jehovah swore to your forefathers.[c] 2 Remember the long road that Jehovah your God made you walk these 40 years in the wilderness,[d] to humble you and to put you to the test[e] so as to know what was in your heart,[f] whether you would keep his commandments or not. 3 So he humbled you and let you go hungry[g] and fed you with the manna,[h] which neither you had known nor your fathers had known, in order to make you know that man does not live by bread alone but man lives by every expression from Jehovah's mouth.[i] The clothing you wore did not wear out, nor did your feet become swollen these 40 years.[j] 5 You well know in your heart that just as a man corrects his son, Jehovah your God was correcting you.[k]

6 "Now you must keep the commandments of Jehovah your God by walking in his ways and by fearing him. 7 For Jehovah your God is bringing you into a good land,[l] a land of streams of water,* springs and fountains# flowing in the valley plain and in the mountainous region, 8 a land of wheat and barley, of grapevines, fig trees, and pomegranates,[m] a land of olive oil and

---

CHAP. 7

a De 7:1, 2
 De 20:16
 Jos 10:28
b Ge 15:16
 Le 18:25
 De 9:5
c Ex 20:3
d Ex 23:33
 De 12:30
 Jg 2:2, 3
 Ps 106:36
e Nu 13:31
f De 1:29
 De 31:6
 Ps 27:1
 Isa 41:10
g Ex 14:13
h Ne 9:10, 11
 Jer 32:20
i De 4:34
j Ex 23:28
 Jos 3:10
k Ex 23:29
 De 2:25
 Jos 2:9
 Jos 24:12
l Nu 14:9
m De 10:17
 1Sa 4:7, 8
n Ex 23:30
o De 9:3
p Jos 10:24
 Jos 12:1
q Ex 17:14
 Ps 9:5
r De 11:25
 Jos 1:5
 Ro 8:31
s Jos 11:14
t De 12:3
 1Ch 14:12
u Isa 30:22

Second Col.

a De 27:15

CHAP. 8

b Pr 3:1, 2
c Ge 15:18
d De 2:7
e Ex 16:4
 Ex 20:20
f De 13:3
 Pr 17:3
g Ex 16:3
h Ex 16:31
 Ps 78:24
i Mt 4:4
j De 29:5
 Ne 9:21
k Pr 3:12
 1Co 11:32
 Heb 12:5-7
 Re 3:19
l Ex 3:8
 Le 26:4
 De 11:11, 12
m Nu 13:23

7:16 *Lit., "Your eye." 7:19 *Or "trials." 7:20 *Or possibly, "panic; terror."

8:7 *Or "wadis of water." #Or "deep water sources."

honey,[a] **9** a land where food will not be scarce and you will lack nothing, a land where the stones contain iron and from its mountains you will mine copper.

10 "When you have eaten and are satisfied, you must praise Jehovah your God for the good land that he has given you.[b] **11** Be careful not to forget Jehovah your God by failing to keep his commandments, his judicial decisions, and his statutes that I am commanding you today. **12** When you eat and are satisfied and you build fine houses and dwell in them,[c] **13** when your herd and your flocks multiply and your silver and gold increase and you have an abundance of everything, **14** do not let your heart become proud[d] and cause you to forget Jehovah your God, who brought you out of the land of Egypt, out of the house of slavery,[e] **15** who caused you to walk through the great and fearsome wilderness,[f] with poisonous serpents and scorpions and with parched ground that has no water. He made water flow out of the flinty rock[g] **16** and fed you with manna[h] in the wilderness, which your fathers had not known, in order to humble you[i] and to put you to the test so as to benefit you in the future.[j] **17** If you should say in your heart, 'My own power and the strength of my own hand have produced this wealth for me,'[k] **18** remember that it is Jehovah your God who gives power to you to make wealth,[l] in order to carry out his covenant that he swore to your forefathers, as it is today.[m]

19 "If you should ever forget Jehovah your God and you walk after other gods and serve them and bow down to them, I do bear witness against you today that you will surely perish.[n] **20** Like

the nations that Jehovah is destroying before you, that is how you will perish, because you would not listen to the voice of Jehovah your God.[a]

9 "Hear, O Israel, today you are crossing the Jordan[b] to go in and dispossess nations greater and mightier than you,[c] cities great and fortified to the heavens,*[d] **2** a people great and tall, the sons of the An′a-kim,[e] about whom you know and have heard it said, 'Who can stand up to the sons of A′nak?' **3** Therefore, you should know this day that Jehovah your God will cross ahead of you.[f] He is a consuming fire,[g] and he will annihilate them. He will subdue them before your eyes so that you may quickly drive them out* and destroy them, just as Jehovah has promised you.[h]

4 "Do not say in your heart when Jehovah your God drives them away from before you, 'It was because of my own righteousness that Jehovah has brought me in to take possession of this land.'[i] Rather, it is because of the wickedness of these nations[j] that Jehovah is driving them away from before you. **5** It is not because of your righteousness or the uprightness of your heart that you are going in to take possession of their land. Instead, it is because of the wickedness of these nations that Jehovah your God is driving them away from before you[k] and in order to carry out the word that Jehovah swore to your forefathers, Abraham,[l] Isaac,[m] and Jacob.[n] **6** Know, then, that it is not because of your righteousness that Jehovah your God is giving you this good land to take possession of, because you are an obstinate* people.[o]

CHAP. 8	
a	Eze 20:6
b	De 6:10-12
c	Ho 13:6
d	De 9:4
	De 32:15
e	Ps 106:21
f	De 1:19
	Jer 2:6
g	Nu 20:11
h	Ex 16:35
i	De 8:2
j	Heb 12:11
k	Ho 12:8
l	Ps 127:1
	Ho 2:8
m	De 7:12
n	De 4:25, 26
	De 30:17, 18
	Jos 23:12, 13

Second Col.	
a	Da 9:11, 12
CHAP. 9	
b	Jos 4:19
c	De 7:1
d	Nu 13:28
e	Nu 13:33
f	De 1:30
	De 20:4
	De 31:3
g	De 4:24
	Heb 12:29
h	Ex 23:31
	De 7:23, 24
i	De 7:7, 8
	Eze 36:22
j	Ge 15:16
	De 12:31
	De 18:9, 12
k	Le 18:25
l	Ge 13:14, 15
	Ge 17:1, 8
m	Ge 26:3
n	Ge 28:13
o	Ex 34:9
	Ps 78:8

9:1 *That is, with towering walls. **9:3** *Or "dispossess them." **9:6** *Lit., "stiff-necked."

7 "Remember—never forget—the way you provoked Jehovah your God in the wilderness.[a] From the day that you left the land of Egypt until your coming to this place, you have rebelled against Jehovah.[b] 8 Even in Ho′reb you provoked Jehovah, and Jehovah was so angry with you that he was ready to annihilate you.[c] 9 When I went up the mountain to receive the stone tablets,[d] the tablets of the covenant that Jehovah made with you,[e] I remained on the mountain 40 days and 40 nights,[f] eating no food and drinking no water. 10 Then Jehovah gave me the two tablets of stone written on with God's finger, and on them were all the words that Jehovah had spoken to you on the mountain out of the fire in the day of the assembly.*[g] 11 At the end of the 40 days and 40 nights, Jehovah gave me the two tablets of stone, the tablets of the covenant, 12 and Jehovah told me, 'Get up, go down quickly from here, because your people whom you brought out of Egypt have acted corruptly.[h] They have quickly turned aside from the path I commanded them to follow. They have made a metal image* for themselves.'[i] 13 Jehovah then said to me, 'I have seen this people, and look! it is an obstinate* people.[j] 14 Let me be, and I will annihilate them and wipe out their name from under the heavens, and let me make you a nation mightier and more numerous than they are.'[k]

15 "Then I turned and went down the mountain while the mountain was burning with fire,[l] and the two tablets of the covenant were in both my hands.[m]

16 Then I looked and saw that you had sinned against Jehovah your God! You had made a metal* calf for yourselves. You had turned aside quickly from the path Jehovah had commanded you to follow.[a] 17 So I took hold of the two tablets and threw them down with both my hands and shattered them before your eyes.[b] 18 Then I prostrated myself before Jehovah, as at first, for 40 days and 40 nights. I neither ate food nor drank water,[c] because of all the sins that you had committed by your doing what was evil in Jehovah's eyes and offending him. 19 For I was terrified because of Jehovah's great anger against you,[d] in that he was ready to annihilate you. However, Jehovah listened to me that time also.[e]

20 "Jehovah was so angry with Aaron that he was ready to annihilate him,[f] but I made supplication for Aaron at that time also. 21 Then I took the sinful thing you made, the calf,[g] and burned it up in the fire; I crushed it and ground it thoroughly until it was fine like dust, and I threw the dust into the stream that flows down from the mountain.[h]

22 "Further, at Tab′e·rah,[i] at Mas′sah,[j] and at Kib′roth-hat·ta′a·vah,[k] you also provoked Jehovah to anger. 23 When Jehovah sent you out of Ka′desh-bar′ne·a[a] and said, 'Go up and take possession of the land that I will certainly give you!' you again rebelled against the order of Jehovah your God,[m] and you did not exercise faith[n] in him and did not obey him. 24 You have rebelled against Jehovah ever since I have known you.

25 "So I kept prostrating myself before Jehovah 40 days and 40 nights,[o] for I prostrated my-

---

CHAP. 9

a De 9:22
  Ps 78:40
  Heb 3:16

b Ex 17:2
  Nu 11:4
  Nu 16:1, 2
  Nu 25:2, 3
  De 31:27

c Ex 32:4, 10

d Ex 24:12
  Ex 31:18
  Ex 32:16

e Ex 24:7

f Ex 24:18

g Ex 19:19
  De 4:10-13

h Ex 32:7

i Ex 32:4

j Ex 32:9

k Ex 32:10

l Ex 19:18

m Ex 32:15

Second Col.

a Ex 20:3, 4

b Ex 32:19

c Ex 34:28

d Ex 32:10

e Ex 32:11, 14
  Ps 106:23

f Ex 32:2, 21

g Ex 32:4

h Ex 32:20

i Nu 11:3

j Ex 17:7

k Nu 11:4, 34

l Nu 13:26

m Nu 14:3, 4

n De 1:32
  Ps 106:24, 25
  Heb 3:19

o Ex 34:28

9:10 *Or "congregation." 9:12 *Or "molten statue." 9:13 *Lit., "stiffnecked."

9:16 *Or "molten."

self in this way because Jehovah said he would annihilate you. **26** I began to make supplication to Jehovah and to say, 'O Sovereign Lord Jehovah, do not bring your people to ruin. They are your personal possession,*[a] whom you redeemed through your greatness and brought out of Egypt with a mighty hand.[b] **27** Remember your servants Abraham, Isaac, and Jacob.[c] Do not pay attention to the stubbornness of this people, their wickedness, and their sin.[d] **28** Otherwise the people of the land from which you brought us may say: "Jehovah was unable to bring them into the land that he promised them, and because he hated them, he brought them out to put them to death in the wilderness."[e] **29** For they are your people and your personal possession,*[f] whom you brought out with your great power and your outstretched arm.'[g]

10 "At that time Jehovah said to me, 'Carve out for yourself two tablets of stone like the first ones,[h] and come up to me on the mountain; also you must make for yourself an ark* of wood. **2** And I will write on the tablets the words that appeared on the first tablets, which you shattered, and you should place them in the ark.' **3** So I made an ark of acacia wood and carved out two tablets of stone like the first ones and went up the mountain with the two tablets in my hand.[i] **4** Then he wrote on the tablets the words he had written before,[j] the Ten Commandments,*[k] which Jehovah had spoken to you on the mountain out of the fire[l] on the day of the assembly;*[m] and Je-

hovah gave them to me. **5** Then I turned and went down the mountain[a] and placed the tablets in the ark that I had made, where they remain, just as he had commanded me.

6 "The Israelites then departed from Be·er'oth Ben'e·ja'a·kan for Mo·se'rah. There Aaron died and was buried,[b] and his son El·e·a'zar began to serve as priest in his place.[c] **7** From there they departed for Gud'go·dah, and from Gud'go·dah for Jot'ba·thah,[d] a land flowing with streams of water.*

8 "At that time Jehovah set apart the tribe of Le'vi[e] to carry the ark of Jehovah's covenant,[f] to stand before Jehovah in order to minister to him, and to bless in his name,[g] as they do to this day. **9** That is why Le'vi has no share or inheritance with his brothers. Jehovah is his inheritance, just as Jehovah your God had said to him.[h] **10** I myself stayed on the mountain as I did the first time, 40 days and 40 nights,[i] and Jehovah listened to me on that occasion also.[j] Jehovah did not want to destroy you. **11** Then Jehovah said to me, 'Go ahead of the people, and prepare to depart, so that they may go in and take possession of the land that I have sworn to their forefathers to give to them.'[k]

12 "Now, O Israel, what is Jehovah your God asking of you?[l] Only this: to fear Jehovah your God,[m] to walk in all his ways,[n] to love him, to serve Jehovah your God with all your heart and all your soul,*[o] **13** and to keep the commandments and statutes of Jehovah that I am commanding you today for your own good.[p] **14** Look, to Jehovah your God belong the heavens, even the

---

9:26, 29 *Or "your inheritance." 10:1 *Or "chest." 10:4 *Lit., "the Ten Words." Also known as the Decalogue. #Or "congregation."

CHAP. 9
a Ex 19:5
Ps 135:4
b Ex 32:11
c Ex 3:6
Ex 6:8
De 9:5
d Ex 32:31, 32
e Ex 32:12
Nu 14:15, 16
f 1Ki 8:51
Ne 1:10
g Ex 6:6
De 4:20, 34

CHAP. 10
h Ex 34:1
i Ex 34:4
j Ex 32:15
k Ex 20:1
Ex 34:28
l De 4:36
De 5:4
m Ex 19:17
De 5:22

Second Col.
a Ex 34:29
b Nu 20:23, 24
Nu 33:31, 38
c Nu 20:28
d Nu 33:33
e Nu 1:50
Nu 3:6
Nu 8:14
f Nu 3:30, 31
g Nu 6:23-27
De 21:5
2Ch 30:27
h Nu 18:20, 24
De 18:1
i Ex 24:18
Ex 34:28
j Ex 32:14
k Ge 15:18
l Mic 6:8
m De 5:29
n De 5:33
Jos 22:5
o De 6:5
Lu 10:27
p De 6:24

10:7 *Or "wadis of water." 10:12 *See Glossary.

heavens of the heavens,* and
the earth with all that is in it.[a]
15 But only to your forefathers
did Jehovah draw close and express his love, and he has chosen you, their offspring,[b] out of
all the peoples, as you are today. **16** You must now cleanse*
your hearts[c] and stop being
so stubborn.#[d] **17** For Jehovah
your God is the God of gods[e]
and the Lord of lords, the God
great, mighty, and awe-inspiring,
who treats none with partiality[f] and does not accept a bribe.
18 He executes justice for the
fatherless child* and the widow[g] and loves the foreign resident,[h] giving him food and clothing. **19** You too must love the
foreign resident, for you became
foreign residents in the land of
Egypt.[i]

20 "Jehovah your God you
should fear, him you should
serve,[j] to him you should cling,
and by his name you should
swear. **21** He is the One you
are to praise.[k] He is your God,
who has done all these great
and awe-inspiring things for you
that your own eyes have seen.[l]
22 With 70 people* your forefathers went down into Egypt,[m]
and now Jehovah your God has
made you as numerous as the
stars of the heavens.[n]

11 "You must love Jehovah
your God[o] and always
keep your obligation to him and
his statutes, his judicial decisions, and his commandments.
2 You know that today I am addressing you, not your sons
who have not known or seen
the discipline of Jehovah your
God,[p] his greatness,[q] his mighty
hand[r] and his outstretched arm.
3 They did not see his signs and
his deeds that he did in Egypt
to Phar′aoh king of Egypt and to
all his land;[a] **4** or what he did
to the armies of Egypt, to Phar′-
aoh's horses and war chariots,
which were overwhelmed by the
waters of the Red Sea when they
were chasing after you, and Jehovah destroyed them once and
for all.*[b] **5** They did not see
what he has done for* you in the
wilderness until your coming to
this place, **6** or what he did to
Da′than and A·bi′ram, the sons
of E·li′ab the son of Reu′ben,
when the earth opened and swallowed them up, along with their
households and their tents and
every living thing that followed
them, before the eyes of all Israel.[c] **7** Your own eyes have seen
all the great deeds that Jehovah
did.

8 "You must keep the whole
commandment that I am giving
you today, so that you may grow
strong and cross over into the
land to take possession of it,
9 and so that you may live long[d]
in the land that Jehovah swore
to give to your forefathers and
their offspring,*[e] a land flowing
with milk and honey.[f]

10 "The land you are going
to take possession of is not like
the land of Egypt, out of which
you came, where you used to
sow your seed and irrigate it
with your foot,* like a garden of
vegetables. **11** But the land you
are about to cross into and possess is a land of mountains and
valley plains.[g] It drinks the water that rains from the heavens;[h]
12 it is a land that Jehovah your
God is caring for. The eyes of
Jehovah your God are constant-

10:14 *Or "the highest heavens." **10:16** *Lit., "circumcise the foreskin of." #Lit., "and do not harden your neck any longer." **10:18** *Or "the orphan." **10:22** *Or "souls."

11:4 *Or "until this day." **11:5** *Or "to." **11:9** *Lit., "seed." **11:10** *Or "water it with your foot," that is, by some form of foot power, whether on a waterwheel or by forming and opening water channels.

CHAP. 10
a 1Ch 29:11, Ps 24:1, Ps 115:16
b De 4:37
c De 30:6
d Ex 34:9, De 9:6, De 31:27
e Ex 18:11, 2Ch 2:5, Ps 97:9
f Ac 10:34, Ro 2:11
g Ps 68:5, Jas 1:27
h Le 19:10, De 24:14, Ps 146:9
i Ex 22:21, Le 19:34
j Lu 4:8
k Ex 15:2, Re 19:6
l 2Sa 7:23
m Ge 46:27, Ex 1:5, Ac 7:14
n Ge 15:1, 5

CHAP. 11
o De 6:5, De 10:12, Mr 12:30
p De 8:5, Heb 12:6
q De 5:24, De 9:26
r Ex 13:3

Second Col.
a De 4:34
b Ex 14:23, 28, Heb 11:29
c Nu 16:1, 32
d De 4:40, Pr 3:1, 2
e Ge 13:14, 15, Ge 26:3, Ge 28:13
f Ex 3:8, Eze 20:6
g De 1:7
h De 8:7

ly upon it, from the beginning of the year to the close of the year.

13 "And if you will diligently obey my commandments that I am commanding you today and love Jehovah your God and serve him with all your heart and all your soul,*[a] 14 I will also give rain for your land at its appointed time, autumn rain and spring rain, and you will gather your grain and your new wine and your oil.[b] 15 And I will provide vegetation in your fields for your livestock, and you will eat and be satisfied.[c] 16 Be careful not to let your heart be enticed to go astray and worship other gods and bow down to them.[d] 17 Otherwise, Jehovah's anger will blaze against you, and he will shut up the heavens so that it will not rain[e] and the ground will not give its produce and you will quickly perish from the good land that Jehovah is giving you.[f]

18 "You must impress these words of mine on your heart and your soul* and bind them as a reminder on your hand, and they should be like a headband on your forehead."[g] 19 Teach them to your children, speaking about them when you sit in your house and when you walk on the road and when you lie down and when you get up.[h] 20 Write them on the doorposts of your house and on your gates, 21 so that you and your sons may live long[i] in the land that Jehovah swore to give to your forefathers,[j] for as long as the heavens are over the earth.

22 "If you strictly observe this commandment that I am giving you and carry it out, to love Jehovah your God,[k] to walk in all his ways and to cling to him,[l] 23 Jehovah will drive away all these nations

from before you,[a] and you will dispossess nations greater and more numerous than you are.[b] 24 Every place you set your foot will become yours.[c] From the wilderness up to Leb′a·non, from the River, the river Eu·phra′tes, to the western sea,* your boundary will become.[d] 25 Nobody will stand up to you.[e] Jehovah your God will spread the dread and the fear of you over the whole land on which you walk,[f] just as he promised you.

26 "See, I am putting before you today a blessing and a curse:[g] 27 the blessing if you obey the commandments of Jehovah your God that I am commanding you today,[h] 28 and the curse if you do not obey the commandments of Jehovah your God[i] and you turn aside from the way I am commanding you to follow today and you follow gods that you have not known.

29 "When Jehovah your God brings you into the land you are to possess, you must pronounce* the blessing on Mount Ger′i·zim and the curse on Mount E′bal.[j] 30 Are they not on the other side of the Jordan toward the west,* in the land of the Ca′naan·ites who live in the Ar′a·bah, opposite Gil′gal, beside the big trees of Mo′reh?[k] 31 For you are crossing the Jordan to enter and take possession of the land that Jehovah your God is giving you.[l] When you take possession of it and live in it, 32 you must be careful to carry out all the regulations and the judicial decisions that I am putting before you today.[m]

12 "These are the regulations and the judicial decisions that you should be careful to carry out all the days that

---

CHAP. 11

a De 4:29
  De 6:5
  De 10:12
  Mt 22:37

b Le 26:4
  De 8:7-9
  De 28:12
  Jer 14:22

c De 8:10

d De 8:19
  De 29:18
  Heb 3:12

e De 28:15, 23
  1Ki 8:35, 36
  2Ch 7:13, 14

f De 8:19

g Pr 7:1-3

h De 6:6-9
  Pr 22:6
  Eph 6:4

i De 4:40
  Pr 4:10

j Ge 13:14, 15

k De 6:5
  Lu 10:27

l De 10:20
  De 13:4
  Jos 22:5

Second Col.

a Ex 23:28
  Jos 3:10

b De 7:1
  De 9:1, 5

c Jos 14:9

d Ge 15:18
  Ex 23:31

e De 7:24
  Jos 1:5

f Ex 23:27
  Jos 2:9, 10
  Jos 5:1

g De 30:15

h De 28:1, 2
  Ps 19:8, 11

i Le 26:15, 16
  Isa 1:20

j De 27:12, 13
  Jos 8:33, 34

k Ge 12:6

l Jos 1:11

m De 5:32
  De 12:32

11:13, 18 *See Glossary. 11:18 "Lit., "between your eyes." 11:24 *That is, the Great Sea, the Mediterranean. 11:29 *Or "give." 11:30 *Or "sunset."

you are alive in the land that Jehovah the God of your forefathers will give you to possess. **2** You should completely destroy all the places where the nations you will dispossess have served their gods,[a] whether on the high mountains or on the hills or under any luxuriant tree. **3** You should pull down their altars, shatter their sacred pillars,[b] burn their sacred poles* in the fire, and cut down the graven images of their gods,[c] obliterating their very names from that place.[d]

4 "You must not worship Jehovah your God in that way.[e] **5** Rather, seek Jehovah your God wherever he chooses to establish his name and his place of residence among all your tribes, and go there.[f] **6** That is where you are to bring your burnt offerings,[g] your sacrifices, your tithes,*[h] the contribution from your hand,[i] your vow offerings, your voluntary offerings,[j] and the firstborn of your herd and flock.[k] **7** You and your households must eat there before Jehovah your God[l] and rejoice in all your undertakings,[m] because Jehovah your God has blessed you.

8 "You must not do as we are doing here today, with everyone doing whatever is right in his own eyes,* **9** because you have not yet come into the resting-place[n] and the inheritance that Jehovah your God is giving you. **10** When you do cross the Jordan[o] and dwell in the land that Jehovah your God is giving you to possess, he will certainly give you rest from all your enemies around you, and you will dwell in security.[p] **11** You will bring all that I am commanding you to the place that Jehovah your God chooses to have his name reside[a]—your burnt offerings, your sacrifices, your tithes,[b] the contribution from your hand, and every vow offering that you vow to Jehovah. **12** You will rejoice before Jehovah your God,[c] you and your sons, your daughters, your male and female slaves, and the Levite inside your cities,* for he has no share or inheritance with you.[d] **13** Be careful not to offer up your burnt offerings in any other place you may see.[e] **14** You should offer your burnt offerings only in the place that Jehovah chooses in one of your tribal territories, and there you should do everything I am commanding you.[f]

15 "But whenever you desire it,* you may slaughter and eat meat,[g] according to the blessing that Jehovah your God has given you in all your cities.[#] The unclean person and the clean person may eat it, as you would eat a gazelle or a deer. **16** But you must not eat the blood;[h] you should pour it out on the ground like water.[i] **17** You will not be allowed to eat within your cities* the tenth part of your grain, your new wine, your oil, the firstborn of your herd and flock,[j] any of your vow offerings that you vow, your voluntary offerings, or the contribution from your hand. **18** These you are to eat before Jehovah your God in the place Jehovah your God will choose[k]—you and your son, your daughter, your male and female servant, and the Levite inside your cities;* and you will rejoice before Jehovah your God in all your undertakings. **19** Be careful not to neglect the Levite[l] as long as you live in your land.

CHAP. 12
a Ex 34:13
b Ex 23:24
c De 7:25
d Ex 23:13
  Jos 23:7
e Le 18:3
  De 12:31
f 2Ch 7:12
g Le 1:3
h De 14:22
i Nu 18:19
  De 12:11
j 1Ch 29:3
  Ezr 2:68
k De 12:17
  De 15:19
l De 15:19, 20
m Le 23:40
  De 12:12, 18
  De 14:23, 26
  Ps 32:11
  Ps 100:2
  Php 4:4
n 1Ki 8:56
  1Ch 23:25
o Jos 3:17
p De 33:28
  1Ki 4:25

Second Col.
a De 16:2
  De 26:2
b De 14:22, 23
c De 14:26
  1Ki 8:66
  Ne 8:10
d Nu 18:20, 24
  De 10:9
  De 14:28, 29
  Jos 13:14
e Le 17:3, 4
  1Ki 12:28
f 2Ch 7:12
g De 12:21
h Ge 9:4
  Le 7:26
  Le 17:10
  Ac 15:20, 29
i Le 17:13
  De 15:23
j De 14:22, 23
k De 12:11
l Nu 18:21
  De 14:27
  2Ch 31:4
  Ne 10:38, 39
  Mal 3:8

12:3 *See Glossary. **12:6** *Or "tenth parts." **12:8** *Or "what he thinks is right."

12:12, 18 *Lit., "gates." **12:15** *Or "in all the desire of your soul." #Lit., "inside all your gates." **12:17** *Lit., "inside your gates."

20 "When Jehovah your God enlarges your territory,[a] just as he has promised you,[b] and you say, 'I want to eat meat,' because you desire* to eat meat, you may eat meat whenever you desire it.*[c] **21** If the place that Jehovah your God chooses to put his name[d] is far away from you, you should then slaughter some of your herd or some of your flock that Jehovah has given you, just as I have commanded you, and you should eat inside your cities* whenever you desire it.# **22** You may eat it as you would eat the gazelle and the deer;[e] both the unclean person and the clean person may eat it. **23** Just be firmly resolved not to eat the blood,[f] because the blood is the life,*[g] and you must not eat the life* with the flesh. **24** You must not eat it. You should pour it out on the ground like water.[h] **25** You must not eat it, so that it may go well with you and your children after you, because you are doing what is right in Jehovah's eyes. **26** You should take only the holy things that are yours and your vow offerings when you come to the place that Jehovah will choose. **27** There you will offer your burnt offerings, the flesh and the blood,[i] on the altar of Jehovah your God, and the blood of your sacrifices should be poured out against the altar[j] of Jehovah your God, but the flesh you may eat.

28 "Be careful to obey all these words that I am commanding you, so that it may always go well with you and your sons after you, because you are doing what is good and right in the eyes of Jehovah your God.

29 "When Jehovah your God annihilates the nations that you are to dispossess,[a] and you are living in their land, **30** be careful not to be entrapped after they have been annihilated from before you. Do not ask about their gods, saying, 'How were these nations accustomed to serve their gods? I too will do the same.'[b] **31** You must not do this to Jehovah your God, because they do for their gods every detestable thing that Jehovah hates, even burning their sons and their daughters in the fire to their gods.[c] **32** Every word that I am commanding you is what you should be careful to do.[d] You must not add to it nor take away from it.[e]

13 "In case a prophet or one who foretells by dreams arises in your midst and gives you a sign or a portent, **2** and the sign or the portent about which he spoke to you comes true while he is saying, 'Let us walk after other gods, gods that you have not known, and let us serve them,' **3** you must not listen to the words of that prophet or that dreamer,[f] for Jehovah your God is testing you[g] to know whether you love Jehovah your God with all your heart and all your soul.*[h] **4** After Jehovah your God you should walk, him you should fear, his commandments you should keep, to his voice you should listen; he is the one you should serve, and to him you should hold fast.[i] **5** But that prophet or that dreamer should be put to death,[j] because he encouraged rebellion against Jehovah your God—who brought you out of the land of Egypt and redeemed you from the house of slavery—to turn you from the way in which Jehovah your God has commanded you to walk. And you must remove what is evil from your midst.[k]

CHAP. 12
a 1Ki 4:21
b Ge 15:18 Ex 34:24 De 11:24
c Le 11:2-4
d De 14:23 2Ch 7:12
e De 14:4, 5
f Le 3:17 De 12:16
g Ge 9:4 Le 17:11, 14
h Le 17:13 De 15:23
i Le 17:11
j Le 4:29, 30

Second Col.
a Ex 23:23 Ps 44:2 Ps 78:55
b De 7:16 Ps 106:36 Eze 20:28
c Le 18:3, 21 Le 20:2 De 18:10-12 Jer 32:35
d Jos 22:5
e De 4:2 Jos 1:7

CHAP. 13
f Isa 8:19 Jer 27:9
g De 8:2
h De 6:5 De 10:12 Mt 22:37
i De 10:20
j De 18:20
k De 17:2, 3, 7 1Co 5:13

12:20 *Or "your soul desires." 12:20, 21 #Or "in all the desire of your soul." 12:21 *Lit., "gates." 12:23 *Or "soul."

13:3 *See Glossary.

6 "If your brother, the son of your mother, or your son or your daughter or your cherished wife or your closest companion* should try to entice you in secrecy, saying, 'Let us go and serve other gods,'[a] gods that neither you nor your forefathers have known, **7** from the gods of the peoples all around you, whether near you or those far away from you, from one end of the land to the other end of the land, **8** you must not give in to him or listen to him,[b] nor should you show pity or feel compassion or protect him; **9** instead, you should kill him without fail.[c] Your hand should be the first to come upon him to put him to death, and the hand of all the people afterward.[d] **10** And you must stone him to death,[e] because he has sought to turn you away from Jehovah your God, who has brought you out of the land of Egypt, out of the house of slavery. **11** Then all Israel will hear and become afraid, and they will never again do anything bad like this among you.[f]

12 "In case you hear it said in one of your cities that Jehovah your God is giving you to occupy, **13** 'Good-for-nothing men have gone out among you to turn away the inhabitants of their city, saying: "Let us go and serve other gods," gods that you have not known,' **14** you should look into the matter, making a thorough investigation and inquiry;[g] and if it is confirmed to be true that this detestable thing has been done among you, **15** you should without fail strike down the inhabitants of that city with the sword.[h] Devote it and everything that is in it, including its livestock, to destruction[i] by the sword. **16** You should then collect all its spoil into the mid-

dle of its public square and burn the city with fire, and its spoil will serve as a whole offering to Jehovah your God. It will become a permanent heap of ruins. It should never be rebuilt. **17** Your hand should take nothing that was set apart for destruction,*[a] so that Jehovah may turn away from his burning anger and show you mercy and compassion and multiply you, just as he has sworn to your forefathers.[b] **18** For you should obey* Jehovah your God by keeping all his commandments that I am commanding you today, thus doing what is right in the eyes of Jehovah your God.[c]

14 "You are sons of Jehovah your God. Do not cut yourselves[d] or shave your foreheads bald* for a dead person.[e] **2** For you are a holy people[f] to Jehovah your God, and Jehovah has chosen you to become his people, his special property,* out of all the peoples who are on the face of the earth.[g]

3 "You must not eat anything that is detestable.[h] **4** These are the animals that you may eat:[i] the bull, the sheep, the goat, **5** the deer, the gazelle, the roebuck, the wild goat, the antelope, the wild sheep, and the mountain sheep. **6** You may eat any animal that has a split hoof divided into two and that chews the cud. **7** However, you must not eat the following animals that chew the cud or that have split hooves: the camel, the hare, and the rock badger, because they chew the cud but do not have split hooves. They are unclean for you.[j] **8** Also the pig because it has a split hoof but does not chew the cud. It is un-

---

CHAP. 13
a 1Ki 11:4
2Pe 2:1

b Ga 1:8

c Ex 22:20
Ex 32:27
Nu 25:5

d De 17:2, 3, 7

e Le 20:2, 27

f De 17:13
1Ti 5:20

g De 19:15
1Ti 5:19

h De 17:4, 5
2Ch 28:6

i Ex 22:20

Second Col.
a Jos 6:18

b Ge 22:15, 17
Ge 26:3, 4

c De 6:18

CHAP. 14
d Le 19:28

e Le 21:1, 5

f Le 19:2
Le 20:26
De 28:9
1Pe 1:15

g Ex 19:5, 6
De 7:6

h Le 11:43
Le 20:25
Ac 10:14

i Le 11:2, 3

j Le 11:4-8

13:17 *Or "made sacred by ban." 13:18 *Or "listen to the voice of." 14:1 *Lit., "put (make) baldness between your eyes." 14:2 *Or "treasured possession."

13:6 *Or "your companion who is like your own soul."

clean for you. You must not eat their flesh or touch their carcasses.

9 "Of everything that is living in the waters, you may eat these: Anything with fins and scales, you may eat.[a] 10 But you must not eat anything that has no fins and scales. It is unclean for you.

11 "You may eat any clean bird. 12 But you must not eat these: the eagle, the osprey, the black vulture,[b] 13 the red kite, the black kite, every kind of glede, 14 every kind of raven, 15 the ostrich, the owl, the gull, every kind of falcon, 16 the little owl, the long-eared owl, the swan, 17 the pelican, the vulture, the cormorant, 18 the stork, every kind of heron, the hoopoe, and the bat. 19 Every winged swarming creature* also is unclean for you. They should not be eaten. 20 Any clean flying creature you may eat.

21 "You must not eat any animal that was found dead.[c] You may give it to the foreign resident who is inside your cities,* and he may eat it, or it may be sold to a foreigner. For you are a holy people to Jehovah your God.

"You must not boil a young goat in its mother's milk.[d]

22 "You must without fail give a tenth* of everything your seed produces in the field year by year.[e] 23 You will eat the tenth part of your grain, your new wine, your oil, and the firstborn of your herd and your flock before Jehovah your God in the place that he chooses to have his name reside,[f] so that you may learn to fear Jehovah your God always.[g]

24 "But if the journey should be too long for you and you are not able to carry it to the place

that Jehovah your God chooses as the place for his name[a] because it is far away from you (because Jehovah your God will bless you), 25 you may then convert it into money, and with your money in hand, travel to the place that Jehovah your God will choose. 26 You may then spend the money on whatever you desire*—cattle, sheep, goats, wine and other alcoholic beverages, and anything you please;* and you will eat there before Jehovah your God and rejoice, you and your household.[b] 27 And do not neglect the Levite who is inside your cities,[c] for he has no share or inheritance with you.[d]

28 "At the end of every three years, you should bring out the entire tenth part of your produce for that year and deposit it inside your cities.[e] 29 Then the Levite, who has no share or inheritance with you, the foreign resident, the fatherless child,* and the widow who are in your cities will come and eat their fill,[f] so that Jehovah your God may bless you in all that you do.[g]

15 "At the end of every seven years, you should grant a release.[h] 2 This is the nature of the release: Every creditor will release his neighbor from the debt he incurred. He should not demand payment from his neighbor or his brother, for it will be proclaimed a release to Jehovah.[i] 3 You may demand payment from the foreigner,[j] but you should release your claim on whatever your brother owes you. 4 However, no one among you should become poor, for Jehovah will surely bless you[k] in the land that Jehovah your God is giving you to possess as an inheritance, 5 but only if you

CHAP. 14
a Le 11:9, 10

b Le 11:13-20

c Ex 22:31
Le 17:15

d Ex 23:19
Ex 34:26

e De 12:11
De 26:12

f De 12:5, 17
De 15:19, 20

g Ps 111:10

Second Col.
a De 12:5, 6

b De 12:7
De 26:11
Ps 100:2

c Nu 18:21
2Ch 31:4
1Co 9:13

d Nu 18:20
De 10:9

e De 26:12

f Ex 22:21
De 10:18
Jas 1:27

g De 15:10
Ps 41:1
Pr 11:24
Pr 19:17
Mal 3:10
Lu 6:35

CHAP. 15
h Le 25:2

i De 31:10

j Ex 12:43
De 14:21
De 23:20

k De 28:8

14:19 *Or "insect." 14:21 *Lit., "gates." 14:22 *Or "a tithe."

14:26 *Or "your soul desires." *Or "anything your soul may ask of you." 14:29 *Or "the orphan."

strictly obey the voice of Jehovah your God and carefully observe all this commandment that I am giving you today.[a] **6** For Jehovah your God will bless you just as he has promised you, and you will lend* to many nations, but you will not need to borrow;[b] and you will dominate many nations, but they will not dominate you.[c]

7 "If one of your brothers becomes poor among you in one of your cities of the land that Jehovah your God is giving you, do not harden your heart or be tightfisted toward your poor brother.[d] **8** For you should generously open your hand to him[e] and by all means lend* whatever he needs or is lacking. **9** Be careful not to harbor this evil idea in your heart, 'The seventh year, the year of the release, has approached,'[f] and hold back your generosity toward your poor brother and give him nothing. If he calls out to Jehovah against you, it will be a sin on your part.[g] **10** You should generously give to him,[h] and you* should not give to him grudgingly, for this is why Jehovah your God will bless your every deed and undertaking.[i] **11** For there will always be poor people in the land.[j] That is why I am commanding you, 'You should generously open up your hand to your afflicted and poor brother in your land.'

12 "If one of your brothers, a Hebrew man or woman, is sold to you and has served you for six years, then in the seventh year you should set him free.[l] **13** And if you should set him free, do not send him away empty-handed. **14** You should supply him generously with something from your flock, your threshing floor, and your press

for oil and wine. Just as Jehovah your God has blessed you, you should give to him. **15** Remember that you became a slave in the land of Egypt and that Jehovah your God redeemed you. That is why I am commanding you to do this today.

16 "But if he says to you, 'I will not go out from your company!' because he loves you and your household, since he has been happy while with you,[a] **17** you should then take an awl and put it through his ear into the door, and he will become your slave for life. You should do the same with your slave girl. **18** Do not consider it a hardship when you set him free and he leaves you, because his service to you for six years was worth twice as much as that of a hired worker, and Jehovah your God has blessed you in everything that was done.

19 "You should sanctify every firstborn male of your herd and your flock to Jehovah your God.[b] You must not do any work with the firstborn of your herd* nor shear the firstborn of your flock. **20** You and your household should eat it before Jehovah your God year by year in the place that Jehovah will choose.[c] **21** But if it has a defect—lameness, blindness, or any other serious defect—you must not sacrifice it to Jehovah your God.[d] **22** You should eat it inside your cities,* the unclean and clean person together, as though it were a gazelle or a deer.[e] **23** But you must not eat its blood;[f] you should pour it out on the ground like water.[g]

16 "Observe the month of A'bib,* and celebrate the Passover to Jehovah your God,[h] for in the month of A'bib, Jeho-

---

CHAP. 15
a Jos 1:7, 8
　Isa 1:19

b De 28:12

c De 28:13
　1Ki 4:24, 25

d Pr 21:13
　Jas 2:15, 16
　1Jo 3:17

e Le 25:35
　Pr 19:17
　Mt 5:42
　Lu 6:34, 35
　Ga 2:10

f De 15:1

g Ex 22:22, 23
　De 24:14, 15
　Pr 21:13

h Ac 20:35
　2Co 9:7
　1Ti 6:18
　Heb 13:16

i De 24:19
　Ps 41:1

j Mt 26:11

k Pr 3:27
　Mt 5:42
　Lu 12:33

l Ex 21:2
　Le 25:39

Second Col.
a Ex 21:5, 6

b Ex 13:2
　Ex 22:30
　Nu 3:13
　Nu 18:15, 17

c De 12:5, 6
　De 14:23
　De 16:11

d Le 22:20
　De 17:1
　Mal 1:8
　Heb 9:14

e De 12:15
　De 14:4, 5

f Ge 9:4
　Le 7:26
　Ac 15:20, 29

g Le 17:10, 13
　De 12:16

CHAP. 16
h Ex 12:14
　Le 23:5
　Nu 9:2
　Nu 28:16
　1Co 5:7

15:6, 8 *Or "lend on pledge." 15:10 *Lit., "your heart." 　　15:19 *Lit., "bull." 15:22 *Lit., "gates." 16:1 *See App. B15.

vah your God brought you out of Egypt by night.[a] **2** And you should sacrifice the Passover offering to Jehovah your God,[b] from the flock and the herd,[c] in the place that Jehovah chooses to have his name reside.[d] **3** You must not eat anything leavened along with it;[e] for seven days you should eat unleavened bread, the bread of affliction, because you came out of the land of Egypt in haste.[f] Do this so that you may remember the day you came out of the land of Egypt as long as you live.[g] **4** No sourdough should be found with you in all your territory for seven days,[h] nor should any of the meat that you will sacrifice in the evening on the first day remain all night until the next morning.[i] **5** You will not be allowed to sacrifice the Passover offering in just any of the cities that Jehovah your God is giving you. **6** But it should be done at the place that Jehovah your God chooses to have his name reside. You should sacrifice the Passover offering in the evening as soon as the sun sets,[j] at the appointed time of your coming out of Egypt. **7** You must cook it and eat it[k] in the place that Jehovah your God will choose,[l] and in the morning you may return to your own tents. **8** Six days you should eat unleavened bread, and on the seventh day there will be a solemn assembly to Jehovah your God. You must do no work.[m]

9 "You should count off seven weeks. You should begin counting off seven weeks from the time you first put the sickle to the standing grain.[n] **10** Then you are to celebrate the Festival of Weeks to Jehovah your God[o] with the voluntary offering from your hand, given in proportion to how Jehovah your God blesses you.[p] **11** And you are to re-

joice before Jehovah your God, you and your son, your daughter, your male slave, your female slave, the Levite who is inside your cities,* the foreign resident, the fatherless child,# and the widow, who are in your midst, in the place that Jehovah your God chooses to have his name reside.[a] **12** Remember that you became a slave in Egypt,[b] and observe and carry out these regulations.

13 "You should celebrate the Festival of Booths*[c] for seven days when you make an ingathering from your threshing floor and from your press for oil and wine. **14** Rejoice during your festival,[d] you and your son, your daughter, your male slave, your female slave, the Levite, the foreign resident, the fatherless child, and the widow, who are inside your cities. **15** Seven days you will celebrate the festival[e] to Jehovah your God in the place that Jehovah chooses, for Jehovah your God will bless all your produce and all that you do,[f] and you will become nothing but joyful.[g]

16 "Three times a year, all your males should appear before Jehovah your God: at the place that he chooses: at the Festival of Unleavened Bread,[h] the Festival of Weeks,[i] and the Festival of Booths,*[j] and none of them should appear before Jehovah empty-handed. **17** The gift that each one brings should be in proportion to the blessing that Jehovah your God has given you.[k]

18 "You should appoint judges[l] and officers for each tribe in all the cities* that Jehovah your God is giving you, and they must judge the

---

CHAP. 16
a Ex 34:18
b Mt 26:17
c Ex 12:5, 6
  2Ch 35:7
d 1Ki 8:29
e Ex 13:3
  Le 23:6
  Nu 28:17
  1Co 5:8
f Ex 12:33
g Ex 12:14
  Ex 13:8, 9
h Ex 12:15
  Ex 13:7
i Ex 12:10
  Ex 34:25
j Ex 12:3, 6
  Nu 9:2, 3
  Mt 26:19, 20
k Ex 12:8
  2Ch 35:13
l Joh 2:13
  Joh 11:55
m Ex 12:16
  Le 23:8
n Ex 23:16
  Ex 34:22
  Le 23:15
o Nu 28:26
p De 16:17
  1Co 16:2
  2Co 8:12

Second Col.
a De 12:5-7
b Ex 3:7
  De 5:15
c Ex 23:16
  Le 23:34
  Nu 29:12
  De 31:10, 11
  Joh 7:2
d De 12:12
  Ne 8:10, 17
  Ec 5:18
e Le 23:36, 40
  Ne 8:18
f De 7:13
  De 28:8
  De 30:16
g Php 4:4
  1Th 5:16
h Ex 23:14, 15
i De 16:10
j De 16:13
k 2Co 8:12
l Ex 18:25, 26
  De 1:16
  2Ch 19:4, 5

16:11 *Lit., "gates." #Or "the orphan."
16:13, 16 *Or "Temporary Shelters."
16:18 *Lit., "inside all your gates."

people with righteous judgment. **19** You must not pervert justice,[a] show partiality,[b] or accept a bribe, for the bribe blinds the eyes of the wise[c] and distorts the words of the righteous. **20** Justice—justice you should pursue,[d] so that you may keep living and take possession of the land that Jehovah your God is giving you.

21 "You should not plant any sort of tree as a sacred pole[*e] near the altar of Jehovah your God that you make for yourself. **22** "Neither should you set up a sacred pillar for yourself,[f] something Jehovah your God hates.

17 "You must not sacrifice to Jehovah your God a bull or a sheep that has a defect or anything wrong with it, for it would be detestable to Jehovah your God.[g]

2 "Suppose a man or a woman is found among you, in any of your cities that Jehovah your God is giving you, who is practicing what is bad in the eyes of Jehovah your God and violating his covenant,[h] **3** and he goes astray and worships other gods and he bows down to them or to the sun or the moon or all the army of the heavens,[i] a thing that I have not commanded.[j] **4** When it is reported to you or you hear about it, then you should investigate the matter thoroughly. If it is confirmed to be true[k] that this detestable thing has been done in Israel, **5** you must bring the man or the woman who has done this evil thing out to the city gates, and the man or the woman must be stoned to death.[l] **6** On the testimony* of two witnesses or of three witnesses[m] the one who is to die should be put to death. He must not be put to death on

16:21 *See Glossary. 17:6 *Lit., "mouth."

the testimony of one witness.[a] **7** The hand of the witnesses should be the first to come against him to put him to death, and the hand of all the people afterward. You must remove what is bad from your midst.[b]

8 "If a case arises in one of your cities that is too difficult for you to judge, whether it is a case involving bloodshed[c] or a legal claim that has been raised or a violent deed that has been committed or other matters of dispute, you should rise up and go to the place that Jehovah your God chooses.[d] **9** Go to the Levitical priests and to the judge[e] serving in those days, and make your inquiry, and they will hand down the decision to you.[f] **10** Then you must act according to the decision that they hand down to you from the place that Jehovah chooses. Be careful to do according to all that they instruct you. **11** You must act according to the law that they show you and according to the decision that they declare to you.[g] Do not deviate from the decision that they will hand down to you, either to the right or to the left.[h] **12** The man who acts presumptuously by not listening to the priest who is ministering to Jehovah your God or to the judge must die.[i] You must remove what is bad from Israel.[j] **13** All the people will then hear and become afraid, and they will not act presumptuously anymore.[k]

14 "When you enter the land that Jehovah your God is giving you and you have taken possession of it and are living in it, and you say, 'Let me appoint a king over myself like all the nations around me,'[l] **15** in that case, you should without fail appoint a king whom Jehovah your God chooses.[m] You should appoint a king from among your

CHAP. 16

a Ex 23:2
  Le 19:15

b De 1:17

c Ex 23:8
  1Sa 12:3
  Ec 7:7

d Mic 6:8

e Ex 34:13

f Ex 23:24
  Le 26:1
  De 12:3

CHAP. 17

g Le 22:20
  De 15:21
  Mal 1:8

h De 4:23
  De 13:6-9

i De 4:19

j De 13:12-15

k Joh 7:51

l De 13:6, 10

m Mt 18:16
  Joh 8:17
  1Ti 5:19
  Heb 10:28

Second Col.

a Nu 35:30
  De 19:15

b De 13:5
  1Co 5:13

c Nu 35:11

d De 12:5
  1Ki 3:16, 28
  Ps 122:2, 5

e 1Sa 7:15, 16

f De 19:17
  De 21:5

g Mal 2:7

h De 5:32
  De 12:32

i Pr 11:2
  Heb 10:28

j De 13:5
  1Co 5:13

k De 13:11
  De 19:20

l 1Sa 8:5, 20
  1Sa 10:19

m 1Sa 9:17
  1Sa 10:24
  1Sa 16:12, 13

brothers. You are forbidden to appoint over yourself a foreigner who is not your brother. **16** However, he should not acquire many horses for himself[a] or make the people go back to Egypt in order to obtain more horses,[b] since Jehovah told you, 'You must never go back again by this way.' **17** Neither should he take many wives for himself, so that his heart may not go astray;[c] nor should he acquire vast amounts of silver and gold for himself.[d] **18** When he takes his seat on the throne of his kingdom, he must write for himself in a book* a copy of this Law, taken from the one kept by the Levitical priests.[e]

19 "It is to remain with him, and he must read from it all the days of his life,[f] so that he may learn to fear Jehovah his God and observe all the words of this Law and these regulations by carrying them out.[g] **20** Thus his heart will not exalt itself above his brothers, and he will not deviate from the commandment, either to the right or to the left, so that he may remain a long time over his kingdom, he and his sons in the midst of Israel.

18 "The Levitical priests, and indeed the entire tribe of Le'vi, will have no share or inheritance with Israel. They will eat of the offerings made by fire to Jehovah, which is their inheritance.[h] **2** So they should have no inheritance in the midst of their brothers. Jehovah is their inheritance, just as he has spoken to them.

3 "Now this will be the due right of the priests from the people: Whoever makes a sacrifice, whether a bull or a sheep, is to give the shoulder, the jaws, and the stomach to the priest.

4 The firstfruits of your grain, your new wine, your oil, and the first wool that is shorn from your flock you should give him.[a] **5** Jehovah your God has chosen him and his sons from all your tribes to minister in the name of Jehovah always.[b]

6 "But if a Levite leaves one of your cities in Israel where he was living[c] and he* desires to go to the place that Jehovah chooses,[#d] **7** he may minister there in the name of Jehovah his God the same as all his brothers, the Levites, who are stationed there before Jehovah.[e] **8** He will receive an equal share of food with them,[f] in addition to what he receives from selling his ancestral possessions.

9 "When you have entered into the land that Jehovah your God is giving you, you must not learn to imitate the detestable practices of those nations.[g] **10** There should not be found in you anyone who makes his son or his daughter pass through the fire,[h] anyone who employs divination,[i] anyone practicing magic,[j] anyone who looks for omens,[k] anyone who is a sorcerer,[l] **11** anyone binding others with a spell, anyone who consults a spirit medium[m] or a fortune-teller,[n] or anyone who inquires of the dead.[o] **12** For whoever does these things is detestable to Jehovah, and on account of these detestable practices Jehovah your God is driving them away from before you. **13** You should prove yourself blameless before Jehovah your God.[p]

14 "For these nations that you are dispossessing used to listen to those practicing magic[q] and divination,[r] but Jehovah your God has not allowed you to

CHAP. 17
a De 20:1 2Sa 8:4 Ps 20:7 Pr 21:31
b Isa 31:1
c 1Ki 11:1-3 Ne 13:26
d Job 31:24, 28 1Ti 6:9
e De 31:9, 26 2Ki 22:8
f 2Ch 34:18
g Ps 1:2 Ps 119:97

CHAP. 18
h Nu 18:20, 24 De 10:9 Jos 13:14, 33 1Co 9:13

Second Col.

a Ex 23:19 Nu 18:8, 12 2Ch 31:4 Ne 12:44
b Ex 28:1 Nu 3:10 De 10:8
c Nu 35:2
d De 12:5, 6 De 16:2 Ps 26:8
e 2Ch 31:2
f Le 7:10
g Le 18:26 De 12:30
h De 12:31 2Ki 16:1, 3 2Ch 28:1, 3 Ps 106:35-37 Jer 32:35
i 2Ki 17:17 Ac 16:16
j Le 19:26 Ac 19:19
k Eze 21:21
l Ex 22:18
m Le 20:27 1Ch 10:13
n Le 19:31
o 1Sa 28:7-11 Isa 8:19 Ga 5:19, 20
p Mt 5:48 2Pe 3:14
q Le 19:26 2Ki 21:1, 2, 6
r Jos 13:22

17:18 *Or "a scroll."

18:6 *Or "his soul." #That is, the place Jehovah selects as the center for worship.

do anything like this. **15** Jehovah your God will raise up for you from among your brothers a prophet like me. You must listen to him.ᵃ **16** This is in response to what you asked of Jehovah your God in Ho′reb on the day of the assembly*ᵇ when you said, 'Do not let me hear the voice of Jehovah my God or see this great fire anymore, so that I do not die.'ᶜ **17** Then Jehovah said to me, 'What they have said is good. **18** I will raise up for them from the midst of their brothers a prophet like you,ᵈ and I will put my words in his mouth,ᵉ and he will speak to them all that I command him.ᶠ **19** Indeed, I will require an account from the man who will not listen to my words that he will speak in my name.ᵍ

20 "'If any prophet presumptuously speaks a word in my name that I did not command him to speak or speaks in the name of other gods, that prophet must die.ʰ **21** However, you may say in your heart: "How will we know that Jehovah has not spoken the word?" **22** When the prophet speaks in the name of Jehovah and the word is not fulfilled or does not come true, then Jehovah did not speak that word. The prophet spoke it presumptuously. You should not fear him.'

19 "When Jehovah your God destroys the nations whose land Jehovah your God is giving you and you have dispossessed them and have settled in their cities and their houses,ⁱ **2** you should set apart three cities in the midst of your land that Jehovah your God is giving you to possess.ʲ **3** You should divide the territory of the land that Jehovah your God has given you to possess into three parts,

and prepare the roads so that any manslayer can flee to one of those cities.

4 "Now this is what should take place regarding the manslayer who may flee there in order to live: When he strikes his fellow man unintentionally and he did not previously hate him;ᵃ **5** as when he goes with his fellow man into the forest to gather wood and he raises his hand to cut the tree with the ax, but the axhead flies off the handle and hits his fellow man and he dies, the manslayer should flee to one of these cities to live.ᵇ **6** Otherwise, in the heat of anger,* the avenger of bloodᶜ may chase after the manslayer, overtake him, and kill him, because the distance to the city was too far. However, he did not deserve to die, since he did not previously hate his fellow man.ᵈ **7** That is why I am commanding you: 'Set three cities apart.'

8 "If Jehovah your God enlarges your territory as he swore to your forefathersᵉ and he has given you all the land that he promised to give to your forefathersᶠ **9** —provided you faithfully observe all this commandment that I am giving you today, to love Jehovah your God and always to walk in his waysᵍ—then you are to add three other cities to these three.ʰ **10** In this way no innocent blood will be spilledⁱ in your land that Jehovah your God is giving you as an inheritance, and no bloodguilt will come upon you.ʲ

11 "But if a man hated his fellow manᵏ and he was waiting to attack him and he fatally wounded him* and he died, and the man has fled to one of these cities, **12** the elders of his city should then sum-

---

CHAP. 18	
a	Ge 49:10
	Nu 24:17
	Lu 7:16
	Joh 1:45
	Joh 6:14
	Ac 3:22
	Ac 7:37
b	Ex 19:17
c	Ex 20:19
d	Ex 34:28
	Nu 12:3
	Mt 4:1, 2
	Mt 11:29
	Joh 5:46
e	Joh 17:8
f	Joh 12:49
	Heb 1:2
g	Ac 3:23
h	De 13:1-5
	Jer 28:11-17
CHAP. 19	
i	De 7:1
	De 9:1
j	Nu 35:14
	Jos 20:7, 9
Second Col.	
a	Nu 35:15
	De 4:42
b	Nu 35:25
c	Nu 35:12, 19
d	Jos 20:4, 5
e	Ge 15:18
	Ex 23:31
	De 11:24
f	Ge 28:14
g	De 11:22, 23
h	Jos 20:7, 8
i	Pr 6:16, 17
j	De 21:6-9
k	1Jo 3:15

18:16 *Or "congregation."

19:6 *Lit., "because his heart is hot."
19:11 *Or "his soul."

mon him from there and deliver him into the hand of the avenger of blood, and he must die.[a] **13** You* should not feel sorry for him, and you must remove the guilt of innocent blood out of Israel,[b] so that it may go well for you.

14 "When you receive your inheritance in the land that Jehovah your God is giving you to possess, you must not move your neighbor's boundary marker[c] from the place where the ancestors set the boundaries.

15 "No single witness may convict* another for any error or any sin that he may commit.[d] On the testimony* of two witnesses or on the testimony of three witnesses the matter should be established.[e] **16** If a malicious witness testifies against a man and charges him with some transgression,[f] **17** the two men who have the dispute will stand before Jehovah, the priests and the judges who will be serving in those days.[g] **18** The judges will thoroughly investigate,[h] and if the man who testified is a false witness and has brought a false charge against his brother, **19** you should do to him just as he had schemed to do to his brother,[i] and you must remove what is bad from your midst.[j] **20** Those who remain will hear and be afraid, and they will never again do anything bad like this among you.[k] **21** You* should not feel sorry;[l] Life* will be for life,[Δ] eye for eye, tooth for tooth, hand for hand, foot for foot.[m]

20 "If you go to war against your enemies and you see their horses and chariots and troops that outnumber yours, do not be afraid of them, for

Jehovah your God who brought you up out of the land of Egypt is with you.[a] **2** When you are about to go into battle, the priest should approach and address the people.[b] **3** He should tell them, 'Hear, O Israel, you are about to do battle with your enemies. Do not be fainthearted. Do not be afraid or be terrified or tremble because of them, **4** for Jehovah your God is marching with you to fight for you against your enemies and to save you.'[c]

5 "The officers too should tell the people, 'Who has built a new house and has not inaugurated it? Let him return to his house. Otherwise, he may die in the battle and another man will inaugurate it. **6** And who has planted a vineyard and not begun to use it? Let him go and return to his house. Otherwise, he may die in the battle and another man will begin to use it. **7** And who has become engaged to a woman and has not married her? Let him go and return to his house.[d] Otherwise, he might die in the battle and another man will marry her.' **8** The officers should also ask the people, 'Who is fearful and fainthearted?[e] He should return to his house, so that he may not cause his brothers to lose heart as he has.'*[f] **9** When the officers have finished speaking to the people, they should appoint chiefs of the armies to lead the people.

10 "If you approach a city to fight against it, you should also announce to it terms of peace.[g] **11** If it gives a peaceful answer to you and opens up to you, all the people found there will become yours for forced labor, and they will serve you.[h] **12** But if it refuses to make peace with you and instead goes

---

CHAP. 19
a Ge 9:6
　Ex 21:12
　Nu 35:16
　De 27:24

b Le 24:17, 21
　Nu 35:33
　2Sa 21:1

c De 27:17

d Nu 35:30
　De 17:6

e Mt 18:16
　Job 8:17
　2Co 13:1
　1Ti 5:19

f Ex 23:1
　1Ki 21:13
　Mr 14:56

g De 17:8, 9

h De 13:14
　De 17:4
　2Ch 19:6

i Pr 19:5

j De 21:20, 21
　De 24:7
　1Co 5:13

k De 13:11
　De 17:13
　1Ti 5:20

l De 19:13

m Ex 21:23-25
　Le 24:20
　Mt 5:38

Second Col.

CHAP. 20
a De 3:22
　De 31:6
　Ps 20:7
　Pr 21:31

b Nu 31:6

c Ex 14:14
　Jos 23:10

d De 24:5

e Jg 7:3

f Nu 13:33
　Nu 14:1-3
　Nu 32:9
　De 1:28

g Jos 11:19

h Le 25:44, 46
　Jos 9:22, 27

19:13, 21 *Lit., "Your eye." 19:15 *Lit., "rise up against." *Lit., "mouth." 19:21 *Or "Soul." Δ Or "soul."

20:8 *Or "cause the heart of his brothers to melt as his own heart."

to war with you, you should besiege it, **13** and Jehovah your God will certainly give it into your hand, and you must strike down every male in it with the sword. **14** However, the women, the children, the livestock, and everything that is in the city, all its spoil, you may plunder for yourself,ᵃ and you will eat the spoil of your enemies, which Jehovah your God has given to you.ᵇ

15 "That is what you will do to all the cities very far away from you that are not of the cities of these nearby nations. **16** But in the cities of these peoples, which Jehovah your God is giving you as an inheritance, you must not allow any breathing thing to live.ᶜ **17** Instead, you should devote them completely to destruction, the Hitʹtites, the Amʹor·ites, the Caʹnaan·ites, the Perʹiz·zites, the Hiʹvites, and the Jebʹu·sites,ᵈ just as Jehovah your God has commanded you; **18** so that they may not teach you to follow all their detestable practices that they have done for their gods, causing you to sin against Jehovah your God.ᵉ

19 "If you lay siege to a city and capture it after fighting against it for many days, you should not destroy its trees by wielding an ax against them. You may eat from them, but you should not cut them down.ᶠ For should you besiege a tree of the field as you would a man? **20** You may destroy only a tree that you know is not used for food. You may cut it down and build siegeworks against the city that is making war against you, until it falls.

21 "If someone is found slain in a field of the land that Jehovah your God is giving you to possess and it is not known who killed him, **2** your elders and judgesᵍ should go out and measure the distance from the dead body to the cities that surround it. **3** Then the elders of the city nearest to the body should take from the herd a young cow that has never been put to work, that has never pulled in a yoke, **4** and the elders of that city should lead the young cow down to a valley* running with water where no tilling or sowing of seed has been done, and they should break the neck of the young cow there in the valley.ᵃ

5 "And the priests, the Leʹvites, will approach because Jehovah your God has chosen them to minister to him,ᵇ to pronounce blessings in the name of Jehovah.ᶜ They will declare how every dispute involving violence should be resolved.ᵈ **6** Then all the elders of the city who are nearest to the dead body should wash their handsᵉ over the young cow whose neck was broken in the valley, **7** and they should declare, 'Our hands did not shed this blood, nor did our eyes see it shed. **8** Do not hold this against your people Israel, whom you redeemed,ᶠ O Jehovah, and do not let guilt for innocent blood remain among your people Israel.'ᵍ Then the bloodguilt will not be held against them. **9** In this way you will remove the guilt of innocent blood from your midst by doing what is right in Jehovah's eyes.

10 "If you go to war against your enemies and Jehovah your God defeats them for you and you take them captive,ʰ **11** and you see among the captives a beautiful woman and you are attracted to her and you want to take her as your wife, **12** you may bring her into your house. She should then shave her head, attend to her nails, **13** and re-

---

CHAP. 20
a 2Ch 14:13

b Jos 22:8

c Jos 6:17
  Jos 10:28
  Jos 11:11

d De 7:1

e Ex 34:15
  De 7:4
  Jos 23:12, 13
  Isa 2:6
  1Co 5:6
  1Co 15:33

f Ne 9:25

CHAP. 21
g De 16:18

Second Col.
a Nu 35:33

b Ex 28:1

c Nu 6:23-27
  1Ch 23:13

d De 17:8, 9

e Ps 26:6
  Mt 27:24

f 2Sa 7:23

g Isa 26:21
  Jer 26:15

h Nu 31:9
  De 20:13, 14

21:4 *Or "wadi."

move the clothing of her captivity, and dwell in your house. She will weep for her father and her mother a whole month,[a] and afterward you may have relations with her; you will become her husband and she will become your wife. **14** But if you are not pleased with her, you should then let her go[b] wherever she wishes.* But you may not sell her for money or treat her harshly, since you have humiliated her.

15 "If a man has two wives and he loves one more than the other* and both have borne sons to him and the firstborn son belongs to the unloved one,[c] **16** on the day that he gives his inheritance to his sons, he will not be allowed to treat the son of the loved one as his firstborn at the expense of the son of the unloved one, the firstborn. **17** He should recognize as the firstborn the unloved one's son by giving him the double portion of everything he has, for that one is the beginning of his procreative power. The right of the firstborn's position belongs to him.[d]

18 "If a man has a son who is stubborn and rebellious and he does not obey his father or his mother,[e] and they have tried to correct him but he refuses to listen to them,[f] **19** his father and his mother should take hold of him and bring him out to the elders at the gate of his city **20** and say to the elders of his city, 'This son of ours is stubborn and rebellious, and he refuses to obey us. He is a glutton[g] and a drunkard.'[h] **21** Then all the men of his city must stone him to death. So you must remove what is bad from your midst, and all Israel will hear and become afraid.[i]

21:14 *Or "according to her soul."
21:15 *Lit., "two wives, one loved and one hated."

CHAP. 21
a Nu 20:29
  De 34:8

b De 24:1

c Ge 29:30, 33

d Ge 25:31
  2Ch 21:3

e Ex 20:12
  De 27:16
  Pr 1:8
  Eph 6:1

f De 8:5
  Pr 13:24
  Pr 19:18
  Pr 23:13
  Heb 12:9

g Pr 28:7

h Ro 13:13
  1Co 6:10
  Eph 5:18

i De 13:10, 11

Second Col.
a Nu 25:5

b Jos 10:26
  Ac 10:39

c Jos 8:29
  Joh 19:31

d Ga 3:13

e Nu 35:34

CHAP. 22
f Ex 23:4

g Mt 7:12

h Ex 23:5
  Le 19:18
  Lu 10:27
  Ga 6:10

i Le 22:28
  Ps 145:9
  Pr 12:10
  Mt 10:29

22 "If a man commits a sin deserving the sentence of death and he has been put to death[a] and you have hung him on a stake,[b] **23** his dead body should not remain all night on the stake.[c] Instead, you should be sure to bury him on that day, because the one hung up is something accursed of God,[d] and you should not defile your land that Jehovah your God is giving you as an inheritance.[e]

22 "If you see your brother's bull or his sheep going astray, do not deliberately ignore it.[f] You should without fail lead it back to your brother. **2** But if your brother does not live near you or you do not know him, you should bring the animal to your house, and it will remain with you until your brother searches for it. Then you should return it to him.[g] **3** That is what you should do with his donkey, with his clothing, and with anything that your brother has lost and you have found. You must not ignore it.

4 "If you see your brother's donkey or his bull fall down on the road, you must not deliberately ignore it. You should without fail help him raise the animal up.[h]

5 "A woman must not put on the clothing of a man, nor should a man wear the clothing of a woman. For anyone doing so is detestable to Jehovah your God.

6 "If you happen upon a bird's nest along the road with young ones or eggs, whether in a tree or on the ground, and the mother is sitting on the young ones or the eggs, you must not take the mother together with her young. **7** Be sure to send the mother away, but you may take the young for yourself. Do this so that it may go well with you and you may live long.

8 "If you build a new house, you must also make a parapet for your roof,[a] so that you may not bring bloodguilt on your house because of someone falling from it.

9 "You must not sow your vineyard with two sorts of seed.[b] Otherwise, everything produced from the seed you sow as well as the product of the vineyard will be forfeited to the sanctuary.

10 "You must not plow with a bull and a donkey together.[c]

11 "You must not wear clothing made of wool and linen mixed together.[d]

12 "You should make tassels on the four corners of the clothing you wear.[e]

13 "If a man takes a wife and has relations with her but then comes to hate her* **14** and he accuses her of misconduct and gives her a bad name by saying: 'I have taken this woman, but when I had relations with her, I did not find evidence that she was a virgin,' **15** the father and mother of the girl should produce the evidence of the girl's virginity for the elders at the gate of the city. **16** The girl's father must say to the elders, 'I gave my daughter to this man as a wife, but he hates* her **17** and is accusing her of misconduct by saying: "I have found out that your daughter does not have evidence of virginity." Now this is the evidence of my daughter's virginity.' They will then spread out the cloth before the elders of the city. **18** The city elders[f] will take the man and discipline him.[g] **19** They will fine him 100 silver shekels* and give them to the girl's father, because the man defamed a virgin of Israel,[h] and she will continue to be

his wife. He will not be allowed to divorce her as long as he lives.

20 "If, though, the accusation is true, and there is no evidence that the girl was a virgin, **21** they should bring the girl out to the entrance of her father's house, and the men of her city should stone her to death, because she has committed a disgraceful act[a] in Israel by committing sexual immorality* in the house of her father.[b] So you must remove what is bad from your midst.[c]

22 "If a man is found lying down with a woman who is the wife of another man, both of them must die together, the man who lay down with the woman as well as the woman.[d] So you must remove what is bad out of Israel.

23 "If a virgin is engaged to a man, and another man happens to meet her in the city and lies down with her, **24** you should bring them both out to the gate of that city and stone them to death, the girl because she did not scream in the city and the man because he humiliated the wife of his fellow man.[e] So you must remove what is evil from your midst.

25 "If, however, the man happened to meet the engaged girl in the field and the man overpowered her and lay down with her, the man who lay down with her is to die by himself, **26** and you must do nothing to the girl. The girl has not committed a sin deserving of death. This case is the same as when a man attacks his fellow man and murders him.*[f] **27** For he happened to meet her in the field, and the engaged girl screamed, but there was no one to rescue her.

28 "If a man happens to meet a virgin girl who is not en-

CHAP. 22
a 2Sa 11:2
  Ac 10:9

b Le 19:19

c Pr 12:10

d Le 19:19

e Nu 15:38
  Mt 23:2, 5

f Ex 18:21
  De 1:13
  De 16:18

g De 25:2
  Pr 10:13
  Pr 19:29

h Mal 2:16

Second Col.
a Heb 13:4

b Le 21:9

c Le 11:45
  1Co 5:13

d Ge 20:3
  Ex 20:14
  Le 20:10
  1Co 6:9, 10
  1Co 6:18

e Le 20:10
  De 5:18
  1Th 4:3, 6
  Heb 13:4

f Ge 4:8
  Nu 35:20, 21
  Jas 2:11

22:13 *Or "then rejects her." 22:16 *Or "rejects." 22:19 *A shekel equaled 11.4 g (0.367 oz t). See App. B14.

22:21 *Or "prostitution." 22:26 *Or "murders him, a soul."

gaged and he seizes her and lies down with her and they are discovered,[a] **29** the man who lay down with her must give the girl's father 50 silver shekels, and she will become his wife.[b] Because he humiliated her, he will not be allowed to divorce her as long as he lives.

30 "No man should take his father's wife, so that he may not dishonor his father.*[c]

23 "No man who has been castrated by having his testicles crushed or who has had his male organ cut off may come into the congregation of Jehovah.[d]

2 "No illegitimate son may come into the congregation of Jehovah.[e] Even to the tenth generation, none of his descendants may come into the congregation of Jehovah.

3 "No Am'mon·ite or Mo'ab·ite may come into the congregation of Jehovah.[f] Even to the tenth generation, none of their descendants may ever come into the congregation of Jehovah, **4** because they did not come to your aid with food and water when you were on the way going out of Egypt,[g] and because they hired against you Ba'laam the son of Be'or from Pe'thor of Mes·o·po·ta'mi·a to curse* you.[h] **5** But Jehovah your God refused to listen to Ba'laam.[i] Rather, Jehovah your God changed the curse into a blessing for you,[j] because Jehovah your God loved you.[k] **6** You should never seek their welfare or their prosperity all your days.[l]

7 "You must not hate an E'dom·ite, for he is your brother.[m]

"You must not hate an Egyptian, for you became a foreign

resident in his country.[a] **8** The third generation of children born to them may enter the congregation of Jehovah.

9 "When you are encamped against your enemies, you should avoid anything bad.*[b] **10** If a man becomes unclean because of a nocturnal emission,[c] he should go outside the camp and not reenter the camp. **11** When evening falls, he should wash with water, and then he may return to the camp at sunset.[d] **12** A private place* should be designated for use outside the camp, and there is where you should go. **13** A peg should be part of your equipment. When you squat outside, you should dig a hole with it and then cover your excrement. **14** For Jehovah your God is walking about within your camp[e] to deliver you and to hand over your enemies to you, and your camp must be holy,[f] so that he does not see anything indecent in you and turn away from accompanying you.

15 "You should not hand over a slave to his master when he escapes from his master and comes to you. **16** He may dwell among you in whatever place he chooses in one of your cities, wherever he likes. You must not mistreat him.[g]

17 "None of the daughters of Israel may become a temple prostitute,[h] neither may anyone of the sons of Israel become a temple prostitute.[i] **18** You must not bring the price paid to a female prostitute or the price paid to* a male prostitute* into the house of Jehovah your God to fulfill a vow, for both of them are something detestable to Jehovah your God.

CHAP. 22
a Ge 34:2, 5

b Ge 34:11, 12
Ex 22:16

c Le 18:8
Le 20:11
De 27:20
1Co 5:1

CHAP. 23
d Le 21:18, 20
Isa 56:4, 5

e Ex 20:14
Le 20:10

f Ne 13:1, 2

g Jg 11:18

h Nu 22:6
Jos 24:9

i Nu 22:35

j Nu 23:11, 25
Nu 24:10

k De 7:7, 8

l 2Sa 8:2
2Sa 12:31

m Ge 25:25, 26
Ge 36:1
Nu 20:14

Second Col.
a Ge 46:6
Le 19:34
Ps 105:23

b 1Sa 21:5
2Sa 11:11

c Le 15:16

d Le 15:31

e Le 26:12

f 1Pe 1:16

g Ex 22:21

h Le 19:29
Le 21:9

i 1Ki 14:24
2Ki 23:7

22:30 *Lit., "uncover the skirt of his father." 23:4 *Or "call down evil upon."

23:9 *Or "defiling." 23:12 *That is, a latrine. 23:18 *Or "the earnings of." *Lit., "a dog."

19 "You must not make your brother pay interest,[a] whether interest on money, on food, or on anything on which interest may be charged. **20** You may make a foreigner pay interest,[b] but you must not make your brother pay interest,[c] so that Jehovah your God may bless you in every undertaking of yours in the land you are going to take possession of.[d]

21 "If you make a vow to Jehovah your God,[e] do not be slow about paying it.[f] For Jehovah your God will surely require it of you; otherwise, it will be a sin on your part.[g] **22** But if you refrain from making a vow, you will not be guilty of sin.[h] **23** The word of your lips you should keep,[i] and you must carry out what your own mouth vowed as a voluntary offering to Jehovah your God.[j]

24 "If you enter your neighbor's vineyard, you may eat enough grapes to satisfy your appetite,* but you should not put any in your container.[k]

25 "If you go into your neighbor's field of standing grain, you may pluck the ripe ears with your hand, but you should not put a sickle to your neighbor's grain.[l]

24 "If a man marries a woman but she does not please him because he found something indecent about her, he must write out a certificate of divorce for her,[m] hand it to her, and dismiss her from his house.[n] **2** After she leaves his house, she may go and become another man's wife.[o] **3** If the second man hates* her and writes out a certificate of divorce for her, hands it to her, and dismisses her from his house or if the second man who married her should die, **4** her first husband who dis-

missed her will not be allowed to take her back again as his wife after she has been defiled, for that is something detestable to Jehovah. You must not bring sin into the land that Jehovah your God is giving you as an inheritance.

5 "When a man is newly married, he should not serve in the army or be given any other duties. He should remain exempt for one year and stay at home and bring joy to his wife.[a]

6 "No one should seize a hand mill or its upper millstone as security for a loan,*[b] for that would be taking someone's livelihood# as security.

7 "If someone is found to have kidnapped one* of his Israelite brothers and he has mistreated him and sold him,[c] the kidnapper must die.[d] You should remove what is bad from your midst.[e]

8 "When there is an outbreak of leprosy,* be very careful to do according to all that the Levitical priests will instruct you.[f] Be careful to do exactly as I commanded them. **9** Remember what Jehovah your God did to Mir′i·am on the way when you were coming out of Egypt.[g]

10 "If you make any sort of loan to your neighbor,[h] you must not enter into his house to seize from him what he has offered as security. **11** You should stand outside, and the man who received the loan should bring outside to you what he is giving as security. **12** And if the man is in need, you must not go to bed with what he gave as secu-

CHAP. 23	
a	Ex 22:25
	Le 25:36, 37
	Ne 5:10
	Ps 15:5
b	De 15:6
c	Pr 28:8
d	De 15:4
	De 15:7, 10
	Pr 19:17
	Lu 6:34, 35
e	Jg 11:30, 31
	1Sa 1:11
f	Jon 2:9
g	Ec 5:4, 6
h	Ec 5:5
i	Nu 30:2
	Ps 15:4
	Pr 20:25
j	Jg 11:35
	1Sa 14:24
	Mt 5:33
k	Mt 6:11
	Ro 13:10
l	Mt 12:1
	Lu 6:1
CHAP. 24	
m	Mt 5:31, 32
	Mt 10:4, 11
n	Mal 2:16
	Mt 1:19
	Mt 19:3-8
o	Le 21:7
Second Col.	
a	De 20:7
	Pr 5:18
	Ec 9:9
b	Ex 22:26, 27
c	Ge 37:28
	Ge 40:15
d	Ex 21:16
e	De 19:18, 19
	De 21:20, 21
f	Le 13:2, 15
	Mr 1:44
	Lu 17:14
g	Nu 12:10, 15
h	De 15:7, 8
	Pr 3:27

23:24 * Or "soul."   24:3 * Lit., "rejects."

24:6 * Or "as a pledge."   # Or "taking a life; taking a soul."   24:7 * Or "a soul."   24:8 * The Hebrew word rendered "leprosy" is broad in meaning and can include various contagious skin diseases. It may also include certain infections found on clothing and in houses.

rity still in your possession.[a]
13 You should by all means return to him what he has given as security as soon as the sun sets, and he will go to bed with his garment,[b] and he will bless you; and it will mean righteousness for you before Jehovah your God.

14 "You must not defraud a hired worker who is in need and poor, whether one of your brothers or a foreign resident in your land, within your cities.*[c]
15 You should give him his wages that very day,[d] before the sun sets, because he is in need and his life* depends on his wages. Otherwise, he will cry out to Jehovah against you, and you will be guilty of sin.[e]

16 "Fathers should not be put to death for what their children do, and children should not be put to death for what their fathers do.[f] A person should be put to death only for his own sin.[g]

17 "You must not pervert the judgment of the foreign resident or of the fatherless child,*[h] and you must not seize the garment of a widow as security for a loan.*[i] **18** Remember that you became a slave in Egypt, and Jehovah your God redeemed you from there.[j] That is why I am commanding you to do this.

19 "When you reap your harvest from your field and you have forgotten a sheaf in the field, do not go back to get it. It should be left for the foreign resident, the fatherless child, and the widow,[k] so that Jehovah your God may bless you in all that you do.[l]

20 "When you beat your olive tree, you should not repeat the procedure on its branches.

24:14 *Lit., "gates." 24:15 *Or "soul." 24:17 *Or "the orphan." #Or "as a pledge."

What is left should remain for the foreign resident, the fatherless child, and the widow.[a]
21 "When you gather the grapes of your vineyard, you must not return to gather the leftovers. They should be left for the foreign resident, the fatherless child, and the widow. **22** Remember that you became a slave in the land of Egypt. That is why I am commanding you to do this.

25 "When a dispute arises between men, they may present themselves before the judges,[b] and they will judge them and pronounce the righteous one innocent and the wicked one guilty.[c] **2** If the wicked one deserves to be beaten,[d] the judge will have him lie down prostrate, and he will be beaten in his presence. The number of strokes should correspond to the wickedness of his deed. **3** He may beat him with up to 40 strokes,[e] but no more. If he would continue beating him with more strokes than this, your brother would be disgraced before your eyes.

4 "You must not muzzle a bull when it is threshing out grain.[f]

5 "If brothers dwell together and one of them dies without having a son, the wife of the dead one should not marry someone from outside the family. Her brother-in-law should go to her, take her as his wife, and perform brother-in-law marriage with her.[g] **6** The firstborn whom she will bear will carry on the name of his dead brother,[h] so that his name may not be wiped out of Israel.[i]

7 "Now if the man does not want to marry his brother's widow, his brother's widow should then go to the elders at the city gate and say, 'My husband's brother has refused to preserve his brother's name in Israel. He

---

CHAP. 24

a Job 24:9, 10

b Ex 22:26, 27

c Le 25:39, 43
  Pr 14:31

d Le 19:13
  Jer 22:13
  Mt 20:8

e Pr 22:22, 23
  Jas 5:4

f 2Ch 25:3, 4

g Eze 18:20

h Ex 22:21, 22

i Ex 22:26, 27

j De 5:15

k Le 19:9
  Le 23:22
  Ru 2:16
  Ps 41:1

l De 15:7, 10
  Pr 11:24
  Pr 19:17
  Lu 6:38
  2Co 9:6
  1Jo 3:17

Second Col.

a Le 19:10
  De 26:13

CHAP. 25

b De 16:18
  De 17:8, 9
  De 19:16, 17

c Ex 23:6
  2Ch 19:6
  Pr 17:15
  Pr 31:9

d Pr 10:13
  Pr 20:30
  Pr 26:3
  Lu 12:48
  Heb 2:2

e 2Co 11:24

f Pr 12:10
  1Co 9:9
  1Ti 5:18

g Ge 38:7, 8
  Ru 4:5
  Mt 22:19

h Ge 38:9
  Ru 4:10, 17

i Nu 27:1, 4

has not consented to perform brother-in-law marriage with me.' **8** The elders of his city must call him and speak to him. Should he insist and say, 'I do not want to marry her,' **9** then his brother's widow should approach him before the elders, remove his sandal from his foot,ᵃ spit in his face, and say, 'That is what should be done to the man who will not build up his brother's household.' **10** After that his family name* in Israel will be known as 'The house of the one who had his sandal removed.'

11 "If two men get into a fight with each other and the wife of the one intervenes to protect her husband from the one striking him and she reaches out her hand and grabs hold of him by his private parts, **12** you must amputate her hand. You* should not feel sorry.

13 "You must not have in your bag two different stone weights,ᵇ a large one and a small one. **14** You must not have in your house two different measuring containers,*ᶜ a large one and a small one. **15** You should keep an accurate and honest weight and an accurate and honest measure, so that you will live long in the land that Jehovah your God is giving you.ᵈ **16** For every unjust person who does such things is detestable to Jehovah your God.ᵉ

17 "Remember what Amʹa·lek did to you on the way as you were coming out of Egypt,ᶠ **18** how he met you along the way and attacked all those straggling behind you when you were exhausted and weary. He did not fear God. **19** When Jehovah your God has given you rest from all your enemies

around you in the land that Jehovah your God is giving you as an inheritance to possess,ᵃ you should wipe out the mention of Amʹa·lek from under the heavens.ᵇ You must not forget.

26 "When eventually you enter into the land that Jehovah your God is giving you as an inheritance and you have taken possession of it and are dwelling in it, **2** you are to take some of the firstfruits of all the produce* of the ground, which you will gather from your land that Jehovah your God is giving you, and put them in a basket and go to the place that Jehovah your God chooses to have his name reside.ᶜ **3** You must go to the priest who will be serving in those days and say to him, 'Today I am reporting to Jehovah your God that I have come into the land that Jehovah swore to our forefathers to give to us.'ᵈ

4 "The priest will then take the basket out of your hand and deposit it before the altar of Jehovah your God. **5** Then you are to declare before Jehovah your God, 'My father was a wandering* A·ra·maeʹan,ᵉ and he went down to Egyptᶠ and resided there as a foreigner, with few in his household.ᵍ But there he became a great nation, mighty and numerous.ʰ **6** And the Egyptians mistreated and oppressed us and imposed harsh slavery on us.ⁱ **7** So we began to cry out to Jehovah, the God of our forefathers, and Jehovah heard our voice and looked upon our affliction and our trouble and our oppression.ʲ **8** Finally Jehovah brought us out of Egypt with a mighty hand and an outstretched armᵏ and with terrifying deeds and with signs and miracles.ˡ **9** Then he brought us to this place and gave us

CHAP. 25
ᵃ Ru 4:7

ᵇ Pr 11:1
Pr 20:10
Mic 6:11

ᶜ Le 19:36

ᵈ De 4:40

ᵉ Le 19:35

ᶠ Ex 17:8
Nu 24:20

Second Col.
ᵃ Jos 22:4

ᵇ Ex 17:14
1Sa 14:47, 48
1Sa 15:1-3
1Ch 4:42, 43

CHAP. 26
ᶜ Ex 23:19
Le 23:10
Nu 18:8, 12
2Ch 6:6
2Ch 31:5
Pr 3:9

ᵈ Ge 17:1, 8
Ge 26:3

ᵉ Ge 28:5
Ho 12:12

ᶠ Ge 46:3
Ac 7:15

ᵍ Ge 46:27

ʰ Ex 1:7
De 10:22
Ps 105:24

ⁱ Ex 1:11

ʲ Ex 3:9
Ex 4:31
Ac 7:34

ᵏ Ex 6:6

ˡ Ex 7:3
De 4:33, 34

25:10 *Or "the name of his household." Lit., "his name." **25:12** *Lit., "Your eye." **25:14** *Lit., "in your house an ephah and an ephah." See App. B14.

26:2 *Lit., "fruit." **26:5** *Or possibly, "perishing."

this land, a land flowing with milk and honey.[a] **10** Now I have brought the firstfruits of the produce of the ground that Jehovah has given me.'[b]

"You must deposit it before Jehovah your God and bow down before Jehovah your God. **11** You will then rejoice over all the good that Jehovah your God has given you and your household, you and the Levite and the foreign resident who is among you.[c]

12 "When you finish tithing[d] the entire tenth of your produce in the third year, the year of the tenth, you will give it to the Levite, the foreign resident, the fatherless child,* and the widow, and they will eat their fill within your cities.#[e] **13** You will then say before Jehovah your God, 'I have cleared the holy portion out of my house and given it to the Levite, the foreign resident, the fatherless child, and the widow,[f] just as you have commanded me. I have not violated or neglected your commandments. **14** I have not eaten of it while mourning or removed any of it while unclean or given any of it for the dead. I have obeyed the voice of Jehovah my God and have done all that you commanded me. **15** Now look down from your holy dwelling, the heavens, and bless your people Israel and the land that you have given us,[g] just as you swore to our forefathers,[h] the land flowing with milk and honey.'[i]

16 "This day Jehovah your God is commanding you to carry out these regulations and judicial decisions. You must observe them and carry them out with all your heart[j] and all your soul.* **17** Today you have obtained Jehovah's declaration that he will become your God

as you walk in his ways and observe his regulations,[a] his commandments,[b] and his judicial decisions,[c] and as you listen to his voice. **18** And today Jehovah has obtained your declaration that you will become his people, his special property,*[d] just as he has promised you, and that you will observe all his commandments **19** and that he will put you high above all the other nations that he has made,[e] giving you praise and fame and glory as you prove yourself a people holy to Jehovah your God,[f] just as he has promised."

27 Then Moses together with the elders of Israel commanded the people, saying: "Observe every commandment that I am giving you today. **2** And in the day when you will cross the Jordan into the land that Jehovah your God is giving you, set up large stones and cover them with plaster.*[g] **3** Then write on them all the words of this Law when you have crossed over, so that you may enter into the land that Jehovah your God is giving you, a land flowing with milk and honey, just as Jehovah, the God of your forefathers, has promised you.[h] **4** When you have crossed the Jordan, you should set up these stones on Mount E′bal[i] and cover them with plaster,* just as I am commanding you today. **5** You are also to build an altar there to Jehovah your God, an altar of stones. You should not use iron tools on them.[j] **6** You should build the altar of Jehovah your God with whole stones and offer burnt offerings to Jehovah your God on it. **7** You are to offer communion sacrifices[k] and eat them there,[l] and you will rejoice before Jehovah your God.[m] **8** And clearly write

	CHAP. 26
a	Ex 3:8
	De 8:7, 8
	Eze 20:6
b	De 26:2
c	De 12:7
	De 16:14
d	De 12:5, 6
	De 14:22
e	De 14:28, 29
	Pr 14:21
	1Jo 3:17
f	Jas 1:27
g	Ex 23:25
h	Ge 15:18
	Ge 26:3
i	De 8:7, 8
j	De 6:6
	De 11:1
	Ps 119:34
	1Jo 5:3

Second Col.	
a	Le 26:46
b	Ec 12:13
c	Le 19:37
d	De 14:2
	De 29:10-13
e	De 4:8
f	De 7:6
	De 28:1, 9

	CHAP. 27
g	Jos 8:30-32
h	Nu 13:26, 27
i	De 11:29
j	Ex 20:25
k	Le 3:1
l	Le 7:15
m	De 12:7

26:12 *Or "the orphan." #Lit., "gates."
26:16 *See Glossary.

26:18 *Or "treasured possession."
27:2, 4 *Or "whitewash them with lime."

on the stones all the words of this Law."[a]

9 Then Moses and the Levitical priests spoke to all Israel, saying: "Keep silent and listen, O Israel. This day you have become the people of Jehovah your God.[b] **10** You must listen to the voice of Jehovah your God and carry out his commandments[c] and his regulations, which I am commanding you today."

11 On that day Moses commanded the people, saying: **12** "The following tribes will stand on Mount Ger′i·zim[d] to bless the people when you have crossed the Jordan: Sim′e·on, Le′vi, Judah, Is′sa·char, Joseph, and Benjamin. **13** And the following will stand on Mount E′bal[e] to pronounce the curse: Reu′ben, Gad, Ash′er, Zeb′u·lun, Dan, and Naph′ta·li. **14** And the Levites will answer every man of Israel with a loud voice:[f]

15 "'Cursed is the man who makes a carved image[g] or a metal statue,*[h] a thing detestable to Jehovah,[i] the workmanship of the hands of a craftsman,# and who has hidden it.' (And all the people will respond, saying, 'Amen!'[A])

16 "'Cursed is the one who treats his father or his mother with contempt.'[j] (And all the people will say, 'Amen!')

17 "'Cursed is the one who moves his neighbor's boundary marker.'[k] (And all the people will say, 'Amen!')

18 "'Cursed is the one who causes a blind person to lose his way on the road.'[l] (And all the people will say, 'Amen!')

19 "'Cursed is the one who perverts the judgment[m] of a foreign resident, a fatherless

child,* or a widow.'[a] (And all the people will say, 'Amen!')

20 "'Cursed is the one who lies down with his father's wife, for he has dishonored his father.'*[b] (And all the people will say, 'Amen!')

21 "'Cursed is the one who lies down with any animal.'[c] (And all the people will say, 'Amen!')

22 "'Cursed is the one who lies down with his sister, the daughter of his father or the daughter of his mother.'[d] (And all the people will say, 'Amen!')

23 "'Cursed is the one who lies down with his mother-in-law.'[e] (And all the people will say, 'Amen!')

24 "'Cursed is the one who ambushes and kills his neighbor.'[f] (And all the people will say, 'Amen!')

25 "'Cursed is the one who accepts a bribe to kill* an innocent person.'#[g] (And all the people will say, 'Amen!')

26 "'Cursed is the one who will not uphold the words of this Law by carrying them out.'[h] (And all the people will say, 'Amen!')

28 "And if you will without fail listen to the voice of Jehovah your God by being careful to do all his commandments that I am commanding you today, Jehovah your God will certainly put you high above all other nations of the earth.[i] **2** All these blessings will come upon you and overtake you,[j] because you keep listening to the voice of Jehovah your God:

3 "Blessed you will be in the city, and blessed you will be in the field.[k]

4 "Blessed will be your children*[l] and the fruit of your

CHAP. 27
a Ex 24:12
b Ex 19:5
  De 26:18
c 1Ki 2:3
  Mt 19:17
  1Jo 5:3
d De 11:29
e Jos 8:33
f De 33:10
g Ex 20:4
  De 4:15, 16
  Isa 44:9
h Ex 34:17
  Le 19:4
i De 7:25
  De 29:17
j Ex 20:12
  De 21:18-21
  Pr 20:20
  Pr 30:17
  Mt 15:4
k De 19:14
  Pr 23:10
l Le 19:14
m De 16:20
  Pr 17:23
  Mic 3:11

Second Col.
a Ex 22:21, 22
  De 10:17, 18
  Mal 3:5
  Jas 1:27
b Le 18:8
  1Co 5:1
c Ex 22:19
  Le 18:23
  Le 20:15
d Le 18:9
  Le 20:17
e Le 18:17
  Le 20:14
f Ex 20:13
  Ex 21:12
  Nu 35:31
g Mt 27:3, 4
h De 28:15
  Ga 3:10

CHAP. 28
i De 26:18, 19
j De 26:3, 4
  Pr 10:22
  Isa 1:19
k De 11:14
l Le 26:9
  Ps 127:3
  Ps 128:3

27:15 *Or "molten statue." #Or "a wood-and-metal worker." △Or "So be it!" 27:19 *Or "an orphan." 27:20 *Lit., "uncovered the skirt of his father." 27:25 *Or "strike down." #Or "a soul of innocent blood." 28:4 *Lit., "the fruit of your womb."

ground and the offspring of your livestock, your young cattle and sheep.[a]

5 "Blessed will be your basket[b] and your kneading bowl.[c]

6 "Blessed you will be when you come in, and blessed you will be when you go out.

7 "Jehovah will cause your enemies who rise up against you to be defeated before you.[d] They will attack you from one direction, but they will flee from you in seven different directions.[e] **8** Jehovah will decree for you a blessing on your storehouses[f] and every undertaking of yours, and he will certainly bless you in the land that Jehovah your God is giving you. **9** Jehovah will establish you as a holy people to himself,[g] just as he swore to you,[h] because you continue to keep the commandments of Jehovah your God and walk in his ways. **10** All the peoples of the earth will have to see that Jehovah's name has been called upon you,[i] and they will be afraid of you.[j]

11 "Jehovah will make you overflow with many children and much livestock and fruitful ground[k] in the land that Jehovah swore to your forefathers to give you.[l] **12** Jehovah will open up to you his good storehouse, the heavens, to give your land rain in its season[m] and to bless all that you do. You will lend to many nations, while you yourself will not need to borrow.[n] **13** Jehovah will make you the head, and not the tail; and you will be on top,[o] and not on the bottom, if you keep obeying the commandments of Jehovah your God that I am commanding you today to observe and to do. **14** You must not deviate from all the words that I am commanding you today, to the right or to the left,[p] to walk after other gods to serve them.[q]

15 "But if you will not listen to the voice of Jehovah your God by taking care to do all his commandments and his statutes that I am commanding you today, all these curses will come upon you and overtake you:[a]

16 "Cursed you will be in the city, and cursed you will be in the field.[b]

17 "Cursed will be your basket[c] and your kneading bowl.[d]

18 "Cursed will be your children*[e] and the fruit of your ground and your young cattle and sheep.[f]

19 "Cursed you will be when you come in, and cursed you will be when you go out.

20 "Jehovah will send upon you the curse, confusion and punishment in every undertaking of yours until you have been annihilated and have quickly perished, because of your bad practices and your forsaking me.[g] **21** Jehovah will cause the disease to cling to you until he has exterminated you from the land you are going to take possession of.[h] **22** Jehovah will strike you with tuberculosis, burning fever,[i] inflammation, feverish heat, the sword,[j] scorching blight, and mildew;[k] and they will pursue you until you have perished. **23** The skies over your head will be copper, and the earth beneath you, iron.[l] **24** Jehovah will make the rain of your land powder and dust that will come down on you from the heavens until you have been annihilated. **25** Jehovah will cause you to be defeated before your enemies.[m] You will attack them from one direction, but you will flee from them in seven different directions; and you will become an object of horror to all the earth's kingdoms.[n] **26** And your carcasses will become food for every bird

CHAP. 28
a De 7:13
b De 26:2
c Ex 23:25
d De 32:30; Jos 10:11
e De 7:23; 2Ch 14:13
f Le 26:10; Pr 3:9, 10; Mal 3:10
g De 7:6
h Ex 19:6
i Isa 43:10; Da 9:19; Ac 15:17
j Nu 22:3; De 11:25; Jos 5:1
k De 30:9; Ps 65:9
l Ge 15:18
m Le 26:4; De 11:14
n De 15:6
o 1Ki 4:21
p De 5:32; Jos 1:7; Isa 30:21
q Le 19:4

Second Col.
a Le 26:16, 17; Da 9:11
b 1Ki 17:1
c De 26:2
d Le 26:26
e La 2:11, 19; La 4:10
f Le 26:20, 22
g Jos 23:16
h Le 26:25; Jer 24:10
i Le 26:16
j Le 26:33
k Am 4:9
l Le 26:19; De 11:17; 1Ki 17:1
m Le 26:14, 17; 1Sa 4:10
n Jer 29:18; Lu 21:24

28:18 *Lit., "the fruit of your womb."

of the sky and animal of the ground, with no one to frighten them away.[a]

27 "Jehovah will strike you with the boils of Egypt, piles, eczema, and skin lesions, from which you cannot be healed. 28 Jehovah will strike you with madness and blindness[b] and confusion.* 29 You will grope about at midday, just as a blind man gropes about in darkness,[c] and you will not succeed in anything you do; and you will be constantly defrauded and robbed, with no one to save you.[d] 30 You will become engaged to a woman, but another man will rape her. You will build a house, but you will not live in it.[e] You will plant a vineyard, but you will not begin to use it.[f] 31 Your bull will be slaughtered before your eyes, but you will not eat any of it. Your donkey will be stolen right in front of you, but it will not return to you. Your sheep will be given to your enemies, but you will have no savior. 32 Your sons and your daughters will be given to another people[g] while you look on, and you will always long for them, but your hands will be powerless. 33 The fruitage of your ground and all that you produce will be eaten by a people whom you have not known,[h] and you will always be defrauded and crushed. 34 You will be driven mad by what your eyes see.

35 "Jehovah will strike you with painful and incurable boils on your knees and legs, from the sole of your foot to the crown of your head. 36 Jehovah will drive you and the king whom you set up over yourself to a nation that you and your forefathers have not known,[i] and there you will serve other gods, gods of wood and of stone.[j] 37 And you

will become an object of horror and of scorn,* and a cause for ridicule among all the peoples to whom Jehovah drives you.[a]

38 "You will take much seed out into the field, but you will gather little,[b] because the locust will devour it. 39 Vineyards you will plant and cultivate, but you will drink no wine and gather nothing,[c] because the worm will consume it. 40 You will have olive trees in all your territory, but you will rub no oil on yourself, because your olives will drop off. 41 Sons and daughters you will bear, but they will not remain yours, because they will go off into captivity.[d] 42 Swarms of insects* will overwhelm all your trees and the fruitage of your ground. 43 The foreign resident who is in your midst will keep ascending higher and higher over you, while you yourself will keep descending lower and lower. 44 He will lend to you, but you will not lend to him.[e] He will become the head, while you yourself will become the tail.[f]

45 "All these curses[g] will certainly come upon you and pursue you and overtake you until you have been annihilated,[h] because you did not listen to the voice of Jehovah your God by keeping his commandments and his statutes that he commanded you.[i] 46 And they will continue on you and your offspring as a permanent sign and portent,[j] 47 because you did not serve Jehovah your God with rejoicing and joy of heart when you had such an abundance of everything.[k] 48 Jehovah will send your enemies against them[l] while you are hungry[m] and thirsty and poorly clothed and lacking everything. He will put

---

CHAP. 28
a Jer 7:33
b Ex 4:11
c Isa 59:10
d Jg 3:14
  Jg 6:1-5
  Ne 9:27
e Isa 5:9
  La 5:2
f Am 5:11
  Mic 6:15
g 2Ch 29:9
h Ne 9:37
  Isa 1:7
i 2Ki 17:6
  2Ki 25:7
  2Ch 33:11
  2Ch 36:5, 6
j Jer 16:13

Second Col.
a 1Ki 9:8
  2Ch 7:20
  Jer 24:9
  Jer 25:9
b Isa 5:10
  Hag 1:6
c Zep 1:13
d 2Ki 24:14
  Jer 52:15, 30
e Pr 22:7
f Ezr 9:7
g De 28:15
  De 29:27
h 2Ki 17:20
  Jer 24:10
i De 11:26-28
j 1Co 10:11
k De 12:7
  Ne 9:35
l 2Ch 12:8, 9
  Jer 5:19
m Jer 44:27

28:28 *Or "bewilderment of heart." 28:37 *Lit., "a proverb." 28:42 *Or "Whirring insects."

an iron yoke on your neck until he has annihilated you.

49 "Jehovah will raise up against you a distant nation,[a] from the end of the earth; it will pounce like an eagle,[b] a nation whose language you will not understand,[c] 50 a nation fierce in appearance that will show no regard to the old or favor to the young.[d] 51 They will eat the offspring of your livestock and the fruitage of your ground until you have been annihilated. They will not leave any grain, new wine or oil, young cattle or sheep for you until they have destroyed you.[e] 52 They will besiege you, shutting you up inside all your cities* throughout your land until your high and fortified walls that you are trusting in fall down. Yes, they will certainly besiege you within all your cities throughout your land that Jehovah your God has given you.[f] 53 Then you will have to eat your own children,* the flesh of your sons and your daughters[g] whom Jehovah your God has given you, because of the severity of the siege and the distress your enemy inflicts on you.

54 "Even the most delicate and sensitive man among you will have no pity on his brother or his cherished wife or his sons who remain, 55 and he will not share with them any of the flesh of his sons that he will eat, because he has nothing else on account of the severity of the siege and the distress your enemy inflicts on your cities.[h] 56 And the delicate and sensitive woman among you who would not even think of putting the sole of her foot on the ground because she is so delicate[i] will show no pity to her cherished husband or her son or her daughter, 57 even toward the afterbirth that comes from between her legs and toward the sons she bears, for she will secretly eat them because of the severity of the siege and the distress your enemy inflicts on your cities.

58 "If you will not carefully observe all the words of this Law that are written in this book[a] and you do not fear this glorious and awe-inspiring name,[b] that of Jehovah[c] your God, 59 Jehovah will inflict very severe plagues on you and your offspring, great and enduring plagues,[d] and grievous and enduring sicknesses. 60 He will bring back upon you all the diseases of Egypt that you used to fear, and they will certainly cling to you. 61 Moreover, Jehovah will even bring upon you every sickness or plague not written in the book of this Law until you have been annihilated. 62 Although you have become as numerous as the stars of the heavens,[e] very few of your number will be left,[f] because you did not listen to the voice of Jehovah your God.

63 "And just as Jehovah once delighted to make you prosper and to multiply you, so Jehovah will delight to destroy you and to annihilate you; and you will be torn from the land you are about to possess.

64 "Jehovah will scatter you among all the nations, from the one end of the earth to the other end of the earth,[g] and there you will have to serve gods of wood and of stone, which you and your forefathers have not known.[h] 65 You will have no peace among those nations[i] nor a place of rest for the sole of your foot. Rather, Jehovah will give you there an anxious heart[j] and failing eyes and a feeling of despair.*[k] 66 Your life will be in great peril, and you will feel dread night and day; and you

---

CHAP. 28

a Jer 6:22
  Hab 1:6

b Jer 4:13
  Ho 8:1

c Jer 5:15

d 2Ch 36:17
  Isa 47:6
  Lu 19:44

e Le 26:26
  Jer 15:13

f 2Ki 17:5
  2Ki 25:1
  Lu 19:43

g 2Ki 6:28
  La 4:10
  Eze 5:10

h Jer 52:6

i La 4:5

Second Col.

a Ex 24:7
  De 31:26

b De 10:17
  Ps 99:3

c Ex 3:15
  Ex 6:3
  Ex 20:2
  Ps 83:18
  Ps 113:3
  Isa 42:8

d Le 26:21
  Da 9:12

e De 10:22

f De 4:27

g Le 26:33
  Ne 1:8
  Lu 21:24

h De 4:27, 28

i Am 9:4

j Eze 12:19

k Le 26:16, 36

28:52 *Lit., "gates." 28:53 *Lit., "the fruit of your womb."

28:65 *Or "and despair of soul."

will be uncertain of your survival. **67** In the morning you will say, 'If only it were evening!' and in the evening you will say, 'If only it were morning!' because of the dread you will feel in your heart and because of what your eyes will see. **68** And Jehovah will certainly bring you back to Egypt by ship, by the way that I told you, 'You will never see it again,' and there you will have to sell yourselves to your enemies as male and female slaves, but there will be no buyer."

29 These are the words of the covenant that Jehovah commanded Moses to make with the people of Israel in the land of Mo'ab, in addition to the covenant that he made with them at Ho'reb.[a]

2 Moses then called together all Israel and said to them: "You have seen all that Jehovah did before your eyes in the land of Egypt to Phar'aoh and all his servants and all his land,[b] **3** the great judgments* that your eyes saw, those great signs and miracles.[c] **4** But Jehovah has not given you a heart to understand and eyes to see and ears to hear, down to this day.[d] **5** 'While I kept guiding you for 40 years in the wilderness,[e] your garments did not wear out on you and your sandals did not wear out on your feet.[f] **6** You did not eat bread, and you did not drink wine or anything alcoholic, so that you would know that I am Jehovah your God.' **7** You eventually came to this place, and Si'hon the king of Hesh'bon[g] and Og the king of Ba'shan[h] came out to meet us in battle, but we defeated them.[i] **8** After that we took their land and gave it as an inheritance to the Reu'ben-ites, the Gad'ites, and the half tribe of the Ma·nas'sites.[j]

29:3 *Or "trials."

CHAP. 29
a Ex 24:8

b Ex 19:4
  Jos 24:5

c De 4:34
  Ne 9:10

d Ro 11:8

e De 1:3
  De 8:2

f De 8:4
  Ne 9:21
  Mt 6:31

g Nu 21:26

h Nu 21:33

i Ps 135:10, 11

j Nu 32:33
  De 3:12, 13

Second Col.
a De 4:6
  De 8:18
  Jos 1:7, 8
  1Ki 2:3
  Ps 103:17, 18
  Lu 11:28

b Ne 8:2

c Ex 12:38

d De 1:3
  De 29:1

e Ex 19:5
  De 7:6
  De 28:9

f Ex 6:7
  Ex 29:45

g Ge 17:1, 7
  Ge 22:16, 17

h Ge 26:3

i Ge 28:13

j De 2:4

k Nu 25:1, 2

l De 11:16
  Heb 3:12

m Heb 12:15

9 Therefore, observe the words of this covenant and obey them, so that everything you do will turn out well.[a]

10 "All of you are stationed today before Jehovah your God, the heads of your tribes, your elders, your officers, every man of Israel, **11** your children, your wives,[b] and your foreign resident[c] who is in the midst of your camp, from the one gathering your wood to the one drawing your water. **12** You are here in order to enter into the covenant of Jehovah your God and his oath, which Jehovah your God is making with you today[d] **13** in order that he may establish you today as his people[e] and that he may be your God,[f] just as he has promised you and just as he swore to your forefathers, Abraham,[g] Isaac,[h] and Jacob.[i]

14 "Now it is not with you alone that I am making this covenant and this oath, **15** but it is with those standing here with us today before Jehovah our God and with those who are not here with us today. **16** (For you well know how we lived in the land of Egypt and how we passed through the midst of various nations on our journey.[j] **17** And you used to see their detestable things and their disgusting idols*[k] of wood and stone, silver and gold, that were among them.) **18** Beware that there may not be a man or a woman, a family or a tribe among you today whose heart turns away from Jehovah our God to go serve the gods of those nations,[l] that there may not be a root among you producing poisonous fruit and wormwood.[m]

19 "But if someone hears the words of this oath and boasts in his heart, saying, 'I will have

---

29:17 *The Hebrew term may be related to a word for "dung" and is used as an expression of contempt.

peace, though I insist on walking in the ways of my own heart,' to the ruin of everything* in his path, 20 Jehovah will not be willing to forgive him.ᵃ Instead, Jehovah's great anger will blaze against that man, and the entire curse written in this book will certainly come upon him,ᵇ and Jehovah will indeed wipe out his name from under the heavens. 21 Jehovah will then single him out from all the tribes of Israel for calamity in accord with the entire curse of the covenant that is written in this book of the Law.

22 "When the future generation of your sons and the foreigner from a distant land see the plagues of the land, the maladies that Jehovah has brought upon it— 23 sulfur and salt and burning, so that its whole land will not be sown or sprout, nor will any vegetation spring up in it, like the overthrow of Sod'om and Go·mor'rah,ᶜ Ad'mah and Ze·boi'im,ᵈ which Jehovah overthrew in his anger and in his wrath— 24 they and all the nations will say, 'Why did Jehovah do this to this land?ᵉ What caused this great, burning anger?' 25 Then they will say, 'It was because they abandoned the covenant of Jehovah,ᶠ the God of their forefathers, which he made with them when he brought them out of the land of Egypt.ᵍ 26 But they went and served other gods and bowed down to them, gods that they had not known and that he had not permitted them to worship.*ʰ 27 Then Jehovah's burning anger came against that land by bringing upon it the entire curse written in this book.ⁱ 28 Therefore, Jehovah uprooted them from their soil in his angerʲ and

fury and great indignation and deported them to another land, where they are today.'ᵃ

29 "The things concealed belong to Jehovah our God,ᵇ but the things revealed belong to us and to our descendants forever, so that we may carry out all the words of this Law.ᶜ

30 "When all these words come upon you, the blessing and the curse that I have put before you,ᵈ and you call them to mind*ᵉ in all the nations where Jehovah your God has dispersed you,ᶠ 2 and you return to Jehovah your Godᵍ and listen to his voice according to all that I am commanding you today, you and your sons, with all your heart and all your soul,*ʰ 3 Jehovah your God will then bring back your captivesⁱ and show you mercyʲ and regather you from all the peoples where Jehovah your God has scattered you.ᵏ 4 Even if your people are dispersed to the extremity of the heavens, from there Jehovah your God will gather you and bring you back.ˡ 5 Jehovah your God will bring you into the land your fathers took possession of, and you will possess it; and he will make you prosper and will multiply you more than your fathers.ᵐ 6 Jehovah your God will cleanse# your heart and the heart of your offspring,ⁿ so that you will love Jehovah your God with all your heart and all your soul* and you may live.ᵒ 7 Then Jehovah your God will bring all these curses upon your enemies, who hated and persecuted you.ᵖ

8 "You will then return and listen to the voice of Jehovah and observe all his commandments that I am commanding you today. 9 Jehovah your God

---

CHAP. 29
a Jos 24:19
b De 27:26
  De 28:15
c Ge 19:24
  Jude 7
d Ge 10:19
  Ge 14:2
e 1Ki 9:8, 9
  2Ch 7:21, 22
  Jer 22:8, 9
f 1Ki 19:10
g Jer 31:32
h Jg 2:12
i Le 26:16
  De 27:26
j De 28:45, 63
  1Ki 14:15
  2Ki 17:18
  Lu 21:24

Second Col.
a Ezr 9:7
  Da 9:7
b Ro 11:33
c Ps 78:5
  Ec 12:13

CHAP. 30
d De 11:26-28
  De 28:2, 15
e 1Ki 8:47
  Ne 1:9
  Eze 18:28
  Joe 2:13
f 2Ki 17:6
  2Ch 36:20
g Isa 55:7
  1Jo 1:9
h De 4:29
i Jer 29:14
j La 3:22
k Ezr 1:2, 3
  Ps 147:2
  Jer 32:37
  Eze 34:13
l De 28:64
  Zep 3:20
m Ne 1:9
n Jer 32:37, 39
o De 6:5
p Ge 12:2, 3
  Jer 25:12
  La 3:64
  Ro 12:19

29:19 *Lit., "the well-watered one along with the dry one." 29:26 *Lit., "not apportioned to them."

30:1 *Lit., "and you bring them back to your heart." 30:2, 6 *See Glossary. 30:6 #Lit., "circumcise."

will make you abundantly prosperous in all the work of your hands,[a] multiplying your children and your livestock and the produce of your ground, for Jehovah will again delight to make you prosper, just as he delighted in your forefathers.[b] **10** For then you will listen to the voice of Jehovah your God and keep his commandments and statutes written in this book of the Law, and you will return to Jehovah your God with all your heart and all your soul.*[c]

11 "Now this commandment that I am commanding you today is not too difficult for you, nor is it beyond your reach.*[d] **12** It is not in the heavens, so that you have to say, 'Who will ascend to the heavens and get it for us, so that we may hear it and observe it?'[e] **13** Nor is it on the other side of the sea, so that you have to say, 'Who will cross over to the other side of the sea and get it for us, so that we may hear it and observe it?' **14** For the word is very near you, in your own mouth and in your own heart,[f] so that you may do it.[g]

15 "See, I do put before you today life and good, and death and bad.[h] **16** If you listen to the commandments of Jehovah your God that I am commanding you today, by loving Jehovah your God,[i] by walking in his ways, and by keeping his commandments and his statutes and his judicial decisions, then you will live[j] and multiply, and Jehovah your God will bless you in the land you are going to possess.[k]

17 "But if your heart turns away[l] and you do not listen and you are enticed and bow down to other gods and serve them,[m] **18** I tell you today that you will certainly perish.[n] You will not

live long in the land you are crossing the Jordan to possess. **19** I take the heavens and the earth as witnesses against you today that I have put life and death before you, the blessing and the curse;[a] and you must choose life so that you may live,[b] you and your descendants,[c] **20** by loving Jehovah your God,[d] by listening to his voice, and by sticking to him,[e] for he is your life and by him you will endure a long time in the land that Jehovah swore to give to your forefathers, Abraham, Isaac, and Jacob."[f]

31 Then Moses went out and spoke these words to all Israel, **2** saying to them: "I am 120 years old today.[g] I can no longer lead you,* for Jehovah has said to me, 'You will not cross this Jordan.'[h] **3** Jehovah your God is the one crossing before you, and he himself will annihilate these nations before you, and you will drive them away.[i] Joshua is the one who will lead you across,[j] just as Jehovah has spoken. **4** Jehovah will do to them just as he did to Si'hon[k] and to Og,[l] the kings of the Am'or·ites, and to their land when he annihilated them.[m] **5** Jehovah will defeat them for you, and you are to do to them according to the whole commandment that I have given you.[n] **6** Be courageous and strong.[o] Do not be afraid or struck with terror before them,[p] for Jehovah your God is the one marching with you. He will neither desert you nor abandon you."[q]

7 Moses then called Joshua and said to him before the eyes of all Israel: "Be courageous and strong,[r] for you are the one who will bring this people into the land that Jehovah swore to their forefathers to give to them, and

---

CHAP. 30
a Isa 65:21, 22
  Mal 3:10
b Jer 32:37, 41
c Ne 1:9
  Ac 3:19
d Isa 45:19
e Ro 10:6
f Ro 10:8
g Mt 7:21
  Jas 1:25
h De 11:26
i De 6:5
j Le 18:5
k Le 25:18
  De 30:5
l De 29:18
  Heb 3:12
m De 4:19
n De 8:19
  Jos 23:15
  1Sa 12:25

Second Col.
a De 11:26
  De 27:26
  De 28:2, 15
b De 32:47
c Jos 24:15
d De 10:12
e De 4:4
f Ge 12:7
  Ge 15:18

CHAP. 31
g Ex 7:7
  De 34:7
  Ac 7:23
h Nu 20:12
  De 3:27
i De 9:3
j Nu 27:18
  De 3:28
  Jos 1:2
k Nu 21:23, 24
l Nu 31:33, 35
m Ex 23:23
n Nu 33:52
  De 7:2, 24
  De 20:16
o Jos 1:6
  Ps 27:14
  Ps 118:6
p Nu 14:9
  De 7:18
q De 4:31
  Jos 1:5
  Heb 13:5
r Jos 10:25

30:10 *See Glossary. 30:11 *Lit., "nor is it far away."

31:2 *Lit., "go out and come in."

you will give it to them as an inheritance.[a] **8** Jehovah is the one marching before you, and he will continue with you.[b] He will neither desert you nor abandon you. Do not be afraid or be terrified."[c]

9 Then Moses wrote this Law[d] and gave it to the priests, the Levites, who carry the ark of Jehovah's covenant, and to all the elders of Israel. **10** Moses commanded them, saying: "At the end of every seven years, at the appointed time in the year of the release,[e] during the Festival of Booths,[f] **11** when all Israel appears before the presence of Jehovah[g] your God in the place that he chooses, you should read this Law for all Israel to hear it.[h] **12** Gather the people together,[i] the men, the women, the children,* and your foreign resident who is within your cities,[#] in order that they may listen and learn about and fear Jehovah your God and take care to carry out all the words of this Law. **13** Then their sons who have not known this Law will listen[j] and learn to fear Jehovah your God all the days that you live in the land that you are crossing the Jordan to possess."[k]

14 Jehovah then said to Moses: "Look! The time has drawn near for you to die.[l] Call Joshua, and present yourselves* at the tent of meeting, so that I may commission him."[m] So Moses and Joshua went and presented themselves at the tent of meeting. **15** Then Jehovah appeared at the tent in the pillar of cloud, and the pillar of cloud stood by the entrance of the tent.[n]

16 Jehovah now said to Moses: "Look! You are about to die,* and this people will begin to commit spiritual prostitution with the foreign gods that are around them in the land to which they are going.[a] They will forsake me[b] and break my covenant that I have made with them.[c] **17** At that time my anger will blaze against them,[d] and I will forsake them[e] and hide my face from them[f] until they are devoured. Then after many calamities and distresses have come upon them,[g] they will say, 'Is it not because our God is not in our midst that these calamities have come upon us?'[h] **18** But I will keep my face hidden in that day because of all the wickedness that they have done in turning to other gods.[i]

19 "Now write down this song for yourselves[j] and teach it to the Israelites.[k] Have them learn it* in order that this song may serve as my witness against the people of Israel.[l] **20** When I bring them to the land that I have sworn about to their forefathers[m]—one flowing with milk and honey[n]—and they eat their fill and prosper,* they will turn to other gods and serve them and treat me with disrespect and break my covenant.[p] **21** When many calamities and distresses come upon them,[q] this song will serve as a witness to them (for their descendants should not forget it), for I already know the inclination that they have developed[r] even before I bring them into the land about which I have sworn."

22 So Moses wrote down this song in that day and taught it to the Israelites.

23 He* then commissioned Joshua[s] the son of Nun and said:

CHAP. 31
a De 1:38
b Ex 33:14
c Jos 1:9
d Ex 34:27
e De 15:1
f Le 23:34
g De 16:16
h Ne 8:7
i De 4:10
  Heb 10:25
j De 6:6, 7
  Eph 6:4
k De 30:16
l Nu 27:13
m De 3:28
n Ex 33:9
  Ex 40:38

Second Col.
a Jg 2:17
  Ps 106:37-39
b 1Ki 11:33
c Jg 2:12, 20
d De 29:20
e 1Ch 28:9
  2Ch 15:2
  2Ch 24:20
f De 32:20
  Ps 104:29
  Eze 39:23
g Ne 9:27
h Jg 6:13
i Isa 59:2
j De 31:30
  De 32:44
k De 4:9
  De 11:19
l De 31:21
m Ge 15:18
n Ex 3:8
  Nu 13:26, 27
o Ne 9:25
p Ex 24:7
  De 8:12-14
  De 29:1
  Ne 9:26
q De 28:59
r Ex 16:4
s Nu 27:18
  De 31:14

31:16 *Lit., "lie down with your fathers." **31:19** *Lit., "Place it in their mouths." **31:20** *Lit., "grow fat." **31:23** *Evidently God.

"Be courageous and strong,[a] for you are the one who will bring the Israelites into the land about which I have sworn to them,[b] and I will continue with you."

24 As soon as Moses had completed writing the words of this Law in a book in their entirety,[c] 25 Moses commanded the Levites who carry the ark of Jehovah's covenant, saying: 26 "Take this book of the Law[d] and place it at the side of the ark[e] of the covenant of Jehovah your God, and it will serve as a witness there against you. 27 For I myself will know your rebelliousness[f] and your stubbornness.*[g] If you have been so rebellious against Jehovah while I am still alive with you, then how much more so will you be after my death! 28 Gather together to me all the elders of your tribes and your officers, and let me speak these words in their hearing, and let me take the heavens and the earth as witnesses against them.[h] 29 For I well know that after my death you will surely act wickedly[i] and turn aside from the way about which I have commanded you. And calamity will certainly befall you[j] at the close of the days, because you will do what is bad in the eyes of Jehovah and you will offend him by the works of your hands."

30 Then in the hearing of the entire congregation of Israel, Moses recited the words of this song from beginning to end:[k]

32 "Give ear, O heavens, and I will speak,
And let the earth hear the words of my mouth.
2 My instruction will fall as the rain;
My words will trickle as the dew,
As gentle rains upon grass

And as copious showers upon vegetation.
3 For I will declare the name of Jehovah.[a]
Tell about the greatness of our God![b]
4 The Rock, perfect is his activity,[c]
For all his ways are justice.[d]
A God of faithfulness[e] who is never unjust;[f]
Righteous and upright is he.[g]
5 They are the ones who have acted corruptly.[h]
They are not his children, the defect is their own.[i]
They are a crooked and twisted generation![j]
6 Is this the way that you should treat Jehovah,[k]
O foolish and unwise people?[l]
Is he not your Father who caused your existence,[m]
The One who made you and firmly established you?
7 Remember the days of old;
Consider the years of past generations.
Ask your father, and he can tell you;[n]
Your elders, and they will inform you.
8 When the Most High gave the nations their inheritance,[o]
When he divided the sons of Adam* from one another,[p]
He fixed the boundary of the peoples[q]
With regard for the number of the sons of Israel.[r]
9 For Jehovah's people are his portion;[s]
Jacob is his inheritance.[t]
10 He found him in a wilderness land[u]
And in an empty, howling desert.[v]
He protectively encircled him, took care of him,[w]

CHAP. 31
a Jos 1:6, 9
b De 1:38
   De 3:28
c Ex 34:27
d De 17:18
   2Ch 34:14
e 1Ki 8:9
f De 9:24
   Ne 9:26
g Ex 32:9
   Ps 78:8
h De 30:19
i Jg 2:19
j De 28:15
k De 32:44

Second Col.

CHAP. 32
a Joh 17:26
b 1Ch 29:11
   Ps 145:3
c 2Sa 22:31
   Ps 18:2
   Ps 19:7
   Jas 1:17
d Ps 33:5
e De 7:9
   1Pe 4:19
f De 25:16
g Ge 18:25
h De 31:27
   Jg 2:19
   Ps 14:1
i Isa 1:4
j Ps 78:8
   Lu 9:41
k Isa 1:2
l Jer 4:22
m Ex 4:22
   De 32:18
   Isa 63:16
n Ex 13:14
   Ps 44:1
o Ge 10:5
   Ps 115:16
p Ge 11:9
q De 2:5, 19
   Ac 17:26
r Ge 15:18
   Ex 23:31
s Ex 19:5
   De 7:6
t Ps 78:71
u De 8:14, 15
v Jer 2:6
w Ne 9:19, 20

31:27 *Lit., "stiff neck."   32:8 *Or possibly, "the human race."

And safeguarded him as
the pupil of his eye.[a]

11 Just as an eagle stirs up
its nest,
Hovers over its fledglings,
Spreading out its wings,
taking them,
Carrying them on its
pinions,[b]

12 Jehovah alone kept leading
him;*[c]
No foreign god was with
him.[d]

13 He made him ride upon
earth's high places,[e]
So that he ate the produce
of the field.[f]
He nourished him with honey
from the crag
And oil out of a flinty rock,

14 Butter of the herd and milk
of the flock,
Together with the choicest*
sheep,
And rams of Ba'shan, and
he-goats,
Together with the finest#
wheat;[g]
And you drank wine from
the blood△ of grapes.

15 When Jesh'u·run* grew fat,
he kicked out rebelliously.
You have grown fat, you
have become stout, you
have become bloated.[h]
So he forsook God, who
made him,[i]
And despised the Rock of
his salvation.

16 They incited him to fury
with foreign gods;[j]
They were offending him
with detestable things.[k]

17 They were sacrificing to
demons, not to God,[l]
To gods that they had not
known,

New ones that came along
recently,
To gods that your fore-
fathers did not know.

18 You forgot the Rock[a] who
fathered you,
And you did not remember
the God who gave birth
to you.[b]

19 When Jehovah saw it, he
rejected them[c]
Because his sons and his
daughters offended him.

20 So he said, 'I will hide my
face from them;[d]
I will see what will become
of them.
For they are a perverse
generation,[e]
Sons in whom there is no
faithfulness.[f]

21 They have incited me to
fury* with what is not a
god;[g]
They have offended me with
their worthless idols.[h]
So I will incite them to
jealousy with what is not
a people;[i]
I will offend them with a
foolish nation.[j]

22 For my anger has kindled
a fire[k]
That will burn to the depths
of the Grave,*[l]
And it will consume the
earth and its produce
And will set ablaze the foundations of mountains.

23 I will increase their
calamities;
I will use up my arrows on
them.

24 They will be exhausted from
hunger[m]
And eaten up by burning fever and bitter destruction.[n]
I will send the teeth of beasts
against them[o]

CHAP. 32
a Zec 2:8
b Ex 19:4
c De 1:31
d Isa 43:12
e De 33:29
f De 8:7, 8
g Ps 147:14
h De 31:20
Ne 9:25
i Isa 1:4
Ho 13:6
j Jg 2:12
1Ki 14:22
1Co 10:21, 22
k 2Ki 23:13
Eze 8:17
l Le 17:7
Ps 106:37
1Co 10:20

_____

Second Col.
a Ps 106:21
Isa 17:10
Jer 2:32
b De 4:34
c Jg 2:14
Ps 78:59
d De 31:17
e De 32:5
Isa 65:2
Mt 17:17
f Isa 1:2
g Ps 96:5
1Co 10:21, 22
h 1Sa 12:10, 21
i Ho 2:23
Ro 9:25
Ro 11:11
1Pe 2:10
j Ro 10:19
k La 4:11
l Am 9:2
m De 28:53
n De 28:21, 22
o Le 26:22

_____

32:12 *That is, Jacob.   32:14 *Lit., "fat of." #Lit., "kidney fat of." △Or "juice."   32:15 *Meaning "Upright One," an honorary title for Israel.

32:21 *Or "jealousy."   32:22 *Or "Sheol," that is, the common grave of mankind. See Glossary.

And the venom of reptiles
of the dust.

25 Outside, a sword will
bereave them;[a]
Inside, there is terror[b]
For both young man and
virgin,
Infant together with gray-
haired man.[c]

26 I would have said: "I will
scatter them;
I will make the memory of
them cease from among
men,"

27 If not for my dread of the
enemy's reaction,[d]
Because the adversaries
might misconstrue it.[e]
They might say: "Our power
has triumphed;[f]
It was not Jehovah who did
all of this."

28 For they are a nation devoid
of sense,*
And there is no understanding among them.[g]

29 If only they were wise![h] They
would ponder over this.[i]
They would think about their
outcome.[j]

30 How could one chase after
1,000,
And two put 10,000 to flight?[k]
Not unless their Rock had
sold them[l]
And Jehovah had surren-
dered them.

31 For their rock is not like
our Rock,[m]
Even our enemies have
understood this.[n]

32 For their vine is from the
vine of Sod'om
And from the terraces
of Go·mor'rah.[o]
Their grapes are grapes
of poison,
Their clusters are bitter.[p]

33 Their wine is the venom
of serpents,

The cruel poison of cobras.

34 Is this not stored up with me,
Sealed up in my storehouse?[a]

35 Vengeance is mine, and
retribution,[b]
At the appointed time when
their foot slips,[c]
For the day of their disaster
is near,
And what awaits them will
come quickly.'

36 For Jehovah will judge his
people,[d]
And he will feel pity for*
his servants[e]
When he sees that their
strength has waned,
And that only the helpless
and weak remain.

37 Then he will say, 'Where are
their gods,[f]
The rock in whom they
sought refuge,

38 Who used to eat the fat
of their sacrifices,*
To drink the wine of their
drink offerings?[g]
Let them rise up and help
you.
Let them become your place
of refuge.

39 See now that I—I am he,[h]
And there are no gods apart
from me.[i]
I put to death, and I make
alive.
I wound,[k] and I will heal,[l]
And no one can rescue from
my hand.[m]

40 For I raise my hand to
heaven,
And I swear: "As surely as
I live forever,"[n]

41 If I sharpen my flashing
sword
And prepare my hand for
judgment,[o]
I will pay back vengeance
on my adversaries[p]

CHAP. 32
a La 1:20
b Eze 7:15
c 2Ch 36:17
La 2:21
d 1Sa 12:22
Eze 20:14
e Ex 32:12
Nu 14:15, 16
f Ps 115:2
g Mt 13:15
h Ps 81:13
i Ho 14:9
j Jer 2:19
k 2Ch 24:24
l Jg 2:14
1Sa 12:9
m 1Sa 2:2
n Ex 14:25
1Sa 4:8
Ezr 1:2, 3
o Jude 7
p Isa 5:4
Jer 2:21

Second Col.
a Ro 2:5
b Na 1:2
Ro 12:19
Heb 10:30
c Ps 73:12, 18
d Heb 10:30
e Jg 2:18
Ps 90:13
Ps 106:45
Ps 135:14
f Jg 10:14
g Ho 2:8
1Co 10:20, 21
h Isa 41:4
Isa 48:12
i De 4:35
j 1Sa 2:6
Ps 68:20
k 2Ch 21:16, 18
l Nu 12:13
Jer 17:14
m Isa 43:13
n 1Ti 1:17
Re 10:5, 6
o Na 1:3
p Isa 1:24
Isa 59:18

32:28 *Or possibly, "deaf to advice."

32:36 *Or "feel regret over." **32:38**
*Or "eat their finest sacrifices."

And bring retribution to
those who hate me.

42 I will make my arrows drunk
with blood,
And my sword will eat flesh,
With the blood of the slain
and the captives,
With the heads of the leaders
of the enemy.'

43 Be glad, you nations, with his
people,[a]
For he will avenge the blood
of his servants,[b]
And he will repay vengeance
to his adversaries[c]
And will make atonement
for* the land of his people."

44 Thus Moses came and recited all the words of this song
in the hearing of the people,[d] he
and Ho·she′a*[e] the son of Nun.
45 After Moses finished speaking all these words to all Israel, **46** he said to them: "Take to
heart all the words of my warning to you today,[f] so that you
may command your sons to take
care to do all the words of this
Law.[g] **47** For this is no empty
word for you, but it means your
life,[h] and by this word you may
live long in the land that you are
crossing the Jordan to possess."

48 Jehovah spoke to Moses on this same day, saying:
49 "Go up into this mountain of
Ab′a·rim,[i] Mount Ne′bo,[j] which is
in the land of Mo′ab, which faces
toward Jer′i·cho, and view the
land of Ca′naan, which I am giving to the Israelites as a possession.[k] **50** Then you will die on
the mountain you are about to
ascend, and be gathered to your
people,* just as Aaron your
brother died on Mount Hor[l] and

was gathered to his people,
51 because both of you were
unfaithful to me among the Israelites at the waters of Mer′i·bah[a]
of Ka′desh in the wilderness of
Zin, because you did not sanctify me before the people of Israel.[b] **52** You will see the land
from a distance, but you will not
enter the land that I am giving to
the people of Israel."[c]

33 Now this is the blessing
that Moses the man of the
true God pronounced on the Israelites before his death.[d] **2** He
said:

"Jehovah—from Si′nai he
came,[e]
And he shone upon them
from Se′ir.
He shone forth in glory from
the mountainous region
of Pa′ran,[f]
And with him were holy
myriads,*[g]
At his right hand his
warriors.[h]

3 He had affection for his
people;[i]
All their holy ones are in
your hand.[j]
They were sitting at your
feet;[k]
They began to listen to your
words.[l]

4 (Moses gave us a command,
a law,[m]
As a possession of the
congregation of Jacob.)[n]

5 And He became king in
Jesh′u·run,*[o]
When the heads of the
people gathered together,[p]
Along with all the tribes
of Israel.[q]

6 Let Reu′ben live and not die
off,[r]
And may his men not become
few."[s]

CHAP. 32
a Ge 12:2, 3
1Ki 8:43
Ro 3:29
Ro 15:10
b 2Ki 9:7
Re 6:10
c Mic 5:15
d Re 15:3
e Nu 11:28
De 31:22, 23
f De 11:18
g De 6:6, 7
h Le 18:5
De 30:19
Ro 10:5
i Nu 27:12
j De 34:1
k Ge 10:19
Ge 15:18
Jos 1:3
l Nu 20:28
Nu 33:38

Second Col.
a Nu 20:12, 13
b Le 22:32
Isa 8:13
c Nu 27:13, 14
De 3:27
De 34:4, 5

CHAP. 33
d Ge 49:28
e Ex 19:18
f Hab 3:3
g Da 7:10
Jude 14
h Ps 68:17
i De 7:8
Ho 11:1
j Ex 19:6
k Ex 19:23
l Ex 20:19
m Ex 24:8
n De 4:8
Ac 7:53
o Isa 44:2
p Ex 18:25
Ex 19:7
q Nu 1:44, 46
r Ge 49:3
s Nu 26:7
Jos 13:15

32:43 *Or "will cleanse." 32:44 *The
original name of Joshua. Hoshea is
a shortened form of Hoshaiah, which
means "Saved by Jah; Jah Has Saved."
32:50 *This is a poetic expression for
death.

33:2 *Or "were tens of thousands of
holy ones." 33:5 *Meaning "Upright
One," an honorary title for Israel.

7 And he pronounced this blessing on Judah:[a]

"Hear, O Jehovah, the voice of Judah,[b]
And may you bring him back to his people.
His arms have defended* what belongs to him,
And may you help him against his adversaries."[c]

8 Of Le'vi he said:[d]

"Your* Thum'mim and your U'rim[e] belong to the man loyal to you,
Whom you put to the test at Mas'sah.[g]
You began to contend with him by the waters of Mer'i·bah,[h]

9 The man who said to his father and his mother, 'I have not shown regard to them.'
Even his brothers he did not acknowledge,[i]
And he ignored his own sons.
For they kept your word,
And they observed your covenant.[j]

10 Let them instruct Jacob in your judicial decisions[k]
And Israel in your Law.[l]
Let them offer up incense as a pleasant aroma for you*[m]
And a whole offering on your altar.[n]

11 Bless, O Jehovah, his strength,
And may you show pleasure in the work of his hands.
Crush the legs* of those who rise up against him,
So that those who hate him may rise up no more."

12 Of Benjamin he said:[o]

"Let the beloved one of Jehovah reside in security by him;

While he shelters him the whole day,
He will reside between his shoulders."

13 Of Joseph he said:[a]

"May his land be blessed by Jehovah[b]
With the choice things of heaven,
With dew and the waters from the springs below,[c]

14 With choice things produced by the sun
And the choice yield each month,[d]

15 With the choicest things from the ancient mountains*[e]
And choice things of the enduring hills,

16 With the choice things of the earth and what fills it,[f]
And with the approval of the One residing in the thornbush.[g]
May they come upon the head of Joseph,
On the crown of the head of the one singled out from his brothers.[h]

17 His splendor is like that of a firstborn bull,
And his horns are the horns of a wild bull.
With them he will push* peoples
All together to the ends of the earth.
They are the tens of thousands of E'phra·im,[i]
And they are the thousands of Ma·nas'seh."

18 Of Zeb'u·lun he said:[j]

"Rejoice, O Zeb'u·lun, in your going out,
And you, Is'sa·char, in your tents.[k]

19 They will call peoples to the mountain.

CHAP. 33

a Ge 49:8
1Ch 5:2

b Ps 78:68

c Jg 1:2
2Sa 7:8, 9

d Ge 49:5
Nu 3:12

e Ex 28:30
Le 8:6, 8

f Ex 32:26

g Ex 17:7

h Nu 20:13

i Ex 32:27
Le 10:6, 7

j Mal 2:4, 5

k De 17:9

l 2Ch 17:8, 9
Mal 2:7

m Ex 30:7
Nu 16:40

n Le 1:9

o Ge 49:27

Second Col.

a Ge 49:22

b Jos 16:1

c Ge 49:25

d Le 26:5
Ps 65:9

e Jos 17:17, 18

f De 8:7, 8

g Ex 3:4
Ac 7:30

h Ps 37:7
Ge 49:26
1Ch 5:1, 2

i Ge 48:19, 20

j Ge 49:13

k Ge 49:14

33:7 *Or "contended for." 33:8 *"Your" and "you" in this verse refer to God. 33:10 *Lit., "in your nose." 33:11 *Or "hips."

33:15 *Or possibly, "the mountains of the east." 33:17 *Or "gore."

There they will offer the sacrifices of righteousness.
For they will draw from the abundant wealth of* the seas
And the hidden hoards" of the sand."

20 Of Gad he said:[a]

"Blessed is the one widening the borders of Gad.[b]
He lies there like a lion,
Ready to tear off the arm, yes, the crown of the head.

21 He will select the first portion for himself,[c]
For there the allotment of a lawgiver is reserved.[d]
The heads of the people will gather together.
The righteousness of Jehovah he will execute,
And his judicial decisions with Israel."

22 Of Dan he said:[e]

"Dan is a lion cub.[f]
He will leap out from Ba'shan."[g]

23 Of Naph'ta·li he said:[h]

"Naph'ta·li is satisfied with the approval
And full of the blessing of Jehovah.
Take possession of the west and south."

24 Of Ash'er he said:[i]

"Blessed with sons is Ash'er.
May he be favored by his brothers,
And may he dip* his feet in oil.

25 Iron and copper are your gate locks,[j]
And you will be secure all your days.*

26 There is none like the true God[k] of Jesh'u·run,[l]
Who rides through heaven to help you
And who rides upon the clouds in his majesty.[a]

27 God is a refuge from ancient times,[b]
His everlasting arms are beneath you.[c]
And he will drive away the enemy from before you,[d]
And he will say, 'Annihilate them!'[e]

28 Israel will reside in security,
And the fountain of Jacob will be secluded
In a land of grain and new wine,[f]
Whose skies will drip with dew.[g]

29 Happy you are, O Israel![h]
Who is there like you,[i]
A people enjoying salvation in Jehovah,[j]
Your protective shield[k]
And your majestic sword?
Your enemies will cringe before you,[l]
And you will tread on their backs."*

34 Then Moses went up from the desert plains of Mo'ab to Mount Ne'bo,[m] to the top of Pis'gah,[n] which faces Jer'i·cho.[o] And Jehovah showed him all the land, from Gil'e·ad to Dan.[p] **2** and all Naph'ta·li and the land of E'phra·im and Ma·nas'seh, and all the land of Judah as far as the western sea,*[q] **3** and the Neg'eb[r] and the District,[s] the valley plain of Jer'i·cho, the city of the palm trees, as far as Zo'ar.[t]

4 Jehovah then said to him: "This is the land about which I have sworn to Abraham, Isaac, and Jacob, saying, 'To your offspring* I will give it.'[u] I have let you see it with your own

---

CHAP. 33
a Ge 49:19
b Jos 13:24-28
c Nu 32:1-5
d Jos 22:1, 4
e Ge 49:16
f Jg 13:2, 24
  Jg 15:8, 20
  Jg 16:30
g Jos 19:47
h Ge 49:21
i Ge 49:20
j De 8:7, 9
k Ex 15:11
l Isa 44:2

Second Col.
a Ps 68:32-34
b Ps 46:11
  Ps 91:2
c Isa 40:11
d De 9:3
e De 31:3, 4
f De 8:7, 8
g De 11:11
h Ps 33:12
  Ps 144:15
  Ps 146:5
i De 4:7
  2Sa 7:23
  Ps 147:20
j Ex 23:31
  Isa 12:2
k Ps 115:9
l Ps 66:3

CHAP. 34
m De 32:49
n De 3:27
o Nu 36:13
p Jg 18:29
q Ex 23:31
  Nu 34:2, 6
  De 11:24
r Jos 15:1
s Ge 13:10
t Ge 19:22, 23
u Ge 12:7
  Ge 26:3
  Ge 28:13

33:19 *Lit., "will suck the abundance of." "Or "treasures." **33:24** *Or "bathe." **33:25** *Lit., "And like your days will be your strength."

33:29 *Or possibly, "high places." **34:2** *That is, the Great Sea, the Mediterranean. **34:4** *Lit., "seed."

eyes, but you will not cross over there."[a]

5 After that Moses the servant of Jehovah died there in the land of Mo′ab just as Jehovah had said.[b] **6** He buried him in the valley in the land of Mo′ab, opposite Beth-pe′or, and nobody knows where his grave is down to this day.[c] **7** Moses was 120 years old at his death.[d] His eyes had not grown dim, and his strength had not departed. **8** The people of Israel wept for Moses on the desert plains of Mo′ab for 30 days.[e] Then the days of weeping and mourning for Moses were completed.

9 Joshua the son of Nun was full of the spirit of wisdom, for Moses had laid his hand on him;[a] and the Israelites began to listen to him, and they did just as Jehovah had commanded Moses.[b] **10** But there has never again arisen a prophet in Israel like Moses,[c] whom Jehovah knew face-to-face.[d] **11** He performed all the signs and the miracles that Jehovah had sent him to do in the land of Egypt to Phar′aoh and all his servants and all his land,[e] **12** along with the mighty hand and the awesome power that Moses displayed before the eyes of all Israel.[f]

CHAP. 34
a Nu 20:12
b De 32:50
  Jos 1:2
c Jude 9
d De 31:1, 2
  Ac 7:23
  Ac 7:30, 36
e Nu 20:29

Second Col.
a De 31:14
  1Ti 4:14
b Nu 27:18, 21
  Jos 1:16
c Ac 3:22
  Ac 7:37
d Ex 33:11
  Nu 12:8
e De 4:34
f De 26:8
  Lu 24:19

JOSHUA

OUTLINE OF CONTENTS

1

After the death of Moses the servant of Jehovah, Jehovah said to Joshua*[a] the son of Nun, the minister[b] of Moses: **2** "Moses my servant is dead.[c] Now get up, cross the Jordan, you and all this people, and go into the land that I am giving to them, to the people of Israel.[d] **3** I will give you every place on which you set your foot, just as I promised Moses.[e] **4** Your territory will extend from the wilderness up to Leb·a·non and to the great river, the Eu·phra′tes —all the land of the Hit′tites*— and to the Great Sea* on the west.*[g] **5** No one will be able to take a stand against you as long as you live.[h] Just as I was with Moses, so I will be with you.[i] I will neither desert you nor abandon you.[j] **6** Be courageous

and strong,[a] for you are the one who will cause this people to inherit the land that I swore to their forefathers I would give to them.[b]

7 "Only be courageous and very strong, and observe carefully the entire Law that Moses my servant commanded you. Do not deviate from it either to the right or to the left,[c] so that you may act wisely wherever you go.[d] **8** This book of the Law should not depart from your mouth,[e] and you must read it in an undertone* day and night, in order to observe carefully all that is written in it;[f] for then your way will be successful and then you will act wisely.[g] **9** Have I not commanded you? Be courageous and strong. Do not be struck with terror or fear, for Jehovah your God is with you wherever you go."[h]

CHAP. 1
a De 31:14
b Ex 24:13
   Nu 11:28
c De 34:5
d De 3:28
e De 11:24
f Nu 13:29
g Ge 15:18
   Ex 23:31
   Nu 34:2, 3
   De 1:7
   Jos 15:1, 4
h De 7:24
   De 11:25
i Ex 3:12
   Jos 3:7
j De 31:6

Second Col.
a De 31:23
b Ge 12:7
   Ge 15:18
   Ge 26:3
c De 5:32
   De 29:9
   1Ki 2:3
e De 6:6
   De 30:14
f De 17:18, 19
   Ps 1:1, 2
   1Ti 4:15
   Jas 1:25
g 1Ch 22:13
h Ex 23:27
   De 31:7, 8

1:1 *Or "Jehoshua," meaning "Jehovah Is Salvation." **1:4** *That is, the Mediterranean. #Or "toward the sunset."

1:8 *Or "meditate on it."

10 Then Joshua commanded the officers of the people: **11** "Pass throughout the camp and give this command to the people, 'Get provisions ready, because in three days you will cross the Jordan to go in and take possession of the land that Jehovah your God is giving you to possess.'"[a]

12 And to the Reu'ben·ites, the Gad'ites, and the half tribe of Ma·nas'seh, Joshua said: **13** "Remember what Moses the servant of Jehovah commanded you:[b] 'Jehovah your God is giving you rest and has given you this land. **14** Your wives, your children, and your livestock will dwell in the land that Moses has given you on this side* of the Jordan,[c] but all your mighty warriors[d] should cross over in battle formation ahead of your brothers.[e] You must help them **15** until Jehovah gives your brothers rest, just as he has given you, and they also take possession of the land that Jehovah your God is giving them. Then return to the land you were given to occupy and take possession of it, the land that Moses the servant of Jehovah gave you on the east side of the Jordan.'"[f]

16 They answered Joshua: "We will do all that you have commanded, and we will go wherever you send us.[g] **17** Just as we listened to everything Moses said, so we will listen to you. Only may Jehovah your God be with you just as he was with Moses.[h] **18** Any man who rebels against your order and does not obey every command you give him will be put to death.[i] Only be courageous and strong."[j]

2 Then Joshua the son of Nun secretly sent two men out from Shit'tim[k] as spies. He told them: "Go and inspect the land,

1:14; 2:10 *That is, the east side.

CHAP. 1
a De 9:1
  Jos 3:2, 3

b Nu 32:20-22
  Jos 22:1-4

c De 3:19, 20
  De 29:8
  Jos 13:8

d Nu 1:3
  Nu 26:2

e De 3:18

f Nu 32:33
  Jos 22:4, 9

g Nu 32:17, 25

h Nu 27:18, 20
  De 34:9

i De 17:12

j De 31:7
  Jos 1:6, 9

CHAP. 2
k Nu 25:1
  Nu 33:49

Second Col.
a Jos 6:17
  Mt 1:5
  Heb 11:31
  Jas 2:25

b Jg 3:28
  Jg 12:5

c Ex 3:8

d Ex 23:27
  De 2:25
  De 11:25

e Ex 15:15
  Jos 5:1

f Ex 14:21
  Ex 15:13, 14

g Nu 21:21-24

h Nu 21:33, 34
  De 3:3
  Jos 9:9, 10

especially Jer'i·cho." So they went on and came to the house of a prostitute named Ra'hab,[a] and they stayed there. **2** The king of Jer'i·cho was told: "Look! Israelite men have come in here tonight to spy out the land." **3** At that the king of Jer'i·cho sent word to Ra'hab: "Bring out the men who came and are staying in your house, for they have come to spy out the entire land."

4 But the woman took the two men and hid them. Then she said: "Yes, the men came to me, but I did not know where they were from. **5** And at dark when the city gate was about to be closed, the men went out. I do not know where the men went, but if you quickly chase after them, you will catch up with them." **6** (However, she had taken them up to the roof and hidden them among stalks of flax laid in rows on the roof.) **7** So the men chased after them in the direction of the Jordan at the fords,[b] and the city gate was shut once the pursuers had gone out.

8 Before the men lay down to sleep, she came up to them on the roof. **9** She said to the men: "I do know that Jehovah will give you the land[c] and that the fear of you has fallen upon us.[d] All the inhabitants of the land are disheartened because of you,[e] **10** for we heard how Jehovah dried up the waters of the Red Sea before you when you left Egypt[f] and what you did to the two kings of the Am'or·ites, Si'hon[g] and Og,[h] whom you devoted to destruction on the other side* of the Jordan. **11** When we heard about it, we lost heart,* and no one has any courage# because of you, for Jehovah your God is

2:11 *Lit., "our hearts melted." #Lit., "and spirit no longer arose in a man."

God in the heavens above and on the earth beneath.[a] **12** Now, please, swear to me by Jehovah that, because I showed loyal love to you, you will also show loyal love to my father's household; and you must give me a sign of good faith.* **13** You must spare the lives of my father and mother, my brothers and sisters, and all who belong to them, and you must save us* from death."[b]

14 At that the men said to her: "We will give our lives for yours!* If you do not tell about our mission, then we will show loyal love and faithfulness toward you when Jehovah gives us the land." **15** After that she let them down by a rope through the window, for her house was on a side of the city wall. In fact, she was dwelling on the wall.[c] **16** Then she said to them: "Go to the mountainous region and hide there for three days, so that those pursuing you may not find you. Then, after your pursuers have come back, you can go on your way."

17 The men said to her: "We will be free from guilt respecting this oath that you made us swear[d] **18** unless, when we come into the land, you tie this cord of scarlet thread in the window by which you let us down. You should gather your father, your mother, your brothers, and all your father's household with you into the house.[e] **19** Then if anyone goes out the doors of your house into the open, his blood will be on his own head, and we will be free from guilt. But if harm comes to* anyone who remains with you in the house, his blood will be on our heads. **20** But if you report our mission,[f] we will be free from

guilt respecting your oath that you made us swear." **21** She replied: "Let it be according to your words."

With that she sent them off, and they went their way. Afterward, she tied the scarlet cord in the window. **22** So they left and went to the mountainous region and stayed there for three days, until the pursuers returned. The pursuers had been looking for them on every road but did not find them. **23** The two men then descended from the mountainous region and crossed the river and came to Joshua the son of Nun. They related to him all the things that had happened to them. **24** Then they said to Joshua: "Jehovah has handed over the entire land to us.[a] In fact, all the inhabitants of the land are disheartened because of us."[b]

3 Then Joshua got up early in the morning, and he and all the Israelites* departed from Shit′tim and came to the Jordan. They spent the night there before crossing over.

2 After three days, the officers[d] passed throughout the camp **3** and commanded the people: "As soon as you see the ark of the covenant of Jehovah your God being carried by the Levitical priests,[e] you should depart from your place and follow it. **4** But keep a distance of about 2,000 cubits* from it; do not come any nearer to it, so that you may know which is the way to go, for you have not traveled on this way before."

5 Joshua now said to the people: "Sanctify yourselves,[f] for tomorrow Jehovah will do wonderful things among you."[g]

6 Then Joshua said to the priests: "Take up the ark[h] of the

---

CHAP. 2
a De 4:39
  2Ch 20:6
  Da 4:35

b Jos 6:23

c Heb 11:31

d Nu 30:2

e Jos 6:23

f Jos 2:14

Second Col.
a Ex 23:31
  Jos 6:2
  Jos 21:44

b Ex 15:14-16
  Jos 2:9-11
  Jos 5:1

CHAP. 3
c Nu 25:1
  Jos 2:1

d De 1:15
  Jos 1:10, 11

e Nu 4:15
  1Ch 15:2

f Ex 19:10
  Le 20:7

g Ex 34:10

h Ex 25:10
  Nu 4:15

2:12 *Or "a reliable sign." 2:13 *Or "our souls." 2:14 *Or "Our souls will die instead of you!" 2:19 *Or "if a hand is laid on."

3:1 *Lit., "sons of Israel." 3:4 *About 890 m (2,920 ft). See App. B14.

covenant and pass ahead of the people." So they took up the ark of the covenant and went ahead of the people.

7 Then Jehovah said to Joshua: "This day I will start to exalt you in the eyes of all Israel,[a] so that they may know that I will be with you[b] just as I was with Moses.[c] **8** You should give this command to the priests carrying the ark of the covenant: 'When you reach the edge of the waters of the Jordan, you should stand still in the Jordan.'"[d]

9 And Joshua said to the Israelites: "Come here and listen to the words of Jehovah your God." **10** Joshua then said: "By this you will know that a living God is among you,[e] and that he will without fail drive away from before you the Ca'naan·ites, the Hit'tites, the Hi'vites, the Per'iz·zites, the Gir'ga·shites, the Am'or·ites, and the Jeb'u·sites.[f] **11** Look! The ark of the covenant of the Lord of the whole earth is passing ahead of you into the Jordan. **12** Now take 12 men from the tribes of Israel, one man for each tribe,[g] **13** and as soon as the soles of the feet of the priests carrying the Ark of Jehovah, the Lord of the whole earth, touch* the waters of the Jordan, the waters of the Jordan flowing from upstream will be halted and they will stand still like a dam."[#h]

14 So when the people departed from their tents just before crossing the Jordan, the priests carrying the ark[i] of the covenant went ahead of the people. **15** As soon as the carriers of the Ark reached the Jordan and the priests carrying the Ark dipped their feet into the edge of the waters (now the Jordan overflows its banks[j] all the days of harvest), **16** the waters

flowing from upstream stood still. They rose up like a dam" very far away at Adam, the city near Zar'e·than, while the waters descending toward the Sea of the Ar'a·bah, the Salt Sea,* drained away. They were halted, and the people crossed over opposite Jer'i·cho. **17** While the priests carrying the ark of Jehovah's covenant kept standing still on dry ground[a] in the middle of the Jordan, all Israel crossed over on dry ground[b] until the whole nation had finished crossing the Jordan.

4 As soon as the whole nation had finished crossing the Jordan, Jehovah said to Joshua: **2** "Take 12 men from the people, one man from each tribe,[c] **3** and give them this command: 'Take up 12 stones from the middle of the Jordan, from the place where the priests' feet stood still,[d] and carry them over with you and set them down in the place where you will spend the night.'"[e]

4 So Joshua called the 12 men whom he had appointed from the Israelites, one man from each tribe, **5** and Joshua said to them: "Pass ahead of the Ark of Jehovah your God to the middle of the Jordan, and each of you should lift up a stone on his shoulder, according to the number of the tribes of the Israelites, **6** to serve as a sign among you. If your children* should later ask you, 'Why do you have these stones?'[f] **7** you must tell them: 'Because the waters of the Jordan were halted from before the ark[g] of Jehovah's covenant. When it crossed the Jordan, the waters of the Jordan were halted. These stones will serve as a lasting memorial* to the people of Israel.'"[h]

CHAP. 3	
a	Jos 4:14
b	Jos 1:5, 17
c	Ex 3:12 Ex 14:31
d	Jos 3:17
e	De 7:21
f	Ex 3:8 De 7:1 Ps 44:2
g	Jos 4:2, 3
h	Ps 114:1, 3
i	Ex 25:10 Jos 3:6 Ac 7:44, 45
j	Jos 4:18 1Ch 12:15
Second Col.	
a	Jos 4:3
b	Ps 66:6
CHAP. 4	
c	Jos 3:12, 13
d	Jos 3:17
e	Jos 4:19, 20
f	Ex 13:14 De 6:20, 21 Ps 78:3, 4
g	Jos 3:13, 16
h	De 4:9

3:13 *Lit., "rest in." 3:13, 16 #Or "wall." 3:16 *That is, the Dead Sea. 4:6 *Lit., "sons." 4:7 *Or "reminder."

8 So the Israelites did just as Joshua had commanded. They took up 12 stones from the middle of the Jordan, just as Jehovah had instructed Joshua, to correspond to the number of the tribes of the Israelites. They took them over to the place where they would spend the night and set them down there. **9** Joshua also set up 12 stones in the middle of the Jordan at the place where the feet of the priests who carried the ark of the covenant stood,[a] and the stones are there to this day. **10** The priests carrying the Ark remained standing in the middle of the Jordan until everything that Jehovah had ordered Joshua to tell the people to do was completed, in harmony with all that Moses had commanded Joshua. All the while, the people hurried across. **11** As soon as all the people had finished crossing over, the Ark of Jehovah and the priests crossed over in the sight of the people.[b] **12** And the Reu′ben·ites, the Gad′ites, and the half tribe of Ma·nas′seh crossed over in battle formation[c] ahead of the other Israelites, just as Moses had instructed them.[d] **13** About 40,000 soldiers armed for battle crossed over before Jehovah onto the desert plains of Jer′i·cho.

14 On that day Jehovah exalted Joshua in the eyes of all Israel,[e] and they deeply respected* him all the days of his life, just as they had deeply respected Moses.[f]

15 Then Jehovah said to Joshua: **16** "Command the priests carrying the ark[g] of the Testimony to come up out of the Jordan." **17** So Joshua commanded the priests: "Come up out of the Jordan." **18** When the priests carrying the ark[h] of

the covenant of Jehovah came up from the middle of the Jordan and the soles of the feet of the priests stepped onto dry ground, the waters of the Jordan resumed their course and overflowed the banks[a] as before.

19 The people came up from the Jordan on the tenth day of the first month and camped at Gil′gal[b] on the eastern border of Jer′i·cho.

20 As for the 12 stones that they had taken out of the Jordan, Joshua set these up at Gil′gal.[c] **21** Then he said to the Israelites: "In the future when your children ask their fathers, 'What do these stones mean?'[d] **22** you must explain to your children: 'Israel crossed the Jordan on dry land[e] **23** when Jehovah your God dried up the waters of the Jordan before them until they had crossed it, just as Jehovah your God did to the Red Sea when he dried it up before us until we crossed it.[f] **24** He did this so that all the peoples of the earth may know how mighty Jehovah's hand is[g] and so that you may always fear Jehovah your God.'"

5 As soon as all the kings of the Am′or·ites[h] who were on the west side* of the Jordan and all the kings of the Ca′naan·ites[i] who were by the sea heard that Jehovah had dried up the waters of the Jordan before the Israelites until they had crossed over, they lost heart,*[j] and they lost all courage[△] because of the Israelites.[k]

2 At that time Jehovah said to Joshua: "Make for yourself flint knives and circumcise[l] the men of Israel again, a second time." **3** So Joshua made flint knives and circumcised the men of

CHAP. 4	
a	Jos 3:17
b	Jos 3:8, 17
c	Jos 1:12, 14
d	Nu 32:20-22
	Nu 32:25-29
e	Jos 3:7
f	Ex 14:31
g	Ex 25:22
h	Nu 4:15
Second Col.	
a	Jos 3:13, 15
b	Jos 4:3
	Jos 5:8, 9
	Jos 10:6
c	Jos 4:8
d	Ps 44:1
e	Jos 3:17
	Ps 66:6
f	Ex 14:21
	Isa 63:12
	Heb 11:29
g	Ex 9:16
	Ex 15:6
	De 28:10
	1Sa 17:46
	2Ki 19:19
	Ps 106:8
CHAP. 5	
h	Ge 10:15, 16
i	Nu 13:29
j	Ex 15:15
	Jos 2:24
k	Jos 2:9-11
l	Ge 17:9-11

4:14 *Lit., "they feared."

5:1 *Lit., "the side toward the sea." *Lit., "their hearts melted." △Lit., "and there was no spirit in them any longer."

Israel at Gib'e·ath-ha·ar'a·loth.*[a]
4 This is why Joshua circumcised them: All the males of the people who left Egypt, all the men of war,* had died in the wilderness on the journey after they left Egypt.[b] **5** All the people who left Egypt were circumcised, but all the people born in the wilderness on the journey after they left Egypt were not circumcised. **6** The Israelites had walked for 40 years[c] in the wilderness until the entire nation had died off, that is, the men of war who left Egypt who did not obey the voice of Jehovah.[d] Jehovah swore to them that he would never let them see the land[e] that Jehovah had sworn to their forefathers to give to us,[f] a land flowing with milk and honey.[g] **7** So he raised up their sons instead of them.[h] These Joshua circumcised; they were uncircumcised because they had not circumcised them during the journey.

8 When they finished circumcising the entire nation, they remained where they were in the camp until they recovered.

9 Then Jehovah said to Joshua: "Today I have rolled away from you the reproach of Egypt." So that place has been called Gil'gal*[i] until this day.

10 The Israelites continued to camp at Gil'gal, and they observed the Passover on the 14th day of the month,[j] in the evening, on the desert plains of Jer'i·cho. **11** And they began to eat the produce of the land the day after the Passover, unleavened bread[k] and roasted grains, on this same day. **12** Then the manna stopped on the day following when they had eaten some of the produce of the land; there was no longer manna for

the Israelites,[a] but they began to eat the produce of the land of Ca'naan in that year.[b]

13 When Joshua was near Jer'i·cho, he looked up and saw a man[c] standing in front of him with a drawn sword in his hand.[d] Joshua walked up to him and asked: "Are you on our side or on the side of our adversaries?" **14** To this he said: "No, but I have come as prince* of Jehovah's army."[e] With that Joshua fell with his face to the ground and prostrated himself and said to him: "What does my lord have to say to his servant?" **15** The prince of Jehovah's army replied to Joshua: "Remove your sandals from your feet, because the place where you are standing is holy." At once Joshua did so.[f]

6 Now Jer'i·cho was tightly shut up because of the Israelites; no one was leaving and no one was entering.[g]

2 Jehovah then said to Joshua: "See, I have handed over to you Jer'i·cho and its king and its mighty warriors.[h] **3** All you fighting men should march around the city, going around the city once. That is what you should do for six days. **4** Have seven priests carry seven ram's horns before the Ark. But on the seventh day, you should march around the city seven times and the priests should blow the horns.[i] **5** When the ram's horn is sounded—as soon as you hear the sound* of the horn—all the people should shout a great war cry. Then the wall of the city will fall down flat,[j] and the people must go up, each one straight ahead."

6 So Joshua the son of Nun called the priests together and told them: "Take up the ark of the covenant, and seven priests should carry seven ram's horns

---

CHAP. 5
a Jos 5:8, 9

b Nu 14:29
  Nu 26:65
  De 2:14

c Nu 14:33
  De 1:3

d Nu 14:22, 23

e De 1:35

f Ge 13:14, 15
  Ex 33:1

g Ex 3:8
  Nu 13:26, 27
  Eze 20:6

h Nu 14:31

i Jos 4:19
  Jos 5:3

j Ex 12:24, 25
  Nu 9:5

k Ex 12:18

Second Col.
a Ex 16:35

b De 6:10-12
  De 8:10

c Ge 18:2
  Jg 13:6
  Ac 1:10

d Ex 23:23
  Nu 22:23
  1Ch 21:16

e Ex 23:20
  1Ki 22:19
  Da 10:13

f Ex 3:4, 5

CHAP. 6
g Jos 2:9

h Nu 14:9
  De 7:24
  Ne 9:24

i Jg 7:22

j Heb 11:30

5:3 *Meaning "Hill of the Foreskins."
5:4 *Or "the men of military age." 5:9 *Meaning "Rolling; Rolling Away."

5:14 *Or "chief." 6:5 *Or "long blast."

before the Ark of Jehovah."[a] **7** Then he told the people: "Move on and march around the city, and the armed troops[b] should go ahead of the Ark of Jehovah." **8** And just as Joshua had spoken to the people, the seven priests carrying seven ram's horns before Jehovah went forward and blew the horns, and the ark of the covenant of Jehovah was following them. **9** And the armed troops went ahead of the priests who were blowing the horns, and the rear guard followed the Ark as the horns were blown continuously.

10 Now Joshua had commanded the people: "Do not shout nor let your voices be heard. Not a word should come out of your mouths until the day I say to you, 'Shout!' Then shout." **11** He had the Ark of Jehovah go around the city, going around it once, after which they returned to the camp and spent the night there.

12 The next morning Joshua got up early, and the priests took up the Ark[c] of Jehovah, **13** and seven priests carrying seven ram's horns walked before the Ark of Jehovah, continuously blowing the horns. The armed troops were walking ahead of them while the rear guard was following the Ark of Jehovah as the horns were blown continuously. **14** They marched around the city on the second day once, after which they returned to the camp. That was what they did for six days.[d]

15 On the seventh day they got up early, as soon as the dawn broke, and they marched around the city in the same manner seven times. It was only on that day that they marched around the city seven times.[e] **16** And on the seventh time, the priests blew the horns, and Joshua told

the people: "Shout,[a] for Jehovah has given you the city! **17** The city and everything in it is to be devoted to destruction;[b] it all belongs to Jehovah. Only Raʹ-hab[c] the prostitute may keep living, she and all who are with her in the house, because she hid the messengers we sent out.[d] **18** But keep away from what is devoted to destruction,[e] so that you do not desire something devoted to destruction and take it,[f] making the camp of Israel something devoted to destruction by bringing disaster* on it.[g] **19** But all the silver and the gold and the articles of copper and iron are holy to Jehovah.[h] They should go into the treasury of Jehovah."[i]

20 Then the people shouted when the horns were blown.[j] As soon as the people heard the sound of the horn and shouted a great war cry, the wall fell down flat.[k] After that the people went up into the city, each one straight ahead, and they captured the city. **21** They devoted all that was in the city to destruction by the sword, man and woman, young and old, bull, sheep, and donkey.[l]

22 Joshua said to the two men who had spied out the land: "Go into the house of the prostitute and bring out the woman and all who belong to her, just as you swore to her."[m] **23** So the young spies went in and brought out Raʹhab, along with her father, her mother, her brothers, and all who belonged to her; yes, they brought out her whole family,[n] and they brought them safely to a place outside the camp of Israel.

24 Then they burned the city and everything in it with fire. But the silver, the gold, and the articles of copper and iron,

CHAP. 6
a Nu 4:15

b Nu 10:14, 18, 22
  Jos 1:12, 14

c 1Ch 15:2

d Jos 6:3

e Jos 6:4

_____

Second Col.
a Jos 6:5, 10

b Le 27:29
  De 7:2
  De 20:16

c Jos 2:1
  Mt 1:5
  Heb 11:31

d Ge 12:3
  Jos 2:4, 6
  Jas 2:25

e De 7:26

f De 13:17
  Jos 7:11, 21

g Jos 7:25

h Nu 31:22, 23

i Jos 6:24
  1Ki 7:51
  1Ch 18:11

j Jos 6:4, 16

k Jos 6:5
  Heb 11:30

l De 7:2
  De 20:16

m Jos 2:14
  Heb 11:31

n Jos 2:12, 13
  Jos 2:17-19

_____
6:18 *Or "trouble; ostracism."

they gave to the treasury of Jehovah's house.[a] **25** Only Ra'hab the prostitute and her father's household and all who belonged to her were spared by Joshua;[b] and she lives in Israel to this day,[c] because she hid the messengers whom Joshua sent out to spy on Jer'i·cho.[d]

26 At that time Joshua pronounced this oath:* "Cursed be the man before Jehovah who undertakes to rebuild this city of Jer'i·cho. At the cost of his firstborn he will lay its foundation, and at the cost of his youngest he will put up its doors."[e]

27 So Jehovah was with Joshua,[f] and his fame spread through all the earth.[g]

7 But the Israelites were unfaithful with regard to what had been devoted to destruction, for A'chan[h] son of Car'mi, son of Zab'di, son of Ze'rah, of the tribe of Judah, took some of what was devoted to destruction.[i] At this Jehovah's anger blazed against the Israelites.[j]

2 Then Joshua sent men out from Jer'i·cho to A'i,[k] which is close by Beth-a'ven and east of Beth'el,[l] telling them: "Go up and spy on the land." So the men went up and spied on A'i. **3** When they returned to Joshua, they told him: "Not all the people need to go up. About two or three thousand men are enough to defeat A'i. Do not tire out all the people by making them go, for there are only a few of them." **4** So about 3,000 men went up there, but they had to flee from the men of A'i.[m] **5** The men of A'i struck down 36 men, and they pursued them from outside the city gate as far as Sheb'a·rim,* and they continued striking

them down on the descent. So the courage* of the people melted and flowed away like water.

6 At this Joshua ripped his garments and fell with his face to the ground before the Ark of Jehovah until the evening, he and the elders of Israel, and they kept throwing dust on their heads. **7** Joshua said: "Alas, Sovereign Lord Jehovah, why did you bring this people all the way across the Jordan just to hand us over to the Am'or·ites to be destroyed? If only we had been satisfied to remain on the other side* of the Jordan! **8** Pardon me, O Jehovah, what can I say now that Israel has retreated* before his enemies? **9** When the Ca'naan·ites and all the inhabitants of the land hear about it, they will surround us and wipe out our very name from the earth, and what will you do about your great name?"[a]

10 Jehovah replied to Joshua: "Get up! Why are you lying on your face? **11** Israel has sinned. They have violated my covenant[b] that I commanded them to keep. They took some of what was devoted to destruction,[c] stealing[d] it and secretly putting it among their own possessions.[e] **12** Therefore, the Israelites will not be able to stand against their enemies. They will turn their backs and flee from their enemies, because they have become something devoted to destruction. I will not be with you again unless you annihilate from your midst what was devoted to destruction.[f] **13** Get up and sanctify the people![g] Tell them, 'Sanctify yourselves tomorrow, for this is what Jehovah the God of Israel says: "What is devoted to destruction is among you, O Israel. You will not be

---

CHAP. 6
a Jos 6:19

b Jos 2:14
Jos 6:17, 22

c Mt 1:5

d Heb 6:10
Jas 2:25

e 1Ki 16:34

f De 31:6
Jos 1:5

g Jos 9:1, 2
Jos 9:9, 10

CHAP. 7
h Jos 22:20
1Ch 2:7

i De 7:26

j Jos 6:17, 18

k Ge 12:8

l Ge 28:19

m Le 26:14, 17
De 28:15, 25
De 32:30

Second Col.
a De 32:26, 27
Ps 106:8
Ps 143:11
Eze 20:9

b Ex 24:7

c Jos 6:17

d Ex 20:15

e Jos 7:21

f De 7:26
Jos 6:18
Isa 59:2

g Ex 19:10

6:26 *Or possibly, "made the people swear this oath."   7:5 *Meaning "Quarries."

7:5 *Lit., "heart."   7:7 *That is, the east side.   7:8 *Or "turned his back."

able to stand against your enemies until you remove from your midst the thing devoted to destruction. **14** You are to present yourselves in the morning, tribe by tribe, and the tribe that Jehovah selects[a] will come near, family by family, and the family that Jehovah selects will come near, household by household, and the household that Jehovah selects will come near, man by man. **15** And the one who is caught with the thing devoted to destruction will be burned with fire,[b] he and all that belongs to him, because he has violated the covenant[c] of Jehovah and because he has committed a disgraceful act in Israel.'"

16 So Joshua rose early the next morning and had Israel come near, tribe by tribe, and the tribe of Judah was selected. **17** He had the families of Judah come near and the family of the Ze′rah·ites[d] was selected, after which he had the family of the Ze′rah·ites come near, man by man, and Zab′di was selected. **18** Finally he had the household of Zab′di come near, man by man, and A′chan son of Car′mi, son of Zab′di, son of Ze′rah, of the tribe of Judah, was selected.[e] **19** Then Joshua said to A′chan: "My son, please, honor Jehovah the God of Israel and make confession to him. Tell me, please, what you have done. Do not hide it from me."

20 A′chan answered Joshua: "For a fact I am the one who sinned against Jehovah the God of Israel, and this is what I have done. **21** When I saw among the spoil a good-looking official garment from Shi′nar[f] and 200 shekels* of silver and one gold bar weighing 50 shekels, I desired them, so I took them. They are now hidden in the

ground inside my tent, with the money underneath."

22 At once Joshua sent messengers, and they ran to the tent, and there the garment was hidden in his tent, with the money underneath it. **23** So they took the things out of the tent and brought them to Joshua and all the Israelites and placed them before Jehovah. **24** Joshua and all Israel with him then took A′chan[a] the son of Ze′rah, the silver, the official garment, and the bar of gold,[b] along with his sons, his daughters, his bull, his donkey, his flock, his tent, and everything that was his, and they brought them up to the Valley* of A′chor.[c] **25** Joshua said: "Why have you brought disaster* upon us?[d] Jehovah will bring disaster upon you on this day." With that all Israel stoned him,[e] after which they burned them with fire.[f] Thus they stoned all of them. **26** And they raised a huge pile of stones over him that remains to this day. At this Jehovah's hot anger subsided.[g] That is why the name of that place is Valley of A′chor* to this day.

8 Then Jehovah said to Joshua: "Do not be afraid or be terrified.[h] Take with you all the fighting men and go up against A′i. See, I have handed over to you the king of A′i, his people, his city, and his land.[i] **2** Do to A′i and to its king just as you did to Jer′i·cho and its king,[j] except you may plunder its spoil and its livestock for yourselves. Set an ambush behind the city."

3 So Joshua and all the fighting men went up against A′i. Joshua chose 30,000 mighty warriors and sent them off by night. **4** He gave them this command: "See, you are to lie in

---

CHAP. 7
a Pr 16:33

b Jos 1:18
Jos 7:25

c Ex 24:7

d Ge 38:30
Nu 26:20
1Ch 2:4, 6

e Pr 16:33
Ac 5:3

f Ge 10:10

Second Col.
a Jos 22:20

b Jos 6:19

c Jos 15:7, 12
Isa 65:10
Ho 2:15

d Jos 6:18
1Ch 2:7

e Le 24:14
Jos 1:18

f Jos 7:15

g De 13:17

CHAP. 8
h De 7:18
De 31:8
Jos 1:9
Isa 12:2
Ro 8:31

i Ps 44:3

j Jos 6:2, 21

7:21 *A shekel equaled 11.4 g (0.367 oz t). See App. B14. 7:24 *Or "Low Plain." 7:25 *Or "trouble; ostracism." 7:26 *Meaning "Disaster; Ostracism."

ambush behind the city. Do not go very far from the city, and all of you be ready. 5 I and all the people with me will approach the city, and when they come out against us as before,[a] we will retreat from them. 6 When they come out after us, we will draw them away from the city, for they will say, 'They are retreating from us just as before.'[b] And we will retreat from them. 7 Then you should rise up from the ambush and capture the city; Jehovah your God will hand it over to you. 8 As soon as you have seized the city, you should set it on fire.[c] You should do according to Jehovah's word. See, I have given you your orders."

9 Then Joshua sent them out, and they marched to the place of ambush; they took a position between Beth'el and A'i, to the west of A'i, while Joshua spent that night with the people.

10 After Joshua rose up early in the morning and gathered* the troops, he and the elders of Israel led them to A'i. 11 All the fighting men[d] who were with him marched up and advanced to the front of the city. They camped to the north of A'i, with the valley between them and A'i. 12 In the meantime, he had taken about 5,000 men and had set them as an ambush[e] between Beth'el[f] and A'i, to the west of the city. 13 So the people set the main camp to the north of the city[g] and the rear guard west of the city,[h] and Joshua went that night into the middle of the valley.*

14 And as soon as the king of A'i saw this, he and the men of the city hurried out early in the morning to meet Israel in battle at a certain place overlooking the desert plain. But he did not know that there was an ambush

set against him to the rear of the city. 15 When the men of A'i attacked, Joshua and all Israel fled along the road in the direction of the wilderness.[a] 16 Then all the people who were in the city were summoned to pursue them; and as they pursued Joshua they were drawn away from the city. 17 Not a man was remaining in A'i and Beth'el who did not go out after Israel. They left the city wide open and pursued Israel.

18 Jehovah now said to Joshua: "Stretch out the javelin that is in your hand toward A'i,[b] for into your hand I will give it."[c] So Joshua stretched out the javelin that was in his hand toward the city. 19 The moment he stretched out his hand, the ambush rose up quickly from its place and ran into the city and captured it. They immediately set the city on fire.[d]

20 When the men of A'i turned around, they saw the smoke of the city rising to the sky, and they had no strength to flee in any direction. Then the people who had been fleeing toward the wilderness turned on their pursuers.[a] 21 When Joshua and all Israel saw that the ambush had captured the city and saw the smoke of the city rising, they turned around and attacked the men of A'i. 22 And the others came out of the city to meet them, so that the men of A'i were trapped in the middle, with some Israelites on this side and some on that side, and they struck them down until there was not one survivor or escapee remaining.[e] 23 But they caught the king of A'i[f] alive and brought him before Joshua.

24 After Israel finished killing all the inhabitants of A'i in the field, in the wilderness where they had pursued them, and every last one of them had fallen by the sword, then all Isra-

---

8:10 *Or "mustered." 8:13 *Or "low plain."

CHAP. 8
a Jos 7:5

b Jos 8:16

c Jos 8:19, 28

d Jos 8:1, 3

e Jos 8:2

f Ge 28:19

g Jos 8:5

h Jos 8:4

Second Col.
a Jos 8:6

b Ex 17:11
  Jos 8:26

c De 7:24

d Jos 8:8, 28

e Le 27:29
  De 7:2

f Jos 8:29
  Jos 12:7, 9

el returned to A'i and struck it with the sword. **25** All those who fell on that day, from man to woman, amounted to 12,000, all the people of A'i. **26** Joshua did not draw back his hand with which he had stretched out the javelin[a] until he had devoted all the inhabitants of A'i to destruction.[b] **27** However, Israel took the livestock and the spoil of that city for themselves, according to the orders that Jehovah had given to Joshua.[c]

28 Then Joshua burned A'i and reduced it to a permanent mound of ruins,[d] as it remains to this day. **29** He hung the king of A'i on a stake* until the evening, and as the sun was about to set, Joshua gave the order to take his dead body down from the stake.[e] Then they pitched it at the entrance of the city gate and raised up a great pile of stones over him, which is there to this day.

30 It was then that Joshua built an altar on Mount E'bal[f] to Jehovah the God of Israel, **31** just as Moses the servant of Jehovah had commanded the Israelites and as it is written in the book of the Law[g] of Moses: "An altar of whole stones on which no iron tool has been wielded."[h] On it they offered up burnt offerings to Jehovah as well as communion sacrifices.[i]

32 Then he wrote there on the stones a copy of the Law[j] that Moses had written before the Israelites.[k] **33** All Israel, their elders, the officers, and their judges were standing on both sides of the Ark in front of the Levitical priests who were carrying the ark of the covenant of Jehovah. The foreign residents were there as well as the natives.[l] Half of them stood in front of Mount Ger'i·zim, and the other half in front of

8:29 *Or "tree."

CHAP. 8
a Ex 17:11
   Jos 8:18
b Ex 27:29
c Jos 8:2
d Jos 8:8
e De 21:22, 23
f De 11:29
   De 27:4, 5
g De 31:9
   Jos 1:8
h Ex 20:25
i De 27:6, 7
j De 27:2, 3
k Ex 24:4
   Ex 34:27
l Le 24:22
   Nu 15:16

Second Col.
a De 27:12, 13
b De 11:29
c De 31:9
   Ne 8:3
d De 28:2
e De 27:15
   De 28:15
f De 4:2
   De 12:32
g Le 24:22
   Nu 15:16
h De 29:10, 11
   De 31:12
   Ne 8:2

CHAP. 9
i Jos 12:7, 8
j Nu 34:2, 6
k Ge 15:18-21
   Ex 3:17
   Ex 23:23
   De 7:1
l Jos 24:11
m Jos 10:2
   Jos 11:19
n Jos 6:20
o Jos 8:24
p Jos 5:10
   Jos 10:43
q Ge 10:15, 17
   Ge 34:2
   Ex 3:8
r Ex 34:12
   De 7:2
   De 20:16-18

Mount E'bal[a] (just as Moses the servant of Jehovah had previously commanded),[b] to bless the people of Israel. **34** After this he read aloud all the words of the Law,[c] the blessings[d] and the curses,[e] according to all that is written in the book of the Law. **35** There was not a word of all that Moses had commanded that Joshua did not read aloud in front of all the congregation of Israel,[f] including the women and children and the foreign residents[g] who were living* among them.[h]

9 When all the kings who were on the west side of the Jordan[i] heard what had happened, those in the mountainous region, in the She·phe'lah, along the entire coast of the Great Sea,*[j] and in front of Leb'a·non—the Hit'tites, the Am'or·ites, the Ca'naan·ites, the Per'iz·zites, the Hi'vites, and the Jeb'u·sites[k]— **2** they formed an alliance to fight against Joshua and Israel.[l]

3 The inhabitants of Gib'e·on[m] also heard what Joshua had done to Jer'i·cho[n] and A'i.[o] **4** So they acted shrewdly and put provisions into worn-out sacks on their donkeys, along with worn-out wineskins that had burst and had been mended; **5** they also had worn-out and patched sandals on their feet, and they were wearing worn-out garments. All the bread of their provisions was dry and crumbly. **6** Then they went to Joshua at the camp at Gil'gal[p] and said to him and the men of Israel: "We have come from a distant land. Now make a covenant with us." **7** But the men of Israel said to the Hi'vites:[q] "Perhaps you are living near us. So how can we make a covenant with you?"[r] **8** They replied to Joshua: "We are your servants."*

8:35 *Lit., "walking." 9:1 *That is, the Mediterranean. 9:8 *Or "slaves."

Then Joshua said to them: "Who are you, and where do you come from?" **9** At this they said to him: "Your servants have come from a very distant land[a] out of regard for the name of Jehovah your God, because we have heard about his fame and about all he did in Egypt[b] **10** and about all he did to the two kings of the Am′or·ites who were on the other side* of the Jordan, King Si′hon[c] of Hesh′-bon and King Og[d] of Ba′shan, who was in Ash′ta·roth. **11** So our elders and all the inhabitants of our land told us, 'Take provisions with you for the journey and go to meet them. Tell them: "We will be your servants;[e] now make a covenant with us."'[f] **12** This bread that we took as our provisions was still hot on the day we left our houses to come here to you. Now you can see it is dry and crumbly.[g] **13** And these wineskins were new when we filled them, but now they have burst.[h] And our garments and sandals have worn out because of the great length of the journey."

14 At that the men took* some of their provisions, but they did not inquire of Jehovah.[i] **15** So Joshua made peace with them[j] and made a covenant with them to let them live, and that is what the chieftains of the assembly swore to them in an oath.[k]

16 At the end of three days, after they made a covenant with them, they heard that they lived nearby, in their vicinity. **17** Then the Israelites set out and came to their cities on the third day; their cities were Gib′e·on,[l] Che·phi′rah, Be·er′oth, and Kir′i·ath-je′a·rim.[m] **18** But the Israelites did not attack them, because the chieftains of

the assembly had sworn an oath to them by Jehovah[a] the God of Israel. So all the assembly began to murmur against the chieftains. **19** At this all the chieftains said to the entire assembly: "Since we swore an oath to them by Jehovah the God of Israel, we are not allowed to hurt them. **20** This is what we will do: We will let them live, so that there is no indignation against us because of the oath that we swore to them."[b] **21** And the chieftains added: "Let them live, but let them become gatherers of wood and drawers of water for all the assembly." This is what the chieftains promised them.

22 Joshua now called them and said to them: "Why did you trick us by saying, 'We are from a place very far away from you,' when you really live right among us?[c] **23** From now on you are cursed,[d] and you will always occupy a slave's position as gatherers of wood and drawers of water for the house of my God." **24** They answered Joshua: "It was because your servants were plainly told that Jehovah your God had commanded Moses his servant to give you all the land and to annihilate all its inhabitants from before you.[e] So we were afraid for our lives* because of you,[f] and that is why we did this.[g] **25** Now we are at your mercy.* Do to us whatever you think is good and right." **26** And that is what he did with them; he saved them from the hands of the Israelites, and they did not kill them. **27** But that day Joshua made them gatherers of wood and drawers of water for the assembly[h] and for Jehovah's altar at the place that He should choose,[i] and they remain so to this day.[j]

CHAP. 9
a De 20:10, 15

b Ex 9:16
Ex 15:13, 14
Jos 2:9, 10

c Nu 21:21-24
De 2:32-34

d Nu 21:33-35
De 3:3

e De 20:10, 11

f Jos 9:6

g Jos 9:5

h Jos 9:4

i Nu 27:18, 21
1Sa 30:7, 8

j Jos 11:19

k 2Sa 21:2

l Jos 10:2

m Jos 18:11, 14
1Sa 7:1
1Ch 13:5

Second Col.
a Nu 30:2
De 6:13

b 2Sa 21:1
Ps 15:4
Ec 5:4, 6

c Jos 9:6, 16

d Ge 9:25, 26

e De 7:1
De 20:16

f De 2:25
De 11:25
Jos 5:1

g Heb 11:31

h Jos 9:21

i 1Ki 8:29
2Ch 6:6

j 1Ch 9:2
Ezr 7:24
Ezr 8:17
Ne 3:26
Ne 7:60

9:10 *That is, the east side. **9:14** *Or "examined."

9:24 *Or "souls." **9:25** *Lit., "in your hands."

10 As soon as King A·do′ni·ze′dek of Jerusalem heard that Joshua had captured A′i and devoted it to destruction, doing to A′i and its king^a just as he had done to Jer′i·cho and its king,^b and how the inhabitants of Gib′e·on had made peace with Israel^c and remained among them, **2** he was greatly alarmed,^d because Gib′e·on was a great city, like one of the royal cities. It was greater than A′i,^e and all its men were warriors. **3** So A·do′ni·ze′dek king of Jerusalem sent this message to Ho′ham king of Heb′ron,^f Pi′ram king of Jar′muth, Japhi′a king of La′chish, and De′bir king of Eg′lon:^g **4** "Come to my aid, and let us attack Gib′e·on, because it has made peace with Joshua and the Israelites."^h **5** At this the five kings of the Am′or·itesⁱ—the king of Jerusalem, the king of Heb′ron, the king of Jar′muth, the king of La′chish, and the king of Eg′lon—gathered together along with their armies, and they marched on and encamped against Gib′e·on to fight against it.

6 Then the men of Gib′e·on sent word to Joshua at the camp at Gil′gal:^j "Do not forsake* your slaves.^k Come quickly! Rescue us and help us! All the kings of the Am′or·ites from the mountainous region have gathered against us." **7** So Joshua went up from Gil′gal with all the fighting men and the mighty warriors.^l

8 Jehovah then said to Joshua: "Do not be afraid of them,^m for I have handed them over to you.ⁿ Not one of them will be able to stand against you."^o **9** Joshua came against them by surprise after marching all night long from Gil′gal. **10** Jehovah threw them into confusion before Israel,^p and they inflicted a

great slaughter on them at Gib′e·on, pursuing them by way of the ascent of Beth-ho′ron and striking them down as far as A·ze′kah and Mak·ke′dah. **11** While they were fleeing from Israel and were on the descent of Beth-ho′ron, Jehovah hurled great hailstones from the sky on them as far as A·ze′kah, and they perished. In fact, more died from the hail than from the sword of the Israelites.

12 It was then, on the day that Jehovah routed the Am′or·ites before the eyes of the Israelites, that Joshua said to Jehovah before Israel:

"Sun, stand still^a over
　　Gib′e·on,^b
And moon, over the Valley*
　　of Ai′ja·lon!"

13 So the sun stood still and the moon did not move until the nation could take vengeance on its enemies. Is it not written in the book of Ja′shar?^c The sun stood still in the middle of the sky and did not hasten to set for about a whole day. **14** There has never been a day like that one, either before it or after it, when Jehovah listened to the voice of a man,^d for Jehovah was fighting for Israel.^e

15 After that Joshua together with all Israel returned to the camp at Gil′gal.^f

16 Meanwhile, the five kings fled and hid in the cave at Mak·ke′dah.^g **17** Then it was reported to Joshua: "The five kings have been found hiding in the cave at Mak·ke′dah."^h **18** So Joshua said: "Roll large stones over the mouth of the cave and assign men to guard them. **19** But the rest of you should not stop. Pursue your enemies and strike them from the rear.ⁱ Do not allow them to enter into their cities, for Jehovah your

---

CHAP. 10
a Jos 8:24, 29
b Jos 6:2, 21
c Jos 9:9, 15
　Jos 11:19
d De 2:25
　De 11:25
　Jos 2:10, 11
　Jos 5:1
e Jos 8:25
f Ge 23:2
　Nu 13:22
g Jos 12:7,
　10-12
h Jos 9:9, 15
　Jos 11:19
i Ge 15:16
j Jos 5:10
k Jos 9:25, 27
l Jos 8:3
m De 3:2
　De 20:1
n Jos 7:24
　Jos 11:6
o Jos 1:3-5
p Ps 44:3

Second Col.
a 2Ki 20:10
　Ps 135:6
　Isa 38:8
b Isa 28:21
c 2Sa 1:17, 18
d De 9:18, 19
　1Ki 17:22
　Jas 5:16
e De 1:30
　Jos 23:3
f Jos 5:10
　Jos 9:6
g Jos 10:10
h Jos 10:28
i De 28:7

10:6 *Lit., "let your hand drop from."

10:12 *Or "Low Plain."

God has given them into your hands."

20 After Joshua and the Israelites had finished inflicting a very great slaughter on them, to the point of wiping them out except for some survivors who escaped and entered into the fortified cities, **21** all the people returned safely to Joshua at the camp at Mak·ke'dah. Not a man dared to utter a word* against the Israelites. **22** Then Joshua said: "Open the mouth of the cave and bring the five kings out of the cave to me." **23** So they brought to him from the cave these five kings: the king of Jerusalem, the king of Heb'ron, the king of Jar'muth, the king of La'chish, and the king of Eg'lon.[a] **24** When they brought these kings to Joshua, he summoned all the men of Israel and said to the commanders of the fighting men who had gone with him: "Come forward. Place your feet on the backs of the necks of these kings." So they came forward and placed their feet on the backs of their necks.[b] **25** Then Joshua said to them: "Do not be afraid or be terrified.[c] Be courageous and strong, for this is what Jehovah will do to all your enemies against whom you are fighting."[d]

26 Then Joshua struck them and put them to death and hung them on five stakes,* and they remained hanging on the stakes until the evening. **27** At sunset Joshua ordered that they be taken down off the stakes[e] and thrown into the cave where they had hidden themselves. Then large stones were placed at the mouth of the cave, and these remain to this very day.

28 Joshua captured Mak·ke'dah[f] on that day and struck it with the sword. He devoted its

king and everyone* in it to destruction, letting no survivor remain.[a] He did to the king of Mak·ke'dah[b] just as he had done to the king of Jer'i·cho.

29 Then Joshua together with all Israel went from Mak·ke'dah to Lib'nah and fought against Lib'nah.[c] **30** Jehovah also gave it and its king[d] into Israel's hand, and they struck it and everyone* in it with the sword, not letting a survivor remain in it. So they did to its king just as they had done to the king of Jer'i·cho.[e]

31 Next Joshua together with all Israel went from Lib'nah to La'chish[f] and camped there and fought against it. **32** Jehovah gave La'chish into Israel's hand, and they captured it on the second day. They struck it and everyone* in it with the sword,[g] just as they had done to Lib'nah.

33 Then Ho'ram king of Ge'zer[h] went up to help La'chish, but Joshua struck him and his people down until not one survivor remained.

34 Then Joshua together with all Israel went from La'chish to Eg'lon[i] and camped there and fought against it. **35** They captured it on that day and struck it with the sword. They devoted everyone* in it to destruction on that day, just as they had done to La'chish.[j]

36 Then Joshua together with all Israel went up from Eg'lon to Heb'ron[k] and fought against it. **37** They captured it and struck it, its king, its towns, and everyone* in it with the sword, not letting any survivor remain. Just as he had done to Eg'lon, he devoted it and everyone* in it to destruction.

38 Finally Joshua together with all Israel turned toward De'bir[l] and fought against it.

CHAP. 10

a Jos 10:3-5
Jos 12:7,
10-12

b Ex 23:27

c De 31:6
Jos 1:9

d De 3:21
De 7:18, 19

e De 21:22, 23
Jos 8:29

f Jos 10:10
Jos 15:20, 41

Second Col.

a De 20:16

b Jos 12:7, 16

c Jos 15:20, 42
Jos 21:13

d Jos 12:7, 15

e Jos 6:2, 21

f Jos 10:3, 4
Jos 12:7, 11
Jos 15:20, 39

g De 20:16

h Jos 12:7, 12
Jos 16:10
Jos 21:20, 21
1Ki 9:16

i Jos 10:3, 4
Jos 12:7, 12
Jos 15:20, 39

j De 20:16
Jos 10:32

k Ge 13:18
Ge 23:19
Nu 13:22
Jos 10:3, 4
Jos 15:13
Jos 21:13

l Jos 12:7, 13
Jos 15:15

10:21 *Lit., "sharpened his tongue."
10:26 *Or "trees."
10:28, 30, 32, 35, 37 *Or "every soul."

39 He captured it, its king, and all its towns, and they struck them down with the sword, devoting everyone* in it to destruction,[a] not letting any survivor remain.[b] He did to De'bir and its king just as he had done to Heb'ron and to Lib'nah and its king.

40 Joshua conquered all the land of the mountainous region, the Neg'eb, the She·phe'lah,[c] and the slopes, and all their kings, not letting any survivor remain; he devoted everything that breathed to destruction,[d] just as Jehovah the God of Israel had commanded.[e] **41** Joshua conquered them from Ka'desh-bar'ne·a[f] to Gaz'a[g] and all the land of Go'shen[h] and up to Gib'e·on.[i] **42** Joshua captured all these kings and their land, all at the same time, because it was Jehovah the God of Israel who was fighting for Israel.[j] **43** Then Joshua returned with all Israel to the camp at Gil'gal.[k]

11 As soon as Ja'bin king of Ha'zor heard of it, he sent word to Jo'bab king of Ma'don,[l] and to the king of Shim'ron, the king of Ach'shaph,[m] **2** the kings who were in the northern mountainous region, those in the plains* south of Chin'ne·reth, those in the She·phe'lah and on the slopes of Dor[n] to the west, **3** the Ca'naan·ites[o] to the east and the west, the Am'or·ites,[p] the Hit'tites, the Per'iz·zites, the Jeb'u·sites in the mountainous region, and the Hi'vites[q] at the base of Her'mon[r] in the land of Miz'pah. **4** So they came out with all their armies, a vast multitude as numerous as the grains of sand on the seashore, together with very many horses and war chariots. **5** All these kings agreed to meet, and they came and camped together at the wa-

---

ters of Mer'om to fight against Israel.

6 At this Jehovah said to Joshua: "Do not be afraid because of them,[a] for about this time tomorrow, I am giving over all of them slain to Israel. Their horses you must hamstring,[b] and their chariots you must burn in the fire." **7** Joshua together with all the fighting men then launched a surprise attack against them along the waters of Mer'om. **8** Jehovah gave them into Israel's hand,[c] and they defeated them and pursued them as far as Great Si'don[d] and Mis're·photh-ma'im[e] and the Valley of Miz'peh to the east, and they struck them down until no survivors remained.[f] **9** Joshua then did to them just as Jehovah had told him; he hamstrung their horses and burned their chariots in the fire.[g]

10 Moreover, Joshua then returned and captured Ha'zor and struck down its king with the sword,[h] because Ha'zor had formerly been the head of all these kingdoms. **11** They struck down everyone* in it with the sword, devoting them to destruction.[i] Not a breathing thing was left.[j] Then he burned Ha'zor in the fire. **12** Joshua captured all the cities of these kings and defeated all their kings with the sword.[k] He devoted them to destruction,[l] just as Moses the servant of Jehovah had commanded. **13** However, Israel did not burn any of the cities that stood on their mounds except Ha'zor; it was the only one Joshua burned. **14** All the spoil of these cities and the livestock, the Israelites plundered for themselves.[m] But they struck every human with the sword until they had annihilated each one.[n] They did not let anyone who breathed remain.[o] **15** Just as Jehovah had

---

CHAP. 10
a De 7:2
b Jos 11:14
c Jos 9:1, 2
  Jg 1:9
d Le 27:29
  De 20:16
  Jos 11:14
e De 7:2
  De 9:5
f Nu 34:2, 4
  De 9:23
g De 2:23
h Jos 15:20, 51
i Jos 11:16, 19
j Ex 14:14
  De 1:30
k Jos 4:19

CHAP. 11
l Jos 12:7, 19
m Jos 12:7, 20
n Jos 17:11
  Jg 1:27
o Nu 13:29
p Ge 15:16
q De 7:1
  De 20:17
r De 4:48

Second Col.
a Jos 10:8
b De 17:16
  Pr 21:31
c Jos 21:44
d Ge 10:19
  Jos 19:28, 31
e Jos 13:1, 6
f De 20:16
g Jos 11:6
h Jos 12:7, 19
i Le 27:29
j De 20:16
  Jos 11:14
k De 9:5
l De 7:2, 16
m Jos 8:2, 27
n De 7:2
o De 20:16

commanded Moses his servant, so Moses commanded Joshua,[a] and so Joshua did. He left nothing undone of all that Jehovah had commanded Moses.[b]

16 Joshua conquered all this land, the mountainous region, all the Neg'eb,[c] all the land of Go'shen, the She·phe'lah,[d] the Ar'a·bah,[e] and the mountainous region of Israel and its Shephe'lah,* 17 from Mount Ha'lak, which goes up to Se'ir, and as far as Ba'al·gad[f] in the Valley of Leb'a·non at the base of Mount Her'mon,[g] and he captured all their kings and defeated them, putting them to death. 18 Joshua waged war with all these kings for quite some time. 19 There was no city that made peace with the Israelites except the Hi'vites inhabiting Gib'e·on.[h] They conquered all the others by war.[i] 20 It was Jehovah who allowed their hearts to become stubborn[j] so that they waged war against Israel, in order for him to devote them to destruction without any favorable consideration.[k] They were to be annihilated, just as Jehovah had commanded Moses.[l]

21 At that time Joshua wiped out the An'a·kim[m] from the mountainous region, from Heb'ron, De'bir, A'nab, and all the mountainous region of Judah and all the mountainous region of Israel. Joshua devoted them and their cities to destruction.[n] 22 There were no An'a·kim left in the land of the Israelites; they remained[o] only in Gaz'a,[p] in Gath,[q] and in Ash'dod.[r] 23 So Joshua took control of all the land, just as Jehovah had promised Moses,[s] and then Joshua gave it as an inheritance to Israel by their shares to be divided among their tribes.[t] And the land had rest from war.[u]

11:16 *Or "its foothills."

---

12 Now these are the kings of the land whom the Israelites defeated, whose land they took possession of on the east side of the Jordan, from the Ar'non Valley*[a] up to Mount Her'mon[b] and all the Ar'a·bah toward the east:[c] 2 King Si'hon[d] of the Am'or·ites, who lived in Hesh'bon and ruled from A·ro'er,[e] which was on the rim of the Ar'non Valley,*[f] and from the middle of the valley, and half of Gil'e·ad as far as the Valley[g] of Jab'bok, the boundary of the Am'mon·ites. 3 He also ruled over the Ar'a·bah as far as the Sea of Chin'ne·reth*[g] toward the east and as far as the Sea of the Ar'a·bah, the Salt Sea,# to the east in the direction of Beth-jesh'i·moth, and toward the south under the slopes of Pis'gah.[h]

4 Also the territory of King Og[i] of Ba'shan, who was one of the last of the Reph'a·im[j] and who lived in Ash'ta·roth and Ed're·i 5 and ruled in Mount Her'mon, in Sal'e·cah, and in all Ba'shan,[k] as far as the boundary of the Gesh'ur·ites and the Ma·ac'a·thites,[l] and half of Gil'e·ad, to the territory of King Si'hon of Hesh'bon.[m]

6 Moses the servant of Jehovah and the Israelites defeated them,[n] after which Moses the servant of Jehovah gave their land as a possession to the Reu'ben·ites, the Gad'ites, and the half tribe of Ma·nas'seh.[o]

7 These are the kings of the land whom Joshua and the Israelites defeated on the west side of the Jordan, from Ba'al·gad[p] in the Valley of Leb'a·non[q] and as far as Mount Ha'lak,[r] which goes up to Se'ir,[s] after which Joshua gave their land to the tribes

---

CHAP. 11
a De 3:28
  De 7:1
  De 31:7
b De 4:2, 5
c Nu 13:17
  De 1:7
d Jos 10:40, 41
e Jos 12:7, 8
f Jos 13:1, 5
g De 4:48
  Jos 13:8, 11
h Jos 9:7, 15
i Jos 11:19
j De 20:17
j De 2:30
k Ex 34:12
  De 7:2
l De 20:16
m Nu 13:22
  De 1:28
  Jos 15:13, 14
n Le 27:29
  Jos 11:12
  Jos 24:11
o Ex 23:28-30
p Jg 1:18
q 1Sa 17:4
r 2Ch 26:1, 6
s Ex 23:27
  De 11:23
t Nu 26:53, 54
  Jos 14:1
u Jos 14:15
  Jos 21:44
  Jos 23:1

Second Col.

CHAP. 12
a De 2:24
b De 3:8
c De 4:47-49
d Nu 21:23, 24
e De 3:12
f Nu 21:13
g Joh 6:1
h De 3:27
i Nu 21:33-35
j De 3:11
k De 29:7
l Jos 13:13
m Nu 21:26
n Nu 21:23, 24
  Nu 21:33-35
o Nu 32:33
  De 3:12, 13
p Jos 13:1, 5
q Jos 1:4
r Jos 11:16, 17
s De 2:12

12:1, 2 *Or "Wadi Arnon." 12:2 #Or "Wadi." 12:3 *That is, the lake of Gennesaret, or the Sea of Galilee. #That is, the Dead Sea.

of Israel as a possession by their shares,[a] **8** in the mountainous region, in the She·phe'lah, in the Ar'a·bah, on the slopes, in the wilderness, and in the Neg'eb[b]—the land of the Hit'tites, the Am'or·ites,[c] the Ca'naan·ites, the Per'iz·zites, the Hi'vites, and the Jeb'u·sites:[d]

9 The king of Jer'i·cho,[e] one; the king of A'i,[f] which was beside Beth'el, one;

10 the king of Jerusalem, one; the king of Heb'ron,[g] one;

11 the king of Jar'muth, one; the king of La'chish, one;

12 the king of Eg'lon, one; the king of Ge'zer,[h] one;

13 the king of De'bir,[i] one; the king of Ge'der, one;

14 the king of Hor'mah, one; the king of A'rad, one;

15 the king of Lib'nah,[j] one; the king of A·dul'lam, one;

16 the king of Mak·ke'dah,[k] one; the king of Beth'el,[l] one;

17 the king of Tap'pu·ah, one; the king of He'pher, one;

18 the king of A'phek, one; the king of Las·shar'on, one;

19 the king of Ma'don, one; the king of Ha'zor,[m] one;

20 the king of Shim'ron-me'ron, one; the king of Ach'shaph, one;

21 the king of Ta'a·nach, one; the king of Me·gid'do, one;

22 the king of Ke'desh, one; the king of Jok'ne·am[n] in Car'mel, one;

23 the king of Dor on the slopes of Dor,[o] one; the king of Goi'im in Gil'gal, one;

24 the king of Tir'zah, one; a total of 31 kings.

13 Now Joshua had grown old and was advanced in years.[a] So Jehovah said to him: "You have grown old and are advanced in years; but much of the land remains to be taken in possession.* **2** This is the land remaining:[b] all the regions of the Phi·lis'tines and all the Gesh'ur·ites[c] **3** (from the branch of the Nile* that is east of* Egypt up to the border of Ek'ron to the north, which used to be considered Ca'naan·ite territory)[d] including that of the five lords of the Phi·lis'tines[e]—the Gaz'ites, the Ash'dod·ites,[f] the Ash'ke·lon·ites,[g] the Git'tites,[h] and the Ek'ron·ites;[i] that of the Av'vim[j] **4** to the south; all the land of the Ca'naan·ites; Me·ar'ah, which belongs to the Si·do'ni·ans,[k] as far as A'phek, to the border of the Am'or·ites; **5** the land of the Ge'bal·ites[l] and all of Leb'a·non toward the east, from Ba'al-gad at the base of Mount Her'mon to Le'bo-ha'math;*[m] **6** all the inhabitants of the mountainous region from Leb'a·non[n] to Mis're·photh-ma'im;[o] and all the Si·do'ni·ans.[p] I will drive them out* before the Israelites.[q] You have only to assign it to Israel as an inheritance, just as I have commanded you.[r] **7** Now you must apportion this land as an inheritance to the nine tribes and the half tribe of Ma·nas'seh."[s]

8 With the other half tribe, the Reu'ben·ites and the Gad'ites took their inheritance that Moses gave them on the east side of the Jordan, just as Moses the servant of Jehovah had given them;[t] **9** from A·ro'er,[u] which is on the rim of the Ar'non Valley,*[v] and the city that

13:1 *Or "be conquered." 13:3 *Or "from Shihor." *Lit., "in front of." 13:5 *Or "the entrance of Hamath." 13:6 *Or "dispossess them." 13:9 *Or "Wadi Arnon."

is in the middle of the valley, and all the tableland* of Med′e-ba as far as Di′bon; **10** and all the cities of King Si′hon of the Am′or·ites, who reigned in Hesh′bon, up to the border of the Am′mon·ites;[a] **11** also Gil′e-ad and the territory of the Gesh′ur·ites and the Ma·ac′a-thites[b] and all Mount Her′mon and all Ba′shan[c] as far as Sal′e-cah;[d] **12** all the royal realm of Og in Ba′shan, who reigned in Ash′ta·roth and in Ed′re·i. (He was one of the last of the Reph′a·im.)[e] Moses defeated them and drove them out.*[f] **13** But the Israelites did not drive out*[g] the Gesh′ur·ites and the Ma·ac′a-thites, for Gesh′ur and Ma′a·cath live in the midst of Israel to this day.

14 It was only to the tribe of the Levites that he did not give an inheritance.[h] The offerings made by fire to Jehovah the God of Israel are their inheritance,[i] just as he promised them.[j]

15 Then Moses gave an inheritance to the tribe of the Reu′ben·ites by their families, **16** and their territory was from A·ro′er, which is on the rim of the Ar′non Valley,* and the city in the middle of the valley, and all the tableland by Med′e-ba; **17** Hesh′bon and all its towns[k] on the tableland, Di′bon, Ba′moth-ba′al, Beth-ba′al-me′on,[l] **18** Ja′haz,[m] Ked′e-moth,[n] Meph′a·ath,[o] **19** Kir·i·a·tha′im, Sib′mah,[p] and Ze′reth-sha′har on the mountain of the valley,* **20** Beth-pe′or, the slopes of Pis′gah,[q] Beth-jesh′i·moth,[r] **21** all the cities of the tableland, and all the royal realm of King Si′hon of the Am′or·ites, who reigned in Hesh′bon.[s] Moses defeated him[t]

CHAP. 13
a Nu 21:23, 24
b De 3:14
c Jos 17:1
d 1Ch 5:11
e De 3:11
f Nu 21:23, 24
Nu 21:33-35
g Nu 33:55
Jos 23:12, 13
h Nu 18:20
De 10:9
De 12:12
i Le 7:33-35
De 18:1
j Nu 18:24
k Nu 21:25, 26
l Nu 32:37, 38
m Nu 21:23
n De 2:26
o Jos 21:8, 37
p Nu 32:37, 38
q De 3:16, 17
r Nu 33:48, 49
s Nu 21:25
t De 2:30

Second Col.
a Nu 31:7, 8
b Nu 22:5
2Pe 2:15
c Nu 22:7
d Nu 32:34, 35
e Jos 12:2
Jg 11:13
f 2Sa 11:1
g Nu 21:26
h Ge 32:2
Jos 21:8, 38
i Nu 32:34, 36
j Ge 33:17
k Nu 21:26
l Nu 34:2, 11
De 3:16, 17
Joh 6:1
m De 3:13
n 1Ch 6:77, 80
o Nu 32:40, 41
De 3:14
p Nu 21:33
q Nu 32:39

and the Mid′i·an·ite chieftains E′vi, Re′kem, Zur, Hur, and Re′ba,[a] vassals* of Si′hon who were dwelling in the land. **22** Ba′laam[b] the son of Be′or, the diviner,[c] was one whom the Israelites killed with the sword along with the rest who were slain. **23** The boundary of the Reu′ben·ites was the Jordan; and this territory was the inheritance of the Reu′ben·ites by their families, with the cities and their settlements.

24 Furthermore, Moses gave an inheritance to the tribe of Gad, the Gad′ites by their families, **25** and their territory included Ja′zer[d] and all the cities of Gil′e·ad and half of the land of the Am′mon·ites[e] as far as A·ro′er, which faces Rab′bah;[f] **26** and from Hesh′bon[g] to Ra′math-miz′peh and Bet′o-nim, and from Ma·ha·na′im[h] to the border of De′bir; **27** and in the valley,* Beth-ha′ram, Beth-nim′rah,[i] Suc′coth,[j] and Za′phon, the rest of the royal realm of King Si′hon of Hesh′bon,[k] with the Jordan as the border from the lower end of the Sea of Chin′ne·reth*[l] on the east side of the Jordan. **28** This was the inheritance of the Gad′ites by their families, with the cities and their settlements.

29 Further, Moses gave an inheritance to the half tribe of Ma·nas′seh, to half of the tribe of Ma·nas′seh by their families.[m] **30** And their territory extended from Ma·ha·na′im[n] and took in all of Ba′shan, all the royal realm of King Og of Ba′shan, and all the tent villages of Ja′ir[o] in Ba′shan, 60 towns. **31** And half of Gil′e-ad, and Ash′ta·roth and Ed′re·i,[p] the cities of the royal realm of Og in Ba′shan, went to the sons of Ma′chir[q] the son of Ma·nas′-

13:9 *Or "plateau." 13:12 *Or "dispossessed them." 13:13 *Or "dispossess." 13:16 *Or "Wadi Arnon." 13:19, 27 *Or "low plain."

13:21 *That is, kings who were subject to Sihon. 13:27 *That is, the lake of Gennesaret, or the Sea of Galilee.

seh, to half of the sons of Ma'-chir by their families.

32 These were the inheritances that Moses gave them on the desert plains of Mo'ab beyond the Jordan, east of Jer'i-cho.[a]

33 But to the tribe of the Levites, Moses did not give an inheritance.[b] Jehovah the God of Israel is their inheritance, just as he promised them.[c]

14 Now this is what the Israelites took as an inheritance in the land of Ca'naan, which El·e·a'zar the priest and Joshua the son of Nun and the heads of the paternal houses of the tribes of Israel gave them to inherit.[d] **2** Their inheritance was by lot,[e] just as Jehovah had commanded through Moses for the nine and a half tribes.[f] **3** Moses had given the inheritance of the other two and a half tribes on the other side* of the Jordan,[g] and to the Levites he did not give an inheritance among them.[h] **4** The descendants of Joseph were considered two tribes,[i] Ma·nas'seh and E'phra·im;[j] and they did not give a share in the land to the Levites, except cities[k] to dwell in and their pastures for their livestock and their property.[l] **5** So the Israelites apportioned the land just as Jehovah had commanded Moses.

6 Then the men of Judah approached Joshua in Gil'gal,[m] and Ca'leb[n] the son of Je·phun'neh the Ken'iz·zite said to him: "You well know what Jehovah said[o] to Moses the man of the true God[p] about you and me at Ka'desh-bar'ne·a.[q] **7** I was 40 years old when Moses the servant of Jehovah sent me out of Ka'desh-bar'ne·a to spy out the land,[r] and I returned with a forthright

report.*[a] **8** Although my brothers who went up with me caused the people to lose heart,* I followed Jehovah my God wholeheartedly.*[b] **9** Moses swore on that day, saying: 'The land on which your foot has walked will become a lasting inheritance for you and your sons, because you have followed Jehovah my God wholeheartedly.'[c] **10** Now just as he promised,[d] Jehovah has preserved me alive[e] these 45 years since Jehovah made this promise to Moses when Israel walked in the wilderness;[f] I am still here today, 85 years old. **11** And today I am as strong as on the day Moses sent me out. My strength is now as it was then, for war and for other activities. **12** Therefore, give me this mountainous region that Jehovah promised on that day. Though you heard on that day that there were An'a·kim[g] there with great fortified cities,[h] surely* Jehovah will be with me,[i] and I will drive them out,# just as Jehovah promised.[j]

13 So Joshua blessed him and gave Heb'ron to Ca'leb the son of Je·phun'neh as an inheritance.[k] **14** That is why Heb'ron belongs to Ca'leb the son of Je·phun'neh the Ken'iz·zite as an inheritance to this day, because he followed Jehovah the God of Israel wholeheartedly.[l] **15** The name of Heb'ron was previously Kir'i·ath-ar'ba[m] (Ar'ba was the great man among the An'a·kim). And the land had rest from war.[n]

15 The land allotted*[o] to the tribe of Judah for their families extended to the boundary of E'dom,[p] the wilderness of

---

14:3 *That is, the east side.

14:7 *Lit., "with a word just as with my heart." **14:8** *Lit., "caused the heart of the people to melt." #Lit., "fully; completely." **14:12** *Or "likely." #Or "dispossess them." **15:1** *Or "given by lot."

Zin, to the Neg'eb at its southern end. **2** Their southern boundary ran from the extremity of the Salt Sea,*[a] from the bay that faces southward. **3** And it extended south to the ascent of A·krab'bim,[b] passed over to Zin, then went up from the south to Ka'desh-bar'ne·a,[c] over to Hez'ron, up to Ad'dar, and went around toward Kar'ka. **4** Then it passed on to Az'mon[d] and extended to the Wadi* of Egypt,[e] and the boundary ended at the Sea.*[f] This was their southern boundary.

5 The eastern boundary was the Salt Sea* up to the end of the Jordan, and the boundary at the northern corner was at the bay of the sea, at the end of the Jordan.[f] **6** The boundary went up to Beth-hog'lah[g] and passed over at the north of Beth-ar'a·bah,[h] and the boundary went up to the stone of Bo'han[i] the son of Reu'ben. **7** The boundary went up to De'bir at the Valley* of A'chor[j] and turned northward to Gil'gal,[k] which is in front of the ascent of A·dum'mim that is south of the wadi, and the boundary passed over to the waters of En-she'mesh[l] and ended at En-ro'gel.[m] **8** The boundary went up to the Valley of the Son of Hin'nom[n] to the slope of the Jeb'u·site[o] at the south, that is, Jerusalem,[p] and the boundary went up to the top of the mountain that faces the Valley of Hin'nom to the west, which is at the extremity of the Valley* of Reph'a·im to the north. **9** And the boundary was marked from the top of the mountain to the spring of the waters of Neph·to'ah[q] and extended to the cities of Mount E'phron; and the boundary was marked to Ba'al·ah, that

is, Kir'i·ath-je'a·rim.[a] **10** The boundary went around from Ba'al·ah westward to Mount Se'ir and passed over to the slope of Mount Je'a·rim at the north, that is, Ches'a·lon, and it went down to Beth-she'mesh[b] and passed over to Tim'nah.[c] **11** And the boundary extended to the slope of Ek'ron[d] to the north, and the boundary was marked to Shik'ke·ron and passed over to Mount Ba'al·ah and extended to Jab'ne·el, and the boundary ended at the sea.

12 The western boundary was at the Great Sea*[e] and its coast. This was the boundary of the descendants of Judah by their families on all sides.

13 And to Ca'leb[f] the son of Je·phun'neh, he gave a share among the descendants of Judah at the order of Jehovah to Joshua, namely, Kir'i·ath-ar'ba (Ar'ba was the father of A'nak), that is, Heb'ron.[g] **14** So Ca'leb drove out from there the three sons of A'nak:[h] She'shai, A·hi'man, and Tal'mai,[i] descendants of A'nak. **15** Then he went up from there against the inhabitants of De'bir.[j] (The name of De'bir was previously Kir'i·ath-se'pher.) **16** Ca'leb then said: "To the man who strikes Kir'i·ath-se'pher and captures it, I will give my daughter Ach'sah as a wife." **17** And Oth'ni·el[k] the son of Ke'naz,[k] Ca'leb's brother, captured it. So he gave him his daughter Ach'sah[m] as a wife. **18** While she was going home, she urged him to ask her father for a field. Then she dismounted from her donkey.* Ca'leb asked her: "What do you want?"[n] **19** She said: "Please grant me a blessing, for you have given me a piece of land in the south;* give me also

---

CHAP. 15
a Nu 34:2, 3
b Jg 1:36
c Nu 34:4
d Nu 34:2, 5
e 1Ki 8:65
f Nu 34:12
g Jos 18:19, 20
h Jos 18:21, 22
i Jos 18:17, 20
j Jos 7:26
k Jos 5:8, 9
l Jos 18:17, 20
m 1Ki 1:9
n Jos 18:16, 20 2Ki 23:10 Jer 7:31
o Jg 1:21
p Jos 18:28 Jg 19:10
q Jos 18:15, 20

Second Col.
a Jos 9:16, 17 2Sa 6:2 1Ch 13:6
b Jos 21:8, 16
c Jos 19:43, 48 Jg 14:1, 2 2Ch 28:18
d 1Sa 5:10 1Sa 7:14 2Ki 1:2
e Nu 34:2, 6 De 11:24
f Nu 13:30 De 1:36
g Ge 23:2 Ge 35:27 Jos 20:7 Jos 21:11, 12
h Nu 13:33 Jos 11:21
i Nu 13:22 Jg 1:10, 20
j Jos 10:38, 39
k Jg 3:9-11
l 1Ch 4:13
m 1Ch 2:49
n Jg 1:14, 15

15:2, 5 *That is, the Dead Sea. 15:4 *See Glossary. *That is, the Great Sea, the Mediterranean. 15:7, 8 *Or "Low Plain."

15:12 *That is, the Mediterranean. 15:18 *Or possibly, "she clapped her hands while on the donkey." 15:19 *Or "the Negeb."

Gul'loth-ma'im."* So he gave her Upper Gul'loth and Lower Gul'-loth.

20 This was the inheritance of the tribe of Judah by their families.

21 The cities at the extremity of the tribe of Judah toward the boundary of E'dom[a] in the south were: Kab'ze-el, E'der, Ja'gur, **22** Ki'nah, Di·mo'-nah, A·da'dah, **23** Ke'desh, Ha'-zor, Ith'nan, **24** Ziph, Te'lem, Be·a'loth, **25** Ha'zor-ha·dat'tah, and Ke'ri·oth-hez'ron, that is, Ha'zor, **26** A'mam, She'ma, Mo·la'dah,[b] **27** Ha'zar-gad'dah, Hesh'-mon, Beth-pel'et,[c] **28** Ha'zar-shu'al, Be'er-she'ba,[d] Biz·i·o·thi'ah, **29** Ba'al·ah, I'im, E'zem, **30** El·to'lad, Che'sil, Hor'mah,[e] **31** Zik'-lag,[f] Mad·man'nah, San·san'nah, **32** Le·ba'oth, Shil'him, A'in, and Rim'mon[g]—a total of 29 cities together with their settlements.

33 In the She·phe'lah,[h] there were: Esh'ta·ol, Zo'rah,[i] Ash'-nah, **34** Za·no'ah, En·gan'nim, Tap'pu·ah, E'nam, **35** Jar'muth, A·dul'lam,[j] So'coh, A·ze'kah,[k] **36** Sha·a·ra'im,[l] Ad·i·tha'im, and Ge·de'rah and Ged·e·ro·tha'im*—14 cities and their settlements.

37 Ze'nan, Ha·dash'ah, Mig'dal-gad, **38** Di'le·an, Miz'peh, Jok'-the·el, **39** La'chish,[m] Boz'kath, Eg'lon, **40** Cab'bon, Lah'mam, Chit'lish, **41** Ge·de'roth, Beth-da'gon, Na'a·mah, and Mak·ke'dah[n]—16 cities and their settlements.

42 Lib'nah,[o] E'ther, A'shan,[p] **43** Iph'tah, Ash'nah, Ne'zib, **44** Kei'lah, Ach'zib, and Ma·re'-shah—nine cities and their settlements.

45 Ek'ron and its dependent* towns and its settlements; **46** from Ek'ron westward, all that is alongside Ash'dod and their settlements.

47 Ash'dod,[a] its dependent* towns and its settlements; Gaz'a,[b] its dependent towns and its settlements, down to the Wadi of Egypt, the Great Sea,[#] and the adjacent region.[c]

48 And in the mountainous region, Sha'mir, Jat'tir,[d] So'coh, **49** Dan'nah, Kir'i·ath-san'nah, that is, De'bir, **50** A'nab, Esh'-te·moh,[e] A'nim, **51** Go'shen,[f] Ho'lon, and Gi'loh[g]—11 cities and their settlements.

52 Arab, Du'mah, E'shan, **53** Ja'nim, Beth-tap'pu·ah, A·phe'-kah, **54** Hum'tah, Kir'i·ath-ar'ba, that is, Heb'ron,[h] and Zi'or—nine cities and their settlements.

55 Ma'on,[i] Car'mel, Ziph,[j] Jut'tah, **56** Jez're·el, Jok'de-am, Za·no'ah, **57** Ka'in, Gib'e-ah, and Tim'nah[k]—ten cities and their settlements.

58 Hal'hul, Beth-zur, Ge'dor, **59** Ma'a·rath, Beth-a'noth, and El'te·kon—six cities and their settlements.

60 Kir'i·ath-ba'al, that is, Kir'i·ath-je'a·rim,[l] and Rab'bah—two cities and their settlements.

61 In the wilderness, Beth-ar'a·bah,[m] Mid'din, Se·ca'cah, **62** Nib'shan, the City of Salt, and En-ged'i[n]—six cities and their settlements.

63 As for the Jeb'u·sites[o] who were dwelling in Jerusalem,[p] the men of Judah were not able to drive them away,[q] so the Jeb'u-sites continue dwelling with the people of Judah in Jerusalem to this day.

16 And the land that fell by lot*[r] to the descendants of Joseph[s] was from the Jordan at Jer'i·cho to the waters east of

CHAP. 15
a Nu 34:2, 3
  De 2:5
b Jos 19:1, 2
c Ne 11:25, 26
  Jos 19:1-3
d Ge 21:31
  Jos 19:1, 4
e Nu 14:44, 45
  Jos 19:1, 4
  Jg 1:17
f Jos 19:1, 5
  1Sa 27:5, 6
  1Ch 12:1
g Jos 19:1, 7
  Ne 11:25, 29
h Jg 1:9
i Jos 19:40, 41
  Jg 16:31
j 1Sa 22:1
k 1Sa 17:1
l 1Sa 17:52
m 2Ki 18:14
n Jos 10:28
o Jos 10:29
  2Ki 8:22
p Jos 19:1, 7

Second Col.
a 1Sa 5:1
b Ge 10:19
c Nu 34:2, 5
d Jos 21:8, 14
e 1Ch 6:57
f Jos 11:16
g 2Sa 15:12
h Jos 14:15
i Jos 23:25
  1Sa 25:2, 3
j 1Sa 23:14
k Ge 38:12
l Jos 9:16, 17
  Jos 18:11, 14
  1Sa 7:1
m Jos 18:21, 22
n 1Sa 23:29
o Ge 10:15, 16
p 1Ch 11:4
q Nu 33:55
  Jg 1:8, 21
  Jg 19:11
  2Sa 5:6

CHAP. 16
r Nu 26:55
  Nu 33:54
  Pr 16:33
s Ge 49:22
  De 33:13

15:19 *Meaning "Basins (Bowls) of Water." 15:36 *Or possibly, "Gederah and its sheepfolds." 15:45, 47 *Or "surrounding."

15:47 #That is, the Mediterranean. 16:1 *Or "was allotted."

Jer'i·cho, through the wilderness going up from Jer'i·cho into the mountainous region of Beth'el.[a] **2** It extended from Beth'el belonging to Luz and continued to the boundary of the Ar'chites at At'a·roth, **3** then it went down westward to the boundary of the Japh'le·tites as far as the boundary of Lower Beth-ho'ron[b] and Ge'zer,[c] and it ended at the sea.

4 So Joseph's descendants,[d] Ma·nas'seh and E'phra·im, took possession of their land.[e] **5** The boundary of the descendants of E'phra·im by their families was as follows: The boundary of their inheritance to the east was At'a·roth-ad'dar,[f] as far as Upper Beth-ho'ron,[g] **6** and the boundary extended to the sea. Mich'me'thath[h] was on the north, and the boundary went around east to Ta'a·nath-shi'loh, and it passed on the east to Ja·no'ah. **7** Then it went down from Ja·no'ah to At'a·roth and Na'a·rah and reached to Jer'i·cho[i] and extended to the Jordan. **8** From Tap'pu·ah[j] the boundary continued westward to the Wadi of Ka'nah, and it ended at the sea.[k] This is the inheritance of the tribe of E'phra·im by their families; **9** the descendants of E'phra·im also had enclave cities in the midst of the inheritance of Ma·nas'seh,[l] all the cities and their settlements.

10 But they did not drive away the Ca'naan·ites who were dwelling in Ge'zer,[m] and the Ca'naan·ites continue to dwell among E'phra·im to this day[n] and have been subjected to forced labor.[o]

17 Then the lot[p] fell for the tribe of Ma·nas'seh,[q] because he was Joseph's firstborn.[r] Since Ma'chir,[s] the firstborn of Ma·nas'seh and the father of Gil'e·ad, was a man of war, he received Gil'e·ad and Ba'shan.[t] **2** And the lot fell for the rest

of the descendants of Ma·nas'seh according to their families, for the sons of Abi·e'zer,[a] the sons of He'lek, the sons of As'ri·el, the sons of She'chem, the sons of He'pher, and the sons of She·mi'da. These were the descendants of Ma·nas'seh the son of Joseph, the males according to their families.[b] **3** But Ze·lo'phe·had[c] the son of He'pher, the son of Gil'e·ad, the son of Ma'chir, the son of Ma·nas'seh, did not have sons, only daughters, and these were the names of his daughters: Mah'lah, Noah, Hog'lah, Mil'cah, and Tir'zah. **4** So they presented themselves before El·e·a'zar[d] the priest, Joshua the son of Nun, and the chieftains, saying: "It was Jehovah who commanded Moses to give us an inheritance among our brothers."[e] So at the order of Jehovah, he gave them an inheritance among the brothers of their father.[f]

5 There were also ten allotments that fell to Ma·nas'seh apart from the land of Gil'e·ad and Ba'shan, which were on the other side* of the Jordan,[g] **6** for the daughters of Ma·nas'seh received an inheritance along with his sons, and the land of Gil'e·ad became the property of the rest of the descendants of Ma·nas'seh.

7 And the boundary of Ma·nas'seh was from Ash'er to Mich'me'thath,[h] which faces She'chem,[i] and the boundary continued toward the south* to the land of the inhabitants of En-Tap'pu·ah. **8** The land of Tap'pu·ah[j] became Ma·nas'seh's, but Tap'pu·ah on Ma·nas'seh's boundary belonged to the descendants of E'phra·im. **9** And the boundary went down to the Wadi of Ka'nah, southward to the wadi. There were cit-

CHAP. 16

a Jos 18:11, 13

b Jos 18:11, 13
1Ch 7:24

c 1Ch 7:20, 28

d Ge 48:5

e De 33:13-15
Jos 17:17, 18

f Jos 18:11, 13

g 2Ch 8:1, 5

h Jos 17:7

i Jos 6:20, 26

j Jos 17:8

k Nu 34:2, 6

l Jos 17:9

m Jg 1:29

n Nu 33:52, 55

o Jos 17:13

CHAP. 17

p Nu 26:55
Nu 33:54
Pr 16:33

q Ge 41:51
Nu 46:20
Ge 48:17, 18

r De 21:17

s Ge 50:23
Nu 26:29
1Ch 7:14

t De 3:13
Jos 13:31

Second Col.

a Jg 6:11

b Nu 26:29-32

c Nu 26:33

d Nu 27:1, 2
Nu 34:17
Jos 14:1

e Nu 27:7, 11

f Nu 36:6, 12

g Jos 13:29

h Jos 16:5, 6

i Jos 20:7
Jos 24:1
1Ch 6:66, 67

j Jos 16:8

17:5 * That is, the east side.   17:7 * Lit., "to the right."

ies of E'phra·im among the cities of Ma·nas'seh,[a] and the boundary of Ma·nas'seh was on the north of the wadi, and it ended at the sea.[b] **10** To the south it belonged to E'phra·im, and to the north it belonged to Ma·nas'seh, and the sea was his boundary,[c] and on the north they* reached to Ash'er, and on the east, to Is'sa·char.

11 In the territories of Is'sa·char and Ash'er, Ma·nas'seh was given* Beth-she'an and its dependent* towns, Ib'le·am[d] and its dependent towns, the inhabitants of Dor[e] and its dependent towns, the inhabitants of En-dor[f] and its dependent towns, the inhabitants of Ta'a·nach[g] and its dependent towns, and the inhabitants of Me·gid'do and its dependent towns, three of the heights.

12 But the descendants of Ma·nas'seh were not able to take possession of these cities; the Ca'naan·ites persisted in dwelling in this land.[h] **13** When the Israelites grew strong, they subjected the Ca'naan·ites to forced labor,[i] but they did not drive them out* entirely.[j]

14 The descendants of Joseph said to Joshua: "Why have you given us* as an inheritance only one lot[k] and one allotment? We are a numerous people, for Jehovah has blessed us until now."[l] **15** Joshua replied to them: "If you are such a numerous people, go up to the forest and clear out a place for yourself there in the land of the Per'iz·zites[m] and the Reph'a·im,[n] since the mountainous region of E'phra·im[o] is too cramped for you." **16** Then the descendants of Joseph said: "The mountain-

ous region is not enough for us, and all the Ca'naan·ites who are dwelling in the land of the valley* have war chariots[a] with iron scythes,[Δ] both those in Beth-she'an[b] and its dependent* towns and those in the Valley[s] of Jez're·el."[c] **17** So Joshua said this to the house of Joseph, to E'phra·im and Ma·nas'seh: "You are a numerous people, and you have great power. You will not receive only one lot,[d] **18** but the mountainous region will also be yours.[e] Although it is a forest, you will clear it, and it will be the extremity of your territory. For you will drive away the Ca'naan·ites, even though they are strong and have war chariots with iron scythes."[Δf]

18 Then all the assembly of the Israelites congregated at Shi'loh,[g] and they set up the tent of meeting there,[h] as the land was now subdued before them.[i] **2** But there were still seven tribes left of the Israelites whose inheritance had not been allotted. **3** So Joshua said to the Israelites: "How long will you put off going in to take possession of the land that Jehovah the God of your forefathers has given you?[j] **4** Give me three men from each tribe to send out; they should go out and walk throughout the land and map it out according to their inheritance. Then they should return to me. **5** They must apportion it among themselves into seven shares.[k] Judah will remain in his territory to the south,[l] and the house of Joseph will remain in their territory to the north.[m] **6** As for you, map out the land into seven shares, and bring them here to me, and I will cast lots[n] here for you before Jehovah our God.

CHAP. 17

a Jos 16:9
b Jos 16:8
c Nu 34:2, 6
d 2Ki 9:27
e Jos 12:7, 23
f 1Sa 28:7
g Jos 12:7, 21
h Jg 1:27
i Jos 16:10
  Jg 1:30
  2Ch 8:8
j Ex 23:33
  Nu 33:55
  De 20:16, 17
  Jos 23:12, 13
  Jg 1:28
k Nu 33:54
l Ge 48:19
  Nu 26:34, 37
m Ex 33:2
n Ge 15:18-20
o Jos 24:33

Second Col.

a De 20:1
  Jg 1:19
b Jos 17:11
c Jos 19:17, 18
  Jg 6:33
d Jos 17:14
e Nu 33:53
  Jos 20:7
  Jg 4:5
f De 20:1
  De 31:6
  Jos 13:6
  Pr 21:31

CHAP. 18

g Jos 19:51
  Jos 22:9
  Jg 21:19
h 1Sa 1:3
  1Sa 4:3
  Ps 78:60
  Jer 7:12
  Ac 7:44, 45
i Nu 14:8
  De 7:22
  De 33:29
j Nu 33:53, 55
k Nu 34:13
  Jos 19:51
l Jos 15:1
m Nu 16:1, 4
n Nu 26:55
  Nu 33:54
  Nu 14:2
  Pr 16:33
  Ac 13:19

17:10 *That is, the people of Manasseh or Manasseh's territory. 17:11, 16 *Or "surrounding." 17:13 *Or "not dispossess them." 17:14 *Lit., "me."

17:16 #Or "low plain." 17:16, 18 ΔLit., "chariots of iron." 17:16 SOr "Low Plain."

7 But the Levites have no share among you,[a] because the priesthood of Jehovah is their inheritance;[b] and Gad, Reu'ben, and the half tribe of Ma·nas'seh[c] have already taken their inheritance on the east side of the Jordan, which Moses the servant of Jehovah gave them."

8 The men prepared to go, and Joshua commanded those who were to map out the land: "Go and walk through the land and map it out and return to me, and I will cast lots for you here before Jehovah in Shi'loh."[d] **9** With that the men went and traveled through the land and mapped it out by cities into seven shares, recording it in a book. After that they returned to Joshua at the camp in Shi'loh. **10** Joshua then cast lots for them in Shi'loh before Jehovah.[e] There Joshua apportioned the land to the Israelites by their shares.[f]

11 The lot came up for the tribe of Benjamin by their families, and the territory of their lot was between the people of Judah[g] and the people of Joseph.[h] **12** On the north side, their boundary started at the Jordan, and the boundary went up to the slope of Jer'i·cho[i] on the north and went up on the mountain westward, and it extended to the wilderness of Beth-a'ven.[j] **13** And the boundary continued from there to Luz, at the southern slope of Luz, that is, Beth'el;[k] the boundary went down to At'a·roth-ad'dar[l] on the mountain that is south of Lower Beth-ho'ron.[m] **14** And the boundary was marked at the western side and went around toward the south from the mountain that faces Beth-ho'ron to the south; it ended at Kir'i·ath-ba'al, that is, Kir'i·ath-je'a·rim,[n] a city of Judah. This is the western side.

15 The south side was from the extremity of Kir'i·ath-je'a·rim, and the boundary extended westward; it went out to the spring of the waters of Neph·to'ah.[a] **16** The boundary went down to the extremity of the mountain that faces the Valley of the Son of Hin'nom,[b] which is in the Valley* of Reph'a·im[c] to the north, and it went down to the Valley of Hin'nom, to the slope of the Jeb'u·site[d] on the south, and down to En-ro'gel.[e] **17** And it was marked northward and extended to En-she'mesh and then out to Gel·i'loth, which is in front of the ascent of A·dum'mim,[f] and it went down to the stone[g] of Bo'han[h] the son of Reu'ben. **18** And it continued to the northern slope in front of the Ar'a·bah and went down to the Ar'a·bah. **19** And the boundary continued to the northern slope of Beth-hog'lah,[i] and the boundary ended at the northern bay of the Salt Sea*[j] at the southern end of the Jordan. This was the southern boundary. **20** And the Jordan served as its boundary on the eastern side. This was the inheritance of the descendants of Benjamin by their families, according to its boundaries on all sides.

21 And the cities of the tribe of Benjamin by their families were: Jer'i·cho, Beth-hog'lah, E'mek-ke'ziz, **22** Beth-ar'a·bah,[k] Zem·a·ra'im, Beth'el,[l] **23** Av'vim, Pa'rah, Oph'rah, **24** Che'phar-am'mo·ni, Oph'ni, and Ge'ba[m]—12 cities and their settlements.

25 Gib'e·on,[n] Ra'mah, Be·er'oth, **26** Miz'peh, Che·phi'rah, Mo'zah, **27** Re'kem, Ir'pe·el, Tar'a·lah, **28** Ze'lah,[o] Ha-e'leph, Je·bu'si, that is, Jerusalem,[p] Gib'e·ah,[q] and Kir'i·ath—14 cities and their settlements.

18:16 *Or "Low Plain." 18:19 *That is, the Dead Sea.

CHAP. 18

a Nu 18:20
  Jos 13:33

b De 10:9
  De 18:1

c De 3:12, 13

d Jos 19:51
  Jg 21:19

e Pr 16:33

f Nu 33:54
  Ac 13:19

g Jos 15:1

h Jos 16:1

i Jos 2:1
  Jos 16:1

j Jos 7:2

k Ge 28:18, 19

l Jos 16:5

m Jos 10:11
  Jos 21:20, 22

n Jos 15:9

Second Col.

a Jos 15:9, 12

b Jos 15:8, 12
  Jer 7:31
  Jer 19:2
  Mt 5:22

c De 2:11

d Jos 15:63

e Jos 15:7, 12
  1Ki 1:9

f Jos 15:7, 12

g De 19:14

h Jos 15:6, 12

i Jos 15:6, 12

j Nu 34:12

k Jos 15:6, 12

l Ge 12:8
  1Ki 12:28, 29

m Jos 21:8, 17

n Jos 9:16, 17
  1Ki 3:4

o 2Sa 21:14

p Jos 15:8, 12
  1Ch 11:4
  2Ch 3:1

q 1Sa 10:26

This was the inheritance of the descendants of Benjamin by their families.

19 Then the second lot[a] came out for Sim'e·on, for the tribe of Sim'e·on[b] by their families. And their inheritance was within the inheritance of Judah.[c] **2** Their inheritance was Be'er-she'ba[d] with She'ba, Mo·la'dah,[e] **3** Ha'zar-shu'al,[f] Ba'lah, E'zem,[g] **4** El·to'lad,[h] Be'thul, Hor'mah, **5** Zik'lag,[i] Beth-mar'ca·both, Ha'-zar-su'sah, **6** Beth-le·ba'oth,[j] and Sha·ru'hen—13 cities and their settlements; **7** A'in, Rim'-mon, E'ther, and A'shan[k]—four cities and their settlements; **8** and all the settlements that were around these cities as far as Ba'al·ath-be'er, Ra'mah of the south. This was the inheritance of the tribe of Sim'e·on by their families. **9** The inheritance of the descendants of Sim'e·on was taken out of the allotment of Judah, because the share of Judah was too large for them. So the descendants of Sim'e·on received a possession within their inheritance.[l]

10 Next the third lot[m] came up for the descendants of Zeb'-u·lun[n] by their families, and the boundary of their inheritance went as far as Sa'rid. **11** Their boundary went up westward to Mar'e·al and reached to Dab'be-sheth and then to the valley* in front of Jok'ne·am. **12** And it went from Sa'rid eastward toward the sunrise, to the border of Chis'loth-ta'bor and out to Dab'e·rath[o] and then up to Ja·phi'a. **13** And from there it continued eastward toward the sunrise to Gath-he'pher,[p] to Eth-ka'zin, and out to Rim'-mon, and it extended to Ne'-ah. **14** And the boundary went around it on the north to Han'na-

19:11 *Or "wadi."

CHAP. 19
a Jos 18:6
b Ge 46:10
c Ge 49:5, 7
d Ge 21:31
  Ge 26:32, 33
  Jos 15:21, 28
e Jos 15:21, 26
  1Ch 4:28-31
f Jos 15:21, 28
g Jos 15:20, 29
h Jos 15:21, 30
i Jos 15:21, 31
  1Sa 27:6
j Jos 15:21, 32
k Jos 15:20, 42
  1Ch 4:24, 32
  1Ch 6:59, 64
l Jg 1:3
m Jos 18:6
n Ge 49:13
o Jos 21:27, 28
p 2Ki 14:25

Second Col.
a Jos 12:7, 20
b Jg 12:8
c Nu 26:27
d Nu 33:54
e Ge 49:14
f Jos 17:16
  Jg 6:33
  1Ki 21:1
g 1Sa 28:4
  1Ki 1:3
  2Ki 4:8
h Jos 21:8, 29
i Jg 4:6
j Nu 26:25
k Nu 26:55
  Jos 18:6
l Ge 49:20
m Jos 21:8, 31
n 1Ki 18:19
o Ge 10:15
  Jg 1:31
p 2Sa 5:11
  1Ki 5:1
q Jg 1:31
r Jos 21:8, 31

thon, and it ended at the Valley of Iph'tah-el, **15** and Kat'tath, Na·hal'al, Shim'ron,[a] I'da-lah, and Beth'le·hem[b]—12 cities and their settlements. **16** This was the inheritance of the descendants of Zeb'u·lun by their families.[c] These were the cities and their settlements.

17 The fourth lot[d] came out for Is'sa·char,[e] for the descendants of Is'sa·char by their families. **18** And their boundary was to Jez're·el,[f] Che·sul'loth, Shu'nem,[g] **19** Haph'a·ra'im, Shi'on, An·a·ha'rath, **20** Rab'bith, Kish'i·on, E'bez, **21** Re'meth, En-gan'nim,[h] En-had'dah, and Beth-paz'zez. **22** And the boundary reached to Ta'bor[i] and Sha·ha·zu'mah and Beth-she'mesh, and the end of their border was at the Jordan —16 cities and their settlements. **23** This was the inheritance of the tribe of Is'sa·char by their families,[j] the cities and their settlements.

24 Then the fifth lot[k] came out for the tribe of Ash'er[l] by their families. **25** And their boundary was Hel'kath,[m] Ha'-li, Be'ten, Ach'shaph, **26** Al-lam'me·lech, A'mad, and Mi'shal. It reached westward to Car'mel[n] and to Shi'hor-lib'nath, **27** and it went back toward the east to Beth-da'gon and reached to Zeb'-u·lun and the Valley of Iph'tah-el to the north, to Beth-e'mek and Ne·i'el, and it extended to Ca'bul on the left, **28** and to E'bron, Re'hob, Ham'mon, and Ka'nah as far as Great Si'don.[o] **29** And the boundary went back to Ra'-mah and as far as the fortified city of Tyre.[p] Then the boundary went back to Ho'sah, and it ended at the sea in the region of Ach'zib, **30** Um'mah, A'phek,[q] and Re'hob[r]—22 cities and their settlements. **31** This was the inheritance of the tribe of Ash'er by their families.[a] These were the cities and their settlements.

32 The sixth lot[b] came out for the descendants of Naph'ta-li, for the descendants of Naph'ta-li by their families. **33** Their boundary was from He'leph, from the big tree in Za·a·nan'-nim,[c] and Ad'a·mi·ne'keb and Jab'ne·el as far as Lak'kum; and it ended at the Jordan. **34** The boundary went back westward to Az'noth-ta'bor and extended from there to Huk'-kok and reached to Zeb'u·lun on the south and to Ash'er on the west and to Judah at the Jordan toward the east. **35** And the fortified cities were Zid'dim, Zer, Ham'math,[d] Rak'kath, Chin'-ne·reth, **36** Ad'a·mah, Ra'mah, Ha'zor,[e] **37** Ke'desh,[f] Ed're·i, En-ha'zor, **38** Yi'ron, Mig'dal-el, Ho'rem, Beth-a'nath, and Beth-she'mesh[g]—19 cities and their settlements. **39** This was the inheritance of the tribe of Naph'ta·li by their families,[h] the cities and their settlements.

40 The seventh lot[i] came out for the tribe of Dan[j] by their families. **41** And the border of their inheritance was Zo'rah,[k] Esh'ta·ol, Ir-she'mesh, **42** Sha-al·ab'bin,[l] Ai'ja·lon,[m] Ith'lah, **43** E'lon, Tim'nah,[n] Ek'ron,[o] **44** El'te·keh, Gib'be·thon,[p] Ba'-al·ath, **45** Je'hud, Ben'e-be'rak, Gath-rim'mon,[q] **46** Me-jar'kon, and Rak'kon, with the border facing Jop'pa.[r] **47** But the territory of Dan was too cramped for them.[s] So they went up and fought against Le'shem[t] and captured it and struck it with the sword. Then they took possession of it and settled in it, and they changed the name of Le'-shem to Dan, after the name of Dan their forefather.[u] **48** This was the inheritance of the tribe of Dan by their families. These were the cities and their settlements.

49 Thus they finished dividing the land for inheritance by its territories. Then the Israelites gave Joshua the son of Nun an inheritance in their midst. **50** At the order of Jehovah they gave him the city he asked for, Tim'nath-se'rah,[a] in the mountainous region of E'phra·im, and he built up the city and settled in it.

51 These were the inheritances that El·e·a'zar the priest, Joshua the son of Nun, and the heads of the paternal houses of the tribes of Israel distributed[b] by lot in Shi'loh[c] before Jehovah, at the entrance of the tent of meeting.[d] So they finished apportioning the land.

20 Then Jehovah said to Joshua: **2** "Tell the Israelites, 'Select for yourselves the cities of refuge[e] about which I spoke to you through Moses, **3** so that the manslayer who unintentionally or accidentally* kills someone[g] may flee there. And they will serve as a refuge for you from the avenger of blood.[f] **4** He must flee to one of these cities[g] and stand at the entrance of the city gate[h] and present his case in the hearing of the elders of that city. Then they must receive him into the city and give him a place and he will live with them. **5** If the avenger of blood chases after him, they should not surrender the manslayer into his hand, for he killed his fellow man accidentally* and he did not previously hate him.[i] **6** He must dwell in that city until he stands trial before the assembly[j] and remain there until the death of the high priest[k] who is in office at that time. Then the manslayer may return to the city from which he fled, and he may enter his city and his house.'"[l]

CHAP. 19
a Nu 26:47
b Nu 26:55
  Jos 18:6
c Jg 4:11
d Jos 21:32
e Jos 11:10
  Jg 4:2
  1Sa 12:9
f Jos 20:7
g Jg 1:33
h Nu 26:50
i Jos 18:6
j Ge 49:17
k Jos 15:20, 33
  Jg 13:2
l Jg 1:35
m Jos 10:12
  Jos 21:8, 24
n Jg 14:1
o Jos 15:20, 45
p Jos 21:8, 23
q Jos 21:8, 24
r Jon 1:3
  Ac 9:36
s Nu 26:54
  Nu 33:54
t Jg 18:7
u Jg 18:29

Second Col.
a Jos 24:29, 30
b Nu 34:17
  Jos 14:1
c Jg 21:19
  Jer 7:12
d Jos 18:1, 8

CHAP. 20
e Ex 21:12, 13
  Nu 35:14, 15
  De 4:41
f Ge 9:6
  Ex 21:23
  Nu 35:26, 27
g De 19:3
h Pr 31:23
i Nu 35:22-24
  De 19:4-6
j Nu 35:12, 24
k Nu 35:25
l Nu 35:28

20:3, 5 *Or "unknowingly." **20:3** [g] Or "strikes a soul."

7 So they gave a sacred status to* Ke'desh[a] in Gal'i·lee in the mountainous region of Naph'ta·li, She'chem[b] in the mountainous region of E'phra·im, and Kir'i·ath·ar'ba,[c] that is, Heb'ron, in the mountainous region of Judah. **8** In the region of the Jordan, east of Jer'i·cho, they selected Be'zer[d] in the wilderness on the tableland* out of the tribe of Reu'ben, Ra'moth[e] in Gil'e·ad out of the tribe of Gad, and Go'lan[f] in Ba'shan out of the tribe of Ma·nas'seh.[g]

9 These became the cities appointed for all the Israelites and for the foreign residents residing among them, so that anyone who unintentionally killed someone* could flee there[h] and not die by the hand of the avenger of blood prior to standing trial before the assembly.[i]

21 The heads of the paternal houses of the Levites now approached El·e·a'zar[j] the priest, Joshua the son of Nun, and the heads of the paternal houses of the tribes of Israel, **2** and they spoke to them in Shi'loh[k] in the land of Ca'naan, saying: "Jehovah through Moses commanded that we be given cities in which to dwell, along with their pastures for our livestock."[l] **3** So at the order of Jehovah, the Israelites gave the Levites these cities[m] and their pastures out of their own inheritance.[n]

4 The lot came out for the families of the Ko'hath·ites,[o] and the Levites who were descendants of Aaron the priest were given by lot* 13 cities out of the tribe of Judah,[p] the tribe of Sim'e·on,[q] and the tribe of Benjamin.[r]

5 And for the rest of the Ko'hath·ites, there were allotted*

20:7 *Or "they set apart." 20:8 *Or "plateau." 20:9 *Or "a soul." 21:4 *Or "were allotted." 21:5 *Or "given by lot."

ten cities out of the families of the tribe of E'phra·im,[a] the tribe of Dan, and the half tribe of Ma·nas'seh.[b]

6 And for the Ger'shon·ites,[c] there were allotted 13 cities out of the families of the tribe of Is'sa·char, the tribe of Ash'er, the tribe of Naph'ta·li, and the half tribe of Ma·nas'seh in Ba'shan.[d]

7 For the Me·rar'ites[e] by their families, there were 12 cities out of the tribe of Reu'ben, the tribe of Gad, and the tribe of Zeb'u·lun.[f]

8 Thus the Israelites gave the Levites these cities and their pastures by lot, just as Jehovah had commanded through Moses.[g]

9 So from the tribe of Judah and the tribe of Sim'e·on, they gave these cities here mentioned by name,[h] **10** and they were given to the sons of Aaron of the Ko'hath·ite families of the Levites, because they received the first lot. **11** They gave them Kir'i·ath·ar'ba[i] (Ar'ba was the father of A'nak), that is, Heb'ron,[j] in the mountainous region of Judah, and its surrounding pastures. **12** But the field of the city and its settlements they gave to Ca'leb the son of Je·phun'neh as his possession.[k]

13 And to the sons of Aaron the priest, they gave the city of refuge for the manslayer,[l] namely, Heb'ron[m] with its pastures, also Lib'nah[n] with its pastures, **14** Jat'tir[o] with its pastures, Esh·te·mo'a[p] with its pastures, **15** Ho'lon[q] with its pastures, De'bir[r] with its pastures, **16** A'in[s] with its pastures, Jut'tah[t] with its pastures, and Beth-she'mesh with its pastures—nine cities out of these two tribes.

17 And from the tribe of Benjamin: Gib'e·on[u] with its pastures, Ge'ba with its pastures,[v]

CHAP. 20
a Jos 21:32
b Ge 33:18
  Jos 21:20, 21
c Jos 14:15
  Jos 21:13
d Jos 21:8, 36
  1Ch 6:77, 78
  Jos 21:8, 38
  1Ch 6:77, 80
f Jos 21:27
  1Ch 6:71
g De 4:41-43
h Nu 35:11, 15
i Nu 35:12, 24
  De 21:5

CHAP. 21
j Nu 34:17
k Jos 18:1
l Le 25:33, 34
  Nu 35:2-4
  Jos 14:4
m Nu 35:8
n Ge 49:5, 7
o Ge 46:11
  Nu 3:27-31
p 1Ch 6:54, 55
q Jos 19:1
r 1Ch 6:60, 64

Second Col.
a 1Ch 6:66
b 1Ch 6:61, 70
c Ex 6:17
  Nu 3:21, 22
d Nu 32:33
  1Ch 6:62
e Ex 6:19
f 1Ch 6:63
g Nu 35:2, 5
h 1Ch 6:64, 65
i Ge 23:2
  Ge 35:27
  Jos 15:13, 14
  Jos 20:7
  Jg 1:10
j 2Sa 2:1
  2Sa 15:10
  1Ch 6:54-56
k Jg 1:20
l Nu 35:6, 15
m Jos 15:20, 54
n Jos 15:20, 42
o Jos 15:20, 48
p Jos 15:20, 50
q Jos 15:20, 51
r Jos 15:20, 49
  1Ch 6:57, 58
s Jos 19:1, 7
t Jos 15:20, 55
u Jos 9:3
  Jos 18:21, 25
v 1Ch 6:57, 60

18 An'a·thoth[a] with its pastures, and Al'mon with its pastures —four cities.

19 All the cities given to the descendants of Aaron, the priests, were 13 cities with their pastures.[b]

20 And the rest of the Ko'hath·ite families among the Levites were given by lot cities from the tribe of E'phra·im. **21** They gave them the city of refuge for the manslayer,[c] namely, She'chem[d] with its pastures in the mountainous region of E'phra·im, Ge'zer[e] with its pastures, **22** Kib'za·im with its pastures, and Beth-ho'ron[f] with its pastures—four cities.

23 And from the tribe of Dan: El'te·ke with its pastures, Gib'bethon with its pastures, **24** Ai'jalon[g] with its pastures, Gath-rim'mon with its pastures—four cities.

25 And from the half tribe of Ma·nas'seh: Ta'a·nach[h] with its pastures and Gath-rim'mon with its pastures—two cities.

26 All the cities together with their pastures that the rest of the families of the Ko'hath·ites received were ten.

27 And the Ger'shon·ites[i] of the families of the Levites received from the half tribe of Ma·nas'seh the city of refuge for the manslayer, namely, Go'lan,[j] in Ba'shan, with its pastures and Be·esh'te·rah with its pastures —two cities.

28 And from the tribe of Is'sa·char:[k] Kish'i·on with its pastures, Dab'e·rath[l] with its pastures, **29** Jar'muth with its pastures, and En-gan'nim with its pastures—four cities.

30 And from the tribe of Ash'er:[m] Mi'shal with its pastures, Ab'don with its pastures, **31** Hel'kath[n] with its pastures, and Re'hob[o] with its pastures —four cities.

32 And from the tribe of Naph'ta·li: the city of refuge[a] for the manslayer, namely, Ke'desh[b] in Gal'i·lee with its pastures, Ham'moth-dor with its pastures, and Kar'tan with its pastures—three cities.

33 All the cities of the Ger'shon·ites by their families were 13 cities with their pastures.

34 And the families of the Me·rar'ites,[c] the rest of the Levites, received from the tribe of Zeb'u·lun:[d] Jok'ne·am[e] with its pastures, Kar'tah with its pastures, **35** Dim'nah with its pastures, and Na·hal'al[f] with its pastures —four cities.

36 And from the tribe of Reu'ben: Be'zer[g] with its pastures, Ja'haz with its pastures,[h] **37** Ked'e·moth with its pastures, and Meph'a·ath with its pastures—four cities.

38 And from the tribe of Gad:[i] the city of refuge for the manslayer, namely, Ra'moth in Gil'e·ad[j] with its pastures, Ma·ha·na'im[k] with its pastures, **39** Hesh'bon[l] with its pastures, and Ja'zer[m] with its pastures—a total of four cities.

40 All the cities that were allotted to the Me·rar'ites by their families, the rest of the families of the Levites, were 12 cities.

41 All the cities of the Levites within the possession of the Israelites were 48 cities together with their pastures.[n] **42** Each of these cities had its pastures all around it—this was the case for all these cities.

43 So Jehovah gave Israel all the land that he had sworn to give to their forefathers,[o] and they took possession of it and settled in it.[p] **44** Furthermore, Jehovah gave them rest on every side, just as he had sworn to their forefathers,[q] and not one of all their enemies could stand against them.[r] Jehovah gave all

CHAP. 21

a Jer 1:1

b Le 25:33, 34
  Nu 35:4

c Nu 35:11, 15

d Jos 20:7
  1Ki 12:1

e Jos 16:10

f Jos 16:1, 3
  Jos 18:11, 13

g Jos 10:12
  Jg 1:35
  2Ch 28:18

h Jos 17:11

i Jos 21:6

j 1Ch 6:71

k 1Ch 6:72, 73

l Jos 19:12, 16

m 1Ch 6:74, 75

n Jos 19:25, 31

o Jos 19:28, 31
  Jg 1:31

Second Col.

a Nu 35:14, 15

b Jos 20:7

c Jos 21:7

d 1Ch 6:77

e Jos 19:10, 11

f Jg 1:30

g De 4:41-43
  Jos 20:8

h 1Ch 6:78, 79

i 1Ch 6:80, 81

j Jos 20:8, 9
  1Ki 22:3

k Ge 32:2
  2Sa 2:8

l Nu 21:26
  Nu 32:37

m Nu 32:1

n Nu 35:5, 7

o Ge 13:14, 15
  Ge 15:18
  Ge 26:3
  Ge 28:4

p Ex 23:30

q Ex 33:14
  De 12:10
  Jos 1:13
  Jos 11:23
  Jos 22:4

r De 28:7

their enemies into their hand.[a] **45** Not a promise* failed out of all the good promises that Jehovah had made to the house of Israel; all of them came true.[b]

22 Then Joshua summoned the Reu′ben·ites, the Gad′ites, and the half tribe of Ma·nas′seh **2** and said to them: "You have done all that Moses the servant of Jehovah commanded you,[c] and you have obeyed my voice in all that I commanded you.[d] **3** You have not forsaken your brothers all this time, down to this day;[e] and you have kept the obligation of the commandment of Jehovah your God.[f] **4** Now Jehovah your God has given your brothers rest, just as he promised them.[g] So now you may return to your tents in the land that Moses the servant of Jehovah gave you to possess on the other side* of the Jordan.[h] **5** Only be very careful to carry out the commandment and the Law that Moses the servant of Jehovah gave you,[i] by loving Jehovah your God,[j] by walking in all his ways,[k] by keeping his commandments,[l] by sticking to him,[m] and by serving him[n] with all your heart and with all your soul."*[o]

6 Then Joshua blessed them and sent them away, and they went to their tents. **7** And to the half tribe of Ma·nas′seh, Moses had given an inheritance in Ba′shan,[p] and to the other half of the tribe, Joshua gave land on the west side of the Jordan,[q] along with their brothers. Moreover, when Joshua sent them away to their tents, he blessed them **8** and said to them: "Return to your tents with many riches, with very much livestock, with silver and gold, copper and iron, and garments in very great

---

CHAP. 21
a De 7:24
　De 31:3

b Jos 23:14
　1Ki 8:56
　Heb 6:18

CHAP. 22
c Nu 32:20-22
　De 3:18

d Jos 1:16

e Jos 11:18

f Nu 32:25-27

g Jos 21:44

h Nu 32:33

i De 6:6
　De 12:32
　2Ki 21:8

j De 6:5
　De 11:1
　Mt 22:37

k De 10:12

l De 13:4
　1Jo 5:3

m De 4:4
　De 10:20
　Jos 23:8

n De 6:13
　Jos 24:15
　Lu 4:8

o De 4:29
　De 11:13
　Mr 12:30, 33

p Jos 13:29, 30

q Jos 17:5

Second Col.
a De 28:8

b Nu 31:27

c Nu 32:1

d Nu 32:33

e De 13:12-15

f Jos 18:1
　Jos 19:51

g Ex 6:25
　Nu 25:11
　Jg 20:28

h Nu 1:16
　De 1:13

i Jos 22:11, 12

---

quantity.[a] Take your share of the spoil[b] of your enemies, along with your brothers."

9 After that the Reu′ben·ites, the Gad′ites, and the half tribe of Ma·nas′seh departed from the other Israelites, from Shi′loh in the land of Ca′naan, and they returned to the land of Gil′e·ad,[c] the land of their possession where they had settled at the order of Jehovah through Moses.[d] **10** When they came to the regions of the Jordan in the land of Ca′naan, the Reu′ben·ites, the Gad′ites, and the half tribe of Ma·nas′seh built an altar there by the Jordan, a large, impressive altar. **11** Later the other Israelites heard about it[e] and said: "Look! The Reu′ben·ites, the Gad′ites, and the half tribe of Ma·nas′seh have built an altar on the frontier of the land of Ca′naan in the regions of the Jordan on the side belonging to the Israelites." **12** When the Israelites heard about it, the whole assembly of the Israelites congregated at Shi′loh[f] to go to war against them.

13 Then the Israelites sent Phin′e·has[g] the son of El·e·a′zar the priest to the Reu′ben·ites, the Gad′ites, and the half tribe of Ma·nas′seh in the land of Gil′e·ad, **14** and ten chieftains were with him, one chieftain of each paternal house of all the tribes of Israel, each a head of his paternal house among the thousands* of Israel.[h] **15** When they came to the Reu′ben·ites, the Gad′ites, and the half tribe of Ma·nas′seh in the land of Gil′e·ad, they said to them:

16 "This is what all the assembly of Jehovah says: 'What is this act of unfaithfulness[i] that you have committed against the God of Israel? You have turned back today from following

---

21:45 *Or "word." **22:4** *That is, the east side. **22:5** *See Glossary. **22:14** *Or "clans."

Jehovah by building yourselves an altar and rebelling against Jehovah.ᵃ 17 Was the error of Pe'or not enough for us? We have not cleansed ourselves from it down to this day, even though a plague came upon the assembly of Jehovah.ᵇ 18 And you would turn back today from following Jehovah! If you rebel today against Jehovah, then tomorrow he will be indignant against the entire assembly of Israel.ᶜ 19 Now if it is because the land of your possession is unclean, cross over to the land of Jehovah's possessionᵈ where the tabernacle of Jehovah residesᵉ and settle among us, but do not rebel against Jehovah, and do not make us rebels by building yourselves an altar in addition to the altar of Jehovah our God.ᶠ 20 When A'chanᵍ the son of Ze'rah committed an act of unfaithfulness regarding what was devoted to destruction, did not indignation come against all the assembly of Israel?ʰ And he was not the only man to die for his error.'"

21 At this the Reu'ben·ites, the Gad'ites, and the half tribe of Ma·nas'seh said in answer to the heads of the thousands* of Israel:ʲ 22 "The God of gods, Jehovah!* The God of gods, Jehovah!ᵏ He knows, and Israel will also know. If we were rebellious and unfaithful to Jehovah, do not spare us this day. 23 If we built ourselves an altar to turn back from following Jehovah and to offer burnt offerings, grain offerings, and communion sacrifices on it, Jehovah will exact the penalty.ˡ 24 No, it was because of another concern that we did this, for we said, 'In the future, your sons will say to our sons: "What do you have to do with Jehovah the God of Isra-

el? 25 Jehovah has put the Jordan as a boundary between us and you, the Reu'ben·ites and the Gad'ites. You have no share in Jehovah." And your sons will hinder our sons from worshipping* Jehovah.'

26 "So we said, 'Let us by all means take action by building an altar, not for burnt offerings or sacrifices, 27 but to be a witness between you and usᵃ and our descendants* after us that we will carry out our service to Jehovah before him with our burnt offerings and our sacrifices and our communion sacrifices,ᵇ so that your sons may not say to our sons in the future: "You have no share in Jehovah."' 28 So we said, 'If they should say that to us and to our descendants* in the future, we will then say: "See the replica of Jehovah's altar that our forefathers made, not for burnt offerings or sacrifices, but to be a witness between you and us."' 29 It is unthinkable for us to rebel against Jehovah and to turn back today from following Jehovahᶜ by building an altar for burnt offerings, grain offerings, and sacrifices, other than the altar of Jehovah our God that is before his tabernacle!"ᵈ

30 When Phin'e·has the priest, the chieftains of the assembly, and the heads of the thousands* of Israel who were with him heard the words that the descendants of Reu'ben, Gad, and Ma·nas'seh spoke, they were satisfied.ᵉ 31 So Phin'e·has the son of El·e·a'zar the priest said to the descendants of Reu'ben, Gad, and Ma·nas'seh: "Today we know that Jehovah is among us, because you have not committed this act of unfaithfulness against Jehovah. Now you

---

CHAP. 22
a De 12:13, 14

b Nu 25:3, 9
  De 4:3

c Jos 7:1
  1Ch 21:14

d Nu 34:2
  Jos 1:11

e Jos 18:1

f De 12:13, 14

g Jos 7:1

h Jos 7:11, 15

i Jos 7:5
  Jos 7:24, 25

j Jos 22:13, 14

k De 10:17

l De 12:11, 13

Second Col.
a Ge 31:48
  Jos 24:27

b De 12:5, 6

c De 6:14

d De 12:14

e Jos 22:13, 14

22:21, 30 *Or "clans." 22:22 *Or "The Divine One, God, Jehovah."

22:25 *Lit., "fearing." 22:27, 28 *Lit., "generations."

have saved the Israelites out of the hand of Jehovah."

32 Then Phin'e·has the son of El·e·a'zar the priest and the chieftains returned from the Reu'ben·ites and the Gad'ites in the land of Gil'e·ad to the land of Ca'naan, and they brought back word to the other Israelites. **33** And the Israelites were satisfied with the report. The Israelites then praised God, and they said nothing more about going to war against the Reu'ben·ites and the Gad'ites to destroy the land in which they were dwelling.

34 So the Reu'ben·ites and the Gad'ites named the altar,* because "it is a witness between us that Jehovah is the true God."

23 Many days after Jehovah had given Israel rest[a] from all its surrounding enemies, when Joshua was old and advanced in years,[b] **2** Joshua summoned all Israel,[c] its elders, its heads, its judges, and its officers,[d] and he said to them: "I have grown old; I am advanced in years. **3** And you have seen for yourselves all that Jehovah your God did to all these nations in your behalf because Jehovah your God was the one who was fighting for you.[e] **4** See, I assigned to you by lot*[f] the land of the nations that remain as an inheritance for your tribes,[g] as well as that of all the nations that I destroyed,[h] from the Jordan to the Great Sea# on the west.△ **5** And Jehovah your God was the one who kept thrusting them away from before you,[i] and he drove them out* for you, and you took possession of their land, just as Jehovah your God promised you.[j]

6 "Now you must be very courageous to observe and carry out all that is written in the book of the Law[a] of Moses so never deviating from it to the right or to the left,[b] **7** by never mingling with these nations[c] that remain with you. You must not even mention the names of their gods[d] nor swear by them, and you must never serve them nor bow down to them.[e] **8** But you must stick to Jehovah your God,[f] just as you have done down to this day. **9** Jehovah will drive away great and mighty nations from before you,[g] for not a man has been able to stand before you to this day.[h] **10** Just one man of you will chase a thousand,[i] because Jehovah your God is fighting for you,[j] just as he promised you.[k] **11** So be on guard constantly*[l] by loving Jehovah your God.[m]

12 "But if you should turn back at all and stick to what is left of these nations that remain[n] with you and you form marriage alliances*[o] with them and associate with them and they with you, **13** you should know for sure that Jehovah your God will not continue to drive out* these nations for you.[p] They will become a trap and a snare and a scourge on your flanks[q] and thorns in your eyes until you have perished from this good land that Jehovah your God has given you.

14 "Now look! I am about to die,* and you well know with all your heart and with all your soul# that not one word out of all the good promises that Jehovah your God has spoken to you has failed. They have all come true for you. Not one word of them has failed.[r] **15** But just as all

CHAP. 23
a Ex 33:14
  Le 26:6
  Jos 21:44
b Jos 13:1
c De 31:28
d De 16:18
e De 20:4
  Jos 10:11-14
  Jos 10:40, 42
f Jos 18:10
g Jos 13:2-6
h De 7:1
i Ex 23:30
  Ex 33:2
  De 11:23
j Nu 33:53

Second Col.
a Ex 24:7
  De 17:18
  De 31:26
b De 5:32
  De 12:32
  Jos 1:7, 8
c Ex 23:33
  De 7:2
d Ex 23:13
e Ex 20:5
f De 10:20
  Jos 22:5
g De 11:23
h Jos 1:3-5
i Le 26:8
  Jg 3:31
  2Sa 23:8
j Ex 23:27
  De 3:22
k De 28:7
l De 4:9
  Jos 22:5
m De 6:5
n Ex 23:29
  Jos 13:2-6
o Ex 34:16
  De 7:3
  Jg 3:6
  1Ki 11:4
  Ezr 9:2
p Jg 2:3, 21
q Nu 33:55
r Jos 21:45
  1Ki 8:56

22:34 *From the explanation given, the altar was likely named Witness. **23:4** *Or "I allotted to you." #That is, the Mediterranean. △Or "toward the sunset." **23:5** *Or "dispossessed them."

23:11 *Or "So watch your souls carefully." **23:12** *Or "you intermarry." **23:13** *Or "dispossess." **23:14** *Lit., "I am going today in the way of all the earth." #See Glossary.

the good promises that Jehovah your God has spoken to you have come upon you,[a] so Jehovah will bring upon you all the calamity that he promised* and will annihilate you from this good land that Jehovah your God has given you.[b] **16** If you violate the covenant of Jehovah your God that he commanded you to keep and if you go and serve other gods and bow down to them, then Jehovah's anger will blaze against you[c] and you will quickly perish from the good land that he has given you."[d]

24 Joshua then assembled all the tribes of Israel together at She'chem and summoned the elders of Israel, its heads, its judges, and its officers,[e] and they stood before the true God. **2** Joshua said to all the people: "This is what Jehovah the God of Israel says, 'It was on the other side of the River* that your forefathers[f] lived a long time ago[g] —Te'rah the father of Abraham and the father of Na'hor—and they used to serve other gods.[h] **3** "'In time I took your forefather Abraham[i] from the other side of the River* and had him walk through all the land of Ca'naan and made his offspring* many.[j] I gave him Isaac;[k] **4** then to Isaac I gave Jacob and E'sau.[l] Later to E'sau I gave Mount Se'ir as his possession;[m] and Jacob and his sons went down to Egypt.[n] **5** I later sent Moses and Aaron,[o] and I plagued Egypt with what I did among them,[p] and then I brought you out. **6** When I was bringing your fathers out of Egypt[q] and you came to the sea, the Egyptians were chasing after your fathers with war chariots and cavalrymen as far as the Red Sea.[r] **7** They began to cry out to Jeho-

vah,[a] so he placed a darkness between you and the Egyptians and brought the sea over them and covered them,[b] and your own eyes saw what I did in Egypt.[c] Then you dwelled in the wilderness many years.*[d]

8 "'And I brought you to the land of the Am'or·ites who were dwelling on the other side* of the Jordan, and they fought against you.[e] But I gave them into your hand so that you could take possession of their land, and I annihilated them from before you.[f] **9** Then Ba'lak son of Zip'por, the king of Mo'ab, rose up and fought against Israel. So he summoned Ba'laam the son of Be'or to curse you.[g] **10** But I would not listen to Ba'laam.[h] So I blessed you repeatedly,[i] and I rescued you from his hand.[j]

11 "'Then you crossed the Jordan[k] and came to Jer'i·cho.[l] And the leaders* of Jer'i·cho, the Am'or·ites, the Per'iz·zites, the Ca'naan·ites, the Hit'tites, the Gir'ga·shites, the Hi'vites, and the Jeb'u·sites fought against you, but I gave them into your hand.[m] **12** So I sent the feeling of dejection* ahead of you, and it drove them out from before you[n]—two kings of the Am'or·ites. It was not by your sword and not by your bow.[o] **13** Thus I gave you a land for which you had not toiled and cities that you had not built,[p] and you settled in them. You are eating from vineyards and olive groves that you did not plant.'[q]

14 "Therefore, fear Jehovah and serve him with integrity* and faithfulness,*[r] and remove the gods that your forefathers served on the other side of the

CHAP. 23
a Le 26:3-12
  De 28:1
b Le 26:14-17
  De 28:15, 63
c 2Ki 24:20
d Jos 23:12, 13

CHAP. 24
e Ex 18:25
  Jos 23:2
f Ge 11:26, 27
g Ge 11:28, 31
h Jos 24:15
i Ge 12:1
  Ne 9:7
  Ac 7:2
j Ge 15:1, 5
k Ge 21:3
l Ge 25:26
m Ge 36:8
  De 2:5
n Ge 46:2, 3
o Ex 3:10
p Ex 11:1
q Ex 12:37
r Ex 14:9

Second Col.
a Ex 14:10
b Ex 14:20, 27
  Ps 106:11
c Ex 3:20
  De 4:34
d Nu 14:34
e Nu 21:23
f Ne 9:22
g Nu 22:2, 5
  De 23:3, 4
h Nu 22:12
i Nu 23:11, 25
  Nu 24:10
j Nu 31:7, 49
k Jos 3:17
l Jos 5:10
m Jos 11:16
  Jos 21:44
  Heb 11:30
n Ex 23:28
  Jos 2:9, 10
o Ps 44:3
p Jos 11:14
q De 6:10, 11
  De 8:7, 8
r Ge 17:1
  De 10:12
  De 18:13
  1Sa 12:24

23:15 *Or "all the evil word." 24:2, 3 *That is, the Euphrates. 24:3 *Lit., "seed."

24:7 *Lit., "days." 24:8 *That is, the east side. 24:11 *Or possibly, "landowners." 24:12 *Or possibly, "panic; terror." 24:14 *Or "in a blameless way." #Or "in truth."

River* and in Egypt,[a] and serve Jehovah. **15** Now if it seems bad to you to serve Jehovah, choose for yourselves today whom you will serve,[b] whether the gods that your forefathers served on the other side of the River*[c] or the gods of the Am'or·ites in whose land you are dwelling.[d] But as for me and my household, we will serve Jehovah."

16 At this the people answered: "It is unthinkable for us to abandon Jehovah and to serve other gods. **17** It is Jehovah our God who brought us and our fathers up out of the land of Egypt,[e] out of the house of slavery,[f] and who performed these great signs before our eyes[g] and who kept guarding us the entire way in which we walked and among all the peoples through whom we passed.[h] **18** Jehovah drove out all the peoples, including the Am'or·ites, who lived in the land before us. Therefore, we too will serve Jehovah, because he is our God."

19 Then Joshua said to the people: "You are not able to serve Jehovah, for he is a holy God;[i] he is a God who requires exclusive devotion.[j] He will not pardon your transgressions* and your sins.[k] **20** If you abandon Jehovah and serve foreign gods, he will also turn against you and exterminate you after doing good for you."[l]

21 But the people said to Joshua: "No, but we will serve Jehovah!"[m] **22** So Joshua said to the people: "You are witnesses against yourselves that of your own accord, you have chosen for yourselves to serve Jehovah."[n] To this they said: "We are witnesses."

23 "Therefore, remove the foreign gods that are among you,

and incline your hearts to Jehovah the God of Israel." **24** The people said to Joshua: "We will serve Jehovah our God, and we will obey his voice!"

25 So Joshua made a covenant with the people on that day and established a regulation and a ruling for them in She'chem. **26** Then Joshua wrote these words in the book of God's Law[a] and took a great stone[b] and set it up under the large tree that is by the sanctuary of Jehovah.

27 Joshua went on to say to all the people: "Look! This stone will serve as a witness against us,[c] because it has heard everything Jehovah said to us, and it will serve as a witness against you, so that you may not deny your God." **28** With that Joshua sent the people away, each one to his inheritance.[d]

29 After these things, Joshua the son of Nun, the servant of Jehovah, died at the age of 110.[e] **30** So they buried him in the territory of his inheritance in Tim'nath-se'rah,[f] which is in the mountainous region of E'phra·im, north of Mount Ga'ash. **31** Israel continued to serve Jehovah all the days of Joshua and all the days of the elders who outlived Joshua and who had known all of Jehovah's deeds in behalf of Israel.[g]

32 The bones of Joseph,[h] which the Israelites had brought up out of Egypt, were buried in She'chem in the portion of the field that Jacob had acquired from the sons of Ha'mor,[i] She'chem's father, for 100 pieces of money;[j] and it became the inheritance of the sons of Joseph.[k]

33 Also, El·e·a'zar the son of Aaron died.[l] So they buried him in the Hill of Phin'e·has his son,[m] which had been given to him in the mountainous region of E'phra·im.

24:14, 15 *That is, the Euphrates.
24:19 *Or "rebellion."

CHAP. 24
a Le 17:7
  Eze 23:8

b De 30:19, 20
  1Ki 18:21

c Jos 24:2

d Ex 23:32
  De 7:25
  Jg 6:10
  Jg 10:6

e Ex 19:4
  De 32:12

f De 6:12

g Ex 14:31
  De 4:34
  De 29:2

h Ex 23:23

i Le 19:2
  Ps 99:5
  Isa 6:3
  1Pe 1:15

j Ex 20:5
  Ex 34:14
  Nu 25:11
  Mt 4:10

k Ex 23:20, 21
  Nu 14:35

l De 28:15, 20
  Jos 23:16
  2Ch 15:2
  Isa 63:10
  Jer 17:13

m Ex 19:8

n De 26:17
  Jos 24:15

Second Col.
a De 31:26

b Ge 31:45

c Ge 31:48

d Jg 2:6

e Jg 2:8, 9

f Jos 19:49, 50

g De 31:12, 13
  Jg 2:7

h Ge 50:25
  Ex 13:19
  Heb 11:22

i Ac 7:15, 16

j Ge 33:18, 19

k Jos 20:7

l Nu 3:4
  Nu 20:26

m Ex 6:25
  Jg 20:28

JUDGES

1 After the death of Joshua,[a] the Israelites* inquired of Jehovah:[b] "Who of us will go up first to fight against the Ca′naan‐ites?" **2** Jehovah replied: "Judah will go up.[c] Look! I am giving* the land into his hand." **3** Then Judah said to his brother Sim′e‐on: "Come up with me into my assigned territory*[d] to fight against the Ca′naan‐ites. Then I will go with you into your assigned territory." So Sim′e‐on went with him.

4 When Judah went up, Jehovah gave the Ca′naan‐ites and the Per′iz‐zites into their hands,[e] and they defeated 10,000 men in Be′zek. **5** They found A‐do′ni‐be′zek in Be′zek, and there they fought against him and defeated the Ca′naan‐ites[f] and the Per′iz‐zites.[g] **6** When A‐do′ni‐be′zek fled, they chased him and caught him and cut off his thumbs and his big toes. **7** Then A‐do′ni‐be′zek said: "There are 70 kings whose thumbs and big toes were cut off and who are picking up food under my table. Just as I have done, so God has repaid me." After that they brought him to Jerusalem,[h] and he died there.

8 Furthermore, the men of Judah fought against Jerusalem[i] and captured it; they struck it with the sword and set the city on fire. **9** Afterward, the men of Judah went down to fight against the Ca′naan‐ites inhabiting the mountainous region and the Neg′eb and the She·phe′lah.[j] **10** So Judah marched against the Ca′naan‐ites who were dwelling in He′bron (the name of He′bron was previously Kir′i·ath·ar′ba), and they struck down She′shai, A·hi′man, and Tal′mai.[k]

11 They marched from there against the inhabitants of De′bir.[l] (The name of De′bir was previously   Kir′i·ath·se′pher.)[a] **12** Then Ca′leb[b] said: "To the man who strikes Kir′i·ath·se′pher and captures it, I will give my daughter Ach′sah as a wife."[c] **13** And Oth′ni·el[d] the son of Ke′naz,[e] Ca′leb's younger brother, captured it. So he gave him his daughter Ach′sah as a wife. **14** While she was going home, she urged him to ask her father for a field. Then she dismounted from her donkey.* Ca′leb asked her: "What do you want?" **15** She said to him: "Please grant me a blessing, for you have given me a piece of land in the south;* give me also Gul′loth·ma′im."# So Ca′leb gave her Upper Gul′loth and Lower Gul′loth.

16 And the descendants of the Ken′ite,[f] Moses' father‐in‐law,[g] came up from the city of palm trees[h] with the people of Judah to the wilderness of Judah south of A′rad.[i] They went there and settled among the people.[j] **17** But Judah marched on with his brother Sim′e‐on, and they attacked the Ca′naan‐ites inhabiting Ze′phath and devoted it to destruction.[k] So they named the city Hor′mah.*[l] **18** Then Judah captured Gaz′a[m] and its territory, Ash′ke·lon[n] and its territory, and Ek′ron[o] and its territory. **19** Jehovah was with Judah, and they took possession of the mountainous region, but they could not drive out the inhabitants of the plain,* because they had war chariots with iron scythes.#[p] **20** They gave He′bron to Ca′leb, just as Moses had promised,[q] and he drove out from there the three sons of A′nak.[r]

CHAP. 1
a Jos 24:29
b Nu 27:18, 21
   Jg 20:18
c Ge 49:8
   De 33:7
   1Ch 5:2
d Jos 15:1
   Jos 19:1, 9
e De 9:3
f Ge 10:6
   De 20:17
g Ge 15:18-21
   Ex 3:8
   Jg 3:5
   1Ki 9:20, 21
h Jos 15:8, 12
i Jos 15:63
   Jg 1:21
j Jos 11:16
   Jos 15:20, 33
k Jos 11:21
   Jos 15:13, 14
l Jos 10:38

Second Col.
a Jos 15:15
b Nu 13:3, 6
   Nu 14:24
   De 1:35, 36
   Jos 14:13
c Jos 15:16-19
d Jg 3:9
e 1Ch 4:13
f Nu 24:21
   Jg 4:11
g Ex 3:1
   Ex 4:18
   Ex 18:1
   Nu 10:29
h De 34:3
   Jg 3:13
i Nu 21:1
j Nu 10:29-32
k Le 27:29
   De 20:16
l Jos 19:1, 4
m Ge 10:19
   Jos 11:22
   Jg 14:19
n Jos 13:1-3
o Jos 15:20, 45
p De 20:1
   Jos 17:16
q Nu 14:24
   Jos 14:9
r Nu 13:22

1:1 *Lit., "sons of Israel." **1:2** *Or "have given." **1:3** *Lit., "my lot." **1:14** *Or possibly, "she clapped her hands while on the donkey." **1:15** *Or "the Negeb." #Meaning "Basins (Bowls) of Water." **1:17** *Meaning "A Devoting to Destruction." **1:19** *Or "low plain." #Lit., "chariots of iron."

21 But the Ben'ja·min·ites did not drive out the Jeb'u·sites inhabiting Jerusalem, so the Jeb'u·sites continue dwelling with the Ben'ja·min·ites in Jerusalem down to this day.[a]

22 Meantime, the house of Joseph[b] went up against Beth'el, and Jehovah was with them.[c] **23** The house of Joseph was spying on Beth'el (incidentally, the name of the city was previously Luz),[d] **24** and the spies saw a man going out of the city. So they said to him: "Show us, please, the way into the city, and we will treat you kindly."* **25** So the man showed them the way into the city, and they struck the city with the sword, but they let the man and all his family go free.[e] **26** The man went to the land of the Hit'tites and built a city and named it Luz, which is its name to this day.

27 Ma·nas'seh did not take possession of Beth-she'an and its dependent* towns, Ta'a·nach[f] and its dependent towns, the inhabitants of Dor and its dependent towns, the inhabitants of Ib'le·am and its dependent towns, and the inhabitants of Me·gid'do and its dependent towns.[g] The Ca'naan·ites persisted in dwelling in this land. **28** When Israel grew stronger, they subjected the Ca'naan·ites to forced labor,[h] but they did not drive them out completely.[i]

29 Nor did E'phra·im drive out the Ca'naan·ites who were dwelling in Ge'zer. The Ca'naan·ites continued to dwell among them in Ge'zer.[j]

30 Zeb'u·lun did not drive out the inhabitants of Kit'ron and the inhabitants of Na'ha·lol.[k] The Ca'naan·ites continued to dwell among them and were subjected to forced labor.[l]

31 Ash'er did not drive out the inhabitants of Ac'co and the inhabitants of Si'don,[a] Ah'lab, Ach'zib,[b] Hel'bah, A'phik,[c] and Re'hob.[d] **32** So the Ash'er·ites continued to dwell among the Ca'naan·ites inhabiting the land, because they did not drive them out.

33 Naph'ta·li did not drive out the inhabitants of Beth-she'mesh and the inhabitants of Beth-a'nath,[e] but they continued to dwell among the Ca'naan·ites inhabiting the land.[f] The inhabitants of Beth-she'mesh and Beth-a'nath became forced laborers for them.

34 The Am'or·ites confined the Dan'ites to the mountainous region, for they would not let them come down into the plain.*[g] **35** So the Am'or·ites persisted in dwelling in Mount He'res, Ai'ja·lon,[h] and Sha·al'bim.[i] But when the power* of the house of Joseph increased,# they were forced into hard labor. **36** The territory of the Am'or·ites was from the ascent of A·krab'bim,[j] from Se'la upward.

2 Then Jehovah's angel[k] went up from Gil'gal[l] to Bo'chim and said: "I brought you up out of Egypt into the land about which I swore to your forefathers.[m] Furthermore, I said, 'I will never break my covenant with you.[n] **2** For your part, you must not make a covenant with the inhabitants of this land[o] and you should pull down their altars.'[p] But you have not obeyed my voice.[q] Why have you done this? **3** That is why I also said, 'I will not drive them away from before you,[r] and they will ensnare you,[s] and their gods will lure you away.'"[t]

4 When Jehovah's angel spoke these words to all the Isra-

1:24 *Lit., "show you loyal love." **1:27** *Or "surrounding." **1:34** *Or "low plain." **1:35** *Lit., "hand." #Lit., "became heavy."

elites, the people began to weep loudly. **5** So they named that place Bo'chim,* and they sacrificed there to Jehovah.

6 When Joshua sent the people away, each of the Israelites went to his inheritance to take possession of the land.[a] The people continued to serve Jehovah all the days of Joshua and all the days of the elders who outlived Joshua and who had seen all of Jehovah's great deeds in behalf of Israel.[b] **8** Then Joshua the son of Nun, the servant of Jehovah, died at the age of 110.[c] **9** So they buried him in the territory of his inheritance in Tim'nath-he'res,[d] in the mountainous region of E'phra·im, north of Mount Ga'ash.[e] **10** All that generation were gathered to their ancestors,* and another generation arose after them that did not know Jehovah or what he had done for Israel.

11 So the Israelites did what was bad in the eyes of Jehovah and served* the Ba'als.[f] **12** Thus they abandoned Jehovah, the God of their fathers, who brought them out of the land of Egypt.[g] And they followed other gods, the gods of the peoples who were all around them,[h] and they bowed down to them and offended Jehovah.[i] **13** They abandoned Jehovah and served Ba'al and the Ash'to·reth images.[j] **14** At this Jehovah's anger blazed against Israel, so he handed them over to plunderers who pillaged them.[k] He sold them into the hand of the enemies around them,[l] and they were no longer able to hold their own against their enemies.[m] **15** Wherever they went, the hand of Jehovah was against them, bringing disaster on them,[n] just as Jehovah had said

and just as Jehovah had sworn to them,[a] and they were in great distress.[b] **16** So Jehovah would raise up judges who would save them from the hand of their plunderers.[c]

17 But they refused to listen even to the judges and would prostitute themselves to other gods and bow down to them. They quickly turned aside from the way in which their forefathers had walked, those who had obeyed the commandments of Jehovah.[d] They failed to do that. **18** Whenever Jehovah did raise up judges for them,[e] Jehovah would be with the judge and save them from the hand of their enemies all the days of the judge; for Jehovah was moved to pity*[f] over their groaning caused by those who oppressed them[g] and those who were treating them abusively.

19 But when the judge died, they would again act more corruptly than their fathers by following other gods, serving them and bowing down to them.[h] They did not abandon their practices and their stubborn behavior. **20** Finally Jehovah's anger blazed against Israel,[i] and he said: "Because this nation has violated my covenant[j] that I commanded their forefathers and they have disobeyed me,[k] **21** I for my part will not drive out from before them even one of the nations that Joshua left behind when he died.[l] **22** This is to test whether Israel will keep Jehovah's way[m] by walking in it as their fathers did." **23** So Jehovah allowed these nations to remain. He did not drive them out quickly, and he did not give them into Joshua's hand.

3 These are the nations that Jehovah allowed to remain so that they could test all those of Israel who had not

---

CHAP. 2
a Jos 24:28
b Jos 23:3
  Jos 24:31
c Jos 24:29
d Jos 19:49, 50
e Jos 24:30
f Jg 3:7
  Jg 10:6
  1Ki 18:17, 18
g De 31:16
h De 6:14
i Ex 20:5
j Jg 3:7
  Jg 10:6
  1Ki 11:5
k Jg 3:8
  2Ki 17:20
  Ps 106:40, 41
l Jg 4:2
m Le 26:17, 37
  De 28:15, 25
n De 28:15

Second Col.
a De 4:25, 26
b Jg 10:9
c Jg 3:9
  1Sa 12:11
  Ne 9:27
  Ps 106:43
d Jg 2:7
e Jg 3:9
f De 32:36
  Ps 106:45
g Jg 4:3
h Jg 4:1
  Jg 8:33
i De 7:4
  Jg 10:7
  Ps 106:40
j Ex 24:3, 8
  Ex 34:27
  De 29:1
  Jos 23:16
k Le 26:14, 17
l Jos 13:1, 2
m Nu 33:55
  De 8:2
  Jos 23:12, 13
  Jg 3:4

2:5 *Meaning "Weepers." 2:10 *This is a poetic expression for death. 2:11 *Or "worshipped."

2:18 *Or "felt regret."

experienced any of the wars of Ca'naan[a] **2** (this was so that succeeding generations of Israelites would experience war, those who had not experienced such things before): **3** the five lords of the Phi·lis'tines,[b] and all the Ca'naan·ites, the Si·do'ni·ans,[c] and the Hi'vites[d] inhabiting Mount Leb'a·non[e] from Mount Ba'al-her'mon as far as Le'bo-ha'math.[f] **4** They served as a means of testing Israel to determine whether Israel would obey Jehovah's commandments that he had given their fathers through Moses.[g] **5** So the Israelites lived among the Ca'naan·ites,[h] the Hit'tites, the Am'or·ites, the Per'iz·zites, the Hi'vites, and the Jeb'u·sites. **6** They would take their daughters as wives, and their own daughters they gave to their sons, and they began serving their gods.[i]

7 So the Israelites did what was bad in Jehovah's eyes, and they forgot Jehovah their God and were serving the Ba'als[j] and the sacred poles.[k] **8** At this Jehovah's anger blazed against Israel, and he sold them into the hand of Cu'shan-rish·a·tha'im the king of Mes·o·po·ta'mi·a.[*] The Israelites served Cu'shan-rish·a·tha'im for eight years. **9** When the Israelites called to Jehovah for help,[l] Jehovah raised up a savior to rescue the Israelites,[m] Oth'ni·el[n] the son of Ke'naz, the younger brother of Ca'leb. **10** The spirit of Jehovah came upon him,[o] and he became the judge of Israel. When he went out to battle, Jehovah gave Cu'shan-rish·a·tha'im the king of Mes·o·po·ta'mi·a[*] into his hand so that he prevailed over Cu'shan-rish·a·tha'im. **11** After

that the land had rest[*] for 40 years. Then Oth'ni·el the son of Ke'naz died.

12 And once again the Israelites began doing what was bad in Jehovah's eyes.[a] So Jehovah let Eg'lon the king of Mo'ab[b] prevail over Israel, because they did what was bad in Jehovah's eyes. **13** Furthermore, he brought against them the Am'mon·ites[c] and the A·mal'ek·ites.[d] They attacked Israel and captured the city of palm trees.[e] **14** The Israelites served Eg'lon the king of Mo'ab for 18 years.[f] **15** Then the Israelites called to Jehovah for help,[g] so Jehovah raised up for them a savior,[h] E'hud[i] the son of Ge'ra, a Ben'ja·min·ite[j] who was left-handed.[k] In time the Israelites sent tribute through him to Eg'lon the king of Mo'ab. **16** Meanwhile, E'hud made for himself a two-edged sword, a cubit[*] long, and he strapped it underneath his garment on his right thigh. **17** He then presented the tribute to Eg'lon the king of Mo'ab. Now Eg'lon was a very fat man.

18 When E'hud finished presenting the tribute, he sent away the people who had carried the tribute. **19** But after reaching the carved images[*] at Gil'gal,[l] he himself went back and said: "I have a secret message for you, O king." So the king said: "Silence!" With that all his attendants left him. **20** So E'hud came to him as he was sitting alone in his cool roof chamber. Then E'hud said: "I have a message from God for you." So he rose up from his throne.[*] **21** Then E'hud drew the sword from his right thigh with his left hand and plunged it into his bel-

CHAP. 3	
a	De 8:2
	Jg 2:10
b	Jg 1:18, 19
c	Jos 13:1, 4
	Jg 1:31
d	Jos 9:1, 2
e	Jos 13:1, 6
f	Nu 34:2, 8
	Jos 13:1, 5
g	Ex 23:33
	Jg 2:21, 22
h	Jg 1:29
	Ps 106:34
i	Ex 34:15, 16
	Nu 25:1, 2
	De 7:3, 4
	1Ki 11:1, 4
j	De 31:16
	Jg 2:11
	Jg 10:6
k	Ex 34:13
	De 12:3
	De 16:21
l	De 4:30
	Jg 10:10, 15
m	Jg 2:16, 18
	Jg 3:15
n	1Ch 4:13
o	Nu 11:16, 17
	Jg 6:34
	Jg 11:29
	Jg 14:5, 6
	Jg 15:14
	1Sa 11:6
	1Sa 16:13
	2Ch 15:1

Second Col.	
a	Jg 2:19
b	Ge 19:36, 37
c	Ge 19:36, 38
	Jg 11:4, 5
d	Ex 17:8
	Jg 6:3
e	De 34:3
f	De 28:48
g	Ps 78:34
h	Jg 3:9
i	Jg 4:1
j	Ge 49:27
k	Jg 20:15, 16
l	Jos 4:19
	Jos 5:8, 9

3:3 *Or "the entrance of Hamath." **3:7** *See Glossary. **3:8** *Lit., "Aram-naharaim." **3:10** *Lit., "Aram." **3:11** *Or "peace." **3:16** *Perhaps a short cubit of about 38 cm (15 in.). See App. B14. **3:19** *Or possibly, "the quarries." **3:20** *Or "seat."

ly. **22** The handle went in after the blade, and the fat closed in over the blade, for he did not draw the sword out of his belly, and the fecal matter came out. **23** E'hud went out through the porch,* closing the doors of the roof chamber behind him and locking them. **24** After he left, the servants returned and saw that the doors of the roof chamber were locked. So they said: "He must be relieving himself* in the cool interior room." **25** They kept waiting until they were embarrassed, but when they saw that he was still not opening the doors of the roof chamber, they took the key and opened them and saw their lord fallen to the floor* dead!

26 E'hud escaped while they were lingering, and he passed by the carved images*ᵃ and made it safely to Se·i'rah. **27** When he arrived, he sounded the hornᵇ in the mountainous region of E'phra·im;ᶜ and the Israelites went down out of the mountainous region, with him at their head. **28** Then he said to them: "Follow me, because Jehovah has given your enemies, the Mo'ab·ites, into your hand." So they followed him and captured the fords of the Jordan against the Mo'ab·ites, and they did not allow anyone to cross. **29** At that time they struck down about 10,-000 Mo'ab·ites,ᵈ all strong and valiant men; not a single one escaped.ᵉ **30** So Mo'ab was subdued on that day under Israel's hand; and the land had rest* for 80 years.ᶠ

31 After him was Sham'garᵍ the son of A'nath, who struck down 600 Phi·lis'tine menʰ with a cattle goad;ⁱ he too saved Israel.

4 But after E'hud died, the Israelites again did what was bad in Jehovah's eyes.ᵃ **2** So Jehovah sold them into the hand of Ja'bin the king of Ca'naan,ᵇ who reigned in Ha'zor. The chief of his army was Sis'e·ra, who lived in Ha·ro'shethᶜ of the nations.* **3** The Israelites cried out to Jehovah,ᵈ because Ja'bin* had 900 war chariots with iron scythes,*ᵉ and he harshly oppressed the Israelitesᶠ for 20 years.

4 Now Deb'o·rah, a prophetess,ᵍ the wife of Lap'pi·doth, was judging Israel at that time. **5** She used to sit under Deb'o·rah's palm tree between Ra'mahʰ and Beth'elⁱ in the mountainous region of E'phra·im; the Israelites would go up to her for judgment. **6** She sent for Ba'rakʲ the son of A·bin'o·am out of Ke'desh-naph'ta·liᵏ and said to him: "Has not Jehovah the God of Israel given the command? 'Go and march to* Mount Ta'bor, and take 10,000 men of Naph'ta·li and Zeb'u·lun with you. **7** I will bring to you Sis'e·ra, the chief of Ja'bin's army, along with his war chariots and his troops to the stream* of Ki'shon,ⁱ and I will give him into your hand.'"ᵐ

8 At this Ba'rak said to her: "If you go with me, I will go, but if you do not go with me, I will not go." **9** To this she said: "I will certainly go with you. However, the campaign you are going on will not bring you glory, for it will be into the hand of a woman that Jehovah will give Sis'e·ra."ⁿ Then Deb'o·rah got up and went with Ba'rak to Ke'desh.ᵒ **10** Ba'rak summoned Zeb'u·lun and Naph'ta·liᵖ to Ke'desh, and 10,000 men followed his steps. Deb'o·rah also went up with him.

CHAP. 3
a Jg 3:19

b Jg 6:34
  1Sa 13:3

c Jg 7:24

d De 28:7

e Le 26:7, 8

f Jg 3:11

g Jg 5:6

h Jos 13:1, 2

i Jg 15:3, 15
  1Sa 17:47, 50

Second Col.

CHAP. 4
a Jg 2:19

b Jg 2:14
  Jg 3:8
  Jg 10:7

c Jg 4:18

d Jg 2:18
  Jg 3:9
  Ps 107:19

e Jos 17:16
  Jg 1:19

f De 28:48

g Ex 15:20
  2Ki 22:14
  Lu 2:36
  Ac 21:8, 9

h Jos 18:21, 25

i Ge 28:17, 19

j Heb 11:32

k Jos 21:32

l 1Ki 18:40
  Ps 83:9

m De 20:1

n Jg 4:21, 22
  Jg 5:24, 26

o Jos 20:7, 9
  Jos 21:32

p Jg 5:18

3:23 *Or possibly, "air vent." **3:24** *Lit., "covering his feet." **3:25** *Lit., "earth." **3:26** *Or possibly, "the quarries." **3:30** *Or "peace."

4:2 *Or "Harosheth-ha-goiim." **4:3** *Lit., "he." #Lit., "chariots of iron." **4:6** *Or "Deploy your men on." **4:7** *Or "wadi."

11 Incidentally, He'ber the Ken'ite had separated from the Ken'ites,[a] the descendants of Ho'bab, Moses' father-in-law,[b] and his tent was pitched near the big tree in Za·a·nan'nim, which is at Ke'desh.

12 They reported to Sis'e·ra that Ba'rak the son of A·bin'o·am had gone up to Mount Ta'bor.[c] **13** At once Sis'e·ra assembled all his war chariots—900 chariots with iron scythes*—and all the troops that were with him from Ha·ro'sheth of the nations to go to the stream# of Ki'shon.[d] **14** Deb'o·rah now said to Ba'rak: "Rise up, for this is the day that Jehovah will give Sis'e·ra into your hand. Is Jehovah not going out before you?" And Ba'rak descended from Mount Ta'bor with 10,000 men following him. **15** Then Jehovah threw Sis'e·ra and all his war chariots and all the army into confusion[e] before the sword of Ba'rak. Finally Sis'e·ra got down from his chariot and fled on foot. **16** Ba'rak chased after the war chariots and the army as far as Ha·ro'sheth of the nations. So Sis'e·ra's whole army fell by the sword; not even one remained.[f]

17 But Sis'e·ra fled on foot to the tent of Ja'el[g] the wife of He'ber[h] the Ken'ite, for there was peace between Ja'bin[i] the king of Ha'zor and the house of He'ber the Ken'ite. **18** Then Ja'el came out to meet Sis'e·ra and said to him: "Come in, my lord, come in here. Do not be afraid." So he went into her tent, and she covered him with a blanket. **19** Then he said to her: "Give me, please, a little water to drink, for I am thirsty." So she opened a skin bottle of milk and gave him a drink,[j] after which she again covered him. **20** He told her: "Stand at the entrance

of the tent, and if anybody comes and asks you, 'Is there a man here?' say, 'No!'"

21 But Ja'el the wife of He'ber took a tent pin and a hammer in her hand. Then while he was fast asleep and exhausted, she stealthily approached him and drove the pin through his temples and beat it into the ground, and he died.[a]

22 Ba'rak went there in pursuit of Sis'e·ra, and Ja'el now came out to meet him and said: "Come and I will show you the man you are looking for." He went in with her and saw Sis'e·ra lying dead, with the tent pin through his temples.

23 So on that day, God subdued Ja'bin the king of Ca'naan before the Israelites.[b] **24** The hand of the Israelites came down harder and harder against Ja'bin the king of Ca'naan,[c] until they destroyed Ja'bin the king of Ca'naan.[d]

5 On that day Deb'o·rah[e] along with Ba'rak[f] the son of A·bin'o·am sang this song:[g]

2 "Because of the unbound hair* in Israel,
Because of the people's volunteering,[h]
Praise Jehovah!

3 Listen, you kings! Give ear, you rulers!
To Jehovah I will sing.
I will sing praises* to Jehovah,[i] Israel's God.[j]

4 Jehovah, when you went out from Se'ir,[k]
When you marched out of the territory of E'dom,
The earth shook, and the heavens poured,
The clouds poured down water.

5 Mountains melted* before the face of Jehovah,[l]

Reference column:

CHAP. 4
a Nu 24:21
Jg 1:16
1Sa 15:6

b Nu 10:29

c Jg 4:6

d Jg 5:20, 21

e Ex 14:24
Jos 10:10

f Le 26:7

g Jg 5:24

h Jg 4:11

i Jg 4:1, 2

j Jg 5:25

Second Col.
a Jg 4:9
Jg 5:26, 27

b Heb 11:32, 33

c Ge 9:25

d De 7:24

CHAP. 5
e Jg 4:4

f Jg 4:6
Heb 11:32

g Ex 15:1
Ps 18:Sup

h Jg 4:10

i 2Sa 22:50
Ps 7:17

j Ex 20:2

k De 33:2

l De 4:11

4:13 *Lit., "chariots of iron." #Or "wadi." **5:2** *Or "the warriors with unbound hair." **5:3** *Or "make music." **5:5** *Or possibly, "quaked."

Even Si′nai before the face
of Jehovah,[a] Israel's God.[b]

6 In the days of Sham′gar[c]
the son of A′nath,
In the days of Ja′el,[d] the
roads were deserted;
Travelers kept to the back
roads.

7 The villagers in Israel were
no more;*
They were no more until I,
Deb′o·rah,[e] rose up,
Until I arose as a mother
in Israel.[f]

8 They chose new gods;[g]
Then there was war in the
gates.[h]
A shield could not be seen,
nor a lance,
Among 40,000 in Israel.

9 My heart is with the commanders of Israel,[i]
Who went as volunteers
with the people.[j]
Praise Jehovah!

10 You riders on tawny donkeys,
You who sit on fine carpets,
And you who walk on the
road,
Consider!

11 The voices of the water
distributors were heard
at the watering places;
There they were recounting
the righteous acts of
Jehovah,
The righteous acts of his
villagers in Israel.
Then Jehovah's people went
down to the gates.

12 Awake, awake, O Deb′o·rah![k]
Awake, awake, sing a song![l]
Rise up, Ba′rak![m] Lead your
captives away, you son of
A·bin′o·am!

13 Then those who were left
came down to the nobles;
Jehovah's people came down
to me against the mighty.

14 Out of E′phra·im was their
origin, those in the valley;*
They are following you,
O Benjamin, among your
peoples.
From Ma′chir[a] the commanders went down,
And from Zeb′u·lun those
who bear the recruiter's
staff.#

15 The princes in Is′sa·char
were with Deb′o·rah,
As was Is′sa·char, so was
Ba′rak.[b]
Into the valley plain* he was
sent on foot.[c]
Among the divisions of
Reu′ben there was intense
heart-searching.

16 Why did you sit down between the two saddlebags,
Listening to them playing
their pipes for the flocks?[d]
For the divisions of Reu′ben,
there was intense heart-
searching.

17 Gil′e·ad remained beyond
the Jordan;[e]
And Dan, why did he stay
with the ships?[f]
Ash′er sat idle at the
seashore,
And by his harbors* he
remained.[g]

18 Zeb′u·lun was a people who
risked their lives* to the
point of death;
Naph′ta·li also,[h] on the open
heights.[i]

19 Kings came, they fought;
The kings of Ca′naan then
fought[j]
In Ta′a·nach, by the waters
of Me·gid′do.[k]
No spoil of silver did they
take.[l]

20 From heaven the stars
fought;

CHAP. 5
a Ex 19:18
Ne 9:13

b Ex 20:2

c Jg 3:31

d Jg 4:17

e Jg 4:4

f Jg 4:5

g De 32:16, 17
Jg 2:12

h Jg 4:1-3

i Jg 4:6

j Jg 4:10

k Jg 4:4

l Jg 5:1

m Jg 4:6

Second Col.
a Nu 32:39

b Jg 4:6
Heb 11:32

c Jg 4:14

d Nu 32:1

e Jos 22:9

f Jos 19:46, 48

g Jos 19:24, 29

h Jg 4:6, 10

i Jg 4:14

j Jg 4:13

k Jg 1:27

l Jg 4:16

5:7 *Or "ceased."

5:14, 15 *Or "low plain." 5:14 #Or possibly, "those handling the equipment of
a scribe." 5:17 *Or "landing places."
5:18 *Or "scorned their souls."

From their orbits they fought against Sis·e·ra.

21 The torrent* of Ki'shon washed them away,[a]

The ancient torrent,* the torrent* of Ki'shon.

You trampled down the powerful, O my soul.[#]

22 Then the hooves of horses pounded

As his stallions galloped furiously.[b]

23 'Curse Me'roz,' said the angel of Jehovah,

'Yes, curse its inhabitants,

For they did not come to the assistance of Jehovah,

To the assistance of Jehovah with the mighty ones.'

24 Most blessed of women is Ja'el[c]

The wife of He'ber[d] the Ken'ite;

She is most blessed of women living in tents.

25 He asked for water; she gave him milk.

In a majestic banquet bowl she offered curdled milk.*[e]

26 With her hand she reached for the tent pin,

Her right hand for the workman's mallet.

And she hammered Sis'e·ra, she crushed his head,

And she smashed and pierced his temples.[f]

27 Between her feet he collapsed; he fell and lay still;

Between her feet he collapsed and fell;

Where he collapsed, there he fell defeated.

28 From the window a woman looked out,

Sis'e·ra's mother peered out from the lattice,

'Why is his chariot delayed in coming?

Why are the hoofbeats of his chariots so late?'[a]

29 The wisest of her noble ladies would answer her;

Yes, she too would repeat to herself,

30 'They must be dividing the spoil they found,

A girl,* two girls,[#] to every warrior,

Spoil of dyed cloth for Sis'e·ra, spoil of dyed cloth,

An embroidered garment, dyed cloth, two embroidered garments

For the necks of the plunderers.'

31 So let all your enemies perish,[b] O Jehovah,

But let those who love you be like the sun rising in its glory."

And the land had rest* for 40 years.[c]

6 But the Israelites again did what was bad in the eyes of Jehovah,[d] so Jehovah gave them into the hand of Mid'i·an for seven years.[e] 2 The hand of Mid'i·an dominated over Israel. Because of Mid'i·an, the Israelites made hiding places* for themselves in the mountains, in the caves, and in the places difficult to approach.[g] 3 If Israel sowed seed, Mid'i·an and Am'a·lek[h] and the Easterners[i] would attack them. 4 They would camp against them and ruin the produce of the land all the way to Gaz'a, and they left nothing for Israel to eat and no sheep or bull or donkey.[j] 5 For they would come up with their livestock and tents as numerous as the locusts,[k] and they and their camels could not be numbered,[l] and they would come into the land to destroy it. 6 So Israel became greatly impoverished on account

---

CHAP. 5
a Jg 4:7, 13
Ps 83:9

b Ps 20:7
Pr 21:31

c Jg 4:17

d Jg 4:11

e Jg 4:19

f Jg 4:21, 22

Second Col.
a Jg 4:15, 16

b Ps 83:9

c Jg 3:10, 11
Jg 3:30

CHAP. 6
d Jg 2:19

e De 28:15, 48
Jg 2:14
Ne 9:28

f Nu 33:55

g 1Sa 13:5, 6

h Jg 3:13

i Jg 8:10

j De 28:15, 33
De 28:31, 48

k Jg 8:10

l Jg 7:12

5:21 *Or "stream." [#]See Glossary.
5:25 *Or "offered cream."
5:30 *Lit., "womb." [#]Lit., "wombs."
5:31 *Or "peace." 6:2 *Or possibly, "underground storage places."

of Mid'i·an; and the Israelites called to Jehovah for help.[a]

7 When the Israelites called to Jehovah for help because of Mid'i·an,[b] **8** Jehovah sent to the Israelites a prophet who said to them: "This is what Jehovah the God of Israel says, 'I brought you up from Egypt and thus brought you out of the house of slavery.[c] **9** So I rescued you from the hand of Egypt and from all your oppressors and drove them out from before you and gave you their land.[d] **10** And I said to you: "I am Jehovah your God.[e] You must not fear the gods of the Am'or·ites in whose land you are dwelling."[f] But you did not obey me.'"*[g]

11 Later Jehovah's angel came[h] and sat under the big tree that was in Oph'rah, which belonged to Jo'ash the Abi-ez'rite.[i] His son Gid'e·on[j] was beating out wheat in the winepress in order to hide it from Mid'i·an. **12** Jehovah's angel appeared to him and said: "Jehovah is with you,[k] you mighty warrior." **13** At this Gid'e·on said to him: "Pardon me, my lord, but if Jehovah is with us, why has all of this come upon us?[l] Where are all his wonderful acts that our fathers related to us,[m] saying, 'Did Jehovah not bring us up out of Egypt?'[n] Now Jehovah has deserted us[o] and given us into Mid'i·an's hand." **14** Jehovah faced him and said: "Go with the strength you have, and you will save Israel out of Mid'i·an's hand.[p] Is it not I who send you?" **15** Gid'e·on answered him: "Pardon me, Jehovah. How can I save Israel? Look! My clan* is the least in Ma·nas'seh, and I am the most insignificant in my father's house." **16** But Jehovah said to him: "Because I will be with

you,[a] you will strike down Mid'i·an as if they were one man."

17 Then he said to him: "If, now, I have found favor in your eyes, show me a sign that you are the one speaking with me. **18** Please do not depart from here until I return with my gift and set it before you."[b] So he said: "I will stay here until you return." **19** And Gid'e·on went in and prepared a young goat and made unleavened bread from an e'phah* of flour.[c] He put the meat in the basket and the broth in the cooking pot; then he brought them out to him and served them under the big tree.

20 The angel of the true God now said to him: "Take the meat and the unleavened bread and place them on the big rock there, and pour out the broth." And he did so. **21** Then Jehovah's angel stretched out the tip of the staff that was in his hand and touched the meat and the unleavened bread, and fire flared up from the rock and consumed the meat and the unleavened bread.[d] Jehovah's angel vanished from his sight. **22** Gid'e·on now realized that it was Jehovah's angel.[e]

At once Gid'e·on said: "Alas, Sovereign Lord Jehovah, for I have seen Jehovah's angel face-to-face!"[f] **23** But Jehovah said to him: "Peace be with you. Have no fear;[g] you will not die." **24** So Gid'e·on built an altar there to Jehovah, and it is called Je·ho'vah-sha'lom*[h] down to this day. It is still in Oph'rah of the Abi-ez'rites.

25 That night Jehovah said to him: "Take the young bull that belongs to your father, the second young bull that is seven years old, and tear down the

---

CHAP. 6

a De 4:30

b Jg 2:18
  Ps 107:19

c Ex 20:2
  Le 26:13
  Jg 2:1

d Jos 10:42
  Ne 9:24

e De 6:4

f Jos 24:15

g De 28:15
  Jg 2:2
  Jer 3:13

h Jg 2:1

i Jos 17:2
  Jg 6:24
  Jg 8:32

j Ge 49:22, 24
  Heb 11:32

k Jg 2:18

l Jg 6:2

m De 4:9
  Ps 44:1

n Ex 13:14

o De 31:17
  2Ch 15:2

p Jg 8:22
  Heb 11:32

Second Col.

a De 20:3, 4
  Jg 2:18

b Ge 18:3, 5
  Jg 13:15

c Ge 18:6, 7
  Jg 13:15

d Le 9:24
  Jg 13:19, 20
  1Ki 18:38
  1Ch 21:26
  2Ch 7:1

e Jg 13:8, 9
  Heb 13:2

f Ge 16:7, 13
  Ge 32:24, 30
  Jg 13:21, 22
  Lu 1:11, 12

g Da 10:19

h Ge 22:14
  Ex 17:15

6:10 *Lit., "listen to my voice." 6:15 *Lit., "thousand."

6:19 *About 22 L (20 dry qt). See App. B14. 6:24 *Meaning "Jehovah Is Peace."

altar of Ba′al that belongs to your father, and cut down the sacred pole* next to it.ᵃ **26** After you build an altar to Jehovah your God on top of this stronghold with the row of stones, take the second young bull and offer it as a burnt offering on the pieces of wood from the sacred pole* that you cut down." **27** So Gid′e·on took ten men of his servants and did just as Jehovah told him. But he feared the household of his father and the men of the city too much to do it by day, so he did it at night.

28 When the men of the city got up early the next morning, they saw that the altar of Ba′al had been pulled down and the sacred pole* beside it had been cut down and the second young bull had been offered up on the altar that had been built. **29** They asked one another: "Who did this?" After they investigated, they said: "Gid′e·on the son of Jo′ash did this." **30** So the men of the city said to Jo′ash: "Bring your son out that he may die, because he pulled down the altar of Ba′al and cut down the sacred pole* next to it." **31** Jo′ashᵇ then said to all those who confronted him: "Do you have to defend Ba′al? Do you have to save him? Whoever defends him should be put to death this morning.ᶜ If he is a god, let him defend himself,ᵈ since someone pulled down his altar." **32** And he called Gid′e·on Jer·ub·ba′al* on that day, saying: "Let Ba′al defend himself, for someone has pulled down his altar."

33 All Mid′i·anᵉ and Am′a·lekᶠ and the Easterners joined forces;ᵍ and they crossed over*

into the Valley* of Jez′re·el and camped. **34** Then Jehovah's spirit came upon* Gid′e·onᵃ and he sounded the horn,ᵇ and the Abi·ez′ritesᶜ rallied behind him. **35** He sent out messengers through all of Ma·nas′seh, and they too rallied behind him. He also sent out messengers through Ash′er, Zeb′u·lun, and Naph′ta·li, and they came up to meet him.

36 Then Gid′e·on said to the true God: "If you are saving Israel by means of me, just as you have promised,ᵈ **37** here I am laying a fleece of wool on the threshing floor. If there is dew on the fleece only but all the ground around it is dry, then I will know that you will save Israel by means of me, just as you have promised." **38** And that is how it happened. When he rose up early the next day and wrung the fleece, he squeezed off enough dew from the fleece to fill a large banquet bowl with water. **39** However, Gid′e·on said to the true God: "Do not let your anger burn against me, but let me ask just once more. Let me, please, make just one more test with the fleece. Please let the fleece alone be dry while there is dew all over the ground." **40** So that is what God did that night; only the fleece was dry, and there was dew all over the ground.

7 Then Jer·ub·ba′al, that is, Gid′e·on,ᵉ and all the people with him rose early and encamped at the well of Ha′rod, while the camp of Mid′i·an was north of him at the hill of Mo′reh in the valley plain.* **2** Jehovah now said to Gid′e·on: "There are too many people with you for me to give Mid′i·an into their hand.ᶠ Otherwise, Israel might

---

CHAP. 6
a Ex 23:24
De 12:3

b Jg 6:11

c De 13:5
De 17:2-5

d 1Ki 18:26, 27
Ps 115:5
Jer 10:5

e Nu 25:17, 18
Jg 6:2

f Ex 17:16
Nu 24:20
De 25:19

g Jg 6:3
Jg 7:12

Second Col.
a Jg 3:9, 10
Jg 11:29
Jg 13:24, 25
Jg 14:6
Jg 15:14
Zec 4:6

b Jg 3:26, 27

c Jos 17:2

d Jg 6:14

CHAP. 7
e Jg 6:11, 32

f 1Sa 14:6
2Ch 14:11

6:25, 26, 28, 30 *See Glossary. **6:32** *Meaning "Let Baal Make a Legal Defense (Contend)." **6:33** *Or "crossed the river."

6:33 *Or "Low Plain." **6:34** *Lit., "clothed." **7:1** *Or "low plain."

brag about itself against me and say, 'My own hand saved me.'[a] **3** Now, please, announce in the presence of the people: 'Whoever is afraid and trembling, let him return home.'"[b] So Gid'e·on put them to the test. With that, 22,000 of the people returned home, and 10,000 remained.

4 Still Jehovah said to Gid'e·on: "There are yet too many people. Have them go down to the water so that I may test them for you there. When I say to you, 'This one will go with you,' he will go with you, but when I say to you, 'This one will not go along with you,' he will not go along." **5** So he took the people down to the water.

Then Jehovah said to Gid'e·on: "Separate everyone who laps up the water with his tongue just as a dog laps, from those who bend down on their knees to drink." **6** The number of those lapping up the water, putting their hand to their mouth, was 300 men. The rest of the people bent down on their knees to drink.

7 Jehovah now said to Gid'e·on: "I will save you with the 300 men who lapped the water, and I will give Mid'i·an into your hand.[c] But let all the other people go back home." **8** So after they took the provisions and the horns from the people, he sent all the other men of Israel back home, and he kept only the 300 men. The camp of Mid'i·an was below him in the valley plain.[d]

9 During that night, Jehovah said to him: "Get up, attack the camp, for I have given it into your hand.[e] **10** But if you are afraid to attack, go down to the camp with Pu'rah your attendant. **11** Listen to what they say, and afterward you will have the courage* to attack the

camp." At that he and Pu'rah his attendant went down to the edge of the encamped army.

12 Now Mid'i·an and Am'a·lek and all the Easterners[a] covered the valley plain like a swarm of locusts, and their camels were without number,[b] as many as the grains of sand on the seashore. **13** Gid'e·on now came, and there was a man relating a dream to his companion, and he said: "This is the dream I had. There was a round loaf of barley bread rolling into the camp of Mid'i·an. It came to a tent and struck it so hard that it collapsed.[c] Yes, it turned the tent upside down, and the tent fell flat." **14** At this his companion said: "This can only be the sword of Gid'e·on[d] the son of Jo'ash, a man of Israel. God has given Mid'i·an and all the camp into his hand."[e]

15 As soon as Gid'e·on heard him relate the dream and its interpretation,[f] he bowed down to worship. After that he returned to the camp of Israel and said: "Get up, for Jehovah has given the camp of Mid'i·an into your hand." **16** Then he divided the 300 men into three bands and gave all of them horns[g] and large empty jars with torches inside the jars. **17** Then he said to them: "Watch me and do exactly what I do. When I come to the edge of the camp, you should do just as I do. **18** When I blow the horn, I and all who are with me, you also must blow the horns all around the camp and shout, 'For Jehovah and for Gid'e·on!'"

19 Gid'e·on and the 100 men who were with him came to the edge of the camp at the start of the middle night watch,* just after the sentries were posted. They blew the horns[h] and

---

CHAP. 7
a 1Sa 17:47

b De 20:8

c Jg 7:2

d Jg 6:33

e Jg 3:9, 10
Jg 4:14

Second Col.
a Jg 6:33

b Jg 6:3, 5

c Jg 6:16

d Jg 6:14

e Jg 7:7

f Jg 7:11

g Jg 7:8

h Jg 7:8

7:11 *Lit., "your hands will grow strong."

7:19 *From about 10:00 p.m. to about 2:00 a.m.

smashed the large water jars that were in their hands.ᵃ 20 So the three bands blew the horns and shattered the large jars. They held the torches in their left hands and blew the horns in their right hands and they called out: "The sword of Jehovah and of Gid'e·on!" 21 All the while each man stood in his place all around the camp, and the whole army ran away, shouting as they fled.ᵇ 22 The 300 continued to blow the horns, and Jehovah turned the sword of each one against the other throughout the camp;ᶜ and the army fled as far as Beth-shit'tah, on to Zer'e·rah, as far as the outskirts of A'bel-me·ho'lahᵈ by Tab'bath.

23 And the men of Israel were called together from Naph'ta·li, Ash'er, and all of Ma·nas'seh,ᵉ and they chased after Mid'i·an. 24 Gid'e·on sent messengers into all the mountainous region of E'phra·im, saying: "Go down to attack Mid'i·an, and capture the access to the waters as far as Beth-bar'ah and the Jordan." So all the men of E'phra·im were gathered together, and they captured the waters as far as Beth-bar'ah and the Jordan. 25 They also captured the two princes of Mid'i·an, O'reb and Ze'eb; they killed O'reb on the rock of O'reb,ᶠ and they killed Ze'eb at the winepress of Ze'eb. They kept on pursuing Mid'i·an,ᵍ and they brought the heads of O'reb and Ze'eb to Gid'e·on in the region of the Jordan.

8 Then the men of E'phra·im said to him: "What have you done to us? Why did you not call us when you went to fight against Mid'i·an?"ʰ And they quarreled bitterly with him.ⁱ 2 But he said to them: "What have I done compared with you? Are not the gleanings of E'phra·imʲ better than the grape har-

vest of Abi-e'zer?ᵃ 3 It was into your hand that God gave Mid'i·an's princes O'reb and Ze'eb,ᵇ and what have I done compared with you?" When he spoke this way,* they calmed down.#

4 Gid'e·on then came to the Jordan and crossed it. He and the 300 men with him were tired, but they kept up the pursuit. 5 So he said to the men of Suc'coth: "Please give loaves of bread to the people following me, for they are tired and I am chasing after Ze'bah and Zal·mun'na, the kings of Mid'i·an." 6 But the princes of Suc'coth said: "Are the palms of Ze'bah and Zal·mun'na already in your hand so that we should give bread to your army?" 7 At this Gid'e·on said: "Just for that, when Jehovah gives Ze'bah and Zal·mun'na into my hand, I will give you a thrashing with the thorns and the briars of the wilderness."ᶜ 8 And he went up from there to Pe·nu'el and made the same request, but the men of Pe·nu'el gave him the same answer as the men of Suc'coth. 9 So he said also to the men of Pe·nu'el: "When I return in peace, I will pull down this tower."ᵈ

10 Now Ze'bah and Zal·mun'na were in Kar'kor with their armies, about 15,000 men. These were all who remained of the entire army of the Easterners,ᵉ for 120,000 men armed with swords had fallen. 11 Gid'e·on continued up by the way of the tent dwellers east of No'bah and Jog'be·hahᶠ and attacked the camp, which was off guard. 12 When Ze'bah and Zal·mun'na fled, he pursued and captured the two Mid'i·an·ite kings, Ze'bah and Zal·mun'na, throwing the whole camp into a panic.

8:3 *Lit., "word." #Lit., "their spirit relaxed from against him."

CHAP. 7
ᵃ Jg 7:16

ᵇ Ex 14:25
　2Ki 7:6, 7

ᶜ 2Ch 20:23

ᵈ 1Ki 19:16

ᵉ Jg 6:35

ᶠ Ps 83:11
　Isa 10:26

ᵍ Jg 8:4

CHAP. 8
ʰ Jg 7:2

ⁱ Jg 12:1
　2Ch 25:10

ʲ Jg 7:24

Second Col.
ᵃ Jg 6:11, 34

ᵇ Jg 7:24, 25

ᶜ Jg 8:16

ᵈ Jg 8:17

ᵉ Jg 7:12

ᶠ Nu 32:34, 35

13 Gid′e·on the son of Jo′ash then returned from the war by way of the pass that goes up to He′res. **14** En route he captured and interrogated a young man from Suc′coth. So the young man wrote out for him the names of the princes and elders of Suc′coth, 77 men. **15** With that he went to the men of Suc′coth and said: "Here are Ze′bah and Zal·mun′na about whom you taunted me, saying, 'Are the palms of Ze′bah and Zal·mun′na already in your hand so that we should give bread to your exhausted men?'"[a] **16** Then he took the elders of the city and with thorns and briars of the wilderness, he taught the men of Suc′coth a lesson.[b] **17** And he pulled down the tower of Pe·nu′el[c] and killed the men of the city.

18 He asked Ze′bah and Zal·mun′na: "What sort of men did you kill in Ta′bor?" To this they said: "They were like you, each one looked like the son of a king." **19** At that he said: "They were my brothers, the sons of my mother. As surely as Jehovah lives, if you had spared their lives, I would not have to kill you." **20** Then he said to Je′ther his firstborn: "Get up, kill them." But the young man did not draw his sword; he was afraid, for he was still a young man. **21** So Ze′bah and Zal·mun′na said: "Get up yourself and slay us, for a man is judged by his mightiness."* So Gid′e·on got up and killed Ze′bah and Zal·mun′na[d] and took the crescent-shaped ornaments that were on the necks of their camels.

22 Later the men of Israel said to Gid′e·on: "Rule over us, you and your son and your grandson as well, for you saved us out of the hand of Mid′i·an."[e]

23 But Gid′e·on said to them: "I will not rule over you, nor will my son rule over you. Jehovah is the one who will rule over you."[a] **24** Gid′e·on continued: "Let me make one request of you: that each of you give me a nose ring from his spoil." (For they had gold nose rings because they were Ish′ma·el·ites.)[b] **25** They replied: "We will surely give them." With that they spread out a robe and each man threw a nose ring from his spoil on it. **26** The weight of the gold nose rings that he had requested amounted to 1,700 gold shekels,* besides the crescent-shaped ornaments, the pendants, the purple wool garments worn by the kings of Mid′i·an, and the necklaces from the camels.[c]

27 Gid′e·on made it into an eph′od[d] and exhibited it in his city Oph′rah;[e] and all Israel committed spiritual prostitution with it there,[f] and it served as a snare to Gid′e·on and to his household.[g]

28 Thus Mid′i·an[h] was subdued before the Israelites, and they did not challenge them* again; and the land had rest# for 40 years in the days of Gid′e·on.[i]

29 So Jer·ub·ba′al[i] the son of Jo′ash returned to his home and stayed there.

30 Gid′e·on became father to 70 sons,* for he had many wives. **31** His concubine in She′chem also bore him a son, and he named him A·bim′e·lech.[k] **32** And Gid′e·on the son of Jo′ash died at a good old age and was buried in the tomb of Jo′ash his father in Oph′rah of the Abi·ez′rites.

33 As soon as Gid′e·on died, the Israelites again committed

CHAP. 8
a Jg 8:5, 6

b Jg 8:7

c Jg 8:8, 9

d Ps 83:11

e Jg 6:14

Second Col.
a Ex 15:18
1Sa 10:19
Isa 33:22
Isa 43:15

b Ge 16:11
Ge 25:13
Ge 28:9
Ge 37:28

c Jg 8:21

d Ex 28:6
Jg 17:5

e Jg 6:11

f Jg 2:17

g Ps 106:36

h Jg 6:1

i Jg 3:11
Jg 5:31

j Jg 6:32
1Sa 12:11

k Jg 9:1, 2
2Sa 11:21

l Jg 6:11, 24

8:21 *Or "for as a man is, so is his strength."

8:26 *A shekel equaled 11.4 g (0.367 oz t). See App. B14. **8:28** *Lit., "did not lift up their head." #Or "peace." **8:30** *Lit., "had 70 sons who came out from his thigh."

spiritual prostitution with the Ba'als,[a] and they appointed Ba'al-be'rith as their god.[b] 34 The Israelites did not remember Jehovah their God,[c] who had rescued them from the hand of all their enemies around them;[d] 35 nor did they show loyal love toward the household of Jer·ub·ba'al, that is Gid'e·on, in return for all the good that he had done for Israel.[e]

9 In time A·bim'e·lech[f] the son of Jer·ub·ba'al went to his mother's brothers in She'chem, and he said to them and to all the family of his grandfather:* 2 "Please ask all the leaders* of She'chem, 'Which is better for you, for all 70 sons of Jer·ub·ba'al to rule over you or for one man to rule over you? And remember that I am your own bone and flesh.'"#

3 So his mother's brothers said this in his behalf to all the leaders of She'chem, and their hearts were inclined to follow A·bim'e·lech, for they said: "He is our own brother." 4 Then they gave him 70 pieces of silver from the house* of Ba'al-be'rith,[h] and A·bim'e·lech used it to hire idle and insolent men to accompany him. 5 After that he went to his father's house at Oph'rah[i] and killed his brothers,[j] the sons of Jer·ub·ba'al, 70 men, on one stone. The only survivor was Jo'tham, the youngest son of Jer·ub·ba'al, because he hid.

6 Then all the leaders of She'chem and all Beth-mil'lo gathered together and made A·bim'e·lech king,[k] close by the big tree, by the pillar that was in She'chem.

7 When they reported it to Jo'tham, he at once went and stood on the top of Mount Ger'-

i·zim[a] and called out in a loud voice to them: "Listen to me, you leaders of She'chem, and then God will listen to you.

8 "Once there were trees that went to anoint a king over them. So they said to the olive tree, 'Rule over us.'[b] 9 But the olive tree said to them, 'Must I give up my oil,* which they use to glorify God and men, to go and wave over the other trees?' 10 Then the trees said to the fig tree, 'Come and rule over us.' 11 But the fig tree said to them, 'Must I give up my sweetness and my good fruitage to go and wave over the other trees?' 12 Next the trees said to the vine, 'Come and rule over us.' 13 The vine replied to them, 'Must I give up my new wine that makes God and men rejoice to go and wave over the trees?' 14 Finally all the other trees said to the bramble, 'Come and rule over us.'[c] 15 At this the bramble said to the trees, 'If you are really anointing me as king over you, come and seek refuge under my shadow. But if not, let fire come out of the bramble and consume the cedars of Leb'a·non.'

16 "Now have you acted sincerely and honorably in making A·bim'e·lech king,[d] and have you shown goodness toward Jer·ub·ba'al and his household, and have you treated him as he deserves? 17 When my father fought for you,[e] he risked his life* to save you from Mid'i·an's hand.[f] 18 But today you have risen up against my father's household and killed his sons, 70 men, on one stone.[g] Then you made A·bim'e·lech, the son of his slave girl,[h] king over the leaders of She'chem just because he is your brother. 19 Yes, if you are acting sincerely and honor-

---

CHAP. 8
a Jg 2:17, 19
 Jg 10:6

b Jg 9:4

c Jg 3:7

d Ps 106:43

e Jg 9:16-18

CHAP. 9
f Jg 8:30, 31

g Jg 8:30

h Jg 8:33
 Jg 9:46

i Jg 6:11
 Jg 8:27

j 2Ki 11:1
 2Ch 21:4

k De 17:14
 1Sa 8:7

Second Col.
a De 11:29
 Jos 8:33
 Joh 4:20

b Jg 8:22

c Jg 9:6

d Jg 9:6

e Jg 7:9

f Jg 8:28

g Jg 9:5

h Jg 8:30, 31

9:1 *Lit., "the family of the house of the father of his mother." 9:2 *Or possibly, "landowners." #Or "your blood relative." 9:4 *Or "temple."

9:9 *Or "fruitfulness." 9:17 *Or "soul."

ably toward Jer·ub·ba′al and his household this day, rejoice over A·bim′e·lech and let him also rejoice over you. 20 But if not, may fire come out of A·bim′e·lech and consume the leaders of She′chem and Beth-mil′lo,[a] and may fire come out of the leaders of She′chem and Beth-mil′lo and consume A·bim′e·lech."[b]

21 Then Jo′tham[c] fled and escaped to Be′er, and he lived there because of his brother A·bim′e·lech.

22 A·bim′e·lech ruled* over Israel for three years. 23 Then God let hostility develop* between A·bim′e·lech and the leaders of She′chem, and they dealt treacherously with A·bim′e·lech. 24 This was so that the violence done to the 70 sons of Jer·ub·ba′al might be avenged, so as to place responsibility for their blood on their brother A·bim′e·lech for killing them[d] and on the leaders of She′chem for helping him to kill his brothers. 25 So the leaders of She′chem set men to ambush him on the mountaintops, and they would rob everyone who passed by them on the road. In time it was reported to A·bim′e·lech.

26 Then Ga′al son of E′bed and his brothers crossed over into She′chem,[e] and the leaders of She′chem put their trust in him. 27 They went out into the field and gathered the grapes of their vineyards, trod them out, and held a festival, after which they went into the house of their god[f] and ate and drank and cursed A·bim′e·lech. 28 Then Ga′al the son of E′bed said: "Who is A·bim′e·lech, and who is She′chem that we should serve him? Is he not the son of Jer·ub·ba′al,[g] and is not Ze′bul his commissioner? Serve the men of Ha′mor, She′chem's father! But

why should we serve him? 29 If only this people were under my command, I would depose A·bim′e·lech." Then he said to A·bim′e·lech: "Increase your army and come out."

30 When Ze′bul the prince of the city heard the words of Ga′al the son of E′bed, his anger blazed. 31 So he secretly* sent messengers to A·bim′e·lech, saying: "Look! Ga′al the son of E′bed and his brothers are now in She′chem, and here they are inciting the city against you. 32 Now come up by night, you and your men, and lie in wait in the field. 33 As soon as the sun rises in the morning, you should get up early and attack the city; and when he and his men come out against you, do whatever you can to defeat him."*

34 So A·bim′e·lech and all the people with him rose up by night, and in four bands they lay in wait against She′chem. 35 When Ga′al the son of E′bed went out and stood at the entrance of the city gate, A·bim′e·lech and the people with him rose up from the ambush. 36 When Ga′al saw the people, he said to Ze′bul: "Look! There are people coming down from the mountaintops." But Ze′bul said to him: "You are seeing the shadows of the mountains as if they were men."

37 Ga′al later said: "Look! People are coming down from the center of the land, and one band is coming by the way of the big tree of Me·on′e·nim." 38 Ze′bul replied to him: "Where now is your boast, 'Who is A·bim′e·lech that we should serve him?'[a] Are these not the people you rejected? Go out now and fight against them." 39 So Ga′al went out at the head of the leaders of She′chem

---

CHAP. 9
a Jg 9:6, 49

b Jg 9:39, 53

c Jg 9:5

d Ge 9:6
Jg 9:5

e Jos 21:20, 21
Jos 24:1

f Jg 8:33

g Jg 6:32

Second Col.
a Jg 9:28, 29

9:22 *Or "played the prince." 9:23 *Lit., "sent a bad spirit."

9:31 *Or "cunningly." 9:33 *Or "do to him what your hand finds possible."

and fought against A·bim'e·lech.
40 A·bim'e·lech pursued him, and Ga'al fled from him, and many fell slain as far as the entrance of the city gate.

41 And A·bim'e·lech continued to dwell in A·ru'mah, and Ze'bul[a] drove Ga'al and his brothers out of She'chem. **42** The next day the people went out into the field, and A·bim'e·lech was told about it. **43** So he took the people and divided them into three bands and lay in wait in the field. When he saw the people going out of the city, he attacked them and struck them down. **44** A·bim'e·lech and the bands with him charged forward and took a position at the entrance of the city gate, while two bands attacked all who were in the field, and they struck them down. **45** A·bim'e·lech fought against the city all that day and captured it. He killed the people in it, and then he pulled the city down[b] and sowed it with salt.

46 When all the leaders of the tower of She'chem heard about this, they immediately went to the vault* of the house# of El·be'rith.[c] **47** As soon as it was reported to A·bim'e·lech that all the leaders of the tower of She'chem had gathered together, **48** A·bim'e·lech and all the men with him went up Mount Zal'mon. A·bim'e·lech took an ax in his hand and cut off a tree branch and lifted it on his shoulder and said to the people with him: "What you saw me do, hurry and do the same!" **49** So all the people also cut off branches and followed A·bim'e·lech. Then they put the branches against the vault and set the vault on fire. So all the people of the tower of She'chem also died, about 1,000 men and women.

50 A·bim'e·lech then went to The'bez; he camped against The'bez and captured it. **51** There was a strong tower in the middle of the city, and all the men and women and all the city leaders fled there. They shut themselves in and climbed onto the roof of the tower. **52** A·bim'e·lech made his way to the tower and attacked it. He approached the entrance of the tower to set it on fire. **53** Then one of the women dropped an upper millstone on A·bim'e·lech's head and crushed his skull.[a] **54** He quickly called the attendant bearing his weapons and said to him: "Draw your sword and put me to death, so that they may not say about me, 'A woman killed him.'" So his attendant ran him through, and he died.

55 When the men of Israel saw that A·bim'e·lech was dead, they all went back home. **56** Thus God repaid A·bim'e·lech for the evil that he had done to his father by killing his 70 brothers.[b] **57** God also made all the evil of the men of She'chem come back on their own heads. So the curse of Jo'tham[c] the son of Jer·ub·ba'al[d] came upon them.

10 After A·bim'e·lech, To'la the son of Pu'ah, the son of Do'do, a man of Is'sa·char, rose up to save Israel.[e] He lived in Sha'mir in the mountainous region of E'phra·im. **2** He judged Israel for 23 years. Then he died and was buried in Sha'mir.

3 After him Ja'ir the Gil'e·ad·ite rose up and judged Israel for 22 years. **4** He had 30 sons who rode on 30 donkeys, and they had 30 cities, which to this day are called Hav'voth-ja'ir;[f] they are in the land of Gil'e·ad. **5** After that Ja'ir died and was buried in Ka'mon.

CHAP. 9
a Jg 9:30

b 1Ki 12:25

c Jg 8:33
Jg 9:4, 27

Second Col.
a 2Sa 11:21

b Ge 9:6
Jg 9:5, 24

c Jg 9:7, 20

d Jg 6:32

CHAP. 10
e Jg 2:16

f De 3:14

9:46 *Or "stronghold." #Or "temple."

6 Again the Israelites did what was bad in the eyes of Jehovah,[a] and they began to serve the Ba′als,[b] the Ash′to·reth images, the gods of A′ram,* the gods of Si′don, the gods of Mo′ab,[c] the gods of the Am′mon·ites,[d] and the gods of the Phi·lis′tines.[e] They abandoned Jehovah and did not serve him. **7** Then Jehovah's anger blazed against Israel, and he sold them into the hands of the Phi·lis′tines and the Am′mon·ites.[f] **8** So they crushed and greatly oppressed the Israelites in that year—for 18 years they oppressed all the Israelites on the side of the Jordan that had been the land of the Am′or·ites in Gil′e·ad. **9** The Am′mon·ites would also cross the Jordan to fight against Judah and Benjamin and the house of E′phra·im; and Israel was greatly distressed. **10** Then the Israelites called to Jehovah for help,[g] saying: "We have sinned against you, for we abandoned our God and served the Ba′als."[h]

11 But Jehovah said to the Israelites: "Did I not save you from Egypt[i] and from the Am′or·ites,[j] the Am′mon·ites, the Phi·lis′tines,[k] **12** the Si·do′ni·ans, Am′a·lek, and Mid′i·an when they oppressed you? When you cried out to me, I saved you out of their hand. **13** But you abandoned me and served other gods.[l] That is why I will not save you again.[m] **14** Go to the gods whom you have chosen and call for help.[n] Let them save you in your time of distress."[o] **15** But the Israelites said to Jehovah: "We have sinned. Do to us whatever is good in your eyes. Only save us, please, this day." **16** And they removed the foreign gods from their midst and served Jehovah,[p] so that he could no longer tolerate* Israel's suffering.[q]

10:6 *Or "Syria." 10:16 *Or "and his soul became impatient because of."

17 In time the Am′mon·ites[a] were called together, and they pitched camp in Gil′e·ad. So the Israelites gathered together and pitched camp in Miz′pah. **18** The people and the princes of Gil′e·ad said to one another: "Who will take the lead in fighting against the Am′mon·ites?[b] Let him become the chief over all the inhabitants of Gil′e·ad."

11 Now Jeph′thah[c] the Gil′e·ad·ite was a mighty warrior; he was the son of a prostitute, and Gil′e·ad was Jeph′thah's father. **2** But Gil′e·ad's wife also bore him sons. When the sons of his wife grew up, they drove Jeph′thah out and said to him: "You will have no inheritance in our father's household, for you are the son of another woman." **3** So Jeph′thah fled from his brothers and settled in the land of Tob. And idle men joined company with Jeph′thah, and they followed him.

4 After a while, the Am′mon·ites fought against Israel.[d] **5** And when the Am′mon·ites fought against Israel, the elders of Gil′e·ad immediately went to bring Jeph′thah back from the land of Tob. **6** They said to Jeph′thah: "Come and serve as our commander, so that we can fight against the Am′mon·ites." **7** But Jeph′thah said to the elders of Gil′e·ad: "Was it not you who hated me so much that you drove me out of my father's house?[e] Why have you come to me now when you are in distress?" **8** At this the elders of Gil′e·ad said to Jeph′thah: "That is why we have returned to you. If you go with us and fight against the Am′mon·ites, you will become our leader over all the inhabitants of Gil′e·ad."[f] **9** So Jeph′thah said to the elders of Gil′e·ad: "If you bring me back to fight against the Am′mon·ites and Jehovah defeats them for me, then I will indeed become your leader!" **10** The elders of Gil′e·ad said to Jeph′thah: "Let Jehovah be the witness* between us if we do not do as you say." **11** So Jeph′thah went with the elders of Gil′e·ad, and the people made him their leader and commander. And Jeph′thah repeated all his words before Jehovah in Miz′pah.[a]

12 Jeph′thah then sent messengers to the king of the Am′mon·ites,[b] saying: "What do you have against me* that you have come to attack my land?" **13** So the king of the Am′mon·ites said to the messengers of Jeph′thah: "It is because Israel took my land when they came up out of Egypt,[c] from the Ar′non[d] to the Jab′bok and as far as the Jordan.[e] Now return it peaceably." **14** But Jeph′thah sent messengers back to the king of the Am′mon·ites **15** to say to him:

"This is what Jeph′thah says: 'Israel did not take the land of the Mo′ab·ites[f] and the land of the Am′mon·ites,[g] **16** for when they came up out of Egypt, Israel walked through the wilderness as far as the Red Sea[h] and came to Ka′desh.[i] **17** Then Israel sent messengers to the king of E′dom,[j] saying: "Please let us pass through your land," but the king of E′dom did not listen. Also to the king of Mo′ab[k] they sent word, but he did not consent. So Israel kept dwelling in Ka′desh.[l] **18** When they walked through the wilderness, they bypassed the land of E′dom[m] and the land of Mo′ab. They traveled east of the land of Mo′ab[n] and camped in the region of the Ar′non; they did not come within the boundary of Mo′ab,[o] for the Ar′non was the boundary of Mo′ab.

11:10 *Lit., "the one who hears." 11:12 *Lit., "What to me and to you?"

19 "'After that Israel sent messengers to Si′hon king of the Am′or·ites, king of Hesh′bon, and Israel said to him: "Please let us pass through your land to our own place."[a] **20** But Si′hon did not trust Israel to cross through his territory, so Si′hon gathered all his people together and encamped in Ja′haz and fought against Israel.[b] **21** At this Jehovah the God of Israel gave Si′hon and all his people into Israel's hand, so that they defeated them and Israel took possession of all the land of the Am′or·ites, the inhabitants of that land.[c] **22** Thus they took possession of all the territory of the Am′or·ites from the Ar′non to the Jab′bok and from the wilderness to the Jordan.[d]

23 "'It was Jehovah the God of Israel who drove out the Am′or·ites from before his people Israel,[e] and now would you drive them out? **24** Do you not possess whatever your god Che′mosh[f] gives you to possess? So everyone whom Jehovah our God has driven out from before us is the one we will drive out.[g] **25** Now are you any better than Ba′lak[h] the son of Zip′por, the king of Mo′ab? Did he ever contend with Israel, or did he ever fight against them? **26** While Israel was dwelling in Hesh′bon and its dependent* towns[i] and in A·ro′er and its dependent towns and in all the cities that are by the banks of the Ar′non for 300 years, why did you never try to take them back during that time?[j] **27** I have not sinned against you, but you are wrong to attack me. Let Jehovah the Judge[k] be judge today between the people of Israel and the people of Am′mon.'"

28 But the king of the Am′mon·ites would not listen to the

11:26 *Or "surrounding."

CHAP. 11

a Jg 10:17
   Jg 11:34

b Ge 19:36, 38

c Nu 21:23, 24

d Nu 21:26

e De 3:16, 17

f Ge 19:36, 37
   De 2:9

g De 2:19, 37

h Nu 14:25

i Nu 20:1

j Ge 36:1
   Nu 20:14
   De 2:4

k Ge 19:36, 37

l Nu 20:22

m Nu 21:4

n Nu 21:11

o Nu 21:13

Second Col.

a Nu 21:21-26
   De 2:26, 27

b De 2:32, 33

c Jos 13:15, 21

d De 2:36

e Ne 9:22

f 1Ki 11:7

g Ex 23:28
   Ex 34:11
   Nu 33:53
   De 9:5
   De 18:12

h Nu 22:2, 3
   Jos 24:9

i Nu 21:25

j Nu 21:26

k Isa 33:22

message that Jeph'thah sent to him.

29 Jehovah's spirit came upon Jeph'thah,[a] and he passed through Gil'e·ad and Ma·nas'seh to go to Miz'peh of Gil'e·ad,[b] and from Miz'peh of Gil'e·ad he continued on to the Am'mon·ites.

30 Then Jeph'thah made a vow[c] to Jehovah and said: "If you give the Am'mon·ites into my hand, **31** then whoever comes out of the door of my house to meet me when I return in peace from the Am'mon·ites will become Jehovah's,[d] and I will offer that one up as a burnt offering."[e]

32 So Jeph'thah went to fight against the Am'mon·ites, and Jehovah gave them into his hand. **33** He struck them down with a very great slaughter from A·ro'er all the way to Min'nith—20 cities—and as far as A'bel·ker'a·mim. Thus the Am'mon·ites were subdued before the Israelites.

34 Finally Jeph'thah came to his home in Miz'pah,[f] and look! his daughter was coming out to meet him, playing the tambourine and dancing! Now she was his one and only child. Besides her, he had neither son nor daughter. **35** When he saw her, he ripped his garments and said: "Oh no, my daughter! You have broken my heart,* for you have become the one I have banished. Now I have opened my mouth to Jehovah, and I am unable to turn back."[g]

36 But she said to him: "My father, if you have opened your mouth to Jehovah, do to me as you have promised,[h] since Jehovah has executed vengeance for you upon your enemies, the Am'mon·ites." **37** She then said to her father: "Let this be done for me: Let me be alone for two months, and let me go away into the mountains, and let me weep

over my virginity with my female companions."*

38 At this he said: "Go!" So he sent her away for two months, and she went to the mountains with her companions to weep over her virginity. **39** At the end of two months, she returned to her father, after which he carried out the vow he had made regarding her.[a] She never had relations with a man. And it became a custom* in Israel: **40** From year to year, the young women of Israel would go to give commendation to the daughter of Jeph'thah the Gil'e·ad·ite four days in the year.

12 Then the men of E'phra·im were summoned, and they crossed over to Za'phon* and said to Jeph'thah: "Why did you not call us to go with you when you crossed over to fight against the Am'mon·ites?[b] We will burn your house down with you in it." **2** But Jeph'thah said to them: "Along with my people, I was engaged in a great conflict with the Am'mon·ites. I did call to you for help, but you did not save me from their hand. **3** When I saw that you would not save me, then I decided to risk my life* and go against the Am'mon·ites,[c] and Jehovah handed them over to me. So why have you come today to fight against me?"

4 Jeph'thah then gathered all the men of Gil'e·ad,[d] and they fought E'phra·im; the men of Gil'e·ad defeated E'phra·im, who had said: "You are only fugitives from E'phra·im, you Gil'e·ad·ites in E'phra·im and Ma·nas'seh." **5** Gil'e·ad captured the fords of the Jordan[e] ahead of E'phra·im; and when the men of E'phra·im

---

CHAP. 11

a Jg 3:9, 10
Zec 4:6

b Jg 10:17

c De 23:21

d 1Sa 1:11

e 1Sa 1:24

f Jg 10:17
Jg 11:11

g Nu 30:2
Ps 15:4
Ec 5:4

h Jg 11:30, 31

Second Col.
a 1Sa 1:22, 24

CHAP. 12

b Jg 8:1

c Jg 11:29

d De 3:12, 13

e Jg 3:28
Jg 7:24

11:35 *Lit., "You brought me very low."

11:37 *Or "weep with my friends because I will never marry." **11:39** *Or "regulation." **12:1** *Or possibly, "crossed over northward." **12:3** *Or "I put my soul in my hand."

were trying to escape, they would say, "Let me cross over"; then the men of Gil'e·ad would ask each one, "Are you an E'phra·im·ite?" When he would reply, "No!" **6** they would say to him, "Please say Shib'bo·leth." But he would say, "Sib'bo·leth," as he was unable to say the word correctly. Then they would seize him and slay him at the fords of the Jordan. So 42,000 E'phra·im·ites fell at that time.

7 Jeph'thah judged Israel for six years, after which Jeph'thah the Gil'e·ad·ite died and was buried in his city in Gil'e·ad.

8 Ib'zan from Beth'le·hem judged Israel after him.[a] **9** He had 30 sons and 30 daughters. He sent his daughters to marry men outside his clan, and he brought in 30 women to marry his sons. He judged Israel for seven years. **10** Then Ib'zan died and was buried in Beth'le·hem.

11 After him E'lon the Ze·bu'lu·nite judged Israel; he judged Israel for ten years. **12** Then E'lon the Ze·bu'lu·nite died and was buried in Ai'ja·lon in the land of Zeb'u·lun.

13 After him Ab'don the son of Hil'lel the Pir'a·thon·ite judged Israel. **14** He had 40 sons and 30 grandsons who rode on 70 donkeys. He judged Israel for eight years. **15** Then Ab'don the son of Hil'lel the Pir'a·thon·ite died and was buried in Pir'a·thon in the land of E'phra·im in the mountain of the A·mal'ek·ite.[b]

13 Again the Israelites did what was bad in Jehovah's eyes,[c] and Jehovah gave them into the hand of the Phi·lis'tines[d] for 40 years.

2 Meanwhile, there was a man of Zo'rah[e] of the family of the Dan'ites,[f] whose name was Ma·no'ah.[g] His wife was barren and childless.[h] **3** In time Jehovah's

---

angel appeared to the woman and said to her: "Look, you are barren and childless. But you will conceive and give birth to a son.[a] **4** Now be careful not to drink wine or anything alcoholic,[b] and do not eat anything unclean.[c] **5** Look! You will conceive and give birth to a son, and no razor should touch his head,[d] because the child will be a Naz'i·rite of God from birth,* and he will take the lead in saving Israel out of the hand of the Phi·lis'tines."[e]

6 Then the woman went and told her husband: "A man of the true God came to me, and his appearance was like an angel of the true God, very awe-inspiring. I did not ask him where he was from, nor did he tell me his name.[f] **7** But he said to me, 'Look! You will conceive and give birth to a son. Now do not drink wine or anything alcoholic, and do not eat anything unclean, because the child will be a Naz'i·rite of God from birth* until the day of his death.'"

8 Ma·no'ah pleaded with Jehovah and said: "Pardon me, Jehovah. Please let the man of the true God whom you just sent come again to instruct us about what we should do with the child who will be born." **9** So the true God listened to Ma·no'ah, and the angel of the true God came again to the woman while she was sitting in the field; her husband Ma·no'ah was not with her. **10** The woman quickly ran and told her husband: "Look! The man who came to me the other day has appeared to me."[g]

11 Then Ma·no'ah got up and went with his wife. He came to the man and said to him: "Are you the man who spoke to my wife?" He said: "I am." **12** Then Ma·no'ah said: "May your words come true! What will be the

---

CHAP. 12
a Jg 2:16

b Ge 36:12
Ex 17:16
Nu 13:29
1Sa 15:2

CHAP. 13
c Jg 2:11, 19
Jg 10:6

d Jos 13:1-3
Jg 10:7

e Jos 15:20, 33
Jos 19:41, 48

f Ge 49:16

g Jg 16:31

h Ge 30:22, 23

Second Col.
a Ge 18:10
1Sa 1:20
Lu 1:11, 13

b Nu 6:2, 3
Lu 1:15

c Le 11:26, 27

d Nu 6:2, 5

e Jg 2:16
Jg 13:1
Ne 9:27

f Jg 13:17, 18

g Jg 13:3

13:5, 7 *Lit., "from the womb."

child's manner of life, and what will be his work?"[a] **13** So Jehovah's angel said to Ma·no'ah: "Your wife should keep herself from everything that I mentioned to her.[b] **14** She should not eat anything that the grapevine produces, she should not drink wine or anything alcoholic,[c] and she should not eat anything unclean.[d] Everything that I commanded her, let her observe."

15 Ma·no'ah now said to Jehovah's angel: "Please stay, and let us prepare a young goat for you."[e] **16** But Jehovah's angel said to Ma·no'ah: "If I stay, I will not eat your food; but if you wish to present a burnt offering to Jehovah, you may offer it up." Ma·no'ah did not know that he was Jehovah's angel. **17** Then Ma·no'ah said to Jehovah's angel: "What is your name,[f] so that we may honor you when your word comes true?" **18** However, Jehovah's angel said to him: "Why are you asking about my name, seeing that it is a wonderful one?"

19 Then Ma·no'ah took the young goat and the grain offering and offered them on the rock to Jehovah. And He was doing something amazing while Ma·no'ah and his wife were looking on. **20** As the flame ascended from the altar heavenward, Jehovah's angel ascended in the flame from the altar while Ma·no'ah and his wife were looking on. At once they fell with their faces to the ground. **21** Jehovah's angel did not appear again to Ma·no'ah and his wife. Then Ma·no'ah realized that he was Jehovah's angel.[g] **22** Ma·no'ah then said to his wife: "We are sure to die, because it is God whom we have seen."[h] **23** But his wife said to him: "If Jehovah wanted to put us to death, he would not have accepted a burnt offering[i] and a

grain offering from our hand, he would not have shown us all these things, and he would not have told us any of these things."

24 The woman later gave birth to a son and named him Samson;[a] and as the boy grew, Jehovah continued to bless him. **25** In time Jehovah's spirit started to impel him[b] in Ma'ha·neh-dan,[c] between Zo'rah and Esh'ta·ol.[d]

14 Then Samson went down to Tim'nah, and in Tim'nah he saw a Phi·lis'tine woman.* **2** So he went up and told his father and mother: "In Tim'nah a Phi·lis'tine woman caught my eye, and I want you to get her for me as a wife." **3** But his father and mother said to him: "Can you not find a woman among your relatives and among all our people?[e] Must you go and take a wife from among the uncircumcised Phi·lis'tines?" But Samson said to his father: "Get her for me, because she is the right one for me."* **4** His father and mother did not realize that this was from Jehovah, for He was looking for an opportunity against the Phi·lis'tines, as the Phi·lis'tines were ruling over Israel at that time.[f]

5 So Samson went down with his father and mother to Tim'nah. When he reached the vineyards of Tim'nah, why look! a lion* came roaring at him. **6** Then Jehovah's spirit empowered him,[g] and he tore it in two, just as someone tears a young goat in two with his bare hands. But he did not tell his father or mother what he had done. **7** Then he went down and spoke to the woman, and she was still the right one in Samson's eyes.[h]

CHAP. 13
a Jg 13:8
b Jg 13:4
c Nu 6:2, 3
d Le 11:26, 27
e Ge 18:5, 7
  Jg 6:18, 19
  Heb 13:2
f Ge 32:29
  Jg 13:6
g Jg 6:22, 23
h Ex 33:20
  Joh 1:18
i Jg 13:16

Second Col.
a Heb 11:32
b Jg 3:9, 10
  Jg 6:34
  Jg 11:29
  1Sa 11:6
c Jg 18:11, 12
d Jos 15:20, 33

CHAP. 14
e De 7:3
f Jg 13:1
g Jg 13:24, 25
h Jg 14:2

14:1 *Lit., "a woman of the daughters of the Philistines." **14:3** *Lit., "she is right in my eyes." **14:5** *Or "a maned young lion."

8 Later when he was going back to take her home,[a] he turned aside to look at the dead body of the lion, and there in the lion's carcass was a swarm of bees and honey. **9** So he scraped the honey out into his hands and ate it as he walked along. When he rejoined his father and mother, he gave them some to eat. But he did not tell them that he had scraped the honey out of the carcass of a lion.

10 His father went down to the woman, and Samson held a banquet there, for that was what the young men used to do. **11** When they saw him, they brought 30 groomsmen to accompany him. **12** Then Samson said to them: "Please let me tell you a riddle. If during the seven days of the banquet you solve it and tell me the answer, I will have to give you 30 linen garments and 30 outfits of clothing. **13** But if you are unable to tell me the answer, you must give me 30 linen garments and 30 outfits of clothing." They said: "Tell us your riddle; we want to hear it." **14** So he said to them:

"Out of the eater came something to eat,
And out of the strong came something sweet."[b]

They were unable to solve the riddle for three days. **15** On the fourth day, they said to Samson's wife: "Trick your husband[c] so that he will tell us the answer to the riddle. Otherwise, we will burn you and your father's house with fire. Did you invite us here to take our possessions?" **16** So Samson's wife wept over him and said: "You must hate me; you do not love me.[d] You told a riddle to my people, but you have not told the answer to me." At this he said to her: "Why, I have not told it even to my own father and mother!

Should I tell it to you?" **17** But she kept weeping over him the rest of the seven-day banquet. He finally told her on the seventh day, because she had pressured him. Then she told her people the answer to the riddle.[a] **18** So on the seventh day before the sun set,[*] the men of the city said to him:

"What is sweeter than honey,
And what is stronger than a lion?"[b]

He replied to them:

"If you had not plowed with my young cow,[c]
You would not have solved my riddle."

19 Then Jehovah's spirit empowered him,[d] and he went down to Ash′ke·lon[e] and struck down 30 of their men and took their clothing and gave the outfits to those who had answered the riddle.[f] He was furious as he went back up to his father's house.

20 Samson's wife[g] was then given to one of his groomsmen who had accompanied him.[h]

15 After a while, in the days of the wheat harvest, Samson went to visit his wife, bringing a young goat. He said: "I wish to go in to my wife in the bedroom."[*] But her father did not allow him to go in. **2** Her father said: "I thought, 'You must surely hate her.'[i] So I gave her to your groomsman.[j] Is not her younger sister more attractive than she is? Please, take her instead." **3** However, Samson said to them: "This time I cannot be blamed by the Phi·lis′tines for harming them."

4 So Samson went and caught 300 foxes. Then he took torches, turned the foxes tail to

---

CHAP. 14
a Ge 24:67
  Mt 1:24

b Jg 14:8, 9

c Jg 16:5

d Jg 16:15

Second Col.
a Jg 16:16, 18

b Jg 14:14

c Jg 14:15

d Jg 13:24, 25
  Jg 14:6
  Jg 15:14

e Jos 13:2, 3
  Jg 1:18

f Jg 14:12

g Jg 14:2

h Jg 14:11
  Jg 15:1, 2

CHAP. 15
i Jg 14:17

j Jg 14:11, 20

14:18 *Or possibly, "before he went into the interior room." 15:1 *Or "the interior room."

tail, and put one torch between each pair of tails. **5** Then he set fire to the torches and sent the foxes out into the fields of standing grain of the Phi·lis'-tines. He set on fire everything from sheaf to standing grain, as well as the vineyards and the olive groves.

6 The Phi·lis'tines asked: "Who did this?" They were told: "It was Samson, the son-in-law of the Tim'nite, because he took his wife and gave her to his groomsman."[a] At that the Phi·lis'tines went up and burned her and her father with fire.[b] **7** Then Samson said to them: "If this is how you act, I will not quit until I take revenge on you."[c] **8** Then he struck them down one after the other* with a great slaughter, after which he went down and stayed in a cave* of the crag E'tam.

9 Later the Phi·lis'tines came up and camped in Judah and were tramping about in Le'hi.[d] **10** Then the men of Judah said: "Why have you come up against us?" to which they answered: "We have come up to capture* Samson, to do to him just as he did to us." **11** So 3,000 men of Judah went down to the cave* of the crag E'tam and said to Samson: "Do you not know that the Phi·lis'tines are ruling over us?[e] So why have you done this to us?" He said to them: "As they did to me, so I did to them." **12** But they said to him: "We have come to capture* you and to hand you over to the Phi·lis'tines." Then Samson said: "Swear to me that you yourselves will not assault me." **13** They said to him: "No, we will only tie you and hand you over to them, but we will not put you to death."

15:8 *Lit., "struck them leg on thigh." 15:8, 11 *Or "cleft." 15:10, 12 *Or "tie."

CHAP. 15

a Jg 14:11, 20

b Jg 14:15

c Jg 14:4

d 2Sa 23:11, 12

e Jg 13:1

Second Col.

a Jg 13:24, 25
Jg 14:5, 6

b Jg 16:9, 12

c Jg 3:31

d Jg 16:30

e Jg 15:9

f Ex 17:6

g Ge 49:16
Jg 2:16
Jg 13:1, 5
Jg 16:31
Heb 11:32

So they bound him with two new ropes and brought him up from the crag. **14** When he came to Le'hi, the Phi·lis'tines shouted triumphantly at meeting him. Then Jehovah's spirit empowered him,[a] and the ropes on his arms became like linen threads that were scorched with fire, and his fetters melted off his hands.[b] **15** He now found a fresh jawbone of a male donkey; he reached out and grabbed it and struck down 1,000 men with it.[c] **16** Then Samson said:

"With the jawbone of a donkey—one heap, two heaps!
With the jawbone of a donkey I struck down 1,000 men."[d]

17 When he finished speaking, he threw the jawbone away and called that place Ra'math-le'hi.*[e] **18** Then he became very thirsty, and he called on Jehovah and said: "It was you who gave this great salvation into the hand of your servant. But now am I to die of thirst and fall into the hand of the uncircumcised?" **19** So God split open a hollow that was in Le'hi, and water flowed from it.[f] When he drank, his spirit* returned and he revived. That is why he named the place En-hak·kor'e,* which is in Le'hi to this day.

20 And he judged Israel in the days of the Phi·lis'tines for 20 years.[g]

16 One time Samson went to Gaz'a and saw a prostitute there, and he went in to her. **2** The Gaz'ites were told: "Samson has come here." So they surrounded him and lay in ambush for him all night long in the city gate. They stayed quiet the whole night, saying

---

15:17 *Meaning "Lofty Place of the Jawbone." 15:19 *Or "strength." *Meaning "Spring of the One Calling."

to themselves: "When daylight comes, we will kill him."

3 However, Samson kept lying there until midnight. Then he got up at midnight and grabbed the doors of the city gate and the two side posts and pulled them out along with the bar. He put them on his shoulders and carried them up to the top of the mountain that faces Heb'ron.

4 After that he fell in love with a woman in the Valley* of So'rek whose name was De·li'·lah.[a] **5** So the lords of the Phi·lis'tines approached her and said: "Trick* him[b] and find out what gives him such great strength and how we can overpower him and tie him and subdue him. For this we will each give you 1,100 silver pieces."

6 De·li'lah later said to Samson: "Please tell me where your great power comes from and what can be used to tie you and subdue you." **7** Samson said to her: "If they tie me with seven fresh bowstrings* that have not been dried out, I will grow as weak as an ordinary man." **8** So the lords of the Phi·lis'tines brought up to her seven fresh bowstrings that had not been dried out, and she tied him with them. **9** Now they set an ambush in the inner room, and she called out to him: "The Phi·lis'tines are upon you, Samson!" At that he tore apart the bowstrings, just as easily as a thread of flax* comes apart when it touches fire.[c] The secret of his power did not become known.

10 Then De·li'lah said to Samson: "Look! You have fooled me* and told me lies. Now tell me, please, what can be used to tie you." **11** So he said to her: "If they tie me up with new ropes

that have not been used for work, I will grow as weak as an ordinary man." **12** So De·li'lah took new ropes and tied him with them and called out: "The Phi·lis'tines are upon you, Samson!" (All the while the ambush was set in the inner room.) At that he tore them off his arms like threads.[a]

13 After that De·li'lah said to Samson: "Up until now you have fooled me and told me lies.[b] Tell me what can be used to tie you." Then he said to her: "If you weave the seven braids of my head with the warp thread." **14** So she fixed them with a pin and called out to him: "The Phi·lis'tines are upon you, Samson!" So he woke up from his sleep and pulled out the loom pin and the warp thread.

15 She now said to him: "How can you say, 'I love you,'[c] when your heart is not with me? These three times you have fooled me and have not told me the source of your great power."[d] **16** Because day after day she kept nagging him and pressuring him, he* was weary to the point of dying.[e] **17** So he finally opened his heart to her, saying: "A razor has never touched my head, because I am a Naz'i·rite of God from birth.*[f] If I am shaved, my power will leave me and I will grow weak and become like all other men."

18 When De·li'lah saw that he had opened his heart to her, she immediately summoned the Phi·lis'tine lords,[g] saying: "Come up this time, for he has opened his heart to me." So the Phi·lis'tine lords came up to her, bringing the money with them. **19** She made him fall asleep on her knees; then she called the man and had him shave off the seven braids of his head. After that

---

CHAP. 16
a Jg 16:18

b Jg 14:15

c Jg 15:14

Second Col.
a Jg 16:9

b Jg 16:7, 11

c Jg 14:16

d Jg 16:7
Jg 16:11
Jg 16:13

e Jg 14:17

f Nu 6:5
Jg 13:5, 7

g Jg 16:5

16:4 *Or "Wadi." **16:5** *Or "Persuade." **16:7** *Or "sinews." **16:9** *Or "tow." **16:10** *Or "trifled with me."

16:16 *Or "his soul." **16:17** *Lit., "from my mother's womb."

she began to have control over him, for his power was leaving him. **20** Now she called out: "The Phi·lis'tines are upon you, Samson!" He woke up from his sleep and said: "I will go out as at other times[a] and shake myself free." But he did not know that Jehovah had left him. **21** So the Phi·lis'tines seized him and bored his eyes out. Then they brought him down to Gaz'a and bound him with two copper fetters, and he became a grinder of grain in the prison. **22** But the hair of his head started to grow back again after he had been shaved.[b]

23 The Phi·lis'tine lords gathered together to offer a great sacrifice to Da'gon[c] their god and to celebrate, for they were saying: "Our god has given Samson our enemy into our hand!" **24** When the people saw him, they praised their god and said: "Our god has given into our hand our enemy, the one who devastated our land[d] and killed so many of us."[e]

25 Because their heart was cheerful, they said: "Call Samson to provide us some amusement." So they called Samson out of the prison to entertain them; they made him stand between the pillars. **26** Then Samson said to the boy holding him by the hand: "Let me feel the pillars that support the house, so that I can lean against them." **27** (Incidentally, the house was full of men and women. All the Phi·lis'tine lords were there, and on the roof there were about 3,000 men and women who were looking on while Samson provided amusement.)

28 Samson[f] now called out to Jehovah: "Sovereign Lord Jehovah, remember me, please, and strengthen me,[g] please, just this once, O God, and let me take re-

venge on the Phi·lis'tines for one of my two eyes."[a]

29 Then Samson braced himself against the two middle pillars that supported the house, and he leaned on them with his right hand on one and his left hand on the other. **30** Samson called out: "Let me* die with the Phi·lis'tines!" Then he pushed with all his might, and the house fell on the lords and all the people in it.[b] So he killed more at his death than he had killed during his life.[c]

31 Later his brothers and all his father's family came down to take him back. They brought him up and buried him between Zo'rah[d] and Esh'ta·ol in the tomb of Ma·no'ah[e] his father. He had judged Israel for 20 years.[f]

17 There was a man of the mountainous region of E'phra·im[g] named Mi'cah. **2** He said to his mother: "The 1,100 silver pieces that were taken from you about which you pronounced a curse, which I heard —look! the silver is with me. I was the one who took it." At that his mother said: "May Jehovah bless my son." **3** So he gave the 1,100 pieces of silver back to his mother, but his mother said: "I will without fail sanctify the silver to Jehovah from my hand for my son to use in making a carved image and a metal statue.*[h] Now I give it back to you."

4 After he returned the silver to his mother, his mother took 200 silver pieces and gave them to the silversmith. He made a carved image and a metal statue;* and they were put in Mi'cah's house. **5** This man Mi'cah had a house of gods, and he made an eph'od[i] and teraphim statues*[j] and installed# one of

---

CHAP. 16
a Jg 16:9
  Jg 16:12
  Jg 16:14

b Jg 13:5

c 1Sa 5:4

d Jg 15:4, 5

e Jg 15:7, 8
  Jg 15:15, 16

f Heb 11:32

g Jg 14:5, 6
  Jg 14:19
  Jg 15:14

Second Col.
a Jg 16:21

b Jg 16:27

c Jg 14:19
  Jg 15:7, 8
  Jg 15:15, 16

d Jg 13:2

e Jg 13:8

f Jg 2:16
  Jg 15:20

CHAP. 17
g Jos 17:14, 15

h Ex 20:4
  Le 26:1
  De 27:15

i Ex 28:6
  Jg 8:27

j Ge 31:19

16:30 *Or "my soul." **17:3, 4** *Or "molten statue." **17:5** *Or "household gods; idols." #Lit., "filled the hand of."

his sons to serve as priest for him.[a] **6** In those days, there was no king in Israel.[b] Each one was doing what was right in his own eyes.*[c]

7 Now there was a young man of Beth'le·hem[d] in Judah who was of the family of Judah. He was a Levite[e] who had been living there for a time. **8** The man left the city of Beth'le·hem in Judah to find a place to live. While on his journey, he came to the mountainous region of E'phra·im, to the house of Mi'cah.[f] **9** Then Mi'cah said to him: "Where do you come from?" He replied: "I am a Levite from Beth'le·hem in Judah, and I am on my way to find a place to live." **10** So Mi'cah said to him: "Stay with me and serve as a father* and a priest for me. I will give you ten silver pieces a year and a set of garments and your food." So the Levite went in. **11** Thus the Levite agreed to stay with the man, and the young man became like one of his sons. **12** Furthermore, Mi'cah installed* the Levite to serve as a priest for him,[g] and he lived in the house of Mi'cah. **13** Then Mi'cah said: "Now I know that Jehovah will be good to me, for the Levite has become my priest."

18 In those days there was no king in Israel.[h] And in those days the tribe of the Dan'ites[i] was looking for an inheritance to dwell in, because until then they had not received an inheritance among the tribes of Israel.[j]

2 The Dan'ites sent five men from among their family, capable men from Zo'rah and Esh'ta·ol,[k] to spy out the land and to explore it. They said to them: "Go,

explore the land." When they came to the mountainous region of E'phra·im, to the house of Mi'cah,[a] they spent the night there. **3** While they were near the house of Mi'cah, they recognized the voice* of the young Levite man, so they went over to him and asked: "Who brought you here? What are you doing in this place? What is keeping you here?" **4** He replied to them: "Thus and so Mi'cah did for me, and he hired me to serve as priest for him."[b] **5** Then they said to him: "Please ask God whether our journey will be successful." **6** The priest said to them: "Go in peace. Jehovah is with you on your journey."

7 So the five men went on and came to La'ish.[c] They saw how the people in it were dwelling in self-reliance in the manner of the Si·do'ni·ans. They were quiet and unsuspecting,[d] and no oppressive conqueror was in the land to disturb them. They were far away from the Si·do'ni·ans, and they had no dealings with anyone else.

8 When they returned to their brothers at Zo'rah and Esh'ta·ol,[e] their brothers said to them: "How did it go?" **9** They replied: "Let us go up against them, for we have seen that the land is very good. Why are you hesitant? Do not delay to go in to take possession of the land. **10** When you arrive, you will find an unsuspecting people,[f] and the land is spacious. God has given it into your hand, a place where there is no lack of anything on the earth."[g]

11 Then 600 men armed for battle from the family of the Dan'ites departed from Zo'rah and Esh'ta·ol.[h] **12** They went up and camped at Kir'i·ath-je'a·rim[i] in Judah. That is why

---

CHAP. 17
a Nu 3:10
De 12:11, 13
2Ch 13:8, 9

b 1Sa 8:4, 5

c Jg 21:25

d Mic 5:2

e Nu 3:45
Jos 14:3
Jos 18:7

f Jg 17:1, 5

g Nu 3:10
Jg 17:5

CHAP. 18
h Jg 8:23
1Sa 8:4, 5

i Jos 19:40

j Jos 19:47, 48
Jg 1:34

k Jos 19:41, 48

Second Col.
a Jg 17:1, 5

b Jg 17:9, 10

c Jos 19:47, 48
Jg 18:29

d Jg 18:27

e Jos 15:20, 33
Jg 18:2

f Jg 18:7, 27

g Ex 3:8
De 8:7-9

h Jg 18:2

i 1Sa 7:1

17:6 *Or "what he thought was right."
17:10 *Or "an adviser." 17:12 *Lit., "filled the hand of."
18:3 *Or "accent."

that place, which is west of Kir'i·ath-je'a·rim, is called Ma'ha·neh-dan*ª to this day. 13 They went from there to the mountainous region of E'phra·im and came to the house of Mi'cah.ᵇ

14 Then the five men who had gone to spy out the land of La'ish ᶜ said to their brothers: "Did you know that there are in these houses an eph'od, teraphim statues,* a carved image, and a metal statue?"ᵈ Think about what you should do." 15 So they stopped there and came to the house of the young Levite manᵉ at the house of Mi'cah and asked how he was. 16 All the while the 600 men of Dan,ᶠ armed for battle, stood at the entrance of the gate. 17 The five men who had gone to spy out the landᵍ went inside to take the carved image, the eph'od,ʰ the teraphim statues,*ⁱ and the metal image.*ʲ (The priestᵏ was standing at the entrance of the gate with the 600 men armed for battle.) 18 They went into the house of Mi'cah and took the carved image, the eph'od, the teraphim statues,* and the metal image." The priest said to them: "What are you doing?" 19 But they said to him: "Be quiet. Put your hand over your mouth, and come with us to be a father* and a priest for us. Which is better—for you to be a priest to the house of one manˡ or to become a priest to a tribe and family in Israel?"ᵐ 20 So the priest was satisfied, and he took the eph'od, the teraphim statues,* and the carved imageⁿ and went off with the people.

21 Then they turned to go on their way, putting the children, the livestock, and the valuable

things ahead of them. 22 They had gone some distance away from the house of Mi'cah when the men who lived in the houses near the house of Mi'cah gathered together and caught up with the Dan'ites. 23 When they cried out to the Dan'ites, they turned to face them and said to Mi'cah: "What is the matter? Why have you been gathered together?" 24 So he said: "You have taken my gods that I made, and you have gone off with the priest too. What do I have left? How, then, can you ask me, 'What is the matter with you?'" 25 The Dan'ites replied: "Do not raise your voice against us; otherwise, angry men* may assault you, and that would cost you your life" and the livesᐃ of your household." 26 So the Dan'ites went on their way; and Mi'cah, seeing that they were stronger than he was, turned and went back to his house.

27 After they took what Mi'cah had made, as well as his priest, they went to La'ish,ª to a people quiet and unsuspecting.ᵇ They struck them down with the sword and burned the city with fire. 28 There was no one to rescue it, for it was far from Si'don and they had no dealings with anyone else and it was in the valley plain* that belonged to Beth-re'hob.ᶜ Then they rebuilt the city and settled in it. 29 Furthermore, they named the city Danᵈ after the name of their father, Dan, who was born to Israel.ᵉ But La'ish was the city's former name.ᶠ 30 After that the Dan'ites set up the carved imageᵍ for themselves, and Jon'a·thanʰ the son of Ger'shom,ⁱ the son of Moses, and his sons became priests to the tribe of the Dan'ites until the day that

---

CHAP. 18
a Jg 13:24, 25

b Jg 17:1, 5

c Jg 18:2
  Jg 18:29

d De 27:15
  Jg 17:4, 5

e Jg 17:7, 12
  Jg 18:30

f Jg 18:11

g Jg 18:2

h Ex 28:6
  Jg 8:27

i Ge 31:19

j Le 19:4
  De 27:15
  Jg 17:3-5

k Jg 17:12

l Jg 17:12

m Jg 18:30

n Jg 17:4, 5

Second Col.
a Jos 19:47, 48
  Jg 18:29

b Jg 18:7, 10

c Nu 13:17, 21

d Jos 19:47, 48
  Jg 20:1
  1Ki 4:25
  1Ki 12:28, 29

e Ge 30:6
  Ge 32:28

f Jg 18:7

g Jg 17:1, 4
  Jg 18:18

h Jg 17:12

i Ex 2:21, 22

18:12 *Meaning "Camp of Dan." 18:14, 17, 18, 20 *Or "household gods; idols." 18:14, 17, 18 "Or "molten statue." 18:19 *Or "an adviser."

18:25 *Or "men bitter of soul." "Or "soul." ᐃOr "souls." 18:28 *Or "low plain."

the inhabitants of the land went into exile. **31** And they set up the carved image that Mi′cah had made, and it remained there all the days that the house of the true God was in Shi′loh.[a]

19 In those days, when there was no king in Israel,[b] a Levite who was then living in a remote part of the mountainous region of E′phra·im[c] took a concubine from Beth′le·hem[d] in Judah as his wife. **2** But his concubine was unfaithful to him, and she left him to go to her father's house at Beth′le·hem in Judah. She remained there for four months. **3** Then her husband went after her to persuade her to come back; he had his male attendant and a couple of donkeys with him. So she brought him into her father's house. When her father saw him, he was glad to meet him. **4** So his father-in-law, the young woman's father, convinced him to stay with him three days; and they would eat and drink, and he would spend the night there.

5 On the fourth day, when they got up early in the morning to go, the father of the young woman said to his son-in-law: "Eat something to give you strength,* and then you may go." **6** So they sat down, and they both ate and drank together; after that the father of the young woman said to the man: "Please, stay overnight and enjoy yourself."* **7** When the man rose to go, his father-in-law kept begging him, so he stayed overnight again.

8 When he got up early in the morning on the fifth day to go, the father of the young woman said: "Please, eat something to give you strength." And they lingered until it was late in the

day, and they both kept eating. **9** When the man rose to go with his concubine and his attendant, his father-in-law, the young woman's father, said to him: "Look, now! It is almost evening. Please, stay overnight. Here the day is coming to an end. Stay here overnight and enjoy yourself. Tomorrow you can get up early for your journey and go to your home."* **10** However, the man did not want to stay another night, so he got up and traveled as far as Je′bus, that is, Jerusalem.[a] He had with him the two saddled donkeys, his concubine, and his attendant.

11 When they were close to Je′bus, the daylight was nearly gone. So the attendant said to his master: "Should we stop at this city of the Jeb′u·sites and stay overnight here?" **12** But his master said to him: "We should not stop at a city of foreigners who are not Israelites. We will go on as far as Gib′e·ah."[b] **13** Then he said to his attendant: "Come and let us try to reach one of those places; we will stay overnight either in Gib′e·ah or in Ra′mah."[c] **14** So they went on their way, and the sun began to set when they were near Gib′e·ah, which belongs to Benjamin.

15 So they stopped there and went in to stay overnight in Gib′e·ah. Once inside, they sat down in the public square of the city, but nobody took them into his house to stay overnight.[d] **16** Eventually that evening, an old man came in from his work in the field. He was from the mountainous region of E′phra·im,[e] and he was living for a time in Gib′e·ah; but the residents of the city were Ben′ja·min·ites.[f] **17** When he looked up and saw the traveler in the public square of the city, the old

---

CHAP. 18
a Ex 40:2
Jos 18:1
1Sa 3:3

CHAP. 19
b 1Sa 8:4, 5

c Jos 17:14, 15

d Ge 35:19
Mic 5:2

Second Col.
a Jos 15:8, 63
Jos 18:28
Jg 1:8

b Jos 18:28

c Jos 18:21, 25

d Ge 19:2

e Jg 19:1

f Jos 18:21, 28

19:5, 8 *Or "to sustain your heart."
19:6 *Or "make your heart feel good."
19:9 *Lit., "tent."

man said: "Where are you going, and where do you come from?" **18** He replied: "We are traveling from Beth'le·hem in Judah to a remote area of the mountainous region of E'phra·im, where I am from. I went to Beth'le·hem in Judah,[a] and I am going to the house of Jehovah,* but nobody is taking me into his house. **19** We have enough straw and fodder for our donkeys,[b] and bread[c] and wine for me, the woman, and our attendant. There is nothing lacking." **20** However, the old man said: "May you have peace! Let me take care of anything you need. Just do not stay overnight in the public square." **21** So he brought him into his house and gave feed* to the donkeys. Then they washed their feet and ate and drank.

22 While they were enjoying themselves, some worthless men of the city surrounded the house and were pounding on the door, and they kept saying to the old man who owned the house: "Bring out the man who came into your house, so that we may have sex with him."[d] **23** At that the owner of the house went out and said to them: "No, my brothers, do not act wickedly. Please, this man is a guest in my house. Do not commit this disgraceful act. **24** Here are my virgin daughter and this man's concubine. Let me bring them out, and you can humiliate them if you must.*[e] But you must not commit this disgraceful act toward this man."

25 But the men refused to listen to him, so the man grabbed hold of his concubine[f] and brought her outside to them. They raped her and abused her all night long until the morning. Then they sent her away at the break of dawn. **26** Early in the morning, the woman came and fell down at the entrance of the man's house where her master was and lay there until it was light. **27** When her master got up in the morning and opened the doors of the house to go out to resume his journey, he saw the woman, his concubine, lying at the entrance of the house with her hands on the threshold. **28** So he said to her: "Get up; let us go." But there was no answer. The man then put her on the donkey and set out for his home.

29 When he reached his house, he took the slaughtering knife and took hold of his concubine and cut her up limb by limb into 12 pieces and sent one piece into each territory of Israel. **30** All who saw it said: "Such a thing has never happened or been seen from the day that the Israelites went up out of the land of Egypt down to this day. Consider it,* take counsel,[a] and tell us what to do."

20 Consequently, all the Israelites came out from Dan[b] down to Be'er-she'ba and from the land of Gil'e·ad,[c] and the entire assembly gathered unitedly* before Jehovah at Miz'pah.[d] **2** So the chiefs of the people and all the tribes of Israel took their places in the congregation of God's people—400,000 foot soldiers armed with swords.[e]

3 The Ben'ja·min·ites heard that the men of Israel had gone up to Miz'pah.

Then the men of Israel said: "Tell us, how did this terrible thing happen?"[f] **4** At this the Levite man,[g] the husband of the murdered woman, said in

CHAP. 19
a Jg 19:1, 2

b Ge 24:32

c Ge 18:5
Ge 19:3

d Ge 19:4, 5
Le 20:13
Ro 1:27
1Co 6:9, 10
Jude 7

e Ge 19:6-8

f Jg 19:2

Second Col.
a Jg 20:7

CHAP. 20
b Jos 19:47, 48
Jg 18:29

c Jos 22:9

d 1Sa 7:5
1Sa 10:17
2Ki 25:23

e Jg 20:17
2Sa 24:9

f Jg 19:22

g Jg 19:1, 2

19:18 *Or possibly, "and I serve at the house of Jehovah." 19:21 *Or "gave mixed fodder." 19:24 *Or "abuse them and do what is good in your eyes."

19:30 *Or "Set your hearts on it." 20:1 *Lit., "as one man."

answer: "I came to Gib'e·ah[a] of Benjamin with my concubine to stay overnight. **5** And the inhabitants* of Gib'e·ah rose up against me and surrounded the house by night. They meant to kill me, but they raped my concubine instead, and she died.[b] **6** So I took my concubine's body and cut it up and sent the pieces into every part of Israel's inheritance,[c] because they had committed a shameful and disgraceful act in Israel. **7** Now all you people of Israel, give your advice and counsel[d] here."

8 Then all the people rose up in unison* and said: "Not one of us will go to his tent or return to his house. **9** Now this is what we will do to Gib'e·ah: We will go up against it by lot.[e] **10** We will take 10 men out of 100 from all the tribes of Israel, and 100 out of 1,000 and 1,000 out of 10,000 to collect provisions for the army, so that they may take action against Gib'e·ah of Benjamin, in view of the disgraceful act that they committed in Israel." **11** Thus all the men of Israel were gathered against the city united* as allies.

12 Then the tribes of Israel sent men to all the tribesmen of Benjamin, saying: "What is this terrible thing that has happened among you? **13** Now hand over the worthless men from Gib'e·ah,[f] so that we may put them to death and clear out what is bad from Israel."[g] But the Ben'ja·min·ites refused to listen to their Israelite brothers.

14 Then the Ben'ja·min·ites gathered together out of the cities to Gib'e·ah to go out to battle against the men of Israel. **15** That day the Ben'ja·min·ites mustered from their cities 26,000 men armed with swords, apart

from the 700 chosen men of Gib'e·ah. **16** In this army were 700 chosen men who were left-handed. Every one of these men could sling a stone to within a hairbreadth and would not miss.

17 The men of Israel apart from Benjamin mustered 400,000 men armed with swords,[a] and each one was an experienced warrior. **18** They rose up and went up to Beth'el to inquire of God.[b] Then the people of Israel said: "Who of us should go up in the lead to the battle against the Ben'ja·min·ites?" Jehovah replied: "Judah is to take the lead."

19 After that the Israelites rose up in the morning and camped against Gib'e·ah.

20 The men of Israel now went out to battle against Benjamin; they drew up in battle formation against them at Gib'e·ah. **21** So the Ben'ja·min·ites came out from Gib'e·ah and struck down 22,000 men of Israel on that day. **22** However, the army of the men of Israel showed themselves courageous and again drew up in battle formation in the same place as on the first day. **23** Then the Israelites went up and wept before Jehovah until the evening and inquired of Jehovah: "Should we again go into battle against our brothers, the people of Benjamin?"[c] To this Jehovah said: "Go up against them."

24 So the Israelites drew near to the Ben'ja·min·ites on the second day. **25** In turn Benjamin came out from Gib'e·ah to meet them on the second day and struck down another 18,000 Israelites,[d] all of them armed with swords. **26** At that all the men of Israel went up to Beth'el. They wept and sat there before Jehovah,[e] and they fasted[f] on that day until the evening and offered up burnt offerings[g] and

CHAP. 20
a Jg 19:12, 14

b Jg 19:25, 26

c Jg 19:29

d Jg 19:30

e Jg 20:18
  Pr 16:33

f Jg 19:22, 25

g De 13:5
  De 17:7
  De 22:22
  1Co 5:6, 13

Second Col.
a Jg 20:2

b Ex 28:30
  Nu 27:21
  Jg 20:27

c Jg 20:28

d Jg 20:21

e Jg 20:23

f 2Ch 20:3
  Ezr 8:21

g Le 1:3

communion offerings[a] before Jehovah. **27** After that the men of Israel inquired of Jehovah,[b] for the ark of the covenant of the true God was there in those days. **28** Now Phin′e·has[c] the son of El·e·a′zar, the son of Aaron, was ministering* before it in those days. They asked: "Should we go out yet again to battle against our brothers, the men of Benjamin, or should we stop?"[d] Jehovah replied: "Go up, because tomorrow I will give them into your hand." **29** Then Israel set men in ambush[e] all around Gib′e·ah.

30 The Israelites went up against the Ben′ja·min·ites on the third day, and they drew up in formation against Gib′e·ah the same as at the other times.[f] **31** When the Ben′ja·min·ites went out to meet the army, they were drawn away from the city.[g] Then, as at the other times, they started to attack and kill some of the men on the highways, one of which goes up to Beth′el and the other to Gib′e·ah, leaving about 30 men of Israel dead in the open field.[h] **32** So the Ben′ja·min·ites said: "They are suffering defeat before us the same as before."[i] But the Israelites said: "We will retreat and draw them away from the city onto the highways." **33** So all the men of Israel rose up from their places and drew up in formation at Ba′al-ta′mar while the Israelite ambush charged out of their places in the vicinity of Gib′e·ah. **34** Thus 10,000 chosen men out of all Israel came in front of Gib′e·ah, and the fighting was heavy. But the Ben′ja·min·ites did not know that disaster was near at hand.

35 Jehovah defeated Benjamin[j] before Israel, and on that

day the Israelites struck down 25,100 men in Benjamin, all of them armed with swords.[a]

36 However, the Ben′ja·min·ites imagined that the men of Israel would be defeated when they retreated from Benjamin,[b] but they retreated because they trusted in the ambush that was set against Gib′e·ah.[c] **37** The ambush acted quickly and charged toward Gib′e·ah. Then the ambush spread out and struck down the whole city with the sword.

38 Now the men of Israel had arranged that the men who ambushed the city would make a smoke signal go up from there. **39** When the Israelites turned around in the battle, the men of Benjamin started by attacking and killing about 30 men of Israel,[d] and they said: "They are clearly suffering another defeat before us, just as in the previous battle."[e] **40** But the signal started to go up from the city as a pillar of smoke. When the men of Benjamin turned to look, they saw the whole city going up in flames to the sky. **41** Then the men of Israel made an about-face, and the men of Benjamin were dismayed, for they saw that disaster had overtaken them. **42** So they retreated from the men of Israel toward the wilderness, but the battle followed them; the men coming out of the cities joined in striking them down. **43** They surrounded the Ben′ja·min·ites and pursued them relentlessly. They trampled them down directly in front of Gib′e·ah toward the east. **44** Finally 18,000 men of Benjamin fell, all mighty warriors.[f]

45 The men of Benjamin turned and fled into the wilderness to the crag of Rim′mon,[g]

CHAP. 20
a Le 3:1

b Nu 27:21
  Jg 20:18

c Ex 6:25
  Nu 25:7

d Jg 20:23

e Jos 8:3, 4

f Jg 20:20, 22

g Jg 20:36

h Jg 20:39

i Jg 20:21, 25

j Jg 20:28, 48

Second Col.
a Jg 20:14, 15
  Jg 20:46

b Jg 20:31

c Jg 20:29

d Jg 20:31

e Jg 20:21, 25

f Jg 20:15

g Jg 21:13

20:28 *Lit., "standing."

and the Israelites killed* 5,000 of them on the highways, and they kept pursuing them as far as Gi′dom; so they struck down 2,000 more men. **46** All those of Benjamin who fell on that day amounted to 25,000 men armed with swords,[a] all mighty warriors. **47** But 600 retreated into the wilderness to the crag of Rim′mon, and they stayed on the crag of Rim′mon for four months.

48 And the men of Israel turned back against the Ben′ja·min·ites and struck those of the city with the sword, from men to livestock, all that remained. Also, they set all the cities in their path on fire.

21 Now the men of Israel had sworn this oath in Miz′pah:[b] "Not one of us will give his daughter to a man from Benjamin as a wife."[c] **2** Consequently, the people came to Beth′el[d] and sat there before the true God until evening, crying out and weeping bitterly. **3** And they were saying: "Why, O Jehovah the God of Israel, has this happened in Israel? Why should one tribe be missing today from Israel?" **4** And the next day the people got up early and built an altar there to offer up burnt offerings and communion offerings.[e]

5 Then the people of Israel said: "Who of all the tribes of Israel did not come up to assemble before Jehovah?" for they had taken a great oath that anyone who did not come up to Jehovah at Miz′pah would be put to death without fail. **6** So the people of Israel felt sorrow over what had happened to Benjamin their brother. They said: "Today one tribe has been chopped off from Israel. **7** What should we do to provide wives for those who are left, now that we have sworn by

Jehovah[a] not to give them any of our daughters as wives?"[b]

8 They asked: "Who among the tribes of Israel did not come up to Jehovah at Miz′pah?"[c] It so happened that no one had come from Ja′besh-gil′e·ad into the camp where the congregation was. **9** When the people were counted, they saw that none of the inhabitants of Ja′besh-gil′e·ad were there. **10** So the assembly sent there 12,000 of the mightiest men. They commanded them: "Go and strike down the inhabitants of Ja′besh-gil′e·ad with the sword, even the women and the children.[d] **11** This is what you should do: Every male as well as every woman who has had sexual relations with a male, you should devote to destruction." **12** Among the inhabitants of Ja′besh-gil′e·ad, they found 400 girls who were virgins, who had never had sexual relations with a man. So they brought them to the camp at Shi′loh,[e] which is in the land of Ca′naan.

13 Then all the assembly sent a message to the Ben′ja·min·ites on the crag of Rim′mon[f] and offered them peace. **14** So Benjamin came back at that time. They gave them the women whom they had kept alive from the women of Ja′besh-gil′e·ad,[g] but they did not find enough for them. **15** And the people felt sorrow over what had happened to Benjamin[h] because Jehovah had made a division among the tribes of Israel. **16** The elders of the assembly said: "What should we do to provide wives for the remaining men, since all the women were annihilated out of Benjamin?" **17** They replied: "There should be an inheritance for the survivors of Benjamin, so that a tribe may not be wiped out of Israel. **18** But we are not allowed to give them wives from our daughters, because the peo-

---

CHAP. 20
a Jg 20:15, 35

CHAP. 21
b Jg 20:1

c Jg 21:18

d Jg 20:18, 26

e Le 3:1

Second Col.
a Le 5:4
  Le 19:12
  Mt 5:33

b Jg 21:1, 18

c Jg 20:1

d Jg 21:5

e Jos 18:1

f Jg 20:46, 47

g Jg 21:8, 12

h Jg 21:6

20:45 *Lit., "they made a gleaning of."

ple of Israel have sworn: 'Cursed is the one who gives a wife to Benjamin.'"[a]

19 Then they said: "Look! There is a festival of Jehovah from year to year in Shi'loh,[b] which is north of Beth'el and east of the highway that goes up from Beth'el to She'chem and south of Le·bo'nah." **20** So they commanded the men of Benjamin: "Go and set an ambush in the vineyards. **21** And when you see the young women* of Shi'loh come out to join in their circle dances, each of you should come out from the vineyards and seize a wife from the young women of Shi'loh, and you should return to the land of Benjamin. **22** And should their fathers or their brothers come to make a complaint against us, we

will then tell them, 'Show us favor for their sakes, because we could not provide each one a wife by war[a] and you could not give a wife to them without becoming guilty.'"[b]

23 So the men of Benjamin did just that, and they each carried off a wife from the women who were dancing. After that they went back to their inheritance and rebuilt their cities[c] and settled in them.

24 And the Israelites dispersed from there at that time, each one to his tribe and his family, and they departed from there, each one to his inheritance.

25 In those days there was no king in Israel.[d] Each one was doing what was right in his own eyes.*

21:21 *Lit., "the daughters."

21:25 *Or "what he thought was right."

CHAP. 21
a Le 19:12
  Jg 21:1

b Jos 18:1

Second Col.
a Jg 21:12, 14

b Jg 21:1, 18

c Jg 20:48

d Jg 17:6
  1Sa 8:4, 5

RUTH

OUTLINE OF CONTENTS

---

1 Now in the days when the judges[a] administered justice,* a famine occurred in the land; and a man went from Beth'le·hem[b] in Judah to reside as a

foreigner in the fields* of Mo'ab,[a] he along with his wife and his two sons. **2** The man's name was E·lim'e·lech,* his wife's

---

1:1 *Or "ruled."

1:1 *Or "region." 1:2 *Meaning "My God Is King."

CHAP. 1
a Jg 2:16
b Mic 5:2

Second Col.
a Ge 19:36, 37
  De 2:9
  Jg 3:30

name was Na·o'mi,* and the names of his two sons were Mah'lon# and Chil'i·on.^ They were Eph'rath·ites from Beth'le·hem in Judah. And they came to the fields of Mo'ab and remained there.

3 After some time E·lim'e·lech, Na·o'mi's husband, died, and she was left with her two sons. 4 The men later married Mo'ab·ite women; one was named Or'pah, and the other was named Ruth.ª They remained there for about ten years. 5 Then the two sons, Mah'lon and Chil'i·on, also died, and the woman was left without her two children and her husband. 6 So she started out with her daughters-in-law to return from the fields of Mo'ab, for she had heard in Mo'ab that Jehovah had turned his attention to his people by giving them food.*

7 She left the place where she had been living with both of her daughters-in-law. As they were walking on the road to return to the land of Judah, 8 Na·o'mi said to both of her daughters-in-law: "Go, return, each of you to your mother's home. May Jehovah show loyal love to you,b just as you have shown it to the men who have died and to me. 9 May Jehovah grant* that each of you finds security# in the home of your husband."c Then she kissed them, and they wept loudly. 10 They kept saying to her: "No, but we will go with you to your people." 11 But Na·o'mi said: "Return, my daughters. Why should you go with me? Can I still give birth to sons who could become your husbands?d 12 Return, my daugh-

ters. Go, for I have grown too old to marry. Even if I could hope to find a husband tonight and could also bear sons, 13 would you keep waiting for them until they could grow up? Would you refrain from getting remarried for their sakes? No, my daughters, I feel very bitter for you, because the hand of Jehovah has turned against me."ª

14 Again they wept loudly, after which Or'pah kissed her mother-in-law and departed. But Ruth stuck with her. 15 So Na·o'mi said: "Look! Your widowed sister-in-law has returned to her people and her gods. Return with your sister-in-law."

16 But Ruth said: "Do not plead with me to abandon you, to turn back from accompanying you; for where you go I will go, and where you spend the night, I will spend the night. Your people will be my people, and your God my God.b 17 Where you die I will die, and there I will be buried. May Jehovah do so to me and add to it if anything but death should separate me from you."

18 When Na·o'mi saw that Ruth insisted on going with her, she stopped trying to convince her. 19 And they both continued on their way until they came to Beth'le·hem.c As soon as they arrived in Beth'le·hem, the whole city became stirred up over them, and women were saying: "Is this Na·o'mi?" 20 She would say to the women: "Do not call me Na·o'mi.* Call me Ma'ra,# for the Almighty has made life very bitter for me.d 21 I was full when I went, but Jehovah made me return empty-handed. Why should you call me Na·o'mi, when it is Jehovah who opposed me and the Almighty who caused me calamity?"e

---

CHAP. 1
a Mt 1:5

b Ex 34:6
Ru 2:20

c Ru 3:1

d De 25:5, 6

Second Col.
a Ru 1:20

b Ru 2:11, 12

c Ru 1:1, 2

d Ru 1:13

e Ru 1:3, 5

1:2, 20 *Meaning "My Pleasantness." 1:2 #Possibly from a Hebrew word meaning "grow weak; fall sick." ^Meaning "One Failing; One Coming to an End." 1:6 *Lit., "bread." 1:9 *Or "make a gift." #Lit., "a resting-place." 1:20 #Meaning "Bitter."

22 This is how Na·o'mi returned from the fields of Mo'ab,[a] along with her Mo'ab·ite daughter-in-law Ruth. They came to Beth'le·hem at the beginning of the barley harvest.[b]

2 Now Na·o'mi had a relative on her husband's side who was very wealthy; his name was Bo'az,[c] and he was of the family of E·lim'e·lech.

2 Ruth the Mo'ab·i·tess said to Na·o'mi: "Let me go out, please, to the fields and glean[d] among the ears of grain behind whoever looks on me with favor." So Na·o'mi said to her: "Go, my daughter." **3** At that she went out and began to glean in the field behind the harvesters. By chance she came upon a plot of land belonging to Bo'az,[e] who was of the family of E·lim'e·lech.[f] **4** Just then Bo'az arrived from Beth'le·hem and said to the harvesters: "Jehovah be with you." And they replied: "Jehovah bless you."

5 Bo'az then asked the young man in charge of the harvesters: "To whom does this young woman belong?" **6** The young man in charge of the harvesters answered: "The young woman is a Mo'ab·i·tess[g] who returned with Na·o'mi from the fields of Mo'ab.[h] **7** She asked, 'Please, may I glean[i] and gather among the cut-off ears* of grain left behind by the harvesters?' And she has been on her feet since she came this morning until just now, when she sat in the shelter for a short rest."

8 Then Bo'az said to Ruth: "Listen, my daughter. Do not go away to glean in another field, and do not go anywhere else; stay close by my young women.[j] **9** Keep your eyes on the field that they harvest, and go with them. I have commanded

2:7, 15 * Or possibly, "the sheaves."

the young men not to touch* you. When you are thirsty, go to the water jars and drink from what the young men have drawn."

10 At that she fell facedown and bowed down to the ground and said to him: "How have I found favor in your eyes, and why have you taken notice of me, when I am a foreigner?"[a] **11** Bo'az answered her: "A full report was made to me of all you have done for your mother-in-law after the death of your husband and how you left your father and your mother and the land of your relatives to go to a people whom you had not known before.[b] **12** May Jehovah reward you for what you have done,[c] and may there be a perfect wage* for you from Jehovah the God of Israel, under whose wings you have come to seek refuge."[d] **13** To this she said: "Let me find favor in your eyes, my lord, because you have comforted me and spoken reassuringly to* your servant, although I am not even one of your servants."

14 Bo'az said to her at mealtime: "Come here, eat some of the bread, and dip your piece in the vinegar." So she sat down beside the harvesters. He then handed her some roasted grain, and she ate and was satisfied, and she had something left over. **15** When she got up to glean,[e] Bo'az commanded his young men: "Let her glean even among the cut-off ears* of grain, and do not mistreat her.[f] **16** You should also be sure to pull out some ears of grain from the bundles for her and leave them behind for her to glean, and do not say anything to stop her."

17 So she continued to glean in the field until evening.[g] When

2:9 * Or "disturb." 2:12 * Or "a full reward." 2:13 * Lit., "spoken to the heart of."

Cross references (center column):

CHAP. 1
a Nu 21:13
  Ru 1:1

b Ru 2:23

CHAP. 2
c Ru 2:20
  Ru 4:21, 22
  Mt 1:5
  Lu 3:23, 32

d Le 23:22
  De 24:19

e Ru 2:20

f Ru 1:2

g Ru 1:3, 4

h Ru 1:16, 22

i Le 23:22
  De 24:19

j Ru 2:22

Second Col.
a Ex 23:9
  Le 19:34

b Ru 1:14, 16

c Ru 4:11, 17
  Mt 1:5, 16

d Ps 17:8
  Ps 36:7
  Ps 57:1
  Ps 63:7

e Le 19:9
  Ru 2:2

f Ru 2:9

g Ru 2:7

she beat out what she had gleaned, it came to about an e′phah* of barley. 18 Then she took it and went into the city, and her mother-in-law saw what she had gleaned. Ruth also took out and gave to her the food that was left over[a] after she had eaten her fill.

19 Her mother-in-law then said to her: "Where did you glean today? Where did you work? May the one who took notice of you be blessed."[b] So she told her mother-in-law about whom she had worked with, saying: "The name of the man I worked with today is Bo′az." 20 At that Na·o′mi said to her daughter-in-law: "May he be blessed by Jehovah, who has not failed in his loyal love toward the living and the dead."[c] Na·o′mi continued: "The man is related to us.[d] He is one of our repurchasers."*[e] 21 Then Ruth the Mo′ab·i·tess said: "He also told me, 'Stay close by my young people until they have finished my entire harvest.'"[f] 22 Na·o′mi said to her daughter-in-law Ruth: "It is better, my daughter, for you to go out with his young women than to be harassed in another field."

23 So she stayed close to the young women of Bo′az and gleaned until the barley harvest[g] and the wheat harvest came to an end. And she kept dwelling with her mother-in-law.[h]

3 Na·o′mi, her mother-in-law, now said to her: "My daughter, should I not look for a home* for you,[i] so that it may go well with you? 2 Is not Bo′az our relative? He is the one whose young women you were with. Tonight he is winnowing barley at

the threshing floor. 3 So wash yourself and rub on some perfumed oil; then dress up* and go down to the threshing floor. Do not make your presence known to the man until he has finished eating and drinking. 4 When he lies down, take note of the place where he lies down; then go and uncover his feet and lie down. He will tell you what you should do."

5 At that she replied: "All that you say to me I will do." 6 So she went down to the threshing floor and did all that her mother-in-law had instructed her to do. 7 Meanwhile, Bo′az ate and drank and was feeling good at heart. Then he went to lie down at the end of the grain heap. After that she quietly came and uncovered his feet and lay down. 8 At midnight the man began to shiver, and he leaned forward and saw a woman lying at his feet. 9 He said: "Who are you?" She replied: "I am Ruth, your servant. Spread out your garment* over your servant, for you are a repurchaser."[a] 10 At that he said: "May Jehovah bless you, my daughter. You have shown your loyal love more in this last instance than in the first instance,[b] by not going after the young men, whether poor or rich. 11 And now, my daughter, have no fear. I will do for you everything that you say,[c] for everyone in the city* knows that you are an excellent woman. 12 While it is true that I am a repurchaser,[d] there is a repurchaser more closely related than I am.[e] 13 Stay here tonight, and if he will repurchase you in the morning, fine! Let him repurchase you.[f] But if he does not want to repurchase you, I will then repurchase you myself, as

CHAP. 2
a Ru 2:14

b Ps 41:1

c Ex 34:6
Ru 1:8
Ps 36:7

d Ru 2:1

e Le 25:25
De 25:5, 6
Ru 3:9, 12

f Ru 2:8

g Ru 1:22

h Ru 1:16

CHAP. 3
i Ru 1:9

j Ru 2:1, 20

Second Col.
a Le 25:25
De 25:5, 6
Ru 2:20

b Ru 1:14, 16

c Ru 3:9

d Le 25:25
Ru 2:20

e Ru 4:1

f Ru 4:5

___

2:17 *About 22 L (20 dry qt). See App. B14. 2:20 *Or "one of our relatives with the right to repurchase (redeem)." 3:1 *Lit., "resting-place."

3:3 *Or "put on your outer garments."
3:9 *Or "the skirt of your garment."
3:11 *Lit., "all the gate of my people."

surely as Jehovah lives. Lie down here until the morning."

14 So she lay at his feet until the morning and then got up before it was light enough for anyone to be recognized. He then said: "Do not let it be known that a woman came to the threshing floor." **15** He also said: "Bring the cloak that you are wearing, and hold it out." So she held it out, and he put six measures* of barley in it and put it on her, after which he went into the city.

16 She went her way to her mother-in-law, who now said: "How did it go for you,* my daughter?" She told her everything that the man had done for her. **17** She added: "He gave me these six measures of barley and said to me, 'Do not go empty-handed to your mother-in-law.'" **18** At that she said: "Sit here, my daughter, until you learn how the matter will turn out, for the man will not rest until he settles the matter today."

4 Now Boʹaz went up to the city gate[a] and sat there. And look! the repurchaser whom Boʹaz had mentioned[b] passed by. At that Boʹaz said: "Come here and sit down, So-and-so." And he went over and sat down. **2** Then Boʹaz took ten of the city elders[c] and said: "Sit down here." So they sat down.

3 Boaz now said to the repurchaser:[d] "Naʹoʹmi, who has returned from the fields of Moʹab,[e] must sell the plot of land that belonged to our brother Elimʹe-lech.[f] **4** So I thought I should disclose it to you and say, 'Buy it in front of the inhabitants and the elders of my people.[g] If you will repurchase it, repurchase it. But if you will not repurchase it, tell me so that I will know, for you have the claim to repur-

chase it, and I am next in line after you.'" He replied: "I am willing to repurchase it."[a] **5** Then Boʹaz said: "On the day you buy the field from Naʹoʹmi, you must also buy it from Ruth the Moʹab·iʹtess, the wife of the dead man, in order to restore the name of the dead man to his inheritance."[b] **6** To this the re-purchaser said: "I am unable to repurchase it, for I may ruin my own inheritance. Repurchase it for yourself with my right of re-purchase, because I am not able to repurchase it."

7 Now this was the custom of former times in Israel concerning the right of repurchase and exchange to validate every sort of transaction: A man had to remove his sandal[c] and give it to the other party, and this was the manner of confirming an agreement* in Israel. **8** So when the repurchaser said to Boʹaz, "Buy it for yourself," he removed his sandal. **9** Then Boʹaz said to the elders and all the people: "You are witnesses[d] today that I am buying from Naʹoʹmi all that belonged to Elimʹe-lech and all that belonged to Chilʹi·on and Mahʹlon. **10** I am also acquiring Ruth the Moʹab·iʹtess, the wife of Mahʹlon, as a wife to restore the name of the dead man to his inheritance,[e] so that the name of the dead man will not be cut off from among his brothers and from the city gate of his home. You are witnesses today."[f]

11 At this all the people who were in the city gate and the elders said: "We are witnesses! May Jehovah grant the wife who is entering your house to be like Rachel and like Leʹah, both of whom built the house of Israel.[g] May you prosper in Ephʹra·thah[h] and make a good name* in Bethʹle·hem.[i]

CHAP. 4
a De 25:7
  Pr 31:23

b Ru 3:12

c De 16:18

d Le 25:25
  De 25:5, 6
  Ru 2:20
  Ru 3:9, 12

e Ru 1:1, 6

f Ru 1:2

g Ge 23:18
  Jer 32:9, 10

Second Col.
a Ru 3:13

b Ge 38:7, 8
  De 25:5, 6

c De 25:7, 9

d Ge 23:18
  Ru 4:4
  Jer 32:12

e Ge 38:7, 8
  De 25:5, 6

f Ru 4:4

g Ge 28:3
  Ge 35:23-26
  Ge 46:15, 18
  Ge 46:22, 25

h Ge 35:19

i Ru 1:1
  Mic 5:2

3:15 *Possibly six seah measures, or about 44 L (40 dry qt). See App. B14. 3:16 *Lit., "Who are you?"

4:7 *Or "the attestation." 4:11 *Lit., "proclaim a name."

12 May your house become like the house of Peʹrez,[a] whom Taʹmar bore to Judah, through the offspring that Jehovah will give you by this young woman."[b]

13 So Boʹaz took Ruth and she became his wife. He had relations with her, and Jehovah let her conceive and she gave birth to a son. **14** Then the women said to Na·oʹmi: "Praised be Jehovah, who has not left you without a repurchaser today. May his name be proclaimed in Israel! **15** He* has restored# your life△ and will sustain you in your old age, because he has been born to your daughter-in-law, who loves you[c] and is better to you than seven sons." **16** Na·oʹ-

---

4:15 *That is, Naomi's grandson. #Or "has become a restorer of." △Or "soul."

CHAP. 4
a Ge 38:29
Nu 26:20
Mt 1:3
b Ps 127:3
c Ru 1:14, 16

Second Col.
a Mt 1:5
Lu 3:23, 32
b 1Sa 17:12
Isa 11:1
Ro 15:12
c Ru 4:12
Mt 1:2-6
d Ge 46:12
Nu 26:21
1Ch 2:5
e 1Ch 2:9-15
f Ex 6:23
g Ru 4:17
1Sa 16:1
h 2Sa 7:8
1Ch 2:13, 15

mi took the child and held him to her bosom, and she cared for him.* **17** Then the neighbor women gave him a name. They said, "A son has been born to Na·oʹmi," and they named him Oʹbed.[a] He is the father of Jesʹse,[b] David's father.

18 Now this is the family line* of Peʹrez:[c] Peʹrez became father to Hezʹron;[d] **19** Hezʹron became father to Ram; Ram became father to Am·minʹa·dab;[e] **20** Am·minʹa·dab[f] became father to Nahʹshon; Nahʹshon became father to Salʹmon; **21** Salʹmon became father to Boʹaz; Boʹaz became father to Oʹbed; **22** Oʹbed became father to Jesʹse;[g] and Jesʹse became father to David.[h]

4:16 *Or "became his nurse." 4:18 *Lit., "these are the generations."

THE FIRST OF

SAMUEL

1 Now there was a man of Ra·math·a·im-zo'phim*[a] of the mountainous region of E'phra·im[b] whose name was El·ka'nah,[c] the son of Je·ro'ham, the son of E·li'hu, the son of To'hu, the son of Zuph, an E'phra·im·ite. **2** He had two wives; one was named Han'nah, and the other was named Pe·nin'nah. Pe·nin'nah had children, but Han'nah had no children. **3** That man went up from his city year after year to worship* and to sacrifice to Jehovah of armies in Shi'-loh.[a] That is where the two sons of E'li, Hoph'ni and Phin'e·has,[b] served as priests to Jehovah.[c]

4 One day when El·ka'nah offered a sacrifice, he gave portions to his wife Pe·nin'nah as well as to all her sons and

CHAP. 1
a 1Sa 1:19
  1Sa 7:15, 17
b Jos 16:5
c 1Ch 6:22, 27

Second Col.
a Ex 23:14
  Ex 34:23
  De 12:5, 6
  Jos 18:1
  Jg 21:19
  Lu 2:41
b 1Sa 2:12, 22
  1Sa 4:17
c Nu 3:10
  De 33:10
  Mal 2:7

1:1 *Or "of Ramah, a Zuphite."

1:3 *Or "bow down."

her daughters,[a] 5 but to Han'-nah he gave a special portion, because Han'nah was the one he loved; but Jehovah had not given her children.* 6 Moreover, her rival wife taunted her relentlessly in order to upset her because Jehovah had not given her children. 7 That is what she would do year after year; whenever Han'nah went up to the house of Jehovah,[b] her rival would taunt her so much that she would weep and not eat. 8 But her husband El·ka'-nah said to her: "Han'nah, why do you weep, and why do you not eat, and why are you so sad?* Am I not better to you than ten sons?"

9 Then Han'nah got up after they had finished eating and drinking in Shi'loh. At the time, E'li the priest was sitting on the seat by the doorpost of the temple*[c] of Jehovah. 10 Han'nah was extremely bitter,* and she began to pray to Jehovah[d] and to weep uncontrollably. 11 And she made this vow: "O Jehovah of armies, if you look upon the affliction of your servant and remember me and you do not forget your servant and give to your servant a male child,[e] I will give him to Jehovah all the days of his life, and no razor will touch his head."[f]

12 While she prayed for a long time before Jehovah, E'li was watching her mouth. 13 Han'nah was speaking in her heart, only her lips were trembling, but her voice was not heard. So E'li thought she was drunk. 14 E'li said to her: "How long will you stay drunk? Stop drinking your wine." 15 At this Han'nah answered: "No, my lord!

I am a woman under great stress;* I have not drunk wine or anything alcoholic, but I am pouring out my soul* before Jehovah.[a] 16 Do not take your servant for a worthless woman, for I have been speaking until now out of my great anguish and distress." 17 Then E'li answered: "Go in peace, and may the God of Israel grant your petition that you have asked of him."[b] 18 To this she said: "Let your servant find favor in your eyes." And the woman went on her way and ate, and her face was no longer downcast.

19 Then they got up early in the morning and bowed before Jehovah, after which they returned to their house in Ra'-mah.[c] El·ka'nah had sexual relations with his wife Han'nah, and Jehovah gave attention to* her.[d] 20 Within a year* Han'nah became pregnant and gave birth to a son and named[e] him Samuel,* because, as she said, "it is from Jehovah that I have asked him."

21 In time El·ka'nah went up with all his household to offer the yearly sacrifice to Jehovah[f] and to present his vow offering. 22 But Han'nah did not go up,[g] for she said to her husband: "As soon as the boy is weaned, I will bring him; then he will appear before Jehovah and remain there from then on."[h] 23 El·ka'nah her husband then said to her: "Do what you think is best.* Stay at home until you wean him. May Jehovah carry out what you have said." So the woman stayed at home and nursed her son until she weaned him.

24 As soon as she had weaned him, she took him

CHAP. 1
a Le 7:15

b De 16:16
1Sa 2:18, 19

c Ex 25:8
1Sa 3:3
2Sa 7:2

d Ps 55:22
Ps 65:2

e Ge 30:22

f Nu 6:5

Second Col.
a Ps 42:6
Ps 62:8
Ps 142:2

b 1Sa 1:11

c 1Sa 1:1

d 1Sa 1:11
Ps 66:19
Pr 15:29

e Ge 5:29
Ge 41:51
Ex 2:21, 22
Mt 1:21

f 1Sa 1:3

g De 16:16

h 1Sa 1:11
1Sa 2:11
2Ch 31:16

1:5 *Lit., "had closed her womb." 1:8 *Or "why does your heart feel bad?" 1:9 *That is, the tabernacle. 1:10 *Or "bitter of soul."

1:15 *Or "a woman hard-pressed in spirit." #See Glossary. 1:19 *Lit., "remembered." 1:20 *Or possibly, "In due time." #Meaning "Name of God." 1:23 *Lit., "what is good in your eyes."

up to Shi'loh, along with a three-year-old bull, one e'phah* of flour, and a large jar of wine,[a] and she came to the house of Jehovah in Shi'loh[b] and brought the young boy with her. **25** Then they slaughtered the bull and brought the boy to E'li. **26** With that she said: "Pardon me, my lord! As surely as you live,* my lord, I am the woman who was standing with you in this place to pray to Jehovah.[c] **27** It was for this boy that I prayed, and Jehovah granted my petition that I asked of him.[d] **28** I, in turn, now lend him to Jehovah. For all his days, he is lent to Jehovah."

And he* bowed down there to Jehovah.

2 Then Han'nah said in prayer: "My heart rejoices in Jehovah;[e]
My horn* is exalted by Jehovah.
My mouth is opened wide against my enemies,
For I rejoice in your acts of salvation.

2 There is no one holy like Jehovah,
There is no one but you,[f]
And there is no rock like our God.[g]

3 Do not keep speaking with haughtiness;
Let nothing arrogant come from your mouth,
For Jehovah is a God of knowledge,[h]
And by him deeds are rightly evaluated.

4 The bows of mighty men are shattered,
But those who are stumbling are given strength.[i]

5 The well-fed must hire themselves out for bread,
But the hungry hunger no more.[a]
The barren has given birth to seven,[b]
But she who had many sons has become desolate.*

6 Jehovah kills, and he preserves life;*
He brings down to the Grave,[#] and he raises up.[c]

7 Jehovah impoverishes, and he enriches;[d]
He abases, and he exalts.[e]

8 He raises the lowly one from the dust;
He lifts up the poor from the ash heap,*[f]
To make them sit with princes,
Giving them a seat of honor.
To Jehovah belong earth's supports,[g]
And he places the productive land upon them.

9 He guards the steps of his loyal ones,[h]
But the wicked will be silenced in darkness,[i]
For not by power does a man prevail.[j]

10 Jehovah will shatter those fighting against him;*[k]
He will thunder against them from the heavens.[l]
Jehovah will judge to the ends of the earth,[m]
He will give power to his king[n]
And exalt the horn* of his anointed one."[o]

11 Then El·ka'nah went to his house in Ra'mah, but the boy

CHAP. 1
a Nu 15:8-10
b Jos 18:1
c 1Sa 1:15
d 1Sa 1:11, 17
  Ps 66:19

CHAP. 2
e Ps 13:6
  Lu 1:46
f Ex 15:11
  De 4:35
  Ps 73:25
  Ps 86:8
  Ps 89:6
g De 32:4
h Job 36:4
  Job 37:16
  Ro 11:33
i Isa 40:29

Second Col.
a Lu 1:53
b 1Sa 1:11, 20
c De 32:39
  Job 14:13
  Ps 30:3
  Ps 49:15
  Ps 68:20
  Ho 13:14
  Joh 11:24
  1Co 15:55
d De 8:18
  De 28:12
  2Ch 1:11, 12
  Job 42:12
  Pr 10:22
e Ps 75:7
f Ps 113:5, 7
  Lu 1:52
g Ps 102:25
h Ps 91:11
  Ps 97:10
  Ps 121:3
i Ps 37:28
j Ps 33:16
  Zec 4:6
k Ex 15:6
l 1Sa 7:10
  2Sa 22:14
  Ps 18:13
m Ps 96:13
  Ac 17:31
n Ps 2:6
  Ps 110:1
  Mt 28:18
o Lu 1:69
  Ac 4:27

1:24 *About 22 L (20 dry qt). See App. B14. **1:26** *Or "By the life of your soul." **1:28** *Evidently referring to Elkanah. **2:1, 10** *Or "strength." See Glossary. **2:5** *Lit., "has withered." **2:6** *Or "brings to life." [#]Or "Sheol," that is, the common grave of mankind. See Glossary. **2:8** *Or possibly, "garbage dump." **2:10** [#]Or possibly, "Those contending against Jehovah will be terrified."

became a minister of* Jehovah[a] before E'li the priest.

12 Now the sons of E'li were wicked men;[b] they had no regard for Jehovah. 13 This is what they did with the due right of the priests from the people:[c] Whenever any man was offering a sacrifice, an attendant of the priest came with a three-pronged fork in his hand when the meat was boiling, 14 and he would thrust it into the basin, the two-handled cooking pot, the cauldron, or the one-handled cooking pot. Whatever the fork brought up, the priest would take for himself. That is what they would do in Shi'loh to all the Israelites coming there. 15 Also, even before the man sacrificing could make the fat smoke,[d] an attendant of the priest would come and say to him: "Give the priest meat to roast. He will not take boiled raw meat from you, only raw meat." 16 When the man would say to him: "Let them first be sure to make the fat smoke,[e] then take for yourself whatever you desire,"* he would say: "No, give it to me now; if not, I will take it by force!" 17 Thus the sin of the attendants came to be very great before Jehovah,[f] for the men treated the offering of Jehovah with disrespect.

18 Now Samuel was ministering[g] before Jehovah, wearing* a linen eph'od,[h] though he was just a boy. 19 Also, his mother would make for him a little sleeveless coat, and she brought it up to him year after year when she came up with her husband to offer the yearly sacrifice.[i] 20 And E'li blessed El-ka'nah and his wife and said: "May Jehovah grant you a child from this wife in place of the one who was lent to Jehovah."[j] And

they went back home. 21 Jehovah turned his attention to Han'nah, so that she could conceive;[a] and she gave birth to three more sons and two daughters. And the boy Samuel continued growing up before Jehovah.[b]

22 Now E'li was very old, but he had heard about everything that his sons were doing[c] to all Israel and how they would lie down with the women who served at the entrance of the tent of meeting.[d] 23 He used to say to them: "Why do you keep doing things like these? For the things I am hearing about you from all the people are bad. 24 No, my sons, the report that I hear circulating among the people of Jehovah is not good. 25 If a man should sin against another man, someone may appeal to Jehovah for him;* but if a man should sin against Jehovah,[e] who can pray for him?" But they refused to listen to their father, for Jehovah had determined to put them to death.[f] 26 Meanwhile, the boy Samuel kept growing in stature and in favor both with Jehovah and with the people.[g]

27 A man of God came to E'li and said to him: "This is what Jehovah says: 'Did I not plainly reveal myself to your father's house while they were in Egypt as slaves to the house of Phar'aoh?[h] 28 And he was chosen out of all the tribes of Israel[i] to serve as my priest and to go up on my altar[j] to make sacrifices, to offer incense,* and to bear an eph'od before me; and I gave to the house of your forefather all the offerings made by fire of the Israelites.'#[k] 29 Why do you men scorn* my sacrifice

CHAP. 2
a 1Sa 1:11
1Sa 3:1, 15

b 1Sa 2:22

c Le 7:34

d Le 3:3-5

e Le 3:16
Le 7:25, 31

f 1Sa 2:29

g 1Sa 2:11
1Sa 3:15

h 2Sa 6:14

i Ex 23:14
1Sa 1:3, 21

j 1Sa 1:27, 28

Second Col.
a Ge 21:1, 2
1Sa 1:19

b 1Sa 2:26
1Sa 3:19

c 1Sa 2:12-17

d Ex 38:8
Le 21:6

e Nu 15:31
1Sa 2:17
1Sa 3:13, 14

f Pr 29:1
Pr 30:17

g 1Sa 2:21

h Ex 4:14, 27

i Ex 28:1
Le 8:12
Nu 17:5, 8

j Nu 18:7

k Le 2:3
Le 6:16
Le 10:14
Nu 5:9
Nu 18:9

2:11 *Or "was serving." 2:16 *Or "your soul craves." 2:18 *Lit., "girded with."

2:25 *Or possibly, "God will arbitrate for him." 2:28 *Or possibly, "to make sacrificial smoke billow up." #Lit., "sons of Israel." 2:29 *Lit., "kick at."

and my offering that I have commanded in my place of dwelling?[a] Why do you keep honoring your sons more than me by fattening yourselves from the best portions of every offering of my people Israel?[b]

30 "'That is why the word of Jehovah the God of Israel is: "I did indeed say that your house and the house of your forefather would always walk before me."[c] But now Jehovah declares: "It is unthinkable, on my part, because those honoring me I will honor,[d] but those despising me will be treated with contempt." **31** Look! Days are coming when I will cut off your strength* and that of your father's house, so that no man in your house will live to old age.[e] **32** And you will look upon a rival in my dwelling amid all the good that is done to Israel,[f] and never again will there be an old man in your house. **33** The man of yours whom I do not cut off from serving at my altar will cause your eyes to fail and will bring you grief,* but the greater number of your house will die by the sword of men.[g] **34** And what happens to your two sons, Hophʹni and Phinʹeʹhas, will be the sign for you: On one day both of them will die.[h] **35** Then I will raise up for myself a faithful priest.[i] He will act in harmony with what is my heart's desire;* and I will build for him a lasting house, and he will walk before my anointed one always. **36** Anyone who remains in your house will come and bow down to him for the payment of money and a loaf of bread, and will say: "Assign me, please, to one of the priestly offices to eat a piece of bread."'"[j]

2:31 *Lit., "arm." 2:33 *Or "will cause your soul to pine away." 2:35 *Or "is in my heart and in my soul."

CHAP. 2
a Ex 25:8
  Jos 18:1
  1Sa 1:3

b 1Sa 2:14-16

c Ex 28:43

d Ps 18:20
  Ps 91:14

e 1Sa 3:14
  1Sa 4:11, 18
  1Sa 22:18
  1Ki 2:27

f Ps 78:60, 61

g 1Sa 22:18, 21

h 1Sa 4:11, 17

i 1Ki 2:27, 35
  1Ch 29:22

j Le 2:3
  Nu 5:9

Second Col.

CHAP. 3
a 1Sa 2:11, 18

b Nu 12:6
  1Ch 17:15

c 1Sa 4:15

d Le 24:2

e 1Sa 1:9
  1Sa 3:15

f Am 3:7

g 1Sa 4:17

3 Meanwhile, the boy Samuel was ministering[a] to Jehovah before Eʹli, but word from Jehovah had become rare in those days; visions[b] were not widespread.

2 One day Eʹli was lying down in his usual place, and his eyes had grown dim; he was not able to see.[c] **3** The lamp of God[d] had not yet been extinguished, and Samuel was lying in the temple*[e] of Jehovah, where the Ark of God was. **4** Jehovah then called Samuel. He answered: "Here I am." **5** He ran to Eʹli and said: "Here I am, for you called me." But he said: "I did not call. Lie down again." So he went and lay down. **6** Jehovah called once again: "Samuel!" At this Samuel got up and went to Eʹli and said: "Here I am, for you called me." But he said: "I did not call, my son. Lie down again." **7** (Now Samuel had not yet come to know Jehovah, and the word of Jehovah had not yet been revealed to him.)[f] **8** So Jehovah called again, a third time: "Samuel!" At that he got up and went to Eʹli and said: "Here I am, for you called me."

Eʹli then realized that it was Jehovah who was calling the boy. **9** So Eʹli said to Samuel: "Go, lie down, and if he calls you, you should say, 'Speak, Jehovah, for your servant is listening.'" And Samuel went and lay down in his place.

10 Jehovah came and stood there, and he called as at the other times: "Samuel, Samuel!" At this Samuel said: "Speak, for your servant is listening." **11** Jehovah said to Samuel: "Look! I am doing something in Israel that will make both ears of anyone who hears about it tingle.[g] **12** On that day I will carry out toward Eʹli all that I said

---

3:3 *That is, the tabernacle.

about his house, from start to finish.[a] **13** You must tell him that I am bringing a lasting judgment on his house for the error that he has known about,[c] for his sons are cursing God,[c] but he has not rebuked them.[d] **14** That is why I have sworn to the house of E′li that the error of the house of E′li will never be atoned for by sacrifices or by offerings."[e]

15 Samuel lay down until the morning; then he opened the doors of Jehovah's house. Samuel was afraid to tell E′li of the vision. **16** But E′li called for Samuel: "Samuel, my son!" At this he said: "Here I am." **17** He asked: "What message did he speak to you? Please, do not hide it from me. May God do so to you and add to it if you hide from me a single word of all that he said to you." **18** So Samuel told him everything, and he did not hide anything from him. Eli said: "It is Jehovah. Let him do what is good in his eyes."

19 Samuel continued growing up, and Jehovah himself was with him[f] and did not let any of all his words go unfulfilled.[*] **20** All Israel from Dan to Be′er-she′ba became aware that Samuel had been confirmed as Jehovah's prophet. **21** And Jehovah continued to appear in Shi′loh, for Jehovah revealed himself to Samuel in Shi′loh by the word of Jehovah.[g]

4 And the word of Samuel went out to all Israel.

Then Israel went out to meet the Phi·lis′tines in battle; they camped beside Eb·en·e′zer, and the Phi·lis′tines were encamped at A′phek. **2** The Phi·lis′tines drew up in battle formation to meet Israel, but the battle went badly and Israel was defeated by the Phi·lis′tines, who struck

down about 4,000 men from the battle line in the field. **3** When the people returned to the camp, the elders of Israel said: "Why did Jehovah allow us to be defeated* today by the Phi·lis′-tines?[a] Let us take the ark of Jehovah's covenant with us from Shi′loh,[b] so that it may be with us and save us from the hand of our enemies." **4** So the people sent men to Shi′loh, and they carried from there the ark of the covenant of Jehovah of armies, who sits enthroned above* the cherubs.[c] The two sons of E′li, Hoph′ni and Phin′e·has,[d] were also there with the ark of the covenant of the true God.

5 As soon as the ark of the covenant of Jehovah came into the camp, all the Israelites broke out into loud shouting, so that the earth shook. **6** When the Phi·lis′tines heard the sound of the shouting, they said: "Why is there such loud shouting in the camp of the Hebrews?" Finally they learned that the Ark of Jehovah had come into the camp. **7** The Phi·lis′tines became afraid, for they said: "God has come into the camp!"[e] So they said: "Too bad for us, for nothing like this has ever happened before! **8** Too bad for us! Who will save us from the hand of this majestic God? This is the God who struck Egypt with every sort of slaughter in the wilderness.[f] **9** Be courageous and act like men, you Phi·lis′tines, so that you may not serve the Hebrews just as they have served you.[g] Act like men and fight!" **10** So the Phi·lis′-tines fought and Israel was defeated,[h] and each one fled to his tent. The slaughter was very great; on Israel's side, 30,-000 foot soldiers fell. **11** More-

---

CHAP. 3

a Nu 23:19
  1Sa 2:31-34
  Isa 55:10, 11

b 1Sa 2:22, 23
  Joh 15:22
  Jas 4:17

c Nu 15:30
  1Sa 2:12, 17

d Ec 8:11

e 1Sa 4:11
  1Sa 22:21
  1Ki 2:27

f 1Sa 2:21

g 1Sa 3:1, 4
  Ps 99:6

Second Col.

CHAP. 4

a De 28:15, 25
  De 32:30
  Jg 2:14

b 2Sa 15:25

c Ex 25:18
  Nu 7:89
  2Ki 19:15
  Ps 80:1

d 1Sa 2:12

e Ex 14:25
  Ex 15:14

f Ex 7:5
  Ps 78:43, 51

g De 28:48
  Jg 10:7
  Jg 13:1

h Le 26:14, 17
  De 28:25
  1Sa 4:2

3:19 *Lit., "fall to the earth."

4:3 *Lit., "Why has Jehovah defeated us?" 4:4 *Or possibly, "between."

over, the Ark of God was captured, and the two sons of E'li, Hoph'ni and Phin'e·has, died.[a]

12 A man of Benjamin ran from the battle line and arrived at Shi'loh on that day with his garments ripped apart and dirt on his head.[b] **13** When the man arrived, E'li was sitting on the seat by the roadside watching, because his heart was trembling over the Ark of the true God.[c] The man went into the city to report the news, and the whole city began crying out. **14** When E'li heard the sound of the outcry, he asked: "What does the sound of this turmoil mean?" The same man hurried in and reported the news to E'li. **15** (Now E'li was 98 years old, and his eyes stared straight ahead, and he could not see.)[d] **16** Then the man said to E'li: "I am the one who came from the battle line! Just today I fled from the battle line." At this he asked: "What happened, my son?" **17** So the bearer of the news related: "Israel has fled from the Phi·lis'tines, and there was a great defeat among the people;[e] also your own two sons, Hoph'ni and Phin'e·has, have died,[f] and the Ark of the true God has been captured."[g]

18 At the moment he mentioned the Ark of the true God, E'li fell backward from his seat beside the gate, and his neck was broken and he died, for he was old and heavy. He had judged Israel for 40 years. **19** His daughter-in-law, the wife of Phin'e·has, was pregnant and close to giving birth. When she heard the report that the Ark of the true God had been captured and that her father-in-law and her husband had died, she doubled over and unexpectedly went into labor and gave birth. **20** As she was dying, the women standing by her said: "Do not be

afraid, for you have given birth to a son." She did not answer and did not pay attention to it.* **21** But she named the boy Ich'a·bod,*[a] saying: "Glory has gone away from Israel into exile,"[b] referring to the capture of the Ark of the true God and what happened to her father-in-law and her husband.[c] **22** She said: "Glory has gone away from Israel into exile, because the Ark of the true God has been captured."[d]

5 When the Phi·lis'tines captured the Ark[e] of the true God, they brought it from Eb·en·e'zer to Ash'dod. **2** The Phi·lis'tines took the Ark of the true God and brought it into the house* of Da'gon and set it beside Da'gon.[f] **3** When the Ash'dod·ites got up early the next day, there was Da'gon fallen facedown on the ground before the Ark of Jehovah.[g] So they took Da'gon and returned him to his place.[h] **4** When they got up early in the morning on the following day, there was Da'gon fallen facedown on the ground before the Ark of Jehovah. The head of Da'gon and the palms of both his hands were cut off and were lying on the threshold. Only the fish part* had been left intact. **5** That is why to this day, the priests of Da'gon and all those who enter the house of Da'gon do not walk on the threshold of Da'gon in Ash'dod.

6 The hand of Jehovah was heavy against the Ash'dod·ites, and he devastated them by striking Ash'dod and its territories with piles.*[i] **7** When the men of Ash'dod saw what was happening, they said: "Do not let the

---

CHAP. 4
a 1Sa 2:31, 34
  1Sa 4:3, 17
  Ps 78:61, 64

b Jos 7:6

c 1Sa 4:4

d 1Sa 3:2

e 1Sa 3:11

f 1Sa 2:34

g 1Sa 4:10, 11

Second Col.
a 1Sa 14:3

b Ps 78:61

c 1Sa 2:32, 34
  1Sa 4:5, 11

d 1Sa 4:11
  Jer 7:12

CHAP. 5
e 1Sa 4:11

f Jg 16:23
  1Ch 10:8-10

g Ex 12:12
  1Ch 16:26
  Ps 97:7

h Isa 46:6, 7

i 1Sa 6:5, 6

4:20 *Or "and did not set her heart on it." 4:21 *Meaning "Where Is the Glory?" 5:2 *Or "temple." 5:4 *Lit., "Only Dagon." 5:6 *Or "hemorrhoids."

Ark of the God of Israel remain with us, for his hand has dealt harshly with us and our god Daʹ-gon." **8** So they sent for and gathered all the lords of the Phi-lisʹtines and asked them: "What should we do with the Ark of the God of Israel?" They replied: "Let the Ark of the God of Isra-el be moved to Gath."[a] So they moved the Ark of the God of Is-rael there.

9 After they moved it there, the hand of Jehovah came against the city, bringing great panic. He struck the men of the city, from small to great, and piles broke out on them.[b] **10** So they sent the Ark of the true God to Ekʹron,[c] but as soon as the Ark of the true God came to Ekʹron, the Ekʹron-ites began to cry out: "They have brought the Ark of the God of Israel to us to put us and our people to death!"[d] **11** Then they sent for and gath-ered all the lords of the Phi-lisʹ-tines and said: "Send the Ark of the God of Israel away; let it re-turn to its place so that we and our people may not be put to death." For the terror of death had spread through the whole city; the hand of the true God had been very heavy there,[e] **12** and the men who did not die had been struck with piles. And the city's cry for help ascended to the heavens.

6 The Ark[f] of Jehovah was in Phi-lisʹtine territory for sev-en months. **2** The Phi-lisʹtines called the priests and the divin-ers[g] and asked: "What should we do with the Ark of Jehovah? Let us know how we should send it back to its place." **3** They re-plied: "If you send the ark of the covenant of Jehovah the God of Israel away, do not send it back without an offering. You should by all means return to him a guilt offering.[h] Only then will you be healed, and it will

be made known to you why his hand has not turned away from you." **4** So they asked: "What guilt offering should we send to him?" They said: "According to the number of the lords of the Phi-lisʹtines,[a] send five golden piles* and five golden mice, for the same scourge has afflicted every one of you and your lords. **5** You should make images of your piles and images of your mice[b] that are bringing the land to ruin, and you should honor the God of Israel. Perhaps he will lighten the weight of his hand that is on you and your god and your land.[c] **6** Why should you harden your heart as Egypt and Pharʹaoh hardened their hearts?[d] When He dealt harsh-ly with them,[e] they had to send Israel away, and they departed.[f] **7** Now prepare a new wagon and two cows that have calves and have never been under a yoke. Then hitch the cows to the wag-on, but take their calves back home, away from them. **8** Take the Ark of Jehovah and place it on the wagon, and put the gold-en articles that you are sending to him as a guilt offering in a box next to it.[g] Then send it on its way **9** and watch: If it goes up the road to Beth-sheʹmesh,[h] to its own territory, then it is the one who has done this great evil to us. But if not, we will know that it was not his hand that struck us; it happened to us by coincidence."

10 The men did according-ly. They took two cows that had calves and hitched them to the wagon, and the calves they penned up at home. **11** Then they put the Ark of Jeho-vah on the wagon, as well as the box containing the gold-en mice and the images of their piles. **12** And the cows went straight ahead on the road to

---

CHAP. 5
a 1Sa 17:4

b 1Sa 5:6

c Jos 15:20, 45
2Ki 1:2
Am 1:8

d 1Sa 5:7

e 1Sa 5:6, 9

CHAP. 6
f 1Sa 4:11
1Sa 5:1
Ps 78:61

g De 18:9, 10
Isa 2:6

h 1Sa 6:4, 17

Second Col.
a Jos 13:2, 3
1Sa 6:16

b 1Sa 6:18

c 1Sa 5:6, 11

d Ex 7:13
Ex 8:15
Ex 14:17

e Ex 9:14, 16
Ro 9:17, 18

f Ex 6:1
Ex 11:1
Ex 12:33

g 1Sa 6:3, 4

h Jos 15:10, 12
Jos 21:8, 16
2Ch 28:18

6:4 *Or "hemorrhoids."

Beth-she'mesh.[a] They stayed on the one highway, mooing as they went; they did not turn either to the right or to the left. All the while the lords of the Phi·lis'tines were walking behind them as far as the boundary of Beth-she'mesh. **13** The people of Beth-she'mesh were reaping the wheat harvest in the valley plain.* When they raised their eyes and saw the Ark, they were overjoyed at seeing it. **14** The wagon came into the field of Joshua the Beth-she'mite and stopped there near a large stone. So they chopped up the wood of the wagon, and they offered the cows[b] as a burnt offering to Jehovah.

15 The Levites[c] took down the Ark of Jehovah and the box that was with it, which contained the golden articles, and they put them on the large stone. The men of Beth-she'mesh[d] offered up burnt offerings and made sacrifices on that day to Jehovah.

16 When the five lords of the Phi·lis'tines saw it, they returned to Ek'ron on that day. **17** Now these are the golden piles that the Phi·lis'tines sent as a guilt offering to Jehovah:[e] one for Ash'dod,[f] one for Gaz'a, one for Ash'ke·lon, one for Gath,[g] one for Ek'ron.[h] **18** And the number of the golden mice corresponded to the number of all the cities of the Phi·lis'tines that belonged to the five lords—both the fortified cities and the villages in the open country.

And the large stone upon which they rested the Ark of Jehovah serves as a witness down to this day in the field of Joshua the Beth-she'mite. **19** But God struck down the men of Beth-she'mesh, because they had looked upon the Ark of Jehovah.

6:13 *Or "low plain."

He struck down 50,070* among the people, and the people began mourning because Jehovah had struck them down with a great slaughter.[a] **20** So the men of Beth-she'mesh asked: "Who will be able to stand before Jehovah, this holy God,[b] and to whom will he go away from us?"[c] **21** So they sent messengers to the inhabitants of Kir'i·ath-je'a·rim,[d] saying: "The Phi·lis'tines have returned the Ark of Jehovah. Come down and take it up with you."[e]

7 So the men of Kir'i·ath-je'a·rim came and took the Ark of Jehovah up into the house of A·bin'a·dab[f] on the hill, and they sanctified his son El·e·a'zar to guard the Ark of Jehovah.

2 A long time elapsed, 20 years in all, from the day of the Ark's coming to Kir'i·ath-je'a·rim, and all the house of Israel began to seek* after Jehovah.[g] **3** Samuel then said to all the house of Israel: "If you are returning to Jehovah with all your heart,[h] put away the foreign gods[i] and the Ash'to·reth images[j] from among you, and direct your heart unswervingly to Jehovah and serve only him,[k] and he will rescue you from the hand of the Phi·lis'tines."[l] **4** At that the Israelites got rid of the Ba'als and the Ash'to·reth images and served only Jehovah.[m]

5 Then Samuel said: "Gather all Israel together at Miz'pah,[n] and I will pray to Jehovah in your behalf."[o] **6** So they gathered together at Miz'pah, and they drew water and poured it out before Jehovah and kept a fast on that day.[p] There they said: "We have sinned against Jehovah."[q] And Samuel began serving as judge* over the Israelites in Miz'pah.

6:19 *Lit., "70 men, 50,000 men." 7:2 *Or "mourn."

CHAP. 6
a 1Sa 6:8, 9
b 1Sa 6:7
c Nu 3:30, 31
d Jos 21:8, 16
e 1Sa 6:4
f 1Sa 5:1
g 1Sa 5:8
h Jg 1:18
  1Sa 5:10

Second Col.
a Nu 4:15, 20
  1Ch 13:10
b Le 11:45
c Nu 17:12, 13
  2Sa 6:8, 9
  Ps 76:7
d Jos 18:14
  1Ch 13:5, 6
e 1Ch 16:1
  2Ch 1:4

CHAP. 7
f 2Sa 6:2, 4
  1Ch 13:5, 7
g Ne 9:28
h 1Sa 12:24
i Jos 24:14, 23
  Jg 3:7
j Jg 2:13
  Jg 10:6
  1Ki 11:33
k De 10:20
  De 13:4
  Lu 4:8
l De 28:1
m Jg 10:16
n Jg 20:1
  1Sa 10:17
  2Ki 25:23
  Jer 40:6
o 1Sa 12:23
  Jas 5:16
p 2Ch 20:3
  Ne 9:1
  Joe 2:12
q Jg 10:10
r Jg 2:18

7 When the Phi·lis'tines heard that the Israelites had gathered together at Miz'pah, the lords of the Phi·lis'tines[a] went up against Israel. When the Israelites heard of it, they were afraid because of the Phi·lis'tines. **8** So the Israelites said to Samuel: "Do not stop calling to Jehovah our God to help us[b] and to save us from the hand of the Phi·lis'tines." **9** Then Samuel took a suckling lamb and offered it up as a whole burnt offering[c] to Jehovah; and Samuel called to Jehovah for help in behalf of Israel, and Jehovah answered him.[d] **10** As Samuel was offering up the burnt offering, the Phi·lis'tines advanced for battle against Israel. Jehovah now caused it to thunder loudly[e] on that day against the Phi·lis'tines, and He threw them into confusion,[f] and they were defeated before Israel.[g] **11** At that the men of Israel went out from Miz'pah and pursued the Phi·lis'tines, striking them down as far as south of Beth-car. **12** Then Samuel took a stone[h] and set it between Miz'pah and Jesh'a·nah and named it Eb·en·e'zer,[*] for he said: "Until now Jehovah has helped us."[i] **13** Thus the Phi·lis'tines were subdued, and they did not come again into the territory of Israel;[j] and the hand of Jehovah continued against the Phi·lis'tines all the days of Samuel.[k] **14** Also, the cities that the Phi·lis'tines had taken from Israel were returned to Israel, from Ek'ron to Gath, and Israel recovered their territory from the hand of the Phi·lis'tines.

There was also peace between Israel and the Am'or·ites.[l]

15 Samuel kept on judging Israel throughout his life.[m] **16** Each year he traveled in a circuit to Beth'el,[n] Gil'gal,[o] and Miz'pah,[a] and he judged Israel in all these places. **17** But he would return to Ra'mah,[b] because his house was there, and there he also judged Israel. He built an altar there to Jehovah.[c]

8 When Samuel had grown old, he appointed his sons as judges for Israel. **2** The name of his firstborn son was Joel, and the name of his second, A·bi'jah;[d] they were judges in Be'er-she'ba. **3** But his sons did not walk in his ways; they were inclined to pursue dishonest profit,[e] they accepted bribes,[f] and they perverted justice.[g]

4 In time all the elders of Israel gathered together and came to Samuel at Ra'mah. **5** They said to him: "Look! You have grown old, but your sons are not walking in your ways. Now appoint for us a king to judge us like all the other nations."[h] **6** But it displeased[*] Samuel when they said: "Give us a king to judge us." Then Samuel prayed to Jehovah, **7** and Jehovah said to Samuel: "Listen to everything the people say to you; for it is not you whom they have rejected, but it is I whom they have rejected as their king.[i] **8** They are doing just as they have done from the day I brought them up out of Egypt until this day; they keep forsaking me[j] and serving other gods,[k] and that is what they are doing to you. **9** Now listen to them. However, you should solemnly warn them; tell them what the king who rules over them will have the right to demand."

10 So Samuel told the people who were asking him for a king all the words of Jehovah. **11** He said: "This is what the king who rules over you will have the right to demand:[l] He will take your sons[m] and put

Cross references

7:12 *Meaning "Stone of Help."

8:6 *Lit., "was bad in the eyes of."

them in his chariots[a] and make them his horsemen,[b] and some will have to run before his chariots. **12** And he will appoint for himself chiefs over thousands[c] and chiefs over fifties,[d] and some harvest will do his plowing,[e] reap his harvest,[f] and make his weapons of war and equipment for his chariots.[g] **13** He will take your daughters to be ointment mixers,* cooks, and bakers.[h] **14** He will take the best of your fields, your vineyards, and your olive groves,[i] and he will give them to his servants. **15** He will take the tenth of your grainfields and your vineyards, and he will give it to his court officials and his servants. **16** And he will take your male and female servants, your best herds, and your donkeys, and he will use them for his work.[j] **17** He will take the tenth of your flocks,[k] and you will become his servants. **18** The day will come when you will cry out because of the king you have chosen for yourselves,[l] but Jehovah will not answer you in that day."

19 However, the people refused to listen to what Samuel told them, and they said: "No, we are determined to have a king over us. **20** Then we will be like all the other nations, and our king will judge us and lead us and fight our battles." **21** After Samuel heard all the words of the people, he repeated them in the hearing of Jehovah. **22** Jehovah said to Samuel: "Listen to them, and appoint a king to reign over them."[m] Samuel then said to the men of Israel: "Each of you should return to his city."

9 There was a man of Benjamin named Kish,[n] the son of A·bi′el, the son of Ze′ror son of Be·co′rath son of A·phi′-

ah, a Ben′ja·min·ite[a] and a very wealthy man. **2** He had a son named Saul,[b] who was young and handsome—there was no man among the Israelites more handsome than he—and he stood head and shoulders taller than all the people.

3 When the donkeys* belonging to Saul's father Kish got lost, Kish said to his son Saul: "Please take with you one of the attendants and go look for the donkeys." **4** They passed through the mountainous region of E′phra·im and through the land of Shal′i·shah, and they did not find them. They traveled through the land of Sha′a·lim, but the donkeys were not there. They passed through the entire land of the Ben′ja·min·ites, and they did not find them.

5 They came into the land of Zuph, and Saul said to his attendant who was with him: "Come, let us return, so that my father does not start worrying about us rather than the donkeys."[c] **6** But the attendant replied: "Look, there is a man of God in this city, a man who is held in honor. All that he says is sure to come true.[d] Let us go there now. Perhaps he can tell us which way to go." **7** At this Saul said to his attendant: "If we go, what can we take to the man? There is no bread in our bags; there is nothing to take as a gift to the man of the true God. What do we have?" **8** So the attendant answered Saul again: "Look! There is a quarter of a shekel* of silver in my hand. I will give it to the man of the true God, and he will tell us which way to go." **9** (In former times in Israel, this was what a man would say when going to

---

CHAP. 8
a 1Ki 9:22
  1Ki 10:26

b 1Ki 4:26

c 2Sa 18:1
  1Ch 27:1

d 2Ki 1:14

e 1Ch 27:26

f 1Ki 4:7

g 1Ki 4:26

h 1Ki 4:22

i 1Ch 27:28, 31

j 1Ki 5:15, 16

k 1Ki 4:22, 23

l 1Ki 12:3, 4

m 1Sa 8:7
  Ho 13:11

CHAP. 9
n 1Sa 14:51
  1Ch 8:33
  Ac 13:21

Second Col.
a Jg 21:17

b 1Sa 11:15
  1Sa 13:13
  1Sa 15:26
  1Sa 28:7
  1Sa 31:4
  2Sa 1:23

c 1Sa 10:2

d 1Sa 3:19

8:13 *Or "perfume makers."

9:3 *Lit., "female donkeys." 9:8 *A shekel equaled 11.4 g (0.367 oz t). See App. B14.

seek God: "Come, and let us go to the seer."ª For the prophet of today used to be called a seer in former times.) **10** Then Saul said to his attendant: "What you said is good. Let us go." So they went to the city where the man of the true God was.

11 While they were going up the ascent to the city, they met girls going out to draw water. So they said to them: "Is the seerᵇ in this place?" **12** They answered: "He is. Look, he is just ahead of you. Hurry now, for today he has come to the city, because the people are making a sacrificeᶜ today on the high place.ᵈ **13** As soon as you come into the city, you will find him before he goes up to the high place to eat. The people will not eat until he comes, for he is the one who blesses the sacrifice. Once that is done, those who are invited may eat. So now go up right away, and you will find him." **14** So they went up to the city. As they were coming into the middle of the city, there was Samuel coming out to meet them to go up to the high place.

15 The day before Saul came, Jehovah had told* Samuel: **16** "Tomorrow about this time, I will send to you a man from the land of Benjamin.ᵉ You must anoint him as leader over my people Israel,ᶠ and he will save my people from the hand of the Phi·lis′tines. For I have seen the affliction of my people, and their outcry has reached me."ᵍ **17** When Samuel saw Saul, Jehovah told him: "Here is the man of whom I said to you, 'This is the one who will govern my people.'"*ʰ

18 Then Saul approached Samuel in the middle of the gate and said: "Tell me, please,

---

9:15 *Lit., "uncovered the ear of." **9:17** *Or "keep my people within bounds."

CHAP. 9

a 1Sa 9:19
2Sa 15:27
1Ch 9:22
1Ch 29:29

b 1Sa 9:19

c 1Sa 7:9
1Sa 16:5

d 1Ki 3:2
1Ch 16:39
2Ch 1:3

e Jos 18:11

f 1Sa 10:1
1Sa 15:1

g Ps 106:43, 44
Ps 107:19

h 1Sa 10:24
1Sa 15:17
Ac 13:21

Second Col.

a 1Sa 9:13, 24

b 1Sa 9:3

c 1Sa 8:5, 19
1Sa 12:13

d Jg 20:46, 47

e 1Sa 9:13, 24

f 1Sa 9:3, 10

---

where is the house of the seer?" **19** Samuel answered Saul: "I am the seer. Go up ahead of me to the high place, and you will eat with me today.ª I will send you away in the morning, and I will tell you all that you want to know.* **20** As for the donkeys that were lost three days ago,ᵇ do not worry about them, for they have been found. And to whom does all that is desirable of Israel belong? Is it not to you and to the whole house of your father?"ᶜ **21** At this Saul answered: "Am I not a Ben′ja·min·ite of the smallest of the tribes of Israel,ᵈ and my family the most insignificant of all the families of the tribe of Benjamin? So why have you spoken to me in this way?"

22 Then Samuel took Saul and his attendant and brought them to the dining hall and gave them a place at the head of those invited; there were about 30 men. **23** Samuel said to the cook: "Bring the portion that I gave you and told you, 'Set it aside.'" **24** At that the cook lifted up the leg and what was on it, and set it before Saul. And Samuel said: "What has been reserved has been set before you. Eat, because they have reserved it for you for this occasion. For I told them, 'I invited guests.'" So Saul ate with Samuel on that day. **25** Then they went down from the high placeᵉ to the city, and he continued to speak with Saul on the housetop. **26** They rose early, and at daybreak Samuel called to Saul on the housetop, saying: "Get ready, so that I may send you away." So Saul got ready and both he and Samuel went outside. **27** While they were descending toward the outskirts of the city, Samuel said to Saul: "Tell the attendantᶠ to go

---

9:19 *Lit., "all that is in your heart."

on ahead of us," so he went on ahead. "But you, stand still now, so that I may let you hear the word of God."

10 Samuel then took the flask of oil and poured it out on Saul's head.[a] He kissed him and said: "Has not Jehovah anointed you as a leader[b] over his inheritance?[c] **2** When you leave me today, you will find two men near the tomb of Rachel[d] in the territory of Benjamin at Zel′zah, and they will say to you, 'The donkeys that you went to look for have been found, but now your father has forgotten about the donkeys[e] and is worried about you. He is saying: "What should I do about my son?"' **3** Go on from there until you come to the big tree of Ta′bor, where you will meet three men going up to the true God at Beth′el,[f] one carrying three young goats, one carrying three loaves of bread, and one carrying a large jar of wine. **4** They will ask about your welfare and give you two loaves, and you must accept the loaves from them. **5** After that you will come to the hill of the true God, where there is a garrison of the Phi·lis′tines. When you come to the city, you will meet a group of prophets coming down from the high place, and a stringed instrument and tambourine and flute and harp will be played ahead of them while they are prophesying. **6** The spirit of Jehovah will empower you,[g] and you will prophesy along with them and be changed into a different person.[h] **7** When these signs have taken place, do whatever your hand finds possible, because the true God is with you. **8** Then go down ahead of me to Gil′gal,[i] and I will go down to you there to offer up burnt sacrifices and communion sacrifices. You

should wait for seven days until I come to you. Then I will let you know what you should do."

9 As soon as Saul turned around to leave Samuel, God began changing his heart to be like that of someone else, and all these signs came true on that day. **10** So they went from there to the hill, and a group of prophets met him. At once the spirit of God empowered him,[a] and he began to prophesy[b] among them. **11** When all those who previously knew him saw him prophesying with the prophets, they said to one another: "What has happened to the son of Kish? Is Saul also among the prophets?" **12** Then a man from there said: "But who is their father?" So it became a saying:* "Is Saul also among the prophets?"[c]

13 When he finished prophesying, he came to the high place. **14** The brother of Saul's father later said to him and to his attendant: "Where did you go?" At that he said: "To look for the donkeys,[d] but we saw that they were not there, so we went to Samuel." **15** Saul's uncle asked: "Please tell me, what did Samuel say to you?" **16** Saul replied to his uncle: "He told us that the donkeys had already been found." But Saul did not tell him what Samuel said about the matter of the kingship.

17 Samuel then called the people together to Jehovah at Miz′pah[e] **18** and said to the Israelites: "This is what Jehovah the God of Israel says: 'It was I who brought Israel up out of Egypt and who rescued you from the hand of Egypt[f] and from the hand of all the kingdoms that were oppressing you. **19** But today you have rejected your God[g] who was your Savior out

---

CHAP. 10
a 1Sa 16:13
　2Ki 9:2, 3

b 1Sa 9:16
　Ac 13:21

c Ex 19:5
　De 32:9

d Ge 35:19

e 1Sa 9:3, 5

f Ge 28:19, 22

g Nu 11:25

h 1Sa 10:10

i 1Sa 7:15, 16
　1Sa 11:14

Second Col.
a Jg 14:5, 6
　1Sa 11:6
　1Sa 16:13

b 1Sa 10:6
　1Sa 19:23

c 1Sa 19:24

d 1Sa 9:3

e 1Sa 7:5

f Ex 13:14
　De 4:34

g 1Sa 8:7
　1Sa 12:12

10:12 *Or "a proverb."

of all your evils and distresses, and you said: "No, you should appoint a king over us." Now take your stand before Jehovah by your tribes and by your thousands."*

20 So Samuel had all the tribes of Israel draw near,ᵃ and the tribe of Benjamin was selected.ᵇ 21 Then he had the tribe of Benjamin draw near by its families, and the family of the Mat′rites was selected. Finally Saul the son of Kish was selected.ᶜ But when they went to look for him, he was nowhere to be found. 22 So they inquired of Jehovah:ᵈ "Has the man come here yet?" Jehovah answered: "There he is hiding himself among the luggage." 23 So they ran and brought him from there. When he stood in the middle of the people, he was head and shoulders taller than all the other people.ᵉ 24 Samuel said to all the people: "Do you see the one whom Jehovah has chosen,ᶠ that there is none like him among all the people?" And all the people began to shout: "Long live the king!"

25 Samuel spoke to the people about the rightful due of kingsᵍ and wrote it in a book and deposited it before Jehovah. Then Samuel sent all the people away, everyone to his house. 26 Saul also went to his home in Gib′e·ah, accompanied by the warriors whose hearts Jehovah had touched. 27 But some worthless men said: "How will this one save us?"ʰ So they despised him, and they did not bring any gift to him.ⁱ But he said nothing about it.*

11 Then Na′hash the Am′mon·iteʲ came up and camped against Ja′beshᵏ in Gil′e·ad. All the men of Ja′besh said

to Na′hash: "Make a covenant* with us, and we will serve you." 2 Na′hash the Am′mon·ite said to them: "I will make it with you on this condition: that all your right eyes be bored out. I will do this to humiliate all Israel." 3 The elders of Ja′besh replied to him: "Give us seven days' time so that we can send messengers into all the territory of Israel, and, if there is no one to rescue us, we will surrender to you." 4 In time the messengers came to Gib′e·ahᵃ of Saul and spoke these words in the hearing of the people, and all the people wept at the top of their voice.

5 But Saul was coming from the field behind the herd, and Saul said: "What is the matter with the people? Why are they weeping?" So they related to him the words of the men of Ja′besh. 6 The spirit of God empowered Saulᵇ when he heard these words, and he burned with anger. 7 So he took a pair of bulls and cut them into pieces, and he sent these into all the territory of Israel by the hand of the messengers, who said: "Whoever does not follow Saul and Samuel should expect this to be done to his cattle!" And the fear of Jehovah fell upon the people, so that they came out with one accord.* 8 Then he counted them in Be′zek, and there were 300,000 Israelites and 30,000 men of Judah. 9 They now said to the messengers who had come: "This is what you should say to the men of Ja′besh in Gil′e·ad, 'Tomorrow when the sun gets hot, you will be saved.'" With that the messengers came and told the men of Ja′besh, and they were overjoyed. 10 So the men of Ja′besh said: "Tomorrow we will surrender to you, and you may

CHAP. 10
a Jos 7:16-18
  Ac 1:24

b 1Sa 9:21

c Ac 13:21

d Jg 1:1
  Jg 20:18, 28
  1Sa 23:2

e 1Sa 9:2

f De 17:14, 15
  1Sa 9:17

g 1Sa 8:11-18

h 1Sa 11:12

i 1Ki 10:1, 10
  2Ch 17:5

CHAP. 11
j De 2:19

k Jg 21:8
  1Sa 31:11, 12

Second Col.
a 1Sa 10:26
  1Sa 14:2

b Jg 3:9, 10
  Jg 6:34
  Jg 11:29
  Jg 14:5, 6
  1Sa 10:10, 11
  1Sa 16:13

10:19 *Or "clans." 10:27 *Lit., "And he was like someone speechless." 11:1 *Or "an agreement." 11:7 *Lit., "as one man."

do to us whatever seems good to you."[a]

11 On the next day, Saul divided the people into three bands, and they made their way into the middle of the camp during the morning watch* and struck down the Am′mon·ites[b] until the day grew hot. Those who survived were scattered, so that no two of them were left together. 12 Then the people said to Samuel: "Who was saying, 'Is Saul to be king over us?'[c] Hand the men over, and we will put them to death." 13 However, Saul said: "Not a man should be put to death on this day,[d] for today Jehovah has rescued Israel."

14 Samuel later said to the people: "Come and let us go to Gil′gal[e] to reconfirm the kingship."[f] 15 So all the people went to Gil′gal, and in Gil′gal they made Saul king before Jehovah. Then they offered communion sacrifices there before Jehovah,[g] and Saul and all the men of Israel celebrated with great joy.[h]

12 Finally Samuel said to all Israel: "Here I have done* all that you asked of me, and I appointed a king to reign over you.[i] 2 Now here is the king who is leading* you![j] As for me, I have grown old and gray, and my sons are here with you,[k] and I have led you from my youth until this day.[l] 3 Here I am. Testify against me before Jehovah and before his anointed one:[m] Whose bull or whose donkey have I taken?[n] Or whom have I defrauded or crushed? From whose hand have I accepted a bribe* to make me look the other way?[o] If I have, I will re-

store it to you."[a] 4 To this they said: "You have not defrauded us or crushed us or accepted anything at all from anyone's hand." 5 So he said to them: "Jehovah is a witness against you, and his anointed one is a witness this day that you have found nothing to accuse me of."* To this they said: "He is a witness."

6 So Samuel said to the people: "Jehovah, who used Moses and Aaron and who brought your forefathers up out of the land of Egypt,[b] is a witness. 7 And now take your positions, and I will judge you before Jehovah in view of all the righteous acts that Jehovah has done for you and for your forefathers.

8 "As soon as Jacob had come into Egypt[c] and your forefathers began calling to Jehovah for help,[d] Jehovah sent Moses[e] and Aaron to lead your forefathers out of Egypt and to cause them to dwell in this place.[f] 9 But they forgot Jehovah their God, and he sold them[g] into the hand of Sis′e·ra[h] the chief of the army of Ha′zor and into the hand of the Phi·lis′tines[i] and into the hand of the king of Mo′ab,[j] and they fought against them. 10 And they called to Jehovah for help[k] and said, 'We have sinned,[l] for we have left Jehovah to serve the Ba′als[m] and the Ash′to·reth[n] images; now rescue us out of the hand of our enemies so that we may serve you.' 11 Then Jehovah sent Jer·ub·ba′al[o] and Be′dan and Jeph′thah[p] and Samuel[q] and rescued you from the hand of the enemies all around you, so that you could live in security.[r] 12 When you saw that Na′hash,[s] the king of the Am′mon·ites, had come against you, you kept saying to me, 'No, we are

CHAP. 11
a 1Sa 11:3
b 1Sa 11:1
c 1Sa 10:26, 27
d 2Sa 19:22
e 1Sa 7:15, 16
f 1Sa 10:17, 24
g Le 7:11
h 1Ki 1:39, 40
  2Ki 11:12, 14
  1Ch 12:39, 40

CHAP. 12
i 1Sa 8:5
  1Sa 10:24
  1Sa 11:14, 15
j 1Sa 8:20
k 1Sa 8:1, 3
l 1Sa 3:19
m 1Sa 9:16, 17
  1Sa 10:1
n Nu 16:15
o De 16:19

Second Col.
a Ex 22:4
  Le 6:4
b Ex 6:26
c Ge 46:6
d Ex 2:23
e Ex 3:9, 10
f Jos 11:23
g De 32:18, 30
  Jg 2:12, 14
h Jg 4:2
i Jg 10:7
  Jg 13:1
j Jg 3:12
k Jg 2:18
  Jg 3:9
l Jg 10:10, 15
m Jg 3:7
n Jg 2:13
o Jg 6:32
p Jg 11:1
q Heb 11:32
r Le 26:6
s 1Sa 11:1

11:11 *That is, about 2:00 a.m. until 6:00 a.m. 12:1 *Lit., "listened to your voice as respects." 12:2 *Lit., "walking before." 12:3 *Or "hush money."

12:5 *Lit., "have not found anything in my hand."

determined to have a king over us!"[a] even though Jehovah your God is your King.[b] **13** Now here is the king whom you have chosen, the one you asked for. Look! Jehovah has appointed a king over you.[c] **14** If you fear Jehovah[d] and serve him[e] and obey his voice[f] and you do not rebel against the order of Jehovah, and both you and the king who reigns over you follow Jehovah your God, fine. **15** But if you do not obey the voice of Jehovah and you rebel against the order of Jehovah, the hand of Jehovah will be against you and your fathers.[g] **16** Now take your positions and see this great thing that Jehovah is doing before your eyes. **17** Is it not the wheat harvest today? I will call on Jehovah to make it thunder and rain; then know and understand what an evil thing you have done in the eyes of Jehovah in asking for a king for yourselves."[h]

18 At that Samuel called to Jehovah, and Jehovah made it thunder and rain on that day, so that all the people were greatly in fear of Jehovah and of Samuel. **19** And all the people said to Samuel: "Pray to Jehovah your God for your servants,[i] as we do not want to die, for we have added to all our sins another evil by asking for a king."

20 So Samuel said to the people: "Do not be afraid. You have indeed done all this evil. Only do not turn away from following Jehovah,[j] and serve Jehovah with all your heart.[k] **21** Do not turn away to follow the empty things,*[l] which are of no benefit[m] and cannot rescue, because they are empty.* **22** For the sake of his great name,[n] Jehovah will not abandon his people,[o] for Jehovah has taken it

upon himself to make you his people.[a] **23** As for me, it is unthinkable for me to sin against Jehovah by ceasing to pray in your behalf, and I will continue to instruct you in the good and right way. **24** Only fear Jehovah,[b] and serve him faithfully* with all your heart, for see what great things he has done for you.[c] **25** But if you flagrantly do what is bad, you will be swept away,[d] both you and your king."[e]

13 Saul was . . .* years old when he became king,[f] and for two years he reigned over Israel. **2** Saul chose 3,000 men out of Israel; 2,000 of these were with Saul at Mich'mash and in the mountainous region of Beth'el and 1,000 were with Jon'a·than[g] at Gib'e·ah[h] of Benjamin. He sent the rest of the people away, each one to his tent. **3** Then Jon'a·than struck down the garrison of the Phi·lis'tines[i] that was in Ge'ba,[j] and the Phi·lis'tines heard about it. And Saul had the horn blown[k] throughout all the land, saying: "Let the Hebrews hear!" **4** All Israel heard the news: "Saul has struck down a garrison of the Phi·lis'tines, and now Israel has become a stench among the Phi·lis'tines." So the people were summoned to follow Saul at Gil'gal.[l]

5 The Phi·lis'tines also gathered together to fight against Israel, with 30,000 war chariots and 6,000 horsemen and troops as numerous as the grains of sand on the seashore;[m] and they went up and camped in Mich'mash to the east of Beth-a'ven.[n] **6** And the men of Israel saw that they were in trouble, because they were hard-pressed; so the people hid in the caves,[o] the hol-

---

12:21 *Or "unrealities."

12:24 *Or "in truth." **13:1** *The number is missing in the Hebrew text.

lows, the crags, the cellars,* and the cisterns. **7** Some of the Hebrews even crossed the Jordan to the land of Gad and Gil′e·ad.ᵃ But Saul was still in Gil′gal, and all the people following him were trembling. **8** He continued waiting for seven days until the designated* time that Samuel had set, but Samuel did not come to Gil′gal, and the people were scattering from him. **9** Finally Saul said: "Bring to me the burnt sacrifice and the communion sacrifices." And he offered up the burnt sacrifice.ᵇ

10 But as soon as he had finished offering up the burnt sacrifice, Samuel arrived. So Saul went out to meet him and bless him. **11** Then Samuel said: "What have you done?" Saul replied: "I saw that the people were deserting me,ᶜ and you did not come within the designated time, and the Phi·lis′tines were gathering together at Mich′mash.ᵈ **12** So I said to myself, 'Now the Phi·lis′tines will come down against me at Gil′gal, and I have not sought the favor* of Jehovah.' So I felt obligated to offer up the burnt sacrifice."

13 At this Samuel said to Saul: "You have acted foolishly. You have not obeyed the commandment that Jehovah your God gave you.ᵉ If you had, Jehovah would have made your kingdom firm over Israel forever. **14** But now your kingdom will not last.ᶠ Jehovah will find a man agreeable to his heart,ᵍ and Jehovah will commission him as a leader over his people,ʰ because you did not obey what Jehovah commanded you."ⁱ

15 Then Samuel rose and went his way up from Gil′gal to Gib′e·ah of Benjamin, and Saul took the count of the peo-

ple; those still with him were about 600 men.ᵃ **16** Saul, his son Jon′a·than, and the people still with them were dwelling in Ge′baᵇ of Benjamin, and the Phi·lis′tines had encamped at Mich′mash.ᶜ **17** And the raiding parties would go out from the camp of the Phi·lis′tines in three bands. One band would turn toward the road to Oph′rah, to the land of Shu′al; **18** another band would turn toward the road of Beth-ho′ron;ᵈ and the third band would turn toward the road leading to the boundary that overlooks the valley of Ze·bo′im, toward the wilderness.

19 Now there was not a metalworker to be found in all the land of Israel, because the Phi·lis′tines had said: "So that the Hebrews may not make a sword or a spear." **20** And all the Israelites had to go down to the Phi·lis′tines to get their plowshares, mattocks, axes, or sickles sharpened. **21** The price for sharpening was a pim* for the plowshares, for the mattocks, for the three-toothed instruments, for the axes, and for fixing fast the oxgoad. **22** And on the day of battle, not a sword or a spear was found in the hand of any of the people who were with Saul and his son Jon′a·than;ᵉ only Saul and his son Jon′a·than had weapons.

23 Now a garrison* of the Phi·lis′tines had gone out to the ravine pass of Mich′mash.ᶠ

14 One day Jon′a·thanᵍ the son of Saul said to the attendant carrying his weapons: "Come and let us cross over to the Phi·lis′tines outpost on the other side." But he did not tell his father. **2** Saul was staying on the outskirts of Gib′e·ahʰ under the pomegranate tree in

---

CHAP. 13
a Nu 32:1, 33
  Jos 13:24, 25

b 1Sa 15:22, 23

c 1Sa 13:6, 8

d 1Sa 13:5

e 1Sa 15:11

f 1Sa 15:28

g 1Sa 16:1
  2Sa 7:15
  Ps 78:70
  Ac 13:22

h Ge 49:10
  2Sa 5:2
  2Sa 7:8
  1Ch 28:4

i Pr 11:2

Second Col.
a 1Sa 13:7
  1Sa 14:2

b 1Sa 13:3

c 1Sa 13:2

d Jos 10:11

e 1Sa 17:47, 50

f 1Sa 13:2
  1Sa 14:4, 5

CHAP. 14
g 1Sa 14:49
  1Sa 18:1
  2Sa 1:4

h 1Sa 10:26

13:6 *Or "vaults." **13:8** *Or "appointed." **13:12** *Or "softened the face."

13:21 *An ancient weight, approximately two thirds of a shekel. **13:23** *Or "an outpost."

Mig'ron, and there were about 600 men with him.[a] 3 (And A·hi'jah the son of A·hi'tub,[b] the brother of Ich'a·bod,[c] the son of Phin'e·has,[d] the son of E'li,[e] the priest of Jehovah in Shi'loh,[f] was carrying the eph'od.)[g] And the people did not know that Jon'a·than had gone. 4 Now between the passages that Jon'a·than was trying to cross over to reach the outpost of the Phi·lis'tines, there was a toothlike crag on one side and a toothlike crag on the other side; the name of the one was Bo'zez, and the name of the other was Se'neh. 5 The one crag was a pillar on the north facing Mich'mash, and the other was on the south facing Ge'ba.[h]

6 So Jon'a·than said to his armor-bearer: "Come and let us cross over to the outpost of these uncircumcised men.[i] Perhaps Jehovah will act in our behalf, for nothing can hinder Jehovah from saving by many or by few."[j] 7 At this his armor-bearer said to him: "Do whatever your heart impels you to do. Turn wherever you wish, and I will follow you wherever your heart impels you." 8 Then Jon'a·than said: "We will cross over to those men and reveal our presence to them. 9 If they say to us, 'Stand still until we come to you!' we will stand where we are and not go up to them. 10 But if they say, 'Come up against us!' we will go up, because Jehovah will give them into our hand. This will be our sign."[k]

11 Then both of them revealed their presence to the outpost of the Phi·lis'tines. The Phi·lis'tines said: "Look! The Hebrews are coming out from the holes where they have been hiding."[l] 12 So the men of the outpost said to Jon'a·than and his armor-bearer: "Come up to us, and we will teach you a les-

son!"[a] At once Jon'a·than said to his armor-bearer: "Follow me, for Jehovah will give them into the hand of Israel."[b] 13 And Jon'a·than climbed up on his hands and feet, and his armor-bearer was behind him; and the Phi·lis'tines began to fall before Jon'a·than, and his armor-bearer was putting them to death behind him. 14 In the first attack that Jon'a·than and his armor-bearer made, they struck down about 20 men within about half the plowing line in an acre of field.*

15 Then terror spread in the field camp and among all the people of the outpost, and even the raiding parties[c] were terrified. The earth began quaking, and a terror from God ensued. 16 Saul's watchmen in Gib'e·ah[d] of Benjamin saw that the turmoil was spreading in every direction.[e]

17 Saul said to the people with him: "Take a count, please, and see who has left us." When they took the count, they saw that Jon'a·than and his armor-bearer were not there. 18 Saul now said to A·hi'jah:[f] "Bring the Ark of the true God near!" (For the Ark of the true God was with the Israelites at that time.*) 19 And while Saul was speaking to the priest, the turmoil in the camp of the Phi·lis'tines was growing greater and greater. Then Saul said to the priest: "Stop what you are doing."* 20 So Saul and all the people with him assembled and went into the battle, where they found that the Phi·lis'tines had turned their swords against one another, and the confusion was

---

CHAP. 14
a 1Sa 13:15
b 1Sa 22:9
c 1Sa 4:21
d 1Sa 2:12
  1Sa 4:17
e 1Sa 1:9
f Jos 18:1
  1Sa 1:3
g Ex 29:5
  Nu 27:21
h 1Sa 13:2, 3
i Ge 17:9, 10
  Jg 14:3
  Jg 15:18
  1Sa 17:36
  1Ch 10:4
j Jg 7:2
  2Ki 6:15, 16
  2Ch 14:11
k Ge 24:14
  Jg 7:11
  1Sa 10:7
l 1Sa 13:6
  1Sa 14:22

Second Col.
a 1Sa 14:10
b 1Sa 14:6
  2Sa 5:23, 24
  2Ki 6:15, 16
c 1Sa 13:17
d 1Sa 10:26
  1Sa 14:2
e 1Sa 14:20
f 1Sa 14:3

14:14 *Lit., "a span of a field," that is, the measure of land that a span of bulls can plow in a day. 14:18 *Lit., "on that day." 14:19 *Lit., "Withdraw your hand."

very great. **21** Also, the Hebrews who had previously sided with the Phi·lis′tines and who had come up with them into the camp were going over to Israel under Saul and Jon′a·than. **22** All the men of Israel who had hidden[a] in the mountainous region of E′phra·im heard that the Phi·lis′tines had fled, and they too joined in pursuing them in the battle. **23** So Jehovah saved Israel on that day,[b] and the battle extended as far as Beth-a′ven.[c]

24 But the men of Israel were hard-pressed on that day, for Saul had put the people under this oath: "Cursed is the man who eats any food* before the evening and until I have taken vengeance on my enemies!" So none of the people ate any food.[d]

25 And all the people* came into the forest, and there was honey on the ground. **26** When the people came into the forest, they saw the honey dripping, but no one would put his hand to his mouth, because they feared the oath. **27** But Jon′a·than had not heard his father put the people under an oath,[e] so he stretched out the tip of the staff that was in his hand and dipped it into the honeycomb. When he drew his hand back to his mouth, his eyes brightened. **28** At this one of the people said: "Your father put the people under a strict oath, saying, 'Cursed is the man who eats food today!'[f] That is why the people are so tired." **29** However, Jon′a·than said: "My father has brought great trouble* on the land. Look at how my eyes brightened because I tasted this little bit of honey. **30** How much better if the people had eaten freely[g] to-

day from the spoil of their enemies that they found! For then the slaughter of the Phi·lis′tines would have been even greater."

31 On that day they kept striking down the Phi·lis′tines from Mich′mash to Ai′ja·lon,[a] and the people became very tired. **32** So the people began rushing greedily at the spoil, and they took sheep and cattle and calves and slaughtered them on the ground, and they ate the meat along with the blood.[b] **33** So it was reported to Saul: "Look! The people are sinning against Jehovah by eating meat with the blood."[c] At this he said: "You have acted faithlessly. Roll a large stone to me immediately." **34** Saul then said: "Spread out among the people and say to them, 'Each of you must bring his bull and his sheep and slaughter them here and then eat them. Do not sin against Jehovah by eating meat with the blood.'"[d] So each of them brought his bull with him that night and slaughtered it there. **35** And Saul built an altar to Jehovah.[e] This was the first altar he built to Jehovah.

36 Saul later said: "Let us go down after the Phi·lis′tines by night and plunder them until the morning light. We will not leave a single survivor." To this they said: "Do whatever seems good in your eyes." Then the priest said: "Let us approach the true God here."[f] **37** And Saul inquired of God: "Should I go down after the Phi·lis′tines?[g] Will you give them into the hand of Israel?" But God did not answer him on that day. **38** So Saul said: "Come here, all you chiefs of the people, and find out what sin has been committed today. **39** For as surely as Jehovah is alive, who rescued Israel, even if it turns out to be Jon′a·than my

---

14:24 *Lit., "bread." **14:25** *Lit., "land." **14:29** *Or "brought ostracism."

CHAP. 14
a 1Sa 13:6

b De 33:29
  Jg 2:18

c 1Sa 13:5

d Le 5:4
  Nu 30:2
  De 23:21

e 1Sa 14:17

f 1Sa 14:24

g 1Sa 14:26

Second Col.
a Jos 10:12

b Ge 9:4
  Le 3:17
  Le 17:10
  De 12:16
  Ac 15:29

c De 12:23

d 1Sa 14:32

e 1Sa 7:15, 17

f Nu 27:21
  1Sa 30:7, 8

g Jg 1:1
  1Sa 30:8
  2Sa 5:19

son, he must die." But none of the people would answer him. **40** Then he said to all Israel: "You will be on one side, and my son Jon′a·than and I will be on the other side." At this the people said to Saul: "Do whatever seems good in your eyes."

41 Saul then said to Jehovah: "O God of Israel, answer with the Thum′mim!"[a] Then Jon′a·than and Saul were selected, and the people went free. **42** Saul now said: "Cast lots[b] to decide between me and my son Jon′a·than." And Jon′a·than was selected. **43** Then Saul said to Jon′a·than: "Tell me, what have you done?" So Jon′a·than told him: "I merely tasted a little honey on the tip of the staff in my hand.[c] Here I am! I am ready to die!"

44 At this Saul said: "Thus may God do and may he add to it if you do not die, Jon′a·than."[d] **45** But the people said to Saul: "Should Jon′a·than die—the one who brought this great victory*[e] to Israel? It is unthinkable! As surely as Jehovah is alive, not even a single hair of his head should fall to the ground, for it was with God that he acted this day."[f] With that the people rescued[g] Jon′a·than, and he did not die.

46 So Saul stopped pursuing the Phi·lis′tines, and the Phi·lis′tines went to their own territory.

47 Saul secured the kingship over Israel and fought against all his enemies on every side, against the Mo′ab·ites,[g] the Am′mon·ites,[h] the E′dom·ites,[i] the kings of Zo′bah,[j] and the Phi·lis′tines;[k] and wherever he went he defeated them. **48** And he fought bravely and conquered the A·mal′ek·ites[l] and rescued Israel from the hand of their plunderers.

49 The sons of Saul were Jon′a·than, Ish′vi, and Mal′chi·shu′a.[a] And he had two daughters; the name of the older one was Me′rab,[b] and the name of the younger one, Mi′chal.[c] **50** The name of Saul's wife was A·hin′o·am the daughter of A·him′a·az. The name of the chief of his army was Ab′ner[d] the son of Ner, the uncle of Saul. **51** Kish[e] was the father of Saul, and Ner[f] the father of Ab′ner was the son of A·bi′el.

52 There was fierce warfare with the Phi·lis′tines all the days of Saul.[g] When Saul saw any strong or courageous man, he would recruit him into his service.[h]

15 Then Samuel said to Saul: "Jehovah sent me to anoint you as king over his people Israel;[i] now listen to what Jehovah has to say.[j] **2** This is what Jehovah of armies says: 'I will call to account the A·mal′ek·ites for what they did to Israel when they opposed them along their way coming up from Egypt.[k] **3** Now go, and strike down the A·mal′ek·ites,[l] and devote them to destruction[m] along with all that they have. You must not spare* them; you are to put them to death,[n] man as well as woman, child as well as infant, bull as well as sheep, camel as well as donkey.'"[o] **4** Saul summoned the people and counted them in Te·la′im: There were 200,000 foot soldiers and 10,000 men of Judah.[p]

5 Saul advanced as far as the city of Am′a·lek and set an ambush by the valley.* **6** Saul then said to the Ken′ites:[q] "Go, depart from among the A·mal′ek·ites, so that I do not sweep you away with them.[r] For you showed loyal love to all the peo-

CHAP. 14
a Ex 28:30
  De 33:8
  Ezr 2:62, 63
b Pr 16:33
c 1Sa 14:27
d 1Sa 14:24
e 1Sa 14:14
f 1Sa 14:6
g 1Sa 12:9
h 1Sa 11:11
i Ge 36:8
j 2Sa 10:6
k 1Sa 9:16, 17
l Ex 17:14
  De 25:19
  1Sa 15:3

Second Col.
a 1Sa 31:2
  1Ch 8:33
b 1Sa 18:17
c 1Sa 18:27
  1Sa 25:44
  2Sa 3:13
  2Sa 6:20
d 1Sa 17:55
  2Sa 2:8
  2Sa 3:27
e 1Sa 9:1
f 1Ki 2:5
g Ge 49:27
  1Sa 9:16, 17
h 1Sa 8:11
  1Sa 10:26

CHAP. 15
i 1Sa 9:16
  1Sa 10:1
j 1Sa 12:14
k Ex 17:8
  Nu 24:20
  De 25:17, 18
l Ex 17:14
  De 25:19
  1Ch 4:43
m Le 27:29
  1Sa 15:18
n De 9:1, 3
o De 13:17
  Jos 6:18
p 1Sa 11:8
  1Sa 13:15
q Nu 10:29, 32
  Nu 24:21
  Jg 1:16
r Ge 18:25
  Ge 19:12, 13
  Jos 6:17

14:45 *Or "salvation." *Lit., "redeemed."   **15:3** *Or "show compassion to." **15:5** *Or "wadi."

ple of Israel[a] at the time they came up out of Egypt." So the Ken'ites departed from the midst of Am'a·lek. **7** After that Saul struck down the A·mal'ek·ites[b] from Hav'i·lah[c] as far as Shur,[d] which is next to Egypt. **8** He caught A'gag[e] the king of Am'a·lek alive, but all the other people he devoted to destruction with the sword.[f] **9** However, Saul and the people spared* A'gag and the best of the flock, the herd, the fattened animals, the rams, and all that was good.[g] They did not want to devote them to destruction. But all the goods that were worthless and unwanted, these they devoted to destruction.

10 Then the word of Jehovah came to Samuel: **11** "I regret* that I have made Saul king, for he has turned away from following me and he has not carried out my words."[h] Samuel became very upset, and he kept crying out to Jehovah all night long.[i] **12** When Samuel got up early in the morning to meet Saul, Samuel was told: "Saul went to Car'mel,[j] and there he erected a monument for himself.[k] Then he turned around and went down to Gil'gal." **13** When Samuel finally came to him, Saul said to him: "May Jehovah bless you. I have carried out the word of Jehovah." **14** But Samuel said: "Then what is this sound of the flock in my ears and the sound of the cattle that I hear?"[l] **15** To this Saul said: "They were brought from the A·mal'ek·ites, because the people spared* the best of the flock and the herd for sacrificing them to Jehovah your God; but what was left we devoted to destruction." **16** At this Samuel said to Saul: "Stop! Let me tell you what Jehovah said

to me last night."[a] So he said to him: "Speak!"

17 Samuel continued: "Were you not insignificant in your own eyes[b] when you were made head of the tribes of Israel and when Jehovah anointed you as king over Israel?[c] **18** Jehovah later sent you on a mission and said, 'Go, and devote the sinful A·mal'ek·ites to destruction.[d] Fight against them until you have exterminated them.'[e] **19** So why did you not obey the voice of Jehovah? Instead, you rushed greedily toward the spoil[f] and did what was bad in the eyes of Jehovah!"

20 However, Saul said to Samuel: "But I have obeyed the voice of Jehovah! I went on the mission to which Jehovah sent me, and I brought back A'gag the king of Am'a·lek, and I devoted the A·mal'ek·ites to destruction.[g] **21** But the people took sheep and cattle from the spoil, the best of what was devoted to destruction, to sacrifice to Jehovah your God at Gil'gal."[h]

22 Samuel then said: "Does Jehovah take as much pleasure in burnt offerings and sacrifices[i] as in obeying the voice of Jehovah? Look! To obey is better than a sacrifice,[j] and to pay attention than the fat[k] of rams; **23** for rebelliousness[l] is the same as the sin of divination,[m] and pushing ahead presumptuously the same as using magical power and idolatry.* Because you have rejected the word of Jehovah,[n] he has rejected you from being king."[o]

24 Then Saul said to Samuel: "I have sinned, for I have overstepped the order of Jehovah and your words, because I feared the people and listened to what they said. **25** And now,

---

CHAP. 15
a Ex 18:9, 12

b De 25:19
  1Sa 14:47, 48

c Ge 25:17, 18

d 1Sa 27:8

e 1Sa 15:33

f Le 27:29
  1Sa 15:3

g Jos 7:12

h 1Sa 13:13
  1Sa 15:3

i 1Sa 16:1

j Jos 15:20, 55

k 2Sa 18:18

l 1Sa 15:3

Second Col.
a 1Sa 15:10, 11

b 1Sa 9:21
  1Sa 10:22

c 1Sa 9:16
  1Sa 10:1

d 1Sa 15:3

e De 25:19

f De 13:17
  1Sa 15:9

g Le 27:29
  De 7:16
  1Sa 15:3, 9

h 1Sa 15:15

i Isa 1:11

j Pr 21:3
  Ho 6:6
  Mr 12:33

k Le 3:16

l 1Sa 12:15

m Le 20:6
  De 18:10, 12
  1Ch 10:13

n 1Sa 15:3

o 1Sa 13:14
  1Sa 16:1
  Ac 13:22

15:9, 15 *Or "showed compassion to."
15:11 *Or "am grieved."

15:23 *Lit., "teraphim statues," that is, household gods; idols.

please, pardon my sin, and return with me so that I may bow down to Jehovah."[a] **26** But Samuel said to Saul: "I will not return with you, for you have rejected the word of Jehovah, and Jehovah has rejected you from continuing as king over Israel."[b] **27** As Samuel was turning to go, Saul grabbed hold of the hem of his sleeveless coat, but it ripped away. **28** At this Samuel said to him: "Jehovah has ripped away the royal rule of Israel from you today, and he will give it to one of your fellow men who is better than you.[c] **29** Moreover, the Excellency of Israel[d] will not prove false[e] or change his mind,* for He is not a mere man that he should change his mind."*[f]

30 At this he said: "I have sinned. But honor me, please, in front of the elders of my people and in front of Israel. Return with me, and I will bow down to Jehovah your God."[g] **31** So Samuel returned behind Saul, and Saul bowed down to Jehovah. **32** And Samuel said: "Bring A'gag the king of Am'a·lek near to me." Then A'gag went to him reluctantly,* for A'gag had been saying to himself: 'Surely the threat* of death is past.' **33** However, Samuel said: "Just as your sword has bereaved women of children, so your mother will be most bereaved among women." With that Samuel hacked A'gag to pieces before Jehovah at Gil'gal.[h]

34 Samuel now went to Ra'mah, and Saul went up to his own house at Gib'e·ah of Saul. **35** Samuel did not see Saul again until the day of his death, for Samuel went into mourning for Saul.[i] And Jehovah regretted that he had made Saul king over Israel.[j]

15:29 *Or "feel regret." **15:32** *Or possibly, "confidently." *Lit., "bitterness."

16 Jehovah eventually said to Samuel: "How long will you mourn for Saul[a] now that I have rejected him from ruling as king over Israel?[b] Fill your horn with oil[c] and go. I will send you to Jes'se[d] the Beth'le·hem·ite, because I have selected from among his sons a king for myself."[e] **2** But Samuel said: "How can I go? When Saul hears about it, he will kill me."[f] Jehovah replied: "Take a young cow with you and say, 'I have come to sacrifice to Jehovah.' **3** Invite Jes'se to the sacrifice; then I will make known to you what to do. You must anoint for me the one whom I designate to you."[g]

4 Samuel did what Jehovah said. When he came to Beth'le·hem,[h] the elders of the city were trembling at meeting him, and they said: "Does your coming mean peace?" **5** To this he said: "It means peace. I have come to sacrifice to Jehovah. Sanctify yourselves, and come with me to the sacrifice." Then he sanctified Jes'se and his sons, after which he summoned them to the sacrifice. **6** As they came in and he saw E·li'ab,[i] he said: "Surely here before Jehovah stands his anointed one." **7** But Jehovah said to Samuel: "Do not pay attention to his appearance and how tall he is,[j] for I have rejected him. For the way man sees is not the way God sees, because mere man sees what appears to the eyes, but Jehovah sees into the heart."[k] **8** Then Jes'se called A·bin'a·dab[l] and had him pass before Samuel, but he said: "Jehovah has not chosen this one either." **9** Next Jes'se presented Sham'mah,[m] but he said: "Jehovah has not chosen this one either." **10** So Jes'se had seven of his sons pass before Samuel, but Samuel said to Jes'se: "Jehovah has not chosen any of these."

CHAP. 15
a 1Sa 15:30

b 1Sa 13:14
1Sa 16:1

c 1Sa 13:14
1Sa 16:12, 13
Ac 13:22

d 1Ch 29:11

e Tit 1:2
Heb 6:18

f Nu 23:19

g 1Sa 15:25

h Ex 17:14
De 25:19
1Sa 15:3

i 1Sa 16:1

j 1Sa 15:11

Second Col.

CHAP. 16
a 1Sa 15:35

b 1Sa 15:23, 26

c 1Ki 1:39

d Ru 4:17
1Ch 2:12

e Ge 49:10
1Sa 13:14
Ps 78:70
Ac 13:22

f 1Sa 22:17

g Ps 89:20

h Ru 4:11
1Sa 20:6

i 1Sa 17:28
1Ch 2:13

j 1Sa 10:21, 23

k 1Ki 8:39
1Ch 28:9
Ps 7:9
Pr 24:12
Jer 17:10
Ac 1:24

l 1Sa 17:13
1Ch 2:13

m 2Sa 13:3

11 Finally Samuel said to Jes'se: "Are these all of your boys?" To this he said: "The youngest[a] has been left out until now; he is pasturing the sheep."[b] Then Samuel said to Jes'se: "Send for him, because we will not sit down for the meal until he comes here." **12** So he sent for him and brought him in. Now he was ruddy, with beautiful eyes, and handsome in appearance.[c] Then Jehovah said: "Get up, anoint him, for this is the one!"[d] **13** So Samuel took the horn of oil[e] and anointed him in the presence of his brothers. And the spirit of Jehovah began to empower David from that day forward.[f] Samuel later rose and went his way to Ra'mah.[g]

14 Now the spirit of Jehovah had departed from Saul,[h] and a bad spirit from Jehovah terrorized him.[i] **15** The servants of Saul said to him: "You see that a bad spirit from God is terrorizing you. **16** Let our lord, please, command your servants before you to look for a man who is skilled at playing the harp.[j] Whenever a bad spirit from God comes upon you, he will play it, and you will feel better." **17** So Saul said to his servants: "Find me, please, a man who plays well, and bring him to me."

18 One of the attendants said: "Look! I have seen how a son of Jes'se the Beth'lehem-ite plays skillfully, and he is a courageous, mighty warrior.[k] He can speak well, and he is handsome,[l] and Jehovah is with him."[m] **19** Saul then sent messengers to Jes'se and said: "Send to me your son David, who is with the flock."[n] **20** So Jes'se loaded a donkey with bread, a skin bottle of wine, and a young goat and sent them to Saul with his son David. **21** Thus David came to Saul and began serving him.[o] Saul grew to love

him very much, and he became his armor-bearer. **22** Saul sent a message to Jes'se: "Please let David remain in my service, for he has found favor in my eyes." **23** Whenever a bad spirit from God came upon Saul, David took the harp and played it, and Saul found relief and felt better, and the bad spirit would depart from him.[a]

17 And the Phi·lis'tines[b] assembled their armies* for war. They assembled at So'coh,[c] which belongs to Judah, and they camped between So'coh and A·ze'kah,[d] in E'phes-dam'mim.[e] **2** Saul and the men of Israel assembled and camped in the Valley* of E'lah,[f] and they drew up in battle formation to meet the Phi·lis'tines. **3** The Phi·lis'tines occupied the mountain on one side, and the Israelites occupied the mountain on the other side, with the valley between them.

4 Then a champion came out from the camps of the Phi·lis'tines; his name was Go·li'ath,[g] from Gath,[h] and his height was six cubits and a span.* **5** He had a helmet of copper on his head, and he was wearing a coat of mail of overlapping scales. The weight of the copper coat of mail* was 5,000 shekels.* **6** He had shin guards of copper on his legs and a javelin[j] of copper slung between his shoulders. **7** The wooden shaft of his spear was like the beam of loom workers,[k] and the iron blade of his spear weighed 600 shekels;* and his shield-bearer was marching ahead of him. **8** Then he stood and called out to the battle line

---

CHAP. 16
a 1Sa 17:14

b 2Sa 7:8
Ps 78:70

c 1Sa 17:42

d 1Sa 13:14
Ps 89:20
Ac 13:22

e 1Sa 16:1
1Ki 1:39

f Nu 11:17
Jg 3:9, 10
1Sa 18:12
2Sa 23:2

g 1Sa 1:1, 19

h 1Sa 18:12
1Sa 28:15

i 1Sa 18:10
1Sa 19:9

j Pr 22:29

k 1Sa 17:32, 36
1Sa 17:45, 46

l 1Sa 16:12

m 1Sa 18:12

n 1Sa 17:15

o Pr 22:29

Second Col.
a 1Sa 16:14
1Sa 18:10
1Sa 19:9

CHAP. 17
b Jg 3:1, 3
Jos 9:16
1Sa 14:52

c 2Ch 28:18

d Jos 15:20, 35
Jer 34:7

e 1Ch 11:12, 13

f 1Sa 21:9

g 1Sa 17:23

h Jos 11:22
2Sa 21:20, 21

i 1Sa 17:38, 39
1Ki 22:34

j 1Sa 17:45

k 1Ch 20:5

17:1 *Lit., "camps." **17:2** *Or "Low Plain." **17:4** *His height was about 2.9 m (9 ft 5.75 in.). See App. B14. **17:5** *About 57 kg (125 lb). See App. B14. **17:7** *About 6.84 kg (15 lb). See App. B14.

of Israel[a] and said to them: "Why have you come out to draw up in battle formation? Am I not the Phi·lis'tine, and are you not the servants of Saul? Choose a man for yourselves, and let him come down to me. **9** If he is able to fight with me and strike me down, we will then become your servants. But if I prevail against him and strike him down, you will become our servants and serve us." **10** The Phi·lis'tine then said: "I do taunt* the battle line of Israel[b] this day. Give me a man, and let us fight it out!"

11 When Saul and all Israel heard these words of the Phi·lis'tine, they became terrified and greatly afraid.

12 Now David was the son of the Eph'rath·ite[c] from Beth'·le·hem[d] of Judah named Jes'se,[e] who had eight sons[f] and who in the days of Saul was already an old man. **13** The three oldest sons of Jes'se had followed Saul to the war.[g] The names of his three sons who went to war were E·li'ab[h] the firstborn, his second son A·bin'a·dab,[i] and the third Sham'mah.[j] **14** David was the youngest,[k] and the three oldest followed Saul.

15 David was going back and forth from Saul to tend the sheep[l] of his father at Beth'·le·hem. **16** Meanwhile, the Phi·lis'tine would come forward and take his position each morning and each evening for 40 days.

17 Then Jes'se said to his son David: "Take, please, this e'phah* of roasted grain and these ten loaves of bread, and carry them quickly to your brothers in the camp. **18** And take these ten portions of cheese* to the chief of the thousand; also, you should check

on the welfare of your brothers and bring back some token from them." **19** They were with Saul and all the other men of Israel in the Valley* of E'lah,[a] fighting against the Phi·lis'tines.[b]

20 So David got up early in the morning and left someone in charge of the sheep; then he packed up and went just as Jes'se had commanded him. When he came to the camp enclosure, the army was going out to the battle line, shouting a battle cry. **21** Israel and the Phi·lis'tines drew up so that one battle line faced the other battle line. **22** David immediately left his baggage in the care of the baggage keeper and ran to the battle line. When he arrived, he began asking about the welfare of his brothers.[c]

23 While he was speaking with them, there came the champion named Go·li'ath,[d] the Phi·lis'tine from Gath. He came out from the battle line of the Phi·lis'tines, and he spoke the same words as before,[e] and David heard him. **24** When all the men of Israel saw the man, they fled from him, terrified.[f] **25** The men of Israel were saying: "Have you seen this man who is coming out? He comes to taunt* Israel.[g] The king will give great riches to the man who strikes him down, he will give him his own daughter,[h] and he will give the house of his father exemption in Israel."

26 David began to say to the men who were standing near him: "What will be done for the man who strikes down that Phi·lis'tine over there and takes away reproach from Israel? For who is this uncircumcised Phi·lis'tine that he should taunt* the battle line of the living God?"[i] **27** Then the people told

---

CHAP. 17

a Nu 33:55

b 1Sa 17:26
2Ki 19:22

c Ge 35:16, 19
Ru 1:2

d 1Sa 17:58
Mic 5:2
Mt 2:6

e Ru 4:22

f 1Ch 2:13-15

g Nu 1:3

h 1Sa 16:6

i 1Sa 16:8

j 1Sa 16:9

k 1Ch 2:13, 15

l 1Sa 16:11, 19

Second Col.

a 1Sa 17:2
1Sa 21:9

b 1Sa 9:16, 17

c 1Sa 17:17, 18

d 1Sa 17:4

e 1Sa 17:10

f 1Sa 17:11

g 1Sa 17:10

h Jos 15:16
1Sa 14:49
1Sa 18:17, 21

i 1Sa 17:10
Jer 10:10

17:10, 25, 26 *Or "challenge." 17:17 *About 22 L (20 dry qt). See App. B14. 17:18 *Lit., "milk."

17:19 *Or "Low Plain."

him the same thing as before: "This is what will be done for the man who strikes him down." **28** When his oldest brother E·li′ab[a] heard him speak to the men, he became angry with David and said: "Why have you come down? And with whom did you leave those few sheep in the wilderness?[b] I well know your presumptuousness and the bad intentions of your heart; you came down just to see the battle." **29** To this David said: "What have I done now? I was only asking a question!" **30** So he turned from him toward someone else and asked the same thing as before,[c] and the people gave him the same reply as before.[d]

31 The words that David had spoken were overheard and reported to Saul. So he sent for him. **32** David said to Saul: "Let no one lose heart* because of him. Your servant will go and fight with this Phi·lis′tine."[e] **33** But Saul said to David: "You are not able to go fight against this Phi·lis′tine, for you are but a boy,[f] and he has been a soldier* from his youth." **34** David then said to Saul: "Your servant became a shepherd of his father's flock, and a lion[g] came, also a bear, and each carried off a sheep from the flock. **35** I went out after it and struck it down and rescued it from its mouth. When it rose up against me, I grabbed it by its fur* and struck it down and put it to death. **36** Your servant struck down both the lion and the bear, and this uncircumcised Phi·lis′tine will become like one of them, for he has taunted* the battle lines of the living God."[h]

17:32 *Or "courage." **17:33** *Or "a man of war." **17:35** *Or "by the jaw." Lit., "by its beard." **17:36, 45** *Or "challenged."

CHAP. 17
a 1Sa 16:6,11
  1Ch 2:13

b 1Sa 17:20

c 1Sa 17:26

d 1Sa 17:25

e 1Sa 16:18

f 1Sa 17:42

g Isa 31:4

h 1Sa 17:10
  Jer 10:10

Second Col.
a De 7:21
  2Ki 6:16
  Heb 11:32-34

b Jg 20:15, 16

c 1Sa 16:12
  1Sa 17:33

d 1Sa 24:14
  2Sa 16:9
  2Ki 8:13

e 1Sa 17:4, 6

f 2Sa 5:10
  Heb 11:32-34

g 1Sa 17:10
  2Ki 19:22

h De 9:1-3
  Jos 10:8

---

37 Then David added: "Jehovah, who rescued me from the claws of the lion and the bear, he is the one who will rescue me from the hand of this Phi·lis′tine."[a] At this Saul said to David: "Go, and may Jehovah be with you."

38 Saul now clothed David with his garments. He put a copper helmet on his head, after which he clothed him with a coat of mail. **39** Then David strapped on his sword over his garments and tried to go but could not, for he was not used to them. David said to Saul: "I am unable to go in these things, for I am not used to them." So David took them off. **40** He then took his staff in his hand and chose five smooth stones from the streambed* and placed them in the pouch of his shepherd's bag, and his sling[b] was in his hand. And he began approaching the Phi·lis′tine.

41 The Phi·lis′tine came closer and closer to David, and his shield-bearer was ahead of him. **42** When the Phi·lis′tine looked and saw David, he sneered at him in contempt because he was just a ruddy and handsome boy.[c] **43** So the Phi·lis′tine said to David: "Am I a dog,[d] so that you are coming against me with sticks?" With that the Phi·lis′tine cursed David by his gods. **44** The Phi·lis′tine said to David: "Just come to me, and I will give your flesh to the birds of the heavens and to the beasts of the field."

45 David replied to the Phi·lis′tine: "You are coming against me with sword and spear and javelin,[e] but I am coming against you in the name of Jehovah of armies,[f] the God of the battle line of Israel, whom you have taunted.*[g] **46** This very day Jehovah will surrender you into my hand,[h] and I will strike you down

---

17:40 *Or "wadi."

and cut off your head; and on this day I will give the corpses of the camp of the Phi·lis′tines to the birds of the heavens and to the wild beasts of the earth; and people of all the earth will know that there is a God in Israel.[a] 47 And all those gathered here* will know that it is not with the sword or the spear that Jehovah saves,[b] for the battle belongs to Jehovah,[c] and he will give all of you into our hand."[d]

48 Then the Phi·lis′tine rose and drew steadily closer to meet David, but David ran quickly toward the battle line to meet the Phi·lis′tine. 49 David thrust his hand into his bag and took a stone from there and slung it. He struck the Phi·lis′tine in the forehead, and the stone sank into his forehead and he fell facedown on the ground.[e] 50 So David prevailed over the Phi·lis′tine with a sling and a stone; he struck down the Phi·lis′tine and put him to death, though there was no sword in David's hand.[f] 51 David continued running and stood over him. Then he took hold of the Phi·lis′tine's sword and pulled it out of its sheath and made sure that he was dead by cutting off his head with it. When the Phi·lis′tines saw that their mighty one had died, they fled.[h]

52 At that the men of Israel and of Judah rose and broke into shouting and pursued the Phi·lis′tines all the way from the valley[i] to the gates of Ek′ron,[j] and the slain of the Phi·lis′tines lay fallen along the road from Sha′a·ra′im,[k] as far as Gath and Ek′ron. 53 After the Israelites returned from hotly pursuing the Phi·lis′tines, they pillaged their camps. 54 Then David took the head of the Phi·lis′tine and brought it to Jerusalem, but he put the

Phi·lis′tine's weapons in his own tent.[a]

55 At the moment that Saul saw David go out to meet the Phi·lis′tine, he said to Ab′ner,[b] the chief of the army: "Whose son is this boy,[c] Ab′ner?" Ab′ner replied: "As surely as you live,* O king, I do not know!" 56 The king said: "Find out whose son the young man is." 57 So as soon as David returned from striking down the Phi·lis′tine, Ab′ner took him and brought him before Saul with the head of the Phi·lis′tine[d] in his hand. 58 Saul now said to him: "Whose son are you, boy?" to which David said: "The son of your servant Jes′se[e] the Beth′le·hem·ite."[f]

18 As soon as David had finished speaking to Saul, Jon′a·than[g] and David became bound together in close friendship,* and Jon′a·than began to love him as himself.*[h] 2 From that day, Saul kept David with him, and he did not allow him to return to his father's house.[i] 3 And Jon′a·than and David made a covenant,[j] because he loved him as himself.*[k] 4 Jon′a·than took off the sleeveless coat that he wore and gave it to David, along with his gear, his sword, his bow, and his belt. 5 David began going out and was successful*[l] wherever Saul would send him. So Saul put him in charge of the fighting men,[m] and this pleased all the people and the servants of Saul.

6 When David and the others would return from striking down the Phi·lis′tines, the women would come out from all the cities of Israel with song[n] and danc-

---

CHAP. 17
a Ex 9:16
　 De 28:10
　 1Ki 8:43
　 2Ki 19:19
　 Da 3:29

b Ps 44:6, 7
　 Zec 4:6

c 2Ch 20:15
　 Pr 21:31

d De 20:4

e 1Sa 17:37
　 2Sa 21:22

f Jg 3:31
　 Jg 15:15, 16
　 1Sa 17:47

g 1Sa 21:9

h De 28:7
　 Jos 23:10
　 Heb 11:32-34

i 1Sa 17:2, 19

j Jos 15:20, 45

k Jos 15:20, 36

Second Col.
a 1Sa 21:9

b 1Sa 14:50

c 1Sa 16:19, 21

d 1Sa 17:54

e Ru 4:22
　 1Sa 16:1
　 1Ch 2:13, 15
　 Mt 1:6
　 Lu 3:23, 32
　 Ac 13:22

f 1Sa 17:12

CHAP. 18
g 1Sa 14:1, 49

h 1Sa 19:2
　 1Sa 20:17, 41
　 2Sa 1:26

i 1Sa 8:11
　 1Sa 16:22
　 1Sa 17:15

j 1Sa 20:8, 42
　 1Sa 23:18
　 2Sa 9:1
　 2Sa 21:7

k Pr 17:17
　 Pr 18:24

l 1Sa 18:30

m 1Sa 14:52

n Ex 15:20, 21
　 Jg 5:1

17:47 *Lit., "all this congregation."
17:55 *Or "By the life of your soul." 18:1 *Or "Jonathan's soul became bound with David's soul." 18:1, 3 *Or "as his own soul." 18:5 *Or "acted wisely."

es to meet King Saul with tambourines,[a] with rejoicing, and with lutes. **7** The women who were celebrating would sing:

"Saul has struck down his thousands,
And David his tens of thousands."[b]

8 Saul became very angry,[c] and this song displeased him, for he said: "They have credited David with tens of thousands, but to me they have credited thousands. The only thing left to give him is the kingship!"[d] **9** From that day on, Saul was always looking at David suspiciously.

10 The next day a bad spirit from God gripped Saul,[e] and he started to act strangely* inside the house, while David was playing music on the harp[f] as on other occasions. Saul had a spear in his hand,[g] **11** and he hurled the spear,[h] saying to himself: 'I will pin David to the wall!' But David escaped from him twice. **12** Then Saul was afraid of David because Jehovah was with him[i] but had departed from Saul.[j] **13** So Saul removed him from his presence and appointed him as chief of a thousand, and David would lead the army into battle.*[k] **14** David continued to have success*[l] in all he did, and Jehovah was with him.[m] **15** And when Saul saw that he was very successful, he became afraid of him. **16** But all Israel and Judah loved David, because he would lead them in their campaigns.

17 Saul later said to David: "Here is my oldest daughter Me'rab.[n] I will give her to you as a wife.[o] However, you should continue to display your courage for me and fight the wars of Jeho-

vah."[a] For Saul said to himself: 'Do not let my hand come against him. Let the hand of the Phi·lis'tines strike him.'[b] **18** At this David said to Saul: "Who am I and who are my relatives, my father's family in Israel, for me to become son-in-law to the king?"[c] **19** However, when the time came to give Saul's daughter Me'rab to David, she had already been given to be the wife of A'dri·el[d] the Me·hol'ath·ite.

20 Now Saul's daughter Mi'chal[e] was in love with David, and it was reported to Saul, and this pleased him. **21** So Saul said: "I will give her to him to serve as a snare to him, so that the hand of the Phi·lis'tines may come upon him."[f] Saul then said to David a second time: "You will form a marriage alliance with me* today." **22** Further, Saul ordered his servants: "Speak to David secretly and say, 'Look! The king is pleased with you, and all his servants are fond of you. So now form a marriage alliance with the king.'" **23** When Saul's servants told David these things, David said: "Is it a trivial matter to you to form a marriage alliance with the king when I am a man poor and lightly esteemed?"[g] **24** Then Saul's servants reported to him: "These are the words that David spoke."

25 At that Saul said: "This is what you should say to David, 'The king does not want any bride price[h] except 100 foreskins[i] of the Phi·lis'tines, to take revenge on the enemies of the king.'" For Saul was scheming to have David fall by the hand of the Phi·lis'tines. **26** So his servants reported these words to David, and it was pleasing to David to form a marriage alliance with the king.[j] Before the allotted time, **27** David

---

CHAP. 18
a Jg 11:34

b 1Sa 21:11
  1Sa 29:5

c Ge 4:5
  Pr 14:30

d 1Sa 13:14
  1Sa 15:27, 28
  1Sa 16:13
  1Sa 20:31
  1Sa 24:17, 20

e 1Sa 16:14

f 1Sa 16:16, 23

g 1Sa 19:9, 10

h 1Sa 20:33

i 1Sa 18:28, 29

j 1Sa 16:14

k 2Sa 5:2

l 1Sa 18:5

m Ge 39:2
  Jos 6:27
  1Sa 10:7
  1Sa 16:18

n 1Sa 14:49

o 1Sa 17:25

Second Col.
a 1Sa 25:28

b 1Sa 18:25

c 2Sa 7:18

d 2Sa 21:8

e 1Sa 14:49
  1Sa 19:11
  1Sa 25:44
  2Sa 3:13
  2Sa 6:16

f 1Sa 18:17

g 1Sa 18:18

h Ge 29:18

i 1Sa 17:26, 36
  2Sa 3:14

j 1Sa 18:21

18:10 *Or "behaved like a prophet." **18:13** *Lit., "and he went out and came in before the people." **18:14** *Or "act wisely."

18:21 *Or "will become my son-in-law."

went with his men and struck down 200 Phi·lis′tine men, and David brought the full number of their foreskins to the king, to form a marriage alliance with the king. Therefore, Saul gave him his daughter Mi′chal as a wife.[a] 28 Saul realized that Jehovah was with David[b] and that his daughter Mi′chal loved him.[c] 29 This made Saul even more afraid of David, and Saul became an enemy of David for the rest of his life.[d]

30 The princes of the Phi·lis′tines would go out to battle, but as often as they went out, David was more successful* than all the servants of Saul;[e] and his name was highly esteemed.[f]

19 Saul later spoke to Jon′a·than his son and to all his servants about putting David to death.[g] 2 Since Saul's son Jon′a·than was very fond of David,[h] Jon′a·than told David: "My father Saul wants to have you put to death. Please be on your guard in the morning, and go to a secret place, and remain hidden. 3 I will go out and stand next to my father in the field where you will be. I will talk about you to my father, and if I learn anything, I will be sure to tell you."[i]

4 So Jon′a·than spoke well of David[j] to his father Saul. He said to him: "The king should not sin against his servant David, for he has not sinned against you and what he has done for you has benefited you. 5 He risked his life* to strike down the Phi·lis′tine,[k] so that Jehovah brought about a great victory# for all Israel. You saw it, and you were overjoyed. So why should you sin against innocent blood in having David put to death for no reason?"[l] 6 Saul listened to

Jon′a·than, and Saul swore: "As surely as Jehovah is living, he will not be put to death." 7 Afterward Jon′a·than called David and told him all these things. So Jon′a·than brought David to Saul, and he continued to serve him as before.[a]

8 In time war broke out again, and David went out and fought against the Phi·lis′tines and struck them down with a great slaughter, and they fled from before him.

9 And a bad spirit from Jehovah[b] came upon David when he was sitting in his house with his spear in his hand, while David was playing music on the harp.[c] 10 Saul tried to pin David to the wall with the spear, but he eluded Saul, who drove the spear into the wall. David fled and escaped during that night. 11 Saul later sent messengers to David's house to watch it and to kill him in the morning,[d] but David's wife Mi′chal told him: "If you do not escape* tonight, tomorrow you will be a dead man." 12 Immediately Mi′chal let David down through the window, so that he could run away and escape. 13 Mi′chal took the teraphim statue* and placed it on the bed, and she put a net of goat hair at the place of his head, and she covered it with a garment.

14 Saul now sent messengers to take David, but she said: "He is sick." 15 So Saul sent the messengers to see David and told them: "Bring him to me on his bed to have him put to death."[e] 16 When the messengers came in, there was the teraphim statue* on the bed and a net of goat hair where his head would have been. 17 Saul said to Mi′chal: "Why did you trick

---

CHAP. 18
a 1Sa 17:25
b 1Sa 16:13
1Sa 24:17, 20
c 1Sa 18:20
d 1Sa 18:9, 12
1Sa 20:33
e 1Sa 18:5
f 2Sa 7:9
CHAP. 19
g 1Sa 18:9
Pr 27:4
h 1Sa 18:1
Pr 18:24
i 1Sa 20:9, 13
Pr 17:17
j 1Sa 22:14
k 1Sa 17:49
l 1Sa 20:32
Second Col.
a 1Sa 16:21
1Sa 18:2, 13
b 1Sa 16:14
c 1Sa 18:10, 11
d Ps 59:Sup, 3
e 1Sa 18:9

18:30 *Or "acted more wisely." 19:5 *Or "put his soul in his hand." #Or "salvation."

19:11 *Or "If you do not let your soul escape." 19:13, 16 *Or "the household god; the idol."

me like this and send my enemy[a] away and escaped, and he came to "He said to me, 'Send me away, or I will kill you!'"

18 Now David had run away and escaped, and he came to Samuel at Ra′mah.[b] He told him all that Saul had done to him. Then he and Samuel went away, and they stayed in Nai′oth.[c] **19** In time it was reported to Saul: "Look! David is in Nai′oth in Ra′mah." **20** At once Saul sent messengers to seize David. When they saw the elderly ones of the prophets prophesying and Samuel standing and presiding over them, the spirit of God came to be upon Saul's messengers, and they began behaving as prophets as well.

21 When they told it to Saul, he immediately sent other messengers, and they too began behaving as prophets. So Saul sent messengers again, a third group, and they too began behaving as prophets. **22** Finally he also went to Ra′mah. When he reached the great cistern that is in Se′cu, he asked: "Where are Samuel and David?" They replied: "There in Nai′oth[d] in Ra′mah." **23** While Saul was on his way from there to Nai′oth in Ra′mah, the spirit of God came upon him as well, and he walked along behaving as a prophet until he came into Nai′oth in Ra′mah. **24** He also stripped off his garments, and he too behaved as a prophet before Samuel, and he lay there naked* all that day and all that night. That is why they say: "Is Saul also among the prophets?"[e]

20 Then David ran away from Nai′oth in Ra′mah. However, he came to Jon′a·than and said: "What have I done?[f] What is my offense, and how have I

sinned against your father for him to seek my life?"* **2** At this Jon′a·than said to him: "It is unthinkable![a] You will not die. Look! My father will not do anything, great or small, without disclosing it to me. Why should my father hide this matter from me? This will not happen." **3** But David swore further and said: "Your father surely knows that I have found favor in your eyes[b] and would say, 'Do not let Jon′a·than know this or he will be upset.' But as surely as Jehovah is living and as surely as you are* living, there is only a step between me and death!"[c]

4 Then Jon′a·than said to David: "Whatever you say,* I will do for you." **5** David said to Jon′a·than: "Tomorrow is the new moon,[d] and I am certainly expected to sit with the king to eat; you must send me away, and I will hide in the field until the evening on the third day. **6** If your father misses me at all, then say, 'David begged me for permission to go quickly to his city Beth′le·hem,[e] because there is a yearly sacrifice there for all the family.'[f] **7** If his response is, 'That is fine,' it means peace to your servant. But if he becomes angry, you can be sure that he is determined to harm me. **8** Show loyal love to your servant,[g] for you have brought your servant into Jehovah's covenant with you.[h] But if I am guilty,[i] put me to death yourself. Why turn me over to your father?"

9 To this Jon′a·than said: "It is unthinkable to suggest that about you! If I learn that my father is determined to harm you, would I not tell you?"[j] **10** Then David said to Jon′a·than: "Who will tell me whether your father

---

CHAP. 19
a 1Sa 18:29

b 1Sa 7:15, 17

c 1Sa 20:1

d 1Sa 19:18

e 1Sa 10:11

CHAP. 20
f 1Sa 24:11
Ps 18:20

Second Col.
a 1Sa 19:6

b 1Sa 18:1
1Sa 19:2

c 1Sa 27:1

d Nu 10:10
2Ch 2:4

e 1Sa 16:4, 18

f 1Sa 20:28, 29

g Pr 17:17

h 1Sa 18:3
1Sa 23:18

i 1Sa 20:1

j 1Sa 19:2

19:24 *Or "lightly clad."

20:1 *Or "soul." 20:3 *Or "your soul is." 20:4 *Or "your soul says."

gives you a harsh answer?" 11 Jon'a·than said to David: "Come, let us go out into the field." So both of them went out into the field. 12 And Jon'a·than said to David: "Let Jehovah the God of Israel be a witness that I will sound out my father about this time tomorrow or by the third day. If he is favorably disposed toward David, will I not then send you word and disclose it to you? 13 But if my father intends to harm you, may Jehovah do that and more to Jon'a·than if I do not disclose it to you and send you away in peace. May Jehovah be with you,ᵃ just as he was with my father.ᵇ 14 And will you not show me the loyal love of Jehovah while I am alive and even when I die?ᶜ 15 Never withdraw your loyal love from my household,ᵈ even when Jehovah wipes out all the enemies of David from the face of the earth." 16 So Jon'a·than made a covenant with the house of David, saying, "Jehovah will require it and call David's enemies to account." 17 So Jon'a·than had David swear again by his love for him, for he loved him as he loved himself.*ᵉ

18 Jon'a·than then said to him: "Tomorrow is the new moon,ᶠ and you will be missed, for your seat will be vacant. 19 By the third day, you will be missed even more, and you must go to the place where you hid the other day* and stay near the stone here. 20 I will then shoot three arrows to one side of it, as though I were shooting at a target. 21 When I send the attendant, I will say, 'Go, find the arrows.' If I say to the attendant, 'Look! The arrows are on this side of you, get them,' then you may come back, for as sure-

ly as Jehovah is living, it means everything is peaceful for you and there is no danger. 22 But if I should say to the boy, 'Look! The arrows are beyond you,' then go, for Jehovah has sent you away. 23 As for the promise that we have made,ᵃ you and I, may Jehovah be between us forever."ᵇ

24 So David hid in the field. When the new moon came, the king took his seat at the meal to eat.ᶜ 25 The king was sitting in his usual seat by the wall. Jon'a·than was facing him, and Ab'nerᵈ was sitting at Saul's side, but David's place was vacant. 26 Saul did not say anything that day, for he said to himself: 'Something has happened so that he is not clean.ᵉ Yes, he must be unclean.' 27 And the day after the new moon, on the second day, David's place continued vacant. Saul then said to Jon'a·than his son: "Why has the son of Jes'seᶠ not come to the meal either yesterday or today?" 28 Jon'a·than answered Saul: "David begged me for permission to go to Beth'le·hem.ᵍ 29 He said, 'Please permit me to go, because we have a family sacrifice in the city, and my own brother summoned me. So if I have found favor in your eyes, please let me slip away to see my brothers.' That is why he has not come to the king's table." 30 Then Saul became enraged with Jon'a·than, and he said to him: "You son of a rebellious woman, do you think I do not know that you are choosing to side with the son of Jes'se, to your own shame and to the shame of your mother?* 31 As long as the son of Jes'se is alive on the earth, you and your kingship will not be firmly established.ʰ So now send some-

---

CHAP. 20
a 1Sa 16:13
  1Sa 17:37

b 1Sa 10:7
  1Sa 11:6

c 2Sa 9:1, 3
  2Sa 9:6, 7

d 2Sa 21:7

e 1Sa 18:1, 3
  2Sa 1:26
  Pr 18:24

f 1Sa 20:5

Second Col.
a 1Sa 20:13, 14

b 1Sa 20:42

c 1Sa 20:5

d 1Sa 14:50

e Le 11:23, 24
  Le 15:4, 5
  Le 15:16, 18
  Nu 19:16

f 1Sa 17:12

g 1Sa 20:6

h 1Sa 18:8

20:17 *Or "his own soul." 20:19 *Lit., "on the working day."

20:30 *Lit., "to the shame of your mother's nakedness?"

one to bring him to me, for he must die."*[a]

32 However, Jon'a·than said to Saul his father: "Why should he be put to death?[b] What has he done?" **33** At that Saul hurled the spear at him to strike him,[c] so Jon'a·than knew that his father was determined to put David to death.[d] **34** Jon'a·than immediately rose up from the table in the heat of anger, and he did not eat any food on the second day after the new moon, for he was upset over David[e] and his own father had humiliated him.

35 In the morning Jon'a·than went out to the field for the appointment with David, and a young attendant was with him.[f] **36** And he said to his attendant: "Please run and find the arrows that I shoot." The attendant ran, and Jon'a·than shot the arrow beyond him. **37** When the attendant reached the place where Jon'a·than had shot the arrow, Jon'a·than called out to the attendant: "Is not the arrow beyond you?" **38** Jon'a·than called out to the attendant: "Hurry! Go quickly! Do not delay!" And Jon'a·than's attendant picked up the arrows and came back to his master. **39** The attendant did not understand anything about the matter; only Jon'a·than and David knew what was meant. **40** Then Jon'a·than gave his weapons to his attendant and told him: "Go, take them to the city."

41 When the attendant left, David rose up from a place nearby that was to the south. Then he fell with his face to the ground and bowed three times, and they kissed each other and wept for each other, but David wept the most. **42** Jon'a·than said to David: "Go in peace, since we have both sworn[g] in the

name of Jehovah, saying, 'May Jehovah be between you and me and between your offspring* and my offspring* forever.'"[a]

Then David rose up and left, and Jon'a·than went back to the city.

21 David later came to Nob[b] to A·him'e·lech the priest. A·him'e·lech began to tremble when he met David, and he said to him: "Why are you by yourself and no one is with you?"[c] **2** David replied to A·him'e·lech the priest: "The king instructed me to do something, but he said, 'Do not let anyone know anything about the mission on which I am sending you and about the instructions I have given you.' I made an appointment with my young men to meet at a certain place. **3** Now if there are five loaves of bread at your disposal, just give them to me, or whatever is available." **4** But the priest answered David: "There is no ordinary bread on hand, but there is holy bread[d]—provided that the young men have kept away from women."*[e] **5** David answered the priest: "Women have certainly been kept away from us as on previous occasions when I went out on a campaign.[f] If the bodies of the young men are holy even when the mission is ordinary, how much more so today should they be holy!" **6** So the priest gave him the holy bread,[g] because there was no bread there except the showbread, which had been removed from Jehovah's presence to be replaced by fresh bread on the day it was taken away.

7 Now one of Saul's servants was there on that day, detained before Jehovah. His name was Do'eg[h] the E'dom·ite,[i] the chief of Saul's shepherds.

CHAP. 20
a 1Sa 19:6, 10

b 1Sa 19:5
Pr 17:17
Pr 18:24

c 1Sa 18:11
1Sa 19:10

d 1Sa 20:6, 7

e 1Sa 18:1

f 1Sa 20:19-22

g 1Sa 20:17, 23

Second Col.
a 1Sa 23:18
2Sa 9:7

CHAP. 21
b 1Sa 22:9, 19

c 1Sa 18:13

d Ex 25:30
Le 24:5, 9
Mt 12:3, 4

e Ex 19:15
Le 15:16
2Sa 11:11

f Le 15:18

g Le 24:7-9
Mt 2:25, 26
Lu 6:3, 4

h 1Sa 22:9
Ps 52:Sup

i Ge 36:1

20:31 *Lit., "for he is a son of death." 20:42 *Lit., "seed." 21:4 *Or "have abstained from sexual relations."

8 David then said to A·him′e·lech: "Is there a spear or a sword here at your disposal? I did not take my own sword or my weapons with me, because the king's mission was urgent." **9** To this the priest said: "The sword of Go·li′ath[a] the Phi·lis′tine, whom you struck down in the Valley* of E′lah,[b] is here, wrapped up in a cloth behind the eph′od.[c] If you want to take it for yourself, take it, because it is the only one here." David said: "There is none like it. Give it to me."

10 That day David rose up and continued his flight[d] from Saul, and he eventually came to King A′chish of Gath.[e] **11** The servants of A′chish said to him: "Is this not David, the king of the land? Is he not the one they sang about when they danced, saying,

'Saul has struck down his thousands,
And David his tens of thousands'?"[f]

12 David took these words to heart, and he became very much afraid[g] of King A′chish of Gath. **13** So he disguised his sanity[h] in their presence and acted insane while among them.* He was making marks on the doors of the gate and letting his saliva run down his beard. **14** Finally A′chish said to his servants: "You see that this man is crazy! Why bring him to me? **15** Do I have a shortage of crazy men that I need to have this one acting crazy before me? Should this man enter my house?"

22 So David went from there,[i] escaping to the cave of A·dul′lam.[j] When his brothers and his father's entire house heard of it, they went down there to him. **2** And all those who were in trouble and in debt

and who had a grievance* gathered to him, and he became their chief. There were about 400 men with him.

3 David later went from there to Miz′peh in Mo′ab and said to the king of Mo′ab:[a] "Please let my father and mother stay with you until I know what God will do for me." **4** So he left them with the king of Mo′ab, and they stayed with him the whole time that David was in the stronghold.[b]

5 In time Gad[c] the prophet said to David: "Do not stay in the stronghold. Go from there into the land of Judah."[d] So David left and went into the forest of He′reth.

6 Saul heard that David and the men with him had been found. Saul was then sitting in Gib′e·ah[e] under the tamarisk tree on the high place with his spear in his hand, and all his servants were stationed around him. **7** Then Saul said to his servants stationed around him: "Listen, please, you Ben′ja·min·ites. Will the son of Jes′se[f] also give fields and vineyards to all of you? Will he appoint all of you as chiefs of thousands and chiefs of hundreds?[g] **8** All of you have conspired against me! No one informed me when my own son made a covenant with the son of Jes′se![h] Not one of you has sympathy for me and informs me that my own son has incited my own servant against me to ambush me, as is now the case."

9 Then Do′eg[i] the E′dom·ite, who was stationed there over the servants of Saul, answered:[j] "I saw the son of Jes′se come to Nob to A·him′e·lech the son of A·hi′tub.[k] **10** And he inquired of Jehovah for him and gave him provisions. He even gave him the sword of Go·li′ath the Phi·lis′-

---

CHAP. 21
a 1Sa 17:51, 54

b 1Sa 17:2, 50

c Ex 28:6

d 1Sa 27:1

e Jos 11:22
  1Sa 5:8
  1Sa 17:4
  1Sa 27:2
  Ps 56:Sup

f 1Sa 18:6-8
  1Sa 29:4, 5

g Ps 56:3, 6

h Ps 34:Sup

_____

CHAP. 22
i 1Sa 21:10

j Jos 15:20, 35
  2Sa 23:13
  Ps 34:19
  Ps 56:13

_____

Second Col.
a Ru 4:10, 17
  1Sa 14:47

b 1Sa 22:1

c 2Sa 24:11, 12
  1Ch 21:9, 10
  1Ch 29:29
  2Ch 29:25

d 1Sa 23:3

e 1Sa 10:26

f Ru 4:22

g 1Sa 8:11, 12

h 1Sa 18:3
  1Sa 20:17

i 1Sa 21:1, 7
  Ps 52:Sup

j Ps 52:2, 3

k 1Sa 14:3
  1Sa 22:20

21:9 *Or "Low Plain." 21:13 *Lit., "in their hand."

22:2 *Or "were bitter of soul."

tine."[a] **11** At once the king sent for A·him′e·lech son of A·hi′tub the priest and all the priests of his father's house, who were in Nob. So all of them came to the king.

12 Saul now said: "Listen, please, you son of A·hi′tub!" to which he replied: "Here I am, my lord." **13** Saul said to him: "Why have you conspired against me, you and the son of Jes′se, by giving him bread and a sword and by making an inquiry of God for him? He opposes me and waits in ambush, as is now the case." **14** At this A·him′e·lech answered the king: "Who among all your servants is as trustworthy* as David?[b] He is the king's son-in-law[c] and a chief over your bodyguard and honored in your house.[d] **15** Was today the first time I inquired of God for him?[e] What you are saying is unthinkable on my part! Do not let the king hold anything against his servant and against my father's entire house, for your servant did not know a single thing about any of this."[f]

16 But the king said: "You will surely die,[g] A·him′e·lech, you along with all your father's house."[h] **17** With that the king said to the guards* stationed around him: "Turn and kill the priests of Jehovah, because they have sided with David! They knew that he was a runaway, and they did not inform me!" But the king's servants did not want to lift their hands to assault the priests of Jehovah. **18** Then the king said to Do′eg:[i] "You turn and assault the priests!" Immediately Do′eg the E′dom·ite[j] went and assaulted the priests himself. He killed on that day 85 men wearing the linen eph′od.[k] **19** He also struck Nob,[l] the city

of the priests, with the sword; man as well as woman, child as well as infant, bull, donkey, and sheep, he put to the sword.

20 However, one son of A·him′e·lech the son of A·hi′tub, whose name was A·bi′a·thar,[a] escaped and ran away to follow David. **21** A·bi′a·thar told David: "Saul has killed the priests of Jehovah." **22** At this David said to A·bi′a·thar: "I knew on that day,[b] when Do′eg the E′dom·ite was there, that he would be sure to tell Saul. I am personally responsible for the death of everyone* in your father's house. **23** Stay with me. Do not be afraid, for whoever seeks your life* seeks my life;* you are under my protection."[c]

23 In time David was told: "The Phi·lis′tines are fighting against Kei′lah,[d] and they are raiding the threshing floors." **2** So David inquired of Jehovah:[e] "Should I go and strike down these Phi·lis′tines?" Jehovah said to David: "Go, strike down the Phi·lis′tines and rescue Kei′lah." **3** But the men of David said to him: "Look! We are afraid while here in Judah;[f] how much more so if we go to Kei′lah against the battle line of the Phi·lis′tines!"[g] **4** So David inquired once again of Jehovah.[h] Jehovah now answered him: "Rise up; go down to Kei′lah because I will give the Phi·lis′tines into your hand."[i] **5** So David went with his men to Kei′lah and fought against the Phi·lis′tines; he carried off their livestock and struck them down with a great slaughter, and David rescued the inhabitants of Kei′lah.[j]

6 Now when A·bi′a·thar[k] the son of A·him′e·lech ran away to David at Kei′lah, he had an eph′od with him. **7** Saul was told:

CHAP. 22
a 1Sa 21:6, 9

b 1Sa 19:4
1Sa 20:32
1Sa 24:11
1Sa 26:23

c 1Sa 17:25
1Sa 18:27

d 1Sa 18:5, 13

e 1Sa 22:10

f 1Sa 21:1, 2

g 1Sa 14:44
1Sa 20:31

h 2Sa 2:27, 32

i Ps 52:Sup

j Ge 25:30

k 2Sa 2:27, 31

l 1Sa 21:1
1Sa 22:9

Second Col.
a 1Sa 23:6
1Sa 30:7
2Sa 20:25
1Ki 2:27

b 1Sa 21:1, 7

c 1Ki 2:26

CHAP. 23
d Jos 15:20, 44

e 1Sa 30:8
2Sa 5:19
Ps 37:5

f 1Sa 22:5

g 1Sa 13:5
1Sa 14:52

h Jg 6:39

i 1Sa 14:6
2Sa 5:19

j 1Sa 23:1

k 1Sa 22:20

22:14 *Or "faithful." 22:17 *Lit., "runners."

22:22 *Or "every soul." 22:23 *Or "soul."

"David has come to Kei'lah." Then Saul said: "God has handed him over to me,*[a] for he has trapped himself by entering a city with gates and bars." **8** So Saul summoned all the people to war, to go down to Kei'lah and besiege David and his men. **9** When David learned that Saul was plotting against him, he said to A·bi'a·thar the priest: "Bring the eph'od here."[b] **10** Then David said: "O Jehovah the God of Israel, your servant has indeed heard that Saul intends to come to Kei'lah to destroy the city because of me.[c] **11** Will the leaders* of Kei'lah surrender me into his hand? Will Saul come down as your servant has heard? O Jehovah the God of Israel, please tell your servant." To this Jehovah said: "He will come down." **12** David asked: "Will the leaders of Kei'lah surrender me and my men into Saul's hand?" Jehovah replied: "They will surrender you."

13 At once David rose up with his men, about 600 in number,[d] and they left Kei'lah and moved about wherever they could. When Saul was told that David had escaped from Kei'lah, he did not go out after him. **14** David stayed in the wilderness in places difficult to approach, in the mountainous region of the wilderness of Ziph.[e] Saul searched for him constantly,[f] but Jehovah did not give him into his hand. **15** David was aware that* Saul had gone out to seek his life[g] while David was in the wilderness of Ziph at Ho'resh.

16 Jon'a·than the son of Saul now went out to David at Ho'resh, and he helped him find

strength* in Jehovah.[a] **17** He said to him: "Do not be afraid, for my father Saul will not find you; you will be king over Israel,[b] and I will become second to you; and my father Saul also knows that."[c] **18** Then the two of them made a covenant[d] before Jehovah, and David stayed in Ho'resh, and Jon'a·than went to his home.

19 The men of Ziph later went up to Saul at Gib'e·ah[e] and said: "Is not David hiding near us* in the places difficult to approach at Ho'resh,[g] on the hill of Hach·i'lah,[h] which is south* of Je·shi'mon?*[i] **20** Whenever it pleases you* to come down, O king, come, and we will surrender him into the hand of the king."[j] **21** At this Saul said: "May you be blessed by Jehovah, for you have shown compassion to me. **22** Please go and try to find out exactly where he is and who saw him there, for I have been told that he is very cunning. **23** Carefully ascertain where all his hiding places are and return to me with the evidence. I will then go with you, and if he is in the land, I will search him out among all the thousands* of Judah."

24 So they left and went to Ziph[k] ahead of Saul, while David and his men were in the wilderness of Ma'on,[l] in the Ar'a·bah[m] to the south of Je·shi'mon. **25** Then Saul came with his men to look for him.[n] When David was told, he at once went down to the crag[o] and stayed in the wilderness of Ma'on. When Saul heard this, he chased after David into the wilderness of Ma'on. **26** As Saul came to one

CHAP. 23
a 1Sa 23:14

b Nu 27:21
1Sa 30:7

c 1Sa 22:19

d 1Sa 22:1, 2
1Sa 25:13
1Sa 30:9

e Jos 15:20, 55
1Sa 23:19
1Sa 26:1

f 1Sa 18:29
1Sa 20:33
1Sa 27:1

Second Col.
a Ps 37:5
Pr 17:17

b 1Sa 16:13
2Sa 2:4
2Sa 5:3

c 1Sa 20:31
1Sa 24:17, 20

d 1Sa 18:3
1Sa 20:42

e 1Sa 10:26

f 1Sa 26:1
Ps 54:Sup

g 1Sa 23:15

h 1Sa 26:3

i 1Sa 23:24

j Ps 54:3

k 1Sa 23:14

l Jos 15:20, 55
1Sa 25:2, 3

m De 1:7

n 1Sa 26:2
Ps 54:3

o 1Sa 23:28

23:7 *Lit., "sold him into my hand."
23:11 *Or possibly, "landowners."
23:15 *Or possibly, "was fearful because." "Or "soul."

23:16 *Lit., "he strengthened his hand."
23:19 *Lit., "on the right side." "Or possibly, "the desert; the wilderness."
23:20 *Or "your soul." 23:23 *Or "clans."

side of the mountain, David and his men were on the other side of the mountain. David was hurrying to get away[a] from Saul, but Saul and his men were closing in on David and his men to capture them.[b] 27 But a messenger came to Saul, saying: "Come quickly, for the Phi·lis'tines have made a raid on the land!" 28 At that Saul stopped chasing after David[c] and went to confront the Phi·lis'tines. That is why that place was named the Crag of the Divisions.

29 Then David made his way up from there and stayed in the places difficult to approach at En·ged'i.[d]

24 As soon as Saul returned from pursuing the Phi·lis'tines, they told him: "Look! David is in the wilderness of En·ged'i."[e]

2 So Saul took 3,000 men chosen from all Israel and went to look for David and his men on the rocky cliffs of the mountain goats. 3 Saul came to the stone sheepfolds along the road, where there was a cave, and he went in to relieve himself* while David and his men were sitting in the recesses at the back of the cave.[f] 4 David's men said to him: "This is the day on which Jehovah is saying to you, 'Look! I am giving your enemy into your hand,[g] and you can do to him whatever seems good to you.'" So David rose up and quietly cut off the edge of Saul's sleeveless coat. 5 But afterward David's heart* kept striking him[h] because he had cut off the edge of Saul's sleeveless coat. 6 He said to his men: "It is unthinkable from Jehovah's standpoint that I should do such a thing to my lord, the anointed of Jehovah, by lifting my hand

against him, for he is the anointed of Jehovah."[a] 7 So David restrained* his men with these words, and he did not allow them to attack Saul. As for Saul, he rose up from the cave and went on his way.

8 Then David got up and went out from the cave and called out after Saul: "My lord the king!"[b] When Saul looked behind him, David bowed down low with his face to the ground and prostrated himself. 9 David said to Saul: "Why do you listen to the words of men who say, 'Look! David is seeking to harm you'?[c] 10 This very day your own eyes have seen how Jehovah gave you into my hand in the cave. But when someone said to kill you,[d] I had pity on you and said, 'I will not lift my hand against my lord, for he is the anointed of Jehovah.'[e] 11 And look, my father, yes, see the edge of your sleeveless coat in my hand; for when I cut off the edge of your sleeveless coat, I did not kill you. You can now see and understand that I do not intend to harm you or to rebel, and I have not sinned against you,[f] whereas you are hunting me down to take my life.*[g] 12 May Jehovah judge between you and me,[h] and may Jehovah take vengeance on you for me,[i] but my hand will not come against you.[j] 13 Just as the ancient proverb says, 'From the wicked comes wickedness,' but my hand will not come against you. 14 After whom has the king of Israel gone out? Whom are you chasing? A dead dog? A single flea?[k] 15 May Jehovah be the judge, and he will judge between you and me, and he will see and will plead my case[l] and judge me and rescue me from your hand."

CHAP. 23	
a	Ps 31:22
b	Ps 17:9
c	Ps 54:7
d	Jos 15:20, 62 Ca 1:14
CHAP. 24	
e	1Sa 23:28, 29
f	Ps 57:Sup Ps 142:Sup
g	1Sa 26:8, 23
h	2Sa 24:10

Second Col.

a	Ex 22:28 1Sa 26:11 2Sa 1:14 1Ch 16:22
b	1Sa 26:17
c	1Sa 26:19
d	1Sa 24:4
e	1Sa 9:16 1Sa 10:1 1Sa 26:9 Ps 105:15
f	1Sa 26:18 Ps 35:7
g	1Sa 23:14
h	1Sa 26:23
i	De 32:35
j	1Sa 26:11
k	1Sa 26:20
l	1Sa 25:39 Ps 35:1

24:3 *Lit., "to cover his feet." 24:5 *Or "conscience."

24:7 *Or possibly, "dispersed." 24:11 *Or "soul."

16 At the moment that David finished speaking these words to him, Saul said: "Is this your voice, my son David?"[a] And Saul began to weep loudly. **17** He said to David: "You are more righteous than I am, for you have treated me well and I have repaid you with evil.[b] **18** Yes, today you have told me of the good you did by not killing me when Jehovah surrendered me into your hand.[c] **19** For what man finds his enemy and sends him on his way unharmed? Jehovah will reward you with good[d] because of what you have done for me today. **20** And now look! I know that you will surely rule as king[e] and that in your hand the kingdom of Israel will endure. **21** Now swear to me by Jehovah[f] that you will not wipe out my descendants* after me and that you will not annihilate my name out of my father's house."[g] **22** So David swore to Saul, after which Saul went home.[h] But David and his men went up to the stronghold.[i]

25 In time Samuel[j] died; and all Israel gathered together to mourn for him and to bury him at his house in Ra'mah.[k] Then David rose and went down to the wilderness of Pa'ran.

2 Now there was a man in Ma'on[l] whose work was in Car'mel.*[m] The man was very wealthy; he had 3,000 sheep and 1,000 goats, and he was then shearing his sheep at Car'mel. **3** The man's name was Na'bal,[n] and his wife's name was Ab'i-gail.[o] The wife was discerning and beautiful, but the husband, a Ca'leb·ite,[p] was harsh, and he behaved badly.[q] **4** David heard in the wilderness that Na'bal was shearing his sheep. **5** So David sent ten young men to

him, and David told the young men: "Go up to Car'mel, and when you come to Na'bal, ask him in my name about his welfare. **6** Then say, 'May you live long and may you be well* and may your household be well and may all that you have be well. **7** Now I hear that you are doing your shearing. When your shepherds were with us, we did not harm them,[a] and they found nothing missing the whole time they were in Car'mel. **8** Ask your young men, and they will tell you. May my young men find favor in your eyes, because we have come at a joyous time.* Please give to your servants and to your son David whatever you can spare.'"[b]

9 So David's young men went and told all of this to Na'bal in David's name. When they finished, **10** Na'bal answered David's servants: "Who is David, and who is the son of Jes'se? Nowadays many servants are breaking away from their masters.[c] **11** Do I have to take my bread and my water and the meat that I butchered for my shearers and give it to men who come from who knows where?"

12 At that moment David's young men returned and reported all these words to him. **13** David immediately said to his men: "Everyone strap on your sword!"[d] So they all strapped on their swords, and David also strapped on his own sword, and about 400 men went up with David, while 200 men stayed with the baggage.

14 Meanwhile, one of the servants reported to Ab'i·gail, Na'bal's wife: "Look! David sent messengers from the wilderness to wish our master well, but he screamed insults at them.[e] **15** Those men were

---

CHAP. 24
a 1Sa 26:17

b 1Sa 26:21

c 1Sa 24:4, 10

d 1Sa 26:25
Ps 18:20

e 1Sa 13:14
1Sa 15:28
1Sa 18:8
1Sa 20:31
1Sa 23:17

f Le 19:12
De 6:13

g 2Sa 9:1
2Sa 21:7

h 1Sa 15:34

i 1Sa 23:29

CHAP. 25
j 1Sa 1:20
1Sa 2:18
1Sa 3:20
Ps 99:6

k 1Sa 7:15, 17

l 1Sa 23:24

m Jos 15:20, 55

n 1Sa 25:25

o 1Sa 27:3

p Nu 13:6
Nu 32:11, 12

q 1Sa 25:17, 21

Second Col.
a 1Sa 25:14-16

b De 15:7

c 1Sa 22:2

d Ps 37:8
Pr 15:1
Ec 7:9

e 1Sa 25:10

24:21 *Lit., "seed." **25:2** *A city in Judah; not the same as Mount Carmel.

25:6 *Or "may you have peace." **25:8** *Lit., "a good day."

very good to us. They never harmed us, and we did not miss a single thing the whole time we were together with them in the fields.[a] **16** They were like a protective wall around us, both by night and by day, the whole time we were with them shepherding the flock. **17** Now decide what you are going to do, for disaster has been determined against our master and against all his house,[b] and he is such a worthless* man[c] that no one can speak to him."

18 So Ab'i·gail[d] quickly took 200 loaves of bread, two large jars of wine, five dressed sheep, five seah measures* of roasted grain, 100 cakes of raisins, and 200 cakes of pressed figs and put all of it on the donkeys.[e] **19** Then she said to her servants: "Go on ahead of me; I will follow you." But she said nothing to her husband Na'bal.

20 While she was riding on the donkey and going down under cover of the mountain, just then David and his men were coming down toward her, and she met them. **21** Now David had been saying: "It was for nothing that I guarded everything that belongs to this fellow in the wilderness. Not a single thing belonging to him went missing,[f] and yet he repays me evil for good.[g] **22** May God do the same and more to the enemies of David* if I allow a single male* of his to survive until the morning."

23 When Ab'i·gail caught sight of David, she hurried down off the donkey and threw herself facedown before David, bowing to the ground. **24** She then fell

at his feet and said: "My lord, let the blame be on me; let your servant girl speak to you, and listen to the words of your servant girl. **25** Please, do not let my lord pay attention to this worthless Na'bal,[a] for he is just like his name. Na'bal* is his name, and senselessness is with him. But I, your servant girl, did not see my lord's young men whom you sent. **26** And now, my lord, as surely as Jehovah is living and as you are* living, it is Jehovah who has held you back[b] from incurring bloodguilt[c] and from taking revenge* with your own hand. May your enemies and those seeking injury to my lord become like Na'bal. **27** Now let this gift*[d] that your servant girl has brought to my lord be given to the young men who are following my lord.[e] **28** Pardon, please, the transgression of your servant girl, for Jehovah will without fail make for my lord a lasting house,[f] because my lord is fighting the wars of Jehovah,[g] and no evil has been found in you all your days.[h] **29** When someone rises up to pursue you and seeks your life,* the life* of my lord will be wrapped securely in the bag of life with Jehovah your God, but the lives* of your enemies he will hurl away like stones from a sling.△ **30** And when Jehovah has done for my lord all the good things he has promised and he appoints you as leader over Israel,[i] **31** you will have no remorse or regret* in your heart for shedding blood without cause and for letting the hand of my lord take revenge.*[j] When Jehovah confers

---

CHAP. 25
a 1Sa 25:7

b 1Sa 25:13

c 1Sa 25:3

d 1Sa 25:3

e 2Sa 16:1
2Sa 17:27-29

f 1Sa 25:7

g 1Sa 25:10
Ps 35:12

Second Col.
a 1Sa 25:17

b Ge 20:6

c Ge 9:6

d 1Sa 25:18

e 1Sa 22:2
1Sa 25:13

f 1Sa 15:28
2Sa 7:8, 11
1Ki 9:5

g 1Sa 17:45
1Sa 18:17

h 1Sa 24:11
1Ki 15:5

i 1Sa 13:13, 14
1Sa 23:17
2Sa 6:21
2Sa 7:8
Ps 89:20

j De 32:35
1Sa 24:15

25:17 *Or "good-for-nothing." 25:18 *A seah equaled 7.33 L (6.66 dry qt). See App. B14. 25:22 *Or possibly, "to David." #Lit., "anyone urinating against a wall." A Hebrew expression of contempt referring to males.

25:25 *Meaning "Senseless; Stupid." 25:26 *Or "your soul is." #Or "bringing salvation." 25:27 *Lit., "blessing." 25:29 *Or "soul." #Or "souls." △Or "as from the hollow of a sling." 25:31 *Lit., "staggering or stumbling." #Or "bring salvation."

good upon my lord, remember your servant girl."

32 At this David said to Ab'i·gail: "Praise Jehovah the God of Israel, who sent you this day to meet me! **33** And blessed be your good sense! May you be blessed for restraining me this day from incurring bloodguilt[a] and from taking revenge* with my own hands. **34** Otherwise, as surely as Jehovah the God of Israel who held me back from harming you[b] is living, if you had not come quickly to meet me,[c] by morning there would not have remained a single male* belonging to Na'bal."[d] **35** With that David accepted from her what she had brought him and said to her: "Go up in peace to your house. See, I have listened to you, and I will grant your request."

36 Ab'i·gail later went back to Na'bal, who was feasting like a king in his house, and Na'bal* was in a good mood and was as drunk as could be. She did not tell him a single thing until the morning light. **37** In the morning, when Na'bal was sober, his wife told him these things. And his heart became like a dead man's, and he lay paralyzed like a stone. **38** About ten days later, Jehovah struck Na'bal, and he died.

39 When David heard that Na'bal had died, he said: "Praise Jehovah, who has pleaded my case[e] of reproach from Na'bal and has kept his servant from doing anything bad,[g] and Jehovah has brought the badness of Na'bal back on his own head!" Then David sent word to propose to Ab'i·gail to take her as his wife. **40** So David's ser-

vants came to Ab'i·gail at Car'mel and said to her: "David has sent us to you to take you as his wife." **41** She immediately rose up and bowed with her face to the ground and said: "Here is your slave as a servant to wash the feet[a] of the servants of my lord." **42** Then Ab'i·gail[b] quickly rose up and rode on her donkey with five of her female servants walking behind her; she accompanied the messengers of David and became his wife.

43 David had also married A·hin'o·am[c] from Jez're·el,[d] and both women became his wives.[e]

44 But Saul had given his daughter Mi'chal,[f] David's wife, to Pal'ti[g] the son of La'ish, who was from Gal'lim.

26 In time the men of Ziph[h] came to Saul at Gib'e·ah,[i] saying: "Is David not hiding on the hill of Hach·i'lah facing Je·shi'mon?"*[j] **2** So Saul rose up and went down to the wilderness of Ziph with 3,000 chosen men of Israel to look for David in the wilderness of Ziph.[k] **3** Saul camped on the hill of Hach·i'lah, which faces Je·shi'mon, by the road. David was then living in the wilderness, and he learned that Saul had come into the wilderness after him. **4** So David sent spies to verify that Saul had indeed come. **5** David later went to the place where Saul had encamped, and David saw the place where Saul and Ab'ner[l] the son of Ner, the chief of his army, were lying asleep; Saul lay asleep in the camp enclosure with the troops camping all around him. **6** Then David said to A·him'e·lech the Hit'tite[m] and A·bish'ai[n] the son of Ze·ru'iah,[o] the brother of Jo'ab: "Who will go down with me into the camp to Saul?" A·bish'ai replied: "I will

---

25:33 *Or "bringing salvation." 25:34 *Lit., "anyone urinating against a wall." A Hebrew expression of contempt referring to males. 25:36 *Lit., "Nabal's heart."

26:1 *Or possibly, "the desert; the wilderness."

CHAP. 25

a De 19:10
  1Sa 25:26

b 1Sa 25:24

c 1Sa 25:18

d 1Sa 25:22

e 1Sa 24:15
  Ps 35:1

f 1Sa 25:10, 14

g 1Sa 25:34

Second Col.

a Ge 18:3, 4
  Lu 7:44

b 1Sa 25:3

c 1Sa 27:3
  2Sa 3:2
  1Ch 3:1

d Jos 15:20, 56

e 1Sa 30:5
  2Sa 5:13

f 1Sa 18:20

g 2Sa 3:14, 15

CHAP. 26

h Jos 15:20, 55

i Jg 19:14
  1Sa 10:26

j 1Sa 23:14
  1Sa 23:19, 24
  Ps 54:Sup

k 1Sa 24:2

l 1Sa 14:50
  1Sa 17:55
  2Sa 2:8
  2Sa 3:27

m Ge 10:15

n 2Sa 16:9
  2Sa 18:5
  2Sa 23:18

o 2Sa 2:18
  1Ch 2:15, 16

go down with you." **7** So David and A·bish'ai made their way to the troops by night, and they found Saul lying asleep in the camp enclosure with his spear stuck into the ground next to his head; Ab'ner and the troops were lying all around him.

8 A·bish'ai now said to David: "Today God has surrendered your enemy into your hand.[a] And now, please, let me pin him to the ground with the spear just once, and I will not need to do it twice. **9** However, David said to A·bish'ai: "Do not harm him, for who can lift his hand against the anointed of Jehovah[b] and remain innocent?"[c] **10** David continued: "As surely as Jehovah is living, Jehovah himself will strike him down,[d] or his day will come[e] and he will die, or he will go down into battle and perish.[f] **11** It is unthinkable from Jehovah's standpoint for me to lift my hand against the anointed of Jehovah![g] So now take, please, the spear next to his head and the water jug, and let us be on our way." **12** So David took the spear and the water jug from next to Saul's head, and they went away. No one saw[h] or noticed them or woke up, for they were all asleep, because a deep sleep from Jehovah had fallen upon them. **13** Then David crossed to the other side and stood on the top of the mountain some distance away, with a considerable space between them.

14 David called out to the troops and to Ab'ner[i] the son of Ner, saying: "Ab'ner, will you not answer?" Ab'ner answered: "Who are you who calls to the king?" **15** David said to Ab'ner: "Are you not a man? And who is like you in Israel? So why did you not keep watch over your lord the king? For one of the soldiers came in to do away with your lord the king.[j] **16** What you

have done is not good. As surely as Jehovah is living, you deserve to die, because you have not kept watch over your lord, the anointed of Jehovah.[a] Now look around! Where are the king's spear and the water jug[b] that were next to his head?"

17 Then Saul recognized the voice of David and said: "Is this your voice, my son David?"[c] David replied: "It is my voice, my lord the king." **18** He added: "Why is my lord chasing after his servant,[d] for what have I done, and what am I guilty of?[e] **19** My lord the king, please, listen to the words of his servant: If it is Jehovah who incited you against me, let him accept* my grain offering. But if men have incited you,[f] they are cursed before Jehovah, because they have driven me away today from being united with Jehovah's inheritance,[g] saying, 'Go, serve other gods!' **20** And now do not let my blood fall to the ground away from the presence of Jehovah, for the king of Israel has gone out to look for a single flea,[h] as if he were chasing a partridge on the mountains."

21 In turn Saul said: "I have sinned.[i] Come back, my son David, for I will do you no more harm, because you regarded my life* as precious[j] this day. Yes, I have acted foolishly and have made a terrible mistake." **22** David answered: "Here is the spear of the king. Let one of the young men come over and take it. **23** It is Jehovah who will repay each one for his own righteousness[k] and his own faithfulness, for today Jehovah gave you into my hand, but I was unwilling to lift my hand against the anointed of Jehovah.[l] **24** Look! Just as your life* was

---

CHAP. 26
a 1Sa 24:4
1Sa 26:23

b 1Sa 10:1

c 1Sa 24:6
2Sa 1:14
1Ch 16:22
Ps 20:6

d De 32:35
1Sa 24:12
1Sa 25:38
Ps 94:1, 23

e Ps 37:12, 13

f 1Sa 31:3, 6

g Le 19:18
1Sa 24:6
1Ch 16:22
Ps 105:15

h 1Sa 24:4

i 1Sa 14:50
1Sa 17:55
2Sa 2:8
2Sa 3:8

j 1Sa 26:8

Second Col.

a 1Sa 9:16, 17
1Sa 10:1

b 1Sa 26:11

c 1Sa 24:8, 16

d Ps 35:7

e 1Sa 24:9, 11

f 1Sa 24:9

g Ex 19:5
De 26:18

h 1Sa 24:14

i 1Sa 24:17

j 1Sa 24:10
1Sa 26:11

k Ps 7:8
Ps 18:20

l 1Sa 24:6
1Sa 26:9

26:19 *Lit., "smell." 26:21, 24 *Or "soul."

precious to me this day, so may my life* be precious in the eyes of Jehovah, and may he rescue me out of all distress."[a] **25** Saul replied to David: "May you be blessed, my son David. You will surely do great things, and you will surely prevail."[b] Then David went on his way, and Saul returned to his place.[c]

27 However, David said in his heart: "One day I will perish by Saul's hand. The best thing for me is to escape[d] to the land of the Phi·lis′tines; then Saul will give up looking for me in all the territory of Israel,[e] and I will escape from his hand." **2** So David rose up with the 600 men[f] who were with him and went over to A′chish[g] the son of Ma′och, the king of Gath. **3** David stayed with A′chish in Gath, he and his men, each man with his household. With David were his two wives, A·hin′o·am[h] of Jez′re·el and Ab′i·gail[i] the Car′mel·ite, Na′bal's widow. **4** When report was made to Saul that David had run away to Gath, he stopped searching for him.[j]

5 Then David said to A′chish: "If I have found favor in your eyes, let them give me a place in one of the cities of the countryside, so that I may live there. Why should your servant live in the royal city with you?" **6** So A′chish gave him Zik′lag[k] on that day. That is why Zik′lag belongs to the kings of Judah down to this day.

7 The length of time* that David lived in the countryside of the Phi·lis′tines was a year and four months.[l] **8** David would go up with his men to raid the Gesh′ur·ites,[m] the Gir′zites, and the A·mal′ek·ites,[n] for they were inhabiting the land that extended from Te′lam as far as

Shur[a] and down to the land of Egypt. **9** When David would attack the land, he preserved neither man nor woman alive,[b] but he took the flocks, herds, donkeys, camels, and clothing, after which he would return to A′chish. **10** Then A′chish would ask: "Where did you make a raid today?" David would reply: "Against the south* of Judah"[c] or "Against the south of the Je·rah′me·el·ites"[d] or "Against the south of the Ken′ites."[e] **11** David did not spare alive any man or woman to be brought to Gath, saying: "That they may not tell them about us and say, 'This is what David did.'" (And that was his practice the whole time he lived in the countryside of the Phi·lis′tines.) **12** So A′chish believed David, saying to himself: 'He has certainly become a stench among his people Israel, so he will always be my servant.'

28 In those days the Phi·lis′tines assembled their armies for war against Israel.[f] So A′chish said to David: "You know, of course, that you and your men will go out into battle with me."[g] **2** At that David said to A′chish: "You surely know what your servant will do." A′chish said to David: "That is why I will appoint you as my permanent bodyguard."*[h]

3 Now Samuel had died, and all Israel had mourned him and had buried him in Ra′mah, his own city.[i] And Saul had removed the spirit mediums and the fortune-tellers from the land.[j]

4 The Phi·lis′tines assembled and went and set up camp in Shu′nem.[k] So Saul assembled all Israel, and they set up camp in Gil·bo′a.[l] **5** When Saul saw the camp of the Phi·lis′tines,

CHAP. 26
a Ps 34:19
b 1Sa 24:19
c 1Sa 24:22
  1Sa 27:4

CHAP. 27
d 1Sa 19:18
  1Sa 22:1, 5
e 1Sa 18:29
  1Sa 23:23
f 1Sa 25:13
  1Sa 30:9
g 1Sa 21:10, 14
  1Sa 27:12
h 1Sa 25:43
i 1Sa 25:39, 42
  1Sa 30:5
j 1Sa 23:14
  1Sa 26:25
k 1Sa 19:5
  1Sa 30:1
  2Sa 1:1
  1Ch 12:1, 20
l 1Sa 29:3
m Jos 13:1, 2
n Ge 36:12
  Ex 17:8, 14
  Nu 13:29
  1Sa 15:2
  2Sa 1:1

Second Col.
a Ge 25:17, 18
  Ex 15:22
  1Sa 15:7
b De 25:19
  1Sa 15:3
c Jos 15:1, 2
d 1Ch 2:9
e Nu 24:21
  1Sa 15:6

CHAP. 28
f 1Sa 14:52
g 1Sa 27:12
  1Sa 29:3
h 1Sa 29:2
i 1Sa 25:1
j Ex 22:18
  Le 19:31
  Le 20:6, 27
  De 18:10, 11
  Re 21:8
k Jos 19:17, 18
  2Ki 4:8
l 1Sa 31:1
  2Sa 1:21
  2Sa 21:12

he was afraid, and his heart trembled greatly.[a] **6** Although Saul would inquire of Jehovah,[b] Jehovah never answered him, either in dreams or by the U'rim[c] or through the prophets. **7** Finally Saul said to his servants: "Find me a woman who is a spirit medium,[d] and I will go and consult her." His servants replied: "Look! There is a woman who is a spirit medium in Endor."[e]

8 So Saul disguised himself and put on other garments and went to the woman by night with two of his men. He said: "Use divination, please, by acting as a spirit medium,[f] and bring up for me the one whom I designate to you." **9** However, the woman said to him: "You must know what Saul did, how he removed the spirit mediums and the fortune-tellers from the land.[g] Why, then, are you trying to trap me* to have me put to death?"[h] **10** Saul then swore to her by Jehovah, saying: "As surely as Jehovah is alive, you will not incur any guilt in this matter!" **11** At this the woman said: "Whom should I bring up for you?" He replied: "Bring up Samuel for me." **12** When the woman saw "Samuel,"*[i] she cried out at the top of her voice and said to Saul: "Why did you trick me? You are Saul!" **13** The king said to her: "Do not be afraid, but what do you see?" The woman replied to Saul: "I see one like a god coming up out of the earth." **14** At once he asked her: "What does he look like?" to which she said: "It is an old man coming up, and he is clothed in a sleeveless coat."[i] At that Saul realized that it was "Samuel," and he bowed low with his face to the ground and prostrated himself.

15 Then "Samuel" said to Saul: "Why have you disturbed me by having me brought up?" Saul replied: "I am in great trouble. The Phi·lis'tines are fighting against me, and God has departed from me and no longer answers me, either through the prophets or in dreams;[a] so that is why I am calling on you to let me know what I should do."[b]

16 And "Samuel" said: "Why do you inquire of me now that Jehovah has departed from you[c] and has become your adversary? **17** Jehovah will do for himself what he foretold through me: Jehovah will rip the kingdom out of your hands and give it to one of your fellow men, David.[d] **18** Because you did not obey the voice of Jehovah and you did not execute his burning anger against the A·mal'ek·ites,[e] that is why Jehovah is doing this to you this day. **19** Jehovah will also give both Israel and you into the hand of the Phi·lis'tines,[f] and tomorrow you[g] and your sons[h] will be with me. Jehovah will also give the army of Israel into the hands of the Philis'tines."[i]

20 At once Saul fell full length on the ground and became very much afraid because of "Samuel's" words. And there was no strength left in him, because he had not eaten food all day and all night. **21** When the woman came to Saul and saw that he had been greatly disturbed, she said to him: "Here your servant has obeyed what you said, and I risked my life*[j] and did what you told me to do. **22** Now, please, listen to what your servant has to say. Let me set before you a piece of bread; then eat so that you will have some strength to go on your way." **23** But he refused and said: "I am not going to

---

CHAP. 28
a 1Sa 28:20

b 1Sa 14:37

c Ex 28:30
  Nu 27:21

d Ex 22:18
  Le 19:31
  Le 20:6
  1Sa 15:23
  1Sa 28:3

e Jos 17:11

f De 18:10, 11
  1Ch 10:13

g 1Sa 28:3

h Ex 22:18
  Le 20:27

i 1Sa 28:3

j 1Sa 15:27

Second Col.
a 1Sa 28:6

b Le 19:31

c 1Sa 15:23
  1Sa 16:14

d 1Sa 13:14
  1Sa 15:28
  1Sa 16:13
  1Sa 24:20

e 1Sa 15:9
  1Ch 10:13

f 1Sa 28:1
  1Sa 31:1

g 1Sa 31:5

h 1Sa 31:2
  2Sa 2:8

i 1Sa 31:7

j Le 20:27

28:9 *Or "my soul." **28:12** *Or "what appeared to be Samuel."

28:21 *Or "took my soul in my hand."

eat." However, his servants and also the woman kept urging him. Finally he listened to them and got up from the ground and sat on the bed. **24** The woman had a fattened calf in the house, so she quickly slaughtered* it and took flour and kneaded dough and baked it into unleavened bread. **25** She served them to Saul and his servants, and they ate. After that they rose up and left during the night.[a]

29 The Phi·lis′tines[b] assembled all their armies at A′phek, while the Israelites were camping by the spring in Jez′re·el.[c] **2** And the lords of the Phi·lis′tines were passing by with their hundreds and their thousands, and David and his men were marching at the rear with A′chish.[d] **3** But the princes of the Phi·lis′tines said: "Why are these Hebrews here?" A′chish replied to the princes of the Phi·lis′tines: "This is David, the servant of King Saul of Israel, who has been with me for a year or more.[e] I have not found any fault in him from the day he deserted to me until today." **4** But the princes of the Phi·lis′tines became indignant at him, and they said to him: "Make the man go back.[f] Let him return to the place where you assigned him. Do not let him go down with us into the battle, so that he will not turn against us during the battle.[g] For what better way to put himself in favor with his lord than with the heads of our men? **5** Is this not the David about whom they sang when they danced, saying:

'Saul has struck down his
  thousands,
And David his tens of thousands'?"[h]

6 So A′chish[i] summoned David and said to him: "As surely

as Jehovah is living, you are upright, and I am pleased to have you go on the campaign with my army,[a] for I have not found any fault with you from the day you came to me until today.[b] But the lords do not trust you.[c] **7** So return in peace, and do not do anything to displease the lords of the Phi·lis′tines." **8** However, David said to A′chish: "Why, what have I done? What fault have you found in your servant from the day that I came to you until today? Why should I not come with you and fight against the enemies of my lord the king?" **9** A′chish answered David: "From my standpoint, you have been as good as an angel of God.[d] But the princes of the Phi·lis′tines have said, 'Do not let him go up with us into the battle.' **10** Now get up early in the morning with the servants of your lord who came with you; rise up and leave early in the morning as soon as it is light."

11 So David and his men rose up early in the morning to return to the land of the Phi·lis′tines, and the Phi·lis′tines went up to Jez′re·el.[e]

30 When David and his men came to Zik′lag[f] on the third day, the A·mal′ek·ites[g] had made a raid on the south* and on Zik′lag, and they had attacked Zik′lag and burned it with fire. **2** They had taken captive the women[h] and all who were in it, from the smallest to the greatest. They had not killed anyone, but they had carried them off and gone on their way. **3** When David and his men came to the city, they found it burned down, and their wives and their sons and their daughters had been carried off captive. **4** So David and the men with him began

---

CHAP. 28
a 1Sa 28:8

CHAP. 29
b 1Sa 28:1

c Jos 19:17, 18
  1Sa 29:11

d 1Sa 28:2

e 1Sa 27:7, 12

f 1Ch 12:19

g 1Sa 14:21

h 1Sa 18:7
  1Sa 21:11

i 1Sa 21:10
  1Sa 27:2

Second Col.
a 1Sa 28:2

b 1Sa 27:11, 12

c 1Sa 29:3, 9

d 1Sa 27:12

e Jos 19:17, 18
  1Sa 29:1

CHAP. 30
f Jos 15:21, 31
  1Sa 27:5, 6

g Ge 36:12
  Ex 17:14
  1Sa 15:2
  1Sa 27:8

h 1Sa 27:3

28:24 *Or "sacrificed."

30:1 *Or "the Negeb."

weeping loudly until they had no strength left to weep. **5** David's two wives had also been carried off captive, A·hin'o·am of Jez're·el and Ab'i·gail the widow of Na'bal the Car'mel·ite.ᵃ **6** David was very distressed, because the men were talking of stoning him, for all the men* had become very bitter over the loss of their sons and daughters. But David strengthened himself by Jehovah his God.ᵇ

7 David then said to A·bi'a·thar the priest, the son of A·him'e·lech: "Please bring the eph'od here."ᵈ So A·bi'a·thar brought the eph'od to David. **8** David inquired of Jehovah:ᵉ "Should I chase after this marauder band? Will I overtake them?" At this He said to him: "Go in pursuit, for you will certainly overtake them, and you will make the rescue."ᶠ

9 David immediately set out with the 600 menᵍ who were with him, and they went on as far as the Wadi* Be'sor, where some of the men stayed behind. **10** David kept up the chase with 400 men, but the 200 men who were too tired to cross the Wadi Be'sor stayed behind.ʰ

11 They found an Egyptian man in the field and took him to David. They gave him food to eat and water to drink, **12** as well as a slice of a cake of pressed figs and two cakes of raisins. After he ate, he regained his strength,* for he had not eaten any food or drunk any water for three days and three nights. **13** David now asked him: "To whom do you belong, and where are you from?" to which he said: "I am an Egyptian attendant, a slave of an A·mal'ek·ite man, but my master left me because I got

sick three days ago. **14** We made a raid on the south* of the Cher'e·thitesᵃ and on the territory of Judah and on the south* of Ca'leb,ᵇ and Zik'lag we burned with fire." **15** At this David said to him: "Will you lead me down to this marauder band?" He replied: "If you swear to me by God that you will not put me to death and that you will not hand me over to my master, I will lead you down to this marauder band."

16 So he led him down to where they were spread out all over the land, eating and drinking and celebrating because of all the great spoil that they had taken from the land of the Phi·lis'tines and the land of Judah. **17** Then David struck them down from the morning darkness until the following evening; not a man escapedᶜ except 400 men who fled on camels. **18** David recovered all that the A·mal'ek·ites had taken,ᵈ and David rescued his two wives. **19** Nothing of theirs was missing, from the smallest to the greatest. They recovered their sons and daughters and the spoil;ᵉ David recovered everything that they had taken. **20** So David took all the flocks and the herds, which they drove before their own livestock. They said: "This is David's spoil."

21 Then David came to the 200 men who had been too tired to go along with David and who had stayed behind by the Wadi Be'sor,ᶠ and they came out to meet David and the people with him. When David came near to the men, he asked them how they were. **22** However, every bad and worthless man among those who had gone with David said: "Since they did not go with us, we will not give them any of the spoil that

---

CHAP. 30
ᵃ 1Sa 25:42
  1Sa 25:43

ᵇ Ps 18:6
  Ps 31:1, 9
  Ps 34:19
  Ps 143:5

ᶜ 1Sa 22:20
  1Ki 2:26

ᵈ 1Sa 23:9

ᵉ Nu 27:21
  Jg 20:28
  1Sa 23:2, 11
  1Sa 28:6

ᶠ 1Sa 30:18
  Ps 34:19

ᵍ 1Sa 23:13
  1Sa 27:2

ʰ 1Sa 30:21

Second Col.
ᵃ 2Sa 8:18
  1Ki 1:38
  1Ch 18:17
  Eze 25:16
  Zep 2:5

ᵇ Jos 14:13

ᶜ Ex 17:14

ᵈ 1Sa 30:3

ᵉ 1Sa 30:8
  Ps 34:19

ᶠ 1Sa 30:10

30:6 *Or "for the souls of all the people." 30:9 *See Glossary. 30:12 *Lit., "his spirit returned to him."

30:14 *Or "the Negeb."

we recovered except that each one may take his wife and his sons and go away." **23** But David said: "You must not do this, my brothers, with what Jehovah has given us. He protected us and gave into our hand the marauder band that came against us.[a] **24** Who would agree with you on this? The share of the one who went down into the battle will be the same as the share of the one who sat by the baggage.[b] All will have a share together."[c] **25** And from that day forward, he kept it set as a regulation and a rule for Israel down to this day.

26 When David returned to Zik′lag, he sent some of the spoil to the elders of Judah who were his friends, saying: "Here is a gift[*] for you from the spoil of Jehovah's enemies." **27** He sent it to those who were in Beth′el,[d] to those in Ra′moth of the Neg′eb,[*] to those in Jat′tir,[e] **28** to those in A·ro′er, to those in Siph′moth, to those in Esh·te·mo′a,[f] **29** to those in Ra′cal, to those in the cities of the Je·rah′me·el·ites,[g] to those in the cities of the Ken′ites,[h] **30** to those in Hor′mah,[i] to those in Bor′a·shan, to those in A′thach, **31** to those in Heb′ron,[j] and to all the places that David and his men had frequented.

31 Now the Phi·lis′tines were fighting against Israel.[k] And the men of Israel fled from before the Phi·lis′tines, and many fell slain on Mount Gil·bo′a.[l] **2** The Phi·lis′tines kept in close range of Saul and his sons, and the Phi·lis′tines struck down Jon′a·than,[m] A·bin′a·dab, and Mal′chi·shu′a, Saul's sons.[n] **3** The fighting grew fierce against Saul, and the archers found him, and he was severely wounded by the archers.[o]

4 Then Saul said to his armor-bearer: "Draw your sword and run me through with it, so that these uncircumcised men[*] may not come and run me through and deal ruthlessly[*] with me." But his armor-bearer was unwilling, because he was very much afraid. So Saul took the sword and fell on it.[b] **5** When his armor-bearer saw that Saul was dead,[c] he too fell on his own sword and died with him. **6** Thus Saul, his three sons, his armor-bearer, and all his men died together on that day.[d] **7** When the people of Israel who were in the region of the valley[*] and in the region of the Jordan saw that the men of Israel had fled and that Saul and his sons had died, they began to abandon the cities and flee;[e] the Phi·lis′tines then came and occupied them.

8 The next day, when the Phi·lis′tines came to strip the slain, they found Saul and his three sons fallen on Mount Gil·bo′a.[f] **9** So they cut off his head and stripped off his armor and sent word throughout the land of the Phi·lis′tines to spread the news[g] in the houses[*] of their idols[h] and among the people. **10** Then they put his armor in the house of the Ash′to·reth images and fastened his corpse to the wall of Beth-shan.[i] **11** When the inhabitants of Ja′besh-gil′e·ad[j] heard what the Phi·lis′tines had done to Saul, **12** all the warriors rose and traveled all night and took the bodies of Saul and his sons off the wall of Beth-shan. They returned to Ja′besh and burned them there. **13** Then they took their bones[k] and buried them under the tamarisk tree in Ja′besh,[l] and they fasted for seven days.

CHAP. 30
a 1Sa 30:8
b 1Sa 30:10
c Nu 31:27
Jos 22:8
Ps 68:12
d Jos 19:4, 8
e Jos 15:20, 48
Jos 21:8, 14
f Jos 15:20, 50
Jos 21:8, 14
g 1Sa 27:10
1Ch 2:9
h Jg 1:16
1Sa 15:6
i Nu 21:3
Jos 19:1, 4
Jg 1:17
j Jos 14:13
2Sa 2:1

CHAP. 31
k 1Sa 14:52
1Sa 29:1
l 1Sa 28:4
2Sa 1:21
1Ch 10:1-5
m 1Sa 13:2
n 1Ch 8:33
o 2Sa 1:4, 6

Second Col.
a 1Sa 17:26
2Sa 1:20
b 1Ch 10:4
c 1Sa 26:10
1Ch 10:13
d 1Sa 28:19
1Ch 10:6, 7
e 1Sa 13:6
f 1Sa 28:4
1Sa 31:1
2Sa 1:6
1Ch 10:8-12
g 2Sa 1:20
h Jg 16:23
i Jos 17:11
Jg 1:27
j 1Sa 11:1, 9-11
k 2Sa 21:12
l 2Sa 2:4, 5

30:26 *Lit., "blessing." **30:27** *Or "the south."

31:4 *Or "abusively." **31:7** *Or "low plain." **31:9** *Or "temples."

THE SECOND OF
SAMUEL

OUTLINE OF CONTENTS

1 After Saul's death, when David had returned from defeating* the A·mal′ek·ites, David stayed at Zik′lag[a] for two days. **2** On the third day, a man came from the camp of Saul with his garments ripped apart and dirt on his head. When he approached David, he fell down to the ground and prostrated himself.

3 David asked him: "Where are you coming from?" He replied: "I have escaped from the camp of Israel." **4** David asked him: "How did things turn out? Please tell me." To this he said: "The people have fled from the battle and many have fallen and died. Even Saul and his son Jon′a·than have died."[b] **5** Then David asked the young man who brought him the news: "How do you know that Saul and his son Jon′a·than are dead?" **6** The young man replied: "By chance I was on Mount Gil·bo′a,[c] and there was Saul supporting himself on his spear, and the chariots and horsemen had caught up with him.[d] **7** When he turned around and saw me, he called me, and I said, 'Here I am!' **8** He asked me, 'Who are you?' I replied, 'I am an A·mal′ek·ite.'[e] **9** Then he said, 'Please stand over me and put me to death, for I am in great agony, but I am still alive.'* **10** So I stood over him and put him to death,[f] for I knew that he could not survive after he had fallen down wounded. Then I took the crown* that was on his head and the bracelet that was on his arm, and I brought them here to my lord."

11 At this David took hold of his garments and ripped them apart, and so did all the men who were with him. **12** And they wailed and wept and fasted[a] until evening for Saul, for his son Jon′a·than, for the people of Jehovah, and for the house of Israel,[b] because they had fallen by the sword.

13 David asked the young man who brought him the news: "Where are you from?" He said: "I am the son of a foreign resident, an A·mal′ek·ite." **14** Then David said to him: "Why did you not fear to lift your hand to do away with the anointed of Jehovah?"[c] **15** With that David called one of the young men and said: "Step forward and strike him." So he struck him down, and he died.[d] **16** David said to him: "Your blood is on your own head, because your own mouth testified against you by saying, 'I myself put the anointed of Jehovah to death.'"[e]

17 Then David chanted this dirge* over Saul and his son Jon′a·than[f] **18** and said that the people of Judah should be taught the dirge called "The Bow," which is written in the book of Ja′shar:[g]

19　"The beauty, O Israel, lies
　　　slain upon your high
　　　places.[h]
　　How the mighty have fallen!
20　Do not tell it in Gath;[i]
　　Do not announce it in the
　　　streets of Ash′ke·lon,
　　Or the daughters of the Phi·
　　　lis′tines will rejoice,
　　Or the daughters of the un·
　　　circumcised men will exult.
21　You mountains of Gil·bo′a,[j]
　　May there be no dew or rain
　　　upon you,
　　Nor fields producing holy
　　　contributions,[k]
　　Because there the shield of
　　　mighty ones was defiled,
　　The shield of Saul is no lon·
　　　ger anointed with oil.

1:1 *Or "striking down." **1:9** *Or "because all my soul is still in me." **1:10** *Or "diadem."

1:17 *Or "song of mourning."

CHAP. 1
a 1Sa 27:5, 6

b 1Sa 31:1, 6
　1Ch 10:4, 6

c 1Sa 28:4
　1Ch 10:1

d 1Sa 31:3
　1Ch 10:3

e Ex 17:16
　De 25:19
　1Sa 15:20
　1Sa 30:1

f 1Sa 31:4

Second Col.
a 1Sa 31:11, 13

b 1Sa 31:1

c Nu 12:8
　1Sa 24:6
　1Sa 26:9
　1Sa 31:4

d 2Sa 4:10

e 2Sa 1:6, 10

f 1Sa 31:6

g Jos 10:13

h 1Sa 31:8

i 1Sa 31:9

j 1Sa 31:1
　1Ch 10:1

k Le 27:16

22 From the blood of the slain,
from the fat of mighty
ones,
The bow of Jon′a·than did
not turn back,ᵃ
And the sword of Saul would
not return without suc-
cess.ᵇ

23 Saul and Jon′a·than,ᶜ beloved and cherished* dur-
ing their life,
And in death they were not
separated.ᵈ
Swifter than the eagles they
were,ᵉ
Mightier than the lions.ᶠ

24 O daughters of Israel, weep
over Saul,
Who clothed you in scarlet
and finery,
Who put gold ornaments
upon your clothing.

25 How the mighty have fallen
in battle!
Jon′a·than lies slain upon
your high places!ᵍ

26 I am distressed over you,
my brother Jon′a·than;
You were very dear to me.ʰ
More wonderful was your
love to me than the love of
women.ⁱ

27 How the mighty have fallen
And the weapons of war
have perished!"

2 Afterward David inquired of
Jehovah,ʲ saying: "Should I
go up into one of the cities of Judah?" Jehovah said to him: "Go
up." David then asked: "Where
should I go?" He replied: "To
Heb′ron."ᵏ **2** So David went up
there with his two wives, A·hin′-
o·am′ of Jez′re·el and Ab′i·gail ᵐ
the widow of Na′bal the Car′mel-
ite. **3** David also brought the
men who were with him,ⁿ each
with his household, and they settled in the cities around Heb′ron.
4 Then the men of Judah came,

CHAP. 1
a 1Sa 18:4
   1Sa 20:20
b 1Sa 14:47
c 1Sa 18:1
d 1Sa 31:6
   1Ch 10:6
e Job 9:26
f Pr 30:30
g 1Sa 31:8
h 1Sa 18:1, 3
i 1Sa 19:2
   1Sa 20:17, 41
   1Sa 23:16-18
   Pr 17:17
   Pr 18:24

CHAP. 2
j Nu 27:21
   1Sa 28:6
k Ge 23:2
   Nu 13:22
   Jos 14:14
   Jos 20:7
   2Sa 5:1
   1Ki 2:11
l 1Sa 25:43
m 1Sa 25:42
   1Sa 30:5
n 1Sa 22:1, 2
   1Sa 27:2
   1Ch 12:1

Second Col.
a Ge 49:10
   1Sa 15:24, 28
   1Sa 16:13
   2Sa 5:4, 5
   1Ch 11:3
b 1Sa 31:11-13
c 2Sa 9:7
   2Sa 10:2
d 1Sa 14:50
   1Sa 17:55
   1Sa 26:5
   2Sa 4:1
   1Ki 2:5
e 2Sa 4:5-8
   2Sa 4:12
f Ge 32:1, 2
   1Sa 13:29, 30
g Jos 13:8, 11
h 1Sa 19:17, 18
i Jos 16:5-8
j 2Sa 2:4
k 1Ch 3:4
l 2Sa 2:8
m 1Sa 10:12
   Jos 18:21, 25
   1Sa 21:8, 17
   2Sa 20:8
   2Ch 1:3
n 2Sa 8:16
   2Sa 20:23
   1Ki 1:5, 7
o 1Ch 2:15, 16

---

and there they anointed David as
king over the house of Judah.ᵃ
They told David: "The men
of Ja′besh-gil′e·ad were the ones
who buried Saul." **5** So David sent messengers to the
men of Ja′besh-gil′e·ad and said
to them: "May you be blessed by
Jehovah, because you showed
loyal love to your lord Saul
by burying him.ᵇ **6** May Jehovah show loyal love and faithfulness to you. I will also show you
kindness because you have done
this.ᶜ **7** Now let your hands be
strong and be courageous men,
for your lord Saul is dead, and
the house of Judah has anointed
me as king over them."

8 But Ab′nerᵈ the son of Ner,
the chief of Saul's army, had tak-
en Saul's son Ish-bo′shethᵉ and
brought him across to Ma·ha·na′-
imᶠ **9** and made him king over
Gil′e·ad,ᵍ the Ash′ur·ites, Jez′-
re·el,ʰ E′phra·im,ⁱ Benjamin, and
over all Israel. **10** Ish-bo′sheth,
Saul's son, was 40 years old
when he became king over Israel, and he reigned for two years.
The house of Judah, however,
supported David.ʲ **11** The time*
that David was king in Heb′ron
over the house of Judah was sev-
en years and six months.ᵏ

12 In time Ab′ner the son of
Ner and the servants of Ish-
bo′sheth, Saul's son, went out
from Ma·ha·na′imˡ to Gib′e·on.ᵐ
13 Jo′abⁿ the son of Ze·ru′iahᵒ
and the servants of David also
went out and encountered them
at the pool of Gib′e·on; and one
group sat on this side of the
pool, and the other group on
that side of the pool. **14** Finally Ab′ner said to Jo′ab: "Let the
young men get up and engage in
combat* before us." To this Jo′-
ab said: "Let them get up."
15 So they got up and crossed
over by number, 12 for Benjamin

and Saul's son Ish-bo'sheth and 12 from the servants of David. **16** They grabbed one another by the head and each of them thrust his sword into the side of his opponent, and they all fell down together. So that place, which is in Gib'e·on, was called Hel'kath-haz·zu'rim.

17 The fighting that ensued was extremely fierce that day, and Ab'ner and the men of Israel were finally defeated before the servants of David. **18** Now the three sons of Ze·ru'iah[b] were there—Jo'ab,[b] A·bish'ai,[c] and As'a·hel;[d] and As'a·hel was as swift on his feet as a gazelle in the open field. **19** As'a·hel chased after Ab'ner, and he would not veer to the right or to the left in his pursuit of Ab'ner. **20** When Ab'ner looked behind, he asked, "Is that you, As'a·hel?" to which he replied, "Yes, it is." **21** Then Ab'ner said to him: "Veer to your right one or to your left and capture one of the young men, and take whatever you strip off him for yourself." But As'a·hel did not want to stop chasing him. **22** So Ab'ner said to As'a·hel once again: "Stop chasing me. Why should I strike you down? How could I look your brother Jo'ab in the face?" **23** But he kept refusing to stop, so Ab'ner struck him in the abdomen with the butt end of the spear,[e] and the spear came out from his back; and he fell there and died on the spot. Everyone who came to the place where As'a·hel fell and died would stop and pause there.

24 Then Jo'ab and A·bish'ai went in pursuit of Ab'ner. As the sun was setting, they came to the hill of Am'mah, which faces Gi'ah on the way to the wilderness of Gib'e·on. **25** There the Ben'ja·min·ites gathered together behind Ab'ner, and they formed one company and made a stand on the top of a certain hill. **26** Then Ab'ner called out to Jo'ab: "Is the sword going to devour endlessly? Do you not know that the outcome will only be bitterness? How long, then, will it be before you tell the people to turn back from pursuing their brothers?" **27** At that Jo'ab said: "As surely as the true God is living, if you had not spoken, then only by the morning would the people have stopped pursuing their brothers." **28** Jo'ab now blew the horn, and his men stopped chasing after Israel, and the fighting ceased.

29 Ab'ner and his men then marched through the Ar'a·bah[a] all that night and crossed the Jordan and marched through the entire ravine* and finally came to Ma·ha·na'im.[b] **30** After Jo'ab turned back from pursuing Ab'ner, he gathered all the people together. Of David's servants, 19 were missing, in addition to As'a·hel. **31** But the servants of David had defeated the Ben'ja·min·ites and the men of Ab'ner, and 360 of their men had died. **32** They took As'a·hel[c] and buried him in his father's tomb, which is at Beth'le·hem.[d] Then Jo'ab and his men marched all night long, and they reached Heb'ron[e] at daybreak.

3 The war between the house of Saul and the house of David dragged on; and David kept getting stronger,[f] and the house of Saul grew steadily weaker.[g]

2 Meanwhile, sons were born to David in Heb'ron.[h] His firstborn was Am'non[i] by A·hin'o·am[i] of Jez're·el. **3** His second was Chil'e·ab by Ab'i·gail,[k] the widow of Na'bal the Car'mel·ite; and the third was Ab'sa·lom[l] the son of Ma'a·cah, the daughter of Tal'-

CHAP. 2
a 1Ch 2:15, 16

b 2Sa 10:7
  2Sa 24:2
  1Ki 11:15
  1Ch 11:6

c 1Sa 26:6
  2Sa 20:6
  1Ch 11:20

d 2Sa 3:27
  2Sa 23:24
  1Ch 27:1, 7

e 2Sa 3:27

Second Col.
a De 1:7
  Jos 12:2, 3

b Jos 21:8, 38
  2Sa 2:8

c 2Sa 2:18
  1Ch 2:15, 16

d Ge 35:19
  Ru 4:11
  1Sa 16:1

e 2Sa 2:1, 3
  1Ch 11:1

CHAP. 3
f 1Sa 15:27, 28
  1Sa 24:17, 20
  1Sa 26:25

g 2Sa 2:17

h 1Ch 3:1-4

i 2Sa 13:1

j 1Sa 25:43

k 1Sa 25:42

l 2Sa 15:12

2:29 *Or possibly, "through all of Bithron."

mai[a] the king of Gesh'ur. **4** The fourth was Ad·o·ni'jah[b] the son of Hag'gith, and the fifth was Sheph·a·ti'ah the son of A·bi'tal. **5** The sixth was Ith're·am by David's wife Eg'lah. These were born to David in Heb'ron.

6 While the war between the house of Saul and the house of David continued, Ab'ner[c] kept strengthening his position in the house of Saul. **7** Now Saul had had a concubine whose name was Riz'pah,[d] the daughter of A'iah. Ish-bo'sheth[e] later said to Ab'ner: "Why did you have relations with the concubine of my father?"[f] **8** Ab'ner grew very angry over the words of Ish-bo'sheth and said: "Am I a dog's head from Judah? Until this very day, I have shown loyal love toward the house of your father Saul and to his brothers and his friends, and I have not betrayed you into the hand of David; yet today you call me to account for an error concerning a woman. **9** May God do so to Ab'ner and add to it if I do not do for David just as Jehovah swore to him:[g] **10** to transfer the kingdom from the house of Saul and to establish the throne of David over Israel and over Judah, from Dan to Be'er·she'ba."[h] **11** He was not able to say one more word in reply to Ab'ner, for he was afraid of him.[i]

12 Ab'ner immediately sent messengers to David, saying: "To whom does the land belong?" He added: "Make a covenant with me, and I will do whatever I can* to turn all Israel to your side."[j] **13** To this he replied: "Good! I will make a covenant with you. The only thing I ask of you is that you do not try to see my face unless first you bring Mi'chal,[k] Saul's daugh-

ter, when you come to see me." **14** Then David sent messengers to Ish-bo'sheth,[a] Saul's son, saying: "Give me my wife Mi'chal, to whom I became engaged for 100 foreskins of the Phi·lis'tines."[b] **15** So Ish-bo'sheth sent to take her from her husband, Pal'ti·el[c] the son of La'ish. **16** But her husband kept walking with her, weeping as he followed her as far as Ba·hu'rim.[d] Then Ab'ner said to him: "Go, return!" At that he returned.

17 Meanwhile, Ab'ner sent word to the elders of Israel, saying: "For some time you wanted to have David as king over you. **18** Now act, for Jehovah said to David: 'By the hand of my servant David[e] I will save my people Israel from the hand of the Phi·lis'tines and from the hand of all their enemies.'" **19** Then Ab'ner spoke to the people of Benjamin.[f] Ab'ner also went to speak privately to David at Heb'ron to tell him what Israel and the whole house of Benjamin had agreed upon.

20 When Ab'ner came to David at Heb'ron with 20 men, David held a feast for Ab'ner and for the men with him. **21** Then Ab'ner said to David: "Let me go and gather all Israel together to my lord the king, so that they may make a covenant with you, and you will become king over all that you desire."* So David sent Ab'ner off, and he went his way in peace.

22 Just then, David's servants and Jo'ab returned from a raid, bringing a great quantity of spoil back with them. Ab'ner was no longer with David in Heb'ron, for he had sent him on his way in peace. **23** When Jo'ab[g] and all the army that was with him arrived, Jo'ab was told: "Ab'ner[h] the son of Ner[i] came to

---

CHAP. 3
a 2Sa 13:37

b 1Ki 1:5

c 2Sa 2:8

d 2Sa 21:8-11

e 2Sa 2:10

f 2Sa 16:21
  1Ki 2:22

g 1Sa 15:27, 28
  Ps 78:70
  Ps 89:20

h Jg 20:1
  2Sa 24:2

i 2Sa 3:39

j 2Sa 5:3

k 1Sa 18:20
  1Sa 9:11
  1Ch 15:29

Second Col.
a 2Sa 2:10

b 1Sa 18:25, 27

c 1Sa 25:44

d 2Sa 16:5
  1Ki 2:8

e 1Sa 13:14
  1Sa 15:27, 28
  1Sa 16:1, 13
  Ps 89:3, 20
  Ps 132:17
  Ac 13:22

f 1Sa 10:20, 21
  1Ch 12:29

g 2Sa 8:16

h 1Sa 14:50
  2Sa 2:8, 22

i 1Sa 14:51

3:12 *Lit., "and look! my hand is with you."

3:21 *Or "your soul desires."

the king, and he sent him off, and he went his way in peace." 24 So Jo'ab went in to the king and said: "What have you done? Here Ab'ner came to you. Why did you send him off so that he successfully got away? 25 You know Ab'ner the son of Ner! He came here to fool you and to get to know your every move and to find out everything that you are doing."

26 So Jo'ab left David and sent messengers after Ab'ner, and they brought him back from the cistern of Si'rah; but David did not know anything about it. 27 When Ab'ner returned to Heb'ron,[a] Jo'ab took him aside inside the gate to speak with him privately. However, there he stabbed him in the abdomen, and he died;[b] this was for killing[*] his brother As'a·hel.[c] 28 When David heard about it later, he said: "I and my kingdom are forever innocent before Jehovah of the bloodguilt[d] for Ab'ner the son of Ner. 29 May it turn back on the head of Jo'ab[e] and on the entire house of his father. May Jo'ab's house never be without a man suffering from a discharge[f] or a leper[g] or a man working at the spindle[*] or one falling by the sword or one in need of food!"[h] 30 So Jo'ab and his brother A·bish'ai[i] killed Ab'ner[j] because he had put As'a·hel their brother to death in the battle[k] at Gib'e·on.

31 Then David said to Jo'ab and all the people with him: "Rip your garments apart and tie on sackcloth and wail over Ab'ner." King David himself was walking behind the funeral bier. 32 They buried Ab'ner in Heb'ron; and the king wept loudly at Ab'ner's tomb, and all the people

gave way to weeping. 33 The king chanted over Ab'ner and said:

"Should Ab'ner die the death
    of a senseless person?
34 Your hands had not been
    bound,
And your feet were not in
    fetters.[*]
You fell like one falling
    before criminals."[#a]

At that all the people wept over him again.

35 Later all the people came to give David bread for consolation[*] while it was still daytime, but David swore: "May God do so to me and add to it if before the sun sets I taste bread or anything at all!"[b] 36 All the people took notice, and it pleased them. Like everything that the king did, it pleased all the people. 37 So all the people and all Israel knew on that day that the king was not responsible for having Ab'ner the son of Ner put to death.[c] 38 Then the king said to his servants: "Do you not know that a prince and a great man has fallen this day in Israel?[d] 39 Today I am weak, although anointed as king,[e] and these men, the sons of Ze·ru'iah,[f] are too brutal for me.[g] May Jehovah repay the evildoer according to his own evil."[h]

4 When Saul's son Ish·bo'sheth[*][i] heard that Ab'ner had died in Heb'ron,[j] his courage failed him[#] and all the Israelites were disturbed. 2 There were two men in charge of the marauder bands that belonged to the son of Saul: one was named Ba'a·nah and the other Re'chab. They were sons of Rim'mon the Be·er'oth·ite, of the tribe of Benjamin. (For Be·er'oth[k] too used

---

CHAP. 3
a 2Sa 3:20

b 1Ki 2:5

c 2Sa 2:22, 23

d Ge 9:6
Ex 21:12
Nu 35:33
De 21:9

e Ps 7:16
Ps 55:23
Pr 5:22

f Le 15:2

g Le 13:44
Nu 5:2

h De 27:24
Ps 109:2, 10

i 2Sa 2:24

j 2Sa 2:8

k 2Sa 2:23

Second Col.
a 1Ki 2:31, 32

b Jg 20:26

c 2Sa 3:28
1Ki 2:5

d 1Sa 14:50
2Sa 2:8
2Sa 3:12

e 2Sa 2:4

f 1Ch 2:15, 16

g 2Sa 19:13
2Sa 20:10

h 2Sa 3:29
1Ki 2:5, 34

CHAP. 4
i 2Sa 2:8

j 2Sa 3:27

k Jos 9:17
Jos 18:21, 25

3:27 *Lit., "for the blood of." 3:29 *Perhaps referring to a crippled man required to do women's work. 3:34 *Lit., "copper." #Lit., "the sons of unrighteousness." 3:35 *Or "bread of mourning." 4:1 *Lit., "the son of Saul." #Lit., "his hands became feeble."

to be counted as part of Benjamin. **3** The Be·er′oth·ites ran away to Git′ta·im,[a] and they are foreign residents there down to this day.)

4 Now Saul's son Jon′a·than[b] had a son whose feet were crippled.*[c] He was five years old when the report about Saul and Jon′a·than came from Jez′re·el,[d] and his nurse picked him up and fled, but as she was fleeing in panic, he fell and was crippled. His name was Me·phib′o·sheth.[e]

5 The sons of Rim′mon the Be·er′oth·ite, Re′chab and Ba′a·nah, went to the house of Ish-bo′sheth during the hot part of the day, as he was taking his midday rest. **6** They went into the house as if they were getting wheat, and they struck him in the abdomen; then Re′chab and his brother Ba′a·nah[f] escaped. **7** When they had entered the house, he was lying on his bed in his bedroom, and they struck him and put him to death, after which they cut off his head. Then they took his head and walked all night long on the road to the Ar′a·bah. **8** And they brought the head of Ish-bo′sheth[g] to David at Heb′ron and said to the king: "Here is the head of Ish-bo′sheth the son of Saul your enemy[h] who sought your life.*[i] This day Jehovah gives to my lord the king revenge on Saul and his descendants."

9 However, David answered Re′chab and his brother Ba′a·nah, the sons of Rim′mon the Be·er′oth·ite, and said to them: "As surely as Jehovah is living, the one who rescued me* out of all distress,[j] **10** when someone reported to me, 'Here Saul is dead,'[k] and he thought he was bringing me good news, I took hold of him and killed him[l] in

Zik′lag. That was the messenger's reward he received from me! **11** How much more so when wicked men have killed a righteous man in his own house on his bed! Should I not require his blood from your hands[a] and rid the earth of you?" **12** David then ordered the young men to kill them.[b] They cut off their hands and feet and hung them[c] by the pool in Heb′ron. But they took the head of Ish-bo′sheth and buried it in the burial place of Ab′ner in Heb′ron.

5 In time all the tribes of Israel came to David at Heb′ron[d] and said: "Look! We are your own bone and flesh.*[e] **2** In times past while Saul was our king, you were the one who was leading Israel on its campaigns.*[f] And Jehovah said to you: 'You will shepherd my people Israel, and you will become leader over Israel.'"[g] **3** So all the elders of Israel came to the king at Heb′ron, and King David made a covenant with them[h] in Heb′ron before Jehovah. Then they anointed David as king over Israel.[i]

4 David was 30 years old when he became king, and he reigned for 40 years.[j] **5** In Heb′ron he reigned over Judah for 7 years and 6 months, and in Jerusalem[k] he reigned for 33 years over all Israel and Judah. **6** And the king and his men set out for Jerusalem against the Jeb′u·sites[l] who were inhabiting the land. They taunted David: "You will never come in here! Even the blind and the lame will drive you away." They thought, 'David will never get in here.'[m] **7** However, David captured the stronghold of Zion, which is now the City of David.[n] **8** So David

---

CHAP. 4
a Ne 11:31, 33
b 1Sa 20:16
c 2Sa 9:3
d 1Sa 29:1, 11
e 2Sa 9:13
　1Ch 8:34
f 2Sa 4:2
g 2Sa 2:10
h 1Sa 18:28, 29
i 1Sa 18:10, 11
　1Sa 20:1, 33
　1Sa 23:15
j 1Sa 24:12
　1Sa 26:25
　2Sa 12:7
　Ps 34:7
k 2Sa 1:2, 4
l 1Sa 1:13-15

Second Col.
a Ge 9:6
　Ex 21:12
　Nu 35:16, 30
b Ps 55:23
c De 21:22

CHAP. 5
d 2Sa 2:1, 11
　1Ch 12:23
e 1Ch 11:1-3
f 1Sa 18:13
　1Sa 25:28
g Ge 49:10
　1Sa 16:1
　1Sa 25:30
　2Sa 6:21
　2Sa 7:8
　1Ch 28:4
　Ps 78:71
h 2Ki 11:17
i 1Sa 16:13
　2Sa 2:4
　Ac 13:22
j 1Ch 29:26, 27
k Ge 14:18
l Ex 23:23
　Jos 15:63
　Jg 1:8, 21
m 1Ch 11:4-6
n 1Ki 2:10
　Ne 12:37

4:4 *Or "lame." 4:8 *Or "soul." 4:9 *Lit., "redeemed my soul."

5:1 *Or "your blood relatives." 5:2 *Lit., "the one bringing out and the one bringing in Israel."

said on that day: “Those who attack the Jeb′u·sites should go through the water tunnel to strike down both ‘the lame and the blind,’ who are hateful to David!”* That is why it is said: “The blind and the lame will never enter the house.” **9** Then David took up residence in the stronghold, and it was called* the City of David; and David began to build all around from the Mound#[a] inward.[b] **10** Thus David became greater and greater,[c] and Jehovah the God of armies was with him.[d]

11 King Hi′ram[e] of Tyre sent messengers to David, also cedar timbers,[f] woodworkers, and stonemasons for building walls, and they began to build a house* for David.[g] **12** And David knew that Jehovah had firmly established him as king over Israel[h] and had exalted his kingdom[i] for the sake of His people Israel.[j]

13 David took more concubines[k] and wives in Jerusalem after he came from Heb′ron, and more sons and daughters were born to David.[l] **14** These are the names of those born to him in Jerusalem: Sham·mu′a, Sho′bab, Nathan,[m] Sol′o·mon,[n] **15** Ib′har, E·li′shu·a, Ne′pheg, Ja·phi′a, **16** E·lish′a·ma, E·li′a·da, and E·liph′e·let.

17 When the Phi·lis′tines heard that David had been anointed as king over Israel,[o] all the Phi·lis′tines came up to search for David.[p] When David heard about it, he went down to the stronghold.[q] **18** Then the Phi·lis′tines came in and spread out in the Valley* of Reph′a·im.[r] **19** David inquired of Jehovah,[s] saying: “Should I go up against the Phi·lis′tines? Will you give them into my hand?” At this Jehovah said to David: “Go up, for I will surely give the Phi·lis′tines into your hand.”[a] **20** So David came to Ba′al-pe·ra′zim, and David struck them down there. At that he said: “Jehovah has broken through my enemies[b] before me, like a breach made by waters.” That is why he named that place Ba′al-pe·ra′zim.*[c] **21** The Phi·lis′tines abandoned their idols there, and David and his men took them away.

22 Later the Phi·lis′tines came up once again and spread out in the Valley* of Reph′a·im.[d] **23** David inquired of Jehovah, but He said: “Do not go directly up. Instead, go around behind them, and come against them in front of the ba′ca bushes. **24** And when you hear the sound of marching in the tops of the ba′ca bushes, then act decisively, for Jehovah will have gone out before you to strike down the army of the Phi·lis′tines.” **25** So David did just as Jehovah commanded him, and he struck down the Phi·lis′tines[e] from Ge′ba[f] all the way to Ge′zer.[g]

6 David again gathered all the best troops in Israel, 30,000 men. **2** Then David and all the men with him set out for Ba′al·e-ju′dah to bring up from there the Ark of the true God,[h] before which people call on the name of Jehovah of armies,[i] who sits enthroned above* the cherubs.[j] **3** However, they placed the Ark of the true God on a new wagon[k] to transport it from the house of A·bin′a·dab,[l] which was on the hill; and Uz′zah and A·hi′o, the sons of A·bin′a·dab, were leading the new wagon.

4 So they transported the Ark of the true God from A·bin′-

5:8 *Or “the soul of David.” 5:9 *Or possibly, “and he called it.” #Or “Millo.” A Hebrew term meaning “fill.” 5:11 *Or “palace.” 5:18, 22 *Or “Low Plain.”

5:20 *Meaning “Master of Breakings Through.” 6:2 *Or possibly, “between.”

CHAP. 5
a 1Ki 9:15, 24; 1Ki 11:27; 2Ch 32:5
b 1Ch 11:7-9
c 1Sa 16:13; 2Sa 3:1
d 1Sa 17:45
e 1Ki 5:1, 8
f 2Ch 2:3
g 2Sa 7:2; 1Ch 14:1, 2
h 2Sa 7:16; Ps 41:11; Ps 89:21
i Ps 89:27
j 1Ki 10:9; 2Ch 2:11
k 2Sa 15:16
l 1Ch 3:5-9; 1Ch 14:3-7
m Lu 3:23, 31
n 2Sa 12:24
o 2Sa 5:3
p Ps 2:2
q 1Sa 22:1, 5; 1Sa 24:22; 2Sa 23:14; 1Ch 14:8
r Jos 15:8, 12; 1Ch 11:15; 1Ch 14:9
s Nu 27:21

Second Col.
a 1Ch 14:10-12
b 2Sa 22:41
c Isa 28:21
d Jos 15:8, 12; 1Ch 11:15; 1Ch 14:13-17
e Le 26:7
f Jos 18:21, 24
g Jos 16:10

CHAP. 6
h 1Sa 7:2; 1Ki 8:1; 1Ch 13:1-5
i De 20:4; 1Sa 1:3; 1Ch 17:24
j Ex 25:22; 1Sa 4:4; 1Ch 13:6-11; Ps 80:1
k Ex 25:14; Nu 7:9; Jos 3:14
l 1Sa 7:1

a·dab's house on the hill, and A·hi'o was walking ahead of the Ark. **5** David and all the house of Israel were celebrating before Jehovah with all sorts of juniper-wood instruments, harps, other stringed instruments,[a] tambourines,[b] sistrums, and cymbals.[c] **6** But when they came to the threshing floor of Na'con, Uz'zah thrust his hand out to the Ark of the true God and grabbed hold of it,[d] for the cattle nearly upset it. **7** At that Jehovah's anger blazed against Uz'zah, and the true God struck him down[e] there for his irreverent act,[f] and he died there beside the Ark of the true God. **8** But David became angry[*] because Jehovah's wrath had broken through against Uz'zah; and that place has been called Pe'rez-uz'zah[#] down to this day. **9** So David became fearful of Jehovah[g] on that day and said: "How can the Ark of Jehovah come to me?"[b] **10** David was not willing to bring the Ark of Jehovah to where he was in the City of David.[i] Instead, David had it taken to the house of O'bed-e'dom[j] the Git'tite.

11 The Ark of Jehovah remained at the house of O'bed-e'dom the Git'tite for three months, and Jehovah kept blessing O'bed-e'dom and all his household.[k] **12** The report was made to King David: "Jehovah has blessed the house of O'bed-e'dom and all that belongs to him because of the Ark of the true God." So David went to bring the Ark of the true God from the house of O'bed-e'dom up to the City of David with rejoicing.[l] **13** When the carriers[m] of the Ark of Jehovah had marched six steps, he sacrificed a bull and a fattened animal.

14 David was dancing around before Jehovah with all his might; all the while David wore[*] a linen eph'od.[a] **15** David and all the house of Israel were bringing up the Ark[b] of Jehovah with joyful shouting[c] and with the sound of the horn.[d] **16** But when the Ark of Jehovah came into the City of David, Saul's daughter Mi'chal[e] looked down through the window and saw King David leaping and dancing around before Jehovah; and she began to despise him in her heart.[f] **17** So they brought the Ark of Jehovah in and set it in its place inside the tent that David had pitched for it.[g] Then David offered up burnt offerings[h] and communion sacrifices[i] before Jehovah.[j] **18** When David finished offering up the burnt offerings and the communion sacrifices, he blessed the people in the name of Jehovah of armies. **19** Further, he distributed to all the people, to the whole multitude of Israel, to each man and woman, a ring-shaped loaf of bread, a date cake, and a raisin cake, and then all the people left, each to his own house.

20 When David returned to bless his own household, Saul's daughter Mi'chal[k] came out to meet him. She said: "How glorious the king of Israel made himself when he uncovered himself today before the eyes of the slave girls of his servants, just as an empty-headed man openly uncovers himself!"[l] **21** At this David said to Mi'chal: "My celebration was before Jehovah, who chose me rather than your father and all his household and who appointed me as leader over Jehovah's people, Israel."[m] Therefore, I will celebrate before Jehovah, **22** and I will humble myself even more than this and

---

CHAP. 6

a 1Sa 10:5

b Ex 15:20

c Ps 150:3-5

d Nu 4:15
  1Ch 15:2

e Le 10:1, 2
  1Sa 6:19

f Pr 11:2

g 1Sa 6:20
  Ps 119:120

h 1Ch 13:12-14

i 2Sa 5:7

j 1Ch 15:25

k Ge 30:27
  Ge 39:5

l 1Ch 15:25, 26
  Ps 24:7
  Ps 68:24

m Nu 4:15
  Nu 7:9
  Jos 3:3
  1Ch 15:2, 15

Second Col.

a 1Ch 15:27, 28

b Ex 37:1
  Ps 132:8

c 1Ch 15:16

d Ps 150:3

e 1Sa 14:49
  1Sa 18:20, 27
  2Sa 3:14

f 1Ch 15:29

g 1Ch 15:1

h Le 1:3

i Le 3:1

j 1Ch 16:1-3

k 1Sa 18:27

l Ex 22:28

m 1Sa 13:13, 14
  1Sa 15:27, 28
  1Sa 16:1, 12

6:8 *Or "upset." #Meaning "Breach Against Uzzah."

6:14 *Lit., "was girded with."

become low even in my own eyes. But by the slave girls whom you mentioned, I will be glorified." **23** So Saul's daughter Mi′chal[a] had no children down to the day of her death.

7 When the king was settled in his own house[*b] and Jehovah had given him rest from all his surrounding enemies, **2** the king said to Nathan[c] the prophet: "Here I am living in a house of cedars[d] while the Ark of the true God sits in the midst of tent cloths."[e] **3** Nathan replied to the king: "Go and do whatever is in your heart, for Jehovah is with you."[f]

4 On that very night, the word of Jehovah came to Nathan, saying: **5** "Go and say to my servant David, 'This is what Jehovah says: "Should you build me a house to dwell in?[g] **6** For I have not dwelled in a house from the day I brought the people of Israel out of Egypt to this day,[h] but I have been moving[*] about in a tent and in a tabernacle.[i] **7** During all the time that I went with all the Israelites,[*] did I ever say one word to any of the tribal leaders of Israel whom I appointed to shepherd my people Israel, saying, 'Why did you not build a house of cedars for me?'"[i] **8** Now say this to my servant David, 'This is what Jehovah of armies says: "I took you from the pastures, from following the flock,[j] to become a leader over my people Israel.[k] **9** And I will be with you wherever you go,[l] and I will do away with[*] all your enemies from before you;[m] and I will make a great name for you[n] like the name of the great men of the earth. **10** I will appoint a place for my people Israel and settle them, and they will live

there and not be disturbed anymore; and wicked men will not oppress them again as they did in the past,[a] **11** from the day that I appointed judges[b] over my people Israel. And I will give you rest from all your enemies.[c]

'"Also, Jehovah has told you that Jehovah will make a house[*] for you.[d] **12** When your days come to an end[e] and you are laid to rest with your forefathers, then I will raise up your offspring[*] after you, your own son,[*] and I will firmly establish his kingdom.[f] **13** He is the one who will build a house for my name,[g] and I will firmly establish the throne of his kingdom forever.[h] **14** I will become his father, and he will become my son.[i] When he does wrong, I will reprove him with the rod of men and with the strokes of the sons of men.[*j] **15** My loyal love will not be taken away from him the way I took it away from Saul,[k] whom I removed from before you. **16** Your house and your kingdom will be secure forever before you; your throne will be firmly established forever."'"[l]

17 Nathan told David all these words and this entire vision.[m]

18 At that King David came in and sat down before Jehovah and said: "Who am I, O Sovereign Lord Jehovah? And what is my house that you have brought me this far?[n] **19** As if this were not enough, O Sovereign Lord Jehovah, you also speak about the house of your servant down to a distant future time; and this is instruction[*] for all mankind, O Sovereign Lord Jehovah. **20** What more can your servant David say to you when you

CHAP. 6
a 1Sa 14:49
  2Sa 6:16

CHAP. 7
b 1Ch 17:1
c 2Sa 12:1
  1Ch 29:29
d 2Sa 5:11
e 2Sa 6:17
f 1Ki 8:17
  1Ch 17:2
  1Ch 22:7
g 1Ki 5:3
  1Ki 8:17-19
  1Ch 17:4-6
  1Ch 22:7,8
h Jos 18:1
i Ex 40:18, 34
j 1Sa 16:11
k 2Sa 5:2
  1Ch 17:7-10
  1Ch 28:4
  Ps 78:70, 71
l 1Sa 18:14
  2Sa 5:10
m 2Sa 22:1
  Ps 18:37
n 1Ch 14:2, 17

Second Col.
a Jg 2:14
  Ps 89:20, 22
b Jg 2:16
c De 25:19
d 1Ki 2:24
  Ps 89:4
e 1Ki 2:1
f Ge 49:10
  1Ki 8:20
  1Ch 17:11-14
  Ps 132:11
  Isa 9:7
  Isa 11:1
  Mt 21:9
  Mt 22:42
  Lu 1:32, 33
  Joh 7:42
  Ac 2:30
g 1Ki 5:5
  1Ki 6:12
  Zec 6:12, 13
h 1Ki 1:37
  1Ch 22:10
  1Ch 28:7
  Ps 89:4, 36
i 1Ch 28:6
  Mt 3:17
j Ps 89:30, 32
  Jer 52:3
k 1Sa 15:23, 26
l Ps 45:6
  Ps 89:36
  Da 2:44
  Heb 1:8
  Re 11:15
m 1Ch 17:15
n 1Ch 17:16-22

7:1 *Or "palace." 7:6 *Lit., "walking." 7:7 *Lit., "sons of Israel." 7:9 *Lit., "cut off." 7:11 *Or "dynasty." 7:12 *Lit., "seed." #Lit., "one who will come out of your inward parts." 7:14 *Or possibly, "Adam." 7:19 *Or "law."

know me so well,[a] O Sovereign Lord Jehovah? **21** For the sake of your word and in agreement with your heart* you have done all these great things and have revealed them to your servant.[b] **22** That is why you are truly great,[c] O Sovereign Lord Jehovah. There is no one like you,[d] and there is no God except you;[e] everything we have heard with our ears confirms this. **23** And what other nation on earth is like your people Israel?[f] God went and redeemed them as his people,[g] making a name for himself[h] by doing great and awe-inspiring things for them.[i] You drove out the nations and their gods in behalf of your people, whom you redeemed to yourself from Egypt. **24** You established your people Israel as your own people for all time;[j] and you, O Jehovah, have become their God.[k]

25 "Now, O Jehovah God, carry out the promise you have made concerning your servant and his house for all time, and may you do just as you have promised.[l] **26** May your name be exalted forever,[m] so that people may say, 'Jehovah of armies is God over Israel,' and may the house of your servant David be firmly established before you.[n] **27** For you, Jehovah of armies, the God of Israel, have made a revelation to your servant by saying, 'I will build a house* for you.'[o] That is why your servant has the courage# to pray this prayer to you. **28** And now, O Sovereign Lord Jehovah, you are the true God, and your words are truth,[p] and you have promised these good things to your servant. **29** So may it please you to bless the house of

your servant, and may it continue forever before you;[a] for you, O Sovereign Lord Jehovah, have promised, and with your blessing may the house of your servant be blessed forever."[b]

8 Some time later, David defeated the Phi·lis′tines[c] and subdued them,[d] and David took Meth′eg-am′mah out of the hands of the Phi·lis′tines.

2 He defeated the Mo′ab·ites[e] and made them lie down on the ground and measured them with a line. He measured out two lines to be put to death, and one full line to be kept alive.[f] And the Mo′ab·ites became David's servants and brought tribute.[g]

3 David defeated Had·ad·e′zer the son of Re′hob the king of Zo′bah[h] as he was on his way to restore his authority at the Eu·phra′tes River.[i] **4** David captured 1,700 horsemen and 20,000 foot soldiers from him. Then David hamstrung all but 100 of the chariot horses.[j]

5 When the Syrians of Damascus[k] came to help King Had·ad·e′zer of Zo′bah, David struck down 22,000 of the Syrians.[l] **6** David then established garrisons in Syria of Damascus, and the Syrians became David's servants and brought tribute. Jehovah gave David victory* wherever he went.[m] **7** Moreover, David took the circular shields of gold from the servants of Had·ad·e′zer and brought them to Jerusalem.[n] **8** From Be′tah and Be·ro′thai, cities of Had·ad·e′zer, King David took a great quantity of copper.

9 Now King To′i of Ha′math[o] heard that David had defeated the entire army of Had·ad·e′zer.[p] **10** So To′i sent his son Jo′ram to King David to ask about his welfare and to congratulate him because he had fought

---

CHAP. 7
a 1Sa 16:7
  Ps 17:3
b Ps 25:14
  1Ch 16:25
c De 3:24
d Ex 15:11
  Ps 83:18
e De 4:35
f De 4:7
  Ps 147:19, 20
g Ex 3:8
  Ex 19:5
  Isa 63:9
h Ex 9:16
i De 10:21
j De 26:18
k Ex 15:2
l 1Ch 17:23-27
  Ps 89:20, 28
m 1Ch 29:11
  Ps 72:19
  Mt 6:9
  Joh 12:28
n Isa 9:7
  Jer 33:22
o 2Sa 7:11
p Nu 23:19
  Ps 89:35
  Ps 132:11
  Joh 17:17

Second Col.
a Ps 89:20, 36
  Ps 132:12
b 2Sa 22:51
  Ps 72:17

CHAP. 8
c Jos 13:2, 3
  2Sa 21:15
d 1Ch 18:1
e Nu 24:17
  Jg 3:29
  1Sa 14:47
  Ps 60:8
f De 23:3-6
g 2Ki 3:4
  1Ch 18:2
h 2Sa 10:6
  1Ki 11:23
  Ps 60:Sup
i Ge 15:18
  Ex 23:31
  1Ki 4:21
  1Ch 18:3, 4
j De 17:16
  Ps 20:7
  Ps 33:17
k Isa 7:8
l 1Ch 18:5, 6
m De 7:24
  2Sa 8:14
n 1Ch 18:7, 8
o 2Ki 14:28
p 1Ch 18:9-11

7:21 *Or "in harmony with your will."
7:27 *Or "dynasty." #Lit., "has found his heart."

8:6 *Or "salvation."

and defeated Had·ad·e′zer (for Had·ad·e′zer had often fought against To′i), and he brought articles of silver, gold, and copper. **11** King David sanctified these to Jehovah, along with the silver and the gold that he had sanctified from all the nations that he had subdued:[a] **12** from Syria and Mo′ab,[b] from the Am′mon·ites, the Phi·lis′tines,[c] the A·mal′ek·ites,[d] and from the spoil of Had·ad·e′zer[e] the son of Re′hob the king of Zo′bah. **13** David also made a name for himself when he came back from striking down 18,000 E′dom·ites in the Valley of Salt.[f] **14** He established garrisons in E′dom. In all E′dom he established garrisons, and all the E′dom·ites became David's servants.[g] Jehovah gave David victory* wherever he went.[h]

15 David kept reigning over all Israel,[i] and David was administering justice and righteousness[j] for all his people.[k] **16** Jo′ab[l] the son of Ze·ru′iah was over the army, and Je·hosh′a·phat[m] the son of A·hi′lud was recorder. **17** Za′dok[n] the son of A·hi′tub and A·him′e·lech the son of A·bi′a·thar were priests, and Se·rai′ah was secretary. **18** Be·nai′ah[o] the son of Je·hoi′a·da was over the Cher′e·thites and the Pel′e·thites.[p] And David's sons became chief ministers.*

9 David then said: "Is there anyone still left of the house of Saul to whom I may show loyal love for the sake of Jon′a·than?"[q] **2** Now there was a servant of the house of Saul named Zi′ba.[r] So they called him to David, and the king asked him: "Are you Zi′ba?" He replied: "I am your servant." **3** The king continued: "Is there anyone left of the house of Saul to whom I may extend God's loyal love?" Zi′-

ba replied to the king: "There is still one son of Jon′a·than; he is crippled* in both feet."[a] **4** The king asked him: "Where is he?" Zi′ba replied to the king: "He is in the house of Ma′chir[b] the son of Am′mi·el at Lo-de′bar."

5 King David immediately sent for him and took him from the house of Ma′chir the son of Am′mi·el at Lo-de′bar. **6** When Me·phib′o·sheth the son of Jon′a·than the son of Saul came in to David, he at once fell facedown and prostrated himself. Then David said: "Me·phib′o·sheth!" to which he replied: "Here is your servant." **7** David said to him: "Do not be afraid, for I will certainly show loyal love[c] to you for the sake of your father Jon′a·than, and I will return to you all the land of Saul your grandfather, and you will always dine* at my table."[d]

8 At that he prostrated himself and said: "What is your servant, that you have turned your attention* to a dead dog[e] like me?" **9** The king now sent for Zi′ba, Saul's attendant, and said to him: "Everything that belonged to Saul and to all his house I give to the grandson of your master.[f] **10** You will cultivate the land for him —you and your sons and your servants—and you will gather its produce to provide food for those who belong to the grandson of your master to eat. But Me·phib′o·sheth, the grandson of your master, will always dine at my table."[g]

Now Zi′ba had 15 sons and 20 servants.[h] **11** Then Zi′ba said to the king: "Your servant will do all that my lord the king commands his servant to do." So Me·phib′o·sheth ate at David's* table like one of the sons of the king.

CHAP. 8

a Jos 6:19
　1Ki 7:51
　1Ch 22:14
　1Ch 26:27

b 2Sa 8:2

c 2Sa 8:1

d 1Sa 30:18

e 2Sa 8:7

f 1Ch 18:12, 13
　Ps 60:Sup

g Ge 25:23, 26
　Ge 27:29, 37
　Nu 24:18

h Ps 60:12

i 2Sa 5:3, 5

j 1Ki 3:6

k 1Ch 18:14-17

l 2Sa 20:23
　1Ch 11:6

m 2Sa 20:24
　1Ki 4:3

n 2Sa 15:27
　1Ch 6:8
　1Ch 24:3

o 2Sa 23:20
　1Ki 1:44
　1Ki 2:35

p 2Sa 15:18
　2Sa 20:7

CHAP. 9

q 1Sa 18:1, 3
　1Sa 20:15, 42

r 2Sa 16:1
　2Sa 19:17

Second Col.

a 2Sa 4:4
　2Sa 9:13
　2Sa 19:26

b 2Sa 17:27-29

c Pr 11:17

d 2Sa 19:28
　Pr 11:25

e 1Sa 24:14

f 2Sa 9:1
　2Sa 16:4
　2Sa 19:29

g 2Sa 19:28

h 2Sa 19:17

8:14 *Or "salvation." 8:18 *Lit., "became priests."

9:3 *Or "lame." 9:7 *Lit., "eat bread." 9:8 *Lit., "face." 9:11 *Or possibly, "my."

12 Now Me·phib'o·sheth also had a young son named Mi'ca;[a] and all those who lived in Zi'ba's house became servants of Me·phib'o·sheth. **13** And Me·phib'o·sheth lived in Jerusalem, for he always ate at the table of the king;[b] and he was crippled in both feet.[c]

10 Later the king of the Am'mon·ites[d] died, and his son Ha'nun became king in his place.[e] **2** At that David said: "I will show loyal love toward Ha'nun the son of Na'hash as his father showed loyal love toward me." So David sent his servants to offer him comfort over the loss of his father. But when David's servants came into the land of the Am'mon·ites, **3** the princes of the Am'mon·ites said to Ha'nun their lord: "Do you think that David is honoring your father by sending comforters to you? Is it not to search through the city and to spy it out and to overthrow it that David has sent his servants to you?" **4** So Ha'nun took the servants of David and shaved off half their beards[f] and cut their garments in half at their buttocks and sent them away. **5** When David was told, he at once sent men to meet them, because the men had been deeply humiliated; and the king told them: "Stay in Jer'i·cho[g] until your beards grow back, and then return."

6 In time the Am'mon·ites saw that they had become a stench to David, so the Am'mon·ites sent and hired Syrians of Beth-re'hob[h] and Syrians of Zo'bah,[i] 20,000 foot soldiers; and the king of Ma'a·cah,[j] with 1,000 men; and from Ish'tob,* 12,000 men.[k] **7** When David heard about it, he sent Jo'ab and the entire army, including his mightiest warriors.[l] **8** And the Am'-

10:6, 8 *Or "the men of Tob."

mon·ites went out and drew up in battle formation at the entrance of the city gate while the Syrians of Zo'bah and of Re'hob, along with Ish'tob* and Ma'a·cah, were by themselves in the open field.

9 When Jo'ab saw that the battle charges were coming against him from the front and the rear, he chose some of the best troops in Israel and drew them up in battle formation to meet the Syrians.[a] **10** He put the rest of the men under the command* of his brother A·bish'ai,[b] in order to draw them up in battle formation to meet the Am'mon·ites.[c] **11** Then he said: "If the Syrians become too strong for me, then you must come to my rescue; but if the Am'mon·ites become too strong for you, I will come to your rescue. **12** We must be strong and courageous[d] for our people and for the cities of our God, and Jehovah will do what is good in his eyes."[e]

13 Then Jo'ab and his men advanced to meet the Syrians in battle, and they fled from before him.[f] **14** When the Am'mon·ites saw that the Syrians had fled, they fled from A·bish'ai and went into the city. After that Jo'ab returned from the Am'mon·ites and came to Jerusalem.

15 When the Syrians saw that they had been defeated by Israel, they regrouped.[g] **16** So Had·ad·e'zer[h] sent for the Syrians in the region of the River,*[i] and then they came to He'lam, with Sho'bach the chief of the army of Had·ad·e'zer leading them.

17 When the report was made to David, he immediately gathered all Israel and crossed the Jordan and came to He'lam. The

10:10 *Lit., "in the hand." 10:16 *That is, the Euphrates.

CHAP. 9
a 1Ch 8:34
1Ch 9:40

b 2Sa 9:7
2Sa 19:28

c 2Sa 4:4

CHAP. 10
d Ge 19:36, 38
Jg 10:7
Jg 11:12, 33
1Sa 11:1

e 1Ch 19:1-5

f Le 19:27

g Jos 18:21

h Nu 13:21

i 2Sa 8:5

j Jos 13:13

k 1Ch 19:6, 7

l 2Sa 23:8
1Ch 19:8, 9

Second Col.
a 1Ch 19:10-13

b 1Sa 26:6
2Sa 2:18
2Sa 23:18
1Ch 2:15, 16

c Nu 21:24

d De 31:6

e Ps 37:5
Ps 44:5
Pr 29:25

f 1Ch 19:14, 15

g 1Ch 19:16

h 2Sa 8:3-5

i Ge 15:18
Ex 23:31

Syrians then drew up in battle formation to meet David and fought against him.[a] **18** But the Syrians fled from Israel; and David killed 700 charioteers and 40,000 horsemen of the Syrians, and he struck down Sho'bach the chief of their army, who died there.[b] **19** When all the kings, the servants of Had·ad·e'zer, saw that they had been defeated by Israel, they promptly made peace with Israel and became their subjects;[c] and the Syrians were afraid to help the Am'monites anymore.

11 At the start of the year,* at the time when kings go on campaigns, David sent Jo'ab and his servants and the entire army of Israel to bring the Am'monites to ruin, and they besieged Rab'bah,[d] while David stayed in Jerusalem.[e]

2 One evening* David got up from his bed and walked around on the rooftop of the king's house.[f] From the rooftop he saw a woman bathing, and the woman was very beautiful. **3** David sent someone to inquire about the woman, and he reported: "Is this not Bath-she'ba[f] the daughter of E·li'am[g] and the wife of U·ri'ah[h] the Hit'tite?"[i] **4** Then David sent messengers to bring her.[j] So she came in to him, and he lay down with her.[k] (This happened while she was purifying herself from her uncleanness.*)[l] Afterward, she returned to her house.

5 The woman became pregnant, and she sent a message to David: "I am pregnant." **6** At this David sent a message to Jo'ab: "Send to me U·ri'ah the Hit'tite." So Jo'ab sent U·ri'ah to David. **7** When U·ri'ah came to him, David asked him how Jo'ab

was getting along, how the troops were getting along, and how the war was going. **8** David then said to U·ri'ah: "Go down to your house and relax."* When U·ri'ah left the king's house, the king's courtesy gift* was sent after him. **9** However, U·ri'ah slept at the entrance of the king's house with all the other servants of his lord, and he did not go down to his own house. **10** So David was told: "U·ri'ah did not go down to his own house." At that David said to U·ri'ah: "Have you not just returned from a journey? Why did you not go down to your own house?" **11** U·ri'ah replied to David: "The Ark[a] and Israel and Judah are dwelling in temporary shelters, and my lord Jo'ab and the servants of my lord are camping in the open field. So should I go into my own house to eat and drink and lie down with my wife?[b] As surely as you live and are alive,* I will not do this thing!"

12 Then David said to U·ri'ah: "Stay here also today, and tomorrow I will send you away." So U·ri'ah stayed in Jerusalem on that day and the following day. **13** David then sent for him to come and eat and drink with him, and he got him drunk. But in the evening, he went out to sleep on his bed with the servants of his lord, and he did not go down to his house. **14** In the morning David wrote a letter to Jo'ab and sent it by the hand of U·ri'ah. **15** He wrote in the letter: "Put U·ri'ah in the front lines where the fighting is fiercest. Then retreat from behind him, so that he will be struck down and die."[c]

CHAP. 10
a 1Ch 19:17-19

b De 20:1
Ps 18:37, 38

c Ge 15:18
De 20:10, 11

CHAP. 11
d 2Sa 12:26

e 1Ch 20:1

f 2Sa 12:24
1Ki 1:11

g 1Ch 3:5, 9

h 2Sa 23:8, 39
1Ki 15:5

i Ge 10:15
De 20:17

j Ex 20:14, 17

k Le 18:20
Le 20:10
Pr 6:32
Heb 13:4

l Le 12:2
Le 15:19
Le 18:19

Second Col.
a 2Sa 6:17
2Sa 7:2

b Le 15:16
1Sa 21:5

c Ps 51:14
Pr 3:29

11:1 *That is, in the spring. **11:2** *Or "Late one afternoon." #Or "palace." **11:4** *Possibly her menstrual uncleanness.

11:8 *Lit., "wash your feet." #Or "the king's portion," that is, the portion sent by the host to the honored guest. **11:11** *Or "and as your soul is living."

16 Jo'ab had been carefully watching the city, and he stationed U·ri'ah where he knew there were mighty warriors. **17** When the men of the city came out and fought against Jo'ab, some of David's servants fell, and U·ri'ah the Hit'tite was among those who died.[a] **18** Jo'ab now reported to David all the news about the war. **19** He instructed the messenger: "When you finish speaking to the king about all the news of the war, **20** the king may become angry and say to you, 'Why did you have to go so near to the city to fight? Did you not know that they would shoot from the top of the wall? **21** Who struck down A·bim'e·lech[b] the son of Je·rub'-be·sheth?[c] Was it not a woman who threw an upper millstone on him from the top of the wall, causing his death at The'bez? Why did you have to go so close to the wall?' Then say, 'Your servant U·ri'ah the Hit'tite also died.'"

22 So the messenger went and told David everything that Jo'ab had sent him to tell. **23** Then the messenger told David: "Their men overpowered us, and they came out against us in the field; but we drove them back to the entrance of the city gate. **24** And the archers were shooting at your servants from the top of the wall, and some of the servants of the king died; your servant U·ri'ah the Hit'tite also died."[d] **25** At that David said to the messenger: "Say this to Jo'ab: 'Do not let this matter trouble you, for the sword devours one as well as another. Intensify your battle against the city and conquer it.' And encourage him."

26 When U·ri'ah's wife heard that her husband U·ri'ah had died, she began to mourn her husband. **27** As soon as the

mourning period was over, David sent for her and brought her to his house, and she became his wife[a] and bore him a son. But what David had done was very displeasing to* Jehovah.[b]

12 So Jehovah sent Nathan[c] to David. He came in to him[d] and said: "There were two men in one city, the one rich and the other poor. **2** The rich man had very many sheep and cattle;[e] **3** but the poor man had nothing but one small female lamb, which he had bought.[f] He cared for it, and it grew up together with him and his sons. It would eat from the little food he had and drink from his cup and sleep in his arms. It became as a daughter to him. **4** Later a visitor came to the rich man, but he would not take any of his own sheep and cattle to prepare a meal for the traveler who had come to him. Instead, he took the poor man's lamb and prepared it for the man who had come to him."[g]

5 At this David grew very angry against the man, and he said to Nathan: "As surely as Jehovah is living,[h] the man who did this deserves to die! **6** And he should pay for the lamb four times over,[i] because he did this and showed no compassion."

7 Then Nathan said to David: "You are the man! This is what Jehovah the God of Israel says: 'I myself anointed you as king over Israel,[j] and I rescued you from the hand of Saul.[k] **8** I was willing to give you your master's house[l] and put your master's wives[m] in your arms, and I gave you the house of Israel and of Judah.[n] And as if that were not enough, I was willing to do much more for you.[o] **9** Why did you despise the word of Jehovah by doing what is bad in

---

CHAP. 11
a 2Sa 12:9

b Jg 9:50-53

c Jg 6:32
  Jg 7:1

d 2Sa 11:17

e 2Sa 12:26

Second Col.
a 2Sa 5:13
  2Sa 12:9

b Ge 39:7-9
  1Ki 15:5
  Ps 5:6
  Ps 11:4
  Heb 13:4

CHAP. 12
c 1Ki 1:8
  1Ch 17:1
  1Ch 29:29

d Ps 51:Sup

e 2Sa 5:13
  2Sa 15:16

f 2Sa 11:3

g 2Sa 11:4

h De 6:13

i Ex 22:1

j 1Sa 16:13
  2Sa 7:8

k 1Sa 18:10, 11
  1Sa 19:10
  1Sa 23:14

l 1Sa 13:13, 14
  1Sa 15:26, 28

m 2Sa 3:7
  1Ki 2:22

n 2Sa 2:4
  2Sa 5:5

o 2Sa 7:19

11:27 *Lit., "was bad in the eyes of."

his eyes? You struck down U·ri′ah the Hit′tite with the sword!ᵃ Then you took his wife as your wifeᵇ after you killed him by the sword of the Am′mon·ites.ᶜ 10 Now a sword will never depart from your own house,ᵈ because you despised me by taking the wife of U·ri′ah the Hit′tite as your wife.’ 11 This is what Jehovah says: ‘Here I am bringing against you calamity from within your own house;ᵉ and before your own eyes, I will take your wives and give them to another man,*ᶠ and he will lie down with your wives in broad daylight.*ᵍ 12 Although you acted in secret,ʰ I will do this in front of all Israel and in broad daylight.’”*

13 David then said to Nathan: “I have sinned against Jehovah.”ⁱ Nathan replied to David: “Jehovah, in turn, forgives your sin.*ʲ You will not die.ᵏ 14 Nevertheless, because you have treated Jehovah with utter disrespect in this matter, the son just born to you will certainly die.”

15 Then Nathan went to his own house.

And Jehovah struck the child whom U·ri′ah’s wife had borne to David, and he became sick. 16 David pleaded with the true God in behalf of the boy. David went on a strict fast and would go in and spend the night lying on the ground.ˡ 17 So the elders of his house stood over him and tried to raise him up from the ground, but he refused and would not eat with them. 18 On the seventh day the child died, but David’s servants were afraid to tell him that the child was dead. They said: “While the child was alive we

spoke to him, and he did not listen to us. So how can we tell him that the child has died? He may do something terrible.”

19 When David saw that his servants were whispering to one another, he discerned that the child had died. David said to his servants: “Has the child died?” They replied: “He has died.” 20 So David got up from the ground. He washed, rubbed himself with oil,ᵃ changed his clothing, and went to the houseᵇ of Jehovah and prostrated himself. Afterward, he went to his house* and asked for food to be brought to him, and he ate. 21 His servants asked him: “Why have you acted in this way? While the child was alive, you fasted and kept weeping; but as soon as the child died, you got up and ate food.” 22 He replied: “While the child was alive, I fastedᶜ and kept weeping because I said to myself, ‘Who knows whether Jehovah may show me favor and let the child live?’ᵈ 23 Now that he has died, why should I fast? Can I bring him back?ᵉ I will go to him,ᶠ but he will not return to me.”ᵍ

24 Then David comforted his wife Bath-she′ba.ʰ He went in to her and lay down with her. In time she bore a son, and he was named Sol′o·mon.*ⁱ And Jehovah loved him,ʲ 25 and he sent word through Nathanᵏ the prophet to name him Jed·i·di′ah,* for the sake of Jehovah.

26 Jo′ab continued fighting against Rab′bah of the Am′mon·ites,ᵐ and he captured the royal city.*ⁿ 27 So Jo′ab sent messengers to David and said: “I have fought against Rab′bah,ᵒ and I have captured the city

CHAP. 12
a Ex 20:13
b Ex 20:14, 17
c 2Sa 11:15, 27
d Nu 14:18
  2Sa 13:32
  2Sa 18:33
  Ga 6:7
e 2Sa 12:15, 19
  2Sa 13:10-15
  2Sa 15:14
f Ex 21:24
  Job 31:9-11
  Job 34:11
g 2Sa 16:21, 22
h 2Sa 11:4, 15
i Ge 39:9
  Ps 32:5
  Ps 38:3
  Ps 51:up, 4
  Pr 28:13
j Ex 34:6
  Ps 32:1
k Le 20:10
  Ps 103:10
l 2Sa 12:22
  Jon 3:8, 9

Second Col.
a Ru 3:3
  2Sa 14:2
b 2Sa 6:17
c 2Sa 12:16
  Joe 1:14
d Isa 38:3, 5
  Joe 2:13, 14
  Am 5:15
  Jon 3:8, 9
e Ec 9:6
f Job 30:23
  Ec 3:20
  Ac 2:29, 34
  Ac 13:36
g Ec 9:5, 10
h 2Sa 11:3
i 1Ch 3:5, 9
  1Ch 22:9
  1Ch 28:5
  Mt 1:6
j 2Sa 7:12
  1Ch 29:1
k 2Sa 7:4, 5
  2Sa 12:1
  1Ki 1:8
l De 3:11
  Jos 13:24, 25
m De 23:3, 6
n 2Sa 11:25
  1Ch 20:1
o 2Sa 11:1

of waters.* 28 Now gather the rest of the troops and encamp against the city and capture it. Otherwise, I will be the one to capture the city, and it will be credited to me."*

29 So David gathered all the troops and went to Rab'bah and fought against it and captured it. 30 Then he took the crown of Mal'cam from its head. The weight of it was a talent* of gold, along with precious stones, and it was placed on David's head. He also took a vast amount of spoil[a] from the city.[b] 31 And he brought out the people who were in it and put them to work at sawing stones, at working with sharp iron instruments and with iron axes, and at brickmaking. That was what he did to all the cities of the Am'mon·ites. Finally David and all the troops returned to Jerusalem.

13 Now David's son Ab'salom had a beautiful sister named Ta'mar,[c] and David's son Am'non[d] fell in love with her. 2 Am'non was so distressed that he became sick because of his sister Ta'mar, for she was a virgin and it seemed impossible for Am'non to do anything to her. 3 Now Am'non had a companion named Je·hon'a·dab,[e] the son of Shim'e·ah,[f] David's brother; and Je·hon'a·dab was a very clever man. 4 So he said to him: "Why are you, the king's son, so depressed every morning? Why not tell me?" Am'non replied to him: "I am in love with Ta'mar, the sister[g] of my brother Ab'salom." 5 Je·hon'a·dab replied to him: "Lie down on your bed and pretend to be sick. When your father comes to see you, say to

him, 'Please, let my sister Ta'mar come and serve me some food. If she prepares the food given to the sick* before my eyes, I will eat it from her hand.'"

6 So Am'non lay down and pretended to be sick, and the king came in to see him. Then Am'non said to the king: "Please, let my sister Ta'mar come in and bake two heart-shaped cakes before my eyes so that I may take food from her hand." 7 At that David sent a message to Ta'mar at the house, saying: "Please go to the house of your brother Am'non and prepare food* for him." 8 So Ta'mar went to the house of her brother Am'non, where he was lying down. She took the dough and kneaded it into cakes before his eyes and cooked the cakes. 9 Then she took the pan and served him. But Am'non refused to eat and said: "Have everybody leave me!" So everybody left him.

10 Am'non now said to Ta'mar: "Bring the food* into the bedroom, so that I may eat it from your hand." So Ta'mar took the heart-shaped cakes that she had made and brought them to her brother Am'non in the bedroom. 11 When she brought them for him to eat, he grabbed her and said: "Come, lie down with me, my sister." 12 But she said to him: "No, my brother! Do not humiliate me, for such a thing is not done in Israel.[a] Do not do this disgraceful thing.[b] 13 How could I live down my shame? And you will be regarded as one of the disgraceful men in Israel. Now speak, please, to the king, for he will not withhold me from you." 14 But he refused to listen to her, and he overpowered her and humiliated her by raping her. 15 Then

CHAP. 12
a 2Sa 8:11, 12

b 1Ch 20:2, 3

CHAP. 13
c 1Ch 3:9

d 2Sa 3:2

e 2Sa 13:35

f 1Sa 16:9
1Ch 2:13

g Le 18:9
Le 20:17

Second Col.
a Le 18:9, 29
Le 20:17
De 27:22

b Ge 34:2, 7
Jg 20:5, 6

12:27 *Possibly referring to the water resources of the city. 12:28 *Lit., "and my name will be called upon it." 12:30 *A talent equaled 34.2 kg (1,101 oz t). See App. B14.

13:5, 7, 10 *Or "the bread of consolation."

Am'non began hating her with a very intense hatred, so that his hatred for her became greater than the love he had felt for her. Am'non said to her: "Get up; go away!" 16 At this she said to him: "No, my brother, for sending me away now is worse than what you have done with me!" But he refused to listen to her.

17 With that he called his young attendant and said: "Get this person out of my presence, please, and lock the door behind her." 18 (Now she was wearing a special* robe, for those were the garments that the virgin daughters of the king wore.) So his attendant led her outside, and he locked the door behind her. 19 Then Ta'mar put ashes on her head,ᵃ and she ripped apart the fine robe she was wearing; and she kept her hands on her head and walked off, crying out as she walked.

20 At this her brother Ab'-sa·lomᵇ asked her: "Was it your brother Am'non who was with you? And now keep silent, my sister. He is your brother.ᶜ Do not let your heart dwell on this matter." Then Ta'mar lived in isolation at the house of her brother Ab'sa·lom. 21 When King David heard about all these things, he became very angry.ᵈ But he would not hurt the feelings of Am'non his son, because he loved him, for he was his firstborn. 22 And Ab'sa·lom said nothing to Am'non, either bad or good; for Ab'sa·lom hatedᵉ Am'non because he had humiliated his sister Ta'mar.ᶠ

23 After two full years, Ab'-sa·lom's sheepshearers were at Ba'al-ha'zor, near E'phra·im,ᵍ and Ab'sa·lom invited all the sons of the king.ʰ 24 So Ab'-sa·lom came in to the king and said: "Your servant is having his sheep sheared. Please

let the king and his servants go with me." 25 But the king said to Ab'sa·lom: "No, my son. If all of us go, we will be a burden to you." Although he kept urging him, he did not consent to go, but he blessed him. 26 Ab'sa·lom then said: "If not you, please let my brother Am'non go with us."ᵃ The king replied to him: "Why should he go with you?" 27 But Ab'sa·lom urged him, so he sent Am'non and all the king's sons with him.

28 Then Ab'sa·lom ordered his attendants: "Watch, and when Am'non's heart is in a cheerful mood from the wine, I will say to you, 'Strike down Am'non!' You must then put him to death. Do not be afraid. Is it not I who commands you? Be strong and courageous." 29 So Ab'sa·lom's attendants did to Am'non exactly as Ab'sa·lom had ordered; then all the other sons of the king got up, and each one mounted his mule and fled. 30 While they were on the way, the report reached David: "Ab'-sa·lom has struck down all the sons of the king, and not one of them survived." 31 At this the king got up and ripped his clothes apart and lay on the ground, and all his servants were standing by with their garments ripped apart.

32 However, Je·hon'a·dabᵇ the son of Shim'e·ah,ᶜ David's brother, said: "Do not let my lord think that they have killed all the young sons of the king, for only Am'non has died.ᵈ This is by the order of Ab'sa·lom, who decided to do thisᵉ from the day that Am'non humiliated his sisterᶠ Ta'mar.ᵍ 33 Now do not let my lord the king pay attention to* the report that says, 'All the king's sons have died'; only Am'-non has died."

CHAP. 13

a Jos 7:6
  Es 4:1
  Jer 6:26

b 2Sa 3:3
  2Sa 13:1

c Le 18:9
  De 27:22

d Pr 19:13

e Pr 18:19

f Ge 34:7

g Joh 11:54

h 1Ki 1:9, 19

Second Col.

a Ps 55:21
  Pr 10:18
  Pr 26:24-26

b 2Sa 13:3

c 1Sa 16:9
  1Ch 2:13

d 2Sa 12:10

e Ge 27:41
  Ps 7:14
  Pr 18:19

f Le 18:9, 29

g 2Sa 13:12-14

13:18 *Or "an ornamented."

13:33 *Lit., "take to his heart."

34 Meanwhile, Ab'sa·lom ran away.[a] Later the watchman raised his eyes and saw that there were many people coming from the road behind him next to the mountain. **35** At this Je·hon'a·dab[b] said to the king: "Look! The king's sons have returned. It is just as your servant said." **36** As he finished speaking, the king's sons came in, weeping loudly; also the king and all his servants wept very bitterly. **37** But Ab'sa·lom fled and went to Tal'mai[c] the son of Am·mi'hud the king of Gesh'ur. David mourned his son for many days. **38** After Ab'sa·lom fled and went to Gesh'ur,[d] he stayed there for three years.

39 Finally King David longed to go to Ab'sa·lom, for he had become reconciled to* the death of Am'non.

14 Now Jo'ab the son of Ze·ru'iah[e] learned that the king's heart longed for Ab'sa·lom.[f] **2** So Jo'ab sent to Te·ko'a[g] and summoned from there a clever woman and told her: "Act like you are in mourning, please, and put on garments of mourning, and do not rub yourself with oil.[h] Behave like a woman who has been mourning over someone dead for a long time. **3** Then go in and speak to the king like this." With that Jo'ab put the words in her mouth.*

4 The Te·ko'ite woman went in to the king and fell with her face to the ground and prostrated herself and said: "Help me, O king!" **5** The king replied to her: "What is the matter?" To this she said: "Alas, I am a widow; my husband is dead. **6** And I, your servant, had two sons, and the two of them fought with each other in the field. There was no one to separate them, and one struck the oth-

er down and killed him. **7** Now the whole family has risen up against me, your servant, and they are saying, 'Hand over the one who struck his brother, so that we may put him to death for the life* of his brother whom he killed,[a] even if it means wiping out the heir!' They would extinguish the last glowing coal that I have left# and leave to my husband neither a name nor a survivor△ on the surface of the earth."

8 Then the king said to the woman: "Go to your home, and I will issue an order regarding you." **9** At this the Te·ko'ite woman said to the king: "O my lord the king, let the guilt be on me and on my father's house, while the king and his throne are innocent." **10** The king then said: "If anyone speaks further to you, bring him to me, and he will never trouble you again." **11** But she said: "Please, let the king remember Jehovah your God, so that the avenger of blood[b] does not bring ruin and annihilate my son." To this he said: "As surely as Jehovah is living,[c] not one of your son's hairs will fall to the ground." **12** The woman now said: "Let your servant, please, speak a word to my lord the king." So he said: "Speak!"

13 The woman said: "Why, then, have you thought to do something like this against the people of God?[d] When the king speaks this way, he makes himself guilty, for the king does not bring back his own banished son.[e] **14** We will surely die and be like waters that are poured out on the ground, which cannot be recovered. But God would not take away a life,* and he considers reasons

---

CHAP. 13
a 2Sa 13:38

b 2Sa 13:3

c 2Sa 3:3

d De 3:14
Jos 12:4, 5
2Sa 14:23

CHAP. 14
e 2Sa 2:18
1Ch 2:15, 16

f 2Sa 13:39
2Sa 18:33
2Sa 19:2

g 2Ch 11:5, 6
2Ch 20:20
Am 1:1

h Ec 9:8
Da 10:3

Second Col.
a Nu 35:19
De 19:11, 12

b Nu 35:19, 27
De 19:6

c De 6:13
Ec 8:4

d Ex 19:5
Nu 6:27

e 2Sa 13:38

13:39 *Or "had found consolation over."
14:3 *Or "told her what to say."

14:7, 14 *Or "soul." 14:7 #That is, the last hope for descendants. △Lit., "remnant."

why the banished one should not always be banished from him. **15** I have come in to say this to my lord the king because the people made me afraid. So your servant said, 'Let me speak, please, to the king. Perhaps the king will act on the request of his slave. **16** The king may listen and rescue his slave from the hand of the man seeking to annihilate me and my only son from the inheritance God gave us.'[a] **17** Then your servant said, 'May the word of my lord the king please give me relief,' for my lord the king is just like an angel of the true God in distinguishing what is good from what is bad. May Jehovah your God be with you."

18 The king now answered the woman: "Please do not hide from me anything I ask you." The woman replied: "Let my lord the king speak, please." **19** The king then asked: "Did Jo'ab put you up to all of this?"[b] The woman answered: "As surely as you are* living, O my lord the king, it is just as# my lord the king says, for it was your servant Jo'ab who instructed me and put all these words in the mouth of your servant. **20** Your servant Jo'ab has done this to change the appearance of things, but my lord has wisdom like that of the angel of the true God and knows all that is happening in the land."

21 The king then said to Jo'ab: "All right, I will do this thing.[c] Go and bring back the young man Ab'sa·lom."[d] **22** At this Jo'ab fell with his face to the ground and prostrated himself and praised the king. Jo'ab said: "Today your servant knows that I have found favor in your eyes, O my lord the king, because the king has acted on the request

of his servant." **23** Then Jo'ab got up and went to Gesh'ur[a] and brought Ab'sa·lom to Jerusalem. **24** However, the king said: "Let him return to his own house, but he may not see my face." So Ab'sa·lom returned to his own house, and he did not see the face of the king.

25 Now in all Israel, no man was as highly praised for his handsome appearance as Ab'sa·lom. From the sole of his foot to the crown of his head, there was no flaw in him. **26** When he shaved his head —he had to shave it at the end of every year because it was so heavy for him—the hair of his head weighed 200 shekels* by the royal stone weight.# **27** To Ab'sa·lom were born three sons[b] and one daughter, whose name was Ta'mar. She was a very beautiful woman.

28 And Ab'sa·lom continued living in Jerusalem for two full years, but he did not see the face of the king.[c] **29** So Ab'sa·lom summoned Jo'ab in order to send him to the king, but Jo'ab would not come to him. Then he sent for him again, a second time, and he still refused to come. **30** Finally he said to his servants: "Jo'ab's plot of land is next to mine, and he has some barley there. Go and set it on fire." So the servants of Ab'sa·lom set the plot of land on fire. **31** At this Jo'ab got up and came to Ab'sa·lom's house and said to him: "Why did your servants set my plot of land on fire?" **32** Ab'sa·lom replied to Jo'ab: "Look! I sent this message to you, 'Come and let me send you to the king to ask: "Why have I come from Gesh'ur?[d] It

CHAP. 14
a 2Sa 14:2, 7

b 2Sa 14:1-3

c 2Sa 14:13

d 2Sa 13:38

_____

Second Col.
a De 3:14
  2Sa 3:3
  2Sa 13:37

b 2Sa 18:18

c 2Sa 14:24

d 2Sa 14:23

_____

14:19 *Or "your soul is." #Or "no one can go to the left or right from what."

14:26 *About 2.3 kg (5 lb). See App. B14. #This may have been a standard weight kept at the royal palace or a "royal" shekel that was different from the common shekel.

would have been better for me to stay there. Now let me see the face of the king, and if there is guilt in me, then he should put me to death.'"'"

33 So Jo'ab went in to the king and told him. Then he called Ab'sa·lom, who came in to the king and prostrated himself before him, falling with his face to the ground before the king. Then the king kissed Ab'sa·lom.[a]

15 After all these things, Ab'-sa·lom acquired for himself a chariot and horses and 50 men to run before him.[b] **2** Ab'sa·lom would rise up early and stand at the side of the road to the city gate.[c] Whenever any man had a legal case that was to come to the king for judgment,[d] Ab'sa·lom would call him and say: "From what city are you?" and he would say: "Your servant is from one of the tribes of Israel." **3** Ab'sa·lom would say to him: "See, your claims are right and proper, but there is no one from the king to hear your case." **4** Ab'sa·lom would say: "If only I were appointed judge in the land! Then every man who has a legal case or judgment could come to me, and I would see that he receives justice."

5 And when a man came near to bow down to him, Ab'sa·lom would extend his hand and grab hold of him and kiss him.[e] **6** Ab'sa·lom would do this to all the Israelites who would come in to the king for judgment; so Ab'sa·lom kept stealing the hearts of the men of Israel.[f]

7 At the end of four years,* Ab'sa·lom said to the king: "Let me go, please, to Heb'ron[g] to pay my vow that I made to Jehovah. **8** For your servant made this solemn vow[h] when I was dwelling in Gesh'ur[i] in Syria: 'If Jehovah will bring me back to Jeru-

salem, I will make an offering to* Jehovah.'" **9** So the king said to him: "Go in peace." With that he rose up and went to Heb'ron.

10 Ab'sa·lom now sent spies through all the tribes of Israel, saying: "As soon as you hear the sound of the horn, announce, 'Ab'sa·lom has become king in Heb'ron!'"[a] **11** Now 200 men from Jerusalem had gone there with Ab'sa·lom; they were invited and went unsuspectingly, unaware of what was happening. **12** Further, when he offered the sacrifices, Ab'sa·lom sent for A·hith'o·phel[b] the Gi'lon·ite, David's adviser,*[c] from his city Gi'-loh.[d] The conspiracy kept gaining momentum, and the people who supported Ab'sa·lom were growing in number.[e]

13 In time an informer came to David, saying: "The heart of the men of Israel has turned to Ab'sa·lom." **14** At once David said to all his servants with him in Jerusalem: "Get up, and let us run away,[f] for none of us will escape from Ab'sa·lom! Hurry, for fear he may quickly overtake us and bring disaster on us and strike the city with the sword!"[g] **15** The king's servants replied to the king: "Whatever my lord the king decides, your servants are ready to do."[h] **16** So the king went out with all his household following him, but the king left ten concubines[i] to take care of the house.* **17** And the king continued on his way out with all the people following, and they stopped at Beth·mer'hak.

18 All his servants leaving with him* and all the Cher'e·thites, the Pel'e·thites,[j] and the Git'tites,[k] 600 men who had followed him from Gath,[l] were

---

CHAP. 14
a Ge 45:15

CHAP. 15
b 1Sa 8:11
  1Ki 1:5
  Pr 11:2

c De 25:7
  Ru 4:1

d 1Sa 8:20
  2Sa 8:15

e Ps 10:9
  Ps 55:21
  Pr 26:25

f Pr 11:9

g 2Sa 3:2

h Le 22:21

i 2Sa 13:38
  2Sa 14:23

Second Col.
a 2Sa 2:1
  2Sa 5:1, 5
  1Ch 3:4

b 2Sa 16:23
  2Sa 17:14
  2Sa 23:8, 34

c Ps 41:9
  Ps 55:12, 13
  Joh 13:18

d Jos 15:20, 51

e Ps 3:1
  Pr 24:21

f 2Sa 19:9
  Ps 3:Sup

g 2Sa 12:11

h Pr 18:24

i 2Sa 12:11
  2Sa 16:21
  2Sa 20:3

j 2Sa 8:18
  2Sa 20:7
  1Ki 1:38
  1Ch 18:17

k Jos 13:2, 3

l 1Sa 27:4
  1Ch 18:1

15:8 *Or "worship." Lit., "render service to." 15:12 *Or "counselor." 15:16 *Or "palace." 15:18 *Or "crossing at his side."

15:7 *Or possibly, "40 years."

passing by as the king reviewed them.* **19** Then the king said to It'tai[a] the Git'tite: "Why should you also go with us? Go back and dwell with the new king, for you are a foreigner and also an exile from your place. **20** Yesterday you came, so today should I make you wander with us, to go when I must go and where I must go? Go back and take your brothers with you, and may Jehovah show you loyal love and faithfulness!"[b] **21** But It'tai answered the king: "As surely as Jehovah is living and as surely as my lord the king is living, wherever my lord the king may be, whether for death or for life, there your servant will be!"[c] **22** At that David said to It'tai:[d] "Go and cross over." So It'tai the Git'tite crossed over, together with all his men and children.

23 Everyone in the land was weeping loudly while all these people crossed over, and the king was standing by the Kid'ron Valley;[e] all the people were crossing over to the road leading to the wilderness. **24** Za'dok[f] was also there and with him were all the Levites[g] carrying the ark[h] of the covenant of the true God;[i] and they set the Ark of the true God down; and A·bi'a·thar[j] went up, while all the people completed crossing over from the city. **25** But the king said to Za'dok: "Take the Ark of the true God back to the city.[k] If I find favor in the eyes of Jehovah, he will also bring me back and let me see it and its dwelling place.[l] **26** But if he should say, 'I have found no pleasure in you,' then let him do to me whatever seems good in his eyes." **27** The king said to Za'dok the priest: "Are you not a seer?[m] Return to the city in peace, and

take the two sons of you men with you, A·him'a·az your own son and Jon'a·than[a] the son of A·bi'a·thar. **28** See, I will linger by the fords of the wilderness until word comes from you to inform me."[b] **29** So Za'dok and A·bi'a·thar took the Ark of the true God back to Jerusalem, and they remained there.

30 As David was going up the Mount* of Olives,[c] he was weeping as he went up; his head was covered, and he was walking barefoot. All the people with him also covered their heads and were weeping as they went up. **31** David was then told: "A·hith'o·phel is among those conspiring[d] with Ab'sa·lom."[e] At this David said: "Turn, please, the advice* of A·hith'o·phel into foolishness,[f] O Jehovah!"[g]

32 When David came to the summit where people used to bow down to God, Hu'shai[h] the Ar'chite[i] was there to meet him, with his robe ripped apart and dirt on his head. **33** However, David said to him: "If you go across with me, you will be a load on me. **34** But if you return to the city and you say to Ab'sa·lom, 'I am your servant, O King. I was the servant of your father in the past, but now I am your servant,'[j] you can then frustrate the advice of A·hith'o·phel for me.[k] **35** Are not Za'dok and A·bi'a·thar the priests there with you? You must tell Za'dok and A·bi'a·thar the priests everything that you hear from the house of the king.[l] **36** Look! There with them are their two sons, A·him'a·az[m] the son of Za'dok and Jon'a·than[n] the son of A·bi'a·thar, and through them send to me everything that you hear." **37** So Hu'shai, David's friend,*[o] went into the city as Ab'sa·lom was entering into Jerusalem.

CHAP. 15
a 2Sa 18:2

b 2Sa 2:5, 6
Ps 25:10
Ps 57:3
Ps 61:7
Ps 89:14

c Pr 17:17
Pr 18:24

d 2Sa 18:2

e 1Ki 2:36, 37
2Ch 30:14
Joh 18:1

f 2Sa 8:17
2Sa 20:25
1Ki 1:8
1Ki 2:35
1Ch 6:8

g Nu 8:19

h Ex 37:1
Le 16:2

i Nu 4:15
Nu 7:9

j 1Sa 22:20
1Sa 30:7

k 2Sa 6:17

l 2Sa 7:2
Ps 26:8
Ps 27:4

m 1Sa 9:9

Second Col.

a 2Sa 17:17

b 2Sa 15:36
2Sa 17:16, 21

c Mt 21:1
Mt 24:3
Ac 1:12

d Ps 41:9
Ps 55:12, 13
Joh 13:18

e Ps 3:Sup

f 2Sa 16:23
2Sa 17:14

g Ps 3:7

h 2Sa 16:16

i Jos 16:1, 2

j 2Sa 16:18, 19

k 2Sa 17:7, 14

l 2Sa 17:15, 16

m 2Sa 18:19

n 2Sa 17:17
1Ki 1:42

o 2Sa 16:16
1Ch 27:33

15:18 *Or "crossing before the king's face."

15:30 *Or "ascent." 15:31 *Or "counsel." 15:37 *Or "confidant."

16 When David had passed a little beyond the summit,[a] Zi′ba,[b] the attendant of Me·phib′o·sheth,[c] was there to meet him with a couple of saddled donkeys, and on them were 200 loaves of bread, 100 cakes of raisins, 100 cakes of summer fruit,* and a large jar of wine.[d] **2** Then the king said to Zi′ba: "Why have you brought these things?" Zi′ba replied: "The donkeys are for the household of the king to ride, the bread and the summer fruit are for the young men to eat, and the wine is for those who get exhausted in the wilderness to drink."[e] **3** The king now said: "And where is the son* of your master?"[f] At this Zi′ba said to the king: "He is staying in Jerusalem, for he said, 'Today the house of Israel will give back the royal rule of my father to me.'"[g] **4** The king then said to Zi′ba: "Look! Everything that belongs to Me·phib′o·sheth is yours."[h] Zi′ba replied: "I bow down before you. May I find favor in your eyes, my lord the king."[i]

5 When King David reached Ba·hu′rim, a man of the family of Saul's house named Shim′e·i,[j] the son of Ge′ra, came out shouting curses as he approached.[k] **6** He was throwing stones at David and at all the servants of King David, as well as at all the people and the mighty men on his right and on his left. **7** Shim′e·i said as he cursed: "Get out, get out, you bloodguilty man! You worthless man! **8** Jehovah has brought back on you all the bloodguilt for the house of Saul, in whose place you have ruled as king, but Jehovah gives the kingship into the hand of Ab′sa·lom your son. Now calamity has overtaken you because you are a bloodguilty man!"[l]

9 Then A·bish′ai the son of Ze·ru′iah[a] said to the king: "Why should this dead dog[b] curse my lord the king?[c] Let me go over, please, and take off his head."[d] **10** But the king said: "What do I have to do with you, you sons of Ze·ru′iah?[e] Let him curse me,[f] for Jehovah has said to him,[g] 'Curse David!' So who should say, 'Why are you doing this?'" **11** David then said to A·bish′ai and all his servants: "Here my own son, who came from my own body, is seeking my life,*[h] and how much more now a Ben′ja·min·ite![i] Leave him alone so that he may curse me, for Jehovah told him to! **12** Perhaps Jehovah will see my affliction,[j] and Jehovah will restore goodness to me instead of the curses shouted at me this day."[k] **13** With that David and his men kept going down the road while Shim′e·i was walking alongside the mountain abreast of him, shouting curses[l] and throwing stones and a lot of dust.

14 At length the king and all the people with him arrived at their destination exhausted, and they refreshed themselves.

15 Meanwhile, Ab′sa·lom and all the men of Israel arrived in Jerusalem, and A·hith′o·phel[m] was with him. **16** When Hu′shai[n] the Ar′chite,[o] David's friend,* came in to Ab′sa·lom, Hu′shai said to Ab′sa·lom: "Long live the king![p] Long live the king!" **17** At this Ab′sa·lom said to Hu′shai: "Is this your loyal love toward your friend? Why did you not go with your friend?" **18** So Hu′shai said to Ab′sa·lom: "No, I am on the side of the one who has been chosen by Jehovah, this people, and all the men of Israel. I will stay with him. **19** And again I say, Whom

---

CHAP. 16

a 2Sa 15:30

b 2Sa 9:2, 9

c 2Sa 9:6

d 1Sa 25:18

e 2Sa 17:27-29

f 2Sa 9:3

g 2Sa 19:25-27

h 2Sa 9:9, 10

i Pr 26:22

j 2Sa 19:16
  1Ki 2:8, 44

k Ex 22:28
  Ec 10:20

l 1Sa 24:6, 7
  1Sa 26:9, 11
  Ps 3:1, 2
  Ps 7:1
  Ps 71:10, 11

Second Col.

a 1Ch 2:15, 16

b 1Sa 24:14

c Ex 22:28

d 1Sa 26:8

e 2Sa 19:22
  1Ki 2:5

f Ps 37:8
  1Pe 2:23

g 2Sa 12:10

h 2Sa 12:11
  2Sa 15:14
  2Sa 17:12

i 2Sa 19:16

j Ge 29:32
  Ex 3:7
  Ps 25:18

k Ps 109:28

l 2Sa 16:5

m 2Sa 15:12, 31

n 2Sa 15:32, 37
  1Ch 27:33

o Jos 16:1, 2

p 1Ki 1:25

16:1 *Especially figs and perhaps also dates. **16:3** *Or "grandson."

16:11 *Or "soul." **16:16** *Or "confidant."

should I serve? Should it not be his son? Just as I served your father, so I will serve you."[a]

20 Ab·sa·lom then said to A·hith′o·phel: "Give me your advice.*[b] What should we do?" 21 At that A·hith′o·phel said to Ab′sa·lom: "Have relations with your father's concubines,[c] those whom he left behind to take care of the house.*[d] Then all Israel will hear that you have made yourself a stench to your father, and those who support you will be strengthened." 22 So they pitched a tent for Ab′sa·lom on the roof,[e] and Ab′sa·lom had relations with the concubines of his father[f] before the eyes of all Israel.[g]

23 In those days the advice that A·hith′o·phel gave was considered as* the word of the true God. That was how all the advice of A·hith′o·phel was esteemed, both by David and by Ab′sa·lom.

17 A·hith′o·phel then said to Ab′sa·lom: "Please let me choose 12,000 men and rise up and chase after David tonight. 2 I will come upon him when he is weary and powerless,*[i] and I will throw him into a panic; and all the people who are with him will flee, and I will strike down only the king.[j] 3 Then I will bring all the people back to you. The return of all the people depends on what happens with the man you are seeking. Then all the people will be at peace." 4 The proposal was just right in the eyes of Ab′sa·lom and all the elders of Israel.

5 However, Ab′sa·lom said: "Please call Hu′shai[k] the Ar′chite as well, and let us hear what he has to say." 6 So Hu′shai came in to Ab′sa·lom. Then Ab′sa·lom

said to him: "This is the advice A·hith′o·phel gave. Should we act on his advice? If not, you tell us." 7 At this Hu′shai said to Ab′sa·lom: "The advice that A·hith′o·phel gave is not good in this instance!"[a]

8 Hu′shai continued: "You well know that your father and his men are mighty,[b] and they are desperate,* like a bear that has lost her cubs in the field.[c] Moreover, your father is a warrior,[d] and he will not spend the night with the people. 9 At this very moment he is hiding in one of the caves* or in some other place;[e] and if he attacks first, those hearing of it will say, 'The people following Ab′sa·lom have been defeated!' 10 Even the courageous man whose heart is like that of a lion[f] will surely melt in fear, for all Israel knows that your father is a mighty man[g] and that the men with him are courageous. 11 I give this advice: Let all Israel be gathered to you, from Dan to Be′er-she′ba,[h] as many as the grains of sand by the sea,[i] and you should lead them into the fight. 12 We will come against him wherever he is found, and we will come upon him just like the dew that falls on the ground; and not one of them will survive, not he nor any of the men with him. 13 If he retreats into a city, all Israel will carry ropes to that city, and we will drag it down into the valley until not even a pebble is left."

14 Then Ab′sa·lom and all the men of Israel said: "The advice of Hu′shai the Ar′chite is better[j] than the advice of A·hith′o·phel!" For Jehovah had determined* to frustrate the sound advice of A·hith′o·phel,[k] so that

---

CHAP. 16
a 2Sa 15:34
b Ps 37:12
c Le 18:8
  Le 20:11
  1Ki 2:22
d 2Sa 15:16
e 2Sa 11:2
f De 22:30
  2Sa 20:3
g 2Sa 12:11, 12
h 2Sa 15:12
  2Sa 17:14, 23

CHAP. 17
i 2Sa 16:14
j Ps 37:12
  Ps 41:9
  Ps 55:12, 13
k 2Sa 15:32
  2Sa 16:16

Second Col.
a 2Sa 15:34
b 1Sa 16:18
  2Sa 15:18
  2Sa 23:8, 18
  1Ch 11:26
c Pr 17:12
d 1Sa 17:50
  1Sa 18:7
  1Sa 19:8
  2Sa 10:18
e 1Sa 22:1
  1Sa 23:19
f Ge 49:9
  2Sa 1:23
  Isa 31:4
g 1Sa 18:5
h Jg 20:1
i 1Ki 4:20
j Pr 21:1
k 2Sa 15:31, 34
  2Sa 16:23
  Pr 19:21
  Pr 21:30

16:20 *Or "counsel." 16:21 *Or "palace." 16:23 *Or "was as if someone were inquiring of." 17:2 *Or "feeble in both hands."

17:8 *Or "bitter of soul." 17:9 *Or "pits; ravines." 17:14 *Or "commanded."

Jehovah could bring disaster on Ab′sa·lom.[a]

15 Hu′shai later said to Za′dok and A·bi′a·thar[b] the priests: "This is what A·hith′o·phel has advised Ab′sa·lom and the elders of Israel, and this is what I have advised. **16** Now quickly send word to David and warn him: 'Do not stay at the fords* of the wilderness tonight, but cross over without fail, or the king and all the people with him may be wiped out.'"[#c]

17 Jon′a·than[d] and A·him′a·az[e] were staying at En-ro′gel;[f] so a servant girl went off and told them and they went to tell King David, for they did not dare to be seen entering the city. **18** However, a young man saw them and told Ab′sa·lom. So the two of them quickly went off and came to the house of a man in Ba·hu′rim[g] who had a well in his courtyard. They went down into it, **19** and the man's wife spread a covering over the top of the well and covered it with cracked grain; no one knew about it. **20** The servants of Ab′sa·lom came to the woman at her house and asked: "Where are A·him′a·az and Jon′a·than?" The woman replied: "They passed by toward the water."[h] Then the men searched for them but did not find them, so they returned to Jerusalem.

21 After the men were gone, they came up out of the well and went and informed King David. They said to him: "Rise up and quickly cross the water, for this is what A·hith′o·phel advised against you."[i] **22** Immediately David and all the people with him rose up and crossed the Jordan. By daybreak, there was no one left who had not crossed the Jordan.

23 When A·hith′o·phel saw that his advice had not been acted on, he saddled a donkey and went to his house in his hometown.[a] After he gave instructions to his household,[b] he hanged* himself.[c] So he died and was buried in the burial place of his forefathers.

24 Meanwhile, David went to Ma·ha·na′im,[d] and Ab′sa·lom crossed the Jordan with all the men of Israel. **25** Ab′sa·lom put A·ma′sa[e] in charge of the army in place of Jo′ab;[f] A·ma′sa was the son of a man named Ith′ra the Israelite, who had relations with Ab′i·gail[g] the daughter of Na′hash, the sister of Ze·ru′iah, Jo′ab's mother. **26** Israel and Ab′sa·lom camped in the land of Gil′e·ad.[h]

27 As soon as David came to Ma·ha·na′im, Sho′bi the son of Na′hash from Rab′bah[i] of the Am′mon·ites, Ma′chir[j] the son of Am′mi·el from Lo-de′bar, and Bar·zil′lai[k] the Gil′e·ad·ite from Ro·ge′lim **28** brought beds, basins, clay pots, wheat, barley, flour, roasted grain, broad beans, lentils, parched grain, **29** honey, butter, sheep, and cheese.* They brought all of this out for David and the people with him to eat,[l] for they said: "The people are hungry and tired and thirsty in the wilderness."[m]

18 Then David numbered the men who were with him and placed over them chiefs of thousands and chiefs of hundreds.[n] **2** And David sent one third of the men under the command* of Jo′ab,[o] one third under the command of Jo′ab's brother A·bish′ai[p] the son of Ze·ru′iah,[q] and one third under the command of It′tai[r] the Git′tite. The king then said to the men: "I will

CHAP. 17

a De 2:30
2Ch 25:20

b 2Sa 8:17
2Sa 15:35

c Ps 35:24, 25

d 1Ki 1:42

e 2Sa 15:27, 36
2Sa 18:19

f Jos 15:7, 12
Jos 18:16, 20
1Ki 1:9

g 2Sa 16:5
2Sa 19:16

h Ex 1:19
Jos 2:3-5
1Sa 19:12, 14
1Sa 21:2

i 2Sa 17:1, 2

Second Col.

a Jos 15:20, 51
2Sa 15:12

b 2Ki 20:1

c 1Sa 31:4
1Ki 16:18
Ps 5:10
Ps 55:23
Mt 27:3, 5
Ac 1:18

d Ge 32:1, 2
Jos 13:24, 26

e 2Sa 19:13
2Sa 20:4, 10

f 2Sa 8:16

g 1Ch 2:16, 17

h Nu 32:1
De 3:15

i De 3:11
Jos 13:24, 25
2Sa 12:26, 29

j 2Sa 9:3-5

k 2Sa 19:31, 32
1Ki 2:7

l Pr 11:25

m 1Sa 25:18
2Sa 16:2

CHAP. 18

n Pr 20:18

o 2Sa 8:16
2Sa 10:7

p 2Sa 23:18, 19

q 1Ch 2:15, 16

r 2Sa 15:19, 21

also go out with you." **3** But they said: "You must not go out,[a] for if we flee, they would not care about* us; and if half of us would die, they would not care about us, because you are worth 10,000 of us.[b] Therefore, it would be better if you would send us help from the city." **4** The king said to them: "Whatever seems best to you, I will do." So the king stood next to the city gate, and all the men went out by hundreds and by thousands. **5** Then the king gave Jo'ab and A·bish'ai and It'tai this order: "Deal gently with the young man Ab'sa·lom for my sake."[c] All the men heard it when the king gave all the chiefs the order about Ab'sa·lom.

6 The men went out to the field to meet Israel, and the battle took place in the forest of E'phra·im.[d] **7** There the people of Israel[e] were defeated by the servants of David,[f] and a great slaughter took place on that day—20,000 men. **8** The battle spread through the whole region. Furthermore, the forest devoured more of the people than the sword did on that day.

9 Ab'sa·lom eventually found himself facing the servants of David. Ab'sa·lom was riding on a mule, and the mule went under the thick branches of a large tree, and his head got entangled in the big tree, so that he was suspended in midair* while the mule he had been riding kept going. **10** Then someone saw it and told Jo'ab:[g] "Look! I have seen Ab'sa·lom hanging in a big tree." **11** Jo'ab replied to the man who told him: "If you saw it, why did you not strike him down to the ground on the spot? Then I would have gladly given you ten pieces of silver and a belt."

12 But the man said to Jo'ab: "Even if I were handed* 1,000 pieces of silver, I could not lift my hand against the king's son, for we heard the king order you and A·bish'ai and It'tai, 'Whoever you are, watch over the young man Ab'sa·lom.'[a] **13** If I had disobeyed and taken his life,* it could never have remained hidden from the king, and you would not have protected me." **14** To this Jo'ab said: "I am not going to waste any more time with you!" So he took three spikes* in his hand and drove them through the heart of Ab'sa·lom while he was still alive in the midst of the big tree. **15** Then ten attendants who carried Jo'ab's weapons came and struck Ab'sa·lom until he was dead.[b] **16** Jo'ab now blew the horn, and the men returned from chasing after Israel; Jo'ab called for them to halt. **17** They took Ab'sa·lom and threw him into a big pit in the forest and piled up over him a very big heap of stones.[c] And all Israel fled to their homes.

18 Now Ab'sa·lom, while he was alive, had taken and set up for himself a pillar in the Valley* of the King,[d] for he said: "I have no son to preserve the memory of my name."[e] So he named the pillar after himself, and it is called Ab'sa·lom's Monument to this day.

19 A·him'a·az[f] the son of Za'dok said: "Let me run, please, and break the news to the king, for Jehovah has given him justice by freeing him from his enemies."[g] **20** But Jo'ab said to him: "You will not be a bearer of news this day. You may break the news on another day, but to-

CHAP. 18
a 2Sa 21:17

b 2Sa 17:1-3
La 4:20

c 2Sa 18:12

d 2Sa 17:26

e 2Sa 16:15

f Ps 3:7
Pr 24:21, 22

g 2Sa 8:16
2Sa 18:2

_____
Second Col.
a 2Sa 18:5

b 2Sa 12:10
Pr 2:22
Pr 20:20
Pr 30:17

c Jos 7:24, 26
Jos 8:29
Jos 10:23, 27

d Ge 14:17

e 2Sa 14:27

f 2Sa 15:35, 36
2Sa 17:17

g Ps 9:4

18:3 *Lit., "set heart toward." 18:9 *Lit., "between the heavens and the earth." 18:12 *Lit., "were weighing upon my palms." 18:13 *Or "if I had dealt treacherously against his soul." 18:14 *Or possibly, "darts; spears." Lit., "rods." 18:18 *Or "Low Plain."

day you will not break the news, because the king's own son has died."[a] **21** Then Jo'ab said to a Cush'ite:[b] "Go, tell the king what you have seen." At that the Cush'ite bowed to Jo'ab and ran off. **22** A·him'a·az the son of Za'dok said once again to Jo'ab: "Whatever happens, please let me also run behind the Cush'ite." However, Jo'ab said: "Why should you run, my son, when there is no news for you to tell?" **23** Still he said: "Whatever happens, let me run." So Jo'ab said to him: "Run!" And A·him'a·az ran by the way of the district of the Jordan,* and he eventually overtook the Cush'ite.

24 Now David was sitting between the two city gates,[c] and the watchman[d] went up to the roof of the gate by the wall. He looked up and saw a man running by himself. **25** So the watchman called out and told the king. The king said: "If he is by himself, he has news to tell." As he came steadily nearer, **26** the watchman saw another man running. The watchman then called to the gatekeeper: "Look! Another man running by himself!" The king said: "This one is also bringing news." **27** The watchman said: "I can see that the first man runs like A·him'a·az[e] the son of Za'dok," so the king said: "He is a good man, and he comes with good news." **28** A·him'a·az then called out to the king: "All is well!" With that he bowed to the king with his face to the ground. Then he said: "May Jehovah your God be praised, who has surrendered the men who rebelled* against my lord the king!"[f]

29 However, the king said: "Is everything all right with the young man Ab'sa·lom?" To this A·him'a·az said: "I saw the great commotion when Jo'ab sent the king's servant and your servant, but I did not know what it was."[a] **30** So the king said: "Step aside, stand here." At that he stepped aside and stood there.

31 Then the Cush'ite arrived,[b] and the Cush'ite said: "Let my lord the king accept this news: Today Jehovah has brought justice by freeing you from the hand of all those who rebelled against you."[c] **32** But the king said to the Cush'ite: "Is everything all right with the young man Ab'sa·lom?" To this the Cush'ite said: "May all the enemies of my lord the king and all those who rebelled against you to harm you become like the young man!"[d]

33 This disturbed the king, and he went up to the roof chamber over the gateway and wept, saying as he walked: "My son Ab'sa·lom, my son, my son Ab'sa·lom! If only I had died instead of you, Ab'sa·lom my son, my son!"[e]

19 It was reported to Jo'ab: "The king is weeping and mourning for Ab'sa·lom."[f] **2** So the victory* on that day was turned into mourning for all the people, because they heard that the king was grieving over his son. **3** The people quietly returned to the city[g] that day like people who are ashamed because they fled in the battle. **4** The king covered his face and kept crying out with a loud voice: "My son Ab'sa·lom! Ab'sa·lom my son, my son!"[h]

5 Then Jo'ab went in to the king at the house and said: "Today you have put to shame all your servants who this day saved your life* and the lives* of your sons,[i] your daughters,[j] your wives, and your concubines.[k] **6** You love those who hate you and hate those who love you,

---

CHAP. 18
a 2Sa 18:5

b Ge 10:6

c 2Sa 18:4

d 2Ki 9:17

e 2Sa 18:19

f 2Sa 22:47
  Ps 144:1

Second Col.
a 2Sa 18:22

b 2Sa 18:21

c 2Sa 22:49
  Ps 55:18
  Ps 94:1
  Ps 124:2, 3

d Ps 27:2

e 2Sa 12:10
  2Sa 17:14
  2Sa 19:1
  Pr 19:13

CHAP. 19
f 2Sa 18:5
  2Sa 18:14

g 2Sa 17:24

h 2Sa 18:33

i 2Sa 3:2-5
  2Sa 5:14-16

j 2Sa 13:1

k 2Sa 5:13
  2Sa 15:16

18:23 *Lit., "the district." **18:28** *Lit., "lifted up their hand."

19:2 *Or "salvation." **19:5** *Or "soul." #Or "souls."

for you have made it clear today that your chiefs and servants mean nothing to you, because I am sure that if only Ab'sa·lom were alive today and the rest of us were dead, it would be all right with you. **7** Now get up, go out and reassure* your servants, because by Jehovah I swear that if you do not go out, not a man will remain with you tonight. This will be worse for you than all the injury that has come upon you from your youth until now." **8** So the king rose up and sat in the city gate, and all the people were informed: "Now the king is sitting in the gate." Then all the people came before the king.

But Israel had fled, each to his home.[a] **9** All the people in all the tribes of Israel were disputing, saying: "The king saved us from our enemies,[b] and he rescued us from the Phi·lis'tines; but now he has fled the land because of Ab'sa·lom.[c] **10** And Ab'sa·lom, whom we anointed over us,[d] has died in the battle.[e] So now, why are you doing nothing to bring the king back?"

11 King David sent this message to Za'dok[f] and A·bi'a·thar[g] the priests: "Speak to the elders of Judah,[h] saying, 'Why should you be the last ones to bring the king back to his house, when the word of all Israel has come to the king at his house? **12** You are my brothers; you are my own bone and flesh.* Why should you be the last ones to bring the king back?' **13** And you should say to A·ma'sa,[i] 'Are you not my own bone and flesh? So may God do to me and add to it if you will not become my army chief from now on instead of Jo'ab.'"[j]

14 So he won over* the hearts of all the men of Judah as

19:7 *Lit., "speak to the heart of." 19:12 *Or "my blood relatives." 19:14 *Lit., "he bent."

CHAP. 19
a 2Sa 18:17

b 1Sa 17:50
1Sa 18:7
1Sa 19:5
2Sa 5:25
2Sa 8:5

c 2Sa 15:14

d 2Sa 15:10, 12

e 2Sa 18:14

f 2Sa 8:17
2Sa 15:25
1Ki 1:8

g 1Sa 22:20
1Sa 30:7
2Sa 15:24
1Ch 15:11, 12

h 2Sa 2:4

i 2Sa 17:25
1Ch 2:16, 17

j 2Sa 8:16
2Sa 18:5, 14

Second Col.
a Jos 5:9
1Sa 11:14

b 2Sa 16:5
1Ki 2:8, 9

c 2Sa 9:2, 10
2Sa 16:1

d 2Sa 16:5

e 2Sa 23:18

f 2Sa 2:18

g Ex 22:28
2Sa 16:7
1Ki 21:13

h 2Sa 3:39
2Sa 16:10

i 1Ki 2:8, 9

j 2Sa 9:3, 6
2Sa 16:3, 4

---

one man, and they sent word to the king: "Come back, you and all your servants."

15 The king started back and reached the Jordan, and the people of Judah came to Gil'gal[a] to meet the king and to escort him across the Jordan. **16** Then Shim'e·i[b] the son of Ge'ra, the Ben'ja·min·ite from Ba·hu'rim, hurried down with the men of Judah to meet King David, **17** and there were 1,000 men from Benjamin with him. Also Zi'ba,[c] the attendant of the house of Saul, with his 15 sons and 20 servants, rushed down to the Jordan ahead of the king. **18** He* crossed the ford to bring the king's household across and to do whatever he desired. But Shim'e·i the son of Ge'ra fell down before the king when he was about to cross the Jordan. **19** He said to the king: "Do not let my lord hold me guilty, and do not remember the wrong your servant did[d] on the day that my lord the king went out of Jerusalem. May the king not take it to heart, **20** for your servant well knows that I have sinned; so today I have been the first of all the house of Joseph to come down to meet my lord the king."

21 At once A·bish'ai[e] the son of Ze·ru'iah[f] said: "Should not Shim'e·i be put to death for this, because he cursed the anointed of Jehovah?"[g] **22** But David said: "What does this have to do with you, you sons of Ze·ru'iah,[h] that you should act against me today? Should anyone be put to death today in Israel? For do I not know that today I am king over Israel?" **23** Then the king said to Shim'e·i: "You will not die." And the king gave him his oath.[i]

24 Me·phib'o·sheth,[j] the grandson of Saul, also came down to

---

19:18 *Or possibly, "They."

meet the king. He had not cared for his feet or trimmed his mustache or washed his garments from the day the king left until the day he returned in peace. 25 When he came to* Jerusalem to meet the king, the king said to him: "Why did you not go with me, Me·phib'o·sheth?" 26 To this he said: "My lord the king, my servant[a] tricked me. For your servant had said, 'Let me get my donkey saddled so that I may ride on it and go with the king,' for your servant is crippled.[b] 27 But he slandered your servant to my lord the king.[c] However, my lord the king is like an angel of the true God, so do whatever seems good to you. 28 All the household of my father could have been doomed to death by my lord the king, and yet you placed your servant among those eating at your table.[d] So what right do I have to cry out further to the king?"

29 However, the king said to him: "Why keep on speaking like this? I have decided that you and Zi'ba should share the field."[e] 30 At this Me·phib'o·sheth said to the king: "Let him take it all, now that my lord the king has come to his house in peace."

31 Then Bar·zil'lai[f] the Gil'e·ad·ite came down from Ro·ge'lim to the Jordan to escort the king to the Jordan. 32 Bar·zil'lai was very old, 80 years of age, and he supplied the king with food while he was staying in Ma·ha·na'im,[g] for he was a very wealthy man. 33 So the king said to Bar·zil'lai: "Cross over with me, and I will supply you with food in Jerusalem."[h] 34 But Bar·zil'lai said to the king: "How many days* of my life are left that I should go up with the king to Jerusalem? 35 I am 80 years old today.[i] Can

19:25 *Or possibly, "from." 19:34 *Lit., "days of years."

I discern between good and bad? Can I, your servant, taste what I eat and drink? Can I still listen to the voice of male and female singers?[a] So why should your servant be an added burden to my lord the king? 36 It is enough that your servant could bring the king to the Jordan. Why should the king repay me with this reward? 37 Let your servant return, please, and let me die in my city near the burial place of my father and my mother.[b] But here is your servant Chim'ham.[c] Let him cross over with my lord the king, and you may do for him what seems good to you."

38 So the king said: "Chim'ham will go across with me, and I will do for him what seems good to you; whatever you ask of me I will do for you." 39 All the people now began to cross the Jordan, and when the king crossed, the king kissed Bar·zil'lai[d] and blessed him; and Bar·zil'lai returned home. 40 When the king went across to Gil'gal,[e] Chim'ham crossed with him. All the people of Judah and half the people of Israel brought the king across.[f]

41 Then all the men of Israel approached the king and said to him: "Why did our brothers the men of Judah steal you away and bring the king and his household over the Jordan, along with all of David's men?"[g] 42 All the men of Judah answered the men of Israel: "Because the king is related to us.[h] Why are you angry over this? Have we eaten anything at the king's expense, or has a gift been given to us?"

43 However, the men of Israel answered the men of Judah: "We have ten parts in the king, so that we have a greater claim in David than you have. Why, then, have you treated us with contempt? Should we not have been

---

CHAP. 19
a 2Sa 9:9

b 2Sa 4:4

c Le 19:16
  2Sa 16:3

d 2Sa 9:7-10

e 2Sa 16:4

f 2Sa 17:27-29
  1Ki 2:7

g Pr 3:27

h Pr 11:25

i Ps 90:10

Second Col.
a Ec 2:8

b Ge 50:13

c 1Ki 2:7

d Ge 31:55
  1Sa 20:41
  Ac 20:37

e 1Sa 11:14

f 2Sa 2:4

g Jg 8:1
  Jg 12:1
  2Sa 19:15

h Ps 78:68, 70

first to bring our king back?" But the word of the men of Judah prevailed over* that of the men of Israel.

20 Now there was a trouble-maker named She'ba[a] the son of Bich'ri, a Ben'ja·min·ite. He blew the horn[b] and said: "We have no share in David, and we have no inheritance in the son of Jes'se.[c] Everyone to his gods,* O Israel!"[d] **2** At that all the men of Israel quit following David to follow She'ba the son of Bich'-ri;[e] but the men of Judah stuck to their king, from the Jordan to Jerusalem.[f]

3 When David came to his house* at Jerusalem,[g] the king took the ten concubines he had left behind to take care of the house,[h] and he put them in a house under guard. He supplied food to them, but he did not have any relations with them.[j] They remained in confinement until the day of their death, living as if they were widows, even though they had a living husband.

4 The king now said to A·ma'-sa:[j] "Call the men of Judah together to me within three days, and you also should be here." **5** So A·ma'sa went to call Judah together, but he came later than the set time that had been appointed for him. **6** Then David said to A·bish'ai:[k] "She'ba[l] the son of Bich'ri may do us more harm than Ab'sa·lom did.[m] Take the servants of your lord and chase after him, so that he may not find fortified cities and escape from us." **7** So the men of Jo'ab,[n] the Cher'e·thites, the Pel'e·thites,[o] and all the mighty men went out after him; they left Jerusalem to chase after She'ba the son of Bich'ri. **8** When they

were near the great stone in Gib'e·on,[a] A·ma'sa[b] came to meet them. Now Jo'ab was wearing his battle clothing, and he had a sword in its sheath strapped to his hip. When he stepped forward, the sword fell out.

9 Jo'ab said to A·ma'sa: "Are you all right, my brother?" Then with his right hand, Jo'ab took hold of A·ma'sa's beard as if to kiss him. **10** A·ma'sa was not on guard against the sword that was in Jo'ab's hand, and Jo'ab stabbed him with it in the abdomen,[c] and his intestines spilled out on the ground. He did not have to stab him again; once was enough to kill him. Then Jo'ab and his brother A·bish'ai chased after She'ba the son of Bich'ri.

11 One of Jo'ab's young men stood by him and was saying: "Whoever is on Jo'ab's side and whoever belongs to David, let him follow Jo'ab!" **12** All the while A·ma'sa was wallowing in his blood in the middle of the road. When the man saw that all the people were stopping, he moved A·ma'sa from the road to the field. Then he threw a garment over him, because he saw that everyone was stopping when they came up to him. **13** After he had removed him from the road, all the men followed Jo'ab to chase after She'ba[d] the son of Bich'ri.

14 She'ba passed through all the tribes of Israel to Abel of Beth-ma'a·cah.[e] The Bich'rites gathered together and also went in after him.

15 Joab and his men* came and besieged him in Abel of Beth-ma'a·cah and raised up a siege rampart against the city, as it was standing within a rampart. And all the men with Jo'ab were undermining the wall to knock it down. **16** And a wise

---

CHAP. 20
a 2Sa 20:21

b Jg 3:26, 27
2Sa 15:10

c 2Sa 19:43

d 1Ki 12:16

e Pr 24:21

f 2Sa 19:15
2Sa 19:41, 42

g 2Sa 5:11

h 2Sa 15:16

i 2Sa 16:21, 22

j 2Sa 17:25
2Sa 19:13
1Ch 2:17

k 1Sa 26:6
2Sa 10:10
2Sa 23:18
1Ch 18:12

l 2Sa 20:1

m 2Sa 15:12

n 2Sa 8:16

o 2Sa 8:18
2Sa 15:18
1Ki 1:38

Second Col.
a Jos 18:21, 25
Jos 21:8, 17

b 2Sa 17:25
2Sa 19:13

c 2Sa 3:27
1Ki 2:5

d 2Sa 20:1

e 1Ki 15:20
2Ki 15:29

19:43 *Or "was more severe than." 20:1 *Or possibly, "tents." 20:3 *Or "palace."

20:15 *Lit., "They."

woman called out from the city: "Listen, men, listen! Please tell Jo'ab, 'Come here, and let me speak to you.'" **17** So he went near to her, and the woman said: "Are you Jo'ab?" He replied: "I am." At this she said to him: "Listen to the words of your servant." He said: "I am listening." **18** She continued: "They would always say in the past, 'Let them inquire in Abel, and that was the end of the matter.' **19** I represent the peaceable and faithful ones of Israel. You are seeking to destroy a city that is like a mother in Israel. Why should you do away with* the inheritance of Jehovah?"[a] **20** Jo'ab answered: "It is unthinkable for me to do away with it and destroy it. **21** That is not the case at all. Rather, a man named She'ba[b] the son of Bich'ri from the mountainous region of E'phra·im[c] has rebelled* against King David. If you hand over this one man, I will withdraw from the city." Then the woman said to Jo'ab: "Look! His head will be thrown over the wall to you!"

22 At once the wise woman went in to all the people, and they cut off the head of She'ba the son of Bich'ri and threw it to Jo'ab. At that he blew the horn, and they dispersed from the city, each one to his home;[d] and Jo'ab returned to Jerusalem to the king.

23 Now Jo'ab was in charge of all the army of Israel;[e] Be·nai'ah[f] the son of Je·hoi'a·da[g] was over the Cher'e·thites and the Pel'e·thites.[h] **24** A·do'ram[i] was over those conscripted for forced labor; Je·hosh'a·phat[j] the son of A·hi'lud was the recorder. **25** She'va was the secretary; Za'dok[k] and A·bi'a·thar[l] were priests. **26** And I'ra the

CHAP. 20
a Ex 19:5
　De 32:9

b 2Sa 20:1

c Jos 17:14, 15
　Jg 2:8, 9

d Ec 9:14, 15
　Ec 9:18

e 2Sa 8:16
　2Sa 19:13

f 2Sa 23:20
　1Ch 27:5

g 1Ch 12:27

h 2Sa 8:18
　2Sa 15:18
　1Ki 1:38, 44

i 1Ki 4:6
　1Ki 12:18

j 1Ki 4:3

k 2Sa 15:27

l 2Sa 17:15
　2Sa 19:11
　1Ki 4:4

Second Col.

CHAP. 21
a Le 26:18, 20

b Ge 9:6
　Ex 20:13
　Nu 35:30, 33

c Jos 9:3, 27

d Ge 10:15, 16

e Jos 9:15

f Nu 35:31

g 2Sa 21:1

h Nu 25:4
　De 21:22

i 1Sa 10:26

j 1Sa 9:17

k 2Sa 4:4
　2Sa 9:10
　2Sa 19:24

l 1Sa 18:3
　1Sa 20:42

m 2Sa 3:7

Ja'ir·ite also became a chief minister* for David.

21 Now there was a famine[a] in the days of David for three consecutive years, so David consulted Jehovah, and Jehovah said: "There is bloodguilt on Saul and on his house, because he put the Gib'e·on·ites to death."[b] **2** So the king called the Gib'e·on·ites[c] and spoke to them. (Incidentally, the Gib'e·on·ites were not Israelites but Am'or·ites[d] who remained, and the Israelites had sworn to spare them,[e] but Saul sought to strike them down in his zeal for the people of Israel and Judah.) **3** David said to the Gib'e·on·ites: "What should I do for you, and how can I make atonement, so that you will bless the inheritance of Jehovah?" **4** The Gib'e·on·ites said to him: "It is not a matter of silver or gold* for us in connection with Saul and his household; nor can we put any man to death in Israel." At that he said: "Whatever you say, I will do for you." **5** They said to the king: "The man who exterminated us and schemed to annihilate us from living anywhere in the territory of Israel[g]— **6** let seven of his sons be given to us. We will hang their dead bodies*[h] before Jehovah in Gib'e·ah[i] of Saul, the chosen one of Jehovah."[j] The king then said: "I will hand them over."

7 However, the king showed compassion for Me·phib'o·sheth,[k] the son of Jon'a·than the son of Saul, because of the oath made before Jehovah between David and Jon'a·than,[l] the son of Saul. **8** So the king took Ar·mo'ni and Me·phib'o·sheth, the two sons of Riz'pah[m] the daughter of A'iah whom she bore to

---

20:19 *Lit., "swallow up." 20:21 *Lit., "lifted up his hand."

20:26 *Lit., "became a priest." 21:6 *Lit., "will expose them," that is, with arms and legs broken.

Saul, and the five sons of Mi'-chal*[a] the daughter of Saul whom she bore to A'dri·el[b] the son of Bar·zil'lai the Me·hol'-ath·ite. **9** Then he handed them over to the Gib'e·on·ites, and they hung their dead bodies on the mountain before Jehovah.[c] All seven of them died togeth-er; they were put to death in the first days of harvest, at the start of the barley harvest. **10** Then Riz'pah[d] the daughter of A'iah took sackcloth and spread it out on the rock from the start of harvest until rain poured down from the heavens on the bodies; she did not allow the birds of the heavens to land on them by day nor the wild beasts of the field to come near by night.

11 David was told what Saul's concubine Riz'pah the daughter of A'iah had done. **12** So Da-vid went and took the bones of Saul and the bones of his son Jon'a·than from the leaders* of Ja'besh-gil'e·ad,[e] who had sto-len them from the public square of Beth-shan, where the Phi·lis'-tines had hung them on the day that the Phi·lis'tines struck down Saul on Gil·bo'a.[f] **13** He brought the bones of Saul and the bones of his son Jon'-a·than up from there, and they also gathered the bones of the men who had been execut-ed.*[g] **14** Then they buried the bones of Saul and of Jon'a·than his son in the land of Benjamin in Ze'lah[h] in the tomb of Kish[i] his father. After they did everything that the king had commanded, God listened to their entreaties for the land.[j]

15 Once again there was war between the Phi·lis'tines and Is-rael.[k] So David and his ser-vants went down and fought

the Phi·lis'tines, but David be-came exhausted. **16** A descen-dant of the Reph'a·im[a] named Ish'bi·be'nob, whose copper spear weighed 300 shekels*[b] and who was armed with a new sword, intended to strike David down. **17** At once A·bish'ai[c] the son of Ze·ru'iah came to his aid[d] and struck the Phi·lis'tine down and put him to death. At that time the men of David swore this oath to him: "You must not go out with us to battle anymore![e] You must not extinguish the lamp of Israel!"[f]

18 After this, war broke out again with the Phi·lis'tines[g] at Gob. At that time Sib'be·cai[h] the Hu'shath·ite struck down Saph, who was a descendant of the Reph'a·im.[i]

19 And war broke out again with the Phi·lis'tines[j] at Gob, and El·ha'nan the son of Ja'a·re·or'e·gim the Beth'le·hem-ite struck down Go·li'ath the Git'tite, whose spear had a shaft like the beam of loom workers.[k]

20 War broke out yet again at Gath, where there was a man of extraordinary size, with 6 fin-gers on each hand and 6 toes on each foot, 24 in all; and he too was a descendant of the Reph'a·im.[l] **21** He kept taunting Israel.[m] So Jon'a·than the son of Shim'e·i,[n] David's brother, struck him down.

22 These four were descen-dants of the Reph'a·im in Gath, and they fell by the hand of Da-vid and by the hand of his ser-vants.[o]

22 And David spoke to Je-hovah the words of this song[p] in the day that Jehovah rescued him out of the hand of all his enemies[q] and out of Saul's hand.[r] **2** He said:

CHAP. 21

a 1Sa 18:20
  1Sa 25:44
  2Sa 3:14
  2Sa 6:23

b 1Sa 18:19

c Nu 35:31
  De 19:21

d 2Sa 3:7

e 2Sa 2:5

f 1Sa 28:4
  1Sa 31:1
  1Sa 31:11, 12
  2Sa 1:6
  1Ch 10:8

g 2Sa 21:9

h Jos 18:28

i 1Sa 9:1
  1Sa 10:11

j Jos 7:24-26
  2Sa 24:25

k 2Sa 5:17, 22

_____

Second Col.

a De 2:11

b 1Sa 17:4, 7
  1Ch 11:23

c 2Sa 23:18, 19

d 2Sa 22:19

e 2Sa 18:3

f 1Ki 11:36
  1Ki 15:4
  2Ki 8:19

g 1Ch 20:4

h 1Ch 11:26, 29
  1Ch 27:1, 11

i Ge 14:5

j 1Ch 20:5

k 1Sa 17:4, 7

l 1Ch 20:6-8

m 1Sa 17:10, 45
  2Ki 19:22

n 1Sa 16:9
  1Sa 17:13
  1Ch 2:13

o Ps 60:12

_____

CHAP. 22

p Ex 15:1
  Jg 5:1

q Ps 34:19

r 1Sa 23:14
  Ps 18:Sup

21:8 *Or possibly, "Merab." **21:12** *Or possibly, "landowners." **21:13** *Lit., "exposed."

21:16 *About 3.42 kg (7.5 lb). See App. B14.

"Jehovah is my crag and my
    stronghold[a] and the One
    who rescues me.[b]

3 My God is my rock,[c] in whom
    I take refuge,
My shield[d] and my horn*
    of salvation,[#] my secure
    refuge[△e]
And my place to flee,[f] my
    savior;[g] you who save me
    from violence.

4 I call on Jehovah, who is
    worthy of praise,
And I will be saved from
    my enemies.

5 The waves of death broke
    all around me;[h]
Flash floods of worthless
    men terrified me.[i]

6 The ropes of the Grave*
    surrounded me;[j]
The snares of death
    confronted me.[k]

7 In my distress I called
    on Jehovah,[l]
To my God I kept calling.
Then from his temple he
    heard my voice,
And my cry for help reached
    his ears.[m]

8 Back and forth the earth
    began to shake and rock;[n]
The foundations of the
    heavens trembled[o]
And shook back and forth
    because he had been
    angered.[p]

9 Smoke ascended from his
    nostrils,
And a consuming fire came
    from his mouth;[q]
Glowing coals blazed from
    him.

10 He made the heavens bend
    as he descended,[r]
And thick gloom was
    beneath his feet.[s]

11 He rode on a cherub[a] and
    came flying.
He was visible on the wings
    of a spirit.*[b]

12 Then he put darkness
    around him as a shelter,[c]
In dark waters and thick
    clouds.

13 From the brightness before
    him fiery coals blazed.

14 Then Jehovah began to
    thunder from heaven;[d]
The Most High made his
    voice heard.[e]

15 He shot his arrows[f] and
    scattered them;
Lightning, and he threw
    them into confusion.[g]

16 The bed of the sea became
    visible;[h]
The foundations of the
    land were exposed by
    the rebuke of Jehovah,
By the blast of the breath
    from his nostrils.[i]

17 He reached down from
    on high;
He took hold of me
    and pulled me from deep
    waters.[j]

18 He rescued me from my
    strong enemy,[k]
From those hating me, who
    were stronger than I was.

19 They confronted me on the
    day of my disaster,[l]
But Jehovah was my
    support.

20 He brought me out into
    a place of safety;*[m]
He rescued me because he
    was pleased with me.[n]

21 Jehovah rewards me accord-
    ing to my righteousness;[o]
He repays me according
    to the innocence* of my
    hands.[p]

22 For I have kept the ways
    of Jehovah,

CHAP. 22
a Ps 31:3
b Ps 18:2, 3
c De 32:4
   1Sa 2:1, 2
d Ge 15:1
   De 33:29
   Ps 3:3
e Ps 9:9
   Pr 18:10
f Ps 59:16
g Isa 12:2
   Lu 1:46, 47
   Tit 3:4
h Ps 69:14
i Ps 18:4
j Ps 116:3, 4
k Ps 18:5
l Ps 142:1
   Jon 2:2
m Ex 3:7
   Ps 18:6
   Ps 34:15
n Jg 5:4
o Job 26:11
p Ps 18:7-12
   Ps 77:18
q Isa 30:27
r Ps 144:5
   Isa 64:1
s De 4:11
   1Ki 8:12
   Ps 18:9
   Ps 97:2

_____

Second Col.
a 1Sa 4:4
   Ps 80:1
   Ps 99:1
b Heb 1:7
c Job 36:29
d Ex 19:16
   1Sa 2:10
e Ps 18:13-16
   Isa 30:30
f Ps 7:13
   Ps 77:17
g Ps 144:6
h Ex 14:21
   Ps 106:9
   Ps 114:3
i Ex 15:8
j Ps 18:16-19
   Ps 124:2-4
   Ps 144:7
k Ps 3:7
   Ps 56:9
l Ps 19:11
   1Sa 23:26
   2Sa 15:10
m Ps 31:8
n Ps 149:4
o Isa 26:23
   1Ki 8:32
p Ps 18:20-24
   Ps 24:3, 4

_____

22:3 *See Glossary. [#]Or "my powerful savior." [△]Or "secure height." 22:6
*Or "Sheol," that is, the common grave
of mankind. See Glossary.

_____

22:11 *Or "of the wind." 22:20 *Or "a
roomy place." 22:21 *Lit., "the cleanness."

And I have not wickedly
abandoned my God.

23 All his judgments[a] are
before me;
I will not deviate from his
statutes.[b]

24 I will remain blameless[c]
before him,
And I will keep myself from
error.[d]

25 May Jehovah repay me according to my righteous-
ness,[e]
According to my innocence
before him.[f]

26 With someone loyal you act
in loyalty;[g]
With the blameless, mighty
man, you deal blamelessly;[h]

27 With the pure you show
yourself pure,[i]
But with the crooked you
show yourself shrewd.*[j]

28 For you save those who are
humble,[k]
But your eyes are against
the haughty, and you abase
them.[l]

29 For you are my lamp,
O Jehovah;[m]
It is Jehovah who lights up
my darkness.[n]

30 With your help I can charge
against a marauder band;
By God's power I can scale
a wall.[o]

31 The way of the true God
is perfect;[p]
The saying of Jehovah
is refined.[q]
He is a shield to all those
taking refuge in him.[r]

32 For who is a God besides
Jehovah?[s]
And who is a rock except our
God?[t]

33 The true God is my strong
fortress,[u]
And he will make my way
perfect.[v]

CHAP. 22

a De 6:1
  Ps 19:9
b De 8:11
c Ps 84:11
d Ps 18:23
  Pr 14:16
e Job 34:11
  Isa 3:10
  Heb 11:6
f Ps 18:24
  Pr 5:21
g Ps 37:28
  Ps 97:10
h Ps 18:25-30
i Mt 5:8
  1Pe 1:16
j Ps 125:5
k Job 34:28
l Da 4:37
  1Pe 5:5
m Ps 27:1
n Ps 97:11
o Ps 18:29
  Php 4:13
  Heb 11:33, 34
p De 32:4
q Ps 12:6
  Pr 30:5
r Ps 35:2
  Ps 91:4
s Isa 44:6
t De 32:31
  Ps 18:31-42
u Ps 27:1
  Isa 12:2
v Isa 26:7

Second Col.

a Isa 33:15, 16
  Hab 3:19
b Ps 18:35
  Ps 113:6-8
c Ps 17:5
d Ex 14:13
e 1Sa 23:5
f 1Sa 17:49
  Ps 44:3, 5
g Ge 49:8
h Ps 18:40
i 1Sa 28:6
  Pr 1:28
  Isa 1:15
  Mic 3:4
j 1Sa 30:6
  2Sa 15:12
k 2Sa 8:3
  Ps 2:8
  Ps 60:8
l Ps 18:43-45
m De 33:29

34 He makes my feet like those
of a deer;
He makes me stand on high
places.[a]

35 He trains my hands for
warfare;
My arms can bend a bow
of copper.

36 You give me your shield
of salvation,
And your humility makes
me great.[b]

37 You widen the path for my
footsteps;
My feet* will not slip.[c]

38 I will pursue my enemies
and annihilate them;
I will not return until they
are wiped out.

39 And I will wipe them out and
crush them, so that they
will not rise up;[d]
They will fall under my feet.

40 You will equip me with
strength for the battle;[e]
You will make my foes collapse under me.[f]

41 You will make my enemies
retreat from me;*[g]
I will put an end to# those
who hate me.[h]

42 They cry for help, but there
is no one to save them;
They even cry to Jehovah,
but he does not answer
them.[i]

43 I will pound them as fine as
the dust of the earth;
I will pulverize and trample
them like mud in the
streets.

44 You will rescue me from the
faultfinding of my people.[j]
You will safeguard me to be
the head of nations;[k]
A people whom I have not
known will serve me.[l]

45 Foreigners will come cringing before me;[m]

What they hear about me will make them obey me.*

46 Foreigners will lose courage;*
They will come trembling from their strongholds.

47 Jehovah is alive! Praised be my Rock![a]
Let the God of the rock of my salvation be exalted.[b]

48 The true God executes vengeance for me;[c]
He subdues the peoples under me;[d]

49 He rescues me from my enemies.
You lift me high[e] above those who attack me;
You save me from the man of violence.[f]

50 That is why I will thank you, O Jehovah, among the nations,[g]
And to your name I will sing praises:*[h]

51 He performs great acts of salvation* for his king;[i]
He displays loyal love to his anointed one,
To David and his offspring# forever."[j]

23 These are the last words of David:[k]

"The word of David the son of Jes'se,[l]
And the word of the man who was raised on high,[m]
The anointed[n] of the God of Jacob,
The pleasant singer* of the songs[o] of Israel.

2 The spirit of Jehovah spoke through me;[p]
His word was on my tongue.[q]

3 The God of Israel spoke;

To me the Rock of Israel[a] said:
'When the one ruling over mankind is righteous,[b]
Ruling in the fear of God,[c]

4 It is like the morning light when the sun shines,[d]
A morning without clouds.
It is like the brightness after the rain,
Making grass sprout from the earth.'[e]

5 Is not my house like that before God?
For he has made an eternal covenant with me,[f]
Arranged in every detail and secured.
Because it means my complete salvation and all my delight,
Is that not why he makes it flourish?[g]

6 But worthless men are all thrown away[h] like thornbushes,
For they cannot be taken with the hand.

7 When a man touches them, He should be fully armed with iron and the shaft of a spear,
And they should be completely burned up with fire in their place."

8 These are the names of David's mighty warriors:[i] Jo'sheb-bas'she'beth a Tah'che'mo·nite, the head of the three.[j] He brandished his spear over 800 slain at one time. 9 Next to him, El-e·a'zar[k] the son of Do'do[l] the son of A·ho'hi was among the three mighty warriors with David when they taunted the Phi·lis'tines. They had gathered there for the battle, and when the men of Israel retreated, 10 he stood his ground and kept striking down the Phi·lis'tines until his arm grew weary and his hand became stiff from gripping the sword.[m] So Jehovah brought

---

CHAP. 22

a De 32:4
b Ps 18:46
　Ps 89:26
c 1Sa 25:29
　2Sa 18:19
d Ps 18:47
　Ps 110:1
　Ps 144:1, 2
e 2Sa 5:12
　2Sa 7:9
f Ps 18:48
g De 32:43
　Ps 117:1
h 1Ch 16:9
　Ps 145:2
　Ro 15:9
i Ps 2:6
　Ps 21:1
j Ps 89:20, 29
　Lu 1:32, 33

CHAP. 23

k Ge 49:1
　De 33:1
l 1Sa 17:58
　Mt 1:6
m 2Sa 7:8
n 1Sa 16:13
o 1Ch 16:9
p Mr 12:36
　2Ti 3:16
q Ac 1:16
　2Pe 1:21

Second Col.

a De 32:4
　Ps 144:1
b Pr 29:2
　Isa 9:7
　Isa 32:1
c Ex 18:21
　Isa 11:3
d Mal 4:2
　Mt 17:2
　Re 1:16
e Ps 72:1, 6
f 2Sa 7:16, 19
　1Ch 17:11
　Ps 89:3
　Ps 89:28, 29
　Ps 132:11
g Isa 9:7
　Isa 11:1
　Am 9:11
h Ps 37:10
i 2Sa 10:7
　2Sa 20:7
　1Ch 11:10
j 1Ch 11:11
k 1Ch 11:12-14
l 1Ch 27:1, 4
m Jg 8:4

22:45 *Lit., "At the hearing of the ear, they will obey me." 22:46 *Or "fade away." 22:50 *Or "make music." 22:51 *Or "great victories." #Lit., "seed." 23:1 *Or "The pleasant one."

about a great victory* on that day;[a] and the people returned behind him to strip the slain.

11 Next to him was Sham'mah the son of A'gee the Har'a·rite. The Phi·lis'tines gathered together at Le'hi, where there was a plot of land full of lentils; and the people fled because of the Phi·lis'tines. **12** But he took his stand in the middle of the field and defended it and kept striking down the Phi·lis'tines, so that Jehovah brought about a great victory.*[b]

13 Three of the 30 headmen went down during the harvest to David at the cave of A·dul'lam,[c] and a company* of the Phi·lis'tines was camped in the Valley# of Reph'a·im.[d] **14** David was then in the stronghold,[e] and an outpost of the Phi·lis'tines was in Beth'le·hem. **15** Then David expressed his longing: "If only I could have a drink of the water from the cistern by the gate of Beth'le·hem!" **16** At that time the three mighty warriors forced their way into the camp of the Phi·lis'tines and drew water from the cistern by the gate of Beth'le·hem and brought it to David; but he refused to drink it and poured it out to Jehovah.[f] **17** He said: "It is unthinkable on my part, O Jehovah, that I should do this! Should I drink the blood[g] of the men going at the risk of their lives?"* So he refused to drink it. These are the things that his three mighty warriors did.

18 A·bish'ai[h] the brother of Jo'ab the son of Ze·ru'iah[i] was the head of another three; he brandished his spear over 300 slain, and he had a reputation like the three.[j] **19** Although he was the most distinguished of

the other three and he was their chief, he did not attain to the rank of the first three.

20 Be·nai'ah[a] the son of Je·hoi'a·da was a courageous man* who performed many exploits in Kab'ze·el.[b] He struck down the two sons of Ar'i·el of Mo'ab, and he descended into a water-pit on a snowy day and killed a lion.[c] **21** He also struck down an Egyptian man of extraordinary size. Though the Egyptian had a spear in his hand, he went against him with a rod and snatched the spear away from the Egyptian's hand and killed him with his own spear. **22** These things Be·nai'ah the son of Je·hoi'a·da did, and he had a reputation like that of the three mighty warriors. **23** Although he was distinguished even more than the thirty, he did not attain to the rank of the three. However, David appointed him over his own bodyguard.

24 As'a·hel[d] the brother of Jo'ab was among the thirty: El·ha'nan the son of Do'do of Beth'le·hem,[e] **25** Sham'mah the Ha'rod·ite, E·li'ka the Ha'rod·ite, **26** He'lez[f] the Pal'tite, I'ra[g] the son of Ik'kesh the Te·ko'ite, **27** Abi·e'zer[h] the An'a·thoth·ite,[i] Me·bun'nai the Hu'shath·ite, **28** Zal'mon the A·ho'hite, Ma'ha·rai[j] the Ne·toph'a·thite, **29** He'leb the son of Ba'a·nah the Ne·toph'a·thite, It'tai the son of Ri'bai of Gib'e·ah of the Ben'ja·min·ites, **30** Be·nai'ah[k] a Pir'a·thon·ite, Hid'dai of the wa·dis* of Ga'ash,[l] **31** A'bi·al'bon the Ar'bath·ite, Az'ma·veth the Bar·hu'mite, **32** E·li'ah·ba the Sha·al'bo·nite, the sons of Ja'shen, Jon'a·than, **33** Sham'mah the Har'a·rite, A·hi'am the son of Sha'rar the Har'a·rite,

---

CHAP. 23
a Jg 15:14, 16
  1Sa 14:6
  1Sa 19:5

b Ps 3:8
  Ps 44:3

c Jos 15:20, 35
  1Sa 22:1

d Jos 15:1, 8
  2Sa 5:22
  1Ch 11:15-19

e 1Sa 22:1, 4
  1Ch 12:16

f Le 9:9
  Le 17:13

g Ge 9:4
  Le 17:10

h 1Sa 26:6
  2Sa 21:17

i 2Sa 2:18
  1Ch 2:15, 16

j 1Ch 11:20, 21

Second Col.
a 2Sa 8:18
  2Sa 20:23
  1Ki 1:8
  1Ki 2:29
  1Ch 27:5, 6

b Jos 15:21

c 1Ch 11:22-25
  Pr 30:30

d 2Sa 2:18, 23
  1Ch 2:15, 16
  1Ch 27:1, 7

e 1Ch 11:26-41

f 1Ch 27:1, 10

g 1Ch 27:1, 9

h 1Ch 27:1, 12

i Jos 21:8, 18
  Jer 1:1

j 1Ch 27:1, 13

k 1Ch 27:1, 14

l Jg 2:8, 9

23:10, 12 *Or "salvation." 23:13 *Or "tent village." #Or "Low Plain." 23:17 *Or "souls?"

23:20 *Lit., "the son of a man of valor." 23:30 *See Glossary.

34 E·liph′e·let the son of A·has′·bai the son of the Ma·ac′a·thite, E·li′am the son of A·hith′·o·phel[a] the Gi′lon·ite, **35** Hez′ro the Car′mel·ite, Pa′a·rai the Ar′bite, **36** I′gal the son of Nathan of Zo′bah, Ba′ni the Gad′ite, **37** Ze′lek the Am′mon·ite, Na′ha·rai the Be·er′oth·ite, the armor-bearer of Jo′ab the son of Ze·ru′iah, **38** I′ra the Ith′rite, Ga′reb the Ith′rite,[b] **39** and U·ri′ah[c] the Hit′tite—37 in all.

24 The anger of Jehovah again blazed against Israel[d] when one incited David* against them, saying: "Go, take a count[e] of Israel and Judah."[f] **2** So the king said to Jo′ab[g] the chief of the army who was with him: "Please go through all the tribes of Israel, from Dan to Be′er-she′ba,[h] and register the people, so that I may know the number of the people." **3** But Jo′ab said to the king: "May Jehovah your God multiply the people 100 times, and may the eyes of my lord the king see it, but why does my lord the king want to do such a thing?"

4 But the king's word prevailed over Jo′ab and the chiefs of the army. So Jo′ab and the chiefs of the army went out from before the king to register the people of Israel.[i] **5** They crossed the Jordan and camped at A·ro′er,[j] to the right* of the city in the middle of the valley,# toward the Gad′ites, and on to Ja′zer.[k] **6** After that they went on to Gil′e·ad[l] and the land of Tah′tim-hod′shi and continued to Dan-ja′an and went around to Si′don.[m] **7** Then they went to the fortress of Tyre[n] and all the cities of the Hi′vites[o] and of the Ca′naan·ites, and finally they ended up in the Neg′eb[p] of Judah at Be′er-she′ba.[q] **8** Thus

they went through all the land and came to Jerusalem at the end of nine months and 20 days. **9** Jo′ab now gave to the king the number of the people who were registered. Israel amounted to 800,000 warriors armed with swords, and the men of Judah were 500,000.[a]

10 But David's heart* was struck with remorse[b] after he had numbered the people. David then said to Jehovah: "I have sinned[c] greatly by doing this. And now, Jehovah, please forgive your servant's error,[d] for I have acted very foolishly."[e] **11** When David got up in the morning, Jehovah's word came to Gad[f] the prophet, David's visionary, saying: **12** "Go and say to David, 'This is what Jehovah says: "I am giving you three options. Choose the one that I should bring on you."'"[g] **13** So Gad came in to David and told him: "Should seven years of famine come on your land?[h] Or should you flee for three months from your adversaries while they pursue you?[i] Or should there be three days of pestilence in your land?[j] Now consider carefully what I should reply to the One who sent me." **14** So David said to Gad: "It is very distressing to me. Let us fall, please, into the hand of Jehovah,[k] for his mercy is great;[l] but do not let me fall into the hand of man."[m]

15 Then Jehovah sent a pestilence[n] on Israel from the morning until the designated time, so that 70,000 of the people from Dan to Be′er-she′ba[o] died.[p] **16** When the angel stretched out his hand toward Jerusalem to destroy it, Jehovah felt regret* over the calamity,[q] and he said to the angel bringing destruction among the people: "It is

---

CHAP. 23
a 2Sa 15:31
   2Sa 16:23
   2Sa 17:23
   1Ch 27:33
b 1Ch 2:53
c 2Sa 11:3
   1Ki 15:5

CHAP. 24
d 2Sa 21:1
e 1Ch 27:23, 24
f 1Ch 21:1-3
g 2Sa 8:16
   2Sa 20:23
h Jg 20:1
i Nu 1:2
   1Ch 21:4
j De 2:36
   Jos 13:8, 9
k Nu 32:34, 35
l Nu 32:40
m Ge 10:15
   Ge 49:13
   Jos 11:8
n Jos 19:24, 29
o Jos 11:19
p Jos 15:1
q Ge 21:31
   Jos 15:21, 28

Second Col.
a Nu 2:32
   Nu 26:51
   1Ch 21:5, 6
   1Ch 27:23
b 1Sa 24:5
   Ro 2:15
c 2Sa 12:13
d Ps 130:3
   Ho 14:2
   1Jo 1:9
e 1Ch 21:8-13
f 1Sa 22:5
   1Ch 29:29
g Pr 3:12
h Le 26:18, 20
   2Sa 21:1
i Le 26:14, 17
j Le 26:16
k Heb 12:6
l Ps 103:8
   Ps 119:156
m 2Ch 28:1, 5
n Nu 16:46
   1Ch 27:24
o 2Sa 24:2
p 1Ch 21:14, 15
q Ps 78:38
   Jer 26:19
   Joe 2:13

24:1 *Or "when David was incited." 24:5 *Or "the south." #Or "wadi."

24:10 *Or "conscience." 24:16 *Or "grieved."

enough! Now let your hand drop." Jehovah's angel was close to the threshing floor of A·rau′-nah[a] the Jeb′u·site.[b]

17 When David saw the angel who was striking the people down, he said to Jehovah: "I am the one who sinned, and I am the one who did wrong; but these sheep[c]—what have they done? Let your hand, please, come against me and my father's house."[d]

18 So Gad came in to David on that day and said to him: "Go up, set up for Jehovah an altar on the threshing floor of A·rau′-nah the Jeb′u·site."[e] **19** So David went up at the word of Gad, as Jehovah had commanded. **20** When A·rau′nah looked down and saw the king and his servants coming toward him, A·rau′-nah immediately went out and bowed down to the king with his face to the ground. **21** A·rau′-nah asked: "Why has my lord the king come to his servant?" David replied: "To buy from you the threshing floor in order to build an altar to Jehovah, so that the scourge against the people may be halted."[a] **22** But A·rau′-nah said to David: "Let my lord the king take it and offer up what seems good to him.* Here are cattle for the burnt offering and the threshing sledge and the equipment of the cattle for the wood. **23** All of this, O king, A·rau′nah gives to the king." Then A·rau′nah said to the king: "May Jehovah your God show you favor."

24 However, the king said to A·rau′nah: "No, I must buy it from you for a price. I will not offer up to Jehovah my God burnt sacrifices that cost me nothing." So David bought the threshing floor and the cattle for 50 silver shekels.*[b] **25** And David built an altar[c] there to Jehovah and offered up burnt sacrifices and communion sacrifices. Jehovah then responded to the entreaty for the land,[d] and the scourge against Israel was halted.

CHAP. 24
a 2Ch 3:1

b Ge 10:15, 16
Jos 15:8

c Ps 95:7

d 1Ch 21:16, 17

e 1Ch 21:18-23
2Ch 3:1

___

Second Col.
a Nu 16:46, 47
Nu 25:8
2Sa 24:15

b 1Ch 21:24-28

c Ex 20:25
1Ch 22:1

d 2Sa 21:14
2Ch 33:13

24:22 *Lit., "what is good in his eyes." 24:24 *A shekel equaled 11.4 g (0.367 oz t). See App. B14.

THE FIRST OF
KINGS

OUTLINE OF CONTENTS

1 Now King David was old,[a] advanced in years,[*] and although they would cover him with garments, he could not get warm. **2** So his servants said to him: "Let a girl, a virgin, be found for my lord the king, and she will wait on the king as his nurse. She will lie in your arms so that my lord the king may feel warm." **3** They searched throughout all the territory of Israel for a beautiful girl, and they found Ab'i·shag[b] the Shu'nam·mite[c] and brought her in to the king. **4** The girl was extremely beautiful, and she became the king's nurse and waited on him, but the king did not have sexual relations with her.

5 Meanwhile, Ad·o·ni'jah[d] the son of Hag'gith was exalting himself, saying: "I am going to be king!" He had a chariot made for himself with horsemen and 50 men to run before him.[e] **6** But his father had never confronted him[*] by saying: "Why have you done this?" He was also very handsome, and his mother had given birth to him after Ab'salom. **7** He conferred with Jo'ab the son of Ze·ru'iah and A·bi'a·thar[f] the priest, and they offered Ad·o·ni'jah help and support.[g] **8** But Za'dok[h] the priest, Be·nai'ah[i] the son of Je·hoi'a·da, Nathan[j] the prophet, Shim'e·i,[k] Re'i, and David's mighty warriors[l] did not support Ad·o·ni'jah.

9 Eventually Ad·o·ni'jah held a sacrifice[m] of sheep, cattle, and fattened animals by the stone of Zo'he·leth, which is near En·ro'gel, and he invited all his brothers the king's sons, and all the men of Judah the king's servants. **10** But he did not invite Nathan the prophet, Be·nai'ah and the mighty warriors, or Sol'-

o·mon his brother. **11** Nathan[a] then said to Bath·she'ba,[b] Sol'o·mon's mother:[c] "Have you not heard that Ad·o·ni'jah[d] the son of Hag'gith has become king, and our lord David does not know anything about it? **12** So now come, please, and let me advise you, so that you may save your own life and the life of[*] your son Sol'o·mon. **13** Go in to King David and say to him, 'Was it not you, my lord the king, who swore to your servant, saying: "Your son Sol'o·mon will become king after me, and he is the one who will sit on my throne"?[f] So why has Ad·o·ni'jah become king?' **14** While you are still there speaking with the king, I will come in after you and confirm your words."

15 So Bath-she'ba went in to the king, into his private room. The king was very old, and Ab'i·shag[g] the Shu'nam·mite was waiting on the king. **16** Then Bath-she'ba bowed low and prostrated herself to the king, and the king said: "What is your request?" **17** She replied: "My lord, it was you who swore to Jehovah your God to your servant, 'Your son Sol'o·mon will become king after me, and he is the one who will sit on my throne.'[h] **18** But look! Ad·o·ni'jah has become king, and my lord the king does not know anything about it.[i] **19** He sacrificed bulls, fattened animals, and sheep in great quantity and invited all the sons of the king and A·bi'a·thar the priest and Jo'ab the chief of the army;[j] but he did not invite your servant Sol'o·mon.[k] **20** And now, my lord the king, the eyes of all Israel are upon you to tell them who will sit on the throne of my lord the king after him. **21** Otherwise, as soon

---

CHAP. 1

a 2Sa 5:4
1Ch 29:26, 27

b 1Ki 2:17, 22

c Jos 19:17, 18

d 2Sa 3:2, 4
1Ch 3:1, 2

e 2Sa 15:1

f 2Sa 20:25

g 1Ki 2:22

h 2Sa 8:17

i 2Sa 20:23
1Ch 27:5

j 2Sa 7:2
2Sa 12:1

k 1Ki 4:7, 18

l 2Sa 23:8
1Ch 11:10

m 2Sa 15:12

Second Col.

a 2Sa 7:4, 5

b 2Sa 11:3, 27

c 2Sa 12:24

d 2Sa 3:2, 4

e Jg 9:4-6
1Ki 1:21
2Ki 11:1

f 1Ch 22:9
1Ch 28:5
1Ch 29:1

g 1Ki 1:1, 3

h 1Ki 1:13
1Ch 22:9, 10

i 1Ki 1:5, 11

j 1Ki 1:7

k 1Ki 1:9, 10

as my lord the king is laid to rest with his forefathers, I and also my son Sol'o·mon will be considered traitors."

22 And while she was still speaking to the king, Nathan the prophet came in.[a] **23** At once the king was told: "Here is Nathan the prophet!" He came in before the king and prostrated himself to the king with his face to the ground. **24** Then Nathan said: "My lord the king, did you say, 'Ad·o·ni'jah will become king after me, and he is the one who will sit on my throne'?[b] **25** For today he has gone down to sacrifice[c] bulls, fattened animals, and sheep in great quantity, and he has invited all the sons of the king and the chiefs of the army and A·bi'a·thar the priest.[d] They are there eating and drinking with him, and they keep saying, 'Long live King Ad·o·ni'jah!' **26** But he did not invite me, your servant, or Za'dok the priest, or Be·nai'ah[e] the son of Je·hoi'a·da, or your servant Sol'o·mon. **27** Has my lord the king authorized this without telling your servant who should sit on the throne of my lord the king after him?"

28 King David now answered: "Call Bath-she'ba for me." At that she came in and stood before the king. **29** The king then swore an oath: "As surely as Jehovah is living, the one who rescued me* out of all distress,[f] **30** just as I swore to you by Jehovah the God of Israel, saying, 'Your son Sol'o·mon will become king after me, and he is the one who will sit on my throne in my place!' that is what I will bring about this day." **31** Then Bath-she'ba bowed low with her face to the ground and prostrated herself to the king and said:

"May my lord King David live forever!"

32 Immediately King David said: "Call for me Za'dok the priest, Nathan the prophet, and Be·nai'ah[a] the son of Je·hoi'a·da."[b] So they came in before the king. **33** The king said to them: "Take with you the servants of your lord, and have my son Sol'o·mon ride on my own mule,*[c] and lead him down to Gi'hon.[d] **34** Za'dok the priest and Nathan the prophet will anoint him[e] there as king over Israel; then blow the horn and say, 'Long live King Sol'o·mon!'[f] **35** Then follow him back, and he will come in and sit on my throne; and he will be king in my place, and I will commission him as leader over Israel and over Judah." **36** At once Be·nai'ah the son of Je·hoi'a·da said to the king: "Amen! May Jehovah the God of my lord the king confirm it. **37** Just as Jehovah was with my lord the king, so let him be with Sol'o·mon,[g] and may He make his throne greater than the throne of my lord King David."[h]

38 Then Za'dok the priest, Nathan the prophet, Be·nai'ah[i] the son of Je·hoi'a·da, and the Cher'e·thites and the Pel'e·thites[j] went down and had Sol'o·mon ride on the mule of King David,[k] and they brought him to Gi'hon.[l] **39** Za'dok the priest now took the horn of oil[m] out of the tent[n] and anointed Sol'o·mon,[o] and they began to blow the horn, and all the people began shouting: "Long live King Sol'o·mon!" **40** After that all the people followed him and went up, playing flutes and rejoicing greatly, so that the earth was split open by their noise.[p]

41 Ad·o·ni'jah and all those invited by him heard it when they had finished eating.[q] As

---

CHAP. 1
a 1Ki 1:14

b 1Ki 1:5

c 2Sa 15:12

d 1Ki 1:5, 7

e 1Ch 27:5

f Ps 71:23
  Ps 103:4

Second Col.
a 2Sa 20:23
  2Sa 23:20
  1Ch 27:5

b 1Ki 1:8

c 1Ki 1:38
  Lu 19:33-35

d 2Ch 32:30

e 1Sa 16:13

f 1Sa 10:1, 24
  2Sa 15:10
  2Ki 11:12

g 1Ch 28:20

h 1Ki 3:12
  1Ki 10:23
  Ps 72:8

i 1Ch 27:5

j 2Sa 15:18
  1Ch 18:17

k 1Ki 1:33
  Mt 21:7

l 2Ch 32:30

m Ex 30:23-25
  1Sa 16:13

n 2Sa 6:17

o 1Ch 29:22

p 1Sa 4:5

q 1Ki 1:9, 25

1:29 *Or "redeemed my soul."

1:33 *Or "she-mule."

soon as Jo'ab heard the sound of the horn, he said: "Why is there such a noisy uproar in the city?" **42** While he was still speaking, Jon'a·than[a] the son of A·bi'a·thar the priest came. Then Ad·o·ni'·jah said: "Come in, for you are a good* man, and you must bring good news." **43** But Jon'a·than answered Ad·o·ni'jah: "No! Our lord King David has made Sol'o·mon king. **44** The king sent with him Za'dok the priest, Nathan the prophet, Be·nai'ah the son of Je·hoi'a·da, and the Cher'e·thites and the Pel'e·thites, and they had him ride on the mule of the king.[b] **45** Then Za'dok the priest and Nathan the prophet anointed him as king in Gi'hon. After that they came up from there rejoicing, and the city is in an uproar. That was the noise that you heard. **46** Moreover, Sol'o·mon has sat down on the royal throne. **47** Another thing, the servants of the king have come in to congratulate our lord King David, saying, 'May your God make Sol'o·mon's name more splendid than your name, and may He make his throne greater than your throne!' At that the king bowed down on the bed. **48** And the king also said, 'May Jehovah the God of Israel be praised, who today has granted someone to sit on my throne and has allowed my own eyes to see it!'"

49 And all those invited by Ad·o·ni'jah became terrified, and each of them rose up and went his own way. **50** Ad·o·ni'jah was also afraid because of Sol'o·mon, so he got up and went and grabbed hold of the horns of the altar.[c] **51** The report was made to Sol'o·mon: "Here Ad·o·ni'jah has become afraid of King Sol'·o·mon; and he has taken hold of the horns of the altar, saying,

'Let King Sol'o·mon first swear to me that he will not put his servant to death by the sword.'" **52** To this Sol'o·mon said: "If he behaves in a worthy manner, not a single hair of his will fall to the ground; but if what is bad is found in him,[a] he will have to die." **53** So King Sol'o·mon sent for him to be brought down from the altar. Then he came in and bowed down to King Sol'o·mon, after which Sol'o·mon said to him: "Go to your own house."

2 When the time of David's death drew near, he gave his son Sol'o·mon these instructions: **2** "I am about to die.* Therefore, be strong[b] and prove yourself a man.[c] **3** You must keep your obligation to Jehovah your God by walking in his ways and by observing his statutes, his commandments, his judgments, and his reminders as they are written in the Law of Moses;[d] then you will succeed* in everything you do and everywhere you turn. **4** And Jehovah will carry out his promise that he made concerning me: 'If your sons pay attention to their way by walking faithfully before me with all their heart and soul,*[e] there will never fail to be a man of your line# sitting on the throne of Israel.'[f]

5 "You also well know what Jo'ab the son of Ze·ru'iah did to me, what he did to two chiefs of the armies of Israel—Ab'ner[g] the son of Ner and A·ma'sa[h] the son of Je'ther. He killed them, shedding the blood[i] of war in peacetime, and he put the blood of war on the belt around his waist and on the sandals on his feet. **6** You must act according to your wisdom and not let his gray

---

CHAP. 1	
a	2Sa 15:36 2Sa 17:17
b	1Ki 1:33, 34
c	Ex 21:14 Ex 38:1, 2 1Ki 2:28
Second Col.	
a	1Ki 2:23
CHAP. 2	
b	De 31:6 Jos 1:6 1Ch 28:20
c	1Ki 3:7
d	De 17:18-20 Ec 12:13
e	De 6:5 2Ki 20:3 2Ki 23:3 2Ch 17:3 Mt 22:37
f	2Sa 7:12, 16 1Ki 8:25 1Ch 17:11 Ps 132:11, 12
g	2Sa 3:27, 30
h	2Sa 17:25 2Sa 20:10 1Ch 2:17
i	Nu 35:33 2Sa 3:28

1:42 *Or "worthy."

2:2 *Lit., "I am going in the way of all the earth." **2:3** *Or "act wisely." **2:4** *See Glossary. #Lit., "will not be cut off from you a man."

hairs go down in peace to the Grave.*ª

7 "But toward the sons of Bar·zil'lai[b] the Gil'e·ad·ite, you should show loyal love, and they should be among those eating at your table, for that was how they stood by me[c] when I ran away from your brother Ab'sa·lom.[d]

8 "There is also with you Shim'e·i the son of Ge'ra the Ben'ja·min·ite from Ba·hu'rim. He was the one who cursed me with a vicious curse[e] on the day that I was going to Ma·ha·na'im;[f] but when he came down to meet me at the Jordan, I swore to him by Jehovah: 'I will not put you to death by the sword.'[g] **9** Now do not leave him unpunished,[h] for you are a wise man and you know what you should do to him; you must bring his gray hairs down to the Grave* with blood."[i]

10 Then David was laid to rest with his forefathers and was buried in the City of David.[j] **11** The length* of David's reign over Israel was 40 years. In Heb'ron[k] he reigned for 7 years, and in Jerusalem he reigned for 33 years.[l]

12 Sol'o·mon then sat down on the throne of David his father, and gradually his kingship became firmly established.[m]

13 In time Ad·o·ni'jah the son of Hag'gith came to Bath-she'ba, Sol'o·mon's mother. She asked: "Is your coming peaceable?" He replied: "It is peaceable." **14** He then said: "I have something to say to you." So she said: "Speak." **15** He continued: "You well know that the kingship was to become mine, and all Israel expected* me to become king;[n] but the kingship eluded me and became my brother's, for it was

from Jehovah that it became his.[a] **16** But now there is just one request that I am making of you. Do not turn me away." So she said to him: "Speak." **17** He then said: "Please, ask Sol'o·mon the king—for he will not turn you away—to give me Ab'i·shag[b] the Shu'nam·mite as a wife." **18** To this Bath-she'ba said: "Very well! I will speak for you to the king."

19 So Bath-she'ba went in to King Sol'o·mon to speak to him for Ad·o·ni'jah. At once the king rose to meet her and bowed down to her. Then he sat down on his throne and had a throne set for the king's mother, so that she could sit at his right. **20** She then said: "There is one small request that I am making of you. Do not turn me away." So the king said to her: "Make it, my mother; for I will not turn you away." **21** He said: "Let Ab'i·shag the Shu'nam·mite be given as a wife to your brother Ad·o·ni'jah." **22** At this King Sol'o·mon answered his mother: "Why are you requesting Ab'i·shag the Shu'nam·mite for Ad·o·ni'jah? You may as well request the kingship for him,[c] for he is my older brother,[d] and supporting him are A·bi'a·thar the priest and Jo'ab[e] the son of Ze·ru'iah."[f]

23 With that King Sol'o·mon swore by Jehovah: "So may God do to me and add to it if it was not at the cost of his own life* that Ad·o·ni'jah made this request. **24** And now, as surely as Jehovah is living, who has firmly established me[g] and seated me on the throne of David my father and who made a house* for me,[h] just as he promised, Ad·o·ni'jah will be put to death[i] today." **25** King Sol'o·mon immediately sent Be·nai'ah[j] the son of Je·hoi'a·da, who went out and

---

CHAP. 2

a 2Sa 3:29
1Ki 2:31-34

b 2Sa 19:31

c 2Sa 17:27-29

d 2Sa 15:14

e 2Sa 16:5-7

f 2Sa 17:24

g 2Sa 19:23

h Ex 22:28

i 1Ki 2:44, 46

j 2Sa 5:7
1Ch 11:7
1Ch 29:26, 27
Ac 2:29

k 1Ch 12:23

l 2Sa 5:4, 5

m 2Sa 7:8, 12
1Ch 29:23
2Ch 1:1
Ps 89:36, 37
Ps 132:12

n 1Ki 1:5, 25

Second Col.

a 1Ch 22:9

b 1Ki 1:1, 3

c 2Sa 16:21

d 1Ch 3:1, 2, 5

e 2Sa 8:16

f 1Ki 1:7

g 1Ch 22:9, 10

h 2Sa 7:11
1Ch 17:10

i 1Ki 1:51, 52

j 2Sa 8:18
1Ki 1:8
1Ch 27:5

2:6, 9 *Or "Sheol," that is, the common grave of mankind. See Glossary. 2:11 *Lit., "The days." 2:15 *Lit., "had set their faces on."

2:23 *Or "not against his own soul." 2:24 *Or "dynasty."

struck Ad·o·ni′jah down,* and he died.

26 To A·bi′a·thar[a] the priest, the king said: "Go to your fields in An′a·thoth![b] You deserve to die, but on this day I will not put you to death because you carried the Ark of the Sovereign Lord Jehovah before David my father[c] and because you shared in all the hardships that my father suffered.[d] 27 So Sol′o·mon drove A·bi′a·thar out from serving as a priest of Jehovah, to fulfill Jehovah's word against the house of E′li[e] in Shi′loh.[f]

28 When the news reached Jo′ab—for Jo′ab had supported Ad·o·ni′jah[g] but he had not supported Ab′sa·lom[h]—Jo′ab fled to the tent of Jehovah[i] and grabbed hold of the horns of the altar. 29 Then King Sol′o·mon was told: "Jo′ab has fled to the tent of Jehovah, and he is there beside the altar." So Sol′o·mon sent Be·nai′ah the son of Je·hoi′a·da, saying: "Go, strike him down!" 30 So Be·nai′ah went to the tent of Jehovah and said to him: "This is what the king says, 'Come out!'" But he said: "No! I will die here." Be·nai′ah brought word back to the king: "This is what Jo′ab said, and this is what he answered me." 31 Then the king said to him: "Do just as he said; strike him down and bury him and remove from me and from the house of my father the blood that Jo′ab spilled without just cause.[j] 32 Jehovah will bring his blood back on his own head, for without my father David's knowledge, he struck down and killed with the sword two men more righteous and better than he was: Ab′ner[k] the son of Ner, the chief of the army of Israel,[l] and A·ma′sa[m] the son of Je′ther, the chief of the army of Judah.[n]

33 Their blood will come back on the head of Jo′ab and on the head of his offspring* forever;[a] but for David, his offspring,* his house, and his throne, may there be peace from Jehovah forever." 34 Then Be·nai′ah the son of Je·hoi′a·da went up and struck Jo′ab down and put him to death, and he was buried at his own house in the wilderness. 35 Then the king appointed Be·nai′ah[b] the son of Je·hoi′a·da over the army in his place, and the king appointed Za′dok[c] the priest in place of A·bi′a·thar.

36 Then the king summoned Shim′e·i[d] and said to him: "Build yourself a house in Jerusalem, and live there; do not go out from there to any other place. 37 On the day you go out and cross the Kid′ron Valley,[e] you can be sure that you will die. Your blood will be on your own head." 38 Shim′e·i replied to the king: "What you have said is fair. Your servant will do just as my lord the king has said." So Shim′e·i stayed in Jerusalem for many days.

39 But at the end of three years, two of Shim′e·i's slaves ran away to A′chish[f] the son of Ma′a·cah the king of Gath. When Shim′e·i was told: "Look! Your slaves are in Gath," 40 Shim′e·i immediately saddled his donkey and went to see A′chish in Gath to find his slaves. When Shim′e·i returned from Gath with his slaves, 41 Sol′o·mon was told: "Shim′e·i has gone out of Jerusalem to Gath and has returned." 42 At that the king summoned Shim′e·i and said to him: "Did I not put you under oath by Jehovah and warn you: 'On the day you go out from here to any other place, you can be sure that you will die'? And did you not say to me,

---

CHAP. 2

a 1Sa 22:20
  1Ki 1:7

b Jos 21:8, 18
  Jer 1:1

c 1Sa 23:6
  2Sa 15:24
  1Ch 15:11, 12

d 1Sa 22:22, 23

e 1Sa 2:31
  1Sa 3:12

f Jos 18:1

g 1Ki 1:7

h 2Sa 18:14

i 1Ch 21:29

j Ge 9:6
  Ex 21:14
  Nu 35:33
  De 19:13
  1Ki 2:5

k 2Sa 3:26, 27

l 2Sa 2:8

m 2Sa 20:10

n 2Sa 17:25

Second Col.

a 2Sa 3:29

b 1Ch 11:24
  1Ch 27:5

c 1Sa 2:35
  1Ch 6:50, 53
  1Ch 12:28
  1Ch 16:37, 39
  1Ch 24:3

d 1Ki 2:8

e 2Sa 15:23
  2Ki 23:6
  Joh 18:1

f 1Sa 21:10
  1Sa 27:2

2:25 *Or "who fell upon Adonijah."

2:33 *Or "descendants."

'What you are saying is fair; I will obey'?[a] **43** Why, then, did you not keep the oath of Jehovah and the commandment that I imposed on you?" **44** The king then said to Shim′e·i: "You know in your heart all the injury that you did to David my father,[b] and Jehovah will bring back that injury on your own head.[c] **45** But King Sol′o·mon will be blessed,[d] and the throne of David will be firmly established before Jehovah forever." **46** With that the king commanded Be·nai′ah the son of Je·hoi′a·da, who went out and struck him down, and he died.[e]

Thus the kingdom was firmly established in the hand of Sol′o·mon.[f]

3 Sol′o·mon made a marriage alliance with Phar′aoh king of Egypt. He married* Phar′aoh's daughter[g] and brought her to the City of David[h] until he finished building his own house,[i] and the house of Jehovah,[j] and the wall around Jerusalem.[k] **2** But the people were still sacrificing on the high places,[l] because until that time a house for the name of Jehovah had not yet been built.[m] **3** Sol′o·mon continued to love Jehovah by walking in the statutes of David his father, except that he was sacrificing and making offerings smoke on the high places.[n]

4 The king went to Gib′e·on to sacrifice there, for that was the most prominent* high place.[o] Sol′o·mon offered 1,000 burnt sacrifices on that altar.[p] **5** In Gib′e·on Jehovah appeared to Sol′o·mon in a dream by night, and God said: "Ask what you would like me to give you."[q] **6** At this Sol′o·mon said: "You have shown great loyal love toward your servant David my father as he walked before you

in faithfulness and in righteousness and in uprightness of heart. You have continued to show him this great loyal love down to this day by giving him a son to sit on his throne.[a] **7** And now, Jehovah my God, you have made your servant king in the place of David my father, though I am just a youth* and I am inexperienced.#[b] **8** Your servant is among your people whom you have chosen,[c] a people so vast that they cannot be numbered or counted. **9** So grant your servant an obedient heart to judge your people,[d] to discern between good and bad,[e] for who is able to judge this numerous* people of yours?"

10 It was pleasing to Jehovah that Sol′o·mon had requested this.[f] **11** God then said to him: "Because you requested this and you did not request for yourself long life* or riches or the death# of your enemies, but you requested understanding to hear judicial cases,[g] **12** I will do what you asked.[h] I will give you a wise and understanding heart,[i] so that just as there has never been anyone like you before, there will never be anyone like you again.[j] **13** Furthermore, what you have not requested I will give you,[k] both riches and glory,[l] so that there will be no other king like you in your lifetime.*[m] **14** And if you walk in my ways by keeping my regulations and my commandments, just as David your father walked,[n] I will also give you a long life."*[o]

15 When Sol′o·mon awoke, he realized that it had been a

CHAP. 2
a 1Ki 2:38
b 2Sa 16:5, 13
c Ps 7:16
  Pr 5:22
d Ps 21:6
  Ps 72:17
e 1Ki 2:8, 9
  2Ch 1:1
  Pr 16:12

CHAP. 3
g De 7:3, 4
  1Ki 7:8
  1Ki 9:24
  1Ki 11:1
  Ne 13:25-27
h 2Sa 5:7
  1Ch 11:7
i 1Ki 7:1
j 1Ki 8:17-19
k 1Ki 9:15
  2Ch 33:17
l De 12:5, 6
  1Ki 5:3
  1Ch 28:6
m 1Sa 7:9
  1Sa 10:8
  1Ch 21:26
o 1Ch 16:39, 40
  1Ch 21:29
p 2Ch 1:3-6
q 2Ch 1:7-10

Second Col.
a 1Ki 2:1, 4
b 1Ch 29:1
  Jer 1:6
c Ex 19:5, 6
d Ps 72:1
  Ps 119:34
e Heb 5:14
f Pr 15:8
g 1Ch 22:12
  1Ch 29:19
  2Ch 1:11, 12
  Pr 16:16
h Ec 1:16
  1Jo 5:14
i 1Ki 4:29
  Pr 2:3-5
  Jas 1:5
j Mt 12:42
k Ps 84:11
  Mt 6:33
  Eph 3:20
l 1Ki 4:21
  Ec 7:11
m 1Ki 10:23
n 1Ki 15:5
o Ps 21:4
  Ps 91:14, 16
  Pr 3:13, 16

3:1 *Or "took." **3:4** *Lit., "the great."

3:7 *Or "little boy." #Lit., "and I do not know going out and coming in." **3:9** *Or possibly, "difficult." Lit., "heavy." **3:11** *Lit., "many days." #Or "souls." **3:13** *Lit., "all your days." **3:14** *Lit., "lengthen your days."

dream. Then he went to Jerusalem and stood before the ark of the covenant of Jehovah and offered up burnt sacrifices and communion offerings[a] and spread a feast for all his servants.

16 At that time two prostitutes came in to the king and stood before him. 17 The first woman said: "Please, my lord, this woman and I live in one house, and I gave birth while she was in the house. 18 On the third day after I gave birth, this woman also gave birth. We were together, just the two of us; there was no one else with us in the house. 19 During the night this woman's son died, because she lay on him. 20 So she got up in the middle of the night and took my son from my side while your slave girl was asleep and laid him in her arms,* and she laid her dead son in my arms. 21 When I got up in the morning to nurse my son, I saw that he was dead. So I examined him closely in the morning and saw that it was not my son whom I had given birth to." 22 But the other woman said: "No, my son is the living one, and your son is the dead one!" But the first woman was saying: "No, your son is the dead one, and my son is the living one." That is how they argued before the king.

23 Finally the king said: "This one says, 'This is my son, the living one, and your son is the dead one!' and that one says, 'No, your son is the dead one, and my son is the living one!'" 24 The king said: "Bring me a sword." So they brought a sword to the king. 25 The king then said: "Cut the living child in two, and give half to one woman and half to the other." 26 At once the woman whose son was the living one pleaded with the king, for her compassions were stirred toward her son. She said: "Please, my lord! You should give her the living child! By no means put him to death!" But the other woman was saying: "He will be neither mine nor yours! Let them cut him in two!" 27 At that the king answered: "Give the living child to the first woman! By no means put him to death, for she is his mother."

28 So all Israel heard about the judgment that the king had handed down, and they were in awe* of the king,[a] for they saw that the wisdom of God was with him to execute justice.[b]

4 King Sol'o·mon ruled over all Israel.[c] 2 These were his high officials:* Az·a·ri'ah the son of Za'dok[d] was the priest; 3 El·i·hor'eph and A·hi'jah the sons of Shi'sha were secretaries;[e] Je·hosh'a·phat[f] the son of A·hi'lud was the recorder; 4 Be·nai'ah[g] the son of Je·hoi'a·da was in charge of the army; Za'dok and A·bi'a·thar[h] were priests; 5 Az·a·ri'ah the son of Nathan[i] was over the deputies; Za'bud the son of Nathan was a priest and the king's friend;[j] 6 A·hi'shar was over the household; and Ad·o·ni'ram[k] the son of Ab'da was over those conscripted for forced labor.[l]

7 Sol'o·mon had 12 deputies in charge of all Israel who provided the king and his household with food. Each one was responsible for providing the food for one month of the year.[m] 8 These were their names: The son of Hur, in the mountainous region of E'phra·im; 9 the son of De'ker, in Ma'kaz, Sha·al'bim,[n] Beth-she'mesh, and E'lon-beth-ha'nan; 10 the son of He'sed, in A·rub'both (he

---

CHAP. 3
a Le 7:11

Second Col.
a 1Ch 29:23-25
Ps 72:5

b 1Ki 3:9, 10

CHAP. 4
c 2Ch 9:30
Ec 1:12

d 1Ch 6:8
1Ch 27:16, 17

e 2Sa 8:17
1Ch 27:32

f 2Sa 8:16
2Sa 20:24

g 1Ki 1:8
1Ki 2:35
1Ch 27:5

h 1Ki 2:26

i 1Ki 1:9, 10

j 2Sa 15:37
1Ch 27:33

k 2Sa 20:24
1Ki 5:14
1Ki 12:18

l 1Ki 9:15

m 1Ch 27:1

n Jos 19:42, 48

3:20 *Lit., "her bosom." 3:28 *Lit., "fear." 4:2 *Or "his princes."

had So'coh and all the land of He'pher); **11** the son of A·bin'a·dab, in all the slopes of Dor (Sol'o·mon's daughter Ta'phath became his wife); **12** Ba·a'na the son of A·hi'lud, in Ta'a·nach, Me·gid'do,[a] and all Beth-she'an,[b] which is beside Zar'e·than below Jez're·el, from Beth-she'an to A'bel-me·ho'lah to the region of Jok'me·am;[c] **13** the son of Ge'ber, in Ra'moth-gil'e·ad[d] (he had the tent villages of Ja'ir[e] the son of Ma·nas'seh, which are in Gil'e·ad;[f] he also had the region of Ar'gob,[g] which is in Ba'shan:[h] 60 large cities with walls and copper bars); **14** A·hin'a·dab the son of Id'do, in Ma·ha·na'im;[i] **15** A·him'a·az, in Naph'ta·li (he took Bas'e·math, another of Sol'o·mon's daughters, as his wife); **16** Ba·a'na the son of Hu'shai, in Ash'er and Be·a'loth; **17** Je·hosh'a·phat the son of Pa·ru'ah, in Is'sa·char; **18** Shim'e·i[i] the son of E'la, in Benjamin;[k] **19** Ge'ber the son of U'ri, in the land of Gil'e·ad,[l] the land of Si'hon[m] king of the Am'or·ites and of Og[n] king of Ba'shan. There was also one deputy in charge of all these other deputies in the land.

20 Judah and Israel were as numerous as the grains of sand by the sea;[o] they were eating and drinking and rejoicing.[p]

21 Sol'o·mon ruled over all the kingdoms from the River*[q] to the land of the Phi·lis'tines and to the boundary of Egypt. They brought tribute and served Sol'o·mon all the days of his life.[r]

22 Sol'o·mon's food for each day was 30 cor measures* of fine flour and 60 cor measures of flour, **23** 10 fattened cattle, 20 pastured cattle, and 100 sheep,

---

4:21 *That is, the Euphrates. **4:22** *A cor equaled 220 L (200 dry qt). See App. B14.

besides some stags, gazelles, roebucks, and fattened cuckoos. **24** For he controlled everything this side of the River,*[a] from Tiph'sah to Gaz'a,[b] including all the kings on this side of the River; and he enjoyed peace in every region, all around him.[c] **25** Judah and Israel lived in security, everyone under his own vine and under his own fig tree, from Dan to Be'er-she'ba, all the days of Sol'o·mon.

26 And Sol'o·mon had 4,000* stalls of horses for his chariots and 12,000 horses.#[d]

27 These deputies supplied food to King Sol'o·mon and to everyone who ate at the table of King Sol'o·mon. Each was responsible for his month and saw to it that nothing was lacking.[e] **28** They also brought barley and straw wherever it was needed for the horses and for the teams of horses, each according to his quota.

29 And God gave Sol'o·mon wisdom and discernment in very great measure and a broadness of heart* like the sand on the seashore.[f] **30** Sol'o·mon's wisdom surpassed the wisdom of all the people of the East and all the wisdom of Egypt.[g] **31** He was wiser than any other man, wiser than E'than[h] the Ez'ra·hite and He'man,[i] Cal'col,[j] and Dar'da, the sons of Ma'hol; his fame spread among all the surrounding nations.[k] **32** He composed* 3,000 proverbs[l] and his songs[m] numbered 1,005. **33** He would speak about the trees, from the cedar in Leb'a·non to the hyssop[n] that grows on the wall; he would speak about

---

4:24 *That is, west of the Euphrates. **4:26** *This figure is found in some manuscripts and in the parallel account. Other manuscripts say 40,000. #Or "horsemen." **4:29** *Or "heart with understanding." **4:32** *Or "spoke."

CHAP. 4

a 2Ki 23:29

b Jos 17:11
  1Sa 31:8, 10

c Jos 21:34

d De 4:41-43
  1Ki 22:3

e Nu 32:41
  De 3:14

f Nu 32:1

g De 3:4

h Jos 13:8, 11

i Ge 32:1, 2
  2Sa 2:8, 9

j 1Ki 1:8

k Jos 18:11

l Jos 17:1

m Nu 21:21

n De 3:4

o Ge 22:15, 17

p Ec 2:24

q Ge 15:18
  Ex 23:31
  2Sa 8:3
  Ps 72:8-10

r Ps 72:10

Second Col.

a Jos 1:4

b Ge 10:19

c 1Ki 5:4
  1Ch 22:9
  Ps 72:7

d De 17:15, 16
  1Ki 10:24-26
  2Ch 1:14, 17

e 1Ki 4:7

f 1Ki 10:23
  2Ch 1:10
  Pr 2:6

g Ac 7:22

h Ps 89:Sup

i Ps 88:Sup

j 1Ch 2:4, 6

k 1Ki 10:1, 7
  Lu 11:31

l Pr 1:1
  Ec 12:9

m Ca 1:1

n Ex 12:22

the animals,[a] the birds,*[b] the creeping things,*[c] and the fish. **34** People from all the nations came to hear Sol'o·mon's wisdom, including kings from all over the earth who had heard about his wisdom.[d]

5 When Hi'ram the king of Tyre[e] heard that Sol'o·mon had been anointed as king in place of his father, he sent his servants to Sol'o·mon, for Hi'ram had always been a friend of David's.*[f] **2** In turn Sol'o·mon sent word to Hi'ram:[g] **3** "You well know that David my father was not able to build a house for the name of Jehovah his God because of the wars waged against him from every side until Jehovah put his enemies under the soles of his feet.[h] **4** But now Jehovah my God has given me rest on all sides.[i] There is no one opposing me and nothing bad happening.[j] **5** So I intend to build a house for the name of Jehovah my God, just as Jehovah promised to David my father, saying: 'Your son whom I will put on your throne in your place, he is the one who will build the house for my name.'[k] **6** Now command your people to cut cedars of Leb'a·non[l] for me. My servants will work with your servants, and I will pay the wages of your servants according to the rate you set, for you are aware that not one of us knows how to cut trees like the Si·do'ni·ans."[m]

7 When Hi'ram heard Sol'o·mon's words, he rejoiced greatly and said: "May Jehovah be praised today, for he has given David a wise son over this great* people!"[n] **8** So Hi'ram sent word to Sol'o·mon: "I have heard the message you sent to me. I will do all you desire in providing the cedar and juniper timbers.[a] **9** My servants will bring them down from Leb'a·non to the sea, and I will make them into log rafts to go by sea to the place that you designate to me. I will have them broken up there, and you can carry them away. In exchange, you will provide the food that I request for my household."[b]

10 So Hi'ram supplied all the timbers of cedar and juniper that Sol'o·mon desired. **11** And Sol'o·mon gave Hi'ram 20,000 cor measures* of wheat as food supplies for his household and 20 cor measures of very fine olive oil.* That was what Sol'o·mon gave Hi'ram year after year.[c] **12** And Jehovah gave Sol'o·mon wisdom, just as He had promised him.[d] And there was peace between Hi'ram and Sol'o·mon, and the two of them made a treaty.*

13 King Sol'o·mon conscripted men for forced labor out of all Israel; 30,000 men were conscripted.[e] **14** He would send them to Leb'a·non in shifts of 10,000 each month. They would spend a month in Leb'a·non and two months at their homes; and Ad·o·ni'ram[f] was over those conscripted for forced labor. **15** Sol'o·mon had 70,000 common laborers* and 80,000 stonecutters[g] in the mountains,[h] **16** as well as Sol'o·mon's 3,300 princely deputies[i] who served as foremen to supervise the workmen. **17** At the king's order, they quarried large stones, expensive stones,* to lay the foundation[k] of the house with hewn stones.[l] **18** So Sol'o-

CHAP. 4
a Pr 30:30
b Pr 30:19
c Pr 6:6
  Pr 30:25
d 2Ch 9:1, 23

CHAP. 5
e Eze 27:3
f 2Sa 5:11
g 2Ch 2:3
h 2Sa 7:5
  1Ch 22:7, 8
i 1Ki 4:24, 25
j Pr 16:7
k 2Sa 7:12, 13
  1Ch 22:9, 10
  2Ch 2:4
l 1Ki 6:9, 20
m 2Ch 2:8
n 2Ch 2:11, 12

Second Col.
a 2Sa 6:5
  1Ki 6:15
  2Ch 3:5
b 2Ch 2:15, 16
  Ezr 3:7
c 2Ch 2:10
d 1Ki 3:12
  1Ki 4:29
  Jas 1:5
e 1Ki 9:15
f 2Sa 20:24
  1Ki 4:6
  1Ki 12:18
g 1Ch 22:15
h Jos 16:10
  1Ki 9:20-22
  2Ch 2:2
  2Ch 2:17, 18
  2Ch 8:7-9
i 1Ki 9:23
j 1Ki 7:9
  1Ch 22:2
k Re 21:14
l 1Ki 6:7

4:33 *Or "flying creatures." #Possibly including reptiles and insects. **5:1** *Or "had always loved David." **5:7** *Or "numerous."

5:11 *A cor equaled 220 L (200 dry qt). See App. B14. #Lit., "of beaten oil." **5:12** *Or "covenant." **5:15** *Or "burden bearers."

mon's builders and Hi'ram's builders and the Ge'bal·ites[a] did the cutting, and they prepared the timbers and the stones to build the house.

6 In the 480th year after the Israelites* came out of the land of Egypt,[b] in the fourth year after Sol'o·mon became king over Israel, in the month of Ziv*[c] (that is, the second month), he began to build the house of Jehovah.[Ad] **2** The house that King Sol'o·mon built for Jehovah was 60 cubits* long, 20 cubits wide, and 30 cubits high.[e] **3** The porch[f] in front of the temple* was 20 cubits long,* corresponding to the width of the house.[Δ] Its depth was ten cubits from the front of the house.

4 He made windows of narrowing frames*[g] for the house. **5** Further, he built a side structure against the wall of the house; it went around the walls of the house, those of the temple* and the innermost room,[h] and he made side chambers all around.[i] **6** The lowest level of the side chambers was five cubits wide, the middle level was six cubits wide, and the third level was seven cubits wide, for he made offsets* all around the house, so that nothing was attached to the walls of the house.[j]

7 The house was built with quarry stone that had already been prepared,[k] so that no hammers or axes or any iron tools were heard in the house while it was being built. **8** The entrance of the lowest side chamber was on the south* side of the house,[a] and a winding staircase led up to the middle floor, and from the middle floor up to the third floor. **9** He continued building the house and finished it[b] and covered the house with cedar beams and rows of cedar planks.[c] **10** He built the side chambers all around the house,[d] each five cubits high, and they were joined to the house by cedar timbers.

11 Meanwhile, the word of Jehovah came to Sol'o·mon, saying: **12** "As for this house that you are building, if you walk in my statutes and carry out my judgments and observe all my commandments by walking in them,[e] I will also carry out with you my promise that I made to David your father,[f] **13** and I will reside in the midst of the Israelites,[g] and I will not forsake my people Israel."[h]

14 Sol'o·mon continued building the house to finish it. **15** He built the inside walls of the house with cedar boards. He paneled the inside walls with timber, from the floor of the house up to the rafters of the ceiling, and he overlaid the floor of the house with juniper boards.[i] **16** And he built a section of 20 cubits at the rear of the house with cedar boards, from the floor up to the rafters, and he built inside of it* the innermost room,[j] the Most Holy.[k] **17** And the temple*[l]—the part of the house in front of it—was 40 cubits. **18** The cedar inside the house was carved with gourds[m] and flowers in bloom.[n] All of it was cedar; no stone was seen.

19 And he prepared the innermost room[o] inside the house

CHAP. 5
a Jos 13:1, 5

CHAP. 6
b Ex 12:14, 51

c 1Ki 6:37

d 1Ch 28:11, 12
2Ch 3:1, 2

e 2Ch 3:3
Ezr 6:3

f 2Ch 3:4

g Eze 41:26

h Le 16:2
2Ch 5:7
Heb 9:3

i 1Ki 6:10
Eze 41:5, 26

j Eze 41:6, 7

k 1Ki 5:17

Second Col.
a Eze 41:11

b 1Ki 6:38

c 1Ki 5:6
1Ki 6:20

d 1Ki 6:5

e De 17:18, 19
1Ki 8:25
1Ch 28:9

f 2Sa 7:13
1Ch 22:9

g Ex 25:8
Le 26:12
Ps 132:13

h 1Ch 28:20

i 1Ki 5:8
2Ch 3:5

j 1Ki 6:5

k 2Ch 3:8, 9
Heb 9:3

l Heb 9:2

m 1Ki 7:24

n Ex 25:33

o Heb 9:3

6:1 *Lit., "sons of Israel." #See App. B15. ΔSee App. B8. **6:2** *A cubit equaled 44.5 cm (17.5 in.). See App. B14. **6:3** *Lit., "temple of the house." #Or "wide." ΔOr "20 cubits extending across the width of the house." **6:4** *Or "beveled (splayed) windows." **6:5** *Here referring to the Holy. **6:6** *Or "recesses."

6:8 *Lit., "right." **6:16** *That is, inside the house. **6:17** *That is, the Holy, which was in front of the Most Holy.

to put there the ark of the covenant of Jehovah.[a] **20** The innermost room was 20 cubits long, 20 cubits wide, and 20 cubits high;[b] and he overlaid it with pure gold; he overlaid the altar[c] with cedar. **21** Sol'o·mon overlaid the interior of the house with pure gold,[d] and he stretched gold chains in front of the innermost room,[e] which was overlaid with gold. **22** He overlaid the whole house with gold until all the house was completed; he also overlaid with gold the entire altar[f] near the innermost room.

23 In the innermost room he made two cherubs[g] of pinewood,* each ten cubits high.[h] **24** One wing of the cherub measured five cubits, and the other wing was five cubits. From the tip of one wing to the tip of the other wing was ten cubits. **25** The second cherub was also ten cubits. The two cherubs had the same size and shape. **26** The height of the one cherub was ten cubits, as was that of the other cherub. **27** Then he put the cherubs[i] inside the inner house.* The wings of the cherubs were extended so that the wing of the one cherub reached to one wall and the wing of the other cherub reached to the other wall, and their wings extended toward the middle of the house, so that the wings touched. **28** And he overlaid the cherubs with gold.

29 And on all the walls of the house all around both the inner and outer rooms,* he carved figures of cherubs,[k] palm trees,[k] and flowers in bloom.[l] **30** He overlaid the floor of the house with gold in the inner and outer rooms. **31** And for the en-

trance of the innermost room he made doors of pinewood, side pillars, and doorposts, as a fifth part.* **32** The two doors were of pinewood, and he carved on them cherubs, palm trees, and flowers in bloom, and he overlaid them with gold; and he hammered the gold down over the cherubs and the palm trees. **33** For the entrance of the temple,* that was how he made the doorposts of pinewood, belonging to a fourth part.* **34** And he made two doors of juniper wood. The one door had two leaves that turned on pivots, and the other door had two leaves that turned on pivots.[a] **35** He carved cherubs, palm trees, and flowers in bloom, and overlaid gold foil on the carvings.

36 He built the inner courtyard[b] with three rows of hewn stone and a row of cedar beams.[c]

37 In the 4th year, in the month of Ziv,* the house of Jehovah had its foundation laid;[d] **38** and in the 11th year, in the month of Bul* (that is, the eighth month), the house was finished in all its details and according to its plan.[e] So he spent seven years building it.

7 And it took Sol'o·mon 13 years to build his own house,*[f] until his whole house was completed.[g]

2 And he built the House of the Forest of Leb'a·non* 100 cubits* long, 50 cubits wide, and 30 cubits high on four rows of cedar pillars; and there were cedar beams[i] on the pillars. **3** It was paneled above with cedar on the girders that rested on the pillars; they numbered 45, with

6:23 *Lit., "oil wood," possibly the Aleppo pine. 6:27 *That is, the Most Holy. 6:29 *Lit., "inside and outside."

6:31, 33 *Perhaps referring to the construction of the doorframe or to the size of the doors. 6:33 *Here referring to the Holy. 6:37, 38 *See App. B15. 7:1 *Or "palace." 7:2 *A cubit equaled 44.5 cm (17.5 in.). See App. B14.

15 to a row. **4** There were three rows of framed windows, and each window was opposite another window in three tiers. **5** All the entrances and the doorposts had square* frames, as did the front of the windows that were opposite each other in three tiers.

6 And he built the Hall* of Pillars 50 cubits long and 30 cubits wide, and there was a porch in front of it with pillars and a canopy.

7 He also built the Hall* of the Throne,[a] where he would judge—the Hall of Judgment[b]—and they paneled it with cedar from the floor to the rafters.

8 The house* where he was to live, at the other courtyard,[c] was set back from the Hall,[#] and it was similar in workmanship. He also built a house similar to this Hall for Phar′aoh's daughter, whom Sol′o·mon had taken as a wife.[d]

9 All of these were made of expensive stones[e] hewn according to measure, trimmed with stonesaws inside and out, from the foundation up to the coping, and outside as far as the great courtyard.[f] **10** And the foundation was laid with very large, expensive stones; some stones measured ten cubits, and other stones, eight cubits. **11** And above these were expensive stones, hewn according to measure, as well as cedar. **12** Around the great courtyard were three rows of hewn stone and a row of cedar beams, like that for the inner courtyard[g] of the house of Jehovah and the porch of the house.[h]

13 King Sol′o·mon sent for Hi′ram[i] and brought him from Tyre. **14** He was the son of a

widow from the tribe of Naph′ta·li, and his father was a Tyr′i·an coppersmith;[a] and he had great skill, understanding,[b] and experience for all kinds of work in copper.* So he came to King Sol′o·mon and did all his work.

15 He cast the two pillars of copper;[c] each pillar was 18 cubits high, and it took a measuring cord 12 cubits long to encircle each of the two pillars.*[d] **16** And he made two capitals cast in copper to put on the tops of the pillars. One capital was five cubits high, and the other capital was five cubits high. **17** The capital on top of each pillar had mesh network with wreathed chains;[e] seven for the one capital and seven for the other capital. **18** And he made pomegranates in two rows around the one network to cover the capitals that were on the top of the pillars; he did the same for both capitals. **19** The capitals on top of the pillars at the porch were of a lily pattern four cubits high. **20** The capitals were on the two pillars, just above the rounded portion adjoining the network; and there were 200 pomegranates in rows all around on each capital.[f]

21 He set up the pillars of the porch of the temple.*[g] He set up the right-hand[#] pillar and named it Ja′chin,[△] and then he set up the left-hand[※] pillar and named it Bo′az.[□h] **22** And the top of the pillars were of a lily pattern. So the work of the pillars was completed.

CHAP. 7
a 1Ki 10:18
  Ps 122:2, 5

b 1Ki 3:9, 28
  Pr 20:8

c 2Ki 20:4

d 1Ki 3:1
  1Ki 9:24
  2Ch 8:11

e 1Ki 5:17

f 2Ch 4:9

g 1Ki 6:36
  2Ch 4:9
  2Ch 7:7

h 1Ki 6:3

i 1Ki 7:40
  2Ch 2:13, 14

Second Col.
a 2Ch 4:16

b Ex 36:1

c 1Ki 7:21

d 2Ki 25:13, 17
  2Ch 3:15
  Jer 52:21

e 2Ki 25:17
  2Ch 4:12, 13

f 2Ki 25:17
  2Ch 3:16
  Jer 52:22, 23

g 1Ki 6:3
  Eze 40:48

h 2Ch 3:17

7:5 *Or "four-sided; rectangular." 7:6, 7 *Or "Porch." 7:8 *Or "palace." #Lit., "house of the Hall." 7:14 *Or "bronze," here and in subsequent occurrences in this chapter. 7:15 *Or "each of the two pillars was 12 cubits in circumference." 7:21 *Here referring to the Holy. #Or "southern." △Meaning "May He [that is, Jehovah] Firmly Establish." ※Or "northern." □Possibly meaning "In Strength."

23 Then he made the Sea* of cast metal.[a] It was circular in shape, 10 cubits from brim to brim and 5 cubits high, and it took a measuring line 30 cubits long to encircle it.#[b] 24 And there were ornamental gourds[c] below its brim, completely encircling it, ten to a cubit all around the Sea, with two rows of the gourds cast in one piece with it. 25 It stood on 12 bulls,[d] 3 facing north, 3 facing west, 3 facing south, and 3 facing east; and the Sea rested on them, and all their hindquarters were toward the center. 26 And its thickness was a handbreadth;* and its brim was made like the brim of a cup, like a lily blossom. It would hold 2,000 bath measures.#

27 Then he made the ten carriages*[e] of copper. Each carriage was four cubits long, four cubits wide, and three cubits high. 28 And this was how the carriages were constructed: They had side panels, and the side panels were between the crossbars. 29 And on the side panels between the crossbars were lions,[f] bulls, and cherubs,[g] and the same design was above the crossbars. Above and beneath the lions and the bulls were wreaths in relief. 30 And each carriage had four copper wheels and copper axles, and its four cornerpieces served as supports for them. Beneath the basin were the supports, cast with wreaths at the side of each. 31 Its opening was inside the crown, extending upward one cubit; and its opening was round, making up a stand of one and a half cubits, and on its mouth were engravings. And

their side panels were square, not round. 32 The four wheels were below the side panels, and the supports of the wheels were attached to the carriage, and the height of each wheel was one and a half cubits. 33 And the wheels were made like chariot wheels. Their supports, rims,* spokes, and hubs were all of cast metal. 34 There were four supports on the four corners of each carriage; its supports were cast as part of* the carriage. 35 On top of the carriage was a circular band half a cubit high, and on the top of the carriage, its framing pieces and its side panels were cast as part of* it. 36 On the surfaces of its framing pieces and on its side panels he engraved cherubs, lions, and palm trees according to the amount of space on each, with wreaths all around.[a] 37 This is how he made the ten carriages;[b] they were all cast alike,[c] with the same measure and shape.

38 He made ten copper basins;[d] each could hold 40 bath measures. Each basin measured four cubits.* There was one basin for each of the ten carriages. 39 Then he put five carriages on the right side of the house and five on the left side of the house, and he placed the Sea on the right side of the house, toward the southeast.[e]

40 Hi'ram[f] also made the basins, the shovels,[g] and the bowls.[h] So Hi'ram finished all the work that he did for King Sol'o·mon on the house of Jehovah:[i] 41 the two pillars[j] and the bowl-shaped capitals that were on top of the two pillars; the two networks[k] to cover the two bowl-shaped capitals that were on top of the pillars;

CHAP. 7
a Ex 30:18
  2Ki 25:13

b 2Ch 4:2-5

c 1Ki 6:18

d Jer 52:20

e 2Ki 25:16
  Jer 52:17

f Eze 41:19

g Ge 3:24
  Ex 25:18
  1Ki 6:27
  2Ch 3:7
  Eze 41:17,18

Second Col.
a 1Ki 6:29
  1Ki 6:32

b 1Ki 7:27

c 1Ki 7:15, 46
  2Ch 4:3

d Ex 30:18

e 2Ch 4:6, 10

f 1Ki 7:13
  2Ch 2:13

g Ex 27:3
  2Ki 25:14

h Ex 24:6

i 2Ch 4:11-17

j 1Ki 7:15

k 1Ki 7:17

7:23 *Or "reservoir." #Or "it was 30 cubits in circumference." 7:26 *About 7.4 cm (2.9 in.). See App. B14. #A bath equaled 22 L (5.81 gal). See App. B14. 7:27 *Or "water carts."

7:33 *Or "fellies." 7:34, 35 *Or "were one piece with." 7:38 *Or "four cubits in diameter."

42 the 400 pomegranates[a] for the two networks, two rows of pomegranates for each network, to cover the two bowl-shaped capitals that were on the two pillars; **43** the ten carriages[b] and the ten basins[c] on the carriages; **44** the Sea[d] and the 12 bulls beneath the Sea; **45** and the cans, the shovels, the bowls, and all the utensils, which Hi'ram made of polished copper for King Sol'o·mon for the house of Jehovah. **46** The king cast them in clay molds in the district of the Jordan, between Suc'coth and Zar'e·than.

47 Sol'o·mon left all the utensils unweighed because they were in such great quantities. The weight of the copper was not ascertained.[e] **48** Sol'o·mon made all the utensils for the house of Jehovah: the altar[f] of gold; the gold table[g] on which to put the showbread; **49** the lampstands[h] of pure gold, five on the right and five on the left before the innermost room; and the blossoms,[i] the lamps, and the snuffers,[*] of gold;[j] **50** the basins, the extinguishers,[k] the bowls, the cups,[l] and the fire holders,[m] of pure gold; and the sockets for the doors of the inner house,[n] that is, the Most Holy, and for the doors of the house of the temple,[o] of gold.

51 So King Sol'o·mon completed all the work he had to do for the house of Jehovah. Sol'o·mon then brought in the things that David his father had made holy,[p] and he put the silver, the gold, and the articles into the treasuries of the house of Jehovah.[q]

8 At that time Sol'o·mon congregated[r] the elders of Israel, all the heads of the tribes, the chieftains of the paternal hous-

es of Israel.[a] They came to King Sol'o·mon at Jerusalem to bring up the ark of the covenant of Jehovah from the City of David,[b] that is, Zion.[c] **2** All the men of Israel assembled before King Sol'o·mon at the festival[*] in the month of Eth'a·nim,[#] that is, the seventh month.[d] **3** So all the elders of Israel came, and the priests lifted up the Ark.[e] **4** They brought up the Ark of Jehovah, the tent of meeting,[f] and all the holy utensils that were in the tent. The priests and the Levites brought them up. **5** King Sol'o·mon and the entire assembly of Israel, who had been summoned to meet with him, were before the Ark. So many sheep and cattle were being sacrificed[g] that they could not be counted or numbered.

6 Then the priests brought the ark of the covenant of Jehovah to its place,[h] into the innermost room of the house, the Most Holy, underneath the wings of the cherubs.[i]

7 Thus the wings of the cherubs were spread out over the place of the Ark, so that the cherubs overshadowed the Ark and its poles.[j] **8** The poles[k] were so long that the tips of the poles were visible from the Holy in front of the innermost room, but they were not visible from outside. And they are there to this day. **9** There was nothing in the Ark but the two stone tablets[l] that Moses placed there[m] at Ho'reb, when Jehovah made a covenant[n] with the people of Israel while they were coming out of the land of Egypt.[o]

10 When the priests came out from the holy place, the cloud[p] filled the house of Jehovah.[q] **11** The priests were not able to stand to minister because of

---

CHAP. 7
a 1Ki 7:20
b 1Ki 7:27
c 1Ki 7:38
d 1Ki 7:23
e 1Ch 22:14, 16
  2Ch 4:18-22
f Ex 37:25
g Ex 37:10
h Ex 37:17
  Re 1:20
i 1Ki 6:18
j Ex 37:23
k Jer 52:18
l Ex 25:29
m Le 16:12
n 1Ki 6:31
o 1Ki 6:33
p 2Sa 8:10-12
q 2Ch 5:1

CHAP. 8
r Ec 1:1

Second Col.
a 2Ch 5:2, 3
b 2Sa 6:17
c 2Sa 5:7
  1Ch 11:5
d Le 23:34
  De 16:13
e 1Ch 15:2, 15
  2Ch 5:4-6
f Ex 40:2
  2Ch 1:13
g 1Ch 16:1
h Ex 26:33
  Ex 40:21
  2Sa 6:17
  Re 11:19
i 1Ki 6:27
  2Ch 5:7
  Ps 80:1
  Eze 10:5
j Ex 25:20
  2Ch 5:8-10
k Ex 25:14
  Ex 37:4
l De 4:13
  Heb 9:4
m Ex 40:20
  De 10:5
n Ex 24:8
o Ex 19:1
  Nu 10:11, 12
p Ex 40:34
  Le 16:2
q 2Ch 5:11-14

7:49 *Or "tongs."

8:2 *That is, the Festival of Booths. #See App. B15.

the cloud, for the glory of Jehovah filled the house of Jehovah.[a] **12** At that time Sol′o·mon said: "Jehovah said he would reside in the thick gloom.[b] **13** I have successfully built a lofty house for you, an established place for you to dwell in forever."[c]

14 Then the king turned around and began to bless all the congregation of Israel while all the congregation of Israel stood.[d] **15** He said: "May Jehovah the God of Israel be praised, the one who by his own mouth promised my father David, and by his own hand has given fulfillment, saying, **16** 'From the day I brought my people Israel out of Egypt, I have not chosen a city out of all the tribes of Israel in which to build a house for my name to remain there,[e] but I have chosen David to be over my people Israel.' **17** And it was the heart's desire of my father David to build a house for the name of Jehovah the God of Israel.[f] **18** But Jehovah said to my father David, 'It was your heart's desire to build a house for my name, and you did well to desire this in your heart. **19** However, you will not build the house, but your own son who is to be born to you* is the one who will build the house for my name.'[g] **20** Jehovah has carried out the promise that he made, for I have succeeded my father David and I sit on the throne of Israel, just as Jehovah promised. I have also built the house for the name of Jehovah the God of Israel[h] **21** and have set up a place there for the Ark containing the covenant[i] that Jehovah made with our forefathers when he was bringing them out of the land of Egypt."

8:19 *Lit., "your son, the one coming out of your loins."

CHAP. 8
a Ex 40:35
  Eze 10:4
  Eze 43:4
  Eze 44:4
  Ac 7:55
  Re 21:23

b Ex 20:21
  De 5:22
  2Ch 6:1, 2
  Ps 18:11
  Ps 97:2

c Ps 78:69
  Ps 132:13, 14

d 2Ch 6:3-11

e De 12:11

f 2Sa 7:1-3
  1Ch 17:1, 2

g 2Sa 7:12, 13

h 1Ch 28:5, 6

i Ex 34:28
  De 9:9
  De 31:26

Second Col.
a 2Ch 6:12

b Ex 15:11
  1Sa 2:2
  2Sa 7:22

c De 7:9

d 2Ch 6:14-17

e 2Sa 7:12, 13

f 1Ki 2:4
  Ps 132:12

g Isa 66:1

h Ps 148:13
  Jer 23:24

i 2Ch 2:6
  2Ch 6:18-21
  Ne 9:6
  Ac 17:24

j Ex 20:24
  2Sa 7:13

k Da 6:10
  1Pe 3:12

22 Then Sol′o·mon stood before the altar of Jehovah in front of all the congregation of Israel, and he spread his hands out to the heavens,[a] **23** and he said: "O Jehovah the God of Israel, there is no God like you[b] in the heavens above or on the earth beneath, keeping the covenant and showing loyal love[c] to your servants who are walking before you with all their heart.[d] **24** You have kept the promise that you made to your servant David my father. You made the promise with your own mouth, and this day you have fulfilled it with your own hand.[e] **25** And now, O Jehovah the God of Israel, keep the promise you made to your servant David my father when you said: 'There will never fail to be a man of your line before me to sit on the throne of Israel, if only your sons will pay attention to their way by walking before me, just as you have walked before me.'[f] **26** And now, O God of Israel, let the promise that you made to your servant David my father prove trustworthy, please.

27 "But will God really dwell on the earth?[g] Look! The heavens, yes, the heaven of the heavens, cannot contain you;[h] how much less, then, this house that I have built![i] **28** Now pay attention to the prayer of your servant and to his request for favor, O Jehovah my God, and listen to the cry for help and to the prayer that your servant is praying before you today. **29** May your eyes be open toward this house night and day, toward the place of which you said, 'My name will be there,'[j] to listen to the prayer that your servant prays toward this place.[k] **30** And listen to your servant's request for favor and to the request by your people Israel that they pray toward this place, and may you hear from your dwelling place in the heavens;[a] yes, may you hear and forgive.[b]

31 "When a man sins against his fellow man and is made to take an oath* and is brought under liability to the oath,# and while under the oath# he comes before your altar in this house,[c] **32** may you then hear from the heavens and act and judge your servants by pronouncing the wicked one guilty* and bringing what he did on his own head, and by pronouncing the righteous one innocent# and rewarding him according to his own righteousness.[d]

33 "When your people Israel are defeated by an enemy because they kept sinning against you,[e] and they return to you and glorify your name[f] and pray and beg you for favor in this house,[g] **34** may you then hear from the heavens and forgive the sin of your people Israel and bring them back to the land that you gave to their forefathers.[h]

35 "When the heavens are shut up and there is no rain[i] because they kept sinning against you,[j] and they pray toward this place and glorify your name and turn back from their sin because you humbled* them,[k] **36** may you then hear from the heavens and forgive the sin of your servants, of your people Israel, for you will instruct them[l] about the good way in which they should walk; and bring rain on your land[m] that you gave to your people as an inheritance.

37 "If a famine occurs in the land,[n] or a pestilence, a scorching blight, mildew,[o] swarming lo-

custs, or voracious locusts;* or if their enemy besieges them in any of the cities of the land# or if any other sort of plague or disease occurs,[a] **38** whatever prayer, whatever request for favor[b] may be made by any man or by all your people Israel (for each one knows the plague of his own heart)[c] when they spread out their hands toward this house, **39** then may you hear from the heavens, your dwelling place,[d] and may you forgive[e] and take action; and reward each one according to all his ways,[f] for you alone truly know every human heart),[g] **40** so that they may fear you all the days they live on the land that you gave to our forefathers.

41 "Also concerning the foreigner who is not part of your people Israel and who comes from a distant land because of your name*[h] **42** (for they will hear about your great name[i] and your mighty hand and your outstretched arm), and he comes and prays toward this house, **43** may you then listen from the heavens, your dwelling place,[j] and do all that the foreigner asks of you, so that all the peoples of the earth may know your name and fear you,[k] as your people Israel do, and may know that your name has been called on this house that I have built.

44 "If your people go to war against their enemy in the way that you send them,[l] and they pray[m] to Jehovah in the direction of the city that you have chosen[n] and toward the house that I have built for your name,[o] **45** then hear from the heavens their prayer and their request for favor and execute judgment for them.

CHAP. 8
a Ps 33:13
b 2Ch 7:13, 14
  Da 9:19
c 2Ch 6:22, 23
d Job 34:11
e Le 26:14, 17
  Jos 7:8, 11
  2Ki 17:6, 7
f Ne 1:11
g 2Ki 19:19, 20
  2Ch 6:24, 25
h Ps 106:47
i Le 26:19
  De 28:23
j Eze 14:13
k 2Ch 6:26, 27
l Isa 30:20
  Isa 54:13
m 1Ki 18:1
n Le 26:16
  2Ki 6:25
o De 28:21, 22
  Am 4:9

Second Col.
a 2Ch 6:28-31
b 2Ch 33:12, 13
c Pr 14:10
d Isa 63:15
e Ps 130:4
f Job 34:11
  Ps 18:20
g 1Sa 16:7
  1Ch 28:9
  Jer 17:10
h Nu 9:14
  Ru 1:16
  2Ki 5:15
  2Ch 6:32, 33
  Isa 56:6, 7
  Ac 8:27
i Ne 9:10
j Ps 11:4
k Ps 67:2
  Ps 102:15
l Ex 23:31
  1Ki 20:13
m 2Ch 14:11
  2Ch 20:5, 6
n Ps 78:68
  Ps 132:13
o 2Ch 6:34, 35

8:31 *Or "and the latter lays a cursing on him." That is, an oath that carried with it a curse as its penalty if sworn falsely or violated. #Lit., "curse." **8:32** *Lit., "wicked." #Lit., "righteous." **8:35** *Or "afflicted."

8:37 *Or "grasshoppers." #Lit., "in the land of his gates." **8:41** *Or "reputation."

46 "If they sin against you (for there is no man who does not sin),[a] and you are furious with them and you abandon them to an enemy, and their captors carry them off captive to the land of the enemy, far or near;[b] **47** and they come to their senses in the land where they were carried off captive,[c] and they return to you[d] and beg you for favor in the land of their captors,[e] saying, 'We have sinned and done wrong; we have acted wickedly;'[f] **48** and they return to you with all their heart[g] and all their soul* in the land of their enemies who carried them off captive, and they pray to you in the direction of their land that you gave to their forefathers and of the city that you have chosen and the house that I have built for your name,[h] **49** then hear from the heavens, your dwelling place,[i] their prayer and their request for favor, and execute judgment for them **50** and forgive your people who have sinned against you, forgiving all their transgressions they committed against you. You will make them objects of pity before their captors, and they will pity them[j] **51** (for they are your people and your inheritance,[k] whom you brought out of Egypt,[l] from inside the iron-smelting furnace).[m] **52** May your eyes be opened to your servant's request for favor[n] and to the request for favor by your people Israel by listening whenever they call to you.*[o] **53** For you set them apart as your inheritance out of all the peoples of the earth,[p] just as you declared through Moses your servant when you were bringing our forefathers out of

Egypt, O Sovereign Lord Jehovah."

54 And as soon as Sol·o·mon finished offering to Jehovah this entire prayer and request for favor, he rose up from before the altar of Jehovah, where he had been kneeling with his hands spread out to the heavens.[a] **55** He then stood and blessed all the congregation of Israel with a loud voice, saying: **56** "Praised be Jehovah, who has given a resting-place to his people Israel, just as he promised.[b] Not one word of all his good promise that he made through Moses his servant has failed.[c] **57** May Jehovah our God be with us just as he was with our forefathers.[d] May he not abandon us nor forsake us.[e] **58** May he draw our heart toward himself,[f] to walk in all his ways and to keep his commandments, his regulations, and his judgments, which he commanded our forefathers to observe. **59** And may these words of mine with which I have begged Jehovah for favor be near to Jehovah our God by day and night, that he may execute judgment for his servant and for his people Israel as each day requires, **60** so that all the peoples of the earth may know that Jehovah is the true God.[g] There is no other![h] **61** So let your heart be complete[i] with* Jehovah our God by walking in his regulations and by keeping his commandments as on this day."

62 Now the king and all Israel with him offered a grand sacrifice before Jehovah.[j] **63** Sol·o·mon offered the communion sacrifices[k] to Jehovah: He offered 22,000 cattle and 120,000 sheep. Thus the king and all the Israelites inaugurated the house of Jehovah.[l] **64** On that day the king

---

CHAP. 8
a Ps 51:5
  Ps 130:3
  Ec 7:20
  Ro 3:23
  1Jo 1:8
b De 28:15, 36
  2Ki 17:6
  2Ki 25:21
  2Ch 6:36-39
c Le 26:40
d De 30:1, 2
e De 4:27, 29
  2Ch 33:12, 13
f Ne 1:6
  Ps 106:6
  Pr 28:13
  Da 9:5
g 1Sa 7:3
h Da 6:10
i Isa 63:15
j 2Ch 30:9
  Ezr 7:28
  Ne 2:7, 8
k Ne 19:5
  De 9:26
l Ex 14:30
m De 4:20
n 2Ch 6:40
o Ps 86:5
  Ps 145:18
p Ex 19:6
  De 4:34
  De 32:9

Second Col.
a 2Ch 6:12, 13
b 1Ki 4:24, 25
c De 10:11
  Jos 21:45
d De 31:6
  Jos 1:5
  2Ch 32:7
  Ps 46:7
e Isa 41:10
  Heb 13:5
f Ps 86:11
  Ps 119:36
  2Th 3:5
g Jos 4:24
  1Sa 17:46
  Eze 36:23
  Eze 39:7
h De 4:35, 39
  Isa 44:6
i De 18:13
  2Ki 20:3
  1Ch 28:9
  Mt 22:37
j 2Ch 7:4, 5
k Le 3:1
l Ezr 6:16
  Ne 12:27

8:48 *See Glossary. 8:52 *Or "listening to them whatever they ask of you." 8:61 *Or "completely devoted to."

had to sanctify the middle of the courtyard that is before the house of Jehovah, for there he had to offer up the burnt sacrifices, the grain offerings, and the fat pieces of the communion sacrifices, because the copper altar[a] that is before Jehovah was too small to contain the burnt sacrifices, the grain offerings, and the fat[b] pieces of the communion sacrifices. **65** At that time Sol′o·mon held the festival[c] together with all Israel, a great congregation from Le′bo·ha′math* down to the Wadi* of Egypt,[d] before Jehovah our God for 7 days and then another 7 days, 14 days in all. **66** On the following* day, he sent the people away, and they blessed the king and went to their homes rejoicing and feeling glad of heart over all the goodness[e] that Jehovah had shown to David his servant and Israel his people.

9 As soon as Sol′o·mon had finished building the house of Jehovah, the house* of the king,[f] and everything Sol′o·mon desired to make,[g] **2** Jehovah appeared to Sol′o·mon a second time, just as he had appeared to him in Gib′e·on.[h] **3** Jehovah said to him: "I have heard your prayer and your request for favor that you made before me. I have sanctified this house that you built by permanently putting my name there,[i] and my eyes and my heart will always be there.[j] **4** And you, if you walk before me as your father David walked,[k] with integrity of heart[l] and with uprightness,[m] by doing everything I have commanded you,[n] and you obey my regulations and my judgments,[o]

5 then I will establish the throne of your kingdom over Israel forever, just as I promised your father David, saying, 'There will never fail to be a man of your line sitting on the throne of Israel.'[a] **6** But if you and your sons turn away from following me and do not keep my commandments and my statutes that I have put before you, and you go and serve other gods and bow down to them,[b] **7** I will cut Israel off from the surface of the land that I have given to them,[c] and the house that I have sanctified for my name I will cast out of my sight,[d] and Israel will become an object of scorn* and a cause for ridicule among all the peoples.[e] **8** And this house will become heaps of ruins.[f] Everyone passing by it will stare in amazement and will whistle and say, 'Why did Jehovah do that to this land and this house?'[g] **9** Then they will say, 'It was because they abandoned Jehovah their God, who had brought their forefathers out of the land of Egypt, and they embraced other gods and bowed down to them and served them. That is why Jehovah brought all this calamity on them.'"[h]

10 At the end of 20 years, during which Sol′o·mon built the two houses, the house of Jehovah and the house* of the king,[i] **11** Hi′ram[j] the king of Tyre had supplied Sol′o·mon with cedar and juniper timbers and with as much gold as he desired,[k] and King Sol′o·mon gave to Hi′ram 20 cities in the land of Gal′i·lee. **12** So Hi′ram went out from Tyre to see the cities that Sol′o·mon had given him, but he was not satisfied with them.* **13** He said: "What sort of cities are these that you have given me,

---

8:65 *Or "the entrance of Hamath." *See Glossary. **8:66** *Lit., "eighth," that is, the day after the second seven-day period. **9:1, 10** *Or "palace."

9:7 *Lit., "a proverb." **9:12** *Lit., "they were not right in his eyes."

CHAP. 8
a 2Ch 4:1
b Le 3:16
c Le 23:34
d Ge 15:18
  Nu 34:5, 8
  Ps 31:19
  Isa 63:7
  Jer 31:12

CHAP. 9
f 2Ch 8:1
  Ec 2:4
g 2Ch 7:11
h 1Ki 3:5
i De 12:5, 6
  Isa 8:28, 29
j 2Ch 6:40
  2Ch 16:9
  Ps 132:13
k 1Ki 3:6
l Ps 78:70, 72
m 1Ch 29:17
n Ec 12:13
o 2Ch 7:17, 18

Second Col.
a 2Sa 7:16, 17
  1Ki 2:4
  Ps 89:20, 29
b 1Ki 11:4
  2Ch 7:19-22
c Le 18:28
  De 4:26
  2Sa 7:14
  2Ki 17:22, 23
  Ps 89:30-32
d 2Ki 25:9, 10
  2Ch 15:2
e De 28:37
  Ps 44:14
f 2Ch 36:19
  Isa 64:11
g De 29:24, 25
  Jer 22:8, 9
h De 28:64
  Jer 5:19
  Jer 12:7
i 1Ki 6:37-7:1
  2Ch 8:1, 2
j 1Ki 5:1, 7
k 1Ki 5:8

my brother?" So they came to be called the Land of Ca'bul* down to this day. **14** In the meantime, Hi'ram sent to the king 120 talents* of gold.[a]

15 This is the account of those whom King Sol'o·mon conscripted for forced labor[b] to build the house of Jehovah,[c] his own house,* the Mound,*[d] the wall of Jerusalem, Ha'zor,[e] Me·gid'do,[f] and Ge'zer.[g] **16** (Phar'aoh king of Egypt had come up and captured Ge'zer and had burned it with fire, and he had also killed the Ca'naan·ites[h] dwelling in the city. So he gave it as a parting gift* to his daughter,* the wife of Sol'o·mon.) **17** Sol'o·mon built up* Ge'zer, Lower Beth-ho'ron,[j] **18** Ba'al·ath,[k] and Ta'mar in the wilderness, within the land, **19** as well as all of Sol'o·mon's storage cities, the chariot cities,[l] the cities for the horsemen, and whatever Sol'o·mon desired to build in Jerusalem, in Leb'a·non, and in all the land of his dominion. **20** As for all the people who were left from the Am'or·ites, the Hit'tites, the Per'iz·zites, the Hi'vites, and the Jeb'u·sites,[m] who were not part of the people of Israel,[n] **21** their descendants who were left in the land—those whom the Israelites had been unable to devote to destruction—were conscripted by Sol'o·mon for forced labor as slaves until this day.[o] **22** But Sol'o·mon did not make any of the Israelites slaves,[p] for they were his warriors, servants, princes, adjutants, and the chiefs of his charioteers and horsemen.

23 There were 550 chiefs of the deputies who were over the work of Sol'o·mon, the foremen over the people who were doing the work.[a]

24 But Phar'aoh's daughter[b] came up from the City of David[c] to her own house that he had built for her; then he built the Mound.*[d]

25 Three times a year[e] Sol'o·mon offered up burnt sacrifices and communion sacrifices on the altar that he had built for Jehovah,[f] also making sacrificial smoke on the altar, which was before Jehovah, so he completed the house.[g]

26 King Sol'o·mon also made a fleet of ships in E'zi·on-ge'ber,[h] which is by E'loth, on the shore of the Red Sea in the land of E'dom.[i] **27** Hi'ram sent his own servants with the fleet of ships,[j] experienced seamen, to serve along with the servants of Sol'o·mon. **28** They went to O'phir[k] and took from there 420 talents of gold and brought it to King Sol'o·mon.

10 Now the queen of She'ba heard the report about Sol'o·mon in connection with the name of Jehovah,[l] so she came to test him with perplexing questions.*[m] **2** She arrived in Jerusalem with a very impressive entourage,*[n] with camels carrying balsam oil[o] and great quantities of gold and precious stones. She went in to Sol'o·mon and spoke to him about everything that was close to her heart. **3** Sol'o·mon then answered all her questions. There was nothing too difficult for* the king to explain to her.

4 When the queen of She'ba had seen all the wisdom of Sol'o·mon,[p] the house that he built,[q] **5** the food of his table,[r]

CHAP. 9
a 1Ki 10:21
b 1Ki 4:6
  1Ki 5:13
c 1Ki 6:37
d 2Sa 5:9
  1Ki 11:27
  2Ki 12:20
e Jos 19:32, 36
f 1Ki 17:11
  Jg 5:19
  2Ki 9:27
g Jg 1:29
h Jos 16:10
i 1Ki 3:1
j Jos 16:1, 3
  2Ch 8:4-6
k Jos 19:44, 48
  1Ki 4:26
m Nu 13:29
  De 7:1
  Jg 1:21
n 2Ch 8:7-10
o Ge 9:25
p Le 25:39

Second Col.
a 1Ki 5:16
  2Ch 2:18
b 1Ki 3:1
  1Ki 7:8
  2Ch 8:11
c 2Sa 5:9
d 1Ki 9:15
e Ex 23:14
f 2Ch 8:12, 13
g 2Ch 8:36
h De 2:8
i 2Ch 8:17, 18
j 1Ki 5:12
k Ge 10:29
  1Ch 29:3, 4
  Ps 45:9

CHAP. 10
l 1Ki 4:29
m 2Ch 9:1, 2
  Mt 12:42
n Ps 72:10
o 2Ch 25:3, 6
  2Ki 20:13
p 1Ki 3:28
  Ec 12:9
q 2Ch 9:3-8
r 1Ki 4:22

9:13 *Or possibly, "the Land as Good as Nothing." 9:14 *A talent equaled 34.2 kg (1,101 oz t). See App. B14. 9:15 *Or "palace." 9:15, 24 *Or "Millo." A Hebrew term meaning "fill." 9:16 *Or "a wedding gift; a dowry." 9:17 *Or "fortified."

10:1 *Or "with riddles." 10:2 *Or "train." 10:3 *Lit., "nothing hidden from."

the seating of his servants, the table service of his waiters and their attire, his cupbearers, and his burnt sacrifices that he regularly offered up at the house of Jehovah, she was left completely breathless.* 6 So she said to the king: "The report that I heard in my own land about your achievements* and about your wisdom was true. 7 But I did not put faith in the reports until I had come and had seen it with my own eyes. And look! I had not been told the half. You have far surpassed in wisdom and prosperity the report that I heard. 8 Happy are your men, and happy are your servants who stand before you constantly, listening to your wisdom!ᵃ 9 May Jehovah your God be praised,ᵇ who has taken pleasure in you by putting you on the throne of Israel. Because of Jehovah's everlasting love for Israel, he appointed you as king to administer justice and righteousness."

10 Then she gave the king 120 talents* of gold and a great amount of balsam oilᶜ and precious stones.ᵈ Never again was such a quantity of balsam oil brought in as what the queen of She′ba gave to King Sol′o·mon.

11 Hi′ram's fleet of ships that carried gold from O′phirᵉ also brought from O′phir algum timbersᶠ in very great quantity, and precious stones.ᵍ 12 The king made from the algum timbers supports for the house of Jehovah and for the king's house,* as well as harps and stringed instruments for the singers.ʰ Such algum timbers have never again been brought in or seen down to this day.

13 King Sol′o·mon also gave the queen of She′ba whatever she desired and asked for, in addition to what he gave her out of his own generosity.* After that she left and returned to her own land, together with her servants.ᵃ

14 And the weight of the gold that came to Sol′o·mon in one year amounted to 666 talents of gold,ᵇ 15 besides that from the merchants and the profit from the traders and from all the kings of the Arabs and the governors of the land.

16 King Sol′o·mon made 200 large shields of alloyed goldᶜ (600 shekels* of gold went on each shield)ᵈ 17 and 300 bucklers* of alloyed gold (three mi′nasᵘ of gold went on each buckler). Then the king put them in the House of the Forest of Leb′a·non.ᵉ

18 The king also made a great ivory throneᶠ and overlaid it with refined gold.ᵍ 19 There were six steps to the throne, and the throne had a round canopy behind it, and there were armrests on both sides of the seat, and two lionsʰ were standing beside the armrests. 20 And there were 12 lions standing on the six steps, one at each end of the six steps. No other kingdom had made anything like it.

21 All the drinking vessels of King Sol′o·mon were of gold, and all the utensils of the House of the Forest of Leb′a·nonⁱ were of pure gold. There was nothing made of silver, for silver was considered as nothing in the days of Sol′o·mon.ʲ 22 For

CHAP. 10
a Pr 8:34

b 1Ki 5:7

c Ge 43:11

d Ps 72:10

e 1Ki 9:27, 28
Ps 45:9

f 2Ch 2:8

g 2Ch 9:10, 11

h 2Ch 5:12
Ps 150:3

__Second Col.__
a 2Ch 9:12

b 2Ch 9:13, 14

c 1Ki 14:25, 26

d 2Ch 9:15, 16

e 1Ki 7:2

f Ps 122:2, 5

g 2Ch 9:17-19

h Ge 49:9
Nu 23:24
Nu 24:9

i 1Ki 7:2

j 2Ch 9:20, 21

10:5 *Lit., "there was no more spirit in her." 10:6 *Or "words." 10:10 *A talent equaled 34.2 kg (1,101 oz t). See App. B14. 10:12 *Or "palace."

10:13 *Lit., "according to the hand of King Solomon." 10:16 *A shekel equaled 11.4 g (0.367 oz t). See App. B14. 10:17 *A small shield, often carried by archers. ᵘA mina in the Hebrew Scriptures equaled 570 g (18.35 oz t). See App. B14.

the king had a fleet of ships of Tar'shish[a] on the sea along with Hi'ram's fleet. Once every three years, the fleet of ships of Tar'shish would come loaded with gold and silver, ivory,[b] apes, and peacocks.

23 So King Sol'o·mon was greater than all the other kings of the earth in riches[c] and wisdom.[d] 24 And people of all the earth sought an audience with* Sol'o·mon to hear his wisdom that God had put in his heart.[e] 25 They would each bring a gift—articles of silver, articles of gold, garments, armor, balsam oil, horses, and mules—and this continued year after year.

26 And Sol'o·mon kept accumulating chariots and horses;* he had 1,400 chariots and 12,000 horses,*[f] and he kept them stationed in the chariot cities and close to the king in Jerusalem.[g] 27 The king made the silver in Jerusalem as plentiful as the stones, and cedarwood as plentiful as the sycamore trees in the She·phe'lah.[h] 28 The horses of Sol'o·mon had been imported from Egypt, and the company of the king's merchants would obtain the horses in droves* for one price.[i] 29 Each chariot imported from Egypt cost 600 silver pieces, and a horse cost 150; in turn, they would export them to all the kings of the Hit'tites[j] and the kings of Syria.

11 But King Sol'o·mon loved many foreign women[k] besides the daughter of Phar'aoh:[l] Mo'ab·ite,[m] Am'mon·ite,[n] E'dom·ite, Si·do'ni·an,[o] and Hit'tite[p] women. 2 They were from the nations about whom Jehovah

had said to the Israelites: "You must not go in among them,* and they should not come in among you, for they will surely incline your heart to follow their gods."[a] But Sol'o·mon clung to them and loved them. 3 And he had 700 wives who were princesses and 300 concubines, and his wives gradually inclined his heart.* 4 In Sol'o·mon's old age,[b] his wives inclined* his heart to follow other gods,[c] and his heart was not complete with# Jehovah his God like the heart of David his father. 5 And Sol'o·mon followed after Ash'to·reth,[d] the goddess of the Si·do'ni·ans, and Mil'com,[e] the disgusting god of the Am'mon·ites. 6 And Sol'o·mon did what was bad in the eyes of Jehovah, and he did not follow Jehovah completely* as David his father had done.[f]

7 It was then that Sol'o·mon built a high place* to Che'mosh, the disgusting god of Mo'ab, on the mountain in front of Jerusalem and to Mo'lech,[h] the disgusting god of the Am'mon·ites.[i] 8 That was what he did for all his foreign wives who were making sacrificial smoke and sacrificing to their gods.

9 Jehovah became furious at Sol'o·mon, because his heart had inclined away from Jehovah the God of Israel,[j] who had appeared to him twice[k] 10 and had warned him about this very thing, that he should not go after other gods.[l] But he did not obey what Jehovah had commanded. 11 Jehovah now said to Sol'o·mon: "Because you have done this and you have not kept my covenant and my statutes as I commanded you, I will surely

---

CHAP. 10
a Ge 10:4
  Ps 72:10
  Eze 27:12
  Jon 1:3
b 1Ki 10:18
c Ec 5:19
d 1Ki 3:12, 13
  1Ki 4:29
  2Ch 9:22-24
e Pr 2:6
f De 17:15, 16
  1Ki 4:26
g 2Ch 1:14
  2Ch 9:25
h 2Ch 1:15
  2Ch 9:27
i 2Ch 1:16, 17
  2Ch 9:28
j Jos 1:4

CHAP. 11
k De 17:15, 17
  Ne 13:26
l 1Ki 3:1
m Ge 19:36, 37
n 1Ki 14:21
o 1Ki 16:30, 31
p Ge 26:34, 35

Second Col.
a Ex 34:16
  De 7:3
  Jos 23:12, 13
  2Co 6:14
b 1Ki 11:42
c De 7:3, 4
  Ne 13:26
d Jg 2:11, 13
  Jg 10:6
  1Sa 7:3
e Zep 1:5
f 1Ki 15:5
g Le 26:30
  Nu 33:52
  2Ki 21:1, 3
h Le 18:21
  Ac 7:43
i 2Ki 23:13
j De 7:3, 4
  Pr 4:23
k 1Ki 3:5
  1Ki 9:2
l 2Ch 7:19, 20

10:24 *Lit., "sought the face of." 10:26 *Or "horsemen." 10:28 *Or possibly, "from Egypt and from Kue; the king's merchants would buy them from Kue," perhaps referring to Cilicia.

11:2 *Or "You must not intermarry with them." 11:3 *Or "his wives had a powerful influence over him." 11:4 *Or "turned away." #Or "completely devoted to." 11:6 *Lit., "fully."

rip the kingdom away from you, and I will give it to one of your servants.[a] **12** However, for the sake of your father David, I will not do it in your lifetime. I will rip it out of the hand of your son,[b] **13** but I will not rip away the entire kingdom.[c] One tribe I will give to your son,[d] for the sake of David my servant and for the sake of Jerusalem, which I have chosen."[e]

14 Jehovah then raised up a resister against Sol′o·mon,[f] Ha′dad the E′dom·ite, of the royal family of E′dom.[g] **15** When David defeated E′dom,[h] Jo′ab the chief of the army went up to bury the slain, and he tried to strike down every male in E′dom. **16** (For Jo′ab and all Israel stayed there for six months until he had done away with* every male in E′dom.) **17** But Ha′dad fled with some of his father's E′dom·ite servants, and they went to Egypt; Ha′dad was then a young boy. **18** So they set out from Mid′i·an and came to Pa′ran. They took men with them from Pa′ran[i] and came to Egypt, to Phar′aoh king of Egypt, who gave him a house, assigned him a food allowance, and gave him land. **19** Ha′dad found favor in the eyes of Phar′aoh, so much so that he gave him in marriage the sister of his own wife, Tah′pe·nes the queen.* **20** In time the sister of Tah′pe·nes bore him a son, Ge·nu′bath, and Tah′pe·nes brought him up* in the house of Phar′aoh, and Ge·nu′bath remained in the house of Phar′aoh among the sons of Phar′aoh.

21 Ha′dad heard in Egypt that David had been laid to rest with his forefathers[j] and that Jo′ab the chief of the army had died.[k]

So Ha′dad said to Phar′aoh: "Send me away, so that I may go to my own land." **22** But Phar′aoh said to him: "What have you lacked with me that you now seek to go to your own land?" To this he said: "Nothing, but please send me away."

23 God also raised up against Sol′o·mon another resister,[a] Re′zon the son of E·li′a·da, who had fled from his lord, Had·ad·e′zer[b] the king of Zo′bah. **24** He gathered men to himself and became chief of a marauder band when David defeated* them.[c] So they went to Damascus[d] and settled there and began reigning in Damascus. **25** And he became a resister of Israel all the days of Sol′o·mon, adding to the harm done by Ha′dad, and he abhorred Israel while he reigned over Syria.

26 And there was Jer·o·bo′am[e] the son of Ne′bat, an E′phra·im·ite from Zer′e·dah, a servant of Sol′o·mon's[f] whose mother's name was Ze·ru′ah, a widow. He too began to rebel* against the king.[g] **27** This is why he rebelled against the king: Sol′o·mon had built the Mound*[h] and had closed up the gap of the City of David his father.[i] **28** Now this Jer·o·bo′am was a capable man. When Sol′o·mon saw that the young man was a hard worker, he made him overseer[j] over all the compulsory service of the house of Joseph. **29** During that time Jer·o·bo′am went out from Jerusalem, and the prophet A·hi′jah[k] the Shi′lo·nite found him on the road. A·hi′jah was wearing a new garment, and the two of them were by themselves in the field. **30** A·hi′jah took hold of the new garment he was wearing and ripped it

---

CHAP. 11
a 2Ki 17:21

b 2Ch 10:18, 19

c 2Sa 7:12, 15

d 1Ki 12:20
2Ch 11:1

e De 12:11

f 2Sa 7:12, 14

g Ge 27:40

h 2Sa 8:13

i Nu 10:12

j 1Ki 2:10

k 1Ki 2:34

Second Col.
a 1Ki 11:14

b 2Sa 8:3

c 2Sa 10:18

d 2Sa 8:5
1Ki 19:15
Isa 7:8

e 1Ki 11:31
1Ki 12:32
1Ki 14:10
2Ch 11:14
2Ch 13:3, 20

f 1Ki 9:22

g 2Ch 13:6

h 1Ki 9:15, 24

i 2Sa 5:7

j 1Ki 5:16

k 1Ki 12:15
1Ki 14:2
2Ch 9:29

11:16 *Lit., "cut off." 11:19 *Not a ruling queen. 11:20 *Or possibly, "weaned him."

11:24 *Lit., "killed." 11:26 *Lit., "lift his hand." 11:27 *Or "Millo." A Hebrew term meaning "fill."

into 12 pieces. **31** Then he said to Jer·o·bo′am:

"Take ten pieces for yourself, for this is what Jehovah the God of Israel says: 'Here I am ripping the kingdom out of the hand of Sol′o·mon, and I will give you ten tribes.[a] **32** But one tribe will remain his[b] for the sake of my servant David[c] and for the sake of Jerusalem, the city I have chosen out of all the tribes of Israel.[d] **33** I will do this because they have left me[e] and are bowing down to Ash′to·reth the goddess of the Si·do′ni·ans, to Che′mosh the god of Mo′ab, and to Mil′com the god of the Am′monites, and they have not walked in my ways by doing what is right in my eyes and observing my statutes and my judgments as his father David did. **34** But I will not take the entire kingdom out of his hand, and I will keep him as a chieftain for all the days of his life, for the sake of David my servant whom I chose,[f] because he obeyed my commandments and my statutes. **35** But I will take the kingship out of the hand of his son and give it to you, that is, ten tribes.[g] **36** To his son I will give one tribe, so that David my servant may always have a lamp before me in Jerusalem,[h] the city that I have chosen for myself as the place to put my name. **37** I will take you, and you will reign over all that you desire,* and you will become king over Israel. **38** And if you obey all that I command you and walk in my ways and do what is right in my eyes by obeying my statutes and my commandments, just as David my servant did,[i] I will also be with you. I will build you a lasting house, just as I have built for David,[j] and I will give you Israel. **39** And I will humiliate the off-

spring of David because of this,[a] but not always.'"[b]

40 So Sol′o·mon tried to put Jer·o·bo′am to death, but Jer·o·bo′am fled to Egypt, to Shi′shak[c] the king of Egypt,[d] and he remained in Egypt until Sol′o·mon's death.

41 As for the rest of the history of Sol′o·mon, all that he did and his wisdom, is it not written in the book of the history of Sol′o·mon?[e] **42** The length* of Sol′o·mon's reign in Jerusalem over all Israel was 40 years. **43** Then Sol′o·mon was laid to rest with his forefathers and was buried in the City of David his father; and his son Re·ho·bo′am[f] became king in his place.

12 Re·ho·bo′am went to She′chem, for all Israel had come to She′chem[g] to make him king.[h] **2** As soon as Jer·o·bo′am the son of Ne′bat heard of it (he was still in Egypt because he had run off on account of King Sol′o·mon and was living in Egypt),[i] **3** they sent for him. After that Jer·o·bo′am and all the congregation of Israel came to Re·ho·bo′am and said: **4** "Your father made our yoke harsh.[j] But if you make the harsh service of your father easier and you lighten the heavy* yoke he put on us, we will serve you."

5 At this he said to them: "Go away for three days; then return to me." So the people went away.[k] **6** King Re·ho·bo′am then consulted with the older men* who had served his father Sol′o·mon while he was alive, saying: "What advice would you give on how to reply to this people?" **7** They answered him: "If today you would become a servant to this people and submit to their request and give them a favorable answer, they will always be your servants."

CHAP. 11
a 1Ki 12:16

b 1Ki 12:20
2Ch 11:1

c Ge 49:10

d De 12:5, 6
1Ki 11:13
Ps 132:13

e De 28:15
2Ch 15:2

f 1Ki 9:4, 5
Ps 89:49
Ps 132:17
Isa 9:7

g 1Ki 12:20
2Ch 10:16

h 2Sa 7:29
1Ki 15:4
2Ki 8:19

i 1Ki 15:5

j 2Sa 7:11

Second Col.
a 1Ki 12:16

b Ge 49:10
Isa 11:1
Lu 1:32, 33

c 1Ki 14:25

d 2Ch 10:2

e 2Ch 9:29-31

f 1Ch 3:10
2Ch 13:7
Mt 1:7

CHAP. 12
g Ge 12:6
Jos 20:7, 9
Jg 9:1, 2
Ac 7:15, 16

h 2Ch 10:1-4

i 1Ki 11:26, 40

j 1Sa 8:11-18
1Ki 4:7

k 2Ch 10:5-7

11:37 *Or "your soul desires."

11:42 *Lit., "The days." 12:4 *Or "oppressive." 12:6 *Or "the elders."

8 However, he rejected the advice that the older men* gave him, and he consulted with the young men who had grown up with him and who were now his attendants.[a] **9** He asked them: "What advice do you offer on how we should reply to this people who have said to me, 'Make the yoke your father put on us lighter'?" **10** The young men who had grown up with him said to him: "This is what you should say to this people who have said to you, 'Your father made our yoke heavy, but you should make it lighter for us'; this is what you should tell them, 'My little finger will be thicker than my father's hips. **11** My father imposed a heavy yoke on you, but I will add to your yoke. My father punished you with whips, but I will punish you with scourges.'"

12 Jer·o·bo′am and all the people came to Re·ho·bo′am on the third day, just as the king had said: "Return to me on the third day."[b] **13** But the king answered the people harshly, rejecting the advice that the older men* had given him. **14** He spoke to them according to the advice of the young men, saying: "My father made your yoke heavy, but I will add to your yoke. My father punished you with whips, but I will punish you with scourges." **15** So the king did not listen to the people, for this turn of events was caused by Jehovah,[c] in order to carry out the word that Jehovah had spoken through A·hi′jah[d] the Shi′lo·nite to Jer·o·bo′am the son of Ne′bat.

16 When all Israel saw that the king refused to listen to them, the people replied to the king: "What share do we have in David? We have no inheritance in the son of Jes′se. To your gods, O Israel. Now look af-

ter your own house, O David!" With that Israel returned to their homes.*[a] **17** But Re·ho·bo′am continued to reign over the Israelites living in the cities of Judah.[b]

18 Then King Re·ho·bo′am sent A·do′ram,[c] who was in charge of those conscripted for forced labor, but all Israel stoned him to death. King Re·ho·bo′am managed to mount his chariot to flee to Jerusalem.[d] **19** And the Israelites have been in revolt[e] against the house of David down to this day.

20 As soon as all Israel heard that Jer·o·bo′am had returned, they summoned him to the assembly and made him king over all Israel.[f] None of the people followed the house of David except the tribe of Judah.[g]

21 When Re·ho·bo′am arrived in Jerusalem, he immediately congregated all the house of Judah and the tribe of Benjamin, 180,000 trained* warriors, to fight against the house of Israel in order to restore the kingship to Re·ho·bo′am the son of Sol′o·mon.[h] **22** Then the word of the true God came to She·mai′ah[i] the man of the true God, saying: **23** "Say to Re·ho·bo′am the son of Sol′o·mon the king of Judah and to all the house of Judah and Benjamin and the rest of the people, **24** 'This is what Jehovah says: "You must not go up and fight against your Israelite brothers. Each one of you must return to his house, for I have caused this to happen."'" So they obeyed the word of Jehovah and went back home, as Jehovah had told them.

25 Jer·o·bo′am then built up* She′chem[k] in the mountainous region of E′phra·im and lived there. From there he went out

---

CHAP. 12

a 2Ch 10:8-11

b 2Ch 10:12-15

c De 2:30
2Ch 22:7
Ro 9:18

d 1Ki 11:31

Second Col.

a 2Ch 10:16, 17

b 1Ki 11:12, 13
2Ch 11:13, 16

c 2Sa 20:24
1Ki 4:6
1Ki 5:13, 14

d 2Ch 10:18, 19

e 2Ki 17:21

f 1Ki 11:30, 31

g 1Ki 11:12, 13
Ho 11:12

h 2Ch 11:1-4
2Ch 25:5

i 2Ch 12:5

j 1Ki 11:30, 31

k 1Ki 12:1

12:8, 13 *Or "the elders." 12:16 *Lit., "tents." 12:21 *Lit., "chosen." 12:25 *Or "fortified."

and built up* Pe·nu'el.[a] **26** Jer·o·bo'am said in his heart: "Now the kingdom will return to the house of David.[b] **27** If this people continues to go up to offer sacrifices at the house of Jehovah in Jerusalem,[c] the heart of this people will also return to their lord, King Re·ho·bo'am of Judah. Yes, they will kill me and return to King Re·ho·bo'am of Judah." **28** After consultation, the king made two golden calves[d] and said to the people: "It is too much for you to go up to Jerusalem. Here is your God, O Israel, who brought you up out of the land of Egypt."[e] **29** Then he placed one in Beth'el,[f] and the other he put in Dan.[g] **30** And this caused them to sin,[h] and the people went as far as Dan to worship the one there.

31 And he made houses of worship on the high places and appointed priests from the people in general, those who were not Levites.[i] **32** Jer·o·bo'am also established a festival in the eighth month, on the 15th day of the month, like the festival in Judah.[j] On the altar that he made at Beth'el,[k] he sacrificed to the calves he had made, and at Beth'el he assigned priests for the high places that he had made. **33** And he began to make offerings on the altar that he had made at Beth'el on the 15th day in the eighth month, in the month that he had devised on his own; and he established a festival for the people of Israel, and he ascended the altar to make offerings and sacrificial smoke.

13 By the word of Jehovah, a man of God[l] came from Judah to Beth'el while Jer·o·bo'am was standing by the altar[m] to make sacrificial smoke. **2** Then he called out against the altar

by the word of Jehovah and said: "O altar, altar! This is what Jehovah says: 'Look! A son named Jo·si'ah[a] will be born to the house of David! He will sacrifice on you the priests of the high places, those making sacrificial smoke on you, and he will burn human bones on you.'"[b] **3** He gave a sign* on that day, saying: "This is the sign* that Jehovah has declared: Look! The altar will be ripped apart, and the ashes[#] that are on it will be spilled out."

4 As soon as the king heard the word that the man of the true God had called out against the altar at Beth'el, Jer·o·bo'am stretched out his hand from the altar and said: "Seize him!"[c] Immediately, the hand that he had stretched out against him dried up,* and he could not draw it back.[d] **5** Then the altar was ripped apart and the ashes were spilled out from the altar according to the sign* that the man of the true God had given by the word of Jehovah.

6 The king now said to the man of the true God: "Please, beg for the favor* of Jehovah your God, and pray in my behalf that my hand may be restored to me."[e] At this the man of the true God begged for the favor of Jehovah, and the king's hand was restored to its former condition. **7** The king then said to the man of the true God: "Come home with me and take some food, and let me give you a gift." **8** But the man of the true God said to the king: "Even if you gave me half your house, I would not come with you and eat bread or drink water in this place. **9** For this is what I was commanded by

CHAP. 12
a Ge 32:30
  Jg 8:13, 17

b 1Ki 11:38

c De 12:5, 6

d Ex 20:4
  2Ki 10:29

e Ex 32:4, 8
  2Ch 11:15, 16

f Ge 12:8, 9
  Ge 28:19

g Ge 14:14
  De 34:1
  Jg 18:29
  Jg 20:1

h 2Ki 10:31
  2Ki 17:21-23

i Nu 3:10
  1Ki 13:33
  2Ch 11:14
  2Ch 13:9

j Le 23:34

k Am 7:13

CHAP. 13
l 2Ki 23:16, 17

m 1Ki 12:32
  Am 3:14

Second Col.
a 2Ki 21:24
  2Ki 22:1

b 2Ki 23:15, 16
  2Ch 34:33

c 2Ch 16:10
  Jer 20:2

d 2Ki 6:18

e Ex 10:16, 17
  Nu 21:7
  Jer 37:3
  Ac 8:24

12:25 *Or "fortified."

13:3, 5 *Or "portent." **13:3** #Or "fatty ashes," that is, ashes soaked with the fat of the sacrifices. **13:4** *Or "was paralyzed." **13:6** *Or "soften the face."

the word of Jehovah: 'You must not eat bread or drink water, and you must not return by the way you came.'" **10** So he left by another way, and he did not return by the way he had come to Beth'el.

11 There was a certain old prophet dwelling in Beth'el, and his sons came home and related to him all the things that the man of the true God had done that day in Beth'el and the words he had spoken to the king. After they related this to their father, **12** their father asked them: "Which way did he go?" So his sons showed him the way that the man of the true God from Judah had gone. **13** He now said to his sons: "Saddle the donkey for me." They saddled the donkey for him, and he mounted it.

14 He followed the man of the true God and found him sitting under a big tree. Then he said to him: "Are you the man of the true God who came from Judah?"[a] He replied: "I am." **15** He said to him: "Come home with me and eat bread." **16** But he said: "I cannot go back with you or accept your invitation, nor may I eat bread or drink water with you in this place. **17** For I was told by the word of Jehovah, 'You must not eat bread or drink water there. You must not return by the way you came.'" **18** At this he said to him: "I too am a prophet like you, and an angel told me by the word of Jehovah, 'Have him come back with you to your house so that he may eat bread and drink water.'" (He deceived him.) **19** So he went back with him to eat bread and drink water in his house.

20 While they were sitting at the table, the word of Jehovah came to the prophet who had brought him back, **21** and he called out to the man of the true God from Judah, saying, "This

is what Jehovah says: 'Because you rebelled against the order of Jehovah and did not keep the commandment that Jehovah your God gave you, **22** but you went back to eat bread and drink water in the place about which you were told, "Do not eat bread or drink water," your dead body will not come into the tomb of your forefathers.'"[a]

23 After the man of the true God ate bread and drank, the old prophet saddled the donkey for the prophet whom he had brought back. **24** Then he got on his way, but a lion came across him on the road and killed him.[b] His dead body was thrown onto the road, and the donkey stood beside it; the lion was also standing beside the dead body. **25** There were men passing by who saw the dead body thrown onto the road and the lion standing beside the dead body. They came in and told about it in the city where the old prophet lived.

26 When the prophet who had brought him back from the road heard of it, he immediately said: "It is the man of the true God who rebelled against the order of Jehovah;[c] so Jehovah gave him over to the lion, to maul and to kill him, according to the word of Jehovah that he spoke to him."[d] **27** He then said to his sons: "Saddle the donkey for me." So they saddled it. **28** Then he went on his way and found the dead body thrown onto the road, with the donkey and the lion standing beside it. The lion had not eaten the dead body, nor had it mauled the donkey. **29** The prophet lifted up the dead body of the man of the true God and put him on the donkey, and he brought him back into his own city to mourn and bury him. **30** So he laid the dead body in his own tomb, and

---

CHAP. 13
a 1Ki 13:1

Second Col.
a 1Ki 13:30
  2Ki 23:17, 18

b 2Sa 6:7
  1Ki 20:35, 36
  2Ki 17:25

c 1Ki 13:9

d 1Ki 13:21, 22

they kept crying out over him: "Too bad, my brother!" **31** After burying him, he told his sons: "When I die, you must bury me in the place where the man of the true God is buried. Lay my bones next to his bones.ᵃ **32** The word that he called out by the word of Jehovah against the altar in Beth'el and against all the houses of worship on the high placesᵇ in the cities of Sa-mar'i·a is sure to take place."ᶜ

33 Even after this happened, Jer·o·bo'am did not turn back from his bad way, but he kept appointing priests for the high places for the people in general.ᵈ He would install as priests* anyone who so desired, saying: "Let him become one of the priests for the high places."ᵉ **34** This sin on the part of the household of Jer·o·bo'amᶠ led to their destruction and annihilation from the face of the earth.ᵍ

14 At that time A·bi'jah the son of Jer·o·bo'am fell sick. **2** So Jer·o·bo'am said to his wife: "Rise up, please, and disguise yourself so that they will not know that you are Jer·o·bo'am's wife, and go to Shi'-loh. Look! A·hi'jah the prophet is there. He is the one who spoke of me becoming king over this people.ʰ **3** Take with you ten loaves of bread, sprinkled cakes, and a flask of honey, and go to him. He will then tell you what is going to happen to the boy."

4 Jer·o·bo'am's wife did what he said. She rose up and went to Shi'lohⁱ and came to the house of A·hi'jah. A·hi'jah's eyes stared straight ahead, and he could not see because of his age.

5 But Jehovah had told A·hi'-jah: "Here is the wife of Jer·o·bo'am coming to inquire of you regarding her son, for he is sick.

I will tell you what to say to her.* When she arrives, she will conceal her identity."

6 As soon as A·hi'jah heard the sound of her footsteps as she was coming into the entrance, he said: "Come in, wife of Jer·o·bo'am. Why are you concealing your identity? I have been assigned to give you a harsh message. **7** Go, tell Jer·o·bo'am, 'This is what Jehovah the God of Israel says: "I raised you up from among your people to make you a leader over my people Israel.ᵃ **8** Then I ripped the kingdom away from the house of David and gave it to you.ᵇ But you have not become like my servant David, who kept my commandments and who walked after me with all his heart, doing only what was right in my eyes.ᶜ **9** But you have done worse than all those who were prior to you, and you made for yourself another god and metal images* to offend me,ᵈ and it is I whom you have turned your back on.ᵉ **10** For that reason I am bringing calamity on the house of Jer·o·bo'am, and I will annihilate* from Jer·o·bo'am every male,* including the helpless and weak in Israel, and I will make a clean sweep of the house of Jer·o·bo'am,ᶠ just as one clears away the dung until it is all gone! **11** Anyone belonging to Jer·o·bo'am who dies in the city, the dogs will eat; and anyone who dies in the field, the birds of the heavens will eat, for Jehovah has spoken it."'

12 "Now rise up; go to your house. When you set foot in the city, the child will die. **13** All

---

CHAP. 13

a 2Ki 23:17, 18

b Le 26:30
1Ki 12:29, 31

c 2Ki 23:15, 19

d 1Ki 12:25, 31

e 2Ch 11:14, 15

f 1Ki 16:30, 31
2Ki 3:1, 3
2Ki 10:31
2Ki 13:1, 2

g 1Ki 14:10
1Ki 15:25-29
2Ki 17:22, 23

CHAP. 14

h 1Ki 11:30, 31

i Jos 18:1
1Sa 4:3

Second Col.

a 1Ki 11:30, 31
1Ki 12:20

b 1Ki 12:16

c 1Ki 15:5
Ac 13:22

d De 27:15
2Ch 11:15

e Ne 9:26
Ps 50:17

f 1Ki 15:25-29

13:33 *Lit., "fill the hand of."

14:5 *Or "You should tell her such and such." 14:9 *Or "molten statues." 14:10 *Lit., "cut off." *Lit., "anyone urinating against a wall." A Hebrew expression of contempt referring to males.

Israel will mourn him and bury him, for he alone of Jer·o·bo'am's family will be laid in a grave, because he is the only one of the house of Jer·o·bo'am in whom Jehovah the God of Israel has found something good. **14** Jehovah will raise up for himself a king over Israel who will do away with* the house of Jer·o·bo'am[a] from that day forward, yes, even now. **15** Jehovah will strike Israel down like a reed that sways in the water, and he will uproot Israel off this good land that he gave to their forefathers,[b] and he will scatter them beyond the River,*[c] because they made their sacred poles,*[d] offending Jehovah. **16** And he will abandon Israel because of the sins that Jer·o·bo'am has committed and has caused Israel to commit."[e]

17 At that Jer·o·bo'am's wife rose up and went on her way and came to Tir'zah. As she came to the threshold of the house, the boy died. **18** So they buried him, and all Israel mourned him, according to Jehovah's word that he had spoken through his servant A·hi'jah the prophet.

19 And the rest of the history of Jer·o·bo'am, how he waged war[f] and how he reigned, is written in the book of the history of the times of the kings of Israel. **20** And the length* of Jer·o·bo'am's reign was 22 years, after which he was laid to rest with his forefathers;[g] and his son Na'dab became king in his place.[h]

21 Meanwhile, Re·ho·bo'am the son of Sol'o·mon had become king in Judah. Re·ho·bo'am was 41 years old when he became king, and he reigned for 17 years in Jerusalem, the city that Jehovah had chosen[i] out

of all the tribes of Israel as the place to put his name.[a] The name of Re·ho·bo'am's mother was Na'a·mah the Am'mon·it·ess.[b] **22** And Judah was doing what was bad in the eyes of Jehovah,[c] and by the sins they committed they provoked him more than their forefathers had done.[d] **23** They too kept building for themselves high places, sacred pillars, and sacred poles*[e] on every high hill[f] and under every luxuriant tree.[g] **24** There were also male temple prostitutes in the land.[h] They acted according to all the detestable things of the nations that Jehovah had driven out before the Israelites.

25 In the fifth year of King Re·ho·bo'am, King Shi'shak[i] of Egypt came up against Jerusalem.[j] **26** He took the treasures of the house of Jehovah and the treasures of the king's house.*[k] He took everything, including all the gold shields that Sol'o·mon had made.[l] **27** So King Re·ho·bo'am made copper shields to replace them, and he entrusted them to the chiefs of the guard,* who guarded the entrance of the king's house. **28** Whenever the king came to the house of Jehovah, the guards would carry them, and then they would return them to the guard chamber.

29 And the rest of the history of Re·ho·bo'am, all that he did, is it not written in the book of the history of the times of the kings of Judah?[m] **30** There was constant warfare between Re·ho·bo'am and Jer·o·bo'am.[n] **31** Then Re·ho·bo'am was laid to rest with his forefathers and was buried with his forefathers in the City of David.[o] His mother's name was Na'a·mah the

---

CHAP. 14

a 1Ki 15:25-29

b De 8:7-9
De 29:28
Jos 23:15
2Ki 17:6

c De 28:64
2Ki 15:29
2Ki 18:11

d De 12:3

e 1Ki 12:28-30
1Ki 13:33, 34

f 2Ch 12:15
2Ch 13:3

g 2Ch 13:20

h 1Ki 15:25

i Ps 78:68
Ps 132:13

Second Col.

a Ex 20:24
De 12:5, 6
1Ki 8:16, 17

b 1Ki 11:1
2Ch 12:13

c 1Ki 11:7
2Ch 12:1

d Isa 65:2

e Le 26:1

f Isa 65:7

g De 12:2, 3
Isa 57:5
Jer 2:20
Ho 4:13

h De 23:17, 18
1Ki 15:11, 12
1Ki 22:46
2Ki 23:7
Ho 4:14

i 1Ki 11:40

j 2Ch 12:2-4

k 1Ki 7:51
1Ki 15:18
2Ki 18:14, 15
2Ki 24:12, 13

l 1Ki 10:16, 17
2Ch 12:9-11

m 1Ch 27:24
2Ch 12:15

n 1Ki 15:6

o 1Ki 11:43

14:14 *Lit., "cut off." **14:15** *That is, the Euphrates. **14:15, 23** #See Glossary. **14:20** *Lit., "days."

14:26 *Or "palace." **14:27** *Lit., "runners."

Am′mon·it·ess.ᵃ And his son A·bi′jam*ᵇ became king in his place.

15 In the 18th year of King Jer·o·bo′amᶜ the son of Ne′bat, A·bi′jam became king over Judah.ᵈ 2 He reigned for three years in Jerusalem. His mother's name was Ma′a·cahᵉ the granddaughter of A·bish′a·lom. 3 He went on walking in all the sins that his father committed prior to him, and his heart was not complete with* Jehovah his God like the heart of David his forefather. 4 However, on account of David,ᶠ Jehovah his God gave him a lamp in Jerusalemᵍ by raising up his son after him and keeping Jerusalem in existence. 5 For David did what was right in the eyes of Jehovah, and he did not turn aside from anything that He had commanded him all the days of his life, except in the matter of U·ri′ah the Hit′tite.ʰ 6 And there was warfare between Re·ho·bo′am and Jer·o·bo′am all the days of his life.ⁱ

7 As for the rest of the history of A·bi′jam, all that he did, is it not written in the book of the history of the times of the kings of Judah?ʲ There was also war between A·bi′jam and Jer·o·bo′am.ᵏ 8 Then A·bi′jam was laid to rest with his forefathers, and they buried him in the City of David; and his son A′saˡ became king in his place.ᵐ

9 In the 20th year of King Jer·o·bo′am of Israel, A′sa began to reign over Judah. 10 He reigned in Jerusalem for 41 years. His grandmother's name was Ma′a·cahⁿ the granddaughter of A·bish′a·lom. 11 A′sa did what was right in the eyes of Jehovah,ᵒ like David his forefather. 12 He expelled

the male temple prostitutes from the landᵃ and removed all the disgusting idols* that his forefathers had made.ᵇ 13 He even removed Ma′a·cahᶜ his grandmother from her position as queen mother,* because she had made an obscene idol for the worship of the sacred pole.# A′sa cut down her obscene idolᵈ and burned it in the Kid′ron Valley.ᵉ 14 But the high places were not removed.ᶠ Nevertheless, A′sa's heart was complete with* Jehovah all his life.# 15 And he brought the things that he and his father had made holy into the house of Jehovah —silver, gold, and various utensils.ᵍ

16 There was constant warfare between A′sa and Ba′a·shaʰ the king of Israel. 17 So King Ba′a·sha of Israel came up against Judah and began to build up* Ra′mahⁱ to prevent anyone from going out or coming in to# King A′sa of Judah.ʲ 18 At that A′sa took all the silver and the gold that were left in the treasuries of the house of Jehovah and the treasuries of the house* of the king and handed them over to his servants. King A′sa then sent them to Ben-ha′dad the son of Tab·rim′mon the son of He′zi·on, the king of Syria,ᵏ who was dwelling in Damascus, saying: 19 "There is a treaty* between me and you and between my father and your father. I am sending you a gift of silver and gold. Come, break your treaty* with King Ba′a·sha of Israel, so that he will withdraw from me." 20 Ben-

CHAP. 14
a 1Ki 11:1
2Ch 12:13

b 1Ch 3:10
Mt 1:7

CHAP. 15
c 1Ki 12:20

d 2Ch 13:1, 2

e 2Ch 11:20-22

f 2Sa 7:8, 12
Ps 89:33-37
Isa 37:35
Jer 33:20, 21

g 1Ki 11:36
2Ch 21:7
Ps 132:13, 17

h 2Sa 11:4, 15
Ps 51:Sup

i 1Ki 14:30
2Ch 12:15

j 2Ch 13:3

k 2Ch 13:3
1Ch 3:10
Mt 1:7

m 2Ch 14:1

n 2Ch 11:21, 22

o 2Ch 14:2-5
2Ch 14:11
2Ch 15:17

Second Col.
a De 23:17, 18
1Ki 14:24
1Ki 22:45, 46

b 1Ki 11:7
1Ki 14:22, 23

c 2Ch 11:18, 20

d De 7:5
2Ki 18:1, 4
2Ch 34:1, 4

e 2Sa 15:23
2Ch 15:16-18
Joh 18:1

f Nu 33:52
De 12:2
1Ki 22:41, 43

g 1Ch 26:26, 27

h 1Ki 16:3, 12

i Jos 18:21, 25

j 2Ch 16:1-6

k 2Ch 16:7

15:12 *The Hebrew term may be related to a word for "dung" and is used as an expression of contempt. 15:13 *Or "as lady." #See Glossary. 15:14 *Or "was completely devoted to." #Lit., "days." 15:17 *Or "fortify; rebuild." #Or "leaving or entering the territory of." 15:18 *Or "palace." 15:19 *Or "covenant."

14:31 *Also called Abijah. 15:3 *Or "not completely devoted to."

ha'dad listened to King A'sa and sent the chiefs of his armies against the cities of Israel, and they struck down I'jon,[a] Dan,[b] A'bel-beth-ma'a·cah, all Chin'ne·reth, and all the land of Naph'ta·li. **21** When Ba'a·sha heard of it, he immediately quit building* Ra'mah and continued dwelling in Tir'zah.[c] **22** King A'sa then summoned all Judah—no one was exempt—and they carried off the stones and timbers of Ra'mah that Ba'a·sha had been building with, and with them King A'sa built up* Ge'ba[d] in Benjamin, and Miz'pah.[e]

23 As for all the rest of the history of A'sa, all his mightiness and all that he did and the cities that he built,* is it not written in the book of the history of the times of the kings of Judah? But in his old age he suffered from a disease in his feet.[f] **24** Then A'sa was laid to rest with his forefathers and was buried with them in the City of David his forefather; and his son Je·hosh'a·phat[g] became king in his place.

25 Na'dab[h] the son of Jer·o·bo'am became king over Israel in the second year of King A'sa of Judah, and he reigned over Israel for two years. **26** He kept doing what was bad in the eyes of Jehovah and walked in the way of his father[i] and in his sin that he caused Israel to commit.[j] **27** Ba'a·sha the son of A·hi'jah of the house of Is'sa·char conspired against him, and Ba'a·sha struck him down at Gib'be·thon,[k] which belonged to the Phi·lis'tines, while Na'dab and all Israel were besieging Gib'be·thon. **28** So Ba'a·sha put him to death in the third year of King A'sa of Judah and became king in his place. **29** And as soon as he be-

came king, he struck down all the house of Jer·o·bo'am. He did not let remain anyone breathing who belonged to Jer·o·bo'am; he had them annihilated according to Jehovah's word that he had spoken through his servant A·hi'jah the Shi'lo·nite.[a] **30** This was because of the sins that Jer·o·bo'am had committed and had caused Israel to commit and because he had greatly offended Jehovah the God of Israel. **31** As for the rest of the history of Na'dab, all that he did, is it not written in the book of the history of the times of the kings of Israel? **32** And there was constant warfare between A'sa and King Ba'a·sha of Israel.[b]

33 In the third year of King A'sa of Judah, Ba'a·sha the son of A·hi'jah became king in Tir'zah over all Israel and reigned for 24 years.[c] **34** But he kept doing what was bad in the eyes of Jehovah,[d] and he walked in the way of Jer·o·bo'am and in his sin that he caused Israel to commit.[e]

16 The word of Jehovah against Ba'a·sha then came to Je'hu[f] the son of Ha·na'ni,[g] saying: **2** "I raised you up out of the dust and made you leader over my people Israel,[h] but you kept walking in the way of Jer·o·bo'am and caused my people Israel to sin so that they offended me with their sins.[i] **3** So I am making a clean sweep of Ba'a·sha and his house, and I will make his house like the house of Jer·o·bo'am[the son of Ne'bat. **4** Anyone belonging to Ba'a·sha who dies in the city the dogs will eat; and anyone belonging to him who dies in the field the birds of the heavens will eat."

5 As for the rest of the history of Ba'a·sha, what he did and his mightiness, is it not written

---

CHAP. 15
a 2Ki 15:29

b Jg 18:29
  1Ki 12:28, 29

c 1Ki 14:17
  Ca 6:4

d Jos 21:8, 17

e Jos 18:21, 26
  Jg 20:1
  1Sa 7:5
  Jer 40:6

f 2Ch 16:11-14

g 1Ki 22:42
  2Ch 17:3, 4
  2Ch 18:1
  2Ch 19:4
  Mt 1:8

h 1Ki 14:20

i 1Ki 14:7, 9

j 1Ki 12:28-30
  1Ki 13:33

k Jos 19:44, 48
  Jos 21:20, 23
  1Ki 16:15

Second Col.
a 1Ki 14:9, 10

b 2Ch 12:15

c 1Ki 16:8

d 1Ki 16:7

e 1Ki 12:28-30
  1Ki 13:33

CHAP. 16
f 2Ch 19:2
  2Ch 20:34

g 2Ch 16:7

h 1Sa 2:8

i 1Ki 13:33

j 1Ki 14:10, 11
  1Ki 15:29

in the book of the history of the times of the kings of Israel? **6** Then Ba'a·sha was laid to rest with his forefathers and was buried in Tir'zah;[a] and E'lah his son became king in his place. **7** Also through the prophet Je'hu the son of Ha·na'ni, Jehovah's word came against Ba'a·sha and his house, both because of all the badness that he committed in the eyes of Jehovah by offending him with the work of his hands, becoming like the house of Jer·o·bo'am, and also because of his striking him* down.[b]

8 In the 26th year of King A'sa of Judah, E'lah the son of Ba'a·sha became king over Israel in Tir'zah, and he reigned for two years. **9** His servant Zim'ri, the chief of half of his chariot forces, conspired against him while he was in Tir'zah drinking himself drunk at the house of Ar'za, who was over the household in Tir'zah. **10** Zim'ri came in and struck him down[c] and put him to death in the 27th year of King A'sa of Judah, and he became king in his place. **11** When he became king, as soon as he sat down on his throne, he struck down all the house of Ba'a·sha. He did not spare a single male,* whether of his relatives* or of his friends. **12** Thus Zim'ri annihilated the whole house of Ba'a·sha, according to the word that Jehovah had spoken against Ba'a·sha through Je'hu the prophet.[d] **13** This was for all the sins that Ba'a·sha and his son E'lah had committed and the sins they had caused Israel to commit by offending Jehovah the God of Israel with their worthless idols.[e]

14 As for the rest of the history of E'lah, all that he did, is it not written in the book of the history of the times of the kings of Israel?

15 In the 27th year of King A'sa of Judah, Zim'ri became king for seven days in Tir'zah while the troops were camped against Gib'be·thon,[a] which belonged to the Phi·lis'tines. **16** In time the troops who were encamped heard it being said: "Zim'ri has conspired and has also struck down the king." So all Israel made Om'ri,[b] the chief of the army, king over Israel on that day in the camp. **17** Om'ri and all Israel with him went up from Gib'be·thon and laid siege to Tir'zah. **18** When Zim'ri saw that the city had been captured, he went into the fortified tower of the king's house* and burned the house down over himself, and he died.[c] **19** This was for his own sins that he had committed by doing what was bad in the eyes of Jehovah by walking in the way of Jer·o·bo'am and for the sin he had caused Israel to commit.[d] **20** As for the rest of the history of Zim'ri and his conspiracy, is it not written in the book of the history of the times of the kings of Israel?

21 It was then that the people of Israel were divided into two factions. One part of the people became followers of Tib'ni the son of Gi'nath, wanting to make him king, and the other part followed Om'ri. **22** But the people who were following Om'ri prevailed over the people following Tib'ni the son of Gi'nath. So Tib'ni died, and Om'ri became king.

23 In the 31st year of King A'sa of Judah, Om'ri became king over Israel, and he reigned for 12 years. In Tir'zah he reigned for six years. **24** He

---

16:7 *That is, Nadab, the son of Jeroboam. **16:11** *Lit., "anyone urinating against a wall." A Hebrew expression of contempt referring to males. #Or "his avengers of blood."

16:18 *Or "palace."

CHAP. 16
a 1Ki 15:21, 33

b 1Ki 15:25-29

c 2Ki 9:31

d 1Ki 16:1-3

e De 32:21
1Sa 12:21
2Ki 17:15
Isa 41:29

Second Col.
a Jos 19:44, 48
Jos 21:20, 23
1Ki 15:27

b 2Ki 8:26
Mic 6:16

c Jg 9:53, 54
1Sa 31:4
2Sa 17:23

d 1Ki 12:28-30
1Ki 14:7, 9

bought the mountain of Sa·mar'i·a from She'mer for two talents* of silver, and he built a city on the mountain. He named the city that he built Sa·mar'i·a,#ª after She'mer the ownerᵃ of the mountain. 25 Om'ri kept doing what was bad in the eyes of Jehovah, and he was worse than all who were prior to him.ᵇ 26 He walked in all the ways of Jer·o·bo'am the son of Ne'bat and in the sin he had caused Israel to commit by offending Jehovah the God of Israel with their worthless idols.ᶜ 27 As for the rest of the history of Om'ri, what he did and his mighty exploits, is it not written in the book of the history of the times of the kings of Israel? 28 Then Om'ri was laid to rest with his forefathers and was buried in Sa·mar'i·a; and his son A'habᵈ became king in his place.

29 A'hab the son of Om'ri became king over Israel in the 38th year of King A'sa of Judah, and A'hab the son of Om'ri reigned over Israel in Sa·mar'i·aᵉ for 22 years. 30 A'hab the son of Om'ri was worse in the eyes of Jehovah than all those who were prior to him.ᶠ 31 As if it were a trivial thing for him to walk in the sins of Jer·o·bo'amᵍ the son of Ne'bat, he also took as wife Jez'e·belʰ the daughter of Eth·ba'al, the king of the Si·do'ni·ans,ⁱ and began to serve Ba'alʲ and to bow down to him. 32 Further, he set up an altar to Ba'al at the house* of Ba'alᵏ that he built in Sa·mar'i·a. 33 A'hab also made the sacred pole.*ˡ A'hab did more to offend Jehovah the God of Israel than all the kings of Israel prior to him.

34 In his days, Hi'el the Beth'el·ite rebuilt Jer'i·cho. At the cost of A·bi'ram his firstborn he laid its foundation, and at the cost of Se'gub his youngest he put up its doors, according to the word of Jehovah spoken through Joshua the son of Nun.ᵃ

17 Now E·li'jah*ᵇ the Tish'bite, an inhabitant of Gil'e·ad,ᶜ said to A'hab: "As surely as Jehovah the God of Israel whom I serve# is living, during these years there will be no dew or rain except by my word!"ᵈ

2 The word of Jehovah came to him, saying: 3 "Leave here, and turn eastward and hide at the Valley of Che'rith,* east of the Jordan. 4 You should drink from the stream, and I will command the ravens to supply you food there."ᵉ 5 He immediately went and did according to the word of Jehovah; he went and stayed by the Valley of Che'rith,* east of the Jordan. 6 And the ravens were bringing him bread and meat in the morning and bread and meat in the evening, and he drank from the stream.ᶠ 7 But after some days, the stream ran dry,ᵍ because there was no rain in the land.

8 The word of Jehovah then came to him: 9 "Rise up, go to Zar'e·phath, which belongs to Si'don, and stay there. Look! I will command a widow there to supply you with food."ʰ 10 So he rose up and went to Zar'e·phath. When he came to the entrance of the city, there was a widow gathering pieces of wood. So he called to her and said: "Please, bring me a little water in a cup so that I may drink."ⁱ 11 As she went to get it, he called to her: "Please, bring me a piece of bread in your hand."

CHAP. 16
a 1Ki 20:1
  2Ki 17:24
  Am 6:1
  Ac 8:5

b Mic 6:16

c 1Ki 12:28-30
  1Ki 13:33

d 1Ki 16:33
  1Ki 21:4
  1Ki 21:20-22
  2Ki 10:1

e 1Ki 16:23, 24
  Isa 7:9

f 1Ki 16:25
  1Ki 21:25
  2Ki 3:1, 2

g 1Ki 12:28-30

h 1Ki 18:4, 19
  1Ki 21:7
  2Ki 9:30
  Re 2:20

i Ge 10:15

j Jg 2:11
  Jg 10:6
  2Ki 10:19
  2Ki 17:16

k 2Ki 10:21, 27

l Ex 34:13
  2Ki 10:26, 28
  2Ki 13:6

Second Col.
a Jos 6:26

CHAP. 17
b 1Ki 17:15, 16
  1Ki 17:22, 24
  1Ki 18:36, 38
  1Ki 18:46
  2Ki 2:8, 11
  Lu 1:17
  Joh 1:19, 21

c Jos 22:9

d De 28:15, 23
  Jer 14:22
  Lu 4:25
  Jas 5:17

e Ps 37:25
  Mt 6:11

f Nu 11:23
  Jg 15:19

g 1Ki 18:5

h Lu 4:25, 26

i Heb 11:32, 37

16:24 *A talent equaled 34.2 kg (1,101 oz t). See App. B14. #Meaning "Belonging to the Clan Shemer." ᵃLit., "lord." 16:32 *Or "temple." 16:33 *See Glossary.

17:1 *Meaning "My God Is Jehovah." #Lit., "before whom I stand." 17:3, 5 *Or "Wadi Cherith."

12 At this she said: "As surely as Jehovah your God is living, I have no bread, only a handful of flour in the large jar and a little oil in the small jar.ᵃ Now I am gathering a few pieces of wood, and I will go in and make something for me and my son. After we have eaten, we will die."

13 Then E·li′jah said to her: "Do not be afraid. Go in and do as you said. But first make me a small round loaf of bread with what is there, and bring it out to me. Then you can make something afterward for you and your son. **14** For this is what Jehovah the God of Israel says: 'The large jar of flour will not run out, and the small jar of oil will not run dry until the day Jehovah makes it rain on the surface of the ground.'"ᵇ **15** So she went and did as E·li′jah said, and she together with him and her household ate for many days.ᶜ **16** The large jar of flour did not run out, and the small jar of oil did not run dry, according to Jehovah's word that he had spoken through E·li′jah.

17 After these things, the son of the woman who owned the house fell sick, and his sickness became so severe that he stopped breathing.ᵈ **18** At this she said to E·li′jah: "What do you have against me,* O man of the true God? Have you come to remind me of my guilt and to put my son to death?"ᵉ **19** But he said to her: "Give me your son." Then he took him from her arms and carried him up to the roof chamber, where he was staying, and he laid him on his own bed.ᶠ **20** He called out to Jehovah: "O Jehovah my God,ᵍ are you also bringing harm to the widow with whom I am staying by putting her son to

death?" **21** Then he stretched himself out over the child three times and called out to Jehovah: "O Jehovah my God, please, let this child's life* come back into him." **22** Jehovah listened to E·li′jah's request,ᵃ and the life* of the child came back into him, and he revived.*ᵇ **23** E·li′jah took the child and brought him down from the roof chamber into the house and gave him to his mother; and E·li′jah said: "See, your son is alive."ᶜ **24** At that the woman said to E·li′jah: "Now I know that you truly are a man of Godᵈ and that Jehovah's word in your mouth is truth."

18 After some time, in the third year,ᵉ Jehovah's word came to E·li′jah, saying: "Go, present yourself to A′hab, and I will send rain on the surface of the ground."ᶠ **2** So E·li′jah went to present himself to A′hab, while the famine was severeᵍ in Sa·mar′i·a.

3 Meanwhile, A′hab called O·ba·di′ah, who was over the household. (Now O·ba·di′ah greatly feared Jehovah, **4** and when Jez′e·belʰ was doing away with* Jehovah's prophets, O·ba·di′ah took 100 prophets and hid them 50 to a cave, and he supplied them with bread and water.) **5** A′hab then said to O·ba·di′ah: "Go through the land to all the springs of water and to all the valleys.* Perhaps we can find enough grass to keep the horses and mules alive and not have all our animals die." **6** So they divided between themselves the land they were going to pass through. A′hab went alone by one way, and O·ba·di′ah went alone by another way.

7 As O·ba·di′ah was on his way, E·li′jah was there to meet

CHAP. 17
a 2Ki 4:2

b Ps 34:10
　Ps 37:17, 19
　Php 4:19

c Mt 10:41, 42
　Lu 4:25, 26

d 2Ki 4:19, 20

e Job 13:26

f 2Ki 4:21, 32

g Ps 99:6

_____
Second Col.
a Jas 5:16

b De 32:39
　1Sa 2:6
　2Ki 4:32, 34
　2Ki 13:21
　Lu 7:15
　Lu 8:54, 55
　Joh 5:28, 29
　Joh 11:44
　Ac 9:40, 41
　Ac 20:9, 10
　Ro 14:9
　Heb 11:17, 19

c Heb 11:35

d Joh 3:2

CHAP. 18
e Lu 4:25
　Jas 5:17

f Ps 65:9, 10
　Jer 14:22

g Le 26:26
　De 28:24

h 1Ki 16:31

17:18 *Or "What do I have to do with you, . . .?" 17:21, 22 *Or "soul." 17:22 #Or "came to life." 18:4 *Lit., "cutting off." 18:5 *Or "wadis."

him. At once he recognized him and fell facedown and said: "Is this you, my lord E·liʹjah?"[a] 8 He replied to him: "It is I. Go and tell your lord: 'E·liʹjah is here.'" 9 But he said: "What sin have I committed that you should hand your servant over to Aʹhab to put me to death? 10 As surely as Jehovah your God is living, there is not a nation or a kingdom where my lord has not sent to look for you. After they said, 'He is not here,' he made the kingdom and the nation swear that they could not find you.[b] 11 Now you are saying, 'Go and tell your lord: "E·liʹjah is here."' 12 When I depart from you, the spirit of Jehovah will carry you away[c] to a place I will not know, and when I tell Aʹhab and he does not find you, he will surely kill me. Yet, your servant has feared Jehovah from his youth. 13 Has my lord not been told what I did when Jezʹe·bel was killing the prophets of Jehovah, how I hid 100 of the prophets of Jehovah by groups of 50 in a cave and kept supplying them bread and water?[d] 14 But now you are saying, 'Go and tell your lord: "E·liʹjah is here."' He will certainly kill me." 15 However, E·liʹjah said: "As surely as Jehovah of armies whom I serve* is living, today I will present myself to him."

16 So O·ba·diʹah went off to meet Aʹhab and told him, and Aʹhab went to meet E·liʹjah.

17 As soon as Aʹhab saw E·liʹjah, he said to him: "Is this you, the one bringing great trouble* on Israel?"

18 To this he said: "I have not brought trouble on Israel, but you and the house of your father have, by abandoning the commandments of Jehovah and by

following the Baʹals.[a] 19 And now summon all Israel to me at Mount Carʹmel,[b] as well as the 450 prophets of Baʹal and the 400 prophets of the sacred pole,*[c] who are eating at the table of Jezʹe·bel." 20 So Aʹhab sent word among all the people of Israel and collected the prophets together at Mount Carʹmel.

21 Then E·liʹjah approached all the people and said: "How long will you be limping between two different opinions?*[d] If Jehovah is the true God, follow him;[e] but if Baʹal is, follow him!" But the people did not say a word in answer to him. 22 E·liʹjah then said to the people: "I am the only prophet of Jehovah left,[f] while the prophets of Baʹal are 450 men. 23 Let them give us two young bulls, and let them choose one young bull and cut it into pieces and put it on the wood, but they should not put fire to it. I will prepare the other young bull, and I will place it on the wood, but I will not put fire to it. 24 Then you must call on the name of your god,[g] and I will call on the name of Jehovah. The God who answers by fire will show that he is the true God."[h] To this all the people answered: "What you say is good."

25 E·liʹjah now said to the prophets of Baʹal: "Choose one young bull and prepare it first, because you are the majority. Then call on the name of your god, but you must not put fire to it." 26 So they took the young bull that was given to them, prepared it, and kept calling on the name of Baʹal from morning until noon, saying: "O Baʹal, answer us!" But there was no voice and no one answering.[i] They kept limping around the altar

---

CHAP. 18

a 2Ki 1:8

b 1Ki 17:2, 3

c 2Ki 2:15, 16
  Mt 4:1
  Ac 8:39

d 1Ki 18:4

Second Col.

a Ex 20:4
  1Ki 9:9
  1Ki 16:30-33

b Jos 19:26, 31

c 1Ki 16:33

d Jer 2:11
  Ho 10:2
  Mt 12:30
  1Co 10:21
  2Co 6:14, 15

e Ex 20:5
  Jos 24:15
  1Sa 7:3
  Ps 100:3

f 1Ki 19:9, 10

g Jg 6:31

h Le 9:23, 24
  De 4:24
  Jg 6:21
  1Ch 21:26
  2Ch 7:1

i Isa 45:20
  Jer 10:5
  Da 5:23
  Hab 2:18, 19
  1Co 8:4

18:15 *Lit., "before whom I stand."
18:17 *Or "bringing ostracism."

18:19 *See Glossary. 18:21 *Or "on two crutches."

that they had made. **27** About noon E·li′jah began to mock them and say: "Call out at the top of your voice! After all, he is a god![a] Perhaps he is deep in thought or he has gone to relieve himself.* Or maybe he is asleep and someone needs to wake him up!" **28** They were calling out at the top of their voice and cutting themselves with daggers and lances, according to their custom, until their blood gushed out all over them. **29** Noon was past and they continued in a frenzy* until the time the evening grain offering is presented, but there was no voice and no one answering; no one was paying attention.[b]

30 At length E·li′jah said to all the people: "Approach me." So all the people approached him. Then he repaired the altar of Jehovah that had been torn down.[c] **31** E·li′jah then took 12 stones, corresponding to the number of the tribes of the sons of Jacob, to whom Jehovah's word had come, saying: "Israel will be your name."[d] **32** With the stones he built an altar[e] in the name of Jehovah. Then he made a trench all around the altar, an area large enough to sow with two seah measures* of seed. **33** After that he put the pieces of wood in order, cut the young bull into pieces, and placed it on the wood.[f] He now said: "Fill four large jars with water and pour it on the burnt offering and on the pieces of wood." **34** Then he said: "Do it again." So they did it again. Once more he said: "Do it a third time." So they did it a third time. **35** And the water ran all around the altar, and he also filled the trench with water.

36 About the time when the evening grain offering is presented,[a] E·li′jah the prophet stepped forward and said: "O Jehovah, the God of Abraham,[b] Isaac,[c] and Israel, today let it be known that you are God in Israel and that I am your servant and that it is by your word that I have done all these things.[d] **37** Answer me, O Jehovah! Answer me so that this people may know that you, Jehovah, are the true God and that you are turning their hearts back to you."[e]

38 At that the fire of Jehovah fell from above and consumed the burnt offering,[f] the pieces of wood, the stones, and the dust, and it licked up the water from the trench.[g] **39** When all the people saw it, they immediately fell facedown and said: "Jehovah is the true God! Jehovah is the true God!" **40** Then E·li′jah said to them: "Seize the prophets of Ba′al! Do not let a single one of them escape!" At once they seized them, and E·li′jah brought them down to the stream* of Ki′shon[h] and slaughtered them there.[i]

41 E·li′jah now said to A′hab: "Go up, eat and drink, for there is the sound of a heavy downpour."[j] **42** So A′hab went up to eat and drink, while E·li′jah went up to the top of Car′mel and crouched on the ground, keeping his face between his knees.[k] **43** Then he said to his attendant: "Go up, please, and look toward the sea." So he went up and looked and said: "There is nothing at all." Seven times E·li′jah said, "Go back." **44** The seventh time his attendant said: "Look! There is a small cloud like a man's hand ascending out of the sea." He now said: "Go, say to A′hab, 'Hitch up the char-

---

CHAP. 18

a Isa 41:23

b Isa 44:19, 20

c 1Ki 19:14

d Ge 32:28, 30
Ge 35:10
Isa 48:1

e Ex 20:25
De 27:6

f Ge 22:9
Le 1:7, 8

Second Col.

a Ex 29:41

b Ge 26:24

c Ge 28:13

d Nu 16:28
Joh 11:42

e Jer 31:18
Eze 33:11

f Le 9:23, 24
Jg 6:21
2Ch 7:1

g 1Ki 18:23, 24

h Jg 5:20, 21
Ps 83:9

i De 13:1-5
De 18:20

j 1Ki 17:1

k Jas 5:17, 18

18:27 *Or possibly, "he has gone on a journey." 18:29 *Or "behaving like prophets." 18:32 *A seah equaled 7.33 L (6.66 dry qt). See App. B14. 18:40 *Or "wadi."

iot! Go down so that the downpour may not detain you!" **45** Meanwhile, the sky grew dark with clouds, the wind blew, and a heavy downpour fell;[a] and A'hab kept riding and made his way to Jez're·el.[b] **46** But the hand of Jehovah came on E·li'jah, and he wrapped his garment around* his hips and ran ahead of A'hab all the way to Jez're·el.

19 Then A'hab[c] told Jez'e·bel[d] all that E·li'jah had done and how he had killed all the prophets with the sword.[e] **2** At that Jez'e·bel sent a messenger to E·li'jah, saying: "So may the gods do to me and add to it if by this time tomorrow I do not make you like each one* of them!" **3** At that he became afraid, so he got up and ran for his life.*[f] He came to Be'er-she'ba,[g] which belongs to Judah,[h] and he left his attendant there. **4** He went a day's journey into the wilderness and came and sat down under a broom tree, and he asked that he* might die. He said: "It is enough! Now, O Jehovah, take my life* away,[i] for I am no better than my forefathers."

5 Then he lay down and fell asleep under the broom tree. But suddenly an angel touched him[j] and said to him: "Get up and eat."[k] **6** When he looked, there at his head was a round loaf on heated stones and a jug of water. He ate and drank and lay down again. **7** Later the angel of Jehovah came back a second time and touched him and said: "Get up and eat, for the journey will be too much for you." **8** So he got up and ate and drank, and in the strength of that nourishment he went on for 40 days and 40

nights until he reached Ho'reb, the mountain of the true God.[a]

9 There he entered a cave[b] and spent the night; and look! Jehovah's word came to him, telling him: "What are you doing here, E·li'jah?" **10** To this he said: "I have been absolutely zealous for Jehovah the God of armies;[c] for the people of Israel have forsaken your covenant,[d] your altars they have torn down, and your prophets they have killed with the sword,[e] and I am the only one left. Now they are seeking to take my life* away."[f] **11** But He said: "Go out and stand on the mountain before Jehovah." And look! Jehovah was passing by,[g] and a great and strong wind was splitting mountains and breaking crags before Jehovah,[h] but Jehovah was not in the wind. After the wind, there was an earthquake,[i] but Jehovah was not in the earthquake. **12** After the earthquake, there was a fire,[j] but Jehovah was not in the fire. After the fire, there was a calm, low voice.[k] **13** As soon as E·li'jah heard it, he wrapped his face in his official garment[l] and went out and stood at the entrance of the cave. Then a voice asked him: "What are you doing here, E·li'jah?" **14** To this he said: "I have been absolutely zealous for Jehovah the God of armies; for the people of Israel have forsaken your covenant,[m] your altars they have torn down, and your prophets they have killed with the sword, and I am the only one left. Now they are seeking to take my life* away."[n]

15 Jehovah said to him: "Return, and go to the wilderness of Damascus. When you arrive, anoint Haz'a·el[o] as king over Syria. **16** And you should anoint Je'hu[p] the grandson of Nim'shi as king over Israel, and you

---

CHAP. 18
a 1Sa 12:18
  Job 38:37

b Jos 19:17, 18
  1Ki 21:1

CHAP. 19
c 1Ki 16:29
  1Ki 21:25

d 1Ki 16:31

e 1Ki 18:40

f Ex 2:15
  1Sa 27:1

g Ge 21:31

h Jos 15:21, 28

i Nu 11:15
  Job 3:21
  Jon 4:3

j Da 10:8-10
  Ac 12:7

k Ps 34:7
  Heb 1:7, 14

Second Col.
a Ex 3:1
  Ex 19:18
  Mal 4:4

b Heb 11:32, 38

c Ex 20:4, 5
  Nu 25:11
  Ps 69:9

d De 29:24, 25
  Jg 2:20
  1Ki 18:19
  2Ki 17:15

e 1Ki 18:4

f 1Ki 19:2
  Ro 11:2, 3

g Ex 33:22

h Ps 50:3
  Isa 29:6

i 1Sa 14:15
  Job 9:6
  Ps 68:8
  Na 1:5

j De 4:11

k Ex 34:5, 6

l Ex 3:6

m De 31:20
  Ps 78:37
  Isa 1:4
  Jer 22:9

n Ro 11:2, 3

o 2Ki 8:7, 8
  Am 1:4

p 2Ki 9:1-3
  2Ki 9:30-33

18:46 *Or "he girded." 19:2 *Or "make your soul like the soul of each one." 19:3, 4, 10, 14 *Or "soul." 19:4 *Or "his soul."

should anoint E·li′sha* the son of Sha′phat from A′bel-me·ho′lah as prophet to take your place.ᵃ **17** Anyone escaping from Haz′a·el's sword,ᵇ Je′hu will put to death;ᶜ and anyone escaping from Je′hu's sword, E·li′sha will put to death.ᵈ **18** And I still have left 7,000 in Israel,ᵉ all whose knees have not bent down to Ba′al′ and whose mouths have not kissed him."ᵍ

19 So he went from there and found E·li′sha the son of Sha′phat while he was plowing with 12 pairs of bulls ahead of him, and he was with the 12th pair. So E·li′jah went over to him and threw his official garmentʰ on him. **20** At that he left the bulls and ran after E·li′jah and said: "Please, let me kiss my father and my mother. Then I will follow you." He replied to him: "Go, return, for what have I done to stop you?" **21** So he went back and took a pair of bulls and sacrificed them, and he used the plowing gear to boil the meat of the bulls and gave it to the people, and they ate. After that he rose up and followed E·li′jah and began to minister to him.ⁱ

20 Now King Ben-ha′dadʲ of Syriaᵏ gathered his whole army together along with 32 other kings and their horses and chariots, and he went up and laid siegeˡ to Sa·mar′i·aᵐ and fought against it. **2** Then he sent messengers to King A′habⁿ of Israel at the city and said to him: "This is what Ben-ha′dad says, **3** 'Your silver and your gold are mine, as well as the best of your wives and your sons.'" **4** To this the king of Israel answered: "According to your word, my lord the king, I am yours along with all that belongs to me."ᵒ

5 The messengers later came back and said: "This is what

Ben-ha′dad says, 'I sent this message to you: "Your silver, your gold, your wives, and your sons you will give me." **6** But about this time tomorrow I will send my servants to you, and they will carefully search your house and the houses of your servants, and all your desirable things they will seize and take away.'"

7 At that the king of Israel called all the elders of the land and said: "Take note, please, and see that this man is bent on bringing calamity, for he demanded my wives, my sons, my silver, and my gold, and I did not refuse him." **8** Then all the elders and all the people said to him: "Do not obey, and do not consent." **9** So he said to the messengers of Ben-ha′dad: "Say to my lord the king, 'All that you first demanded of your servant I will do, but this I cannot do.'" With that the messengers went off and brought word back to him.

10 Ben-ha′dad now sent him this message: "So may the gods do to me and add to it if there is enough dust in Sa·mar′i·a to give each of the people following me a handful!" **11** The king of Israel answered: "Tell him, 'The one who puts on his armor should not boast about himself like one who takes it off.'"ᵃ **12** As soon as he heard this reply, while he and the kings were drinking in their tents,* he said to his servants: "Get ready to attack!" So they got ready to attack the city.

13 But a prophet approached King A′habᵇ of Israel and said: "This is what Jehovah says, 'Have you seen all this large crowd? Here I am giving it into your hand today, and then you will know that I am Jehovah.'"ᶜ **14** A′hab asked: "By whom?" to

---

CHAP. 19
ᵃ 2Ki 2:9, 15

ᵇ 2Ki 8:12
　2Ki 10:32
　2Ki 13:3

ᶜ 2Ki 9:14, 24
　2Ki 10:6, 7
　2Ki 10:23, 25

ᵈ 2Ki 2:23, 24

ᵉ Ro 11:4

ᶠ Ex 20:5

ᵍ Ho 13:2

ʰ 2Ki 2:8

ⁱ Ex 24:13
　2Ki 2:3
　2Ki 3:11

CHAP. 20
ʲ 2Ki 8:7

ᵏ 2Sa 8:6
　2Ki 5:2
　Isa 9:12

ˡ De 28:52

ᵐ 2Ki 6:24
　2Ki 17:5

ⁿ 1Ki 16:29

ᵒ De 28:15, 48

Second Col.
ᵃ Pr 16:18
　Pr 27:1
　Ec 7:8

ᵇ 1Ki 16:29

ᶜ Ex 14:18
　Ps 37:20

which he said: "This is what Jehovah says, 'By the attendants of the princes of the provinces.'"* So he asked: "Who will start the battle?" to which he said: "You!"

15 A'hab then counted the attendants of the princes of the provinces, and they were 232; after that, he counted all the Israelite men, 7,000. 16 They went out at noon while Ben-ha'dad was drinking himself drunk in the tents* along with the 32 kings who were helping him. 17 When the attendants of the princes of the provinces came out first, Ben-ha'dad at once sent messengers. They reported to him: "Men have come out from Sa·mar'i·a." 18 At that he said: "If they have come out for peace, take them alive; or if they have come out for battle, you should still take them alive." 19 But when these came out of the city—the attendants of the princes of the provinces and the armies that were following them— 20 each one struck down his opponent. Then the Syrians fled,[a] and Israel pursued them, but King Ben-ha'dad of Syria escaped on a horse with some of the horsemen. 21 But the king of Israel went out and kept striking down the horses and the chariots, and he inflicted a great defeat* on the Syrians.

22 Later the prophet[b] approached the king of Israel and said to him: "Go, strengthen yourself and consider what you are going to do,[c] for at the start of the next year* the king of Syria will come up against you."[d]

23 Now the servants of the king of Syria said to him: "Their God is a God of mountains. That

is why they overpowered us. But if we fight against them on level land, we will overpower them. 24 Also do this: Remove all the kings[a] from their places, and replace them with governors. 25 Then gather* an army equal to the army you lost, horse for horse and chariot for chariot. Let us fight against them on level land, and we will surely overpower them." So he listened to their advice and did just that.

26 At the start of the year,* Ben-ha'dad mustered the Syrians and went up to A'phek[b] for battle against Israel. 27 The people of Israel were also mustered and supplied, and they went out to meet them. When the people of Israel camped in front of them, they were like two tiny flocks of goats, while the Syrians filled the whole land.[c] 28 Then the man of the true God approached the king of Israel and said: "This is what Jehovah says, 'Because the Syrians have said: "Jehovah is a God of mountains, and he is not a God of plains," I will give all this large crowd into your hand,[d] and you will certainly know that I am Jehovah.'"[e]

29 They remained encamped opposite each other for seven days, and on the seventh day the battle began. The people of Israel struck down 100,000 Syrian foot soldiers in one day. 30 And the rest fled to A'phek,[f] into the city. But the wall fell down on 27,000 of the men who were left. Ben-ha'dad also fled and came into the city, and he hid in an inner room.

31 So his servants said to him: "Look, we have heard that the kings of the house of Israel are merciful kings.* Please, let us wear sackcloth on our hips

CHAP. 20
a Le 26:8
  De 28:7

b 1Ki 20:13

c Pr 20:18

d 2Sa 11:1

Second Col.
a 1Ki 20:1, 16

b 2Ki 13:17

c Jg 6:5, 6
  1Sa 13:5
  2Ch 32:7

d De 32:26, 27
  Eze 20:9
  Eze 36:22

e Ex 6:7
  Ex 7:5
  Ps 83:18
  Eze 6:14
  Eze 39:7

f 1Ki 20:26

20:14 *Or "the jurisdictional districts." 20:16 *Or "booths." 20:21 *Or "slaughter." 20:22 *That is, next spring.

20:25 *Lit., "number." 20:26 *That is, in the spring. 20:31 *Or "are kings of loyal love."

and put ropes on our heads and go out to the king of Israel. Perhaps he will spare your life."*[a] 32 So they wore sackcloth around their hips and ropes on their heads and came in to the king of Israel and said: "Your servant Ben·ha′dad says, 'Please, let me* live.'" He replied: "Is he still alive? He is my brother." 33 The men took it as an omen and quickly took him at his word, so they said: "Ben·ha′dad is your brother." At that he said: "Go and get him." Then Ben·ha′dad went out to him, and he had him get up into the chariot.

34 Ben·ha′dad now said to him: "The cities that my father took from your father I will return, and you may establish markets* for yourself in Damascus, just as my father did in Sa·mar′i·a."

A′hab replied: "On the basis of this agreement,* I will let you go."

With that he made an agreement with him and let him go.

35 By the word of Jehovah, one of the sons of the prophets*[b] said to his companion: "Strike me, please." But the man refused to strike him. 36 So he said to him: "Because you did not listen to the voice of Jehovah, as soon as you leave me, a lion will kill you."* After he left him, a lion came upon him and killed him.

37 He found another man and said: "Strike me, please." So the man struck him and wounded him.

38 Then the prophet went and waited for the king by the road, disguising himself with a

bandage over his eyes. 39 As the king was passing by, he cried out to the king: "Your servant went into the thick of the battle, and there was a man coming out who brought a man to me and said, 'Guard this man. If he is found missing, your life will have to take the place of his life,*[a] or else you will pay a talent# of silver.' 40 And while your servant was busy here and there, suddenly the man was gone." The king of Israel said to him: "So your own judgment will be; you have decided it yourself." 41 Then he quickly removed the bandage from his eyes, and the king of Israel recognized that he was one of the prophets.[b] 42 He said to him: "This is what Jehovah says, 'Because you have let the man whom I said should be destroyed escape from your hand,[c] your life must take the place of his life,*[d] and your people the place of his people.'"*[e] 43 At that the king of Israel went home to Sa·mar′i·a,[f] sullen and dejected.

21 After these things, an incident took place concerning a vineyard that belonged to Na′both the Jez′re·el·ite; it was in Jez′re·el,[g] next to the palace of A′hab the king of Sa·mar′i·a. 2 A′hab said to Na′both: "Give me your vineyard for me to use as a vegetable garden, for it is near my house. Then I will give you a better vineyard to replace it. Or if you prefer, I will give you its value in money." 3 But Na′both said to A′hab: "It is unthinkable, from Jehovah's standpoint, for me to give you the inheritance of my forefathers."[h] 4 So A′hab came into his house, sullen and dejected over the answer that Na′both the Jez′re·el-

---

CHAP. 20
a Jon 3:8, 9

b 2Ki 2:3

Second Col.
a 2Ki 10:24
Ac 12:19
Ac 16:27

b 1Ki 20:35

c Le 27:29
1Sa 15:9
Jer 48:10

d 1Ki 22:31, 35
2Ch 18:33

e 2Ki 6:24
2Ki 8:12
2Ch 18:16

f 1Ki 16:29

CHAP. 21
g Jos 19:17, 18

h Le 25:23
Nu 36:7

20:31 *Or "soul." 20:32 *Or "my soul." 20:34 *Or "assign streets." #Or "covenant." 20:35 *"The sons of the prophets" seems to refer to a school of instruction for prophets or to an association of prophets. 20:36 *Or "strike you down."

20:39, 42 *Or "your soul will be in place of his soul." 20:39 #A talent equaled 34.2 kg (1,101 oz t). See App. B14.

ite had given him when he said: "I will not give you the inheritance of my forefathers." Then he lay down on his bed, kept his face turned away, and refused to eat.

5 His wife Jez′e·bel[a] came in to him and asked him: "Why are you[*] so sad that you refuse to eat?" **6** He replied to her: "Because I said to Na′both the Jez′-re·el·ite, 'Give me your vineyard for money. Or if you prefer, let me give you another vineyard to replace it.' But he said, 'I will not give you my vineyard.'" **7** His wife Jez′e·bel said to him: "Are you not the one ruling as king over Israel? Get up, eat something, and let your heart be cheerful. I will give you the vineyard of Na′both the Jez′re·el·ite."[b] **8** So she wrote letters in A′hab's name and sealed them with his seal[c] and sent the letters to the elders[d] and the nobles who lived in Na′both's city. **9** She wrote in the letters: "Proclaim a fast, and have Na′-both sit at the head of the people. **10** And have two good-for-nothing men sit in front of him and testify against him,[e] saying, 'You have cursed God and the king!'[f] Then bring him out and stone him to death."[g]

11 So the men of his city, the elders and the nobles who lived in his city, did just as was written in the letters that Jez′e·bel sent to them. **12** They proclaimed a fast and had Na′both sit at the head of the people. **13** Then two of the good-for-nothing men came in and sat down in front of him and began to testify against Na′both in front of the people, saying: "Na′both has cursed God and the king!"[h] After that they brought him to the outskirts of the city and stoned him to death.[i] **14** They now sent word

to Jez′e·bel, saying: "Na′both has been stoned to death."[a]

15 As soon as Jez′e·bel heard that Na′both had been stoned to death, she said to A′hab: "Get up, take possession of the vineyard of Na′both the Jez′re·el·ite,[b] which he refused to give you for money, for Na′both is no longer alive. He is dead." **16** As soon as A′hab heard that Na′both was dead, A′hab got up to go down to the vineyard of Na′both the Jez′-re·el·ite to take possession of it.

17 But Jehovah's word came to E·li′jah[c] the Tish′bite, saying: **18** "Get up, go down to meet A′hab the king of Israel, who is in Sa·mar′i·a.[d] There he is in the vineyard of Na′both, where he has gone to take possession of it. **19** You must tell him, 'This is what Jehovah says: "Have you murdered a man[e] and also taken his property?"'[*f] Then say to him, 'This is what Jehovah says: "In the place where the dogs licked up the blood of Na′both, the dogs will lick up your own blood."'"[g]

20 A′hab said to E·li′jah: "So you have found me, O my enemy!"[h] He replied: "I have found you. 'Because you are determined[*] to do what is bad in the eyes of Jehovah,[i] **21** here I am bringing calamity upon you, and I will make a clean sweep after you and will annihilate from A′hab every male,[*j] including the helpless and weak in Israel.[k] **22** And I will make your house like the house of Jer·o·bo′am[l] the son of Ne′bat and like the house of Ba′a·sha[m] the son of A·hi′jah, for you have provoked my anger and have caused Israel to sin.' **23** Also concerning Jez′e·bel,

---

CHAP. 21
a 1Ki 16:31
  1Ki 18:4
  1Ki 19:2
  1Ki 21:25

b Mic 2:1
  Mic 7:3

c Ne 9:38
  Es 8:8

d De 16:18

e Ex 20:16
  De 17:6

f Ex 22:28

g Le 24:16
  Joh 10:33

h Am 5:12
  Hab 1:4

i 2Ki 9:25, 26
  Ec 4:1

Second Col.

a Ec 5:8
  Ec 8:14
  Hab 1:13

b 1Ki 21:7

c 1Ki 17:1

d 1Ki 16:29

e Ge 4:8, 10

f De 5:21
  Hab 2:9

g 1Ki 22:37, 38
  2Ki 9:25, 26

h 1Ki 18:17
  Am 5:10

i 1Ki 16:30

j 1Ki 10:7, 17

k 2Ki 9:7-9

l 1Ki 15:25-29

m 1Ki 16:3, 11

21:5 *Lit., "is your spirit." 21:19 *Lit., "taken possession?" 21:20 *Lit., "you have sold yourself." 21:21 *Lit., "anyone urinating against a wall." A Hebrew expression of contempt referring to males.

Jehovah has said: 'The dogs will eat up Jez'e·bel in the plot of land of Jez're·el.ᵃ 24 Anyone belonging to A'hab who dies in the city the dogs will eat up, and anyone who dies in the field the birds of the heavens will eat up.ᵇ 25 Indeed, there has never been anyone like A'hab,ᶜ who was so determined* to do what was so bad in the eyes of Jehovah, egged on by his wife Jez'e·bel.ᵈ 26 He acted in the most detestable way by going after the disgusting idols,* just as all the Am'or·ites had done, whom Jehovah drove out from before the Israelites.'"ᵉ

27 As soon as A'hab heard these words, he ripped his garments apart and put sackcloth on his body; and he went on a fast and kept lying down in sackcloth and walking despondently. 28 Jehovah's word then came to E·li'jah the Tish'bite: 29 "Have you seen how A'hab has humbled himself on my account?ᶠ Because he has humbled himself before me, I will not bring the calamity during his lifetime. I will bring the calamity upon his house in the days of his son."ᵍ

22 For three years there was no war between Syria and Israel. 2 In the third year King Je·hosh'a·phatʰ of Judah went down to the king of Israel.ⁱ 3 Then the king of Israel said to his servants: "Do you know that Ra'moth-gil'e·adʲ belongs to us? And yet we are hesitating to take it back from the king of Syria." 4 He then said to Je·hosh'a·phat: "Will you go with me to fight at Ra'moth-gil'e·ad?" Je·hosh'a·phat replied to the king of Israel: "I am the same as you. My

21:25 *Lit., "who sold himself." 21:26 *The Hebrew term may be related to a word for "dung" and is used as an expression of contempt.

people are the same as your people. My horses are the same as your horses."ᵃ

5 But Je·hosh'a·phat said to the king of Israel: "First inquire,ᵇ please, for the word of Jehovah."ᶜ 6 So the king of Israel gathered the prophets together, about 400 men, and said to them: "Should I go to war against Ra'moth-gil'e·ad, or should I refrain?" They said: "Go up, and Jehovah will give it into the king's hand."

7 Je·hosh'a·phat then said: "Is there not here a prophet of Jehovah? Let us also inquire through him."ᵈ 8 At that the king of Israel said to Je·hosh'a·phat: "There is still one more man through whom we can inquire of Jehovah;ᵉ but I hate him,ᶠ for he never prophesies good things concerning me, only bad.ᵍ He is Mi·cai'ah the son of Im'lah." However, Je·hosh'a·phat said: "The king should not say such a thing."

9 So the king of Israel called a court official and said: "Bring Mi·cai'ah the son of Im'lah quickly."ʰ 10 Now the king of Israel and Je·hosh'a·phat the king of Judah were each sitting on his throne, dressed in royal attire, at the threshing floor at the entrance of the gate of Sa·mar'i·a, and all the prophets were prophesying before them.ʲ 11 Then Zed·e·ki'ah the son of Che·na'a·nah made for himself iron horns and said: "This is what Jehovah says, 'With these you will gore* the Syrians until you exterminate them.'" 12 All the other prophets were prophesying the same way, saying: "Go up to Ra'moth-gil'e·ad and you will be successful; Jehovah will give it into the king's hand."

13 So the messenger who went to call Mi·cai'ah said to

22:11 *Or "push."

CHAP. 21
a 2Ki 9:10, 35

b 1Ki 14:11
1Ki 16:4

c 1Ki 16:30

d 1Ki 16:31
2Ch 22:2, 3
Re 2:20

e Ex 23:28
De 9:5

f Ps 78:34

g 2Ki 9:25, 26
2Ki 10:7, 11

CHAP. 22
h 1Ki 15:24

i 2Ch 18:2, 3

j Jos 20:8, 9
1Ki 4:7, 13

Second Col.
a 2Ki 3:7
2Ch 19:2

b Nu 27:21

c 2Ch 18:4, 5

d 2Ki 3:11
2Ch 18:6, 7

e 1Ki 18:4

f 1Ki 21:20
2Ch 36:16

g Isa 30:9, 10
Jer 38:4

h 2Ch 18:8-11

i Eze 13:2, 3

him: "Look! The words of the prophets are unanimously favorable to the king. Let your word, please, become like their words, and speak favorably."[a] **14** But Mi·cai′ah said: "As surely as Jehovah is living, whatever Jehovah says to me is what I will speak." **15** Then he came in to the king, and the king asked him: "Mi·cai′ah, should we go to war against Ra′moth-gil′e·ad, or should we refrain?" At once he replied: "Go up and you will be successful; Jehovah will give it into the king's hand." **16** At that the king said to him: "How many times must I put you under oath not to speak to me anything but the truth in the name of Jehovah?" **17** So he said: "I see all the Israelites scattered on the mountains,[b] like sheep that have no shepherd. Jehovah said: 'These have no master. Let each one go back to his house in peace.'"

18 Then the king of Israel said to Je·hosh′a·phat: "Did I not tell you, 'He will not prophesy good things concerning me, only bad'?"[c]

19 Mi·cai′ah then said: "Therefore, hear the word of Jehovah: I saw Jehovah sitting on his throne[d] and all the army of the heavens standing by him, to his right and to his left.[e] **20** Jehovah then said, 'Who will fool A′hab, so that he will go up and fall at Ra′moth-gil′e·ad?' And one was saying one thing while another said something else. **21** Then a spirit*[f] came forward and stood before Jehovah and said, 'I will fool him.' Jehovah asked him, 'How will you do it?' **22** He replied, 'I will go out and become a deceptive spirit in the mouth of all his prophets.'[g] So he said, 'You will fool

him, and what is more, you will be successful. Go out and do that.' **23** And now Jehovah has put a deceptive spirit in the mouth of all these prophets of yours,[a] but Jehovah has declared calamity for you."[b]

24 Zed·e·ki′ah the son of Che·na′a·nah now approached and struck Mi·cai′ah on the cheek and said: "Which way did the spirit of Jehovah pass from me to speak with you?"[c] **25** Mi·cai′ah replied: "Look! You will see which way on the day when you will enter the innermost room to hide." **26** Then the king of Israel said: "Take Mi·cai′ah and turn him over to A′mon the chief of the city and to Jo′ash the king's son. **27** Tell them, 'This is what the king says: "Put this fellow in the prison[d] and feed him with a reduced allowance of bread and water until I return in peace."'" **28** But Mi·cai′ah said: "If you do return in peace, Jehovah has not spoken with me."[e] Then he added: "Take note, all you peoples."

29 So the king of Israel and Je·hosh′a·phat the king of Judah went up to Ra′moth-gil′e·ad.[f] **30** The king of Israel now said to Je·hosh′a·phat: "I will disguise myself and will go into the battle, but you should put on your royal attire." So the king of Israel disguised himself[g] and entered the battle. **31** Now the king of Syria had ordered his 32 chariot commanders:[h] "Do not fight with anyone, small or great, except the king of Israel." **32** And as soon as the chariot commanders saw Je·hosh′a·phat, they said to themselves: "Surely it is the king of Israel." So they turned to fight against him; and Je·hosh′a·phat began to cry for help. **33** When the chariot commanders saw that it was not the king of Israel, they immediately turned back from following him.

CHAP. 22
a 2Ch 18:12-16

b De 28:15, 25

c 2Ch 18:17

d Isa 6:1
Eze 1:26

e 2Ch 18:18-22
Job 1:6
Da 7:9, 10
Mt 18:10
Re 5:11

f Ps 104:4
Heb 1:7, 14

g 1Ki 22:6

Second Col.
a Eze 14:9

b 1Ki 20:42

c 2Ch 18:23-27

d Heb 11:32, 36

e Nu 16:28, 29

f 2Ch 18:28-32

g 2Ch 35:22

h 1Ki 20:1

22:21 *Or "an angel."

34 But one man shot his
bow at random,* and he struck
the king of Israel between the
joints of his coat of mail. So
the king said to his charioteer:
"Turn around and take me out of
the battle,# for I have been badly wounded."[a] **35** The fighting
raged throughout that day, and
the king had to be propped up in
the chariot, facing the Syrians.
The blood of the wound poured
out into the interior of the war
chariot, and he died in the evening.[b] **36** Around sunset a cry
passed through the camp, saying: "Everyone to his city! Everyone to his land!"[c] **37** Thus the
king died, and he was brought to
Sa·mar′i·a; they buried the king
in Sa·mar′i·a. **38** When they
washed off the war chariot by
the pool of Sa·mar′i·a, the dogs
licked up his blood and the prostitutes bathed there,* according
to the word that Jehovah had
spoken.[d]

39 As for the rest of the history of A′hab, all that he did and
the house* of ivory[e] that he built
and all the cities that he built,
is it not written in the book of
the history of the times of the
kings of Israel? **40** Then A′hab
was laid to rest with his forefathers;[f] and his son A·ha·zi′ah[g]
became king in his place.

41 Je·hosh′a·phat[h] the son
of A′sa had become king over
Judah in the fourth year of
King A′hab of Israel. **42** Je-
hosh′a·phat was 35 years old
when he became king, and he
reigned for 25 years in Jerusalem. His mother's name was
A·zu′bah the daughter of Shil′-
hi. **43** He kept walking in all
the way of A′sa[i] his father. He
did not deviate from it, and he
did what was right in Jehovah's
eyes.[a] However, the high places
were not removed, and the people were still sacrificing and
making sacrificial smoke on the
high places.[b] **44** Je·hosh′a·phat
kept peaceful relations with the
king of Israel.[c] **45** As for the
rest of the history of Je·hosh′-
a·phat, his mighty exploits and
how he waged war, is it not written in the book of the history of
the times of the kings of Judah?
46 He also cleared out of the
land the rest of the male temple
prostitutes[d] who had been left
over in the days of A′sa his father.[e]

47 Then there was no king in
E′dom;[f] a deputy was acting as
king.[g]

48 Je·hosh′a·phat also made
Tar′shish ships* to go to O′phir
for gold,[h] but they did not go because the ships were wrecked at
E′zi·on-ge′ber.[i] **49** It was then
that A·ha·zi′ah the son of A′hab
said to Je·hosh′a·phat: "Let my
servants go with your servants
in the ships," but Je·hosh′a·phat
did not consent.

50 Then Je·hosh′a·phat was
laid to rest with his forefathers[j]
and was buried with his forefathers in the City of David his
forefather; and his son Je·ho′-
ram[k] became king in his place.

51 A·ha·zi′ah[l] the son of A′hab
became king over Israel in Sa-
mar′i·a in the 17th year of
King Je·hosh′a·phat of Judah,
and he reigned over Israel for
two years. **52** And he kept doing what was bad in Jehovah's
eyes and walking in the way of
his father[m] and his mother[n] and
in the way of Jer·o·bo′am the son
of Ne′bat, who had caused Israel
to sin.[o] **53** He continued serving Ba′al[p] and bowing down to
him and kept offending Jehovah
the God of Israel,[q] just as his father had done.

22:34 *Or "in his innocence." #Lit., "camp." **22:38** *Or possibly, "where the prostitutes bathed, the dogs licked up his blood." **22:39** *Or "palace."

22:48 *See Glossary.

CHAP. 22
- a 2Ch 18:33, 34
- b 1Ki 20:42
- c 1Ki 22:17
- d 1Ki 21:18, 19
- e 1Ki 10:22; Eze 27:15
- f 1Ki 16:28
- g 2Ki 1:2; 2Ch 20:35
- h 1Ch 3:10; 2Ch 17:1; 2Ch 20:31; Mt 1:8
- i 1Ki 15:11; 2Ch 14:11; 2Ch 15:8

Second Col.
- a 2Ch 17:3
- b De 12:14; 1Ki 14:23; 1Ki 15:14
- c 2Ch 18:1; 2Ch 19:2
- d De 23:17, 18; 1Ki 14:24
- e 1Ki 15:11, 12
- f Ge 36:1, 9
- g 2Sa 8:14; 2Ki 8:20-22; Ps 108:9
- h 1Ki 10:22
- i 1Ki 9:26; 2Ch 20:35-37
- j 1Ki 2:10
- k 2Ki 8:16; 2Ch 21:1, 5
- l 2Ki 1:2
- m 1Ki 16:30
- n 1Ki 21:25
- o 1Ki 12:28-30; 1Ki 13:33
- p 1Ki 16:31, 32; 2Ki 1:2
- q Ex 20:3; Ex 34:14

KINGS

OUTLINE OF CONTENTS

1 After the death of A'hab, Mo'ab[a] revolted against Israel.

2 It was then that A·ha·zi'ah fell down through the grating in his roof chamber in Sa·mar'i·a and was injured. So he sent messengers and said to them: "Go, inquire of Ba'al-ze'bub the god of Ek'ron[b] to find out whether I will recover from this injury."[c] **3** But the angel of Jehovah said to E·li'jah*[d] the Tish'bite: "Rise up, go to meet the messengers of the king of Sa·mar'i·a and say to them, 'Is it because there is no God in Israel that you are going to inquire of Ba'al-ze'bub the god of Ek'ron?[e] **4** Therefore this is what Jehovah says: "You will not leave the bed on which you are lying, for you will certainly die."'" With that E·li'jah went off.

5 When the messengers returned to him, he immediately said to them: "Why have you come back?" **6** They replied to him: "There was a man who came up to meet us, and he said

to us, 'Go, return to the king who sent you and tell him, "This is what Jehovah says: 'Is it because there is no God in Israel that you are sending to inquire of Ba'al-ze'bub the god of Ek'ron? Therefore, you will not leave the bed on which you are lying, for you will certainly die.'"'"[a] **7** At this he asked them: "What did the man look like who came up to meet you and spoke these words to you?" **8** So they said to him: "He was a man with a garment of hair[b] and a leather belt around his waist."[c] Immediately he said: "It was E·li'jah the Tish'bite."

9 The king then sent him a chief of 50 with his 50 men. When he went up to him, he was sitting on the top of the mountain. He said to him: "Man of the true God,[d] the king says, 'Come down.'" **10** But E·li'jah answered the chief of the 50: "Well, if I am a man of God, let fire come down from the heavens[e] and consume you and your 50 men." And fire came down from the heavens and consumed him and his 50 men.

CHAP. 1
a Ge 19:36, 37
  2Sa 8:2
  Ps 60:8

b Jos 13:2, 3
  1Sa 5:10

c 2Ki 1:16

d 1Ki 17:1
  1Ki 18:36

e Isa 8:19
  Jer 2:11

Second Col.
a 1Ch 10:13, 14

b 1Ki 19:19
  Zec 13:4
  Heb 11:32, 37

c Mt 3:4

d De 33:1

e Nu 11:1
  Nu 16:35
  Lu 9:54
  Jude 7

1:3 *Meaning "My God Is Jehovah."

11 So the king sent again to him another chief of 50 with his 50 men. He went and said to him: "Man of the true God, this is what the king says, 'Come down quickly.'" **12** But E·li′jah answered them: "If I am a man of the true God, let fire come down from the heavens and consume you and your 50 men." And fire of God came down from the heavens and consumed him and his 50 men.

13 Then the king sent again a third chief of 50 and his 50 men. But the third chief of 50 went up and bowed down on his knees in front of E·li′jah and began to beg for favor and say to him: "Man of the true God, please, let my life and the lives of* these 50 servants of yours be precious in your eyes. **14** Fire has already come down from the heavens and consumed the two former chiefs of 50 and their groups of 50, but now let me* life* be precious in your eyes."

15 At that the angel of Jehovah told E·li′jah: "Go down with him. Do not be afraid of him." So he rose and went down with him to the king. **16** E·li′jah then said to the king, "This is what Jehovah says: 'You sent messengers to inquire of Ba′al·ze′bub the god of Ek′ron.ᵃ Is it because there is no God in Israel?ᵇ Why did you not inquire of his word? Therefore, you will not leave the bed on which you are lying, for you will certainly die.'" **17** So he died, according to the word of Jehovah that E·li′jah had spoken; and because he did not have a son, Je·ho′ram*ᶜ became king in his place, in the second year of Je·ho′ramᵈ the son of Je·hosh′a·phat the king of Judah.

18 As for the rest of the history of A·ha·zi′ah,ᵉ what he did,

is it not written in the book of the history of the times of the kings of Israel?

2 When Jehovah was about to take E·li′jahᵃ up to the heavens* in a windstorm,ᵇ E·li′jah and E·li′shaᶜ went out from Gil′gal.ᵈ **2** E·li′jah said to E·li′sha: "Stay here, please, because Jehovah has sent me on to Beth′el." But E·li′sha said: "As surely as Jehovah is living and as you are* living, I will not leave you." So they went down to Beth′el.ᵉ **3** Then the sons of the prophets* in Beth′el came out to E·li′sha and said to him: "Do you know that today Jehovah is taking your master away from headship over you?"ᶠ At this he said: "I already know it. Be silent."

4 E·li′jah now said to him: "E·li′sha, stay here, please, because Jehovah has sent me on to Jer′i·cho."ᵍ But he said: "As surely as Jehovah is living and as you are* living, I will not leave you." So they came to Jer′i·cho. **5** Then the sons of the prophets who were in Jer′i·cho approached E·li′sha and said to him: "Do you know that today Jehovah is taking your master away from headship over you?" At this he said: "I already know it. Be silent."

6 E·li′jah now said to him: "Stay here, please, because Jehovah has sent me on to the Jordan." But he said: "As surely as Jehovah is living and as you are* living, I will not leave you." So both of them went on. **7** And 50 of the sons of the prophets also went and stood watching from a distance while the two of them stood by the Jordan. **8** Then E·li′jah took his official garmentʰ and rolled it up and struck the

---

CHAP. 1
a Jos 13:2, 3

b 2Ki 1:3

c 2Ki 3:1
2Ki 9:22

d 2Ki 8:16

e 1Ki 22:51

Second Col.

CHAP. 2
a 1Ki 17:1

b 2Ki 2:11

c 1Ki 19:16

d 2Ki 4:38

e Ge 28:18, 19
1Ki 12:28, 29
2Ki 2:23

f 1Ki 19:16

g Jos 6:26
1Ki 16:34

h 1Ki 19:19

1:13 *Or "let my soul and the souls of." 1:14 *Or "soul." 1:17 *That is, Ahaziah's brother.

2:1 *Or "sky." 2:2, 4, 6 *Or "your soul is." 2:3 *"The sons of the prophets" seems to refer to a school of instruction for prophets or to an association of prophets.

waters, and they were divided to the left and to the right, so that both of them went across on the dry ground.[a]

9 As soon as they had gone across, E·li′jah said to E·li′sha: "Ask what you want me to do for you before I am taken from you." So E·li′sha said: "Please, may I receive a double portion*[b] of your spirit?"[c] **10** He replied: "You have asked a difficult thing. If you see me when I am taken from you, it will happen for you that way; but if you do not, it will not happen."

11 As they were walking along, speaking as they walked, suddenly a fiery chariot and fiery horses[d] made a separation between the two of them, and E·li′jah ascended to the heavens* in the windstorm.[e] **12** While E·li′sha was watching, he was crying out: "My father, my father! The chariot of Israel and his horsemen!"[f] When he could no longer see him, he took hold of his own garments and ripped them into two pieces.[g] **13** After that he picked up the official garment[h] of E·li′jah that had fallen off him and went back and stood by the bank of the Jordan. **14** Then he took the official garment of E·li′jah that had fallen off him and struck the waters and said: "Where is Jehovah, the God of E·li′jah?" When he struck the waters, they were divided to the left and to the right, so that E·li′sha went across.[i]

15 When the sons of the prophets at Jer′i·cho saw him from a distance, they said: "The spirit of E·li′jah has settled down on E·li′sha."[j] So they went to meet him and bowed down to the ground before him. **16** They said to him: "Here are 50 capable men with your servants. Let them go, please, to look for your master. Perhaps the spirit* of Jehovah has lifted him up and then thrown him on one of the mountains or in one of the valleys."[a] But he said: "Do not send them." **17** However, they kept urging him until he was embarrassed, so he said: "Send them." They sent the 50 men, who kept looking for three days but did not find him. **18** When they returned to him, he was staying in Jer′i·cho.[b] Then he said to them: "Did I not tell you not to go?"

19 In time the men of the city said to E·li′sha: "My master can see that the city is well-situated;[c] but the water is bad, and the land is barren."* **20** At that he said: "Bring me a small new bowl and put salt in it." So they brought it to him. **21** Then he went out to the source of the water and threw salt into it[d] and said: "This is what Jehovah says, 'I have healed this water. No more will it cause death or barrenness.'"* **22** And the water has been healed down to this day, according to the word spoken by E·li′sha.

23 He went up from there to Beth′el. As he was going along the way, some young boys came out from the city and began to jeer at him,[e] and they kept saying to him: "Go up, you baldhead! Go up, you baldhead!" **24** Finally he turned around and looked at them and cursed them in the name of Jehovah. Then two she-bears[f] came out of the forest and tore 42 of the children to pieces.[g] **25** He kept going from there to Mount Car′mel,[h] and from there he returned to Sa·mar′i·a.

3 Je·ho′ram[i] the son of A′hab became king over Israel in Sa·mar′i·a in the 18th year of King Je·hosh′a·phat of Judah,

---

CHAP. 2
a Ex 14:21, 22
  Jos 3:17
  2Ki 2:13, 14

b De 21:17

c De 34:9
  1Ki 19:16
  Lu 1:17

d 2Ki 6:17
  Ps 68:17

e 2Ch 21:5, 12
  Joh 3:13

f 2Ki 13:14

g 2Sa 1:11, 12
  Job 1:19, 20

h 1Ki 19:19
  2Ki 1:8
  Zec 13:4
  Mt 3:4

i Jos 3:13
  2Ki 2:8

j Nu 11:24, 25
  Nu 27:18, 20
  2Ki 2:9

Second Col.
a 1Ki 18:11, 12

b Jos 6:26
  1Ki 16:34

c De 34:1-3

d Ex 15:23-25
  2Ki 4:38-41

e 2Ch 36:15, 16
  Lu 10:16

f Pr 17:12

g 2Ki 1:10

h 2Ki 4:25

CHAP. 3
i 2Ki 1:17

2:9 *Or "two parts." 2:11 *Or "sky."
2:16 *Or "wind." 2:19 *Or possibly, "causing miscarriages." 2:21 *Or possibly, "miscarriages."

and he reigned for 12 years. **2** He kept doing what was bad in Jehovah's eyes, but not to the extent of his father or his mother, for he removed the sacred pillar of Ba′al that his father had made.ᵃ **3** However, he clung to the sins that Jer·o·bo′am the son of Ne′bat had caused Israel to commit.ᵇ He did not depart from them.

4 Now Me′sha the king of Mo′ab was a sheep raiser, and he used to pay 100,000 lambs and 100,000 unshorn rams as tribute to the king of Israel. **5** As soon as A′hab died,ᶜ the king of Mo′ab revolted against the king of Israel.ᵈ **6** So King Je·ho′ram went out on that day from Sa·mar′i·a and mustered all Israel. **7** He also sent a message to King Je·hosh′a·phat of Judah, saying: "The king of Mo′ab has revolted against me. Will you go with me to war against Mo′ab?" To this he said: "I will go.ᵉ I am the same as you. My people are the same as your people. My horses are the same as your horses."ᶠ **8** Then he asked: "By which way should we go up?" He replied: "By the way of the wilderness of E′dom."

9 The king of Israel then set out with the king of Judah and the king of E′dom.ᵍ After they journeyed roundabout for seven days, there was no water for the camp and for the domestic animals that were following behind them. **10** The king of Israel said: "How terrible! Jehovah has called these three kings, only to give them into the hand of Mo′ab!" **11** At that Je·hosh′a·phat said: "Is there no prophet of Jehovah here through whom we may inquire of Jehovah?"ʰ So one of the servants of the king of Israel answered: "There is E·li′shaʲ the son of Sha′phat, who used to pour out water on the hands of E·li′jah."*ʲ **12** Then Je-

hosh′a·phat said: "The word of Jehovah is with him." So the king of Israel and Je·hosh′a·phat and the king of E′dom went down to him.

13 E·li′sha said to the king of Israel: "What do I have to do with you?"ᵃ Go to the prophets of your father and to the prophets of your mother."ᵇ But the king of Israel said to him: "No, for it is Jehovah who has called these three kings to give them into the hand of Mo′ab." **14** To this E·li′sha said: "As surely as Jehovah of armies whom I serve* is living, if I did not have regard for King Je·hosh′a·phatᶜ of Judah, I would not look at you or take notice of you.ᵈ **15** Now bring me a harpist."*ᵉ As soon as the harpist started playing, the hand of Jehovah came on him.ᶠ **16** He said, "This is what Jehovah says: 'Dig trench after trench in this valley,* **17** for this is what Jehovah says: "You will not see wind, and you will not see rain; yet this valley* will be filled with water,ᵍ and you will drink from it, you, your livestock, and your other animals."' **18** But this is a trivial thing in the eyes of Jehovah,ʰ for he will also give Mo′ab into your hand.ⁱ **19** You must strike down every fortified cityʲ and every choice city, you should cut down every good tree, you should stop up all the springs of water, and you should ruin every good plot of land with stones."ᵏ

20 And in the morning, at the time of the morning grain offering,ˡ water was suddenly coming from the direction of E′dom, and the land became filled with the water.

21 All the Mo′ab·ites heard that the kings had come up to fight against them, so they

---

CHAP. 3
a 1Ki 16:30-33

b 1Ki 12:28-30

c 1Ki 22:37

d 2Sa 8:2

e 2Ch 19:2

f 1Ki 22:3, 4

g 2Sa 8:14

h 1Ki 22:7

i 1Ki 19:16
2Ki 2:15

j 1Ki 19:19, 21

Second Col.
a 1Sa 2:30
Eze 14:3

b Jg 10:14
1Ki 18:19
1Ki 22:6

c 2Ch 17:3, 4
2Ch 19:3, 4

d Pr 15:29

e 1Sa 10:5
1Ch 25:1

f 1Ki 18:46
Eze 1:3
Ac 11:21

g Ps 107:35

h Jer 32:17
Mr 10:27

i De 28:7

j De 3:5

k 2Ki 3:25

l Ex 29:39, 40

3:11 *Or "who was Elijah's servant." 3:13 *Lit., "What to me and to you?" 3:14 *Lit., "before whom I stand." 3:15 *Or "musician." 3:16, 17 *Or "wadi."

called together all the men who could bear arms,* and they stationed themselves at the border. **22** When they got up early in the morning, the sun was shining on the water, and to the Mo′ab·ites on the opposite side, the water looked red like blood. **23** They said: "This is blood! The kings have surely slaughtered one another with the sword. So, then, to the spoil,ᵃ O Mo′ab!" **24** When they came into the camp of Israel, the Israelites rose up and began striking down the Mo′ab·ites, who fled from them.ᵇ They advanced into Mo′ab, striking the Mo′ab·ites down as they went. **25** They tore down the cities, and each man threw a stone into every good plot of land, filling it with stones; they stopped up every spring of water,ᶜ and they cut down every good tree.ᵈ Finally only the stone walls of Kir-har′e·sethᵉ remained standing, and the slingers surrounded it and struck it down.

26 When the king of Mo′ab saw that the battle was lost, he took with him 700 men armed with swords to break through to the king of E′dom;ᶠ but they were not able to. **27** So he took his firstborn son who was going to reign in his place and offered him up as a burnt sacrificeᵍ on the wall. And there came to be great indignation against Israel, so they withdrew from against him and returned to their land.

4 Now one of the wives of the sons of the prophetsʰ cried out to E·li′sha, saying: "Your servant my husband is dead, and you well know that your servant had always feared Jehovah.ⁱ Now a creditor has come to take both of my children as his slaves." **2** At this E·li′sha said to her: "What can I do for you? Tell me, what do you have in the house?" She replied: "Your servant has nothing at all in the house but a jar* of oil."ᵃ **3** Then he said: "Go outside, ask for containers from all your neighbors, empty containers. Do not limit yourself to a few. **4** Then go in and close the door behind you and your sons. Fill all these containers, and set the full ones aside." **5** So she left him.

When she closed the door behind her and her sons, they passed the containers to her, and she kept pouring.ᵇ **6** When the containers were full, she said to one of her sons: "Bring another container to me."ᶜ But he said to her: "There are no more containers." At that the oil stopped.ᵈ **7** So she came in and told the man of the true God, and he said: "Go, sell the oil and pay off your debts, and you and your sons can live from what is left."

8 One day E·li′sha went to Shu′nem,ᵉ where there was a prominent woman, and she urged him to eat a meal there.ᶠ As often as he would pass by, he would stop there to eat. **9** So she said to her husband: "I know that it is a holy man of God who comes this way regularly. **10** Please, let us make a small room on the roofᵍ and put there for him a bed, a table, a chair, and a lampstand. Then, whenever he comes to us, he can stay there."ʰ

11 One day he came there, and he went to the room on the roof to lie down. **12** He then said to Ge·ha′ziⁱ his attendant: "Call this Shu′nam·miteʲ woman." So he called her, and she stood before him. **13** Then he said to Ge·ha′zi: "Please tell her, 'Here you have gone to all this trouble for us.ᵏ What can be done for

CHAP. 3
ᵃ Ex 15:9, 10

ᵇ Le 26:7

ᶜ Ge 26:15
2Ch 32:4

ᵈ 2Ki 3:19

ᵉ Isa 16:7

ᶠ 2Ki 3:9

ᵍ De 12:31
2Ch 28:1, 3
Ps 106:37, 38

CHAP. 4
ʰ 2Ki 2:3, 5

ⁱ 1Ki 19:18

_____
Second Col.
ᵃ 1Ki 17:9, 12

ᵇ Mr 6:41
Mr 8:6-8
Joh 2:7-9

ᶜ Mt 14:19

ᵈ Jos 5:12
1Ki 17:14

ᵉ Jos 19:17, 18

ᶠ Ge 19:1-3
Jg 13:15

ᵍ Jg 3:20
1Ki 17:19

ʰ Mt 10:41
Ro 12:13
Heb 13:2

ⁱ 2Ki 5:25-27
2Ki 8:4

ʲ Jos 19:17, 18

ᵏ Ro 16:6

3:21 *Or "all who girded on a belt."   **4:2** *Or "spouted jar."

you?[a] Should I speak in your behalf to the king[b] or to the chief of the army?'" But her reply was: "I am living among my own people." 14 So he said: "Then what can be done for her?" Geha′zi now said: "Well, she does not have a son,[c] and her husband is old." 15 Immediately he said: "Call her." So he called her, and she stood at the doorway. 16 Then he said: "At this time next year, you will be embracing a son."[d] But she said: "No, my master, man of the true God! Do not tell lies to your servant."

17 However, the woman became pregnant and gave birth to a son at the same time the next year, just as E·li′sha had told her. 18 The child grew up, and one day he went out to his father, who was with the reapers. 19 He kept saying to his father: "My head, O my head!" Then his father said to the attendant: "Carry him to his mother." 20 So he carried him back to his mother, and he sat on her lap until noon, and then he died.[e] 21 Then she went up and laid him on the bed of the man of the true God,[f] and she shut the door behind her and left. 22 She now called her husband and said: "Send me, please, one of the attendants and one of the donkeys, and let me go quickly to the man of the true God and return." 23 But he said: "Why are you going to see him today? It is not a new moon[g] or a sabbath." However, she said: "Everything is all right." 24 So she saddled the donkey and said to her attendant: "Go quickly. Do not slow down for me unless I tell you to."

25 So she went to the man of the true God at Mount Car′mel. As soon as the man of the true God saw her from afar, he said to Ge·ha′zi his attendant: "Look! The Shu′nam·mite

woman is over there. 26 Please run to meet her and ask her, 'Are you well? Is your husband well? Is your child well?'" To this she said: "All is well." 27 When she came to the man of the true God at the mountain, she at once grabbed hold of his feet.[a] At this Ge·ha′zi came near to push her away, but the man of the true God said: "Let her alone, for she is in bitter distress,* and Jehovah has hidden it from me and has not told me." 28 She then said: "Did I ask my lord for a son? Did I not say, 'You must not give me a false hope'?"[b]

29 He immediately said to Ge·ha′zi: "Wrap your garments around your waist[c] and take my staff in your hand and go. If you encounter anyone, do not greet him; and if anyone should greet you, do not answer him. Go and place my staff on the boy's face." 30 At this the boy's mother said: "As surely as Jehovah is living and as you yourself are* living, I will not leave you."[d] So he got up and went with her. 31 Ge·ha′zi went before them and put the staff on the boy's face, but there was no sound or response.[e] He went back to meet E·li′sha and told him: "The boy did not wake up."

32 When E·li′sha came into the house, the boy was lying dead on his bed.[f] 33 He went in and closed the door behind them both and began to pray to Jehovah.[g] 34 Then he got up on the bed and lay down on the child and put his own mouth on the boy's mouth, his own eyes on his eyes, and his own palms on his palms and kept bent over him, and the child's body started to grow warm.[h] 35 He walked back and forth in the house, and he got up on the bed and bent over him again.

CHAP. 4
a 2Ki 4:1, 2
  Heb 6:10

b 2Ki 8:3

c Ge 15:2
  Ge 30:1

d Ge 18:10

e 1Ki 17:17

f 2Ki 4:9, 10

g Nu 10:10
  Nu 28:11

Second Col.
a Mt 28:9

b 2Ki 4:16

c 1Ki 18:46

d Mt 15:22, 28

e Mt 17:15, 16
  Mr 9:17, 18

f 2Ki 4:21

g 1Ki 17:19, 20
  Joh 11:41
  Ac 9:40

h 1Ki 17:21, 22
  Ac 20:9, 10

4:27 *Or "for her soul is bitter within her." 4:30 *Or "your soul is."

The boy sneezed seven times, after which he opened his eyes.[a] 36 E·li′sha now called Ge·ha′zi and said: "Call the Shu′nam·mite woman." So he called her and she came in to him. Then he said: "Pick up your son."[b] 37 And she came in and fell at his feet and bowed down to the ground before him, after which he picked up her son and went out.

38 When E·li′sha returned to Gil′gal, there was famine in the land.[c] The sons of the prophets[d] were sitting before him, and he said to his attendant:[e] "Put the large pot on and boil stew for the sons of the prophets." 39 So one of them went out to the field to pick mallows, and he found a wild vine and picked wild gourds from it, filling his garment. He then returned and sliced them into the stewpot, not knowing what they were. 40 They later served it to the men to eat, but as soon as they ate from the stew, they cried out: "There is death in the pot, O man of the true God." And they could not eat it. 41 So he said: "Bring some flour." After he threw it into the pot, he said: "Serve it to the people." And nothing harmful was in the pot.[f]

42 A man came from Ba′al-shal′i·shah,[g] and he brought the man of the true God 20 loaves of barley bread[h] made from the first ripe fruits, as well as a bag of new grain.[i] Then E·li′sha said: "Give it to the people so that they may eat." 43 However, his attendant said: "How can I set this before 100 men?"[j] To this he said: "Give it to the people so that they may eat, for this is what Jehovah says, 'They will eat and have some left over.'"[k] 44 At that he put it before them, and they ate and they had some left over,[l] according to the word of Jehovah.

5 Now Na′a·man the army chief of the king of Syria was a prominent man who was held in esteem by his lord, because through him Jehovah had given victory* to Syria. He was a mighty warrior, although he was a leper.# 2 On one of their raids, the Syrians had taken captive from the land of Israel a little girl who became a servant to Na′a·man's wife. 3 She said to her mistress: "If only my lord would visit the prophet[a] in Sa·mar′i·a! Then he would cure him of his leprosy."[b] 4 So he* went and reported to his lord, telling him what the girl from Israel had said.

5 Then the king of Syria said: "Go now! And I will send a letter to the king of Israel." So he went, taking with him ten talents* of silver, 6,000 pieces of gold, and ten changes of garments. 6 He brought to the king of Israel the letter, which read: "Along with this letter that has come to you, I send my servant Na′a·man so that you may cure him of his leprosy." 7 As soon as the king of Israel read the letter, he ripped his garments apart and said: "Am I God, to put to death and to keep alive?[c] For he is sending this man to me, telling me to cure him of his leprosy! You can see for yourselves that he is seeking a quarrel with me."

8 But when E·li′sha the man of the true God heard that the king of Israel had ripped his garments apart, he at once sent word to the king: "Why did you rip your garments apart? Please let him come to me so that he may know that there is a prophet in Israel."[d] 9 So Na′a·man came with his horses and his war char-

---

CHAP. 4
a 2Ki 8:1, 5

b Heb 11:35

c De 28:23, 24
2Ki 8:1
Eze 14:13

d 2Ki 2:3, 5

e 2Ki 4:12

f Ex 15:23-25
2Ki 2:19-21

g 1Sa 9:3, 4

h Joh 6:9

i 1Sa 9:6, 7

j Mt 14:17
Mr 8:4

k Mt 14:20
Mr 8:8

l Lu 9:17
Joh 6:13

Second Col.

CHAP. 5
a 1Ki 19:16

b Mt 8:2
Mt 11:5
Lu 4:27

c De 32:39

d 1Ki 17:24
1Ki 19:16
2Ki 3:11, 12
2Ki 8:4

5:1 *Or "salvation." #Or "struck with a skin disease." 5:4 *Possibly referring to Naaman. 5:5 *A talent equaled 34.2 kg (1,101 oz t). See App. B14.

iots and stood at the entrance of the house of E·li′sha. 10 However, E·li′sha sent a messenger to tell him: "Go, wash seven times[a] in the Jordan,[b] and your flesh will be restored, and you will be clean." 11 At this Na′a·man became indignant and started to leave, saying: "Here I said to myself, 'He will come out to me and stand here and call on the name of Jehovah his God, moving his hand back and forth over the leprosy to cure it.' 12 Are not the A·ba′nah and the Phar′par, the rivers of Damascus,[c] better than all the waters of Israel? Can I not wash in them and become clean?" With that he turned and went away in a rage.

13 His servants now approached him and said: "My father, if the prophet had told you to do something extraordinary, would you not do it? How much more, then, since he only said to you, 'Wash and be clean'?" 14 At that he went down and plunged*[d] into the Jordan seven times, according to the word of the man of the true God.[d] Then his flesh was restored like the flesh of a little boy,[e] and he became clean.[f]

15 After that he went back to the man of the true God,[g] he and all his entourage,* and he stood before him and said: "Now I know that there is no God anywhere in all the earth but in Israel.[h] Now accept, please, a gift* from your servant." 16 However, E·li′sha said: "As surely as Jehovah whom I serve* is living, I will not accept it.[i] He urged him to accept it, but he kept refusing. 17 Finally Na′a·man said: "If not, please, let your servant be given two mule-loads of soil from this land, for

your servant will no longer offer a burnt offering or a sacrifice to any gods other than Jehovah. 18 But may Jehovah forgive your servant for this one thing: When my lord goes into the house* of Rim′mon to bow down there, he supports himself on my arm, so I have to bow down at the house of Rim′mon. When I bow down at the house of Rim′mon, may Jehovah, please, forgive your servant for this." 19 At this he said to him: "Go in peace." After he departed from him and had traveled for some distance, 20 Ge·ha′zi[a] the attendant of E·li′sha the man of the true God[b] said to himself: 'Here my master has spared this Syrian Na′a·man[c] by not accepting from him what he brought. As surely as Jehovah is living, I will run after him and take something from him.' 21 So Ge·ha′zi chased after Na′a·man. When Na′a·man saw someone running after him, he got down from his chariot to meet him and said: "Is everything all right?" 22 To this he said: "All is well. My master has sent me, saying, 'Look! Just now two young men from the mountainous region of E′phra·im from the sons of the prophets came to me. Give them, please, a talent of silver and two changes of garments.'"[d] 23 Na′a·man said: "Go on, take two talents." He kept urging him,[e] and he wrapped up two talents of silver in two bags, with two changes of garments, and gave them to two of his attendants, who carried them before him.

24 When he reached O′phel,* he took them from their hand and put them in the house and sent the men away. After they left, 25 he went in and stood

CHAP. 5
a Le 14:7
Nu 19:4

b Joh 9:6, 7

c Isa 7:8

d 2Ki 5:10

e Job 33:25

f Lu 4:27
Lu 5:13

g Lu 17:15, 16

h Ps 96:4, 5
Isa 43:10

i Mt 10:8

Second Col.
a 2Ki 4:12
2Ki 8:4

b 1Ki 17:24

c 2Ki 5:1
Lu 4:27

d 2Ki 5:5

e 2Ki 5:16

5:14 *Or "immersed himself in." 5:15 *Lit., "camp." *Lit., "blessing." 5:16 *Lit., "before whom I stand."

5:18 *Or "temple." 5:24 *A location in Samaria, possibly a hill or a fortification.

by his master. E·li'sha now said to him: "Where did you come from, Ge·ha'zi?" But he said: "Your servant did not go anywhere."[a] **26** E·li'sha said to him: "Was my heart not there with you when the man got down from his chariot to meet you? Is it a time to accept silver or to accept garments or olive groves or vineyards or sheep or cattle or male or female servants?[b] **27** Now Na'a·man's leprosy[c] will stick to you and to your descendants forever." Immediately he went out from before him a leper, white as snow.[d]

6 The sons of the prophets[e] said to E·li'sha: "Look! The place where we are staying with you is too cramped for us. **2** Please let us go to the Jordan. Let each of us take a log from there and make a place there where we can dwell." He said: "Go." **3** One of them said: "Will you please come along with your servants?" At that he said: "I will come." **4** So he went with them, and they came to the Jordan and began to cut down the trees. **5** As one of them was cutting down a tree, the axhead fell into the water, and he cried out: "Alas, my master, it was borrowed!" **6** The man of the true God said: "Where did it fall?" So he showed him the place. He then cut off a piece of wood and threw it there and made the axhead float. **7** He said: "Lift it out." So he reached out his hand and took it.

8 Now the king of Syria went to war against Israel.[f] He consulted with his servants and said: "I will encamp at such and such a place with you." **9** Then the man of the true God[g] sent word to the king of Israel, saying: "Beware of passing by this place, because that is where the Syrians are coming down." **10** So the king of Israel sent

word to the place that the man of the true God had warned him about. He kept warning him, and he stayed away from there on several occasions.*[a]

11 This enraged the king* of Syria, so he summoned his servants and said to them: "Tell me! Who among us is on the side of the king of Israel?" **12** Then one of his servants said: "None of us, my lord the king! It is E·li'sha the prophet in Israel who tells the king of Israel the things that you say in your own bedroom."[b] **13** He said: "Go and find out where he is, so that I may send men to capture him." Later the report was made to him: "He is in Do'than."[c] **14** He immediately sent horses and war chariots there, as well as a large army; they came by night and surrounded the city.

15 When the attendant* of the man of the true God rose early and went outside, he saw that an army with horses and war chariots was surrounding the city. At once the attendant said to him: "Alas, my master! What are we to do?" **16** But he said: "Do not be afraid![d] For there are more who are with us than those who are with them."[e] **17** Then E·li'sha began to pray and say: "O Jehovah, open his eyes, please, that he may see."[f] Immediately Jehovah opened the attendant's eyes and he saw, and look! the mountainous region was full of horses and war chariots of fire[g] all around E·li'sha.

18 When the Syrians came down to him, E·li'sha prayed to Jehovah and said: "Please, strike this nation with blindness."[i] So he struck them with blindness, just as E·li'sha had requested. **19** E·li'sha now said to them:

CHAP. 5
a Ac 5:8, 9

b Mt 10:8
Lu 12:15
Ac 20:33
1Ti 6:10

c 2Ki 5:1

d Ex 4:6
Nu 12:10

CHAP. 6
e 2Ki 2:3, 5
2Ki 9:1

f 1Ki 20:1, 34
1Ki 22:31

g 1Ki 17:24

Second Col.
a Mt 2:12

b Da 2:22, 28

c Ge 37:16, 17

d Ex 14:13
Ps 3:6

e 2Sa 22:31
2Ch 32:7
Ps 18:2
Ps 27:3
Ps 46:7
Ps 55:18
Ps 118:11
Ro 8:31

f Ac 7:56

g 2Ki 2:11
Ps 68:17
Zec 6:1

h Ps 34:7
Mt 26:53

i Ge 19:10, 11

6:10 *Or "more than once or twice." **6:11** *Lit., "the heart of the king." **6:15** *Or "minister."

"This is not the way, and this is not the city. Follow me, and let me lead you to the man you are looking for." However, he led them to Sa·mar'i·a.ᵃ

20 When they arrived in Sa·mar'i·a, E·li'sha said: "O Jehovah, open their eyes so that they may see." So Jehovah opened their eyes, and they saw that they were in the middle of Sa·mar'i·a. **21** When the king of Israel saw them, he said to E·li'sha: "Should I strike them down, should I strike them down, my father?" **22** But he said: "You must not strike them down. Do you strike down those whom you have taken captive with your sword and with your bow? Give them bread and water so they may eat and drinkᵇ and return to their lord." **23** So he spread a great feast for them, and they ate and drank, after which he sent them away to return to their lord. And not once did the marauder bands of the Syriansᶜ come again into the land of Israel.

24 Afterward Ben-ha'dad the king of Syria gathered all his army* together and went up and besieged Sa·mar'i·a.ᵈ **25** So there was a great famineᵉ in Sa·mar'i·a, and they besieged it until a donkey's headᶠ was worth 80 silver pieces, and a fourth of a cab measure* of dove's droppings was worth 5 silver pieces. **26** As the king of Israel was passing by on the wall, a woman cried out to him: "Help us, O my lord the king!" **27** To this he said: "If Jehovah does not help you, where can I get help for you? From the threshing floor? Or from the wine or oil press?" **28** The king asked her: "What is the matter with you?"

She replied: "This woman said to me, 'Hand over your son, and we will eat him today, and we will eat my son tomorrow.'ᵃ **29** So we boiled my son and ate him.ᵇ The next day I said to her, 'Hand over your son so that we may eat him.' But she hid her son."

30 As soon as the king heard the woman's words, he ripped his garments apart.ᶜ When he passed by on the wall, the people saw that he was wearing sackcloth under his clothes.* **31** Then he said: "So may God do to me and add to it if the head of E·li'sha the son of Sha'phat remains on him today!"ᵈ

32 E·li'sha was sitting in his house, and the elders were sitting with him. The king sent a man ahead of him, but before the messenger arrived, E·li'sha said to the elders: "Have you seen how this son of a murdererᵉ has sent to take off my head? Watch when the messenger comes, close the door, and hold the door shut against him. Is not the sound of his lord's footsteps behind him?" **33** While he was still speaking with them, the messenger came to him, and the king said: "This calamity is from Jehovah. Why should I wait any longer for Jehovah?"

7 E·li'sha now said, "Listen to the word of Jehovah. This is what Jehovah says: 'Tomorrow about this time at the gate* of Sa·mar'i·a, a seah measure# of fine flour will be worth a shekel,△ and two seah measures of barley will be worth a shekel.'"ᶠ **2** At that the adjutant whom the king relied on said to the man of the true God: "Even if Jehovah

---

CHAP. 6
a 1Ki 16:29

b Pr 25:21
Ro 12:20

c 2Ki 5:2

d De 28:52
1Ki 20:1

e Le 26:26
De 28:15, 17

f De 14:3
Eze 4:14

Second Col.
a Le 26:29
De 28:53-57
Eze 5:10

b La 4:10

c Ge 37:29
1Ki 21:27

d Jer 38:4

e 1Ki 18:13
1Ki 21:9, 10

CHAP. 7
f De 32:36
2Ki 7:18

6:24 *Lit., "camp." 6:25 *A cab equaled 1.22 L (1.11 dry qt). See App. B14.

6:30 *Or "underneath, next to his skin." 7:1 *Or "markets." #A seah equaled 7.33 L (6.66 dry qt). See App. B14. △A shekel equaled 11.4 g (0.367 oz t). See App. B14.

should open floodgates in the heavens, could this* possibly take place?"ᵃ To that he said: "You will see it with your own eyes,ᵇ but you will not eat from it."ᶜ

3 There were four lepers at the entrance of the city gate,ᵈ and they said to one another: "Why are we sitting here until we die? **4** If we say, 'Let us go into the city,' while the famine is in the city,ᵉ we would die there. And if we sit here, we will die anyway. So now let us go over to the camp of the Syrians. If they spare our lives, we will live, but if they put us to death, then we will die." **5** They then got up in the evening darkness and entered the camp of the Syrians. When they reached the outskirts of the Syrian camp, there was nobody there.

6 For Jehovah had caused the Syrian camp to hear the sound of war chariots and horses, the sound of a huge army.ᶠ So they said to one another: "Look! The king of Israel has hired the kings of the Hit′tites and the kings of Egypt to come against us!" **7** They immediately got up and fled in the evening darkness, leaving their tents, horses, donkeys, and the whole camp just as it was, and they fled for their lives.*

8 When these lepers reached the outskirts of the camp, they entered into one of the tents and began to eat and drink. They carried away from there silver, gold, and garments and went and hid them. Then they returned and entered another tent and carried things away from there and went and hid them.

9 Finally they said to one another: "What we are doing is not right. This day is a day of good news! If we hesitate and wait un-

til dawn, we will deserve to be punished. Let us now go and report this at the king's house." **10** So they went and called out to the gatekeepers of the city and reported to them: "We went into the camp of the Syrians, but nobody was there—we did not hear anyone at all. There were only the horses and donkeys tied and the tents left just as they were." **11** At once the gatekeepers called out, and it was reported inside the king's house.

12 Immediately the king got up by night and said to his servants: "Please let me tell you what the Syrians have done to us. They know that we are hungry,ᵃ so they left the camp to hide in the field, saying, 'They will come out of the city, and we will catch them alive and enter into the city.'"ᵇ **13** Then one of his servants said: "Please, let some men take five of the remaining horses that are in the city. Look! They will end up the same as all the crowd of Israel that remain here. Look! They will end up the same as all the crowd of Israel that perished. Let us then send them out and see." **14** So they took two chariots with horses, and the king sent them out to the camp of the Syrians, saying: "Go and see." **15** They followed them as far as the Jordan, and the entire way was covered with garments and utensils that the Syrians had thrown away as they fled in panic. The messengers returned and reported it to the king.

16 The people then went out and plundered the camp of the Syrians, so that a seah measure of fine flour came to be worth a shekel, and two seah measures of barley came to be worth a shekel, according to the word of Jehovah.ᶜ **17** The king had appointed the adjutant whom he relied on to be in charge of the

---

CHAP. 7
a Nu 14:11

b Nu 11:23

c 2Ki 7:17

d Le 13:45, 46

e 2Ki 6:25

f De 28:7
2Sa 5:24

Second Col.
a 2Ki 6:25
2Ki 6:28, 29

b Jos 8:4, 12
Jg 20:29, 37

c Nu 23:19
2Ki 7:1
Isa 55:10, 11

7:2 *Lit., "this word."   7:7 *Or "souls."

gate, but the people trampled him to death at the gate, just as the man of the true God had told the king when he came down to him. **18** It happened just as the man of the true God had said to the king: "Two seah measures of barley will be worth a shekel, and a seah measure of fine flour will be worth a shekel tomorrow at this time at the gate of Sa·mar′i·a."[a] **19** But the adjutant had said to the man of the true God: "Even if Jehovah should open floodgates in the heavens, could such a thing* take place?" To this E·li′sha had said: "You will see it with your own eyes, but you will not eat from it." **20** That is exactly what happened to him, because the people trampled him to death at the gate.

8 E·li′sha said to the woman whose son he had restored to life:*[b] "Rise up and go, you with your household, and live as a foreigner wherever you can, for Jehovah has declared a famine,[c] and it will come on the land for seven years." **2** So the woman got up and did what the man of the true God said. She went with her household and settled in the land of the Phi·lis′tines[d] for seven years.

3 At the end of seven years, the woman returned from the land of the Phi·lis′tines and went to appeal to the king for her house and her field. **4** Now the king was speaking to Ge·ha′zi the attendant of the man of the true God, saying: "Relate to me, please, all the great things that E·li′sha has done."[e] **5** Just as he was relating to the king how he had restored the dead one to life,[f] the woman whose son he had restored to life came to the king, appealing for her house

---

7:19 *Lit., "such a word as this." 8:1 *Or "had revived."

CHAP. 7
a 2Ki 7:1, 2

CHAP. 8
b 2Ki 4:32-35

c Le 26:19
De 28:15, 23
1Ki 17:1

d Jos 13:2, 3

e 2Ki 2:14
2Ki 2:20, 21
2Ki 3:17
2Ki 4:4, 7
2Ki 6:5-7
2Ki 7:1

f 2Ki 4:32-35

Second Col.
a Nu 36:9

b Isa 7:8

c 1Ki 20:1
2Ki 6:24

d 1Ki 17:24

e 1Ki 19:15

f 1Sa 9:8
1Ki 14:2, 3

g 2Ki 8:15

h 2Ki 10:32
2Ki 12:17
2Ki 13:3
Am 1:3

i De 28:63
Am 1:13

j 1Ki 19:15

---

and her field.[a] At once Ge·ha′zi said: "My lord the king, this is the woman, and this is her son, whom E·li′sha restored to life." **6** At that the king asked the woman, and she related the story to him. Then the king assigned her a court official, telling him: "Return all that belongs to her and all the products of the field from the day she left the land until now."

7 E·li′sha came to Damascus[b] when Ben-ha′dad[c] the king of Syria was sick. So the report was made to him: "The man of the true God[d] has come here." **8** At that the king said to Haz′a·el:[e] "Take a gift with you and go and meet the man of the true God.[f] Inquire of Jehovah through him, asking, 'Will I recover from this sickness?'" **9** Haz′a·el went to meet him and took a gift with him, every sort of good thing of Damascus, the load of 40 camels. He came and stood before him and said: "Your son, Ben-ha′dad the king of Syria, has sent me to you, asking, 'Will I recover from this sickness?'" **10** E·li′sha replied to him: "Go and tell him, 'You will certainly recover,' but Jehovah has shown me that he will certainly die."[g] **11** And he kept staring at him to the point of embarrassment. Then the man of the true God gave way to weeping. **12** Haz′a·el asked: "Why is my lord weeping?" He replied: "Because I know what harm you will do to the people of Israel.[h] Their fortified places you will set on fire, their choice men you will kill with the sword, their children you will dash to pieces, and their pregnant women you will rip open."[i] **13** Haz′a·el said: "How could your servant, who is a mere dog, do such a deed?" But E·li′sha said: "Jehovah has shown me that you will be king over Syria."[j]

14 Then he left E·li'sha and returned to his own lord, who said to him: "What did E·li'sha say to you?" He replied: "He told me that you will certainly recover."[a] **15** But the next day, Haz'a·el took a coverlet, dipped it in water, and held* it over his face until he died.[b] And Haz'a·el became king in his place.[c]

16 In the fifth year of Je·ho'ram[d] the son of A'hab the king of Israel, while Je·hosh'a·phat was king of Judah, Je·ho'ram[e] the son of King Je·hosh'a·phat of Judah became king. **17** He was 32 years old when he became king, and he reigned for eight years in Jerusalem. **18** He walked in the way of the kings of Israel, just as those of the house of A'hab had done,[g] for A'hab's daughter had become his wife;[h] and he kept doing what was bad in Jehovah's eyes.[i] **19** But Jehovah did not want to bring Judah to ruin for the sake of David his servant,[j] since he had promised to give him a lamp to him[k] and to his sons always.

20 In his days E'dom revolted against Judah[l] and then set up its own king.[m] **21** So Je·ho'ram crossed over to Za'ir with all his chariots, and he rose up by night and defeated the E'domites who were surrounding him and the chariot commanders; and the troops fled to their tents. **22** But E'dom has kept up its revolt against Judah to this day. Lib'nah[n] also revolted at that time.

23 And the rest of the history of Je·ho'ram, all that he did, is it not written in the book of the history of the times of the kings of Judah? **24** Then Je·ho'ram was laid to rest with his forefathers and was buried with his forefathers in the City of David.[o] And his son A·ha·zi'ah[p] became king in his place.

25 In the 12th year of Je·ho'ram the son of A'hab the king of Israel, A·ha·zi'ah the son of King Je·ho'ram of Judah became king. **26** A·ha·zi'ah was 22 years old when he became king, and he reigned for one year in Jerusalem. His mother's name was Ath·a·li'ah[b] the granddaughter* of King Om'ri[c] of Israel. **27** He walked in the way of the house of A'hab[d] and kept doing what was bad in Jehovah's eyes, like the house of A'hab, for he was related to the house of A'hab by marriage.[e] **28** So he went with Je·ho'ram the son of A'hab to wage war against King Haz'a·el of Syria at Ra'moth-gil'e·ad,[f] but the Syrians wounded Je·ho'ram.[g] **29** So King Je·ho'ram returned to Jez're·el[h] to recover from the wounds that the Syrians had inflicted on him at Ra'mah when he fought against King Haz'a·el of Syria.[i] A·ha·zi'ah the son of Je·ho'ram the king of Judah went down to Jez're·el to see Je·ho'ram the son of A'hab, because he had been wounded.*

9 E·li'sha the prophet then called one of the sons of the prophets and said to him: "Wrap your garments around your waist, and quickly take this flask of oil with you and go to Ra'moth-gil'e·ad.[j] **2** When you arrive there, look for Je'hu[k] the son of Je·hosh'a·phat the son of Nim'shi; go in and have him get up from among his brothers and take him into the innermost room. **3** Then take the flask of oil and pour it out on his head and say, 'This is what Jehovah says: "I anoint you as king over Israel."'[l] Then open the door and flee without delay."

4 So the prophet's attendant got on his way to Ra'moth-gil'e·ad. **5** When he arrived, the army chiefs were seated there. He said: "I have a message for you, O chief." Je'hu asked: "For which one of us?" He said: "For you, O chief." **6** So Je'hu got up and went into the house; the attendant poured the oil out on his head and said to him, "This is what Jehovah the God of Israel says: 'I anoint you as king over Jehovah's people, over Israel.[a] **7** You must strike down the house of A'hab your lord, and I will avenge the blood of my servants the prophets and of all the servants of Jehovah who died at the hands of Jez'e·bel.[b] **8** And the whole house of A'hab will perish; and I will annihilate from A'hab every male,* including the helpless and weak in Israel.[c] **9** And I will make the house of A'hab like the house of Jer·o·bo'am[d] the son of Ne'bat and like the house of Ba'a·sha[e] the son of A·hi'jah. **10** As for Jez'e·bel, the dogs will eat her up in the plot of land at Jez're·el,[f] and no one will bury her.'" With that he opened the door and fled.[g]

11 When Je'hu went back to the servants of his lord, they asked him: "Is everything all right? Why did this crazy man come to you?" He answered them: "You know that sort of man and his sort of talk." **12** But they said: "That is not true! Tell us, please." Then he said: "This is what he said to me, and then he added, 'This is what Jehovah says: "I anoint you as king over Israel."'"[h] **13** At this each of them quickly took his garment and put it under him on the bare steps,[i] and they blew the horn and said: "Je'hu has become king!"[j] **14** Then Je'hu[k] the son of Je·hosh'a·phat the son

of Nim'shi conspired against Je-ho'ram.

Je·ho'ram had been on guard at Ra'moth-gil'e·ad,[a] he with all Israel, because of King Haz'a·el[b] of Syria. **15** King Je·ho'ram later returned to Jez're·el[c] to recover from the wounds that the Syrians inflicted on him when he fought King Haz'a·el of Syria.[d]

Je'hu now said: "If you agree,* do not let anyone escape from the city to go and report this in Jez're·el." **16** Then Je'hu mounted his chariot and went to Jez're·el, for Je·ho'ram was lying there wounded, and King A·ha·zi'ah of Judah had gone down to see Je·ho'ram. **17** As the watchman was standing on the tower in Jez're·el, he saw the throng of Je'hu's men approaching. At once he said: "I see a throng of men." Je·ho'ram said: "Take a cavalryman and send him to meet them, and let him say, 'Are you coming in peace?'" **18** So a horseman went to meet him and said: "This is what the king says, 'Are you coming in peace?'" But Je'hu said: "What do you have to do with 'peace'? Fall in behind me!"

The watchman then reported: "The messenger reached them, but he has not returned." **19** So he sent out a second horseman, who said when he came to them: "This is what the king says, 'Are you coming in peace?'" But Je'hu said: "What do you have to do with 'peace'? Fall in behind me!"

20 The watchman then reported: "He reached them, but he has not returned, and the driving is like the driving of Je'hu the grandson* of Nim'shi, for he drives like a madman." **21** Je·ho'ram said: "Hitch up!" So his war chariot was hitched

---

CHAP. 9
a 1Ki 19:16

b 1Ki 18:4
1Ki 19:2
1Ki 21:15, 25
Lu 18:7

c 1Ki 21:20, 21

d 1Ki 15:28, 29

e 1Ki 16:11, 12

f 1Ki 21:23

g 2Ki 9:3

h 2Ki 9:6

i Mt 21:7

j 2Sa 15:10
1Ki 1:34, 39

k 1Ki 19:16

Second Col.
a 2Ki 8:28

b 1Ki 19:15
2Ki 8:15
2Ki 10:32

c Jos 19:17, 18
1Ki 21:1

d 2Ch 22:6

9:8 *Lit., "anyone urinating against a wall." A Hebrew expression of contempt referring to males. **9:15** *Or "your soul agrees." **9:20** *Lit., "son."

up and King Je·ho'ram of Isra-el and King A·ha·zi'ah[a] of Judah each went out in his own war chariot to meet Je'hu. They en-countered him in the plot of land of Na'both[b] the Jez're·el·ite.

22 As soon as Je·ho'ram saw Je'hu, he said: "Are you coming in peace, Je'hu?" But he said: "What peace could there be as long as there is the prostitution of Jez'e·bel[c] your mother and her many sorceries?"[d] **23** At once Je·ho'ram turned his char-iot to flee, and he said to A·ha·zi'-ah: "We have been tricked, A·ha-zi'ah!" **24** Je'hu took his bow in hand and shot Je·ho'ram be-tween the shoulders, and the ar-row came out at his heart, and he collapsed in his war chariot. **25** He then said to Bid'kar his adjutant: "Pick him up and throw him into the field of Na'-both the Jez're·el·ite.[e] Remem-ber, you and I were riding to-gether* behind A'hab his father when Jehovah himself made this pronouncement against him:[f] **26** "'As surely as I saw the blood of Na'both[g] and the blood of his sons yesterday," declares Jeho-vah, "I will repay[h] you in this very plot of land," declares Je-hovah.' So now pick him up and throw him into the plot of land, according to the word of Jeho-vah."[i]

27 When King A·ha·zi'ah[j] of Judah saw what was happening, he fled by way of the garden house. (Later Je'hu pursued him and said: "Strike him down also!" So they struck him down in the chariot on his way up to Gur, which is by Ib'le·am.[k] But he con-tinued his flight to Me·gid'do and died there. **28** Then his ser-vants carried him in a chariot to Jerusalem, and they buried him in his grave with his forefathers in the City of David.[l] **29** It was

9:25 *Lit., "riding teams."

CHAP. 9
a 2Ki 8:25
  2Ki 8:29
  2Ch 22:7

b 1Ki 21:1, 15

c 1Ki 16:31
  1Ki 18:4
  1Ki 19:2
  1Ki 21:7

d Le 20:6
  De 18:10
  1Ki 18:19

e 1Ki 21:19

f 1Ki 21:29

g Ge 4:8, 10
  Ps 9:12
  Ps 72:14

h Ge 9:5
  Le 24:17

i 1Ki 21:24

j 2Ki 8:29
  2Ch 22:7

k Jos 17:11

l 2Sa 5:7

Second Col.
a 2Ki 8:24
  2Ch 22:2

b 1Ki 21:1

c 1Ki 16:31
  1Ki 21:25

d 1Ki 16:15-19

e Ex 32:26
  Ps 94:16

f 1Ki 16:31

g 2Ki 9:10

h Isa 55:10, 11

i 1Ki 21:23

CHAP. 10
j 1Ki 16:29

k 1Ki 21:8

in the 11th year of Je·ho'ram the son of A'hab that A·ha·zi'ah[a] had become king over Judah.)

30 When Je'hu came to Jez'-re·el,[b] Jez'e·bel[c] heard of it. So she painted her eyes with black paint* and adorned her head and looked down through the window. **31** As Je'hu came in through the gate, she said: "Did it go well with Zim'ri, the killer of his lord?"[d] **32** Looking up to the window, he said: "Who is on my side? Who?"[e] Immedi-ately two or three court officials looked down at him. **33** He said: "Throw her down!" So they threw her down, and some of her blood splattered on the wall and on the horses, and he tram-pled her. **34** After that he went in and ate and drank. He then said: "Please, take care of this accursed woman and bury her. After all, she is the daughter of a king."[f] **35** But when they went to bury her, they did not find anything but her skull and her feet and the palms of her hands.[g] **36** When they returned and told him, he said: "This ful-fills the word of Jehovah[h] that he spoke through his servant E·li'jah the Tish'bite, saying, 'In the plot of land of Jez're·el, the dogs will eat the flesh of Jez'e-bel.[i] **37** And the dead body of Jez'e·bel will become as manure on the surface of the field in the plot of land of Jez're·el, so that they may not say: "This is Jez'e-bel."'"

10 Now A'hab[j] had 70 sons in Sa·mar'i·a. So Je'hu wrote letters and sent them to Sa-mar'i·a, to the princes of Jez'-re·el, the elders,[k] and the guard-ians of A'hab's children,* saying: **2** "Now when this letter comes to you, the sons of your lord will be with you, as well as the

9:30 *Or "eye shadow." 10:1 *Lit., "the guardians of Ahab."

war chariots, the horses, a fortified city, and weapons. **3** Select the best and most suitable* of the sons of your lord and put him on the throne of his father. Then fight for the house of your lord."

4 But they were overcome with fear and said: "Look! If two kings could not stand before him,[a] how can we stand?" **5** So the overseer of the palace,* the governor of the city, the elders, and the guardians sent this message to Je′hu: "We are your servants, and we will do everything that you tell us. We will not make anyone king. Do whatever seems good in your eyes."

6 Then he wrote them a second letter, saying: "If you belong to me and are willing to obey me, bring the heads of the sons of your lord and come to me tomorrow at this time at Jez′re·el."

Now the 70 sons of the king were with the distinguished men of the city who were raising them. **7** As soon as the letter came to them, they took the sons of the king and slaughtered them, 70 men,[b] and they put their heads in baskets and sent them to him at Jez′re·el. **8** The messenger came in and told him: "They have brought the heads of the sons of the king." So he said: "Put them in two heaps at the entrance of the city gate until morning." **9** When he went out in the morning, he stood before all the people and said: "You are innocent.* Yes, I conspired against my lord, and I killed him,[c] but who struck down all of these? **10** Know, then, that not a single word of Jehovah's that Jehovah has spoken against the house of A′hab will go unfulfilled,*[d] and Jehovah has

done what he spoke through his servant E·li′jah."[a] **11** Moreover, Je′hu struck down all who were left of the house of A′hab in Jez′re·el, as well as all his distinguished men, his acquaintances, and his priests,[b] until he had left him no survivor.[c]

12 Then he got up and went on his way to Sa·mar′i·a. The binding house* of the shepherds was on the way. **13** There Je′hu encountered the brothers of King A·ha·zi′ah[d] of Judah, and he said to them, "Who are you?" They said: "We are the brothers of A·ha·zi′ah, and we are on our way down to ask if all is well with the sons of the king and the sons of the queen mother."* **14** Immediately he said: "Capture them alive!" So they captured them alive and slaughtered them at the cistern of the binding house, 42 men. He did not let a single one of them survive.[e]

15 As he went from there, he encountered Je·hon′a·dab[f] the son of Re′chab,[g] who was coming to meet him. When he greeted* him, he said to him: "Is your heart fully# with me, just as my heart is with your heart?"

Je·hon′a·dab replied: "It is."

"If so, give me your hand."

So he gave him his hand, and Je′hu pulled him up into the chariot with him. **16** Then he said: "Come along with me, and see my toleration of no rivalry toward* Jehovah."[h] So they had him ride with him in his war chariot. **17** Then he came to Sa·mar′i·a, and he struck down all who were left over of A′hab's house in Sa·mar′i·a until he had annihilated them,[i] according to

---

CHAP. 10

a 2Ki 9:24, 27

b 1Ki 21:21

c 2Ki 9:14, 21

d 1Sa 15:29
Isa 14:27

Second Col.

a 1Ki 21:19-24
2Ki 9:7, 36

b 1Ki 18:19
2Ki 23:19, 20

c 1Ki 21:21

d 2Ki 8:29
2Ki 9:21, 27
2Ch 22:1

e 2Ch 22:8

f Jer 35:6, 19

g 1Ch 2:55

h Nu 25:11
1Ki 19:10

i 2Ki 9:8
2Ch 22:7

10:3 *Or "upright." **10:5** *Lit., "house." **10:9** *Or "righteous." **10:10** *Lit., "will fall to the earth."

10:12 *Apparently a place where sheep were bound in order to be sheared. **10:13** *Or "the lady." **10:15** *Or "blessed." #Lit., "upright." **10:16** *Or "my zeal for."

Jehovah's word that he had spoken to E·li′jah.[a]

18 Further, Je′hu collected all the people together and said to them: "A′hab worshipped Ba′al a little,[b] but Je′hu will worship him much more. **19** So summon all the prophets of Ba′al,[c] all his worshippers, and all his priests[d] to me. Do not let a single one be absent, because I have a great sacrifice for Ba′al. Anyone who is absent will not live." But Je′hu was acting with cunning to destroy the worshippers of Ba′al.

20 Je′hu continued: "Declare* a solemn assembly for Ba′al." So they proclaimed it. **21** After that Je′hu sent word throughout Israel, and all the worshippers of Ba′al came. Not a single one was left out who did not come. They entered the house* of Ba′al,[e] and the house of Ba′al was filled from end to end. **22** He said to the one who was in charge of the wardrobe: "Bring out garments for all the worshippers of Ba′al." So he brought out the clothing for them. **23** Then Je′hu and Je·hon′a·dab[f] the son of Re′chab went into the house of Ba′al. He now said to the worshippers of Ba′al: "Search carefully and see that there are no worshippers of Jehovah here, only worshippers of Ba′al." **24** Finally they came in to offer up sacrifices and burnt offerings. Je′hu had stationed 80 of his men outside and said: "If any one of the men I am putting into your hands escapes, it will be your life for his."*

25 As soon as he finished offering up the burnt offering, Je′hu said to the guards* and the adjutants: "Come in and strike them down! Do not let a single

one escape!"* So the guards and the adjutants struck them down with the sword and threw them out, and they kept going as far as the inner sanctuary* of the house of Ba′al. **26** Then they brought out the sacred pillars[b] of the house of Ba′al and burned each one.[c] **27** They tore down the sacred pillar[d] of Ba′al, and they tore down the house of Ba′al[e] and turned it into latrines, as it remains to this day.

28 Thus Je′hu annihilated Ba′al out of Israel. **29** However, Je′hu did not turn away from the sins that Jer·o·bo′am the son of Ne′bat had caused Israel to commit as regards the golden calves that were in Beth′el and in Dan.[f] **30** So Jehovah said to Je′hu: "Because you have acted well and have done what is right in my eyes by carrying out all that was in my heart to do to the house of A′hab,[g] four generations of your sons will sit on the throne of Israel."[h] **31** But Je′hu did not take care to walk in the Law of Jehovah the God of Israel with all his heart.[i] He did not turn away from the sins that Jer·o·bo′am had caused Israel to commit.[j]

32 In those days Jehovah started to cut off* Israel piece by piece. Haz′a·el kept attacking them throughout the territory of Israel,[k] **33** from the Jordan eastward, all the land of Gil′e·ad—of the Gad′ites, the Reu′ben·ites, and the Ma·nas′sites[l]—from A·ro′er, which is by the Ar′non Valley,* to Gil′e·ad and Ba′shan.[m]

34 And the rest of the history of Je′hu, all that he did and all his mightiness, is it not written in the book of the history of the times of the kings of Israel?

CHAP. 10

a 1Ki 21:20, 21
2Ki 9:26

b 1Ki 16:32, 33
1Ki 18:22

c 2Ki 3:13

d 2Ki 10:11

e 1Ki 16:30, 32

f 2Ki 10:15
Jer 35:6, 19

Second Col.

a Ex 32:26, 27
De 13:6-9
Eze 9:5

b Le 26:1

c De 7:25

d Le 26:30
De 7:5

e 1Ki 16:30, 32

f 1Ki 12:28-30
1Ki 13:33
Ho 8:6

g 1Ki 21:21

h 2Ki 13:1, 10
2Ki 14:23
2Ki 15:8, 12

i De 10:12
Ho 1:4

j 1Ki 12:28-30
1Ki 13:34
1Ki 14:16

k 1Ki 19:17
2Ki 8:12
2Ki 13:22

l Nu 32:33
Jos 22:9

m De 3:13-16
De 28:63
Jos 13:8-12

10:20 *Lit., "Sanctify." 10:21 *Or "temple." 10:24 *Or "it will be your soul for his soul." 10:25 *Lit., "runners."

10:25 *Lit., "the city," perhaps a fortresslike structure. 10:32 *Or "reduce." 10:33 *Or "Wadi Arnon."

35 Then Je'hu was laid to rest with his forefathers, and they buried him in Sa·mar'i·a; and his son Je·ho'a·haz[a] became king in his place. **36** The length* of Je'hu's reign over Israel was 28 years in Sa·mar'i·a.

11 Now when Ath·a·li'ah,[b] A·ha·zi'ah's mother, saw that her son had died,[c] she rose up and destroyed the entire royal line.*[d] **2** However, Je·hosh'e·ba the daughter of King Je·ho'ram, A·ha·zi'ah's sister, took Je·ho'ash[e] the son of A·ha·zi'ah and stole him away from among the sons of the king who were to be put to death, keeping him and his nurse in an inner bedroom. They managed to keep him concealed from Ath·a·li'ah, so he was not put to death. **3** He remained with her for six years, hidden at the house of Jehovah, while Ath·a·li'ah was ruling over the land.

4 In the seventh year, Je·hoi'a·da sent for the chiefs of hundreds of the Ca'ri·an bodyguard and of the palace guards*[f] and had them come to him at the house of Jehovah. He made a pact* with them and had them swear to it at the house of Jehovah, and then he showed them the son of the king.[g] **5** He ordered them: "This is what you are to do: One third of you will be on duty on the Sabbath and will keep strict watch over the king's house,*[h] **6** another third will be at the Gate of the Foundation, and another third will be at the gate behind the palace guards. You will take turns watching over the house. **7** Your two divisions that are supposed to be off duty on the Sabbath must keep strict watch over the house of Jehovah to protect the king. **8** You must surround the king on every side, each with his weapons in hand. Anyone entering within the ranks will be put to death. Stay with the king wherever he goes."*

9 The chiefs of hundreds[a] did exactly what Je·hoi'a·da the priest had commanded. So each one took his men who were on duty on the Sabbath, together with those who were off duty on the Sabbath, and they came in to Je·hoi'a·da the priest.[b] **10** The priest then gave the chiefs of hundreds the spears and the circular shields that had belonged to King David, which were in the house of Jehovah. **11** And the palace guards[c] took their positions, each with his weapons in hand, from the right side of the house to the left side of the house, by the altar[d] and by the house, all around the king. **12** Then Je·hoi'a·da brought the king's son[e] and put on him the crown* and the Testimony,*[f] and they made him king and anointed him. They began to clap their hands and say: "Long live the king!"[g]

13 When Ath·a·li'ah heard the sound of the people running, she immediately came to the people at the house of Jehovah.[h] **14** Then she saw the king standing there by the pillar according to the custom.[i] The chiefs and the trumpeters[j] were with the king, and all the people of the land were rejoicing and blowing the trumpets. At this Ath·a·li'ah ripped her garments apart and cried out: "Conspiracy! Conspiracy!" **15** But Je·hoi'a·da the priest commanded the chiefs of

---

CHAP. 10
a 2Ki 13:1

CHAP. 11
b 2Ki 8:26
  2Ki 11:20
  2Ch 21:5, 6
  2Ch 24:7

c 2Ki 9:27

d 2Ch 21:4
  2Ch 22:10-12

e 2Ki 12:1

f 1Ki 14:27

g 2Ch 23:1-3

h 1Ki 7:1
  2Ch 23:4-7

Second Col.
a 2Ki 11:4

b 2Ch 23:8-11

c 1Ki 14:27

d 1Ki 8:22
  2Ch 4:1

e 2Ki 11:2

f Ex 25:21
  Ex 31:18

g 1Ki 1:39, 40

h 2Ch 23:12-15

i 2Ki 23:3

j 2Ch 5:12

10:36 *Lit., "The days." 11:1 *Lit., "all seed of the kingdom." 11:4 *Lit., "the runners." #Or "covenant." 11:5 *Or "palace."

11:8 *Lit., "when he goes out and when he comes in." 11:12 *Or "diadem." #Possibly a scroll containing the Law of God.

hundreds,[a] those appointed over the army, and said to them: "Take her out from among the ranks, and if anyone follows her, put him to death with the sword!" For the priest had said: "Do not put her to death in the house of Jehovah." **16** So they seized her, and when she reached the place where the horses enter the king's house,*[b] she was put to death there.

17 Then Je·hoi′a·da made a covenant between Jehovah and the king and the people,[c] that they would continue as the people of Jehovah, and he also made a covenant between the king and the people.[d] **18** After that all the people of the land came to the house* of Ba′al and tore down his altars,[e] completely smashed his images,[f] and killed Mat′tan the priest of Ba′al[g] in front of the altars.

Then the priest appointed overseers over the house of Jehovah.[h] **19** Further, he took the chiefs of hundreds,[i] the Ca′ri·an bodyguard, the palace guards,[j] and all the people of the land to escort the king down from the house of Jehovah, and they came to the king's house* by the way of the gate of the palace guard. He then sat on the throne of the kings.[k] **20** So all the people of the land rejoiced and the city was quiet, for they had put Ath·a·li′ah to death with the sword at the king's house.

21 Je·ho′ash[l] was seven years old when he became king.[m]

12 In the seventh year of Je′hu,[n] Je·ho′ash[o] became king, and he reigned for 40 years in Jerusalem. His mother's name was Zib′i·ah from Be′er-she′ba.[p] **2** Je·ho′ash continued doing what was right in Jehovah's eyes all the days

that Je·hoi′a·da the priest instructed him. **3** However, the high places[a] were not removed, and the people were still sacrificing and making sacrificial smoke on the high places.

4 Je·ho′ash said to the priests: "Take all the money that is brought to the house of Jehovah for the holy offerings,[b] the money for which each one is assessed,[c] the money given as an estimated value for a person,* and all the money that each person's heart is moved to bring to the house of Jehovah.[d] **5** The priests will personally take it from their donors* and use it to repair the house, wherever any damage is* found."[e]

6 By the 23rd year of King Je·ho′ash, the priests had not yet repaired the damage to the house.[f] **7** So King Je·ho′ash called Je·hoi′a·da[g] the priest and the other priests and said to them: "Why are you not repairing the damage to the house? Therefore, do not take any more money from your donors unless it is used to repair the house."[h] **8** At that the priests agreed not to take any more money from the people and not to be responsible for repairing the house.

9 Je·hoi′a·da the priest then took a chest[i] and bored a hole in its lid and put it next to the altar on the right as one enters the house of Jehovah. That is where the priests who served as doorkeepers would put all the money that was brought into the house of Jehovah.[j] **10** Whenever they saw that there was a great deal of money in the chest, the secretary of the king and the high priest would come up and collect* and count the money that had been brought to the house

---

CHAP. 11

a 2Ki 11:4
  2Ch 23:9

b 1Ki 7:1

c 1Sa 10:25
  2Sa 5:3

d 2Ch 23:16, 17

e De 12:3

f De 7:25

g De 13:5

h 2Ch 23:18-21

i 2Ki 11:4, 15

j 1Ki 14:27

k 2Sa 7:8, 16

l 2Ki 11:2

m 2Ch 24:1

CHAP. 12

n 1Ki 19:16
  2Ki 10:30

o 2Ki 11:2
  1Ch 3:10, 11

p 2Ch 24:1, 2

Second Col.

a Nu 33:52

b 2Ch 31:12

c Ex 30:13
  2Ch 24:9

d Ex 25:2
  Ex 35:21

e 2Ch 24:7

f 2Ch 24:5

g 2Ki 11:4
  2Ch 23:1
  2Ch 24:15

h 2Ch 24:6

i 2Ch 24:8
  Mr 12:41
  Lu 21:1

j 2Ch 24:10

11:16, 19 *Or "palace." 11:18 *Or "temple."

12:4 *Or "soul." 12:5 *Or "acquaintances." "Or "cracks are." 12:10 *Or "put into bags." Lit., "bind."

of Jehovah.[a] 11 They would give the money that had been counted to those appointed over the work being done in the house of Jehovah. They, in turn, paid it to the woodworkers and to the builders who were working at the house of Jehovah,[b] 12 as well as to the masons and the stonecutters. They also bought timbers and hewn stones for repairing the damage to the house of Jehovah and used the money for all the other expenses incurred in repairing the house.

13 However, none of the money brought to the house of Jehovah was used to make basins of silver, extinguishers, bowls, trumpets,[c] or any sort of gold or silver article for the house of Jehovah.[d] 14 They would give it only to those who did the work, and with it they repaired the house of Jehovah. 15 They would not call for an accounting from the men to whom they gave the money to give to the workers, for they were trustworthy.[e] 16 However, the money for guilt offerings[f] and the money for sin offerings was not brought to the house of Jehovah; it belonged to the priests.[g]

17 It was then that Haz′a·el[h] the king of Syria went up to fight against Gath,[i] and he captured it, after which he decided to attack* Jerusalem.[j] 18 At that King Je·ho′ash of Judah took all the holy offerings that his forefathers Je·hosh′a·phat, Je·ho′ram, and A·ha·zi′ah, the kings of Judah, had sanctified, as well as his own holy offerings and all the gold to be found in the treasuries of the house of Jehovah and the king's house,* and sent them to Haz′a·el the king of Syria.[k] So he withdrew from Jerusalem.

19 As for the rest of the history of Je·ho′ash, all that he did, is it not written in the book of the history of the times of the kings of Judah? 20 However, his servants joined in a conspiracy against him[a] and struck Je·ho′ash down at the house of the Mound,*[b] on the way that goes down to Sil′la. 21 His servants Jo′za·car the son of Shim′e·ath and Je·hoz′a·bad the son of Sho′mer were the ones who struck him and put him to death.[c] They buried him with his forefathers in the City of David, and his son Am·a·zi′ah became king in his place.[d]

13 In the 23rd year of Je·ho′ash[e] the son of A·ha·zi′ah[f] the king of Judah, Je·ho′a·haz the son of Je′hu[g] became king over Israel in Sa·mar′i·a, and he reigned for 17 years. 2 He continued to do what was bad in Jehovah's eyes, and he persisted in the sin that Jer·o·bo′am the son of Ne′bat had caused Israel to commit.[h] He did not turn away from it. 3 So Jehovah's anger[i] grew hot against Israel,[j] and he gave them into the hand of King Haz′a·el[k] of Syria and into the hand of Ben-ha′dad[l] the son of Haz′a·el all their days.

4 In time Je·ho′a·haz begged for the favor* of Jehovah, and Jehovah listened to him, for he had seen the oppression the king of Syria had inflicted on Israel.[m] 5 So Jehovah provided Israel with a savior[n] to free them from Syria's grip, and the Israelites were able to dwell in their homes as before.* 6 (However, they did not depart from the sin of the house of Jer·o·bo′am that he had caused Israel to commit.[o] They continued in this sin,* and

---

CHAP. 12
a 2Ch 24:11

b 2Ki 22:4-6
2Ch 24:12

c Nu 10:2
2Ch 5:12

d 2Ch 24:14

e 2Ki 22:7

f Le 5:15

g Le 7:7
Nu 18:8

h 1Ki 19:15
2Ki 8:13
2Ki 10:32

i 1Ch 18:1

j 2Ch 24:23

k 1Ki 15:18
2Ki 16:8
2Ki 18:15

Second Col.
a 2Ch 24:25,
26
2Ch 25:27

b 2Sa 5:9
1Ki 9:15, 24
2Ch 32:5

c 2Ki 14:1, 5

d 2Ch 24:27

CHAP. 13
e 2Ki 11:2, 21

f 2Ki 8:26
2Ki 9:27

g 2Ki 10:30, 35

h 1Ki 12:28-30
1Ki 13:33
1Ki 14:16

i Heb 12:29

j Le 26:14, 17

k 1Ki 19:17
2Ki 8:12

l 2Ki 13:24

m Ex 3:7
Jg 10:16
2Ki 14:26, 27

n Ne 9:27

o 2Ki 10:29
2Ki 17:21

12:17 *Lit., "Hazael set his face to go up against." 12:18 *Or "palace."

12:20 *Or "at Beth-millo." 13:4 *Or "softened the face." 13:5 *That is, in peace and security. 13:6 *Lit., "In it he walked."

the sacred pole*[a] continued to stand in Sa·mar'i·a.) 7 Je·ho'a·haz was left with an army of only 50 horsemen, 10 chariots, and 10,000 foot soldiers, because the king of Syria had destroyed them,[b] trampling them like the dust at threshing time.[c]

8 As for the rest of the history of Je·ho'a·haz, all that he did and his mightiness, is it not written in the book of the history of the times of the kings of Israel? 9 Then Je·ho'a·haz was laid to rest with his forefathers, and they buried him in Sa·mar'i·a;[d] and his son Je·ho'ash became king in his place.

10 In the 37th year of King Je·ho'ash of Judah, Je·ho'ash[e] the son of Je·ho'a·haz became king over Israel in Sa·mar'i·a, and he reigned for 16 years. 11 He continued to do what was bad in Jehovah's eyes, not departing from all the sins that Jer·o·bo'am the son of Ne'bat had made Israel commit.[f] He continued* in these sins.

12 As for the rest of the history of Je·ho'ash, all that he did and his mightiness and how he fought against King Am·a·zi'ah of Judah,[g] is it not written in the book of the history of the times of the kings of Israel? 13 Then Je·ho'ash was laid to rest with his forefathers, and Jer·o·bo'am*[h] sat on his throne. And Je·ho'ash was buried in Sa·mar'i·a with the kings of Israel.[i]

14 Now when E·li'sha[j] became ill with the sickness from which he eventually died, Je·ho'ash the king of Israel came down to him and wept over him, saying: "My father, my father! The chariot of Israel and his horsemen!"[k] E·li'sha then said to him: "Take a bow and arrows." So he took a bow and arrows.

16 Then he said to the king of Israel: "Put your hand to the bow." So he put his hand to it, after which E·li'sha laid his hands on the king's hands. 17 Then he said: "Open the window toward the east." So he opened it. E·li'sha said: "Shoot!" So he shot. He now said: "Jehovah's arrow of victory,* the arrow of victory over[#] Syria! You will strike down[△] Syria at A'phek[a] until you finish it off."

18 He continued: "Take the arrows," and he took them. Then he said to the king of Israel: "Strike the ground." So he struck the ground three times and stopped. 19 At that the man of the true God grew indignant at him and said: "You should have struck the ground five or six times! Then you would have struck down Syria until you finished it off, but now you will strike down Syria only three times."[b]

20 After that E·li'sha died and was buried. There were Mo'abite marauder bands[c] that would come into the land at the beginning of the year.* 21 As some men were burying a man, they saw the marauder band, so they quickly threw the man into E·li'sha's burial place and ran off. When the man touched the bones of E·li'sha, he came to life[d] and stood on his feet.

22 Now King Haz'a·el[e] of Syria oppressed Israel[f] all the days of Je·ho'a·haz. 23 However, Jehovah extended favor and mercy to them[g] and showed his concern for them for the sake of his covenant with Abraham,[h] Isaac,[i] and Jacob.[j] He did not want to bring them to ruin, and he has not cast them away from his

---

CHAP. 13

a De 7:5
  1Ki 14:15
  1Ki 16:33

b 2Ki 8:12
  2Ki 10:32

c Am 1:3

d 2Ki 10:35

e 2Ki 14:1

f 2Ki 10:29

g 2Ki 14:8, 13

h 2Ki 14:28

i 2Ki 10:35
  2Ki 13:9

j 1Ki 19:16

k 2Ki 2:11, 12

Second Col.

a 1Sa 29:1
  1Ki 20:26

b 2Ki 13:25

c 2Ki 1:1
  2Ki 24:2

d Joh 11:44
  Heb 11:35

e 1Ki 19:15

f 2Ki 8:12
  2Ki 10:32

g 2Ki 14:26, 27

h Ge 13:14-16

i Ge 26:3

j Ge 28:13
  Ps 105:8
  Mic 7:20

13:17 *Or "salvation." [#]Or "salvation against." [△]Or "defeat." 13:20 *Lit., "at the coming in of the year," likely in the spring.

13:6 *See Glossary. 13:11 *Lit., "walked." 13:13 *That is, Jeroboam II.

presence to this day. **24** When King Haz·a′el of Syria died, his son Ben-ha′dad became king in his place. **25** Je·ho′ash the son of Je·ho′a·haz then took back from Ben-ha′dad the son of Haz′a·el the cities that he had taken in war from Je·ho′a·haz his father. Three times Je·ho′ash struck him down,*[a] and he recovered the cities of Israel.

14 In the second year of Je·ho′ash[b] the son of Je·ho′a·haz the king of Israel, Am·a·zi′ah the son of King Je·ho′ash of Judah became king. **2** He was 25 years old when he became king, and he reigned for 29 years in Jerusalem. His mother's name was Je·ho·ad′din of Jerusalem.[c] **3** He continued to do what was right in Jehovah's eyes, but not like David[d] his forefather. He did everything as Je·ho′ash his father had done.[e] **4** However, the high places were not removed,[f] and the people were still sacrificing and making sacrificial smoke on the high places.[g] **5** As soon as he had the kingdom firmly in his control, he struck down his servants who had struck down his father the king.[h] **6** But he did not put the sons of the murderers to death, in harmony with Jehovah's commandment written in the book of Moses′ Law: "Fathers should not be put to death for their sons, and sons should not be put to death for their fathers; but each one should be put to death for his own sin."[i] **7** He struck down the E′dom·ites[j] in the Valley of Salt,[k] 10,000 men, and captured Se′la in the war,[l] and its name became Jok′the·el to this day.

8 Then Am·a·zi′ah sent messengers to Je·ho′ash son of Je·ho′a·haz son of Je′hu the king of Israel, saying: "Come, let us confront each other in battle."*[a] **9** King Je·ho′ash of Israel sent this message to King Am·a·zi′ah of Judah: "The thorny weed in Leb′a·non sent a message to the cedar in Leb′a·non, 'Give your daughter to my son as a wife.' However, a wild beast of Leb′a·non passed by and trampled down the thorny weed. **10** True, you have struck down E′dom,[b] so your heart has become arrogant. Enjoy your glory, but stay in your own house.* Why should you provoke disaster and fall, bringing Judah down with you?" **11** But Am·a·zi′ah did not listen.[c]

So King Je·ho′ash of Israel went up, and he and King Am·a·zi′ah of Judah confronted each other in battle at Beth-she′mesh,[d] which belongs to Judah.[e] **12** Judah was defeated by Israel, so each one fled to his home.* **13** King Je·ho′ash of Israel captured King Am·a·zi′ah of Judah, son of Je·ho′ash son of A·ha·zi′ah, at Beth-she′mesh. Then they came to Jerusalem, and he made a breach in the wall of Jerusalem from the Gate of E′phra·im[f] to the Corner Gate,[g] 400 cubits.* **14** He took all the gold and the silver and all the articles that were found in the house of Jehovah and in the treasuries of the house* of the king, as well as hostages. Then he returned to Sa·mar′i·a.

15 As for the rest of the history of Je·ho′ash, what he did and his mightiness and how he fought against King Am·a·zi′ah of Judah, is it not written in the book of the history of the times of the kings of Israel? **16** Then Je·ho′ash was laid to rest with his forefathers and was buried in

---

CHAP. 13
a 2Ki 13:19

CHAP. 14
b 2Ki 13:10

c 2Ch 25:1-4

d 1Ki 15:5

e 2Ch 24:2

f 1Ki 15:14

g 2Ki 12:1, 3

h 2Ki 12:20
2Ch 24:25

i De 24:16

j 2Ki 8:20

k 2Sa 8:13
1Ch 18:12

l 2Ch 25:11, 12

Second Col.
a 2Ch 25:17-19

b 2Ki 14:7

c 2Ch 25:15, 16

d Jos 15:10, 12
Jos 21:8, 16

e 2Ch 25:20-24

f Ne 8:16
Ne 12:38, 39

g Jer 31:38
Zec 14:10

13:25 *Or "defeated him."

14:8 *Or "meet face-to-face." 14:10, 14 *Or "palace." 14:12 *Lit., "tent." 14:13 *About 178 m (584 ft). See App. B14.

Sa·mar'i·a[a] with the kings of Israel; and his son Jer·o·bo'am*[b] became king in his place.

17 Am·a·zi'ah[c] the son of Jeho'ash the king of Judah lived for 15 years after the death of Je·ho'ash[d] the son of Je·ho'a·haz the king of Israel.[e] **18** As for the rest of the history of Am·a·zi'ah, is it not written in the book of the history of the times of the kings of Judah? **19** Later a conspiracy was formed against him[f] at Jerusalem, and he fled to La'chish, but they sent men after him to La'chish and put him to death there. **20** So they carried him back on horses, and he was buried in Jerusalem with his forefathers in the City of David.[g] **21** Then all the people of Judah took Az·a·ri'ah,*[h] who was 16 years old,[i] and made him king in place of his father Am·a·zi'ah.[j] **22** He rebuilt E'lath[k] and restored it to Judah after the king* was laid to rest with his forefathers.[l]

23 In the 15th year of Am·a·zi'ah the son of Je·ho'ash the king of Judah, Jer·o·bo'am[m] the son of King Je·ho'ash of Israel became king in Samar'i·a, and he reigned for 41 years. **24** He continued to do what was bad in Jehovah's eyes. He did not depart from all the sins that Jer·o·bo'am the son of Ne'bat had caused Israel to commit.[n] **25** He restored the boundary of Israel from Le'bo-ha'math*[o] clear to the Sea of the Ar'a·bah,*[p] according to the word that Jehovah the God of Israel spoke through his servant Jo'nah[q] the son of A·mit'tai,

the prophet from Gath-he'pher.[a] **26** For Jehovah had seen the very bitter affliction of Israel.[b] There was no one left to help Israel, not even the helpless or the weak. **27** But Jehovah had promised not to wipe out the name of Israel from under the heavens.[c] So he saved them by the hand of Jer·o·bo'am the son of Je·ho'ash.[d]

28 As for the rest of the history of Jer·o·bo'am, all that he did and his mightiness, how he fought and how he restored Damascus[e] and Ha'math[f] to Judah in Israel, is it not written in the book of the history of the times of the kings of Israel? **29** Then Jer·o·bo'am was laid to rest with his forefathers, with the kings of Israel; and his son Zech·a·ri'ah[g] became king in his place.

15 In the 27th year of King Jer·o·bo'am* of Israel, Az·a·ri'ah*[h] the son of King Am·a·zi'ah[i] of Judah became king.[j] **2** He was 16 years old when he became king, and he reigned for 52 years in Jerusalem. His mother's name was Je·co·li'ah of Jerusalem. **3** He continued to do what was right in Jehovah's eyes, just as his father Am·a·zi'ah had done.[k] **4** However, the high places were not removed,[l] and the people were still sacrificing and making sacrificial smoke on the high places.[m] **5** Jehovah afflicted the king, and he remained a leper[n] until the day of his death; and he stayed in a separate house,[o] while the king's son Jo'tham[p] was in charge of the house,* judging the people of the land.[q] **6** As for the rest of the history of Az·a·ri'ah,[r] all that he did, is it not written in the book of the history of the times of the kings of Judah? **7** Then Az·a·ri'ah was laid to rest with

CHAP. 14

a 2Ki 10:35
  2Ki 13:9

b Ho 1:1
  Am 1:1
  Am 7:10

c 2Ki 14:1

d 2Ki 13:10

e 2Ch 25:25-28

f 2Ki 12:20

g 1Ki 2:10

h Mt 1:8

i 2Ki 15:1, 2

j 2Ch 26:1

k De 2:8
  1Ki 9:26
  2Ki 16:6

l 2Ch 26:2

m Ho 1:1
  Am 1:1

n 1Ki 12:28-30
  1Ki 13:34
  Ps 106:20

o Nu 13:21
  Nu 34:2, 7, 8

p De 3:16, 17

q Jon 1:1
  Mt 12:39

Second Col.

a Jos 19:10, 13

b Ex 3:7
  Jg 10:16
  Ps 106:43, 44

c Jer 31:20

d 2Ki 13:4, 5

e 2Sa 8:6

f 2Ch 8:3

g 2Ki 15:8

CHAP. 15

h 2Ki 14:21

i 2Ki 14:1

j 2Ch 26:1, 3

k 2Ch 26:4, 5

l Nu 33:52

m De 12:13, 14
  1Ki 22:41, 43
  2Ki 14:1, 4

n Nu 12:10
  2Ki 5:27

o Le 13:45, 46

p 2Ki 15:32

q 2Ch 26:16-21

r 2Ch 26:22, 23

14:16; 15:1 *That is, Jeroboam II. **14:21; 15:1** #Meaning "Jehovah Has Helped." He is called Uzziah at 2Ki 15:13; 2Ch 26:1-23; Isa 6:1; and Zec 14:5. **14:22** *That is, his father Amaziah. **14:25** *Or "the entrance of Hamath." #That is, the Salt Sea, or the Dead Sea.

15:5 *Or "palace."

his forefathers,[a] and they buried him with his forefathers in the City of David; and his son Jo'tham became king in his place.

8 In the 38th year of King Az·a·ri'ah[b] of Judah, Zech·a·ri'ah[c] the son of Jer·o·bo'am became king over Israel in Sa·mar'i·a, and he reigned for six months. **9** He did what was bad in Jehovah's eyes, just as his forefathers had done. He did not depart from the sins that Jer·o·bo'am the son of Ne'bat had caused Israel to commit.[d] **10** Then Shal'lum the son of Ja'besh conspired against him and struck him down[e] at Ib'le·am.[f] After putting him to death, he became king in his place. **11** As for the rest of the history of Zech·a·ri'ah, it is written in the book of the history of the times of the kings of Israel. **12** That fulfilled Jehovah's word spoken to Je'hu: "Four generations of your sons[g] will sit on the throne of Israel."[h] And that is how it happened.

13 Shal'lum the son of Ja'besh became king in the 39th year of King Uz·zi'ah[i] of Judah, and he reigned for a full month in Sa·mar'i·a. **14** Then Men'a·hem the son of Ga'di came up from Tir'zah[j] to Sa·mar'i·a and struck down Shal'lum[k] the son of Ja'besh in Sa·mar'i·a. After putting him to death, he became king in his place. **15** As for the rest of the history of Shal'lum and the conspiracy that he formed, it is written in the book of the history of the times of the kings of Israel. **16** It was then that Men'a·hem came from Tir'zah and struck down Tiph'sah and all who were in it and its territory, because it did not open its gates to him. He struck it down and ripped open its pregnant women.

17 In the 39th year of King Az·a·ri'ah of Judah, Men'-

a·hem the son of Ga'di became king over Israel, and he reigned for ten years in Sa·mar'i·a. **18** He continued to do what was bad in Jehovah's eyes. He did not depart from all the sins that Jer·o·bo'am the son of Ne'bat had caused Israel to commit,[a] all his days. **19** King Pul[b] of As·syr'i·a came into the land, and Men'a·hem gave Pul 1,000 talents* of silver in return for his support in strengthening his hold on the kingdom.[c] **20** So Men'a·hem raised the silver from Israel by exacting it from the prominent, wealthy men.[d] He gave the king of As·syr'i·a 50 silver shekels* for each man. Then the king of As·syr'i·a turned back and did not stay in the land. **21** As for the rest of the history of Men'a·hem,[e] all that he did, is it not written in the book of the history of the times of the kings of Israel? **22** Then Men'a·hem was laid to rest with his forefathers; and his son Pek·a·hi'ah became king in his place.

23 In the 50th year of King Az·a·ri'ah of Judah, Pek·a·hi'ah the son of Men'a·hem became king over Israel in Sa·mar'i·a, and he reigned for two years. **24** He continued to do what was bad in Jehovah's eyes. He did not depart from the sins that Jer·o·bo'am the son of Ne'bat had caused Israel to commit.[f] **25** Then his adjutant Pe'kah[g] the son of Rem·a·li'ah conspired against him and struck him down in Sa·mar'i·a in the fortified tower of the king's house* with Ar'gob and Ar'i·eh. He had 50 men of Gil'e·ad with him; and after he put him to death, he became king in his place. **26** As for the rest of the history of Pek·a·hi'ah,

---

CHAP. 15

a Isa 6:1

b 2Ki 14:21

c 2Ki 14:29

d 1Ki 12:28-30
1Ki 13:33
1Ki 14:16

e Ho 1:4
Am 7:9

f Jos 17:11

g 2Ki 13:1, 10
2Ki 14:23, 29

h 2Ki 10:30

i 2Ch 26:1

j 1Ki 14:17
1Ki 15:21
1Ki 16:8, 17

k 2Ki 15:10

Second Col.

a 1Ki 12:28-30
1Ki 13:33
1Ki 14:16

b 1Ch 5:26

c 2Ki 12:18
2Ki 16:8

d 2Ki 23:35

e 2Ki 15:14

f 1Ki 12:28-30
1Ki 13:33
1Ki 14:16

g 2Ch 28:6

15:19 *A talent equaled 34.2 kg (1,101 oz t). See App. B14. **15:20** *A shekel equaled 11.4 g (0.367 oz t). See App. B14. **15:25** *Or "palace."

all that he did, it is written in the book of the history of the times of the kings of Israel.

27 In the 52nd year of King Az·a·ri′ah of Judah, Pe′kah[a] the son of Rem·a·li′ah became king over Israel in Sa·mar′i·a, and he reigned for 20 years. **28** He continued to do what was bad in Jehovah's eyes, and he did not depart from the sins that Jer·o·bo′am the son of Ne′bat had caused Israel to commit.[b] **29** In the days of King Pe′kah of Israel, King Tig′lath-pil·e′ser[c] of As·syr′i·a invaded and captured I′jon, A′bel-beth-ma′a·cah,[d] Ja·no′ah, Ke′desh,[e] Ha′zor, Gil′e·ad,[f] and Gal′i·lee—all the land of Naph′ta·li[g]—and he took the inhabitants into exile in As·syr′i·a.[h] **30** Then Ho·she′a[i] the son of E′lah formed a conspiracy against Pe′kah the son of Rem·a·li′ah, and he struck him and put him to death; and he became king in his place in the 20th year of Jo′tham[j] the son of Uz·zi′ah. **31** As for the rest of the history of Pe′kah, all that he did, it is written in the book of the history of the times of the kings of Israel.

32 In the second year of Pe′kah the son of Rem·a·li′ah the king of Israel, Jo′tham[k] the son of King Uz·zi′ah[l] of Judah became king. **33** He was 25 years old when he became king, and he reigned for 16 years in Jerusalem. His mother's name was Je·ru′sha the daughter of Za′dok.[m] **34** He kept doing what was right in Jehovah's eyes, just as his father Uz·zi′ah had done.[n] **35** However, the high places were not removed, and the people were still sacrificing and making sacrificial smoke on the high places.[o] He was the one who built the upper gate of the house of Jehovah.[p] **36** As for the rest of the history of Jo′tham, what he did, is it not writ-

ten in the book of the history of the times of the kings of Judah? **37** In those days Jehovah began sending Re′zin the king of Syria and Pe′kah[a] the son of Rem·a·li′ah against Judah.[b] **38** Then Jo′tham was laid to rest with his forefathers and was buried with his forefathers in the City of David his forefather. And his son A′haz became king in his place.

16 In the 17th year of Pe′kah the son of Rem·a·li′ah, A′haz[c] the son of King Jo′tham of Judah became king. **2** A′haz was 20 years old when he became king, and he reigned for 16 years in Jerusalem. He did not do what was right in the eyes of Jehovah his God as David his forefather had done.[d] **3** Instead, he walked in the way of the kings of Israel,[e] and he even made his own son pass through the fire,[f] following the detestable practices of the nations[g] that Jehovah had driven out from before the Israelites. **4** He also kept sacrificing and making sacrificial smoke on the high places,[h] on the hills, and under every luxuriant tree.[i]

5 It was then that King Re′zin of Syria and Pe′kah son of Rem·a·li′ah the king of Israel came up to wage war against Jerusalem.[j] They laid siege against A′haz but were not able to capture the city. **6** At that time King Re′zin of Syria restored E′lath[k] to E′dom, after which he drove the Jews* out of E′lath. And the E′dom·ites entered E′lath, and they have occupied it down to this day. **7** So A′haz sent messengers to King Tig′lath-pil·e′ser[l] of As·syr′i·a, saying: "I am your servant and your son. Come up and save me from the hand of the king of Syria and the hand of the king of Israel, who are attacking me." **8** A′haz then took the silver and the gold that was

CHAP. 15
a 2Ch 28:6
  Isa 7:1, 4

b 1Ki 12:28-30
  1Ki 13:33
  1Ki 14:16

c 2Ki 16:7
  1Ch 5:6
  1Ch 5:26
  2Ch 28:19, 20

d 1Ki 15:20

e Jos 20:7, 9

f Nu 32:40

g Isa 9:1

h Le 26:38
  De 28:64
  2Ki 17:22, 23
  Isa 8:4

i 2Ki 17:1

j 2Ch 27:1

k 2Ch 27:7
  Mt 1:9

l 2Ki 14:21

m 2Ch 27:1

n 2Ch 27:2

o Nu 33:52
  De 12:14

p 2Ch 27:3

Second Col.
a 2Ki 15:27
  2Ch 28:6

b 2Ki 16:5
  Isa 7:1, 2

CHAP. 16
c Isa 1:1
  Isa 7:1
  Ho 1:1
  Mic 1:1
  Mt 1:9

d 2Ch 28:1-4

e 1Ki 12:28-30
  1Ki 16:33

f Le 20:2, 3
  2Ch 33:1, 6
  Jer 7:31

g De 12:29-31

h Nu 33:52

i De 12:2

j 2Ki 15:37
  2Ch 28:5, 6

k 2Ki 14:21, 22

l 2Ki 15:29

16:6 *Or "the men of Judah."

to be found at the house of Jehovah and in the treasuries of the king's house* and sent the king of As·syr'i·a a bribe.[a] **9** The king of As·syr'i·a responded to his request, and he went up to Damascus and captured it and led its people into exile to Kir,[b] and he put Re'zin to death.[c]

10 Then King A'haz went to meet King Tig'lath-pil·e'ser of As·syr'i·a at Damascus. When he saw the altar that was in Damascus, King A'haz sent U·ri'jah the priest a plan of the altar, showing its pattern and how it was made,[d] **11** U·ri'jah[f] the priest built an altar[f] according to all the directions that King A'haz had sent from Damascus. U·ri'jah the priest finished building it before King A'haz returned from Damascus. **12** When the king returned from Damascus and saw the altar, he approached the altar and made offerings on it.[g] **13** And on that altar he continued to make his burnt offerings and his grain offerings smoke; he also poured out his drink offerings and sprinkled the blood of his communion sacrifices on it. **14** Then he moved the copper altar[h] that was before Jehovah from its place in front of the house, from between his own altar and the house of Jehovah, and he put it at the north side of his own altar. **15** King A'haz commanded U·ri'jah[i] the priest: "Make the morning burnt offering smoke on the great altar,[j] also the evening grain offering,[k] the king's burnt offering, and his grain offering, as well as the burnt offerings, the grain offerings, and the drink offerings of all the people. You should also sprinkle on it all the blood of the burnt offerings and all the blood of the other sacrifices. As for the copper altar, let me decide what to do with it." **16** And

U·ri'jah the priest did everything that King A'haz had commanded.[a]

17 Furthermore, King A'haz cut the side panels of the carriages[b] into pieces and removed the basins from them,[c] and he took the Sea down off the copper bulls[d] that supported it and put it on a stone pavement.[e] **18** And the covered structure for the Sabbath that had been built in the house and the king's outer entryway he shifted away from the house of Jehovah; he did so because of the king of As·syr'i·a.

19 As for the rest of the history of A'haz, what he did, is it not written in the book of the history of the times of the kings of Judah?[f] **20** Then A'haz was laid to rest with his forefathers and was buried with his forefathers in the City of David; and his son Hez·e·ki'ah*[g] became king in his place.

17 In the 12th year of King A'haz of Judah, Ho·she'a[h] the son of E'lah became king over Israel in Sa·mar'i·a; he ruled for nine years. **2** He continued to do what was bad in Jehovah's eyes, only not to the extent of the kings of Israel prior to him. **3** King Shal·man·e'ser of As·syr'i·a came up against him,[i] and Ho·she'a became his servant and began to pay tribute to him.[j] **4** However, the king of As·syr'i·a learned that Ho·she'a was involved in a conspiracy, for he had sent messengers to King So of Egypt[k] and did not bring the tribute up to the king of As·syr'i·a as in former years. Therefore, the king of As·syr'i·a kept him confined and bound in prison.

5 The king of As·syr'i·a invaded the entire land, and he came to Sa·mar'i·a and laid siege to it

CHAP. 16
a 1Ki 15:18, 19

b Am 1:4, 5

c Isa 9:11

d De 12:30

e Isa 8:2

f Jer 23:11
  Eze 22:26

g 2Ch 28:22,
  23
  2Ch 28:25

h 2Ch 4:1

i Isa 8:2

j 2Ch 28:23

k Ex 29:39-41

Second Col.
a 2Ki 16:11

b 1Ki 7:27, 28

c 1Ki 7:38
  2Ch 4:6

d 1Ki 7:23, 25

e 2Ch 28:24
  2Ch 29:19

f 2Ch 28:26,
  27

g 2Ki 18:1
  2Ch 29:1
  Isa 1:1
  Ho 1:1
  Mt 1:9

CHAP. 17
h 2Ki 15:30

i 2Ki 18:9
  Isa 10:5, 6
  Ho 10:14, 15

j 2Ki 18:14

k Isa 31:1

16:8 *Or "palace."

16:20 *Meaning "Jehovah Strengthens."

for three years. **6** In the ninth year of Ho·she′a, the king of As·syr′i·a captured Sa·mar′i·a.ᵃ He then led the people of Israel into exileᵇ in As·syr′i·a and made them dwell in Ha′lah and in Ha′bor at the river Go′zanᶜ and in the cities of the Medes.ᵈ

7 This happened because the people of Israel had sinned against Jehovah their God, who brought them up out of the land of Egypt from under the control of Phar′aoh king of Egypt.ᵉ They worshipped* other gods,ᶠ **8** they followed the customs of the nations that Jehovah had driven out from before the Israelites, and they followed the customs that the kings of Israel had established.

9 The Israelites were pursuing the things that were not right according to Jehovah their God. They kept building high places in all their cities,ᵍ from watchtower to fortified city.* **10** They kept setting up for themselves sacred pillars and sacred poles*ʰ on every high hill and under every luxuriant tree;ⁱ **11** and on all the high places they would make sacrificial smoke just as the nations did that Jehovah had driven into exile from before them.ʲ They kept doing wicked things to offend Jehovah.

12 They continued to serve disgusting idols,*ᵏ about which Jehovah had told them: "You must not do this!"ˡ **13** Jehovah kept warning Israel and Judah through all his prophets and every visionary,ᵐ saying: "Turn back from your wicked ways!ⁿ Keep my commandments and my statutes according to all the law that I commanded your forefathers and that I sent to you through my servants the prophets." **14** But they did not listen, and they remained just as stubborn as* their forefathers who had not shown faith in Jehovah their God.ᵃ **15** They continued rejecting his regulations and his covenantᵇ that he had made with their forefathers and his reminders that he had given to warn them,ᶜ and they kept following worthless idolsᵈ and became worthless themselves,ᵉ imitating the nations all around them that Jehovah had commanded them not to imitate.ᶠ

16 They kept leaving all the commandments of Jehovah their God, and they made metal statuesᵍ of two calvesᵍ and a sacred pole,*ʰ and they bowed down to all the army of the heavensⁱ and served Ba′al.ʲ **17** They also made their sons and their daughters pass through the fire,ᵏ they practiced divinationˡ and looked for omens, and they kept devoting* themselves to do what was bad in the eyes of Jehovah, to offend him.

18 So Jehovah was very angry with Israel, so that he removed them from his sight.ᵐ He did not let any remain but the tribe of Judah alone.

19 Even Judah did not keep the commandments of Jehovah their God;ⁿ they also walked in the customs that Israel followed.ᵒ **20** Jehovah rejected all the descendants of Israel and humiliated them and gave them into the hand of plunderers, until he had cast them away from before him. **21** He ripped Israel away from the house of David, and they made

17:7 *Lit., "feared." **17:9** *That is, in every place, whether sparsely inhabited or populous. **17:10, 16** *See Glossary. **17:12** *The Hebrew term may be related to a word for "dung" and is used as an expression of contempt. **17:14** *Lit., "hardened their neck like the neck of." **17:16** "Or "molten statues." **17:17** *Lit., "selling."

Jer·o·bo'am the son of Ne'bat king.[a] But Jer·o·bo'am caused Israel to stray from following Jehovah, and he caused them to commit a great sin. **22** And the people of Israel kept walking in all the sins that Jer·o·bo'am had committed.[b] They did not depart from them **23** until Jehovah removed Israel from his sight, just as he had declared through all his servants the prophets.[c] So Israel was taken into exile from its land to As·syr'i·a,[d] where they remain to this day.

24 The king of As·syr'i·a then brought people from Babylon, Cu'thah, Av'va, Ha'math, and Seph·ar·va'im[e] and settled them in the cities of Sa·mar'i·a in place of the Israelites; they took possession of Sa·mar'i·a and lived in its cities. **25** When they first began dwelling there, they did not fear* Jehovah. So Jehovah sent lions among them,[f] and they killed some of the people. **26** It was reported to the king of As·syr'i·a: "The nations that you have taken into exile and resettled in the cities of Sa·mar'i·a do not know the religion* of the God of the land. So he keeps sending lions among them, which are putting them to death, because none of them know the religion of the God of the land."

27 At that the king of As·syr'i·a commanded: "Have one of the priests whom you took into exile from there return to live there and to teach them the religion of the God of the land." **28** So one of the priests whom they had taken into exile from Sa·mar'i·a came back to live in Beth'el,[g] and he began to teach them how they should fear* Jehovah.[h]

29 However, each different nation made their own god,*

which they placed in the houses of worship on the high places that the Sa·mar'i·tans had made; each different nation did so in their cities where they were living. **30** So the men of Babylon made Suc'coth-be'noth, the men of Cuth made Ner'gal, the men of Ha'math[a] made A·shi'ma, **31** and the Av'vites made Nib'haz and Tar'tak. The Se'phar·vites would burn their sons in the fire to A·dram'me·lech and A·nam'me·lech, the gods of Seph·ar·va'im.[b] **32** Although they feared Jehovah, they appointed priests for the high places from the people in general, and these officiated for them at the houses of worship on the high places.[c] **33** Thus, they feared Jehovah, but they worshipped their own gods according to the religion* of the nations from which they had been deported.[d]

34 To this day they follow their former religions.* None of them worship* Jehovah,* and none follow his statutes, his judgments, the Law, and the commandment that Jehovah gave the sons of Jacob, whose name he changed to Israel.[e] **35** When Jehovah made a covenant with them,[f] he commanded them: "You must not fear other gods, and you must not bow down to them or serve them or sacrifice to them.[g] **36** But Jehovah, who brought you up out of the land of Egypt with great power and an outstretched arm,[h] is the One you should fear,[i] and to him you should bow down, and to him you should sacrifice. **37** And the regulations, the judgments, the Law, and the commandment that he wrote for you,[j] you should always follow carefully, and you must not fear other gods. **38** And you must

---

CHAP. 17
a 1Ki 12:20

b 1Ki 12:28-30

c De 28:45, 63
1Ki 14:16
Ho 1:4
Am 5:27
Mic 1:6

d 2Ki 18:11

e 2Ki 19:11, 13

f Ex 23:29

g Ge 28:18, 19
Jos 16:1
1Ki 12:28, 29

h Joh 4:20-22

_____
Second Col.
a 2Ki 17:24

b 2Ki 18:34

c 1Ki 12:31, 32
1Ki 13:33

d 2Ki 17:24, 41

e Ge 32:28

f Ex 19:5
Ex 24:7
De 29:1

g Ex 20:3-5
Ex 23:24
Ex 34:14
De 5:9

h Ex 6:6

i De 6:12, 13

j De 31:9

17:25, 28 *Or "worship." 17:26, 33, 34 *Or "religious customs." 17:29 *Or "gods."

17:34 *Lit., "fear."

not forget the covenant that I made with you,[a] and you must not fear other gods. **39** But it is Jehovah your God whom you should fear, as he is the one who will rescue you out of the hand of all your enemies."

40 But they did not obey, and they followed their former religion.*[b] **41** So these nations came to fear Jehovah,[c] but they were also serving their own graven images. Both their sons and their grandsons have done just as their forefathers did, down to this day.

18 In the third year of Ho·she′a[d] the son of E′lah the king of Israel, Hez·e·ki′ah[e] the son of King A′haz[f] of Judah became king. **2** He was 25 years old when he became king, and he reigned for 29 years in Jerusalem. His mother's name was A′bi* the daughter of Zech·a·ri′ah.[g] **3** He kept doing what was right in Jehovah's eyes,[h] just as David his forefather had done.[i] **4** He was the one who removed the high places,[j] smashed the sacred pillars, and cut down the sacred pole.*[k] He also crushed the copper serpent that Moses had made;[l] for down to that time the people of Israel had been making sacrificial smoke to it and it used to be called the copper serpent-idol.*# **5** He trusted in Jehovah[m] the God of Israel; there was no one like him among all the kings of Judah after him nor among those prior to him. **6** He held fast to Jehovah.[n] He did not turn away from following him; he continued to keep the commandments that Jehovah had given to Moses. **7** And Jehovah was with him. Wherever he went, he acted wisely. He rebelled against the king of As·syr′-

i·a and refused to serve him.[a] **8** He also defeated the Phi·lis′tines[b] clear to Gaz′a and its territories, from watchtower to fortified city.*

9 In the fourth year of King Hez·e·ki′ah, that is, the seventh year of Ho·she′a[c] the son of E′lah the king of Israel, King Shal·man·e′ser of As·syr′i·a came up against Sa·mar′i·a and began to lay siege to it.[d] **10** They captured it[e] at the end of three years; in the sixth year of Hez·e·ki′ah, which was the ninth year of King Ho·she′a of Israel, Sa·mar′i·a was captured. **11** Then the king of As·syr′i·a took Israel into exile[f] in As·syr′i·a and settled them in Ha′lah and in Ha′bor at the river Go′zan and in the cities of the Medes.[g] **12** This was because they had not listened to the voice of Jehovah their God but kept violating his covenant, all that Moses the servant of Jehovah had commanded.[h] They neither listened nor obeyed.

13 In the 14th year of King Hez·e·ki′ah, Sen·nach′er·ib the king of As·syr′i·a[a] came up against all the fortified cities of Judah and captured them.[j] **14** So King Hez·e·ki′ah of Judah sent word to the king of As·syr′i·a at La′chish: "I am at fault. Withdraw from against me, and I will give whatever you may impose on me." The king of As·syr′i·a imposed on King Hez·e·ki′ah of Judah a fine of 300 silver talents* and 30 gold talents. **15** So Hez·e·ki′ah gave all the silver that could be found in the house of Jehovah and in the treasuries of the king's house.*[k] **16** At that time Hez·e·ki′ah removed* the doors of the temple[l]

CHAP. 17
a De 4:23

b 2Ki 17:34

c Ezr 4:1, 2

CHAP. 18
d 2Ki 15:30
  2Ki 17:1

e 2Ch 28:27
  Mt 1:9

f 2Ki 16:2, 20

g 2Ch 29:1, 2

h 2Ki 20:3
  2Ch 31:20, 21
  Ps 119:128

i 1Ki 15:5

j Nu 33:52
  1Ki 3:2
  2Ki 14:1, 4

k De 7:5
  De 12:3
  2Ch 31:1

l Nu 21:8, 9

m 2Ki 19:15
  2Ch 32:7, 8

n De 10:20
  Jos 23:8

Second Col.
a 2Ki 16:7

b 2Ch 28:18, 19
  Isa 14:28, 29

c 2Ki 17:1

d 2Ki 17:3-6

e Ho 13:16
  Am 3:11
  Mic 1:6

f Isa 8:4
  Am 6:1, 7

g 2Ki 19:36
  1Ch 5:26

h De 8:20
  1Ki 14:15

i Isa 10:5

j 2Ki 18:17
  Isa 36:1

k 2Ki 12:18
  2Ki 16:8
  2Ch 16:2, 3

l 1Ki 6:33-35

17:40 *Or "religious customs." **18:2** *An abbreviated form of Abijah. **18:4** *See Glossary. #Or "called Nehushtan."

18:8 *That is, in every place, whether sparsely inhabited or populous. **18:14** *A talent equaled 34.2 kg (1,101 oz t). See App. B14. **18:15** *Or "palace." **18:16** *Lit., "cut off."

of Jehovah and the doorposts that King Hez·e·ki'ah of Judah himself had overlaid,*[a] and he gave them to the king of As·syr'i·a.

17 The king of As·syr'i·a then sent the Tar'tan,* the Rab'sa·ris,# and the Rab'sha·keh△ with a vast army from La'chish[b] to King Hez·e·ki'ah in Jerusalem.[c] They went up to Jerusalem and took up a position by the conduit of the upper pool, which is at the highway of the laundryman's field.[d] **18** When they called for the king to come out, E·li'a·kim[e] son of Hil·ki'ah, who was in charge of the household,* Sheb'nah[f] the secretary, and Jo'ah son of A'saph the recorder came out to them.

19 So the Rab'sha·keh said to them: "Please, say to Hez·e·ki'ah, 'This is what the great king, the king of As·syr'i·a, says: "What is the basis for your confidence?[g] **20** You are saying, 'I have a strategy and the power to wage war,' but these are empty words. In whom have you put your trust, so that you dare to rebel against me?[h] **21** Look! You trust in the support of this crushed reed, Egypt,[i] which if a man should lean on it would enter into his palm and pierce it. That is the way Phar'aoh king of Egypt is to all those who trust in him. **22** And if you should say to me, 'We trust in Jehovah our God,'[j] is he not the one whose high places and altars Hez·e·ki'ah has removed,[k] while he says to Judah and Jerusalem, 'You should bow down before this altar in Jerusalem'?"[l] **23** So now make this wager, please, with my lord the king of As·syr'i·a: I will give you 2,000 horses if you are able to find enough riders for them.[a] **24** How, then, could you drive back even one governor who is the least of my lord's servants, while you put your trust in Egypt for chariots and for horsemen? **25** Now is it without authorization from Jehovah that I have come up against this place to destroy it? Jehovah himself said to me, 'Go up against this land and destroy it.'"

26 At this E·li'a·kim son of Hil·ki'ah, and Sheb'nah[b] and Jo'ah said to the Rab'sha·keh:[c] "Speak to your servants, please, in the Ar·a·ma'ic* language,[d] for we can understand it; do not speak to us in the language of the Jews in the hearing of the people on the wall."[e] **27** But the Rab'sha·keh said to them: "Is it just to your lord and to you that my lord sent me to speak these words? Is it not also to the men who sit on the wall, those who will eat their own excrement and drink their own urine along with you?"

28 Then the Rab'sha·keh stood and called out loudly in the language of the Jews, saying: "Hear the word of the great king, the king of As·syr'i·a.[f] **29** This is what the king says, 'Do not let Hez·e·ki'ah deceive you, for he is not able to rescue you out of my hand.[g] **30** And do not let Hez·e·ki'ah cause you to trust in Jehovah by saying: "Jehovah will surely rescue us, and this city will not be given into the hand of the king of As·syr'i·a."[h] **31** Do not listen to Hez·e·ki'ah, for this is what the king of As·syr'i·a says: "Make peace with me and surrender,* and each of you will eat from his own vine and from his own fig tree and will drink the water of his own cistern, **32** until I come and take you to a land like your own land,[i] a land of grain and new wine,

---

CHAP. 18
a 2Ch 29:1, 3

b Jos 15:20, 39
  2Ch 11:5, 9

c 2Ch 32:9

d Isa 36:2, 3

e 2Ki 19:2
  Isa 22:20-24

f Isa 22:15-19

g 2Ch 32:10
  Isa 36:4-10

h 2Ki 18:7

i Isa 30:1, 2

j 2Ch 32:8

k Isa 31:1

l De 12:11, 13
  2Ch 32:12

Second Col.
a Isa 10:12, 13

b 2Ki 18:18

c 2Ki 18:17

d Ezr 4:7
  Da 2:4

e Isa 36:11, 12

f Isa 36:13-20

g 2Ch 32:15

h 2Ki 19:32-34

i 2Ki 17:6

18:16 *That is, overlaid with gold. 18:17 *Or "the commander." #Or "the chief court official." △Or "the chief cupbearer." 18:18 *Or "palace."

18:26 *Or "Syrian." 18:31 *Lit., "Make a blessing with me and come out to me."

a land of bread and vineyards, a land of olive trees and honey. Then you will live and not die. Do not listen to Hez·e·ki′ah, for he misleads you by saying, 'Jehovah will rescue us.' **33** Have any of the gods of the nations rescued their land out of the hand of the king of As·syr′i·a? **34** Where are the gods of Ha′math[a] and Ar′pad? Where are the gods of Seph·ar·va′im,[b] He′na, and Iv′vah? Have they rescued Sa·mar′i·a out of my hand?[c] **35** Who among all the gods of the lands have rescued their land out of my hand, so that Jehovah should rescue Jerusalem out of my hand?"[d]

36 But the people kept silent and did not say a word to him in reply, for the order of the king was, "You must not answer him."[e] **37** But E·li′a·kim son of Hil·ki′ah, who was in charge of the household,[*] Sheb′nah the secretary, and Jo′ah son of A′saph the recorder came to Hez·e·ki′ah with their garments ripped apart and told him the words of the Rab′sha·keh.

19 As soon as King Hez·e·ki′ah heard this, he ripped his garments apart and covered himself with sackcloth and went into the house of Jehovah.[f] **2** Then he sent E·li′a·kim, who was in charge of the household,[*] Sheb′nah the secretary, and the elders of the priests, covered with sackcloth, to the prophet Isaiah,[g] the son of A′moz. **3** They said to him: "This is what Hez·e·ki′ah says, 'This day is a day of distress, of rebuke,[*] and of disgrace; for the children are ready to be born,[″] but there is no strength to give birth.[h] **4** Perhaps Jehovah your God will hear all the words of the Rab′sha·keh, whom the king

of As·syr′i·a his lord sent to taunt the living God,[a] and he will call him to account for the words that Jehovah your God has heard. So offer up a prayer[b] in behalf of the remnant who have survived.'"

5 So the servants of King Hez·e·ki′ah went in to Isaiah,[c] **6** and Isaiah said to them: "This is what you should say to your lord, 'This is what Jehovah says: "Do not be afraid[d] because of the words that you heard, the words with which the attendants of the king of As·syr′i·a blasphemed me.[e] **7** Here I am putting a thought in his mind,[*] and he will hear a report and return to his own land; and I will make him fall by the sword in his own land."'"[f]

8 After the Rab′sha·keh heard that the king of As·syr′i·a had pulled away from La′chish,[g] he returned to him and found him fighting against Lib′nah.[h] **9** Now the king heard it said about King Tir·ha′kah of E·thi·o′pi·a: "Here he has come out to fight against you." So he sent messengers[i] again to Hez·e·ki′ah, saying: **10** "This is what you should say to King Hez·e·ki′ah of Judah, 'Do not let your God in whom you trust deceive you by saying: "Jerusalem will not be given into the hand of the king of As·syr′i·a."[j] **11** Look! You have heard what the kings of As·syr′i·a did to all the lands by devoting them to destruction.[k] Will you alone be rescued? **12** Did the gods of the nations that my forefathers destroyed rescue them? Where are Go′zan, Ha′ran,[l] Re′zeph, and the people of E′den who were in Tel·as′sar? **13** Where is the king of Ha′math, the king of Ar′pad, and the king of the cities of Seph·ar·va′im, and of He′na, and of Iv′vah?"[m]

CHAP. 18
a Nu 13:21

b 2Ki 17:24

c 2Ki 17:6

d 2Ki 19:17-19
   2Ch 32:15
   Isa 37:23

e Isa 36:21, 22

CHAP. 19
f Isa 37:1-4

g Isa 1:1

h Isa 26:17, 18

Second Col.
a Isa 17:45
   2Ki 18:35

b 2Sa 22:7
   2Ch 20:9
   2Ch 32:20
   Ps 50:15

c Isa 37:5-7

d De 20:3
   Isa 41:10
   Isa 51:7

e 2Ki 18:17

f 2Ch 32:21
   Isa 37:37, 38

g 2Ki 18:14

h Isa 37:8-13

i 2Ki 18:17

j 2Ch 32:15

k 2Ki 17:5
   2Ch 32:10, 13
   Isa 10:8-11

l Ge 11:31

m 2Ki 17:24
   2Ki 18:33, 34

18:37; 19:2 *Or "palace." 19:3 *Or "insult." ″Lit., "have come to the opening of the womb."

19:7 *Lit., "a spirit in him."

14 Hez·e·ki'ah took the letters out of the hand of the messengers and read them. Hez·e·ki'ah then went up to the house of Jehovah and spread them* out before Jehovah.[a] **15** And Hez·e·ki'ah began to pray[b] before Jehovah and say: "O Jehovah the God of Israel, sitting enthroned above* the cherubs,[c] you alone are the true God of all the kingdoms of the earth.[d] You made the heavens and the earth. **16** Incline your ear, O Jehovah, and hear![e] Open your eyes,[f] O Jehovah, and see! Hear the words that Sen·nach'er·ib has sent to taunt the living God. **17** It is a fact, O Jehovah, that the kings of As·syr'i·a have devastated the nations and their lands.[g] **18** And they have thrown their gods into the fire, because they were not gods[h] but the work of human hands,[i] wood and stone. That is why they could destroy them. **19** But now, O Jehovah our God, please save us out of his hand, so that all the kingdoms of the earth may know that you alone are God, O Jehovah."[j]

20 Isaiah son of A'moz then sent this message to Hez·e·ki'ah: "This is what Jehovah the God of Israel says, 'I have heard your prayer[k] to me concerning King Sen·nach'er·ib of As·syr'i·a.[l] **21** This is the word that Jehovah has spoken against him:

"The virgin daughter of Zion
    despises you, she scoffs
    at you.
The daughter of Jerusalem
    shakes her head at you.
22 Whom have you taunted
    and blasphemed?[m]
Against whom have you
    raised your voice[n]
And lifted your arrogant
    eyes?

It is against the Holy One
    of Israel![a]
23 Through your messengers[b]
    you have taunted Jehovah[c]
    and said,
'With the multitude of my
    war chariots
I will ascend the heights
    of mountains,
The remotest parts of
    Leb'a·non.
I will cut down its lofty
    cedars, its choice juniper
    trees.
I will enter its farthest re-
    treats, its densest forests.
24 I will dig wells and drink
    foreign waters;
I will dry up all the streams*
    of Egypt with the soles
    of my feet.'
25 Have you not heard? From
    long ago it was deter-
    mined.*[d]
From days gone by I have
    prepared# it.[e]
Now I will bring it about.[f]
You will turn fortified cities
    into desolate piles of
    ruins.[g]
26 Their inhabitants will
    be helpless;
They will be terrified
    and put to shame.
They will become as
    vegetation of the field
    and green grass,[h]
As grass of the roofs that is
    scorched by the east wind.
27 But I well know when you
    sit, when you go out, when
    you come in,[i]
And when you are enraged
    against me,[j]
28 Because your rage against
    me[k] and your roaring have
    reached my ears.[l]
So I will put my hook in
    your nose and my bridle[m]
    between your lips,

CHAP. 19
a 1Ki 8:30
  Isa 37:14-20

b 2Ch 32:20

c Ex 25:22

d 1Ch 29:10, 11

e 1Ki 8:29
  Ps 65:2

f 2Ch 16:9
  Da 9:18

g 2Ki 16:8, 9
  2Ki 17:6, 24

h Isa 41:29

i Jer 10:3

j Ps 83:17, 18
  Isa 45:5, 6

k 2Ki 19:15

l Isa 37:21, 22

m 2Ki 19:10

n 2Ki 18:30
  Isa 10:12, 13

Second Col.
a Isa 37:23-25

b 2Ki 18:17

c 2Ch 32:17
  Isa 10:10, 11

d Isa 14:24

e Ps 33:11

f Isa 46:10

g Isa 10:5
  Isa 37:26, 27

h Isa 40:7

i Pr 5:21
  Heb 4:13

j Isa 37:28, 29

k Ps 46:6
  Isa 10:5, 15

l 2Ki 18:35
  Isa 10:12, 13

m Ps 32:9

19:14 *Lit., "it." 19:15 *Or possibly, "between."

19:24 *Or "the Nile canals." 19:25 *Lit., "done." #Or "formed."

And I will lead you back the
way you came."[a]

29 "'And this will be the sign
for you:* This year you will eat
what grows on its own;" and
in the second year you will eat
grain that sprouts from that;[b]
but in the third year you will sow
seed and reap, and you will plant
vineyards and eat their fruitage.[c]
30 Those of the house of Judah
who escape, those who are left,[d]
will take root downward and
produce fruit upward. **31** For a
remnant will go out of Jerusalem
and survivors from Mount Zion.
The zeal of Jehovah of armies
will do this.[e]

32 "'Therefore this is what
Jehovah says about the king of
As·syr'i·a:[f]

"He will not come into this
city[g]
Or shoot an arrow there
Or confront it with a shield
Or cast up a siege rampart
against it.[h]

33 By the way he came he will
return;
He will not come into this
city," declares Jehovah.

34 "I will defend this city[i] and
save it for my own sake[j]
And for the sake of my
servant David."'[k]

35 On that very night the angel of Jehovah went out and
struck down 185,000 men in the
camp of the As·syr'i·ans.[l] When
people rose up early in the
morning, they saw all the dead
bodies.[m] **36** So King Sen·nach'-
er·ib of As·syr'i·a departed and
returned to Nin'e·veh[n] and
stayed there.[o] **37** And as he
was bowing down at the house*
of his god Nis'roch, his own
sons A·dram'me·lech and Shar·
e'zer struck him down with the

19:29 *That is, Hezekiah. "Or "the
growth from spilled kernels of grain."
19:37 *Or "temple."

CHAP. 19
a 2Ki 19:33
b Le 25:4-6
c Isa 37:30-32
d 2Ch 32:22
  Isa 10:20
e Isa 59:17
  Zec 1:14, 15
f Isa 10:24
g 2Ch 32:22
h Isa 37:33-35
i Isa 31:5
j 1Sa 12:22
  Isa 43:25
  Eze 36:22
k 2Ki 20:6
  Jer 23:5
l 2Ch 32:21
  Isa 31:8
m Eze 12:30
  Isa 37:36-38
n Jon 1:2
o 2Ki 19:7, 28

Second Col.
a 2Ch 32:21
b Ge 8:4
c Ezr 4:2

CHAP. 20
d 2Ch 32:24
e Isa 38:1-3
f 2Ch 31:20, 21
  Ps 25:7
  Ps 119:49
g Isa 38:4-6
h Ps 39:12
i De 32:39
  Ps 41:3
  Ps 103:3
  Ps 147:3
j Ps 66:13
  Ps 116:12-14
k 2Ch 32:22
  Isa 10:24
l 2Ki 19:34
  Isa 37:35
m Isa 38:21, 22
n Jg 6:17
  Isa 7:11

20:6 *Lit., "days."

sword[a] and then escaped to the
land of Ar'a·rat.[b] And his son
E'sar-had'don[c] became king in
his place.

20 In those days Hez·e·ki'ah
became sick and was at
the point of death.[d] The prophet Isaiah the son of A'moz came
and said to him, "This is what Jehovah says: 'Give instructions to
your household, for you will die;
you will not recover.'"[e] **2** At
that he turned his face to the
wall and began to pray to Jehovah: **3** "I beg you, O Jehovah,
remember, please, how I have
walked before you faithfully
and with a complete heart, and
I have done what was good in
your eyes."[f] And Hez·e·ki'ah began to weep profusely.

4 Isaiah had not yet gone out
to the middle courtyard when
Jehovah's word came to him,
saying:[g] **5** "Go back and say to
Hez·e·ki'ah, the leader of my
people, 'This is what Jehovah
the God of David your forefather
says: "I have heard your prayer.
I have seen your tears.[h] Here
I am healing you.[i] On the third
day you will go up to the house
of Jehovah.[j] **6** I will add 15
years to your life,* and I will rescue you and this city out of the
hand of the king of As·syr'i·a,[k]
and I will defend this city for my
own sake and for the sake of David my servant."'"[l]

7 Isaiah then said: "Bring a
cake of pressed dried figs." So
they brought it and applied it to
the boil, after which he gradually recovered.[m]

8 Hez·e·ki'ah had asked Isaiah: "What is the sign[n] to show
that Jehovah will heal me and
that I will go up on the third
day to the house of Jehovah?"
9 Isaiah replied: "This is the
sign from Jehovah to show you
that Jehovah will carry out the

word that he has spoken: Do you
want the shadow on the stairway* to move forward ten steps
or back ten steps?"[a] **10** Hez·e-
ki'ah said: "It is an easy thing
for the shadow to extend itself
ten steps but not to go back ten
steps." **11** So Isaiah the prophet called out to Jehovah, and He
made the shadow on the stairway of A'haz go back ten steps
after it had already descended
the steps.[b]
12 At that time the king
of Babylon, Be·ro'dach-bal'a·dan
son of Bal'a·dan, sent letters
and a gift to Hez·e·ki'ah, for he
had heard that Hez·e·ki'ah had
been sick.[c] **13** Hez·e·ki'ah welcomed* them and showed them
his entire treasure-house[d]—the
silver, the gold, the balsam oil
and other precious oil, his armory, and everything that was to
be found in his treasuries. There
was nothing that Hez·e·ki'ah did
not show them in his own house#
and in all his dominion.
14 After that Isaiah the
prophet came in to King Hez·e-
ki'ah and asked him: "What did
these men say, and where did
they come from?" So Hez·e·ki'ah
said: "They came from a distant
land, from Babylon."[e] **15** Next
he asked: "What did they see
in your house?"# Hez·e·ki'ah replied: "They saw everything in
my house.# There was nothing
that I did not show them in my
treasuries."
16 Isaiah now said to Hez·e-
ki'ah: "Hear the word of Jehovah,[f] **17** 'Look! Days are coming, and all that is in your house#
and all that your forefathers
have stored up to this day will
be carried off to Babylon.[g] Nothing will be left,' says Jehovah.
18 'And some of your own sons
to whom you will become father
will be taken[a] and will become
court officials in the palace of
the king of Babylon.'"[b]
19 At that Hez·e·ki'ah said to
Isaiah: "The word of Jehovah
that you have spoken is good."[c]
Then he added: "It is good if
there will be peace and stability*
during my lifetime."#[d]
20 As for the rest of the
history of Hez·e·ki'ah, all his
mightiness and how he made
the pool[e] and the conduit and
brought the water into the city,[f]
is it not written in the book of
the history of the times of the
kings of Judah? **21** Then Hez-
e·ki'ah was laid to rest with
his forefathers;[g] and his son
Ma·nas'seh[h] became king in his
place.[i]

21

Ma·nas'seh[j] was 12 years
old when he became king,
and he reigned for 55 years in
Jerusalem.[k] His mother's name
was Heph'zi·bah. **2** He did what
was bad in Jehovah's eyes,
following the detestable practices of the nations[l] that Jehovah had driven out from before
the people of Israel.[m] **3** He rebuilt the high places that his father Hez·e·ki'ah had destroyed,[n]
and he set up altars to Ba'al
and made a sacred pole,*[o] just
as A'hab the king of Israel had
done.[p] And he bowed down to
all the army of the heavens and
served them.[q] **4** He also built
altars in the house of Jehovah,[r] about which Jehovah had
said: "In Jerusalem, I will put my
name."[s] **5** And he built altars
to all the army of the heavens[t] in
two courtyards of the house
of Jehovah.[u] **6** And he made
his own son pass through the
fire; he practiced magic, looked
for omens,[v] and appointed spirit

20:9 *Perhaps these stairs were used to count time, as on a sundial. 20:13 *Or "listened to." 20:13, 15, 17 #Or "palace."

20:19 *Or "truth." #Lit., "days." 21:3 *See Glossary.

CHAP. 20
a Isa 38:7, 8
b Jos 10:12; 2Ch 32:31
c Isa 39:1, 2
d 2Ch 32:27
e Isa 39:3, 4
f Isa 39:5-7
g 2Ki 24:12, 13; 2Ki 25:13; 2Ch 36:7, 18; Jer 27:21, 22; Da 1:2

Second Col.
a 2Ki 24:12
b Da 1:19; Da 2:49
c Ps 141:5
d Isa 39:8
e Joh 9:11
f 2Ch 32:30
g 1Ki 2:10
h 2Ki 21:16; 2Ki 23:26; 2Ch 33:11-13
i 2Ch 32:33

CHAP. 21
j 1Ch 3:13; Mt 1:10
k 2Ch 33:1
l De 12:30, 31; 2Ch 36:14; Eze 16:51
m 2Ch 33:2-6
n 2Ki 18:1, 4
o 2Ki 23:4
p 1Ki 16:30, 32
q De 4:19
r Jer 32:34
s De 12:5; 2Sa 7:12, 13; 1Ki 8:29; 1Ki 9:3
t Eze 8:16
u 1Ki 6:36; 1Ki 7:12
v Le 19:26

mediums and fortune-tellers.[a] He did on a grand scale what was bad in Jehovah's eyes, to offend him.

7 He put the carved image of the sacred pole*[b] that he made into the house about which Jehovah had said to David and to his son Sol′o·mon: "In this house and in Jerusalem, which I have chosen out of all the tribes of Israel, I will permanently put my name.[c] 8 And I will never again make the feet of Israel wander from the land that I gave to their forefathers,[d] provided they carefully observe all that I have commanded them,[e] the entire Law that my servant Moses ordered them to follow." 9 But they did not obey, and Ma·nas′seh kept leading them astray, causing them to do greater evil than the nations that Jehovah had annihilated from before the Israelites.[f]

10 Jehovah kept speaking through his servants the prophets,[g] saying: 11 "Ma·nas′seh the king of Judah has done all these detestable things; he has acted more wickedly than all the Am′or·ites[h] before him,[i] and he has made Judah sin with his disgusting idols.* 12 Therefore this is what Jehovah the God of Israel says: 'Here I am bringing such a disaster on Jerusalem[j] and Judah that it will make both ears of anyone who hears about it tingle.[k] 13 And I will stretch out on Jerusalem the measuring line[l] applied to Sa·mar′i·a[m] and use the leveling tool* applied to the house of A′hab,[n] and I will wipe Jerusalem clean, just as one wipes a bowl clean, wiping it and turning it upside down.[o] 14 I will forsake the remnant of my inheritance[p] and give them

into the hand of their enemies, and they will become plunder and spoil to all their enemies,[a] 15 because they did what was bad in my eyes and were continually offending me from the day that their forefathers came out of Egypt to this day.'"[b]

16 Ma·nas′seh also shed innocent blood in very great quantity until he had filled Jerusalem from one end to the other,[c] besides his sin of causing Judah to sin by doing what was bad in the eyes of Jehovah. 17 As for the rest of the history of Ma·nas′seh and all that he did and the sins that he committed, are they not written in the book of the history of the times of the kings of Judah? 18 Then Ma·nas′seh was laid to rest with his forefathers and was buried in the garden of his house, in the garden of Uz′za;[d] and his son A′mon became king in his place.

19 A′mon[e] was 22 years old when he became king, and he reigned for two years in Jerusalem.[f] His mother's name was Me·shul′le·meth the daughter of Ha′ruz from Jot′bah. 20 He continued to do what was bad in Jehovah's eyes, just as his father Ma·nas′seh had done.[g] 21 He kept walking in all the ways that his father walked, and he continued serving and bowing down to the disgusting idols that his father had served.[h] 22 So he abandoned Jehovah the God of his forefathers, and he did not walk in the way of Jehovah.[i] 23 Eventually A′mon's servants conspired against him and put the king to death in his own house. 24 But the people of the land struck down all those who conspired against King A′mon, and they made his son Jo·si′ah king in his place.[j] 25 As for the rest of the history of A′mon, what he did, is it not written in the book of the history

---

CHAP. 21
a Le 20:27
   De 18:10, 11

b 2Ki 23:6

c 2Ch 33:7-9

d 1Ch 17:9

e De 28:1

f De 7:1

g 2Ch 33:10
   2Ch 36:15, 16
   Jer 7:25
   Mt 23:37

h Ge 15:16

i Le 18:24, 25
   2Ki 23:26
   2Ki 24:3
   Jer 15:4

j 2Ki 22:16, 17
   Mic 3:12

k Jer 19:3

l Isa 28:17
   La 2:8

m 2Ki 17:6
   Eze 23:33

n 1Ki 21:21
   2Ki 10:11

o Jer 25:9

p De 32:9
   2Ki 17:18

Second Col.
a Le 26:25
   De 28:63

b De 9:21
   De 31:29
   Jg 2:11, 13

c 2Ki 24:3, 4
   Jer 2:34
   Mt 23:30
   Heb 11:37

d 2Ki 21:23, 26

e Mt 1:10

f 2Ch 33:21

g 2Ch 33:22, 23

h 2Ki 21:1, 3

i 2Ki 22:16, 17
   Jer 2:13

j 2Ch 33:25

of the times of the kings of Judah? **26** So they buried him in his grave in the garden of Uz'za,[a] and his son Jo·si'ah[b] became king in his place.

22 Jo·si'ah[c] was eight years old when he became king, and he reigned for 31 years in Jerusalem.[d] His mother's name was Je·di'dah the daughter of A·dai'ah from Boz'kath. **2** He did what was right in Jehovah's eyes and walked in all the ways of David his forefather,[f] and he did not deviate to the right or to the left.

3 In the 18th year of King Jo·si'ah, the king sent Sha'phan the secretary, the son of Az·a·li'ah the son of Me·shul'lam, to the house of Jehovah,[g] saying: **4** "Go up to Hil·ki'ah[h] the high priest, and let him collect all the money that is being brought into the house of Jehovah,[i] which the doorkeepers have collected from the people.[j] **5** Have them give it to those appointed over the work in the house of Jehovah who, in turn, will give it to the workers in the house of Jehovah who are to repair the damage to* the house,[k] **6** that is, to the craftsmen, the builders, and the masons; and they are to use it to buy timbers and hewn stones to repair the house.[l] **7** But no accounting should be required of them for the money that they are given, because they are trustworthy."[m]

8 Later Hil·ki'ah the high priest said to Sha'phan the secretary:[n] "I have found the book of the Law[o] in the house of Jehovah." So Hil·ki·ah gave the book to Sha'phan, who began to read it.[p] **9** Then Sha'phan the secretary went to the king and told him: "Your servants have poured out the money that was found in the house, and they have handed

it over to those appointed over the work in the house of Jehovah."[a] **10** Sha'phan the secretary also told the king: "There is a book[b] that Hil·ki'ah the priest has given me." Then Sha'phan began to read it before the king.

11 As soon as the king heard the words of the book of the Law, he ripped his garments apart.[c] **12** Then the king gave this order to Hil·ki'ah the priest, A·hi'kam[d] the son of Sha'phan, Ach'bor the son of Mi·cai'ah, Sha'phan the secretary, and A·sai'ah the king's servant: **13** "Go, inquire of Jehovah in my behalf, in behalf of the people, and in behalf of all Judah concerning the words of this book that has been found; for Jehovah's rage that has been set ablaze against us is great,[e] because our forefathers did not obey the words of this book by observing all that is written concerning us."

14 So Hil·ki'ah the priest, A·hi'kam, Ach'bor, Sha'phan, and A·sai'ah went to Hul'dah the prophetess.[f] She was the wife of Shal'lum son of Tik'vah son of Har'has, the caretaker of the wardrobe, and she was dwelling in the Second Quarter of Jerusalem; and they spoke to her there.[g] **15** She said to them: "This is what Jehovah the God of Israel says, 'Tell the man who sent you to me: **16** "This is what Jehovah says, 'I will bring calamity on this place and its inhabitants, all the words of the book that the king of Judah has read.[h] **17** Because they have abandoned me and are making sacrifices smoke to other gods[i] in order to offend me with all the work of their hands,[j] my rage will be set ablaze against this place and it will not be extinguished.'"[k] **18** But to the king of Judah who sent you to inquire of Jehovah, this is what you

---

22:5 *Or "the cracks in."

should say to him, "This is what Jehovah the God of Israel says: 'Regarding the words that you have heard, **19** because your heart was responsive* and you humbled yourself[a] before Jehovah on hearing what I have spoken against this place and its inhabitants—that they would become an object of horror and a curse—and you ripped your garments apart[b] and wept before me, I also have heard you, declares Jehovah. **20** That is why I will gather you to your ancestors,* and you will be laid in your grave in peace, and your eyes will not see all the calamity that I will bring on this place.'"'" Then they brought the reply to the king.

23 So the king sent word, and they summoned all the elders of Judah and Jerusalem.[c] **2** After that the king went up to the house of Jehovah with all the men of Judah, all the inhabitants of Jerusalem, the priests, and the prophets—all the people, from small to great. He read in their hearing all the words of the book[d] of the covenant[e] that had been found in the house of Jehovah.[f] **3** The king stood by the pillar and made a covenant* before Jehovah,[g] that he would follow Jehovah and keep his commandments, his reminders, and his statutes with all his heart and with all his soul[#] by carrying out the words of this covenant that were written in this book. And all the people agreed to the covenant.[h]

4 The king then ordered Hilki′ah[i] the high priest, the priests of the second rank, and the doorkeepers to bring out from the temple of Jehovah all the utensils made for Ba′al, for the sacred pole,[#a] and for all the army of the heavens. Then he burned them outside Jerusalem on the terraces of Kid′ron, and he took their ashes to Beth′el.[b] **5** So he put out of business the foreign-god priests, whom the kings of Judah had appointed to make sacrificial smoke on the high places in the cities of Judah and the surroundings of Jerusalem, as well as those making sacrificial smoke to Ba′al, to the sun, to the moon, to the constellations of the zodiac, and to all the army of the heavens.[c] **6** He brought the sacred pole[#d] out from the house of Jehovah to the outskirts of Jerusalem, to the Kid′ron Valley, and he burned it[e] in the Kid′ron Valley and ground it to dust and scattered its dust on the graves of the common people.[f] **7** He also tore down the houses of the male temple prostitutes,[g] which were in the house of Jehovah and where the women were weaving tent shrines for the sacred pole.[#]

8 Then he brought all the priests out of the cities of Judah, and he made unfit for worship the high places where the priests had been making sacrificial smoke, from Ge′ba[h] to Be′er-she′ba.[i] He also tore down the high places of the gates that were at the entrance of the gate of Joshua the chief of the city, which were on the left as one entered the city gate. **9** The priests of the high places did not serve at the altar of Jehovah in Jerusalem,[j] but they did eat unleavened bread along with their brothers. **10** He also made unfit for worship To′pheth,[k] which is in the Valley of the Sons of Hin′nom,*[l] so that no one could make his son or his daughter pass through the fire to Mo′lech.[m] **11** And he prohib-

---

CHAP. 22

a 1Ki 21:29
Jas 4:6

b 2Ki 22:11

CHAP. 23

c 2Ch 34:29, 30

d De 31:26

e Ex 24:8

f 2Ki 22:8

g 2Ki 11:17
2Ch 15:10, 12

h Jos 24:24, 25
2Ch 34:31, 32

i 2Ki 22:4

Second Col.

a 2Ki 21:1, 7
2Ch 34:4

b 1Ki 12:28, 29

c 2Ki 21:1, 3
Jer 8:1, 2

d 2Ki 21:1, 7

e De 7:25

f 2Ch 34:4

g Le 18:22
De 23:17,18
1Ki 5:11, 12
1Ki 22:46

h Jos 21:17, 19
1Ki 15:22

i Ge 21:31

j Eze 44:10
Mal 2:7, 8

k Jer 7:31

l Jos 15:8

m 2Ki 16:2, 3
Jer 32:35

22:19 *Lit., "soft." **22:20** *This is a poetic expression for death. **23:3** *Or "renewed the covenant." **23:3, 4, 6, 7** [#]See Glossary.

23:10 *See Glossary, "Gehenna."

ited the horses that the kings of Judah had dedicated* to the sun from entering the house of Jehovah by the chamber# of Na'than-mel'ech the court official, which was in the porticoes; and he burned the chariots of the sun[a] in the fire. **12** The king also tore down the altars that the kings of Judah had set up on the roof[b] of A'haz's upper chamber, as well as the altars that Ma-nas'seh had set up in two courtyards of the house of Jehovah.[c] He crushed them and scattered their dust in the Kid'ron Valley. **13** And the king made unfit for worship the high places that were in front of Jerusalem that were to the south* of the Mount of Ruination,# which Sol'o-mon the king of Israel had built to Ash'to-reth the disgusting goddess of the Si-do'ni-ans; and to Che'mosh the disgusting god of Mo'ab; and to Mil'com[d] the detestable god of the Am'mon-ites.[e] **14** He broke the sacred pillars to pieces and cut down the sacred poles*[f] and filled their places with human bones. **15** He also tore down the altar in Beth'el, the high place that Jer-o-bo'am the son of Ne'bat had made that caused Israel to sin.[g] After tearing down that altar and the high place, he burned the high place, ground it to dust, and burned the sacred pole.*[h]

16 When Jo-si'ah turned and saw the graves on the mountain, he had the bones taken from the graves and burned them on the altar, making it unfit for worship, according to Jehovah's word that had been proclaimed by the man of the true God who foretold that these things would happen.[a] **17** Then he said: "What is the gravestone over there that I am looking at?" At this the men of the city said to him: "It is the grave of the man of the true God from Ju-dah[b] who foretold these things that you have done against the altar of Beth'el." **18** So he said: "Let him rest. Do not let anyone disturb his bones." So they left his bones undisturbed, as well as the bones of the prophet who had come from Sa-mar'i-a.[c]

19 Jo-si'ah also removed all the houses of worship on the high places that were in the cities of Sa-mar'i-a,[d] which the kings of Israel had built to offend God, and he did the same thing to them that he had done at Beth'el.[e] **20** So he sacrificed on the altars all the priests of the high places who were there, and he burned human bones on them.[f] After that he returned to Jerusalem.

21 The king now commanded all the people: "Hold a Passover[g] to Jehovah your God as is written in this book of the covenant."[h] **22** No Passover like this had been held since the days when the judges had judged Israel or in all the days of the kings of Israel and the kings of Judah.[i] **23** But in the 18th year of King Jo-si'ah, this Passover to Jehovah was held in Jerusalem.

24 Jo-si'ah also cleared out the spirit mediums, the fortune-tellers,[j] the teraphim statues,*[k] the disgusting idols,# and all the disgusting things that had appeared in the land of Judah and in Jerusalem, in order to carry out the words of the Law[l] that were written in the book that Hil-ki'ah the priest had

---

CHAP. 23
a De 4:19
  Eze 8:16

b Jer 19:13
  Zep 1:4, 5

c 2Ki 21:1, 5

d Zep 1:4, 5

e 1Ki 11:5, 7

f Ex 23:24
  De 7:5
  2Ch 34:1, 3

g 1Ki 12:28, 33

h 2Ch 34:6, 7

Second Col.
a 1Ki 13:2

b 1Ki 13:1

c 1Ki 13:30, 31

d 1Ki 12:25, 31
  1Ki 13:32
  2Ki 17:9

e 2Ch 34:6, 7

f 1Ki 13:2

g 2Ch 35:1

h Ex 12:3-14

i 2Ch 35:18, 19

j Le 19:31
  De 18:10, 11
  2Ki 21:1, 6
  Isa 8:19

k Ge 31:19

l Nu 33:52
  De 12:2

23:11 *Lit., "given." #Or "dining room." 23:13 *Lit., "right." That is, south, when one faces east. #That is, the Mount of Olives, particularly the southern extremity also known as the Mount of Offense. 23:14, 15 *See Glossary.

23:24 *Or "household gods; idols." #The Hebrew term may be related to a word for "dung" and is used as an expression of contempt.

found in the house of Jehovah.[a]
25 There was no king like him prior to him, who returned to Jehovah with all his heart and with all his soul*[b] and with all his strength, according to all the Law of Moses; nor did anyone like him rise up after him.

26 Nevertheless, Jehovah did not turn away from his burning anger that blazed against Judah because of all the offensive things that Ma·nas'seh had done to offend Him.[c] **27** Jehovah said: "I will also remove Judah from my sight,[d] just as I removed Israel;[e] and I will reject this city that I chose, Jerusalem, and the house about which I said, 'My name will continue there.'"[f]

28 As for the rest of the history of Jo·si'ah, all that he did, is it not written in the book of the history of the times of the kings of Judah? **29** In his days Phar'aoh Ne'choh the king of Egypt came to meet the king of As·syr'i·a by the Eu·phra'tes River, and King Jo·si'ah went out to confront him; but when Ne'choh saw him, he put him to death at Me·gid'do.[g] **30** So his servants transported his dead body in a chariot from Me·gid'do and brought him to Jerusalem and buried him in his grave. Then the people of the land took Jo·si'ah's son Je·ho'a·haz and anointed him and made him king in place of his father.[h]

31 Je·ho'a·haz[i] was 23 years old when he became king, and he reigned for three months in Jerusalem. His mother's name was Ha·mu'tal[j] the daughter of Jeremiah from Lib'nah. **32** He began to do what was bad in Jehovah's eyes, according to all that his forefathers had done.[k] **33** Phar'aoh Ne'choh[l] imprisoned him at Rib'lah[m] in the land

of Ha'math, to keep him from reigning in Jerusalem, and then imposed on the land a fine of 100 silver talents* and a gold talent.[a] **34** Furthermore, Phar'aoh Ne'choh made Jo·si'ah's son E·li'a·kim king in place of his father Jo·si'ah and changed his name to Je·hoi'a·kim; but he took Je·ho'a·haz and brought him to Egypt,[b] where he eventually died.[c] **35** Je·hoi'a·kim gave the silver and the gold to Phar'aoh, but he had to tax the land to give the silver that Phar'aoh demanded. He exacted an assessed amount of silver and gold from each of the people of the land to give to Phar'aoh Ne'choh.

36 Je·hoi'a·kim[d] was 25 years old when he became king, and he reigned for 11 years in Jerusalem.[e] His mother's name was Ze·bi'dah the daughter of Pe·dai'ah from Ru'mah. **37** He continued to do what was bad in Jehovah's eyes,[f] according to all that his forefathers had done.[g]

24 In Je·hoi'a·kim's days King Neb·u·chad·nez'zar[h] of Babylon came against him, and Je·hoi'a·kim became his servant for three years. However, he turned against him and rebelled. **2** Then Jehovah began to send against him marauder bands of Chal·de'ans,[i] Syrians, Mo'ab·ites, and Am'mon·ites. He kept sending them against Judah to destroy it, according to Jehovah's word[j] that he had spoken through his servants the prophets. **3** Surely it was by the order of Jehovah that this happened to Judah, to remove them from his sight[k] because of all the sins that Ma·nas'seh had committed,[l] **4** and also the innocent blood that he had shed,[m] for he had filled Jerusalem with innocent blood and Jehovah was not willing to forgive.[n]

CHAP. 23
a 2Ki 22:8
b De 4:29
c 2Ki 21:11, 12
  2Ki 24:3, 4
  Jer 15:4
d De 29:28
  2Ki 25:11
  Eze 23:33
e 2Ki 18:11
  2Ki 21:13
f De 12:5
  1Ki 8:29
  1Ki 9:3
g 1Ki 9:15
  2Ch 35:20-25
  Zec 12:11
h 2Ch 36:1, 2
i Jer 22:11
j 2Ki 24:18
k 2Ki 21:1, 2
  2Ki 21:19-21
l 2Ki 23:29
m Jer 39:5
  Jer 52:10

Second Col.
a 2Ch 36:3
b 2Ch 36:4, 5
c 2Ki 22:11, 12
d Jer 1:3
  Jer 22:18, 19
e 2Ch 36:5
f Jer 26:21
  Jer 36:22-24
g 2Ch 28:24, 25
  2Ch 33:1, 4

CHAP. 24
h Jer 25:1
  Jer 46:2
  Da 1:1
  Da 3:1
  Da 4:33
i Hab 1:6
j Le 26:27, 28
  De 28:15
  2Ki 23:27
k Le 26:33
  De 4:26
l 2Ki 21:11
  2Ki 23:26
m 2Ki 21:16
  Jer 2:34
  Jer 19:4
n Jer 15:1
  La 3:42

23:33 *A talent equaled 34.2 kg (1,101 oz t). See App. B14.

5 As for the rest of the history of Je·hoi′a·kim, all that he did, is it not written in the book of the history of the times of the kings of Judah?[a] **6** Then Je·hoi′a·kim was laid to rest with his forefathers;[b] and his son Je·hoi′a·chin became king in his place.

7 Never again did the king of Egypt venture out of his land, for the king of Babylon had taken all that belonged to the king of Egypt,[c] from the Wadi* of Egypt[d] up to the Eu·phra′tes River.[e]

8 Je·hoi′a·chin[f] was 18 years old when he became king, and he reigned for three months in Jerusalem.[g] His mother's name was Ne·hush′ta the daughter of El·na′than of Jerusalem. **9** He continued to do what was bad in Jehovah's eyes, according to all that his father had done. **10** During that time the servants of King Neb·u·chad·nez′zar of Babylon came up against Jerusalem, and the city came under siege.[h] **11** King Neb·u·chad·nez′zar of Babylon came to the city while his servants were laying siege to it. **12** King Je·hoi′a·chin of Judah went out to the king of Babylon,[i] along with his mother, his servants, his princes, and his court officials;[j] and the king of Babylon took him captive in the eighth year of his reign.[k] **13** Then he took out from there all the treasures of the house of Jehovah and the treasures of the king's house.*[l] He cut into pieces all the gold utensils that Sol′o·mon the king of Israel had made in the temple of Jehovah,[m] just as Jehovah had foretold. **14** He took into exile all Jerusalem, all the princes,[n] all the mighty warriors, and every craftsman

and metalworker*[a]—he took 10,-000 into exile. No one was left behind except the poorest people of the land.[b] **15** Thus he took Je·hoi′a·chin[c] into exile to Babylon;[d] he also led away the king's mother, the king's wives, his court officials, and the foremost men of the land, taking them into exile from Jerusalem to Babylon. **16** The king of Babylon also took into exile to Babylon all the warriors, 7,000, as well as 1,000 craftsmen and metalworkers,* all of them mighty men and trained for war. **17** The king of Babylon made Mat·ta·ni′ah, Je·hoi′a·chin's uncle,[e] king in his place and changed his name to Zed·e·ki′ah.[f]

18 Zed·e·ki′ah was 21 years old when he became king, and he reigned for 11 years in Jerusalem. His mother's name was Ha·mu′tal[g] the daughter of Jeremiah from Lib′nah. **19** He continued to do what was bad in Jehovah's eyes, according to all that Je·hoi′a·kim had done.[h] **20** It was because of Jehovah's anger that these things took place in Jerusalem and in Judah, until he cast them out of his sight.[i] And Zed·e·ki′ah rebelled against the king of Babylon.[j]

25 In the ninth year of Zed·e·ki′ah's reign, in the tenth month, on the tenth day of the month, King Neb·u·chad·nez′-zar[k] of Babylon came with all his army against Jerusalem.[l] He camped against it and built a siege wall all around it,* **2** and the city was under siege until the 11th year of King Zed·e·ki′ah. **3** On the ninth day of the fourth month the famine was severe[n] in the city, and there was no food for the people of the land.[o] **4** The city wall

---

24:14 *Or possibly, "builder of bulwarks." **24:16** *Or possibly, "builders of bulwarks."

CHAP. 24

a 2Ch 36:8
b Jer 22:18, 19
    Jer 36:30
c Jer 46:2
d Nu 34:2, 5
    Ge 15:18
    1Ki 4:21
e Jer 24:1
    Jer 37:1
f 2Ch 36:8
g Da 1:1
i 2Ch 36:9, 10
    Jer 24:1
    Eze 17:12
j Jer 29:1, 2
k Jer 52:28
l 2Ki 20:13, 17
m 1Ki 7:48-50
    Ezr 1:7
    Da 5:2
n Da 1:3, 6

Second Col.

a Jer 24:1
b 2Ki 25:12
c 2Ki 25:27
    1Ch 3:17
d 2Ki 22:24, 25
e 1Ch 3:15
f 2Ch 36:10-12
    Jer 37:1
    Jer 52:1
g 2Ki 23:31
h 2Ki 23:36, 37
    Jer 24:8
    Jer 37:1, 2
    Jer 38:5, 6
    Eze 21:25
i 2Ki 23:27
j 2Ch 36:11, 13
    Jer 27:12
    Jer 38:17
    Eze 17:12-15

CHAP. 25

k Jer 27:8
    Jer 43:10
    Da 4:1
l 2Ch 36:17
    Jer 34:2
    Eze 24:1, 2
m Isa 29:3
    Jer 32:2, 28
    Jer 39:1
    Jer 52:4, 5
    Eze 4:1, 2
    Eze 21:21, 22
n Le 26:26
    De 28:53
    Jer 37:21
    Jer 38:2
    La 4:4
    Eze 4:16
    Eze 5:10, 12
o Jer 52:6-11

was broken through,[a] and all the soldiers fled by night through the gate between the double wall near the king's garden, while the Chal·de'ans were surrounding the city; and the king went by the way of the Ar'a·bah.[b] **5** But the Chal·de'an army pursued the king, and they overtook him in the desert plains of Jer'i·cho, and all his troops were scattered from his side. **6** Then they seized the king[c] and brought him up to the king of Babylon at Rib'-lah, and they passed sentence on him. **7** They slaughtered Zed·e·ki'ah's sons before his eyes; then Neb·u·chad·nez'zar blinded Zed·e·ki'ah's eyes, bound him with copper fetters, and brought him to Babylon.[d]

8 In the fifth month, on the seventh day of the month, that is, in the 19th year of King Neb·u·chad·nez'zar the king of Babylon, Neb·u'zar·ad'an[e] the chief of the guard, the servant of the king of Babylon, came to Jerusalem.[f] **9** He burned down the house of Jehovah,[g] the king's house,*[h] and all the houses of Jerusalem;[i] he also burned down the house of every prominent man.[j] **10** And the walls surrounding Jerusalem were pulled down by the entire Chal·de'-an army that was with the chief of the guard.[k] **11** Neb·u'zar·ad'-an the chief of the guard took into exile the rest of the people who were left in the city, the deserters who had gone over to the king of Babylon, and the rest of the population.[l] **12** But the chief of the guard left some of the poorest people of the land to serve as vinedressers and as compulsory laborers.[m] **13** And the Chal·de'ans broke into pieces the copper pillars[n] of the house of Jehovah and the carriages[o] and the copper Sea[p] that were in

the house of Jehovah, and they carried the copper away to Babylon.[a] **14** They also took the cans, the shovels, the extinguishers, the cups, and all the copper utensils used in the temple service. **15** The chief of the guard took the fire holders and the bowls that were of genuine gold[b] and silver.[c] **16** As for the two pillars, the Sea, and the carriages that Sol'o·mon had made for the house of Jehovah, the copper of all these articles was beyond weighing.[d] **17** Each pillar was 18 cubits* high,[e] and the capital on it was of copper; and the height of the capital was three cubits, and the network and pomegranates all around on the capital were all made of copper.[f] The second pillar with its network was like it.

18 The chief of the guard also took Se·rai'ah[g] the chief priest, Zeph·a·ni'ah[h] the second priest, and the three doorkeepers.[i] **19** And he took from the city one court official who was the commissioner over the soldiers, five close associates of the king who were found in the city, as well as the secretary of the chief of the army, the one mustering the people of the land, and 60 men of the common people of the land who were yet found in the city. **20** Neb·u'zar·ad'an[j] the chief of the guard took them and brought them to the king of Babylon at Rib'lah.[k] **21** The king of Babylon struck them down and put them to death at Rib'lah in the land of Ha'math.[l] Thus Judah went into exile from its land.[m]

22 King Neb·u·chad·nez'zar of Babylon appointed Ged·a·li'ah[n] the son of A·hi'kam[o] the son of Sha'phan[p] over the people whom he had left behind in the land of Judah.[q] **23** When all the army

---

25:9 *Or "palace."

25:17 *A cubit equaled 44.5 cm (17.5 in.). See App. B14.

CHAP. 25

a Jer 21:4
  Jer 39:2, 4-7
  Eze 33:21
b Eze 12:12
c Jer 21:7
d Eze 32:4, 5
  Eze 12:12, 13
  Eze 17:16
e Jer 40:1
f Jer 52:12-14
  La 4:12
g 1Ki 9:8
  Ps 74:3
  Ps 79:1
  Isa 64:11
  Jer 7:14
  La 1:10
  La 2:7
  Mic 3:12
h 1Ki 7:1
i Jer 34:22
j 2Ch 36:19
k Ne 1:3
  Jer 39:8
l Jer 15:2
  Jer 39:9
  Jer 52:15, 30
  Eze 5:2
m Jer 39:10
  Jer 52:16
n 1Ki 7:15
o 1Ki 7:27
p 1Ki 7:23

Second Col.

a 2Ki 20:17
  Jer 52:17-20
b 1Ki 7:48, 50
c 2Ch 24:14
  2Ch 36:18
  Ezr 1:7, 10, 11
  Da 5:2
d 1Ki 7:47
e 1Ki 7:15
f 1Ki 7:16, 20
  Jer 52:21-23
g Ezr 7:1
h Jer 21:1, 2
  Jer 29:25, 29
i Jer 52:24-27
j 2Ki 25:8
  Jer 39:9
  Jer 40:1
k Jer 39:5
l Nu 34:2, 8
  1Ki 8:65
m De 28:36, 64
  2Ki 23:27
  2Ki 25:11
n Jer 39:13, 14
o Jer 26:24
p 2Ki 22:8
q Jer 40:5, 6

chiefs and their men heard that the king of Babylon had appointed Ged·a·liʹah, they immediately came to Ged·a·liʹah at Mizʹpah. They were Ishʹma·el the son of Neth·a·niʹah, Jo·haʹnan the son of Ka·reʹah, Se·raiʹah the son of Tan·huʹmeth the Ne·tophʹa·thite, and Ja·az·a·niʹah the son of the Ma·acʹa·thite, together with their men.[a] 24 Ged·a·liʹah swore an oath to them and their men and said to them: "Do not be afraid of being servants to the Chal·deʹans. Live in the land and serve the king of Babylon, and it will go well with you."[b]

25 And in the seventh month, Ishʹma·el[c] son of Neth·a·niʹah son of E·lishʹa·ma, who was of the royal line,* came with ten other men, and they struck down Ged·a·liʹah and he died, along with the Jews and the Chal·deʹans

25:25 *Lit., "the seed of the kingdom."

CHAP. 25
a Jer 40:7-9

b Jer 27:12

c Jer 40:15

Second Col.
a Jer 41:1, 2

b Jer 42:14
Jer 43:4, 7

c Jer 41:17, 18

d 2Ki 24:8, 12
Jer 24:1
Mt 1:11

e Jer 52:31-34

who were with him in Mizʹpah.[a] 26 After that all the people, from small to great, including the army chiefs, rose up and went to Egypt,[b] for they were afraid of the Chal·deʹans.[c]

27 And in the 37th year of the exile of King Je·hoiʹa·chin[d] of Judah, in the 12th month, on the 27th day of the month, King Eʹvil-merʹo·dach of Babylon, in the year he became king, released* King Je·hoiʹa·chin of Judah from prison.[e] 28 He spoke kindly with him and put his throne higher than the thrones of the other kings who were with him in Babylon. 29 So Je·hoiʹa·chin took off his prison garments, and he regularly ate before him all the days of his life. 30 A regular allowance of food was given him from the king, day after day, all the days of his life.

25:27 *Lit., "raised up the head of."

THE FIRST OF
CHRONICLES

OUTLINE OF CONTENTS

1

Adam,
Seth,[a]
E'nosh,
2 Ke'nan,
Ma·hal'a·lel,[b]
Ja'red,[c]
3 E'noch,[d]
Me·thu'se·lah,
La'mech,[e]
4 Noah,[f]
Shem,[g] Ham, and Ja'pheth.[h]

5 The sons of Ja'pheth were Go'mer, Ma'gog, Ma'da·i, Ja'van, Tu'bal,[i] Me'shech,[j] and Ti'ras.[k]

6 The sons of Go'mer were Ash'ke·naz, Ri'phath, and To·gar'mah.[l]

7 The sons of Ja'van were E·li'shah, Tar'shish, Kit'tim, and Ro'da·nim.

8 The sons of Ham were Cush,[a] Miz'ra·im, Put, and Ca'naan.[b]

9 The sons of Cush were Se'ba,[c] Hav'i·lah, Sab'tah, Ra'a·mah,[d] and Sab'te·ca.

The sons of Ra'a·mah were She'ba and De'dan.[e]

10 Cush became father to Nim'rod.[f] He was the first to become a mighty one on the earth.

11 Miz'ra·im became father to Lu'dim,[g] An'a·mim, Le·ha'bim, Naph·tu'him,[h] 12 Path-

CHAP. 1
a Ge 4:25
b Ge 5:12, 15
c Ge 5:18
d Heb 11:5
e Ge 5:25, 28
f Ge 5:29
g Ge 11:10
h Ge 6:10
i Isa 66:19
j Eze 27:13
k Ge 10:2
l Ge 10:3
  Eze 27:14

Second Col.
a Isa 11:11
b Ge 10:6
c Ps 72:10
d Eze 27:22
e Ge 10:7
f Ge 10:8, 9
g Jer 46:9
h Ge 10:13, 14

ru'sim,[a] Cas·lu'him (from whom the Phi·lis'tines[b] came), and Caph'to·rim.[c]

13 Ca'naan became father to Si'don,[d] his firstborn, and Heth,[e] **14** as well as the Jeb'u·site,[f] the Am'or·ite,[g] the Gir'ga·shite,[h] **15** the Hi'vite,[i] the Ark'ite, the Si'nite, **16** the Ar'vad·ite,[j] the Zem'a·rite, and the Ha'math·ite.

17 The sons of Shem were E'lam,[k] As'shur,[l] Ar·pach'shad, Lud, and A'ram,

and* Uz, Hul, Ge'ther, and Mash.[m]

18 Ar·pach'shad became father to She'lah,[n] and She'lah became father to E'ber.

19 Two sons were born to E'ber. The name of the one was Pe'leg,*[o] because in his lifetime the earth# was divided. The name of his brother was Jok'tan.

20 Jok'tan became father to Al·mo'dad, She'leph, Ha·zar·ma'veth, Je'rah,[p] **21** Ha·do'ram, U'zal, Dik'lah, **22** O'bal, A·bim'a·el, She'ba, **23** O'phir,[q] Hav'i·lah,[r] and Jo'bab; all of these were the sons of Jok'tan.

24 Shem,
   Ar·pach'shad,
   She'lah,
25 E'ber,
   Pe'leg,[s]
   Re'u,[t]
26 Se'rug,[u]
   Na'hor,[v]
   Te'rah,[w]
27 A'bram, that is, Abraham.[x]

28 The sons of Abraham were Isaac[y] and Ish'ma·el.[z]

29 These are their family origins: Ish'ma·el's firstborn Neba'ioth,[a] then Ke'dar,[b] Ad'be·el, Mib'sam,[c] **30** Mish'ma, Du'mah,

Mas'sa, Ha'dad, Te'ma, **31** Je'tur, Na'phish, and Ked'e·mah. These were the sons of Ish'ma·el.

32 The sons that Ke·tu'rah,[a] Abraham's concubine, gave birth to were Zim'ran, Jok'shan, Me'dan, Mid'i·an,[b] Ish'bak, and Shu'ah.[c]

The sons of Jok'shan were She'ba and De'dan.[d]

33 The sons of Mid'i·an were E'phah,[e] E'pher, Ha'noch, A·bi'da, and El·da'ah.

All of these were the sons of Ke·tu'rah.

34 Abraham became father to Isaac.[f] The sons of Isaac were E'sau[g] and Israel.[h]

35 The sons of E'sau were El'i·phaz, Reu'el, Je'ush, Ja'lam, and Kor'ah.[i]

36 The sons of El'i·phaz were Te'man,[j] O'mar, Ze'pho, Ga'tam, Ke'naz, Tim'na, and Am'a·lek.[k]

37 The sons of Reu'el were Na'hath, Ze'rah, Sham'mah, and Miz'zah.[l]

38 The sons of Se'ir[m] were Lo'tan, Sho'bal, Zib'e·on, A'nah, Di'shon, E'zer, and Di'shan.[n]

39 The sons of Lo'tan were Ho'ri and Ho'mam. Lo'tan's sister was Tim'na.[o]

40 The sons of Sho'bal were Al'van, Man'a·hath, E'bal, She'pho, and O'nam.

The sons of Zib'e·on were A'iah and A'nah.[p]

41 The son* of A'nah was Di'shon.

The sons of Di'shon were Hem'dan, Esh'ban, Ith'ran, and Che'ran.[q]

42 The sons of E'zer[r] were Bil'han, Za'a·van, and A'kan.

The sons of Di'shan were Uz and A'ran.[s]

43 These are the kings who reigned in the land of E'dom[t]

CHAP. 1
a Eze 29:14
b Jos 13:2, 3
c De 2:23
   Am 9:7
d Isa 23:2
e Ge 10:15-18
f Jg 1:21
g Ge 15:16
   Nu 13:29
   De 3:8
h De 7:1
i Jos 9:3, 7
j Eze 27:11
k Ezr 4:9
l Eze 27:23
m Ge 10:22, 23
n Ge 11:14
o Ge 11:19
p Ge 10:26-29
q 1Ki 9:28
r Ge 2:11
   Ge 25:18
s Ge 11:19
t Ge 11:21
u Ge 11:23
v Ge 11:25
w Ge 11:26
x Ge 17:5
y Ge 21:3
z Ge 16:11, 12
a Ge 28:9
b Eze 27:21
c Ge 25:13-15

Second Col.
a Ge 25:1-4
b Ge 37:28
c Job 2:11
d Isa 21:13
e Isa 60:6
f Ac 7:8
g Ge 25:25
h Ge 32:28
i Ge 36:4, 5
   Ob 9
k Ge 36:11, 12
l Ge 36:13
m Ge 36:8
n Ge 36:20, 21
o Ge 36:22
p Ge 36:23, 24
q Ge 36:25, 26
r 1Ch 1:38
s Ge 36:27, 28
t Ge 32:3

1:17 *The following are the sons of Aram. See Ge 10:23. **1:19** *Meaning "Division." #Or "earth's population."

1:41 *Lit., "sons."

before any king reigned over the Israelites:*[a] Be'la the son of Be'or; the name of his city was Din'ha·bah. 44 When Be'la died, Jo'bab the son of Ze'rah from Boz'rah[b] began to reign in his place. 45 When Jo'bab died, Hu'sham from the land of the Te'man·ites began to reign in his place. 46 When Hu'sham died, Ha'dad the son of Be'dad, who defeated Mid'i·an in the territory* of Mo'ab, began to reign in his place. The name of his city was A'vith. 47 When Ha'dad died, Sam'lah from Mas·re'kah began to reign in his place. 48 When Sam'lah died, Sha'ul from Re·ho'both by the River began to reign in his place. 49 When Sha'ul died, Ba'al·ha'nan the son of Ach'bor began to reign in his place. 50 When Ba'al-ha'nan died, Ha'dad began to reign in his place. The name of his city was Pa'u, and the name of his wife was Me·het'a·bel the daughter of Ma'tred, the daughter of Me'za·hab. 51 Then Ha'dad died.

The sheikhs* of E'dom were Sheikh Tim'na, Sheikh Al'vah, Sheikh Je'theth,[c] 52 Sheikh O·hol·i·ba'mah, Sheikh E'lah, Sheikh Pi'non, 53 Sheikh Ke'naz, Sheikh Te'man, Sheikh Mib'zar, 54 Sheikh Mag'di·el, Sheikh I'ram. These were the sheikhs of E'dom.

2 These were the sons of Israel:[d] Reu'ben,[e] Sim'e·on,[f] Le'vi,[g] Judah,[h] Is'sa·char,[i] Zeb'u·lun,[j] 2 Dan,[k] Joseph,[l] Benjamin,[m] Naph'ta·li,[n] Gad,[o] and Ash'er.[p]

3 The sons of Judah were Er, O'nan, and She'lah. These three were born to him from Shu'a's daughter, the Ca'naan·it·ess.[q] But Er, Judah's firstborn, was

---

CHAP. 1

a Ge 36:31-39
b Jer 49:13
c Ge 36:40-43

CHAP. 2

d Ge 32:28
e Ge 29:32
Ge 49:3, 4
f Ge 29:33
g Ge 29:34
Ge 49:5-7
h Ge 29:35
Ge 49:8-12
Heb 7:14
i Ge 30:18
Ge 49:14, 15
j Ge 49:20
Ge 49:13
k Ge 30:4-6
Ge 49:16-18
l Ge 30:22, 24
Ge 49:22-26
m Ge 35:16, 18
Ge 49:27
n Ge 30:7, 8
Ge 49:21
o Ge 30:9-11
Ge 49:19
p Ge 30:12, 13
Ge 49:20
q Ge 38:2-5

Second Col.

a Ge 38:7
b Ge 38:11
c Lu 3:23, 33
d Nu 26:21
e Jos 7:15, 18
f De 7:26
Jos 6:18
Jos 22:20
g 1Sa 27:10
h Ru 4:19-21
Mt 1:3
i Mt 1:4, 5
j Nu 2:3
k Lu 3:23, 32
Ru 2:1
m Ru 4:17, 22
1Sa 16:1
n 1Sa 17:13
o 1Sa 16:6-10
p 1Sa 16:13
1Sa 17:12
Mt 1:6
q 2Sa 17:25
r 2Sa 21:17
2Sa 23:18, 19
s 2Sa 8:16
1Ch 11:6
t 2Sa 2:18
2Sa 3:30
2Sa 23:24
u 2Sa 19:13
1Ki 2:5

---

displeasing to Jehovah, so He put him to death.[a] 4 Ta'mar,[b] Judah's daughter-in-law, bore to him Pe'rez[c] and Ze'rah. Judah had five sons in all.

5 The sons of Pe'rez were Hez'ron and Ha'mul.[d]

6 The sons of Ze'rah were Zim'ri, E'than, He'man, Cal'col, and Da'ra. There were five of them in all.

7 The son* of Car'mi was A'char,[g] who brought disaster[△] on Israel,[e] who was unfaithful with regard to what had been devoted to destruction.[f]

8 The son* of E'than was Az·a·ri'ah.

9 The sons of Hez'ron who were born to him were Je·rah'me·el,[g] Ram,[h] and Che·lu'bai.*

10 Ram became father to Am·min'a·dab.[i] Am·min'a·dab became father to Nah'shon[i] the chieftain of the descendants of Judah. 11 Nah'shon became father to Sal'ma.[k] Sal'ma became father to Bo'az.[l] 12 Bo'az became father to O'bed. O'bed became father to Jes'se.[m] 13 Jes'se became father to his firstborn E·li'ab, A·bin'a·dab[n] the second, Shim'e·a the third,[o] 14 Ne·than'el the fourth, Rad'dai the fifth, 15 O'zem the sixth, and David[p] the seventh. 16 Their sisters were Ze·ru'iah and Ab'i·gail.[q] The sons of Ze·ru'iah were A·bish'ai,[r] Jo'ab,[s] and As'a·hel,[t] three. 17 Ab'i·gail gave birth to A·ma'sa,[u] and the father of A·ma'sa was Je'ther the Ish'ma·el·ite.

18 Ca'leb* the son of Hez'ron became father to sons by his wife A·zu'bah and by Jer'i-

---

1:43 *Lit., "sons of Israel." 1:46 *Lit., "field." 1:51 *A sheikh was a tribal chief.

2:7, 8 *Lit., "sons." 2:7 *Meaning "Bringer of Disaster; Bringer of Ostracism." In Jos 7:1, also called Achan. △Or "trouble; ostracism." 2:9 *Also called Caleb in vss. 18, 19, 42. 2:18 *Also called Chelubai in vs. 9.

oth; and these were her sons: Je'sher, Sho'bab, and Ar'don. **19** When A·zu'bah died, Ca'leb married Eph'rath,[a] and she bore Hur[b] to him. **20** Hur became father to U'ri. U'ri became father to Bez'al·el.[c]

21 Afterward Hez'ron had relations with the daughter of Ma'chir[d] the father of Gil'e·ad.[e] He married her when he was 60 years old, and she bore Se'gub to him. **22** Se'gub became father to Ja'ir,[f] who had 23 cities in the land of Gil'e·ad.[g] **23** Later Gesh'ur[h] and Syria[i] took Hav'voth-ja'ir[j] from them, along with Ke'nath[k] and its dependent* towns, 60 cities. All of these were the descendants of Ma'chir the father of Gil'e·ad.

24 After the death of Hez'ron[l] in Ca'leb-eph'ra·thah, A·bi'jah the wife of Hez'ron bore him Ash'hur[m] the father of Te·ko'a.[n]

25 The sons of Je·rah'me·el the firstborn of Hez'ron were Ram the firstborn, Bu'nah, O'ren, O'zem, and A·hi'jah. **26** Je·rah'me·el had another wife, whose name was At'a·rah. She was the mother of O'nam. **27** The sons of Ram the firstborn of Je·rah'me·el were Ma'az, Ja'min, and E'ker. **28** The sons of O'nam were Sham'mai and Ja'da. The sons of Sham'mai were Na'dab and A·bi'shur. **29** The name of A·bi'shur's wife was Ab'i·ha·il, who bore him Ah'ban and Mo'lid. **30** The sons of Na'dab were Se'led and Ap'pa·im. But Se'led died without sons. **31** The son* of Ap'pa·im was Ish'i. And the son* of Ish'i was She'shan, and the son* of She'shan, Ah'lai. **32** The sons of Ja'da the brother of Sham'mai were Je'ther and Jon'a·than. But Je'ther died without

sons. **33** The sons of Jon'a·than were Pe'leth and Za'za. These were the descendants of Je·rah'me·el.

34 She'shan had no sons, only daughters. Now She'shan had an Egyptian servant whose name was Jar'ha. **35** She'shan gave his daughter to be the wife of his servant Jar'ha, and she bore him At'tai. **36** At'tai became father to Nathan. Nathan became father to Za'bad. **37** Za'bad became father to Eph'lal. Eph'lal became father to O'bed. **38** O'bed became father to Je'hu. Je'hu became father to Az·a·ri'ah. **39** Az·a·ri'ah became father to He'lez. He'lez became father to El·e·a'sah. **40** El·e·a'sah became father to Sis'mai. Sis'mai became father to Shal'lum. **41** Shal'lum became father to Jek·a·mi'ah. Jek·a·mi'ah became father to E·lish'a·ma.

42 The sons of Ca'leb*[a] the brother of Je·rah'me·el were Me'sha his firstborn, who was the father of Ziph, and the sons of Ma·re'shah the father of Heb'ron. **43** The sons of Heb'ron were Kor'ah, Tap'pu·ah, Re'kem, and She'ma. **44** She'ma became father to Ra'ham the father of Jor'ke·am. Re'kem became father to Sham'mai. **45** The son of Sham'mai was Ma'on. Ma'on was the father of Beth-zur.[b] **46** Ca'leb's concubine E'phah gave birth to Ha'ran, Mo'za, and Ga'zez. Ha'ran became father to Ga'zez. **47** The sons of Jah'dai were Re'gem, Jo'tham, Ge'shan, Pel'et, E'phah, and Sha'aph. **48** Ca'leb's concubine Ma'a·cah gave birth to She'ber and Tir'ha·nah. **49** In time she bore Sha'aph the father of Mad·man'nah,[c] She'va the father of Mach·be'nah,

CHAP. 2
a 1Ch 4:4

b Ex 17:12
Ex 24:14

c Ex 31:2-5
Ex 36:1
Ex 37:1

d Ge 50:23
1Ch 7:14

e Nu 26:29
Jos 17:1

f De 3:14
Jos 13:29, 30

g Nu 32:40, 41

h 2Sa 3:3
2Sa 13:38

i 2Sa 8:6

j 1Ki 4:13

k Nu 32:42

l Ge 46:12

m 1Ch 4:5

n Ne 3:5

Second Col.
a 1Ch 2:9

b Jos 15:20, 58
Ne 3:16

c Jos 15:21, 31

2:23 *Or "surrounding." 2:31 *Lit., "sons." | 2:42 *Also called Chelubai in vs. 9.

and Gib'e·a.[a] Ca'leb's[b] daughter was Ach'sah.[c] **50** These were the descendants of Ca'leb.

The sons of Hur[d] the first-born of Eph'ra·thah[e] were Sho'bal the father of Kir'i·ath-je'a·rim,[f] **51** Sal'ma the father of Beth'le·hem,[g] and Ha'reph the father of Beth-ga'der. **52** Sho'bal the father of Kir'i·ath-je'a·rim had sons: Ha·ro'eh and half of the Me·nu'hoth. **53** The families of Kir'i·ath-je'a·rim were the Ith'rites,[h] the Pu'thites, the Shu'math·ites, and the Mish'ra·ites. It was from these that the Zo'rath·ites[i] and the Esh'ta·ol·ites[j] came. **54** The sons of Sal'ma were Beth'le·hem,[k] the Ne·toph'a·thites, At'roth-beth-jo'ab, half of the Man·a·ha'thites, and the Zor'ites. **55** The families of the scribes dwelling at Ja'bez were the Ti'rath·ites, the Shim'e·ath·ites, and the Su'cath·ites. These were the Ken'ites[l] who came from Ham'math the father of the house of Re'chab.[m]

3 These were the sons of David who were born to him in Heb'ron:[n] the firstborn Am'non,[o] whose mother was A·hin'o·am[p] of Jez're·el; the second, Daniel, whose mother was Ab'i·gail[q] the Car'mel·ite; **2** the third, Ab'sa·lom[r] the son of Ma'a·cah the daughter of Tal'mai the king of Gesh'ur; the fourth, Ad·o·ni'jah[s] the son of Hag'gith; **3** the fifth, Sheph·a·ti'ah, whose mother was A·bi'tal; and the sixth, Ith're·am, whose mother was David's wife Eg'lah. **4** These six were born to him in Heb'ron; he reigned there for 7 years and 6 months, and for 33 years he reigned in Jerusalem.[t]

5 These were born to him in Jerusalem:[u] Shim'e·a, Sho'bab, Nathan,[v] and Sol'o·mon;[w] the mother of these four was Bath-she'ba[x] the daughter of

Am'mi·el. **6** And nine other sons were Ib'har, E·lish'a·ma, E·liph'e·let, **7** No'gah, Ne'pheg, Ja·phi'a, **8** E·lish'a·ma, E·li'a·da, and E·liph'e·let. **9** All of these were the sons of David, besides the sons of the concubines, and Ta'mar[a] was their sister.

10 The son of Sol'o·mon was Re·ho·bo'am;[b] A·bi'jah[c] was his son, A'sa[d] his son, Je·hosh'a·phat[e] his son, **11** Je·ho'ram[f] his son, A·ha·zi'ah[g] his son, Je·ho'ash[h] his son, **12** Am·a·zi'ah[i] his son, Az·a·ri'ah[i] his son, Jo'tham[k] his son, **13** A'haz[l] his son, Hez·e·ki'ah[m] his son, Ma·nas'seh[n] his son, **14** A'mon[o] his son, Jo·si'ah[p] his son. **15** The sons of Jo·si'ah were the firstborn, Jo·ha'nan, the second, Je·hoi'a·kim,[q] the third, Zed·e·ki'ah,[r] the fourth, Shal'lum. **16** The sons of Je·hoi'a·kim were Jec·o·ni'ah[s] his son and Zed·e·ki'ah his son. **17** The sons of Jec·o·ni'ah the prisoner were She·al'ti·el, **18** Mal·chi'ram, Pe·dai'ah, She·naz'zar, Jek·a·mi'ah, Hosh'a·ma, and Ned·a·bi'ah. **19** The sons of Pe·dai'ah were Ze·rub'ba·bel[t] and Shim'e·i; and the sons of Ze·rub'ba·bel were Me·shul'lam and Han·a·ni'ah (and She·lo'mith was their sister); **20** and five other sons were Ha·shu'bah, O'hel, Ber·e·chi'ah, Has·a·di'ah, and Ju'shab-he'sed. **21** And the sons of Han·a·ni'ah were Pel·a·ti'ah and Je·sha'iah; the son* of Je·sha'iah was Re·pha'iah; the son* of Re·pha'iah was Ar'nan; the son* of Ar'nan was O·ba·di'ah; the son* of O·ba·di'ah was Shec·a·ni'ah; **22** and the sons of Shec·a·ni'ah were She·mai'ah and the sons of She·mai'ah: Hat'tush, I'gal, Ba·ri'ah, Ne·a·ri'ah, and Sha'phat—six in all. **23** And the sons of Ne·a·ri'ah were Eli·o·e'nai, Hiz·ki'ah, and Az·ri'kam, three. **24** And the sons of Eli·o·e'nai were Hod·a·vi'-

CHAP. 2
a Jos 15:20, 57
b 1Ch 2:18
c Jos 15:16, 17
d Ex 17:12
  Ex 24:14
e 1Ch 2:19
f Jos 15:9, 12
  1Ch 13:5
g Jos 15:19
  Joh 7:42
h 1Ch 11:10, 40
i 1Ch 4:2
j Jos 15:20, 33
k Ge 35:19
  Mt 2:1
l Jg 1:16
  Jg 4:11
  1Sa 15:6
m 2Ki 10:15
  Jer 35:6, 19

CHAP. 3
n 2Sa 3:2-5
o 1Sa 13:32
p 1Sa 25:43
q 1Sa 25:2, 39
r 1Sa 13:28, 37
  2Sa 15:10
  2Sa 18:14
s 1Ki 1:5, 11
  1Ki 2:24
t 2Sa 5:5
u 2Sa 5:13-16
  1Ch 14:3-7
v Lu 3:23, 31
w Mt 1:7
x 2Sa 11:3, 27

Second Col.
a 2Sa 13:1
b 1Ki 11:43
c 2Ch 13:1
d 2Ch 14:1
e 2Ch 20:31
f 2Ch 21:5
g 2Ch 22:2
h 2Ch 24:1
i 2Ch 25:1
j 2Ki 14:21
k 2Ch 27:1
l 2Ch 28:1
m 2Ch 29:1
n 2Ki 21:1
o 2Ki 21:19
p 2Ki 22:1
q 2Ki 23:34
  2Ch 36:5
r 2Ch 36:11
s 2Ki 24:6, 8
  2Ki 25:27
  Es 2:6
t Ezr 5:2
  Mt 1:12
  Lu 3:23, 27

3:21 *Lit., "sons."

ah, E·li′a·shib, Pe·la′iah, Ak′kub, Jo·ha′nan, De·la′iah, and A·na′ni, seven.

4 The sons of Judah were Pe′rez,ᵃ Hez′ron,ᵇ Car′mi, Hur,ᶜ and Sho′bal.ᵈ **2** Re·a′iah the son of Sho′bal became father to Ja′hath; Ja′hath became father to A·hu′mai and La′had. These were the families of the Zo′rath·ites.ᵉ **3** These were the sons of the father of E′tam:ᶠ Jez′re·el, Ish′ma, and Id′bash (and the name of their sister was Haz·ze·lel·po′ni), **4** and Pe·nu′el was the father of Ge′dor, and E′zer was the father of Hu′shah. These were the sons of Hur,ᵍ the firstborn of Eph′ra·thah and the father of Beth′le·hem.ʰ **5** Ash′hurⁱ the father of Te·ko′aʲ had two wives, He′lah and Na′a·rah. **6** Na′a·rah bore to him A·huz′zam, He′pher, Te′me·ni, and Ha·a·hash′ta·ri. These were the sons of Na′a·rah. **7** And the sons of He′lah were Ze′reth, Iz′har, and Eth′nan. **8** Koz became father to A′nub, Zo·be′bah, and the families of A·har′hel the son of Ha′rum.

9 Ja′bez was more honorable than his brothers; and his mother named him Ja′bez,* saying: "I gave birth to him in pain." **10** Ja′bez called on the God of Israel, saying: "O that you would bless me and enlarge my territory and let your hand be with me and preserve me from calamity, so that it may bring no harm to me!" So God brought about what he had asked for.

11 Che′lub the brother of Shu′hah became father to Me′hir, who was the father of Esh′ton. **12** Esh′ton became father to Beth-ra′pha, Pa·se′ah, and Te·hin′nah, the father of Ir-na′hash. These were the men of Re′cah. **13** And the sons of Ke′naz were

CHAP. 4

ᵃ Ge 38:29
  Nu 26:20
  Ru 4:18
  Mt 1:3

ᵇ Ge 46:12
  1Ch 2:5

ᶜ Ex 17:12
  Ex 24:14
  1Ch 2:19

ᵈ 1Ch 2:50

ᵉ 1Ch 2:53

ᶠ 2Ch 11:5, 6

ᵍ 1Ch 2:19

ʰ Mic 5:2

ⁱ 1Ch 2:24

ʲ 2Ch 11:5, 6

Second Col.

ᵃ Jos 15:16, 17
  Jg 3:9, 11

ᵇ Nu 32:11, 12
  Jos 15:13

ᶜ Ge 38:2, 5
  Nu 26:20

Oth′ni·elᵃ and Se·rai′ah, and the son* of Oth′ni·el was Ha′thath. **14** Me·o′no·thai became father to Oph′rah. Se·rai′ah became father to Jo′ab the father of Ge·har′a·shim,* so called because they were craftsmen.

15 The sons of Ca′lebᵇ the son of Je·phun′neh were I′ru, E′lah, and Na′am; and the son* of E′lah was Ke′naz. **16** The sons of Je·hal′le·lel were Ziph, Zi′phah, Tir′i·a, and As′a·rel. **17** The sons of Ez′rah were Je′ther, Me′red, E′pher, and Ja′lon; she* conceived and bore Mir′i·am, Sham′mai, and Ish′bah the father of Esh·te·mo′a. **18** (And his Jewish wife gave birth to Je′red the father of Ge′dor, He′ber the father of So′co, and Je·ku′thi·el the father of Za·no′ah.) These were the sons of Bi·thi′ah, the daughter of Phar′aoh, whom Me′red married.

19 The sons of Ho·di′ah's wife, the sister of Na′ham, were the fathers of Kei′lah the Gar′mite and Esh·te·mo′a the Ma·ac′a·thite. **20** And the sons of Shi′mon were Am′non, Rin′nah, Ben-ha′nan, and Ti′lon. And the sons of Ish′i were Zo′heth and Ben-zo′heth.

21 The sons of She′lahᶜ the son of Judah were Er the father of Le′cah, La′a·dah the father of Ma·re′shah, and the families of the workers of fine fabric of the house of Ash·be′a, **22** and Jo′kim, the men of Co·ze′ba, Jo′ash, and Sa′raph, who became husbands of Mo′ab·ite women, and Jash′u·bi-le′hem. These records are ancient.* **23** They were potters who lived in Ne·ta′im and Ge·de′rah. They lived there and worked for the king.

24 The sons of Sim'e·on[a] were Nem'u·el, Ja'min, Ja'rib, Ze'rah, and Sha'ul.[b] **25** Shal'lum was his son, Mib'sam his son, and Mish'ma his son. **26** And the sons of Mish'ma were Ham'mu·el his son, Zac'cur his son, Shim'e·i his son. **27** And Shim'e·i had 16 sons and 6 daughters; but his brothers did not have many sons, and none of their families had as many as the men of Judah had.[c] **28** They lived in Be'er-she'ba,[d] Mo·la'dah,[e] Ha'zar-shu'al,[f] **29** Bil'hah, E'zem,[g] To'lad, **30** Be·thu'el,[h] Hor'mah,[i] Zik'lag,[j] **31** Beth-mar'ca·both, Ha'zar-su'sim,[k] Beth-bir'i, and Sha'a·ra'im. These were their cities until the reign of David.

32 Their settlements were E'tam, A'in, Rim'mon, To'chen, and A'shan,[l] five cities, **33** along with their settlements that were all around these cities as far as Ba'al. These were their genealogical enrollments and the places where they lived. **34** And Me·sho'bab, Jam'lech, Jo'shah the son of Am·a·zi'ah, **35** Joel, Je'hu son of Josh·i·bi'ah son of Se·rai'ah son of As'i·el, **36** and Eli·o·e'nai, Ja·a·ko'bah, Jesh·o·hai'ah, A·sai'ah, Ad'i·el, Je·sim'i·el, Be·nai'ah, **37** and Zi'za son of Shi'phi son of Al'lon son of Je·da'iah son of Shim'ri son of She·mai'ah; **38** these mentioned by name were the chieftains among their families, and the household of their forefathers increased in number. **39** And they went to the entrance of Ge'dor, to the east side of the valley, to look for pastures for their flocks. **40** They eventually found rich and good pastures, and the land was spacious, quiet, and undisturbed. Those who previously lived there were Ham'ites.[m] **41** These whose names are listed came during the days of

King Hez·e·ki'ah[a] of Judah and struck down the tents of the Ham'ites and the Me·u'nim who were there. They devoted them to destruction down to this day; and they settled in their place because there were pastures for their flocks there.

42 Some of the Sim'e·on·ites, 500 men, went to Mount Se'ir[b] with Pel·a·ti'ah, Ne·a·ri'ah, Re·pha'iah, and Uz'zi·el, the sons of Ish'i who led them. **43** And they struck down the rest of the A·mal'ek·ites[c] who had escaped, and they have lived there down to this day.

5 These are the sons of Reu'ben,[d] Israel's firstborn. He was the firstborn, but because he defiled* the bed of his father,[e] his right as firstborn was given to the sons of Joseph[f] the son of Israel, so he was not enrolled genealogically for the right of the firstborn. **2** Though Judah[g] was superior to his brothers and from him came the one to be the leader,[h] the right as firstborn belonged to Joseph. **3** The sons of Reu'ben the firstborn of Israel were Ha'noch, Pal'lu, Hez'ron, and Car'mi.[i] **4** The sons of Joel were She·mai'ah his son, Gog his son, Shim'e·i his son, **5** Mi'cah his son, Re·a'iah his son, Ba'al his son, **6** and Be·er'ah his son, whom King Til'gath-pil·ne'ser[j] of As·syr'i·a took into exile; he was a chieftain of the Reu'ben·ites. **7** His brothers by their families in the genealogical enrollment by their descendants were, as the head, Je·i'el, Zech·a·ri'ah, **8** and Be'la son of A'zaz son of She'ma son of Joel, who lived in A·ro'er[k] and as far as Ne'bo and Ba'al-me'on.[l] **9** To the east he settled as far as the beginning of the wilderness at the Eu·phra'tes River,[m] for their livestock had become numerous in the land of Gil'e·ad.[n] **10** In the days

---

CHAP. 4
a Ge 46:10
b Nu 26:12, 13
c Nu 26:22
d Jos 19:1, 2
e Jos 15:21, 26
f Jos 15:21, 28
  Jos 19:1, 3
  Ne 11:25-27
g Jos 15:21, 29
h Jos 19:1, 4
i Jg 1:17
j Jos 15:20, 31
  Jos 19:1, 5
  1Sa 27:5, 6
k Jos 19:1, 5
l Jos 19:1, 7
m Ge 10:6, 20

Second Col.
a 2Ch 29:1
b Ge 36:8
c Ex 17:14, 16
  1Sa 15:7

CHAP. 5
d Ge 29:32
  Ge 49:3, 4
e Ge 35:22
f Ge 49:22, 26
  Jos 14:4
g Ge 49:8, 10
  Nu 2:3
  Nu 10:14
  Jg 1:1, 2
  Ps 60:7
h Mt 2:6
  Heb 7:14
i Ge 46:9
  Ex 6:14
j 2Ki 16:7
k De 2:36
l Nu 32:34, 38
  Jos 13:15, 17
  Eze 25:9, 10
m Ge 15:18
  De 1:7
  Jos 1:4
  2Sa 8:3
n Jos 22:9

5:1 *Or "profaned."

of Saul, they waged war against the Hag'rites, who were defeated before them, so they dwelled in their tents throughout all the territory east of Gil'e·ad.

11 Now the descendants of Gad lived next to them in the land of Ba'shan as far as Sal'e·cah.[a] 12 Joel was the head, Sha'pham the second, and Ja'nai and Sha'phat in Ba'shan. 13 And their brothers belonging to their paternal houses were Mi'cha·el, Me·shul'lam, She'ba, Jo'rai, Ja'can, Zi'a, and E'ber, seven in all. 14 These were the sons of Ab'i·ha·il son of Hu'ri son of Ja·ro'ah son of Gil'e·ad son of Mi'cha·el son of Je·shish'ai son of Jah'do son of Buz. 15 A'hi son of Ab'di·el son of Gu'ni was head of their paternal house. 16 They lived in Gil'e·ad,[b] in Ba'shan[c] and its dependent* towns, and in all the pastures of Shar'on as far as they extended. 17 They were all enrolled genealogically in the days of King Jo'tham[d] of Judah and in the days of King Jer·o·bo'am*[e] of Israel.

18 The Reu'ben·ites, the Gad'ites, and the half tribe of Ma·nas'seh had 44,760 mighty warriors in their army who carried shields and swords and were armed with bows,* and they were trained in war. 19 They waged war against the Hag'rites,[f] Je'tur, Na'phish,[g] and No'dab. 20 And they were helped in fighting them, so that the Hag'rites and all who were with them were given into their hand, for they called to God for help in the war, and he responded to their entreaty because they trusted in him.[h] 21 They captured their livestock—50,000 camels, 250,000 sheep, and 2,000 donkeys—as well as 100,000 peo-

ple.* 22 Many had fallen slain, because the war was waged by the true God.[a] And they lived in their place until the time of the exile.[b]

23 The descendants of the half tribe of Ma·nas'seh[c] lived in the land from Ba'shan to Ba'al-her'mon and Se'nir and Mount Her'mon.[d] They were numerous. 24 These were the heads of their paternal houses: E'pher, Ish'i, E'li·el, Az'ri·el, Jeremiah, Hod·a·vi'ah, and Jah'di·el; they were mighty warriors, men of fame, and heads of their paternal houses. 25 But they acted unfaithfully toward the God of their forefathers and prostituted themselves to the gods of the peoples of the land,[e] whom God had annihilated from before them. 26 So the God of Israel stirred up the spirit of King Pul of As·syr'i·a[f] (that is, King Til'gath-pil·ne'ser[g] of As·syr'i·a) so that he took into exile those of the Reu'ben·ites, the Gad'ites, and the half tribe of Ma·nas'seh and brought them to Ha'lah, Ha'bor, Ha'ra, and the river Go'zan,[h] where they are until this day.

6 The sons of Le'vi[i] were Ger'shon, Ko'hath,[j] and Me·rar'i.[k] 2 The sons of Ko'hath were Am'ram, Iz'har,[l] Heb'ron, and Uz'zi·el.[m] 3 The children* of Am'ram[n] were Aaron,[o] Moses,[p] and also Mir'i·am.[q] And the sons of Aaron were Na'dab, A·bi'hu,[r] El·e·a'zar,[s] and Ith'a·mar.[t] 4 El·e·a'zar became father to Phin'e·has;[u] Phin'e·has became father to Ab·i·shu'a. 5 Ab·i·shu'a became father to Buk'ki; Buk'ki became father to Uz'zi. 6 Uz'zi became father to Zer·a·hi'ah; Zer·a·hi'ah became father to Me·ra'ioth. 7 Me·ra'ioth became father to Am·a·ri'ah; Am·a·ri'ah became father to A·hi'tub.[v]

CHAP. 5
a De 3:8, 10
  Jos 12:4, 5
b Nu 32:1
c De 3:3, 13
  De 32:14
d 2Ki 15:32
  2Ch 27:1
  Isa 1:1
  Ho 1:1
  Mic 1:1
e 2Ki 14:16, 28
f 1Ch 5:10
g Ge 25:13, 15
  1Ch 1:31
h Ps 20:7
  Ps 22:4

Second Col.
a Jos 10:42
  1Sa 17:45, 47
  2Ch 20:15
b 2Ki 15:29
  2Ki 17:6
c Jos 13:29, 30
d De 4:47, 48
e De 5:7-9
  Jg 2:17
  Jg 8:33
  2Ki 17:10, 11
f Ezr 1:1
  Pr 21:1
g 2Ki 15:19, 29
h 2Ki 17:6
  2Ki 18:11

CHAP. 6
i Ge 29:34
  Ex 6:16
j Ex 6:18
  Nu 3:27
k Nu 3:17
  Nu 26:57
l Ex 6:21
m Ex 6:22
  Le 10:4
n Ex 6:20
o 1Ch 23:13
p Ex 6:26
  Ac 7:37, 38
q Ex 15:20
r Ex 24:1
  Le 10:1
s Nu 3:32
  De 10:6
t Ex 6:23
  Ex 28:1
  Nu 4:28
  1Ch 24:2, 4
u Ex 6:25
  Nu 25:11
v 2Sa 8:17

5:16 *Or "surrounding." 5:17 *That is, Jeroboam II. 5:18 *Lit., "and tread the bow."

5:21 *Or "human souls." 6:3 *Lit., "sons."

8 A·hi'tub became father to Za'dok;[a] Za'dok became father to A·him'a·az.[b] **9** A·him'a·az became father to Az·a·ri'ah; Az·a·ri'ah became father to Jo·ha'nan. **10** Jo·ha'nan became father to Az·a·ri'ah. He served as priest in the house that Sol'o·mon built in Jerusalem.

11 Az·a·ri'ah became father to Am·a·ri'ah; Am·a·ri'ah became father to A·hi'tub. **12** A·hi'tub became father to Za'dok;[c] Za'dok became father to Shal'lum. **13** Shal'lum became father to Hil·ki'ah;[d] Hil·ki'ah became father to Az·a·ri'ah. **14** Az·a·ri'ah became father to Se·rai'ah;[e] Se·rai'ah became father to Je·hoz'a·dak.[f] **15** And Je·hoz'a·dak went into exile when Jehovah took Judah and Jerusalem into exile by the hand of Neb·u·chad·nez'zar.

16 The sons of Le'vi were Ger'shom,* Ko'hath, and Me·rar'i. **17** These are the names of the sons of Ger'shom: Lib'ni and Shim'e·i.[g] **18** The sons of Ko'hath were Am'ram, Iz'har, He'bron, and Uz'zi·el.[h] **19** The sons of Me·rar'i were Mah'li and Mu'shi.

These were the families of the Levites by their forefathers:[i] **20** Of Ger'shom,[j] Lib'ni his son, Ja'hath his son, Zim'mah his son, **21** Jo'ah his son, Id'do his son, Ze'rah his son, Je·ath'e·rai his son. **22** The sons* of Ko'hath were Am·min'a·dab his son, Kor'ah[k] his son, As'sir his son, **23** El·ka'nah his son, E·bi'a·saph[l] his son, As'sir his son, **24** Ta'hath his son, U·ri'el his son, Uz·zi'ah his son, and Sha'ul his son. **25** The sons of El·ka'nah were A·ma'sai and A·hi'moth. **26** As for El·ka'nah, the sons of El·ka'nah were Zo'phai his son, Na'hath his son, **27** E·li'ab his son, Je·ro'ham his son, El·ka'nah[m] his son. **28** The sons of Samuel[a] were Joel the firstborn and A·bi'jah the second.[b] **29** The sons* of Me·rar'i were Mah'li,[c] Lib'ni his son, Shim'e·i his son, Uz'zah his son, **30** Shim'e·a his son, Hag·gi'ah his son, and A·sai'ah his son.

31 These were the ones whom David appointed to direct the singing at the house of Jehovah after the Ark came to rest there.[d] **32** They were responsible for the singing at the tabernacle of the tent of meeting until Sol'o·mon built the house of Jehovah in Jerusalem,[e] and they carried out their service as prescribed for them.[f] **33** These are the men who served with their sons: Of the Ko'hath·ites, He'man[g] the singer, son of Joel[h] son of Samuel **34** son of El·ka'nah[i] son of Je·ro'ham son of E'li·el son of To'ah **35** son of Zuph son of El·ka'nah son of Ma'hath son of A·ma'sai **36** son of El·ka'nah son of Joel son of Az·a·ri'ah son of Zeph·a·ni'ah **37** son of Ta'hath son of As'sir son of E·bi'a·saph son of Kor'ah **38** son of Iz'har son of Ko'hath son of Le'vi son of Israel.

39 His brother A'saph[j] stood at his right hand; A'saph was son of Ber·e·chi'ah son of Shim'e·a **40** son of Mi'cha·el son of Ba·a·se'iah son of Mal·chi'jah **41** son of Eth'ni son of Ze'rah son of A·dai'ah **42** son of E'than son of Zim'mah son of Shim'e·i **43** son of Ja'hath son of Ger'shom son of Le'vi.

44 The descendants of Me·rar'i[k] their brothers were at the left hand; there was E'than[l] son of Kish'i son of Ab'di son of Mal'luch **45** son of Hash·a·bi'ah son of Am·a·zi'ah son of Hil·ki'ah **46** son of Am'zi son of Ba'ni son of She'mer **47** son of Mah'li son of Mu'shi son of Me·rar'i son of Le'vi.

CHAP. 6
a 1Ki 1:8
  1Ki 2:35
b 2Sa 15:27, 36
c Ne 11:11
d 2Ch 34:14
e 2Ki 25:18
f Hag 1:1
g Nu 3:18
h Nu 3:19, 20
i Nu 26:57
j Nu 3:18
k Nu 16:1, 32
  Nu 26:10, 11
  Jude 11
l Ex 6:24
m 1Sa 1:1

Second Col.
a 1Sa 1:20
b 1Sa 8:1, 2
c Ex 6:19
  1Ch 23:21
d 2Sa 6:17
  1Ch 15:16
e 1Ki 6:14
f 2Ch 35:15
g 1Ch 15:16, 17
h 1Sa 8:1, 2
i 1Sa 1:1
j 1Ch 25:1
  2Ch 5:12
  Ps 50:Sup
k 1Ch 23:6
l 1Ch 15:16, 17

6:16 *Also called Gershon in vs. 1.
6:22, 29 *Or "descendants."

48 Their brothers the Levites were appointed* for all the service of the tabernacle, the house of the true God.[a] **49** Aaron and his sons[b] made the sacrifices smoke on the altar of burnt offering[c] and on the altar of incense,[d] performing the duties connected with the most holy things, to make atonement for Israel,[e] according to all that Moses the servant of the true God had commanded. **50** These were the descendants of Aaron:[f] El·e·a′zar[g] his son, Phin′e·has his son, Ab·i·shu′a his son, **51** Buk′ki his son, Uz′zi his son, Zer·a·hi′ah his son, **52** Me·ra′ioth his son, Am·a·ri′ah his son, A·hi′tub[h] his son, **53** Za′dok[i] his son, and A·him′a·az his son.

54 These were their settlements by their encampments* in their territory: for the descendants of Aaron belonging to the family of the Ko′hath·ites, as the first lot fell to them, **55** they gave them Heb′ron[j] in the land of Judah, with its surrounding pastures. **56** But the field of the city and its settlements they gave to Ca′leb[k] the son of Je·phun′neh. **57** And to the descendants of Aaron they gave the cities* of refuge,[l] Heb′ron,[m] also Lib′nah[n] with its pastures, Jat′tir,[o] Esh·te·mo′a with its pastures,[p] **58** Hi′len with its pastures, De′bir[q] with its pastures, **59** A′shan[r] with its pastures, and Beth-she′mesh[s] with its pastures; **60** and from the tribe of Benjamin, Ge′ba[t] with its pastures, Al′e·meth with its pastures, and An′a·thoth[u] with its pastures. All their cities for their families were 13 cities.[v]

61 To the rest of the Ko′hath·ites, there were allotted* ten cit-

ies, from the family of the tribe, from the half tribe, the half of Ma·nas′seh.[a]

62 To the Ger′shom·ites by their families they assigned 13 cities from the tribe of Is′sa·char, the tribe of Ash′er, the tribe of Naph′ta·li, and the tribe of Ma·nas′seh in Ba′shan.[b]

63 To the Me·rar′ites by their families they assigned by lot 12 cities from the tribe of Reu′ben, the tribe of Gad, and the tribe of Zeb′u·lun.[c]

64 Thus the Israelites gave the Levites these cities with their pastures.[d] **65** Furthermore, they assigned by lot these cities from the tribe of Judah, the tribe of Sim′e·on, and the tribe of Benjamin, which are mentioned by their names.

66 Some of the Ko′hath·ite families had cities from the tribe of E′phra·im as their territory.[e] **67** They gave them the cities* of refuge, She′chem[f] with its pastures in the mountainous region of E′phra·im, Ge′zer[g] with its pastures, **68** Jok′me·am with its pastures, Beth-ho′ron[h] with its pastures, **69** Ai′ja·lon[i] with its pastures, and Gath-rim′mon[j] with its pastures; **70** and from half of the tribe of Ma·nas′seh, A′ner with its pastures and Bil′e·am with its pastures, to the rest of the families of the Ko′hath·ites.

71 To the Ger′shom·ites they assigned from the family of the half tribe of Ma·nas′seh, Go′lan[k] in Ba′shan with its pastures and Ash′ta·roth with its pastures;[l] **72** and from the tribe of Is′sa·char, Ke′desh with its pastures, Dab′e·rath[m] with its pastures,[n] **73** Ra′moth with its pastures, and A′nem with its pastures; **74** and from the tribe of Ash′er, Ma′shal with its pastures, Ab′don

CHAP. 6
a Nu 3:5-7
b Ex 28:1
  Nu 3:10
c Ex 29:38
d Ex 30:7
e Ex 30:10
  Le 4:20
  Le 17:11
  2Ch 29:24
f Ex 6:23
g Ex 28:1
  Nu 3:32
h 2Sa 8:17
i 1Ki 2:35
j Nu 13:22
  Jos 21:8, 11
k Jos 14:13
  Jg 1:20
l Nu 35:12, 13
m Jos 20:7, 9
n Jos 15:20, 42
o Jos 15:20, 48
p Jos 21:13-16
q Jg 1:11
r 1Ch 4:24, 32
s Jos 15:10, 12
t Jos 18:21, 24
u Jos 21:8, 18
  Jer 1:1
v Jos 21:4

Second Col.
a Jos 21:5
b Jos 21:27-33
c Jos 21:34-40
d Nu 35:2-4
e Jos 21:20-26
f Jos 20:7, 9
g Jos 16:10
h Jos 10:11
i Jos 10:12
  Jg 1:35
j Jos 19:45, 48
k De 4:41-43
l Jos 21:27
m Jos 19:12, 16
n Jos 21:8, 28

6:48 *Lit., "were the ones given." 6:54 *Or "walled camps." 6:57 *Or possibly, "city," in agreement with Jos 21:13. 6:61 *Or "given by lot."

6:67 *Or possibly, "city," in agreement with Jos 21:21.

with its pastures,[a] **75** Hu'kok with its pastures, and Re'hob[b] with its pastures; **76** and from the tribe of Naph'ta·li, Ke'desh[c] in Gal'i·lee[d] with its pastures, Ham'mon with its pastures, and Kir·i·a·tha'im with its pastures.

77 To the rest of the Me·rar'ites they assigned from the tribe of Zeb'u·lun,[e] Rim'mo·no with its pastures, Ta'bor with its pastures; **78** and in the region of the Jordan at Jer'i·cho, to the east of the Jordan, from the tribe of Reu'ben, they were given Be'zer in the wilderness with its pastures, Ja'haz[f] with its pastures, **79** Ked'e·moth[g] with its pastures, and Meph'a·ath with its pastures; **80** and from the tribe of Gad, Ra'moth in Gil'e·ad with its pastures, Ma·ha·na'im[h] with its pastures, **81** Hesh'bon[i] with its pastures, and Ja'zer[j] with its pastures.

7 Now the sons of Is'sa·char were To'la, Pu'ah, Ja'shub, and Shim'ron[k]—four. **2** And the sons of To'la were Uz'zi, Re·pha'iah, Je'ri·el, Jah'mai, Ib'sam, and She·mu'el, the heads of their paternal houses. Descended from To'la were mighty warriors, whose number in the days of David was 22,600. **3** And the descendants* of Uz'zi were Iz·ra·hi'ah and the sons of Iz·ra·hi'ah: Mi'cha·el, O·ba·di'ah, Joel, and Is·shi'ah—all five of them were chiefs.# **4** And with them by their descendants, according to their paternal houses, there were 36,000 soldiers in their army available for war, for they had many wives and sons. **5** And their brothers of all the families of Is'sa·char were mighty warriors, 87,000 as listed in the genealogical enrollment.[l]

6 The sons of Benjamin[m] were Be'la,[n] Be'cher,[o] and Je·di'a·el[p]—three. **7** And the sons of

Be'la were Ez'bon, Uz'zi, Uz'zi·el, Jer'i·moth, and I'ri—five—heads of their paternal houses, mighty warriors, and 22,034 were in their genealogical enrollment.[a] **8** And the sons of Be'cher were Ze·mi'rah, Jo'ash, E·li·e'zer, Eli·o·e'nai, Om'ri, Jer'e·moth, A·bi'jah, An'a·thoth, and Al'e·meth—all of these were the sons of Be'cher. **9** Their genealogical enrollment by their descendants as respects the heads of their paternal houses was 20,200 mighty warriors. **10** And the sons of Je·di'a·el[b] were Bil'han and the sons of Bil'han: Je'ush, Benjamin, E'hud, Che·na'a·nah, Ze'than, Tar'shish, and A·hish'a·har. **11** All of these were the sons of Je·di'a·el, according to the heads of their forefathers, 17,200 mighty warriors ready to go out to the army for war.

12 The Shup'pim and the Hup'pim were the sons of Ir;[c] the Hu'shim were the sons of A'her.

13 The sons of Naph'ta·li[d] were Jah'zi·el, Gu'ni, Je'zer, and Shal'lum—descendants* of Bil'hah.[e]

14 The sons of Ma·nas'seh:[f] As'ri·el, whom his Syrian concubine bore. (She bore Ma'chir[g] the father of Gil'e·ad. **15** Ma'chir took a wife for Hup'pim and for Shup'pim, and the name of his sister was Ma'a·cah.) The name of the second was Ze·lo'phe·had,[h] but Ze·lo'phe·had had daughters.[i] **16** Ma'a·cah, Ma'chir's wife, bore a son and named him Pe'resh; and the name of his brother was She'resh; and his sons were U'lam and Re'kem. **17** And the son* of U'lam was Be'dan. These were the sons of Gil'e·ad son of Ma'chir son of Ma·nas'seh. **18** And his sister was Ham·mo'le·cheth. She gave birth to Ish'hod, Abi·e'zer, and Mah'lah. **19** And the sons of She·mi'da were A·hi'an, She'chem, Lik'hi, and A·ni'am.

7:3, 13, 17 *Lit., "sons." 7:3 #Lit., "heads."

CHAP. 6

a Jos 21:8, 30

b Jos 19:28, 31
  Jg 1:31

c Jos 20:7, 9
  Jos 21:32, 33

d Mt 3:13

e Jos 21:34-39

f Nu 21:23

g De 2:26

h Ge 32:1, 2
  2Sa 8:8

i Nu 21:26

j Nu 32:1

CHAP. 7

k Ge 46:13
  Nu 26:23, 24

l Nu 26:25

m Ge 35:16, 18
  Nu 26:38, 39

n 1Ch 8:1

o Ge 46:21

p 1Ch 7:10

Second Col.

a Nu 26:41

b 1Ch 7:6

c 1Ch 7:7

d Nu 26:48, 49

e Ge 30:3, 8
  Ge 46:24, 25

f Ge 41:50, 51

g Ge 50:23
  Nu 26:29
  De 3:15

h Nu 26:33

i Nu 27:1, 7

20 The sons of E'phra·im[a] were Shu'the·lah,[b] Be'red his son, Ta'hath his son, E·le·a'dah his son, Ta'hath his son, **21** Za'bad his son, Shu'the·lah his son, E'zer, and E'le·ad. The men of Gath[c] who were born in the land killed them because they went down to take their livestock. **22** E'phra·im their father carried on mourning for many days, and his brothers kept coming in to comfort him. **23** Afterward he had relations with his wife, and she became pregnant and gave birth to a son. But he named him Be·ri'ah* because it was with calamity that she was in his house. **24** And his daughter was She'e·rah, who built Lower[d] and Upper Beth-ho'ron[e] and Uz'zen-she'e·rah. **25** And there was Re'phah his son, Re'sheph, Te'lah his son, Ta'han his son, **26** La'dan his son, Am·mi'hud his son, E·lish'a·ma his son, **27** Nun his son, and Joshua*[f] his son.

28 Their possession and their settlements were Beth'el[g] and its dependent* towns, and to the east Na'a·ran, and to the west Ge'zer and its dependent towns, and She'chem and its dependent towns, as far as Ay'yah* and its dependent towns; **29** and next to the descendants of Ma·nas'seh, Beth-she'an[h] and its dependent towns, Ta'a·nach[i] and its dependent towns, Me·gid'do[j] and its dependent towns, and Dor[k] and its dependent towns. In these the descendants of Joseph the son of Israel lived.

30 The sons of Ash'er were Im'nah, Ish'vah, Ish'vi, and Be·ri'ah,[l] and their sister was Se'rah.[m] **31** The sons of Be·ri'ah were He'ber and Mal'chi·el,

who was the father of Bir'za·ith. **32** He'ber became father to Japh'let, Sho'mer, and Ho'tham, and to Shu'a their sister. **33** The sons of Japh'let were Pa'sach, Bim'hal, and Ash'vath. These were the sons of Japh'let. **34** The sons of She'mer* were A'hi, Roh'gah, Je·hub'bah, and A'ram. **35** The sons of He'lem* his brother were Zo'phah, Im'na, She'lesh, and A'mal. **36** The sons of Zo'phah were Su'ah, Har'ne·pher, Shu'al, Be'ri, Im'rah, **37** Be'zer, Hod, Sham'ma, Shil'shah, Ith'ran, and Be·e'ra. **38** The sons of Je'ther were Je·phun'neh, Pis'pah, and A'ra. **39** The sons of Ul'la were A'rah, Han'ni·el, and Ri·zi'a. **40** All of these were the sons of Ash'er, heads of their paternal houses, select, mighty warriors, heads of the chieftains; and their number listed in the genealogical enrollment[a] was 26,000 men[b] in the army available for war.

8 Benjamin[c] became father to Be'la[d] his firstborn, Ash'bel[e] the second, A·har'ah the third, **2** No'hah the fourth, and Ra'pha the fifth. **3** Be'la's sons were Ad'dar, Ge'ra,[f] A·bi'hud, **4** Ab·i·shu'a, Na'a·man, A·ho'ah, **5** Ge'ra, She·phu'phan, and Hu'ram. **6** These were the sons of E'hud, the heads of the paternal houses of the inhabitants of Ge'ba,[g] who were taken into exile to Man'a·hath: **7** Na'a·man, A·hi'jah, and Ge'ra—he was the one who took them into exile and he became father to Uz'za and A·hi'hud. **8** Sha·ha·ra'im became father to children in the territory* of Mo'ab after he sent them away. Hu'shim and Ba'a·ra were his wives.# **9** And by his wife

---

CHAP. 7
a Nu 1:33

b Nu 26:35

c 1Sa 7:14
1Sa 17:4

d Jos 16:1, 3

e Jos 16:5
Jos 21:20, 22
2Ch 8:3, 5

f Ex 33:11
Nu 11:28
Nu 32:11, 12
De 34:9
Jos 1:1

g Ge 28:16, 19
Jos 16:1, 2

h Jos 17:11
1Sa 31:8, 10

i Jg 5:1, 19

j Jg 1:27
1Ki 9:15

k 1Ki 4:7, 11

l Nu 26:44, 45

m Ge 46:17

Second Col.
a Ex 30:14

b Nu 1:41
Nu 26:47

CHAP. 8
c Ge 35:16, 18

d 1Ch 7:6

e Ge 46:21

f Ge 46:21

g Jos 21:8, 17
1Sa 13:16

7:23 *Meaning "With Calamity." 7:27 *Or "Jehoshua," meaning "Jehovah Is Salvation." 7:28 *Or "surrounding." #Or possibly, "Gaza," though not the Gaza in Philistia.

7:34 *Also called Shomer in vs. 32. 7:35 *Likely the same as "Hotham" in vs. 32. 8:8 *Lit., "field." #Or possibly, "after he sent away his wives Hushim and Baara."

Ho'desh, he became father to Jo'bab, Zib'i·a, Me'sha, Mal'cam, **10** Je'uz, Sa·chi'a, and Mir'mah. These were his sons, heads of the paternal houses.

11 By Hu'shim he became father to A·bi'tub and El·pa'al. **12** And the sons of El·pa'al were E'ber, Mi'sham, She'med (who built O'no*ᵃ* and Lod*ᵇ* and its dependent* towns), **13** Be·ri'ah, and She'ma. These were heads of the paternal houses of the inhabitants of Ai'ja·lon.*ᶜ* These drove out the inhabitants of Gath. **14** And there were A·hi'o, Sha'shak, Jer'e·moth, **15** Zeb·a·di'ah, A'rad, E'der, **16** Mi'cha·el, Ish'pah, Jo'ha, the sons of Be·ri'ah; **17** and Zeb·a·di'ah, Me·shul'lam, Hiz'ki, He'ber, **18** Ish'me·rai, Iz·li'ah, Jo'bab, the sons of El·pa'al; **19** and Ja'kim, Zich'ri, Zab'di, **20** E·li·e'nai, Zil'le·thai, E'li·el, **21** A·dai'ah, Be·ra'iah, Shim'rath, the sons of Shim'e·i; **22** and Ish'pan, E'ber, E'li·el, **23** Ab'don, Zich'ri, Ha'nan, **24** Han·a·ni'ah, E'lam, An·tho·thi'jah, **25** Iph·de'iah, Pe·nu'el, the sons of Sha'shak; **26** and Sham'she·rai, She·ha·ri'ah, Ath·a·li'ah, **27** Ja·a·re·shi'ah, E·li'jah, Zich'ri, the sons of Je·ro'ham. **28** These were heads of the paternal houses by their descendants. These headmen lived in Jerusalem.

29 The father of Gib'e·on, Je·i'el, lived in Gib'e·on.*ᵈ* His wife's name was Ma'a·cah.*ᵉ* **30** And his firstborn son was Ab'don, followed by Zur, Kish, Ba'al, Na'dab, **31** Ge'dor, A·hi'o, and Ze'cher. **32** Mik'loth became father to Shim'e·ah. And they all lived near their brothers in Jerusalem, along with their other brothers.

33 Ner*ᶠ* became father to Kish; Kish became father to Saul;*ᵍ* Saul became father

to Jon'a·than,*ᵃ* Mal'chi-shu'a,*ᵇ* A·bin'a·dab,*ᶜ* and Esh-ba'al.*ᵈ* **34** And Jon'a·than's son was Mer'ib-ba'al.*ᵉ* Mer'ib-ba'al became father to Mi'cah.*ᶠ* **35** And the sons of Mi'cah were Pi'thon, Mel'ech, Ta·re'a, and A'haz. **36** A'haz became father to Je·ho'ad·dah; Je·ho'ad·dah became father to Al'e·meth, Az'ma·veth, and Zim'ri. Zim'ri became father to Mo'za. **37** Mo'za became father to Bin'e·a, Ra'phah his son, El·e·a'sah his son, A'zel his son. **38** A'zel had six sons, and their names were Az·ri'kam, Bo'che·ru, Ish'ma·el, She·a·ri'ah, O·ba·di'ah, and Ha'nan. All of these were the sons of A'zel. **39** And the sons of his brother E'shek were U'lam his firstborn, Je'ush the second, and E·liph'e·let the third. **40** And the sons of U'lam were mighty warriors who could handle* the bow, and they had many sons and grandsons, numbering 150. All of these were descendants of Benjamin.

9 All the Israelites were enrolled genealogically, and they are written in the Book of the Kings of Israel. And Judah was taken into exile to Babylon for their unfaithfulness.*ᵍ* **2** The first inhabitants to return to their possession in their cities were some Israelites, the priests, the Levites, and the temple servants.*ʰ* **3** And some of the descendants of Judah,*ⁱ* of Benjamin,*ʲ* of E'phra·im, and of Ma·nas'seh settled in Jerusalem: **4** U'thai son of Am·mi'hud son of Om'ri son of Im'ri son of Ba'ni, of the descendants of Pe'rez*ᵏ* son of Judah. **5** And of the Shi'lo·nites, A·sai'ah the firstborn and his sons. **6** And of the sons of Ze'rah,*ˡ* Je·u'el and 690 of their brothers.

Center column references:

CHAP. 8
a Ne 6:2

b Ezr 2:1, 33

c Jos 19:42, 48
Jos 21:8, 24

d Jos 9:15, 17
Jos 21:8, 17
1Ch 21:29

e 1Ch 9:35-38

f 1Sa 14:50

g 1Sa 9:1, 2
1Sa 11:15

Second Col.
a 1Sa 14:45

b 1Sa 14:49

c 1Sa 31:2

d 2Sa 2:8
1Ch 9:39-44

e 2Sa 4:4

f 2Sa 9:12

CHAP. 9
g Jer 39:9

h Jos 9:3, 27
Ezr 2:43-54
Ezr 2:70
Ezr 8:20
Ne 7:73
Ne 11:3

i Ne 11:4, 5

j Ne 11:7-9

k Ge 46:12
1Ch 2:4

l 1Ch 2:4, 6

8:33 *Also called Ishbosheth. **8:34** *Also called Mephibosheth. **8:40** *Lit., "who tread." **9:2** *Or "the Nethinim. Lit., "the given ones."

8:12 *Or "surrounding."

7 And of the descendants of Benjamin, Sal'lu son of Me·shul'lam son of Hod·a·vi'ah son of Has·se·nu'ah, **8** Ib·ne'iah son of Je·ro'ham, E'lah son of Uz'zi son of Mich'ri, and Me·shul'lam son of Sheph·a·ti'ah son of Reu'el son of Ib·ni'jah. **9** And their brothers by line of descent were 956. All these men were heads of their paternal houses.*

10 And of the priests, there were Je·da'iah, Je·hoi'a·rib, Ja'chin,[a] **11** Az·a·ri'ah son of Hil·ki'ah son of Me·shul'lam son of Za'dok son of Me·ra'ioth son of A·hi'tub, a leader of the house* of the true God, **12** A·dai'ah son of Je·ro'ham son of Pash'hur son of Mal·chi'jah, Ma'a·sai son of Ad'i·el son of Jah'ze·rah son of Me·shul'lam son of Me·shil'le·mith son of Im'mer, **13** and their brothers, heads of the paternal houses, 1,760 mighty, capable men available for the service of the house of the true God.

14 And of the Levites, there were She·mai'ah[b] son of Has'shub son of Az·ri'kam son of Hash·a·bi'ah from the descendants of Me·rar'i; **15** and Bak·bak'kar, He'resh, Ga'lal, Mat·ta·ni'ah son of Mi'ca son of Zich'ri son of A'saph, **16** O·ba·di'ah son of She·mai'ah son of Ga'lal son of Je·du'thun, and Ber·e·chi'ah son of A'sa son of El·ka'nah, who was dwelling in the settlements of the Ne·toph'a·thites.[c]

17 The gatekeepers[d] were Shal'lum, Ak'kub, Tal'mon, A·hi'man, and their brother Shal'lum the head, **18** and until then he was at the king's gate to the east.[e] These were the gatekeepers of the camps of the Levites. **19** And Shal'lum son of Ko're son of E·bi'a·saph son of Kor'ah, and his brothers of his pater-

nal house, the Kor'ah·ites, were over the duties of the service, the doorkeepers of the tent, and their fathers had been over the camp of Jehovah as the keepers of the entryway. **20** It was Phin'e·has[a] the son of El·e·a'zar[b] who had been their leader in the past; Jehovah was with him. **21** Zech·a·ri'ah[c] the son of Me·shel·e·mi'ah was the gatekeeper of the entrance of the tent of meeting.

22 All those selected as gatekeepers at the thresholds numbered 212. They were in their settlements by their genealogical enrollment.[d] David and Samuel the seer[e] appointed these to their office of trust. **23** They and their sons were over the guard service for the gates of the house of Jehovah,[f] the house of the tent. **24** The gatekeepers were on the four sides —east, west, north, and south.[g] **25** From time to time, their brothers were to come in from their settlements for seven days to serve along with them. **26** There were four chief* gatekeepers in the office of trust. They were Levites, and they were in charge of the chambers" and of the treasuries of the house of the true God.[h] **27** They would spend the night in their stations all around the house of the true God, for they cared for the guard service and were in charge of the key and would open up the house from morning to morning.

28 Some of them were in charge of the utensils[i] of the service; they would count them when they brought them in and count them when they took them out. **29** Some of them were appointed over the utensils, over all the holy utensils,[j] and over the fine flour,[k] the wine,[l] the oil,[m]

CHAP. 9

a Ne 11:10-14

b Ne 11:15

c 1Ch 2:54
  Ne 12:28

d Ezr 2:1, 42
  Ne 11:19

e Ne 3:29

Second Col.

a Nu 25:11, 13
  Jos 22:30
  Jg 20:28

b Ex 6:25
  Nu 3:32

c 1Ch 26:14, 19

d 1Ch 9:1

e 1Sa 9:9

f 2Ch 23:16, 19
  Ne 12:45

g 1Ch 26:14-16

h 1Ch 26:20
  1Ch 28:11, 12
  2Ch 31:12

i Nu 1:50

j 1Ki 8:4

k Le 2:1
  1Ch 23:29

l Le 23:12, 13

m Ex 27:20

9:9 *Lit., "heads of fathers for the house of their fathers." **9:11** *Or "temple."

9:26 *Lit., "mighty." "Or "dining rooms."

the frankincense,[a] and the balsam oil.[b] **30** Some of the sons of the priests mixed the ointment of balsam oil. **31** And Mat·ti·thi'ah of the Levites, who was the firstborn of Shal'lum the Kor'ah·ite, was in the office of trust over the things baked in pans.[c] **32** Some of their brothers of the Ko'hath·ites were in charge of the layer bread,*[d] to prepare it every sabbath.[e]

33 These were the singers, the heads of the paternal houses of the Levites in the chambers,* those set free from other duties; for by day and by night it was their responsibility to be on duty. **34** These were the heads of the paternal houses of the Levites by their line of descent, headmen. These lived in Jerusalem.

35 The father of Gib'e·on, Je·i'el, lived in Gib'e·on.[f] His wife's name was Ma'a·cah. **36** And his firstborn son was Ab'don, followed by Zur, Kish, Ba'al, Ner, Na'dab, **37** Ge'dor, A·hi'o, Zech·a·ri'ah, and Mik'loth. **38** Mik'loth became father to Shim'e·am. And they all lived near their brothers in Jerusalem, along with their other brothers. **39** Ner[g] became father to Kish; Kish became father to Saul;[h] Saul became father to Jon'a·than,[i] Mal'chi·shu'a,[j] A·bin'a·dab,[k] and Esh·ba'al. **40** And Jon'a·than's son was Mer'ib·ba'al.[l] Mer'ib·ba'al became father to Mi'cah.[m] **41** And the sons of Mi'cah were Pi'thon, Mel'ech, Tahr'e·a, and A'haz. **42** A'haz became father to Ja'rah; Ja'rah became father to Al'e·meth, Az'ma·veth, and Zim'ri. Zim'ri became father to Mo'za. **43** Mo'za became father to Bin'e·a and Re·pha'iah his son, El·e·a'sah his son, A'zel his son.

44 A'zel had six sons, and their names were Az·ri'kam, Bo'che·ru, Ish'ma·el, She·a·ri'ah, O·ba·di'ah, and Ha'nan. These were the sons of A'zel.

10 Now the Phi·lis'tines were fighting against Israel. And the men of Israel fled from before the Phi·lis'tines, and many fell slain on Mount Gil·bo'a.[a] **2** The Phi·lis'tines kept in close range of Saul and his sons, and the Phi·lis'tines struck down Jon'a·than, A·bin'a·dab, and Mal'chi·shu'a,[b] Saul's sons. **3** The fighting grew fierce against Saul, and the archers found him, and he was wounded by the archers.[c] **4** Then Saul said to his armor-bearer: "Draw your sword and run me through with it, so that these uncircumcised men may not come and deal ruthlessly*[d] with me." But his armor-bearer was unwilling, because he was very much afraid. So Saul took the sword and fell on it.[e] **5** When his armor-bearer saw that Saul was dead, he too fell on his own sword and died. **6** Thus Saul and his three sons died, and all those of his house died together.[f] **7** When all the people of Israel in the valley* saw that everyone had fled and that Saul and his sons had died, they began to abandon their cities and flee; the Phi·lis'tines then came and occupied them.

8 The next day, when the Phi·lis'tines came to strip the slain, they found Saul and his sons fallen on Mount Gil·bo'a.[g] **9** So they stripped him and took off his head and his armor, and they sent word throughout the land of the Phi·lis'tines to spread the news to their idols[h] and the people. **10** Then they put his armor in the house* of their god

---

CHAP. 9
a Le 2:1, 2

b Ex 25:3, 6

c Le 2:5, 7

d 2Ch 2:4
2Ch 13:11

e Le 24:6, 8

f Jos 21:8, 17

g 1Sa 14:50

h 1Sa 9:1, 2
1Sa 11:15

i 1Sa 14:45
1Sa 18:1
2Sa 1:23

j 1Sa 14:49

k 1Sa 31:2

l 2Sa 4:4

m 2Sa 9:12

Second Col.

CHAP. 10
a 1Sa 31:1-5
2Sa 1:21, 25

b 1Ch 8:33

c 1Sa 26:9, 10

d Jg 16:21, 23

e 1Ch 10:13

f 1Sa 31:6, 7

g 1Sa 28:4
1Sa 31:8-10

h Jg 16:23, 24

9:32 *That is, the showbread. 9:33 *Or "dining rooms."

10:4 *Or "abusively." 10:7 *Or "low plain." 10:10 *Or "temple."

and fastened his skull to the house of Da'gon.[a]

11 When all those of Ja'besh[b] in Gil'e·ad heard about all that the Phi·lis'tines had done to Saul,[c] **12** all the warriors rose up and carried off the corpse of Saul and the corpses of his sons. They brought them to Ja'besh and buried their bones under the big tree in Ja'besh,[d] and they fasted for seven days.

13 Thus Saul died for the unfaithfulness he had shown against Jehovah because he had not obeyed the word of Jehovah,[e] also for consulting a spirit medium[f] **14** instead of inquiring of Jehovah. So He put him to death and turned the kingship over to David the son of Jes'se.[g]

11 In time all the Israelites gathered to David at Heb'ron[h] and said: "Look! We are your own bone and flesh.*[i] **2** In times past while Saul was king, you were the one who was leading Israel on its campaigns.*[j] And Jehovah your God said to you: 'You will shepherd my people Israel, and you will become leader over my people Israel.'"[k] **3** So all the elders of Israel came to the king at Heb'ron, and David made a covenant with them in Heb'ron before Jehovah. Then they anointed David as king over Israel,[l] according to Jehovah's word through Samuel.[m]

4 Later David and all Israel set out for Jerusalem, that is, Je'bus,[n] where the Jeb'u·sites[o] were inhabiting the land. **5** The inhabitants of Je'bus taunted David: "You will never come in here!"[p] However, David captured the stronghold of Zion,[q] which is now the City of David.[r] **6** So David said: "Whoever is the

first to strike the Jeb'u·sites will become chief* and prince." And Jo'ab[a] the son of Ze·ru'iah went up first, and he became the chief. **7** Then David took up residence in the stronghold. That is why they called it the City of David. **8** He began to build up the city all around, from the Mound* to the areas around it, and Jo'ab restored the rest of the city. **9** Thus David became greater and greater,[b] and Jehovah of armies was with him.

10 Now these are the heads of David's mighty warriors, who gave him strong support in his kingship, together with all Israel, to make him king according to Jehovah's word concerning Israel.[c] **11** This is the list of David's mighty warriors: Ja·sho'be·am[d] the son of a Hach'mon·ite, the head of the three.[e] He brandished his spear over 300 slain at one time.[f] **12** Next to him was El·e·a'zar[g] the son of Do'do the A·ho'hite.[h] He was among the three mighty warriors. **13** He was with David at Pas-dam'mim,[i] where the Phi·lis'tines had gathered together for war. Now there was a plot of land full of barley, and the people had fled because of the Phi·lis'tines. **14** But he took his stand in the middle of the field and defended it and kept striking down the Phi·lis'tines, so that Jehovah brought about a great victory.*[j]

15 Three of the 30 headmen went down to the rock, to David at the cave of A·dul'lam,[k] while a Phi·lis'tine army was camped in the Valley* of Reph'a·im.[l] **16** David was then in the stronghold, and a garrison of the Phi·lis'tines was in Beth'le·hem. **17** Then David expressed

---

CHAP. 10
a 1Sa 5:2
b 1Sa 11:1
c 1Sa 31:11-13
d 2Sa 2:5
  2Sa 21:12
e 1Sa 13:13
  1Sa 15:22, 23
f Le 20:6
  1Sa 28:7
g Ru 4:17
  1Sa 13:14
  1Sa 15:27, 28
  2Sa 5:3

CHAP. 11
h Nu 13:22
  2Sa 2:1
  2Sa 5:5
  1Ch 12:23
i 2Sa 5:1, 2
j 1Sa 18:6, 13
k 2Sa 6:21
  2Sa 7:8, 9
  Ps 78:70, 71
l 1Ch 16:13
  2Sa 2:4
  2Sa 5:3
m 1Sa 15:27, 28
n Jos 15:63
  Jg 1:21
  Jg 19:10
o Ge 10:15, 16
  Ge 15:18, 21
  Ex 3:17
p 2Sa 5:6-10
q 1Ki 8:1
  Ps 2:6
  Ps 48:2
r 1Ki 2:10

Second Col.
a 2Sa 2:18
b 2Sa 3:1
c 1Sa 16:12, 13
d 1Ch 27:1, 2
e 2Sa 23:8
f Jos 23:10
g 2Sa 23:9, 10
  2Sa 23:15-17
h 1Ch 8:1, 4
i 1Sa 17:1
j Ps 18:50
k 2Sa 22:1
l Jos 15:8, 10
  2Sa 23:13-17

11:1 *Or "your blood relatives." 11:2 *Lit., "the one bringing out and the one bringing in Israel."

11:6 *Lit., "head." 11:8 *Or "Millo." A Hebrew term meaning "fill." 11:14 *Or "salvation." 11:15 *Or "Low Plain."

his longing: "If only I could have a drink of the water from the cistern by the gate of Beth'-le·hem!"[a] **18** At that the three forced their way into the camp of the Phi·lis'tines and drew water from the cistern by the gate of Beth'le·hem and brought it to David; but David refused to drink it and poured it out to Jehovah. **19** He said: "It is unthinkable on my part from the standpoint of my God to do this! Should I drink the blood of these men who risked their lives?*[b] For it was at the risk of their lives* that they brought it." So he refused to drink it. These are the things that his three mighty warriors did.

20 A·bish'ai[c] the brother of Jo'ab[d] became head of another three; he brandished his spear over 300 slain, and he had a reputation like the three.[e] **21** Of the other three, he was more distinguished than two of them, and he was their chief; yet he did not attain to the rank of the first three.

22 Be·nai'ah[f] the son of Je·hoi'a·da was a courageous man* who performed many exploits in Kab'ze·el.[g] He struck down the two sons of Ar'i·el of Mo'ab, and he descended into a waterpit on a snowy day and killed a lion.[h] **23** He also struck down an Egyptian man of extraordinary size—five cubits* tall.[i] Though the Egyptian had a spear in his hand like the beam of loom workers,[j] he went against him with a rod and snatched the spear away from the Egyptian's hand and killed him with his own spear.[k] **24** These things Be·nai'ah the son of Je·hoi'a·da did, and he had a reputation like that of the three mighty warriors. **25** Although he was dis-

tinguished even more than the thirty, he did not attain to the rank of the three.[a] However, David appointed him over his own bodyguard.

26 The mighty warriors of the military forces were As'a·hel[b] the brother of Jo'ab, El·ha'nan the son of Do'do of Beth'le·hem,[c] **27** Sham'moth the Ha'ro·rite, He'lez the Pel'o·nite, **28** I'ra[d] the son of Ik'kesh the Te·ko'ite, Abi·e'zer[e] the An'a·thoth·ite, **29** Sib'be·cai[f] the Hu'shath·ite, I'lai the A·ho'hite, **30** Ma'ha·rai[g] the Ne·toph'a·thite, He'led[h] the son of Ba'a·nah the Ne·toph'a·thite, **31** I'thai the son of Ri'bai of Gib'e·ah of the Ben'ja·min·ites,[i] Be·nai'ah the Pir'a·thon·ite, **32** Hu'rai of the wadis* of Ga'ash,[j] A·bi'el the Ar'bath·ite, **33** Az'ma·veth the Ba·ha'rum·ite, E·li'ah·ba the Sha·al'bo·nite, **34** the sons of Ha'shem the Gi'zo·nite, Jon'a·than the son of Sha'gee the Har'a·rite, **35** A·hi'am the son of Sa'car the Har'a·rite, E·li'phal the son of Ur, **36** He'pher the Me·che'rath·ite, A·hi'jah the Pel'o·nite, **37** Hez'ro the Car'mel·ite, Na'a·rai the son of Ez'bai, **38** Joel the brother of Nathan, Mib'har the son of Hag'ri, **39** Ze'lek the Am'mon·ite, Na'ha·rai the Be·roth'ite, the armor-bearer of Jo'ab the son of Ze·ru'iah; **40** I'ra the Ith'rite, Ga'reb the Ith'rite, **41** U·ri'ah[k] the Hit'tite, Za'bad the son of Ah'lai, **42** Ad'i·na the son of Shi'za the Reu'ben·ite, a head of the Reu'ben·ites, and 30 with him; **43** Ha'nan the son of Ma'a·cah, Josh'a·phat the Mith'nite, **44** Uz·zi'a the Ash'te·rath·ite, Sha'ma and Je·i'el, the sons of Ho'tham the A·ro'er·ite; **45** Je·di'a·el the son of Shim'ri, and Jo'ha his brother the Ti'zite; **46** E'li·el the Ma'ha·vite, Jer'i·bai and Josh·a·vi'ah the sons of El'na·am, and Ith'mah the Mo'ab-

---

CHAP. 11
a 1Sa 20:6

b Ge 9:4
  Le 17:10

c 1Sa 26:6
  2Sa 2:18
  2Sa 18:2

d 2Sa 3:30

e 2Sa 23:18, 19

f 1Ki 4:4
  1Ch 27:1, 5

g Jos 15:21

h Jg 14:5, 6
  1Sa 17:36, 37
  2Sa 23:20-23

i 1Sa 17:4

j 1Sa 17:7

k 1Sa 17:51

Second Col.
a 1Ch 11:19

b 2Sa 2:18, 23
  1Ch 27:1, 7

c 2Sa 23:24-39

d 1Ch 27:1, 9

e 1Ch 27:1, 12

f 2Sa 21:18
  1Ch 27:1, 11

g 1Ch 27:1, 13

h 1Ch 27:1, 15

i Jg 20:15
  1Ch 12:1, 2

j Jos 24:30

k 2Sa 11:3, 17
  2Sa 12:9
  1Ki 15:5

11:19 *Or "souls." 11:22 *Lit., "the son of a man of valor." 11:23 *His height was about 2.23 m (7.3 ft). See App. B14.

11:32 *See Glossary.

ite; **47** E′li·el, O′bed, and Ja·a-si′el the Me·zo′ba·ite.

12 These were the men who came to David at Zik′lag[a] while he was unable to move about freely because of Saul[b] the son of Kish, and they were among the mighty warriors who supported him in battle.[c] **2** They were armed with the bow, and they could use both the right hand and the left hand[d] to sling stones[e] or to shoot arrows with the bow. They were of the brothers of Saul, from Benjamin.[f] **3** The head was A·hi·e′-zer, along with Jo′ash, both sons of She·ma′ah the Gib′e·ath-ite;[g] Je′zi·el and Pel′et the sons of Az′ma·veth,[h] Ber′a·cah, Je′hu the An′a·thoth·ite, **4** Ish·ma′iah the Gib′e·on·ite,[i] a mighty warrior among the thirty[j] and over the thirty; also Jeremiah, Ja-ha·zi′el, Jo·ha′nan, Jo′za·bad the Ge·de′rath·ite, **5** E·lu′zai, Jer′i-moth, Be·a·li′ah, Shem·a·ri′ah, Sheph·a·ti′ah the Har′i·phite, **6** El·ka′nah, Is·shi′ah, Az′ar·el, Jo·e′zer, and Ja·sho′be·am, the Kor′ah·ites;[k] **7** and Jo·e′lah and Zeb·a·di′ah the sons of Je·ro′ham of Ge′dor.

8 Some of the Gad′ites went over to David's side at the stronghold in the wilderness;[l] they were mighty warriors, soldiers trained for war, standing ready with the large shield and the lance, whose faces were like those of lions and who were as swift as the gazelles on the mountains. **9** E′zer was the head, O·ba·di′ah the second, E·li′ab the third, **10** Mish·man′-nah the fourth, Jeremiah the fifth, **11** At′tai the sixth, E′li-el the seventh, **12** Jo·ha′nan the eighth, El·za′bad the ninth, **13** Jeremiah the tenth, Mach′-ban·nai the eleventh. **14** These were of the Gad′ites,[m] heads of the army. The least one was equal to 100, and the greatest

to 1,000.[a] **15** These are the men who crossed the Jordan in the first month when it was overflowing its banks, and they chased away all those living in the lowlands, to the east and to the west.

16 Some of the men of Benjamin and Judah also came to David at his stronghold.[b] **17** Then David went out before them and said to them: "If you have come to me in peace to help me, my heart will be united with you. But if it is to betray me to my adversaries when my hands have done no wrong, let the God of our forefathers see it and judge."[c] **18** Then the spirit came upon* A·ma′sai,[d] the head of the thirty:

> "We are yours, O David, and
>   we are with you, O son of
>   Jes′se.[e]
> Peace, peace be yours, and
>   peace to the one helping
>   you,
> For your God is helping
>   you."[f]

So David received them and appointed them among the heads of the troops.

19 Some from Ma·nas′seh also deserted to David when he came with the Phi·lis′tines to battle against Saul; but he did not help the Phi·lis′tines, for after consultation, the lords of the Phi·lis′tines[g] sent him away, saying: "He will desert to his lord Saul, and it will cost us our heads."[h] **20** When he went to Zik′lag,[i] these deserted to him from Ma·nas′seh: Ad′nah, Jo′za-bad, Je·di′a·el, Mi′cha·el, Jo′za-bad, E·li′hu, and Zil′le·thai, heads of the thousands of Ma·nas′seh.[j] **21** They helped David against the marauder band, because all of them were mighty, courageous men,[k] and they became chiefs in the army. **22** Day after

---

CHAP. 12
a 1Sa 27:5, 6
  2Sa 1:1
a 1Sa 27:1
c 1Ch 11:10
d Jg 3:15
  Jg 20:15, 16
e 1Sa 17:49
f Ge 49:27
g 1Sa 11:4
h 1Ch 11:26, 33
i Jos 9:3
j 1Ch 11:15
k Nu 26:10, 11
l 1Sa 23:14, 29
  1Sa 24:22
  1Ch 11:16
m Ge 49:19
  De 33:20

Second Col.
a Le 26:8
b 1Sa 22:1
  1Sa 23:14
  1Sa 24:22
c 1Sa 24:12, 15
  1Sa 26:23
  Ps 7:6
d Jg 6:34
  Jg 13:24, 25
e 2Sa 15:21
f Ps 54:4
g Jg 3:1, 3
h 1Sa 29:2-4
i 1Sa 30:1
j De 33:17
k 1Ch 5:23, 24
  1Ch 11:10

12:18 *Lit., "clothed."

day people kept coming to David[a] to help him until it was a camp as great as the camp of God.[b]

23 This is the number of the heads of those armed for battle who came to David at Heb′ron[c] to turn the kingship of Saul over to him according to Jehovah's order.[d] **24** The men of Judah carrying the large shield and the lance were 6,800, armed for battle. **25** Of the Sim′e·on·ites, the mighty, courageous men of the army were 7,100.

26 Of the Levites, 4,600. **27** Je·hoi′a·da[e] was the leader of the sons of Aaron,[f] and with him were 3,700, **28** as well as Za′dok,[g] a mighty and courageous young man, along with 22 chiefs from his paternal house.

29 Of the Ben′ja·min·ites, the brothers of Saul,[h] there were 3,000, of whom the greater number had previously been guarding the interests of the house of Saul. **30** Of the E′phra·im·ites, there were 20,800 mighty, courageous men of fame among their paternal houses.

31 Of the half tribe of Ma·nas′seh, there were 18,000 who had been designated by name to come to make David king. **32** Of the tribe of Is′sa·char, who understood the times and knew what Israel should do, there were 200 of their headmen, and all their brothers were under their command. **33** Of Zeb′u·lun, there were 50,000 who could serve in the army, drawing up in battle formation with all the weapons of war, all joining David with undivided loyalty.* **34** Of Naph′ta·li, there were 1,000 chiefs, and with them were 37,000 with the large shield and the spear. **35** Of the Dan′ites,

those drawing up in battle formation were 28,600. **36** And of Ash′er, those who could serve in the army for drawing up in battle formation were 40,000.

37 From across the Jordan,[a] of the Reu′ben·ites, the Gad′ites, and the half tribe of Ma·nas′seh, there were 120,000 soldiers with all kinds of weapons of war. **38** All of these were men of war, joining together in battle line; they came with a complete heart to Heb′ron to make David king over all Israel, and also all the rest of Israel were united in wanting* to make David king.[b] **39** And they remained there with David for three days, eating and drinking, for their brothers had made preparation for them. **40** Also those near them, and even those as far as Is′sa·char, Zeb′u·lun, and Naph′ta·li, were bringing food on donkeys, camels, mules, and cattle—provisions of flour, cakes of pressed figs and raisins, wine, oil, and cattle and sheep in great quantity, for there was rejoicing in Israel.

13 David consulted with the chiefs of the thousands and of the hundreds and with every leader.[c] **2** Then David said to all the congregation of Israel: "If it seems good to you and it is acceptable to Jehovah our God, let us send word to our remaining brothers in all regions of Israel and also to the priests and the Levites in their cities[d] with pastures to come and join us. **3** And let us bring back the Ark[e] of our God." For they had not cared for it in the days of Saul.[f] **4** All the congregation agreed to do that, for it seemed right to all the people. **5** So David congregated all Israel, from the river* of

---

CHAP. 12
a 2Sa 2:3

b 2Sa 3:1

c 2Sa 2:1
2Sa 5:1

d 1Sa 16:1, 13
1Ch 11:10

e 1Ch 27:1, 5

f 1Ch 6:49

g 2Sa 8:17
1Ki 1:8
1Ki 2:35
1Ch 6:1, 8
1Ch 27:16, 17

h 1Ch 8:1, 33
1Ch 12:1, 2

Second Col.
a Nu 32:33
Jos 13:8

b Ge 49:8, 10
1Ch 11:10

CHAP. 13
c 1Ch 15:25

d Nu 35:2

e 1Sa 7:2

f 1Sa 14:18

12:33 *Or "all those joining David were not doublehearted."

12:38 *Lit., "were of one heart." 13:5 *Or "from Shihor."

Egypt as far as Le′bo-ha′math,*ᵃ to bring the Ark of the true God from Kir′i·ath-je′a·rim.ᵇ

6 David and all Israel went up to Ba′al·ah,ᶜ to Kir′i·ath-je′a·rim, which belongs to Judah, to bring up from there the Ark of the true God, Jehovah, who sits enthroned above* the cherubs,ᵈ where his name is called on. **7** However, they placed the Ark of the true God on a new wagonᵉ and brought it from the house of A·bin′a·dab, and Uz′zah and A·hi′o were leading the wagon.ᶠ **8** David and all Israel were celebrating before the true God with all their might, accompanied by songs, harps, other stringed instruments, tambourines,ᵍ cymbals,ʰ and trumpets.ⁱ **9** But when they came to the threshing floor of Chi′don, Uz′zah thrust his hand out and grabbed hold of the Ark, for the cattle nearly upset it. **10** At that Jehovah's anger blazed against Uz′zah, and He struck him down because he had thrust his hand out to the Ark,ʲ and he died there before God.ᵏ **11** But David became angry* because Jehovah's wrath had broken through against Uz′zah; and that place has been called Pe′rez-uz′zah* down to this day.

12 So David became fearful of the true God on that day and said: "How can I bring the Ark of the true God to me?"ˡ **13** David did not bring the Ark to where he was in the City of David, but he had it taken to the house of O′bed-e′dom the Git′tite. **14** The Ark of the true God was with the household of O′bed-e′dom, remaining at his house for three months, and Jehovah kept blessing the house-

hold of O′bed-e′dom and all he had.ᵃ

14 King Hi′ramᵇ of Tyre sent messengers to David, along with cedar timbers, stonemasons,* and woodworkers to build a house* for him.ᶜ **2** And David knew that Jehovah had firmly established him as king over Israel,ᵈ for his kingship was highly exalted for the sake of His people Israel.ᵉ

3 David took more wivesᶠ in Jerusalem, and David became father to more sons and daughters.ᵍ **4** These are the names of the children born to him in Jerusalem:ʰ Sham·mu′a, Sho′bab, Nathan,ⁱ Sol′o·mon,ʲ **5** Ib′har, E·li′shu·a, El′pe·let, **6** No′gah, Ne′pheg, Ja·phi′a, **7** E·lish′a·ma, Be·e·li′a·da, and E·liph′e·let.

8 When the Phi·lis′tines heard that David had been anointed as king over all Israel,ᵏ all the Phi·lis′tines came up to search for David.ˡ When David heard about it, he went out against them. **9** Then the Phi·lis′tines came in and kept making raids in the Valley* of Reph′a·im.ᵐ **10** David inquired of God, saying: "Should I go up against the Phi·lis′tines? Will you give them into my hand?" At this Jehovah said to him: "Go up, and I will surely give them into your hand."ⁿ **11** So David went up to Ba′al-pe·ra′zim,ᵒ and he struck them down there. At that David said: "The true God has broken through my enemies by my hand, like a breach made by waters." That is why they named that place Ba′al-pe·ra′zim.* **12** The Phi·lis′tines abandoned their gods there, and when David gave the order, these were burned in the fire.ᵖ

CHAP. 13
a Nu 34:2, 8

b 1Sa 6:21–7:1
2Sa 6:1, 2
1Ch 15:3

c Jos 15:9, 12

d Ex 25:22
Nu 7:89
1Sa 4:4
2Sa 6:2

e Ex 37:5

f 2Sa 6:3-8

g Ex 15:20

h 1Ch 25:1

i 2Ch 5:13

j Nu 4:15

k Le 10:1, 2

l 2Sa 6:9-11

Second Col.
a Ge 30:27
Ge 39:5

CHAP. 14
b 1Ki 5:6, 8

c 2Sa 5:11, 12

d Ps 89:20, 21

e 2Sa 7:8

f De 17:17

g 2Sa 5:13-16

h 1Ch 3:5-9

i Lu 3:23, 31

j 1Ki 1:47
Mt 1:6

k 1Ch 11:3

l 2Sa 5:17
Ps 2:2

m 2Sa 5:18, 22
2Sa 23:13

n 2Sa 5:19-21

o Isa 28:21

p De 7:25

13:5 *Or "the entrance of Ha-math." 13:6 *Or possibly, "between." 13:11 *Or "upset." #Meaning "Breach Against Uzzah."

14:1 *Or "builders of walls." #Or "palace." 14:9 *Or "Low Plain." 14:11 *Meaning "Master of Breakings Through."

13 Later the Phi·lis′tines once again made a raid in the valley.*[a] **14** David again inquired of God, but the true God said to him: "Do not go directly up after them. Instead, go around behind them, and come against them in front of the ba′ca bushes.[b] **15** And when you hear the sound of marching in the tops of the ba′ca bushes, launch your attack, for the true God will have gone out before you to strike down the army of the Phi·lis′tines."[c] **16** So David did just as the true God commanded him,[d] and they struck down the Phi·lis′tine army from Gib′e·on to Ge′zer.[e] **17** And David's fame spread into all the lands, and Jehovah put the dread of him upon all the nations.[f]

15 And he continued building houses for himself in the City of David, and he prepared a place for the Ark of the true God and pitched a tent for it.[g] **2** It was then that David said: "No one is to carry the Ark of the true God except the Levites, for Jehovah has chosen them to carry the Ark of Jehovah and to minister to him always."[h] **3** Then David congregated all Israel at Jerusalem to bring the Ark of Jehovah up to the place that he had prepared for it.[i]

4 David gathered the descendants of Aaron[j] and the Levites:[k] **5** from the Ko′hath·ites, U·ri′el the chief and 120 of his brothers; **6** from the Me·rar′ites, A·sai′ah[l] the chief and 220 of his brothers; **7** from the Ger′shom·ites, Joel[m] the chief and 130 of his brothers; **8** from the descendants of E·li·za′phan,[n] She·mai′ah the chief and 200 of his brothers; **9** from the descendants of Heb′ron, E′li·el the chief and 80 of his brothers; **10** from the de-

scendants of Uz′zi·el,[a] Am·min′a·dab the chief and 112 of his brothers. **11** Furthermore, David called the priests Za′dok[b] and A·bi′a·thar[c] and the Levites U·ri′el, A·sai′ah, Joel, She·mai′ah, E′li·el, and Am·min′a·dab, **12** and he said to them: "You are the heads of the paternal houses of the Levites. Sanctify yourselves, you and your brothers, and bring the Ark of Jehovah the God of Israel up to the place that I have prepared for it. **13** Since you did not carry it the first time,[d] the anger of Jehovah our God broke out against us,[e] because we did not search out the proper procedure."[f] **14** So the priests and the Levites sanctified themselves to bring up the Ark of Jehovah the God of Israel.

15 Then the Levites carried the Ark of the true God on their shoulders with the poles,[g] just as Moses had commanded by Jehovah's word. **16** David then told the chiefs of the Levites to appoint their brothers the singers to sing out joyfully, accompanied by musical instruments: stringed instruments, harps,[h] and cymbals.[i]

17 So the Levites appointed He′man[j] the son of Joel and, of his brothers, A′saph[k] the son of Ber·e·chi′ah and, of the Me·rar′ites their brothers, E′than[l] the son of Kush·a′iah. **18** Together with them were their brothers of the second division,[m] Zech·a·ri′ah, Ben, Ja·a′zi·el, She·mir′a·moth, Je·hi′el, Un′ni, E·li′ab, Be·nai′ah, Ma·a·sei′ah, Mat·ti·thi′ah, E·liph′e·le·hu, and Mik·ne′iah and O′bed-e′dom and Je·i′el the gatekeepers. **19** The singers He′man,[n] A′saph,[o] and E′than were to play the copper cymbals;[p] **20** and Zech·a·ri′ah, A′zi·el, She·mir′a·moth, Je·hi′el, Un′ni, E·li′ab, Ma·a·sei′ah, and Be·nai′ah

---

CHAP. 14
a 2Sa 5:22-25

b Jos 8:2
Ps 18:34

c De 23:14
Jg 4:14

d Ge 6:22
Ex 39:32

e Jos 16:10

f De 2:25
De 11:25
Jos 2:9

CHAP. 15
g 2Sa 7:1, 2
1Ch 16:1
Ps 132:1-5

h Nu 4:15
De 10:8

i 2Sa 6:12
1Ch 13:5

j Nu 3:2, 3

k 1Ch 6:1

l 1Ch 6:29, 30

m 1Ch 23:6-8

n Ex 6:18, 22

Second Col.
a Ex 6:16, 18

b 2Sa 8:17

c 1Sa 22:20
1Ki 2:27, 35

d 2Sa 6:3

e 2Sa 6:8

f Nu 4:15
De 31:9

g Ex 25:14
Nu 4:6
2Ch 5:9

h Ps 33:2

i 1Ch 16:5
2Ch 5:12, 13

j 1Ch 6:31, 33
1Ch 25:5

k 1Ch 6:31, 39
1Ch 25:1, 2
Ps 83:Sup

l 1Ch 6:31, 44

m 1Ch 25:9

n 1Ch 6:31-33

o 1Ch 25:1

p 1Ch 13:8

14:13 *Or "low plain."

played stringed instruments tuned to Al'a·moth;*[a] 21 and Mat·ti·thi'ah,[b] E·liph'e·le·hu, Mik·ne'iah, O'bed-e'dom, Je·i'el, and Az·a·zi'ah played harps tuned to Shem'i·nith,*[c] to act as directors. 22 Chen·a·ni'ah[d] the chief of the Levites supervised the transport, for he was an expert, 23 and Ber·e·chi'ah and El·ka'nah were gatekeepers for the Ark. 24 The priests Sheb·a·ni'ah, Josh'a·phat, Ne·than'el, A·ma'sai, Zech·a·ri'ah, Be·nai'ah, and E·li·e'zer loudly sounded the trumpets before the Ark of the true God,[e] and O'bed-e'dom and Je·hi'ah also served as gatekeepers for the Ark.

25 Then David and the elders of Israel and the chiefs of the thousands were walking along to bring the ark of the covenant of Jehovah up from the house of O'bed-e'dom[f] with rejoicing.[g] 26 When the true God helped the Levites who were carrying the ark of the covenant of Jehovah, they sacrificed seven young bulls and seven rams.[h] 27 David was dressed in a sleeveless coat of fine fabric, as were all the Levites carrying the Ark, the singers, and Chen·a·ni'ah the chief of the transport and the singers; David was also wearing a linen eph'od.[i] 28 All the Israelites were bringing up the ark of the covenant of Jehovah with joyful shouting,[j] with the sound of the horn, with trumpets,[k] with cymbals, playing loudly on stringed instruments and harps.[l]

29 But when the ark of the covenant of Jehovah came to the City of David,[m] Saul's daughter Mi'chal[n] looked down through the window and saw King David skipping about and celebrating; and she began to despise him in her heart.[o]

15:20, 21 *See Glossary.

CHAP. 15

a Ps 46:Sup

b 1Ch 16:4, 5

c Ps 6:Sup

d 1Ch 15:27

e 1Ch 16:4, 6

f 1Ch 13:14

g 2Sa 6:4, 5
2Sa 6:12

h 2Sa 6:13

i 2Sa 6:14, 15

j 1Ch 13:8

k 1Ch 16:4, 6

l 2Sa 6:5

m 1Ch 17:1

n 1Sa 18:27
2Sa 3:13, 14

o 2Sa 6:16

Second Col.

CHAP. 16

a 1Ki 8:1
1Ch 15:1

b 2Sa 6:17-19
1Ki 8:5

c Le 1:3

d Le 3:1

e Nu 18:2

f 1Ch 6:31, 39

g 1Ch 15:18

h 1Ch 15:21

i 1Ch 15:17, 19

j 1Ch 6:31, 39

k Ps 106:1

l Ps 67:2
Ps 105:1-6
Isa 12:4

m 2Sa 23:1
Eph 5:19

n Ps 107:43

o Le 22:32
Isa 45:25
Jer 9:24

p 1Ch 28:9
Php 4:4

q Am 5:4
Zep 2:3

r Ps 24:5, 6

16 So they brought the Ark of the true God in and placed it inside the tent that David had pitched for it;[a] and they presented burnt offerings and communion sacrifices before the true God.[b] 2 When David finished offering up the burnt offerings[c] and the communion sacrifices,[d] he blessed the people in the name of Jehovah. 3 Further, he distributed to all the Israelites, to each man and woman, a round loaf of bread, a date cake, and a raisin cake. 4 Then he appointed some of the Levites to minister before the Ark of Jehovah,[e] to honor,* thank, and praise Jehovah the God of Israel. 5 A'saph[f] was the head, and second to him was Zech·a·ri'ah; and Je·i'el, She·mir'a·moth, Je·hi'el, Mat·ti·thi'ah, E·li'ab, Be·nai'ah, O'bed-e'dom, and Je·i'el[g] played stringed instruments and harps;[h] and A'saph played the cymbals,[i] 6 and Be·nai'ah and Ja·ha·zi'el the priests blew the trumpets constantly before the ark of the covenant of the true God.

7 It was on that day that David first contributed a song of thanks to Jehovah through A'saph[j] and his brothers:

8 "Give thanks to Jehovah,[k] call on his name, Make his deeds known among the peoples![l]

9 Sing to him, sing praises* to him,[m] Ponder over# all his wonderful works.[n]

10 Boast about his holy name.[o] Let the hearts of those seeking Jehovah rejoice.[p]

11 Search for Jehovah[q] and his strength. Seek his face* constantly.[r]

16:4 *Lit., "to remember." 16:9 *Or "make music." #Or possibly, "Speak about." 16:11 *Or "presence."

12 Remember the wonderful
     works he has performed,[a]
   His miracles and the judg-
     ments he has pronounced,
13 You offspring* of Israel his
     servant,[b]
   You sons of Jacob, his cho-
     sen ones.[c]
14 He is Jehovah our God.[d]
   His judgments are through-
     out the earth.[e]
15 Remember his covenant
     forever,
   The promise he made,* to a
     thousand generations,[f]
16 The covenant he made with
     Abraham,[g]
   And the oath he swore to
     Isaac,[h]
17 Which he established as a
     decree to Jacob[i]
   And as a lasting covenant to
     Israel,
18 Saying, 'I will give you the
     land of Ca′naan[j]
   As your allotted
     inheritance.'[k]
19 This was when you were few
     in number,
   Yes, very few, and you were
     foreigners in the land.[l]
20 They walked about from na-
     tion to nation,
   From one kingdom to anoth-
     er people.[m]
21 He did not allow any man to
     oppress them,[n]
   But on their account he re-
     proved kings,[o]
22 Saying, 'Do not touch my
     anointed ones,
   And to my prophets do noth-
     ing bad.'[p]
23 Sing to Jehovah, all the
     earth!
   Announce his salvation day
     after day![q]
24 Declare his glory among the
     nations,

His wonderful works among
     all the peoples.
25 For Jehovah is great and
     most worthy of praise.
   He is more awe-inspiring
     than all other gods.[a]
26 All the gods of the peoples
     are worthless gods,[b]
   But Jehovah is the one who
     made the heavens.[c]
27 In his presence are majesty*
     and splendor;[d]
   Strength and joy are in his
     dwelling place.[e]
28 Give Jehovah his due, you
     families of the peoples,
   Give Jehovah his due for his
     glory and strength.[f]
29 Give Jehovah the glory due
     his name;[g]
   Bring a gift and come in be-
     fore him.[h]
   Bow down to* Jehovah in
     holy adornment.*[i]
30 Tremble before him, all the
     earth!
   The earth* is firmly es-
     tablished; it cannot be
     moved.*[j]
31 Let the heavens rejoice, and
     let the earth be joyful;[k]
   Declare among the nations:
     'Jehovah has become
     King!'[l]
32 Let the sea thunder and all
     that fills it;
   Let the fields and everything
     in them rejoice.
33 At the same time let the trees
     of the forest shout joyfully
     before Jehovah,
   For he is coming* to judge
     the earth.
34 Give thanks to Jehovah, for
     he is good;[m]

CHAP. 16
a Ps 111:2-4
b Isa 41:8
c Ps 135:4
d Ps 95:7
e Ps 105:7-11
f De 7:9
g Ge 15:18
  Ge 17:1, 2
h Ge 26:3-5
i Ge 28:14
j Ge 12:7
  Ge 17:8
  Ge 35:12
k De 32:8
l Ge 34:30
  De 26:5
  Ps 105:12-15
m Ge 20:1
  Ge 46:6
n Ge 31:7, 42
o Ge 12:17
  Ge 20:3
p Ge 20:7
q Ps 40:10
  Ps 96:1-6

Second Col.
a Ex 15:11
b Isa 45:20
  1Co 8:4
c Isa 44:24
d De 33:26
  Ps 8:1
e 1Ti 1:11
f Ps 68:34
  Ps 96:7-13
g De 28:58
  Ne 9:5
  Ps 148:13
h 1Ch 29:3-5
  Mt 5:23
i De 26:10
j Ps 104:5
  Ec 1:4
k Ps 97:1
l Re 19:6
m 2Ch 5:13
  Lu 18:19

16:13 *Or "descendants." Lit., "seed."
16:15 *Lit., "The word he commanded."

16:27 *Or "dignity." 16:29 *Or "Worship." *Or possibly, "because of the
splendor of his holiness." 16:30 *Or
"The productive land." *Or "be shak-
en; be made to totter." 16:33 *Or "has
come."

His loyal love endures forever.[a]

35 And say, 'Save us, O God of our salvation,[b]
Gather us and rescue us from the nations,
So that we may give thanks to your holy name[c]
And exult in praising you.*[d]

36 May Jehovah, the God of Israel, be praised
Throughout all eternity.'"*

And all the people said, "Amen!"# and they praised Jehovah.

37 Then David left A'saph[e] and his brothers there before the ark of the covenant of Jehovah to minister continually before the Ark,[f] according to the daily routine.[g] 38 O'bed-e'dom and his brothers, numbering 68, and O'bed-e'dom, the son of Je·du'thun, and Ho'sah were gatekeepers; 39 and Za'dok[h] the priest and his fellow priests were before the tabernacle of Jehovah on the high place at Gib'e·on[i] 40 to offer up burnt offerings to Jehovah regularly on the altar of burnt offering, morning and evening, and to do all that is written in the Law of Jehovah that he commanded Israel.[j] 41 With them were He'man and Je·du'thun[k] and the rest of the selected men who were designated by their names to thank Jehovah,[l] because "his loyal love endures forever";[m] 42 and with them were He'man[n] and Je·du'thun to sound the trumpets, cymbals, and the instruments used to praise* the true God; and the sons of Je·du'thun[o] were at the gate. 43 Then all the people went to their homes, and David went to bless his own household.

17 As soon as David was settled in his own house,* he said to Nathan[a] the prophet: "Here I am living in a house of cedars[b] while the ark of the covenant of Jehovah is under tent cloths."[c] 2 Nathan replied to David: "Do whatever is in your heart, for the true God is with you."

3 On that very night, the word of God came to Nathan, saying: 4 "Go and say to my servant David, 'This is what Jehovah says: "You are not the one who will build the house for me to dwell in.[d] 5 For I have not dwelled in a house from the day I brought Israel out to this day, but I continued going from tent to tent and from one tabernacle to another.*[e] 6 During all the time that I went with all Israel, did I ever say one word to any of the judges of Israel whom I appointed to shepherd my people, saying, 'Why did you not build a house of cedars for me?'"'

7 "Now say this to my servant David, 'This is what Jehovah of armies says: "I took you from the pastures, from following the flock, to become a leader over my people Israel.[f] 8 And I will be with you wherever you go,[g] and I will do away with* all your enemies from before you;[h] and I will make a name for you like the name of the great men of the earth.[i] 9 I will appoint a place for my people Israel and settle them, and they will live there and not be disturbed anymore; and wicked men will not oppress them* again as they did in the past,[j] 10 from the day that

CHAP. 16
a Ps 103:17
Jer 31:3
La 3:22
b Ps 68:20
c Ps 122:4
d Isa 43:21
e 1Ch 15:16, 17
f 1Ch 16:4-6
g Ex 29:38
2Ch 13:11
Ezr 3:4
h 1Ch 12:28
i 1Ki 3:4
j Ex 29:39
2Ch 2:4
k 1Ch 25:1
l 1Ch 16:4
m 2Ch 5:13
Ezr 3:11
n 1Ch 6:31, 33
1Ch 15:16, 17
o 1Ch 25:1, 3

Second Col.

CHAP. 17
a 1Ki 1:8
1Ch 29:29
b 1Ch 14:1
c 2Sa 7:1-3
1Ch 15:1
2Ch 1:4
d 2Sa 7:4-7
1Ki 8:17-19
1Ch 22:7, 8
e Ex 40:2
Nu 4:24, 25
2Sa 6:17
Ps 78:60
f 1Sa 16:11, 12
1Sa 17:15
1Sa 25:30
2Sa 7:8-11
Ps 78:70, 71
g 1Sa 18:14
2Sa 8:6
h 1Sa 25:29
1Sa 26:10
Ps 89:20, 22
i 1Sa 18:30
j Ex 2:23

16:35 *Or "exult in your praise." 16:36 *Or "From eternity to eternity." #Or "So be it!" 16:42 *Or "instruments of the song of."

17:1 *Or "palace." 17:5 *Possibly meaning "from one tent site to another and from one dwelling place to another." 17:8 *Lit., "cut off." 17:9 *Lit., "wear them out."

I appointed judges over my people Israel.[a] And I will subdue all your enemies.[b] Moreover, I tell you, 'Jehovah will build a house* for you.'

11 "'"When your days come to an end and you go to be with your forefathers, I will raise up your offspring* after you, one of your sons,[c] and I will firmly establish his kingship.[d] **12** He is the one who will build a house for me,[e] and I will firmly establish his throne forever.[f] **13** I will become his father, and he will become my son.[g] I will not remove my loyal love from him[h] the way I removed it from the one who was prior to you.[i] **14** I will cause him to stand in my house and in my kingship forever,[j] and his throne will last forever."'"[k]

15 Nathan told David all these words and this entire vision.

16 At that King David came in and sat down before Jehovah and said: "Who am I, O Jehovah God? And what is my house that you have brought me this far?[l] **17** As if this were not enough, O God, you also speak about the house of your servant down to a distant future time,[m] and you have looked on me as if I were a man who should be further exalted,* O Jehovah God. **18** What more can your servant David say to you about the honor given me when you know your servant so well?[n] **19** O Jehovah, for the sake of your servant and in agreement with your heart* you have done all these great things by revealing your greatness.[o] **20** O Jehovah, there is no one like you,[p] and there is no God except you;[q] everything we have heard with our ears confirms this. **21** And

what other nation on earth is like your people Israel?[a] The true God went and redeemed them as his people.[b] You made a name for yourself by your great and awe-inspiring deeds,[c] driving out nations from before your people,[d] whom you redeemed from Egypt. **22** You made your people Israel your own people for all time;[e] and you, O Jehovah, became their God.[f] **23** Now, O Jehovah, may the promise you have made concerning your servant and his house prove faithful for all time, and may you do just as you have promised.[g] **24** May your name endure* and be exalted[h] forever, so that people may say, 'Jehovah of armies, the God of Israel, is God to Israel,' and may the house of your servant David be firmly established before you.[i] **25** For you, my God, have revealed to your servant your purpose to build him a house.* That is why your servant has the confidence to offer this prayer to you. **26** And now, O Jehovah, you are the true God, and you have promised these good things concerning your servant. **27** So may it please you to bless the house of your servant, and may it continue forever before you, for you, O Jehovah, have blessed, and it is blessed forever."

18 Some time later, David defeated the Phi·lis′tines and subdued them and took Gath[j] and its dependent* towns out of the hands of the Phi·lis′tines.[k] **2** Then he defeated Mo′ab,[l] and the Mo′ab·ites became David's servants and brought tribute.[m]

3 David defeated King Had·ad·e′zer[n] of Zo′bah[o] near Ha′-math[p] as he was on his way to establish his authority at the Eu-

---

CHAP. 17
a Jg 2:16
b Ps 18:40
c 1Ki 8:20
1Ch 22:10
d 2Sa 7:12-17
1Ki 9:5
1Ch 28:5
Jer 23:5
e 1Ki 5:5
1Ch 22:10
f Ps 89:3, 4
Isa 9:7
Da 2:44
g 2Sa 7:14
Lu 9:35
Heb 1:5
h Isa 55:3
i 1Sa 15:24, 28
1Ch 10:13, 14
j Da 2:44
Joh 1:49
2Pe 1:11
k Ps 89:36
Jer 33:20, 21
Lu 1:32, 33
Heb 1:8
Re 3:21
l 2Sa 7:8
2Sa 7:18-20
m Mt 22:42
Ac 13:34
Re 22:16
n Ps 139:1
o 2Sa 7:21-24
p Ex 15:11
q Isa 43:10

Second Col.
a De 4:7
Ps 147:20
b Ex 19:5
Ps 77:15
c De 4:34
Ne 9:10
Isa 63:12
Eze 20:9
d De 7:1
Jos 10:42
Jos 21:44
e 1Sa 12:22
f Ge 17:7
De 7:6, 9
g 2Sa 7:25-29
h 2Ch 6:33
Ps 72:19
Mt 6:9
Joh 12:28
i Ps 89:35, 36

CHAP. 18
j 1Sa 5:8
2Sa 1:20
k 2Sa 8:1
l Nu 24:17
Ps 60:8
m 2Sa 8:2
2Ki 3:4
n 1Ki 11:23
o 1Sa 14:47
2Sa 10:6
Ps 60:Sup
p 2Ch 8:3

17:10, 25 *Or "dynasty." 17:11 *Lit., "seed." 17:17 *Or "a man of high station." 17:19 *Or "in harmony with your will."

17:24 *Or "prove faithful." 18:1 *Or "surrounding."

phra'tes River.[a] **4** David captured 1,000 chariots, 7,000 horsemen, and 20,000 foot soldiers from him.[b] Then David hamstrung all but 100 of the chariot horses.[c] **5** When the Syrians of Damascus came to help King Had·ad·e'zer of Zo'bah, David struck down 22,000 of the Syrians.[d] **6** David then established garrisons in Syria and Damascus, and the Syrians became David's servants and brought tribute. Jehovah gave David victory* wherever he went.[e] **7** Moreover, David took the circular shields of gold from the servants of Had·ad·e'zer and brought them to Jerusalem. **8** From Tib'hath and Cun, cities of Had·ad·e'zer, David took a great quantity of copper. With it Sol'o·mon made the copper Sea,[f] the pillars, and the copper utensils.[g]

9 When King To'u of Ha'math heard that David had defeated the entire army of King Had·ad·e'zer[h] of Zo'bah,[i] **10** he immediately sent his son Ha·do'ram to King David to ask about his welfare and to congratulate him because he had fought and defeated Had·ad·e'zer (for Had·ad·e'zer had often fought against To'u), and he brought all sorts of articles of gold, silver, and copper. **11** King David sanctified these to Jehovah,[j] along with the silver and the gold that he had carried off from all the nations: from E'dom and Mo'ab, from the Am'mon·ites,[k] the Phi·lis'tines,[l] and the A·mal'ek·ites.[m]

12 A·bish'ai[n] the son of Ze·ru'iah[o] struck down 18,000 E'domites in the Valley of Salt.[p] **13** He established garrisons in E'dom, and all the E'dom·ites became David's servants.[q] Jehovah gave David victory* wherever he went.[r] **14** David kept reign-

ing over all Israel,[a] and he was administering justice and righteousness for all his people.[b] **15** Jo'ab the son of Ze·ru'iah was over the army,[c] Je·hosh'a·phat[d] the son of A·hi'lud was recorder, **16** Za'dok the son of A·hi'tub and A·him'e·lech the son of A·bi'a·thar were priests, and Shav'sha was secretary. **17** Be·nai'ah the son of Je·hoi'a·da was over the Cher'e·thites[e] and the Pel'e·thites.[f] And David's sons were first in position next to the king.

19 Later Na'hash the king of the Am'mon·ites died, and his son became king in his place.[g] **2** At that David said: "I will show loyal love[h] toward Ha'nun the son of Na'hash, because his father showed loyal love toward me." So David sent messengers to offer him comfort over the loss of his father. But when David's servants came into the land of the Am'mon·ites[i] to comfort Ha'nun, **3** the princes of the Am'mon·ites said to Ha'nun: "Do you think that David is honoring your father by sending comforters to you? Is it not to make a thorough search and to overthrow you and to spy out the land that his servants have come to you?" **4** So Ha'nun took the servants of David and shaved them[j] and cut their garments in half at their buttocks and sent them away. **5** When David was told about the men, he at once sent others to meet them, because the men had been deeply humiliated; and the king told them: "Stay in Jer'i·cho[k] until your beards grow back, and then return."

6 In time the Am'mon·ites saw that they had become a stench to David, so Ha'nun and the Am'mon·ites sent 1,000 silver talents* to hire chariots

---

18:6, 13 *Or "salvation."

19:6 *A talent equaled 34.2 kg (1,101 oz t). See App. B14.

and horsemen from Mes·o·po·taʹ-mi·a,* Aʹram·maʹa·cah, and Zoʹbah.ᵃ 7 Thus they hired 32,000 chariots, along with the king of Maʹa·cah and his people. Then they came and camped before Medʹe·ba.ᵇ The Amʹmon·ites gathered together from their cities and came out for the battle.

8 When David heard about it, he sent Joʹabᶜ and the entire army, including his mightiest warriors.ᵈ 9 And the Amʹmon-ites went out and drew up in battle formation at the entrance of the city while the kings who had come were by themselves in the open field.

10 When Joʹab saw that the battle charges were coming against him from the front and the rear, he chose some of the best troops in Israel and drew them up in battle formation to meet the Syrians.ᵉ 11 He put the rest of the men under the command* of his brother A·bishʹai,ᶠ in order to draw them up in battle formation to meet the Amʹmon·ites. 12 Then he said: "If the Syriansᵍ become too strong for me, then you must come to my rescue; but if the Amʹmon·ites become too strong for you, I will rescue you. 13 We must be strong and courageousʰ for our people and for the cities of our God, and Jehovah will do what is good in his eyes."

14 Then Joʹab and his men advanced to meet the Syrians in battle, and they fled from before him.ⁱ 15 When the Amʹmon·ites saw that the Syrians had fled, they also fled from his brother A·bishʹai and went into the city. After that Joʹab came to Jerusalem.

16 When the Syrians saw that they had been defeated by Isra-

el, they sent messengers to summon the Syrians in the region of the River,*ᵃ with Shoʹphach the chief of the army of Had·ad·eʹzer leading them.ᵇ

17 When the report was made to David, he immediately gathered all Israel and crossed the Jordan and came to them and drew up in battle formation against them. David drew up in battle formation to meet the Syrians, and they fought against him.ᶜ 18 But the Syrians fled from Israel; and David killed 7,000 charioteers and 40,000 foot soldiers of the Syrians, and he put Shoʹphach the chief of the army to death. 19 When the servants of Had·ad·eʹzer saw that they had been defeated by Israel,ᵈ they promptly made peace with David and became his subjects;ᵉ and Syria did not want to help the Amʹmon·ites anymore.

20 At the start of the year,* at the time when kings go on campaigns, Joʹabᶠ led a military expedition and devastated the land of the Amʹmon·ites; he came and besieged Rabʹbah,ᵍ while David stayed in Jerusalem.ʰ Joʹab attacked Rabʹbah and tore it down.ⁱ 2 Then David took the crown of Malʹcam from its head, and found that it weighed a talent* of gold, and in it there were precious stones; and it was placed on David's head. He also took a vast amount of spoil from the city.ʲ 3 And he brought out the people who were in it and put them to workᵏ at sawing stones and at working with sharp iron instruments and with axes. That was what David did to all the cities of the Amʹmon·ites. Finally David and all the troops returned to Jerusalem.

CHAP. 19
a 1Sa 14:47
  2Sa 8:3
  2Sa 10:6

b Jos 13:8, 9

c 2Sa 8:16

d 2Sa 10:7, 8
  2Sa 23:8

e 2Sa 10:9-12

f 1Ch 11:20, 21

g 2Sa 8:5

h De 31:6
  Jos 1:9

i Le 26:7, 8
  De 28:7
  2Sa 10:13, 14

Second Col.
a 2Sa 8:3

b 2Sa 10:15, 16

c 2Sa 10:17-19

d Ps 18:39

e 1Ch 14:17
  Ps 18:44

CHAP. 20
f 1Ch 11:6

g De 3:11

h 2Sa 11:1

i 2Sa 12:26

j 2Sa 8:11, 12
  2Sa 12:30, 31

k 1Ki 9:20, 21

19:6 *Lit., "Aram-naharaim." 19:11 *Lit., "in the hand." 19:16 *That is, the Euphrates. 20:1 *That is, in the spring. 20:2 *About 34.2 kg (1,101 oz t). See App. B14.

4 After this, war broke out at Ge′zer with the Phi·lis′tines. At that time Sib′be·cai[a] the Hu′shath·ite struck down Sip′pai, who was a descendant of the Reph′a·im,[b] and they were subdued.

5 And there was war again with the Phi·lis′tines, and El·ha′nan the son of Ja′ir struck down Lah′mi the brother of Go·li′ath[c] the Git′tite, whose spear had a shaft like the beam of loom workers.[d]

6 War broke out yet again at Gath,[e] where there was a man of extraordinary size,[f] with 6 fingers on each hand and 6 toes on each foot, 24 in all; and he too was a descendant of the Reph′a·im.[g] **7** He kept taunting[h] Israel. So Jon′a·than the son of Shim′e·a,[i] David's brother, struck him down.

8 These were descendants of the Reph′a·im[j] in Gath,[k] and they fell by the hand of David and by the hand of his servants.

21 Then Satan* stood up against Israel and incited David to number Israel.[l] **2** So David said to Jo′ab[m] and the chiefs of the people: "Go, count Israel from Be′er-she′ba to Dan;[n] then report to me so that I may know their number." **3** But Jo′ab said: "May Jehovah multiply his people 100 times! My lord the king, are not all of them already servants of my lord? Why does my lord want to do this? Why should he become a cause of guilt to Israel?"

4 But the king's word prevailed over Jo′ab. So Jo′ab went out and traveled throughout Israel, after which he came to Jerusalem.[o] **5** Jo′ab now gave to David the number of the people who were registered. All Israel amounted to 1,100,000 men armed with swords, and Ju-

dah, 470,000 men armed with swords.[a] **6** But Le′vi and Benjamin were not registered among them,[b] because the king's word was detestable to Jo′ab.[c]

7 Now this was very displeasing to the true God, so he struck Israel. **8** David then said to the true God: "I have sinned[d] greatly by doing this. And now, please, forgive your servant's error,[e] for I have acted very foolishly."[f] **9** Jehovah then spoke to Gad,[g] David's visionary, saying: **10** "Go and say to David, 'This is what Jehovah says: "I am giving you three options. Choose the one that I should bring on you."'" **11** So Gad came in to David and said to him: "This is what Jehovah says, 'Take your pick **12** whether there should be three years of famine,[h] or three months of being swept away by your adversaries while the sword of your enemies overtakes you,[i] or three days of the sword of Jehovah—pestilence in the land[j]—with Jehovah's angel bringing destruction[k] in all the territory of Israel.' Now consider what I should reply to the One who sent me." **13** So David said to Gad: "It is very distressing to me. Please, let me fall into the hand of Jehovah, for his mercy is very great;[l] but do not let me fall into the hand of man."[m]

14 Then Jehovah sent a pestilence[n] on Israel, so that 70,000 people out of Israel fell.[o] **15** Moreover, the true God sent an angel to Jerusalem to destroy it; but as he was about to do so, Jehovah saw it and felt regret* over the calamity,[p] and he said to the angel bringing destruction: "It is enough![q] Now let your hand drop." Jehovah's angel was standing close to the threshing floor of Or′nan[r] the Jeb′u·site.[s]

16 When David raised his eyes, he saw Jehovah's angel

CHAP. 20

a 2Sa 21:18
1Ch 11:26, 29
b De 3:13
c 1Sa 17:4, 7
1Sa 21:9
d 2Sa 21:19
1Ch 11:23, 24
e Jos 11:22
1Sa 7:14
f Nu 13:33
De 2:10
De 3:11
g 2Sa 21:16
2Sa 21:20-22
h 1Sa 17:10
2Ki 19:22
i 1Ch 2:13
j De 2:11
k 1Sa 17:4

CHAP. 21

l 2Sa 24:1-3
m 2Sa 8:16
n Jg 18:29
2Sa 17:11
o 2Sa 24:4, 8

Second Col.

a 2Sa 24:9
b Nu 1:47
c 1Ch 27:23, 24
d 2Sa 12:13
e Ps 25:11
Ps 51:1
f 2Sa 24:10-14
g 1Ch 29:29
h Le 26:26
i Le 26:14, 17
j Le 26:25
k 2Ki 19:35
l Ex 34:6
Ps 51:1
Isa 55:7
La 3:22
m 2Ch 28:9
n Nu 16:46
o 2Sa 24:15, 16
p Ex 32:14
De 32:36
q Ps 90:13
r 2Ch 3:1
s 2Sa 5:6

21:1 *Or possibly, "a resister."

21:15 *Or "grieved."

standing between the earth and the heavens with a drawn sword[a] in his hand extended toward Jerusalem. David and the elders, covered with sackcloth,[b] at once threw themselves down with their faces to the ground.[c] **17** David said to the true God: "Was it not I who said to number the people? I am the one who sinned, and I am the one who did wrong;[d] but these sheep—what have they done? O Jehovah my God, let your hand, please, come against me and my father's house; but do not bring this scourge on your people."[e]

18 Jehovah's angel then told Gad[f] to tell David to go up and erect an altar to Jehovah on the threshing floor of Or′nan the Jeb′u·site.[g] **19** So David went up at the word of Gad, which he had spoken in the name of Jehovah. **20** Meanwhile, Or′nan turned around and saw the angel, and his four sons who were with him hid themselves. Now Or′nan had been threshing wheat. **21** When David came up to him, Or′nan looked and saw David, and he immediately went out from the threshing floor and bowed down to David with his face to the ground. **22** David said to Or′nan: "Sell* me the site of the threshing floor, so that I may build an altar to Jehovah on it. Sell it to me for the full price, so that the scourge against the people may be halted."[h] **23** But Or′nan said to David: "Take it as your own, and let my lord the king do what seems good to him.* Here, I am providing the cattle for burnt offerings and the threshing sledge[i] for the wood and the wheat as a grain offering. I give all of it."

24 However, King David said to Or′nan: "No, I must buy it

for the full price, because I will not take what is yours and give it to Jehovah or offer up burnt sacrifices that cost me nothing."[a] **25** So David gave Or′nan 600 gold shekels* by weight for the site. **26** And David built an altar[b] there to Jehovah and offered up burnt sacrifices and communion sacrifices, and he called on Jehovah, who now answered him with fire[c] from the heavens on the altar of burnt offering. **27** Then Jehovah ordered the angel[d] to return his sword to its sheath. **28** At that time, when David saw that Jehovah had answered him at the threshing floor of Or′nan the Jeb′u·site, he continued to sacrifice there. **29** However, the tabernacle of Jehovah that Moses had made in the wilderness and the altar of burnt offering were at that time on the high place at Gib′e·on.[e] **30** But David had not been able to go before it to consult God, for he was terrified because of the sword of Jehovah's angel.

22 David then said: "This is the house of Jehovah the true God, and this is an altar for burnt offering for Israel."[f]

2 David then gave orders to bring together the foreign residents[g] who were in the land of Israel, and he assigned them to be stonecutters to cut and shape stones for building the house of the true God.[h] **3** David also prepared iron in great quantity for nails for the doors of the gates and for clamps, and so much copper that it was beyond weighing,[i] **4** and also cedar timbers[j] without number, for the Si·do′ni·ans[k] and the Tyr′i·ans[l] brought great quantities of cedar timbers to David. **5** And David said: "My son Sol′o·mon is

---

CHAP. 21
a Nu 22:31
   Jos 5:13

b 2Ki 19:1

c 2Sa 24:17

d Ps 51:4

e Ex 32:12
   Nu 16:22

f 2Sa 24:11

g 2Sa 24:18-23
   2Ch 3:1

h Nu 25:8

i Isa 28:27

Second Col.
a 2Sa 24:24, 25

b Ex 20:25

c Le 9:23, 24
   1Ki 18:38
   2Ch 7:1

d 2Sa 24:16
   Ps 103:20

e 1Ki 3:4
   1Ch 16:39
   2Ch 1:3

CHAP. 22
f De 12:5, 6
   2Sa 24:18
   2Ch 3:1

g 1Ki 9:20, 21
   2Ch 2:17, 18

h 1Ki 5:15, 17
   1Ki 6:7
   1Ki 7:9

i 1Ki 7:47

j 2Sa 5:11

k 1Ki 5:6, 8

l 2Ch 2:3

21:22 *Lit., "Give." **21:23** *Lit., "what is good in his eyes."

21:25 *A shekel equaled 11.4 g (0.367 oz t). See App. B14.

young and inexperienced,*[a] and the house to be built for Jehovah is to be exceedingly magnificent,[b] so that its fame and beauty[c] will be known in all lands.[d] Therefore, I will make preparation for him." So David prepared materials in great quantity before his death.

6 Moreover, he summoned his son Sol'o·mon and instructed him to build a house for Jehovah the God of Israel. **7** David told his son Sol'o·mon: "As for me, it was my heart's desire to build a house for the name of Jehovah my God.[e] **8** But Jehovah's word came to me, saying, 'You have shed a great deal of blood, and you have fought great wars. You will not build a house for my name,[f] for you have shed a great deal of blood on the earth before me. **9** Look! You will have a son[g] who will be a man of peace,* and I will give him rest from all his enemies who surround him,[h] for Sol'o·mon*[i] will be his name and I will grant Israel peace and quiet in his days.[j] **10** He is the one who will build a house for my name.[k] He will become my son, and I will be his father.[l] I will firmly establish the throne of his kingship over Israel forever.'"[m]

11 "Now, my son, may Jehovah be with you, and may you be successful and build the house of Jehovah your God, just as he has spoken concerning you.[n] **12** Only may Jehovah give you discretion and understanding[o] when he gives you authority over Israel, so that you may keep the law of Jehovah your God.[p] **13** Then you will be successful if you carefully observe the regulations[q] and the judgments that Jehovah ordered Moses to give Israel.[r] Be courageous

and strong. Do not be afraid or be terrified.[a] **14** Here I have taken great pains to prepare for Jehovah's house 100,000 talents* of gold and 1,000,000 talents of silver and such great quantities of copper and iron[b] that they cannot be weighed, and I have prepared timbers and stones,[c] but you will add to them. **15** A great number of workmen are with you—stonecutters, stonemasons,[d] woodworkers, and all kinds of skilled workers.[e] **16** The gold, silver, copper, and iron are beyond measure.[f] Get up and begin the work, and may Jehovah be with you."[g]

17 David then ordered all the princes of Israel to help his son Sol'o·mon: **18** "Is not Jehovah your God with you, and has he not given you rest on every side? For he handed over to me the inhabitants of the land, and the land has been subdued before Jehovah and before his people. **19** Now determine with all your heart and soul* to seek Jehovah your God,[h] and start building the sanctuary of Jehovah the true God,[i] in order to bring the ark of the covenant of Jehovah and the holy utensils of the true God[j] to the house built for the name of Jehovah."[k]

23 When David had grown old and was near the end of his life,* he made his son Sol'o·mon king over Israel.[l] **2** He then gathered all the princes of Israel, the priests,[m] and the Levites.[n] **3** The Levites who were 30 years old and up were numbered;[o] their number, their head count man by man, was 38,000. **4** Of these, 24,000

CHAP. 22
a 1Ki 3:7
b 2Ch 2:5
c Hag 2:3
d Ps 68:29
e De 12:5, 6
   2Sa 7:2
   Ps 132:3-5
f 1Ch 17:4
g 1Ch 28:5
h 2Sa 7:12, 13
   1Ki 4:25
   1Ki 5:4
i 2Sa 12:24
j Ps 72:7
k 1Ki 5:5
l 2Sa 7:14
   Heb 1:5
m 1Ch 17:12-14
   Ps 89:35, 36
n 1Ch 28:20
o 2Ch 1:10
   Ps 72:1
p De 4:6
q Le 19:37
   1Ch 28:7
r De 12:1
   De 17:18, 19
   Jos 1:8
   1Ki 2:3
   1Ch 28:7
   Ps 19:8, 11

Second Col.
a Jos 1:6, 9
   1Ch 28:20
b 1Ch 29:6, 7
c 1Ch 29:2-4
d 1Ki 5:17
   1Ki 6:7
   1Ki 7:9
e 1Ki 7:13, 14
f 1Ch 22:3
g 2Ch 1:1
h De 4:29
   2Ch 20:3
   Da 9:3
i 1Ki 6:1
j 1Ki 8:6, 21
k De 12:21
   1Ki 8:29
   1Ki 9:3

CHAP. 23
l 1Ki 1:33, 39
   1Ch 28:5
m Ex 29:8, 9
n Nu 3:6
o Nu 4:2, 3

22:5 *Or "delicate." 22:9 *Lit., "rest." *From a Hebrew word meaning "Peace."

22:14 *A talent equaled 34.2 kg (1,101 oz t). See App. B14. 22:19 *See Glossary. 23:1 *Lit., "old and full of days."

served as supervisors over the work of Jehovah's house, and there were 6,000 officers and judges,[a] **5** and there were 4,000 gatekeepers,[b] and 4,000 gave praise[c] to Jehovah on the instruments about which David said, "I made them for giving praise."

6 Then David organized* them into divisions[d] according to the sons of Le′vi: Ger′shon, Ko′hath, and Me·rar′i.[e] **7** Of the Ger′shon·ites were La′dan and Shim′e·i. **8** The sons of La′dan were Je·hi′el the headman, Ze′tham, and Joel,[f] three. **9** The sons of Shim′e·i were She·lo′moth, Ha′zi·el, and Ha′ran, three. These were the heads of the paternal houses for La′dan. **10** And the sons of Shim′e·i were Ja′hath, Zi′na, Je′ush, and Be·ri′ah. These four were the sons of Shim′e·i. **11** Ja′hath was the head and Zi′zah, the second. But since Je′ush and Be·ri′ah did not have many sons, they were counted as one paternal house with one area of responsibility.

12 The sons of Ko′hath were Am′ram, Iz′har,[g] Heb′ron, and Uz′zi·el,[h] four. **13** The sons of Am′ram were Aaron[i] and Mo′ses.[j] But Aaron was permanently set apart* to sanctify the Most Holy, he and his sons, to offer sacrifices before Jehovah, to minister to him, and to pronounce blessings in his name always.[l] **14** As for Moses the man of the true God, his sons were named among the tribe of the Levites. **15** The sons of Moses were Ger′shom[m] and E·li·e′zer.[n] **16** Of the sons of Ger′shom, Sheb′u·el[o] was the head. **17** Of the descendants* of E·li·e′zer, Re·ha·bi′ah[p] was the head; E·li·e′zer did not have other sons, but the sons of Re·ha·bi′ah were very many. **18** Of the

sons of Iz′har,[a] She·lo′mith[b] was the headman. **19** The sons of Heb′ron were Je·ri′ah the head, Am·a·ri′ah the second, Ja·ha·zi′el the third, and Jek·a·me′am[c] the fourth. **20** The sons of Uz′zi·el[d] were Mi′cah the head and Is·shi′ah the second.

21 The sons of Me·rar′i were Mah′li and Mu′shi.[e] The sons of Mah′li were El·e·a′zar and Kish. **22** El·e·a′zar died, but he had no sons, only daughters. So the sons of Kish, their relatives,* took them as wives. **23** The sons of Mu′shi were Mah′li, E′der, and Jer′e·moth, three.

24 These were the sons of Le′vi according to their paternal houses, the heads of the paternal houses, by those registered who were counted and listed by their names and who carried out the work for the service of the house of Jehovah, from 20 years old and up. **25** For David had said: "Jehovah the God of Israel has given rest to his people,[f] and he will reside in Jerusalem forever.[g] **26** Also the Levites will not have to carry the tabernacle or any of its utensils for its service."[h] **27** For according to the last instructions of David, the Levites from 20 years old and up were numbered. **28** Their function was to assist the sons of Aaron[i] for the service of the house of Jehovah, to be in charge of the courtyards,[j] the dining rooms, the purification of every holy thing, and any work needed for the service of the house of the true God. **29** They assisted with the layer bread,*[k] the fine flour for the grain offering, the wafers of unleavened bread,[l] the griddle cakes, the mixed dough,[m] and all measures of quantity and size. **30** They were to stand morning by morn-

---

CHAP. 23
a De 16:18
  1Ch 26:29
  2Ch 19:8
b 1Ch 26:12
c 1Ch 6:31, 32
d 2Ch 8:14
  2Ch 31:2
e Ex 6:16
f 1Ch 26:21, 22
g Ex 6:21
h Ex 6:18
i Ex 4:14
j Ex 6:20, 26
k Ex 28:1
l Le 9:22
  Nu 6:23-27
  De 21:5
m Ex 2:21, 22
n Ex 18:3, 4
o 1Ch 26:24
p 1Ch 26:25

Second Col.
a Nu 3:27
b 1Ch 24:20, 22
c 1Ch 24:20, 23
d Ex 6:22
e Ex 6:19
f 2Sa 7:1
g 1Ki 8:12, 13
  Ps 135:21
h Nu 4:15
i Nu 3:9
j 1Ki 6:36
k Le 24:5, 6
  1Ch 9:32
l Ex 29:1, 2
  Le 2:4
m Le 7:12

23:6 *Or "divided." 23:17 *Lit., "sons."

23:22 *Lit., "brothers." 23:29 *That is, the showbread.

ing[a] to thank and praise Jehovah and likewise in the evening.[b] **31** They assisted whenever the burnt sacrifices were offered to Jehovah on the Sabbaths,[c] the new moons,[d] and during the festival seasons,[e] according to the number required by the rules concerning them, doing so regularly before Jehovah. **32** They also took care of their responsibilities toward the tent of meeting, toward the holy place, and toward their brothers the sons of Aaron for the service of the house of Jehovah.

24 Now the divisions of the descendants of Aaron were these: The sons of Aaron were Na′dab, A·bi′hu,[f] El·e·a′zar, and Ith′a·mar.[g] **2** However, Na′dab and A·bi′hu died before their father,[h] and they did not have any sons; but El·e·a′zar[i] and Ith′a·mar continued to serve as priests. **3** David, along with Za′dok[j] from the sons of El·e·a′zar and A·him′e·lech from the sons of Ith′a·mar, made divisions of them for the office of their service. **4** Since the sons of El·e·a′zar had more headmen than the sons of Ith′a·mar had, they divided them accordingly: The sons of El·e·a′zar had 16 as heads of their paternal houses, and the sons of Ith′a·mar had 8 as heads of their paternal houses.

5 Further, they divided them by lots,[k] the one group along with the other, for there were chiefs of the holy place and chiefs of the true God from both the sons of El·e·a′zar and the sons of Ith′a·mar. **6** Then Shemai′ah the son of Ne·than′el the secretary of the Levites recorded their names before the king, the princes, Za′dok[l] the priest, A·him′e·lech[m] the son of A·bi′a·thar,[n] and the heads of the paternal houses of the priests and of the Levites, one paternal house

CHAP. 23
a Ex 29:39

b 1Ch 16:4, 37

c Ex 20:10

d Nu 10:10
Ps 81:3

e De 16:16

CHAP. 24
f Le 10:1

g Ex 6:23
Ex 28:1

h Nu 26:61

i Nu 16:39, 40

j 2Sa 8:17

k Pr 16:33

l 1Ki 2:35

m 2Sa 8:17

n 2Sa 19:11
1Ki 1:5, 7

Second Col.
a Lu 1:5

b 2Ki 11:9
Lu 1:8, 23

c Ex 6:18

d 1Ch 23:16
1Ch 26:24

e 1Ch 23:17

f 1Ch 23:18

g 1Ch 26:31

h Ge 46:11

i 1Ch 23:22

being selected for El·e·a′zar and one being selected for Ith′a·mar.

7 The first lot came out to Je·hoi′a·rib; the second to Je·da′iah, **8** the third to Ha′rim, the fourth to Se·o′rim, **9** the fifth to Mal·chi′jah, the sixth to Mij′a·min, **10** the seventh to Hak′koz, the eighth to A·bi′jah,[a] **11** the ninth to Jesh′u·a, the tenth to Shec·a·ni′ah, **12** the 11th to E·li′a·shib, the 12th to Ja′kim, **13** the 13th to Hup′pah, the 14th to Je·sheb′e·ab, **14** the 15th to Bil′gah, the 16th to Im′mer, **15** the 17th to He′zir, the 18th to Hap′piz·zez, **16** the 19th to Peth·a·hi′ah, the 20th to Je·hez′kel, **17** the 21st to Ja′chin, the 22nd to Ga′mul, **18** the 23rd to De·la′iah, the 24th to Ma·a·zi′ah.

19 These were their offices for their service[b] when they would come into the house of Jehovah according to the procedure set by their forefather Aaron, just as Jehovah the God of Israel had commanded him.

20 And of the rest of the Levites: of the sons of Am′ram,[c] there was Shu′ba·el;[d] of the sons of Shu′ba·el, Jeh·de′iah; **21** of Re·ha·bi′ah:[e] of the sons of Re·ha·bi′ah, Is·shi′ah the head; **22** of the Iz′har·ites, She·lo′moth;[f] of the sons of She·lo′moth, Ja′hath; **23** and of the sons of Heb′ron, Je·ri′ah[g] the head, Am·a·ri′ah the second, Ja·ha·zi′el the third, Jek·a·me′am the fourth; **24** of the sons of Uz′zi·el, Mi′cah; of the sons of Mi′cah, Sha′mir. **25** The brother of Mi′cah was Is·shi′ah; of the sons of Is·shi′ah, Zech·a·ri′ah. **26** The sons of Me·rar′i[h] were Mah′li and Mu′shi; of the sons of Ja·a·zi′ah, Be′no. **27** The sons of Me·rar′i: of Ja·a·zi′ah, Be′no, Sho′ham, Zac′cur, and Ib′ri; **28** of Mah′li, El·e·a′zar, who did not have any sons;[i] **29** of Kish: the sons of Kish, Je·rah′me·el;

30 and the sons of Mu'shi were Mah'li, E'der, and Jer'i·moth.

These were the sons of Le'vi by their paternal houses. 31 And they also cast lots[a] just as their brothers the sons of Aaron did in the presence of King David, Za'dok, A·him'e·lech, and the heads of the paternal houses of the priests and of the Levites. Regarding the paternal houses, the head one was just as his younger brother.

25 Further, David and the chiefs of the groups for the service separated some of the sons of A'saph, He'man, and Je·du'thun[b] to serve by prophesying with the harps, the stringed instruments,[c] and the cymbals.[d] The list of the official men for this service was, 2 of the sons of A'saph: Zac'cur, Joseph, Neth·a·ni'ah, and Ash·a·re'lah, the sons of A'saph under the direction of A'saph, who prophesied under the direction of the king. 3 Of Je·du'thun,[e] the sons of Je·du'thun: Ged·a·li'ah, Ze'ri, Je·sha'iah, Shim'e·i, Hash·a·bi'ah, and Mat·ti·thi'ah,[f] six, under the direction of their father Je·du'thun, who prophesied with the harp, thanking and praising Jehovah.[g] 4 Of He'man,[h] the sons of He'man: Buk·ki'ah, Mat·ta·ni'ah, Uz'zi·el, Sheb'u·el, Jer'i·moth, Han·a·ni'ah, Ha·na'ni, E·li'a·thah, Gid·dal'ti, Ro·mam'ti·e'zer, Josh·be·kash'ah, Mal·lo'thi, Ho'thir, and Ma·ha'zi·oth. 5 All of these were sons of He'man, a visionary of the king in matters pertaining to the true God to his glory;* thus the true God gave He'man 14 sons and 3 daughters. 6 All of these were under the direction of their father for singing at the house of Jehovah, with cymbals, stringed instruments, and harps[i] for the service of the house of the true God.

Under the king's direction were A'saph, Je·du'thun, and He'man.

7 The number of them and their brothers who were trained in song to Jehovah, all experts, was 288. 8 So they cast lots[a] for their duties, the small and the great alike, the expert along with the learner.

9 The first lot to come out belonged to A'saph for Joseph,[b] the second for Ged·a·li'ah[c] (he and his brothers and his sons were 12); 10 the third for Zac'cur,[d] his sons and his brothers, 12; 11 the fourth for Iz'ri, his sons and his brothers, 12; 12 the fifth for Neth·a·ni'ah,[e] his sons and his brothers, 12; 13 the sixth for Buk·ki'ah, his sons and his brothers, 12; 14 the seventh for Jesh·a·re'lah, his sons and his brothers, 12; 15 the eighth for Je·sha'iah, his sons and his brothers, 12; 16 the ninth for Mat·ta·ni'ah, his sons and his brothers, 12; 17 the tenth for Shim'e·i, his sons and his brothers, 12; 18 the 11th for Az'ar·el, his sons and his brothers, 12; 19 the 12th for Hash·a·bi'ah, his sons and his brothers, 12; 20 for the 13th, Shu'ba·el,[f] his sons and his brothers, 12; 21 for the 14th, Mat·ti·thi'ah, his sons and his brothers, 12; 22 for the 15th, for Jer'e·moth, his sons and his brothers, 12; 23 for the 16th, for Han·a·ni'ah, his sons and his brothers, 12; 24 for the 17th, for Josh·be·kash'ah, his sons and his brothers, 12; 25 for the 18th, for Ha·na'ni, his sons and his brothers, 12; 26 for the 19th, for Mal·lo'thi, his sons and his brothers, 12; 27 for the 20th, for E·li'a·thah, his sons and his brothers, 12; 28 for the 21st, for Ho'thir, his sons and his brothers, 12; 29 for the 22nd, for Gid·dal'ti,[g] his sons

---

25:5 *Lit., "to raise up his horn."

CHAP. 24
a Pr 16:33

CHAP. 25
b 1Ch 16:41, 42
2Ch 5:11, 12
2Ch 35:15

c 1Sa 10:5

d 1Ch 15:16

e 1Ch 16:41, 42

f 1Ch 15:16, 18

g Eph 5:19

h 1Ch 15:16, 19

i 1Ch 13:8
1Ch 15:16
1Ch 16:5

Second Col.
a Pr 16:33

b 1Ch 25:1, 2

c 1Ch 25:1, 3

d 1Ch 25:1, 2

e 1Ch 25:1, 2

f 1Ch 25:1, 4

g 1Ch 25:1, 4

and his brothers, 12; **30** for the 23rd, for Ma·ha′zi·oth,[a] his sons and his brothers, 12; **31** for the 24th, for Ro·mam′ti-e′zer,[b] his sons and his brothers, 12.

26 The divisions of gatekeepers[c] were as follows: of the Kor′ah·ites, Me·shel·e·mi′ah[d] the son of Ko′re of the sons of A′saph. **2** And Me·shel·e·mi′ah had sons: Zech·a·ri′ah the firstborn, Je·di′a·el the second, Zeb·a·di′ah the third, Jath′ni·el the fourth, **3** E′lam the fifth, Je·ho·ha′nan the sixth, El′ie·ho·e′nai the seventh. **4** And O′bed-e′dom had sons: She·mai′ah the firstborn, Je·hoz′a·bad the second, Jo′ah the third, Sa′car the fourth, Ne·than′el the fifth, **5** Am′mi·el the sixth, Is′sa·char the seventh, and Pe·ul′le·thai the eighth; for God had blessed him.

6 And to his son She·mai′ah, there were sons born who were rulers of their paternal house, for they were mighty, capable men. **7** The sons of She·mai′ah: Oth′ni, Reph′a·el, O′bed, and El·za′bad; and his brothers E·li′hu and Sem·a·chi′ah were also capable men. **8** All of these were of the sons of O′bed-e′dom; they and their sons and their brothers were capable men and qualified for the service, 62 belonging to O′bed-e′dom. **9** And Me·shel·e·mi′ah[e] had sons and brothers, 18 capable men. **10** And Ho′sah of the sons of Me·rar′i had sons. Shim′ri was the head, for although he was not the firstborn, his father appointed him as head, **11** Hil·ki′ah the second, Teb·a·li′ah the third, Zech·a·ri′ah the fourth. All the sons and brothers of Ho′sah were 13.

12 Of these divisions of the gatekeepers, the headmen had duties just as their brothers did, to minister at the house of Jehovah. **13** So they cast lots,[f] the small and the great alike by

their paternal houses, for the different gates. **14** Then the lot to the east fell to Shel·e·mi′ah. For Zech·a·ri′ah his son, a discreet adviser, they cast the lots, and his lot came out to the north. **15** O′bed-e′dom had his to the south, and his sons[a] were assigned the storehouses. **16** Shup′pim and Ho′sah[b] had theirs to the west, near the Shal′lech·eth Gate by the highway that goes up, guard group corresponding to guard group; **17** there were six Levites to the east; to the north, four each day and to the south, four each day; and for the storehouses,[c] two by two; **18** for the portico to the west, there were four at the highway[d] and two at the portico. **19** These were the divisions of the gatekeepers from the sons of the Kor′ah·ites and of the Me·rar′ites.

20 As regards the Levites, A·hi′jah was in charge of the treasuries of the house of the true God and the treasuries of the things made holy.*[e] **21** The sons of La′dan: the sons of the Ger′shon·ite belonging to La′dan, the heads of the paternal houses belonging to La′dan the Ger′shon·ite, Je·hi′e·li[f] **22** and the sons of Je·hi′e·li, Ze′tham and his brother Joel. They were in charge of the treasuries of the house of Jehovah.[g] **23** From the Am′ram·ites, the Iz′har·ites, the Heb′ron·ites, and the Uz·zi′el·ites,[h] **24** Sheb′u·el son of Ger′shom son of Moses was a leader in charge of the storehouses. **25** As regards his brothers, of E·li·e′zer,[i] there was Re·ha·bi′ah[j] his son, Je·sha′iah his son, Jo′ram his son, Zich′ri his son, and She·lo′moth his son. **26** This She·lo′moth and his brothers were in charge of all the treasuries

---

CHAP. 25
a 1Ch 25:1, 4

b 1Ch 25:1, 4

CHAP. 26
c 1Ch 9:2, 22
2Ch 23:16, 19

d 1Ch 26:14, 19

e 1Ch 26:14, 19

f Pr 16:33

Second Col.
a 1Ch 26:4, 5

b 1Ch 26:10, 11

c 1Ch 26:15

d 1Ch 26:16

e 1Ki 7:51
1Ki 14:25, 26
1Ch 9:26
1Ch 18:10, 11

f 1Ch 29:8

g 1Ki 15:18

h Nu 3:27

i Ex 18:3, 4

j 1Ch 23:17

26:20 *Or "the things dedicated."

of the things made holy,[a] which King David,[b] the heads of the paternal houses,[c] the chiefs of the thousands and of the hundreds, and the chiefs of the army had made holy. **27** From the wars[d] and from the spoil,[e] they had made things holy to maintain the house of Jehovah; **28** also, all that Samuel the seer,[f] Saul the son of Kish, Ab'ner[g] the son of Ner, and Jo'ab[h] the son of Ze·ru'iah[i] had made holy. Whatever anyone made holy was put in the care of She·lo'mith and his brothers.

29 Of the Iz'har·ites,[j] Chen·a·ni'ah and his sons were assigned outside administrative duties as officers and as judges[k] over Israel.

30 Of the Heb'ron·ites,[l] Hash·a·bi'ah and his brothers, 1,700 capable men, were over the administration of Israel in the region west of the Jordan for all the work of Jehovah and for the king's service. **31** Of the Heb'ron·ites, Je·ri'jah[m] was the head of the Heb'ron·ites by line of descent of their paternal house. In the 40th year of David's kingship,[n] they were sought out, and mighty, capable men were found among them in Ja'zer[o] in Gil'e·ad. **32** And his brothers numbered 2,700 capable men, heads of the paternal houses. So King David assigned them over the Reu'ben·ites, the Gad'ites, and the half tribe of the Ma·nas'sites, for every matter of the true God and matter of the king.

27 This is the number of Israelites, the heads of the paternal houses, the chiefs of the thousands and of the hundreds,[p] and their officers who ministered to the king[q] in every matter of the divisions that would come in and go out month by month during all the months of the year; there were 24,000 in each division.

CHAP. 26

a Nu 31:50
　1Ch 18:10, 11

b 1Ch 29:3, 4

c 1Ch 29:6, 7

d Jos 6:19

e Nu 31:28

f 1Sa 9:9

g 1Sa 14:50

h 2Sa 20:23

i 2Sa 2:18

j 1Ch 23:12

k De 17:9
　2Ch 19:8

l 1Ch 23:12

m 1Ch 23:19

n 1Ch 29:26, 27

o Jos 13:24, 25
　Jos 21:8, 39

CHAP. 27

p Ex 18:25
　De 1:15
　1Sa 8:11, 12

q 1Ch 28:1

Second Col.

a 1Ch 11:11

b Nu 26:20, 21

c 2Sa 23:9

d 1Ch 8:1, 4

e 2Sa 23:20-23
　1Ki 4:4

f 1Ch 12:27

g 2Sa 2:18
　2Sa 23:8, 24

h 1Ch 2:15, 16

i 2Sa 23:8, 26

j 2Ch 11:5, 6
　Am 1:1

k 1Ch 11:10, 27

l 2Sa 21:18

m Nu 26:20

n 2Sa 23:8, 27

o 1Ch 6:60, 64

p 2Sa 23:8, 28

q Nu 26:20

r 2Sa 23:8, 30

2 Over the first division of the first month was Ja·sho'be·am[a] the son of Zab'di·el, and 24,000 were in his division. **3** Of the sons of Pe'rez,[b] he was the head of all the chiefs of the groups assigned to serve during the first month. **4** Over the division of the second month was Do'dai[c] the A·ho'hite[d] with his division, and Mik'loth was the leader, and 24,000 were in his division. **5** The chief of the third group assigned to serve during the third month was Be·nai'ah[e] the son of Je·hoi'a·da[f] the chief priest, and 24,000 were in his division. **6** This Be·nai'ah was a mighty warrior of the thirty and in charge of the thirty, and over his division was his son Am·miz'a·bad. **7** The fourth for the fourth month was As'a·hel,[g] Jo'ab's brother,[h] and his son Zeb·a·di'ah after him, and 24,000 were in his division. **8** The fifth chief for the fifth month was Sham'huth the Iz'rah·ite, and 24,000 were in his division. **9** The sixth for the sixth month was I'ra[i] the son of Ik'kesh the Te·ko'ite,[j] and 24,000 were in his division. **10** The seventh for the seventh month was He'lez[k] the Pel'o·nite of the E'phra·im·ites, and 24,000 were in his division. **11** The eighth for the eighth month was Sib'be·cai[l] the Hu'shath·ite of the Ze'rah·ites,[m] and 24,000 were in his division. **12** The ninth for the ninth month was Abi·e'zer[n] the An'a·thoth·ite[o] of the Ben'ja·min·ites, and 24,000 were in his division. **13** The tenth for the tenth month was Ma'ha·rai[p] the Ne·toph'a·thite of the Ze'rah·ites,[q] and 24,000 were in his division. **14** The 11th for the 11th month was Be·nai'ah[r] the Pir'a·thon·ite of the sons of E'phra·im, and 24,000 were in his division. **15** The 12th for the 12th month was Hel'dai the Ne·toph'a·thite,

of Oth′ni·el, and 24,000 were in
his division.

16 These were the leaders of
the tribes of Israel: Of the Reu′-
ben·ites, E·li·e′zer the son of
Zich′ri was leader; of the Sim′e-
on·ites, Sheph·a·ti′ah the son of
Ma′a·cah; **17** of Le′vi, Hash·a-
bi′ah the son of Kem·u′el; of Aaron, Za′dok; **18** of Judah, E·li′-
hu,[a] one of David's brothers; of
Is′sa·char, Om′ri the son of Mi′-
cha·el; **19** of Zeb′u·lun, Ish·ma′-
iah the son of O·ba·di′ah; of
Naph′ta·li, Jer′i·moth the son
of Az′ri·el; **20** of the E′phra·im-
ites, Ho·she′a the son of Az·a·zi′-
ah; of the half tribe of Ma·nas′-
seh, Joel the son of Pe·dai′ah;
21 of the half tribe of Ma·nas′-
seh in Gil′e·ad, Id′do the son of
Zech·a·ri′ah; of Benjamin, Ja·a-
si′el the son of Ab′ner;[b] **22** of
Dan, Az′ar·el the son of Je·ro′-
ham. These were the princes of
the tribes of Israel.

23 David did not count those
20 years of age and under, because Jehovah had promised to
make Israel as many as the
stars of the heavens.[c] **24** Jo′ab
the son of Ze·ru′iah had started to take the count, but he did
not finish; and God's anger came
against Israel* because of this,[d]
and the number was not entered
into the account of the history of
the times of King David.

25 Over the treasuries of the
king[e] was Az′ma·veth the son of
Ad′i·el. Jon′a·than the son of Uz-
zi′ah was over the storehouses*
in the fields, in the cities, in
the villages, and in the towers.
26 Over the field workers who
cultivated the soil was Ez′ri the
son of Che′lub. **27** Shim′e·i the
Ra′math·ite was over the vineyards; over the produce of
the vineyards for the wine supplies was Zab′di the Shiph′mite.
28 Over the olive groves and
the sycamore trees[a] in the She-
phe′lah[b] was Ba′al-ha′nan the Ge-
de′rite; over the oil supplies was
Jo′ash. **29** Over the herds that
grazed in Shar′on[c] was Shit′-
rai the Shar′on·ite, and Sha′-
phat the son of Ad′lai was over
the herds in the valley plains.*
30 Over the camels was O′bil
the Ish′ma·el·ite; over the donkeys* was Jeh·de′iah the Me·ron′-
o·thite. **31** Over the flocks was
Ja′ziz the Hag′rite. All of these
were the chiefs of King David's
property.

32 Jon′a·than,[d] David's neph-
ew, was an adviser, a man of
understanding and a secretary,
and Je·hi′el the son of Hach′mo-
ni looked after the king's sons.[e]
33 A·hith′o·phel[f] was an adviser to the king, and Hu′shai[g]
the Ar′chite was the king's
friend.* **34** After A·hith′o·phel
there were Je·hoi′a·da the son of
Be·nai′ah[h] and A·bi′a·thar;[i] and
Jo′ab[j] was chief of the king's
army.

28 David then congregated
all the princes of Isra-
el to Jerusalem: the princes of
the tribes, the chiefs of the divisions[k] ministering to the king,
the chiefs of thousands and the
chiefs of hundreds,[l] the chiefs of
all the property and livestock of
the king[m] and of his sons,[n] together with the court officials
and every mighty and capable
man.[o] **2** Then King David rose
to his feet and said:

"Hear me, my brothers and
my people. It was my heart's
desire to build a house as
the resting-place for the ark of
the covenant of Jehovah and
as the footstool of our God,[p] and
I made preparations to build.[q]
3 But the true God told me,

CHAP. 27
a 1Sa 16:1, 6; 1Sa 17:28
b 1Sa 14:50; 2Sa 3:27
c Ge 15:5
d 2Sa 24:2, 15; 1Ch 21:6, 7
e 2Ki 18:15

Second Col.
a 2Ch 9:27
b 2Ch 26:9, 10
c Isa 35:2
d 2Sa 13:3; 2Sa 21:21
e 1Ch 3:1-9
f 2Sa 15:12; 2Sa 16:23; 2Sa 17:23
g 2Sa 15:37; 2Sa 16:16, 17
h 2Sa 23:20-23; 1Ki 2:35
i 1Ki 1:7
j 1Ch 11:6

CHAP. 28
k 1Ch 27:1
l Ex 18:25
m 1Ch 27:25, 29
n 1Ch 3:1-9
o 1Ch 11:10
p Ps 132:3-5
q 1Ch 22:2-4

27:24 *Lit., "and anger was on Israel." **27:25** *Or "treasuries."
27:29 *Or "low plains." **27:30** *Lit., "female donkeys." **27:33** *Or "confidant."

'You will not build a house for my name,[a] for you are a man of wars, and you have shed blood.'[b] 4 However, Jehovah the God of Israel chose me out of all the house of my father to become king over Israel forever,[c] for he chose Judah as leader[d] and of the house of Judah, my father's house,[e] and of my father's sons, I was the one whom he approved, to make me king over all Israel.[f] 5 And of all my sons —for Jehovah has given me many sons[g]—he chose my son Sol'o·mon[h] to sit on the throne of the kingship of Jehovah over Israel.[i]

6 "He said to me, 'Your son Sol'o·mon is the one who will build my house and my courtyards, for I have chosen him as my son and I will become his father.[j] 7 I will firmly establish his kingship forever[k] if he resolutely observes my commandments and my judicial decisions,[l] as he is now doing.' 8 So I say before the eyes of all Israel, Jehovah's congregation, and in the ears of our God: Carefully observe and search for all the commandments of Jehovah your God, so that you may possess the good land[m] and pass it on as a permanent inheritance to your sons after you.

9 "And you, Sol'o·mon my son, know the God of your father and serve him with a complete* heart[n] and with a delightful# soul,[a] for Jehovah searches through all hearts,[o] and he discerns every inclination of the thoughts.[p] If you search for him, he will let himself be found by you,[q] but if you leave him, he will reject you forever.[r] 10 See, now, for Jehovah has chosen you to build a house as a sanctuary. Be courageous and go to work."

11 David then gave to his son Sol'o·mon the architectural plan[a] of the porch[b] and of its houses, its storerooms, its roof chambers, its inner rooms, and the house of the propitiatory cover.*[c] 12 He gave him the architectural plan of everything that had been conveyed to him through inspiration* for the courtyards[d] of Jehovah's house, for all the dining rooms around it, for the treasuries of the house of the true God, and for the treasuries of the things made holy;#[e] 13 also for the divisions of the priests[f] and of the Levites, for all the duties of the service of Jehovah's house, and for all the utensils of the service of Jehovah's house; 14 also for the weight of the gold, the gold for all the utensils for the different services, the weight of all the utensils of silver, and for all the utensils for the different services; 15 also the weight for the gold lampstands[g] and their gold lamps, the weight of the different lampstands and their lamps, and the weight of the silver lampstands, for each lampstand and its lamps according to its use; 16 also the weight of the gold for the tables of the layer bread,*[h] for each table, as well as the silver for the tables of silver, 17 for the forks, the bowls, the pitchers of pure gold, and the weight of the small gold bowls,[i] for each small bowl, and the weight of the small silver bowls, for each small bowl. 18 He also gave the weight for the refined gold for the incense altar[j] and for the representation of the chariot,[k] namely, the cherubs[l] of gold that spread their wings out and overshadow the

CHAP. 28
a 1Ch 17:4
b 1Ch 22:7, 8
c 1Sa 16:1, 13
  2Sa 7:8
  Ps 89:20
d Ge 49:10
  1Ch 5:2
  Ps 60:7
e Ru 4:22
f 1Sa 13:14
  1Sa 16:11, 12
g 1Ch 3:1-9
h 1Ch 22:9
i 1Ch 17:14
  2Ch 1:8
j 2Sa 7:13, 14
k 1Ch 17:13, 14
  Ps 72:8
l De 12:1
  1Ki 6:12
m De 6:3
n De 10:12
o 1Sa 16:7
  1Ch 29:17
  Pr 17:3
  Re 2:23
p De 31:21
  Ps 139:2
q Mt 7:7
  Heb 11:6
  Jas 4:8
r De 31:17
  2Ch 15:2
  Heb 10:38

Second Col.
a Heb 8:5
b 2Ch 3:4
c Le 16:2
  1Ki 6:19
d 1Ki 6:36
  1Ki 7:12
e 1Ch 9:26
  1Ch 26:20
f 1Ch 24:1
g 2Ch 4:7
h 2Ch 4:8, 19
i 1Ki 7:48, 50
j 1Ki 7:48
k Ps 18:10
l Ex 25:20
  1Sa 4:4
  1Ki 6:23

28:9 *Or "completely devoted." #Or "willing." ^See Glossary.

28:11 *Or "house of the atonement." 28:12 *Lit., "by the spirit." #Or "things dedicated." 28:16 *That is, the showbread.

ark of the covenant of Jehovah. **19** David said: "The hand of Jehovah was upon me, and he gave me insight to put all the details of the architectural plan[a] in writing."[b]

20 Then David said to his son Sol'o·mon: "Be courageous and strong and go to work. Do not be afraid or be terrified, for Jehovah God, my God, is with you.[c] He will not desert you or abandon you,[d] but he will be with you until all the work for the service of Jehovah's house is finished. **21** And here are the divisions of the priests[e] and of the Levites[f] for all the service of the house of the true God. You have willing, skilled workers to perform every kind of service,[g] as well as the princes[h] and all the people who will carry out all your instructions."

29 King David now said to all the congregation: "My son Sol'o·mon, the one whom God has chosen,[i] is young and inexperienced,*[j] and the work is great, for it is not a temple[#] for man but for Jehovah God.[k] **2** And I have spared no effort to prepare for the house of my God, providing the gold for the goldwork, the silver for the silverwork, the copper for the copperwork, the iron for the ironwork,[l] the timbers[m] for the timberwork, onyx stones, and stones to be set with mortar, mosaic pebbles, every kind of precious stone, and alabaster stones in great quantity. **3** Moreover, because of my delight in the house of my God,[n] there is also my private treasure[o] of gold and silver that I am giving to the house of my God, in addition to all that I have prepared for the holy house, **4** including

3,000 talents* of gold from O'phir[a] and 7,000 talents of refined silver, for coating the walls of the houses, **5** the gold for the goldwork and the silver for the silverwork, and for all the work to be done by the craftsmen. Now who volunteers to come forward today with a gift in hand for Jehovah?"[b]

6 So the princes of the paternal houses, the princes of the tribes of Israel, the chiefs of thousands and of hundreds,[c] and the chiefs of the business of the king[d] came forward voluntarily. **7** And they gave to the service of the house of the true God: 5,000 talents of gold, 10,000 darics,* 10,000 talents of silver, 18,000 talents of copper, and 100,000 talents of iron. **8** Whoever had precious stones gave them to the treasury of the house of Jehovah, under the care of Je·hi'el[e] the Ger'shon·ite.[f] **9** The people rejoiced over making these voluntary offerings, for they made the voluntary offerings to Jehovah with a complete heart,[g] and David the king also rejoiced greatly.

10 Then David praised Jehovah before the eyes of all the congregation. David said: "May you be praised, O Jehovah the God of Israel our father, throughout all eternity.* **11** Yours, O Jehovah, are the greatness[h] and the mightiness[i] and the beauty and the splendor and the majesty,*[j] for everything in the heavens and on the earth is yours.[k] Yours is the kingdom, O Jehovah.[l] You are the One exalting yourself as head over all. **12** The riches and the glory are from you,[m] and you rule over

---

CHAP. 28
a 1Ch 28:11
b Ex 25:9, 40
c De 31:6
  Jos 1:6, 9
  Ro 8:31
d Jos 1:5
e 1Ch 24:1
f 1Ch 24:20
g Ex 36:1, 2
h 1Ch 22:17
  1Ch 28:1

CHAP. 29
i 1Ch 28:5
j 1Ki 3:7
k 2Ch 2:4
l 1Ch 22:3, 16
m 1Ch 22:4, 14
n Ps 26:8
  Ps 27:4
  Ps 122:1
o 1Ch 21:24

Second Col.
a Job 28:16
b Ex 35:5
c Ex 18:25
d 1Ch 27:25, 29
  1Ch 27:31
e 1Ch 26:22
f 1Ch 6:1
g 2Co 9:7
h Ps 145:3
  1Ti 1:17
i Re 5:13
j 1Ch 16:27
  Ps 8:1
k Ps 24:1
  Isa 42:5
l Ps 103:19
  Mt 6:10
m De 8:18
  Pr 10:22
  Php 4:19

29:1 *Or "delicate." #Or "citadel; palace." **29:4** *A talent equaled 34.2 kg (1,101 oz t). See App. B14. **29:7** *A daric was a Persian gold coin. See App. B14. **29:10** *Or "from eternity to eternity." **29:11** *Or "dignity."

everything,[a] and in your hand there are power[b] and mightiness,[c] and your hand is able to make great[d] and to give strength to all.[e] **13** And now, O our God, we thank you and praise your beautiful name.

14 "And yet, who am I and who are my people that we should be in a position to make voluntary offerings like this? For everything is from you, and we have given to you what comes from your own hand. **15** For we are foreign residents in your presence and settlers, just like all our forefathers.[f] For our days on the earth are like a shadow[g]—without hope. **16** O Jehovah our God, all this wealth that we have prepared to build for you a house for your holy name is from your own hand, and it all belongs to you. **17** I well know, O my God, that you examine the heart[h] and that you take pleasure in integrity.*[i] In the uprightness* of my heart, I have voluntarily offered all these things, and I am overjoyed to see your people who are present here make voluntary offerings to you. **18** O Jehovah, the God of Abraham, Isaac, and Israel, our forefathers, keep these inclinations and thoughts in the hearts of your people forever, and direct their hearts to you.[j] **19** And give a complete* heart[k] to my son Sol'o·mon, so that he may observe your commandments,[l] your reminders, and your regulations and do all these things and build the temple# for which I have made preparation."[m]

20 David then said to all the congregation: "Now praise Jehovah your God." And all the congregation praised Jehovah the God of their forefathers and bowed low and prostrated themselves to Jehovah and to the king. **21** And they continued to offer sacrifices to Jehovah and to offer up burnt offerings[a] to Jehovah on the following day, 1,000 young bulls, 1,000 rams, 1,000 male lambs, and their drink offerings;[b] they offered sacrifices in great number for all Israel.[c] **22** They continued eating and drinking before Jehovah on that day with great rejoicing,[d] and for a second time they made Sol'o·mon the son of David king and anointed him before Jehovah as leader,[e] and also Za'dok as priest.[f] **23** And Sol'o·mon sat on Jehovah's throne[g] as king in place of David his father, and he was successful, and all the Israelites were obedient to him. **24** All the princes,[h] the mighty warriors,[i] and also all the sons of King David[j] submitted themselves to Sol'o·mon the king. **25** And Jehovah made Sol'o·mon exceedingly great before the eyes of all Israel and bestowed on him such royal majesty as no king over Israel ever had before.[k]

26 Thus David the son of Jes'se reigned over all Israel, **27** and the length* of his reign over Israel was 40 years. In Heb'ron he reigned for 7 years,[l] and in Jerusalem he reigned for 33 years.[m] **28** And he died at a good old age,[n] satisfied with long life,* wealth, and glory; and his son Sol'o·mon became king in his place.[o] **29** As for the history of King David, from beginning to end, it is written among the words of Samuel the seer, Nathan[p] the prophet, and Gad[q] the visionary, **30** together with all his kingship, his mightiness, and the events of the times involving him and Israel and all the surrounding kingdoms.

CHAP. 29
a 2Ch 20:6
b Isa 40:26
c De 3:24
  Eph 1:19
  Re 15:3
d 2Ch 1:11, 12
e 2Ch 16:9
  Ps 18:32
  Isa 40:29
f Le 25:23
  Heb 11:13
g Job 14:1, 2
  Jas 4:13, 14
h 1Ch 28:9
i Pr 11:20
  Pr 15:8
  Heb 1:9
j Ps 10:17
  Ps 86:11
k Mr 12:30
l 1Ki 6:12
m 1Ch 22:14

Second Col.
a Le 1:3
b Le 23:12, 13
  Nu 15:5
c 1Ki 8:63, 64
d De 12:7
  2Ch 7:10
  Ne 8:12
e 1Ki 1:38-40
  1Ch 23:1
f 1Ki 2:35
g 1Ch 28:5
h 1Ch 22:17
i 1Ch 28:1
j 1Ch 3:1-9
k 1Ki 3:12
  2Ch 1:1, 12
  Ec 2:9
l 2Sa 2:11
m 2Sa 5:4, 5
n 1Ki 1:1
o 1Ki 2:10-12
p 2Sa 7:2
  2Sa 12:1
q 1Ch 21:9, 10

29:17 *Or "rectitude; uprightness." #Or "sincerity." 29:19 *Or "completely devoted." #Or "citadel; palace."

29:27 *Lit., "the days." 29:28 *Lit., "with days."

THE SECOND OF

CHRONICLES

OUTLINE OF CONTENTS

1 Sol′o·mon the son of David grew ever stronger in his kingship, and Jehovah his God was with him and made him exceedingly great.[a]

2 Sol′o·mon sent for all Israel, the chiefs of the thousands and of the hundreds, the judges, and all the chieftains of all Israel, the heads of the paternal houses. **3** Then Sol′o·mon and all the congregation went to the high place at Gib′e·on,[b] for that was where the tent of meeting of the true God was, which tent Moses the servant of Jehovah had made in the wilderness. **4** However, David had brought the Ark of the true God up from Kir′i·ath-je′a·rim[c] to the place that David had prepared for it; he had pitched a tent for it in Jerusalem.[d] **5** And the copper altar[e] that Bez′al·el[f] the son of U′ri the son of Hur had made had been put before the tabernacle of Jehovah; and Sol′o·mon and the congregation would pray before it.* **6** Sol′o·mon now made

offerings there before Jehovah, and he offered up 1,000 burnt offerings on the copper altar[a] of the tent of meeting.

7 That night God appeared to Sol′o·mon and said to him: "Ask what you would like me to give you."[b] **8** At this Sol′o·mon said to God: "You have shown great loyal love toward my father David,[c] and you have made me king in his place.[d] **9** Now, O Jehovah God, let your promise to David my father prove faithful,[e] for you have made me king over a people as numerous as the dust particles of the earth.[f] **10** Give me now wisdom and knowledge[g] to lead this people,* for who can possibly judge this great people of yours?"[h]

11 Then God said to Sol′o·mon: "Because this is your heart's desire and you have not asked for wealth, riches, and honor or for the death* of those hating you, nor have you asked

CHAP. 1
a 1Ch 29:25
Ec 2:9
Mt 6:28, 29
Mt 12:42

b 1Ki 3:4
1Ch 21:29

c 1Ch 13:5

d 1Ch 16:1

e Ex 38:1, 2

f Ex 31:2-5

Second Col.
a 1Ki 3:4

b 1Ki 3:5-9

c 2Sa 7:8

d 1Ch 28:5
Ps 89:28, 29

e 2Sa 7:12
1Ch 28:6
Ps 132:11

f Ge 13:14, 16

g Pr 2:6
Jas 1:5

h Ps 72:1, 2

1:5 *Or "would inquire of Him there."　　1:10 *Lit., "to go out before this people and to come in."　　1:11 *Or "soul."

for a long life,* but you have asked for wisdom and knowledge to judge my people over whom I have made you king, **12** wisdom and knowledge will be given you; but I will also give you wealth and riches and honor such as no kings before you have had and none after you will have."[b]

13 So Sol′o·mon came from the high place at Gib′e·on,[c] from before the tent of meeting, to Jerusalem; and he reigned over Israel. **14** Sol′o·mon kept accumulating chariots and horses;* he had 1,400 chariots and 12,000 horses,*[d] and he kept them stationed in the chariot cities[e] and close by the king in Jerusalem.[f] **15** The king made the silver and the gold in Jerusalem as plentiful as the stones,[g] and cedarwood as plentiful as the sycamore trees in the She·phe′lah.[h] **16** The horses of Sol′o·mon had been imported from Egypt,[i] and the company of the king's merchants would obtain the horses in droves* for one price.[j] **17** Each chariot imported from Egypt cost 600 silver pieces, and a horse cost 150; in turn, they would export them to all the kings of the Hit′tites and the kings of Syria.

2 Sol′o·mon now gave the order to build a house for Jehovah's name[k] and a house* for his kingdom.[l] **2** Sol′o·mon enlisted 70,000 men as common laborers,* 80,000 men as stonecutters in the mountains,[m] and 3,600 as overseers over them.[n] **3** Further, Sol′o·mon sent word to Hi′ram[o] the king of Tyre: "Do for me as you did for David my fa-

ther when you sent him cedarwood to build a house* to live in.[a] **4** Now I am building a house for the name of Jehovah my God, to sanctify it to him, to burn perfumed incense[b] before him, and also for the constant layer bread*[c] and the burnt offerings, morning and evening,[d] on the Sabbaths,[e] on the new moons,[f] and at the festival seasons[g] of Jehovah our God. This is a lasting obligation for Israel. **5** The house that I am building will be great, for our God is greater than all the other gods. **6** And who is up to the task of building him a house? For the heavens and the heaven of the heavens cannot contain him,[h] so who am I that I should build him a house except as a place for making sacrifices smoke before him? **7** Now send me a craftsman who is skilled in working in gold, silver, copper,[i] iron, purple wool, crimson, and blue thread and who knows how to cut engravings. He will work in Judah and in Jerusalem with my skilled craftsmen, whom David my father has provided.[j] **8** And send me timbers of cedar, juniper,[k] and algum[l] from Leb′a·non, for I well know that your servants are experienced at cutting down the trees of Leb′a·non.[m] My servants will work along with your servants[n] **9** to prepare for me great quantities of timber, for the house that I am to build will be extraordinarily great. **10** Now look! I will supply the food for your servants,[o] the woodcutters who cut down the trees: 20,000 cors* of wheat, 20,000 cors of barley, 20,000 baths* of wine, and 20,000 baths of oil."

11 At that Hi′ram the king of Tyre sent this written message

CHAP. 1
a 1Ki 3:10-13
　1Ki 3:28

b 1Ch 29:25
　2Ch 9:22
　Ec 2:9

c 1Ki 3:4

d De 17:16
　1Ki 4:26

e 2Ch 8:5, 6

f 2Ch 9:25

g 1Ki 10:21

h 1Ki 10:27
　2Ch 9:27

i 2Ch 9:28

j 1Ki 10:28, 29

CHAP. 2
k De 12:11
　1Ch 22:10

l 1Ki 7:1

m 1Ki 5:15

n 1Ki 5:16
　1Ki 9:22
　2Ch 2:17,18

o 1Ki 5:1

Second Col.
a 2Sa 5:11

b Ex 30:7

c Ex 25:30

d Nu 28:4

e Nu 28:9

f Nu 28:11

g De 16:16

h 1Ki 8:27
　Isa 66:1
　Ac 17:24

i 1Ki 7:13, 14

j 1Ch 22:15

k 1Ki 5:6, 8
　2Ch 3:5

l 1Ki 10:11

m 1Ki 5:9

n 1Ki 5:14

o 1Ki 5:11

1:11 *Lit., "many days." **1:14** *Or "horsemen." **1:16** *Or possibly, "from Egypt and from Kue; the king's merchants would buy them from Kue," perhaps referring to Cilicia. **2:1, 3** *Or "palace." **2:2** *Or "as burden bearers."

2:4 *That is, the showbread. **2:10** *A cor equaled 220 L (200 dry qt). See App. B14. "A bath equaled 22 L (5.81 gal). See App. B14.

to Sol'o·mon: "Because Jehovah loves his people, he has made you their king." **12** Hi'ram then said: "May Jehovah the God of Israel be praised, who made the heavens and the earth, because he has given to King David a wise son,[a] endowed with discretion and understanding,[b] who will build a house for Jehovah and a house for his kingdom. **13** Now I am sending a skilled craftsman, endowed with understanding, Hi'ram-a'bi,[c] **14** who is the son of a Dan'ite woman but whose father was a man of Tyre; he has experience in working in gold, silver, copper, iron, stones, timbers, purple wool, blue thread, fine fabric, and crimson.[d] He can do every sort of engraving and make any design he is given.[e] He will work with your own skilled craftsmen and the skilled craftsmen of my lord David your father. **15** Now let my lord send the wheat, barley, oil, and wine he has promised to his servants.[f] **16** And we will cut down trees from Leb'a·non,[g] as many as you need, and we will bring them to you as rafts by sea to Jop'pa;[h] and you will take them up to Jerusalem."[i]

17 Sol'o·mon then took a count of all the men who were foreign residents in the land of Israel,[j] after the census taken by David his father,[k] and there were found 153,600. **18** So he assigned 70,000 of them as common laborers,* 80,000 as stone-cutters[l] in the mountains, and 3,600 as overseers for putting the people to work.[m]

3 Then Sol'o·mon started to build the house of Jehovah[n] in Jerusalem on Mount Mo·ri'ah,[o] where Jehovah had appeared to his father David,[p] in the place that David had prepared on the threshing floor of Or'nan[q]

2:18 *Or "as burden bearers."

the Jeb'u·site. **2** He started to build on the second day of the second month, in the fourth year of his reign. **3** And the foundation that Sol'o·mon laid for building the house of the true God was 60 cubits long and 20 cubits wide,[a] according to the former measurement.* **4** The porch in front was 20 cubits long, corresponding to the width of the house,* and its height was 120;* and he overlaid it inside with pure gold.[b] **5** He paneled the great house with juniper wood, after which he covered it with fine gold,[c] and then he decorated it with palm-tree figures[d] and chains.[e] **6** Further, he overlaid the house with beautiful precious stones;[f] and the gold[g] he used was gold from Par·va'im. **7** He covered the house, the rafters, the thresholds, its walls, and its doors with gold;[h] and he engraved cherubs on the walls.[i]

8 He now made the Most Holy compartment;*[j] its length matched the width of the house, 20 cubits, and its width was 20 cubits. He covered it with 600 talents* of fine gold.[k] **9** The weight of the gold for the nails was 50 shekels;* and he covered the roof chambers with gold.

10 Then he made in the Most Holy compartment* two cherub sculptures, and he covered them with gold.[l] **11** The overall length of the wings of the cherubs[m] was 20 cubits; one wing of the first cherub was five

---

CHAP. 2
a 1Ki 5:7

b 2Ch 1:11, 12

c 1Ki 7:13, 14
2Ch 4:11-16

d 2Ch 3:14

e Ex 31:2-5

f 2Ch 2:10

g 1Ki 5:6, 8

h Jos 19:46, 48
Ezr 3:7

i 1Ki 5:9

j 2Ch 8:7, 8

k 1Ch 22:2

l 1Ki 5:17, 18
1Ch 22:15

m 1Ki 5:15, 16

CHAP. 3
n 1Ki 6:1
1Ki 6:37

o Ge 22:2, 14

p 2Sa 24:25
1Ch 21:18

q 2Sa 24:18
1Ch 21:22

Second Col.
a 1Ki 6:2

b 1Ki 6:3

c 1Ki 6:15, 22

d 1Ki 6:29

e 1Ki 6:21

f 1Ch 29:2, 8

g 1Ch 29:3, 4

h Ex 26:29

i Ex 26:1
1Ki 6:29

j Ex 26:33
1Ki 8:6
Heb 9:24

k 1Ki 6:20

l 1Ki 6:23-28

m 1Ki 8:6
1Ch 28:18

3:3 *A standard cubit equaled 44.5 cm (17.5 in.), but some feel that "the former measurement" refers to the long cubit that equaled 51.8 cm (20.4 in.). See App. B14. 3:4 *Or "20 cubits extending across the width of the house." *An uncertain dimension. 3:8, 10 *Lit., "house." 3:8 *A talent equaled 34.2 kg (1,101 oz t). See App. B14. 3:9 *A shekel equaled 11.4 g (0.367 oz t). See App. B14.

cubits long and touched the wall of the house, and its other wing was five cubits long and touched one of the other cherub's wings. **12** And one wing of the other cherub was five cubits long and touched the other wall of the house, and its other wing was five cubits long and touched one of the first cherub's wings. **13** The wings of these cherubs were spread out 20 cubits; and they stood on their feet, and they faced inward.*

14 He also made the curtain[a] of blue thread, purple wool, crimson, and fine fabric, and incorporated cherub designs into it.[b]

15 Then he made two pillars[c] at the front of the house, 35 cubits in length, and the capital on top of each pillar was five cubits.[d] **16** And he made chains, like necklaces, and put them on the tops of the pillars, and he made 100 pomegranates and put them on the chains. **17** He set up the pillars in front of the temple, one to the right* and one to the left;[e] he named the one on the right Ja′chin[△] and the one on the left Bo′az.[⊠]

4 Then he made the copper altar,[e] 20 cubits long, 20 cubits wide, and 10 cubits high.

2 He made the Sea*[f] of cast metal. It was circular in shape, 10 cubits from brim to brim and 5 cubits high, and it took a measuring line 30 cubits long to encircle it.[g] **3** And there were ornamental gourds[h] under it, completely encircling it, ten to a cubit all around the Sea. The gourds were in two rows and were cast in one piece with it. **4** It stood on 12 bulls,[i] 3 fac-

ing north, 3 facing west, 3 facing south, and 3 facing east; and the Sea rested on them, and all their hindquarters were toward the center. **5** And its thickness was a handbreadth;* and its brim was made like the brim of a cup, like a lily blossom. The reservoir could hold# 3,000 bath measures.[△]

6 Further, he made ten basins for washing and put five to the right and five to the left.[a] They would rinse in them the things used for the burnt offering.[b] But the Sea was for the priests for washing.[c]

7 He then made ten lampstands of gold,[d] as specified,[e] and put them in the temple, five on the right and five on the left.[f]

8 He also made ten tables and placed them in the temple, five on the right and five on the left;[g] and he made 100 golden bowls.

9 Then he made the courtyard[h] of the priests[i] and the great court*[j] and the doors for the court, and he overlaid their doors with copper. **10** And he placed the Sea on the right side, toward the southeast.[k]

11 Hi′ram also made the cans, the shovels, and the bowls.[l]

So Hi′ram finished the work that he did for King Sol′o·mon on the house of the true God:[m] **12** the two pillars[n] and the bowl-shaped capitals that were on top of the two pillars; the two networks[o] to cover the two bowl-shaped capitals that were on top of the pillars; **13** the 400 pomegranates[p] for the two networks, two rows of pomegranates for each network, to cover the two bowl-shaped capitals that were on the pillars;[q] **14** the ten carriages* and the ten basins on

---

CHAP. 3
a Mt 27:51
  Heb 10:19, 20

b Ex 26:31, 33

c 2Ki 25:13

d 1Ki 7:15-22
  2Ki 25:17
  2Ch 4:11-13
  Jer 52:22, 23

CHAP. 4
e Ex 38:1, 2
  1Ki 8:22

f Ex 30:20
  Ex 38:8

g 1Ki 7:23-26

h 1Ki 6:18

i Jer 52:20

Second Col.
a 1Ki 7:38, 39

b Le 1:9
  Le 9:14

c Ex 29:4

d Ex 37:17

e 1Ch 28:12, 15

f Ex 40:24

g 2Ch 4:19

h Ex 27:9
  Le 6:16

i 1Ki 6:36

j 1Ki 7:12

k 1Ki 7:39

l Ex 27:3

m 1Ki 7:40-46

n 2Ch 3:17

o 1Ki 7:17

p 1Ki 7:20

q Jer 52:22

3:13 *That is, toward the Holy. **3:17** *Or "south." #Or "north." △Meaning "May He [that is, Jehovah] Firmly Establish." ⊠Possibly meaning "In Strength." **4:2** *Or "reservoir."

4:5 *About 7.4 cm (2.9 in.). See App. B14. #Or "Its capacity was." △A bath equaled 22 L (5.81 gal). See App. B14. **4:9** *Or "enclosure." **4:14** *Or "water carts."

the carriages;[a] **15** the Sea and the 12 bulls beneath it;[b] **16** and the cans, the shovels, the forks,[c] and all their utensils Hi′ram-a′biv[d] made of polished copper for King Sol′o·mon for the house of Jehovah. **17** The king cast them in the district of the Jordan in the thick clay between Suc′coth[e] and Zer′e·dah. **18** Sol′o·mon made all these utensils in great quantities; the weight of the copper was not ascertained.[f]

19 Sol′o·mon made all the utensils[g] for the house of the true God: the altar of gold;[h] the tables[i] with the showbread on them;[j] **20** the lampstands and their lamps of pure gold,[k] to burn before the innermost room according to the requirements; **21** and the blossoms, the lamps, and the snuffers,* of gold, the purest gold; **22** the extinguishers, the bowls, the cups, and the fire holders, of pure gold; and the entrance of the house, its inner doors for the Most Holy,[l] and the doors of the house of the temple, of gold.[m]

5 So Sol′o·mon completed all the work he had to do for the house of Jehovah.[n] Sol′o·mon then brought in the things that David his father had made holy,[o] and he put the silver, the gold, and all the articles into the treasuries of the house of the true God.[p] **2** At that time Sol′o·mon congregated the elders of Israel, all the heads of the tribes, the chieftains of the paternal houses of Israel. They came to Jerusalem to bring up the ark of the covenant of Jehovah from the City of David,[q] that is, Zion.[r] **3** All the men of Israel assembled before the king at the festival* that is held in the seventh month.[s]

4 So all the elders of Israel came, and the Levites lifted up the Ark.[a] **5** They brought up the Ark, the tent of meeting,[b] and all the holy utensils that were in the tent. The priests and the Levites* brought them up. **6** King Sol′o·mon and the entire assembly of Israel who had been summoned to meet with him were before the Ark. So many sheep and cattle were being sacrificed[c] that they could not be counted or numbered. **7** Then the priests brought the ark of the covenant of Jehovah to its place, into the innermost room of the house, the Most Holy, underneath the wings of the cherubs.[d] **8** Thus the wings of the cherubs were spread out over the place of the Ark, so that the cherubs covered over the Ark and its poles[e] from above. **9** The poles were so long that the tips of the poles were visible from the Holy in front of the innermost room, but they were not visible from outside. And they are there to this day. **10** There was nothing in the Ark but the two tablets that Moses placed in it at Ho′reb,[f] when Jehovah made a covenant[g] with the people of Israel while they were coming out of Egypt.[h]

11 When the priests came out from the holy place (for all the priests who were present had sanctified themselves,[i] regardless of their divisions),[j] **12** all the Levite singers[k] who belonged to A′saph,[l] to He′man,[m] to Je·du′thun,[n] and to their sons and their brothers were clothed in fine fabric, holding cymbals, stringed instruments, and harps; they were standing east of the altar, and along with them 120 priests were sounding the trumpets.[o] **13** At the moment when the trumpeters and the singers

---

CHAP. 4
a 1Ki 7:27, 38
b 1Ki 7:23, 25
c Ex 38:3
d 2Ch 2:13, 14
e Jos 13:27, 28
f 1Ki 7:47
  1Ch 22:3, 14
  Jer 52:20
g 2Ki 24:13
h Ex 37:25, 26
  Re 8:3
i Ex 25:23, 24
  2Ch 4:8
j 1Ki 7:48-50
k Ex 25:31, 37
l 1Ki 6:31, 32
m 1Ki 6:33-35

CHAP. 5
n 1Ki 6:38
o 1Ch 22:14
p 1Ki 7:51
  1Ch 26:26
q 2Sa 6:12
  2Ch 1:4
r 1Ki 8:1, 2
  Ps 2:6
s Le 23:34
  2Ch 7:8

Second Col.
a Ex 25:14
  Nu 4:15
  1Ki 8:3-5
  1Ch 15:2, 15
b Ex 40:35
  Nu 4:29, 31
c 2Sa 6:13
d 1Ki 6:20, 23
  1Ki 8:6-9
e Ex 25:14
f Ex 34:1
  Ex 40:20
g Ex 19:5
  Ex 24:7
h Ex 19:1
i Ex 19:10
  Nu 8:21
j 1Ch 24:1
k 1Ch 15:16
l 1Ch 6:31, 39
m 1Ch 6:31, 33
n 1Ch 16:41
  1Ch 25:1, 6
  1Ch 25:3
o 1Ch 15:24

4:21 *Or "tongs." **5:3** *That is, the Festival of Booths.

5:5 *Or "The Levitical priests."

were praising and thanking Jehovah in unison, and as the sound ascended from the trumpets, the cymbals, and the other musical instruments as they were praising Jehovah, "for he is good; his loyal love endures forever,"[a] then the house, the house of Jehovah, was filled with a cloud.[b] **14** The priests were not able to stand to minister because of the cloud, for the glory of Jehovah filled the house of the true God.[c]

6 At that time Sol'o·mon said: "Jehovah said he would reside in the thick gloom.[d] **2** Now I have built a lofty house for you, an established place for you to dwell in forever."[e]

3 Then the king turned around and began to bless all the congregation of Israel while all the congregation of Israel stood.[f] **4** He said: "May Jehovah the God of Israel be praised, the one who by his own mouth promised my father David and by his own hands has given fulfillment, saying, **5** 'From the day I brought my people out of the land of Egypt, I have not chosen a city out of all the tribes of Israel in which to build a house for my name to remain there,[g] and I have not chosen a man to become leader over my people Israel. **6** But I have chosen Jerusalem[h] for my name to remain there, and I have chosen David to be over my people Israel.'[i] **7** And it was the heart's desire of my father David to build a house for the name of Jehovah the God of Israel.[j] **8** But Jehovah said to my father David, 'It was your heart's desire to build a house for my name, and you did well to desire this in your heart. **9** However, you will not build the house, but your own son who is to be born to you* is

---

6:9 *Lit., "your son, the one coming out of your loins."

CHAP. 5
a 1Ch 16:34

b Ex 40:34, 35
  1Ki 8:10, 11

c 2Ch 7:1, 2
  Eze 10:4
  Re 21:23

CHAP. 6
d Ex 20:21
  1Ki 8:12, 13
  Ps 97:2

e Ps 132:13, 14

f 1Ki 8:14-21

g De 12:5, 6

h Ps 48:1

i 2Sa 7:8
  1Ch 28:4

j 2Sa 7:2
  1Ki 5:3

Second Col.
a 1Ch 17:4

b 1Ch 28:5
  1Ch 29:23

c 1Ch 17:11

d Ex 40:20
  1Ki 8:9

e 1Ki 8:22

f 1Ki 6:36

g 1Ki 8:54

h De 7:9
  1Ki 8:23-26

i 1Ki 3:6

j 2Sa 7:12, 13
  1Ch 22:10

k Ps 132:12

l 1Ki 2:4

the one who will build the house for my name.'[a] **10** Jehovah has carried out the promise that he made, for I have succeeded my father David and I sit on the throne of Israel,[b] just as Jehovah promised.[c] I have also built the house for the name of Jehovah the God of Israel, **11** and there I have placed the Ark containing the covenant[d] that Jehovah made with the people of Israel."

12 Then he stood before the altar of Jehovah in front of all the congregation of Israel, and he spread out his hands.[e] **13** (For Sol'o·mon had made a platform of copper and put it in the middle of the court.*[f] It was five cubits* long, five cubits wide, and three cubits high; and he stood on it.) And he knelt down in front of all the congregation of Israel and spread his hands out to the heavens,[g] **14** and he said: "O Jehovah the God of Israel, there is no God like you in the heavens or on the earth, keeping the covenant and showing loyal love to your servants who are walking before you with all their heart.[h] **15** You have kept the promise that you made to your servant David my father.[i] You made the promise with your own mouth, and this day you have fulfilled it with your own hand.[j] **16** And now, O Jehovah the God of Israel, keep the promise you made to your servant David my father when you said: 'There will never fail to be a man of your line before me to sit on the throne of Israel, if only your sons will pay attention to their way by walking in my law,[k] just as you have walked before me.'[l] **17** And now, O Jehovah the God

---

6:13 *Or "enclosure." *A cubit equaled 44.5 cm (17.5 in.). See App. B14.

of Israel, let the promise that you made to your servant David prove trustworthy.

18 "But will God really dwell with mankind on the earth?[a] Look! The heavens, yes, the heaven of the heavens, cannot contain you;[b] how much less, then, this house that I have built![c] **19** Now pay attention to the prayer of your servant and to his request for favor, O Jehovah my God, and listen to the cry for help and to the prayer that your servant is praying before you. **20** May your eyes be open toward this house day and night, toward the place where you said that you would put your name,[d] to listen to the prayer that your servant prays toward this place. **21** And listen to your servant's pleas for help and to the pleas of your people Israel when they pray toward this place,[e] and may you hear from your dwelling place, from the heavens;[f] yes, may you hear and forgive.[g]

22 "If a man sins against his fellow man and is made to take an oath* and is brought under liability to the oath,# and while under the oath# he comes before your altar in this house,[h] **23** may you then hear from the heavens and act and judge your servants by paying back the wicked one and bringing what he did on his own head[i] and by pronouncing the righteous one innocent* and rewarding him according to his own righteousness.[j]

24 "And if your people Israel are defeated by an enemy because they kept sinning against you,[k] and they return and glo-

---

6:22 *Or "and the latter lays a curs-ing on him." That is, an oath that carried with it a curse as its penal-ty if sworn falsely or violated. #Lit., "curse." 6:23 *Lit., "righteous."

CHAP. 6
a Ac 7:48
b 2Ch 2:6
  Isa 40:12
  Ac 17:24
c 1Ki 8:27-30
  Isa 66:1
d De 26:2
e Da 6:10
f 2Ki 19:20
  2Ch 30:27
g 2Ch 7:12-14
  Mic 7:18
h 1Ki 8:31, 32
i Job 34:11
j Isa 3:10, 11
  Eze 18:20
k Le 26:14, 17
  Jos 7:8, 11
  Jg 2:14

Second Col.
a Da 9:3, 19
b Ezr 9:5
c 1Ki 8:33, 34
d Isa 57:15
e Ps 106:47
f Le 26:19
  De 28:23
g Eze 14:13
h 1Ki 8:35, 36
i Isa 30:20, 21
  Isa 54:13
j 1Ki 18:1
k Ru 1:1
  2Ki 6:25
l Le 26:14, 16
  De 28:21, 22
m Am 4:9
  Hag 2:17
n De 28:38
  Joe 1:4
o 2Ch 12:2
  2Ch 32:1
p 1Ki 8:37-40
q 2Ch 20:5, 6
r 2Ch 33:13
s Pr 14:10
t Da 6:10
u Isa 63:15
v Ps 130:4
w 1Sa 16:7
  1Ch 28:9
  Jer 11:20
  Jer 17:10

rify your name[a] and pray[b] and beg for favor before you in this house,[c] **25** may you then hear from the heavens[d] and forgive the sin of your people Israel and bring them back to the land that you gave to them and their fore-fathers.[e]

26 "When the heavens are shut up and there is no rain[f] because they kept sinning against you,[g] and they pray toward this place and glorify your name and turn back from their sin because you humbled* them,[h] **27** may you then hear from the heavens and forgive the sin of your servants, of your people Israel, for you will instruct them about the good way in which they should walk;[i] and bring rain[j] on your land that you gave to your people as an inheritance.

28 "If a famine occurs in the land,[k] or a pestilence,[l] a scorch-ing blight, mildew,[m] swarming lo-custs, or voracious locusts*[n] or if their enemies besiege them in any of the cities of the land#[o] or if any other sort of plague or disease occurs,[p] **29** what-ever request,[q] whatever request for favor[r] may be made by any man or by all your people Isra-el (for each one knows his own plague and his own pain)[s] when they spread out their hands to-ward this house,[t] **30** then may you hear from the heavens, your dwelling place,[u] and may you forgive;[v] and reward each one according to all his ways, for you know his heart (you alone truly know the human heart),[w] **31** so that they may fear you by walk-ing in your ways all the days they live on the land that you gave to our forefathers.

32 "Also concerning the for-eigner who is not part of your

6:26 *Or "afflicted." 6:28 *Or "grass-hoppers." #Lit., "in the land of his gates."

people Israel and who comes from a distant land because of your great name*[a] and your mighty hand and your outstretched arm, and he comes and prays toward this house,[b] **33** may you then listen from the heavens, your dwelling place, and do all that the foreigner asks of you, so that all the peoples of the earth may know your name[c] and fear you, as your people Israel do, and may know that your name has been called on this house that I have built.

34 "If your people go to war against their enemies in the way that you send them[d] and they pray[e] to you in the direction of this city that you have chosen and toward the house that I have built for your name,[f] **35** then hear from the heavens their prayer and their request for favor and execute judgment for them.[g]

36 "If they sin against you (for there is no man who does not sin),[h] and you are furious with them and you abandon them to an enemy, and their captors carry them off captive to a land, far or near,[i] **37** and they come to their senses in the land where they were carried off captive, and they return to you and beg you for favor in the land where they are captives, saying, 'We have sinned and done wrong; we have acted wickedly,'[j] **38** and they return to you with all their heart[k] and all their soul* in the land of their captivity[l] where they were carried off captive, and they pray in the direction of their land that you gave to their forefathers and the city that you have chosen[m] and the house that I have built for your name, **39** then hear from the heavens, your dwelling

place, their prayer and their request for favor, and execute judgment for them[a] and forgive your people who have sinned against you.

40 "Now, O my God, please, may your eyes be opened and your ears attentive to the prayer offered in* this place.[b] **41** And now go up, O Jehovah God, to your resting-place,[c] you and the Ark of your strength. Let your priests, O Jehovah God, be clothed with salvation, and let your loyal ones rejoice in your goodness.[d] **42** O Jehovah God, do not reject* your anointed one.[e] May you remember your loyal love to David your servant."[f]

7 Now as soon as Sol·o·mon had finished praying,[g] fire came down from the heavens[h] and consumed the burnt offering and the sacrifices, and Jehovah's glory filled the house.[i] **2** The priests were unable to enter the house of Jehovah because Jehovah's glory had filled the house of Jehovah.[j] **3** And all the people of Israel were looking on when the fire came down and the glory of Jehovah was upon the house, and they bowed low with their faces to the ground on the pavement and prostrated themselves and thanked Jehovah, "for he is good; his loyal love endures forever."

4 Now the king and all the people offered sacrifices before Jehovah.[k] **5** King Sol·o·mon offered the sacrifice of 22,000 cattle and 120,000 sheep. Thus the king and all the people inaugurated the house of the true God.[l] **6** The priests were standing at their posts of duty, as were the Levites who had the instruments used to accompany the song to

---

CHAP. 6

a Ex 12:48
　Ru 1:16
　2Ki 5:15
　Isa 56:6, 7
　Ac 8:27

b 1Ki 8:41-43

c Ps 22:27
　Ps 46:10

d Nu 31:2
　Jos 8:1
　Jg 1:1, 2
　1Sa 15:3

e 2Ch 14:11
　2Ch 20:5, 6

f 1Ki 8:44, 45

g Isa 37:36

h Ps 130:3
　Ec 7:20
　Ro 3:23

i Le 26:34
　1Ki 8:46-50

j Le 26:40
　Ezr 9:6
　Ne 1:6
　Ps 106:6
　Da 9:5

k 1Sa 7:3

l De 30:1-3
　Da 9:2, 3

m Da 6:10

Second Col.

a Jer 51:36, 37

b 2Ch 7:15
　2Ch 16:9
　Ps 65:2
　Isa 37:17

c 1Ch 28:2

d Ps 65:4
　Ps 132:8-10

e 1Ki 1:34
　Ps 18:50

f Ac 13:34

CHAP. 7

g 1Ki 8:54

h Le 9:24
　1Ch 21:26

i Ex 40:34, 35

j 1Ki 8:11

k 1Ki 8:62, 63

l Ezr 6:16

6:32 *Or "reputation." 6:38 *See Glossary.

6:40 *Or "respecting." 6:42 *Lit., "turn away the face of."

Jehovah.[a] (King David had made these instruments for giving thanks to Jehovah—"for his loyal love endures forever"—when David would offer praise with them.*) And the priests were loudly sounding the trumpets[b] in front of them, while all the Israelites were standing.

7 Then Sol'o·mon sanctified the middle of the courtyard that was before the house of Jehovah, for there he had to offer up the burnt offerings[c] and the fat pieces of the communion sacrifices, because the copper altar[d] that Sol'o·mon had made could not contain the burnt sacrifices, the grain offerings,[e] and the fat pieces.[f] 8 At that time Sol'o·mon held the festival for seven days[g] together with all Israel, a very great congregation from Le'bo-ha'math* down to the Wadi* of Egypt.[h] 9 But on the eighth day* they held a solemn assembly,[i] because they had held the inauguration of the altar for seven days and the festival for seven days. 10 Then on the 23rd day of the seventh month, he sent the people away to their homes rejoicing[j] and feeling glad of heart over the goodness that Jehovah had shown to David and Sol'o·mon and Israel his people.[k]

11 Thus Sol'o·mon finished the house of Jehovah and the house* of the king;[l] and everything that came into Sol'o·mon's heart to do regarding the house of Jehovah and his own house he accomplished successfully.[m] 12 Jehovah then appeared to Sol'o·mon[n] during the night and said to him: "I have heard your prayer, and I have chosen this place for myself as a house of sacrifice.[o] 13 When I shut up

the heavens and there is no rain and when I command the grasshoppers to devour the land and if I send a pestilence among my people, 14 if my people on whom my name has been called[a] humble themselves[b] and pray and seek my face and turn away from their evil ways,[c] then I will hear from the heavens and forgive their sin and heal their land.[d] 15 Now my eyes will be open and my ears attentive to prayer at this place.[e] 16 And now I have chosen and sanctified this house so that my name may be there permanently,[f] and my eyes and my heart will always be there.[g]

17 "And you, if you walk before me as your father David walked by doing everything I have commanded you, and you obey my regulations and my judgments,[h] 18 then I will establish the throne of your kingship,[i] just as I made a covenant with your father David,[j] saying, 'There will never fail to be a man of your line ruling over Israel.'[k] 19 But if you turn away and forsake my statutes and my commandments that I have put before you and you go and serve other gods and bow down to them,[l] 20 I will uproot Israel from my land that I have given them,[m] and this house that I have sanctified for my name I will cast out of my sight, and I will make it an object of scorn* and a cause for ridicule among all the peoples.[n] 21 And this house will become heaps of ruins. Everyone passing by it will stare in amazement[o] and will say, 'Why did Jehovah do that to this land and this house?'[p] 22 Then they will say, 'It was because they abandoned Jehovah[q] the God of their forefathers, who had brought them out of the land

CHAP. 7
a 1Ch 25:7
  2Ch 5:11, 12
b 2Ch 5:13
c Le 1:3
d 2Ch 4:1
e Le 2:1
f Le 4:8-10
  1Ki 8:64-66
g Le 23:34
  De 16:13
h Nu 34:2, 5, 8
i Le 23:36
j De 16:15
k 2Ch 6:41
l Ec 2:4
m 1Ki 9:1-3
n 2Ch 1:7
o De 12:5, 6
  Ps 78:68

Second Col.
a Isa 43:10
b Le 26:41
  2Ch 33:12, 13
c Isa 55:7
d 2Ch 6:39
e 2Ch 6:40
f De 12:21
g 2Ch 6:20
h 1Ki 9:4, 5
i 2Sa 7:12, 13
j Ps 89:28, 29
k 1Ki 2:4
l Ex 20:5
  1Ki 9:6-9
m De 4:25, 26
  2Ki 17:20
n De 28:37
  Jer 24:9
o 2Ch 29:8
  Da 9:12
p De 29:24, 25
  2Ki 25:8, 9
  Jer 22:8, 9
q 2Ch 15:2

7:6 *Possibly referring to the Levites. 7:8 *Or "the entrance of Hamath." # See Glossary. 7:9 *The day after the festival, or the 15th day. 7:11 *Or "palace."

7:20 *Lit., "a proverb."

of Egypt,[a] and they embraced other gods and bowed down to them and served them.[b] That is why he brought all this calamity on them.'"[c]

8 At the end of 20 years, during which Sol'o·mon built the house of Jehovah and his own house,*[d] **2** Sol'o·mon rebuilt the cities that Hi'ram[e] had given Sol'o·mon and settled Israelites* there. **3** Furthermore, Sol'o·mon went to Ha'math-zo'bah and captured it. **4** Then he built up* Tad'mor in the wilderness and all the storage cities[f] that he had built in Ha'math.[g] **5** He also built up Upper Beth-ho'ron[h] and Lower Beth-ho'ron,[i] fortified cities with walls, gates, and bars, **6** and Ba'al·ath[j] as well as all of Sol'o·mon's storage cities, all the chariot cities,[k] the cities for the horsemen, and whatever Sol'o·mon desired to build in Jerusalem, in Leb'a·non, and in all the land of his dominion.

7 As for all the people who were left from the Hit'tites, the Am'or·ites, the Per'iz·zites, the Hi'vites, and the Jeb'u·sites,[l] who were not part of Israel,[m] **8** their descendants who were left in the land—those whom the Israelites had not exterminated[n]—were conscripted by Sol'o·mon for forced labor until this day.[o] **9** But Sol'o·mon did not make any of the Israelites slaves for his work,[p] for they were his warriors, the chiefs of his adjutants, and the chiefs of his charioteers and horsemen.[q] **10** There were 250 chiefs of the deputies of King Sol'o·mon, the foremen over the people.[r]

11 Sol'o·mon also brought Phar'aoh's daughter[s] up from the City of David to the house that he had built for her,[t] for

he said: "Although she is my wife, she should not dwell in the house of King David of Israel, for the places to which the Ark of Jehovah has come are holy."[a]

12 Then Sol'o·mon offered up burnt sacrifices[b] to Jehovah on the altar[c] of Jehovah that he had built in front of the porch.[d] **13** He followed the daily routine and made offerings according to the commandment of Moses for the Sabbaths,[e] the new moons,[f] and the appointed festivals three times in the year[g]—the Festival of Unleavened Bread,[h] the Festival of Weeks,[i] and the Festival of Booths.*[j] **14** Further, he appointed the divisions of the priests[k] for their services according to the rule of his father David, and the Levites for their posts of duty, to praise[l] and to minister in the presence of the priests according to the daily routine, and the gatekeepers in their divisions for the different gates,[m] for such was the commandment of David, the man of the true God. **15** And they did not deviate from the king's commandment to the priests and the Levites concerning any matter or concerning the storehouses. **16** So Sol'o·mon's work was all well-organized,* from the day the foundation of the house of Jehovah was laid[n] until it was finished. So the house of Jehovah was completed.[o]

17 It was then that Sol'o·mon went to E'zi·on-ge'ber[p] and to E'loth[q] on the seashore in the land of E'dom.[r] **18** Hi'ram[s] sent him ships and experienced seamen by means of his own servants. They went with Sol'o·mon's servants to O'phir[t] and took from there 450 talents* of

---

CHAP. 7
a Ex 12:51
b Isa 2:8
  Jer 2:11
c 2Ch 36:17

CHAP. 8
d 1Ki 6:37, 38
  1Ki 7:1
  1Ki 9:10
e 1Ki 5:1
f 1Ki 9:17-19
g 2Ki 14:28
h Jos 16:5
i Jos 16:1, 3
  1Ch 7:24
j Jos 19:44, 48
k 1Ki 4:26
l Ge 15:18-21
  Nu 13:29
m 1Ki 9:20-23
n Jos 15:63
  Jos 17:12
o Jos 16:10
  2Ch 2:17, 18
p Le 25:39
q 1Sa 8:11, 12
r 1Ki 5:16
  1Ki 9:23
  2Ch 2:18
s 1Ki 3:1
t 1Ki 7:8
  1Ki 9:24

Second Col.
a Ex 29:43
b Le 1:3
c 2Ch 4:1
d 1Ki 6:3
e Nu 28:9
f Nu 28:11-15
g De 16:16
h Le 23:6
i Le 23:15, 16
j Le 23:34
k 1Ch 24:1
l 1Ch 6:31, 32
  1Ch 15:16
  1Ch 16:37, 42
  1Ch 25:1
m 1Ch 26:1
n 1Ki 6:1
o 1Ki 7:51
p Nu 33:1, 35
  1Ki 22:48
q De 2:8
  2Ki 14:21, 22
  2Ki 16:6
r 1Ki 9:26-28
s 2Sa 5:11
t 1Ki 22:48
  Ps 45:9

8:13 *Or "Temporary Shelters." 8:16 *Or "well-arranged; completed." 8:18 *A talent equaled 34.2 kg (1,101 oz t). See App. B14.

8:1 *Or "palace." 8:2 *Lit., "sons of Israel." 8:4 *Or "rebuilt."

gold[a] and brought it to King Sol'o·mon.[b]

9 Now the queen of She'ba[c] heard the report about Sol'o·mon, so she came to Jerusalem to test Sol'o·mon with perplexing questions.* She was accompanied by a very impressive entourage,[d] with camels carrying balsam oil and great quantities of gold[d] and precious stones. She went in to Sol'o·mon and spoke to him about everything that was close to her heart.[e] **2** Sol'o·mon then answered all her questions. There was nothing too difficult for* Sol'o·mon to explain to her.

3 When the queen of She'ba had seen Sol'o·mon's wisdom,[f] the house that he built,[g] **4** the food of his table,[h] the seating of his servants, the table service of his waiters and their attire, his cupbearers and their attire, and his burnt sacrifices that he regularly offered up at the house of Jehovah,[i] she was left completely breathless.* **5** So she said to the king: "The report that I heard in my own land about your achievements* and about your wisdom was true. **6** But I did not put faith in the reports until I had come and had seen it with my own eyes.[j] And look! I had not been told the half of your great wisdom.[k] You have far surpassed the report that I heard.[l] **7** Happy are your men, and happy are your servants who stand before you constantly, listening to your wisdom! **8** May Jehovah your God be praised, who has taken pleasure in you by putting you on his throne as king for Jehovah your God. Because your God loves Israel,[m] in order to make it continue forever, he appointed you

over it as king to administer justice and righteousness."

9 Then she gave the king 120 talents* of gold[a] and a great quantity of balsam oil and precious stones. Never again was such balsam oil brought in as what the queen of She'ba gave to King Sol'o·mon.[b]

10 Moreover, the servants of Hi'ram and the servants of Sol'o·mon who brought gold from O'phir[c] also brought algum timbers and precious stones.[d] **11** The king made from the algum timbers stairs for the house of Jehovah[e] and for the king's house,*[f] as well as harps and stringed instruments for the singers.[g] Nothing like them had ever been seen before in the land of Judah.

12 King Sol'o·mon also gave the queen of She'ba whatever she desired and asked for, more than* what she had brought to the king. Then she left and returned to her own land, together with her servants.[h]

13 And the weight of the gold that came to Sol'o·mon in one year amounted to 666 talents of gold,[i] **14** besides that brought in by the merchants and the traders and all the kings of the Arabs and the governors of the land who were bringing gold and silver in to Sol'o·mon.[j]

15 King Sol'o·mon made 200 large shields of alloyed gold[k] (600 shekels* of alloyed gold went on each shield)[l] **16** and 300 bucklers* of alloyed gold (three mi'nas* of gold went on each

---

CHAP. 8
a 1Ki 10:22

b Ec 2:8

CHAP. 9
c Mt 12:42
Lu 11:31

d Ps 72:15

e 1Ki 10:1-3

f 1Ki 3:28
Ec 12:9

g 1Ki 10:4-9

h 1Ki 4:22, 23

i 2Ch 8:12, 13

j Lu 11:31

k Ec 1:16

l 1Ki 4:31, 34
2Ch 1:11, 12

m 2Ch 2:11

__Second Col.__
a Ps 72:10

b 1Ki 10:10

c 1Ki 9:27, 28
1Ki 10:22
2Ch 8:18

d 1Ki 10:11, 12

e 1Ki 6:8

f 1Ki 7:1

g 1Ch 25:1
Ps 92:3

h 1Ki 10:13

i 1Ki 10:14, 15
2Ch 1:15
Ps 68:29
Ps 72:15

j Ps 72:10

k 2Ch 12:9

l 1Ki 10:16, 17

9:1 *Or "with riddles." *Or "train." **9:2** *Lit., "nothing hidden from." **9:4** *Lit., "there was no more spirit in her." **9:5** *Or "words."

9:9 *A talent equaled 34.2 kg (1,101 oz t). See App. B14. **9:11** *Or "palace." **9:12** *Or possibly, "in addition to gifts corresponding to the value of." **9:15** *A shekel equaled 11.4 g (0.367 oz t). See App. B14. **9:16** *A small shield, often carried by archers. *A mina in the Hebrew Scriptures equaled 570 g (18.35 oz t). See App. B14.

buckler). Then the king put them in the House of the Forest of Leb'a·non.[a]

17 The king also made a great ivory throne and overlaid it with pure gold.[b] **18** There were six steps to the throne, and there was a gold footstool attached to the throne, and there were armrests on both sides of the seat, and two lions[c] were standing beside the armrests. **19** And there were 12 lions[d] standing on the six steps, one at each end of the six steps. No other kingdom had made anything like it. **20** All the drinking vessels of King Sol'o·mon were of gold, and all the utensils of the House of the Forest of Leb'a·non were of pure gold. There was nothing made of silver, for silver was considered as nothing in the days of Sol'o·mon.[e] **21** For the king's ships would go to Tar'shish[f] with the servants of Hi'ram.[g] Once every three years, the ships of Tar'shish would come loaded with gold and silver, ivory,[h] apes, and peacocks.

22 So King Sol'o·mon was greater than all the other kings of the earth in riches and wisdom.[i] **23** And the kings of all the earth sought an audience with* Sol'o·mon to hear his wisdom that the true God had put in his heart.[j] **24** They would each bring a gift—articles of silver, articles of gold, garments,[k] armor, balsam oil, horses, and mules—and this continued year after year. **25** And Sol'o·mon had 4,000 stalls for his horses and chariots and 12,000 horses,*[l] and he kept them stationed in the chariot cities and close by the king in Jerusalem.[m] **26** And he ruled over all the kings from the River* to the land of the Phi·lis'tines and to the boundary of

Egypt.[a] **27** The king made the silver in Jerusalem as plentiful as the stones, and cedarwood as plentiful as the sycamore trees in the She·phe'lah.[b] **28** And they would bring horses to Sol'o·mon from Egypt[c] and from all the other lands.

29 As for the rest of the history of Sol'o·mon,[d] from beginning to end, is it not written among the words of Nathan[e] the prophet, in the prophecy of A·hi'jah[f] the Shi'lo·nite, and in the record of visions of Id'do[g] the visionary concerning Jer·o·bo'am[h] the son of Ne'bat? **30** Sol'o·mon reigned in Jerusalem over all Israel for 40 years. **31** Then Sol'o·mon was laid to rest with his forefathers. So they buried him in the City of David his father;[i] and his son Re·ho·bo'am became king in his place.

10 Re·ho·bo'am went to She'chem,[k] for all Israel had come to She'chem to make him king.[l] **2** As soon as Jer·o·bo'am[m] the son of Ne'bat heard of it (he was still in Egypt because he had fled on account of King Sol'o·mon),[n] Jer·o·bo'am came back from Egypt. **3** Then they sent for him, and Jer·o·bo'am and all Israel came to Re·ho·bo'am and said: **4** "Your father made our yoke harsh.[o] But if you make the harsh service of your father easier and you lighten the heavy* yoke he put on us, we will serve you."

5 At this he said to them: "Return to me after three days." So the people went away.[p] **6** King Re·ho·bo'am then consulted with the older men* who had served his father Sol'o·mon while he was alive, saying: "What advice would you give on how to reply to this people?" **7** They answered him: "If you are good to this people

---

CHAP. 9
a 1Ki 7:2
b 1Ki 10:18-20
c Ge 49:9
d Nu 23:24
e 1Ki 10:21, 22
  1Ki 10:27
f Ps 72:10
  Jon 1:3
g 1Ki 9:27
h 1Ki 10:18
i 1Ki 3:12, 13
  1Ki 4:29
  1Ki 10:23-25
j 1Ki 3:28
  1Ki 4:34
  2Ch 1:12
  Pr 2:6
k Mt 6:29
l De 17:16
  1Ki 4:26
m 1Ki 10:26

Second Col.
a 1Ki 4:21
b 1Ki 10:27
  1Ch 27:28
c 1Ki 10:28
  2Ch 1:16
d 1Ki 11:41-43
e 2Sa 7:2
  2Sa 12:1
  1Ki 1:8
  1Ch 29:29
f 1Ki 11:30, 31
  1Ki 14:2
  1Ki 14:6, 10
g 2Ch 12:15
  2Ch 13:22
h 1Ki 11:26
i 2Sa 5:9
  1Ki 2:10
j 1Ki 14:21

CHAP. 10
k Jos 20:7
  Jos 24:1
  Jg 9:1
l 1Ki 12:1-4
m 1Ki 11:28
n 1Ki 11:40
o 1Sa 8:11-18
  1Ki 4:7
p 1Ki 12:5-7

9:23 *Lit., "sought the face of." 9:25 *Or "horsemen." 9:26 *That is, the Euphrates.

10:4 *Or "oppressive." 10:6 *Or "the elders."

and please them and give them a favorable answer, they will always be your servants."

8 However, he rejected the advice that the older men* gave him, and he consulted with the young men who had grown up with him and who were now his attendants.[a] **9** He asked them: "What advice do you offer on how we should reply to this people who have said to me, 'Make the yoke your father put on us lighter'?" **10** The young men who had grown up with him said to him: "This is what you should say to the people who have said to you, 'Your father made our yoke heavy, but you should make it lighter for us'; this is what you should tell them, 'My little finger will be thicker than my father's hips. **11** My father imposed a heavy yoke on you, but I will add to your yoke. My father punished you with whips, but I will do so with scourges.'"

12 Jer·o·bo'am and all the people came to Re·ho·bo'am on the third day, just as the king had said: "Return to me on the third day."[b] **13** But the king answered them harshly. Thus King Re·ho·bo'am rejected the advice of the older men.* **14** He spoke to them according to the advice of the young men, saying: "I will make your yoke heavier, and I will add to it. My father punished you with whips, but I will do so with scourges." **15** So the king did not listen to the people, for this turn of events was caused by the true God,[c] in order to carry out the word that Jehovah had spoken through A·hi'jah[d] the Shi'lo·nite to Jer·o·bo'am the son of Ne'bat.

16 As for all Israel, because the king refused to listen to them, the people replied to the king: "What share do we have in

David? We have no inheritance in the son of Jes'se. Each one to your gods, O Israel! Now look after your own house, O David."[a] With that all Israel returned to their homes.*[b]

17 But Re·ho·bo'am continued to reign over the Israelites living in the cities of Judah.[c]

18 Then King Re·ho·bo'am sent Ha·do'ram,[d] who was in charge of those conscripted for forced labor, but the Israelites stoned him to death. King Re·ho·bo'am managed to mount his chariot to flee to Jerusalem.[e] **19** And the Israelites have been in revolt against the house of David down to this day.

11 When Re·ho·bo'am arrived in Jerusalem, he immediately congregated the house of Judah and Benjamin,[f] 180,000 trained* warriors, to fight against Israel in order to restore the kingdom to Re·ho·bo'am.[g] **2** Then the word of Jehovah came to She·mai'ah[h] the man of the true God, saying: **3** "Say to Re·ho·bo'am the son of Sol'o·mon the king of Judah and to all Israel in Judah and Benjamin, **4** 'This is what Jehovah says: "You must not go up and fight against your brothers. Each of you return to his house, for I have caused this to happen."'"[i] So they obeyed the word of Jehovah and returned and did not go against Jer·o·bo'am.

5 Re·ho·bo'am lived in Jerusalem and built fortified cities in Judah. **6** Thus he built up* Beth'le·hem,[j] E'tam, Te·ko'a,[k] **7** Beth-zur, So'co,[l] A·dul'lam,[m] **8** Gath,[n] Ma·re'shah, Ziph,[o] **9** Ad·o·ra'im, La'chish,[p] A·ze'kah,[q] **10** Zo'rah, Ai'ja·lon,[r] and He'bron,[s] fortified cities that were in Judah and Benjamin. **11** Further, he reinforced the

---

CHAP. 10
a 1Ki 12:8-11
b 1Ki 12:12-15
c De 2:30 2Sa 17:14
d 1Ki 11:29-31

Second Col.
a 1Ki 11:32
b 1Ki 12:16, 17
c 1Ki 11:35, 36
d 2Sa 20:24 1Ki 4:6
e 1Ki 12:18, 19

CHAP. 11
f Ge 49:27 2Ch 14:8
g 1Ki 12:21-24
h 2Ch 12:15
i 1Ki 11:31 2Ch 10:15
j Ge 35:19 Mt 2:1
k Am 1:1
l 2Ch 28:18
m 1Sa 22:1
n 1Ch 18:1
o 1Sa 23:14
p 2Ch 32:9
q Jos 10:10 Jer 34:7
r Jos 19:42, 48
s Jos 14:14, 15 2Sa 2:1

10:8, 13 *Or "the elders."

10:16 *Lit., "tents." **11:1** *Lit., "chosen." **11:6** *Or "fortified."

fortified places and put commanders in them and supplied them with food and oil and wine, **12** and he supplied all the different cities with large shields and lances; he reinforced them to a very great degree. And Judah and Benjamin remained his.

13 And the priests and the Levites who were in all Israel took their stand with him, coming out of all their territories. **14** The Levites left their pastures and their possession[a] and came to Judah and Jerusalem, because Jer·o·bo'am and his sons had dismissed them from serving as priests to Jehovah.[b] **15** Jer·o·bo'am then appointed his own priests for the high places[c] and for the goatlike demons*[d] and for the calves that he had made.[e] **16** And those from all the tribes of Israel who had their heart set on seeking Jehovah the God of Israel followed them to Jerusalem to sacrifice to Jehovah the God of their forefathers.[f] **17** For three years they strengthened the kingship of Judah and supported Re·ho·bo'am the son of Sol'o·mon, for they walked in the way of David and Sol'o·mon for three years.

18 Then Re·ho·bo'am took as his wife Ma'ha·lath the daughter of David's son Jer'i·moth and of Ab'i·ha·il the daughter of Jes'se's son E·li'ab.[g] **19** In time she bore him sons: Je'ush, Shem·a·ri'ah, and Za'ham. **20** After her, he married Ma'a·cah the granddaughter of Ab'sa·lom.[h] In time she bore him A·bi'jah,[i] At'tai, Zi'za, and She·lo'mith. **21** Re·ho·bo'am loved Ma'a·cah the granddaughter of Ab'sa·lom more than all his other wives and concubines,[j] for he took 18 wives and 60 concubines, and he became father to 28 sons and 60 daugh-

ters. **22** So Re·ho·bo'am appointed A·bi'jah the son of Ma'a·cah as head and leader among his brothers, for he intended to make him king. **23** However, he acted with understanding and sent* some of his sons to all the regions of Judah and Benjamin, to all the fortified cities,[a] and gave them abundant provisions and acquired many wives for them.

12 Soon after the kingship of Re·ho·bo'am was firmly established[b] and he had become strong, he abandoned the Law of Jehovah,[c] and also all Israel with him. **2** In the fifth year of King Re·ho·bo'am, King Shi'shak[d] of Egypt came up against Jerusalem, for they had behaved unfaithfully toward Jehovah. **3** He had 1,200 chariots, 60,000 horsemen, and countless troops who came with him from Egypt—Lib'y·ans, Suk'ki·im, and E·thi·o'pi·ans.[e] **4** He captured the fortified cities of Judah and finally reached Jerusalem.

5 She·mai'ah[f] the prophet came to Re·ho·bo'am and the princes of Judah who had gathered at Jerusalem because of Shi'shak, and he said to them: "This is what Jehovah says, 'You have abandoned me, so I have also abandoned you[g] to the hand of Shi'shak.'" **6** At that the princes of Israel and the king humbled themselves[h] and said: "Jehovah is righteous." **7** When Jehovah saw that they had humbled themselves, the word of Jehovah came to She·mai'ah, saying: "They have humbled themselves. I will not destroy them,[i] and in a little while I will rescue them. I will not pour out my wrath on Jerusalem through Shi'shak. **8** But they will become his servants, so that they will know the difference

---

CHAP. 11
a Nu 35:2, 3

b 1Ki 12:31, 32

c 1Ki 13:33

d Le 17:7

e 1Ki 12:26, 28

f De 12:11
1Ch 22:1
2Ch 15:8, 9
2Ch 30:10, 11

g 1Sa 16:6
1Sa 17:13

h 2Sa 13:1
2Sa 18:33

i 1Ki 15:1
2Ch 12:16
Mt 1:7

j De 17:17

Second Col.
a 2Ch 11:5, 11

CHAP. 12
b 2Ch 11:17

c De 32:15
2Ch 26:11, 16

d 1Ki 11:40
1Ki 14:25

e Na 3:9

f 1Ki 12:22-24

g De 28:15
2Ch 15:2

h 2Ch 33:10, 12

i 1Ki 21:29
2Ch 34:26, 27

11:15 *Lit., "the goats."

11:23 *Or "dispersed."

between serving me and serving the kings* of other lands."

9 So King Shi′shak of Egypt came up against Jerusalem. He took the treasures of the house of Jehovah[a] and the treasures of the king's house.* He took everything, including the gold shields that Sol′o·mon had made.[b] **10** So King Re·ho·bo′am made copper shields to replace them, and he entrusted them to the chiefs of the guard,* who guarded the entrance of the king's house. **11** Whenever the king came to the house of Jehovah, the guards would come in and carry them, and then they would return them to the guard chamber. **12** Because the king humbled himself, Jehovah's anger turned away from him,[c] and he did not destroy them completely.[d] Moreover, there were some good things found in Judah.[e]

13 King Re·ho·bo′am strengthened his position in Jerusalem and continued to reign; Re·ho·bo′am was 41 years old when he became king, and he reigned for 17 years in Jerusalem, the city that Jehovah had chosen out of all the tribes of Israel as the place to put his name. The name of the king's mother was Na′a·mah the Am′mon·it·ess.[f] **14** But he did what was bad, for he had not resolved in his heart to search for Jehovah.[g]

15 As for Re·ho·bo′am's history, from beginning to end, is it not written among the words of She·mai′ah[h] the prophet and of Id′do[i] the visionary in the genealogical record? And there were constant wars between Re·ho·bo′am and Jer·o·bo′am.[j] **16** Then Re·ho·bo′am was laid to rest with his forefathers and was buried in the City of David;[k] and

his son A·bi′jah[a] became king in his place.

13 In the 18th year of King Jer·o·bo′am, A·bi′jah became king over Judah.[b] **2** He reigned for three years in Jerusalem. His mother's name was Mi·cai′ah[c] the daughter of U·ri′el of Gib′e·ah.[d] And there was war between A·bi′jah and Jer·o·bo′am.[e]

3 So A·bi′jah went to war with an army of 400,000 mighty, trained* warriors.[f] And Jer·o·bo′am drew up in battle formation against him with 800,000 trained* men, mighty warriors. **4** A·bi′jah now stood on Mount Zem·a·ra′im, which is in the mountainous region of E′phra·im, and said: "Hear me, O Jer·o·bo′am and all Israel. **5** Do you not know that Jehovah the God of Israel gave to David a kingdom over Israel forever,[g] to him and to his sons,[h] by a covenant of salt?*[i] **6** But Jer·o·bo′am[j] the son of Ne′bat, the servant of David's son Sol′o·mon, rose up and rebelled against his lord.[k] **7** And idle, worthless men kept gathering to him. And they proved superior to Re·ho·bo′am the son of Sol′o·mon when Re·ho·bo′am was young and fainthearted, and he could not hold his own against them.

8 "And now you think you can hold your own against the kingdom of Jehovah in the hand of the sons of David because you are a large crowd and you have the golden calves that Jer·o·bo′am made as gods for you.[l] **9** Have you not driven out Jehovah's priests,[m] the descendants of Aaron, and the Levites, and have you not appointed your own priests just like the peoples of the other lands?[n] Anyone who came along

---

CHAP. 12

a 1Ki 7:51

b 1Ki 10:16, 17
 1Ki 14:25-28

c 2Ch 33:10, 12

d La 3:22

e Ge 18:23-25
 1Ki 14:1, 13
 2Ch 19:2, 3

f De 23:3
 1Ki 11:1
 1Ki 14:21

g 1Sa 7:3
 1Ki 18:21
 Mr 12:30

h 1Ki 12:22-24

i 2Ch 9:29
 2Ch 13:22

j 1Ki 14:30, 31

k 2Sa 5:9

Second Col.

a Mt 1:7

CHAP. 13

b 1Ki 15:1, 2

c 2Ch 11:20, 21

d Jos 18:28
 1Sa 10:26

e 1Ki 15:6

f 2Ch 11:1

g Ge 49:10
 2Sa 7:8
 Ps 78:70, 71

h 2Sa 7:12, 13
 1Ch 17:11, 14
 Lu 1:32

i Ps 89:28, 29

j 2Ch 10:2

k 1Ki 11:26, 27
 1Ki 12:20

l 1Ki 12:26, 28
 2Ch 11:15

m 2Ch 11:14

n 1Ki 12:31, 33
 1Ki 13:33

12:8 *Lit., "kingdoms." 12:9 *Or "palace." 12:10 *Lit., "runners."

13:3 *Lit., "chosen." 13:5 *That is, a permanent and unchanging covenant.

with* a young bull and seven rams could become a priest of what are not gods. **10** As for us, Jehovah is our God,[a] and we have not abandoned him; our priests, the descendants of Aaron, are ministering to Jehovah, and the Levites assist in the work. **11** They are making burnt offerings smoke to Jehovah each morning and each evening[b] along with perfumed incense,[c] and the layer bread*[d] is on the table of pure gold, and they light up the golden lampstand[e] and its lamps each evening,[f] because we are caring for our responsibility to Jehovah our God; but you have abandoned him. **12** Now look! the true God is with us, leading us, with his priests and the signal trumpets for sounding the battle alarm against you. O men of Israel, do not fight against Jehovah the God of your forefathers, for you will not be successful."[g]

13 But Jer·o·bo'am dispatched an ambush to come from behind them, so that they were in front of Judah and the ambush was behind them. **14** When the men of Judah turned around, they saw that they had to fight the battle both in front and from behind. So they began to cry out to Jehovah,[h] while the priests were loudly sounding the trumpets. **15** The men of Judah broke out in a war cry, and when the men of Judah shouted the war cry, the true God defeated Jer·o·bo'am and all Israel before A·bi'jah and Judah. **16** The Israelites fled before Judah, and God gave them into their hand. **17** A·bi'jah and his people inflicted a great slaughter on them, and the slain of Israel kept falling, 500,000 trained*

men. **18** Thus the men of Israel were humbled at that time, but the men of Judah proved superior because they relied* on Jehovah the God of their forefathers.[a] **19** A·bi'jah kept chasing after Jer·o·bo'am and captured cities from him, Beth'el[b] and its dependent* towns, Jesh'a·nah and its dependent towns, and E'phra·in[c] and its dependent towns. **20** And Jer·o·bo'am never regained his power during the time of A·bi'jah; then Jehovah struck him down and he died.[d]

21 But A·bi'jah grew in strength. In time he took 14 wives,[e] and he became father to 22 sons and 16 daughters. **22** And the rest of A·bi'jah's history, his deeds and his words, is recorded in the writings* of the prophet Id'do.[f]

14 Then A·bi'jah was laid to rest with his forefathers, and they buried him in the City of David;[g] and his son A'sa became king in his place. In his days the land had rest for ten years.

2 A'sa did what was good and right in the eyes of Jehovah his God. **3** He removed the foreign altars[h] and the high places, smashed the sacred pillars,[i] and cut down the sacred poles.*[j] **4** Further, he told Judah to search for Jehovah the God of their forefathers and to observe the Law and the commandment. **5** So he removed from all the cities of Judah the high places and the incense stands,[k] and under him, the kingdom continued without disturbance. **6** He built fortified cities in Judah,[l] since the land had no disturbance and there was no war against him during these years, for Jehovah

---

CHAP. 13

a 2Ch 11:16

b Ex 29:39

c Ex 30:1

d Ex 25:30

e Ex 25:31

f Ex 27:20

g Nu 10:9

h 2Ch 14:11
  2Ch 18:31

Second Col.

a 2Ki 18:1, 5
  1Ch 5:20
  2Ch 16:8
  Ps 22:5
  Ps 37:5
  Na 1:7

b 1Ki 12:28, 29

c Joh 11:54

d 1Sa 25:38
  1Ki 14:20
  Ac 12:21-23

e De 17:17

f 2Ch 9:29
  2Ch 12:15

CHAP. 14

g 2Sa 5:9

h De 7:5

i Ex 23:24

j 1Ki 14:22, 23
  2Ki 18:1, 4

k 2Ch 34:1, 4

l 2Ch 11:5

13:9 *Lit., "came to fill his hand with." **13:11** *That is, the showbread. **13:17** *Lit., "chosen." **13:18** *Lit., "leaned." **13:19** *Or "surrounding." **13:22** *Or "exposition; commentary." **14:3** *See Glossary.

gave him rest.[a] **7** He said to Judah: "Let us build these cities and surround them with walls and towers,[b] gates* and bars. For the land is still at our disposal, because we have searched for Jehovah our God. We have searched, and he has given us rest all around." So their building was successful.[c]

8 A'sa had an army of 300,000 men from Judah, equipped with large shields and lances. And out of Benjamin were 280,000 mighty warriors who carried bucklers* and were armed with bows.*[d]

9 Later Ze'rah the E·thi·o'pi·an came against them with an army of 1,000,000 men and 300 chariots.[e] When he reached Ma·re'shah,[f] **10** A'sa went out against him and they drew up in battle formation in the Valley of Zeph'a·thah at Ma·re'shah. **11** A'sa then called to Jehovah his God[g] and said: "O Jehovah, it does not matter to you whether those you help are many or have no power.[h] Help us, O Jehovah our God, for we are relying* on you,[i] and in your name we have come against this crowd.[j] O Jehovah, you are our God. Do not let mortal man prevail against you."[k]

12 So Jehovah defeated the E·thi·o'pi·ans before A'sa and before Judah, and the E·thi·o'pi·ans fled.[l] **13** A'sa and the people with him pursued them as far as Ge'rar,[m] and the E·thi·o'pi·ans continued falling until not one of them was alive, for they were crushed by Jehovah and by his army. Afterward they carried off a very great deal of spoil. **14** Further, they struck all the cities around Ge'rar, for

the dread of Jehovah had come upon them; and they plundered all the cities, for there was much to plunder in them. **15** They also attacked the tents of those with livestock, and they captured a great number of flocks and camels, after which they returned to Jerusalem.

15 Now the spirit of God came upon Az·a·ri'ah the son of O'ded. **2** So he went out to meet A'sa and said to him: "Hear me, O A'sa and all Judah and Benjamin! Jehovah is with you as long as you remain with him;[a] and if you search for him, he will let himself be found by you,[b] but if you abandon him, he will abandon you.[c] **3** For a long time* Israel had been without the true God, without a priest teaching, and without law.[d] **4** But when in their distress they returned to Jehovah the God of Israel and searched for him, he let himself be found by them.[e] **5** In those times no one could travel safely,* for there was much unrest among all the inhabitants of the lands. **6** Nation was being crushed by nation and one city by another city, because God kept them in disorder with every sort of distress.[f] **7** But you, be strong and do not become discouraged,*[g] for your activity will be rewarded."

8 As soon as A'sa heard these words and the prophecy of O'ded the prophet, he took courage and removed the disgusting idols from all the land of Judah[h] and Benjamin and from the cities that he had captured from the mountainous region of E'phra·im, and he restored Jehovah's altar that was before the porch of

---

CHAP. 14
a 2Ch 15:15
  Pr 16:7

b 2Ch 32:2, 5

c Ps 127:1

d 2Ch 11:1, 12
  2Ch 13:3

e 2Ch 16:8

f Jos 15:20, 44
  2Ch 11:5, 8

g Ex 14:10
  1Ch 5:20
  2Ch 32:20

h Jg 7:7
  1Sa 14:6

i 2Ch 13:12
  2Ch 32:7, 8

j 1Sa 17:45
  Ps 20:5
  Pr 18:10

k Jos 7:9
  Ps 9:19

l De 28:7

m Ge 20:1

Second Col.

CHAP. 15
a Jas 4:8

b Isa 55:6

c 1Ch 28:9
  Heb 10:38

d De 33:8, 10
  2Ch 17:8, 9
  Mal 2:7

e Ps 106:43, 44
  Isa 55:7

f De 28:15, 48

g Jos 1:9
  1Ch 28:20

h 2Ki 23:24

14:7 *Lit., "double doors." 14:8 *A small shield, often carried by archers. *Lit., "and tread the bow." 14:11 *Lit., "we lean."

15:3 *Lit., "And many days." 15:5 *Lit., "there was no peace for the one going out or the one coming in." 15:7 *Lit., "do not let your hands drop."

Jehovah.[a] **9** And he gathered together all Judah and Benjamin and the foreign residents with them from E′phra·im and Ma·nas′seh and Sim′e·on,[b] for they had deserted to him from Israel in great number when they saw that Jehovah his God was with him. **10** So they were gathered together at Jerusalem in the third month of the 15th year of A′sa's reign. **11** On that day they sacrificed to Jehovah from the spoil they had brought, 700 cattle and 7,000 sheep. **12** Furthermore, they entered into a covenant to search for Jehovah the God of their forefathers with all their heart and with all their soul.*[c] **13** Whoever would not search for Jehovah the God of Israel was to be put to death, whether small or great, man or woman.[d] **14** So they took an oath to Jehovah with a loud voice, with joyful shouting, and with the trumpets and horns. **15** And all Judah rejoiced over the oath, for they had taken the oath with all their heart and they eagerly sought him and he let himself be found by them,[e] and Jehovah continued to give them rest on every side.[f]

16 A′sa the king even removed Ma′a·cah[g] his grandmother from her position as queen mother,* because she had made an obscene idol for the worship of the sacred pole.*[h] A′sa cut down her obscene idol and pulverized it and burned it in the Kid′ron Valley.[i] **17** But the high places were not removed[j] from Israel.[k] Nevertheless, A′sa's heart was complete* all his life.*[l] **18** And he brought the things that he and his father had made holy into the house of the true God—silver, gold, and vari-

ous utensils.[a] **19** There was no war until the 35th year of A′sa's reign.[b]

16 In the 36th year of the reign of A′sa, King Ba′a·sha[c] of Israel came up against Judah and began to build up* Ra′mah[d] to prevent anyone from going out or coming in to* King A′sa of Judah.[e] **2** At that A′sa brought out silver and gold from the treasuries of Jehovah's house[f] and the king's house* and sent them to King Ben-ha′dad of Syria,[g] who was dwelling in Damascus, saying: **3** "There is a treaty* between me and you and between my father and your father. I am sending you silver and gold. Come, break your treaty* with King Ba′a·sha of Israel, so that he will withdraw from me."

4 Ben-ha′dad listened to King A′sa and sent the chiefs of his armies against the cities of Israel, and they struck down I′jon,[h] Dan,[i] A′bel-ma′im, and all the storage places of the cities of Naph′ta·li.[j] **5** When Ba′a·sha heard of it, he immediately quit building* Ra′mah and abandoned his work on it. **6** King A′sa then took all Judah, and they carried off the stones and timbers of Ra′mah[k] that Ba′a·sha had been building with,[l] and with them he built up* Ge′ba[m] and Miz′pah.[n]

7 At that time Ha·na′ni[o] the seer came to King A′sa of Judah and said to him: "Because you relied* on the king of Syria and did not rely* on Jehovah your God, the army of the king of Syria has escaped out of your hand.[p] **8** Were not the E·thi·o′pi·ans and the Lib′y·ans a very great army with many chariots

CHAP. 15	
a	2Ch 8:12
b	2Ch 11:16
	2Ch 30:25
c	De 4:29
	2Ki 23:3
	Ne 10:28, 29
d	Ex 22:20
e	2Ch 15:2
f	Pr 16:7
g	1Ki 15:9, 10
h	De 13:6-9
i	1Ki 15:13, 14
j	1Ki 22:43
k	1Ki 14:22, 23
	2Ki 14:3, 4
	2Ki 23:19, 20
l	1Ki 8:61
Second Col.	
a	1Ki 7:51
	1Ki 15:15
	1Ch 26:26
b	2Ch 14:1
CHAP. 16	
c	1Ki 15:25, 27
d	Jos 18:21, 25
e	1Ki 15:17-19
f	1Ki 7:51
g	1Ki 20:1
	2Ki 12:18
	2Ki 16:8
h	2Ki 15:29
i	Jg 18:29
j	1Ki 15:20-22
k	Jos 18:21, 25
l	1Ki 15:17
m	Jos 18:21, 24
	1Ch 6:60, 64
n	Jos 18:21, 26
	Jg 20:1
o	1Ki 16:1
	2Ch 19:2
	2Ch 20:34
p	Jer 17:5

16:1 *Or "fortify; rebuild." #Or "leaving or entering the territory of." **16:2** *Or "palace." **16:3** *Or "covenant." **16:5** *Or "fortifying; rebuilding." **16:6** *Or "fortified; rebuilt." **16:7** *Lit., "leaned." #Lit., "lean."

15:12, 16 *See Glossary. **15:16** #Or "as lady." **15:17** *Or "completely devoted." #Lit., "days."

and horsemen? But because you relied on Jehovah, he gave them into your hand.[a] 9 For the eyes of Jehovah are roving about through all the earth[b] to show his strength* in behalf of those whose heart is complete toward# him.[c] You have acted foolishly in this matter; from now on there will be wars against you."[d]

10 However, A'sa became offended at the seer and put him in prison* because he was enraged at him over this. And A'sa began to mistreat others among the people at that same time. 11 Now the history of A'sa, from beginning to end, is written in the Book of the Kings of Judah and of Israel.[e]

12 In the 39th year of his reign, A'sa developed an ailment in his feet until he became very sick; and even in his sickness, he turned, not to Jehovah, but to the healers. 13 Then A'sa was laid to rest with his forefathers;[f] he died in the 41st year of his reign. 14 So they buried him in the grand burial place that he had excavated for himself in the City of David,[g] and they laid him on a bier that had been filled with balsam oil and different sorts of ingredients mixed into a specially made ointment.[h] Further, they made an extraordinarily great funeral burning for him.*

17 And his son Je·hosh'a·phat[i] became king in his place, and he strengthened his position over Israel. 2 He stationed military forces in all the fortified cities of Judah and put garrisons in the land of Judah and in the cities of E'phra·im that A'sa his father had

captured.[a] 3 Jehovah continued with Je·hosh'a·phat because he walked in the former ways of his forefather David[b] and did not search for the Ba'als. 4 For he searched for the God of his father[c] and followed* his commandment and not the practices of Israel.[d] 5 Jehovah kept the kingdom firmly established in his hand;[e] and all Judah continued to give gifts to Je·hosh'a·phat, and he had riches and glory in abundance.[f] 6 His heart became bold in the ways of Jehovah, and he even removed the high places[g] and the sacred poles*[h] from Judah.

7 In the third year of his reign he sent for his princes, Ben-ha'il, O·ba·di'ah, Zech·a·ri'-ah, Ne·than'el, and Mi·cai'ah, to teach in the cities of Judah. 8 There were Levites with them: She·mai'ah, Neth·a·ni'ah, Zeb·a·di'ah, As'a·hel, She·mir'a·moth, Je·hon'a·than, Ad·o·ni'jah, To·bi'jah, and Tob·ad·o·ni'jah, and along with them E'lish'a·ma and Je·ho'ram the priests.[i] 9 They began teaching in Judah, taking with them the book of Jehovah's Law,[j] and they went around through all the cities of Judah teaching among the people.

10 And the dread of Jehovah came upon all the kingdoms of the lands surrounding Judah, and they did not fight against Je·hosh'a·phat. 11 And the Phi·lis'tines brought to Je·hosh'a·phat gifts and money as tribute. The Arabs brought him 7,700 rams and 7,700 male goats from their flocks.

12 Je·hosh'a·phat grew greater and greater,[k] and he continued building fortified places[l] and storage cities[m] in Judah. 13 He carried out extensive projects in the cities of Judah, and

CHAP. 16
a 2Ch 14:9, 11
  Ps 37:39, 40

b Zec 4:10

c 1Pe 3:12

d 1Ki 15:32

e 1Ki 15:23

f 1Ki 15:24

g 2Sa 5:7

h Mr 16:1
  Lu 23:55, 56
  Joh 19:40

CHAP. 17
i 1Ki 15:24
  1Ki 22:41

Second Col.
a 2Ch 15:8

b 2Sa 8:15

c De 4:29
  2Ch 26:1, 5

d 1Ki 12:28-30
  1Ki 13:33

e 1Ki 9:4, 5
  Ps 132:12

f 2Ch 18:1

g 1Ki 22:42, 43

h De 7:5

i De 33:8, 10
  Mal 2:7

j De 31:11
  Jos 1:7, 8
  Ne 8:7

k 2Ch 18:1

l 2Ch 14:2, 6

m 1Ki 9:19
  2Ch 8:3, 4

16:9 *Or "support." #Or "completely devoted to." 16:10 *Lit., "in the house of the stocks." 16:14 *Evidently, not a cremation of Asa, but a burning of spices.

17:4 *Lit., "walked in." 17:6 *See Glossary.

he had soldiers, mighty warriors, in Jerusalem. **14** These were grouped by their paternal houses: of Judah the chiefs of thousands, Ad′nah the chief, and with him were 300,000 mighty warriors.[a] **15** And under his command was Je·ho·ha′nan the chief, and with him were 280,000. **16** And also under his command was Am·a·si′ah the son of Zich′ri, who volunteered for Jehovah's service, and with him were 200,000 mighty warriors. **17** And out of Benjamin[b] was E·li′a·da, a mighty warrior, and with him were 200,000 men equipped with the bow and shield.[c] **18** And under his command was Je·hoz′a·bad, and with him were 180,000 men equipped for the army. **19** These were ministering to the king in addition to those whom the king put in the fortified cities throughout all Judah.[d]

18 Je·hosh′a·phat had riches and glory in abundance,[e] but he made a marriage alliance with A′hab.[f] **2** So years later he went down to A′hab at Sa·mar′i·a,[g] and A′hab sacrificed sheep and cattle in abundance for him and for the people with him. And he urged* him to go up against Ra′moth-gil′e·ad.[h] **3** Then King A′hab of Israel said to King Je·hosh′a·phat of Judah: "Will you go with me to Ra′moth-gil′e·ad?" He replied to him: "I am the same as you, and my people are the same as your people and will support you in the war."

4 But Je·hosh′a·phat said to the king of Israel: "First inquire, please, for the word of Jehovah."[i] **5** So the king of Israel gathered the prophets together, 400 men, and said to them: "Should we go to war against Ra′moth-gil′e·ad, or should I re-

frain?" They said: "Go up, and the true God will give it into the king's hand."

6 Je·hosh′a·phat then said: "Is there not here a prophet of Jehovah?[a] Let us also inquire through him."[b] **7** At that the king of Israel said to Je·hosh′a·phat: "There is still one more man[c] through whom we can inquire of Jehovah; but I hate him, for he never prophesies good things concerning me, but always bad.[d] He is Mi·cai′ah the son of Im′lah." However, Je·hosh′a·phat said: "The king should not say such a thing."

8 So the king of Israel called a court official and said: "Bring Mi·cai′ah the son of Im′lah quickly."[e] **9** Now the king of Israel and Je·hosh′a·phat the king of Judah were each sitting on his throne, dressed in royal attire; they were sitting at the threshing floor at the entrance of the gate of Sa·mar′i·a, and all the prophets were prophesying before them. **10** Then Zed·e·ki′ah the son of Che·na′a·nah made for himself iron horns and said: "This is what Jehovah says, 'With these you will gore* the Syrians until you exterminate them.'" **11** All the other prophets were prophesying the same way, saying: "Go up to Ra′moth-gil′e·ad and you will be successful;[f] Jehovah will give it into the king's hand."

12 So the messenger who went to call Mi·cai′ah said to him: "Look! The words of the prophets are unanimously favorable to the king. Let your word, please, become like theirs,[g] and speak favorably."[h] **13** But Mi·cai′ah said: "As surely as Jehovah is living, whatever my God says is what I will speak."[i] **14** Then he came in to the king, and the king asked him:

CHAP. 17
a 2Ch 13:3
　2Ch 26:11-13

b Ge 49:27

c 2Ch 14:8

d 2Ch 11:5, 23

CHAP. 18
e 2Ch 17:5

f 1Ki 16:28, 33
　1Ki 21:25

g 1Ki 22:2-4
　2Ch 19:2

h De 4:41-43
　1Ch 6:77, 80

i 2Sa 2:1
　1Ki 22:5, 6

Second Col.
a 2Ki 3:11

b 1Ki 22:7, 8

c 1Ki 18:4
　1Ki 19:9, 10

d Jer 38:4

e 1Ki 22:9-12

f Mic 3:5

g Isa 30:9, 10

h 1Ki 22:13-17

i Jer 23:28
　Ac 20:27

18:2 *Or "persuaded."

18:10 *Or "push."

"Mi·cai'ah, should we go to war against Ra'moth-gil'e·ad, or should I refrain?" At once he replied: "Go up and you will be successful; they will be given into your hand." **15** At that the king said to him: "How many times must I put you under oath not to speak to me anything but the truth in the name of Jehovah?" **16** So he said: "I see all the Israelites scattered on the mountains, like sheep that have no shepherd.ᵃ Jehovah said: 'These have no master. Let each one go back to his house in peace.'"

17 Then the king of Israel said to Je·hosh'a·phat: "Did I not tell you, 'He will not prophesy good things concerning me, only bad'?"ᵇ

18 Mi·cai'ah then said: "Therefore, hear the word of Jehovah: I saw Jehovah sitting on his throneᶜ and all the army of the heavensᵈ standing at his right and at his left.ᵉ **19** Jehovah then said, 'Who will fool King A'hab of Israel, so that he will go up and fall at Ra'moth-gil'e·ad?' And one was saying one thing while another said something else. **20** Then a spirit*ᶠ came forward and stood before Jehovah and said, 'I will fool him.' Jehovah asked him, 'How will you do it?' **21** He replied, 'I will go out and become a deceptive spirit in the mouth of all his prophets.' So he said, 'You will fool him, and what is more, you will be successful. Go out and do that.' **22** And now Jehovah has put a deceptive spirit in the mouth of these prophets of yours,ᵍ but Jehovah has declared calamity for you."

23 Zed·e·ki'ahʰ the son of Che·na'a·nah now approached and struck Mi·cai'ahⁱ on the cheekʲ and said: "Which way did

the spirit of Jehovah pass from me to speak with you?"ᵃ **24** Mi·cai'ah replied: "Look! You will see which way on the day when you will enter the innermost room to hide." **25** Then the king of Israel said: "Take Mi·cai'ah and turn him over to A'mon the chief of the city and to Jo'ash the king's son. **26** Tell them, 'This is what the king says: "Put this fellow in the prisonᵇ and feed him with a reduced allowance of bread and water until I return in peace."'" **27** But Mi·cai'ah said: "If you do return in peace, Jehovah has not spoken with me."ᶜ Then he added: "Take note, all you peoples."

28 So the king of Israel and Je·hosh'a·phat the king of Judah went up to Ra'moth-gil'e·ad.ᵈ **29** The king of Israel now said to Je·hosh'a·phat: "I will disguise myself and will go into the battle, but you should put on your royal attire." So the king of Israel disguised himself, and they entered the battle. **30** Now the king of Syria had ordered his chariot commanders: "Do not fight with anyone, small or great, except the king of Israel." **31** And as soon as the chariot commanders saw Je·hosh'a·phat, they said to themselves: "It is the king of Israel." So they turned to fight against him; and Je·hosh'a·phat began to cry for help,ᵉ and Jehovah helped him, and God at once diverted them from him. **32** When the chariot commanders saw that it was not the king of Israel, they immediately turned back from following him.

33 But one man shot his bow at random,* and he struck the king of Israel between the joints of his coat of mail. So the king said to his charioteer: "Turn around and take me out of the battle,# for I have been

CHAP. 18

a Le 26:14, 17
  Nu 27:16, 17

b 1Ki 22:18

c Isa 6:1
  Eze 1:26
  Re 20:11

d Job 1:6
  Da 7:9, 10

e 1Ki 22:19-23

f Ps 104:4

g Isa 19:14
  Eze 14:9

h 2Ch 18:10

i 2Ch 18:7

j Jer 20:2
  Mr 14:65

Second Col.

a 1Ki 22:24-28

b 2Ch 16:10
  Ac 5:18

c Nu 16:29

d Jos 20:8
  1Ki 22:29-33
  2Ch 18:2

e Ex 14:10
  2Ch 13:14

___

18:20 *Or "an angel."

18:33 *Or "in his innocence." #Lit., "camp."

badly wounded."[a] **34** The fighting raged throughout that day,
and the king of Israel had to be
propped up in the chariot, facing the Syrians until the evening;
and he died at sunset.[b]

19 Then King Je·hosh'a·phat
of Judah returned safe-
ly*[c] to his own house# in Jerusalem. **2** Je'hu[d] the son of Ha-
na'ni[e] the visionary went out to
meet him and said to King Je-
hosh'a·phat: "Is it the wicked you should be helping,[f] and
is it those who hate Jehovah
you should love?[g] Because of
this the indignation of Jehovah
is against you. **3** Nevertheless,
there are good things that have
been found in you,[h] because you
cleared out the sacred poles*
from the land and you have prepared your heart# to search for
the true God."[i]

4 Je·hosh'a·phat continued
living in Jerusalem, and he went
out again among the people from
Be'er-she'ba to the mountainous
region of E'phra·im,[j] to bring
them back to Jehovah the God
of their forefathers.[k] **5** He also
appointed judges throughout the
land in all the fortified cities of
Judah, city by city.[l] **6** And he
said to the judges: "Pay attention
to what you are doing, for you do
not judge for man but for Jehovah, and he is with you when you
pass judgment.[m] **7** Now let the
fear of Jehovah be upon you.[n]
Be careful about what you do,
for with Jehovah our God there
is no injustice,[o] no partiality,[p] no
bribe-taking."[q]

8 In Jerusalem also, Je·hosh'-
a·phat appointed some of the Levites and the priests and some of
the heads of the paternal houses
of Israel to serve as judges for
Jehovah and to settle legal cases for the inhabitants of Jerusalem.[a] **9** And he commanded them: "This is what you
should do in the fear of Jehovah, with faithfulness and a
complete* heart: **10** Whenever
your brothers living in their cities bring a legal case that involves the shedding of blood[b] or
a question about a law, a commandment, regulations, or judgments, you should warn them so
that they may not become guilty
before Jehovah; otherwise his
indignation will come against
you and your brothers. This is
what you should do, so that you
may not incur guilt. **11** Here is
Am·a·ri'ah the chief priest who
is over you for every matter
of Jehovah.[c] Zeb·a·di'ah the son
of Ish'ma·el is the leader of the
house of Judah for every matter
pertaining to the king. And the
Levites will serve as officers for
you. Be strong and act, and let
Jehovah be with those who do
what is good."*[d]

20 Afterward the Mo'ab·ites[e]
and the Am'mon·ites,[f] together with some of the Am'-
mon·im,* came to wage war
against Je·hosh'a·phat. **2** So
Je·hosh'a·phat was told: "A large
crowd has come against you
from the region of the sea,*
from E'dom,[g] and there they are
in Haz'a·zon-ta'mar, that is, En-
ged'i."[h] **3** At that Je·hosh'a·phat
became afraid, and he resolved*
to search for Jehovah.[i] So he
proclaimed a fast for all Judah.
4 The people of Judah then
gathered together to inquire of
Jehovah;[j] they came from all the
cities of Judah to consult Jehovah.

5 Then Je·hosh'a·phat stood
up in the congregation of Judah

19:1 *Or "in peace." #Or "palace." **19:3** *See Glossary. #Or "your heart is resolved."

19:9 *Or "completely devoted." **19:11** *Or "with what is good." **20:1** *Or possibly, "the Meunites." **20:2** *Evidently, the Dead Sea. **20:3** *Lit., "set his face."

CHAP. 18
a 1Ki 22:34, 35
b 2Ch 18:22

CHAP. 19
c 2Ch 18:31, 32
d 1Ki 16:1
e 2Ch 16:7
f 1Ki 21:25
g Ps 139:21
h 1Ki 14:1, 13
i 2Ch 17:3-6
j Jos 17:14, 15
k 2Ch 15:8
l De 16:18
m De 1:16, 17; Ps 82:1
n Ex 18:21
o Ge 18:25; De 32:4
p Ac 10:34; Ro 2:11; 1Pe 1:17
q De 10:17; De 16:19

Second Col.
a De 17:9; De 21:5; De 25:1
b De 17:8
c Mal 2:7
d 2Ch 15:2

CHAP. 20
e Jg 3:14; 2Sa 8:2; Ps 83:2, 6
f Ge 19:36-38
g Jos 15:1
h Jos 15:20, 62
i 2Ch 19:1, 3
j De 4:29-31

and Jerusalem in the house of Jehovah before the new courtyard, **6** and he said:

"O Jehovah the God of our forefathers, are you not God in the heavens;[a] do you not have dominion over all the kingdoms of the nations?[b] In your hand are power and might, and no one can stand against you.[c] **7** O our God, did you not drive away the inhabitants of this land from before your people Israel and then give it as a lasting possession to the offspring* of your friend Abraham?[d] **8** And they settled in it, and they built for you there a sanctuary for your name,[e] saying, **9** 'If disaster should come on us, whether by sword, adverse judgment, pestilence, or famine, let us stand before this house and before you (for your name is in this house)[f] and call to you for help out of our distress, and may you hear and save us.'[g] **10** Now here are the men of Am′mon, Mo′ab, and the mountainous region of Se′ir,[h] whom you did not allow Israel to invade when they came out of the land of Egypt. They turned away from them and did not annihilate them.[i] **11** Now they are repaying us by coming in to drive us out from your possession that you gave us as an inheritance.[j] **12** O our God, will you not execute judgment on them?[k] For we are powerless before this large crowd that is coming against us; and we do not know what we should do,[l] but our eyes are toward you."[m]

13 Meanwhile, all those of Judah were standing before Jehovah, along with their little ones, their wives, and their children.*

14 Then in the middle of the congregation, the spirit of Jehovah came upon Ja·ha·zi′el son of Zech·a·ri′ah son of Be·nai′ah

son of Je·i′el son of Mat·ta·ni′ah the Levite of the sons of A′saph. **15** He said: "Pay attention, all Judah and you inhabitants of Jerusalem and King Je·hosh′a·phat! Here is what Jehovah says to you, 'Do not be afraid or be terrified because of this large crowd, for the battle is not yours but God's.[a] **16** Tomorrow go down against them. They will be coming up by the pass of Ziz, and you will find them at the end of the valley* before the wilderness of Je·ru′el. **17** You will not need to fight this battle. Take your position, stand still,[b] and see the salvation of Jehovah in your behalf.*[c] O Judah and Jerusalem, do not be afraid or be terrified.[d] Tomorrow go out against them, and Jehovah will be with you.'"[e]

18 At once Je·hosh′a·phat bowed low with his face to the ground, and all Judah and the inhabitants of Jerusalem fell down before Jehovah to worship Jehovah. **19** Then the Levites who were descendants of the Ko′hath·ites[f] and the Kor′ah·ites rose up to praise Jehovah the God of Israel with a very loud voice.[g]

20 They rose up early the next morning and went out to the wilderness of Te·ko′a.[h] As they went out, Je·hosh′a·phat stood up and said: "Listen to me, O Judah and you inhabitants of Jerusalem! Put faith in Jehovah your God so that you may be able to stand firm.* Put faith in his prophets,[i] and you will be successful."

21 After he consulted with the people, he appointed men to sing[j] to Jehovah and to offer praise in holy adornment as they went out ahead of the armed

---

CHAP. 20
a 1Ki 8:23
  Mt 6:9

b 1Ch 29:11
  Da 4:17

c 1Ch 29:12
  Isa 40:15, 17
  Da 4:35

d Ge 12:7
  Ne 9:7, 8
  Isa 41:8
  Jas 2:23

e 2Ch 2:4

f 2Ch 6:20

g 1Ki 8:33, 34
  2Ch 6:28-30

h Ge 36:8

i Nu 20:17, 18
  De 2:5, 9, 19

j Jg 11:23, 24
  Ps 83:2, 4

k Jg 11:27, 28
  Ps 7:6

l 2Ki 6:15, 16

m 2Ch 14:11
  Ps 25:15
  Ps 62:1

Second Col.
a De 1:29, 30
  Jos 11:4, 6
  2Ch 32:7, 8

b Isa 30:15

c Ex 14:13, 14
  Ex 15:2
  1Sa 2:1
  1Ch 16:23
  La 3:26

d De 31:8
  Jos 10:25

e Nu 14:9
  2Ch 15:2

f 1Ch 23:12

g 1Ch 15:16

h 2Ch 11:5, 6

i Ex 14:31
  Ex 19:9

j 1Ch 15:16

20:7 *Lit., "seed." 20:13 *Lit., "sons."

20:16 *Or "wadi." 20:17 *Or "see how Jehovah rescues you." 20:20 *Or "to endure."

men, saying: "Give thanks to Jehovah, for his loyal love endures forever."[a]

22 When they began joyfully singing praises, Jehovah set an ambush against the men of Am′mon, Mo′ab, and the mountainous region of Se′ir who were invading Judah, and they struck each other down.[b] **23** And the Am′mon·ites and the Mo′ab·ites turned against the inhabitants of the mountainous region of Se′ir[c] to destroy and annihilate them; and when they finished with the inhabitants of Se′ir, they helped to destroy one another.[d]

24 But when Judah came to the watchtower of the wilderness[e] and looked toward the crowd, there they saw their carcasses fallen to the ground;[f] there were no survivors. **25** So Je·hosh′a·phat and his people came to carry off the spoil from them, and they found among them an abundance of goods, clothing, and desirable articles, which they stripped off for themselves until they could carry no more.[g] It took three days to carry off the spoil, for it was abundant. **26** On the fourth day they congregated together at the Valley* of Ber′a·cah, for there they praised# Jehovah. That is why they named that place Valley of Ber′a·cahᐃʰ—until today.

27 Then all the men of Judah and Jerusalem, with Je·hosh′a·phat at their head, returned to Jerusalem with rejoicing, for Jehovah had made them rejoice over their enemies.[i] **28** So they came into Jerusalem with stringed instruments, harps,[j] and trumpets[k] and went to the house of Jehovah.[l] **29** And the dread of God came upon all the kingdoms of the lands when they heard that Jehovah had fought against the enemies of Israel.[a]

30 Thus the kingdom of Je·hosh′a·phat had no disturbance, and his God continued to give him rest on every side.[b]

31 And Je·hosh′a·phat continued reigning over Judah. He was 35 years old when he became king, and he reigned for 25 years in Jerusalem. His mother's name was A·zu′bah the daughter of Shil′hi.[c] **32** He kept walking in the way of his father A′sa.[d] He did not deviate from it, and he did what was right in Jehovah's eyes.[e] **33** However, the high places were not removed,[f] and the people had not yet prepared their heart for the God of their forefathers.[g]

34 As for the rest of the history of Je·hosh′a·phat, from beginning to end, there it is written among the words of Je′hu[h] the son of Ha·na′ni,[i] which were included in the Book of the Kings of Israel. **35** After this King Je·hosh′a·phat of Judah made an alliance with King A·ha·zi′ah of Israel, who acted wickedly.[j] **36** So he made him his partner in making ships to go to Tar′shish,[k] and they built the ships in E′zi·on·ge′ber.[l] **37** However, E·li·e′zer the son of Dod·av′a·hu of Ma·re′sha spoke prophetically against Je·hosh′a·phat, saying: "Because you have made an alliance with A·ha·zi′ah, Jehovah will destroy your works."[m] So the ships were wrecked,[n] and they were unable to go to Tar′shish.

21 Then Je·hosh′a·phat was laid to rest with his forefathers and was buried with his forefathers in the City of David; and his son Je·ho′ram became king in his place.[o] **2** His brothers, Je·hosh′a·phat's sons, were Az·a·ri′ah, Je·hi′el, Zech·a·ri′ah, Az·a·ri′ah, Mi′cha·el, and Sheph·a·ti′ah; all of these were the sons of King Je·hosh′a·phat of

---

CHAP. 20
a Ex 34:6

b Jg 7:22
1Sa 14:20

c De 2:5

d Ex 14:25
Eze 38:21

e 2Ch 20:16

f Ex 14:30
Ps 110:5, 6
Isa 37:36

g Ex 12:35
2Ki 7:15, 16

h Ex 17:14, 15
1Sa 7:12

i 1Sa 2:1
Ps 20:5
Ps 30:1

j 2Sa 6:5
1Ch 16:5

k Nu 10:8
1Ch 13:8
2Ch 29:26

l Ps 116:19

Second Col.
a Ex 15:13, 14
Jos 9:3, 9
2Ch 17:10

b Jos 23:1
2Sa 7:1
2Ch 15:15

c 1Ki 22:41, 42

d 1Ki 15:11

e 2Ch 17:3, 4
2Ch 19:2, 3

f 1Ki 15:14
1Ki 22:43
2Ch 17:1, 6

g 1Ki 18:21

h 1Ki 16:1
2Ch 19:2

i 2Ch 16:7

j 2Ki 1:2, 16

k 1Ki 10:22; 23

l Nu 33:1, 35
De 2:8
1Ki 9:26

m 2Ch 19:2
Ps 127:1

n 1Ki 22:48

CHAP. 21
o 1Ki 22:50

20:26 *Or "Low Plain." #Lit., "blessed." ᐃMeaning "Blessing."

Israel. **3** And their father had given them many gifts in silver and gold, and valuable things, along with fortified cities in Judah;[a] but he gave the kingdom to Je·ho'ram,[b] for he was the first-born.

4 When Je·ho'ram had taken control of the kingdom of his father, he strengthened his position by killing all his brothers[c] with the sword, as well as some of the princes of Israel. **5** Je·ho'ram was 32 years old when he became king, and he reigned for eight years in Jerusalem.[d] **6** He walked in the way of the kings of Israel,[e] just as those of the house of A'hab had done, for A'hab's daughter had become his wife;[f] and he kept doing what was bad in Jehovah's eyes. **7** But Jehovah did not want to bring the house of David to ruin for the sake of the covenant that he had made with David,[g] since he had promised to give a lamp to him and to his sons always.[h]

8 In his days E'dom revolted against Judah[i] and then set up its own king.[j] **9** So Je·ho'ram and his commanders crossed over with all his chariots, and he rose up by night and defeated the E'dom·ites who were surrounding him and the chariot commanders. **10** But E'dom has kept up its revolt against Judah to this day. Lib'nah[k] also revolted against him at that time, because he had abandoned Jehovah the God of his forefathers.[l] **11** He had also made high places[m] on the mountains of Judah to cause the inhabitants of Jerusalem to commit spiritual prostitution, and he led Judah astray.

12 Eventually a written message came to him from E·li'jah[n] the prophet, saying: "This is what Jehovah the God of David your forefather says, 'You have

not walked in the ways of your father Je·hosh'a·phat[a] or in the ways of King A'sa[b] of Judah. **13** But you walk in the way of the kings of Israel[c] and cause Judah and the inhabitants of Jerusalem to commit spiritual prostitution[d] like the prostitution of the house of A'hab,[e] and you even killed your own brothers,[f] the household of your father, who were better than you. **14** Therefore, Jehovah is dealing a great blow to your people, to your sons, to your wives, and to all your possessions. **15** And you will suffer with many sicknesses, including a disease of your intestines, until your intestines come out because of the disease, day after day.'"

16 Then Jehovah stirred up[g] against Je·ho'ram the Phi·lis'-tines*[h] and the Arabs[i] who were near the E·thi·o'pi·ans. **17** So they invaded Judah, forcing their way in, and carried off all the possessions that were found in the king's house,*[j] as well as his sons and his wives; and the only son left to him was Je·ho'a·haz,#[k] his youngest son. **18** And after all of this, Jehovah afflicted him with an incurable disease in his intestines.[l] **19** Some time later, when two full years had passed, his intestines came out because of his disease, and he died while suffering severely from his disease; and his people did not make a burning for him like the burning that was made for his forefathers.[m] **20** He was 32 years old when he became king, and he reigned for eight years in Jerusalem. No one regretted it when he died. So they buried him in the City of David,[n] but not in the burial places of the kings.[o]

21:16 *Lit., "the spirit of the Philistines." **21:17** *Or "palace." #Also called Ahaziah.

CHAP. 21
a 2Ch 11:5, 23
b 2Ki 8:16
c Jg 9:5, 6
d 2Ki 8:17-19
e 1Ki 14:7, 9
   Ho 4:1
f 2Ch 22:2
   Ne 13:26
g 2Sa 23:5
   Ps 89:20, 28
   Jer 33:20, 21
h 2Sa 7:12, 16
   1Ki 11:36
   Ps 132:11
i Ge 27:40
j 1Ki 22:47
   2Ki 8:20-22
k Jos 21:13
   2Ki 19:8
l 2Ch 15:2
   Jer 2:13
m De 12:2
n 2Ki 2:1, 11

Second Col.
a 2Ch 17:3
b 1Ki 15:11
   2Ch 14:2, 5
c 1Ki 16:25, 33
d Ex 34:15
   Jer 3:8
e 2Ki 9:22
f 2Ch 21:4
g 1Ki 11:14
   2Ch 33:11
   Isa 10:5
h Jos 13:1, 2
   2Sa 8:1
i 2Ch 17:11
j 1Ki 14:25, 26
k 2Ch 22:1
l Ac 12:21-23
m 2Ch 16:13, 14
   Jer 34:4, 5
n 1Ki 2:10
o 2Ch 24:24, 25
   2Ch 28:27

22 Then the inhabitants of Jerusalem made his youngest son A·ha·zi′ah king in his place, for the marauder band that came with the Arabs to the camp had killed all the older ones.[a] So A·ha·zi′ah the son of Je·ho′ram began to reign as king of Judah.[b] **2** A·ha·zi′ah was 22 years old when he became king, and he reigned for one year in Jerusalem. His mother's name was Ath·a·li′ah[c] the granddaughter* of Om′ri.[d]

3 He too walked in the ways of the house of A′hab,[e] for his mother became his adviser in acting wickedly. **4** And he kept doing what was bad in Jehovah's eyes, like the house of A′hab, for they became his advisers after the death of his father, to his destruction. **5** He followed their advice and went with Je·ho′ram the son of King A′hab of Israel to wage war against King Haz′a·el[f] of Syria at Ra′moth-gil′e·ad,[g] where the archers wounded Je·ho′ram. **6** He returned to Jez′re·el[h] to recover from the wounds that they had inflicted on him at Ra′mah when he fought against King Haz′a·el of Syria.[i]

A·ha·zi′ah* the son of Je·ho′ram[j] the king of Judah went down to Jez′re·el to see Je·ho′ram[k] the son of A′hab, because he had been wounded.*[l] **7** But God brought about the downfall of A·ha·zi′ah by his coming to Je·ho′ram; and when he came, he went out with Je·ho′ram to meet Je′hu[m] the grandson* of Nim′shi, whom Jehovah had anointed to do away with# the house of A′hab.[n] **8** When Je′hu began to execute judgment on the house of A′hab, he found the princes of Judah and the sons of A·ha·zi′ah's brothers, ministers of A·ha·zi′ah, and he killed them.[a] **9** Then he looked for A·ha·zi′ah; they captured him where he was hiding in Sa·mar′i·a, and they brought him to Je′hu. Then they put him to death and buried him,[b] for they said: "He is the grandson of Je·hosh′a·phat, who searched for Jehovah with all his heart."[c] There was no one of the house of A·ha·zi′ah who had the power to rule the kingdom.

10 When Ath·a·li′ah,[d] A·ha·zi′ah's mother, saw that her son had died, she rose up and destroyed the entire royal line* of the house of Judah.[e] **11** However, Je·ho·shab′e·ath the daughter of the king took Je·ho′ash[f] the son of A·ha·zi′ah and stole him away from among the sons of the king who were to be put to death, and she put him and his nurse in an inner bedroom. Je·ho·shab′e·ath the daughter of King Je·ho′ram[g] (she was the wife of Je·hoi′a·da[h] the priest and a sister of A·ha·zi′ah) managed to keep him concealed from Ath·a·li′ah, so that she did not put him to death.[i] **12** He remained with them for six years, hidden in the house of the true God, while Ath·a·li′ah was ruling over the land.

23 In the seventh year, Je·hoi′a·da acted courageously and made a pact* with the chiefs of hundreds,[j] namely, Az·a·ri′ah the son of Je·ro′ham, Ish′ma·el the son of Je·ho·ha′nan, Az·a·ri′ah the son of O′bed, Ma·a·sei′ah the son of A·dai′ah, and E·li·sha′phat the son of Zich′ri. **2** Then they went throughout Judah and gathered together the Levites[k] from all the cities of Judah and the heads of the paternal houses of Israel. When

---

22:2 *Lit., "daughter." 22:6 *In some Hebrew manuscripts, "Azariah." #Or "he was sick." 22:7 *Lit., "son." #Lit., "cut off."

22:10 *Lit., "all seed of the kingdom." 23:1 *Or "covenant."

CHAP. 22
a 2Ch 21:16, 17

b 2Ki 8:24-26

c 2Ki 11:1
2Ki 11:13, 16
2Ch 24:7

d 1Ki 16:28

e 1Ki 16:33
2Ki 8:27, 28
Mic 6:16

f 2Ki 8:15
2Ki 10:32

g 1Ki 22:3
2Ch 18:14

h Jos 19:18, 23

i 2Ki 9:15

j 2Ki 8:16

k 2Ki 3:1

l 2Ki 9:16

m 1Ki 19:16
2Ki 9:20, 21

n 2Ki 9:6, 7

Second Col.
a 2Ki 10:10-14

b 2Ki 9:27, 28

c 2Ch 17:3, 4

d 2Ch 22:2

e 2Ki 11:1-3

f 2Ki 11:21

g 2Ki 8:16

h 2Ch 23:1

i 2Sa 7:12, 13
1Ki 15:4
2Ch 21:7

CHAP. 23
j 2Ki 11:4

k 2Ch 8:14

they came to Jerusalem, **3** the entire congregation made a covenant[a] with the king in the house of the true God, after which he said to them:

"Look! The king's son will reign, just as Jehovah promised concerning the sons of David.[b] **4** This is what you are to do: One third of the priests and of the Levites who will be on duty[c] on the Sabbath will be doorkeepers;[d] **5** another third will be at the house* of the king,[e] and the other third will be at the Gate of the Foundation, and all the people will be in the courtyards of the house of Jehovah.[f] **6** Do not let anyone enter the house of Jehovah except the priests and the Levites who are ministering.[g] These may enter because they are a holy group, and all the people will keep the obligation to Jehovah. **7** The Levites must surround the king on every side, each with his weapons in hand. Anyone entering the house will be put to death. Stay with the king wherever he goes."*

8 The Levites and all Judah did exactly what Je·hoi′a·da the priest had commanded. So each one took his men who were on duty on the Sabbath, together with those who were off duty on the Sabbath,[h] for Je·hoi′a·da the priest had not dismissed the divisions[i] from their duty. **9** Je·hoi′a·da the priest then gave the chiefs of hundreds[j] the spears and the bucklers* and the circular shields that had belonged to King David,[k] which were in the house of the true God.[l] **10** He then stationed all the people, each with his weapon* in hand, from the right side of the house to the left side of the house, by the altar and by the house, all around the king. **11** Then they brought the king's son* out and put on him the crown* and the Testimony*[b] and made him king, and Je·hoi′a·da and his sons anointed him. Then they said: "Long live the king!"[c]

12 When Ath·a·li′ah heard the sound of the people running and praising the king, she immediately came to the people at the house of Jehovah.[d] **13** Then she saw the king standing there by his pillar at the entrance. The princes[e] and the trumpeters were with the king, and all the people of the land were rejoicing[f] and blowing the trumpets, and the singers with musical instruments were leading* the praises. At this Ath·a·li′ah ripped her garments apart and cried out: "Conspiracy! Conspiracy!" **14** But Je·hoi′a·da the priest brought out the chiefs of hundreds, those appointed over the army, and said to them: "Take her out from among the ranks, and if anyone follows her, put him to death with the sword!" For the priest had said: "Do not put her to death in the house of Jehovah." **15** So they seized her, and when she reached the entrance of the Horse Gate of the king's house,* they immediately put her to death there.

16 Then Je·hoi′a·da made a covenant between himself and all the people and the king, that they would continue as the people of Jehovah.[g] **17** After that all the people came to the house* of Ba′al and tore it down,[h] and they smashed his altars and his images,[i] and they killed Mat′tan the priest of Ba′al[j]

CHAP. 23
a 2Sa 5:3

b 2Sa 7:8, 12
1Ki 2:4
1Ki 9:5
Ps 89:20, 29

c 1Ch 24:3

d 2Ki 11:5-8
1Ch 9:22-25
1Ch 26:1

e 1Ki 7:1

f 1Ki 7:12

g 1Ch 23:28, 32

h 2Ki 11:9-12

i 1Ch 24:1
1Ch 26:1

j 1Ki 11:4

k 2Sa 8:7

l 1Ch 26:26, 27
2Ch 5:1

Second Col.
a 2Ki 11:2

b De 17:18

c 1Sa 10:1, 24

d 2Ki 11:13-16

e 2Ch 23:1

f 1Ki 1:39, 40

g 2Ki 11:17, 18
2Ch 34:1, 31

h 2Ki 10:27, 28

i De 12:3
2Ch 34:1, 4

j De 13:5
1Ki 18:40

23:5, 15 *Or "palace." 23:7 *Lit., "when he goes out and when he comes in." 23:9 *A small shield, often carried by archers. 23:10 *Or "missile." 23:11 *Or "diadem." #Possibly a scroll containing the Law of God. 23:13 *Or "giving the signal for." 23:17 *Or "temple."

in front of the altars. **18** Then Je·hoi′a·da put the oversight of the house of Jehovah in the hands of the priests and the Levites, whom David had assigned in divisions over the house of Jehovah to offer up the burnt sacrifices of Jehovah[a] according to what is written in the Law of Moses,[b] with rejoicing and with song, as directed by* David. **19** He also stationed the gatekeepers[c] by the gates of the house of Jehovah, so that no one unclean in any respect could enter. **20** He now took the chiefs of hundreds,[d] the nobles, the rulers of the people, and all the people of the land and escorted the king down from the house of Jehovah. Then they came through the upper gate to the king's house* and seated the king on the throne[e] of the kingdom.[f] **21** So all the people of the land rejoiced and the city was quiet, for they had put Ath·a·li′ah to death with the sword.

24 Je·ho′ash was seven years old when he became king,[g] and he reigned for 40 years in Jerusalem. His mother's name was Zib′i·ah from Be′er-she′ba.[h] **2** Je·ho′ash continued doing what was right in Jehovah's eyes all the days of Je·hoi′a·da the priest.[i] **3** Je·hoi′a·da chose two wives for him, and he became father to sons and daughters.

4 Afterward it was the heart's desire of Je·ho′ash to renovate the house of Jehovah.[j] **5** So he gathered the priests and the Levites together and said to them: "Go out to the cities of Judah and collect money from all Israel to repair the house of your God[k] from year to year; and you should act quickly in the matter." But the Levites did not act quickly.[l] **6** So the king called

Je·hoi′a·da the chief and said to him:[a] "Why have you not required the Levites to bring in from Judah and Jerusalem the sacred tax ordered by Moses[b] the servant of Jehovah, the sacred tax of the congregation of Israel, for the tent of the Testimony?[c] **7** For the sons of Ath·a·li′ah,[d] that wicked woman, had broken into the house of the true God,[e] and they had used all the holy things of the house of Jehovah for the Ba′als." **8** Then, at the king's order, a chest[f] was made and placed outside at the gate of the house of Jehovah.[g] **9** After that a proclamation was issued throughout Judah and Jerusalem to bring to Jehovah the sacred tax[h] that Moses the servant of the true God had imposed on Israel in the wilderness. **10** All the princes and all the people rejoiced,[i] and they kept bringing contributions and dropping them into the chest until it was full.*

11 Whenever the Levites brought the chest in to be turned over to the king and they saw that there was a great deal of money in it, the secretary of the king and the commissioner of the chief priest would come and empty the chest,[j] and then they would take it back to its place. That was what they did from day to day, and they gathered money in abundance. **12** Then the king and Je·hoi′a·da would give it to those supervising the work of the service of Jehovah's house, and they would hire the stonecutters and the craftsmen for renovating Jehovah's house,[k] and also workers in iron and copper to repair Jehovah's house. **13** And those supervising the work got it started, and the repair work

---

CHAP. 23
a 1Ch 23:6
 1Ch 23:30, 31

b Ex 29:38
 Nu 28:2

c 1Ch 9:26
 1Ch 26:1, 13

d 2Ki 11:9

e 1Ki 7:7

f 2Ki 11:19, 20

CHAP. 24
g 2Ki 11:21

h Ge 21:14
 2Sa 3:10
 2Ki 12:1

i 2Ki 12:2

j 2Ki 22:3-5

k 2Ki 12:4, 5
 2Ch 29:1, 3
 2Ch 34:9, 10

l 2Ki 12:6

Second Col.
a 2Ki 12:7

b Ex 30:12-16

c Nu 1:50

d 2Ch 22:2, 3

e 2Ch 28:24

f Mr 12:41

g 2Ki 12:9

h Ex 30:12-16
 Ne 10:32
 Mt 17:24

i 1Ch 29:5

j 2Ki 12:10

k 2Ki 12:11, 12
 2Ch 34:10, 11

23:18 *Lit., "by the hands of." 23:20 *Or "palace."

24:10 *Or possibly, "until they all had given."

progressed under their supervision, and they restored the house of the true God to its proper condition and reinforced it. **14** And as soon as they finished, they brought the money that was left over to the king and Je·hoi′a·da, and they used it to make utensils for the house of Jehovah, utensils for the ministry and for making offerings and cups and utensils of gold and of silver.[a] And they would offer up burnt sacrifices[b] at the house of Jehovah regularly all the days of Je·hoi′a·da.

15 When Je·hoi′a·da was old and satisfied with years, he died; he was 130 years old at his death. **16** So they buried him in the City of David along with the kings,[c] because he had done good in Israel[d] with respect to the true God and His house.

17 After Je·hoi′a·da's death the princes of Judah came and bowed down to the king, and the king listened to them. **18** They abandoned the house of Jehovah the God of their forefathers and began serving the sacred poles* and the idols, so that God's anger came* against Judah and Jerusalem because of their guilt. **19** He kept sending prophets among them to bring them back to Jehovah, and they kept warning* them, but they refused to listen.[e]

20 God's spirit came upon* Zech·a·ri′ah the son of Je·hoi′a·da′ the priest, and he stood above the people and said to them: "This is what the true God says, 'Why are you violating the commandments of Jehovah? You will not be successful! Because you have abandoned Jehovah, he will, in turn, abandon you.'"[g] **21** But they conspired against him[h] and stoned him at the king's

order in the courtyard of Jehovah's house.[a] **22** Thus King Je·ho′ash did not remember the loyal love that his father* Je·hoi′a·da had shown toward him, and he killed his son, who said as he was dying: "May Jehovah see to it and call you to account."[b]

23 At the beginning of the year* the Syrian army came up against Je·ho′ash, and they invaded Judah and Jerusalem.[c] Then they did away with all the princes[d] of the people, and they sent all their spoil to the king of Damascus. **24** For although the invading Syrian army had a small number of men, Jehovah handed over to them a very large army,[e] because they had abandoned Jehovah the God of their forefathers; so they* executed judgment on Je·ho′ash. **25** And when they withdrew from him (for they left him severely wounded*), his own servants conspired against him because he had shed the blood of the sons* of Je·hoi′a·da′ the priest. They killed him on his own bed.[g] So he died and they buried him in the City of David,[h] but they did not bury him in the burial places of the kings.[i]

26 These were the conspirators[j] against him: Za′bad the son of Shim′e·ath the Am′mon·it·ess and Je·hoz′a·bad the son of Shim′rith the Mo′ab·i·tess. **27** Regarding his sons and the many pronouncements against him[k] and the renovation* of the house of the true God,[l] all these things are recorded in the writings* of the Book of the Kings. And his son Am·a·zi′ah became king in his place.

24:22 *That is, Zechariah's father.
24:23 *Lit., "the turn of the year."
24:24 *That is, the Syrians. **24:25** *Or "with many diseases." #Or "son." Possibly the plural form denotes excellence. **24:27** *Lit., "founding." #Or "exposition; commentary."

24:18 *See Glossary. #Lit., "there was anger." **24:19** *Or "bearing witness against." **24:20** *Lit., "clothed."

CHAP. 24
a Ex 37:16
Nu 7:84

b Nu 28:3

c 1Ki 2:10

d 2Ch 23:1

e 2Ki 17:13, 14
2Ch 36:15, 16
Jer 7:25, 26

f 2Ch 23:11

g De 29:24, 25
1Ch 28:9
2Ch 15:2

h Jer 11:19

Second Col.
a Mt 23:35
Lu 11:51

b Ge 9:5
Ps 94:1
Jer 11:20
Heb 10:30

c 2Ki 12:17

d 2Ch 24:17, 18

e Le 26:17, 37
De 32:30

f 2Ch 24:20, 21

g 2Ki 12:20

h 2Sa 5:9
1Ki 2:10

i 2Ch 21:16, 20
2Ch 28:27

j 2Ki 12:21

k 2Ch 24:20

l 2Ch 24:13

25 Am·a·zi′ah was 25 years old when he became king, and he reigned for 29 years in Jerusalem. His mother's name was Je·ho·ad′dan of Jerusalem.ª **2** He continued to do what was right in Jehovah's eyes, but not with a complete heart. **3** As soon as he had the kingdom firmly in his control, he killed his servants who had killed his father the king.ᵇ **4** But he did not put their sons to death, for he acted in harmony with what is written in the Law, in the book of Moses, where Jehovah commanded: "Fathers should not die for their sons, and sons should not die for their fathers; but each one should die for his own sin."ᶜ

5 And Am·a·zi′ah gathered Judah together and had them stand according to the paternal houses, by the chiefs of thousands and by the chiefs of hundreds for all Judah and Benjamin.ᵈ He registered them from 20 years old and up,ᵉ and he found them to be 300,000 trained* warriors to serve in the army, able to handle the lance and the large shield. **6** Further, he hired from Israel 100,000 mighty warriors for 100 silver talents.* **7** But a man of the true God came to him, saying: "O king, do not let the army of Israel go with you, for Jehovah is not with Israel,ᶠ not with any of the E′phra·im·ites. **8** But go by yourself, act, and be courageous in battle. Otherwise, the true God could cause you to stumble before an enemy, for God has the power to helpᵍ and to cause stumbling." **9** At this Am·a·zi′ah said to the man of the true God: "But what about the 100 talents that I have given to the troops of Israel?" The man of

the true God replied: "Jehovah has the means to give you much more than that."ª **10** So Am·a·zi′ah dismissed the troops that had come to him from E′phra·im, sending them to their own place. However, they were very angry with Judah, so they returned to their own place in the heat of anger.

11 Then Am·a·zi′ah took courage and led his own troops to the Valley of Salt,ᵇ and he struck down 10,000 men of Se′ir.ᶜ **12** And the men of Judah captured 10,000 alive. So they brought them to the top of the crag and threw them down from the top of the crag, and they were all dashed to pieces. **13** But the members of the troop whom Am·a·zi′ah had sent back from accompanying him to the warᵈ were making raids on the cities of Judah, from Sa·mar′i·aᵉ clear to Beth-ho′ron;ᶠ they struck down 3,000 of them and took much spoil.

14 But after Am·a·zi′ah returned from striking down the E′dom·ites, he brought the gods of the men of Se′ir and set them up for himself as gods,ᵍ and he began to bow down before them and to make sacrificial smoke to them. **15** So Jehovah grew very angry with Am·a·zi′ah, and he sent a prophet who said to him: "Why are you following the people's gods that did not rescue their own people out of your hand?"ʰ **16** As he spoke to him, the king said: "Did we appoint you as an adviser to the king?ⁱ Stop!ʲ Why should they strike you down?" Then the prophet quit, but he added: "I know that God has decided to bring you to ruin, because you have done this and you have not listened to my advice."ᵏ

17 After consulting with his advisers, King Am·a·zi′ah of Judah sent a message to Je·ho′ash

---

CHAP. 25
a 2Ki 14:1-6

b 2Ch 24:26

c De 24:16

d 1Sa 8:11, 12

e Nu 1:2, 3

f 2Ch 19:2

g 2Ch 14:11
  2Ch 20:6

Second Col.
a 1Sa 2:7
  Pr 10:22
  Hag 2:8

b 2Sa 8:13
  Ps 60:Sup

c 2Ki 14:7
  2Ch 20:10, 11

d 2Ch 25:9

e 1Ki 16:29

f 2Ch 8:3, 5

g Ex 20:3, 5
  De 7:25
  2Ch 28:22, 23

h 2Ch 24:20
  Ps 115:8
  Jer 2:5
  Jer 10:5

i 2Ch 16:10
  2Ch 18:25, 26

j Isa 30:10

k 1Sa 2:25
  Pr 29:1

25:5 *Lit., "chosen." **25:6** *A talent equaled 34.2 kg (1,101 oz t). See App. B14.

son of Je·ho′a·haz son of Je′hu the king of Israel, saying: "Come! Let us confront each other in battle."*[a] 18 King Je·ho′ash of Israel sent this message to King Am·a·zi′ah of Judah: "The thorny weed in Leb′a·non sent a message to the cedar in Leb′a·non, 'Give your daughter to my son as a wife.' However, a wild beast of Leb′a·non passed by and trampled down the thorny weed. 19 You have said, 'Look! I* have struck down E′dom.'[b] So your heart has become arrogant, wanting to be glorified. But now stay in your own house.[c] Why should you provoke disaster and fall, bringing Judah down with you?"

20 But Am·a·zi′ah did not listen,[c] for this was from the true God to give them into the hand of the enemy,[d] because they had followed the gods of E′dom.[e] 21 So King Je·ho′ash of Israel went up, and he and King Am·a·zi′ah of Judah confronted each other in battle at Beth-she′mesh,[f] which belongs to Judah. 22 Judah was defeated by Israel, so each one fled to his home.* 23 King Je·ho′ash of Israel captured King Am·a·zi′ah of Judah, son of Je·ho′ash son of Je·ho′a·haz,* at Beth-she′mesh. Then he brought him to Jerusalem and made a breach in the wall of Jerusalem from the Gate of E′phra·im[g] to the Corner Gate,[h] 400 cubits.* 24 He took all the gold and the silver and all the articles that were found in the house of the true God with* O′bed-e′dom and in the treasuries of the king's house,*[i] as well as hostages. Then he returned to Sa·mar′i·a.

25 Am·a·zi′ah[a] the son of Je·ho′ash the king of Judah lived for 15 years after the death of Je·ho′ash[b] the son of Je·ho′a·haz the king of Israel.[c] 26 As for the rest of the history of Am·a·zi′ah, from beginning to end, look! is it not written in the Book of the Kings of Judah and of Israel? 27 From the time that Am·a·zi′ah turned away from following Jehovah, they formed a conspiracy[d] against him in Jerusalem, and he fled to La′chish, but they sent men after him to La′chish and put him to death there. 28 So they carried him back on horses and buried him with his forefathers in the city of Judah.

26 Then all the people of Judah took Uz·zi′ah,[e] who was 16 years old, and made him king in place of his father Am·a·zi′ah.[f] 2 He rebuilt E′loth[g] and restored it to Judah after the king* was laid to rest with his forefathers.[h] 3 Uz·zi′ah[i] was 16 years old when he became king, and he reigned for 52 years in Jerusalem. His mother's name was Je·co·li′ah of Jerusalem.[j] 4 He continued to do what was right in Jehovah's eyes, just as his father Am·a·zi′ah had done.[k] 5 And he kept searching for God in the days of Zech·a·ri′ah, who taught him to fear the true God. During the time he was searching for Jehovah, the true God made him prosper.[l]

6 He went out and fought against the Phi·lis′tines[m] and broke through the wall of Gath,[n] the wall of Jab′neh,[o] and the wall of Ash′dod.[p] Then he built cities in the territory of Ash′dod and among the Phi·lis′tines. 7 The true God continued to help him against the Phi·lis′tines, against the Arabians[q] who were dwelling in Gur·ba′al, and against the Me-

CHAP. 25	
a	2Ki 14:8-10
b	2Ch 25:11
c	2Ki 14:11-14
d	2Ch 22:7
e	2Ch 25:14
f	Jos 21:8, 16 1Sa 6:19
g	Ne 8:16 Ne 12:38, 39
h	2Ch 26:9 Jer 31:38 Zec 14:10
i	1Ki 7:51 1Ki 15:18 2Ki 24:12, 13 2Ki 25:13-15 2Ch 12:9
Second Col.	
a	2Ki 14:1
b	2Ki 13:10
c	2Ki 14:17-20
d	2Ki 12:20 2Ki 15:8, 10 2Ki 21:23
CHAP. 26	
e	Mt 1:8
f	2Ki 14:21
g	1Ki 9:26 2Ki 16:6
h	2Ki 14:22
i	Isa 1:1 Isa 6:1
j	2Ki 15:2
k	2Ki 14:1, 3
l	1Ch 14:7 Ps 1:2, 3
m	2Sa 8:1 2Ch 21:16 Isa 14:29
n	1Ch 18:1
o	Jos 15:11, 12
p	Jos 15:20, 46 1Sa 5:1
q	2Ch 17:11

25:17 *Or "meet face-to-face." 25:19 *Lit., "You." 25:19, 24 *Or "palace." 25:22 *Lit., "tents." 25:23 *Also called Ahaziah. *About 178 m (584 ft). See App. B14. 25:24 *Or "under the care of."

26:2 *That is, his father Amaziah.

u'nim. **8** The Am'mon·ites[a] began to give tribute to Uz·zi'ah. His fame eventually spread as far as Egypt, for he became extremely powerful. **9** Moreover, Uz·zi'ah built towers[b] in Jerusalem by the Corner Gate,[c] the Valley Gate,[d] and the Buttress, and he fortified them. **10** Further, he built towers[e] in the wilderness and dug* many cisterns (for he had a great deal of livestock); he also did so in the She·phe'lah and on the plain.# He had farmers and vinedressers in the mountains and in Car'mel, for he loved agriculture.

11 Moreover, Uz·zi'ah came to have an army equipped for war. They would go out on military campaigns, organized in divisions. They were numbered and registered[f] by Je·i'el the secretary[g] and Ma·a·sei'ah the officer, under the command of Han·a·ni'ah, one of the king's princes. **12** The entire number of the heads of the paternal houses who were over these mighty warriors was 2,600. **13** The armed forces under their command numbered 307,500 men ready for war, a powerful military force to support the king against the enemy.[h] **14** Uz·zi'ah equipped the entire army with shields, lances,[i] helmets, coats of mail,[j] bows, and slingstones.[k] **15** Further, in Jerusalem he made engines of war designed by engineers; they were set on the towers[l] and on the corners of the walls and could shoot arrows and large stones. So his fame spread far and wide, for he received tremendous help and he became strong.

16 However, as soon as he was strong, his heart became haughty to his own ruin, and he acted unfaithfully against Jeho-

vah his God by entering the temple of Jehovah to burn incense on the altar of incense.[a] **17** Immediately Az·a·ri'ah the priest and 80 other courageous priests of Jehovah went in after him. **18** They confronted King Uz·zi'ah and said to him: "It is not proper for you, Uz·zi'ah, to burn incense to Jehovah![b] It is only the priests who should burn incense, for they are the descendants of Aaron,[c] those who have been sanctified. Go out from the sanctuary, for you have acted unfaithfully and you will receive no glory from Jehovah God for this."

19 But Uz·zi'ah, who had a censer in his hand to burn incense, became enraged;[d] and during his rage against the priests, leprosy[e] broke out on his forehead in the presence of the priests in the house of Jehovah next to the altar of incense. **20** When Az·a·ri'ah the chief priest and all the priests turned toward him, they saw that he had been stricken with leprosy in his forehead! So they rushed him out of there, and he himself hurried out, because Jehovah had struck him.

21 King Uz·zi'ah remained a leper until the day of his death, and he kept staying in a separate house as a leper,[f] for he had been excluded from the house of Jehovah. His son Jo'tham was in charge of the king's house,* judging the people of the land.[g]

22 And the rest of the history of Uz·zi'ah, from beginning to end, was recorded by the prophet Isaiah[h] the son of A'moz. **23** Then Uz·zi'ah was laid to rest with his forefathers, and they buried him with his forefathers, but in the burial field that belonged to the kings, for they said: "He is a leper." And his

---

CHAP. 26
a Ge 19:36, 38
  Jg 11:15

b 2Ch 14:2, 7

c 2Ki 14:13
  Jer 31:38
  Zec 14:10

d Ne 3:13

e 2Ki 9:17

f Nu 1:2, 3
  2Sa 24:9

g 2Ch 24:11

h 2Ch 11:1
  2Ch 13:3
  2Ch 14:8
  2Ch 17:14
  2Ch 25:5

i 2Ch 11:5, 12

j 1Sa 17:4, 5

k Jg 20:16
  1Sa 17:49
  1Ch 12:1, 2

l 2Ch 14:2, 7

Second Col.
a Nu 1:51

b Nu 16:39, 40
  Nu 18:7

c Ex 30:7
  1Ch 23:13

d 2Ch 16:10
  2Ch 25:15, 16

e Nu 12:10
  2Ki 5:27

f Le 13:45, 46
  Nu 5:2
  Nu 12:14, 15

g 2Ki 15:5-7

h Isa 1:1
  Isa 6:1

26:10 *Or "hewed out," likely from rock. # Or "tableland."

26:21 *Or "palace."

son Jo'tham[a] became king in his place.

27 Jo'tham[b] was 25 years old when he became king, and he reigned for 16 years in Jerusalem. His mother's name was Je·ru'shah the daughter of Za'dok.[c] **2** He kept doing what was right in Jehovah's eyes, just as his father Uz·zi'ah had done,[d] except that he did not invade the temple of Jehovah.[e] But the people were still acting ruinously. **3** He built the upper gate of Jehovah's house,[f] and he did much building on the wall of O'phel.[g] **4** He also built cities[h] in the mountainous region of Judah,[i] and he built fortified places[j] and towers[k] in the wooded areas. **5** He waged war against the king of the Am'mon·ites[l] and eventually prevailed against them, so that the Am'mon·ites gave him in that year 100 silver talents,* 10,-000 cor measures# of wheat, and 10,000 of barley. The Am'monites also paid this to him in the second and third years.[m] **6** So Jo'tham kept growing strong, for he established* his ways before Jehovah his God.

7 As for the rest of the history of Jo'tham, all his wars and his ways, it is written in the Book of the Kings of Israel and of Judah.[n] **8** He was 25 years old when he became king, and he reigned for 16 years in Jerusalem.[o] **9** Then Jo'tham was laid to rest with his forefathers, and they buried him in the City of David.[p] And his son A'haz became king in his place.[q]

28 A'haz[r] was 20 years old when he became king, and he reigned for 16 years in Jerusalem. He did not do what was right in Jehovah's eyes as David

his forefather had done.[a] **2** Instead, he walked in the ways of the kings of Israel,[b] and he even made metal statues*[c] of the Ba'als. **3** Moreover, he made sacrificial smoke in the Valley of the Son of Hin'nom* and burned up his sons in the fire,[d] following the detestable practices of the nations[e] that Jehovah had driven out from before the Israelites. **4** He also kept sacrificing and making sacrificial smoke on the high places,[f] on the hills, and under every luxuriant tree.[g]

5 So Jehovah his God gave him into the hand of the king of Syria,[h] so that they defeated him and carried off a great number of captives and brought them to Damascus.[i] He was also given into the hand of the king of Israel, who inflicted on him a great slaughter. **6** For Pe'kah[j] the son of Rem·a·li'ah killed in Judah 120,000 in one day, all brave men, because they had abandoned Jehovah the God of their forefathers.[k] **7** And Zich'ri, an E'phra·im·ite warrior, killed the king's son Ma·a·sei'ah and Az·ri'kam, who was in charge of the palace,* and El·ka'nah, who was second to the king. **8** Moreover, the Israelites took 200,000 of their brothers captive—women, sons, and daughters; they also seized a great deal of spoil, and they took the spoil to Sa·mar'i·a.[l]

9 But a prophet of Jehovah named O'ded was there. He went out before the army that was coming to Sa·mar'i·a and said to them: "Look! It was because Jehovah the God of your forefathers was angry with Judah that he gave them into your hand,[m] and you slaughtered them with a fury that has

---

CHAP. 26
a 2Ki 15:32

CHAP. 27
b Isa 1:1
  Ho 1:1
  Mic 1:1
  Mt 1:9
c 2Ki 15:33
d 2Ki 15:34, 35
  2Ch 26:3, 4
e 2Ch 26:16-18
f Jer 26:10
g 2Ch 33:1, 14
  Ne 3:26
h 2Ch 11:5
  2Ch 14:2, 7
i Jos 14:12, 13
j 2Ch 17:12
k 2Ki 9:17
  2Ch 26:9, 10
l Jg 11:4
  2Sa 10:6
  2Ch 20:1
  Jer 49:1
m 2Ch 26:8
n 2Ki 15:36
o 2Ki 15:33
p 2Sa 5:9
q 2Ki 15:38

CHAP. 28
r Ho 1:1
  Mic 1:1
  Mt 1:9

Second Col.
a 2Ki 16:2
b 1Ki 12:26, 28
  1Ki 16:33
c Ex 34:17
d 2Ch 33:1, 6
  Jer 7:31
e De 12:31
f Le 26:30
g Isa 57:4, 5
h 2Ki 16:5, 6
  2Ch 24:24
i 2Sa 8:6
  1Ch 18:5
j 2Ki 15:37
  Isa 7:1
k 2Ki 15:2
  Ps 73:27
l 1Ki 16:23, 24
  1Ki 22:51
m Jg 2:14
  Jg 3:8

27:5 *A talent equaled 34.2 kg (1,101 oz t). See App. B14. #A cor equaled 220 L (200 dry qt). See App. B14. 27:6 *Or "prepared."

28:2 *Or "molten statues." 28:3 *See Glossary, "Gehenna." 28:7 *Lit., "house."

reached clear to the heavens. **10** And now you intend to make the people of Judah and Jerusalem your male and female servants.[a] Nevertheless, are you not also guilty before Jehovah your God? **11** Now listen to me and return the captives whom you took from your brothers, for Jehovah's burning anger is against you."

12 At that some of the chiefs of the E'phra·im·ites, Az·a·ri'ah the son of Je·ho·ha'nan, Ber·e·chi'ah the son of Me·shil'le·moth, Je·hiz·ki'ah the son of Shal'lum, and A·ma'sa the son of Had'lai, confronted those coming in from the military campaign, **13** and they said to them: "Do not bring the captives in here, for it will make us guilty before Jehovah. What you intend to do will add to our sins and to our guilt, for our guilt is already great and there is burning anger against Israel." **14** So the armed soldiers handed over the captives and the plunder[b] to the princes and the entire congregation. **15** Then the men who had been designated by name rose up and took hold of the captives, and they provided clothes from the spoil for all those among them who were naked. So they clothed them and gave them sandals, food and drink, and oil for their skin. Furthermore, they transported the feeble on donkeys and brought them to their brothers in Jer'i·cho, the city of palm trees. After that they returned to Sa·mar'i·a.

16 At that time King A'haz asked the kings of As·syr'i·a for help.[c] **17** And once again the E'dom·ites invaded and attacked Judah and carried off captives. **18** The Phi·lis'tines[d] also made a raid on the cities of the She·phe'lah[e] and the Neg'eb of Judah and captured Beth-she'mesh,[f] Ai'ja·lon,[g] Ge·de'roth, So'co and its

dependent* towns, Tim'nah[a] and its dependent towns, and Gim'zo and its dependent towns; and they settled there. **19** Jehovah humbled Judah because of King A'haz of Israel, for he had let Judah go unrestrained, resulting in great unfaithfulness toward Jehovah.

20 King Til'gath-pil·ne'ser[b] of As·syr'i·a eventually came against him and caused him distress[c] rather than strengthening him. **21** For A'haz had stripped the house of Jehovah and the house* of the king[d] and the houses of the princes and made a gift to the king of As·syr'i·a; but it was of no help to him. **22** And during his time of distress, King A'haz acted even more unfaithfully toward Jehovah. **23** He began to sacrifice to the gods of Damascus[e] that had defeated him,[f] and he went on to say: "Because the gods of the kings of Syria are helping them, I will sacrifice to them so that they may help me."[g] But they caused him and all Israel to stumble. **24** Furthermore, A'haz collected the utensils of the house of the true God; he then cut to pieces the utensils of the house of the true God,[h] closed the doors of the house of Jehovah,[i] and made altars for himself in every corner of Jerusalem. **25** And in all the cities of Judah, he made high places for making sacrificial smoke to other gods,[j] and he offended Jehovah the God of his forefathers.

26 As for the rest of his history, all his dealings from beginning to end, there it is written in the Book of the Kings of Judah and of Israel.[k] **27** Then A'haz was laid to rest with his forefathers, and they buried him in

CHAP. 28	
a	Le 25:39, 46 2Ch 8:9
b	2Ch 28:8
c	2Ki 16:7, 8 Isa 7:10-12
d	2Ch 26:1, 6
e	2Ch 26:10
f	Jos 15:10, 12
g	2Ch 11:10
Second Col.	
a	Jg 14:1
b	2Ki 15:29 2Ki 16:7, 8 1Ch 5:26
c	2Ki 17:5 Isa 7:20
d	2Ki 18:15, 16 2Ch 12:9
e	2Ch 25:14
f	2Ki 16:10-13
g	Jer 44:18
h	2Ki 16:17
i	1Ki 6:33, 34 2Ch 29:7
j	1Ki 14:22, 23 2Ki 15:32, 35 2Ch 21:5, 11 2Ch 33:1, 3
k	2Ki 16:19

28:18 *Or "surrounding." **28:21** *Or "palace."

the city, in Jerusalem, for they did not bring him into the burial places of the kings of Israel.[a] And his son Hez·e·ki′ah became king in his place.

29 Hez·e·ki′ah[b] became king at the age of 25, and he reigned for 29 years in Jerusalem. His mother's name was A·bi′jah the daughter of Zech·a·ri′ah.[c] **2** He kept doing what was right in Jehovah's eyes,[d] just as David his forefather had done.[e] **3** In the first year of his reign, in the first month, he opened the doors of the house of Jehovah and repaired them.[f] **4** Then he brought the priests and the Levites and assembled them in the square to the east. **5** He said to them: "Listen to me, you Levites. Now sanctify yourselves[g] and sanctify the house of Jehovah the God of your forefathers, and remove what is impure from the holy place.[h] **6** For our fathers have been unfaithful and have done what was bad in the eyes of Jehovah our God.[i] They abandoned him and turned their faces away from the tabernacle of Jehovah and turned their back on him.[j] **7** They also closed the doors of the porch[k] and extinguished the lamps.[l] They stopped burning incense[m] and offering up burnt sacrifices[n] in the holy place to the God of Israel. **8** Therefore, Jehovah's indignation came against Judah and Jerusalem,[o] so that he made them an object of horror and astonishment and a cause for whistling,* as you can see with your own eyes.[p] **9** Here our forefathers fell by the sword,[q] and our sons, our daughters, and our wives went into captivity for this.[r] **10** Now it is my heart's desire to make a covenant with Jehovah the God of Israel,[s] so that his burning anger may turn away from us. **11** My sons, now is not the time to be negligent,* for Jehovah has chosen you to stand before him, to serve you as his ministers,[a] and to make his sacrifices to smoke."[b]

12 At that the Levites rose up: Ma′hath the son of A·ma′sai and Joel the son of Az·a·ri′ah of the Ko′hath·ites;[c] from the Me·rar′ites,[d] Kish the son of Ab′di and Az·a·ri′ah the son of Je·hal′le·lel; from the Ger′shon·ites,[e] Jo′ah the son of Zim′mah and E′den the son of Jo′ah; **13** from the sons of E·li·za′phan, Shim′ri and Je·u′el; from the sons of A′saph,[f] Zech·a·ri′ah and Mat·ta·ni′ah; **14** from the sons of He′man,[g] Je·hi′el and Shim′e·i; from the sons of Je·du′thun,[h] She·mai′ah and Uz′zi·el. **15** Then they gathered their brothers together and sanctified themselves and came, as the king had commanded by the words of Jehovah, to cleanse the house of Jehovah.[i] **16** The priests then went inside the house of Jehovah to do the cleansing and brought out all the uncleanness that they found in the temple of Jehovah and took it to the courtyard[j] of the house of Jehovah. In turn the Levites took it and carried it outside to the Kid′ron Valley.[k] **17** Thus they began the sanctification on the first day of the first month, and on the eighth day of the month they reached the porch of Jehovah.[l] They sanctified the house of Jehovah for eight days, and on the 16th day of the first month they finished.

18 After that they went in to King Hez·e·ki′ah and said: "We have cleansed the whole house of Jehovah, the altar of burnt offering[m] and all its utensils,[n] and the table of the layer bread*[o]

CHAP. 28
a 2Ch 21:16, 20
   2Ch 33:20

CHAP. 29
b Isa 1:1
   Ho 1:1
   Mt 1:10
c 2Ki 18:1, 2
d 2Ch 31:20
e 1Ki 15:5
   2Ki 18:3
f 1Ki 6:33, 34
   2Ch 28:24
g 1Ch 15:11, 12
h 2Ki 18:4
i 2Ch 28:22, 23
   Jer 44:21
j Jer 2:27
   Eze 8:16
k 1Ki 6:33, 34
l Le 24:2
m Ex 30:8
n Ex 29:38
o 2Ch 24:18
p Le 26:32
   De 28:15, 25
q Le 26:14, 17
r 2Ch 28:5-8
s 2Ch 15:10-13

Second Col.
a Nu 3:6
   De 10:8
b 1Ch 23:13
c Nu 4:2, 3
   1Ch 23:12
d 1Ch 23:21
e 1Ch 23:7
f 1Ch 15:16, 17
   1Ch 25:1, 2
g 1Ch 25:5
h 1Ch 25:1
i 2Ch 29:5
j 1Ki 15:13
k 2Ki 23:4, 6
   2Ch 15:16
   Joh 18:1
l 1Ki 6:3
   1Ch 28:11
m 2Ch 4:1
n 1Ki 7:40
o 1Ki 7:48

29:8 *Or "mocking."

29:11 *Or "to rest." **29:18** *That is, the showbread.

and all its utensils. **19** And all the utensils that King A'haz cast aside during his reign when he acted unfaithfully[a] we have made ready and sanctified,[b] and they are before the altar of Jehovah."

20 And King Hez·e·ki'ah got up early and gathered the princes of the city together, and they went up to the house of Jehovah. **21** They brought seven bulls, seven rams, seven male lambs, and seven male goats as a sin offering for the kingdom, for the sanctuary, and for Judah.[c] So he told the priests, the descendants of Aaron, to offer them up on the altar of Jehovah. **22** Then they slaughtered the cattle,[d] and the priests took the blood and sprinkled it on the altar;[e] next they slaughtered the rams and sprinkled the blood on the altar, and they slaughtered the male lambs and sprinkled the blood on the altar. **23** Then they brought the male goats of the sin offering before the king and the congregation and laid their hands on them. **24** The priests slaughtered them and made a sin offering with their blood on the altar, to make atonement for all Israel, because the king said that the burnt offering and the sin offering should be for all Israel.

25 Meanwhile, he had the Levites stationed at the house of Jehovah with cymbals, stringed instruments, and harps,[f] by the commandment of David[g] and of Gad[h] the king's visionary and of Nathan[i] the prophet, for the commandment was from Jehovah through his prophets. **26** So the Levites were standing with the instruments of David, and the priests with the trumpets.[j]

27 Then Hez·e·ki'ah ordered that the burnt sacrifice be offered on the altar.[k] When the burnt offering started, the song of Jehovah started and also the trumpets, following the direction of the instruments of King David of Israel. **28** And the whole congregation bowed down while the song was sung and the trumpets were sounding—all this continued until the burnt offering was finished. **29** And as soon as they finished making the offering, the king and all those with him bowed low and prostrated themselves. **30** King Hez·e·ki'ah and the princes now told the Levites to praise Jehovah with the words of David[a] and of A'saph[b] the visionary. So they offered praise with great rejoicing, and they bowed down and prostrated themselves.

31 Then Hez·e·ki'ah said: "Now that you have been set apart* for Jehovah, come and bring sacrifices and thanksgiving offerings to the house of Jehovah." So the congregation began to bring sacrifices and thanksgiving offerings, and everyone with a willing heart brought burnt offerings.[c] **32** The number of burnt offerings that the congregation brought was 70 cattle, 100 rams, 200 male lambs—all of these as a burnt offering to Jehovah[d]— **33** and the holy offerings were 600 cattle and 3,000 of the flock. **34** But there were not enough priests to skin all the burnt offerings, so their brothers the Levites helped them out[e] until the work was finished and until the priests could sanctify themselves,[f] for the Levites were more conscientious* about sanctifying themselves than the priests were. **35** Also, there were many burnt offerings,[g] as well as the fat pieces of the communion sacrifices[h] and the drink

---

CHAP. 29

a 2Ch 28:1, 2
  2Ch 28:24

b 2Ch 29:5

c Le 4:3
  Le 4:13, 14
  Nu 15:22-24

d Le 4:4

e Le 4:7, 18

f 1Ch 25:1, 6
  2Ch 9:11

g 1Ch 28:12, 13
  2Ch 8:12, 14

h 2Sa 24:11, 12
  1Ch 29:29

i 2Sa 7:2
  2Sa 12:1

j Nu 10:8
  1Ch 15:24

k Le 1:3, 4

Second Col.

a 2Sa 23:1

b 1Ch 16:7

c Le 1:3

d 1Ki 3:4
  1Ki 8:63
  1Ch 29:21, 22

e Nu 8:19
  2Ch 30:17
  2Ch 35:10, 11

f 2Ch 30:2, 3

g 2Ch 29:32

h Le 3:1
  Le 3:14-16

29:31 *Lit., "Now you have filled your hand." 29:34 *Lit., "upright of heart."

offerings for the burnt offerings.[a] Thus the service of the house of Jehovah was restored.* **36** So Hez·e·ki′ah and all the people rejoiced over what the true God had established for the people,[b] for this had all happened so suddenly.

30 Hez·e·ki′ah sent word to all Israel[c] and Judah, and even wrote letters to E′phra·im and Ma·nas′seh,[d] to come to the house of Jehovah in Jerusalem to observe the Passover to Jehovah the God of Israel.[e] **2** However, the king, his princes, and the whole congregation in Jerusalem decided to observe the Passover in the second month,[f] **3** for they had not been able to observe it at the regular time,[g] because not enough priests had sanctified themselves[h] nor had the people gathered in Jerusalem. **4** This arrangement seemed right in the eyes of the king and the entire congregation. **5** So they decided to make an announcement throughout Israel, from Be′er-she′ba to Dan,[i] that the people should come and observe the Passover to Jehovah the God of Israel at Jerusalem, for as a group they had not observed it according to what is written.[j]

6 Then the couriers* went throughout all Israel and Judah with the letters from the king and his princes, as the king had commanded, saying: "People of Israel, return to Jehovah the God of Abraham, Isaac, and Israel, so that he may return to the remnant who escaped out of the hand of the kings of As·syr′i·a.[k] **7** Do not be like your forefathers and your brothers who acted unfaithfully toward Jehovah the God of their forefathers,

so that he made them an object of horror, just as you are seeing.[a] **8** Now do not be obstinate like your forefathers.[b] Submit to Jehovah and come to his sanctuary[c] that he has sanctified forever and serve Jehovah your God, so that his burning anger may turn away from you.[d] **9** For when you return to Jehovah, your brothers and your sons will be shown mercy by their captors[e] and will be allowed to return to this land,[f] for Jehovah your God is compassionate* and merciful,[g] and he will not turn his face away from you if you return to him."[h]

10 So the couriers* went from city to city throughout the land of E′phra·im and Ma·nas′-seh,[i] even to Zeb′u·lun, but the people were making fun of them and mocking them.[j] **11** However, some individuals from Ash′er, Ma·nas′seh, and Zeb′u·lun humbled themselves and came to Jerusalem.[k] **12** The hand of the true God was also in Judah to unite them* to carry out what the king and the princes had commanded by the word of Jehovah.

13 A multitude of people gathered together at Jerusalem to observe the Festival of Unleavened Bread[l] in the second month;[m] it was a very large congregation. **14** They rose up and removed the altars that were in Jerusalem,[n] and they removed all the incense altars[o] and threw them into the Kid′ron Valley. **15** Then they slaughtered the Passover sacrifice on the 14th day of the second month. The priests and the Levites felt ashamed, so they sanctified themselves and brought burnt offerings to the house of Jehovah. **16** They took their

---

CHAP. 29
a Nu 15:5

b 2Ch 30:12

CHAP. 30
c 2Ch 11:14, 16

d 2Ch 34:1, 6, 7

e Ex 12:43
Le 23:5
De 16:2
2Ch 35:1

f Nu 9:10, 11

g Ex 12:18

h 2Ch 29:34

i Jg 18:29

j 2Ch 35:18

k 2Ki 15:29
1Ch 5:26
2Ch 28:20, 21

Second Col.
a 2Ch 29:8, 9

b Ex 32:9

c De 12:5, 6
Ps 132:13

d 2Ch 29:10

e 1Ki 8:49, 50

f De 30:1-3

g Ex 34:6
Ps 86:5
Mic 7:18

h 2Ch 15:2
Isa 55:7
Jas 4:8

i 2Ch 30:1

j 2Ch 36:15, 16

k 2Ch 11:14, 16

l Le 23:6

m Nu 9:10, 11

n 2Ki 18:22

o 2Ch 28:24

29:35 *Or "prepared." 30:6, 10 *Lit., "runners."

30:9 *Or "gracious." 30:12 *Lit., "to give them one heart."

customary places, according to the Law of Moses the man of the true God; then the priests sprinkled the blood[a] received from the hand of the Levites. **17** There were many in the congregation who had not sanctified themselves, and the Levites were in charge of slaughtering the Passover sacrifices for all who were not clean,[b] to sanctify them to Jehovah. **18** For a great number of the people, especially those from E'phra·im, Ma·nas'seh,[c] Is'sa·char, and Zeb'u·lun, had not cleansed themselves, but they still ate the Passover, contrary to what is written. But Hez·e·ki'ah prayed for them, saying: "May Jehovah, who is good,[d] make allowance for **19** everyone who has prepared his heart to search for the true God,[e] Jehovah, the God of his forefathers, although he has not been purified according to the standard of holiness."[f] **20** And Jehovah listened to Hez·e·ki'ah and pardoned* the people.

21 So the Israelites who were in Jerusalem observed the Festival of Unleavened Bread[g] for seven days with great rejoicing,[h] and the Levites and the priests were praising Jehovah day by day, loudly playing their instruments to Jehovah.[i] **22** Moreover, Hez·e·ki'ah spoke to and encouraged* all the Levites who served Jehovah with discretion. And they ate throughout the festival for seven days,[j] sacrificing communion sacrifices[k] and giving thanks to Jehovah the God of their forefathers.

23 Then all the congregation decided to observe it for seven more days, so they observed it for seven more days with rejoicing.[l] **24** And King Hez·e·ki'-

ah of Judah contributed for the congregation 1,000 bulls and 7,000 sheep, and the princes contributed for the congregation 1,000 bulls and 10,000 sheep;[a] and priests were sanctifying themselves in great number.[b] **25** And all the congregation of Judah, the priests, the Levites, all the congregation that came from Israel,[c] and the foreign residents[d] who came from the land of Israel and those living in Judah continued rejoicing. **26** And there was great rejoicing in Jerusalem, for from the days of Sol'o·mon the son of David the king of Israel, nothing like this had happened in Jerusalem.[e] **27** Finally the Levite priests stood up and blessed the people;[f] and God heard their voice, and their prayer reached his holy dwelling, the heavens.

31 As soon as they had finished all of this, all the Israelites who were present went out to the cities of Judah, and they smashed the sacred pillars,[g] cut down the sacred poles,*[h] and tore down the high places[i] and the altars[j] throughout Judah and Benjamin, as well as in E'phra·im and Ma·nas'seh,[k] until they had destroyed them completely, after which all the Israelites returned to their cities, each one to his own possession.

2 Then Hez·e·ki'ah appointed the priests in their divisions[l] and the Levites in their divisions,[m] each of the priests and Levites for their service,[n] for the burnt offerings and the communion sacrifices, to minister and to give thanks and praise in the gates of the courtyards* of Jehovah.[o] **3** A portion of the king's own goods was given for the burnt offerings,[p] including the

---

CHAP. 30
a Le 1:5
b 2Ch 29:34
c 2Ch 30:1
d Ps 86:5
e 2Ch 19:2, 3
  Ezr 7:10
f Nu 9:6, 10
g Le 23:6
h De 12:5, 7
  Ne 8:10
i 2Ch 29:25
j Le 23:6
k Le 3:1
l 1Ki 8:65

Second Col.
a 2Ch 35:7, 8
b 2Ch 29:34
c 2Ch 30:11, 18
d Ex 12:49
e 1Ki 8:65, 66
f Nu 6:23-26
  De 10:8

CHAP. 31
g Ex 23:24
h De 7:5
  2Ki 18:1, 4
  2Ch 14:2, 3
  2Ch 34:1, 3
i De 12:2
j 2Ch 23:16, 17
k 2Ch 30:1, 18
l 1Ch 24:1
m 1Ch 23:6
n 2Ch 8:14
o 1Ch 23:13
  1Ch 27:27-30
p 2Ch 30:24

30:20 *Lit., "healed." **30:22** *Lit., "spoke to the heart of."

31:1 *See Glossary. **31:2** *Lit., "camps."

morning and evening offerings,[a] as well as the burnt offerings for the Sabbaths,[b] the new moons,[c] and the festivals,[d] according to what is written in the Law of Jehovah.

4 Furthermore, he commanded the people living in Jerusalem to give the portion due the priests and the Levites,[e] so that they might adhere strictly* to the law of Jehovah. **5** As soon as the order was issued, the Israelites gave in great quantities the firstfruits of the grain, new wine, oil,[f] and honey, and of all the produce of the field;[g] they brought in abundantly the tenth of everything.[h] **6** And the people of Israel and of Judah living in the cities of Judah also brought in the tenth of cattle and sheep and the tenth of the holy things[i] that were sanctified to Jehovah their God. They brought it in and put it in many heaps. **7** In the third month[j] they began laying their contributions in heaps; and in the seventh month[k] they finished. **8** When Hez·e·ki′ah and the princes came and saw the heaps, they praised Jehovah and blessed his people Israel.

9 Hez·e·ki′ah asked the priests and the Levites about the heaps, **10** and Az·a·ri′ah the chief priest of the house of Za′dok said to him: "From the time they started bringing the contributions into the house of Jehovah,[l] the people have been eating to satisfaction and there is still an abundant surplus, for Jehovah has blessed his people, and this great plenty is left over."[m]

11 At this Hez·e·ki′ah told them to prepare storerooms*[n] in the house of Jehovah, so they prepared them. **12** They kept

faithfully bringing in the contributions, tenth parts,*[a] and the holy things; Con·a·ni′ah the Levite was put in charge of all of this as supervisor, and his brother Shim′e·i was second. **13** Je·hi′el, Az·a·zi′ah, Na′hath, As′a·hel, Jer′i·moth, Jo′za·bad, E′li·el, Is·ma·chi′ah, Ma′hath, and Be·nai′ah were commissioners assisting Con·a·ni′ah and his brother Shim′e·i, by the order of King Hez·e·ki′ah, and Az·a·ri′ah was supervisor of the house of the true God. **14** And Ko′re the son of Im′nah, the Levite gatekeeper on the east side,[b] was in charge of the voluntary offerings[c] of the true God, and he distributed the contribution made to Jehovah[d] and the most holy things.[e] **15** And under his direction were E′den, Mi·ni′a·min, Jesh′u·a, She·mai′ah, Am·a·ri′ah, and Shec·a·ni′ah, in the cities of the priests,[f] in their office of trust, to distribute equally to their brothers in the divisions,[g] to great and small alike. **16** This was in addition to the distribution made to the males from three years old and up who were listed in the genealogical enrollment, who came daily to serve in the house of Jehovah and to carry out the duties of their divisions.

17 The genealogical enrollment of the priests was by their paternal house,[h] as was that of the Levites who were 20 years old and up,[i] by the duties of their divisions.[j] **18** The genealogical enrollment included all their children, their wives, their sons, and their daughters—their entire congregation—for they kept themselves sanctified for what was holy because of their office of trust— **19** as well as the descendants of Aaron, the priests who were living in the fields of

---

CHAP. 31
a Ex 29:39
b Nu 28:9
c Nu 10:10
d De 16:16
e Nu 18:21
  Ne 10:38, 39
f Nu 18:12
g Ex 22:29
  Ex 23:19
  Ne 10:37
h Pr 3:9
i Le 27:30
  De 14:28
j Le 23:16
k Le 23:24
l Nu 18:8
m Mal 3:10
n Ne 10:38, 39
  Ne 12:44

Second Col.
a Le 27:30
  De 14:28
b 1Ch 26:17, 19
c De 12:5, 6
  De 16:10
d Nu 18:8
e Le 2:10
  Le 7:1
f Jos 21:19
g 1Ch 24:1
h 1Ch 24:4
i Nu 4:2, 3
  Nu 8:24
  1Ch 23:24
j 1Ch 23:6

31:4 *Or "devote themselves fully."
31:11 *Or "dining rooms."

31:12 *Or "tithes."

the pastures surrounding their cities.[a] In all the cities, men had been designated by name to give portions to every male among the priests and to everyone included in the genealogical enrollment of the Levites.

20 Hez·e·ki′ah did this throughout Judah, and he continued to do what was good and right and faithful before Jehovah his God. **21** And every work that he undertook to search for his God, whether in connection with the service of the house of the true God[b] or in the Law and the commandment, he did wholeheartedly, and he was successful.

32 After these things and these acts of faithfulness,[c] King Sen·nach′er·ib of As·syr′i·a came and invaded Judah. He besieged the fortified cities, intent on breaking through and capturing them.[d]

2 When Hez·e·ki′ah saw that Sen·nach′er·ib had come and intended to wage war against Jerusalem, **3** he decided, after consulting with his princes and his warriors, to stop up the waters of the springs outside the city,[e] and they gave him their support. **4** Many people were gathered together, and they stopped up all the springs and the stream that flowed through the land, saying: "Why should the kings of As·syr′i·a come and find plenty of water?"

5 Furthermore, with determination he rebuilt the entire broken-down wall and raised towers on it, and outside he made another wall. He also repaired the Mound*[f] of the City of David, and he made a large number of weapons[#] and shields. **6** He then appointed military chiefs over the people and as-

sembled them at the public square of the city gate and encouraged them,* saying: **7** "Be courageous and strong. Do not be afraid or be terrified because of the king of As·syr′i·a[a] and all the multitude with him, for there are more with us than there are with him.[b] **8** With him is an arm of flesh,* but with us is Jehovah our God to help us and to fight our battles."[c] And the people were strengthened by the words of King Hez·e·ki′ah of Judah.[d]

9 After this, while King Sennach′er·ib of As·syr′i·a was at La′chish* with all his imperial might,* he sent his servants to Jerusalem, to King Hez·e·ki′ah of Judah and to all the Ju·de′ans in Jerusalem,[f] saying:

10 "This is what King Sennach′er·ib of As·syr′i·a says, 'In what are you trusting that you remain in Jerusalem while it is besieged?[g] **11** Is not Hez·e·ki′ah misleading you and handing you over to die by famine and thirst, saying: "Jehovah our God will rescue us from the hand of the king of As·syr′i·a"?[h] **12** Is this not the same Hez·e·ki′ah who removed your God's* high places[i] and His altars[j] and then said to Judah and Jerusalem: "You should bow down before one altar and on it you should make your sacrifices smoke"?[k] **13** Do you not know what I and my forefathers did to all the peoples of the lands?[l] Were the gods of the nations of the lands able to rescue their land from my hand?[m] **14** Who among all the gods of these nations that my forefathers devoted to destruction was able to rescue his people from my hand, so that your

---

CHAP. 31
a Le 25:33, 34
  Nu 35:2
  Jos 21:13

b 2Ch 29:35

CHAP. 32
c 2Ch 31:20

d 2Ki 18:7, 13
  Isa 36:1

e 2Ki 20:20

f 2Sa 5:9
  1Ki 9:24
  1Ki 11:27
  2Ki 12:20

Second Col.
a 2Ki 19:6

b De 31:6, 8
  Jos 1:6, 9
  2Ki 6:16, 17
  2Ch 20:15

c Nu 14:9
  De 20:1, 4
  Jos 10:42
  Jer 17:5

d 2Ch 20:20

e Isa 37:8

f 2Ki 18:17
  Isa 36:2

g 2Ki 18:19
  Isa 36:4

h 2Ki 18:29, 30
  2Ki 19:10

i 2Ki 18:1, 4

j 2Ch 31:1

k 2Ki 18:22
  Isa 36:7

l 2Ki 15:29
  2Ki 17:5
  Isa 37:12

m 2Ki 18:33, 34
  2Ki 19:17, 18

32:5 *Or "Millo." A Hebrew term meaning "fill." [#] Or "missiles."   **32:6** *Lit., "spoke to their heart."   **32:8** *Or "is human strength."   **32:9** *Or "all his military might and splendor."   **32:12** *Lit., "his."

God should be able to rescue you from my hand?[a] **15** Now do not let Hez·e·ki′ah deceive you or mislead you like this![b] Do not put faith in him, for no god of any nation or kingdom was able to rescue his people from my hand and from the hand of my forefathers. How much less, then, will your own God rescue you from my hand!'"[c]

16 His servants said even more against Jehovah the true God and against Hez·e·ki′ah his servant. **17** He also wrote letters[d] to insult Jehovah the God of Israel[e] and to speak against him, saying: "Like the gods of the nations of the lands who could not rescue their people from my hand,[f] so the God of Hez·e·ki′ah will not rescue his people from my hand." **18** They kept calling loudly in the language of the Jews to the people of Jerusalem who were on the wall, to make them afraid and to terrify them, in order to capture the city.[g] **19** They spoke against the God of Jerusalem the same way as against the gods of the peoples of the earth, which are the work of man's hands. **20** But King Hez·e·ki′ah and the prophet Isaiah[h] the son of A′moz kept praying about this and crying out to the heavens for help.[i]

21 Then Jehovah sent an angel and wiped out every mighty warrior,[j] leader, and chief in the camp of the king of As·syr′i·a, so that he went back to his own land in disgrace. He later entered the house* of his god, and there some of his own sons struck him down with the sword.[k] **22** So Jehovah saved Hez·e·ki′ah and the inhabitants of Jerusalem from the hand of King Sen·nach′er·ib of As·syr′i·a and from the hand of all others and gave them rest

on every side. **23** And many brought gifts to Jehovah at Jerusalem and choice things to King Hez·e·ki′ah of Judah,[a] and he was greatly respected by all the nations after that.

24 In those days Hez·e·ki′ah became sick and was at the point of death, and he prayed to Jehovah,[b] who answered him and gave him a sign.*[c] **25** But Hez·e·ki′ah did not respond appreciatively to the good done to him, for his heart became haughty, bringing indignation against him and against Judah and Jerusalem. **26** However, Hez·e·ki′ah humbled himself for the haughtiness of his heart,[d] he and the inhabitants of Jerusalem, and Jehovah's indignation did not come upon them in the days of Hez·e·ki′ah.[e]

27 And Hez·e·ki′ah came to have vast riches and glory;[f] and he made storehouses[g] for himself for silver, gold, precious stones, balsam oil, shields, and for all the desirable articles. **28** He also made storage places for the produce of grain and new wine and oil, as well as stalls for all the different kinds of livestock and stalls for the flocks. **29** He also acquired cities for himself, and an abundance of livestock, flocks, and herds, for God gave him very many possessions. **30** It was Hez·e·ki′ah who stopped up the upper source of the waters[h] of Gi′hon[i] and directed them straight down to the west to the City of David,[j] and Hez·e·ki′ah was successful in every work of his. **31** However, when the spokesmen of the princes of Babylon were sent to ask him about the sign*[k] that had occurred in the land,[l] the true God left him alone to put him to the test,[m] to get to know all that was in his heart.[n]

CHAP. 32

a Ex 14:3
　 Ex 15:9

b 2Ki 18:29

c Ex 5:2
　 De 32:27
　 Da 3:14, 15

d 2Ki 19:14

e Isa 37:29

f 2Ki 17:6
　 2Ki 19:12

g 2Ki 18:26, 28
　 Isa 36:11, 13

h 2Ki 19:2, 20
　 Isa 37:2

i 2Ki 19:14, 15
　 2Ch 14:11

j Ps 76:5

k 2Ki 19:35-37
　 Isa 37:37, 38

Second Col.

a 1Ki 4:21
　 2Ch 17:1, 5

b 2Ki 20:1, 2
　 Isa 38:1, 2

c 2Ki 20:5, 9
　 2Ch 32:31
　 Isa 38:8

d Jer 26:18, 19

e 2Ki 20:19

f 2Ch 1:11, 12
　 2Ch 17:1, 5

g 1Ki 9:17-19

h 2Ch 32:4

i 1Ki 1:33, 45

j 2Sa 5:9

k 2Ki 20:8-11
　 Isa 38:8

l 2Ki 20:12
　 Isa 39:1

m Ge 22:1

n De 8:2
　 Ps 7:9
　 Ps 139:23

32:21 *Or "temple."

32:24, 31 *Or "portent."

32 As for the rest of the history of Hez·e·ki'ah and his acts of loyal love,[a] they are written in the vision of Isaiah[b] the prophet, the son of A'moz, in the Book of the Kings of Judah and of Israel.[c] **33** Then Hez·e·ki'ah was laid to rest with his forefathers, and they buried him in the ascent to the burial places of the sons of David;[d] and all Judah and the inhabitants of Jerusalem honored him at his death. And his son Ma·nas'seh became king in his place.

33 Ma·nas'seh[e] was 12 years old when he became king, and he reigned for 55 years in Jerusalem.[f]

2 He did what was bad in Jehovah's eyes, following the detestable practices of the nations that Jehovah had driven out from before the people of Israel.[g] **3** He rebuilt the high places that his father Hez·e·ki'ah had torn down,[h] he set up altars to the Ba'als and made sacred poles,* and he bowed down to all the army of the heavens and served them.[i] **4** He also built altars in the house of Jehovah,[j] about which Jehovah had said: "In Jerusalem my name will be forever."[k] **5** And he built altars to all the army of the heavens in two courtyards of the house of Jehovah.[l] **6** And he made his own sons pass through the fire[m] in the Valley of the Son of Hin'nom;[n] he practiced magic,[o] used divination, practiced sorcery, and appointed spirit mediums and fortune-tellers.[p] He did on a grand scale what was bad in Jehovah's eyes, to offend him.

7 He put the carved image that he made into the house of the true God[q] about which God had said to David and to his son Sol'o·mon: "In this house and in Jerusalem, which I have cho-

sen out of all the tribes of Israel, I will permanently put my name.[a] **8** And I will never again remove the feet of Israel from the land that I assigned to their forefathers, provided they carefully observe all that I have commanded them, the entire Law, the regulations and the judicial decisions given through Moses." **9** Ma·nas'seh kept leading Judah and the inhabitants of Jerusalem astray, causing them to do worse than the nations that Jehovah had annihilated from before the Israelites.[b]

10 Jehovah kept speaking to Ma·nas'seh and his people, but they paid no attention.[c] **11** So Jehovah brought against them the army chiefs of the king of As·syr'i·a, and they captured Ma·nas'seh with hooks* and bound him with two copper fetters and took him to Babylon. **12** In his distress, he begged Jehovah his God for favor* and kept humbling himself greatly before the God of his forefathers. **13** He kept praying to Him, and He was moved by his entreaty and heard his request for favor, and He restored him to Jerusalem to his kingship.[d] Then Ma·nas'seh came to know that Jehovah is the true God.[e]

14 After this he built an outer wall for the City of David[f] west of Gi'hon[g] in the valley* and as far as the Fish Gate,[h] and he continued it around to O'phel,[i] and he made it very high. Further, he appointed army chiefs in all the fortified cities in Judah. **15** He then removed the foreign gods and the idol image from the house of Jehovah[j] and all the altars that he had built in the mountain of the house of Jehovah[k] and in Jerusalem, and

---

CHAP. 32
a 2Ch 31:20, 21
b Isa 1:1
c 2Ki 20:20
d 1Ki 11:43

CHAP. 33
e Mt 1:10
f 2Ki 21:1
g 2Ki 21:2-6
h 2Ki 18:1, 4
i De 4:19
  2Ki 23:5
j 2Ki 16:10, 11
k De 12:11
  2Ch 6:6
l 1Ki 6:36
  1Ki 7:12
m 2Ki 16:1, 3
n Jos 15:8, 12
  2Ki 23:10
o Le 19:26
p Le 20:6
  De 18:10, 11
q 2Ki 23:6

Second Col.
a 2Ki 21:7-9
  2Ki 23:27
  2Ch 7:16
b Le 18:24
  Jos 24:8
  2Ki 21:11, 16
c 2Ch 36:15, 16
d Isa 1:18
e Da 4:25
f 2Sa 5:9
  2Ch 32:2, 5
g 2Ch 32:30
h Ne 3:3
i 2Ch 27:1, 3
j 2Ki 21:7, 17
k 2Ki 21:1, 4, 5

33:3 * See Glossary.

33:11 *Or possibly, "in the hollows." 33:12 *Or "softened the face of Jehovah his God." 33:14 *Or "wadi."

he had them thrown outside the city. **16** He also prepared the altar of Jehovah[a] and began to offer up communion sacrifices[b] and thanksgiving sacrifices[c] on it, and he told Judah to serve Jehovah the God of Israel. **17** Nevertheless, the people were still sacrificing on the high places, although only to Jehovah their God.

18 As for the rest of the history of Ma·nas′seh, his prayer to his God, and the words of the visionaries who spoke to him in the name of Jehovah the God of Israel, they are recorded in the history of the kings of Israel. **19** Also his prayer[d] and how his entreaty was granted him, all his sins and his unfaithfulness,[e] the locations where he built high places and set up the sacred poles*[f] and the graven images before he humbled himself, they are written among the words of his visionaries. **20** Then Ma·nas′seh was laid to rest with his forefathers, and they buried him at his house; and his son A′mon became king in his place.[g]

21 A′mon[h] was 22 years old when he became king, and he reigned for two years in Jerusalem.[i] **22** And he continued to do what was bad in Jehovah's eyes, just as his father Ma·nas′seh had done;[j] and A′mon sacrificed to all the graven images that his father Ma·nas′seh had made,[k] and he kept serving them. **23** But he did not humble himself before Jehovah[l] as Ma·nas′seh his father had humbled himself;[m] instead, A′mon greatly increased his guilt. **24** Eventually his servants conspired against him[n] and put him to death in his own house. **25** But the people of the land struck down all those who conspired against King A′mon,[o]

and they made his son Jo·si′ah[a] king in his place.

34 Jo·si′ah[b] was eight years old when he became king, and he reigned for 31 years in Jerusalem.[c] **2** He did what was right in Jehovah's eyes and walked in the ways of David his forefather, and he did not deviate to the right or to the left.

3 In the 8th year of his reign, while he was still a boy, he started to search for the God of David his forefather;[d] and in the 12th year, he started to cleanse Judah and Jerusalem[e] of the high places[f] and the sacred poles,* the graven images,[g] and the metal statues.# **4** Further, they tore down the altars of the Ba′als in his presence, and he cut down the incense stands that were up above them. He also broke into pieces the sacred poles,* the graven images, and the metal statues# and reduced them to powder and sprinkled it over the graves of those who used to sacrifice to them.[h] **5** And he burned the bones of priests on their altars.[i] Thus he cleansed Judah and Jerusalem.

6 And in the cities of Ma·nas′seh, E′phra·im,[j] Sim′e·on, and clear to Naph′ta·li, in their surrounding ruins, **7** he tore down the altars and he crushed the sacred poles* and the graven images,[k] reducing them to powder; and he cut down all the incense stands in all the land of Israel,[l] after which he returned to Jerusalem.

8 In the 18th year of his reign, when he had cleansed the land and the temple, he sent Sha′phan[m] the son of Az·a·li′ah, Ma·a·sei′ah the chief of the city, and Jo′ah the son of Jo′a·haz the recorder to repair the house of Jehovah his God.[n] **9** They came

CHAP. 33
a 2Ch 29:18
b Le 3:1
c Le 7:12
d 2Ch 33:12, 13
e 2Ki 21:2, 9
f 2Ki 21:3, 7
g 2Ki 21:18, 19
h Mt 1:10
i 2Ki 21:19-24
j 2Ch 33:1, 2
k 2Ki 21:1, 7
l Jer 8:12
m 2Ch 33:12, 13
n 2Ki 12:20
  2Ch 25:27
o 2Ch 25:1, 3

Second Col.
a 2Ki 21:25, 26

CHAP. 34
b 1Ki 13:2
  Zep 1:1
  Mt 1:10
c 2Ki 22:1, 2
d 2Ch 15:2
e 2Ch 23:4, 14
f 2Ch 33:17
g 2Ch 33:21, 22
h 2Ki 23:6
i 1Ki 13:2
  2Ki 23:16
j 2Ki 23:19
  2Ch 30:1
k 2Ki 17:41
l 2Ch 31:1
m 2Ki 22:12
n 2Ki 22:3-6

33:19; 34:3, 4, 7 *See Glossary.

34:3, 4 #Or "molten statues." 34:8 *Lit., "house."

to Hil·ki′ah the high priest and gave him the money that had been brought to the house of God, which the Levites serving as doorkeepers had collected from Ma·nas′seh, E′phra·im, and all the rest of Israel,ᵃ as well as from Judah, Benjamin, and the inhabitants of Jerusalem. **10** Then they gave it to those who were appointed over the work in the house of Jehovah. In turn the workers in the house of Jehovah used it to mend and repair the house. **11** They gave it to the craftsmen and the builders to buy hewn stones and timbers for braces and to build with beams the houses that the kings of Judah had allowed to fall into ruin.ᵇ

12 And the men did the work faithfully.ᶜ Over them were appointed the Levites Ja′hath and O·ba·di′ah of the Me·rar′ites,ᵈ and Zech·a·ri′ah and Me·shul′lam of the Ko′hath·ites,ᵉ to serve as overseers. And the Levites, all of whom were skilled musicians,ᶠ **13** were in charge of the common laborers* and were overseers of all those who were doing the work in every kind of service; and some of the Levites were secretaries, officers, and gatekeepers.ᵍ

14 While they were taking out the money that had been brought to the house of Jehovah,ʰ Hil·ki·ah the priest found the book of Jehovah's Law given through* Moses.ʲ **15** So Hil·ki′ah said to Sha′phan the secretary: "I have found the book of the Law in the house of Jehovah." With that Hil·ki′ah gave the book to Sha′phan. **16** Then Sha′phan brought the book to the king and told him: "Your servants are doing everything that was assigned to them.

34:13 *Or "the burden bearers." 34:14 *Lit., "by the hand of."

CHAP. 34
a 2Ch 30:11, 18

b 2Ki 12:11, 12

c 2Ki 12:15

d 1Ch 23:6

e 2Ch 20:19

f 1Ch 25:1

g 2Ch 8:14

h 2Ki 22:4

i De 17:18
De 31:24-26
Jos 1:8
2Ki 22:8

j Le 26:46

Second Col.
a 2Ki 22:8

b De 17:18, 19

c 2Ki 22:11-13

d 2Ki 25:22
Jer 40:14

e De 30:17, 18
De 31:16
De 31:24-26
Jos 1:8

f Ex 15:20
Jg 4:4
Lu 2:36
Ac 21:8, 9

g 2Ki 22:14-20

h Jer 35:17

i Le 26:16
De 28:15
De 30:17, 18
Da 9:11

j De 28:20

k 2Ki 21:1, 3, 6
2Ch 28:1, 3

17 They have poured out the money that was found in the house of Jehovah, and they have handed it over to the appointed men and to those doing the work." **18** Sha′phan the secretary also told the king: "There is a book that Hil·ki′ah the priest has given me."ᵃ Then Sha′phan began to read from it before the king.ᵇ

19 As soon as the king heard the words of the Law, he ripped his garments apart.ᵃ **20** Then the king gave this order to Hil·ki′ah, A·hi′kamᵈ the son of Sha′phan, Ab′don the son of Mi′cah, Sha′phan the secretary, and A·sai′ah the king's servant: **21** "Go, inquire of Jehovah in my behalf and in behalf of those who remain in Israel and in Judah concerning the words of the book that has been found; for Jehovah's rage that will be poured out against us is great because our forefathers did not carry out the word of Jehovah by observing all that is written in this book."ᵉ

22 So Hil·ki′ah, along with those sent by the king, went to Hul′dah the prophetess.ᶠ She was the wife of Shal′lum son of Tik′vah son of Har′has, the caretaker of the wardrobe, and she was dwelling in the Second Quarter of Jerusalem; and they spoke to her there.ᵍ **23** She said to them: "This is what Jehovah the God of Israel says, 'Tell the man who sent you to me: **24** "This is what Jehovah says, 'I will bring calamity on this place and its inhabitants,ʰ all the curses that are written in the bookⁱ that they read before the king of Judah. **25** Because they have abandoned meʲ and are making sacrifices smoke to other gods in order to offend meᵏ with all the works of their hands, my rage will pour out on this place and it will not be extinguished.'"[a] **26** But to the king of Judah who sent you to inquire of Jehovah, this is what you should say to him, "This is what Jehovah the God of Israel says: 'Regarding the words that you have heard,[b] **27** because your heart was responsive* and you humbled yourself before God on hearing his words concerning this place and its inhabitants and you humbled yourself before me and ripped your garments apart and wept before me, I also have heard you,[c] declares Jehovah. **28** That is why I will gather you to your ancestors,* and you will be laid in your grave in peace, and your eyes will not see all the calamity that I will bring on this place and its inhabitants.'"'"[d]

Then they brought the reply to the king. **29** So the king sent word and summoned all the elders of Judah and Jerusalem.[e] **30** After that the king went up to the house of Jehovah with all the men of Judah, the inhabitants of Jerusalem, the priests, the Levites—all the people, the great as well as the small. He read in their hearing all the words of the book of the covenant that had been found in the house of Jehovah.[f] **31** The king stood in his place and made a covenant*[g] before Jehovah that he would follow Jehovah and keep his commandments, his reminders, and his regulations with all his heart and with all his soul*[h] by carrying out the words of the covenant that were written in this book.[i] **32** Furthermore, he had all those who were in Jerusalem and Benjamin to agree to it. And the inhabitants of Jerusalem acted according to the covenant of

God, the God of their forefathers.[a] **33** Jo·si'ah then removed all the detestable things* out of all the lands that belonged to the Israelites,[b] and he made everyone in Israel serve Jehovah their God. Throughout his lifetime* they did not deviate from following Jehovah the God of their forefathers.

35 Jo·si'ah held a Passover[c] to Jehovah in Jerusalem, and they slaughtered the Passover sacrifice[d] on the 14th day of the first month.[e] **2** He assigned the priests to their duties and encouraged them to carry out their service of the house of Jehovah.[f] **3** Then he said to the Levites, the instructors of all Israel,[g] those who were holy to Jehovah: "Put the holy Ark in the house that Sol'o·mon the son of David the king of Israel built;[h] you are no longer to carry it on your shoulders.[i] Now serve Jehovah your God and his people Israel. **4** And prepare yourselves by your paternal houses according to your divisions, following what was written by King David[j] of Israel and by his son Sol'o·mon.[k] **5** Stand in the holy place grouped by the paternal houses of your brothers, the rest of the people,* with a corresponding group of the paternal house of the Levites. **6** Slaughter the Passover sacrifice[l] and sanctify yourselves and make preparation for your brothers to carry out the word of Jehovah[m] through Moses."

7 Jo·si'ah contributed flocks to the people, male lambs and young male goats, for the Passover sacrifices for all who were present, a total of 30,000, as well as 3,000 cattle. These were from the king's own property. **8** His princes also made a contribution

---

CHAP. 34

a De 29:22, 23
  Jer 7:20

b 2Ch 34:19

c 2Ch 32:26
  2Ch 33:11, 13

d 1Ki 21:29
  Isa 39:8

e 2Ki 23:1

f 2Ki 23:2
  2Ch 17:3, 9
  Ne 8:3

g Ezr 10:3

h De 6:5

i De 31:24-26
  2Ki 22:8

Second Col.

a 2Ch 30:1, 12
  2Ch 33:1, 16

b 2Ki 23:5

CHAP. 35

c Ex 12:3-11
  2Ki 23:21

d Ex 12:21

e Le 23:5
  De 16:1

f 2Ch 23:18
  2Ch 31:2

g De 33:10
  2Ch 17:8, 9
  Ne 8:7, 8

h 1Ki 6:38
  2Ch 5:7

i Nu 4:15
  1Ch 23:25, 26

j 1Ch 23:6

k 2Ch 8:14

l Ex 12:21
  2Ch 30:1, 15

m 2Ch 30:24

34:27 *Lit., "soft." **34:28** *This is a poetic expression for death. **34:31** *Or "renewed the covenant." *See Glossary.

34:33 *Or "idols." *Lit., "All his days." **35:5** *Lit., "the sons of the people."

as a voluntary offering for the people, the priests, and the Levites. Hil·ki′ah,[a] Zech·a·ri′ah, and Je·hi′el, the leaders of the house of the true God, gave to the priests 2,600 Passover sacrifices and 300 cattle. **9** Con·a·ni′ah and his brothers She·mai′ah and Ne·than′el, along with Hash·a·bi′ah, Je·i′el, and Jo′za·bad, the chiefs of the Levites, contributed to the Levites 5,000 Passover sacrifices and 500 cattle.

10 The service was prepared, and the priests stood at their places and the Levites by their divisions,[b] as the king had commanded. **11** They slaughtered the Passover sacrifices,[c] and the priests sprinkled the blood they received from them,[d] while the Levites were skinning the animals.[e] **12** Next they prepared the burnt offerings so as to distribute them to the rest of the people, who were grouped by paternal house, so that they could be presented to Jehovah as it is written in the book of Moses; and they did the same with the cattle. **13** They cooked* the Passover offering over the fire according to the custom;[f] and they cooked the holy offerings in pots, cauldrons, and pans, after which they brought it quickly to all the rest of the people. **14** Then they made preparations for themselves and for the priests, because the priests, the descendants of Aaron, were offering up the burnt sacrifices and the fat pieces until nightfall, so the Levites made preparations for themselves and for the priests, the descendants of Aaron.

15 And the singers, the sons of A′saph,[g] were at their positions by the commandment of David,[h] A′saph,[i] He′man, and Je·du′thun[a] the visionary of the king; and the gatekeepers were at the different gates.[b] There was no need for them to leave their service, because their brothers the Levites made preparations for them. **16** So all the service of Jehovah was prepared on that day to hold the Passover[c] and to offer up the burnt offerings on the altar of Jehovah, according to the order of King Jo·si′ah.[d]

17 The Israelites who were present held the Passover at that time and the Festival of Unleavened Bread for seven days.[e] **18** There had never been held a Passover like it in Israel since the days of Samuel the prophet; nor had any of the other kings of Israel held a Passover like that held by Jo·si′ah,[f] the priests, the Levites, all Judah and Israel who were present, and the inhabitants of Jerusalem. **19** This Passover was held in the 18th year of Jo·si′ah's reign.

20 After all of this, when Jo·si′ah had prepared the temple,* King Ne′cho[g] of Egypt came up to fight at Car′che·mish by the Eu·phra′tes. Then Jo·si′ah went out against him.[h] **21** So he sent messengers to him, saying: "What does this have to do with you, O king of Judah? I am not coming against you today, but my fight is against another house, and God says that I should hurry. For your own sake, refrain from opposing God, who is with me, or he will bring you to ruin." **22** However, Jo·si′ah would not turn away from him, but he disguised himself* to fight against him and would not listen to the words of Ne′cho, which were from the mouth of God. So he came to fight in the Plain of Me·gid′do.[j]

CHAP. 35	
a	2Ki 23:4 2Ch 34:14
b	1Ch 23:6
c	Ex 12:3, 6
d	2Ch 30:16
e	2Ch 29:34
f	Ex 12:8 De 16:6, 7
g	1Ch 16:37
h	1Ch 23:5
i	1Ch 25:1, 2
Second Col.	
a	1Ch 16:41, 42 1Ch 25:3
b	1Ch 26:12, 13
c	Le 23:5
d	2Ki 23:21
e	Ex 12:15 Le 23:6 De 16:3 2Ch 30:1, 21
f	2Ki 23:22, 23 2Ch 30:5, 26
g	Jer 46:2
h	2Ki 23:29
i	1Ki 22:30
j	Jg 1:27 Jg 5:19 Zec 12:11 Re 16:16

35:13 *Or possibly, "roasted."   35:20 *Lit., "house."

23 And the archers shot King Jo·si′ah, and the king said to his servants: "Get me out of here, for I am severely wounded." **24** So his servants took him out of the chariot and had him ride in his second war chariot and brought him to Jerusalem. Thus he died and was buried in the tomb of his forefathers,[a] and all Judah and Jerusalem mourned Jo·si′ah. **25** And Jeremiah[b] chanted over Jo·si′ah, and all the male and female singers[c] keep singing about Jo·si′ah in their dirges* down to this day; and a decision was made that they should be sung in Israel, and they are written among the dirges.

26 As for the rest of the history of Jo·si′ah and his deeds of loyal love, in keeping with what is written in the Law of Jehovah, **27** and what he did, from beginning to end, they are written in the Book of the Kings of Israel and of Judah.[d]

36 Then the people of the land took Jo·si′ah's son Je·ho′a·haz[e] and made him king in Jerusalem in place of his father.[f] **2** Je·ho′a·haz was 23 years old when he became king, and he reigned for three months in Jerusalem. **3** However, the king of Egypt deposed him in Jerusalem and fined the land 100 silver talents* and a gold talent.[g] **4** Furthermore, the king of Egypt made Je·ho′a·haz' brother E·li′a·kim king over Judah and Jerusalem and changed his name to Je·hoi′a·kim; but Ne′cho[h] took his brother Je·ho′a·haz and brought him to Egypt.[i]

5 Je·hoi′a·kim* was 25 years old when he became king, and he reigned for 11 years in Jerusalem. He continued to do what

was bad in the eyes of Jehovah his God.[a] **6** King Neb·u·chad·nez′zar[b] of Babylon came up against him in order to bind him with two copper fetters to take him off to Babylon.[c] **7** And Neb·u·chad·nez′zar took some of the utensils of the house of Jehovah to Babylon and put them in his palace in Babylon.[d] **8** As for the rest of the history of Je·hoi′a·kim, the detestable things that he did and what was found against him, it is written in the Book of the Kings of Israel and of Judah; and his son Je·hoi′a·chin became king in his place.[e]

9 Je·hoi′a·chin* was 18 years old when he became king, and he reigned for three months and ten days in Jerusalem; and he continued to do what was bad in Jehovah's eyes.[g] **10** At the start of the year,* King Neb·u·chad·nez′zar sent to have him brought to Babylon,[h] along with valuable articles of the house of Jehovah.[i] And he made his father's brother Zed·e·ki′ah king over Judah and Jerusalem.[j]

11 Zed·e·ki′ah[k] was 21 years old when he became king, and he reigned for 11 years in Jerusalem.[l] **12** He continued to do what was bad in the eyes of Jehovah his God. He did not humble himself before the prophet Jeremiah,[m] who spoke at the order of Jehovah. **13** He also rebelled against King Neb·u·chad·nez′zar,[n] who had made him take an oath by God, and he remained stubborn* and hardhearted and refused to turn to Jehovah the God of Israel. **14** All the chiefs of the priests as well as the people were exceedingly unfaithful, practicing all the detestable things of the nations, and they defiled the house of Jehovah[o] that he had sanctified in Jerusalem.

CHAP. 35
a 2Ki 23:30
  2Ch 34:28

b Jer 1:1

c Jer 9:17, 20

d 2Ki 23:28

CHAP. 36
e 1Ch 3:15
  Jer 22:11

f 2Ki 23:30, 31

g 2Ki 18:14
  2Ki 23:33

h 2Ki 23:29
  Jer 46:2

i 2Ki 23:34
  Jer 22:11, 12

j Jer 26:20, 21
  Jer 36:32

Second Col.
a 2Ki 23:36, 37

b 2Ki 24:1
  2Ki 25:1
  Jer 25:1

c 2Ki 24:16
  Da 1:1

d Ezr 1:7
  Jer 27:16
  Da 1:2
  Da 5:2

e 2Ki 24:5, 6

f Jer 22:24
  Mt 1:12

g 2Ki 24:8, 9

h 2Ki 24:10
  Jer 29:1, 2
  Eze 1:2

i 2Ki 24:13
  Jer 27:17, 18

j 2Ki 24:17

k Jer 37:1

l 2Ki 24:18-20
  Jer 52:1-3

m Jer 21:1, 2
  Jer 34:2
  Jer 38:14, 24

n 2Ki 24:20
  Eze 17:12-15

o 2Ki 16:11
  Eze 8:10, 11

35:25 *Or "songs of mourning." **36:3** *A talent equaled 34.2 kg (1,101 oz t). See App. B14.

36:10 *Possibly, in the spring. **36:13** *Lit., "he hardened his neck."

15 Jehovah the God of their forefathers kept warning them by means of his messengers, warning them again and again, because he felt compassion for his people and for his dwelling place. **16** But they kept ridiculing the messengers of the true God,[a] and they despised his words[b] and mocked his prophets,[c] until the rage of Jehovah came up against his people,[d] until they were beyond healing.

17 So he brought against them the king of the Chal·de′-ans,[e] who killed their young men with the sword[f] in the house of their sanctuary;[g] he felt no compassion for young man or virgin, old or infirm.[h] God gave everything into his hand.[i] **18** All the utensils of the house of the true God, great and small, as well as the treasures of the house of Jehovah and the treasures of the king and his princes, everything he brought to Babylon.[j] **19** He burned down the house of the true God,[k] tore down the wall of Jerusalem,[l] burned all its fortified towers with fire, and destroyed everything of value.[m]

20 He carried off captive to Babylon those who escaped the sword,[a] and they became servants to him[b] and his sons until the kingdom* of Persia began to reign,[c] **21** to fulfill Jehovah's word spoken by Jeremiah,[d] until the land had paid off its sabbaths.[e] All the days it lay desolate it kept sabbath, to fulfill 70 years.[f]

22 In the first year of King Cyrus[g] of Persia, in order that Jehovah's word spoken by Jeremiah[h] would be fulfilled, Jehovah stirred the spirit of King Cyrus of Persia to make a proclamation throughout his kingdom, which he also put in writing,[i] saying: **23** "This is what King Cyrus of Persia says, 'Jehovah the God of the heavens has given me all the kingdoms of the earth,[j] and he has commissioned me to build him a house in Jerusalem, which is in Judah.[k] Whoever there is among you of all his people, may Jehovah his God be with him, and let him go up.'"

36:20 *Or "royalty."

CHAP. 36
a 2Ch 30:1, 10
b Jer 5:12
c Jer 20:7
d Ps 74:1
e 2Ki 24:2
f Le 26:31
   De 28:25
   Ps 79:2
g Eze 9:7
h La 2:21
i De 28:49-51
j 2Ki 20:16, 17
   Isa 39:6
   Jer 27:19-22
   Jer 52:17
k Ps 74:4-7
l Jer 52:14
m 1Ki 9:7
   2Ki 25:9, 10
   Ps 79:1

Second Col.
a 2Ki 25:21
   Ps 137:1
b Jer 27:6, 7
c Jer 1:1-3
d Jer 25:9
e Le 26:34
f Jer 25:12
   Zec 1:12
g Isa 44:28
   Isa 45:1
h Jer 29:14
   Jer 32:42
   Jer 33:10, 11
i Ezr 1:1-4
j Da 5:18
k Isa 44:28
l Ezr 7:12, 13

EZRA

OUTLINE OF CONTENTS

1 In the first year of King Cyrus[a] of Persia, in order that Jehovah's word spoken by Jeremiah[b] would be fulfilled, Jehovah stirred the spirit of King Cyrus of Persia to make a proclamation throughout his kingdom, which he also put in writing, saying:

2 "This is what King Cyrus of Persia says, 'Jehovah the God of the heavens has given me all the kingdoms of the earth,[d] and he has commissioned me to build him a house in Jerusalem,[e] which is in Judah. **3** Whoever there is among you of all his people, may his God be with him, and let him go up to Jerusalem, which is in Judah, and rebuild the house of Jehovah the God of Israel—he is the true God—whose house was in Jerusalem.* **4** Anyone who is residing as a foreigner,[f] wherever he may be, let him be helped by his neighbors* by their giving him silver and gold, goods and livestock, along with the voluntary offering for the house of the true God,[g] which was in Jerusalem.'"

5 Then the heads of the paternal houses of Judah and of Benjamin and the priests and the Levites—everyone whose spirit the true God had stirred—prepared to go up and rebuild the

house of Jehovah, which was in Jerusalem. **6** All those around them supported them by giving them* utensils of silver and of gold, goods, livestock, and valuable things, besides all the voluntary offerings.

7 King Cyrus also brought out the utensils of the house of Jehovah that Neb·u·chad·nez′zar had taken from Jerusalem and had put in the house of his god.[a] **8** King Cyrus of Persia brought them out under the supervision of Mith′re·dath the treasurer, who made an inventory of them for Shesh·baz′zar*[b] the chieftain of Judah.

9 Now this was the inventory: 30 basket-shaped vessels of gold, 1,000 basket-shaped vessels of silver, 29 replacement vessels, **10** 30 small gold bowls, 410 small silver bowls, 1,000 other utensils. **11** All the utensils of gold and of silver were 5,400. Shesh·baz′zar brought all of these up when the exiles[c] were brought up out of Babylon to Jerusalem.

2 And these were the people of the province* who came up from the captives of the exile,[d] those whom King Neb·u·chad-

---

CHAP. 1
a Isa 45:1
Da 10:1

b Jer 25:12
Jer 29:14
Jer 33:10, 11

c 2Ch 36:22, 23

d Da 4:34, 35

e Isa 44:28

f 2Ki 17:6
Jer 9:16

g Ex 35:21
1Ch 29:9
Ezr 7:14-16

Second Col.
a 2Ki 24:11, 13
2Ch 36:7, 18
Ezr 6:5
Da 1:1, 2
Da 5:2

b Ezr 5:14, 16
Hag 1:1, 14
Hag 2:23

c 2Ki 24:14, 15
2Ch 36:20

CHAP. 2
d Ezr 8:1

1:3 *Or possibly, "who is in Jerusalem."
1:4 *Lit., "the men of his place."
1:6 *Lit., "strengthened their hands with." 1:8 *Possibly Zerubbabel at Ezr 2:2; 3:8. 2:1 *Or "jurisdictional district."

nez'zar of Babylon had exiled to Babylon[a] and who later returned to Jerusalem and Judah, each to his own city,[b] 2 those who came with Ze·rub'ba·bel,[c] Jesh'u·a,[d] Ne·he·mi'ah, Se·rai'ah, Re·el·ai'ah, Mor'de·cai, Bil'shan, Mis'par, Big'vai, Re'hum, and Ba'a·nah.

The number of the Israelite men included:[e] 3 the sons of Pa'rosh, 2,172; 4 the sons of Sheph·a·ti'ah, 372; 5 the sons of A'rah,[f] 775; 6 the sons of Pa'hath-mo'ab,[g] of the sons of Jesh'u·a and Jo'ab, 2,812; 7 the sons of E'lam,[h] 1,254; 8 the sons of Zat'tu,[i] 945; 9 the sons of Zac'cai, 760; 10 the sons of Ba'ni, 642; 11 the sons of Be'bai, 623; 12 the sons of Az'gad, 1,222; 13 the sons of Ad·o·ni'kam, 666; 14 the sons of Big'vai, 2,056; 15 the sons of A'din, 454; 16 the sons of A'ter, of Hez·e·ki'ah, 98; 17 the sons of Be'zai, 323; 18 the sons of Jo'rah, 112; 19 the sons of Ha'shum,[j] 223; 20 the sons of Gib'bar, 95; 21 the sons of Beth'le·hem, 123; 22 the men of Ne·to'phah, 56; 23 the men of An'a·thoth,[k] 128; 24 the sons of Az'ma·veth, 42; 25 the sons of Kir'i·ath-je'a·rim, Che·phi'rah, and Be·er'oth, 743; 26 the sons of Ra'mah[l] and Ge'ba,[m] 621; 27 the men of Mich'mas, 122; 28 the men of Beth'el and A'i,[n] 223; 29 the sons of Ne'bo,[o] 52; 30 the sons of Mag'bish, 156; 31 the sons of the other E'lam, 1,254; 32 the sons of Ha'rim, 320; 33 the sons of Lod, Ha'did, and O'no, 725; 34 the sons of Jer'i·cho, 345; 35 the sons of Se·na'ah, 3,630.

36 The priests:[p] the sons of Je·da'iah[q] of the house of Jesh'u·a,[r] 973; 37 the sons of Im'mer,[s] 1,052; 38 the sons of Pash'hur,[t] 1,247; 39 the sons of Ha'rim,[u] 1,017.

40 The Levites:[a] the sons of Jesh'u·a and Kad'mi·el,[b] of the sons of Hod·a·vi'ah, 74. 41 The singers:[c] the sons of A'saph,[d] 128. 42 The sons of the gatekeepers:[e] the sons of Shal'lum, the sons of A'ter, the sons of Tal'mon,[f] the sons of Ak'kub,[g] the sons of Ha·ti'ta, the sons of Sho'bai, altogether 139.

43 The temple servants:*[h] the sons of Zi'ha, the sons of Ha·su'pha, the sons of Tab·ba'oth, 44 the sons of Ke'ros, the sons of Si'a·ha, the sons of Pa'don, 45 the sons of Le·ba'nah, the sons of Hag'a·bah, the sons of Ak'kub, 46 the sons of Ha'gab, the sons of Sal'mai, the sons of Ha'nan, 47 the sons of Gid'del, the sons of Ga'har, the sons of Re·a'iah, 48 the sons of Re'zin, the sons of Ne·ko'da, the sons of Gaz'zam, 49 the sons of Uz'za, the sons of Pa·se'ah, the sons of Be'sai, 50 the sons of As'nah, the sons of Me·u'nim, the sons of Ne·phu'sim, 51 the sons of Bak'buk, the sons of Ha·ku'pha, the sons of Har'hur, 52 the sons of Baz'luth, the sons of Me·hi'da, the sons of Har'sha, 53 the sons of Bar'kos, the sons of Sis'e·ra, the sons of Te'mah, 54 the sons of Ne·zi'ah, the sons of Ha·ti'pha.

55 The sons of the servants of Sol'o·mon: the sons of So'tai, the sons of So'phe'reth, the sons of Pe·ru'da,[i] 56 the sons of Ja'a·lah, the sons of Dar'kon, the sons of Gid'del, 57 the sons of Sheph·a·ti'ah, the sons of Hat'til, the sons of Po'che·reth-haz·ze·ba'im, the sons of A'mi.

58 All the temple servants* and the sons of the servants of Sol'o·mon were 392.

59 And these went up from Tel-me'lah, Tel-har'sha, Che'rub,

CHAP. 2
a 2Ki 24:15, 16
   2Ki 25:11
   2Ch 36:20
b Ne 7:6, 7
c Ezr 1:8, 11
   Hag 1:14
   Mt 1:12
d Ezr 3:8
   Ezr 5:2
   Zec 3:1
e Ne 7:8-38
f Ne 6:17, 18
g Ezr 10:30, 44
   Ne 3:11
h Ezr 10:26, 44
i Ezr 10:27, 44
j Ezr 10:33, 44
k Jos 21:8, 18
   Jer 1:1
l Jos 18:21, 25
m Jos 18:21, 24
n Jos 7:2
o Ezr 10:43, 44
p Ne 7:39-42
q 1Ch 9:2, 10
   Ne 11:3, 10
r 1Ch 24:3, 11
s 1Ch 24:3, 14
   Ezr 10:20, 44
t Ezr 10:22, 44
u 1Ch 24:3, 8
   Ezr 10:21, 44

Second Col.
a Ne 7:43
b Ezr 3:9
   Ne 12:8, 24
c Ne 7:44
d 1Ch 15:16, 17
   Ne 11:3, 17
e Ne 7:45
f 1Ch 9:2, 17
   Ne 11:3, 19
g Ne 12:25, 26
h Jos 9:3, 27
   1Ch 9:2
   Ne 3:26
   Ne 7:46-56
i Ne 7:57-60

2:43 *Or "The Nethinim." Lit., "The given ones." 2:58 *Or "the Nethinim." Lit., "the given ones."

Ad'don, and Im'mer, but they were unable to verify their paternal house and their origin, as to whether they were Israelites:[a] 60 the sons of De·la'iah, the sons of To·bi'ah, the sons of Ne·ko'da, 652. 61 And of the sons of the priests: the sons of Ha·bai'ah, the sons of Hak'koz,[b] the sons of Bar·zil'lai, who took a wife from the daughters of Bar·zil'lai[c] the Gil'e·ad·ite and was called by their name. 62 These looked for their records to establish their genealogy, but they did not find them, so they were disqualified from the priesthood.*[d] 63 The governor* told them that they could not eat from the most holy things[e] until there was a priest who could consult the U'rim and Thum'mim.[f]

64 The total number of the entire congregation was 42,360,[g] 65 apart from their male and female slaves, who were 7,337; they also had 200 male and female singers. 66 Their horses were 736, their mules 245, 67 their camels 435, their donkeys 6,720.

68 When they arrived at the house of Jehovah in Jerusalem, some of the heads of the paternal houses made voluntary offerings[h] for the house of the true God, to rebuild it* on its own site.[i] 69 According to their means, they gave to the project treasury 61,000 gold drachmas,* 5,000 silver mi'nas,*[j] and 100 robes for the priests. 70 And the priests, the Levites, some of

the people, the singers, the gatekeepers, and the temple servants* settled in their cities, and all the rest of Israel# settled in their cities.[a]

3 When the seventh month[b] arrived and the Israelites* were in their cities, they gathered together with one accord in Jerusalem. 2 Jesh'u·a[c] the son of Je·hoz'a·dak and his fellow priests and Ze·rub'ba·bel[d] the son of She·al'ti·el[e] and his brothers rose up and built the altar of the God of Israel, so that they could offer up burnt sacrifices on it, as it is written in the Law of Moses[f] the man of the true God.

3 So they set the altar up on its former site, despite their fear of the peoples of the surrounding lands,[g] and they began offering up burnt sacrifices to Jehovah on it, the morning and the evening burnt sacrifices.[h] 4 Then they held the Festival of Booths* according to what is written,[i] and day by day they offered up the specified number of burnt sacrifices that were required each day.[j] 5 Afterward they offered up the regular burnt offering[k] and the offerings for the new moons[l] and those for all the sanctified festival seasons[m] of Jehovah, as well as those from everyone who willingly offered a voluntary offering[n] to Jehovah. 6 From the first day of the seventh month[o] they started to offer up burnt sacrifices to Jehovah, though the foundation of Jehovah's temple had not yet been laid.

7 They gave money to the stonecutters[p] and the craftsmen,[q] and food and drink and oil to the Si·do'ni·ans and the Tyr'i·ans for bringing cedar timbers

---

CHAP. 2
a Ne 7:61-65
b 1Ch 24:3, 10
  Ne 3:21
c 2Sa 17:27-29
  1Ki 2:7
d Nu 3:10
e Le 2:3
  Le 6:26
  Nu 18:11
f Ex 28:30
  Nu 27:21
  1Sa 28:6
g Ne 7:66-69
  Isa 10:21
  Jer 23:3
h Ex 35:5
  1Ch 29:5
  Ne 7:70-72
i 2Ch 3:1
j Ezr 8:25

Second Col.
a Ne 7:73

CHAP. 3
b 1Ki 8:2
c Hag 1:1
d Ezr 1:7, 8
  Lu 3:23, 27
e 1Ch 3:17
  Mt 1:12
f Ex 20:24
  Ex 40:29
g Ezr 4:4
h Nu 28:3, 4
i Ex 23:16
  Le 23:34
j Ex 29:38
  Nu 29:12, 13
k Ex 29:39, 42
l Nu 10:10
  Ps 81:3
m De 16:16
n De 12:5, 6
o Nu 29:1
p 1Ki 5:17
q Ezr 5:8

2:62 *Or "were excluded from the priesthood as unclean." 2:63 *Or "the Tirshatha," a Persian title for a governor of a province. 2:68 *Or "make it stand." 2:69 *Generally equated with the Persian gold daric that weighed 8.4 g (0.27 oz t). Not the drachma of the Greek Scriptures. See App. B14. #A mina in the Hebrew Scriptures equaled 570 g (18.35 oz t). See App. B14.

2:70 *Or "the Nethinim." Lit., "the given ones." #Lit., "all Israel." 3:1 *Lit., "sons of Israel." 3:4 *Or "Temporary Shelters."

by sea from Leb'a·non to Jop'pa,[a] according to the authorization granted them by King Cyrus of Persia.[b]

8 In the second year after they came to the house of the true God at Jerusalem, in the second month, Ze·rub'ba·bel the son of She·al'ti·el, Jesh'u·a the son of Je·hoz'a·dak and the rest of their brothers, the priests and the Levites, and all those who had come to Jerusalem out of the captivity[c] started the work; they appointed the Levites from 20 years old and up to serve as supervisors over the work of the house of Jehovah. **9** So Jesh'u·a, his sons and his brothers, and Kad'mi·el and his sons, the sons of Judah, joined together to supervise those doing the work in the house of the true God, along with the sons of Hen'a·dad,[d] their sons and their brothers, the Levites.

10 When the builders laid the foundation of the temple of Jehovah,[e] then the priests in official clothing, with the trumpets,[f] and the Levites, the sons of A'saph, with the cymbals, stood up to praise Jehovah according to the direction of King David of Israel.[g] **11** And they began to sing in response[h] by praising and giving thanks to Jehovah, "for he is good; his loyal love toward Israel endures forever."[i] Then all the people shouted with a loud shout of praise to Jehovah because the foundation of the house of Jehovah had been laid. **12** Many of the priests, the Levites, and the heads of the paternal houses —the old men who had seen the former house[j]—wept with a loud voice when they saw the foundation of this house being laid, while many others shouted joyfully at the top of their voice.[k] **13** So the people could not distinguish the sound of the joyful shouts from the sound of

the weeping, for the people were shouting so loudly that the sound was heard from a great distance.

4 When the enemies of Judah and Benjamin[a] heard that the returned exiles[b] were building a temple to Jehovah the God of Israel, **2** they immediately approached Ze·rub'ba·bel and the heads of the paternal houses and said to them: "Let us build along with you; for like you, we worship* your God[c] and we have been sacrificing to him since the days of King E'sar-had'don[d] of As·syr'i·a, who brought us here."[e] **3** However, Ze·rub'ba·bel and Jesh'u·a and the rest of the heads of the paternal houses of Israel said to them: "You have no share with us in building a house to our God,[f] for we alone will build it to Jehovah the God of Israel, just as King Cyrus the king of Persia has commanded us."[g]

4 Then the people of the land were continually discouraging* the people of Judah and disheartening them from building.[h] **5** They hired advisers against them to frustrate their plans[i] all the days of King Cyrus of Persia until the reign of King Da·ri'us[j] of Persia. **6** At the beginning of the reign of A·has·u·e'rus, they wrote an accusation against the inhabitants of Judah and Jerusalem. **7** And in the days of King Ar·ta·xerx'es of Persia, Bish'lam, Mith're·dath, Tab'e·el, and the rest of his colleagues wrote to Ar·ta·xerx'es the king; they translated the letter into Ar·a·ma'ic,[k] writing it with Ar·a·ma'ic characters.*

8 * Re'hum the chief government official and Shim'shai the

CHAP. 3
a Jos 19:46, 48
1Ch 22:3, 4
2Ch 2:10, 16

b Ezr 1:2, 3
Ezr 6:3, 4

c Ne 7:6, 7

d Ne 3:18

e Zec 4:9

f Nu 10:8

g 1Ch 6:31, 32
1Ch 23:5
1Ch 25:1

h Ex 15:21
Ne 12:24

i 1Ch 16:34
2Ch 7:3

j 1Ki 6:22
Hag 2:3

k Ps 126:1, 6
Isa 35:10
Zec 4:9

Second Col.

CHAP. 4
a Ezr 4:6-8
Ne 4:7, 8

b Ezr 2:1, 64

c 2Ki 17:33, 34

d 2Ki 19:36, 37

e 2Ki 17:24

f Ne 2:19, 20
Joh 4:9, 22

g 2Ch 36:23
Ezr 1:1-3
Ezr 6:3, 4

h Ne 6:9

i Ne 6:10-12

j Ezr 4:24
Ezr 5:5
Ezr 6:1

k 2Ki 18:26

4:2 *Lit., "search for." 4:4 *Lit., "weakening the hands of." 4:7 *Or possibly, "it was written in Aramaic and then translated." 4:8 *Ezr 4:8 through 6:18 was originally written in Aramaic.

scribe wrote a letter against Jerusalem to King Ar·ta·xerx′es, as follows: 9 (It was from Re′hum the chief government official and Shim′shai the scribe and the rest of their colleagues, the judges and the lesser governors, the secretaries, the people of E′rech,[a] the Babylonians, the inhabitants of Su′sa,[b] that is, the E′lam·ites,[c] 10 and the rest of the nations that the great and honorable As′e·nap·par took into exile and settled in the cities of Sa·mar′i·a,[d] and the rest in the region Beyond the River,* and now 11 this is a copy of the letter that they sent him.)

"To King Ar·ta·xerx′es from your servants, the men of the region Beyond the River: And now 12 let it be known to the king that the Jews who came up here from you to us have arrived at Jerusalem. They are rebuilding the rebellious and wicked city, and they are finishing the walls[e] and repairing the foundations. 13 Now let it be known to the king that if this city should be rebuilt and its walls finished, they will not give tax, tribute,[f] or toll, and it will result in a loss to the treasuries of the kings. 14 Since we eat the salt of the palace* and it is not proper for us to see the king's interests harmed, we have therefore sent to make this known to the king, 15 so that there may be an investigation of the book of records of your ancestors.[g] You will find in the book of records and learn that this city is a rebellious city, injurious to kings and provinces,* and within it have been those stirring up sedition from ancient times. That is why this city was destroyed.[h] 16 We

are making known to the king that if this city is rebuilt and its walls are finished, you will have no control* of the region Beyond the River."[a]

17 The king sent word to Re′hum the chief government official and Shim′shai the scribe and the rest of their colleagues who were dwelling in Sa·mar′i·a and the rest of the region Beyond the River:

"Greetings! And now 18 the official document that you sent us has been clearly read* before me. 19 By my order an investigation was made, and it was found that from long ago the city has had uprisings against kings, and rebellions and revolts have taken place there.[b] 20 There were powerful kings over Jerusalem who ruled the whole region Beyond the River, and tax, tribute, and toll were paid to them. 21 Now issue an order for these men to stop work, so that the city may not be rebuilt until I issue an order. 22 Be careful not to neglect acting in this regard, so that the king's interests are not harmed any further."[c]

23 Now after the copy of the official document of King Ar·ta·xerx′es had been read before Re′hum and Shim′shai the scribe and their colleagues, they quickly went to Jerusalem to the Jews and used force to stop them. 24 It was then that the work on the house of God, which was in Jerusalem, came to a halt; and it remained at a standstill until the second year of the reign of King Da·ri′us of Persia.[d]

5 Then the prophets Hag′gai[e] and Zech·a·ri′ah[f] the grandson of Id′do[g] prophesied to the Jews who were in Judah and

4:10 *Or "in Trans-Euphrates." 4:14 *Or "we receive our salary from the palace." 4:15 *Or "jurisdictional districts."

4:16 *Lit., "share." 4:18 *Or possibly, "has been translated and read."

in Jerusalem, in the name of the God of Israel who was over them. **2** It was then that Ze·rub'ba·bel[a] the son of She·al'ti·el and Jesh'u·a[b] the son of Je·hoz'a·dak started to rebuild the house of God,[c] which was in Jerusalem; and the prophets of God were with them and supported them.[d] **3** At that time Tat'te·nai the governor of the region Beyond the River* and She'thar-boz'e·nai and their colleagues came to them and asked them: "Who issued an order to you to build this house and to finish this structure?"* **4** Then they asked them: "What are the names of the men who are working on this building?" **5** But God was watching over* the elders of the Jews,[e] and they did not stop them until the report could be sent to Da·ri'us and an official document could be sent back concerning this.

6 Here is a copy of the letter that Tat'te·nai the governor of the region Beyond the River and She'thar-boz'e·nai and his colleagues, the lesser governors of the region Beyond the River, sent to King Da·ri'us; **7** they sent the report to him, and this is what they wrote:

"To King Da·ri'us:

"All peace! **8** Let it be known to the king that we went to the province* of Judah to the house of the great God, and it is being built with large stones rolled into place, and timbers are being laid in the walls. The work is being eagerly done by the people and is making progress through their efforts. **9** Then we questioned their elders, asking them: 'Who issued an order to you to

build this house and to finish this structure?'*[#a] **10** We also asked them their names to inform you, so that we could write the names of the men who are taking the lead.

11 "This is the response they gave us: 'We are the servants of the God of the heavens and the earth, and we are rebuilding the house that was built many years ago, which a great king of Israel built and finished.[b] **12** However, because our fathers angered the God of the heavens,[c] he gave them into the hand of King Neb·u·chad·nez'zar[d] of Babylon, the Chal·de'an, who demolished this house* and took the people into exile to Babylon.[f] **13** Nevertheless, in the first year of King Cyrus of Babylon, King Cyrus issued an order to rebuild this house of God.[g] **14** Moreover, King Cyrus took out of the temple of Babylon the gold and silver vessels of the house of God that Neb·u·chad·nez'zar had taken from the temple in Jerusalem and had brought to the temple of Babylon.[h] They were given to a man named Shesh·baz'zar,*[i] whom Cyrus made governor.[j] **15** Cyrus said to him: "Take these vessels. Go, deposit them in the temple that is in Jerusalem, and let the house of God be rebuilt in its former place."[k] **16** Then this Shesh·baz'zar came, and he laid the foundations of the house of God,[l] which is in Jerusalem; and it has been under construction from then until now, but it has not been completed.'[m]

17 "Now if it seems good to the king, let an investigation be made in the royal treasury there in Babylon, to determine whether King Cyrus issued an order to rebuild that house of God in

---

CHAP. 5
a Mt 1:12

b Zec 6:11

c Ezr 3:2, 8

d Ezr 6:14
  Hag 2:4, 21
  Zec 4:7

e Ezr 7:6, 28
  Ezr 8:22

Second Col.
a Ezr 5:3, 4

b 1Ki 7:51

c De 31:17
  2Ch 34:24,
  25

d 2Ki 24:1
  2Ki 25:1

e 2Ki 25:8, 9

f 2Ki 25:11

g Ezr 1:1-3

h 2Ki 25:14, 15
  2Ch 36:7, 18

i Ezr 1:8, 11

j Hag 1:1, 14

k Ezr 1:2, 7

l Ezr 3:10
  Hag 2:18
  Zec 4:9

m Ezr 4:23, 24

5:3 *Or "of Trans-Euphrates." **5:3, 9** #Or "these beams." **5:5** *Lit., "the eye of their God was on." **5:8** *Or "jurisdictional district."

5:14 *Possibly Zerubbabel at Ezr 2:2; 3:8.

Jerusalem;[a] and let the decision of the king concerning this be sent to us."

6 It was then that King Da·ri′us issued an order, and they made an investigation in the archives* where the treasures were deposited in Babylon. **2** And a scroll was found in the citadel at Ec·bat′a·na, in the province* of Me′di·a, and the following memorandum was written on it:

3 "In the first year of King Cyrus, King Cyrus issued an order concerning the house of God in Jerusalem:[b] 'Let the house be rebuilt as the place where they are to offer sacrifices, and its foundations are to be set in place; its height is to be 60 cubits,* its width 60 cubits,[c] **4** with three layers of large stones rolled into place and one layer of timbers;[d] and let the expense be paid from the king's house.[e] **5** Also, let the gold and silver vessels of the house of God that Neb·u·chad·nez′zar took out of the temple that was in Jerusalem and brought to Babylon[f] be returned, so that they may be put in their place in the temple in Jerusalem and be deposited in the house of God.'[g]

6 "So now Tat′te·nai the governor of the region Beyond the River,* She′thar-boz′e·nai, and your colleagues, the lesser governors of the region Beyond the River[h]—stay away from there. **7** Do not interfere with the work on that house of God. The governor of the Jews and the elders of the Jews will rebuild that house of God in its former place. **8** Furthermore, I am issuing an order as to what you are to do for these elders of the

Jews for rebuilding that house of God: From the royal treasury,[a] from the tax collected in the region Beyond the River, the expenses are to be promptly given to these men to continue without interruption.[b] **9** And whatever is needed—young bulls[c] as well as rams[d] and lambs[e] for the burnt offerings to the God of heaven, wheat,[f] salt,[g] wine,[h] and oil,[i] just as the priests who are in Jerusalem say—is to be given them continually day by day without fail, **10** so that they may continually present offerings that please the God of the heavens and pray for the life of the king and his sons.[j] **11** I have also issued an order that if anyone violates this decree, a timber will be pulled out of his house and he will be lifted up and fastened to it,* and his house will be turned into a public latrine# for this offense. **12** And may the God who has caused his name to reside there[k] overthrow any king and people who lift a hand to violate this order and destroy that house of God, which is in Jerusalem. I, Da·ri′us, issue this order. Let it be done promptly."

13 Then Tat′te·nai the governor of the region Beyond the River, She′thar-boz′e·nai,[l] and their colleagues promptly carried out everything that King Da·ri′us had ordered. **14** And the elders of the Jews continued building and making progress,[m] urged on by the prophesying of Hag′gai[n] the prophet and Zech·a·ri′ah[o] the grandson of Id′do; they finished building it by the order of the God of Israel[p] and by the order of Cyrus[q] and Da·ri′us[r] and King Ar·ta·xerx′es[s] of Persia. **15** They completed the house by the third day of the month of

---

CHAP. 5
a 2Ch 36:22, 23
   Ezr 6:3, 4

CHAP. 6
b 2Ch 36:22, 23
   Ezr 1:1-3
c 1Ki 6:2
d Ezr 3:7
   Ezr 5:8
e Ezr 7:20
   Isa 49:23
f 2Ki 25:13-15
   2Ch 36:7, 18
   Da 1:1, 2
   Da 5:2
g Ezr 1:8, 11
h Ezr 5:3, 6

Second Col.
a Ezr 7:20
   Hag 2:7, 8
b Ezr 5:5
c Le 1:3, 5
d Le 1:10
e Nu 28:3
f Le 2:1
g Le 2:13
h Nu 15:5
i Ex 27:20
   Le 2:4
j Ezr 7:23
k De 12:5, 6
   2Ch 7:16
l Ezr 5:6
m Ezr 3:8
   Ezr 4:3
n Hag 1:12
o Ezr 5:1, 2
   Zec 1:1, 7
   Zec 6:15
p Hag 1:8
q 2Ch 36:23
   Ezr 1:2, 3
   Isa 44:28
r Ezr 6:12
s Ezr 7:12, 13

6:1 *Lit., "the house of the records."
6:2 *Or "jurisdictional district." 6:3
*About 26.7 m (87.6 ft). See App. B14.
6:6 *Or "of Trans-Euphrates."

6:11 *Or "and he will be impaled on it." #Or possibly, "a garbage dump; a dunghill."

A'dar,* in the sixth year of the reign of King Da·ri'us.

16 Then the Israelites, the priests, the Levites,[a] and the rest of the former exiles held the inauguration* of this house of God with joy. 17 And they presented for the inauguration of this house of God 100 bulls, 200 rams, 400 lambs, and as a sin offering for all Israel 12 male goats, corresponding to the number of the tribes of Israel.[b] 18 And they appointed the priests in their groups and the Levites in their divisions for the service of God in Jerusalem,[c] according to what is written in the book of Moses.[d]

19 And the former exiles held the Passover on the 14th day of the first month.[e] 20 The priests and the Levites, without exception, had cleansed themselves,[f] so they were all clean; they slaughtered the Passover sacrifice for all the former exiles, for their fellow priests, and for themselves. 21 Then the Israelites who had returned from the exile ate of it, along with everyone who had joined them and had separated himself from the uncleanness of the nations of the land to worship* Jehovah the God of Israel.[g] 22 They also joyfully held the Festival of Unleavened Bread[h] for seven days, for Jehovah caused them to rejoice and he had made the heart of the king of As·syr'i·a favorable toward them,[i] so that he supported them* in the work of the house of the true God, the God of Israel.

7 After these things, during the reign of King Ar·ta·xerx'es[j] of Persia, Ez'ra*[k] returned. He was the son of Se·rai'ah,[l] son of Az·a·ri'ah, son of Hil·ki'ah,[a] 2 son of Shal'lum, son of Za'dok, son of A·hi'tub, 3 son of Am·a·ri'ah, son of Az·a·ri'ah,[b] son of Me·ra'ioth, 4 son of Zer·a·hi'ah, son of Uz'zi, son of Buk'ki, 5 son of Ab·i·shu'a, son of Phin'e·has,[c] son of El·e·a'zar,[d] son of Aaron[e] the chief priest. 6 This Ez'ra came up from Babylon. He was a copyist* who was well-versed in* the Law of Moses,[f] which Jehovah the God of Israel had given. The king granted everything he requested, for the hand of Jehovah his God was upon him.

7 Some of the Israelites, the priests, the Levites,[g] the singers,[h] the gatekeepers,[i] and the temple servants,*[j] went up to Jerusalem in the seventh year of King Ar·ta·xerx'es. 8 And Ez'ra came to Jerusalem in the fifth month, in the seventh year of the king. 9 On the first day of the first month, he began the journey from Babylon, and he arrived in Jerusalem on the first day of the fifth month, for the good hand of his God was upon him.[k] 10 Ez'ra had prepared his heart* to consult the Law of Jehovah and to practice it,[l] and to teach its regulations and judgments in Israel.[m]

11 This is a copy of the letter that King Ar·ta·xerx'es gave to Ez'ra the priest and copyist,* an expert in the study* of the commandments of Jehovah and of his regulations to Israel:

12 * "Ar·ta·xerx'es,[n] the king of kings, to Ez'ra the priest, the copyist* of the Law of the God of the heavens: May you have perfect peace. And

---

CHAP. 6

a 1Ch 9:2
Ne 7:73

b 2Ch 7:5

c 1Ch 23:6

d Nu 3:6

e Ex 12:2, 14
Le 23:5
De 16:1
Es 3:7

f Ex 30:19, 20
Le 21:8
Le 22:2, 3

g Ex 12:48
Nu 9:14

h Ex 12:17
Le 23:6

i Ezr 7:27
Pr 21:1

CHAP. 7

j Ne 2:1

k Ne 8:2
Ne 12:26

l 1Ch 6:14

Second Col.

a 2Ki 22:8

b 2Ch 31:10

c Nu 25:11
Jg 20:28

d Ex 6:23, 25
Nu 3:32
De 10:6

e Ex 7:1
Ex 28:1

f Ne 8:1, 4

g Ezr 8:18, 19

h 1Ch 6:31, 32

i 1Ch 9:22-27

j 1Ch 9:2
Ezr 8:20

k Ezr 8:22

l De 5:1
De 17:10

m De 33:8, 10
Mal 2:7

n Ezr 6:14
Ne 2:1

6:15 *See App. B15. 6:16 *Or "dedication." 6:21 *Lit., "search for." 6:22 *Lit., "strengthened their hands." 7:1 *Meaning "Help."

7:6, 11, 12 *Or "scribe." 7:6 #Or "He was a skilled copyist of." 7:7 *Or "the Nethinim." Lit., "the given ones." 7:10 *Or "had determined in his heart." 7:11 #Or "a copyist of the words." 7:12 #Ezr 7:12 through 7:26 was originally written in Aramaic.

now 13 I have issued an or- der that everyone in my realm of the people of Israel and their priests and Levites who is will- ing to go with you to Jerusalem should go.[a] 14 For you are sent by the king and his seven ad- visers to investigate whether the Law of your God, which is with you,* is being applied in Judah and Jerusalem, 15 and to take the silver and the gold that the king and his advisers have vol- untarily given to the God of Is- rael, whose residence is in Je- rusalem, 16 with all the silver and the gold that you receive* in all the province# of Babylon, along with the gift that the peo- ple and the priests voluntarily give to the house of their God, which is in Jerusalem.[b] 17 And you are to buy promptly with this money bulls,[c] rams,[d] lambs,[e] along with their grain offerings[f] and their drink offerings,[g] and you are to present them on the altar of the house of your God in Jerusalem.

18 "And whatever seems good to you and to your brothers to do, you may do with the rest of the silver and the gold, ac- cording to the will of your God. 19 And all the vessels that are given to you for the service of the house of your God, you are to deliver before God at Jeru- salem.[h] 20 And the rest of the necessities of the house of your God that you are required to give, you will give out of the roy- al treasury.

21 "I, King Ar·ta·xerxʹes, have issued an order to all the trea- surers in the region Beyond the River,* that everything that Ezʹ- ra[j] the priest, the copyist# of the Law of the God of the heavens,

CHAP. 7
a Ezr 1:2, 3

b Ezr 1:5, 6
  Ezr 8:25

c Le 1:3

d Le 1:10

e Nu 28:3

f Nu 15:4

g Nu 15:5

h Ezr 8:30

i Ezr 6:3, 4
  Ezr 6:8

j Ezr 7:6
  Ne 8:2

Second Col.
a Nu 15:5

b Ex 27:20
  Le 2:1

c Le 2:13

d Ezr 1:2

e Ezr 6:9, 10

f Ne 5:4

g 1Ch 15:16

h 1Ch 9:2

i Ne 8:2, 3

j Ezr 6:22
  Pr 21:1
  Isa 60:13

k Ezr 9:9
  Ne 1:11

l Ezr 7:14

requests of you is to be done promptly, 22 up to 100 talents* of silver, 100 cor measures# of wheat, 100 bath measures△ of wine,[a] 100 bath measures of oil,[b] and salt[c] without limit. 23 Let everything that is ordered by the God of the heavens be done with zeal for the house of the God of the heavens,[d] so that there may be no wrath against the king's realm and his sons.[e] 24 And you are further advised that it is not permitted to impose any tax, tribute,[f] or toll on any of the priests and Levites, musicians,[g] doorkeepers, temple servants,*[h] and workers of this house of God.

25 "And you, Ezʹra, according to the wisdom that you possess from your God,* appoint magis- trates and judges to judge all the people in the region Be- yond the River, all those who know the laws of your God; and you should instruct anyone who does not know them.[i] 26 And everyone who does not observe the Law of your God and the law of the king should have judg- ment executed on him promptly, whether it is death, banishment, a fine, or imprisonment."

27 May Jehovah the God of our forefathers be praised, who put it into the heart of the king to beautify the house of Jehovah in Jerusalem![j] 28 And he has shown me loyal love be- fore the king[k] and his advisers[l] and all the mighty princes of the king. So I took courage* because the hand of Jehovah my God

7:14 *Lit., "in your hand." 7:16 *Lit., "find." #Or "jurisdictional district." 7:21 *Or "in Trans-Euphrates." #Or "scribe."

7:22 *A talent equaled 34.2 kg (1,101 oz t). See App. B14. #A cor equaled 220 L (200 dry qt). See App. B14. △A bath equaled 22 L (5.81 gal). See App. B14. 7:24 *Or "Nethinim." Lit., "given ones." 7:25 *Lit., "according to the wisdom of your God that is in your hand." 7:28 *Or "strengthened myself."

was upon me, and I gathered out of Israel leading men* to go up with me.

8 Now these were the heads of their paternal houses and the genealogical enrollment of those who went up with me out of Babylon during the reign of King Ar·ta·xerx′es:[a] **2** of the sons of Phin′e·has,[b] Ger′shom; of the sons of Ith′a·mar,[c] Daniel; of the sons of David, Hat′tush; **3** of the sons of Shec·a·ni′ah, of the sons of Pa′rosh, Zech·a·ri′ah, and with him there was an enrollment of 150 males; **4** of the sons of Pa′hath-mo′ab,[d] El′ie·ho·e′nai the son of Zer·a·hi′ah, and with him 200 males; **5** of the sons of Zat′tu,[e] Shec·a·ni′ah the son of Ja·ha·zi′el, and with him 300 males; **6** of the sons of A′din,[f] E′bed the son of Jon′a·than, and with him 50 males; **7** of the sons of E′lam,[g] Je·sha′iah the son of Ath·a·li′ah, and with him 70 males; **8** of the sons of Sheph·a·ti′ah,[h] Zeb·a·di′ah the son of Mi′cha·el, and with him 80 males; **9** of the sons of Jo′ab, O·ba·di′ah the son of Je·hi′el, and with him 218 males; **10** of the sons of Ba′ni, She·lo′mith the son of Jo·si·phi′ah, and with him 160 males; **11** of the sons of Be′bai,[j] Zech·a·ri′ah the son of Be′bai, and with him 28 males; **12** of the sons of Az′gad,[j] Jo·ha′nan the son of Hak′ka·tan, and with him 110 males; **13** of the sons of Ad·o·ni′kam,[k] those who were the last, and these were their names: E·liph′e·let, Je·i′el, and She·mai′ah, and with them 60 males; **14** and of the sons of Big′vai, U′thai and Zab′bud, and with them 70 males.

15 I assembled them at the river that comes to A·ha′va,[m] and we camped there for three days. But when I examined the people and the priests, I did not find any of the Levites there. **16** So I sent for E·li·e′zer, Ar′i·el, She·mai′ah, El·na′than, Ja′rib, El·na′than, Nathan, Zech·a·ri′ah, and Me·shul′lam, who were leading men, and for Joi′a·rib and El·na′than, who were instructors. **17** Then I gave them a command concerning Id′do the leader in the place called Ca·si·phi′a. I told them to tell Id′do and his brothers, the temple servants* who were in Ca·si·phi′a, to bring to us ministers for the house of our God. **18** Since the good hand of our God was upon us, they brought a discreet man from the sons of Mah′li[a] the grandson of Le′vi the son of Israel, namely, She·re·bi′ah,[b] and his sons and his brothers, 18 men; **19** and Hash·a·bi′ah, and with him Je·sha′iah from the Me·rar′ites,[c] his brothers and their sons, 20 men. **20** And there were 220 of the temple servants,* whom David and the princes gave to the service of the Levites, all of whom had been designated by name.

21 Then I proclaimed a fast there at the river A·ha′va, to humble ourselves before our God, to seek guidance from him for our journey, for us and for our children and for all our goods. **22** I was ashamed to ask the king for soldiers and horsemen to protect us against the enemies along the way, because we had said to the king: "The good hand of our God is over all those seeking him,[d] but his strength and his anger are against all those abandoning him."[e] **23** So we fasted and made request of our God concerning this, and he listened to our entreaty.[f]

24 I now set apart 12 of the chiefs of the priests, namely,

CHAP. 8
a Ezr 7:7

b 1Ch 6:3, 4

c Ex 6:23

d Ezr 2:1, 6

e Ezr 2:1, 8
Ezr 10:27, 44

f Ezr 2:1, 15

g Ezr 2:1, 7

h Ezr 2:1, 4

i Ezr 2:1, 11
Ezr 10:28, 44

j Ezr 2:1, 12

k Ne 7:6, 18

l Ezr 2:1, 14

m Ezr 8:31

_____
Second Col.
a Nu 3:20

b Ezr 8:24, 25

c 1Ch 6:16

d 2Ch 16:9
Ezr 7:6
Ezr 7:28
Zec 4:6

e 2Ch 15:2

f 2Ch 7:14
Jer 29:10, 12
Jer 50:4, 5

7:28 *Lit., "heads."

8:17, 20 *Or "the Nethinim." Lit., "the given ones."

She·re·bi′ah and Hash·a·bi′ah,[a] along with ten of their brothers. **25** Then I weighed out to them the silver and the gold and the utensils, the contribution that the king and his advisers and his princes and all the Israelites who were present there had made to the house of our God.[b] **26** Thus I weighed out into their hand 650 talents* of silver, 100 silver utensils worth 2 talents, 100 talents of gold, **27** 20 small gold bowls worth 1,000 darics,* and 2 utensils of fine copper, gleaming red, as desirable as gold.

28 Then I said to them: "You are holy to Jehovah,[c] and the utensils are holy, and the silver and the gold are a voluntary offering to Jehovah the God of your forefathers. **29** Guard them carefully until you weigh them out before the chiefs of the priests and the Levites and the princes of the paternal houses of Israel in Jerusalem,[d] in the chambers* of the house of Jehovah." **30** And the priests and the Levites took the silver and the gold and the utensils that had been weighed out to them, in order to bring them to Jerusalem to the house of our God.

31 Finally we pulled away from the river A·ha′va[e] on the 12th day of the first month[f] to go to Jerusalem, and the hand of our God was over us, and he rescued us from the hand of the enemy and from ambush along the way. **32** So we came to Jerusalem[g] and stayed there for three days. **33** And on the fourth day, we weighed out the silver and the gold and the utensils in the house of our God[h] and handed them over to Mer′e·moth[i] son of U·ri′jah the

priest, and with him was El·e·a′zar son of Phin′e·has, and with them were the Levites Jo′za·bad[a] son of Jesh′u·a and No·a·di′ah son of Bin′nu·i.[b] **34** Everything was numbered and weighed, and all the weight was recorded. **35** Those coming out of the captivity, the former exiles, presented burnt sacrifices to the God of Israel, 12 bulls[c] for all Israel, 96 rams,[d] 77 male lambs, and 12 male goats[e] as a sin offering; all of this was a burnt offering to Jehovah.[f]

36 Then we gave the decrees of the king[g] to the satraps* of the king and the governors of the region Beyond the River,*[h] and they supported the people and the house of the true God.[i]

9 And as soon as these things had been done, the princes approached me and said: "The people of Israel and the priests and the Levites have not separated themselves from the peoples of the lands and their detestable practices,[j] those of the Ca′naan·ites, the Hit′tites, the Per′iz·zites, the Jeb′u·sites, the Am′mon·ites, the Mo′ab·ites, the Egyptians,[k] and the Am′or·ites.[l] **2** They have taken some of their daughters as wives for themselves and for their sons.[m] Now they, the holy offspring,*[n] have become mingled with the peoples of the lands.[o] The princes and the deputy rulers have been the foremost offenders in this unfaithfulness."

3 Now as soon as I heard of this, I ripped apart my garment and my sleeveless coat and pulled out some of the hair of my head and my beard, and I sat

---

CHAP. 8
a Ezr 8:18, 19

b Ezr 7:14-16
　Ezr 7:19

c Le 21:6-8
　Isa 52:11

d Ezr 7:19
　Ezr 8:33

e Ezr 8:15, 21

f Es 3:7

g Ezr 7:8

h Ezr 7:19
　Ezr 8:29

i Ne 3:4, 21

Second Col.
a Ne 8:7

b Ne 12:1, 8

c Le 1:3

d Le 1:10

e Le 22:18, 19

f Ezr 7:17

g Ezr 7:21

h Ge 15:18

i Ezr 6:13

CHAP. 9
j Le 20:23
　De 12:29, 30

k Le 18:3

l Ge 15:16

m Ex 34:15, 16
　Ezr 10:44

n Ezr 19:5, 6

o Ne 13:1, 3

8:26 *A talent equaled 34.2 kg (1,101 oz t). See App. B14. 8:27 *A daric was a Persian gold coin. See App. B14. 8:29 *Or "dining halls." 8:36 *Title meaning "protectors of the realm," here applied to governors of provinces in the Persian Empire. *Or "of Trans-Euphrates." 9:2 *Lit., "seed."

down in shock. **4** Then every-one who had reverence for* the words of the God of Israel gath-ered around me because of the unfaithfulness of the exiled peo-ple, while I was sitting in shock until the evening grain offering.[a]

5 And at the time of the eve-ning grain offering,[b] I stood up from my humiliation, with my garment and my sleeveless coat torn apart, and I got down on my knees and spread out my hands to Jehovah my God. **6** And I said: "O my God, I feel ashamed and embarrassed to raise my face to you, O my God, for our errors have multiplied over our heads and our guilt has mounted up to the heavens.[c] **7** From the days of our forefathers until this day our guilt has been great;[d] and because of our errors, we, our kings, and our priests have been given into the hand of the kings of the lands, to the sword,[e] to captivity,[f] to plunder,[g] and to disgrace, as is the case today.[h] **8** But now for a brief moment, favor has come from Jehovah our God by letting a remnant es-cape and by giving us a secure position* in his holy place,[i] to make our eyes shine, O our God, and to revive us a little in our slavery. **9** For although we are slaves,[j] our God has not aban-doned us in our slavery; but he has extended his loyal love to-ward us before the kings of Per-sia,[k] to revive us so as to raise up the house of our God[l] and to restore its ruins and to give us a stone wall* in Judah and in Je-rusalem.

10 "But now what can we say, O our God, after this? For we have left your commandments, **11** which you gave us through your servants the prophets, say-ing: 'The land that you are going

in to take possession of is an im-pure land because of the impu-rity of the peoples of the lands, because of their detestable prac-tices with which they have filled it from end to end with their uncleanness.[a] **12** Therefore, do not give your daughters to their sons, neither accept their daugh-ters for your sons;[b] and you must never seek their peace and their prosperity,[c] so that you may grow strong and eat the good of the land and take pos-session of it for your sons for-ever.' **13** And after all that has come upon us for our bad deeds and our great guilt—for you, O our God, have not dealt with us according to our er-ror,[d] and you have allowed those of us here to escape[e]— **14** are we to break your com-mandments again and form mar-riage alliances* with the peoples who practice these detestable things?[f] Would you not become so angry with us that you would completely destroy us, leaving no remnant or survivor? **15** O Jehovah the God of Is-rael, you are righteous,[g] for we have survived as a remnant to this day. Here we are before you in our guilt, for it is impossible to stand before you because of this."[h]

10 While Ez'ra was praying[i] and making confession, weeping and lying prostrate be-fore the house of the true God, a large crowd of men, women, and children of Isra-el gathered around him, for the people were weeping profuse-ly. **2** Then Shec·a·ni'ah the son of Je·hi'el[j] of the sons of E'lam[k] said to Ez'ra: "We have acted unfaithfully against our God by marrying* foreign women from the peoples of the land.[l] Despite

---

CHAP. 9	
a	Ex 29:41
b	Nu 28:4, 5
c	Da 9:7
d	Nu 32:14
	2Ch 29:6
e	2Ki 10:32
	2Ch 36:17
f	2Ki 17:22, 23
	2Ki 25:6, 7
g	2Ki 17:20
h	Ne 9:32
i	Ne 9:31
	Ps 138:7
j	Ne 9:36, 37
k	Ezr 1:1-3
l	Ezr 6:14
	Zec 4:9
Second Col.	
a	Le 18:24
	De 12:30, 31
	De 18:9-11
b	Ex 23:32
	Ex 34:15, 16
	De 7:3, 4
	Jos 23:12, 13
c	De 23:3, 6
d	Ps 103:8, 10
	La 3:22
e	Ps 106:46
f	Ezr 9:1
	Ne 13:23
g	Ne 9:33
	Da 9:7
h	Ps 130:3
	Ps 143:2
CHAP. 10	
i	Ezr 9:5, 6
j	Ezr 10:26, 44
k	Ezr 2:1, 7
l	Ezr 9:2

9:4 *Lit., "who trembled at." **9:8** *Lit., "a peg." **9:9** *Or "a wall of protection."

9:14 *Or "and intermarry." **10:2** *Or "by taking into our houses."

this, there is still hope for Israel. **3** Now let us make a covenant with our God[a] to send away all the wives and those born from them, in harmony with the direction of Jehovah and of those who have reverence for* the commandment of our God.[b] Let us act according to the Law. **4** Get up, for this matter is your responsibility, and we are with you. Be strong and take action."

5 At that Ez'ra rose and had the chiefs of the priests, the Levites, and all Israel take an oath to do what had been said.[c] So they took an oath. **6** Ez'ra now got up from before the house of the true God and went to the chamber* of Je·ho·ha'nan the son of E·li'a·shib. Although he went there, he ate no food and drank no water, for he was in mourning because of the unfaithfulness of the exiled people.[d]

7 Then they made a proclamation throughout Judah and Jerusalem that all the former exiles gather together at Jerusalem; **8** and according to the decision of the princes and the elders, anyone who did not come within three days' time would have all his goods confiscated,* and he would be banished from the congregation of the exiled people.[e] **9** So all the men of Judah and Benjamin gathered together at Jerusalem within three days, that is, in the ninth month, on the 20th day of the month. All the people were sitting in a courtyard of the house of the true God, shivering because of the matter at hand and because of the heavy rain.

10 Then Ez'ra the priest rose and said to them: "You have acted unfaithfully by marrying for-

CHAP. 10
a 2Ki 11:17
  2Ch 29:10
  2Ch 34:31

b Ezr 9:4

c Ne 10:28-30

d Ezr 9:3, 4
  Da 9:3-5

e Ezr 7:26

Second Col.
a Ne 13:23

b De 7:3, 4
  Ne 13:3
  2Co 6:17

c Ezr 9:1

d Ne 8:7
  Ne 11:16

e Ezr 9:1, 2
  Ne 13:28
  Eze 44:22
  Mal 2:7, 8

f Ezr 2:1, 2
  Ezr 3:2
  Zec 6:11

eign women,[a] and so you have added to the guilt of Israel. **11** Now make confession to Jehovah the God of your forefathers and do his will. Separate yourselves from the peoples of the land and from these foreign wives."[b] **12** To this the whole congregation answered with a loud voice: "It is our duty to do exactly as you say. **13** However, there are many people, and it is the rainy season. It is not possible to stand outside, and the matter will not take just one or two days, for we have rebelled extensively in this matter. **14** So, please, let our princes represent the entire congregation;[c] and let all those in our cities who have married foreign women come at an appointed time, along with the elders and judges of each city, until we turn back the burning anger of our God from us concerning this matter."

15 However, Jon'a·than the son of As'a·hel and Jah·zei'ah the son of Tik'vah objected to this, and the Levites Me·shul'lam and Shab'be·thai[d] supported them. **16** But the former exiles did what was agreed on; and Ez'ra the priest and the family heads of their paternal houses, all designated by name, convened separately on the first day of the tenth month to look into the matter; **17** and by the first day of the first month they finished dealing with all the men who had married foreign women. **18** And it was discovered that some of the sons of the priests had married foreign women:[e] of the sons of Jesh'u·a[f] the son of Je·hoz'a·dak and his brothers, Ma·a·sei'ah, E·li·e'zer, Ja'rib, and Ged·a·li'ah. **19** But they promised* to send their wives away, and since they were guilty, they would offer a ram of the flock for their guilt.[a]

20 Of the sons of Im'mer,[b] there were Ha·na'ni and Zeb·a·di'ah; **21** and of the sons of Ha'rim,[c] Ma·a·sei'ah, E·li'jah, She·mai'ah, Je·hi'el, and Uz·zi'ah; **22** and of the sons of Pash'hur,[d] Eli·o·e'nai, Ma·a·sei'ah, Ish'ma·el, Ne·than'el, Jo'za·bad and El·e·a'sah. **23** And of the Levites, there were Jo'za·bad, Shim'e·i, Ke·lai'ah (that is, Ke·li'ta), Peth·a·hi'ah, Judah, and E·li·e'zer; **24** and of the singers, E·li'a·shib; and of the gatekeepers, Shal'lum, Te'lem, and U'ri.

25 And of Israel, of the sons of Pa'rosh,[e] there were Ra·mi'ah, Iz·zi'ah, Mal·chi'jah, Mij'a·min, El·e·a'zar, Mal·chi'jah, and Be·nai'ah; **26** and of the sons of E'lam,[f] Mat·ta·ni'ah, Zech·a·ri'ah, Je·hi'el,[g] Ab'di, Jer'e·moth, and E·li'jah; **27** and of the sons of Zat'tu,[h] Eli·o·e'nai, E·li'a·shib, Mat·ta·ni'ah, Jer'e·moth, Za'bad, and A·zi'za; **28** and of the sons of Be'bai,[i] Je·ho·ha'nan, Han·a·ni'ah, Zab'bai, and Ath'lai; **29** and of the sons of Ba'ni, Me·shul'lam, Mal'luch, A·dai'ah, Ja'-

shub, She'al, and Jer'e·moth; **30** and of the sons of Pa'hath-mo'ab,[a] Ad'na, Che'lal, Be·nai'ah, Ma·a·sei'ah, Mat·ta·ni'ah, Bez'al·el, Bin'nu·i, and Ma·nas'seh; **31** and of the sons of Ha'rim,[b] E·li·e'zer, Is·shi'jah, Mal·chi'jah,[c] She·mai'ah, Shim'e·on, **32** Benjamin, Mal'luch, and Shem·a·ri'ah; **33** and of the sons of Ha'shum,[d] Mat·te'nai, Mat'tat·tah, Za'bad, E·liph'e·let, Jer'e·mai, Ma·nas'seh, and Shim'e·i; **34** of the sons of Ba'ni, Ma·a·da'i, Am'ram, U'el, **35** Be·nai'ah, Be·dei'ah, Chel'u·hi, **36** Va·ni'ah, Mer'e·moth, E·li'a·shib, **37** Mat·ta·ni'ah, Mat·te'nai, and Ja'a·su; **38** and of the sons of Bin'nu·i, Shim'e·i, **39** Shel·e·mi'ah, Nathan, A·dai'ah, **40** Mach·nad'e·bai, Sha'shai, Sha'rai, **41** Az'ar·el, Shel·e·mi'ah, Shem·a·ri'ah, **42** Shal'lum, Am·a·ri'ah, and Joseph; **43** and of the sons of Ne'bo, Je·i'el, Mat·ti·thi'ah, Za'bad, Ze·bi'na, Jad'dai, Joel, and Be·nai'ah. **44** All of these had taken foreign wives,[e] and they sent their wives away, along with their sons.[f]

CHAP. 10
a Le 5:17, 18

b 1Ch 24:3, 14
  Ezr 2:1, 37

c 1Ch 24:3, 8
  Ezr 2:1, 39

d Ezr 2:1, 38

e Ezr 2:1, 3
  Ne 3:25

f Ezr 2:1, 7
  Ezr 8:1, 7

g Ezr 10:2

h Ezr 2:1, 8

i Ezr 2:1, 11
  Ezr 8:1, 11

Second Col.
a Ezr 2:1, 6

b Ezr 2:1, 32

c Ne 3:11

d Ezr 2:1, 19
  Ne 8:4

e De 7:3, 4

f Ezr 10:16, 17

NEHEMIAH

OUTLINE OF CONTENTS

1 The words of Ne·he·mi′ah*[a] the son of Hac·a·li′ah: Now in the month of Chis′lev,[#] in the 20th year, I was in Shu′shan[Δb] the citadel.[☐] **2** At that time Ha·na′ni,[c] one of my brothers, arrived with other men from Judah, and I asked them about the remaining Jews who had escaped the captivity,[d] and also about Jerusalem. **3** They replied: "Those remaining there in the province* who have survived the captivity are in a terrible situation and in disgrace.[e] The walls of Jerusalem are broken down,[f] and its gates have been burned with fire."[g]

4 As soon as I heard these words, I sat down and began to weep and mourn for days, and I kept fasting[h] and praying before the God of the heavens. **5** I said: "O Jehovah, the God of the heavens, the great and awe-inspiring God who keeps his covenant and shows loyal love to those who love him and keep his commandments,[i] **6** please, let your ear be attentive and your eyes open to listen to the prayer of your servant that I am praying to you today, day and night,[j] concerning your servants the Israelites, all the while confessing the sins that the people of Israel have committed against you.

We have sinned, both I and the house of my father.[a] **7** We have certainly acted corruptly against you[b] by not keeping the commandments, regulations, and judicial decisions that you gave to your servant Moses.[c]

8 "Remember, please, the word that you commanded* your servant Moses: 'If you act unfaithfully, I will scatter you among the peoples.[d] **9** But if you return to me and observe my commandments and obey them, though your dispersed people should be at the end of the heavens, I will gather them[e] from there and bring them to the place that I have chosen to have my name reside.'[f] **10** They are your servants and your people, whom you redeemed by your great power and by your mighty hand.[g] **11** O Jehovah, please, let your ear be attentive to the prayer of your servant and to the prayer of your servants who take delight in fearing your name, and please, grant success to your servant today, and may this man show me compassion."[h]

Now I was cupbearer to the king.[i]

2 In the month of Ni′san,[#] in the 20th year[j] of King Ar·ta·xerx′es,[k] wine was set before him, and as usual I took up the wine and gave it to the king.[l] But I had never been gloomy in his presence. **2** So the king said to

CHAP. 1
a Ne 1:11
  Ne 5:14
  Ne 10:1
b Es 1:2
  Es 3:15
  Da 8:2
c Ne 7:2
d Jer 52:30
e 1Ki 9:7
  Ne 9:36, 37
  Ps 79:4
f 2Ki 25:10
g Ne 2:17
  La 1:4
h 2Ch 20:3
  Ezr 8:21
i De 7:9
  Da 9:4
j Ps 88:1
  Lu 18:7

Second Col.
a 2Ch 29:6
  Ezr 9:6
b Ps 106:6
c Le 27:34
  Nu 36:13
  De 12:1
  Ne 9:34
d Le 26:33
  De 4:27
  De 28:64
e De 30:1-4
f De 12:5
  Ps 132:13
g Le 25:42
  De 5:15
  De 9:26, 29
h 1Ki 8:49, 50
  Ezr 7:1
  Ps 106:46
  Pr 21:1
i Ne 2:1

CHAP. 2
j Ne 1:1
k Ezr 7:1
  Ne 13:6
l Ne 1:11

1:1 *Meaning "Jah Comforts." **1:1; 2:1** #See App. B15. **1:1** ΔOr "Susa." ☐Or "palace; fortress." **1:3** *Or "jurisdictional district."

1:8 *Or "the warning you gave to."

me: "Why do you look so gloomy when you are not sick? This can be nothing but gloominess of heart." At this I became very frightened.

3 Then I said to the king: "Long live the king! Why should I not look gloomy when the city, the place where my forefathers are buried, lies in ruins, and its gates have been consumed by fire?"[a] **4** The king then said to me: "What is it that you are seeking?" At once I prayed to the God of the heavens.[b] **5** I then said to the king: "If it pleases the king and if your servant has found favor with you, send me to Judah, to the city where my forefathers are buried, so that I may rebuild it."[c] **6** Then the king, with his royal consort* sitting beside him, said to me: "How long will your journey be, and when will you return?" So it pleased the king to send me,[d] and I gave him a set time.[e]

7 Then I said to the king: "If it pleases the king, let letters be given me for the governors of the region Beyond the River,*[f] granting me safe passage until I reach Judah, **8** as well as a letter to A'saph the keeper of the Royal Park,* so that he may give me timber for beams for the gates of the Fortress[g] of the House* and for the walls of the city[h] and for the house where I will go." So the king gave them to me,[i] for the good hand of my God was upon me.[j]

9 Eventually I came to the governors of the region Beyond the River and gave them the king's letters. The king also sent with me army chiefs and horsemen. **10** When San·bal'lat[k] the Hor'o·nite and To·bi'ah[l] the Am'mon·ite[m] official* heard about it,

they were very displeased that someone had come to do something good for the people of Israel.

11 At length I came to Jerusalem, and I stayed there for three days. **12** I rose up by night, I and a few men with me, and I did not tell anyone what my God had put into my heart to do for Jerusalem, and there was no animal with me except the one I was riding. **13** And I went out at night through the Valley Gate,[a] passing in front of the Fountain of the Big Snake to the Gate of the Ash Heaps,[b] and I inspected the walls of Jerusalem that were broken down and its gates that had been consumed by fire.[c] **14** And I passed along to the Fountain Gate[d] and to the King's Pool, and there was not enough space for the animal I was riding to pass. **15** But I continued up the valley*[e] by night, and I kept inspecting the wall, after which I came back and entered through the Valley Gate, and then I returned.

16 The deputy rulers[f] did not know where I had gone and what I was doing, for I had not yet said anything to the Jews, the priests, the nobles, the deputy rulers, and the rest of the workers. **17** Finally I said to them: "You can see what a terrible situation we are in, how Jerusalem lies in ruins and its gates have been burned with fire. Come, let us rebuild the walls of Jerusalem, so that this disgrace will not continue." **18** Then I told them of how the good hand of my God was upon me[g] and also of the words that the king had spoken to me.[h] At this they said: "Let us get up and build." So they strengthened themselves* for the good work.[i]

CHAP. 2
a Ne 1:2, 3

b 1Sa 1:13

c Da 9:25

d Ne 1:11

e Ne 5:14
　Ne 13:6

f Jos 1:4
　Ezr 5:3

g Ne 7:2

h Ne 1:3

i Ezr 7:21

j Ezr 7:6

k Ne 4:1
　Ne 6:2

l Ne 2:19
　Ne 4:3
　Ne 6:14
　Ne 13:7

m Ne 13:1

Second Col.
a 2Ch 26:9

b Ne 3:13

c Ne 1:3
　La 1:4
　La 2:9

d Ne 3:15
　Ne 12:37

e 2Sa 15:23
　Joh 18:1

f Ne 4:14

g Ezr 7:6, 28
　Ne 2:7, 8

h Da 9:25

i Hag 1:14

19 Now when San·bal′lat the Hor′o·nite, To·bi′ah[a] the Am′mon·ite[b] official,* and Ge′shem the Arabian[c] heard of it, they began to mock us[d] and show us our contempt and say: "What are you doing? Are you rebelling against the king?"[e] **20** However, I replied: "The God of the heavens is the One who will grant us success,[f] and we his servants will get up and build; but you have neither share nor claim nor memorial* in Jerusalem."[g]

3 E·li′a·shib[h] the high priest and his brothers the priests got up to build the Sheep Gate.[i] They sanctified* it[j] and set up its doors; they sanctified it as far as the Tower of Me′ah,[k] as far as the Tower of Ha·nan′el.[l] **2** And next to them the men of Jer′i·cho[m] were building; and next to them Zac′cur the son of Im′ri was building.

3 The sons of Has·se·na′ah built the Fish Gate;[n] they timbered it[o] and then set up its doors, its bolts, and its bars. **4** And next to them Mer′e·moth[p] the son of U·ri′jah the son of Hak′koz did repair work, and next to them Me·shul′lam[q] the son of Ber·e·chi′ah the son of Me·shez′a·bel did repair work, and next to them Za′dok the son of Ba′a·na did repair work. **5** And next to them the Te·ko′ites[r] did repair work, but their prominent men would not lower themselves to share in* the service of their masters.

6 Joi′a·da the son of Pa·se′ah and Me·shul′lam the son of Bes·o·dei′ah repaired the Gate of the Old City;[s] they timbered it and then set up its doors, its bolts, and its bars. **7** Next to them Mel·a·ti′ah the Gib′e·on·ite[t] and Ja′don the Me·ron′o·thite

did repair work, men of Gib′e·on and Miz′pah[a] who were under the authority of* the governor of the region Beyond the River.[#b] **8** Next to them Uz′zi·el the son of Har·hai′ah, one of the goldsmiths, did repair work, and next to him Han·a·ni′ah, one of the ointment mixers,* did repair work; and they paved[#] Jerusalem as far as the Broad Wall.[c] **9** And next to them Re·pha′iah the son of Hur, a prince of half the district of Jerusalem, did repair work. **10** And next to them Je·da′iah the son of Ha·ru′maph did repair work in front of his own house, and next to him Hat′tush the son of Hash·ab·nei′ah did repair work.

11 Mal·chi′jah the son of Ha′rim[d] and Has′shub the son of Pa′hath-mo′ab[e] repaired another section,* as well as the Tower of the Ovens.[f] **12** And next to them Shal′lum the son of Hal·lo′hesh, a prince of half the district of Jerusalem, did repair work, along with his daughters.

13 Ha′nun and the inhabitants of Za·no′ah[g] repaired the Valley Gate;[h] they built it and then set up its doors, its bolts, and its bars, and they repaired 1,000 cubits* of the wall as far as the Gate of the Ash Heaps.[i] **14** Mal·chi′jah the son of Re′chab, a prince of the district of Beth-hac·che′rem,[j] repaired the Gate of the Ash Heaps; he built it and set up its doors, its bolts, and its bars.

15 Shal′lun the son of Col·ho′zeh, a prince of the district of Miz′pah,[k] repaired the Fountain Gate;[l] he built it and its roof, set up its doors, its bolts, and its bars, and also repaired the wall

---

CHAP. 2
a Ne 6:14
b Ne 13:1, 2
c Ne 4:7
　Ne 6:1, 2
d Ps 79:4
e Ne 6:6
f Ps 127:1
g Ezr 4:1-3

CHAP. 3
h Ne 12:10
　Ne 13:4, 28
i Joh 5:2
j Ne 12:30
k Ne 12:38, 39
l Jer 31:38
　Zec 14:10
m Ezr 2:1, 34
n 2Ch 33:1, 14
　Zep 1:10
o Ne 2:7, 8
p Ezr 8:33
　Ne 3:21
q Ne 3:30
　Ne 6:17, 18
r Ne 3:27
　Am 1:1
s Ne 12:38, 39
t 2Sa 21:2

Second Col.
a Jos 18:21, 26
　2Ch 16:6
　Jer 40:6
b Ge 15:18
c Ne 12:38
d Ezr 2:1, 32
e Ezr 2:1, 6
f Ne 12:38
g Jos 15:20, 34
　Ne 11:25, 30
h 2Ch 26:9
i Ne 2:13
j Jer 6:1
k Jos 18:21, 26
l Ne 2:14
　Ne 12:37

2:19 *Lit., "servant." 2:20 *Or "entitlement." 3:1 *Or "dedicated." 3:5 *Lit., "not bring their neck into."

3:7 *Lit., "belonging to the throne of." #Or "of Trans-Euphrates." 3:8 *Or "the perfume makers." #Or "paved with flagstone." 3:11 *Or "measured section." 3:13 *About 445 m (1,460 ft). See App. B14.

of the Pool[a] of the Canal to the King's Garden[b] and as far as the Stairway[c] that goes down from the City of David.[d]

16 After him Ne·he·mi'ah the son of Az'buk, a prince of half the district of Beth-zur,[e] did repair work from in front of the Burial Places of David[f] as far as the pool[g] that had been built and as far as the House of the Mighty Ones.

17 After him the Levites did repair work: Re'hum the son of Ba'ni; and next to him Hash·a·bi'ah, a prince of half the district of Kei'lah,[h] did repair work for his district. 18 After him their brothers did repair work: Bav'vai the son of Hen'a·dad, a prince of half the district of Kei'lah.

19 And next to him E'zer the son of Jesh'u·a,[i] a prince of Miz'pah, was repairing another section in front of the ascent to the Armory at the Buttress.[j]

20 After him Bar'uch the son of Zab'bai[k] worked with fervor and repaired another section, from the Buttress as far as the entrance of the house of E·li'a·shib[l] the high priest.

21 After him Mer'e·moth[m] the son of U·ri'jah the son of Hak'koz repaired another section, from the entrance of the house of E·li'a·shib as far as the end of E·li'a·shib's house.

22 And after him the priests, men of the district of the Jordan,*[n] did repair work. 23 After them Benjamin and Has'shub did repair work in front of their own house. After them Az·a·ri'ah the son of Ma·a·sei'ah the son of A·na·ni'ah did repair work near his own house. 24 After him Bin'nu·i the son of Hen'a·dad repaired another section, from the house of Az·a·ri'ah as far as the Buttress[o] and as far as the corner.

25 After him Pa'lal the son of U'zai did repair work in front of the Buttress and the tower that goes out from the King's House,*[a] the upper one that belongs to the Courtyard of the Guard.[b] After him there was Pe·dai'ah the son of Pa'rosh.[c]

26 And the temple servants*[d] who lived in O'phel[e] did repair work as far as in front of the Water Gate[f] on the east and the protruding tower.

27 After them the Te·ko'ites[g] repaired another section, from in front of the great protruding tower as far as the wall of O'phel.

28 The priests did repair work above the Horse Gate,[h] each in front of his own house.

29 After them Za'dok[i] the son of Im'mer did repair work in front of his own house.

And after him She·mai'ah the son of Shec·a·ni'ah, the keeper of the East Gate,[j] did repair work.

30 After him Han·a·ni'ah the son of Shel·e·mi'ah and Ha'nun the sixth son of Za'laph repaired another section.

After him Me·shul'lam[k] the son of Ber·e·chi'ah did repair work in front of his own hall.

31 After him Mal·chi'jah, a member of the goldsmith guild, did repair work as far as the house of the temple servants*[l] and the traders, in front of the Inspection Gate and as far as the roof chamber of the corner.

32 And between the roof chamber of the corner and the Sheep Gate,[m] the goldsmiths and the traders did repair work.

4 Now as soon as San·bal'lat[n] heard that we were rebuilding the wall, he became angry and very upset,* and he

kept mocking the Jews. **2** And in the presence of his brothers and the army of Sa·mar′i·a, he said: "What are the feeble Jews doing? Will they do this by themselves? Will they offer sacrifices? Will they finish up in a day? Will they bring the charred stones to life out of the heaps of dusty rubble?"[a]

3 Now To·bi′ah[b] the Am′mon·ite,[c] who was standing beside him, said: "If even a fox would climb up on what they are building, it would knock down their stone wall."

4 Hear, O our God, for we are being treated with contempt,[d] and make their reproach return on their own heads,[e] and give them over as plunder in a land of captivity. **5** And do not cover over their guilt or let their sin be erased from before you,[f] for they have insulted the builders.

6 So we kept building the wall, and the entire wall was joined together and rebuilt up to half its height, and the people continued to put their heart into the work.

7 Now as soon as San·bal′lat, To·bi′ah,[g] the Arabians,[h] the Am′mon·ites, and the Ash′dod·ites[i] heard that the repairing of the walls of Jerusalem was progressing and that the gaps were being filled in, they became very angry. **8** They conspired together to come and fight against Jerusalem and to create a disturbance in it. **9** But we prayed to our God and kept a guard posted against them day and night.

10 However, people of Judah were saying: "The strength of the laborers* has failed, and there is so much rubble; we will never be able to build the wall."

11 And our enemies kept saying: "Before they know it or see

us, we will come right in among them and kill them and stop the work."

12 Whenever the Jews living near them came in, they told us again and again:* "They will come at us from all directions."

13 So I kept men posted at the lowest parts of the space behind the wall at the exposed places, and I posted them by families with their swords, their lances, and their bows. **14** When I saw their fear, I immediately rose and said to the nobles[a] and the deputy rulers and the rest of the people: "Do not be afraid of them.[b] Remember Jehovah, who is great and awe-inspiring;[c] and fight for your brothers, your sons and daughters, your wives and homes."

15 Now after our enemies heard that what they were doing had become known to us and that the true God had frustrated their plan, we all went back to work on the wall. **16** From that day forward, half of my men would do the work[d] and half of them would hold the lances, the shields, the bows, and the coats of mail. And the princes[e] stood behind the whole house of Judah **17** who were building the wall. Those who were carrying the loads did the work with one hand while holding a weapon* in the other hand. **18** And each of the builders had a sword strapped to his hip while building, and the one to blow the horn[f] stood beside me.

19 I then said to the nobles and the deputy rulers and the rest of the people: "The work is large and extensive, and we are spread out on the wall far apart from one another. **20** When you hear the sound of the horn, gather together to where we are. Our God will fight for us."[g]

CHAP. 4
a Ne 4:10

b Ne 2:19

c Ne 13:1, 2

d Ps 123:3

e Ps 79:12

f Jer 18:23

g Ne 4:3

h Ne 2:19

i Jos 13:2, 3
Ne 13:23

Second Col.
a Ne 13:17

b Nu 14:9
De 20:3
Jos 1:9

c De 7:21
De 10:17

d Ne 5:16

e Ne 11:1

f Nu 10:9
2Ch 13:12

g De 1:30
Jos 23:10

4:10 *Or "burden bearers."

4:12 *Lit., "ten times." 4:17 *Or "missile."

21 So we kept working while the other half were holding the lances, from the break of dawn until the stars came out. **22** At that time I said to the people: "Let the men, each along with his attendant, spend the night inside Jerusalem, and they will guard us by night and work during the day." **23** So neither I nor my brothers, my attendants,[a] and the guards who followed me ever took off our garments, and each of us kept his weapon in his right hand.

5 However, there was a great outcry from the people and their wives against their Jewish brothers.[b] **2** Some were saying: "We are many with our sons and our daughters. We must get grain in order to eat and stay alive." **3** Others were saying: "We are giving our fields and our vineyards and our houses as security to get grain during the food shortage." **4** Still others were saying: "We have borrowed money on our fields and our vineyards for the king's tribute.[c] **5** Now we are of the same flesh and blood as our brothers,* and our children are just like their children; yet we have to subject our sons and daughters to slavery, and some of our daughters are already in slavery.[d] But we are powerless to stop this, because our fields and our vineyards belong to others."

6 I became very angry when I heard their outcry and these words. **7** So I considered these things in my heart, and I took issue with the nobles and the deputy rulers and said to them: "Each one of you is demanding interest* from your own brother."[e]

Further, I arranged for a great assembly because of them.

8 And I said to them: "To the extent possible, we have bought back our own Jewish brothers who were sold to the nations; but will you now sell your own brothers,[a] and are they to be sold back to us?" At this they became speechless, and they could find nothing to say. **9** Then I said: "What you are doing is not good. Should you not walk in the fear of our God[b] so that the nations, our enemies, cannot reproach us? **10** Moreover, I, my brothers, and my attendants are lending them money and grain. Let us, please, stop this lending on interest.[c] **11** Please, restore to them on this very day their fields,[d] their vineyards, their olive groves, and their houses, as well as the hundredth* of the money, the grain, the new wine, and the oil that you are demanding as interest from them."

12 To this they said: "We will restore these things to them and ask nothing back. We will do precisely as you say." So I called the priests and made those men swear to keep this promise. **13** Also, I shook out the folds of my garment* and said: "In this manner may the true God shake out from his house and from his possessions every man who does not carry out this promise, and in this manner may he be shaken out and emptied." To this all the congregation said: "Amen!"# And they praised Jehovah, and the people did as they promised.

14 Moreover, from the day that he commissioned me to become their governor[e] in the land of Judah, from the 20th year[f] to the 32nd year[g] of King Ar·ta·xerx′es,[h] 12 years, neither I nor my brothers ate the food allowance due the governor.[i] **15** But

---

CHAP. 4
a Ne 13:19

CHAP. 5
b De 15:9

c De 28:15, 33
Ne 9:36, 37

d Ex 21:7
De 15:12

e Ex 22:25
De 23:19
Ps 15:5
Eze 22:12

Second Col.
a Le 25:35
De 15:7, 8
Jer 34:8, 9

b Le 25:36
Ne 5:15

c Eze 18:5, 8

d Ne 5:3

e Ne 10:1

f Ne 2:1

g Ne 13:6

h Ezr 8:1

i 1Co 9:14, 15
2Th 3:8

5:5 *Lit., "like the flesh of our brothers is our flesh." 5:7 *Or "usury."

5:11 *Or "1 percent," that is, monthly. 5:13 *Lit., "shook out my bosom." #Or "So be it!"

the former governors who were before me had burdened the people and had been taking from them 40 silver shekels* for bread and wine each day. Also, their attendants had oppressed the people. But I did not do that[a] because of the fear of God.

16 Furthermore, I took a hand in the work on this wall, and not a field did we acquire;[c] all my attendants were gathered there for the work. **17** There were 150 Jews and deputy rulers dining at my table, as well as those who came to us from the nations. **18** Every day one bull, six choice sheep, and birds were prepared for me,* and once every ten days we had all sorts of wine in abundance. Despite all this I did not demand the food allowance due the governor, because the people were already bearing their burden of service. **19** Do remember me favorably,* O my God, for all that I have done in behalf of this people.[d]

6 Now as soon as San·bal′lat, To·bi′ah,[e] Ge′shem the Arabian,[f] and the rest of our enemies were told that I had rebuilt the wall[g] and that there were no gaps left in it (although up to that time I had not set up the doors in the gates),[h] **2** San·bal′lat and Ge′shem immediately sent this message to me: "Come, and let us set a time to meet together in the villages of the Valley Plain of O′no."[i] But they were scheming to harm me. **3** So I sent messengers to them, saying: "I am engaged in a great work, and I am not able to go down. Why should the work stop while I leave it to come to you?" **4** They sent me the same message four times, and I gave them the same reply each time.

5:15 *A shekel equaled 11.4 g (0.367 oz t). See App. B14. **5:18** *Or "at my expense." **5:19** *Or "for good."

CHAP. 5
a 2Co 11:9
  2Co 12:14

b Ne 5:9

c Ac 20:33
  2Co 12:17

d Ne 13:14
  Ps 18:24
  Isa 38:3
  Mal 3:16

CHAP. 6
e Ne 2:10
  Ne 4:3

f Ne 2:19
  Ne 4:7

g Da 9:25

h Ne 3:1, 3

i 1Ch 8:12
  Ne 11:31, 35

Second Col.
a Ne 2:19

b Ezr 4:14, 15

c Ezr 4:4

d Ps 68:35
  Ps 138:3
  Isa 41:10

e Nu 1:51
  Nu 18:7
  2Ch 26:18, 19

f Ne 2:10

g Ne 4:3, 4

---

5 Then San·bal′lat sent his attendant to me with the same message a fifth time, with an open letter in his hand. **6** There it was written: "Among the nations it has been heard, and Ge′shem[a] is also saying it, that you and the Jews are scheming to rebel.[b] That is why you are building the wall; and according to these reports you are to become their king. **7** Also, you have appointed prophets to proclaim about you throughout Jerusalem, 'There is a king in Judah!' And now these things will be told to the king. So come, and let us discuss this together."

8 However, I sent him this reply: "None of the things you are saying have taken place; you are making them up out of your own imagination."* **9** For they were all trying to frighten us, saying: "Their hands will slacken in the work, and it will not be done."[c] Now, I pray, strengthen my hands.[d]

10 Then I went to the house of She·mai′ah the son of De·la′iah the son of Me·het′a·bel while he was confined there. He said: "Let us set a time to meet at the house of the true God, within the temple, and let us close the doors of the temple, for they are coming to kill you. They are coming to kill you by night." **11** But I said: "Should a man like me run away? Can a man like me go into the temple and live?[e] I will not go in!" **12** Then I realized that God had not sent him, but that To·bi′ah and San·bal′lat[f] had hired him to speak this prophecy against me. **13** He had been hired to frighten me and to cause me to sin, so that they would have grounds to damage my reputation in order to reproach me.

14 Do remember, O my God, To·bi′ah[g] and San·bal′lat and

6:8 *Lit., "from your heart."

these deeds, and also No·a·di′ah the prophetess and the rest of the prophets who were constantly trying to frighten me.

15 So the wall was completed on the 25th day of E′lul,* in 52 days.

16 As soon as all our enemies heard of it and all the surrounding nations saw it, they became greatly ashamed,*[a] and they realized that it was with our God's help that this work had been done. **17** In those days the nobles[b] of Judah were sending many letters to To·bi′ah, and To·bi′ah would reply to them. **18** Many in Judah swore allegiance to him, for he was a son-in-law of Shec·a·ni′ah the son of A′rah,[c] and his son Je·ho·ha′nan had married the daughter of Me·shul′lam[d] the son of Ber·e·chi′ah. **19** Also, they would constantly tell me good things about him and then report to him what I said. Then To·bi′ah would send letters to frighten me.[e]

7 As soon as the wall had been rebuilt[f] I set up the doors;[g] then the gatekeepers,[h] the singers,[i] and the Levites[i] were appointed. **2** I then put my brother Ha·na′ni[k] in charge of Jerusalem, along with Han·a·ni′ah the chief of the Fortress,[l] for he was a most trustworthy man and feared the true God[m] more than many others. **3** So I said to them: "The gates of Jerusalem should not be opened until the heat of the day, and while they are standing guard, they should shut the doors and bolt them. And assign the inhabitants of Jerusalem as guards, each to his assigned guardpost and each in front of his own house." **4** Now the city was spacious and large, and there were few people inside in it,[n] and the houses had not been rebuilt.

5 But my God put it into my heart to gather together the nobles and the deputy rulers and the people to be enrolled genealogically.[a] Then I found the book of genealogical enrollment of those who first came up, and I found written in it:

6 And these were the people of the province* who came up out of the captivity of the exiles, those whom King Neb·u·chad·nez′zar[b] of Babylon had exiled[c] and who later returned to Jerusalem and Judah, each to his own city,[d] **7** those who came with Ze·rub′ba·bel,[e] Jesh′u·a,[f] Ne·he·mi′ah, Az·a·ri′ah, Ra·a·mi′ah, Na·ham′a·ni, Mor′de·cai, Bil′shan, Mis′pe·reth, Big′vai, Ne′hum, and Ba′a·nah.

The number of the Israelite men included:[g] **8** the sons of Pa′rosh, 2,172; **9** the sons of Sheph·a·ti′ah, 372; **10** the sons of A′rah,[h] 652; **11** the sons of Pa′hath-mo′ab,[i] of the sons of Jesh′u·a and Jo′ab,[j] 2,818; **12** the sons of E′lam,[k] 1,254; **13** the sons of Zat′tu, 845; **14** the sons of Zac′cai, 760; **15** the sons of Bin′nu·i, 648; **16** the sons of Be′bai, 628; **17** the sons of Az′gad, 2,322; **18** the sons of Ad·o·ni′kam, 667; **19** the sons of Big′vai, 2,067; **20** the sons of A′din, 655; **21** the sons of A′ter, of Hez·e·ki′ah, 98; **22** the sons of Ha′shum, 328; **23** the sons of Be′zai, 324; **24** the sons of Ha′riph, 112; **25** the sons of Gib′e·on,[l] 95; **26** the men of Beth′le·hem and Ne·to′phah, 188; **27** the men of An′a·thoth,[m] 128; **28** the men of Beth-az′ma·veth, 42; **29** the men of Kir′i·ath-je′a·rim,[n] Che·phi′rah, and Be·er′oth,[o] 743; **30** the men of Ra′mah and Ge′ba,[p] 621; **31** the men of Mich′mas,[q] 122; **32** the men of Beth′el[r] and A′i,[s] 123; **33** the men of the other Ne′bo, 52; **34** the sons of the other

---

CHAP. 6

a Ne 4:7
  Ps 129:5
b Ne 5:7
c Ezr 2:1, 5
d Ne 3:4
e Ne 6:9
  Ne 6:10, 13

CHAP. 7

f Ne 2:17
  Ne 6:15
  Da 9:25
g Ne 3:1, 6, 13
h 1Ch 26:1
  Ezr 2:1, 42
i 1Ch 9:33
  Ezr 2:1, 41
j Ezr 3:8
k Ne 1:2
l Ne 2:8
m Ne 5:15
n Ne 11:1

Second Col.

a 1Ch 9:1
  Ezr 2:59, 62
b 2Ki 25:1
  Da 3:1
c 2Ki 24:12, 14
  2Ch 36:17, 20
  Jer 39:9
  Jer 52:15, 28
d Ezr 2:1
e Ezr 1:8, 11
  Zec 4:9
  Mt 1:12
f Ezr 3:8
  Ezr 5:2
  Hag 1:14
  Zec 3:1
g Ezr 2:2-35
h Ne 6:17, 18
i Ezr 10:30, 44
j Ezr 8:1, 9
k Ezr 10:26, 44
l Jos 11:19
  2Sa 21:2
  Ne 3:7
m Jos 21:8, 18
  Jer 1:1
n 1Sa 7:2
o Jos 18:25, 28
p Jos 18:21, 24
q 1Sa 13:5
r 1Ki 12:32
s Jos 7:2

6:15 *See App. B15.   **6:16** *Lit., "they fell greatly in their own eyes."

7:6 *Or "jurisdictional district."

E'lam, 1,254; **35** the sons of Ha'rim, 320; **36** the sons of Jer'i-cho, 345; **37** the sons of Lod, Ha'did, and O'no,ᵃ 721; **38** the sons of Se-na'ah, 3,930.

39 The priests:ᵇ the sons of Je-da'iah of the house of Jesh'u-a, 973; **40** the sons of Im'mer, 1,052; **41** the sons of Pash'hur,ᶜ 1,247; **42** the sons of Ha'rim,ᵈ 1,017.

43 The Levites:ᵉ the sons of Jesh'u-a, of Kad'mi-el,ᶠ of the sons of Ho'de-vah, 74. **44** The singers:ᵍ the sons of A'saph,ʰ 148. **45** The gatekeepers:ⁱ the sons of Shal'lum, the sons of A'ter, the sons of Tal'mon, the sons of Ak'kub,ʲ the sons of Ha-ti'ta, the sons of Sho'bai, 138.

46 The temple servants:*ᵏ the sons of Zi'ha, the sons of Ha-su'pha, the sons of Tab-ba'-oth, **47** the sons of Ke'ros, the sons of Si'a, the sons of Pa'don, **48** the sons of Le-ba'nah, the sons of Hag'a-bah, the sons of Sal'mai, **49** the sons of Ha'nan, the sons of Gid'del, the sons of Ga'har, **50** the sons of Re-a'iah, the sons of Re'zin, the sons of Ne-ko'da, **51** the sons of Gaz'zam, the sons of Uz'za, the sons of Pa-se'ah, **52** the sons of Be'-sai, the sons of Me-u'nim, the sons of Ne-phush'e-sim, **53** the sons of Bak'buk, the sons of Ha-ku'pha, the sons of Har'hur, **54** the sons of Baz'lith, the sons of Me-hi'da, the sons of Har'sha, **55** the sons of Bar'kos, the sons of Sis'e-ra, the sons of Te'mah, **56** the sons of Ne-zi'ah, the sons of Ha-ti'pha.

57 The sons of the servants of Sol'o-mon:ˡ the sons of So'-tai, the sons of So-phe'reth, the sons of Pe-ri'da, **58** the sons of Ja'a-la, the sons of Dar'-kon, the sons of Gid'del, **59** the sons of Sheph-a-ti'ah, the sons of

Hat'til, the sons of Po'che-reth-haz-ze-ba'im, the sons of A'mon. **60** All the temple servants*ᵃ and the sons of the servants of Sol'-o-mon were 392.

61 And these went up from Tel-me'lah, Tel-har'sha, Che'rub, Ad'don, and Im'mer, but they were unable to verify their paternal house and their origin, as to whether they were Israel-ites:ᵇ **62** the sons of De-la'iah, the sons of To-bi'ah, the sons of Ne-ko'da, 642. **63** And of the priests: the sons of Ha-bai'ah, the sons of Hak'koz,ᶜ the sons of Bar-zil'lai, who took a wife from the daughters of Bar-zil'laiᵈ the Gil'e-ad-ite and was called by their name. **64** These looked for their records to establish their genealogy, but they could not be found, so they were disqualified from the priesthood.*ᵉ **65** The governor*ᶠ told them that they should not eat from the most holy thingsᵍ until there was a priest who could consult the U'rim and Thum'mim.ʰ

66 The total number of the entire congregation was 42,360,ⁱ **67** apart from their male and female slaves,ʲ who were 7,337; they also had 245 male and female singers.ᵏ **68** Their horses were 736, their mules 245, **69** their camels 435, their donkeys 6,720.

70 Some of the heads of the paternal houses contributed to the work.ˡ The governor* gave to the treasury 1,000 gold drach-mas,# 50 bowls, and 530 priests' robes.ᵐ **71** And some of the

---

CHAP. 7
a Ne 6:2
Ne 11:31, 35

b Ezr 2:36-39

c Ezr 10:22, 44

d 1Ch 24:3, 8

e Ezr 2:40

f Ezr 3:9

g 1Ch 25:7
Ezr 2:41

h 1Ch 6:31, 39

i Ezr 2:42
Ne 7:1

j 1Ch 9:2, 17
Ne 11:19
Ne 12:25

k Jos 9:3, 27
1Ch 9:2
Ezr 2:43-54
Ezr 2:58

l Ezr 2:55-58
Ne 11:3

Second Col.
a Jos 9:3, 27
Ne 3:26

b Ezr 2:59-63

c 1Ch 24:3, 10
Ne 3:21

d 2Sa 17:27-29
2Sa 19:31
1Ki 2:7

e Nu 18:7

f Ne 8:9
Ne 10:1

g Le 2:3
Nu 18:8, 9

h Ex 28:30
1Sa 28:6

i Ezr 2:64-67

j Le 25:44

k Ex 15:21
1Sa 18:6

l Ezr 2:68, 69

m Le 6:10

7:46 *Or "The Nethinim." Lit., "The given ones."

7:60 *Or "the Nethinim." Lit., "the given ones." 7:64 *Or "were excluded from the priesthood as unclean." 7:65 *Or "the Tirshatha," a Persian title for a governor of a province. 7:70 *Or "The Tirshatha," a Persian title for a governor of a province. #Generally equated with the Persian gold daric that weighed 8.4 g (0.27 oz t). Not the drachma of the Greek Scriptures. See App. B14.

heads of the paternal houses gave to the project treasury 20,-000 gold drachmas and 2,200 silver mi′nas.* 72 And the rest of the people gave 20,000 gold drachmas, 2,000 silver mi′nas, and 67 priests' robes.

73 And the priests, the Levites, the gatekeepers, the singers,[a] some of the people, the temple servants,* and all the rest of Israel# settled in their cities.[b] When the seventh month arrived,[c] the Israelites had settled in their cities.[d]

8 All the people then gathered with one accord at the public square in front of the Water Gate,[e] and they told Ez′ra[f] the copyist* to bring the book of the Law of Moses,[g] which Jehovah had commanded Israel.[h] 2 So Ez′ra the priest brought the Law before the congregation[i] of men, women, and all who could listen with understanding, on the first day of the seventh month.[j] 3 And he read aloud from it[k] before the public square in front of the Water Gate, from daybreak until midday, to the men, the women, and all who could understand; and the people listened attentively[l] to the book of the Law. 4 And Ez′ra the copyist* was standing on a wooden podium made for the occasion; and standing alongside him on his right were Mat·ti·thi′ah, She′ma, A·nai′ah, U·ri′ah, Hil·ki′ah, and Ma·a·sei′ah; and on his left were Pedai′ah, Mish′a·el, Mal·chi′jah,[m] Ha′shum, Hash·bad′da·nah, Zecha·ri′ah, and Me·shul′lam.

5 Ez′ra opened the book in the sight of all the people, for he was above all the people. As he opened it, all the people

stood up. 6 Then Ez′ra praised Jehovah the true God, the great One, at which all the people answered, "Amen!* Amen!"[a] and lifted up their hands. They then bowed low and prostrated themselves to Jehovah with their faces to the ground. 7 And Jesh′u·a, Ba′ni, She·re·bi′ah,[b] Ja′min, Ak′kub, Shab′be·thai, Ho·di′ah, Ma·a·sei′ah, Ke·li′ta, Az·a·ri′ah, Jo′za·bad,[c] Ha′nan, and Pe·la′iah, who were Levites, were explaining the Law to the people,[d] while the people remained standing. 8 And they continued reading aloud from the book, from the Law of the true God, clearly explaining it and putting meaning into it; so they helped the people to understand what was being read.*[e]

9 And Ne·he·mi′ah, who was then the governor,# Ez′ra[f] the priest and copyist,* and the Levites who were instructing the people said to all the people: "This day is holy to Jehovah your God.[g] Do not mourn or weep." For all the people were weeping as they heard the words of the Law. 10 He said to them: "Go, eat the choice things* and drink what is sweet, and send portions of food[h] to those who have nothing prepared; for this day is holy to our Lord, and do not feel sad, for the joy of Jehovah is your stronghold."# 11 And the Levites were calming all the people, saying: "Be quiet! for this day is holy, and do not feel sad." 12 So all the people went away to eat and to drink and to send out portions of food and to carry on a great rejoicing,[i] for they understood the words that had been made known to them.[j]

CHAP. 7
a Ne 7:1
b Ne 11:20
c Le 23:24, 27
  1Ki 8:2
  Ezr 3:1
d Ezr 2:70

CHAP. 8
e Ne 3:26
  Ne 12:37
f Ezr 7:6
g De 31:9
  Jos 1:8
h Le 27:34
i De 31:12
  2Ch 17:8, 9
  Mal 2:7
j Le 23:24
  1Ki 8:2
k Ac 13:15
  Ac 15:21
l Ac 16:14
  Ac 17:11
m Ne 12:40, 42

Second Col.
a De 27:26
b Ne 9:4
c Ezr 8:33
  Ne 11:16
d De 33:8, 10
e Lu 24:27
  Ac 8:30, 31
f Ezr 7:11
g Le 23:24
h Es 9:19
i Ps 126:1-3
j Ne 8:8

7:71 *A mina in the Hebrew Scriptures equaled 570 g (18.35 oz t). See App. B14. 7:73 *Or "the Nethinim." Lit., "the given ones." #Lit., "all Israel." 8:1, 4, 9 *Or "scribe."

8:6 *Or "So be it!" 8:8 *Or "they gave understanding in the reading." 8:9 #Or "the Tirshatha," a Persian title for a governor of a province. 8:10 *Lit., "fatty things." #Or "strength."

13 And on the second day, the heads of the paternal houses of all the people, the priests, and the Levites gathered around Ez'ra the copyist* to gain further insight into the words of the Law. **14** Then they found written in the Law that Jehovah had commanded through Moses that the Israelites should dwell in booths* during the festival in the seventh month,ᵃ **15** and that they should make proclamationᵇ and announce throughout all their cities and throughout Jerusalem, saying: "Go out to the mountainous region and bring in leafy branches from olive trees, oil trees, myrtle and palm trees, and the leafy branches of other trees to make booths, according to what is written."

16 So the people went out and brought them in to make booths for themselves, each one on his roof, as well as in their courtyards, in the courtyards of the house of the true God,ᶜ in the public square of the Water Gate,ᵈ and in the public square of the Gate of E'phra·im.ᵉ **17** Thus all those of the congregation who had come back from the captivity made booths and were dwelling in the booths, for the Israelites had not done it this way from the days of Joshuaᶠ the son of Nun until that day, so that there was very great rejoicing.ᵍ **18** And day by day there was a reading from the book of the Law of the true God,ʰ from the first day until the last day. And they held the festival for seven days, and there was a solemn assembly on the eighth day, as was required.ⁱ

9 On the 24th day of this month the Israelites assembled; they were fasting with sackcloth and dust on them-

selves.ᵃ **2** Those of Israelite descent then separated themselves from all the foreigners,ᵇ and they stood and confessed their own sins and the errors of their fathers.ᶜ **3** Then they stood up at their place and read aloud from the book of the Lawᵈ of Jehovah their God for a fourth of the day;* and for another fourth of it they were confessing and bowing down to Jehovah their God.

4 Jesh'u·a, Ba'ni, Kad'mi·el, Sheb·a·ni'ah, Bun'ni, She·re·bi'ah,ᵉ Ba'ni, and Che·na'ni stood on the raised platformᶠ of the Levites, and they cried out with a loud voice to Jehovah their God. **5** And the Levites Jesh'u·a, Kad'mi·el, Ba'ni, Hash·ab·nei'ah, She·re·bi'ah, Ho·di'ah, Sheb·a·ni'ah, and Peth·a·hi'ah said: "Stand up and praise Jehovah your God throughout all eternity.*ᵍ And let them praise your glorious name, which is exalted above all blessing and praise.

6 "You alone are Jehovah;ʰ you made the heavens, yes, the heaven of the heavens and all their army, the earth and all that is on it, the seas and all that is in them. And you preserve all of them alive, and the army of the heavens are bowing down to you. **7** You are Jehovah the true God, who chose A'bramⁱ and brought him out of Urʲ of the Chal·de'ans and gave him the name Abraham.ᵏ **8** You found his heart faithful before you,ˡ so you made a covenant with him to give him the land of the Ca'naan·ites, the Hit'tites, the Am'or·ites, the Per'iz·zites, the Jeb'u·sites, and the Gir'ga·shites, to give it to his offspring;*ᵐ and you kept your promises, because you are righteous.

CHAP. 8
a Le 23:34, 42
De 16:13, 16
Joh 7:2

b Le 23:4

c 1Ki 6:36
1Ki 7:12
2Ch 4:9
2Ch 20:5

d Ne 3:26
Ne 8:1, 3

e 2Ki 14:13
Ne 12:38, 39

f Jos 1:1

g De 16:14, 15

h De 31:10-12

i Le 23:34, 36

Second Col.

CHAP. 9
a Jos 7:6
Jon 3:5, 6

b Ezr 9:1, 2
Ne 13:3

c Le 26:40
Ezr 9:6
Ps 106:6
Da 9:8

d Ne 8:3, 8

e Ne 8:7

f Ne 8:4

g Jer 33:10, 11

h De 6:4

i Ge 12:1, 2

j Ge 11:31

k Ge 17:5

l Ge 22:10-12

m Ge 15:18

8:13 *Or "scribe." 8:14 *Or "temporary shelters." 9:3 *Or "for three hours." 9:5 *Or "from eternity to eternity." 9:8 *Lit., "seed."

9 "So you saw the affliction of our forefathers in Egypt,[a] and you heard their outcry at the Red Sea. **10** Then you performed signs and miracles against Phar'aoh and all his servants and all the people of his land,[b] for you knew that they acted presumptuously[c] against them. You made a name for yourself that remains to this day.[d] **11** And you split the sea before them, so that they crossed through the sea on the dry land,[e] and you hurled their pursuers into the depths like a stone thrown into the turbulent waters.[f] **12** You led them by day with a pillar of cloud, and by night with a pillar of fire, to light up for them the way they should go.[g] **13** And you came down on Mount Si'nai[h] and spoke with them from heaven[i] and gave them righteous judgments, laws of truth,* good regulations and commandments.[j] **14** You made known to them your holy Sabbath,[k] and you gave them commandments, regulations, and a law through your servant Moses. **15** You gave them bread from heaven when they were hungry,[l] and you brought water out of the crag when they were thirsty,[m] and you told them to enter and take possession of the land that you had sworn* to give to them. **16** "But they, our forefathers, acted presumptuously[n] and became stubborn,*[o] and they would not listen to your commandments. **17** They refused to listen,[p] and they did not remember your extraordinary acts that you performed among them, but they became stubborn* and appointed a head to return to their slavery in Egypt.[q] But you are a God ready to forgive,[r] com-

passionate* and merciful, slow to anger and abundant in loyal love,*[a] and you did not abandon them.[b] **18** Even when they made for themselves a metal statue* of a calf and were saying, 'This is your God who led you up out of Egypt,'[c] and they committed great acts of disrespect, **19** even then you, in your great mercy, did not abandon them in the wilderness.[d] The pillar of cloud did not depart from over them by day to lead them in the way, nor the pillar of fire by night to light up for them the way they should go.[e] **20** And you gave your good spirit to give them insight,[f] and you did not hold back your manna from their mouth,[g] and you gave them water when they were thirsty.[h] **21** For 40 years you provided them with food in the wilderness.[i] They lacked nothing. Their garments did not wear out,[j] and their feet did not become swollen.

22 "You gave them kingdoms and peoples, apportioning them piece by piece,[k] so that they took possession of the land of Si'hon,[l] that is, the land of the king of Hesh'bon,[m] as well as the land of Og[n] the king of Ba'shan. **23** And you made their sons as numerous as the stars of the heavens.[o] Then you brought them into the land that you had promised their forefathers that they should enter and possess.[p] **24** So their sons went in and took possession of the land,[q] and you subdued before them the Ca'naan·ites,[r] who were the inhabitants of the land, and you gave them into their hand, both their kings and the peoples of the land, to do with them as they pleased. **25** And they captured fortified cities[s] and a fertile* land,[t] and they took possession

---

CHAP. 9

a Ex 2:23-25
  Ex 3:7
b Ex 7:3
  De 6:22
c Ex 5:2
d Ex 9:16
e Ex 14:21, 22
f Ex 15:1, 5, 10
g Ex 13:21
  Ex 14:19, 20
h Ex 19:11
i De 4:10, 36
j De 4:8
k Ex 16:29
  Ex 20:8-11
  De 5:12-14
l Ex 16:4
m Ex 17:6
n Nu 14:44
o De 9:6
p Nu 14:11, 41
q Nu 14:1, 4

Second Col.

a Ex 34:6
  Nu 14:18
b De 4:31
c Ex 32:1, 4
d Nu 14:19, 20
e Ex 40:38
  Nu 9:15
f Nu 11:17, 25
g Ex 16:14, 15
h Nu 20:8
i Ex 16:35
  Nu 14:33
  De 2:7
j De 29:5
k Jos 11:23
l Nu 21:23, 24
  De 2:31
m Nu 21:26
n Nu 21:33, 35
o Ge 15:1, 5
p Ge 12:7
  Ge 26:3
q Nu 14:29-31
  Jos 21:43
r Jos 18:1
s De 3:4, 5
t De 8:7-9

9:13 *Or "reliable laws." 9:15 *Lit., "lifted your hand." 9:16, 17 *Lit., "hardened their neck." 9:17 *Or "a God of acts of forgiveness."

9:17 *Or "gracious." #Or "lovingkindness." 9:18 *Or "molten statue." 9:25 *Or "rich."

of houses full of all sorts of good things, cisterns already dug, vineyards, olive groves,[a] and fruit trees in abundance. So they ate and grew satisfied and fat, and they basked in your great goodness.

26 "However, they became disobedient and rebelled against you[b] and turned their back on your Law.* They killed your prophets who warned them so as to bring them back to you, and they committed acts of great disrespect.[c] 27 For this you gave them into the hand of their adversaries,[d] who kept causing them distress.[e] But they would cry out to you in the time of their distress, and you would hear from the heavens; and because of your great mercy, you would give them saviors to rescue them out of the hand of their adversaries.[f]

28 "But as soon as they had relief, they would again do what is bad before you,[g] and you would abandon them to the hand of their enemies, who would dominate them.*[h] Then they would return and call to you for help,[i] and you would hear from the heavens and rescue them time and again because of your great mercy.[j] 29 Although you would warn them so as to bring them back to your Law, they behaved presumptuously and refused to listen to your commandments;[k] and they sinned against your regulations, by which a man will live if he observes them.[l] But they stubbornly turned their back and stiffened their neck, and they refused to listen. 30 You extended patience to them[m] for many years and kept warning them by your spirit through your prophets, but they refused to listen.

Finally you gave them into the hand of the peoples of the lands.[a] 31 And in your great mercy, you did not exterminate them[b] or abandon them, for you are a compassionate* and merciful God.[c]

32 "And now, O our God, the God great, mighty, and awe-inspiring, who has kept his covenant and shown loyal love,[d] do not treat lightly all the hardship that has found us, our kings, our princes,[e] our priests,[f] our prophets,[g] our forefathers, and all your people from the days of the kings of As·syr′i·a[h] down to this day. 33 You have been righteous in all that has come upon us, for you have acted faithfully; but we are the ones who have acted wickedly.[i] 34 As for our kings, our princes, our priests, and our forefathers, they have not observed your Law nor paid attention to your commandments or to your reminders* by which you warned them. 35 Even when they were in their kingdom and enjoying the abundant goodness that you gave them and they were in the broad and fertile* land that you bestowed on them, they did not serve you[j] and did not turn away from their bad practices. 36 So here we are today, slaves[k]—yes, slaves in the land that you gave to our forefathers to eat its fruitage and its good things. 37 Its abundant produce is for the kings whom you have put over us because of our sins.[l] They rule over our bodies and over our livestock as they see fit, and we are in great distress.

38 "So in view of all this, we are making a binding agreement[m] in writing, and it is attested by the seal of our princes, our Levites, and our priests."[n]

CHAP. 9
a Jos 24:13
b De 31:20
  De 32:15
  Jg 2:12
c 2Ki 21:11
  Ps 106:38
d Jg 2:14
e De 31:17
f Jg 2:18
  Jg 3:9, 15
  1Sa 12:11
  2Ki 13:4, 5
g Jg 2:19
h Jg 4:1, 2
  Jg 6:1
i Jg 6:6
j Ps 106:43-45
k 2Ki 17:13, 14
  2Ch 24:19
l Le 18:5
m Ro 10:21

Second Col.
a 2Ch 36:15, 16
  Isa 42:24
  Jer 40:2, 3
b Eze 14:22
c Ex 34:6
  De 4:31
d De 7:9
  Da 9:4
e 2Ki 24:12, 14
f Jer 34:18-20
g La 4:13, 14
h 2Ki 17:6
i Da 9:5
j De 28:47
  De 32:15
k De 28:48
  Ezr 9:9
l De 28:15, 33
  Ne 5:4
m 2Ki 23:3
  2Ch 15:12
  Ezr 10:3
n Ne 10:28, 29

9:26 *Lit., "and cast your Law behind their back." 9:28 *Or "crush them." 9:31 *Or "gracious." 9:34 *Or "warnings." 9:35 *Or "rich."

10 Those who attested it by putting their seal to it[a] were:

Ne·he·mi′ah the governor,* the son of Hac·a·li′ah,

And Zed·e·ki′ah, **2** Se·rai′ah, Az·a·ri′ah, Jeremiah, **3** Pash′hur, Am·a·ri′ah, Mal·chi′jah, **4** Hat′tush, Sheb·a·ni′ah, Mal′luch, **5** Ha′rim,[b] Mer′e·moth, O·ba·di′ah, **6** Daniel,[c] Gin′ne·thon, Bar′uch, **7** Me·shul′lam, A·bi′jah, Mij′a·min, **8** Ma·a·zi′ah, Bil′gai, and She·mai′ah; these are the priests.

9 Also the Levites: Jesh′u·a the son of Az·a·ni′ah, Bin′nu·i of the sons of Hen′a·dad, Kad′mi·el,[d] **10** and their brothers Sheb·a·ni′ah, Ho·di′ah, Ke·li′ta, Pe·la′iah, Ha′nan, **11** Mi′ca, Re′hob, Hash·a·bi′ah, **12** Zac′cur, She·re·bi′ah,[e] Sheb·a·ni′ah, **13** Ho·di′ah, Ba′ni, and Be·ni′nu.

14 The heads of the people: Pa′rosh, Pa′hath-mo′ab,[f] E′lam, Zat′tu, Ba′ni, **15** Bun′ni, Az′gad, Be′bai, **16** Ad·o·ni′jah, Big′vai, A′din, **17** A′ter, Hez·e·ki′ah, Az′zur, **18** Ho·di′ah, Ha′shum, Be′zai, **19** Ha′riph, An′a·thoth, Ne′bai, **20** Mag′pi·ash, Me·shul′lam, He′zir, **21** Me·shez′a·bel, Za′dok, Jad′du·a, **22** Pel·a·ti′ah, Ha′nan, A·nai′ah, **23** Ho·she′a, Han·a·ni′ah, Has′shub, **24** Hal·lo′hesh, Pil′ha, Sho′bek, **25** Re′hum, Ha·shab′nah, Ma·a·sei′ah, **26** A·hi′jah, Ha′nan, A′nan, **27** Mal′luch, Ha′rim, and Ba′a·nah.

28 The rest of the people—the priests, the Levites, the gatekeepers, the singers, the temple servants,* and everyone who separated himself from the peoples of the lands to follow the Law of the true God,[g] along with their wives, their sons, and their daughters, all those with knowledge and understanding*— **29** joined their brothers, their prominent men, and bound themselves with a curse and an oath, to walk in the Law of the true God, which had been given through Moses the servant of the true God, and to observe carefully all the commandments of Jehovah our Lord, his judgments, and his regulations. **30** We will not give our daughters to the peoples of the land, and we will not take their daughters for our sons.[a]

31 If the peoples of the land bring in their wares and every kind of grain to sell on the Sabbath day, we will not buy anything from them on the Sabbath[b] or on a holy day.[c] We will also forgo the produce of the seventh year[d] and every outstanding debt.[e]

32 Also, we imposed the obligation on ourselves for each of us to give a third of a shekel* yearly for the service of the house* of our God,[f] **33** for the layer bread,*[g] the regular grain offering,[h] the regular burnt offering of the Sabbaths[i] and the new moons,[j] and for the appointed feasts,[k] for the holy things, for the sin offerings[l] to make atonement for Israel, and for all the work of the house of our God.

34 Also, we cast lots concerning the supply of the wood that the priests, the Levites, and the people should bring to the house of our God by our paternal houses, at the appointed times, year by year, to burn on the altar of Jehovah our God, according to what is written in the Law.[m] **35** We will also bring the first ripe fruits of our land

---

CHAP. 10
a Ne 9:38

b Ezr 2:1, 39

c Ezr 8:1, 2

d Ezr 3:9
Ne 12:8

e Ne 12:24

f Ne 7:6, 11

g Ne 8:1
Ne 9:2

Second Col.
a Ex 34:15, 16
De 7:3, 4

b Ex 20:10

c Ex 12:16
Nu 29:1, 12

d Ex 23:10, 11
Le 25:4, 5

e De 15:1-3

f Ex 30:13

g Le 24:5-7

h Ex 29:40, 41

i Nu 28:9

j Nu 28:11-13
1Ch 23:31

k De 16:16

l Le 16:15

m Le 1:7
Le 6:12, 13

10:1 *Or "the Tirshatha," a Persian title for a governor of a province.   **10:28** *Or "the Nethinim." Lit., "the given ones."   **10:28** *Or possibly, "all those old enough to understand."   **10:32** *A shekel equaled 11.4 g (0.367 oz t). See App. B14.   *Or "temple."   **10:33** *That is, the showbread.

and the first ripe fruits of every sort of fruit tree, year by year, to the house of Jehovah,[a] **36** as well as the firstborn of our sons and of our livestock[b]—according to what is written in the Law—and the firstborn of our herds and of our flocks. We will bring them to the house of our God, to the priests who minister at the house of our God.[c] **37** Also, the firstfruits of our coarse meal,[d] our contributions, the fruitage of every sort of tree,[e] new wine, and oil,[f] we should bring to the priests to the storerooms* of the house of our God,[g] along with the tenth# from our land to the Levites,[h] for the Levites are the ones who collect the tenths in all our agricultural cities.

38 And the priest, the son of Aaron, must be with the Levites when the Levites collect the tenth; and the Levites should offer up a tenth of the tenth to the house of our God,[i] to the rooms* of the storehouse. **39** For it is to the storerooms* that the Israelites and the sons of the Levites should bring the contribution[j] of the grain, the new wine, and the oil,[k] and that is where the utensils of the sanctuary are, as well as the priests who minister, the gatekeepers, and the singers. We will not neglect the house of our God.[l]

11 Now the princes of the people were living in Jerusalem;[m] but the rest of the people cast lots[n] to bring one out of every ten to live in Jerusalem, the holy city, while the other nine stayed in the other cities. **2** Moreover, the people blessed all the men who volunteered to live in Jerusalem.

3 And these are the heads of the province* who lived in Je-

rusalem. (The rest of Israel, the priests, the Levites, the temple servants,*[a] and the sons of the servants of Sol′o·mon,[b] lived in the other cities of Judah, each one in his own possession in his city.[c]

4 Also, there lived in Jerusalem some of the people of Judah and of Benjamin.) Of the people of Judah were A·thai′ah son of Uz·zi′ah son of Zech·a·ri′ah son of Am·a·ri′ah son of Sheph·a·ti′ah son of Ma·hal′a·lel of the sons of Pe′rez,[d] **5** and Ma·a·sei′ah son of Bar′uch son of Col·ho′zeh son of Ha·zai′ah son of A·dai′ah son of Joi′a·rib son of Zech·a·ri′ah son of the She·la′nite. **6** All the sons of Pe′rez who were dwelling in Jerusalem were 468 capable men.

7 And these were the people of Benjamin: Sal′lu[e] son of Me·shul′lam son of Jo′ed son of Pe·dai′ah son of Ko·lai′ah son of Ma·a·sei′ah son of Ith′i·el son of Je·sha′iah, **8** and after him Gab·ba′i and Sal·la′i, 928; **9** and Joel the son of Zich′ri was their overseer, and Judah the son of Has·se·nu′ah was second in charge of the city.

10 Of the priests: Je·da′iah son of Joi′a·rib, Ja′chin,[f] **11** Se·rai′ah son of Hil·ki′ah son of Me·shul′lam son of Za′dok son of Me·ra′ioth son of A·hi′tub,[g] a leader of the house* of the true God, **12** and their brothers who did the work of the house, 822; and A·dai′ah son of Je·ro′ham son of Pel·a·li′ah son of Am′zi son of Zech·a·ri′ah son of Pash′hur[h] son of Mal·chi′jah, **13** and his brothers, heads of paternal houses, 242; and A·mash′sai son of Az′ar·el son of Ah′zai son of Me·shil′le·moth son of Im′mer, **14** and their brothers who were mighty, courageous men, 128; and their

CHAP. 10	
a	Ex 23:19 Nu 18:8, 13 De 26:2
b	Ex 13:2 Nu 18:15
c	Nu 18:8, 11 1Co 9:13
d	Nu 15:20
e	Le 27:30
f	Nu 18:8, 12 De 18:1, 4
g	2Ch 31:11
h	Nu 18:21
i	Nu 18:26
j	De 12:5, 6
k	De 14:23
l	Ne 13:10, 11
CHAP. 11	
m	Ne 7:4
n	Pr 16:33
Second Col.	
a	Jos 9:3, 27 Ezr 8:17
b	Ezr 2:58
c	Ezr 2:70
d	Nu 26:20
e	1Ch 9:3, 7
f	1Ch 9:10-13
g	1Ch 6:12
h	Jer 21:1, 2 Jer 38:1

10:37-39 *Or "dining halls." **10:37** #Or "tithes." **11:3** *Or "jurisdictional district."

11:3 *Or "the Nethinim." Lit., "the given ones." **11:11** *Or "temple."

overseer was Zab′di·el, a member of a prominent family.

15 And of the Levites: She·mai′ah[a] son of Has′shub son of Az·ri′kam son of Hash·a·bi′ah son of Bun′ni, **16** and Shab′be·thai[b] and Jo′za·bad,[c] of the heads of the Levites, who were in charge of the outside business of the house of the true God; **17** and Mat·ta·ni′ah,[d] son of Mi′cah son of Zab′di son of A′saph,[e] the conductor of the singing, who led the praises during prayer,[f] and Bak·bu·ki′ah, the second of his brothers, and Ab′da son of Sham·mu′a son of Ga′lal son of Je·du′thun.[g] **18** All the Levites in the holy city were 284.

19 And the gatekeepers were Ak′kub, Tal′mon,[h] and their brothers who kept guard in the gates, 172.

20 The rest of Israel, the priests, and the Levites were in all the other cities of Judah, each in his own inherited property.* **21** The temple servants*[i] were living in O′phel,[j] and Zi′ha and Gish′pa were in charge of the temple servants.*

22 The overseer of the Levites in Jerusalem was Uz′zi son of Ba′ni son of Hash·a·bi′ah son of Mat·ta·ni′ah[k] son of Mi′ca, of the sons of A′saph, the singers; he was in charge of the work of the house of the true God. **23** For there was a royal order in their behalf,[l] and there was a fixed provision for the singers as each day required. **24** And Peth·a·hi′ah son of Me·shez′a·bel of the sons of Ze′rah son of Judah was the king's adviser* for every matter of the people.

25 Regarding the settlements with their fields, some of the people of Judah lived in

Kir′i·ath-ar′ba[a] and its dependent* towns, in Di′bon and its dependent towns, in Je·kab′ze·el[b] and its settlements, **26** in Jesh′u·a, in Mo·la′dah,[c] in Beth-pel′et,[d] **27** in Ha′zar-shu′al,[e] in Be′er-she′ba and its dependent* towns, **28** in Zik′lag,[f] in Me·co′nah and its dependent* towns, **29** in En-rim′mon,[g] in Zo′rah,[h] and in Jar′muth, **30** in Za·no′ah,[i] in A·dul′lam and their settlements, in La′chish[j] and its fields, and in A·ze′kah[k] and its dependent* towns. They settled# from Be′er-she′ba clear to the Valley of Hin′nom.[l]

31 And the people of Benjamin were in Ge′ba,[m] Mich′mash, Ai′ja, Beth′el[n] and its dependent* towns, **32** An′a·thoth,[o] Nob,[p] A·na·ni′ah, **33** Ha′zor, Ra′mah,[q] Git′ta·im, **34** Ha′did, Ze·bo′im, Ne·bal′lat, **35** Lod, and O′no,[r] the valley of the craftsmen. **36** And some divisions of the Levites from Judah were assigned to Benjamin.

12 These were the priests and the Levites who went up with Ze·rub′ba·bel[s] the son of She·al′ti·el,[t] and Jesh′u·a:[u] Se·rai′ah, Jeremiah, Ez′ra, **2** Am·a·ri′ah, Mal′luch, Hat′tush, **3** Shec·a·ni′ah, Re′hum, Mer′e·moth, **4** Id′do, Gin′ne·thoi, A·bi′jah, **5** Mij′a·min, Ma·a·di′ah, Bil′gah, **6** She·mai′ah, Joi′a·rib, Je·da′iah, **7** Sal′lu, A′mok, Hil·ki′ah, and Je·da′iah. These were the heads of the priests and their brothers in the days of Jesh′u·a.

8 The Levites were Jesh′u·a, Bin′nu·i, Kad′mi·el,[v] She·re·bi′ah, Judah, and Mat·ta·ni′ah,[w] who led the songs of thanksgiving along with his brothers. **9** And Bak·bu·ki′ah and Un′ni their brothers stood opposite them for guard duties.* **10** Jesh′u·a

---

CHAP. 11
a 1Ch 9:2, 14
b 1Ch 10:14, 15
c Ezr 8:33
Ne 8:7
d Ne 11:22
Ne 12:25
e Ne 7:6, 44
f 1Ch 16:4
2Ch 5:13
g 1Ch 16:41, 42
2Ch 35:15
h 1Ch 9:2, 17
Ezr 2:1, 42
Ne 12:25
i Ezr 2:1, 58
2Ch 27:1, 3
j Ne 3:26
k 1Ch 9:2, 15
Ezr 6:3, 9
Ezr 7:21-24

Second Col.
a Ge 23:2
Jos 14:15
b Jos 15:21
2Sa 23:20
c Jos 15:21, 26
Jos 19:1, 2
d Jos 15:21, 27
Jos 19:1, 3
f Jos 15:21, 31
Jos 19:1, 5
1Sa 27:5, 6
g Jos 15:21, 32
h Jos 15:20, 33
Jos 19:40, 41
i Jos 15:20, 34
Ne 3:13
j Jos 15:20, 39
Isa 37:8
k Jos 15:20, 35
Jos 15:8, 12
2Ki 23:10
m Jos 18:21, 24
n Ge 28:19
o Jos 18:11, 13
Jos 21:8, 18
p 1Sa 21:1
q Jos 18:21, 25
r 1Ch 8:12
Ezr 2:1, 33

CHAP. 12
s Ezr 1:8, 11
t Mt 1:12
u Zec 3:1
v Ezr 2:1, 40
Ezr 3:9
w 1Ch 9:2, 15
Ne 11:17
Ne 12:25

11:20 *Or "his own inheritance." 11:21 *Or "the Nethinim." Lit., "the given ones." 11:24 *Lit., "was at the king's hand."

11:25, 27, 28, 30, 31 *Or "surrounding." 11:30 #Or "camped." 12:9 *Or possibly, "during the service."

became father to Joiʹaʹkim, and Joiʹaʹkim became father to Eʹliʹaʹshib,[a] and Eʹliʹaʹshib to Joiʹaʹda.[b] 11 And Joiʹaʹda became father to Jonʹaʹthan, and Jonʹaʹthan became father to Jadʹduʹa.

12 In the days of Joiʹaʹkim, these were the priests, the heads of the paternal houses: for Seʹraiʹah,[c] Meʹraiʹah; for Jeremiah, Hanʹaʹniʹah; 13 for Ezʹra,[d] Meʹshulʹlam; for Amʹaʹriʹah, Jeʹhoʹhaʹnan; 14 for Malʹluʹchi, Jonʹaʹthan; for Shebʹaʹniʹah, Joseph; 15 for Haʹrim,[e] Adʹna; for Meʹraʹioth, Helʹkai; 16 for Idʹdo, Zechʹaʹriʹah; for Ginʹneʹthon, Meʹshulʹlam; 17 for Aʹbiʹjah,[f] Zichʹri; for Miʹniʹaʹmin, . . . ;* for Moʹaʹdiʹah, Pilʹtai; 18 for Bilʹgah,[g] Shamʹmuʹa; for Sheʹmaiʹah, Jeʹhonʹaʹthan; 19 for Joiʹaʹrib, Matʹteʹnai; for Jeʹdaʹiah,[h] Uzʹzi; 20 for Salʹlaʹi, Kalʹlai; for Aʹmok, Eʹber; 21 for Hilʹkiʹah, Hashʹaʹbiʹah; for Jeʹdaʹiah, Neʹthanʹel.

22 The heads of the paternal houses of the Levites in the days of Eʹliʹaʹshib, Joiʹaʹda, Joʹhaʹnan, and Jadʹduʹa[i] were recorded, as were the priests, down to the kingship of Daʹriʹus the Persian. 23 The Levites who were heads of the paternal houses were recorded in the book of the history of the times, down to the days of Joʹhaʹnan the son of Eʹliʹaʹshib. 24 The heads of the Levites were Hashʹaʹbiʹah, Sheʹreʹbiʹah, and Jeshʹuʹa[j] the son of Kadʹmiʹel,[k] and their brothers stood opposite them to offer praise and give thanks according to the instructions of David[l] the man of the true God, guard group corresponding to guard group. 25 Matʹtaʹniʹah,[m] Bakʹbuʹkiʹah, Oʹbaʹdiʹah, Meʹshulʹlam, Talʹmon, and Akʹkub[n] were standing guard as gatekeepers,[o] guarding the store-rooms by the gates. 26 These served in the days of Joiʹaʹkim the son of Jeshʹuʹa[a] the son of Joʹzaʹdak and in the days of Neʹheʹmiʹah the governor and Ezʹra[b] the priest and copyist.*

27 At the inauguration of the walls of Jerusalem, they sought the Levites and brought them to Jerusalem from all the places they lived to celebrate the inauguration with rejoicing, with songs of thanksgiving,[c] and with cymbals, stringed instruments, and harps. 28 And the sons of the singers* gathered together from the district,[d] from all around Jerusalem, from the settlements of the Neʹtophʹaʹthites,[d] 29 from Beth-gilʹgal,[e] and from the fields of Geʹba[f] and Azʹmaveth,[g] for the singers had built settlements for themselves all around Jerusalem. 30 And the priests and the Levites purified themselves, and they purified the people,[h] the gates,[i] and the wall.[j]

31 Then I brought the princes of Judah up on top of the wall. Further, I appointed two large thanksgiving choirs and processions, and the one walked to the right on the wall toward the Gate of the Ash Heaps.[k] 32 Hoshaiʹah and half of the princes of Judah walked behind them, 33 along with Azʹaʹriʹah, Ezʹra, Meʹshulʹlam, 34 Judah, Benjamin, Sheʹmaiʹah, and Jeremiah. 35 With them were some of the sons of the priests with the trumpets;[l] Zechʹaʹriʹah son of Jonʹaʹthan son of Sheʹmaiʹah son of Matʹtaʹniʹah son of Miʹcaiʹah son of Zacʹcur son of Aʹsaph,[m] 36 and his brothers Sheʹmaiʹah, Azʹarʹel, Milʹaʹlai, Gilʹaʹlai, Maʹai, Neʹthanʹel, Judah, and Haʹnaʹni, with the musical instruments of David[n] the

---

CHAP. 12
a Ne 3:1
b Ne 13:28
c Ne 11:3, 11
d Ne 12:1
e Ezr 2:1, 39
f Ne 12:1, 4
g Ne 12:1, 5
h Ne 12:1, 6
i Ne 12:10, 11
j Ne 8:7
k Ezr 2:1, 40
l 1Ch 16:4
  1Ch 23:28, 30
m 1Ch 9:2, 15
n 1Ch 9:17
  Ezr 2:1, 42
  Ne 11:1, 19
o 1Ch 9:22-27

Second Col.
a Ezr 3:2, 8
b Ezr 7:1, 6
c 2Ch 5:13
  2Ch 7:6
d 2Ch 2:54
  1Ch 9:2, 16
  Ne 7:6, 26
e Jos 15:7, 12
f Jos 21:8, 17
  Ne 11:31
g Ezr 2:1, 24
h Ex 19:10
i Ne 7:1
j Ne 6:15
k Ne 2:13
  Ne 3:13
l Nu 10:2
  2Ch 5:12
m 1Ch 25:1, 2
n 1Ch 23:5

12:26 *Or "scribe." 12:28 *Or "And the trained singers." #That is, the district around the Jordan.

man of the true God; and Ez'-ra[a] the copyist* went before them. **37** At the Fountain Gate[b] they went straight ahead up the Stairway[c] of the City of David[d] by the ascent of the wall above the House of David and on to the Water Gate[e] to the east.

38 The other thanksgiving choir walked in the opposite direction,* and I followed it with half of the people, on the wall up over the Tower of the Ovens[f] and on to the Broad Wall[g] **39** and up over the Gate of E'phra·im[h] and on to the Gate of the Old City[i] and on to the Fish Gate,[j] the Tower of Ha·nan'el,[k] the Tower of Me'ah, and on to the Sheep Gate;[l] and they came to a halt at the Gate of the Guard.

40 At length the two thanksgiving choirs stood before the house of the true God; so did I and half of the deputy rulers with me, **41** and the priests E·li'a·kim, Ma·a·sei'ah, Mi·ni'a·min, Mi·cai'ah, Eli·o·e'nai, Zech·a·ri'ah, and Han·a·ni'ah, with the trumpets, **42** and Ma·a·sei'-ah, She·mai'ah, El·e·a'zar, Uz'zi, Je·ho·ha'nan, Mal·chi'jah, E'lam, and E'zer. And the singers sang loudly under the oversight of Iz·ra·hi'ah.

43 On that day they offered great sacrifices and rejoiced,[m] for the true God made them rejoice with great joy. The women and the children also rejoiced,[n] so that the rejoicing of Jerusalem could be heard far away.[o]

44 On that day men were appointed over the storehouses[p] for the contributions,[q] the first-fruits,[r] and the tenths.*[s] Into them they were to gather from the fields of the cities the portions required by the Law[t] for the priests and the Levites,[u] for there was rejoicing in Ju-

dah because of the priests and the Levites who were ministering. **45** And they began taking care of the duties of their God and the obligation of the purification, as did the singers and the gatekeepers, according to the instructions of David and his son Sol'o·mon. **46** For long ago in the days of David and A'saph, there were directors* for the singers and for the songs of praise and thanksgiving to God.[a] **47** And during the days of Ze·rub'ba·bel[b] and during the days of Ne·he·mi'ah, all Israel gave portions to the singers[c] and the gatekeepers,[d] according to the daily need. They also set aside the portion for the Levites,[e] and the Levites set aside the portion for the descendants of Aaron.

13 On that day the book of Moses was read in the hearing of the people,[f] and it was found written that no Am'mon·ite or Mo'ab·ite[g] should ever enter the congregation of the true God,[h] **2** for they had not met the Israelites with bread and water, but instead they had hired Ba'laam against them to curse them.[i] However, our God had changed the curse into a blessing.[j] **3** As soon as they heard the Law, they began to separate from Israel all those of foreign descent.*[k]

4 Now before this, the priest in charge of the storerooms* of the house* of our God[l] was E·li'a·shib,[m] a relative of To·bi'ah.[n] **5** He had made available for him a large storeroom,* where previously they used to put the grain offering, the frankincense, and the utensils and the tenth* of the grain, the new wine, and the oil,[o] to which the Levites,[p]

CHAP. 12
a Ne 8:4
b Ne 2:14
c Ne 3:15
d 2Sa 5:7, 9
e Ne 3:26
Ne 8:1
f Ne 3:11
g Ne 3:8
h 2Ki 14:13
Ne 8:16
i Ne 3:6
j 2Ch 33:14
Ne 3:3
k Jer 31:38
Zec 14:10
l Ne 3:1
Joh 5:2
m Ezr 6:16, 17
n Jer 31:13
o Ezr 3:10, 13
p 2Ch 31:11
q Ne 10:39
r Ne 10:35-37
s Ne 10:38
Ne 13:12, 13
t Ex 34:26
Nu 15:18, 19
De 26:2
u Nu 18:21

Second Col.
a 1Ch 25:1, 6
b Ezr 3:2
Hag 1:12
Lu 3:23, 27
c Ne 11:23
d Ne 10:39
e Nu 18:21

CHAP. 13
f De 31:11
Ne 8:2, 3
Ac 15:21
g Ge 19:36-38
h De 23:3, 6
i Nu 22:4-6
j Nu 23:8
Nu 24:10
k Ezr 10:10, 11
Ne 9:1, 2
l Ne 10:37, 38
m Ne 3:1
n Ne 2:10
o De 18:3, 4
p Nu 18:24

12:36 *Or "scribe." **12:38** *Or "in front." **12:44** *Or "tithes."   **12:46** *Lit., "heads." **13:3** *Or "mixed descent." **13:4** *Or "dining halls." #Or "temple." **13:5** *Or "dining hall." #Or "tithe."

the singers, and the gatekeepers are entitled, along with the contribution for the priests.ᵃ

6 And during all this time I was not in Jerusalem, for I went to the king in the 32nd yearᵇ of King Ar·ta·xerx′esᶜ of Babylon; and sometime later I asked the king for a leave of absence. **7** Then I came to Jerusalem and noticed the terrible thing that E·li′a·shibᵈ had done in behalf of To·bi′ah,ᵉ making a storeroom available for him in the courtyard of the house of the true God. **8** This was very displeasing to me, so I threw all of To·bi′ah's household furniture out of the storeroom.* **9** After that I gave orders, and they cleansed the storerooms;* and I put back there the utensils of the house of the true God,ᶠ with the grain offering and the frankincense.ᵍ

10 I also found out that the portions of the Levitesʰ had not been given them,ⁱ so that the Levites and the singers who did the work had gone off, each to his own field.ʲ **11** So I reprimanded the deputy rulersᵏ and said: "Why has the house of the true God been neglected?"ˡ Then I gathered them together and assigned them back to their posts. **12** And all Judah brought in the tenthᵐ of the grain, the new wine, and the oil to the storerooms.ⁿ **13** Then I put Shel·e·mi′ah the priest, Za′dok the copyist,* and Pe·dai′ah of the Levites in charge of the storerooms, and Ha′nan the son of Zac′cur the son of Mat·ta·ni′ah was their assistant, for these men were considered reliable. It was their responsibility to make the distribution to their brothers.

14 Do remember me,ᵒ O my God, concerning this, and do not wipe out my acts of loyal love

that I have done for the house of my God and its services.*ᵃ

15 In those days I saw people in Judah treading winepresses on the Sabbath,ᵇ bringing in heaps of grain and loading them on donkeys, and bringing wine, grapes, figs, and every sort of load into Jerusalem on the Sabbath day.ᶜ So I warned them against selling provisions on that day.* **16** And the Tyr′i·ans who lived in the city were bringing in fish and all kinds of merchandise, selling them to the people of Judah and in Jerusalem on the Sabbath.ᵈ **17** So I reprimanded the nobles of Judah and said to them: "What is this evil thing that you are doing, even profaning the Sabbath day? **18** Was not this what your forefathers did, so that our God brought all this disaster on us and also on this city? Now you are adding to the burning anger against Israel by profaning the Sabbath."ᵉ

19 So as soon as the shadows began to fall on the gates of Jerusalem before the Sabbath, I ordered that the doors be closed. I also said that they should not open them until after the Sabbath, and I stationed some of my own attendants at the gates so that no loads would be brought in on the Sabbath day. **20** So the traders and the sellers of all kinds of merchandise spent the night outside Jerusalem once or twice. **21** Then I warned them and said to them: "Why are you spending the night in front of the wall? If you do it again, I will use force against you." From that time on they did not come on the Sabbath.

22 And I told the Levites that they should regularly purify

CHAP. 13
a Ne 12:44

b Ne 5:14

c Ezr 7:1
Ne 2:1

d Ne 12:10

e Ne 4:7

f Ne 10:39

g Le 2:14, 15

h Ne 10:37
Ne 12:47

i Mal 3:8

j Nu 35:2

k Ezr 9:2

l Ne 10:39

m Le 27:30
Nu 18:21

n Ne 10:38, 39
Mal 3:10

o Ne 5:19

Second Col.
a Heb 6:10

b Ex 20:10
Ex 34:21
Ex 35:2

c Jer 17:21, 27

d Ne 10:31

e Ex 20:8-10

13:8 *Or "dining hall." 13:9 *Or "dining halls." 13:13 *Or "scribe."

13:14 *Or "guardianship." 13:15 *Or possibly, "warned them on that day not to sell provisions."

themselves and come and guard the gates to keep the Sabbath day holy.[a] This, also, do remember to my credit, O my God, and show me pity according to your abundant loyal love.[b]

23 In those days I also saw Jews who had married* Ash'dod·ite,[c] Am'mon·ite, and Mo'ab·ite[d] women.[e] **24** Half of their sons were speaking Ash'dod·ite and the language of the different peoples, but none of them knew how to speak the language of the Jews. **25** So I reprimanded them and called down a curse on them and struck some of the men[f] and pulled out their hair and made them swear by God: "You should not give your daughters to their sons, and you should not accept any of their daughters for your sons or yourselves.[g] **26** Was it not because of these that King Sol'o·mon of Israel sinned? Among the many nations there was no king like him;[h] and he was loved by his

God,[a] so that God made him king over all Israel. But the foreign wives caused even him to sin.[b] **27** Is it not something unheard of for you to commit this great evil in acting unfaithfully against our God by marrying foreign women?"[c]

28 One of the sons of Joi'a·da[d] the son of E·li'a·shib[e] the high priest had become a son-in-law of San·bal'lat[f] the Hor'o·nite. So I drove him away from me.

29 Do remember them, O my God, because they have defiled the priesthood and the covenant of the priesthood[g] and the Levites.[h]

30 And I purified them from every foreign defilement, and I assigned duties to the priests and to the Levites, each to his own service,[i] **31** and arranged for the supply of the wood[j] at appointed times and for the first ripe fruits.

Do remember me favorably,* O my God.[k]

CHAP. 13

a De 5:12
b Ne 5:19
  Ne 13:14
  Ne 13:30, 31
c Jos 13:2, 3
d De 23:3, 4
e Ezr 9:1, 2
  Ezr 10:10
  2Co 6:14
f De 25:2
  Ezr 7:26
g De 7:3, 4
  Ne 10:30
h 1Ki 3:12, 13
  2Ch 9:22

Second Col.

a 2Sa 12:24
b 1Ki 11:1-5
c Ezr 10:2
d Ne 12:10
e Ne 3:1
  Ne 13:4
f Ne 2:10
  Ne 6:14
g Ex 40:15
  Nu 25:11-13
h Mal 2:4
i 1Ch 23:6
  1Ch 25:1
j Ne 10:34
k Ne 5:19

13:23 *Or "had taken into their houses."

13:31 *Or "for good."

ESTHER

OUTLINE OF CONTENTS

1 Now in the days of A·has·u·e′rus,* that is, the A·has·u·e′rus who ruled over 127 provinces#a from In′di·a to E·thi·o′pi·a,b **2** in those days when King A·has·u·e′rus was sitting on his royal throne in Shu′shan*b the citadel,# **3** in the third year of his reign, he held a banquet for all his princes and his servants. The army of Persiac and Me′di·a,d the nobles, and the princes of the provinces# were before him, **4** and he showed them the wealth of his glorious kingdom and the grandeur and the splendor of his magnificence for many days, 180 days. **5** And when these days were completed, the king held a banquet for seven days for all the people present in Shu′shan* the citadel,# from the greatest to the least, in the courtyard of the garden of the king's palace. **6** There were linen, fine cotton, and blue material held fast in ropes of fine fabric, purple wool in silver rings, pillars of marble, and couches of gold and silver on a pavement of porphyry, marble, pearl, and black marble.

7 Wine was served in gold cups;* each cup was different from the other, and the royal wine was plentiful, according to the means of the king. **8** The drinking was according to the rule that no one was under compulsion,* for the king had arranged with the officials of his palace that each should do as he pleased.

9 Queen Vash′tie also held a banquet for the women at the royal house* of King A·has·u·e′rus.

10 On the seventh day, when the king's heart was in a cheerful mood because of the wine, he told Me·hu′man, Biz′tha, Har·bo′na,a Big′tha, A·bag′tha, Ze′thar, and Car′kas, the seven court officials who were personal attendants to King A·has·u·e′rus, **11** to bring before the king Queen Vash′ti, wearing the royal headdress,* to show the peoples and the princes her beauty, for she was very beautiful. **12** But Queen Vash′ti kept refusing to come at the king's order that was conveyed through the court officials. At this the king became very angry, and his rage flared up within him.

13 The king then spoke to the wise men who had insight with regard to precedents* (for in this way the king's matter came before all those versed in law and legal cases, **14** and those closest to him were Car·she′na, She′thar, Ad·ma′tha, Tar′shish, Me′res, Mar·se′na, and Me·mu′can, seven princesb of Persia and Me′di·a, who had access to the king and who occupied the highest positions in the kingdom). **15** The king asked: "According to law, what is to be done with Queen Vash′ti because she has not obeyed the order of King A·has·u·e′rus conveyed through the court officials?"

16 To this Me·mu′can said in the presence of the king and the princes: "It is not against the king alone that Queen Vash′ti has done wrong,c but against all the princes and against all the peoples in all the provinces# of King A·has·u·e′rus. **17** For what the queen did will become known by all the wives, and they will despise their husbands and say, 'King A·has·u·e′rus said to bring in Queen Vash′ti before

---

CHAP. 1

a Es 8:9
Da 6:1

b Ezr 4:9
Ne 1:1
Da 8:2

c Ezr 1:2

d Isa 21:2
Jer 51:11
Da 5:28

e Es 1:12
Es 2:1, 17

Second Col.

a Es 7:9

b Ezr 7:14

c Es 1:12

1:1 *Understood to be Xerxes I, son of Darius the Great (Darius Hystaspis). 1:1, 3, 16 #Or "jurisdictional districts." 1:2 △Or "Cush." 1:2, 5 *Or "Susa." 1:2, 5 #Or "palace; fortress." 1:7 *Or "vessels; goblets." 1:8 *Or "restriction." 1:9 *Or "palace."

1:11 *Or "turban." 1:13 *Or "procedures." Lit., "the times."

him, but she refused to come.'
18 This very day the princesses of Persia and Me′di·a who know about what the queen did will talk to all the princes of the king, resulting in much contempt and indignation. **19** If it seems good to the king, let a royal decree be issued from him, and let it be written among the laws of Persia and Me′di·a, which cannot be repealed,[a] that Vash′ti may never again come in before King A·has·u·e′rus; and let the king confer her royal position on a woman who is better than she is. **20** And when the decree of the king is heard in all his vast realm, all the wives will give honor to their husbands, from the greatest to the least."

21 This proposal pleased the king and the princes, and the king did what Me·mu′can said. **22** So he sent letters to all the royal provinces,[*b] to each province[*] in its own script[▲] and to each people in its own language, for every husband to be master[🔲] in his own house and to speak in the language of his own people.

2 After these things, when the rage of King A·has·u·e′rus[c] had subsided, he remembered what Vash′ti had done[d] and what had been decided against her.[e] **2** Then the king's personal attendants said: "A search should be made for young, beautiful virgins for the king. **3** And let the king appoint commissioners in all the provinces[*] of his realm[f] to bring together all the beautiful young virgins to Shu′shan[🔲] the citadel,[▲] to the house of the women.[🔲] Let them be put in the care of Heg′a·i[g] the king's eu-

nuch and guardian of the women, and let them be given beauty treatments.[*] **4** And the young woman who is most pleasing to the king will be queen instead of Vash′ti."[a] The suggestion was pleasing to the king, and that is what he did.

5 There was a certain Jewish man in Shu′shan[🔲b] the citadel[▲] whose name was Mor′de·cai[c] son of Ja′ir son of Shim′e·i son of Kish, a Ben′ja·min·ite,[d] **6** who had been taken into exile from Jerusalem with the people who were deported with King Jec·o·ni′ah[*e] of Judah, whom King Neb·u·chad·nez′zar of Babylon took into exile. **7** He was the guardian[*] of Ha·das′sah,[🔲] that is, Esther, the daughter of his father's brother,[f] for she had neither father nor mother. The young woman was beautifully formed and attractive in appearance, and at the death of her father and her mother, Mor′de·cai took her as his daughter. **8** When the king's word and his law were proclaimed and when many young women were brought together at Shu′shan[🔲] the citadel[▲] under the care of Heg′a·i,[g] Esther was also taken to the king's house[*] under the care of Heg′a·i the guardian of the women.

9 Now the young woman was pleasing to him and won his favor,[*] so he promptly arranged for her beauty treatments[🔲h] and her diet, and he assigned to her seven selected young women from the king's house. He also transferred her and her young attendants to the best place in the house of the women.[▲] **10** Esther did not say

---

CHAP. 1
a Es 8:8
  Da 6:8

b Es 3:12, 14

CHAP. 2
c Es 1:1

d Es 1:12

e Es 1:19

f Es 8:9

g Es 2:15

Second Col.
a Es 1:19

b Ezr 4:9
  Ne 1:1
  Es 1:2
  Da 8:2

c Es 3:2
  Es 10:3

d Ge 49:27
  1Sa 9:21

e 2Ki 24:14, 15
  1Ch 3:16
  2Ch 36:9, 10
  Jer 22:28
  Jer 24:1
  Jer 37:1
  Jer 52:31
  Mt 1:11

f Es 2:15

g Es 2:3

h Es 2:12

1:22 *Lit., "the jurisdictional districts of the king." "Or "jurisdictional district." ▲Or "style of writing." 🔲Or "prince." **2:3** *Or "jurisdictional districts." **2:3, 5, 8** "Or "Susa." **2:3, 5, 8** ▲Or "palace; fortress." **2:3** 🔲Or "to the harem."

2:3 *Or "be given massages." **2:6** *Called Jehoiachin at 2Ki 24:8. **2:7** *Or "caretaker." "Meaning "Myrtle." **2:8** *Or "palace." **2:9** *Or "loyal love." "Or "her massages." ▲Or "in the harem."

anything about her people[a] or her relatives, for Mor'de·cai[b] had instructed her not to tell anyone.[c] **11** Day after day Mor'de·cai would walk in front of the courtyard of the house of the women* to learn about Esther's welfare and about what was happening to her.

12 Each young woman had her turn to go in to King A·has·u·e'rus after completing the 12-month treatment that was prescribed for the women, for this was the way they had to fulfill their beauty treatment*—six months with oil of myrrh[d] and six months with balsam oil[e] and various ointments for beauty treatment.# **13** Then the young woman was ready to go in to the king, and whatever she asked for would be given her when she went from the house of the women* to the king's house. **14** In the evening she would go in, and in the morning she would return to the second house of the women,* under the care of Sha·ash'·gaz the king's eunuch,[f] the guardian of the concubines. She would not go to the king again unless the king had been especially pleased with her and she was requested by name.[g]

15 And when the turn came for Esther the daughter of Ab'i·ha·il the uncle of Mor'de·cai, who had taken her as his daughter,[h] to go in to the king, she did not request anything except what Heg'a·i the king's eunuch, the guardian of the women, recommended. (All the while Esther was winning the favor of everyone who saw her.) **16** Esther was taken to King A·has·u·e'rus at his royal house in the tenth month, that is, the month of Te'-

beth,* in the seventh year[a] of his reign. **17** And the king came to love Esther more than all the other women, and she won his favor and approval* more than any of the other virgins. So he put the royal headdress# on her head and made her queen[b] instead of Vash'ti.[c] **18** And the king held a great banquet for all his princes and his servants, the banquet of Esther. He then proclaimed an amnesty for the provinces,* and he kept giving gifts according to the means of the king.

19 Now when virgins*[d] were brought together a second time, Mor'de·cai was sitting in the king's gate. **20** Esther did not say anything about her relatives and her people,[e] just as Mor'de·cai had instructed her; Esther continued to do what Mor'de·cai said, just as when she was under his care.[f]

21 In those days while Mor'de·cai was sitting in the king's gate, Big'than and Te'resh, two court officials of the king, doorkeepers, got angry and plotted to do away with* King A·has·u·e'rus. **22** But Mor'de·cai learned about it, and he immediately told Queen Esther. Esther then spoke to the king in Mor'de·cai's name.* **23** So the matter was investigated and eventually confirmed, and both men were hanged on a stake; and this was all recorded in the book of the history of the times in the presence of the king.[g]

3 After this King A·has·u·e'rus promoted Ha'man[h] the son of Ham·me·da'tha the Ag'ag·ite[i] and exalted him by putting his throne above all the other princes who were with him.[j]

CHAP. 2
a Es 3:8

b Es 2:7

c Es 4:12-14

d Pr 7:17
Ca 3:6

e Ge 43:11
1Ki 10:2
2Ki 20:13

f Es 2:3

g Es 4:11

h Es 2:7

Second Col.
a Es 1:3

b Es 4:14

c Es 1:19

d Es 2:3, 4

e Es 2:5, 6
Es 3:8

f Es 2:7, 10

g Es 6:1, 2

CHAP. 3
h Es 3:10
Es 8:7
Es 9:24

i Ex 17:16
Nu 24:7
De 25:19
1Sa 15:8, 32

j Es 1:14

2:11 *Or "of the harem." **2:12** *Or "their massages." #Or "and with massages of the women." **2:13** *Or "from the harem." **2:14** *Or "the second harem." **2:16** *See App. B15. **2:17** *Or "loyal love." #Or "turban." **2:18** *Or "jurisdictional districts." **2:19** *Or "young women." **2:21** *Lit., "to lay hand on." **2:22** *Or "on behalf of Mordecai."

2 And all the king's servants who were in the king's gate would bow low and prostrate themselves to Ha'man, for this is what the king had commanded respecting him. But Mor'de·cai refused to bow low or prostrate himself. **3** So the king's servants who were in the king's gate said to Mor'de·cai: "Why are you ignoring the king's commandment?" **4** Day after day they would ask him, but he would not listen to them. Then they told Ha'man to see whether Mor'de·cai's conduct would be tolerated;[e] for he had told them that he was a Jew.[b]

5 Now when Ha'man saw that Mor'de·cai refused to bow low and prostrate himself to him, Ha'man became filled with rage.[c] **6** But he despised the thought of doing away with* Mor'de·cai alone, for they had told him about Mor'de·cai's people. So Ha'man began seeking to annihilate all the Jews who were in the entire realm of A·has·u·e'rus, all of Mor'de·cai's people.

7 In the first month, that is, the month of Ni'san,* in the 12th year[d] of King A·has·u·e'rus, they cast Pur* (that is, the Lot) before Ha'man to determine the day and the month, and it fell on the 12th month, that is, A'dar.*[f] **8** Ha'man then said to King A·has·u·e'rus: "There is a certain people scattered and dispersed among the peoples[g] in all the provinces* of your realm,[h] whose laws are different from those of all other peoples; and they do not obey the king's laws, and it is not in the king's interests to let them be. **9** If it pleases the king, let a decree be written that they be destroyed. I will pay 10,000 silver talents* to

the officials to put into the royal treasury."*

10 At that the king removed his signet ring[a] from his own hand and gave it to Ha'man[b] the son of Ham·me·da'tha the Ag'ag·ite,[c] who was the enemy of the Jews. **11** The king said to Ha'man: "The silver and the people are given to you, to do with them as you see fit." **12** The king's secretaries[d] were then called on the 13th day of the first month. They put in writing[e] all of Ha'man's orders to the king's satraps, the governors who were over the provinces,* and the princes of the different peoples, to each province* in its own script△ and to each people in its own language. It was written in the name of King A·has·u·e'rus and sealed with the king's signet ring.[f]

13 The letters were sent by means of couriers to all the king's provinces,* giving the order to annihilate, to kill, and to destroy all the Jews, young and old alike, children and women, on a single day, on the 13th day of the 12th month, that is, the month of A'dar,[g] and to seize their possessions.[h] **14** A copy of the document was to be issued as a law in every province* and proclaimed to all the peoples, so that they would be prepared for that day. **15** The couriers went out quickly[i] by order of the king; the law was issued in Shu'shan*[j] the citadel.* The king and Ha'man then sat down to drink, but the city of Shu'shan* was in confusion.

4 When Mor'de·cai[k] learned of everything that had been done,[l] he ripped his garments

---

CHAP. 3
a Da 6:13

b Es 2:5

c Es 5:9

d Es 1:3
  Es 2:16

e Es 9:24

f Es 9:1

g De 4:27
  Ne 1:8
  Jer 50:17

h Es 1:1

Second Col.
a Ge 41:42

b Es 3:1
  Es 8:2

c Nu 24:7
  1Sa 15:8, 32

d Es 8:9

e Da 6:8

f Es 8:8
  Da 6:17

g Es 9:1

h Es 8:11, 12

i Es 8:14

j Ezr 4:9
  Ne 1:1
  Da 8:2

CHAP. 4
k Es 2:5

l Es 3:8-11

3:6 *Lit., "laying a hand on."   3:7 *See App. B15.   3:8, 12, 13 *Or "jurisdictional districts."   3:9 *A talent equaled 34.2 kg (1,101 oz t). See App. B14.

3:9 *Or possibly, "I will pay 10,000 talents into the royal treasury for those who carry out this work."   3:12, 14 *Or "jurisdictional district."   3:12 △Or "style of writing."   3:15 *Or "Susa." *Or "palace; fortress."

apart and put on sackcloth and ashes. Then he went out into the middle of the city, crying out loudly and bitterly. **2** He went only as far as the king's gate, for no one was to enter the king's gate wearing sackcloth. **3** And in every province*[a] where the king's word and his decree reached, there was great mourning among the Jews, along with fasting[b] and weeping and wailing. Many were lying down in sackcloth and ashes.[c] **4** When Esther's female attendants and her eunuchs came in and told her, the queen was deeply distressed. Then she sent garments for Mor'de·cai to wear instead of his sackcloth, but he refused them. **5** At this Esther summoned Ha'thach, one of the king's eunuchs, whom he had appointed to serve her, and she ordered him to find out from Mor'de·cai what this meant and what was happening.

6 So Ha'thach went out to Mor'de·cai in the public square of the city in front of the king's gate. **7** Mor'de·cai told him about everything that had happened to him and the exact amount of money[d] that Ha'man had promised to pay to the king's treasury for the Jews to be destroyed.[e] **8** He also gave him a copy of the written decree that had been issued in Shu'shan*[f] for their annihilation. He was to show it to Esther and explain it to her and instruct her[g] to go in to the king to beg for his favor and to plead directly with him in behalf of her people.

9 Ha'thach came back and told Esther what Mor'de·cai had said. **10** Esther replied to Ha'thach with instructions to tell Mor'de·cai:[h] **11** "All the king's servants and the people of the

king's provinces* are aware that if any man or woman goes into the king's inner courtyard[a] without being summoned, there is only one law that applies: He is to be put to death; he may live only if the king holds out to him the golden scepter.[b] And I have not been summoned to the king now for 30 days."

12 When Mor'de·cai was told what Esther had said, **13** he replied to Esther: "Do not imagine that because you are in the king's household you are any more likely to escape than all the other Jews. **14** For if you remain silent at this time, relief and deliverance will come to the Jews from another source,[c] but you and your father's house will perish. And who knows whether it is for a time like this that you have attained to your royal status?"[d]

15 Then Esther replied to Mor'de·cai: **16** "Go, gather all the Jews who are found in Shu'shan* and fast[e] in my behalf. Do not eat or drink for three days,[f] night and day. I along with my female attendants will also fast. I will go in to the king, which is against the law, and if I am to perish, I will perish." **17** So Mor'de·cai went his way and did all that Esther had instructed him to do.

5 On the third day[g] Esther put on her royal robes and stood in the inner courtyard of the king's house,* opposite the king's house, while the king was sitting on his royal throne in the royal house opposite the entrance. **2** As soon as the king saw Queen Esther standing in the courtyard, she gained his favor, and the king held out to Esther the golden scepter[h] that

---

CHAP. 4
a Es 1:1

b 2Ch 20:3
Ezr 8:21

c Da 9:3

d Es 3:9

e Es 3:8, 13

f Es 3:14, 15

g Es 2:20

h Es 2:5, 7

Second Col.
a Es 5:1

b Es 5:2
Es 8:4

c 1Sa 12:22
Isa 54:17

d Es 2:17

e 2Ch 20:3
Ezr 8:21

f Es 5:1

CHAP. 5
g Es 4:16

h Es 4:11
Es 8:4

4:3 *Or "jurisdictional district." 4:8, 16 *Or "Susa."

4:11 *Or "jurisdictional districts." 5:1 *Or "palace."

was in his hand. Esther then approached and touched the top of the scepter.

3 The king asked her: "What is the matter, Queen Esther? What is your request? Even to* the half of my kingdom, it will be granted you!" **4** Esther replied: "If it pleases the king, let the king along with Ha'man* come today to the banquet that I have prepared for him." **5** So the king said to his men: "Tell Ha'man to come quickly, as Esther requests." So the king and Ha'man went to the banquet that Esther had prepared.

6 During the banquet of wine, the king said to Esther: "What is your petition? It will be granted you! And what is your request? Even to* the half of my kingdom, it will be done!"* **7** Esther answered: "My petition and my request is, **8** If I have found favor with the king and if it pleases the king to grant my petition and to act on my request, let the king and Ha'man come to the banquet that I will hold for them tomorrow; and tomorrow I will do as the king says."

9 On that day Ha'man went out joyful and with a cheerful heart. But when Ha'man saw Mor'de·cai in the king's gate and noticed that he did not rise and tremble in his presence, Ha'man was filled with rage against Mor'de·cai.* **10** However, Ha'man restrained himself and went to his house. Then he sent for his friends and Ze'resh* his wife. **11** Ha'man boasted about his glorious wealth, his many sons,* and how the king had promoted him and had exalted him over the princes and the servants of the king.*

12 Ha'man added: "What is more, Queen Esther invited no

one else but me to accompany the king to the banquet she prepared.* I am also invited tomorrow to be with her and the king.* **13** But all of this fails to satisfy me as long as I see Mor'de·cai the Jew sitting in the king's gate." **14** So Ze'resh his wife and all his friends said to him: "Have a stake put up, 50 cubits* high. And in the morning tell the king that Mor'de·cai should be hanged on it.* Then go with the king to enjoy yourself at the banquet." This suggestion seemed good to Ha'man, so he had the stake put up.

6 That night the king could not sleep.* So he said to bring the book of the historical records of the times,* and it was read to the king. **2** There it was found written what Mor'de·cai had reported concerning Big'tha·na and Te'resh, two court officials of the king, doorkeepers, who had plotted to do away with* King A·has·u·e'rus.* **3** The king asked: "What honor and recognition has been given to Mor'de·cai for this?" To this the king's personal attendants said: "Nothing has been done for him."

4 Later the king said: "Who is in the courtyard?" Now Ha'man had come into the outer courtyard* of the king's house* to speak to the king about having Mor'de·cai hanged on the stake that he had prepared for him.* **5** The king's attendants said to him: "It is Ha'man* standing in the courtyard." So the king said: "Have him come in."

6 When Ha'man came in, the king said to him: "What should be done for the man whom the king wishes to honor?" Ha'man

---

CHAP. 5
a Es 3:1, 10

b Es 7:2

c Es 3:2-5

d Es 5:14
Es 6:13

e Es 9:7-10

f Es 3:1

Second Col.
a Es 5:5

b Es 5:8

c Es 6:4
Es 7:9

CHAP. 6
d Es 10:2

e Es 2:21, 23

f Es 4:11

g Es 5:14

h Es 3:1

5:3, 6 *Or "for."

5:14 *About 22.3 m (73 ft). See App. B14. **6:1** *Lit., "the king's sleep fled." **6:2** *Lit., "to lay hand on." **6:4** *Or "palace."

said in his heart: "Whom would the king wish to honor more than me?"[a] **7** So Ha′man said to the king: "For the man whom the king wishes to honor, **8** let them bring royal attire[b] that the king wears and a horse on which the king rides, with the royal headdress on its head. **9** Then let the attire and the horse be put into the charge of one of the king's noble princes, and they should clothe the man whom the king wishes to honor and have him ride on the horse in the public square of the city. They should call out before him: 'This is what is done for the man whom the king wishes to honor!'"[c] **10** At once the king said to Ha′man: "Quick! Take the attire and the horse, and do what you just said for Mor′de·cai the Jew who is sitting in the king's gate. Do not leave out anything that you have said."

11 So Ha′man took the attire and the horse, and he clothed Mor′de·cai[d] and made him ride in the public square of the city and called out before him: "This is what is done for the man whom the king wishes to honor!" **12** Afterward Mor′de·cai returned to the king's gate, but Ha′man hurried to his house, mourning with his head covered. **13** When Ha′man related to his wife Ze′resh[e] and to all his friends everything that had happened to him, his wise men and his wife Ze′resh said to him: "If Mor′de·cai, before whom you have started to fall, is of Jewish descent,* you will not prevail against him; you will surely fall before him."

14 While they were still speaking with him, the king's court officials arrived and quickly took Ha′man to the banquet that Esther had made.[f]

7 So the king and Ha′man[a] came in to Queen Esther's banquet. **2** The king said to Esther again on the second day during the banquet of wine: "What is your petition, Queen Esther? It will be granted you. And what is your request? Even to* the half of my kingdom, it will be done!"[b] **3** Queen Esther answered: "If I have found favor with you, O king, and if it pleases the king, let my life* be granted as my petition, and my people[c] as my request. **4** For we have been sold,[d] I and my people, to be annihilated, killed, and destroyed.[e] If we had simply been sold as male and female slaves, I would have kept silent. But the distress is not proper, for it will be damaging to the king."

5 King A·has·u·e′rus then said to Queen Esther: "Who is this, and where is the man who has dared to do such a thing?" **6** Esther said: "The adversary and enemy is this evil Ha′man."

Ha′man became terrified because of the king and the queen. **7** The king rose up in a rage from the banquet of wine and went into the palace garden, but Ha′man stood up to plead with Queen Esther for his life,* for he realized that the king was determined to punish him. **8** The king returned from the palace garden to the house of the wine banquet and saw that Ha′man had thrown himself on the couch where Esther was. The king exclaimed: "Is he also going to rape the queen in my own house?" As soon as these words left the king's mouth, they covered Ha′man's face. **9** Har·bo′na,[f] one of the king's court officials, now said: "Ha′man also prepared a stake for Mor′de·cai,[g] whose report saved the king.[h] It is standing at Ha′man's house,

---

CHAP. 6
a Es 3:2
  Es 5:11

b Es 8:15

c Ge 41:42, 43

d Es 2:5, 6

e Es 5:10, 14

f Es 5:8

Second Col.

CHAP. 7
a Es 3:1

b Es 5:3, 6

c Es 2:5, 7

d Es 3:8, 9

e Es 3:13
  Es 4:7, 8

f Es 1:10

g Es 5:14

h Es 6:2

6:13 *Lit., "from the seed of the Jews."   7:2 *Or "for."   7:3, 7 *Or "soul."

50 cubits* high." At that the king said: "Hang him on it." **10** So they hanged Ha′man on the stake that he had prepared for Mor′de·cai, and the king's rage subsided.

8 On that day King A·has·u·e′rus gave the house of Ha′man,[a] the enemy of the Jews,[b] to Queen Esther; and Mor′de·cai came in before the king, because Esther had revealed how he was related to her.[c] **2** Then the king removed his signet ring[d] that he had taken away from Ha′man and gave it to Mor′de·cai. And Esther put Mor′de·cai in charge of the house of Ha′man.[e]

3 Moreover, Esther spoke again to the king. She fell down at his feet and wept and pleaded with him to undo the harm done by Ha′man the Ag′ag·ite and his scheme against the Jews.[f] **4** The king held the golden scepter out to Esther,[g] at which Esther rose and stood before the king. **5** She said: "If it pleases the king and if I have his favor, and if it seems proper to the king and I am pleasing in his eyes, let an order be written to annul the documents of that schemer Ha′man[h] the son of Ham·me·da′tha the Ag′ag·ite,[i] which he wrote to destroy the Jews in all the king's provinces.* **6** For how can I bear to look upon the disaster that will come upon my people, and how can I bear to see the destruction of my relatives?"

7 So King A·has·u·e′rus said to Queen Esther and to Mor′de·cai the Jew: "Look! I have given the house of Ha′man to Esther[j] and have had him hanged on the stake,[k] because of his plot to attack* the Jews. **8** You may now write in the king's name whatever you see fit in behalf of the Jews and seal it with the king's signet ring, for a decree that is written in the king's name and sealed with the king's signet ring cannot be revoked."[a]

9 So the secretaries of the king were summoned at that time in the third month, that is, the month of Si′van,* on the 23rd day, and they wrote all that Mor′de·cai commanded to the Jews, as well as to the satraps,[b] the governors, and the princes of the provinces*[c] from In′di·a to E·thi·o′pi·a, 127 provinces,* to each province△ in its own script⑧ and to each people in its own language and to the Jews in their own script⑧ and language.

10 He wrote it in the name of King A·has·u·e′rus and sealed it with the king's signet ring[d] and sent the written documents by the hand of couriers on horses; they rode on swift post-horses, bred for royal service. **11** In these documents the king granted permission to the Jews in all the different cities to gather together and defend their lives* and to annihilate, kill, and destroy any forces of any people or province△ that might attack them, including women and children, and to seize their possessions.[e] **12** This was to occur on the same day in all the provinces* of King A·has·u·e′rus, on the 13th day of the 12th month, that is, the month of A′dar.*[f] **13** The text* of the document was to be issued as law throughout all the provinces.* It was to be proclaimed to all the peoples, so that the Jews would be ready on that day to take vengeance on their enemies.[g] **14** The couriers riding the post-horses used in the royal service went out

---

7:9 *About 22.3 m (73 ft). See App. B14. **8:5, 9, 12, 13** *Or "jurisdictional districts." **8:7** *Lit., "because he thrust out his hand against."

8:9, 12 *See App. B15. **8:9, 11** △Or "jurisdictional district." **8:9** ⑧Or "style of writing." **8:11** *Or "souls." **8:13** *Or "copy."

CHAP. 8
a Es 5:11

b Es 3:8
Es 9:24

c Es 2:5, 7

d Ge 41:41, 42
Es 3:10
Da 6:17

e Da 2:48

f Es 3:9
Es 7:4
Es 9:24, 25

g Es 4:11

h Es 3:12, 14

i Ex 17:16
Nu 24:7
De 25:19
1Sa 15:8, 33

j Es 8:1

k Es 7:10

Second Col.
a Da 6:8, 15

b Da 6:1

c Es 9:3

d Es 8:2

e Es 9:5-10

f Es 3:13
Es 9:1, 2
Es 9:16, 17

g Ps 149:6, 7

urgently and speedily at the king's order. The law was also issued in Shu'shan*[a] the citadel.[#]

15 Now Mor'de·cai left the king's presence in royal apparel of blue and linen, wearing a great golden crown and a fine-fabric cloak of purple wool.[b] And the city of Shu'shan* shouted for joy. 16 For the Jews there was relief* and rejoicing and exultation and honor. 17 And in all the provinces△ and all the cities, wherever the decree of the king and his law reached, the Jews were rejoicing and exulting, holding banquets and celebrations. Many of the peoples of the land were declaring themselves Jews,[c] for the dread of the Jews had fallen upon them.

9 On the 13th day of the 12th month, that is, the month of A'dar,*[d] when the king's word and his law were to be carried out,[e] on the day when the enemies of the Jews hoped to overpower them, the opposite happened, and the Jews defeated those who hated them.[f] 2 The Jews gathered together in their cities in all the provinces△ of King A·has·u·e'rus[g] to lay hands on those seeking to harm them, and not a man could stand against them, for the dread of them had fallen upon all the peoples.[h] 3 And all the princes of the provinces,△ the satraps,[i] the governors, and those handling the business of the king were supporting the Jews, for they were in fear of Mor'de·cai. 4 Mor'de·cai had become powerful[j] in the king's house,[#] and his fame was spreading throughout all the provinces,△ because Mor'de·cai was steadily growing more powerful.

5 The Jews struck down all their enemies with the sword, killing and destroying them; they did whatever they wanted to those hating them.[a] 6 In Shu'shan*[b] the citadel[#] the Jews killed and destroyed 500 men. 7 Also, they killed Par·shan·da'tha, Dal'phon, As·pa'tha, 8 Po·ra'tha, A·da·li'a, A·ri·da'tha, 9 Par·mash'ta, Ar'i·sai, Ar'i·dai, and Vai·za'tha, 10 the ten sons of Ha'man the son of Ham·me·da'tha, the enemy of the Jews.[c] But after they killed them, they did not seize any plunder.[d]

11 On that day the number of those killed in Shu'shan* the citadel[#] was reported to the king.

12 The king said to Queen Esther: "In Shu'shan* the citadel[#] the Jews have killed and destroyed 500 men and the ten sons of Ha'man. What, then, have they done in the rest of the king's provinces?△[e] What is your petition now? It will be granted you. And what is your further request? It will be done." 13 Esther replied: "If it pleases the king,[f] let the Jews who are in Shu'shan* be permitted to act tomorrow also according to today's law;[g] and let the ten sons of Ha'man be hanged on the stake."[h] 14 So the king gave orders for that to be done. A law was issued in Shu'shan,* and the ten sons of Ha'man were hanged.

15 The Jews in Shu'shan* gathered together again on the 14th day of the month of A'dar[i] and killed 300 men in Shu'shan,* but they did not seize any plunder.

16 The rest of the Jews in the provinces△ of the king also gathered together and defended their lives.*[j] They got rid of their enemies,[k] killing 75,000 of those who hated them; but they did not seize any plunder. 17 That was on the 13th day of the month

---

CHAP. 8
a Ezr 4:9
  Ne 1:1
  Es 1:2
  Da 8:2

b Es 6:7, 8

c Zec 8:23

CHAP. 9
d Es 3:7
  Es 8:11, 12

e Es 3:13

f De 32:36
  2Sa 22:41

g Es 1:1

h Es 8:17

i Da 6:1

j Es 8:15

Second Col.
a Es 8:11

b Ezr 4:9
  Ne 1:1
  Es 1:2
  Da 8:2

c Es 3:8, 10
  Es 7:4-6

d Es 8:11
  Es 9:16

e Es 9:16

f Es 5:8
  Es 7:3
  Es 8:5

g Es 8:11

h Es 7:10

i Es 9:21, 22

j Es 7:3

k Es 8:13
  Ps 149:6, 7

8:14, 15; 9:6, 11-15 *Or "Susa." 8:14; 9:6, 11, 12 #Or "palace; fortress." 8:16 *Lit., "light." 8:17; 9:2-4, 12, 16 △Or "jurisdictional districts." 9:1 *See App. B15. 9:4 #Or "palace."

9:16 *Or "stood up for their souls."

of A'dar, and they rested on the 14th day and made it a day of feasting and of rejoicing.

18 The Jews in Shu'shan* gathered together on the 13th day[a] and on the 14th day,[b] and they rested on the 15th day and made it a day of feasting and rejoicing. 19 That is why the rural Jews inhabiting the cities of the outlying districts made the 14th day of the month of A'dar a day of rejoicing and feasting, a day of celebration,[c] and a time to send portions of food to one another.[d]

20 Mor'de·cai[e] recorded these events and sent official letters to all the Jews in all the provinces* of King A·has·u·e'rus, both near and far. 21 He instructed them to observe the 14th day of the month of A'dar, as well as the 15th day, each and every year, 22 because on those days the Jews rested from their enemies and in that month their grief was changed to rejoicing and their mourning[f] to a day of celebration. They were to observe them as days of feasting and rejoicing and as a time to send portions of food to one another and gifts to the poor.

23 And the Jews agreed to continue the celebration that they had started and to do what Mor'de·cai wrote to them. 24 For Ha'man[g] the son of Ham·me·da'tha the Ag'ag·ite,[h] the enemy of all the Jews, had schemed against the Jews to destroy them,[i] and he had cast Pur,[j] that is, the Lot, to throw them into a panic and to destroy them. 25 But when Esther came in before the king, he gave orders in writing:[k] "Let his evil scheme against the Jews[l] come back on his own head"; and they hanged him and his sons on the stake.[m]

26 That is why they called these days Pu'rim, after the name of the Pur.*[a] Therefore, because of all that was written in this letter and what they saw concerning this matter and what had come upon them, 27 the Jews obligated themselves and their descendants and all those joining them[b] to celebrate these two days without fail and to carry out what was written concerning them at the appointed time each and every year. 28 These days were to be remembered and observed in every generation, by each family, each province,* and each city; and these days of Pu'rim should not cease among the Jews, and their commemoration should not come to an end among their descendants.

29 Then Queen Esther, the daughter of Ab'i·ha·il, and Mor'de·cai the Jew wrote with full authority to confirm a second letter about Pu'rim. 30 He sent official letters to all the Jews in the 127 provinces,*[c] the realm of A·has·u·e'rus,[d] in words of peace and truth 31 to confirm the observance of the days of Pu'rim at their appointed times, just as Mor'de·cai the Jew and Queen Esther had instructed them to do[e] and just as they had obligated themselves* and their descendants to carry out,[f] including the fasting[g] and supplication.[h] 32 And the command of Esther confirmed these matters concerning Pu'rim,[i] and it was recorded in a book.

10 King A·has·u·e'rus imposed forced labor on the land and the islands of the sea.

CHAP. 9
a Es 9:1, 2

b Es 9:13, 15

c Ps 124:2, 6

d Ne 8:10

e Es 2:5, 6

f Es 4:1-3

g Es 3:1

h Ex 17:16
Nu 24:7
De 25:19
1Sa 15:8, 33

i Es 3:8, 9

j Es 3:7

k Es 8:10

l Es 8:3

m Es 5:14
Es 7:10
Es 9:14

Second Col.
a Es 3:7

b Le 24:22
Es 8:17

c Es 8:9

d Es 1:1

e Es 9:20, 21

f Es 9:27

g 2Ch 20:3

h Es 4:1

i Es 9:26

9:18 *Or "Susa." 9:20, 30 *Or "jurisdictional districts."

9:26 *"Pur," meaning "Lot." The plural form "Purim" came to designate the Jewish festival celebrated in the 12th month of the sacred calendar. See App. B15. 9:28 *Or "jurisdictional district." 9:31 *Or "had imposed upon their soul."

2 And all his powerful and mighty accomplishments, as well as the detailed account of Mor'de·cai's[a] greatness to which the king exalted him,[b] are they not written in the book of the history of the times[c] of the kings of Me'di·a and Persia?[d] **3** For Mor'decai the Jew was second only to King A·has·u·e'rus. He was great* among the Jews and respected by the multitude of his brothers, working for the good of his people and advocating the welfare of# all their descendants.

CHAP. 10
a Es 2:5, 6
b Es 8:15
　Da 2:48
c Ezr 4:15
　Es 6:1
d Es 1:3
　Da 6:15

10:3 * Or "highly regarded."　# Lit., "and speaking peace for."

JOB

OUTLINE OF CONTENTS

1 There was a man in the land of Uz whose name was Job.*[a] He was an upright man of integrity;*[b] he feared God and shunned what was bad.[c] **2** Seven sons and three daughters were born to him. **3** His livestock amounted to 7,000 sheep, 3,000 camels, 1,000 cattle,* and 500 donkeys,* along with a very large number of servants, so

that he became the greatest of all the people of the East.

4 Each of his sons would hold a banquet at his house on his own set day.* They would invite their three sisters to eat and drink with them. **5** After a series of banquet days was complete, Job would send for them in order to sanctify them. Then he would get up early in the morning and offer up burnt sacrifices[a] for each of them. For

---

1:1 *Possibly meaning "Object of Hostility." *Or "a blameless and upright man." 1:3 *Lit., "500 pairs of cattle." *Lit., "female donkeys."

CHAP. 1
a Eze 14:14
Jas 5:10, 11

b Ge 6:9

c Job 2:3

Second Col.
a Ge 8:20
Ge 12:7, 8

1:4 *Or "at the house of each one in his turn."

Job said: "Maybe my sons have sinned and have cursed God in their heart." That is what Job would always do.[a]

6 Now the day came when the sons of the true God[b] entered to take their station before Jehovah,[c] and Satan[d] also entered among them.[e]

7 Then Jehovah said to Satan: "Where have you come from?" Satan answered Jehovah: "From roving about on the earth and from walking about in it."[f] **8** And Jehovah said to Satan: "Have you taken note of* my servant Job? There is no one like him on the earth. He is an upright man of integrity,*[g] fearing God and shunning what is bad." **9** At that Satan answered Jehovah: "Is it for nothing that Job has feared God?[h] **10** Have you not put up a protective hedge around him[i] and his house and everything he has? You have blessed the work of his hands,[j] and his livestock has spread out in the land. **11** But, for a change, stretch out your hand and strike everything he has, and he will surely curse you to your very face." **12** Then Jehovah said to Satan: "Look! Everything that he has is in your hand.* Only do not lay your hand on the man himself!" So Satan went out from the presence* of Jehovah.[k]

13 Now on the day when his sons and daughters were eating and drinking wine in their oldest brother's house,[l] **14** a messenger came to Job and said: "The cattle were plowing and the donkeys were grazing beside them **15** when the Sa·be'ans attacked and took them, and they killed the servants with the sword. I

am the only one who escaped to tell you."

16 While he was still speaking, another one came and said: "Fire from God* fell from the heavens and blazed among the sheep and the servants and consumed them! I am the only one who escaped to tell you."

17 While he was still speaking, another one came and said: "The Chal·de'ans[a] formed three bands and made a raid on the camels and took them, and they killed the servants with the sword. I am the only one who escaped to tell you."

18 While he was still speaking, yet another one came and said: "Your sons and your daughters were eating and drinking wine in their oldest brother's house. **19** Suddenly a great wind came from the wilderness, and it struck the four corners of the house, so that it fell on the young people and they were killed. I am the only one who escaped to tell you."

20 At that Job got up and ripped apart his garment and cut the hair off his head; then he fell to the ground and bowed down **21** and said:

"Naked I came out of my
  mother's womb,
And naked I will return.[b]
Jehovah has given,[c] and
  Jehovah has taken away.
Let the name of Jehovah
  continue to be praised."

22 In all of this, Job did not sin or accuse God of doing anything wrong.*

2 Afterward the day came when the sons of the true God*[d] entered to take their station before Jehovah,[e] and Satan also entered among them to take his station before Jehovah.[f]

CHAP. 1
a Ge 18:17, 19

b Ge 6:2
De 33:2
Job 38:7

c 1Ki 22:19
Ps 103:20
Da 7:13

d Zec 3:1
Mt 4:1, 3
Lu 22:31
Joh 13:2
Re 12:9

e Job 2:1-3

f 1Pe 5:8

g Ge 6:9

h Re 12:10

i Ge 15:1
Ge 31:7

j Ge 26:12

k Job 2:7

l Job 1:4

Second Col.
a Ge 11:28

b Ge 3:19
Ps 49:17
Ec 5:15
Ec 12:7
1Ti 6:7

c Ec 5:19
Jas 1:17

CHAP. 2
d Ge 6:2
De 33:2
Job 38:7

e Ps 103:20
Da 7:13

f Job 1:6-8

1:6; 2:1 *A Hebrew idiom that refers to angelic sons of God. **1:8** *Lit., "set your heart upon." *Or "a blameless and upright man." **1:12** *Or "under your control." *Lit., "face."

1:16 *Or possibly, "Lightning." **1:22** *Or "ascribe anything improper to God."

2 Then Jehovah said to Satan: "Where have you come from?" Satan answered Jehovah: "From roving about on the earth and from walking about in it."[a] **3** And Jehovah said to Satan: "Have you taken note of* my servant Job? There is no one like him on the earth. He is an upright man of integrity,[#b] fearing God and shunning what is bad. He is still holding firmly to his integrity,[c] even though you try to incite me against him[d] to destroy[△] him for no reason." **4** But Satan answered Jehovah: "Skin for skin. A man will give everything that he has for his life.* **5** But, for a change, stretch out your hand and strike his bone and flesh, and he will surely curse you to your very face."[e]

6 Then Jehovah said to Satan: "Look! He is in your hand!"[#] Only do not take his life!"* **7** So Satan went out from the presence* of Jehovah and struck Job with painful boils[#f] from the sole of his foot to the crown of his head. **8** And Job took a piece of broken pottery to scrape himself, and he was sitting among the ashes.[g]

9 Finally his wife said to him: "Are you still holding firmly to your integrity? Curse God and die!" **10** But he said to her: "You are talking like one of the senseless women. Should we accept only what is good from the true God and not accept also what is bad?"[h] In all of this, Job did not sin with his lips.[i]

11 Three companions* of Job heard about all the calamities that had come upon him, and each came from his own place

—El'i·phaz[a] the Te'man·ite, Bil'dad[b] the Shu'hite,[c] and Zo'phar[d] the Na'a·ma·thite. So they agreed to meet together to go and sympathize with Job and comfort him. **12** When they saw him from a distance, they did not recognize him. They began to weep loudly and to rip their garments apart, and they threw dust into the air and onto their heads.[e] **13** Then they sat on the ground with him for seven days and seven nights. No one said a word to him, for they saw that his pain was very great.[f]

3 It was after this that Job began to speak and to curse the day of his birth.*[g] **2** Job said:

3 "Let the day perish on which
      I was born,[h]
   Also the night when someone said: 'A man has been
      conceived!'[i]
4 Let that day be darkness.
   Let God above show no
      concern for it;
   Let no light shine upon it.
5 Let the deepest darkness*
      reclaim it.
   Let a rain cloud settle
      over it.
   Let whatever darkens the
      day terrify it.
6 That night—let the gloom
      seize it;
   Let it not rejoice among
      the days of a year,
   And let it not enter among
      the number of the months.
7 Indeed! Let that night
      become barren;
   Let no joyful cry be heard
      in it.
8 Let those who curse the day
      put a curse on it,
   Those who are able to
      awaken Le·vi'a·than.*[i]

CHAP. 2
a 1Pe 5:8

b Ge 6:9

c Job 27:5

d Job 1:11

e Le 24:15, 16
  Job 1:11, 12
  Re 12:10

f Job 30:30

g Jer 6:26

h Job 1:21

i Jas 5:10, 11

Second Col.
a Job 4:1
  Job 15:1
  Job 22:1
  Job 42:7, 9

b Job 8:1
  Job 18:1
  Job 25:1

c Ge 25:1, 2

d Job 11:1
  Job 20:1

e Eze 27:30, 31

f Job 16:6

CHAP. 3
g Jer 20:14, 15

h Job 10:18, 19
  Jer 15:10

i Job 10:18, 19

j Job 41:1, 10
  Ps 104:25, 26

2:3 *Lit., "set your heart upon." #Or "a blameless and upright man." △Lit., "swallow." 2:4, 6 *Or "soul." 2:6 #Or "under your control." 2:7 *Lit., "face." #Or "with severe ulcers." 2:11 *Or "acquaintances."

3:1 *Lit., "curse his day." 3:5 *Or "darkness and death's shadow." 3:8 *Understood to refer to the crocodile or some other large, powerful aquatic animal.

9 Let the stars of its twilight
　grow dark;
　Let it wait in vain for
　daylight,
　And let it not see the rays
　of dawn.
10 For it did not close the doors
　of my mother's womb;[a]
　Nor did it hide trouble from
　my eyes.
11 Why did I not die at birth?
　Why did I not perish when
　I came from the womb?[b]
12 Why were there knees to
　receive me
　And breasts to nurse me?
13 For now I would be lying
　down undisturbed;[c]
　I would be sleeping and
　at rest[d]
14 With kings of the earth and
　their advisers,
　Who built for themselves
　places that are now in
　ruins,*
15 Or with princes who
　possessed gold,
　Whose houses were filled
　with silver.
16 Or why was I not like a
　hidden miscarriage,
　Like children who have
　never seen the light?
17 There even the wicked have
　ceased from agitation;
　There the weary are at rest.[e]
18 There the prisoners are at
　ease together;
　They do not hear the voice
　of the one forcing them
　to work.
19 Small and great are the same
　there,[f]
　And the slave is set free from
　his master.
20 Why does he give light to one
　who is suffering
　And life to those in bitter
　distress?*[g]

21 Why do they long for death,
　but it does not come?[a]
　They dig for it more than
　for hidden treasures,
22 Those who are rejoicing
　greatly,
　Who are happy when they
　find the grave.
23 Why does he give light to
　a man who has lost his way,
　Whom God has hedged in?[b]
24 For in place of my food
　comes my sighing,[c]
　And my groaning[d] pours out
　like water.
25 For what I have dreaded
　has come upon me,
　And what I have feared
　has befallen me.
26 I have had no peace,
　no quiet, no rest,
　But trouble keeps coming."

4 El´i·phaz[e] the Te´man·ite then
　said in reply:

2 "If someone tries to speak
　to you, will you become
　impatient?
　For who can hold back from
　speaking?
3 True, you have corrected
　many,
　And you used to strengthen
　the weak hands.
4 Your words would raise up
　anyone stumbling,
　And you would strengthen
　those whose knees were
　buckling.
5 But now it has happened
　to you, and you are
　overwhelmed;*
　It touches you, and you are
　dismayed.
6 Does your reverence for God
　not give you confidence?
　Does your way of integrity[f]
　not give you hope?
7 Remember, please: What
　innocent person has ever
　perished?

CHAP. 3
a Job 10:18

b Jer 20:17, 18

c Ec 9:5, 10

d Joh 11:11

e Ps 146:4
　Ec 9:10
　Isa 57:1, 2

f Job 30:23
　Ps 49:10, 12
　Ec 8:8
　Ec 9:2

g 1Sa 1:10
　2Ki 4:27

Second Col.
a Nu 11:11, 15
　1Ki 19:3, 4
　Job 7:15, 16
　Jon 4:2, 3

b Job 12:14
　Job 19:8

c Ps 102:9, 10

d Ps 22:1
　Ps 38:8

CHAP. 4
e Job 2:11
　Job 15:1
　Job 22:1
　Job 42:7, 9

f Job 1:1

3:14 *Or possibly, "who built desolate places for themselves." 3:20 *Or
"those bitter of soul."

4:5 *Lit., "you become weary."

When have the upright ever been destroyed?

8 What I have seen is that those who plow* what is harmful
And those who sow trouble will reap the same.

9 By the breath of God they perish,
And through a blast of his anger they come to an end.

10 The lion roars, and a young lion growls,
But even the teeth of strong lions* are broken.

11 A lion perishes for lack of prey,
And the cubs of a lion are scattered.

12 Now a word was brought to me in secret,
And a whisper of it reached my ear.

13 In troubling thoughts during visions of the night,
When deep sleep falls upon men,

14 A terrible trembling came upon me,
Filling all my bones with dread.

15 A spirit passed over my face;
The hair of my flesh bristled.

16 It then stood still,
But I did not recognize its appearance.
A form was in front of my eyes;
There was a calm, and then I heard a voice:

17 'Can a mortal man be more righteous than God?
Can a man be cleaner than his own Maker?'

18 Look! He has no faith in his servants,
And he finds fault with his angels.*

Second Col.

CHAP. 4
a Ge 3:19

CHAP. 5
b Pr 22:22
Am 5:12

---

19 How much more so with those dwelling in houses of clay,
Whose foundation is in the dust,[a]
Who are crushed as easily as a moth!

20 They are completely crushed from morning to evening;
They perish forever, and no one takes notice.

21 Are they not like a tent whose cord is pulled out?
They die without wisdom.

5 "Call, please! Is there anyone answering you?
To which of the holy ones will you turn?

2 For resentment will kill the foolish one,
And envy will put the simpleminded to death.

3 I have seen the foolish one taking root,
But suddenly his dwelling place is cursed.

4 His sons are far from safety,
And they are crushed at the city gate,[b] with no one to save them.

5 The hungry one eats what he harvests,
Taking it even from among the thorns,
And their possessions are ensnared.

6 For harmful things do not sprout from the dust,
And trouble does not spring from the ground.

7 For man is born for trouble,
As surely as sparks fly upward.

8 But I would appeal to God,
And to God I would submit my case,

9 To the One doing great and unsearchable things,
Wonderful things without number.

10 He gives rain to the earth
And sends waters upon the fields.

4:8 *Or "devise." 4:10 *Or "maned young lions." 4:18 *Or "messengers."

11 He raises the lowly up high,
    And he raises up the deject-
    ed one to salvation.
12 He frustrates the schemes
    of the crafty,
    So that the work of their
    hands does not succeed.
13 He catches the wise in their
    own cunning,[a]
    So that the plans of the
    shrewd are thwarted.
14 They meet with darkness
    during the day,
    And they grope about at
    midday as if it were night.
15 He saves from the sword
    of their mouth,
    Saving the poor from the
    hand of the strong,
16 So that there is hope for
    the lowly,
    But the mouth of unrigh-
    teousness is shut.
17 Look! Happy is the man
    whom God reproves;
    So do not reject the
    discipline of the Almighty!
18 For he causes pain, but binds
    up the wound;
    He breaks apart, but heals
    with his own hands.
19 He will save you from six
    calamities,
    Even the seventh will not
    harm you.
20 During famine he will
    redeem you from death,
    And from the power of
    a sword during war.
21 You will be protected from
    the lash of the tongue,[b]
    And you will not fear
    devastation when it comes.
22 You will laugh at destruction
    and hunger,
    And you will not fear the
    wild beasts of the earth.
23 For the stones of the field
    will not harm you,*

    And the wild beasts of the
    field will be at peace with
    you.
24 You will know that your tent
    is secure,*
    And nothing will be missing
    when you inspect your
    pasture.
25 You will enjoy many children,
    And your descendants will
    be as plentiful as the
    vegetation of the earth.
26 You will still be strong when
    you go to the grave,
    Like sheaves of grain
    gathered in their season.
27 Look! We have investigated
    this, and it is so.
    Listen and accept it."

6 Job then said in reply:
2 "If only my anguish[a] could
    be fully weighed
    And put on scales together
    with my calamity!
3 For now it is heavier than
    the sands of the seas.
    That is why my words have
    been wild talk.*[b]
4 For the arrows of the
    Almighty have pierced me,
    And my spirit is drinking
    their venom;[c]
    The terrors from God are
    lined up against me.
5 Will a wild donkey[d] cry out
    when it has grass,
    Or will a bull bellow when
    it has fodder?
6 Is tasteless food eaten
    without salt,
    Or is there flavor in the juice
    of a mallow?
7 I have* refused to touch
    such things.
    They are like contamination
    in my food.
8 O that my request would be
    realized

CHAP. 5
a 1Co 3:19

b Pr 12:18

Second Col.

CHAP. 6
a Ps 31:9

b Ec 7:7
  Jas 3:2

c Pr 18:14

d Job 24:5

5:23 *Or "will have a covenant (an agreement) with you."   5:24 *Lit., "peace."   6:3 *Or "rash, reckless speech."   6:7 *Or "My soul has."

And that God would grant
    my desire!

9 That God would be willing
    to crush me,
  And that he would reach
    out his hand and do away
    with me![a]

10 For even that would bring
    me comfort;
  I would leap for joy despite
    the unrelenting pain,
  For I have not denied the
    sayings of the Holy One.[b]

11 Do I have the strength to
    keep waiting?[c]
  And what end awaits me,
    that I should continue
    to live?*

12 Is my strength like that
    of rock?
  Or is my flesh made of
    copper?

13 Is there any way that I can
    help myself
  When all my means of
    support has been driven
    from me?

14 Anyone who withholds loyal
    love from his fellow man[d]
  Will forsake the fear of the
    Almighty.[e]

15 My own brothers have been
    as treacherous[f] as a winter
    stream,
  Like the water of winter
    streams that dry up.

16 They are darkened by ice,
  And in them the melting
    snow is hidden.

17 But in due season they
    become waterless and
    come to an end;
  When it becomes hot, they
    dry up.

18 Their course is diverted;
  They flow into the desert
    and vanish.

19 The caravans of Te'ma[g]
    look for them;

The travelers from She'ba*[a]
    wait for them.

20 They are ashamed because
    of their misplaced trust;
  They come there only to be
    disappointed.

21 For this is how you have
    become to me;[b]
  You have seen the terror of
    my calamity, and you are
    afraid.[c]

22 Have I said, 'Give me some-
    thing,'
  Or requested that you make
    a gift for me from your
    wealth?

23 Have I asked to be rescued
    from the hand of an enemy
  Or to be saved* from
    oppressors?

24 Instruct me, and I will be
    silent;[d]
  Help me to understand
    my mistake.

25 Honest words are not
    painful![e]
  But what benefit can be
    found in your reproof?[f]

26 Are you scheming to reprove
    my words,
  A desperate man's sayings,[g]
    which the wind blows
    away?

27 You would also cast lots over
    an orphan[h]
  And sell* your own friend![i]

28 So now turn and look at me,
  For I would not lie to your
    very faces.

29 Reconsider, please—do not
    misjudge me—
  Yes, reconsider, for my
    righteousness is yet intact.

30 Is my tongue speaking
    unjustly?
  Does my palate not discern
    that something is wrong?

CHAP. 6
a Nu 11:11, 15
  1Ki 19:3, 4
  Jon 4:3

b Le 19:2
  Ho 11:9

c Job 7:6, 7
  Ps 103:15, 16

d Pr 3:3
  Pr 19:22
  Ho 6:6
  Zec 7:9

e 1Jo 3:17

f Job 19:19
  Ps 38:11

g Isa 21:13, 14

Second Col.
a Job 1:14, 15

b Job 13:4

c Ps 38:11

d Job 32:11, 12

e Pr 12:18
  Pr 25:11

f Job 16:2, 3
  Job 21:34

g Job 10:1

h Job 31:21, 22
  Mal 3:5

i Ge 37:28

6:11 *Or "that I should prolong my life
(soul)." 6:19 *Or "The traveling company of
the Sabeans." 6:23 *Lit., "redeemed." 6:27
*Or "barter over."

7 "Is not the life of mortal man on earth like compulsory labor,
And are not his days like those of a hired worker?[a]

2 Like a slave, he longs for the shadow,
And like a hired worker, he waits for his wages.[b]

3 Thus I have been assigned months of futility
And nights of misery have been counted out for me.[c]

4 When I lie down I ask, 'When will I get up?'[d]
But as the night drags on, I toss restlessly until the dawning of the day.*

5 My flesh is covered with maggots and clods of dirt;[e]
My skin is full of scabs and pus.[f]

6 My days go by more quickly than a weaver's shuttle,[g]
And they come to an end without hope.[h]

7 Remember that my life is wind,[i]
That my eye will never again see happiness.*

8 The eye that sees me now will see me no more;
Your eyes will look for me, but I will be gone.[j]

9 Like a cloud that fades and vanishes,
The one who goes down to the Grave* does not come back up.[k]

10 He will not return again to his house,
And his place will acknowledge him no more.[l]

11 Therefore, I will not restrain my mouth.
I will speak in the anguish of my spirit;

I will complain in my bitter distress!*[a]

12 Am I the sea or a sea monster,
That you should set a guard over me?

13 When I say, 'My couch will comfort me;
My bed will help ease my misery,'

14 Then you terrify me with dreams
And frighten me with visions,

15 So that I* would choose suffocation,
Yes, death rather than this body of mine.#[b]

16 I loathe my life;[c] I do not want to go on living.
Leave me alone, for my days are like a breath.[d]

17 What is mortal man that you should concern yourself with him
And fix your attention* on him?[e]

18 Why do you inspect him every morning
And test him every moment?[f]

19 Will you not look away from me
And leave me alone long enough to swallow my saliva?[g]

20 If I have sinned, how could I harm you, the Observer of mankind?[h]
Why have you made me your target?
Have I become a burden to you?

21 Why do you not pardon my transgression
And excuse my error?
For soon I will lie down in the dust,[i]
And you will look for me, but I will be gone."

CHAP. 7
a Job 14:5, 6
Ps 39:4

b Le 19:13
De 24:15

c Ps 6:6

d Job 2:8
Job 30:17

e Job 30:19

f Job 30:30

g Ps 102:11
Ps 103:15
Ps 144:4

h Job 17:15

i Ps 89:47
Ec 2:11

j Job 7:21
Jas 4:14

k Job 10:21
Job 14:12
Ps 78:39
Ec 9:10

l Ps 103:15, 16
Ps 146:4
Ec 9:5

Second Col.
a 1Sa 1:10
Job 10:1
Pr 14:10

b Job 3:20, 21

c Ge 27:46
1Ki 19:4
Job 10:1
Jon 4:3

d Ps 62:9
Ps 144:4
Ec 6:12

e Job 8:4
Ps 103:15
Ps 144:3

f Job 23:10

g Job 14:6

h Job 34:21
Pr 5:21
Jer 16:17
Heb 4:13
1Pe 3:12

i Ge 3:19
Ps 104:29
Ec 12:7

7:4 *Or "until morning twilight." 7:7 *Lit., "see good." 7:9 *Or "Sheol," that is, the common grave of mankind. See Glossary.

7:11 *Or "with bitterness of my soul!" 7:15 *Or "my soul." #Lit., "than my bones." 7:17 *Lit., "set your heart."

8 Bilʹdad[a] the Shuʹhite[b] then said in reply:

2 "How long will you keep speaking like this?[c]
The words of your mouth are but a mighty wind!

3 Will God pervert justice,
Or will the Almighty pervert righteousness?

4 If your sons sinned against him,
He let them be punished for their revolt;*

5 But if you would just look to God[d]
And plead with the Almighty for favor,

6 And if you were truly pure and upright,[e]
He would pay attention to you*
And restore you to your rightful place.

7 And though your beginning was small,
Your future would be great.[f]

8 Ask, please, the former generation,
And pay attention to the things their fathers found out.[g]

9 For we were born only yesterday, and we know nothing,
Because our days on earth are a shadow.

10 Will they not instruct you
And tell you what they know?*

11 Will a papyrus plant grow tall where there is no marsh?
Will a reed grow tall without water?

12 While it is still in the bud, not yet plucked off,
It will dry up before any other plant.

13 This is the outcome* of all who forget God,
For the hope of the godless# will perish,

14 Whose confidence is in vain
And whose trust is as fragile as a spider's web.*

15 He will lean against his house, but it will not keep standing;
He will try to hold on to it, but it will not last.

16 He is a moist plant in the sunlight,
And his shoots spread out in the garden.[a]

17 In a heap of stones, his roots become entwined;
He looks for a house among the stones.*

18 But when he is uprooted* from his place,
That place will deny him and say, 'I have never seen you.'[b]

19 Yes, that is how he will disappear;*[c]
Then others will spring up from the dust.

20 Surely God will not reject those who keep integrity;*
Nor will he support# evil men,

21 For he will yet fill your mouth with laughter
And your lips with shouts of joy.

22 Those hating you will be clothed with shame,
And the tent of wicked ones will be no more."

9 Job said in reply:
2 "For a fact I know that this is so.

CHAP. 8
a Job 18:1
Job 25:1

b Ge 25:1, 2
Job 42:9

c Job 11:3

d Job 5:8, 9
Job 11:13
Job 22:23

e Job 1:8

f Job 11:14, 17

g Job 15:17, 18

Second Col.
a Job 5:3

b Job 20:9

c Job 20:5

8:4 *Lit., "He sent them into the hand of their revolt." 8:6 *Or "rouse himself for you." 8:10 *Lit., "And bring forth words from their hearts?" 8:13 *Lit., "So are the paths." #Or "the apostate." 8:14 *Lit., "house." 8:17 *Or "He looks at a house of stones." 8:18 *Or "swallowed up." 8:19 *Or "that is the dissolving of his way." 8:20 *Or "the blameless." #Lit., "take hold of the hand of."

But how can mortal man be in the right in a case with God?[a]

3 If someone wishes to argue with Him,*[b]
That one could not answer one of His questions in a thousand.

4 He is wise in heart and mighty in power.[c]
Who can resist him and come off uninjured?[d]

5 He moves* mountains without anyone knowing it;
He overturns them in his anger.

6 He shakes the earth out of its place,
So that its pillars tremble.[e]

7 He commands the sun not to shine
And seals off the light of the stars;[f]

8 He spreads out the heavens by himself,[g]
And he treads upon the high waves of the sea.[h]

9 He made the Ash,* the Ke′sil,# and the Ki′mah constellations,△[i]
And the constellations of the southern sky;※

10 He does great and unsearchable things,[j]
Wonderful things that cannot be counted.[k]

11 He passes by me, and I cannot see him;
He moves past me, but I do not discern him.

12 When he snatches something, who can resist him?
Who can say to him, 'What are you doing?'[l]

13 God will not restrain his anger;[m]

Even the helpers of Ra′hab*[a] will bow down to him.

14 How much more when I answer him
Must I choose my words carefully to argue with him!

15 Even if I were in the right, I would not answer him.[b]
I could only plead for mercy from my judge.*

16 If I call out to him, will he answer me?
I do not believe that he will listen to my voice,

17 For he crushes me with a storm
And multiplies my wounds for no reason.[c]

18 He does not let me catch my breath;
He keeps filling me with bitter things.

19 If it is a matter of power, he is the strong one.[d]
If it is a matter of justice, he says: 'Who can call me to account?'*

20 If I were in the right, my own mouth would condemn me;
Even if I keep my integrity,* he will declare me guilty.#

21 Even if I keep my integrity,* I am not confident about myself;#
I reject△ this life of mine.

22 It is all the same. That is why I say,
'He destroys the innocent* and the wicked alike.'

23 If a flash flood should cause sudden death,
He would mock at the despair of the innocent.

24 The earth has been handed over to the wicked;[e]

CHAP. 9
a De 32:4
Ps 143:1, 2
Ro 3:23

b Job 40:2
Ro 9:20

c Job 36:5
Ps 104:24
Isa 40:26
Da 2:20

d Pr 14:16
Pr 28:14
Isa 30:1
Da 5:18, 20
Zec 7:12
Ro 2:5

e Ps 75:3

f Ge 1:16

g Ge 1:1
Ps 33:6
Isa 44:24

h Job 38:8-11

i Job 38:31
Am 5:8

j Isa 40:28
Ro 11:33

k Ps 40:5

l Da 4:35
Ro 9:20

m De 32:22

Second Col.
a Job 26:12

b Job 10:15

c Job 2:3
Job 34:5, 6

d Isa 40:28

e 1Jo 5:19

9:3 *Or "to take Him to court." 9:5 *Or "removes." 9:9 *Possibly the Great Bear constellation (Ursa Major). #Possibly the Orion constellation. △Possibly the Pleiades stars in the Taurus constellation. ※Lit., "the interior rooms of the south."

9:13 *Possibly a great sea monster. 9:15 *Or possibly, "my opponent at law." 9:19 *Lit., "summon me?" 9:20, 21 *Or "Even if I am innocent." 9:20 #Lit., "crooked." 9:21 #Or "I do not know my soul." △Or "despise; refuse." 9:22 *Or "those keeping integrity."

He covers the eyes* of its judges.

If it is not he, then, who is it?

25 Now my days are swifter than a runner;[a]

They run away without seeing good.

26 They glide by like reed boats,

Like eagles that swoop down on their prey.

27 If I say, 'I will forget my complaint,

I will change my expression and be cheerful,'

28 I would still be afraid because of all my pains,[b]

And I know you would not find me innocent.

29 I would be found guilty.*

So why should I struggle in vain?[c]

30 If I wash myself in water from melting snow,

And I cleanse my hands in lye,*[d]

31 Then you would dip me in a pit,

So that even my own garments would detest me.

32 For he is not a man like me that I may answer him,

That we should go to court together.[e]

33 There is no person to decide* between us,

Who could serve as our judge.*

34 If he would stop beating me*

And not let his terror frighten me,[f]

35 Then I would speak to him unafraid,

For it is not in me to speak out of fear.

CHAP. 9
a Job 7:6
Ps 90:10
Jas 4:14

b Job 21:6

c Ps 73:13

d Jer 2:22
Mal 3:2

e Isa 45:9
Ro 9:20

f Job 13:21

Second Col.

CHAP. 10
a Nu 11:11, 15
1Ki 19:3, 4
Job 7:16
Jon 4:3

b Job 14:15
Ps 138:8
Isa 64:8

c Ps 90:2

d Job 10:14

e Job 1:8
Ps 139:1

f De 32:39

g Ps 119:73
Ps 139:13-16

h Ge 2:7
Isa 45:9
Isa 64:8
Ro 9:21

i Ge 3:19
Ps 104:29
Ec 12:7

j Ps 139:15

10 "I loathe* my life.[a]

I will give vent to my complaints.

I will speak out in my bitter distress!*

2 I will say to God: 'Do not pronounce me guilty.

Tell me why you are contending with me.

3 Does it benefit you to oppress,

To despise the work of your hands[b]

While you favor the advice of the wicked?

4 Do you have eyes of flesh,

Or do you see as mortal man does?

5 Are your days like the days of mortals,

Or are your years like those of a man,[c]

6 That you should search out my error

And keep looking for my sin?[d]

7 You know that I am not guilty;[e]

And no one can save me from your hand.[f]

8 Your own hands have shaped me and made me,[g]

But now you would completely destroy me.

9 Remember, please, that you made me out of clay,[h]

But now you make me return to dust.[i]

10 Did you not pour me out like milk

And curdle me like cheese?

11 With skin and flesh you clothed me,

And with bones and sinews you wove me together.[j]

12 You have given me life and loyal love;

9:24 *Lit., "faces." 9:29 *Lit., "wicked." 9:30 *Or "potash." 9:33 *Or "no mediator." *Lit., "put his hand upon us both." 9:34 *Lit., "remove his rod from upon me."

10:1 *Or "My soul loathes." *Or "with bitterness of my soul!"

You have guarded my spirit*
with your care.ᵃ

13 But you secretly intended
to do these things.*
I know that these things are
from you.

14 If I sinned, you would
watch me,ᵇ
And you would not acquit me
of my error.

15 If I am guilty, too bad for me!
And even if I am innocent,
I cannot raise my head,ᶜ
For I am filled with dishonor
and affliction.ᵈ

16 If I raise my head up, you
hunt for me like a lionᵉ
And again show your power
against me.

17 You bring new witnesses
against me
And increase your anger
against me,
As hardship after hardship
comes upon me.

18 So why did you bring me out
from the womb?ᶠ
I should have died before
any eye could see me.

19 It would have been as though
I never existed;
I would have been taken
straight from the womb
to the grave.'

20 Are not my days few?ᵍ
Let him leave me alone;
Let him turn his eyes away
from me, so that I may find
some relief*ʰ

21 Before I go away—and I will
not return'—
To the land of deepest
darkness,*ⁱ

22 To the land of utter gloom,
A land of deep shadow and
disorder,
Where even the light is like
the gloom."

CHAP. 10
a Ps 8:4

b Ps 139:1

c Job 9:15

d Ps 119:153

e Isa 38:13

f Job 3:11
Jer 20:18

g Job 7:6
Job 14:1, 2
Ps 39:5, 6
Ps 103:15, 16

h Job 9:27

i Job 7:9
Ps 115:17
Isa 38:11

j Job 38:17
Ps 88:12
Ec 9:10

Second Col.

CHAP. 11
a Job 20:1
Job 42:9

b Job 12:4

c Job 6:10

d Job 6:29
Job 10:7

e Job 38:1

---

11 Zoʹpharᵃ the Naʹa·ma·thite
said in reply:

2 "Will all these words go
unanswered,
Or will a lot of talking make
someone right?*

3 Will your empty talk silence
people?
Will no one rebuke you for
your mocking words?ᵇ

4 For you say, 'My teaching is
pure,ᶜ
And I am clean in your eyes.'ᵈ

5 But if only God would speak
And open his lips to you!ᵉ

6 Then he would reveal to you
the secrets of wisdom,
For practical wisdom has
many sides.
Then you would realize that
God allows some of your
error to be forgotten.

7 Can you discover the deep
things of God
Or discover everything
about* the Almighty?

8 It is higher than heaven.
What can you accomplish?
It is deeper than the Grave.*
What can you know?

9 It is longer than the earth
And broader than the sea.

10 If he passes by and detains
someone and convenes
a court,
Who can resist him?

11 For he knows when men are
deceitful.
When he sees what is evil,
will he not take notice?

12 But an empty-headed man
will understand
Only when a wild donkey can
give birth to a man.*

13 If only you would prepare
your heart

10:12 *Or "breath; life." 10:13 *Lit.,
"And these things you have hidden
in your heart." 10:20 *Or "cheer up
a little." 10:21 *Or "of darkness and
death's shadow."

11:2 *Or "will a boaster be right?" 11:7
*Or "find out the limit of." 11:8 *Or
"Sheol," that is, the common grave
of mankind. See Glossary. 11:12 *Or
"when a wild donkey is born a man."

And stretch out your hands
    to him.

14 If your hand is doing wrong,
    put it far away,
    And let no unrighteousness
    dwell in your tents.

15 For then you could lift up
    your face with no defect;
    You could stand firm, free
    of fear.

16 For then you will forget your
    trouble;
    You will remember it as
    waters that have flowed
    past you.

17 Your life will become
    brighter than midday;
    Even its darkness will be
    like the morning.

18 You will be confident
    because there is hope,
    And you will look around
    and lie down in security.

19 You will lie down, with no
    one to make you afraid,
    And many people will seek
    your favor.

20 But the eyes of the wicked
    will fail;
    And they will find no place
    to escape,
    And their only hope will be
    death."*ᵃ

12 Then Job said in reply:
    2 "Surely you are the
    people who know,*
    And wisdom will die out
    with you!

3 But I too have understand-
    ing.*
    I am not inferior to you.
    Who does not know these
    things?

4 I have become a laughing-
    stock to my companions,ᵇ
    One calling to God for an
    answer.ᶜ
    A righteous and blameless
    man is a laughingstock.

5 The carefree person has
    contempt for calamity,
    Thinking it is only for those
    whose feet are unsteady.*

6 The tents of robbers are
    at peace,ᵃ
    And those who provoke God
    are secure,ᵇ
    Those who have their god
    in their hands.

7 However, ask, please, the
    animals, and they will
    instruct you;
    Also the birds of the heav-
    ens, and they will tell you.

8 Or give consideration*
    to the earth, and it will
    instruct you;
    And the fish of the sea will
    declare it to you.

9 Who among all these does
    not know
    That the hand of Jehovah
    has done this?

10 In his hand is the life of
    every living thing*
    And the spirit# of every
    human.Δᶜ

11 Does not the ear test out
    words
    As the tongue* tastes food?ᵈ

12 Is not wisdom found among
    the aged,ᵉ
    And does not understanding
    come with a long life?

13 With him there are wisdom
    and mightiness;ᶠ
    He has counsel and under-
    standing.ᵍ

14 When he tears something
    down, it cannot be rebuilt;ʰ
    What he has shut, no man
    can open.

15 When he withholds the wa-
    ters, everything dries up;ⁱ
    When he sends them out,
    they overwhelm the earth.ʲ

CHAP. 11
a Job 8:13, 14
  Job 18:5, 14

CHAP. 12
b Job 16:10
  Job 17:2
  Job 30:1
  Ps 22:7
  Heb 11:36

c Ps 91:15
  Mic 7:7

Second Col.
a Ps 37:35
  Ps 73:12
  Jer 12:1

b Job 21:7, 9

c Nu 16:22
  Ps 104:30
  Ec 12:7
  Eze 18:4

d Job 34:3

e Job 32:6, 7

f Job 9:4
  Da 2:20

g Job 36:5
  Ps 147:5
  Isa 40:14
  Jer 10:12
  Ro 11:34

h Jude 7

i Ge 8:1
  Ex 14:21
  Na 1:4

j Ge 6:17

11:20 *Or "the expiring of the soul." 12:2 *Lit., "you are the people." 12:3 *Lit., "a heart." 12:5 *Or "slipping." 12:8 *Or possibly, "speak." 12:10 *Or "the soul of every-one alive." #Or "breath." ΔLit., "of all flesh of man." 12:11 *Lit., "palate."

16 With him there are strength and practical wisdom;[a]

To him belong the one going astray and the one leading astray;

17 He makes counselors go barefoot,*

And he makes fools of judges.[b]

18 He loosens the bonds imposed by kings,[c]

And he binds a belt around their waist.

19 He makes priests walk barefoot,[d]

And he overthrows those who are firmly established in power;[e]

20 He deprives trusted advisers of speech

And takes away the sensibleness of old men;*

21 He pours out contempt upon nobles,[f]

And he makes powerful ones weak;*

22 He reveals deep things from the darkness,[g]

And he brings deep darkness into the light;

23 He makes nations grow great in order to destroy them;

He enlarges nations, that he may lead them into exile.

24 He takes away the understanding* of the leaders of the people

And makes them wander in trackless wastelands.[h]

25 They grope in darkness,[i] where there is no light;

He makes them wander about like drunken men.[j]

13 "Yes, my eye has seen all of this,

My ear has heard and understood it.

2 What you know, I also know; I am not inferior to you.

3 For my part, I would rather speak to the Almighty himself;

I desire to argue my case with God.[a]

4 But you are smearing me with lies;

All of you are useless physicians.[b]

5 If only you would keep absolutely silent,

That would show wisdom on your part.[c]

6 Listen, please, to my arguments,

And pay attention to the pleadings of my lips.

7 Will you speak unjustly on God's behalf,

And will you speak deceitfully for him?

8 Will you take his side,*

Will you try to plead the case of the true God?

9 Would it turn out well if he examined you?[d]

Will you fool him as you would a mortal man?

10 He will surely rebuke you If you secretly try to show favoritism.[e]

11 Will not his very dignity terrify you

And the dread of him fall upon you?

12 Your wise* sayings are proverbs of ashes;

Your defenses# are as fragile as defenses of clay.

13 Keep silent before me, so that I may speak.

Then let whatever may come upon me come!

14 Why do I put myself in danger*

CHAP. 12
a Ro 1:20

b Isa 29:14
Isa 44:25

c Da 2:21

d Jer 14:18

e Lu 1:52

f Ps 107:40

g Da 2:22

h Ps 107:40

i De 28:29

j Ps 107:27

Second Col.

CHAP. 13
a Job 23:3, 4
Job 31:35

b Job 16:2

c Pr 17:28
Jas 1:19

d Ps 139:23
Jer 17:10

e Ps 50:20, 21
Jas 2:9

12:17 *Or "stripped of everything."
12:20 *Or "of elders." **12:21** *Lit., "loosens the belt of powerful ones."
12:24 *Lit., "heart."

13:8 *Or "show partiality toward him."
13:12 *Or "memorable." #Lit., "shield bosses." **13:14** *Lit., "Why do I carry my flesh in my teeth?"

And take my life* in my hands?

15 Though he may slay me,
   I would still wait;[a]
   I would argue my case*
   before his face.

16 He would then become
   my salvation,[b]
   For no godless person*
   may come in before him.[c]

17 Listen closely to my word;
   Pay attention to my
   declaration.

18 See, now, I have prepared
   my legal case;
   I know I am in the right.

19 Who will contend with me?
   I would die if I were to stay
   silent!*

20 Only grant two things to me,
   O God,*
   So that I will not conceal
   myself from before you:

21 Remove your heavy hand far
   away from me,
   And do not let the fear of you
   terrify me.[d]

22 Either call and I will answer,
   Or let me speak, and you
   answer me.

23 What are my errors and sins?
   Reveal to me my transgression and my sin.

24 Why do you hide your face[e]
   And consider me your
   enemy?[f]

25 Will you try to frighten
   a windblown leaf
   Or chase after dry stubble?

26 For you keep recording bitter
   accusations against me,
   And you make me answer
   for the sins of my youth.

27 You have put my feet in
   stocks,
   You scrutinize all my paths,

And you trace out each
   of my footprints.

28 So man* decays like
   something rotten,
   Like a garment eaten
   by moths.

14 "Man, born of woman,
   Is short-lived[a] and filled
   with trouble.*[b]

2 He comes up like a blossom
   and then withers away;*[c]
   He flees like a shadow and
   disappears.[d]

3 Yes, you have fixed your eye
   upon him,
   And you bring him* into
   judgment with yourself.[e]

4 Who can produce someone
   clean from someone
   unclean?[f]
   No one can!

5 If his days are decided,
   The number of his months
   is with you;
   You have set a limit for
   him that he may not go
   beyond.[g]

6 Turn your gaze away from
   him so that he may rest,
   Until, like a hired worker,
   he finishes out his day.[h]

7 For there is hope even for
   a tree.
   If it is cut down, it will sprout
   again,
   And its twigs will continue
   to grow.

8 If its root grows old in the
   ground
   And its stump dies in the
   soil,

9 At the scent of water it will
   sprout;
   And it will produce branches
   like a new plant.

10 But a man dies and lies
   powerless;

CHAP. 13
a Job 19:25
  Ps 23:4

b Ex 15:2
  Ps 27:1
  Isa 12:2

c Job 27:8
  Job 36:13
  Isa 33:14

d Job 9:34, 35
  Job 33:6, 7

e Ps 10:1
  Ps 13:1
  Ps 44:24

f Job 16:9
  Job 19:11
  Job 33:8-11

Second Col.

CHAP. 14
a Ps 39:5, 6
  Jas 4:14

b Ge 3:19
  Ge 47:9
  Ps 90:10
  Ec 2:23

c Ps 103:15, 16
  Isa 40:6
  Jas 1:10, 11
  1Pe 1:24

d 1Ch 29:15
  Ps 102:11
  Ps 144:4

e Ps 143:2

f Ge 5:3
  Ps 51:5
  Ro 5:12

g Ps 39:4

h Ps 39:13

13:14 *Or "soul." **13:15** *Or "defend my ways." **13:16** *Or "no apostate." **13:19** *Or possibly, "If someone can, I will stay silent and die." **13:20** *Lit., "Only two things, do not do to me." **13:28** *Lit., "he," possibly referring to Job. **14:1** *Or "glutted with agitation." **14:2** *Or possibly, "and is cut off." **14:3** *Lit., "me."

When a human expires,
where is he?[a]

11 Waters disappear from the
sea,
And a river drains away and
dries up.

12 Man also lies down and does
not get up.[b]
Until heaven is no more,
they will not wake up,
Nor will they be aroused
from their sleep.[c]

13 O that in the Grave* you
would conceal me,[d]
That you would hide me
until your anger passes by,
That you would set a
time limit for me and
remember me![e]

14 If a man dies, can he live
again?[f]
I will wait all the days of
my compulsory service
Until my relief comes.[g]

15 You will call, and I will
answer you.[h]
You will long* for the work
of your hands.

16 But for now, you keep
counting my every step;
You watch only for my sin.

17 My transgression is sealed
up in a bag,
And you seal up my error
with glue.

18 As a mountain falls and
crumbles away
And a rock is dislodged from
its place,

19 As water wears away stones
And its torrents wash away
earth's soil,
So you have destroyed the
hope of mortal man.

20 You keep overpowering him
until he perishes;[i]
You change his appearance,
and you send him away.

21 His sons are honored, but
he does not know it;
They become insignificant,
but he does not realize it.[a]

22 He feels pain only while he
is still in his flesh;
He* mourns only while he
is still alive."

15 El·i·phaz[b] the Te′man·ite
said in reply:

2 "Will a wise person answer
with empty arguments,*
Or will he fill his belly with
the east wind?

3 Reproving with mere words
is useless,
And talk alone is of no
benefit.

4 For you undermine the fear
of God,
And you diminish any
concern for God.

5 For your error dictates what
you say,*
And you choose crafty
speech.

6 Your own mouth condemns
you, and not I;
Your own lips testify against
you.[c]

7 Were you the first man ever
born,
Or was your birth before
that of the hills?

8 Do you listen to the
confidential talk of God,
Or do you limit wisdom to
yourself?

9 What do you know that we
do not know?[d]
What do you understand that
we do not?

10 Both the gray-haired and
the aged are among us,[e]
Men much older than your
father.

11 Are God's consolations not
enough for you,

CHAP. 14
a Ec 3:19, 20
Ec 9:10

b Ec 9:5
Ec 12:5

c Ps 13:3
Joh 11:11
Ac 7:59, 60

d 1Sa 2:6
Isa 57:1, 2

e Lu 23:42
Joh 5:28, 29
Heb 11:35

f Joh 11:25
Ac 26:8
1Co 15:12
Re 20:13

g Job 19:25

h Da 12:13
Joh 5:28, 29
Joh 11:43, 44

i Ec 8:8
Isa 57:16

Second Col.
a Ec 9:5, 6

CHAP. 15
b Job 2:11
Job 4:1

c Job 42:8

d Job 13:2
Job 16:2

e Job 32:6

14:13 *Or "Sheol," that is, the common
grave of mankind. See Glossary. 14:15
*Or "yearn."

14:22 *Or "His soul." 15:2 *Or "with
blustery knowledge." 15:5 *Or "your
error trains your mouth."

Or words spoken gently
to you?

12 Why does your heart carry
you away,
And why do your eyes flash
with anger?

13 For you turn your spirit
against God himself,
And you allow such words to
go out of your own mouth.

14 What is mortal man that
he should be pure,
Or anyone born of a
woman that he should
be righteous?[a]

15 Look! He has no faith in his
holy ones,
And even the heavens are
not pure in his eyes.[b]

16 How much less so when
a person is detestable and
corrupt,[c]
A man who drinks in unrighteousness just like water!

17 I will inform you; listen
to me!
I will relate what I have seen,

18 What wise men have related
from their fathers,[d]
Things they have not hidden.

19 To them alone the land was
given,
And no stranger passed
among them.

20 A wicked person suffers
torment all his days,
Throughout all the years
reserved for the tyrant.

21 Terrifying sounds are in his
ears;[e]
In a time of peace, marauders attack him.

22 He does not believe that he
will escape from darkness;[f]
He is reserved for a sword.

23 He wanders about in search
of food*—where is it?
He well knows that the day
of darkness is at hand.

15:23 *Lit., "bread."

24 Distress and anguish keep
terrifying him;
They overpower him like
a king ready to launch
an attack.

25 For he raises his hand
against God himself
And tries to defy* the
Almighty;

26 He stubbornly rushes
against Him,
With his thick, strong
shield;*

27 His face is covered with fat,
And his hips bulge with fat;

28 He resides in cities that will
be brought to ruin,
In houses where no one will
dwell,
Which will become heaps
of stones.

29 He will not grow rich,
and his wealth will not
accumulate,
Nor will his possessions
spread over the land.

30 He will not escape from
darkness;
A flame will dry up his twig,*
And he will pass away by
a blast of God's* mouth.[a]

31 He should not go astray and
trust in what is worthless,
For what he gets in exchange
will be worthless;

32 It will happen before his day,
And his branches will never
flourish.[b]

33 He will be like a vine
that shakes off its unripe
grapes,
And like an olive tree that
casts off its blossoms.

34 For the assembly of godless
ones* is sterile,[c]
And fire will consume the
tents of bribery.

15:25 *Or "tries to prevail against."
15:26 *Lit., "his thick shield bosses."
15:30 *That is, any hope of recovery. *Lit., "his." 15:34 *Or "of apostates."

Marginal references:

CHAP. 15
a Job 25:4

b Job 25:5, 6
Job 42:7

c Job 4:18, 19

d Job 8:8

e Job 18:11
Job 20:25

f Job 18:12

Second Col.
a Job 4:9

b Job 22:15, 16

c Job 8:11-13

35 They conceive trouble
   and give birth to what
   is wicked,
   And their womb produces
   deceit."

16

Job said in reply:

2 "I have heard many
   things like these before.
   All of you are troublesome
   comforters!ᵃ

3 Is there an end to empty*
   words?
   What provokes you to
   answer this way?

4 I could also speak as you do.
   If you were in my place,*
   I could make persuasive
   speeches against you
   And shake my head at you.ᵇ

5 Instead, though, I would
   strengthen you with the
   words of my mouth,
   And the consolation of my
   lips would bring relief.ᶜ

6 If I speak, my own pain is
   not relieved,ᵈ
   And if I stop speaking, how
   much is my pain reduced?

7 But now he has made me
   weary;ᵉ
   He has devastated my whole
   household.*

8 You also seize me, and it has
   become a witness,
   So that my own skinniness
   rises up and testifies to my
   face.

9 His anger has torn me to
   pieces, and he harbors
   animosity against me.ᶠ
   He grinds his teeth
   against me.
   My adversary pierces me
   with his eyes.ᵍ

10 They have opened their
   mouth wide against me,ʰ
   And they have scornfully
   struck my cheeks;

In large numbers they gather
   against me.ᵃ

11 God hands me over to young
   boys,
   And he thrusts me into the
   hands of the wicked.ᵇ

12 I was untroubled, but he
   shattered me;ᶜ
   He grabbed me by the
   back of the neck and
   crushed me;
   Then he set me up as his
   target.

13 His archers surround me;ᵈ
   He pierces my kidneysᵉ and
   feels no compassion;
   He pours out my gall on the
   earth.

14 He breaks through against
   me with breach after
   breach;
   He rushes at me like
   a warrior.

15 I have sewn sackcloth
   together to cover my skin,ᶠ
   And I have buried my
   dignity* in the dust.ᵍ

16 My face is red from
   weeping,ʰ
   And on my eyelids is deep
   shadow,*

17 Although my hands have
   done no violence
   And my prayer is pure.

18 O earth, do not cover
   my blood!ⁱ
   And let there be no resting-
   place for my outcry!

19 Even now, my witness is
   in the heavens;
   The one who can testify
   for me is in the heights.

20 My companions ridicule meʲ
   As my eye sheds tears*
   to God.ᵏ

21 Let someone arbitrate
   between a man and God,
   As one would between a man
   and his fellow.ˡ

CHAP. 16
a Job 13:4, 5
  Job 19:2, 3

b Ps 109:25
  Mt 27:39

c Pr 27:9
  Mt 7:12
  Ro 12:15
  1Pe 3:8

d Job 2:13

e Job 7:3

f Job 10:16

g Job 33:8-10

h Ps 22:13

Second Col.
a Ps 35:15

b Ps 27:12

c Job 1:12, 17

d Job 7:20

e Ps 73:21

f 1Ki 21:27
  2Ki 6:30

g Job 30:19
  Ps 7:5

h Ps 6:6
  Ps 31:9
  La 1:16

i Ge 4:8, 10
  Ps 72:14

j Job 12:4

k Ps 40:1
  Ps 142:2

l Job 31:35

16:3 *Or "blustery." 16:4 *Or "If your
soul were in place of my soul." 16:7
*Or "those assembling with me." 16:15 *Or "strength." Lit., "horn."
16:16 *Or "death's shadow." 16:20 *Or
possibly, "looks sleeplessly."

22 For the years to come are
few,
And I will go away on the
path of no return.ᵃ

17 "My spirit has been
broken, my days have
been extinguished;
The graveyard awaits me.ᵇ

2 Mockers surround me,ᶜ
And my eye must gaze at*
their rebellious behavior.

3 Please accept my security,
and keep it with you.
Who else will shake hands
with me and pledge in my
behalf?ᵈ

4 For you have concealed
discernment from their
heart;ᵉ
That is why you do not exalt
them.

5 He may offer to share with
his friends,
While the eyes of his
children fail.

6 He has made me an object of
scorn* among the peoples,ᶠ
So that I became one in
whose face they spit.ᵍ

7 From anguish my eyes grow
dim,ʰ
And all my limbs are but
a shadow.

8 Upright people stare in
amazement at this,
And the innocent one is disturbed over the godless.*

9 The righteous one keeps
holding fast to his way,ⁱ
And the one with clean
hands grows stronger.ʲ

10 However, you may all come
and resume your arguing,
For I have not found anyone
wise among you.ᵏ

11 My days are finished;ˡ
My plans, the desires of
my heart, have been
shattered.ᵐ

12 They keep turning night into
day,
Saying, 'Light must be near
because it is dark.'

13 If I wait, the Grave* will
become my home;ᵃ
I will spread out my bed
in darkness.ᵇ

14 I will call out to the pit,*ᶜ
'You are my father!'
To the maggot, 'My mother
and my sister!'

15 Where, then, is my hope?ᵈ
Who can see hope for me?

16 It# will go down to the barred
gates of the Grave*
When we all descend
together into the dust."ᵉ

18 Bilʹdadᶠ the Shuʹhite said
in reply:

2 "How long before you stop
making such speeches?
Show some understanding
so that we may then speak.

3 Why should we be viewed
as animalsᵍ
And be considered stupid*
in your eyes?

4 Even if you tear yourself*
to pieces in your anger,
Will the earth be abandoned
for your sake,
Or will the rock move away
from its place?

5 Yes, the light of the wicked
will be extinguished,
And the flame of his fire
will not shine.ʰ

6 The light in his tent will
certainly grow dark,
And the lamp over him
will be extinguished.

7 His vigorous stride is
shortened,
And his own counsel
will make him fall.ⁱ

CHAP. 16
a Job 7:9
Job 14:10
Ec 12:5

CHAP. 17
b Ps 88:3, 4
Isa 38:10

c Ps 35:16
Heb 11:36

d Pr 17:18

e 2Sa 17:14
Isa 6:10
Mt 11:25

f Ps 69:11, 12

g Job 30:9, 10

h Job 16:16
Ps 6:7
Ps 31:9

i Ps 119:165

j Job 24:3, 4
Ps 84:5, 7

k Job 6:29

l Job 7:6
Job 9:25
Isa 38:10

m Jas 4:13, 14

Second Col.
a Ec 12:5, 7

b Job 10:21, 22

c Ps 49:7, 9
Ps 143:7

d Job 7:6
Job 14:19
Job 19:10

e Ge 3:19
Job 3:19

CHAP. 18
f Job 2:11
Job 8:1

g Ps 73:22

h Job 8:13, 14
Job 11:20

i Job 5:13

17:2 *Or "dwell on." 17:6 *Lit., "a proverb; a byword." 17:8 *Or "the apostate."

17:13, 16 *Or "Sheol," that is, the common grave of mankind. See Glossary.
17:14 *Or "grave." 17:16 #That is, my
hope. 18:3 *Or possibly, "unclean."
18:4 *Or "your soul."

8 For his feet will lead him into
a net,
And he will wander onto its
mesh.
9 A trap will seize him by the
heel;
A snare will catch him.a
10 A rope is hidden for him
on the ground,
And a trap lies in his path.
11 Terrors frighten him on all
sidesb
And chase him at his feet.
12 His strength fails him,
And disasterc will make him
stagger.*
13 His skin is eaten away;
The most deadly disease*
consumes his limbs.
14 He is torn away from the
security of his tentd
And marched to the king
of terrors.*
15 Strangers* will live in his
tent;
Sulfur will be scattered on
his home.e
16 His roots will dry up beneath
him,
And his branches will wither
above him.
17 The memory of him will fade
from the earth,
And in the street his name
will be unknown.*
18 He will be driven from the
light into the darkness
And chased away from the
productive land.
19 He will have no offspring and
no descendants among his
people,
And he will be without
a survivor in the place
where he lives.*

20 When his day comes, the
people in the West will be
appalled
And the people in the East
will be seized with horror.
21 This is what happens to the
tents of a wrongdoer
And to the place of the one
who has not known God."

19 Job said in reply:
2 "How long will you keep
irritating my soul,*a
Crushing me with words?b
3 These ten times you have
rebuked* me;
You are not ashamed to deal
harshly with me.c
4 And if indeed I made
a mistake,
My error remains with me.
5 If you insist on exalting
yourselves over me,
Claiming that the reproach
against me is justified,
6 Know, then, that it is God
who has misled me,
And he has caught me in his
hunting net.
7 Look! I keep crying out,
'Violence!' but I get no
answer;d
I keep crying for help, but
there is no justice.e
8 My path he has blocked with
a stone wall, and I cannot
pass by;
He has covered my roadways
with darkness.f
9 He has stripped me of my
glory
And removed the crown
from my head.
10 He breaks me down on all
sides until I perish;
My hope he uproots like
a tree.
11 His anger burns against me,
And he views me as his
enemy.g

CHAP. 18
a Job 5:5
  Job 22:5, 10

b Job 15:21
  Job 20:25

c Job 15:23

d Job 11:20

e De 29:22, 23

Second Col.

CHAP. 19
a Ps 42:10

b Ps 55:21
  Pr 12:18

c Pr 18:24

d Ps 22:2
  Hab 1:2

e Lu 18:7

f Job 3:23
  Ps 88:8

g Job 13:24

18:12 *Or "limp." 18:13 *Lit., "The
firstborn of death." 18:14 *Or "a terrible death." 18:15 *Lit., "Something
not his." 18:17 *Lit., "he will have no
name." 18:19 *Or "the place of his
temporary residence."

19:2 *Or "irritating me." See Glossary.
19:3 *Or "insulted."

12 His troops come together
and besiege me,
And they camp around my
tent.
13 My own brothers he has
driven far away from me,
And those who know
me have turned away
from me.[a]
14 My close companions* are
gone,
And those whom I knew well
have forgotten me.[b]
15 Guests in my house[c] and
my slave girls consider me
a stranger;
I am a foreigner in their eyes.
16 I call for my servant, but
he does not respond;
With my mouth I beg him
for compassion.
17 My very breath has become
loathsome to my wife,[d]
And I am a stench to my
own brothers.*
18 Even young children
despise me;
When I rise up, they begin
jeering at me.
19 All my close friends
detest me,[e]
And those whom I loved have
turned against me.[f]
20 My bones stick to my skin
and my flesh,[g]
And I escape with the skin
of my teeth.
21 Show me mercy, my companions, show me mercy,
For God's own hand has
touched me.[h]
22 Why do you keep persecuting me as God does,[i]
Attacking me without letup?*[j]
23 If only my words were
written down,
If only they could be
inscribed in a book!

24 O that they were carved
forever in the rock,
With an iron stylus and lead!
25 For I well know that my
redeemer*[a] is alive;
He will come later and rise
up over the earth.#
26 After my skin has thus been
destroyed,
While yet in my flesh, I will
see God,
27 Whom I will see for myself,
Whom my own eyes will see,
not someone else's.[b]
But deep inside I feel
overwhelmed!*
28 For you say, 'In what way are
we persecuting him?'[c]
Since the root of the problem
is with me.
29 Be in fear of the sword
yourselves,[d]
For the sword brings punishment against errors;
You should know that there
is a judge."[e]

20 Zoʹphar[f] the Naʹa·ma·thite
said in reply:

2 "This is why my own
troubling thoughts urge
me to answer
Because of the agitation
I feel.
3 I have heard a reproof that
insults me;
And my understanding*
impels me to reply.
4 Surely you must have always
known this,
For it has been so since man*
was put on the earth,[g]
5 That the joyful cry of the
wicked is brief
And the rejoicing of the godless one* is for a moment.[h]

CHAP. 19
a Ps 31:11
  Ps 69:8

b Ps 38:11

c Job 31:32

d Job 2:9

e Job 17:6
  Ps 88:8

f Ps 109:5

g Job 30:30
  Ps 102:5

h Job 1:10-12
  Ps 38:2

i Job 2:9, 10

j Ps 69:26

Second Col.
a Job 14:14
  Ps 19:14
  Ps 69:18
  Ps 103:2, 4
  Mt 20:28
  Mr 10:45

b Ps 17:15

c Ps 69:26

d De 32:41

e Ps 58:11
  Mt 7:1
  Ro 14:4
  Jas 4:12

CHAP. 20
f Job 2:11
  Job 11:1

g Job 8:8

h Job 8:13, 19
  Job 21:28

19:14 *Or "My relatives." 19:17 *Lit.,
"the sons of my womb," that is,
the womb that bore me (my mother's
womb). 19:22 *Lit., "And not be satis-
fied with my flesh?" 19:25 *Or "repurchaser." #Lit., "over
(upon) the dust." 19:27 *Or "My kid-
neys have failed within me." 20:3 *Lit.,
"a spirit from my understanding." 20:4
*Or "mankind; Adam." 20:5 *Or "the
apostate."

6 Although his greatness
   ascends to heaven
   And his head reaches to the
   clouds,
7 He will perish forever like
   his own dung;
   Those who used to see him
   will say, 'Where is he?'
8 He will fly off like a dream,
   and they will not find him;
   He will be chased away like
   a vision of the night.
9 The eye that once saw him
   will not do so again,
   And his place will behold
   him no more.ᵃ
10 His own children will seek
   the favor of the poor,
   And his own hands will give
   back his wealth.ᵇ
11 His bones were full of
   youthful vigor,
   But it* will lie down with him
   in mere dust.
12 If what is bad tastes sweet
   in his mouth,
   If he hides it under his
   tongue,
13 If he savors it and does not
   let it go
   But keeps holding it in his
   mouth,
14 His food will turn sour inside
   him;
   It will become like the poison* of cobras within him.
15 He has swallowed down
   wealth, but he will
   vomit it up;
   God will empty it out of his
   belly.
16 The venom of cobras he will
   suck;
   The fangs* of a viper will kill
   him.
17 He will never see the streams
   of water,
   The torrents of honey and
   butter.

CHAP. 20
a Job 8:13, 18

b Job 20:18

Second Col.
a Job 20:10

18 He will give back his goods
   without consuming them;*
   He will not enjoy the wealth
   from his trade.ᵃ
19 For he has crushed and
   abandoned the poor;
   He has seized a house that
   he did not build.
20 But he will feel no peace
   within himself;
   His wealth will not help him
   escape.
21 There is nothing left for him
   to devour;
   That is why his prosperity
   will not last.
22 When his wealth reaches its
   peak, anxiety will overtake
   him;
   The full force of misfortune
   will come against him.
23 As he fills his belly,
   God* will send his burning
   anger upon him,
   Raining it down upon him
   into his bowels.
24 When he flees from weapons
   of iron,
   Arrows from a copper bow
   will pierce him.
25 He pulls an arrow from
   his back,
   A glittering weapon from
   his gall,
   And terror seizes him.ᵇ
26 Total darkness awaits his
   treasures;
   A fire that no one fanned
   will consume him;
   Calamity awaits any
   survivors in his tent.
27 Heaven will uncover his
   error;
   The earth will rise up against
   him.
28 A flood will sweep his house
   away;
   It will be a heavy torrent
   on the day of God's* anger.

20:11 *That is, his vigor. **20:14** *Or
"gall." **20:16** *Lit., "tongue."

b Job 15:21
  Job 18:5, 11

20:18 *Lit., "and he will not swallow."
20:23 *Lit., "He." **20:28** *Lit., "his."

29 This is the wicked man's
　　share from God,
　　The inheritance that God
　　has decreed for him."

21 Job said in reply:
　2 "Listen carefully
　　　to what I say;
　　Let this be the consolation
　　you give me.
3 Bear with me while I speak;
　　After I speak, you may then
　　mock me.[a]
4 Is my complaint directed
　　toward a man?
　　If it were, would I* not lose
　　patience?
5 Look at me and stare in
　　amazement;
　　Put your hand over your
　　mouth.
6 When I think about it,
　　I am disturbed,
　　And my whole body
　　shudders.
7 Why do the wicked live on,[b]
　　Grow old, and become
　　wealthy?*[c]
8 Their children are always
　　in their presence,
　　And they get to see their
　　descendants.
9 Their houses are secure,
　　they are free from fear,[d]
　　And God does not punish
　　them with his rod.
10 Their bulls breed without
　　failure;
　　Their cows give birth and
　　do not miscarry.
11 Their boys run outside just
　　like a flock,
　　And their children skip
　　about.
12 They sing accompanied by
　　tambourine and harp
　　And rejoice at the sound
　　of the flute.*[e]
13 They spend their days in
　　contentment

　　And go down peacefully*
　　　to the Grave.#
14 But they say to the true God,
　　'Leave us alone!
　　We have no desire to know
　　your ways.[a]
15 Who is the Almighty, that
　　we should serve him?[b]
　　What would we gain by being
　　acquainted with him?'[c]
16 But I know that they
　　do not control their
　　own prosperity.[d]
　　The thinking* of the wicked
　　is far from me.[e]
17 How often is the lamp of the
　　wicked extinguished?[f]
　　How often does disaster
　　come upon them?
　　How often does God deal out
　　destruction to them in his
　　anger?
18 Do they ever become like
　　straw before the wind
　　And like chaff that a storm
　　wind carries away?
19 God will store up a man's
　　punishment for his own
　　sons.
　　But may God repay him so
　　that he will know it.[g]
20 May his own eyes see his
　　ruin,
　　And may he be the one to
　　drink from the rage of the
　　Almighty.[h]
21 For what does he care about
　　what happens to his house
　　after him
　　If the number of his months
　　is cut short?*[i]
22 Can anyone teach knowledge
　　to God,*[j]
　　When He is the one who
　　judges even the highest
　　ones?[k]

CHAP. 21
a Job 16:10, 20
　Job 17:2
　Heb 11:36

b Hab 1:3, 13

c Job 12:6
　Ps 37:7
　Ps 73:3
　Ps 73:12
　Jer 12:1

d Ps 73:3, 5

e Isa 5:12
　Isa 22:13
　Am 6:4, 5

Second Col.
a Ps 10:4, 11
　Ps 73:3, 11

b Ex 5:2
　Ps 10:4
　Ho 13:6

c Mal 3:14

d Lu 12:19, 20

e Ps 1:1

f Pr 13:9
　Pr 20:20
　Pr 24:20

g Ps 11:6
　Isa 26:11

h Ps 75:8
　Isa 51:17
　Jer 25:15
　Re 14:10

i Ps 55:23

j Isa 40:13, 14
　Ro 11:34
　1Co 2:16

k Isa 40:23

21:4 *Lit., "my spirit." 21:7 *Or "powerful." 21:12 *Or "pipe."

21:13 *Or "in a moment," that is, a quick
and painless death. #Or "Sheol," that
is, the common grave of mankind. See
Glossary. 21:16 *Or "advice; scheming." 21:21 *Or "cut in two." 21:22
*Or "teach God anything."

23 One man dies in his full vigor[a]
   When he is completely carefree and at ease,[b]

24 When his thighs are padded with fat
   And his bones are strong.*

25 But another man dies deeply distressed,*
   Never having tasted good things.

26 Together they will lie down in the dust,[c]
   And maggots will cover both of them.[d]

27 Look! I know exactly what you are thinking
   And the schemes you devise to wrong me.*[e]

28 For you say, 'Where is the house of the prominent man,
   And where is the tent
   in which the wicked one lived?'[f]

29 Have you not questioned travelers?
   Do you not carefully study their observations,*

30 That an evil person is spared on the day of disaster
   And rescued on the day of fury?

31 Who will confront him about his way,
   And who will repay him for what he has done?

32 When he is carried to the graveyard,
   A vigil will be kept over his tomb.

33 The clods of earth of the valley* will be sweet to him,[g]
   And all mankind follows after him#[h]
   Like the countless number before him.

34 So why offer me meaningless comfort?[a]
   There is nothing but deceit in your answers!"

22 El′i·phaz[b] the Te′man·ite said in reply:

2 "Can a man be of use to God?
   Can anyone with insight be of benefit to him?[c]

3 Does the Almighty care* that you are righteous,
   Or does he gain anything because you follow the course of integrity?[d]

4 Will he punish you
   And enter into judgment with you for your reverence?

5 Is it not because your own wickedness is so great
   And there is no end to your errors?[e]

6 For you seize a pledge from your brothers for no reason,
   And you strip people of their garments, leaving them naked.*[f]

7 You do not give the tired one a drink of water,
   And you hold back food from the hungry.[g]

8 The land belongs to the powerful man,[h]
   And the favored one dwells in it.

9 But you sent away widows empty-handed,
   And you crushed the arms of fatherless children.*

10 That is why you are surrounded by traps,*[i]
   And sudden terrors frighten you;

11 That is why it is so dark that you cannot see,
   And a flood of water covers you.

CHAP. 21
a Ps 49:17
  Lu 12:19, 20

b Ps 73:12, 19
  Mt 24:38, 39

c Job 3:19
  Ec 9:2

d Job 24:20

e Ps 59:3

f Job 20:5, 7

g Job 3:17

h Ro 5:12

Second Col.
a Job 16:2, 3

CHAP. 22
b Job 2:11
  Job 4:1

c Job 15:14, 15

d Job 2:3
  Job 32:3

e Job 1:8
  Job 4:7

f Job 31:19, 22

g Job 31:17, 22

h Job 31:25, 28

i Job 18:5, 9

21:24 *Lit., "the marrow of his bones is moist." 21:25 *Or "with a bitter soul." 21:27 *Or possibly, "to act violently against me." 21:29 *Lit., "signs." 21:33 *Or "wadi." #Lit., "And he will drag all mankind after him."

22:3 *Or "Does it delight the Almighty." 22:6 *Lit., "strip off garments of the naked." 22:9 *Or "of orphans." 22:10 *Lit., "bird traps."

12 Is not God in the heights
  of heaven?
  And see how high all the
  stars are.
13 But you have said: 'What
  does God really know?
  Can he judge through thick
  gloom?
14 Clouds screen him off so that
  he does not see
  As he walks about on the
  vault* of heaven.'
15 Will you follow the ancient
  path
  That wicked men have
  walked,
16 Men who have been snatched
  away* before their time,
  Whose foundation was
  washed away by a flood?*ᵃ
17 They were saying to the true
  God: 'Leave us alone!'
  And 'What can the Almighty
  do to us?'
18 Yet, he is the One who filled
  their houses with good
  things.
  (Such wicked thinking is far
  from my own.)
19 The righteous will see this
  and rejoice,
  And the innocent will mock
  them and say:
20 'Our opponents have been
  destroyed,
  And a fire will consume what
  is left of them.'
21 Get to know Him, and you
  will be at peace;
  Then good things will come
  your way.
22 Accept the law from his
  mouth,
  And keep his sayings in
  your heart.ᵇ
23 If you return to the Almighty,
  you will be restored;ᶜ
  If you remove unrighteousness from your tent,

24 If you would throw your
  gold* into the dust
  And the gold of Oʹphirᵃ into
  the rocky ravines,*
25 Then the Almighty will
  become your gold,*
  And he will be your choicest
  silver.
26 For then your delight will be
  in the Almighty,
  And you will lift up your face
  to God.
27 You will entreat him, and
  he will hear you;
  And your vows you will pay.
28 Whatever you decide to do
  will succeed,
  And light will shine upon
  your path.
29 For you will be humiliated
  when you speak arrogantly,
  But he will save the humble.*
30 He will rescue those who
  are innocent;
  So if your hands are clean,
  you will certainly be
  rescued."

23 Job said in reply:
  2 "Even today I will
    complain stubbornly;*ᵇ
  My strength is exhausted
  because of my sighing.
  3 If only I knew where to find
    God!ᶜ
  I would go to his place
  of dwelling.ᵈ
  4 I would present my case
  before him
  And fill my mouth with
  arguments;
  5 I would learn how he would
  answer me
  And take note of what he
  says to me.
  6 Would he contend with me
  using his great power?
  No, surely he would give me
  a hearing.ᵉ

CHAP. 22
a Job 4:18, 19

b Job 11:13

c Job 8:5, 6

Second Col.
a 1Ki 9:28
  Job 28:16
  Ps 45:9
  Isa 13:12

CHAP. 23
b Job 10:1

c Job 13:3
  Job 16:21

d Job 31:37

e Ps 22:24
  Isa 57:16

22:14 *Or "circle." 22:16 *Or "whose
lives were cut short." #Lit., "river."
22:24, 25 *Or "gold nuggets." 22:24
#Or "wadis." 22:29 *Or "the one with
downcast eyes." 23:2 *Or "my complaint is rebellious."

7 There the upright one could set matters straight with him,
And I would be acquitted once and for all by my Judge.

8 But if I go east, he is not there;
And I return and I cannot find him.

9 When he is working on the left, I cannot look upon him;
Then he turns to the right, but I still do not see him.

10 But he knows the path I have taken.[a]
After he has tested me, I will come out as pure gold.[b]

11 My feet have closely followed his footsteps;
I have kept to his way without deviating.[c]

12 I have not departed from the commandment of his lips.
I have treasured up his sayings[d] even more than what was required of me.*

13 When he is determined, who can resist him?[e]
When he* wants to do something, he does it.[f]

14 For he will carry out completely what has been determined* for me,
And he has many such things in store.

15 That is why I am anxious because of him;
When I think about him, my fear grows.

16 God has made me faint-hearted,
And the Almighty has made me afraid.

17 But I have not yet been silenced by the darkness
Nor by the gloom that has covered my face.

CHAP. 23
a Job 1:8
Ps 1:6
Ps 139:1

b Job 31:6
Ps 17:3

c Ps 18:21
Ps 44:18

d Ps 119:11, 127
Jer 15:16

e Ro 9:19

f Nu 23:19
Ps 135:6
Isa 14:24
Isa 46:10

Second Col.

CHAP. 24
a Hab 1:2

b De 19:14
De 27:17
Pr 23:10
Ho 5:10

c De 24:17

d Ps 109:16
Pr 22:16
Isa 10:1, 2
Jas 5:4

e Isa 32:14
Jer 14:6

f Ex 22:26, 27
De 24:13

g 2Ki 4:1

h Ex 22:26, 27
De 24:13

---

24 "Why does the Almighty not set a time?[a]
Why do those who know him not see his day?*

2 People move boundary markers;[b]
They carry off flocks for their own pasture.

3 They drive away the donkey of fatherless children
And seize the widow's bull as security for a loan.*[c]

4 They force the poor off the road;
The helpless of the earth must hide from them.[d]

5 The poor forage for food like wild donkeys[e] in the wilderness;
They seek food in the desert for their children.

6 They must harvest in another's field*
And glean from the vineyard of the wicked.

7 They spend the night naked, without clothing;[f]
They have no covering for the cold.

8 They are drenched by the mountain rains;
They cling to the rocks for lack of shelter.

9 The fatherless child is snatched away from the breast;[g]
And the garments of the poor are taken as security for a loan,[h]

10 Forcing them to go about naked, without clothing,
And hungry, as they carry the sheaves of grain.

11 They toil among the terrace walls in the heat of the day;*

23:12 *Or "prescribed for me." 23:13 *Or "his soul." 23:14 *Or "prescribed."

24:1 *That is, his day of judgment. 24:3 *Or "as a pledge." 24:6 *Or possibly, "harvest fodder in the field." 24:11 *Or possibly, "they press out oil among the terrace walls."

They tread the winepresses,
yet they go thirsty.[a]

12 The dying keep groaning
in the city;
The fatally wounded* cry
for help,[b]
But God does not regard this
as improper.#

13 There are those who rebel
against light;[c]
They do not recognize its
ways,
And they do not follow its
paths.

14 The murderer rises at
daybreak;
He slays the helpless and
the poor,[d]
While at night he engages
in theft.

15 The eye of the adulterer
waits for the twilight,[e]
Saying, 'No one will see me!'[f]
And he covers his face.

16 In the darkness they break
into* houses;
By day they shut them-
selves in.
They are strangers to
the light.[g]

17 For morning is the same as
deep darkness for them;
They are familiar with the
terrors of deep darkness.

18 But they are swiftly carried
away by the waters.*
Their portion of the land
will be cursed.[b]
They will not return to their
vineyards.

19 Just as drought and heat
take away the melted snow,
The Grave* takes away those
who have sinned![i]

20 His mother* will forget him;
the maggot will feast on
him.
He will be remembered
no more.[a]
And unrighteousness will
be broken just like a tree.

21 He preys on the barren
woman,
And mistreats the widow.

22 God* will use his strength to
do away with the powerful;
Though they may rise up,
they have no assurance
of life.

23 God* lets them become
confident and secure,[b]
But his eyes are on everything they do.#c

24 They are exalted for a little
while, then they are no
more.[d]
They are brought low[e] and
gathered like everyone
else;
They are cut off like heads
of grain.

25 Now who can prove me a liar
Or refute my word?"

25 Bil′dad[f] the Shu′hite said
in reply:

2 "Rulership and fearsome
might are his;
He establishes peace in
heaven.*

3 Can his troops be numbered?
Upon whom does his light
not rise?

4 So how can mortal man be
righteous before God,[g]
Or how can one born of
a woman be innocent?*[h]

5 Even the moon is not bright
And the stars are not pure
in his eyes,

6 How much less so mortal
man, who is a maggot,

CHAP. 24
a Jer 22:13
Jas 5:4

b Ec 4:1

c Joh 3:19

d Ps 10:4, 8

e Pr 7:8-10

f 2Sa 12:9, 12
Ps 94:3, 7
Pr 30:20

g Joh 3:20

h De 28:15, 16
Pr 3:33

i Ps 49:13, 14
Ps 55:15
Lu 12:20

Second Col.
a Pr 10:7
Ec 8:10
Ec 9:5

b Ec 8:11
Isa 56:12
Lu 12:19

c Ps 11:4
Pr 5:21
Pr 15:3

d Ps 37:10
Ps 92:7
Jas 1:11

e Ec 8:12, 13

CHAP. 25
f Job 2:11
Job 8:1

g Job 4:17, 18
Job 22:3

h Job 15:14, 15

24:12 *Or "souls of the wounded." # Or possibly, "God charges no one with wrong." 24:16 *Lit., "dig into." 24:18 *Lit., "He is swift on the surface of the waters." 24:19 *Or "Sheol," that is, the common grave of mankind. See Glossary.

24:20 *Lit., "The womb." 24:22, 23 *Lit., "He." 24:23 #Lit., "on their ways." 25:2 *Lit., "in his heights." 25:4 *Or "pure."

And a son of man, who is a worm!"

26 Job said in reply:

2 "How you have helped the one with no power! How you have saved the arm that has no strength![a]

3 What great advice you have given to the one lacking wisdom![b] How freely* you have revealed your practical wisdom!*

4 To whom are you trying to speak, And who inspired you to say such things?*

5 Those who are powerless in death tremble; They are even lower than the waters and their inhabitants.

6 The Grave* is naked in front of God,*[c] And the place of destruction△ lies uncovered.

7 He stretches out the northern sky* over empty space,*[d] Suspending the earth upon nothing;

8 He wraps up the waters in his clouds,[e] So that the clouds do not burst under their weight;

9 He shuts off the view of his throne, Spreading out his cloud over it.[f]

10 He marks out the horizon* on the surface of the waters;[g] He makes a boundary between light and darkness.

11 The very pillars of heaven shake; They are stunned by his rebuke.

12 He stirs up the sea with his power,[a] And by his understanding he breaks the sea monster* to pieces.[b]

13 With his breath* he makes the skies clear; His hand pierces the elusive* serpent.

14 Look! These are just the fringes of his ways;[c] Only a faint whisper has been heard of him! So who can understand his mighty thunder?"[d]

27 Job continued his discourse,* saying:

2 "As surely as God lives, who has deprived me of justice,[e] As the Almighty lives, who has made me* bitter,[f]

3 As long as my breath is within me And spirit from God is in my nostrils,[g]

4 My lips will not speak unrighteousness; Nor will my tongue mutter deceit!

5 It is unthinkable for me to declare you men righteous! Until I die, I will not renounce* my integrity![h]

6 I will maintain my righteousness and never let it go;[i] My heart will not condemn* me as long as I live.*

7 May my enemy become like the wicked, Those assaulting me like the unrighteous.

CHAP. 26
a Job 16:2, 3

b Job 12:2
  Job 17:10

c Ps 139:8
  Heb 4:13

d Job 9:8
  Ps 104:2
  Isa 42:5

e Pr 30:4
  Ec 11:3

f Ps 97:2

g Pr 8:27
  Jer 5:22

Second Col.
a Ps 74:13
  Isa 51:15

b Job 9:13

c Ps 92:5
  Ec 3:11
  Isa 55:9

d Job 37:5

CHAP. 27
e Job 34:5

f Ru 1:20
  2Ki 4:27

g Ge 2:7
  Isa 42:5
  Ac 17:25

h Job 22:1, 5
  Pr 27:11

i Job 2:3

26:3 *Or "abundantly." *Or "common sense." 26:4 *Lit., "And whose breath (spirit) has come out from you?" 26:6 *Or "Sheol," that is, the common grave of mankind. See Glossary. *Lit., "him." △Or "And Abaddon." 26:7 *Lit., "the north." *Lit., "emptiness." 26:10 *Lit., "a circle."

26:12 *Lit., "Rahab." 26:13 *Or "wind." *Or "gliding." 27:1 *Lit., "proverb." 27:2 *Or "my soul." 27:5 *Or "I will not take away from myself; I will maintain." 27:6 *Or "taunt." *Or "for any of my days."

8 For what hope does the godless man* have when he is destroyed,[a]
   When God takes away his life?#

9 Will God hear his outcry
   When distress comes upon him?[b]

10 Or will he find delight in the Almighty?
   Will he call on God at all times?

11 I will teach you about the power* of God;
   I will not hide anything about the Almighty.

12 Look! If you have all seen visions,
   Why are your speeches completely empty?

13 This is the wicked man's share from God,[c]
   The inheritance that tyrants receive from the Almighty.

14 If his sons become many, they will fall by the sword,[d]
   And his descendants will not have enough food.

15 Those who survive him will be buried by the plague,
   And their widows will not weep for them.

16 Even if he piles up silver like the dust
   And stores up fine clothing like the clay,

17 Though he may gather it, The righteous man will wear it,[e]
   And the innocent will divide up his silver.

18 The house he builds is as fragile as a moth's cocoon,
   Like a shelter[f] made by a watchman.

19 He will go to bed rich but will gather nothing;
   When he opens his eyes, nothing will be there.

20 Terror overtakes him like a flood;
   A storm snatches him away by night.[a]

21 An east wind will carry him off, and he will be gone;
   It sweeps him away from his place.[b]

22 It will hurl itself at him without pity[c]
   As he desperately tries to flee from its force.[d]

23 It claps its hands at him
   And whistles[e] at him from its place.*

28 "There is a place to mine silver
   And a place for gold that they refine;[f]

2 Iron is taken from the ground,
   And copper is smelted* from rocks.[g]

3 Man conquers the darkness;
   He probes to the limit in the gloom and darkness,
   Searching for ore.*

4 He sinks a shaft far from where people reside,
   In forgotten places, far from where people walk;
   Some men descend and swing suspended.

5 Food grows on top of the earth;
   But below, there is an upheaval as if by fire.*

6 There in the stones is sapphire,
   And the dust contains gold.

7 No bird of prey knows the path to it;
   The eye of a black kite has not seen it.

8 No majestic beasts have trodden on it;

27:8 *Or "the apostate." #Or "soul."
27:11 *Or possibly, "by the hand."

27:23 *Or possibly, "They clap their hands at him and whistle at him from their place." 28:2 *Lit., "poured." 28:3 *Lit., "stone." 28:5 *Apparently a reference to mining operations.

CHAP. 27
a Job 13:15, 16
  Job 36:13

b Job 35:12
  Ps 18:37, 41
  Pr 28:9
  Jer 11:11
  Jas 4:3

c Ps 11:6
  Ec 8:13
  Mal 3:5

d Es 9:7-10
  Ho 9:13

e Pr 13:22
  Pr 28:8
  Ec 2:26

f Isa 1:8
  La 2:6

Second Col.
a Ps 73:3, 19

b Mt 7:26, 27

c Ps 83:15

d Isa 10:3
  Am 2:14

e La 2:15

CHAP. 28
f Pr 17:3
  Mal 3:3

g De 8:7, 9

The young lion has not
  prowled there.
9 Man strikes the flinty rock
  with his hand;
  He overturns the mountains
  at their foundation.
10 He cuts water channels[a]
  in the rock;
  His eyes spot every precious
  thing.
11 He dams up the sources
  of rivers
  And brings what was hidden
  to the light.
12 But wisdom—where can it be
  found,[b]
  And where is the source of
  understanding?[c]
13 No man recognizes its value,[d]
  And it cannot be found in
  the land of the living.
14 The deep waters say, 'It is
  not in me!'
  And the sea says, 'It is not
  with me!'[e]
15 It cannot be bought with
  pure gold;
  Nor can silver be weighed
  out in exchange for it.[f]
16 It cannot be bought with gold
  of O'phir[g]
  Nor with rare onyx and
  sapphire.
17 Gold and glass cannot be
  compared to it;
  Nor can a vessel of fine* gold
  be exchanged for it.[h]
18 Coral and crystal are not
  worthy of mention,[i]
  For a bagful of wisdom is
  worth more than one full
  of pearls.
19 The topaz[j] of Cush cannot
  be compared to it;
  It cannot be purchased even
  with pure gold.
20 But from where does wisdom
  come,
  And where is the source
  of understanding?[k]

21 It has been hidden from the
  eyes of every living thing[a]
  And concealed from the
  birds of the heavens.
22 Destruction and death say,
  'Our ears have heard only
  a report of it.'
23 God understands the way
  to find it;
  He alone knows where
  it resides,[b]
24 For he looks to the ends
  of the earth,
  And he sees everything
  under the heavens.[c]
25 When he set the force*
  of the wind[d]
  And measured out the
  waters,[e]
26 When he made a regulation
  for the rain[f]
  And a path for the thunderous storm cloud,[g]
27 Then he saw wisdom and
  explained it;
  He established and tested it.
28 And he said to man:
  'Look! The fear of Jehovah
  —that is wisdom,[h]
  And to turn away from bad
  is understanding.'"[i]

29 Job continued his dis-
  course,* saying:
2 "If only I were in the months
  gone by,
  In the days when God was
  watching over me,
3 When he caused his lamp
  to shine upon my head,
  When I walked through
  darkness by his light,[j]
4 When I was in* my prime,
  When God's friendship was
  felt in my tent,[k]
5 When the Almighty was still
  with me,
  When my children* were all
  around me,

CHAP. 28
a 2Ki 20:20
  2Ch 32:30

b Pr 2:6
  Jas 1:5

c Job 28:28

d Pr 3:15

e Ro 11:34

f Pr 3:13, 14

g Isa 13:12

h Pr 16:16

i Pr 8:11
  Pr 20:15

j Ex 28:15, 17

k Job 28:12

Second Col.
a Ec 8:17
  1Co 2:8, 11

b Jas 1:5

c Pr 15:3
  Zec 4:10
  1Pe 3:12

d Ps 148:8
  Ec 1:6

e Job 5:10
  Job 26:8
  Job 37:10
  Ps 135:7
  Pr 30:4
  Isa 40:12

f Zec 10:1

g Job 38:25

h De 4:6
  Ps 111:10
  Pr 9:10
  Ec 12:13
  Ro 1:20

i Pr 3:7

CHAP. 29
j Ps 18:28
  Ps 119:105

k Ps 25:14
  Pr 3:32

28:17 *Or "refined."

28:25 *Lit., "weight." 29:1 *Lit., "proverb." 29:4 *Lit., "in the days of." 29:5
*Or "attendants."

6 When my steps were awash
in butter,
And the rocks poured out
streams of oil for me.ª

7 When I used to go out to the
city gateᵇ
And take my seat in the
public square,ᶜ

8 The young men would see
me and step aside,*
And even the old men would
rise and remain standing.ᵈ

9 Princes refrained from
speaking;
They would put their hand
over their mouth.

10 The voices of the prominent
men were silenced;
Their tongue was stuck to
the roof of their mouth.

11 Whoever heard me would
speak well of me,
And those who saw me
would testify for me.

12 For I would rescue the poor
who cried for help,ᵉ
Along with the fatherless
child and anyone who had
no helper.ᶠ

13 The one about to perish
would bless me,ᵍ
And I made the heart of
the widow rejoice.ʰ

14 I put on righteousness as
my clothing;
My justice was like a robe*
and a turban.

15 I became eyes to the blind
And feet to the lame.

16 I was a father to the poor;ⁱ
I would investigate the legal
case of those I did not
know.ʲ

17 I would break the jaws of
the wrongdoerᵏ
And tear the prey away from
his teeth.

18 I used to say, 'I will die in
my own home,*ˡ

And my days will be as
numerous as the grains
of sand.

19 My roots will spread out into
the waters,
And dew will stay all night
on my branches.

20 My glory is constantly
renewed,
And the bow in my hand
will keep shooting.'

21 People would listen
expectantly,
Waiting in silence for
my advice.ª

22 After I had spoken, they had
nothing more to say;
My words would fall gently*
on their ears.

23 They waited for me as for
the rain;
They opened their mouth
wide as for the spring
rain.ᵇ

24 When I smiled at them, they
could hardly believe it;
The light of my face would
reassure them.*

25 I gave them direction as their
head,
And I lived like a king among
his troops,ᶜ
Like one who comforts the
mourners.ᵈ

30 "Now they laugh at meᵉ
—Men younger than I am,
Whose fathers I would have
refused
To put with the dogs that
guarded my flock.

2 Of what use was the power
of their hands to me?
Their vigor has perished.

3 They are worn out from want
and hunger;
They gnaw at the parched
ground
That was already ruined
and desolate.

CHAP. 29
a De 32:13
  De 33:24

b Ru 4:1
  Pr 31:23

c Ne 8:1

d Le 19:32

e Pr 21:13
  Pr 24:11

f Jas 1:27

g De 24:12, 13

h De 10:17, 18

i Lu 14:13
  Jas 1:27

j Pr 29:7

k Ps 58:6
  Pr 30:14

l Ge 25:8
  2Ki 22:20

Second Col.
a Job 29:9

b Ps 72:6
  Pr 16:15

c Job 1:3

d Ec 7:2

CHAP. 30
e Job 12:4

29:8 *Lit., "hide themselves." 29:14
*Or "sleeveless coat." 29:18 *Lit., "in
my nest."

29:22 *Lit., "would drip." 29:24 *Or
possibly, "They did not darken the light
of my face."

4 They gather the salt herb
from the bushes;
Their food is the root
of broom trees.

5 They are driven out of the
community;[a]
People shout at them as they
would at a thief.

6 They live on the slopes
of ravines,*
In holes in the ground and
in the rocks.

7 From the bushes they cry out
And huddle together among
the nettles.

8 As sons of the senseless and
the nameless ones,
They have been driven*
out of the land.

9 But now they mock me even
in their songs;[b]
I have become an object
of scorn* to them.[c]

10 They detest me and keep
their distance from me;[d]
They do not hesitate to spit
in my face.[e]

11 Because God has disarmed
me* and humbled me,
They throw off all restraint#
in my presence.

12 On my right they rise up
like a mob;
They put me to flight
And put up barriers of
destruction in my path.

13 They tear up my roadways
And make my calamity
worse,[f]
Without anyone to stop
them.*

14 They come as if through
a wide breach in the wall;
They roll in amid the
devastation.

15 Terror overwhelms me;

My dignity is driven away
like the wind,
And my salvation vanishes
like a cloud.

16 Now my life* ebbs from me;[a]
Days of affliction[b] take hold
of me.

17 Aching pierces my bones*
at night;[c]
The gnawing pain never
stops.[d]

18 With great force my garment
is disfigured;*
Like the collar of my
garment, it chokes me.

19 God has thrown me down
into the mud;
I am reduced to dust and
ashes.

20 I cry to you for help, but you
do not answer me;[e]
I stand up, but you just look
at me.

21 You have cruelly turned
against me;[f]
With the full might of your
hand, you assault me.

22 You pick me up and carry me
off with the wind;
Then you toss me about in
the storm.*

23 For I know that you will
bring me down to death,
To the house where everyone
living will meet.

24 But no one would strike at
a broken man*[g]
As he cries for help during
his time of disaster.

25 Have I not wept for those
who have fallen on hard
times?*
Have I# not grieved for
the poor?[h]

CHAP. 30

a Ge 4:12
Ps 109:10
Da 4:25

b Ps 69:12
La 3:14

c Job 17:6

d Job 19:13

e Nu 12:14
De 25:9
Isa 50:6
Mt 27:30

f Job 16:2
Ps 69:26

Second Col.
a Ps 22:14

b Job 10:15

c Ps 6:2

d Job 2:8, 13
Job 7:4

e Job 19:7
Ps 22:2

f Job 7:20
Job 19:6

g Job 13:25

h Pr 14:21
Pr 14:31
Pr 19:17

30:6 *Or "wadis." **30:8** *Lit.,
"scourged." **30:9** *Lit., "a proverb; a
byword." **30:11** *Lit., "loosened my
bowstring." #Or "They cast off the
bridle." **30:13** *Or possibly, "Without
anyone helping them."

30:16 *Or "soul." **30:17** *Lit., "My
bones are bored through." **30:18** *Or
possibly, "The severity of my affliction disfigures me." **30:22** *Or possibly, "dissolve me with a crash." **30:24**
*Lit., "a heap of ruins." **30:25** *Or
"who are having a hard day?" #Or "Has
my soul."

26 Although I hoped for good,
      bad came;
   I expected the light,
      but darkness came.

27 The churning inside me
      did not stop;
   Days of affliction
      confronted me.

28 I walk about gloomy;[a] there
      is no sunlight.
   In the assembly, I rise and
      cry for help.

29 I have become a brother
      to jackals
   And a companion to the
      daughters of the ostrich.[b]

30 My skin has blackened and
      fallen off;[c]
   My bones burn from the
      heat.*

31 My harp is used only for
      mourning,
   And my flute* for the sound
      of weeping.

31 "I have made a covenant
      with my eyes.[d]
   So how could I show improp-
      er attention to a virgin?[e]

2 What, then, would be my
      share from God above,
   What inheritance from
      the Almighty on high?

3 Does not disaster await
      the wrongdoer
   And calamity those doing
      what is harmful?[f]

4 Does he not see my ways[g]
   And count all my steps?

5 Have I ever walked in
      untruth?*
   Has my foot hurried to
      deceive?[h]

6 Let God weigh me with
      accurate scales;[i]
   Then he will recognize my
      integrity.[j]

7 If my footsteps deviate from
      the way[k]

Or my heart has followed
      after my eyes[a]
   Or my hands have been
      defiled,

8 Then let me sow seed and
      someone else eat,[b]
   And let what I plant be
      uprooted.*

9 If my heart has been enticed
      by a woman[c]
   And I have lain in wait[d] at
      my neighbor's door,

10 Then let my wife grind grain
      for another man,
   And let other men have
      sexual relations with her.*[e]

11 For that would be shameful
      conduct,
   An error deserving punish-
      ment by the judges.[f]

12 It would be a fire that would
      devour and destroy,*[g]
   Consuming even the roots
      of# all my produce.

13 If I denied justice to my male
      or female servants
   When they had a complaint*
      against me,

14 What can I do when God
      confronts me?*
   What can I answer him
      when he calls for an
      accounting?[h]

15 Did not the One who made
      me in the womb also make
      them?[i]
   Was it not the same One
      who formed us before
      our birth?*[j]

16 If I refused to give the poor
      what they desired[k]
   Or saddened the eyes of
      the widow;*[l]

17 If I ate my portion of food
      alone

CHAP. 30
a Ps 38:6
  Ps 42:9
  Ps 43:2
b Mic 1:8
c Job 7:5
  La 4:8

CHAP. 31
d Pr 6:25, 26
  Mt 5:28
e Job 31:9, 10
f Job 20:26-29
  Ps 73:3, 18
  Pr 10:29
g Ge 16:13
  2Ch 16:9
  Ps 139:3
  Pr 5:21
  Jer 32:19
h Ps 26:5
  Pr 6:16, 18
i 1Sa 2:3
j Job 2:3
  Job 27:5
  Ps 7:8
k De 11:16
  Jer 10:23

Second Col.
a Nu 15:39
  Ec 11:9
  Eze 6:9
  Mt 5:29
  1Jo 2:16
b Le 26:16
c Job 31:1
  Mt 5:28
d Job 24:15
e 2Sa 12:9, 11
  Jer 8:10
f Ge 38:24
  Le 20:10
  De 22:22
g Pr 6:25-27
  Pr 7:27
h Pr 22:22, 23
  Isa 1:1-3
i Job 34:19
  Pr 14:31
  Pr 22:2
  Mal 2:10
j Ps 139:16
k De 15:7, 8
l De 10:18
  Pr 28:27

30:30 *Or possibly, "fever." 30:31 *Or
"pipe." 31:5 *Or possibly, "with men of
untruth?"

31:8 *Or "let my descendants be rooted out." 31:10 *Lit., "let other men
kneel down over her." 31:12 *Lit., "eat
(devour) to destruction." #Or "Uprooting." 31:13 *Or "legal case." 31:14
*Lit., "rises up?" 31:15 *Lit., "in the
womb." 31:16 *Lit., "caused the eyes
of the widow to fail."

Without sharing it with the orphans;[a]

18 (For from my youth the orphan* grew up with me as though I were his father,

And I have been a guide for the widow# from childhood.△)

19 If I saw anyone perishing for lack of clothing

Or a poor man with nothing to cover himself;[b]

20 If he* did not bless me[c]

As he warmed himself with the wool of my sheep;

21 If I shook my fist against the orphan[d]

When he needed my assistance in the city gate;*[e]

22 Then let my arm* fall from my shoulder,

And let my arm be broken at the elbow.#

23 For I dreaded disaster from God,

And I could not stand before his dignity.

24 If I put my confidence in gold

Or said to fine gold, 'You are my security!'[f]

25 If I found my joy in my great wealth[g]

Because of the many possessions I acquired;[h]

26 If I saw the sun* shining

Or the moon moving in its splendor;[i]

27 And my heart was secretly enticed,

And my mouth kissed my hand in worship of them;[j]

28 Then that would be an error deserving punishment by the judges,

For I would have denied the true God above.

29 Have I ever rejoiced over the destruction of my enemy[a]

Or gloated because evil befell him?

30 I never allowed my mouth to sin

By asking for his life* in an oath.[b]

31 Have the men of my tent not said,

'Who can find anyone who has not been satisfied with his food?'*[c]

32 No stranger* had to spend the night outside;[d]

I opened my doors to the traveler.

33 Have I ever tried to cover over my transgressions, like other men,[e]

By hiding my error in the pocket of my garment?

34 Have I been in fear of the reaction of the multitude,

Or have I been terrified by the contempt of other families,

Making me silent and afraid to go outside?

35 If only someone would listen to me![f]

I would sign my name to what I have said.*

Let the Almighty answer me![g]

If only my accuser had written out the charges in a document!

36 I would carry it on my shoulder,

And I would bind it around my head like a crown.

37 I would give him an accounting for every step I took;

I would approach him confidently, like a prince.

38 If my own ground would cry out against me

And its furrows would weep together;

CHAP. 31

a Eze 18:5, 7
Jas 1:27
1Jo 3:17

b Isa 58:7
Lu 3:11
Jas 2:15, 16

c De 24:13

d Pr 14:21

e Pr 31:23

f Ps 49:6, 7
1Ti 6:17

g Es 5:11
Ps 62:10
Pr 11:28

h De 8:17, 18

i De 4:19

j De 11:16

Second Col.

a Pr 17:5
Pr 24:17, 18

b Mt 5:44
Ro 12:14

c Ge 18:5
Ro 12:13

d Ge 19:1, 3
Heb 13:2
1Pe 4:9

e Ge 3:8
Pr 28:13
Ac 5:8

f Job 19:7

g Job 13:22

31:18 *Lit., "he." #Lit., "her." △Lit., "from my mother's womb." 31:20 *Lit., "his loins." 31:21 *Or possibly, "When I saw that I had support in the city gate." 31:22 *Or "shoulder blade." #Or "from its socket; from its upper bone." 31:26 *Lit., "light."

31:30 *Or "soul." 31:31 *Lit., "meat." 31:32 *Or "foreign resident." 31:35 *Or "Here is my signature."

39 If I have eaten its fruitage
     without payment,[a]
   Or if I have caused its
     owners* to despair;[b]
40 Then let thorns sprout for
     me instead of wheat
   And foul-smelling weeds
     instead of barley."
   The words of Job end here.

32 So these three men
stopped trying to answer
Job, because he was convinced
of his own righteousness.*[c]
2 But E·li′hu the son of Bar′-
a·chel the Buz′ite[d] of the family of Ram had become very angry. His anger blazed against
Job for trying to prove himself*
right rather than God.[e] **3** He
was also very angry with Job's
three companions because they
could not find an answer but had
declared God wicked.[f] **4** E·li′-
hu had been waiting to respond
to Job, because they were older than he was.[g] **5** When E·li′-
hu saw that the three men had
nothing to say in answer, his anger flared up. **6** So E·li′hu the
son of Bar′a·chel the Buz′ite began to speak, saying:

   "I am young*
   And you men are aged.[h]
   So I respectfully held back,[i]
   And I dared not tell you what
     I know.
7 I thought, 'Let age* speak,
   And let a multitude of years
     declare wisdom.'
8 But it is the spirit in people,
   The breath of the Almighty,
     that gives them under-
     standing.[j]
9 Age alone does not* make
     one wise,
   Nor is it only old men who
     understand what is right.[k]

10 So I say, 'Listen to me,
   And I will also tell you what
     I know.'
11 Look! I have waited for your
     words;
   I kept listening to your
     reasoning[a]
   As you searched for things
     to say.[b]
12 I paid close attention to you,
   But none of you could prove
     Job wrong*
   Or answer his arguments.
13 So do not say, 'We have
     found wisdom;
   It is God who refutes him,
     not a man.'
14 He did not direct his words
     against me,
   So I will not reply to him
     with your arguments.
15 They are dismayed, they
     have no more answers;
   They have nothing left to say.
16 I have waited, but they do not
     continue speaking;
   They just stand there,
     with no further answer.
17 So I too will give an answer;
   I too will tell what I know,
18 For I am full of words;
   The spirit within me
     compels me.
19 My insides are like wine that
     has no vent,
   Like new wineskins ready
     to burst.[c]
20 Let me speak so that I can
     find relief!
   I will open my lips and give
     an answer.
21 I will not show partiality
     to anyone;[d]
   Nor will I flatter* any human,
22 For I do not know how
     to flatter;
   If I did, my Maker would
     quickly do away with me.

CHAP. 31
a Jas 5:4

b 1Ki 21:15

CHAP. 32
c Job 6:29
  Job 27:6

d Ge 22:20, 21

e Job 10:2, 3

f Ex 20:7
  Job 4:18-20
  Job 22:2, 3
  Job 25:5, 6
  Job 42:8

g Le 19:32

h Job 15:10

i 1Ti 5:1
  1Pe 5:5

j 1Ki 3:12
  1Ki 4:29
  Job 35:11
  Pr 2:6
  Ec 2:26
  Da 1:17
  Mt 11:25
  Jas 1:5

k Ps 119:100
  Ec 4:13

Second Col.
a Jas 1:19

b Pr 15:28

c Mt 9:17

d Le 19:15
  Pr 24:23
  Jas 3:17

31:39 *Or "the soul of its owners."
32:1 *Or "because he was righteous
in his own eyes." **32:2** *Or "his soul."
32:6 *Lit., "small in days." **32:7** *Lit.,
"days." **32:9** *Or "Many days alone do
not."

32:12 *Or "reprove Job." **32:21** *Or
"confer an honorary title to."

33 "But now, Job, please hear my words;
Listen to everything I say.

2 Look, please! I must open my mouth;
My tongue* must speak.

3 My words declare the uprightness of my heart,[a]
And my lips sincerely tell what I know.

4 God's own spirit made me,[b]
And the Almighty's own breath brought me to life.[c]

5 Reply to me if you are able;
Present your arguments before me; take your position.

6 Look! I am just like you before the true God;
From the clay I too was shaped.[d]

7 So no fear of me should terrify you,
And no pressure from me should overwhelm you.

8 But you said in my hearing,
Yes, I kept hearing these words,

9 'I am pure, without transgression;[e]
I am clean, without error.[f]

10 But God finds reasons to oppose me;
He considers me his enemy.[g]

11 He puts my feet in stocks;
He scrutinizes all my paths.'[h]

12 But you are not right in saying this, so I will answer you:
God is far greater than mortal man.[i]

13 Why do you complain against Him?[j]
Is it because he did not answer all your words?[k]

14 For God speaks once and a second time,
But no one pays attention,

15 In a dream, a vision of the night,[l]

When deep sleep falls upon people
While they sleep in their beds.

16 Then he uncovers their ears[a]
And impresses* his instruction upon them,

17 To turn a person away from wrongdoing[b]
And to protect a man from pride.[c]

18 God spares his soul* from the pit,[#d]
His life from perishing by the sword.[△]

19 A person is also reproved by pain on his bed
And by the constant distress of his bones,

20 So that his very being* loathes bread,
And he[#] rejects even fine food.[e]

21 His flesh wastes away from sight,
And his bones that were hidden now protrude.*

22 His soul* draws near to the pit;[#]
His life to those who bring death.

23 If there is a messenger* for him,
One advocate out of a thousand,
To tell to man what is upright,

24 Then God shows him favor and says,
'Spare him from going down into the pit![#f]
I have found a ransom![g]

25 Let his flesh become fresher* than in youth;[h]
Let him return to the days of his youthful vigor.'[i]

CHAP. 33

a Mt 12:34
  Lu 6:45

b Ps 119:73

c Ge 2:7
  Ec 12:7
  Ac 17:25

d Ge 2:7

e Job 10:7
  Job 16:16, 17
  Job 23:11

f Job 29:14

g Job 13:24
  Job 16:9
  Job 19:11

h Job 13:27
  Job 14:16
  Job 31:4

i Job 12:13
  Ps 8:4
  Isa 40:25
  Isa 55:9

j Isa 45:9
  Ro 9:20

k Job 13:24

l Nu 12:6
  Da 4:5

Second Col.

a Job 36:10

b Ge 20:6, 7
  Mt 27:19

c Da 4:24, 25

d Ge 31:24

e Ps 107:17, 18

f Job 14:13

g Job 19:25
  Mt 20:28

h 2Ki 5:14

i De 34:7
  Job 42:16
  Ps 103:3-5

33:16 *Lit., "puts a seal on." **33:18, 22** *Or "life." **33:18, 22, 24** *Or "grave." **33:18** △Or "by a weapon (missile)." **33:20** *Lit., "his life." #Or "his soul." **33:21** *Or "are laid bare." **33:23** *Or "an angel." **33:25** *Or "healthier."

26 He will entreat God,[a]
  who will accept him,
  And he will see His face
  with shouts of joy,
  And He will restore His righteousness to mortal man.

27 That person will declare*
  to men,
  'I have sinned[b] and distorted
  what is right,
  But I did not receive what
  I deserved.#

28 He has redeemed my soul*
  from going into the pit,#c
  And my life will see the
  light.'

29 Indeed, God does all these
  things
  Twice, three times, for
  a man,

30 To bring him* back from
  the pit,#
  So that he may be enlightened with the light of life.[d]

31 Pay attention, Job!
  Listen to me!
  Keep silent, and I will
  continue speaking.

32 If you have something to say,
  reply to me.
  Speak, for I want to prove
  you right.

33 If you have nothing to say,
  you should listen to me;
  Keep silent, and I will teach
  you wisdom."

34 So E·li′hu continued to say
  in reply:

2 "Listen to my words, you
  who are wise;
  Hear me, you who know
  so much.

3 For the ear tests words
  Just as the tongue* tastes
  food.

4 Let us evaluate for ourselves
  what is right;

Let us decide among
  ourselves what is good.

5 For Job has said, 'I am in
  the right,[a]
  But God has denied me
  justice.[b]

6 Would I lie about what my
  own judgment should be?
  My wound is incurable,
  though there is no
  transgression.'[c]

7 What other man is like Job,
  Who drinks up derision like
  water?

8 He is in company with
  wrongdoers
  And in association with
  wicked men.[d]

9 For he has said, 'A man does
  not benefit
  From trying to please God.'[e]

10 So listen to me, you men
  of understanding:*
  It is unthinkable for the true
  God to act wickedly,[f]
  For the Almighty to do
  wrong![g]

11 For he will reward a man
  according to what he does[h]
  And bring upon him the
  consequences of his ways.

12 For a certainty, God does not
  act wickedly;[i]
  The Almighty does not
  pervert justice.[j]

13 Who put him in charge
  of the earth,
  And who appointed him
  over the whole world?*

14 If he fixes his attention*
  on them,
  If he gathers their spirit
  and breath to himself,[k]

15 All humans* would perish
  together,
  And mankind would return
  to the dust.[l]

16 So if you have understanding, pay attention to this;

CHAP. 33

a Ps 30:8

b 2Sa 12:13
  Ps 32:5
  Pr 28:13
  Lu 15:21
  1Jo 1:9

c Ps 19:14
  Isa 38:17

d Ps 56:13

Second Col.

CHAP. 34

a Job 29:14
  Job 33:9

b Job 27:2

c Job 9:17, 18

d Pr 1:10, 15
  Pr 4:14

e Job 9:22-24
  Job 35:3

f Ge 18:25
  2Ch 19:7
  Ps 92:15

g De 32:4
  Ro 9:14
  Heb 6:10

h 1Ch 28:9
  Ps 62:12
  Pr 24:12
  Jer 32:19
  Eze 33:20
  Ro 2:6
  2Co 5:10
  Ga 6:7
  1Pe 1:17
  Re 22:12

i Jas 1:13

j Ps 89:14
  Ps 97:2
  Ps 99:4
  Ro 2:11

k Ps 104:29
  Ec 12:7
  Isa 42:5
  Ac 17:25

l Ge 3:19
  Ps 146:4
  Ec 3:20

33:27 *Lit., "sing." #Or possibly, "And it did not profit me." 33:28 *Or "life." 33:28, 30 #Or "grave." 33:30 *Or "his soul." 34:3 *Lit., "palate."

34:10 *Lit., "heart." 34:13 *Or "the inhabited earth." 34:14 *Lit., "his heart." 34:15 *Lit., "flesh."

Listen carefully to what I say.

17 Should someone who hates justice be in control,
Or would you condemn a powerful one who is righteous?

18 Would you say to a king, 'You are good for nothing,'
Or to nobles, 'You are wicked'?[a]

19 There is One who does not show partiality to princes
And who does not favor the rich over the poor,*[b]
For they are all the work of his hands.[c]

20 They may die suddenly,[d] in the middle of the night;[e]
They shake violently and pass away;
Even the powerful are removed, but not by human hands.[f]

21 For God's eyes are upon the ways of a man,[g]
And He sees all his steps.

22 There is no darkness or deep shadow
Where wrongdoers can conceal themselves.[h]

23 For God has not set an appointed time for any man
To appear before him in judgment.

24 He breaks the powerful without needing to investigate
And sets up others in their place.[i]

25 For he knows what they are doing;[j]
He overthrows them during the night, and they are crushed.[k]

26 He strikes them for their wickedness,
In a place where all can see,[l]

27 Because they have turned away from following him[m]
And have no regard for any of his ways;[n]

28 They cause the poor to cry out to him,

So that he hears the outcry of the helpless.[a]

29 When God remains silent, who can condemn him?
When he hides his face, who can see him?
Whether toward a nation or a man, the result is the same,

30 So that a godless person* may not rule[b]
Or lay snares for the people.

31 For will anyone say to God, 'I have been punished, although I have committed no offense;[c]

32 Teach me what I have failed to see;
If I have done anything wrong, I will not do it again'?

33 Should he reward you on your terms when you reject his judgment?
You must decide, not I.
So tell me what you know so well.

34 Men of understanding* will say to me
—Any wise man who hears me—

35 'Job speaks without knowledge,[d]
And his words lack insight.'

36 Let Job be tested* to the limit
Because his replies are like those of wicked men!

37 He adds rebellion to his sin;[e]
He scornfully claps his hands before us
And multiplies his words against the true God!"[f]

35

E·li′hu continued his response:

2 "Are you so convinced that you are right that you would say,
'I am more righteous than God'?[g]

34:19 *Or "the noble over the lowly."

34:30 *Or "an apostate." 34:34 *Lit., "heart." 34:36 *Or possibly, "My father, let Job be tested."

3 For you say, 'What does it
matter to you?*
Am I better off than if I had
sinned?'ᵃ

4 I will reply to you
And to your companionsᵇ
with you.

5 Look up to heaven and see,
Observe the clouds,ᶜ which
are high above you.

6 If you sin, how do you hurt
him?ᵈ
If your transgressions multiply, what do you do to him?ᵉ

7 If you are righteous, what
do you give him;
What does he receive from
you?ᶠ

8 Your wickedness affects only
a human like yourself,
And your righteousness,
a son of man.

9 People cry out when under
great oppression;
They cry for relief from
the domination* of the
powerful.ᵍ

10 But no one says, 'Where is
God, my Grand Maker,ʰ
The one causing songs to be
sung in the night?'ⁱ

11 He teaches us ʲ more than
the beasts of the earth,ᵏ
And he makes us wiser than
the birds of the heavens.

12 People cry out, but he does
not answer,ˡ
Because of the pride of
the wicked.ᵐ

13 Surely God does not hear
an empty cry;*ⁿ
The Almighty does not pay
attention to it.

14 How much less, then, when
you complain that you do
not see him!ᵒ
Your legal case is before
him, so you should wait
anxiously for him.ᵖ

15 For he has not angrily called
for an accounting;
Nor has he taken note of
your extreme rashness.ᵃ

16 Job opens his mouth wide
in vain;
He multiplies words without
knowledge."ᵇ

36
E·liʹhu continued:

2 "Be patient with me
a little longer while
I explain,
For I still have words to
speak on God's behalf.

3 I will speak comprehensively
about what I know,
And I will ascribe righteousness to my Maker.ᶜ

4 Truly my words are not false;
The One perfect in knowl-
edgeᵈ is here before you.

5 Indeed, God is mightyᵉ and
rejects no one;
He is great in his power of
understanding.*

6 He will not preserve the lives
of the wicked,ᶠ
But he gives justice to the
afflicted.ᵍ

7 He does not take his eyes off
the righteous;ʰ
He enthrones them with
kings,*ⁱ and they are
exalted forever.

8 But if they are bound in
shackles
And caught in ropes of
affliction,

9 He reveals to them what they
have done,
Their transgressions caused
by their pride,

10 He opens their ears to
correction
And tells them to turn away
from wrongdoing.ʲ

11 If they obey and serve him,
They will live out their days
in prosperity,

CHAP. 35

a Job 9:22-24
Job 34:9
Ps 73:13

b Job 2:11

c Ps 68:34

d Pr 8:36
Pr 9:12

e Pr 19:3

f Ro 11:35

g Pr 29:2

h Isa 51:12, 13
1Pe 4:19

i Ps 42:8
Ps 149:5
Ac 16:25

j Ps 94:12
Isa 48:17

k Ge 1:26

l Ps 18:41

m Pr 1:28, 29
1Pe 5:5

n Pr 15:29
Isa 1:15
Jer 11:11

o Job 9:11

p Ps 37:5

Second Col.

a Ps 103:10-12

b Job 34:35
Job 38:2

CHAP. 36

c De 32:4
Ps 11:7
Ps 139:14
Da 9:14
Re 15:3

d 1Sa 2:3
Job 37:16

e Ps 24:8
Ps 99:4
Jer 32:18

f Ps 9:17
Ps 68:2
2Pe 2:9

g Ps 10:14
Ps 140:12
Pr 22:22, 23

h Ps 33:18
Ps 34:15

i Ps 78:70, 71
Ps 113:7, 8
Isa 9:7

j Eze 18:30

35:3 *Likely referring to God. 35:9
*Lit., "arm." 35:13 *Or "a lie." 36:5 *Lit., "heart." 36:7 *Or possibly,
"He enthrones kings."

And their years will be pleasant.[a]

12 But if they do not obey, they will perish by the sword*[b]
And die without knowledge.

13 The godless* at heart will harbor resentment.
They do not cry for help even when he binds them.

14 They die* while still young,[c]
Spending# their life among male temple prostitutes.[d]

15 But God* rescues the afflicted during their affliction;
He opens their ear when they are oppressed.

16 He draws you away from the brink of distress[e]
To a broad space, free of restriction,[f]
With rich food on your table as consolation.[g]

17 Then you will be satisfied with the judgment on the wicked,[h]
When judgment is rendered and justice is upheld.

18 But take care that rage does not lead you into spitefulness,*[i]
And do not let a large bribe lead you astray.

19 Would your cry for help
Or any of your strenuous efforts keep you from distress?[j]

20 Do not long for the night,
When people vanish from their place.

21 Beware that you do not turn to wrongdoing,
Choosing this instead of affliction.[k]

22 Look! God is exalted in his power;
What instructor is like him?

23 Who has directed* his way[a]
Or said to him, 'What you have done is wrong'?[b]

24 Remember to magnify his activity,[c]
Of which men have sung.[d]

25 All mankind has seen it,
Mortal man looks on from a distance.

26 Yes, God is greater than we can know;[e]
The number of his years is beyond comprehension.*[f]

27 He draws up the drops of water;[g]
They condense into rain from his mist;

28 Then the clouds pour it down;[h]
They shower down upon mankind.

29 Can anyone understand the layers of clouds,
The thundering from his tent?*[i]

30 See how he spreads his lightning*[i] over it
And covers the depths# of the sea.

31 By these he sustains* the peoples;
He gives them food in abundance.[k]

32 With his hands he covers the lightning,
And he directs it against its target.[l]

33 His thunder tells about him,
Even the livestock tell who* is coming.

37 "At this my heart pounds
And leaps from its place.

2 Listen carefully to the rumbling of his voice
And the thunder that comes from his mouth.

CHAP. 36
a Jer 26:13

b Job 33:16-18
Isa 1:19, 20
Ro 2:8

c Ps 55:23

d 1Ki 14:24

e Isa 30:21

f Ps 18:19

g Isa 55:2

h Pr 2:22
Jer 25:31

i Pr 19:19
Pr 29:22

j Job 34:20
Ps 33:16
Pr 11:4

k Heb 11:24, 25

Second Col.
a Isa 40:14

b Job 34:10
Ro 9:14

c Ps 92:5
Ps 104:24

d Ex 15:1

e Ps 145:3
Ps 148:13
Re 15:3

f Ps 90:2
Ps 102:25-27
1Ti 1:17
Heb 1:10-12

g Ge 2:6
Am 5:8

h Pr 3:20
Isa 55:10
Jer 14:22

i 2Sa 22:12

j Job 37:3

k Ac 14:17

l 2Sa 22:15
Ps 18:14
Ps 144:6

36:12 *Or "by a weapon (missile)." **36:13** *Or "apostate." **36:14** *Or "Their soul dies." #Or possibly, "Ending." **36:15** *Lit., "He." **36:18** *Or "spiteful handclapping."

36:23 *Or possibly, "criticized; called him to account for." **36:26** *Or "is unsearchable." **36:29** *Lit., "booth." **36:30** *Lit., "light." #Lit., "roots." **36:31** *Or possibly, "pleads the cause of." **36:33** *Or possibly, "what."

3 He unleashes it under the
   entire heavens
   And sends his lightning[a]
   to the ends of the earth.

4 After that is a roaring sound;
   He thunders with a majestic
   voice,[b]
   And he does not hold it back
   when his voice is heard.

5 God thunders with his voice[c]
   in a wonderful way;
   He does great things that
   are beyond our under-
   standing.[d]

6 For he says to the snow,
   'Fall to the earth,'[e]
   And to the downpour of rain,
   'Pour down mightily.'[f]

7 God puts a stop to all human
   activity*
   So that every mortal man
   will know His work.

8 The wild animals go into
   their dens
   And remain in their lairs.

9 The storm wind blows from
   its chamber,[g]
   And the cold comes from
   the north winds.[h]

10 By the breath of God, the ice
   is produced,[i]
   And the broad waters are
   frozen solid.[j]

11 Yes, he weighs down the
   clouds with moisture;
   He scatters his lightning[k]
   in the clouds;

12 They swirl around where he
   directs them;
   They carry out whatever he
   commands[l] on the surface
   of the inhabited earth.*

13 Whether it is for
   punishment*[m] or for the
   sake of the land
   Or for loyal love, he causes
   it to happen.[n]

14 Listen to this, Job;
   Stop and consider carefully
   the wonderful works
   of God.[a]

15 Do you know how God
   controls* the clouds
   And how he causes the
   lightning to flash from
   his cloud?

16 Do you know how the clouds
   float?[b]
   These are the wonderful
   works of the One perfect
   in knowledge.[c]

17 Why does your clothing
   become hot
   When the earth is still because of the south wind?[d]

18 Can you, with him, spread
   out* the skies[e]
   As solid as a metal mirror?

19 Tell us what we should say
   to him;
   We cannot answer because
   we are in the dark.

20 Should he be told that I want
   to speak?
   Or has anyone said something that should be
   communicated to him?[f]

21 They cannot even see the
   light,*
   Though it is bright in the sky,
   Until a wind passes by and
   clears away the clouds.

22 Out of the north comes
   golden splendor;
   God's majesty[g] is awe-
   inspiring.

23 Understanding the Almighty
   is beyond our reach;[h]
   He is great in power,[i]
   And he never violates his
   justice[j] and abundant
   righteousness.[k]

24 Therefore, people should
   fear him.[l]
   For he does not favor any
   who think that they are
   wise."*[m]

37:7 *Lit., "puts a seal on the hand of
every human." 37:12 *Or "of the productive land of the earth." 37:13 *Lit.,
"a rod."

37:15 *Or "commands." 37:18 *Or
"beat out." 37:21 *That is, of the sun.
37:24 *Lit., "who are wise of heart."

38 Then Jehovah answered Job out of the windstorm:[a]

2 "Who is this who is obscuring my counsel
And speaking without knowledge?[b]

3 Brace yourself, please, like a man;
I will question you, and you inform me.

4 Where were you when I founded the earth?[c]
Tell me, if you think you understand.

5 Who set its measurements, in case you know,
Or who stretched a measuring line across it?

6 Into what were its pedestals sunk,
Or who laid its cornerstone,[d]

7 When the morning stars[e] joyfully cried out together,
And all the sons of God*[f] began shouting in applause?

8 And who barricaded the sea behind doors[g]
When it burst out from the womb,

9 When I clothed it with clouds
And wrapped* it in thick gloom,

10 When I established my limit for it
And put its bars and doors in place,[h]

11 And I said, 'You may come this far, and no farther;
Here is where your proud waves will stop'?[i]

12 Have you ever* commanded the morning
Or made the dawn know its place,[j]

13 To take hold of the ends of the earth
And to shake the wicked out of it?[k]

14 It is transformed like clay under a seal,
And its features stand out like those of a garment.

15 But the light of the wicked is held back from them,
And their uplifted arm is broken.

16 Have you gone down to the sources of the sea
Or explored the deep waters?[a]

17 Have the gates of death[b] been revealed to you,
Or have you seen the gates of deep darkness?*[c]

18 Have you understood the vast expanse of the earth?[d]
Tell me, if you know all of this.

19 In which direction does the light reside?[e]
And where is the place of darkness,

20 That you should take it to its territory
And understand the paths to its home?

21 Do you know this because you were already born
And the number of your years* is great?

22 Have you entered the storehouses of the snow,[f]
Or have you seen the storehouses of the hail,[g]

23 Which I have reserved for the time of distress,
For the day of battle and war?[h]

24 From what direction is light* dispersed,
And from where does the east wind blow on the earth?[i]

25 Who has cut a channel for the flood
And made a path for the thunderous storm cloud,[j]

CHAP. 38

a Ex 19:16, 19
1Ki 19:11

b Job 42:3

c Ge 1:1
Ne 9:6
Ps 136:6
Pr 8:29
Heb 1:10

d Ps 104:5

e Re 22:16

f Ge 6:2
1Ki 22:19
Job 1:6
Job 2:1
Ps 89:6

g Ps 33:7
Pr 8:29

h Ge 1:9
Jer 5:22

i Pr 8:29

j Ge 1:5
Ps 74:16

k Job 24:15
1Th 5:7

Second Col.

a Ge 1:2
Ps 77:19

b Ps 9:13
Mt 16:18

c Job 10:21, 22

d Ps 74:17
Ps 89:11

e Isa 45:7

f Job 37:6

g Jos 10:11
Isa 30:30

h Ex 9:24
Eze 13:13

i Ps 135:7

j Job 28:26

38:7 *A Hebrew idiom that refers to angelic sons of God. **38:9** *Or "swaddled." **38:12** *Lit., "in your days."

38:17 *Or "death's shadow." **38:21** *Lit., "days." **38:24** *Or possibly, "lightning."

26 To make it rain where
   no man lives,
   On the wilderness where
   there are no humans,[a]

27 To satisfy devastated
   wastelands
   And cause the grass to
   sprout?[b]

28 Does the rain have a father,[c]
   Or who fathered the
   dewdrops?[d]

29 From whose womb did the
   ice emerge,
   And who gave birth to the
   frost of heaven[e]

30 When the waters are covered
   as if with stone,
   And the surface of the deep
   waters is frozen solid?[f]

31 Can you tie the ropes of the
   Ki′mah constellation*
   Or untie the cords of the
   Ke′sil constellation?*[g]

32 Can you lead out a constellation* in its season
   Or guide the Ash constellation* along with its sons?

33 Do you know the laws
   governing the heavens,[h]
   Or can you impose their*
   authority on the earth?

34 Can you raise your voice
   to the clouds
   To cause a flood of water
   to cover you?[i]

35 Can you send out lightning
   bolts?
   Will they come and say
   to you, 'Here we are!'

36 Who put wisdom within the
   clouds*[j]
   Or gave understanding to the
   sky phenomenon?*[k]

37 Who is wise enough to count
   the clouds,
   Or who can tip over the
   water jars of heaven[a]

38 When the dust pours into
   a mass
   And the clods of earth stick
   together?

39 Can you hunt prey for a lion
   Or satisfy the appetites
   of young lions[b]

40 When they crouch in their
   lairs
   Or lie in ambush in their
   dens?

41 Who prepares food for the
   raven[c]
   When its young cry to God
   for help
   And wander about because
   there is nothing to eat?

39 "Do you know the
   time when the mountain
   goats give birth?[d]
   Have you watched the deer
   give birth to their young?[e]

2 Do you count the months
   that they must complete?
   Do you know the time when
   they give birth?

3 They crouch down when they
   give birth to their young,
   And their labor pains end.

4 Their young become strong
   and grow up in the open
   field;
   They go out and do not
   return to them.

5 Who set the wild donkey*
   free,[f]
   And who untied the ropes
   of the wild donkey?

6 I have made the desert plain
   its home
   And the salt land its
   dwelling.

7 It scorns the tumult of the
   city;
   It does not hear the shouts
   of the driver.

CHAP. 38
a Ps 104:13
  Ps 107:35

b Ps 147:7, 8

c 1Sa 12:18
  Isa 30:23
  Jer 5:24

d Ge 27:28

e Ps 147:16

f Job 37:10

g Am 5:8

h Pr 3:19
  Jer 31:35
  Jer 33:25

i Zec 10:1

j Jer 10:12

k Ps 136:5
  Pr 3:20

Second Col.
a Jer 10:13

b Ps 104:21
  Ps 145:15, 16
  Na 2:12

c Ps 147:9
  Mt 6:26
  Lu 12:24

CHAP. 39
d Ps 104:18

e Ps 29:9

f Job 24:5
  Ps 104:10, 11

38:31 *Possibly the Pleiades stars in
the Taurus constellation. #Possibly the
Orion constellation. 38:32 *Lit., "Maz-
zaroth." At 2Ki 23:5, the related term in
plural form refers to the constellations
of the zodiac. #Possibly the Great
Bear constellation (Ursa Major). 38:33
*Or possibly, "His." 38:36 *Or possi-
bly, "within man." #Or possibly, "to the
mind."

39:5 *Or "onager."

8 It roams the hills, seeking
    pasture,
  Looking for every green
    plant.
9 Is the wild bull willing
    to serve you?ᵃ
  Will it spend the night in
    your stable?*
10 Will you hold a wild bull
    to the furrow with a rope,
  Or will it follow you to plow*
    the valley?
11 Will you trust in its great
    strength
  And let it do your heavy
    work?
12 Will you rely on it to bring
    back your harvest,*
  And will it gather it to your
    threshing floor?
13 The wings of the ostrich flap
    joyfully,
  But can her pinions and
    plumage compare with
    the stork's?ᵇ
14 For she leaves her eggs on
    the ground,
  And she keeps them warm
    in the dust.
15 She forgets that some foot
    may crush them
  Or that a wild animal may
    trample them.
16 She treats her sons harshly,
    as if they were not hers;ᶜ
  She has no fear that her
    labor may be in vain.
17 For God has deprived her of*
    wisdom
  And given her no share in
    understanding.
18 But when she rises up and
    flaps her wings,
  She laughs at the horse and
    at its rider.
19 Are you the one who gives
    the horse its strength?ᵈ
  Do you clothe its neck with
    a rustling mane?

20 Can you cause it to leap like
    a locust?
  Its majestic snorting is
    terrifying.ᵃ
21 It paws the ground in the
    valley and exults mightily;ᵇ
  It charges into the battle.*ᶜ
22 It laughs at fear and is afraid
    of nothing.ᵈ
  It does not turn back be-
    cause of the sword.
23 The quiver rattles against it,
  The spear and the javelin
    flash.
24 Trembling with excitement,
    it surges forward,*
  It cannot stand still at#
    the sound of the horn.
25 When the horn blows, it says,
    'Aha!'
  It smells the battle from afar
  And hears the shouting of
    commanders and the battle
    cry.ᵉ
26 Is it by your understanding
    that the falcon soars,
  Spreading its wings to
    the south?
27 Or is it at your order that
    an eagle flies upwardᶠ
  And builds its nest high up,ᵍ
28 Spending the night on a cliff,
  Dwelling in its stronghold
    on a rocky crag?*
29 From there it searches for
    food;ʰ
  Its eyes look far into the
    distance.
30 Its young sip up blood;
  And wherever the slain are,
    there it is."ⁱ

40 Jehovah continued to an-
    swer Job:

2 "Should a faultfinder con-
    tend with the Almighty?ʲ
  Let the one who wants to
    reprove God answer."ᵏ

CHAP. 39
a De 33:17

b Ps 104:17
  Zec 5:9

c La 4:3

d Ps 147:10
  Isa 31:1

Second Col.
a Jer 8:16

b Jg 5:22
  Ps 32:9

c Pr 21:31
  Jer 46:9
  Jer 47:3
  Hab 1:8

d Isa 5:28
  Jer 8:6

e Jer 46:4

f Pr 23:5
  Isa 40:31

g Jer 49:16
  Ob 4

h Job 9:26
  Jer 49:22

i Mt 24:28

CHAP. 40
j Job 33:12, 13
  Isa 45:9

k Job 13:3
  Job 23:3-5
  Job 31:35

39:9 *Or "manger." 39:10 *Or "harrow." 39:12 *Lit., "seed." 39:17 *Lit.,
"made her forget."

39:21 *Lit., "It goes out to meet armor."
39:24 *Lit., "swallows the ground
(earth)." #Or possibly, "It does not believe." 39:28 *Lit., "on the tooth of a
crag."

3 Job said in answer to Jehovah:

4 "Look! I am unworthy.[a]
What can I reply to you?
I put my hand over my mouth.[b]

5 I spoke once, but I will not answer again;
Twice, but I will say no more."

6 Then Jehovah answered Job out of the windstorm:[c]

7 "Brace yourself, please, like a man;
I will question you, and you inform me.[d]

8 Will you call into question* my justice?
Will you condemn me so that you may be right?[e]

9 Do you have an arm as powerful as the true God's,[f]
Or can your voice thunder like his?[g]

10 Adorn yourself, please, with glory and majesty;
Clothe yourself with dignity and splendor.

11 Release the fury of your anger;
Look at everyone who is haughty, and bring him low.

12 Look at everyone who is haughty, and humble him,
And tread down the wicked where they stand.

13 Hide them all in the dust;
Bind them* in the hidden place,

14 Then even I would acknowledge to you*
That your right hand can save you.

15 Here, now, is Be·he′moth,* which I made as I made you.

It eats grass like a bull.

16 Look at the strength in its hips
And the power in the muscles of its belly!

17 It stiffens its tail like a cedar;
The sinews of its thighs are woven together.

18 Its bones are tubes of copper;
Its limbs are like wrought-iron rods.

19 It ranks first* among the works of God;
Only its Maker can approach it with his sword.

20 For the mountains produce food for it,
Where all the wild animals play.

21 It lies down under the lotus trees,
In the shelter of the reeds of the marsh.

22 The lotus trees cast their shadow on it,
And the poplars of the valley* surround it.

23 If the river is turbulent, it does not panic.
It is confident, although the Jordan[a] rushes against its mouth.

24 Can anyone capture it while it is watching,
Or pierce its nose with a hook?*

41 "Can you catch Le·vi′a·than*[b] with a fishhook
Or hold down its tongue with a rope?

2 Can you put a rope* through its nostrils
Or pierce its jaws with a hook?#

3 Will it make many pleas to you,

CHAP. 40
a Job 42:5, 6

b Ps 39:9
Pr 30:32

c Job 38:1

d Job 38:3
Job 42:4

e Ps 51:4
Ro 3:4

f Ex 15:6
Ps 89:13
Isa 40:26
1Co 10:22

g Job 37:4
Ps 29:3

Second Col.
a Jos 3:15

CHAP. 41
b Ps 104:25, 26

40:8 *Or "invalidate." 40:13 *Lit., "their faces." 40:14 *Or "commend you." 40:15 *Possibly the hippopotamus.

40:19 *Lit., "It is the beginning." 40:22 *Or "wadi." 40:24 *Lit., "snare." 41:1 *Possibly the crocodile. 41:2 *Lit., "a rush." #Lit., "thorn."

Or will it speak gently to
you?

4 Will it make a covenant with
you,
So that you may make it your
slave for life?

5 Will you play with it as with
a bird
Or tie it on a leash for your
little girls?

6 Will traders barter for it?
Will they divide it up among
merchants?

7 Will you fill its hide with
harpoons[a]
Or its head with fishing
spears?

8 Lay your hand on it;
You will remember the battle
and never do it again!

9 Any hope of subduing it is
futile.
The mere sight of it would
overwhelm you.*

10 No one dares to stir it up.
So who is it who can stand
up to me?[b]

11 Who has given me anything
first that I should repay
him?[c]
Whatever is under the
heavens is mine.[d]

12 I will not be silent about
its limbs,
About its mightiness and
its well-formed body.

13 Who has removed its outer
covering?
Who will enter its open jaws?

14 Who can pry open the doors
of its mouth?*
Its teeth all around are
fearsome.

15 Its back has rows of scales*
Tightly sealed together.

16 Each one fits so closely
to the other

That no air can come
between them.

17 They are stuck to one
another;
They cling together and
cannot be separated.

18 Its snorting flashes out light,
And its eyes are like the rays
of dawn.

19 Flashes of lightning go out
of its mouth;
Fiery sparks escape.

20 Smoke pours out of its
nostrils,
Like a furnace fueled with
rushes.

21 Its breath sets coals ablaze,
And a flame shoots from its
mouth.

22 There is great strength in
its neck,
And dismay runs before it.

23 The folds of its flesh are
tightly joined together;
They are firm, as though cast
upon it and immovable.

24 Its heart is hard as stone,
Yes, hard as a lower
millstone.

25 When it rises up, even the
mighty are frightened;
Its thrashing causes
bewilderment.

26 No sword that reaches it
will prevail;
Nor will spear, dart,
or arrowhead.[a]

27 It regards iron as straw,
Copper as rotten wood.

28 An arrow does not make
it flee;
Slingstones turn into stubble
against it.

29 It regards a club as stubble,
And it laughs at the rattling
of a javelin.

30 Underneath, it is like sharp
fragments of pottery;
It spreads itself in the mud
like a threshing sledge.[b]

31 It makes the deep boil just
like a pot;

CHAP. 41
a Job 41:26

b 2Ch 20:6
Da 4:35
Ac 11:17
Ro 9:19

c Ro 11:35

d De 10:14
Ps 24:1
Ps 50:12
1Co 10:26

Second Col.
a Job 41:7

b Isa 41:15

41:9 *Or "hurl you down."   41:14 *Lit.,
"face."   41:15 *Or possibly, "Its pride is
its rows of scales."

It stirs up the sea like an ointment pot.
32 It leaves a glistening wake in its path.
One would think that the deep had white hair.
33 There is nothing like it on the earth,
A creature made to have no fear.
34 It glares at everything that is haughty.
It is king over all the majestic wild beasts."

42 Then Job said in reply to Jehovah:

2 "Now I know that you are able to do all things
And that nothing you have in mind to do is impossible for you.[a]

3 You said, 'Who is this who is obscuring my counsel without knowledge?'[b]
Therefore I spoke, but without understanding
About things too wonderful for me, which I do not know.[c]

4 You said, 'Please listen, and I will speak.
I will question you, and you inform me.'[d]

5 My ears have heard about you,
But now I do see you with my eyes.

6 That is why I take back what I said,*[e]
And I repent in dust and ashes."[f]

7 After Jehovah had spoken these words to Job, Jehovah said to El'i·phaz the Te'man·ite:

"My anger burns against you and your two companions,[g] for you have not spoken the truth about me[h] as my servant Job has. 8 Now take seven bulls and seven rams and go to my servant Job, and offer up a burnt

sacrifice for yourselves. And my servant Job will pray for you.[a] I will surely accept his request* not to deal with you according to your foolishness, for you have not spoken the truth about me as my servant Job has."

9 So El'i·phaz the Te'man·ite, Bil'dad the Shu'hite, and Zo'phar the Na'a·ma·thite went and did what Jehovah had told them to do. And Jehovah accepted Job's prayer.

10 After Job had prayed for his companions,[b] Jehovah removed Job's tribulation[c] and restored his prosperity.* Jehovah gave him double what he had before.[d] 11 All his brothers and sisters and all his former friends[e] came to him and ate a meal with him in his house. They sympathized with him and comforted him over all the calamity that Jehovah had allowed to come upon him. Each of them gave him a piece of money and a gold ring.

12 So Jehovah blessed the last part of Job's life more than the beginning,[f] and Job came to have 14,000 sheep, 6,000 camels, 1,000 pairs of cattle, and 1,000 female donkeys.[g] 13 He also came to have seven more sons and three more daughters.[h] 14 He named the first daughter Je·mi'mah, the second Ke·zi'ah, and the third Ker'en-hap'puch. 15 No women in all the land were as beautiful as Job's daughters, and their father gave them an inheritance along with their brothers.

16 After this Job lived for 140 years, and he saw his children and his grandchildren—four generations. 17 Finally Job died, after a long and satisfying life.*

CHAP. 42
a Ge 18:14
Ps 135:6
Isa 43:13
Isa 55:10, 11
Jer 32:17
Mr 10:27
Lu 18:27

b Job 38:2

c Ps 40:5
Ps 139:6

d Job 38:3
Job 40:7

e Job 40:4

f Ezr 9:6
Ps 51:17

g Job 2:11

h Job 11:6
Job 15:14, 15
Job 22:2, 3

Second Col.
a Ge 20:17
Jas 5:15

b Mt 6:14

c Job 2:6, 7
Jas 5:11

d Ge 32:10
1Sa 2:7
2Ch 25:9
Pr 22:4
Isa 61:7

e Job 19:13

f Pr 3:33
Pr 10:22
Heb 11:6
Jas 5:11

g Job 1:3

h Job 1:1, 2

42:6 *Or "make a retraction."

42:8 *Lit., "Surely I will lift up his face." 42:10 *Lit., "Jehovah turned back the captivity of Job." 42:17 *Lit., "old and full of days."

PSALMS

OUTLINE OF CONTENTS

BOOK ONE
(Psalms 1-41)

1 Happy is the man who does
  not walk according to the
advice of the wicked
And does not stand on the
  path of sinners[a]
And does not sit in the seat
  of scoffers.[b]
2 But his delight is in the law
  of Jehovah,[c]
And he reads His law in an
  undertone* day and night.[d]
3 He will be like a tree planted
  by streams of water,
A tree that produces fruit in
  its season,
The foliage of which does
  not wither.
And everything he does will
  succeed.[e]
4 The wicked are not like that;

They are like the chaff that
  the wind blows away.
5 That is why the wicked will
  not remain standing in the
  judgment;[a]
Nor will sinners remain
  standing in the assembly
  of the righteous.[b]
6 For Jehovah is aware of the
  way of the righteous,[c]
But the way of the wicked
  will perish.[d]

2 Why are the nations agitated
  And the peoples muttering*
  an empty thing?[e]
2 The kings of the earth take
  their stand
And high officials gather
  together* as one[f]

CHAP. 1
a Pr 4:14
b Pr 22:10
c Ps 19:7
  Ps 40:8
  Ps 112:1
  Mt 5:3
  Ro 7:22
  Jas 1:25
d Jos 1:8
  Ps 119:97
  1Ti 4:15
e 1Ch 22:13
  Jer 17:7, 8

Second Col.
a Mt 25:41
b Mal 3:18
  Mt 13:49, 50
c Ps 37:18
  Jer 12:3
  1Pe 3:12
d Pr 14:12

CHAP. 2
a Ac 4:25-28
f Mt 27:1, 2
  Lu 23:10, 11
  Re 19:19

1:2 *Or "he meditates on His law."

2:1 *Or "meditating on." 2:2 *Or "take counsel together."

Against Jehovah and against
his anointed one.*a

3 They say: "Let us tear off
their shackles
And throw off their ropes!"

4 The One enthroned in the
heavens will laugh;
Jehovah will scoff at them.

5 At that time he will speak to
them in his anger
And terrify them in his burning anger,

6 Saying: "I myself have installed my king b
On Zion,c my holy mountain."

7 Let me proclaim the decree
of Jehovah;
He said to me: "You are my
son;d
Today I have become your
father.e

8 Ask of me, and I will give nations as your inheritance
And the ends of the earth as
your possession.f

9 You will break them with an
iron scepter,g
And you will smash them
like a piece of pottery."h

10 So now, you kings, show
insight;
Accept correction,* you
judges of the earth.

11 Serve Jehovah with fear,
And rejoice with trembling.

12 Honor* the son,i or God# will
become indignant
And you will perish from the
way,j
For His anger flares up
quickly.
Happy are all those taking
refuge in Him.

A melody of David when he was fleeing
from his son Ab′sa·lom.k

3 O Jehovah, why have
my adversaries become
so numerous?l

Why are so many rising up
against me?a

2 Many are saying about me:*
"God will not save him."b
(Selah)#

3 But you, O Jehovah, are a
shield around me,c
My glory d and the One who
lifts up my head.e

4 I will call aloud to Jehovah,
And he will answer me from
his holy mountain.f (Selah)

5 I will lie down and sleep;
And I will wake up in safety,
For Jehovah continues to
support me.g

6 I am not afraid of the tens
of thousands
Lined up against me on every
side.h

7 Rise up, O Jehovah! Save
me,i O my God!
For you will strike all my
enemies on the jaw;
You will break the teeth
of the wicked.j

8 Salvation belongs to
Jehovah.k
Your blessing is upon your
people. (Selah)

To the director; to be accompanied
with stringed instruments.
A melody of David.

4 When I call, answer me,
O my righteous God.l
Make a way of escape* for
me in my distress.
Show me favor and hear my
prayer.

2 You sons of men, how long
will you turn my honor into
humiliation?
How long will you love what
is worthless and search for
what is false? (Selah)

3 Know that Jehovah will treat
his loyal one in a special
way;*

CHAP. 2
a Ps 89:20
  Isa 61:1

b Ps 45:6
  Eze 21:27
  Da 7:13, 14
  Re 19:16

c 2Sa 5:7
  Re 14:1

d Mt 3:16, 17
  Mr 1:9-11
  Ro 1:4

e Ac 13:33
  Heb 1:5
  Heb 5:5

f Ps 72:8
  Heb 1:2
  Re 11:15

g Re 12:5
  Re 19:15

h Da 2:44
  Re 2:26, 27

i Php 2:9-11

j Joh 3:36

CHAP. 3
k 2Sa 15:14

l 2Sa 15:12
  2Sa 16:15

Second Col.
a 2Sa 12:11

b 2Sa 16:7, 8

c Ge 15:1

d Isa 45:25

e Ps 27:6

f 2Sa 15:25
  Ps 2:6

g Ps 4:8
  Pr 3:24

h 2Ki 6:15, 16
  Ps 27:3
  Ro 8:31

i 1Ti 4:10

j 2Th 1:6

k Ps 37:39
  Isa 43:11
  Re 19:1

CHAP. 4
l Ps 11:7

2:2 *Or "his Christ." 2:10 *Or "Be
warned." 2:12 *Lit., "Kiss." #Lit.,
"he."

3:2 *Or "my soul." #See Glossary.
4:1 *Lit., "Make broad space." 4:3 *Or
"distinguish his loyal one; set his loyal
one apart for himself."

Jehovah will hear when I call
to him.

4 Be agitated, but do not sin.[a]
Have your say in your heart,
upon your bed, and keep
silent. (*Selah*)

5 Offer the sacrifices of righteousness,
And trust in Jehovah.[b]

6 There are many saying:
"Who will show us any-
thing good?"
Let the light of your face
shine upon us, O Jehovah.[c]

7 You have filled my heart with
greater rejoicing
Than those who have an
abundant harvest of grain
and new wine.

8 I will lie down and sleep in
peace,[d]
For you alone, O Jehovah,
make me dwell in security.[e]

To the director for Neʹhiʹloth.*
A melody of David.

5 Listen to my words,
O Jehovah;[f]
Be attentive to my sighing.

2 Pay attention to my cry for
help,
O my King and my God,
because to you I pray.

3 O Jehovah, you will hear my
voice in the morning;[g]
In the morning I will express
my concern to you[h] and
wait expectantly.

4 For you are not a God who
takes pleasure in wicked-
ness;[i]
No one bad may remain with
you.[j]

5 No arrogant person may
stand in your presence.
You hate all those who
behave wickedly;[k]

6 You will destroy those who
speak lies.[l]
Jehovah detests violent and
deceptive people.*[m]

7 But I will come into your
house[a] because of your
great loyal love;[b]
I will bow down before your
holy temple* in reverential
fear of you.[c]

8 Lead me, O Jehovah, in your
righteousness because of
my foes;
Make your way clear for me.[d]

9 For nothing they say can be
trusted;
Within them is nothing but
malice;
Their throat is an open
grave;
They flatter with their
tongue.*[e]

10 But God will declare them
guilty;
Their own schemes will
cause their downfall.[f]
May they be driven away
because of their many
transgressions,
For they have rebelled
against you.

11 But all those who take refuge
in you will rejoice;[g]
They will always shout
joyfully.
You will block approach to
them,
And those loving your name
will rejoice in you.

12 For you will bless anyone
righteous, O Jehovah;
You will surround them with
approval as with a large
shield.[h]

To the director; to be accompanied
with stringed instruments tuned to
Shemʹiʹnith.* A melody of David.

6 O Jehovah, do not reprove
me in your anger,
And do not correct me in
your rage.[i]

2 Show me favor,* O Jehovah,
for I am growing weak.

CHAP. 4
a Eph 4:26

b Ps 37:3
Ps 62:8
Pr 3:5
1Pe 4:19

c Nu 6:26
Ps 80:7
Pr 16:15
1Pe 3:12

d Ps 3:5
Pr 3:24, 26

e Le 25:18

CHAP. 5
f Ps 65:2
1Pe 3:12

g Ps 55:16, 17

h Mr 1:35

i Ps 89:14
Pr 6:16-19
Hab 1:13

j Ps 15:1-5
Pr 12:19

k Ro 12:9
Heb 1:9

l Pr 20:19
Joh 8:44
Col 3:9
Re 21:8

m Ge 9:6
Ps 55:23
Pr 6:16, 17
1Pe 3:10

Second Col.
a 1Sa 3:3
1Ch 16:1

b Ps 69:13

c Ps 28:2
Ps 138:2

d Ps 25:4, 5
Ps 27:11

e Pr 29:5
Ro 3:13

f 2Sa 15:31
2Sa 17:23
Ps 7:14, 15

g Ps 40:16

h Ge 15:1
Ps 3:3

CHAP. 6
i Ps 38:1
Jer 10:24

5:Sup; 6:Sup *See Glossary. 5:6 *Or
"a man of bloodshed and deception."

5:7 *Or "sanctuary." 5:9 *Or "They
use a smooth tongue." 6:2 *Or "mercy."

Heal me, O Jehovah,[a] for my
bones are shaking.
3 Yes, I am* greatly disturbed,[b]
And I ask you, O Jehovah
—how long will it be?[c]
4 Return, O Jehovah, and
rescue me;*[d]
Save me for the sake of your
loyal love.[e]
5 For in death there is no
mention* of you;
In the Grave,# who will praise
you?[f]
6 I have grown weary with my
sighing;[g]
All night long I soak my bed
with tears;*
I flood my couch with weeping.[h]
7 My eye is weak from my
grief;[i]
It has dimmed* because of
all those harassing me.
8 Get away from me, all you
who behave wickedly,
For Jehovah will hear the
sound of my weeping.[j]
9 Jehovah will hear my request for favor;[k]
Jehovah will accept my
prayer.
10 All my enemies will be put
to shame and dismayed;
They will fall back in sudden
disgrace.[l]

A dirge* of David that he sang to
Jehovah regarding the words
of Cush the Ben·ja·min·ite.

7 O Jehovah my God, in you
I have taken refuge.[m]
Save me from all those
persecuting me and
rescue me.[n]
2 Otherwise they will tear me*
to pieces as a lion does,[o]
Carrying me off with no one
to rescue me.

3 O Jehovah my God, if I am
at fault in this,
If I have acted unjustly,
4 If I have wronged the one
doing good to me,[a]
Or if I have plundered my
enemy without cause,*
5 Then let an enemy pursue
and overtake me;*
Let him trample my life down
to the earth
And cause my glory to perish
in the dust. (Selah)
6 Rise up in your anger,
O Jehovah;
Stand up against the fury
of my enemies;[b]
Awake for me, and demand
that justice be done.[c]
7 Let the nations surround
you;
And you will act against
them from on high.
8 Jehovah will pass sentence
on the peoples.[d]
Judge me, O Jehovah,
according to my righteousness
And according to my
integrity.[e]
9 Please put an end to the evil
deeds of the wicked.
But establish the righteous,[f]
Since you are the righteous
God[g] who examines the
hearts[h] and the deepest
emotions.*[i]
10 God is my shield,[j] the Savior
of those upright in heart.[k]
11 God is a righteous Judge,[l]
And God proclaims his judgments* every day.
12 If anyone will not repent,[m]
He sharpens his sword;[n]
He bends his bow and makes
it ready.[o]
13 He prepares his deadly
weapons;

CHAP. 6

a Ps 41:4
b Ps 103:2, 3
b Mt 26:38, 39
c Ps 13:1, 2
d Ps 50:15
e Ps 119:88
  La 3:22
f Ps 30:9
  Ps 115:17
  Ec 9:5, 10
g Ps 69:3
h Ps 39:12
i Ps 31:9
j Ps 3:4
  Ps 145:18, 19
  Heb 5:7
k Ps 31:22
  Ps 40:1
  Jon 2:2
l Ps 40:14
  Jer 20:11

CHAP. 7

m Ps 18:2
  Pr 18:10
n Jer 15:15
  2Co 4:9
  2Pe 2:9
o Ps 10:9

Second Col.

a Pr 17:13
b Ps 3:7
  Ps 35:1
c Ps 103:6
d Ge 18:25
  Ps 9:7, 8
e Ps 18:20
  Ps 26:11
  Ps 41:12
f Ps 37:25
g De 32:4
  Re 15:3
h 1Sa 16:7
i 1Ch 28:9
  Jer 17:10
  Re 2:23
j Ge 15:1
  Pr 30:5
k Pr 2:21
l Ge 18:25
  Ps 9:4
  Ps 98:9
m Isa 55:7
n De 32:41
o De 32:21, 23

6:3 *Or "my soul is." 6:4; 7:2, 5 *Or
"my soul." 6:5 *Or "remembrance."
#Or "Sheol," that is, the common grave
of mankind. See Glossary. 6:6 *Lit.,
"make my bed swim." 6:7 *Or "grown
old." 7:Sup *Or "song of mourning."

7:4 *Or possibly, "While I spared the
one opposing me without cause." 7:9
*Or "tests the hearts and the kidneys."
7:11 *Or "hurls denunciations."

He makes ready his flaming arrows.[a]

14 Look at the one who is pregnant with wickedness;
He conceives trouble and gives birth to lies.[b]

15 He excavates a pit and digs it deep,
But he falls into the very hole he made.[c]

16 The trouble he causes will return on his own head;[d]
His violence will fall on the crown of his head.

17 I will praise Jehovah for his justice;[e]
I will sing praises* to the name of Jehovah[f] the Most High.[g]

To the director; upon the Git′tith.*
A melody of David.

8 O Jehovah our Lord, how majestic your name is throughout the earth;
You have set your splendor even higher than the heavens!*[h]

2 Out of the mouth of children and infants[i] you have established strength
On account of your adversaries,
To silence the enemy and the avenger.

3 When I see your heavens, the works of your fingers,
The moon and the stars that you have prepared,[j]

4 What is mortal man that you keep him in mind,
And a son of man that you take care of him?[k]

5 You made him a little lower than godlike ones,*
And you crowned him with glory and splendor.

6 You gave him dominion over the works of your hands;[i]

You have put everything under his feet:

7 All the flocks and cattle,
As well as the wild animals,*[a]

8 The birds of the heavens and the fish of the sea,
Whatever passes through the paths of the seas.

9 O Jehovah our Lord, how majestic your name is throughout the earth!

To the director; upon Muth-lab′ben.*
A melody of David.

א [Aleph]

9 I will praise you, O Jehovah, with all my heart;
I will tell about all your wonderful works.[b]

2 I will rejoice and exult in you;
I will sing praises* to your name, O Most High.[c]

ב [Beth]

3 When my enemies retreat,[d]
They will stumble and perish from before you.

4 For you defend my just cause;
You sit on your throne judging with righteousness.[e]

ג [Gimel]

5 You have rebuked nations[f] and destroyed the wicked,
Blotting out their name forever and ever.

6 The enemy has been ruined forever;
You uprooted their cities,
And all memory of them will perish.[g]

ה [He]

7 But Jehovah is enthroned forever;[h]
He has firmly established his throne for justice.[i]

8 He will judge the inhabited earth* in righteousness;[j]
He will render righteous legal decisions for the nations.[k]

CHAP. 7
a De 32:42
b Jas 1:15
c Es 7:10
  Ps 10:2
  Ps 35:7, 8
  Ps 57:6
  Pr 26:27
d Es 9:24, 25
e Ps 35:28
f Isa 25:1
  Heb 13:15
  Re 15:4
g Da 4:17

CHAP. 8
h 1Ki 8:27
  Ps 104:1
  Ps 148:13
i Mt 21:16
  Lu 10:21
  1Co 1:27
j Ps 19:1
  Ps 104:19
  Isa 40:26
  Ro 1:20
k Ge 1:29
  Ge 9:3
  Ps 144:3
  Mt 6:25, 30
  Joh 3:16
  Ac 14:17
  Heb 2:6-8
l Ge 1:26
  Ge 9:1, 2

Second Col.
a Ge 1:28
  Ge 9:3

CHAP. 9
b 1Ch 16:12
  1Ch 29:11
  Re 4:11
c Ps 28:7
d Ps 56:9
e Ps 89:14
  1Pe 2:24
f De 9:4
g De 25:19
h Ps 90:2
i Ro 14:10
  Re 20:11
j Ge 18:25
  Ps 85:11
  Isa 26:9
k Ps 96:13
  Ps 98:9
  Ac 17:31

7:17; 9:2 *Or "make music." 8:Sup; 9:Sup *See Glossary. 8:1 *Or possibly, "You whose splendor is recounted above the heavens!" 8:5 *Or "than angels."

8:7 *Lit., "the beasts of the field." 9:8 *Or "the productive land."

ו [Waw]

9 Jehovah will become a
   secure refuge* for the
   oppressed,[a]
   A secure refuge in times
   of distress.[b]

10 Those knowing your name
   will trust in you;[c]
   You will never abandon those
   seeking you, O Jehovah.[d]

ז [Zayin]

11 Sing praises to Jehovah,
   who is dwelling in Zion;
   Make his deeds known
   among the peoples.[e]

12 For the One who avenges
   their blood remembers
   them;[f]
   He will not forget the cry
   of the afflicted.[g]

ח [Heth]

13 Show me favor, O Jehovah;
   see my affliction by those
   hating me,
   You who raise me from the
   gates of death,[h]

14 So that I may declare your
   praiseworthy deeds in
   the gates of the daughter
   of Zion,[i]
   And rejoice in your acts
   of salvation.[j]

ט [Teth]

15 The nations have sunk down
   into the pit they made;
   Their own foot has been
   caught in the net they hid.[k]

16 Jehovah is known by the
   judgment he executes.[l]
   The wicked one has been
   ensnared in the work of
   his own hands.[m]
   Hig·ga′ion.* (Selah)

י [Yod]

17 The wicked will retreat
   toward the Grave,*
   All the nations who forget
   God.

18 But the poor will not always
   be forgotten;[a]
   Nor will the hope of the meek
   ever perish.[b]

כ [Kaph]

19 Rise up, O Jehovah! Do not
   let mortal man prevail.
   May the nations be judged
   in your presence.[c]

20 Strike them with fear,
   O Jehovah,[d]
   Let the nations know that
   they are only mortal men.
   (Selah)

ל [Lamed]

10 Why, O Jehovah, do you
   stand at a distance?
   Why do you hide yourself
   in times of distress?[e]

2 The wicked one arrogantly
   pursues the helpless one,[f]
   But he will be caught in the
   schemes he devises.[g]

3 For the wicked one boasts
   about his selfish desires*[h]
   And blesses the greedy one;#

נ [Nun]

   He disrespects Jehovah.

4 In his haughtiness, the wicked man makes no investigation;
   All his thoughts are: "There
   is no God."[i]

5 His ways keep prospering,[j]
   But your judgments are beyond his understanding;[k]
   He scoffs* at all his adversaries.

6 He says in his heart: "I will
   never be shaken;*
   For generation after generation
   I will never see calamity."[l]

פ [Pe]

7 His mouth is full of curses,
   lies, and threats;[m]
   Under his tongue are trouble
   and injury.[n]

CHAP. 9

a Ps 91:2
b Ps 46:1
  Ps 54:7
c Ps 91:14
  Pr 18:10
  Jer 16:21
d 2Ch 20:12
  Ps 25:15
  2Co 1:10
e Ps 96:10
  Ps 107:19, 22
  Isa 12:3, 4
f Ge 4:9, 10
  Ge 9:5
  De 32:43
  2Ki 9:24, 26
  2Ki 24:3, 4
  Lu 11:49-51
g Ex 3:7
  Ps 72:13, 14
  Lu 18:7
h Ps 30:3
  Isa 38:9, 10
  Re 1:17, 18
i Jer 17:19, 20
j Ps 13:5
  Ps 20:5
k De 32:35
  Pr 5:22
l Ex 14:4
  Jos 2:10
  2Ki 19:19
m Pr 26:27
  Isa 3:11

Second Col.

a Ps 12:5
  Ps 72:4
b Ps 10:17
  Mt 5:5
c Ge 18:25
  Ps 82:8
d Ex 15:16
  Ex 23:27

CHAP. 10

e Ps 13:1
  Ps 22:1
  Jer 14:8
f Ex 14:17
g Ps 7:14, 16
  Ps 37:7
  Pr 5:22
  Pr 26:27
h Ex 15:9
  Ho 12:8
i Ps 14:1, 2
  Ps 53:1
  Zep 1:12
j Ps 37:35
k Isa 26:11
  Ho 14:9
l Pr 14:16
  Ec 8:11
m Ro 3:14
n Ps 7:14
  Ps 12:2
  Ps 55:21

9:9 *Or "secure height." **9:16** *See
Glossary. **9:17** *Or "Sheol," that is, the
common grave of mankind. See Glossary.

10:3 *Or "the desire of his soul." #Or
possibly, "The greedy one blesses himself." **10:5** *Or "puffs." **10:6** *Or "will
never stagger (totter)."

8 He waits in ambush near the settlements;

From his hiding place he kills an innocent one.[a]

ע [Ayin]

His eyes are watching for an unfortunate victim.[b]

9 He waits in his hiding place like a lion in its lair.*[c]

He waits to seize the helpless one.

He seizes the helpless one when he pulls his net shut.[d]

10 The victim is crushed and brought down;

The unfortunate ones fall into his clutches.*

11 He says in his heart: "God has forgotten.[e]

He has turned away his face. He never notices."[f]

ק [Qoph]

12 Rise up, O Jehovah.[g] O God, lift up your hand.[h]

Do not forget the helpless ones.[i]

13 Why has the wicked one disrespected God?

He says in his heart: "You will not hold me accountable."

ר [Resh]

14 But you do see trouble and distress.

You look on and take matters in hand;[j]

To you the unfortunate victim turns;[k]

You are the helper for the fatherless child.*[l]

ש [Shin]

15 Break the arm of the wicked and evil man,[m]

So that when you search for his wickedness,

You will find it no more.

16 Jehovah is King forever and ever.[n]

The nations have perished from the earth.[a]

ת [Taw]

17 But you will hear the request of the meek, O Jehovah.[b]

You will make their hearts firm[c] and pay close attention to them.[d]

18 You will render justice to the fatherless and to those who are crushed,[e]

So that mortal man of the earth may no longer make them afraid.[f]

To the director. Of David.

11 In Jehovah I have taken refuge.[g]

So how can you say to me:*

"Flee like a bird to your mountain!

2 See how the wicked bend the bow;

They set their arrow on the bowstring,

To shoot from the darkness those upright in heart.

3 When the foundations* are torn down,

What can the righteous do?"

4 Jehovah is in his holy temple.[h]

Jehovah's throne is in the heavens.

His own eyes see, his watchful* eyes examine the sons of men.[i]

5 Jehovah examines the righteous one as well as the wicked one;[k]

He* hates anyone who loves violence.[l]

6 Upon the wicked, he will rain down snares;*

Fire and sulfur[m] and a scorching wind will be the portion of their cup.

CHAP. 10

a Pr 1:10, 11
b Ps 17:9, 11
c Job 38:39, 40
  Ps 17:12
  Ps 59:3
d Ps 140:5
  Jer 5:26
e Ec 8:11
f Ps 73:3, 11
  Ps 94:3, 7
  Eze 8:12
  Eze 9:9
g Ps 3:7
h Mic 5:9
i Ps 9:12
  Ps 35:10
j 2Ki 9:26
  2Ch 6:23
k 1Pe 4:19
l De 10:17, 18
  Ps 146:9
  Heb 13:6
m Job 38:15
n Ex 15:18
  Ps 145:13
  Jer 10:10
  Da 4:34
  1Ti 1:17

Second Col.

a Ps 9:5
  Ps 44:2
b Ps 9:18
c 1Ch 29:18, 19
d Pr 15:8
  1Pe 3:12
e Ps 72:4
f Isa 51:12

CHAP. 11

g 2Ch 14:11
  Ps 7:1
  Ps 56:11
h Mic 1:2
  Hab 2:20
i 2Ch 20:6
  Ps 103:19
  Re 4:2, 3
j 2Ch 16:9
  Pr 15:3
  Zec 4:10
  Heb 4:13
k Ge 6:5
  Ge 7:1
l Pr 3:31
  Pr 6:16, 17
m Ge 19:24
  Eze 38:22

10:9 *Or "thicket." **10:10** *Or "strong claws." **10:14** *Or "the orphan."

11:1 *Or "my soul." **11:3** *Or "the foundations of justice." **11:4** *Or "beaming." **11:5** *Or "His soul; His very being." **11:6** *Or possibly, "burning coals."

7 For Jehovah is righteous;[a]
 he loves righteous acts.[b]
The upright will see his
 face.*[c]

To the director; tuned to Shem′i·nith.*
 A melody of David.

12 Save me, O Jehovah, for
 the loyal one is no more;
Faithful people have van-
 ished from among men.

2 They speak lies to one another;
They flatter with their lips*
 and speak with deceitful
 hearts.#[d]

3 Jehovah will cut off all flattering lips
And the tongue that makes
 great boasts,[e]

4 Those who say: "We will pre-
 vail with our tongues.
We use our lips as we please;
 Who will be our master?"[f]

5 "Because the afflicted are
 oppressed,
Because of the sighing of the
 poor,[g]
I will rise up to act," says
 Jehovah.
"I will save them from those
 who treat them with con-
 tempt."*

6 The sayings of Jehovah are
 pure;[h]
They are like silver refined
 in an earthen furnace,*
 purified seven times.

7 You will guard them,
 O Jehovah;[i]
You will protect each one of
 them from this generation
 forever.

8 The wicked walk around unrestrained
Because the sons of men
 promote depravity.[j]

11:7 *Or "experience his favor." 12:Sup
*See Glossary. 12:2 *Lit., "speak with
a smooth lip." #Lit., "with a heart and a
heart." 12:5 *Or "puff at them." 12:6
*Or possibly, "a smelting furnace set on
the ground."

CHAP. 11
a De 32:4

b Ps 146:8

c Job 36:7
 Ps 34:15
 1Pe 3:12

CHAP. 12
d Ps 28:3

e Ex 15:9, 10
 1Sa 2:3
 Eze 28:2

f Ps 10:5

g Ex 3:7

h 2Sa 22:31
 Ps 19:8

i 1Sa 2:9

j Ec 8:11

Second Col.

CHAP. 13
a Job 13:24
 Ps 6:3
 Ps 22:2

b Ps 22:7, 8

c Ps 25:2
 Ps 35:19

d Ps 52:8
 Ps 147:11
 1Pe 5:6, 7

e 1Sa 2:1

f Ps 116:7
 Ps 119:17

CHAP. 14
g Ps 10:4
 Isa 29:16

h Ps 53
 Ro 3:10-12

i 2Ch 16:9
 Ps 33:13-15
 Heb 11:6

j Ec 7:29

To the director. A melody of David.

13 How long, O Jehovah, will
 you forget me? Forever?
How long will you hide your
 face from me?[a]

2 How long will I* have anxious
 concern,
With grief in my heart each
 day?
How long will my enemy
 triumph over me?[b]

3 Look upon me and answer
 me, O Jehovah my God.
Give light to my eyes, so that
 I may not fall asleep in
 death,

4 So that my enemy will not
 say: "I have defeated him!"
Do not let my opponents rejoice over my downfall.[c]

5 As for me, I trust in your
 loyal love;[d]
My heart will rejoice in your
 acts of salvation.[e]

6 I will sing to Jehovah, for he
 has richly rewarded me.*[f]

To the director. Of David.

14 The foolish* one says in
 his heart:
"There is no Jehovah."[g]
Their actions are corrupt,
 and their dealings are detestable;
No one is doing good.[h]

2 But Jehovah looks
 down from heaven on the
 sons of men
To see whether anyone has
 insight, whether anyone
 is seeking Jehovah.[i]

3 They have all turned aside;[j]
They are all alike corrupt.
No one is doing good,
Not even one.

4 Do none of the wrongdoers
 understand?
They devour my people as if
 they were eating bread.
They do not call on Jehovah.

13:2 *Or "my soul." 13:6 *Or "he has
dealt rewardingly with me." 14:1 *Or
"senseless."

5 But they will be filled with great terror,[a]

For Jehovah is with the generation of the righteous.

6 You wrongdoers try to frustrate the plans of the lowly one,

But Jehovah is his refuge.[b]

7 O that Israel's salvation may come from Zion![c]

When Jehovah gathers back his captive people,

Let Jacob be joyful, let Israel rejoice.

A melody of David.

15 O Jehovah, who may be a guest in your tent?

Who may reside in your holy mountain?[d]

2 The one who is walking faultlessly,*[e]

Practicing what is right[f]

And speaking the truth in his heart.[g]

3 He does not slander with his tongue,[h]

He does nothing bad to his neighbor,[i]

And he does not defame* his friends.[j]

4 He rejects anyone who is contemptible,[k]

But he honors those fearing Jehovah.

He does not go back on his promise,* even when it is bad for him.[l]

5 He does not lend his money on interest,[m]

And he does not accept a bribe against the innocent.[n]

Whoever does these things will never be shaken.*[o]

A mik'tam of David.*

16 Protect me, O God, for I have taken refuge in you.[p]

15:2 *Or "with integrity." **15:3** *Or "shame." **15:4** *Lit., "oath." **15:5; 16:8** *Or "will never stagger (totter)." **16:Sup** *See Glossary.

CHAP. 14

a Ex 15:16
b Ps 9:9
   Ps 142:5
c Ro 11:26, 27

CHAP. 15

d Ps 2:6
   Ps 24:3, 4
e Ps 1:1
f Isa 33:15, 16
   Ac 10:34, 35
g Pr 3:32
   Eph 4:25
h Le 19:16
   Ps 101:5
   Pr 20:19
i Pr 14:21
   Ro 12:17
j Ex 23:1
k Es 3:2
l Jos 9:18-20
   Jg 11:34, 35
   Ps 50:14
   Mt 5:33
m Ex 22:25
n Ex 23:8
o Ps 16:7, 8
   Pr 12:3
   2Pe 1:10

CHAP. 16

p Ps 25:20

Second Col.

a Ps 119:63
b De 8:19
   Ps 97:7
   Jon 2:8
c Ex 23:13
   Jos 23:6, 7
d Ps 73:26
e Ps 23:5
f Ps 78:55
g Isa 48:17
h Ps 17:3
   Ps 26:2
i Ps 139:17, 18
j Ps 73:23
   Ac 2:25-28
k Ps 49:15
   Ac 2:31
   Ac 3:15
   Re 1:17, 18
l Job 14:13, 14
   Ac 13:34-37
m Pr 12:28
n Ps 21:6
   Mt 5:8

---

2 I have said to Jehovah: "You are Jehovah, my Source of goodness.

3 And the holy ones in the earth,

The majestic ones, bring me great delight."[a]

4 Those who pursue other gods multiply their sorrows.[b]

I will never pour out their drink offerings of blood,

Nor will my lips mention their names.[c]

5 Jehovah is my portion, my allotted share,[d] and my cup.[e]

You safeguard my inheritance.

6 Pleasant places have been measured out to me.

Yes, I am content with my inheritance.[f]

7 I will praise Jehovah, who has given me advice.[g]

Even during the night, my innermost thoughts* correct me.[h]

8 I keep Jehovah before me constantly.[i]

Because he is at my right hand, I will never be shaken.*[i]

9 So my heart rejoices, my whole being* is joyful.

And I reside* in security.

10 For you will not leave me in* the Grave.*[k]

You will not allow your loyal one to see the pit.^[l]

11 You make known to me the path of life.[m]

In your presence* is abundant joy;[n]

16:7 *Or "my deepest emotions." Lit., "my kidneys." **16:9** *Lit., "my glory." #Or "my flesh resides." **16:10** *Or "abandon my soul to." #Or "Sheol," that is, the common grave of mankind. See Glossary. ^Or possibly, "to see corruption." **16:11** *Lit., "With your face."

There is happiness* at your right hand forever.

A prayer of David.

17 Hear my plea for justice, O Jehovah;

Pay attention to my cry for help;

Listen to my prayer spoken without deceit.[a]

2 May you make a just decision in my behalf;[b]

May your eyes see what is right.

3 You have examined my heart, you have inspected me by night;[c]

You have refined me,[d]

You will find that I have not schemed anything bad,

And my mouth has not transgressed.

4 As for the activities of men, In accord with the word of your lips, I avoid the paths of the robber.[e]

5 Let my steps stay on your tracks

So that my feet will not stumble.[f]

6 I do call on you, because you will answer me,[g] O God.

Incline your ear* to me. Hear my words.[h]

7 Show your loyal love in a wonderful way,[i]

O Savior of those seeking refuge at your right hand

From those who rebel against you.

8 Guard me like the pupil of your eye;[j]

Conceal me in the shadow of your wings.[k]

9 Guard me from the wicked who attack me,

From my mortal enemies* who surround me.[l]

10 They have become insensitive;*

With their mouth they speak arrogantly;

11 Now they hem us in;[a]

They watch for the chance to cause our downfall.*

12 He is like a lion eager to tear its prey to pieces,

Like a young lion crouching in ambush.

13 Rise up, O Jehovah, to confront him[b] and bring him down;

Rescue me* from the wicked with your sword;

14 Rescue me with your hand, O Jehovah,

From men of this world,* whose share is in this life,[c]

Those whom you fill with the good things you provide[d]

And who leave an inheritance to their many sons.

15 But as for me, in righteousness I will see your face;

I am satisfied to awaken in your presence.*[e]

To the director. By Jehovah's servant David, who addressed the words of this song to Jehovah in the day that Jehovah rescued him from the hand of all his enemies and from the hand of Saul. He said:[f]

18 I have affection for you, O Jehovah, my strength.[g]

2 Jehovah is my crag and my stronghold and the One who rescues me.[h]

My God is my rock,[i] in whom I take refuge,

My shield and my horn* of salvation,* my secure refuge.[Δj]

CHAP. 17
a Ps 145:18

b Ps 37:5, 6

c Ps 11:5
Ps 16:7
1Co 4:4

d Ps 26:2
Mal 3:3
1Pe 1:6, 7

e Ps 119:9

f Ps 18:36
Ps 94:18
Ps 119:133
Ps 121:3

g Ps 55:16

h Isa 37:17

i Ps 31:21
La 3:22

j De 32:9, 10
Zec 2:8

k Ru 2:12
Ps 36:7
Ps 57:1

l 1Sa 24:11
Ps 35:4

Second Col.
a 1Sa 23:26

b Ps 7:6

c Ps 73:12

d Mt 5:45

e Ps 65:4

CHAP. 18
f 2Sa 22:1

g Ps 18:32
Isa 12:2

h Ps 3:3
Ps 37:39, 40
Ps 40:17

i De 32:4

j Ge 15:1
2Sa 22:2-4

17:10 *Or "They are enclosed in their own fat." 17:11 *Or "throw us down to the ground." 17:13 *Or "my soul." 17:14 *Or "system of things." 17:15 *Or "to see your form." 18:2 *See Glossary. #Or "my powerful savior." ΔOr "secure height."

16:11 *Or "pleasantness." 17:6 *Or "Bend down and listen." 17:9 *Or "my enemies against the soul."

3 I call on Jehovah, who is worthy of praise,
   And I will be saved from my
   enemies.[a]
4 The ropes of death encircled me;[b]
   Flash floods of worthless
   men terrified me.[c]
5 The ropes of the Grave*
   surrounded me;
   The snares of death confronted me.[d]
6 In my distress I called on
   Jehovah,
   To my God I kept crying for
   help.
   From his temple he heard my
   voice,[e]
   And my cry to him for help
   reached his ears.[f]
7 Then the earth began to
   shake and rock;[g]
   The foundations of the
   mountains trembled
   And shook back and forth
   because he had been
   angered.[h]
8 Smoke ascended from his
   nostrils,
   And a consuming fire came
   from his mouth;[i]
   Glowing coals blazed from
   him.
9 He made the heavens bend
   as he descended,[j]
   And thick gloom was
   beneath his feet.[k]
10 He rode on a cherub and
   came flying.[l]
   He swooped down on the
   wings of a spirit.*[m]
11 He then covered himself in
   darkness,[n]
   All around him as a shelter,
   Dark waters and thick
   clouds.[o]
12 From the brightness
   before him

Hail and fiery coals broke
   through the clouds.
13 Then Jehovah began to
   thunder in the heavens;[a]
   The Most High made his
   voice heard[b]
   With hailstones and fiery
   coals.
14 He shot his arrows and
   scattered them;[c]
   He hurled his lightning
   and threw them into
   confusion.[d]
15 The streambeds* became
   visible;[e]
   The foundations of the land
   were exposed by your
   rebuke, O Jehovah,
   By the blast of the breath
   from your nostrils.[f]
16 He reached down from on
   high;
   He took hold of me and
   pulled me from deep
   waters.[g]
17 He rescued me from my
   strong enemy,[h]
   From those hating me, who
   were stronger than I was.[i]
18 They confronted me on the
   day of my disaster,[j]
   But Jehovah was my support.
19 He brought me out into a
   place of safety;*
   He rescued me because he
   was pleased with me.[k]
20 Jehovah rewards me according to my righteousness;[l]
   He repays me according
   to the innocence* of my
   hands.[m]
21 For I have kept the ways
   of Jehovah,
   And I have not wickedly
   abandoned my God.
22 All his judgments are
   before me;

CHAP. 18
a Ps 50:15
b 1Sa 20:3 Ps 116:3
c 2Sa 20:1 2Sa 22:5, 6 Ps 22:16
d Ec 9:12
e Ps 11:4
f 2Sa 22:7 Ps 10:17 Ps 34:15 1Pe 3:12
g Jg 5:4
h 2Sa 22:8-16 Ps 77:18
i Isa 30:27
j Ps 144:5 Isa 64:1
k 2Sa 22:10
l Ps 99:1
m Ps 104:3 Heb 1:7
n Ps 97:2
o Job 36:29

Second Col.
a 1Sa 2:10 1Sa 7:10
b 2Sa 22:14 Ps 29:3
c Isa 30:30
d Job 36:32 Ps 144:6
e Ps 74:15 Ps 106:9 Ps 114:1, 3
f Ex 15:8 2Sa 22:16
g 2Sa 22:17-20 Ps 124:2-4
h Ps 3:7
i Ps 35:10
j 1Sa 19:11 1Sa 23:26
k Ps 149:4
l 1Sa 26:23 1Ki 8:32
m 1Sa 24:11 2Sa 22:21-25 Ps 24:3, 4

18:5 *Or "Sheol," that is, the common grave of mankind. See Glossary. 18:10 *Or "the wind."

18:15 *Or "water channels." 18:19 *Or "a roomy place." 18:20 *Lit., "the cleanness."

I will not disregard his statutes.

23 I will remain blameless before him,[a]
And I will keep myself from error.[b]

24 May Jehovah repay me according to my righteousness,[c]
According to the innocence of my hands before him.[d]

25 With someone loyal you act in loyalty;[e]
With the blameless man you deal blamelessly;[f]

26 With the pure you show yourself pure,[g]
But with the crooked you show yourself shrewd.[h]

27 For you save those who are lowly*[i]
But you abase the haughty.#[j]

28 For it is you who light my lamp, O Jehovah,
My God lights up my darkness.[k]

29 With your help I can charge against a marauder band;[l]
By God's power I can scale a wall.[m]

30 The way of the true God is perfect;[n]
The saying of Jehovah is refined.[o]
He is a shield to all those taking refuge in him.[p]

31 For who is a God besides Jehovah?[q]
And who is a rock except our God?[r]

32 The true God is the one who clothes me with strength,[s]
And he will make my way perfect.[t]

33 He makes my feet like those of a deer;
He makes me stand on high places.[u]

34 He trains my hands for warfare;

35 You give me your shield of salvation,[a]
Your right hand supports* me,
And your humility makes me great.[b]

36 You widen the path for my footsteps;
My feet* will not slip.[c]

37 I will pursue my enemies and overtake them;
I will not return until they are wiped out.

38 I will crush them so that they cannot rise up;[d]
They will fall under my feet.

39 You will equip me with strength for the battle;
You will make my foes collapse under me.[e]

40 You will make my enemies retreat from me,*
And I will put an end to# those who hate me.[f]

41 They cry for help, but there is no one to save them;
They even cry to Jehovah, but he does not answer them.

42 I will pound them as fine as dust in the wind;
I will throw them out like mud in the streets.

43 You will rescue me from the faultfinding of the people.[g]
You will appoint me the head of nations.[h]
A people whom I have not known will serve me.[i]

44 At a mere report they will obey me;
Foreigners will come cringing before me.[j]

45 Foreigners will lose courage;*

My arms can bend a bow of copper.

CHAP. 18
a Ps 84:11
b 2Sa 22:24
Pr 14:16
c Isa 3:10
Heb 11:6
d 2Sa 22:25
Pr 5:21
e Ps 97:10
f 2Sa 22:26-31
Job 34:11
Jer 32:19
g Mt 5:8
h Ps 125:5
i Job 34:28
j Pr 6:16, 17
Isa 2:11
Lu 18:14
k Ps 97:11
Isa 42:16
l 2Sa 5:19
Heb 11:32-34
m 2Sa 22:30
Php 4:13
n De 32:4
Da 4:37
Re 15:3
o Ps 12:6
Ps 19:8
p Ps 18:2
Ps 84:11
q Ps 86:8
Isa 45:5
r De 32:31
1Sa 2:2
2Sa 22:32-43
s Ps 84:5, 7
t Isa 26:7
u Hab 3:19

Second Col.
a Ge 15:1
De 33:29
Ps 28:7
b 2Sa 22:36
Ps 113:6-8
c Ps 17:5
d Ps 2:8, 9
e Ps 44:5
f 2Sa 22:41
Ps 34:21
g 1Sa 30:6
h 2Sa 22:41
Ps 2:8
i 2Sa 22:44-46
j De 33:29

18:35 *Or "sustains." 18:36 *Or "ankles." 18:40 *Or "You will give me the back of my enemies." #Lit., "silence." 18:45 *Or "fade away."

18:27 *Or "afflicted." #Lit., "haughty eyes."

They will come trembling
from their strongholds.

46 Jehovah is alive! Praised be
my Rock![a]

Let the God of my salvation
be exalted.[b]

47 The true God executes vengeance for me;[c]

He subdues the peoples
under me.

48 He rescues me from my
angry enemies;

You lift me high above those
who attack me;[d]

You save me from the man
of violence.

49 That is why I will glorify
you among the nations,
O Jehovah,[e]

And to your name I will sing
praises.*[f]

50 He performs great acts of
salvation* for his king;[g]

He displays loyal love to his
anointed one,[h]

To David and his offspring"
forever.[i]

To the director. A melody of David.

19 The heavens are declaring
the glory of God;[j]

The skies above* proclaim
the work of his hands.[k]

2 Day after day their speech
bubbles forth,

And night after night they
reveal knowledge.

3 There is no speech, and
there are no words;

Their voice is not heard.

4 But into all the earth their
sound* has gone out,

And to the ends of the inhabited earth" their message.[l]

In the heavens he has
pitched a tent for the sun;

18:49 *Or "make music." 18:50 *Or
"great victories." "Lit., "seed." 19:1
*Or "expanse." 19:4 *Or possi-
bly, "measuring line." "Or "productive
land."

CHAP. 18

a De 32:4
b Ex 15:2
   2Sa 22:47-49
c De 32:35
   Na 1:2
   Ro 12:19
d 2Sa 7:9
   Ps 59:1
e De 32:43
   Ps 117:1
   Isa 11:10
f 2Sa 22:50,
   51
   1Ch 16:9
   Ro 15:9
g Ps 2:6
   Ps 144:10
h 2Sa 7:15-17
   1Ki 3:6
i Ps 89:20, 36
   Isa 9:7
   Lu 1:32, 33
   Re 5:5

CHAP. 19

j Ps 8:3, 4
   Isa 40:22
   Ro 1:20
k Ps 150:1
   Re 4:11
l Ro 10:18

Second Col.

a Ps 104:19
b Ps 119:72
c Ps 23:3
d Ps 119:111,
   129
e Pr 1:5
   2Ti 3:15
f 2Ch 24:9, 10
g Pr 4:4
   Pr 6:23
   Mt 6:22
h De 10:12
   Pr 1:7
   Mal 3:16
i Ps 119:137,
   160
   Re 16:7
j Ps 119:127
   Pr 8:10
k Ps 119:103
   Pr 16:24
l Ps 119:11
m Ps 119:165
n 1Co 4:4
o Ge 20:6
   De 17:12
   1Sa 15:23
   2Sa 6:7
   2Ch 26:16-18
p Ps 119:133
q Isa 38:3

---

5 It is like a bridegroom emerg-
ing from the bridal cham-
ber;

It rejoices like a mighty man
running his course.

6 It emerges from one end of
the heavens,

And it circles to their other
end;[a]

And nothing is concealed
from its heat.

7 The law of Jehovah is perfect,[b] restoring strength.*[c]

The reminder of Jehovah is
trustworthy,[d] making the
inexperienced one wise.[e]

8 The orders from Jehovah
are righteous, causing the
heart to rejoice;[f]

The commandment of
Jehovah is clean, making
the eyes shine.[g]

9 The fear of Jehovah[h] is pure,
lasting forever.

The judgments of Jehovah
are true, altogether righteous.[i]

10 They are more desirable than
gold,

Than much fine* gold,[j]

And sweeter than honey,[k]
the honey that drips from
the combs.

11 By them your servant has
been warned;[l]

In keeping them, there is a
large reward.[m]

12 Who can discern mistakes?[n]

Pronounce me innocent from
sins I am unaware of.

13 And hold your servant back
from presumptuous acts;[o]

Do not let them domi-
nate me.[p]

Then I will be complete,[q]

And innocent of blatant
sins.*

19:7 *Or "restoring (bringing back) the
soul." 19:10 *Or "refined." 19:13 *Or
"much transgression."

14 May the words of my mouth
and the meditation of my
heart
Be pleasing to you,[a]
O Jehovah, my Rock[b]
and my Redeemer.[c]

To the director. A melody of David.

20 May Jehovah answer you
in the day of distress.
May the name of the God of
Jacob protect you.[d]

2 May he send you help from
the holy place[e]
And sustain you from Zion.[f]

3 May he remember all your
gift offerings;
May he accept with favor*
your burnt offering. (*Selah*)

4 May he grant you the desires
of your heart[g]
And give success to all your
plans.*

5 We will shout joyfully over
your acts of salvation;[h]
We will lift our banners in
the name of our God.[i]
May Jehovah fulfill all your
requests.

6 Now I do know that Jehovah
saves his anointed one.[j]
He answers him from his
holy heavens
With great salvation* by his
right hand.[k]

7 Some rely on chariots and
others on horses,[l]
But we call on the name
of Jehovah our God.[m]

8 They have collapsed and
fallen,
But we have risen up and
been restored.[n]

9 O Jehovah, save the king![o]
He will answer us in the day
we call for help.[p]

To the director. A melody of David.

21 O Jehovah, in your
strength the king re-
joices;[q]

How greatly he rejoices in
your acts of salvation![a]

2 You have granted him the
desire of his heart,[b]
And you have not withheld
the request of his lips.
(*Selah*)

3 For you meet him with rich
blessings;
You place a crown of fine*
gold on his head.[c]

4 He asked you for life, and
you gave it to him,[d]
A long life,* forever and ever.

5 Your acts of salvation bring
him great glory.[e]
Dignity and splendor you
bestow on him.

6 You make him blessed
forever;[f]
You make him glad with the
joy of your presence.*[g]

7 For the king trusts in
Jehovah;[h]
Because of the loyal love
of the Most High, he will
never be shaken.*[i]

8 Your hand will find all your
enemies;
Your right hand will find
those hating you.

9 You will make them like
a fiery furnace at the
appointed time when
you give them attention.
Jehovah will swallow them
up in his anger, and fire
will consume them.

10 Their descendants* you will
destroy from the earth,
And their offspring from the
sons of men.

11 For they intended to do what
is bad against you;[k]
They have devised schemes
that will not succeed.[l]

12 For you will make them
retreat[m]

CHAP. 19
a Ps 49:3
  Ps 51:15
  Ps 143:5
  Php 4:8
b Ps 18:2
c Job 19:25
  Isa 43:14

CHAP. 20
d Ps 9:10
  Pr 18:10
e 2Ch 20:8, 9
f 2Sa 5:7
  Ps 50:2
  Ps 134:3
g Ps 21:1, 2
h Ps 59:16
i 1Sa 17:45
j Ps 2:2, 4
k Ps 17:7
l Ps 33:17
  Isa 31:1
m 2Ch 14:11
  2Ch 20:12
  2Ch 32:8
n Jg 5:31
  Ps 125:1
o Ps 18:50
p Ps 44:7

CHAP. 21
q Ps 63:11

Second Col.
a Ps 28:7
b Ps 2:8
  Ps 20:4
c 2Sa 12:30
d Ps 13:3
  Ps 61:6
e 2Sa 7:8, 9
f Ps 72:17
g Ps 16:11
  Ps 45:7
h 1Sa 30:6
i Ps 16:8
j De 32:22
  Ps 110:5
  Mal 4:1
k Ps 34:16
l Ps 2:1
m Ps 9:3
  Ps 56:9

20:3 *Lit., "consider as being fat."
20:4 *Or "counsel." 20:6 *Or "victories."

21:3 *Or "refined." 21:4 *Lit., "Length
of days." 21:6 *Lit., "face." 21:7 *Or
"will never stagger (totter)." 21:10
*Lit., "fruitage."

By aiming your bow* at them.#

13 Rise up, O Jehovah, in your strength.
We will sing praises* to your mightiness.

To the director; set to "The Doe of the Dawn."* A melody of David.

22 My God, my God, why have you forsaken me?[a]
Why are you far from saving me,
Far from my cries of anguish?[b]

2 My God, I keep calling by day, and you do not answer;[c]
And by night there is no silence on my part.

3 But you are holy,[d]
Surrounded by* the praises of Israel.

4 In you our fathers put their trust;[e]
They trusted, and you kept rescuing them.[f]

5 To you they cried out, and they were saved;
They trusted in you, and they were not disappointed.*[g]

6 But I am a worm and not a man,
Scorned by* men and despised by the people.[h]

7 All those seeing me mock me;[i]
They sneer and shake their heads in derision:[j]

8 "He entrusted himself to Jehovah. Let Him rescue him!
Let Him save him, for he is so dear to Him!"[k]

9 You were the One who brought me out of the womb,[l]

The One who made me feel secure on my mother's breasts.

10 I have been entrusted to your care* from birth;
From my mother's womb, you have been my God.

11 Do not stay far off from me, for trouble is near[a]
And I have no other helper.[b]

12 Many young bulls surround me;[c]
Powerful bulls of Ba'shan encircle me.[d]

13 They open their mouth wide against me,[e]
Like a roaring lion that tears its prey to pieces.[f]

14 I am poured out like water;
All my bones are out of joint.
My heart has become like wax;[g]
It melts deep within me.[h]

15 My strength has dried up like a piece of pottery;[i]
My tongue sticks to my gums;[j]
You are bringing me down to the dust of death.[k]

16 For dogs surround me;[l]
They close in on me like a pack of evildoers,[m]
Like a lion they are at my hands and feet.[n]

17 I can count all my bones.[o]
They look on and stare at me.

18 They divide my garments among themselves,
And they cast lots for my clothing.[p]

19 But you, O Jehovah, do not remain far away.[q]
You are my strength; hurry to help me.[r]

20 Save me* from the sword,
My precious life# from the paws△ of dogs;[s]

CHAP. 22

a Ps 22:16
  Mt 27:46
  Mr 15:34
b Heb 5:7
c Ps 42:3
d Isa 6:3
  1Pe 1:15
e Ge 15:1, 6
f Ex 14:13
  Heb 11:32-34
g Ps 25:2
  Ps 99:6
  Ro 10:11
h Ps 31:11
  Isa 53:3
i Ps 35:16
j Ps 109:25
k Mt 27:41-43
  Lu 23:35, 36
l Ps 71:6
  Ps 139:16

Second Col.

a Ps 10:1
b Lu 23:46
  Heb 5:7
c Ps 68:30
d Eze 39:18
e Mt 26:4
f Ps 57:4
  1Pe 5:8
g Lu 22:44
  Joh 12:27
h Mt 26:38
  Mr 14:33
i Pr 17:22
j Joh 19:28
k Isa 53:12
  1Co 15:3, 4
l Ps 59:5, 6
  Lu 22:63
m Ps 86:14
n Mt 27:35
  Joh 20:25
o Ps 34:20
  Joh 19:36
p Mr 15:24
  Lu 23:34
  Joh 19:23, 24
q Ps 10:1
r Ps 40:13
s Ps 22:16

21:12 *Lit., "bowstrings." #Lit., "their faces." 21:13 *Lit., "sing and make music." 22:Sup *Possibly a tune or a musical style. 22:3 *Or "Enthroned among (upon)." 22:5 *Or "were not put to shame." 22:6 *Or "A reproach to."

22:10 *Lit., "thrown upon you." 22:20 *Or "my soul." #Lit., "My only one," referring to his soul, or life. △Lit., "hand."

21 Save me from the mouth
of the lion[a] and the horns
of wild bulls;
Answer and save me.

22 I will declare your name to
my brothers;[b]
In the midst of the congregation I will praise you.[c]

23 You who fear Jehovah,
praise him!
All you offspring* of Jacob,
glorify him![d]
Stand in awe of him, all you
offspring* of Israel.

24 For he has not despised nor
loathed the suffering of the
oppressed one;[e]
He has not hidden his face
from him.[f]
When he cried to him for
help, he heard.[g]

25 I will praise you in the large
congregation;[h]
I will pay my vows before
those who fear him.

26 The meek will eat and be
satisfied;[i]
Those seeking Jehovah will
praise him.[j]
May you enjoy life* forever.

27 All the ends of the earth
will remember and turn to
Jehovah.
All the families of the
nations will bow down
before you.[k]

28 For the kingship belongs
to Jehovah;[l]
He rules over the nations.

29 All the prosperous ones* of
the earth will eat and will
bow down;
All those going down to the
dust will kneel before him;
None of them can preserve
their lives.#

30 Their descendants* will
serve him;

The generation to come will
be told about Jehovah.

31 They will come and tell of his
righteousness.
They will tell the people yet
to be born what he has
done.

A melody of David.

23

Jehovah is my Shepherd.[a]
I will lack nothing.[b]

2 In grassy pastures he makes
me lie down;
He leads me to well-watered
resting-places.*[c]

3 He refreshes me.*[d]
He leads me in the paths# of
righteousness for the sake
of his name.[e]

4 Though I walk in the valley
of deep shadow,[f]
I fear no harm,[g]
For you are with me;[h]
Your rod and your staff
reassure me.*

5 You prepare a table for me
before my enemies.[i]
You refresh* my head with
oil;[j]
My cup is well-filled.[k]

6 Surely goodness and loyal
love will pursue me all the
days of my life,[l]
And I will dwell in the house
of Jehovah for all my
days.[m]

Of David. A melody.

24

To Jehovah belong the
earth and everything
in it,[n]
The productive land and
those dwelling on it.

2 For he has solidly fixed it on
the seas[o]
And firmly established it on
the rivers.

3 Who may ascend to the
mountain of Jehovah,[p]

CHAP. 22
a Ps 35:17
b Joh 17:6
c Ps 40:9
Heb 2:11, 12
d Ps 50:23
e Ps 34:6
Ps 69:33
f Nu 6:25
g Heb 5:7
h Ps 35:18
40:10
Ps 111:1
i Ps 37:11
Isa 65:13
j Zep 2:3
k Ge 22:18
Re 7:9
Re 15:4
l 1Ch 29:11
Re 11:17

Second Col.

CHAP. 23
a Ps 80:1
Jer 23:3
Eze 34:12
1Pe 2:25
b Ps 34:9
Ps 84:11
Mt 6:33
Php 4:19
Heb 13:5
c Eze 34:13, 14
d Ps 19:7
Ps 51:12
e Ps 31:3
f Job 38:17
g Ps 3:6
Ps 27:1
Isa 41:10
h Isa 43:2
Ro 8:31
i Ps 22:26
Ps 31:19
j Lu 7:46
Jas 5:14
k Ps 16:5
l Ps 103:17
m Ps 15:1-5
Ps 27:4
Ps 65:4
Ps 122:1

CHAP. 24
n 1Ch 29:11
Job 41:11
1Co 10:26
o Ge 1:9
Job 38:11
Ps 136:6
Jer 5:22
p Ps 15:1-5

22:23 *Lit., "seed." 22:26 *Lit., "May
your heart live." 22:29 *Lit., "fat
ones." #Or "souls." 22:30 *Lit., "A
seed."

23:2 *Or possibly, "to tranquil waters."
23:3 *Or "my soul." #Lit., "tracks."
23:4 *Or "comfort me." 23:5 *Or
"grease."

And who may stand up in his holy place?

4 Anyone with innocent hands and a pure heart,[a]
Who has not sworn a false oath by My life,*
Nor taken an oath deceitfully.[b]

5 He will receive blessings from Jehovah[c]
And righteousness* from his God of salvation.[d]

6 This is the generation of those seeking him,
Of those seeking your face, O God of Jacob. (Selah)

7 Lift up your heads, you gates;[e]
Open up,* you ancient doorways,
That the glorious King may enter![f]

8 Who is this glorious King?
Jehovah, strong and mighty,[g]
Jehovah, mighty in battle.[h]

9 Lift up your heads, you gates;[i]
Open up, you ancient doorways,
That the glorious King may enter!

10 Who is he, this glorious King?
Jehovah of armies—he is the glorious King.[j] (Selah)

Of David.

ℵ [Aleph]

25 To you, O Jehovah, I turn.*

ב [Beth]

2 My God, I trust in you;[k]
Do not let me be put to shame.[l]
Do not let my enemies gloat over me.[m]

ג [Gimel]

3 Surely none who hope in you will be put to shame,[n]

But shame awaits those who are treacherous without cause.[a]

ד [Daleth]

4 Make me know your ways, O Jehovah;[b]
Teach me your paths.[c]

ה [He]

5 Cause me to walk in your truth and teach me,[d]
For you are my God of salvation.

ו [Waw]

In you I hope all day long.

ז [Zayin]

6 Remember your mercy, O Jehovah, and your loyal love,[e]
Which you have always shown.*[f]

ח [Heth]

7 Do not remember the sins of my youth and my transgressions.
Remember me according to your loyal love,[g]
For the sake of your goodness, O Jehovah.[h]

ט [Teth]

8 Good and upright is Jehovah.[i]
That is why he instructs sinners in the way to live.[j]

י [Yod]

9 He will guide the meek in what is right,*[k]
And he will teach the meek ones his way.[l]

כ [Kaph]

10 All the paths of Jehovah are loyal love and faithfulness
For those observing his covenant[m] and his reminders.[n]

ל [Lamed]

11 For the sake of your name, O Jehovah,[o]
Forgive my error, though it is great.

CHAP. 24
a 2Sa 22:21
Isa 33:15, 16
Mt 5:8
b Ps 34:12, 13
Mal 3:5
c Ps 128:1-5
d Isa 12:2
e Ps 118:19
Ps 122:2
f 2Sa 6:15
Ps 48:1-3
g Ps 93:1
h Ex 15:3
1Sa 17:47
2Ch 20:15
Isa 42:13
i Ps 118:19
j 1Ch 29:11

CHAP. 25
k Isa 26:3
l Ro 10:11
m Ps 41:11
n Ps 69:6

Second Col.
a Ps 31:17
b Ex 33:13
Ps 86:11
Ps 143:8
c Ps 27:11
d Ps 43:3
e Ex 34:6
Isa 55:3
f Ps 103:17
Ps 136:1
g Ps 6:4
Ps 51:1
h Ex 33:19
Ps 27:13
i Ps 92:15
Ps 119:68
Ps 145:9
Ac 14:17
j Ps 19:33
Isa 30:20
Mic 4:2
k Zep 2:3
l Ps 32:8
m De 29:1
n Ps 19:7
o Ps 31:3
Ps 79:9
Ps 109:21
Ps 143:11
Eze 36:22
Da 9:19
Mt 6:9

24:4 *Or "My soul," referring to Jehovah's life by which an individual swears.
24:5 *Or "justice."   24:7 *Or "Rise up."
25:1 *Or "I raise my soul."

25:6 *Or "Which are from ancient times."   25:9 *Lit., "in judgment."

ℤ [Mem]

12 Who is the man fearing
Jehovah?[a]
He will instruct him about
the way he should choose.[b]

ℤ [Nun]

13 He* will experience what is
good,[c]
And his descendants# will
take possession of the
earth.[d]

ℤ [Samekh]

14 Close friendship with
Jehovah belongs to those
who fear him,[e]
And he makes his covenant
known to them.[f]

ℤ [Ayin]

15 My eyes are always toward
Jehovah,[g]
For he will free my feet from
the net.[h]

ℤ [Pe]

16 Turn your face to me and
show me favor,
For I am alone and helpless.

ℤ [Tsade]

17 The distresses of my heart
have multiplied;[i]
Free me from my anguish.

ℤ [Resh]

18 See my affliction and my
trouble,[j]
And pardon all my sins.[k]

19 See how numerous my enemies are
And how violent their hatred
is for me.

ℤ [Shin]

20 Guard my life* and save me.[l]
Do not let me be put to
shame, for I have taken refuge in you.

ℤ [Taw]

21 May integrity and uprightness safeguard me,[m]
For my hope is in you.[n]

22 O God, rescue* Israel out of
all his distresses.

25:13 *Or "His soul." #Lit., "seed."
25:20; 26:9 *Or "my soul." 25:22 *Lit.,
"redeem."

CHAP. 25

a Ps 111:10

b Ps 37:23

c Ps 31:19

d Ps 37:11

e Pr 3:32
Joh 15:15

f Ge 18:17
Ge 22:17
Am 3:7

g Ps 141:8

h Ps 91:3
Ps 124:6-8

i Ps 73:21

j 2Sa 16:12

k Ps 32:5
Ps 51:9

l Ps 17:8
Ps 121:7

m Ps 41:12

n Ps 37:34

Second Col.

CHAP. 26

a 2Ki 20:3

b Ps 21:7

c Ps 17:3
Ps 66:10

d Ps 43:3
Ps 86:11

e Jer 15:17

f Ps 139:21

g Ps 1:1

h Ps 50:23
Ps 95:2

i 1Sa 3:3
1Ch 16:1
Ps 27:4

j Ps 63:2

k 1Sa 25:29

l 1Sa 2:9
Pr 10:9

Of David.

26 Judge me, O Jehovah, for
I have walked in my in-
tegrity;[a]
In Jehovah I have trusted
without wavering.[b]

2 Examine me, O Jehovah, and
put me to the test;
Refine my innermost
thoughts* and my heart.[c]

3 For your loyal love is always
in front of me,
And I walk in your truth.[d]

4 I do not associate* with deceitful men,[e]
And I avoid those who hide
what they are.#

5 I hate the company of evil
men,[f]
And I refuse to associate*
with the wicked.[g]

6 I will wash my hands in innocence,
And I will march around your
altar, O Jehovah,

7 To cause the sound of
thanksgiving to be heard[h]
And to declare all your wonderful works.

8 Jehovah, I love the house
where you dwell,[i]
The place where your glory
resides.[j]

9 Do not sweep me* away with
sinners[k]
Nor take my life away with
violent men,#

10 Whose hands engage in
shameful conduct,
And whose right hand is full
of bribes.

11 But as for me, I will walk in
my integrity.
Rescue* me and show me
favor.

12 My foot is standing on level
ground;[l]

26:2 *Or "my deepest emotions." Lit.,
"my kidneys." 26:4, 5 *Lit., "sit."
26:4 #Or "I do not mingle with hypocrites." 26:9 #Or "with men of bloodshed." 26:11 *Lit., "Redeem."

In the great congregation,*
I will praise Jehovah.[a]

Of David.

27 Jehovah is my light[b] and
my salvation.
Whom should I fear?[c]
Jehovah is the stronghold
of my life.[d]
Whom should I dread?

2 When evil men attacked me
to devour my flesh,[e]
My adversaries and my en-
emies were the ones who
stumbled and fell.

3 Though an army should set
up camp against me,
My heart will not fear.[f]
Though war should break out
against me,
Even then I will remain confident.

4 One thing I have asked from
Jehovah
—It is what I will look for—
That I may dwell in the house
of Jehovah all the days of
my life,[g]
To gaze upon the pleasant-
ness of Jehovah
And to look with apprecia-
tion* upon his temple.[#h]

5 For he will hide me in his
shelter on the day of ca-
lamity;[i]
He will conceal me in the
secret place of his tent;[j]
High on a rock he will
place me.[k]

6 Now my head is high
above my enemies who
surround me;
I will offer sacrifices at his
tent with joyful shouting;
I will sing praises* to
Jehovah.

7 Hear me, O Jehovah, when
I cry out;[l]
Show me favor and
answer me.[m]

8 Speaking for you, my heart
has said:
"Seek to find my face."
Your face, O Jehovah, I will
seek to find.[a]

9 Do not hide your face
from me.[b]
Do not turn your servant
away in your anger.
You are my helper;[c]
Do not forsake me or leave
me, my God of salvation.

10 Even if my own father and
mother abandon me,[d]
Jehovah himself will take
me in.[e]

11 Instruct me in your way,
O Jehovah,[f]
Lead me in the path of uprightness because of my
foes.

12 Do not hand me over to my
adversaries,*[g]
For false witnesses have
risen up against me,[h]
And they threaten me with
violence.

13 Where would I be if I did not
have faith
That I would see Jehovah's
goodness in the land of the
living?*[i]

14 Hope in Jehovah;[j]
Be courageous and strong
of heart.[k]
Yes, hope in Jehovah.

Of David.

28 To you I keep calling,
O Jehovah my Rock;[l]
Do not turn a deaf ear to me.
If you keep silent toward me,
I will become like those
going down to the pit.*[m]

2 Hear my pleas when I cry
to you for help

CHAP. 26
a Ps 111:1

CHAP. 27
b Ps 36:9
Ps 43:3
Ps 119:105
c Ps 23:4
Ro 8:31
Heb 13:6
d Ps 62:6
Isa 12:2
e Ps 22:16
f 2Ch 20:15
2Ch 32:7
Ps 3:6
g Ps 23:6
Ps 65:4
h 1Sa 3:3
1Ch 16:1
Ps 26:8
i Ps 32:7
Ps 57:1
Zep 2:3
j Ps 61:4
k Ps 40:2
l Ps 130:2
m Ps 4:1
Ps 5:2

Second Col.
a Ps 63:1
Ps 105:4
Zep 2:3
b Ps 69:17
Ps 143:7
c Ps 46:1
d Ps 69:8
e Isa 49:15
f Ps 25:4
Ps 86:11
Isa 30:20
Isa 54:13
g Ps 31:8
Ps 41:2
Ps 41:11
h Mt 26:59-61
i Job 33:28-30
j Ps 25:3
Ps 62:5
k Isa 40:31

CHAP. 28
l De 32:4
Isa 26:4
m Job 33:28

26:12 *Lit., "In assemblies." 27:4 *Or
"to look contemplatively." #Or "sanc-
tuary." 27:6 *Or "make music." 27:12 *Or "to the soul of my adversaries." 27:13 *Or possibly, "Surely I
do have faith that I will see Jehovah's
goodness in the land of the living."
28:1 *Or "grave."

As I lift up my hands
toward the innermost room
of your sanctuary.[a]

3 Do not drag me away with
the wicked, with those
practicing what is hurtful,[b]

Those who are speaking
words of peace with their
fellow man while evil is in
their hearts.[c]

4 Pay them back for their
deeds,[d]

According to their evil practices.

Repay them for the work of
their hands,

According to what they have
done.[e]

5 For they pay no attention to
the activities of Jehovah,[f]

Nor to the work of his
hands.[g]

He will tear them down and
not build them up.

6 May Jehovah be praised,
For he has heard my pleas
for help.

7 Jehovah is my strength[h] and
my shield;[i]

In him my heart trusts.[j]

I have received his help, and
my heart rejoices,

So I will praise him with my
song.

8 Jehovah is a strength for his
people;

He is a stronghold, bringing
grand salvation to his
anointed one.[k]

9 Save your people, and bless
your inheritance.[l]

Shepherd them and carry
them in your arms
forever.[m]

A melody of David.

29 Give Jehovah his due, you
sons of mighty ones,

Give Jehovah his due for his
glory and strength.[n]

2 Give Jehovah the glory due
his name.

Bow down to* Jehovah in
holy adornment.[#]

3 The voice of Jehovah is
heard over the waters;

The glorious God thunders.[a]

Jehovah is over many wa-
ters.[b]

4 The voice of Jehovah is powerful;[c]

The voice of Jehovah is
splendid.

5 The voice of Jehovah is
breaking the cedars;

Yes, Jehovah shatters the
cedars of Leb′a·non.[d]

6 He makes Leb′a·non* skip
like a calf,

And Sir′i·on[e] like a young
wild bull.

7 The voice of Jehovah strikes
with flames of fire;[f]

8 The voice of Jehovah makes
the wilderness shudder;[g]

Jehovah makes the wilder-
ness of Ka′desh[h] shudder.

9 The voice of Jehovah makes
the deer shudder and give
birth

And strips bare the forests.[i]

And all in his temple say:
"Glory!"

10 Jehovah sits enthroned
above the flooding
waters;*[j]

Jehovah sits enthroned as
King forever.[k]

11 Jehovah will give strength to
his people.[l]

Jehovah will bless his people
with peace.[m]

A melody. A song of inauguration
of the house. Of David.

30 I will exalt you,
O Jehovah, for you
have lifted* me up;

You did not let my enemies
rejoice over me.[n]

CHAP. 28
a Ps 5:7
b Nu 16:25, 26
Ps 26:9
c Ps 62:4
d Ps 59:12
Jer 18:22
e Ps 62:12
2Th 1:6
f Job 34:26, 27
g Isa 5:12
h Isa 12:2
i Ge 15:1
2Sa 22:3
Ps 3:3
j Ps 56:4
k 1Sa 16:13
2Sa 22:3
Ps 20:6
l De 9:29
m Isa 40:11

CHAP. 29
n 1Ch 16:28, 29

Second Col.
a 1Sa 7:10
Ps 18:13
b Ps 104:3
c Job 26:11
Job 40:9
d Isa 2:12, 13
e De 3:8, 9
f Ex 19:18
Ps 77:18
g Isa 13:13
Heb 12:26
h Nu 13:26
i Isa 10:17, 18
Eze 20:47
j Job 38:25
k 1Ti 1:17
l Isa 40:29
m Ps 72:7

CHAP. 30
n Ps 25:2
Ps 41:11

29:2 *Or "Worship." #Or possibly, "because of the splendor of his holiness."
29:6 *Evidently, the Lebanon mountain range. 29:10 *Or "the heavenly
ocean." 30:1 *Or "drawn."

2 O Jehovah my God, I cried
to you for help, and you
healed me.[a]

3 O Jehovah, you have lifted
me* up from the Grave,[#b]
You kept me alive; you
spared me from sinking
into the pit.[Δc]

4 Sing praises* to Jehovah,
you his loyal ones,[d]
Give thanks to his holy
name;[#e]

5 Because being under his anger is only for a moment,[f]
But being in his favor* is for
a lifetime.[g]
Weeping may come in the
evening, but in the morn-
ing, there is a joyful cry.[h]

6 When I was untroubled,
I said:
"I will never be shaken."*

7 O Jehovah, while I was in
your favor,* you made me
as strong as a mountain.[i]
But when you hid your face,
I became terrified.[j]

8 To you, O Jehovah, I kept
calling;[k]
And to Jehovah, I kept pleading for favor.

9 What profit is there in my
death,* in my going down
to the pit?[Δl]
Will the dust praise you?[m]
Will it tell of your faithfulness?[n]

10 Hear, O Jehovah, and show
me favor.[o]
O Jehovah, become my
helper.[p]

11 You have changed my
mourning into dancing;
You have removed my sack-
cloth, and you clothe me
with rejoicing,

12 So that I* may sing your
praise and not keep silent.
O Jehovah my God, I will
praise you forever.

To the director. A melody of David.

31
In you, O Jehovah, I have
taken refuge.[a]
May I never be put to shame.[b]
Rescue me because of your
righteousness.[c]

2 Incline your ear* to me.
Come quickly to my rescue.[d]
Become for me a mountain
stronghold,
A fortified place to save me.[e]

3 For you are my crag and my
stronghold;[f]
For the sake of your name,[g]
you will lead me and
guide me.[h]

4 You will free me from the net
that they have secretly laid
for me,[i]
For you are my fortress.[j]

5 Into your hand I entrust my
spirit.[k]
You have redeemed me,
O Jehovah, the God of
truth.*[l]

6 I hate those who are devoted
to worthless, vain idols,
But as for me, I trust in
Jehovah.

7 I will rejoice greatly in your
loyal love,
For you have seen my affliction;[m]
You are aware of my deep
distress.*

8 You have not handed me
over to the enemy,
But you make me stand in a
place of safety.*

9 Show me favor, O Jehovah,
for I am in distress.
Anguish has made my eyes
weak,[n] my whole body* as
well.[o]

CHAP. 30
a 2Ki 20:5
Ps 6:2
Ps 103:3

b Ps 86:13

c Ps 16:10
Ps 28:1
Isa 38:17
Jon 2:6

d Ps 32:11

e Ex 3:15

f Isa 12:1

g Isa 54:8

h Ps 126:5

i 2Sa 5:12
Ps 89:17

j Ps 10:1
Ps 143:7

k Ps 34:6
Ps 77:1

l Ps 28:1

m Ps 6:5
Ps 115:17
Ec 9:10

n Ps 88:11
Isa 38:18

o Ps 143:1

p Ps 28:7

Second Col.

CHAP. 31
a Ps 18:2

b Ps 22:4, 5
Ro 10:11

c Ps 143:1

d Ps 40:17
Ps 70:1
Ps 71:2

e 2Sa 22:3
Ps 18:2

f 2Sa 22:2

g Ps 25:11
Jer 14:7

h Ps 23:3

i Ps 91:3
Mt 6:13

j Pr 18:10

k Lu 23:46
Ac 7:59

l De 32:4

m Ps 9:13

n Ps 6:7

o Ps 22:14

30:3 *Or "my soul." #Or "Sheol," that
is, the common grave of mankind. See
Glossary. **30:3, 9** ΔOr "grave." **30:4**
*Or "Make music." #Lit., "memorial."
30:5, 7 *Or "goodwill." **30:6** *Or "will
never stagger (totter)." **30:9** *Lit.,
"blood."

30:12 *Or "my glory." **31:2** *Or "Bend
down and listen." **31:5** *Or "the faithful God." **31:7** *Or "the distresses of
my soul." **31:8** *Or "a roomy place."
31:9 *Or "my soul and my belly."

10 My life is consumed with grief[a]
And my years with groaning.[b]
My strength is waning because of my error;
My bones grow weak.[c]

11 I am scorned by all my adversaries,[d]
Especially my neighbors.
And I am dreaded by my acquaintances;
When they see me in public, they flee from me.[e]

12 I am put out of their heart* and forgotten, as if I were dead;
I am like a broken jar.

13 I have heard many evil rumors;
Terror surrounds me.[f]
When they gather together as one against me,
They scheme to take away my life.*[g]

14 But I trust in you, O Jehovah.[h]
I declare: "You are my God."[i]

15 My days* are in your hand.
Rescue me from the hand of my enemies and from those persecuting me.[j]

16 Make your face shine upon your servant.[k]
Save me by your loyal love.

17 O Jehovah, may I not be put to shame when I call on you.[l]
May the wicked be put to shame;
May they be silenced in the Grave.*[n]

18 May lying lips become speechless,[o]
Lips that speak arrogantly against the righteous, with haughtiness and contempt.

19 How abundant your goodness is![a]
You have stored it up for those who fear you,[b]
And you have shown it before all men, in behalf of those taking refuge in you.[c]

20 You will conceal them in the secret place of your presence[d]
From the schemes of men;
You will hide them in your shelter
From malicious attacks.*[e]

21 May Jehovah be praised,
For in a wonderful way, he has shown his loyal love to me[f] in a besieged city.[g]

22 As for me, I panicked and said:
"I will perish from before you."[h]
But you heard my pleas for help when I cried out to you.[i]

23 Love Jehovah, all you who are loyal to him![j]
Jehovah protects the faithful,[k]
But he repays exceedingly anyone showing haughtiness.[l]

24 Be courageous, and may your heart be strong,[m]
All you who are waiting for Jehovah.[n]

Of David. Mas′kil.*

32 Happy is the one whose transgression is pardoned, whose sin is covered.*[o]

2 Happy is the man whom Jehovah does not charge with guilt,[p]
In whose spirit there is no deceit.

3 When I kept silent, my bones wasted away because of my groaning all day long.[q]

CHAP. 31
a Pr 15:13
b Ps 71:9
c Ps 32:3
Ps 102:3, 5
d Ps 22:6
Ps 42:10
Ps 102:8
e Ps 38:11
f Jer 20:10
g Ps 57:4
h Ps 56:4
i Ps 43:5
j Ps 142:6
k Nu 6:25
l Ps 25:2
Isa 50:7
m Ne 6:16
Isa 41:11
Jer 20:11
n 1Sa 2:9
o Ps 12:3
Ps 63:11

Second Col.
a Ps 73:1
Isa 63:7
b Isa 64:4
1Co 2:9
c Ps 126:2
Isa 26:12
d Ps 27:5
Ps 32:7
e Ps 64:2, 3
f Ps 17:7
g 1Sa 23:7
h Jon 2:4
i 2Ch 33:13
j Ps 6:9
Pr 15:29
Heb 5:7
k 1Sa 2:9
Ps 145:20
l 2Sa 22:28
Isa 2:11
Jas 4:6
m Isa 35:4
n Ps 62:1
La 3:20, 21
Mic 7:7

CHAP. 32
o Isa 1:18
Ac 3:19
p Ro 4:7, 8
q Pr 28:13

31:12 *Or "mind." 31:13 *Or "soul." 31:15 *Lit., "times." 31:17 *Or "Sheol," that is, the common grave of mankind. See Glossary.

31:20 *Lit., "From the quarreling of tongues." 32:Sup *See Glossary. 32:1 *Or "forgiven."

4 For day and night your hand*
was heavy upon me.[a]
My strength evaporated# like
water in the dry summer
heat. (*Selah*)

5 Finally I confessed my sin
to you;
I did not cover my error.[b]
I said: "I will confess
my transgressions to
Jehovah."[c]
And you pardoned the error
of my sins.[d] (*Selah*)

6 This is why every loyal one
will pray to you[e]
While you may yet be found.[f]
Then even the floodwaters
will not reach him.

7 You are a hiding place
for me;
You will safeguard me from
distress.[g]
You will surround me with
joyful shouts of deliver-
ance.[h] (*Selah*)

8 "I will give you insight and
instruct you in the way
you should go.[i]
I will give you advice with my
eye upon you.[j]

9 Do not become like a horse
or a mule, without under-
standing,[k]
Whose spiritedness must be
controlled with a bridle or
a halter
Before it will come near to
you."

10 Many are the pains of the
wicked;
But the one trusting in
Jehovah is surrounded
by His loyal love.[l]

11 Rejoice in Jehovah and be
joyful, you righteous ones;
Shout joyfully, all you who
are upright in heart.

33 Shout joyfully, you righteous ones, because of
Jehovah.[m]

It is fitting for the upright to
praise him.

2 Give thanks to Jehovah with
the harp;
Sing praises* to him with a
ten-stringed instrument.

3 Sing to him a new song;[a]
Play skillfully on the strings,
along with shouts of joy.

4 For the word of Jehovah is
upright,[b]
And everything he does is
trustworthy.

5 He loves righteousness and
justice.[c]
The earth is filled with
Jehovah's loyal love.[d]

6 By the word of Jehovah the
heavens were made,[e]
And by the spirit* of his
mouth everything in them.#

7 He gathers the seawaters
like a dam;[f]
He puts the surging waters
in storehouses.

8 Let the whole earth fear
Jehovah.[g]
Let the inhabitants of the
productive land be in awe
of him.

9 For he spoke, and it came
to be;[h]
He commanded, and it stood
firm.[i]

10 Jehovah has frustrated the
schemes* of the nations;[j]
He has thwarted the plans#
of the peoples.[k]

11 But the decisions* of
Jehovah will stand
forever;[l]
The thoughts of his heart are
from generation to generation.

12 Happy is the nation whose
God is Jehovah,[m]
The people he has chosen
as his own possession.[n]

CHAP. 32
a Ps 38:2
b Ps 38:18
Ps 51:4
1Jo 1:9
c Le 5:5
Ps 41:4
d 2Sa 12:13
Ps 86:5
Ps 103:3
Isa 44:22
e Ps 65:2, 3
f Ps 69:13
Isa 55:6
g Ps 9:9
h Ex 15:1
2Sa 22:1
i Ps 86:11
j Pr 3:6
k Ps 26:3
Jer 8:6
l Ps 34:8
Pr 13:21
Pr 16:20

CHAP. 33
m Php 4:4

Second Col.
a Ps 40:3
Ps 98:1
Ps 149:1
Isa 42:10
Re 5:9
b Ps 12:6
c Job 37:23
Ps 11:7
Ps 45:7
d Ps 145:16
Ac 14:17
e Heb 11:3
f Ge 1:9
Job 38:8-11
Pr 8:29
Jer 5:22
g Re 14:7
h Ps 148:4, 5
i Ps 119:90
j Isa 8:10
Isa 19:3
k Ps 21:8, 11
l Pr 19:21
Isa 46:10
m De 33:29
n Ps 65:4
Ps 135:4
1Pe 2:9

32:4 *Or "displeasure." #Or "My life's
moisture changed."

33:2 *Or "Make music." **33:6** *Or
"breath." #Lit., "all their army."
33:10, 11 *Or "counsel." **33:10** #Or
"thoughts."

13 Jehovah looks down from heaven;
   He sees all the sons of men.[a]

14 From his place of residence,
   He gazes on the inhabitants of the earth.

15 He is the one forming the hearts of all;
   He examines all their works.[b]

16 No king is saved by a large army;[c]
   A mighty man is not saved by his great power.[d]

17 The horse is a false hope for salvation;*[e]
   Its great strength does not ensure escape.

18 Look! The eye of Jehovah watches over those fearing him,[f]
   Those waiting for his loyal love,

19 To rescue them* from death
   And to keep them alive during famine.[g]

20 We are* in expectation of Jehovah.
   He is our helper and our shield.[h]

21 Our hearts rejoice in him,
   For we trust in his holy name.[i]

22 May your loyal love rest upon us, O Jehovah,[j]
   While we keep waiting for you.[k]

Of David, when he disguised his sanity[l] before A·bimʹe·lech, who drove him away, and he left.

34 א [Aleph]
   I will praise Jehovah at all times;
   His praise will be on my lips constantly.

ב [Beth]
2 I* will boast in Jehovah;[m]
   The meek will hear and rejoice.

ג [Gimel]
3 Magnify Jehovah along with me;[a]
   Let us exalt his name together.

ד [Daleth]
4 I inquired of Jehovah, and he answered me.[b]
   He rescued me from all my fears.[c]

ה [He]
5 Those who looked to him became radiant;
   Their faces could not be put to shame.

ז [Zayin]
6 This lowly one called, and Jehovah heard.
   He saved him from all his distresses.[d]

ח [Heth]
7 The angel of Jehovah camps all around those fearing Him,[e]
   And he rescues them.[f]

ט [Teth]
8 Taste and see that Jehovah is good;[g]
   Happy is the man who takes refuge in him.

י [Yod]
9 Fear Jehovah, all you his holy ones,
   For those who fear him lack nothing.[h]

כ [Kaph]
10 Even strong young lions* have been reduced to hunger,
   But those seeking Jehovah will lack nothing good.[i]

ל [Lamed]
11 Come, my sons, listen to me;
   I will teach you the fear of Jehovah.[j]

מ [Mem]
12 Who among you takes pleasure in life
   And would love to see many good days?[k]

CHAP. 33
a Ps 11:4
  Ps 14:2
  Ps 15:3
  Heb 4:13

b 1Ch 28:9
  Job 34:21
  Pr 24:12

c Jos 11:6

d 2Ch 32:21
  Ps 44:4, 5

e 2Ki 7:6, 7
  Ps 20:7
  Pr 21:31
  Isa 31:1

f Job 36:7
  Ps 34:15

g Isa 33:15, 16

h De 33:29

i Ps 28:7
  Pr 18:10

j Ps 32:10

k Mic 7:7

CHAP. 34
l 1Sa 21:12, 13

m Jer 9:24
  1Co 1:31

Second Col.
a Ps 35:27

b Heb 5:7

c Ps 18:48

d 2Sa 22:1

e 2Ki 6:17
  Ps 91:11
  Mt 18:10
  Heb 1:7, 14

f 2Ki 19:35
  Da 6:22
  Ac 5:18, 19
  Ac 12:11

g 1Pe 2:3

h Ps 23:1
  Php 4:19

i Ps 23:6
  Ps 84:11

j Job 28:28
  Pr 1:7
  Pr 8:13

k De 6:1, 2
  De 30:19, 20
  1Pe 3:10-12

33:17 *Or "for victory." 33:19 *Or "their soul." 33:20 *Or "Our soul is."
34:2 *Or "My soul."

34:10 *Or "maned young lions."

ב [Nun]

13 Then guard your tongue
　　from what is bad,[a]
　　Your lips from speaking de-
　　ception.[b]

ס [Samekh]

14 Turn away from what is bad
　　and do what is good;[c]
　　Seek peace and pursue it.[d]

ע [Ayin]

15 The eyes of Jehovah are on
　　the righteous,[e]
　　And his ears listen to their
　　cry for help.[f]

פ [Pe]

16 But the face of Jehovah is
　　against those doing what
　　is bad,
　　To erase all memory of them
　　from the earth.[g]

צ [Tsade]

17 They cried out, and Jehovah
　　heard;[h]
　　He rescued them from all
　　their distresses.[i]

ק [Qoph]

18 Jehovah is close to the
　　brokenhearted;[j]
　　He saves those who are
　　crushed in spirit.*[k]

ר [Resh]

19 Many are the hardships* of
　　the righteous one,[l]
　　But Jehovah rescues him
　　from them all.[m]

ש [Shin]

20 He is guarding all his bones;
　　Not one of them has been
　　broken.[n]

ת [Taw]

21 Disaster will put the wicked
　　to death;
　　Those hating the righteous
　　will be found guilty.

22 Jehovah is redeeming the
　　life* of his servants;
　　None of those taking refuge
　　in him will be found guilty.[o]

34:18 *Or "are discouraged." **34:19**
*Or "calamities." **34:22** *Or "soul."

CHAP. 34

a Jas 1:26
　Jas 3:8

b Pr 12:19
　Pr 15:4
　1Pe 2:1

c Ps 37:27
　Ps 97:10
　Am 5:15
　Ro 12:9

d Mt 5:9
　Heb 12:14

e Job 36:7
　Ps 33:18

f Ps 18:6
　Isa 59:1

g Ps 37:10
　Pr 10:7

h Ps 145:18, 19

i 2Ch 32:22
　Ac 12:11

j Ps 147:3
　Isa 61:1

k Ps 51:17
　Isa 57:15
　Isa 66:2

l Pr 24:16
　2Ti 3:12

m Da 6:21, 22
　1Co 10:13

n Joh 19:36

o Ps 84:11

Second Col.

CHAP. 35

a 1Sa 24:15

b Ps 3:7

c Ex 15:3

d Isa 42:13

e 1Sa 23:26

f Isa 12:2

g Jer 17:18

h Ex 14:19, 20
　Isa 37:36

i Ps 57:6
　Ps 141:10

j Ps 18:17

k Ps 40:17
　Pr 22:22, 23

l Ps 27:12
　Mt 26:59

Of David.

35

O Jehovah, defend my
　case against my oppos-
　ers;[a]
Fight against those who fight
　against me.[b]

2 Take up your buckler* and
　　large shield,[c]
　　And rise up to my defense.[d]

3 Lift up your spear and battle-
　　ax* against my pursuers.[e]
　　Say to me:# "I am your salva-
　　tion."[f]

4 May those who are hunting
　　for my life# be put to
　　shame and humiliated.[g]
　　May those who are plotting
　　to destroy me retreat in
　　disgrace.

5 May they become like chaff
　　in the wind;
　　May Jehovah's angel drive
　　them away.[h]

6 May their path be dark and
　　slippery
　　As Jehovah's angel pursues
　　them.

7 For without cause they have
　　hidden a net to trap me;
　　Without cause they have dug
　　a pit for me.#

8 May disaster come upon him
　　by surprise;
　　May the net that he hid catch
　　him;
　　May he fall into it and be de-
　　stroyed.[i]

9 But I# will rejoice in Jehovah;
　　I will be joyful in his acts of
　　salvation.

10 All my bones will say:
　　"O Jehovah, who is like you?
　　You rescue the helpless from
　　those who are stronger,[j]
　　The helpless and the poor
　　from those who rob them."[k]

11 Malicious witnesses come
　　forward,[l]

35:2 *A small shield, often carried by
archers. **35:3** *Or "double ax." **35:3,
4, 7, 9** #Or "my soul."

Asking me things I know
nothing about.
12 They repay me with bad for
good,[a]
Making me* feel bereaved.
13 But when they were ill, I
clothed myself with sack-
cloth;
I afflicted myself* by fasting,
And when my prayer would
return unanswered,[#]
14 I walked about mourning as
for a friend or a brother of
mine;
I bowed down in sorrow,
like one mourning for his
mother.
15 But when I stumbled, they
rejoiced and gathered to-
gether;
They gathered together to
strike me down in ambush;
They tore me to pieces and
did not keep silent.
16 The ungodly scornfully mock
me,*
They grind their teeth
against me.[b]
17 O Jehovah, how long will you
just look on?[c]
Rescue me* from their at-
tacks,[d]
My precious life[#] from the
young lions.[Δe]
18 Then I will give thanks to you
in the great congregation;[f]
I will praise you among the
throngs of people.
19 Do not let those who for
no reason are my enemies
gloat over me;
Do not let those hating me
without cause[g] wink their
eyes maliciously.[h]
20 For they do not speak words
of peace,

But they deceptively scheme
against the peaceful ones
of the land.[a]
21 They open their mouth wide
to accuse me,
Saying: "Aha! Aha! Our eyes
have seen it."
22 You have seen this,
O Jehovah. Do not
remain silent.[b]
O Jehovah, do not stay
far from me.[c]
23 Awake and rise to my
defense,
My God, Jehovah, defend me
in my legal case.
24 Judge me according to your
righteousness,[d] O Jehovah
my God;
Do not let them gloat
over me.
25 May they never say to themselves: "Aha! We got what
we wanted."*
May they never say: "We
have swallowed him up."[e]
26 Let all of them be put to
shame and disgraced,
Those who gloat over my
calamity.
Let those who exalt them-
selves over me be clothed
with shame and humilia-
tion.
27 But let those who take pleasure in my righteousness
shout joyfully;
May they constantly say:
"May Jehovah be magnified,
who takes pleasure in the
peace of his servant."[f]
28 Then my tongue will recount* your righteousness[g]
And praise you all day long.[h]

To the director. Of Jehovah's
servant, David.

36 Transgression speaks to
the wicked one deep
within his heart;

CHAP. 35
a 1Sa 19:4, 5
1Sa 20:33
Jer 18:20

b Ps 37:12

c Hab 1:13

d Ps 142:6

e Ps 22:20
Ps 57:4

f Ps 22:22

g Ps 69:4
Joh 15:24, 25

h Pr 6:12, 13

Second Col.
a Ps 31:13
Jer 11:19
Mt 26:4

b Ps 28:1

c Ps 10:1
Ps 71:12

d Ps 26:1
Ps 96:13

e Ps 41:1, 2

f Ps 84:11
Ps 149:4

g Ps 51:14

h Ps 71:24

35:12, 13, 17 *Or "my soul." 35:13 #Or
"would return upon my bosom." 35:16
*Or possibly, "The ungodly mock for a
cake." 35:17 #Lit., "My only one," referring to his soul, or life. ΔOr "maned
young lions."

35:25 *Or "Aha! Our soul." 35:28 *Or
"meditate on."

There is no fear of God before his eyes.[a]

2 For in his own eyes he flatters himself too much
To detect and hate his error.[b]

3 The words of his mouth are hurtful and deceptive;
He shows no insight for doing what is good.

4 He plots hurtful schemes even on his bed.
He is set on a path that is not good;
He does not reject what is bad.

5 O Jehovah, your loyal love reaches to the heavens,[c]
Your faithfulness up to the clouds.

6 Your righteousness is like majestic mountains;*[d]
Your judgments are like vast, deep waters.[e]
Man and beast you preserve,# O Jehovah.

7 How precious your loyal love is, O God![g]
In the shadow of your wings,
The sons of men take refuge.[h]

8 They drink their fill of the rich bounty* of your house,[i]
And you cause them to drink of the torrent of your delights.[j]

9 With you is the source of life;[k]
By your light we can see light.[l]

10 Continue showing your loyal love to those who know you,[m]
And your righteousness, to the upright in heart.[n]

11 Do not let the foot of the haughty tread on me
Or the hand of the wicked drive me away.

12 There the wrongdoers have fallen;
They have been knocked down and cannot get up.[a]

Of David.

א [Aleph]

37 Do not be upset* because of evil men
Or envious of wrongdoers.[b]

2 They will quickly wither like grass[c]
And shrivel like green new grass.

ב [Beth]

3 Trust in Jehovah and do what is good;[d]
Reside in the earth,* and act with faithfulness.[e]

4 Find exquisite delight* in Jehovah,
And he will grant you the desires of your heart.

ג [Gimel]

5 Commit your way to* Jehovah;[f]
Rely on him, and he will act in your behalf.[g]

6 He will make your righteousness shine like daybreak,
And your justice like the midday sun.

ד [Daleth]

7 Keep silent before Jehovah[h]
And wait expectantly* for him.
Do not be upset by the man
Who succeeds in carrying out his schemes.[i]

ה [He]

8 Let go of anger and abandon rage;[j]
Do not become upset and turn to doing evil.*

9 For evil men will be done away with,[k]

CHAP. 36
a Ro 3:18
b De 29:19, 20
c Ps 103:11
d Ps 71:19
e Ro 11:33
f Ps 145:9
  1Ti 4:10
g Mic 7:18
h Ru 2:12
  Ps 17:8
  Ps 91:4
i Ps 65:4
j Ps 16:11
k Job 33:4
  Jer 2:13
  Ac 17:28
  Re 4:11
l Ps 27:1
  Ps 43:3
  Jas 1:17
  1Pe 2:9
m Ps 103:17
n Ps 7:10
  Ps 97:11

Second Col.
a Ps 1:5

CHAP. 37
b Ps 73:3
  Pr 23:17
c Ps 73:12, 19
d Isa 1:17
  Heb 13:16
e Pr 28:20
f Ps 55:22
  Pr 16:3
g Mt 6:33
  Php 4:6
  1Pe 5:6, 7
h Ps 62:1
  La 3:26
i Job 21:7
  Ps 73:3
  Jer 12:1
j Pr 14:29
  Eph 4:26
k Ps 55:23

36:6 *Lit., "like mountains of God." # Or "save." 36:8 *Lit., "the fatness."

37:1 *Or "show yourself heated up." 37:3 *Or "land." *Or "Find your greatest joy." 37:5 *Lit., "Roll your way upon." 37:7 *Or "patiently." 37:8 *Or possibly, "Do not become upset, for it can only lead to harm."

But those hoping in Jehovah will possess the earth.[a]

ו [Waw]

10 Just a little while longer, and the wicked will be no more;[b]
You will look at where they were,
And they will not be there.[c]

11 But the meek will possess the earth,[d]
And they will find exquisite delight in the abundance of peace.[e]

ז [Zayin]

12 The wicked man plots against the righteous;[f]
He grinds his teeth at him.

13 But Jehovah will laugh at him,
For He knows that his day will come.[g]

ח [Heth]

14 The wicked draw their swords and bend* their bows
To bring down the oppressed and the poor,
To slaughter those whose way is upright.

15 But their sword will pierce their own heart;[h]
Their bows will be broken.

ט [Teth]

16 Better is the little of the righteous one
Than the abundance of many wicked ones.[i]

17 For the arms of the wicked will be broken,
But Jehovah will support the righteous.

י [Yod]

18 Jehovah is aware of what the blameless go through,*
And their inheritance will last forever.[j]

19 They will not be put to shame in the time of disaster;

In the time of famine they will have plenty.

כ [Kaph]

20 But the wicked will perish;[a]
The enemies of Jehovah will vanish like glorious pastures;
They will vanish like smoke.

ל [Lamed]

21 The wicked one borrows and does not repay,
But the righteous one is generous* and giving.[b]

22 Those blessed by Him will possess the earth,
But those cursed by Him will be done away with.[c]

מ [Mem]

23 Jehovah guides* the steps of a man[d]
When He finds pleasure in his way.[e]

24 Although he may fall, he will not be hurled down,[f]
For Jehovah supports him by the hand.*[g]

נ [Nun]

25 I was once young and now I am old,
But I have not seen anyone righteous abandoned,[h]
Nor his children looking for bread.*[i]

26 He always lends freely,[j]
And his children are in line for a blessing.

ס [Samekh]

27 Turn away from bad and do what is good,[k]
And you will remain forever.

28 For Jehovah loves justice,
And he will not abandon his loyal ones.[l]

ע [Ayin]

They will always be guarded;[m]
But the descendants of the wicked will be done away with.[n]

CHAP. 37

a Ps 25:12, 13
Ps 37:29
Mt 5:5
2Pe 2:9

b Job 24:24

c 1Sa 25:39
Ps 52:4, 5

d Isa 45:18
Mt 5:5
Re 21:3

e Ps 72:7
Ps 119:165
Isa 48:18

f 1Sa 18:21, 25

g 1Sa 26:9, 10

h 2Sa 17:23
Es 7:10
Ps 7:15

i Pr 16:8
Pr 30:8, 9
1Ti 6:6

j Ps 16:11

Second Col.

a Pr 10:7

b De 15:11
Job 31:16, 22
Ps 112:9
Pr 19:17

c Ps 37:9

d Pr 16:9

e Pr 11:20

f Ps 34:19
Pr 24:16

g Ps 91:11, 12

h Ps 94:14
Mt 6:33
Heb 13:5

i De 24:19
Ps 145:15
Pr 10:3

j De 15:7, 8
Ps 112:5

k Ps 34:14
Isa 1:17

l 2Sa 22:26

m Ps 97:10
Pr 2:7, 8

n Pr 2:22

37:14 *Or "string." 37:18 *Lit., "the days of the blameless."

37:21 *Or "showing favor." 37:23 *Or "makes firm." 37:24 *Or "with His hand." 37:25 *Or "food."

29 The righteous will possess
the earth,[a]
And they will live forever
on it.[b]

 פ [Pe]

30 The mouth of the righteous
one imparts wisdom,*
And his tongue speaks about
justice.[c]

31 The law of his God is in his
heart;[d]
His steps will not falter.[e]

צ [Tsade]

32 The wicked watches the righteous,
Seeking to put him to death.

33 But Jehovah will not abandon him to the hand of
that one[f]
Or find him guilty when he is
judged.[g]

ק [Qoph]

34 Hope in Jehovah and follow
his way,
And he will exalt you to take
possession of the earth.
When the wicked are done
away with,[h] you will see it.[i]

ר [Resh]

35 I have seen the ruthless,
evil man
Spreading out like a luxuriant tree in its native soil.[j]

36 But he suddenly passed away
and was gone;[k]
I kept searching for him, and
he could not be found.[l]

ש [Sin]

37 Take note of the blameless
one,*
And keep the upright one[m] in
sight,
For the future of that man
will be peaceful.[n]

38 But all the transgressors will
be destroyed;
The future of wicked people
will be cut off.[o]

37:30 *Or "utters wisdom in an undertone." **37:37** *Or "the one who keeps
integrity."

CHAP. 37
a De 30:20
Ps 37:9
Pr 2:21
Mt 5:5

b Mt 25:46
Re 21:3, 4

c Mt 12:35
Eph 4:29
Col 4:6

d De 6:6
Ps 40:8

e Ps 121:3

f 2Pe 2:9

g Ps 109:31

h Ps 37:22

i Ps 52:5, 6

j Es 5:11
Job 21:7

k Ex 15:9, 10

l Ps 37:10

m Job 1:1

n Job 42:12, 16

o Ps 1:4
Pr 10:7
2Pe 2:9

Second Col.
a Isa 12:2

b Ps 9:9
Isa 33:2

c Isa 46:4
1Co 10:13

d Ps 22:4
Da 3:17
Da 6:23

CHAP. 38
e Jer 10:24

f Ps 32:4

g Ps 6:2
Ps 41:4
Ps 51:8

h Ezr 9:6
Ps 40:12

i Ps 38:3

ת [Taw]

39 The salvation of the righteous is from Jehovah;[a]
He is their fortress in the
time of distress.[b]

40 Jehovah will help them and
rescue them.[c]
He will rescue them from the
wicked and save them,
Because they take refuge in
him.[d]

A melody of David,
to serve as a reminder.*

38 O Jehovah, do not reprove
me in your anger,
Nor correct me in your
wrath.[e]

2 For your arrows have pierced
deep into me,
And your hand presses down
on me.[f]

3 My whole body is sick* because of your indignation.
There is no peace within my
bones because of my sin.[g]

4 For my errors loom over my
head;[h]
Like a heavy burden, they
are too much for me to
bear.

5 My wounds stink and fester
Because of my foolishness.

6 I am distressed and extremely downcast;
I walk around sad all day
long.

7 There is a burning within
me;*
My whole body is sick.[i]

8 I have grown numb and become completely crushed;
My anguished heart makes
me groan aloud.*

9 O Jehovah, all my desires
are before you,
And my sighing is not hidden
from you.

38:Sup *Or "to bring to remembrance."
38:3 *Lit., "There is no sound spot in my
flesh." **38:7** *Lit., "My loins are full of
burning." **38:8** *Or "roar."

10 My heart pounds, my
strength is gone,
And the light of my eyes has
left me.[a]
11 My friends and my companions avoid me because of
my plague,
And my close acquaintances
keep their distance.
12 Those seeking my life* set
traps;
Those trying to harm me
speak of ruin;[b]
They mutter deception all
day long.
13 But like someone deaf,
I would not listen;[c]
Like someone speechless,
I would not open my
mouth.[d]
14 I have become like a man
who cannot hear,
Whose mouth has nothing
to say in defense.
15 For on you, O Jehovah,
I waited,[e]
And you answered me,
O Jehovah my God.[f]
16 For I said: "May they not
gloat over me
Or exalt themselves over me
if my foot slips."
17 For I was ready to collapse,
And my pain was always
with me.[g]
18 I confessed my error;[h]
I was troubled by my sin.[i]
19 But my enemies are vigorous* and mighty,[a]
Those hating me for no
reason have become
numerous.
20 They repaid me with bad
for good;
They were resisting me for
pursuing what is good.
21 Do not abandon me,
O Jehovah.

O God, do not remain far
away from me.[a]
22 Do hurry to help me,
O Jehovah, my salvation.[b]

To the director; of Je·du´thun.*[c]
A melody of David.

39 I said: "I will guard my
step
To avoid sinning with my
tongue.[d]
I will guard my mouth with
a muzzle[e]
As long as anyone wicked is
in my presence."
2 I was speechless and silent;[f]
I kept quiet even about what
is good,
But my pain was intense.*
3 My heart smoldered*
inside me.
As I pondered,* the fire kept
burning.
Then my tongue spoke:
4 "O Jehovah, help me to know
what my end will be,
And the measure of my
days,[g]
So that I may know how
short my life is.*
5 Indeed, you have made my
days just a few;*[h]
And my life span is as nothing before you.[i]
Surely every man, though he
seems secure, is nothing
but a mere breath.[j] (Selah)
6 Surely every man walks
about like a shadow.
He rushes around* for nothing.
He piles up wealth, not
knowing who will enjoy it.[k]
7 What, then, can I hope for,
O Jehovah?
You are my only hope.

Second Col.

a Ps 22:11
Ps 35:22

b Ps 27:1
Ps 62:2
Isa 12:2

CHAP. 39

c 1Ch 16:41
1Ch 25:1

d Pr 18:21

e Ps 141:3

f Ps 38:13
Mt 27:12
1Pe 2:23

g Ps 90:12

h Ps 90:9
Jas 4:14

i Ps 90:4

j Ps 62:9
Ps 144:4

k Ps 49:10
Ec 2:18, 19
Ec 4:8
Lu 12:19, 20

CHAP. 38

a Ps 6:7

b 2Sa 16:7
Ps 62:4

c 2Sa 16:11

d Ps 39:2, 9

e 2Sa 16:12
Ps 123:2

f Ps 138:3

g Ps 77:2

h Ps 32:5

i Ps 51:3

38:12 *Or "my soul." **38:19** *Lit.,
"alive." *Or possibly, "But my enemies
without cause are many."

39:Sup *See Glossary. **39:2** *Or
"stirred up." **39:3** *Lit., "grew hot."
*Or "sighed." **39:4** *Or "how transient
I am." **39:5** *Lit., "handbreadths."
39:6 *Lit., "makes noise."

8 Save me from all my trans-
  gressions.[a]
  Do not let the foolish one
    make me an object of con-
    tempt.
9 I remained speechless;
  I could not open my mouth,[b]
  Because this was your
    doing.[c]
10 Remove your plague
    from me.
  I am worn down because
    your hand strikes me.
11 You correct man with pun-
    ishment for his error;[d]
  You consume the things he
    treasures just as a moth
    does.
  Surely every man is but a
    mere breath.[e] (Selah)
12 Hear my prayer, O Jehovah,
  Listen to my cry for help.[f]
  Do not ignore my tears.
  For I am but a foreign resi-
    dent to you,[g]
  A traveler passing through,*
    just like all my
    forefathers.[h]
13 Turn your harsh gaze away
    from me so that I may
    cheer up
  Before I pass away and I am
    gone."

To the director. Of David. A melody.

40 I earnestly hoped in*
    Jehovah,
  And he inclined his ear#
    to me and heard my cry
    for help.[i]
2 He brought me up out of
    a roaring pit,
  Out of the slimy mire.
  And he set my feet upon
    a crag;
  He made my footing secure.
3 Then he put a new song in
    my mouth,[j]

Praise to our God.
  Many will look on in awe
  And put their trust in
    Jehovah.
4 Happy is the man who trusts
    in Jehovah
  And who does not look to the
    defiant or to those who are
    false.*
5 How many things you have
    done,
  O Jehovah my God,
  Your wonderful works and
    your thoughts toward us.[a]
  None can compare to you;[b]
  If I were to try to tell and
    speak of them,
  They would be too numerous
    to recount![c]
6 Sacrifice and offering you
    did not desire,*[d]
  But you opened up my ears
    to hear.[e]
  You did not ask for burnt of-
    ferings and sin offerings.[f]
7 Then I said: "Look, I have
    come.
  In the scroll* it is written
    about me.[g]
8 To do your will, O my God,
    is my delight,*[h]
  And your law is deep
    within me.[i]
9 I proclaim the good news of
    righteousness in the great
    congregation.[j]
  Look! I do not restrain my
    lips,[k]
  O Jehovah, as you well know.
10 I do not cover over your righ-
    teousness in my heart.
  I declare your faithfulness
    and salvation.
  I do not hide your loyal love
    and your truth in the great
    congregation."[l]
11 O Jehovah, do not withhold
    your mercy from me.

CHAP. 39
a Ps 25:11
  Mic 7:19

b Job 40:4
  Ps 38:13

c 2Sa 16:10

d Ps 90:8

e Ps 39:5
  Ps 102:11

f Ps 28:1

g Le 25:23
  1Ch 29:15

h Heb 11:13

CHAP. 40
i Ps 34:15

j Ps 33:3
  Ps 98:1

Second Col.
a Re 15:3

b Ex 15:11

c Ps 139:17, 18

d 1Sa 15:22
  Ps 51:16, 17
  Ho 6:6

e Isa 50:5

f Heb 10:5-9

g Lu 24:44

h Joh 4:34

i Ps 37:31
  Ro 7:22

j Ps 22:22

k Heb 13:15

l Heb 2:12

39:12 *Or "A settler." **40:1** *Or "waited
patiently for." #Or "bent down to listen."

40:4 *Or "to liars." **40:6** *Or "delight
in." **40:7** *Lit., "the scroll of the book."
40:8 *Or "desire."

May your loyal love and
   your truth constantly
   safeguard me.[a]

12 The calamities surrounding
   me are too many to count.[b]
So many of my errors overwhelm me that I cannot see
   my way;[c]
They are more numerous
   than the hairs of my head,
And I have lost heart.

13 Please be willing, O Jehovah,
   to save me.[d]
O Jehovah, hurry to
   help me.[e]

14 May all those seeking to take
   my life*
Be put to shame and dis-
   graced.
May those who delight in
   my calamity
Retreat in humiliation.

15 May those who are saying to
   me: "Aha! Aha!"
Be appalled because of their
   own shame.

16 But let those seeking you[f]
Exult and rejoice in you.[g]
May those who love your acts
   of salvation always say:
   "May Jehovah be magni-
   fied."[h]

17 But I am helpless and poor;
May Jehovah pay attention
   to me.
You are my helper and my
   rescuer;[i]
My God, do not delay.[j]

To the director. A melody of David.

41 Happy is anyone who
   shows consideration to
   the lowly one;[k]
Jehovah will rescue him in
   the day of calamity.

2 Jehovah will guard him and
   keep him alive.
He will be pronounced happy
   in the earth;[l]
You will never turn him over
   to the will* of his enemies.[m]

3 Jehovah will sustain him on
   his sickbed;[a]
During his sickness you will
   completely change his bed.

4 For I said: "O Jehovah, show
   me favor.[b]
Heal me,*[c] for I have sinned
   against you."[d]

5 But my enemies speak evil
   about me:
"When will he die and his
   name perish?"

6 If one of them comes to
   see me, his heart speaks
   falsely.
He gathers something harmful to say;
Then he goes out and
   spreads it abroad.

7 All those who hate me whisper to one another;
They are scheming some-
   thing bad against me:

8 "A dreadful thing has overtaken him;
Now that he is down, he will
   not rise again."[e]

9 Even the man at peace with
   me, one whom I trusted,[f]
Who was eating my bread,
   has lifted his heel against
   me.*[g]

10 But you, O Jehovah, show
   me favor and raise me up,
So that I may repay them.

11 By this I will know that you
   are pleased with me:
When my enemy cannot
   shout in triumph over me.[h]

12 As for me, you uphold me
   because of my integrity;[i]
You will keep me in your
   presence forever.[j]

13 May Jehovah, the God of
   Israel, be praised
Throughout all eternity.*[k]
Amen and Amen.

CHAP. 40
a Ps 61:6, 7
b Ps 71:20
c Ps 38:4
d Ps 25:17
e Ps 38:22
  Ps 70:1-5
f De 4:29
g Ps 13:5
h Ps 35:27
i Ps 54:4
  Isa 50:7
  Heb 13:6
j Ps 143:7

CHAP. 41
k De 15:7, 8
  Ps 112:9
  Pr 14:21
  Pr 22:9
l Mt 5:7
m 2Pe 2:9

Second Col.
a 2Ki 20:5
  Ps 103:3
b Ps 51:1
c Ps 6:2
  Ps 147:3
d Ps 32:5
  Ps 38:3
  Pr 28:13
e Ps 3:2
  Ps 71:10, 11
f 2Sa 15:12
  Job 19:19
  Ps 55:12, 13
g Mr 14:18
  Joh 13:18
  Joh 13:26
h Ps 31:8
  Jer 20:13
i Ps 25:21
  Pr 7:7
j Ps 34:15
k 1Ch 16:36
  1Ch 29:10

40:14 *Or "soul." **41:2** *Or "desire;
soul." See Glossary.

41:4 *Or "my soul." **41:9** *Or "turned
against me." **41:13** *Or "From eternity
to eternity."

BOOK TWO
(Psalms 42-72)

To the director.
Mas'kil* of the sons of Kor'ah.[a]

42 As a deer that longs for
streams of water,
So I long* for you, O God.

2 I do thirst* for God, for the
living God.[b]
When may I come and appear
before God?[c]

3 My tears are my food day and
night;
All day long people taunt me:
"Where is your God?"[d]

4 These things I remember,
and I pour out my soul,*
For I once walked along with
the multitude;
I used to walk solemnly*
before them to the house
of God,
With sounds of rejoicing and
thanksgiving,
Those of a crowd celebrating
a festival.[e]

5 Why am I* in despair?[f]
Why is this turmoil
within me?
Wait for God,[g]
For I will yet praise him as
my Grand Savior.[h]

6 My God, I am* in despair.[i]
That is why I remember you,[j]
From the land of Jordan and
the peaks of Her'mon,
From Mount Mi'zar'.[#]

7 Deep waters call to deep
waters
At the sound of your water-
falls.
All your surging waves have
overwhelmed me.[k]

8 By day Jehovah will grant me
his loyal love,
And by night his song will
be with me—a prayer to the
God of my life.[l]

9 I will say to God, my crag:
"Why have you forgot-
ten me?[a]
Why should I walk about sad
because of the oppression
by my enemy?"[b]

10 With murderous hostility*
my enemies taunt me;
All day long they taunt me:
"Where is your God?"[c]

11 Why am I* in despair?
Why is this turmoil
within me?
Wait for God,[d]
For I will yet praise him as
my Grand Savior and my
God.[e]

43 Judge me, O God,[f]
Defend my legal case[g]
against a disloyal nation.
Rescue me from the man
of deception and unrigh-
teousness.

2 For you are my God, my fortress.[h]
Why have you cast me off?
Why must I walk about sad
because of the oppression
by my enemy?[i]

3 Send out your light and your
truth.[j]
May these lead me;[k]
May they guide me to your
holy mountain and to your
grand tabernacle.[l]

4 Then I will come to the altar
of God,[m]
To God, my exceeding joy.
And I will praise you with the
harp,[n] O God, my God.

5 Why am I* in despair?
Why is this turmoil
within me?
Wait for God,[o]
For I will yet praise him as
my Grand Savior and my
God.[p]

CHAP. 42
a 2Ch 20:19
b Ps 63:1
c Ps 27:4
  Ps 84:2
d Ps 3:2
  Ps 42:10
  Ps 79:10
e De 16:14, 16
  2Ch 30:23,
  24
f Ps 55:4
  Mr 14:34
g Ps 37:7
  La 3:24
  Mic 7:7
h Ps 43:5
i Ps 22:1
  Joh 12:27
j Jon 2:7
k Ps 88:7
l Ps 27:1

Second Col.
a Ps 13:1
b Ps 38:6
  Ps 43:2
c Ps 3:2
  Ps 42:3
  Ps 79:10
d Ps 37:7
e Ps 42:5
  Ps 43:5

CHAP. 43
f Ps 26:1
  Ps 35:24
g Ps 35:1
  Pr 22:22, 23
h Ps 28:7
  Ps 140:7
i Ps 42:9
j Ps 40:11
  Pr 6:23
k Ps 5:8
  Ps 27:11
  Ps 143:10
l 1Ch 16:1
  Ps 78:68, 69
m Ps 84:3
n 2Sa 6:5
o Ps 37:7
p Ps 42:5, 11

42:Sup; 42:4 *See Glossary. **42:1** *Or
"my soul longs." **42:2** *Or "My soul
thirsts." **42:4** #Or "slowly." **42:5, 11;
43:5** *Or "is my soul." **42:6** *Or "my
soul is." #Or "the little mountain."

42:10 *Or possibly, "As if crushing my
bones."

To the director.
Of the sons of Kor′ah.[a] Mas′kil.*

44 O God, we have heard
with our own ears,
Our forefathers have re-
counted to us,[b]
The deeds you accomplished
in their days,
In the days of long ago.

2 With your hand you drove
away nations[c]
And settled our forefathers
there.[d]
You crushed nations and
drove them out.[e]

3 It was not by their own sword
that they took possession
of the land,[f]
And their own arm did not
bring them victory.[g]
Rather, it was by your right
hand and your arm[h] and
the light of your face,
For you took pleasure in
them.[i]

4 You are my King, O God;[j]
Command* complete victory#
for Jacob.

5 By your power we will drive
back our adversaries;[k]
In your name we will trample
down those who rise up
against us.[l]

6 For I do not trust in my bow,
And my sword cannot
save me.[m]

7 It was you who saved us from
our adversaries,[n]
You who humiliated those
who hate us.

8 To God we will offer praise
all day long,
And we will give thanks to
your name forever. (Selah)

9 But now you have cast us off
and humiliated us,
And you do not go out with
our armies.

10 You keep making us retreat
from our adversary;[o]

Those who hate us take
whatever they want.

11 You hand us over to be
devoured like sheep;
You have scattered us among
the nations.[a]

12 You sell your people for next
to nothing;[b]
You make no profit from the
sale.*

13 You make us a reproach to
our neighbors,
An object of ridicule
and jeering to those all
around us.

14 You make us an object of
scorn* among the nations,[c]
Something for the peoples to
shake their heads at.

15 I feel humiliated all day long,
And I am overwhelmed by
my shame,

16 On account of the sound of
their taunts and insults,
Because of our enemy who is
taking revenge.

17 All of this has come upon us,
yet we have not forgotten
you,
And we have not violated
your covenant.[d]

18 Our heart has not deviated;
Our footsteps do not stray
from your path.

19 But you have crushed us
where the jackals dwell;
You have covered us with
deep shadow.

20 If we have forgotten the
name of our God
Or if we spread out our
hands in prayer to a
foreign god,

21 Will not God discover this?
He is aware of the secrets
of the heart.[e]

22 For your sake we are being
put to death all day long;
We have been accounted as
sheep for slaughtering.[f]

CHAP. 44
a 2Ch 20:19

b Ex 13:14
Nu 21:14
Jg 6:13

c De 7:1

d Ex 15:17
Ps 78:55
Ps 80:8, 9

e Jos 10:5, 11
Ps 135:10, 11

f De 4:38
Jos 24:12

g 1Sa 12:22

h Isa 63:11-13

i De 7:7, 8

j Ps 74:12
Isa 33:22

k Ps 18:39
Php 4:13

l Ps 60:12

m 1Sa 17:45
Ps 20:7
Ps 33:16

n Jos 24:8

o De 28:15, 25

_____
Second Col.
a De 28:64

b De 32:30

c De 28:37
2Ch 7:20

d Ex 34:10

e Ps 139:1
Ec 12:14
Jer 17:10

f Ro 8:36

_____
44:Sup *See Glossary. **44:4** *Or
"Grant." #Or "grand salvation."

44:12 *Or "by the price for them."
44:14 *Lit., "a proverb."

23 Rouse yourself. Why do you
keep sleeping, O Jehovah?[a]
Awake! Do not keep casting
us off forever.[b]
24 Why do you hide your face?
Why do you forget our affliction and our oppression?
25 For we* have been brought
down to the dust;
Our bodies are pressed to
the ground.[c]
26 Rise up as our helper![d]
Rescue* us because of your
loyal love.[e]

To the director; set to "The Lilies."
Of the sons of Kor′ah.[f] Mas′kil.*
A song of love.

45 My heart is stirred by
something good.
I say: "My song is* about a
king."[g]
May my tongue be the
stylus*[h] of a skilled copyist.[Δi]
2 You are the most handsome
of the sons of men.
Gracious speech flows from
your lips.[j]
That is why God has blessed
you forever.[k]
3 Strap your sword[l] on your
side, O mighty one,[m]
In your dignity and your
splendor.[n]
4 And in your splendor go on
to victory;*[o]
Ride in the cause of truth
and humility and righ-
teousness,[p]
And your right hand will
accomplish# awe-inspiring
things.
5 Your arrows are sharp, making peoples fall before
you;[q]
They pierce the hearts of the
king's enemies.[r]

CHAP. 44	
a	Ps 7:6
	Ps 78:65, 66
b	Job 13:24
	Ps 13:1
	Ps 88:14
c	Ps 119:25
d	Ps 33:20
e	Ps 130:7
CHAP. 45	
f	2Ch 20:19
g	Ps 2:6
h	Isa 8:1
i	2Sa 23:2
	Ezr 7:6
j	Joh 7:46
k	Ps 72:17
l	Re 1:16
	Re 19:15
m	Isa 9:6
n	Heb 1:3
o	Re 6:2
p	Re 19:11
q	Ps 2:9
	2Th 1:7, 8
r	Re 17:14
	Re 19:19

Second Col.	
a	Ps 89:29, 36
b	Isa 11:4
	Jer 33:15
	Heb 1:8, 9
c	Heb 7:26
d	Mt 7:23
e	Isa 61:1
	Ac 10:38
f	Ps 21:6
g	Isa 13:12

6 God is your throne forever
and ever;[a]
The scepter of your
kingdom is a scepter
of uprightness.*[b]
7 You loved righteousness,[c]
and you hated
wickedness.[d]
That is why God, your God,
has anointed you[e] with the
oil of exultation[f] more than
your companions.
8 All your garments are scented with myrrh and aloes-
wood and cassia;
From the grand ivory palace,
stringed instruments make
you rejoice.
9 The daughters of kings
are among your ladies of
honor.
The royal consort* has taken
her stand at your right
hand, adorned in gold of
O′phir.[g]
10 Listen, O daughter, pay attention and incline your
ear;
Forget your people and your
father's house.
11 And the king will long for
your beauty,
For he is your lord,
So bow down to him.
12 The daughter of Tyre will
come with a gift;
The wealthiest of men will
seek your favor.*
13 Inside the palace* the king's
daughter is absolutely
magnificent;
Her clothing is adorned
with# gold.
14 She will be brought to
the king in richly woven
garments.*

44:25 *Or "our souls." 44:26 *Lit.,
"Redeem." 45:Sup *See Glossary.
45:1 *Lit., "My works are." #Or "pen."
ΔOr "scribe." 45:4 *Or "success."
#Lit., "teach you."

45:6 *Or "justice." 45:9 *Or "The
queen." 45:12 *Or "soften your face."
45:13 *Lit., "house." #Lit., "with settings of." 45:14 *Or possibly, "in embroidered robes."

The virgin companions following her are brought in before you.

15 They will be brought with rejoicing and joy;
They will enter into the king's palace.

16 Your sons will take the place of your forefathers.
You will appoint them as princes in all the earth.[a]

17 I will make your name known throughout all generations to come.[b]
That is why peoples will praise you forever and ever.

To the director.
Of the sons of Korʹah.[c]
According to the Alʹaʹmoth style.*
A song.

46 God is our refuge and strength,[d]
A help that is readily found in times of distress.[e]

2 That is why we will not fear, though the earth undergoes change,
Though the mountains topple into the depths of the sea,[f]

3 Though its waters roar and foam over,[g]
Though the mountains rock on account of its turbulence. (Selah)

4 There is a river the streams of which make the city of God rejoice,[h]
The holy grand tabernacle of the Most High.

5 God is in the city;[i] it cannot be overthrown.
God will come to its aid at the break of dawn.[j]

6 The nations were in an uproar, the kingdoms were overthrown;
He raised his voice, and the earth melted.[k]

7 Jehovah of armies is with us;[l]

The God of Jacob is our secure refuge.* (Selah)

8 Come and witness the activities of Jehovah,
How he has done astonishing things on the earth.

9 He is bringing an end to wars throughout the earth.[a]
He breaks the bow and shatters the spear;
He burns the military wagons* with fire.

10 "Give in and know that I am God.
I will be exalted among the nations;[b]
I will be exalted in the earth."[c]

11 Jehovah of armies is with us;[d]
The God of Jacob is a secure refuge for us.[e] (Selah)

To the director.
Of the sons of Korʹah.[f] A melody.

47 All you peoples, clap your hands.
Shout in triumph to God with joyful cries.

2 For Jehovah the Most High is awe-inspiring;[g]
He is the great King over all the earth.[h]

3 He subdues peoples under us;
He puts nations under our feet.[i]

4 He chooses our inheritance for us,[j]
The pride of Jacob, whom he loves.[k] (Selah)

5 God has ascended amid joyful shouting;
Jehovah, amid the sound of the horn.*

6 Sing praises* to God, sing praises.
Sing praises to our King, sing praises.

CHAP. 45
a Isa 32:1

b Ps 72:17

CHAP. 46
c 2Ch 20:19

d Pr 14:26
  Isa 25:4

e De 4:7
  Ps 145:18, 19
  Na 1:7

f Isa 54:10

g Ps 93:4
  Jer 5:22

h 2Ch 6:6

i De 23:14
  Ps 132:13
  Isa 12:6

j Ex 14:24

k Jos 2:24

l Jos 1:9
  Jer 1:19
  Ro 8:31

Second Col.
a Isa 11:9
  Mic 4:3

b Isa 2:11

c 1Ch 29:11

d 2Ch 20:17

e Ps 48:3
  Ps 125:2

CHAP. 47
f 2Ch 20:19

g Ps 76:12

h Ps 22:28

i De 33:29

j De 9:5

k De 7:6
  Mal 1:2

46:7 *Or "secure height." **46:9** *Or possibly, "the shields." **47:5** *Or "ram's horn; trumpet." **47:6** *Or "Make music."

46:Sup *See Glossary.

7 For God is King of all the earth;[a]
Sing praises, and show insight.

8 God has become King over the nations.[b]
God sits on his holy throne.

9 The leaders of the peoples have gathered together
With the people of the God of Abraham.
For the rulers* of the earth belong to God.
He is highly exalted.[c]

A song.
A melody of the sons of Kor′ah.[d]

48 Jehovah is great and most worthy of praise
In the city of our God, in his holy mountain.

2 Beautiful in its loftiness, the joy of the whole earth,[e]
Is Mount Zion in the far north,
The city of the Grand King.[f]

3 In her fortified towers, God has made known that he is a secure refuge.*[g]

4 For look! kings have assembled;*
Together they have advanced.

5 When they saw it, they were amazed.
They panicked and fled in terror.

6 Trembling seized them there, Anguish like that of a woman giving birth.

7 With an east wind you wreck the ships of Tar′shish.

8 What we heard about, we have now seen for ourselves
In the city of Jehovah of armies, in the city of our God.
God will firmly establish it forever.[h] (Selah)

47:9 *Lit., "shields." 48:3 *Or "secure height." 48:4 *Or "met by appointment."

CHAP. 47
a Jer 10:7
  Zec 14:9

b 1Ch 16:31
  Ps 96:10
  Ps 97:1
  Re 19:6

c Ps 97:9

CHAP. 48
d 2Ch 20:19

e La 2:15

f Ps 47:8
  Ps 135:21
  Mt 5:34, 35

g Ps 125:1

h Ps 87:5
  Isa 2:2
  Mic 4:1

Second Col.
a Ps 26:3
  Ps 40:10
  Ps 63:3

b Ps 113:3

c Ps 17:7
  Ps 60:5
  Ps 98:2

d Ps 78:68

e Ps 97:8

f Ne 12:38, 39

g Isa 26:1

h Ps 31:14

i Isa 58:11

CHAP. 49
j 2Ch 20:19

k Ps 143:5

l Ps 27:1

---

9 We ponder your loyal love, O God,[a]
Within your temple.

10 Like your name, O God, your praise
Reaches to the ends of the earth.[b]
Your right hand is filled with righteousness.[c]

11 May Mount Zion[d] rejoice, May the towns* of Judah be joyful, because of your judgments.[e]

12 March around Zion; go all around it;
Count its towers.[f]

13 Set your hearts upon its ramparts.*[g]
Inspect its fortified towers,
So that you may tell about it to future generations.

14 For this God is our God[h] forever and ever.
He will guide us forevermore.*[i]

To the director.
Of the sons of Kor′ah.[j] A melody.

49 Hear this, all you peoples.
Pay attention, all you inhabitants of the world,*

2 Both small and great,*
Rich and poor alike.

3 My own mouth will speak wisdom,
And the meditation of my heart[k] will show understanding.

4 I will pay attention to a proverb;
I will expound my riddle with the harp.

5 Why should I fear during times of trouble,[l]
When I am surrounded by the evil* of those trying to overthrow me?

48:11 *Lit., "daughters." 48:13 *Or "fortified walls." 48:14 *Or possibly, "until we die." 49:1 *Or "system of things." 49:2 *Lit., "both sons of humankind as well as sons of man." 49:5 *Lit., "error."

6 Those who are trusting in
   their wealth[a]
   And who boast about their
   great riches,[b]

7 None of them can ever redeem a brother
   Or give to God a ransom for
   him,[c]

8 (The ransom* price for their
   life# is so precious
   That it is always beyond their
   reach);

9 That he should live forever
   and not see the pit.*[d]

10 He sees that even wise
    people die;
    The stupid and the unreason-
    ing perish together,[e]
    And they must leave their
    wealth to others.[f]

11 Their inner wish is that their
    houses will last forever,
    Their tents to generation
    after generation.
    They have named their
    estates after themselves.

12 But man, although honored,
    will not remain;[g]
    He is no better than the
    beasts that perish.[h]

13 This is the way of the stupid
    ones[i]
    And of those who follow
    them, who take pleasure in
    their empty words. (Selah)

14 They are assigned like sheep
    to the Grave.*
    Death will shepherd them;
    The upright will rule over
    them[j] in the morning.
    Every trace of them will fade
    away;[k]
    The Grave*[l] rather than a
    palace will be their home.[m]

15 But God will redeem me#
    from the power△ of the
    Grave,*[n]

For he will take hold of me.
(Selah)

16 Do not be afraid because
    a man becomes rich,
    Because the splendor of his
    house increases,

17 For when he dies he can take
    nothing with him;[a]
    His splendor will not go
    down with him.[b]

18 For during his lifetime he
    congratulates himself.*[c]
    (People praise you when you
    prosper.)[d]

19 But he finally joins the gener-
    ation of his forefathers.
    They will never again see the
    light.

20 A man who does not under-
    stand this, although
    honored,[e]
    Is no better than the beasts
    that perish.

A melody of A'saph.[f]

50 The God of gods,
    Jehovah,*[g] has spoken;
    He summons the earth
    From the rising of the sun
    until its setting.#

2 Out of Zion, the perfection
   of beauty,[h] God shines
   forth.

3 Our God will come and cannot remain silent.[i]
   Before him is a consuming
   fire,[j]
   And a great storm rages all
   around him.[k]

4 He summons the heavens
   above and the earth,[l]
   So as to judge his people:[m]

5 "Gather to me my loyal ones,
   Those making a covenant
   with me over sacrifice."[n]

6 The heavens proclaim his
   righteousness,
   For God himself is Judge.[o]
   (Selah)

CHAP. 49
a De 8:17, 18
  Pr 18:11
b Jer 9:23
  1Ti 6:17
c Pr 11:4
  Mt 16:26
d Ps 89:48
e Ec 2:16
  Ro 5:12
f Ps 39:6
  Pr 11:4
  Pr 23:4
  Ec 2:18
  Lu 12:19, 20
g Ps 39:5
  Jas 1:11
h Ps 49:20
i Lu 12:19, 20
j Mal 4:3
k Ps 39:11
l Job 24:19
m 1Sa 2:6
  Job 7:9
n Job 33:28
  Ps 16:10
  Ps 30:3
  Ps 86:13

Second Col.
a Job 1:21
  Ec 5:15
  1Ti 6:17
b Isa 10:3
c Lu 12:19
d Pr 14:20
e Ps 49:12

CHAP. 50
f 1Ch 25:1
g Ps 95:3
h Ps 48:2
  La 2:15
i Isa 65:6
j Ex 19:18
  Da 7:9, 10
  Heb 12:29
k Ps 97:3, 4
l De 30:19
  De 32:1
  Isa 1:2
m Mic 6:2
n Ex 24:8
o Ps 75:7

49:8 *Or "redemption." #Or "soul."
49:9 *Or "grave." 49:14, 15 *Or "Sheol," that is, the common grave of mankind. See Glossary. 49:15 #Or "my
soul." △Lit., "hand."

49:18 *Or "his soul." 50:1 *Or "The
Divine One, God, Jehovah." #Or "From
east to west."

7 "Listen, O my people, and
    I will speak;
  Israel, I will bear witness
    against you.[a]
  I am God, your God.[b]

8 I do not reprove you because
    of your sacrifices,
  Nor because of your whole
    burnt offerings that are
    constantly before me.[c]

9 I do not need to take a bull
    from your house,
  Nor goats* from your pens.[d]

10 For every wild animal of the
    forest is mine,[e]
  Even the beasts upon a thou-
    sand mountains.

11 I know every bird of the
    mountains;[f]
  The countless animals of the
    field are mine.

12 If I were hungry, I would not
    tell you,
  For the productive land and
    everything in it is mine.[g]

13 Will I eat the flesh of bulls
  And drink the blood of
    goats?[h]

14 Offer thanksgiving as your
    sacrifice to God,[i]
  And pay your vows to the
    Most High;[j]

15 Call on me in the time of
    distress.[k]
  I will rescue you, and you
    will glorify me."

16 But God will say to the
    wicked:
  "What right do you have to
    relate my regulations[m]
  Or to speak about my cove-
    nant?[n]

17 For you hate discipline,*
  And you keep turning your
    back on my words.[#][o]

18 When you see a thief, you
    approve of him,*[p]

And you keep company with
    adulterers.

19 You use your mouth to
    spread what is bad,
  And deception is attached to
    your tongue.[a]

20 You sit and speak against
    your own brother;[b]
  You reveal the faults of*
    your own mother's son.

21 When you did these things,
    I remained silent,
  So you thought that I would
    be just like you.
  But now I will reprove you,
  And I will state my case
    against you.[c]

22 Please consider this, you
    who forget God,[d]
  So that I may not tear you to
    pieces with no one to res-
    cue you.

23 The one who offers thanks-
    giving as his sacrifice glori-
    fies me,[e]
  And as for the one who fol-
    lows a set course,
  I will cause him to see salva-
    tion by God."[f]

To the director. A melody of David,
when Nathan the prophet came in to
him after David had relations
with Bath-she′ba.[g]

51 Show me favor, O God,
    according to your loyal
    love.[h]
  Blot out my transgressions
    according to your great
    mercy.[i]

2 Thoroughly wash me from
    my error,[j]
  And cleanse me from my
    sin.[k]

3 For I am well-aware of my
    transgressions,
  And my sin is always before
    me.*[l]

4 Against you—you above all*—
    I have sinned;[m]
  What is bad in your eyes
    I have done.[n]

CHAP. 50
a Ne 9:30
  Ps 81:8
b Ex 20:2
c 1Sa 15:22
  Isa 1:11
  Jer 7:22, 23
  Ho 6:6
d Mic 6:7
e 1Ch 29:14
  Ac 17:24
f Job 38:41
g De 10:14
  Job 41:11
  1Co 10:26
h Mic 6:6-8
i Ps 69:30, 31
  Pr 21:3
  Ho 6:6
  Heb 13:15
j De 23:21
  Ps 76:11
  Ec 5:4
k 2Ch 33:12, 13
  Ps 91:15
l Ps 22:21-23
  Ps 50:23
m Ps 7:4
  Mt 7:22, 23
  Ro 2:21
n De 31:20
  Heb 8:9
o Ps 9:26
  Isa 5:24
p Isa 5:22, 23

Second Col.
a Jer 9:5
b Le 19:16
c Ps 50:4
  Ec 12:14
d Ps 9:17
  Jer 2:32
  Ho 4:6
e 1Th 5:18
  Heb 13:15
f Mic 6:8

CHAP. 51
g 2Sa 11:3
h Nu 14:18
  Ps 25:7
  Ps 41:4
i Ps 103:13
  Pr 28:13
  Isa 43:25
  Isa 44:22
j Isa 1:18
  1Co 6:11
k Heb 9:13, 14
  1Jo 1:7
l Ps 32:5
  Ps 40:12
m Ge 39:9
  2Sa 12:13
n 2Sa 12:9
  Ps 38:18

50:9 *Lit., "male goats." 50:17 *Or
"instruction." #Lit., "throwing my
words behind you." 50:18 *Or possibly, "you join him."

50:20 *Or "defame." 51:3 *Or "on my
mind." 51:4 *Lit., "only you."

So that you might prove righteous when you speak
And be right in your judgment.[a]

5 Look! I was born guilty of error,
And my mother conceived me in sin.*[b]

6 Look! You find pleasure in truth in the inner person;[c]
Teach my innermost self* true wisdom.

7 Purify me from my sin with hyssop, so that I will be clean;[d]
Wash me, so that I will be whiter than snow.[e]

8 Let me hear sounds of joy and rejoicing,
So that the bones you crushed will rejoice.[f]

9 Turn your face away* from my sins,[g]
And wipe away# all my errors.[h]

10 Create in me a pure heart, O God,[i]
And put within me a new spirit,[j] a steadfast one.

11 Do not cast me out from your presence;
And do not take your holy spirit away from me.

12 Restore to me the joy of your salvation;[k]
Stir within me a willingness to obey you.*

13 I will teach transgressors your ways,[l]
So that sinners will return to you.

14 Save me from bloodguilt,[m]
O God, the God of my salvation,[n]
So that my tongue may joyfully declare your righteousness.[o]

15 O Jehovah, open my lips,
So that my mouth may declare your praise.[a]

16 For you do not want a sacrifice—otherwise I would give it;[b]
You do not find delight in a whole burnt offering.[c]

17 The sacrifices pleasing to God are a broken spirit;
A heart broken and crushed, O God, you will not reject.*[d]

18 In your goodwill do what is good for Zion;
Build up the walls of Jerusalem.

19 Then you will take delight in the sacrifices of righteousness,
The burnt sacrifices and the whole offerings;
Then bulls will be offered up on your altar.[e]

To the director. Mas'kil.* Of David, when Do'eg the E'dom·ite came and told Saul that David had come to the house of A·him'e·lech.[f]

52 Why do you boast about your evil acts, you mighty one?[g]
The loyal love of God lasts all day long.[h]

2 Your tongue, as sharp as a razor,[i]
Schemes harm and works deceitfully.[j]

3 You love evil more than what is good,
Lying more than speaking what is right. (Selah)

4 You love every harmful word,
O you deceitful tongue!

5 That is why God will pull you down once and for all;[k]
He will snatch you up and tear you away from your tent;[l]

CHAP. 51
a Ro 3:4
b Job 14:4
  Ro 3:23
  Ro 5:12
c 1Sa 16:7
  2Ki 20:3
  1Ch 29:17
d Le 14:3, 4
  Heb 9:13, 14
e Isa 1:18
f Ps 6:2
  Ps 38:3
  Isa 57:15
g Ps 103:12
  Isa 38:17
h Mic 7:19
i Jer 32:39
j Eze 11:19
  Eph 4:23
k Ps 21:1
l Ac 2:38
m Ge 9:6
n Ps 38:22
  Isa 12:2
  Re 7:10
o Ne 9:33
  Ps 35:28
  Ps 59:16
  Da 9:7

Second Col.
a Ps 34:1
  Ps 109:30
  Heb 13:15
b Pr 21:3
c 1Sa 15:22
  Ps 40:6
  Ho 6:6
d 2Ki 22:18, 19
  2Ch 33:13
  Ps 22:24
  Ps 34:18
  Pr 28:13
  Isa 57:15
  Lu 15:22-24
  Lu 18:13, 14
e Ho 14:2

CHAP. 52
f 1Sa 22:9
g 1Sa 21:7
  Ps 94:3, 4
h Ps 103:17
i Ps 57:4
  Ps 59:7
j 1Sa 22:9, 18
  Ps 109:2
k Pr 12:19
  Pr 19:9
l Ps 37:9

51:5 *Or "And sinful from the moment my mother conceived me." 51:6 *Or "my secret self." 51:9 *Or "Hide your face." #Or "blot out." 51:12 *Lit., "May you support me with a willing spirit."

51:17 *Or "despise." 52:Sup *See Glossary.

He will uproot you from the land of the living.[a] (Selah)

6 The righteous ones will see it and be filled with awe,[b]
And they will laugh at him.[c]

7 "Here is a man who did not make God his refuge,*[d]
But he trusted in his great riches[e]
And relied on# his own evil plots."△

8 But I will be like a luxuriant olive tree in God's house;
My trust is in God's loyal love,[f] forever and ever.

9 I will praise you forever because you have taken action;[g]
In the presence of your loyal ones,
I will hope in your name,[h] for it is good.

To the director; in the style of Ma′ha·lath.* Mas′kil.* Of David.

53 The foolish* one says in his heart:
"There is no Jehovah."[i]
Their unrighteous actions are corrupt and detestable;
No one is doing good.[j]

2 But God looks down from heaven on the sons of men
To see whether anyone has insight, whether anyone is seeking Jehovah.[l]

3 They have all turned away;
They are all alike corrupt.
No one is doing good,
Not even one.[m]

4 Do none of the wrongdoers understand?
They devour my people as if they were eating bread.
They do not call on Jehovah.[n]

5 But they will be filled with great terror,

Terror they have never felt before,*
For God will scatter the bones of those attacking you.#
You will put them to shame, for Jehovah has rejected them.

6 O that Israel's salvation may come from Zion![a]
When Jehovah gathers back his captive people,
Let Jacob be joyful, let Israel rejoice.

To the director; to be accompanied with stringed instruments. Mas′kil.* Of David, when the Ziph′ites came in and said to Saul: "David is hiding among us."[b]

54 O God, save me by your name,[c]
And defend me*[d] with your power.

2 O God, hear my prayer;[e]
Pay attention to the words of my mouth.

3 For strangers rise up against me,
And ruthless men seek my life.*[f]
They have no regard for God.#[g] (Selah)

4 Look! God is my helper;[h]
Jehovah is with those supporting me.*

5 He will repay my foes[i] with their own evil;
In your faithfulness, put an end to* them.[j]

6 I will sacrifice to you[k] willingly.
I will praise your name,
O Jehovah, for it is good.[l]

7 For he saves me from every distress,[m]
And I will look in triumph on my enemies.[n]

CHAP. 52
a Pr 2:22
b Ps 37:34
c Ps 58:10
d Jer 17:5
e Ps 49:6, 7
  Ps 11:28
f Ps 13:5
  Ps 147:11
g Ps 50:15
h Ps 27:14
  Ps 123:2
  Pr 18:10

CHAP. 53
i Ps 10:4
  Ro 1:21
j Ps 14:1-7
  Ro 3:10
k Ps 11:4
  Ps 33:13-15
  Jer 16:17
  Jer 23:24
l 1Ch 28:9
  2Ch 15:2
  2Ch 19:1, 3
  Isa 55:6
  Pr 3:12
m Ec 7:20
  Ro 3:12
n Job 21:7, 14

Second Col.
a Isa 12:6

CHAP. 54
b 1Sa 23:19
  1Sa 26:1
c Ps 20:1
  Ps 79:9
  Pr 18:10
d Ps 43:1
e Ps 13:3
  Ps 65:2
f Ps 22:16
  Ps 59:3
g Ps 36:1
h 1Ch 12:18
  Heb 13:6
i Ro 12:19
j Ps 143:12
k Ps 50:14
  Heb 13:15
l Ps 7:17
  Ps 52:9
m 2Sa 4:9
  Ps 34:19
  Ps 37:39
n Ps 37:34
  Ps 59:10

52:7 *Or "fortress." #Or "took shelter in." △Lit., "adversities by him." **53:Sup; 54:Sup** *See Glossary. **53:1** *Or "senseless." **53:5** *Or possibly, "Fear where there was nothing to fear." #Lit., "camping against you." **54:1** *Or "plead my cause." **54:3** *Or "soul." #Or "They do not keep God before them." **54:4** *Or "my soul." **54:5** *Lit., "silence."

To the director; to be accompanied with stringed instruments. Mas'kil.* Of David.

55 Listen to my prayer, O God,[a]

And do not ignore my request for mercy.*[b]

2 Do pay attention to me and answer me.[c]

My concern makes me restless,[d]

And I am distraught

3 Because of what the enemy is saying

And the pressure from the wicked one.

For they heap trouble upon me,

And in anger they harbor animosity against me.[e]

4 My heart is in anguish within me,[f]

And the terrors of death overwhelm me.[g]

5 Fear and trembling come upon me,

And shuddering grips me.

6 I keep saying: "If only I had wings like a dove!

I would fly away and reside in safety.

7 Look! I would flee far away.[h]

I would lodge in the wilderness.[i] (Selah)

8 I would hurry to a place of shelter

Away from the raging wind, away from the storm."

9 Confuse them, O Jehovah, and frustrate their plans,*[j]

For I have seen violence and conflict in the city.

10 Day and night they walk around on its walls;

Within it are malice and trouble.[k]

11 Ruin is in its midst;

Oppression and deception never depart from its public square.[l]

12 For it is not an enemy who taunts me;[a]

Otherwise I could put up with it.

It is not a foe who has risen up against me;

Otherwise I could conceal myself from him.

13 But it is you, a man like me,*[b]

My own companion whom I know well.[c]

14 We used to enjoy a warm friendship together;

Into the house of God we used to walk along with the multitude.

15 May destruction overtake them![d]

Let them go down alive into the Grave;*

For evil resides among them and within them.

16 As for me, I will call out to God,

And Jehovah will save me.[e]

17 Evening and morning and noontime, I am troubled and I groan,*[f]

And he hears my voice.[g]

18 He will rescue* me and give me# peace from those fighting against me,

For multitudes come against me.[h]

19 God will hear and respond to them,[i]

The one who sits enthroned from of old.[j] (Selah)

They will refuse to change, Those who have not feared God.[k]

20 He* attacked those at peace with him;[l]

He violated his covenant.[m]

21 His words are smoother than butter,[n]

CHAP. 55

a 1Pe 3:12

b Ps 28:2
Ps 143:7

c Ps 17:1

d Isa 38:14

e 2Sa 16:5-7

f Ps 69:29

g Ps 18:4
Ps 116:3
Isa 38:10

h 2Sa 15:14

i 1Sa 23:14

j 2Sa 15:31
2Sa 17:7

k 2Sa 17:1

l Ps 109:2

Second Col.

a Ps 41:9
Mt 26:21
Joh 13:18

b Ps 55:12
2Sa 16:23

c Lu 22:21
Lu 22:48

d 2Sa 17:23
2Sa 18:14
Ps 109:15
Mt 27:3, 5
Ac 1:16, 18

e Ps 91:15

f Ps 119:147
Da 6:10

g Ps 5:3

h 2Ch 32:7
Ps 3:6

i Ps 143:12

j De 33:27
Ps 90:2

k Ps 36:1

l 2Sa 15:12

m 2Sa 5:3
Ec 8:2

n 2Sa 16:23

55:Sup *See Glossary.   55:1 *Or "And do not hide yourself when I pray for help."   55:9 *Lit., "divide their tongue."

55:13 *Or "a man, my equal."   55:15 *Or "Sheol," that is, the common grave of mankind. See Glossary.   55:17 *Or "I am boisterous."   55:18 *Lit., "redeem." #Or "my soul."   55:20 *That is, the former friend mentioned in vss. 13 and 14.

But conflict is in his heart.
His words are softer than oil,
But they are drawn swords.[a]

22 Throw your burden on
Jehovah,[b]
And he will sustain you.[c]
Never will he allow the
righteous one to fall.*[d]

23 But you, O God, will bring
them down to the deep-
est pit.[e]
Those bloodguilty and
deceitful men will not
live out half their days.[f]
But as for me, I will trust
in you.

To the director; set to "The Silent
Dove That Is Far Away."
Of David. Mik'tam.* When the
Phi·lis'tines captured him in Gath.[g]

56 Show me favor, O God,
because mortal man
is attacking* me.
All day long they keep fighting and oppressing me.

2 My foes keep snapping at me
all day long;
Many arrogantly fight
against me.

3 When I am afraid,[h] I put
my trust in you.[i]

4 In God—whose word
I praise—
In God I put my trust;
I am not afraid.
What can mere man* do
to me?[j]

5 All day long they hurt my
interests;
Their only thought is to
harm me.[k]

6 They conceal themselves
to attack;
They watch my every step,[l]
Hoping to take away my
life.*[m]

7 Reject them because of their
wickedness.
Bring down the nations in
your anger, O God.[a]

8 You keep track of my wandering.[b]
Do collect my tears in your
skin bottle.[c]
Are they not recorded in
your book?[d]

9 My enemies will retreat on
the day that I call for help.[e]
Of this I am confident: God
is on my side.[f]

10 In God—whose word
I praise—
In Jehovah—whose word
I praise—

11 In God I put my trust;
I am not afraid.[g]
What can a mere human
do to me?[h]

12 I am bound by my vows
to you, O God;[i]
I will offer you expressions
of thanksgiving.[j]

13 For you have rescued me*
from death[k]
And prevented my feet from
stumbling,[l]
So that I may walk before
God in the light of the
living.[m]

To the director; set to "Do Not Bring
to Ruin." Of David. Mik'tam.* When he
ran away from Saul into the cave.[n]

57 Show me favor, O God,
show me favor,
For I take* refuge in you,[o]
And in the shadow of your
wings I take refuge until
the troubles pass.[p]

2 I call to God the Most High,
To the true God, who brings
them to an end for me.

3 He will send help from heav-
en and save me.[q]
He will frustrate the one
snapping at me. (Selah)

CHAP. 55
a Ps 28:3
  Ps 62:4
b Ps 43:5
  1Pe 5:6, 7
c Ps 37:5
  Ps 68:19
  Php 4:6, 7
d Ps 37:23, 24
  Ps 62:2
  Ps 121:3
e Ps 55:15
f Ps 5:6
  Pr 10:27

CHAP. 56
g 1Sa 21:10
h 1Sa 21:12
i Ps 18:2
j Ps 27:1
  Ps 56:10, 11
  Ro 8:31
  Heb 13:6
k Jer 18:18
l Lu 20:20
m Ps 59:3
  Ps 71:10

Second Col.
a Jer 18:23
b 1Sa 27:1
c Ps 39:12
d Mal 3:16
e Ps 18:40
f Ro 8:31
g Ps 27:1
h Ps 56:4
  Isa 51:7, 12
i Nu 30:2
  Ec 5:4
j Ps 50:23
k 2Co 1:10
l Ps 94:18
  Ps 116:8
m Job 33:29, 30

CHAP. 57
n 1Sa 22:1
  1Sa 24:3
  Ps 142:Sup
o Ps 18:2
p Ru 2:12
  Ps 17:8
q Ps 144:7
  Ac 12:11

55:22 *Or "stagger; totter." 56:Sup;
57:Sup *See Glossary. 56:1 *Or
"snapping at." 56:4 *Lit., "flesh."
56:6, 13 *Or "my soul."

57:1 *Or "my soul takes."

God will send his loyal love
and his faithfulness.[a]

4 I am* surrounded by lions;[b]
I must lie among men who
want to devour me,
Whose teeth are spears and
arrows
And whose tongue is a sharp
sword.[c]

5 Be exalted above the heavens, O God;
May your glory be over all
the earth.[d]

6 They have prepared a net to
ensnare my feet;[e]
I am* bowed down with distress.[f]
They have dug a pit ahead
of me,
But they fell into it themselves.[g] (Selah)

7 My heart is steadfast,
O God,[h]
My heart is steadfast.
I will sing and make music.

8 Do awake, my glory.
Do awake, O stringed instru-
ment; you too, O harp.
I will awaken the dawn.[i]

9 I will praise you among the
peoples, O Jehovah;[j]
I will sing praises* to you
among the nations.[k]

10 For your loyal love is great,
as high as the heavens,[l]
And your faithfulness, up to
the skies.

11 Be exalted above the heavens, O God;
May your glory be over all
the earth.[m]

To the director;
set to "Do Not Bring to Ruin."
Of David. Mikʹtam.*

58 Can you speak about righteousness when you are
silent?[n]
Can you judge in upright-
ness, you sons of men?[o]

2 Instead, you devise unrighteousness in your heart,[a]
And your hands dispense
violence in the land.[b]

3 The wicked go astray* from
birth;[#]
They are wayward, liars from
the time they are born.

4 Their venom is like the
venom of serpents;[c]
They are deaf like the cobra
that stops up its ear.

5 It will not listen to the voice
of charmers,
No matter how skillful their
spells.

6 O God, knock the teeth out
of their mouth!
Break the jaws of these
lions,* O Jehovah!

7 May they disappear like
waters that drain away.
May He bend his bow and
make them fall by his
arrows.

8 May they be like a snail that
melts away as it moves
along;
Like a woman's stillborn
child who never sees the
sun.

9 Before your cooking pots
feel the heat of the bramble,
He will sweep away both the
moist and the burning twig,
as in a storm wind.[d]

10 The righteous one will rejoice because he has seen
the vengeance;[e]
His feet will be drenched
with the blood of the
wicked.[f]

11 Then men will say: "Surely
there is a reward for the
righteous.[g]
There is indeed a God who
judges in the earth."[h]

CHAP. 57
a Ps 40:11
  Ps 61:7

b Ps 22:13
  Ps 35:17

c Ps 52:2
  Ps 64:3
  Pr 25:18

d Ps 57:11
  Ps 108:5

e Ps 35:7

f Ps 42:6

g 1Sa 24:4
  Pr 26:27

h Ps 112:7

i Ps 108:2-5

j Ps 9:11
  Ps 145:11, 12

k Ro 15:9

l Ps 36:5
  Ps 103:11

m Ps 8:1
  Ps 57:5
  Ps 108:5

CHAP. 58
n 2Ch 19:6

o Ps 82:2

Second Col.
a Ec 3:16
  Mic 3:9

b Ec 5:8
  Isa 10:1, 2

c Ps 140:3
  Jas 3:8

d Pr 10:25
  Jer 23:19

e Ps 52:5, 6
  Ps 64:10
  Eze 25:17
  Re 18:20

f Pr 21:18

g Isa 3:10

h Ps 9:16
  Ps 98:9

57:4, 6 *Or "My soul is." **57:9** *Or "make music." **58:Sup** *See Glossary.

58:3 *Or "are corrupt." #Lit., "from the womb." **58:6** *Or "maned young lions."

To the director; set to "Do Not Bring to Ruin." Of David. Mik'tam.*
When Saul sent men to watch David's house to put him to death.[a]

59 Rescue me from my ene-mies, O my God;[b]
Protect me from those rising up against me.[c]

2 Rescue me from those who act wickedly,
And save me from violent* men.

3 Look! They wait to ambush me;*[d]
Strong men attack me
But not because I have revolted or sinned,[e]
O Jehovah.

4 Though I did no wrong, they run and prepare to attack.
Do arise at my calling and see.

5 For you, O Jehovah God of armies, are the God of Israel.[f]
Awake to turn your attention to all the nations.
Do not show mercy to any malicious traitors.[g] (Selah)

6 They return each evening;[h]
They growl* like dogs[i] and prowl around the city.[j]

7 Look what pours* forth from their mouth;
Their lips are like swords,[k]
For they say: "Who is listen-ing?"[l]

8 But you, O Jehovah, will laugh at them;[m]
You will scoff at all the na-tions.[n]

9 O my Strength, I will keep watch for you;[o]
For God is my secure refuge.*[p]

10 The God who shows loyal love to me will come to my aid;[q]

God will cause me to look in triumph on my foes.[a]

11 Do not kill them, so that my people may not forget.
By your power make them wander about;
Cause their downfall, O Jehovah, our shield.[b]

12 For the sin of their mouth, the word of their lips,
May they be trapped by their pride,[c]
Because of the cursing and deception that they speak.

13 Finish them off in your wrath;[d]
Finish them off, so that they are no more;
Make them know that God is ruling in Jacob and to the ends of the earth.[e] (Selah)

14 Let them return in the eve-ning;
Let them growl* like dogs and prowl around the city.[f]

15 Let them wander about for something to eat;[g]
Do not let them be satisfied or find a lodging place.

16 But as for me, I will sing about your strength;[h]
In the morning I will joyfully tell about your loyal love.
For you are my secure refuge[i]
And a place for me to flee in my time of distress.[j]

17 O my Strength, to you I will sing praises,*[k]
For God is my secure refuge, the God who shows loyal love to me.[l]

To the director; set to "The Lily of Reminder." Mik'tam.* Of David.
For teaching. When he fought with A'ram-na·ha·ra'im and A'ram-Zo'bah, and Jo'ab returned and struck down 12,000 E'dom·ites in the Valley of Salt.[m]

60 O God, you rejected us; you broke through our defenses.[n]

CHAP. 59
a 1Sa 19:11
b 1Sa 19:12
  Ps 18:48
  Ps 71:4
c Ps 12:5
  Ps 91:14
d 1Sa 19:1
  Ps 10:9
  Ps 71:10
e 1Sa 24:11
  1Sa 26:18
  Ps 69:4
f De 33:29
g Pr 2:22
h 1Sa 19:11
i Ps 22:16
j Ps 59:14
k Ps 57:4
  Ps 64:3
l Ps 10:4, 11
  Ps 73:3, 11
m Ps 37:12, 13
n Ps 33:10
o Ps 27:1
  Ps 46:1
p Ps 9:9
  Ps 62:2
q Ps 6:4

Second Col.
a Ps 54:7
b Ge 15:1
  De 33:29
  Ps 3:3
c Ps 64:8
  Pr 12:13
  Pr 16:18
d Ps 7:9
e 1Sa 17:46
  Ps 9:16
  Ps 83:17, 18
f Ps 59:6
g Ps 109:2, 10
h Job 37:23
  Ps 21:13
  Ps 145:10-12
i 1Sa 17:37
  Ps 61:3
j Pr 18:10
k Isa 12:2
l Ps 59:10

CHAP. 60
m 2Sa 8:13
  1Ch 18:3
n Ps 60:10

59:Sup; 60:Sup *See Glossary.
59:Sup *Lit., "the." 59:2 *Or "blood-thirsty." 59:3 *Or "my soul." 59:6, 14 *Or "bark." 59:7 *Or "bubbles." 59:9 *Or "secure height."

59:17 *Or "make music."

You were angry with us;
but now accept us back!

2 You caused the earth to
quake; you split it open.
Repair its breaches, for it
is falling.

3 You caused your people to
suffer hardship.
You made us drink wine that
makes us stagger.[a]

4 Give* a signal to those fear-
ing you
To flee and dodge the bow.
(Selah)

5 So that your loved ones may
be rescued,
Save us with your right hand
and answer us.[b]

6 God has spoken in his holiness:*
"I will exult, I will give
out She'chem as an inheritance,[c]
And I will measure off the
Valley# of Suc'coth.[d]

7 Gil'e·ad belongs to me, as
does Ma·nas'seh,[e]
And E'phra·im is the helmet*
for my head;
Judah is my commander's
staff.[f]

8 Mo'ab is my washbasin.[g]
Over E'dom I will throw my
sandal.[h]
Over Phi·lis'ti·a I will shout in
triumph."[i]

9 Who will bring me to the be-
sieged* city?
Who will lead me as far as
E'dom?[j]

10 Is it not you, O God, who
have rejected us,
Our God, who no longer goes
out with our armies?[k]

11 Help us in our distress,
For salvation by humans is
worthless.[l]

12 By God we will gain power,[a]
And he will trample on our
adversaries.[b]

To the director; to be accompanied
with stringed instruments. Of David.

61 Hear, O God, my cry for
help.
Do pay attention to my
prayer.[c]

2 From the ends of the earth
I will cry out to you
When my heart is in
despair.*[d]
Lead me onto a rock that is
higher than I am.[e]

3 For you are my refuge,
A strong tower that protects
me from the enemy.[f]

4 I will be a guest in your tent
forever;[g]
I will take refuge in the shelter of your wings.[h] (Selah)

5 For you, O God, have heard
my vows.
You have given me the inheritance belonging to those
who fear your name.[i]

6 You will add days to the life*
of the king,[j]
And his years will be from
generation to generation.

7 He will sit enthroned* forever before God;[k]
Grant him# loyal love and
faithfulness, so that these
may safeguard him.[l]

8 Then I will sing praises* to
your name forever[m]
As I pay my vows day after
day.[n]

To the director; of Je·du'thun.*
A melody of David.

62 Indeed, I wait* silently for
God.
My salvation comes from
him.[o]

CHAP. 60
a Isa 51:17
b Ps 18:35
  Ps 21:8
  Ps 108:6
  Ps 118:15
  Isa 41:10
c Ge 12:6, 7
d Jos 13:27, 28
  Ps 108:7-9
e Jos 13:29-31
f Ge 49:10
g Nu 24:17
  2Sa 8:2
h Nu 24:18
  2Sa 8:14
i 2Sa 8:1
j 2Sa 8:14
  Ps 108:10-13
k De 1:42
  De 20:4
  Jos 7:12
l Ps 62:9
  Ps 118:8
  Ps 146:3

Second Col.
a Ps 18:32
b 2Sa 10:12
  Ps 44:5

CHAP. 61
c Ps 5:2
  Ps 17:1
  Ps 28:2
  Ps 55:1
d Jon 2:2
e Ps 27:5
  Ps 40:2
f 1Sa 17:45
  Ps 18:2
  Pr 18:10
g Ps 23:6
  Ps 27:4
h Ps 63:7
i Ps 115:13
j Ps 18:50
  Ps 21:1, 4
k 2Sa 7:16, 17
  Ps 41:12
l Ps 40:11
  Ps 143:12
  Pr 20:28
m Ps 146:2
n Ps 65:1
  Ps 66:13
  Ec 5:4

CHAP. 62
o Ps 37:39
  Ps 68:19
  Isa 12:2

60:4 *Or possibly, "You have given."
60:6 *Or possibly, "in his holy place."
#Or "Low Plain." 60:7 *Lit., "strong-
hold." 60:9 *Or possibly, "fortified."

61:2 *Or "grows feeble." 61:6 *Lit.,
"days." 61:7 *Or "will dwell." #Or
"Assign." 61:8 *Or "make music."
62:Sup *See Glossary. 62:1 *Or "my
soul waits."

2 Indeed, he is my rock and
   my salvation, my secure
   refuge;*[a]
   I will never be greatly
   shaken.[b]
3 How long will you assault a
   man in order to murder
   him?[c]
   All of you are as dangerous
   as a leaning wall, a stone
   wall ready to collapse.*
4 For they consult together to
   topple him from his high
   position;*
   They take pleasure in lying.
   With their mouth they
   bless, but inside they are
   cursing.[d] (*Selah*)
5 Indeed, I wait silently*
   for God[e]
   Because my hope comes
   from him.[f]
6 Indeed, he is my rock and
   my salvation, my secure
   refuge;
   I will never be shaken.[g]
7 Upon God depends my salvation and my glory.
   My strong rock, my refuge,
   is God.[h]
8 Trust in him at all times,
   O people.
   Pour out your hearts before
   him.[i]
   God is a refuge for us.[j]
   (*Selah*)
9 The sons of men are a mere
   breath,
   The sons of mankind are
   a delusion.[k]
   When laid together on the
   scales, they are lighter
   than a mere breath.[l]
10 Do not trust in extortion
   Or put false hopes in robbery.

If your wealth increases, do
   not set your heart on it.[a]
11 Once God has spoken, twice
   I have heard this:
   That strength belongs to
   God.[b]
12 Also loyal love is yours,
   O Jehovah,[c]
   For you repay each one ac-
   cording to his deeds.[d]

*A melody of David, when he was
in the wilderness of Judah.*[e]

63
O God, you are my God,
   I keep looking for you.[f]
I do thirst* for you.[g]
I am[#] faint with longing
   for you
In a dry and parched land,
   where there is no water.[h]
2 So I have looked upon you
   in the holy place;
   I have seen your strength
   and your glory.[i]
3 Because your loyal love is
   better than life,[j]
   My own lips will glorify you.[k]
4 Thus I will praise you all my
   life;
   In your name I will lift up my
   hands.
5 I am* satisfied with the best
   and choicest portion,[#]
   So my mouth will praise you
   with joy on my lips.[l]
6 I remember you while upon
   my bed;
   I meditate on you during the
   watches of the night.[m]
7 For you are my helper,[n]
   And I shout joyfully in the
   shadow of your wings.[o]
8 I cling* to you;
   Your right hand keeps fast
   hold on me.[p]
9 But those who seek to
   destroy my life*

CHAP. 62
a Ps 18:2
b Ps 37:23, 24
  2Co 4:8, 9
c Ps 38:12
d Ps 5:9
  Ps 28:3
  Ps 55:21
e Ps 43:5
  Mic 7:7
f Ps 62:1, 2
  Ps 71:5
g Ps 16:8
  Pr 10:30
h Ps 95:1
  Isa 26:4
i 1Sa 1:15
j Pr 14:26
k Ps 60:11
l Isa 40:15

Second Col.
a De 6:10-12
  Job 31:24, 28
  Pr 11:4, 28
  Pr 23:4, 5
  Mt 6:19, 24
  Mr 8:36
  Lu 12:15
  1Ti 6:17
  1Jo 2:16
b Job 9:4
  Na 1:3
  Re 19:1
c Ps 36:7
  Ps 86:15
  Mic 7:18
d Job 34:11
  Pr 24:12
  Ro 2:6
  2Co 5:10
  Ga 6:7
  2Ti 4:14
  Re 20:12, 13
  Re 22:12

CHAP. 63
e 1Sa 23:14
f Isa 26:9
g Ps 42:2
h Ps 63:Sup
  Ps 143:6
i 1Ch 16:28
  Ps 96:6
j Ps 30:5
  Ps 100:5
k Ps 66:16, 17
l Ps 71:23
  Ps 135:3
m Ps 119:55,
  148
n 1Sa 17:37
o Ps 5:11
  Ps 57:1
  Ps 61:4
p Isa 41:10

62:2 *Or "secure height." **62:3** *Or
possibly, "All of you, as if he were a
leaning wall, a stone wall ready to collapse." **62:4** *Or "his dignity." **62:5**
*Or "wait silently, O my soul."

63:1 *Or "My soul thirsts." #Lit., "My
flesh is." **63:5** *Or "My soul is." #Lit.,
"as with fat and fatness." **63:8** *Or
"My soul clings." **63:9** *Or "destroy my
soul; kill me."

Will descend into the depths
of the earth.

10 They will be handed over to
the power of the sword;
They will become food for
jackals.*

11 But the king will rejoice in
God.
Every person swearing by
Him will exult,*
For the mouth of those
speaking lies will be si-
lenced.

To the director. A melody of David.

64 Hear my voice, O God, as
I plead.[a]
Safeguard my life from the
dreadfulness of the enemy.

2 Shield me from the secret
plots of wicked men,[b]
From the crowd of wrong-
doers.

3 They sharpen their tongue
just like a sword;
They aim their cruel words
like arrows,

4 To shoot at the innocent
from their hiding places;
They shoot at him suddenly,
without fear.

5 They hold fast to their evil
intent;*
They discuss how to hide
their traps.
They say: "Who will see
them?"[c]

6 They search out new ways of
wrongdoing;
They secretly devise their
shrewd strategy;[d]
The thinking within each
one's heart is unfathom-
able.

7 But God will shoot at them;[e]
Suddenly they will be
wounded by an arrow.

8 Their own tongue will cause
their downfall;[f]

63:10 *Or "foxes." 63:11; 64:10 *Or
"boast." 64:5 *Or "They encourage
one another to do evil."

CHAP. 64
a Ps 55:1

b Ps 56:6
Ps 109:2

c Ps 10:4, 11
Ps 59:7

d Ps 140:5

e Ps 7:11, 12

f Pr 12:13
Pr 18:7

Second Col.
a Ps 107:40, 43

b Ps 58:10
Ps 68:2, 3

CHAP. 65
c Ps 76:2

d Ps 116:18
Ec 5:4

e Ps 145:18
Ac 10:31
1Jo 5:14

f Ps 40:12
Ro 7:23, 24
Ga 5:17

g Ps 51:2
Isa 1:18
1Jo 1:7

h Ps 15:1-5
Ps 27:4
Ps 84:1-4
Ps 84:10

i Ps 36:7, 8

j 1Sa 3:3
1Ch 16:1

k De 10:21
Re 15:3

l Ps 22:27

m Ps 93:1

n Ps 89:9
Ps 107:29

o Isa 17:12, 13
Isa 57:20

p Ps 66:3

All those looking on will
shake their head.

9 Then all men will become
afraid,
And they will proclaim what
God has done,
And they will have insight
into his deeds.[a]

10 The righteous one will rejoice in Jehovah and take
refuge in him;[b]
All the upright in heart will
exult.*

To the director.
A melody of David. A song.

65 Praise awaits you, O God,
in Zion;[c]
We will pay our vows to you.[d]

2 O Hearer of prayer, to you
people of all sorts* will
come.[e]

3 My errors have over-
whelmed me,[f]
But you cover over our transgressions.[g]

4 Happy is the one whom you
choose and bring near
To reside in your
courtyards.[h]
We will be satisfied with the
goodness of your house,[i]
Your holy temple.*[j]

5 You will answer us with awe-
inspiring deeds[k] of righteousness,
O God of our salvation;
You are the Confidence of all
the ends of the earth[l]
And of those distant across
the sea.

6 You* firmly established the
mountains by your power;
You* are clothed with mightiness.[m]

7 You* calm the raging seas,[n]
The crash of their waves and
the turmoil of the nations.[o]

8 The inhabitants of remote
places will be awestruck by
your signs;[p]

65:2 *Lit., "all flesh." 65:4 *Or "sanctuary." 65:6, 7 *Lit., "He."

You will cause those from the sunrise to the sunset to shout joyfully.

9 You care for the earth,
Making it abundantly fruitful* and very rich.[a]
The stream from God is full of water;
You provide grain for them,[b]
For that is how you prepared the earth.

10 You drench its furrows and level off its plowed soil;*
You soften it with showers of rain; you bless its growth.[c]

11 You crown the year with your goodness;
Your tracks overflow with abundance.*[d]

12 The pastures of the wilderness keep overflowing,*[e]
And the hills are clothed with joyfulness.[f]

13 The pastures are covered with flocks,
And the valleys* are carpeted with grain.[g]
They shout in triumph, yes, they sing.[h]

To the director. A song. A melody.

66 Shout in triumph to God, all the earth.[i]

2 Sing praises* to his glorious name.
Make his praise glorious.[j]

3 Say to God: "How awe-inspiring your works are![k]
Because of your great power,
Your enemies will cringe before you.[l]

4 All the earth will bow down to you;[m]
They will sing praises to you;
They will sing praises to your name."[n] (Selah)

5 Come and see the works of God.
His deeds toward the sons of men are awe-inspiring.[a]

6 He changed the sea into dry land;[b]
They crossed the river on foot.[c]
There we rejoiced in him.[d]

7 He rules forever[e] by his might.
His eyes keep watch on the nations.[f]
Those who are stubborn should not exalt themselves.[g] (Selah)

8 Praise our God, you peoples,[h]
And let the sound of his praise be heard.

9 He preserves us alive;*[i]
He does not allow our feet to stumble.#[j]

10 For you have examined us, O God;[k]
As silver is refined, so you have refined us.

11 You brought us into a hunting net;
You put a crushing burden upon us.*

12 You allowed mortal man to ride over us;*
We came through fire and through water;
Then you brought us to a place of relief.

13 I will come into your house with whole burnt offerings;[l]
I will pay my vows to you[m]

14 That my lips promised[n]
And my mouth spoke when I was in distress.

15 I will offer burnt offerings of fattened animals to you
With the smoke of sacrificial rams.

CHAP. 65
a De 11:11, 12
  Ac 14:17

b Ps 104:14, 15

c Ps 147:7, 8

d Ge 27:28
  De 33:16
  Mal 3:10

e Isa 35:1

f Isa 55:12

g Isa 30:23

h Ac 14:17

CHAP. 66
i Ps 98:4

j Ps 72:19
  Re 4:11

k Ex 15:16
  Ps 76:12
  Isa 2:19
  Jer 10:10

l Ps 81:15

m Ps 22:27
  Mal 1:11

n Isa 42:10
  Re 15:4

Second Col.
a Ps 46:8
  Zep 2:11

b Ex 14:21, 22

c Jos 3:15, 16

d Ex 15:1

e Da 4:34
  1Ti 1:17

f Ps 11:4
  Pr 15:3
  Heb 4:13

g Isa 37:29

h De 32:43
  Ro 15:10

i 1Sa 25:29

j 1Sa 2:9
  Ps 121:3

k De 8:2

l Nu 15:3

m Ps 56:12
  Ps 116:14
  Ec 5:4, 5

n Nu 30:2
  Jg 11:35

65:9 *Lit., "making it overflow." 65:10 *Or "its ridges." 65:11 *Lit., "drip with fatness." 65:12 *Lit., "dripping." 65:13 *Or "low plains." 66:2 *Or "Make music."

66:9 *Or "sets our soul in life." #Or "stagger; totter." 66:11 *Lit., "on our hips." 66:12 *Lit., "our head."

I will offer bulls along with male goats. (Selah)

16 Come and listen, all you who fear God,
And I will tell you what he has done for me.*[a]

17 I called to him with my mouth
And glorified him with my tongue.

18 If I had harbored anything hurtful in my heart,
Jehovah would not have heard me.[b]

19 But God did hear;[c]
He paid attention to my prayer.[d]

20 Praise to God, who did not reject my prayer
Or withhold his loyal love from me.

To the director; to be accompanied with stringed instruments. A melody. A song.

67 God will show us favor and bless us;
He will make his face shine upon us*[e] (Selah)

2 So that your way may be known throughout the earth,[f]
Your acts of salvation among all the nations.[g]

3 Let peoples praise you, O God;
Let all the peoples praise you.

4 Let nations rejoice and shout joyfully,[h]
For you will judge the peoples fairly,[i]
You will guide the nations of the earth. (Selah)

5 Let peoples praise you, O God;
Let all the peoples praise you.

6 The earth will give its produce;[j]
God, our God, will bless us.[k]

CHAP. 66
a Ps 22:24
b Job 27:8, 9
Pr 15:29
Pr 28:9
Isa 1:15
Joh 9:31
c Ps 34:6
Ps 65:2
Ps 116:1
1Jo 3:22
d Heb 5:7

CHAP. 67
e Nu 6:25
Pr 16:15
f Ro 10:18
Col 1:23
g Ps 98:2
Isa 49:6
Lu 2:30, 31
Ac 28:28
Tit 2:11
h Isa 42:10
i Ps 9:8
Ps 96:10
Ps 98:9
Ro 2:5
j Le 26:4
Ps 85:12
Isa 30:23
Eze 34:27
k Ge 17:7

Second Col.
a Ps 22:27
Re 15:4

CHAP. 68
b Nu 10:35
Ps 21:8
c Na 1:6
d Ps 32:11
e Isa 12:4
f Ex 6:3
g Ex 22:22-24
De 10:17, 18
Ps 10:14
Ps 146:9
h Isa 57:15
i Ps 113:9
j Isa 61:1
k De 28:15, 23
Ps 107:33, 34
l Ex 13:21
m Ps 114:1, 4
Heb 12:26
n Ex 19:18
Jg 5:4, 5

---

7 God will bless us,
And all the ends of the earth will fear* him.[a]

To the director. Of David. A melody. A song.

68 Let God rise up, let his enemies be scattered,
And let those who hate him flee from before him.[b]

2 As smoke is driven away, may you drive them away;
As wax melts before the fire,
So let the wicked perish before God.[c]

3 But let the righteous rejoice;[d]
May they be overjoyed before God;
May they exult with rejoicing.

4 Sing to God; sing praises* to his name.[e]
Sing to the One riding through the desert plains.*
Jah△ is his name!* Rejoice before him!

5 A father of the fatherless and a protector* of widows*
Is God in his holy dwelling.[h]

6 God gives those who are alone a home to dwell in;[i]
He leads prisoners out into prosperity.[j]
But the stubborn* must live in a parched land.[k]

7 O God, when you led* your people,[l]
When you marched through the desert, (Selah)

8 The earth quaked;[m]
Heaven poured down rain* because of God;
This Si'nai quaked because of God, the God of Israel.[n]

9 You made it rain in abundance, O God;

66:16 *Or "my soul." 67:7 *Or "honor." 68:4 *Or "make music." *Or possibly, "on the clouds." △"Jah" is a shortened form of the name Jehovah. 68:5 *Lit., "judge." 68:6 *Or "rebellious." 68:7 *Lit., "went out before." 68:8 *Lit., "dripped."

You reinvigorated your exhausted people.*

10 They dwelled in your tent
community;[a]

In your goodness, you provided for the poor, O God.

11 Jehovah gives the command;

The women proclaiming the
good news are a large
army.[b]

12 The kings of armies flee,[c]
they flee!

She who remains at home
shares in the spoil.[d]

13 Although you men were lying
among the campfires,*

There will be the wings of a
dove covered with silver,

With pinions of fine[#] gold.

14 When the Almighty One
scattered its kings,[e]

Snow fell in Zal′mon.*

15 The mountain of Ba′shan[f]
is a mountain of God;*

The mountain of Ba′shan
is a mountain of peaks.

16 Why do you look with envy,
you mountains of peaks,

Toward the mountain that
God has chosen* as his
dwelling?[g]

Indeed, Jehovah will reside
there forever.[h]

17 The war chariots of God are
tens of thousands, thou-
sands upon thousands.[i]

Jehovah has come from
Si′nai into the holy place.[j]

18 You ascended on high;[k]

You carried away captives;

You took gifts in the form of
men,[l]

Yes, even stubborn ones,[m]
to reside among them,
O Jah God.

19 May Jehovah be praised, who
daily carries our load,[a]

The true God of our salvation. (Selah)

20 The true God is for us a God
who saves;[b]

And Jehovah the Sovereign
Lord provides escape from
death.[c]

21 Yes, God will smash the
heads of his enemies,

The hairy crown of the head
of anyone who continues*
in his guilt.[d]

22 Jehovah has said: "I will
bring them back from
Ba′shan;[e]

I will bring them back from
the depths of the sea,

23 So that your foot may be
awash in blood[f]

And the tongue of your dogs
may have its portion from
the enemies."

24 They see your processions,
O God,

The processions of my God,
my King, into the holy
place.[g]

25 The singers walk in front, the
musicians playing stringed
instruments after them;[h]

In between are the young
women playing tambou-
rines.[i]

26 In congregated throngs,*
praise God;

Praise Jehovah, you who are
from the Source of Israel.[j]

27 There Benjamin,[k] the youngest, is subduing them,

Also the princes of Judah
with their noisy crowd,

The princes of Zeb′u·lun,
the princes of Naph′ta·li.

28 Your God has decreed that
you will be strong.

Show your strength, O God,
you who have acted in our
behalf.[l]

CHAP. 68

a Nu 10:34

b Ex 15:20
Jg 5:1
Jg 11:34
1Sa 18:6

c Nu 31:25-27
Jos 10:12, 16
Jos 12:7
Jg 5:19

d Nu 31:27
1Sa 30:23-25

e Nu 21:3
Jos 10:5, 10

f Nu 21:33
De 3:8, 10

g 1Ch 11:5
Ps 48:2, 3
Ps 132:13

h De 12:5, 6
1Ki 9:3
Heb 12:22

i 2Ki 6:16, 17
Mt 26:53

j Ex 19:23
De 33:2

k 2Sa 5:7

l Eph 4:8, 11

m De 2:36
De 7:22

Second Col.

a Ps 55:22
1Pe 5:6, 7

b Isa 12:2
Isa 45:17

c Ge 32:39

d Ps 55:23
Eze 18:26

e Nu 21:33

f Ps 58:10

g 1Ch 15:25, 28
Ps 24:7

h 1Ch 15:16
Ps 87:7
Ps 150:3

i Jg 11:34
1Sa 18:6

j Ps 95:6
Isa 44:2

k Ge 49:27
1Sa 9:21

l Ps 138:8

68:9 *Lit., "inheritance." 68:13 *Or
possibly, "the sheepfolds." #Or
"yellowish-green." 68:14 *Or "It was
as if it snowed in Zalmon." 68:15 *Or
"a majestic mountain." 68:16 *Or "desires."

68:21 *Or "walks about." 68:26 *Lit.,
"In assemblies."

29 Because of your temple at
  Jerusalem,[a]
  Kings will bring gifts to you.[b]
30 Rebuke the wild beasts of the
  reeds,
  The assembly of bulls[c] and
  their calves,
  Until the peoples bow down
  bringing* pieces of silver.
  But he scatters the peoples
  who delight in war.
31 Bronze articles will be
  brought* out of Egypt;[d]
  Cush will hasten to offer
  gifts to God.
32 O kingdoms of the earth,
  sing to God,[e]
  Sing praises* to Jehovah,
  (*Selah*)
33 To the one who rides the ancient heaven of heavens.[f]
  Look! He thunders with his
  voice, his mighty voice.
34 Acknowledge God's
  strength.[g]
  His majesty is over Israel,
  And his strength is in the
  skies.*
35 God is awe-inspiring from
  his* grand sanctuary.[h]
  He is the God of Israel,
  Who gives strength and power to the people.[i]
  Praise to God.

To the director; set to "The Lilies."
  Of David.

69 Save me, O God, for
  the waters threaten my
  life.*[j]
2 I have sunk down into the
  deep mud, where there is
  no solid ground.[k]
  I have come into deep
  waters,
  And the rushing stream has
  swept me away.[l]

3 I am exhausted from calling
  out;[a]
  My throat has become
  hoarse.
  My eyes have grown weary
  while waiting for my God.[b]
4 Those hating me without
  cause[c]
  Are more numerous than the
  hairs of my head.
  Those who would do away
  with me,
  My treacherous enemies,*
  have become many.
  I was forced to hand over
  what I had not stolen.
5 O God, you are aware of my
  foolishness,
  And my guilt is not hidden
  from you.
6 May those hoping in you
  not be put to shame
  because of me,
  O Sovereign Lord, Jehovah
  of armies.
  May those seeking you
  not be humiliated because
  of me,
  O God of Israel.
7 I suffer reproach on your
  account;[d]
  Humiliation covers my face.[e]
8 I have become a stranger to
  my brothers,
  A foreigner to the sons of my
  mother.[f]
9 Zeal for your house has
  consumed me,[g]
  And the reproaches of those
  reproaching you have fall-
  en upon me.[h]
10 When I humbled myself* with
  fasting,*
  I was reproached for it.
11 When I made sackcloth my
  clothing,
  I became an object of scorn*
  to them.

CHAP. 68
a 1Ki 6:1
  1Ch 16:1
  Ezr 5:14

b 1Ki 10:10
  2Ch 32:23
  Ps 72:10

c Eze 39:18

d Isa 45:14
  Isa 60:5

e De 32:43

f Ps 104:3

g Ps 96:7

h Ps 47:2
  Ps 66:5

i Ps 29:11
  Isa 40:29-31

CHAP. 69
j Ps 144:7
  La 3:54
  Jon 2:5

k Ps 40:2

l Ps 32:6
  Jon 2:3

Second Col.
a Ps 22:2

b Ps 119:82
  Ps 119:123
  Isa 38:14

c Lu 23:22
  Joh 15:24, 25

d Ps 22:6
  Jer 15:15

e Isa 50:6
  Mt 26:67
  Mt 27:29

f Job 19:13
  Ps 31:11
  Joh 1:11
  Joh 7:5

g 1Ki 19:10
  Ps 119:139
  Mt 21:12, 13
  Mr 11:15-17
  Joh 2:13-17

h Ro 15:3

68:30 *Or possibly, "stamping down
on." **68:31** *Or possibly, "Ambassadors will come." **68:32** *Or "Make
music." **68:34** *Lit., "clouds." **68:35**
*Lit., "your." **69:1** *Or "have come to
my soul."

69:4 *Or "enemies for no reason."
69:10 *Lit., "my soul." *Or possibly,
"When I wept and fasted." **69:11** *Lit.,
"a proverb."

12 I am the talk of those sitting
   in the city gate,
   And the drunkards make me
   the subject of their songs.
13 But may my prayer come to
   you,
   O Jehovah, at an acceptable
   time.[a]
   In your abundant loyal love,
   O God,
   Answer me with your sure
   acts of salvation.[b]
14 Rescue me from the mire;
   Do not let me sink down.
   Rescue me from those who
   hate me
   And from the deep waters.[c]
15 Do not let the rushing floodwaters sweep me away,[d]
   Or let the deep swallow me,
   Or let the well* close its
   mouth over me.[e]
16 Answer me, O Jehovah, for
   your loyal love is good,[f]
   According to your abundant
   mercy turn toward me,[g]
17 And do not hide your face
   from your servant.[h]
   Answer me quickly, for I am
   in distress.[i]
18 Come near to me and rescue
   me;*
   Redeem me on account of my
   enemies.
19 You know my reproach and
   my disgrace and my humiliation.[j]
   You see all my foes.
20 Reproach has broken my
   heart, and the wound is
   incurable.*
   I was hoping for sympathy,
   but there was none,[k]
   And for comforters, but
   I found none.[l]
21 But for food they gave me
   poison,*[m]

And for my thirst they gave
   me vinegar to drink.[a]
22 Let their table become a trap
   for them,
   And their prosperity,
   a snare.[b]
23 Let their eyes become darkened so that they cannot
   see,
   And make their hips tremble
   constantly.
24 Pour out upon them your
   indignation,*
   And may your burning anger
   overtake them.[c]
25 Let their encampment*
   become desolate;
   Let there be no inhabitant
   in their tents.[d]
26 For they pursue the one
   whom you struck,
   And they keep recounting
   the pains of those you
   wounded.
27 Add more guilt to their guilt,
   And may they have no share
   in your righteousness.
28 Let them be erased from the
   book of the living,*[e]
   And may they not be
   enrolled among the
   righteous.[f]
29 But I am afflicted and in
   pain.[g]
   May your saving power,
   O God, protect me.
30 I will sing praises to the
   name of God,
   And I will magnify him with
   thanksgiving.
31 This will please Jehovah
   more than a bull,
   More than a young bull with
   horns and hooves.[h]
32 The meek will see it and
   rejoice.
   You who are seeking God,
   may your hearts revive.
33 For Jehovah is listening to
   the poor,[i]

CHAP. 69

a Isa 49:8
  Heb 5:7

b Ps 68:20

c Ps 144:7

d Ps 69:2

e Ps 16:10

f Ps 63:3
  Ps 109:21

g Ps 25:16

h Ps 27:9
  Ps 102:2

i Ps 31:9
  Ps 40:13

j Ps 22:6

k Ps 142:4

l Job 19:14

m Mt 27:34
  Mr 15:23

Second Col.

a Mt 27:48
  Mr 15:36
  Lu 23:36
  Joh 19:29

b Ro 11:9, 10

c Ps 21:9

d Ac 1:20

e Ex 32:33

f Php 4:3
  Re 3:5
  Re 13:8

g Ps 109:22

h Ps 50:13-15
  Ho 14:2

i Ps 10:17
  Ps 102:17
  Isa 66:2

69:15 *Or "pit." 69:18 *Or "Come near
to my soul and reclaim it." 69:20 *Or
"and I am to the point of despair."
69:21 *Or "a poisonous plant."

69:24 *Or "wrath." 69:25 *Or "walled
camp." 69:28 *Or "book of life."

And he will not despise his captive people.[a]

34 Let heaven and earth praise him,[b]

The seas and everything that moves in them.

35 For God will save Zion[c]

And will rebuild the cities of Judah,

And they will dwell there and possess it.*

36 The descendants of his servants will inherit it,[d]

And those who love his name[e] will reside in it.

To the director. Of David, to serve as a reminder.*

70 O God, save me;

O Jehovah, hurry to help me.[f]

2 May those seeking to take my life*

Be put to shame and disgraced.

May those who delight in my calamity

Retreat in humiliation.

3 May those who are saying: "Aha! Aha!"

Be driven back in shame.

4 But let those who are seeking you

Exult and rejoice in you.[g]

May those who love your acts of salvation always say:

"May God be magnified!"

5 But I am helpless and poor;[h]

O God, act quickly in my behalf.[i]

You are my helper and my rescuer;[j]

O Jehovah, do not delay.[k]

71 In you, O Jehovah, I have taken refuge.

May I never be put to shame.[l]

2 In your righteousness save me and rescue me.

Incline your ear* to me and save me.[a]

3 Become for me a rock fortress

Where I can always enter.

Give the command to save me,

For you are my crag and my stronghold.[b]

4 O my God, rescue me from the hand of the wicked,[c]

From the grasp of the unjust oppressor.

5 For you are my hope, O Sovereign Lord Jehovah;

I have trusted in you* since my youth.[d]

6 I have depended on you from birth;

It was you who took me from my mother's womb.[e]

I praise you constantly.

7 I have become like a miracle to many,

But you are my strong refuge.

8 My mouth is filled with your praise;[f]

All day long I tell about your splendor.

9 Do not cast me off in my old age;[g]

Do not abandon me when my strength fails.[h]

10 My enemies speak against me,

And those seeking to take my life* conspire together,[i]

11 Saying: "God has abandoned him.

Chase after him and seize him, for there is no one to save him."[j]

12 O God, do not remain far away from me.

O my God, hurry to help me.[k]

13 May those who are resisting me*

CHAP. 69

a Ps 146:7
Isa 61:1
Lu 4:18

b Ps 96:11
Isa 49:13

c Ps 51:18

d Isa 61:9
Isa 66:22

e Ps 91:14
Jas 1:12

CHAP. 70

f Ps 40:13-17

g Ps 5:11
La 3:25

h Ps 109:22

i Ps 141:1

j Ps 18:2

k Ps 13:3

CHAP. 71

l Ps 25:2
Ps 31:1-3
Isa 45:17
Jer 17:18

Second Col.

a Ps 34:15

b 2Sa 22:2, 3
Ps 18:2
Ps 144:2

c Ps 17:8, 9
Ps 59:1
Ps 140:4
Mt 6:13

d 1Sa 17:45
Jer 17:7

e Ps 22:9, 10
Ps 139:16
Isa 46:3

f Ps 51:15
Heb 13:15

g Ps 92:14

h Ps 73:26
Ec 12:3

i 2Sa 17:1, 2

j Ps 3:2
Ps 42:10
Mt 27:42, 43

k Ps 22:11
Ps 35:22
Ps 38:21, 22

69:35 *That is, "the land." 70:Sup *Or "to bring to remembrance." 70:2 *Or "soul."

71:2 *Or "Bend down and listen." 71:5 *Or "You are my confidence." 71:10 *Or "seeking my soul." 71:13 *Or "my soul."

Be put to shame and perish.[a]
May those seeking my ca-
lamity
Be covered with disgrace
and humiliation.[b]

14 But as for me, I will continue
to wait;
I will add to your praise.

15 My mouth will recount your
righteousness,[c]
All day long your acts of salvation,
Though they are too many
for me to grasp.*[d]

16 I will come and tell about
your mighty acts,
O Sovereign Lord Jehovah;
I will mention your righ-
teousness, yours alone.

17 O God, you have taught me
from my youth,[e]
And until now I keep declaring your wonderful works.[f]

18 Even when I am old and
gray, O God, do not
abandon me.[g]
Let me tell the next generation about your power*
And about your mightiness
to all those who are to
come.[h]

19 Your righteousness, O God,
reaches to the heights;[i]
You have done great things;
O God, who is like you?[j]

20 Though you have made me
experience much distress
and calamity,[k]
Revive me again;
Bring me up from the
depths* of the earth.[l]

21 May you increase my greatness
And surround and
comfort me.

22 Then I will praise you on a
stringed instrument
Because of your faithful-
ness, O my God.[m]

CHAP. 71

a 2Sa 17:23

b Ps 109:29

c Ps 35:28
  Ps 40:9

d Ps 40:5

e Ps 71:5

f 2Sa 22:1
  1Ch 16:4
  Ps 9:1

g Ps 37:25
  Ps 71:9

h Ex 13:8
  1Ch 29:10, 11
  Ps 78:2-4

i Ps 36:6

j Ex 15:11
  Ps 86:8
  Ps 89:6
  Jer 10:7

k 2Sa 12:10, 11

l Ps 40:2
  Ps 86:13

m Ps 25:10
  Ps 108:4
  Ps 146:6

Second Col.

a Ps 63:5
  Ps 104:33

b 2Sa 4:9
  Ps 103:4

c Ps 71:8

d Ps 71:13

CHAP. 72

e 1Ch 22:11, 12
  1Ch 29:19
  Jer 23:5

f 1Ki 3:9, 28

g Isa 11:4

h Ps 89:36, 37
  Lu 1:32, 33
  Re 11:15

i 2Sa 23:3, 4
  Pr 16:15
  Pr 19:12

j Isa 61:11

k 1Ki 4:25
  1Ch 22:9
  Isa 2:4
  Isa 9:6

I will sing your praises* with
the harp,
O Holy One of Israel.

23 My lips will shout joyfully as
I sing praises to you,[a]
For you have saved my life.*[b]

24 My tongue will speak about*
your righteousness all day
long,[c]
For those seeking my de-
struction will be ashamed
and disgraced.[d]

Regarding Solomon.

72 O God, give your judgments to the king,
And endow the son of the
king with your righteous-
ness.[e]

2 May he plead the cause
of your people with righ-
teousness,
And of your lowly ones with
justice.[f]

3 May the mountains bring
peace to the people,
And may the hills bring righteousness.

4 Let him defend* the lowly
among the people,
Let him save the sons of the
poor,
And let him crush the de-
frauder.[g]

5 They will fear you as long as
there is a sun
And as long as the moon remains,
For generation after generation.[h]

6 He will be like the rain that
falls on the mown grass,
Like showers of rain that water the earth.[i]

7 In his days the righteous will
flourish,*[j]
And peace will abound[k] until
the moon is no more.

71:15 *Or "number." 71:18 *Lit.,
"arm." 71:20 *Or "watery deeps."
71:22 *Or "make music to you." 71:23
*Or "redeemed my soul." 71:24 *Or
"meditate on." 72:4 *Lit., "judge."
72:7 *Lit., "sprout."

8 He will have subjects* from
   sea to sea
   And from the River# to the
   ends of the earth.ᵃ
9 The desert dwellers will bow
   down before him,
   And his enemies will lick the
   dust.ᵇ
10 The kings of Tarʹshish and
   of the islands will pay
   tribute.ᶜ
   The kings of Sheʹba and of
   Seʹba will present gifts.ᵈ
11 All the kings will bow down
   before him,
   And all the nations will serve
   him.
12 For he will rescue the poor
   who cry for help,
   Also the lowly one and whoever has no helper.
13 He will have pity on the lowly
   and the poor,
   And the lives* of the poor he
   will save.
14 From oppression and from
   violence he will rescue
   them,*
   And their blood will be precious in his eyes.

72:8 *Or "will rule." #That is, the Euphrates. 72:13 *Or "souls." 72:14
*Or "redeem their souls."

15 May he live and be given the
   gold of Sheʹba.ᵃ
   May prayers be said for him
   continually,
   And may he be blessed all
   day long.
16 There will be an abundance
   of grain on the earth;ᵇ
   On the top of the mountains
   it will overflow.
   His fruit will flourish as in
   Lebʹa·non,ᶜ
   And in the cities people will
   blossom like the vegetation
   of the earth.ᵈ
17 May his name endure forever,ᵉ
   And may it prosper as long
   as the sun.
   May people obtain a blessing
   for themselves by means of
   him;ᶠ
   May all nations pronounce
   him happy.
18 May Jehovah God be
   praised, Israel's God,ᵍ
   Who alone does wonderful
   things.ʰ
19 May his glorious name be
   praised forever,ⁱ
   And may his glory fill the
   whole earth.ʲ
   Amen and Amen.
20 This completes the prayers
   of David, the son of Jesʹse.ᵏ

CHAP. 72
a Ex 23:31
  1Ki 4:21
  Ps 2:8
  Ps 22:27, 28
  Da 2:35
  Zec 9:10

b Ps 2:9
  Ps 110:1

c 1Ki 4:21

d 1Ki 10:1, 2

Second Col.
a 1Ki 10:10

b Isa 30:23

c Isa 35:1, 2

d 1Ki 4:20

e Ps 45:17
  Ps 89:35, 36

f Ge 22:18
  Ga 3:14

g 1Ch 29:10

h Ex 15:11

i Re 5:13

j Nu 14:21
  Hab 2:14

k 1Sa 17:58

BOOK THREE
(Psalms 73-89)

A melody of Aʹsaph.ᵃ

73 God is truly good to Israel,
   to those pure in heart.ᵇ
2 As for me, my feet had almost strayed;
   My steps had nearly slipped.ᶜ
3 For I became envious of the
   arrogant*
   When I would see the peace
   of the wicked.ᵈ
4 For they have no pain in their
   death;

73:3 *Or "boasters."

Their bodies are healthy.*ᵃ
5 They are not troubled like
   other humans,ᵇ
   Nor do they suffer like other
   men.ᶜ
6 Therefore, haughtiness is
   their necklace;ᵈ
   Violence clothes them as a
   garment.
7 Their prosperity* makes
   their eyes bulge;

CHAP. 73
a 2Ch 35:15

b Ps 84:11
  Mt 5:8

c Ps 94:18

d Job 21:7
  Jer 12:1

Second Col.
a Ec 7:15

b Job 12:6
  Job 21:7, 9

c Jer 12:1

d Job 21:14, 15

73:4 *Or "Their paunch is fat." 73:7
*Lit., "fat."

They have exceeded the imaginations of the heart.

8 They scoff and say evil things.[a]
They arrogantly threaten oppression.[b]

9 They speak as if they were as high as heaven,
And their tongues swagger about in the earth.

10 So his people turn aside to them,
And they drink from their abundant water.

11 They say: "How does God know?[c]
Does the Most High really have knowledge?"

12 Yes, these are the wicked, who always have it easy.[d]
They keep increasing their wealth.

13 Surely in vain I have kept my heart pure
And washed my hands in innocence.[f]

14 And I was troubled all day long;[g]
Every morning I was chastised.[h]

15 But if I had said these things, I would have betrayed your people.*

16 When I tried to understand it,
It was troubling to me

17 Until I entered the grand sanctuary of God,
And I discerned their future.

18 Surely you place them on slippery ground.[i]
You make them fall to their ruin.[j]

19 How suddenly they are devastated![k]
How sudden is their finish as they come to a terrible end!

20 Like a dream when one wakes up, O Jehovah,

When you rouse yourself, you will dismiss* their image.

21 But my heart was sour,[a]
And deep inside* I felt sharp pain.

22 I was unreasoning and lacked understanding;
I was like a senseless beast before you.

23 But now I am continually with you;
You have taken hold of my right hand.[b]

24 You guide me with your advice,[c]
And afterward you will lead me to glory.[d]

25 Whom do I have in the heavens?
And besides you I desire nothing on earth.[e]

26 My body and my heart may fail,
But God is the rock of my heart and my portion forever.[f]

27 Truly, those keeping far from you will perish.
You will put an end to* everyone who immorally# leaves you.[g]

28 But as for me, drawing near to God is good for me.[h]
I have made the Sovereign Lord Jehovah my refuge,
To declare all your works.[i]

A mas′kil.* Of A′saph.[j]

74

Why, O God, have you rejected us forever?[k]
Why does your anger burn* against the flock of your pasture?[l]

2 Remember the people* you acquired long ago,[m]

CHAP. 73
a Ps 53:1

b 1Ki 21:7

c Ps 10:4, 11
Ps 94:3, 7
Eze 8:12
Zep 1:12

d Ps 37:35

e Ps 17:14

f Job 34:7, 9
Job 35:3

g Ps 34:19

h Job 7:17, 18

i Ps 35:6, 7
Jer 23:11, 12

j Ps 37:10, 20
Ps 55:23
Pr 3:33

k Job 21:23
Ps 37:1, 2
Isa 30:13

Second Col.
a Ps 73:3

b Ps 16:8
Ps 63:8
Isa 41:10

c Ps 25:9
Ps 32:8
Ps 73:23
Ps 143:10
Pr 3:6

d Ps 37:34

e Ps 42:2
Ps 84:2
Isa 26:9

f Ps 16:5
La 3:24

g Nu 15:39
Jas 4:4

h Ps 65:4
Jas 4:8

i Ps 118:17

CHAP. 74
j 1Ch 25:1
2Ch 35:15

k La 5:20

l De 29:19, 20
Ps 100:3

m De 9:23

73:15 *Lit., "the generation of your sons."

73:20 *Lit., "despise." 73:21 *Lit., "in my kidneys." 73:27 *Lit., "silence." #Or "unfaithfully." 74:Sup *See Glossary. 74:1 *Lit., "smoke." 74:2 *Lit., "your assembly."

The tribe you redeemed as your inheritance.[a]

Remember Mount Zion, where you have resided.[b]

3 Direct your steps to the perpetual ruins.[c]

The enemy has devastated everything in the holy place.[d]

4 Your foes roared inside your meeting place.*[e]

They have set up their own banners as signs there.

5 They were like men wielding axes against a thick forest.

6 They broke up all its engravings[f] with axes and iron bars.

7 They set your sanctuary on fire.[g]

They profaned the tabernacle bearing your name, casting it to the ground.

8 They and their offspring have said in their hearts: "All the meeting places of God* in the land must be burned."

9 There are no signs for us to see;

There is no longer any prophet,

And no one among us knows how long this will last.

10 How long, O God, will the adversary keep taunting?[h]

Will the enemy treat your name with disrespect forever?[i]

11 Why do you hold back your hand, your right hand?[j]

Draw it out of your bosom* and put an end to them.

12 But God is my King from long ago,

The one performing acts of salvation on the earth.[k]

13 You stirred up the sea with your strength;[a]

You smashed the heads of the sea monsters in the waters.

14 You crushed the heads of Le·vi′a·than;*

You gave it as food to the people, to those inhabiting the deserts.

15 You cut openings for the springs and the streams;[b]

You dried up ever-flowing rivers.[c]

16 The day belongs to you, also the night.

You made the light* and the sun.[d]

17 You set up all the boundaries of the earth;[e]

You made summer and winter.[f]

18 Remember the enemy's taunts, O Jehovah,

How a foolish people treats your name with disrespect.[g]

19 Do not surrender the life* of your turtledove to the wild beasts.

Do not forget the life of your afflicted people forever.

20 Remember the covenant,

For the dark places of the earth have become full of the haunts of violence.

21 May the crushed one not turn away disappointed;[h]

May the lowly and the poor praise your name.[i]

22 Rise up, O God, and plead your legal case.

Remember how the foolish taunt you all day long.[j]

23 Do not forget what your foes are saying.

The uproar of those who defy you is ascending constantly.

CHAP. 74
a De 4:20
  De 32:9

b Ps 48:2
  Ps 132:13

c Da 9:17

d Ps 79:1

e La 2:7

f 1Ki 6:18, 35

g 2Ki 25:9
  Isa 64:11

h Ps 13:2
  Ps 79:4

i Eze 36:23

j Ps 44:23
  Isa 64:12
  La 2:3

k Ex 15:2
  Isa 33:22

Second Col.
a Ex 14:21
  Ne 9:10, 11

b Isa 48:21

c Jos 3:13

d Ge 1:3, 5
  Ps 136:7, 8

e Ac 17:26

f Ge 8:22

g Isa 52:5

h Ps 12:5

i Ezr 3:11

j Ps 89:50, 51
  Isa 52:5

74:4 *Or "your place of assembly." 74:8 *Or "All places where God is worshipped." 74:11 *Or "from the folds of your garment."

74:14 *See Glossary. 74:16 *Or "the luminary." 74:19 *Or "soul."

To the director. Set to the melody "Do Not Bring to Ruin." Of A'saph.[a] A song.

75 We give thanks to you,
O God, we give thanks to you;
Your name is near,[b]
And people declare your wondrous works.

2 You say: "When I set a time, I judge with fairness.

3 When the earth and all its inhabitants were dissolved, It was I who kept its pillars firm." (*Selah*)

4 I say to the boastful, "Do not boast,"
And to the wicked, "Do not exalt your strength.*

5 Do not exalt your strength* up high
Or speak with arrogance.

6 For exaltation does not come From the east or the west or the south.

7 For God is Judge.[c]
He puts one man down and exalts another.[d]

8 For there is a cup in Jehovah's hand;[e]
The wine is foaming and is fully mixed.
He will surely pour it out,
And all the wicked of the earth will drink it, down to the dregs."[f]

9 But as for me, I will proclaim it forever;
I will sing praises* to the God of Jacob.

10 For he says: "I will cut off all the strength* of the wicked,
But the strength* of the righteous will be exalted."

To the director; to be accompanied with stringed instruments. A melody of A'saph.[g] A song.

76 God is known in Judah;[h]
In Israel his name is great.[i]

2 His shelter is in Sa'lem,[j]
And his dwelling is in Zion.[k]

3 There he broke the flaming arrows of the bow,
The shield and the sword and the weapons of war.[a] (*Selah*)

4 You shine brightly;*
You are more majestic than the mountains of prey.

5 The courageous of heart have been plundered.[b]
They have fallen asleep;
The warriors were all helpless.[c]

6 From your rebuke, O God of Jacob,
Both the charioteer and the horse have fallen fast asleep.[d]

7 You alone are awe-inspiring.[e]
Who can withstand your intense anger?[f]

8 From heaven you pronounced judgment;[g]
The earth was afraid and was silent[h]

9 When God rose up to execute judgment,
To save all the meek of the earth.[i] (*Selah*)

10 For the rage of man will serve to your praise;[j]
With the remnants of their rage you will adorn yourself.

11 Make your vows to Jehovah your God and pay them,[k]
Let all who are around him bring their gift in fear.[l]

12 He will humble the pride* of leaders;
He inspires fear in the kings of the earth.

To the director; on Je·du'thun.* Of A'saph.[m] A melody.

77 With my voice I will cry out to God;
To God I will cry out, and he will hear me.[n]

CHAP. 75
a 2Ch 35:15

b Isa 30:27

c Ps 50:6
Ps 58:11

d 1Sa 2:7
Da 2:21
Da 4:17
Lu 1:52

e Ps 11:5, 6

f Job 21:19, 20
Jer 25:15, 28
Jer 49:12
Re 14:9, 10
Re 16:19
Re 18:6

CHAP. 76
g 2Ch 35:15

h Ps 48:1, 3

i 2Ch 2:5

j Ge 14:18

k Ps 74:2
Ps 132:13
Ps 135:21

Second Col.
a 2Ch 32:21
Ps 46:9

b Lu 1:51

c Isa 31:8
Isa 37:36

d Na 2:13

e Ps 89:7

f Jer 10:10
Na 1:6

g 1Ki 8:49

h 2Ch 20:29
Ps 2:4, 5

i Ps 147:6
Pr 3:34
Zep 2:3

j Pr 16:4
Da 3:19, 28

k Nu 30:2

l 2Ch 32:23
Ps 89:7

CHAP. 77
m 2Ch 35:15

n Ps 34:6
Pr 15:29

75:4, 5 *Lit., "horn." 75:9 *Or "make music." 75:10 *Lit., "horns." 76:4 *Or "You are enveloped with light." 76:12 *Lit., "spirit." 77:Sup *See Glossary.

2 In the day of my distress
   I search for Jehovah.[a]
At night my hands are
   stretched out to him with-
   out ceasing.*
I[#] cannot be comforted.

3 When I remember God,
   I groan;[b]
I am troubled and my
   strength fails.*[c] (Selah)

4 You hold my eyelids open;
I am agitated and cannot
   speak.

5 My thoughts turn to the days
   of long ago,[d]
The years of the distant past.

6 During the night I remember
   my song;*[e]
I ponder in my heart;[f]
I make[#] a diligent search.

7 Will Jehovah cast us off forever?[g]
Will he never again show his
   favor?[h]

8 Has his loyal love ceased
   forever?
Will his promise come to
   nothing for all generations?

9 Has God forgotten to show
   his favor,[i]
Or has his anger caused his
   mercy to cease? (Selah)

10 Must I keep saying: "This is
   what distresses me:*[j]
The Most High has changed
   his position[#] toward us"?

11 I will remember the works
   of Jah;
I will remember your marvelous deeds of long ago.

12 And I will meditate on all
   your activity
And ponder over your dealings.[k]

13 O God, your ways are holy.
What god is as great as you,
   O God?[l]

14 You are the true God, who
   does marvelous things.[a]
You have revealed your
   strength to the peoples.[b]

15 With your power* you have
   rescued[#] your people,[c]
The sons of Jacob and of
   Joseph. (Selah)

16 The waters saw you, O God;
The waters saw you and
   were disturbed.[d]
And the deep waters became
   agitated.

17 The clouds poured down
   water.
The cloudy skies thundered,
And your arrows flew here
   and there.[e]

18 The sound of your thunder[f]
   was like chariot wheels;
Flashes of lightning lit up
   the inhabited earth;*[g]
The earth trembled and
   quaked.[h]

19 Your way was through the
   sea,[i]
Your path through many
   waters;
But your footprints could
   not be traced.

20 You led your people just like
   a flock,[j]
In the care* of Moses and
   Aaron.[k]

Mas′kil.* Of A′saph.[l]

78 Listen, my people, to my
   law;*
Incline your ear to the words
   of my mouth.

2 I will open my mouth in a
   proverb.
I will propound riddles of
   long ago.[m]

3 The things we have heard
   and know,
Which our fathers have
   related to us,[n]

CHAP. 77
a Ps 18:6
  Ps 50:15
b Ps 42:5
c Ps 143:4
d Ps 143:5
  Isa 51:9
e Ps 42:8
f Ps 77:12
g Ps 74:1
h Ps 79:5
i Isa 49:14
  Isa 63:15
j Ps 31:22
k 1Ch 16:9
  Ps 143:5
l Ex 15:11
  Ps 89:8

Second Col.
a Ps 72:18
  Re 15:3
b Ex 9:16
  Isa 52:10
  Da 3:29
  Da 6:26, 27
c Ex 6:6
  De 9:29
d Ex 14:21
  Jos 3:16
  Ps 114:1-3
e 2Sa 22:15
  Ps 144:6
f Ps 29:3
g Ps 97:4
h Ex 19:18
  2Sa 22:8
i Ne 9:10, 11
  Hab 3:15
j Ex 13:21
  Ps 78:52
k Isa 63:11
  Ac 7:35, 36

CHAP. 78
l 1Ch 25:1
m Pr 1:5, 6
  Mt 13:34, 35
n Ex 13:8
  Ps 44:1

77:2 *Lit., "growing numb." [#]Or "My soul." 77:3 *Lit., "my spirit faints." 77:6 *Or "string music." [#]Lit., "My spirit makes." 77:10 *Or "pierces me." [#]Lit., "right hand."

77:15 *Lit., "arm." [#]Lit., "redeemed." 77:18 *Or "the productive land." 77:20 *Lit., "By the hand." 78:Sup *See Glossary. 78:1 *Or "instruction."

4 We will not hide from their sons;
  We will relate to the generation to come[a]
  The praiseworthy deeds of Jehovah and his strength,[b]
  The wonderful things he has done.[c]

5 He established a reminder in Jacob
  And set a law in Israel;
  He commanded our forefathers
  To make these things known to their children,[d]

6 So that the next generation,
  The children yet to be born, might know them.[e]
  They in turn would relate them to their children.[f]

7 Then these would put their confidence in God.
  They would not forget God's works[g]
  But would observe his commandments.[h]

8 Then they would not be like their forefathers,
  A stubborn and rebellious generation,[i]
  A generation whose heart was unsteady*[j]
  And whose spirit was not faithful to God.

9 The E′phra·im·ites were armed with the bow,
  But they retreated in the day of battle.

10 They did not keep the covenant of God[k]
   And refused to walk in his law.[l]

11 They also forgot what he had done,[m]
   His wonderful works that he showed them.[n]

12 He did marvelous things in the sight of their forefathers,[o]
   In the land of Egypt, the region of Zo′an.[p]

78:8 *Lit., "unprepared."

CHAP. 78

a De 4:9
  De 6:6, 7
  De 6:21
  De 11:18, 19
  Jos 4:6, 7

b Isa 63:7

c Ps 98:1

d Ge 18:19
  De 6:6, 7

e Ps 71:17, 18
  Ps 102:18

f De 4:10

g De 4:9
  Ps 103:2

h De 5:29

i Ex 32:9
  De 1:43
  De 31:27
  2Ki 17:13, 14
  Eze 20:18
  Ac 7:51

j Ps 81:11, 12
  Jer 7:24-26

k De 31:16

l 2Ch 13:8, 9
  Ne 9:26

m De 32:18
  2Ch 13:12
  Jer 2:32

n Ps 106:21, 22

o De 4:34
  Ne 9:10

p Nu 13:22

Second Col.

a Ex 14:21, 22
  Ex 15:8

b Ex 13:21
  Ex 14:20, 24

c Ex 17:6
  Nu 20:11
  Ps 105:41
  Isa 48:21
  1Co 10:4

d De 8:14, 15

e De 9:21, 22
  Ps 95:8
  Heb 3:16

f Ps 106:14

g Ex 16:8

h Ex 17:6

i Ex 16:3

j Nu 11:10

k Heb 12:29

l Nu 11:1

m Ps 106:24
  Heb 3:10
  Jude 5

---

13 He split the sea to let them pass through,
   And he made the waters stand up like a dam.*[a]

14 He led them with a cloud by day
   And the whole night with the light of a fire.[b]

15 He split rocks in the wilderness,
   He let them drink their fill as if from deep waters.[c]

16 He brought streams out of a crag
   And caused waters to flow down like rivers.[d]

17 But they continued to sin against him
   By rebelling against the Most High in the desert;[e]

18 They challenged* God in their heart[f]
   By demanding food that they craved.#

19 So they spoke against God,
   Saying: "Can God spread a table in the wilderness?"[g]

20 Look! He struck a rock
   So that waters flowed and streams flooded out.[h]
   "Can he also give us bread,
   Or can he provide meat for his people?"[i]

21 When Jehovah heard them, he became furious;[j]
   A fire[k] blazed against Jacob,
   And his anger flared up against Israel[l]

22 Because they did not put faith in God;[m]
   They did not trust in his ability to save them.

23 So he commanded the cloudy skies above,
   And he opened the doors of heaven.

24 He kept raining down manna for them to eat;

78:13 *Or "wall."   78:18 *Lit., "tested."
#Or "food for their soul."

He gave them the grain of
heaven.[a]

25 Men ate the bread of mighty
ones;*[b]
He provided enough to satisfy them.[c]

26 He stirred up the east wind
in the heavens
And made a south wind blow
by his power.[d]

27 And he rained down meat on
them like dust,
Birds like the sand of the
seashore.

28 He made them fall in the
midst of his camp,
All around his tents.

29 And they ate and gorged
themselves;
He gave them what they
desired.[e]

30 But before they fully satisfied their craving,
While their food was yet in
their mouth,

31 God's wrath flared up against
them.[f]
He put to death their stron-
gest men;[g]
He brought down the young
men of Israel.

32 Despite this they sinned even
more[h]
And did not put faith in his
wonderful works.[i]

33 So he brought their days to
an end as if a mere breath,[j]
And their years by sudden
terrors.

34 But as often as he killed
them, they would search
for him;[k]
They would return and look
for God,

35 Remembering that God was
their Rock[l]
And that the Most High God
was their Redeemer.*[m]

36 But they tried to deceive him
with their mouth

And lied to him with their
tongue.

37 Their heart was not steadfast
toward him;[a]
And they were not faithful to
his covenant.[b]

38 But he was merciful;[c]
He would forgive* their error
and not bring them to
ruin.[d]
He often held back his anger[e]
Instead of stirring up all his
wrath.

39 For he remembered that they
were flesh,[f]
A wind that blows past and
does not return.*

40 How often they rebelled
against him in the wilderness[g]
And made him feel hurt in
the desert![h]

41 Again and again they put
God to the test,[i]
And they grieved* the Holy
One of Israel.

42 They did not remember his
power,*
The day that he rescued#
them from the adversary,[j]

43 How he displayed his signs
in Egypt[k]
And his miracles in the
region of Zo'an,

44 And how he turned the Nile
canals into blood[l]
So that they could not drink
from their streams.

45 He sent swarms of gadflies
to devour them[m]
And frogs to bring them to
ruin.[n]

46 He gave their crops to the
voracious locusts,
The fruit of their labor to the
swarming locusts.[o]

CHAP. 78

a Ex 16:14, 35
Ex 16:31, 32
Nu 11:7
De 8:3
Joh 6:31
1Co 10:2, 3

b Ps 103:20

c Ex 16:12

d Nu 11:31-34

e Nu 11:19, 20

f Nu 11:10

g Nu 11:34

h Nu 14:2-4
Nu 25:3
1Co 10:8-10

i Ex 16:15
De 8:14, 15

j Nu 14:29, 35
De 2:14

k Nu 21:7
Jg 4:3

l De 32:4

m Ex 6:6

Second Col.

a Ps 95:10
Heb 3:10

b De 31:20
Jer 31:32

c Ex 34:6
Nu 14:18
Ne 9:31

d Nu 14:19, 20
Jer 30:11
La 3:22

e Ne 9:27
Isa 48:9
Eze 20:9

f Ps 103:14

g Nu 14:11

h Isa 63:10
Eph 4:30
Heb 3:16

i Nu 14:22
De 6:16
Ps 95:8, 9

j Ex 14:30

k De 4:34
Ne 9:10
Ps 105:27-36

l Ex 7:19

m Ex 8:24

n Ex 8:6

o Ex 10:14, 15

78:38 *Lit., "cover." 78:39 *Or possibly, "That the spirit is going forth
and does not come back." 78:41 *Or
"pained." 78:42 *Lit., "hand." #Lit.,
"redeemed."

78:25 *Or "of angels." 78:35 *Or
"Avenger."

47 He destroyed their vines
with hail[a]
And their sycamore trees
with hailstones.

48 He gave their beasts of
burden over to the hail[b]
And their livestock to the
lightning bolts.*

49 He inflicted his burning
anger on them,
Fury and indignation and
distress,
Companies of angels bringing calamity.

50 He cleared a pathway for his
anger.
He did not spare them* from
death;
And he gave them* over to
pestilence.

51 Finally he struck down all
the firstborn of Egypt,[c]
The beginning of their procreative power in the tents
of Ham.

52 Then he brought his people
out like a flock[d]
And guided them like a drove
in the wilderness.

53 He led them in security,
And they felt no fear;[e]
The sea covered their
enemies.[f]

54 And he brought them to his
holy territory,[g]
This mountainous region
that his right hand
acquired.[h]

55 He drove out the nations
from before them;[i]
He allotted to them
an inheritance by the
measuring line;[j]
He settled the tribes of Israel
in their homes.[k]

56 But they kept challenging*
God the Most High, and
rebelling against him;[l]
They did not pay attention
to his reminders.[m]

CHAP. 78

a Ex 9:23
b Ex 9:25
c Ex 12:29
   Ps 105:36
d Ps 77:20
   Ps 105:37
e Ex 14:20
   Heb 11:29
f Ex 14:27
   Ex 15:10
g Ex 15:17
h Ps 44:3
i Jos 24:12
   Ps 44:2
j Jos 13:7
k Ne 9:24, 25
l De 31:16
   De 32:15
   Ps 2:11
   2Sa 20:1
   Ne 9:26
m 2Ki 17:15
   Jer 44:23

Second Col.

a De 9:7
   Jg 3:6
b Ho 7:16
c De 12:2
   Jg 2:2
   Eze 20:28
d Jg 2:12
   1Sa 7:3
e Jg 2:20
f Jos 18:1
   1Sa 4:11
g Jer 7:12
h 1Sa 4:21
   1Sa 5:1
i 1Sa 4:2, 10
j 1Sa 2:33, 34
   1Sa 4:11
k 1Sa 4:19
l Ps 44:23
m Isa 42:13
n 1Sa 5:6
o Ge 49:10
p Ps 87:2
   Ps 132:13
   Ps 135:21
q Ps 76:2

---

57 They also turned away and
were as treacherous as
their forefathers.[a]
They were as unreliable as
a loose bow.[b]

58 They kept offending him with
their high places,[c]
And they incited him to fury*
with their carved images.[d]

59 God heard and became
furious,[e]
So he utterly rejected Israel.

60 He finally forsook the tabernacle of Shi'loh,[f]
The tent where he had resided among men.[g]

61 He let the symbol of his
strength go into captivity;
His splendor into the hand
of the adversary.[h]

62 He handed his people over
to the sword[i]
And became furious with his
inheritance.

63 Fire consumed his young
men,
And to his virgins no wedding songs were sung.*

64 His priests fell by the sword,[j]
And their own widows did
not weep.[k]

65 Then Jehovah woke up as
from sleep,[l]
Like a mighty man[m] waking
up from wine.

66 And he drove his adversaries
back;[n]
He put them to lasting disgrace.

67 He rejected the tent of
Joseph;
He did not choose the tribe
of E'phra·im.

68 But he chose the tribe of
Judah,[o]
Mount Zion, which he loves.[p]

69 He made his sanctuary as enduring as the heavens,*[q]

78:48 *Or possibly, "the burning fever."
78:50 *Or "their soul." *Lit., "their
life." **78:56** *Or "testing."

78:58 *Or "to jealousy." **78:63** *Lit.,
"And his virgins were not praised."
78:69 *Lit., "He built his sanctuary like
the heights."

Like the earth that he has established forever.[a]

70 He chose David[b] his servant
And took him from the sheep pens,[c]

71 From tending the nursing ewes;
He made him the shepherd over Jacob, his people,[d]
And over Israel, his inheritance.[e]

72 He shepherded them with integrity of heart,[f]
And with skillful hands he led them.[g]

A melody of A'saph.[h]

79 O God, the nations have invaded your inheritance;[i]
They have defiled your holy temple;[j]
They have turned Jerusalem into a heap of ruins.[k]

2 They have given the dead bodies of your servants as food to the birds of the heavens
And the flesh of your loyal ones to the wild beasts of the earth.[l]

3 They have poured out their blood like water around Jerusalem,
And no one is left to bury them.[m]

4 We have become an object of reproach to our neighbors;[n]
Those around us ridicule and jeer us.

5 How long, O Jehovah, will you be furious? Forever?[o]
How long will your indignation burn just like fire?[p]

6 Pour out your wrath on the nations that do not know you
And on the kingdoms that do not call on your name.[q]

7 For they have devoured Jacob

And have desolated his homeland.[a]

8 Do not hold us accountable for the errors of our ancestors.[b]
Quickly show us your mercy,[c]
For we have been brought very low.

9 Help us, O God of our salvation,[d]
For the sake of your glorious name;
Rescue us and forgive* our sins for the sake of your name.[e]

10 Why should the nations say: "Where is their God?"[f]
Before our eyes may it become known among the nations
That the shed blood of your servants has been avenged.[g]

11 May you hear the sighing of the prisoner.[h]
Use your great power* to preserve# those sentenced to death.△[i]

12 Repay our neighbors sevenfold[j]
For the taunts they have leveled at you, O Jehovah.[k]

13 Then we, your people and the flock of your pasture,[l]
Will give thanks to you forever;
And we will declare your praise from generation to generation.[m]

To the director; set to "The Lilies." A reminder. Of A'saph.[n] *A melody.*

80 O Shepherd of Israel, listen,
You who are guiding Joseph just like a flock.[o]
You who sit enthroned above* the cherubs,[p]
Shine forth.#

79:9 *Lit., "cover." **79:11** *Lit., "arm." #Or possibly, "set free." △Lit., "the sons of death." **80:1** *Or possibly, "between." #Or "Reveal your radiance."

CHAP. 78
a Ps 104:5
  Ps 119:90
  Ec 1:4
b 1Sa 16:12, 13
c 1Sa 17:15
d 2Sa 7:8
e 2Sa 6:21
f 2Sa 8:15
  1Ki 3:6
  1Ki 9:4
  1Ki 15:5
g 1Sa 18:14

CHAP. 79
h 1Ch 25:1
i Ex 15:17
j 2Ki 24:12, 13
  Ps 74:3, 7
  La 1:10
k 2Ki 25:9, 10
  2Ch 36:17-19
  Jer 52:13
  Jer 7:33
  Jer 15:3
  Jer 34:20
m Jer 14:16
  Jer 16:4
n De 28:37
  Eze 36:4
o Ps 74:1
  Ps 85:5
  Isa 64:9
p Zep 1:18
q Jer 10:25

Second Col.
a 2Ch 36:20, 21
b Ne 9:34
c Ps 69:17
  La 3:22
d 1Ch 16:35
e Jos 7:9
  1Sa 12:22
  2Ch 14:11
  Ps 115:1, 2
  Isa 48:9
  Jer 14:7
f Joe 2:17
g Jer 51:35
  Eze 36:23
h Ex 2:23
  Isa 42:6, 7
i Ps 102:19, 20
j Jer 12:14
k Ps 74:18
l Ps 74:1
  Ps 95:7
  Ps 100:3
m Ps 145:4
  Isa 43:21

CHAP. 80
n 1Ch 25:1
o Ps 77:20
  Isa 40:11
  Jer 31:10
  Eze 34:12
  1Pe 2:25
p Ex 25:20, 22
  1Sa 4:4

2 Before E′phra·im and Benjamin and Ma·nas′seh,
Do stir up your mightiness;[a]
Come and save us.[b]

3 O God, restore us;[c]
Let your face shine upon us,
so that we may be saved.[d]

4 Jehovah God of armies, how long will you be hostile toward* the prayer of your people?[e]

5 You feed them tears as their bread,
And you make them drink tears beyond measure.

6 You let our neighbors quarrel over us;
Our enemies keep mocking us as they please.[f]

7 O God of armies, restore us;
Let your face shine upon us,
so that we may be saved.[g]

8 You made a vine[h] depart from Egypt.
You drove out the nations and planted it.[i]

9 You cleared a space for it,
And it took root and filled the land.

10 The mountains were covered by its shadow,
And the cedars of God by its branches.

11 Its branches reached as far as the sea,
And its shoots to the River.*[k]

12 Why have you broken down the stone walls of the vineyard,[l]
So that all those passing by pluck its fruit?[m]

13 The boars of the forest ravage it,
And the wild animals of the field feed on it.[n]

14 O God of armies, please return.
Look down from heaven and see!

Take care of this vine,[a]

15 The stock* that your right hand has planted,[b]
And look upon the son whom# you made strong for yourself.[c]

16 It is burned with fire,[d] cut down.
They perish at your rebuke.*

17 May your hand give support to the man at your right hand,
To the son of man you have made strong for yourself.[e]

18 Then we will not turn away from you.
Preserve us alive, so that we may call on your name.

19 O Jehovah God of armies, restore us;
Let your face shine upon us,
so that we may be saved.[f]

To the director; upon the Git′tith.*
Of A′saph.[g]

81

Shout joyfully to God our strength.[h]
Shout in triumph to the God of Jacob.

2 Begin the music and take a tambourine,
The melodious harp together with the stringed instrument.

3 Blow the horn on the new moon,[i]
On the full moon, for the day of our festival.[j]

4 For it is a decree for Israel,
A ruling of the God of Jacob.[k]

5 He established it as a reminder for Joseph[l]
When He went out against the land of Egypt.[m]
I heard a voice* that I did not recognize:

CHAP. 80
a Isa 42:13
b Isa 25:9
c Ps 85:4
La 5:21
d Nu 6:25
Ps 67:1, 2
e Ps 74:1
Ps 85:5
La 3:44
f Ps 44:13
Ps 79:4
g Ps 80:3, 19
h Isa 5:7
i Ps 44:2
Ps 78:55
Jer 2:21
j Ex 23:28, 30
Jos 24:12, 13
1Ki 4:25
k Ge 15:18
Ex 23:31
1Ki 4:21
Ps 72:8
l Isa 5:5
m Na 2:2
n 2Ki 18:9
2Ki 24:1
2Ki 25:1
2Ch 32:1
Jer 39:1

Second Col.
a Isa 63:15
b Isa 5:7
Jer 2:21
c Ex 4:22
Isa 49:5
d Ps 79:5
Jer 52:12, 13
e Ps 89:20, 21
f Ps 80:7

CHAP. 81
g 1Ch 25:1
h Ps 28:8
i Nu 29:1
j Ex 23:16
Nu 10:10
k Le 23:23, 24
l Ex 12:14
m Ex 12:12

80:4 *Lit., "fume against." 80:11 *That is, the Euphrates. 80:15 *Or "main stem of the vine." #Or "branch that." 80:16 *Lit., "the rebuke of your face." 81:Sup *See Glossary. 81:5 *Or "language."

6 "I lifted the burden from his
    shoulder;[a]
  His hands were freed from
    the basket.
7 In your distress you called,
    and I rescued you;[b]
  I answered you from the
    thundercloud.*[c]
  I tested you at the waters of
    Mer'i·bah.#[d] (Selah)
8 Hear, my people, and I will
    testify against you.
  O Israel, if you would only
    listen to me.[e]
9 Among you, there will be no
    strange god,
  And you will not bow down
    to a foreign god.[f]
10 I, Jehovah, am your God,
  The one who brought you out
    of the land of Egypt.[g]
  Open your mouth wide, and
    I will fill it.[h]
11 But my people did not listen
    to my voice;
  Israel would not submit
    to me.[i]
12 So I let them follow their
    stubborn hearts;
  They did what they thought
    was right.*[j]
13 If only my people would lis-
    ten to me,[k]
  If only Israel would walk in
    my ways![l]
14 Their enemies I would quick-
    ly subdue;
  I would turn my hand against
    their adversaries.*
15 Those who hate Jehovah will
    cringe in his presence,
  And their outcome* will be
    forever.
16 But he will feed you* with the
    finest# wheat[n]
  And satisfy you with honey
    from the rock."[o]

81:7 *Lit., "in the hidden place of thunder." #Meaning "Quarreling." **81:12**
*Lit., "They walked in their counsels."
81:15 *Lit., "time." **81:16** *Lit., "him,"
that is, God's people. #Lit., "the fat of."

CHAP. 81

a Ex 1:13, 14
   Ex 6:6

b Ex 14:10, 13
   Ps 91:15

c Ex 19:16, 19

d Ex 17:6, 7

e Ex 15:26

f Ex 20:2-5
   De 6:13, 14

g De 5:6

h De 32:13, 14

i Ex 32:1
   De 32:15

j Jer 7:23, 24
   Jer 11:7, 8
   Mic 6:16

k De 32:29

l De 5:29
   Isa 48:17, 18

m Nu 14:9

n Ps 147:14

o De 32:13, 14

Second Col.

CHAP. 82

a 1Ch 25:1

b 2Ch 19:6

c Ex 18:21, 22
   Ps 82:6
   Joh 10:34, 35

d Le 19:15
   Ec 5:8

e De 1:16, 17
   2Ch 19:7
   Pr 18:5

f De 24:17

g Pr 22:3

h Mic 3:1

i Ps 11:3
   Pr 29:4

j Joh 10:34, 35
   1Co 8:5

k Ps 49:12

l Ps 146:3, 4

m Ps 96:13

CHAP. 83

n 2Ch 20:14

o Ps 28:1

p Ps 2:1, 2

A melody of A'saph.[a]

82 God takes his place in the
        divine assembly;*[b]
  In the middle of the gods# he
    judges:[c]
2 "How long will you continue
    to judge with injustice[d]
  And show partiality to the
    wicked?[e] (Selah)
3 Defend* the lowly and the
    fatherless.[f]
  Render justice to the help-
    less and destitute.[g]
4 Rescue the lowly and the
    poor;
  Save them out of the hand
    of the wicked."
5 They do not know, nor do
    they understand;[h]
  They are walking about in
    darkness;
  All the foundations of the
    earth are being shaken.[i]
6 "I have said, 'You are gods,#[j]
  All of you are sons of the
    Most High.
7 But you will die just as
    men do;[k]
  And like any other prince
    you will fall!'"[l]
8 Rise up, O God, and judge
    the earth,[m]
  For all the nations belong to
    you.

A song. A melody of A'saph.[n]

83 O God, do not be silent;[o]
  Do not keep quiet* or still,
    O Divine One.
2 For look! your enemies are
    in an uproar;[p]
  Those who hate you act
    arrogantly.*
3 With cunning they secretly
    plot against your people;
  They conspire against your
    treasured ones.*

82:1 *Or "in the assembly of the Divine One." **82:1, 6** #Or "godlike ones."
82:3 *Or "Judge." **83:1** *Or "keep
speechless." **83:2** *Or "raise their
heads." **83:3** *Lit., "concealed ones."

4 They say: "Come, let us anni-
    hilate them as a nation,[a]
  So that the name of Israel
    may be remembered no
    more."
5 They devise a unified
    strategy;*
  They have made an alliance[#]
    against you[b]—
6 The tents of E'dom and the
    Ish'ma·el·ites, Mo'ab[c] and
    the Hag'rites,[d]
7 Ge'bal and Am'mon[e] and
    Am'a·lek,
  Phi·lis'ti·a[f] together with the
    inhabitants of Tyre.[g]
8 As·syr'i·a[h] too has joined
    them;
  They give support to* the
    sons of Lot.[i] (Selah)
9 Do to them as you did to
    Mid'i·an,[j]
  As you did to Sis'e·ra and
    Ja'bin at the stream* of
    Ki'shon.[k]
10 They were annihilated
    at En-dor;[l]
  They became manure for the
    ground.
11 Make their nobles like O'reb
    and Ze'eb[m]
  And their princes* like
    Ze'bah and Zal·mun'na,[n]
12 For they said: "Let us take
    possession of the land
    where God dwells."
13 O my God, make them like
    a whirling thistle,*[o]
  Like stubble blown about
    by the wind.
14 Like a fire that burns up the
    forest,
  Like a flame that scorches
    the mountains,[p]
15 So may you pursue them
    with your tempest[q]

And terrify them with your
    windstorm.[a]
16 Cover* their faces with dis-
    honor,
  So that they may search for
    your name, O Jehovah.
17 May they be put to shame
    and be terrified forever;
  May they be disgraced and
    perish;
18 May people know that you,
    whose name is Jehovah,[b]
  You alone are the Most High
    over all the earth.[c]

For the director; upon the Git'tith.*
Of the sons of Kor'ah.[d] A melody.

84

How lovely* your grand
    tabernacle is,[e]
  O Jehovah of armies!
2 My whole being* yearns,
  Yes, I am faint with longing,
  For the courtyards of
    Jehovah.[f]
  My heart and my flesh shout
    joyfully to the living God.
3 Even the bird finds a home
    there
  And the swallow a nest for
    herself,
  Where she cares for her
    young
  Near your grand altar,
    O Jehovah of armies,
  My King and my God!
4 Happy are those dwelling
    in your house![g]
  They continue to praise you.[h]
    (Selah)
5 Happy are the men who find
    their strength in you,[i]
  Whose hearts are set on the
    highways.
6 When they pass through the
    Ba'ca Valley,*
  They make it into a place of
    springs;

CHAP. 83
a Ex 1:8-10 2Ch 20:1 Es 3:6
b 2Sa 10:6 Isa 7:2, 5
c 2Ch 20:1, 10
d 1Ch 5:10
e Jer 49:2
f Ex 15:14 Ps 60:8
g Am 1:9
h 2Ki 17:5
i Ge 19:36-38 De 2:9
j Jg 8:10, 12
k Jg 4:2, 7, 15
l Jos 17:11
m Jg 7:25
n Jg 8:21
o Isa 17:13
p Ps 144:5 Na 1:6
q Isa 30:30

Second Col.
a Ps 11:6
b Ex 6:3 Ps 68:4 Isa 42:8 Isa 54:5
c Ps 59:13 Ps 92:8 Da 4:17
CHAP. 84
d 2Ch 20:19
e Ps 27:4 Ps 43:3 Ps 46:4
f Ps 42:1, 2 Ps 63:1, 2
g Ps 23:6 Ps 65:4
h 1Ch 25:7 Ps 150:1
i Ps 28:7

83:5 *Lit., "They consult with a heart together." #Or "a covenant." 83:8 *Lit.,
"have become an arm to." 83:9 *Or
"wadi." 83:11 *Or "leaders." 83:13
*Or "like tumbleweed."

83:16 *Lit., "Fill." 84:Sup *See Glossary. 84:1 *Or "deeply loved." 84:2
*Or "My soul." 84:6 *Or "the valley of
baca bushes."

And the early rain clothes it*
with blessings.

7 They will walk on from
strength to strength;[a]
Each one appears before
God in Zion.

8 O Jehovah God of armies,
hear my prayer;
Listen, O God of Jacob.
(Selah)

9 Look, our shield[b] and our
God,*
Look upon the face of your
anointed one.[c]

10 For a day in your courtyards
is better than a thousand
anywhere else![d]
I choose to stand at the
threshold of the house
of my God
Rather than to dwell in the
tents of wickedness.

11 For Jehovah God is a sun[e]
and a shield;[f]
He gives favor and glory.
Jehovah will not hold back
anything good
From those walking in integrity.[g]

12 O Jehovah of armies,
Happy is the man who trusts
in you.[h]

For the director. Of the sons of
Korʹah.[i] A melody.

85 You have shown favor,
O Jehovah, to your
land;[j]
You brought back those of
Jacob who were taken
captive.[k]

2 You have pardoned the error
of your people;
You forgave* all their sin.[l]
(Selah)

3 You held back all your fury;
You turned away from your
hot anger.[m]

4 Restore us,* O God of our
salvation,
And set aside your displeasure with us.[a]

5 Will you be furious with us
forever?[b]
Will you prolong your anger
to generation after generation?

6 Will you not revive us again
So that your people may
rejoice in you?[c]

7 Show us your loyal love to us,
O Jehovah,[d]
And grant us your salvation.

8 I will listen to what the true
God Jehovah says,
For he will speak peace to his
people,[e] to his loyal ones,
But let them not return to
overconfidence.[f]

9 Surely his salvation is near
to those who fear him,[g]
So that his glory may reside
in our land.

10 Loyal love and faithfulness
will meet together;
Righteousness and peace
will kiss each other.[h]

11 Faithfulness will sprout from
the earth,
And righteousness will look
down from the heavens.[i]

12 Yes, Jehovah will give what
is good,*[j]
And our land will yield its
harvest.[k]

13 Righteousness will walk
before him[l]
And make a path for his footsteps.

A prayer of David.

86 Incline your ear,*
O Jehovah, and an-
swer me,
For I am afflicted and poor.[m]

2 Guard my life,* for I am
loyal.[n]

CHAP. 84
a Ps 18:32
  Isa 40:29-31
  Hab 3:19
b Ge 15:1
c 1Sa 2:10
d Ps 26:8
  Ps 27:4
  Ps 43:3, 4
e Ps 27:1
  Isa 60:19, 20
f De 33:29
  2Sa 22:3
  Ps 144:2
g Ps 34:9
  Ps 37:18
h Ps 146:5
  Jer 17:7

CHAP. 85
i 2Ch 20:19
j Le 26:42
  Joe 2:18
k Ezr 2:1
  Jer 30:18
  Eze 39:25
l Jer 50:20
  Mic 7:18
m Ps 103:9
  Isa 12:1

Second Col.
a Ps 80:3, 4
b Ps 74:1
  Ps 79:5
c Ezr 3:11
  Jer 33:10, 11
d La 3:22
e Isa 57:19
f De 8:17, 18
  Ps 78:7
g Isa 46:13
h Ps 72:3
  Isa 32:17
i Isa 26:9
  Isa 45:8
j Ps 84:11
  Jas 1:17
k Le 26:4
  Ps 67:6
  Isa 25:6
  Isa 30:23
l Ps 89:14

CHAP. 86
m Ps 34:6
  Isa 66:2
n Ps 37:128

84:6 *Or possibly, "And the instructor
enwraps himself." 84:9 *Or possibly,
"Look at our shield, O God." 85:2 *Lit.,
"covered."

85:4 *Or "Gather us back." 85:12 *Or
"prosperity." 86:1 *Or "Bend down and
listen." 86:2 *Or "soul."

Save your servant who is
   trusting in you,
For you are my God.[a]

3 Show me favor, O Jehovah,[b]
For I call to you all day long.[c]

4 Make your servant* rejoice,
For to you, O Jehovah,
   I turn.[#]

5 For you, O Jehovah,
   are good[d] and ready
   to forgive;[e]
You abound in loyal love for
   all those who call on you.[f]

6 Listen, O Jehovah, to my
   prayer;
And pay attention to my
   pleas for help.[g]

7 I call on you in the day of my
   distress,[h]
For you will answer me.[i]

8 There is none like you among
   the gods, O Jehovah,[j]
There are no works like
   yours.[k]

9 All the nations that you made
Will come and bow down
   before you, O Jehovah,[l]
And they will give glory to
   your name.[m]

10 For you are great and do
   wondrous things;[n]
You are God, you alone.[o]

11 Instruct me, O Jehovah,
   about your way.[p]
I will walk in your truth.[q]
Unify my heart* to fear your
   name.[r]

12 I praise you, O Jehovah my
   God, with all my heart,[s]
And I will glorify your name
   forever.

13 For your loyal love toward
   me is great,
And you have saved my life*
   from the depths of the
   Grave.[#t]

14 O God, presumptuous men
   rise up against me;[a]
A band of ruthless men seek
   to take my life,*
And they have no regard for
   you.[#b]

15 But you, O Jehovah, are a
   God merciful and compassionate,*
Slow to anger and abundant
   in loyal love and faithfulness.[#c]

16 Turn to me and show me
   favor.[d]
Give your strength to your
   servant,[e]
And save the son of your
   slave girl.

17 Show me a sign* of your
   goodness,
So that those who hate me
   may see it and be put to
   shame.
For you, O Jehovah, are my
   helper and comforter.

Of the sons of Kor'ah.[f]
A melody. A song.

87 His city's foundation is in
   the holy mountains.[g]

2 Jehovah loves the gates of
   Zion[h]
More than all the tents of
   Jacob.

3 Glorious things are being
   said about you, O city of
   the true God.[i] (Selah)

4 I will count Ra'hab[j] and
   Babylon among those who
   know* me;
Here are Phi·lis'ti·a and Tyre,
   together with Cush.
It will be said: "This is one
   who was born there."

5 And about Zion it will be
   said:
"Each and every one was
   born in her."

CHAP. 86
a 2Ch 16:9
b Ps 57:1
c Ps 25:5
d Ps 25:8
   Ps 145:9
   Lu 18:19
e Isa 55:7
   Mic 7:18
f Ps 130:7
g Ps 17:1
h Ps 18:6
i Ps 116:1
j Ex 15:11
   Ps 96:5
   1Co 8:5, 6
k De 3:24
   Ps 104:24
l Isa 2:2, 3
   Zec 14:9
   Re 7:9, 10
m Re 15:4
n Ps 72:18
   Da 6:27
o De 6:4
   Ps 83:18
   Isa 44:6
   1Co 8:4
p Ps 27:11
   Ps 119:33
   Ps 143:8
   Isa 54:13
q Ps 43:3
r Ec 12:13
   Jer 32:39
s Mt 22:37
t Job 33:28
   Ps 56:13
   Ps 116:8

Second Col.
a 2Sa 15:12
b Ps 10:4
   Ps 54:3
c Ex 34:6
   Ne 9:17
   Jon 4:2
d Ps 25:16
e Ps 28:7

CHAP. 87
f 2Ch 20:19
g Ps 48:1
h Ps 78:68
   Ps 132:13
i Ps 48:2
   Isa 60:14
j Ps 89:10
   Isa 30:7

86:4 *Or "the soul of your servant."
#Or "I raise my soul." 86:11 *Or "Give
me an undivided heart." 86:13 *Or
"soul." #Or "Sheol," that is, the common grave of mankind. See Glossary.

86:14 *Or "seek my soul." #Or "have
not set you in front of themselves."
86:15 *Or "gracious." #Or "and truth."
86:17 *Or "evidence." 87:4 *Or "acknowledge."

And the Most High will firmly establish her.

6 Jehovah will declare, when recording the peoples:
"This is one who was born there." (*Selah*)

7 Singers[a] and those performing circle dances[b] will say:
"All my springs are in you."*[c]

A song. A melody of the sons of Korʹah.[d] To the director; in the style of Maʹha·lath,* to be sung alternately. Masʹkil* of Heʹman[e] the Ezʹra·hite.

88 O Jehovah, the God of my salvation,[f]
By day I cry out,
And by night I come before you.[g]

2 Let my prayer come to you,[h]
Incline your ear* to my cry for help.[i]

3 For my soul* has been filled with calamity,[j]
And my life is on the brink of the Grave.*[k]

4 I am already counted among those going down to the pit;*[l]
I have become a helpless man,*[m]

5 Left among the dead
Like the slain lying in a grave,
Whom you remember no longer
And who have been separated from your care.*

6 You have put me in the lowest pit,
In dark places, in a large abyss.

7 Your rage weighs heavily on me,[n]
And you overwhelm me with your crashing waves. (*Selah*)

8 You have driven my acquaintances far away from me;[a]
You have made me something detestable to them.
I am trapped and cannot escape.

9 My eye is worn out because of my affliction.[b]
I call on you, O Jehovah, all day long;[c]
To you I spread out my hands.

10 Will you perform wonders for the dead?
Can those powerless in death rise up to praise you?[d] (*Selah*)

11 Will your loyal love be declared in the grave,
Your faithfulness in the place of destruction?*

12 Will your wonders be known in the darkness
Or your righteousness in the land of oblivion?[e]

13 But I still cry to you for help, O Jehovah,[f]
Each morning my prayer comes before you.[g]

14 Why, O Jehovah, do you reject me?*[h]
Why do you hide your face from me?[i]

15 From my youth on,
I have been afflicted and ready to perish;[j]
I am numb from the terrible things you allow me to suffer.

16 Your burning anger overwhelms me;[k]
Your terrors destroy me.

17 They surround me like waters all day long;
They close in on me from all sides.*

18 You have driven my friends and companions far away from me;[l]

CHAP. 87
a 1Ch 15:16

b Ps 150:4

c Ps 46:4

CHAP. 88
d 2Ch 20:19

e 1Ki 4:30, 31
   1Ch 2:6

f Ps 27:9
   Isa 12:2

g Ps 22:2

h 1Ki 8:30

i Ps 141:1

j Ps 71:20

k Isa 38:10

l Ps 143:7

m Ps 31:12

n Ps 90:7
   Ps 102:10

Second Col.
a Job 19:13, 19
   Ps 31:11
   Ps 142:4

b Job 17:7
   Ps 42:3
   La 3:49

c Ps 55:17

d Job 14:14
   Ps 115:17
   Isa 38:18

e Ec 2:16
   Ec 8:10
   Ec 9:5

f Ps 46:1

g Ps 55:17
   Ps 119:147

h Ps 43:2

i Job 13:24
   Ps 13:1

j Job 17:1

k Ps 102:10

l Job 19:13
   Ps 31:11
   Ps 38:11
   Ps 142:4

87:7 *Or "For me, you are the source of all things." 88:Sup; 88:3 *See Glossary. 88:2 *Or "Bend down and listen." 88:3 *Or "Sheol," that is, the common grave of mankind. See Glossary. 88:4 *Or "grave." #Or "like a man without strength." 88:5 *Lit., "hand."

88:11 *Or "in Abaddon." 88:14 *Or "my soul." 88:17 *Or possibly, "all at once."

Darkness has become my companion.

Mas'kil.* Of E'than[a] the Ez'ra·hite.

89 I will sing about Jehovah's expressions of loyal love forever.

With my mouth I will make known your faithfulness to all generations.

2 For I have said: "Loyal love will be built up* forever,[b]

And you have firmly established your faithfulness in the heavens."

3 "I have made a covenant with my chosen one;[c]

I have sworn to David my servant:[d]

4 'I will firmly establish your offspring* forever,[e]

And I will build up your throne for all generations.'"[f] (Selah)

5 The heavens praise your marvels, O Jehovah,

Yes, your faithfulness in the congregation of the holy ones.

6 For who in the skies can compare to Jehovah?[g]

Who among the sons of God[h] is like Jehovah?

7 God is held in awe in the council* of holy ones;[i]

He is grand and awe-inspiring to all who are around him.[j]

8 O Jehovah God of armies, Who is mighty like you, O Jah?[k]

Your faithfulness surrounds you.[l]

9 You rule over the raging of the sea;[m]

When its waves surge, you calm them.[n]

10 You have crushed Ra'hab* like one who is slain.[p]

With your strong arm you have scattered your enemies.[a]

11 The heavens are yours, and the earth is yours;[b]

The productive land and what fills it[c]—you have founded them.

12 The north and the south—you created them;

Ta'bor[d] and Her'mon[e] joyously praise your name.

13 Your arm is mighty;[f]

Your hand is strong;[g]

Your right hand is exalted.[h]

14 Righteousness and justice are the foundation of your throne;[i]

Loyal love and faithfulness stand before you.[j]

15 Happy are the people who know the joyful shouting.[k]

O Jehovah, they walk in the light of your face.

16 They rejoice in your name all day long,

And in your righteousness they are exalted.

17 For you are the glory of their strength,[l]

And by your approval our strength* is exalted.[m]

18 For our shield belongs to Jehovah,

Our king belongs to the Holy One of Israel.[n]

19 At that time you spoke in a vision to your loyal ones and said:

"I have granted strength to a mighty one;[o]

I have exalted a chosen one from among the people.[p]

20 I have found David my servant;[q]

With my holy oil I have anointed him.[r]

21 My hand will support him,[s]

And my arm will strengthen him.

CHAP. 89

a 1Ki 4:30, 31
1Ch 2:6

b 1Ch 16:41
Isa 54:10

c 2Sa 7:8
1Ki 8:16
Lu 1:32, 33

d Ps 132:11
Eze 34:23
Ho 3:5
Joh 7:42

e 1Ch 17:11
Re 22:16

f 2Sa 7:12, 13
Heb 1:8

g Ps 40:5
Ps 71:19

h Job 38:7

i Isa 6:2, 3

j Da 7:9, 10

k 1Sa 2:2
Ps 84:12

l De 32:4

m Jer 31:35

n Ps 65:7
Ps 107:29

o Isa 30:7

p Ex 14:26
Ex 15:4

Second Col.

a Ex 3:20
De 4:34
Lu 1:51

b 1Co 10:26

c 1Ch 29:11
Ps 50:12

d Jos 19:22, 23

e De 3:8
Jos 12:1

f Ex 6:6

g Ex 13:3

h Ps 44:3

i De 32:4
Ps 71:19
Re 15:3

j Ex 34:6
Jer 9:24

k Nu 10:10
Ps 98:6

l Ps 28:7

m 1Sa 2:10

n Ps 2:6

o 1Sa 18:14

p 2Sa 7:8

q Ac 13:22

r 1Sa 16:12, 13
Ac 10:38

s Ps 80:17
Isa 42:1

89:Sup *See Glossary. **89:2** *Or "endure." **89:4** *Lit., "seed." **89:7** *Or "assembly."

89:17 *Lit., "horn."

22 No enemy will exact tribute
   from him,
   And no unrighteous man will
   oppress him.[a]

23 I will crush to pieces his adversaries from before him[b]
   And strike down those who
   hate him.[c]

24 My faithfulness and loyal
   love are with him,[d]
   And in my name his
   strength* will be exalted.

25 I will put his hand* over
   the sea
   And his right hand over the
   rivers.[e]

26 He will call out to me:
   'You are my Father,
   My God and the Rock of my
   salvation.'[f]

27 And I will place him as firstborn,[g]
   The highest of the kings of
   the earth.[h]

28 I will maintain my loyal love
   for him forever,[i]
   And my covenant with him
   will never fail.[j]

29 I will establish his offspring*
   forever
   And make his throne as enduring as the heavens.[k]

30 If his sons leave my law
   And do not walk according to
   my decrees,*

31 If they violate my statutes
   And do not keep my commandments,

32 Then I will punish their disobedience* with a rod[l]
   And their error with flogging.

33 But I will never abandon my
   loyal love for him[m]
   Nor be untrue to my
   promise.*

34 I will not violate my
   covenant[a]
   Or change what my lips have
   spoken.[b]

35 I have sworn in my holiness,
   once and for all;
   I will not tell lies to David.[c]

36 His offspring* will endure
   forever;[d]
   His throne will endure like
   the sun before me.[e]

37 Like the moon, it will be
   firmly established forever
   As a faithful witness in the
   skies." (Selah)

38 But you yourself have cast
   off and rejected him;[f]
   You have become furious
   with your anointed one.

39 You have spurned the covenant with your servant;
   You have profaned his
   crown* by throwing it to
   the ground.

40 You have broken down all his
   stone walls;*
   You have reduced his fortifications to ruins.

41 All who pass by have pillaged
   him;
   He is a reproach to his neighbors.[g]

42 You have made his adversaries victorious;*[h]
   You have caused all his
   enemies to rejoice.

43 You have also driven back
   his sword,
   And you have made him lose
   ground in the battle.

44 You have brought an end to
   his splendor
   And hurled his throne to the
   ground.

45 You have cut short the days
   of his youth;
   You have clothed him with
   shame. (Selah)

CHAP. 89

a 1Ch 17:9

b 2Sa 3:1
  2Sa 7:9

c Ps 110:1

d 2Sa 7:15
  1Ch 17:13
  Ac 13:34

e 1Ki 4:21
  Ps 72:8

f 2Sa 22:47
  Ps 18:2

g Ps 2:7
  Heb 1:5

h 1Ti 6:15
  Re 1:5
  Re 19:16

i Ac 13:34

j 2Sa 23:5
  Ps 89:34

k Isa 9:7
  Jer 33:17
  Heb 1:8

l 2Sa 7:14
  1Ki 11:14, 31

m 2Sa 7:15
  1Ki 11:32, 36

Second Col.

a Jer 33:20, 21

b Jas 1:17

c Nu 23:19
  Ps 132:11

d 2Sa 7:16, 17
  Ps 72:17
  Isa 11:1
  Jer 23:5
  Joh 12:34
  Re 22:16

e Da 7:14
  Lu 1:32, 33

f 1Ch 28:9

g De 28:37

h De 28:25

89:24 *Lit., "horn." 89:25 *Or "authority." 89:29, 36 *Lit., "seed." 89:30
*Or "judgments." 89:32 *Or "rebel-
lion." 89:33 *Lit., "Nor be false with
my faithfulness."

89:39 *Or "diadem." 89:40 *Or "his
shelters of stone." 89:42 *Lit., "lifted
up the right hand of his adversaries."

46 How long, O Jehovah, will
you hide yourself? Will it
be forever?[a]
Will your rage continue to
burn like a fire?

47 Remember how short my
life is![b]
Was it to no purpose that you
created all humans?

48 What man can live and never
see death?[c]
Can he save himself* from
the power of the Grave?[#]
(*Selah*)

89:48 *Or "his soul." [#]Lit., "the hand
of Sheol," that is, the common grave of
mankind. See Glossary.

49 Where are your former acts
of loyal love, O Jehovah,
That you swore about to David in your faithfulness?[a]

50 Remember, O Jehovah, the
taunts hurled at your
servants;
How I have to bear* the
taunts of all the peoples;

51 How your enemies have
hurled insults, O Jehovah;
How they have insulted
every footstep of your
anointed one.

52 May Jehovah be praised
forever. Amen and Amen.[b]

89:50 *Lit., "carry in my bosom."

CHAP. 89
a Ps 13:1

b Job 7:7
  Ps 39:5

c Job 30:23
  Ps 49:7, 9

Second Col.
a 2Sa 7:12-15
  Ps 132:11
  Isa 55:3

b Ps 41:13
  Ps 72:18

BOOK FOUR
(Psalms 90-106)

A prayer of Moses,
the man of the true God.[a]

90 O Jehovah, you have been
our dwelling place*[b]
throughout all genera-
tions.

2 Before the mountains were
born
Or you brought forth* the
earth and the productive
land,[c]
From everlasting to everlasting,[#] you are God.[d]

3 You make mortal man return
to dust;
You say: "Return, you sons of
men."[e]

4 For a thousand years are in
your eyes just as yesterday
when it is past,[f]
Just as a watch during the
night.

5 You sweep them away;[g] they
become like mere sleep;
In the morning they are like
grass that sprouts.[h]

6 In the morning it blossoms
and is renewed,

90:1 *Or possibly, "our refuge." 90:2
*Or "brought forth as with labor pains."
[#]Or "From eternity to eternity."

CHAP. 90
a De 33:1

b De 33:27
  Ps 91:1

c Jer 10:12

d Ps 93:2
  Isa 40:28
  Hab 1:12
  1Ti 1:17
  Re 1:8
  Re 15:3

e Ge 3:19
  Ps 104:29
  Ps 146:3, 4
  Ec 3:20
  Ec 12:7

f 2Pe 3:8

g Job 9:25

h Ps 103:15
  1Pe 1:24

Second Col.
a Job 14:2

b Nu 17:12, 13
  De 32:22

c Jer 16:17

d Pr 24:12
  Heb 4:13

e 2Sa 19:34, 35

f Job 14:10
  Ps 78:39
  Lu 12:20
  Jas 4:13, 14

g Isa 33:14
  Lu 12:5

h Ps 39:4

But by evening it withers and
dries up.[a]

7 For we are consumed by
your anger[b]
And terrified by your rage.

8 You place our errors in front
of you;*[c]
Our secrets are exposed by
the light of your face.[d]

9 Our days ebb* away because
of your fury;
And our years come to an
end like a whisper.[#]

10 The span of our life is
70 years,
Or 80[e] if one is especially
strong.*
But they are filled with trouble and sorrow;
They quickly pass by, and
away we fly.[f]

11 Who can fathom the power
of your anger?
Your fury is as great as the
fear you deserve.[g]

12 Teach us how to count our
days[h]

90:8 *Or "You are aware of our errors."
90:9 *Or "Our life ebbs." [#]Or "a sigh."
90:10 *Or "because of special mightiness."

So that we may acquire a heart of wisdom.

13 Return, O Jehovah![a] How long will this last?[b]
Have pity on your servants.[c]

14 Satisfy us with your loyal love[d] in the morning,
So that we may shout joyfully and rejoice[e] during all our days.

15 Make us rejoice in proportion to the days you have afflicted us,[f]
For as many years as we have experienced calamity.[g]

16 May your servants see your activity,
And may their sons see your splendor.[h]

17 May the favor of Jehovah our God be upon us;
May you prosper* the work of our hands.
Yes, prosper* the work of our hands.[i]

91 Anyone dwelling in the secret place of the Most High[j]
Will lodge under the shadow of the Almighty.[k]

2 I will say to Jehovah: "You are my refuge and my stronghold,[l]
My God in whom I trust."[m]

3 For he will rescue you from the trap of the birdcatcher,
From the destructive pestilence.

4 With his pinions he will cover* you,
And under his wings you will take refuge.[n]
His faithfulness[o] will be a large shield[p] and a protective wall.#

5 You will not fear the terrors of the night,[q]
Nor the arrow that flies by day,[r]

6 Nor the pestilence that stalks in the gloom,
Nor the destruction that ravages at midday.

7 A thousand will fall at your side
And ten thousand at your right hand,
But to you it will not come near.[a]

8 You will only see it with your eyes
As you witness the punishment* of the wicked.

9 Because you said: "Jehovah is my refuge,"
You have made the Most High your dwelling;*[b]

10 No disaster will befall you,[c]
And no plague will come near your tent.

11 For he will give his angels[d] a command concerning you,
To guard you in all your ways.[e]

12 They will carry you on their hands,[f]
So that you may not strike your foot against a stone.[g]

13 On the young lion and the cobra you will tread;
You will trample underfoot the maned lion and the big snake.[h]

14 God said: "Because he has affection for me,* I will rescue him.[i]
I will protect him because he knows# my name.[j]

15 He will call on me, and I will answer him.[k]
I will be with him in distress.[l]
I will rescue him and glorify him.

16 I will satisfy him with long life,[m]
And I will cause him to see my acts of salvation."*[n]

CHAP. 90
a Ps 6:4
b Ps 89:46
c De 32:36
  Ps 135:14
d Ps 36:7
  Ps 51:1
  Ps 63:3
  Ps 85:7
e Ps 149:2
f Ps 30:5
g De 2:14
h Nu 14:31
  Jos 23:14
i Ps 127:1
  Pr 16:3
  Isa 26:12
  1Co 3:7

CHAP. 91
j Ps 27:5
  Ps 31:20
  Ps 32:7
k Ps 57:1
l Ps 18:2
  Pr 18:10
m Pr 3:5
n Ex 19:4
  De 32:11
  Ru 2:12
o Ps 57:3
  Ps 86:15
p Ge 15:1
  Ps 84:11
q Ps 121:4, 6
  Isa 60:2
r Ps 64:2, 3
  Isa 54:17

Second Col.
a Ex 12:13
b Ps 71:3
  Ps 90:1
c Pr 12:21
d 2Ki 6:17
  Ps 34:7
  Mt 18:10
e Ex 23:20
  Heb 1:7, 14
f Isa 63:9
g Ps 37:24
  Mt 4:6
h Lu 4:10, 11
i Lu 10:19
j Ps 18:2
k Ps 9:10
  Pr 18:10
l Ro 10:13
  Heb 5:7
m Ps 138:7
  Isa 43:2
n Ps 21:1, 4
  Pr 3:1, 2
o Isa 45:17

90:17 *Or "firmly establish." 91:4 *Or "block approach to." #Or "a bulwark."

91:8 *Lit., "retribution." 91:9 *Or possibly, "fortress; refuge." 91:14 *Lit., "he has joined himself to me." #Or "acknowledges." 91:16 *Or "see salvation from me."

A melody.
A song for the Sabbath day.

92 It is good to give thanks to Jehovah[a]
And to sing praises* to your name, O Most High,

2 To declare your loyal love[b] in the morning
And your faithfulness during the nights,

3 Accompanied by a ten-stringed instrument and a lute,
By the melodious sound of a harp.[c]

4 For you have made me rejoice, O Jehovah, because of your deeds;
Because of the works of your hands I shout joyfully.

5 How great your works are, O Jehovah![d]
How very deep your thoughts are![e]

6 No unreasoning man can know them;
And no foolish person can understand this:[f]

7 When the wicked sprout like weeds*
And all the wrongdoers flourish,
It is that they may be annihilated forever.[g]

8 But you are exalted forever, O Jehovah.

9 Indeed, look in triumph on your enemies, O Jehovah,
Look at how your enemies will perish;
All the wrongdoers will be scattered.[h]

10 But you will exalt my strength* like that of a wild bull;
I will moisten my skin with fresh oil.[i]

11 My eyes will look in triumph on my foes;[j]

My ears will hear about the downfall of the evil men who attack me.

12 But the righteous will flourish like a palm tree
And grow big like a cedar in Leb′a·non.[a]

13 They are planted in the house of Jehovah;
They flourish in the courtyards of our God.[b]

14 Even in old age* they will still be thriving;[c]
They will remain vigorous* and fresh,[d]

15 Declaring that Jehovah is upright.
He is my Rock;[e] in whom there is no unrighteousness.

93 Jehovah has become King![f]
With grandeur he is clothed;
Jehovah is clothed with strength;
He wears it like a belt.
The earth* is firmly established;
It cannot be moved.*

2 Your throne was firmly established long ago;[g]
From eternity you have existed.[h]

3 The rivers have surged, O Jehovah,
The rivers have surged and roared;
The rivers keep surging and pounding.

4 Above the sound of many waters,
Mightier than the breaking waves of the sea,[i]
Jehovah is majestic in the heights.[j]

5 Your reminders are very trustworthy.[k]

CHAP. 92
a Ps 50:23

b Isa 63:7

c 1Ch 15:16
1Ch 25:6
2Ch 29:25

d Ps 40:5
Ps 145:4
Ec 3:11
Re 15:3

e Job 26:14
Ro 11:33

f Ps 14:1
1Co 2:14

g Ps 37:35, 38
Jer 12:1-3

h De 28:7
Ps 68:1

i Ps 23:5

j Ps 37:34

Second Col.
a Ps 52:8
Isa 61:3
Isa 65:22

b Ps 100:4

c Ps 71:18
Pr 16:31
Isa 40:31
Isa 46:4

d Jer 17:7, 8

e De 32:4

CHAP. 93
f Ps 96:10
Ps 97:1
Isa 52:7
Re 11:17
Re 19:6

g Ps 145:13

h Ps 90:2

i Ps 65:7

j Ps 8:1
Ps 76:4

k Ps 19:7
Ps 119:111

92:1 *Or "make music." 92:7 *Or "grass." 92:10 *Lit., "horn." 92:14 *Or "during gray-headedness." *Lit., "fat." 93:1 *Or "productive land." *Or "cannot totter."

Holiness adorns* your house,[a] O Jehovah, for all times.

94

O God of vengeance, Jehovah,[b]

O God of vengeance, shine forth!

2 Rise up, O Judge of the earth.[c]

Repay to the haughty what they deserve.[d]

3 How long will the wicked, O Jehovah,

How long will the wicked continue to exult?[e]

4 They babble and speak arrogantly;

All the wrongdoers brag about themselves.

5 They crush your people, O Jehovah,[f]

And oppress your inheritance.

6 They kill the widow and the foreign resident,

And they murder the fatherless children.

7 They say: "Jah does not see;[g]

The God of Jacob does not take notice of it."[h]

8 Understand this, you who are unreasoning;

You foolish ones, when will you ever show insight?[i]

9 The One who made* the ear, can he not hear?

The One who formed the eye, can he not see?[j]

10 The One correcting the nations, can he not reprove?[k]

He is the One who imparts knowledge to people![l]

11 Jehovah knows the thoughts of men,

That they are but a mere breath.[m]

12 Happy is the man whom you correct, O Jah,[n]

Whom you teach from your law,[a]

13 To give him tranquillity during days of calamity,

Until a pit is dug for the wicked.[b]

14 For Jehovah will not forsake his people,[c]

Nor will he abandon his inheritance.[d]

15 For judgment will once again be righteous,

And all the upright in heart will follow it.

16 Who will rise up for me against the wicked?

Who will take a stand for me against the wrongdoers?

17 If Jehovah had not been my helper,

I* would soon have perished.*[e]

18 When I said: "My foot is slipping,"

Your loyal love, O Jehovah, kept supporting me.[f]

19 When anxieties* overwhelmed me,*

You comforted and soothed me.△[g]

20 Can a throne* of corruption be allied with you

While it is framing trouble in the name of the law?*[h]

21 They make vicious attacks on the righteous one*[i]

And condemn the innocent one to death.*[j]

22 But Jehovah will become a secure refuge* for me,

My God is my rock of refuge.[k]

CHAP. 93

a Eze 43:12
  1Pe 1:16

CHAP. 94

b De 32:35
  Na 1:2
  Ro 12:19

c Ge 18:25
  Ac 17:31

d Ps 31:23

e Ps 73:3
  Ps 74:10

f Ps 14:4

g Ps 59:2, 7
  Eze 8:12

h Ps 10:4, 11
  Ps 73:3, 11
  Isa 29:15

i Pr 1:22

j Ps 34:15

k Ps 9:5
  Isa 10:12

l Ps 25:8
  Isa 28:26
  Joh 6:45

m 1Co 3:20

n Ps 119:71
  Pr 3:11
  1Co 11:32
  Heb 12:5, 6

Second Col.

a Ps 19:8

b Ps 55:23
  2Pe 2:9

c 1Sa 12:22
  Ps 37:28
  Heb 13:5

d De 32:9

e Ps 124:2, 3
  2Co 1:10

f 1Sa 2:9
  Ps 37:24
  Ps 121:3
  La 3:22

g Ps 86:17
  Php 4:6, 7

h Isa 10:1
  Da 6:7
  Ac 5:27, 28

i Ps 59:3

j 1Ki 21:13

k Ps 18:2

94:17 *Or "My soul." *Lit., "resided in silence." 94:19 *Or "disquieting thoughts." *Or "became many inside of me." △Or "Your consolations soothed my soul." 94:20 *Or "rulers; judges." *Or "by decree." 94:21 *Or "the soul of the righteous one." *Lit., "And the blood of the innocent they declare guilty (wicked)." 94:22 *Or "secure height."

93:5 *Or "befits." 94:9 *Lit., "planted."

23 He will make their wicked
   deeds come back upon
   them.[a]
   He will do away with* them
   by means of their own evil.
   Jehovah our God will do
   away with* them.[b]

95
Come, let us shout joyfully
to Jehovah!
   Let us shout in triumph to
   our Rock of salvation.[c]

2 Let us come into his presence* with thanksgiving;[d]
   Let us sing and shout in
   triumph to him.

3 For Jehovah is a great God,
   A great King over all other
   gods.[e]

4 In his hand are the depths
   of the earth;
   The mountain peaks belong
   to him.[f]

5 The sea, which he made,
   belongs to him,[g]
   And his hands formed the
   dry land.[h]

6 Come, let us worship and
   bow down;
   Let us kneel before Jehovah
   our Maker.[i]

7 For he is our God,
   And we are the people of his
   pasture,
   The sheep in his care.*[j]
   Today if you listen to his
   voice,[k]

8 Do not harden your heart
   as at Mer′i·bah,*[l]
   As in the day of Mas′sah#
   in the wilderness,[m]

9 When your forefathers tested me;[n]
   They challenged me, though
   they had seen my works.[o]

10 For 40 years I felt a loathing
   toward that generation,
   and I said:

"They are a people who always go astray in their
   hearts;
   They have not come to know
   my ways."

11 So I swore in my anger:
   "They will not enter into my
   rest."[a]

96
Sing to Jehovah a new
song.[b]
   Sing to Jehovah, all the
   earth![c]

2 Sing to Jehovah; praise his
   name.
   Proclaim the good news of
   his salvation day after day.[d]

3 Declare his glory among the
   nations,
   His wonderful works among
   all the peoples.[e]

4 Jehovah is great and most
   worthy of praise.
   He is more awe-inspiring
   than all other gods.

5 All the gods of the peoples
   are worthless gods,[f]
   But Jehovah is the one who
   made the heavens.[g]

6 In his presence are majesty*
   and splendor;[h]
   Strength and beauty are in
   his sanctuary.[i]

7 Give Jehovah his due, you
   families of the peoples,
   Give Jehovah his due for his
   glory and strength.[j]

8 Give Jehovah the glory due
   his name;[k]
   Bring a gift and come into his
   courtyards.

9 Bow down to* Jehovah in
   holy adornment;#
   Tremble before him, all the
   earth!

10 Declare among the nations:
   "Jehovah has become
   King![l]

CHAP. 94
a Pr 5:22
  2Th 1:6
b 1Sa 26:9, 10

CHAP. 95
c 2Sa 22:47
d Ps 50:23
  Ps 100:4
e Ex 18:11
  Jer 10:10
  1Co 8:5, 6
f Am 4:13
  Am 9:3
g Jer 5:22
h Ge 1:9, 10
i Ps 100:3
  Mt 4:10
  Re 14:7
j Ps 23:1
  Isa 40:11
k Heb 3:7-11
  Heb 4:7
l Heb 3:15
m Ex 17:7
n Ps 78:18
  1Co 10:9
o Nu 14:22, 23

Second Col.
a Ge 2:3
  Nu 14:22, 23
  Heb 4:3

CHAP. 96
b Ps 33:3
  Ps 40:3
  Ps 98:1
  Ps 149:1
  Isa 42:10
c 1Ch 16:23-25
  Ps 66:4
d Ps 40:10
  Ps 71:15
  Isa 52:7
e Mt 28:19
  1Pe 2:9
  Re 14:6
f Ps 97:7
  Isa 44:10
g 1Ch 16:26
  Ex 8:4
h Ex 24:9, 10
  Isa 6:1-3
  Eze 1:27, 28
  Re 4:2, 3
i 1Ch 16:27
  1Ch 29:11
j 1Ch 16:28-33
  Ps 29:1
k Ps 29:2
  Ps 72:19
l Ps 93:1
  Ps 97:1
  Re 11:15
  Re 19:6

94:23 *Lit., "will silence." 95:2 *Lit.,
"before his face." 95:7 *Lit., "of his
hand." 95:8 *Meaning "Quarreling."
#Meaning "Testing; Trial."

96:6 *Or "dignity." 96:9 *Or "Worship." #Or possibly, "because of the
splendor of his holiness."

The earth* is firmly es-
tablished, it cannot be
moved.#

He will judge△ the peoples
fairly."^a

11 Let the heavens rejoice, and
let the earth be joyful;

Let the sea thunder and all
that fills it;^b

12 Let the fields and everything
in them rejoice.^c

At the same time let all the
trees of the forest shout
joyfully^d

13 Before Jehovah, for he is
coming,*

He is coming to judge the
earth.

He will judge the inhabited
earth# with righteousness^e

And the peoples with his
faithfulness.^f

97 Jehovah has become
King!^g

Let the earth be joyful.^h

Let the many islands rejoice.^i

2 Clouds and thick gloom are
all around him;^j

Righteousness and justice
are the foundation of his
throne.^k

3 Fire goes before him^l

And consumes his adver-
saries on every side.^m

4 His lightning bolts light up
the land;

The earth sees it and trembles.^n

5 The mountains melt like wax
before Jehovah,^o

Before the Lord of the whole
earth.

6 The heavens proclaim his
righteousness,

And all the peoples see his
glory.^p

7 Let all those serving any
carved image be put to
shame,^a

Those who boast about their
worthless gods.^b

Bow down to* him, all you
gods.^c

8 Zion hears and rejoices;^d

The towns* of Judah are
joyful

Because of your judgments,
O Jehovah.^e

9 For you, O Jehovah, are
the Most High over all the
earth;

You are exalted far above all
other gods.^f

10 O you who love Jehovah,
hate what is bad.^g

He is guarding the lives* of
his loyal ones;^h

He rescues them from the
hand# of the wicked.^i

11 Light has flashed up for the
righteous^j

And rejoicing for those
upright in heart.

12 Rejoice in Jehovah, you
righteous ones,

And give thanks to his holy
name.*

A melody.

98 Sing to Jehovah a new
song,^k

For he has done wonderful
things.^l

His right hand, his holy arm,
has brought about salva-
tion.*^m

2 Jehovah has made known his
salvation;^n

He has revealed his righ-
teousness before the
nations.^o

3 He has remembered his loyal
love and faithfulness to the
house of Israel.^p

CHAP. 96
a Ps 67:4
Ps 98:9
b Ps 98:7
c Ps 65:13
d 1Ch 16:33
e Ge 18:25
Ps 9:8
Ps 98:9
Ac 17:31
2Pe 3:7
f De 32:4

CHAP. 97
g Ps 96:10
Re 11:16, 17
Re 19:6
h Isa 49:13
i Isa 60:9
j Ex 20:21
k Ps 99:4
l Ps 50:3
Da 7:9, 10
m Na 1:2, 6
Mal 4:1
n Ex 19:16, 18
Ps 77:18
Ps 104:32
o Jg 5:5
Na 1:5
Hab 3:6
p Hab 2:14

Second Col.
a Jer 10:14
b Isa 37:19
c Ex 12:12
Ex 18:11
d Isa 51:3
e Ps 48:11
f Ex 18:11
Isa 44:8
g Ps 34:14
Ps 101:3
Ps 119:104
Ro 12:9
Heb 1:9
h Ps 37:28
Ps 145:20
i Da 3:28
Mt 6:13
j Ps 112:4
Pr 4:18
Isa 30:26
Mic 7:9

CHAP. 98
k Ps 33:3
Ps 96:1
Ps 149:1
Isa 42:10
l Ex 15:11
Ps 111:2
m Ex 15:6
Isa 52:10
Isa 59:16
Isa 63:5
n Lu 2:30, 31
o Isa 5:16
p Le 26:42
Lu 1:54, 55

96:10 *Or "productive land." #Or
"cannot totter." △Or "plead the cause
of." 96:13 *Or "has come." #Or "the
productive land."

97:7 *Or "Worship." 97:8 *Lit.,
"daughters." 97:10 *Or "souls."
#Or "power." 97:12 *Lit., "memorial."
98:1 *Or "has won him victory."

All the ends of the earth
have seen the salvation by
our God.*[a]

4 Shout in triumph to
Jehovah, all the earth.
Be cheerful and shout joyful-
ly and sing praises.*[b]

5 Sing praises* to Jehovah
with the harp,
With the harp and the melodious song.

6 With the trumpets and the
sound of the horn,[c]
Shout in triumph before the
King, Jehovah.

7 Let the sea thunder and all
that fills it,
The earth* and those dwelling in it.

8 Let the rivers clap their
hands;
Let the mountains shout joyfully together[d]

9 Before Jehovah, for he is
coming* to judge the earth.
He will judge the inhabited
earth*[] with righteousness[e]
And the peoples with fairness.[f]

99 Jehovah has become
King.[g] Let the peoples
tremble.
He sits enthroned above*
the cherubs.[h] Let the earth
shake.

2 Jehovah is great in Zion,
And he is high over all the
peoples.[i]

3 Let them praise your great
name,[j]
For it is awe-inspiring and
holy.

4 He is a mighty king who
loves justice.[k]
You have firmly established
what is upright.

You have brought about
justice and righteousness[a]
in Jacob.

5 Exalt Jehovah our God[b]
and bow down* at his footstool;[c]
He is holy.[d]

6 Moses and Aaron were
among his priests,[e]
And Samuel was among
those calling on his name.[f]
They would call to Jehovah,
And he would answer them.[g]

7 He would speak to them from
the pillar of cloud.[h]
They kept his reminders and
the decree that he gave
to them.[i]

8 O Jehovah our God, you
answered them.[j]
You were a God who par-
doned them,[k]
But you punished* them for
their sinful deeds.

9 Exalt Jehovah our God[m]
And bow down* before his
holy mountain,[n]
For Jehovah our God is holy.[o]

A melody of thanksgiving.

100 Shout in triumph to
Jehovah, all the
earth.[p]

2 Serve Jehovah with rejoicing.[q]
Come into his presence with
joyful shouting.

3 Know* that Jehovah is God.[r]
He is the one who made us,
and we belong to him.*[s]
We are his people and the
sheep of his pasture.[t]

4 Come into his gates with
thanksgiving,[u]
Into his courtyards with
praise.[v]
Give thanks to him; praise
his name.[w]

CHAP. 98
a Isa 49:6
  Ac 28:28
  Ro 10:18
b Ps 47:1
  Ps 67:4
c Nu 10:10
  1Ch 15:28
  2Ch 29:27
d Isa 44:23
e Ps 9:8
  Ac 17:31
f Ps 67:4
  Ps 96:10
  Ro 2:6

CHAP. 99
g Ps 93:1
  Re 11:17
h Ex 25:22
i Ps 83:18
j Ps 8:1
  Ps 148:13
  Re 15:4
k Job 36:6

Second Col.
a De 10:17, 18
  Jer 9:24
b Ex 15:2
c 1Ch 28:2
  Ps 132:7
d Le 19:2
e Ex 24:6
  Nu 14:19, 20
f 1Sa 7:9
g Ex 15:24, 25
  1Sa 15:10
h Ex 19:9
i Ex 40:16
  1Sa 12:3
j De 9:19
k Mic 7:18
l Ex 34:6, 7
m Ex 15:2
n Ps 2:6
o 1Sa 2:2
  Isa 6:3

CHAP. 100
p Ps 95:1, 2
  Ps 98:4
q De 12:12
  Ne 8:10
r De 6:4
s Ps 149:2
t Ps 95:6, 7
  Eze 34:31
  1Pe 2:25
u Ps 50:23
  Ps 66:13
  Ps 122:1, 2
v Ps 65:4
w Ps 96:2
  Heb 13:15

98:3 *Or "the victory of our God." **98:4** *Or "make music." **98:5** *Or "Make music." **98:7** *Or "productive land." **98:9** *Or "has come." *[] Or "the productive land." **99:1** *Or possibly, "between."

99:5, 9 *Or "worship." **99:8** *Lit., "executed vengeance against." **100:3** *Or "Acknowledge." *[] Or possibly, "and not we ourselves."

5 For Jehovah is good;[a]
His loyal love endures forever,
And his faithfulness through
all generations.[b]

Of David. A melody.

101 I will sing about loyal
love and justice.
To you, O Jehovah, I will sing
praises.*

2 I will act with discretion and
blamelessness.*
When will you come to me?
I will walk with integrity of
heart[c] inside my house.

3 I will not set anything worthless* before my eyes.
I hate the deeds of those who
deviate from what is right;[d]
I will have nothing to do with
them.#

4 A crooked heart is far
from me;
I will not accept* what is bad.

5 Anyone slandering his neigh-
bor in secret,[e]
I will silence.*
Anyone with haughty eyes
and an arrogant heart,
I will not tolerate.

6 I will look to the faithful ones
of the earth,
So that they may dwell
with me.
The one walking in
blamelessness* will minister to me.

7 No deceitful person will
dwell in my house,
And no liar will stand in my
presence.*

8 Every morning I will silence*
all the wicked of the earth,

To cut off all wrongdoers
from the city of Jehovah.[a]

A prayer of the oppressed one when
he is in despair* and pours out his
concern before Jehovah.[b]

102 O Jehovah, hear my
prayer;[c]
Let my cry for help reach
you.[d]

2 Do not hide your face from
me in my time of distress.[e]
Incline your ear* to me;
Do answer me quickly when
I call.[f]

3 For my days are vanishing
like smoke,
And my bones are charred
like a fireplace.[g]

4 My heart has been struck
down like grass and has
withered,[h]
For I forget to eat my food.

5 Because of my loud groaning,[i]
My bones cling to my flesh.[j]

6 I resemble the pelican of the
wilderness;
I am like a little owl among
the ruins.

7 I lie awake;*
I am like a solitary bird on
a roof.[k]

8 All day long my enemies
taunt me.[l]
Those who mock me* use my
name as a curse.

9 For I eat ashes as my bread,[m]
And my drink is mingled with
tears,[n]

10 Because of your anger and
your indignation,
For you lifted me up only
to cast me aside.

11 My days are like a fading
shadow,*[o]
And I am withering like
grass.[p]

Middle column references:

CHAP. 100
a Ps 86:5
  Lu 18:19

b Ex 34:6, 7
  De 7:9
  Ps 98:3

CHAP. 101
c 1Ki 9:4
  Ps 78:70, 72

d Ps 97:10

e Pr 20:19

Second Col.
a Pr 20:8

CHAP. 102
b Ps 61:2
  Ps 142:2

c Ps 55:1
  Da 9:17

d Ex 2:23

e Ps 27:9
  La 1:20

f Ps 143:7
  Isa 65:24

g La 1:13

h Ps 143:4

i Ps 6:6
  Ps 38:8

j Job 19:20
  Pr 17:22

k Ps 38:11

l Ps 31:11
  Ps 74:10
  Ps 79:4

m La 3:15

n Ps 80:5

o Ps 39:5

p Job 14:1, 2
  Ps 102:4

101:1 *Or "make music." 101:2 *Or
"integrity." 101:3 *Or "good-for-
nothing." #Or "Their deeds do
not cling to me." 101:4 *Lit., "know."
101:5, 8 *Or "do away with." 101:6 *Or
"in integrity." 101:7 *Lit., "in front of
my eyes."

102:Sup *Or "he grows weak." 102:2
*Or "Bend down and listen." 102:7 *Or
possibly, "I am emaciated." 102:8 *Or
"make a fool of me." 102:11 *Or "a
lengthening shadow."

12 But you remain forever,
　　O Jehovah,[a]
　　And your fame* will endure
　　　for all generations.[b]
13 Surely you will rise up and
　　show mercy on Zion,[c]
　　For it is time to show her
　　　your favor;[d]
　　The appointed time has
　　　come.[e]
14 For your servants find
　　pleasure in her stones[f]
　　And have affection even for
　　　her dust.[g]
15 The nations will fear the
　　name of Jehovah,
　　And all the kings of the earth
　　　your glory.[h]
16 For Jehovah will rebuild
　　Zion;[i]
　　He will appear in his glory.[j]
17 He will pay attention to the
　　prayer of the destitute;[k]
　　He will not despise their
　　　prayer.[l]
18 This is written for the future
　　generation,[m]
　　So that a people yet to be
　　　brought forth* will praise
　　　Jah.
19 For he looks down from his
　　holy height,[n]
　　From the heavens Jehovah
　　　views the earth,
20 To hear the sighing of the
　　prisoner,[o]
　　To release those sentenced
　　　to death,[p]
21 So that the name of Jehovah
　　will be declared in Zion[q]
　　And his praise in Jerusalem,
22 When the peoples and
　　kingdoms
　　Gather together to serve
　　　Jehovah.[r]
23 He prematurely robbed me
　　of my strength;
　　He cut short my days.

24 I said: "O my God,
　　Do not do away with me
　　　in the middle of my life,
　　You whose years span all
　　　generations.[a]
25 Long ago you laid the foun-
　　dations of the earth,
　　And the heavens are the
　　　work of your hands.[b]
26 They will perish, but you will
　　remain;
　　Just like a garment they will
　　　all wear out.
　　Just like clothing you will
　　　replace them, and they will
　　　pass away.
27 But you are the same, and
　　your years will never end.[c]
28 The children of your ser-
　　vants will dwell securely,
　　And their offspring will be
　　　firmly established before
　　　you."[d]

Of David.

103
Let me* praise
　　Jehovah;
　　Let everything within me
　　　praise his holy name.
2 Let me* praise Jehovah;
　　May I never forget all that
　　　he has done.[e]
3 He forgives all your errors[f]
　　And heals all your ailments;[g]
4 He reclaims your life from
　　the pit*[h]
　　And crowns you with his
　　　loyal love and mercy.[i]
5 He satisfies you with good
　　things[j] all your life,
　　So that your youth is
　　　renewed like that of an
　　　eagle.[k]
6 Jehovah acts with righteous-
　　ness[l] and justice
　　For all who are oppressed.[m]
7 He made known his ways
　　to Moses,[n]
　　His deeds to the sons of
　　　Israel.[o]

CHAP. 102
a Ps 90:2
b Ex 3:15
c Isa 49:15
d Isa 60:10
e Ezr 1:1, 2
　Isa 40:2
　Da 9:2
f Ne 2:3
　Ps 137:5
g Ps 79:1
h Isa 60:3
　Zec 8:22
i Ps 147:2
　Jer 33:7
j Isa 60:1
k Da 9:20, 21
l Ps 22:24
m Ps 78:4
　Ro 15:4
n 2Ch 16:9
o Ex 3:7
　Isa 61:1
p 2Ch 33:12, 13
　Ps 79:11
q Ps 9:13, 14
　Ps 22:22
　Isa 51:11
r Isa 11:10
　Isa 49:22
　Isa 60:3

Second Col.
a Ps 90:2
　Hab 1:12
　Re 1:8
b Ps 8:3
　Isa 48:13
　Heb 1:10-12
c Job 36:26
　Mal 3:6
　Jas 1:17
d Isa 66:22

CHAP. 103
e De 8:2
　Ps 105:5
f 2Sa 12:13
　Isa 43:25
g Ex 15:26
　Ps 41:3
　Ps 147:3
　Isa 33:24
　Jas 5:15
　Re 21:4
h Ps 56:13
i Mic 7:18
j Ps 23:5
　Ps 65:4
k Ps 51:12
　Isa 40:31
l Ps 9:8
m Ps 12:5
　Pr 22:22, 23
　Jas 5:4
n Ex 24:4
　Nu 12:8
o Ps 147:19

102:12 *Or "name." Lit., "memorial."
102:18 *Lit., "be created."

103:1, 2 *Or "my soul." **103:4** *Or "grave."

8 Jehovah is merciful and compassionate,*[a]
Slow to anger and abundant in loyal love.#[b]
9 He will not always find fault,[c]
Nor will he stay resentful forever.[d]
10 He has not dealt with us according to our sins,[e]
Nor has he repaid us what our errors deserve.[f]
11 For as the heavens are higher than the earth,
So great is his loyal love toward those who fear him.[g]
12 As far off as the sunrise is from the sunset,
So far off from us he has put our transgressions.[h]
13 As a father shows mercy to his sons,
Jehovah has shown mercy to those who fear him.[i]
14 For he well knows how we are formed,[j]
Remembering that we are dust.[k]
15 As for mortal man, his days are like those of grass;[l]
He blooms like a blossom of the field.[m]
16 But when a wind blows, it is no more,
As though it was never there.*
17 But the loyal love of Jehovah is for all eternity*
Toward those who fear him,[n]
And his righteousness toward their children's children,[o]
18 Toward those who keep his covenant[p]
And those who are careful to observe his orders.
19 Jehovah has firmly established his throne in the heavens;[q]
And his kingship rules over everything.[a]
20 Praise Jehovah, all you his angels,[b] mighty in power,
Who carry out his word,[c] obeying his voice.*
21 Praise Jehovah, all his armies,[d]
His ministers who do his will.[e]
22 Praise Jehovah, all his works,
In all the places where he rules.*
Let my whole being# praise Jehovah.

104

Let me# praise Jehovah.[f]
O Jehovah my God, you are very great.[g]
With majesty* and splendor you are clothed.[h]
2 You are wrapped in light[i] as with a garment;
You stretch out the heavens like a tent cloth.[j]
3 He lays beams of his upper rooms in the waters above,*[k]
Making the clouds his chariot,[l]
Moving on the wings of the wind.[m]
4 He makes his angels spirits,
His ministers a consuming fire.[n]
5 He has established the earth on its foundations;[o]
It will not be moved from its place* forever and ever.[p]
6 You covered it with deep waters as with a garment.[q]
The waters stood above the mountains.
7 At your rebuke they fled;[r]

CHAP. 103
a Isa 55:7, Jas 5:11
b Ex 34:6, Joe 2:13, Jon 4:2
c Ps 30:5
d Isa 57:16
e Ne 9:31
f Ezr 9:13, Ps 130:3, Isa 55:7
g Ps 103:17, Isa 55:9
h Le 16:21, 22, Isa 43:25, Jer 31:34
i Ps 78:38, Isa 49:15, Mal 3:17, Jas 5:15
j Ps 78:39
k Ge 2:7
l Ps 90:5, 6, 1Pe 1:24
m Job 14:1, 2
n Lu 1:50
o Ex 20:6
p Ex 19:5, De 7:9, Ps 25:10
q 2Ch 20:6, Isa 66:1

Second Col.
a Ps 47:2, Ps 145:13, Da 4:25
b Da 7:10
c 2Ki 19:35, Lu 1:19
d 1Ki 22:19, Ps 148:2, Lu 2:13, 14
e Mt 13:41, Heb 1:7

CHAP. 104
f Ps 103:1
g Ps 86:10
h 1Ch 16:27, Eze 1:27, 28, Da 7:9
i Jas 1:17, 1Jo 1:5
j Isa 40:22
k Ps 18:11, Am 9:6
l De 33:26, Isa 19:1
m 2Sa 22:11, Job 38:1
n Eze 1:13, Heb 1:7, 14
o Job 38:4, 6, Ps 24:1, 2
p Ec 1:4
q Ge 1:2
r Ge 1:9

103:8 *Or "gracious." #Or "loving-kindness." **103:16** *Lit., "And its place no longer knows it." **103:17** *Or "from eternity to eternity." **103:20** *Lit., "hearing the voice (sound) of his word." **103:22** *Or "the places of his sovereignty." **103:22; 104:1** #Or "my soul." **104:1** *Or "dignity." **104:3** *Lit., "in the waters." **104:5** *Or "will not totter."

At the sound of your thunder
they ran away in panic

8 —Mountains ascended[a] and
valleys descended—
To the place you established
for them.

9 You set a boundary that they
should not pass,[b]
That they should never again
cover the earth.

10 He sends springs into the
valleys;*
Between the mountains they
flow.

11 They provide water for all
the wild beasts of the field;
The wild donkeys quench
their thirst.

12 Above them roost the birds
of the sky;
They sing among the thick
foliage.

13 He is watering the mountains
from his upper rooms.[c]
With the fruitage of your
works the earth is satis-
fied.[d]

14 He is making grass grow for
the cattle
And vegetation for man-
kind's use,[e]
To grow food from the land

15 And wine that makes man's
heart rejoice,[f]
Oil that makes the face
shine,
And bread that sustains the
heart of mortal man.[g]

16 The trees of Jehovah are
satisfied,
The cedars of Leb'a·non that
he planted,

17 Where the birds make nests.
The home of the stork[h] is in
the juniper trees.

18 The high mountains are for
the mountain goats;[i]
The crags are a refuge for
the rock badgers.[j]

19 He has made the moon to
mark the appointed times;

The sun well knows when to
set.[a]

20 You bring darkness, and
night falls,[b]
When all the wild animals
of the forest roam about.

21 The young lions* roar for
their prey[c]
And seek their food from
God.[d]

22 When the sun rises,
They withdraw and lie down
in their dens.

23 Man goes to his work,
And he labors until evening.

24 How many your works are,
O Jehovah![e]
You have made all of them
in wisdom.[f]
The earth is full of what you
have made.

25 There is the sea, so great
and wide,
Teeming with countless living things, both small and
great.[g]

26 There the ships travel,
And Le·vi'a·than,*[h] which you
formed to play in it.

27 All of them wait for you
To give them their food in
its season.[i]

28 What you give them, they
gather.[j]
When you open your hand,
they are satisfied with
good things.[k]

29 When you hide your face,
they are disturbed.
If you take away their spirit,
they die and return to the
dust.[l]

30 If you send out your spirit,
they are created,[m]
And you renew the surface
of the ground.

31 The glory of Jehovah will
last forever.
Jehovah will rejoice in his
works.[n]

CHAP. 104

a Pr 8:25

b Job 38:8-10
Ps 33:7
Pr 8:29
Jer 5:22

c Job 38:37
Ps 147:8
Jer 10:13
Am 9:6
Mt 5:45

d Ps 65:9
Ac 14:17

e Ge 1:29, 30
Ge 9:3

f Ec 9:7

g Ec 10:19

h Jer 8:7

i Job 39:1

j Pr 30:26

Second Col.

a Ge 1:16
Ps 19:6
Jer 31:35

b Ge 1:5
Ps 74:16
Isa 45:7

c Am 3:4

d Ps 147:9

e Ne 9:6

f Pr 3:19
Jer 10:12

g Ge 1:21

h Job 41:1

i Ps 136:25
Ps 145:15
Ps 147:9
Mt 6:26

j Lu 12:24

k Ps 107:9
Ps 145:16

l Ge 3:19
Job 34:14, 15
Ps 146:3, 4
Ec 3:19, 20
Ec 12:7

m Job 33:4
Ac 17:28

n Ge 1:31

104:10 *Or "wadis."

104:21 *Or "maned young lions."
104:26 *See Glossary.

32 He looks at the earth, and it
   trembles;
   He touches the mountains,
   and they smoke.[a]
33 I will sing to Jehovah[b]
   throughout my life;
   I will sing praises* to my God
   as long as I live.[c]
34 Let my thoughts be pleasing
   to him.*
   I will rejoice in Jehovah.
35 The sinners will vanish from
   the earth,
   And the wicked will no longer exist.[d]
   Let me* praise Jehovah.
   Praise Jah!*

105 Give thanks to
   Jehovah,[e] call on his
   name,
   Make his deeds known
   among the peoples![f]
2 Sing to him, sing praises*
   to him,
   Ponder over* all his wonderful works.[g]
3 Boast about his holy name.[h]
   Let the hearts of those seeking Jehovah rejoice.[i]
4 Search for Jehovah[j] and his
   strength.
   Seek his face* constantly.
5 Remember the wonderful
   works he has performed,
   His miracles and the judgments he has pronounced,[k]
6 You offspring* of Abraham
   his servant,[l]
   You sons of Jacob, his
   chosen ones.[m]
7 He is Jehovah our God.[n]
   His judgments are throughout the earth.[o]
8 He remembers his covenant
   forever,[p]

The promise he made,* to
   a thousand generations,[a]
9 The covenant he made with
   Abraham,[b]
   And the oath he swore to
   Isaac,[c]
10 Which he established as a
   decree to Jacob
   And as a lasting covenant
   to Israel,
11 Saying, "I will give you the
   land of Ca′naan[d]
   As your allotted inheritance."[e]
12 This was when they were few
   in number,[f]
   Yes, very few, and they were
   foreigners in the land.[g]
13 They walked about from
   nation to nation,
   From one kingdom to another people.[h]
14 He did not allow any man
   to oppress them,[i]
   But on their account he
   reproved kings,[j]
15 Saying, "Do not touch my
   anointed ones,
   And to my prophets do
   nothing bad."[k]
16 He called down a famine on
   the land;[l]
   He cut off their supply of
   bread.*
17 He sent ahead of them a man
   Who was sold to be a slave,
   Joseph.[m]
18 With fetters they bound* his
   feet;[n]
   His neck was put in irons*
19 Until the time that his word
   proved true,[o]
   The saying of Jehovah is
   what refined him.
20 The king sent to release
   him,[p]
   The ruler of the peoples set
   him free.

CHAP. 104
a Ex 19:18
b Ps 13:6
c Ps 146:2
d Ps 37:10, 38
  Pr 2:22

CHAP. 105
e Ps 136:1
f 1Ch 16:8-13
  Ps 96:3
  Ps 145:11, 12
  Isa 12:4
g Ps 77:12
  Ps 119:27
h Jer 9:24
i Ps 119:2
j Am 5:4
  Zep 2:3
k De 7:18, 19
l Ex 3:6
m Ex 19:5, 6
  Isa 41:8
n Ex 20:2
  Ps 100:3
o 1Ch 16:14-18
  Isa 26:9
  Re 15:4
p Ne 1:5

Second Col.
a De 7:9
  Lu 1:72, 73
b Ge 17:1, 2
  Ge 22:15-18
c Ge 26:3
d Ge 12:7
  Ge 13:14, 15
  Ge 15:18
  Ge 26:3
  Ge 28:13
e Ps 78:55
f Ge 34:30
g Ge 17:8
  Ge 23:4
  1Ch 16:19-22
  Ac 7:4, 5
h Ge 20:1
  Ge 46:6
i Ge 31:7, 42
j Ge 12:17
  Ge 20:2, 3
k Ge 26:9, 11
l Ge 41:30, 54
  Ge 42:5
  Ac 7:11
m Ge 37:28, 36
  Ge 45:4, 5
  Ge 50:20
n Ge 39:20
o Ac 7:10
p Ge 41:14

104:33; 105:2 *Or "make music."
104:34 *Or possibly, "Let my meditation about him be pleasurable."
104:35 *Or "my soul." *Or "Hallelujah!" "Jah" is a shortened form of the
name Jehovah. 105:2 *Or possibly,
"Speak about." 105:4 *Or "presence."
105:6 *Or "descendants." Lit., "seed."

105:8 *Lit., "The word he commanded." 105:16 *Lit., "broke every bread
rod." Possibly referring to rods used for
storing bread. 105:18 *Lit., "afflicted."
*Or "His soul came into iron."

21 He made him master of his household,
Ruler over all his property,[a]
22 To have authority over* his princes as he pleased[#]
And to teach his elders wisdom.[b]
23 Then Israel came into Egypt,[c]
And Jacob lived as a foreigner in the land of Ham.
24 God made his people very fruitful;[d]
He made them mightier than their adversaries,[e]
25 Whose hearts he let change to hate his people,
To plot against his servants.[f]
26 He sent his servant Moses,[g]
And Aaron,[h] whom he had chosen.
27 They performed his signs among them,
His miracles in the land of Ham.[i]
28 He sent darkness and the land became dark;[j]
They did not rebel against his words.
29 He changed their waters into blood
And killed their fish.[k]
30 Their land swarmed with frogs,[l]
Even in the royal chambers.
31 He ordered the gadflies to invade
And gnats in all their territories.[m]
32 He turned their rain to hail
And sent lightning* on their land.[n]
33 He struck their vines and their fig trees
And shattered the trees of their territory.
34 He said that the locusts should invade,
Young locusts without number.[o]

35 They devoured all the vegetation in the land,
And they devoured the produce of the ground.
36 Then he struck down every firstborn in their land,[a]
The beginning of their procreative power.
37 He brought his people out with silver and gold;[b]
And no one among his tribes stumbled.
38 Egypt rejoiced when they left,
For the dread of Israel* had fallen on them.[c]
39 He spread a cloud to screen them off[d]
And fire to give light by night.[e]
40 They asked, and he brought quail;[f]
He kept satisfying them with bread from heaven.[g]
41 He opened a rock, and waters flowed out;[h]
These flowed through the desert like a river.[i]
42 For he remembered the holy promise he had made to Abraham his servant.[j]
43 So he brought out his people with exultation,[k]
His chosen ones with a joyful cry.
44 He gave them the lands of nations;[l]
They inherited what other peoples had worked hard to produce,[m]
45 So that they would keep his decrees[n]
And observe his laws.
Praise Jah!*

106 Praise Jah!*
Give thanks to Jehovah, for he is good;[o]
His loyal love endures forever.[p]

CHAP. 105
a Ge 41:39-41
  Ge 41:48
  Ge 45:8
b Ge 41:33, 38
c Ge 46:4, 6
d Ex 1:7
  Ac 7:17
e Ex 1:8, 9
f Ex 1:10
  Ac 7:18, 19
g Ex 3:10
  Ex 4:12
  Ex 6:11
h Ex 4:14
  Ex 7:1
i Ne 9:10
  Ps 78:43-51
j Ex 10:22, 23
k Ex 7:20, 21
  Ex 8:6
m Ex 8:17, 24
n Ex 9:23-26
o Ex 10:13-15

Second Col.
a Ex 12:29
b Ge 15:13, 14
  Ex 3:22
  Ex 12:35, 36
c Ex 12:33
d Ex 14:19, 20
e Ex 13:21
f Ps 78:27
g Ex 16:12-15
  Ps 78:24
h Ex 17:6
  1Co 10:1, 4
i Ps 78:15, 16
j Ge 12:7
  Ge 15:13, 14
  Ex 2:24
  De 9:5
k Nu 33:3
l Jos 11:23
  Jos 21:43
  Ne 9:22
  Ps 78:55
  Ac 13:19
m De 6:10, 11
  Jos 5:11, 12
n De 4:40

CHAP. 106
o Lu 18:19
p 1Ch 16:34
  Ezr 3:11
  Ps 103:17
  Ps 107:1

2 Who can fully declare
   Jehovah's mighty acts
   Or proclaim all his praise-
   worthy deeds?[a]

3 Happy are those who act
   with justice,
   Who always do what is right.[b]

4 Remember me, O Jehovah,
   when you show favor*
   toward your people.[c]
   Take care of me with your
   acts of salvation,

5 So that I may enjoy the goodness you show your chosen
   ones,[d]
   That I may rejoice along with
   your nation,
   That I may proudly praise*
   you along with your inheritance.

6 We have sinned just as our
   forefathers did;[e]
   We have done wrong; we
   have acted wickedly.[f]

7 Our forefathers in Egypt did
   not appreciate* your wonderful works.
   They did not remember your
   abundant loyal love,
   But they rebelled at the sea,
   by the Red Sea.[g]

8 But he saved them for the
   sake of his name,[h]
   To make his mightiness
   known.[i]

9 He rebuked the Red Sea,
   and it dried up;
   He led them through its
   depths as through a
   desert;*[j]

10 He saved them from the hand
   of their foe[k]
   And reclaimed them from
   the hand of the enemy.[l]

11 The waters covered their
   adversaries;
   Not one of them survived.*[m]

12 Then they had faith in his
   promise;[a]
   They began to sing his
   praise.[b]

13 But they quickly forgot what
   he did;[c]
   They did not wait for his
   counsel.

14 They gave way to their selfish desires in the wilderness;[d]
   They tested God in the
   desert.[e]

15 He gave them what they
   requested,
   But then struck them with
   disease that made them*
   waste away.[f]

16 In the camp they grew
   jealous of Moses
   And of Aaron,[g] the holy one
   of Jehovah.[h]

17 The earth then opened up
   and swallowed Da'than
   And covered those assembled with A·bi'ram.[i]

18 A fire blazed among their
   group;
   A flame consumed the
   wicked.[j]

19 They made a calf in Ho'reb
   And bowed down to a statue
   of metal;*[k]

20 They exchanged my glory
   For the representation of
   a grass-eating bull.[l]

21 They forgot God[m] their
   Savior,
   Who did great things in
   Egypt,[n]

22 Wonderful works in the land
   of Ham,[o]
   Awe-inspiring deeds at the
   Red Sea.[p]

23 He was about to order their
   annihilation,
   But Moses his chosen one
   interceded with him*

CHAP. 106

a Ps 40:5

b Ps 15:1, 2
  Isa 64:5

c Ne 5:19
  Ps 51:18
  Ps 119:132

d Ex 19:5

e Ne 9:16
  Ps 78:8

f Ezr 9:6
  Da 9:5

g Ex 14:11, 12

h Ps 143:11
  Eze 20:14

i Ex 9:16
  Ro 9:17

j Ex 14:21, 22

k Ex 14:30

l Isa 49:26

m Ex 14:13, 28

_____

Second Col.

a Ex 14:31

b Ex 15:1

c Ex 15:24
  Ex 16:2, 3
  Ex 17:7

d Nu 11:4
  De 9:22
  1Co 10:6

e Ex 17:2
  Ps 78:18
  1Co 10:9
  Heb 3:8, 9

f Nu 11:31, 33
  Ps 78:29-31

g Nu 16:3

h Le 21:8
  Nu 16:5-7

i Nu 16:27, 32

j Nu 16:35

k Ex 32:4
  De 9:12

l Ex 20:4

m De 32:18

n De 4:34

o Ps 78:51

p Ex 14:25

_____

106:4 *Or "goodwill." 106:5 *Or "may boast about." 106:7 *Or "grasp the meaning of." 106:9 *Or "wilderness." 106:11 *Or "was left."

_____

106:15 *Or "their soul." 106:19 *Or "molten statue." 106:23 *Lit., "stood in the breach before him."

To avert his destructive
anger.[a]

24 Then they despised the
desirable land;[b]
They had no faith in his
promise.[c]

25 They kept grumbling in their
tents;[d]
They did not listen to the
voice of Jehovah.[e]

26 So he raised his hand in an
oath concerning them
That he would make them
fall in the wilderness;[f]

27 He would make their
descendants fall among
the nations,
And he would scatter them
throughout the lands.[g]

28 Then they joined in worship
of* Ba'al of Pe'or,[h]
And they ate sacrifices
offered to the dead.[#]

29 They provoked Him by their
actions,[i]
And a scourge broke out
among them.[j]

30 But when Phin·e·has stood
up and intervened,
The scourge was halted.[k]

31 And it was counted to him
as righteousness
Through all generations forever.[l]

32 They provoked Him at the
waters of Mer'i·bah,*
And it went badly for Moses
because of them.[m]

33 They embittered his spirit,
And he spoke rashly with
his lips.[n]

34 They did not annihilate the
peoples,[o]
As Jehovah had commanded
them.[p]

35 But they mingled with the
nations[q]
And adopted* their ways.[r]

36 They kept serving their
idols,[a]
And these became a snare
to them.[b]

37 They would sacrifice their
sons
And their daughters to
demons.[c]

38 They kept spilling innocent
blood,[d]
The blood of their own sons
and daughters
Whom they sacrificed to the
idols of Ca'naan;[e]
And the land was polluted
with bloodshed.

39 They became unclean by
their works;
They committed spiritual
prostitution by their
deeds.[f]

40 So the anger of Jehovah
blazed against his people,
And he grew to detest his
inheritance.

41 He repeatedly handed them
over to the nations,[g]
So that those who hated
them might rule over
them.[h]

42 Their enemies oppressed
them,
And they were subject to
their power.*

43 Many times he rescued
them,[i]
But they would rebel and
disobey,[j]
And they would be brought
low for their error.[k]

44 But he would see their
distress[l]
And hear their cry for help.[m]

45 For their sake he would
remember his covenant,
And he would feel pity,*
moved by his great[#] loyal
love.[n]

46 He would cause them to be
pitied

CHAP. 106

a Ex 32:10, 11
De 9:14, 19
b Nu 13:32
De 8:7-9
c Nu 14:11
d Nu 14:2
De 1:27
e Nu 14:22, 23
f Nu 14:28, 29
Heb 3:11
g Le 26:33
De 4:27
h Nu 25:3
Ho 9:10
i Nu 25:6
De 32:16
j Nu 25:9
1Co 10:8
k Nu 25:7, 8
l Nu 25:11-13
m Nu 20:2, 12
Nu 27:13, 14
n Nu 20:10
o Jos 16:10
Jos 17:12
Jg 1:21
p Nu 33:52
De 7:1, 2
q Jos 15:63
Jg 1:33
r Isa 2:6

Second Col.

a Jg 2:11, 12
2Ki 17:12
b Ex 23:32, 33
c De 12:31
2Ki 16:1, 3
2Ki 17:17, 18
Jer 7:30, 31
1Co 10:20
d 2Ki 21:16
e Eze 16:20
f Jer 3:9
g De 32:30
Jg 3:8
h Jg 10:6-8
i Jg 10:11, 12
1Sa 12:11
j Jg 4:1
k Jg 6:1-5
l Jg 2:18
m Jg 3:9
n Ex 34:6
De 32:36
Isa 63:7
La 3:32
Joe 2:13

106:28 *Or "attached themselves to."
#That is, sacrifices offered either to
dead people or to lifeless gods.
106:32 *Meaning "Quarreling." 106:35
*Or "learned."

106:42 *Lit., "hand." 106:45 *Or "feel
regret." #Or "abundant."

By all who held them
captive.[a]

47 Save us, O Jehovah our
God,[b]
And gather us from the
nations[c]
So that we may give thanks
to your holy name
And exult in praising you.*[d]

106:47 *Or "exult in your praise."

CHAP. 106
a Ezr 9:9
b Ps 79:9
c Jer 32:37
d 1Ch 16:35

Second Col.
a 1Ch 29:10
Ps 41:13
Lu 1:68

48 May Jehovah, the God of
Israel, be praised
Throughout all eternity.*[a]
And let all the people say,
"Amen!"[#]
Praise Jah![△]

106:48 *Or "From eternity to eternity."
#Or "So be it!" △Or "Hallelujah!" "Jah"
is a shortened form of the name Jehovah.

BOOK FIVE
(Psalms 107-150)

107 Give thanks to Jehovah,
for he is good;[a]
His loyal love endures forever.[b]

2 Let those reclaimed* by
Jehovah say this,
Those whom he reclaimed
from the hand# of the
adversary,[c]

3 Whom he gathered together
from the lands,[d]
From the east and from the
west,*
From the north and from the
south.[e]

4 They wandered about in the
wilderness, in the desert;
They did not find a way to a
city where they could live.

5 They were hungry and
thirsty;
They were* faint from
exhaustion.

6 They kept crying out to
Jehovah in their distress;[f]
He rescued them from their
plight.[g]

7 He had them walk in the
right way[h]
To come to a city where they
could live.[i]

8 Let people give thanks to
Jehovah[j] for his loyal love

107:2 *Or "repurchased." #Or "power."
107:3 *Or "From sunrise and from sunset." 107:5 *Or "Their soul was."

CHAP. 107
a Lu 18:19
b 1Ch 16:34
Ps 103:17
c Isa 35:10
Jer 15:21
Mic 4:10
d Ps 106:47
Jer 29:14
e Isa 43:5, 6
Jer 31:8
f Ho 5:14, 15
g Isa 41:17
h Isa 30:21
i Ne 11:3
j 1Ch 16:8

Second Col.
a Ps 40:5
b Ps 34:10
Isa 55:2
Lu 1:53
c Ps 106:43
La 3:42
d Le 26:21
e Ps 68:6
Ps 146:7
Isa 49:8, 9
Isa 61:1
f La 3:22

And for his wonderful works
in behalf of the sons of
men.[a]

9 For he has satisfied the
thirsty*
And filled the hungry# with
good things.[b]

10 Some were living in deepest
darkness,
Prisoners in affliction and
in irons.

11 For they had rebelled against
the word of God;
They disrespected the counsel of the Most High.[c]

12 So he humbled their hearts
through hardship;[d]
They stumbled, and there
was no one to help them.

13 They called to Jehovah for
help in their distress;
He saved them from their
plight.

14 He brought them out of
deepest darkness,
And he tore off their
shackles.[e]

15 Let people give thanks to
Jehovah for his loyal love[f]
And for his wonderful works
in behalf of the sons of
men.

16 For he has broken down the
doors of copper

107:9 *Or "the parched soul." #Or "the
hungry soul."

And cut through the bars of iron.[a]

17 They were foolish and suffered affliction[b]
On account of their transgressions and their errors.[c]

18 They lost their appetite for* all food;
They drew near the gates of death.

19 They would call to Jehovah for help in their distress;
He would save them from their plight.

20 He would send his word and heal them[d]
And rescue them from the pits they were trapped in.

21 Let people give thanks to Jehovah for his loyal love
And for his wonderful works in behalf of the sons of men.

22 Let them offer the sacrifices of thanksgiving[e]
And declare his works with a joyful cry.

23 Those who travel on the sea in ships,
Who ply their trade over the vast waters,[f]

24 They have seen the works of Jehovah
And his wonderful works in the deep;[g]

25 How by his word a windstorm arises,[h]
Lifting up the waves of the sea.

26 They rise up to the sky;
They plunge down to the depths.
Their courage* melts away because of the impending calamity.

27 They reel and stagger like a drunken man,
And all their skill proves useless.[i]

28 Then they cry out to Jehovah in their distress,[a]
And he rescues them from their plight.

29 He calms the windstorm;
The waves of the sea grow quiet.[b]

30 They rejoice when these grow still,
And he leads them to their desired harbor.

31 Let people give thanks to Jehovah for his loyal love
And for his wonderful works in behalf of the sons of men.[c]

32 Let them exalt him in the congregation of the people,[d]
And let them praise him in the council* of the elders.

33 He turns rivers into a desert
And springs of water into parched ground,[e]

34 Fruitful land into salty wasteland,[f]
Because of the wickedness of those dwelling in it.

35 He turns the desert into reedy pools of water,
And dry land into springs of water.[g]

36 He causes the hungry to dwell there,[h]
So that they may establish a city where they can live.[i]

37 They sow fields and plant vineyards[j]
That yield fruitful crops.[k]

38 He blesses them and they increase greatly;
He does not let their cattle diminish.[l]

39 But again they become few and are humiliated
Because of oppression, calamity, and grief.

40 He pours out contempt upon nobles

CHAP. 107

a Isa 45:1, 2

b Jer 2:19

c La 3:39

d Ps 147:3

e Le 7:12
   Ps 50:14

f 2Ch 9:21
   Eze 27:9

g Ge 1:21
   Ps 104:25

h Ps 135:7
   Jer 10:13
   Jon 1:4

i Jon 1:4, 13

Second Col.

a Jon 1:14

b Ps 65:7
   Ps 89:9
   Jon 1:15

c Ps 105:5

d Ps 111:1

e 1Ki 17:1, 7
   Isa 42:15
   Am 4:7

f Ge 13:10
   De 29:22, 23

g 2Ki 3:17
   Isa 35:7
   Isa 41:18

h Ps 146:7
   Lu 1:53

i Ps 107:7

j Isa 65:21

k Ac 14:17

l De 7:13, 14

107:18 *Or "Their soul detested."
107:26 *Or "soul."

107:32 *Lit., "seat."

And makes them wander in trackless wastelands.[a]

41 But he protects* the poor from oppression[b]
And makes their families as numerous as a flock.

42 The upright see this and rejoice;[c]
But all the unrighteous shut their mouths.[d]

43 Whoever is wise will observe these things[e]
And will carefully consider Jehovah's acts of loyal love.[f]

A song. A melody of David.

108

My heart is steadfast, O God.
I will sing and make music with my whole being.*[g]

2 Do awake, O stringed instrument; you too, O harp.[h]
I will awaken the dawn.

3 I will praise you among the peoples, O Jehovah,
And I will sing praises* to you among the nations.

4 For your loyal love is great, as high as the heavens,[i]
And your faithfulness, up to the skies.

5 Be exalted above the heavens, O God;
May your glory be over all the earth.[j]

6 So that your loved ones may be rescued,
Save us with your right hand and answer me.[k]

7 God has spoken in his holiness:*
"I will exult, I will give out She′chem[l] as an inheritance,
And I will measure off the Valley# of Suc′coth.[m]

8 Gil′e·ad[a] belongs to me, as does Ma·nas′seh,
And E′phra·im is the helmet* for my head;[b]
Judah is my commander's staff.[c]

9 Mo′ab is my washbasin.[d]
Over E′dom I will throw my sandal.[e]
Over Phi·lis′ti·a I will shout in triumph."[f]

10 Who will bring me to the fortified city?
Who will lead me as far as E′dom?[g]

11 Is it not you, O God, who have rejected us,
Our God, who no longer goes out with our armies?[h]

12 Help us in our distress,[i]
For salvation by humans is worthless.[j]

13 By God we will gain power,[k]
And he will trample on our adversaries.[l]

To the director. Of David. A melody.

109

O God whom I praise,[m] do not remain silent.

2 For the wicked and the deceitful open their mouths against me.
They speak about me with lying tongues;[n]

3 They surround me with hateful words,
And they attack me without cause.[o]

4 They resist me in response to my love;[p]
But I continue to pray.

5 They repay me with bad for good[q]
And hatred for my love.[r]

6 Appoint a wicked man over him;
May a resister* stand at his right hand.

7 When he is judged, may he be found guilty;*

CHAP. 107
a Job 12:21, 24
b 1Sa 2:8
c Ps 58:10
d Ex 11:7
   Ps 63:11
e Ps 64:9
   Ho 14:9
f Ps 77:12
   Ps 143:5
   Jer 9:24

CHAP. 108
g Ps 57:7-11
   Ps 104:33
h Ps 81:2
i Ps 36:5
   Ps 103:11
j Ps 8:1
   Ps 57:5, 11
k Ps 20:6
   Ps 60:5
l Jos 17:7
m Ge 33:17
   Ps 60:6-8

Second Col.
a Jos 13:8, 11
b De 33:17
c Ge 49:10
d 2Sa 8:13
e Nu 24:18
   2Sa 8:14
f 2Sa 8:1
g Ps 60:9-12
h De 23:14
i Ps 18:6
j Ps 118:8
   Ps 146:3, 4
k 1Sa 2:4
   2Sa 22:40
   Isa 40:29-31
l Ps 44:5

CHAP. 109
m Ps 33:1
n 2Sa 15:2, 3
   Ps 31:18
o Ps 15:12
   2Sa 16:5-7
   Ps 69:4
p 2Sa 13:39
q Ps 35:11, 12
   Ps 38:19, 20
r Ps 55:12-14

107:41 *Or "puts on high," that is, out of reach. 108:1 *Lit., "even my glory." 108:3 *Or "make music." 108:7 *Or possibly, "in his holy place." #Or "Low Plain."

108:8 *Lit., "stronghold." 109:6 *Or "an accuser." 109:7 *Or "wicked."

May even his prayer be counted as a sin.[a]

8 Let his days be few;[b]
His office of oversight let someone else take.[c]

9 Let his children* become fatherless,
And his wife, a widow.

10 May his children* become wandering beggars,
Foraging for food from their ruined homes.

11 May his creditor seize* all that he has,
And may strangers plunder his possessions.

12 May no one extend kindness* to him,
And may no one show favor to his fatherless children.

13 Let his descendants* be cut off;[d]
May their name be erased within a generation.

14 Let the error of his forefathers be remembered by Jehovah,[e]
And may the sin of his mother not be erased.

15 May Jehovah always be mindful of what they have done;
And may he cut off the memory of them from the earth.[f]

16 For he did not remember to show kindness,*[g]
But he kept pursuing the oppressed,[h] poor, and brokenhearted man
To put him to death.[i]

17 He loved to pronounce a curse, so that is what came upon him;
He had no desire to bless, so he received no blessing.

18 He was clothed with curses as his garment.

And they were poured into his body like water,
Into his bones like oil.

19 May his curses be like the clothing in which he wraps himself[a]
And like a belt he always wears.

20 This is the payment from Jehovah for the one who resists me[b]
And for those who speak evil things against me.*

21 But you, Jehovah the Sovereign Lord,
Act in my behalf for the sake of your name.[c]
Rescue me, because your loyal love is good.[d]

22 For I am helpless and poor,[e]
And my heart has been pierced within me.[f]

23 I am passing away like a fading shadow;
I have been shaken off like a locust.

24 My knees give way from fasting;
My body is thin, and I am wasting away.*

25 I have become the object of their taunts.[g]
When they see me, they shake their heads.[h]

26 Help me, O Jehovah my God;
Save me by your loyal love.

27 May they know that this is by your hand;
That you, O Jehovah, have done it.

28 Let them pronounce a curse, but may you give a blessing.
When they rise up against me, may they be put to shame,
But let your servant rejoice.

29 Let those who resist me be clothed with humiliation;

CHAP. 109

a Isa 1:15
Mic 3:4

b Ps 55:23
Mt 27:5

c Ac 1:16-20

d Ps 37:28

e 2Sa 3:28, 29
2Sa 21:1

f Ps 34:16

g Jas 2:13

h Ps 10:2

i 2Sa 16:11
2Sa 17:1, 2
Ps 37:32

Second Col.
a Ps 109:29

b 2Sa 17:23

c Ps 25:11
Ps 31:3

d Ps 36:7
Ps 69:16
Ps 86:5

e Ps 40:17

f Ps 102:4

g Ps 31:11

h Ps 22:7
Mt 27:39

109:9, 10 *Lit., "sons." 109:11 *Or "May usurers lay out traps for." 109:12, 16 *Or "loyal love." 109:13 *Or "posterity."

109:20 *Or "my soul." 109:24 *Lit., "My flesh has grown lean, without fatness (oil)."

May they be wrapped in their shame as in a robe.*ᵃ

30 My mouth will fervently praise Jehovah;
I will praise him in front of many people.ᵇ

31 For he will stand at the right hand of the poor
To save him from those who condemn him.*

Of David. A melody.

110 Jehovah declared to my Lord:
"Sit at my right handᶜ
Until I place your enemies as a stool for your feet."ᵈ

2 Jehovah will extend the scepter of your power out of Zion, saying:
"Go subduing in the midst of your enemies."ᵉ

3 Your people will offer themselves willingly on the day of your military force.*
In splendid holiness, from the womb of the dawn,
You have your company of young men just like dew-drops.

4 Jehovah has sworn an oath, and he will not change his mind:*
"You are a priest foreverᶠ
In the manner of Mel·chiz′e·dek!"ᵍ

5 Jehovah will be at your right hand;ʰ
He will crush kings on the day of his anger.ⁱ

6 He will execute judgment against* the nations;ʲ
He will fill the land with dead bodies.ᵏ
He will crush the leader# of a vast land.△

CHAP. 109

a Ps 35:26
b Ps 22:22

CHAP. 110

c Ro 8:34
Eph 1:20
Heb 8:1
Heb 12:2

d Mt 22:43, 44
Mr 12:36
Lu 20:42, 43
Ac 2:34, 35
1Co 15:25
Heb 1:3, 13
Heb 10:12, 13

e Ps 2:8, 9
Ps 45:4, 5
Mt 28:18
Re 6:2
Re 12:5
Re 19:11, 15

f Heb 7:21, 28

g Ge 14:18
Heb 5:5, 6
Heb 6:19, 20
Heb 7:3, 11

h Ps 16:8

i Ps 2:2
Ro 2:5
Re 11:18
Re 19:19

j Ps 79:6

k Jer 25:31-33

Second Col.

CHAP. 111

a Ps 68:4
Ps 113:1
Re 19:1

b Ps 9:1

c Ps 98:1
Ps 139:14
Re 15:3

d Ps 77:12
Ps 143:5

e Ps 103:17

f De 31:19
Jos 4:5-7

g Ex 34:6
Jas 5:11

h Ps 37:25
Mt 6:33

i Ps 89:34
Ps 105:8

j Ps 44:2
Ps 105:44

k De 32:4

---

7 He* will drink from the stream along the road.
Therefore, he will hold his head high.

111 Praise Jah!*ᵃ
א [Aleph]
I will praise Jehovah with all my heartᵇ
ב [Beth]
In the assembled group of upright ones and in the congregation.
ג [Gimel]

2 The works of Jehovah are great;ᶜ
ד [Daleth]
They are studied by all those finding pleasure in them.ᵈ
ה [He]

3 His activity is glorious and splendid,
ו [Waw]
And his righteousness endures forever.ᵉ
ז [Zayin]

4 He causes his wonderful works to be remembered.ᶠ
ח [Heth]
Jehovah is compassionate* and merciful.ᵍ
ט [Teth]

5 Food he gives to those fearing him.ʰ
י [Yod]
He remembers his covenant forever.ⁱ
כ [Kaph]

6 He has revealed to his people his powerful works
ל [Lamed]
By giving them the inheritance of the nations.ʲ
מ [Mem]

7 The works of his hands are truth and justice;ᵏ

109:29 *Or "sleeveless coat." 109:31 *Or "his soul." 110:3 *Or "on the day your army mobilizes." 110:4 *Or "he will feel no regret." 110:6 *Or "among." #Lit., "head." △Or "of the entire earth."

110:7 *Referring to "my Lord" in vs. 1. 111:1 *Or "Hallelujah!" "Jah" is a shortened form of the name Jehovah. 111:4 *Or "gracious."

נ [Nun]

Trustworthy are all his orders.[a]

ס [Samekh]

8 They are always reliable,* now and forever;

ע [Ayin]

They are made in truth and righteousness.[b]

פ [Pe]

9 He has given redemption to his people.[c]

צ [Tsade]

He commanded that his covenant should last forever.

ק [Qoph]

His name is holy and awe-inspiring.[d]

ר [Resh]

10 The fear of Jehovah is the beginning of wisdom.[e]

ש [Sin]

All those observing his orders* show good insight.[f]

ת [Taw]

His praise endures forever.

112 Praise Jah!*[g]

א [Aleph]

Happy is the man who fears Jehovah,[h]

ב [Beth]

Who takes great pleasure in his commandments.[i]

ג [Gimel]

2 His descendants will be mighty in the earth,

ד [Daleth]

And the generation of the upright will be blessed.[j]

ה [He]

3 Wealth and riches are in his house,

ו [Waw]

And his righteousness continues forever.

ז [Zayin]

4 To the upright he shines like a light in the darkness.[k]

ח [Heth]

He is compassionate* and merciful[a] and righteous.

ט [Teth]

5 It goes well for the man who generously* lends.[b]

י [Yod]

He conducts his affairs with justice.

כ [Kaph]

6 He will never be shaken.[c]

ל [Lamed]

The righteous will be remembered forever.[d]

מ [Mem]

7 He will not fear bad news.[e]

נ [Nun]

His heart is steadfast, trusting in Jehovah.[f]

ס [Samekh]

8 His heart is unshakable;* he is not afraid;[g]

ע [Ayin]

In the end he will look in triumph on his adversaries.[h]

פ [Pe]

9 He has distributed widely;* he has given to the poor.[i]

צ [Tsade]

His righteousness continues forever.[j]

ק [Qoph]

His own strength# will be exalted with glory.

ר [Resh]

10 The wicked one will see and be upset.

ש [Shin]

He will grind his teeth and melt away.

ת [Taw]

The desires of the wicked will perish.[k]

113 Praise Jah!*
Offer praise, you servants of Jehovah,
Praise the name of Jehovah.

2 May Jehovah's name be praised

CHAP. 111

a Ps 19:8
  Isa 55:10, 11
b Ps 19:9
c Ex 15:13
  Lu 1:68
  Re 7:10
d Ps 89:7
  Isa 6:2, 3
  Lu 1:49
  Re 4:8
e Job 28:28
  Pr 1:7
  Ec 12:13
f De 4:6
  Jos 1:7, 8
  1Ki 2:3
  Ps 119:100
  2Ti 3:14, 15

CHAP. 112

g Ex 15:2
  Re 19:1
h Ps 111:10
i Ps 1:1, 3
  Ps 40:8
j Ps 25:12, 13
  Ps 37:25, 26
k Ps 97:11
  1Pe 2:9

Second Col.

a Lu 6:36
  Eph 4:32
b De 15:7, 8
  Ps 41:1
  Pr 19:17
  Lu 6:34, 35
  Ac 20:35
  Heb 13:16
c Ps 15:5
  Ps 125:1
d Ne 5:19
  Pr 10:7
e Ps 27:1
  Pr 3:25
f Ps 62:8
  Isa 26:3
g Pr 28:1
h Ps 59:10
i De 15:11
  Pr 11:24
  Pr 19:17
j De 24:12, 13
  2Co 9:9
  Heb 6:10
k Pr 11:7

111:8 *Or "well-founded." 111:10 *Lit., "them." 112:1; 113:1 *Or "Hallelujah!" "Jah" is a shortened form of the name Jehovah.

112:4 *Or "gracious." 112:5 *Or "graciously." 112:8 *Or "resolute; steady." 112:9 *Or "generously." #Lit., "horn."

From now on and forever.[a]

3 From the rising of the sun to its setting,
Let Jehovah's name be praised.[b]

4 Jehovah is high above all the nations;[c]
His glory is above the heavens.[d]

5 Who is like Jehovah our God,[e]
The one who dwells* on high?

6 He stoops down to look on heaven and earth,[f]

7 Raising the lowly from the dust.
He lifts up the poor from the ash heap*[g]

8 In order to make him sit with nobles,
With the nobles of his people.

9 He gives the barren woman a home
As a happy mother with children.*[h]
Praise Jah!*

114 When Israel went out of Egypt,[i]
The house of Jacob from a people speaking a foreign language,

2 Judah became his sanctuary,*
Israel, his dominion.[j]

3 The sea saw it and fled;[k]
The Jordan turned back.[l]

4 The mountains skipped about like rams,[m]
The hills, like lambs.

5 What made you flee, O sea?[n]
Why, O Jordan, did you turn back?[o]

6 Why did you skip about like rams, O mountains,
Like lambs, O hills?

7 Tremble, O earth, because of the Lord,
Because of the God of Jacob,[a]

8 Who turns the rock into a reedy pool of water,
The flinty rock into springs of water.[b]

115 Not to us, O Jehovah, not to us,*
But to your name give glory[c]
Because of your loyal love and your faithfulness.[d]

2 Why should the nations say: "Where is their God?"[e]

3 Our God is in the heavens;
He does whatever he pleases.

4 Their idols are silver and gold,
The work of human hands.[f]

5 A mouth they have, but they cannot speak;[g]
Eyes, but they cannot see;

6 Ears they have, but they cannot hear;
A nose, but they cannot smell;

7 Hands they have, but they cannot feel;
Feet, but they cannot walk;[h]
They make no sound with their throat.[i]

8 The people who make them will become just like them,[j]
As will all those who trust in them.[k]

9 O Israel, trust in Jehovah[l]
—He is their help and their shield.[m]

10 O house of Aaron,[n] trust in Jehovah
—He is their help and their shield.

11 You who fear Jehovah, trust in Jehovah[o]
—He is their help and their shield.[p]

12 Jehovah remembers us and will bless;

113:5 *Or "sits enthroned." 113:7 *Or possibly, "garbage dump." 113:9 *Lit., "sons." *Or "Hallelujah!" "Jah" is a shortened form of the name Jehovah. 114:2 *Or "holy place."

115:1 *Or "To us belongs nothing, O Jehovah, to us belongs nothing."

CHAP. 113
a 1Ch 16:36
  1Ch 29:10
  Ps 106:48
b Ps 72:19
  Ps 86:9
  Isa 59:19
  Mal 1:11
c Ps 97:9
  Ps 99:2
d 1Ki 8:27
e Ex 15:11
f Ps 18:35
  Ps 138:6
  Isa 57:15
  Isa 66:2
g 1Sa 2:7
h 1Sa 2:5
  Isa 54:1

CHAP. 114
i Ex 12:41
j Ex 6:7
  Ex 19:6
  De 32:9
k Ex 14:21
l Jos 3:16
m Ex 19:18
  Jg 5:4
n Ex 15:8
o Jos 4:23

Second Col.
a 1Ch 16:29, 30
b Ex 17:6
  Nu 20:11
  De 8:14, 15
  Ps 107:35

CHAP. 115
c Isa 48:11
  Joh 12:28
d Ps 138:2
e Ex 32:12
  Nu 14:15, 16
  De 32:26, 27
  Ps 79:10
f Ps 135:15-18
  Isa 40:19
  Isa 46:6
  Jer 10:3, 4
  Jer 10:8, 9
  Ac 19:26
  1Co 10:19
g Hab 2:19
h 1Sa 5:3
  Isa 46:7
i Hab 2:18
j Isa 44:9
k Ps 97:7
l De 33:29
  Ps 33:20
n Ex 28:1
o Pr 16:20
p Ps 84:11

He will bless the house of Israel;[a]

He will bless the house of Aaron.

13 He will bless those who fear Jehovah,

The small as well as the great.

14 Jehovah will give you an increase,

To you and your children.*[b]

15 May you be blessed by Jehovah,[c]

The Maker of heaven and earth.[d]

16 As for the heavens, they belong to Jehovah,[e]

But the earth he has given to the sons of men.[f]

17 The dead do not praise Jah;[g]

Nor do any who go down into the silence of death.*[h]

18 But we will praise Jah

From now on and forever. Praise Jah!

116

I love Jehovah

Because he hears* my voice, my pleas for help.[i]

2 For he inclines his ear* to me,[j]

And I will call on him as long as I live.*

3 The ropes of death encircled me;

The Grave had me in its grip.*[k]

I was overcome by distress and grief.[l]

4 But I called on the name of Jehovah:[m]

"O Jehovah, rescue me!"*

5 Jehovah is compassionate* and righteous;[a]

Our God is merciful.[b]

6 Jehovah is guarding the inexperienced.[c]

I was brought low, and he saved me.

7 Let my soul* rest once again,

For Jehovah has dealt kindly with me.

8 You have rescued me* from death,

My eye from tears, my foot from stumbling.[d]

9 I will walk before Jehovah in the land of the living.

10 I had faith, for I spoke;[e]

I was greatly afflicted.

11 As for me, I panicked and said:

"Every man is a liar."[f]

12 With what will I repay Jehovah

For all the good he has done for me?

13 I will take up the cup of salvation,*

And I will call on the name of Jehovah.

14 I will pay my vows to Jehovah

In the presence of all his people.[g]

15 Costly* in the eyes of Jehovah

Is the death of his loyal ones.[h]

16 I beg you, O Jehovah,

For I am your servant.

I am your servant, the son of your slave girl.

You have freed me from my bonds.[i]

17 I will offer to you the sacrifice of thanksgiving;[j]

I will call on the name of Jehovah.

18 I will pay my vows to Jehovah[k]

CHAP. 115
a Ge 12:2
b Ge 13:16
c Ps 3:8
d Ps 96:5
e Isa 66:1
f Ge 1:28
  Ps 37:29
  Isa 45:18
  Ac 17:26
g Ps 6:5
  Ec 9:5
h Ps 31:17

CHAP. 116
i Ps 18:6
j Ps 34:15
k Isa 38:10
l Ps 18:4
  Ps 38:6
m Ps 34:6
  Ro 10:13

Second Col.
a De 32:4
b Ex 34:6
  Ne 9:17
  Da 9:9
c Ps 19:7
d Ps 56:13
  Ps 94:18
e 2Co 4:13
f Ro 3:4
g Ps 22:25
  Jon 2:9
h 1Sa 25:29
  Job 1:12
  Ps 91:14
  Zec 2:8
  2Pe 2:9
i Ps 107:14
j Le 7:12
  Ps 50:23
k Ps 22:25
  Ps 76:11

115:14 *Lit., "sons." 115:17 *Lit., "into silence." 115:18 *Or "Hallelujah!" "Jah" is a shortened form of the name Jehovah. 116:1 *Or possibly, "I love because Jehovah hears." 116:2 *Or "bends down to listen." #Lit., "in my days." 116:3 *Lit., "The distresses of Sheol found me." 116:4, 8 *Or "my soul."

116:5 *Or "gracious." 116:7 *See Glossary. 116:13 *Or "grand salvation." 116:15 *Lit., "Precious."

In the presence of all his
people,[a]
19 In the courtyards of the
house of Jehovah,[b]
In your midst, O Jerusalem.
Praise Jah!*[c]

117 Praise Jehovah, all you
nations;[d]
Glorify him, all you
peoples.*[e]
2 For his loyal love toward us
is great;[f]
The faithfulness[g] of Jehovah
endures forever.[h]
Praise Jah!*[i]

118 Give thanks to Jehovah,
for he is good;[j]
His loyal love endures
forever.
2 Let Israel now say:
"His loyal love endures
forever."
3 Let those of the house of
Aaron now say:
"His loyal love endures
forever."
4 Let those fearing Jehovah
now say:
"His loyal love endures
forever."
5 I called on Jah* in my
distress;
Jah answered and brought
me into a place of safety.#[k]
6 Jehovah is on my side;
I will not be afraid.[l]
What can man do to me?[m]
7 Jehovah is on my side as
my helper;*[n]
I will look in triumph on
those who hate me.[o]
8 It is better to take refuge in
Jehovah
Than to trust in humans.[p]
9 It is better to take refuge in
Jehovah

Than to trust in princes.[a]
10 All the nations
surrounded me,
But in the name of Jehovah,
I warded them off.[b]
11 They surrounded me,
yes, I was completely surrounded,
But in the name of Jehovah,
I warded them off.
12 They surrounded me like
bees,
But they were extinguished
as quickly as a fire among
thorns.
In the name of Jehovah,
I warded them off.[c]
13 I was pushed hard* to make
me fall,
But Jehovah helped me.
14 Jah is my shelter and my
strength,
And he has become my
salvation.[d]
15 The sound of rejoicing and
salvation*
Is in the tents of the righteous.
The right hand of Jehovah is
demonstrating its power.[e]
16 The right hand of Jehovah
is exalting itself;
The right hand of Jehovah is
demonstrating its power.[f]
17 I will not die, no, I will live,
In order to declare the works
of Jah.[g]
18 Jah disciplined me severely,[h]
But he did not hand me over
to death.[i]
19 Open to me the gates of righteousness;[j]
I will enter them and praise
Jah.
20 This is the gate of Jehovah.
The righteous will enter
through it.[k]
21 I will praise you, for you
answered me[l]
And you became my salva-
tion.

CHAP. 116
a Ps 116:14
b Ps 96:8
c Re 19:1

CHAP. 117
d Re 7:9, 10
e Ro 15:11
f La 3:22
g Ps 25:10
  Ps 91:4
h Ps 100:5
i Ps 111:1

CHAP. 118
j Mt 19:17
k Ps 18:19
l Ps 27:1
m Isa 51:12
  Ro 8:31
  Heb 13:6
n Mt 26:52, 53
o Ps 54:7
p Ps 40:4
  Ps 146:3, 4
  Jer 17:5

Second Col.
a Eze 29:6, 7
b 2Ch 20:15, 17
c 2Ch 14:11
d Ex 15:2
  Ps 18:2
  Isa 12:2
e Ps 89:13
  Isa 63:12
f Ex 15:6
  Isa 40:26
g Ps 6:5
  Ps 71:17
h Ps 66:10
  Ps 94:12
i Ps 16:10
j Isa 26:2
  Re 22:14
k Ps 24:3, 4
l Ps 116:1

116:19; 117:2 *Or "Hallelujah!" "Jah" is
a shortened form of the name Jehovah. 117:1 *Or "clans." 118:5 *"Jah"
is a shortened form of the name Jehovah. #Or "a roomy place." 118:7 *Or
possibly, "along with those helping me."

118:13 *Or possibly, "You pushed me
hard." 118:15 *Or "victory."

22 The stone that the builders rejected
Has become the chief cornerstone.*ᵃ

23 This has come from Jehovah;ᵇ
It is wonderful in our eyes.ᶜ

24 This is the day that Jehovah has made;
We will be joyful and rejoice in it.

25 Jehovah, save us, please, we beg!
Jehovah, grant us victory, please!

26 Blessed is the one who comes in the name of Jehovah;ᵈ
We bless you from the house of Jehovah.

27 Jehovah is God;
He gives us light.ᵉ
Join in the festival procession with branches in hand,ᶠ
Up to the horns of the altar.ᵍ

28 You are my God, and I will praise you;
My God, I will exalt you.ʰ

29 Give thanks to Jehovah,ⁱ for he is good;
His loyal love endures forever.ʲ

א [Aleph]

119 Happy are those who are blameless* in their way,
Who walk in the law of Jehovah.ᵏ

2 Happy are those who observe his reminders,ˡ
Who search for him with all their heart.ᵐ

3 They practice no unrighteousness;
They walk in his ways.ⁿ

4 You have commanded
That your orders be carefully kept.ᵒ

CHAP. 118

a Isa 28:16
Lu 20:17
Ac 4:11
1Co 3:11
Eph 2:19, 20
1Pe 2:4-7

b Ac 5:31

c Mr 12:10, 11

d Mt 21:7-9
Mt 23:39
Mr 11:7-10
Lu 19:37, 38

e Ps 18:28
1Pe 2:9

f Le 23:34
Ps 42:4

g Ex 27:2

h Ex 15:2
Isa 25:1

i Ps 50:23

j Ezr 3:11
Ps 118:1

CHAP. 119

k 2Ki 20:3
Jas 1:25

l Ps 19:7

m 2Ch 31:20, 21

n Isa 38:3

o De 5:33
Jer 7:23
Jas 2:10

Second Col.

a Ps 51:10

b Ps 119:80

c Pr 6:20, 22

d Ps 25:5

e Ps 112:1

f Ps 19:13
Ps 37:31

g Jer 15:16

h Ps 19:8, 10
Ps 119:72

i Ps 119:93
Ps 119:100

j Ps 25:10

k Jas 1:23-25

l Isa 38:20

---

5 If only I could remain steadfast*ᵃ
So as to observe your regulations!

6 Then I would not be put to shameᵇ
When I consider all your commandments.

7 I will praise you with an upright heart
When I learn your righteous judgments.

8 I will observe your regulations.
May you never utterly forsake me.

ב [Beth]

9 How can a young man keep his path clean?
By keeping on guard according to your word.ᶜ

10 With my whole heart I seek you.
Do not let me stray from your commandments.ᵈ

11 In my heart I treasure up your sayingᵉ
So that I may not sin against you.ᶠ

12 May you be praised, O Jehovah;
Teach me your regulations.

13 With my lips I declare
All the judgments that you have spoken.

14 I rejoice over your remindersᵍ
More than over all other valuable things.ʰ

15 I will ponder over* your ordersⁱ
And keep my eyes on your paths.ʲ

16 I am fond of your statutes.
I will not forget your word.ᵏ

ג [Gimel]

17 Deal kindly with your servant,
So that I may live and observe your word.ˡ

118:22 *Lit., "the head of the corner." **119:1** *Or "who keep integrity." **119:5** *Lit., "O that my ways were firmly established." **119:15** *Or "study."

18 Open my eyes so that I may
   see clearly
   The wonderful things from
   your law.

19 I am but a foreigner in the
   land.[a]
   Do not hide your commandments from me.

20 I am* consumed with
   longing
   For your judgments at all
   times.

21 You rebuke the presumptuous,
   The cursed ones who stray
   from your command-
   ments.[b]

22 Remove from me* scorn
   and contempt,
   For I have observed your
   reminders.

23 Even when princes sit
   together and speak
   against me,
   Your servant ponders over*
   your regulations.

24 I am fond of your reminders;[c]
   They are my advisers.[d]

ℸ [Daleth]

25 I lie* prostrate in the dust.[e]
   Preserve me alive according to your word.[f]

26 I told you of my ways, and
   you answered me;
   Teach me your regulations.[g]

27 Make me understand the
   meaning* of your orders,
   So that I may ponder over#
   your wonderful works.[h]

28 I have* been sleepless from
   grief.
   Strengthen me according to
   your word.

29 Remove from me the way
   of deception,[i]

And favor me with your law.

30 The way of faithfulness
   I have chosen.[a]
   I recognize that your judg-
   ments are right.

31 I cling to your reminders.[b]
   O Jehovah, do not let me be
   disappointed.*[c]

32 I will eagerly pursue* the
   way of your command-
   ments
   Because you make room for
   it in my heart.#

ה [He]

33 Teach me, O Jehovah,[d] the
   way of your regulations,
   And I will follow it to the
   end.[e]

34 Give me understanding,
   So that I may observe
   your law
   And keep it with my whole
   heart.

35 Guide me* in the pathway
   of your commandments,[f]
   For in it I take delight.

36 Incline my heart to your
   reminders,
   Not to selfish gain.*[g]

37 Turn my eyes away from
   looking at what is worthless;[h]
   Preserve me alive in your
   way.

38 Fulfill your promise* to
   your servant,
   So that you may be feared.#

39 Remove the disgrace that
   I dread,
   For your judgments are
   good.[i]

40 See how I long for your
   orders.
   Preserve me alive in your
   righteousness.

CHAP. 119

a 1Ch 29:15

b De 28:15

c Ps 119:14
  Ps 119:168

d De 17:18-20
  Ps 119:105
  2Ti 3:16, 17

e Ps 22:15

f Ps 119:154
  Ps 143:11

g Ps 86:11

h Ps 145:5

i Ps 141:4
  Pr 30:8

Second Col.

a Jos 24:15

b Ps 19:7

c Ps 25:20
  Ps 119:80

d Isa 48:17
  Joh 6:45
  Jas 1:5

e Ps 119:112

f Ps 23:3

g Lu 12:15
  1Ti 6:10
  Heb 13:5

h Nu 15:39
  Pr 4:25
  Pr 23:4, 5

i Ps 19:9
  Ps 119:75

119:20 *Or "My soul is." 119:22 *Lit.,
"Roll away from upon me." 119:23
*Or "studies." 119:25 *Or "My soul
lies." 119:27 *Lit., "way." #Or "study."
119:28 *Or "My soul has."

119:31 *Or "be put to shame." 119:32
*Lit., "will run." #Or possibly, "you
make my heart have the confidence."
119:35 *Or "Make me walk." 119:36
*Or "to profits." 119:38 *Or "saying."
#Or possibly, "Which is made to those
who fear you."

ו [Waw]

41 May I experience your loyal love, O Jehovah,[a]

Your salvation in harmony with your promise;*[b]

42 Then I will reply to the one taunting me,

For I put my trust in your word.

43 Do not utterly remove the word of truth from my mouth,

For I have hoped in* your judgment.

44 I will keep your law constantly,

Forever and ever.[c]

45 And I will walk about in a place of safety,*[d]

For I search for your orders.

46 I will speak about your reminders in front of kings,

And I will not be ashamed.[e]

47 I am fond of your commandments,

Yes, I love them.[f]

48 I will raise my hands to your commandments, which I love,[g]

And I will ponder over* your regulations.[h]

ז [Zayin]

49 Remember your word* to your servant,

Through which you give me hope.#

50 This is my comfort in my affliction,[i]

For your saying has preserved me alive.

51 The presumptuous utterly scorn me,

But I do not deviate from your law.[j]

52 I remember your judgments from of old,[k] O Jehovah,

And I find comfort in them.[a]

53 I am seized with burning rage because of the wicked,

Who forsake your law.[b]

54 Your regulations are songs to me

Wherever I dwell.*

55 During the night I remember your name, O Jehovah,[c]

So that I may keep your law.

56 This has been my practice

Because I have observed your orders.

ח [Heth]

57 Jehovah is my portion;[d]

I have promised to keep your words.[e]

58 I appeal to you# with all my heart;[f]

Show me your favor[g] according to your promise.*

59 I have examined my ways,

In order to turn my feet back to your reminders.[h]

60 I hurry and do not delay

To keep your commandments.[i]

61 The ropes of the wicked surround me,

But your law I do not forget.[j]

62 At midnight I get up to give you thanks[k]

For your righteous judgments.

63 I am a friend of all who fear you

And of those who keep your orders.[l]

64 Your loyal love, O Jehovah, fills the earth;[m]

Teach me your regulations.

ט [Teth]

65 You have dealt well with your servant,

CHAP. 119

a Ps 51:1
Ps 90:14

b Ps 119:76

c Ps 119:33

d Ps 118:5

e Ro 1:16

f Job 23:12
Ps 119:174
Ro 7:22

g Ps 119:127

h Ps 119:23
Ps 119:71

i Ps 94:19
Ro 15:4

j Ps 119:157

k Nu 16:5
De 1:35, 36
De 4:3

Second Col.

a Ro 15:4

b Ps 119:158
Ps 139:21
Pr 28:4

c Ps 63:6
Isa 26:9

d Ps 16:5

e Ex 19:8

f Ps 51:17

g Ps 57:1

h Ps 119:101
Eph 5:15

i 2Ch 29:1, 3

j 1Sa 26:8, 9
2Ch 29:1, 2

k Ps 42:8

l Pr 13:20

m Ps 33:5
Ps 104:13

119:41, 58 *Or "saying." **119:43** *Or "I wait for." **119:45** *Or "a roomy place." **119:48** *Or "study." **119:49** *Or "promise." #Or "For which you made me wait."

119:54 *Or "In the house where I dwell as a foreigner." **119:58** #Or "I soften (seek the smile of) your face."

O Jehovah, according to
your word.

66 Teach me good sense and
knowledge,[a]

For I have put my trust in
your commandments.

67 Before I was afflicted,
I used to go astray,*

But now I keep your
saying.[b]

68 You are good[c] and your
works are good.

Teach me your regulations.[d]

69 The presumptuous smear
me with lies,

But I observe your orders
with all my heart.

70 Their heart is insensitive,*[e]
But I am fond of your law.[f]

71 It is good that I have been
afflicted,[g]

So that I may learn your
regulations.

72 The law that you have proclaimed is good for me,[h]

More so than thousands of
pieces of gold and silver.[i]

א [Yod]

73 Your hands made me and
formed me.

Give me understanding,
So that I may learn your
commandments.[j]

74 Those who fear you see me
and rejoice,

For your word is my hope.*[k]

75 I know, O Jehovah, that
your judgments are righ-
teous[l]

And that you have afflicted
me in your faithfulness.[m]

76 May your loyal love[n] please
comfort me,

According to the promise,*
you made to your servant.

77 Show me mercy, so that
I may keep living,[o]

For I am fond of your law.[a]

78 May the presumptuous be
put to shame,

For they wrong me without
cause.*

But I will ponder over* your
orders.[b]

79 Let those who fear you
return to me,

Those who know your
reminders.

80 May my heart be blameless
in following your regula-
tions,[c]

So that I may not be put to
shame.[d]

כ [Kaph]

81 I long for* your salvation,[e]
For your word is my hope.*

82 My eyes long for your
saying[f]

While I say: "When will you
comfort me?"[g]

83 For I am like a skin bottle
dried up in the smoke,

But your regulations I do
not forget.[h]

84 How many days must your
servant wait?

When will you bring judg-
ment against those perse-
cuting me?[i]

85 The presumptuous dig pits
for me,

Those who defy your law.

86 All your commandments
are trustworthy.

Men persecute me without
cause; help me![j]

87 They almost exterminated
me from the earth,

But I did not abandon your
orders.

88 Preserve me alive because
of your loyal love,

So that I may keep the reminders you have spoken.

CHAP. 119
a 1Ki 3:9
  Ps 94:10
  Da 2:21
  Php 1:9

b Ps 119:11

c Ps 86:5
  Mr 10:18

d Isa 48:17

e Isa 6:10

f Ps 40:8
  Ro 7:22

g 1Co 11:32
  Heb 12:9-11

h De 17:18, 19

i Ps 19:7, 10
  Pr 3:13-15

j 1Ch 22:12
  Job 32:8

k Ps 119:147

l Ps 119:160

m De 32:4
  Heb 12:11

n Ex 34:6
  Ps 86:5

o Ps 51:1
  Ps 103:13
  Ps 119:116
  Da 9:18
  Lu 1:50

Second Col.
a Ro 7:22

b Ps 119:45

c 1Ki 8:58

d Ps 119:5, 6
  1Jo 2:28

e Mic 7:7

f Ps 69:3

g Ps 86:17
  Ps 102:2

h Ps 119:61
  Ps 119:176

i Ps 7:6
  Re 6:9, 10

j Ps 142:6

119:67 *Or "I was sinning by mistake." **119:70** *Lit., "unfeeling, like
fat." **119:74, 81** *Or "I wait for your
word." **119:76** *Or "saying."

119:78 *Or possibly, "with lies." #Or
"study." **119:81** #Or "My soul pines
for."

ל [Lamed]

89 Forever, O Jehovah,
Your word will remain in
the heavens.[a]

90 Your faithfulness is through
all generations.[b]
You have firmly established
the earth, so that it continues to stand.[c]

91 By your judgments they*
remain until today,
For they are all your servants.

92 If I had not been fond of
your law,
I would have perished in my
affliction.[d]

93 I will never forget your
orders,
Because by them you have
preserved me alive.[e]

94 I belong to you; save me,[f]
Because I have searched
for your orders.[g]

95 The wicked wait to
destroy me,
But I give close attention to
your reminders.

96 I have seen a limit to all
perfection,
But your commandment has
no limit.*

מ [Mem]

97 How I do love your law![h]
I ponder over* it all day
long.[i]

98 Your commandment makes
me wiser than my ene-
mies,[j]
Because it is with me forever.

99 I have more insight than all
my teachers,[k]
Because I ponder over*
your reminders.

100 I act with more understanding than older men,
Because I observe your
orders.

119:91 *That is, all his creative works.
119:96 *Lit., "is very broad." 119:97,
99 *Or "study."

CHAP. 119

a Ps 89:2
　Ps 119:152

b De 7:9

c Ps 104:5
　Ec 1:4

d Pr 6:23
　Mt 4:4

e Le 18:5
　De 30:16
　Joh 6:63
　Ro 10:5

f Ps 86:2
　Isa 41:10

g Ps 119:15

h Ps 40:8

i Ps 1:2

j Ps 19:7
　Pr 2:6
　Pr 10:8

k Mt 11:25
　Lu 2:46, 47

Second Col.

a Ps 18:23
　Ps 119:59

b Ps 19:7, 10
　Pr 24:13, 14

c Ps 119:100

d Ps 97:10
　Ps 101:3
　Pr 8:13
　Pr 13:5
　Ro 12:9

e Ps 43:3
　Pr 6:23
　Isa 51:4
　Ro 15:4
　2Ti 3:16, 17
　2Pe 1:19

f Ps 34:19

g Ps 119:88
　Ps 143:11

h Ps 50:23
　Ho 14:2
　Heb 13:15

i De 33:10
　Isa 48:17

j Ps 119:61

k Ps 119:87

l Ps 19:8
　Ps 119:129
　Jer 15:16

---

101 I refuse to walk on any evil
path,[a]
So that I may keep your
word.

102 I do not turn aside from
your judgments,
For you have instructed me.

103 How sweet your sayings are
to my palate,
More so than honey to my
mouth![b]

104 By your orders I act with
understanding.[c]
That is why I hate every
false path.[d]

נ [Nun]

105 Your word is a lamp to my
foot,
And a light for my path.[e]

106 I have sworn an oath, and
I will carry it out,
To observe your righteous
judgments.

107 I have been greatly
afflicted.[f]
O Jehovah, preserve me
alive according to your
word.[g]

108 Please take pleasure in
my voluntary offerings
of praise,*[h] O Jehovah,
And teach me your judg-
ments.[i]

109 My life is in constant danger,*
But I have not forgotten
your law.[j]

110 The wicked have set a trap
for me,
But I have not strayed from
your orders.[k]

111 I take your reminders as my
permanent possession,*
For they are the joy of my
heart.[l]

112 I have resolved* to obey
your regulations

119:108 *Lit., "the voluntary offerings
of my mouth." 119:109 *Or "My soul
is in my hand constantly." 119:111 *Or
"my eternal heritage." 119:112 *Lit.,
"have inclined my heart."

At all times, down to the
last.

ᗝ [*Samekh*]

113 I hate the halfhearted
ones,*[a]

But I love your law.[b]

114 You are my shelter and my
shield,[c]

For your word is my hope.*[d]

115 Stay away from me, you evil
men,[e]

So that I may observe
the commandments of my
God.

116 Support me as you promised,*[f]

So that I may keep living;

Do not let my hope turn into
disappointment.#[g]

117 Support me that I may be
saved;[h]

Then I will always concen-
trate on your regulations.[i]

118 You reject all those who
stray from your regula-
tions,[j]

For they are false and
deceitful.

119 You discard all the wicked
of the earth as if they
were worthless dross.[k]

That is why I love your
reminders.

120 The dread of you makes my
body* tremble;

I am in fear of your judgments.

ᗻ [*Ayin*]

121 I have done what is just and
righteous.

Do not abandon me to my
oppressors!

122 Guarantee the welfare of
your servant;

May the presumptuous not
oppress me.

123 My eyes have grown
weary waiting for your
salvation[a]

And for your righteous
promise.*[b]

124 Show your loyal love to
your servant,[c]

And teach me your regula-
tions.[d]

125 I am your servant; give me
understanding,[e]

So that I may know your
reminders.

126 The time has come for
Jehovah to act,[f]

For they have broken your
law.

127 That is why I love your
commandments

More than gold, even fine*
gold.[g]

128 Therefore, I consider every
instruction* from you to
be right;[h]

I hate every false path.[i]

ᗺ [*Pe*]

129 Your reminders are wonderful.

That is why I observe* them.

130 The disclosure of your
words brings light,[j]

Giving understanding to the
inexperienced.[k]

131 I open my mouth wide and
sigh,*

Because I long for your
commandments.[l]

132 Turn to me and show me
favor,[m]

In keeping with your judgment toward those loving
your name.[n]

133 Guide my steps safely*
by your saying;

May nothing wicked domi-
nate me.[o]

CHAP. 119
a 1Ki 18:21
Re 3:16
b Ps 40:8
Ps 119:97
c Ps 32:7
Ps 91:2
d Ps 130:5
e Ps 26:5
f Isa 41:10
g Ps 25:2
Ro 10:11
h Isa 41:13
i Jos 1:8
Ps 119:48
j 1Ch 28:9
Ps 95:10
k Pr 2:22
Pr 25:4, 5
Eze 22:18

Second Col.
a Ps 69:3
Ps 143:7
b Ps 119:81
c Ps 69:16
d Ps 143:10
e Ps 119:34
2Ti 2:7
Jas 1:5
f Ps 9:19
Jer 18:23
g Ps 19:9, 10
Ps 119:72
Pr 3:13, 14
h Ps 19:8
i Ps 119:104
j Ps 119:105
Pr 6:23
2Co 4:6
2Pe 1:19
k Ps 19:7
Pr 1:1, 4
2Ti 3:15
l Ps 42:1
1Pe 2:2
m 1Sa 1:10, 11
2Sa 16:11, 12
Isa 38:9, 20
n Heb 6:10
o Ps 19:13
Ro 6:12

119:113 *Or "men of divided heart." **119:114** *Or "I wait for your word." **119:116** *Or "according to your say-ing." #Or "be put to shame." **119:120** *Lit., "flesh." **119:123** *Or "saying." **119:127** *Or "re-fined." **119:128** *Or "order." **119:129** *Or "my soul observes." **119:131** *Lit., "pant." **119:133** *Or "Make my steps steady."

134 Rescue* me from oppressive men,
And I will keep your orders.

135 Make your face shine* upon your servant,[a]
And teach me your regulations.

136 Tears stream down from my eyes
Because people do not keep your law.[b]

** צ [Tsade]**

137 You are righteous, O Jehovah,[c]
And your judgments are fair.[d]

138 The reminders you give are righteous
And completely reliable.

139 My zeal consumes me,[e]
Because my adversaries have forgotten your words.

140 Your saying is thoroughly refined,[f]
And your servant loves it.[g]

141 I am insignificant and despised;[h]
Yet, I have not forgotten your orders.

142 Your righteousness is an eternal righteousness,[i]
And your law is truth.[j]

143 Though distress and difficulty come upon me,
I remain fond of your commandments.

144 The righteousness of your reminders is eternal.
Give me understanding,[k] so that I may keep living.

ק [Qoph]

145 I call with my whole heart. Answer me, O Jehovah.
Your regulations I will observe.

146 I call on you; save me!
I will keep your reminders.

147 I have been awake before dawn* to cry for help,[l]

CHAP. 119
a Nu 6:25
  Ps 4:6

b Eze 9:4
  2Pe 2:7, 8

c De 32:4

d Re 16:5, 7

e 2Ki 10:16
  Ps 69:9
  Joh 2:17

f Ps 12:6
  Ps 119:160

g Ps 119:97

h Ps 22:6, 7

i Ps 36:6

j Ex 34:6
  Ps 119:160
  Joh 17:17

k Ps 119:34

l Ps 5:3
  Ps 88:13
  Mr 1:35

Second Col.

a Ps 63:6
  Lu 6:12

b Ps 51:1
  Isa 63:7

c De 4:7
  Ps 46:1
  Ps 145:18

d Ps 19:9
  Joh 17:17

e Ps 119:144
  Ec 3:14

f Ps 9:13

g 1Sa 24:15
  Ps 43:1

h 2Ki 17:15, 18
  Ps 73:27
  Pr 15:29

i 1Ch 21:13
  Ps 86:15
  Isa 55:7
  2Co 1:3
  Jas 5:11

j Ps 25:19

k Ps 139:21

For your words are my hope.*

148 My eyes open before the night watches,
So that I can ponder over* your saying.[a]

149 Do listen to my voice because of your loyal love.[b]
O Jehovah, preserve me alive according to your justice.

150 Those who engage in shameful conduct* come near;
They are far away from your law.

151 You are near, O Jehovah,[c]
And all your commandments are truth.[d]

152 Long ago I learned about your reminders,
That you have established them to last forever.[e]

ר [Resh]

153 Look on my affliction and rescue me,[f]
For I have not forgotten your law.

154 Defend me* and rescue me;[g]
Preserve me alive in harmony with your promise.#

155 Salvation is far away from the wicked,
For they have not searched for your regulations.[h]

156 Your mercy is great, O Jehovah.[i]
Preserve me alive in harmony with your justice.

157 My persecutors and my adversaries are many;[j]
But I have not deviated from your reminders.

158 I look on the treacherous with loathing,
Because they do not keep your saying.[k]

119:134 *Lit., "Redeem." 119:135 *Or "smile." 119:147 *Or "in the morning twilight."

119:147 *Or "I wait for your words." 119:148 *Or "study." 119:150 *Or "in obscene conduct." 119:154 *Or "Conduct my legal case." #Or "saying."

159 See how I love your orders!
O Jehovah, preserve me
alive because of your loyal love.[a]
160 The very essence of your
word is truth,[b]
And all your righteous judgments endure forever.

ש [Sin] or [Shin]

161 Princes persecute me[c] for
no cause,
But my heart stands in awe
of your words.[d]
162 I rejoice over your saying[e]
Like someone who finds
great spoil.
163 I hate falsehood
—I detest it[f]—
I love your law.[g]
164 Seven times a day
I praise you
Because of your righteous
judgments.
165 Abundant peace belongs to
those who love your law;[h]
Nothing can make them
stumble.*
166 I hope for your acts of salvation, O Jehovah,
And I observe your com-
mandments.
167 I keep* your reminders,
And I love them dearly.[i]
168 I observe your orders and
your reminders,
For you are aware of all that
I do.[j]

ת [Taw]

169 May my cry for help reach
you, O Jehovah.[k]
According to your word,
make me understand.[l]
170 May my request for favor
come before you.
Save me, as you have promised.*
171 May my lips overflow with
praise,[m]

For you teach me your regulations.
172 May my tongue sing about
your saying,[a]
For all your commandments
are righteous.
173 May your hand be ready
to help me,[b]
Because I choose to obey
your orders.[c]
174 I long for your salvation,
O Jehovah,
And I am fond of your law.[d]
175 Let me* live so that I may
praise you;[e]
May your judgments be my
help.
176 I have strayed like a lost
sheep.[f] Search for your
servant,
For I have not forgotten
your commandments.[g]

A Song of the Ascents.*

120 I called to Jehovah in
my distress,[h]
And he answered me.[i]
2 O Jehovah, rescue me*
from lying lips
And from the deceitful
tongue.
3 What will He do to you, and
how will He punish you,*
You deceitful tongue?[j]
4 With sharp arrows[k] of a
warrior
And burning coals[l] of
broomwood.
5 Woe to me, for I have
lived as a foreigner
in Me′shech![m]
I have been dwelling among
the tents of Ke′dar.[n]
6 I have* been dwelling far
too long
With those who hate peace.[o]
7 I am for peace, but when
I speak,
They are for war.

CHAP. 119

a Ps 119:40, 88
La 3:22

b 2Sa 7:28
Ps 12:6
Joh 17:17

c Ps 119:23

d 2Ki 22:19

e Jer 15:16

f Ps 101:7
Ps 119:29,
104

g Ps 1:2

h Ps 1:2, 3
Pr 3:1, 2
Isa 32:17
Isa 48:18

i Ps 1:2
Ps 40:8
Ro 7:22

j Ps 139:3
Pr 5:21
Pr 15:11
Heb 4:13

k Ps 18:6
1Ch 22:12
Pr 2:3, 5

m Ps 63:5
Ps 71:17
Ps 145:7

Second Col.

a Ps 40:9

b Ps 60:5

c De 30:19
Jos 24:15, 22

d Ps 1:2

e Ps 9:13, 14
Isa 38:19

f Ps 95:7
Lu 15:4
1Pe 2:25

g Ec 12:13

CHAP. 120

h Ps 18:6

i Ps 50:15
Jon 2:1, 2

j Pr 12:22

k Ps 7:13

l Ps 140:10

m Ge 10:2

n Jer 49:28

o Ps 57:4

119:165 *Or "For them there is no stumbling block." 119:167 *Or "My soul
keeps." 119:170 *Or "according to
your saying."

119:175; 120:2 *Or "my soul." 120:Sup
*See Glossary. 120:3 *Lit., "and what
will He add to you?" 120:6 *Or "My
soul has."

A Song of the Ascents.

121 I raise my eyes to the mountains.[a]
From where will my help come?

2 My help comes from Jehovah,[b]
The Maker of heaven and earth.

3 He will never allow your foot to slip.*[c]
The One guarding you will never be drowsy.

4 Look! He will never be drowsy nor go to sleep,
The One guarding Israel.[d]

5 Jehovah is guarding you.
Jehovah is the shade[e] at your right hand.[f]

6 By day the sun will not strike you,[g]
Nor the moon by night.[h]

7 Jehovah will guard you against all harm.[i]
He will guard your life.*[j]

8 Jehovah will guard you in all you do*
From now on and forever.

A Song of the Ascents. Of David.

122 I rejoiced when they said to me:
"Let us go to the house of Jehovah."[k]

2 And now our feet are standing
Within your gates, O Jerusalem.[l]

3 Jerusalem is built as a city
That is joined together as one.[m]

4 The tribes have gone up to it,
The tribes of Jah,*
According to the reminder to Israel,
To give thanks to the name of Jehovah.[n]

5 For thrones for judgment were set up there,[o]

Thrones of the house of David.[a]

6 Ask for the peace of Jerusalem.[b]
Those who love you, O city, will be secure.

7 May peace continue within your ramparts.*
Security within your fortified towers.

8 For the sake of my brothers and my companions I will say:
"May there be peace within you."

9 For the sake of the house of Jehovah our God,[c]
I will seek good for you.

A Song of the Ascents.

123 To you I raise my eyes,[d]
You who are enthroned in the heavens.

2 As the eyes of servants look to the hand of their master,
And the eyes of a servant girl to the hand of her mistress,
So our eyes look to Jehovah our God[e]
Until he shows us favor.[f]

3 Show us favor, O Jehovah, show us favor,
For we have had our full share of contempt.[g]

4 We have had our full share of* ridicule from the self-assured
And the contempt of the arrogant.

A Song of the Ascents. Of David.

124 "If Jehovah had not been with us"[h]
—Let Israel now say—

2 "If Jehovah had not been with us[i]
When men rose up to attack us,[j]

3 Then they would have swallowed us up alive[k]

121:3 *Or "totter."   121:7 *Or "soul." 121:8 *Lit., "your going out and your coming in."   122:4 *"Jah" is a shortened form of the name Jehovah.

122:7 *Or "fortified walls."   123:4 *Or "Our soul has had more than enough."

CHAP. 121
a Ps 125:2
b Ps 46:1
   Isa 41:13
   Jer 20:11
   Heb 13:6
c Ps 91:11, 12
   Pr 3:26
d Isa 27:3
   Isa 40:28
e Ps 91:1
   Isa 25:4
f Ps 16:8
   Ps 109:31
g Isa 49:10
   Re 7:16
h Ps 91:5, 6
i Ps 91:10
   Pr 12:21
j Ps 97:10
   Ps 145:20

CHAP. 122
k 2Sa 6:15
   Ps 27:4
   Ps 42:4
   Ps 84:10
l 2Ch 6:6
   Ps 84:7
   Ps 100:4
m 2Sa 5:9
n Ex 23:17
   De 12:5, 6
o De 17:8, 9
   2Ch 19:8

Second Col.
a 2Sa 7:16
   1Ki 10:18
   1Ch 29:23
b Ps 51:18
c 1Ch 29:3
   Ps 26:8
   Ps 69:9

CHAP. 123
d Ps 25:15
   Ps 121:1
e Ps 119:82
   Ps 130:6
f La 3:25
   Mic 7:7
g Ne 4:4
   Ps 44:13

CHAP. 124
h Ps 46:7
   Ro 8:31
   Heb 13:6
i Ps 54:4
   Ps 118:6
j Ps 3:1
   Ps 22:16
k Ps 27:2

When their anger was burning against us.[a]

4 Then the waters would have washed us away,
The torrent would have swept over us.*[b]

5 The raging waters would have overwhelmed us.*

6 May Jehovah be praised,
For he has not given us as prey to their teeth.

7 We are* like a bird that escaped
From the hunter's trap;[c]
The trap was broken,
And we escaped.[d]

8 Our help is in the name of Jehovah,[e]
The Maker of heaven and earth."

A Song of the Ascents.

125 Those who trust in Jehovah[f]
Are like Mount Zion, which cannot be shaken
But endures forever.[g]

2 Just as mountains surround Jerusalem,[h]
So Jehovah surrounds his people[i]
From now on and forever.

3 The scepter of wickedness will not remain upon the land allotted to the righteous,[j]
So that the righteous do not turn to doing* what is wrong.[k]

4 Do good, O Jehovah, to those who are good,[l]
To those who are upright in heart.[m]

5 As for those who turn aside to their crooked ways,
Jehovah will remove them along with the wrongdoers.[n]
May there be peace upon Israel.

A Song of the Ascents.

126 When Jehovah gathered back the captives of Zion,[a]
We thought we were dreaming.

2 At that time our mouth was filled with laughter
And our tongue with a joyful shout.[b]
At that time they said among the nations:
"Jehovah has done great things for them."[c]

3 Jehovah has done great things for us,[d]
And we are overjoyed.

4 Do gather back* our captives, O Jehovah,
Like streams in the Neg′eb.#

5 Those sowing seed with tears
Will reap with a joyful shout.

6 The one who does go out, though weeping,
Carrying his bag of seed,
Will surely return with a joyful shout,[e]
Carrying in his sheaves.[f]

A Song of the Ascents. Of Solomon.

127 Unless Jehovah builds the house,
It is in vain that its builders work hard on it.[g]
Unless Jehovah guards the city,[h]
It is in vain that the guard stays awake.

2 It is in vain that you rise up early,
That you stay up late,
That you toil for your food,
Since he provides for his loved ones while giving them sleep.[i]

3 Look! Sons* are an inheritance from Jehovah;[j]
The fruit of the womb is a reward.[k]

CHAP. 124

a Ps 56:1
b Ps 18:4
c 1Sa 23:26-28
  2Sa 17:21, 22
d Ps 25:15
  Ps 91:3
e Pr 18:10

CHAP. 125

f Jer 17:7
g 1Ki 8:12, 13
  Ps 48:2
  Ps 132:13, 14
h 1Ki 11:7
  Ac 1:12
i Ps 34:7
  Isa 31:5
  Zec 2:4, 5
j Isa 14:5
k Ec 7:7
l Ps 51:18
m Ps 36:10
  Ps 73:1
n 1Ch 10:13
  Ps 53:5
  Isa 59:8

Second Col.

CHAP. 126

a Ezr 1:2, 3
  Ps 85:1
b Ezr 3:11
  Ps 106:47
  Isa 49:13
  Jer 31:12
c Jos 2:9, 10
  Ne 6:15, 16
d Ezr 7:27, 28
  Isa 11:11
e Ps 30:5
  Isa 61:1-3
f Isa 9:3

CHAP. 127

g Pr 3:6
  Pr 10:22
  Pr 16:3
h Isa 27:3
i Ps 3:5
  Ec 5:12
j Ge 33:4, 5
  Ge 48:3, 4
  1Sa 2:21
k Ge 41:51, 52
  Le 26:9
  Job 42:12, 13
  Ps 128:3

4 Like arrows in the hand of
   a mighty man,
   So are the sons of one's
   youth.[a]
5 Happy is the man who fills
   his quiver with them.[b]
   They will not be put to
   shame,
   For they will speak with
   enemies in the city gate.

A Song of the Ascents.

128 Happy is everyone who
        fears Jehovah,[c]
   Who walks in His ways.[d]
2 You will eat what your hands
   worked hard to produce.
   You will be happy and will
   enjoy prosperity.[e]
3 Your wife will be like a fruitful vine within your house;[f]
   Your sons will be like shoots
   of an olive tree around
   your table.
4 Look! That is how the man
   who fears Jehovah
   Will be blessed.[g]
5 Jehovah will bless you from
   Zion.
   May you see Jerusalem prosper all the days of your
   life[h]
6 And see the sons of your
   sons.
   May there be peace upon
   Israel.

A Song of the Ascents.

129 "Since my youth they
        have constantly at-
        tacked me"[i]
   —Let Israel now say—
2 "Since my youth they have
   constantly attacked me;[j]
   But they have not defeated me.[k]
3 Plowmen have plowed across
   my back;[l]
   They have made their furrows long."
4 But Jehovah is righteous;[m]
   He has cut up the ropes of
   the wicked.[n]

5 They will be put to shame
   and will retreat in disgrace,
   All those who hate Zion.[a]
6 They will become like grass
   on the rooftops
   That withers before it is
   pulled up,
7 That cannot fill the reaper's
   hand
   Nor the arms of the one gathering sheaves.
8 Those passing by will not
   say:
   "May the blessing of Jehovah
   be upon you;
   We bless you in the name of
   Jehovah."

A Song of the Ascents.

130 From the depths I call
        to you, O Jehovah.[b]
2 O Jehovah, hear my voice.
   May your ears pay attention
   to my pleas for help.
3 If errors were what you
   watch,* O Jah,#
   Then who, O Jehovah, could
   stand?[c]
4 For with you there is true
   forgiveness,[d]
   So that you may be held in
   awe.*[e]
5 I hope in Jehovah, my whole
   being* hopes in him;
   I wait for his word.
6 I eagerly wait* for Jehovah,[f]
   More than watchmen wait for
   the morning,[g]
   Yes, more than watchmen
   wait for the morning.
7 Let Israel keep waiting for
   Jehovah,
   For Jehovah is loyal in his
   love,[h]
   And he has great power to
   redeem.
8 He will redeem Israel from
   all their errors.

130:3 *Or "keep track of." #"Jah" is a
shortened form of the name Jehovah.
130:4 *Lit., "be feared." **130:5** *Or
"my soul." **130:6** *Or "My soul eagerly
waits."

CHAP. 127
a Pr 17:6
b Ge 50:23

CHAP. 128
c Ps 112:1
   Heb 5:7
d Ps 119:1
   Mic 6:8
e Ec 5:18
   Isa 65:22
f Ex 23:26
   Ps 127:3
g Ps 127:4, 5
h Ps 122:6
   Isa 33:20

CHAP. 129
i Ex 5:6, 9
j La 1:3
k Ps 118:13
   Ps 125:3
l Ps 66:12
   Isa 51:23
m Ezr 9:15
   Ne 9:33
n Ps 124:7

Second Col.
a Ne 4:4
   Ne 6:15, 16
   Es 6:13
   Es 9:5
   Ps 137:7
   Zec 12:3

CHAP. 130
b La 3:55
   Jon 2:1, 2
c Ps 38:4
   Ps 103:14
   Ps 143:1, 2
   Isa 55:7
   Da 9:18
   Ro 3:20
   Tit 3:5
d Ps 34:6, 7
   Ps 25:11
e Jer 33:8, 9
f Mic 7:7
g Ps 119:147
h Ps 86:5

A Song of the Ascents. Of David.

131 O Jehovah, my heart is
not haughty,
Nor are my eyes lofty;[a]
Nor do I aspire to things too
great,[b]
Or to things that are
beyond me.

2 No, but I have calmed and
quieted my soul*[c]
Like a weaned child with its
mother;
I am[#] contented like a
weaned child.

3 Let Israel wait for Jehovah[d]
From now on and forever.

A Song of the Ascents.

132 O Jehovah, remember
David
And all his suffering;[e]

2 How he swore to Jehovah,
How he vowed to the Powerful One of Jacob:[f]

3 "I will not go into my tent,
my home.[g]
I will not lie upon my couch,
my bed;

4 I will not allow my eyes to
sleep,
Nor my eyelids to slumber

5 Until I find a place for
Jehovah,
A fine residence* for the
Powerful One of Jacob."[h]

6 Look! We heard about it in
Eph·ra·thah;[i]
We found it in the fields of
the forest.[j]

7 Let us come into his residence;*[k]
Let us bow down at his footstool.

8 Rise up, O Jehovah, to come
to your resting-place,[m]
You and the Ark of your
strength.[n]

9 May your priests be clothed
with righteousness,

And may your loyal ones
shout joyfully.

10 For the sake of David your
servant,
Do not reject* your anointed
one.[a]

11 Jehovah has sworn to David;
He will surely not go back on
his word:
"One of your offspring,*
I will place on your throne.[b]

12 If your sons keep my cove-
nant
And my reminders that
I teach them,[c]
Their sons too
Will sit on your throne for-
ever."[d]

13 For Jehovah has chosen
Zion;[e]
He has desired it for his
dwelling place:[f]

14 "This is my resting-place
forever;
Here I will dwell,[g] for this
is my desire.

15 I will richly bless it with
provisions;
I will satisfy its poor with
bread.[h]

16 Its priests I will clothe with
salvation,[i]
And its loyal ones will shout
joyfully.[j]

17 There I will make the
strength* of David grow.
I have prepared a lamp for
my anointed one.[k]

18 I will clothe his enemies with
shame,
But the crown* on his head
will flourish."[l]

A Song of the Ascents. Of David.

133 Look! How good and
how pleasant it is
For brothers to dwell together in unity![m]

CHAP. 131
a Ps 78:70
 Ps 138:6
b 1Sa 18:23
c 1Sa 30:6
 Ps 62:1
 Isa 30:15
 La 3:26
d Ps 130:7
 Mic 7:7

CHAP. 132
e 1Sa 20:1
f 2Sa 7:2, 3
g 2Sa 5:11
h 2Sa 7:2
 1Ki 8:17
 1Ch 15:3, 12
 Ac 7:45, 46
i 1Sa 17:12
j 1Sa 7:1
 1Ch 13:6
k Ps 43:3
l 1Ch 28:2
 Ps 5:7
m Nu 10:35
 2Sa 6:17
n 2Ch 6:41, 42

Second Col.
a 1Ki 15:4
 2Ki 19:34
b 1Ki 8:25
 Ps 89:3, 4
 Ps 89:20, 36
 Isa 9:7
 Jer 33:20, 21
 Mt 9:27
 Lu 1:69
 Ac 2:30, 31
 Ac 13:22, 23
c 1Ch 29:19
d 2Sa 7:12, 16
 1Ch 17:11, 12
 Ps 89:20, 29
e Ps 48:2, 3
 Ps 78:68
 Heb 12:22
f Ps 87:2
g Ps 46:5
 Isa 24:23
h Ps 22:26
 Ps 147:12, 14
i Ps 149:4
j Ps 132:8, 9
k 1Ki 11:36
 1Ki 15:4
 2Ch 21:7
l Ps 2:6
 Ps 72:8
 Isa 9:6
 Re 11:15

CHAP. 133
m Ge 13:8
 Joh 13:35
 Col 3:14
 Heb 13:1

131:2 *Or "myself." See Glossary. #Or
"My soul is." 132:5 *Or "A grand tabernacle." 132:7 *Or "his grand tabernacle."

132:10 *Lit., "turn back the face of."
132:11 *Lit., "of the fruit of your womb."
132:17 *Lit., "horn." 132:18 *Or "diadem."

2 It is like fine oil poured on the head[a]
That runs down the beard, Aaron's beard,[b]
And runs down onto the collar of his garments.

3 It is like the dew of Her′mon[c]
That descends on the mountains of Zion.[d]
That is where Jehovah decreed his blessing
—Life everlasting.

A Song of the Ascents.

134 Praise Jehovah, All you servants of Jehovah,[e]
You who stand in the house of Jehovah during the nights.[f]

2 Raise your hands[g] in holiness*
And praise Jehovah.

3 May Jehovah, the Maker of heaven and earth,
Bless you from Zion.

135 Praise Jah!* Praise the name of Jehovah;
Offer praise, you servants of Jehovah,[h]

2 You who are standing in the house of Jehovah,
In the courtyards of the house of our God.[i]

3 Praise Jah, for Jehovah is good.[j]
Sing praises* to his name, for it is pleasant.

4 For Jah has chosen Jacob for himself,
Israel for his special property.*[k]

5 For I well know that Jehovah is great;
Our Lord is greater than all other gods.[l]

---

6 Jehovah does everything he pleases to do[a]
In heaven and on earth, in the seas and all the depths.

7 He causes clouds* to ascend from the ends of the earth;
He makes lightning for# the rain;
He brings the wind out of his storehouses.[b]

8 He struck down the firstborn of Egypt,
Both man and beast.[c]

9 He sent signs and miracles among you, O Egypt,[d]
Against Phar′aoh and all his servants.[e]

10 He struck down many nations[f]
And killed mighty kings[g]

11 —Si′hon the king of the Am′or·ites,[h]
Og the king of Ba′shan,[i]
And all the kingdoms of Ca′naan.

12 He gave their land as an inheritance,
An inheritance to Israel his people.[j]

13 O Jehovah, your name endures forever.
O Jehovah, your fame* endures for all generations.[k]

14 For Jehovah will defend* his people,[l]
And he will feel compassion# for his servants.[m]

15 The idols of the nations are silver and gold,
The work of human hands.[n]

16 A mouth they have, but they cannot speak;[o]
Eyes, but they cannot see;

17 Ears they have, but they cannot hear.
There is no breath in their mouth.[p]

134:2 *Or possibly, "in the sanctuary." **135:1** *Or "Hallelujah!" "Jah" is a shortened form of the name Jehovah. **135:3** *Or "Make music." **135:4** *Or "treasured possession." **135:7** *Or "vapors." #Or possibly, "makes sluices for." **135:13** *Or "name." Lit., "memorial." **135:14** *Or "plead the cause of." #Or "feel regret."

18 The people who make them
will become just like
them,[a]
As will all those who trust
in them.[b]

19 O house of Israel, praise
Jehovah.
O house of Aaron, praise
Jehovah.

20 O house of Le'vi, praise
Jehovah.[c]
You who fear Jehovah,
praise Jehovah.

21 May Jehovah be praised from
Zion,[d]
The One residing in
Jerusalem.[e]
Praise Jah![f]

136 Give thanks to Jehovah,
for he is good;[g]
His loyal love endures forever.[h]

2 Give thanks to the God of
gods,[i]
For his loyal love endures
forever.

3 Give thanks to the Lord of
lords,
For his loyal love endures
forever.

4 He alone does great wonders,[j]
For his loyal love endures
forever.[k]

5 He skillfully made* the heavens,[l]
For his loyal love endures
forever.

6 He spread out the earth over
the waters,[m]
For his loyal love endures
forever.

7 He made the great lights,[n]
For his loyal love endures
forever,

8 The sun to rule over the day,[o]
For his loyal love endures
forever,

9 The moon and the stars to
rule over the night,[p]

For his loyal love endures
forever.

10 He struck down Egypt's firstborn,[a]
For his loyal love endures
forever.

11 He brought Israel out from
their midst,[b]
For his loyal love endures
forever,

12 With a mighty hand[c] and an
outstretched arm,
For his loyal love endures
forever.

13 He split the Red Sea in two,*[d]
For his loyal love endures
forever.

14 He caused Israel to pass
through the middle of it,[e]
For his loyal love endures
forever.

15 He shook off Phar'aoh and
his army into the Red Sea,[f]
For his loyal love endures
forever.

16 He led his people through
the wilderness,[g]
For his loyal love endures
forever.

17 He struck down great kings,[h]
For his loyal love endures
forever.

18 He killed mighty kings,
For his loyal love endures
forever,

19 Si'hon[i] the king of the
Am'or·ites,
For his loyal love endures
forever,

20 And Og[j] the king of Ba'shan,
For his loyal love endures
forever.

21 He gave their land as an
inheritance,[k]
For his loyal love endures
forever,

22 An inheritance to Israel his
servant,
For his loyal love endures
forever.

CHAP. 135
a Isa 44:9
b Ps 97:7
c De 10:8
d Ps 48:1
Ps 132:13
e Jer 3:17
f Re 19:6

CHAP. 136
g Lu 18:19
h 2Ch 7:3
2Ch 20:21
Ps 106:1
Ps 107:1
i Ps 97:9
Da 2:47
j Ex 15:11
Re 15:3
k Ps 103:17
l Job 38:36
Pr 3:19, 20
m Ge 1:9
Ps 24:1, 2
n Ge 1:14
o Ge 1:16
Jer 31:35
p Ps 8:3

Second Col.
a Ex 12:29
b Ex 12:51
c Ex 13:14
d Ex 14:21
e Ex 14:29
f Ex 14:27, 28
g Ex 13:18
Ex 15:22
h Jos 12:7, 8
i Nu 21:21-24
j Nu 21:33-35
k Nu 32:33

136:5 *Or "made with understanding."   **136:13** *Lit., "into pieces."

23 He remembered us when we were low,[a]

For his loyal love endures forever.[b]

24 He kept rescuing us from our adversaries,[c]

For his loyal love endures forever.

25 He gives food to every living thing,*[d]

For his loyal love endures forever.

26 Give thanks to the God of the heavens,

For his loyal love endures forever.

137

By the rivers of Babylon,[e] there we sat.

We wept when we remembered Zion.

2 Upon the poplar trees in her* midst,

We hung our harps.[g]

3 For there our captors asked us for a song,[h]

Those mocking us wanted amusement:

"Sing for us one of the songs of Zion."

4 How can we sing the song of Jehovah

On foreign soil?

5 If I should forget you, O Jerusalem,

Let my right hand be forgetful.*[i]

6 Let my tongue stick to my palate

If I do not remember you,

If I do not place Jerusalem above

My greatest reasons for rejoicing.[j]

7 Remember, O Jehovah,

What the E′dom·ites said on the day Jerusalem fell:

"Tear it down! Tear it down to its foundations!"[k]

8 O daughter of Babylon, who is soon to be devastated,[a]

Happy will be the one who rewards you

With the treatment you inflicted on us.[b]

9 Happy will be the one who seizes your children

And dashes them against the rocks.[c]

Of David.

138

I will praise you with all my heart.[d]

In the face of other gods, I will sing praises.*

2 I will bow down toward your holy temple,*[e]

And I will praise your name[f]

Because of your loyal love and your faithfulness.

For you have magnified your saying and your name above everything else.*

3 On the day I called, you answered me;[g]

You made me bold* and strong.[h]

4 All the kings of the earth will praise you, O Jehovah,[i]

For they will have heard the promises you have spoken.

5 They will sing about the ways of Jehovah,

For the glory of Jehovah is great.[j]

6 Though Jehovah is high, he takes note of the humble,[k]

But the haughty he knows only from a distance.[l]

7 Even when I walk in the midst of danger, you will preserve me alive.[m]

You stretch out your hand against the anger of my enemies;

Your right hand will save me.

CHAP. 136
a De 32:36
b Ne 9:32
c Jg 3:9
  Jg 6:9
d Ps 145:15
  Ps 147:9

CHAP. 137
e Jer 51:13
  Eze 3:15
  Da 10:4
f Da 9:2, 3
g Isa 24:8
h Ps 123:4
i Ne 2:3
  Ps 84:2
  Ps 102:13, 14
  Isa 62:1
  Jer 51:50
j Ps 122:1
k Jer 49:7
  La 4:22
  Eze 25:12
  Ob 10-13

Second Col.
a Isa 47:1
  Jer 25:12
  Jer 50:2
b Jer 50:29
  Re 18:6
c Isa 13:1, 16

CHAP. 138
d Ps 9:1
e 1Sa 3:3
  1Ch 16:1
  Ps 28:2
f Joh 17:6
g Ps 18:6
h Ps 29:11
  Isa 12:2
  Isa 41:10
i Ps 102:15
  Isa 60:3
j 1Ki 8:10, 11
k 1Sa 2:8
  Ps 113:6-8
  Isa 57:15
l Jas 4:6
  1Pe 5:5
m Ps 71:20

136:25 *Lit., "all flesh." 137:2 *Referring to Babylon. 137:5 *Or possibly, "wither."

138:1 *Or possibly, "In defiance of other gods, I will make music to you." 138:2 *Or "sanctuary." *Or possibly, "you have magnified your saying above all your name." 138:3 *Or "bold in my soul."

8 Jehovah will accomplish all
things in my behalf.
O Jehovah, your loyal love
endures forever;[a]
Do not forsake the works of
your hands.[b]

For the director. Of David. A melody.

139 O Jehovah, you have
searched through me,
and you know me.[c]
2 You know when I sit down
and when I rise up.[d]
You discern my thoughts
from afar.[e]
3 You observe* me when I travel and when I lie down;
You are familiar with all my
ways.[f]
4 There is not a word on my
tongue,
But look! O Jehovah, you
already know it well.[g]
5 Behind and before me, you
surround me;
And you lay your hand
upon me.
6 Such knowledge is beyond
my comprehension.*
It is too high for me to
reach.*[h]
7 Where can I escape from
your spirit,
And where can I run away
from your face?[i]
8 If I were to ascend to heaven,
you would be there,
And if I were to make my bed
in the Grave,* look! you
would be there.[j]
9 If I would fly away with the
wings of the dawn
To reside by the most remote
sea,
10 Even there your hand would
lead me

And your right hand would
take hold of me.[a]
11 If I say: "Surely darkness will
conceal me!"
Then the night around me
would become light.
12 Even the darkness would not
be too dark for you,
But night would be as bright
as the day;[b]
Darkness is the same as light
to you.[c]
13 For you produced my kidneys;
You kept me screened off*
in my mother's womb.[d]
14 I praise you because in an
awe-inspiring way I am
wonderfully made.[e]
Your works are wonderful,[f]
I know* this very well.
15 My bones were not hidden
from you
When I was made in secret,
When I was woven in the
depths of the earth.[g]
16 Your eyes even saw me as
an embryo;
All its parts were written in
your book
Regarding the days when
they were formed,
Before any of them existed.
17 So to me, how precious your
thoughts are![h]
O God, how vast is the sum
of them![i]
18 If I try to count them, they
outnumber the grains of
sand.[j]
When I awake, I am still with
you.*[k]
19 O God, if only you would slay
the wicked![l]
Then the violent* men would
depart from me,

CHAP. 138
a Ps 103:17

b Job 14:15
Ps 71:18

CHAP. 139
c 1Sa 16:6, 7
1Ch 28:9
Ps 17:3
Ps 139:23
Jer 20:12

d Ge 16:13

e Ps 94:11

f Ge 28:15
2Sa 8:14
Job 31:4
Ps 121:8
Pr 5:21

g Heb 4:12

h Job 26:14
Job 42:3
Ps 40:5
Ro 11:33

i Jon 1:3

j Job 26:6
Pr 15:11

Second Col.
a Ps 63:8
Ps 73:23
Isa 41:13

b Da 2:22

c Heb 4:13

d Ps 22:9
Ps 71:6
Jer 1:5

e Ge 1:26

f Ps 19:1
Ps 104:24
Ps 111:2
Re 15:3

g Job 10:10, 11

h Isa 55:9

i Ro 11:33

j Ps 40:5

k Ps 63:6

l Ps 5:6

139:3 *Lit., "measure." **139:6** *Or "is
too amazing for me." #Or "too much
for me to fathom." **139:8** *Or "Sheol,"
that is, the common grave of mankind.
See Glossary.

139:13 *Or possibly, "wove me together." **139:14** *Or "My soul knows."
139:18 *Or possibly, "I would still be
counting them." **139:19** *Or "bloodguilty."

20 Those who say things
　against you with evil in-
　tent;*
　They are your adversaries
　who take up your name
　in a worthless way.ᵃ
21 Do I not hate those who hate
　you, O Jehovah,ᵇ
　And loathe those who revolt
　against you?ᶜ
22 I have nothing but hatred
　for them;ᵈ
　They have become real
　enemies to me.
23 Search through me, O God,
　and know my heart.ᵉ
　Examine me, and know my
　anxious* thoughts.ᶠ
24 See whether there is in me
　any harmful way,ᵍ
　And lead meʰ in the way
　of eternity.

For the director. A melody of David.

140 Rescue me, O Jehovah,
　　　from evil men;
　Protect me from violent
　men,ⁱ
2 Those who scheme evil in
　their heartsʲ
　And stir up conflict all day
　long.
3 They sharpen their tongue
　like that of a serpent;ᵏ
　Venom of vipers is behind
　their lips.ˡ (Selah)
4 Protect me, O Jehovah, from
　the hands of the wicked;ᵐ
　Safeguard me from violent
　men,
　Those who scheme to
　trip me.
5 The haughty ones hide a trap
　for me;
　With ropes they spread out a
　net beside the path.ⁿ
　They set snares for me.ᵒ
　(Selah)
6 I say to Jehovah: "You are
　my God.

Listen, O Jehovah, to my
　pleas for help."ᵃ
7 O Jehovah the Sovereign
　Lord, my strong Savior,
　You shield my head in the
　day of battle.ᵇ
8 Do not grant, O Jehovah,
　the desires of the wicked.
　Do not let their plots suc-
　ceed, so that they are not
　exalted. (Selah)ᶜ
9 May the heads of those sur-
　rounding me
　Be covered with the evil
　spoken by their lips.ᵈ
10 May burning coals rain down
　on them.ᵉ
　May they be hurled into the
　fire,
　Into deep pits,*ᶠ never to rise
　again.
11 May the slanderer find no
　place on the earth.*ᵍ
　May evil pursue men of
　violence and strike them
　down.
12 I know that Jehovah will
　defend the lowly
　And give justice to the poor.ʰ
13 Surely the righteous will give
　thanks to your name;
　The upright will dwell before
　your face.*ⁱ

A melody of David.

141 O Jehovah, I call on
　　　you.ʲ
　Come quickly to help me.ᵏ
　Do pay attention when I call
　to you.ˡ
2 May my prayer be as
　incenseᵐ prepared before
　you,ⁿ
　My uplifted hands like the
　evening grain offering.ᵒ
3 Station a guard for my
　mouth, O Jehovah,
　Do set a watch over the door
　of my lips.ᵖ

CHAP. 139
a Ex 20:7
b 2Ch 19:2
　2Co 6:14
c Ps 119:158
d Ps 101:3
e Jer 20:12
f Ps 94:19
g Ps 17:3
h Ps 5:8
　Ps 143:8
　Ps 143:10

CHAP. 140
i Ps 18:48
　Ps 59:1
j Ps 64:2, 6
k Ps 52:1, 2
　Ps 58:3, 4
l Ro 3:13
　Jas 3:8
m Ps 17:8
　Ps 36:11
　Ps 71:4
n Ps 10:9
o Jer 18:22

Second Col.
a Ps 28:2
　Ps 55:1
b 1Sa 17:37
c 2Sa 15:31
　Ps 27:12
d Ps 7:16
　Pr 12:13
e Ps 11:5, 6
　Ps 55:23
f Ps 12:3
g Ps 10:17, 18
　Ps 22:24
i Ps 23:6

CHAP. 141
j Ps 31:17
k Ps 40:13
　Ps 70:5
l Ps 39:12
m Ex 30:34-36
n Lu 1:9, 10
　Re 5:8
　Re 8:3, 4
o Ex 29:41
p Pr 13:3
　Pr 21:23
　Jas 1:26

139:20 *Or "according to their idea." 139:23 *Or "disquieting."

140:10 *Or "Into watery pits." 140:11 *Or "in the land." 140:13 *Or "in your presence."

4 Do not let my heart incline to
   anything bad,[a]
   To share in vile deeds with
      evil men;
   May I never feast on their
      delicacies.

5 Should the righteous one
   strike me, it would be an
   act of loyal love;[b]
   Should he reprove me, it
   would be like oil on my
   head,[c]
   Which my head would never
   refuse.[d]
   My prayer will continue even
   during their calamities.

6 Though their judges are
   thrown down from the cliff,
   The people will pay attention
   to my words, for they are
   pleasant.

7 Just as when someone plows
   and breaks up the soil,
   So our bones have been scattered at the mouth of the
   Grave.*

8 But my eyes look to
   you, O Sovereign Lord
   Jehovah.[e]
   In you I have taken refuge.
   Do not take away my life.*

9 Protect me from the jaws
   of the trap they have laid
   for me,
   From the snares of evildoers.

10 The wicked will fall into their
   own nets all together[f]
   While I pass by safely.

   Mas′kil.* Of David when he was
   in the cave.[g] A prayer.

142 With my voice I call to
      Jehovah for help;[h]
   With my voice I plead with
      Jehovah for favor.

2 Before him I pour out my
   concern;
   Before him I tell about my
   distress[i]

3 When my spirit* fails
   within me.
   Then you watch my
   roadway.[a]
   In the path where I walk,
   They hide a trap for me.

4 Look at my right hand
   and see
   That no one cares
   about* me.[b]
   There is nowhere I can flee;[c]
   No one is concerned
   about me.#

5 I call to you, O Jehovah,
   for help.
   I say: "You are my refuge,[d]
   All I have* in the land of the
   living."

6 Pay attention to my cry for
   help,
   For I have been brought very
   low.
   Rescue me from my persecu-
   tors,[e]
   For they are stronger than
   I am.

7 Bring me# out of the dungeon
   To praise your name.
   May the righteous gather
   around me
   Because you deal kindly
   with me.

   A melody of David.

143 O Jehovah, hear my
      prayer;[f]
   Listen to my plea for help.
   In your faithfulness and
   in your righteousness,
   answer me.

2 Do not enter into judgment
   with your servant,
   For no one living can be righteous before you.[g]

3 For the enemy pursues me;#
   He has crushed my life into
   the ground.

CHAP. 141
a 1Ki 8:58
  Ps 119:36

b 2Sa 12:7, 9
  Pr 17:10
  Ga 6:1

c Pr 6:23
  Jas 5:14

d Pr 9:8
  Pr 19:25
  Pr 25:12

e 2Ch 20:12
  Ps 25:15

f Es 7:10
  Ps 7:14, 15
  Ps 9:15
  Ps 57:6

CHAP. 142
g 1Sa 22:1
  1Sa 24:3
  Heb 11:32, 38

h Ps 28:2
  Ps 141:1

i Ps 18:6
  Jon 2:7
  Mt 26:38, 39
  Mr 15:34
  Heb 5:7

Second Col.
a Ps 139:3

b Ps 31:11
  Ps 69:20

c 1Sa 23:11

d Pr 18:10

e 1Sa 20:33
  1Sa 23:26
  1Sa 25:29

CHAP. 143
f Ps 65:2

g Job 9:2
  Ps 130:3
  Ec 7:20
  Ro 3:20
  Ga 2:16
  1Jo 1:10

141:7 *Or "Sheol," that is, the common
grave of mankind. See Glossary. **141:8**
*Or "pour out my soul." **142:Sup** *See
Glossary.

142:3 *Or "strength." **142:4** *Lit., "recognizes." **142:4, 7; 143:3** # Or "my
soul." **142:5** *Lit., "My share."

He has caused me to dwell
  in darkness like those long
  dead.
4 My spirit* is failing;[a]
  My heart is numb within me.[b]
5 I remember the days of old;
  I meditate on all your
    activity;[c]
  I eagerly ponder over* the
    work of your hands.
6 I spread out my hands to you;
  I am* like a parched land that
    thirsts for you.[d] (Selah)
7 Do answer me quickly,
    O Jehovah;
  My strength* has come to an
    end.[f]
  Do not hide your face
    from me,[g]
  Or I will be like those going
    down into the pit.*[h]
8 Let me hear your loyal love
    in the morning,
  For I trust in you.
  Make known to me the way
    I should walk,[i]
  For to you I turn.*
9 Rescue me from my enemies,
    O Jehovah.
  I seek your protection.[j]
10 Teach me to do your will,[k]
  For you are my God.
  Your spirit is good;
  May it lead me on level
    ground.*
11 For the sake of your name,
    O Jehovah, preserve me
    alive.
  In your righteousness, res-
    cue me* from distress.[l]
12 In your loyal love, put an end
    to* my enemies;[m]
  Destroy all those harassing
    me,*[n]
  For I am your servant.[o]

143:4 *Or "strength." 143:5 *Or
"study." 143:6 *Or "My soul is."
143:7 *Lit., "spirit." *Or "grave."
143:8 *Or "For I lift up my soul to
you." 143:10 *Or "in the land of uprightness." 143:11, 12 *Or "my soul."
143:12 *Lit., "silence."

CHAP. 143

a Ps 143:3

b Ps 102:4

c Ps 77:5, 6
  Ps 77:11, 12
  Ps 111:2, 3

d Ps 63:1

e Ps 40:13
  Ps 70:5

f Ps 142:3

g Ps 27:9

h Ps 28:1

i Ps 5:8
  Pr 3:6

j Ps 59:1
  Ps 61:3, 4
  Ps 91:1

k Ps 25:4

l Ps 31:1

m 1Sa 25:29
  1Sa 26:9, 10

n 1Sa 24:12

o Ps 89:20

Second Col.

CHAP. 144

a De 32:4

b 2Sa 22:35
  Ps 18:2, 34

c 2Sa 22:2, 3

d Ps 18:47

e Ps 8:4
  Heb 2:6

f Ps 39:5

g 1Ch 29:15
  Job 14:1, 2

h Ps 18:9

i Ex 19:18

j Job 36:32

k 2Sa 22:15

l 2Sa 22:17, 18
  Ps 18:16, 17
  Ps 54:3

m Ps 33:3
  Ps 40:3
  Ps 96:1
  Isa 42:10
  Re 5:9
  Re 14:3

Of David.

144 May Jehovah, my
  Rock,[a] be praised,
  Who trains my hands for bat-
    tle,
  My fingers for warfare.[b]
2 He is my loyal love and my
    stronghold,
  My secure refuge* and my
    rescuer,
  My shield and the One in
    whom I have taken shelter,[c]
  The One subduing peoples
    under me.[d]
3 O Jehovah, what is man that
    you should notice him,
  The son of mortal man that
    you should pay attention to
    him?[e]
4 Man resembles a mere
    breath;[f]
  His days are like a passing
    shadow.[g]
5 O Jehovah, lower* your
    heavens and descend;[h]
  Touch the mountains and
    make them smoke.[i]
6 Make lightning flash and
    scatter the enemy;[j]
  Shoot your arrows
    and throw them into confu-
    sion.[k]
7 Stretch out your hands from
    above;
  Rescue me and save me from
    the surging waters,
  From the hand* of the for-
    eigners,[l]
8 Whose mouths speak lies
  And who raise their right
    hand to swear to what is
    false.*
9 O God, I will sing to you
    a new song.[m]
  I will sing praises* to you,
    accompanied by a ten-
    stringed instrument,

144:2 *Or "secure height." 144:5 *Or
"bend." 144:7 *Or "grip." 144:8 *Lit.,
"And their right hand is a right hand of
falsehood." 144:9 *Or "make music."

10 To the One who gives victory* to kings,[a]
  The One rescuing his servant David from the deadly
  sword.[b]

11 Rescue me and save me from
  the hand of the foreigners,
  Whose mouths speak lies
  And who raise their right
  hand to swear to what is
  false.

12 Then our sons will be like
  young plants that grow up
  quickly,
  Our daughters like corner
  pillars carved for a palace.

13 Our storehouses will overflow with every kind of
  produce;
  Our flocks in our fields will
  multiply by the thousands,
  by the tens of thousands.

14 Our cattle, heavy with
  young, will suffer no mis-
  hap* or miscarriage;
  There will be no cry of distress in our public squares.

15 Happy is the people for
  whom it is this way!
  Happy is the people whose
  God is Jehovah![c]

A praise of David.

א [Aleph]

145 I will exalt you, O my
  God the King,[d]
  I will praise your name for-
  ever and ever.[e]

ב [Beth]

2 All day long I will praise you;[f]
  I will praise your name forever and ever.[g]

ג [Gimel]

3 Jehovah is great and most
  worthy of praise;[h]
  His greatness is unsearchable.*[i]

ד [Daleth]

4 Generation after generation
  will praise your works;

They will tell about your
  mighty acts.[a]

ה [He]

5 Of the glorious splendor
  of your majesty they will
  speak[b]
  And on your wonderful
  works I will meditate.

ו [Waw]

6 They will speak about your
  awe-inspiring deeds,*
  And I will declare your greatness.

ז [Zayin]

7 They will bubble over as they
  recall your abundant goodness,[c]
  And they will shout joyfully
  because of your righteousness.[d]

ח [Heth]

8 Jehovah is compassionate*
  and merciful,[e]
  Slow to anger and great in
  loyal love.[f]

ט [Teth]

9 Jehovah is good to all,[g]
  And his mercy is evident in
  all his works.

י [Yod]

10 All your works will glorify
  you, O Jehovah,[h]
  And your loyal ones will
  praise you.[i]

כ [Kaph]

11 They will proclaim the glory
  of your kingship[j]
  And speak about your
  mightiness,[k]

ל [Lamed]

12 To make known to men your
  mighty acts[l]
  And the glorious splendor of
  your kingship.[m]

מ [Mem]

13 Your kingship is an eternal
  kingship,
  And your dominion
  endures throughout all
  generations.[n]

CHAP. 144
a 2Sa 5:19
  Ps 18:50

b 1Sa 17:45, 46
  2Sa 21:15, 17

c Ps 33:12
  Ps 37:9
  Ps 37:37
  Ps 146:5

CHAP. 145
d Isa 33:22
  Re 11:17

e 1Ch 29:10

f Ps 119:164

g Ps 146:2

h Ps 150:2
  Ro 1:20
  Re 15:3

i Job 26:14
  Ps 139:6
  Ro 11:33

Second Col.
a Ex 12:26, 27

b Ps 8:1

c 1Ki 8:66
  Ps 13:6
  Ps 31:19
  Isa 63:7
  Jer 31:12

d Ps 51:14
  Re 15:3

e 2Ch 30:9
  Eph 2:4

f Ex 34:6
  Ne 9:17

g Ps 25:8
  Na 1:7
  Mt 5:44, 45
  Ac 14:17
  Jas 1:17

h Ps 19:1

i Ps 30:4
  Heb 13:15

j Lu 10:8, 9

k De 3:24
  1Ch 29:11
  Re 15:3

l Ps 98:1

m Ps 103:19

n Ps 146:10
  1Ti 1:17

144:10 *Or "salvation." 144:14 *Or
"rupture." 145:3 *Or "beyond understanding."

145:6 *Or "power." 145:8 *Or "gracious."

ס [Samekh]

14 Jehovah supports all who
   are falling[a]
   And raises up all who are
   bowed down.[b]

ע [Ayin]

15 All eyes look hopefully to
   you;
   You give them their food in
   its season.[c]

פ [Pe]

16 You open your hand
   And satisfy the desire of
   every living thing.[d]

צ [Tsade]

17 Jehovah is righteous in all
   his ways[e]
   And loyal in all that he does.[f]

ק [Qoph]

18 Jehovah is near to all those
   calling on him,[g]
   To all who call on him in
   truth.*[h]

ר [Resh]

19 He satisfies the desire of
   those who fear him;[i]
   He hears their cry for help,
   and he rescues them.[j]

ש [Shin]

20 Jehovah guards all those
   who love him,[k]
   But all the wicked he will annihilate.[l]

ת [Taw]

21 My mouth will declare the
   praise of Jehovah;[m]
   Let every living thing* praise
   his holy name forever and
   ever.[n]

146 Praise Jah!*[o]
        Let my whole being#
        praise Jehovah.[p]

 2 I will praise Jehovah all my
   life.
   I will sing praises# to my God
   as long as I live.

3 Do not put your trust in
   princes*
   Nor in a son of man, who
   cannot bring salvation.[a]

4 His spirit* goes out, he returns to the ground;[b]
   On that very day his
   thoughts perish.[c]

5 Happy is the one who has
   the God of Jacob as his
   helper,[d]
   Whose hope is in Jehovah
   his God,[e]

6 The Maker of heaven and
   earth,
   Of the sea, and of all that is
   in them,[f]
   The One who always remains
   faithful,[g]

7 The One securing justice for
   those defrauded,
   The One giving bread to the
   hungry.[h]
   Jehovah is releasing the
   prisoners.*[i]

8 Jehovah is opening the eyes
   of the blind;[j]
   Jehovah is raising up those
   bowed down;[k]
   Jehovah loves the righteous.

9 Jehovah is protecting the
   foreign residents;
   He sustains the fatherless
   child and the widow,[l]
   But he thwarts the plans of
   the wicked.*[m]

10 Jehovah will be King
   forever,[n]
   Your God, O Zion, for generation after generation.
   Praise Jah!*

147 Praise Jah!*
        It is good to sing prais-
        es# to our God;
        How pleasant and fitting it is
        to praise him![o]

 2 Jehovah is building Jerusalem;[p]

145:18 *Or "in sincerity." 145:21 *Lit.,
"all flesh." 146:1, 10; 147:1 *Or "Hallelujah!" "Jah" is a shortened form of the
name Jehovah. 146:1 #Or "my soul."
146:2; 147:1 #Or "make music."

146:3 *Or "nobles." 146:4 *Or
"breath." 146:7 *Lit., "bound ones."
146:9 *Or "makes the way of the wicked
crooked."

He gathers together the dispersed ones of Israel.[a]

3 He heals the brokenhearted;
He binds up their wounds.[b]

4 He counts the number of the stars;
He calls all of them by name.[c]

5 Our Lord is great and is mighty in power;[c]
His understanding is beyond measure.[d]

6 Jehovah raises up the meek,[e]
But he hurls the wicked to the ground.

7 Sing to Jehovah with thanksgiving;
Sing praises to our God, accompanied by the harp,

8 The One who covers the heavens with clouds,
The One providing rain for the earth,[f]
The One making grass sprout[g] on the mountains.

9 To the animals he gives food,[h]
To the young ravens that call out for it.[i]

10 He does not delight in the power of the horse;[j]
Nor is he impressed by the strong legs of a man.[k]

11 Jehovah finds pleasure in those who fear him,[l]
In those waiting for his loyal love.[m]

12 Glorify Jehovah, O Jerusalem.
Praise your God, O Zion.

13 He makes the bars of your city gates strong;
He blesses your sons within you.

14 He brings peace to your territory;[n]
He satisfies you with the finest* wheat.[o]

15 He sends his command to the earth;
His word runs swiftly.

16 He sends the snow like wool;[a]
He scatters the frost just like ashes.[b]

17 He hurls down his hailstones* like morsels of bread.[c]
Who can withstand his cold?[d]

18 He sends out his word, and they melt.
He makes his wind blow,[e] and the waters flow.

19 He declares his word to Jacob,
His regulations and judgments to Israel.[f]

20 He has not done so with any other nation;[g]
They know nothing about his judgments.
Praise Jah!*[h]

148

Praise Jah!*
Praise Jehovah from the heavens;[i]
Praise him in the heights.

2 Praise him, all his angels.[j]
Praise him, all his army.[k]

3 Praise him, sun and moon.
Praise him, all shining stars.[l]

4 Praise him, O highest heavens*
And waters above the heavens.

5 Let them praise the name of Jehovah,
For he commanded, and they were created.[m]

6 He keeps them established forever and ever;[n]
He has issued a decree that will not pass away.[o]

7 Praise Jehovah from the earth,
You great sea creatures and all deep waters,

8 You lightning and hail, snow and thick clouds,

CHAP. 147
a De 30:1-3
  Eze 36:24
b Isa 40:26
c Na 1:3
d Isa 40:28
  Ro 11:33
e Ps 37:11
f 1Ki 18:45
  Jer 14:22
  Mt 5:45
g Job 38:25-27
  Isa 30:23
h Ps 136:25
i Job 38:41
  Lu 12:24
j Isa 31:1
  Ho 1:7
k 1Sa 16:7
l Mal 3:16
m Ps 33:18
n Le 26:6
  Isa 60:17
o De 8:7, 8
  Ps 132:14, 15

Second Col.
a Job 37:6
b Job 38:29
c Jos 10:11
d Job 37:10
e Ps 148:8
f De 4:5
g Ex 19:5
  Ex 31:16, 17
  De 4:8
  1Ch 17:21
  Ro 3:1, 2
h Re 19:6

CHAP. 148
i Ps 89:5
j Ps 103:20
  Lu 2:13
k Jer 32:18
  Jude 14
l Ps 19:1
m Ps 33:6
n Ps 89:37
o Ps 119:91
  Jer 31:35, 36
  Jer 33:25

147:14 *Lit., "the fat of."

147:17 *Or "ice." 147:20; 148:1 *Or "Hallelujah!" "Jah" is a shortened form of the name Jehovah. 148:4 *Lit., "heavens of the heavens."

You storm wind, carrying out his word,[a]

9 You mountains and all you hills,[b]

You fruit trees and all you cedars,[c]

10 You wild animals[d] and all you domestic animals,

You creeping things and winged birds,

11 You kings of the earth and all you nations,

You princes and all you judges of the earth,[e]

12 You young men and young women,*

Old men and young together.#

13 Let them praise the name of Jehovah,

For his name alone is unreachably high.[f]

His majesty is above earth and heaven.[g]

14 He will exalt the strength* of his people,

For the praise of all his loyal ones,

Of the sons of Israel, the people close to him.

Praise Jah!#

149 Praise Jah!#
Sing to Jehovah a new song;[h]

Praise him in the congregation of the loyal ones.[i]

2 Let Israel rejoice in its Grand Maker;[j]

Let the sons of Zion be joyful in their King.

3 Let them praise his name with dancing[k]

And sing praises* to him, accompanied by the tambourine and the harp.[l]

4 For Jehovah takes pleasure in his people.[a]

He adorns the meek with salvation.[b]

5 Let the loyal ones exult in glory;

Let them shout for joy upon their beds.[c]

6 Let the songs praising God be in their throat,

And a two-edged sword be in their hand,

7 To execute vengeance on the nations

And punishment on the peoples,

8 To bind their kings with shackles

And their nobles with iron fetters,

9 To execute the judgment written against them.[d]

This honor belongs to all his loyal ones.

Praise Jah!#

150 Praise Jah!#[e]
Praise God in his holy place.[f]

Praise him in the expanse of* his strength.[g]

2 Praise him for his mighty works.[h]

Praise him for his exceeding greatness.[i]

3 Praise him with the sounding of the horn.[j]

Praise him with the stringed instrument and the harp.[k]

4 Praise him with the tambourine[l] and the circle dance.

Praise him with strings[m] and the flute.*[n]

5 Praise him with ringing cymbals.

Praise him with crashing cymbals.[o]

6 Every breathing thing—let it praise Jah.

Praise Jah!#[p]

CHAP. 148

a Ex 9:23
Ps 107:25
Isa 30:30

b Ps 98:8

c 1Ch 16:33
Isa 44:23

d Isa 43:20

e Ps 2:10, 11

f Ps 8:1
Isa 12:4

g 1Ki 8:27
1Ch 29:11

CHAP. 149

h Ps 33:3
Ps 96:1
Isa 42:10
Re 5:9

i Ps 22:22

j Ps 100:3
Isa 54:5

k Jg 11:34

l Ex 15:20
Ps 150:4

Second Col.

a Ps 84:11

b Ps 132:16
Isa 61:10

c Ps 63:6

d De 7:1

CHAP. 150

e Re 19:6

f Ps 116:19

g Ps 19:1

h Ps 107:15
Re 15:3

i De 3:24
Ps 145:3

j Ps 81:3

k 1Ch 15:28

l Ex 15:20

m Ps 92:1, 3
Ps 144:9

n 1Sa 10:5

o 2Sa 6:5
1Ch 15:19
1Ch 16:5

p Re 5:13

148:12 *Lit., "virgins." #Or "Old and young together." **148:14** *Lit., "the horn." **148:14; 149:1, 9; 150:1, 6** #Or "Hallelujah!" "Jah" is a shortened form of the name Jehovah. **149:3** *Or "make music."

150:1 *Or "the sky that bears witness to." **150:4** *Or "pipe."

PROVERBS

1 The proverbs of Sol'o·mon,[a] the son of David,[b] the king of Israel:[c]

2 To learn* wisdom[d] and discipline;
  To understand wise sayings;

3 To acquire the discipline[e] that gives insight,
  Righteousness,[f] good judgment,*[g] and uprightness;[#]

4 To impart shrewdness[h] to the inexperienced;
  To give a young man knowledge and thinking ability.[i]

5 A wise person listens and takes in more instruction;[j]
  A man of understanding acquires skillful direction*[k]

6 To understand a proverb and a puzzling saying,*
  The words of the wise and their riddles.[l]

7 The fear of* Jehovah is the beginning of knowledge.[m]
  Only fools despise wisdom and discipline.[n]

8 Listen, my son, to the discipline of your father,[o]
  And do not forsake the instruction* of your mother.[p]

9 They are an attractive wreath for your head[q]
  And a fine ornament for your neck.[r]

10 My son, if sinners try to entice you, do not consent.[s]

11 If they say: "Come with us,
  Let us set an ambush to shed blood,
  We will lie hidden, waiting for innocent victims without cause.

12 We will swallow them alive as the Grave* does,
  Whole, like those going down to the pit.

13 Let us seize all their precious treasures;
  We will fill our houses with spoil.

14 You should join us,*
  And we will all share equally what we steal."[#]

15 My son, do not follow them.
  Keep your feet off their path,[a]

16 For their feet run to do evil;
  They hurry to shed blood.[b]

17 It is surely in vain to spread a net in full sight of a bird.

18 That is why these lie in ambush to shed blood;
  They lie hidden to take the lives* of others.

19 These are the ways of those seeking dishonest profit,
  Which will take away the life* of those who obtain it.[c]

20 True wisdom[d] cries aloud in the street.[e]
  It keeps raising its voice in the public squares.[f]

21 At the corner* of the busy streets it calls out.
  At the entrances of the city gates it says:[g]

22 "How long will you inexperienced ones love inexperience?
  How long will you ridiculers take pleasure in ridicule?
  And how long will you foolish ones hate knowledge?[h]

23 Respond to my reproof.*[i]
  Then I will pour out my spirit for you;
  I will make my words known to you.[j]

24 Because I called out, but you kept refusing,
  I stretched out my hand, but no one was paying attention.[k]

CHAP. 1
a 1Ki 4:29, 32
  Ec 12:9
b 2Sa 12:24
c 1Ki 2:12
d Pr 8:11
e Pr 3:11, 12
f Heb 12:11
g 1Ki 3:28
h Pr 15:5
i Pr 2:11
  Pr 3:21
  Pr 8:12
j Pr 9:9
k 1Sa 25:32, 33
  Pr 24:6
l Ec 12:11
m Job 28:28
  Pr 9:10
n Pr 5:12, 13
  Pr 18:2
o De 6:6, 7
  Eph 6:4
  Heb 12:9
p Le 19:3
  Pr 31:26
  2Ti 1:5
q Pr 4:7, 9
r Pr 3:21, 22
s Ge 39:7, 8
  De 13:6-8

Second Col.
a Pr 4:14
  Pr 13:20
  1Co 15:33
b Pr 6:16-18
  Ro 3:15
c Pr 15:27
d Ro 16:27
  1Co 1:20
  Jas 3:17
e Mt 10:27
f Pr 8:1-3
  Pr 9:1, 3
g Joh 18:20
  Ac 20:20
h Pr 5:12, 13
  Joh 3:20
i Ps 141:5
  Re 3:19
j Isa 54:13
k Isa 65:12

1:2 *Lit., "To know." 1:3 *Or "what is just." #Or "fairness." 1:5 *Or "wise guidance." 1:6 *Or "a parable." 1:7 *Or "reverence for." 1:8 *Or "law." 1:12 *Or "Sheol," that is, the common grave of mankind. See Glossary.

1:14 *Or "Throw in your lot with us." #Or "share a common bag (purse)." 1:18 *Or "souls." 1:19 *Or "soul." 1:21 *Lit., "head." 1:23 *Or "Turn back when I reprove."

25 You kept neglecting all my
   advice
   And rejecting my reproof.
26 I also will laugh when disaster strikes you;
   I will mock when what you
   dread comes,[a]
27 When what you dread comes
   like a storm,
   And your disaster arrives
   like a storm wind,
   When distress and trouble
   come upon you.
28 At that time they will keep
   calling me, but I will not
   answer;
   They will eagerly look for
   me, but they will not
   find me,[b]
29 Because they hated knowledge,[c]
   And they did not choose to
   fear Jehovah.[d]
30 They refused my advice;
   They disrespected all my
   reproof.
31 So they will bear the consequences* of their way,[e]
   And they will be glutted with
   their own counsel.#
32 For the waywardness of
   the inexperienced will kill
   them,
   And the complacency of
   fools will destroy them.
33 But the one listening to me
   will dwell in security[f]
   And be undisturbed by the
   dread of calamity."[g]

2 My son, if you accept my
   sayings
   And treasure up my commandments,[h]
2 By making your ear attentive
   to wisdom[i]
   And inclining your heart to
   discernment;[j]
3 Moreover, if you call out for
   understanding[k]

And raise your voice for
   discernment;[a]
4 If you keep seeking for it as
   for silver,[b]
   And you keep searching for
   it as for hidden treasures;[c]
5 Then you will understand the
   fear of Jehovah,[d]
   And you will find the knowledge of God.[e]
6 For Jehovah himself gives
   wisdom;[f]
   From his mouth come knowledge and discernment.
7 He treasures up practical
   wisdom for the upright;
   He is a shield for those walking in integrity.[g]
8 He watches over the paths
   of justice,
   And he will guard the way
   of his loyal ones.[h]
9 Then you will understand
   what is righteous and just
   and fair,
   The entire course of what
   is good.[i]
10 When wisdom enters your
   heart[j]
   And knowledge becomes
   pleasant to your soul,*[k]
11 Thinking ability will keep
   watch over you,[l]
   And discernment will safeguard you,
12 To save you from the bad
   course,
   From the man speaking
   perverse things,[m]
13 From those leaving the
   upright paths
   To walk in the ways of darkness,[n]
14 From those who rejoice in
   wrongdoing,
   Who find joy in the perverse-
   ness of evil,
15 Those whose paths are
   crooked
   And whose entire course
   is devious.

CHAP. 1
a Jg 10:13, 14
b La 3:44
c Ho 4:6
d Jg 5:8
e Jer 6:19
  Ga 6:7
f Isa 48:18
g 2Ki 6:15, 16
  Isa 26:3
  2Pe 2:9

CHAP. 2
h De 6:6, 8
i Pr 1:5
j Heb 5:14
k 1Ki 3:11, 12
  Pr 9:10
  2Ti 2:7

Second Col.
a Php 1:9
b Ps 19:9, 10
c Job 28:15-18
d Job 28:28
  Pr 8:13
  Jer 32:40
e Jer 9:24
  1Jo 5:20
f Ex 31:2, 3
  1Ki 4:29
  2Ti 3:16, 17
  Jas 3:17
g Ps 41:12
  Pr 28:18
h Ps 97:10
i Ec 12:13
  Mic 6:8
  Mt 22:37-40
j Ps 119:111
k Ac 17:11
l Ec 7:12
m Pr 8:13
n Joh 3:19

1:31 *Lit., "eat from the fruit." #Or
"schemes; plans."

2:10 *See Glossary.

16 It will save you from the wayward* woman,

From the smooth# words of the immoral△ woman,ᵃ

17 Who abandons the close companion* of her youthᵇ

And forgets the covenant of her God;

18 For her house sinks down into death,

And her paths* lead to those powerless in death.ᶜ

19 None of those having relations with* her will return,

Nor will they regain the pathways of life.ᵈ

20 So follow the way of good people

And stay on the paths of the righteous,ᵉ

21 For only the upright will reside in the earth,

And the blameless* will remain in it.ᶠ

22 As for the wicked, they will be cut off from the earth,ᵍ

And the treacherous will be torn away from it.ʰ

3 My son, do not forget my teaching,*

And may your heart observe my commandments,

2 Because they will add many days

And years of life and peace to you.ⁱ

3 Do not let loyal love and faithfulness* leave you.ʲ

Tie them around your neck;

Write them on the tablet of your heart;ᵏ

4 Then you will find favor and good insight

In the eyes of God and man.ˡ

5 Trust in Jehovahᵃ with all your heart,

And do not rely* on your own understanding.ᵇ

6 In all your ways take notice of him,ᶜ

And he will make your paths straight.ᵈ

7 Do not become wise in your own eyes.ᵉ

Fear Jehovah and turn away from bad.

8 It will be a healing to your body*

And refreshment for your bones.

9 Honor Jehovah with your valuable things,ᶠ

With the firstfruits* of all your produce;#ᵍ

10 Then your storehouses will be completely filled,ʰ

And your vats* will overflow with new wine.

11 My son, do not reject the discipline of Jehovah,ⁱ

And do not loathe his reproof,ʲ

12 For those whom Jehovah loves he reproves,ᵏ

Just as a father does a son in whom he delights.

13 Happy is the man who finds wisdomᵐ

And the man who acquires discernment;

14 To gain it is better than gaining silver,

And having it as profit is better than having gold.ⁿ

15 It is more precious than corals;*

Nothing you desire can compare to it.

16 Long life is in its right hand;

Riches and glory are in its left hand.

CHAP. 2

a Ge 39:10-12
  Pr 6:23, 24
  Pr 7:4, 5

b Ge 2:24
  Pr 5:18

c Pr 5:3, 5
  Pr 5:20, 23
  Pr 9:16-18
  Eph 5:5

d Ec 7:26
  Re 22:15

e Pr 13:20

f Ps 37:11, 29

g Ps 104:35
  Pr 10:7
  Mt 25:46

h De 28:45, 63

CHAP. 3

i De 5:16

j Ho 12:6

k De 6:6, 8

l 2Co 8:21

Second Col.

a Isa 26:4
  Jer 17:7

b Pr 28:26
  Jer 10:23
  1Co 3:18

c 1Sa 23:2, 4
  Ne 1:11
  Php 4:6

d Jos 1:7
  Ps 25:9
  Jas 1:5

e Pr 26:12
  Ro 12:16

f Nu 31:50
  De 16:16
  Lu 16:9
  1Ti 6:18

g Ex 23:19

h 2Ch 31:10
  Mal 3:10

i Pr 15:32
  Heb 12:5, 6

j Ps 94:12

k Re 3:19

l De 8:5
  Heb 12:7, 9

m Ec 7:12

n Job 28:15, 18

2:16 *Lit., "strange." Evidently, one morally estranged from God. #Or "seductive." △Lit., "foreign." Evidently, one morally alienated from God. **2:17** *Or "the husband." **2:18** *Lit., "tracks." **2:19** *Lit., "going in to." **2:21** *Or "the one who keeps integrity." **3:1** *Or "law." **3:3** *Or "truth."

3:5 *Lit., "lean." **3:8** *Lit., "navel." **3:9** *Or "very best." #Or "income." **3:10** *Or "winepresses." **3:15** *See Glossary.

17 Its ways are pleasant,
And all its paths are peaceful.[a]

18 It is a tree of life to those who take hold of it,
And those who keep firm hold of it will be called happy.[b]

19 Jehovah founded the earth in wisdom.[c]
He solidly established the heavens in discernment.[d]

20 By his knowledge the watery deeps were split apart
And the cloudy skies dripped with dew.[e]

21 My son, do not lose sight of them.*
Safeguard practical wisdom and thinking ability;

22 They will give you* life
And be an adornment for your neck;

23 Then you will walk on your way in safety,
And your foot will never stumble.*[f]

24 When you lie down, you will have no fear;[g]
You will lie down, and your sleep will be pleasant.[h]

25 You will not fear any sudden terror[i]
Nor the storm that is coming on the wicked.[j]

26 For Jehovah will prove to be your source of confidence;[k]
He will keep your foot from being caught.[l]

27 Do not withhold good from those to whom you should give it*[m]
If it is within your power# to help.[n]

28 Do not say to your neighbor, "Go away; come back later! I will give it to you tomorrow,"
If you can give it now.

29 Do not plot harm against your neighbor[a]
When he lives in a sense of security with you.

30 Do not quarrel with a man for no reason[b]
If he has done nothing bad to you.[c]

31 Do not envy the violent man[d]
Nor choose any of his ways,

32 For Jehovah detests a devious person,[e]
But His close friendship is with the upright.[f]

33 The curse of Jehovah is on the house of the wicked one,[g]
But he blesses the home of the righteous.[h]

34 For he mocks those who ridicule,[i]
But he shows favor to the meek.[j]

35 The wise will inherit honor,
But the stupid ones glorify dishonor.[k]

4 Listen, my sons, to the discipline of a father;[l]
Pay attention in order to gain understanding,

2 For I will give you good instruction;
Do not forsake my teaching.*[m]

3 I was a true son to my father[n]
And the one especially loved by my mother.[o]

4 He taught me and said:
"May your heart hold fast to my words.[p]
Keep my commandments and continue living.[q]

5 Acquire wisdom, acquire understanding.[r]
Do not forget, and do not turn aside from what I say.

CHAP. 3
a Php 4:9
b Ps 1:1, 2
c Ps 104:24
d Pr 8:27
  Jer 10:12
e Job 36:27
  Job 38:37
  Jer 10:13
f Isa 26:7
g Ps 3:5
  Pr 6:22
h Ec 5:12
i Ps 27:1
j Ps 73:12, 19
k Pr 10:29
  Pr 28:1
l Ps 91:14
m Jas 2:15, 16
n De 15:7, 8
  Pr 28:27

Second Col.
a Pr 6:16, 18
b Pr 18:6
  Pr 20:3
c Ro 12:18
d Ps 37:1
  Pr 23:17
e Pr 6:16, 17
f Ps 15:1, 2
  Pr 24:3, 4
  Ps 25:14
g De 28:15
  Jos 7:24, 25
  Es 9:24, 25
h Job 42:12, 13
  Ps 37:25
i Pr 19:29
j Ps 37:11
  Ps 138:6
  Isa 57:15
  Jas 4:6
k Es 6:11, 12
  Pr 12:8

CHAP. 4
l De 6:6, 7
  Pr 19:20
  Eph 6:1
m 1Ch 28:9
n 1Ki 2:12
o 1Ki 1:16-21
p De 4:9
q Le 18:5
r Ne 8:3, 8
  Pr 9:10

3:21 *Evidently referring to God's qualities mentioned in the previous verses. 3:22 *Or "your soul." 3:23 *Or "strike against anything." 3:27 *Or "to whom it is owing." #Or "within the power of your hand."

4:2 *Or "law."

6 Do not forsake it, and it will
   protect you.
   Love it, and it will safeguard
   you.
7 Wisdom is the most important* thing,[a] so acquire
   wisdom,
   And with all you acquire,
   acquire understanding.[b]
8 Highly esteem it, and it will
   exalt you.[c]
   It will honor you because you
   embrace it.[d]
9 It will place an attractive
   wreath on your head;
   It will adorn you with a
   crown of beauty."
10 Listen, my son, and accept
   my sayings,
   And the years of your life
   will be many.[e]
11 I will instruct you in the way
   of wisdom;[f]
   I will lead you in the tracks
   of uprightness.[g]
12 When you walk, your steps
   will not be hindered;
   And if you run, you will not
   stumble.
13 Hold on to discipline; do not
   let it go.[h]
   Safeguard it, for it means
   your life.[i]
14 Do not enter the path of the
   wicked,
   And do not walk in the way
   of evil men.[j]
15 Shun it, do not take it;[k]
   Turn away from it, and pass
   it by.[l]
16 For they cannot sleep unless
   they do what is bad.
   They are robbed of sleep unless they cause someone's
   downfall.
17 They feed themselves with
   the bread of wickedness,
   And they drink the wine of
   violence.

18 But the path of the righteous
   is like the bright morning
   light
   That grows brighter
   and brighter until full daylight.[a]
19 The way of the wicked is like
   the darkness;
   They do not know what
   makes them stumble.
20 My son, pay attention to my
   words;
   Listen carefully* to my
   sayings.
21 Do not lose sight of them;
   Keep them deep within your
   heart,[b]
22 For they are life to those who
   find them[c]
   And health to their whole
   body.*
23 Above all the things that
   you guard, safeguard your
   heart,[d]
   For out of it are the sources
   of life.
24 Put crooked speech away
   from you,[e]
   And keep devious talk far
   away from you.
25 Your eyes should look
   straight ahead,
   Yes, fix your gaze* straight
   ahead of you.[f]
26 Smooth out* the course of
   your feet,[g]
   And all your ways will be
   sure.
27 Do not incline to the right
   or the left.[h]
   Turn your feet away from
   what is bad.

5 My son, pay attention to
   my wisdom.
   Listen carefully* to my
   discernment,[i]
2 So that you may guard your
   thinking abilities

Cross references

CHAP. 4
a Ec 7:12

b Pr 15:14
  Mt 13:23
  Heb 5:14

c Da 1:17, 20

d 1Ki 4:29

e De 5:16

f 1Ki 4:29

g Isa 26:7

h Pr 8:10
  Heb 2:1
  Heb 12:5, 6

i De 32:45-47
  Heb 12:11

j Ps 1:1
  1Co 15:33

k Am 5:15
  Eph 5:11

l Pr 5:3, 8
  1Th 5:22

Second Col.
a 2Sa 23:3, 4
  Ps 119:105
  1Co 13:12
  2Co 4:6
  2Pe 1:19

b Ps 40:8
  Pr 2:1

c 1Ti 4:8

d Jer 17:9
  Mr 7:21-23
  Eph 6:14

e 1Pe 2:1

f Mt 6:22

g Eph 5:15

h De 12:32
  Jos 1:7

CHAP. 5
i 1Ki 4:29
  Jas 1:19

Footnotes

4:7 *Or "the prime." 4:20; 5:1 *Lit., "Incline your ear." 4:22 *Lit., "to all their flesh." 4:25 *Or "beaming eyes." 4:26 *Or possibly, "Carefully consider."

And safeguard knowledge with your lips.[a]

3 For the lips of a wayward* woman drip like a honeycomb,[b]

And her mouth is smoother than oil.[c]

4 But in the end she is as bitter as wormwood[d]

And as sharp as a two-edged sword.[e]

5 Her feet descend into death. Her steps lead straight to the Grave.*

6 She gives no thought to the path of life.

Her course wanders, but she does not know where.

7 Now, my sons, listen to me And do not turn away from what I am saying.

8 Stay far away from her; Do not go near the entrance of her house,[f]

9 So that you may not give your dignity to others[g]

Nor reap years of what is cruel;[h]

10 So that strangers may not drain your resources*[i]

And what you labored for go to the house of a foreigner.

11 Otherwise, you will groan at the end of your life

When your flesh and body waste away[j]

12 And you say: "How I hated discipline!

How my heart despised reproof!

13 I did not listen to the voice of my instructors

Or pay attention to my teachers.

14 I have come to the brink of complete ruin

In the midst of the entire congregation."*[k]

15 Drink water from your own cistern

And flowing* water from your own well.[b]

16 Should your springs be dispersed outside,

Your streams of water in the public squares?[b]

17 Let them be for you alone, And not for strangers with you.[c]

18 May your own fountain* be blessed,

And may you rejoice with the wife of your youth,[d]

19 A loving doe, a graceful mountain goat.*[e]

Let her breasts satisfy# you at all times.

May you be captivated by her love constantly.[f]

20 So why, my son, should you be captivated by a wayward* woman

Or embrace the bosom of an immoral# woman?[g]

21 For the ways of man are before the eyes of Jehovah; He examines all his paths.[h]

22 The wicked one is ensnared by his own errors,

And he will be caught in the ropes of his own sin.[i]

23 He will die for lack of discipline

And go astray because of his excessive foolishness.

6 My son, if you have put up security* for your neighbor,[j]

If you have given your handshake# to a stranger,[k]

2 If you have been ensnared by your promise,

Caught by the words of your mouth,[l]

3 Do this, my son, and free yourself,

CHAP. 5
a Pr 15:7
b Pr 7:14-21
c Pr 9:16, 17
d Ec 7:26
e Pr 6:32, 33
f Pr 9:14, 15
g Pr 29:3
h Pr 6:33-35
  Pr 7:23
i Pr 31:3
  Lu 15:30
j Pr 7:22, 23
k Pr 6:27-29

Second Col.
a 1Co 7:3
  Heb 13:4
b Pr 5:20
c Ge 2:24
d De 24:5
  Ec 9:9
e Ca 2:9
f Ge 26:8
  Ge 29:20
  Ca 8:6
g Pr 22:14
h 2Ch 16:9
  Ps 11:4
  Ps 17:3
  Jer 17:10
  Heb 4:13
i Ps 7:14-16
  Ga 6:7

CHAP. 6
j Pr 17:18
k Pr 11:15
  Pr 20:16
l Pr 18:7

5:3, 20 *Lit., "strange." See Pr 2:16. 5:5 *Or "Sheol," that is, the common grave of mankind. See Glossary. 5:10 *Or "power." 5:14 *Lit., "In the midst of the assembly and the congregation." 5:15 *Or "fresh." 5:18 *Or "water source." 5:19 *Or "ibex." #Or "intoxicate." 5:20 #Lit., "foreign." See Pr 2:16. 6:1 *Lit., "gone surety." #That is, in a pledge.

For you have fallen into the hand of your neighbor:

Go and humble yourself and urgently plead with your neighbor.[a]

4 Do not allow your eyes to sleep,

Nor your eyelids to slumber.

5 Free yourself like a gazelle from the hunter's hand,

Like a bird from the hand of the birdcatcher.

6 Go to the ant, you lazy one;[b]

Observe its ways and become wise.

7 Although it has no commander, officer, or ruler,

8 It prepares its food in the summer,[c]

And it gathers its food supplies in the harvest.

9 How long, you lazy one, will you lie there?

When will you rise up from your sleep?

10 A little sleep, a little slumbering,

A little folding of the hands to rest,[d]

11 And your poverty will come like a bandit,

And your want like an armed man.[e]

12 A useless and wicked man walks about with crooked speech;[f]

13 He winks with his eye,[g] signals with his foot, and motions with his fingers.

14 With a perverted heart, He is always scheming evil[h] and spreading contentions.[i]

15 Therefore, his disaster will come suddenly;

In a moment he will be broken beyond healing.[j]

16 There are six things that Jehovah hates;

Yes, seven things that he* detests:

17 Haughty eyes,[a] a lying tongue,[b] and hands that shed innocent blood,[c]

18 A heart plotting wicked schemes,[d] and feet that run quickly to evil,

19 A false witness who lies with every breath,[e]

And anyone sowing contentions among brothers.[f]

20 Observe, my son, the commandment of your father,

And do not forsake the instruction* of your mother.[g]

21 Always bind them around your heart;

Tie them about your neck.

22 When you walk about, it will lead you;

When you lie down, it will stand guard over you;

And when you awaken, it will speak to you.*

23 For the commandment is a lamp,[h]

And the law is a light,[i]

And the reproofs of discipline are the way to life.[j]

24 They will guard you against the bad woman,[k]

Against the seductive tongue of the immoral* woman.[l]

25 Do not desire her beauty in your heart[m]

Or allow her to captivate you with her alluring eyes,

26 For because of a prostitute, a man is reduced to a loaf of bread,[n]

But the wife of another man preys on a precious life.*

27 Can a man rake fire to his chest and not burn his garments?[o]

28 Or can a man walk on hot coals without scorching his feet?

29 It is the same with anyone having relations with his neighbor's wife;

CHAP. 6

a Mt 5:25

b Pr 10:26
  Pr 26:13-15

c Pr 30:24, 25

d Pr 20:13
  Pr 24:33, 34
  Ec 4:5

e Pr 13:4
  Pr 20:4
  Pr 24:30-34

f Pr 16:27
  Jas 3:6

g Pr 10:10
  Pr 16:30

h Ps 36:1, 4
  Isa 32:7
  Mic 2:1

i Pr 16:28
  Ro 16:17

j Ps 73:12, 18

Second Col.

a Ps 101:5
  Pr 8:13
  Pr 16:5

b Pr 12:22
  Re 21:8

c Ge 4:8, 10
  Nu 35:31
  De 27:25

d Pr 11:20
  Zec 8:17
  Mal 2:16

e Ex 23:1

f Le 19:16
  Ga 5:20, 21
  Jas 3:14, 15

g De 21:18, 21
  Eph 6:1

h Ps 119:105

i Isa 51:4

j Pr 4:13
  Heb 12:11

k Ec 7:26

l Pr 5:3
  Pr 7:4, 5

m Mt 5:28
  Jas 1:14, 15

n Pr 29:3
  Lu 15:16, 30

o Ga 6:7

6:16 *Or "his soul."

6:20 *Or "law." 6:22 *Or "instruct you." 6:24 *Lit., "foreign." See Pr 2:16. 6:26 *Or "soul."

No one who touches her will go unpunished.[a]

30 People do not despise a thief
If he steals to satisfy himself* when he is hungry.

31 Yet, when found, he will repay sevenfold;
He will give up all the valuables of his house.[b]

32 Anyone committing adultery with a woman is lacking good sense;*
The one who does so brings ruin on himself.[#c]

33 He will get only wounds and dishonor,[d]
And his disgrace will not be wiped away.[e]

34 For jealousy makes a husband furious;
He will show no compassion when he takes revenge.[f]

35 He will accept no compensation;*
He will not be appeased, no matter how large you make the gift.

7 My son, keep my sayings,
And treasure up my commandments.[g]

2 Keep my commandments and live;[h]
Guard my instruction* like the pupil of your eye.

3 Tie them around your fingers;
Write them on the tablet of your heart.[i]

4 Say to wisdom, "You are my sister,"
And call understanding "my relative,"

5 To guard you against the wayward* woman,[j]
Against the immoral# woman and her smooth△ words.[k]

---

6 From the window of my house,
Through my lattice, I looked down,

7 And as I observed the naive# ones,
I discerned among the youths a young man lacking good sense.*[a]

8 He passed along the street near her corner,
And he marched in the direction of her house

9 In the twilight, in the evening,[b]
At the approach of night and darkness,

10 Then I saw a woman meet him,
Dressed like* a prostitute,[c] with a cunning heart.

11 She is loud and defiant.[d]
She never stays* at home.

12 One moment she is outside, next she is in the public squares,
She lurks near every corner.[e]

13 She grabs hold of him and gives him a kiss;
With a bold face, she says to him:

14 "I had to offer communion sacrifices.[f]
Today I paid my vows.

15 That is why I came out to meet you,
To look for you, and I found you!

16 I have spread fine covers upon my bed,
Colorful linen from Egypt.[g]

17 I have sprinkled my bed with myrrh, aloes, and cinnamon.[h]

18 Come, let us drink our fill of love until the morning;
Let us enjoy passionate love together,

CHAP. 6
a 2Sa 11:4
2Sa 12:10, 11
Pr 6:32-35
Heb 13:4

b Ex 22:1, 4

c Pr 2:18, 19
Pr 5:20, 23
Mal 3:5
1Co 6:9, 10
Heb 13:4

d Pr 5:8, 9

e 1Ki 15:5
1Ch 5:1
Mt 1:6

f Ge 39:19, 20

CHAP. 7
g Pr 10:14

h Le 18:5
De 5:16
Isa 55:3
Joh 12:50

i Pr 2:10, 11

j Pr 23:27, 28

k Pr 2:11, 16
Pr 5:3
Pr 6:23, 24

Second Col.
a Pr 6:32
Pr 9:16, 17

b Job 24:15

c Jer 4:30

d Pr 9:13-18

e Pr 23:27, 28

f Le 19:5

g Eze 27:7

h Ca 3:6
Ca 4:14

6:30 *Or "fill his soul." 6:32 *Lit., "in want of heart." 6:32 #Or "his soul." 6:35 *Or "ransom." 7:2 *Or "law." 7:5 *Lit., "strange." See Pr 2:16. #Lit., "foreign." See Pr 2:16. △Or "seductive."

7:7 #Or "inexperienced." 7:10 *Or "with the garment of." 7:11 *Lit., "Her feet never stay."

19 For my husband is not at
home;

He has gone on a distant
journey.

20 He took a bag of money with
him,

And he will not return until
the day of the full moon."

21 She misleads him with great
persuasiveness.*

She seduces him with
smooth speech.

22 Suddenly he goes after her,
like a bull to the slaughter,

Like a fool to be punished in
the stocks,*b

23 Until an arrow pierces his
liver;

Like a bird rushing into a
trap, he does not know
that it will cost him his
life.*c

24 And now, my sons, listen
to me;

Pay attention to the words
I speak.

25 Do not let your heart turn
aside to her ways.

Do not stray onto her paths,d

26 For she has caused many to
fall down slain,e

And those she has killed are
numerous.f

27 Her house leads to the
Grave;*

It goes down to the inner
chambers of death.

8 Is not wisdom calling out?

Is not discernment raising
its voice?g

2 On the heightsh along the
road,

It takes its position at the
crossroads.

3 Next to the gates leading into
the city,

At the entrances of the doorways,

It keeps crying out loudly:a

4 "To you, O people, I am
calling;

I raise my voice to everyone.*

5 You inexperienced ones,
learn shrewdness;b

You stupid ones, acquire an
understanding heart.*

6 Listen, for what I say is
important,

My lips speak what is right;

7 For my mouth softly utters
truth,

And my lips detest what is
wicked.

8 All the sayings of my mouth
are righteous.

None of them are twisted or
crooked.

9 They are all straightforward
to the discerning

And right to those who have
found knowledge.

10 Take my discipline instead
of silver,

And knowledge rather than
the finest gold,c

11 For wisdom is better than
corals;*

All other desirable things
cannot compare to it.

12 I, wisdom, dwell together
with shrewdness;

I have found knowledge and
thinking ability.d

13 The fear of Jehovah means
the hating of bad.e

I hate self-exaltation and
pridef and the evil way and
perverse speech.g

14 I possess good advice and
practical wisdom;h

Understandingi and poweri
are mine.

15 By me kings keep reigning,

And high officials decree
righteousness.k

CHAP. 7

a Pr 5:3

b 1Co 6:18

c Pr 5:8-11

d Pr 5:8

e Ec 7:26

f 1Co 10:8

CHAP. 8

g Pr 1:20, 21

h Mt 10:27

Second Col.

a Ac 20:20

b Ps 19:7

c Ps 19:9, 10
Ps 119:72,
127
Pr 3:13-15

d Pr 2:11
Pr 5:1, 2

e Ps 97:10
Ps 101:3
Pr 16:6
Ro 12:9

f Ps 101:5
1Pe 5:5

g Pr 4:24

h Pr 2:7

i Pr 4:7

j Pr 24:5

k Ps 72:1

7:22 *Or "fetters." **7:23** *Or "soul."
7:27 *Or "Sheol," that is, the common
grave of mankind. See Glossary.

8:4 *Lit., "to the sons of men." **8:5**
*Lit., "understand heart." **8:11** *See
Glossary.

16 By me princes keep ruling,
And nobles judge in righteousness.

17 I love those loving me,
And those seeking me will find me.[a]

18 Riches and glory are with me,
Lasting wealth* and righteousness.

19 My fruitage is better than gold, even refined gold,
And what I produce is better than the finest silver.[b]

20 I walk in the path of righteousness,
In the middle of the pathways of justice;

21 I give a rich inheritance to those who love me,
And I fill up their storehouses.

22 Jehovah produced me as the beginning of his way,[c]
The earliest of his achievements of long ago.[d]

23 From ancient times* I was installed,[e]
From the start, from times earlier than the earth.[f]

24 When there were no deep waters,[g] I was brought forth,*
When there were no springs overflowing with water.

25 Before the mountains were set in place,
Before the hills, I was brought forth,

26 When he had not yet made the earth and its fields
Or the first clods of earth's soil.

27 When he prepared the heavens,[h] I was there;
When he marked out the horizon* on the surface of the waters,[i]

28 When he established* the clouds above,
When he founded the fountains of the deep,

29 When he set a decree for the sea
That its waters should not pass beyond his order,[a]
When he established* the foundations of the earth,

30 Then I was beside him as a master worker.[b]
I was the one he was especially fond of[c] day by day;
I rejoiced before him all the time;[d]

31 I rejoiced over his habitable earth,
And I was especially fond of the sons of men.*

32 And now, my sons, listen to me;
Yes, happy are those who keep my ways.

33 Listen to discipline[e] and become wise,
And never neglect it.

34 Happy is the man who listens to me
By coming early to* my doors day by day,
By waiting next to my doorposts;

35 For the one finding me will find life,[f]
And he receives approval from Jehovah.

36 But the one who ignores me harms himself,*
And those who hate me love death."[g]

9 True wisdom has built its house;
It has carved* out its seven pillars.

2 It has fully prepared its meat;*

CHAP. 8
a Pr 2:4, 5

b Pr 3:13, 14

c Joh 1:1-3, 14

d Col 1:15-17

e Mic 5:2

f Joh 8:58
Joh 17:5

g Ge 1:2

h Ps 33:6
Jer 10:12

i Ge 1:6, 7
Job 26:10

Second Col.
a Job 38:8-11
Ps 33:7
Ps 104:6-9
Jer 5:22

b Ge 1:26
Joh 1:1, 3
Joh 17:5
Col 1:15, 16

c Isa 42:1
Mt 3:17

d Job 38:7

e Pr 3:11
Pr 4:13
Heb 12:7, 9

f Pr 13:14

g Pr 5:23

8:18 *Or "Hereditary values." 8:23 *Or "From time immemorial." 8:24 *Or "brought forth as with labor pains." 8:27 *Lit., "a circle." 8:28 *Lit., "made strong." 8:29 *Or "decreed." 8:31 *Or "mankind." 8:34 *Or "By keeping awake at." 8:36 *Or "his soul." 9:1 *Or "hewed." 9:2 *Lit., "She has slaughtered her slaughtering."

It has mixed its wine;
It has also arranged its table.

3 It has sent out its female
servants
To call out from the heights
above the city:[a]

4 "Whoever is inexperienced,
let him come in here."
She says to the one lacking
good sense:*

5 "Come, eat my bread
And share in drinking the
wine that I have mixed.

6 Leave behind your inexperience* and live;[b]
Walk forward in the way of
understanding."[c]

7 The one who corrects a ridiculer invites dishonor,[d]
And whoever reproves someone wicked will get hurt.

8 Do not reprove a ridiculer,
or he will hate you.[e]
Reprove a wise person, and
he will love you.[f]

9 Share with a wise person,
and he will become wiser.[g]
Teach someone righteous,
and he will add to his
learning.

10 The fear of Jehovah is the
beginning of wisdom,[h]
And knowledge of the Most
Holy One[i] is understanding.

11 For by me your days will
be many,[j]
And years will be added
to your life.

12 If you become wise, you
are wise to your own
advantage,
But if you are a ridiculer,
you alone will bear it.

13 A stupid woman is loud.[k]
She is ignorant and knows
absolutely nothing.

14 She sits at the entrance
of her house

On a seat in the high places
of the city,[a]

15 Calling out to those
passing by,
To those walking straight
ahead on their way:

16 "Whoever is inexperienced,
let him come in here."
She says to those lacking
good sense:*[b]

17 "Stolen waters are sweet,
And food eaten in secret is
pleasant."[c]

18 But he does not know that
those powerless in death
are there,
That her guests are in the
depths of the Grave.*[d]

10 Proverbs of Sol′o·mon.[e]
A wise son makes his
father rejoice,[f]
But a foolish son is the grief
of his mother.

2 The treasures gained by
wickedness will be of no
benefit,
But righteousness is what
rescues from death.[g]

3 Jehovah will not cause
the righteous one* to go
hungry,[h]
But he will deny the wicked
what they crave.

4 Idle hands will cause
poverty,[i]
But diligent hands bring
riches.[j]

5 The son acting with insight
gathers the crop in
summer,
But the son acting shame-
fully is fast asleep during
the harvest.[k]

6 Blessings are on the head of
the righteous one,[l]
But the mouth of the wicked
conceals violence.

CHAP. 9
a Pr 1:20-22
b Ps 119:130
c Pr 4:5
  Pr 13:20
d Pr 15:12
e 1Ki 21:20, 21
  1Ki 22:8
  2Ch 25:15, 16
  Mt 7:6
f Ps 141:5
  Pr 27:6
  Pr 28:23
g Pr 1:5
  Pr 15:31
  Pr 17:10
  Pr 25:12
h Ps 111:10
i 1Ch 28:9
  Mt 11:27
  Joh 17:3
j De 6:1, 2
  Pr 8:35
  Pr 10:27
k Pr 7:10, 11

Second Col.
a Pr 23:27, 28
b Pr 6:32
c Pr 7:18, 19
d Pr 2:18, 19
  Pr 7:23, 26
  Pr 23:27, 28

CHAP. 10
e Pr 1:1
f Pr 13:1
  Pr 27:11
g Pr 11:4
h Ps 33:18, 19
  Ps 37:25
  Mt 6:33
i Pr 20:4
  Ec 10:18
j Pr 12:24
  Pr 13:4
  Pr 21:5
k Pr 6:6, 9
l Ex 23:25
  Pr 28:20

9:4, 16 *Lit., "in want of heart." 9:6
*Or "the inexperienced ones."

9:18 *Or "Sheol," that is, the common
grave of mankind. See Glossary. 10:3
*Or "the soul of the righteous one."

7 The memory* of the righteous one is due for a blessing,[a]

But the name of the wicked will rot.[b]

8 The wisehearted person will accept instructions,*[c]

But the one speaking foolishly will be trodden down.[d]

9 The one walking in integrity will walk in security,[e]

But the one making his ways crooked will be found out.[f]

10 The one who slyly winks his eye causes grief,[g]

And the one who speaks foolishly will be trodden down.[h]

11 The mouth of the righteous one is a source of life,[i]

But the mouth of the wicked conceals violence.[j]

12 Hatred is what stirs up contentions,

But love covers over all transgressions.[k]

13 Wisdom is found on the lips of the discerning person,[l]

But the rod is for the back of one lacking good sense.*[m]

14 Those who are wise treasure up knowledge,[n]

But the mouth of the fool invites ruin.[o]

15 The wealth* of a rich man is his fortified city.

The ruin of the poor is their poverty.[p]

16 The activity of the righteous one leads to life;

But the produce of the wicked one leads to sin.[q]

17 The one who heeds discipline is a path to life,*

But the one who ignores reproof leads others astray.

18 The one who conceals his hatred speaks lies,[a]

And the one spreading malicious reports* is stupid.

19 When words are many, transgression cannot be avoided,[b]

But whoever controls his lips acts discreetly.[c]

20 The tongue of the righteous one is like the finest silver,[d]

But the heart of the wicked one is worth little.

21 The lips of the righteous one nourish* many,[e]

But the foolish die for lack of sense.[f]

22 It is the blessing of Jehovah that makes one rich,[g]

And He adds no pain* with it.

23 Engaging in shameful conduct is like a game to the stupid one,

But wisdom is for the man of discernment.[h]

24 What the wicked one fears will come upon him;

But the desire of the righteous one will be granted.[i]

25 When the storm passes by, the wicked one will be no more,[j]

But the righteous one is a foundation forever.[k]

26 Like vinegar to the teeth and smoke to the eyes,

So the lazy person is to the one who sends him.*

27 The fear of Jehovah prolongs life,[l]

But the years of the wicked will be cut short.[m]

28 The expectation* of the righteous brings joy,[n]

But the hope of the wicked will perish.[o]

29 The way of Jehovah is a stronghold for the blameless one,[p]

10:7 *Or "reputation." **10:8** *Lit., "commandments." **10:13** *Lit., "in want of heart." **10:15** *Or "valuable thing." **10:17** *Or possibly, "is on the path to life."

10:18 *Or "rumors." **10:21** *Or "guide." **10:22** *Or "sorrow; hardship." **10:26** *Or "to his employer." **10:28** *Or "hope."

But it means ruin for evil-doers.[a]

30 The righteous one will never be made to fall,[b]

But the wicked will no longer inhabit the earth.[c]

31 The mouth of the righteous one produces* wisdom,

But the perverse tongue will be cut off.

32 The lips of the righteous one know what is pleasing,

But the mouth of the wicked is perverse.

11 Dishonest* scales are detestable to Jehovah,

But an accurate weight# brings pleasure to him.[d]

2 When presumptuousness comes, dishonor will follow,[e]

But wisdom is with the modest ones.[f]

3 The integrity of the upright is what guides them,[g]

But the deviousness of the treacherous will destroy them.[h]

4 Wealth* will be of no benefit on the day of fury,[i]

But righteousness is what will rescue from death.[j]

5 The righteousness of the blameless one makes his path straight,

But the wicked one will fall because of his own wickedness.[k]

6 The righteousness of the upright will rescue them,[l]

But the treacherous will be caught by their own desires.[m]

7 When a wicked man dies, his hope perishes;

And expectations based on his power also perish.[n]

8 The righteous one is rescued from distress,

And the wicked one takes his place.[a]

9 By his mouth the apostate* brings his neighbor to ruin,

But by knowledge the righteous are rescued.[b]

10 The goodness of the righteous makes a city rejoice,

And when the wicked perish, there is a joyful cry.[c]

11 Because of the blessing of the upright a city is exalted,[d]

But the mouth of the wicked tears it down.[e]

12 Whoever is lacking good sense* shows contempt for# his neighbor,

But the man of true discernment remains silent.[f]

13 A slanderer goes about revealing confidential talk,[g]

But the trustworthy person* keeps a confidence.#

14 When there is no skillful direction,* the people fall,

But there is success* through many advisers.△[h]

15 Whoever guarantees a loan* for a stranger is sure to fare badly,[i]

But whoever avoids# shaking hands in a pledge will be secure.

16 A gracious* woman acquires glory,[j]

But ruthless men seize riches.

17 A kind man* benefits himself,#[k]

But the cruel person brings trouble△ on himself.[l]

CHAP. 10
a Ro 2:6-8
b Ps 16:8
c Ps 37:9

CHAP. 11
d Le 19:36
e Pr 16:18
  Lu 14:8, 9
f Mic 6:8
  1Pe 5:5
g Ps 26:1
  Pr 13:6
h Pr 28:18
i Eze 7:19
  Mt 16:26
j Ge 7:1
k 2Sa 17:23
  Es 7:10
  Pr 5:22
l Jer 39:18
m Pr 1:32
n Ex 15:9, 10
  Lu 12:18-20

Second Col.
a Es 7:9
  Pr 21:18
  Da 6:23, 24
b Pr 2:10-12
c Ex 15:20, 21
  Es 9:19, 22
d Pr 14:34
e Jas 3:6
f Pr 17:27
  1Pe 2:23
g Le 19:16
  Pr 20:19
  Pr 26:22
h Pr 15:22
  Pr 20:18
  Pr 24:6
i Pr 6:1, 5
  Pr 20:16
j 1Sa 25:39
  1Pe 3:3, 4
k Lu 6:38
l Jas 5:3, 4

10:31 *Or "bears the fruit of." **11:1** *Or "Cheating." #Or "a complete stone weight." **11:4** *Or "Valuable things." **11:9** *Or "godless man." **11:12** *Lit., "in want of heart." #Or "despises." **11:13** *Lit., "the one faithful in spirit." #Lit., "covers over a matter." **11:14** *Or "wise guidance." #Or "salvation." △Or "counselors." **11:15** *Or "puts up security." #Lit., "hates." **11:16** *Or "charming." **11:17** *Or "A man of loyal love." #Or "does good to his soul." △Or "disgrace."

18 The wicked one earns deceptive wages,[a]
But the one who sows righteousness receives a true reward.[b]

19 The one standing firmly for righteousness is in line for life,[c]
But the one chasing after evil is in line for death.

20 Those crooked at heart are detestable to Jehovah,[d]
But those whose way is blameless bring pleasure to him.[e]

21 Be assured of this:* An evil person will not go unpunished,[f]
But the children of the righteous will escape.

22 Like a gold ring in the snout of a pig
Is a beautiful woman who rejects good sense.

23 The desire of the righteous leads to good,[g]
But what the wicked hope for leads to fury.

24 One gives generously* and ends up with more;[h]
Another withholds what should be given, but he comes to poverty.[i]

25 The generous person* will prosper,*[j]
And whoever refreshes△ others will himself be refreshed.[k]

26 The people will curse the one who withholds grain,
But they will bless the one who sells it.

27 The one who diligently seeks to do good seeks favor,[l]
But the one searching for bad—that is what will surely come upon him.[m]

28 The one trusting in his riches will fall,[n]

But the righteous will flourish like the foliage.[a]

29 Anyone who brings trouble* on his household will inherit the wind,[b]
And the fool will be a servant to the wisehearted one.

30 The fruitage of the righteous one is a tree of life,[c]
And the one who wins souls* is wise.[d]

31 If, indeed, the righteous one on earth is rewarded,
How much more the wicked one and the sinner![e]

12 The one who loves discipline loves knowledge,[f]
But the one who hates reproof is unreasoning.*[g]

2 The good person obtains Jehovah's approval,
But He condemns the man of wicked schemes.[h]

3 No man is made secure by wickedness,[i]
But the righteous will never be uprooted.

4 A capable wife is a crown to her husband,[j]
But the wife who acts shamefully is like rottenness in his bones.[k]

5 The thoughts of the righteous are just,
But the guidance of the wicked is deceptive.

6 The words of the wicked are a deadly ambush,*[l]
But the mouth of the upright saves them.[m]

7 When the wicked are overthrown, they are no more,
But the house of the righteous will keep standing.[n]

8 A man is praised for the discretion of his mouth,[o]

CHAP. 11
a Job 27:13, 14
b Ga 6:7, 8
c Ac 10:34, 35
Re 2:10
d Ps 18:26
Pr 3:32
e Ps 51:6
Pr 15:8
f Ec 8:13
Eze 18:4
g Isa 26:9
Mt 5:6
h De 15:10
Pr 19:17
Ec 11:1, 2
i Hag 1:6
j Ac 20:35
2Co 9:6
k Lu 6:38
l Pr 12:2
m Es 7:10
Ps 10:2
n Job 31:24, 28
Ps 52:5, 7

Second Col.
a Ps 1:2, 3
Ps 52:8
b Jos 7:15
c Pr 15:4
d 1Co 9:20-22
Jas 5:19, 20
e Eze 18:24
2Th 1:6
1Pe 4:18

CHAP. 12
f Pr 4:13
g Ps 32:9
h De 25:1
1Ki 8:31, 32
i Ps 37:10, 38
j Pr 18:22
Pr 19:14
k 1Ki 21:25
l 2Sa 17:1, 2
m Es 7:3, 4
Pr 14:3
n Pr 24:3
Mt 7:24, 25
o Ge 41:39
1Sa 16:18

11:21 *Lit., "Hand to hand." 11:24 *Lit., "scatters." 11:25 *Or "soul." #Lit., "will be made fat." △Lit., "freely waters."

11:29 *Or "disgrace." 11:30 *See Glossary. 12:1 *Or "has no sense." 12:6 *Lit., "lie in wait for blood."

But one with a twisted heart will be treated with contempt.[a]

9 Better to be lightly esteemed and have a servant
Than to glorify oneself and have no food.*[b]

10 The righteous one takes care of his domestic animals,*[c]
But even the mercy of the wicked is cruel.

11 The one who cultivates his land will be satisfied with food,[d]
But the one pursuing worthless things is lacking good sense.*

12 The wicked man envies what other evil men have caught,
But the root of the righteous bears fruit.

13 The evil man is ensnared by his own sinful speech,[e]
But the righteous one escapes from distress.

14 From the fruitage of his speech* a man is satisfied with good,[f]
And the work of his hands will reward him.

15 The way of the fool is right in his own eyes,[g]
But the wise one accepts advice.*[h]

16 A fool immediately* shows his annoyance,[i]
But the shrewd man overlooks# an insult.

17 The one who testifies faithfully will tell the truth,*
But a false witness speaks deceit.

18 Thoughtless speech is like the stabs of a sword,

But the tongue of the wise is a healing.[a]

19 Truthful lips will endure forever,[b]
But a lying tongue will last for only a moment.[c]

20 Deceit is in the heart of those who plot mischief,
But those who promote* peace have joy.[d]

21 No harm will befall the righteous one,[e]
But the wicked will have their fill of calamity.[f]

22 Lying lips are detestable to Jehovah,[g]
But those acting faithfully bring pleasure to him.

23 A shrewd man conceals what he knows,
But the heart of the fool blurts out his foolishness.[h]

24 The hand of the diligent ones will rule,[i]
But idle hands will be put to forced labor.[j]

25 Anxiety in a man's heart weighs it down,*[k]
But a good word cheers it up.[l]

26 The righteous one searches out his pastures,
But the course of the wicked leads them astray.

27 The lazy do not chase after the prey,[m]
But diligence is a man's precious treasure.

28 The path of righteousness leads to life;[n]
Along its pathway there is no death.

13 A wise son accepts his father's discipline,[o]
But the scoffer does not listen to a rebuke.*[p]

2 From the fruitage of his speech* a man will eat what is good,[q]

CHAP. 12
a 1Sa 25:14, 17
　Mt 27:3, 4

b Pr 13:7

c Ge 33:12-14
　Ex 23:12
　De 22:4, 10
　De 25:4
　Jon 4:11

d Pr 28:19
　Eph 4:28

e 1Ki 2:23, 24
　Ps 5:6
　Ec 5:6

f Pr 13:2
　Pr 18:20

g Pr 3:7
　Pr 26:12

h Pr 1:5

i Pr 29:11

Second Col.
a Pr 16:24

b 1Pe 3:10

c Pr 19:9
　Ac 5:3, 5

d Mt 5:9

e Ps 91:9, 10

f Pr 1:30, 31
　Isa 48:22

g Ps 5:6
　Pr 6:16, 17
　Re 21:8

h Pr 10:19

i Ge 39:4
　1Ki 11:28

j Pr 19:15

k Ps 38:6
　Pr 13:12
　Pr 15:13

l Pr 16:24
　Isa 50:4

m Pr 26:13-15

n Ps 37:27
　Pr 10:7
　Hab 2:4

CHAP. 13
o Heb 12:7, 9

p 1Sa 2:2-25
　Pr 9:7

q Pr 12:14
　Pr 18:20

12:9 *Lit., "bread." 12:10 *Or "the soul of his domestic animal." 12:11 *Lit., "in want of heart." 12:14; 13:2 *Lit., "mouth." 12:15 *Or "counsel." 12:16 *Or "in the same day." #Lit., "covers over." 12:17 *Lit., "what is righteous." 12:20 *Lit., "those who are counselors of." 12:25 *Or "depresses him." 13:1 *Or "correction."

But the very desire* of the treacherous is for violence.

3 The one guarding his mouth# protects his life,*a
But the one opening his lips wide will come to ruin.b

4 The lazy person has his cravings, yet he# has nothing,c
But the diligent one* will be fully satisfied.△d

5 The righteous one hates lies,e
But the actions of the wicked bring shame and disgrace.

6 Righteousness protects the one whose way is innocent,f
But wickedness brings down the sinner.

7 There is one who pretends to be rich, yet has nothing;g
There is another who pretends to be poor, yet has great wealth.

8 Riches are the ransom for a man's life,*h
But the poor are not even threatened.#i

9 The light of the righteous shines brightly,*j
But the lamp of the wicked will be extinguished.k

10 Presumptuousness leads only to strife,l
But wisdom belongs to those who seek advice.*m

11 Wealth quickly gained* will dwindle,n
But the wealth of the one who gathers it little by little# will increase.

12 Expectation* postponed makes the heart sick,o
But a desire realized is a tree of life.p

13:2-4, 8, 19 *Or "soul." 13:3 #Or "what he says." 13:4 #Or "his soul." △Lit., "will be made fat." 13:8 *Lit., "hear no rebuke." 13:9 *Lit., "rejoices." 13:10 *Or "those consulting together." 13:11 *Or "Wealth from vanity." #Lit., "gathers by hand." 13:12 *Or "Hope."

CHAP. 13

a Ps 39:1
  Ps 141:3
  Pr 21:23

b Pr 10:19
  Mt 12:36

c Pr 26:13-15

d Pr 10:4
  Pr 12:24

e Ps 119:163
  Pr 8:13
  Eph 4:25

f Pr 25:21

g Pr 12:9

h Jer 41:8

i Jer 39:10

j Ps 97:11

k Pr 24:20

l Jg 8:1

m Pr 11:2
  Pr 24:6
  Ac 15:5, 6

n Pr 28:8
  Jer 17:11

o Ps 143:7

p Ge 21:5-7
  Lu 2:29, 30

Second Col.

a 2Ch 36:15, 16

b Pr 19:8, 11
  Pr 13:18

c Pr 24:14

d Pr 14:15

e 1Sa 25:25

f 2Sa 4:9, 10

g Pr 25:25

h Ps 141:5
  Pr 15:32
  Heb 12:11

i 1Ki 1:47, 48

j Am 5:10

k Ac 4:13

l Ge 34:1, 2

m De 28:20

n Ro 2:9, 10

o De 6:10, 11

p 1Sa 3:12, 13
  1Ki 1:5, 6
  Pr 29:15

---

13 Whoever despises instruction* will pay the penalty,a
But the one who respects the commandment will be rewarded.b

14 The teaching* of the wise one is a source of lifec
To turn one away from the snares of death.

15 Keen insight wins favor,
But the way of the treacherous is harsh.

16 The shrewd person acts with knowledge,d
But the fool exposes his own foolishness.e

17 A wicked messenger falls into trouble,f
But a faithful envoy brings healing.g

18 Whoever neglects discipline comes to poverty and disgrace,
But the one accepting correction* will be glorified.h

19 Desire when realized is sweet to a person,*i
But the stupid hate to turn away from bad.j

20 The one walking with the wise will become wise,k
But the one who has dealings with the stupid will fare badly.l

21 Calamity pursues sinners,m
But prosperity rewards the righteous.n

22 The good person leaves an inheritance to his grandchildren,
But the sinner's wealth will be stored up for the righteous one.o

23 The plowed field of the poor yields much food,
But it* may be swept away by injustice.

24 Whoever holds back his rod* hates his son,p

13:13 *Or "the word." 13:14 *Or "law." 13:18 *Or "reproof." 13:23 *Or "he." 13:24 *Or "discipline; punishment."

But the one who loves him
disciplines him diligently.*ᵃ

25 The righteous one eats and
satisfies his appetite,*ᵇ
But the stomach of the
wicked is empty.ᶜ

14 The truly wise woman
builds up her house,ᵈ
But the foolish one tears it
down with her own hands.

2 The one walking in his uprightness fears Jehovah,
But the one whose ways are
devious* despises Him.

3 The rod of haughtiness is in
the mouth of the fool,
But the lips of the wise will
protect them.

4 Where there are no cattle the
manger is clean,
But the power of a bull yields
an abundant harvest.

5 A faithful witness will not lie,
But a false witness lies with
every breath.ᵉ

6 The scoffer seeks wisdom
and finds none,
But knowledge comes easily
to the person with under-
standing.ᶠ

7 Stay away from the foolish
man,
For you will not find knowledge on his lips.ᵍ

8 By wisdom the shrewd man
understands the way he is
going,
But the stupid are deceived*
by their foolishness.ʰ

9 Fools make fun of guilt,*ⁱ
But among the upright, there
is a willingness to reconcile.#

10 The heart knows its own
bitterness,*

And no outsider can share in
its joy.

11 The house of the wicked will
be destroyed,ᵃ
But the tent of the upright
will flourish.

12 There is a way that seems
right to a man,
But in the end it leads to
death.ᶜ

13 Even in laughter the heart
may feel pain,
And rejoicing may end in
grief.

14 The one wayward at heart
will reap the results of
his ways,ᵈ
But the good man reaps the
reward of his dealings.ᵉ

15 The naive* person believes
every word,
But the shrewd one ponders
each step.ᶠ

16 The wise one is cautious
and turns away from evil,
But the stupid one is reckless* and overconfident.

17 The one who is quick to
anger acts foolishly,ᵍ
But the man who thinks
things out* is hated.

18 The naive* will inherit
foolishness,
But the shrewd are crowned
with knowledge.ʰ

19 Bad people will have to bow
down before the good,
And the wicked will bow at
the gates of the righteous.

20 The poor man is hated even
by his neighbors,ⁱ
But many are the friends
of the rich person.ʲ

21 The one who despises his
neighbor sins,
But whoever shows compas-
sion to the lowly is happy.ᵏ

22 Will not those who plot
mischief go astray?

CHAP. 13
a De 6:6, 7
Pr 19:18
Pr 22:15
Eph 6:4
Heb 12:6

b Ps 34:10
Ps 37:25

c Isa 65:13

CHAP. 14
d Pr 24:3
Pr 31:26

e Pr 6:16, 19
Pr 19:5

f Pr 18:15

g Pr 13:20

h Pr 14:12

i Pr 10:23
Pr 30:20

Second Col.
a Pr 21:12

b Pr 30:12

c Pr 16:25

d Pr 1:32

e Ga 6:7, 8
Pr 27:12

f Ne 6:2, 3
Pr 27:12

g Pr 12:16
Pr 16:32

h Pr 4:7-9

i Pr 19:7

j Pr 19:4

k Ps 41:1
Pr 19:17
Isa 58:7, 8

13:24 *Or possibly, "promptly." 13:25
*Or "soul." 14:2 *Or "crooked." 14:8
*Or possibly, "the stupid deceive oth-
ers." 14:9 *Or "of making amends."
#Or "there is goodwill." 14:10 *Or "the
bitterness of its soul."

14:15, 18 *Or "inexperienced." 14:16
*Or "furious." 14:17 *Or "the man of
thinking abilities."

But those intent on doing good will receive loyal love and faithfulness.[a]

23 There is benefit in every kind of hard work,

But mere talk leads to want.[b]

24 The crown of the wise is their wealth;

But the foolishness of the stupid is only foolishness.[c]

25 A true witness saves lives,*

But a deceitful one lies with every breath.

26 There is strong confidence in the fear of Jehovah,[d]

And it will be a refuge for his children.[e]

27 The fear of Jehovah is a fountain of life,

To turn one away from the snares of death.

28 A multitude of people are a king's majesty,[f]

But a ruler without subjects is ruined.

29 The one who is slow to anger has great discernment,[g]

But the impatient one displays his foolishness.[h]

30 A calm heart gives life* to the body,

But jealousy is rottenness to the bones.[i]

31 The one who defrauds the lowly one insults his Maker,[j]

But whoever shows compassion to the poor glorifies Him.[k]

32 The wicked one will be brought down by his own evil,

But the righteous one will find refuge in his integrity.[l]

33 Wisdom rests quietly in the heart of an understanding person,[m]

But among the stupid it must make itself known.

34 Righteousness exalts a nation,[n]

But sin is disgraceful to a people.

35 The king finds pleasure in a servant who acts with insight,[a]

But his fury is against the one who acts shamefully.[b]

15 A mild* answer turns away rage,[c]

But a harsh# word stirs up anger.[d]

2 The tongue of the wise makes good use of knowledge,[e]

But the mouth of the stupid blurts out foolishness.

3 The eyes of Jehovah are everywhere,

Watching both the bad and the good.[f]

4 A calm tongue* is a tree of life,[g]

But twisted speech causes despair.#

5 A fool disrespects his father's discipline,[h]

But a shrewd person accepts correction.*[i]

6 In the house of the righteous one there is abundant treasure,

But the produce* of the wicked one brings him trouble.[j]

7 The lips of the wise spread knowledge,[k]

But not so the heart of the stupid one.[l]

8 The sacrifice of the wicked is detestable to Jehovah,[m]

But the prayer of the upright is a pleasure to Him.[n]

9 Jehovah detests the way of the wicked one,[o]

But he loves the one who pursues righteousness.[p]

10 Discipline seems bad* to one forsaking the way,[q]

CHAP. 14
a Job 42:10
  Ps 25:10
b Pr 28:19
c Pr 27:22
d Ps 34:9
  Ro 8:31
e Pr 18:10
  Jer 15:11
f 1Ki 4:21
g Pr 17:27
  Jas 1:19
h Pr 25:28
  Pr 29:11
  Ec 7:9
i Ge 37:3, 4
  1Sa 18:8, 9
j De 24:14, 15
  Ps 12:5
k Mt 19:21
l Pr 2:7
  Pr 10:9
m Pr 15:28
n De 4:6

Second Col.
a 2Sa 15:32-34
  Pr 22:29
b 1Ki 2:44, 46

CHAP. 15
c Jg 8:2, 3
  1Sa 25:32, 33
  Pr 25:15
d 1Ki 12:14, 16
e Pr 16:23
  Isa 50:4
f 2Ch 16:9
  Ps 11:4
  Heb 4:13
g Pr 12:18
  Pr 16:24
  Pr 17:27
h 1Sa 2:2-25
i Ps 141:5
  Pr 13:1
  Heb 12:11
j Jas 5:3, 4
k Ps 37:30
  Mt 10:27
l Mt 12:34, 35
m Isa 1:11
n Jas 5:16
  1Pe 3:12
  1Jo 3:21, 22
o Ps 146:9
p Isa 26:7
q 1Ki 18:17, 18

14:25 *Or "souls." 14:30 *Or "health."

15:1 *Or "gentle." #Or "painful." 15:4 *Or "A tongue of healing." #Lit., "the crushing of the spirit." 15:5 *Or "reproof." 15:6 *Or "income." 15:10 *Or "severe."

But whoever hates reproof will die.[a]

11 The Grave* and the place of destruction* are in full view of Jehovah.[b]

How much more so the hearts of men![c]

12 The scoffer does not love the one correcting* him.[d]

He will not consult the wise.[e]

13 A joyful heart makes for a cheerful countenance,

But heartache crushes the spirit.[f]

14 The understanding heart seeks knowledge,[g]

But the mouth of the stupid feeds on* foolishness.[h]

15 All the days of the afflicted one are bad,[i]

But the one with a cheerful* heart has a continual feast.[j]

16 Better is a little in the fear of Jehovah[k]

Than great wealth along with anxiety.*[l]

17 Better is a dish of vegetables where there is love[m]

Than a fattened* bull where there is hatred.[n]

18 A hot-tempered man stirs up strife,[o]

But one who is slow to anger calms a quarrel.[p]

19 The way of the lazy one is like a hedge of thorns,[q]

But the path of the upright is like a level highway.[r]

20 A wise son makes his father rejoice,[s]

But a stupid man despises his mother.[t]

21 Foolishness is a joy to one lacking good sense,*[u]

22 Plans fail when there is no consultation,*

But there is accomplishment through many advisers.*[b]

23 A man rejoices in giving the right answer,*[c]

And a word spoken at the right time—how good it is![d]

24 The path of life leads upward to one with insight,[e]

To turn him away from the Grave* below.[f]

25 Jehovah will tear down the house of the haughty,[g]

But he will preserve the boundary of the widow.[h]

26 Jehovah detests the schemes of the wicked one,[i]

But pleasant sayings are pure to Him.[j]

27 The one making dishonest profit brings trouble* on his own household,[k]

But the one hating bribes will keep living.[l]

28 The heart of the righteous one meditates before answering,*[m]

But the mouth of the wicked blurts out bad things.

29 Jehovah is far away from the wicked,

But he hears the prayer of the righteous.[n]

30 Bright eyes make* the heart rejoice;

A good report invigorates the bones.*[o]

31 The one who listens to life-giving reproof

Is at home among the wise.[p]

32 Anyone refusing discipline despises his life,*[q]

But the man of discernment walks straight ahead.[a]

CHAP. 15

a Le 26:21
Pr 1:32
b Ps 139:8
c Jer 17:10
Heb 4:13
d Pr 9:7
Joh 3:20
Joh 7:7
e 2Ch 18:6, 7
f Pr 12:25
Pr 17:22
g Ps 119:97
Ac 17:11
h Isa 30:9, 10
i Job 3:11
j Ac 16:23-25
k Ps 37:16
l Pr 15:17
m Ps 133:1
n Pr 17:1
o Pr 10:12
p Ge 13:8, 9
1Sa 25:23, 24
Pr 25:15
Jas 1:19
q Pr 26:13-15
r Isa 30:21
s Pr 27:11
t Pr 23:22
Pr 30:17
u Pr 26:18, 19
Ec 7:4

Second Col.

a Pr 10:23
Eph 5:15, 16
Jas 3:13
b Pr 20:18
c Eph 4:29
d 1Sa 25:32, 33
Pr 25:11
e Mt 7:13, 14
f Pr 8:35, 36
g Lu 18:14
h Ps 146:9
i Pr 6:16, 18
Ps 19:14
j De 16:19
1Sa 8:1, 3
Pr 1:19
l Isa 33:15, 16
m Pr 16:23
n Ps 34:15, 16
Ps 138:6
Ps 145:19
Joh 9:31
o Pr 16:24
Pr 25:25
p Pr 9:8
Pr 19:20
q Pr 5:12, 14
Heb 12:25

15:11, 24 *Or "Sheol," that is, the common grave of mankind. See Glossary. 15:11 *Or "and Abaddon." 15:12 *Or "reproving." 15:14 *Or "pursues." 15:15 *Or "good." 15:16 *Or "confusion." 15:17 *Lit., "manger-fed." 15:21 *Lit., "in want of heart."

15:22 *Or "confidential talk." *Or "counselors." 15:23 *Lit., "in the answer of his mouth." 15:27 *Or "disgrace." 15:28 *Or "carefully considers how to answer; thinks before speaking." 15:30 *Or "A cheerful glance makes." *Lit., "makes the bones fat." 15:32 *Or "soul."

But whoever listens to reproof acquires understanding.*[a]

33 The fear of Jehovah is a training in wisdom,[b]
And before glory there is humility.[c]

16 A man prepares the thoughts of his heart,*
But the answer he gives# is from Jehovah.[d]

2 All of a man's ways seem right* to him,[e]
But Jehovah examines the motives.*[f]

3 Commit to Jehovah whatever you do,*[g]
And your plans will succeed.

4 Jehovah has made everything work for his purpose,
Even the wicked for the day of disaster.[h]

5 Everyone proud in heart is detestable to Jehovah.[i]
Be assured* that he will not go unpunished.

6 By loyal love and faithfulness, error is atoned for,[j]
And by fearing Jehovah one turns away from bad.[k]

7 When Jehovah is pleased with a man's ways,
He causes even his enemies to be at peace with him.[l]

8 Better is a little with righteousness[m]
Than a large income without justice.[n]

9 A man may plot out his course in his heart,
But it is Jehovah who directs his steps.[o]

10 Inspired* decision should be on the lips of a king;[p]
He must never betray justice.[q]

11 Honest balances and scales are from Jehovah;
All the weights in the bag are his doing.[a]

12 Wicked practices are detestable to kings,[b]
For the throne is firmly established by righteousness.[c]

13 Righteous speech is a pleasure to kings.
They love someone who speaks honestly.[d]

14 The king's rage is like a messenger of death,[e]
But the wise man appeases* it.[f]

15 In the light of the king's face there is life;
His favor is like a cloud of rain in spring.[g]

16 How much better to acquire wisdom than gold![h]
To gain understanding is to be chosen over silver.[i]

17 The highway of the upright avoids what is bad.
Whoever safeguards his way preserves his life.*[j]

18 Pride is before a crash,
And a haughty spirit before stumbling.[k]

19 Better to be humble* among the meek[l]
Than to share the spoil of the haughty.

20 The one who shows insight in a matter will find success,*
And happy is the one trusting in Jehovah.

21 The wise in heart will be called understanding,[m]
And the one kind in speech* adds persuasiveness.[n]

22 Insight is a fountain of life to those possessing it,
But fools are disciplined by their own foolishness.

CHAP. 15
a Pr 13:18
  Mt 7:24, 25
b Ps 111:10
c Pr 18:12
  Jas 4:10

CHAP. 16
d Jer 1:9
  Lu 12:11, 12
e 1Sa 15:13, 14
  Ps 36:1, 2
  Pr 21:2
  Jer 17:9
f 1Sa 16:6, 7
  Pr 24:12
g Ps 37:5
  Php 4:6, 7
h Ex 14:4
  Ro 9:21
i Pr 6:16, 17
  Pr 8:13
  Pr 21:4
j Ac 3:19
k Ne 5:8, 9
  2Co 7:1
l Ge 31:24
  Ex 34:24
m 1Ti 6:6
n Ps 37:16
  Jer 17:11
o Pr 16:1
  Jer 10:23
p De 17:18, 19
  1Ki 3:28
q Ps 72:1, 14

Second Col.
a Le 19:36
  Pr 11:1
b Pr 20:26
c Pr 29:14
  Re 19:11
d Ps 101:6
e 1Sa 22:17, 18
  1Ki 2:29
f Ec 10:4
g Ps 72:1, 6
h Ec 7:12
i Pr 4:7
j Pr 10:9
k Pr 11:2
  Da 4:30-32
l Isa 57:15
m Pr 4:7
n Lu 4:22
  Col 4:6

15:32 *Lit., "heart." 16:1 *Lit., "The arrangings of the heart belong to a man." #Or "the right answer." Lit., "the answer of the tongue." 16:2 *Lit., "pure." #Lit., "spirits." 16:3 *Lit., "Roll to Jehovah your works." 16:5 *Lit., "Hand to hand." 16:10 *Or "Divine."

16:14 *Or "avoids." 16:17 *Or "soul." 16:19 *Lit., "lowly of spirit." 16:20 *Lit., "good." 16:21 *Or "And appealing speech." Lit., "And sweetness of lips."

23 The heart of the wise one
      gives his mouth insight[a]
  And adds persuasiveness to
      his speech.

24 Pleasant sayings are a honey-
      comb,
  Sweet to the soul* and a
      healing to the bones.[b]

25 There is a way that seems
      right to a man,
  But in the end it leads to
      death.[c]

26 The appetite* of a laborer
      makes him work hard
  For his hunger# urges
      him on.[d]

27 A worthless man digs up
      what is bad;[e]
  His speech is like a scorching
      fire.[f]

28 A troublemaker* causes
      dissension,[g]
  And a slanderer separates
      close friends.[h]

29 A violent man entices his
      neighbor
  And leads him in the wrong
      way.

30 He winks his eye as he
      schemes harm.
  He pinches his lips together
      as he carries out mischief.

31 Gray hair is a crown of
      beauty*[i]
  When it is found in the way
      of righteousness.[j]

32 The one slow to anger[k] is
      better than a mighty man,
  And the one controlling his
      temper* than one conquer-
      ing a city.[l]

33 The lot is cast into the lap,[m]
  But every decision by it is
      from Jehovah.[n]

17 Better is a piece of dry
      bread where there is
      peace*[o]

Than a house full of feasting*
      along with quarreling.[a]

2 A servant with insight will
      rule over a son who acts
      shamefully;
  He will share in the inheri-
      tance as one of the broth-
      ers.

3 The refining pot is for silver
      and the furnace for gold,[b]
  But Jehovah is the examiner
      of hearts.[c]

4 A wicked man pays attention
      to hurtful speech,
  And a deceptive man listens
      to a malicious tongue.[d]

5 Whoever mocks the poor
      insults his Maker,[e]
  And whoever rejoices over
      another's disaster will not
      go unpunished.[f]

6 Grandsons* are a crown to
      the aged,
  And fathers# are the glory
      of their sons.[Δ]

7 Upright* speech does not
      befit a fool.[g]
  How much less does false
      speech befit a ruler!*[h]

8 A gift is like a precious
      stone* to its owner;[i]
  Everywhere he turns, it
      brings him success.[j]

9 Whoever forgives* a trans-
      gression seeks love,[k]
  But the one who keeps harp-
      ing on a matter separates
      close friends.[l]

10 A rebuke makes a deeper
      impression on one having
      understanding[m]
  Than striking a stupid
      person a hundred times.[n]

11 A bad man seeks only
      rebellion,
  But a cruel messenger will
      be sent to punish him.[o]

CHAP. 16

a Pr 22:17, 18
  Mt 12:35

b Pr 4:20-22
  Pr 12:18

c Pr 14:12
  Mt 7:22, 23

d Ec 6:7

e Pr 6:12, 14

f Jas 3:6

g Jas 3:16

h Ge 3:1
  1Sa 24:9
  Ro 16:17

i Le 19:32
  Job 32:7
  Pr 20:29

j Ps 92:12-14

k Pr 14:29
  Jas 1:19

l Pr 25:28

m Nu 26:55
  Pr 18:18

n 1Sa 14:41, 42
  Ac 1:24, 26

CHAP. 17

o Ps 37:16

Second Col.

a Pr 15:16, 17
  Pr 21:9, 19

b Pr 27:21

c Pr 26:2
  Pr 21:2
  Pr 24:12

d Jer 5:31

e Pr 14:31

f Pr 24:17
  Ob 12

g Pr 26:7

h Pr 16:10

i Ge 32:20
  2Sa 16:1

j 1Sa 25:18, 35
  Pr 18:16
  Pr 19:6

k Pr 10:12
  1Pe 4:8

l Pr 16:28

m Ps 141:5
  Pr 9:8

n Pr 27:22

o 2Sa 18:15
  2Sa 20:1, 22
  1Ki 2:22, 24

16:24 *Or "taste." See Glossary. **16:26**
*Or "soul." #Lit., "mouth." **16:28** *Or
"A schemer." **16:31** *Or "glory." **16:32**
*Lit., "ruling over his spirit." **17:1** *Or
"quietness."

17:1 *Lit., "sacrifices." **17:6** *Or
"Grandchildren." #Or "parents." ΔOr
"children." **17:7** *Or "Fine." #Or "noble." **17:8** *Or "is a stone that brings
favor." **17:9** *Lit., "covers over."

12 Better to meet a bear
      bereaved of her cubs
   Than to encounter someone
      stupid in his foolishness.*

13 If anyone repays bad for
      good,
   Bad will not depart from his
      house.*

14 Beginning a fight is like
      opening a floodgate;*
   Before the quarrel breaks
      out, take your leave.*

15 Anyone who acquits the
      wicked one and anyone
      who condemns the righ-
      teous one*
   —Both of them are detestable
      to Jehovah.

16 What good is it that the
      stupid one has the means
      to acquire wisdom
   When he has no heart for
      acquiring it?*

17 A true friend shows love
      at all times,*
   And is a brother who is born
      for times of distress.*

18 A man lacking good sense*
      shakes hands and agrees
   To put up security* in the
      presence of his neighbor.*

19 The one who loves conflict
      loves transgression.*
   Anyone who makes his entry-
      way high invites a crash.*

20 The one who is crooked
      at heart will not find
      success,*
   And the one who speaks de-
      ceitfully will fall into ruin.

21 The one who fathers a stupid
      child will experience grief;
   And the father of a senseless
      child has no joy.*

22 A joyful heart is good
      medicine,*

But a crushed spirit saps
      one's strength.*

23 A wicked man will take a
      bribe in secret*
   To pervert the course of
      justice.*

24 Wisdom is directly in front
      of the discerning person,
   But the eyes of the stupid
      wander to the ends of the
      earth.*

25 A stupid son brings grief
      to his father
   And heartache* to the one
      who gave birth to him.*

26 To punish* the righteous one
      is not good,
   And to flog honorable people
      goes against what is right.

27 A man of knowledge
      restrains his words,*
   And a discerning man will
      remain calm.*

28 Even a fool who keeps silent
      will be considered wise,
   And the one who seals his
      lips, discerning.

18 Whoever isolates himself
      pursues his own selfish
      desires;
   He rejects* all practical
      wisdom.

2 A stupid person takes no
      pleasure in understanding;
   He would rather disclose
      what is in his heart.*

3 When a wicked person
      comes, contempt also
      comes,
   And along with dishonor
      there is disgrace.*

4 The words of a man's mouth
      are deep waters.*
   The fountain of wisdom is
      a bubbling brook.

5 It is not good to show partial-
      ity to the wicked one*

CHAP. 17
a Pr 27:3

b 2Sa 12:8-10

c Ge 13:8, 9
  Pr 25:8
  Mt 5:39
  Ro 12:18

d Ex 23:7
  1Ki 21:13
  Isa 5:22, 23

e Pr 1:22
  Ro 1:20, 21

f Pr 18:24
  Joh 15:13

g Ru 1:16, 17
  1Sa 19:2

h Pr 11:15
  Pr 22:26, 27

i Jas 3:16

j 2Sa 15:2-4

k Ps 18:26
  Pr 6:14, 15

l 1Sa 2:22-25
  1Sa 8:1-3
  2Sa 15:14

m Pr 12:25
  Pr 15:13

Second Col.
a Pr 18:14

b Ex 23:8

c Ec 2:14

d Pr 15:20

e Pr 10:19
  Jas 1:19

f Pr 15:4
  Ec 9:17
  Jas 3:13

CHAP. 18
g Pr 10:19

h Pr 11:2

i Pr 10:11

j De 1:16, 17
  Pr 28:21

17:14 *Or "like opening a dam." Lit.,
"letting out waters." 17:16 *Or "When
he is lacking good sense?" 17:18 *Lit.,
"in want of heart." #Or "go surety."
17:20 *Lit., "good." 17:22 *Or "good
for healing."

17:22 *Or "dries up the bones." 17:23
*Lit., "a bribe from the bosom." 17:25
*Lit., "bitterness." 17:26 *Or "impose
a fine on." 17:27 *Lit., "cool of spirit."
18:1 *Or "shows contempt for."

Or to deprive the righteous
one of justice.[a]
6 The speech of the stupid one
leads to quarrels,[b]
And his mouth invites a beating.[c]
7 The mouth of the stupid is
his ruin,[d]
And his lips are a snare for
his life.*
8 The words of a slanderer are
like tasty morsels;*[e]
They are gulped right down
into the stomach.[f]
9 Whoever is lazy in his work
Is a brother to the one who
causes ruin.[g]
10 The name of Jehovah is a
strong tower.[h]
Into it the righteous one runs
and receives protection.*[i]
11 The wealth of the rich is his
fortified city;
It is like a protective wall in
his imagination.[j]
12 Before a crash a man's heart
is lofty,[k]
And before glory there is
humility.[l]
13 When anyone replies to a
matter before he hears the
facts,
It is foolish and humiliating.[m]
14 A person's spirit can sustain
him through illness,[n]
But who can bear a crushed
spirit?*[o]
15 The heart of the understanding one acquires knowl-
edge,[p]
And the ear of the wise seeks
to find knowledge.
16 A man's gift opens the way
for him;[q]
It gives him access to great
people.
17 The first to state his case
seems right,[a]
Until the other party comes
and cross-examines him.*[b]
18 Casting lots puts an end to
disputes[c]
And decides between* strong
opponents.
19 A brother offended is more
unyielding than a fortified
city,[d]
And there are disputes like
the bars of a fortress.[e]
20 From the fruitage of a man's
speech* his stomach will
be filled;[f]
He will be satisfied with what
his lips produce.
21 Death and life are in the
power of the tongue;[g]
Those who love to use it will
eat its fruitage.[h]
22 The one who finds a good
wife has found something
good,[i]
And he receives Jehovah's
favor.*[j]
23 The poor man implores when
speaking,
But the rich man answers
harshly.
24 There are companions ready
to crush one another,[k]
But there is a friend who
sticks closer than a
brother.[l]

19 It is better to be poor and
walk in integrity[m]
Than to be stupid and speak
lies.[n]
2 A person* without knowledge is not good,[o]
And the one who acts rashly#
is sinning.
3 It is a man's own foolishness
that distorts his way,
And his heart becomes
enraged against Jehovah.

18:7; 19:2 *Or "soul." 18:8 *Or "like things to be swallowed greedily." 18:10 *Lit., "is raised high," that is, out of reach, safe. 18:14 *Or "complete despair?"

18:17 *Or "searches him through." 18:18 *Lit., "separates." 18:20 *Lit., "mouth." 18:22 *Or "goodwill." 19:2 #Lit., "hastens with his feet."

CHAP. 18
a 1Ki 21:9, 10
b Pr 13:10
c Pr 19:19
d Pr 13:3
e Le 19:16
f Pr 26:22
g Pr 10:4
h 1Sa 17:45, 46 Ps 20:1
i Ps 18:2 Ps 91:14
j Ps 49:6, 7 Pr 11:4 Jer 9:23 Lu 12:19-21
k Pr 11:2 Da 5:23, 30 Ac 12:21-23
l Pr 22:4 1Pe 5:5
m Pr 25:8
n Job 1:21 2Co 4:16 2Co 12:10
o Pr 17:22
p 1Ki 3:7-9 Pr 9:9
q Ge 43:11 Pr 17:8

Second Col.
a 2Sa 16:3, 4
b 2Sa 19:25-27 Pr 25:8
c Jos 14:1, 2 Ne 11:1 Pr 16:33
d Ge 27:41 2Sa 13:22
e 2Sa 14:28 Ac 15:37-39
f Pr 12:14 Pr 13:2
g Mt 15:18 Eph 4:29 Jas 3:6, 9
h Ec 10:12
i Pr 31:10
j Pr 19:14 Ec 9:9
k 2Sa 15:31 Mt 26:49
l 1Sa 19:2, 4 Pr 17:17

CHAP. 19
m Pr 15:16 Jas 2:5
n Pr 28:6
o Ro 10:2

4 Wealth attracts many friends,
   But the poor man will be deserted even by his friend.[a]
5 A false witness will not go unpunished,[b]
   And the one who lies with every breath will not escape.[c]
6 Many seek the favor of a noble,*
   And everyone is a friend to the man who gives gifts.
7 All the brothers of a poor man hate him;[d]
   How much more he is shunned by his friends![e]
   He pursues them with requests, but no one responds.
8 Whoever acquires good sense* loves himself.*[f]
   Whoever treasures discernment will find success.^[g]
9 A false witness will not go unpunished,
   And the one who lies with every breath will perish.[h]
10 It is not fitting for a fool to live in luxury;
   How much less for a servant to rule over princes![i]
11 The insight of a man certainly slows down his anger,[j]
   And it is beauty on his part to overlook* an offense.*[k]
12 The king's rage is like the growling of a lion,*[l]
   But his favor is like dew on the vegetation.
13 A stupid son brings adversity on his father,[m]
   And a quarrelsome* wife is like a roof that never stops leaking.[n]
14 A house and wealth are inherited from fathers,
   But a discreet wife is from Jehovah.[a]
15 Laziness brings on a deep sleep,
   And a sluggish person* will go hungry.[b]
16 The one who keeps the commandment keeps his life;*[c]
   The one who is reckless about his ways will die.[d]
17 The one showing favor to the lowly is lending to Jehovah,[e]
   And He will repay* him for what he does.[f]
18 Discipline your son while there is hope,[g]
   And do not become responsible for* his death.[h]
19 The hot-tempered man will pay the penalty;
   If you try to spare him, you will have to do it again and again.[i]
20 Listen to counsel and accept discipline,[j]
   In order to become wise in your future.[k]
21 Many are the plans in a man's heart,
   But the counsel* of Jehovah is what will prevail.[l]
22 The desirable thing in a man is his loyal love;[m]
   And it is better to be poor than to be a liar.
23 The fear of Jehovah leads to life;[n]
   The one who has it will have a pleasant rest, free from harm.[o]
24 The lazy one buries his hand in the banquet bowl,
   But he does not even bother to bring it back to his mouth.[p]
25 Strike the ridiculer,[q] so that the inexperienced one may become shrewd,[r]

CHAP. 19
a Pr 14:20
b Pr 19:18, 19
c Pr 19:9
d Pr 14:20
e Ec 9:14, 15
   Jas 2:2, 3
f Pr 15:32
g Pr 2:2, 5
h Pr 19:5
   Re 21:8
i 2Sa 3:24
   2Sa 3:38, 39
   Pr 30:21, 22
   Ec 10:7
j Pr 14:29
   Pr 16:32
   Jas 1:19
k Ge 50:19-21
   Mt 18:21, 22
   Eph 4:32
l Pr 16:14
   Pr 20:2
   Da 2:12
m 2Sa 16:21, 22
n Pr 21:9, 19
   Pr 27:15

Second Col.
a Ge 24:14
   Pr 18:22
   Pr 31:10
b Pr 23:21
   Pr 24:33, 34
   2Th 3:10
c Pr 16:17
d Pr 15:32
e Ge 15:7, 8
   Ps 37:25, 26
   Heb 13:16
f Pr 11:24
   Mt 5:7
   Heb 6:10
g Pr 13:24
   Pr 22:6, 15
h 1Sa 3:12, 13
i 1Sa 24:16-18
   1Sa 26:21
j Pr 4:13
k De 8:14, 16
   Heb 12:7, 11
l Ge 11:6, 7
   Ge 50:19, 20
   Pr 21:30
   Da 4:35
   Ac 5:38, 39
m Mic 6:8
n Pr 14:27
   Mal 3:16
o Pr 12:21
p Pr 6:9-11
   Pr 15:19
q Pr 24:30, 31
   Pr 26:14, 15
   De 25:2
r Pr 15:5

19:6 *Or "generous man." 19:8 *Lit., "acquires heart." *Or "his soul." ^Lit., "good." 19:11 *Lit., "pass over." *Or "a transgression." 19:12 *Or "a maned young lion." 19:13 *Or "nagging."

19:15, 16 *Or "soul." 19:17 *Or "reward." 19:18 *Or "desire." Lit., "raise your soul to." 19:21 *Or "purpose."

And reprove the understanding one, so that he will increase in knowledge.[a]

26 The one who mistreats his father and drives away his mother

Is a son causing shame and disgrace.[b]

27 My son, if you stop listening to discipline,

You will stray from the sayings of knowledge.

28 A worthless witness mocks justice,[c]

And the mouth of the wicked gulps down evil.[d]

29 Judgment is in store for ridiculers,[e]

And beatings for the back of the stupid ones.[f]

20 Wine is a ridiculer,[g] alcohol is unruly;[h]

Whoever goes astray by them is not wise.[i]

2 The terror* of a king is like the growling of a lion;[#j]

Whoever provokes his anger risks his own life.[k]

3 It is honorable for a man to refrain from a dispute,[l]

But every fool will become embroiled in it.[m]

4 The lazy one does not plow in winter,

So he will be begging during the harvest when he has nothing.*[n]

5 The thoughts* of a man's heart are like deep waters,

But the discerning man draws them out.

6 Many men proclaim their loyal love,

But who can find a faithful man?

7 The righteous one is walking in his integrity.[o]

Happy are his children* who come after him.[a]

8 When the king sits on the throne to judge,[b]

He sifts out all evil with his eyes.[c]

9 Who can say: "I have cleansed my heart;[d]

I am pure from my sin"?[e]

10 Dishonest weights and false measures*

—Both are detestable to Jehovah.[f]

11 Even a child* is known by his actions,

Whether his behavior is pure and right.[g]

12 The hearing ear and the seeing eye

—Jehovah has made both of them.[h]

13 Do not love sleep, or you will come to poverty.[i]

Open your eyes, and you will be satisfied with bread.[j]

14 "It is no good, it is no good!" says the buyer;

Then he goes away and boasts about himself.[k]

15 There is gold, also much coral,*

But the lips of knowledge are something precious.[l]

16 Take a man's garment if he has given security for a stranger;[m]

Seize the pledge from him if he did so for a foreign woman.*[n]

17 Bread gained by deceit tastes good to a man,

But afterward his mouth will be full of gravel.[o]

18 By consultation,* plans will succeed,*[p]

CHAP. 19
a Pr 9:9
  Pr 21:11
b Ex 20:12
  Le 20:9
  Pr 20:20
  Pr 30:17
c 1Ki 21:9, 10
d Pr 4:16, 17
e Pr 9:12
f Pr 10:13
  Pr 26:3

CHAP. 20
g Ge 9:20, 21
  Pr 23:29-35
h Isa 28:7
i 1Co 6:10
  Ga 5:21
  Eph 5:18
j Pr 19:12
  Ec 10:4
k 1Ki 2:22-24
l Pr 14:29
  2Ti 2:23
m Pr 18:6
  Ec 7:9
n Pr 6:10, 11
  2Th 3:10
o Job 1:1
  Lu 1:5, 6

Second Col.
a Ps 37:25, 26
b 1Ki 7:7
c 1Ki 3:28
  Ps 72:1, 4
  Pr 16:12
d Job 14:4
e Ps 51:5
  Ec 7:20
  Jas 3:2
f Pr 11:1
  Am 8:5
  Mic 6:11
g Pr 22:15
h Ex 4:11
i Pr 10:4
j Pr 12:11
k Le 19:13
  Pr 21:6
l Pr 3:13-15
m Pr 11:15
n Pr 27:13
o Pr 6:30, 31
p Pr 15:22

20:2 *Or "fearsomeness." #Or "a maned young lion." 20:4 *Or possibly, "They will look during the harvest but find nothing." 20:5 *Or "intentions." Lit., "counsel." 20:7 *Lit., "sons." 20:10 *Or "Two different stone weights and two different measuring containers." 20:11 *Or "boy." 20:15 *See Glossary. 20:16 *Or "a foreigner." 20:18 *Or "counsel." #Or "be made firm."

And by skillful direction*
wage your war.ª

19 A slanderer goes about
revealing confidential
talk;ᵇ

Do not associate with one
who loves to gossip.*

20 Whoever curses his father
and his mother,

His lamp will be extinguished
when darkness comes.ᶜ

21 An inheritance obtained first
by greed

Will not be a blessing in the
end.ᵈ

22 Do not say: "I will pay back
evil!"ᵉ

Hope in Jehovah,ᶠ and he will
save you.ᵍ

23 Dishonest weights* are
detestable to Jehovah,

And deceptive scales are not
good.

24 A man's footsteps are
directed by Jehovah;ʰ

How can a man understand
his own way?*

25 It is a snare for a man to cry
out rashly, "Holy!"ⁱ

And only later to give consideration to what he vowed.ʲ

26 A wise king sifts out the
wickedᵏ

And drives the threshing
wheel over them.ˡ

27 The breath of a man is the
lamp of Jehovah,

Searching through his
innermost being.

28 Loyal love and faithfulness
safeguard the king;ᵐ

By loyal love he sustains his
throne.ⁿ

29 The glory of young men is
their strength,ᵒ

And the splendor of old men
is their gray hair.ᵖ

CHAP. 20

a Pr 11:14
Pr 24:6
Lu 14:31, 32

b Le 19:16
Pr 11:13
Pr 25:9, 23

c Ex 20:12
Le 20:9
Pr 19:26

d Pr 28:8, 20
1Ti 6:9, 10

e De 32:35
Pr 24:29
Mt 5:38, 39
Ro 12:17, 19
1Th 5:15

f Ps 37:34

g Ps 34:7
1Pe 4:19

h Ps 37:23
Jer 10:23

i Le 27:9

j Nu 30:2
Ec 5:4, 6
Mt 5:33

k Ps 101:8

l Isa 28:27

m Ps 61:6, 7

n Ps 21:7

o Ec 11:9

p Le 19:32
Pr 16:31

Second Col.

a Ps 119:71

CHAP. 21

b Ex 14:4
Ezr 7:27

c Ne 2:7, 8
Isa 44:28
Re 17:17

d Ps 36:1, 2
Pr 16:2

e 1Sa 16:6, 7
Pr 24:12
Jer 17:10

f 1Sa 15:22, 23
Ho 6:6
Mic 6:7, 8
Mt 12:7

g Ps 10:4

h Pr 13:4

i Pr 14:29

j Pr 1:19
Pr 20:21

k Ps 7:14-16
Ps 37:37
Pr 16:17
1Pe 1:22

m Pr 17:1
Pr 21:19
Pr 25:24
Pr 27:15

n Ge 6:5
Ps 36:1, 4

o 1Sa 25:10, 11

---

30 Bruises and wounds purge*
away evil,ª

And beatings cleanse one's
innermost being.

21 A king's heart is like
streams of water in
Jehovah's hand.ᵇ

He directs it wherever
He pleases.ᶜ

2 All of a man's ways seem
right to him,ᵈ

But Jehovah examines the
hearts.*ᵉ

3 To do what is right and just
Is more pleasing to Jehovah
than a sacrifice.ᶠ

4 Haughty eyes and an
arrogant heart

—The lamp that guides the
wicked is sin.ᵍ

5 The plans of the diligent
surely lead to success,*ʰ

But all who are hasty surely
head for poverty.ⁱ

6 Gaining treasures by a lying
tongue

Is like a vanishing mist,
a deadly snare.*ʲ

7 The violence of the wicked
will sweep them away,ᵏ

For they refuse to act with
justice.

8 The way of a guilty man is
crooked,

But the activity of the pure
man is upright.ˡ

9 Better to dwell on a corner
of the roof

Than in the same house with
a quarrelsome* wife.ᵐ

10 The wicked man* craves
what is bad;ⁿ

He shows no favor toward
his neighbor.ᵒ

11 When a ridiculer is punished,
the inexperienced become
wiser,

20:18 *Or "wise guidance." **20:19** *Or
"who entices with his lips." **20:23** *Or
"Two different stone weights." **20:24**
*Or "the way to go?"

20:30 *Or "scour." **21:2** *Or "motives." **21:5** *Or "advantage." **21:6**
*Or possibly, "for those seeking death."
21:9 *Or "nagging." **21:10** *Or "The
soul of the wicked one."

And when a wise person receives insight, he gains knowledge.*[a]

12 The Righteous One observes the house of the wicked one;

He overthrows the wicked to their ruin.[b]

13 Whoever stops up his ear to the cry of the lowly one

Will himself call and not be answered.[c]

14 A secret gift subdues anger,[d]

And a hidden bribe,* fierce rage.

15 It is a joy for the righteous one to act with justice,[e]

But it is something terrible to those who practice evil.

16 The man who strays from the way of insight

Will rest in the company of those powerless in death.[f]

17 The one who loves having a good time* will come to poverty;[g]

The one who loves wine and oil will not grow rich.

18 The wicked one is a ransom for the righteous one,

And the treacherous one will be taken in place of the upright.[h]

19 Better to dwell in the wilderness

Than with a quarrelsome* and irritable wife.[i]

20 Precious treasure and oil are found in the house of the wise,[j]

But the stupid man will squander* what he has.[k]

21 Whoever pursues righteousness and loyal love

Will find life, righteousness, and glory.[l]

22 A wise man can scale* the city of the mighty

And undermine the strength in which they trust.[a]

23 The one guarding his mouth and his tongue

Keeps himself* out of trouble.[b]

24 A presumptuous, arrogant braggart is what you call

The man who acts with reckless presumptuousness.[c]

25 What the lazy man craves will put him to death,

For his hands refuse to work.[d]

26 All day long he greedily craves,

But the righteous one gives, holding nothing back.[e]

27 The sacrifice of the wicked is detestable.[f]

How much more when he offers it with evil intent!*

28 A lying witness will perish,[g]

But the man who listens will testify with success.*

29 The wicked man puts on a bold face,[h]

But it is the upright one whose course is sure.*[i]

30 There is no wisdom, nor discernment, nor counsel in opposition to Jehovah.[j]

31 The horse is prepared for the day of battle,[k]

But salvation belongs to Jehovah.[l]

22 A good name* is to be chosen rather than great wealth;[m]

To be respected# is better than silver and gold.

2 The rich and the poor have this in common:*

CHAP. 21

a Pr 9:9
Pr 19:25

b Ge 19:29
Ps 37:10, 20
2Pe 2:4
2Pe 3:5, 6

c De 15:9
Pr 28:27
Jas 5:4

d Pr 18:16

e Ps 106:3

f Jas 1:15
2Pe 2:21

g Ec 7:4
Lu 15:13, 14

h Es 7:10

i Pr 17:1
Pr 21:9
Pr 25:24
Pr 27:15

j Pr 15:6
Ec 5:19

k Lu 15:13, 14

l Pr 15:9
Pr 22:4
Mt 5:6
Ro 2:6, 7

Second Col.

a Ec 7:19
2Co 10:4

b Ps 141:3
Pr 10:19
Ec 10:20

c Nu 14:44
Es 6:4

d Pr 6:6-11
Pr 13:4
Pr 19:24

e Ps 37:25, 26
Ps 112:9
Lu 6:30

f 1Sa 15:22, 23
Pr 15:8
Isa 1:11

g De 19:18, 19
Pr 19:5

h Pr 28:14
Pr 29:1

i Pr 11:5

j Nu 23:7, 8
Pr 19:21
Ac 5:38, 39

k Ps 20:7
Ps 33:17
Isa 31:1

l 2Ch 20:15, 17
Ps 68:20
Re 7:10

CHAP. 22

m Ec 7:1

21:11 *Or "he knows what to do."   21:14 *Lit., "a bribe in the bosom."   21:17 *Or "loves pleasure."   21:19 *Or "nagging."   21:20 *Lit., "swallow."

21:22 *Or "prevail over."   21:23 *Or "his soul."   21:27 *Or "along with shameful conduct!"   21:28 *Lit., "speak forever."   21:29 *Or "who makes his way sure."   22:1 *Or "A good reputation." Lit., "A name." #Lit., "Favor."   22:2 *Lit., "meet together."

Jehovah made them both.[a]

3 The shrewd one sees the danger and conceals himself,
But the inexperienced keep right on going and suffer the consequences.*

4 The result of humility and the fear of Jehovah
Is riches and glory and life.[b]

5 Thorns and traps are in the crooked man's path,
But whoever values his life* keeps far away from them.[c]

6 Train a boy* in the way he should go;[d]
Even when he grows old he will not depart from it.[e]

7 The rich one rules the poor,
And the borrower is a slave to the lender.[f]

8 Whoever sows unrighteousness will reap disaster,[g]
And the rod of his fury will come to its end.[h]

9 The generous person* will be blessed,
For he shares his food with the poor.[i]

10 Drive away the scornful man,
And contention will disappear;
Disputes* and insults will cease.

11 The one who loves a pure heart and whose speech is gracious
Will have the king as his friend.[j]

12 The eyes of Jehovah safeguard knowledge,
But He overturns the words of the treacherous.[k]

13 The lazy one says: "There is a lion outside!
I will be killed in the middle of the public square!"[l]

14 The mouth of wayward* women is a deep pit.[a]
The one condemned by Jehovah will fall into it.

15 Foolishness is bound up in the heart of a boy,*[b]
But the rod of discipline will remove it far from him.[c]

16 The one defrauding the poor to increase his wealth[d]
And the one giving gifts to the rich
Will end up in poverty.

17 Incline your ear and listen to the words of the wise,[e]
In order to apply your heart to my knowledge,[f]

18 For it is pleasant to keep them deep within you,[g]
So that all of them may constantly be on your lips.[h]

19 For your confidence to be in Jehovah,
I am giving you knowledge today.

20 Have I not already written you,
Imparting advice and knowledge,

21 To teach you true and reliable words,
So that you can return with an accurate report to the one who sent you?

22 Do not rob the poor man because he is poor,[i]
And do not crush the lowly man in the city gate,[j]

23 For Jehovah himself will plead their cause[k]
And he will take the life* of those who defraud them.

24 Do not keep company with a hot-tempered man
Or get involved with one disposed to rage,

25 So that you never learn his ways
And ensnare yourself.*[l]

CHAP. 22
a Ac 17:26

b Ps 34:9
Pr 18:12

c Pr 4:14, 15

d Ge 18:19
De 6:6, 7
Eph 6:4

e 2Ti 3:14, 15

f 2Ki 4:1
Mt 18:25

g Ga 6:7, 8

h Ps 125:3

i De 15:7, 8
Pr 11:25
Heb 6:10

j Ps 45:2
Pr 16:13
Mt 5:8

k Ac 13:8-10

l Pr 26:13-15

Second Col.
a Pr 5:3
Ec 7:26

b Ge 8:21

c Pr 13:24
Pr 19:18

d Ps 12:5
Pr 14:31

e Pr 13:20

f Pr 15:14

g Pr 2:10
Pr 24:14

h Pr 15:7

i Pr 23:10

j Ex 23:6
Am 5:12

k 1Sa 24:12
Ps 12:5

l Pr 13:20

22:3 *Or "penalty." 22:5 *Or "soul." 22:6, 15 *Or "child; youth." 22:9 *Lit., "He with a good eye." 22:10 *Or "Lawsuits."

22:14 *Lit., "strange." See Pr 2:16. 22:23 *Or "rob the soul." 22:25 *Or "your soul."

26 Do not be among those who shake hands in a pledge,
Who put up security for loans.[a]

27 If you have nothing to pay,
Your bed will be taken right out from under you!

28 Do not move an ancient boundary marker
That your forefathers put in place.[b]

29 Have you seen a man skillful at his work?
He will stand before kings;[c]
He will not stand before common men.

23 When you sit down to eat with a king,
Carefully consider what is before you;

2 Put a knife to your throat*
If you have a large appetite.#

3 Do not crave his delicacies,
For it is deceptive food.

4 Do not wear yourself out to gain wealth.[d]
Stop and show understanding.*

5 When you cast your eyes on it, it is not there,[e]
For it will surely sprout wings like an eagle and fly off into the sky.[f]

6 Do not eat the food of a stingy person;*
Do not crave his delicacies,

7 For he is like one keeping accounts.*
"Eat and drink," he says to you, but he does not mean it.#

8 You will vomit up the morsels you have eaten
And will have wasted your compliments.

9 Do not speak in the ears of the stupid one,[a]
For he will despise the wisdom of your words.[b]

10 Do not move an ancient boundary marker[c]
Or encroach on the field of the fatherless.

11 For their Defender* is strong;
He will take up their cause against you.[d]

12 Apply your heart to discipline
And your ear to the sayings of knowledge.

13 Do not hold back discipline from a boy.*[e]
If you strike him with the rod, he will not die.

14 With the rod you should strike him,
In order to save him* from the Grave.#

15 My son, if your heart becomes wise,
Then my own heart will rejoice.[f]

16 My innermost being* will find joy
When your lips speak what is right.

17 Let your heart not envy sinners,[g]
But be in the fear of Jehovah all day long,[h]

18 For then you will have a future[i]
And your hope will not be cut off.

19 Listen, my son, and become wise,
And direct your heart in the right way.

20 Do not be among those who drink too much wine,[j]

CHAP. 22
a Pr 6:1-3

b De 19:14
Pr 23:10
Ho 5:10

c 1Sa 16:18, 19
1Ki 7:13, 14

CHAP. 23
d Pr 28:20
Joh 6:27
1Ti 6:9, 10

e 1Jo 2:16, 17

f Pr 27:24

Second Col.
a Pr 9:7
Pr 26:4

b Mt 7:6

c De 19:14
Pr 22:28

d Ex 22:22, 23
Ps 10:14

e Pr 13:24
Pr 19:18
Eph 6:4

f Pr 27:11
3Jo 4

g Ps 37:1

h Ps 111:10
2Co 7:1

i Ps 37:37
Pr 24:14

j Pr 20:1
Isa 5:11
Ro 13:13
1Pe 4:3

23:2 *Or "Restrain yourself." #Or "a soul full of desire." **23:4** *Or possibly, "Cease from your own understanding." **23:6** *Or "of anyone whose eye is evil." **23:7** *Or "calculating in his soul." #Lit., "his heart is not with you."

23:11 *Lit., "Redeemer." **23:13** *Or "child; youth." **23:14** *Or "his soul." #Or "Sheol," that is, the common grave of mankind. See Glossary. **23:16** *Lit., "My kidneys."

Among those who gorge themselves on meat,[a]

21 For a drunkard and a glutton will come to poverty,[b]
And drowsiness will clothe one with rags.

22 Listen to your father who caused your birth,
And do not despise your mother just because she has grown old.[c]

23 Buy* truth and never sell it,[d]
Also wisdom and discipline and understanding.[e]

24 The father of a righteous one will surely be joyful;
Whoever fathers a wise son will rejoice in him.

25 Your father and your mother will rejoice,
And she who gave birth to you will be joyful.

26 My son, do give your heart to me,
And may your eyes take pleasure in my ways.[f]

27 For a prostitute is a deep pit,
And an immoral* woman is a narrow well.[g]

28 She lies in wait like a robber;[h]
She increases the number of unfaithful men.

29 Who has woe? Who has uneasiness?
Who has quarrels? Who has complaints?
Who has wounds for no reason? Who has bleary* eyes?

30 Those lingering long over wine;[i]
Those searching out* mixed wine.

31 Do not look at the wine's red color
As it sparkles in the cup and goes down smoothly,

32 For in the end it bites like a serpent,
And it secretes poison like a viper.

33 Your eyes will see strange things,
And your heart will speak perverse things.[a]

34 And you will be like one lying down in the middle of the sea,
Like one lying at the top of a ship's mast.

35 You will say: "They have struck me, but I did not feel it.*
They beat me, but I did not know it.
When will I wake up?[b]
I need another drink."[#]

24 Do not envy evil men,
And do not crave their company,[c]

2 For their heart meditates on violence,
And their lips speak of trouble.

3 By wisdom a house* is built up,[d]
And by discernment it is made secure.

4 By knowledge its rooms are filled
With all sorts of precious and pleasant treasures.[e]

5 A wise man is powerful,[f]
And with knowledge a man increases his power.

6 By skillful direction* you will wage your war,[g]
And through many advisers[#] there is victory.[^h]

7 True wisdom is unattainable for a fool;[i]
He has nothing to say in the city gate.

CHAP. 23
a Pr 28:7
1Co 10:31

b De 21:20, 21
Pr 21:17

c Ex 20:12
Ex 21:17
Mt 15:5, 6
Eph 6:1

d Php 3:7, 8

e Pr 4:5
Pr 16:16

f Ps 107:43

g Pr 22:14

h Pr 7:10, 12
Ec 7:26

i Pr 20:1
Eph 5:18

Second Col.
a Ho 4:11

b Ge 19:33

CHAP. 24
c Ps 26:5
Pr 1:10

d Pr 9:1
Pr 14:1

e 1Ki 10:23
Pr 15:6

f Pr 8:14
Pr 21:22

g Pr 20:18
Lu 14:31, 32

h Pr 11:14
Pr 13:10
Pr 15:22
Ac 15:5, 6

i Pr 14:6
1Co 2:14

23:23 *Or "Acquire." 23:27 *Lit., "foreign." See Pr 2:16. 23:29 *Or "dullness of." 23:30 *Or "who gather to try out."

23:35 *Or "I felt no pain." #Or "I will seek it again." 24:3 *Or "household." 24:6 *Or "wise guidance." #Or "counselors." ^Or "success; salvation."

8 Anyone who plots evil
    Will be called a master
    schemer.[a]
9 Foolish schemes* are sinful,
    And people detest a ridi-
    culer.[b]
10 If you become discouraged
    in the day of distress,*
    Your strength will be meager.
11 Rescue those who are being
    taken away to death,
    And hold back those stagger-
    ing to the slaughter.[c]
12 If you say, "But we did not
    know about this,"
    Does not the One who exam-
    ines hearts* discern it?[d]
    Yes, the One who watches
    you# will know
    And will repay each man
    according to his activity.[e]
13 My son, eat honey, because
    it is good;
    Honey from the comb is
    sweet to the taste.
14 Likewise, know that wisdom
    is good for you.*[f]
    If you find it, you will have
    a future
    And your hope will not be
    cut off.[g]
15 Do not wickedly lie in
    ambush near the home
    of the righteous one;
    Do not destroy his place
    of rest.
16 For the righteous one may
    fall seven times, and he
    will get up again,[h]
    But the wicked will be made
    to stumble by calamity.[i]
17 When your enemy falls, do
    not rejoice,
    And when he stumbles,
    do not let your heart be
    joyful;[j]
18 Otherwise, Jehovah will see
    and be displeased,

And He will turn away his
    anger from him.*[a]
19 Do not be upset* because of
    evil men;
    Do not envy wicked people.
20 For there is no future for
    anyone evil;[b]
    The lamp of the wicked will
    be extinguished.[c]
21 My son, fear Jehovah and the
    king.[d]
    And do not associate with
    dissenters,*[e]
22 For their disaster will arise
    suddenly.[f]
    Who knows what ruin both*
    will bring upon them?[g]
23 These sayings also belong
    to the wise:
    Partiality in judgment is not
    good.[h]
24 Whoever says to the wicked
    one, "You are righteous,"[i]
    Will be cursed by the peo-
    ples and denounced by the
    nations.
25 But it will go well for those
    reproving him;[j]
    Blessings of good things will
    come upon them.[k]
26 People will kiss the lips of
    the one replying honestly.*[l]
27 Prepare your outside work,
    and get everything ready
    in the field;
    Then build your house.*
28 Do not testify against
    your neighbor without
    grounds.[m]
    Do not use your lips to
    deceive others.[n]
29 Do not say: "I will do to him
    just as he has done to me;
    I will repay him for what
    he did."*[o]

CHAP. 24
a Pr 6:12-14
b Pr 22:10
c Ps 82:4
d Pr 5:21
    Pr 17:3
    Pr 21:2
e Ps 62:12
    Mt 16:27
    Ro 2:5, 6
f Pr 19:9, 10
    Ps 119:103
g Pr 23:18
h Ps 34:19
    2Co 1:10
i 1Sa 26:9, 10
    Es 7:10
j Job 31:29
    Pr 17:5
    Pr 25:21, 22

Second Col.
a Eze 26:2, 3
    Zec 1:15
b Ps 73:18, 27
    Pr 10:7
c Pr 13:9
d 1Sa 24:6, 7
    1Pe 2:17
e 2Sa 15:12
f Nu 16:2, 31
g Pr 20:2
h Le 19:15
    De 1:16, 17
    De 16:19
    2Ch 19:7
    1Ti 5:21
i Pr 17:15
j Le 19:17
    1Ti 5:20
k Pr 28:23
l Pr 27:5
m Ex 20:16
n Eph 4:25
o Pr 20:22
    Ro 12:17, 19
    1Th 5:15

24:9 *Or "The schemes of a fool."
24:10 *Or "in times of trouble." 24:12
*Or "motives." #Or "your soul."
24:14 *Or "is sweet to your soul."

24:18 *That is, the enemy. 24:19 *Or
"show yourself heated up." 24:21 *Or
"those who are for a change." 24:22
*That is, Jehovah and the king. 24:26
*Or possibly, "Replying in a straight-
forward way is like giving a kiss."
24:27 *Or "household." 24:29 *Or
"I will get even with him."

30 I passed by the field of the lazy one,[a]

By the vineyard of the man lacking good sense.*

31 I saw that it was overgrown with weeds;

The ground was covered with nettles,

And its stone wall was broken down.[b]

32 I observed this and took it to heart;

I saw it and learned this lesson:*

33 A little sleep, a little slumbering,

A little folding of the hands to rest,

34 And your poverty will come like a bandit,

And your want like an armed man.[c]

25 These also are the proverbs of Sol′o·mon,[d] which the men of Hez·e·ki′ah[e] the king of Judah transcribed:*

2 It is the glory of God to keep a matter secret,[f]

And the glory of kings is to search through a matter.

3 As the heavens are high and the earth is deep,

So the heart of kings is unsearchable.

4 Remove the dross from the silver,

And it will emerge completely refined.[g]

5 Remove the wicked one from the king's presence,

And his throne will be firmly established in righteousness.[h]

6 Do not honor yourself before the king,[i]

And do not take a place among the prominent,[j]

7 For it is better for him to say to you, "Come up here,"

Than to humiliate you in the presence of a noble.[a]

8 Do not rush into a legal dispute,

For what will you do later if your neighbor humiliates you?[b]

9 Plead your case with your neighbor,[c]

But do not reveal what you were told confidentially,*[d]

10 So that the one listening will not put you to shame

And you spread a bad report* that cannot be recalled.

11 Like apples of gold in silver carvings*

Is a word spoken at the right time.[e]

12 Like an earring of gold and an ornament of fine gold

Is a wise reprover to the receptive ear.[f]

13 Just like the coldness of snow on the day of harvest

Is a faithful messenger to those who sent him,

For he refreshes his master.*[g]

14 Like clouds and wind that bring no rain

Is a man who boasts about a gift never given.*[h]

15 By patience a commander is won over,

And a gentle* tongue can break a bone.[i]

16 If you find honey, eat only what you need,

For if you take too much, you may vomit it up.[j]

17 Rarely set foot in your neighbor's house,

So that he does not get tired of you and hate you.

CHAP. 24
a Pr 6:10, 11

b Pr 20:4
Pr 22:13
Ec 10:18

c Pr 10:4
Pr 23:21

CHAP. 25
d 1Ki 4:29, 32
Ec 12:9

e 2Ch 29:1

f De 29:29
Ro 11:33

g Pr 17:3

h 1Ki 2:44, 46
Pr 20:28
Pr 29:14

i Pr 27:2

j Ps 131:1

Second Col.
a Lu 14:8-10
1Pe 5:5

b Pr 18:17
Mt 5:25

c Mt 18:15

d Pr 11:13

e Pr 15:23
Isa 50:4

f Ps 141:5
Pr 1:8, 9
Pr 9:8

g Pr 13:17

h Mt 5:37

i Ge 32:4, 5
Pr 15:1

j Pr 25:27

24:30 *Lit., "in want of heart." 24:32 *Lit., "I took the discipline:" 25:1 *Or "copied and compiled." 25:9 *Or "the secrets of others." 25:10 *Or "a malicious rumor." 25:11 *Or "settings." 25:13 *Or "the soul of his master." 25:14 *Lit., "a gift of falsehood." 25:15 *Or "mild."

18 Like a war club and a sword
and a sharp arrow
Is a man bearing false witness against his neighbor.[a]

19 Like a broken tooth or an unsteady foot
Is confidence in an unreliable* person in times of trouble.

20 Like one who removes a garment on a cold day
And like vinegar poured on soda*
Is the one who sings songs to a gloomy heart.[b]

21 If your enemy* is hungry, give him bread to eat;
If he is thirsty, give him water to drink,[c]

22 For you will be heaping burning coals on his head,*[d]
And Jehovah will reward you.

23 The north wind brings a downpour,
And a gossiping tongue brings an angry face.[e]

24 Better to dwell on a corner of the roof
Than in the same house with a quarrelsome* wife.[f]

25 Like cold water on a tired soul*
Is a good report from a distant land.[g]

26 Like a muddied spring and a ruined well
Is a righteous person who gives in to* a wicked one.

27 It is not good to eat too much honey,[h]
Nor is it glorious to seek one's own glory.[i]

28 As a city broken through, without a wall,

Is the man who cannot control his temper.*[a]

26 Like snow in summer and rain at harvesttime,
Honor is not fitting for someone stupid.[b]

2 Just as a bird has reason to flee and a swallow to fly,
So a curse does not come without a real reason.*

3 A whip is for the horse, a bridle is for the donkey,[c]
And the rod is for the back of stupid people.[d]

4 Do not answer the stupid one according to his foolishness,
So that you do not put yourself on his level.*

5 Answer the stupid one according to his foolishness,
So that he does not think he is wise.[e]

6 Like someone who cripples his own feet and harms himself*
Is the one who entrusts matters to someone stupid.

7 Like the limp* legs of the lame,
So is a proverb in the mouth of stupid people.[f]

8 Like tying a stone to a sling,
So is giving glory to someone stupid.[g]

9 Like a thorn plant that comes into the hand of a drunkard,
So is a proverb in the mouth of stupid people.

10 Like an archer who wounds at random,*
So is the one who hires the stupid one or those passing by.

CHAP. 25
a Ex 20:16

b Ps 137:3, 4

c Ex 23:5
2Ki 6:21, 22
Pr 24:17
Mt 5:44

d Ro 12:20

e Ps 101:5

f Pr 21:9, 19
Pr 27:15

g Pr 15:30
Isa 52:7

h Pr 25:16

i Pr 27:2
Joh 5:44
Php 2:3

Second Col.
a 1Sa 20:33
Pr 16:32
Pr 22:24, 25
Pr 29:11

CHAP. 26
b Pr 30:21, 22
Ec 10:7

c Ps 32:9

d Pr 27:22

e Mt 21:23-25

f Pr 17:7

g Pr 19:10
Pr 26:1

25:19 *Or possibly, "a treacherous." **25:20** *Or "alkali." **25:21** *Lit., "the one hating you." **25:22** *That is, to soften the person and melt his hardness. **25:24** *Or "nagging." **25:25** *See Glossary. **25:26** *Or "compromises with." Lit., "staggers before."

25:28 *Or "who has no restraint for his spirit." **26:2** *Or possibly, "So an undeserved curse does not come to pass." **26:4** *Or "So that you do not make yourself his equal." **26:6** *Lit., "drinks violence." **26:7** *Or "dangling." **26:10** *Or "who wounds everyone."

11 Like a dog that returns to
   its vomit,
      The stupid one repeats his
      foolishness.[a]

12 Have you seen a man who
   thinks he is wise?[b]
      There is more hope for some-
      one stupid than for him.

13 The lazy one says: "There is
   a young lion in the road,
      A lion in the public square!"[c]

14 A door keeps turning on its
   hinges,*
      And the lazy one on his bed.[d]

15 The lazy one buries his hand
   in the banquet bowl,
      But he is too tired to bring
      it back to his mouth.[e]

16 The lazy one thinks he is
   wiser
      Than seven people who give
      a sensible reply.

17 Like someone grabbing hold
   of a dog's ears
      Is the one passing by who
      becomes furious about*
      a quarrel that is not his.[f]

18 Like a madman who shoots
   fiery missiles, arrows,
   and death*

19 Is the man who plays a trick
   on his neighbor and says,
   "I was only joking!"[g]

20 Where there is no wood,
   the fire goes out,
      And where there is no slan-
      derer, quarreling ceases.[h]

21 As charcoal for the embers
   and wood for the fire,
      So a contentious man kindles
      a quarrel.[i]

22 The words of a slanderer are
   like tasty morsels;*
      They are gulped right down
      into the stomach.[j]

23 Like a silver glazing over
   a piece of earthenware

Are affectionate words from*
an evil heart.[a]

24 The one who hates others
   disguises it with his lips,
      But inside he harbors deceit.

25 Although he speaks graciously, do not trust him,
      For there are seven detest-
      able things in his heart.*

26 Though his hatred is
   concealed by deceit,
      His evil will be exposed
      in the congregation.

27 The one who digs a pit will
   fall into it,
      And whoever rolls away a
      stone—it will come back
      on him.[b]

28 A lying tongue hates those
   crushed by it,
      And a flattering mouth caus-
      es ruin.[c]

27 Do not boast about tomorrow,
      For you do not know what
      a day will bring.*[d]

2 Let someone else* praise
   you, and not your own
   mouth;
      Others,[#] and not your own
      lips.[e]

3 A stone is heavy and sand
   is weighty,
      But the irritation caused by
      a fool is heavier than both.[f]

4 There is the cruelty of rage
   and the flood of anger,
      But who can withstand
      jealousy?[g]

5 Open reproof is better than
   concealed love.[h]

6 The wounds inflicted by
   a friend are faithful,[i]
      But an enemy's kisses are
      plentiful.*

CHAP. 26
a 2Pe 2:22

b Pr 12:15
1Co 3:18
1Co 8:2

c Pr 22:13

d Pr 6:9
Pr 19:15
Pr 24:33, 34

e Pr 19:24

f 1Th 4:11
1Pe 4:15

g Pr 15:21

h Pr 22:10
Jas 3:6

i Pr 3:30
Pr 16:28
Pr 17:14

j Pr 18:8

Second Col.
a 2Sa 20:9, 10

b Es 7:10
Ps 9:15
Pr 28:10
Ec 10:8

c Pr 29:5

CHAP. 27
d Lu 12:19, 20
Jas 4:13, 14

e Pr 25:27
Jer 9:23
2Co 10:18

f 1Sa 25:25

g Ge 37:9-11
Pr 14:30
Ac 17:5

h Le 19:17
Mt 18:15

i 2Sa 12:7, 9
Ps 141:5
Re 3:19

26:23 *Lit., "fervent lips with." 26:25
*Or "For his heart is completely detest-
able." 27:1 *Lit., "will give birth to."
27:2 *Lit., "a stranger." #Lit., "A foreigner." 27:6 *Or possibly, "insincere;
forced."

26:14 *Or "pivot." 26:17 *Or possibly,
"who meddles in." 26:18 *Or "deadly
arrows." 26:22 *Or "like things to be
swallowed greedily."

7 One whose appetite* is
   satisfied turns down[#]
   honey from the comb,
   But to the hungry,[△] even
   what is bitter tastes sweet.

8 Like a bird that strays* from
   its nest
   Is a man who strays from his
   home.

9 Oil and incense make the
   heart rejoice;
   So does sweet friendship
   springing from sincere
   counsel.*[a]

10 Do not forsake your friend
   or your father's friend,
   And do not enter your own
   brother's house on the day
   of your disaster;
   Better is a neighbor nearby
   than a brother far away.[b]

11 Be wise, my son, and make
   my heart rejoice,[c]
   So that I can make a reply
   to him who taunts me.[d]

12 The shrewd person sees
   the danger and conceals
   himself,[e]
   But the inexperienced keep
   right on going and suffer
   the consequences.*

13 Take a man's garment if he
   has given security for a
   stranger;
   Seize the pledge from him
   if he did so for a foreign
   woman.*[f]

14 When someone blesses his
   fellow man with a loud
   voice early in the morning,
   It will be counted as a curse
   to him.

15 A quarrelsome* wife is like a
   constantly leaking roof on
   a rainy day.[g]

16 Whoever can restrain her
   can restrain the wind
   And can grip oil with his
   right hand.

17 As iron sharpens iron,
   So one man sharpens his
   friend.*[a]

18 The one who cares for a fig
   tree will eat its fruit,[b]
   And the one who takes
   care of his master will
   be honored.[c]

19 As water reflects one's face,
   So the heart of one man
   reflects another's.

20 The Grave and the place
   of destruction* are never
   satisfied,[d]
   Nor are a man's eyes ever
   satisfied.

21 As the refining pot is for
   silver and the furnace for
   gold,[e]
   So a person is tested by the
   praise he receives.*

22 Even if you pound a fool with
   a pestle
   Like crushed grain in a
   mortar,
   His foolishness will not leave
   him.

23 You should know well the
   appearance of your flock.
   Take good care of* your
   sheep,[f]

24 For wealth does not last
   forever,[g]
   Nor a crown* for all generations.

25 The green grass disappears,
   new grass appears,
   And the vegetation of the
   mountains is gathered in.

26 The young rams provide your
   clothing,
   And the male goats provide
   the price of a field.

CHAP. 27
a 1Sa 23:16
  Pr 15:23
  Pr 16:24

b Pr 17:17
  Pr 18:24

c Pr 10:1
  Pr 23:15
  2Jo 4

d Job 1:8, 9

e Pr 18:10
  Isa 26:20
  Heb 11:7

f Pr 20:16

g Pr 21:9, 19

Second Col.
a 1Sa 23:16
  Heb 10:24,
  25

b Pr 13:4

c Ge 39:2
  Pr 17:2

d Pr 30:15, 16

e Pr 17:3

f Col 3:23

g Pr 23:4, 5
  1Ti 6:17

27:7 *Or "A soul who." [#]Lit., "treads
down." [△]Or "the hungry soul." 27:8
*Or "is fleeing away." 27:9 *Or "from
counsel of the soul." 27:12 *Or "penalty." 27:13 *Or "a foreigner." 27:15
*Or "nagging."

27:17 *Lit., "the face of his friend."
27:20 *Or "Sheol and Abaddon." 27:21
*Or "So a man is according to his
praise." 27:23 *Or "Set your heart on;
Pay attention to." 27:24 *Or "diadem."

27 And there will be enough
goat's milk to feed you,
To feed your household, and
to sustain your servant
girls.

28 The wicked flee when no
one pursues them,
But the righteous are as
confident as a lion.*ᵃ

2 When there is transgression*
in the land, it will have one
prince after another,ᵇ
But with the help of a man
of discernment and knowl-
edge, a prince# will long
endure.ᶜ

3 A poor man who defrauds
the lowlyᵈ
Is like a rain that sweeps
away all the food.

4 Those who abandon the law
praise the wicked one,
But those who observe the
law are indignant with
them.ᵉ

5 Evil men cannot understand
justice,
But those who seek Jehovah
can understand every-
thing.ᶠ

6 Better is a poor man who
walks in his integrity
Than a rich man whose ways
are corrupt.ᵍ

7 An understanding son
observes the law,
But a companion of gluttons
disgraces his father.ʰ

8 The one who increases his
wealth by interestⁱ and
usury
Amasses it for the one who
shows favor to the poor.ʲ

9 The one refusing to listen
to the law
—Even his prayer is detest-
able.ᵏ

10 The one misleading the upright into an evil course
will fall into his own pit,ˡ

But the blameless will inherit
what is good.ᵃ

11 A rich man is wise in his own
eyes,ᵇ
But a poor man with discernment can see through him.ᶜ

12 When the righteous triumph,
there is great glory,
But when the wicked rise
to power, people go into
hiding.ᵈ

13 The one covering over
his transgressions will not
succeed,ᵉ
But whoever confesses and
abandons them will be
shown mercy.ᶠ

14 Happy is the man who is
always on guard,*
But whoever hardens
his heart will fall into
calamity.ᵍ

15 Like a growling lion and
a charging bear
Is a wicked ruler over a
helpless people.ʰ

16 A leader without discernment abuses his power,ⁱ
But the one hating dishonest
profit will prolong his life.ʲ

17 A man burdened with bloodguilt for taking someone's
life* will keep fleeing until
the grave.#ᵏ
Let no one support him.

18 The one walking faultlessly
will be saved,ˡ
But the one whose ways
are crooked will suddenly
fall.ᵐ

19 The one cultivating his
ground will have plenty
of bread,
But the one taking up worthless pursuits will have his
fill of poverty.ⁿ

20 A faithful man will receive
many blessings,ᵒ

CHAP. 28
a Da 3:16, 17
Ac 4:13

b 1Ki 16:8, 15
1Ki 16:22

c Da 4:27

d Pr 14:31

e Nu 25:6-8
1Sa 15:22, 23
Eph 5:11

f Ps 25:14
Mr 4:11, 12
Jas 1:5

g Pr 16:8
Pr 19:1

h Pr 23:20
1Co 15:33

i De 23:19

j Pr 13:22
Pr 19:17

k Ps 66:18
Pr 15:29
Isa 1:15

l Ps 7:14-16

Second Col.
a De 7:12
Ps 37:11, 18
Ps 84:11

b Pr 18:11

c Mr 10:21

d 1Ki 17:1-3
Pr 29:2

e 1Sa 15:13-15

f 2Sa 12:13
2Ch 33:12, 13
Ps 32:3, 5
Ps 51:1

g Ex 7:22
Ne 9:29
Pr 29:1
Jer 16:12, 13

h Zep 3:3
Mt 2:16

i Ne 5:15
Am 4:1

j Isa 33:15, 16

k Ge 9:6
1Ki 21:19
Mt 27:3-5

l Ps 5:21

m Ps 73:12, 18
1Th 5:3
Re 3:3

n Pr 23:21
Lu 15:13, 14

o 1Sa 18:5
Ne 7:2
Ps 101:6

28:1 *Or "a young lion." 28:2 *Or "revolt." #Lit., "he."

28:14 *Or "who is never without fear."
28:17 *Or "with the blood of a soul."
#Or "pit."

But the one hastening to get rich will not remain innocent.[a]

21 It is not good to show partiality;[b]
But a man might do wrong for a piece of bread.

22 An envious* man is eager for wealth,
Not knowing that poverty will overtake him.

23 Whoever reproves a man[c] will afterward find more favor[d]
Than someone who flatters with his tongue.

24 Whoever robs his father and mother and says, "It is not wrong,"[e]
Is a partner of the man who causes ruin.[f]

25 The greedy person* stirs up dissension,
But whoever relies on Jehovah will prosper.[#g]

26 Whoever trusts in his own heart is stupid,[h]
But the one who walks in wisdom will escape.[i]

27 Whoever gives to the poor will lack nothing,[j]
But the one who closes his eyes to them will receive many curses.

28 When the wicked rise to power, a man hides himself,
But when they perish, the righteous increase.[k]

29 A man who stiffens his neck* after much reproof[l]
Will suddenly be broken beyond healing.[m]

2 When the righteous are many, the people rejoice,
But when the wicked one rules, the people groan.[n]

3 A man who loves wisdom makes his father rejoice,[a]
But the one who keeps company with prostitutes squanders his wealth.[b]

4 By justice a king brings stability to a land,[c]
But a man seeking bribes brings it to ruin.

5 A man who flatters his neighbor
Spreads out a net for his feet.[d]

6 A bad man's transgression ensnares him,[e]
But the righteous one cries out joyfully and rejoices.[f]

7 The righteous one is concerned about the legal rights of the poor,[g]
But the wicked one has no such concern.[h]

8 Boastful men inflame a town,[i]
But those who are wise turn away anger.[j]

9 When a wise man enters into a controversy with a fool,
There will be ranting and ridicule, but no satisfaction.[k]

10 Bloodthirsty men hate anyone innocent,*[l]
And they seek to take the life# of the upright.△

11 A stupid person gives vent to all his feelings,*[m]
But the wise one calmly keeps them in check.[n]

12 When a ruler pays attention to lies,
All his servants will be wicked.[o]

13 The poor man and the oppressor have this in common:*
Jehovah gives light to the eyes of both.#

CHAP. 28
a 2Ki 5:20-22
  Jer 17:11
  1Ti 6:9
b Le 19:15
  Pr 18:5
  Jas 2:1
c 2Sa 12:7, 9
  Ga 2:11
d Ps 141:5
  Pr 27:6
e Mr 7:10, 11
f Pr 19:26
g 1Ki 3:11-13
h Pr 3:5
  Jer 17:9
i Job 28:28
j De 15:7, 10
  Ps 41:1
  Pr 19:17
  Heb 13:16
k Es 8:17

CHAP. 29
l Ex 11:10
  2Ch 36:11-13
m 1Sa 2:22-25
  2Ch 36:15, 16
n Es 3:13, 15

Second Col.
a Pr 27:11
b Pr 5:8-10
  Pr 6:26
  Lu 15:13, 14
c 2Sa 8:15
  Ps 89:14
  Isa 9:7
d Pr 26:28
  Ro 16:18
e Pr 5:22
f Ps 97:11
g Ps 41:1
h Jer 5:28
i Jas 3:6
j Ac 19:29, 35
k Pr 26:4
l Ge 27:41
  1Sa 20:31
  1Jo 3:11, 12
m Pr 12:16
  Pr 25:28
n Pr 14:29
o 1Ki 21:8-11
  Jer 38:4, 5

28:22 *Or "greedy." 28:25 *Or possibly, "The arrogant soul." #Lit., "will be made fat." 29:1 *Or "who remains stubborn."

29:10 *Or "blameless." #Or "soul." △Or possibly, "But the upright seeks to protect his life." 29:11 *Lit., "spirit." 29:13 *Lit., "meet together." #That is, He gives them life.

14 When a king judges the poor fairly,[a]

His throne will always be secure.[b]

15 The rod* and reproof impart wisdom,[c]

But a child left unrestrained brings shame on his mother.

16 When the wicked increase, transgression increases,

But the righteous will see their downfall.[d]

17 Discipline your son and he will bring you rest;

And he will give you* great pleasure.[e]

18 Where there is no vision,* the people go unrestrained,[f]

But happy are those who observe the law.[g]

19 A servant will not let himself be corrected by words,

For though he understands, he does not obey.[h]

20 Have you seen a man hasty with his words?[i]

There is more hope for a fool than for him.[j]

21 If a servant is pampered from his youth,

He will become thankless later on.

22 A man prone to anger stirs up strife;[k]

Anyone disposed to rage commits many transgressions.[l]

23 The haughtiness of a man will humble him,[m]

But whoever is humble in spirit will obtain glory.[n]

24 The partner of a thief hates himself.*

He may hear the call to testify,[ᵁ] but he reports nothing.[o]

25 Trembling at* men is[ᵁ] a snare,[a]

But the one trusting in Jehovah will be protected.[b]

26 Many seek an audience with* a ruler,

But it is from Jehovah that a man gets justice.[c]

27 An unjust man is detestable to the righteous,[d]

But the one whose way is upright is detestable to the wicked one.[e]

30 The weighty message contained in the words of A'gur son of Ja'keh, which he spoke to Ith'i·el, to Ith'i·el and U'cal.

2 I am more ignorant than anyone else,[f]

And I lack the understanding a man should have.

3 I have not learned wisdom,

And I do not possess the knowledge of the Most Holy One.

4 Who has ascended to heaven and then descended?[g]

Who has gathered the wind in the palms of both hands?

Who has wrapped up the waters in his garment?[h]

Who has established* all the ends of the earth?[i]

What is his name and the name of his son—if you know?

5 Every saying of God is refined.[j]

He is a shield to those taking refuge in him.[k]

6 Add nothing to his words,[l]

Or he will reprove you,

And you will be proved a liar.

7 Two things I ask of you.

Do not withhold them from me before I die.

CHAP. 29

a Ps 72:1, 2

b Pr 20:28
Pr 25:5
Isa 9:7

c Pr 22:6
Pr 22:15
Pr 23:13
Eph 6:4

d Ps 37:34
Re 18:20

e Heb 12:11

f Ho 4:6

g Pr 19:16
Joh 13:17
Jas 1:25

h Pr 26:3

i Ec 5:2
Jas 1:19

j Pr 14:29
Pr 21:5

k Pr 15:18

l 1Sa 18:8, 9
Jas 3:16

m Es 6:6, 10
Jas 4:6

n Pr 18:12
Mt 18:4
Php 2:8, 9

o Le 5:1

Second Col.

a Mt 10:28
Mt 26:75

b 2Ch 14:11
Pr 18:10

c Ps 62:12
Lu 18:6, 7

d Ps 119:115
Ps 139:21

e Joh 7:7
1Jo 3:13

CHAP. 30

f Job 42:3

g Joh 3:13

h Isa 40:12

i Job 38:4

j Ps 12:6

k Ge 15:1
2Sa 22:31
Ps 84:11

l De 4:2
Re 22:18

29:15 *Or "discipline; punishment." **29:17** *Or "your soul." **29:18** *Or "prophetic vision; revelation." **29:24** *Or "his own soul." ᵁOr "an oath involving a curse."

29:25 *Or "Fear of." ᵁOr "lays." **29:26** *Or possibly, "seek the favor of." Lit., "seek the face of." **30:4** *Lit., "raised."

8 Remove untruth and lies far
  from me.ᵃ
  Give me neither poverty nor
    riches.
  Just let me consume my
    portion of food,ᵇ
9 So that I do not become
  satisfied and deny you and
  say, "Who is Jehovah?"ᶜ
  Nor let me become poor
    and steal and dishonor*
    the name of my God.
10 Do not slander a servant to
  his master,
  Or he may curse you and you
    will be found guilty.ᵈ
11 There is a generation that
  curses its father
  And does not bless its
    mother.ᵉ
12 There is a generation that
  is pure in its own eyesᶠ
  But has not been cleansed
    from its filth.*
13 There is a generation whose
  eyes are so haughty
  And whose eyes look so
    arrogantly!ᵍ
14 There is a generation whose
  teeth are swords
  And whose jaws are slaugh-
    tering knives;
  They devour the lowly ones
    of the earth
  And the poor from among
    mankind.ʰ
15 The leeches have two daughters that cry, "Give! Give!"
  There are three things that
    do not get satisfied,
  Four that never say,
    "Enough!"
16 —The Grave*ⁱ and a barren
  womb,
  A land that is deprived of
    water,

  And fire that never says,
    "Enough!"
17 The eye that mocks a father
  and despises obedience to
  a motherᵃ
  —The ravens of the valley*
    will peck it out,
  And the young eagles will eat
    it up.ᵇ
18 There are three things that
  are beyond my comprehension,*
  And four that I do not under-
    stand:
19 The way of an eagle in the
  heavens,
  The way of a serpent on a
    rock,
  The way of a ship in the open
    sea,
  And the way of a man with
    a young woman.
20 This is the way of an adulterous woman:
  She eats, she wipes her
    mouth;
  Then she says, "I have done
    nothing wrong."ᶜ
21 There are three things that
  make the earth shudder
  And four things it cannot
    endure:
22 When a slave rules as king,ᵈ
  When a fool is glutted with
    food,
23 When a hated* woman is
  taken as a wife,
  And when a servant girl
    takes the place of* her
    mistress.ᵉ
24 Four things on earth are
  among the smallest,
  But they are instinctively
    wise:*ᶠ
25 The ants are not strong
  creatures,*

CHAP. 30
ᵃ Pr 12:22

ᵇ Mt 6:11
  1Ti 6:8

ᶜ De 6:10-12

ᵈ Da 6:24

ᵉ Le 20:9
  Pr 19:26
  Mr 7:10, 11

ᶠ Ps 36:1, 2
  Isa 65:5
  1Jo 1:8

ᵍ Ps 101:5
  Pr 6:16, 17

ʰ Ps 14:3
  Pr 22:16
  Isa 32:7

ⁱ Pr 27:20

Second Col.
ᵃ Pr 23:22

ᵇ Le 20:9
  De 21:18, 21
  Pr 20:20

ᶜ Pr 7:10, 11

ᵈ Pr 19:10
  Ec 10:7
  Isa 3:4

ᵉ Ge 16:5

ᶠ Job 35:11

30:9 *Or "assail." 30:12 *Lit., "excrement." 30:16 *Or "Sheol," that is, the
common grave of mankind. See Glossary. 30:17 *Or "wadi." 30:18 *Or "are too
wonderful for me." 30:23 *Or "an unloved." #Or "supplants." 30:24 *Or
"exceedingly wise." 30:25 *Lit., "a
people not strong."

Yet they prepare their food
in the summer.[a]

26 The rock badgers*[b] are not
mighty creatures,[#]
Yet they make their house
in the crags.[c]

27 The locusts[d] have no king,
Yet they all go forward in
formation.*[e]

28 The gecko lizard[f] clings with
its feet,
And it goes into the palace
of a king.

29 There are three things that
have an impressive stride,
Four that are impressive as
they move:

30 The lion, the mightiest
among beasts,
Which does not retreat from
anyone;[g]

31 The greyhound; the male
goat;
And a king whose army is
with him.

32 If you have foolishly exalted
yourself[h]
Or if you have schemed to
do so,
Put your hand over your
mouth.[i]

33 For as the churning of milk
produces butter
And the squeezing of the
nose produces blood,
So the stirring up of anger
produces quarrels.[j]

31 The words of King Lem'-
u·el, the weighty message
his mother gave to instruct him:[k]

2 What should I tell you, O my
son,
What, O son of my womb,
And what, O son of my
vows?[l]

3 Do not give your vigor to
women,[m]
Nor follow ways that destroy
kings.[n]

4 It is not for kings,
O Lem'u·el,
It is not for kings to drink
wine
Nor for rulers to say, "Where
is my drink?"[a]

5 So that they do not drink and
forget what is decreed
And pervert the rights of the
lowly ones.

6 Give alcohol to those who
are perishing[b]
And wine to those in bitter
distress.*[c]

7 Let them drink and forget
their poverty;
Let them remember their
trouble no more.

8 Speak up in behalf of the
speechless;
Defend the rights of all
who are perishing.[d]

9 Speak up and judge
righteously;
Defend the rights* of the
lowly and the poor.[e]

א [Aleph]

10 Who can find a capable*
wife?[f]
Her value is far more than
that of corals.[#]

ב [Beth]

11 Her husband trusts her from
his heart,
And he lacks nothing of
value.

ג [Gimel]

12 She rewards him with good,
not bad,
All the days of her life.

ד [Daleth]

13 She obtains wool and linen;
She delights to work with
her hands.[g]

ה [He]

14 She is like the ships of
a merchant,[h]

CHAP. 30	
a	Pr 6:6-8
b	Le 11:5
c	Ps 104:18
d	Ex 10:14 Joe 1:4
e	Joe 2:7
f	Le 11:29, 30
g	Nu 23:24 Isa 31:4
h	Pr 26:12
i	Pr 27:2
j	Pr 26:21
CHAP. 31	
k	Pr 1:8 2Ti 1:5
l	1Sa 1:11, 28
m	Ho 4:11
n	De 17:15, 17 1Ki 11:1-3 Ne 13:26
Second Col.	
a	Ec 10:17 Isa 28:7
b	Ps 104:15 Mt 27:34
c	Jer 16:7
d	Ps 82:4
e	De 1:16, 17 2Sa 8:15 Ps 72:1, 2 Isa 11:4
f	Ru 3:10, 11 Pr 12:4 Pr 19:14
g	1Sa 2:18, 19 Tit 2:3-5
h	2Ch 9:21

30:26 *Or "The hyraxes." #Lit., "a people not mighty." **30:27** *Or "divided in
groups."

31:6 *Or "those bitter of soul." **31:9**
*Or "Plead the cause." **31:10** *Or "an
excellent." #See Glossary.

Bringing her food in from
afar.

֖ [Waw]

15 She also rises while it is still
night,
Providing food for her
household
And portions for her female
servants.ᵃ

֖ [Zayin]

16 She sets her mind on a field
and buys it;
She plants a vineyard from
her own labors.*

֖ [Heth]

17 She prepares herself for
hard work,*ᵇ
And she strengthens her
arms.

֖ [Teth]

18 She sees that her trading
is profitable;
Her lamp does not go out
at night.

֖ [Yod]

19 Her hands seize the distaff,
And her hands take hold of
the spindle.*ᶜ

֖ [Kaph]

20 She extends her palm to the
lowly one,
And she opens her hands
to the poor.ᵈ

֖ [Lamed]

21 She does not worry about
her household because
of the snow,
For her whole household
is clothed in warm*
garments.

֖ [Mem]

22 She makes her own bed
covers.
Her clothing is of linen and
purple wool.

CHAP. 31

a 1Ti 5:9, 10

b Ge 24:15, 20

c Ex 35:25

d 1Sa 25:18
Pr 19:17
1Ti 2:10
Heb 13:16

Second Col.

a Ru 4:1
Job 29:7, 8

b Jg 13:22, 23
1Sa 25:30, 31
Es 5:8
Tit 2:3

c Pr 14:1
1Ti 5:9, 10
Tit 2:3-5

d 2Ki 9:30
Es 1:10-12
Pr 6:25, 26

e Ge 24:60
Jg 5:7
1Pe 3:3, 4

f Ru 3:10, 11

g Ro 16:1, 2

֖ [Nun]

23 Her husband is well-known
in the city gates,ᵃ
Where he sits among the
elders of the land.

֖ [Samekh]

24 She makes and sells linen
garments*
And supplies belts to the
merchants.

֖ [Ayin]

25 She is clothed with strength
and splendor,
And she looks to the future
with confidence.*

֖ [Pe]

26 She opens her mouth in
wisdom;ᵇ
The law of kindness* is on
her tongue.

֖ [Tsade]

27 She watches over the activity of her household,
And the bread of laziness
she does not eat.ᶜ

֖ [Qoph]

28 Her children rise up and
declare her happy;
Her husband rises up and
praises her.

֖ [Resh]

29 There are many capable*
women,
But you—you surpass
them all.

֖ [Shin]

30 Charm may be false, and
beauty may be fleeting,*ᵈ
But the woman who fears
Jehovah will be praised.ᵉ

֖ [Taw]

31 Give her the reward for what
she does,*ᶠ
And let her works praise her
in the city gates.ᵍ

31:16 *Or "with her earnings." Lit.,
"from the fruitage of her hands." **31:17**
*Lit., "girds her hips with strength."
31:19 *The distaff and the spindle were
sticks used to spin or make thread and
yarn. **31:21** *Lit., "double."

31:24 *Or "undergarments." **31:25**
*Or "laughs at a future day." **31:26**
*Or "Loving instruction; The law of loy-
al love." **31:29** *Or "excellent." **31:30**
*Or "empty." **31:31** *Lit., "Give her
from the fruit of her hands."

ECCLESIASTES

OUTLINE OF CONTENTS

---

1 The words of the congregator,*ᵃ the son of David, the king in Jerusalem.ᵇ

2 "The greatest futility!"*
  says the congregator,
"The greatest futility!
  Everything is futile!"ᶜ

3 What does a person gain
  from all his hard work
At which he toils under
  the sun?ᵃ
4 A generation is going, and
  a generation is coming,
But the earth remains*
  forever.ᵇ

CHAP. 1
a 1Ki 8:1, 22
b 1Ki 2:12
  2Ch 9:30
c Ps 39:5
  Ro 8:20

Second Col.
a Ec 2:11
  Mt 16:26
  Joh 6:27
b Ps 78:69
  Ps 104:5
  Ps 119:90

1:1 *Or "assembler; convener."   **1:2** *Or "vanity."

1:4 *Lit., "is standing."

5 The sun rises,* and the sun
  sets;
  Then it hurries back# to the
    place where it rises again.ᵃ
6 The wind goes south and
    circles around to the north;
  Round and round it contin-
    uously circles; the wind
    keeps making its rounds.
7 All the streams* flow into the
    sea, yet the sea is not full.ᵇ
  To the place from which the
    streams flow, there they
    return so as to flow again.ᶜ
8 All things are wearisome;
  No one can even speak of it.
  The eye is not satisfied at
    seeing;
  Nor is the ear filled from
    hearing.
9 What has been is what
    will be,
  And what has been done
    will be done again;
  There is nothing new under
    the sun.ᵈ
10 Is there anything of which
    one may say, "Look at this
    —it is new"?
  It already existed from long
    ago;
  It already existed before
    our time.
11 No one remembers people
    of former times;
  Nor will anyone remember
    those who come later;
  Nor will they be remem-
    bered by those who come
    still later.ᵉ

12 I, the congregator, have
been king over Israel in Jerusa-
lem.ᶠ **13** I set my heart to study
and explore with wisdomᵍ everything that has been done under
the heavensʰ—the miserable occupation that God has given to
the sons of men that keeps them
occupied.

14 I saw all the works that were
    done under the sun,
  And look! everything was
    futile, a chasing after the
    wind.ᵃ
15 What is crooked cannot
    be made straight,
  And what is lacking cannot
    possibly be counted.

16 Then I said in my heart:
"Look! I have acquired great wisdom, more than anyone who was
before me in Jerusalem,ᵇ and my
heart gained a great deal of wisdom and knowledge."ᶜ **17** I applied my heart to knowing wisdom and to knowing madness*
and to knowing folly,ᵈ and this
too is a chasing after the wind.
18 For an abundance of wisdom
    brings an abundance of
    frustration,
  So that whoever increases
    knowledge increases pain.ᵉ

2 Then I said in my heart:
  "Come and let me try out
pleasure* and see what good
comes." But look! that too was
futility.
2 I said about laughter,
    "It is madness!"
  And about pleasure,*
    "What use is it?"

3 I explored with my heart by
indulging myself with wine,ᶠ all
the while maintaining my own
wisdom; I even embraced foolishness to find out what was the
best thing for humans to do during their few days of life under the heavens. **4** I undertook
great works.ᵍ I built houses for
myself;ʰ I planted vineyards for
myself.ⁱ **5** I made gardens and
parks for myself, and I planted
in them all sorts of fruit trees.
6 I made pools of water for myself, to irrigate a grove* of flourishing trees. **7** I acquired male
and female servants,ʲ and I had

CHAP. 1
a Ge 8:22
  Ps 19:6

c Job 38:8, 10

c Job 36:27, 28
  Isa 55:10
  Am 5:8

d Ge 8:22
  Ec 1:4

e Ec 2:16
  Ec 9:5
  Isa 40:6

f 1Ki 11:42
  Ec 1:1

g 1Ki 4:29, 30

h Ec 8:16

Second Col.
a Ps 39:5, 6
  Ec 2:11, 18
  Ec 2:26
  Lu 12:15

b Ec 2:9

c 1Ki 3:28
  1Ki 4:29-31
  2Ch 1:10-12

d Ec 2:2, 3
  Ec 2:12
  Ec 7:25

e Ec 2:15
  Ec 12:12

CHAP. 2
f Ps 104:15
  Ec 10:19

g 1Ki 9:17-19
  2Ch 9:15, 16

h 1Ki 7:1, 8

i 1Ki 4:25
  Ca 8:11

j 1Sa 8:10, 13
  1Ki 9:22

1:5 *Or "shines forth." #Or "returns
panting." 1:7 *Or "winter streams;
seasonal streams."

1:17 *Or "extreme foolishness." 2:1, 2
*Or "rejoicing." 2:6 *Or "forest."

servants born in my household.* I also acquired much livestock —cattle and flocks[a]—more than any of my predecessors in Jerusalem. **8** I accumulated silver and gold for myself,[b] the treasures of* kings and of provinces.[c] I gathered male and female singers for myself, as well as what brings great pleasure to the sons of men—a woman, yes, many women.# **9** So I grew great and surpassed anyone prior to me in Jerusalem.[d] And my wisdom remained with me.

10 I did not deny myself anything that I desired.*[e] I did not withhold from my heart any sort of pleasure,# for my heart was joyful because of all my hard work, and this was my reward△ for all my hard work.[f] **11** But when I reflected on all the works that my own hands had done and on all the hard work that I had toiled to accomplish,[g] I saw that everything was futile, a chasing after the wind;[h] there was nothing of real value* under the sun.[i]

12 Then I turned my attention to wisdom and madness and folly.[j] (For what can the man do who comes after the king? Only what has already been done.) **13** And I saw that there is an advantage to wisdom over folly,[k] just as there is an advantage to light over darkness.

14 The wise one has his eyes in his head;*[l] but the stupid one is walking in darkness.[m] I have also come to realize that there is one outcome* that befalls all of them.[n] **15** Then I said in my heart: "What happens to the stupid one will also happen to me."*[o]

What, then, did I gain by becoming excessively wise? So I said in my heart: "This too is futility." **16** For there is no lasting memory either of the wise one or of the stupid one.[a] In the days to come, everyone will be forgotten. And how will the wise one die? Along with the stupid one.[b]

17 So I came to hate life,[c] because everything being done under the sun seemed distressing to me, for everything was futile,[d] a chasing after the wind.[e] **18** I came to hate all that I had worked so hard for under the sun,[f] because I must leave it behind for the man coming after me.[g] **19** And who knows whether he will be wise or foolish?[h] Yet he will take control over all the things I spent great effort and wisdom to acquire under the sun. This too is futility. **20** So I began to despair in my heart over all the hard work at which I had toiled under the sun. **21** For a man may work hard, guided by wisdom and knowledge and skill, but he must hand over his portion* to a man who did not work for it.[i] This too is futility and a great tragedy.#

22 What does a man really gain from all his hard work and ambition that drives him* to work hard under the sun?[j] **23** For during all his days, his occupation brings pain and frustration,[k] and even at night his heart does not rest.[l] This too is futility.

24 There is nothing better for a man than to eat and drink and find enjoyment* in his hard work.[m] This too, I have realized, is from the hand of the true God,[n] **25** for who eats and who drinks better than I do?[o]

CHAP. 2

a 1Ki 4:22, 23
b 1Ki 9:14, 28
  1Ki 10:10
  2Ch 1:15
c 1Ki 10:14, 15
  2Ch 9:13, 14
d 1Ki 3:13
  1Ki 10:23
e 1Ki 11:9
f Ec 3:22
  Ec 5:18
  Ec 9:9
g 1Ki 7:1
h Ps 49:10
  Ec 1:14
  Ec 2:16
  1Ti 6:7
i Ec 1:3
  Ec 2:17
j Ec 1:17
  Ec 7:25
k Pr 4:7
  Ec 7:11, 12
l Pr 4:25
m Pr 14:8
  Pr 17:24
  Joh 3:19
  1Jo 2:11
n Ec 3:19, 20
  Ec 9:2, 3
  Ec 9:11
o Ps 49:10

Second Col.

a Ex 1:8
  Ec 1:11
b Ec 6:8
  Ro 5:12
c 1Ki 19:2, 4
  Jer 20:17, 18
d Job 7:6
  Ec 2:21
  Ro 8:20
e Ec 1:14
  Ec 5:16
f Ec 2:4-8
g Ps 39:6
  Lu 12:20
h 1Ki 12:6, 8
  2Ch 12:1, 9
i Ec 2:18
  Ec 5:15, 16
j Ec 1:3
  Ec 3:9
k Job 14:1, 2
  Lu 12:29
l Ge 31:40, 41
m De 12:18
  Ec 3:22
  Ec 8:15
  Ac 14:17
n Ec 3:12, 13
  Ec 5:18, 19
o 1Ki 4:7
  1Ki 4:22, 23
  1Ki 10:4, 5
  1Ki 10:21

2:7 *Lit., "sons of the house." 2:8 *Or "property peculiar to." #Or "a lady, yes, ladies." 2:10 *Lit., "that my eyes asked for." #Or "rejoicing." △Or "portion." 2:11 *Or "of advantage." 2:14 *Or "has his eyes open." #Or "eventuality."

2:21 *Or "hand over everything." #Or "calamity." 2:22 *Lit., "and the striving of his heart." 2:24 *Or "cause his soul to see good."

26 To the man who pleases him he gives wisdom and knowledge and rejoicing,[a] but to the sinner he gives the occupation of gathering and merely collecting to give to the one who pleases the true God.[b] This too is futility, a chasing after the wind.

3 There is an appointed time for everything,

A time for every activity under the heavens:

2 A time for birth and a time to die;

A time to plant and a time to uproot what was planted;

3 A time to kill and a time to heal;

A time to tear down and a time to build up;

4 A time to weep and a time to laugh;

A time to wail and a time to dance;*

5 A time to throw stones away and a time to gather stones together;

A time to embrace and a time to refrain from embracing;

6 A time to search and a time to give up as lost;

A time to keep and a time to throw away;

7 A time to rip apart[c] and a time to sew together;

A time to be silent[d] and a time to speak;[e]

8 A time to love and a time to hate;[f]

A time for war and a time for peace.

9 What does the worker gain from all his efforts?[g] **10** I have seen the occupation that God has given to the sons of men to keep them occupied. **11** He has made everything beautiful* in its time.[h] He has even put eternity in their heart; yet mankind will never find out the work that the true God has made from start to finish.

12 I have concluded that there is nothing better for them than to rejoice and to do good during their life,[a] **13** also that everyone should eat and drink and find enjoyment for all his hard work. It is the gift of God.[b]

14 I have come to know that everything the true God makes will endure forever. There is nothing to add to it and nothing to subtract from it. The true God has made it this way, so that people will fear him.[c]

15 Whatever happens has already happened, and what is to come has already been;[d] but the true God seeks what has been pursued.*

16 I have also seen this under the sun: In the place of justice there was wickedness, and in the place of righteousness there was wickedness.[e] **17** So I said in my heart: "The true God will judge both the righteous and the wicked,[f] for there is a time for every activity and every action."

18 I also said in my heart about the sons of men that the true God will test them and show them that they are like animals, **19** for there is an outcome* for humans and an outcome for animals; they all have the same outcome.[g] As the one dies, so the other dies; and they all have but one spirit.[h] So man has no superiority over animals, for everything is futile. **20** All are going to the same place.[i] They all come from the dust,[j] and they all are returning to the dust.[k] **21** Who really knows whether the spirit of humans ascends upward, and whether the spirit of animals descends down to the earth?[l] **22** And I saw that there is noth-

---

CHAP. 2
a 1Sa 18:14
  Pr 3:32, 33
  Isa 3:10

b De 6:10, 11
  Pr 13:22
  Pr 28:8

CHAP. 3
c 2Sa 3:31

d Ps 39:1

e 1Sa 19:4
  1Sa 25:23, 24
  Es 4:13, 14
  Ps 145:11
  Pr 9:8

f Ps 139:21
  Ro 12:9

g Ec 1:3
  Ec 5:15, 16

h Ge 1:31
  Ro 1:20

Second Col.
a Ps 37:3
  1Th 5:15

b Ec 5:18, 19
  Isa 65:21, 22

c Jer 10:7
  Re 15:4

d Ec 1:9

e Ps 82:2
  Ps 94:16, 21

f Ec 12:14
  Ac 17:31
  Ro 2:5, 6

g Job 14:10
  Ps 39:5
  Ps 89:48

h Ge 7:22
  Ps 104:29
  Ec 12:7

i Ec 9:10

j Ge 2:7, 19

k Ge 3:19
  Job 10:9

l Ps 146:3, 4
  Ec 3:19
  Ec 9:10

3:4 *Lit., "leap; skip about." 3:11 *Or "well-arranged; proper; appropriate."

3:15 *Or possibly, "what has passed away." 3:19 *Or "eventuality."

ing better than for a man to find enjoyment in his work,[a] because that is his reward;* for who can enable him to see what will happen after he is gone?[b]

4 Again I turned my attention to all the acts of oppression that go on under the sun. I saw the tears of the oppressed, and there was no one to comfort them.[c] And their oppressors had the power, and there was no one to comfort them. **2** And I congratulated the dead who had already died rather than the living who were still alive.[d] **3** And better off than both of them is the one who has not yet been born,[e] who has not seen the distressing deeds that are done under the sun.[f]

4 And I have seen how much effort* and skillful work spring from rivalry between people;[g] this too is futility, a chasing after the wind.

5 The stupid one folds his hands while his flesh wastes away.*[h]

6 Better is a handful of rest than two handfuls of hard work and chasing after the wind.[i]

7 I turned my attention to another example of futility under the sun: **8** There is a man who is all alone, without any companion; he has no son or brother, but there is no end to all his hard work. His eyes are never satisfied with riches.[j] But does he ask himself, 'For whom am I working hard and depriving myself* of good things'?[k] This too is futility and a miserable occupation.

9 Two are better than one[m] because they have a good reward* for their hard work. **10** For if one of them falls, the other can help his partner up.

But what will happen to the one who falls with no one to help him up?

11 Moreover, if two lie down together, they will stay warm, but how can just one keep warm? **12** And someone may overpower one alone, but two together can take a stand against him. And a threefold cord cannot quickly* be torn apart.

13 Better is a poor but wise child than an old but stupid king,[a] who no longer has enough sense to heed a warning.[b] **14** For he* went out from prison to become king,[c] although in that one's kingship he was born poor.[d] **15** I considered all those alive who walk about under the sun, as well as how it goes with the young successor who stands up in the other's place. **16** Although there is no end to all his supporters, those who come later will not be happy with him.[e] This too is futility, a chasing after the wind.

5 Watch your step whenever you go to the house of the true God;[f] it is better to draw near to listen[g] than to give a sacrifice as the stupid ones do,[h] for they are not aware that what they are doing is bad.

2 Do not be quick with your mouth, nor let your heart speak rashly before the true God,[i] for the true God is in the heavens but you are on the earth. That is why your words should be few.[j] **3** For a dream comes from too many preoccupations,*[k] and the chatter of the stupid one comes from too many words.[l] **4** Whenever you make a vow to God, do not delay to pay it,[m] for he finds no pleasure in the stupid ones.[n] What you vow, pay.[o] **5** Better for you not to vow than to vow

CHAP. 3
[a] De 12:7
Ec 5:18
[b] Job 14:21
Ec 6:12

CHAP. 4
[c] Ps 69:20
Ps 142:4
[d] Job 3:17
Ec 2:17
[e] Jer 20:18
[f] Ec 1:14
[g] Ga 5:26
[h] Pr 6:10, 11
Pr 20:4
[i] Ps 37:16
Pr 15:16
Pr 16:8
Pr 17:1
[j] Pr 7:20
Ec 5:10
[k] Ps 39:6
Lu 12:18-20
[l] Ec 2:22, 23
[m] Ge 2:18
Pr 27:17

Second Col.
[a] Pr 19:1
Pr 28:6, 16
[b] 1Ki 22:8
2Ch 25:15, 16
[c] Ge 41:14, 40
[d] 2Sa 7:8
Job 5:11
[e] 2Sa 20:1

CHAP. 5
[f] Ps 15:1, 2
[g] De 31:12
Ac 17:11
[h] 1Sa 13:12, 13
1Sa 15:22
Pr 21:27
Isa 1:13
Ho 6:6
[i] Nu 30:2
1Sa 14:24
[j] Pr 10:19
[k] Mt 6:25, 34
Lu 12:18-20
[l] Pr 10:19
Pr 15:2
[m] De 23:21
Ps 76:11
Mt 5:33
[n] Ec 10:12
[o] Nu 30:2
Ps 66:13

3:22 *Or "portion." 4:4 *Or "hard work." 4:5 *Lit., "and is eating his own flesh." 4:8 *Or "my soul." 4:9 *Or "greater benefit."

4:12 *Or "easily." 4:14 *Perhaps referring to the wise child. 5:3 *Or "too many cares."

and not pay.ᵃ **6** Do not allow your mouth to cause you* to sin,ᵇ and do not say before the angel*ᶻ that it was a mistake.ᶜ Why make the true God indignant over what you say so that he has to destroy the work of your hands?ᵈ **7** For just as many preoccupations lead to dreams,ᵉ so, too, many words lead to futility. But fear the true God.ᶠ

8 If you see any oppression of the poor and a violation of justice and righteousness in your district, do not be surprised about the matter.ᵍ For that high official is being watched by one who is higher than he is, and there are others who are still higher than them.

9 Also, the profit of the land is divided among them all; even the king is served by the field.ʰ

10 A lover of silver will never be satisfied with silver, nor a lover of wealth with income.ⁱ This too is futility.ʲ

11 When good things increase, those consuming them increase.ᵏ And what advantage is it to the owner, except to look at them with his eyes?ˡ

12 Sweet is the sleep of the one serving, whether he eats little or much, but the plenty belonging to the rich one does not permit him to sleep.

13 There is a great tragedy* that I have seen under the sun: riches that were hoarded by their owner to his own harm.
14 Those riches were lost because of a disastrous venture,* and when he becomes a father to a son, he has nothing left in his possession.ᵐ

15 Just as one came from his mother's womb, naked he will go away, just as he came.ⁿ And he cannot carry away anything for all his hard work.ᵃ

16 This too is a great tragedy:* Exactly as he came, so he will go away; and what profit is there to the one who keeps working hard for the wind?ᵇ **17** Also, every day he eats in darkness, with a great deal of frustration and sickness and anger.ᶜ

18 This is what I have seen to be good and proper: that one should eat and drink and find enjoyment for all the hard workᵈ at which he toils under the sun during the few days of life that the true God has given him, for that is his reward.*ᵉ **19** Also, when the true God gives a man riches and material possessionsᶠ along with the ability to enjoy them, he should take his reward* and rejoice in his hard work. This is the gift of God.ᵍ **20** For he will hardly notice* the passing days of his life, because the true God keeps him preoccupied with the rejoicing of his heart.ʰ

6 There is another tragedy* that I have seen under the sun, and it is common among men: **2** The true God gives a man riches and material possessions and glory, so that he lacks nothing that he desires;* yet the true God does not enable him to enjoy them, although a stranger may enjoy them. This is futility and a severe affliction. **3** If a man should become a father a hundred times and live for many years and reach old age, yet he* does not enjoy his good things before he reaches the grave,ᶻ I must say that a stillborn child is better off than he is.ⁱ **4** For this one came in vain and went away

---

Cross-references (center column):

CHAP. 5
a De 23:22
  Pr 20:25

b Jg 11:35

c Le 5:4

d Ps 127:1
  Hag 1:11

e Ec 5:3

f Ec 12:13

g Ec 3:16

h 1Sa 8:11, 12
  1Ki 4:7
  2Ch 26:9, 10
  Ca 8:11

i Ec 4:8

j Mt 6:24
  Lu 12:15
  1Ti 6:10

k 1Ki 4:22, 23

l Pr 23:4, 5
  1Jo 2:16

m Pr 23:4, 5
  Mt 6:19

n Job 1:21

Second Col.
a Ps 49:17
  Lu 12:20
  1Ti 6:7

b Mt 16:26
  Joh 6:27

c 1Ti 6:10

d 1Ki 4:20

e Ec 2:24
  Ec 3:22
  Isa 65:21, 22

f 1Ki 3:12, 13
  Job 42:12

g De 8:10
  Ec 3:12, 13
  1Ti 6:17
  Jas 1:17

h De 28:8
  Ps 4:7

CHAP. 6
i Ec 4:2, 3

5:6 *Lit., "your flesh." #Or "messenger." **5:13, 16; 6:1** *Or "calamity." **5:14** *Or "occupation." **5:18, 19** *Or "portion." **5:20** *Or "remember." **6:2** *Or "lacks nothing for his soul." **6:3** *Or "his soul." #Or "and even the grave has not become his."

in darkness, and his name is shrouded in darkness. **5** Even though he never saw the sun or knew anything, he is still better off* than the former one.ᵃ **6** What is the benefit of living a thousand years twice over but not experiencing enjoyment? Do not all go to the same place?ᵇ

7 All the hard work of a man is to fill his mouth;ᶜ yet his appetite* is never satisfied. **8** For what advantage does the wise one have over the stupid one,ᵈ or of what benefit is it that the poor man knows how to survive?* **9** Better to enjoy what the eyes see than to wander after one's desires.* This too is futility, a chasing after the wind.

10 Whatever has come to be has already been named, and it is known what man is; and he is not able to dispute* with the one more powerful than he. **11** The more words,* the more futility; and what advantage do they bring to man? **12** Who knows what is best for a man to do in life during the few days of his futile life, which he spends like a shadow?ᵉ For who can tell man what will happen under the sun after he is gone?

7 A good name* is better than good oil,ᶠ and the day of death is better than the day of birth. **2** Better to go to the house of mourning than to the house of feasting,ᵍ for that is the end of every man, and the living should take it to heart. **3** Better is distress than laughter,ʰ for the sadness of the face makes the heart better.ⁱ **4** The heart of the wise is in the house of

mourning, but the heart of the stupid is in the house of rejoicing.*ᵃ

5 Better to listen to a wise man's rebukeᵇ than to listen to the song of fools. **6** For as the crackling of thorns burning under the pot, so is the laughter of the fool;ᶜ and this too is futility. **7** But oppression can drive the wise one into madness, and a bribe corrupts the heart.ᵈ

8 Better is the end of a matter than its beginning. Better to be patient than to be haughty in spirit.ᵉ **9** Do not be quick* to take offense,ᶠ for the taking of offense lodges in the bosom of fools.#ᵍ

10 Do not say, "Why were the former days better than these?" for it is not out of wisdom that you ask this.ʰ

11 Wisdom together with an inheritance is a good thing and an advantage to those who see the light of day.* **12** For wisdom is a protectionⁱ just as money is a protection,ʲ but the advantage of knowledge is this: Wisdom preserves the life of its owner.ᵏ

13 Consider the work of the true God, for who can straighten out what he has made crooked?ˡ **14** On a good day, reflect this goodness,ᵐ but on the day of adversity,* consider that God made the one as well as the other,ⁿ so that men cannot be certain of# anything that will happen to them in the future.ᵒ

15 During my futile lifeᵖ I have seen everything—from the righteous one who perishes in his righteousnessᵠ to the wicked one who lives long despite his badness.ʳ

CHAP. 6
a Job 3:11, 13
  Job 14:1
b Job 30:23
  Ec 3:20
  Ro 5:12
c Ge 3:19
  Pr 16:26
d Ps 49:10
  Ec 2:15, 16
e 1Ch 29:15
  Job 8:9
  Job 14:1, 2
  Ps 102:11

CHAP. 7
f Pr 10:7
  Pr 22:1
  Isa 56:5
  Lu 10:20
g Isa 5:11, 12
  Ps 119:71
  Lu 6:21
i 2Co 7:10
  Heb 12:11

Second Col.
a 1Sa 25:36
  Pr 21:17
b Ps 141:5
  Pr 15:31
c Ec 2:2
d Ex 23:8
  De 16:19
  1Sa 8:1-3
  Pr 17:23
e Pr 13:10
  Jas 5:10
  1Pe 5:5
f Pr 16:32
  Jas 1:19
g Ge 4:5
  Es 5:9
  Pr 14:17, 29
  Pr 29:11
h Lu 9:62
i Pr 4:5, 6
j Pr 10:15
k Pr 3:13, 18
  Pr 8:35
  Pr 9:11
l Job 9:12
  Isa 14:27
m Jas 5:13
n Job 2:10
  Isa 45:7
o Pr 27:1
  Ec 9:11
  Jas 4:13, 14
p Ps 39:5
q Ge 4:8
  1Sa 22:18
r Job 21:7
  Ps 73:12

6:5 *Lit., "has more rest." 6:7 *Or "soul." 6:8 *Lit., "to walk in front of the living." 6:9 *Or "than the walking about of the soul." 6:10 *Or "plead his cause." 6:11 *Or possibly, "things." 7:1 *Or "A good reputation." Lit., "A name."

7:4 *Or "amusement." 7:9 *Lit., "hurry in your spirit." #Or possibly, "is the mark of a fool." 7:11 *That is, those alive. 7:14 *Or "calamity." #Or "discover."

16 Do not be overly righteous,[a] nor show yourself excessively wise.[b] Why should you bring ruin to yourself?[c] **17** Do not be excessively wicked, nor be foolish.[d] Why should you die before your time?[e] **18** It is best to grasp one warning without letting go of the other;[f] for the one who fears God will heed them both.

19 Wisdom makes a wise man more powerful than ten strong men in a city.[g] **20** For there is no righteous man on earth who always does good and never sins.[h]

21 Also, do not take to heart every word that people say;[i] otherwise, you may hear your servant calling down evil on[*] you; **22** for you well know in your heart that many times you yourself have called down evil on others.[j]

23 All of this I tested with wisdom, and I said: "I will become wise." But it was beyond me. **24** What has come to be is out of reach and exceedingly deep. Who can understand it?[k] **25** I directed my heart to know and to explore and to search for wisdom and the reason behind things, and to understand the wickedness of stupidity and the folly of madness.[l] **26** Then I discovered this: More bitter than death is the woman who is like a hunter's net, whose heart is like dragnets, and whose hands are like prison chains. The one who pleases the true God will escape her,[m] but the sinner is captured by her.[n]

27 "See, this is what I found," says the congregator.[o] "I investigated one thing after another to reach my conclusion, **28** but what I[*] continually sought, I have not found. One man[#] out of

a thousand I found, but a woman among them I have not found. **29** This alone I have found: The true God made mankind upright,[a] but they have sought out many schemes."[b]

8 Who is like the wise man? Who knows the solution to a problem?[*] A man's wisdom lights up his face and softens his stern appearance.

2 I say: "Obey the king's orders[c] out of regard for the oath to God.[d] **3** Do not rush to depart from his presence.[e] Do not take a stand for anything bad;[f] for he can do whatever he pleases, **4** because the word of the king is absolute;[g] who can say to him, 'What are you doing?'"

5 The one who observes the commandment will not experience harm,[h] and the wise heart will know the right time and procedure.[*][i] **6** For every matter there is a time and procedure,[*][j] because the troubles of mankind are so abundant. **7** Since no one knows what will happen, who can tell him how it will happen?

8 Just as no man has power over the spirit[*] or can restrain the spirit, so no one has power over the day of death.[k] Just as no one is discharged during a war, so wickedness will not allow those who practice it to escape.[#]

9 All of this I have seen, and I applied my heart to every work that has been done under the sun, during the time that man has dominated man to his harm.[*][l] **10** And I saw the wicked being buried, those who used to go in and out of the holy place, but they were soon forgot-

---

CHAP. 7
a Isa 65:5
　Mt 6:1
　Ro 10:3
　Ro 14:10
b Pr 3:7
　Ro 12:3
c Pr 16:18
d Ps 14:1
　Pr 14:9
e Ps 55:23
　Pr 10:27
f Php 4:5
g Pr 21:22
　Pr 24:5
h 2Ch 6:36
　Ps 51:5
　Ro 3:23
　1Jo 1:8
i 1Sa 24:9
j Jas 3:2, 8, 9
k Ps 36:6
　Ps 139:6
　Isa 55:9
　Ro 11:33
l Ec 1:17
　Ec 2:12
m Ge 39:7-9
n Pr 5:3, 14
　Pr 7:22, 23
　Pr 22:14
o Ec 1:1

Second Col.
a Ge 1:26, 31
b Ge 3:6
　Ge 6:12
　De 32:5

CHAP. 8
c Pr 24:21, 22
　Ro 13:1
　Tit 3:1
　1Pe 2:13
d 2Sa 5:3
e Ec 10:4
f 1Ki 1:5, 7
　Pr 20:2
g 1Ki 2:24, 25
h Ro 13:5
　1Pe 3:13
i 1Sa 24:12, 13
　1Sa 26:8-10
　Ps 37:7
j Ec 3:17
k Ps 89:48
l Ex 1:13, 14
　Mic 7:3

7:21 *Lit., "cursing." 7:28 *Or "my soul." #Or "upright man."

8:1 *Or "the interpretation of a matter?" 8:5, 6 *Or "judgment." 8:8 *Or "breath; wind." #Or possibly, "their wickedness cannot rescue the wicked." 8:9 *Or "injury; detriment."

ten in the city where they acted that way.[a] This too is futility.

11 Because sentence against a bad deed has not been executed speedily,[b] the heart of men becomes emboldened to do bad.[c] **12** Although a sinner may do bad a hundred times and still live a long time, yet I am aware that it will turn out well for those who fear the true God, because they fear him.[d] **13** But it will not turn out well for the wicked one,[e] nor will he prolong his days that are like a shadow,[f] because he does not fear God.

14 There is something futile* that takes place on the earth: There are righteous people who are treated as if they had acted wickedly,[g] and there are wicked people who are treated as if they had acted righteously.[h] I say that this too is futility.

15 So I recommended rejoicing,[i] because there is nothing better for man under the sun than to eat and drink and rejoice; this should accompany him as he works hard during the days of his life,[j] which the true God gives him under the sun.

16 I applied my heart to acquire wisdom and to see all the activity* happening on the earth,[k] even going without sleep day and night.# **17** Then I considered all the work of the true God, and I realized that mankind cannot comprehend what happens under the sun.[l] No matter how hard men try, they cannot comprehend it. Even if they claim that they are wise enough to know, they cannot really comprehend it.[m]

9 So I took all of this to heart and concluded that the righteous and the wise, as well as

their works, are in the hands of the true God.[a] Men are not aware of the love and the hate that took place prior to them. **2** All have the very same outcome,*[b] the righteous and the wicked,[c] the good and the clean and the unclean, those sacrificing and those not sacrificing. The good one is the same as the sinner; the one who swears an oath is the same as the one who is cautious about swearing an oath. **3** This is a distressing thing that happens under the sun: Because all have the same outcome,*[d] the heart of humans is also full of bad; and there is madness in their heart during their life, and then they die!#

4 There is hope for whoever is among the living, because a live dog is better off than a dead lion.[e] **5** For the living know* that they will die,[f] but the dead know nothing at all,[g] nor do they have any more reward,# because all memory of them is forgotten.[h] **6** Also, their love and their hate and their jealousy have already perished, and they no longer have any share in what is done under the sun.[i]

7 Go, eat your food with rejoicing, and drink your wine with a cheerful heart,[j] for already the true God has found pleasure in your works.[k] **8** May your clothing always be white,* and do not fail to put oil on your head.[l] **9** Enjoy life with your beloved wife[m] all the days of your futile life, which He has given you under the sun, all the days of your futility, for that is your lot* in life and in your hard work at which you toil under the sun.[n] **10** Whatever your hand finds to

---

CHAP. 8
a Pr 10:7
b Ps 10:4, 6
c 1Sa 2:22, 23
d Ps 34:9
  Ps 103:13
  Ps 112:1
  Isa 3:10
  2Pe 2:9
e Ps 37:10
  Isa 57:21
f Job 24:24
g Ec 7:15
h Ps 37:7
  Ps 73:12
i Ps 100:2
j Ec 2:24
  Ec 3:12, 13
k Ec 1:13
  Ec 7:25
l Ec 3:11
  Ro 11:33
m Job 28:12
  Ec 7:24
  Ec 11:5

Second Col.

CHAP. 9
a De 33:3
  1Sa 2:9
  Ps 37:5
b Ec 5:15
c Ec 8:10
d Job 3:17-19
  Ec 2:15
e Isa 38:19
f Ge 3:19
  Ro 5:12
g Ps 88:10
  Ps 115:17
  Ps 146:4
  Isa 38:18
  Joh 11:11
h Job 7:9, 10
  Ec 2:16
i Ec 9:10
j De 12:7
  Ps 104:15
  Ec 2:24
k De 16:15
  Ac 14:17
l Da 10:2, 3
m Pr 5:18
n Ec 5:18

8:14 *Or "frustrating." 8:16 *Or "occupation." #Or possibly, "that people do not see sleep either by day or by night."

9:2, 3 *Or "eventuality." 9:3 #Lit., "and after it—to the dead ones!" 9:5 *Or "are conscious." #Or "wages." 9:8 *That is, bright clothing reflecting a joyful mood, not clothing of mourning. 9:9 *Or "portion."

do, do with all your might, for there is no work nor planning nor knowledge nor wisdom in the Grave,*[a] where you are going.

11 I have seen something further under the sun, that the swift do not always win the race, nor do the mighty win the battle,[b] nor do the wise always have the food, nor do the intelligent always have the riches,[c] nor do those with knowledge always have success,[d] because time and unexpected events* overtake them all. **12** For man does not know his time.[e] Just as fish are caught in an evil net and birds are caught in a trap, so the sons of men are ensnared in a time of disaster,* when it suddenly overtakes them.

13 I also observed this about wisdom under the sun—and it impressed me: **14** There was a small city with a few men in it; and a mighty king came against it and surrounded it and built great siegeworks against it. **15** In it was found a poor but wise man, and he saved the city by his wisdom. But no one remembered that poor man.[f] **16** And I said to myself: 'Wisdom is better than mightiness;[g] yet a poor man's wisdom is despised, and his words are not heeded.'[h]

17 Better to heed the calm words of the wise than the shouts of the one ruling among fools.

18 Wisdom is better than weapons of war, but just one sinner can destroy much good.[i]

10 As dead flies cause the perfumer's oil to stink and bubble, so a little foolishness outweighs wisdom and glory.[j]

2 The heart of the wise one leads him in the right way,* but the heart of the stupid one leads him in the wrong way.*[a] **3** In whatever way the fool walks, he is lacking good sense,*[b] and he lets everyone know that he is a fool.*

4 If the anger* of a ruler should flare up against you, do not leave your place,[d] for calmness allays great sins.[e]

5 There is something distressing that I have seen under the sun, the sort of mistake made by those in power:[f] **6** Foolishness is put in many high positions, but the rich* remain in low positions.

7 I have seen servants on horseback but princes walking on foot just like servants.[g]

8 The one who digs a pit may fall into it;[h] and the one who breaks through a stone wall may be bitten by a snake.

9 The one who quarries stones may be hurt by them, and the one who splits logs may be endangered by them.*

10 If an iron tool is dull and one does not sharpen its edge, he will need to exert much effort. But wisdom helps to achieve success.

11 If the snake bites before it is charmed, there is no advantage to the skilled charmer.*

12 The words from the mouth of the wise one bring favor,[i] but the lips of the stupid one are his ruin.[j] **13** The first words out of his mouth are foolishness,[k] and his last words are disastrous madness. **14** But the fool keeps on speaking.[l]

CHAP. 9
a Ps 115:17
Ps 146:3, 4
Isa 38:18

b 1Sa 17:50
Ps 33:16

c Ec 2:15

d 2Sa 17:23

e Ec 8:8
Jas 4:13, 14

f Ec 9:11

g Pr 21:22
Pr 24:5
Ec 7:12, 19
Ec 9:18

h Mr 6:3
1Co 2:8

i Jos 22:20
1Co 5:6
Heb 12:15

CHAP. 10
j Nu 20:10, 12
2Sa 12:9-11

Second Col.
a Pr 14:8
Pr 17:16

b Pr 10:23

c Pr 13:16
Pr 18:7

d Ec 8:2, 3

e 1Sa 25:23, 24
Pr 25:15

f 1Sa 26:21
1Ki 12:13, 14

g Pr 30:21-23

h Pr 26:27

i 1Ki 10:6, 8
Ps 37:30
Lu 4:22
Eph 4:29

j Ps 64:2, 8
Pr 10:14, 21
Pr 14:3

k 1Sa 25:10, 11

l Pr 10:19
Pr 15:2

9:10 *Or "Sheol," that is, the common grave of mankind. See Glossary. 9:11 *Or "unforeseen occurrence." 9:12 *Or "calamity."

10:2 *Lit., "is at his right hand." #Lit., "is at his left hand." 10:3 *Lit., "his heart is lacking." 10:4 *Lit., "spirit; breath." 10:6 *Or "the capable." 10:9 *Or possibly, "should be careful with them." 10:11 *Lit., "the master of the tongue."

A man does not know what will happen; who can tell him what will come after him?[a]

15 The hard work of the stupid one wears him out, for he does not even know how to find his way to the city.

16 How terrible for a land when the king is a boy[b] and the princes start their feasting in the morning! **17** How happy for the land when the king is the son of nobles and the princes eat at the proper time for strength, not for drunkenness![c]

18 Because of extreme laziness the roof beams sag, and because of idle hands the house leaks.[d]

19 Bread* is made for laughter, and wine makes life enjoyable;[e] but money answers every need.[f]

20 Even in your thoughts,* do not curse# the king,[g] and do not curse the rich in your bedroom; for a bird△ may convey the sound,⊠ or a creature with wings may repeat what was said.

11 Cast* your bread on the waters,[h] for after many days you will find it again.[i] **2** Give a share to seven or even to eight,[j] for you do not know what disaster* will occur on the earth.

3 If the clouds are filled with water, they will pour down rain on the earth; and if a tree falls to the south or to the north, the place where the tree falls is where it will lie.

4 The one who watches the wind will not sow seed, and the one who looks at the clouds will not reap.[k]

5 Just as you do not know how the spirit operates in the

bones of the child inside* a pregnant woman,[a] so you do not know the work of the true God, who does all things.[b]

6 Sow your seed in the morning and do not let your hand rest until the evening;[c] for you do not know which will have success, whether this one or that one, or whether they will both do well.

7 Light is sweet, and it is good for the eyes to see the sun. **8** For if a man should live many years, let him enjoy them all.[d] But he should remember that the days of darkness may be many; all that is to come is futility.[e]

9 Rejoice, young man, while you are young, and let your heart be glad in the days of your youth. Follow the ways of your heart and go where your eyes lead you; but know that the true God will bring you into judgment* for all these things.[f] **10** So remove troublesome things from your heart, and ward off harmful things from your body,* for youth and the prime of life are futility.[g]

12 Remember, then, your Grand Creator in the days of your youth,[h] before the days of distress* come[i] and the years arrive when you will say: "I have no pleasure in them"; **2** before the sun and the light and the moon and the stars grow dark,[j] and the clouds return after* the downpour; **3** in the day when the guards* of the house become shaky,# and the strong men stoop over, and the women quit grinding because they have become few, and the ladies looking out the windows find it dark;[k] **4** when the doors to the street have been closed, when

---

CHAP. 10
a Pr 27:1
  Ec 6:12
  Jas 4:13, 14

b 2Ch 13:7
  2Ch 36:9

c Pr 31:4, 5

d Pr 21:25
  Pr 24:33, 34

e Ps 104:15
  Ec 9:7

f Ec 7:12

g Ex 22:28

CHAP. 11
h Pr 22:9

i De 15:10, 11
  Pr 19:17
  Lu 14:13, 14
  Heb 6:10

j Ps 37:21
  Lu 6:38
  2Co 9:7
  1Ti 6:18

k Pr 20:4

Second Col.
a Ps 139:15

b Job 26:14
  Ps 40:5
  Ec 8:17
  Ro 11:33

c Ec 9:10
  2Co 9:6
  Col 3:23

d Ec 5:18
  Ec 8:15

e Ec 12:1

f Ec 3:17
  Ec 12:14
  Ro 2:6

g Ps 25:7
  2Ti 2:22

CHAP. 12
h Ps 71:17
  Ps 148:7, 12
  Lu 2:48, 49
  2Ti 3:15

i Ps 90:10

j 1Sa 4:15

k Ge 48:10

10:19 *Or "Food." **10:20** *Or possibly, "on your bed." #Or "call down evil upon." △Lit., "flying creature of the heavens." ⊠Or "message." **11:1** *Or "Send out." **11:2** *Or "calamity."

11:5 *Lit., "bones in the womb of." **11:9** *Or "call you to account." **11:10** *Lit., "flesh." **12:1** *Or "the calamitous days." **12:2** *Or possibly, "with." **12:3** *Or "keepers." #Or "tremble."

the sound of the grinding mill becomes low, when one gets up at the sound of a bird, and all the daughters of song grow faint.[a] **5** Also, one is afraid of heights, and there are terrors in the street. And the almond tree blossoms,[b] and the grasshopper drags itself along, and the caper berry bursts, because man is walking to his lasting house[c] and the mourners walk about in the street;[d] **6** before the silver cord is removed, and the golden bowl is crushed, and the jar at the spring is broken, and the waterwheel for the cistern is crushed. **7** Then the dust returns to the earth,[e] just as it was, and the spirit* returns to the true God who gave it.[f]

8 "The greatest futility!"* says the congregator.[g] "Everything is futile."[h]

9 Not only had the congregator become wise but he con-

tinually taught the people what he knew,[a] and he pondered and made a thorough search in order to compile* many proverbs.[b] **10** The congregator sought to find delightful words[c] and to record accurate words of truth.

11 The words of the wise are like oxgoads,[d] and their collected sayings are like firmly embedded nails; they have been given from one shepherd. **12** As for anything besides these, my son, be warned: To the making of many books there is no end, and much devotion to them is wearisome to the flesh.[e]

13 The conclusion of the matter, everything having been heard, is: Fear the true God[f] and keep his commandments,[g] for this is the whole obligation of man.[h] **14** For the true God will judge every deed, including every hidden thing, as to whether it is good or bad.[i]

CHAP. 12
a 2Sa 19:34, 35
b Pr 16:31
c Job 30:23
  Ec 9:10
d Ge 50:7, 10
e Ge 3:19
  Ps 146:4
f Ge 2:7
  Job 27:3
  Job 34:14, 15
  Ps 104:29
  Isa 42:5
g 1Ki 8:1
h Ec 1:2, 14

Second Col.
a 1Ki 10:1, 3
  1Ki 10:6, 8
b 1Ki 4:29, 32
  Pr 1:1
c Pr 16:24
  Pr 25:11
d Ac 2:37
  Heb 4:12
e Ec 1:18
f Job 28:28
  Ps 111:10
  Pr 1:7
g 1Jo 5:3
h De 6:1, 2
  De 10:12
i Ps 62:12
  Ec 11:9
  Mt 12:36, 37
  Ac 17:31
  2Co 5:10
  1Ti 5:24

12:7 *Or "life force."   12:8 *Or "vanity."

12:9 *Or "arrange in order."

THE SONG OF SOLOMON

OUTLINE OF CONTENTS

---

1 The song of songs,* which is
    Sol·o·mon's:[a]

2 "May he kiss me with the
     kisses of his mouth,
   For your expressions of
     affection are better than
     wine.[b]

3 The fragrance of your oils
     is pleasant.[c]
   Your name is like a fragrant
     oil poured out.[d]
   That is why the young
     women love you.

4 Take me with you;* let us
     run.
   The king has brought me
     into his interior rooms!
   Let us be joyful and rejoice
     in you.
   Let us praise# your
     expressions of affection
     more than wine.
   Rightly they△ love you.

5 I am dark,* but lovely,
     O daughters of Jerusalem,

CHAP. 1
a 1Ki 4:29, 32

b Ca 4:10

c Pr 27:9
   Ec 9:8
   Ca 5:5

d Ec 7:1

1:1 *Or "The superlative song."

1:4 *Lit., "Draw me after you." #Or
"recount." △That is, the young women.
1:5 *Lit., "black."

Like the tents of Ke′dar,[a]
like the tent cloths[b]
of Sol′o·mon.

6 Do not stare at me because
I am swarthy,
Because the sun has gazed
upon me.
The sons of my mother
were angry with me;
They appointed me the
keeper of the vineyards,
But my own vineyard I did
not keep.

7 Tell me, you whom I love*
so much,
Where you pasture your
flock,[c]
Where you have them lie
down at midday.
Why should I be like a
woman wrapped in a veil#
Among the flocks of your
companions?"

8 "If you do not know, O most
beautiful of women,
Go follow the tracks of the
flock
And pasture your young
goats next to the tents
of the shepherds."

9 "I liken you, my beloved,
to a* mare among the
chariots of Phar′aoh.[d]

10 Your cheeks are lovely
with ornaments,*
Your neck with strings
of beads.

11 We will make for you gold
ornaments*
Studded with silver."

12 "While the king sits at his
round table,
My perfume*[e] gives off its
fragrance.

13 My dear one is to me like
a fragrant bag of myrrh[f]

Spending the night between
my breasts.

14 My dear one is to me like
a cluster of henna[a]
Among the vineyards
of En-ged′i."[b]

15 "Look! You are beautiful,
my beloved.
Look! You are beautiful.
Your eyes are those
of doves."[c]

16 "Look! You are beautiful,*
my dear one, and
delightful.[d]
Our bed is among the foliage.

17 The beams of our house*
are cedars,
Our rafters are juniper trees.

2 "I am but a saffron*
of the coastal plain,
A lily of the valleys."[e]

2 "Like a lily among thorns
Is my beloved among the
daughters."

3 "Like an apple tree among
the trees of the forest,
So is my dear one among
the sons.
I passionately desire to sit
in his shade,
And his fruit is sweet
to my taste.

4 He brought me into the
banquet house,*
And his banner over me
was love.

5 Refresh me with raisin
cakes;[f]
Sustain me with apples,
For I am lovesick.

6 His left hand is under
my head,
And his right hand
embraces me.[g]

7 I put you under oath,
O daughters of Jerusalem,
By the gazelles[h] and the
does of the field:

CHAP. 1
a Ps 120:5
Eze 27:21

b Ex 36:14

c Ca 6:3

d 1Ki 10:28
2Ch 1:16, 17
Ca 6:4

e Ca 4:13, 14

f Ex 30:23, 25
Es 2:12
Ps 45:8
Ca 4:6
Ca 5:13

Second Col.
a Ca 4:13

b Jos 15:20, 62
1Sa 23:29
2Ch 20:2

c Ca 4:1
Ca 5:2

d Ca 5:10

CHAP. 2
e Ca 2:16

f 1Sa 30:11, 12

g Ca 8:3

h 2Sa 2:18

1:7 *Or "my soul loves." #Or "a veil
of mourning." 1:9 *Or "my." 1:10 *Or
possibly, "among the braids of hair."
1:11 *Or "circlets." 1:12 *Lit., "spikenard."

1:16 *Or "handsome." 1:17 *Or "grand
house." 2:1 *Or "crocus." 2:4 *Lit.,
"the house of wine."

Do not try to awaken or
  arouse love in me until
  it feels inclined.*[a]

8 The sound of my dear one!
  Look! Here he comes,
  Climbing the mountains,
  leaping over the hills.
9 My dear one is like a gazelle,
  like a young stag.[b]
  There he is, standing behind
  our wall,
  Gazing through the windows,
  Looking through the lattices.
10 My dear one speaks, he says
  to me:
  'Rise up, my beloved,
  My beautiful one, come
  away with me.
11 Look! The winter* has
  passed.
  The rains are over and gone.
12 Blossoms have appeared
  in the land,[c]
  The time of pruning has
  arrived,[d]
  And the song of the turtledove is heard in our land.[e]
13 The fig tree ripens its early
  figs;[f]
  The vines are in blossom and
  give off their fragrance.
  Rise up, my beloved, and
  come.
  My beautiful one, come away
  with me.
14 O my dove, in the retreats
  of the crag,[g]
  In the recesses of the cliff,
  Let me see you and hear
  your voice,[h]
  For your voice is pleasant
  and your appearance is
  lovely.'"[i]
15 "Catch the foxes for us,
  The little foxes that ruin
  the vineyards,
  For our vineyards are
  in bloom."
16 "My dear one is mine and
  I am his.[j]

He is shepherding[a] among
  the lilies.[b]
17 Until the day grows breezy*
  and the shadows flee,
  Return quickly, O my
  dear one,
  Like the gazelle[c] or the
  young stag[d] upon the
  mountains of separation.#

3 "Upon my bed during the
  nights,
  I sought the one I love.*[e]
  I sought him, but I did not
  find him.[f]
2 I will arise and roam the city;
  In the streets and in the
  public squares,
  Let me seek the one I love.*
  I sought him, but I did not
  find him.
3 The watchmen making
  their rounds in the city
  found me.[g]
  'Have you seen the one
  I love?'*
4 Scarcely had I passed by
  them
  When I found the one I love.*
  I held on to him, I would not
  let him go
  Until I brought him into my
  mother's house,[h]
  Into the interior room of her
  who conceived me.
5 I put you under oath,
  O daughters of Jerusalem,
  By the gazelles and the does
  of the field:
  Do not try to awaken or
  arouse love in me until
  it feels inclined."[i]
6 "What is this coming up
  from the wilderness like
  columns of smoke,
  Perfumed with myrrh and
  frankincense,
  With all the fragrant
  powders of a merchant?"[j]

CHAP. 2
a Ca 3:5
  Ca 8:4

b Ca 2:17
  Ca 8:14

c Ca 6:11

d Isa 18:5
  Joh 15:2

e Jer 8:7

f Isa 28:4
  Na 3:12

g Ca 5:2
  Jer 48:28

h Ca 8:13

i Ca 1:5
  Ca 6:10

j Ca 7:10

Second Col.
a Ca 1:7

b Ca 2:1
  Ca 6:3

c 2Sa 2:18

d Ca 2:9
  Ca 8:14

CHAP. 3
e Ca 1:7

f Ca 5:6

g Ca 5:7

h Ca 8:2

i Ca 2:7
  Ca 8:4

j Ex 30:23, 24
  Ex 30:34

2:11 *Or "rainy season."

2:17 *Lit., "the day breathes." #Or
possibly, "the cleft mountains." Or "the
mountains of Bether." 3:1-4 *Or "my
soul loves."

7 "Look! It is the couch
     belonging to Sol'o·mon.
Sixty mighty men
     surround it,
Of the mighty men of Israel,[a]
8 All of them armed with
     a sword,
All trained in warfare,
Each with his sword
     at his side
To guard against the terrors
     of the night.
9 "It is the royal litter*
     of King Sol'o·mon
That he made for himself
     from the trees of
     Leb'a·non.[b]
10 Its pillars he made of silver,
     Its supports of gold.
Its seat is of purple wool;
     Its interior was lovingly
     decorated
By the daughters
     of Jerusalem."
11 "Go out, O daughters
     of Zion,
Gaze at King Sol'o·mon
Wearing the wedding crown*
     his mother[c] made for him
On the day of his marriage,
On the day of his heart's
     rejoicing."

4 "Look! You are beautiful,
     my beloved.
Look! You are beautiful.
Your eyes are those of doves
     behind your veil.
Your hair is like a flock
     of goats
Streaming down the
     mountains of Gil'e·ad.[d]
2 Your teeth are like a flock
     of newly shorn sheep
That have come up from
     being washed,
All of them bearing twins,
And not one has lost her
     young.

3:9 *A covered couch used to carry a
person of importance. 3:11 *Or "the
wreath; the garland."

CHAP. 3
a 1Ki 9:22

b 1Ki 5:8, 9

c 2Sa 12:24
  Pr 4:3

CHAP. 4
d Nu 32:1
  De 3:12
  Ca 6:5-7

Second Col.
a Ca 1:10

b Ne 3:25
  Ca 7:4

c 2Sa 8:7
  2Ki 11:10

d Ca 7:3

e Ec 2:5

f Ca 4:1

g De 3:25

h De 3:8, 9
  Ps 133:3

i Pr 5:18, 19

j Ca 7:12

k Ca 1:2, 4

3 Your lips are like a
     scarlet thread,
And your speech is
     delightful.
Like a segment of
     pomegranate
Are your cheeks* behind
     your veil.
4 Your neck[a] is like the tower
     of David,[b]
Built with courses of stone
Upon which are hung a
     thousand shields,
All the circular shields
     of the mighty men.[c]
5 Your two breasts are like
     two fawns,
The twins of a gazelle,[d]
That feed among the lilies."
6 "Until the day grows breezy*
     and the shadows flee,
I will go my way to the
     mountain of myrrh
And to the hill of
     frankincense."[e]
7 "You are altogether
     beautiful, my beloved,[f]
There is no blemish in you.
8 Come with me from
     Leb'a·non, my bride,
Come with me from
     Leb'a·non.[g]
Descend from the peak
     of A·ma'nah,*
From the peak of Se'nir,
     the peak of Her'mon,[h]
From the lairs of lions, from
     the mountains of leopards.
9 You have captured my heart,[i]
     my sister, my bride,
You have captured my heart
     with one glance of your
     eyes,
With one pendant of your
     necklace.
10 How beautiful your
     expressions of affection
     are,[j] my sister, my bride!
Your expressions of affection
     are far better than wine,[k]

4:3 *Or "temples." 4:6 *Lit., "the day
breathes." 4:8 *Or "Anti-Lebanon."

And the fragrance of your perfume than any spice![a]

11 Your lips, my bride, drip with comb honey.[b]

Honey and milk are under your tongue,[c]

And the fragrance of your garments is like the fragrance of Leb′a·non.

12 My sister, my bride, is like a locked garden,

A locked garden, a spring sealed shut.

13 Your shoots* are a paradise# of pomegranates

With the choicest fruits, with henna along with spikenard plants,

14 Spikenard[d] and saffron, cane*[e] and cinnamon,[f]

With all sorts of trees of frankincense, myrrh, and aloes,[g]

Along with all the finest perfumes.[h]

15 You are a garden spring, a well of fresh water,

And flowing streams from Leb′a·non.[i]

16 Awake, O north wind; Come in, O south wind.

Breathe* upon my garden. Let its fragrance spread."

"Let my dear one come into his garden

And eat its choicest fruits."

5 "I have entered my garden,[j] O my sister, my bride.

I have picked my myrrh and my spice.[k]

I have eaten my honeycomb and my honey;

I have drunk my wine and my milk."[l]

"Eat, dear friends! Drink and become intoxicated with expressions of affection!"[m]

2 "I am asleep, but my heart is awake.[a]

There is the sound of my dear one knocking!"

"Open to me, O my sister, my beloved,

My dove, my flawless one! For my head is wet with dew,

The locks of my hair with the moisture of the night."[b]

3 "'I have taken off my robe. Must I put it back on?

I have washed my feet. Must I soil them again?'

4 My dear one withdrew his hand from the hole of the door,

And my feelings for him were stirred.

5 I got up to open to my dear one;

My hands dripped with myrrh,

And my fingers with liquid myrrh,

Onto the handles of the lock.

6 I opened to my dear one, But my dear one had turned away, he had gone.

I felt despair* when he departed.#

I sought him, but I did not find him.[c]

I called him, but he did not answer me.

7 The watchmen making their rounds in the city found me.

They struck me, they wounded me.

The watchmen of the walls took my shawl* away from me.

8 I put you under oath, O daughters of Jerusalem:

If you find my dear one, Tell him that I am lovesick."

9 "How is your dear one better than any other dear one,

CHAP. 4
a Es 2:12
  Ca 1:12

b Pr 16:24

c Ca 5:1

d Joh 12:3

e Isa 43:24

f Pr 7:17

g Ps 45:8

h Ex 30:23, 24
  Ex 30:34
  Eze 27:2, 22

i Jer 18:14

CHAP. 5
j Ca 4:16

k Ca 4:13, 14

l Ca 4:11

m Ca 1:2

Second Col.
a Ca 3:1

b Lu 2:8

c Ca 3:1, 3

4:13 *Or possibly, "skin." #Or "garden." 4:14 *An aromatic reed. 4:16 *Or "Blow gently."

5:6 *Or "My soul went out." #Or possibly, "My soul left me when he spoke." 5:7 *Or "veil."

You most beautiful of
women?

How is your dear one better
than any other dear one,

That you put us under such
an oath?"

10 "My dear one is dazzling
and ruddy;

He stands out among ten
thousand.

11 His head is gold, the finest
gold.

The locks of his hair are
like waving palm fronds,*

As black as the raven.

12 His eyes are like doves
by streams of water,

Bathing themselves in milk,

Sitting by a brimming pool.*

13 His cheeks are like a bed
of spices,[a]

Mounds of scented herbs.

His lips are lilies, dripping
with liquid myrrh.[b]

14 His hands are cylinders of
gold, set with chrys·o·lite.

His abdomen is polished
ivory covered with
sapphires.

15 His legs are pillars of marble
set on pedestals of the
finest gold.

His appearance is like
Leb′a·non, as unrivaled
as the cedars.[c]

16 His mouth* is sweetness
itself,

And everything about him
is desirable.[d]

This is my dear one, this is
my beloved, O daughters
of Jerusalem."

6 "Where has your dear one
gone,

O most beautiful of women?

Which way did your dear one
turn?

Let us seek him with you."

CHAP. 5
a Ca 6:2

b Ca 1:13

c Ps 92:12

d Ca 2:3

Second Col.

CHAP. 6
a Ca 1:7
  Ca 2:16

b Ca 7:10

c Ca 2:16

d 1Ki 14:17
  1Ki 15:33

e Ca 1:9

f Ps 48:2

g Ca 6:10

h Ca 1:15
  Ca 4:9
  Ca 7:4

i Ca 4:1-3

j 1Ki 11:1

k Ca 2:14

2 "My dear one has gone down
to his garden,

To the beds of spice plants,

To shepherd among the
gardens

And to pick lilies.[a]

3 I am my dear one's,

And my dear one is mine.[b]

He is shepherding among
the lilies."[c]

4 "You are as beautiful as
Tir′zah,*[d] my beloved,[e]

As lovely as Jerusalem,[f]

As breathtaking as armies
around their banners.[g]

5 Turn your eyes[h] away
from me,

For they overwhelm me.

Your hair is like a flock
of goats

Streaming down the slopes
of Gil′e·ad.[i]

6 Your teeth are like a flock
of sheep

That have come up from
being washed,

All of them bearing twins,

And not one has lost her
young.

7 Like a segment of
pomegranate

Are your cheeks* behind
your veil.

8 There may be 60 queens

And 80 concubines

And young women without
number.[j]

9 But only one is my dove,[k]
my flawless one.

The only one of her mother.

She is the favorite* of the
one who bore her.

The daughters see her, and
they pronounce her happy;

Queens and concubines,
and they praise her.

10 'Who is she who shines*
like the dawn,

5:11 *Or possibly, "like date clusters."
5:12 *Or possibly, "the fountain rims."
5:16 *Lit., "palate."

6:4 *Or "Pleasant City." 6:7 *Or "temples." 6:9 *Lit., "the pure one." 6:10
*Lit., "looks down."

As beautiful as the full
moon,
As pure as the sunlight,
As breathtaking as armies
around their banners?"[a]

11 "I went down to the garden
of nut trees[b]
To see the new growth
in the valley,*
To see whether the vine
had sprouted,#
Whether the pomegranate
trees had blossomed.

12 Before I knew it,
My desire* had put me
At the chariots of my noble#
people."

13 "Return, return,
O Shu′lam·mite!
Return, return,
That we may look upon you!"
"Why do you gaze upon the
Shu′lam·mite?"[c]
"She is like the dance of
two companies!"*

7 "How beautiful your feet
are in your sandals,
O noble daughter!
The curves of your thighs
are like ornaments,
The work of an artisan's
hands.

2 Your navel is a round bowl.
May it never lack mixed
wine.
Your belly is a heap of
wheat,
Encircled by lilies.

3 Your two breasts are like
two fawns,
The twins of a gazelle.[d]

4 Your neck[e] is like an ivory
tower.[f]
Your eyes[g] are like the pools
in Hesh′bon,[h]
By the gate of Bath-rab′bim.
Your nose is like the tower
of Leb′a·non,

Which looks toward
Damascus.

5 Your head crowns you
like Car′mel,[a]
And the locks of your hair*[b]
are like purple wool.[c]
The king is captivated#
by the flowing tresses.

6 How beautiful you are,
and how pleasant you are,
O beloved girl, above all
exquisite delights!

7 Your stature is like a palm
tree,
And your breasts are like
date clusters.[d]

8 I said, 'I will climb the palm
tree
To take hold of its stalks
of fruit.'
May your breasts be like
clusters of grapes,
Your breath as fragrant
as apples,

9 And your mouth* like the
best wine."
"May it go down smoothly
for my dear one,
Softly flowing over the lips
of those asleep.

10 I am my dear one's,[e]
And his desire is for me.

11 Come, O my dear one,
Let us go out to the fields;
Let us lodge among the
henna plants.[f]

12 Let us rise early and go
to the vineyards
To see if the vine has
sprouted,#
If the blossoms have
opened,[g]
If the pomegranates are
in bloom.[h]
There I will express my
affection for you.[i]

13 The mandrakes[j] give off
their fragrance;
At our doors are all sorts
of choice fruits.[k]

CHAP. 6
a Ca 6:4

b Ec 2:5

c Ca 1:6

CHAP. 7
d Ca 4:5

e Ca 1:10

f Ca 4:4

g Ca 4:1

h Nu 21:25
Jos 21:8, 39

Second Col.
a Isa 35:2

b Ca 6:5

c Es 8:15

d Ca 7:3
Ca 8:10

e Ca 2:16
Ca 6:3

f Ca 1:14

g Ca 2:13

h Ca 6:11

i Ca 1:2
Ca 4:10

j Ge 30:14

k Ca 4:16

6:11 *Or "wadi." 6:11; 7:12 #Or "budded." 6:12 *Or "soul." #Or "willing."
6:13 *Or "dance of Mahanaim."

7:5 *Lit., "your head." #Or "held
bound." 7:9 *Lit., "palate."

The new as well as the old,
O my dear one, I have kept
    in store for you.

8 "If only you were like my
    brother,
Who nursed at my mother's
    breasts!
Then if I found you outside,
    I would kiss you,[a]
And no one would
    despise me.

2 I would lead you;
I would bring you into the
    house of my mother,[b]
She who taught me.
I would give you spiced
    wine to drink,
The fresh juice of
    pomegranates.

3 His left hand would be under
    my head,
And his right hand would
    embrace me.[c]

4 I put you under oath,
    O daughters of Jerusalem:
Do not try to awaken or
    arouse love in me until
    it feels inclined."[d]

5 "Who is this coming up from
    the wilderness,
Leaning upon her dear one?"
"Under the apple tree
    I awakened you.
There your mother was in
    labor with you.
There she who gave birth
    to you was in labor.

6 Place me as a seal upon your
    heart,
As a seal upon your arm,
For love is as strong as
    death is,[e]
And exclusive devotion is as
    unyielding as the Grave.*
Its flames are a blazing fire,
    the flame of Jah.#[f]

7 Surging waters cannot
    extinguish love,[a]
Nor can rivers wash it away.[b]
If a man would offer all
    the wealth of his house
    for love,
It* would be utterly
    despised."

8 "We have a little sister,[c]
And she has no breasts.
What will we do for our
    sister
On the day when she is
    spoken for?"

9 "If she is a wall,
We will build upon her
    a battlement of silver,
But if she is a door,
We will board her up with
    a cedar plank."

10 "I am a wall,
And my breasts are like
    towers.
So in his eyes I have become
    As one who finds peace.

11 Sol'o·mon had a vineyard[d]
    in Ba'al-ha'mon.
He entrusted the vineyard
    to caretakers.
Each one would bring in a
    thousand pieces of silver
    for its fruit.

12 I have my own vineyard at
    my disposal.
The thousand pieces of
    silver* belong to you,
O Sol'o·mon,
And two hundred to those
    who care for its fruit."

13 "O you who are dwelling
    in the gardens,[e]
The companions listen
    for your voice.
Let me hear it."[f]

14 "Hurry, my dear one,
And be swift like a gazelle[g]
Or a young stag
Upon the mountains
    of spices."

8:6 *Or "Sheol," that is, the common grave of mankind. See Glossary. #"Jah" is a shortened form of the name Jehovah.

8:7 *Or possibly, "He." **8:12** *Lit., "The thousand."

CHAP. 8
a Ca 1:2

b Ca 3:4

c Ca 2:6

d Ca 2:7
  Ca 3:5

e Joh 15:13
  Eph 5:25
  Re 12:11

f De 4:24
  1Jo 4:8

Second Col.
a 1Co 13:8, 13

b Ro 8:38, 39

c Ca 1:6

d Ec 2:4

e Ca 1:6
  Ca 6:11

f Ca 2:14

g Ca 2:9, 17

ISAIAH

OUTLINE OF CONTENTS

1 The vision that Isaiah*[a] the son of A′moz saw concerning Judah and Jerusalem in the days of Uz·zi′ah,[b] Jo′tham,[c] A′haz,[d] and Hez·e·ki′ah,[e] kings of Judah:[f]

2 Hear, O heavens, and pay attention, O earth,[g]
For Jehovah has spoken:
"Sons I have brought up and raised,[h]
But they have revolted against me.[i]
3 A bull well knows its buyer,
And a donkey the manger of its owner;
But Israel does not know me,*[j]
My own people do not behave with understanding."
4 Woe to the sinful nation,[k]
The people weighed down with error,
A brood of wicked men, corrupt children!
They have abandoned Jehovah;[l]
They have treated the Holy One of Israel with disrespect;
They have turned their backs on him.
5 Where will you be struck next as you add to your rebellion?[m]
The whole head is sick,
And the whole heart is diseased.[n]
6 From the sole of the foot to the head, nothing is healthy.
There are wounds and bruises and open sores
—They have not been treated* or bound up or softened with oil.[o]
7 Your land is desolate.
Your cities are burned with fire.

Foreigners devour your land right in front of you.[a]
It is like a wasteland overthrown by foreigners.[b]
8 The daughter of Zion has been left like a shelter* in a vineyard,
Like a hut in a cucumber field,
Like a city under siege.[c]
9 Unless Jehovah of armies had left us a few survivors,
We should have become just like Sod′om,
And we should have resembled Go·mor′rah.[d]
10 Hear the word of Jehovah, you dictators* of Sod′om.[e]
Pay attention to the law# of our God, you people of Go·mor′rah.[f]
11 "Of what benefit to me are your many sacrifices?"[g] says Jehovah.
"I have had enough of your burnt offerings of rams[h] and the fat of well-fed animals,[i]
And I have no delight in the blood[j] of young bulls[k] and lambs and goats.[l]
12 When you come to appear before me,[m]
Who has required this from you,
This trampling of my courtyards?[n]
13 Stop bringing in any more worthless grain offerings.
Your incense is detestable to me.[o]
New moons,[p] sabbaths,[q] the calling of conventions[r]
—I cannot put up with the use of magical power[s] along with your solemn assembly.
14 I have* hated your new moons and your festivals.

1:8 *Or "booth." 1:10 *Or "rulers." #Or "instruction." 1:14 *Or "My soul has."

CHAP. 1
a 2Ch 32:32
b 2Ch 26:22
  Isa 6:1
c 2Ch 27:1, 2
d 2Ch 28:1
e 2Ch 29:1, 2
  2Ch 32:20
f Mt 1:9
g Ps 50:4
h De 1:31
i De 4:25, 26
  Eze 20:8
j Ho 4:6
k Da 9:11
l De 31:16
  Jer 2:5
m Jer 5:3
n Ne 9:34, 35
  Da 9:8
o Lu 10:34

Second Col.
a De 28:33, 63
b 2Ki 18:11
c 2Ki 18:13, 14
  Isa 8:7, 8
d Ge 19:24, 25
  De 29:22, 23
  Ro 9:29
e Ge 13:13
  Isa 3:8, 9
f De 32:32
  Jude 7
g 1Sa 15:22
  Pr 15:8
  Ho 6:6
  Mic 6:7
h Ex 29:38
i Le 3:14-16
j Le 17:11
k Le 4:18, 21
l Le 16:5
m De 16:16
n Ec 5:1
  Mal 1:8
o Pr 21:27
  Eze 8:11, 12
p Nu 28:11
q Ex 31:13
r Le 23:2
s Le 19:26

They have become a burden to me;
I am tired of bearing them.

15 And when you spread out your palms,
I hide my eyes from you.[a]
Although you offer many prayers,[b]
I am not listening;[c]
Your hands are filled with blood.[d]

16 Wash yourselves, make yourselves clean;[e]
Remove your evil deeds from my sight;
Stop doing bad.[f]

17 Learn to do good, seek justice,[g]
Correct the oppressor,
Defend the rights of the fatherless child,*
And plead the cause of the widow."[h]

18 "Come, now, and let us set matters straight between us," says Jehovah.[i]
"Though your sins are like scarlet,
They will be made as white as snow;[j]
Though they are as red as crimson cloth,
They will become like wool.

19 If you show willingness and listen,
You will eat the good things of the land.[k]

20 But if you refuse and rebel,
You will be devoured by the sword,[l]
For the mouth of Jehovah has spoken it."

21 How the faithful city[m] has become a prostitute![n]
She was full of justice;[o]
Righteousness used to lodge in her,[p]
But now murderers.[q]

22 Your silver has become dross,[r]

And your beer* is diluted with water.

23 Your princes are stubborn and partners with thieves.[a]
Every one of them loves a bribe and chases after gifts.[b]
They do not grant justice to the fatherless,*
And the legal case of the widow never reaches them.[c]

24 Therefore the true Lord, Jehovah of armies,
The Powerful One of Israel, declares:
"Ah! I will rid myself of my adversaries,
And I will take revenge on my enemies.[d]

25 I will turn my hand against you,
I will smelt away your dross as with lye,
And I will remove all your impurities.[e]

26 I will restore your judges as in the beginning
And your advisers as at the start.[f]
After this you will be called City of Righteousness, Faithful Town.[g]

27 With justice Zion will be redeemed,[h]
And her people who return, with righteousness.

28 The rebels and the sinners will be broken together,[i]
And those leaving Jehovah will come to their finish.[j]

29 For they will be ashamed of the mighty trees that you desired,[k]
And you will be disgraced because of the gardens* that you chose.[l]

30 For you will become like a big tree with withering leaves,[m]

CHAP. 1
a Pr 15:29
b Mt 6:7
c Pr 28:9
  Isa 59:2
  La 3:44
d Mic 3:2-4
e Jer 4:14
f Isa 55:7
g Mic 6:8
h De 10:18
  Jer 22:3
i Mic 6:2
  Jas 4:8
j Ps 51:7
  Isa 44:22
  Mic 7:19
k De 28:1, 2
  Joe 2:19
l Le 26:33
  Pr 29:1
m Ps 48:2
n Jer 2:20
o 2Sa 8:15
  1Ki 3:28
p 2Ch 19:9, 10
q Mic 3:1-3
  Lu 13:34
r Eze 22:18

Second Col.
a Isa 3:14
  Mic 3:9-11
b Ex 23:8
c Ex 22:22
  Jer 5:28
d Eze 5:13
e Jer 6:29, 30
  Jer 9:7
  Mal 3:3
f Nu 12:3
  1Sa 12:1, 3
  Isa 32:1
  Eze 34:23
g Isa 62:1
h Jer 31:11
i Eze 20:38
j 1Ki 9:6, 7
k Eze 6:13
l Isa 65:3
  Isa 66:17
m Jer 17:5, 6

1:17 *Or "the orphan."   1:22 *Or "wheat beer."   1:23 *Or "the orphans."   1:29 *Apparently trees and gardens connected with idolatrous worship.

And like a garden without water.

31 The strong man will become tow,*

And his work a spark;

Both of them will go up in flames together,

With no one to extinguish them."

2 This is what Isaiah the son of A'moz saw concerning Judah and Jerusalem:[a]

2 In the final part of the days,*

The mountain of the house of Jehovah

Will become firmly established above the top of the mountains,[b]

And it will be raised up above the hills,

And to it all the nations will stream.[c]

3 And many peoples will go and say:

"Come, let us go up to the mountain of Jehovah,

To the house of the God of Jacob.[d]

He will instruct us about his ways,

And we will walk in his paths."[e]

For law* will go out of Zion,

And the word of Jehovah out of Jerusalem.[f]

4 He will render judgment among the nations

And set matters straight* respecting many peoples.

They will beat their swords into plowshares

And their spears into pruning shears.[g]

Nation will not lift up sword against nation,

Nor will they learn war anymore.[h]

1:31 *A flammable ropelike fiber. **2:2** *Or "In the last days." **2:3** *Or "instruction." **2:4** *Or "correct matters."

CHAP. 2

a Isa 1:1

b Zec 8:3

c Ps 72:1, 8
Ps 86:9
Mic 4:1-3
Hag 2:7
Ac 10:34, 35

d Zec 8:23

e Isa 54:13

f Isa 51:4

g Ps 46:9

h Ps 72:7
Isa 60:18
Mt 26:52

Second Col.

a Isa 60:19, 20

b De 31:16, 17

c De 18:10

d De 17:15, 16

e 2Ch 28:1, 2
2Ch 33:1, 7

f Ex 20:18

g Zep 1:4, 7

h Isa 66:16

---

5 O house of Jacob, come,

Let us walk in the light of Jehovah.[a]

6 For you have forsaken your people, the house of Jacob,[b]

Because they have become full of things from the East;

They practice magic[c] like the Phi·lis'tines,

And they abound with the children of foreigners.

7 Their land is filled with silver and gold,

And there is no limit to their treasures.

Their land is filled with horses,

And there is no limit to their chariots.[d]

8 Their land is filled with worthless gods.[e]

They bow down to the work of their own hands,

To what their own fingers have made.

9 So man bows down, he becomes low,

And you cannot possibly pardon them.

10 Enter into the rock and hide yourself in the dust

Because of the terrifying presence of Jehovah

And his majestic splendor.[f]

11 The haughty eyes of man will be brought low,

And the arrogance of men will bow down.*

Jehovah alone will be exalted in that day.

12 For it is the day belonging to Jehovah of armies.[g]

It is coming upon everyone who is haughty and lofty,

Upon everyone, whether exalted or lowly,[h]

13 Upon all the cedars of Leb'a·non that are lofty and exalted

---

2:11 *Or "be humbled."

And upon all the oaks of
Ba'shan,

14 Upon all the lofty mountains
And upon all the high hills,

15 Upon every high tower and
every fortified wall,

16 Upon all the ships of
Tar'shish[a]
And upon all desirable boats.

17 Man's haughtiness will be
brought down,
And the arrogance of men
will bow low.*
Jehovah alone will be
exalted in that day.

18 The worthless gods will
completely disappear.[b]

19 And people will enter into
the caves of the rocks
And into the holes in the
ground,[c]
Because of the terrifying
presence of Jehovah
And his majestic splendor,[d]
When he arises to make the
earth tremble in terror.

20 In that day men will take
their worthless gods of
silver and of gold
That they had made for
themselves to bow down to
And throw them away to
the shrewmice* and to
the bats,[e]

21 In order to enter into
the holes in the rocks
And into the clefts of
the crags,
Because of the terrifying
presence of Jehovah
And his majestic splendor,
When he arises to make the
earth tremble in terror.

22 For your own sakes, quit
trusting in mere man,
Who is only the breath in
his nostrils.*
Why should he be taken
into account?

CHAP. 2
a 1Ki 10:22
Eze 27:25

b Isa 27:9

c Re 6:15

d Isa 2:10
2Th 1:9

e Isa 30:22
Isa 31:7

Second Col.

CHAP. 3
a Le 26:26
De 28:49, 51
Jer 37:21
Eze 4:16

b Eze 13:9

c Ex 18:21

d De 18:10, 12
Isa 8:19

e Jer 9:4, 5
Mic 3:2, 3

f Le 19:32

g 2Ch 33:1, 6
Eze 9:9

3 For look! the true Lord,
Jehovah of armies,
Is removing from Jerusalem
and Judah every kind of
support and supply,
All support of bread and
water,[a]

2 Mighty man and warrior,
Judge and prophet,[b] diviner
and elder,

3 Chief of 50,[c] dignitary,
and adviser,
The expert magician and
the skilled charmer.[d]

4 I will make boys their
princes,
And the unstable* will rule
over them.

5 The people will oppress
one another,
Each one his fellow man.[e]
The boy will assault the
old man,
And the lightly esteemed
one will defy the respected
one.[f]

6 Each one will take hold of
his brother in his father's
house and say:
"You have a cloak—you be
our commander.
Take charge of this over-
thrown pile of ruins."

7 But he will protest in
that day:
"I will not be your wound
dresser;*
I have no food or clothing
in my house.
Do not make me commander
over the people."

8 For Jerusalem has stumbled,
And Judah has fallen,
Because in word and deed
they are against Jehovah;
They behave defiantly in his
glorious presence.*[g]

9 The expression of their faces
testifies against them,

2:17 *Or "be humbled." **2:20** *Voracious rodents. **2:22** *Or "Whose
breath is in his nostrils."

3:4 *Or "fickle." **3:7** *Or "your healer."
3:8 *Lit., "in the eyes of his glory."

And they proclaim their sin
like Sod'om;[a]
They do not try to hide it.
Woe to them,* for they
are bringing disaster on
themselves!

10 Tell the righteous that it
will go well for them;
They will be rewarded for
what they do.*[b]

11 Woe to the wicked one!
Disaster will befall him,
For what his hands have
done will be done to him!

12 As for my people, their
taskmasters are abusive,
And women rule over them.
My people, your leaders are
causing you to wander,
And they confuse the
direction of your paths.[c]

13 Jehovah is taking his
position to accuse;
He is standing up to pass
sentence on peoples.

14 Jehovah will enter into
judgment with the elders
and princes of his people.
"You have burned down
the vineyard,
And what you have stolen
from the poor is in your
houses.[d]

15 How dare you crush my
people
And grind the faces of the
poor in the dirt?"[e] declares
the Sovereign Lord,
Jehovah of armies.

16 Jehovah says: "Because
the daughters of Zion are
haughty,
Walking with their heads
high,*
Flirting with their eyes,
skipping along,
Making a tinkling sound
with their anklets,

17 Jehovah will also strike the
head of the daughters of
Zion with scabs,
And Jehovah will make their
forehead bare.[a]

18 In that day Jehovah will take
away the beauty of their
bangles,
The headbands and the
crescent-shaped
ornaments,[b]

19 The earrings,* the bracelets,
and the veils,

20 The headdresses, the ankle chains, and the
breastbands,*
The perfume receptacles#
and the charms,△

21 The finger rings and the
nose rings,

22 The ceremonial robes, the
overtunics, the cloaks,
and the purses,

23 The hand mirrors[c] and the
linen garments,*
The turbans and the veils.

24 Instead of balsam oil,[d] there
will be a rotten smell;
Instead of a belt, a rope;
Instead of a beautiful
hairstyle, baldness;[e]
Instead of a rich garment,
a garment of sackcloth;[f]
And a brand mark instead
of beauty.

25 By the sword your men will
fall,
And your mighty men in
battle.[g]

26 Her entrances will mourn
and grieve,[h]
And she will sit on the
ground desolate."[i]

4 And seven women will grab
hold of one man in that day,[j]
saying:

"We will eat our own bread
And wear our own clothing;

CHAP. 3
a Ge 18:20
  Isa 1:10
  Jude 7

b Ec 8:12
  Zep 2:3

c Jer 5:31
  Hab 1:4

d Isa 1:23
  Jer 5:26-28
  Mic 2:1, 2
  Mic 6:10

e Mic 3:2, 3

Second Col.
a Isa 3:24

b Jg 8:26

c Ex 38:8

d Es 2:12

e Mic 1:16

f La 2:10

g La 2:21

h La 1:4

i La 2:10

CHAP. 4
j Isa 3:25

3:9 *Or "their soul." 3:10 *Lit., "will
eat the fruitage of their deeds."
3:16 *Lit., "with an outstretched neck
(throat)."

3:19 *Or "pendants." 3:20 *Or "sashes." #Lit., "houses of the soul." △Or
"ornamental humming shells." 3:23
*Or "the undergarments."

Only let us be called by your name
To take away our disgrace."*ᵃ

2 In that day when Jehovah makes sprout will be splendid and glorious, and the fruitage of the land will be the pride and beauty of the survivors of Israel.ᵇ **3** Whoever remains in Zion and is left over in Jerusalem will be called holy, all of those in Jerusalem written down for life.ᶜ

4 When Jehovah washes away the filth* of the daughters of Zionᵈ and rinses away the bloodshed of Jerusalem from her midst by the spirit of judgment and by a spirit of burning,#ᵉ **5** Jehovah will also create over the whole site of Mount Zion and over the place of her conventions a cloud and smoke by day and a bright flaming fire by night;ᶠ for over all the glory there will be a shelter. **6** And there will be a booth for shade by day from the heat,ᵍ and for refuge and protection from storms and the rain.ʰ

5 Let me sing, please, to my beloved
A song about my loved one and his vineyard.ⁱ
My beloved had a vineyard on a fruitful hillside.

2 He dug it up and rid it of stones.
He planted it with a choice red vine,
Built a tower in the middle of it,
And hewed out a winepress in it.ʲ
Then he kept hoping for it to produce grapes,
But it produced only wild grapes.ᵏ

3 "And now, you inhabitants of Jerusalem and men of Judah,

Please judge between me and my vineyard.ᵃ

4 What more could I have done for my vineyard
That I have not already done?ᵇ
Why, when I hoped for grapes,
Did it produce only wild grapes?

5 Now, please, let me tell you What I will do to my vineyard:
I will remove its hedge,
And it will be burned down.ᶜ
I will break down its stone wall,
And it will be trampled on.

6 I will make it a wasteland;ᵈ
It will not be pruned or hoed.
It will be overgrown with thornbushes and weeds,ᵉ
And I will command the clouds not to send any rain on it.ᶠ

7 For the vineyard of Jehovah of armies is the house of Israel;ᵍ
The men of Judah are the plantation* he was fond of.
He kept hoping for justice,ʰ
But look! there was injustice;
For righteousness,
But look! a cry of distress."ⁱ

8 Woe to those who join one house to another houseʲ
And who annex one field to another fieldᵏ
Until there is no more room
And you live by yourselves on the land!

9 Jehovah of armies has sworn in my ears
That many houses, though great and beautiful,
Will become an object of horror,
Without an inhabitant.ˡ

CHAP. 4	
a	Ge 30:22, 23 Lu 1:24, 25
b	Isa 30:23 Joe 3:18 Zec 9:17
c	Ex 32:32, 33
d	Eze 36:25
e	Eze 22:20-22
f	Ex 13:21 Nu 9:15 Zec 2:4, 5
g	Ps 121:5
h	Isa 25:4

CHAP. 5	
i	Ps 80:8 Isa 5:7 Jer 2:21 Lu 20:9
j	Mt 21:33 Mr 12:1
k	Ho 10:1

Second Col.	
a	Mic 6:2
b	2Ch 36:15 Eze 24:13
c	Le 26:31, 33 Ne 2:3 Ps 79:1
d	De 29:22, 23 Jer 25:11 Jer 45:4
e	Isa 32:13
f	De 11:16, 17
g	Ps 80:8 Jer 12:10
h	Mic 6:8
i	De 15:9
j	Mic 2:1, 2
k	1Ki 21:15, 16
l	2Ch 36:20, 21 Isa 27:10

4:1 *That is, the humiliation of being unmarried and childless. **4:4** *Lit., "excrement." #Or "purging."

5:7 *Or "planting."

10 For ten acres* of vineyard
   will produce but one bath
   measure,#
   And a ho′mer measure# of
   seed will produce only
   an e′phah.#a
11 Woe to those who get up
   early in the morning to
   drink alcohol,b
   Who linger late into the
   evening darkness until
   wine inflames them!
12 They have harp and stringed
   instrument,
   Tambourine, flute, and wine
   at their feasts;
   But they do not consider the
   activity of Jehovah,
   And they do not see the work
   of his hands.
13 So my people will go into
   exile
   For lack of knowledge;c
   Their glorious men will
   go hungry,d
   And all their people will be
   parched with thirst.
14 So the Grave* has enlarged
   itself#
   And has opened its mouth
   wide without limit;e
   And her splendor,△ her
   noisy multitudes, and
   her revelers
   Will certainly go down
   into it.
15 And man will bow down,
   Man will be brought low,
   And the eyes of the haughty
   will be brought low.
16 Jehovah of armies will be
   exalted by his judgment;*
   The true God, the Holy
   One,f will sanctify himself
   through righteousness.g
17 And the lambs will graze
   as in their pasture;

Foreign residents will feed
   on the desolate places
   of well-fed animals.
18 Woe to those who drag along
   their guilt with ropes of
   deception
   And their sin with wagon
   cords;
19 Those who say: "Let Him
   speed up his work;
   Let it come quickly that we
   may see it.
   Let the purpose* of the Holy
   One of Israel take place
   That we may know it!"a
20 Woe to those who say that
   good is bad and bad is
   good,b
   Those who substitute
   darkness for light and
   light for darkness,
   Those who put bitter for
   sweet and sweet for bitter!
21 Woe to those wise in their
   own eyes
   And discreet in their own
   sight!c
22 Woe to those who are mighty
   in drinking wine
   And to the men who are
   masters at mixing alcoholic
   drinks,d
23 Those who acquit the wicked
   for a bribee
   And who deny justice to the
   righteous!f
24 Therefore, just as the
   tongue of fire consumes
   the stubble
   And dry grass shrivels
   in the flames,
   Their very roots will rot,
   And their blossoms will
   scatter like powder,
   Because they rejected the
   law* of Jehovah of armies
   And disrespected the word
   of the Holy One of Israel.g
25 That is why the anger of
   Jehovah burns against his
   people,

CHAP. 5
a De 28:15, 17
  Joe 1:17

b Lu 21:34
  Ro 13:13

c Isa 27:11
  Jer 8:7
  Ho 4:6

d La 4:9

e De 28:63

f Isa 6:3
  Re 4:8

g De 32:4

Second Col.
a Jer 5:12
  Jer 17:15
  Eze 12:22

b Pr 17:15
  Mal 2:17

c Pr 3:7
  Ro 12:16

d Pr 23:20
  Pr 31:4, 5

e De 16:19
  Isa 1:23
  Mic 3:11

f 1Ki 21:13
  Pr 17:15

g De 31:20
  2Ki 17:13, 14
  Ne 9:26
  Isa 1:4

5:10 *Lit., "ten spans." #See App. B14.
5:14 *Or "Sheol," that is, the common
grave of mankind. See Glossary. #Or
"its soul." △Or "her nobles." 5:16 *Or
"justice."

5:19 *Or "decision; counsel." 5:24 *Or
"instruction."

And he will stretch out
his hand against them
and strike them.[a]

The mountains will quake,
And their corpses will be like
refuse in the streets.[b]

In view of all this, his anger
has not turned back,
But his hand is still stretched
out to strike.

26 He has raised up a signal*
to a distant nation;[c]

He has whistled for them
to come from the ends
of the earth;[d]
And look! they are coming
very swiftly.[e]

27 None among them are tired
or stumbling.

No one is drowsy or sleeps.
The belt around their waist
is not loosened,
Nor are their sandal laces
broken.

28 All their arrows are sharp,
And all their bows are bent.*

The hooves of their horses
are like flint,
And their wheels like a storm
wind.[f]

29 Their roaring is like that
of a lion;

They roar like young lions.*[g]
They will growl and seize
the prey
And carry it off with no one
to rescue it.

30 In that day they will growl
over it
Like the growling of the sea.[h]

Anyone who gazes at the
land will see distressing
darkness;

Even the light has grown
dark because of the
clouds.[i]

6 In the year that King Uz·zi′ah
died,[j] I saw Jehovah sitting
on a lofty and elevated throne,[k]

5:26 *Or "signal pole." 5:28 *Or
"ready to shoot." 5:29 *Or "maned
young lions."

CHAP. 5
a De 31:16, 17
2Ch 36:15, 16
La 2:2

b Jer 16:4

c Jer 52:4

d De 28:49, 50
Jer 5:15

e Jer 4:13

f Hab 1:8

g Jer 50:17

h Jer 6:23

i Jer 4:23

CHAP. 6
j 2Ch 26:23

k 1Ki 22:19
Da 7:9

Second Col.
a Ex 15:11
Re 4:8

b Re 15:8

c Isa 29:13

d Eze 10:2

e Re 8:5

f Ge 1:26
Joh 1:1, 2
Joh 12:41

g Ps 110:3
Mt 4:19, 20

h Jer 5:21
Mt 13:14, 15
Lu 8:9, 10
Ac 28:25-27

---

and the skirts of his robe
filled the temple. 2 Seraphs
were standing above him; each
had six wings. Each* covered his
face with two and covered his
feet with two, and each of them
would fly about with two.

3 And one called to the other:
"Holy, holy, holy is Jehovah
of armies.[a]
The whole earth is filled
with his glory."

4 And the pivots of the
thresholds quivered at the sound
of the shouting,* and the house
was filled with smoke.[b]

5 Then I said: "Woe to me!
I am as good as dead,*
For I am a man of unclean
lips,
And I live among a people
of unclean lips;[c]
For my eyes have seen the
King, Jehovah of armies
himself!"

6 At that, one of the seraphs
flew to me, and in his hand was
a glowing coal[d] that he had tak-
en with tongs from the altar.[e]
7 He touched my mouth and
said:
"Look! This has touched
your lips.
Your guilt is removed,
And your sin is atoned for."

8 Then I heard the voice of
Jehovah saying: "Whom shall
I send, and who will go for us?"[f]
And I said: "Here I am! Send
me!"[g]

9 And he replied, "Go, and say
to this people:
'You will hear again and
again,
But you will not understand;
You will see again and again,
But you will not get any
knowledge.'[h]

6:2 *Lit., "He." 6:4 *Lit., "the voice of
the one calling." 6:5 *Lit., "I have been
brought to silence."

10 Make the heart of this people
unreceptive,[a]
Make their ears unrespon-
sive,[b]
And paste their eyes
together,
So that they may not see
with their eyes
And hear with their ears,
So that their heart may not
understand
And they may not turn back
and be healed."

11 At this I said: "How long,
O Jehovah?" Then he said:

"Until the cities crash in
ruins without an inhabitant
And the houses are without
people
And the land is ruined and
desolate;[c]
12 Until Jehovah removes men
far away[d]
And the deserted condition
of the land becomes very
extensive.

13 "But there will still be a
tenth in it, and it will again be
burned, like a big tree and like
an oak, which after they are
cut down leave a stump; a holy
seed* will be its stump."

7 Now in the days of A'haz[e]
son of Jo'tham son of Uz·zi'-
ah, the king of Judah, King Re'-
zin of Syria and Pe'kah[f] son of
Rem·a·li'ah, the king of Israel,
came up to wage war against Jerusalem, but he* could not capture it.[g] 2 A report was made
to the house of David: "Syria has
joined forces with E'phra·im."

And the heart of A'haz and
the heart of his people began to
tremble, like the trees of the forest shaking in the wind.

3 Jehovah then said to Isaiah: "Go out, please, to meet
A'haz, you and your son She'ar-

ja'shub,*[a] at the end of the con-
duit# of the upper pool[b] by
the highway of the laundryman's
field. 4 You must say to him,
'Take care to stay calm. Do not
be afraid, and do not lose heart
because of these two stumps of
smoldering logs, because of the
hot anger of Re'zin and Syria and
the son of Rem·a·li'ah.[c] 5 For
Syria with E'phra·im and the son
of Rem·a·li'ah have plotted harm
against you, saying: 6 "Let us
go up against Judah and tear it
apart* and conquer it# for ourselves, and let us appoint the son
of Tab'e·el as its king."[d]

7 "'This is what the Sovereign
Lord Jehovah says:

"It will not succeed,
Nor will it take place.
8 For the head of Syria is
Damascus,
And the head of Damascus
is Re'zin.
Within just 65 years
E'phra·im will be completely
shattered and cease to be
a people.[e]
9 The head of E'phra·im is
Sa·mar'i·a,[f]
And the head of Sa·mar'i·a
is the son of Rem·a·li'ah.[g]
Unless you have firm faith,
You will not be firmly
established."'"

10 Jehovah continued speaking to A'haz: 11 "Ask for a sign
from Jehovah your God;[h] it may
be as deep as the Grave* or as
high as the sky." 12 But A'haz
said: "I will not ask, nor will I put
Jehovah to the test."

13 Isaiah then said: "Listen, please, O house of David.
Is it not enough that you try

CHAP. 6
a Eze 3:7

b Jer 6:10
Joh 3:20

c 2Ch 36:20, 21
Isa 3:26
Isa 24:1

d 2Ki 25:11

CHAP. 7
e 2Ki 16:1, 2

f 2Ki 15:37
2Ch 28:6

g 2Ki 16:5

Second Col.
a Isa 8:18

b 2Ki 18:17

c 2Ki 15:30
Isa 8:6, 7

d 2Ki 16:5

e 2Ki 17:6
Ho 1:6

f 1Ki 16:23, 24

g 2Ki 15:27

h Jg 6:36, 37
Isa 37:30
Isa 38:7, 8

6:13 *Or "offspring." 7:1 *Or possibly,
"they." 7:3 *Meaning "Only a Remnant Will Return." #Or "water channel." 7:6 *Or
possibly, "terrorize it." #Or "make a
breach in its walls." Lit., "split it open."
7:11 *Or "Sheol," that is, the common
grave of mankind. See Glossary.

the patience of men? Must you also try the patience of God?[a] 14 Therefore, Jehovah himself will give you a sign: Look! The young woman* will become pregnant and will give birth to a son,[b] and she will name him Im·man′u·el.*[c] 15 He will eat butter and honey by the time that he knows how to reject the bad and choose the good. 16 For before the boy knows how to reject the bad and choose the good, the land of the two kings whom you dread will be completely abandoned.[d] 17 Jehovah will bring against you and against your people and against the house of your father a time such as has not come since the day E′phra·im broke away from Judah,[e] for He will bring the king of As·syr′i·a.[f]

18 "In that day Jehovah will whistle for the flies from the distant streams of the Nile of Egypt and for the bees in the land of As·syr′i·a, 19 and they will all come and settle down on the steep valleys,* on the rocky clefts, on all the thornbushes, and on all the watering places.

20 "In that day by means of a hired razor from the region of the River,* by means of the king of As·syr′i·a,[g] Jehovah will shave the head and the hair of the legs, and it will sweep away the beard as well.

21 "In that day a man will keep alive a young cow of the herd and two sheep. 22 And because of the abundance of milk, he will eat butter, for everyone remaining in the land will eat butter and honey.

23 "In that day wherever there used to be 1,000 vines worth 1,000 pieces of silver, there will be only thornbushes and weeds. 24 Men will

go there with bow and arrow, because all the land will become thornbushes and weeds. 25 And all the mountains that used to be cleared with a hoe, you will not go near for fear of thornbushes and weeds; they will become a grazing place for bulls and a trampling ground of sheep."

8 Jehovah said to me: "Take a large tablet[a] and write on it with an ordinary stylus,* 'Ma′her-shal′al-hash-baz.'* 2 And let me have it confirmed in writing* by faithful witnesses, U·ri′ah[b] the priest and Zech·a·ri′ah the son of Je·ber·e·chi′ah."

3 Then I had relations with* the prophetess,# and she became pregnant and in time gave birth to a son.[c] Jehovah then said to me: "Name him Ma′her-shal′al-hash-baz, 4 for before the boy knows how to call out, 'My father!' and 'My mother!' the resources of Damascus and the spoil of Sa·mar′i·a will be carried away before the king of As·syr′i·a."[d]

5 Jehovah spoke to me again:

6 "Because this people has rejected the gently flowing waters of the Shi·lo′ah*[e] And they rejoice over Re′zin and the son of Rem·a·li′ah,[f]

7 Therefore look! Jehovah will bring against them The mighty and vast waters of the River,* The king of As·syr′i·a[g] and all his glory. He will come up over all his streambeds And overflow all his banks

---

Cross references (center column):

CHAP. 7
a 2Ch 36:15, 16

b Isa 9:6
Joh 1:14
1Ti 3:16

c Mt 1:23
Lu 1:30-35

d 2Ki 15:29
2Ki 16:8, 9
Isa 8:3, 4
Isa 17:1

e 1Ki 12:20

f 2Ki 18:13, 14
2Ch 28:19, 20
Isa 36:1

g 2Ki 16:7

Second Col.

CHAP. 8
a Isa 30:8

b 2Ki 16:10

c Isa 8:18

d 2Ki 15:29
2Ki 16:8, 9
2Ki 17:6
Isa 7:16
Isa 17:1

e 2Ki 17:16
Jer 17:13

f Isa 7:1

g 2Ki 17:5
2Ki 18:9

7:14 *Or "The maiden." #Meaning "With Us Is God." 7:19 *Or "wadis." 7:20; 8:7 *That is, the Euphrates. 8:1 *Lit., "with the stylus of a mortal man." #Possibly meaning "Hurrying to the Spoil, Coming Quickly to the Plunder." 8:2 *Or "witnessed; attested." 8:3 *Lit., "went near to." #That is, the wife of Isaiah. 8:6 *The Shiloah was a water conduit.

8 And sweep through Judah.
　　He will flood and pass
　　　through, reaching to
　　　the neck;[a]
　　His outspread wings will fill
　　　the breadth of your land,
　　O Im·man′u·el!"*[b]
9 Cause harm, you peoples,
　　but you will be shattered
　　　to pieces.
　　Listen, all you from distant
　　　parts of the earth!
　　Prepare for battle,* but
　　　you will be shattered
　　　to pieces![c]
　　Prepare for battle, but you
　　　will be shattered to pieces!
10 Devise a plan, but it will
　　be thwarted!
　　Say what you like, but it will
　　　not succeed,
　　For God is with us!*[d]

11 With his strong hand on
me, this is what Jehovah said to
me to warn me away from following the course of this people:
12 "You should not call a con-
　　spiracy what this people
　　calls a conspiracy!
　　Do not fear what they fear;
　　Do not tremble at it.
13 Jehovah of armies—he is
　　the One you should regard
　　as holy,[e]
　　He is the One you should
　　fear,
　　And he is the One who
　　should cause you
　　to tremble."[f]
14 He will become as a
　　sanctuary,
　　But as a stone to strike
　　against
　　And as a rock to stumble
　　over[g]
　　To both houses of Israel,
　　As a trap and a snare
　　To the inhabitants of
　　Jerusalem.

15 Many of them will stumble
　　and fall and be broken;
　　They will be ensnared
　　and caught.
16 Wrap up the written
　　confirmation;*
　　Seal up the law# among
　　my disciples!

17 I will keep in expectation
of* Jehovah,[a] who is hiding his
face from the house of Jacob,[b]
and I will hope in him.
18 Look! I and the children
whom Jehovah has given me[c]
are as signs[d] and as miracles in
Israel from Jehovah of armies,
who resides on Mount Zion.
19 And if they say to you: "Inquire of the spirit mediums or
of the fortune-tellers who chirp
and mutter," is it not of their God
that a people should inquire?
Should they inquire of the dead
in behalf of the living?[e] 20 Instead, they should inquire of the
law and of the written confirmation!*
　When they do not speak according to this word, they have
no light.#[f] 21 And each one will
pass through the land afflicted and hungry;[g] and because he
is hungry and indignant, he will
curse his king and his God as he
looks upward. 22 Then he will
look to the earth and see only
distress and darkness, obscuri-
ty and hard times, gloom and no
brightness.

9 However, the gloom will not
be as when the land had distress, as in former times when
the land of Zeb′u·lun and the
land of Naph′ta·li were treated
with contempt.[h] But at a later
time He will cause it to be honored—the way by the sea, in the
region of the Jordan, Gal′i·lee of
the nations.

CHAP. 8
a 2Ch 28:19, 20
　Isa 7:17, 20
　Isa 10:28-32

b Isa 7:14
　Mt 1:23

c 2Ch 32:21

d De 20:1
　Ps 44:3

e Le 10:3
　Le 22:32

f Ec 12:13
　Mt 10:28

g Mt 21:42, 44
　Lu 20:17, 18
　Ro 9:31-33
　1Co 1:23
　1Pe 2:7, 8

Second Col.
a Ps 33:20

b De 31:16, 17
　Mic 3:4

c Heb 2:13

d Isa 7:14, 16
　Isa 8:3, 4

e Le 20:6
　De 18:10, 11
　Ps 146:4
　Ec 9:5, 10

f Pr 4:19

g De 28:15, 48

CHAP. 9
h 2Ki 15:29

8:8 *See Isa 7:14.   8:9 *Or "Gird yourselves."   8:10 *The Hebrew for "God is
with us" is Immanuel. See Isa 7:14; 8:8.
  8:16, 20 *Or "the attestation."   8:16
#Or "instruction."   8:17 *Or "eagerly
wait for."   8:20 #Lit., "dawn."

2 The people who were
    walking in the darkness
Have seen a great light.
As for those dwelling in the
    land of deep shadow,
Light has shone on them.[a]

3 You have made the nation
    populous;
You have made its rejoicing
    great.
They rejoice before you
As people rejoice in the
    harvesttime,
As those who joyfully divide
    up the spoil.

4 For you have shattered to
    pieces the yoke of their
    load,
The rod on their shoulders,
    the staff of the taskmaster,
As in the day of Mid'i·an.[b]

5 Every boot that shakes the
    earth as it marches
And every garment soaked
    in blood
Will become fuel for the fire.

6 For a child has been born
    to us,[c]
A son has been given to us;
And the rulership* will rest
    on his shoulder.[d]
His name will be
    called Wonderful Counsel-
    or,[e] Mighty God,[f] Eternal
    Father, Prince of Peace.

7 To the increase of his
    rulership*
And to peace, there will be
    no end,[g]
On the throne of David[h]
    and on his kingdom
In order to establish it
    firmly[i] and to sustain it
Through justice[j] and
    righteousness,[k]
From now on and forever.
The zeal of Jehovah of
    armies will do this.

8 Jehovah sent a word against
    Jacob,

And it has come against
    Israel.[a]

9 And all the people will
    know it
    —E'phra·im and the inhabi-
    tants of Sa·mar'i·a—
Who say in their haughtiness
    and in their insolence
    of heart:

10 "Bricks have fallen,
But we will build with hewn
    stone.[b]
Sycamore trees have been
    cut down,
But we will replace them
    with cedars."

11 Jehovah will raise up Re'zin's
    adversaries against him
And will stir his enemies
    to action,

12 Syria from the east and
    the Phi·lis'tines from
    the west,[c]
They will devour Israel with
    open mouths.[d]
In view of all this, his anger
    has not turned back,
But his hand is still stretched
    out to strike.[e]

13 For the people have not
    returned to the One who
    strikes them;
They have not sought
    Jehovah of armies.[f]

14 Jehovah will cut off from
    Israel
Head and tail, shoot and
    rush,* in one day.[g]

15 The elder and highly
    respected one is the head,
And the prophet giving false
    instruction is the tail.[h]

16 Those leading this people are
    causing them to wander,
And those who are being led
    are confused.

17 That is why Jehovah will not
    rejoice over their young
    men,

CHAP. 9
a Mt 4:13-16
  Lu 1:78, 79
  Lu 2:30-32
  Joh 1:9
  Joh 8:12

b Jg 8:12, 28
  Isa 10:26, 27

c Lu 1:35
  Lu 2:11

d Ge 49:10
  Ps 2:6
  Zec 6:13
  Lu 22:29
  Re 19:16

e Isa 11:2
  Mt 7:28, 29
  Mt 12:42

f Ps 45:3
  Joh 1:18

g Ps 72:1, 7
  Da 2:44

h Lu 1:32, 33

i 2Sa 7:16, 17
  Re 11:15

j Isa 42:1
  Mt 12:18

k Ps 45:6
  Isa 32:1
  Jer 23:5
  Heb 1:8

_____
Second Col.
a 2Ki 17:6

b Am 5:11

c 2Ch 28:18

d De 31:17

e Isa 5:25
  Isa 10:4

f 2Ki 17:13, 14
  Ho 7:10
  Am 4:6
  Am 5:6

g 2Ki 17:6
  Ho 10:15

h De 13:1-3

_____
9:6, 7 *Or "government; princely rule." 9:12 *Lit., "from behind." 9:14 *Or possibly, "palm branch and reed."

And he will have no mercy on
　their fatherless children*
　and their widows
Because all of them are
　apostates and evildoers[a]
And every mouth is speaking
　senselessness.
In view of all this, his anger
　has not turned back,
But his hand is still stretched
　out to strike.[b]

18 For wickedness burns like
　　a fire,
Consuming thornbushes and
　weeds.
It will set fire to the thickets
　of the forest,
And they will go up in clouds
　of smoke.

19 In the fury of Jehovah of
　　armies
The land has been set on fire,
And the people will become
　fuel for the fire.
No one will spare even his
　brother.

20 One will cut down on the
　　right
But still be hungry;
And one will eat on the left
But will not be satisfied.
Each will devour the flesh
　of his own arm,

21 Ma·nas'seh will devour
　　E'phra·im,
And E'phra·im Ma·nas'seh.
Together they will be against
　Judah.[c]
In view of all this, his anger
　has not turned back,
But his hand is still stretched
　out to strike.[d]

10 Woe to those who enact
　　harmful regulations,[e]
Who constantly draft
　oppressive decrees,
2 To deny the legal claim of
　　the poor,
To deprive the lowly among
　my people of justice,[f]

Making widows their spoil
And fatherless children*
　their plunder![a]

3 What will you do on the day
　　of reckoning,*[b]
When destruction comes
　from afar?[c]
To whom will you flee for
　assistance,[d]
And where will you leave
　your wealth?[#]

4 Nothing remains except
　　to crouch among the
　　prisoners
Or to fall among the slain.
In view of all this, his anger
　has not turned back,
But his hand is still stretched
　out to strike.[e]

5 "Aha! the As·syr'i·an,[f]
The rod to express my
　anger[g]
And the staff in their hand
　for my denunciation!

6 I will send him against
　　an apostate nation,[h]
Against the people who
　infuriated me;
I will command him to
　take much spoil and much
　plunder
And to trample them like
　mud in the streets.[i]

7 But he will not be inclined
　　this way
And his heart will not
　scheme this way;
For it is in his heart to
　annihilate,
To cut off many nations,
　not a few.

8 For he says,
'Are not my princes all
　kings?[j]

9 Is not Cal'no[k] just like
　Car'che·mish?[l]
Is not Ha'math[m] like Ar'pad?[n]
Is not Sa·mar'i·a[o] like
　Damascus?[p]

CHAP. 9
a De 4:25, 26

b Isa 5:25

c 2Ch 28:6

d Isa 5:25

CHAP. 10
e Le 19:15
　De 1:16, 17

f Am 2:7, 8

Second Col.
a De 27:19
　Jas 1:27

b Ho 9:7

c De 28:49, 50

d Ho 5:13

e Isa 5:25
　Isa 9:12

f Ge 10:9, 11

g 2Ki 17:3
　Isa 8:3, 4
　Isa 10:24

h 2Ki 17:6

i De 28:45, 63
　2Ki 17:22, 23

j 2Ki 18:19, 24

k Am 6:2

l 2Ch 35:20

m 2Ki 17:24

n 2Ki 19:11, 13

o 2Ki 17:5
　2Ki 18:9, 10

p 2Ki 16:8, 9

9:17 *Or "their orphans."

10:2 *Or "And orphans." 10:3 *Or "punishment." #Or "glory,"

10 My hand has seized the
kingdoms of the worthless
gods,
Whose graven images were
more than those of
Jerusalem and Sa·mar′i·a!ᵃ
11 Will I not also do to
Jerusalem and her idols
Just as I have done
to Sa·mar′i·a and to her
worthless gods?′ᵇ
12 "When Jehovah finishes
all his work on Mount Zion and
in Jerusalem, He* will punish
the king of As·syr′i·a for his insolent heart and his proud, arrogant gaze.ᶜ 13 For he says,
'I will do this by the strength
of my hand
And with my wisdom, for
I am wise.
I will remove the boundaries
of peoplesᵈ
And pillage their treasures,ᵉ
And I will subdue the inhabitants like a mighty one.ᶠ
14 Like a man reaching into
a nest,
My hand will seize the
resources of the peoples;
And like one gathering
abandoned eggs,
I will gather the whole earth!
No one will flutter his wings
or open his mouth or
chirp.'"
15 Will the ax exalt itself over
the one who chops with it?
Will the saw exalt itself over
the one who saws with it?
Could a staffᵍ wave the one
who lifts it?
Or could a rod lift up the one
who is not made of wood?
16 Therefore the true Lord,
Jehovah of armies,
Will inflict emaciation on
his fat ones,ʰ
And beneath his glory he
will kindle a blazing fire.ⁱ

10:12 *Lit., "I."

CHAP. 10
a 2Ki 19:17, 18

b 2Ki 18:33, 34
2Ch 32:16, 19

c 2Ki 18:19
2Ki 18:28, 35

d 2Ki 15:29
2Ki 17:6
2Ki 18:11
1Ch 5:26

e 2Ki 16:8
2Ki 18:16

f 2Ki 18:19, 25

g Isa 10:5

h 2Ch 32:21

i Isa 30:30, 31

Second Col.
a Ps 84:11

b Isa 9:5
Isa 30:27
Isa 31:8, 9
Na 1:6

c Isa 37:36

d 2Ch 28:20, 21
Ho 5:13
Ho 14:3

e Isa 65:9
Ho 1:10, 11

f Isa 1:9

g Isa 28:22

h Ro 9:27, 28

i De 28:45, 63

17 Israel's Lightᵃ will become
a fire,ᵇ
And his Holy One a flame;
It will blaze up and consume
his weeds and his thorn-
bushes in one day.
18 He will utterly* do away with
the glory of his forest and
his orchard;
It will be as when a sick man
wastes away.ᶜ
19 The rest of the trees of his
forest
Will be so few that a boy
could list them.
20 In that day those remaining
of Israel
And the survivors of the
house of Jacob
Will no longer support
themselves on the one
who struck them;ᵈ
But they will support
themselves on Jehovah,
The Holy One of Israel,
with faithfulness.
21 Only a remnant will return,
The remnant of Jacob,
to the Mighty God.ᵉ
22 For though your people,
O Israel,
Are as the grains of sand
of the sea,
Only a remnant of them
will return.ᶠ
An extermination has been
decided on,ᵍ
And justice* will engulf
them.ʰ
23 Yes, the extermination decided on by the Sovereign
Lord, Jehovah of armies,
Will be carried out in the
entire land.ⁱ
24 Therefore this is what the
Sovereign Lord, Jehovah of armies, says: "Do not be afraid, my
people who are dwelling in Zion,
because of the As·syr′i·an, who

10:18 *Or "from soul to flesh." 10:22
*Or "punishment."

used to strike you with the rod[a] and to lift up his staff against you as Egypt did.[b] **25** For in a very little while the denunciation will come to an end; my anger will be directed to their destruction.[c] **26** Jehovah of armies will brandish a whip against him,[d] as when he defeated Mid'i·an by the rock O'reb.[e] And his staff will be over the sea, and he will raise it as he did with Egypt.[f]

27 In that day his load will depart from on your shoulder,[g]
And his yoke from on your neck,[h]
And the yoke will be broken[i] because of the oil."

28 He has come to Ai'ath;[j]
He has passed through Mig'ron;
At Mich'mash[k] he deposits his baggage.

29 They have passed over the ford;
They spend the night at Ge'ba;[l]
Ra'mah trembles, Gib'e·ah[m] of Saul has fled.[n]

30 Cry out and scream, O daughter of Gal'lim!
Pay attention, O La'i·shah!
O poor An'a·thoth![o]

31 Mad·me'nah has run away.
The inhabitants of Ge'bim have sought shelter.

32 This very day he will halt in Nob.[p]
He shakes his fist at the mountain of the daughter of Zion,
The hill of Jerusalem.

33 Look! The true Lord, Jehovah of armies,
Is chopping off branches with a terrible crash;[q]
The tallest trees are being cut down,
And the lofty are brought low.

34 He strikes down the thickets of the forest with an iron tool,*
And Leb'a·non will fall by a mighty one.

11 A twig[a] will grow out of the stump of Jes'se,[b]
And a sprout[c] from his roots will bear fruit.

2 And the spirit of Jehovah will settle upon him,[d]
The spirit of wisdom[e] and of understanding,
The spirit of counsel and of mightiness,[f]
The spirit of knowledge and of the fear of Jehovah.

3 And he will find delight in the fear of Jehovah.[g]
He will not judge by what appears to his eyes,
Nor reprove simply according to what his ears hear.[h]

4 He will judge the lowly with fairness,*
And with uprightness he will give reproof in behalf of the meek ones of the earth.
He will strike the earth with the rod of his mouth[i]
And put the wicked to death with the breath# of his lips.[j]

5 Righteousness will be the belt around his waist,
And faithfulness the belt of his hips.[k]

6 The wolf will reside for a while with the lamb,[l]
And with the young goat the leopard will lie down,
And the calf and the lion* and the fattened animal will all be together;#[m]
And a little boy will lead them.

CHAP. 10
a 2Ki 18:13
  Isa 10:5
b Ex 14:3, 9
c 2Ki 19:35
d 2Ch 32:21
  Isa 30:32
  Na 3:7
e Jg 7:25
  Jg 8:21
  Ps 83:11
f Ex 14:21, 27
g Isa 9:4
  Na 1:13
h Isa 14:25
i 2Ki 19:35
  Isa 37:35, 36
j Jos 7:2
k 1Sa 13:2
  1Sa 14:31
l Jos 21:8, 17
  2Ch 16:6
m Jg 20:13
n Ho 5:8
o Jos 21:8, 18
  Jer 1:1
p 1Sa 22:18, 19
q 2Ch 32:21
  Isa 37:36

Second Col.

CHAP. 11
a Ps 132:11
  Isa 53:2
  Re 5:5
  Re 22:16
b Ru 4:17
  1Sa 17:58
  Mt 1:1, 6
  Lu 3:23, 32
  Ac 13:22, 23
  Ro 15:12
c Jer 23:5
  Jer 33:15
  Zec 3:8
  Zec 6:12
d Isa 42:1
  Joh 1:32
  Ac 10:38
e Lu 2:52
f Isa 9:6
g Heb 5:7
h Joh 7:24
  Joh 8:16
i Ps 2:9
  Ps 110:2
  Re 19:11, 15
j 2Th 2:8
k Re 3:14
l Isa 65:25
m Eze 34:25

10:34 *Or "an ax." **11:4** *Or "righteousness." #Or "spirit." **11:6** *Or "the maned young lion." #Or possibly, "And the calf and the lion will feed together."

7 The cow and the bear will
    feed together,
  And their young will lie down
    together.
  The lion will eat straw like
    the bull.[a]

8 The nursing child will play
    over the lair of a cobra,
  And a weaned child will
    put his hand over the den
    of a poisonous snake.

9 They will not cause any
    harm[b]
  Or any ruin in all my holy
    mountain,[c]
  Because the earth will
    certainly be filled with the
    knowledge of Jehovah
  As the waters cover the sea.[d]

10 In that day the root of Jes'se
    will stand up as a signal*
    for the peoples.[f]
  To him the nations will turn
    for guidance,[#g]
  And his resting-place will
    become glorious.

  11 In that day Jehovah will
again offer his hand, a second
time, to reclaim the remnant of
his people who are left from As-
syr'i·a,[h] from Egypt,[i] from Path'-
ros,[j] from Cush,[k] from E'lam,
from Shi'nar,* from Ha'math,
and from the islands of the sea.[m]
12 He will raise up a signal* for
the nations and gather the dispersed ones of Israel,[n] and he
will gather together the scattered ones of Judah from the
four corners of the earth.[o]

13 The jealousy of E'phra·im
    will be gone,[p]
  And those who show
    hostility to Judah will
    be done away with.
  E'phra·im will not be jealous
    of Judah,
  Nor will Judah show hostility
    toward E'phra·im.[q]

14 And they will swoop down
    on the slopes* of the
    Phi·lis'tines to the west;
  Together they will plunder
    the people of the East.
  They will thrust out their
    hand against# E'dom[a] and
    Mo'ab,[b]
  And the Am'mon·ites will
    become their subjects.[c]

15 Jehovah will divide* the
    gulf# of the Egyptian sea[d]
  And wave his hand over
    the River.△e
  With his scorching breath⊠
    he will strike it in its□
    seven torrents,
  And he will cause people
    to walk across in their
    sandals.

16 And there will be a highway[f]
    out of As·syr'i·a for the
    remnant of his people
    who are left,[g]
  As there was for Israel in the
    day he came out of the land
    of Egypt.

12 In that day you will cer-
    tainly say:

  "I thank you, O Jehovah,
  For although you were angry
    with me,
  Your anger gradually sub-
    sided, and you comforted
    me.[h]

2 Look! God is my salvation.[i]
  I will trust and feel no dread;[j]
  For Jah* Jehovah is my
    strength and my might,
  And he has become my
    salvation."[k]

3 With rejoicing you will draw
    water
  From the springs of
    salvation.[l]

4 And in that day you will say:

CHAP. 11
a Ho 2:18
b Isa 2:4
  Isa 35:9
  Isa 60:18
  Mic 4:4
c Isa 51:3
  Isa 56:7
  Isa 65:25
d Ps 22:27
  Hab 2:14
e Ro 15:12
  Re 22:16
f Ge 49:10
  Isa 49:22
  Isa 62:10
g Ac 11:18
  Ac 28:28
h Isa 11:16
i Isa 27:13
  Jer 44:28
  Mic 7:12
j Jer 44:15
k Zep 3:10
l Da 8:2
m Isa 66:19
n Ezr 1:2, 3
  Isa 49:22
  Isa 62:10
o Ps 147:2
  Isa 66:20
p 2Ch 30:1, 10
  Jer 31:6
q Jer 3:18
  Eze 37:16, 19
  Ho 1:11

Second Col.
a Am 9:11, 12
  Ob 18
b Isa 25:10
c Jer 49:2
d Ex 14:22
e Ge 15:18
f Isa 19:23
  Isa 27:13
  Isa 35:8
  Isa 40:3
  Isa 57:14
  Jer 31:21
g Ezr 1:2, 3

CHAP. 12
h De 30:3
  Ps 30:5
  Ps 85:1
  Ps 126:1
  Isa 40:2
  Isa 66:13
i Isa 45:17
j Isa 26:4
k Ps 118:14
  Ho 1:7
l Isa 49:10

11:10, 12 *Or "signal pole." **11:10** #Or
"The nations will search for him." **11:11**
*That is, Babylonia.

11:14 *Lit., "shoulder." #Or "extend
their power over." **11:15** *Or possibly,
"dry up." #Lit., "tongue." △That is,
the Euphrates. ⊠Or "spirit." □Or possibly, "strike it into." **12:2** *"Jah" is a
shortened form of the name Jehovah.

"Give thanks to Jehovah,
call on his name,
Make his deeds known
among the peoples![a]
Declare that his name is
exalted.[b]

5 Sing praises* to Jehovah,[c]
for he has done
magnificent things.[d]
Let this be made known in
all the earth.

6 Cry out and shout for joy,
you inhabitant* of Zion,
For great in your midst is the
Holy One of Israel."

13 A pronouncement against
Babylon[e] that Isaiah[f] the
son of A′moz saw in vision:

2 "Raise up a signal*[g] on a
mountain of bare rocks.
Call out to them, wave your
hand,
So that they may come
into the entrances of the
nobles.

3 I have issued the command
to those whom I have
appointed.*[h]
I have summoned my war-
riors to express my anger,
My proudly exultant ones.

4 Listen! A crowd in the
mountains;
It sounds like a numerous
people!
Listen! The uproar of
kingdoms,
Of nations gathered
together![i]
Jehovah of armies is mustering the army for war.[j]

5 They are coming from
a distant land,[k]
From the extremity of the
heavens,
Jehovah and the weapons
of his wrath,

To bring ruin to all the
earth.[a]

6 Wail, for the day of Jehovah
is near!
It will come as a destruction
from the Almighty.[b]

7 That is why all hands will go
limp,
And every man's heart will
melt with fear.[c]

8 The people are panic-
stricken.[d]
They are seized with
convulsions and pain,
Like a woman in labor.
They look at one another
in horror,
With faces inflamed by
anguish.

9 Look! The day of Jehovah
is coming,
Cruel both with fury and
with burning anger,
To make the land an object
of horror,[e]
And to annihilate the land's
sinners from it.

10 For the stars of the heavens
and their constellations*[f]
Will not give off their light;
The sun will be dark when
it rises,
And the moon will not shed
its light.

11 I will call the inhabited earth
to account for its badness,[g]
And the wicked for their
error.
I will put an end to the pride
of the presumptuous,
And I will humble the
haughtiness of tyrants.[h]

12 I will make mortal man
scarcer than refined gold,[i]
And humans scarcer than
the gold of O′phir.[j]

13 That is why I will make the
heavens tremble,

CHAP. 12
a 1Ch 16:8
  Ps 105:1, 2

b Ex 15:2

c Ps 149:3

d Ps 98:1

CHAP. 13
e Jer 25:12
  Jer 50:1-3
  Re 18:2

f Isa 1:1

g Jer 51:12
  Jer 51:27, 28

h Isa 45:1

i Da 5:28

j Jer 50:15

k Jer 50:9
  Jer 51:28

Second Col.
a Jer 51:11

b Isa 13:18
  Jer 50:13

c Jer 50:43

d Da 5:6

e Jer 50:23, 29

f Job 9:9
  Job 38:31
  Am 5:8

g Ps 137:8
  Jer 51:37
  Re 18:2

h Jer 50:29
  Da 5:22, 23

i Jer 50:30
  Jer 51:3, 4

j 1Ki 10:11

12:5 *Or "Make music." 12:6 *Lit., "inhabitress," referring to the population
collectively as a woman. 13:2 *Or "signal pole." 13:3 *Lit., "to my sanctified
ones."

13:10 *Lit., "and their Kesils," perhaps
referring to Orion and surrounding constellations.

And the earth will be shaken out of its place[a]

At the fury of Jehovah of armies in the day of his burning anger.

14 Like a hunted gazelle and like a flock with no one to gather them,

Each will return to his own people;

Each will flee to his own land.[b]

15 Whoever is found will be pierced through,

And whoever is caught will fall by the sword.[c]

16 Their children will be dashed to pieces before their eyes,[d]

Their houses will be looted,

And their wives will be raped.

17 Here I am raising up against them the Medes,[e]

Who regard silver as nothing

And who take no delight in gold.

18 Their bows will shatter young men;[f]

They will show no pity on the fruit of the womb

Nor mercy to children.

19 And Babylon, the most glorious* of kingdoms,[g]

The beauty and the pride of the Chal·de′ans,[h]

Will be like Sod′om and Go·mor′rah when God overthrew them.[i]

20 She will never be inhabited,

Nor will she be a place to reside in throughout all generations.[j]

No Arab will pitch his tent there,

And no shepherds will rest their flocks there.

21 The desert creatures will lie down there;

Their houses will be filled with eagle owls.

The ostriches will reside there,[a]

And wild goats* will skip about there.

22 Howling creatures will cry out in her towers,

And jackals in her luxurious palaces.

Her time is near, and her days will not be prolonged."[b]

14 For Jehovah will show mercy to Jacob,[c] and he will again choose Israel.[d] He will settle them* in their land,[e] and the foreign residents will join them and attach themselves to the house of Jacob.[f] 2 And peoples will take them and bring them to their own place, and the house of Israel will possess them as male and female servants[g] in Jehovah's land; and they will be the captors of those who held them captive, and they will have in subjection those who were forcing them to work.*

3 In the day when Jehovah gives you rest from your pain and from your turmoil and from the hard slavery imposed on you,[h] 4 you will recite this proverb* against the king of Babylon:

"How the one forcing others to work# has met his end!

How the oppression has ended![i]

5 Jehovah has broken the rod of the wicked,

The staff of the rulers,[j]

6 The one furiously striking peoples with unceasing blows,[k]

The one angrily subduing nations with relentless persecution.[l]

CHAP. 13
a Jer 51:29
b Jer 50:16
c Jer 51:3, 4
d Ps 137:8, 9
e Isa 21:2
Jer 50:9
Jer 51:11
Da 5:30, 31
f Jer 50:14
g Isa 47:5
Da 4:30
h Isa 47:1
i Ge 19:24, 25
Jer 50:40
j Jer 50:3, 13
Jer 51:29, 37
Re 18:21

Second Col.
a Re 18:2
b Jer 51:33

CHAP. 14
c Le 26:42
d Zec 1:17
e De 30:1-3
Isa 66:20
Jer 24:6
Eze 36:24
f Isa 56:6, 7
Isa 60:3
Zec 8:22, 23
g Isa 61:5
Zec 2:8, 9
h Ezr 3:1
Ezr 9:8
Jer 30:10
i Jer 50:23
j Ps 125:3
k 2Ch 36:17
Jer 50:17
l Hab 1:6
Zec 1:15

13:19 *Or "the decoration."

13:21 *Or possibly, "And goatlike demons." 14:1 *Or "give them rest." 14:2 *Or "their taskmasters." 14:4 *Or "taunt." #Or "the taskmaster."

7 The whole earth now rests,
   free of disturbance.
 People cry out for joy.[a]
8 Even the juniper trees
   rejoice over you,
 Along with the cedars of
   Leb′a·non.
 They say, 'Ever since you
   have fallen,
 No woodcutter comes up
   against us.'
9 Even the Grave* underneath
   is stirred up
 To meet you when you come.
 Because of you, it awakens
   those powerless in death,
 All the oppressive leaders#
   of the earth.
 It makes all the kings of
   the nations rise from their
   thrones.
10 All of them speak up and say
   to you,
 'Have you also become weak
   like us?
 Have you become like us?
11 Down to the Grave* your
   pride has been brought,
 The sound of your stringed
   instruments.[b]
 Maggots are spread beneath
   you as a bed,
 And worms are your
   covering.'
12 How you have fallen from
   heaven,
 O shining one, son of the
   dawn!
 How you have been cut down
   to the earth,
 You who vanquished
   nations![c]
13 You said in your heart, 'I will
   ascend to the heavens.[d]
 Above the stars of God
   I will lift up my throne,[e]
 And I will sit down on the
   mountain of meeting,

 In the remotest parts
   of the north.[a]
14 I will go up above the tops
   of the clouds;
 I will make myself resemble
   the Most High.'
15 Instead, you will be brought
   down to the Grave,*
 To the remotest parts
   of the pit.
16 Those seeing you will stare
   at you;
 They will closely examine
   you, saying,
 'Is this the man who was
   shaking the earth,
 Who made kingdoms
   tremble,[b]
17 Who made the inhabited
   earth like the wilderness
 And overthrew its cities,[c]
 Who refused to let his
   prisoners go home?'[d]
18 All other kings of the
   nations,
 Yes, all of them, lie down
   in glory,
 Each one in his own tomb.*
19 But you are discarded
   without a grave,
 Like a detested sprout,*
 Clothed with the slain who
   were stabbed with the
   sword,
 Who go down to the stones
   of a pit,
 Like a carcass trampled
   underfoot.
20 You will not join them in
   a grave,
 For you destroyed your own
   land,
 You killed your own people.
 The offspring of evildoers
   will never again be named.
21 Prepare a slaughtering block
   for his sons
 Because of the guilt of their
   forefathers,

CHAP. 14
a Ps 126:2
  Isa 49:13
  Jer 51:48
  Re 18:20

b Re 18:22

c 2Ch 36:17
  Jer 51:7
  Eze 29:19
  Da 5:18, 19

d Isa 47:7
  Da 4:30

e Da 5:22, 23

_____
Second Col.
a Ps 48:1, 2

b Jer 51:25

c 2Ki 25:21
  Isa 64:10

d 2Ki 24:12, 14
  2Ki 25:11

14:9, 11, 15 *Or "Sheol," that is, the common grave of mankind. See Glossary. **14:9** #Lit., "the he-goats." **14:18** *Lit., "house." **14:19** *Or "branch."

So that they will not rise up
  and take over the earth
And fill the land with their
  cities."

22 "I will rise up against
them,"[a] declares Jehovah of armies.

"And I will wipe out from
Babylon name and remnant and
descendants and posterity,"[b] declares Jehovah.

23 "And I will make her a possession of porcupines and a region of marshes, and I will sweep
her with the broom of annihilation,"[c] declares Jehovah of armies.

24 Jehovah of armies has
  sworn:
"Just as I have intended,
  so it will occur,
And just as I have decided,
  that is what will come true.
25 I will crush the As·syr'i·an
  in my land,
And I will trample him on
  my mountains.[d]
His yoke will be removed
  from them,
And his load will be removed
  from their shoulder."[e]
26 This is what has been decided* against all the earth,
And this is the hand that is
  stretched out# against all
  the nations.
27 For Jehovah of armies has
  decided,
And who can thwart it?[f]
His hand is stretched out,
And who can turn it back?[g]
28 In the year that King A'haz
  died,[h] this pronouncement
  was made:
29 "Do not rejoice, Phi·lis'ti·a,
  any of you,
Just because the staff of the
  one striking you has been
  broken.

For from the root of
  the serpent[a] will come a
  poisonous snake,[b]
And its offspring will be
  a flying fiery snake.*
30 While the firstborn of the
  lowly feed
And the poor lie down in
  security,
I will put your root to death
  with famine,
And what is left of you will
  be killed.[c]
31 Wail, O gate! Cry out, O city!
All of you will lose heart,
  O Phi·lis'ti·a!
For a smoke is coming from
  the north,
And there are no stragglers
  in his ranks."
32 How should they answer the
  messengers of the nation?
That Jehovah has laid the
  foundation of Zion,[d]
And that the lowly ones of
  his people will take refuge
  in her.

15 A pronouncement against
  Mo'ab:[e]
Because it has been
  devastated in a night,
Ar[f] of Mo'ab has been
  silenced.
Because it has been
  devastated in a night,
Kir[g] of Mo'ab has been
  silenced.
2 He has gone up to the
  House* and to Di'bon,[h]
To the high places to weep.
Mo'ab wails over Ne'bo[i]
  and over Med'e·ba.[j]
Every head is shaved bald,[k]
  every beard is clipped.[l]
3 In its streets they have put
  on sackcloth.
On their roofs and in their
  public squares they all
  wail;
They go down weeping.[m]

CHAP. 14

a Isa 43:14
  Jer 50:25
  Jer 51:56

b Jer 51:62

c Isa 13:1, 21
  Jer 50:35, 39
  Re 18:2

d 2Ch 32:21, 22
  Isa 30:31
  Isa 31:8
  Isa 37:36, 37

e Isa 10:24

f Ps 33:11
  Pr 19:21
  Pr 21:30
  Isa 46:11

g 2Ch 20:5, 6
  Isa 43:13

h 2Ki 16:20
  2Ch 28:27

Second Col.

a 2Ch 26:3, 6

b 2Ki 18:1, 8

c Jer 47:1
  Eze 25:16
  Joe 3:4
  Am 1:6-8
  Zep 2:4
  Zec 9:5

d Ps 48:1-3
  Ps 87:1, 2
  Ps 132:13, 14

CHAP. 15

e Jer 9:25, 26
  Eze 25:11

f Nu 21:28
  De 2:9

g 2Ki 3:24, 25
  Jer 48:31

h Jer 48:18

i Jer 48:1

j Nu 21:30
  Jos 13:15-17

k De 14:1

l Jer 48:36, 37

m Jer 48:38

14:26 *Lit., "the counsel that is coun-
seled." #Or "is ready to strike."

14:29 *Or "a darting poisonous snake."
15:2 *Or "the Temple."

4 Hesh'bon and E·le·a'leh[a]
cry out;
Their voice is heard as far
as Ja'haz.[b]
That is why the armed men
of Mo'ab keep shouting.
He* is trembling.
5 My heart cries out over
Mo'ab.
Its fugitives have fled as
far as Zo'ar[c] and Eg'lath-
she·li'shi·yah.[d]
On the ascent of Lu'hith they
weep as they go up;
On the way to Hor·o·na'im
they cry out over the
catastrophe.[e]
6 For the waters of Nim'rim
are desolate;
The green grass has
dried up,
The grass is gone and
nothing green is left.
7 That is why they are carrying
away what is left of their
stores and their riches;
They are crossing the valley*
of poplars.
8 For the outcry echoes
throughout the territory
of Mo'ab.[f]
The wailing reaches
to Eg·la'im;
The wailing reaches
to Be'er·e'lim.
9 For the waters of Di'mon
are full of blood,
And I have more in store
for Di'mon:
A lion for those of Mo'ab
who escape
And for those remaining
in the land.[g]

16 Send a ram to the ruler
of the land,
From Se'la through the
wilderness
To the mountain of the
daughter of Zion.
2 Like a bird chased away
from its nest,[h]

CHAP. 15

a Nu 32:37
Isa 16:9

b Jg 11:20

c Ge 13:10

d Jer 48:34

e Jer 48:3, 5

f Jer 48:20

g 2Ki 17:25, 26

CHAP. 16

h Jer 48:19

Second Col.

a Nu 21:13

b Jer 48:8, 42

c 2Sa 7:16, 17

d Ps 45:6
Ps 72:1, 2
Isa 9:6, 7
Isa 32:1
Jer 23:5

e Jer 48:26, 29
Zep 2:9, 10

f Am 2:1

g Isa 15:2
Jer 48:20

h 2Ki 3:24, 25

i Jos 13:15, 17

j Nu 32:37, 38
Jos 13:15, 19

k Jos 13:24, 15
Jer 48:32

So the daughters of Mo'ab
will be at the fords of
Ar'non.[a]
3 "Offer counsel, carry out
the decision.
Make your shadow at high
noon like the night.
Conceal the dispersed and
do not betray those fleeing.
4 May my dispersed ones
reside in you, O Mo'ab.
Become a place of concealment to them because of
the destroyer.[b]
The oppressor will reach
his end,
The destruction will come
to an end,
And those trampling others
down will perish from the
earth.
5 Then a throne will be firmly
established in loyal love.
The one who sits on it in the
tent of David will be faithful;[c]
He will judge fairly and will
swiftly execute righteousness."[d]
6 We have heard about the
pride of Mo'ab—he is very
proud[e]—
His haughtiness and his
pride and his fury;[f]
But his empty talk will come
to nothing.
7 So Mo'ab will wail for Mo'ab;
They will all wail.[g]
Those who are stricken will
moan for the raisin cakes
of Kir-har'e·seth.[h]
8 For the terraces of Hesh'bon[i]
have withered,
The vine of Sib'mah,[j]
The rulers of the nations
have trampled its bright-
red branches;*
They had reached as far as
Ja'zer;[k]
They had extended into the
wilderness.

15:4 *Or "His soul." **15:7** *Or "wadi."   **16:8** *Or "its branches laden with red grapes."

Its shoots had spread out and gone as far as the sea.

9 That is why I will weep over the vine of Sib′mah as I weep for Ja′zer.

With my tears I will drench you, O Hesh′bon and E·le·a′leh,[a]

Because the shouting over your summer fruit and your harvest has ended.*

10 Rejoicing and joyfulness have been taken away from the orchard,

And there are no songs of joy or shouting in the vineyards.[b]

The treader no longer treads out wine in the presses, For I have caused the shouting to cease.[c]

11 That is why deep within me I am boisterous over Mo′ab,[d]

Like the strumming of a harp,

And my innermost being over Kir-har′e·seth.[e]

12 Even when Mo′ab wears himself out on the high place and goes to pray in his sanctuary, he will accomplish nothing.[f]

13 This is the word that Jehovah previously spoke concerning Mo′ab. **14** And now Jehovah says: "Within three years, like the years of a hired worker,* the glory of Mo′ab will be disgraced with much tumult of every sort, and those who remain will be very few and insignificant."[g]

17 A pronouncement against Damascus:[h]

"Look! Damascus will cease to be a city, And it will become a heap of ruins.[i]

CHAP. 16
a Isa 15:4
  Jer 48:34

b Jer 48:33

c Zep 2:9

d Isa 15:5
  Jer 48:36

e Isa 15:1

f Jer 48:7, 35

g Isa 25:10
  Jer 48:46, 47
  Zep 2:9

CHAP. 17
h Jer 49:23
  Zec 9:1

i 2Ki 16:8, 9
  Isa 8:4
  Am 1:5

Second Col.
a Nu 32:34
  Jos 13:15, 16
  2Ki 10:32, 33

b 2Ki 17:6
  Isa 7:8
  Isa 28:1, 2
  Ho 5:14

c 2Ki 16:8, 9

d Jos 15:8, 12
  Jos 18:11, 16

e De 4:27
  De 24:20

f 2Ch 31:1

g Ho 8:6, 11

h Ho 10:14
  Am 3:11

---

2 The cities of A·ro′er[a] will be abandoned;

They will become places for flocks to lie down

With no one to make them afraid.

3 Fortified cities will disappear from E′phra·im,[b]

And the kingdom from Damascus;[c]

And those remaining of Syria Will be like the glory of the Israelites,* declares Jehovah of armies.

4 "In that day the glory of Jacob will diminish,

And his healthy body* will grow thin.

5 It will be as when the harvester is gathering the standing grain

And his arm harvests the ears of grain,

Like when one gleans grain in the Valley* of Reph′a·im.[d]

6 Only gleanings will be left, As when an olive tree is beaten:

Only two or three ripe olives remain on the highest branch,

Only four or five on its fruit-bearing branches," declares Jehovah the God of Israel.

7 In that day man will look up to his Maker, and his eyes will gaze at the Holy One of Israel. **8** He will not look to the altars,[f] the work of his hands;[g] and he will not gaze at what his fingers have made, either the sacred poles* or the incense stands.

9 In that day his fortress cities will become like an abandoned site in the woodland,[h]

16:9 *Or possibly, "Because the battle cry has descended on your summer fruit and your harvest." **16:14** *Or "counted as carefully as a hired worker does"; that is, in exactly three years.

17:3 *Lit., "sons of Israel." **17:4** *Lit., "the fat of his flesh." **17:5** *Or "Low Plain." **17:8** *See Glossary.

Like a branch that was
abandoned before the
Israelites;
It will become a wasteland.

10 For you have forgotten the
God[a] of your salvation;
You have failed to remember
the Rock[b] of your fortress.
That is why you plant
beautiful* plantations
And set it with the shoot of
a stranger.#

11 In the day you carefully
fence in your plantation,
In the morning you make
your seed sprout,
But the harvest will vanish
in the day of disease and
incurable pain.[c]

12 Listen! There is a commotion
of many peoples,
Who are as boisterous as
the seas!
There is an uproar of
nations,
Whose sound is like the roar
of mighty waters!

13 The nations will make a
sound like the roar of
many waters.
He will rebuke them, and
they will flee far away,
Chased like the chaff of the
mountains before a wind,
Like a whirling thistle*
before a storm wind.

14 In the evening there is terror.
Before morning they are
no more.
This is the share of those
pillaging us
And the lot of those
plundering us.

18 Woe to the land of
whirring insect wings
In the region of the rivers
of E·thi·o'pi·a![d]

2 It sends envoys by sea,
Across the waters in papyrus
vessels, saying:

"Go, you swift messengers,
To a tall and smooth-skinned
nation,*
To a people feared every-
where,[a]
To a strong, conquering
nation,#
Whose land is washed away
by rivers."

3 All you inhabitants of the
land and you residents of
the earth,
What you see will be like
a signal* raised on the
mountains,
And you will hear a sound
like the blowing of a horn.

4 For this is what Jehovah
said to me:
"I will remain undisturbed
and look on* my estab-
lished place,
Like the shimmering heat
along with the sunlight,
Like the cloud of dew in
the heat of harvest.

5 For before the harvest,
When the blossom is finished
and the bloom becomes a
ripening grape,
The shoots will be cut off
with pruning shears
And the tendrils will be
lopped off and removed.

6 They will all be left for
the birds of prey of the
mountains
And for the beasts of the
earth.
The birds of prey will spend
the summer on them,
And all the beasts of the
earth will spend the har-
vesttime on them.

7 At that time a gift will
be brought to Jehovah
of armies,

CHAP. 17
a Ps 50:22
Ho 8:14

b De 32:4
2Sa 22:32

c De 28:30
Ho 8:7

CHAP. 18
d Isa 20:3,4
Eze 30:4

Second Col.
a 2Ch 12:2, 3
2Ch 14:9
2Ch 16:8

17:10 *Or "pleasant." #Or "a foreign
god." 17:13 *Or "Like tumbleweed." 18:2 *Lit., "a nation drawn out
and scoured." #Or "a nation of ten-
sile strength that treads down." 18:3
*Or "signal pole." 18:4 *Or possibly,
"from."

From a tall and smooth-
skinned nation,*

From a people feared
everywhere,

From a strong, conquering
nation,#

Whose land is washed away
by rivers

To the place that bears
the name of Jehovah of
armies, Mount Zion."[a]

19 A pronouncement against
Egypt:[b]

Look! Jehovah is riding on a
swift cloud and is coming
into Egypt.

The worthless gods of Egypt
will tremble before him,[c]

And the heart of Egypt will
melt within it.

2 "I will incite Egyptians
against Egyptians,

And they will fight one
another,

Each against his brother and
his neighbor,

City against city, kingdom
against kingdom.

3 And the spirit of Egypt
will become bewildered
within it,

And I will confuse its plans.[d]

They will resort to the
worthless gods,

To the charmers and to
the spirit mediums and to
the fortune-tellers.[e]

4 I will hand Egypt over to
a hard master,

And a harsh king will rule
over them,"[f] declares the
true Lord, Jehovah of ar-
mies.

5 The water of the sea will be
dried up,

And the river will become
parched and run dry.[g]

6 And the rivers will stink;

The Nile canals of Egypt will
become low and parched.

The reeds and the rushes
will decay.[a]

7 The plants along the Nile River, at the mouth of the Nile,

And all the land sown with
seed along the Nile[b] will
dry up.[c]

It will be blown away, and it
will be no more.

8 And the fishermen will
mourn,

Those casting fishhooks into
the Nile will lament,

And those who spread their
nets on the water will
dwindle.

9 Those who work in combed
flax[d]

And those making white
fabric on the loom will be
put to shame.

10 Her weavers will be crushed;

All the hired workers will
grieve.*

11 The princes of Zo'an[e] are
foolish.

The wisest advisers of
Phar'aoh give unreason-
able advice.[f]

How can you say to
Phar'aoh:

"I am a descendant of wise
ones,

A descendant of ancient
kings"?

12 Where, then, are your wise
men?[g]

Let them tell you if they
know what Jehovah of
armies has decided
concerning Egypt.

13 The princes of Zo'an have
acted foolishly;

The princes of Noph*[h] have
been deceived;

The chiefs of her tribes have
led Egypt astray.

14 Jehovah has poured out on
her a spirit of confusion;[i]

CHAP. 18
a Isa 8:18
 Isa 24:23

CHAP. 19
b Jer 25:17, 19
 Eze 29:2
 Joe 3:19

c Ex 12:12
 Jer 43:12
 Jer 46:25
 Eze 30:13

d Isa 19:11, 13

e Isa 8:19
 Ac 16:16
 Re 18:23

f Isa 20:3, 4
 Jer 46:25, 26
 Eze 29:19

g Eze 30:12
 Zec 10:11

Second Col.
a Ex 2:3

b De 11:10

c Eze 29:10

d Ex 9:25, 31
 Pr 7:16

e Ps 78:12
 Eze 30:14

f Isa 44:25

g Ge 41:8
 1Ki 4:30
 Ac 7:22

h Jer 46:14
 Eze 30:13

i Job 12:20, 24
 Isa 19:3

18:7 *Lit., "a nation drawn out and
scoured." #Or "a nation of tensile
strength that treads down."

19:10 *Or "be grieved in soul." 19:13
*Or "Memphis."

And they have led Egypt
astray in whatever she
does,
Like a drunk staggering
in his vomit.
15 And Egypt will not have any
work to do,
Whether for the head or the
tail, the shoot or the rush.*

16 In that day Egypt will become like women, trembling and terrified because of the threatening hand that Jehovah of armies raises against it.ᵃ 17 And the land of Judah will become a cause for terror to Egypt. They will feel dread at the mention of it because of the decision that Jehovah of armies has made against them.ᵇ

18 In that day there will be five cities in the land of Egypt speaking the language of Ca'naanᶜ and swearing loyalty to Jehovah of armies. One city will be called The City of Tearing Down.

19 In that day there will be an altar to Jehovah in the middle of the land of Egypt and a pillar to Jehovah at its boundary. 20 It will be for a sign and for a witness to Jehovah of armies in the land of Egypt; for they will cry out to Jehovah because of the oppressors, and he will send them a savior, a grand one, who will save them. 21 And Jehovah will become known to the Egyptians, and the Egyptians will know Jehovah in that day, and they will offer sacrifices and gifts and make a vow to Jehovah and pay it. 22 Jehovah will strike Egypt,ᵈ striking and healing it; and they will return to Jehovah, and he will respond to their entreaties and heal them.

23 In that day there will be a highwayᵉ out of Egypt to As·syr'i·a. Then As·syr'i·a will come into Egypt, and Egypt into As·syr'i·a,

and Egypt will serve God together with As·syr'i·a. 24 In that day Israel will be the third along with Egypt and with As·syr'i·a,ᵃ a blessing in the midst of the earth, 25 for Jehovah of armies will have blessed it, saying: "Blessed be my people, Egypt, and the work of my hands, As·syr'i·a, and my inheritance, Israel."ᵇ

20 In the year that King Sar'gon of As·syr'i·a sent the Tar'tan* to Ash'dod,ᶜ he fought against Ash'dod and captured it.ᵈ 2 At that time Jehovah spoke through Isaiahᵉ the son of A'moz, saying: "Go, remove the sackcloth from your hips, and take your sandals off your feet." And he did so, walking about naked* and barefoot.

3 Jehovah then said: "Just as my servant Isaiah has walked about naked and barefoot for three years as a signᶠ and a portent against Egyptᵍ and E·thi·o'pi·a,ʰ 4 so the king of As·syr'i·a will lead the captives of Egyptⁱ and the exiles of E·thi·o'pi·a, boys and old men, naked and barefoot and with exposed buttocks, the nakedness* of Egypt. 5 And they will be terrified and will be ashamed of E·thi·o'pi·a their hope and of Egypt their pride.* 6 The inhabitants of this coastland will say in that day, 'Look at what happened to our hope, to which we fled for help and rescue from the king of As·syr'i·a! How will we escape now?'"

21 A pronouncement against the wilderness of the sea:*ʲ

It is coming like storm winds
that sweep through in the
south,

20:1 *Or "the commander." 20:2 *Or "lightly clad." 20:4 *Or "to the shame." 20:5 *Or "whose beauty they admired." 21:1 *Apparently refers to the region of ancient Babylonia.

CHAP. 19	
a	Isa 11:15
b	Isa 20:3, 4
	Jer 25:17, 19
	Jer 43:10, 11
	Eze 29:6
c	Jer 43:4, 7
	Jer 44:1
d	Isa 19:1
	Jer 46:13
e	Isa 11:16
	Isa 35:8
	Isa 40:3
Second Col.	
a	Zec 2:11
b	De 32:9
	Ps 115:12
	Isa 61:9
CHAP. 20	
c	Jos 13:2, 3
d	Am 1:8
e	Isa 1:1
f	Isa 8:18
g	Isa 19:1
h	Isa 18:1
i	Isa 19:4
CHAP. 21	
j	Isa 13:1, 20

From the wilderness, from
 a fearsome land.ᵃ

2 A harsh vision has been told
 to me:

The treacherous one is
 acting treacherously,
And the destroyer is
 destroying.
Go up, O E'lam! Lay siege,
 O Me'di·aⁱᵇ
I will put an end to all the
 sighing she caused.ᶜ

3 That is why I am in great
 anguish.*ᵈ

Convulsions have seized me,
Like those of a woman giving
 birth.
I am too distressed to hear;
I am too disturbed to see.

4 My heart falters; I shudder
 in terror.

The twilight I longed for
 makes me tremble.

5 Set the table and arrange
 the seats!

Eat and drink!ᵉ
Get up, you princes, anoint*
 the shield!

6 For this is what Jehovah said
 to me:

"Go, post a lookout and have
 him report what he sees."

7 And he saw a war chariot
 with a team of horses,

A war chariot of donkeys,
A war chariot of camels.
He watched carefully, with
 great attentiveness.

8 Then he called out like
 a lion:

"Upon the watchtower,
 O Jehovah, I am standing
 constantly by day,
And I am stationed at my
 guardpost every night.ᶠ

9 Look at what is coming:
Men in a war chariot with
 a team of horses!"ᵍ

Then he spoke up and said:

21:3 *Lit., "my hips are full of pain."
21:5 *Or "oil."

CHAP. 21
a Isa 13:4, 18

b Jer 51:11, 28
 Da 5:28, 30

c Ps 137:1
 Isa 14:4, 7
 Isa 35:10

d Hab 3:16

e Da 5:1

f Eze 3:17
 Hab 2:1

g Jer 50:3, 9
 Jer 51:27, 28

Second Col.
a Isa 13:19
 Isa 14:4
 Isa 45:1
 Jer 51:8
 Da 5:28, 30
 Re 14:8
 Re 18:2

b Jer 50:2
 Jer 51:44, 52

c 1Ki 8:46

d Ge 32:3
 De 2:8
 Ps 137:7

e Jer 25:17, 23

f Job 6:19
 Jer 25:17, 23

g Ge 25:13
 Ps 120:5
 Ca 1:5
 Isa 42:11
 Jer 49:28
 Eze 27:21

"She has fallen! Babylon
 has fallen!ᵃ

All the graven images of her
 gods he has shattered to
 the ground!"ᵇ

10 O my people who have been
 threshed,

The product* of my
 threshing floor,ᶜ
I have reported to you what
 I have heard from Jehovah
 of armies, the God of
 Israel.

11 A pronouncement against
Du'mah:*

Someone is calling out to me
 from Se'ir:ᵈ
"Watchman, what of the
 night?
Watchman, what of the
 night?"

12 The watchman said:

"The morning is coming,
 and also the night.
If you would inquire, inquire.
Come again!"

13 A pronouncement against
the desert plain:

In the forest in the desert
 plain you will spend the
 night,
O caravans of De'dan.ᵉ

14 Bring water to meet the
 thirsty one,

You inhabitants of the land
 of Te'ma,ᶠ
And bring bread for the one
 fleeing.

15 For they have fled from the
 swords, from the drawn
 sword,

From the bent bow, and from
 the cruelty of the war.

16 For this is what Jehovah
said to me: "Within one year, like
the years of a hired worker,* all
the glory of Ke'darᵍ will come to

21:10 *Lit., "son." 21:11 *Meaning "Silence." 21:16 *Or "counted as carefully as a hired worker does"; that is, in exactly one year.

an end. **17** The remaining bowmen of the warriors of Ke′dar will be few, for Jehovah the God of Israel has spoken.”

22 A pronouncement about the Valley of Vision:*[a]

What is the matter with you
    that you have all gone up
    to the roofs?
2 You were full of turmoil,
    A boisterous city, an exultant
    town.
Your slain were not slain
    with the sword,
    Nor did they die in battle.[b]
3 All your dictators have fled
    together.[c]
They were taken prisoner
    without need of a bow.
All who were found were
    taken prisoner,[d]
Even though they had fled
    far away.
4 That is why I said: “Turn
    your eyes away from me,
    And I will weep bitterly.[e]
Do not insist on
    comforting me
Over the destruction of the
    daughter of* my people.[f]
5 For it is a day of confusion
    and of defeat and of panic,[g]
From the Sovereign Lord,
    Jehovah of armies,
    In the Valley of Vision.
There is a demolishing of
    the wall[h]
    And a cry to the mountain.
6 E′lam[i] picks up the quiver
    With manned chariots
    and horses,*
And Kir[j] uncovers# the
    shield.
7 Your choicest valleys#
    Will become full of war
    chariots,

And the horses* will take
    their positions at the gate,
8 And the screen* of Judah
    will be removed.

“In that day you will look toward the armory of the House of the Forest,[a] **9** and you will see the many breaches of the City of David.[b] And you will collect the waters of the lower pool.[c] **10** You will count the houses of Jerusalem, and you will pull down the houses to reinforce the wall. **11** And you will make a basin between the two walls for the water of the old pool, but you will not look to its Grand Maker, and you will not see the One who formed it long ago.

12 In that day the Sovereign
    Lord, Jehovah of armies,
Will call for weeping and
    mourning,[d]
For shaved heads and the
    wearing of sackcloth.
13 But instead, there is
    celebration and rejoicing,
The killing of cattle and the
    slaughtering of sheep,
The eating of meat and the
    drinking of wine.[e]
‘Let us eat and drink, for
    tomorrow we will die.’”[f]

14 Then Jehovah of armies revealed himself in my ears: “‘This error will not be atoned in your behalf until you people die,’ says the Sovereign Lord, Jehovah of armies.”

15 This is what the Sovereign Lord, Jehovah of armies, says: “Go in to this steward, to Sheb′na,[h] who is in charge of the house,* and say, **16** ‘What is your interest here, and who is there of interest to you here, that you hewed out a burial place here for yourself?’ He is hewing out his burial place in a high place; he is cutting out

CHAP. 22
a Jer 6:6

b Isa 3:1
  Jer 38:2
  La 4:9

c 2Ki 25:4, 5

d 2Ki 25:11

e Jer 4:19
  Jer 8:18, 19
  Jer 9:1

f Mic 1:8, 9

g Mic 7:4

h 2Ki 25:10
  Ne 1:3

i Ge 10:22

j 2Ki 16:9

Second Col.
a 1Ki 7:1, 2

b 2Ki 25:9, 10
  Jer 52:7

c Ne 3:15

d Joe 2:17

e Isa 5:12
  Isa 56:12
  Am 6:1, 4
  Lu 17:27
  Jas 5:5

f 1Co 15:32

g Le 26:31
  Isa 1:11
  Jer 15:1
  Eze 24:13

h 2Ki 18:37
  2Ki 19:2

22:1 *Evidently referring to Jerusalem.
22:4 *A poetic personification, perhaps expressing pity or sympathy. 22:6, 7 *Or “horsemen.” 22:6 #Or “prepares.”
22:7 #Or “low plains.”

22:8 *Or “protection.” 22:15 *Or “palace.”

a resting-place* for himself in a crag. **17** 'Look! Jehovah will hurl you down violently, O man, and seize you forcibly. **18** He will certainly wrap you up tightly and hurl you like a ball into a wide land. There you will die, and there your glorious chariots will be, a disgrace to your master's house. **19** And I will depose you from your position and throw you out of your office.

20 "'In that day I will call my servant E·liʹa·kimᵃ the son of Hil·kiʹah, **21** and I will clothe him with your robe and firmly bind your sash around him,ᵇ and I will give your authority* into his hand. And he will be a father to the inhabitants of Jerusalem and to the house of Judah. **22** And I will put the key of the house of Davidᶜ on his shoulder. He will open and no one will shut; and he will shut and no one will open. **23** I will drive him in as a peg in a lasting place, and he will become as a throne of glory to the house of his father. **24** And they will hang on him all the glory* of the house of his father, the descendants and the offspring,ᵘ all the small vessels, the bowl-shaped vessels, as well as all the large jars.

25 "'In that day,' declares Jehovah of armies, 'the peg that is driven in a lasting place will be removed,ᵈ and it will be cut down and fall, and the load that it supported will fall to ruin, for Jehovah himself has spoken.'"

23 A pronouncement about Tyre:ᵉ

Wail, you ships of Tarʹshish!ᶠ
For the port has been destroyed; it cannot be entered.
From the land of Kitʹtimᵍ it has been revealed to them.

2 Be silent, you inhabitants of the coastland.
The merchants from Siʹdonᵃ who cross the sea have filled you.

3 Over many waters went the grain* of Shiʹhor,*ᵇ
The harvest of the Nile, her revenue,
Bringing the profit of the nations.ᶜ

4 Be ashamed, O Siʹdon, you stronghold of the sea,
Because the sea has said:
"I have not had birth pains, and I have not given birth,
Nor have I brought up young men or raised young women."*ᵈ

5 As when they heard the report about Egypt,ᵉ
People will be in anguish over the report about Tyre.ᶠ

6 Cross over to Tarʹshish!
Wail, you inhabitants of the coastland!

7 Is this your city that was exultant from long ago, from her early times?
Her feet used to take her to distant lands to reside.

8 Who has decided this against Tyre,
The bestower of crowns,
Whose merchants were princes,
Whose tradesmen were honored in all the earth?ᵍ

9 Jehovah of armies himself has decided this,
To profane her pride over all her beauty,
To humiliate all those who were honored throughout the earth.ʰ

10 Cross over your land like the Nile River, O daughter of Tarʹshish.

CHAP. 22
a 2Ki 18:26, 37

b Ge 41:41, 42
Es 8:15

c Re 3:7

d Isa 22:15, 17

CHAP. 23
e Jer 25:17, 22
Jer 47:4
Eze 26:3
Eze 27:2
Joe 3:4
Am 1:9, 10
Zec 9:3, 4

f 2Ch 9:21
Eze 27:25

g Ge 10:2, 4
Jer 2:10
Eze 27:6

Second Col.
a Ge 10:15
Eze 27:8

b Jer 2:18

c Eze 27:32, 33
Eze 28:4

d Jer 47:4

e Isa 19:1, 16

f Eze 27:35
Eze 28:19

g Eze 28:2

h Da 4:37
Jas 4:6

22:16 *Lit., "a residence." **22:21** *Or "dominion." **22:24** *Lit., "weight." ᵘOr "offshoots."

23:3 *Lit., "seed." ᵘThat is, a branch of the Nile River. **23:4** *Lit., "virgins."

There is no longer any
shipyard.*[a]

11 He has stretched his hand
out over the sea;
He has shaken kingdoms.
Jehovah has ordered the annihilation of Phoe·ni′cia's
strongholds.[b]

12 And he says: "You will exult
no more,[c]
O oppressed one, the virgin
daughter of Si′don.
Get up, cross over to
Kit′tim.[d]
Even there you will find
no rest."

13 Look! The land of the
Chal·de′ans.[e]
This is the people—As·syr′i·a[f]
was not the one—
They made her a place for
those haunting the desert.
They have erected their
siege towers;
They have stripped bare her
fortified towers,[g]
Reducing her to a crumbling
ruin.

14 Wail, you ships of Tar′shish,
For your stronghold has
been destroyed.[h]

15 In that day Tyre will be
forgotten for 70 years,[i] the same
as the lifetime* of one king. At
the end of 70 years, it will happen to Tyre as in the song of a
prostitute:

16 "Take a harp, go around
the city, O forgotten
prostitute.
Play your harp skillfully;
Sing many songs,
So that they will remember
you."

17 At the end of 70 years, Jehovah will turn his attention to
Tyre, and she will return to her
hire and prostitute herself with
all the world's kingdoms on the

face of the earth. 18 But her
profit and her hire will become
something holy to Jehovah. It
will not be stored or laid away,
because her hire will be for
those dwelling before Jehovah,
so that they may eat to satisfaction and wear elegant clothing.[a]

24 Look! Jehovah is emptying the land* and making
it desolate.[b]
He turns it upside
down*[c] and scatters its
inhabitants.[d]

2 It will be the same for
everyone:
The people as well as the
priest,
The servant and his master,
The servant and her
mistress,
The buyer and the seller,
The lender and the borrower,
The creditor and the debtor.[e]

3 The land will be completely
emptied;
It will be completely
plundered,[f]
For Jehovah has spoken
this word.

4 The land mourns;*[g] it is
wasting away.
The productive land withers;
it is fading away.
The prominent people of the
land wither.

5 The land has been polluted
by its inhabitants,[h]
For they have bypassed
the laws,[i]
Changed the regulation,[j]
And broken the lasting*
covenant.[k]

6 That is why the curse
devours the land,[l]
And those inhabiting it are
held guilty.
That is why the inhabitants
of the land have dwindled,

CHAP. 23
a Isa 23:1
  Eze 26:14, 17
b Eze 26:5, 15
c Eze 26:13
d Eze 27:6
e Isa 13:19
  Hab 1:6
f Isa 10:12
  Na 3:18
  Zep 2:13
g Eze 26:8, 9
h Isa 23:1
i Jer 25:8, 11
  Jer 27:3, 6

Second Col.
a Isa 60:5

CHAP. 24
b Isa 5:5
  Jer 4:6
  Eze 6:6
c 2Ki 21:13
d De 28:63, 64
  Ne 1:8
  Jer 9:16
e Eze 7:12, 13
f Le 26:31
  De 29:28
g Jer 4:28
  La 1:4
h Le 18:24
  Nu 35:33, 34
  2Ch 33:9
  Jer 3:1
  Jer 23:10, 11
  La 4:13
i 2Ki 22:13
  Da 9:5
j Mic 3:11
k Ex 19:3, 5
  Ex 24:7
  Jer 31:32
  Jer 34:18-20
l Le 26:15, 16

23:10 *Or possibly, "harbor." 23:15
*Lit., "days." 24:1 *Or "earth." #Or "He twists the
face of it." 24:4 *Or possibly, "dries
up." 24:5 *Or "ancient."

And very few men are left.[a]

7 The new wine mourns,* the vine withers,[b]
   And all those cheerful at heart are sighing.[c]

8 The joy of the tambourines has ceased;
   The noise of the revelers has ended;
   The happy sound of the harp has ceased.[d]

9 They drink wine without song,
   And alcohol tastes bitter to those drinking it.

10 The deserted town is broken down;[e]
   Every house is shut up so that no one can enter.

11 They cry out for wine in the streets.
   All rejoicing has disappeared;
   The joy of the land has gone.[f]

12 The city is left in ruins;
   The gate has been crushed to a heap of rubble.[g]

13 For this is how it will be in the land, among the peoples:
   As when an olive tree is beaten,[h]
   Like the gleaning when the grape harvest comes to an end.[i]

14 They will raise their voice,
   They will shout joyfully.
   From the sea* they will proclaim the majesty of Jehovah.[j]

15 That is why they will glorify Jehovah in the region of light;*[k]
   In the islands of the sea they will glorify the name of Jehovah the God of Israel.[l]

16 From the ends of the earth we hear songs:

"Glory* to the Righteous One!"[a]

But I say: "I am wasting away, I am wasting away!
Woe to me! The treacherous have acted treacherously;
With treachery the treacherous have acted treacherously."[b]

17 Terror and pits and traps await you, inhabitant of the land.[c]

18 Anyone fleeing from the sound of terror will fall into the pit,
   And anyone coming up from the pit will be caught in the trap.[d]
   For the floodgates above will be opened,
   And the foundations of the land will quake.

19 The land has burst apart;
   The land has been shaken up;
   The land convulses violently.[e]

20 The land staggers like a drunken man,
   And it sways back and forth like a hut in the wind.
   Its transgression weighs heavily on it,[f]
   And it will fall, so that it will not rise up again.

21 In that day Jehovah will turn his attention to the army of the heights above
   And to the kings of the earth upon the earth.

22 And they will be gathered together
   Like prisoners gathered into a pit,
   And they will be shut up in the dungeon;
   After many days they will be given attention.

23 The full moon will be abashed,

CHAP. 24

a De 4:27
   De 28:15, 62

b Jer 8:13
   Joe 1:10

c Isa 32:12

d Jer 7:34

e 2Ki 25:8-10

f La 5:15

g Isa 32:14
   Jer 9:11
   La 1:4
   La 2:8, 9

h De 24:20

i Jer 6:9
   Eze 6:8

j Isa 40:9
   Jer 31:12
   Jer 33:10, 11

k Isa 43:5

l Isa 11:11
   Isa 60:9

Second Col.

a Ex 15:11
   Ezr 9:15
   Ps 145:7
   Re 15:3

b Jer 9:2, 3

c Jer 8:3
   Eze 14:21

d Jer 48:44

e Jer 4:24

f 2Ki 21:16
   2Ch 36:15, 16
   Jer 14:20

24:7 *Or possibly, "dries up." 24:14 *Or "the west." 24:15 *Or "in the east."

24:16 *Or "Decoration."

And the shining sun will be ashamed,[a]
For Jehovah of armies has become King[b] in Mount Zion[c] and in Jerusalem,
Glorious before the elders of his people.*[d]

25
O Jehovah, you are my God.
I exalt you, I praise your name,
For you have done wonderful things,[e]
Things purposed* from ancient times,[f]
In faithfulness,[g] in trustworthiness.

2 For you have turned a city into a pile of stones,
A fortified town into a crumbling ruin.
The foreigner's tower is a city no more;
It will never be rebuilt.

3 That is why a strong people will glorify you;
The city of tyrannical nations will fear you.[h]

4 For you have become a stronghold to the lowly,
A stronghold to the poor in his distress,[i]
A refuge from the rainstorm,
And a shade from the heat.[j]
When the blast of the tyrants is like a rainstorm against a wall,

5 As the heat in a parched land,
You subdue the uproar of strangers.
Like heat is subdued by the shadow of a cloud,
So the song of the tyrants is silenced.

6 In this mountain[k] Jehovah of armies will make for all the peoples
A banquet of rich dishes,[a]
A banquet of fine wine,*
Of rich dishes filled with marrow,
Of fine, filtered wine.

7 In this mountain he will do away with* the shroud that is enveloping all the peoples
And the covering# that is woven over all the nations.

8 He will swallow up* death forever,[b]
And the Sovereign Lord Jehovah will wipe away the tears from all faces.[c]
The reproach of his people he will take away from all the earth,
For Jehovah himself has spoken it.

9 In that day they will say:
"Look! This is our God![d]
We have hoped in him,[e]
And he will save us.[f]
This is Jehovah!
We have hoped in him.
Let us be joyful and rejoice in the salvation by him."[g]

10 For the hand of Jehovah will rest on this mountain,[h]
And Mo'ab will be trampled on in its place[i]
Like straw trampled into a pile of manure.

11 He will slap out his hands into it
Like a swimmer slapping out his hands to swim,
And he will bring down its haughtiness[j]
With the skillful movements of his hands.

12 And the fortified city, with your high walls of security,
He will bring down;
He will knock it down to the ground, to the very dust.

CHAP. 24
a Re 21:23
b Ps 97:1
  Re 11:17
c Ps 132:13
  Isa 12:6
  Joe 3:17
  Mic 4:7
  Zec 2:10
d 1Ki 8:11

CHAP. 25
e Ps 40:5
  Ps 98:1
  Ps 107:8
  Ps 145:1, 4
f Ps 33:11
g De 32:4
  Ne 9:33
h Ps 46:10
  Ps 66:3
  Eze 38:23
i Ps 46:1
  Na 1:7
  Zep 3:12
j Ps 91:1
  Ps 121:5-7
  Isa 49:10
k Isa 11:9
  Isa 65:25

Second Col.
a Ps 72:16
  Ps 85:11, 12
  Jer 31:12
b Ho 13:14
  1Co 15:54
  2Ti 1:10
  Re 20:14
c Isa 35:10
  Re 7:17
  Re 21:4
d Isa 25:1
e Ps 37:34
  Ps 146:5
f Mic 7:7
g Ps 20:5
  Zep 3:14, 15
h Ps 132:13, 14
  Isa 12:6
i Isa 15:1
  Zep 2:9
j Jer 48:29
  Jas 4:6

24:23 *Lit., "before his elders." 25:1 *Or "Counsels." 25:6 *Or "of wine kept on the dregs." 25:7 *Lit., "swallow up." #Or "veil." 25:8 *Or "do away with."

26 In that day this song will be sung[a] in the land of Judah:[b]

"We have a strong city.[c]
He makes salvation its walls
and its ramparts.[d]

2 Open up the gates[e] so that
the righteous nation may
enter,
A nation that is keeping
faithful conduct.

3 You will safeguard those
who fully lean on you;*
You will give them
continuous peace,[f]
Because it is in you that they
trust.[g]

4 Trust in Jehovah forever,[h]
For Jah* Jehovah is the
eternal Rock.[i]

5 For he has brought low those
inhabiting the height,
the lofty city.
He brings it down,
He brings it down to the
earth;
He casts it down to the dust.

6 The foot will trample it,
The feet of the afflicted,
the steps of the lowly."

7 The path of the righteous
one is upright.*
Because you are upright,
You will smooth out the
course of the righteous.

8 As we follow the path of your
judgments, O Jehovah,
Our hope is in you.
We* long for your name
and your memorial.#

9 In the night I long for you
with my whole being,*
Yes, my spirit keeps looking
for you;[j]

26:3 *Or possibly, "those whose inclination is unshakable." 26:4 *"Jah" is a shortened form of the name Jehovah. 26:7 *Or "level." 26:8 *Or "With our soul we." #That is, that God and his name be remembered, made known. 26:9 *Or "with my soul."

For when there are
judgments from you
for the earth,
The inhabitants of the
land learn about
righteousness.[a]

10 Even if the wicked is shown
favor,
He will not learn
righteousness.[b]
Even in the land of uprightness* he will act wickedly,[c]
And he will not see the
majesty of Jehovah.[d]

11 O Jehovah, your hand is
raised, but they do not
see it.[e]
They will see your zeal for
your people and be put
to shame.
Yes, the fire for your adversaries will consume them.

12 O Jehovah, you will grant us
peace,[f]
Because everything we have
done
You have accomplished
for us.

13 O Jehovah our God, other
masters besides you have
ruled over us,[g]
But we make mention of your
name alone.[h]

14 They are dead; they will not
live.
Powerless in death, they will
not rise up.[i]
For you have turned your
attention to them
To annihilate them and destroy all mention of them.

15 You have enlarged the
nation, O Jehovah,
You have enlarged the
nation;
You have glorified yourself.[j]
You have greatly extended
all the borders of the land.[k]

16 O Jehovah, during distress
they turned to you;

26:10 *Or "straightforwardness."

They poured out their prayer in a whisper when you disciplined them.[a]

17 Just as a pregnant woman about to give birth
Has labor pains and cries out in pain,
So we have been because of you, O Jehovah.

18 We became pregnant, we had labor pains,
But it is as if we have given birth to wind.
We have not brought salvation to the land,
And no one is born to inhabit the land.

19 "Your dead will live.
My corpses* will rise up.[b]
Awake and shout joyfully,
You residents in the dust![c]
For your dew is as the dew of the morning,#
And the earth will let those powerless in death come to life.△

20 Go, my people, enter your inner rooms,
And shut your doors behind you.[d]
Hide yourself for a brief moment
Until the wrath* has passed by.[e]

21 For look! Jehovah is coming from his place
To call the inhabitants of the land to account for their error,
And the land will expose her bloodshed
And will no longer cover over her slain."

27 In that day Jehovah, with his harsh and great and strong sword,[f]

Will turn his attention to Le·vi′a·than,* the gliding serpent,
To Le·vi′a·than, the twisting serpent,
And he will kill the monster that is in the sea.

2 In that day sing to her:*
"A vineyard of foaming wine![a]

3 I, Jehovah, am safeguarding her.[b]
Every moment I water her.[c]
I safeguard her night and day,
So that no one may harm her.[d]

4 There is no wrath in me.[e]
Who will confront me with thornbushes and weeds in the battle?
I will trample them and set them on fire all together.

5 Otherwise, let him hold fast to my stronghold.
Let him make peace with me;
Peace let him make with me."

6 In the coming days Jacob will take root,
Israel will blossom and sprout,[f]
And they will fill the land with produce.[g]

7 Must he be struck with the stroke of the one striking him?
Or must he be killed as with the slaughter of his slain?

8 With a startling cry you will contend with her when sending her away.
He will expel her with his fierce blast in the day of the east wind.[h]

9 So in this way the error of Jacob will be atoned for,[i]
And this will be the full fruitage when his sin is taken away:

CHAP. 26

a Ps 78:34, 35
Ho 5:15

b Isa 25:8
Ho 13:14
Mr 12:26
Joh 5:28, 29
Joh 11:24, 25
Ac 24:15
1Co 15:21
1Th 4:14
Re 20:12, 13

c Ge 3:19

d Ge 7:15, 16
Ex 12:22, 23
Pr 18:10

e Ps 27:5
Ps 91:4

CHAP. 27

f De 32:41
Jer 47:6

Second Col.

a Ps 80:8
Isa 5:1
Jer 2:21

b De 33:29

c Isa 35:6
Isa 41:18
Isa 58:11

d Ps 121:4
Isa 46:3, 4

e Ps 85:2, 3
Isa 12:1

f Eze 39:25
Ho 14:5

g Isa 60:21, 22
Jer 30:18, 19

h Jer 4:11
Eze 13:13

i Isa 4:4
Isa 48:10

26:19 *Lit., "A corpse of mine." #Or possibly, "the dew of herbs (mallows)." △Or "will give birth to those powerless in death." **26:20** *Or "denunciation."

27:1 *See Glossary. **27:2** *Apparently referring to Israel, here personified as a woman and likened to a vineyard.

He will make all the stones
of the altar
Like chalkstones that have
been pulverized,
And no sacred poles* or
incense stands will be left.ᵃ

10 For the fortified city will be
deserted;
The pastures will be
forsaken and abandoned
like a wilderness.ᵇ
There the calf will graze
and lie down
And will consume her
branches.ᶜ

11 When her twigs have
dried up,
Women will come and break
them off,
Making fires with them.
For this people is without
understanding.ᵈ
That is why their Maker will
show them no mercy,
And the One who formed
them will show them no
favor.ᵉ

12 In that day Jehovah will
beat out the fruit from the flowing stream of the River* to the
Wadi* of Egypt,ᶠ and you will be
gathered up one after the other,
O people of Israel.ᵍ **13** In that
day a great horn will be blown,ʰ
and those who are perishing in
the land of As·syrʹi·aⁱ and those
dispersed in the land of Egyptʲ
will come and bow down to Jehovah in the holy mountain in
Jerusalem.ᵏ

28 Woe to the showy* crown*
of the drunkards of
Eʹphra·im!ˡ
And the fading blossom of its
glorious beauty,
Which is on the head of
the fertile valley of those
overcome with wine!

_____
27:9, 12 *See Glossary. 27:12 *That is,
the Euphrates. 28:1, 3 *Or "haughty;
proud." 28:1 *Apparently referring to
the capital city, Samaria.

2 Look! Jehovah has someone
strong and mighty.
Like a thundering hailstorm,
a destructive windstorm,
Like a thunderstorm of
powerful floodwaters,
He will forcefully hurl it
down to the earth.

3 The showy* crowns of the
drunkards of Eʹphra·im
Will be trampled underfoot.ᵃ

4 And the fading flower of
its glorious beauty,
Which is on the head of the
fertile valley,
Will become like the early fig
before summer.
When someone sees it, he
swallows it as soon as it is
in his hand.

5 In that day Jehovah of armies will become a glorious
crown and a beautiful garland to
those left of his people.ᵇ **6** And
he will become a spirit of justice to the one who sits in judgment and a source of mightiness
to those who repel the attack at
the gate.ᶜ

7 And these also go astray
because of wine;
Their alcoholic beverages
make them stagger.
Priest and prophet go astray
because of alcohol;
The wine confuses them,
And they stagger from their
alcohol;
Their vision makes them
go astray,
And they stumble in
judgment.ᵈ

8 For their tables are full
of filthy vomit
—There is no place
without it.

9 To whom will one impart
knowledge,
And to whom will one
explain the message?
To those who have just been
weaned from milk,

CHAP. 27
a Mic 5:13, 14

b Isa 6:11, 12
Jer 26:18
La 2:5
Eze 36:4

c Isa 32:14

d De 32:28
Isa 1:3
Jer 4:22
Ho 4:6

e 2Ch 36:15, 16
Eze 9:9, 10

f Nu 34:2, 5

g De 30:3
Ne 1:9
Isa 11:11, 12
Am 9:14

h Isa 49:22
Isa 62:10

i 2Ki 17:6
Isa 11:16
Ho 9:3

j Jer 43:4, 7
Zec 10:10

k Isa 2:3
Isa 25:6
Isa 52:1
Jer 3:17

CHAP. 28
l Isa 7:2

Second Col.
a 2Ki 17:6
Isa 17:3

b Isa 11:16

c Ps 18:34
Ps 68:35

d 2Ki 16:10, 11
Jer 5:31

Those just taken away from
the breasts?

10 For it is "command after
command, command after
command,

Line by line, line by line,*[a]

A little here, a little there."

11 So by means of those with
stammering speech* and a foreign language, he will speak to
this people.[b] **12** He once told
them: "This is the resting-place.
Let the weary one rest; this is
the place of refreshment," but
they refused to listen.[c] **13** So
to them the word of Jehovah
will be:

"Command after command,
command after command,

Line by line, line by line,*[d]

A little here, a little there,"

So that when they walk,

They will stumble and fall
backward

And be broken and ensnared
and caught.[e]

14 So hear the word of Jehovah,
you boasters,

You rulers of this people
in Jerusalem,

15 For you men say:

"We have made a covenant
with Death,[f]

And with the Grave* we have
made an agreement.[#]

When the raging flash flood
passes through,

It will not reach us,

For we have made a lie
our refuge

And we have hidden
ourselves in falsehood."[g]

16 Therefore this is what the
Sovereign Lord Jehovah
says:

"Here I am laying as
a foundation in Zion
a tested stone,[a]

The precious cornerstone[b]
of a sure foundation.[c]

No one exercising faith will
panic.[d]

17 And I will make justice the
measuring line[e]

And righteousness the
leveling tool.*[f]

The hail will sweep away
the refuge of lies,

And the waters will flood out
the hiding place.

18 Your covenant with Death
will be dissolved,

And your agreement with
the Grave* will not stand.[g]

When the raging flash flood
passes through,

You will be crushed by it.

19 As often as it passes
through,

It will sweep you away;[h]

For it will pass through
morning after morning,

During the day and during
the night.

Only terror will make
them understand what was
heard."*

20 For the bed is too short to
stretch out on,

And the woven sheet is too
narrow to wrap up in.

21 For Jehovah will rise up
as at Mount Pe·ra′zim;

He will rouse himself as in
the valley* near Gib′e·on,[i]

That he may do his deed
—his strange deed—

And that he may carry
out his work—his
unusual work.[j]

22 Now do not scoff,[k]

So that your bonds may not
be further tightened,

CHAP. 28
a 2Ki 21:13
  Isa 28:17
  La 2:8

b De 28:49, 50
  Jer 5:15
  1Co 14:21

c Ps 81:10, 11

d Isa 28:17

e 2Ch 36:15, 16
  Isa 8:14, 15

f Isa 28:18

g Isa 30:9, 10

Second Col.
a Ps 118:22

b Mt 21:42
  Mr 12:10
  Lu 20:17
  Ac 4:11

c Eph 2:19, 20

d Ro 9:33
  Ro 10:11
  1Pe 2:4, 6

e 2Ki 21:13

f Jer 11:20

g Isa 28:15

h Isa 24:1

i Jos 10:8-14
  2Sa 5:20
  1Ch 14:10-16

j La 2:15
  Hab 1:5-7

k 2Ch 36:15, 16
  Jer 20:7

28:10, 13 *Or "Measuring line upon measuring line, measuring line upon measuring line." **28:11** *Lit., "lip." **28:15, 18** *Or "Sheol," that is, the common grave of mankind. See Glossary. **28:15** #Or possibly, "effected a vision." **28:17** *Or "plumb line." **28:19** *Or possibly, "When they understand, they will feel sheer terror." **28:21** *Or "low plain."

For I have heard from the
Sovereign Lord, Jehovah
of armies,
That an extermination has
been determined for all
the land.*[a]

23 Give ear and listen to my
voice;
Pay attention and listen
to what I say.
24 Does the plower keep
plowing all day before he
sows seed?
Does he continually break up
and harrow his ground?[b]
25 When he has smoothed out
its surface,
Does he not then
scatter black cumin and
sow cumin,
And does he not plant wheat,
millet, and barley in their
places
And spelt[c] around the edges?
26 For He teaches* him the
right way;
His God instructs him.[d]
27 For black cumin is not
crushed with a threshing
sledge,[e]
And a wagon wheel is not
driven over cumin.
Rather, black cumin is
beaten out with a rod,
And cumin with a staff.
28 Does a person crush grain
for bread?
No, he does not thresh it
incessantly;[f]
And when he drives the
roller of his wagon over it
with his horses,
He does not crush it.[g]
29 This also comes from
Jehovah of armies,
Whose counsel* is wonderful
And whose achievements are
great.#[h]

CHAP. 28
a Isa 10:23
  Isa 24:1

b Ps 30:5
  Ps 103:9
  Mic 7:18

c Ex 9:31, 32
  Eze 4:9

d Ps 119:71

e Isa 41:15
  Am 1:3

f Ps 103:9
  Isa 21:10
  Mic 7:18

g Le 26:44
  Jer 10:24

h Ps 40:5
  Jer 32:19
  Ro 11:33

Second Col.

CHAP. 29
a 2Sa 5:7, 9

b De 16:16

c De 28:53-55

d Isa 51:19
  La 1:4

e Jer 15:14
  Zep 1:7

f 2Ki 24:11
  2Ki 25:1

g Isa 51:23

h Isa 13:19
  Isa 14:22
  Isa 21:9

i Isa 13:11
  Isa 17:13

j Isa 47:9
  Isa 48:3

k 1Sa 2:10
  Jer 50:25
  Na 1:3

l Jer 25:12, 14

29 "Woe to Ar′i·el,* Ar′i·el,
the city where David
encamped![a]
Continue year after year;
Let the cycle of festivals[b]
continue.
2 But I will bring distress on
Ar′i·el,[c]
And there will be mourning
and lamentation,[d]
And she will become to
me like an altar hearth
of God.[e]
3 I will encamp on all sides
against you,
And I will besiege you with
a palisade
And raise up siegeworks
against you.[f]
4 You will be brought low;
From the ground you will
speak,
And what you say will be
muffled by dust.
Your voice will come from
the ground[g]
Like the voice of a spirit
medium,
And your words will chirp
from the dust.
5 The crowd of your enemies*
will be like fine powder,[h]
The crowd of the tyrants just
like the blowing chaff.[i]
And it will happen in an
instant, suddenly.[j]
6 Jehovah of armies will give
you his attention
With thunder and earth-
quake and a great noise,
With storm wind and
tempest and the flames
of a consuming fire."[k]
7 Then the crowd of all the
nations waging war against
Ar′i·el[l]
—All those waging war
against her,

28:22 *Or "for the whole earth." 28:26
*Or "disciplines; chastises." 28:29
*Or "purpose." #Or "And whose prac-
tical wisdom is great."

29:1 *Possibly meaning "The Altar
Hearth of God," apparently referring to
Jerusalem. 29:5 *Lit., "strangers."

The siege towers against her,
And those bringing distress
  on her—
Will become like a dream,
  a vision of the night.
8 Yes, it will be just as when
  someone hungry dreams
  that he is eating,
But he wakes up hungry,*
And as when someone
  thirsty dreams that he
  is drinking,
But he wakes up tired and
  thirsty.#
So it will happen with the
  crowd of all the nations
That wage war against
  Mount Zion.ᵃ
9 Be stunned and amazed;ᵇ
Blind yourselves and be
  blinded.ᶜ
They are drunk, but not
  with wine;
They are staggering, but not
  from alcohol.
10 For Jehovah has poured a
  spirit of deep sleep on
  you;ᵈ
He has closed your eyes,
  the prophets,ᵉ
And he has covered your
  heads, the visionaries.ᶠ

11 Every vision becomes for
you like the words of a sealed
book.ᵍ When they give it to
someone who can read, saying:
"Read this out loud, please," he
will say: "I cannot, for it is
sealed up." 12 And when they
give the book to someone who
cannot read, saying: "Read this,
please," he will say: "I cannot
read at all."

13 Jehovah says: "This people
approaches me with their
  mouth
And they honor me with
  their lips,ʰ
But their heart is far
  removed from me;

And their fear of me is based
  on commands of men that
  they have been taught.ᵃ
14 Therefore, I am the One who
  will again do wonderful
  things with this people,ᵇ
With wonder upon wonder;
And the wisdom of their wise
  men will perish,
And the understanding of
  their discreet men will be
  hidden."ᶜ
15 Woe to those who go to great
  lengths to conceal their
  plans* from Jehovah.ᵈ
Their deeds are done in a
  dark place,
While they say:
  "Who sees us?
Who knows about us?"ᵉ
16 How you twist things!*
Should the potter be regarded the same as the clay?ᶠ
Should what is made say
  about its maker:
"He did not make me"?ᵍ
And does what is formed
  say about its former:
"He shows no understand-
  ing"?ʰ
17 In just a short time, Leb′-
  a·non will be turned into
  an orchard,ⁱ
And the orchard will be
  regarded as a forest.ʲ
18 In that day the deaf will hear
  the words of the book,
And out of the gloom and
  darkness the eyes of the
  blind will see.ᵏ
19 The meek will rejoice greatly
  in Jehovah,
And the poor among men will
  be joyful in the Holy One
  of Israel.ˡ
20 For the tyrant will be
  no more,
The boaster will come
  to his finish,

29:8 *Or "and his soul is empty." #Or
"and his soul is parched."

29:15 *Or "counsel." 29:16 *Or "How
perverse of you!"

CHAP. 29
a Isa 10:12
  Jer 51:24

b Hab 1:5

c Isa 6:9

d Isa 6:10
  Ro 11:8

e Jer 14:14
  Jer 27:15

f Mic 3:7

g Isa 8:16

h Isa 48:1
  Jer 5:2

Second Col.
a Mt 15:7-9
  Mr 7:6-8

b Isa 28:21
  Hab 1:5

c Jer 8:9
  1Co 1:19

d Isa 30:1

e Eze 8:12

f Isa 64:8

g Jer 18:6

h Ro 9:20, 21

i Isa 35:1
  Isa 41:19

j Isa 32:14, 15

k Isa 35:5
  Isa 42:16

l Isa 41:16

And all those keeping alert
     to do harm will be de-
     stroyed,[a]
21 Those who with a false word
     make others guilty,
   Who lay traps for the defend-
     er* in the city gate,[b]
   And who with empty
     arguments deny justice to
     the righteous one.[c]

22 So this is what Jehovah,
who redeemed Abraham,[d] says
to the house of Jacob:

   "Jacob will no longer be
     ashamed,
   And no more will his face
     grow pale.*[e]
23 For when he sees his
     children,
   Who are the work of my
     hands, in his midst,[f]
   They will sanctify my name;
   Yes, they will sanctify the
     Holy One of Jacob,
   And they will stand in awe
     of the God of Israel.[g]
24 Those who are wayward
     in spirit will acquire
     understanding,
   And those who complain will
     accept instruction."

30 "Woe to the stubborn
     sons,"[h] declares
     Jehovah,
   "Who carry out plans that
     are not mine,[i]
   Who make alliances,* but
     not by my spirit,
   In order to add sin to sin.
2 They go down to Egypt[j]
     without consulting me,*[k]
   To take shelter under
     Phar′aoh's protection*
   And to take refuge in the
     shadow of Egypt!

3 But the protection of
     Phar′aoh will become for
     you a reason for shame,
   And refuge in Egypt's
     shadow a cause for
     humiliation.[a]
4 For his princes are in Zo′an,[b]
   And his envoys have reached
     Ha′nes.
5 They will all be put to shame
   By a people who can bring
     no benefit to them,
   Who offer no help and no
     benefit,
   Only shame and disgrace."[c]

6 A pronouncement against
the beasts of the south:

   Through the land of distress
     and hardship,
   Of the lion, the roaring lion,
   Of the viper and the flying
     fiery snake,*
   They carry their wealth on
     the backs of donkeys
   And their supplies on the
     humps of camels.
   But these things will not
     benefit the people.
7 For Egypt's help is
     completely useless.[d]
   So I have called this one:
     "Ra′hab,[e] who sits still."
8 "Now go, write it on a tablet
     in their presence,
   And inscribe it in a book,[f]
   So that it may serve for a
     future day
   As a permanent witness.[g]
9 For they are a rebellious
     people,[h] deceitful sons,[i]
   Sons who are unwilling to
     hear the law* of Jehovah.[j]
10 They say to the seers,
     'Do not see,'
   And to the visionaries, 'Do
     not tell us truthful visions.[k]
   Tell us flattering* things; en-
     vision deceptive illusions.[l]

CHAP. 29
a Mic 2:1
b Am 5:10
c Eze 13:19
d Ne 9:7
  Mic 7:20
e Joe 2:27
f Isa 45:11
g Isa 8:13
  Ho 3:5

CHAP. 30
h Isa 1:2
  Isa 63:10
  Isa 65:2
i Isa 29:15
j Isa 31:1
  Eze 29:6
k Nu 27:21
  1Ki 22:7

Second Col.
a Jer 17:5
b Isa 19:11
  Eze 30:14
c Isa 31:3
  Jer 2:36
d Isa 31:1
  Jer 37:7, 8
e Ps 87:4
  Ps 89:10
f Isa 8:1
  Jer 36:2
g Ro 15:4
h De 31:27
  Isa 1:4
  Jer 44:3
i Isa 59:3
  Jer 9:3
j 2Ch 33:10
  2Ch 36:15, 16
  Ne 9:29
  Jer 7:13
k 2Ch 16:10
  2Ch 18:7
  Jer 11:21
  Jer 26:11
l Jer 23:16, 17
  Eze 13:7
  Mic 2:11

29:21 *Lit., "the one reproving." 29:22
*That is, from shame and disappoint-
ment. 30:1 *Lit., "pour out a libation,"
evidently referring to making an agreement. 30:2 *Or "without inquiring of
my mouth." #Lit., "in the stronghold of
Pharaoh."

30:6 *Or "the darting poisonous
snake." 30:9 *Or "instruction."
30:10 *Lit., "smooth."

11 Turn aside from the way;
deviate from the path.
Quit putting before us the
Holy One of Israel.'"[a]

12 Therefore this is what the
Holy One of Israel says:
"Since you reject this word[b]
And you trust in fraud and
deceit
And you rely on these,[c]

13 So this error will be for you
like a broken wall,
Like a bulging high wall
ready to fall.
It will crash suddenly, in an
instant.

14 It will be broken like a large
potter's jar,
So completely smashed that
no fragment among its
pieces will be left
To rake the fire from the
fireplace
Or to scoop water from a
puddle."*

15 For this is what the Sovereign Lord Jehovah, the
Holy One of Israel, says:
"By returning to me and
resting, you will be saved;
Your strength will be in
keeping calm and showing
trust."[d]
But you were unwilling.[e]

16 Instead, you said: "No, we
will flee on horses!"
So flee you will.
"And on swift horses we
will ride!"[f]
So those pursuing you will
be swift.[g]

17 A thousand will tremble at
the threat of one;[h]
At the threat of five you
will flee
Until what is left of you is
like a mast on the top of
a mountain,
Like a signal pole on a hill.[i]

18 But Jehovah is waiting patiently* to show you favor,[a]
And he will rise up to show
you mercy.[b]
For Jehovah is a God of
justice.[c]
Happy are all those keeping
in expectation of# him.[d]

19 When the people dwell in
Zion, in Jerusalem,[e] you will by
no means weep.[f] He will surely show you favor at the sound
of your cry for help; he will answer you as soon as he hears it.[g]
20 Though Jehovah will give
you bread in the form of distress and water in the form of
oppression,[h] your Grand Instructor will no longer hide himself,
and you will see your Grand Instructor[i] with your own eyes.
21 And your own ears will hear
a word behind you saying, "This
is the way.[j] Walk in it," in case
you should go to the right or in
case you should go to the left.[k]

22 And you will defile the silver overlay of your graven images and the golden plating of
your metal statues.*[l] You will
cast them away like a menstrual cloth and say to them, "Be
gone!"#[m] 23 And he will give
the rain for the seed you sow
in the ground,[n] and the bread
that the ground produces will
be abundant and rich.*[o] In that
day your livestock will graze in
spacious pastures.[p] 24 And the
cattle and the donkeys that work
the ground will eat fodder seasoned with sorrel, which was
winnowed with the shovel and
the pitchfork. 25 And on every
tall mountain and on every high
hill will be streams and watercourses,[q] in the day of the great
slaughter when the towers fall.

CHAP. 30

a Am 7:13, 16
b Am 2:4, 5
c Jer 13:25
  Mic 3:11
d 1Ch 5:20
  2Ch 16:8
  Isa 26:3
e Mt 23:37
  Ac 7:51
f Isa 31:1, 3
g De 28:49, 50
  Jer 4:13
  La 4:19
  Hab 1:6, 8
h Le 26:36
  De 32:30
i Eze 12:16

Second Col.

a Ex 34:6
  Eze 36:9, 10
b Ps 102:13
  Ro 9:15
c Ps 99:4
  Jer 10:24
d Jer 17:7
e Ne 11:1
  Isa 44:28
  Isa 62:1
  Jer 31:6
  Zec 1:17
f Ne 12:27
  Isa 61:3
g Jer 29:11, 12
h Le 26:26
  Ps 80:5
i Job 36:22
  Ps 32:8
  Ps 71:17
  Ps 119:102
j Ps 25:8, 9
k De 5:32
  Jos 1:7, 8
  Pr 4:27
l Ex 32:4
  De 7:5, 25
  Jg 17:3, 4
m Ho 14:8
  Zec 13:2
n Ps 65:9
  Zec 10:1
o Ho 2:21, 22
p Isa 65:10
q Isa 41:18
  Isa 44:3

30:14 *Or possibly, "a cistern." 30:18 *Or "keeping in expectation." #Or "eagerly waiting for." 30:22 *Or "molten statues." #Or possibly, "and call them filth." 30:23 *Lit., "fat and well-oiled."

26 And the light of the full moon will become like the light of the sun; and the light of the sun will become seven times stronger,[a] like the light of seven days, in the day that Jehovah binds up the breakdown* of his people[b] and heals the severe wound from the blow he inflicted.[c]

27 Look! The name of Jehovah
is coming from far away,
Burning with his anger and with heavy clouds.
His lips are full of indignation,
And his tongue is like a consuming fire.[d]

28 His spirit* is like a flooding torrent that reaches clear to the neck,
To shake the nations in a sieve of destruction;#
And the peoples will have a bridle in their jaws[e] that leads them astray.

29 But your song will be like the one sung in the night
When you prepare* for a festival,[f]
And your heart will rejoice like one
Who walks with# a flute
On his way to the mountain of Jehovah, to the Rock of Israel.[g]

30 Jehovah will make his majestic voice[h] heard
And reveal his arm[i] as it descends in the heat of anger,[j]
With the flame of a consuming fire,[k]
A cloudburst[l] and a thunderstorm and hailstones.[m]

31 For because of the voice of Jehovah, As·syr′i·a will be struck with terror;[n]

He will strike it with a rod.[a]

32 And every swing of his rod of punishment
That Jehovah will bring down on As·syr′i·a
Will be accompanied by tambourines and harps[b]
As he brandishes his arm against them in battle.[c]

33 For his To′pheth*[d] is already prepared;
It is also made ready for the king.[e]
He has made the woodpile deep and wide,
With an abundance of fire and wood.
The breath of Jehovah, like a torrent of sulfur,
Will set fire to it.

31 Woe to those who go down to Egypt for assistance,[f]
Who rely on horses,[g]
Who trust in war chariots because they are numerous,
And in warhorses* because they are mighty.
But they do not look to the Holy One of Israel,
And they do not search for Jehovah.

2 But he is also wise and will bring calamity,
And he will not take back his words.
He will rise up against the house of evildoers
And against those who help wrongdoers.[h]

3 The Egyptians, though, are mere men and not God;
Their horses are flesh and not spirit.[i]
When Jehovah stretches out his hand,
Whoever offers help will stumble

CHAP. 30
a Isa 60:20
  Re 21:23
  Re 22:5

b La 2:13

c Jer 33:6
  Am 9:11

d Isa 10:17
  Na 1:6
  Zep 3:8

e 2Ki 19:28
  Ps 32:9

f De 16:14
  Ps 42:4
  Jer 33:10, 11

g De 32:4
  Isa 26:4

h Ps 29:3, 4

i Ex 15:16
  Ps 98:1

j Na 1:2

k Ps 18:13

l Jg 5:4

m Jos 10:11

n Isa 37:36

Second Col.
a Isa 10:12

b Ex 15:20
  Jg 11:34

c Isa 10:24, 26

d 2Ki 23:10
  Jer 7:32

e Isa 37:37, 38
  Eze 32:22

CHAP. 31
f Isa 30:2

g De 17:15, 16

h Eze 29:6, 7

i Ps 33:17
  Pr 21:31

30:26 *Or "fracture." 30:28 *Or "breath." #Lit., "a sieve of worthlessness." 30:29 *Or "sanctify yourself." #Or "to the sound of."

30:33 *"Topheth" is here used as a figurative place of burning, representing destruction. 31:1 *Or "in horsemen."

And whoever is helped will fall;
They will all perish at the same time.

4 For this is what Jehovah has said to me:
"Just as the lion growls,
a strong young lion,* over its prey,
When a whole group of shepherds is called together against it,
And it is not terrified by their voice
Or daunted by their commotion,
So will Jehovah of armies come down to wage war
Over Mount Zion and over her hill.

5 Like swooping birds, so Jehovah of armies will defend Jerusalem.[a]
He will defend her and save her.
He will spare her and rescue her."

6 "Return to the One against whom you have blatantly revolted, O people of Israel.[b] 7 For in that day each one will reject his worthless gods of silver and his valueless gods of gold, which your own hands sinfully made.

8 And the As·syr′i·an will fall by the sword, not of a man;
And a sword, not of a human, will devour him.[c]
He will flee because of the sword,
And his young men will be put to forced labor.

9 His crag will pass away because of sheer fright,
And his princes will be terrified because of the signal pole," declares Jehovah,
Whose light* is in Zion and whose furnace is in Jerusalem.

CHAP. 32

32 Look! A king[a] will reign for righteousness,[b]
And princes will rule for justice.

2 And each one will be like a hiding place* from the wind,
A place of concealment# from the rainstorm,
Like streams of water in a waterless land,[c]
Like the shadow of a massive crag in a parched land.

3 Then the eyes of those seeing will no longer be pasted shut,
And the ears of those hearing will pay attention.

4 The heart of those who are impetuous will ponder over knowledge,
And the stammering tongue will speak fluently and clearly.[d]

5 The senseless one will no longer be called generous,
And the unprincipled man will not be called noble;

6 For the senseless one will speak nonsense,
And his heart will devise harmful things,[e]
To promote apostasy* and to speak what is wayward against Jehovah,
To cause the hungry one# to go unfed
And to deprive the thirsty one of something to drink.

7 The devices of the unprincipled man are bad;[f]
He promotes shameful conduct
To ruin the afflicted one with lies,[g]
Even when the poor speaks what is right.

8 But the generous one has generous intentions,

Footnotes (references, column and center):

CHAP. 31
a De 32:11, 12
  Ps 91:4

b Isa 55:7
  Joe 2:12

c 2Ki 19:35
  2Ch 32:21
  Isa 37:36

Second Col.

CHAP. 32
a Ge 49:10
  Ps 2:6
  Lu 1:32, 33
  Joh 1:49

b Ps 45:6
  Ps 72:1
  Isa 9:7
  Isa 11:4, 5
  Jer 23:5
  Zec 9:9
  Heb 1:9
  Re 19:11

c Isa 35:6

d Isa 35:6

e Mic 2:1

f Jer 5:26
  Mic 7:3

g 1Ki 21:9, 10

31:4 *Or "a maned young lion." 31:9 *Or "fire."

32:2 *Or "a shelter." #Or "A refuge." 32:6 *Or "act in an irreverent way." #Or "the soul of the hungry one."

And in generous* endeavors
he perseveres.

9 "You complacent women, get
up and listen to my voice!
You carefree daughters,ᵃ pay
attention to what I say!

10 In a little over a year,
you who are carefree will
shudder,
Because no fruit will have
been gathered when the
grape harvest ends.ᵇ

11 Tremble, you complacent
women!
Shudder, you who are
carefree!
Strip yourselves bare,
And put sackcloth around
your hips.ᶜ

12 Beat your breasts in
lamentation
Over the desirable fields and
the fruitful vine.

13 For the ground of my people
will be covered with thorns
and briars;
They will cover all the houses of rejoicing,
Yes, the city of exultation.ᵈ

14 For the fortified tower has
been forsaken;
The noisy city has been
abandoned.ᵉ
Oʹphelᶠ and the watchtower
have become a permanent
wasteland,
A delight for wild donkeys,
A pasture for the flocks,ᵍ

15 Until the spirit is poured out
on us from above,ʰ
And the wilderness becomes
an orchard,
And the orchard is regarded
as a forest.ⁱ

16 Then justice will reside in
the wilderness,
And righteousness will dwell
in the orchard.ʲ

17 The result of true righteousness will be peace,ᵏ

And the fruitage of true righteousness will be lasting
tranquillity and security.ᵃ

18 My people will dwell in a
peaceful abiding place,
In secure dwellings and in
tranquil resting-places.ᵇ

19 But the hail will flatten the
forest,
And the city will be
completely leveled.

20 Happy are you who sow seed
alongside all waters,
Who send out* the bull and
the donkey."ᶜ

33 Woe to you, you destroyer
who has not been
destroyed;ᵈ
You betrayer who has not
been betrayed!
When you finish destroying,
you will be destroyed.ᵉ
When you finish betraying,
you will be betrayed.

2 O Jehovah, show us favor.ᶠ
Our hope is in you.
Become our arm*ᵍ every
morning,
Yes, our salvation in the
time of distress.ʰ

3 At the sound of turmoil
peoples flee.
When you rise up, nations
scatter.ⁱ

4 As the voracious locusts
gather, so your spoil will
be gathered;
People will rush on it like
swarms of locusts.

5 Jehovah will be exalted,
For he resides in the heights
above.
He will fill Zion with justice
and righteousness.

6 He is the stability of your
times;
An abundance of salvation,ʲ
wisdom, knowledge, and
the fear of Jehovahᵏ
—This is his treasure.

CHAP. 32
a Isa 3:16

b La 2:12
Zep 1:13

c Isa 3:24

d Isa 22:2
La 2:15

e 2Ki 25:9, 10

f 2Ch 27:1, 3
Ne 3:26

g Isa 27:10

h Isa 44:3

i Isa 29:17
Isa 35:1, 2

j Isa 42:1, 4
Isa 60:21

k Ps 119:165
Ps 55:12

Second Col.
a Eze 37:26
Mic 4:3, 4

b Isa 60:18
Isa 65:22
Jer 23:6
Eze 34:25
Ho 2:18

c Isa 30:23, 24

CHAP. 33
d 2Ki 18:13
Isa 10:5

e Isa 10:12
Na 3:7

f Ps 123:2

g Ps 44:3
Isa 52:10

h Ps 46:1
Na 1:7

i Ps 46:6
Ps 68:1
Isa 17:13

j Ps 27:1

k Pr 19:23

32:8 *Or "noble." 32:20 *Or "let loose." 33:2 *Or "strength."

7 Look! Their heroes cry out in
   the street;
   The messengers of peace
   weep bitterly.
8 The highways are deserted;
   There is no one traveling on
   the pathways.
   He* has broken the covenant;
   He has rejected the cities;
   He shows no regard for
   mortal man.ᵃ
9 The land mourns* and
   withers away.
   Leb'a·non is ashamed;ᵇ it has
   decayed.
   Shar'on has become like
   the desert,
   And Ba'shan and Car'mel
   shake off their leaves.ᶜ
10 "Now I will rise up," says
    Jehovah,
    "Now I will exalt myself;ᵈ
    Now I will magnify myself.
11 You conceive dried grass
    and give birth to stubble.
    Your own spirit will consume
    you like a fire.ᵉ
12 And peoples will become as
    the burnings of lime.
    As thorns cut down, they will
    be set ablaze with fire.ᶠ
13 You who are far away, listen
    to what I will do!
    And you who are nearby,
    acknowledge my might!
14 The sinners in Zion are in
    dread;ᵍ
    Trembling has seized the
    apostates:
    'Who of us can live where
    there is a consuming fire?ʰ
    Who of us can live with
    unquenchable flames?'
15 The one who walks in
    continual righteousness,ⁱ
    Who speaks what is upright,ʲ
    Who rejects dishonest,
    fraudulent gain,
    Whose hands refuse a bribe
    rather than grabbing it,ᵏ

Who closes his ear to talk
   of bloodshed,
And who shuts his eyes to
   avoid seeing what is bad
16 —He will reside in the
    heights;
    His secure refuge* will be in
    rocky strongholds,
    His bread will be provided,
    And his water supply will
    never fail."ᵃ
17 Your eyes will behold a king
    in his splendor;
    They will see a land far away.
18 In your heart you will recall*
    the terror:
    "Where is the secretary?
    Where is the one who
    weighed out the tribute?ᵇ
    Where is the one who
    counted the towers?"
19 You will no more see the
    insolent people,
    A people whose language
    is too obscure* to
    comprehend,
    Whose stammering tongue
    you cannot understand.ᶜ
20 Behold Zion, the city of our
    festivals!ᵈ
    Your eyes will see Jerusalem
    as a tranquil dwelling
    place,
    A tent that will not be
    moved.ᵉ
    Never will its tent pins be
    pulled out,
    And none of its ropes will
    be torn apart.
21 But there the Majestic One,
    Jehovah,
    Will be for us a region of
    rivers, of wide canals,
    Where no galley fleet will go
    And no majestic ships will
    pass by.
22 For Jehovah is our Judge,ᶠ
    Jehovah is our Lawgiver,ᵍ
    Jehovah is our King;ʰ

CHAP. 33
a 2Ki 18:19, 20

b Isa 37:24

c Na 1:4

d Ps 46:10

e Isa 5:24

f Isa 9:18

g De 28:66, 67

h De 32:22
  Na 1:6
  Heb 12:29

i Eze 18:17

j 1Ch 29:17

k Ex 23:8
  De 16:19

_____
Second Col.
a 1Ki 19:5, 6
  Ps 34:9, 10
  Isa 65:13

b 2Ki 15:19

c De 28:49, 50
  Isa 28:11
  Jer 5:15

d De 12:5, 6

e Ps 125:1

f Ge 18:25
  Ps 50:6
  Ps 98:9

g Le 26:3
  Jas 4:12

h Ps 44:4
  Ps 97:1
  Re 11:15, 17

33:8 *Referring to the enemy. **33:9** *Or possibly, "dries up." **33:16** *Or "secure height." **33:18** *Or "meditate on." **33:19** *Lit., "deep."

He is the One who will
save us.[a]

23 Your ropes will hang loose;
They cannot hold up the
mast nor spread the sail.
At that time an abundance of
spoil will be divided up;
Even the lame will take much
plunder.[b]

24 And no resident* will say:
"I am sick."[c]
The people dwelling in the
land will be pardoned for
their error.[d]

34 Come close to hear,
you nations,
And pay attention, you
peoples.
Let the earth and that which
fills it listen,
The land and all its produce.

2 For Jehovah's indignation
is against all the nations,[e]
And his wrath is against
all their army.[f]
He will devote them to
destruction;
He will give them to the
slaughter.[g]

3 Their slain will be thrown
out,
And the stench of their
carcasses will ascend;[h]
The mountains will melt
because of* their blood.[i]

4 All the army of the heavens
will rot away,
And the heavens will be
rolled up like a scroll.
All their army will wither
away,
As a withered leaf falls from
the vine
And a shriveled fig from
the fig tree.

5 "For in the heavens my
sword will be drenched.[j]
It will descend on E′dom
in judgment,[k]

On the people whom
I devoted to destruction.

6 Jehovah has a sword; it will
be covered with blood.
It will be covered with the
fat,[a]
With the blood of young
rams and goats,
With the kidney fat of rams.
For Jehovah has a sacrifice
in Boz′rah,
A great slaughter in the land
of E′dom.[b]

7 The wild bulls will go down
with them,
The young bulls with the
powerful ones.
Their land will be drenched
in blood,
And their dust will be soaked
with fat."

8 For Jehovah has a day of
vengeance,[c]
A year of retribution for the
legal case over Zion.[d]

9 Her* streams will be changed
into pitch,
And her dust into sulfur,
And her land will become
like burning pitch.

10 By night or by day it will not
be extinguished;
Its smoke will keep
ascending forever.
From generation to gener-
ation she will remain
devastated;
No one will pass through her
forever and ever.[e]

11 The pelican and the porcupine will possess her,
And long-eared owls and
ravens will reside in her.
He will stretch out over
her the measuring line of
emptiness
And the plumb line* of
desolation.

12 None of her nobles will be
called to the kingship,

33:24 *Or "inhabitant." 34:3 *Or "will
flow with."

34:9 *Evidently referring to Bozrah,
the capital of Edom. 34:11 *Lit., "the
stones."

And all her princes will come
to nothing.

13 Thorns will grow in her
fortified towers,
Nettles and thorny weeds in
her fortresses.
She will become a lair of
jackals,[a]
An enclosure for ostriches.

14 Desert creatures will meet
up with howling animals,
And the wild goat* will call
to its companion.
Yes, there the nightjar will
settle and find a place of
rest.

15 There the arrow snake will
make its nest and lay eggs,
And it will hatch them and
gather them in its shadow.
Yes, there the kites will gather, each one with her mate.

16 Search in the book of
Jehovah and read it out
loud:
Not one of them will be
missing;
None of them will be lacking
a mate,
For it is the mouth of
Jehovah that has given
the order,
And it is his spirit that has
gathered them together.

17 He is the One who has cast
the lot for them,
And his own hand has mea-
sured out their assigned
place.*
They will possess it for all
time;
They will reside in it
throughout all generations.

35 The wilderness and the
parched land will exult,[b]
And the desert plain will be
joyful and blossom as the
saffron.*[c]

2 Without fail it will blossom;[a]
It will rejoice and shout for
joy.
The glory of Leb′a·non will
be given to it,[b]
The splendor of Car′mel[c]
and of Shar′on.[d]
They will see the glory of
Jehovah, the splendor of
our God.

3 Strengthen the weak hands,
And make firm the knees
that are shaking.[e]

4 Say to those who are anxious
at heart:
"Be strong. Do not be afraid.
Look! Your own God will
come with vengeance,
God will come with
retribution.[f]
He will come and save you."[g]

5 At that time the eyes of the
blind will be opened,[h]
And the ears of the deaf will
be unstopped.[i]

6 At that time the lame will
leap like the deer,[j]
And the tongue of the
speechless will shout for
joy.[k]
For waters will burst forth
in the wilderness,
And streams in the desert
plain.

7 The heat-parched ground
will become a reedy pool,
And the thirsty ground
springs of water.[l]
In the lairs where jackals
rested,[m]
There will be green grass
and reeds and papyrus.

8 And a highway will be there,[n]
Yes, a way called the Way of
Holiness.
The unclean one will not
travel on it.[o]
It is reserved for the one
walking on the way;
No one foolish will stray
onto it.

CHAP. 34
a Mal 1:3

CHAP. 35
b Isa 29:17
Isa 32:14, 15

c Isa 4:2
Isa 27:6
Isa 35:6
Isa 51:3
Eze 36:35

Second Col.
a Ho 14:5, 6

b Isa 60:13

c Jer 50:19

d Isa 65:10

e Heb 12:12

f Jer 51:56

g Isa 25:9
Zep 3:16, 17

h Ps 146:8
Isa 42:16
Mt 9:28-30

i Isa 29:18
Jer 6:10
Mr 7:32-35
Lu 7:22

j Mt 11:5
Ac 8:7
Ac 14:8-10

k Mt 15:30

l Isa 44:3

m Jer 9:11

n Ezr 1:3
Isa 11:16
Isa 49:11
Isa 62:10
Jer 31:21

o Isa 52:1

34:14 *Or possibly, "the goatlike demon." 34:17 *Lit., "divided it for them
with a measuring line." 35:1 *Or "crocus."

9 No lion will be there,
  And no vicious wild beasts
    will come on it.
  They will not be found
    there;[a]
  Only the repurchased ones
    will walk there.[b]

10 Those redeemed by Jehovah
    will return[c] and come to
    Zion with a joyful cry.[d]
  Unending joy will crown
    their heads.[e]
  Exultation and rejoicing
    will be theirs,
  And grief and sighing
    will flee away.[f]

36 In the 14th year of King
  Hez·e·ki′ah, Sen·nach′er·ib
the king of As·syr′i·a[g] came
up against all the fortified cities of Judah and captured them.[b]
2 The king of As·syr′i·a then
sent the Rab′sha·keh*[i] with a vast
army from La′chish[j] to King Hez-
e·ki′ah in Jerusalem. They took
up a position by the conduit of
the upper pool,[k] which is at
the highway of the laundry-
man's field.[l] **3** Then E·li′a·kim[m]
son of Hil·ki′ah, who was in
charge of the household,* Sheb′-
na[n] the secretary, and Jo′ah son
of A′saph the recorder came out
to him.

4 So the Rab′sha·keh said to
them: "Please, say to Hez·e·ki′ah,
'This is what the great king, the
king of As·syr′i·a, says: "What is
the basis for your confidence?[o]
5 You are saying, 'I have a strategy and the power to wage war,'
but these are empty words. In
whom have you put trust, so that
you dare to rebel against me?[p]
6 Look! You trust in the support of this crushed reed, Egypt,
which if a man should lean on it
would enter into his palm and
pierce it. That is the way Phar′-
aoh king of Egypt is to all those

36:2 *Or "the chief cupbearer." 36:3
*Or "palace."

---

who trust in him.[a] **7** And if you
should say to me, 'We trust in
Jehovah our God,' is he not the
one whose high places and altars
Hez·e·ki′ah has removed,[b] while
he says to Judah and Jerusalem,
'You should bow down before
this altar'?"[c] **8** So now make
this wager, please, with my lord
the king of As·syr′i·a:[d] I will give
you 2,000 horses if you are able
to find enough riders for them.
9 How, then, could you drive
back even one governor who is
the least of my lord's servants,
while you put your trust in Egypt
for chariots and for horsemen?
10 Now is it without authorization from Jehovah that I have
come up against this land to destroy it? Jehovah himself said to
me, 'Go up against this land and
destroy it.'"

11 At this E·li′a·kim[e] and
Sheb′na[e] and Jo′ah said to the
Rab′sha·keh:[f] "Speak to your servants, please, in the Ar·a·ma′-
ic* language,[g] for we can understand it; do not speak to us in
the language of the Jews in the
hearing of the people on the
wall."[h] **12** But the Rab′sha·keh
said: "Is it just to your lord and
to you that my lord sent me to
speak these words? Is it not also
to the men who sit on the wall,
those who will eat their own excrement and drink their own
urine along with you?"

13 Then the Rab′sha·keh
stood and called out loudly in
the language of the Jews,[i] saying: "Hear the word of the
great king, the king of As·syr′i·a.[j]
14 This is what the king says,
'Do not let Hez·e·ki′ah deceive
you, for he is not able to rescue
you.[k] **15** And do not let Hez·e-
ki′ah cause you to trust in Jehovah[l] by saying: "Jehovah will
surely rescue us, and this city
will not be given into the hand

36:11 *Or "Syrian."

of the king of As·syr'i·a." **16** Do not listen to Hez·e·ki'ah, for this is what the king of As·syr'i·a says: "Make peace with me and surrender,* and each of you will eat from his own vine and from his own fig tree and will drink the water of his own cistern, **17** until I come and take you to a land like your own land,*ᵃ a land of grain and new wine, a land of bread and vineyards. **18** Do not let Hez·e·ki'ah mislead you by saying, 'Jehovah will rescue us.' Have any of the gods of the nations rescued their land out of the hand of the king of As·syr'-i·a?ᵇ **19** Where are the gods of Ha'math and Ar'pad?ᶜ Where are the gods of Seph·ar·va'im?ᵈ And have they rescued Sa·mar'i·a out of my hand?ᵉ **20** Who among all the gods of these lands have rescued their land out of my hand, so that Jehovah should rescue Jerusalem out of my hand?"'"ᶠ

21 But they kept silent and did not say a word to him in reply, for the order of the king was, "You must not answer him."ᵍ **22** But E·li'a·kim son of Hil·ki'ah, who was in charge of the household,* Sheb'naʰ the secretary, and Jo'ah son of A'saph the recorder came to Hez·e·ki'ah with their garments ripped apart and told him the words of the Rab'sha·keh.

37 As soon as King Hez·e·ki'ah heard this, he ripped his garments apart and covered himself with sackcloth and went into the house of Jehovah.ⁱ **2** Then he sent E·li'a·kim, who was in charge of the household,* Sheb'na the secretary, and the elders of the priests, covered with sackcloth, to the prophet Isaiah,ʲ the son of A'moz. **3** They said to him: "This is what

Hez·e·ki'ah says, 'This day is a day of distress, of rebuke,* and of disgrace; for the children are ready to be born,⁺ but there is no strength to give birth.ᵃ **4** Perhaps Jehovah your God will hear the words of the Rab'sha·keh, whom the king of As·syr'i·a his lord sent to taunt the living God,ᵇ and he will call him to account for the words that Jehovah your God has heard. So offer up a prayerᶜ in behalf of the remnant who have survived.'"ᵈ

5 So the servants of King Hez·e·ki'ah went in to Isaiah,ᵉ **6** and Isaiah said to them: "This is what you should say to your lord, 'This is what Jehovah says: "Do not be afraidᶠ because of the words that you heard, the words with which the attendants of the king of As·syr'i·aᵍ blasphemed me. **7** Here I am putting a thought in his mind,* and he will hear a report and return to his own land;ʰ and I will make him fall by the sword in his own land."'"ⁱ

8 After the Rab'sha·keh heard that the king of As·syr'i·a had pulled away from La'chish, he returned to him and found him fighting against Lib'nah.ʲ **9** Now the king heard it said about King Tir·ha'kah of E·thi·o'-pi·a: "He has come out to fight against you." When he heard this, he sent messengers again to Hez·e·ki'ah,ᵏ saying: **10** "This is what you should say to King Hez·e·ki'ah of Judah, 'Do not let your God in whom you trust deceive you by saying: "Jerusalem will not be given into the hand of the king of As·syr'-i·a."ˡ **11** Look! You have heard what the kings of As·syr'i·a did to all the lands by devoting them to destruction.ᵐ Will you alone

---

CHAP. 36
a 2Ki 17:6
  2Ki 17:22, 23

b 2Ki 19:11, 12
  2Ch 32:14
  Isa 37:11, 12

c Jer 49:23

d 2Ki 17:24

e 2Ki 17:6
  2Ki 17:22, 23
  Isa 10:11

f 2Ki 19:17, 18
  2Ch 32:15
  Isa 37:23

g 2Ki 18:36, 37
  Pr 9:7

h Isa 22:15

CHAP. 37
i 2Ki 19:1-4

j 2Ch 26:22
  Isa 1:1

Second Col.
a Isa 26:17, 18

b 1Sa 17:45
  2Ki 18:28, 35

c 2Ki 32:20
  Ps 50:15
  Joe 2:17

d 2Ki 17:18

e 2Ki 19:5-7

f De 20:1

g 2Ki 18:17

h Pr 21:1

i 2Ch 32:21
  Isa 37:37, 38

j Jos 10:29, 30
  2Ki 8:22
  2Ki 19:8-13

k 2Ki 18:17

l 2Ch 32:15

m 2Ki 17:5, 6
  2Ch 32:13
  Isa 10:11

36:16 *Lit., "Make with me a blessing and come out to me." **36:22; 37:2** *Or "palace."

37:3 *Or "insult." ⁺Lit., "have come to the opening of the womb." **37:7** *Lit., "a spirit in him."

be rescued? **12** Did the gods of the nations that my forefathers destroyed rescue them?[a] Where are Go'zan, Ha'ran,[b] Re'zeph, and the people of E'den who were in Tel-as'sar? **13** Where is the king of Ha'math, the king of Ar'pad, and the king of the cities of Seph·ar·va'im,[c] and of He'na, and of Iv'vah?'"

14 Hez·e·ki'ah took the letters out of the hand of the messengers and read them. Hez·e·ki'ah then went up to the house of Jehovah and spread them* out before Jehovah.[d] **15** And Hez·e·ki'ah began to pray to Jehovah[e] and say: **16** "O Jehovah of armies,[f] the God of Israel, sitting enthroned above* the cherubs, you alone are the true God of all the kingdoms of the earth. You made the heavens and the earth. **17** Incline your ear, O Jehovah, and hear![g] Open your eyes, O Jehovah, and see![h] Hear all the words that Sen·nach'er·ib has sent to taunt the living God.[i] **18** It is a fact, O Jehovah, that the kings of As·syr'i·a have devastated all the lands,[j] as well as their own land. **19** And they have thrown their gods into the fire,[k] because they were not gods but the work of human hands,[l] wood and stone. That is why they could destroy them. **20** But now, O Jehovah our God, save us out of his hand, so that all the kingdoms of the earth may know that you alone are God, O Jehovah."[m]

21 Isaiah son of A'moz then sent this message to Hez·e·ki'ah: "This is what Jehovah the God of Israel says, 'Because you prayed to me concerning King Sen·nach'er·ib of As·syr'i·a,[n] **22** this is the word that Jehovah has spoken against him:

"The virgin daughter of Zion despises you, she scoffs at you.
The daughter of Jerusalem shakes her head at you.
23 Whom have you taunted[a] and blasphemed?
Against whom have you raised your voice[b]
And lifted your arrogant eyes?
It is against the Holy One of Israel![c]
24 Through your servants you have taunted Jehovah[d] and said,
'With the multitude of my war chariots
I will ascend the heights of mountains,[e]
The remotest parts of Leb'a·non.
I will cut down its lofty cedars, its choice juniper trees.
I will enter its highest retreats, its densest forests.
25 I will dig wells and drink waters;
I will dry up the streams* of Egypt with the soles of my feet.'
26 Have you not heard?
From long ago it was determined.*
From days gone by I have prepared# it.[f]
Now I will bring it about.[g]
You will turn fortified cities into desolate piles of ruins.[h]
27 Their inhabitants will be helpless;
They will be terrified and put to shame.
They will become as vegetation of the field and green grass,
As grass of the roofs that is scorched by the east wind.

CHAP. 37

a Isa 36:19

b Ge 11:31

c 2Ki 17:24
   Isa 36:19

d 2Ki 19:14-19

e 1Ki 8:30
   2Ch 6:20
   2Ch 20:9
   Da 9:3

f Ps 46:7
   Isa 8:13

g 2Ch 6:40
   Ps 65:2

h 2Ch 16:9
   1Pe 3:12

i Isa 37:4

j 2Ki 15:29
   2Ki 16:8, 9
   1Ch 5:26

k Isa 10:11

l Isa 40:19
   Isa 41:7
   Jer 10:3
   Ho 8:6
   Ac 17:29

m De 32:31, 39
   Ps 83:18
   Ps 96:5

n 2Ki 19:20, 21

Second Col.

a 2Ki 19:4, 16

b 2Ki 18:30, 35
   Isa 10:12, 13

c Ex 15:11
   2Ki 19:22-24
   Isa 10:20
   Eze 39:7

d 2Ch 32:17

e Isa 10:10, 11

f Ps 33:11
   Isa 46:10

g Isa 55:10, 11

h 2Ki 19:25, 26

37:14 *Lit., "it." **37:16** *Or possibly, "between."

37:25 *Or "the Nile canals." **37:26** *Lit., "done." #Or "formed."

28 But I well know when you sit,
     when you go out, when you
     come in,[a]
     And when you are enraged
         against me,[b]
29 Because your rage against
     me[c] and your roaring have
     reached my ears.[d]
     So I will put my hook in
         your nose and my bridle[e]
         between your lips,
     And I will lead you back
         the way you came."

30 "'And this will be the sign
for you:* This year you will eat
what grows on its own;[f] and
in the second year, you will eat
grain that sprouts from that; but
in the third year you will sow
seed and reap, and you will plant
vineyards and eat their fruitage.[f]
31 Those of the house of Judah
who escape, those who are left,[g]
will take root downward and
produce fruit upward. 32 For a
remnant will go out of Jerusalem
and survivors from Mount Zion.[h]
The zeal of Jehovah of armies
will do this.[i]

33 "'Therefore this is what
Jehovah says about the king of
As·syr'i·a:[j]

     "He will not come into
         this city[k]
     Or shoot an arrow there
     Or confront it with a shield
     Or cast up a siege rampart
         against it."[l]
34 'By the way he came he will
     return;
     He will not come into this
         city,' declares Jehovah.
35 'I will defend this city[m] and
     save it for my own sake[n]
     And for the sake of my
         servant David.'"[o]

36 And the angel of Jehovah
went out and struck down 185,-
000 men in the camp of the As-
syr'i·ans. When people rose up

early in the morning, they saw
all the dead bodies.[a] 37 So
King Sen·nach'er·ib of As·syr'i·a
departed and returned to Nin'e-
veh[b] and stayed there.[c] 38 And
as he was bowing down at the
house* of his god Nis'roch, his
own sons A·dram'me·lech and
Shar·e'zer struck him down with
the sword[d] and then escaped to
the land of Ar'a·rat.[e] And his
son E'sar-had'don[f] became king
in his place.

38 In those days Hez·e·ki'ah
became sick and was at
the point of death.[g] The prophet Isaiah[h] the son of A'moz came
and said to him, "This is what
Jehovah says: 'Give instructions
to your household, for you will
die; you will not recover.'"[i] 2 At
that Hez·e·ki'ah turned his face
to the wall and began to pray
to Jehovah: 3 "I beg you, O Jehovah, remember,[j] please, how
I have walked before you faithfully and with a complete heart,[k]
and I have done what was good
in your eyes." And Hez·e·ki'ah began to weep profusely.

4 Then the word of Jehovah
came to Isaiah, saying: 5 "Go
back and say to Hez·e·ki'ah,[l]
'This is what Jehovah the God
of David your forefather says:
"I have heard your prayer.[m]
I have seen your tears.[n] Here
I am adding 15 years to your
life,*[o] 6 and I will rescue you
and this city out of the hand
of the king of As·syr'i·a, and
I will defend this city.[p] 7 This
is the sign from Jehovah to
show you that Jehovah will carry out the word that he has spoken:[q] 8 Here I will make the declining shadow of the sun on the
stairway* of A'haz go back ten
steps."'"[r] So the sun went back
ten steps on the stairway that it
had already descended.

CHAP. 37
a Pr 5:21
   Pr 15:3
   Heb 4:13
b 2Ki 19:27, 28
c Ps 46:6
   Isa 10:15
   Isa 37:23
d Isa 36:4, 20
e Ps 32:9
f 2Ki 19:29-31
g Isa 1:9
   Isa 10:20, 21
h 2Ki 19:4
i Isa 59:17
   Joe 2:18
   Zec 1:14, 15
j Isa 10:24
k 2Ch 32:22
   Isa 10:32
   2Ki 19:32-34
m Isa 31:5
n De 32:27
   1Sa 12:22
   2Ki 20:6
   Eze 36:22
o 1Ki 15:4

Second Col.
a 2Ki 19:35-37
   2Ch 32:21
b Ge 10:8, 11
   Jon 1:2
c 2Ki 19:7, 28
d 2Ch 32:21
e Ge 8:4
f Ezr 4:1, 2

CHAP. 38
g 2Ch 32:24
h 2Ki 19:20
   Isa 1:1
i 2Ki 20:1-3
j Ne 13:22
   Ps 20:1-3
   Heb 6:10
k 2Ki 31:20, 21
l 2Ki 20:4-6
m Pr 15:29
   1Jo 5:14
n Ps 39:12
   Ps 56:8
o De 32:39
   1Sa 2:6
p 2Ch 32:22
q 2Ki 20:8-11
r Jos 10:12, 13

37:30 *That is, Hezekiah. #Or "the
growth from spilled kernels of grain."
37:38 *Or "temple." 38:5 *Lit., "days."
38:8 *Perhaps these stairs were used to
count time, as on a sundial.

9 A writing* of King Hez·e·ki'ah of Judah when he became sick and recovered from his sickness.

10 I said: "In the middle of my life
I must go into the gates of the Grave.*
I will be deprived of my remaining years."

11 I said: "I will not see Jah,*
Jah in the land of the living.ª
I will look no more on mankind
When I am with the inhabitants of the place where everything ceases.

12 My own dwelling has been pulled out and removed from meᵇ
Like the tent of a shepherd.
I have rolled up my life like a loom worker;
He cuts me off like the threads of the warp.
From daylight to nightfall you keep bringing me to an end.ᶜ

13 I calm myself until the morning.
Like a lion, he keeps breaking all my bones;
From daylight to nightfall you keep bringing me to an end.ᵈ

14 Like the swift or the thrush,*
so I keep chirping;ᵉ
I keep cooing like the dove.ᶠ
My eyes look wearily to the height:ᵍ
'O Jehovah, I am in great distress;
Be my support!'*ʰ

15 What can I say?
He has spoken to me and acted.

16 'O Jehovah, by these things* every man lives,
And in them is the life of my spirit.
You will restore me to health and preserve me alive.ª

17 Look! Instead of peace, I had great bitterness;
But in your fondness for me,*
You preserved me from the pit of destruction.ᵇ
You have thrown all my sins behind your back.*ᶜ

18 For the Grave* cannot glorify you,ᵈ
Death cannot praise you.ᵉ
Those who go down into the pit cannot hope for your faithfulness.ᶠ

19 The living, the living can praise you,
Just as I can this day.
A father can give his sons knowledge about your faithfulness.ᵍ

20 O Jehovah, save me,
And we will play my songs on stringed instrumentsʰ
All the days of our life at the house of Jehovah.'"ⁱ

21 Isaiah then said: "Bring a cake of pressed dried figs and apply it to the boil, so that he may recover."ʲ **22** Hez·e·ki'ah had asked: "What is the sign that I will go up to the house of Jehovah?"ᵏ

39 At that time the king of Babylon, Mer'o·dach-bal'a·dan son of Bal'a·dan, sent letters and a gift to Hez·e·ki'ah,ˡ for he had heard that he had been sick and had recovered.ᵐ

CHAP. 38
a Ps 6:5
  Ec 9:5

b Ps 146:4
  Ec 8:8

c Job 17:1

d Ps 39:10

e Ps 102:7

f Isa 59:11

g Ps 39:7

h Ps 39:12
  Ps 119:82, 123

Second Col.
a 1Sa 2:6
  Job 33:28
  Ps 71:20

b Ps 30:3
  Ps 86:13
  Jon 2:6

c Isa 43:25
  Mic 7:18

d Ps 30:9

e Ps 6:5
  Ps 115:17

f Ec 9:5, 10

g Ge 18:19
  De 4:9
  Jos 4:21-24

h Ps 30:11, 12

i 2Ki 20:5
  Ps 84:2

j 2Ki 20:7

k 2Ki 20:8

CHAP. 39
l 2Ch 32:23

m 2Ki 20:5
  2Ki 20:12, 13

38:9 *Or "composition." **38:10, 18** *Or "Sheol," that is, the common grave of mankind. See Glossary. **38:11** *"Jah" is a shortened form of the name Jehovah. **38:14** *Or possibly, "crane." #Lit., "Be my surety."

38:15 *Or "solemnly." #Or "the bitterness of my soul." **38:16** *That is, God's words and deeds. **38:17** *Or "my soul." #Or "removed all my sins from your sight."

2 Hez·e·ki′ah gladly welcomed* them and showed them his treasure-house[a]—the silver, the gold, the balsam oil and other precious oil, his whole armory, and everything that was to be found in his treasuries. There was nothing that Hez·e·ki′ah did not show them in his own house[a] and in all his dominion.

3 After that Isaiah the prophet came in to King Hez·e·ki′ah and asked him: "What did these men say, and where did they come from?" So Hez·e·ki′ah said: "They came from a distant land, from Babylon."[b] **4** Next he asked: "What did they see in your house?"[a] Hez·e·ki′ah replied: "They saw everything in my house.[a] There was nothing that I did not show them in my treasuries."

5 Isaiah now said to Hez·e·ki′ah: "Hear the word of Jehovah of armies, **6** 'Look! Days are coming, and all that is in your house[a] and all that your forefathers have stored up to this day will be carried off to Babylon. Nothing will be left,'[c] says Jehovah.[d] **7** 'And some of your own sons to whom you will become father will be taken and will become court officials in the palace of the king of Babylon.'"[e]

8 At that Hez·e·ki′ah said to Isaiah: "The word of Jehovah that you have spoken is good." Then he added: "Because there will be peace and stability* during my lifetime."[#f]

40 "Comfort, comfort my people," says your God.[g]
2 "Speak to the heart of* Jerusalem,
And proclaim to her that her compulsory service has been fulfilled,

CHAP. 39
a 2Ch 32:27

b 2Ki 20:14, 15

c 2Ki 24:11, 13
2Ki 25:13
2Ch 36:18
Da 1:1, 2

d 2Ki 20:16-18

e 2Ki 24:12
Da 2:49
Da 5:29

f 2Ki 20:19

CHAP. 40
g Isa 49:13
Isa 51:3
2Co 1:3, 4

Second Col.
a Ps 79:8, 9
Jer 31:34
Jer 33:8

b Jer 16:18
Da 9:11, 12

c Isa 35:8
Isa 57:14
Mal 3:1

d Isa 11:16

e Mt 3:1, 3
Mr 1:2-4
Lu 3:3-6
Joh 1:23

f Isa 42:16

g Isa 24:15

h Isa 49:6
Isa 52:10

i Job 14:1, 2
Ps 90:5, 6

j Jas 1:11

k Ps 103:15, 16

l Isa 46:10
1Pe 1:24, 25

m Isa 52:7

That her guilt has been paid off.[a]
From the hand of Jehovah she has received a full amount* for all her sins."[b]
3 A voice of one calling out in the wilderness:
"Clear up* the way of Jehovah![c]
Make a straight highway[d] through the desert for our God.[e]
4 Let every valley be raised up,
And every mountain and hill be made low.
The rough ground must become level,
And the rugged ground a valley plain.[f]
5 The glory of Jehovah will be revealed,[g]
And all flesh* will see it together,[h]
For the mouth of Jehovah has spoken."
6 Listen! Someone is saying: "Call out!"
Another asks: "What should I call out?"
"All flesh* is* green grass.
All their loyal love is like the blossom of the field.[i]
7 The green grass dries up, The blossom withers,[j]
Because the breath* of Jehovah blows upon it.[k]
Surely the people are but green grass.
8 The green grass dries up, The blossom withers,
But the word of our God endures forever."[l]
9 Go up onto a high mountain, You woman bringing good news for Zion.[m]
Raise your voice with power,

39:2 *Lit., "rejoiced over." **39:2, 4, 6** #Or "palace." **39:8** *Or "truth." #Lit., "days." **40:2** *Or "Speak consolingly to."

40:2 *Or "received double." **40:3** *Or "Prepare." **40:5** *Or "all humans." **40:6** *Or "All humans are." **40:7** *Or "spirit."

You woman bringing good news for Jerusalem.
Raise it, do not be afraid.
Announce to the cities of Judah: "Here is your God."[a]

10 Look! The Sovereign Lord Jehovah will come with power,
And his arm will rule for him.[b]
Look! His reward is with him,
And the wage he pays is before him.[c]

11 Like a shepherd he will care for* his flock.[d]
With his arm he will gather together the lambs,
And in his bosom he will carry them.
He will gently lead those nursing their young.[e]

12 Who has measured the waters in the hollow of his hand[f]
And taken the measurements* of the heavens with a span of his hand?#
Who has gathered in a measure the dust of the earth[g]
Or weighed the mountains in the balances
And the hills in the scales?

13 Who has taken the measurements of* the spirit of Jehovah,
And who can instruct him as his adviser?[h]

14 With whom did he consult to gain understanding,
Or who teaches him in the path of justice,
Or teaches him knowledge,
Or shows him the way of true understanding?[i]

15 Look! The nations are like a drop from a bucket,

And as the film of dust on the scales they are regarded.[a]
Look! He lifts up the islands like fine dust.

16 Even Leb'a·non is not sufficient to keep a fire burning,*
And its wild animals are not sufficient for a burnt offering.

17 All the nations are as something nonexistent in front of him;[b]
He regards them as nothing, as an unreality.[c]

18 To whom can you compare God?[d]
What likeness can you put next to him?[e]

19 The craftsman casts an idol,*
The metalworker overlays it with gold,[f]
And he forges silver chains.

20 He chooses a tree for his contribution,[g]
A tree that will not rot.
He searches for a skilled craftsman
To prepare a carved image that will not topple over.[h]

21 Do you not know?
Have you not heard?
Has it not been told to you from the beginning?
Have you not understood from the foundations of the earth?[i]

22 There is One who dwells above the circle* of the earth,[j]
And its inhabitants are like grasshoppers.
He is stretching out the heavens like a fine gauze,
And he spreads them out like a tent to dwell in.[k]

23 He reduces high officials to nothing

CHAP. 40
a Isa 12:2
  Isa 25:9

b Isa 53:1
  Joh 12:37, 38

c Isa 62:11
  Re 22:12

d Isa 49:10
  Eze 34:15, 16
  1Pe 2:25

e Ge 33:13
  1Pe 5:2, 3

f Pr 30:4

g Job 38:4, 5

h Job 36:22, 23
  Ro 11:34
  1Co 2:16

i Ps 147:5

Second Col.
a Ps 62:9

b Da 4:35

c Isa 41:11, 12

d Ex 8:10
  Ps 86:8
  Jer 10:6, 7

e De 4:15, 16
  Ac 17:29

f Ps 115:4-8

g Isa 44:14, 15

h Isa 41:7
  Isa 46:6, 7
  Jer 10:3, 4

i Ps 19:1
  Ro 1:20

j Isa 66:1

k Isa 44:24
  Jer 10:12
  Zec 12:1

40:11 *Or "will shepherd." 40:12 *Or "the proportions." #The distance between the end of the thumb and the little finger when the hand is spread. See App. B14. 40:13 *Or possibly, "has comprehended."

40:16 *Or "cannot provide sufficient firewood." 40:19 *Or "a molten statue." 40:22 *Or "sphere."

And makes the judges* of the earth an unreality.

24 They are hardly planted,
They are hardly sown,
Their stem has hardly taken root in the earth,
And they are blown on and dry up,
And the wind carries them away like stubble.ᵃ

25 "To whom can you liken me to make me his equal?" says the Holy One.

26 "Lift up your eyes to heaven and see.
Who has created these things?ᵇ
It is the One who brings out their army by number;
He calls them all by name.ᶜ
Because of his vast dynamic energy and his awe-inspiring power,ᵈ
Not one of them is missing.

27 Why do you say, O Jacob,
and why do you declare, O Israel,
'My way is hidden from Jehovah,
And I receive no justice from God'?ᵉ

28 Do you not know? Have you not heard?
Jehovah, the Creator of the ends of the earth, is a God for all eternity.ᶠ
He never tires out or grows weary.ᵍ
His understanding is unsearchable.*ʰ

29 He gives power to the tired one
And full might to those lacking strength.*ⁱ

30 Boys will tire out and grow weary,
And young men will stumble and fall,

31 But those hoping in Jehovah will regain power.
They will soar on wings like eagles.ᵃ
They will run and not grow weary;
They will walk and not tire out."ᵇ

41 "Listen to me in silence,* you islands;
Let the nations regain their strength.
Let them approach; then let them speak.ᶜ
Let us come together for judgment.

2 Who has raised up someone from the sunrise,*ᵈ
Calling him in righteousness to His feet,#
To hand over nations to him
And to make him subdue kings?ᵉ
Who reduces them to dust before his sword,
Like windblown stubble before his bow?

3 He pursues them, passing along unhindered
Over paths that his feet have not traveled.

4 Who has acted and done this,
Summoning the generations from the beginning?
I, Jehovah, am the First One;ᶠ
And with the last ones I am the same."ᵍ

5 The islands have seen it and have become afraid.
The ends of the earth began to tremble.
They draw near and come forward.

6 Each one helps his companion
And says to his brother: "Be strong."

CHAP. 40

a 1Ki 21:20, 21
2Ki 10:10, 11
Jer 22:24, 30

b Ps 102:25

c Ps 147:4

d Ps 89:13

e Isa 49:14
Eze 37:11

f Ge 21:33
Ps 90:2
Jer 10:10
1Ti 1:17

g Ps 121:4
Isa 27:3

h Ps 139:4, 6
Ps 147:5
Isa 55:9
Ro 11:33
1Co 2:16

i Ps 29:11
Isa 40:26
Php 4:13
Heb 11:33, 34

Second Col.

a Ps 103:5

b 1Ki 18:46
Ps 84:7

CHAP. 41

c Isa 41:21

d Isa 44:28
Isa 46:11
Re 16:12

e Isa 45:1

f Isa 43:10
Isa 44:6
Isa 48:12
Re 1:8

g Isa 46:4
Mal 3:6
Jas 1:17

40:23 *Or "rulers." 40:28 *Or "cannot be fathomed." 40:29 *Or "dynamic energy."

41:1 *Or "Keep silence before me." 41:2 *Or "from the east." #That is, to serve Him.

7 So the craftsman strengthens the metalworker;[a]
The one who flattens with the forge hammer
Strengthens the one hammering at the anvil.
He says about the soldering: "It is good."
Then it is fastened with nails so that it will not topple over.

8 "But you, O Israel, are my servant,[b]
You, O Jacob, whom I have chosen,[c]
The offspring* of Abraham my friend,[d]

9 You, whom I took from the ends of the earth,[e]
And you, whom I called from its most distant parts.
I said to you, 'You are my servant;[f]
I have chosen you; I have not rejected you.[g]

10 Do not be afraid, for I am with you.[h]
Do not be anxious, for I am your God.[i]
I will fortify you, yes, I will help you,[j]
I will really hold on to you with my right hand of righteousness.'

11 Look! All those getting enraged against you will be put to shame and humiliated.[k]
Those who fight with you will be brought to nothing and perish.[l]

12 You will search for men who struggle with you, but you will not find them;
The men at war with you will become as something nonexistent, as nothing at all.[m]

13 For I, Jehovah your God, am grasping your right hand,

The One saying to you, 'Do not be afraid. I will help you.'[a]

14 Do not be afraid, you worm* Jacob,[b]
You men of Israel, I will help you," declares Jehovah, your Repurchaser,[c] the Holy One of Israel.

15 "Look! I have made you a threshing sledge,[d]
A new threshing instrument with double-edged teeth.
You will tread down the mountains and crush them
And make the hills like chaff.

16 You will winnow them,
And the wind will carry them away;
A windstorm will scatter them.
You will be joyful in Jehovah,[e]
And you will boast in the Holy One of Israel."[f]

17 "The needy and the poor are seeking water, but there is none.
Their tongue is dry from thirst.[g]
I, Jehovah, will answer them.[h]
I, the God of Israel, will not abandon them.[i]

18 I will make rivers flow on the bare hills[j]
And springs in the valley plains.[k]
I will turn the wilderness into a reedy pool of water
And the waterless land into springs of water.[l]

19 In the desert I will plant the cedar tree,
The acacia and the myrtle and the oil tree.[m]
In the desert plain I will plant the juniper tree,
Together with the ash and the cypress tree,[n]

CHAP. 41
a Isa 44:12
  Isa 46:6
b Ex 19:5, 6
  Le 25:42
c De 7:6
  Ps 33:12
d 2Ch 20:7
  Jas 2:23
e Ps 107:2, 3
f Isa 43:10
g 1Sa 12:22
  Jer 33:25, 26
h De 20:1
  Ps 46:1
  Ro 8:31
i Isa 60:19, 20
j De 33:27
  Ps 115:9
k Isa 45:24
l Isa 40:17
  Isa 60:12
m Isa 54:17

Second Col.
a De 33:29
b De 7:7
c Isa 43:14
  Isa 47:4
d Mic 4:13
e Isa 25:9
f Isa 12:6
g De 28:48
  Am 8:11
h Isa 30:19
  Isa 55:1
i Ps 94:14
  Isa 42:16
  Heb 13:5
j Isa 30:25
k Joe 3:18
l Ps 107:35
m Isa 32:14, 15
  Isa 60:21
n Isa 51:3
  Isa 55:13

41:8 *Lit., "seed."

41:14 *That is, defenseless and lowly.

20 So that all people may see
    and know

And pay attention and under-
    stand

That the hand of Jehovah
    has done this,

And the Holy One of Israel
    has created it."[a]

21 "Present your case," says
    Jehovah.

"Produce your arguments,"
    says the King of Jacob.

22 "Produce evidence and tell
    us the things that will
    happen.

Do tell us about the former*
    things,

So that we may reflect on
    them# and know their out-
    come.

Or declare to us the things
    that are coming.[b]

23 Tell us what will happen
    in the future,

So that we may know that
    you are gods.[c]

Yes, do something, good or
    bad,

So that we may be amazed
    when we see it.[d]

24 Look! You are something
    nonexistent,

And your achievement is
    nothing.[e]

Anyone who chooses you
    is detestable.[f]

25 I have raised up someone
    from the north, and he will
    come,[g]

One from the rising of the
    sun*[h] who will call on my
    name.

He will trample rulers# as if
    they were clay,[i]

Like a potter who treads
    moist clay.

26 Who told about this from
    the beginning, so that
    we could know,

Or from times past, so that
    we could say, 'He is right'?[a]

Indeed, no one announced it!

No one declared it!

No one heard anything from
    you!"[b]

27 I was the first to say to Zion:
    "Look! Here they are!"[c]

And to Jerusalem I will send
    a bearer of good news.[d]

28 But I kept looking, and there
    was no one;

There was not one among
    them to give advice.

And I kept asking them to
    reply.

29 Look! All of them are a
    delusion.*

Their works are nothing.

Their metal images# are wind
    and unreality.[e]

42 Look! My servant,[f] whom
    I support!

My chosen one,[g] whom
    I have* approved![h]

I have put my spirit in him;[i]

He will bring justice to the
    nations.[j]

2 He will not cry out or raise
    his voice,

And he will not make his
    voice heard in the street.[k]

3 No crushed reed will he
    break,

And no smoldering wick will
    he extinguish.[l]

In faithfulness will he bring
    justice.[m]

4 He will not grow dim or be
    crushed until he establish-
    es justice in the earth;[n]

And the islands keep waiting
    for his law.*

5 This is what the true God,
    Jehovah, says,

The Creator of the heavens
    and the Grand One who
    stretched them out,[o]

CHAP. 41

a Eze 39:28

b Isa 42:9
  Isa 46:9, 10
  Isa 48:5

c Isa 44:6, 7

d Jer 10:5

e Isa 44:10
  Jer 10:14, 15

f De 7:26
  De 27:15
  Ps 115:4, 8

g Isa 44:28
  Isa 45:1
  Jer 51:28, 29

h Isa 46:11
  Re 16:12

i Mic 7:10

Second Col.

a Isa 43:9
  Isa 44:7
  Isa 45:21

b Hab 2:18, 19

c Isa 43:10

d Ezr 1:1, 2
  Isa 40:9

e Ps 115:4-8
  Isa 44:9
  1Co 8:4

CHAP. 42

f Isa 52:13

g Isa 49:7
  Lu 9:35

h Mt 3:17
  Joh 6:27
  2Pe 1:17

i Isa 61:1
  Mt 3:16

j Mt 12:15-18

k Zec 9:9
  Mt 12:16, 19

l Mt 11:28, 29
  Heb 2:17

m Isa 11:3, 4
  Mt 12:20
  Joh 5:30
  Re 19:11

n Isa 9:7
  Isa 49:8

o Isa 40:22, 26

41:22 *Lit., "first." #Or "apply our heart." 41:25 *Or "from the east." #Or "deputy rulers." 41:29 *Or "something nonexistent." #Or "molten statues." 42:1 *Or "my soul has." 42:4 *Or "instruction."

The One who spread out the earth and its produce,[a]

The One who gives breath to the people on it[b]

And spirit to those who walk on it:[c]

6 "I, Jehovah, have called you in righteousness;

I have taken hold of your hand.

I will safeguard you and give you as a covenant for the people[d]

And as a light of the nations,[e]

7 For you to open the blind eyes,[f]

To bring the prisoner out of the dungeon

And those sitting in darkness out of the prison.[g]

8 I am Jehovah. That is my name;

I give my glory to no one else,*

Nor my praise to graven images.[h]

9 See, the first things have come to pass;

Now I am declaring new things.

Before they spring up, I tell you about them."[i]

10 Sing to Jehovah a new song,[j]

His praise from the ends of the earth,[k]

You who go down to the sea and all that fills it,

You islands and their inhabitants.[l]

11 Let the wilderness and its cities raise their voice,[m]

The settlements where Ke'dar[n] dwells.

Let the inhabitants of the crag shout joyfully;

Let them cry out from the top of the mountains.

12 Let them attribute glory to Jehovah

And declare his praise in the islands.[a]

13 Jehovah will go out like a mighty man.[b]

He will awaken his zeal like a warrior.[c]

He will shout, yes, he will let out a war cry;

He will show himself mightier than his enemies.[d]

14 "I have kept quiet for a long time.

I remained silent and restrained myself.

Like a woman giving birth, I will groan, pant, and gasp all at once.

15 I will devastate mountains and hills

And dry up all their vegetation.

I will turn rivers into islands*

And dry up reedy pools of water.[e]

16 I will lead the blind in a way that they do not know[f]

And cause them to tread on unfamiliar paths.[g]

I will turn the darkness before them into light[h]

And turn the rugged terrain into level land.[i]

This is what I will do for them, and I will not abandon them."

17 They will be turned back and will be utterly put to shame,

Those who trust in carved images,

Those who say to metal statues:* "You are our gods."[j]

18 Listen, you who are deaf;

Look and see, you who are blind.[k]

19 Who is blind except my servant,

So deaf as the messenger I send?

CHAP. 42

a Jer 10:12

b Ge 2:7
Ac 17:24, 25

c Job 12:10

d Isa 49:8

e Isa 49:6
Lu 2:29-32
Joh 8:12

f Isa 35:5

g Isa 61:1
1Pe 2:9

h Ex 34:14

i Isa 41:23
Isa 43:19
2Pe 1:21

j Ps 96:1
Ps 98:1
Re 14:3

k Isa 44:23

l Isa 51:5

m Isa 35:1

n Ge 25:13
Isa 60:7

Second Col.

a Ps 22:27
Isa 24:15
Isa 66:19

b Isa 59:17

c Ex 15:3

d 1Sa 2:10

e Ps 107:33
Isa 44:27
Isa 50:2

f Isa 29:18
Isa 35:5
Jer 31:8

g Isa 30:21

h Isa 60:1, 20

i Isa 40:4

j Isa 44:10, 11
Isa 45:16

k Isa 6:9, 10
Isa 43:8

42:8 *Or "I do not share my glory with anyone else." 42:15 *Or "coastlands." 42:17 *Or "molten statues."

Who is so blind as the one
  rewarded,
So blind as the servant of
  Jehovah?[a]

20 You see many things,
  but you do not keep watch.
You open your ears,
  but you do not listen.[b]

21 For the sake of his
  righteousness,
Jehovah has taken pleasure
  in magnifying the law*
  and making it glorious.

22 But this is a people
  plundered and pillaged;[c]
All of them are trapped
  in the holes and hidden
  in the prisons.[d]
They have been plundered
  with no one to rescue
  them,[e]
And pillaged with no one to
  say: "Bring them back!"

23 Who among you will hear
  this?
Who will pay attention and
  listen for the time to come?

24 Who has given Jacob for
  pillage
And Israel to the plunderers?
Is it not Jehovah, the One
  against whom we sinned?
In His ways they refused
  to walk,
And His law* they would not
  obey.[f]

25 So He kept pouring out on
  him wrath,
His anger and the fury of
  war.[g]
It consumed everything
  around him, but he paid
  no attention.[h]
It blazed up against him,
  but he would not take it
  to heart.[i]

43 Now this is what Jehovah
  says,
Your Creator, O Jacob, the
  One who formed you,
  O Israel:[j]

"Do not be afraid, for I have
  repurchased you.[a]
I have called you by your
  name.
You belong to me.

2 When you pass through the
  waters, I will be with you,[b]
And through the rivers, they
  will not flood over you.[c]
When you walk through the
  fire, you will not be
  scorched,
Nor will the flame singe you.

3 For I am Jehovah your God,
The Holy One of Israel,
  your Savior.
I have given Egypt as a
  ransom for you,
E·thi·o'pi·a and Se'ba in
  exchange for you.

4 For you became precious
  in my eyes,[d]
You were honored, and
  I have loved you.[e]
So I will give people in place
  of you
And nations in exchange for
  your life.*

5 Do not be afraid, for I am
  with you.[f]
I will bring your offspring*
  from the east
And gather you together
  from the west.[g]

6 I will say to the north,
  'Give them up!'[h]
And to the south, 'Do not
  hold them back.'
Bring my sons from afar,
  and my daughters from
  the ends of the earth,[i]

7 Everyone who is called
  by my name[j]
And whom I created for my
  own glory,
Whom I have formed and
  made.'[k]

8 Bring out a people who are
  blind, though they have
  eyes,

CHAP. 42
a Isa 56:10
  Jer 4:22
  Eze 12:2

b Eze 33:31

c De 28:15, 33
  Jer 50:17

d Ps 102:19, 20

e De 28:29, 52

f Jg 2:12, 14
  2Ch 15:3, 6
  Ps 106:41

g De 32:22
  Na 1:6

h Isa 9:13
  Jer 5:3
  Ho 7:9

i Isa 57:11

CHAP. 43
j Ps 100:3
  Isa 43:15
  Isa 44:2, 21

Second Col.
a Isa 44:23
  Jer 50:34

b Ex 14:29

c Jos 3:15, 16
  2Ki 2:8

d Ex 19:5, 6

e De 7:8
  Jer 31:3

f Isa 41:10
  Isa 44:2
  Jer 30:10

g De 30:1-3
  Ps 106:47
  Isa 66:20
  Eze 36:24
  Mic 2:12
  Zec 8:7

h Jer 3:18

i Jer 31:8

j Jer 33:16

k Ps 100:3
  Isa 29:23

___

42:21, 24 *Or "instruction."   43:4 *Or "soul."   43:5 *Lit., "seed."

And who are deaf, though they have ears.[a]

9 Let all the nations assemble in one place,
And let the peoples be gathered together.[b]
Who among them can tell this?
Or can they cause us to hear the first things?*[c]
Let them present their witnesses to prove themselves right,
Or let them hear and say, 'It is the truth!'"[d]

10 "You are my witnesses,"[e] declares Jehovah,
"Yes, my servant whom I have chosen,[f]
So that you may know and have faith in me*
And understand that I am the same One.[g]
Before me no God was formed,
And after me there has been none.[h]

11 I—I am Jehovah,[i] and besides me there is no savior."[j]

12 "I am the One who declared and saved and made known
When there was no foreign god among you.[k]
So you are my witnesses," declares Jehovah, "and I am God.[l]

13 Also, I am always the same One;[m]
And no one can snatch anything out of my hand.[n]
When I act, who can prevent it?"[o]

14 This is what Jehovah says, your Repurchaser,[p] the Holy One of Israel:[q]
"For your sakes I will send to Babylon and bring down all the bars of the gates,[r]

And the Chal·de'ans, in their ships, will cry out in distress.[a]

15 I am Jehovah, your Holy One,[b] the Creator of Israel,[c] your King."[d]

16 This is what Jehovah says,
The One making a way through the sea
And a path even through turbulent waters,[e]

17 The One who draws out the war chariot and the horse,[f]
The army together with the mighty warriors:
"They will lie down and not get up.[g]
They will be extinguished, snuffed out like a burning wick."

18 "Do not remember the former things,
And do not dwell on the past.

19 Look! I am doing something new;[h]
Even now it is springing up.
Do you not recognize it?
I will make a way through the wilderness[i]
And rivers through the desert.[j]

20 The wild beast of the field will honor me,
The jackals and the ostriches,
For I provide water in the wilderness,
Rivers in the desert,[k]
For my people, my chosen one,[l] to drink,

21 The people whom I formed for myself
So that they might declare my praise.[m]

22 But you have not called on me, O Jacob,[n]
Because you grew weary of me, O Israel.[o]

23 You have not brought me sheep for your whole burnt offerings

---

43:9 *Possibly referring to the first things to come in the future. 43:10 *Or "and trust me."

Or glorified me with your
sacrifices.
I have not compelled you
to bring me a gift,
Nor have I made you
weary by demanding
frankincense.[a]

24 You did not buy me sweet
cane* with your money,
And with the fat of your
sacrifices you did not
satisfy me.[b]
Instead, you have burdened
me with your sins
And made me weary with
your errors.[c]

25 I, I am the One who is blotting out your transgres-
sions*[d] for my own sake,[e]
And I will not remember
your sins.[f]

26 Remind me; let us bring our
case against each other;
Tell your side of it to prove
you are in the right.

27 Your first forefather sinned,
And your own spokesmen*
have rebelled against me.[g]

28 So I will profane the princes
of the holy place,
And I will give Jacob over
to destruction
And subject Israel to
insulting words.[h]

44 "Now listen, O Jacob my
servant,
And you, O Israel, whom
I have chosen.[i]

2 This is what Jehovah says,
Your Maker and the One
who formed you,[j]
Who has helped you from
the womb:*
'Do not be afraid, my servant
Jacob,[k]
And you, Jesh·u·run,*[l] whom
I have chosen.

3 For I will pour out water on
the thirsty one*[a]
And flowing streams on the
dry ground.
I will pour out my spirit on
your offspring*[b]
And my blessing on your
descendants.

4 And they will spring up as
among the green grass,[c]
Like poplars by the streams
of water.

5 One will say: "I belong to
Jehovah."[d]
Another will call himself
by the name of Jacob,
And yet another will write
on his hand: "Belonging
to Jehovah."
And he will adopt the name
of Israel.'

6 This is what Jehovah says,
The King of Israel[e] and his
Repurchaser,[f] Jehovah
of armies:
'I am the first and I am the
last.[g]
There is no God but me.[h]

7 Who is there like me?[i]
Let him call out and tell it
and prove it to me!
From the time I established
the people of long ago,
Let them tell both the things
to come
And what will yet happen.

8 Do not be in dread,
And do not become
paralyzed with fear.[k]
Have I not told each of
you beforehand and
declared it?
You are my witnesses.[l]
Is there any God but me?
No, there is no other Rock;[m]
I know of none.'"

9 All who form carved images
amount to nothing,
And their cherished objects
will be of no benefit.[n]

CHAP. 43
a Isa 66:3
b Le 3:14-16
c Isa 1:14, 15
d Isa 1:18
  Jer 50:20
e Ps 25:7
  Ps 79:8, 9
  Eze 20:9
f Jer 31:34
g Isa 28:7
  Jer 5:31
h Ps 79:4
  Ps 137:3

CHAP. 44
i Ge 17:1, 7
  Ge 35:10, 11
  Isa 41:8
j Isa 43:1
  Isa 44:21
k Isa 41:10
  Jer 30:10
l De 32:15
  De 33:5, 26

Second Col.
a Isa 41:17
b Isa 32:14, 15
c Isa 61:11
d Zec 13:9
e De 28:5
  Isa 33:22
f Ex 6:6
  Jer 50:34
g Isa 41:4
  Isa 48:12
  Re 22:13
h De 4:35, 39
  Isa 43:10
i Isa 46:9
j Isa 43:9
  Isa 45:21
k Isa 41:10
l Isa 43:10
m De 32:4
  2Sa 22:32
n Jg 10:14
  1Ki 18:26
  1Co 8:4

43:24 *An aromatic reed. 43:25 *Or
"rebellious acts." 43:27 *Possibly referring to teachers of the Law. 44:2
*Or "from birth." #Meaning "Upright
One," an honorary title for Israel.

44:3 *Or "thirsty land." #Lit., "seed."

As their witnesses, they*
see nothing and know
nothing,[a]
So those who made them will
be put to shame.[b]

10 Who would form a god or
cast a metal image*
That can bring no benefit?[c]

11 Look! All his associates will
be put to shame![d]
The craftsmen are mere
humans.
Let them all assemble and
take their stand.
They will be terrified and
be put to shame together.

12 The metalsmith works the
iron over the coals with
his tool.*
He forms it with hammers,
Working it with his powerful
arm.[e]
Then he grows hungry and
his strength fails;
He drinks no water and
grows tired.

13 The wood-carver stretches
the measuring line, tracing
out the pattern with red
chalk.
He works it with a wood
scraper and traces it with
a compass.
He patterns it after a man,[f]
With the beauty of a man,
To sit in a house.*[g]

14 There is one whose work is
to cut down cedars.
He selects a certain type
of tree, an oak,
And he lets it grow strong
among the trees of the
forest.[h]
He plants a laurel tree, and
the rain makes it grow.

15 Then it becomes fuel for
a man to make fires.
He takes part of it to warm
himself;

He builds a fire and bakes
bread.
But he also makes a god and
worships it.
He makes it into a carved
image, and he bows down
before it.[a]

16 Half of it he burns up in a
fire;
With that half he roasts the
meat that he eats, and he
is satisfied.
He also warms himself and
says:
"Ah! I am warm as I watch
the fire."

17 But the rest of it he makes
into a god, into his carved
image.
He bows down to it and
worships it.
He prays to it and says:
"Save me, for you are my
god."[b]

18 They know nothing, they
understand nothing,[c]
Because their eyes are
sealed shut and they
cannot see,
And their heart has no
insight.

19 No one reflects in his heart
Or has knowledge or understanding, saying:
"Half of it I burned up in a
fire,
And on its coals I baked
bread and roasted meat
to eat.
Should I, then, make the
rest of it into a detestable
thing?[d]
Should I worship a block*
of wood from a tree?"

20 He feeds on ashes.
His own deluded heart has
led him astray.
He cannot save himself,*
nor does he say:

CHAP. 44
a Ps 115:4, 5

b Jer 51:17

c Jer 10:5
Ac 19:26

d 1Sa 5:3, 7

e Isa 40:19
Isa 41:7
Isa 46:6

f Ex 20:4
De 4:15, 16
Ac 17:29

g De 27:15

h Isa 40:20
Jer 10:3

Second Col.
a Ex 20:4, 5
Le 26:1
Hab 2:18, 19

b Isa 37:37, 38
Isa 45:20
Isa 46:7

c Jer 10:8, 14
Ro 1:21-23

d De 27:15

44:9 *That is, the images. 44:10 *Or
"molten statue." 44:12 *Or "billhook."
44:13 *Or "shrine."

44:19 *Or "a dry piece." 44:20 *Or
"his soul."

"Is there not a lie in my right hand?"

21 "Remember these things,
O Jacob, and you, O Israel,
For you are my servant.
I formed you, and you are my servant.[a]
O Israel, I will not forget you.[b]

22 I will blot out your transgressions as with a cloud[c]
And your sins as with a thick cloud.
Return to me, for I will repurchase you.[d]

23 Shout joyfully, you heavens,
For Jehovah has acted!
Shout in triumph, you depths of the earth!
Shout for joy, you mountains,[e]
You forest, and all your trees!
For Jehovah has repurchased Jacob,
And on Israel he displays his splendor."[f]

24 This is what Jehovah says, your Repurchaser,[g]
Who formed you since you were in the womb:
"I am Jehovah, who made everything.
I stretched out the heavens by myself,[h]
And I spread out the earth.[i]
Who was with me?

25 I am frustrating the signs of the empty talkers,*
And I am the One who makes diviners act like fools;[j]
The One confounding the wise men
And turning their knowledge into foolishness;[k]

26 The One making the word of his servant come true
And completely fulfilling the predictions of his messengers;[l]

The One saying of Jerusalem, 'She will be inhabited,'[a]
And of the cities of Judah, 'They will be rebuilt,'[b]
And I will restore her ruins';[c]

27 The One saying to the deep waters, 'Be evaporated,
And I will dry up all your rivers';[d]

28 The One saying of Cyrus,[e]
'He is my shepherd,
And he will completely carry out all my will';[f]
The One saying of Jerusalem, 'She will be rebuilt,'
And of the temple, 'Your foundation will be laid.'"[g]

45 This is what Jehovah says to his anointed one, to Cyrus,[h]
Whose right hand I have taken hold of[i]
To subdue nations before him,[j]
To disarm* kings,
To open before him the double doors,
So that the gates will not be shut:

2 "Before you I will go,[k]
And the hills I will level.
The copper doors I will break in pieces,
And the iron bars I will cut down.[l]

3 I will give you the treasures in the darkness
And the hidden treasures in the concealed places,[m]
So that you may know that I am Jehovah,
The God of Israel, who is calling you by your name.[n]

4 For the sake of my servant Jacob and of Israel my chosen one,
I am calling you by your name.

CHAP. 44

a Isa 43:1
   Isa 44:1

b Isa 49:15

c Ps 51:1
   Ps 103:12
   Isa 1:18
   Isa 43:25
   Jer 33:8
   Ac 3:19

d Isa 1:27
   Isa 48:20
   Isa 59:20

e Isa 49:13
   Isa 55:12

f Isa 60:21

g Isa 44:6

h Job 26:7
   Isa 40:22

i Isa 42:5
   Isa 48:13

j Ho 9:7

k 2Sa 15:31
   Isa 29:14

l Jos 23:14
   Isa 55:10, 11
   Zec 1:6

Second Col.

a Ps 147:2

b Isa 60:10

c Isa 61:4

d Isa 42:15
   Jer 50:38
   Re 16:12

e Ezr 1:1, 2
   Isa 41:25
   Isa 45:1
   Isa 46:11
   Da 10:1

f Isa 48:14

g 2Ch 36:22, 23
   Ezr 6:3
   Isa 45:13

CHAP. 45

h Ezr 1:1, 2
   Isa 44:28

i Isa 45:4

j Isa 13:17
   Isa 41:25

k Isa 13:4

l Ps 107:16

m Jer 50:35, 37

n Ezr 1:1, 2
   Isa 44:28

I am giving you a name of honor, although you did not know me.

5 I am Jehovah, and there is no one else.
There is no God except me.[a]
I will strengthen* you, although you did not know me,

6 In order that people may know
From the rising of the sun to its setting*
That there is none besides me.[b]
I am Jehovah, and there is no one else.[c]

7 I form light[d] and create darkness,[e]
I make peace[f] and create calamity;[g]
I, Jehovah, am doing all these things.

8 You heavens, rain down from above;[h]
Let the clouds pour down righteousness.
Let the earth open up and be fruitful with salvation,
And let it cause righteousness to spring up at the same time.[i]
I, Jehovah, have created it."

9 Woe to the one who contends* with his Maker,"
For he is just an earthenware fragment
Among the other earthenware fragments lying on the ground!
Should the clay say to the Potter:ᐃ "What are you making?"[j]
Or should your work say: "He has no hands"?ᵍ

10 Woe to the one who says to a father: "What do you become father to?"
And to a woman: "What are you giving birth to?"*

11 This is what Jehovah says, the Holy One of Israel,[a] the One who formed him:
"Would you question me about the things coming
And command me about my sons[b] and the works of my hands?

12 I made the earth[c] and created man on it.[d]
I stretched out the heavens with my own hands,[e]
And I give orders to all their army."[f]

13 "I have raised up a man in righteousness,[g]
And I will make all his ways straight.
He is the one who will build my city[h]
And set my exiles free[i] without a price or a bribe,"[j] says Jehovah of armies.

14 This is what Jehovah says: "The profit* of Egypt and the merchandise# of E·thi·o′pi·a and the Sa·be′ans, tall of stature,
Will come over to you and become yours.
They will walk behind you in chains.
They will come over and bow down to you.[k]
To you they will say in prayer, 'Surely God is with you,[l]
And there is no one else; there is no other God.'"

15 Truly you are a God who conceals himself,
O God of Israel, the Savior.[m]

16 They will all be put to shame and be humiliated;

Cross References

CHAP. 45
a De 4:35, 39
  De 32:39
b 1Sa 17:46
  Ps 102:15, 16
  Isa 37:20
c Ps 83:18
d Ge 1:3
  Jer 31:35
e Ex 10:21
  Ps 104:20
f Isa 26:12
g Ec 7:14
  Am 3:6
h Eze 34:26
i Isa 61:11
j Isa 29:16
  Jer 18:6
  Ro 9:20

Second Col.
a Isa 43:3
b Ho 1:10
c Ge 1:1
  Isa 40:28
d Ge 1:27
e Isa 44:24
  Jer 32:17
  Zec 12:1
f Ne 9:6
g Isa 42:6
h 2Ch 36:23
  Ezr 1:2, 3
  Isa 44:28
i Isa 14:16, 17
  Isa 43:14
  Isa 49:25
j Isa 13:17
k Es 8:17
  Isa 14:1, 2
  Isa 49:23
  Isa 60:14
  Isa 61:5
l Zec 8:23
m Isa 43:11
  Isa 60:16
  Tit 1:3

45:5 *Lit., "closely gird." 45:6 *Or "From east to west." 45:9 *Or "argues." "Or "with the One who formed him." ᐃOr "the One who formed it." ᵍOr possibly, "Or should the clay say: 'Your work has no handles'?"

45:10 *Or "What are you in birth pains with?" 45:14 *Or possibly, "laborers." #Or possibly, "merchants."

The makers of idols will all
go off in disgrace.ᵃ

17 But Israel will be saved
by Jehovah with an
everlasting salvation.ᵇ
You will not be put to shame
or disgraced for all
eternity.ᶜ

18 For this is what Jehovah
says,
The Creator of the heavens,ᵈ
the true God,
The One who formed the
earth, its Maker who firmly
established it,ᵉ
Who did not create it simply
for nothing,* but formed it
to be inhabited:ᶠ
"I am Jehovah, and there is
no one else.

19 I did not speak in a
concealed place,ᵍ in a
land of darkness;
I did not say to the offspring*
of Jacob,
'Seek me simply for
nothing.'#
I am Jehovah, who speaks
what is righteous and de-
clares what is upright.ʰ

20 Gather together and come.
Approach together, you
escapees from the nations.ⁱ
They know nothing, those
who carry around carved
images
And pray to a god that
cannot save them.ʲ

21 Make your report, present
your case.
Let them consult together
in unity.
Who foretold this long ago
And declared it from times
past?
Is it not I, Jehovah?
There is no other God
but me;

A righteous God and
a Savior,ᵃ there is none
besides me.ᵇ

22 Turn to me and be saved,ᶜ
all the ends of the earth,
For I am God, and there is
no one else.ᵈ

23 By myself I have sworn;
The word has gone out of my
mouth in righteousness,
And it will not return:ᵉ
To me every knee will bend,
Every tongue will swear
loyaltyᶠ

24 And say, 'Surely in Jehovah
are true righteousness and
strength.
All those enraged against
him will come before him
in shame.

25 In Jehovah all the offspring*
of Israel will prove to be
right,ᵍ
And in him they will make
their boast.'"

46 Bel bends down,ʰ Neʹbo
stoops over.
Their idols are loaded on animals, on beasts of burden,ⁱ
Like baggage that burdens
the weary animals.

2 They stoop and bend down
together;
They cannot rescue the
loads,*
And they themselves#
go into captivity.

3 "Listen to me, O house of
Jacob, and all you who
remain of the house of
Israel,ʲ
You whom I have supported
from birth and carried
from the womb,ᵏ

4 Until you grow old I will be
the same;ˡ
Until your hair is gray I will
keep bearing you.

CHAP. 45

a Ps 97:7
  Isa 44:9

b Isa 26:4
  Isa 51:6

c Isa 29:22
  Isa 54:4
  Joe 2:26
  Zep 3:11

d Isa 42:5
  Jer 10:12

e Ps 78:69
  Ps 104:5
  Ps 119:90
  Pr 3:19

f Ge 1:28
  Ge 9:1
  Ps 37:29
  Ps 115:16

g Isa 48:16

h Ps 111:7, 8
  Ps 119:137

i Isa 66:20
  Jer 50:28

j Isa 42:17
  Jer 50:2

Second Col.

a Isa 43:3

b De 4:39
  Isa 44:8
  Mr 12:32

c Mic 7:7

d De 4:35

e Isa 55:10, 11

f De 6:13
  Ro 14:11

g Isa 61:9

CHAP. 46

h Jer 50:2
  Jer 51:44

i Isa 45:20

j Isa 1:9

k Ex 19:4
  De 1:31
  Isa 44:2

l Isa 41:4

45:18 *Or possibly, "to be empty."
45:19, 25 *Lit., "seed." 45:19 #Or "in vain."

46:2 *That is, the idols loaded on the animals. #Or "their souls."

As I have done, I will carry you and bear you and rescue you.[a]

5 To whom will you liken me or make me equal or compare me,[b]
So that we should resemble each other?[c]

6 There are those who lavish gold from their purse;
They weigh out the silver on the scale.
They hire a metalworker, and he makes it into a god.[d]
Then they prostrate themselves, yes, they worship it.*[e]

7 They lift it to their shoulders;[f]
They carry it and put it in its place, and it just stands there.
It does not move from its place.[g]
They cry out to it, but it does not answer;
It cannot rescue anyone from distress.[h]

8 Remember this, and take courage.
Take it to heart, you transgressors.

9 Remember the former* things of long ago,
That I am God,[#] and there is no other.
I am God, and there is no one like me.[i]

10 From the beginning I foretell the outcome,
And from long ago the things that have not yet been done.[j]
I say, 'My decision* will stand,[k]
And I will do whatever I please.'[l]

11 I am calling a bird of prey from the sunrise,[#][m]

From a distant land the man to carry out my decision.*[a]
I have spoken, and I will bring it about.
I have purposed it, and I will also carry it out.[b]

12 Listen to me, you who are stubborn* of heart,
You who are far away from righteousness.

13 I have brought my righteousness near;
It is not far away,
And my salvation will not delay.[c]
I will grant salvation in Zion, my splendor to Israel."[d]

47 Come down and sit in the dust,
O virgin daughter of Babylon.[e]
Sit down on the ground where there is no throne,[f]
O daughter of the Chal·de′ans,
For never again will people call you delicate and pampered.

2 Take a hand mill and grind flour.
Remove your veil.
Strip off your skirt, uncover your legs.
Cross over the rivers.

3 Your nakedness will be uncovered.
Your shame will be exposed.
I will take vengeance,[g] and no man will stand in my way.*

4 "The One repurchasing us —Jehovah of armies is his name—
Is the Holy One of Israel."[h]

5 Sit there silently and go into darkness,
O daughter of the Chal·de′ans;[i]

CHAP. 46
a Isa 43:13

b Ex 15:11

c Ac 17:29

d Isa 40:19
  Jer 10:8, 9

e Isa 44:16, 17
  Da 3:1, 5

f Jer 10:5

g 1Sa 5:3

h 1Ki 18:26
  Isa 37:37, 38
  Jon 1:5

i De 33:26

j Isa 42:9
  Isa 45:21

k Ps 33:11

l Ps 135:6
  Isa 55:10, 11

m Isa 41:2
  Isa 45:1

Second Col.
a Ezr 1:1, 2
  Isa 44:28
  Isa 48:14

b Nu 23:19
  Job 23:13

c Isa 12:2
  Isa 51:5
  Isa 62:11

d Isa 44:23
  Isa 60:21

CHAP. 47
e Ps 137:8
  Jer 50:41, 42

f Da 5:30

g De 32:35, 41
  Ps 94:1

h Isa 41:14
  Isa 43:3
  Isa 44:6

i Isa 47:1

46:6 *Lit., "bow down to it." 46:9 *Lit., "first." #Or "the Divine One." 46:10, 11 *Or "purpose; counsel." 46:11 #Or "east."

46:12 *Lit., "powerful." 47:3 *Or possibly, "and I will not meet anyone kindly."

No more will they call you
Mistress* of Kingdoms.[a]

6 I grew indignant at my
  people.
I profaned my inheritance,[c]
And I gave them into your
  hand.[d]
But you showed them no
  mercy.[e]
Even on the elderly you
  placed a heavy yoke.[f]

7 You said: "I will always be
  the Mistress,* forever."[g]
You did not take these things
  to heart;
You did not consider how
  the matter would end.

8 Now hear this, O lover of
  pleasure,[h]
Who sits in security, who
  says in her heart:
"I am the one, and there is
  no one else.[i]
I will not become a widow.
I will never know the loss
  of children."[j]

9 But these two things will
  come upon you suddenly,
  in one day:[k]
Loss of children and
  widowhood.
In full measure they will
  come upon you[l]
Because of* your many
  sorceries and all your
  powerful spells.[m]

10 You trusted in your
  wickedness.
You said: "No one sees me."
Your wisdom and knowledge
  are what led you astray,
And you say in your heart:
"I am the one, and there
  is no one else."

11 But calamity will come upon
  you,
And none of your charms
  will stop it.*

Adversity will befall you; you
  will not be able to avert it.
Sudden ruin will come upon
  you like you have never
  known.[a]

12 Go ahead, then, with your
  spells and your many
  sorceries,[b]
With which you have toiled
  from your youth.
Perhaps you may be able
  to benefit;
Perhaps you may strike
  people with awe.

13 You have grown weary with
  the multitude of your
  advisers.
Let them stand up now and
  save you,
Those who worship the
  heavens,* who gaze at the
  stars,[c]
Those giving out knowledge
  at the new moons
About the things that will
  come upon you.

14 Look! They are like stubble.
A fire will burn them up.
They cannot save them-
  selves* from the power
  of the flame.
These are not charcoals for
  keeping warm,
And this is not a fire to sit
  in front of.

15 So your charmers will
  become to you,
Those with whom you toiled
  from your youth.
They will wander, each one
  in his own direction.*
There will be no one to save
  you.[d]

48 Hear this, O house of
  Jacob,
You who call yourselves by
  the name of Israel[e]

CHAP. 47
a Isa 13:19
  Isa 14:4
  Re 17:5

b 2Ch 36:15, 16
  Isa 42:24, 25
  Zec 1:15

c De 28:63
  Eze 24:21

d Jer 52:14

e 2Ki 25:18-21
  Ps 137:8

f De 28:49, 50

g Da 4:30
  Re 18:7

h Re 18:3

i Da 5:22, 23

j Re 18:7

k Re 18:10

l Jer 51:29

m Eze 21:21
  Da 5:7
  Re 18:23

Second Col.
a Re 18:10

b Da 2:2

c Da 5:7

d Jer 51:6

CHAP. 48
e Ge 32:28

And who have come from
the waters of* Judah,
You who swear by the name
of Jehovah[a]
And who call on the God
of Israel,
Though not in truth and
righteousness.[b]

2 For they call themselves
after the holy city[c]
And seek the support of the
God of Israel,[d]
Whose name is Jehovah of
armies.

3 "The former* things I told
you long ago.
From my own mouth they
went out,
And I made them known.[e]
Suddenly I took action,
and they came about.[f]

4 Because I knew how
stubborn you are
—That your neck is an iron
sinew and your forehead
is copper[g]—

5 I told you long ago.
Before it came about,
I caused you to hear it,
So that you could not say,
'My idol did this;
My carved image and my
metal image* commanded
this.'

6 You have heard and seen
all of this.
Will you not declare it?[h]
From now on I am announc-
ing new things to you,[i]
Guarded secrets that you
have not known.

7 Only now are they being
created, and not long ago,
Things that you never heard
before today,
So that you cannot say,
'Look! I already know
them.'

8 No, you have not heard,[a]
you have not known,
And in the past your ears
were not opened.
For I know that you are very
treacherous,[b]
And you have been called a
transgressor from birth.[c]

9 But for the sake of my name
I will hold back my anger;[d]
For my own praise I will re-
strain myself toward you,
And I will not do away with
you.[e]

10 Look! I have refined you, but
not in the form of silver.[f]
I have tested* you in the
smelting furnace of
affliction.[g]

11 For my own sake, for my own
sake I will act,[h]
For how could I let myself
be profaned?[i]
I give my glory to no one
else.*

12 Listen to me, O Jacob, and
Israel, whom I have called.
I am the same One.[j] I am the
first; I am also the last.[k]

13 My own hand laid the
foundation of the earth,[l]
And my right hand spread
out the heavens.[m]
When I call to them, they
stand up together.

14 Gather together, all of you,
and listen.
Who among them has
announced these things?
Jehovah has loved him.[n]
He will carry out his delight
against Babylon,[o]
And his arm will come
against the Chal·de′ans.[p]

15 I myself have spoken, and
I have called him.[q]
I have brought him, and his
way will be successful.[r]

CHAP. 48
a De 6:13
b Le 19:12
  Zep 1:4, 5
c Isa 52:1
d Jer 21:1, 2
e Isa 42:9
f Jos 21:45
  Isa 55:10, 11
g Ex 32:9
  2Ki 17:13, 14
  2Ch 36:15, 16
  Ps 78:8
  Eze 3:7
h Isa 43:10
i Isa 42:9
  Isa 65:17

Second Col.
a Isa 29:10
b Jer 5:11
  Jer 9:2
c De 9:7
  Ps 95:10
d 1Sa 12:22
  Ps 25:11
  Ps 79:9
  Jer 14:7
e Ne 9:30, 31
  Ps 78:38
f Pr 17:3
g Isa 1:25
  Jer 9:7
h Isa 48:9
i Eze 20:9
j Isa 43:13
  Isa 46:4
k Isa 44:6
  Re 1:8
  Re 22:13
l Job 38:4
m Isa 40:22
  Isa 42:5
n Isa 45:1
o Isa 44:28
p Isa 13:19
  Jer 50:13
q Isa 41:2
r Isa 45:5

48:1 *Or possibly, "who are descended from." 48:3 *Lit., "first." 48:5 *Or
"molten statue."

48:10 *Or "examined." Or possibly,
"chosen." 48:11 *Or "I do not share my
glory with anyone else."

16 Come near to me, and hear
      this.
  From the very start I have
      not spoken in secret.ᵃ
  From the time it happened
      I was there."
  And now the Sovereign Lord
      Jehovah has sent me, and*
      his spirit.
17 This is what Jehovah says,
      your Repurchaser, the Holy
      One of Israel:ᵇ
  "I, Jehovah, am your God,
  The One teaching you
      to benefit yourself,*ᶜ
  The One guiding you in the
      way you should walk.ᵈ
18 If only you would pay at-
      tention to my
      commandments!ᵉ
  Then your peace would
      become just like a riverᶠ
  And your righteousness like
      the waves of the sea.ᵍ
19 Your offspring* would be as
      many as the sand
  And your descendants as its
      grains.ʰ
  Their name would never be
      cut off or annihilated from
      before me."
20 Go out from Babylon!ⁱ
  Flee from the Chal·de′ans!
  Announce it with a joyful
      cry! Proclaim it!ʲ
  Make it known to the ends
      of the earth.ᵏ
  Say: "Jehovah has repur-
      chased his servant Jacob.ˡ
21 They did not become thirsty
      when he led them through
      devastated places.ᵐ
  He caused water to flow out
      of the rock for them;
  He split a rock and made
      water gush out."ⁿ
22 "There is no peace," says
      Jehovah, "for the wicked."ᵒ

48:16 *Or "along with." 48:17 *Or "for
your own good." 48:19 *Lit., "seed."

CHAP. 48
a Isa 45:19

b Isa 43:14
  Isa 44:6
  Isa 54:5

c 1Ki 8:36
  Ps 25:8
  Isa 54:13
  Mic 4:2

d Ps 32:8
  Isa 30:20, 21
  Isa 49:10

e De 5:29
  Ps 81:13, 14

f Ps 119:165
  Isa 32:18
  Isa 66:12

g Am 5:23, 24

h Ge 22:15, 17
  Jer 33:22
  Ho 1:10

i Jer 50:8
  Re 18:4

j Isa 49:13

k Jer 50:2

l Jer 31:10, 11

m Ex 15:24, 25
  De 8:14, 15
  Isa 43:19

n Ex 17:5, 6
  Nu 20:11

o Isa 57:20, 21

Second Col.

CHAP. 49
a Isa 55:4

b Isa 44:2
  Isa 46:3

c Isa 51:16

d Isa 43:10

e Isa 44:23

f Isa 40:10

g Isa 56:8

h Isa 42:6
  Mt 12:18
  Lu 2:30, 32

---

49 Listen to me, you islands,
      And pay attention, you
      faraway nations.ᵃ
  Jehovah has called me
      before I was born.*ᵇ
  From the time I was in
      my mother's womb he has
      made mention of my name.
2 He made my mouth like
      a sharp sword;
  He has hidden me in the
      shadow of his hand.ᶜ
  He made me a polished
      arrow;
  He concealed me in his
      quiver.
3 He said to me: "You are
      my servant, O Israel,ᵈ
  Through whom I will show
      my splendor."ᵉ
4 But I said: "I have toiled
      for nothing.
  I used up my strength for
      an unreality, in vain.
  But surely my judgment
      is with Jehovah,*
  And my wages# with
      my God."ᶠ
5 And now Jehovah, the One
      who formed me from the
      womb as his servant,
  Has said for me to bring
      Jacob back to him,
  So that Israel may be
      gathered to him.ᵍ
  I will be glorified in the eyes
      of Jehovah,
  And my God will have
      become my strength.
6 And he said: "It is not enough
      that you are my servant
  To raise up the tribes of
      Jacob
  And to bring back those who
      were preserved of Israel.
  I have also given you as a
      light of nations,ʰ

49:1 *Lit., "from the womb." 49:4 *Or
"Jehovah will grant me justice." #Or
"reward."

So that my salvation may
reach the ends of the
earth."ᵃ

7 This is what Jehovah, the
Repurchaser of Israel, his Holy
One,ᵇ says to the one who is despised,*ᶜ to the one who is detested by the nation, to the servant of rulers:

"Kings will see and rise up,
And princes will bow down
Because of Jehovah, who is
faithful,ᵈ
The Holy One of Israel, who
has chosen you."ᵉ

8 This is what Jehovah says:
"In a time of favor*
I answered you,ᶠ
And in a day of salvation
I helped you;ᵍ
I kept safeguarding you to
give you as a covenant
for the people,ʰ
To rehabilitate the land,
To cause them to possess
their desolate inheri-
tances,ⁱ

9 To say to the prisoners,
'Come out!'ʲ
And to those in the dark-
ness,ᵏ 'Show yourselves!'
By the roadways they will
feed,
Along all the worn paths*
will be their pastures.

10 They will not go hungry,
nor will they thirst,ˡ
Nor will scorching heat or
the sun beat down on
them.ᵐ
For the One who has mercy
on them will lead them,ⁿ
And he will guide them by
the springs of water.ᵒ

11 I will make all my mountains
into a road,
And my highways will be
raised up.ᵖ

49:7 *Or "despised in soul." 49:8 *Or
"goodwill." 49:9 *Or possibly, "the
bare hills."

12 Look! These are coming
from far away,ᵃ
And look! these from the
north and from the west,
And these from the land
of Si'nim."ᵇ

13 Shout for joy, you heavens,
and rejoice, you earth.ᶜ
Let the mountains become
cheerful with a joyful cry.ᵈ
For Jehovah has comforted
his people,ᵉ
And he shows mercy to his
own afflicted ones.ᶠ

14 But Zion kept saying:
"Jehovah has abandoned
me,ᵍ and Jehovah has
forgotten me."ʰ

15 Can a woman forget her
nursing child
Or have no compassion for
the son of her womb?
Even if these women forget,
I would never forget you.ⁱ

16 Look! On my palms I have
engraved you.
Your walls are always
before me.

17 Your sons hurry back.
Those who tore you down
and devastated you will
depart from you.

18 Raise your eyes and look all
around.
They are all gathering
together.ʲ
They are coming to you.
"As surely as I am living,"
declares Jehovah,
"You will clothe yourself
with all of them as with
ornaments,
And you will fasten them on
yourself as a bride does.

19 Although your places were
devastated and desolate
and your land was in
ruins,ᵏ
Now it will become
too cramped for those
dwelling there,ˡ

And those who swallowed you down[a] will be far away.[b]

20 The sons born when you were bereaved will say in your hearing,

'This place is too cramped for me.

Make room for me to dwell here.'[c]

21 And you will say in your heart,

'Who has fathered these for me,

Since I am a woman bereaved of children and barren,

Exiled and taken prisoner?

Who has raised these?[d]

Look! I was left all alone,[e]

So where have these come from?'"[f]

22 This is what the Sovereign Lord Jehovah says:

"Look! I will raise up my hand to the nations,

And I will lift up my signal* to the peoples.[g]

They will bring your sons in their arms#

And carry your daughters on their shoulders.[h]

23 Kings will become caretakers for you,[i]

And their princesses will be your nurses.

They will bow down to you with their faces to the ground[j]

And lick the dust of your feet,[k]

And you will have to know that I am Jehovah;

Those hoping in me will not be put to shame."[l]

24 Can those already captured be taken from a mighty man,

Or can the captives of the tyrant be rescued?

25 But this is what Jehovah says:

"Even the captives of a mighty man will be taken away,[a]

And those captured by the tyrant will be rescued.[b]

I will oppose those who oppose you,[c]

And I will save your own sons.

26 I will make those who mistreat you eat their own flesh,

And as with sweet wine, they will become drunk with their own blood.

And all people* will have to know that I am Jehovah,[d]

Your Savior[e] and your Repurchaser,[f]

The Powerful One of Jacob."[g]

50 This is what Jehovah says:

"Where is the divorce certificate[h] of your mother, whom I sent away?

Or to which of my creditors did I sell you?

Look! It was because of your own errors[i] you were sold,

And because of your own transgressions your mother was sent away.[j]

2 Why, then, was no one here when I came?

Why did no one answer when I called?[k]

Is my hand too short to redeem,

Or is there no power in me to rescue?

Look! With my rebuke I dry up the sea;[m]

I make rivers a desert.[n]

Their fish rot for lack of water,

And they die because of thirst.

3 I clothe the heavens with gloom,[o]

49:22 *Or "signal pole." #Lit., "bosom." 49:26 *Lit., "all flesh."

And I make sackcloth their covering."

4 The Sovereign Lord Jehovah has given me the tongue of those taught,*[a]

So that I may know how to answer# the tired one with the right word.△[b]

He awakens me morning by morning;

He awakens my ear to listen like the taught ones.[c]

5 The Sovereign Lord Jehovah has opened my ear,

And I was not rebellious.[d]

I did not turn in the opposite direction.[e]

6 I offered my back to those striking me

And my cheeks to those who plucked them bare.*

I did not hide my face from humiliating things and from spit.[f]

7 But the Sovereign Lord Jehovah will help me.[g]

That is why I will not feel humiliated.

That is why I have set my face like a flint,[h]

And I know that I will not be put to shame.

8 The One who declares me righteous is near.

Who can accuse* me?[i]

Let us stand up together.#

Who has a case against me?

Let him approach me.

9 Look! The Sovereign Lord Jehovah will help me.

Who will pronounce me guilty?

Look! They will all wear out like a garment.

A moth will eat them up.

10 Who among you fears Jehovah

And listens to the voice of his servant?[a]

Who has walked in deep darkness, without any brightness?

Let him trust in the name of Jehovah and support himself on* his God.

11 "Look! All of you who are igniting a fire,

Making sparks fly,

Walk in the light of your fire,

Among the sparks you have set ablaze.

This is what you will have from my hand:

In sheer pain you will lie down.

51 "Listen to me, you who are pursuing righteousness,

You who are seeking Jehovah.

Look to the rock from which you were hewn

And to the quarry from which you were dug.

2 Look to Abraham your father

And to Sarah[b] who gave birth to you.*

For he was only one when I called him,[c]

And I blessed him and made him many.[d]

3 For Jehovah will comfort Zion.[e]

He will bring comfort to all her ruins,[f]

And he will make her wilderness like E'den[g]

And her desert plain like the garden of Jehovah.[h]

Exultation and rejoicing will be found in her,

Thanksgiving and melodious song.[i]

4 Pay attention to me, O my people,

And give ear to me, my nation.[j]

CHAP. 50
a Ex 4:11
  Jer 1:9

b Joh 7:15, 46

c Mt 13:54

d Ps 40:6-8

e Mt 26:39
  Php 2:8

f Mt 26:67
  Mr 14:65
  Lu 22:63
  Joh 18:22

g Isa 49:8

h Eze 3:8, 9

i Ro 8:33

Second Col.
a Isa 42:1
  Isa 53:11

CHAP. 51
b Ge 21:2

c Ge 12:1
  Ge 15:2

d 1Ki 4:20

e Ps 102:13
  Isa 66:13
  Jer 31:12

f Isa 44:26
  Isa 61:4

g Ge 2:8

h Isa 35:1
  Isa 41:18

i Jer 33:10, 11

j Ex 19:6
  De 7:6

50:4 *Or "a well-trained tongue." #Or possibly, "strengthen." △Lit., "with a word." 50:6 *Or "who plucked the beard." 50:8 *Or "contend with." #Or "face each other."

50:10 *Or "rely on." 51:2 *Or "brought you forth with labor pains."

For a law will go out
from me,[a]
And my justice I will
establish as a light to the
peoples.[b]

5 My righteousness draws
near.[c]
My salvation will go out,[d]
And my arms will judge the
peoples.[e]
In me the islands will hope,[f]
And for my arm* they will
wait.

6 Raise your eyes to the
heavens,
And look at the earth below.
For the heavens will disperse
in fragments like smoke;
The earth will wear out like
a garment,
And its inhabitants will die
like gnats.
But my salvation will be
eternal,[g]
And my righteousness will
never fail.*[h]

7 Listen to me, you who know
righteousness,
The people with my law*
in their heart.[i]
Do not be afraid of the taunts
of mortal men,
And do not be terrified
because of their insults.

8 For a moth will eat them up
just like a garment;
The clothes moth* will
devour them like wool.[j]
But my righteousness will
last forever,
And my salvation for all
generations."[k]

9 Awake! Awake! Clothe
yourself with strength,
O arm of Jehovah![l]
Awake as in the days of long
ago, as in past generations.

Was it not you who broke
Ra′hab*[a] to pieces,
Who pierced the sea
monster?[b]

10 Are you not the one who
dried up the sea, the
waters of the vast deep?[c]
The one who made the
depths of the sea a road-
way for the repurchased
ones to cross?[d]

11 The redeemed ones of
Jehovah will return.[e]
They will come to Zion with
a joyful cry,[f]
And unending joy will crown
them.*[g]
Exultation and rejoicing will
be theirs,
And grief and sighing will
flee away.[h]

12 "I myself am the One
comforting you.[i]
Why should you be afraid of
a mortal man who will die[j]
And of a son of man who will
wither like green grass?

13 Why do you forget Jehovah
your Maker,[k]
The One who stretched out
the heavens[l] and laid the
foundation of the earth?
And all day long you were in
constant fear of the rage
of the oppressor,*
As though he were in a position to bring you to ruin.
Where, now, is the rage of
the oppressor?

14 The one bent over in chains
will soon be set free;[m]
He will not die and go into
the pit,
Nor will his bread be lacking.

15 But I am Jehovah your God,
Who stirs up the sea
and makes its waves
boisterous[n]
—Jehovah of armies is his
name.[o]

CHAP. 51
a Isa 2:3
  Mic 4:2
b Pr 6:23
c Isa 46:13
d Isa 12:2
  Isa 56:1
e 1Sa 2:10
  Isa 2:4
f Isa 60:9
g Isa 45:17
h Ps 102:25-27
  Mt 24:35
i Jer 31:33
j Isa 50:9
k Isa 45:17
  Lu 1:50
l Lu 1:51

Second Col.
a Ps 87:4
  Ps 89:10
  Isa 30:7
b Ex 15:4
  Ne 9:10, 11
  Ps 106:22
  Eze 29:3
c Ex 14:21, 22
d Ps 106:9
e Jer 31:11
  Zec 10:10
f Isa 35:10
g Isa 61:7
h Isa 25:8
  Isa 65:18, 19
i Isa 49:13
  Isa 66:13
j Ps 118:6
  Da 3:16, 17
  Mt 10:28
k Isa 44:2
l Isa 40:22
m Ezr 1:2, 3
  Isa 48:20
  Isa 52:2
n Jer 31:35, 36
  Jon 1:4
o Isa 47:4

51:5 *Or "power." **51:6** *Or "will not
be shattered." **51:7** *Or "instruction."
51:8 *Or possibly, "The worm."

51:9 *See Glossary. **51:11** *Lit., "be
upon their head." **51:13** *Or "the one
hemming you in."

16 I will put my words in your
      mouth,
   And with the shadow of my
      hand I will cover you,ᵃ
   In order to plant the heavens
      and to lay the foundation
      of the earthᵇ
   And to say to Zion, 'You are
      my people.'ᶜ
17 Awake! Awake! Rise up,
      O Jerusalem,ᵈ
   You who have drunk from
      the hand of Jehovah his
      cup of wrath.
   You have drunk the goblet;
   You have drained out the cup
      causing staggering.ᵉ
18 Not one of all the sons whom
      she bore is there to guide
      her,
   And not one of all the sons
      whom she raised has taken
      hold of her hand.
19 These two things have
      befallen you.
   Who will sympathize with
      you?
   Destruction and devastation,
      hunger and sword!ᶠ
   Who will comfort you?ᵍ
20 Your sons have fainted.ʰ
   They lie down at every street
      corner*
   Like wild sheep in the net.
   They are full of the wrath
      of Jehovah, the rebuke
      of your God."
21 So please listen to this,
      O woman afflicted and
      drunk, though not with
      wine.
22 This is what your Lord
      Jehovah says, your God
      who defends his people:
   "Look! I will take from
      your hand the cup causing
      staggering,ⁱ
   The goblet, my cup of wrath;
   You will never drink it again.ʲ

23 I will put it into the hand
      of your tormentors,ᵃ
   Those who said to you,*
      'Bow down so that we may
      walk over you!'
   So you made your back like
      the ground,
   Like a street for them to walk
      on."

52 Awake! Awake! Clothe
      yourself with strength,ᵇ
      O Zion!ᶜ
   Put on your beautiful
      garments,ᵈ O Jerusalem,
      the holy city!
   For no more will the un-
      circumcised and unclean
      one enter into you.ᵉ
2 Shake off the dust, rise and
      take a seat, O Jerusalem.
   Loosen the bonds on your
      neck, O captive daughter
      of Zion.ᶠ
3 For this is what Jehovah
      says:
   "You were sold for nothing,ᵍ
   And without money you will
      be repurchased."ʰ
4 For this is what the Sover-
      eign Lord Jehovah says:
   "At first my people went
      down to Egypt to live there
      as foreigners;
   Then As·syrʹi·a oppressed
      them without cause."
5 "What, then, should I do
      here?" declares Jehovah.
   "For my people were taken
      for nothing.
   Those ruling over them
      keep howling in triumph,"ʲ
      declares Jehovah,
   "And constantly, all day long,
      my name is treated with
      disrespect.ᵏ
6 For that reason my people
      will know my name;ˡ
   For that reason they will
      know in that day that I am
      the One speaking.
   Look, it is I!"

CHAP. 51
a De 33:27
  Ps 91:1

b Isa 65:17
  Isa 66:8, 22

c Isa 60:14
  Jer 31:33
  Zec 8:8

d Isa 52:1
  Isa 60:1

e Jer 25:15

f Eze 14:21

g La 1:17

h La 2:11

i Isa 51:17

j Isa 54:9
  Isa 62:8

Second Col.
a Isa 49:25

CHAP. 52
b Hag 2:4

c Isa 51:17

d Isa 61:3

e Isa 35:8
  Isa 60:21
  Re 21:27

f Isa 51:14
  Isa 61:1

g Isa 50:1

h Isa 45:13

i Ge 46:5-7

j Ps 137:3
  Jer 50:17

k Ps 74:10
  Ro 2:24

l Eze 20:44

51:20 *Lit., "at the head of all streets."   51:23 *Or "to your soul."

7 How beautiful on the mountains are the feet of the one bringing good news,[a]

The one proclaiming peace,[b]

The one bringing good news of something better,

The one proclaiming salvation,

The one saying to Zion: "Your God has become King!"[c]

8 Listen! Your watchmen raise their voice.

In unison they shout joyfully,

For they will see it clearly* when Jehovah gathers back Zion.

9 Become cheerful, shout joyfully in unison, you ruins of Jerusalem,[d]

For Jehovah has comforted his people;[e] he has repurchased Jerusalem.[f]

10 Jehovah has bared his holy arm before the eyes of all the nations;[g]

All the ends of the earth will see the acts of salvation* of our God.[h]

11 Turn away, turn away, get out of there,[i] touch nothing unclean![j]

Get out from the midst of her,[k] keep yourselves clean,

You who are carrying the utensils of Jehovah.[l]

12 For you will not depart in panic,

Nor will you have to flee,

For Jehovah will go ahead of you,[m]

And the God of Israel will be your rear guard.[n]

13 Look! My servant[o] will act with insight.

He will be raised up high,

He will be elevated and greatly exalted.[p]

14 Just as there were many who stared at him in amazement

—For his appearance was disfigured more than that of any other man

And his stately form more than that of mankind—

15 So he will startle many nations.[a]

Kings will shut their mouths* before him,[b]

Because they will see what they had not been told

And give consideration to what they had not heard.[c]

53 Who has put faith in the thing heard from us?*[d]

And as for the arm of Jehovah,[e] to whom has it been revealed?[f]

2 He will come up like a twig[g] before him,* like a root out of parched land.

No stately form does he have, nor any splendor;[h]

And when we see him, his appearance does not draw us to him.*

3 He was despised and was avoided by men,

A man who was meant for* pains and was familiar with sickness.

It was as if his face were hidden from us.*

He was despised, and we held him as of no account.[j]

4 Truly he himself carried our sicknesses,[k]

And he bore our pains.[l]

But we considered him as plagued, stricken by God and afflicted.

CHAP. 52

a Isa 40:9
  Na 1:15
  Ac 8:4
  Ro 10:15
  Eph 6:14, 15
b Lu 2:14
  Ac 10:36
  Eph 2:17
c Ps 93:1
  Isa 33:22
  Mic 4:7
  Mt 24:14
  Re 11:15, 17
d Isa 61:4
e Isa 66:13
f Isa 44:23
g Isa 51:9
h Ps 22:27
  Isa 49:6
i Isa 48:20
  Jer 50:8
  Jer 51:6
  Zec 2:6
j Le 5:2
  Eze 44:23
k 2Co 6:17
  Re 18:4
l Le 10:3
  Nu 3:6, 8
  Ezr 1:7
  Ezr 8:30
m Ex 13:21
  1Ch 14:15
n Isa 58:8
o Isa 42:1
  Isa 61:1
  Php 2:5-7
p Ps 2:6
  Ps 110:1
  Isa 9:6
  Mt 28:18

Second Col.

a Ps 2:2
b Ps 2:10
  Ps 72:11
c Ro 15:20, 21

CHAP. 53

d Ro 10:16
e Isa 51:9
f Isa 40:5
  Joh 12:37, 38
g Isa 11:1
  Zec 6:12
h Isa 52:14
  Joh 1:10
  Php 2:7
i Ps 22:7
  Mt 26:67, 68
  Joh 6:66
  1Pe 2:4
j Zec 11:13
  Joh 18:39, 40
  Ac 3:13, 14
  Ac 4:11
  Mt 8:14-17
k Mt 8:14-17
l Le 16:21, 22
  1Pe 2:24
  1Jo 2:1, 2

52:8 *Or "eye to eye." 52:10 *Or "the victory."

52:15 *Or "will be speechless." 53:1 *Or possibly, "in what we heard?" 53:2 *"Him" could refer to an observer in general or to God. #Or "there is no special appearance that we should desire him." 53:3 *Or "who understood." #Or possibly, "He was like someone from whom people turned their faces."

5 But he was pierced[a] for our transgression;[b]
He was crushed for our errors.[c]
He bore the punishment for our peace,[d]
And because of his wounds we were healed.[e]

6 Like sheep we have all wandered about,[f]
Each has turned his own way,
And Jehovah has caused the error of us all to meet up with him.[g]

7 He was oppressed[h] and he let himself be afflicted,[i]
But he would not open his mouth.
He was brought like a sheep to the slaughter,[j]
Like a ewe that is silent before its shearers,
And he would not open his mouth.[k]

8 Because of restraint* and judgment he was taken away;
And who will concern himself with the details of his generation?[#]
For he was cut off from the land of the living;[l]
Because of the transgression of my people he received the stroke.[△m]

9 And he was given a burial place* with the wicked,[n]
And with the rich[#] in his death,[o]
Although he had done no wrong[△]
And there was no deception in his mouth.[p]

10 But it was Jehovah's will* to crush him, and he let him become sick.

If you will present his life* as a guilt offering,[a]
He will see his offspring,[#]
he will prolong his days,[b]
And through him the delight[△] of Jehovah will have success.[c]

11 Because of his anguish,* he will see and be satisfied.
By means of his knowledge the righteous one, my servant,[d]
Will bring a righteous standing to many people,[e]
And their errors he will bear.[f]

12 For that reason I will assign him a portion among the many,
And he will apportion the spoil with the mighty,
Because he poured out his life* even to death[g]
And was counted among the transgressors;[h]
He carried the sin of many people,[i]
And he interceded for the transgressors.[j]

54 "Shout joyfully, you barren woman who has not given birth![k]
Become cheerful and cry out for joy,[l] you who never had birth pains,[m]
For the sons* of the desolate one are more numerous
Than the sons of the woman with a husband,"[#n] says Jehovah.

2 "Make the place of your tent more spacious.[o]
Stretch out the tent cloths of your grand tabernacle.
Do not hold back, lengthen your tent cords,
And make your tent pins strong.[p]

CHAP. 53
a Zec 12:10
Joh 19:34
b Da 9:24
Ro 4:25
c Mt 20:28
Ro 5:6, 19
d Col 1:19, 20
e 1Pe 2:24
f 1Pe 2:25
g 1Pe 3:18
h Ps 22:12
Ps 69:4
i 1Pe 2:23
j Joh 1:29
1Co 5:7
k Mt 27:12-14
Ac 8:32, 33
l Da 9:26
Mt 27:50
m Zec 13:7
Joh 11:49, 50
Ro 5:6
Heb 9:26
n Mt 27:38
o Mt 27:57-60
Mr 15:46
Joh 19:41
p 1Pe 2:22

Second Col.
a Le 16:11
2Co 5:21
Heb 7:27
b Isa 9:7
1Ti 6:16
c Col 1:19, 20
d Isa 42:1
e Ro 5:18, 19
f 1Pe 2:24
g Ps 22:14
Mt 26:27, 28
Heb 2:14
h Mr 15:27
Lu 22:37
Lu 23:32, 33
i Mt 20:28
1Ti 2:5, 6
Tit 2:13, 14
Heb 9:28
j Ro 8:34
Heb 7:25
Heb 9:26
1Jo 2:1, 2

CHAP. 54
k Isa 62:4
l Isa 44:23
Isa 49:13
m Isa 66:7, 8
n Ga 4:26, 27
o Isa 49:20
p Isa 33:20

53:8 *Or "oppression." #Or "his manner of life?" △Or "was struck dead." 53:9 *Or "And one will give his burial place." #Lit., "a rich man." △Or "no violence." 53:10 *Or "But Jehovah took delight."

53:10, 12 *Or "soul." 53:10 #Lit., "seed." △Or "will; good pleasure." 53:11 *Or "the trouble of his soul." 54:1 *Or "children." #Or "master."

3 For you will spread out to the right and to the left.
Your offspring will take possession of nations,
And they will inhabit the desolated cities.[a]

4 Do not be afraid,[b] for you will not be put to shame;[c]
And do not feel humiliated, for you will not be disappointed.
For you will forget the shame of your youth,
And the disgrace of your widowhood you will remember no more."

5 "For your Grand Maker[d] is as your husband,*[e]
Jehovah of armies is his name,
And the Holy One of Israel is your Repurchaser.[f]
He will be called the God of the whole earth.[g]

6 For Jehovah called you as if you were an abandoned wife and grief-stricken,*[h]
Like a wife married in youth and then rejected," says your God.

7 "For a brief moment I abandoned you,
But with great mercy I will gather you back.[i]

8 In a flood of indignation I hid my face from you for a moment,[j]
But with everlasting loyal love I will have mercy on you,"[k] says your Repurchaser,[l] Jehovah.

9 "This is like the days of Noah to me.[m]
Just as I have sworn that the waters of Noah will no more cover the earth,[n]
So I swear that I will no more become indignant toward you or rebuke you.[o]

10 For the mountains may be removed
And the hills may be shaken,
But my loyal love will not be removed from you,[a]
Nor will my covenant of peace be shaken,"[b] says Jehovah, the One having mercy on you.[c]

11 "O afflicted woman,[d] storm-tossed, uncomforted,[e]
I am laying your stones with hard mortar
And your foundation with sapphires.[f]

12 I will make your battlements of rubies,
Your gates of sparkling stones,*
And all your boundaries of precious stones.

13 And all your sons* will be taught by Jehovah,[g]
And the peace of your sons* will be abundant.[h]

14 You will be firmly established in righteousness.[i]
You will be far removed from oppression,[j]
You will fear nothing and have no cause for terror,
For it will not come near you.[k]

15 If anyone should attack you, It will not be at my orders.
Whoever makes an attack on you will fall because of you."[l]

16 "Look! I myself created the craftsman,
Who blows on the charcoal fire,
And his work produces a weapon.
I myself also created the destructive man to bring ruin.[m]

17 No weapon formed against you will have any success,[n]

CHAP. 54

a Isa 49:8
  Eze 36:35

b Isa 41:10

c Isa 61:7

d Isa 44:2

e Eze 16:8
  Ho 2:16

f Isa 44:6

g Zec 14:9
  Ro 3:29

h Isa 49:14
  Isa 62:4

i De 30:1, 3
  Ps 30:5
  Ps 106:47
  Isa 27:12
  Jer 29:10

j Isa 47:6
  Eze 39:23

k Isa 55:3

l Isa 48:17
  Isa 49:26

m Ge 7:23

n Ge 8:21

o Jer 31:35, 36
  Eze 39:29

Second Col.

a Isa 51:6

b Isa 55:3

c Isa 14:1

d Isa 52:2

e La 1:2, 17

f Re 21:19

g Jer 31:34
  Joh 6:45

h Ps 119:165
  Isa 66:12
  Jer 33:6

i Isa 1:26
  Isa 60:21

j Isa 52:1

k Jer 23:4
  Zep 3:13

l Eze 38:16, 22
  Zec 2:8
  Zec 12:3

m Isa 10:5

n Ps 2:2, 4
  Isa 41:12

54:5 *Or "master." 54:6 *Lit., "hurt in spirit."

54:12 *Or "of stones of fire." 54:13 *Or "children."

And you will condemn
any tongue that rises up
against you in the
judgment.
This is the heritage* of the
servants of Jehovah,
And their righteousness
is from me," declares
Jehovah.[a]

55 Come, all you thirsty
ones,[b] come to the
water![c]
You with no money, come,
buy and eat!
Yes, come, buy wine and
milk[d] without money and
without cost.[e]

2 Why do you keep paying
out money for what is not
bread,
And why spend your
earnings* for what brings
no satisfaction?
Listen intently to me, and
eat what is good,[f]
And you* will find great delight in what is truly rich.[Δg]

3 Incline your ear and come
to me.[h]
Listen, and you* will keep
alive,
And I will readily make
with you an everlasting
covenant[i]
In harmony with the expressions of loyal love to David,
which are faithful.*[j]

4 Look! I made him a witness[k]
to the nations,
A leader[l] and commander[m]
to the nations.

5 Look! You will call a nation
that you do not know,
And those of a nation who
have not known you will
run to you
For the sake of Jehovah
your God,[n] the Holy One
of Israel,

Because he will glorify you.[a]

6 Search for Jehovah while he
may be found.[b]
Call to him while he is near.[c]

7 Let the wicked man leave
his way[d]
And the evil man his
thoughts;
Let him return to Jehovah,
who will have mercy
on him,[e]
To our God, for he will
forgive in a large way.*[f]

8 "For my thoughts are not
your thoughts,[g]
And your ways are not my
ways," declares Jehovah.

9 "For as the heavens are
higher than the earth,
So my ways are higher than
your ways
And my thoughts than your
thoughts.[h]

10 For just as the rain and
the snow pour down from
heaven
And do not return there until
they saturate the earth,
making it produce and
sprout,
Giving seed to the sower
and bread to the eater,

11 So my word that goes out
of my mouth will be.*[i]
It will not return to me
without results,[j]
But it will certainly
accomplish whatever is
my delight,*[k]
And it will have sure success
in what I send it to do.

12 For you will go out with
rejoicing,[l]
And in peace you will be
brought back.[m]
The mountains and the hills
will become cheerful be-
fore you with a joyful cry,[n]
And the trees of the field
will all clap their hands.[o]

CHAP. 54
a Jer 23:6

CHAP. 55
b Ps 42:2
Ps 63:1
Am 8:11
Mt 5:6

c Isa 41:17

d Joe 3:18

e Re 21:6
Re 22:17

f Isa 25:6

g Ps 36:7, 8
Ps 63:5

h Jas 4:8

i Isa 61:8

j 2Sa 7:8, 16
2Sa 23:5
Ps 89:28, 29
Jer 33:25, 26
Ac 13:34

k Re 1:5
Re 3:14

l Da 9:25
Mt 23:10

m Ge 49:10

n Zec 8:23

Second Col.
a Isa 49:3
Isa 60:9

b 1Ch 28:9

c Ps 145:18
Jas 4:8

d Eze 18:21
Ac 3:19

e Ex 34:6
2Ch 33:12, 13

f Nu 14:18
Ps 103:12, 13
Isa 43:25

g Ps 40:5

h Ps 103:11

i Nu 23:19
Isa 46:11

j Jos 23:14
Isa 45:23

k Ps 135:6
Isa 46:10

l Isa 35:10

m Isa 54:13
Isa 66:12

n Isa 42:11

o Isa 44:23

54:17 *Or "inheritance." 55:2 *Or
"hard-earned money." 55:2, 3 *Or
"your soul." 55:2 Δ Lit., "in fatness."
55:3 *Or "trustworthy; reliable."

55:7 *Or "will freely forgive." 55:11
*Or "will prove to be." *Or "my will."

13 Instead of thornbushes the juniper tree will grow,[a]
And instead of the stinging nettle the myrtle tree will grow.
And it will bring fame to* Jehovah,[b]
An everlasting sign that will never perish."

56 This is what Jehovah says:
"Uphold justice,[c] and do what is righteous,
For my salvation will soon come
And my righteousness will be revealed.[d]

2 Happy is the man who does this
And the son of man who holds fast to it,
Who keeps the Sabbath and does not profane it[e]
And who holds his hand back from any kind of evil.

3 The foreigner who joins himself to Jehovah[f] should not say,
'Jehovah will surely separate me from his people.'
And the eunuch should not say, 'Look! I am a dried-up tree.'"

4 For this is what Jehovah says to the eunuchs who keep my sabbaths and who choose what I delight in and who hold fast to my covenant:

5 "I will give to them in my house and within my walls a monument and a name,
Something better than sons and daughters.
An everlasting name I will give them,
One that will not perish.

6 As for the foreigners who join themselves to Jehovah to minister to him,
To love the name of Jehovah[g]
And to be his servants,
All those who keep the Sabbath and do not profane it
And who hold fast to my covenant,

7 I will also bring them to my holy mountain[a]
And make them rejoice inside my house of prayer.
Their whole burnt offerings and their sacrifices will be accepted on my altar.
For my house will be called a house of prayer for all the peoples."[b]

8 The Sovereign Lord Jehovah, who is gathering the dispersed ones of Israel,[c] declares:
"I will gather to him others besides those already gathered."[d]

9 All you wild animals of the field, come to eat,
All you wild animals in the forest.[e]

10 His watchmen are blind,[f] none of them have taken note.[g]
All of them are speechless dogs, unable to bark.[h]
They are panting and lying down; they love to slumber.

11 They are dogs with a voracious appetite;*
They are never satisfied.
They are shepherds who have no understanding.[i]
They have all gone their own way;
Every last one of them seeks his own dishonest gain and says:

12 "Come, let me take some wine,
And let us drink our fill of alcohol.[j]
And tomorrow will be like today, only far better!"

CHAP. 55
a Isa 41:19
  Isa 60:13

b Jer 33:9

CHAP. 56
c Mic 6:8

d Isa 46:13
  Isa 51:5

e Isa 58:13, 14

f Isa 60:10
  Zec 8:23

g Mal 1:11

Second Col.
a Isa 2:3
  Mic 4:2
  Zec 8:3

b 1Ki 8:29, 43
  Mt 21:13
  Mr 11:17
  Lu 19:46

c De 30:3
  Isa 27:12
  Ho 1:11

d Isa 49:22
  Isa 60:4

e Jer 12:9

f Isa 6:10
  Isa 29:10

g Jer 6:13, 14
  Eze 13:16

h Eze 33:6

i Mic 3:6

j Isa 5:22
  Isa 28:7
  Ho 4:11

55:13 *Or "will make a name for."

56:11 *Or "with a strong soul."

57 The righteous one has perished,
But no one takes it to heart.
Loyal men are taken away,*[a]
With no one discerning that the righteous one has been taken away
Because of# the calamity.

2 He enters into peace.
They rest on their beds,*
all who walk uprightly.

3 "But as for you, come closer,
You sons of a sorceress,
You children of an adulterer and a prostitute.

4 Whom are you making fun of?
Against whom do you open your mouth wide and stick out your tongue?
Are you not the children of transgression,
The children of deceit,[b]

5 Those who are inflamed with passion among big trees,[c]
Under every luxuriant tree,[d]
Who slaughter the children in the valleys,*[e]
Under the clefts of the crags?

6 With the smooth stones of the valley* is your portion.[f]
Yes, these are your lot.
Even to them you pour out drink offerings and offer gifts.[g]
Should I be satisfied# with these things?

7 On a mountain high and lofty you prepared your bed,[h]
And you went up there to offer sacrifice.[i]

8 Behind the door and the doorpost you set up your memorial.
You left me and uncovered yourself;
You went up and made your bed spacious.

And you made a covenant with them.
You loved sharing their bed,[a]
And you gazed at the male organ.*

9 You went down to Mel'ech* with oil
And with an abundance of perfume.
You sent your envoys far off,
So that you descended to the Grave.#

10 You have toiled in following your many ways,
But you did not say, 'It is hopeless!'
You found renewed strength.
That is why you do not give up.*

11 Whom did you dread and fear
So that you started to lie?[b]
You did not remember me.[c]
You took nothing to heart.[d]
Have I not kept silent and withdrawn?*[e]
So you showed no fear of me.

12 I will make known your 'righteousness'[f] and your works,[g]
And they will not benefit you.[h]

13 When you cry for help,
Your collection of idols will not rescue you.[i]
A wind will carry all of them away,
A mere breath will blow them away,
But the one who takes refuge in me will inherit the land
And will take possession of my holy mountain.[j]

14 It will be said, 'Build up, build up a road! Prepare the way![k]

CHAP. 57
a Mic 7:2

b Isa 1:4
Isa 30:9

c Isa 1:29

d De 12:2
1Ki 14:22, 23

e 2Ki 16:1, 3
Jer 7:31

f Jer 3:9

g Jer 7:18

h Jer 2:20
Eze 16:16
Eze 23:17

i Eze 20:28

Second Col.
a Eze 16:25, 33
Eze 23:18

b Isa 30:9, 10
Isa 59:3

c Isa 1:3
Jer 2:32
Jer 9:3

d Isa 42:24, 25

e Ps 50:21

f Isa 58:2

g Isa 66:3

h Jer 7:4
Mic 3:4

i Jg 10:14
Isa 42:17

j Isa 56:6, 7
Isa 66:20
Eze 20:40
Joe 3:17

k Isa 35:8
Isa 40:3
Isa 62:10

57:1 *That is, in death. #Or possibly, "From." **57:2** *That is, in the grave. **57:5** *Or "wadis." **57:6** *Or "wadi." #Or "Should I comfort myself." **57:8** *Possibly referring to idolatrous worship. **57:9** *Or possibly, "the king." #Or "Sheol," that is, the common grave of mankind. See Glossary. **57:10** *Lit., "grow weary." **57:11** *Or "and hidden matters?"

Remove any obstacle from
the way of my people.'"

15 For this is what the High
and Lofty One says,
Who lives* forever*[a] and
whose name is holy:[b]
"I reside in the high and holy
place,[c]
But also with those crushed
and lowly in spirit,
To revive the spirit of the
lowly
And to revive the heart
of those being crushed.[d]

16 For I will not oppose them
forever
Or always remain indignant;[e]
For a man's spirit would
grow feeble because
of me,[f]
Even the breathing creatures
that I have made.

17 I was indignant at his sinful
pursuit of dishonest gain,[g]
So I struck him, I hid my
face, and I was indignant.
But he kept walking as
a renegade,[h] following the
way of his heart.

18 I have seen his ways,
But I will heal him[i] and
lead him[j]
And restore* comfort to him[k]
and to his mourning ones."[l]

19 "I am creating the fruit of the
lips.
Continuous peace will be
given to the one who is far
away and the one who is
near,"[m] says Jehovah,
"And I will heal him."

20 "But the wicked are like the
restless sea that cannot
calm down,
And its waters keep tossing
up seaweed and mire.

21 There is no peace," says my
God, "for the wicked."[n]

CHAP. 57
a Ge 21:33
  Ps 90:2
  Isa 40:28
  1Ti 1:17

b Ex 15:11
  Lu 1:46, 49

c 1Ki 8:27

d Ps 34:18
  Ps 147:3
  Isa 61:1
  Isa 66:2

e Ps 103:9
  Mic 7:18

f Job 34:14, 15

g Jer 6:13
  Jer 8:10

h Jer 3:14

i Jer 33:6
  Ho 14:4

j Isa 49:10

k Isa 12:1

l Isa 61:2
  La 1:4

m Isa 48:18
  Eph 2:17

n Pr 13:9
  Isa 3:11

Second Col.

CHAP. 58
a Isa 1:2
  Isa 31:6
  Isa 59:13

b Isa 29:13
  Eze 33:32

c Isa 1:14, 15

d Mal 3:14

e Le 16:29

f Jer 34:15, 16
  Mic 3:2-4

58 "Call out full-throated;
do not hold back!
Raise your voice like a horn.
Proclaim to my people their
revolt,[a]
To the house of Jacob their
sins.

2 They seek me day after day,
And they express delight to
know my ways,
As if they were a nation that
had practiced righteous-
ness
And had not abandoned the
justice of their God.[b]
They ask me for righteous
judgments,
Delighting to draw close to
God:[c]

3 'Why do you not see when
we fast?[d]
And why do you not
notice when we afflict
ourselves?'*[e]
Because on the day of your
fast, you pursue your own
interests,#
And you oppress your
laborers.[f]

4 Your fasting ends in quarrels
and fights,
And you strike with the fist
of wickedness.
You cannot fast as you do
today and have your voice
heard in heaven.

5 Should the fast that I choose
be like this,
As a day for someone to
afflict himself,*
To bow down his head like
a rush,
To make his bed on sackcloth
and ashes?
Is this what you call a fast
and a day pleasing
to Jehovah?

6 No, this is the fast that
I choose:

57:15 *Or "resides." **57:18** *Or "make
compensation with."

58:3 *Or "our soul?" #Or "delight."
58:5 *Or "his soul."

To remove the fetters of
　wickedness,
To untie the bands of the
　yoke bar,[a]
To let the oppressed go free,[b]
And to break in half every
　yoke bar;

7 It is to share your bread with
　the hungry,[c]
To bring the poor and home-
　less into your house,
To clothe someone naked
　when you see him,[d]
And not to turn your back
　on your own flesh.

8 Then your light will shine
　through like the dawn,[e]
And your healing will spring
　up quickly.
Your righteousness will go
　before you,
And the glory of Jehovah
　will be your rear guard.[f]

9 Then you will call, and
　Jehovah will answer;
You will cry for help, and he
　will say, 'Here I am!'
If you remove from among
　you the yoke bar
And stop pointing your
　finger and speaking
　maliciously,[g]

10 If you grant to the hungry
　what you yourself desire*[g]
And satisfy those who are
　afflicted,"
Then your light will shine
　even in the darkness,
And your gloom will be like
　midday.[i]

11 Jehovah will always lead you
And satisfy you* even in
　a parched land;[j]
He will invigorate your
　bones,
And you will become like
　a well-watered garden,[k]
Like a spring whose waters
　never fail.

12 They will rebuild ancient
　ruins on your account,[a]
And you will restore
　the foundations of past
　generations.[b]
You will be called the repair-
　er of the broken walls,*[c]
The restorer of roadways
　by which to dwell.

13 If because of the Sabbath
　you refrain* from pursuing
　your own interests" on my
　holy day[d]
And you call the Sabbath
　an exquisite delight, a holy
　day of Jehovah, a day to be
　glorified,[e]
And you glorify it rather
　than pursuing your own
　interests and speaking idle
　words,

14 Then you will find your ex-
　quisite delight in Jehovah,
And I will make you ride
　on the high places of the
　earth.[f]
I will cause you to eat from*
　the inheritance of Jacob
　your forefather,[g]
For the mouth of Jehovah
　has spoken."

59 Look! The hand of
　　Jehovah is not too
　short to save,[h]
Nor is his ear too dull*
　to hear.[i]

2 No, your own errors have
　separated you from your
　God.[j]
Your sins have made him
　hide his face from you,
And he refuses to hear you.[k]

3 For your palms are polluted
　with blood[l]
And your fingers with error.
Your lips speak lies,[m]
　and your tongue mutters
　unrighteousness.

CHAP. 58
a Jer 34:8, 9
b Pr 28:27
c Ps 41:1
　Ps 112:9
　Pr 19:17
　Pr 22:9
d Eze 18:7, 8
　Jas 2:15, 16
　1Jo 3:17
e Pr 4:18
f Ex 14:19
　Isa 52:12
g Isa 32:6
　Isa 59:3
h De 15:7, 8
i Ps 37:5, 6
j Isa 49:10
k Isa 61:11
　Jer 31:12

Second Col.
a Ne 2:5
　Jer 31:38
b Isa 61:4
c Ne 6:1
　Am 9:11, 14
d Ne 13:15
　Isa 56:2
　Jer 17:21
e De 5:12-14
f De 32:13
g Ps 105:10, 11
　Jer 3:18

CHAP. 59
h Nu 11:23
　Isa 50:2
i Ps 116:1
j Jer 5:25
k De 31:16, 17
　De 32:20
　Isa 57:17
　Eze 39:23
　Mic 3:4
l Isa 1:15
　Jer 2:34
　Eze 7:23
m Jer 7:9, 10
　Eze 13:8

58:10 *Or "your own soul desires."
"Or "the afflicted souls." **58:11** *Or
"your soul." **58:12** *Lit., "the breach." **58:13** *Lit.,
"turn your foot back." "Or "your own
delights." **58:14** *Or "to enjoy." **59:1**
*Lit., "heavy."

4 No one calls out for
   righteousness,[a]
And no one goes to court
   in truthfulness.
They trust in unreality*[b] and
   speak what is worthless.
They conceive trouble and
   give birth to what is
   harmful.[c]
5 They hatch the eggs of a
   poisonous snake,
And they weave the cobweb
   of a spider.[d]
Anyone who eats their eggs
   would die,
And the egg that is crushed
   hatches a viper.
6 Their cobweb will not
   serve as a garment,
Nor will they cover
   themselves with what
   they make.[e]
Their works are harmful,
And deeds of violence are
   in their hands.[f]
7 Their feet run to do evil,
And they hurry to shed
   innocent blood.[g]
Their thoughts are harmful
   thoughts;
Ruin and misery are in
   their ways.[h]
8 They have not known the
   way of peace,
And there is no justice in
   their tracks.[i]
They make their roadways
   crooked;
No one treading on them
   will know peace.[j]
9 That is why justice is far
   away from us,
And righteousness does not
   overtake us.
We keep hoping for light, but
   look! there is darkness;
For brightness, but we keep
   walking in gloom.[k]
10 We grope for the wall like
   blind men;

59:4 *Or "emptiness."

Like those without eyes we
   keep groping.[a]
We stumble at high noon as
   in evening darkness;
Among the strong we are
   just like the dead.
11 We all keep growling like
   bears
And cooing mournfully like
   doves.
We hope for justice, but
   there is none;
For salvation, but it is far
   away from us.
12 For our revolts are many
   before you;[b]
Each of our sins testifies
   against us.[c]
For our revolts are with us;
We well know our errors.[d]
13 We have transgressed and
   denied Jehovah;
We have turned our backs
   on our God.
We have spoken of
   oppression and revolt;[e]
We have conceived lies
   and muttered false words
   from the heart.[f]
14 Justice is driven back,[g]
And righteousness stands
   far off;[h]
For truth* has stumbled in
   the public square,
And what is upright is unable
   to enter.
15 Truth* has vanished,[i]
And anyone who turns away
   from bad is plundered.
Jehovah saw this and was
   displeased,[#]
For there was no justice.[j]
16 He saw that there was no
   man,
And he was astonished that
   no one interceded,
So his own arm brought
   about salvation,*

59:14, 15 *Or "honesty." 59:15 #Lit.,
"and it was bad in his eyes." 59:16 *Or
"victory for him."

CHAP. 59

a Jer 5:1
  Eze 22:30
  Mic 7:2

b Isa 30:12, 13

c Mic 2:1

d Job 8:13, 14

e Isa 57:12

f Jer 6:7
  Mic 6:12

g Jer 22:17
  Eze 9:9
  Mt 23:35

h Ro 3:15-17

i Isa 5:7
  Isa 59:15
  Jer 5:1
  Am 6:12
  Hab 1:4

j Jer 8:15

k Isa 5:30

Second Col.

a De 28:15, 29

b Isa 1:5
  Eze 5:5, 6

c Jer 14:7
  Ho 5:5

d Ezr 9:13
  Ne 9:33
  Da 9:5

e Isa 31:6
  Isa 32:6
  Jer 17:13

f Jer 5:23

g Ps 82:2
  Hab 1:4

h Isa 5:22, 23

i Isa 48:1

j Mic 3:2

And his own righteousness
   supported him.
17 Then he put on righteousness like a coat of mail
And the helmet of salvation*
   on his head.[a]
He put on the garments of
   vengeance as his clothing[b]
And wrapped himself with
   zeal like a coat.#
18 He will reward them for what
   they have done:[c]
Wrath to his adversaries, retribution to his enemies.[d]
And to the islands he will
   repay their due.
19 From the sunset they will
   fear the name of Jehovah
And from the sunrise his
   glory,
For he will come in like
   a rushing river,
Which the spirit of Jehovah
   drives along.
20 "To Zion the Repurchaser[e]
   will come,[f]
To those in Jacob who
   turn from transgression,"[g]
   declares Jehovah.

21 "As for me, this is my covenant with them,"[h] says Jehovah.
"My spirit that is on you and
my words that I have placed in
your mouth—they will not be removed from your mouth, from
the mouth of your children,* or
from the mouth of your grandchildren,"# says Jehovah, "from
now on and forever."

60 "Arise, O woman,[i] shed
      light, for your light has
   come.
The glory of Jehovah shines
   on you.[j]
2 For look! darkness will cover
   the earth
And thick gloom the nations;
But on you Jehovah will
   shine,

CHAP. 59
a Eph 6:17
1Th 5:8
b De 32:35
Ps 94:1
c Job 34:11
Ps 62:12
Jer 17:10
d Isa 1:24
La 4:11
Eze 5:13
e Isa 48:17
f Isa 62:11
g De 30:1-3
Ro 11:26
h Ro 11:27
CHAP. 60
i Isa 51:17
Isa 52:1
j Isa 60:19, 20
Second Col.
a Isa 11:10
b Isa 49:23
c Re 21:23, 24
d Isa 49:17, 18
Isa 54:1
e Isa 49:21, 22
f Jer 33:9
g Isa 61:6
Hag 2:7, 8
h 1Ch 1:32, 33
i Mal 1:11
j Isa 42:11
k Ge 25:13
l Ex 29:39, 42
Isa 56:6, 7
m Hag 2:9
n Isa 51:5

And on you his glory will
   be seen.
3 Nations will go to your light[a]
And kings[b] to your shining
   splendor.*[c]
4 Raise your eyes and look
   all around you!
They have all been
   assembled; they are
   coming to you.
From far away your sons
   keep coming,[d]
And your daughters being
   supported on the hip.[e]
5 At that time you will see
   and become radiant,[f]
And your heart will throb
   and overflow,
Because the wealth of the
   sea will be directed to you;
The resources of the nations
   will come to you.[g]
6 Throngs of camels will cover
   your land,*
Young male camels of
   Mid′i·an and E′phah.[h]
All those from She′ba—they
   will come;
Gold and frankincense they
   will carry.
They will proclaim the
   praises of Jehovah.
7 All the flocks of Ke′dar[i]
   will be gathered to you.
The rams of Ne·ba′ioth[k]
   will serve you.
They will come on my altar
   with approval,[l]
And I will beautify my
   glorious house.*[m]
8 Who are these that fly along
   like clouds,
Like doves to their dove-
   cotes?*
9 For in me the islands will
   hope;[n]
The ships of Tar′shish are
   in the lead,*

59:17 *Or "victory." #Or "sleeveless
coat." 59:21 *Lit., "seed." #Lit., "of
the seed of your seed."

60:3 *Or "to the brightness of your
dawn." 60:6 *Lit., "you." 60:7 *Or
"my house of beauty." 60:8 *Or "to the
openings in the birdhouse?" 60:9 *Or
"as at the first."

To bring your sons from far
away,[a]

Along with their silver and
their gold,

To the name of Jehovah your
God and to the Holy One
of Israel,

For he will glorify* you.[b]

10 Foreigners will build your
walls,

And their kings will minister
to you,[c]

For in my indignation
I struck you,

But in my favor* I will have
mercy on you.[d]

11 Your gates will be kept open
constantly;[e]

They will not be closed
by day or by night,

To bring to you the
resources of the nations,

And their kings will take
the lead.[f]

12 For any nation and any
kingdom that will not
serve you will perish,

And the nations will be
utterly devastated.[g]

13 To you the glory of Leb′a·non
will come,[h]

The juniper tree, the ash
tree, and the cypress
together,[i]

To beautify the place of my
sanctuary;

I will glorify the place for
my feet.[j]

14 The sons of those who
oppressed you will come
and bow down before you;

All those treating you
disrespectfully must bow
down at your feet,

And they will have to call
you the city of Jehovah,

Zion of the Holy One of
Israel.[k]

15 Instead of your being abandoned and hated, with
nobody passing through,[a]

I will make you a source
of everlasting pride,

A cause for rejoicing
throughout all
generations.[b]

16 And you will actually drink
the milk of nations,[c]

At the breast of kings you
will nurse;[d]

And you will certainly know
that I, Jehovah, am your
Savior,

And the Powerful One
of Jacob is your
Repurchaser.[e]

17 Instead of the copper I will
bring in gold,

And instead of the iron I will
bring in silver,

Instead of the wood, copper,

And instead of the stones,
iron;

And I will appoint peace as
your overseers

And righteousness as your
task assigners.[f]

18 No more will violence be
heard in your land

Or destruction and ruin
within your boundaries.[g]

And you will call your walls
Salvation[h] and your gates
Praise.

19 For you the sun will no
longer be a light by day,

Nor will the shining of the
moon give you light,

For Jehovah will become
to you an eternal light,[i]

And your God will be your
beauty.[j]

20 No more will your sun set,

Nor will your moon wane,

For Jehovah will become
for you an eternal light,[k]

And the days of your mourning will have ended.[l]

21 And all your people will be
righteous;

CHAP. 60

a Isa 60:4
  Isa 66:20

b Ps 149:4
  Isa 52:1
  Isa 55:5

c Ezr 7:27
  Ne 2:7, 8
  Isa 49:23

d De 30:3
  Ps 30:5
  Isa 54:7
  Isa 57:17, 18

e Re 21:25, 26

f Isa 60:3, 5

g Isa 41:11

h Isa 35:1, 2

i Isa 41:19
  Isa 55:13

j Ps 132:7

k Isa 62:12

Second Col.

a 2Ch 36:20, 21
  Isa 49:14
  Jer 30:17
  La 1:4

b Isa 35:10
  Isa 61:7
  Jer 33:10, 11

c Isa 61:6

d Isa 49:23

e Isa 49:26

f Isa 1:26
  Isa 32:1

g Isa 2:4
  Isa 11:9
  Isa 54:14
  Zec 9:8

h Isa 26:1

i Ps 36:9
  Isa 60:1
  Re 21:23
  Re 22:5

j Zec 2:4, 5

k Ps 27:1
  Ps 84:11

l Isa 25:8
  Isa 30:19
  Isa 35:10

60:9 *Or "beautify." 60:10 *Or "goodwill."

They will possess the land
    forever.
They are the sprout that
    I planted,
The work of my hands,[a]
    for me to be beautified.[b]
22 The little one will become
    a thousand
And the small one a mighty
    nation.
I myself, Jehovah, will speed
    it up in its own time."

61 The spirit of the Sovereign Lord Jehovah
        is upon me,[c]
Because Jehovah anointed
    me to declare good news
    to the meek.[d]
He sent me to bind up the
    brokenhearted,
To proclaim liberty to the
    captives
And the wide opening of
    the eyes to the prisoners,[e]
2 To proclaim the year of
    Jehovah's goodwill*
And the day of vengeance
    of our God,[f]
To comfort all who mourn,[g]
3 To provide for those
    mourning over Zion,
To give them a headdress
    instead of ashes,
The oil of exultation instead
    of mourning,
The garment of praise
    instead of a despondent
    spirit.
And they will be called big
    trees of righteousness,
The planting of Jehovah,
    in order to glorify* him.[h]
4 They will rebuild the ancient
    ruins;
They will raise up the desolated places of the past,[i]
And they will restore the
    devastated cities,[j]
The places that lay desolate
    for generation after
    generation.[k]

5 "Strangers will stand and
    shepherd your flocks,
And foreigners[a] will be
    your farmers and your
    vinedressers.[b]
6 As for you, you will be called
    the priests of Jehovah;[c]
They will call you the
    ministers of our God.
You will eat the resources
    of the nations,[d]
And about their glory*
    you will boast.
7 Instead of shame you will
    have a double portion,
And instead of humiliation
    they will shout joyfully
    over their share.
Yes, they will possess a double portion in their land.[e]
Everlasting rejoicing will be
    theirs.[f]
8 For I, Jehovah, love justice;[g]
I hate robbery and
    unrighteousness.[h]
I will faithfully give them
    their wages,
And I will make an everlasting covenant with them.[i]
9 Their offspring* will be
    known among the nations[j]
And their descendants
    among the peoples.
All who see them will
    recognize them,
That they are the offspring*
    whom Jehovah has
    blessed."[k]
10 I will greatly exult in
    Jehovah.
My whole being* will
    rejoice in my God.[l]
For he has clothed me with
    the garments of salvation;[m]
He has wrapped me with the
    robe[#] of righteousness,
Just like a bridegroom who
    wears a turban like that
    of a priest,[n]

CHAP. 60
a Isa 43:6, 7
b Isa 44:23

CHAP. 61
c Isa 42:1
  Mt 3:16
d Mt 11:4, 5
  Ac 10:37, 38
e Lu 4:17-21
  Lu 7:22
  Ac 26:17, 18
f Isa 34:8
g Isa 25:8
  Mt 5:4
  Lu 6:21
h Isa 60:21
i Isa 49:8
  Isa 51:3
j Isa 44:26
  Isa 58:12
k Eze 36:33, 34

Second Col.
a Isa 60:10
b Isa 14:1, 2
c Ex 19:6
d Isa 23:17, 18
  Isa 60:5, 7
e Zec 9:12
f Isa 35:10
g De 32:4
  Ps 33:5
  Ps 37:28
h Pr 6:16-19
i Isa 55:3
  Jer 32:40
j Zec 8:13
k Isa 65:23
l Isa 65:13
m Isa 52:1
  Re 21:2
n Ex 28:39, 41

61:2 *Or "favor." 61:3 *Or "beautify."

61:6 *Or "riches." 61:9 *Lit., "seed." 61:10 *Or "My soul." #Or "sleeveless coat."

And like a bride who adorns herself with her ornaments.

11 For as the earth brings forth its sprouts
And as the garden makes what is sown in it sprout,
So will the Sovereign Lord Jehovah
Cause righteousness[a] and praise to sprout[b] before all the nations.

62 For the sake of Zion I will not keep silent,[c]
And for the sake of Jerusalem I will not keep still
Until her righteousness shines like a bright light[d]
And her salvation burns like a torch.[e]

2 "The nations will see your righteousness, O woman,[f]
And all kings your glory.[g]
And you will be called by a new name,[h]
Which Jehovah's own mouth will designate.

3 You will become a crown of beauty in the hand of Jehovah,
A royal turban in the palm of your God.

4 No more will you be called an abandoned woman,[i]
And your land will no longer be called desolate.[j]
But you will be called My Delight Is in Her,[k]
And your land will be called the Married One.
For Jehovah will take delight in you,
And your land will be as one married.

5 For just as a young man marries a virgin,
Your sons will marry you.
With the rejoicing of a bridegroom over a bride,
Your God will rejoice over you.[l]

6 Upon your walls, O Jerusalem, I have commissioned watchmen.
Continuously, all day long and all night long, they should not be silent.
You who make mention of Jehovah,
Do not rest,

7 And do not give him any rest until he firmly establishes Jerusalem,
Yes, until he makes her the praise of the earth."[a]

8 Jehovah has sworn an oath with his right hand, with his strong arm:
"I will no longer give your grain as food to your enemies,
Nor will foreigners drink your new wine, for which you have toiled.[b]

9 But those gathering it will eat it and they will praise Jehovah;
And those collecting it will drink it in my holy courtyards."[c]

10 Pass through, pass through the gates.
Clear the way for the people.[d]
Build up, build up the highway.
Rid it of stones.[e]
Raise up a signal* for the peoples.[f]

11 Look! Jehovah has proclaimed to the ends of the earth:
"Say to the daughter of Zion,
'Look! Your salvation is coming.[g]
Look! His reward is with him,
And the wage he pays is before him.'"[h]

12 They will be called the holy people, those repurchased by Jehovah,[i]

CHAP. 61
a Isa 45:8
  Isa 62:1

b Isa 58:11
  Isa 60:18
  Isa 62:7

CHAP. 62
c Ps 102:13
  Zec 2:12

d Isa 1:26

e Isa 51:5

f Isa 54:1
  Isa 60:1

g Isa 49:23
  Isa 60:11

h Jer 33:16

i Isa 49:14
  Isa 54:6

j Isa 32:14

k Ps 149:4
  Zep 3:17

l Isa 65:18, 19
  Jer 32:41

Second Col.
a Isa 61:11
  Jer 33:9
  Zep 3:19, 20

b De 28:49-51
  Jer 5:17

c De 14:23
  Isa 65:21, 22

d Isa 40:3
  Isa 48:20

e Isa 57:14

f Ezr 1:1, 3
  Isa 11:12
  Isa 49:22

g Zec 9:9
  Mt 21:5
  Joh 12:15

h Isa 40:9, 10
  Re 22:12

i Ps 107:2, 3

62:10 *Or "signal pole."

And you will be called
Sought After, a City
Not Abandoned.[a]

63 Who is this coming from
E'dom,[b]
From Boz'rah[c] with bright-
colored* garments,
This one with splendid
clothing,
Marching in his great power?
"It is I, the One speaking in
righteousness,
The One with great power
to save."

2 Why is your clothing red,
And why are your garments
like those of one treading
the winepress?[d]

3 "I have trodden the wine
trough alone.
No one from the peoples
was with me.
I kept treading them in my
anger,
And I kept trampling them
in my wrath.[e]
My garments were spattered
with their blood,
And I have stained all my
clothing.

4 For the day of vengeance
is in my heart,[f]
And the year of my repur-
chased ones has come.

5 I looked, but there was no
one to help;
I was appalled that no one
offered support.
So my arm brought me
salvation,*[g]
And my own wrath
supported me.

6 I trampled peoples in my
anger,
I made them drunk with
my wrath[h]
And poured out their blood
on the ground."

7 I will mention Jehovah's acts
of loyal love,

The praiseworthy acts
of Jehovah,
Because of all that Jehovah
has done for us,[a]
The many good things he
has done for the house
of Israel,
According to his mercy and
his great loyal love.

8 For he said: "Surely they are
my people, sons who will
not be disloyal."*[b]
So he became their Savior.[c]

9 During all their distress it
was distressing to him.[d]
And his own personal
messenger* saved them.[e]
In his love and compassion
he repurchased them,[f]
And he lifted them up and
carried them all the days
of old.[g]

10 But they rebelled[h] and
grieved his holy spirit.[i]
He then turned into their
enemy,[j]
And he fought against them.[k]

11 And they remembered the
days of old,
The days of Moses his
servant:
"Where is the One who
brought them up out of
the sea[l] with the shepherds
of his flock?[m]
Where is the One who put
within him His holy spirit,[n]

12 The One who made His
glorious arm go with the
right hand of Moses,[o]
The One who split the waters
before them[p]
To make an everlasting name
for himself,[q]

13 The One who made them
walk through the surging
waters,*
So that they walked without
stumbling,

63:8 *Or "prove false."   63:9 *Or "the
angel of his presence."   63:13 *Or
"deep waters."

CHAP. 62
a Isa 54:7

CHAP. 63
b Ps 137:7
   Isa 34:5, 6

c Am 1:12

d Joe 3:13
   Re 14:19, 20
   Re 19:15

e Isa 34:2

f Isa 34:8
   Isa 35:4
   Isa 61:1, 2

g Isa 51:9
   Isa 52:10
   Isa 59:16

h Jer 25:15, 16

Second Col.
a Ps 78:12
   Ps 105:5

b Ex 24:7

c Ex 14:30

d Ex 3:7

e Ex 14:19
   Ex 23:20

f De 7:8

g Ex 19:4
   De 1:31

h De 9:7

i Ac 7:51
   Eph 4:30

j Le 26:14, 17
   De 28:63

k Jer 21:5

l Ex 14:30
   Isa 51:10

m Ps 77:20

n Nu 11:16, 17

o Ex 6:1, 6
   Ex 15:16

p Ex 14:21, 22

q Ex 9:15, 16
   Ex 14:17
   Ro 9:17

Like a horse in the open
country?*

14 Just like livestock when they
go down into the valley
plain,

The spirit of Jehovah made
them rest."[a]

This is how you led your
people,

To make a majestic* name
for yourself.[b]

15 Look down from heaven
and see

From your lofty abode of
holiness and glory.*

Where are your zeal and
your mightiness,

The stirring of your
compassions*[c] and
your mercy?[d]

They are withheld from me.

16 For you are our Father;[e]

Although Abraham may not
know us

And Israel may not
recognize us,

You, O Jehovah, are our
Father.

Our Repurchaser of long ago
is your name.[f]

17 Why do you, O Jehovah,
let us* wander from
your ways?

Why do you let* our hearts
become hard, so that
we do not fear you?[g]

Return, for the sake of
your servants,

The tribes of your
inheritance.[h]

18 Your holy people possessed
it for a short time.

Our adversaries have trampled on your sanctuary.[i]

19 For too long we have become
like those you never ruled
over,

Like those never called by
your name.

64 If only you had ripped the
heavens apart and come
down,

So that the mountains would
quake because of you,

2 As when a fire ignites the
brushwood,

And the fire makes the water
boil,

Then your name would be
known to your adversaries,

And the nations would
tremble before you!

3 When you did awe-inspiring
things that we dared not
hope for,[a]

You came down, and the
mountains quaked before
you.[b]

4 From of old no one has heard
or given ear,

Nor has any eye seen a God
except you,

Who acts in behalf of those
who keep in expectation
of* him.[c]

5 You have met up with those
who joyfully do what is
right,[d]

Those who remember you
and follow your ways.

Look! You became indignant,
while we kept sinning,[e]

We did so for a long time.

Should we now be saved?

6 And we have all become like
someone unclean,

And all our acts of
righteousness are like
a menstrual cloth.[f]

We will all wither like a leaf,

And our errors will carry us
off like the wind.

7 There is no one calling on
your name,

No one who stirs himself
to take hold of you,

CHAP. 63
a Jos 22:4

b 2Sa 7:23
Ne 9:10

c Jer 31:20

d De 4:31
Ne 9:17

e Ex 4:22

f Isa 41:14

g Isa 6:10

h Ps 74:2
Ps 80:14, 15

i 2Ch 36:19
Isa 64:11
La 1:10

Second Col.

CHAP. 64
a Ex 34:10

b Hab 3:6

c Ps 130:6-8
Isa 25:9
Mic 7:7
1Co 2:9

d Zep 2:3
Ac 10:34, 35

e Isa 1:21
Isa 63:10

f Le 12:2
Le 15:20

63:13 *Or "the wilderness?" 63:14
*Or "beautiful." 63:15 *Or "beauty."
#Lit., "The agitation of your inward
parts." 63:17 *Or "cause us to." #Lit.,
"make."

64:4 *Or "patiently wait for."

For you have hidden your
face from us,[a]
And you cause us to waste
away* because of[#] our
error.

8 But now, O Jehovah, you
are our Father.[b]
We are the clay, and you
are our Potter;*[c]
We are all the work of your
hand.

9 Do not become too
indignant, O Jehovah,[d]
And do not remember our
error forever.
Look at us, please, for we are
all your people.

10 Your holy cities have become
a wilderness.
Zion has become a
wilderness,
Jerusalem a wasteland.[e]

11 Our house* of holiness
and glory,[#]
Where our forefathers
praised you,
Has been burned with fire,[f]
And all the things we
cherished lie in ruins.

12 In view of this, will you
still restrain yourself,
O Jehovah?
Will you remain silent and
let us be afflicted so
severely?[g]

65 "I have let myself be
searched for by those
who did not ask for me;
I have let myself be found
by those who did not look
for me.[h]
I said, 'Here I am, here I am!'
to a nation that was not
calling on my name.[i]

2 I have spread out my hands
all day long to a stubborn
people,[j]

To those walking in the way
that is not good,[a]
Following their own
thoughts;[b]

3 A people who constantly
offend me to my face,[c]
Sacrificing in gardens[d] and
making sacrificial smoke
on bricks.

4 They sit among graves,[e]
And they pass the night
in hidden places,*
Eating the flesh of pigs,[f]
And the broth of foul[#] things
is in their vessels.[g]

5 They say, 'Keep to yourself;
do not approach me,
For I am holier than you.'*
These are a smoke in my
nostrils, a fire burning all
day long.

6 Look! It is written before me;
I will not stand still,
But I will repay them,[h]
I will repay them in full
measure*

7 For their errors and for the
errors of their forefathers
as well,"[i] says Jehovah.
"Because they have made
sacrificial smoke on the
mountains
And have reproached me
on the hills,[j]
I will first measure out their
wages in full."*

8 This is what Jehovah says:
"Just as when new wine is
found in a cluster of grapes
And someone says, 'Do not
destroy it, for there is
some good* in it,'
So I will do for the sake
of my servants;
I will not destroy them all.[k]

9 I will bring out of Jacob
an offspring*

CHAP. 64

a De 31:17
Isa 57:17

b Isa 63:16

c Isa 29:16
Isa 45:9
Jer 18:6

d Ps 74:1
Ps 79:5

e Ps 79:1
La 1:4
La 5:18
Mic 3:12

f 2Ch 36:17, 19
Jer 52:12, 13

g Ps 74:10, 11
Zec 1:12

CHAP. 65

h Isa 55:6, 7

i Ro 10:20, 21

j De 31:27
Ne 9:29
Zec 7:11

Second Col.

a Isa 59:7, 8
Jer 35:15

b Jer 5:23

c 2Ki 17:16, 17
Jer 32:29

d Isa 1:29
Isa 66:17

e Nu 19:16

f Le 11:7, 8
Isa 66:17

g De 14:3

h Ps 50:3, 21
Jer 16:18
Eze 11:21

i Ex 20:4, 5
Le 26:39

j 1Ki 22:41, 43
2Ki 12:3

k Jer 30:11
Am 9:8

64:7 *Lit., "to melt." [#]Lit., "by the
hand of." 64:8 *Or "the One who
formed us." 64:11 *Or "temple." [#]Or
"beauty." 65:4 *Or possibly, "in watch huts."
[#]Or "unclean." 65:5 *Or possibly, "For
I will convey my holiness to you." 65:6,
7 *Lit., "into their bosom." 65:8 *Lit.,
"a blessing." 65:9 *Lit., "a seed."

And out of Judah the one
to inherit my mountains;[a]
My chosen ones will take
possession of it,
And my servants will reside
there.[b]

10 Shar'on[c] will become a
pasture for sheep
And the Valley* of A'chor[d]
a resting-place for cattle,
For my people who search
for me.

11 But you are among those
forsaking Jehovah,[e]
Those forgetting my holy
mountain,[f]
Those setting a table for
the god of Good Luck,
And those filling up cups
of mixed wine for the god
of Destiny.

12 So I will destine you for
the sword,[g]
And all of you will bow down
to be slaughtered,[h]
Because I called, but you did
not answer,
I spoke, but you did not
listen;[i]
You kept doing what was bad
in my eyes,
And you chose what
displeased me."[j]

13 Therefore this is what the
Sovereign Lord Jehovah
says:
"Look! My servants will eat,
but you will go hungry.[k]
Look! My servants will
drink,[l] but you will go
thirsty.
Look! My servants will
rejoice,[m] but you will
suffer shame.[n]

14 Look! My servants will
shout joyfully because
of the good condition
of the heart,
But you will cry out because
of the pain of heart

And you will wail because
of a broken spirit.

15 You will leave behind a name
that my chosen ones will
use as a curse,
And the Sovereign Lord
Jehovah will put each
of you to death,
But his own servants he will
call by another name;[a]

16 So that anyone who seeks
a blessing for himself in
the earth
Will be blessed by the God
of truth,*
And anyone who swears
an oath in the earth
Will swear by the God of
truth.*[b]
For the former distresses[#]
will be forgotten;
They will be concealed from
my eyes.[c]

17 For look! I am creating new
heavens and a new earth;[d]
And the former things will
not be called to mind,*
Nor will they come up into
the heart.[e]

18 So exult and be joyful for-
ever in what I am creating.
For look! I am creating
Jerusalem a cause for joy
And her people a cause for
exultation.[f]

19 And I will rejoice in Jerusalem and exult in my
people;[g]
No more will there be heard
in her the sound of weep-
ing or a cry of distress."[h]

20 "No more will there be an
infant from that place who
lives but a few days,
Nor an old man who fails to
live out his days.
For anyone who dies
at a hundred will be
considered a mere boy,

CHAP. 65
a Isa 60:21
  Eze 37:21
  Ob 17

b Isa 61:7
  Zep 3:20

c Isa 33:9

d Jos 7:24
  Ho 2:15

e Isa 1:4

f 2Ch 28:24
  2Ch 34:25

g Le 26:25
  Eze 6:13

h Eze 9:6

i 2Ch 36:15, 16

j Isa 66:3

k Ps 37:19, 25
  Am 8:11

l Isa 49:10

m Isa 66:14

n Isa 66:5

Second Col.
a Isa 62:2
  Jer 33:16

b De 6:13

c Isa 12:1
  Jer 31:12
  Zep 3:14, 15

d Ezr 5:2
  Isa 51:16
  Isa 66:22
  2Pe 3:13

e Re 21:1, 4

f Isa 51:11

g Isa 62:4
  Jer 32:41

h Isa 25:8
  Jer 31:12

65:10 *Or "Low Plain."

65:16 *Or "faithfulness." Lit., "Amen."
Or "troubles." 65:17 *Or "be remem-
bered."

And the sinner will be
cursed, even though he is
a hundred years of age.*

21 They will build houses and
live in them,[a]

And they will plant vineyards
and eat their fruitage.[b]

22 They will not build for
someone else to inhabit,

Nor will they plant for others
to eat.

For the days of my people
will be like the days of
a tree,[c]

And the work of their hands
my chosen ones will enjoy
to the full.

23 They will not toil* for
nothing,[#d]

Nor will they bear children
for distress,

Because they are the
offspring△ made up of
those blessed by Jehovah,[e]

And their descendants
with them.[f]

24 Even before they call out,
I will answer;

While they are yet speaking,
I will hear.

25 The wolf and the lamb
will feed together,

The lion will eat straw
just like the bull,[g]

And the serpent's food
will be dust.

They will do no harm
nor cause any ruin in
all my holy mountain,"[h]
says Jehovah.

66 This is what Jehovah says:

"The heavens are my
throne, and the earth
is my footstool.[i]

Where, then, is the house
that you could build
for me,[j]

And where is my resting-
place?"[a]

2 "My own hand has made
all these things,

And this is how they all came
to be," declares Jehovah.[b]

"To this one, then, I will look,

To the one humble and
broken in spirit who
trembles at* my word.[c]

3 The one slaughtering the
bull is like one striking
down a man.[d]

The one sacrificing a sheep
is like one breaking the
neck of a dog.[e]

The one offering a gift—like
the blood of a pig![f]

The one presenting a
memorial offering of
frankincense[g] is like one
saying a blessing with
magical words.*[h]

They have chosen their
own ways,

And they take delight[#]
in what is disgusting.

4 So I will choose ways to
punish them,[i]

And the very things they
dread I will bring upon
them.

Because when I called,
no one answered;

When I spoke, there were
none who listened.[j]

They kept doing what was
bad in my eyes,

And they chose to do what
displeased me."[k]

5 Hear the word of Jehovah,
you who tremble at*
his word:

"Your brothers who hate you
and exclude you because
of my name said, 'May
Jehovah be glorified!'[l]

CHAP. 65
a Jer 31:4

b Isa 62:8
  Am 9:14

c Ps 92:12-14

d Le 26:3-5
  De 28:4

e Isa 61:9

f Isa 66:22

g Isa 35:9
  Ho 2:18

h Isa 2:3, 4
  Isa 11:6-9
  Mic 4:2

CHAP. 66
i Mt 5:34, 35

j 2Ch 6:18
  Ac 17:24

Second Col.
a 1Ch 28:2
  Ac 7:48-50

b Isa 40:26

c 2Ki 22:18, 19
  Lu 18:14

d Isa 1:11

e Le 11:27

f De 14:8

g Le 2:1, 2

h Isa 1:13

i De 28:15

j Jer 7:13

k 2Ki 21:9
  Isa 65:3

l Isa 5:18, 19
  Isa 29:13

65:20 *Or possibly, "And the one who
falls short of a hundred will be considered cursed." 65:23 *Or "work hard."
#Or "in vain." △Lit., "seed."

66:2 *Or "is anxious about." 66:3 *Or
possibly, "one praising an idol." #Or
"their soul takes delight." 66:5 *Or
"are anxious about."

But He will appear and bring you joy,
And they are the ones who will be put to shame."[a]

6 There is a sound of uproar from the city, a sound from the temple!
It is the sound of Jehovah repaying his enemies what they deserve.

7 Before she went into labor, she gave birth.[b]
Before birth pangs came to her, she delivered a male child.

8 Who has ever heard of such a thing?
Who has seen such things?
Will a land be brought to birth in one day?
Or will a nation be born all at once?
Yet, as soon as Zion went into labor, she gave birth to her sons.

9 "Will I bring it to the point of birth and then not bring it forth?" says Jehovah.
"Or would I cause the birth and then shut the womb?" says your God.

10 Rejoice with Jerusalem and be joyful with her,[c] all you who love her.[d]
Exult greatly with her, all you who are in mourning over her,

11 For you will nurse and be fully satisfied from her breast of consolation,
And you will drink deeply and find delight in the abundance of her glory.

12 For this is what Jehovah says:
"Here I am extending to her peace just like a river[e]
And the glory of nations like a flooding torrent.[f]
You will nurse and be carried on the hip,
And you will be bounced on the knees.

13 As a mother comforts her son,
So I will keep comforting you;[a]
And over Jerusalem you will be comforted.[b]

14 You will see this, and your heart will rejoice,
Your bones will flourish just like new grass.
And the hand* of Jehovah will become known to his servants,
But he will denounce his enemies."[c]

15 "For Jehovah will come as a fire,[d]
And his chariots are like a storm wind,[e]
To repay in furious anger,
To rebuke with flames of fire.[f]

16 For with fire Jehovah will execute judgment,
Yes, with his sword, against all flesh;*
And the slain of Jehovah will be many.

17 "Those sanctifying themselves and cleansing themselves to enter the gardens*[g] following one who is in the center, those eating the flesh of pigs[h] and loathsome things and mice,[i] they will all come to their end together," declares Jehovah. 18 "Since I know about their works and their thoughts, I am coming to gather people of all nations and languages, and they will come and see my glory."

19 "I will set a sign among them, and I will send some of those who escape to the nations—to Tar′shish,[j] Pul, and Lud,[k] those who draw the bow,

---

CHAP. 66
a Isa 65:13, 14
  Jer 17:13, 18
b Isa 54:1
c Isa 44:23
d Ps 137:6
e Isa 9:7
f Isa 60:3
  Hag 2:7

Second Col.
a Isa 51:3
b Isa 44:28
  Isa 65:18, 19
c Isa 59:18
d De 4:24
e Ps 50:3
  Jer 25:32, 33
f 2Th 1:7, 8
g Isa 1:29
  Isa 65:3
h Le 11:7, 8
  Isa 65:4
i Le 11:29
j Ge 10:4
k Ge 10:6, 13

66:14 *Or "power." 66:16 *Or "all humans." 66:17 *That is, special gardens used in idol worship.

to Tu′bal and Ja′van,[a] and to the faraway islands—who have not heard a report about me or seen my glory; and they will proclaim my glory among the nations.[b] **20** They will bring all your brothers out of all the nations[c] as a gift to Jehovah, on horses, in chariots, in covered wagons, on mules, and on swift camels, up to my holy mountain, Jerusalem," says Jehovah, "just as when the people of Israel bring their gift in a clean vessel into the house of Jehovah."

21 "I will also take some for the priests and for the Levites," says Jehovah.

22 "For just as the new heavens and the new earth[d] that I am making will remain standing before me," declares Jehovah, "so your offspring* and your name will remain."[a]

23 "And from new moon to new moon and from sabbath to sabbath,
All flesh* will come in to bow down before# me,"[b] says Jehovah.

24 "And they will go out and look on the carcasses of the men who rebelled against me;
For the worms on them will not die,
And their fire will not be extinguished,[c]
And they will become something repulsive to all people."*

CHAP. 66

a Ge 10:2
  Eze 27:12, 13

b Isa 60:3
  Mal 1:11

c De 30:1-3
  Isa 11:16
  Isa 43:6
  Isa 60:4, 9

d Isa 65:17, 18
  2Pe 3:13
  Re 21:1

Second Col.

a Isa 65:23
  Jer 31:35, 36

b Ps 86:9
  Zec 14:16
  Mal 1:11

c Isa 34:10
  Mt 25:41
  Mr 9:47, 48
  2Ti 1:9

66:22 *Lit., "seed." **66:23** *Or "all humans." #Or "to worship." **66:24** *Lit., "all flesh."

JEREMIAH

OUTLINE OF CONTENTS

1

These are the words of Jeremiah* the son of Hil·ki′ah,[a] one of the priests in An′a·thoth[b] in the land of Benjamin. **2** The word of Jehovah came to him in the days of Jo·si′ah[b] the son of A′mon,[a] the king of Judah, in the 13th year of his reign. **3** It came also in the days of Je·hoi′a·kim[b] the son of Jo·si′ah, the king of Judah, until the completion of the 11th year of Zed·e·ki′ah[c] the son of Jo·si′ah, the king of Judah, until Jerusalem went into exile in the fifth month.[d]

CHAP. 1
a Jos 21:8, 18
b 2Ki 22:1, 2

Second Col.
a 2Ki 21:19, 20
b 2Ki 24:1
2Ch 36:4
c 2Ki 24:18, 19
d 2Ki 25:8, 11
Jer 52:12, 15

1:1 *Possibly meaning "Jehovah Exalts."

4 The word of Jehovah came to me, saying:

5 "Before I formed you in the womb I knew* you,[a]
And before you were born# I sanctified you.△[b]
I made you a prophet to the nations."

6 But I said: "Alas, O Sovereign Lord Jehovah!
I do not know how to speak,[c] for I am just a boy."*[d]

7 Jehovah then said to me: "Do not say, 'I am just a boy.'
For you must go to all those to whom I send you,
And you should say everything that I command you.[e]

8 Do not be afraid because of their appearance,[f]
For 'I am with you to save you,'[g] declares Jehovah."

9 Then Jehovah stretched out his hand and touched my mouth.[h] And Jehovah said to me: "I have put my words in your mouth.[i] **10** See, I have commissioned you this day to be over the nations and over the kingdoms, to uproot and to pull down, to destroy and to tear down, to build and to plant."[j]

11 The word of Jehovah again came to me, saying: "What do you see, Jeremiah?" So I said: "I see the branch of an almond tree."*

12 Jehovah said to me: "You have seen correctly, for I am wide awake concerning my word to carry it out."

13 The word of Jehovah came to me a second time, saying: "What do you see?" So I said: "I see a boiling* pot,# and its mouth is tilted away from the north." **14** Then Jehovah said to me:

"Out of the north the calamity will break loose
Against all the inhabitants of the land.[a]

15 For 'I am summoning all the families of the kingdoms of the north,' declares Jehovah,[b]
'And they will come; each one will set up his throne
At the entrance of the gates of Jerusalem,[c]
Against her walls all around
And against all the cities of Judah.[d]

16 And I will declare my judgments against them over all their wickedness,
Because they have abandoned me,[e]
And they are making sacrificial smoke to other gods[f]
And bowing down to the works of their own hands.'[g]

17 But you should prepare for action,*
And you must stand up and tell everything that I command you.
Do not be terrified of them,[h]
So that I do not terrify you before them.

18 For today I have made you a fortified city,
An iron pillar, and copper walls against all the land,[i]
Toward the kings of Judah and her princes,
Toward her priests and the people of the land.[j]

19 And they will certainly fight against you,
But they will not prevail against you,*
For 'I am with you,'[k] declares Jehovah, 'to save you.'"

CHAP. 1
a Jg 13:5
Ps 139:15, 16

b Lu 1:13, 15

c Ex 4:10

d 1Ki 3:5, 7

e Ex 7:1, 2

f Eze 2:6

g Ex 3:11, 12
Jer 15:20
Ac 18:9, 10

h Isa 6:7

i Ex 4:12, 15
Eze 33:7

j Jer 18:7-10
Jer 24:5, 6

Second Col.
a Jer 6:1
Jer 10:22

b Jer 5:15
Jer 6:22
Jer 25:9

c Jer 39:3

d De 28:52
Jer 34:22
Jer 44:6

e Jos 24:20
2Ki 22:17
2Ch 7:19, 20

f Eze 8:10, 11
Ho 11:2

g Isa 2:8

h Eze 2:6

i Jer 15:20
Jer 20:11
Eze 3:8
Mic 3:8

j Jer 26:12

k Ge 28:15
Ex 3:12
Jos 1:5

1:5 *Or "chose." #Lit., "before you came out of the womb." △Or "set you apart." **1:6** *Or "young person." **1:11** *Lit., "an awakening one." **1:13** *Lit., "blown upon," indicating a fanned fire underneath. #Or "wide-mouthed cooking pot." **1:17** *Lit., "gird up your hips." **1:19** *Or "defeat you."

2 The word of Jehovah came to me, saying: **2** "Go and proclaim in the ears of Jerusalem, 'This is what Jehovah says:

"I well remember the devotion* of your youth,[a]
The love you showed when you were engaged to marry,[b]
How you followed me in the wilderness,
In a land not sown with seed.[c]

3 Israel was holy to Jehovah,[d] the firstfruits of his harvest."'

'Anyone devouring him would become guilty.
Disaster would come upon them,' declares Jehovah."[e]

4 Hear the word of Jehovah, O house of Jacob,
And all you families of the house of Israel.

5 This is what Jehovah says:
"What fault did your forefathers find in me,[f]
So that they strayed so far from me,
And they walked after worthless idols[g] and became worthless themselves?[h]

6 They did not ask, 'Where is Jehovah,
The One who brought us out of the land of Egypt,[i]
Who led us through the wilderness,
Through a land of deserts[j] and pits,
Through a land of drought[k] and of deep shadow,
Through a land where no man travels
And where no humans dwell?'

7 I then brought you to a land of orchards,
To eat its fruitage and its good things.[l]

But you came in and defiled my land;
You made my inheritance something detestable.[a]

8 The priests did not ask, 'Where is Jehovah?'[b]
Those handling the Law did not know me,
The shepherds rebelled against me,[c]
The prophets prophesied by Ba′al,[d]
And they followed those who could bring no benefit.

9 'So I will contend further with you,'[e] declares Jehovah,
'And I will contend with the sons of your sons.'

10 'But cross over to the coastlands* of the Kit′tim[f] and see.
Yes, send to Ke′dar[g] and consider carefully;
See whether anything like this has happened.

11 Has a nation ever changed its gods for those that are not gods?
But my own people have exchanged my glory for what is useless.[h]

12 Stare in amazement at this, you heavens;
Shudder in absolute horror,' declares Jehovah,

13 'Because my people have done two bad things:
They have abandoned me, the source of living water,[i]
And dug* for themselves cisterns,
Broken cisterns, that cannot hold water.'

14 'Is Israel a servant or a slave born in the household?
Then why has he been given over to plunder?

CHAP. 2
a Ho 2:15

b Ex 24:3

c De 2:7

d Ex 19:6
   De 7:6

e Ex 17:8, 13

f Isa 5:4
   Mic 6:3

g De 32:21

h Ps 115:4, 8

i Ex 14:30

j De 1:1
   De 32:9, 10

k De 8:14, 15

l Nu 13:26, 27
   De 6:10, 11
   De 8:7-9

Second Col.
a Le 18:24
   Nu 35:33
   Ps 78:58
   Ps 106:38
   Jer 16:18

b 1Sa 2:12
   La 4:13

c Eze 34:7, 8

d 1Ki 18:19
   Jer 23:13

e Eze 20:35
   Mic 6:2

f Ge 10:2, 4

g Ge 25:13
   Ps 120:5
   Jer 49:28

h Ps 106:20

i Ps 36:9
   Jer 17:13
   Re 22:1

2:2 *Or "loyal love." 2:10 *Or "islands." 2:13 *Or "hewed out," likely from rock.

15 Against him young lions*
   roar;[a]
   They have raised their voice.
   They made his land an object
   of horror.
   His cities have been set on
   fire, so that there is no
   inhabitant.
16 The people of Noph*[b] and
   Tah·pan·es[c] feed on the
   crown of your head.
17 Have you not brought this
   on yourself
   By abandoning Jehovah
   your God[d]
   While he was leading you in
   the way?
18 Now why do you wish for
   the way to Egypt[e]
   To drink the waters of
   Shi'hor?*
   Why do you wish for the way
   to As·syr'i·a[f]
   To drink the waters of the
   River?#
19 Your wickedness should
   correct you,
   And your own unfaithfulness
   should reprove you.
   Know and realize how bad
   and bitter it is[g]
   To abandon Jehovah your
   God;
   You have shown no fear
   of me,'[h] declares the
   Sovereign Lord, Jehovah
   of armies.
20 'For long ago I smashed your
   yoke[i]
   And tore off your shackles.
   But you said: "I am not going
   to serve,"
   For on every high hill and
   under every luxuriant tree[j]
   You were lying sprawled out,
   prostituting yourself.[k]
21 I planted you as a choice red
   vine,[l] all of it pure seed;

So how have you turned into
   the degenerate shoots of a
   foreign vine before me?'[a]
22 'Though you should wash
   with soda* and use much
   lye,#
   Your guilt would still be a
   stain before me,'[b] declares
   the Sovereign Lord
   Jehovah.
23 How can you say, 'I have not
   defiled myself.
   I have not followed the
   Ba'als'?
   Look at your way in the
   valley.
   Consider what you have
   done.
   You are like a swift, young
   she-camel,
   Aimlessly running back and
   forth in her ways,
24 A wild donkey accustomed
   to the wilderness,
   Sniffing the wind in her lust.*
   Who can restrain her when
   she is in heat?
   None of those looking for
   her will need to weary
   themselves.
   In her season# they will find
   her.
25 Keep your feet from going
   bare
   And your throat from thirst.
   But you said, 'It is hopeless![c]
   No! I have fallen in love with
   strangers,*[d]
   And I will follow them.'[e]
26 Like the shame of a thief
   when he is caught,
   So the house of Israel has
   been put to shame,
   They, their kings and their
   princes,
   Their priests and their
   prophets.[f]
27 They say to a tree, 'You are
   my father,'[g]

CHAP. 2

a Isa 5:29
  Jer 4:7

b Jer 46:19

c Jer 43:4, 7
  Jer 46:14
  Eze 30:18

d 1Ch 28:9
  2Ch 7:19, 20

e Isa 30:2
  Isa 31:1
  La 5:6
  Eze 16:26
  Eze 17:15

f 2Ki 16:7
  Ho 5:13

g Jer 4:18

h Jer 5:22

i Le 26:13

j 1Ki 14:22, 23
  Eze 6:13

k Ex 34:15
  Eze 16:15, 16

l Ex 15:17
  Ps 80:8
  Isa 5:1

Second Col.

a Isa 5:4

b Jer 16:17

c Jer 18:12

d Isa 2:6
  Jer 3:13

e Jer 44:17

f Ezr 9:7

g Isa 44:13

2:15 *Or "maned young lions." 2:16
*Or "Memphis." 2:18 *That is, a
branch of the Nile River. #That is, the
Euphrates.

2:22 *Or "alkali." #Or "soap." 2:24
*Or "at the craving of her soul." #Lit.,
"her month." 2:25 *Or "foreign gods."

And to a stone, 'You gave
   birth to me.'
But to me they turn their
   back and not their face.[a]
And in the time of their
   calamity they will say,
   'Rise up and save us!'[b]
28 Now where are your gods
   that you made for yourself?[c]
Let them rise up if they can
   save you in your time of
   calamity,
For your gods have become
   as numerous as your cities,
   O Judah.[d]
29 'Why do you keep contending
   against me?
Why have all of you rebelled
   against me?'[e] declares
   Jehovah.
30 I have struck your sons
   in vain.[f]
They would accept no
   discipline;[g]
Your own sword devoured
   your prophets,[h]
Like a marauding lion.
31 O generation, consider
   for yourselves the word
   of Jehovah.
Have I become like a
   wilderness to Israel
Or a land of oppressive
   darkness?
Why have these, my people,
   said, 'We roam freely.
We will come to you no
   more'?[i]
32 Can a virgin forget her
   ornaments,
A bride her breastbands?*
And yet my own people have
   forgotten me for countless
   days.[j]
33 How skillfully, O woman,
   you set your course to
   seek love!
You have trained yourself in
   the ways of wickedness.[k]

34 Even your skirts are stained
   with the blood of the
   innocent poor ones,*[a]
Though I did not find them
   in the act of breaking in;
It is on all your skirts.[b]
35 But you say, 'I am innocent.
Surely his anger has turned
   back from me.'
Now I am bringing judgment
   against you
Because you say, 'I have not
   sinned.'
36 Why do you treat so lightly
   your unstable course?
You will become ashamed
   of Egypt too,[c]
Just as you became ashamed
   of As·syr'i·a.[d]
37 For this reason also you will
   go out with your hands on
   your head,[e]
For Jehovah has rejected
   those in whom you put
   confidence;
They will not bring you
   success."

3 People ask: "If a man sends
   his wife away and she leaves
   him and becomes another man's,
   should he return to her anymore?"

Has that land not been
   utterly polluted?[f]
"You have committed
   prostitution with many
   companions,[g]
And should you now return
   to me?" declares Jehovah.
2 "Raise your eyes to the bare
   hills and see.
Where have you not been
   raped?
You sat along the roadways
   for them,
Like a nomad* in the wilderness.
You keep polluting the land

2:32 *Or "her wedding sash?"

2:34 *Or "souls." 3:2 *Lit., "an A·ra·bian."

CHAP. 2
a 2Ch 29:6
  Jer 32:33

b Jg 10:13-15
  Ps 78:34
  Ps 106:47
  Isa 26:16
  Ho 5:15

c De 32:37, 38

d Jer 11:13

e Jer 5:1
  Jer 9:2
  Da 9:11

f 2Ch 28:20-22
  Isa 9:13

g Isa 1:5
  Jer 5:3
  Zep 3:2

h 2Ch 36:15, 16
  Ne 9:26
  Ac 7:52

i De 32:15

j Ps 106:21
  Isa 17:10
  Jer 18:15
  Ho 8:14

k 2Ch 33:9

Second Col.
a 2Ki 21:16
  Ps 106:38
  Isa 10:1, 2
  Mt 23:35

b Ex 22:2

c Isa 30:3
  Jer 37:7

d 2Ch 28:20, 21

e 2Sa 13:19

CHAP. 3
f Isa 24:5
  Jer 2:7

g Jer 2:20
  Eze 16:28, 29

With your prostitution and
your wickedness.ᵃ

3 So showers of rain are
withheld,ᵇ
And there is no rain in the
spring.
You have the brazen look*
of a wife who commits
prostitution;
You refuse to feel shame.ᶜ

4 But now you call out to me,
'My Father, you are the companion of my youth!ᵈ

5 Should one stay resentful
forever,
Or always hold a grudge?'
This is what you say,
But you keep doing all the
evil you are capable of
doing."ᵉ

6 In the days of King Jo·si′-
ah,ᶠ Jehovah said to me: "'Have
you seen what unfaithful Israel
has done? She has gone up on
every high mountain and underneath every luxuriant tree to
commit prostitution.ᵍ 7 Even
after she did all these things, I
kept telling her to return to me,ʰ
but she did not return; and Judah kept watching her treacherous sister.ⁱ 8 When I saw that,
I sent unfaithful Israel away
with a full certificate of di-
vorceʲ because of her adultery.ᵏ
But her treacherous sister Judah
did not become afraid; she too
went out and committed prosti-
tution.ˡ 9 She took her prostitution lightly, and she kept polluting the land and committing
adultery with stones and with
trees.ᵐ 10 Despite all this, her
treacherous sister Judah did not
return to me with all her heart,
only in pretense,' declares Jehovah."

11 Jehovah then said to me:
"Unfaithful Israel has shown
herself* to be more righ-

CHAP. 3

a Eze 16:16
  Eze 20:28

b Le 26:19
  Jer 14:4
  Am 4:7

c Jer 6:15

d Jer 2:2

e Mic 2:1
  Mic 7:3

f 2Ki 22:1

g Eze 20:28
  Ho 4:13

h 2Ki 17:13
  2Ch 30:6
  Ho 14:1

i Eze 16:46
  Eze 23:2, 4

j De 24:1

k Eze 23:4, 5, 9
  Ho 2:2
  Ho 9:15

l 2Ki 17:19
  Eze 23:4, 11

m Isa 57:5, 6
  Jer 2:27

Second Col.

a Eze 16:51
  Eze 23:4, 11

b 2Ki 17:6
  Jer 23:8

c Jer 4:1
  Eze 33:11
  Ho 14:1

d Ho 11:8, 9

e Jer 23:3

f Jer 23:4
  Eze 34:23

g Ho 1:10

h Ps 87:3
  Eze 43:7

i Isa 2:2, 3
  Isa 56:6, 7
  Isa 60:3
  Mic 4:1, 2
  Zec 2:11
  Zec 8:22, 23

j Jer 50:4
  Eze 37:19
  Ho 1:11

k 2Ch 36:23
  Ezr 1:3
  Am 9:15

teous than treacherous Judah.ᵃ
12 Go and proclaim these words
to the north:ᵇ
"'"Return, O renegade Israel,"
declares Jehovah.'ᶜ '"I will not
look down angrily* on you,ᵈ for
I am loyal," declares Jehovah.' '"I
will not stay resentful forever.
13 Only acknowledge your guilt,
for you have rebelled against Jehovah your God. You continued scattering your favors* to
strangers# under every luxuriant
tree, but you would not obey my
voice," declares Jehovah.'"

14 "Return, you renegade
sons," declares Jehovah. "For I
have become your true master;*
and I will take you, one from a
city and two from a fami-
ly, and I will bring you to Zion.ᵉ
15 And I will give you shepherds after my own heart,ᶠ and
they will feed you with knowledge and insight. 16 You will
become many and will bear fruit
in the land in those days," declares Jehovah.ᵍ "No more will
they say, 'The ark of the covenant of Jehovah!' It will not
come up into the heart, nor will
they remember it or miss it, and
it will not be made again. 17 At
that time they will call Jerusalem the throne of Jehovah;ʰ and
all the nations will be brought
together to the name of Jehovah
at Jerusalem,ⁱ and they will no
longer stubbornly follow their
own wicked heart."

18 "In those days they will
walk together, the house of Judah alongside the house of Israel,ʲ and together they will come
from the land of the north
into the land that I gave to
your forefathers as an inheri-
tance.ᵏ 19 And I thought, 'How
I placed you among the sons
and gave you the desirable land,

3:12 *Lit., "make my face fall." 3:13
*Lit., "ways." #Or "foreign gods."
3:14 *Or possibly, "your husband."

the most beautiful inheritance among the nations!'*[a] I also thought that you would call me, 'My Father!' and that you would not turn away from following me. **20** 'Truly as a wife treacherously leaves her husband,* so also you, O house of Israel, have dealt treacherously with me,'[b] declares Jehovah."

21 On the bare hills a sound is heard,
The weeping and the pleading of the people of Israel,
For they have distorted their way;
They have forgotten Jehovah their God.[c]

22 "Return, you renegade sons.
I will heal your renegade condition."[d]
"Here we are! We have come to you,
For you, O Jehovah, are our God.[e]

23 Truly the hills and the turmoil on the mountains are a delusion.[f]
Truly in Jehovah our God is the salvation of Israel.[g]

24 But the shameful thing* has consumed the toil of our forefathers since our youth,[h]
Their flocks and their herds,
Their sons and their daughters.

25 Let us lie down in our shame,
And let our disgrace cover us,
For we have sinned against Jehovah our God,[i]
We and our fathers since our youth until this day,[j]
And we have not obeyed the voice of Jehovah our God."

4 "If you will return, O Israel," declares Jehovah,
"If you will return to me
And if you will remove your disgusting idols from before me,
Then you will not be a fugitive.[a]

2 And if you swear,
'As surely as Jehovah is alive!' in truth, justice, and righteousness,
Then the nations will obtain a blessing for themselves by him,
And in him they will boast."[b]

3 For this is what Jehovah says to the men of Judah and to Jerusalem:

"Plow for yourselves arable land,
And do not keep sowing among thorns.[c]

4 Circumcise yourselves to Jehovah,
And remove the foreskins of your hearts,[d]
You men of Judah and inhabitants of Jerusalem,
So that my wrath may not blaze up like a fire
And burn with no one to extinguish it,
Because of your evil deeds."[e]

5 Declare it in Judah, and proclaim it in Jerusalem.
Shout and blow a horn throughout the land.[f]
Call out loudly and say:
"Gather together,
And let us flee into the fortified cities.[g]

6 Raise a signal* toward Zion.
Seek shelter, and do not stand still,"
For I am bringing in calamity from the north,[h] a great crash.

7 He has emerged like a lion from his thicket;[i]
The destroyer of nations has set out.[j]

CHAP. 3
a Eze 20:6

b Isa 48:8
Ho 3:1
Ho 5:7

c Isa 17:10
Ho 8:14
Ho 13:6

d Ho 14:1, 4

e Jer 31:18
Ho 3:5

f Isa 65:7

g Isa 12:2

h Ho 9:10

i Jer 2:19

j Ezr 9:7
Ps 106:7

Second Col.

CHAP. 4
a Jer 3:22
Joe 2:12, 13

b Isa 65:16

c Ho 10:12

d Jer 9:25, 26

e La 4:11

f Jer 6:1

g Jer 35:11

h Jer 1:14
Jer 21:7
Jer 25:9

i 2Ki 24:1
2Ki 25:1
Jer 5:6
Jer 50:17

j Eze 26:7

3:19 *Lit., "of the armies of the nations." 3:20 *Lit., "companion." 3:24 *Or "the shameful god."

4:6 *Or "signal pole."

He has gone out from his place to make your land an object of horror.
Your cities will be reduced to ruins, without an inhabitant.[a]

8 Therefore, put on sackcloth,[b]
Mourn* and wail,
Because the burning anger of Jehovah has not turned away from us.

9 "In that day," declares Jehovah, "the heart* of the king will fail him,[c]
Also the heart* of the princes;
The priests will be horrified, and the prophets will be amazed."[d]

10 Then I said: "Alas, O Sovereign Lord Jehovah! Truly you have utterly deceived this people[e] and Jerusalem, saying, 'You will have peace,'[f] when the sword is at our throats."*

11 At that time it will be said to this people and to Jerusalem:

"A scorching wind from the barren hills of the desert
Will sweep down on the daughter of* my people;
It is not coming to winnow or to cleanse.

12 The full wind comes from these places at my bidding.
Now I will pronounce judgments against them.

13 Look! He will come like rain clouds,
And his chariots are like a storm wind.[g]
His horses are swifter than eagles.[h]
Woe to us, for we are ruined!

14 Wash your heart clean of wickedness, O Jerusalem, in order to be saved.[i]

How long will you harbor wicked thoughts?

15 For a voice tells the news from Dan,[a]
And it proclaims disaster from the mountains of E'phra·im.

16 Report it, yes, to the nations;
Proclaim it against Jerusalem."
"Sentinels* are coming from a distant land,
And they will raise their voices against the cities of Judah.

17 They come against her on all sides like guards of the open field,[b]
Because she has rebelled against me,"[c] declares Jehovah.

18 "Your own ways and your actions will be brought upon you.[d]
How bitter is your disaster,
For it reaches clear to your heart!"

19 O my anguish,* my anguish!
I feel great pain in my very heart.#
My heart pounds within me.
I cannot keep silent,
For I have△ heard the sound of the horn,
The alarm signal of war.⊠[e]

20 Disaster after disaster has been reported,
For the whole land has been destroyed.
Suddenly my own tents are destroyed,
In a moment my tent cloths.[f]

21 How long will I keep seeing the signal,*

CHAP. 4
a Isa 5:9
  Isa 6:11
  Jer 2:15
  Jer 9:11

b Jer 6:26

c 2Ki 25:5

d Isa 29:9, 10

e Eze 14:9

f Jer 6:13, 14
  Jer 14:13
  Jer 23:16, 17

g Isa 5:26, 28

h De 28:49, 50
  La 4:19
  Hab 1:8

i Isa 1:16
  Eze 18:31

Second Col.
a Jer 8:16

b 2Ki 25:1, 2

c Isa 63:10
  Eze 2:3

d Ps 107:17

e Zep 1:15, 16

f Jer 10:20

4:8 *Or "Beat your chests." 4:9 *Or "courage." 4:10 *Or "when the sword has reached our soul." 4:11 *A poetic personification, perhaps expressing pity or sympathy.

4:16 *Lit., "Watchers," that is, those watching the city to determine when to attack. 4:19 *Lit., "my intestines." #Lit., "in the walls of my heart." △Or "my soul has." ⊠Or possibly, "the sound of the battle cry." 4:21 *Or "signal pole."

Keep hearing the sound of the horn?[a]

22 For my people are foolish;[b]
They take no note of me.
They are stupid sons, with no understanding.
They are clever* enough when it comes to doing bad,
But they do not know how to do good.

23 I saw the land, and look! it was empty and desolate.[c]
I looked at the heavens, and their light was no more.[d]

24 I saw the mountains, and look! they were quaking,
And the hills were shaking.[e]

25 I saw, and look! there was no man,
And the birds of the heavens had all fled.[f]

26 I saw, and look! the orchard had become a wilderness,
And its cities had all been torn down.[g]
It was because of Jehovah,
Because of his burning anger.

27 For this is what Jehovah says: "The whole land will become desolate,[h]
But I will not carry out a complete extermination.

28 For this reason the land will mourn,[i]
And the heavens above will become dark.[j]
It is because I have spoken, I have decided,
And I will not change my mind,* nor will I turn back from it.[k]

29 At the sound of the horsemen and the archers,
The entire city flees.[l]
They enter into the thickets,
And they climb the rocks.[m]

Every city is abandoned,
And no man dwells in them."

30 Now that you are devastated, what will you do?
You used to clothe yourself with scarlet,
To deck yourself with gold ornaments,
And to enlarge your eyes with black paint.*
But it is in vain that you beautified yourself,[a]
For those lusting after you have rejected you;
They are now seeking to take your life.#[b]

31 For I have heard the sound like that of a sick woman,
The distress like that of a woman giving birth to her first child,
The voice of the daughter of Zion who keeps gasping for breath.
She says as she spreads out her palms:[c]
"Woe to me, for I am* exhausted because of the killers!"

5 Roam the streets of Jerusalem.
Look around and take note.
Search her public squares to see
Whether you can find a man who acts with justice,[d]
One who seeks to be faithful,
And I will forgive her.

2 Even if they say: "As surely as Jehovah is alive!"
They would still swear to what is false.[e]

3 O Jehovah, do your eyes not look for faithfulness?[f]
You struck them, but it made no impact on them.*
You exterminated them, but they refused to accept discipline.[g]

CHAP. 4
a Jer 6:1

b De 32:6
  Jer 5:21

c Jer 9:10

d Isa 5:30
  Joe 2:31

e Isa 5:25

f Zep 1:3

g De 29:22, 23

h Le 26:32
  2Ch 36:20, 21
  Isa 6:11
  Jer 10:22
  Eze 33:28

i Isa 24:4
  Joe 1:10

j Isa 5:30
  Joe 2:30, 31

k 2Ki 23:26
  Eze 24:14

l 2Ki 25:4

m Isa 2:19

Second Col.
a Eze 23:22, 26

b La 1:2

c La 1:17

CHAP. 5
d Eze 22:29
  Mic 7:2

e Isa 48:1

f 2Ch 16:9

g 2Ch 28:20-23
  Jer 2:30

4:22 *Or "wise." 4:28 *Or "feel regret." 4:30 *Or "eye shadow." #Or "seeking your soul." 4:31 *Or "my soul is." 5:3 *Lit., "they did not become weak."

They made their faces
  harder than a rock,[a]
And they refused to turn
  around.[b]
4 But I said to myself: "Surely
  these must be the lowly.
They act foolishly, for they
  do not know the way of
  Jehovah,
The judgment of their God.
5 I will go to the prominent
  men and speak with them,
For they must have taken
  note of the way of Jehovah,
The judgment of their God.[c]
But they had all broken the
  yoke
And torn apart the
  restraints."*
6 That is why a lion of the
  forest attacks them,
A wolf of the desert plains
  keeps ravaging them,
A leopard lies awake at
  their cities.
Everyone going out from
  them is torn to pieces.
For their transgressions
  are many;
Their acts of unfaithfulness
  are numerous.[d]
7 How can I forgive you for
  this?
Your sons have
  abandoned me,
And they swear by what
  is no God.[e]
I satisfied their needs,
But they kept committing
  adultery,
And they flocked to the
  house of a prostitute.
8 They are like eager, lustful
  horses,
Each neighing after another
  man's wife.[f]
9 "Should I not call them to
  account for these things?"
  declares Jehovah.
"Should I* not avenge myself
  on such a nation?"[g]

10 "Come up against her
  vineyard terraces
  and bring ruin,
But do not make a complete
  extermination.[a]
Take away her spreading
  shoots,
For they do not belong
  to Jehovah.
11 For the house of Israel and
  the house of Judah
Have been utterly treach-
  erous with me," declares
  Jehovah.[b]
12 "They have denied Jehovah,
  and they keep saying,
'He will do nothing.'*[c]
No calamity will come
  upon us;
We will not see sword or
  famine.'[d]
13 The prophets are full of
  wind,
And the word* is not in them.
Let this happen to them!"
14 Therefore this is what
  Jehovah, the God of
  armies, says:
"Because these men are
  saying this,
Here I am making my words
  a fire in your mouth,[e]
And this people is the wood,
And it will consume them."[f]
15 "Here I am bringing in on
  you a nation from far away,
  O house of Israel,"[g]
  declares Jehovah.
"It is an enduring nation.
It is an ancient nation,
A nation whose language
  you do not know,
And whose speech you
  cannot understand.[h]
16 Their quiver is like an open
  grave;
All of them are warriors.
17 They will devour your
  harvest and your bread.[i]

CHAP. 5
a Zec 7:11

b Ps 50:17
  Isa 42:25
  Eze 3:7
  Zep 3:2

c Mic 3:1

d Ezr 9:6
  Isa 59:12
  Eze 23:19

e Jos 23:6, 7
  Jer 2:11
  Jer 12:16
  Zep 1:4, 5

f Eze 22:11

g Le 26:25
  Jer 9:9
  Jer 44:22
  Na 1:2

Second Col.
a Le 26:44
  Jer 46:28

b Isa 48:8
  Jer 3:20
  Ho 5:7
  Ho 6:7

c 2Ch 36:15, 16
  Isa 28:15

d Jer 23:17

e Jer 1:9

f Jer 23:29

g Jer 1:15
  Jer 4:16
  Jer 25:9
  Eze 7:24
  Hab 1:6

h De 28:49, 50

i Le 26:16

5:5 *Lit., "bands." 5:9 *Or "my soul."

5:12 *Or possibly, "He does not exist."
5:13 *That is, God's word.

They will devour your sons
and your daughters.
They will devour your flocks
and your herds.
They will devour your vines
and your fig trees.
They will destroy with the
sword your fortified cities
in which you trust."

18 "But even in those days,"
declares Jehovah, "I will not carry out a complete extermination of you.[a] **19** And when they
ask, 'Why has Jehovah our God
done all these things to us?' you
should answer them, 'Just as you
abandoned me to serve a foreign god in your land, so you will
serve foreigners in a land that is
not yours.'"[b]

20 Declare this in the house
of Jacob,
And proclaim it in Judah,
saying:

21 "Hear this, you foolish and
senseless people:*[c]
They have eyes but cannot
see;[d]
They have ears but cannot
hear.[e]

22 'Do you not fear me?'
declares Jehovah,
'Should you not tremble
before me?
It is I who placed the sand as
the boundary for the sea,
A permanent regulation that
it cannot pass over.
Although its waves toss,
they cannot prevail;
Although they roar, they still
cannot pass beyond it.[f]

23 But this people has a stubborn and rebellious heart;
They have turned aside and
gone their own way.[g]

24 And they do not say in their
heart:
"Let us now fear Jehovah
our God,

The One who gives the rain
in its season,
Both the autumn rain and
the spring rain,
The One who guards for us
the appointed weeks of
the harvest."[a]

25 Your own errors have
prevented these things
from coming;
Your own sins have deprived
you of what is good.[b]

26 For among my people there
are wicked men.
They keep peering, as when
birdcatchers crouch down.
They set a deadly trap.
It is men whom they catch.

27 Like a cage full of birds,
So their houses are full of
deception.[c]
That is why they have
become powerful and rich.

28 They have grown fat and
smooth;
They overflow with evil.
They do not plead the legal
case of the fatherless,[d]
That they may gain success;
And they deny justice to the
poor.'"[e]

29 "Should I not call them to
account for these things?"
declares Jehovah.
"Should I* not avenge myself
on such a nation?

30 Something appalling and
horrible has occurred in
the land:

31 The prophets prophesy lies,[f]
And the priests dominate
by their own authority.
And my own people love it
that way.[g]
But what will you do when
the end comes?"

6 Take shelter, O sons
of Benjamin, away from
Jerusalem.
Blow the horn[h] in Te·ko′a;[i]

5:21 *Lit., "you foolish people without
heart."

5:29 *Or "my soul."

CHAP. 5
a Jer 4:27

b De 4:27
De 28:48
De 29:24, 25
2Ch 7:21, 22

c Jer 4:22

d Isa 59:10

e Isa 6:9
Eze 12:2
Mt 13:13

f Job 38:8, 11
Ps 33:7
Pr 8:29

g Ps 95:10
Jer 11:8

Second Col.
a De 11:14

b De 28:23, 24
Jer 3:3

c Am 8:5
Mic 6:11, 12

d Isa 1:23

e Ps 82:2

f Jer 14:14
La 2:14
Eze 13:6

g Isa 30:10
Joh 3:19

CHAP. 6
h Jer 4:5

i 2Ch 11:5, 6
Am 1:1

Light a fire signal over
Beth-hac·che′rem!
For a calamity looms from
the north, a great disaster.[a]

2 The daughter of Zion
resembles a beautiful
and delicate woman.[b]

3 The shepherds and their
droves will come.
They will pitch their tents
all around her,[c]
Each grazing the flock in
his care.[d]

4 "Prepare for* war against
her!
Rise up, and let us attack
her at midday!"
"Woe to us, for the day is
declining,
For the shadows of evening
are getting longer!"

5 "Rise up, and let us attack
during the night
And destroy her fortified
towers."[e]

6 For this is what Jehovah of
armies says:
"Cut down wood and raise
up a siege rampart against
Jerusalem.[f]
She is the city that must be
held to account;
There is nothing but
oppression within her.[g]

7 As a cistern keeps its water
cool,*
So she keeps her wickedness
cool.*
Violence and destruction
are heard in her;[h]
Sickness and plague are
constantly before me.

8 Be warned, O Jerusalem,
or I* will turn away from
you in disgust;[i]
I will make you desolate, a
land without inhabitants."[j]

9 This is what Jehovah of
armies says:

"They will thoroughly glean
the remnant of Israel as
the last grapes on a vine.
Pass your hand again like
one gathering grapes from
the vines."

10 "To whom should I speak and
give warning?
Who will listen?
Look! Their ears are closed,*
so that they are unable to
pay attention.
Look! The word of Jehovah
has become something
they scorn;[b]
They find no pleasure in it.

11 So I am filled with the wrath
of Jehovah,
And I am tired of holding
it in."[c]
"Pour it out on the child in
the street,[d]
On the groups of young men
gathered together.
They will all be captured,
a man along with his wife,
The old men along with the
very old.*[e]

12 Their houses will be turned
over to others,
Together with their fields
and their wives.[f]
For I will stretch my hand
out against the inhabitants
of the land," declares
Jehovah.

13 "For from the least to the
greatest, each one is
making dishonest gain;[g]
From the prophet to the
priest, each one is
practicing fraud.[h]

14 And they try to heal the
breakdown* of my people
lightly,# saying,
'There is peace! There is
peace!'
When there is no peace.[i]

CHAP. 6
a Jer 1:14
　Jer 10:22

b Isa 3:16

c 2Ki 25:1

d Jer 4:16, 17

e 2Ch 36:17, 19
　Am 2:5

f Eze 21:21, 22

g 2Ki 21:16
　Eze 7:23

h Eze 7:11
　Mic 2:2

i Eze 23:18

j Le 26:34
　Jer 9:11

_____
Second Col.
a Isa 6:10
　Ac 7:51

b 2Ch 36:15, 16
　Jer 20:8

c Jer 20:9

d Jer 18:21

e Eze 9:6

f De 28:30
　Jer 8:10
　La 5:11
　Zep 1:13

g Eze 22:12

h Jer 2:8
　Jer 8:10-12
　Jer 23:11
　Mic 3:5, 11
　Zep 3:4

i Jer 14:13
　Jer 23:16, 17
　Eze 13:10
　1Th 5:3

6:4 *Lit., "Sanctify."　6:7 *Or "fresh."
6:8 *Or "my soul."　6:10 *Lit., "Their ear is uncircumcised."
6:11 *Lit., "those full of days."　6:14
*Or "fracture."　#Or "superficially."

15 Do they feel ashamed of the
    detestable things they have
    done?
    They feel no shame at all!
    They do not even know
        how to feel humiliated!ᵃ
    So they will fall among
        the fallen.
    When I bring punishment
        on them they will stumble,"
        says Jehovah.
16 This is what Jehovah says:
    "Stand at the crossroads
        and see.
    Ask about the ancient
        roadways,
    Ask where the good way is,
        and walk in it,ᵇ
    And find rest for
        yourselves."*
    But they say: "We will not
        walk in it."ᶜ
17 "And I appointed watchmenᵈ
        who said,
    'Pay attention to the sound
        of the horn!'"ᵉ
    But they said: "We will not
        pay attention."ᶠ
18 "Therefore hear, O nations!
    And know, O assembly,
    What will happen to them.
19 Listen, O earth!
    I am bringing calamity on
        this peopleᵍ
    As the fruitage of their own
        schemes,
    For they paid no attention
        to my words
    And they rejected my law."*
20 "What do I care that you
        bring frankincense from
        She′ba
    And sweet cane* from
        a distant land?
    Your whole burnt offerings
        are not acceptable,
    And your sacrifices do not
        please me."ʰ
21 Therefore this is what
    Jehovah says:

"Here I am setting for this
    people stumbling blocks,
And they will stumble over
    them,
Fathers and sons together,
A neighbor and his
    companion,
And they will all perish."ᵃ
22 This is what Jehovah says:
    "Look! A people is coming
        from the land of the north,
    And a great nation will be
        awakened from the remot-
        est parts of the earth.ᵇ
23 They will grab hold of the
        bow and the javelin.
    They are cruel and will have
        no mercy.
    Their voice will roar like
        the sea,
    And they ride on horses.ᶜ
    They draw up in battle order
        like a man of war against
        you, O daughter of Zion."
24 We have heard the report
        about it.
    Our hands fall limp;ᵈ
    Distress has seized us,
    Anguish* like that of a
        woman giving birth.ᵉ
25 Do not go out into the field,
    And do not walk on the road,
    For the enemy has a sword;
    There is terror all around.
26 O daughter of my people,
    Put on sacklothᶠ and roll
        in the ashes.
    Mourn as for an only son,
        with bitter wailing,ᵍ
    For suddenly the destroyer
        will come upon us.ʰ
27 "I have made you* a metal
        tester among my people,
    One making a thorough
        search;
    You must take note and
        examine their way.
28 All of them are the most
    stubborn men,ⁱ

CHAP. 6
a Jer 3:3

b Isa 30:21

c Jer 18:15

d Jer 25:4
  Eze 3:17
  Hab 2:1

e Isa 58:1

f Zec 7:11

g De 4:25, 26
  Da 9:12

h Isa 1:11
  Isa 66:3
  Jer 7:21
  Am 5:21

Second Col.
a 2Ch 36:17
  La 2:21

b Jer 1:14
  Jer 25:9

c Hab 1:8

d Eze 21:7

e Jer 4:31

f Jer 4:8

g La 1:2, 16

h Jer 15:8

i Isa 30:1
  Isa 48:4
  Jer 5:23

6:16 *Or "your souls." 6:19 *Or "instruction." 6:20 *An aromatic reed.

6:24 *Lit., "Birth pangs." 6:27 *That
is, Jeremiah.

Walking about as
  slanderers.[a]
They are like copper
  and iron;
All of them are corrupt.
29 The bellows have been
  scorched.
Out from their fire there
  is lead.
One keeps refining intensely
  simply for nothing,[b]
And those who are bad have
  not been separated.[c]
30 Rejected silver is what people will certainly call them,
For Jehovah has rejected
  them."[d]

7 This is the word that came to
Jeremiah from Jehovah, saying: **2** "Stand in the gate of the
house of Jehovah and proclaim
there this message, 'Hear the
word of Jehovah, all you people of Judah who enter these
gates to bow down to Jehovah. **3** This is what Jehovah of
armies, the God of Israel, says:
"Reform your ways and your actions, and I will allow you to
keep residing in this place.[e]
4 Do not put your trust in deceptive words and say, 'This is*
the temple of Jehovah, the temple of Jehovah, the temple of Jehovah!'[f] **5** For if you truly reform your ways and actions; if
you truly uphold justice between
a man and his neighbor;[g] **6** if
you do not oppress foreign residents, orphans,* and widows;[h] if
you do not shed innocent blood
in this place; and if you do not
follow other gods to your own
harm;[i] **7** then I will allow you to
keep residing in this place, in the
land I gave to your forefathers
for all time."'"*

8 "But you are putting your
trust in deceptive words[j]—it

7:4 *Lit., "They are," referring to all
the buildings of the temple complex.
7:6 *Or "fatherless children." 7:7 *Or
"from eternity to eternity."

will bring absolutely no benefit. **9** Can you steal,[a] murder,
commit adultery, swear falsely,[b]
make sacrifices* to Ba'al,[c] and
follow after gods you had not
known, **10** and then come and
stand before me in this house
that bears my name and say, 'We
will be saved,' despite your doing all these detestable things?
11 Has this house that bears my
name become a cave of robbers
in your eyes?[d] Here I have seen
it for myself," declares Jehovah.

12 "'However, go now to my
place in Shi'loh,[e] where I first
caused my name to reside,[f] and
see what I did to it because of
the badness of my people Israel.[g]
13 But you kept doing all these
things,' declares Jehovah, 'and
even though I spoke to you again
and again,* you did not listen.[h] I
kept calling you, but you would
not answer.[i] **14** So I will do to
the house that bears my name,[j]
in which you are trusting,[k] and
to this place that I gave to you
and your forefathers, just as I
did to Shi'loh.[l] **15** I will throw
you out of my sight, just as I
threw out all your brothers, all
the descendants of E'phra·im.'[m]

16 "As for you, do not pray
in behalf of this people. Do not
cry out or offer a prayer or plead
with me in their behalf,[n] for I
will not listen to you.[o] **17** Do
you not see what they are doing
in the cities of Judah and in the
streets of Jerusalem? **18** The
sons are gathering wood, the fathers are lighting the fire, and
the wives are kneading dough in
order to make sacrificial cakes
to the Queen of Heaven,*[p] and
they are pouring out drink offerings to other gods to offend me.[q]
19 'But am I the one they are

7:9 *Or "sacrificial smoke." 7:13 *Lit.,
"rising up early and speaking." 7:18
*The title of a goddess worshipped by
apostate Israelites; possibly a fertility
goddess.

hurting?'* declares Jehovah. 'Is it not they themselves, to their own shame?'ᵃ **20** Therefore this is what the Sovereign Lord Jehovah says, 'Look! My anger and my wrath will be poured out on this place,ᵇ on man and beast, on the trees of the field and the fruitage of the ground; it will burn and will not be extinguished.'ᶜ

21 "This is what Jehovah of armies, the God of Israel, says, 'Go ahead, add your whole burnt offerings to your other sacrifices, and eat the flesh yourselves.ᵈ **22** For on the day I brought your forefathers out of the land of Egypt, I did not speak with them or command them concerning whole burnt offerings and sacrifices.ᵉ **23** But I did give them this command: "Obey my voice, and I will become your God, and you will become my people.ᶠ You must walk in all the way that I command, so that it may go well with you."'ᵍ **24** But they did not listen or incline their ear;ʰ instead, they walked in their own schemes,* stubbornly following their wicked heart,ⁱ and they went backward, not forward, **25** from the day your forefathers came out of the land of Egypt until this day.ʲ So I kept sending all my servants the prophets to you, sending them each day, again and again.*ᵏ **26** But they refused to listen to me, and they did not incline their ear.ˡ Instead, they were stubborn,* and they acted worse than their forefathers!

27 "You will speak all these words to them,ᵐ but they will not listen to you; you will call to them, but they will not answer you. **28** And you will say

to them, 'This is the nation that did not obey the voice of Jehovah their God and refused to accept discipline. Faithfulness has perished and is not even mentioned among them.'*ᵃ

29 "Shear off your uncut* hair and throw it away, and on the bare hills raise a dirge,ᵍ for Jehovah has rejected and will abandon this generation that has infuriated him. **30** 'For the people of Judah have done what is bad in my eyes,' declares Jehovah. 'They have set up their disgusting idols in the house that bears my name, in order to defile it.ᵇ **31** They have built the high places of To'pheth, which is in the Valley of the Son of Hin'nom,*ᶜ in order to burn their sons and their daughters in the fire,ᵈ something that I had not commanded and that had never even come into my heart.'*ᵉ

32 "'Therefore look! the days are coming,' declares Jehovah, 'when it will no longer be called To'pheth or the Valley of the Son of Hin'nom* but the Valley of the Slaughter. They will bury in To'pheth until there is no place left.ᶠ **33** And the dead bodies of this people will become food for the birds of the heavens and for the beasts of the earth, with no one to frighten them away.ᵍ **34** I will put an end to the sound of exultation and the sound of rejoicing, the voice of the bridegroom and the voice of the bride,ʰ in the cities of Judah and in the streets of Jerusalem, for the land will be reduced to ruins.'"ⁱ

8 "At that time," declares Jehovah, "the bones of the kings of Judah, the bones of its

---

CHAP. 7
ᵃ Da 9:7

ᵇ La 2:3

ᶜ 2Ki 22:17
  Jer 17:27

ᵈ Isa 1:11
  Jer 6:20
  Ho 8:13
  Am 5:21

ᵉ 1Sa 15:22
  Ho 6:6

ᶠ Ex 19:5
  Le 26:3, 12

ᵍ De 5:29

ʰ Ex 32:8

ⁱ Ho 4:16
  Zec 7:12

ʲ De 9:7
  1Sa 8:8

ᵏ 2Ki 17:13
  2Ch 36:15
  Ne 9:17, 30
  Jer 25:4

ˡ 2Ch 33:10
  Jer 25:3

ᵐ Jer 26:2
  Eze 2:7

Second Col.
ᵃ Jer 5:1
  Mic 7:2

ᵇ 2Ki 21:1, 4
  2Ch 33:1, 4
  Jer 23:11
  Jer 32:34

ᶜ Jos 15:8, 12

ᵈ De 12:29-31
  2Ki 17:17
  2Ch 28:1, 3
  2Ch 33:1, 6
  Eze 20:31

ᵉ Le 18:21
  Le 20:3
  Jer 19:5, 6
  Jer 32:35

ᶠ Jer 19:11
  Eze 6:4, 5

ᵍ De 28:26
  Ps 79:2
  Jer 16:4

ʰ Isa 24:8
  Jer 25:10

ⁱ Le 26:33
  Isa 1:7
  Isa 6:11

7:19 *Or "offending; provoking." **7:24** *Or "advice." **7:25** *Lit., "daily rising up early and sending." **7:26** *Lit., "they hardened their neck."

7:28 *Lit., "is cut off from their mouth." **7:29** *Or "dedicated." ᵍOr "song of mourning." **7:31, 32** *See Glossary, "Gehenna." **7:31** ᵍOr "had never entered my thoughts."

princes, the bones of the priests, the bones of the prophets, and the bones of the inhabitants of Jerusalem will be taken from their graves. **2** They will be spread out to the sun and to the moon and to all the army of the heavens that they loved and served and followed and sought after and bowed down to.[a] They will not be gathered, nor will they be buried. They will become like manure on the surface of the ground."[b]

3 "And the remnant of this evil family who survive will choose death over life in all the places where I disperse them," declares Jehovah of armies.

4 "And you must say to them, 'This is what Jehovah says:

"Will they fall and not get up again?
If one would turn back, will the other not also turn back?
5 Why is this people, Jerusalem, unfaithful with an enduring unfaithfulness?
They hold fast to deception; They refuse to turn back.[c]
6 I paid attention and kept listening, but the way they spoke was not right.
Not a man repented over his wickedness or asked, 'What have I done?'[d]
Each one keeps returning to the popular course, like a horse dashing into the battle.
7 Even the stork in the sky knows its seasons;*
The turtledove and the swift and the thrush[#] keep to the time of their return.[△]
But my own people do not understand the judgment of Jehovah.'"[e]

8 'How can you say: "We are wise, and we have the law* of Jehovah"?
For in fact, the lying[#] stylus[△a] of the scribes[ß] has been used only for falsehood.
9 The wise have been put to shame.[b]
They have become terrified and will be caught.
Look! They have rejected the word of Jehovah,
And what wisdom do they have?
10 So I will give their wives to other men,
Their fields to other owners;[c]
For from the least to the greatest, each one is making dishonest gain;[d]
From the prophet to the priest, each one is practicing fraud.[e]
11 And they try to heal the breakdown* of the daughter of my people lightly,[#] saying,
"There is peace! There is peace!"
When there is no peace.[f]
12 Do they feel ashamed of the detestable things they have done?
They feel no shame at all!
They do not even know how to feel humiliated![g]
So they will fall among the fallen.
When I bring punishment on them they will stumble,'[h] says Jehovah.
13 'When I gather them, I will bring them to their end,' declares Jehovah.
'There will be no grapes left on the vine, no figs on the fig tree, and the leaves will wither.
And what I gave to them will be lost to them.'"

CHAP. 8
a De 4:19
2Ki 17:16
2Ki 21:1, 3
Jer 19:13
Eze 8:16
Zep 1:4, 5

b Jer 16:4

c Jer 5:3

d Jer 5:1

e Isa 1:3

Second Col.
a Isa 8:1

b Isa 29:14

c De 28:30
Zep 1:13

d Isa 56:11
Eze 33:31
Mic 3:11

e Jer 5:31
Jer 6:12-15
Jer 27:9
La 2:14
Eze 22:28

f Jer 23:16, 17
Eze 13:10

g Jer 3:3

h Jer 23:12

8:7 *Or "appointed times." #Or possibly, "crane." △Or "migration." 8:8 *Or "instruction." #Or "false." △Or "pen." ßOr "secretaries." 8:11 *Or "fracture." #Or "superficially."

14 "Why are we sitting here?
Let us gather together and
enter the fortified cities[a]
and perish there.
For Jehovah our God will do
away with us,
And he gives us poisoned
water to drink,[b]
Because we have sinned
against Jehovah.

15 There was a hope for peace,
but nothing good came,
For a time of healing, but
there is terror![c]

16 From Dan is heard the
snorting of his horses.
At the sound of the neighing
of his stallions,
The whole land quakes.
They come in and devour the
land and everything in it,
The city and its inhabitants."

17 "For here I am sending in
serpents among you,
Poisonous snakes that
cannot be charmed,
And they will certainly bite
you," declares Jehovah.

18 My grief is incurable;
My heart is sick.

19 From a distant land there is
a cry for help
From the daughter of my
people:
"Is Jehovah not in Zion?
Or is her king not in her?"
"Why have they offended me
with their graven images,
With their worthless foreign
gods?"

20 "The harvest has passed, the
summer has ended,
But we have not been saved!"

21 I am shattered over the
breakdown of the daughter
of my people;[d]
I am dejected.
Horror has seized me.

22 Is there no balsam* in
Gil'e·ad?[e]

Or is there no healer* there?[a]
Why has the daughter of my
people not been restored
to health?[b]

9 O that my head were waters,
My eyes a fountain of tears![c]
Then I would weep day and
night
For the slain ones of my
people.

2 O that I had a traveler's lodging place in the wilderness!
Then I would leave my people and go away from them,
For they are all adulterers,[d]
A band of treacherous
people.

3 They bend their tongue like
a bow;
Falsehood, not faithfulness,
prevails in the land.[e]
"They advance from evil to
evil,
And they pay no attention to
me," declares Jehovah.

4 "Everyone, be on guard
against your neighbor,
And do not trust even your
brother.
For every brother is a
betrayer,[g]
And every neighbor is a
slanderer.[h]

5 Each one cheats his
neighbor,
And no one speaks truth.
They have taught their
tongue to speak falsehood.[i]
They wear themselves out
doing what is wrong.

6 You are living in the midst
of deception.
In their deception they
refused to know me,"
declares Jehovah.

7 Therefore this is what
Jehovah of armies says:
"I will smelt them and test
them,[j]
For what else can I do with
the daughter of my people?

CHAP. 8
a Jer 4:5

b Jer 9:15
Jer 23:15
La 3:19

c Jer 4:10
Jer 14:19

d Jer 4:19, 20
Jer 14:17

e Ge 37:25

Second Col.
a Jer 30:12, 13

b Jer 30:17
Jer 33:4, 6

CHAP. 9
c Isa 22:4
Jer 13:17

d Jer 5:7
Jer 23:10

e Isa 59:3

f Jer 4:22

g Jer 12:6
Mic 7:2, 5

h Jer 6:28
Eze 22:9

i Ps 50:19
Mic 6:12

j Isa 1:25
Isa 48:10

8:22 *Or "soothing balm."

8:22 *Or "physician."

8 Their tongue is a deadly
   arrow that speaks
   deception.
   With his mouth a person
   speaks of peace to his
   neighbor,
   But inside he lays an
   ambush."

9 "Should I not call them to
   account for these things?"
   declares Jehovah.
   "Should I* not avenge myself
   on such a nation?ᵃ

10 I will weep and lament over
   the mountains
   And take up a dirge* over the
   pastures of the wilderness,
   For they have been burned
   up so that no man passes
   through,
   And the sound of livestock
   is not heard.
   The birds of heaven and the
   beasts have fled; they are
   gone.ᵇ

11 I will make Jerusalem piles
   of stones,ᶜ the lair of
   jackals,ᵈ
   And I will make the cities
   of Judah desolate, without
   an inhabitant.ᵉ

12 Who is wise enough to
   understand this?
   To whom has the mouth of
   Jehovah spoken, that he
   may declare it?
   Why has the land perished?
   Why is it scorched like the
   wilderness,
   So that no one is passing
   through?"

13 Jehovah replied: "Because
of their rejecting my law* that
I set before them, and because they have not followed
it and obeyed my voice. 14 Instead, they stubbornly followed
their own hearts,ᶠ and they followed the Ba'al images, as their
fathers had taught them to do.ᵍ

15 Therefore this is what Jehovah of armies, the God of Israel, says, 'Here I am making this
people eat wormwood, and I will
make them drink poisoned wa-
ter.ᵃ 16 I will scatter them
among the nations that they and
their fathers have not known,ᵇ
and I will send a sword after
them until I will have exterminated them.'ᶜ

17 This is what Jehovah of
   armies says,
   'Behave with understanding.
   Summon the women who
   sing dirges,*ᵈ
   And send for the skilled
   women to come,

18 So that they may hurry and
   raise a lamentation for us,
   So that our eyes may stream
   with tears
   And our eyelids trickle with
   water.ᵉ

19 For the sound of lamentation
   has been heard from Zion:ᶠ
   "How we have been
   devastated!
   How great our shame is!
   For we have left the land,
   and they have thrown
   down our homes."ᵍ

20 You women, hear the word
   of Jehovah.
   May your ear receive the
   word of his mouth.
   Teach your daughters this
   lamentation,
   And teach one another this
   dirge.*ʰ

21 For death has come up
   through our windows;
   It has entered our fortified
   towers
   To take away the children
   from the streets
   And the young men from
   the public squares.ⁱ

22 Say, 'This is what Jehovah
   declares:

CHAP. 9
a Jer 5:9, 29

b Jer 4:25
  Zep 1:3

c Ps 79:1
  Jer 26:18

d Jer 10:22

e Jer 4:27
  Jer 25:11
  Jer 32:43

f Jer 7:24

g Jg 3:7
  1Sa 12:10
  Ho 11:2

Second Col.
a Jer 8:14
  Jer 23:15
  La 3:15, 19

b Le 26:33
  De 28:64
  Ps 106:27
  Zec 7:14

c Jer 29:17
  Eze 5:2

d 2Ch 35:25

e Jer 6:26
  Jer 14:17

f Jer 4:31
  Eze 7:16
  Mic 1:8, 9

g La 4:15
  Mic 2:10

h Isa 29:2
  Jer 7:29

i 2Ch 36:17
  Jer 6:11

9:9 *Or "my soul." 9:10, 20 *Or "song
of mourning." 9:13 *Or "instruction."

9:17 *Or "songs of mourning."

"The dead bodies of people
will fall like manure on
the surface of the field,
Like a row of newly cut grain
after the reaper,
With no one to gather
them up."'"ᵃ

23 This is what Jehovah says:
"Let not the wise man boast
about his wisdom;ᵇ
Let not the mighty man boast
about his mightiness;
And let not the rich man
boast about his riches."ᶜ

24 "But let the one boasting
boast about this:
That he has insight and
knowledge of me,ᵈ
That I am Jehovah, the One
showing loyal love, justice,
and righteousness in the
earth,ᵉ
For in these things I take delight,"ᶠ declares Jehovah.

25 "Look! Days are coming,"
declares Jehovah, "and I will
hold an accounting with everyone circumcised and yet uncircumcised,ᵍ 26 with Egyptʰ
and Judahⁱ and E'domʲ and the
Am'mon·itesᵏ and Mo'abˡ and
with all of those with hair
clipped at the temples who are
dwelling in the wilderness;ᵐ for
all the nations are uncircumcised, and all the house of Israel are uncircumcised in heart."ⁿ

10 Hear the word that Je-
hovah has spoken against
you, O house of Israel. 2 This
is what Jehovah says:

"Do not learn the way of
the nations,ᵒ
And do not be terrified by
the signs of the heavens
Because the nations are
terrified by them.ᵖ

3 For the customs of the
peoples are a delusion.*
It is just a tree of the forest
that is cut down,

Worked by the hands of the
craftsman with his tool.*ᵃ

4 They adorn it with silver
and goldᵇ
And fasten it with hammer
and nails so that it will not
fall over.ᶜ

5 Like a scarecrow in
a cucumber field, they
cannot speak;ᵈ
They have to be carried,
for they cannot walk.ᵉ
Do not fear them, for they
can do no harm,
Nor can they do any good."ᶠ

6 No one is like you,
O Jehovah.ᵍ
You are great, and your
name is great and mighty.

7 Who should not fear you,
O King of the nations,ʰ
for it is fitting;
Because among all the wise
ones of the nations and
among all their kingdoms,
There is no one at all like
you.ⁱ

8 They are all unreasoning
and stupid.ʲ
Instruction from a tree is
an utter delusion.*ᵏ

9 Silver plates are imported
from Tar'shishˡ and gold
from U'phaz,
The work of a craftsman,
of the hands of a metal-
worker.
Their clothing is blue thread
and purple wool.
They are all made by skilled
workers.

10 But Jehovah is truly God.
He is the living Godᵐ and
the eternal King.ⁿ
Because of his indignation
the earth will quake,ᵒ
And no nations will endure
his denunciation.

11 * This is what you should say
to them:

CHAP. 9
a Isa 5:25
  Jer 16:3, 4
b Isa 5:21
c De 8:12-14
  De 8:17, 18
d 1Co 1:31
  2Co 10:17
e Ex 34:6
  Ps 89:14
f Ps 99:4
  Ho 6:6
  Mic 6:8
  Mic 7:18
g Am 3:1, 2
h Isa 19:1
  Eze 29:2
i Isa 1:1
j Jer 27:2, 3
  Eze 32:29
  Ob 1
k Jer 49:1
  Eze 25:2
l Isa 45:20
  Jer 48:1
m Jer 25:17, 23
  Jer 49:32
n Le 26:41
  Jer 4:4

CHAP. 10
o Isa 18:3, 30
  Le 20:23
  De 12:30
p Isa 47:13

Second Col.
a Isa 40:20
  Isa 44:14, 15
  Isa 45:20
  Hab 2:18
b Ps 115:4
  Isa 40:19
c Isa 41:7
d Hab 2:19
e Isa 46:7
f Isa 41:23
  Isa 44:9
  1Co 8:4
g Ex 15:11
  2Sa 7:22
  Ps 86:8
h Ps 22:28
i Ps 89:6
  Da 4:35
j Jer 51:17
  Hab 2:18
k Isa 44:19
l 1Ki 10:22
m Jos 3:10
  Da 6:26
n Da 4:3
  Hab 1:12
  Re 15:3
o Na 1:5

10:3 *Or "billhook."   10:11 *Vs. 11 was
originally written in Aramaic.

10:3, 8 *Or "futility."

"The gods that did not make the heavens and the earth

Will perish from the earth and from under these heavens."[a]

12 He is the Maker of the earth by his power,

The One who established the productive land by his wisdom[b]

And who stretched out the heavens by his understanding.[c]

13 When he makes his voice heard,

The waters in the heavens are in turmoil,[d]

And he causes clouds* to ascend from the ends of the earth.[e]

He makes lightning for# the rain,

And he brings the wind out of his storehouses.[f]

14 Every man acts unreasonably and without knowledge.

Every metalworker will be put to shame because of the carved image;[g]

For his metal image* is a falsehood,

And there is no spirit# in them.[h]

15 They are a delusion,* a work of mockery.[i]

When their day of reckoning comes, they will perish.

16 The Share of Jacob is not like these things,

For he is the One who formed everything,

And Israel is the staff of his inheritance.[j]

Jehovah of armies is his name.[k]

17 Gather up your bundle from the ground,

O woman dwelling under siege.

18 For this is what Jehovah says:

"Here I am hurling* the inhabitants out of the land at this time,[a]

And I will cause them to experience distress."

19 Woe to me because of my breakdown!*[b]

My wound is incurable.

And I said: "Surely this is my sickness, and I must bear it.

20 My tent has been devastated, and my tent cords have all been torn apart.[c]

My sons have left me and are no more.[d]

There is no one left to stretch out my tent or raise up my tent cloths.

21 For the shepherds have behaved senselessly,[e]

And they have not inquired of Jehovah.[f]

That is why they have not acted with insight,

And all their flocks have been scattered."[g]

22 Listen! A report! It is coming!

A great pounding from the land of the north,[h]

To make the cities of Judah desolate, a lair of jackals.[i]

23 I well know, O Jehovah, that man's way does not belong to him.

It does not belong to man who is walking even to direct his step.[j]

24 Correct me, O Jehovah, with judgment,

But not in your anger,[k] that you may not reduce me to nothing.[l]

25 Pour out your wrath on the nations who ignore you[m]

CHAP. 10

a Isa 2:18
  Jer 51:17, 18
  Zep 2:11

b Pr 3:19
  Isa 45:18

c Ps 136:3, 5
  Isa 40:22
  Jer 51:15, 16

d Job 37:2
  Job 38:34

e Job 36:27
  Ps 135:7

f Ge 8:1
  Ex 14:21
  Nu 11:31
  Jon 1:4

g Isa 42:17
  Isa 44:11

h Jer 51:17
  Hab 2:18, 19

i Isa 41:29

j De 32:9
  Ps 135:4

k Isa 47:4

Second Col.

a De 28:63
  Jer 16:13

b Jer 8:21

c Jer 4:20

d Jer 31:15

e Jer 5:31

f Jer 2:8
  Jer 8:9

g Jer 23:1
  Eze 34:5, 6

h Jer 1:15
  Jer 4:6
  Jer 6:22
  Hab 1:6

i Jer 9:11

j Ps 17:5
  Ps 37:23
  Pr 16:3
  Pr 20:24

k Ps 6:1
  Ps 38:1

l Jer 30:11

m Isa 34:2

10:13 *Or "vapors." #Or possibly, "makes sluices for." 10:14 *Or "molten statue." #Or "breath." 10:15 *Or "futility."

10:18 *Or "slinging." 10:19 *Or "fracture!"

And on the families who
  do not call on your name.
For they have devoured
  Jacob,[a]
Yes, they have devoured
  him to the point of
  extermination,[b]
And they have desolated
  his homeland.[c]

11 This is the word that came
  to Jeremiah from Jehovah,
saying: **2** "Hear the words of
this covenant, you people!

"Speak* them to the men of
Judah and to the inhabitants of
Jerusalem **3** and say to them,
'This is what Jehovah the God of
Israel says: "Cursed is the man
who does not obey the words of
this covenant,[d] which I commanded your forefathers on the
day I brought them out of the
land of Egypt,[e] out of the iron-
smelting furnace,[f] saying, 'Obey
my voice, and do all the things
that I command you; and you will
become my people and I will be
your God,[g] **5** so that I may fulfill the oath that I swore to your
forefathers, to give them the
land flowing with milk and honey,[h] as it is this day.'"'"

And I answered: "Amen,*
O Jehovah."

6 Jehovah then said to me:
"Proclaim all these words in the
cities of Judah and in the streets
of Jerusalem: 'Hear the words
of this covenant, and carry them
out. **7** For I solemnly admon-
ished your forefathers in the day
I brought them out of the land of
Egypt and to this day, admonishing them again and again:*
"Obey my voice."[i] **8** But they
did not listen or incline their
ear; instead, each kept stubbornly following his own wicked
heart.[j] So I brought on them all

the words of this covenant that I
commanded them to do, but they
refused to carry them out.'"

9 Jehovah then said to me:
"There is a conspiracy among
the men of Judah and the inhabitants of Jerusalem. **10** They
have returned to the errors of
their forefathers of old, who refused to obey my words.[a] They
too have followed other gods
and have served them.[b] The
house of Israel and the house
of Judah have broken my covenant that I made with their
forefathers.[c] **11** Therefore this
is what Jehovah says, 'Here I
am bringing on them a calamity[d]
that they will not be able to escape. When they call to me for
help, I will not listen to them.[e]
12 Then the cities of Judah and
the inhabitants of Jerusalem will
go to the gods to which they are
making sacrifices* and call for
help,[f] but these will by no means
save them in the time of their calamity. **13** For your gods have
become as many as your cities, O Judah, and you have set
up as many altars to the shameful thing* as there are streets in
Jerusalem, altars to make sacrifices to Ba'al.'[g]

14 "As for you,* do not pray
in behalf of this people. Do not
cry out in their behalf or offer a
prayer for them,[h] for I will not
be listening when they call out to
me because of their calamity.

15 What right does my beloved
  one have to be in my house
When so many have carried
  out evil schemes?
With holy flesh* will they
  avert the calamity when
  it comes upon you?
Will you exult at that time?
16 Jehovah once called you
  a thriving olive tree,

CHAP. 10
a Jer 51:34

b Isa 10:22

c Ps 79:6, 7
  Jer 8:16
  La 2:22

CHAP. 11
d De 27:26
  De 28:15

e Ex 24:3

f Ex 13:3
  De 4:20

g Le 26:3, 12

h Ge 15:18
  Ex 3:8
  Le 20:24
  De 6:3

i Jer 7:13
  Jer 25:4
  Jer 35:15

j Isa 65:2
  Jer 7:24, 26
  Eze 20:8
  Zec 7:11, 12

Second Col.
a Jg 2:11, 17
  1Sa 8:8
  2Ki 22:17

b 2Ch 28:22,
  23

c De 31:16
  2Ki 17:6, 7
  Ho 6:7

d 2Ki 22:16
  Jer 6:19
  Eze 7:5

e Isa 1:15
  Jer 14:12
  Eze 8:18
  Mic 3:4

f De 32:37, 38
  Jer 2:28

g Jer 7:9, 10

h Jer 7:16
  Jer 14:11

11:2 *Apparently addressed to Jeremiah. 11:5 *Or "So be it." 11:7 *Lit.,
"rising up early and admonishing."

11:12 *Or "sacrificial smoke." 11:13
*Or "the shameful god." 11:14 *That
is, Jeremiah. 11:15 *That is, sacrifices
made in the temple.

Beautiful with fine fruit.
With a great roaring sound,
 he has set her on fire,
And they have broken its
 branches.

17 "Jehovah of armies, your Planter,[a] has declared that a calamity will come upon you because of the evil committed by the house of Israel and the house of Judah, who have offended me by making sacrifices to Ba′al."[b]

18 Jehovah informed me so
 that I would know;
At that time you caused me
 to see what they were
 doing.

19 I was like a docile lamb being
 brought to the slaughter.
I did not know that they were
 scheming against me:[c]
"Let us destroy the tree
 with its fruit,
And let us cut him off from
 the land of the living,
So that his name may be
 remembered no more."

20 But Jehovah of armies
 judges with righteousness;
He examines the innermost
 thoughts* and the heart.[d]
Let me see your vengeance
 on them,
For to you I have committed
 my legal case.

21 Therefore this is what Jehovah says against the men of An′a·thoth[e] who are seeking to take your life* and who say: "You must not prophesy in the name of Jehovah,[f] or you will die by our hand"; **22** therefore this is what Jehovah of armies says: "Here I am going to call them to account. The young men will die by the sword,[g] and their sons and their daughters will die by famine.[h] **23** Not even a remnant will be left of them, be-

---

11:20; 12:2 *Or "deepest emotions." Lit., "kidneys." **11:21** *Or "seeking your soul."

cause I will bring calamity on the men of An′a·thoth[a] in the year of their being called to account."

12 You are righteous,
 O Jehovah,[b] when
 I make my complaint
 to you,
When I speak about matters
 of justice with you.
But why is the way of wicked
 ones successful,[c]
And why are the treacherous
 unworried?

2 You planted them, and they
 have taken root.
They have grown and
 produced fruit.
You are on their lips, but far
 away from their innermost
 thoughts.*[d]

3 But you know me well,
 O Jehovah,[e] you see me;
You have examined my heart
 and found it in union with
 you.[f]
Single them out like sheep
 for slaughtering,
And set them apart for the
 day of killing.

4 How much longer should the
 land wither away
And the vegetation of every
 field dry up?[g]
Because of the evil of those
 dwelling in it,
The beasts and the birds
 have been swept away.
For they have said: "He does
 not see what will happen
 to us."

5 If you get tired running with
 footmen,
How can you run a race
 against horses?[h]
Even if you are confident
 in the land of peace,
How will you fare among
 the dense thickets along
 the Jordan?

6 For even your own brothers,
 the household of your own
 father,

CHAP. 11

a Isa 5:2
 Jer 2:21

b Jer 19:5, 15

c Jer 18:18

d 1Ch 28:9
 Jer 17:10
 Jer 20:12

e Jer 1:1

f Isa 30:10
 Am 2:12
 Am 7:16

g 2Ch 36:17
 La 2:21

h Jer 18:21

Second Col.

a Jos 21:8, 18

CHAP. 12

b Ge 18:25

c Job 12:6
 Job 21:7
 Ps 73:3
 Jer 5:28

d Isa 29:13

e Ps 139:1, 2

f 2Ki 20:3
 Ps 17:3
 Jer 11:20

g Jer 14:6
 Jer 23:10

h Jer 4:13

Have dealt treacherously with you.[a]
They have raised a loud cry against you.
Do not put faith in them,
Even if they speak good things to you.

7 "I have abandoned my house;[b] I have deserted my inheritance.[c]
I have given my dearly beloved one* into the hand of her enemies.[d]

8 My inheritance has become to me like a lion in the forest.
She has roared against me.
So I have come to hate her.

9 My inheritance is like a multicolored* bird of prey to me;
The other birds of prey surround it and attack it.[e]
Come, gather together, all you beasts of the field,
Come to eat.[f]

10 Many shepherds have destroyed my vineyard;[g]
They have trampled my portion of land.[h]
They have turned my desirable portion of land into a desolate wilderness.

11 It has become a wasteland.
It has withered;*
It is desolate before me.[i]
The whole land has been made desolate,
But no man takes it to heart.[j]

12 On all the worn paths through the wilderness the destroyers have come,
For the sword of Jehovah is devouring from one end of the land to the other end.[k]
There is no peace for anyone.*

13 They have sown wheat, but they have reaped thorns.[l]

They have worn themselves out, but to no benefit.
They will be ashamed of their produce
Because of the burning anger of Jehovah."

14 This is what Jehovah says against all my wicked neighbors, who are touching the inheritance that I caused my people Israel to possess:[a] "Here I am uprooting them from their land,[b] and I will uproot the house of Judah from among them. 15 But after I uproot them, I will again have mercy on them and bring each of them back to his inheritance and to his land."

16 "And if they make sure to learn the ways of my people and to swear by my name, 'As surely as Jehovah is alive!' just as they taught my people to swear by Ba′al, they will then be built up among my people. 17 But if they refuse to obey, I will also uproot that nation, uprooting and destroying it," declares Jehovah.[c]

13 This is what Jehovah told me: "Go and buy a linen belt for yourself and put it around your waist, but do not dip it in water." 2 So I bought the belt according to the word of Jehovah and put it around my waist. 3 And the word of Jehovah came to me a second time: 4 "Take the belt that you bought and are wearing and get up, go to the Eu·phra′tes, and hide it there in a cleft of the crag." 5 So I went and hid it by the Eu·phra′tes, just as Jehovah had commanded me.

6 But many days later Jehovah said to me: "Get up, go to the Eu·phra′tes, and take from there the belt that I commanded you to hide there." 7 So I went to the Eu·phra′tes and dug up the belt and took it from the place where I had hidden it, and

---

CHAP. 12
a Jer 9:4

b Lu 13:35

c Ex 19:5
Isa 47:6

d La 2:1

e 2Ki 24:2
Eze 16:37

f Isa 56:9
Jer 7:33

g Ps 80:8
Isa 5:1, 7
Jer 6:3

h Isa 63:18
Jer 3:19

i Jer 9:11
Jer 10:22

j Isa 42:24, 25

k Le 26:33
Jer 15:2

l Le 26:16
Mic 6:15

Second Col.
a Ps 79:4
Jer 48:26
Eze 25:3
Zec 1:15
Zec 2:8

b Jer 48:2
Jer 49:2

c Isa 60:12

12:7 *Or "the beloved one of my soul." 12:9 *Or "speckled." 12:11 *Or possibly, "It mourns." 12:12 *Lit., "any flesh."

I saw that the belt had been ruined; it was completely useless.

8 Then the word of Jehovah came to me: **9** "This is what Jehovah says, 'In the same way I will destroy the pride of Judah and the immense pride of Jerusalem.ᵃ **10** These evil people who refuse to obey my words,ᵇ who stubbornly follow their own heart,ᶜ and who are following other gods, serving and bowing down to them, will become just like this belt that is completely useless.' **11** 'For just as a belt clings to the waist of a man, so I made the whole house of Israel and the whole house of Judah cling to me,' declares Jehovah, 'to become to me a people,ᵈ a name,ᵉ a praise, and something beautiful. But they did not obey.'ᶠ

12 "And you must also give this message to them, 'This is what Jehovah the God of Israel says: "Every large jar should be filled with wine."' And they will reply to you, 'Do we not already know that every large jar should be filled with wine?' **13** Then say to them, 'This is what Jehovah says: "Here I am filling with drunkenness all the inhabitants of this land,ᵍ the kings sitting on the throne of David, the priests and the prophets, and all the inhabitants of Jerusalem. **14** And I will smash them against each other, fathers and sons alike," declares Jehovah.ʰ "I will not show compassion or feel any sorrow or have any mercy on them; nothing will stop me from bringing them to ruin."'ⁱ

15 Hear and pay attention.
Do not be haughty, for Jehovah has spoken.
16 Give glory to Jehovah your God
Before he brings darkness
And before your feet stumble on the mountains at dusk.

You will hope for the light,
But he will bring deep shadow;
He will turn it into thick gloom.ᵃ
17 And if you refuse to listen,
I* will weep in secret because of your pride.
I will shed many tears, and my eyes will stream with tears,ᵇ
Because the flock of Jehovahᶜ has been carried away captive.
18 Tell the king and the queen mother,*ᵈ 'Sit in a lower place,
For your beautiful crown will fall from your head.'
19 The cities of the south are shut,* with no one to open them.
All of Judah has been taken into exile, taken completely into exile.ᵉ
20 Raise your eyes and see those coming from the north.ᶠ
Where is the flock you were given, your beautiful sheep?ᵍ
21 What will you say when your punishment comes
From your close friends whom you cultivated from the start?ʰ
Will not birth pains seize you, like those of a woman giving birth?ⁱ
22 And when you say in your heart, 'Why have these things befallen me?'
It is because of your great error that your skirts have been stripped offᵏ
And your heels have been treated violently.
23 Can a Cush′ite* change his skin, or a leopard its spots?ˡ

CHAP. 13
a Le 26:19
   Zep 3:11

b 2Ch 36:15, 16

c Jer 6:28

d Ex 19:5
   De 26:18
   Ps 135:4

e Jer 33:9

f Jer 6:17

g Isa 29:9
   Isa 51:17
   Jer 25:27

h Jer 6:21
   Eze 5:10

i Eze 7:4
   Eze 24:14

Second Col.
a Isa 59:9

b Jer 9:1

c Ps 100:3

d 2Ki 24:12
   Jer 22:24, 26

e De 28:64

f Jer 6:22

g Eze 34:8

h Isa 39:1, 2

i Jer 6:24
   Mic 4:9

j Jer 5:19
   Jer 16:10, 11

k Eze 16:37

l Pr 27:22

13:17 *Or "My soul." **13:18** *Or "the lady." **13:19** *Or "besieged." **13:23** *Or "an Ethiopian."

If so, then you can do good,
You who are trained to do
bad.

24 So I will scatter them like
straw blown by the desert
wind.[a]

25 This is your lot, the portion
that I have measured out
to you," declares Jehovah,
"Because you have forgotten
me[b] and you trust in lies.[c]

26 Therefore, I will lift up your
skirts over your face,
And your shame will be
seen,[d]

27 Your acts of adultery[e] and
your lustful neighing,
Your obscene* prostitution.
On the hills, in the field,
I have seen your disgusting
behavior.[f]
Woe to you, O Jerusalem!
How much longer will you
remain unclean?"[g]

14 This is the word of Jehovah that came to Jeremiah
concerning the droughts:[h]

2 Judah mourns,[i] and its gates
have faded away.
They sink to the ground
dejected,
And a cry goes up from
Jerusalem.

3 And their masters send their
servants* for water.
They go to the water holes#
and find no water.
They return with their
vessels empty.
They are ashamed and
disappointed,
And they cover their heads.

4 Because the ground is
cracked,
For there is no rain on the
land,[j]
The farmers are dismayed
and cover their heads.

13:27 *Or "shameful." 14:3 *Or "their
small ones." #Or "the ditches; the cisterns."

CHAP. 13
a Le 26:33
De 28:64

b Jer 2:32

c De 32:37, 38
Isa 28:15
Jer 10:14

d La 1:8
Eze 16:37
Eze 23:29

e Jer 2:20
Eze 16:15

f Isa 65:7
Eze 6:13

g Eze 24:13

CHAP. 14
h De 28:24

i Joe 1:10

j Le 26:20
De 28:23

Second Col.
a Jer 12:4
Joe 1:18

b Jos 7:9
Ps 25:11
Ps 115:1, 2

c Ezr 9:6
Ne 9:33
Da 9:5, 8

d Ps 106:8
Ps 106:21
Isa 45:15

e Ex 29:45
De 23:14

f Da 9:19

g Jer 2:23

h Jer 2:25

i Jer 6:20

j Ho 8:13

k Jer 7:16
Jer 11:14

l Isa 1:15
Isa 58:3
Jer 11:11
Eze 8:18

m Isa 1:11

n Jer 9:16
Eze 5:12

5 Even the doe in the field
forsakes her newborn
Because there is no grass.

6 The wild donkeys stand on
the bare hills.
They pant for air like jackals;
Their eyes fail because there
is no vegetation.[a]

7 Although our own errors
testify against us,
O Jehovah, act for the sake
of your name.[b]
For our acts of unfaithfulness are many,[c]
And it is against you that
we have sinned.

8 O hope of Israel, his Savior[d]
in times of distress,
Why are you like a stranger
in the land,
Like a traveler who stops
only to spend the night?

9 Why are you like a man
who is stunned,
Like a mighty man who
cannot save?
For you are among us,
O Jehovah,[e]
And your name has been
called on us.[f]
Do not abandon us.

10 This is what Jehovah says
concerning this people: "They
love to wander about;[g] they have
not restrained their feet.[h] So Jehovah finds no pleasure in them.[i]
Now he will remember their error and call them to account for
their sins."[j]

11 Then Jehovah said to me:
"Do not pray for good to come
to this people.[k] 12 When they
fast, I do not listen to their entreaties,[l] and when they offer
whole burnt offerings and grain
offerings, I take no pleasure in
them,[m] for by the sword, by famine, and by pestilence,* I will do
away with them."[n]

13 At this I said: "Alas, O Sovereign Lord Jehovah! Here the

14:12 *Or "disease."

prophets are saying to them, 'You will not see the sword, and famine will not come upon you, but I will give you true peace in this place.'"[a]

14 Jehovah then said to me: "The prophets are prophesying lies in my name.[b] I have not sent them or commanded them or spoken to them.[c] A lying vision and a worthless divination and the deceit of their own heart is what they are prophesying to you.[d] 15 Therefore this is what Jehovah says concerning the prophets who are prophesying in my name, though I did not send them, and who say that no sword or famine will occur in this land: 'By sword and by famine those prophets will perish.[e] 16 And the people to whom they are prophesying will be cast out into the streets of Jerusalem because of the famine and the sword, with no one to bury them[f]—them, their wives, their sons, or their daughters—for I will pour out on them the calamity they deserve.'[g]

17 "You must speak this word to them,

'Let my eyes stream with tears night and day, let them not cease,[h]
For the virgin daughter of my people has been completely crushed and broken,[i]
With an extremely severe wound.

18 If I go out into the field and look,
I see those slain by the sword![j]
And if I come into the city,
I see the diseases from the famine![k]
For both the prophet and the priest have gone around in a land that they do not know.'"[l]

19 Have you completely rejected Judah, or have you* abhorred Zion?[a]
Why have you struck us, so that there is no healing for us?[b]
There was a hope for peace, but nothing good came,
For a time of healing, but there is terror![c]

20 We acknowledge our wickedness, O Jehovah,
And the error of our forefathers,
For we have sinned against you.[d]

21 For the sake of your name, do not reject us;[e]
Do not despise your glorious throne.
Remember, and do not break your covenant with us.[f]

22 Can any of the worthless idols of the nations give rain,
Or can even the heavens send showers of rain on their own?
Are you not the only One, O Jehovah our God?[g]
And we hope in you,
For you alone have done all these things.

15 Then Jehovah said to me: "Even if Moses and Samuel were standing before me,* I would show no favor toward* this people. Drive them out from before me. Let them go. 2 And if they say to you, 'Where should we go?' you must say to them, 'This is what Jehovah says:

"Whoever is for deadly plague, to deadly plague!
Whoever is for the sword, to the sword![i]
Whoever is for the famine, to the famine!
And whoever is for the captivity, to the captivity!"'[j]

14:19 *Or "has your soul." 15:1 *Or "my soul would not be toward."

3 "'And I will appoint over them four calamities,'*[a] declares Jehovah, 'the sword to kill, the dogs to drag away, and the birds of the heavens and the beasts of the earth to devour and to destroy.[b] 4 And I will make them an object of horror to all the kingdoms of the earth[c] because of Ma·nasʹseh the son of Hez·e·kiʹah, the king of Judah, for what he did in Jerusalem.[d]

5 Who will show compassion
  to you, O Jerusalem,
Who will sympathize with
  you,
And who will stop to ask
  about your welfare?'

6 'You have deserted me,'
  declares Jehovah.[e]
'You keep turning your back
  on me.'*[f]
So I will stretch out my hand
  against you and destroy
  you.[g]
I am tired of feeling pity
  for you.#

7 And I will winnow them with
  a fork in the gates of the
  land.
I will bereave them of
  children.[h]
I will destroy my people,
Since they refuse to turn
  back from their ways.[i]

8 Their widows will become
  more numerous before me
  than the sand of the seas.
I will bring a destroyer
  against them at midday,
  against mothers and
  young men.
I will bring agitation and
  terror upon them suddenly.

9 The woman who bore seven
  children has grown faint;
She* struggles for breath.

Her sun has set while it is
  yet day,
Causing shame and
  humiliation.'*
'And those few remaining
  ones of them
I will give to the sword
  before their enemies,'
  declares Jehovah."[a]

10 Woe to me, O my mother,
  because you gave birth
  to me,[b]
A man subject to quarrel
  and strife with all the land.
I have neither loaned nor
  borrowed;
But all of them curse me.

11 Jehovah said: "I will surely
  minister to you for good;
I will surely intercede for
  you in the time of calamity,
In the time of distress
  against the enemy.

12 Can anyone break iron in
  pieces,
Iron from the north, and
  copper?

13 Your resources and your
  treasures I will give as
  plunder,[c]
Not for a price, but because
  of all your sins throughout
  all your territories.

14 I will give them to your
  enemies
To take to a land you do not
  know.[d]
For a fire has been ignited
  by my anger,
And it is burning against
  you."[e]

15 You know, O Jehovah,
Remember me and turn
  your attention to me.
Take vengeance on my
  persecutors for me.[f]
Do not let me perish*
  because of your slowness
  to anger.

CHAP. 15

a Eze 14:21

b De 28:26
  Jer 7:33

c De 28:15, 25
  Jer 24:9
  Eze 23:46

d 2Ki 21:11
  2Ki 23:26
  2Ki 24:3, 4

e Jer 2:13

f Isa 1:4

g Zep 1:4

h De 28:15, 18
  Jer 9:21
  Eze 24:21

i Jer 5:3

_____

Second Col.

a Jer 44:27
  Eze 5:12

b Jer 20:14

c Jer 20:5

d Le 26:38
  Jer 16:13

e De 32:22
  Isa 42:24, 25
  Jer 17:4

f Jer 11:20
  Jer 12:3
  Jer 17:18
  Jer 37:15

15:3 *Or possibly, "four kinds of judgment." Lit., "four families." **15:6** *Or possibly, "keep walking backward." #Or "feeling regret." **15:9** *Or "Her soul."

15:9 *Or possibly, "It has become ashamed and felt abashed." **15:15** *Lit., "Do not take me away."

Know that for your sake
I bear this reproach.[a]
16 Your words were found,
and I ate them;[b]
And your word became to
me the exultation and the
rejoicing of my heart,
For your name has been
called on me, O Jehovah
God of armies.
17 I do not sit in the company of
merrymakers and rejoice.[c]
Because your hand is upon
me, I sit alone,
For you have filled me with
indignation.*[d]
18 Why is my pain chronic and
my wound incurable?
It refuses to be healed.
Will you become to me like
a deceptive water supply
That cannot be relied on?
19 Therefore this is what
Jehovah says:
"If you return, then I will
restore you,
And you will stand
before me.
If you separate what is
precious from what is
worthless,
You will become like my own
mouth.*
They will have to turn to you,
But you will not turn to
them."
20 "I am making you a fortified
copper wall to this people.[e]
They will certainly fight
against you,
But they will not prevail
against you,*[f]
For I am with you, to save
you and to rescue you,"
declares Jehovah.
21 "And I will rescue you from
the hand of the wicked
And redeem you from the
palm of the ruthless."

16 The word of Jehovah
again came to me, saying:
2 "You must not take a wife for
yourself, and you must not have
sons and daughters in this place.
3 For this is what Jehovah says
concerning the sons and daughters who are born here and concerning their mothers who give
birth to them and concerning
their fathers who cause their
birth in this land: 4 'They will
die of deadly diseases,[a] but no
one will mourn them or bury
them; they will become like manure on the surface of the
ground.[b] They will perish by the
sword and by famine,[c] and their
dead bodies will be food for the
birds of the heavens and for the
beasts of the earth.'

5 For this is what Jehovah
says,
'Do not enter a house where
a mourners' feast is held,
And do not go to wail or offer
sympathy.'[d]
'For I have taken away my
peace from this people,'
declares Jehovah,
'As well as my loyal love and
mercy.[e]
6 Both the great and the small
will die in this land.
They will not be buried,
No one will mourn them,
Nor will anyone cut himself
or make himself bald for
them.*
7 And no one will provide food
for those in mourning,
To comfort them over their
dead;
Nor will anyone give them
the cup of consolation
To drink over the loss of
their father or mother.
8 And do not enter a house
of feasting
To sit down with them to eat
and drink.'

CHAP. 15
a Ps 69:7

b Eze 3:1-3
Re 10:9, 10

c Ps 1:1

d Jer 20:8

e Jer 1:18
Eze 3:9

f Jer 20:11

Second Col.

CHAP. 16
a Jer 15:2

b Ps 79:2, 3
Isa 5:25
Jer 7:33
Jer 9:22
Jer 36:30

c Eze 5:12

d Eze 24:16, 17

e De 31:17
Isa 27:11
Isa 63:10

15:17 *Or "a message of denunciation."
15:19 *Or "become my spokesman."
15:20 *Or "defeat you."

16:6 *Pagan mourning customs apparently practiced in apostate Israel.

9 "For this is what Jehovah of armies, the God of Israel, says, 'Here in this place, in your days and before your very eyes, I will put an end to the sounds of exultation and rejoicing, the voice of the bridegroom and the voice of the bride.'[a]

10 "When you tell this people all these words, they will ask you, 'Why has Jehovah spoken of all this great calamity against us? What error and what sin have we committed against Jehovah our God?'[b] **11** You must reply to them, "'Because your forefathers abandoned me,"[c] declares Jehovah, "and they kept following other gods and serving them and bowing down to them.[d] But me they abandoned, and my law they did not keep.[e] **12** And you have behaved far worse than your forefathers,[f] and each one of you follows the stubbornness of his wicked heart instead of obeying me.[g] **13** So I will hurl you out of this land into a land that neither you nor your forefathers have known,[h] and there you will have to serve other gods day and night,[i] because I will show you no favor.'"

14 "'However, the days are coming,' declares Jehovah, 'when they will no longer say: "As surely as Jehovah is alive, who brought the people of Israel out of the land of Egypt!"[j] **15** but rather: "As surely as Jehovah is alive, who brought the people of Israel from the land of the north and from all the lands to which he had dispersed them!" and I will bring them back to their land, which I gave to their forefathers.'[k]

16 'Here I am sending for many fishermen,' declares Jehovah,
'And they will fish for them.
After that I will send for many hunters,
And they will hunt them down on every mountain and every hill
And out of the clefts of the crags.

17 For my eyes are on everything they do.*
They have not been hidden from before me,
Nor has their error been hidden from my eyes.

18 First, I will repay the full amount due for their error and their sin,[a]
For they have profaned my land with the lifeless figures* of their disgusting idols
And have filled my inheritance with their detestable things.'"[b]

19 O Jehovah, my strength and my stronghold,
My place to flee in the day of distress,[c]
To you the nations will come from the ends of the earth,
And they will say: "Our forefathers inherited utter falsehood,
Futility and useless things of no benefit."[d]

20 Can a man make gods for himself
When they are not really gods?[e]

21 "So I will make them know,
At this time I will make them know my power and my might,
And they will have to know that my name is Jehovah."

17 "The sin of Judah is written down with an iron stylus.
With a diamond point it is engraved on the tablet of their heart
And on the horns of their altars,

CHAP. 16
a Isa 24:7, 8
Jer 7:34
Re 18:23

b Jer 5:19

c Jg 2:12

d Jer 8:1, 2

e Da 9:11
Am 2:4

f Jer 7:26

g Ne 9:29
Jer 6:28

h 2Ch 7:20
Jer 15:14
Jer 17:4

i De 4:27, 28
De 28:36

j Ex 20:2
Jer 23:7, 8

k De 30:1-3
Jer 3:18
Jer 24:6
Jer 30:3
Jer 32:37
Am 9:14

Second Col.
a Isa 40:2

b Le 26:30
Ps 106:38

c Jer 17:17

d Jer 10:5, 14

e Ps 115:4
Jer 2:11
1Co 8:4

16:17 *Lit., "on all their ways." **16:18** *Lit., "the corpses."

2 While their sons remember
  their altars and their
  sacred poles*ª
  Beside a luxuriant tree,
  on the high hills,ᵇ
3 On the mountains in the
  open countryside.
  Your resources, all your
  treasures, I will give as
  plunderᶜ
  —Yes, your high places because of sin throughout
  your territories.ᵈ
4 You will forfeit, of your own
  accord, your inheritance
  that I gave you.ᵉ
  And I will make you serve
  your enemies in a land you
  do not know,ᶠ
  For you have kindled my
  anger like a fire.*ᵍ
  It will burn for all time."
5 This is what Jehovah says:
  "Cursed is the man* who
  puts his trust in mere
  humans,ʰ
  Who relies on human
  power,*ⁱ
  And whose heart turns away
  from Jehovah.
6 He will become like a
  solitary tree in the desert.
  He will not see when good
  comes,
  But he will reside in parched
  places in the wilderness,
  In a salt land where no one
  can live.
7 Blessed is the man* who puts
  his trust in Jehovah,
  Whose confidence is in
  Jehovah.ʲ
8 He will become like a tree
  planted by the waters,
  That sends out its roots to
  the stream.
  He will not notice when heat
  comes,

But his leaves will always
  flourish.ª
  And in the year of drought
  he will not be anxious,
  Nor will he quit producing
  fruit.
9 The heart is more treacherous* than anything else
  and is desperate.#ᵇ
  Who can know it?
10 I, Jehovah, am searching
  the heart,ᶜ
  Examining the innermost
  thoughts,*
  To give to each one
  according to his ways,
  According to the fruitage
  of his works.ᵈ
11 Like a partridge that gathers
  what it has not laid,
  So is the one who acquires
  riches dishonestly.*ᵉ
  They will leave him in
  midlife,
  And in the end he will prove
  senseless."
12 A glorious throne, exalted
  from the beginning,
  Is the place of our
  sanctuary.ᶠ
13 O Jehovah, the hope of
  Israel,
  All those who abandon you
  will be put to shame.
  Those apostatizing from
  you* will be written in
  the dust,ᵍ
  Because they have aban-
  doned Jehovah, the source
  of living water.ʰ
14 Heal me, O Jehovah, and
  I will be healed.
  Save me, and I will be saved,ⁱ
  For you are the object of my
  praise.
15 Look! There are those saying
  to me:

CHAP. 17

a Jg 3:7
  2Ch 24:18
  2Ch 33:1, 3

b Isa 1:29
  Eze 6:13

c 2Ki 24:11, 13
  Jer 15:13

d Le 26:30
  Eze 6:3

e La 5:2

f De 28:48
  Jer 16:13

g Isa 5:25
  Jer 15:14

h Isa 30:1, 2

i 2Ki 16:7

j Ps 34:8
  Ps 146:5
  Isa 26:3

Second Col.

a Ps 1:3
  Ps 92:12, 13

b Ge 6:5
  Ge 8:21
  Pr 28:26

c 1Sa 16:7
  1Ch 28:9
  Pr 17:3
  Pr 21:2

d Ro 2:6
  Ga 6:7
  Re 2:23
  Re 22:12

e Pr 28:20
  Isa 1:23
  Jas 5:4

f 2Ch 2:5
  Isa 6:1

g Ps 73:27
  Isa 1:28

h Jer 2:13
  Re 22:1

i Jer 15:20

17:2 *See Glossary. 17:4 *Or possibly,
"For as a fire you have been ignited in
my anger." 17:5, 7 *Or "strong man."
17:5 #Lit., "makes flesh his arm."

17:9 *Or "deceitful." #Or possibly, "incurable." 17:10 *Or "deepest emotions." Lit., "kidneys." 17:11 *Or "but
not with justice." 17:13 *Lit., "from
me," apparently referring to Jehovah.

"Where is the word of
Jehovah?[a]
Let it come, please!"

16 But as for me, I did not run
away from following you
as a shepherd,
Nor did I long for the day of
disaster.
You well know everything my
lips have spoken;
It all took place before your
face!

17 Do not be a cause of terror
to me.
You are my refuge in the day
of calamity.

18 Let my persecutors be put to
shame,[b]
But do not let me be put to
shame.
Let them be struck with
terror,
But do not let me be struck
with terror.
Bring the day of calamity on
them,[c]
And crush them and destroy
them completely.*

19 This is what Jehovah told
me: "Go and stand in the gate of
the people by which the
kings of Judah go in and
out, and in all the gates of
Jerusalem.[d] 20 You must say
to them, 'Hear the word of Jehovah, you kings of Judah, all
people of Judah, and all inhabitants of Jerusalem, who enter by
these gates. 21 This is what Jehovah says: "Watch yourselves,*
and do not carry any load on
the Sabbath day or bring it in
through the gates of Jerusalem.[e]
22 You must not bring any load
out of your homes on the Sabbath day; and you must do no
work at all.[f] Keep the Sabbath
day sacred, just as I commanded
your forefathers.[g] 23 But they
did not listen or incline their ear,

and they stubbornly refused* to
obey or to accept discipline."[a]

24 "'However, if you strictly obey me," declares Jehovah, "and you bring in no load
through the gates of this city on
the Sabbath day, and you keep
the Sabbath day sacred by not
doing any work on it,[b] 25 then
kings and princes who sit on the
throne of David[c] will also enter in through the gates of this
city, riding in the chariot and on
horses, they and their princes,
the men of Judah and the inhabitants of Jerusalem;[d] and this
city will be inhabited for all
time. 26 And people will come
from the cities of Judah, from
the places around Jerusalem,
from the land of Benjamin,[e] from
the lowland,[f] from the mountainous region, and from the
Neg'eb,* bringing whole burnt
offerings,[g] sacrifices,[h] grain offerings,[i] frankincense, and
thanksgiving sacrifices into the
house of Jehovah.[j]

27 "'But if you do not obey
me by keeping the Sabbath day
sacred and by not carrying loads
and bringing them through the
gates of Jerusalem on the Sabbath day, I will set her gates on
fire, and it will certainly consume the fortified towers of Jerusalem[k] and will not be extinguished."'[l]

18 This is the word that came
to Jeremiah from Jeho-
vah: 2 "Rise up and go down
to the house of the potter,[m] and
there I will cause you to hear my
words."

3 So I went down to the
house of the potter, and he was
working on the potter's wheels.
4 But the vessel that the potter was making with the clay
was spoiled in his hand. So the

CHAP. 17
a Isa 5:19
2Pe 3:4

b Jer 15:15
Jer 20:11

c Jer 18:23

d Jer 7:2

e Ne 13:19

f Ex 20:9, 10
Le 23:3

g Ex 31:13

Second Col.
a Isa 48:4
Eze 20:13

b De 5:12-14

c Ps 132:11

d Jer 22:4

e Jer 32:44

f Jer 33:13

g Le 1:3

h Ezr 3:3

i Le 2:1, 2

j Ps 107:22
Ps 116:17
Jer 33:10, 11

k 2Ki 25:9, 10
Jer 39:8

l 2Ki 22:16, 17
La 4:11

CHAP. 18
m Jer 19:1

17:18 *Or "destroy them twice over."
17:21 *Or "your souls."
17:23 *Lit., "they hardened their neck."
17:26 *Or "the south."

potter reworked it into another vessel, just as he saw fit.*

5 Then the word of Jehovah came to me, saying: 6 "'Can I not do to you just as this potter did, O house of Israel?' declares Jehovah. 'Look! As the clay in the hand of the potter, so are you in my hand, O house of Israel.ᵃ 7 Whenever I may speak about uprooting and pulling down and destroying a nation or a kingdom,ᵇ 8 and that nation abandons its wickedness that I spoke against, I will also change my mind concerning* the calamity that I intended to bring against it.ᶜ 9 But whenever I speak about building up and planting a nation or a kingdom, 10 and it does what is bad in my eyes and does not obey my voice, I will change my mind concerning* the good that I intended to do for it.'

11 "Now say, please, to the men of Judah and to the inhabitants of Jerusalem, 'This is what Jehovah says: "Here I am preparing* a calamity and devising a scheme against you. Turn back, please, from your bad ways, and reform your ways and your practices."'"ᵈ

12 But they said: "It is hopeless!ᵉ For we will walk after our own thoughts, and each of us will act according to the stubbornness of his wicked heart."ᶠ

13 Therefore this is what Jehovah says:

"Ask for yourselves, please, among the nations.
Who has heard anything like this?
The virgin of Israel has done a most horrible thing.ᵍ

14 Does the snow of Leb′a·non disappear from the rocks on its slopes?

Or will cool waters flowing from afar dry up?

15 But my people have forgotten me.ᵃ
For they make sacrifices* to something worthless,ᵇ
And they make men stumble in their ways, the ancient paths,ᶜ
To walk on back roads that are not smooth and level,

16 In order to make their land an object of horrorᵈ
And something to whistle at forever.ᵉ
Every last one passing by it will stare in horror and shake his head.ᶠ

17 Like the east wind, I will scatter them before the enemy.
I will show them my back, not my face, in the day of their disaster."ᵍ

18 And they said: "Come, let us devise a plot against Jeremiah,ʰ for the law* will not perish from our priests or counsel from the wise men or the word from the prophets. Come and let us speak against him# and pay no attention to what he says."

19 Do pay attention to me, O Jehovah,
And listen to what my opponents are saying.

20 Should good be repaid with bad?
For they have dug a pit for my life.*ⁱ
Remember how I stood before you to speak good about them,
To turn your wrath away from them.

21 So give their sons over to the famine,

CHAP. 18
a Ro 9:20, 21

b Jer 1:10
Jer 12:14
Jer 25:9
Jer 45:4

c 1Ki 8:33, 34
Ps 106:45
Jer 7:3
Jer 26:3
Eze 18:21
Joe 2:13
Jon 3:5, 10

d Isa 1:16
Eze 18:23

e Jer 2:25

f De 29:19, 20
Jer 7:24

g Jer 2:13

Second Col.
a Jer 2:19
Jer 3:21

b Jer 10:14, 15

c Jer 6:16

d Le 26:33
Eze 6:14

e 1Ki 9:8
Jer 19:8
La 2:15
Mic 6:16

f De 28:37

g De 31:17

h Jer 11:19

i Ps 35:7

18:4 *Lit., "as it was right in the eyes of the potter to make." 18:8, 10 *Or "feel regret over." 18:11 *Lit., "forming." 18:15 *Or "sacrificial smoke." #Or "not built up." 18:18 *Or "instruction." #Lit., "strike him with the tongue." 18:20 *Or "soul."

And hand them over to the power of the sword.[a]
May their wives become bereaved of children and widowed.[b]
May their men be killed with deadly plague,
Their young men struck down with the sword in battle.[c]

22 Let a cry be heard from their houses
When you bring marauders on them suddenly.
For they have dug a pit to capture me
And have laid traps for my feet.[d]

23 But you, O Jehovah,
Well know all their schemes against me to kill me.[e]
Do not cover their error,
And do not wipe out their sin from before you.
Let them stumble before you[f]
When you take action against them in your anger.[g]

19 This is what Jehovah said: "Go and buy an earthenware flask from a potter.[h] Take some of the elders of the people and some of the elders of the priests, **2** and go out to the Valley of the Son of Hin'nom,[i] at the entrance of the Gate of the Potsherds. And there proclaim the words that I speak to you. **3** You will say, 'Hear the word of Jehovah, you kings of Judah and inhabitants of Jerusalem. This is what Jehovah of armies, the God of Israel, says:

"'"I am about to bring a calamity on this place, and the ears of anyone who hears about it will tingle. **4** It is because they abandoned me[j] and made this place unrecognizable.[k] In it they are sacrificing to other gods, whom they and their forefathers and the kings of Judah had not known, and they have filled this place with the blood of the innocent ones.[a] **5** They built the high places of Ba'al in order to burn their sons in the fire as whole burnt offerings to Ba'al,[b] something that I had not commanded or spoken of and that had never even come into my heart."'*[c]

6 "'"Therefore look! the days are coming,' declares Jehovah, "when this place will no longer be called To'pheth or the Valley of the Son of Hin'nom but the Valley of the Slaughter.[d] **7** I will thwart the plans of Judah and Jerusalem in this place, and I will make them fall by the sword before their enemies and by the hand of those seeking to take their life.* And I will give their dead bodies as food to the birds of the heavens and to the beasts of the earth.[e] **8** And I will make this city an object of horror and something to whistle at. Every last one passing by it will stare in horror and whistle over all its plagues.[f] **9** And I will make them eat the flesh of their sons and daughters, and they will each eat the flesh of his fellow man, because of the siege and their desperation when they are hemmed in by their enemies and those seeking to take their life."'*[g]

10 "Then break the flask before the eyes of the men who go with you, **11** and say to them, 'This is what Jehovah of armies says: "This is how I will break this people and this city, like someone who breaks a potter's vessel so that it can never be repaired; and they will bury the dead in To'pheth until there is no more room to bury them."'[h]

12 "'That is what I will do to this place,' declares Jehovah, 'and to its inhabitants, to make this city like To'pheth. **13** And

CHAP. 18
a Jer 12:3
b La 5:3
c 2Ch 36:17
d Ps 38:12
e Jer 11:19, 20
f Ps 35:4
g Jer 15:15

CHAP. 19
h Jer 18:2
i Jos 15:8, 12
  2Ch 28:1, 3
  Jer 7:31
j 2Ki 22:16, 17
  Isa 65:11
k 2Ch 33:1, 4

Second Col.
a 2Ki 21:16
  Isa 59:7
  Jer 2:34
  La 4:13
  Mt 23:34, 35
b 2Ch 28:1, 3
  2Ch 33:1, 6
  Isa 57:5
c Le 18:21
  Jer 7:31
  Jer 32:35
d Jer 7:32
e De 28:25, 26
  Ps 79:2
  Jer 7:33
  Jer 16:4
f 1Ki 9:8
  Jer 18:16
  La 2:15
g Le 26:29
  De 28:53
  La 2:20
  La 4:10
  Eze 5:10
h Jer 7:32

19:5 *Or "had never entered my thoughts." **19:7, 9** *Or "seeking their soul."

the houses of Jerusalem and the houses of the kings of Judah will become unclean like this place, To′pheth,ᵃ yes, all the houses on whose roofs they offered sacrifices to all the army of the heavensᵇ and where they poured out drink offerings to other gods.'"ᶜ

14 When Jeremiah returned from To′pheth where Jehovah sent him to prophesy, he stood in the courtyard of the house of Jehovah and said to all the people: **15** "This is what Jehovah of armies, the God of Israel, says, 'Here I am bringing on this city and on all its towns all the calamity that I have spoken against it, because they stubbornly refused* to obey my words.'"ᵈ

20 Now Pash′hur the son of Im′mer, the priest, who was also the leading commissioner in the house of Jehovah, was listening when Jeremiah prophesied these things. **2** Then Pash′hur struck Jeremiah the prophet and put him in the stocksᵉ that were at the Upper Gate of Benjamin, which was in the house of Jehovah. **3** But on the following day when Pash′hur released Jeremiah from the stocks, Jeremiah said to him:

"Jehovah has named you, not Pash′hur, but Terror All Around.ᶠ **4** For this is what Jehovah says, 'I will make you an object of terror to yourself and to all your friends, and they will fall by the sword of their enemies while your eyes are looking on;ᵍ and I will give all Judah into the hand of the king of Babylon, and he will take them into exile in Babylon and put them to death by the sword.ʰ **5** And I will give all the wealth of this city, all its resources, all its precious things, and all the treasures of the kings of Judah into

---

19:15 *Lit., "hardened their neck so as not."

the hand of their enemies.ᵃ And they will plunder them and seize them and take them to Babylon.ᵇ **6** And as for you, Pash′hur, and all who live in your house, you will go into captivity. You will go off to Babylon and die there, and you will be buried there with all your friends, because you have prophesied lies to them.'"ᶜ

7 You have fooled me,
    O Jehovah, and I was
    fooled.
You used your strength
    against me, and you
    prevailed.ᵈ
I have become a laughingstock all day long;
Everyone ridicules me.ᵉ
8 For whenever I speak, I must
    cry out and proclaim,
    "Violence and destruction!"
For me the word of Jehovah
    has been the cause of insults and jeering all day
    long.ᶠ
9 So I said: "I am not going to
    make mention of him,
And I will speak no more in
    his name."ᵍ
But in my heart it became
    like a burning fire shut up
    in my bones,
And I was tired of holding
    it in;
I could no longer endure it.ʰ
10 For I heard many evil
    rumors;
Terror surrounded me.ⁱ
"Denounce him; let us
    denounce him!"
Every man wishing me peace
    was watching for my
    downfall:ʲ
"Perhaps he will make
    a foolish mistake,
And we can prevail and take
    our revenge against him."
11 But Jehovah was with me
    like a fearsome warrior.ᵏ
That is why those persecuting me will stumble and
    will not prevail.ˡ

CHAP. 19
a Ps 79:1

b Jer 8:1, 2
  Zep 1:4, 5

c Jer 7:18
  Jer 32:29

d Ne 9:17, 29
  Zec 7:12

CHAP. 20
e 2Ch 16:10

f Jer 6:25

g De 28:32

h Jer 25:9
  Jer 39:9

Second Col.
a 2Ki 20:17
  2Ki 24:11, 13
  2Ki 25:13-15
  La 1:10

b 2Ch 36:10
  Jer 15:13

c Jer 14:14
  Jer 28:15
  Jer 29:21

d Eze 3:14
  Mic 3:8

e Ps 22:7
  Jer 15:10, 15

f 2Ch 36:16
  Jer 6:10

g 1Ki 19:2, 4
  Jon 1:3

h Jer 6:11
  Am 3:8
  Ac 4:19, 20

i Ps 31:13

j Jer 38:16

k Jer 1:8
  Ro 8:31

l Ps 27:2
  Jer 15:15, 20
  Jer 17:18

They will be put to great shame, for they will not succeed.

Their everlasting humiliation will not be forgotten.ᵃ

12 But you, O Jehovah of armies, are examining the righteous one;

You see the innermost thoughts* and the heart.ᵇ

Let me see your vengeance on them,ᶜ

For to you I have committed my legal case.ᵈ

13 Sing to Jehovah! Praise Jehovah!

For he has rescued the poor one* from the hand of evildoers.

14 Cursed be the day I was born!

May the day my mother gave birth to me not be blessed!ᵉ

15 Cursed be the man who brought good news to my father, saying:

"A son has been born to you, a boy!"

Making him rejoice greatly.

16 May that man become like cities that Jehovah overthrew without regret.

May he hear an outcry in the morning and the sound of alarm at midday.

17 Why did he not put me to death in the womb,

So that my mother would become my burial place

And her womb would always remain pregnant?ᶠ

18 Why did I have to come out of the womb

To see trouble and grief,

To end my days in shame?ᵍ

21 Jeremiah received the word from Jehovah when King Zed·e·kiʹahʰ sent to him Pashʹhurⁱ son of Mal·chiʹjah

20:12 *Or "deepest emotions." Lit., "kidneys." 20:13 *Or "the soul of the poor one."

CHAP. 20

a Ps 6:10

b Jer 17:10

c Ps 59:10
Jer 17:18

d Jer 11:20
1Pe 2:23

e Job 3:3
Jer 15:10

f Job 10:18

g Job 3:20

CHAP. 21

h 2Ki 24:18
1Ch 3:15
2Ch 36:9, 10

i Jer 38:1

Second Col.

a Jer 29:25
Jer 37:3
Jer 52:24, 27

b 2Ki 25:1
Jer 32:28
Jer 39:1

c 1Sa 7:10
2Ch 14:11
Isa 37:36, 37

d Jer 32:5

e Isa 63:10
La 2:5

f Isa 5:25

g De 28:21, 22
Eze 7:15

h 2Ki 25:6, 7
Jer 37:17
Jer 39:5-7
Jer 52:9-11
Eze 17:20

i De 48:49, 50
2Ch 36:17

---

and Zeph·a·niʹahᵃ son of Ma·a·seiʹah, the priest, requesting: 2 "Please inquire of Jehovah in our behalf, because King Neb·u·chad·nezʹzar* of Babylon is waging war against us.ᵇ Perhaps Jehovah will perform one of his wonderful works in our behalf, so that he will withdraw from us."ᶜ

3 Jeremiah said to them: "This is what you should say to Zed·e·kiʹah, 4 'This is what Jehovah the God of Israel says: "Here I am turning around against you* the weapons of war that are in your own hands, with which you are fighting the king of Babylonᵈ and the Chal·deʹans who are outside the wall besieging you. And I will gather them into the middle of this city. 5 And I myself will fight against youᵉ with an outstretched hand and a mighty arm, with anger and wrath and great indignation.ᶠ 6 I will strike the inhabitants of this city, both man and beast. By a great pestilence* they will die."ᵍ

7 "'"And after that," declares Jehovah, "I will give King Zed·e·kiʹah of Judah and his servants and the people of this city—those who survive the pestilence, the sword, and the famine—into the hand of King Neb·u·chad·nezʹzar* of Babylon, into the hand of their enemies, and into the hand of those who are seeking to take their life.#ʰ He will strike them down with the sword. He will not feel sorry for them, nor will he show compassion or have any mercy."'ⁱ

8 "And to this people you should say, 'This is what Jehovah says: "Here I am putting before you the way of life and the

21:2, 7 *Lit., "Nebuchadrezzar," a variant spelling. 21:4 *Or "turning in reverse." 21:6 *Or "disease." 21:7 #Or "seeking their soul."

way of death. **9** Those who remain in this city will die by the sword, by famine, and by pestilence. But whoever goes out and surrenders to the Chal·de'ans who are besieging you will keep living, and he will have his life* as a spoil."'[a]

10 "'"For I have set my face against this city for calamity and not for good," declares Jehovah. "It will be given into the hand of the king of Babylon,[c] and he will burn it with fire."[d]

11 "'To the household of the king of Judah: Hear the word of Jehovah. **12** O house of David, this is what Jehovah says:

"Uphold justice every morning,

And rescue the one being robbed from the hand of the defrauder,[e]

So that my wrath does not blaze like a fire[f]

And burn with no one to extinguish it

Because of your evil deeds."'[g]

13 'Here I am against you, O inhabitant of the valley,*

O rock of the level land,' declares Jehovah.

'As for you who say: "Who will come down against us? And who will invade our dwellings?"

14 I will hold an accounting against you

As your deeds deserve,'[h] declares Jehovah.

'And I will set her forest ablaze,

And it will consume all the things around her."'[i]

22 This is what Jehovah says: "Go down to the house* of the king of Judah, and deliver this message. **2** You must

say, 'Hear the word of Jehovah, O king of Judah who sits on the throne of David, you with your servants and your people, those who enter through these gates. **3** This is what Jehovah says: "Uphold justice and righteousness. Rescue the one being robbed from the hand of the defrauder. Do not mistreat any foreign resident, and do not harm any fatherless child* or widow.[a] And do not shed any innocent blood in this place. **4** For if you are careful to carry out this word, then the kings who sit on the throne of David[c] will enter through the gates of this house, riding in chariots and on horses, they with their servants and their people."'[d]

5 "'But if you will not obey these words, by myself I do swear,' declares Jehovah, 'that this house will become a devastated place.'[e]

6 "For this is what Jehovah says concerning the house of the king of Judah,

'You are as Gil'e·ad to me, Like the summit of Leb'a·non.

But I will make you a wilderness;

Not one of your cities will be inhabited.[f]

7 And I will appoint* destroyers against you, Each with his weapons.[g]

They will cut down your choicest cedars

And make them fall into the fire.[h]

8 "'And many nations will pass by this city and say to one another: "Why did Jehovah do this to this great city?"[i] **9** And they will reply: "Because they abandoned the covenant of Jehovah their God and bowed

---

CHAP. 21
a Jer 27:12, 13
  Jer 38:2, 17
b Jer 44:11
c Jer 38:3
d 2Ch 36:17, 19
  Jer 17:27
  Jer 34:2
  Jer 37:10
  Jer 39:8
e Isa 1:17
  Jer 22:3
  Eze 22:29
  Mic 2:2
f De 32:22
  Isa 1:31
  Jer 7:20
g Jer 7:5-7
h Jer 5:9
  Jer 9:9
i 2Ch 36:17, 19
  Jer 52:12, 13

Second Col.

CHAP. 22
a Le 19:15
  Isa 1:17
  Eze 22:7
  Mic 2:2
b 2Ki 24:3, 4
  Jer 7:6, 7
c 1Ki 2:12
d Jer 17:24, 25
e Jer 39:8
  Mic 3:12
f Isa 6:11
  Jer 7:34
g Eze 9:1
h Jer 21:14
i De 29:24-26
  1Ki 9:8, 9
  La 2:15

21:9 *Or "soul." "Or "will escape with his life." **21:13** *Or "low plain." **22:1** *Or "palace." | **22:3** *Or "any orphan." **22:7** *Lit., "sanctify."

down to other gods and served them.'"[a]

10 Do not weep for the dead one,
And do not sympathize with him.
Instead, weep profusely for the one going away,
For he will return no more to see the land of his birth.

11 "For this is what Jehovah says concerning Shal′lum*[b] son of Jo·si′ah, the king of Judah who is reigning instead of his father Jo·si′ah[c] and who has gone out of this place: 'He will return there no more. 12 For he will die in the place where they have taken him into exile, and he will see this land no more.'[d]

13 Woe to the one who builds his house without righteousness
And his upper rooms without justice,
Who makes his fellow man serve him for nothing,
Whose wages he refuses to pay;[e]

14 The one saying, 'I will build for myself a roomy house
With spacious upper rooms.
I will fit it with windows
And panel it with cedar and paint it with vermilion.'*

15 Will you continue reigning because you outdo others in your use of cedar?
Your father also ate and drank,
But he upheld justice and righteousness,[f]
And it went well with him.

16 He defended the legal claim of the afflicted one and the poor one,
So that it went well.
'Is that not what it means to know me?' declares Jehovah.

17 'But your eyes and heart are set only on your dishonest gain,
On shedding innocent blood,
And on committing fraud and extortion.'

18 "Therefore this is what Jehovah says concerning Je·hoi′a·kim[a] son of Jo·si′ah, the king of Judah,

'They will not mourn him:
"Alas, my brother! Alas, my sister!"
They will not mourn him:
"Alas, O master! Alas, his majesty!"

19 With the burial of a donkey he will be buried,[b]
Dragged about and thrown away,
Outside the gates of Jerusalem.'[c]

20 Go up to Leb′a·non and cry out,
Raise your voice in Ba′shan,
And cry out from Ab′a·rim,[d]
For all your passionate lovers have been crushed.[e]

21 I spoke to you when you felt secure.
But you said, 'I will not obey.'[f]
This has been your course since youth,
For you have not obeyed my voice.[g]

22 A wind will shepherd all your shepherds,[h]
And your passionate lovers will go into captivity.
Then you will be put to shame and humiliated because of all your calamity.

23 O you who dwell in Leb′a·non,[i]
Nestled among the cedars,[j]
How you will groan when pangs come on you,
Anguish* like that of a woman giving birth!"[k]

CHAP. 22
a 2Ki 22:16, 17

b 1Ch 3:15
2Ch 36:1

c 2Ki 23:29, 30

d 2Ki 23:34
2Ch 36:4

e Le 19:13
Mic 3:9, 10

f 2Ki 22:1, 2
2Ki 23:23, 25

Second Col.
a 2Ki 23:34
2Ch 36:4

b Jer 36:30

c 2Ch 36:5, 6

d De 32:49

e 2Ki 24:7

f Jer 2:31
Jer 6:16

g De 9:7
Jg 2:11

h Jer 23:1
Eze 34:2

i Jer 22:6

j Isa 2:12, 13

k Jer 4:31
Jer 6:24

22:11 *Also called Jehoahaz. 22:14 *Or "red." 22:23 *Lit., "Birth pangs."

24 "'As surely as I am alive,' declares Jehovah, 'even if Co·ni'ah*[a] son of Je·hoi'a·kim,[b] the king of Judah, were the seal ring on my right hand, I would pull you off from there! **25** I will give you into the hand of those seeking to take your life,* into the hand of those whom you fear, into the hand of King Neb·u·chad·nez'zar# of Babylon, and into the hand of the Chal·de'ans.[c] **26** And I will hurl you and your mother who gave birth to you into another land where you were not born, and there you will die. **27** And they will never return to the land they yearn for.*[d]

28 Is this man Co·ni'ah just a
　　despised, broken pot,
　A vessel that nobody wants?
　Why are he and his descen-
　　dants hurled down
　And thrown into a land they
　　do not know?'[e]
29 O earth,* earth, earth, hear
　　the word of Jehovah.
30 This is what Jehovah says:
　'Write down this man as
　　childless,
　As a man who will not have
　　any success during his
　　lifetime,*
　For none of his descendants
　　will succeed
　In sitting on David's throne
　　and ruling again in
　　Judah.'"[f]

23 "Woe to the shepherds who are destroying and scattering the sheep of my pasture!" declares Jehovah.[g]

2 Therefore this is what Jehovah the God of Israel says against the shepherds who are

shepherding my people: "You have scattered my sheep; you kept dispersing them, and you have not turned your attention to them."[a]

"So I will turn my attention to you because of your evil deeds," declares Jehovah.

3 "Then I will gather together the remnant of my sheep from all the lands to which I have dispersed them,[b] and I will bring them back to their pasture,[c] and they will be fruitful and become many.[d] **4** And I will raise up over them shepherds who will really shepherd them.[e] They will no longer be afraid or be terrified, and none will be missing," declares Jehovah.

5 "Look! The days are coming," declares Jehovah, "when I will raise up to David a righteous sprout.*[f] And a king will reign[g] and show insight and uphold justice and righteousness in the land.[h] **6** In his days Judah will be saved,[i] and Israel will reside in security.[j] And this is the name by which he will be called: Jehovah Is Our Righteousness."[k]

7 "However, the days are coming," declares Jehovah, "when they will no longer say, 'As surely as Jehovah is alive, who brought the people of Israel out of the land of Egypt!'[l] **8** but rather, 'As surely as Jehovah is alive, who brought out and brought back the descendants of the house of Israel from the land of the north and from all the lands to which I had dispersed them,' and they will dwell in their own land."[m]

9 Concerning the prophets:
　My heart is broken
　　within me.
　All my bones are shaking.
　I am like a man who is drunk
　And like a man overcome
　　by wine,

CHAP. 22
a 2Ki 24:6
　Jer 22:28
　Jer 37:1
　Mt 1:11

b 2Ki 23:34

c 2Ki 24:12, 15
　2Ch 36:9, 10
　Jer 24:1
　Jer 29:1, 2

d Jer 52:31-34

e 1Ch 3:17, 18

f 2Ch 36:9, 10
　Jer 36:30
　Mt 1:12

CHAP. 23
g Jer 10:21
　Jer 50:6
　Eze 34:2

Second Col.
a Eze 34:5

b Isa 11:11
　Isa 35:10
　Jer 29:14
　Jer 31:8

c Jer 50:19
　Eze 34:14
　Mic 2:12

d Eze 30:3, 5
　Am 9:14
　Zec 10:8

e Jer 3:15
　Joh 21:15
　Ac 20:28

f Isa 11:1
　Isa 53:2
　Jer 33:15, 16
　Zec 3:8
　Mt 2:23

g Lu 1:32, 33

h Isa 9:7
　Isa 11:3, 4
　Isa 32:1

i Zec 10:6

j De 33:28
　Jer 32:37
　Zec 14:11

k Isa 54:17

l Jer 16:14, 15

m Isa 43:5
　Eze 34:13
　Zep 3:20

22:24 *Also called Jehoiachin and Jeconiah. **22:25** *Or "seeking your soul." #Lit., "Nebuchadrezzar," a variant spelling. **22:27** *Or "the land to which they lift up their soul." **22:29** *Or "land." **22:30** *Lit., "days."

23:5 *Or "heir."

Because of Jehovah and
because of his holy words.

10 For the land is full of
adulterers;[a]

Because of the curse
the land has gone into
mourning[b]

And the pastures of the
wilderness have dried up.[c]

Their course is evil, and they
abuse their power.

11 "Both the prophet and the
priest are polluted.*[d]

Even in my own house I have
found their wickedness,"[e]
declares Jehovah.

12 "So their path will become
slippery and dark;[f]

They will be pushed and
will fall.

For I will bring calamity on
them

In the year of reckoning,"
declares Jehovah.

13 "And in the prophets of
Sa·mar′i·a[g] I have seen
what is repulsive.

Their prophecies are incited
by Ba′al,

And they lead my people
Israel astray.

14 And in the prophets of
Jerusalem I have seen
horrible things.

They commit adultery[h] and
walk in falsehood;[i]

They encourage* evildoers,

And they do not turn away
from their wickedness.

To me they are all like
Sod′om,[j]

And her inhabitants are like
Go·mor′rah."[k]

15 Therefore this is what Jehovah of armies says against the
prophets:

"Here I am making them eat
wormwood

And giving them poisoned
water to drink.[a]

For from the prophets of
Jerusalem apostasy has
spread throughout the
land."

16 This is what Jehovah of
armies says:

"Do not listen to the words
of the prophets who are
prophesying to you.[b]

They are deluding you.*

The vision they speak is
from their own heart,[c]

Not from the mouth of
Jehovah.[d]

17 They are saying again
and again to those who
disrespect me,

'Jehovah has said: "You
will enjoy peace."'[e]

And to everyone who follows
his own stubborn heart
they say,

'No calamity will come upon
you.'[f]

18 For who has stood in the
inner circle of Jehovah

To see and hear his word?

Who has paid attention to his
word in order to hear it?

19 Look! The windstorm of
Jehovah will burst out
in fury;

Like a whirling tempest it
will whirl down on the
head of the wicked.[g]

20 The anger of Jehovah will
not turn back

Until he has carried out
and accomplished the
intentions of his heart.

In the final part of the days
you will clearly understand
this.

21 I did not send the prophets,
yet they ran.

I did not speak to them,
yet they prophesied.[h]

CHAP. 23
a Jer 3:8, 9
Jer 5:7
Jer 13:27
Eze 22:11

b Isa 24:4
Joe 1:10

c Jer 12:4

d Isa 28:7
Jer 5:31
Jer 6:13
Eze 22:25
Zep 3:4

e 2Ch 33:1, 5
2Ch 36:14
Jer 7:11
Eze 8:10, 11
Eze 23:39

f Jer 13:16

g Eze 16:46

h Jer 29:21, 23

i Jer 23:26

j Isa 3:9

k Ge 18:20
De 32:32
Isa 1:10
Jude 7

Second Col.
a Jer 8:14
Jer 9:15

b Jer 27:9
Jer 29:8

c La 2:14

d Jer 14:14
Eze 13:3
Eze 22:28

e Jer 4:10
Jer 6:13, 14
Jer 8:11
Eze 13:10

f Mic 3:11

g Jer 25:32
Jer 30:23, 24

h Jer 14:14
Jer 27:15
Jer 29:8, 9

23:11 *Or "apostate." 23:14 *Lit.,
"strengthen the hands of."

23:16 *Or "They are filling you with
empty hopes."

22 But if they had stood in my inner circle,
They would have made my people hear my words
And would have caused them to turn back from their bad way and their evil deeds."[a]

23 "Am I only a God nearby," declares Jehovah, "and not a God also from far away?"

24 "Can any man hide in a concealed place where I cannot see him?"[b] declares Jehovah.

"Do I not fill the heavens and the earth?"[c] declares Jehovah.

25 "I have heard the prophets who are prophesying lies in my name say, 'I had a dream! I had a dream!'[d] 26 How long will this continue in the heart of the prophets, to prophesy lies? They are prophets of the deceit of their own heart.[e] 27 They intend to make my people forget my name by the dreams they relate to one another, just as their fathers forgot my name because of Baʹal.[f] 28 Let the prophet who has a dream relate the dream, but the one who has my word should speak my word truthfully."

"What does the straw have in common with the grain?" declares Jehovah.

29 "Is not my word just like a fire,"[g] declares Jehovah, "and like a forge hammer that smashes the crag?"[h]

30 "So here I am against the prophets," declares Jehovah, "who steal my words from one another."[i]

31 "Here I am against the prophets," declares Jehovah, "those who use their tongue to say, 'He declares!'"[j]

32 "Here I am against the prophets of lying dreams," declares Jehovah, "who relate them and lead my people astray because of their lies and their boasting."[a]

"But I did not send them or command them. So they will not benefit this people at all,"[b] declares Jehovah.

33 "And when this people or a prophet or a priest asks you, 'What is the burden* of Jehovah?' you should reply to them, '"You people are the burden! And I will cast you off,"[c] declares Jehovah.' 34 As for the prophet or the priest or the people who say, 'This is the burden* of Jehovah!' I will turn my attention on that man and on his household. 35 This is what each of you is saying to his fellow and to his brother, 'What has Jehovah answered? And what has Jehovah spoken?' 36 But the burden* of Jehovah you should mention no more, for the burden* is each one's own word, and you have changed the words of the living God, Jehovah of armies, our God.

37 "This is what you will say to the prophet, 'What answer has Jehovah given you? And what has Jehovah spoken? 38 And if you keep saying, "The burden* of Jehovah!" this is what Jehovah says: "Because of your saying, 'This word is the burden* of Jehovah,' after I told you, 'You must not say: "The burden* of Jehovah!"' 39 look! I will lift you up and throw you away from my presence, both you and the city that I gave to you and your forefathers. 40 And I will bring on you everlasting disgrace and everlasting humiliation, which will not be forgotten."'"[d]

CHAP. 23	
a	Jer 25:4, 5
b	Ge 16:7, 13
	Pr 15:3
	Am 9:2
	Heb 4:13
c	Ps 139:7
d	De 18:20
	Jer 27:9
	Jer 29:21, 23
e	Jer 14:14
f	Jg 3:7
	2Ki 21:1, 3
g	Jer 5:14
h	Heb 4:12
i	De 18:20
	Jer 14:15
	Eze 13:2, 3
j	Eze 13:7
Second Col.	
a	Zep 3:4
b	Jer 7:8
	La 2:14
c	Jer 12:7
d	Jer 24:9
	Jer 42:18
	La 5:20
	Da 9:16

23:33 *Or "burdensome message." The Hebrew word has a double meaning: "a weighty divine pronouncement" or "something burdensome." 23:34, 36, 38 *Or "burdensome message."

24 Then Jehovah showed me two baskets of figs set before the temple of Jehovah, after King Neb·u·chad·nez′zar* of Babylon had carried into exile Jec·o·ni′ah*ᵃ son of Je·hoi′a·kim,ᵇ the king of Judah, along with the princes of Judah, the craftsmen, and the metalworkers;ᐃ he took them from Jerusalem to Babylon.ᶜ 2 One basket had very good figs, like early figs, but the other basket had very bad figs, so bad that they could not be eaten.

3 Jehovah then asked me: "What do you see, Jeremiah?" So I said: "Figs; the good figs are very good, but the bad ones are very bad, so bad that they cannot be eaten."ᵈ

4 Then the word of Jehovah came to me, saying: 5 "This is what Jehovah the God of Israel says, 'Like these good figs, so I will regard in a good way the exiles of Judah, whom I have sent away from this place to the land of the Chal·de′ans. 6 I will keep my eye on them for their good, and I will cause them to return to this land.ᵉ I will build them up, and I will not tear down; I will plant them, and I will not uproot.ᶠ 7 And I will give them a heart to know me, that I am Jehovah.ᵍ They will become my people, and I will become their God,ʰ for they will return to me with all their heart.ⁱ

8 "'But concerning the bad figs that are so bad they cannot be eaten,ʲ this is what Jehovah says: "So I will regard King Zed·e·ki′ahᵏ of Judah, his princes, the remnant of Jerusalem who are left in this land, and those who are dwelling in the land of Egypt.ˡ 9 I will make them an object of horror and calamity to all the kingdoms of the earth,ᵃ a reproach, a proverbial saying, a cause for ridicule, and a curseᵇ in all the places to which I disperse them.ᶜ 10 And I will send against them the sword,ᵈ the famine, and the pestilence,*ᵉ until they have perished from the land that I gave to them and to their forefathers."'"

25 The word that came to Jeremiah concerning all the people of Judah in the fourth year of Je·hoi′a·kimᶠ son of Jo·si′ah, the king of Judah, which was the first year of King Neb·u·chad·nez′zar* of Babylon. 2 This is what Jeremiah the prophet spoke concerning* all the people of Judah and all the inhabitants of Jerusalem:

3 "From the 13th year of Jo·si′ahᵍ son of A′mon, the king of Judah, to this day, these 23 years, the word of Jehovah has come to me, and I kept speaking to you again and again,* but you would not listen.ʰ 4 And Jehovah sent all his servants the prophets to you, sending them again and again,* but you would not listen or incline your ear to hear.ⁱ 5 They would say, 'Turn back, please, each of you from your evil ways and your evil deeds;ʲ then you will continue dwelling for a long time to come in the land that Jehovah long ago gave to you and to your forefathers. 6 Do not follow other gods and serve them and bow down to them, offending me with the work of your hands; otherwise I will bring calamity on you.'

7 "'But you would not listen to me,' declares Jehovah. 'Instead you offended me with the

---

CHAP. 24
a Jer 22:24
b 2Ki 24:6
  1Ch 3:16
c 2Ki 24:15, 16
  Jer 29:1, 2
d Jer 24:8
e Ezr 1:3
  Jer 12:15
  Jer 25:11
  Jer 29:10
  Eze 36:24
f Jer 1:10
  Jer 30:18
  Jer 32:41
g De 30:6
  Jer 31:33
  Eze 11:19
h Jer 30:22
  Jer 32:38
  Zec 8:8
i Jer 29:13
j Jer 29:17
k 2Ki 25:6, 7
  Eze 12:12, 13
l Jer 44:1
  Jer 46:13

Second Col.
a Jer 15:4
  Jer 34:17
b Jer 26:4, 6
  Jer 29:22
c De 28:64
  Jer 29:18
d Le 26:33
  Jer 9:16
e De 28:59
  Jer 15:2
  Eze 7:15

CHAP. 25
f 2Ki 24:1
  Jer 36:1
  Jer 46:2
  Da 1:1
g Jer 1:2
h Jer 7:13
  Jer 13:10
i Jer 29:19
j 2Ki 17:13
  Isa 55:7
  Jer 18:11
  Jer 35:15
  Eze 18:30
  Eze 33:11

24:1; 25:1 *Lit., "Nebuchadrezzar," a variant spelling. 24:1 *Also called Jehoiachin and Coniah. ᐃOr possibly, "builders of bulwarks."

24:10 *Or "disease." 25:2 *Or "to." 25:3 *Lit., "rising up early and speaking." 25:4 *Lit., "rising up early and sending."

work of your hands, to your own
calamity.'[a]
8 "Therefore this is what Jehovah of armies says, '"Because
you would not obey my words,
9 I am sending for all the families of the north,"[b] declares Jehovah, "sending for King Neb-
u·chad·nez'zar* of Babylon, my
servant,[c] and I will bring them
against this land[d] and against its
inhabitants and against all these
surrounding nations.[e] I will devote them to destruction and
make them an object of horror and something to whistle at
and a perpetual ruin. 10 I will
put an end to the sound of exultation and the sound of rejoicing from them,[f] the voice of the
bridegroom and the voice of the
bride,[g] the sound of the hand
mill and the light of the lamp.
11 And all this land will be reduced to ruins and will become an object of horror, and
these nations will have to serve
the king of Babylon for 70
years."'[h]
12 "'But when 70 years have
been fulfilled,[i] I will call to account* the king of Babylon and
that nation for their error,'[j] declares Jehovah, 'and I will make
the land of the Chal·de'ans a
desolate wasteland for all time.[k]
13 I will bring on that land
all my words that I have spoken against it, all that is written
in this book that Jeremiah has
prophesied against all the nations. 14 For many nations and
great kings[l] will make slaves of
them,[m] and I will repay them according to their deeds and the
work of their own hands.'"[n]
15 For this is what Jehovah
the God of Israel said to me:
"Take this cup of the wine of
wrath out of my hand, and make
all the nations to whom I send
you drink it. 16 And they will
drink and stagger and act like
madmen because of the sword
that I am sending among them."[a]
17 So I took the cup out of
the hand of Jehovah and made
all the nations to whom Jehovah sent me drink:[b] 18 starting with Jerusalem and the cities of Judah,[c] her kings and her
princes, to make them a ruin,
an object of horror, something
to whistle at and a curse,[d]
as it is today; 19 then Phar'aoh
king of Egypt and his servants, his princes, and all his
people,[e] 20 and all their mixed
populations; all the kings of
the land of Uz; all the kings
of the land of the Phi·lis'-
tines,[f] Ash'ke·lon,[g] Gaz'a, Ek'ron,
and those remaining of Ash'dod;
21 E'dom,[h] Mo'ab,[i] and the Am'-
mon·ites;[j] 22 all the kings of
Tyre, all the kings of Si'don,[k]
and the kings of the island in the
sea; 23 De'dan,[l] Te'ma, Buz,
and all those with hair clipped at
the temples;[m] 24 all the kings
of the Arabians[n] and all the kings
of the mixed populations who
reside in the wilderness; 25 all
the kings of Zim'ri, all the kings
of E'lam,[o] and all the kings of the
Medes;[p] 26 and all the kings of
the north near and far, one after
the other, and all the other kingdoms of the earth that are on the
surface of the ground; and the
king of She'shach*[q] will drink after them.
27 "And you must say to
them, 'This is what Jehovah of
armies, the God of Israel, says:
"Drink and get drunk and vomit
and fall so that you cannot
get up[r] because of the sword
that I am sending among you."'
28 And if they refuse to take the
cup out of your hand to drink,
say to them, 'This is what Je-

CHAP. 25
a De 32:21; Ne 9:26
b Le 26:25; Isa 5:26; Jer 1:15
c Jer 27:6; Jer 43:10
d De 28:49, 50; Jer 5:15; Eze 7:24
e Eze 26:7; Eze 29:19; Hab 1:6
f Isa 24:7; Eze 26:13
g Jer 7:34
h 2Ch 36:20, 21; Da 9:2; Zec 1:12; Zec 7:5
i De 30:3; Ezr 1:1, 2; Jer 29:10
j Isa 47:1; Jer 51:1; Da 5:26, 30
k Isa 13:1, 19; Isa 14:4, 23
l Jer 50:9; Jer 51:27
m Isa 14:2; Hab 2:8
n Ps 137:8; Jer 50:29; Jer 51:6, 24; Re 18:6

Second Col.
a Jer 51:7; La 4:21; Eze 23:32-34; Na 3:7, 11
b Jer 1:10
c Isa 51:17
d Jer 24:9
e Jer 46:2
f Jer 47:1
g Jer 47:5
h Jer 49:17; La 4:21
i Jer 48:1
j Jer 49:1
k Jer 27:2, 3; Jer 47:4
l Jer 49:8
m Jer 9:25, 26; Jer 49:32
n Jer 49:31, 32
o Jer 49:34
p Jer 51:11
q Jer 51:41
r Isa 63:6; Hab 2:16

25:9 *Lit., "Nebuchadrezzar," a variant spelling. 25:12 *Or "punish."

25:26 *This appears to be a cryptographic name for Babel (Babylon).

hovah of armies says: "You must drink it! **29** For look! if I am bringing calamity first on the city that bears my name,[a] should you go unpunished?"'[b]

"'You will not go unpunished, for I am calling for a sword against all the inhabitants of the earth,' declares Jehovah of armies.

30 "And you are to prophesy all these words to them and say to them,

'From on high Jehovah will roar,
And from his holy dwelling he will make his voice heard.
He will roar loudly against his abiding place.
Shouting like those treading the winepress,
He will sing triumphantly against all the inhabitants of the earth.'

31 'A noise will resound to the ends of the earth,
For Jehovah has a controversy with the nations.
He will personally pass judgment on all humans.*[c]
And he will put the wicked to the sword,' declares Jehovah.

32 This is what Jehovah of armies says:
'Look! A calamity is spreading from nation to nation,[d]
And a great tempest will be unleashed from the remotest parts of the earth.[e]

33 "'And those slain by Jehovah in that day will be from one end of the earth clear to the other end of the earth. They will not be mourned, nor will they be gathered up or buried. They will become like manure on the surface of the ground.'

34 Wail, you shepherds, and cry out!

25:31 *Lit., "all flesh."

Wallow about, you majestic ones of the flock,
Because the time of your slaughter and your dispersion has come,
And you will fall like a precious vessel!
35 The shepherds have no place to flee,
And there is no escape for the majestic ones of the flock.
36 Listen! The outcry of the shepherds
And the wailing of the majestic ones of the flock,
For Jehovah is devastating their pasture.
37 And the peaceful dwelling places have been made lifeless
Because of the burning anger of Jehovah.
38 He has left his lair just like a young lion,*[a]
For their land has become an object of horror
Because of the cruel sword
And because of his burning anger."

26 In the beginning of the reign of Je·hoi′a·kim[b] son of Jo·si′ah, the king of Judah, this word came from Jehovah: **2** "This is what Jehovah says, 'Stand in the courtyard of the house of Jehovah and speak concerning* all the people of the cities of Judah who are coming in to worship* at the house of Jehovah. Tell them everything that I command you; do not take away a word. **3** Perhaps they will listen and each one will turn back from his evil way, and I will change my mind concerning* the calamity that I intend to bring on them because of their evil deeds.[c] **4** Say to them: "This is

---

25:38 *Or "a maned young lion." 26:2 *Or "to." *Or "bow down." 26:3 *Or "feel regret over."

CHAP. 25
a 1Ki 9:7
  Jer 7:12, 14
  Da 9:18
  Ho 12:2
  Mic 6:2

b Jer 49:12
  Ob 16

c Joe 3:2

d Isa 34:2, 3
  Jer 25:17

e Zep 3:8

Second Col.
a Ho 5:14

CHAP. 26
b 2Ki 23:34
  2Ch 36:4
  Jer 25:1
  Jer 35:1
  Jer 36:1

c Isa 55:7
  Jer 18:7, 8
  Jer 36:3
  Eze 18:27

what Jehovah says, 'If you will not listen to me by following my law* that I have placed before you, 5 by listening to the words of my servants the prophets, whom I am sending to you again and again,* whom you have not listened to,ᵃ 6 then I will make this house like Shi′loh,ᵇ and I will make this city an object of cursing to all the nations of the earth.'"'"ᶜ

7 And the priests and the prophets and all the people heard Jeremiah speaking these words in the house of Jehovah.ᵈ 8 So when Jeremiah had finished speaking all that Jehovah had commanded him to speak to all the people, then the priests and the prophets and all the people seized him and said: "You will surely die. 9 Why have you prophesied in the name of Jehovah, saying, 'This house will become like Shi′loh, and this city will be devastated and left without an inhabitant'?" And all the people gathered around Jeremiah in the house of Jehovah.

10 When the princes of Judah heard these words, they came up from the house* of the king to the house of Jehovah and sat down at the entrance of the new gate of Jehovah.ᵉ 11 The priests and the prophets said to the princes and to all the people: "This man deserves the death penalty,ᶠ because he has prophesied against this city just as you have heard with your own ears."ᵍ

12 Jeremiah then said to all the princes and to all the people: "It was Jehovah who sent me to prophesy against this house and against this city all the words that you have heard.ʰ 13 So now, reform your ways and your actions and obey the voice of Jehovah your God, and Jehovah

will change his mind concerning* the calamity that he has spoken against you.ᵃ 14 But as for me, I am in your hand. Do to me whatever seems good and right in your eyes. 15 Only know for certain that if you put me to death, you will bring innocent blood upon yourselves and upon this city and upon her inhabitants, for in truth Jehovah sent me to you to speak all these words in your hearing."

16 Then the princes and all the people said to the priests and the prophets: "This man does not deserve the death penalty, for he spoke to us in the name of Jehovah our God."

17 Furthermore, some of the elders of the land rose up and began saying to the entire congregation of the people: 18 "Mi′cahᵇ of Mo′resh·eth was prophesying in the days of King Hez·e·ki′ahᶜ of Judah, and he said to all the people of Judah, 'This is what Jehovah of armies says:

"Zion will be plowed up as
   a field,
Jerusalem will become
   heaps of ruins,ᵈ
And the mountain of the
   House* will become like
   high places in a forest."'"ᵉ

19 "Did King Hez·e·ki′ah of Judah and all Judah then put him to death? Did he not fear Jehovah and beg for Jehovah's favor,* so that Jehovah changed his mind concerningᵍ the calamity that he had spoken against them?ᶠ So we are about to bring a great calamity on ourselves.ᐃ

20 "And there was another man prophesying in the name of Jehovah, U·ri′jah son of She·mai′ah from Kir′i·ath·je′a·rim,ᵍ

CHAP. 26
a 2Ki 17:13, 14
  Jer 7:12-14
  Jer 25:3

b Ps 78:60

c Jer 24:9

d Jer 26:2

e Jer 36:10

f Jer 18:19, 20

g Jer 38:4

h Jer 1:17

Second Col.
a Jer 7:3
  Jer 36:3
  Eze 18:32
  Jon 3:9

b Mic 1:1

c 2Ch 29:1

d Ps 79:1
  Jer 9:11

e Mic 3:12

f 2Ch 32:26

g Jos 15:20, 60
  Jos 18:11, 14
  1Sa 7:2

26:4 *Or "instruction." 26:5 *Lit., "rising up early and sending." 26:10 *Or "palace."

26:13 *Or "feel regret over." 26:18 *Or "the temple mount." #Or "like a wooded ridge." 26:19 *Or "try to soften the face of Jehovah." #Or "felt regret over." ᐃOr "our souls."

who prophesied against this city and against this land with words like those of Jeremiah. **21** King Je·hoi′a·kim[a] and all his mighty men and all the princes heard his words, and the king sought to put him to death.[b] When U·ri′jah heard of it, he at once became afraid and fled to Egypt. **22** Then King Je·hoi′a·kim sent El·na′than[c] the son of Ach′bor and other men with him to Egypt. **23** They brought U·ri′jah from Egypt and took him to King Je·hoi′a·kim, who then struck him down with the sword[d] and cast his dead body into the graveyard of the common people.''

24 But A·hi′kam[e] the son of Sha′phan[f] supported Jeremiah, so that he was not handed over to the people to be put to death.[g]

27 In the beginning of the reign of Je·hoi′a·kim son of Jo·si′ah, the king of Judah, this word came to Jeremiah from Jehovah: **2** "This is what Jehovah has told me, 'Make for yourself straps and yoke bars, and put them on your neck. **3** Then send them to the king of E′dom,[h] the king of Mo′ab,[i] the king of the Am′mon·ites,[j] the king of Tyre,[k] and the king of Si′don[l] by the hand of the messengers who have come to Jerusalem to King Zed·e·ki′ah of Judah. **4** Give them this command for their masters:

"""This is what Jehovah of armies, the God of Israel, says; this is what you should say to your masters, **5** 'It is I who made the earth, mankind, and the beasts that are on the surface of the earth by my great power and by my outstretched arm; and I have given it to whomever I please.[*m] **6** And now I have given all these lands into the hand of my ser-

---

CHAP. 26
a 2Ki 23:34
  2Ch 36:5
b 2Ch 16:10
c Jer 36:11, 12
d Jer 2:30
e 2Ki 22:12, 13
  Jer 39:13, 14
  Jer 40:5
f 2Ki 22:10
g 1Ki 18:4

CHAP. 27
h Eze 25:12, 13
  Ob 1
i Jer 48:1
  Eze 25:8, 9
j Jer 49:1, 2
  Eze 25:2
k Isa 23:1
  Jer 47:4
  Eze 26:3
l Isa 23:4
  Eze 28:21
  Joe 3:4
m Da 4:17

Second Col.
a Jer 25:9
  Jer 28:14
  Jer 43:10
  Da 2:37, 38
b Ps 137:8
  Jer 50:14, 27
  Da 5:26, 30
c Jer 25:12, 14
  Jer 51:11
d Eze 26:7, 8
e 2Ki 24:17
  1Ch 3:15
  Jer 37:1
f Jer 38:2, 20
g 2Ki 25:7
h 2Ki 25:3
i Jer 21:9
  Eze 14:21
j Jer 28:1, 2
  Jer 28:11
  Jer 37:19
k Jer 14:14
  Jer 23:21
  Jer 28:15
  Jer 29:8, 9
  Eze 13:6

---

vant King Neb·u·chad·nez′zar[a] of Babylon; even the wild beasts of the field I have given him to serve him. **7** All the nations will serve him and his son and his grandson until the time for his own land comes,[b] when many nations and great kings will make him their slave.'[c]

8 """If any nation or kingdom refuses to serve King Neb·u·chad·nez′zar of Babylon and refuses to put its neck under the yoke of the king of Babylon, I will punish that nation with the sword,[d] with famine, and with pestilence,'* declares Jehovah, 'until I have finished them off by his hand.'

9 """Therefore, do not listen to your prophets, your diviners, your dreamers, your magicians, and your sorcerers, who are saying to you: "You will not serve the king of Babylon." **10** For they are prophesying lies to you, so that you will be taken far away from your land and I will disperse you and you will perish.

11 """But the nation that brings its neck under the yoke of the king of Babylon and serves him, I will allow to remain* on its land,' declares Jehovah, 'to cultivate it and dwell in it.'"'"

12 Also to King Zed·e·ki′ah[e] of Judah I spoke in the same way, saying: "Bring your necks under the yoke of the king of Babylon and serve him and his people, and you will keep living.[f] **13** Why should you and your people die by the sword,[g] by famine,[h] and by pestilence,[i] as Jehovah has said about the nation that will not serve the king of Babylon? **14** Do not listen to the words of the prophets who are saying to you, 'You will not serve the king of Babylon,'[j] because they are prophesying lies to you.[k]

27:5 *Lit., "to whom it is right in my eyes."

27:8 *Or "disease." 27:11 *Lit., "rest."

15 "'For I have not sent them,' declares Jehovah, 'but they are prophesying lies in my name, with the result that I will disperse you and you will perish, you and the prophets who are prophesying to you.'"[a]

16 And to the priests and to all this people I said: "This is what Jehovah says, 'Do not listen to the words of your prophets who are prophesying to you: "Look! The utensils of the house of Jehovah will be brought back from Babylon very soon!"[b] for they are prophesying lies to you.[c] **17** Do not listen to them. Serve the king of Babylon and you will keep living.[d] Why should this city become a ruin? **18** But if they are prophets and if the word of Jehovah is with them, please let them beg Jehovah of armies that the remaining utensils in the house of Jehovah, in the house* of the king of Judah, and in Jerusalem may not be taken away to Babylon.'

19 "For this is what Jehovah of armies says concerning the pillars,[e] the Sea,*[f] the carriages,[g] and the remaining utensils that are left in this city, **20** which King Neb·u·chad·nez'zar of Babylon did not take when he took into exile Jec·o·ni'ah son of Je·hoi'a·kim, the king of Judah, from Jerusalem to Babylon, together with all the nobles of Judah and Jerusalem;[h] **21** yes, this is what Jehovah of armies, the God of Israel, says concerning the utensils that are left at the house of Jehovah, in the house* of the king of Judah, and in Jerusalem: **22** "'To Babylon they will be brought,[i] and there they will remain until the day I turn my attention to them," declares Jehovah. "Then I will bring them back and restore them to this place."'"[j]

28 In that same year, in the beginning of the reign of King Zed·e·ki'ah[a] of Judah, in the fourth year, in the fifth month, the prophet Han·a·ni'ah the son of Az'zur from Gib'e·on[b] said to me in the house of Jehovah in the presence of the priests and all the people: **2** "This is what Jehovah of armies, the God of Israel, says, 'I will break the yoke of the king of Babylon.[c] **3** Within two years* I am bringing back to this place all the utensils of the house of Jehovah that King Neb·u·chad·nez'zar of Babylon took from this place and brought to Babylon.'"[d] **4** "'And I will bring back to this place Jec·o·ni'ah[e] son of Je·hoi'a·kim,[f] the king of Judah, and all the exiles of Judah who have gone to Babylon,'[g] declares Jehovah, 'for I will break the yoke of the king of Babylon.'"

5 Then Jeremiah the prophet spoke to Han·a·ni'ah the prophet in the presence of the priests and all the people who were standing in the house of Jehovah. **6** Jeremiah the prophet said: "Amen!* May Jehovah do this! May Jehovah fulfill your words that you prophesied by bringing back from Babylon to this place the utensils of the house of Jehovah and all the exiled people! **7** However, hear, please, this message that I am speaking in your ears and in the ears of all the people. **8** Long ago the prophets who were prior to me and prior to you used to prophesy concerning many lands and great kingdoms, about war, calamity, and pestilence.* **9** If a prophet prophesies about peace and the word of that prophet comes true, then it will be known that Jehovah truly sent that prophet."

CHAP. 27
a Jer 20:6
  Jer 29:21
  Eze 13:3

b 2Ki 24:11, 13
  2Ch 36:7
  Jer 28:1-3
  Da 1:1, 2

c Jer 14:13

d Jer 27:11
  Jer 38:17

e 1Ki 7:15
  2Ki 25:17
  2Ch 4:11, 12
  Jer 52:21

f 1Ki 7:23

g 1Ki 7:27
  2Ki 25:16
  2Ch 4:11, 14

h 2Ki 24:14, 15
  2Ch 36:10
  Jer 24:1
  Da 1:2, 3

i 2Ki 25:13, 14
  2Ch 36:18
  Jer 52:17, 18
  Da 5:3

j Ezr 1:7
  Ezr 5:14

Second Col.

CHAP. 28
a 2Ki 24:17
  2Ch 36:10

b Jos 11:19
  2Sa 21:2

c Jer 27:4, 8

d 2Ki 24:11, 13
  Jer 27:16
  Da 1:2

e 2Ki 24:8
  2Ki 25:27
  Jer 37:1

f Jer 23:36
  2Ki 24:6

g 2Ki 24:12, 14
  Jer 24:1

27:18, 21 *Or "palace." 27:19 *That is, the copper Sea of the temple.

28:3 *Lit., "years of days." 28:6 *Or "So be it!" 28:8 *Or "disease."

10 At that Han·a·ni′ah the prophet took the yoke bar off the neck of the prophet Jeremi-ah and broke it.[a] **11** Han·a·ni′-ah then said in the presence of all the people: "This is what Je-hovah says, 'Just like this I will break the yoke of King Neb·u-chad·nez′zar of Babylon from off the neck of all the nations within two years.'"[b] And Jeremiah the prophet went on his way.

12 After Han·a·ni′ah the prophet had broken the yoke bar from off the neck of Jer-emiah the prophet, this message of Jehovah came to Jeremiah: **13** "Go and say to Han·a·ni′ah, 'This is what Jehovah says: "You have broken yoke bars of wood,[c] but instead of them you will make yoke bars of iron." **14** For this is what Jehovah of armies, the God of Israel, says: "I will put an iron yoke bar on the neck of all these nations, to serve King Neb·u·chad·nez′zar of Bab-ylon, and they must serve him.[d] Even the wild beasts of the field I will give him."'"[e]

15 Jeremiah the prophet then said to Han·a·ni′ah[f] the proph-et: "Listen, please, O Han·a·ni′-ah! Jehovah has not sent you, but you have caused this people to trust in a lie.[g] **16** Therefore this is what Jehovah says, 'Look! I am removing you from the face of the ground. This year you will die, for you have urged rebellion against Jehovah.'"[h]

17 So Han·a·ni′ah the prophet died in that year, in the seventh month.

29 These are the words of the letter that Jeremiah the prophet sent from Jeru-salem to the rest of the elders among the exiled people, the priests, the prophets, and all the people, whom Neb·u·chad·nez′-zar had taken into exile from Je-rusalem to Babylon, **2** after

King Jec·o·ni′ah,[a] the queen mother,*[b] the court officials, the princes of Judah and Jerusalem, and the craftsmen and the metal-workers# had gone out of Jeru-salem.[c] **3** He sent the letter by the hand of El·a′sah the son of Sha′phan[d] and Gem·a·ri′ah the son of Hil·ki′ah, whom King Zed·e·ki′ah[e] of Judah sent to Bab-ylon to King Neb·u·chad·nez′zar of Babylon. It said:

4 "This is what Jehovah of ar-mies, the God of Israel, says to all the exiled people, whom I have caused to go into ex-ile from Jerusalem to Babylon, **5** 'Build houses and live in them. Plant gardens and eat their fruit. **6** Take wives and have sons and daughters; take wives for your sons and give your daughters in marriage, so that they too may have sons and daughters. Be-come many there, and do not de-crease. **7** And seek the peace of the city to which I have ex-iled you, and pray in its behalf to Jehovah, for in its peace you will have peace.[f] **8** For this is what Jehovah of armies, the God of Israel, says: "Do not let your prophets and your diviners who are among you deceive you,[g] and do not listen to the dreams that they are dreaming. **9** For 'they are prophesying lies to you in my name. I have not sent them,[h] de-clares Jehovah.'"

10 "For this is what Jehovah says, 'When 70 years at Babylon are fulfilled, I will turn my at-tention to you,[i] and I will make good my promise by bringing you back to this place.'[j]

11 "'For I well know the thoughts that I am thinking to-ward you,' declares Jehovah, 'thoughts of peace, and not of calamity,[k] to give you a future and a hope.'[l] **12** And you will

---

CHAP. 28
a Jer 27:2

b Jer 28:4

c Jer 27:2

d De 28:48
  Jer 5:19

e Jer 27:6
  Da 2:37, 38

f Jer 28:1

g Jer 14:14
  Jer 23:21
  Jer 27:15
  Eze 13:3

h De 13:5
  De 18:20
  Jer 29:32

Second Col.

CHAP. 29
a 2Ki 24:8
  Jer 22:24

b Jer 22:26

c 2Ki 24:15, 16
  Jer 24:1

d 2Ki 22:8
  Jer 26:24
  Jer 39:13, 14
  Eze 8:11

e 2Ki 24:18

f 1Ti 2:1, 2

g Jer 14:14
  Jer 27:14

h Jer 23:21
  Jer 28:15

i 2Ch 36:20, 21
  Ezr 1:1-3
  Da 9:2
  Zec 1:12

j De 30:3
  Ezr 2:1
  Jer 24:6

k Zep 3:15

l Jer 31:17

29:2 *Or "the lady." # Or possibly, "builders of bulwarks."

call me and come and pray to me, and I will listen to you.'[a]

13 "'You will seek me and find me,[b] for you will search for me with all your heart.[c] 14 And I will let you find me,'[d] declares Jehovah. 'And I will gather your captives and collect you together out of all the nations and places to which I have dispersed you,'[e] declares Jehovah. 'And I will bring you back to the place from which I caused you to go into exile.'[f]

15 "But you have said, 'Jehovah has raised up prophets for us in Babylon.'

16 "For this is what Jehovah says to the king sitting on the throne of David[g] and to all the people dwelling in this city, your brothers who have not gone with you into exile, 17 'This is what Jehovah of armies says: "Here I am sending against them the sword, the famine, and the pestilence,*[h] and I will make them like rotten# figs that are so bad they cannot be eaten."'[i]

18 "'And I will pursue them with the sword,[j] with famine, and with pestilence, and I will make them an object of horror to all the kingdoms of the earth,[k] and a curse, and an object of astonishment, something to whistle at,[l] and a reproach among all the nations to which I disperse them,[m] 19 because they have not listened to my words that I sent to them with my servants the prophets,' declares Jehovah, 'sending them again and again.'*[n]

"'But you have not listened,'[o] declares Jehovah.

20 "Therefore, hear the word of Jehovah, all you exiled people, whom I have sent away from Jerusalem to Babylon. 21 This

is what Jehovah of armies, the God of Israel, says concerning A'hab the son of Ko·lai'ah and concerning Zed·e·ki'ah the son of Ma·a·sei'ah, who are prophesying lies to you in my name,[a] 'Here I am giving them into the hand of King Neb·u·chad·nez'zar* of Babylon, and he will strike them down before your eyes. 22 And what happens to them will become a curse spoken by all the exiles of Judah in Babylon: "May Jehovah make you like Zed·e·ki'ah and like A'hab, whom the king of Babylon roasted in the fire!" 23 for they have acted disgracefully in Israel,[b] committing adultery with the wives of their neighbors and speaking false words in my name that I did not command them.[c]

"'"I am the One who knows, and I am a witness,"[d] declares Jehovah."'

24 "And to She·mai'ah[e] of Ne·hel'am you will say, 25 'This is what Jehovah of armies, the God of Israel, says: "Because you sent in your name letters to all the people who are in Jerusalem, to Zeph·a·ni'ah[f] son of Ma·a·sei'ah, the priest, and to all the priests, saying 'Jehovah has made you priest instead of Je·hoi'a·da the priest to become the overseer of the house of Jehovah, to be in charge of any madman who acts like a prophet and to put him into the stocks and into the pillory;*[g] 27 why, then, have you not rebuked Jeremiah of An'a·thoth,[h] who is acting as a prophet for you?[i] 28 For he even sent to us at Babylon, saying: "It will be a long time! Build houses and live in them. Plant gardens and eat their fruit,[j]—"'"'"

29 When Zeph·a·ni'ah[k] the priest read this letter in the

CHAP. 29

a Da 9:3

b Le 26:40

c De 4:29
   De 30:1-4
   1Ki 8:47, 48
   Jer 24:7

d Isa 55:6

e Isa 49:25
   Jer 30:3
   Eze 39:28

f Ps 126:1
   Ho 6:11
   Am 9:14
   Zep 3:20

g Jer 28:1

h Jer 24:10

i Jer 24:2, 8

j Le 26:33

k De 28:25
   Jer 34:17

l 1Ki 9:8
   2Ch 29:8
   Jer 25:9
   La 2:15

m Jer 24:9

n Jer 7:13

o Jer 6:19

Second Col.

a Jer 14:14
   Jer 29:8
   La 2:14

b Jer 23:14

c Jer 7:9, 10
   Jer 27:15

d Jer 16:17
   Jer 23:24

e Jer 29:31, 32

f 2Ki 25:18, 21
   Jer 21:1, 2
   Jer 37:3
   Jer 52:24, 27

g Jer 20:2

h Jer 1:1

i Jer 43:2

j Jer 29:5

k 2Ki 25:18, 21

29:17 *Or "disease." #Or possibly, "burst." 29:19 *Lit., "rising up early and sending."

29:21 *Lit., "Nebuchadrezzar," a variant spelling. 29:26 *Or "neck irons."

hearing of Jeremiah the prophet, **30** the word of Jehovah came to Jeremiah, saying: **31** "Send to all the exiled people, saying, 'This is what Jehovah says concerning She·mai′ah of Ne·hel′am: "Because She·mai′ah prophesied to you, though I did not send him, and he tried to make you trust in lies, **32** therefore this is what Jehovah says, 'Here I am turning my attention to She·mai′ah of Ne·hel′am and his descendants. Not one man of his will survive among this people, and he will not see the good that I will do for my people,' declares Jehovah, 'for he has urged rebellion against Jehovah.'"'"

30 The word that came to Jeremiah from Jehovah, saying: **2** "This is what Jehovah the God of Israel says, 'Write in a book all the words that I speak to you. **3** For "look! the days are coming," declares Jehovah, "when I will gather the captives of my people, Israel and Judah,"*b* says Jehovah, "and I will bring them back to the land that I gave to their forefathers, and they will possess it once again."'"*c*

4 These are the words that Jehovah spoke to Israel and Judah.

5 This is what Jehovah says:
"We have heard the sounds
　of trembling;
There is terror, and no
　peace.
6 Ask, please, whether a man
　can give birth.
Why, then, do I see every
　strong man with his hands
　on his stomach*
Like a woman giving birth?*d*
Why has every face turned
　pale?
7 Alas! For that day is a
　terrible* one.*e*

There is none like it,
　A time of distress for Jacob.
But he will be saved out
　of it."

8 "And in that day," declares Jehovah of armies, "I will break the yoke from off your neck, and your straps* I will tear in two; and no more will strangers*#* make him*△* their slave. **9** They will serve Jehovah their God and David their king, whom I will raise up for them."*a*

10 "And you, my servant Jacob,
　do not be afraid," declares
　Jehovah,
"And do not be terrified,
　O Israel.*b*
For I will save you from far
　away
And your offspring from the
　land of their captivity.*c*
Jacob will return and be
　calm and undisturbed,
With no one to make them
　afraid."*d*
11 "For I am with you," declares
　Jehovah, "to save you.
But I will make an extermina-
　tion among all the nations
　to which I scattered you;*e*
However, you I will not
　exterminate.*f*
I will discipline* you to the
　proper degree,
And I will by no means leave
　you unpunished."*g*
12 For this is what Jehovah
　says:
"There is no cure for your
　breakdown.*h*
Your wound is incurable.
13 There is no one to plead your
　cause,
No means of healing your
　ulcer.
There is no cure for you.
14 All your passionate lovers
　have forgotten you.*i*

CHAP. 29
a Jer 14:14
　Jer 28:15, 16
　Eze 13:8, 9

CHAP. 30
b De 30:3
　Eze 39:25

c Ezr 2:1
　Jer 29:14
　Jer 32:44
　Eze 20:42
　Am 9:14

d Jer 4:31
　Mic 4:9

e Joe 2:11
　Zep 1:14

Second Col.
a Eze 34:23
　Eze 37:24
　Ho 3:5

b Isa 41:13

c Isa 49:25
　Jer 3:18

d Jer 33:16
　Eze 34:25
　Ho 2:18
　Mic 4:4

e Jer 50:29
　Jer 51:24

f Le 26:44
　Ne 9:31
　La 3:22
　Am 9:8

g Ex 34:6, 7
　Jer 46:27, 28

h 2Ch 36:15, 16
　Isa 6:10
　Jer 8:21, 22

i La 1:2, 19

They no longer seek you out.
For with the stroke of an
enemy I have struck you,[a]
With the punishment of
someone cruel,
Because of your great guilt
and your many sins.[b]

15 Why do you cry out because
of your breakdown?
Your pain is incurable!
Because of your great guilt
and your many sins[c]
I have done this to you.

16 Therefore all those devouring you will be devoured,[d]
And all your enemies will
also go into captivity.[e]
Those pillaging you will be
pillaged,
And I will hand all those
plundering you over to
plundering."[f]

17 "But I will restore your
health and heal your
wounds,"[g] declares
Jehovah,
"Though they called you
an outcast:
'Zion, for whom no one
searches.'"[h]

18 This is what Jehovah says:
"Here I am gathering the
captives of the tents
of Jacob,[i]
And I will have pity for his
tabernacles.
The city will be rebuilt
on her mound,[j]
And the fortified tower will
stand on its rightful site.

19 And from them will come
thanksgiving and the
sounds of laughter.[k]
I will multiply them, and
they will not be few;[l]
I will make them numerous,*
And they will not be
insignificant.[m]

20 His sons will become as in
the past,

And before me his assembly
will be firmly established.[a]
I will deal with all his
oppressors.[b]

21 His majestic one will be one
of his own,
And from his midst his ruler
will emerge.
I will cause him to come
near, and he will approach
me."
"For otherwise, who would
dare* to approach me?"
declares Jehovah.

22 "And you will become my
people,[c] and I will be your
God."[d]

23 Look! A windstorm of
Jehovah will burst out
in fury,[e]
A sweeping tempest that
whirls down on the head
of the wicked.

24 The burning anger of
Jehovah will not turn back
Until he has carried out
and accomplished the
intentions of his heart.[f]
In the final part of the days
you will understand this.[g]

31 "At that time," declares Jehovah, "I will become God
to all the families of Israel, and
they will become my people."[h]

2 This is what Jehovah says:
"The people who survived
the sword found favor
in the wilderness
When Israel was walking
to his resting-place."

3 From far away Jehovah
appeared to me and said:
"I have loved you with an
everlasting love.
That is why I have drawn
you to me with loyal love.*[i]

4 Yet again I will rebuild you
and you will be rebuilt.[j]

CHAP. 30
a La 2:5
b Jer 5:6
c 2Ch 36:14
d Jer 41:11
 Jer 25:12
e Jer 51:29, 56
 Mic 5:9
f Zec 2:8, 9
g Ps 102:13
 Jer 33:6, 7
h La 2:15
i Ps 85:1
 Jer 24:6
 Jer 29:10
j Mic 4:8
k Ezr 3:12
 Ne 8:17
 Isa 35:10
l De 30:5
 Isa 27:6
 Zec 10:8
m Isa 60:22
 Mic 4:7

Second Col.
a Isa 1:26
b Isa 49:26
 Jer 50:18
c Ho 2:23
d Jer 31:1
 Eze 11:20
 Eze 36:28
e Jer 25:32
f Jer 4:28
g Jer 23:20

CHAP. 31
h Le 26:12
 Jer 30:22
 Jer 31:33
i De 7:8
j Jer 33:7
 Am 9:11

30:19 *Or possibly, "honored."
30:21 *Lit., "give his heart in pledge."
31:3 *Or "have continued to show loyal
love to you."

O virgin of Israel, you
will again take up your
tambourines
And go forth dancing
joyfully.*a

5 You will again plant vineyards in the mountains
of Sa·mar′i·a;b
The planters will plant
and enjoy their fruit.c

6 For the day will come when
the watchmen in the
mountains of E′phra·im
will call out:
'Rise up, let us go up to Zion,
to Jehovah our God.'"d

7 For this is what Jehovah
says:
"Cry out to Jacob with
rejoicing.
Shout for joy because you
are over the nations.e
Proclaim it; offer praise
and say,
'O Jehovah, save your people, the remnant of Israel.'f

8 I am bringing them back
from the land of the north.g
I will gather them together
from the remotest parts
of the earth.h
Among them will be the blind
and the lame,i
The pregnant woman and
the one giving birth, all
together.
As a great congregation they
will return here.j

9 They will come weeping.k
I will lead them as they beg
for favor.
I will guide them to streams*
of water,l
On a level path that will not
make them stumble.
For I am a Father to Israel,
and E′phra·im is my
firstborn."m

10 Hear the word of Jehovah,
you nations,

And proclaim it among the
islands far away:a
"The One who scattered
Israel will gather him
together.
He will watch over him as a
shepherd does his flock.b

11 For Jehovah will redeem
Jacobc
And rescue* him out of the
hand of the one stronger
than he is.d

12 They will come and shout
joyfully on the height
of Zione
And become radiant over
the goodness of* Jehovah,
Over the grain and the new
winef and the oil,
And over the young of the
flock and the herd.g
They* will become like a
well-watered garden,h
And they will never languish
again."i

13 "At that time the virgin will
dance joyfully,
Also the young men and the
old men together.j
I will change their mourning
into exultation.k
I will comfort them and give
them joy instead of their
grief.l

14 I will satisfy the priests*
with plenty,#
And my people will be satisfied with my goodness,"m
declares Jehovah.

15 "This is what Jehovah says:
'A voice is heard in Ra′mah,n
lamentation and bitter
weeping:
Rachel is weeping over her
sons.*o
She has refused to be
comforted over her sons,
Because they are no more.'"p

CHAP. 31

a Jer 30:18, 19

b Am 9:14
Mic 4:4

c De 30:9
Isa 65:21, 22

d Isa 2:3
Jer 50:4, 5

e De 32:43
Isa 44:23

f Isa 1:9
Jer 23:3
Joe 2:32

g Isa 43:6
Jer 3:12

h De 30:4
Eze 20:34
Eze 34:12

i Isa 35:6
Isa 42:16

j Ezr 2:1, 64

k Jer 50:4

l Isa 35:7
Isa 49:10

m Ge 48:14
Ex 4:22

Second Col.

a Isa 11:11
Isa 42:10

b Isa 40:11
Eze 34:11-13
Mic 2:12

c Isa 44:23
Isa 48:20

d Isa 49:25

e Ezr 3:13
Ps 126:1
Isa 51:11

f Joe 3:18

g Isa 65:10

h Isa 58:11

i Isa 35:10

j Zec 8:4

k Ezr 3:12

l Isa 51:3
Isa 65:19

m De 30:9
Isa 63:7

n Jos 18:21, 25
Jer 40:1

o La 1:16

p Mt 2:16-18

31:4 *Or "go forth in the dance of those
who are laughing." 31:9 *Or "wadis."
31:11 *Or "reclaim." 31:12 *Or "the
good things from." #Or "Their soul."
31:14 *Or "the soul of the priests."
#Lit., "fatness." 31:15 *Or "children."

16 This is what Jehovah says:

"'Hold back your voice from
weeping and your eyes
from tears,
For there is a reward
for your activity,' declares
Jehovah.
'They will return from the
land of the enemy.'ª

17 'And there is a hope for your
future,'ᵇ declares Jehovah.
'Your sons will return to
their own territory.'"ᶜ

18 "I have surely heard
E'phra·im's moaning,
'You have corrected me,
and I have been corrected,
Like a calf that has not been
trained.
Bring me back, and I will
readily turn back,
For you are Jehovah my God.

19 For after my turning back
I felt remorse;ᵈ
After I was made to understand I struck my thigh
in grief.
I was ashamed and
humiliated,ᵉ
For I bore the reproach of
my youth.'"

20 "Is E'phra·im not a precious
son to me, a beloved child?ᶠ
For as often as I speak
against him, I do remember
him still.
That is why my emotions*
are stirred for him.ᵍ
And I will surely have pity on
him," declares Jehovah.ʰ

21 "Set up road markers for
yourself,
And put up signposts.ᶦ
Pay attention to the highway,
the way that you have
to go.ʲ
Return, O virgin of Israel,
return to these cities
of yours.

22 How long will you waver,
O unfaithful daughter?

For Jehovah has created
something new in the
earth:
A woman will eagerly pursue
a man."

23 This is what Jehovah of
armies, the God of Israel, says:
"They will again say these words
in the land of Judah and in its
cities when I gather back their
captives: 'May Jehovah bless
you, O righteous dwelling place,ª
O holy mountain.'ᵇ **24** And in it
Judah and all its cities will dwell
all together, farmers and those
who lead the flocks.ᶜ **25** For I
will satisfy the weary one* and
fill each one* who is languish-
ing."ᵈ

26 At this I awoke and opened
my eyes, and my sleep had been
pleasurable to me.

27 "Look! The days are coming," declares Jehovah, "when I
will sow the house of Israel and
the house of Judah with the
seed* of man and with the seed
of livestock."ᵉ

28 "And just as I watched
over them to uproot, to pull
down, to tear down, to destroy, and to do harm,ᶠ so
I will watch over them to build
up and to plant,"ᵍ declares Jehovah. **29** "In those days they
will no longer say, 'The fathers
ate sour grapes, but the teeth
of the sons were set on edge.'*ʰ
30 But then each one will die for
his own error. Any man eating
sour grapes will have his own
teeth set on edge."

31 "Look! The days are coming," declares Jehovah, "when I
will make with the house of Israel and with the house of Judah
a new covenant.ᶦ **32** It will not
be like the covenant that I made
with their forefathers on the day
I took hold of their hand to lead
them out of the land of Egypt,ʲ

CHAP. 31

a Ezr 1:5
Jer 23:3
Eze 11:17
Ho 1:11

b Jer 29:11

c Jer 46:27

d De 30:1-3

e Ezr 9:6

f Jer 31:9
Ho 14:4

g Ho 11:8

h De 32:36
Mic 7:18

i Isa 62:10

j Isa 35:8

Second Col.

a Isa 1:26

b Zec 8:3

c Jer 33:12
Eze 36:10, 11

d Ps 107:9

e De 30:9
Eze 36:9
Ho 2:23

f Jer 44:27
Jer 45:4

g Ps 102:16
Ps 147:2
Jer 24:6

h Eze 18:2-4

i Mt 26:27, 28
Lu 22:20
1Co 11:25
Heb 8:8-12

j Ex 19:5

31:20 *Lit., "intestines."

31:25 *Or "soul." **31:27** *Or "offspring." **31:29** *Lit., "got blunted."

'my covenant that they broke,[a] although I was their true master,'* declares Jehovah."

33 "For this is the covenant that I will make with the house of Israel after those days," declares Jehovah. "I will put my law within them,[b] and in their heart I will write it.[c] And I will become their God, and they will become my people."[d]

34 "And they will no longer teach each one his neighbor and each one his brother, saying, 'Know Jehovah!'[e] for they will all know me, from the least to the greatest of them,"[f] declares Jehovah. "For I will forgive their error, and I will no longer remember their sin."[g]

35 This is what Jehovah says,
Who gives the sun for light by day,
The laws* of the moon and the stars for light by night,
Who stirs up the sea and makes its waves boisterous,
Whose name is Jehovah of armies:[h]
36 "'If these regulations should ever fail,' declares Jehovah,
'Only then would the offspring of Israel cease as a nation before me always.'"[i]

37 This is what Jehovah says: "'If the heavens above could be measured and the foundations of the earth below could be explored, only then could I reject all the offspring of Israel for all they have done,' declares Jehovah."[j]

38 "Look! The days are coming," declares Jehovah, "when the city will be built[k] to Jehovah from the Tower of Ha·nan'el[l] to the Corner Gate.[m] **39** And the measuring line[n] will go out straight ahead to the hill of

---

31:32 *Or possibly, "their husband." 31:35 *Or "statutes."

CHAP. 31
a Eze 16:59
b Eze 11:19
c Heb 10:16
d Jer 24:7
  Jer 30:22
e Isa 54:13
  Joh 17:3
f Isa 11:9
  Hab 2:14
g Jer 33:8
  Jer 50:20
  Mt 26:27, 28
  Heb 8:10-12
  Heb 9:15
  Heb 10:17
h Isa 51:15
i Isa 54:10
  Jer 33:20, 21
j Jer 30:11
k Ne 12:27
  Isa 44:28
  Jer 30:18
l Ne 3:1
  Zec 14:10
m 2Ch 26:9
n Zec 1:16

Second Col.
a 2Sa 15:23
  2Ki 23:6
  Joh 18:1
b Ne 3:28
c Joe 3:17

CHAP. 32
d Jer 25:1
e Ne 3:25
  Jer 33:1
  Jer 38:28
f Jer 37:18, 21
g Jer 34:2, 3
  Jer 37:8, 17
h 2Ki 25:6, 7
  Jer 38:17, 18
  Jer 39:5
  Eze 12:13
i Jer 21:4
  Eze 17:15
j Jos 21:8, 18
  Jer 1:1
k Le 25:23, 24

Ga'reb, and it will turn toward Go'ah. **40** And all the valley* of the carcasses and of ashes# and all the terraces as far as the Kid'ron Valley,[a] clear to the corner of the Horse Gate[b] toward the east, will be something holy to Jehovah.[c] It will never again be uprooted or torn down."

32 The word that came to Jeremiah from Jehovah in the 10th year of King Zed·e·ki'ah of Judah, that is, the 18th year of Neb·u·chad·nez'zar.*[d] **2** At that time the armies of the king of Babylon were besieging Jerusalem, and Jeremiah the prophet was confined in the Courtyard of the Guard[e] in the house* of the king of Judah. **3** For King Zed·e·ki'ah of Judah had confined him,[f] saying, "Why do you prophesy like this? You say, 'This is what Jehovah says: "I will give this city into the hand of the king of Babylon, and he will capture it,[g] **4** and King Zed·e·ki'ah of Judah will not escape from the Chal·de'ans, for he will surely be given into the hand of the king of Babylon, and he will speak to him face-to-face and see him eye to eye."'[h] **5** 'He will take Zed·e·ki'ah to Babylon, and there he will remain until I turn my attention to him,' declares Jehovah. 'Although you keep fighting against the Chal·de'ans, you will not succeed.'"[i]

6 Jeremiah said: "The word of Jehovah has come to me, saying, **7** 'Here Han'a·mel the son of Shal'lum your uncle* will come to you and say: "Buy for yourself my field in An'a·thoth,[j] because you have the first right to repurchase it."'"[k]

31:40 *Or "low plain." #Or "fatty ashes," that is, ashes soaked with the fat of the sacrifices. 32:1 *Lit., "Nebuchadrezzar," a variant spelling. 32:2 *Or "palace." 32:7 *That is, paternal uncle.

8 Han′a·mel the son of my uncle came to me, just as Jehovah had said, into the Courtyard of the Guard, and he said to me: "Please buy my field in An′a·thoth, in the land of Benjamin, for you have the right to take possession of it and to repurchase it. Buy it for yourself." At that I knew that this was by the word of Jehovah.

9 So I bought the field in An′a·thoth from Han′a·mel the son of my uncle. I weighed out the money[a] to him, seven shekels* and ten silver pieces. **10** Then I recorded it in a deed,[b] affixed the seal, called in witnesses,[c] and weighed the money in the scales. **11** I took the deed of purchase, the one that was sealed according to the commandment and legal requirements, as well as the one that was left unsealed, **12** and I gave the deed of purchase to Bar′uch[d] son of Ne·ri′ah[e] son of Mah·sei′ah in the presence of Han′a·mel the son of my uncle, the witnesses who wrote in the deed of purchase, and all the Jews who were sitting in the Courtyard of the Guard.[f]

13 I now commanded Bar′uch in their presence, saying: **14** "This is what Jehovah of armies, the God of Israel, says, 'Take these deeds, this deed of purchase, the sealed one and the other deed left unsealed, and put them into an earthenware vessel, so that they may be kept for a long time.' **15** For this is what Jehovah of armies, the God of Israel, says, 'Houses and fields and vineyards will again be bought in this land.'"[g]

16 Then I prayed to Jehovah after giving the deed of purchase to Bar′uch the son of Ne·ri′ah, saying: **17** "Alas, O Sovereign Lord Jehovah! Look! You made the heavens and the earth by your great power[a] and by your outstretched arm. Nothing is too wonderful for you, **18** the One showing loyal love to thousands, but repaying the error of the fathers to* their sons after them,[b] the true God, the great and mighty One, whose name is Jehovah of armies. **19** You are great in counsel* and mighty in deed,[c] you whose eyes observe all the ways of men,[d] to give to each one according to his ways and according to what he does.[e] **20** You have performed signs and miracles in the land of Egypt, which are known down to this day, and thus you have made a name for yourself in Israel and among mankind,[f] as it is today. **21** And you brought your people Israel out of the land of Egypt, with signs, with miracles, with a mighty hand, with an outstretched arm, and with terrifying deeds.[g]

22 "In time you gave them this land that you swore to give to their forefathers,[h] a land flowing with milk and honey.[i] **23** And they came in and took possession of it, but they did not obey your voice or walk in your law. They did not do anything you commanded them to do, so that you caused all this calamity to befall them.[j] **24** Look! Men have come with siege ramparts to capture the city,[k] and because of the sword,[l] the famine, and the pestilence,*[m] the city will certainly fall into the hands of the Chal·de′ans who are fighting against it; what you said has all happened, as you now see. **25** But you have told me, O Sovereign Lord Jehovah, 'Buy for yourself the field with money and call in witnesses,' although

CHAP. 32
a Ge 23:16
b Jer 32:44
c Ru 4:9
d Jer 36:4 Jer 36:26
e Jer 51:59
f Jer 33:1
g Am 9:14 Zec 3:10

Second Col.
a Isa 40:26 Re 4:11
b Ex 34:6, 7 Nu 14:18
c Isa 28:29
d Pr 15:3 Heb 4:13
e Ec 12:14 Jer 17:10 Ro 2:6
f Ex 7:3, 5 Ex 9:15, 16 De 4:34 2Sa 7:23 Isa 63:12
g Ex 6:1, 6 Ex 15:16 De 26:8
h Ge 13:14, 15 Ge 26:3
i Ex 3:8
j De 28:15 Jos 23:16
k De 28:52 2Ki 25:1 Jer 33:4 Eze 4:1, 2
l Le 26:31, 33
m Jer 14:12 Jer 15:2

32:9 *A shekel equaled 11.4 g (0.367 oz t). See App. B14. **32:18** *Lit., "into the bosom of." **32:19** *Or "great as regards your purposes." **32:24** *Or "disease."

the city will certainly be given into the hand of the Chal·deʹans."

26 At that the word of Jehovah came to Jeremiah, saying: 27 "Here I am, Jehovah, the God of all mankind.* Is there anything too wonderful for me? 28 So this is what Jehovah says, 'Here I am handing this city over to the Chal·deʹans and into the hand of King Neb·u·chad·nezʹzar* of Babylon, and he will capture it.ᵃ 29 And the Chal·deʹans fighting against this city will come in and set this city on fire and burn it downᵇ along with the houses on whose roofs the people offered sacrifices to Baʹal and poured out drink offerings to other gods to offend me.'ᶜ

30 "'For the people of Israel and of Judah have done only what was bad in my eyes, from their youth on;ᵈ the people of Israel keep offending me by the work of their hands,' declares Jehovah. 31 'For this city, from the day that they built it down to this day, has been nothing but a cause of anger and wrath to me,ᵉ so that it must be removed from before my face,ᶠ 32 because of all the evil that the people of Israel and of Judah have done to offend me—they, their kings,ᵍ their princes,ʰ their priests, their prophets,ⁱ and the men of Judah and the inhabitants of Jerusalem. 33 They kept turning their backs to me, not their faces;ʲ although I tried to teach them again and again,* none of them would listen to receive discipline.ᵏ 34 And they put their disgusting idols in the house that bears my name, in order to defile it.ˡ 35 Furthermore, they built the high places of Baʹal in the Valley of the Son of Hinʹnom,*ᵐ in order to make

their sons and their daughters pass through the fire to Moʹlech,ᵃ something that I had not commanded themᵇ and that had never come into my heart* to do such a detestable thing, causing Judah to sin.'

36 "Therefore this is what Jehovah the God of Israel says concerning this city that you are saying will be given into the hand of the king of Babylon by the sword, the famine, and the pestilence, 37 'Here I will gather them together from all the lands where I dispersed them in my anger and in my wrath and in great indignation,ᶜ and I will bring them back to this place and let them dwell in security.ᵈ 38 And they will be my people, and I will be their God.ᵉ 39 And I will give them one heartᶠ and one way so that they may always fear me, for their own good and the good of their children after them.ᵍ 40 And I will make with them an everlasting covenant,ʰ that I will not turn away from doing good to them;ⁱ and I will put the fear of me in their hearts, so that they will not turn away from me.ʲ 41 I will exult over them to do good to them,ᵏ and I will firmly plant them in this land,ˡ with all my heart and with all my soul.'"*

42 "For this is what Jehovah says, 'Just as I have brought on this people all this great calamity, so I will bring on them all the goodness* that I am promising them.ᵐ 43 And fields will again be bought in this land,ⁿ though you are saying: "It is a wasteland without man and beast, and it has been handed over to the Chal·deʹans."'

44 "'Fields will be bought with money, deeds of purchase will be recorded and sealed, and

---

CHAP. 32
a 2Ki 25:4
Jer 20:5
b 2Ki 25:9, 10
2Ch 36:17, 19
La 4:11
c Jer 7:18
Jer 19:13
Jer 44:25
d De 9:7
2Ki 17:9
e 1Ki 11:7
2Ki 21:1, 4
f 2Ki 23:27
2Ki 24:3, 4
g 1Ki 11:9, 10
2Ki 23:26
1Ch 10:13
h Eze 22:6
i Mic 3:5, 11
j 2Ch 29:6
Jer 2:27
k Jer 25:3
Jer 35:15
l 2Ki 21:1, 4
Jer 23:11
Eze 8:5, 6
m Jos 15:8, 12

Second Col.
a 2Ch 28:1, 3
2Ch 33:1, 6
Jer 7:31
b Le 18:21
De 18:10, 12
c De 30:3
Jer 29:14
Eze 37:21
d Jer 23:3, 6
Jer 33:16
Eze 34:25
e Jer 31:33
Mic 4:5
f Eze 11:19
g De 5:29
h Isa 55:3
Isa 61:8
i Eze 39:29
j Eze 36:26
k Isa 65:19
Zep 3:17
l Isa 58:11
Jer 24:6
Am 9:15
m Jer 31:28
Zec 8:14, 15
n Eze 37:14

32:27 *Lit., "all flesh." 32:28 *Lit., "Nebuchadrezzar," a variant spelling. 32:33 *Lit., "rising up early and teaching." 32:35 *See Glossary, "Gehenna."

32:35 *Or "had never entered my thoughts." 32:41 *See Glossary. 32:42 *Or "the good things."

witnesses will be called in the land of Benjamin,[a] in the areas around Jerusalem, in the cities of Judah,[b] in the cities of the mountainous region, in the cities of the lowland,[c] and in the cities of the south, because I will bring back their captives,'[d] declares Jehovah."

33 The word of Jehovah came to Jeremiah the second time, while he was still confined in the Courtyard of the Guard,[e] saying: **2** "This is what Jehovah the Maker of earth says, Jehovah who formed it and firmly established it; Jehovah is his name, **3** 'Call to me, and I will answer you and readily tell you great and incomprehensible things that you have not known.'"[f]

4 "For this is what Jehovah the God of Israel says concerning the houses of this city and the houses of the kings of Judah that are pulled down because of the siege ramparts and the sword,[g] **5** and concerning those who are coming to fight the Chal·de'ans, filling these places with the carcasses of those whom I struck down in my anger and in my wrath, those whose evil has caused me to hide my face from this city: **6** 'Here I am bringing recuperation and health to her,[h] and I will heal them and reveal to them an abundance of peace and truth.[i] **7** And I will bring back the captives of Judah and the captives of Israel,[j] and I will build them up as I did at the start.[k] **8** And I will purify them from all the guilt of their sins against me,[l] and I will forgive all the guilt of their sins and their transgressions against me.[m] **9** And she will become to me a name of exultation, a praise, and a beauty before all the nations of the earth who will hear of all the goodness that I bestow on

them.[a] And they will be in dread and will tremble[b] because of all the goodness and peace that I will bestow on her.'"[c]

10 "This is what Jehovah says: 'In this place that you will say is a wasteland, without man or livestock, in the cities of Judah and in the streets of Jerusalem that are desolate, without man or inhabitant or livestock, there will again be heard **11** the sound of exultation and the sound of rejoicing,[d] the voice of the bridegroom and the voice of the bride, the voice of those saying: "Give thanks to Jehovah of armies, for Jehovah is good;[e] his loyal love endures forever!"'[f]

"'They will bring thanksgiving offerings into the house of Jehovah,[g] for I will bring back the captives of the land, as at the start,' says Jehovah."

12 "This is what Jehovah of armies says: 'In this wasteland, without man or livestock, and in all its cities, there will again be pastures for the shepherds to rest their flocks.'[h]

13 "'In the cities of the mountainous region, in the cities of the lowland, in the cities of the south, in the land of Benjamin, in the areas around Jerusalem,[i] and in the cities of Judah,[j] flocks will again pass under the hands of the one counting them,' says Jehovah."

14 "'Look! The days are coming,' declares Jehovah, 'when I will fulfill the good promise that I have spoken concerning the house of Israel and the house of Judah.[k] **15** In those days and at that time I will cause to sprout for David a righteous sprout,*[l] and he will execute justice and righteousness in the land.[m] **16** In those days Judah will be saved[n] and Jerusalem will reside

---

CHAP. 32
a Jer 32:10, 25
b Jer 31:23
c Jer 17:26
　Jer 33:13
d Ps 126:1

CHAP. 33
e Ne 3:25
　Jer 32:2
　Jer 37:21
　Jer 38:28
f Isa 48:6
g De 28:52
　Jer 32:24
h Isa 30:26
　Jer 30:17
i Isa 54:13
j De 30:3
　Jer 30:3
k Jer 24:6
l Isa 40:2
　Zec 13:1
m Ps 85:2
　Isa 43:25
　Jer 31:34
　Mic 7:18

Second Col.
a Isa 62:3, 7
b Mic 7:17
c Ne 6:15, 16
d Jer 31:12
e Zec 9:17
f 2Ch 5:13
　Ezr 3:11
　Ps 106:1
　Isa 12:4
　Mic 7:18
g Le 7:12
　Ps 107:22
h Isa 65:10
　Jer 32:43
i Jer 17:26
j Jer 32:44
k Jer 29:10
l Isa 53:2
　Zec 6:12
　Re 22:16
m Isa 11:1, 4
　Jer 23:5
　Heb 1:9
n Isa 45:17

33:15 *Or "heir."

in security.[a] And this is what she will be called: Jehovah Is Our Righteousness.'"[b]

17 "For this is what Jehovah says: 'There will never fail to be a man from David's line to sit on the throne of the house of Israel,[c] 18 nor will the Levitical priests ever fail to have a man stand before me to offer whole burnt offerings, to burn grain offerings, and to offer sacrifices.'"

19 And the word of Jehovah again came to Jeremiah, saying: 20 "This is what Jehovah says, 'If you could break my covenant regarding the day and my covenant regarding the night, to prevent day and night from coming at their proper time,[d] 21 only then could my covenant with my servant David be broken,[e] so that he should not have a son ruling as king on his throne,[f] and so also my covenant with the Levitical priests, my ministers.[g] 22 Just as the army of the heavens cannot be counted and the sand of the sea cannot be measured, so I will multiply the offspring* of my servant David and the Levites who are ministering to me.'"

23 And the word of Jehovah again came to Jeremiah, saying: 24 "Have you not taken note of what this people is saying, 'Jehovah will reject the two families that he chose'? And they are treating my own people with disrespect, and they no longer regard them as a nation.

25 "This is what Jehovah says: 'Just as surely as I have established my covenant regarding the day and the night,[h] the laws* of heaven and earth,[i] 26 so I will never reject the offspring* of Jacob and of my servant David, so as not to take from his

offspring* rulers over the descendants* of Abraham, Isaac, and Jacob. For I will gather back their captives[a] and have pity on them.'"[b]

34 The word that came to Jeremiah from Jehovah, when King Neb·u·chad·nez'zar* of Babylon and all his army and all the kingdoms of the earth under his dominion and all the peoples were fighting against Jerusalem and all her cities:[c]

2 "This is what Jehovah the God of Israel says, 'Go and speak to King Zed·e·ki'ah[d] of Judah and tell him: "This is what Jehovah says, 'Here I am giving this city into the hand of the king of Babylon, and he will burn it with fire.[e] 3 And you will not escape out of his hand, for you will without fail be caught and handed over to him.[f] And you will see the king of Babylon eye to eye, and he will speak to you face-to-face, and you will go to Babylon.'[g] 4 However, hear the word of Jehovah, O King Zed·e·ki'ah of Judah, 'This is what Jehovah says concerning you: "You will not die by the sword. 5 In peace you will die,[h] and they will make a burning ceremony for you as they did for your fathers, the former kings who were before you, and they will mourn you, 'Alas, O master!' for 'I have spoken the word,' declares Jehovah."'"'"

6 Jeremiah the prophet then spoke all these words to King Zed·e·ki'ah of Judah in Jerusalem, 7 when the armies of the king of Babylon were fighting against Jerusalem and against all the cities of Judah that were left,[i] against La'chish[j] and against A·ze'kah;[k] for they were the only fortified cities that remained of the cities of Judah.

CHAP. 33
a Eze 28:26

b Jer 23:6

c 2Sa 7:16, 17
1Ki 2:4
Ps 89:20, 29
Isa 9:7
Lu 1:32, 33

d Ge 1:16
Isa 54:10
Jer 31:35-37

e 2Sa 7:16, 17
2Sa 23:5
Ps 89:34, 35
Ps 132:11
Isa 55:3

f Isa 9:6
Lu 1:32, 33

g De 21:5

h Ge 1:16

i Ps 104:19
Jer 31:35, 36

Second Col.
a Ezr 2:1, 70

b Isa 14:1
Jer 31:20

CHAP. 34
c 2Ki 25:1
Jer 32:2
Jer 39:1
Jer 52:4

d 2Ch 36:11
Jer 37:1

e Jer 21:10
Jer 32:28, 29
Jer 39:8

f Jer 37:17
Jer 39:5

g 2Ki 25:6, 7
Eze 12:13

h Eze 17:16

i Jer 4:5

j Mic 1:13

k Jos 15:20, 35

33:22, 26 *Lit., "seed." 33:25 *Or "statutes."

34:1 *Lit., "Nebuchadrezzar," a variant spelling.

8 The word that came to Jeremiah from Jehovah after King Zed·e·ki'ah had made a covenant with all the people in Jerusalem to proclaim liberty to them,ᵃ **9** that everyone should free his Hebrew slaves, male and female, so that no one would keep a fellow Jew as his slave. **10** So all the princes and all the people obeyed. They had entered into the covenant that everyone should free his male and female slaves and not keep them as slaves any longer. They obeyed and let them go. **11** However, they later brought back the male and female slaves whom they had freed, and they again forced them back into slavery. **12** So the word of Jehovah came to Jeremiah from Jehovah, saying:

13 "This is what Jehovah the God of Israel says, 'I made a covenant with your forefathersᵇ in the day I brought them out of the land of Egypt, out of the house of slavery,ᶜ saying: **14** "At the end of seven years, each of you should free his Hebrew brother who was sold to you and who has served you six years; you must set him free."ᵈ But your forefathers did not listen or incline their ears to me. **15** And recently* you yourselves turned around and did what was right in my eyes by proclaiming liberty to your fellow men, and you made a covenant before me in the house that bears my name. **16** But then you turned around and profaned my nameᵉ by bringing back your male and female slaves whom you had freed according to their desire,* and you forced them back into slavery.'

17 "Therefore this is what Jehovah says: 'You have not obeyed me in proclaiming liberty, each one to his brother and to his fellow man.ᵃ So I will now proclaim liberty to you,' declares Jehovah, 'to the sword, to pestilence,* and to famine,ᵇ and I will make you an object of horror to all the kingdoms of the earth.ᶜ **18** And this is what will happen to the men who violated my covenant by not carrying out the words of the covenant that they made before me when they cut the calf in two and passed between the halves,ᵈ **19** namely, the princes of Judah, the princes of Jerusalem, the court officials, the priests, and all the people of the land who passed between the halves of the calf: **20** I will hand them over to their enemies and to those seeking to take their lives,* and their dead bodies will become food for the birds of the heavens and for the beasts of the earth.ᵉ **21** And I will give King Zed·e·ki'ah of Judah and his princes into the hand of their enemies and into the hand of those seeking to take their lives* and into the hand of the armies of the king of Babylon,ᶠ who are withdrawing from against you.'ᵍ

22 "'Here I will give the order,' declares Jehovah, 'and I will bring them back to this city, and they will fight against it and capture it and burn it with fire;ʰ and the cities of Judah I will make a wasteland, without an inhabitant.'"ⁱ

35 The word that came to Jeremiah from Jehovah in the days of Je·hoi'a·kimʲ son of Jo·si'ah, the king of Judah, saying: **2** "Go to the house of the Re'cha·bitesᵏ and speak with them and bring them into the house of Jehovah, into one of the dining rooms;* then offer them wine to drink."

CHAP. 34
a Ex 21:2
b Ex 24:7
c Ex 13:3
d Ex 21:2
  Le 25:10
  Le 25:39-42
  De 15:12
e Le 19:12

Second Col.
a Ex 21:2
  Le 25:10
b 2Ki 25:3
  Jer 21:7
c Jer 15:2, 4
  Jer 29:18
d Ge 15:10, 17
e De 28:26
  Ps 79:2
  Jer 16:4
f 2Ki 25:6, 7
  La 4:20
g Jer 37:5
h 2Ki 25:9, 10
  Jer 32:29
  Jer 39:8
i Le 26:33
  Jer 44:2

CHAP. 35
j 2Ki 23:34
  2Ch 36:5
  Da 1:1
k 2Ki 10:15
  1Ch 2:55

34:15 *Lit., "today." 34:16 *Or "soul." 34:17 *Or "disease." 34:20, 21 *Or "seeking their souls." 35:2 *Or "the chambers."

3 So I took Ja·az·a·ni'ah the son of Jeremiah the son of Hab·az·zi·ni'ah, his brothers, all his sons, and the entire house of the Re'cha·bites **4** into the house of Jehovah. I brought them to the dining room of the sons of Ha'nan the son of Ig·da·li'ah, a man of the true God, which was next to the dining room of the princes that was above the dining room of Ma·a·sei'ah the son of Shal'lum the doorkeeper. **5** Then I put cups and goblets full of wine before the men of the house of the Re'cha·bites and said to them: "Drink wine."

6 But they said: "We will not drink wine, because Je·hon'a·dab*ᵃ the son of Re'chab, our forefather, gave us this command, 'Neither you nor your sons must ever drink wine. **7** And you must not build a house, sow seed, or plant or obtain a vineyard. Instead, you must always dwell in tents, so that you may live for a long time in the land where you are residing as foreigners.' **8** So we continue to obey the voice of Je·hon'a·dab the son of our forefather Re'chab in all that he commanded us, by never drinking any wine —we, our wives, our sons, and our daughters. **9** And we do not build houses to dwell in, nor do we have vineyards or fields or seed. **10** We keep living in tents and obeying all that Je·hon'a·dab* our forefather commanded us. **11** But when King Neb·u·chad·nez'zar* of Babylon came up against the land,ᵇ we said, 'Come, let us go into Jerusalem to escape the army of the Chal·de'ans and of the Syrians, and now we are living in Jerusalem.'"

12 And the word of Jehovah came to Jeremiah, saying: **13** "This is what Jehovah of armies, the God of Israel, says, 'Go and say to the men of Judah and to the inhabitants of Jerusalem: "Were you not continually urged to obey my words?"ᵃ declares Jehovah. **14** "Je·hon'a·dab the son of Re'chab commanded his descendants not to drink wine, and they have carried out his words by not drinking it to this day, thus obeying the order of their forefather.ᵇ However, I have spoken to you again and again,* but you have not obeyed me.ᶜ **15** And I kept sending all my servants the prophets to you, sending them again and again,*ᵈ saying, 'Turn back, please, each of you from your evil ways,ᵉ and do what is right! Do not walk after other gods and serve them. Then you will keep dwelling in the land that I gave to you and your forefathers.'ᶠ But you did not incline your ear or listen to me. **16** The descendants of Je·hon'a·dab the son of Re'chab have carried out the order that their forefather gave them,ᵍ but these people have not listened to me."'"

17 "Therefore this is what Jehovah, the God of armies, the God of Israel, says: 'Here I am bringing on Judah and on all the inhabitants of Jerusalem all the calamity that I have warned them about,ʰ for I have spoken to them, but they would not listen, and I kept calling to them, but they would not answer.'"ⁱ

18 And Jeremiah said to the household of the Re'cha·bites: "This is what Jehovah of armies, the God of Israel, says, 'Because you have obeyed the order of your forefather Je·hon'a·dab and you continue to observe all his

---

CHAP. 35
a 2Ki 10:15

b 2Ch 36:5, 6
Da 1:1

__Second Col.__
a Jer 32:33

b Jer 35:8

c 2Ch 36:15, 16
Ne 9:26, 30
Jer 25:3

d Jer 7:24, 25

e Isa 1:16
Jer 25:5
Eze 18:30
Ho 14:1

f Jer 7:5-7

g Jer 35:8

h De 28:15
De 29:26, 27
Jos 23:15, 16
2Ki 23:27

i Isa 65:12
Isa 66:4
Jer 7:13, 14

35:6, 10 *Lit., "Jonadab," the shortened form of Jehonadab. **35:11** *Lit., "Nebuchadrezzar," a variant spelling.

35:14 *Lit., "rising up early and speaking." **35:15** *Lit., "rising up early and sending."

orders, doing exactly what he ordered you, 19 this is what Jehovah of armies, the God of Israel, says: "There will never fail to be a descendant of Je·hon′a·dab* the son of Re′chab to serve in my presence."'"

36 Now in the fourth year of Je·hoi′a·kim*a* son of Jo·si′ah, the king of Judah, this word came to Jeremiah from Jehovah, saying: 2 "Take a scroll* and write in it all the words that I have spoken to you against Israel and Judah*b* and all the nations,*c* from the first day I spoke to you in the days of Jo·si′ah to this day.*d* 3 Perhaps when those of the house of Judah hear of all the calamity that I intend to bring on them, they may turn back from their evil ways, so that I may forgive their error and their sin."*e*

4 Jeremiah then called Bar′uch*f* the son of Ne·ri′ah, and Jeremiah dictated all the words that Jehovah had spoken to him, and Bar′uch wrote them in the scroll.*g* 5 Then Jeremiah commanded Bar′uch: "I am confined and unable to enter the house of Jehovah. 6 So you are the one who must go in and read aloud the words of Jehovah from the scroll that you wrote at my dictation. Read them in the hearing of the people at the house of Jehovah on the day of a fast; thus you will read them to all the people of Judah who come in from their cities. 7 Perhaps their request for favor will reach Jehovah, and they will turn back, each one from his evil ways, for great is the anger and the wrath that Jehovah has declared against this people."

8 So Bar′uch the son of Ne·ri′ah did all that Jeremiah the

prophet had commanded him; he read aloud from the scroll* the words of Jehovah at the house of Jehovah.*a*

9 Now in the fifth year of Je·hoi′a·kim*b* son of Jo·si′ah, the king of Judah, in the ninth month, all the people in Jerusalem and all the people who came into Jerusalem from the cities of Judah proclaimed a fast before Jehovah.*c* 10 Bar′uch then read aloud from the scroll* the words of Jeremiah at the house of Jehovah, in the chamber* of Gem·a·ri′ah*d* the son of Sha′phan*e* the copyist,△ in the upper courtyard, at the entrance of the new gate of the house of Jehovah,*f* in the hearing of all the people.

11 When Mi·cai′ah the son of Gem·a·ri′ah the son of Sha′phan heard all the words of Jehovah from the scroll,* 12 he went down to the house* of the king, to the secretary's chamber. All the princes* were sitting there: E·lish′a·ma*g* the secretary, De·la′iah the son of She·mai′ah, El·na′than*h* the son of Ach′bor,*i* Gem·a·ri′ah the son of Sha′phan, Zed·e·ki′ah the son of Han·a·ni′ah, and all the other princes. 13 Mi·cai′ah told them all the words that he had heard when Bar′uch read from the scroll* in the hearing of the people.

14 Then all the princes sent Je·hu′di the son of Neth·a·ni′ah the son of Shel·e·mi′ah the son of Cush′i to Bar′uch, saying: "Come and bring with you the scroll from which you read in the hearing of the people." Bar′uch the son of Ne·ri′ah took the scroll in his hand and went in to them. 15 They said to him: "Sit down, please, and read it aloud to us." So Bar′uch read it to them.

CHAP. 36
a 2Ki 23:36
Jer 25:1

b Jer 4:16
Jer 32:30

c Jer 1:5
Jer 25:9

d Jer 1:1, 2
Jer 25:3

e Isa 55:7
Eze 33:11
Mic 7:18

f Jer 32:12
Jer 45:2-5

g Jer 45:1

Second Col.
a Jer 7:1, 2

b 2Ki 23:36

c 2Ch 20:2, 3
Es 4:15, 16

d Jer 36:25

e 2Ki 22:8
2Ch 34:20, 21
Jer 26:24
Jer 39:13, 14
Eze 8:11

f Jer 26:10

g Jer 36:20

h Jer 36:25

i 2Ki 22:14
Jer 26:22

35:19 *Lit., "Jonadab," the shortened form of Jehonadab. **36:2** *Lit., "a scroll of a book." **36:4** *Lit., "the scroll of the book."

36:8, 10, 11, 13 *Or "book." **36:10** *Or "dining room." △Or "scribe." **36:12** *Or "palace." *Or "court officials."

16 Now as soon as they heard all the words, they looked at one another in dread, and they said to Bar′uch: "We must certainly tell the king all these words." **17** And they asked Bar′uch: "Tell us, please, how you wrote all these words. Was it at his dictation?" **18** Bar′uch replied to them: "He dictated all these words to me, and I wrote them down with ink in this scroll."* **19** The princes said to Bar′uch: "Go and hide yourselves, you and Jeremiah, and do not let anyone know where you are."[a]

20 Then they went in to the king, to the courtyard, and deposited the scroll in the chamber of E·lish′a·ma the secretary, and they told the king everything they had heard.

21 So the king sent Je·hu′di[b] out to get the scroll, and he brought it from the chamber of E·lish′a·ma the secretary. Je·hu′di began to read it in the hearing of the king and of all the princes standing by the king. **22** The king was sitting in the winter house, in the ninth month,* with a fire burning in the brazier before him. **23** After Je·hu′di had read three or four columns, the king would cut off that portion with the secretary's knife and pitch it into the fire that was burning in the brazier, until the entire scroll ended up in the fire that was in the brazier. **24** And they felt no dread; neither the king nor all his servants who heard all these words ripped their garments apart. **25** Although El·na′than,[c] De·la′iah,[d] and Gem·a·ri′ah[e] pleaded with the king not to burn the scroll, he did not listen to them. **26** Further, the king commanded Je·rah′me·el the son of the king, Se·rai′ah the son of Az′ri·el, and Shel·e·mi′ah the son of Ab′de·el to seize Bar′uch the secretary and Jeremiah the prophet, but Jehovah kept them concealed.[a]

27 And the word of Jehovah again came to Jeremiah after the king had burned up the scroll containing the words that Bar′uch had written at Jeremiah's dictation,[b] saying: **28** "Take another scroll and write on it all the same words that were on the first scroll, which King Je·hoi′a·kim of Judah burned up.[c] **29** And you should say against King Je·hoi′a·kim of Judah, 'This is what Jehovah says: "You have burned up this scroll and said, 'Why have you written on it: "The king of Babylon will certainly come and destroy this land and empty it of man and beast"?'[d] **30** Therefore this is what Jehovah says against King Je·hoi′a·kim of Judah, 'He will have no one to sit on the throne of David,[e] and his dead body will be left exposed to the heat by day and the frost by night.[f] **31** I will call him and his descendants* and his servants to account for their error, and I will bring on them and on the inhabitants of Jerusalem and on the men of Judah all the calamity that I have spoken against them,[g] but they did not listen.'"'"[h]

32 Jeremiah then took another scroll and gave it to Bar′uch the son of Ne·ri′ah, the secretary,[i] and at Jeremiah's dictation he wrote on it all the words of the scroll* that King Je·hoi′a·kim of Judah had burned in the fire.[j] And many more words like those were added.

37 And King Zed·e·ki′ah[k] the son of Jo·si′ah began to reign in place of Co·ni′ah*[l] the son of Je·hoi′a·kim, for

---

CHAP. 36
a Jer 36:26

b Jer 36:14

c 2Ki 24:8

d Jer 36:12

e Jer 36:10

Second Col.
a Jer 1:19

b Jer 36:2

c Jer 36:23

d Jer 25:8, 9

e 2Ki 24:6, 8
  2Ki 24:15
  2Ch 36:9, 10
  Jer 22:24, 30

f Jer 22:18, 19

g De 28:15
  Jer 19:15

h 2Ch 36:15, 16

i Jer 36:2, 4

j Jer 36:23

CHAP. 37
k 2Ki 24:17-19
  1Ch 3:15

l 2Ki 24:12
  Jer 22:24

36:18, 32 *Or "book." **36:22** *The last half of November and the first half of December. See App. B15.

36:31 *Lit., "seed." **37:1** *Also called Jehoiachin and Jeconiah.

King Neb·u·chad·nez′zar* of Babylon made him king in the land of Judah.ᵃ 2 But he and his servants and the people of the land did not listen to the words of Jehovah spoken through Jeremiah the prophet.

3 And King Zed·e·ki′ah sent Je·hu′calᵇ the son of Shel·e·mi′ah and Zeph·a·ni′ahᶜ the son of Ma·a·sei′ah the priest to Jeremiah the prophet, saying: "Please pray in our behalf to Jehovah our God." 4 Jeremiah was moving about freely among the people, for they had not yet put him in prison.ᵈ 5 Now Phar′aoh's army had set out from Egypt,ᵉ and the Chal·de′ans who were besieging Jerusalem heard the report about them. So they withdrew from against Jerusalem.ᶠ 6 Then the word of Jehovah came to Jeremiah the prophet, saying: 7 "This is what Jehovah the God of Israel says, 'This is what you should say to the king of Judah, who sent you to me to inquire of me: "Look! The army of Phar′aoh that is coming to assist you will have to go back to their land, Egypt.ᵍ 8 And the Chal·de′ans will come back and fight against this city and capture it and burn it with fire."ʰ 9 This is what Jehovah says, "Do not deceive yourselves* by saying, 'The Chal·de′ans will surely go away from against us,' because they will not go away. 10 Even if you were to strike down the entire army of the Chal·de′ans who are fighting against you and only their wounded men were left, they would still rise up from their tents and burn this city with fire."'"ⁱ

11 When the Chal·de′an army had withdrawn from against Jerusalem because of Phar′aoh's army,ʲ 12 Jeremiah set out

from Jerusalem to the land of Benjaminᵃ to receive his portion there among his people. 13 But when he reached the Gate of Benjamin, the officer in charge of the guard, whose name was I·ri′jah the son of Shel·e·mi′ah the son of Han·a·ni′ah, seized Jeremiah the prophet and said: "You are deserting to the Chal·de′ans!" 14 But Jeremiah said: "It is not true! I am not deserting to the Chal·de′ans." But he did not listen to him. So I·ri′jah arrested Jeremiah and brought him in to the princes. 15 The princes were furious with Jeremiah,ᵇ and they beat him and imprisoned him*ᶜ in the house of Je·hon′a·than the secretary, which had been made into a prison. 16 Jeremiah was put into the dungeon,* into the vaulted rooms, and he remained there many days.

17 Then King Zed·e·ki′ah sent for him, and the king secretly questioned him in his house.*ᵈ He asked, "Is there any word from Jehovah?" Jeremiah said, "There is!" and he continued, "You will be given into the hand of the king of Babylon!"ᵉ

18 Jeremiah also said to King Zed·e·ki′ah: "How have I sinned against you and against your servants and against this people, so that you have put me into the prison? 19 Where, now, are your prophets who prophesied to you, 'The king of Babylon will not come against you and against this land'?ᶠ 20 Now listen, please, O my lord the king. May you grant, please, my request for favor. Do not send me back to the house of Je·hon′a·thanᵍ the secretary, or I will die there."ʰ 21 So King Zed·e·ki′ah ordered that Jeremiah be put in custody in

CHAP. 37
a 2Ch 36:10-12

b Jer 38:1, 4

c 2Ki 25:18, 21
Jer 21:1, 2
Jer 29:25

d Jer 37:15

e Eze 17:15

f Jer 34:21

g Jer 17:5
La 4:17
Eze 17:17

h Jer 32:29
Jer 34:22
Jer 39:8

i Jer 21:4

j Jer 34:21

_____
Second Col.
a Jer 1:1

b Jer 26:11
Jer 38:4

c Jer 20:2
Heb 11:32, 36

d Jer 38:14

e Jer 21:7
Jer 24:8
Jer 34:21
Eze 12:12, 13

f Jer 14:13
Jer 23:16, 17
Jer 27:14
Jer 28:1, 2
La 2:14

g Jer 37:15

h Jer 26:15
Jer 38:8, 9

_____
37:1 *Lit., "Nebuchadrezzar," a variant spelling. 37:9 *Or "your souls."

37:15 *Lit., "put him into the house of the fetters." 37:16 *Lit., "the house of the cistern." 37:17 *Or "palace."

the Courtyard of the Guard,[a] and he was given a round loaf of bread daily from the street of the bakers[b] until all the bread in the city was gone.[c] And Jeremiah remained in the Courtyard of the Guard.

38 Now Sheph·a·ti′ah the son of Mat′tan, Ged·a·li′ah the son of Pash′hur, Ju′cal[d] the son of Shel·e·mi′ah, and Pash′hur[e] the son of Mal·chi′jah heard the words that Jeremiah was speaking to all the people, saying: **2** "This is what Jehovah says, 'The one who remains in this city will die by the sword, by famine, and by pestilence.*[f] But the one who surrenders[g] to the Chal·de′ans will keep living and will have his life[△] as a spoil[⊠] and live.'[g] **3** This is what Jehovah says, 'This city will surely be handed over to the army of the king of Babylon, and he will capture it.'"[h]

4 The princes said to the king: "Please have this man put to death,[i] for this is how he is weakening the morale* of the soldiers who are left in this city, as well as that of all the people, by speaking such words to them. For this man seeks, not the peace of this people, but their calamity." **5** King Zed·e·ki′ah replied: "Look! He is in your hands, for the king cannot do anything to stop you."

6 So they took Jeremiah and threw him into the cistern of Mal·chi′jah the son of the king, which was in the Courtyard of the Guard.[j] They let Jeremiah down by ropes. Now there was no water in the cistern, only mud, and Jeremiah began to sink down into the mud.

7 E′bed-mel′ech[k] the E·thi·o′pi·an, a eunuch* in the king's

CHAP. 37
a Ne 3:25
Jer 32:2
Jer 33:1
Jer 38:13, 28

b 1Ki 17:6

c 2Ki 25:3
Jer 38:9

CHAP. 38
d Jer 37:3

e Jer 21:1, 2

f Jer 27:13
Jer 29:18
Eze 7:15

g Jer 21:8-10

h 2Ki 25:1, 2
2Ch 36:17

i Jer 26:11

j Jer 33:1
Jer 37:21
Jer 38:28

k Jer 39:16

Second Col.
a Jer 37:13

b Jer 52:6

c 2Ki 20:13

d Jer 37:21

house,* heard that they had put Jeremiah into the cistern. Now the king was sitting in the Gate of Benjamin,[a] **8** so E′bed-mel′ech went out of the king's house* and spoke to the king, saying: **9** "O my lord the king, what these men have done to Jeremiah the prophet is evil! They have thrown him into the cistern, and he will die there because of the famine, for there is no bread left in the city."[b]

10 Then the king commanded E′bed-mel′ech the E·thi·o′pi·an: "Take 30 men with you from here, and pull Jeremiah the prophet up out of the cistern before he dies." **11** So E′bed-mel′ech took the men with him and went into the king's house* to a place beneath the treasury,[c] and they took from there some worn-out rags and worn-out pieces of cloth and let them down by ropes to Jeremiah in the cistern. Then E′bed-mel′ech the E·thi·o′pi·an said to Jeremiah: "Please put the rags and the pieces of cloth between your armpits and the ropes." Jeremiah did so, **13** and they drew Jeremiah out with the ropes and pulled him up out of the cistern. And Jeremiah remained in the Courtyard of the Guard.[d]

14 King Zed·e·ki′ah sent for Jeremiah the prophet to come to him at the third entrance, which is in the house of Jehovah, and the king said to Jeremiah: "I have something to ask of you. Do not hide anything from me." **15** Jeremiah then said to Zed·e·ki′ah: "If I tell you, you will certainly put me to death. And if I give you advice, you will not listen to me." **16** So King Zed·e·ki′ah secretly swore to Jeremiah, saying: "As surely as Jehovah is alive, who has given us this life,* I will not put you to death,

---

38:2 *Or "disease." #Lit., "goes out." △Or "soul." ⊠Or "will escape with his life." 38:4 *Lit., "hands." 38:7 *Or "court official."

38:7, 8, 11 *Or "palace." 38:16 *Or "made for us this soul."

and I will not hand you over to these men who are seeking to take your life."*

17 Jeremiah then said to Zed·e·ki'ah: "This is what Jehovah, the God of armies, the God of Israel, says, 'If you surrender* to the princes of the king of Babylon, your life will be spared,* and this city will not be burned with fire, and you and your household will be spared.ᵃ 18 But if you will not surrender* to the princes of the king of Babylon, this city will not be handed over to the Chal·de'ans, and they will burn it with fire,ᵇ and you will not escape out of their hand.'"ᶜ

19 Then King Zed·e·ki'ah said to Jeremiah: "I am afraid of the Jews who have deserted to the Chal·de'ans, for if I am handed over to them, they may deal cruelly with me." 20 But Jeremiah said: "You will not be handed over to them. Obey, please, the voice of Jehovah in what I am telling you, and it will go well with you, and you* will continue to live. 21 But if you refuse to surrender,* this is what Jehovah has revealed to me: 22 Look! All the women remaining in the house* of the king of Judah are being brought out to the princes of the king of Babylon,ᵈ and they are saying,

'The men whom you trusted# have deceived you and overcome you.ᵉ
They have caused your foot to sink into the mud.
Now they have turned away in retreat.'

23 And all your wives and your sons they are bringing out to the Chal·de'ans, and you will not escape out of their hand, but you will be seized by the king of Babylon,* and because of you this city will be burned with fire."ᵇ

24 Zed·e·ki'ah then said to Jeremiah: "Do not let anyone know about these things, so that you do not die. 25 And if the princes hear that I have spoken with you and they come and say to you, 'Tell us, please, what you said to the king. Do not hide anything from us, and we will not put you to death.ᶜ What did the king say to you?' 26 you must answer them, 'I was making a request of the king, that he not send me back to the house of Je·hon'a·than to die there.'"ᵈ

27 In time all the princes came in to Jeremiah and questioned him. He told them everything that the king had commanded him to say. So they said no more to him, for no one had heard the conversation. 28 Until the day that Jerusalem was captured, Jeremiah remained in the Courtyard of the Guard;ᵉ he was still there when Jerusalem was captured.ᶠ

39 In the ninth year of King Zed·e·ki'ah of Judah, in the tenth month, King Neb·u·chad·nez'zar* of Babylon and all his army came to Jerusalem, and they besieged it.ᵍ

2 In the 11th year of Zed·e·ki'ah, in the fourth month, on the ninth day of the month, they broke through the city wall.ʰ 3 And all the princes of the king of Babylon went in and sat down in the Middle Gate,ⁱ namely, Ner'gal·shar·e'zer the Sam'gar, Ne'bo·Sar'se·chim the Rab'sa·ris,* Ner'gal·shar·e'zer the Rab'mag,#

CHAP. 38
a Jer 21:9
  Jer 27:12

b 2Ki 25:8, 9

c 2Ki 25:6
  Jer 39:5

d Jer 39:3

e La 1:2

Second Col.
a 2Ki 25:7

b Jer 52:8, 13

c Jer 38:4

d Jer 37:15

e Jer 15:20
  Jer 32:2
  Jer 33:1
  Jer 37:21
  Jer 39:13, 14

f 2Ki 25:8, 9
  2Ch 36:17

CHAP. 39
g 2Ki 25:1, 2
  Jer 52:4, 5
  Eze 24:1, 2

h 2Ki 25:3, 4
  Jer 52:6, 7
  Eze 33:21

i Jer 1:15

38:16 *Or "seeking your soul." 38:17, 18, 21 *Lit., "go out." 38:17 #Or "your soul will keep living." 38:20 *Or "your soul." 38:22 *Or "palace." #Lit., "The men of your peace."

39:1 *Lit., "Nebuchadrezzar," a variant spelling. 39:3 *Or according to a different word division of the Hebrew text, "Nergal-sharezer, Samgar-nebo, Sarsechim, Rabsaris." #Or "the chief magician (astrologer)."

and all the rest of the princes of the king of Babylon.

4 When King Zed·e·ki′ah of Judah and all the soldiers saw them, they fled,[a] going out of the city by night by way of the king's garden, through the gate between the double wall, and they continued by the way of the Ar′a·bah.[b] **5** But the Chal·de′an army chased after them, and they overtook Zed·e·ki′ah in the desert plains of Jer′i·cho.[c] They captured him and brought him up to King Neb·u·chad·nez′zar* of Babylon at Rib′lah[d] in the land of Ha′math,[e] where he passed sentence on him. **6** The king of Babylon had the sons of Zed·e·ki′ah slaughtered before his eyes there at Rib′lah, and the king of Babylon had all the nobles of Judah slaughtered.[f] **7** Then he blinded the eyes of Zed·e·ki′ah, after which he bound him with copper fetters to bring him to Babylon.[g]

8 The Chal·de′ans then burned down the king's house* and the houses of the people,[h] and they tore down the walls of Jerusalem.[i] **9** Neb·u′zar·ad′an[j] the chief of the guard took into exile to Babylon the rest of the people who were left in the city, the deserters who had defected to him, and anyone who remained.

10 But Neb·u′zar·ad′an the chief of the guard left in the land of Judah some of the poorest people, those who had nothing at all. On that day he also gave them vineyards and fields to work.*[k]

11 Now King Neb·u·chad·nez′zar* of Babylon gave Neb·u′zar·ad′an the chief of the guard these orders concerning Jeremiah: **12** "Take him and look af-

ter him; do him no harm, and grant whatever he asks of you."[a]

13 So Neb·u′zar·ad′an the chief of the guard, Neb·u·shaz′ban the Rab′sa·ris,* Ner′gal·shar·e′zer the Rab′mag,# and all the principal men of the king of Babylon sent **14** and had Jeremiah taken out of the Courtyard of the Guard[b] and handed him over to Ged·a·li′ah[c] the son of A·hi′kam[d] the son of Sha′phan[e] to be brought to his house. So he lived among the people.

15 While Jeremiah was confined in the Courtyard of the Guard,[f] the word of Jehovah came to him, saying: **16** "Go and tell E′bed-mel′ech[g] the E·thi·o′pi·an, 'This is what Jehovah of armies, the God of Israel, says: "Here I am fulfilling my words on this city for calamity and not for good, and in that day you will see it happen."'

17 "'But I will rescue you in that day,' declares Jehovah, 'and you will not be handed over to the men you fear.'

18 "'For I will surely provide you with escape, and you will not fall by the sword. You will have your life* as a spoil,#[h] because you trusted in me,'[i] declares Jehovah."

40 The word that came to Jeremiah from Jehovah after Neb·u′zar·ad′an[j] the chief of the guard let him go free from Ra′mah.[k] He had taken him there bound with handcuffs, and he was among all the exiles of Jerusalem and of Judah who were being deported to Babylon. **2** Then the chief of the guard took Jeremiah and said to him: "Jehovah your God foretold this calamity against this place, **3** and Jehovah has brought it

---

CHAP. 39

a De 28:25

b 2Ki 25:4-7
Jer 52:7-11

c Jer 32:4
Jer 38:18

d 2Ki 23:31, 33

e 2Ki 17:24

f Jer 21:7
Jer 34:18-20

g Eze 12:13

h Isa 5:9
Jer 38:18

i 2Ki 25:9-11
2Ch 36:17, 19
Ne 1:3
Jer 52:13-15

j 2Ki 25:20
Jer 40:1
Jer 52:12

k 2Ki 25:12
Jer 52:16

Second Col.

a Jer 40:2, 4

b Jer 38:28

c 2Ki 25:22
Jer 40:5
Jer 41:2

d 2Ch 34:20, 21
Jer 26:24

e 2Ki 22:8

f Jer 32:2
Jer 37:21

g Jer 38:7

h Jer 45:2, 5

i Ps 37:39, 40
Jer 17:7

CHAP. 40

j Jer 39:9
Jer 52:12, 13

k Jos 18:21, 25

39:5, 11 *Lit., "Nebuchadrezzar," a variant spelling. 39:8 *Or "palace." 39:10 *Or possibly, "compulsory services."

39:13 *Or "the chief court official." #Or "the chief magician (astrologer)." 39:18 *Or "soul." #Or "will escape with your life."

about just as he said, because you people sinned against Jehovah and did not obey his voice. That is why this has happened to you.[a] **4** Now I am releasing you today from the handcuffs that were on your hands. If it seems good to you to come with me to Babylon, come, and I will look after you. But if you do not want to come with me to Babylon, do not come. See! The entire land is before you. Go wherever you choose."[b]

5 While Jeremiah still had not turned back, Neb·u′zar·ad′an said: "Return to Ged·a·li′ah[c] the son of A·hi′kam[d] the son of Sha′phan,[e] whom the king of Babylon has appointed over the cities of Judah, and stay with him among the people; or go wherever you choose."

The chief of the guard then gave him a food allowance and a gift and let him go. **6** So Jeremiah went to Ged·a·li′ah the son of A·hi′kam at Miz′pah[f] and stayed with him among the people who were left in the land.

7 In time all the army chiefs who were in the field with their men heard that the king of Babylon had appointed Ged·a·li′ah the son of A·hi′kam over the land and that he had appointed him over the men, women, and children from the poor people of the land who had not been deported to Babylon.[g] **8** So they came to Ged·a·li′ah at Miz′pah.[h] They were Ish′ma·el the son of Neth·a·ni′ah, Jo·ha′nan[i] and Jon′a·than the sons of Ka·re′ah, Se·rai′ah the son of Tan·hu′meth, the sons of E′phai the Ne·toph′a·thite, and Jez·a·ni′ah[k] the son of the Ma·ac′a·thite, together with their men. **9** Ged·a·li′ah the son of A·hi′kam the son of Sha′phan swore an oath to them and to their men, saying: "Do not be afraid of serving the Chal·de′ans. Live in the land and serve the king

of Babylon, and it will go well with you.[a] **10** As for me, I will stay in Miz′pah to represent you to* the Chal·de′ans who come to us. But you should gather wine, summer fruits, and oil and put them in your storage containers and settle in the cities that you have taken over."[b]

11 And all the Jews who were in Mo′ab, Am′mon, and E′dom, as well as those who were in all the other lands, also heard that the king of Babylon had let a remnant stay in Judah and that he had appointed over them Ged·a·li′ah the son of A·hi′kam the son of Sha′phan. **12** So the Jews began returning from all the places to which they had been dispersed, and they came into the land of Judah, to Ged·a·li′ah at Miz′pah. And they gathered wine and summer fruits in very great quantity.

13 Jo·ha′nan the son of Ka·re′ah and all the army chiefs who were in the field came to Ged·a·li′ah at Miz′pah. **14** They said to him: "Do you not know that Ba′a·lis, the king of the Am′mon·ites,[c] has sent Ish′ma·el the son of Neth·a·ni′ah to kill you?"*[d] But Ged·a·li′ah the son of A·hi′kam did not believe them.

15 Then Jo·ha′nan the son of Ka·re′ah secretly told Ged·a·li′ah in Miz′pah: "I want to go and strike down Ish′ma·el the son of Neth·a·ni′ah, and no one will know. Why should he kill you,* and why should all the people of Judah who have gathered to you be scattered and the remnant of Judah perish?" **16** But Ged·a·li′ah[e] the son of A·hi′kam said to Jo·ha′nan the son of Ka·re′ah: "Do not do this, for what you are saying concerning Ish′ma·el is a lie."

CHAP. 40
a Jer 50:7

b Jer 39:11, 12

c 2Ki 25:22
  Jer 39:13, 14
  Jer 41:2

d 2Ki 22:12, 13
  Jer 26:24

e 2Ki 22:8

f Jg 20:1
  1Ki 15:22

g 2Ki 25:22
  Jer 39:10

h 2Ki 25:23

i 2Ki 25:25

j Jer 41:11, 16
  Jer 43:2

k Jer 42:1, 2

Second Col.
a 2Ki 25:24
  Jer 27:11

b Jer 39:10

c Jer 41:10

d Jer 41:2

e 2Ki 25:22

40:10 *Lit., "to stand before." **40:14** *Or "to strike your soul?" **40:15** *Or "strike your soul."

41 In the seventh month Ish'-ma·el[a] son of Neth·a·ni'ah son of E·lish'a·ma, who was of the royal line* and one of the principal men of the king, came with ten other men to Ged·a·li'ah the son of A·hi'kam at Miz'-pah.[b] As they were eating a meal together in Miz'pah, **2** Ish'ma·el the son of Neth·a·ni'ah and the ten men who were with him rose up and struck down Ged·a·li'ah the son of A·hi'kam the son of Sha'phan with the sword. So he put to death the one whom the king of Babylon had appointed over the land. **3** Ish'ma·el also struck down all the Jews who were with Ged·a·li'ah in Miz'pah, as well as the Chal·de'an soldiers who were there.

4 On the second day after Ged·a·li'ah had been put to death, before anyone knew about it, **5** there came 80 men from She'-chem,[c] from Shi'loh,[d] and from Sa·mar'i·a.[e] Their beards were shaved off, their garments were ripped apart, they had cut themselves,[f] and they had grain offerings and frankincense[g] in their hand to bring to the house of Jehovah. **6** So Ish'ma·el the son of Neth·a·ni'ah went out from Miz'pah to meet them, weeping as he walked along. When he encountered them, he said to them: "Come to Ged·a·li'ah the son of A·hi'kam." **7** But when they came into the city, Ish'ma·el the son of Neth·a·ni'ah and his men slaughtered them and threw them into the cistern.

8 But there were ten men among them who said to Ish'ma·el: "Do not put us to death, for we have hidden stores of wheat, barley, oil, and honey in the field." So he refrained from putting them to death along with their brothers. **9** Now Ish'ma·el threw all the carcasses of the men he had killed into a great cistern, the one that King A'sa had made because of King Ba'a·sha of Israel.[a] This was the cistern that Ish'ma·el the son of Neth·a·ni'ah filled with the slain men.

10 Ish'ma·el took captive all the rest of the people in Miz'-pah,[b] including the daughters of the king and all the people left in Miz'pah, whom Neb·u'zar·ad'-an the chief of the guard had put in the custody of Ged·a·li'-ah[c] the son of A·hi'kam. Ish'ma·el the son of Neth·a·ni'ah took them captive and went off to cross over to the Am'mon·ites.[d]

11 When Jo·ha'nan[e] the son of Ka·re'ah and all the army chiefs who were with him heard about all the evil that Ish'ma·el the son of Neth·a·ni'ah had done, **12** they took all the men and went off to fight against Ish'ma·el the son of Neth·a·ni'ah, and they found him by the great waters* in Gib'e·on.

13 All the people who were with Ish'ma·el rejoiced when they saw Jo·ha'nan the son of Ka·re'-ah and all the army chiefs with him. **14** Then all the people whom Ish'ma·el had taken captive from Miz'pah[f] turned around and went back with Jo·ha'nan the son of Ka·re'ah. **15** But Ish'ma·el the son of Neth·a·ni'ah and eight of his men escaped from Jo·ha'nan and went to the Am'mon·ites.

16 Jo·ha'nan the son of Ka·re'-ah and all the army chiefs who were with him took with them the rest of the people from Miz'pah, those whom they had rescued from Ish'ma·el the son of Neth-a·ni'ah after he had struck down Ged·a·li'ah[g] the son of A·hi'kam. They brought the men, the soldiers, the women, the children, and the court officials back from

---

CHAP. 41
a 2Ki 25:23
  Jer 40:14

b 2Ki 25:25

c 1Ki 12:1

d Jos 18:1

e 1Ki 16:23, 24

f Le 19:27, 28
  De 14:1

g Le 2:1

Second Col.
a 1Ki 15:22
  2Ch 16:6

b Jer 40:12

c Jer 40:7

d Jer 40:14

e Jer 40:13
  Jer 43:2

f Jer 40:6

g Jer 41:2

41:1 *Lit., "the seed of the kingdom."

41:12 *Or possibly, "great pool."

Gib'e·on. **17** So they went and stayed in the lodging place of Chim'ham next to Beth'le·hem,[a] intending to go on into Egypt[b] **18** because of the Chal·de'ans. For they had become afraid of them, since Ish'ma·el the son of Neth·a·ni'ah had struck down Ged·a·li'ah the son of A·hi'kam, whom the king of Babylon had appointed over the land.[c]

42 Then all the army chiefs, and Jo·ha'nan[d] the son of Ka·re'ah, Jez·a·ni'ah the son of Ho·shai'ah, and all the people, from the least to the greatest, approached **2** and said to Jeremiah the prophet: "Hear, please, our request for favor, and pray in our behalf to Jehovah your God, in behalf of all this remnant, for just a few of many are left,[e] as you can see. **3** May Jehovah your God tell us the way we should walk and what we should do."

4 Jeremiah the prophet replied to them: "I have heard you, and I am praying to Jehovah your God according to your request; and every word that Jehovah answers you, I will tell you. I will not hold back a word from you."

5 They replied to Jeremiah: "May Jehovah be a true and faithful witness against us if we do not do exactly as Jehovah your God instructs us through you. **6** Whether good or bad, we will obey the voice of Jehovah our God, to whom we are sending you, so that it may go well with us because we obey the voice of Jehovah our God."

7 Now ten days later the word of Jehovah came to Jeremiah. **8** So he called for Jo·ha'nan the son of Ka·re'ah and for all the army chiefs who were with him and for all the people, from the least to the greatest.[f] **9** He said to them: "This is what Jehovah

the God of Israel says, to whom you sent me to present your request for favor before him: **10** 'If you will indeed remain in this land, then I will build you up and not tear you down, and I will plant you and not uproot you, for I will feel regret* over the calamity I have caused you.[a] **11** Do not be afraid because of the king of Babylon, whom you fear.'[b]

"'Do not be afraid because of him,' declares Jehovah, 'for I am with you, to save you and to rescue you out of his hand. **12** And I will show you mercy,[c] and he will have mercy on you and return you to your own land.

13 "'But if you say, "No, we will not remain in this land!" and you disobey the voice of Jehovah your God **14** by saying, "No, we will go instead to the land of Egypt,[d] where we will not see war or hear the sound of the horn or hunger for bread; there is where we will live," **15** then hear the word of Jehovah, O remnant of Judah. This is what Jehovah of armies, the God of Israel, says: "If you are absolutely determined to go to Egypt and you go there to reside,* **16** then the very sword you are afraid of will catch up with you there in the land of Egypt, and the very famine you fear will follow after you to Egypt, and there you will die.[e] **17** And all the men who are determined to go to Egypt to reside there will die by the sword, by famine, and by pestilence.* None of them will survive or escape the calamity that I will bring on them."'

18 "For this is what Jehovah of armies, the God of Israel, says: 'Just as my anger and my wrath were poured out on

---

CHAP. 41
a Ge 35:19

b 2Ki 25:26
  Jer 42:14
  Jer 43:7

c Jer 41:2

CHAP. 42
d Jer 40:13, 14

e De 28:62

f Jer 41:16

Second Col.
a De 32:36
  Jer 18:7, 8
  Mic 7:18

b Jer 41:17, 18

c Ex 34:6

d Jer 43:4, 7

e De 28:45
  Jer 44:12-14
  Jer 44:27, 28

42:10 *Or "feel grieved." **42:15** *Or "to reside for a while." **42:17** *Or "disease."

the inhabitants of Jerusalem,[a] so my wrath will be poured out on you if you go to Egypt, and you will become a curse, an object of horror, a malediction, and a reproach,[b] and you will never again see this place.'

19 "Jehovah has spoken against you, O remnant of Judah. Do not go to Egypt. You should know for a certainty that I have warned you today **20** that your error will cost you your lives.* For you sent me to Jehovah your God, saying, 'Pray in our behalf to Jehovah our God, and tell us everything that Jehovah our God says, and we will do it.'[c] **21** And I told you today, but you will not obey the voice of Jehovah your God or do anything he sent me to tell you.[d] **22** Therefore, know for a certainty that by the sword, by famine, and by pestilence you will die in the place where you desire to go and reside."[e]

43 When Jeremiah had finished speaking to all the people all these words from Jehovah their God, every single word that Jehovah their God had sent him to tell them, **2** Az·a·riʹah the son of Ho·shaiʹah, Jo·haʹnan[f] the son of Ka·reʹah, and all the presumptuous men said to Jeremiah: "What you are saying is a lie! Jehovah our God has not sent you to say, 'Do not go to Egypt to reside there.' **3** But Barʹuch[g] the son of Ne·riʹah is inciting you against us to hand us over to the Chal·deʹans, to put us to death or to take us into exile in Babylon."[h]

4 So Jo·haʹnan the son of Ka·reʹah and all the army chiefs and all the people disobeyed the voice of Jehovah to remain in the land of Judah. **5** Instead, Jo·haʹnan the son of Ka·reʹah

and all the army chiefs took with them all the remnant of Judah who had returned to reside in the land of Judah from all the nations where they had been dispersed.[a] **6** They took the men, the women, the children, the daughters of the king, and everyone* whom Neb·uʹzar·adʹan[b] the chief of the guard had left with Ged·a·liʹah[c] the son of A·hiʹkam[d] the son of Shaʹphan,[e] as well as Jeremiah the prophet and Barʹuch the son of Ne·riʹah. **7** And they went into the land of Egypt, for they did not obey the voice of Jehovah, and they went as far as Tahʹpan·hes.[f]

8 Then the word of Jehovah came to Jeremiah in Tahʹpanhes, saying: **9** "Take in your hand large stones, and hide them in the mortar in the brick terrace at the entrance of the house of Pharʹaoh in Tahʹpanhes, with the Jewish men looking on. **10** Then say to them, 'This is what Jehovah of armies, the God of Israel, says: "Here I am sending for Neb·u·chad·nezʹzar* the king of Babylon, my servant,[g] and I will place his throne right above these stones that I have hidden, and he will extend his royal tent over them.[h] **11** And he will come in and strike the land of Egypt.[i] Whoever is meant for deadly plague will be for deadly plague, and whoever is meant for captivity will be for captivity, and whoever is meant for the sword will be for the sword.[j] **12** And I will set the houses* of the gods of Egypt on fire,[k] and he will burn them and lead them captive. He will wrap the land of Egypt around himself just as a shepherd wraps himself in his garment, and he will depart from

---

CHAP. 42

a 2Ki 25:8-10
  2Ch 34:24, 25
  2Ch 36:16, 17
  La 2:4

b Jer 29:18

c Jer 42:1, 2

d 2Ch 24:19
  Ne 9:26
  Zec 7:11

e Jer 43:10, 11

CHAP. 43

f Jer 41:16
  Jer 42:1-3

g Jer 36:4
  Jer 45:1

h Jer 38:4, 6

Second Col.

a Jer 40:11, 12

b Jer 39:10

c 2Ki 25:22

d 2Ch 34:20, 21
  Jer 26:24

e 2Ki 22:8

f Jer 2:14, 16
  Jer 44:1
  Eze 30:4, 18

g Jer 25:9
  Jer 27:6
  Eze 29:19, 20

h Da 2:21
  Da 5:18

i Jer 25:17, 19
  Jer 46:13
  Eze 29:19
  Eze 30:4, 18

j Jer 44:13
  Eze 5:12

k Jer 46:25

42:20 *Or "souls." **43:6** *Or "every soul." **43:10** *Lit., "Nebuchadrezzar," a variant spelling. **43:12** *Or "temples."

there in peace.* **13** And he will break to pieces the pillars* of Beth-she'mesh# in the land of Egypt, and he will burn the houses△ of the gods of Egypt with fire.'"'

44 The word that came to Jeremiah for all the Jews living in the land of Egypt,ᵃ those living in Mig'dol,ᵇ Tah'-pan·hes,ᶜ Noph,*ᵈ and the land of Path'ros,ᵉ saying: **2** "This is what Jehovah of armies, the God of Israel, says, 'You have seen all the calamity that I brought on Jerusalemᶠ and on all the cities of Judah, and today they are in ruins, without an inhabitant.ᵍ **3** It is because of the evil things that they did to offend me by going and making sacrificesʰ and serving other gods whom they had not known, neither you nor your forefathers.ⁱ **4** I kept sending all my servants the prophets to you, sending them again and again,* saying: "Please do not do this detestable thing that I hate."ʲ **5** But they did not listen or incline their ear to turn back from their evil by not making sacrifices to other gods.ᵏ **6** So my wrath and my anger were poured out and burned in the cities of Judah and in the streets of Jerusalem, and they became a ruin and a wasteland, as they are today.ˡ

7 "And now this is what Jehovah, the God of armies, the God of Israel, says, 'Why are you causing a great calamity to yourselves,* so that every man and woman, child and infant, will perish from Judah, leaving you without a remnant? **8** Why should you offend me with the

---

works of your hands by sacrificing to other gods in the land of Egypt where you have gone to reside? You will perish and become an object of cursing and a reproach among all the nations of the earth.ᵃ **9** Have you forgotten the wicked deeds of your forefathers and the wicked deeds of the kings of Judahᵇ and the wicked deeds of their wives,ᶜ as well as your own wicked deeds and the wicked deeds of your wives,ᵈ that were done in the land of Judah and in the streets of Jerusalem? **10** Down to this day they have not humbled themselves,* they have shown no fear,ᵉ nor have they walked in my law and my statutes that I set before you and your forefathers.ᶠ

11 "Therefore this is what Jehovah of armies, the God of Israel, says, 'Here I am determined to bring calamity on you, to destroy all Judah. **12** And I will take the remnant of Judah who were determined to go to the land of Egypt to reside there, and they will all perish in the land of Egypt.ᵍ They will fall by the sword and perish by the famine; from the least to the greatest, they will die by the sword and by famine. And they will become a curse, an object of horror, a malediction, and a reproach.ʰ **13** I will punish those dwelling in the land of Egypt just as I punished Jerusalem, with the sword, with famine, and with pestilence.*ⁱ **14** And the remnant of Judah who have gone to reside in the land of Egypt will not escape or survive to return to the land of Judah. They will long* to return and dwell there, but they will not return, except for a few escapees.'"

CHAP. 44

a Jer 43:4, 7

b Eze 29:10
Eze 30:6

c Eze 30:18

d Jer 46:14
Eze 30:16

e Jer 29:14
Eze 30:14

f 2Ki 25:9, 10
Jer 39:8

g La 1:1

h Jer 11:17

i De 13:6-9
De 32:17
Jer 19:4

j 2Ch 36:15, 16
Isa 65:2
Jer 7:24-26
Jer 35:15

k Jer 19:13

l Isa 6:11
Jer 39:8

Second Col.

a 1Ki 9:7
Jer 24:9
Jer 42:18

b 2Ki 21:19, 20
2Ki 24:8, 9

c 1Ki 11:1-3

d Jer 44:19

e Jer 36:22-24

f De 6:1, 2

g Eze 30:13

h Jer 42:17, 18

i Jer 21:9
Jer 42:22
Jer 43:11

43:12 *Or "unharmed." **43:13** *Or "obelisks." #Or "House (Temple) of the Sun," that is, Heliopolis. △Or "temples." **44:1** *Or "Memphis." **44:4** *Lit., "rising up early and sending." **44:7** *Or "your souls."

44:10 *Or "felt crushed." **44:13** *Or "disease." **44:14** *Or "lift up their soul."

15 All the men who knew that their wives had been making sacrifices to other gods and all the wives who were standing there, who formed a large group, and all the people who were living in the land of Egypt,[a] in Path′ros,[b] answered Jeremiah: **16** "We will not listen to the word that you have spoken to us in the name of Jehovah. **17** Instead, we will surely carry out every word that our mouths have spoken, to make sacrifices to the Queen of Heaven* and to pour out drink offerings to her,[c] just as we, our forefathers, our kings, and our princes did in the cities of Judah and in the streets of Jerusalem when we were satisfied with bread and were well-off, when we saw no calamity at all. **18** From the time we quit making sacrifices to the Queen of Heaven* and pouring out drink offerings to her, we have lacked everything and have perished by the sword and by the famine."

19 The women added: "And when we were making sacrifices to the Queen of Heaven* and pouring out drink offerings to her, was it without the consent of our husbands that we made sacrificial cakes shaped in her image and we poured out drink offerings to her?"

20 Then Jeremiah said to all the people, to the men and their wives and to all the people who were speaking to him: **21** "The sacrifices that you, your forefathers, your kings, your princes, and the people of the land made in the cities of Judah and in the streets of Jerusalem[d]—Jehovah remembered them and they came up into his heart! **22** Finally Je-

hovah could no longer put up with your evil practices and the detestable things you had done, and your land became a devastated place, an object of horror and cursing, without an inhabitant, as it is today.[a] **23** It is because you have made these sacrifices and because you have sinned against Jehovah by not obeying the voice of Jehovah and following his law, his statutes, and his reminders that this calamity has come upon you, as is the case today."[b]

24 Jeremiah continued to say to all the people and to all the women: "Hear the word of Jehovah, all you of Judah who are in the land of Egypt. **25** This is what Jehovah of armies, the God of Israel, says, 'What you and your wives have spoken with your mouths, you have fulfilled with your hands, for you said: "We will surely carry out our vows to make sacrifices to the Queen of Heaven* and to pour out drink offerings to her."[c] You women will surely carry out your vows and perform your vows.'

26 "Therefore hear the word of Jehovah, all you of Judah who are living in the land of Egypt: '"Here I swear by my own great name," says Jehovah, "that my name will no longer be called on in an oath by any man of Judah[d] in all the land of Egypt who says, 'As surely as the Sovereign Lord Jehovah is alive!'[e] **27** Now I am watching over them to bring calamity and not something good;[f] all the men of Judah in the land of Egypt will perish by the sword and by the famine, until they cease to exist.[g] **28** Only a few will escape the sword and return from the land of Egypt to the land of Judah.[h] Then all the remnant of Judah who came to the land of Egypt to reside there will know whose word has come true, mine or theirs!"'"

CHAP. 44
a Jer 43:4, 7

b Jer 44:1

c Jer 7:18

d Jer 11:13
Eze 16:24, 25

Second Col.
a 1Ki 9:8, 9
La 2:15
Eze 33:29

b 2Ch 36:15, 16
Da 9:11

c Jer 7:18
Jer 44:15, 17

d Eze 20:39

e Isa 48:1, 2
Jer 5:2

f Jer 1:10

g Jer 44:12

h Le 26:44
Isa 27:13
Jer 44:14

44:17-19, 25 *The title of a goddess worshipped by apostate Israelites; possibly a fertility goddess.

29 "'And this is the sign for you,' declares Jehovah, 'that I will punish you in this place, so that you will know that my words promising calamity against you will surely come true. 30 This is what Jehovah says: "Here I am giving Phar'aoh Hoph'ra, the king of Egypt, into the hand of his enemies and of those seeking to take his life,* just as I gave King Zed·e·ki'ah of Judah into the hand of King Neb·u·chad·nez'zar# of Babylon, who was his enemy and who sought to take his life."'"△a

45 This is the word that Jeremiah the prophet spoke to Bar'uchb the son of Ne·ri'ah when he wrote in a book these words dictated by Jeremiahc in the fourth year of Je·hoi'a·kimd son of Jo·si'ah, the king of Judah:

2 "This is what Jehovah the God of Israel says concerning you, Bar'uch, 3 'You have said: "Woe to me, for Jehovah has added grief to my pain! I am weary from my groaning, and I have found no resting-place."'

4 "You should say to him, 'This is what Jehovah says: "Look! What I have built up I am tearing down, and what I have planted I am uprooting—the entire land.e 5 But you are seeking* great things for yourself. Stop seeking such things."'

"'For I am about to bring a calamity on all flesh,'#f declares Jehovah, 'and wherever you may go, I will grant you your life△ as a spoil.'"⊡g

46 This is the word of Jehovah to Jeremiah the prophet concerning the nations:h

CHAP. 44
a 2Ki 25:7
Jer 34:21
Jer 39:5

CHAP. 45
b Jer 32:12
Jer 43:3

c Jer 36:4, 32

d Jer 25:1
Jer 36:1

e Isa 5:5
Jer 1:1, 10

f Isa 66:16
Jer 25:17, 26
Zep 3:8

g Jer 21:9
Jer 39:18
Jer 43:6

CHAP. 46
h Jer 1:10

Second Col.
a Jer 25:15, 19
Eze 29:2
Eze 32:2

b 2Ch 35:20

c 2Ki 23:36
Jer 25:1
Jer 36:1

d 2Ki 24:7

e Eze 29:3
Eze 32:2

2 For Egypt,a concerning the army of Phar'aoh Ne'chob the king of Egypt, who was along the Eu·phra'tes River and was defeated at Car'che·mish by King Neb·u·chad·nez'zar# of Babylon in the fourth year of Je·hoi'a·kimc son of Jo·si'ah, the king of Judah:

3 "Prepare your bucklers* and large shields,
   And advance to the battle.
4 Harness the horses and mount, you horsemen.
   Take your positions and put on your helmets.
   Polish the lances and put on your coats of mail.
5 'Why do I see them terror-stricken?
   They are retreating, their warriors are crushed.
   They have fled in panic, their warriors have not turned around.
   There is terror all around,' declares Jehovah.
6 'The swift cannot flee, and the warriors cannot escape.
   In the north, by the bank of the Eu·phra'tes River,
   They have stumbled and fallen.'d
7 Who is this coming up like the Nile River,
   Like the rivers of surging waters?
8 Egypt comes up just like the Nile River,e
   Like rivers of surging waters,
   And it says, 'I will go up and cover the earth.
   I will destroy the city and those inhabiting it.'
9 Go up, you horses!
   Drive madly, you chariots!
   Let the warriors advance,

44:30 *Or "seeking his soul." 44:30; 46:2 #Lit., "Nebuchadrezzar," a variant spelling. 44:30 △Or "was seeking his soul." 45:5 *Or "expecting." #Or "people." △Or "soul." ⊡Or "will let you escape with your life."

46:3 *A small shield, often carried by archers.

Cush and Put, who handle
the shield,[a]
And the Lu′dim,[b] who handle
and bend* the bow.[c]

10 "That day belongs to the
Sovereign Lord, Jehovah of armies, the day of vengeance for
taking revenge on his adversaries. And the sword will devour and satisfy itself and take
its fill of their blood, for the Sovereign Lord, Jehovah of armies,
has a sacrifice* in the land of the
north by the Eu·phra′tes River.[d]

11 Go up to Gil′e·ad to get
balsam,[e]
O virgin daughter of Egypt.
In vain you have multiplied
your remedies,
For there is no cure for you.[f]

12 The nations have heard your
dishonor,[g]
And your outcry has filled
the land.
For warrior stumbles against
warrior,
And they both fall down together."

13 This is the word that Jehovah spoke to Jeremiah the
prophet regarding the coming of
King Neb·u·chad·nez′zar* of Babylon to strike down the land of
Egypt:[h]

14 "Declare it in Egypt,
proclaim it in Mig′dol.[i]
Proclaim it in Noph* and
in Tah′pan·hes.[j]
Say, 'Take your positions and
prepare yourselves,
For a sword will devour all
around you.

15 Why have your powerful men
been swept away?
They did not stand their
ground,

For Jehovah has pushed
them down.

16 In great numbers they are
stumbling and falling.
They are saying to one
another:
"Get up! Let us return to our
people and our homeland
Because of the cruel sword."'

17 There they have proclaimed,
'Phar′aoh king of Egypt is
just a meaningless noise
Who has let the opportunity*
pass by.'[a]

18 'As surely as I am alive,'
declares the King, whose
name is Jehovah of armies,
'He* will come in like Ta′bor[b]
among the mountains
And like Car′mel[c] by the sea.

19 Prepare your baggage for
exile,
O daughter inhabiting Egypt.
For Noph* will become an
object of horror;
It will be set afire* and left
without an inhabitant.[d]

20 Egypt is like a good-looking
heifer,
But stinging flies will come
against her from the north.

21 Even her hired soldiers in
her midst are like fattened
calves,
But they have also turned
back and fled together.
They could not stand their
ground,[e]
For the day of their disaster
has come upon them,
Their time of reckoning.'

22 'Her sound is like that of
a slithering serpent,
For they come after her in
force, with axes,
Like men cutting down
trees.*

CHAP. 46
a Eze 27:2, 10

b Ge 10:6, 13
Eze 30:4, 5

c Isa 66:19

d 2Ki 24:7

e Ge 37:25
Jer 8:22

f Eze 30:21

g Eze 32:9

h Jer 43:10
Eze 29:19
Eze 30:10

i Jer 44:1
Eze 29:10
Eze 30:6

j Jer 43:4, 7
Eze 30:18

Second Col.
a Eze 29:3

b Jos 19:17, 22
Jg 4:6
Ps 89:12

c 1Ki 18:42

d Eze 32:15

e Jer 46:5, 15

46:9 *Lit., "tread." 46:10 *Or "slaughter." 46:13 *Lit., "Nebuchadrezzar," a
variant spelling. 46:14, 19 *Or "Memphis."

46:17 *Lit., "appointed time." 46:18
*That is, Egypt's conqueror. 46:19 *Or
possibly, "will become a wasteland."
46:22 *Or "gathering wood."

23 They will cut down her
   forest,' declares Jehovah,
   'though it seemed impene-
   trable.
   For they are more numerous
   than locusts, without
   number.
24 The daughter of Egypt will
   be put to shame.
   She will be handed over to
   the people of the north.'ᵃ
25 "Jehovah of armies, the
God of Israel, says: 'Now I am
turning my attention to A'monᵇ
from No,*ᶜ to Phar'aoh, to Egypt,
to her gods,ᵈ and to her kings
—yes, to Phar'aoh and all those
trusting in him.'ᵉ
26 "'And I will hand them
over to those seeking to take
their life,* to King Neb·u·chad·
nez'zar*ᶠ of Babylonᶠ and his servants. But afterward she will be
inhabited as in times past,' declares Jehovah.ᵍ
27 'As for you, do not be afraid,
   my servant Jacob,
   And do not be terrified,
   O Israel.ʰ
   For I will save you from far
   away
   And your offspring* from the
   land of their captivity.ⁱ
   Jacob will return and be
   calm and undisturbed,
   With no one to make them
   afraid.ʲ
28 So do not be afraid, my
   servant Jacob,' declares
   Jehovah, 'for I am with
   you.
   I will make an extermination
   among all the nations
   where I dispersed you,ᵏ
   But you I will not extermi-
   nate.ˡ
   I will discipline* you to the
   proper degree,ᵐ

But I will by no means leave
   you unpunished.'"

47 This is the word of Jehovah to Jeremiah the
prophet concerning the Phi·lis'-
tines,ᵃ before Phar'aoh struck
down Gaz'a. 2 This is what Jehovah says:

"Look! Waters are coming
   from the north.
They will become a flooding
   torrent.
And they will flood the land
   and everything in it,
The city and those
   inhabiting it.
The men will cry out,
And everyone dwelling in
   the land will wail.
3 At the sound of the pounding
   hooves of his stallions,
   At the rattling of his war
   chariots
   And the rumbling of his
   wheels,
   Fathers will not even turn
   around for their sons,
   For their hands fall limp,
4 Because the day that is
   coming will destroy all
   the Phi·lis'tines;ᵇ
   It will cut off from Tyreᶜ
   and Si'donᵈ every
   remaining ally.
   For Jehovah will destroy
   the Phi·lis'tines,
   Who are the remaining
   ones from the island of
   Caph'tor.*ᵉ
5 Baldness* will come to Gaz'a.
   Ash'ke·lon has been
   silenced.ᶠ
   O remnant of their valley
   plain,*
   How long will you keep
   making cuts on yourself?ᵍ
6 Ah! The sword of Jehovah!ʰ
   How long will you not be
   quiet?

CHAP. 46
a Eze 30:10
b Na 3:8
c Eze 30:14
d Ex 12:12
  Isa 19:1
  Jer 43:12, 13
e Jer 17:5
  Jer 42:14
f Jer 43:10, 11
  Eze 32:11
g Eze 29:13, 14
h Isa 41:13
  Isa 43:1, 2
  Isa 44:2
i Isa 11:11
  Jer 50:19
  Eze 39:27
  Am 9:14
  Zep 3:20
j Jer 23:3, 6
  Jer 30:10, 11
k Jer 25:9
l Jer 5:10
  Am 9:8
m Jer 10:24

Second Col.

CHAP. 47
a Jer 25:17, 20
  Eze 25:15, 16
  Am 1:6
  Zep 2:4
  Zec 9:5, 6
b Jer 25:17, 20
  Am 1:8
  Zep 2:5
c Eze 26:2
  Am 1:9, 10
d Isa 23:1, 4
  Jer 25:17, 22
  Jer 27:2, 3
  Eze 28:21
  Joe 3:4
e Ge 10:13, 14
  De 2:23
f Zep 2:4
g De 14:1
  Jer 16:6
h De 32:41

46:25 *That is, Thebes. 46:26 *Or
"seeking their soul." *Lit., "Nebuchadrezzar," a variant spelling. 46:27
*Lit., "seed." 46:28 *Or "correct."

47:4 *That is, Crete. 47:5 *That is,
they will shave their heads in mourning
and shame. *Or "low plain."

Go back into your sheath.
Take your rest and be silent.

7 How can it be quiet
When Jehovah has given it
a command?
Against Ash'ke·lon and the
seacoast,[a]
There is where he has
assigned it."

48 For Mo'ab,[b] this is what Jehovah of armies, the God
of Israel, says:

"Woe to Ne'bo,[c] for she has
been destroyed!
Kir·i·a·tha'im[d] has been put
to shame and captured.
The secure refuge* has
been put to shame and
shattered.[e]

2 They no longer praise Mo'ab.
In Hesh'bon[f] they have
plotted her downfall:
'Come, let us put an end to
her as a nation.'
You too, O Mad'men, should
keep silent,
For the sword is following
you.

3 There is the sound of an
outcry from Hor·o·na'im,[g]
Of destruction and great
collapse.

4 Mo'ab has been broken
down.
Her little ones cry out.

5 On the ascent of Lu'hith they
weep continually as they
climb.
And on the way down from
Hor·o·na'im they hear
cries of distress over the
catastrophe.[h]

6 Flee, escape for your lives!*
You must become like a juniper tree in the wilderness.

7 Because you trust in your
works and in your
treasures,
You will also be captured.

And Che'mosh[a] will go into
exile,
Together with his priests
and his princes.

8 The destroyer will come in
on every city,
And no city will escape.[b]
The valley* will perish,
And the level land# will
be annihilated, just as
Jehovah has said.

9 Set up a marker for Mo'ab,
For as she falls into ruins
she will flee,
And her cities will become
an object of horror,
Without an inhabitant.[c]

10 Cursed is the one who
carries out the mission
of Jehovah neglectfully!
Cursed is the one who
holds back his sword
from bloodshed!

11 The Mo'ab·ites have been
undisturbed since their
youth,
Like wine that has settled
on the dregs.
They have not been
poured from one vessel
into another,
And they have never gone
into exile.
That is why their taste
has remained the same,
And their aroma has not
changed.

12 "'Therefore look! the days
are coming,' declares Jehovah,
'when I will send men to over-
turn them. They will turn them
over and empty out their vessels, and they will smash their
large jars to pieces. 13 And
the Mo'ab·ites will be ashamed
of Che'mosh, just as the house
of Israel is ashamed of Beth'el,
which was their confidence.[d]

14 How dare you say: "We are
mighty warriors, ready
for battle"?'[e]

CHAP. 47
a Eze 25:16

CHAP. 48
b Ge 19:36, 37
Isa 15:1

c Nu 32:37, 38

d Jos 13:15, 19
Eze 25:9

e Isa 15:2

f Nu 32:37
Isa 16:8

g Isa 15:5
Jer 48:34

h Isa 15:5

Second Col.
a Nu 21:29
1Ki 11:7

b Eze 25:9

c Zep 2:9

d 1Ki 12:28, 29
Ho 10:15
Am 5:5

e Isa 16:6

48:1 *Or "secure height." 48:6 *Or
"souls."

48:8 *Or "low plain." #Or "the tableland; the plateau."

15 'Mo'ab has been destroyed,
   Her cities have been
      invaded,[a]
   And their choicest young
      men have been slaugh-
      tered,'[b]
   Declares the King, whose
      name is Jehovah of
      armies.[c]
16 The disaster on the Mo'ab-
      ites is coming soon,
   And their downfall is ap-
      proaching quickly.[d]
17 All those around them will
      have to sympathize with
      them,
   All those knowing their
      name.
   Tell them: 'O how the mighty
      rod has been broken, the
      staff of beauty!'
18 Come down from your glory,
   And sit down in thirst,*
      O daughter inhabiting
      Di'bon,[e]
   For the destroyer of Mo'ab
      has come against you,
   And he will bring your
      fortified places to ruin.[f]
19 Stand by the road and watch,
      inhabitant of A·ro'er.[g]
   Ask the man fleeing and
      the woman escaping, 'What
      has happened?'
20 Mo'ab has been put to shame
      and struck with terror.
   Wail and cry out.
   Proclaim in Ar'non[h] that
      Mo'ab has been destroyed.

   21 "Judgment has come to
the level land,*[i] against Ho'-
lon, Ja'haz,[j] and Meph'a·ath;[k]
22 against Di'bon,[l] Ne'bo,[m] and
Beth-dib·la·tha'im; 23 against
Kir·i·a·tha'im,[n] Beth-ga'mul, and
Beth-me'on;[o] 24 against Ke'ri-
oth[p] and Boz'rah; and against all
the cities of the land of Mo'ab,
those far and near.

25 'The strength* of Mo'ab has
      been cut down;
   His arm has been broken,'
      declares Jehovah.
26 'Make him drunk,[a] for he
      has exalted himself against
      Jehovah.[b]
   Mo'ab wallows in his vomit,
   And he is an object of
      ridicule.
27 Was Israel not an object of
      ridicule to you?[c]
   Was he found among thieves,
   So that you should shake
      your head and speak
      against him?
28 Leave the cities and live
      on the crag, inhabitants of
      Mo'ab,
   And become like a dove that
      nests along the sides of the
      gorge.'"
29 "We have heard about the
      pride of Mo'ab—he is very
      haughty—
   About his arrogance, his
      pride, his haughtiness, and
      the loftiness of his heart."[d]
30 "'I know his fury,' declares
      Jehovah,
   'But his empty talk will come
      to nothing.
   They will do nothing.
31 That is why I will wail over
      Mo'ab,
   For all Mo'ab I will cry out
   And moan for the men of
      Kir-he'res.[e]
32 With more than the weeping
      for Ja'zer,[f]
   I will weep for you, O vine of
      Sib'mah.[g]
   Your flourishing shoots have
      crossed the sea.
   To the sea, to Ja'zer, they
      have reached.
   Upon your summer fruit and
      your grape harvest
   The destroyer has
      descended.[h]

CHAP. 48
a Jer 48:8

b Isa 34:2

c Ps 24:8

d Eze 25:11

e Nu 21:30
  Jos 13:15, 17
  Isa 15:2

f Jer 48:8

g Nu 32:34
  De 2:36

h Nu 21:13
  Jos 13:8, 9

i Zep 2:9

j Nu 21:23
  Isa 15:4

k Jos 13:15, 18

l Nu 32:34

m Nu 32:3, 4

n Nu 32:37
  Jer 48:1

o Nu 32:37, 38
  Jos 13:15, 17
  Eze 25:9

p Am 2:2

Second Col.
a Jer 25:15, 16

b Jer 48:42

c La 2:15
  Zep 2:8

d Isa 16:6
  Isa 25:10, 11
  Zep 2:9, 10

e 2Ki 3:24, 25
  Isa 16:7

f Nu 21:32
  Nu 32:34, 35
  Jos 21:8, 39

g Nu 32:37, 38
  Jos 13:15, 19

h Isa 16:8, 9
  Jer 48:8

48:18 *Or possibly, "on the dry
ground." 48:21 *Or "the tableland; the
plateau."

48:25 *Lit., "horn."

33 Rejoicing and joyfulness
    have been removed from
    the orchard
    And from the land of Mo'ab.[a]
    I have caused the wine
    to stop flowing from the
    winepress.
    No one will be treading with
    shouts of joy.
    The shouting will be differ-
    ent shouting.'"[b]

34 "'There is an outcry from
    Hesh'bon[c] clear to
    E·le·a'leh.[d]
    They raise their voice clear
    to Ja'haz,[e]
    From Zo'ar to Hor·o·na'im[f]
    to Eg'lath-she·li'shi·yah.
    Even the waters of Nim'rim
    will become desolate.[g]

35 I will cause to cease from
    Mo'ab,' declares Jehovah,
    'The one bringing an offering
    on the high place
    And the one making sacri-
    fices to his god.

36 That is why my heart will
    moan* for Mo'ab like a
    flute,*[h]
    And my heart will moan* for
    the men of Kir-he'res like a
    flute.*
    For the wealth he has pro-
    duced will perish.

37 For every head is bald,[i]
    And every beard is clipped.
    There are cuts on every
    hand,[j]
    And there is sackcloth on
    their hips!"[k]

38 "'On all the roofs of Mo'ab
    And in all her public
    squares,
    There is nothing but wailing.
    For I have broken Mo'ab
    Like a discarded jar,'
    declares Jehovah.

39 'How she is terrified! Wail!
    How Mo'ab has turned his
    back in shame!

48:36 *Or "be boisterous." #That is, a
flute played in lamentation at a funeral.

Mo'ab has become an object
    of ridicule,
    Something terrifying to all
    those around him.'"

40 "For this is what Jehovah
    says:
    'Look! Just like an eagle that
    swoops down,[a]
    He will spread his wings over
    Mo'ab.[b]

41 The towns will be captured,
    And her strongholds will be
    seized.
    In that day the heart of
    Mo'ab's warriors
    Will be like the heart of a
    woman in childbirth.'"

42 "'And Mo'ab will be annihilat-
    ed from being a people,[c]
    For it is against Jehovah that
    he has exalted himself.[d]

43 Terror and the pit and the
    trap are before you,
    O inhabitant of Mo'ab,'
    declares Jehovah.

44 'Anyone fleeing the terror
    will fall into the pit,
    And anyone coming up from
    the pit will be caught in the
    trap.'
    'For I will bring on Mo'ab the
    year of their punishment,'
    declares Jehovah.

45 'In the shadow of Hesh'bon,
    those fleeing stand power-
    less.
    For a fire will come out of
    Hesh'bon
    And a flame from within
    Si'hon.[e]
    It will consume the forehead
    of Mo'ab
    And the skull of the sons
    of tumult.'

46 'Woe to you, O Mo'ab!
    The people of Che'mosh[g]
    have perished.
    For your sons have been
    taken captive,
    And your daughters have
    gone into exile.[h]

CHAP. 48
a Jer 25:10

b Isa 16:10

c Nu 21:25
   Jos 13:15, 17

d Nu 32:37
   Isa 16:9

e Nu 21:23

f Jer 48:2, 3

g Isa 15:4-6

h Isa 16:11

i Jer 16:6

j Le 19:28

k Ge 37:34
   Isa 15:2, 3

Second Col.
a La 4:19
   Hab 1:8

b Jer 49:22

c Jer 30:11

d Jer 48:29

e Nu 21:26, 28

f Nu 24:17
   Am 2:2

g Nu 21:29
   1Ki 11:7

h Jer 48:7

47 But I will gather the
captives of Mo'ab in the
final part of the days,'
declares Jehovah.

'Down to this point is the
judgment on Mo'ab.'ᵃ

49 For the Am'mon·ites,ᵇ this
is what Jehovah says:

"Does Israel have no sons?
Does he have no heir?
Why has Mal'camᶜ taken
possession of Gad?ᵈ
And why are his people
living in Israel's cities?"

2 "'Therefore look! the days
are coming,' declares
Jehovah,

'When I will cause the alarm
signal of war* to be heard
against Rab'bahᵉ of the
Am'mon·ites.ᶠ

She will become a desolate
mound,
And her dependent# towns
will be set on fire.'

'And Israel will take
possession of those
who dispossessed him,'ᵍ
says Jehovah.

3 'Wail, O Hesh'bon, for A'i
has been destroyed!
Cry out, O dependent towns
of Rab'bah.
Put on sackcloth.
Wail and rove about among
the stone pens,*
For Mal'cam will go into
exile,
Together with his priests
and his princes.ʰ

4 Why do you brag about the
valleys,*
About your flowing plain,
O unfaithful daughter,
Who trusts in her treasures
And who says: "Who will
come against me?"'"

49:2 *Or possibly, "the sound of the
battle cry." #Or "surrounding." **49:3**
*Or "sheep pens." **49:4** *Or "low
plains."

CHAP. 48
a Eze 25:11

CHAP. 49
b Ge 19:36, 38
De 2:19
2Ch 20:1

c 1Ki 11:5
Zep 1:4, 5

d Am 1:13

e De 3:11
Jos 13:24, 25
Eze 25:5
Am 1:14

f Eze 21:19, 20

g Isa 14:2
Jer 50:19
Zep 2:9

h Am 1:13, 15

Second Col.
a Ge 36:10, 11
Eze 25:13
Am 1:12
Ob 8

b Isa 21:13
Jer 25:17, 23

c Ob 5

d Ob 6, 9

e Mal 1:3, 4

---

5 "'Here I am bringing something dreadful on you,'
declares the Sovereign
Lord, Jehovah of armies,
'From all those around you.
You will be dispersed in
every direction,
And no one will gather those
who flee.'"

6 "'But afterward I will
gather the captives of
the Am'mon·ites,' declares
Jehovah."

7 For E'dom, this is what Jehovah of armies says:

"Is there no longer any
wisdom in Te'man?ᵃ
Has good advice perished
from those with under-
standing?
Has their wisdom rotted?

8 Flee, turn back!
Go and dwell down in the
depths, O inhabitants
of De'dan!ᵇ
For I will bring disaster
on E'sau
When the time comes to turn
my attention to him.

9 If grape gatherers came in
to you,
Would they not leave some
behind for gleaning?
If thieves came in by night,
They would cause only as
much ruin as they wanted.ᶜ

10 But I will strip E'sau bare.
I will uncover his places
of concealment,
So that he cannot hide.
His children and his brothers
and his neighbors will all
be destroyed,ᵈ
And he will be no more.ᵉ

11 Leave your fatherless
children,
And I will preserve them
alive,
And your widows will trust
in me."

12 For this is what Jehovah says: "Look! If those not

sentenced to drink the cup must drink it, should you be left completely unpunished? You will not be left unpunished, for you must drink it."[a]

13 "For by myself I have sworn," declares Jehovah, "that Boz'rah will become an object of horror,[b] a reproach, a devastation, and a curse; and all her cities will become perpetual ruins."[c]

14 I have heard a report from Jehovah,
An envoy has been sent among the nations, saying:
"Gather yourselves together and come against her;
Prepare for battle."[d]

15 "For look! I have made you insignificant among the nations,
Despised among men.[e]

16 The shuddering you caused has deceived you,
The presumptuousness of your heart,
O you who reside in the retreats of the crag,
Occupying the highest hill.
Although you build your nest high up like an eagle,
I will bring you down from there," declares Jehovah.

17 "And E'dom must become an object of horror.[f] Everyone passing along by her will stare in horror and whistle on account of all her plagues. 18 Just as in the overthrow of Sod'om and Go·mor'rah and of their neighboring towns,"[g] Jehovah says, "no one will dwell there, and no man will settle there.[h]

19 "Look! Someone will come up against the secure pastures like a lion[i] from the dense thickets along the Jordan, but in a moment I will make him run away from her. And I will appoint over her the chosen one. For who is like me, and who

will challenge me? What shepherd can stand before me?[a]
20 Therefore hear, O men, the decision* that Jehovah has made against E'dom and what he has thought out against the inhabitants of Te'man:[b]

Surely the little ones of the flock will be dragged away.
He will make their dwelling place desolate because of them.[c]

21 At the sound of their falling, the earth has quaked.
There is an outcry!
The sound has been heard as far as the Red Sea.[d]

22 Look! Just like an eagle he will ascend and swoop down,[e]
And he will spread out his wings over Boz'rah.[f]
In that day the heart of the warriors of E'dom
Will become like the heart of a woman in childbirth."

23 For Damascus:[g]
"Ha'math[h] and Ar'pad have been put to shame,
For they have heard a bad report.
They melt in fear.
There is anxiety in the sea that cannot be calmed.

24 Damascus has lost courage.
She has turned to flee, but panic has seized her.
Distress and pain have taken hold of her,
Like a woman who is giving birth.

25 How is it that the city of praise has not been abandoned,
The town of exultation?

26 For her young men will fall in her public squares,
And all the soldiers will perish in that day," declares Jehovah of armies.

CHAP. 49
a Jer 25:27, 28
La 4:21
Ob 16

b Isa 34:6
Isa 63:1
Jer 49:22
Am 1:12

c Ob 18
Mal 1:3

d Ob 1

e Ob 2-4

f Jer 49:13

g Ge 19:24, 25

h Isa 34:6, 10

i Jer 4:7

Second Col.
a Ps 76:7
Jer 50:44-46
Na 1:6

b Ob 9

c Mal 1:4

d 1Ki 9:26

e Jer 4:13

f Jer 48:40
Jer 49:13

g Isa 17:1
Am 1:3

h Nu 13:21
2Ki 17:24
Zec 9:1, 2

49:20 *Or "counsel."

27 "I will set the wall of
Damascus on fire,
And it will consume the
fortified towers of
Ben·ha′dad."ᵃ

28 For Ke′darᵇ and the kingdoms of Ha′zor, which King Neb-
u·chad·nez′zar* of Babylon struck
down, this is what Jehovah says:

"Rise up, go up to Ke′dar,
And destroy the sons of the
East.

29 Their tents and their flocks
will be taken,
Their tent cloths and all
their goods.
Their camels will be
carried off,
And they will cry out
to them, 'Terror is all
around!'"

30 "Flee, go far away!
Go and dwell down in the
depths, O inhabitants of
Ha′zor," declares Jehovah.

"For King Neb·u·chad-
nez′zar* of Babylon has
devised a strategy
against you,
And he has thought out
a plan against you."

31 "Rise up, go up against the
nation that is at peace,
Dwelling in security!"
declares Jehovah.

"It has no doors or bars;
they live in isolation.

32 Their camels will become
plunder,
And their abundant livestock
a spoil.
I will scatter them to every
wind,*
Those who clip their hair
at the temples,ᶜ
And I will bring their disaster from every direction,"
declares Jehovah.

33 "And Ha′zor will become
a lair of jackals,
A perpetual desolation.
No one will dwell there,
And no man will settle
in her."

34 This is the word of Jehovah that came to Jeremiah
the prophet concerning E′lamᵃ
in the beginning of the reign
of King Zed·e·ki′ahᵇ of Judah:
35 "This is what Jehovah of
armies says, 'Here I am breaking the bow of E′lam,ᶜ the
source* of their mightiness.
36 I will bring in on E′lam the
four winds from the four extrem-
ities of the heavens, and I will
scatter them to all these winds.
There will not be a nation to
which the dispersed ones of
E′lam will not go.'"

37 "I will shatter the E′lam-
ites before their enemies and before those seeking to take their
life;* and I will bring calamity
on them, my burning anger," declares Jehovah. "And I will send
the sword after them until I have
exterminated them."

38 "And I will set my throne
in E′lam,ᵈ and I will destroy from
there the king and the princes,"
declares Jehovah.

39 "But in the final part of the
days, I will gather the captives
of E′lam," declares Jehovah.

50 The word that Jehovah
spoke concerning Bab-
ylon,ᵉ concerning the land of
the Chal·de′ans, through Jeremiah the prophet:

2 "Declare it among the
nations and proclaim it.
Raise a signal* and
proclaim it.
Do not hide anything!
Say, 'Babylon has been
captured.ᶠ

CHAP. 49
ᵃ Am 1:4

ᵇ Ge 25:13
Isa 42:11
Isa 60:7
Eze 27:21

ᶜ Jer 9:25, 26
Jer 25:17, 23

Second Col.
ᵃ Ge 10:22
Isa 21:2
Jer 25:17, 23
Eze 32:24
Da 8:2
Ac 2:8, 9

ᵇ 2Ki 24:18

ᶜ Isa 22:6

ᵈ Jer 25:17, 25

CHAP. 50
ᵉ Isa 13:1

ᶠ Jer 51:8
Re 14:8

49:28, 30 *Lit., "Nebuchadrezzar," a variant spelling. **49:32** *Or "in every direction." **49:35** *Lit., "beginning." **49:37** *Or "seeking their soul." **50:2** *Or "signal pole."

Bel has been put to shame.[a]
Mer'o·dach has become
terrified.
Her images have been put
to shame.
Her disgusting idols* have
become terrified.'

3 For a nation has come
against her from the
north.[b]
It makes her land an object
of horror;
No one is dwelling in her.
Both man and beast have
taken flight;
They have gone away."

4 "In those days and at that
time," declares Jehovah, "the
people of Israel and the people of Judah will come together.[c]
They will weep as they walk,[d]
and together they will seek Jehovah their God.[e] **5** They will
ask the way to Zion, with
their faces turned in that direction,[f] saying, 'Come and let us
join ourselves to Jehovah that will
not be forgotten.'[g] **6** My people have become a flock of
lost sheep.[h] Their own shepherds
caused them to stray.' They led
them away onto the moun-
tains, roaming from mountain
to hill. They have forgotten their
resting-place. **7** All those finding them have devoured them,[j]
and their enemies have said,
'We are not guilty, because they
sinned against Jehovah, against
the dwelling place of righteousness and the hope of their forefathers, Jehovah.'"

8 "Flee out of the midst of
Babylon,
Go out of the land of the
Chal·de'ans,[k]
And be like the leading
animals before the flock.

50:2 * The Hebrew term may be related
to a word for "dung" and is used as an
expression of contempt.

CHAP. 50
a Isa 46:1
  Jer 51:44

b Isa 13:17
  Jer 51:11, 48

c Jer 11:12
  Jer 3:18
  Ho 1:11

d Jer 31:8, 9

e Ho 3:5

f Isa 35:10

g Jer 31:31

h Isa 53:6

i Jer 10:21
  Jer 23:2
  Eze 34:2, 6

j Ps 79:6, 7

k Jer 48:20
  Jer 51:6, 45
  Zec 2:7
  2Co 6:17
  Re 18:2, 4

Second Col.
a Jer 21:2
  Jer 51:11, 27,
  28, 48
  Da 5:28, 30

b Isa 13:17, 18

c Jer 25:12
  Jer 27:6, 7

d Re 17:16

e La 1:21

f Jer 14:4-6
  Isa 47:6
  Jer 30:16

g Isa 47:8

h Isa 13:20, 21

i Zec 1:15

j Jer 25:12

k Jer 51:37

l Isa 13:18
  Jer 51:11

9 For here I am raising up and
bringing against Babylon
An assembly of great nations
from the land of the north.[a]
They will come against her
in battle formation;
From there she will be
captured.
Their arrows are like those
of a warrior
Causing bereavement of
children;[b]
They do not come back
without results.

10 Chal·de'a will become a
spoil.[c]
All those taking spoil from
her will be fully satisfied,"[d]
declares Jehovah.

11 "For you kept rejoicing,[e] you
kept exulting
When pillaging my own
inheritance.[f]
For you kept pawing like a
heifer in the grass,
And you kept neighing like
stallions.

12 Your mother has been put
to shame.[g]
She who gave birth to you
has been disappointed.
Look! She is the least of the
nations,
A waterless wilderness and
a desert.[h]

13 Because of the indignation
of Jehovah she will not be
inhabited;[i]
She will become utterly
desolate.[j]
Anyone passing by Babylon
will stare in horror
And whistle because of all
her plagues.[k]

14 Come against Babylon in battle formation on every side,
All you who are bending*
the bow.
Shoot at her, spare no
arrow,[l]

50:14 * Lit., "treading."

For it is against Jehovah that
she has sinned.ᵃ

15 Shout a war cry against her
on every side.

She has surrendered.*

Her pillars have fallen, her
walls are torn down,ᵇ

For it is the vengeance of
Jehovah.ᶜ

Take your vengeance on her.

Do to her just as she has
done.ᵈ

16 Cut off the sower from
Babylon

And the one handling the
sickle in harvesttime.ᵉ

Because of the cruel sword,
each will return to his own
people,

Each one will flee to his own
land.ᶠ

17 "The people of Israel are
scattered sheep.ᵍ Lions have dispersed them.ʰ First the king of
As·syr′i·a devoured them;ⁱ then
King Neb·u·chad·nez′zar* of Babylon gnawed on their bones.ʲ
18 Therefore this is what Jehovah of armies, the God of Israel, says: 'Here I will deal with
the king of Babylon and with
his land in the same way that I
dealt with the king of As·syr′i·a.ᵏ
19 And I will bring Israel back
to his pasture,ˡ and he will graze
on Car′mel and on Ba′shan,ᵐ and
on the mountains of E′phra·imⁿ
and of Gil′e·adᵒ he* will be satisfied.'"

20 "In those days and at that
time," declares Jehovah,

"Israel's guilt will be
searched for,

But there will be none,

And the sins of Judah will
not be found,

For I will forgive those whom
I let remain."ᵖ

21 "Go up against the land
of Mer·a·tha′im and against
the inhabitants of Pe′kod.ᵃ

Let them be massacred and
completely destroyed,"*
declares Jehovah.

"Do all that I have commanded you.

22 There is the sound of war
in the land,

A great catastrophe.

23 How the forge hammer of
all the earth has been cut
down and broken!ᵇ

How Babylon has become
an object of horror among
the nations!ᶜ

24 I have laid a snare for you,
and you have been caught,
O Babylon,

And you did not know it.

You were found and
captured,ᵈ

For it was Jehovah whom
you opposed.

25 Jehovah has opened his
storehouse,

And he brings out the weapons of his indignation.ᵉ

For the Sovereign Lord,
Jehovah of armies,
has a work

In the land of the
Chal·de′ans.

26 Come against her from
distant places.ᶠ

Open up her granaries.ᵍ

Pile her up like heaps of
grain.

Destroy her completely.*ʰ

May she have no one left.

27 Massacre all her young
bulls;ⁱ

Let them go down to the
slaughter.

Woe to them, for their day
has come,

Their time of reckoning!

CHAP. 50
a Jer 51:35, 36
b Jer 51:58
c Jer 51:6, 11
d Ps 137:8
  Re 18:6
e Jer 51:23
f Isa 13:14
  Jer 51:9
g Jer 23:1
  Jer 50:6
  Eze 34:5
h Jer 2:15
i 2Ki 17:6
  Isa 8:7
j 2Ki 25:1
  2Ch 36:17
  Jer 4:7
k 2Ki 19:35
  Isa 14:25
  Zep 2:13
l Isa 11:16
  Isa 65:10
  Jer 23:3
  Jer 33:7
  Eze 34:14
  Mic 2:12
m Mic 7:14
n Jer 31:6
o Ob 19
p Isa 44:22
  Jer 31:34
  Mic 7:19

Second Col.
a Eze 23:22, 23
b Isa 14:5, 6
  Jer 51:20
c Jer 51:41
  Re 18:15, 16
d Jer 51:31
  Da 5:30
  Re 18:8
e Isa 13:5
  Jer 51:11
f Jer 51:27
g Jer 50:10
h Isa 14:22, 23
i Isa 34:6, 7
  Eze 39:18

50:15 *Lit., "given her hand." 50:17
*Lit., "Nebuchadrezzar," a variant spell-
ing. 50:19 *Or "his soul." 50:21 *Or "and devote them to destruction." 50:26 *Or "Devote her to de-
struction."

28 There is the sound of those
fleeing,
Those escaping from the
land of Babylon,
To declare in Zion the
vengeance of Jehovah
our God,
The vengeance for his
temple.[a]

29 Summon archers against
Babylon,
All who are bending* the
bow.[b]
Camp all around her; let no
one escape.
Repay her according to her
activity.[c]
Do to her just as she has
done.[d]
For she has acted arrogantly
against Jehovah,
Against the Holy One of
Israel.[e]

30 So her young men will fall in
her public squares,[f]
And all her soldiers will
perish* in that day,"
declares Jehovah.

31 "Look! I am against you,[g]
O defiant one,"[h] declares
the Sovereign Lord,
Jehovah of armies,
"For your day must come,
the time that I will call you
to account.

32 You, O defiant one, will stumble and fall,
With no one to raise you up.[i]
And I will set your cities
on fire,
And it will consume everything around you."

33 This is what Jehovah of
armies says:
"The people of Israel and
Judah are oppressed,
And all those taking them
captive have held onto
them.[j]

They have refused to let
them go.[a]

34 But their Repurchaser is
strong.[b]
Jehovah of armies is his
name.[c]
He will surely plead their
legal case,[d]
In order to give rest to the
land[e]
And to bring agitation to the
inhabitants of Babylon."[f]

35 "There is a sword against
the Chal·de'ans," declares
Jehovah,
"Against the inhabitants of
Babylon and against her
princes and against her
wise ones.[g]

36 There is a sword against the
empty talkers,* and they
will act foolishly.
There is a sword against her
warriors, and they will
become terrified.[h]

37 There is a sword against
their horses and their war
chariots,
And against all the mixed
populations in her midst,
And they will become like
women.[i]
There is a sword against her
treasures, and they will be
plundered.[j]

38 There is a devastation on her
waters, and they will be
dried up.[k]
For it is a land of graven
images,[l]
And because of their fright-
ful visions they keep acting
with madness.

39 Therefore, the desert
creatures will dwell with
the howling animals,
And in her the ostriches will
dwell.[m]
She will never again be
inhabited,

CHAP. 50

a Ps 94:1
Jer 51:11

b Jer 50:14

c Ps 137:8
Jer 51:56

d La 3:64
Re 18:6

e Isa 14:13

f Isa 13:17, 18

g Jer 51:25

h Isa 14:13
Da 4:30

i Jer 51:26

j Isa 47:6

Second Col.

a Isa 14:17

b Isa 41:14
Re 18:8

c Isa 47:4

d La 3:59

e Isa 14:3, 4

f Jer 51:24

g Isa 47:13
Jer 51:57
Da 5:7

h Jer 51:30

i Isa 13:8

j Isa 45:3

k Isa 44:27
Jer 51:36, 37
Re 16:12

l Isa 46:1
Jer 51:44, 52
Da 5:1, 4

m Isa 13:20, 21
Jer 51:37
Re 18:2

50:29 *Lit., "treading." 50:30 *Lit.,
"be silenced."

50:36 *Or "the false prophets."

Nor will she be a place of
residence throughout all
generations."[a]

40 "Just as with God's overthrow of Sod′om and Go·mor′-
rah[b] and of their neighboring
towns,"[c] declares Jehovah, "no
one will dwell there, and no man
will settle there.[d]

41 Look! A people is coming
in from the north;
A great nation and grand
kings[e] will be raised up
From the remotest parts
of the earth.[f]

42 Bow and javelin they wield.[g]
They are cruel and will show
no mercy.[h]
Their sound is like the
roaring sea,[i]
As they ride on their horses.
Like one man, they line
up in battle formation
against you, O daughter
of Babylon.[j]

43 The king of Babylon has
heard the report about
them,[k]
And his hands drop down.[l]
Anguish seizes him,
Pain like that of a woman
giving birth.

44 "Look! Someone will come
up against the secure pastures
like a lion from the dense thickets along the Jordan, but in a
moment I will make them run
away from her. And I will appoint over her the chosen one.[m]
For who is like me, and who
will challenge me? What shepherd can stand before me?[n]
45 Therefore hear, O men, the
decision* that Jehovah has made
against Babylon[o] and what he
has thought out against the land
of the Chal·de′ans.

Surely the little ones of the
flock will be dragged away.

He will make their dwelling
place desolate because
of them.[a]

46 At the sound of Babylon's
capture, the earth will
quake,
And an outcry will be heard
among the nations."[b]

51 This is what Jehovah says:
"Here I am raising up
a destructive wind
Against Babylon[c] and the
inhabitants of Leb·ka′mai.*

2 I will send winnowers to
Babylon,
And they will winnow her
and make her land empty;
They will come against her
on all sides in the day of
calamity.[d]

3 Let the archer not bend*
his bow.
And let no one stand up
in his coat of mail.
Show no compassion for
her young men.[e]
Devote all her army to
destruction.

4 And they will fall slain in the
land of the Chal·de′ans,
Pierced through in her
streets.[f]

5 For Israel and Judah are not
widowed from their God,
from Jehovah of armies.[g]
But their land* is full of guilt
from the standpoint of the
Holy One of Israel.

6 Flee out of the midst of
Babylon,
And escape for your life.*[h]
Do not perish because of
her error.
For it is the time for
Jehovah's vengeance.
He is paying her back for
what she has done.[i]

CHAP. 50
a Jer 25:12
  Jer 51:43, 64

b Isa 13:19

c Ge 19:24, 25
  Jude 7

d Jer 51:26

e Isa 45:1
  Jer 51:11
  Jer 51:27, 28

f Isa 13:5, 17

g Jer 50:9

h Ps 137:8
  Isa 13:17, 18

i Jer 51:42

j Jer 51:27

k Jer 51:31

l Da 5:6

m Isa 41:25

n Jer 49:19-21

o Jer 51:11

Second Col.
a Isa 13:1, 20
  Jer 51:43

b Re 18:9

CHAP. 51
c Jer 50:9

d Jer 50:14, 29

e Isa 13:17, 18
  Jer 50:30

f Isa 13:15

g Ps 94:14
  Isa 44:21
  Jer 46:28
  Zec 2:12

h Jer 50:8
  Zec 2:7
  Re 18:4

i Jer 25:12, 14
  Jer 50:15

50:45 *Or "counsel."   51:1 *This appears to be a cryptographic name for Chaldea.   **51:3** *Lit.,
"tread."   **51:5** *That is, the land of the
Chaldeans.   **51:6** *Or "soul."

7 Babylon has been a golden cup in the hand of Jehovah;
She made all the earth drunk.
From her wine the nations have drunk;[a]
That is why the nations have gone mad.[b]

8 Suddenly Babylon has fallen and is broken.[c]
Wail over her![d]
Get balsam for her pain; perhaps she may be healed."

9 "We tried to heal Babylon, but she could not be healed.
Leave her and let us go, each to his own land.[e]
For her judgment has reached to the heavens;
It is as high as the clouds.[f]

10 Jehovah has brought about justice for us.[g]
Come, let us recount in Zion the work of Jehovah our God."[h]

11 "Polish the arrows;[i] take up the circular shields.*
Jehovah has stirred up the spirit of the kings of the Medes,[j]
Because he intends to bring Babylon to ruin.
For this is the vengeance of Jehovah, the vengeance for his temple.

12 Lift up a signal*[k] against the walls of Babylon.
Strengthen the guard, post the watchmen.
Prepare those in ambush.
For Jehovah has devised the strategy,
And he will carry out what he has promised against the inhabitants of Babylon."[l]

13 "O woman who resides on many waters,[m]

With abundant treasures,[a]
Your end has come, the limit* of your profit-making.[b]

14 Jehovah of armies has sworn by himself,*
'I will fill you with men, as numerous as locusts,
And they will shout in triumph over you.'[c]

15 He is the Maker of the earth by his power,
The One who established the productive land by his wisdom[d]
And who stretched out the heavens by his understanding.[e]

16 When he makes his voice heard,
The waters in the heavens are in turmoil,
And he causes clouds* to ascend from the ends of the earth.
He makes lightning for* the rain,
And he brings the wind out of his storehouses.[f]

17 Every man acts unreasonably and without knowledge.
Every metalworker will be put to shame because of the carved image;[g]
For his metal image* is a falsehood,
And there is no spirit* in them.[h]

18 They are a delusion,*[i] a work of mockery.
When their day of reckoning comes, they will perish.

19 The Share of Jacob is not like these things,
For he is the One who formed everything,

CHAP. 51
a Re 17:1, 2
  Re 18:3

b Jer 25:15, 16

c Isa 21:9
  Isa 47:9
  Re 14:8

d Re 18:2, 9

e Isa 13:14

f Re 18:4, 5

g Mic 7:9

h Jer 50:28

i Jer 50:14

j Isa 13:17
  Isa 45:1

k Isa 13:2

l Re 17:17

m Re 17:1, 15

_____

Second Col.
a Isa 45:3
  Jer 50:37

b Hab 2:9
  Re 18:11, 12
  Re 18:19

c Jer 50:15

d Ps 93:1
  Ps 104:24

e Ps 136:5
  Pr 3:19
  Isa 40:22
  Jer 10:12-16

f Ps 135:7

g Isa 44:11

h Hab 2:19

i Isa 41:29
  Jer 14:22

_____

51:13 *Lit., "measure." 51:14 *Or "his soul." 51:16 *Or "vapors." *Or possibly, "makes sluices for." 51:17 *Or "molten statue." *Or "breath." 51:18 *Or "futility."

_____

51:11 *Or possibly, "fill the quivers." 51:12 *Or "signal pole."

Even the staff of his
inheritance.ᵃ
Jehovah of armies is his
name."ᵇ

20 "You are a war club for me,
a weapon for battle,
For with you I will smash
nations.
With you I will bring
kingdoms to ruin.

21 With you I will smash the
horse and its rider.
With you I will smash the
war chariot and its rider.

22 With you I will smash man
and woman.
With you I will smash old
man and boy.
With you I will smash young
man and woman.

23 With you I will smash
shepherd and his flock.
With you I will smash farmer
and his team of animals.
With you I will smash governors and deputy rulers.

24 And I will repay Babylon
and all the inhabitants
of Chal·de′a
For all the evil that they have
committed in Zion before
your eyes,"ᶜ declares
Jehovah.

25 "Here I am against you,ᵈ
O destructive mountain,"
declares Jehovah,
"You destroyer of the whole
earth.ᵉ
I will stretch out my hand
against you and roll you
down from the crags
And make you a burned-out
mountain."

26 "People will not take from
you a cornerstone or a
foundation stone,
Because you will become
desolate forever,"ᶠ declares
Jehovah.

27 "Lift up a signal* in the landᵍ

51:27 *Or "signal pole."

CHAP. 51
a De 32:9
b Isa 47:4
c Ps 137:8
d Jer 50:31
e Jer 25:9
f Jer 50:13, 40 Re 18:21
g Isa 13:2 Jer 51:12

Second Col.
a Ge 8:4
b Ge 10:2, 3 Jer 50:41
c Isa 13:17 Da 5:30, 31
d Isa 13:13, 19 Jer 50:13 Jer 50:39, 40
e Isa 13:7
f Jer 50:37
g Ps 107:16 Isa 45:2
h Isa 47:11 Jer 50:24, 43
i Isa 44:27 Jer 50:38 Re 16:12

Blow a horn among the
nations.
Appoint* the nations against
her.
Summon against her the
kingdoms of Ar′a·rat,ᵃ
Min′ni, and Ash′ke·naz.ᵇ
Commission against her a
recruiting officer.
Make the horses come up
like bristling locusts.

28 Appoint* against her the
nations,
The kings of Me′di·a,ᶜ
its governors and all
its deputy rulers
And all the lands they rule
over.

29 And the earth will quake and
tremble,
For the thoughts of Jehovah
against Babylon will be
carried out
To make the land of Babylon
an object of horror, without an inhabitant.ᵈ

30 The warriors of Babylon
have quit fighting.
They sit in their strongholds.
Their strength has failed.ᵉ
They have become like
women.ᶠ
Her homes have been set
on fire.
Her bars have been broken.ᵍ

31 One courier runs to meet
another courier,
And one messenger to meet
another messenger,
To report to the king of Babylon that his city has been
captured on every side,ʰ

32 That the fords have been
seized,ⁱ
That the papyrus boats have
been burned with fire,
And that the soldiers are
terrified."

33 For this is what Jehovah
of armies, the God of Israel,
says:

51:27, 28 *Lit., "Sanctify."

"The daughter of Babylon is
like a threshing floor.
It is the time to tread her
down solid.
Very soon the time of the
harvest will come for her."

34 "King Neb·u·chad·nez'zar* of
Babylon has devoured me;[a]
He has thrown me into
confusion.
He has set me down as an
empty vessel.
He has swallowed me down
like a big snake;[b]
He has filled his stomach
with my fine things.
He has rinsed me away.

35 'May the violence done to
me and to my person come
upon Babylon!' says the
inhabitant of Zion.[c]
'And let my blood come
upon the inhabitants of
Chal·de'a!' says Jerusa-
lem."

36 Therefore this is what
Jehovah says:
"Here I am pleading your
legal case,[d]
And I will execute vengeance
for you.[e]
I will dry up her sea and
make her wells dry.[f]

37 And Babylon will become
piles of stones,[g]
A lair of jackals,[h]
An object of horror and
something to whistle at,
Without an inhabitant.[i]

38 All together they will roar
just like young lions.*
They will growl like lion
cubs."

39 "When they are inflamed, I
will set out their banquet
and make them drunk,
In order that they may exult;[j]
Then they will sleep a lasting
sleep,

From which they will
not wake up,"[a] declares
Jehovah.

40 "I will bring them down like
lambs to the slaughter,
Like rams along with the
goats."

41 "O how She'shach* has been
captured,[b]
How the Praise of the whole
earth has been seized![c]
How Babylon has become an
object of horror among the
nations!

42 The sea has come up over
Babylon.
By the multitude of its waves
she has been covered.

43 Her cities have become an
object of horror, a waterless land and a desert.
A land where no one will live
and where no man will pass
through.[d]

44 I will turn my attention to
Bel[e] in Babylon,
And I will take out of his
mouth what he has
swallowed.[f]
To him nations will stream
no more,
And the wall of Babylon will
fall.[g]

45 Get out of her midst, my
people![h]
Escape for your lives*[i] from
the burning anger of
Jehovah![j]

46 Do not be fainthearted or
afraid about the report to
be heard in the land.
In one year the report will
come,
And the next year another
report,
Of violence in the land and of
ruler against ruler.

47 Therefore look! the days are
coming

CHAP. 51
a 2Ch 36:17, 18
  Jer 50:17

b Jer 51:44

c Ps 137:8
  Jer 50:29

d Jer 50:34

e De 32:35

f Isa 44:27
  Jer 50:38

g Jer 25:12
  Jer 50:15

h Isa 13:19, 22

i Jer 50:13, 39

j Da 5:1, 4

Second Col.
a Jer 25:17, 27
  Jer 51:57

b Jer 25:17, 26

c Isa 13:19
  Jer 49:25
  Da 4:30

d Isa 13:1, 20
  Jer 50:39

e Jer 46:1
  Jer 50:2

f 2Ch 36:7
  Ezr 1:7
  Jer 51:34
  Da 1:1, 2

g Jer 51:58

h Isa 48:20
  Re 18:4

i Jer 51:6
  Zec 2:7

j Isa 13:13

51:34 *Lit., "Nebuchadrezzar," a variant
spelling.   51:38 *Or "maned young lions."

51:41 *This appears to be a cryptographic name for Babel (Babylon).
51:45 *Or "souls."

When I will turn my attention
to the graven images of
Babylon.
All her land will be put to
shame,
And all her slain will fall
in her midst.[a]

48 The heavens and the earth
and everything in them
Will shout joyfully over
Babylon,[b]
For the destroyers will come
to her out of the north,"[c]
declares Jehovah.

49 "Not only did Babylon cause
the slain of Israel to fall[d]
But also at Babylon the slain
ones of all the earth have
fallen.

50 You who escape the sword,
keep going, do not stand
still![e]
Remember Jehovah from far
away,
And may Jerusalem come up
into your heart."[f]

51 "We have been put to shame,
for we have heard taunts.
Humiliation has covered our
faces,
For foreigners* have come
against the holy places of
the house of Jehovah."[g]

52 "Therefore look! the days are
coming," declares Jehovah,
"When I will turn my attention to her graven images,
And throughout all her land
the wounded will groan."[h]

53 "Even if Babylon should
ascend to the heavens,[i]
Even if she should fortify
her towering strongholds,
From me her destroyers will
come,"[j] declares Jehovah.

54 "Listen! There is an outcry
from Babylon,[k]
The sound of great disaster
from the land of the
Chal·de'ans,[l]

51:51 *Or "strangers."

CHAP. 51
a Isa 13:15
  Da 5:30

b Isa 44:23
  Isa 48:20
  Isa 49:13
  Re 18:20

c Jer 50:3
  Jer 50:41

d Jer 50:17
  Jer 51:24

e Jer 50:8
  Re 18:4

f Ezr 1:3
  Ps 137:5

g Ps 79:1
  La 1:10

h Isa 13:15

i Isa 14:13
  Da 4:30

j Jer 50:10

k Isa 13:6

l Jer 50:22, 23

Second Col.
a Isa 21:2

b Jer 50:36

c De 32:35
  Ps 94:1
  Isa 34:8
  Jer 50:29
  Re 18:5

d Ps 137:8

e Jer 25:27

f Jer 51:39

g Jer 50:15
  Jer 51:44

h Hab 2:13

i Jer 32:12
  Jer 36:4
  Jer 45:1

55 For Jehovah is destroying
Babylon,
He will silence her great
voice,
And their waves will roar
like many waters.
The sound of their voice
will be heard.

56 For the destroyer will come
upon Babylon;[a]
Her warriors will be
captured,[b]
Their bows will be shattered,
For Jehovah is a God of
retribution.[c]
He will surely repay.[d]

57 I will make her princes and
her wise men drunk,[e]
Her governors and her depu-
ty rulers and her warriors,
And they will sleep a lasting
sleep,
From which they will not
wake up,"[f] declares the
King, whose name is
Jehovah of armies.

58 This is what Jehovah of
armies says:
"The wall of Babylon, though
broad, will be completely
demolished,[g]
And her gates, though high,
will be set on fire.
The peoples will toil for
nothing;
The nations will weary
themselves just to feed
the fire."[h]

59 This is the word that Jeremiah the prophet gave as a command to Se·rai'ah son of Ne·ri'ah[i]
son of Mah·sei'ah when he went
with King Zed·e·ki'ah of Judah to
Babylon in the fourth year of his
reign; Se·rai'ah was the quarter-
master. 60 Jeremiah wrote in
one book all the calamity that
would come upon Babylon, all
these words written against Babylon. 61 Furthermore, Jeremiah said to Se·rai'ah: "When you
come to Babylon and see her,

you must read aloud all these words. **62** Then say, 'O Jehovah, you have said against this place that it will be destroyed and left without an inhabitant, man or beast, and that she will become desolate forever.'ᵃ **63** And when you finish reading this book, tie a stone to it and throw it into the middle of the Euphrates. **64** Then say, 'This is how Babylon will sink down and never rise againᵇ because of the calamity that I am bringing on her; and they will grow weary.'"ᶜ

Down to this point are the words of Jeremiah.

52 Zedekiahᵈ was 21 years old when he became king, and he reigned for 11 years in Jerusalem. His mother's name was Hamutalᵉ the daughter of Jeremiah of Libʹnah. **2** He continued to do what was bad in Jehovah's eyes, according to all that Jehoiʹaᐧkim had done.ᶠ **3** It was because of Jehovah's anger that these things took place in Jerusalem and in Judah, until he cast them out of his sight.ᵍ And Zedekiah rebelled against the king of Babylon.ʰ **4** In the ninth year of Zedekiah's reign, in the tenth month, on the tenth day of the month, King Nebuchadnezʹzar* of Babylon came with all his army against Jerusalem. They camped against it and built a siege wall all around it.ⁱ **5** And the city was under siege until the 11th year of King Zedekiah.

6 In the fourth month, on the ninth day of the month,ʲ the famine was severe in the city, and there was no food for the people of the land.ᵏ **7** Finally the city wall was broken through, and all the soldiers fled from the city by night through the

gate between the double wall near the king's garden, while the Chaldeʹans were surrounding the city; and they continued by the way of the Arʹaᐧbah.ᵃ **8** But the Chaldeʹan army pursued the king, and they overtook Zedekiahᵇ in the desert plains of Jerʹiᐧcho, and all his troops were scattered from his side. **9** Then they seized the king and brought him up to the king of Babylon at Ribʹlah in the land of Haʹmath, and he passed sentence on him. **10** And the king of Babylon slaughtered Zedekiah's sons before his eyes, and he also slaughtered all the princes of Judah there at Ribʹlah. **11** Then the king of Babylon blinded Zedekiah's eyes,ᶜ bound him with copper fetters, brought him to Babylon, and kept him imprisoned until the day of his death.

12 In the fifth month, on the tenth day of the month, that is, in the 19th year of King Nebuchadnezʹzar* the king of Babylon, Nebuʹzaradʹan the chief of the guard, who was an attendant of the king of Babylon, came into Jerusalem.ᵈ **13** He burned down the house of Jehovah,ᵉ the king's house,* and all the houses of Jerusalem; he also burned down every large house. **14** And the walls surrounding Jerusalem were pulled down by the entire Chaldeʹan army that was with the chief of the guard.ᶠ

15 Nebuʹzaradʹan the chief of the guard took into exile some of the lowly people and the rest of the people who were left in the city. He also took the deserters who had defected to the king of Babylon as well as the rest of the master craftsmen.ᵍ **16** But Nebuʹzaradʹan the chief of the guard left some of the poorest people of the land to serve as

---

CHAP. 51
a Isa 13:1, 20
   Isa 14:23
   Jer 50:3, 39
   Jer 51:29, 37

b Re 18:21

c Jer 51:58

CHAP. 52
d 2Ki 24:17-20
   2Ch 36:11, 12

e 2Ki 23:31

f 2Ki 24:1
   2Ch 36:5

g Le 26:33
   De 31:16, 17

h 2Ch 36:11, 13
   Eze 17:15

i De 28:52
   2Ki 25:1, 2
   Isa 29:3
   Jer 39:1
   Eze 4:1, 2
   Eze 21:21, 22

j Jer 39:2

k De 28:53-57
   2Ki 25:3-7
   Isa 3:1
   Eze 4:16

Second Col.
a Jer 39:4-7

b Jer 24:8
   Jer 34:21
   Jer 37:17
   Jer 38:18

c Eze 12:13

d 2Ki 25:8-10

e 1Ki 9:8
   2Ch 36:17, 19
   Ps 74:8
   Ps 79:1
   Jer 26:18
   La 2:7
   Eze 24:21

f Jer 39:8

g 2Ki 25:11, 12
   Jer 39:5, 10

52:4, 12 *Lit., "Nebuchadrezzar," a variant spelling.

52:13 *Or "palace."

vinedressers and as compulsory laborers.[a]

17 And the Chal·de′ans broke into pieces the copper pillars[b] of the house of Jehovah and the carriages[c] and the copper Sea[d] that were in the house of Jehovah, and they carried all the copper away to Babylon.[e] 18 They also took the cans, the shovels, the extinguishers, the bowls,[f] the cups,[g] and all the copper utensils used in the temple service. 19 The chief of the guard took the basins,[h] the fire holders, the bowls, the cans, the lampstands,[i] the cups, and the bowls that were of genuine gold and silver.[j] 20 As for the two pillars, the Sea, the 12 copper bulls[k] under the Sea, and the carriages that King Sol′o·mon had made for the house of Jehovah, the copper of all these articles was beyond weighing.

21 As for the pillars, each pillar was 18 cubits* high, a measuring cord of 12 cubits could encircle it;[l] its thickness was four fingerbreadths,# and it was hollow. 22 And the capital on it was of copper; and the height of the one capital was five cubits;[m] and the network and pomegranates all around on the capital were all made of copper. The second pillar was just like it, also the pomegranates. 23 There were 96 pomegranates on the sides; in all, there were 100 pomegranates around the network.[n]

24 The chief of the guard also took Se·rai′ah[o] the chief priest, Zeph·a·ni′ah[p] the second priest, and the three doorkeepers.[q] 25 And he took from the city one court official who was the commissioner over the soldiers, seven close associates of the king who were found in the city, as well as the secretary of the chief of the army, the one mustering the people of the land, and 60 men of the common people of the land who were yet found in the city. 26 Neb·u′zar·ad′an the chief of the guard took them and brought them to the king of Babylon at Rib′lah. 27 The king of Babylon struck them down and put them to death at Rib′lah[a] in the land of Ha′math. Thus Judah went into exile from its land.[b]

28 These are the people whom Neb·u·chad·nez′zar* took into exile: in the seventh year, 3,023 Jews.[c]

29 In the 18th year of Neb·u·chad·nez′zar,*[d] 832 people# were taken from Jerusalem.

30 In the 23rd year of Neb·u·chad·nez′zar,* Neb·u′zar·ad′an the chief of the guard took Jews into exile, 745 people.#[e]

In all, 4,600 people# were taken into exile.

31 Then in the 37th year of the exile of King Je·hoi′a·chin[f] of Judah, in the 12th month, on the 25th day of the month, King E′vil-mer′o·dach of Babylon, in the year he became king, released* King Je·hoi′a·chin of Judah and brought him out of prison.[g] 32 He spoke kindly with him and put his throne higher than the thrones of the other kings who were with him in Babylon. 33 So Je·hoi′a·chin took off his prison garments, and he regularly ate before him all the days of his life. 34 A regular allowance of food was given him from the king of Babylon, day after day, until the day of his death, all the days of his life.

CHAP. 52
a 2Ki 25:22
b 1Ki 7:15, 21
c 1Ki 7:27
d 1Ki 7:23
2Ch 4:11-15
e 2Ki 25:13-16
Jer 27:19, 22
f 1Ki 7:45
g 2Ch 4:19, 22
h 1Ki 7:38
i 1Ki 7:48, 49
j 2Ch 24:14
2Ch 36:18
k 1Ki 7:23, 25
l 1Ki 7:15-20
m 2Ch 3:15
n 2Ch 3:16
2Ch 4:13
o 1Ch 6:14
Ezr 7:1
p Jer 21:1, 2
Jer 29:25
q 2Ki 25:18-21

Second Col.
a 2Ki 25:6
Jer 52:10
b Le 18:25
Le 26:33
De 28:36
Isa 24:3
Jer 25:9
c 2Ki 24:12, 14
d Jer 32:1
e Jer 6:9
f 2Ki 24:8
Jer 24:1
Jer 37:1
Mt 1:11
g 2Ki 25:27-30

52:21 *A cubit equaled 44.5 cm (17.5 in.). See App. B14. #A fingerbreadth equaled 1.85 cm (0.73 in.). See App. B14.

52:28-30 *Lit., "Nebuchadrezzar," a variant spelling. 52:29, 30 #Or "souls." 52:31 *Lit., "raised up the head of."

LAMENTATIONS

א [Aleph]*

1 How she now sits all alone,
  the city that was full of
  people!*a*
How she has become like a
  widow, she who was populous among the nations!*b*
How she who was a princess
  among the provinces* has
  been put to forced labor!*c*

ב [Beth]

2 She weeps profusely during
  the night,*d* and her tears
  cover her cheeks.
Not one of all her lovers
  is there to comfort her.*e*
All her own companions
  have betrayed her;*f* they
  have become her enemies.

ג [Gimel]

3 Judah has gone into exile*g*
  under affliction and harsh
  slavery.*h*

She must dwell among the
  nations;*a* she finds no
  resting-place.
All her persecutors have
  overtaken her in her
  distress.

ד [Daleth]

4 The roads to Zion are mourning, because no one is
  coming to the festival.*b*
All her gates are desolate;*c*
  her priests are sighing.
Her virgins* are grieving,
  and she is in bitter anguish.

ה [He]

5 Her adversaries are now
  her master;* her enemies
  are carefree.*d*
For Jehovah has brought
  grief to her because of her
  many transgressions.*e*
Her children have gone
  into captivity before the
  adversary.*f*

CHAP. 1
a Ps 122:3, 4

b 1Ki 4:20

c De 28:15, 48
  2Ki 25:11, 12

d La 1:16

e Jer 4:30
  Eze 16:37

f Jer 30:14

g Le 26:33
  2Ki 24:14, 15
  2Ki 25:21
  Jer 39:9
  Jer 52:27

h Jer 17:4

Second Col.
a De 28:64

b Am 8:10

c Isa 3:26

d Zec 1:15

e 2Ch 36:15, 16
  Ne 9:33
  Da 9:7, 16

f Jer 39:9
  Jer 52:30

1:1 *Chapters 1-4 are dirges in Hebrew alphabetic, or acrostic, form. #Or "jurisdictional districts."

1:4 *Or "young women." 1:5 *Lit., "head."

ו [Waw]

6 All the splendor has
  departed from the
  daughter of Zion.[a]

Her princes are like stags
  that have found no
  pasture,
And they walk exhausted
  before the pursuer.

ז [Zayin]

7 In the days of her affliction
  and her homelessness,
  Jerusalem remembers
All the precious things that
  were hers in the days of
  long ago.[b]
When her people fell into
  the hand of the adversary
  and she had no helper,[c]
The adversaries saw her
  and laughed* over her
  collapse.[d]

ח [Heth]

8 Jerusalem has sinned
  greatly.[e]
That is why she has become
  something abhorrent.
All who used to honor her
  now treat her as something
  contemptible, for they
  have seen her nakedness.[f]
She herself groans[g] and
  turns away in shame.

ט [Teth]

9 Her uncleanness is in her
  skirts.
She gave no thought to her
  future.[h]
Her downfall was astound-
  ing; she has no one to
  comfort her.
O Jehovah, see my affliction,
  for the enemy has magnified himself.[i]

י [Yod]

10 The adversary has laid his
  hands on all her treasures.[j]
For she has seen nations
  enter her sanctuary,[k]
Those whom you command-
  ed should not enter into
  your congregation.

1:7 *Or "gloated."

CHAP. 1

a Eze 24:21

b 1Ki 10:27

c Jer 52:4

d Ps 137:7
  La 2:16

e Isa 1:4
  Isa 59:2
  Eze 22:4

f Jer 13:22
  Eze 23:29

g Jer 4:31

h Jer 8:7

i Jer 50:29

j Jer 52:17, 19
  Da 1:1, 2

k 2Ch 36:17, 18
  Ps 74:7
  Jer 52:13

Second Col.

a Jer 38:9
  Jer 52:6
  La 2:12
  La 4:4

b Jer 21:7

c Ps 102:3

d Le 26:37
  Eze 11:9

e 2Ki 24:14, 15

f 2Ch 36:17

g Re 14:19
  Re 19:15

כ [Kaph]

11 All her people are sighing;
  they are looking for bread.[a]
They have given their valuable things for something
  to eat, just to stay alive.*
Look, O Jehovah, and see
  that I have become as a
  worthless woman.#

ל [Lamed]

12 Is it nothing to all of you
  who pass along the road?
Look and see!
Is there any pain like
  the pain that was dealt
  out to me,
Which Jehovah made me
  suffer in the day of his
  burning anger?[b]

מ [Mem]

13 From on high he has sent
  fire into my bones,[c] and
  he subdues each one.
He has spread out a net for
  my feet; he has forced
  me to turn backward.
He has made me a desolate
  woman.
All day long I am ill.

נ [Nun]

14 My transgressions are
  bound as a yoke, fastened
  together by his hand.
They have been placed on
  my neck, and my strength
  has failed.
Jehovah has given me into
  the hand of those whom
  I cannot resist.[d]

ס [Samekh]

15 Jehovah has tossed aside
  all the powerful men in
  my midst.[e]
He has summoned an
  assembly against me to
  crush my young men.[f]
Jehovah has trodden the
  virgin daughter of Judah
  in the winepress.[g]

1:11 *Or "to restore the soul." #A personification referring to Jerusalem.

ע [*Ayin*]

16 I am weeping because of these things;ᵃ my eyes flow with tears.

For anyone who could comfort me or refresh me* is far away from me.

My sons are desolate, for the enemy has prevailed.

פ [*Pe*]

17 Zion has spread out her hands;ᵇ she has no one to comfort her.

Jehovah has given an order against Jacob to all his adversaries around him.ᶜ

Jerusalem has become to them an abhorrent thing.ᵈ

צ [*Tsade*]

18 Jehovah is righteous,ᵉ for it is against his commands* that I have rebelled.ᶠ

Listen, all you peoples, and see my pain.

My virgins# and my young men have gone into captivity.ᵍ

ק [*Qoph*]

19 I have called out to my lovers, but they have betrayed me.ʰ

In the city my priests and my elders have perished,

While they searched for food in order to stay alive.*ⁱ

ר [*Resh*]

20 See, O Jehovah, for I am in great distress.

My insides* are churning.

My heart has turned over within me, for I have been completely rebellious.ʲ

Outside the sword bereaves;ᵏ inside the house it is like death.

ש [*Shin*]

21 People have heard my sighing; there is no one to comfort me.

All my enemies have heard of my calamity.

They are joyful, because you brought it about.ᵃ

But you will bring about the day that you proclaimed,ᵇ when they will become like me.ᶜ

ת [*Taw*]

22 May all their badness come before you, and may you deal harshly with them,ᵈ

Just as you have dealt harshly with me because of all my transgressions.

For my sighs are many, and my heart is sick.

א [*Aleph*]

2 How Jehovah has covered the daughter of Zion in the cloud of his anger!

He has thrown down the beauty of Israel from heaven to earth.ᵉ

He has not remembered his footstoolᶠ in the day of his anger.

ב [*Beth*]

2 Jehovah has swallowed up without compassion all the dwellings of Jacob.

In his fury he has torn down the fortified places of the daughter of Judah.ᵍ

He has brought down to the ground and profaned the kingdomʰ and her princes.ⁱ

ג [*Gimel*]

3 In the heat of anger he has cut down all the strength* of Israel.

He withdrew his right hand when the enemy approached,ʲ

And in Jacob he kept burning like a fire that consumed everything around it.ᵏ

ד [*Daleth*]

4 He has bent* his bow like an enemy; his right hand is poised as an adversary;ˡ

CHAP. 1
a Jer 31:15

b Jer 4:31

c De 28:49
2Ki 24:1, 2
2Ki 25:1

d La 1:8

e Ne 9:33
Da 9:7

f 1Sa 12:14, 15

g De 28:32

h Jer 30:14

i 2Ki 25:3
Jer 38:9

j Ps 107:11
Isa 1:2
Isa 63:10

k De 32:25
Jer 15:2

Second Col.
a Eze 25:6, 7
Ob 12

b Isa 13:19
Jer 25:12-14
Joe 3:19

c Ps 137:8, 9
Isa 51:22, 23

d Jer 51:35

CHAP. 2
e La 2:15

f 1Ch 28:2
Ps 132:7
Isa 60:13

g De 28:52
Mic 5:11

h Eze 21:26, 27

i Isa 39:7
Isa 43:28

j Ps 74:10, 11

k De 32:22
Isa 42:25
Jer 7:20

l De 28:63
Isa 63:10
Jer 21:5

1:16 *Or "my soul." 1:18 *Lit., "mouth." #Or "young women." 1:19 *Or "to restore the soul." 1:20 *Lit., "intestines."

2:3 *Lit., "every horn." 2:4 *Lit., "trodden."

He kept killing all those
desirable to the eyes.ᵃ
And he poured out his wrath
like a fireᵇ into the tent
of the daughter of Zion.ᶜ

ה [He]
5 Jehovah has become like
an enemy;ᵈ
He has swallowed down
Israel.
He has swallowed down all
her towers;
He has destroyed all its
fortified places.
And in the daughter of Judah
he makes mourning and
lamentation abound.

ו [Waw]
6 He treats his booth violently,ᵉ
like a hut in a garden.
He has put an end to* his
festival.ᶠ
Jehovah has caused
festival and sabbath to
be forgotten in Zion,
And in his fierce indignation
he shows no regard for
king and priest.ᵍ

ז [Zayin]
7 Jehovah has rejected his
altar;
He has spurned his
sanctuary.ʰ
He has surrendered the walls
of her fortified towers into
the hand of the enemy.ⁱ
They have raised their voice
in the house of Jehovah,ʲ
as on the day of a festival.

ח [Heth]
8 Jehovah has resolved to
destroy the wall of the
daughter of Zion.ᵏ
He has stretched out the
measuring line.ˡ
He has not held back
his hand from bringing
destruction.*

And he causes rampart and
wall to mourn.
Together they have been
made weak.

ט [Teth]
9 Her gates have sunk down
into the earth.ᵃ
He has destroyed and broken
her bars.
Her king and her princes
are among the nations.ᵇ
There is no law;* even her
prophets find no vision
from Jehovah.ᶜ

י [Yod]
10 The elders of the daughter
of Zion sit on the ground
in silence.ᵈ
They throw dust on their
heads and wear sackcloth.ᵉ
The virgins of Jerusalem
have bowed their heads
down to the ground.

כ [Kaph]
11 My eyes are worn out from
shedding tears.ᶠ
My insides* are churning.
My liver has been poured
out on the ground, because
of the downfall of the
daughter of# my people,ᵍ
Because of the children
and infants fainting away
in the public squares of
the town.ʰ

ל [Lamed]
12 They keep asking their
mothers, "Where are
grain and wine?"ⁱ
As they faint away like
someone wounded in the
public squares of the city,
As their life* ebbs away
in their mothers' arms.

מ [Mem]
13 What can I use as a witness,
Or to what can I liken you,
O daughter of Jerusalem?

CHAP. 2
a 2Ki 25:21

b Jer 4:4

c Jer 10:20

d Jer 30:14

e 2Ki 25:8, 9
2Ch 36:19
Isa 63:18
Isa 64:11

f La 1:4

g Jer 52:24, 27

h Le 26:31
Jer 26:6
Jer 52:12, 13
Eze 24:21
Mic 3:12

i 2Ch 36:19

j Ps 74:4

k 2Ki 25:10
Jer 39:8

l 2Ki 21:13
Isa 28:17

Second Col.
a Ne 1:3
Jer 14:2

b De 28:15, 36
2Ki 24:15
2Ki 25:7
La 4:20
Eze 12:13
Da 1:3, 6

c Ps 74:9
Jer 23:16
Eze 7:26

d Isa 3:26

e Jer 6:26
Eze 7:18

f La 3:48

g Jer 14:17

h Jer 11:22
La 2:19
La 4:4

i De 28:49, 51
2Ki 25:3
Isa 3:1
Jer 18:21

2:9 *Or "instruction." 2:11 *Lit., "intestines." #A poetic personification,
perhaps expressing pity or sympathy.
2:12 *Or "soul."

2:6 *Or "destroyed." 2:8 *Lit., "from
swallowing up."

To what can I compare you,
to comfort you, O virgin
daughter of Zion?

For your breakdown is as
vast as the sea.[a] Who can
heal you?[b]

ב [Nun]

14 The visions your prophets
saw for you were false
and empty,[c]

And they did not expose
your error in order to turn
away your captivity,[d]

But they kept visioning for
you false and misleading
pronouncements.[e]

ס [Samekh]

15 At you all those passing
by on the road scornfully
clap their hands.[f]

They whistle in amazement[g]
and shake their heads at
the daughter of Jerusalem,
saying:

"Is this the city about which
they said, 'It is perfect in
beauty, the joy of all the
earth'?"[h]

פ [Pe]

16 At you all your enemies have
opened their mouth.

They whistle and grind their
teeth and say: "We have
swallowed her down.[i]

This is the day we were
waiting for![j] It has arrived,
and we have seen it!"[k]

ע [Ayin]

17 Jehovah has done what he
intended;[l] he has carried
out his saying,[m]

What he commanded long
ago.[n]

He has torn down without
compassion.[o]

He has let the enemy rejoice
over you; he has exalted
the strength* of your
adversaries.

2:17 *Lit., "horn."

Reference column

CHAP. 2
a Jer 14:17
  Da 9:12

b Jer 30:12

c Jer 2:8
  Jer 27:14
  Eze 13:2, 3

d Jer 23:14

e Jer 23:32
  Jer 27:9
  Mic 3:5
  Zep 3:4

f Eze 25:2, 6

g 1Ki 9:8
  Jer 25:9

h Ps 48:2
  Eze 16:14

i Jer 51:34

j Mic 4:11

k Ob 13

l Jer 18:11
  Mic 2:3

m 2Ki 23:27

n Le 26:14, 17
  De 28:15

o Eze 5:11

Second Col.

a Isa 51:20
  La 4:9
  Eze 5:16

b Le 26:29
  De 28:53
  Jer 19:9
  La 4:10
  Eze 5:10

c Eze 9:6, 7

d De 28:49, 50
  2Ch 36:17

e Jer 9:21
  Jer 18:21

f Jer 13:14
  Jer 21:7
  La 3:43
  Eze 5:11
  Eze 9:6

g De 16:16

h Zep 1:18

צ [Tsade]

18 Their heart cries out to
Jehovah, O wall of the
daughter of Zion.

Let tears stream down like
a torrent day and night.

Give yourself no respite,
give your eye* no rest.

ק [Qoph]

19 Rise up! Cry out during the
night, at the start of the
watches.

Pour out your heart like
water before the face of
Jehovah.

Raise your hands to him for
the lives* of your children,

Who are fainting away
at every street corner#
because of famine.[a]

ר [Resh]

20 See, O Jehovah, and look
upon the one with whom
you have dealt so harshly.

Should women keep eating
their own offspring,*
their own fully formed
children,[b]

Or should priests and
prophets be killed in the
sanctuary of Jehovah?[c]

ש [Shin]

21 Young boy and old man are
lying dead on the ground
in the streets.[d]

My virgins* and my young
men have fallen by the
sword.[e]

You have killed in the day
of your anger; you have
slaughtered without
compassion.[f]

ת [Taw]

22 As if for a festival day,[g]
you summon terrors
from every direction.

In the day of the wrath of
Jehovah, no one escaped
or survived;[h]

2:18 *Lit., "the daughter of your eye."
2:19 *Or "souls." #Lit., "at the head of
all streets." 2:20 *Or "fruitage." 2:21
*Or "young women."

Those whom I gave birth to* and reared, my enemy exterminated.ᵃ

ℵ [Aleph]

3 I am the man who has seen affliction because of the rod of his fury.

2 He has driven me out and makes me walk in darkness, not in light.ᵇ

3 Indeed, he repeatedly brings his hand against me all day long.ᶜ

ב [Beth]

4 He has worn away my flesh and my skin; He has broken my bones.

5 He has besieged me; he has surrounded me with bitter poisonᵈ and hardship.

6 He has forced me to sit in dark places, like men who died long ago.

ג [Gimel]

7 He has walled me in, so that I cannot escape; He has bound me with heavy copper fetters.ᵉ

8 And when I cry out desperately for help, he rejects* my prayer.ᶠ

9 He has blocked up my paths with hewn stones; He has made my roadways crooked.ᵍ

ד [Daleth]

10 He waits to ambush me like a bear, like a lion in hiding.ʰ

11 He has forced me off the paths and torn me to pieces;* He has made me desolate.ⁱ

12 He has bent* his bow, and he sets me up as the target for the arrow.

ה [He]

13 He has pierced my kidneys with the arrows* of his quiver.

14 I have become a laughingstock to all the peoples, the theme of their song all day long.

15 He has filled me with bitter things and saturated me with wormwood.ᵃ

ו [Waw]

16 He breaks my teeth with gravel; He makes me cower in the ashes.ᵇ

17 You deprive me* of peace; I have forgotten what is good.

18 So I say: "My splendor has perished, as well as my expectation in Jehovah."

ז [Zayin]

19 Remember my affliction and my homeless state,ᶜ the wormwood and the bitter poison.ᵈ

20 You* will surely remember and bow low over me.ᵉ

21 I recall this in my heart; that is why I will show a waiting attitude.ᶠ

ח [Heth]

22 It is because of Jehovah's loyal love that we have not come to our finish,ᵍ For his mercies never end.ʰ

23 They are new each morning;ⁱ your faithfulness is abundant.ʲ

24 "Jehovah is my share,"ᵏ I have said,* "that is why I will show a waiting attitude for him."ˡ

ט [Teth]

25 Good is Jehovah to the one hoping in him,ᵐ to the person* who keeps seeking him.ⁿ

26 Good it is to wait in silence* for the salvation of Jehovah.ᵖ

CHAP. 2
a De 28:18

CHAP. 3
b De 28:15, 29
  Jer 13:16
c Isa 63:10
d Jer 8:14
  Jer 9:15
  La 3:19
e Jer 39:7
f Ps 80:4
  Ps 102:2
  Isa 1:15
  Mic 3:4
g Isa 63:17
h Job 38:39, 40
  Ho 5:14
  Am 5:18, 19
i Jer 6:8
  Jer 32:43

Second Col.
a Jer 9:15
  Jer 23:15
b Ps 102:9
  Jer 6:26
c Ne 9:32
  Ps 137:1
d Jer 9:15
  La 3:5
e Ps 113:5-7
f Ps 130:6-8
  Mic 7:7
g Ezr 9:8
h Ne 9:31
  Jer 30:11
  Mic 7:18
i Ps 30:5
j De 32:4
  Ps 36:5
k Ps 16:5
  Ps 73:26
  Ps 142:5
l Ps 130:6-8
m Ps 25:3
  Ps 130:5
  Isa 25:9
  Isa 30:18
  Mic 7:7
n 1Ch 28:9
  Isa 26:9
  Zep 2:3
o Ps 37:7
p Ps 116:6

2:22 *Or "brought forth healthy." **3:8** *Or "hinders; shuts out." **3:11** *Or possibly, "makes me lie fallow." **3:12** *Lit., "trodden." **3:13** *Lit., "sons."

3:17 *Or "my soul." **3:20** *Or "Your soul." **3:24** *Or "my soul says." **3:25** *Or "soul." **3:26** *Or "to wait patiently."

27 Good it is for a man to carry the yoke during his youth.[a]

ׁ [Yod]

28 Let him sit alone and keep silent when He lays it upon him.[b]

29 Let him put his mouth in the very dust;[c] there may yet be hope.[d]

30 Let him give his cheek to the one striking him; let him have his fill of insults.

כּ [Kaph]

31 For Jehovah will not cast us off forever.[e]

32 Although he has caused grief, he will also show mercy according to his abundant loyal love.[f]

33 For it is not in his heart to afflict or grieve the sons of men.[g]

ל [Lamed]

34 To crush beneath one's feet all the prisoners of the earth,[h]

35 To deprive a man of justice in the presence of the Most High,[i]

36 To defraud a man in his legal case
—Jehovah does not tolerate such things.

מ [Mem]

37 Who, then, can speak and have it happen unless Jehovah commands it?

38 From the mouth of the Most High,
Bad things and good things do not go out together.

39 Why should a living person complain about the consequences of his sin?[j]

נ [Nun]

40 Let us examine and scrutinize our ways,[k] and let us return to Jehovah.[l]

41 Let us lift up our hearts along with our hands to God in the heavens:[m]

42 "We have transgressed and rebelled,[a] and you have not forgiven.[b]

ס [Samekh]

43 With anger you have blocked our approach;[c]
You have pursued and killed us without compassion.[d]

44 You have blocked approach to yourself with a cloud, so that our prayer may not pass through.[e]

45 You make us offscouring and refuse among the peoples."

פ [Pe]

46 All our enemies open their mouths against us.[f]

47 Dread and pitfalls have become our lot,[g] desolation and breakdown.[h]

48 Streams of water flow from my eyes over the breakdown of the daughter of my people.[i]

ע [Ayin]

49 My eyes weep without ceasing, without pausing,[j]

50 Until Jehovah looks down and sees from heaven.[k]

51 My eyes have brought me* grief because of all the daughters of my city.[l]

צ [Tsade]

52 Without cause my enemies have hunted me down like a bird.

53 They have silenced my life in the pit; they kept hurling stones at me.

54 Waters flowed over my head, and I said: "I am finished!"

ק [Qoph]

55 I called out your name, O Jehovah, from the depths of the pit.[m]

56 Hear my voice; do not shut your ear to my cry for help, for relief.

57 You drew near in the day that I called you. You said: "Do not be afraid."

3:51 *Or "my soul."

ר [Resh]

58 You have defended my cause,* O Jehovah, you have redeemed my life.[a]

59 You have seen, O Jehovah, the wrong done to me; please grant me justice.[b]

60 You have seen all their vengeance, all their schemes against me.

שׂ [Sin] or [Shin]

61 You have heard their taunts, O Jehovah, all their schemes against me,[c]

62 The lips of my opposers and their whispering against me all day long.

63 Look at them; whether they sit or stand, they mock me in their songs!

ת [Taw]

64 You will repay them, O Jehovah, according to their deeds.

65 You will make them hardhearted, as your curse to them.

66 You will pursue them in your anger and annihilate them from under the heavens of Jehovah.

א [Aleph]

4 How the shining gold has grown dim, the fine gold![d] How the holy stones[e] lie scattered at every street corner!*[f]

ב [Beth]

2 As for the precious sons of Zion, who were weighed against* refined gold, How they have been regarded as earthenware jars, The work of a potter's hands!

ג [Gimel]

3 Even jackals offer the udder to nurse their young, But the daughter of my people has become cruel,[g]

___

CHAP. 3
a Jer 50:34

b Jer 51:36, 37

c Ps 74:18

CHAP. 4
d 1Ki 6:22

e 1Ki 5:17
  1Ki 7:9-12

f Jer 52:12, 13

g Le 26:29
  De 28:53-57
  Jer 19:9
  La 4:10

Second Col.
a Job 39:14-16

b La 1:11
  La 2:11, 12

c Jer 52:6

d Am 6:4, 7

e Jer 6:2, 26

f Eze 16:48

g Ge 19:24, 25
  Da 9:12

h Nu 6:2

i Ps 102:5

j Jer 29:17
  Jer 38:2

k Le 26:29
  La 2:20
  La 4:3

---

like ostriches in the wilderness.[a]

ד [Daleth]

4 The tongue of the nursing infant sticks to its palate because of thirst. Children beg for bread,[b] but no one gives them any.[c]

ה [He]

5 Those who used to eat delicacies lie famished* in the streets.[d] Those who were brought up wearing scarlet[e] have embraced ash heaps.

ו [Waw]

6 The punishment* of the daughter of my people is greater than the punishment for the sin of Sod'om,[f] Which was overthrown in a moment, with no hand to help her.[g]

ז [Zayin]

7 Her Naz'i·rites[h] were purer than snow, whiter than milk. They were more ruddy than corals; they were like polished sapphires.

ח [Heth]

8 Their appearance has become darker than soot;* They are not recognized in the streets. Their skin has shriveled over their bones;[i] it has become like dry wood.

ט [Teth]

9 Those slain with the sword are better off than those slain by famine,[j] Those who waste away, who are pierced through for lack of food from the field.

י [Yod]

10 The hands of compassionate women have boiled their own children.[k]

___

They have become their food of mourning during the breakdown of the daughter of my people.*

 כ [Kaph]

11 Jehovah has expressed his wrath;
   He has poured out his burning anger.*
   And he starts a fire in Zion that consumes her foundations.*

ל [Lamed]

12 The kings of the earth and all the inhabitants of the productive land did not believe
   That the adversary and the enemy would enter the gates of Jerusalem.*

מ [Mem]

13 It was because of the sins of her prophets, the errors of her priests,*
   Who shed the blood of righteous ones in her midst.*

נ [Nun]

14 They have wandered blindly* in the streets.
   They are polluted with blood,*
   So that none are able to touch their garments.

ס [Samekh]

15 "Go away! Unclean!" they call out to them. "Go away! Go away! Do not touch us!"
   For they have gone homeless and wander about.
   People have said among the nations: "They cannot stay here with us."**

פ [Pe]

16 The face of Jehovah has scattered them;*
   He will no longer look favorably on them.
   Men will show no respect for the priests,* no favor to the elders."*

4:15 * Or "reside here as foreigners."

ע [Ayin]

17 Even now our eyes are worn out from looking in vain for help.*
   We looked and looked for help from a nation that could not save us.*

צ [Tsade]

18 They have hunted us down at every step* so that we could not walk in our public squares.
   Our end has drawn near; our days have finished, for our end has come.

ק [Qoph]

19 Our pursuers were swifter than the eagles of the sky.*
   They chased us on the mountains; they ambushed us in the wilderness.

ר [Resh]

20 The breath of our nostrils, the anointed one of Jehovah,* has been captured in their large pit,*
   The one of whom we said: "In his shade we will live among the nations."

ש [Sin]

21 Exult and rejoice, O daughter of E′dom,* living as you do in the land of Uz.
   But to you also the cup will be passed,* and you will become drunk and expose your nakedness.*

ת [Taw]

22 The punishment for your error, O daughter of Zion, has come to its finish.
   He will not carry you off into exile again.*
   But he will turn his attention to your error, O daughter of E′dom.
   He will uncover your sins.*

5 Remember, O Jehovah, what has befallen us.
   Look and see our disgrace.*

2 Our inheritance has been turned over to strangers, our houses to foreigners.*

3 We have become orphans without a father; our mothers are like widows.ᵃ

4 We must pay to drink our own water,ᵇ and our own wood comes at a price.

5 Those pursuing us are at our neck;

We are weary, but we are given no rest.ᶜ

6 We hold out our hand to Egyptᵈ and to As·syrʹi·a,ᵉ to get enough bread to eat.

7 Our forefathers who sinned are no more, but we must bear their errors.

8 Servants now rule over us; there is no one to snatch us from their hand.

9 We bring in our bread at the risk of our life,*ᶠ because of the sword of the wilderness.

10 Our skin has become as hot as a furnace, because of the pangs of hunger.ᵍ

11 The wives in Zion they have humiliated,* the virgins in the cities of Judah.ʰ

12 Princes were hanged by their hand,ⁱ and elders were shown no respect.ʲ

5:9 *Or "soul."   5:11 *Or "raped."

CHAP. 5
a Ex 22:24
  Jer 18:21
b De 28:15, 48
  Isa 3:1
  Eze 4:11, 16
c De 28:65
d Isa 30:2
  Jer 44:12
  Eze 17:17, 18
e 2Ch 28:16
  Jer 2:18, 36
f Eze 4:10
g 2Ki 25:3
h De 28:30
i Jer 39:6
j Isa 47:6
  Jer 6:11
  La 4:16

Second Col.
a Jos 20:4
b Jer 25:10
c Am 8:10
d La 1:22
e De 28:65
f Jer 26:18
g Ps 102:12
  Ps 145:13
  Ps 146:10
h Ps 79:5
  Jer 14:19
i De 4:30
  Ps 80:3
  Ps 85:4
  Jer 31:18
j Jer 33:13
k De 28:15

---

13 Young men carry the hand mill, and boys stumble under loads of wood.

14 The elders are gone from the city gate;ᵃ young men do not play their music.ᵇ

15 The joy is gone from our heart; our dancing has turned into mourning.ᶜ

16 The crown has fallen from our head. Woe to us, because we have sinned!

17 Because of this our heart is sick,ᵈ

And because of these things our eyes have grown dim,ᵉ

18 Because of Mount Zion, which is desolate;ᶠ foxes now roam on it.

19 As for you, O Jehovah, you sit enthroned forever.

Your throne is for generation after generation.ᵍ

20 Why do you forget us forever and abandon us for so long a time?ʰ

21 Bring us back to yourself, O Jehovah, and we will readily return to you.

Renew our days as in those of old.ʲ

22 However, you have utterly rejected us.

You remain intensely angry with us.ᵏ

EZEKIEL

OUTLINE OF CONTENTS

1 In the 30th year, on the fifth day of the fourth month, while I was among the exiled people[a] by the river Che′bar,[b] the heavens were opened and I began to see visions of God. **2** On the fifth day of the month —that is, in the fifth year of the exile of King Je·hoi′a·chin[c]— **3** the word of Jehovah came to Ezekiel* son of Bu′zi the priest by the river Che′bar in the land of the Chal·de′ans.[d] There the hand of Jehovah came upon him.[e]

4 As I was looking, I saw a tempestuous wind[f] coming from the north, and there was a huge cloud and flashing fire*[g] surrounded by a bright light, and from the midst of the fire was something that looked like electrum.*[h] **5** Within it were what looked like four living creatures,[i] and the appearance of each one was like that of a human. **6** Each one had four faces and four wings.[j] **7** Their feet were straight, and the soles of their feet were like those of a calf, and they were shining like the glow of burnished copper.[k] **8** They had human hands under their wings on all four sides, and the four of them had faces and wings. **9** Their wings

were touching one another. They would not turn when they went; they would each go straight forward.[a]

10 Their faces had this appearance: Each of the four had a man's face with a lion's[b] face on the right, a bull's[c] face on the left, and each of the four had an eagle's[d] face.[e] **11** That is how their faces were. Their wings were spread out above them. Each had two wings that were touching one another and two wings covering their bodies.[f]

12 They would each go straight forward, going wherever the spirit would incline them to go.[g] They would not turn as they went. **13** And the living creatures had the appearance of burning coals of fire, and something that looked like torches of bright fire was moving back and forth between the living creatures, and lightning was flashing out from the fire.[h] **14** And when the living creatures would go forth and return, their movement had the appearance of flashes of lightning.

15 As I was watching the living creatures, I saw one wheel on the earth beside each of the living creatures with four faces.[i] **16** The wheels and their structure appeared to glow like chrys′o·lite, and the four of them looked alike. Their appearance and structure looked as

---

CHAP. 1
a 2Ki 24:12, 14
b Eze 3:15
c 2Ch 36:9, 10
d Jer 22:25
e Eze 3:14
f 1Ki 19:11
g Ex 19:18
  Ps 97:2, 3
h Eze 8:2
i Eze 10:9, 15
  Re 4:6
j Isa 6:2
  Eze 10:20, 21
  Re 4:8
k Da 10:5, 6

Second Col.
a Eze 10:11, 15
b 2Sa 17:10
  Pr 28:1
c Pr 14:3
d Job 39:27, 29
e Eze 10:14, 15
  Re 4:7
f Isa 6:2
g Ps 103:20
  Heb 1:7, 14
h Da 7:9, 10
i Eze 10:9-13
  Re 4:7

1:3 *Meaning "God Strengthens." 1:4 *Or "and lightning." #A shining alloy of gold and silver.

though a wheel were within a wheel.* **17** When they moved, they could go in any of the four directions without turning as they went. **18** Their rims were so high that they inspired awe, and the rims of all four were full of eyes all around.[a] **19** Whenever the living creatures moved, the wheels would move along with them, and when the living creatures were lifted up from the earth, the wheels would also be lifted up.[b] **20** They would go where the spirit inclined them to go, wherever the spirit went. The wheels would be lifted up together with them, for the spirit operating on the living creatures* was also in the wheels. **21** When they moved, these would move; and when they stood still, these would stand still; and when they were lifted up from the earth, the wheels would be lifted up together with them, for the spirit operating on the living creatures was also in the wheels.

22 Over the heads of the living creatures was the likeness of an expanse that sparkled like awesome ice, stretched out above their heads.[c] **23** Under the expanse their wings were straight,* one to the other. Each one had two wings for covering one side of their bodies and two for covering the other side. **24** When I heard the sound of their wings, it was like a sound of rushing waters, like the sound of the Almighty.[d] When they moved, it was like the sound of an army. When they stood still, they would let their wings down.

25 There was a voice above the expanse over their heads. (When they stood still, they

would let their wings down.) **26** Above the expanse that was over their heads was what looked like a sapphire stone,[a] and it resembled a throne.[b] Sitting on the throne up above was someone whose appearance resembled that of a human.[c] **27** I saw something glowing like electrum[d] that was like a fire radiating from what appeared to be his waist and upward; and from his waist down, I saw something that resembled fire.[e] There was a brilliance all around him **28** like that of a rainbow[f] in a cloud on a rainy day. That was how the surrounding brilliant light appeared. It was like the appearance of the glory of Jehovah.[g] When I saw it, I fell facedown and began to hear the voice of someone speaking.

2 He then said to me: "Son of man,* stand up on your feet that I may speak with you."[h] **2** When he spoke to me, spirit came into me and made me stand up on my feet[i] so that I could hear the One speaking to me.

3 He went on to say to me: "Son of man, I am sending you to the people of Israel,[j] to rebellious nations that have rebelled against me.[k] They and their forefathers have transgressed against me down to this very day.[l] **4** I am sending you to sons who are defiant* and hardhearted,[m] and you must say to them, 'This is what the Sovereign Lord Jehovah says.' **5** As for them, whether they listen or refuse to listen—for they are a rebellious house*—they will certainly know that a prophet was among them.[o]

6 "But you, son of man, do not be afraid of them,[p] and do

CHAP. 1
a Pr 15:3
  Zec 4:10

b Eze 10:15-17

c Eze 10:1

d Ps 29:3
  Eze 43:2
  Re 14:2

Second Col.
a Ex 24:10
  Ps 96:6
  Eze 10:1

b 1Ki 22:19
  Ps 99:1
  Isa 6:1
  Re 4:2

c Da 7:9

d Eze 8:2

e De 4:24
  Ps 104:1, 2

f Re 4:3

g Ex 24:16, 17
  Eze 8:4

CHAP. 2
h Da 10:11

i Eze 3:24

j 2Ch 36:15
  Eze 33:7

k Isa 1:4
  Jer 16:12

l De 9:24
  Ps 78:8
  Jer 3:25
  Ac 7:51

m Eze 3:7

n Eze 12:2

o Eze 3:11
  Eze 33:4, 15
  Eze 33:33
  Joh 15:22
  Ac 20:26

p 2Ki 1:15
  Lu 12:4

1:16 *Possibly centered at right angles on the same axis. 1:20 *Lit., "the spirit of the living creature." 1:23 *Or possibly, "extended out straight."

2:1 *"Son of man"; the first of 93 occurrences of this expression in Ezekiel. 2:4 *Or "hard of face."

not be afraid of their words, although you are surrounded by briars and thorns*[a] and are dwelling among scorpions. Do not be afraid of their words,[b] and do not be terrified by their faces,[c] for they are a rebellious house. 7 You must speak my words to them, whether they listen or not, for they are a rebellious people.[d]

8 "But you, son of man, listen to what I am telling you. Do not become rebellious like this rebellious house. Open your mouth and eat what I am giving you."[e]

9 When I looked, I saw a hand stretched out to me,[f] and in it I saw a written scroll.*[g] 10 When he spread it out before me, it had writing on both front and back.[h] Dirges* and mourning and wailing were written on it.[i]

3 Then he said to me: "Son of man, eat what is before you.* Eat this scroll, and go, speak to the house of Israel."[j]

2 So I opened my mouth, and he made me eat this scroll. 3 He went on to say to me: "Son of man, eat this scroll that I am giving you, and fill your stomach with it." So I began to eat it, and it was as sweet as honey in my mouth.[k]

4 He said to me: "Son of man, go in among the house of Israel and speak my words to them. 5 For you are not being sent to a people who speak an unintelligible language or an unknown tongue, but to the house of Israel. 6 You are not being sent to many peoples speaking an unintelligible language or an unknown tongue, whose words you

cannot understand. If I would send you to them, they would listen to you.[a] 7 But the house of Israel will refuse to listen to you, for they do not want to listen to me.[b] All those of the house of Israel are hardheaded and hardhearted.[c] 8 Look! I have made your face exactly as hard as their faces and your forehead exactly as hard as their foreheads.[d] 9 I have made your forehead like a diamond, harder than flint.[e] Do not be afraid of them or be terrified by their faces,[f] for they are a rebellious house."

10 He went on to say to me: "Son of man, take to heart and listen to all my words that I speak to you. 11 Go in among the exiles of your people*[g] and speak to them. Tell them, 'This is what the Sovereign Lord Jehovah says,' whether they listen or refuse to listen."[h]

12 A spirit then carried me along[i] and I heard behind me a great rumbling sound that said: "May the glory of Jehovah be praised from his place." 13 There was the sound of the wings of the living creatures as they were brushing against one another,[j] and the sound of the wheels next to them,[k] and the sound of a great rumbling. 14 And the spirit carried me along and took me, and I went in bitterness and in the rage of my spirit, and the hand of Jehovah rested strongly on me. 15 So I went to the exiled people at Tel-a′bib, who were dwelling by the river Che′bar,[l] and I stayed there where they were dwelling; and in a dazed condition,[m] I stayed among them for seven days.

16 At the end of seven days the word of Jehovah came to me:

17 "Son of man, I have appointed you as a watchman to

Reference column (center):

CHAP. 2

a Mic 7:4

b Isa 51:7

c Jer 1:8
　Eze 3:9

d Jer 1:17

e Jer 15:16
　Re 10:9, 10

f Jer 1:9

g Eze 3:1

h Re 5:1

i Eze 19:1

CHAP. 3

j Re 10:9, 10

k Ps 119:103
　Jer 15:16
　Re 10:9, 10

Second Col.

a Jon 3:4, 5
　Mt 11:21

b Lu 10:16

c Ex 34:9
　Jer 3:3
　Jer 5:3

d Jer 1:18, 19
　Jer 15:20
　Mic 3:8

e Isa 50:7

f Jer 17:18

g 2Ki 24:12, 14

h Eze 2:5

i Eze 8:3

j Eze 1:24

k Eze 10:16

l Eze 1:3

m Jer 23:9

Footnotes:

2:6 *Or possibly, "although the people are obstinate and are like things pricking you." 2:9 *Or "a scroll of a book." 2:10 *Or "Songs of mourning." 3:1 *Lit., "eat what you find."

3:11 *Lit., "of the sons of your people."

the house of Israel;[a] and when you hear a word from my mouth, you must warn them from me.[b] **18** When I say to someone wicked, 'You will surely die,' but you do not warn him, and you fail to speak in order to warn the wicked one to turn from his wicked course so that he may stay alive,[c] he will die for his error because he is wicked,[d] but I will ask his blood back from you.*[e] **19** But if you warn someone wicked and he does not turn back from his wickedness and from his wicked course, he will die for his error, but you will certainly save your own life.*[f] **20** But when someone righteous abandons his righteousness and does what is wrong,# I will put a stumbling block before him and he will die.[g] If you did not warn him, he will die for his sin and his righteous acts will not be remembered, but I will ask his blood back from you.*[h] **21** But if you have warned the righteous one not to sin, and he does not sin, he will surely keep alive because he was warned,[i] and you will have saved your own life.*

22 The hand of Jehovah came upon me there, and he said to me: "Get up, go to the valley plain, and I will speak with you there." **23** So I got up and went to the valley plain, and look! the glory of Jehovah was there,[j] like the glory that I saw at the river Cheʹbar,[k] and I fell facedown. **24** Then spirit entered into me and made me stand up on my feet,[l] and he spoke to me and said:

"Go, shut yourself inside your house. **25** As for you, son of man, they will put ropes on you and tie you with them so that you cannot go out among them.

26 And I will make your tongue stick to the roof of your mouth, and you will become mute, unable to reprove them, because they are a rebellious house. **27** But when I speak with you I will open your mouth, and you must say to them,[a] 'This is what the Sovereign Lord Jehovah says.' Let the one listening listen,[b] and let the one refusing to listen refuse, because they are a rebellious house.[c]

4 "And you, son of man, take a brick and put it in front of you. Engrave on it a city—Jerusalem. **2** Lay siege to it,[d] build a siege wall against it,[e] raise up a siege rampart against it,[f] set up camps against it, and surround it with battering rams.[g] **3** Take an iron griddle and place it as an iron wall between you and the city. Then set your face against it, and it will be under siege; you are to besiege it. This is a sign to the house of Israel.[h]

4 "Then you should lie on your left side and lay the guilt of the house of Israel on yourself.*[i] You will carry their guilt for the number of days that you lie on your side. **5** And I will impose on you 390 days, corresponding to the years of their guilt,[j] and you will carry the guilt of the house of Israel. **6** And you must complete them.

"Then for a second time you will lie down, on your right side, and you will carry the guilt of the house of Judah[k] for 40 days. A day for a year, a day for a year, is what I have given you. **7** And you will turn your face toward the siege of Jerusalem[l] with your arm bared, and you must prophesy against it.

8 "Look! I will tie you with ropes so that you cannot turn from your one side to your oth-

CHAP. 3

a Isa 21:8
Isa 62:6
Jer 6:17

b Isa 58:1
Eze 33:7

c Ac 2:40
1Ti 4:16

d Eze 33:4

e Eze 33:8

f Eze 33:9
Ac 18:6
Ac 20:26

g Eze 18:24, 26
Eze 33:12, 18

h Le 19:17
Eze 33:6
Heb 13:17

i Pr 17:10
Eze 33:14, 15
Jas 5:19, 20

j Eze 1:27, 28

k Eze 1:1

l Eze 2:2
Da 10:19

Second Col.

a Eze 24:27
Eze 33:22

b Mt 11:15

c Isa 30:9

CHAP. 4

d 2Ki 24:11
Jer 39:1

e 2Ki 25:1

f Jer 6:6
Jer 32:24

g Jer 21:22

h Eze 12:6
Eze 24:24

i 2Ki 17:21

j Nu 14:34
1Ki 12:19, 20

k 2Ki 23:27

l Jer 52:4

3:18, 20 *Or "I will hold you accountable for his blood." 3:19, 21 *Or "soul." 3:20 #Or "does injustice."

4:4 *Lit., "it," that is, Ezekiel's left side.

er side until you have completed the days of your siege.

9 "And you should take wheat, barley, broad beans, lentils, millet, and spelt and put them in one container and make them into bread for yourself. For the number of the days that you are lying on your side, 390 days, you will eat it.[a] 10 You will weigh out and eat 20 shekels* of food per day. You will eat it at set times.

11 "And you will drink water by measure, a sixth of a hin.* You will drink it at set times.

12 "You will eat it as you would a round barley loaf; you will bake it before their eyes, using dried human excrement as fuel." 13 Jehovah went on to say: "This is how the Israelites will eat their bread—unclean— among the nations where I will disperse them."[b]

14 I then said: "Not that, Sovereign Lord Jehovah! From my youth until now, I have* not been defiled by eating meat from an animal found dead or a torn animal,[c] and no unclean# meat has entered my mouth."[d]

15 So he said to me: "All right, I will allow you to use cattle manure instead of human excrement, and you will bake your bread over it." 16 He then said to me: "Son of man, here I am cutting off your food supply* in Jerusalem,[e] and with great anxiety they will eat their bread ration by weight,[f] and in horror they will drink their water ration by measure.[g] 17 This will happen so that lacking bread and water, they may look in shock at

one another and waste away because of their error.

5 "As for you, son of man, take a sharp sword for yourself to use as a barber's razor. Shave your head and your beard, and then take scales to weigh and divide the hair into portions. 2 You will burn a third of it in the fire inside the city when the days of the siege are completed.[a] Then you will take another third and strike it with the sword all around the city,*[b] and the last third you will scatter to the wind, and I will draw a sword to chase after them.[c]

3 "You must also take a few strands of them and wrap them up in the folds* of your garment. 4 And take some more of them and throw them into the fire and incinerate them. From this a fire will spread to all the house of Israel.[d]

5 "This is what the Sovereign Lord Jehovah says: 'This is Jerusalem. I have set her in the middle of the nations, with lands all around her. 6 But she has rebelled against my judicial decisions and my statutes, acting more wickedly than the nations and the lands all around her.[e] For they have rejected my judicial decisions, and they did not walk in my statutes.'

7 "Therefore this is what the Sovereign Lord Jehovah says: 'Because you were more troublesome than the nations all around you and you did not walk in my statutes or carry out my judicial decisions but, instead, you followed the judicial decisions of the nations all around you,[f] 8 this is what the Sovereign Lord Jehovah says: "Here I am against you, O city,[g] and I myself will execute judgment in your midst before the eyes of the nations.[h] 9 I will do in you what

---

CHAP. 4
a Eze 4:5

b Ho 9:3

c Ex 22:31
Le 7:24
Le 11:40

d De 14:3
Isa 65:4
Isa 66:17

e Le 26:26
Isa 3:1
Eze 5:16

f 2Ki 25:3
Jer 37:21
La 1:11
La 4:9
La 5:9, 10

g Eze 12:18

Second Col.

CHAP. 5
a Jer 9:21
Eze 4:8

b Jer 15:2

c Le 26:33
Eze 5:12

d Jer 4:4

e Eze 16:46, 47

f 2Ki 21:9, 11
Jer 2:11

g Jer 21:5
Eze 15:7

h De 29:22, 24
1Ki 9:8
La 2:15

4:10 *About 230 g (7.3 oz t). See App. B14. 4:11 *About 0.6 L (1.3 pt). See App. B14. 4:14 *Or "my soul has." #Or "foul." 4:16 *Lit., "breaking your bread rods." Possibly referring to rods used for storing bread.

5:2 *Lit., "her." 5:3 *Or "skirts."

I have never done before, and the likes of which I will not do again, because of all your detestable practices.[a]

10 "'So fathers among you will eat their sons,[b] and sons will eat their fathers, and I will execute judgment among you and scatter all the rest of you in every direction.'"*[c]

11 "'Therefore as surely as I am alive,' declares the Sovereign Lord Jehovah, 'because it was my sanctuary that you defiled with all your disgusting idols and with all your detestable practices,[d] I will also reject* you; my eye will not feel sorry, and I will show no compassion.[e] **12** A third of you will die by the pestilence* or perish in your midst by famine. Another third will fall all around you by the sword.[f] And I will scatter the last third in every direction,* and I will draw a sword to chase after them.[g] **13** Then my anger will come to an end, and my wrath against them will subside, and I will be satisfied.[h] And they will have to know that I, Jehovah, have spoken in my insistence on exclusive devotion,[i] when I have finished unleashing my wrath against them.

14 "'I will make you a devastated place and an object of reproach among the surrounding nations and in the eyes of everyone passing by.[j] **15** You will become an object of reproach and scorn,[k] a warning example and a horror to the nations around you, when I execute judgment on you in anger and in wrath and with furious punishments. I, Jehovah, have spoken.

16 "'I will send against them the deadly arrows of famine to destroy them. The arrows that I send will bring you to ruin.[l] I

will make the famine worse for you by cutting off your food supply.*[a] **17** I will send against you famine and vicious wild beasts,[b] and they will bereave you of children. Pestilence and bloodshed will overwhelm you, and I will bring a sword against you.[c] I, Jehovah, have spoken.'"

6 The word of Jehovah again came to me, saying: **2** "Son of man, turn your face toward the mountains of Israel and prophesy against them. **3** You must say, 'O mountains of Israel, hear the word of the Sovereign Lord Jehovah: This is what the Sovereign Lord Jehovah says to the mountains, to the hills, to the streams, and to the valleys: "Look! I will bring a sword against you, and I will destroy your high places. **4** Your altars will be demolished, your incense stands will be broken,[d] and I will throw your slain ones down before your disgusting idols.*[e] **5** I will throw the carcasses of the people of Israel before their disgusting idols, and I will scatter your bones all around your altars.[f] **6** In all the places where you dwell, the cities will be devastated[g] and the high places will be demolished and will lie devastated.[h] Your altars will be demolished and shattered, your disgusting idols will perish, your incense stands will be cut down, and your works will be wiped out. **7** And those slain will fall in your midst,[i] and you will have to know that I am Jehovah.[j]

8 "'But I will leave a remnant, for some of you will escape the sword among the nations when you are scattered throughout the lands.[k] **9** And

CHAP. 5
a La 4:6
  Da 9:12

b Le 26:29
  Jer 19:9
  La 4:10

c Le 26:33
  De 28:64

d Le 20:3
  2Ki 21:1, 7
  2Ch 36:14
  Jer 32:34

e La 2:21
  Eze 7:4

f Jer 14:12
  Jer 15:2
  Jer 21:9

g Le 26:33
  Jer 9:16
  Jer 42:16

h Eze 16:42

i Ex 20:3, 5
  Ex 34:14
  De 6:15

j De 28:37
  1Ki 9:7
  Ne 2:17

k Ps 79:4
  Jer 24:9
  La 2:15
  La 3:61, 62

l De 32:23

Second Col.
a Le 26:26
  Eze 4:16

b Le 26:22
  De 32:24
  Jer 14:21
  Eze 33:27

c Eze 21:3

CHAP. 6
d Isa 27:9

e Le 26:30

f Jer 8:1, 2

g Jer 2:15
  Jer 32:29
  Mic 3:12

h Eze 16:39

i Jer 14:18

j Jer 7:4

k Jer 30:10
  Jer 44:28
  Eze 14:22

5:10, 12 *Lit., "to every wind." **5:11** *Or "diminish." **5:12** #Or "disease."

5:16 *Lit., "breaking your bread rods." Possibly referring to rods used for storing bread. **6:4** *The Hebrew term may be related to a word for "dung" and is used as an expression of contempt.

those who escape will remember me among the nations where they are taken captive.[a] They will realize that I was brokenhearted over their unfaithful[*] heart that turned away from me[b] and at their eyes that are lusting[#] after their disgusting idols.[c] They will be ashamed of and loathe all the evil and detestable things they have done.[d] **10** They will have to know that I am Jehovah and that my threats to bring this calamity on them were not empty.'"[e]

11 "This is what the Sovereign Lord Jehovah says: 'Clap your hands and stamp your foot and bemoan all the evil and detestable things done by the house of Israel, for they will fall by the sword, by famine, and by pestilence.[f] **12** The one far away will die by pestilence, the one nearby will fall by the sword, and whoever escapes these and is left remaining will die by famine; and I will fully unleash my wrath against them.[g] **13** And you will have to know that I am Jehovah,[h] when their slain lie among their disgusting idols, all around their altars,[i] on every high hill, on all the mountaintops, under every luxuriant tree, and under the branches of big trees where they have made fragrant offerings[*] to appease all their disgusting idols.[j] **14** I will stretch out my hand against them and make the land desolate, and all their dwelling places will become more desolate than the wilderness near Dib'lah. And they will have to know that I am Jehovah.'"

7 The word of Jehovah again came to me, saying: **2** "As for you, son of man, this is what the Sovereign Lord Jehovah says to the land of Israel: 'An end! The end has come upon the four corners of the land. **3** The end is now upon you, and I will unleash my anger against you, and I will judge you according to your ways and call you to account for all your detestable deeds. **4** My eye will not feel sorry for you; nor will I feel compassion,[a] for I will bring upon you the results of your own ways, and you will suffer the consequences of your detestable deeds.[b] And you will have to know that I am Jehovah.'[c]

5 "This is what the Sovereign Lord Jehovah says: 'Look! A calamity, a unique calamity, is coming.[d] **6** An end is coming; the end will come; it will rouse itself[*] against you. Look! It is coming. **7** Your turn[*] has come, you who inhabit the land. The time is coming, the day is near.[e] There is confusion and not joyful shouting on the mountains.

8 "'Very soon I will pour out my rage on you,[f] and I will fully unleash my anger against you,[g] and I will judge you according to your ways and call you to account for all your detestable deeds. **9** My eye will not feel sorry; nor will I feel compassion.[h] I will bring on you the results of your ways, and you will suffer the consequences of your own detestable deeds. And you will have to know that I, Jehovah, am striking you.[i]

10 "'Look, the day! Look, it is coming![j] Your turn[*] has come; the rod has blossomed and presumptuousness has sprouted. **11** Violence has grown into a rod of wickedness.[k] Neither they nor their wealth nor their crowds nor their prominence

---

CHAP. 6
a De 30:1, 2
  Ps 137:1

b Ps 78:40, 41
  Isa 63:10

c Nu 15:39

d Eze 20:43
  Eze 36:31

e Eze 33:29
  Da 9:12
  Zec 1:6

f Jer 15:2
  Jer 16:4
  Eze 5:12

g Eze 5:13

h Eze 12:15

i Jer 8:2

j Eze 20:28

Second Col.

CHAP. 7
a Eze 5:11

b Jer 16:18
  Eze 16:43

c Eze 6:13

d 2Ki 21:12
  Da 9:12

e Zep 1:14

f 2Ch 34:21

g Jer 7:20
  Eze 5:13

h Jer 13:14

i Isa 66:6
  Eze 33:29

j Zep 1:14

k Isa 59:6
  Jer 6:7
  Mic 6:12

6:9 *Or "immoral; promiscuous." #Or "are immorally following." 6:13 *Or "offered pleasing aromas."

7:6 *Lit., "awaken." 7:7, 10 *Or possibly, "The garland."

will survive. **12** The time will come, the day will arrive. Let the buyer not rejoice, and let the seller not mourn, for there is wrath against their whole crowd.*[a] **13** For the seller will not return to what was sold, even if his life is spared, for the vision is against the entire multitude. No one will return, and because of his error,* no one will preserve his life.

14 "'They have blown the trumpet,[b] and everyone is ready, but no one is going to the battle, because my wrath is against the whole multitude.[c] **15** The sword is outside,[d] and the pestilence and the famine are inside. Whoever is in the field will die by the sword, and famine and pestilence will consume those in the city.[e] **16** Their survivors who manage to escape will go to the mountains, and like the doves of the valleys, each one will moan over his error.[f] **17** All their hands will hang limp, and all their knees will drip with water.*[g] **18** They have put on sackcloth,[h] and shuddering has seized* them. Everyone will be put to shame, and every head will be bald.*[i]

19 "'They will throw their silver into the streets, and their gold will become abhorrent to them. Neither their silver nor their gold will be able to save them in the day of Jehovah's fury.[j] They* will not be satisfied, nor will they fill their stomachs, for it# has become a stumbling block causing their er-

ror. **20** They took pride in the beauty of their ornaments, and they made with them* their detestable images, their disgusting idols.[a] That is why I will make it an abhorrent thing to them. **21** I will give it* into the hand of the foreigners for plunder and to the wicked ones of the earth for spoil, and they will profane it. **22** "'I will turn my face away from them,[b] and they will profane my concealed place,* and robbers will enter it and profane it.[c]

23 "'Make the chain,*[d] for the land is full of bloodstained judgment[e] and the city is full of violence.[f] **24** I will bring in the worst of the nations,[g] and they will take possession of their houses,[h] and I will put an end to the pride of the strong ones, and their sanctuaries will be profaned.[i] **25** When their anguish comes, they will seek peace, but there will be none.[j] **26** There will come disaster upon disaster, and one report after another, and people will seek a vision from a prophet,[k] but the law* will perish from a priest and advice# from the elders.[l] **27** The king will go into mourning,[m] and the chieftain will be clothed with despair,* and the hands of the people of the land will tremble in terror. I will treat them according to their ways, and I will judge them as they have judged. And they will have to know that I am Jehovah.'"[n]

8 And in the sixth year, in the sixth month, on the fifth day of the month, when I was sit-

CHAP. 7
a Zep 1:18

b Jer 4:5

c Jer 7:20
 Jer 12:12

d Le 26:25

e Jer 14:18
 Eze 5:12

f Isa 59:11

g Eze 21:7

h Isa 3:24

i Isa 22:12

j Pr 11:4
 Zep 1:18

Second Col.
a 2Ki 21:1, 7
 Jer 7:30

b Jer 18:17

c 2Ch 36:19
 La 1:10

d Jer 39:6, 7
 La 3:7

e 2Ki 21:16
 2Ki 24:3, 4
 Jer 2:34
 Eze 9:9

f Isa 59:6
 Mic 2:2

g De 28:48-51
 Eze 21:31
 Hab 1:6

h Jer 6:12
 La 5:2

i Eze 21:2

j Isa 57:21
 Jer 8:15

k Jer 21:1, 2
 Jer 37:17

l Ps 74:9
 La 2:9
 Eze 20:3

m Jer 52:10

n Eze 6:13

7:12 *That is, neither those who buy property nor those who sell it will benefit, since the destruction will come upon all. **7:13** *Or possibly, "by their error." **7:17** *That is, from urination as a result of fear. **7:18** *Lit., "covered." #That is, their heads will be shaved in mourning. **7:19** *Or "Their souls." #That is, their silver and their gold.

7:20 *That is, their objects of gold and silver. **7:21** *That is, their silver and their gold used to make idols. **7:22** *Apparently referring to the innermost part of Jehovah's sanctuary. **7:23** *That is, chains of captivity. **7:26** *Or "instruction." #Or "counsel." **7:27** *Or "desolation."

ting in my house and the elders of Judah were sitting before me, the hand of the Sovereign Lord Jehovah took hold of me there. **2** As I watched, I saw a form similar to the appearance of fire; there was fire below what appeared to be his waist,[a] and from his waist upward his appearance was bright, like the glow of electrum.*[b] **3** Then he stretched out what appeared to be a hand and took me by a tuft of hair of my head, and a spirit carried me between the earth and the heavens and brought me to Jerusalem by means of the visions from God, to the entrance of the inner gate[c] that faces north, where the idolatrous symbol* of jealousy that incites jealousy stood.[d] **4** And look! the glory of the God of Israel was there,[e] like the appearance that I had seen in the valley plain.[f]

5 He then said to me: "Son of man, please raise your eyes toward the north." So I raised my eyes toward the north, and there, north of the gate of the altar, was this symbol* of jealousy in the entryway. **6** And he said to me: "Son of man, do you see what terrible, detestable things the house of Israel is doing here,[g] things that make me go far away from my sanctuary?[h] But you will see detestable things that are even more terrible."

7 Then he brought me to the entrance of the courtyard, and when I looked, I saw a hole in the wall. **8** He said to me: "Son of man, please bore through the wall." So I bored through the wall, and I saw an entryway. **9** He said to me: "Go in and see the evil, detestable things that they are doing here." **10** So I went in and looked, and I saw

all sorts of images of creeping things and loathsome beasts[a] and all the disgusting idols* of the house of Israel;[b] they were carved on the wall all around. **11** And 70 of the elders of the house of Israel were standing before them, with Ja·az·a·ni'ah the son of Sha'phan[c] standing among them. Each one had his censer in his hand, and the perfumed cloud of incense was ascending.[d] **12** He said to me: "Son of man, do you see what the elders of the house of Israel are doing in the darkness, each one in the inner rooms where his idols are displayed?* For they are saying, 'Jehovah is not seeing us. Jehovah has left the land.'"[e]

13 And he went on to say to me: "You will see detestable things that are even more terrible that they are doing." **14** So he brought me to the entrance of the north gate of the house of Jehovah, and there I saw women sitting and weeping over the god Tam'muz.

15 And he further said to me: "Do you see this, O son of man? You will see detestable things that are even more terrible that are worse than these."[f] **16** So he brought me to the inner courtyard of the house of Jehovah.[g] There at the entrance of the temple of Jehovah, between the porch and the altar, were about 25 men with their backs to the temple of Jehovah and their faces to the east; they were bowing down to the sun in the east.[h]

17 He said to me: "Son of man, do you see this? Is it a trivial thing for the house of Judah to do these detestable things, to fill the land with violence[i] and

---

CHAP. 8
a Da 7:9

b Eze 1:4, 27

c Jer 20:2
  Eze 9:2

d De 32:16

e Ex 40:34

f Eze 1:27, 28

g 2Ch 36:14

h Jer 26:4, 6

Second Col.
a Le 11:10

b Ex 20:4, 5

c 2Ki 22:3, 4
  2Ki 25:22
  Jer 26:24

d Eze 16:17, 18

e Isa 29:15
  Eze 9:9

f 2Ch 36:14

g 2Ch 4:9

h De 4:19
  2Ki 17:16
  Jer 8:1, 2

i 2Ki 21:16
  Jer 19:4
  Eze 9:9

8:2 *A shining alloy of gold and silver.
8:3, 5 *Or "image."

8:10 *The Hebrew term may be related to a word for "dung" and is used as an expression of contempt. 8:12 *Or "in the inner rooms of his showpiece?"

keep offending me? Here they are thrusting out the branch* to my nose. **18** So I will act in rage. My eye will not feel sorry; nor will I feel compassion.ᵃ Even though they cry out loudly in my ears, I will not hear them."ᵇ

9 He then called out in my ears with a loud voice, saying: "Summon those who will bring punishment on the city, each one with his weapon for destruction in his hand!"

2 I saw six men coming from the direction of the upper gateᶜ that faces north, each with his weapon for smashing in his hand; and there was one man among them clothed in linen, with a secretary's inkhorn* at his waist, and they came in and stood beside the copper altar.ᵈ

3 Then the glory of the God of Israelᵉ rose from where it had rested above the cherubs and moved to the threshold of the doorway of the house,ᶠ and he began calling out to the man who was clothed in linen, at whose waist was the secretary's inkhorn. **4** Jehovah said to him: "Go through the city, through Jerusalem, and put a mark on the foreheads of the men who are sighing and groaningᵍ over all the detestable things that are being done in the city."ʰ

5 And to the others he said in my hearing: "Go through the city after him and strike. Do not let your eye feel sorry, and do not feel any compassion.ⁱ **6** Old man, young man, virgin, little child, and women you should kill off completely.ʲ But do not go near to any man on whom there is the mark.ᵏ You should start from my sanctuary." So they started with the elders who were in front of the house.ᵐ

7 Then he said to them: "Defile the house and fill the courtyards with the slain.ᵃ Go!" So they went out and struck down people in the city.

8 While they were striking them down, I alone was left, and I fell facedown and cried out: "Alas, O Sovereign Lord Jehovah! Are you going to destroy all the remaining ones of Israel while you pour out your rage on Jerusalem?"ᵇ

9 So he said to me: "The error of the house of Israel and Judah is very, very great.ᶜ The land is filled with bloodshed,ᵈ and the city is full of corruption.ᵉ For they say, 'Jehovah has left the land, and Jehovah is not seeing.'ᶠ **10** But as for me, my eye will not feel sorry; nor will I show compassion.ᵍ The consequences of their way I will bring down on their own head."

11 Then I saw the man clothed in linen with the inkhorn at his waist bringing back word, saying: "I have done just as you have commanded me."

10 As I was watching, I saw above the expanse that was over the heads of the cherubs something like a sapphire stone appearing above them, and its appearance resembled a throne.ʰ **2** Then he said to the man clothed in linen:ⁱ "Enter between the wheelwork,ʲ under the cherubs, and fill both your hands with burning coalsᵏ from between the cherubs and toss them over the city."ˡ So he entered as I watched.

3 The cherubs were standing to the right of the house when the man entered, and the cloud filled the inner courtyard. **4** And the glory of Jehovahᵐ rose up from the cherubs to the threshold of the doorway of the house, and the house gradually became filled with the cloud,ⁿ

CHAP. 8
a Eze 5:11
b Isa 1:15
Mic 3:4

CHAP. 9
c Jer 20:2
Eze 8:3
d 2Ch 4:1
e Eze 3:23
Eze 8:3, 4
Eze 11:22
f Eze 10:4
g Ps 119:53
2Pe 2:7, 8
h Eze 5:11
i Ex 32:26, 27
Eze 7:4
j 2Ch 36:17
k Ex 12:23
Jos 2:17-19
Re 9:4
l 2Ki 25:18, 21
Jer 25:29
m Eze 8:11

Second Col.
a La 2:21
b Ge 18:23
Eze 11:13
c 2Ch 36:14
Isa 1:4
d 2Ki 21:16
Jer 2:34
Mt 23:30
e Eze 22:29
f Isa 29:15
Eze 8:12
g Eze 5:11
Eze 7:4

CHAP. 10
h Isa 6:1
Eze 1:22, 26
Re 4:2, 3
i Eze 9:2
j Eze 1:16
k Eze 1:13
l 2Ki 25:8, 9
m Eze 1:27, 28
Eze 9:3
n Ex 40:35
2Ch 5:13
Eze 43:5

8:17 * Apparently a branch used in idolatrous worship. **9:2** *Or "a scribe's ink holder."

and the courtyard was full of the brightness of the glory of Jehovah. **5** And the sound of the wings of the cherubs could be heard in the outer courtyard, like the sound of God Almighty when he speaks.[a]

6 Then he commanded the man clothed in linen: "Take fire from between the wheelwork, from between the cherubs," and he entered and stood beside the wheel. **7** Then one of the cherubs stretched his hand out toward the fire that was between the cherubs.[b] He took some and put it into both hands of the one clothed in linen,[c] who now took it and went out. **8** The cherubs had what looked like the form of human hands under their wings.[d]

9 As I was watching, I saw four wheels beside the cherubs, one wheel beside each cherub, and the wheels appeared to glow like chrys'o·lite stone.[e] **10** As for their appearance, the four of them were alike, looking as though a wheel were within a wheel. **11** When they moved, they could go in any of the four directions without turning, because they would go to the place where the head would face without turning. **12** Their entire bodies, their backs, their hands, their wings, and the wheels of all four of them, were full of eyes all around.[f] **13** As regards the wheels, I heard a voice that called to them, "Wheelwork!"

14 Each one* had four faces. The first face was the face of the cherub, the second face was the face of a man,# the third was the face of a lion, and the fourth was the face of an eagle.[g] **15** And the cherubs would rise—they were the same living

creatures* that I had seen at the river Che'bar[a]— **16** and when the cherubs moved, the wheels would move alongside them; and when the cherubs lifted up their wings to be high above the earth, the wheels would not turn or move from their side.[b] **17** When these stood still, they would stand still; and when these rose, they would rise with them, for the spirit operating on the living creatures* was in them.

18 Then the glory of Jehovah[c] departed from over the threshold of the doorway of the house and stood still over the cherubs.[d] **19** The cherubs now lifted up their wings and rose from the earth as I watched. The wheels were also alongside them when they departed. They stopped at the entrance of the eastern gate of the house of Jehovah, and the glory of the God of Israel was above them.[e]

20 These were the living creatures* that I had seen under the God of Israel at the river Che'bar,[f] so I came to know that they were cherubs. **21** All four had four faces, four wings, and what appeared to be human hands under their wings.[g] **22** And the appearances of their faces were like the faces I had seen by the river Che'bar.[h] They would each go straight forward.[i]

11 And a spirit lifted me up and brought me to the eastern gate of the house of Jehovah, the gate that faces east.[j] There at the entrance of the gate I saw 25 men, and among them were Ja·az·a·ni'ah the son of Az'zur and Pel·a·ti'ah the son of Be·nai'ah, princes of the people.[k]

CHAP. 10
a Ps 29:3, 4
  Eze 1:24
  Joh 12:28, 29

b Eze 1:13

c Eze 9:2

d Eze 1:8

e Eze 1:15-18

f Re 4:6, 8

g Eze 1:6, 10
  Re 4:7

Second Col.
a Eze 1:3

b Eze 1:19-21

c Eze 1:27, 28

d Eze 9:3
  Eze 10:4

e Eze 11:22

f Eze 1:1, 22

g Eze 1:8

h Eze 1:10

i Eze 1:12
  Eze 10:11

CHAP. 11
j Eze 10:19

k Isa 1:23
  Eze 22:27

10:14 *That is, each of the cherubs. #Or "human."

10:15 *Lit., "it was the living creature." 10:17 *Lit., "the spirit of the living creature." 10:20 *Lit., "This is the living creature."

2 Then He said to me: "Son of man, these are the men who are scheming evil and giving wicked advice in* this city. **3** They are saying, 'Is it not the time for building houses?*ᵃ The city* is the cooking pot,*ᵇ and we are the flesh.'

4 "So prophesy against them. Prophesy, son of man."ᶜ

5 Then the spirit of Jehovah came upon me,ᵈ and he said to me: "Say, 'This is what Jehovah says: "What you have said is correct, O house of Israel, and I know what you are thinking.* **6** You have caused many to die in this city, and you have filled her streets with the dead."'"ᵉ **7** "Therefore this is what the Sovereign Lord Jehovah says: 'The dead bodies that you have strewn about the city are the flesh, and the city is the cooking pot.ᶠ But you yourselves will be taken out of it.'"

8 "'A sword you have feared,ᵍ and a sword I will bring against you,' declares the Sovereign Lord Jehovah. **9** 'I will bring you out of her and give you into the hand of foreigners and execute judgment on you.ʰ **10** You will fall by the sword.ⁱ I will judge you at the border of Israel,ʲ and you will have to know that I am Jehovah.ᵏ **11** The city will not be a cooking pot for you, and you will not be the flesh within it; I will judge you at the border of Israel, **12** and you will have to know that I am Jehovah. For you did not walk in my regulations and carry out my judgments,ˡ but you have acted in harmony with the judgments of the nations around you.'"ᵐ

11:2 *Or "against." **11:3** *Lit., "She," the city of Jerusalem, where the Jews thought they would be protected. #Or "wide-mouthed cooking pot." **11:5** *Or "the things that come up in your spirit."

13 As soon as I prophesied, Pel·a·ti′ah the son of Be·nai′ah died, and I fell facedown and cried with a loud voice: "Alas, O Sovereign Lord Jehovah! Are you going to exterminate the remaining ones of Israel?"ᵃ

14 The word of Jehovah again came to me, saying: **15** "Son of man, your brothers, those of your brothers with the right of repurchase, along with the entire house of Israel, have been told by the inhabitants of Jerusalem, 'Keep far away from Jehovah. The land is ours; it has been given to us as a possession.' **16** Therefore say, 'This is what the Sovereign Lord Jehovah says: "Although I have removed them far away among the nations and I have scattered them among the lands,ᵇ for a little while I will become a sanctuary for them in the lands to which they have gone."'ᶜ

17 "Therefore say, 'This is what the Sovereign Lord Jehovah says: "I will also collect you from the peoples and gather you from the lands to which you have been scattered, and I will give you the land of Israel.ᵈ **18** And they will return there and remove from it all its disgusting things and detestable practices.ᵉ **19** And I will give them a unified heart,*ᶠ and I will put a new spirit in them;ᵍ and I will remove the heart of stone from their bodiesʰ and give them a heart of flesh,#ⁱ **20** in order that they may walk in my statutes and observe my judgments and obey them. Then they will be my people, and I will be their God."'

21 "'But as for those whose hearts are set to continue in their disgusting things and their detestable practices, I will bring the consequences of their way

---

11:19 *Lit., "one heart." #That is, one sensitive to God's guidance.

CHAP. 11

a Eze 12:27

b Eze 24:3

c Eze 3:17
  Eze 20:46
  Eze 21:2

d 2Pe 1:21

e Eze 7:23
  Eze 22:3, 4

f Eze 24:6

g Jer 38:19

h Jer 39:6, 7
  Jer 52:24-27

i 2Ki 25:18-21
  2Ch 36:17

j 2Ki 14:25
  Jer 52:27

k Eze 6:13

l Ezr 9:7
  Ne 9:34

m De 12:29-31
  2Ch 28:1, 3
  Ps 106:34-36

_____
Second Col.

a Eze 9:8

b 2Ki 24:14, 15
  Jer 24:5

c Le 26:44

d Isa 11:11, 12
  Jer 30:10, 11
  Eze 34:13, 14
  Am 9:14, 15

e Eze 37:23

f Jer 24:7
  Jer 31:33
  Jer 32:39

g Ps 51:10
  Eze 36:31

h Zec 7:12

i Eze 36:26

upon their head," declares the Sovereign Lord Jehovah.'"

22 The cherubs now lifted up their wings, and the wheels were close to them,[a] and the glory of the God of Israel was above them.[b] **23** Then the glory of Jehovah[c] ascended from the city and stopped over the mountain to the east of the city.[d] **24** A spirit then lifted me up—through a vision by the spirit of God—and brought me to the exiled people in Chal·de′a. Then the vision that I had seen left me. **25** And I began to tell the exiled people all the things that Jehovah had shown me.

12 The word of Jehovah again came to me, saying: **2** "Son of man, you are living in a rebellious house. They have eyes to see, but they do not see, and ears to hear, but they do not hear,[e] for they are a rebellious house.[f] **3** As for you, son of man, prepare for yourself luggage for going into exile. Then, during the day while they are watching, you must go into exile. Go into exile from your home to another place while they are watching. Perhaps they will take notice, even though they are a rebellious house. **4** Bring out your luggage packed for going into exile during the day while they are watching, and then in the evening while they are watching, you should leave like someone being taken into exile.[g]

5 "While they are watching, bore a hole in the wall, and carry your belongings out through it.[h] **6** While they are watching, put your belongings on your shoulder and carry them out in the darkness. Cover your face so that you cannot see the ground, for I am making you a sign to the house of Israel."[i]

7 I did just as I was commanded. During the day I brought out my luggage as luggage for going into exile, and in the evening I bored a hole through the wall by hand. And when it was dark, I took out my belongings, carrying them on my shoulder right before their eyes.

8 In the morning the word of Jehovah again came to me, saying: **9** "Son of man, did not the house of Israel, the rebellious house, ask you, 'What are you doing?' **10** Tell them, 'This is what the Sovereign Lord Jehovah says: "This pronouncement concerns the chieftain[a] in Jerusalem and all the house of Israel within the city."'

11 "Say, 'I am a sign for you.[b] Just as I have done, that is what will be done to them. They will go into exile, into captivity.[c] **12** The chieftain who is among them will carry his belongings on his shoulder and leave in the darkness. He will bore a hole in the wall and carry his belongings out through it.[d] He will cover his face so that he cannot see the ground.' **13** I will cast my net over him, and he will be caught in my hunting net.[e] Then I will bring him to Babylon, to the land of the Chal·de′ans, but he will not see it; and there he will die.[f] **14** And all those around him, his helpers and his troops, I will scatter in every direction;[g] and I will draw out a sword to chase after them.[h] **15** And they will have to know that I am Jehovah when I disperse them among the nations and I scatter them among the lands. **16** But I will spare a few of them from the sword, the famine, and the pestilence, so that they may tell about all their detestable practices among the nations where they will go; and they will have to know that I am Jehovah."

17 And the word of Jehovah again came to me, saying: **18** "Son of man, you should eat

---

CHAP. 11

a Eze 1:19

b Eze 10:18, 19

c Eze 9:3
  Eze 10:4

d Zec 14:4

CHAP. 12

e Isa 6:9, 10
  Jer 5:21
  Ro 11:8

f Eze 2:3, 5

g 2Ch 36:20
  Jer 52:10, 11

h 2Ki 25:4

i Isa 8:18
  Eze 4:3
  Eze 24:24

Second Col.

a Jer 21:7
  Eze 21:25

b Eze 24:24

c Jer 52:15

d 2Ki 25:4
  Jer 39:4

e Jer 52:9
  Eze 17:20, 21

f 2Ki 25:6, 7
  Jer 34:3
  Jer 52:11
  Eze 17:16

g 2Ki 25:5

h Le 26:33
  Jer 42:15, 16

your bread with trembling and drink your water with agitation and anxiety.[a] **19** Say to the people of the land, 'This is what the Sovereign Lord Jehovah says to the inhabitants of Jerusalem in the land of Israel: "They will eat their bread with anxiety and drink their water with horror, for their land will become completely desolate[b] because of the violence of all those dwelling in it.[c] **20** The inhabited cities will be devastated, and the land will become a wasteland;[d] and you will have to know that I am Jehovah."'"[e]

21 And the word of Jehovah again came to me, saying: **22** "Son of man, what is this proverb that you have in Israel that says, 'The days go by, and every vision comes to nothing'?[f] **23** Therefore say to them, 'This is what the Sovereign Lord Jehovah says: "I will cause this saying to cease, and they will no more use it as a proverb in Israel."' But tell them, 'The days are near,[g] and every vision will take place.' **24** For there will no longer be any false vision or flattering* divination within the house of Israel.[h] **25** "'For I, Jehovah, will speak. Whatever word I speak will be done without any more delay.[i] In your days,[j] O rebellious house, I will say the word and carry it out,' declares the Sovereign Lord Jehovah.'"

26 The word of Jehovah again came to me, saying: **27** "Son of man, this is what the people* of Israel are saying, 'The vision that he sees is for a long time from now, and he is prophesying about the distant future.'[k] **28** Therefore say to them, 'This is what the Sovereign Lord Jehovah says: "'None of my words will be de-

12:24 *Or "deceitful." **12:27** *Lit., "the house."

CHAP. 12
a Le 26:26

b Isa 6:11
  Zec 7:14

c Ps 107:33, 34
  Jer 6:7

d Isa 64:10
  Jer 25:9

e Eze 6:13

f Isa 5:19
  Am 6:3
  2Pe 3:3, 4

g Joe 2:1
  Zep 1:14

h Jer 14:14
  La 2:14
  Eze 13:23

i La 2:17
  Zec 1:6

j Jer 16:9
  Hab 1:5

k Isa 5:19
  Isa 28:15
  2Pe 3:3, 4

Second Col.

CHAP. 13
a Mic 3:5
  Zep 3:4

b Jer 14:14
  Jer 23:16

c Jer 23:32

d Eze 22:30

e Isa 2:12
  Joe 1:15

f Jer 29:31, 32

g Eze 22:28

h Jer 14:14
  Jer 28:15, 16
  Jer 29:8, 9

i Eze 6:13
  Eze 11:10

---

layed; whatever I say will be done,' declares the Sovereign Lord Jehovah."'"

13 And the word of Jehovah again came to me, saying: **2** "Son of man, prophesy against the prophets of Israel,[a] and say to those who fabricate their own prophecies,*[b] 'Hear the word of Jehovah. **3** This is what the Sovereign Lord Jehovah says: "Woe to the stupid prophets, who follow their own spirit, when they have seen nothing![c] **4** O Israel, your prophets have become like foxes among the ruins. **5** You will not go to the broken places in the stone walls to rebuild them for the house of Israel,[d] so that Israel may keep standing in the battle in the day of Jehovah."[e] **6** "They have seen false visions and foretold a lie, those who are saying, 'The word of Jehovah is,' when Jehovah himself has not sent them, and they have waited for their word to come true.[f] **7** Is it not a false vision that you have seen and a lie that you have foretold when you say, 'The word of Jehovah is,' when I have not said anything?'"

8 "'Therefore this is what the Sovereign Lord Jehovah says: "'Because you have spoken what is false and your visions are a lie, I am against you,' declares the Sovereign Lord Jehovah."[g] **9** My hand is against the prophets whose visions are false and who foretell a lie.[h] They will not be among the people with whom I confide; nor will they be written in the registry of the house of Israel; nor will they return to the land of Israel; and you will have to know that I am the Sovereign Lord Jehovah.[i] **10** All of this is because they have led my people astray by saying, "There

13:2 *Or "who prophesy out of their own heart."

is peace!" when there is no peace.ᵃ When a flimsy partition wall is built, they are plastering it with whitewash.'*ᵇ

11 "Tell those plastering with whitewash that it will fall. A torrential downpour will come, hailstones* will fall, and powerful windstorms will break it down.ᶜ 12 And when the wall falls you will be asked, 'Where is your coating of plaster?'ᵈ

13 "Therefore this is what the Sovereign Lord Jehovah says: 'I will cause powerful windstorms to burst forth in my wrath, and a torrential downpour in my anger, and hailstones in destructive fury. 14 I will tear down the wall that you plastered with whitewash and bring it down to the earth, and its foundation will be exposed. When the city falls, you will perish within her; and you will have to know that I am Jehovah.'

15 "'When I fully unleash my wrath upon the wall and upon those who plastered it with whitewash, I will say to you: "The wall is no more, and those plastering it are no more.ᵉ 16 The prophets of Israel are gone, those who prophesy to Jerusalem and who see visions of peace for her, when there is no peace,"ᶠ declares the Sovereign Lord Jehovah.

17 "As for you, son of man, set your face against the daughters of your people who fabricate their own prophecies, and prophesy against them. 18 Tell them, 'This is what the Sovereign Lord Jehovah says: "Woe to the women who sew together bands for all arms* and make veils for heads of every

size in order to hunt down people's lives!* Are you hunting for the lives* of my people and trying to preserve your own lives?* 19 Will you profane me among my people for handfuls of barley and for scraps of bread,ᵃ putting to death those* who should not die and keeping alive those* who should not live, doing so by your lies to my people, who listen to your lies?"'ᵇ

20 "Therefore this is what the Sovereign Lord Jehovah says: 'Here I am against your bands, O women, which you use to hunt down people* as though they were birds, and I will rip them from your arms and release those whom you are hunting down like birds. 21 I will rip away your veils and rescue my people out of your hand, and they will no longer be something for you to catch in the hunt; and you will have to know that I am Jehovah.ᶜ 22 For you have disheartened the righteous one with your falsehoodᵈ when I was not causing him distress,* and you have strengthened the hands of the wicked one,ᵉ so that he does not turn back from his bad way and stay alive.ᶠ 23 Therefore, you women will no longer see false visions and practice divination;ᵍ and I will rescue my people from your hand, and you will have to know that I am Jehovah.'"

14 And some of the elders of Israel came and sat down before me.ʰ 2 Then the word of Jehovah came to me, saying: 3 "Son of man, these men are determined to follow their disgusting idols,* and they have set up a stumbling block that causes

---

CHAP. 13
a Jer 6:13, 14

b Isa 30:10
Eze 22:28

c Isa 27:8

d Jer 37:19

e Isa 30:12, 13

f Jer 6:13, 14
Jer 28:1-4

Second Col.
a Mic 3:11

b Jer 23:14

c Eze 6:13

d Jer 27:14

e Jer 23:14

f Jer 23:16, 17

g De 18:10, 14
Jer 27:9
Mic 3:6

CHAP. 14
h Eze 33:30, 31

13:10 *That is, building a weak interior wall and with whitewash trying to make it look strong. 13:11 *Lit., "and you, O hailstones." 13:18 *That is, magic bands worn around elbows or wrists. 13:18, 20 *Or "souls." 13:19 *Or "the souls." 13:22 *Or "pain." 14:3 *The Hebrew term may be related to a word for "dung" and is used as an expression of contempt.

people to sin. Should I let them inquire of me?[a] **4** Now speak with them and tell them, 'This is what the Sovereign Lord Jehovah says: "If an Israelite is determined to follow his disgusting idols and sets up a stumbling block causing people to sin and he then comes to inquire of a prophet, I, Jehovah, will answer him appropriately according to his many disgusting idols. **5** For I will cause terror in the hearts of the house of Israel* because they have all withdrawn from me and have gone after their disgusting idols."'[b]

6 "So tell the house of Israel, 'This is what the Sovereign Lord Jehovah says: "Come back and turn away from your disgusting idols and turn your faces away from all your detestable practices.[c] **7** For if any Israelite or foreign resident living in Israel separates himself from me and is determined to follow his disgusting idols and sets up a stumbling block that causes people to sin and then comes to inquire of my prophet,[d] I, Jehovah, I will personally answer him. **8** I will set my face against that man and make him a warning sign and a proverbial saying, and I will cut him off from my people;[e] and you will have to know that I am Jehovah."'

9 "'But if the prophet is fooled and gives a response, it is I, Jehovah, who have fooled that prophet.[f] I will then stretch out my hand against him and annihilate him from my people Israel. **10** They will have to bear their guilt; the guilt of the inquirer will be the same as the guilt of the prophet, **11** so that the house of Israel may stop wandering away from me and stop defiling themselves by all their

transgressions. And they will be my people, and I will be their God,'[a] declares the Sovereign Lord Jehovah."

12 And the word of Jehovah again came to me, saying: **13** "Son of man, if a land sins against me by acting unfaithfully, I will stretch out my hand against it and destroy its food supply,*[b] and I will send famine upon it[c] and cut off man and animal from it."[d] **14** "'Even if these three men—Noah,[e] Daniel,[f] and Job[g]—were within it, they would be able to save only themselves* because of their righteousness,'[h] declares the Sovereign Lord Jehovah."

15 "'Or suppose I make vicious wild animals pass through the land and they depopulate it* and make it a wasteland without anyone passing through because of the wild animals.[i] **16** As surely as I am alive,' declares the Sovereign Lord Jehovah, 'even if these three men were in it, they would save neither their sons nor their daughters; they would save only themselves, and the land would become desolate.'"

17 "'Or suppose I bring a sword against that land[j] and say: "Let a sword pass through the land," and cut off from it both man and animal,[k] **18** even if these three men were in it, as surely as I am alive,' declares the Sovereign Lord Jehovah, 'they would save neither their sons nor their daughters; they would save only themselves.'"

19 "'Or suppose I send a pestilence into that land[l] and pour out my rage on it with bloodshed to cut off from it man and animal, **20** even if Noah,[m] Daniel,[n]

CHAP. 14

a 2Ki 3:13
  Isa 1:15
  Jer 11:11

b Jer 2:5

c Isa 55:7

d Jer 21:1, 2
  Eze 33:31

e Le 20:2, 3

f 1Ki 22:21, 22
  Jer 4:10
  2Th 2:10, 11

Second Col.

a Jer 24:7
  Eze 11:19, 20

b Le 26:26

c Isa 3:1
  Jer 15:2

d Jer 7:20

e Ge 6:8, 9
  Heb 11:7

f Da 10:11

g Job 1:8
  Job 42:8

h Pr 11:4
  Jer 15:1
  2Pe 2:9

i Le 26:22
  Jer 15:3

j Le 26:25
  Jer 25:9
  Eze 21:3

k Zep 1:3

l De 28:21, 22

m Ge 7:1

n Da 10:11

14:5 *Lit., "seize the house of Israel in their heart." 14:13 *Lit., "break its bread rods." Possibly referring to rods used for storing bread. 14:14 *Or "their soul." 14:15 *Or "bereave it of children."

and Job[a] were in it, as surely as I am alive,' declares the Sovereign Lord Jehovah, 'they would save neither their sons nor their daughters; they would save only themselves* because of their righteousness.'"[b]

21 "For this is what the Sovereign Lord Jehovah says: 'So it will be when I send my four punishments*[c]—sword, famine, vicious wild animal, and pestilence[d]—against Jerusalem to cut off man and animal from it.[e] 22 However, some left in it will escape and be brought out,[f] both sons and daughters. They are coming to you, and when you see their ways and their deeds, you will certainly be comforted over the calamity that I brought on Jerusalem, over everything that I did to it.'"

23 "'They will comfort you when you see their ways and their deeds, and you will know that it was not without cause that I did what I had to do to it,'[g] declares the Sovereign Lord Jehovah."

15 The word of Jehovah again came to me, saying: 2 "Son of man, how does the wood of the vine compare with that of any other tree or branch from the trees of the forest? 3 Can a pole from it be used to do work? Or do people make a peg from it to hang utensils on? 4 Look! It is thrown into the fire for fuel, and the fire consumes both ends and scorches the middle. Is it now fit for any work? 5 Even when it was whole, it could not be used for anything. How much less useful it will be when the fire has consumed and scorched it!"

6 "Therefore this is what the Sovereign Lord Jehovah says: 'Just like the wood of the vine

among the trees of the forest, which I have given as fuel for the fire, so I will deal with the inhabitants of Jerusalem.[a] 7 I have set my face against them. They have escaped from the fire, but fire will consume them. And you will have to know that I am Jehovah when I set my face against them.'"[b]

8 "'And I will make the land desolate[c] because they have acted unfaithfully,'[d] declares the Sovereign Lord Jehovah."

16 The word of Jehovah again came to me, saying: 2 "Son of man, make known to Jerusalem her detestable practices.[e] 3 You must say, 'This is what the Sovereign Lord Jehovah says to Jerusalem: "Your origin and your birth were in the land of the Ca′naan·ite. Your father was an Am′or·ite,[f] and your mother was a Hit′tite.[g] 4 As for your birth, on the day you were born, your umbilical cord was not cut, you were not washed in water to make you clean, you were not rubbed with salt, and you were not wrapped in cloths. 5 No one pitied you enough to do any of these things. No one had compassion for you. Instead, you were thrown into the open field because you were* hated on the day you were born.

6 "'"When I was passing by, I saw you kicking about in your own blood, and as you lay there in your blood, I said: 'Keep living!' Yes, I said to you lying there in your blood: 'Keep living!' 7 I made you a very great multitude, like plants sprouting in the field, and you grew up and developed and wore the finest ornaments. Your breasts became firm, and your hair grew; but you were still naked and exposed."'

CHAP. 14
a Job 1:8
 Job 42:8

b Eze 18:20
 Zep 2:3

c Jer 15:2

d Eze 5:17
 Eze 33:27

e Jer 32:43

f De 4:31
 2Ch 36:20
 Eze 6:8
 Mic 5:7

g Ne 9:33
 Jer 22:8, 9
 Eze 9:9
 Da 9:7

Second Col.

CHAP. 15
a Ps 80:14-16
 Isa 5:24
 Jer 7:20
 Eze 20:47

b Eze 6:7
 Eze 7:4

c Isa 6:11
 Jer 25:11
 Eze 6:14

d 2Ch 36:14

CHAP. 16
e Eze 8:10
 Eze 20:4

f Jos 10:5
 1Ki 21:25, 26
 2Ki 21:11

g 1Ch 1:13, 14

14:20 *Or "their soul." 14:21 *Or "my four injurious acts of judgment."

16:5 *Or "your soul was."

8 "'When I was passing by and saw you, I noticed that you were old enough for expressions of love. So I spread my garment* over you[a] and covered your nakedness and made an oath and entered into a covenant with you,' declares the Sovereign Lord Jehovah, 'and you became mine. **9** Furthermore, I washed you with water and rinsed away your blood and put oil on you.[b] **10** I then clothed you with an embroidered garment and gave you fine leather* sandals and wrapped you in fine linen, and I clothed you with costly garments. **11** I adorned you with ornaments and put bracelets on your hands and a necklace around your neck. **12** I also put a ring in your nose and earrings on your ears and a beautiful crown on your head. **13** You kept adorning yourself with gold and silver, and your clothing was fine linen, costly material, and an embroidered garment. Fine flour, honey, and oil were what you ate, and you grew to be extremely beautiful,[c] and you became fit to be a queen.'"*

14 "'Your fame* began to spread among the nations[d] because of your beauty, for it was perfect because my own splendor I placed upon you,'[e] declares the Sovereign Lord Jehovah."

15 "'But you began to trust in your beauty,[f] and you became a prostitute because of your fame.[g] You lavished your acts of prostitution on everyone passing by,[h] and your beauty became his. **16** You took some of your garments and made colorful high places where you prostituted yourself[i]—such things should not take place, nor should they ever happen. **17** You also took your

beautiful jewelry* made from the gold and silver that I had given to you and you made for yourself male images and prostituted yourself with them.[a] **18** And you took your embroidered garments and covered them,* and you offered them my oil and my incense.[b] **19** And the bread that I had given to you—made from fine flour, oil, and honey that I gave you to eat—you also offered to them as a pleasing* aroma.[c] That is exactly what happened,' declares the Sovereign Lord Jehovah."

20 "'You took your sons and your daughters whom you had borne to me,[d] and you sacrificed these to idols to be devoured[e]—have your acts of prostitution not gone far enough? **21** You slaughtered my sons, and you offered them as sacrifices by making them pass through the fire.[f] **22** While engaging in all your detestable practices and acts of prostitution, you did not remember the days of your youth when you were naked and exposed, kicking about in your own blood. **23** After all your evil, woe, woe to you,'[g] declares the Sovereign Lord Jehovah. **24** 'You built yourself a mound and made a high place for yourself in every public square. **25** You built your high places at the most prominent place of every street, and you turned your beauty into something detestable by offering yourself* to everyone passing by,[h] and you multiplied your acts of prostitution.[i] **26** You prostituted yourself to the sons of Egypt,[j] your lustful neighbors,* and you of-

---

CHAP. 16
a Ru 3:9

b Ps 23:5

c Ps 48:2

d 1Ki 4:21

e 1Ki 10:1
Ps 50:2
La 2:15

f Jer 7:4
Mic 3:11

g 1Ki 11:5, 7
Ps 106:35, 36
Isa 57:7, 8
Jer 2:20
Jas 4:4

h Jer 3:13

i 1Ki 14:22, 23
2Ch 21:5, 11

Second Col.
a Isa 57:7, 8

b Eze 8:10, 11

c 2Ki 22:16, 17

d Ex 13:2

e Ps 106:37, 38

f Le 18:21
Le 20:2
2Ki 16:1, 3
2Ch 33:1, 6
Jer 7:31
Eze 20:26

g Jer 13:27
Zep 3:1

h Jer 2:23, 24

i Jer 3:2

j Isa 30:2, 3
Jer 2:36

16:8 *Or "skirt." 16:10 *Or "sealskin." 16:13 *Or "fit for a royal position." 16:14 *Lit., "name."

16:17 *Or "ornaments." 16:18 *That is, the male idols. 16:19 *Or "appeasing; soothing." Lit., "restful." 16:25 *Lit., "spreading your legs." 16:26 *Lit., "your neighbors great of flesh."

fended me with your countless acts of prostitution. **27** Now I will bring my hand against you and diminish your food allowance[a] and give you over to the will* of the women who hate you,[b] the daughters of the Phi·lis′tines, who were appalled because of your obscene conduct.[c]

28 "'Because you could not be satisfied, you then prostituted yourself to the sons of As·syr′i·a,[d] but after prostituting yourself to them, you still did not find satisfaction. **29** So you increased your prostitution toward the land of traders* and toward the Chal·de′ans,[e] but even then you did not find satisfaction. **30** How sick* your heart was,[f] declares the Sovereign Lord Jehovah, 'when you did all these things, behaving like a brazen prostitute![f] **31** But when you built your mound at the most prominent place of every street and made your high place in every public square, you were not like a prostitute, because you refused any payment. **32** You are an adulterous wife who takes strangers instead of her own husband![g] **33** People give all prostitutes a gift,[h] but you are the one who has given gifts to all those lusting after you,[i] and you bribe them to come to you from all around to commit prostitution.[j] **34** You are the opposite of other women who engage in prostitution. No one commits prostitution your way! You pay others, and they do not pay you. Your way is the opposite.'

35 "Therefore, O prostitute,[k] hear the word of Jehovah. **36** This is what the Sovereign Lord Jehovah says: 'Because

your lust has been poured out and your nakedness has been exposed during your prostitution with your lovers and all your detestable, disgusting idols*[a] to which you even sacrificed the blood of your sons,[b] **37** therefore I am collecting together all the lovers you have given pleasure to, all those you loved together with all those you hated. I will collect them together against you from all around and expose your nakedness to them, and they will see you completely naked.[c]

38 "'And I will punish you with the judgments that adulteresses[d] and women shedding blood[e] deserve, and your blood will be shed in rage and jealousy.[f] **39** I will give you into their hand, and they will tear down your mounds, and your high places will be pulled down;[g] and they will strip you of your garments[h] and take your beautiful jewelry*[i] and leave you naked and exposed. **40** They will bring against you a crowd,[j] and they will stone you[k] and will slaughter you with their swords.[l] **41** They will burn your houses with fire[m] and execute judgment on you before the eyes of many women; and I will bring an end to your prostitution,[n] and you will stop giving payment. **42** I will satisfy my rage against you,[o] and my indignation will turn away from you;[p] and I will be calm and no longer feel offended.'

43 "'Because you did not remember the days of your youth[q] and you have angered me by doing all these things, I will now bring the consequences of your ways on your own head,'

	CHAP. 16
a	De 28:48
b	Ps 106:41
c	Jer 2:11, 12
d	2Ki 16:7
e	Eze 23:14, 16
f	Jer 3:3
g	Jer 3:1, 20
h	Ge 38:16
i	Isa 57:9
j	2Ch 16:2, 3
k	Isa 1:21
	Jer 3:6

	Second Col.
a	2Ki 21:11
b	Ps 106:37, 38
c	Jer 13:22 La 1:8
d	Ge 38:24 Le 20:10 De 22:22
e	Ge 9:6 Ex 21:12
f	Ps 79:2, 3 Eze 23:25
g	Isa 27:9 Eze 16:24
h	Jer 4:30
i	Isa 3:18-23 Eze 23:26
j	Eze 23:46, 47 Hab 1:6
k	De 22:20, 21
l	2Ch 36:17 Jer 25:9
m	2Ki 25:8, 9
n	Eze 23:27
o	Eze 5:13
p	Isa 40:2
q	Jer 2:32

16:27 * Or "soul." **16:29** * Lit., "land of Canaan." **16:30** * Or "weak." # Or possibly, "O how I am filled up with rage against you."

16:36 * The Hebrew term may be related to a word for "dung" and is used as an expression of contempt. **16:39** * Or "ornaments."

declares the Sovereign Lord Jehovah, 'and you will no longer carry on your obscene conduct and all your detestable practices.

44 "'Look! Everyone who uses proverbs will apply this proverb to you: "Like mother, like daughter!"ª **45** You are the daughter of your mother, who despised her husband and her children. And you are the sister of your sisters, who despised their husbands and their children. Your mother was a Hit'tite, and your father was an Am'or·ite.'"ᵇ

46 "'Your older sister is Sa·mar'i·a,ᶜ who is dwelling to the north of you* with her daughters,#ᵈ and your younger sister, who is dwelling to the south of you,△ is Sod'omᵉ with her daughters.ᶠ **47** Not only did you walk in their ways and follow their detestable practices, but in a short while you were even more corrupt in all your conduct than they were.ᵍ **48** As surely as I am alive,' declares the Sovereign Lord Jehovah, 'Sod'om your sister and her daughters have not done what you and your daughters have done. **49** Look! This was the error of Sod'om your sister: She and her daughtersʰ were proudⁱ and had an abundance of foodʲ and carefree tranquillity;ᵏ yet they did not support the afflicted and the poor.ˡ **50** They remained haughtyᵐ and carried on detestable practices in my sight,ⁿ so I found it necessary to remove them.ᵒ

51 "'Nor did Sa·mar'i·aᵖ commit even half as many sins as you did. You kept making your detestable practices abound more than they have, to the point that your sisters appeared righ-

16:46 *Lit., "on your left." # Probably referring to dependent towns. △ Lit., "on your right."

CHAP. 16
a 1Ki 21:25, 26
  2Ki 21:2, 9
  Ps 106:35, 36

b De 20:17
  Jos 10:5
  2Ki 21:11
  Eze 16:3

c Eze 23:33

d Jer 3:8

e Ge 18:20
  Isa 3:9
  Jer 23:14

f Ge 19:24, 25

g 2Ki 21:2, 9
  Eze 5:5, 6

h Jude 7

i Pr 16:5

j Ge 13:10

k Pr 1:32

l Pr 21:13

m Pr 16:18

n Ge 13:13
  Ge 18:20
  Ge 19:4, 5

o Ge 19:24, 25
  La 4:6
  2Pe 2:6

p 2Ki 21:13
  Jer 23:13
  Eze 23:33

Second Col.

a Jer 3:11

b Ps 126:1

c Eze 36:11

d Eze 21:24

e 2Ch 28:18

f Isa 3:11
  Ga 6:7

g De 29:12
  Jer 22:8, 9

h Jer 32:40
  Jer 50:4, 5

teous because of all your detestable practices.ª **52** You must now bear your humiliation because you have justified the behavior* of your sisters. On account of your sin of acting more detestably than they have, they are more righteous than you. So now, be ashamed and bear the humiliation of making your sisters appear righteous.'

53 "'And I will gather their captives, the captives of Sod'om and her daughters and the captives of Sa·mar'i·a and her daughters; I will also gather your captives along with them,ᵇ **54** so that you may bear your humiliation; and you will feel humiliated because of what you have done by comforting them. **55** Your own sisters, Sod'om and her daughters, will return to their former state, and Sa·mar'i·a and her daughters will return to their former state, and you along with your own daughters will return to your former state.ᶜ **56** Sod'om your sister was not worthy of your mention in the day of your pride, **57** before your own wickedness was exposed.ᵈ Now the daughters of Syria and her neighbors reproach you, and the daughters of the Phi·lis'tines,ᵉ those all around you, treat you with scorn. **58** You will bear the consequences of your obscene conduct and your detestable practices,' declares Jehovah."

59 "For this is what the Sovereign Lord Jehovah says: 'I will now do with you just as you have done,ᶠ for you despised the oath by breaking my covenant.ᵍ **60** But I myself will remember the covenant that I made with you in the days of your youth, and I will establish with you a permanent covenant.ʰ **61** You

16:52 *Or "have argued in favor."

will remember your behavior and feel humiliated[a] when you welcome your sisters, those older than you as well as those younger than you, and I will give them to you as daughters, but not because of your covenant.'

62 "'And I myself will establish my covenant with you; and you will have to know that I am Jehovah. **63** Then you will remember and be too ashamed to open your mouth because of your humiliation,[b] when I make an atonement for you despite all that you have done,'[c] declares the Sovereign Lord Jehovah."

17 The word of Jehovah again came to me, saying: **2** "Son of man, tell a riddle and relate a proverb about the house of Israel.[d] **3** You must say, 'This is what the Sovereign Lord Jehovah says: "The great eagle,[e] with great wings, long pinions, and full, colorful plumage, came to Leb'a·non[f] and took the top of the cedar.[g] **4** He plucked off its topmost shoot and brought it to the land of traders* and set it down in a city of traders.[h] **5** He then took some of the seed of the land[i] and put it in a fertile field. He planted it like a willow by abundant waters. **6** So it sprouted and became a low, sprawling vine[j] with its foliage facing inward and its roots growing under it. Thus it became a vine and produced shoots and sent out branches.[k]

7 "'And there came another great eagle,[l] with great wings and large pinions.[m] This vine then stretched its roots eagerly toward him, away from the garden beds where it was planted, and it sent out its foliage toward him so that he would irrigate it.[n] **8** It had already been planted in a good field near abundant wa-

ters, in order to produce branches, to bear fruit, and to become a majestic vine."'[a]

9 "Say, 'This is what the Sovereign Lord Jehovah says: "Will it prosper? Will someone not tear out its roots[b] and make its fruit rot and cause its sprouts to wither?[c] It will become so dry that neither a strong arm nor many people will be needed to pull it up by the roots. **10** Although it is transplanted, will it prosper? Will it not dry up completely when the east wind blows on it? It will dry up in the garden bed where it sprouted."'"

11 And the word of Jehovah again came to me, saying: **12** "Please tell the rebellious house, 'Do you not realize what these things mean?' Say, 'Look! The king of Babylon came to Jerusalem and took its king and its princes and brought them back with him to Babylon.[d] **13** Furthermore, he took one of the royal offspring*[e] and made a covenant with him and put him under an oath.[f] Then he took away the prominent men of the land,[g] **14** so that the kingdom would be brought low, unable to rise up, so that only by keeping his covenant might it continue to exist.[h] **15** But the king finally rebelled against him[i] by sending his messengers to Egypt to obtain horses[j] and a large army from them.[k] Will he succeed? Will the one doing these things escape punishment? Can he break the covenant and still escape?'[l]

16 "'As surely as I am alive,' declares the Sovereign Lord Jehovah, "he will die in Babylon, in the place where the king* who made him# king lives, the one whose oath he despised and whose covenant he broke.[m]

CHAP. 16
a Eze 20:43
b Ezr 9:6
  Eze 36:31
c Ps 103:12
  Mic 7:18, 19

CHAP. 17
d Ho 12:10
e De 28:49, 50
  Jer 4:13
  La 4:19
f Jer 22:23
g 2Ki 24:12
  2Ch 36:9, 10
  Jer 24:1
h 2Ki 24:15
i 2Ki 24:17
  Jer 37:1
j Eze 17:13, 14
k 2Ch 36:11
l Eze 17:15
m Jer 37:5, 7
n 2Ki 24:20
  2Ch 36:11, 13

Second Col.
a Jer 37:1
b Jer 21:7
c 2Ki 25:7
d 2Ki 24:12, 14
  Isa 39:7
  Jer 22:24, 25
  Jer 52:31, 32
e 2Ki 24:17
  Jer 37:1
f 2Ch 36:11, 13
g 2Ki 24:15
  Jer 24:1
h Jer 27:12
  Jer 38:17
i 2Ki 24:20
  2Ch 36:11, 13
j De 17:16
k Jer 37:5
l Jer 32:3, 4
m Jer 34:2, 3
  Jer 52:11

17:4 *Lit., "land of Canaan." **17:13** *Lit., "seed." **17:16** *That is, Nebuchadnezzar. #That is, Zedekiah.

17 And the great army and numerous troops of Phar′aoh will be of no help in the war,[a] when siege ramparts are raised and siege walls are built to destroy many lives.* **18** He has despised an oath and broken a covenant. Even though he gave his promise,* he has done all these things, and he will not escape.'"

19 "'Therefore this is what the Sovereign Lord Jehovah says: "As surely as I am alive, I will bring upon his head the consequences of despising my oath[b] and breaking my covenant. **20** I will cast my net over him, and he will be caught in my hunting net.[c] I will bring him to Babylon and enter into judgment with him there because of the unfaithfulness he committed against me.[d] **21** All the fugitives of his troops will fall by the sword, and those remaining will be scattered in every direction."*[e] Then you will have to know that I myself, Jehovah, have spoken."'[f]

22 "'This is what the Sovereign Lord Jehovah says: "I will take a shoot from the top of the lofty cedar[g] and plant it, from the top of its twigs I will pluck a tender shoot,[h] and I myself will plant it on a high and lofty mountain.[i] **23** On a high mountain of Israel I will plant it; and its branches will grow, and it will produce fruit and become a majestic cedar. And every kind of bird will live beneath it and reside in the shadow of its foliage. **24** And all the trees of the field will have to know that I myself, Jehovah, have brought down the high tree and exalted the low tree;[j] I have dried up the green tree and made the dry tree blossom.[k] I myself, Jehovah, have spoken and have done it."'"

---

18 And the word of Jehovah again came to me, saying: **2** "What does this proverb that you quote in the land of Israel mean, 'Fathers have eaten sour grapes, but the teeth of the sons are set on edge'?[a]

3 "'As surely as I am alive,' declares the Sovereign Lord Jehovah, 'you will not continue to quote this saying in Israel. **4** Look! All the souls*—to me they belong. As the soul of the father so also the soul of the son —to me they belong. The soul* who sins is the one who will die.

5 "'Suppose that a man is righteous and does what is just and right. **6** He does not eat idolatrous sacrifices on the mountains;[b] he does not look up to the disgusting idols* of the house of Israel; he does not defile his neighbor's wife[c] or have relations with a woman who is menstruating;[d] **7** he does not mistreat anyone,[e] but he returns what a debtor has given him in pledge;[f] he does not rob anyone,[g] but he gives his own food to the hungry one[h] and covers the naked one with a garment;[i] **8** he does not charge interest or engage in usury,[j] but he refrains from acting with injustice;[k] he executes true justice between one man and another;[l] **9** and he keeps walking in my statutes and observing my judicial decisions in order to act in faithfulness. Such a man is righteous and will surely keep living,'[m] declares the Sovereign Lord Jehovah.

10 "'But suppose that he has become father to a son who is a robber[n] or a murderer*[o] or who

---

CHAP. 17
a Jer 37:7, 8
  La 4:17
  Eze 29:6
b De 5:11
c Eze 12:13
d Eze 20:36
e Eze 12:14
f Eze 6:13
g Isa 11:1
  Jer 23:5
h Isa 53:2
i Ps 2:6
j Isa 9:6
  Eze 21:26, 27
  Da 4:17
  Am 9:11
k 1Sa 2:7, 8
  Lu 1:52

Second Col.

CHAP. 18
a Jer 31:29, 30
b De 12:2
  Jer 3:6
c Le 20:10
d Le 18:19
  Le 20:18
e Pr 14:21
f De 24:12, 13
g Le 6:2, 4
h De 15:11
i Isa 58:6, 7
  Jas 2:15, 16
j Ex 22:25
  Ps 15:5
  Lu 6:34, 35
k Le 19:35
l Le 19:15
  Le 25:14
  De 1:16
m Le 18:5
n Le 19:13
o Ge 9:6
  Ex 21:12

17:17 *Or "souls." 17:18 *Lit., "gave his hand." 17:21 *Lit., "to every wind."

18:4 *Or "lives." See Glossary. *Or "person." See Glossary. 18:6 *The Hebrew term may be related to a word for "dung" and is used as an expression of contempt. 18:10 *Lit., "shedder of blood."

does any of these other things
11 (though the father has not
done any of these things)—he
eats idolatrous sacrifices on the
mountains, defiles his neighbor's wife, **12** mistreats the
needy and the poor,[a] takes
things by robbery, does not return a pledge, looks up to the
disgusting idols,[b] engages in detestable practices,[c] **13** engages
in usury and charges interest[d]—
then the son will not keep living.
Because of all these detestable
things that he has done, he will
surely be put to death. His own
blood will be upon him.

14 "'But suppose that a father has a son who sees all the
sins his father has committed,
and though he sees them, he
does not do such things. **15** He
does not eat idolatrous sacrifices on the mountains; he does
not look up to the disgusting idols of the house of Israel;
he does not defile his neighbor's
wife; **16** he does not mistreat
anyone; he does not seize what
was pledged; he does not take
anything in robbery; he gives his
own food to the hungry one and
covers the naked one with a garment; **17** he refrains from oppressing the poor; he does not
engage in usury or charge interest; and he carries out my judicial decisions and walks in my
statutes. Such a man will not die
because of the error of his father. He will surely keep living.
18 But because his father practiced fraud, robbed his brother,
and did what was wrong among
his people, he will die for his
error.

19 "'But you will say: "Why
does the son not bear guilt because of his father's error?"
Since the son has done what is
just and righteous, has kept all
my statutes and has observed
them, he will surely keep living.[e]

20 The soul* who sins is the one
who will die.[a] A son will bear no
guilt because of the error of his
father, and a father will bear no
guilt because of the error of his
son. The righteousness of the
righteous one will be accounted to him alone, and the wickedness of the wicked one will be
accounted to him alone.[b]

21 "'Now if someone wicked turns away from all the sins
he has committed and keeps my
statutes and does what is just
and righteous, he will surely
keep living. He will not die.[c]
22 None of the transgressions
that he has committed will be
held* against him.[d] He will keep
living for doing what is righteous.'[e]

23 "'Do I take any pleasure
at all in the death of a wicked
person?'[f] declares the Sovereign
Lord Jehovah. 'Do I not prefer
that he turn away from his ways
and keep living?'[g]

24 "'But when someone righteous abandons his righteousness and does what is wrong,*
doing all the detestable things
the wicked do, will he live? None
of the righteous acts that he did
will be remembered.[h] For his unfaithfulness and the sin he has
committed, he will die.[i]

25 "'But you will say: "The
way of Jehovah is unjust."[j] Please
listen, O house of Israel! Is it my
way that is unjust?[k] Is it not your
ways that are unjust?'[l]

26 "'When someone righteous abandons his righteousness and does what is wrong and
dies because of it, he will die for
his own wrongdoing.

27 "'And when someone wicked turns away from the wickedness that he has committed and
begins to do what is just and

18:20 *Or "person." **18:22** *Lit., "remembered." **18:24** *Or "does injustice."

CHAP. 18
a De 15:7, 8

b Le 26:30

c 2Ki 21:11

d Eze 22:12

e De 16:20
  Ro 10:5

Second Col.
a De 24:16
  Jer 31:30
  Eze 18:4

b Isa 3:10, 11
  Ga 6:7

c Isa 55:7
  Eze 3:21
  Eze 33:12, 19
  Ac 3:19

d 2Ch 33:12, 13
  Ps 25:7
  Isa 43:25

e Eze 33:16

f La 3:33
  Eze 33:11
  1Ti 2:3, 4
  2Pe 3:9

g Mic 7:18

h Eze 33:12, 18
  Heb 10:38
  2Jo 8

i Pr 21:16
  Eze 3:20

j Job 35:2
  Pr 19:3
  Eze 33:17, 20

k De 32:4

l Isa 55:9
  Jer 2:17

righteous, he will preserve his own life.*[a] 28 When he realizes and turns away from all the transgressions that he has committed, he will surely keep living. He will not die.

29 "'But the house of Israel will say: "The way of Jehovah is unjust." Is it really my ways that are unjust, O house of Israel?[b] Is it not your ways that are unjust?'

30 "'Therefore, I will judge each one of you according to his ways,[c] O house of Israel,' declares the Sovereign Lord Jehovah. 'Turn away, yes, turn completely away from all your transgressions, so that they will not be a stumbling block bringing guilt upon you. 31 Rid yourselves of all the transgressions you have committed[d] and acquire* a new heart and a new spirit,[e] for why should you die,[f] O house of Israel?'

32 "'I do not take any pleasure in the death of anyone,'[g] declares the Sovereign Lord Jehovah. 'So turn back and live.'"[h]

19 "You must sing a dirge* concerning the chieftains of Israel 2 and say,

'What was your mother?
    A lioness among lions.
She lay down among strong
    young lions* and reared
    her cubs.
3 She raised one of her cubs,
    and he became a strong
    young lion.[i]
He learned how to tear prey
    apart,
He even devoured humans.
4 Nations heard about him and
    caught him in their pit,
And they brought him to the
    land of Egypt with hooks.[j]

5 She waited and eventually
    saw that there was no hope
    for his return.
So she took another of her
    cubs and sent him out as
    a strong young lion.
6 He also walked about among
    the lions and became a
    strong young lion.
He learned how to tear
    prey apart, and he even
    devoured humans.[a]
7 He prowled among their
    fortified towers and
    devastated their cities,
So that the desolate land
    was filled with the sound
    of his roaring.[b]
8 Nations from the surround-
    ing districts came against
    him to cast their net
    over him,
And he was caught in
    their pit.
9 With hooks they put him
    in a cage and brought him
    to the king of Babylon.
There they confined him,
    so that his voice would
    no more be heard on the
    mountains of Israel.
10 Your mother was like a vine[c]
    in your blood,* planted
    by waters.
It bore fruit and was full
    of branches because of
    the abundant water.
11 It developed strong
    branches,* fit for the
    scepters of rulers.
It grew and towered over
    the other trees,
And it became visible
    because of its height
    and because of the
    abundance of its foliage.
12 But in fury she was
    uprooted[d] and thrown
    to the earth,
And an east wind dried up
    her fruit.

CHAP. 18
a Isa 55:7
  1Ti 4:16

b Ge 18:25
  Ps 145:17
  Isa 40:14

c Job 34:11
  Ro 2:6

d Ps 34:14
  Isa 1:16

e Ps 51:10
  Jer 32:39
  Eze 11:19
  Eph 4:23, 24

f De 30:15
  Pr 8:36
  Ac 13:46

g Jer 29:11
  La 3:33
  Eze 33:11
  Lu 15:10
  2Pe 3:9

h De 30:16

CHAP. 19
i 2Ch 36:1

j 2Ki 23:31-34
  2Ch 36:4
  Jer 22:11, 12

Second Col.
a Jer 22:17

b Pr 28:15

c Ps 80:8
  Isa 5:7

d Isa 5:5
  Eze 15:6

18:27 *Or "soul." See Glossary. 18:31 *Lit., "make for yourselves." 19:1 *Or "song of mourning." 19:2 *Or "among maned young lions."

19:10 *Or possibly, "like a vine in your vineyard." 19:11 *Or "rods."

Her strong branches were
    torn off and became dry,[a]
    and fire consumed them.[b]
13 Now she is planted in the
    wilderness,
    In a waterless, thirsty land.[c]
14 The fire spread from her
    branches[*] and consumed
    her shoots and her fruit,
And there was no strong
    branch left, no scepter
    for ruling.[d]

    "'That is a dirge, and it will
serve as a dirge.'"

20 Now in the seventh year,
    in the fifth month, on the
tenth day of the month, some
of the elders of Israel came and
sat down before me to inquire
of Jehovah. **2** Then the word
of Jehovah came to me, saying:
3 "Son of man, speak with the
elders of Israel, and tell them,
'This is what the Sovereign Lord
Jehovah says: "Are you coming
to inquire of me? 'As surely as
I am alive, I will not respond to
your inquiry,'[e] declares the Sovereign Lord Jehovah."'

4 "Are you ready to judge
them?[*] Are you ready to judge
them, son of man? Make them
know the detestable things that
their forefathers did.[f] **5** Tell
them, 'This is what the Sovereign Lord Jehovah says: "In the
day I chose Israel,[g] I also swore[*]
to the offspring[#] of the house
of Jacob, and I made myself
known to them in the land of
Egypt.[h] Yes, I swore to them
and said, 'I am Jehovah your
God.' **6** In that day I swore that
I would bring them out of the
land of Egypt to a land that I
had searched out[*] for them,
one flowing with milk and honey.[i] It was the most beautiful[#] of

all the lands. **7** I then said to
them, 'Each of you must throw
away the detestable things that
are before your eyes; do not defile yourselves with the disgusting idols[*] of Egypt.[a] I am Jehovah your God.'[b]

8 "'"But they rebelled against
me and were not willing to listen
to me. They did not throw away
the detestable things that were
before them, and they would not
abandon the disgusting idols of
Egypt.[c] So I promised to pour
out my rage on them and to
unleash my anger fully against
them in the land of Egypt.
9 But I acted for the sake of my
name so that it would not be profaned before the nations among
whom they were living.[d] For I
made myself known to them[*]
before these nations when I
brought them[*] out of the land of
Egypt.[e] **10** So I brought them
out of the land of Egypt and led
them into the wilderness.[f]

11 "'"I then gave them my statutes[*] and made my judicial decisions known to them,[g] so that the
man who follows them may have
life by them.[h] **12** I also gave my
sabbaths to them[i] as a sign between me and them,[j] so that they
would know that I, Jehovah, am
the one sanctifying them.

13 "'"But the house of Israel
rebelled against me in the wilderness.[k] They did not walk in
my statutes, and they rejected
my judicial decisions, which if a
man follows them, he will have
life by them. They utterly profaned my sabbaths. So I promised to pour out my fury on
them in the wilderness to exterminate them.[l] **14** I acted for
the sake of my own name so

CHAP. 19
a 2Ki 23:34
  2Ki 24:6
  2Ki 25:5-7
b De 32:22
  Eze 15:4
c De 28:48
  Jer 17:5, 6
  Jer 52:27
d Eze 17:16, 18

CHAP. 20
e Isa 1:12, 15
  Eze 14:3
f Eze 16:51
  Eze 22:2
  Lu 11:47
g De 7:6
h Ex 4:31
  Ex 6:7, 8
i Ex 3:8

Second Col.
a Le 18:3
  De 29:16, 17
  Jos 24:14
b Le 20:7
c Ex 32:4
d Nu 14:13-16
  De 9:27, 28
  1Sa 12:22
e Ex 32:11, 12
  Jos 2:9, 10
  Jos 9:3, 9
  1Sa 4:7, 8
f Ex 13:17, 18
  Ex 15:22
g De 4:8
h De 8:3
  De 30:16
i Le 20:8-10
  Le 23:3, 24
  Le 25:4, 11
j Ex 31:13
  Ex 35:2
k Ex 32:8
  Nu 14:22, 23
l Nu 14:11, 12

19:14 *Or "rods." 20:4 *Or "to pronounce judgment on them?" 20:5
*Lit., "raised my hand." #Lit., "seed."
20:6 *Or "spied out." #Or "the decoration."

20:7 *The Hebrew term may be related
to a word for "dung" and is used as an
expression of contempt. 20:9 *That
is, Israel.

that it would not be profaned before the nations, in whose sight I brought them* out.[a] 15 I also swore to them in the wilderness that I would not bring them into the land that I had given them[b] —a land flowing with milk and honey,[c] the most beautiful* of all the lands— 16 because they rejected my judicial decisions, they did not walk in my statutes, and they profaned my sabbaths, for their heart was following after their disgusting idols.[d]

17 ""But I* felt sorry for them, and I did not destroy them; I did not exterminate them in the wilderness. 18 I said to their sons in the wilderness,[e] 'Do not walk in the regulations of your forefathers[f] or keep their judgments or defile yourselves with their disgusting idols. 19 I am Jehovah your God. Walk in my statutes, and keep my judicial decisions, and carry them out.[g] 20 And sanctify my sabbaths,[h] and they will serve as a sign between me and you for you to know that I am Jehovah your God.'[i]

21 ""But the sons began to rebel against me.[j] They did not walk in my statutes, and they did not observe and carry out my judicial decisions, which if a man follows them, he will have life by them. My sabbaths they profaned. So I promised to pour out my rage on them and to unleash my anger against them fully in the wilderness.[k] 22 But I refrained[l] and acted for the sake of my own name,[m] so that it should not be profaned before the nations, in whose sight I brought them* out. 23 Also, I swore to them in the wilderness that I would scatter them among the nations and disperse them

among the lands,[a] 24 because they did not carry out my judicial decisions and they rejected my statutes,[b] they profaned my sabbaths, and they followed after* the disgusting idols of their forefathers.[c] 25 I also allowed them to follow regulations that were not good and judicial decisions by which they could not have life.[d] 26 I let them become defiled by their own sacrifices—when they made every firstborn child pass through the fire*—in order to make them desolate, so that they would know that I am Jehovah.''

27 "So speak to the house of Israel, O son of man, and tell them, 'This is what the Sovereign Lord Jehovah says: "In this way also, your forefathers blasphemed me by acting unfaithfully against me. 28 I brought them into the land that I swore to give them.[f] When they saw all the high hills and leafy trees,[g] they began offering their sacrifices and their offensive offerings. They presented the pleasing* aromas of their sacrifices and poured out their drink offerings there. 29 So I asked them, 'What is the meaning of this high place to which you go? (It is still called High Place to this day.)'"'[h]

30 "Now say to the house of Israel, 'This is what the Sovereign Lord Jehovah says: "Are you defiling yourselves the same way your forefathers did by going after their disgusting idols to commit spiritual prostitution with them?[i] 31 And are you still defiling yourselves to this day by offering sacrifices to all your disgusting idols, making your sons pass through the fire?[j] Should I at the same time re-

---

CHAP. 20

a Jos 7:9
  Eze 36:22

b Nu 14:30
  Ps 95:11
  Ps 106:26, 27

c Nu 13:26, 27

d Ex 32:1, 4
  Nu 25:1, 2
  Ac 7:42

e Nu 14:33

f Ps 78:8

g De 4:1

h Jer 17:22

i Ex 31:13

j Nu 25:1
  De 9:23

k Isa 63:10

l Ps 78:38

m Ps 25:11
  Ps 79:9
  Jer 14:7
  Da 9:19

Second Col.

a Le 26:33
  Ps 106:26, 27

b Le 26:15, 16

c Jer 2:7

d Ps 81:12

e Le 18:21
  Jer 7:31

f Jos 23:5

g De 12:2

h Eze 16:24, 25

i Jg 2:19
  2Ch 21:13
  Jer 13:26, 27

j De 8:10, 12
  Ps 106:36-38
  Jer 7:31

20:14, 22 *That is, Israel. 20:15 *Or "the decoration." 20:17 *Lit., "my eye."

20:24 *Lit., "their eyes were after." 20:28 *Or "appeasing; soothing." Lit., "restful."

spond to your inquiry, O house of Israel?"'[a]

"'As surely as I am alive,' declares the Sovereign Lord Jehovah, 'I will not respond to your inquiry.[b] 32 And what you have in mind* when you say, "Let us become like the nations, like the families of the other lands, who worship# wood and stone,"[c] it will never happen.'"

33 "'As surely as I am alive,' declares the Sovereign Lord Jehovah, 'I will rule as king over you with a mighty hand, with an outstretched arm, and with an outpouring of rage.[d] 34 I will bring you out from the peoples and collect you together out of the lands where you have been scattered with a mighty hand, with an outstretched arm, and with an outpouring of rage.[e] 35 I will bring you into the wilderness of the peoples and enter into judgment with you there face-to-face.[f]

36 "'Just as I entered into judgment with your forefathers in the wilderness of the land of Egypt, so I will enter into judgment with you,' declares the Sovereign Lord Jehovah. 37 'I will make you pass under the shepherd's staff[g] and bring you under obligation to* the covenant. 38 But I will remove from you the rebels and those transgressing against me.[h] For I will bring them out of the land of their foreign residence, but they will not enter the land of Israel;[i] and you will have to know that I am Jehovah.'

39 "As for you, O house of Israel, this is what the Sovereign Lord Jehovah says: 'Each of you go and serve his disgusting idols.[j] But afterward if you do not listen to me, you will no longer be able to profane my holy name by your sacrifices and your disgusting idols.'[a]

40 "'For in my holy mountain, on a high mountain of Israel,'[b] declares the Sovereign Lord Jehovah, 'is where the whole house of Israel, all of them, will serve me in the land.[c] I will take pleasure in them there, and I will require your contributions and the firstfruits of your offerings, all your holy things.[d] 41 Because of the pleasing* aroma, I will take pleasure in you when I bring you out from the peoples and collect you together from the lands to which you have been scattered;[e] and I will be sanctified among you before the eyes of the nations.'[f]

42 "'And you will have to know that I am Jehovah[g] when I bring you to the land of Israel,[h] into the land that I swore to give to your forefathers. 43 And there you will remember your conduct and all your deeds by which you defiled yourselves,[i] and you will loathe yourselves* because of all the bad things that you did.[j] 44 Then you will have to know that I am Jehovah when I deal with you for the sake of my name,[k] not according to your wicked conduct or according to your corrupted dealings, O house of Israel,' declares the Sovereign Lord Jehovah."

45 And the word of Jehovah again came to me, saying: 46 "Son of man, turn your face in the direction of the southern quarter and proclaim to the south, and prophesy to the forest of the field of the south. 47 Say to the forest of the south, 'Hear the word of Jehovah. This is what the Sovereign Lord Jehovah says: "Here I am setting a fire ablaze against

CHAP. 20
a Isa 1:15

b Zec 7:13

c Jer 44:17

d Jer 21:5
Eze 8:18

e Isa 27:13
Eze 34:16

f Jer 2:9

g Le 27:32
Eze 34:17

h Eze 34:20, 21

i Eze 13:9

j Jg 10:14
Ps 81:12

Second Col.
a Isa 1:13
Eze 23:39

b Isa 2:2, 3
Isa 66:20

c Isa 56:7
Zec 8:22

d Mal 3:4

e Isa 11:11
Jer 23:3

f Isa 5:16
Eze 38:23

g Eze 36:23

h Eze 11:17

i Le 26:40
Eze 6:9
Eze 16:61

j Jer 31:18

k Ps 79:9
Eze 36:22, 23

20:32 *Lit., "spirit." #Or "minister to; serve." 20:37 *Lit., "into the bond of." 20:41 *Or "appeasing; soothing." Lit., "restful." 20:43 *Lit., "your faces."

you,[a] and it will consume every green tree and every dry tree in you. The burning flame will not be extinguished,[b] and every face will be scorched by it, from south to north. **48** And all flesh* will see that I myself, Jehovah, have set it afire, so that it will not be extinguished."'"[c]

49 And I said: "Alas, O Sovereign Lord Jehovah! They are saying about me, 'Is he not just speaking in riddles?'"*

21 The word of Jehovah again came to me, saying: **2** "Son of man, turn your face toward Jerusalem, and make a proclamation against the holy places, and prophesy against the land of Israel. **3** Say to the land of Israel, 'This is what Jehovah says: "Here I am against you, and I will bring my sword out of its sheath[d] and cut off from you both the righteous and the wicked. **4** Because I will cut off from you the righteous and the wicked, my sword will be drawn from its sheath against all flesh,* from south to north. **5** All people will have to know that I myself, Jehovah, have drawn my sword from its sheath. It will not go back again."'[e]

6 "And you, son of man, sigh while you* tremble, yes, sigh bitterly before them.[f] **7** And if they say to you, 'Why are you sighing?' you will say, 'Because of a report.' For it will certainly come, and every heart will melt with fear and every hand will hang limp and every spirit will become dejected and every knee will drip with water.*[g] 'Look! It will certainly come—it will take place,' declares the Sovereign Lord Jehovah."

20:48; 21:4 *Or "people." 20:49 *Or "proverbial sayings?" 21:6 *Lit., "your hips." 21:7 *That is, from urination as a result of fear.

---

8 The word of Jehovah again came to me, saying: **9** "Son of man, prophesy and say, 'This is what Jehovah says: "Say, 'A sword! A sword[a] is sharpened, and it is polished. **10** It is sharpened to inflict a great slaughter; it is polished to flash like lightning.'"'"

"Should we not rejoice?"

"'Will it* reject the scepter of my own son,[b] as it does every tree?

11 "'It is given to be polished and to be wielded with the hand. This sword is sharpened and polished, to be put into the hand of an executioner.[c]

12 "'Cry out and wail,[d] son of man, for it has come against my people; it is against all the chieftains of Israel.[e] These will be victims of the sword along with my people. So strike your thigh in grief. **13** For an examination has been made,[f] and what will happen if the sword rejects the scepter? It* will cease to exist,'[g] declares the Sovereign Lord Jehovah.

14 "And you, son of man, prophesy and clap your hands and repeat 'A sword!' three times. It is the sword of the slain victims, the sword of great slaughter, that surrounds them.[h] **15** Their hearts will melt with fear[i] and many will fall at their city gates; I will inflict a slaughter by the sword. Yes, it flashes like lightning and is polished for a slaughter! **16** Cut sharply to the right! Swing to the left! Go wherever your blade is directed! **17** I will also clap my hands and satisfy my rage.[j] I myself, Jehovah, have spoken."

18 And the word of Jehovah again came to me, saying: **19** "As for you, son of man,

21:10 *That is, Jehovah's sword. 21:13 *Or "The scepter."

CHAP. 20
a De 32:22
  Jer 21:14

b Isa 66:24

c 2Ch 7:20
  La 2:17

CHAP. 21
d Le 26:33

e Jer 23:20

f Isa 22:4
  Jer 4:19
  Eze 9:8

g Eze 7:15-17

Second Col.
a Isa 66:16
  Jer 12:12
  Am 9:4

b Ge 49:10
  2Sa 7:12, 14

c Jer 25:9
  Jer 51:20

d Eze 9:8
  Mic 1:8

e Eze 19:1

f Jer 6:27

g 2Ki 25:7
  Eze 19:14
  Eze 21:26

h 2Ki 25:1, 2

i Eze 21:7

j Isa 1:24
  Eze 5:13
  Eze 16:42

mark out two ways for the sword of the king of Babylon to come. Both of them will originate from the same land, and a signpost* should be set up where the road branches off to the two cities. **20** You should mark out one way for the sword to come against Rab′bah[a] of the Am′monites, and the other way against fortified Jerusalem[b] in Judah. **21** For the king of Babylon stops to use divination at the fork in the road, where the two roads branch off. He shakes the arrows. He consults his idols;* he examines the liver. **22** The divination in his right hand is pointed toward Jerusalem, to set up battering rams, to give the word for slaughter, to sound the battle cry, to set battering rams against the gates, to throw up a siege rampart, to build a siege wall.[c] **23** But it will seem like false divination in the eyes of those* who had sworn oaths to them.[d] But he remembers their guilt and will capture them.[e]

24 "Therefore this is what the Sovereign Lord Jehovah says: 'You have caused your own guilt to be remembered by exposing your transgressions and causing your sins to be seen in all your actions. Now that you have been remembered, you will be taken by force.'*

25 "But your day has come, O fatally wounded, wicked chieftain of Israel,[f] the time of your final punishment. **26** This is what the Sovereign Lord Jehovah says: 'Remove the turban, and take off the crown.[g] This will not remain the same.[h] Raise up the low one,[i] and bring low the high one.[j] **27** A ruin, a ruin, a ruin I will make it. And it will not

belong to anyone until the one who has the legal right comes,[a] and I will give it to him.'[b]

28 "And you, son of man, prophesy and say, 'This is what the Sovereign Lord Jehovah says about the Am′monites and about their insults.' Say, 'A sword! A sword is drawn for a slaughter; it is polished to devour and to flash like lightning. **29** Despite the false visions and lying divination about you, you will be piled up on the slain,* the wicked men whose day has come, the time of their final punishment. **30** Return it to its sheath. I will judge you in the place that you were created, in the land of your origin. **31** I will pour out my indignation on you. I will blow upon you with the fire of my fury, and I will hand you over to brutal men, the craftsmen of destruction.[c] **32** You will become fuel for the fire;[d] your own blood will be shed in the land, and you will be remembered no more, for I myself, Jehovah, have spoken.'"

22 And the word of Jehovah again came to me, saying: **2** "As for you, son of man, are you prepared to pronounce judgment on* the bloodguilty city[e] and to make known to her all her detestable things?[f] **3** You are to say, 'This is what the Sovereign Lord Jehovah says: "O city that sheds blood[g] within herself, whose time is coming,[h] who makes disgusting idols* to defile herself,[i] **4** your bloodshed has made you guilty,[j] and your disgusting idols have made you unclean.[k] You have hastened the end of your days, and the end of your years has come. That is why

CHAP. 21
a Jer 49:2
  Eze 25:5
  Am 1:14

b 2Sa 5:9
  2Ch 26:9
  2Ch 32:2, 5
  2Ch 33:1, 14

c Jer 32:24
  Jer 52:4

d 2Ch 36:11, 13
  Eze 17:13

e 2Ki 25:6, 7

f 2Ch 36:11, 13
  Jer 24:8
  Jer 52:1, 2
  Eze 17:19

g 2Ki 25:5-7
  Eze 52:8, 11
  Eze 12:12, 13

h Eze 21:13

i Ps 75:7
  Da 4:17

j Da 4:37
  Lu 21:24

Second Col.
a Ge 49:10
  Ps 89:3, 4
  Ps 110:1
  Isa 9:6
  Isa 11:10
  Lu 1:32, 33
  Re 5:5

b Ps 2:6, 8
  Da 7:13, 14
  Lu 22:29

c Eze 25:5

d Jer 49:2, 3

CHAP. 22
e 2Ki 21:16
  Jer 2:34
  Mt 23:37

f Eze 16:51

g Eze 24:6

h Eze 12:25

i 2Ki 21:11

j Ge 9:6

k Le 26:30
  Eze 23:37

I will make you an object of reproach to the nations and an object of mockery to all the lands.[a] **5** The lands nearby and those far away from you will mock you,[b] you whose name is unclean and who are filled with turmoil. **6** Look! Each of the chieftains of Israel among you uses his authority to shed blood.[c] **7** Within you they treat their father and mother with contempt.[d] They defraud the foreign resident, and they mistreat the fatherless child* and the widow."''[e]

8 "'My holy places you despise, and my sabbaths you profane.[f] **9** Within you are slanderers intent on shedding blood.[g] Within you they eat sacrifices on the mountains and carry on obscene conduct in your midst.[h] **10** Within you they dishonor their father's bed,*[i] and they violate a woman unclean in her menstruation.[j] **11** Within you one man acts detestably with his neighbor's wife,[k] another defiles his own daughter-in-law with obscene conduct,[l] and another violates his sister, the daughter of his own father.[m] **12** Within you they take a bribe to shed blood.[n] You lend on interest[o] or for a profit,* and you extort money from your neighbors.[p] Yes, you have entirely forgotten me,' declares the Sovereign Lord Jehovah.

13 "'Look! I clap my hands in disgust at the dishonest gain you have made and over the acts of bloodshed in your midst. **14** Will your courage* endure and your hands remain strong in the days when I take action against you?[q] I myself, Jehovah, have spoken, and I will take action. **15** I will scatter you among the nations and disperse you among the lands,[a] and I will put an end to your uncleanness.[b] **16** And you will be dishonored before the nations, and you will have to know that I am Jehovah.'"[c]

17 And the word of Jehovah again came to me, saying: **18** "Son of man, the house of Israel has become like worthless dross to me. All of them are copper and tin and iron and lead in a furnace. They have become the dross of silver.[d]

19 "Therefore this is what the Sovereign Lord Jehovah says: 'Because all of you have become like worthless dross,[e] I am collecting you together inside Jerusalem. **20** Just as silver and copper and iron and lead and tin are collected inside a furnace in order to blow fire upon them and melt them, so I will collect you together in my anger and in my rage, and I will blow upon you and make you melt.[f] **21** I will bring you together and blow upon you with the fire of my fury,[g] and you will be melted inside of her.[h] **22** Just as silver is melted in a furnace, so you will be melted inside her; and you will have to know that I myself, Jehovah, have poured out my rage on you.'"

23 And the word of Jehovah again came to me, saying: **24** "Son of man, say to her, 'You are a land that will not be cleansed or rained on in the day of indignation. **25** Her prophets have conspired within her,[i] like a roaring lion tearing prey.[j] They are devouring people.* They are seizing treasure and precious things. They have made many widows within her. **26** Her priests have violated my law,[k] and they keep profaning my holy places.[l] They make no

---

CHAP. 22
a De 28:37
  1Ki 9:7
  Ps 80:6
  Eze 23:32
  Da 9:16
b Ps 79:4
c Isa 1:23
  Mic 1:23
  Zep 3:3
d De 27:16
e Ex 22:21, 22
  Ps 82:3
  Isa 1:17
f Le 19:30
g Ex 23:1
  Le 19:16
h Jer 13:27
i Le 18:7
  Le 20:11
j Le 18:19
  Le 20:18
k Le 18:20
  Le 20:10
  Jer 5:8
l Le 18:15
m Le 20:17
n Ex 23:8
  De 27:25
  Isa 1:23
o De 23:19
p Ex 22:25
  Le 6:4, 5
q Eze 21:7

Second Col.
a De 4:27
  De 28:25
b Isa 1:25
  Eze 23:27
c Eze 6:13
d Pr 17:3
  Jer 6:28-30
e Ps 119:119
  Pr 25:4
f Eze 21:31
g De 4:24
  Ps 21:9
  Jer 21:12
h Ps 68:2
i Jer 5:31
j Jer 6:13, 14
j Mic 3:5
k Jer 2:8
  La 4:13
  Mic 3:11
l Le 20:3
  Le 22:2

22:7 *Or "the orphan." **22:10** *Lit., "expose the nakedness of their father." **22:12** *Or "or take usury." **22:14** *Lit., "heart."

22:25 *Or "souls."

distinction between what is holy and what is common,[a] and they fail to make known what is unclean and what is clean,[b] and they refuse to observe my sabbaths, and I am profaned among them. **27** Her princes in the midst are like wolves tearing prey; they shed blood and kill people* to make dishonest gain.[c] **28** But her prophets have plastered over their deeds with whitewash. They see false visions and give lying divination,[d] and they say: "This is what the Sovereign Lord Jehovah says," when Jehovah himself has not spoken. **29** The people of the land have defrauded and committed robbery,[e] they have mistreated the needy and the poor, and they have defrauded the foreign resident and denied him justice.'

30 "'I was looking for a man from among them who would repair the stone wall or stand before me in the breach in behalf of the land, so that it would not be destroyed,[f] but I found no one. **31** So I will pour out my indignation on them and exterminate them with the fire of my fury. I will bring the consequences of their way on their own head,' declares the Sovereign Lord Jehovah."

23 The word of Jehovah again came to me, saying: **2** "Son of man, there were two women who were the daughters of the same mother.[g] **3** They became prostitutes in Egypt;[h] from their youth they engaged in prostitution. Their breasts were squeezed there, and their virgin bosoms were fondled. **4** Their names were O·hoʹlah,* the older one, and her sister O·holʹi·bah.* They became mine and gave

birth to sons and daughters. As for their names, O·hoʹlah is Sa·marʹi·a,[a] and O·holʹi·bah is Jerusalem.

5 "O·hoʹlah began to prostitute herself[b] while she belonged to me. She lusted after her passionate lovers,[c] her neighbors the As·syrʹi·ans.[d] **6** They were governors clothed in blue and deputy rulers—all desirable young men mounted on their horses. **7** She continued to prostitute herself with all the choicest sons of As·syrʹi·a, and she defiled herself[e] with the disgusting idols* of those she lusted after. **8** She did not abandon the prostitution she practiced in Egypt, for in her youth they had lain down with her, and they fondled her virgin bosom and poured out their lust* on her.[f] **9** So I gave her into the hand of her passionate lovers, the sons of As·syrʹi·a,[g] after whom she had lusted. **10** They exposed her nakedness[h] and seized her sons and daughters,[i] and they killed her with a sword. She became notorious among women, and they executed judgment against her.

11 "When her sister O·holʹi·bah saw it, her lust became even more depraved, and her prostitution was worse than that of her sister.[j] **12** She lusted after her neighbors the sons of As·syrʹi·a,[k] the governors and deputy rulers who were clothed in splendor and mounted on horses—all desirable young men. **13** When she defiled herself, I saw that both of them had followed the same course.[l] **14** But she kept adding to her acts of prostitution. She saw men carved on the wall, images of Chal·deʹans

---

CHAP. 22
a Le 10:10

b Le 11:46, 47

c Mic 3:1-3
  Zep 3:3

d Isa 30:10
  Jer 23:25
  La 2:14
  Eze 13:9, 10

e Isa 1:23
  Isa 3:14
  Jer 21:12
  Mic 2:2

f Ex 32:11
  Ps 106:23

CHAP. 23
g Jer 3:6, 7

h Le 17:7
  De 29:16, 17
  Jos 24:14
  Eze 20:8

Second Col.
a 1Ki 16:23, 24

b 1Ki 14:16
  1Ki 21:25, 26

c Ho 2:5

d 2Ki 15:19
  2Ki 17:3
  Ho 5:13
  Ho 7:11

e Ho 5:3

f Ex 32:1, 4
  1Ki 12:28, 29
  2Ki 10:29

g 2Ki 15:29
  1Ch 5:26

h Ho 2:10

i 2Ki 17:6
  2Ki 18:11

j Jer 3:6-8
  Eze 16:46, 47

k 2Ki 16:7

l 2Ki 17:19

22:27 *Or "souls." 23:4 *Meaning "Her Tent." #Meaning "My Tent Is in Her."

23:7 *The Hebrew term may be related to a word for "dung" and is used as an expression of contempt. 23:8 *Or "immoral intercourse."

carved in vermilion,* **15** wearing belts around their waist, with flowing turbans on their heads, having the appearance of warriors, all of them depicting Babylonians, born in the land of the Chal·de′ans. **16** She began to lust after them as soon as she saw them, and she sent messengers to them in Chal·de′a.ᵃ **17** So the sons of Babylon kept coming to her bed of lovemaking, and they defiled her with their lust.* After she was defiled by them, she# turned away from them in disgust.

18 "When she went on brazenly engaging in prostitution and exposing her nakedness,ᵇ I turned away from her in disgust, just as I* had turned away from her sister in disgust.ᶜ **19** And she kept increasing her acts of prostitution,ᵈ calling to mind the days of her youth when she prostituted herself in the land of Egypt.ᵉ **20** She lusted after them like the concubines of men whose male members are like those of a donkey and whose genitals are like those of a horse. **21** You yearned for the obscene conduct of your youth in Egyptᶠ when they fondled your bosom, the breasts of your youth.

22 "Therefore, O·hol′i·bah, this is what the Sovereign Lord Jehovah says: 'Here I am stirring up your loversʰ whom you* turned away from in disgust, and I will bring them against you from every direction,ⁱ **23** the sons of Babylonʲ and all the Chal·de′ans,ᵏ the men of Pe′kodˡ and Sho′a and Ko′a, along with all the sons of As·syr′i·a. All of them are desirable young men, governors and deputy rulers, warriors

and handpicked,* all mounted on horses. **24** They will attack you with rumbling war chariots and wheels and with a great assembly of troops, with large shield and buckler* and helmet. They will take up positions all around you, and I will authorize them to pass judgment, and they will judge you as they see fit.ᵃ **25** I will express my indignation against you, and they will deal with you in their rage. They will cut off your nose and your ears, and those of you who remain will fall by the sword. They will take away your sons and your daughters, and those of you who remain will be consumed by fire.ᵇ **26** They will strip off your garmentsᶜ and seize your beautiful jewelry.*ᵈ **27** I will put an end to your obscene conduct and your prostitution,ᵉ which started in the land of Egypt.ᶠ You will stop looking at them, and you will remember Egypt no more.'

28 "For this is what the Sovereign Lord Jehovah says: 'Here I am about to hand you over to those you hate, those you* turned away from in disgust.ᵍ **29** They will deal with you in hatred and take away all you have toiled forʰ and leave you naked and exposed. The shameful nakedness of your immorality and your obscene conduct and your prostitution will be exposed.ⁱ **30** These things will be done to you because you chased after the nations like a prostitute,ʲ because you defiled yourself with their disgusting idols.ᵏ **31** You have followed the same course as your sister,ˡ and I will put her cup into your hand.'ᵐ

32 This is what the Sovereign Lord Jehovah says:

CHAP. 23

a Eze 16:29

b Jer 3:2
   Eze 16:36, 37

c Ps 106:39, 40
   Jer 6:8
   Jer 12:8

d Eze 16:25

e Eze 20:7

f Jos 24:14

g Eze 23:3

h Eze 16:37
   Hab 1:6

i Jer 6:22
   Jer 12:9

j Eze 21:19

k 2Ki 24:2

l Jer 50:21

_____

Second Col.

a Jer 39:5

b Eze 15:7
   Eze 20:47

c Jer 13:22
   Re 17:16

d Isa 3:18-23
   Jer 4:30
   Eze 16:39

e Isa 27:9
   Eze 16:41
   Eze 22:15

f Eze 23:3

g Jer 21:7

h De 28:49, 51

i Eze 16:36, 37
   Eze 16:39

j Jer 2:18

k Ps 106:35, 36
   Eze 6:9
   Eze 23:7

l Jer 3:8
   Eze 16:46, 47

m 2Ki 21:13
   Jer 25:15
   Da 9:12

23:14 *Or "red." 23:17 *Or "immoral intercourse." #Or "her soul." 23:18 *Or "my soul." 23:22, 28 *Or "your soul."

23:23 *Lit., "summoned ones." 23:24 *A small shield, often carried by archers. 23:26 *Or "ornaments."

'You will drink the deep and wide cup of your sister,[a]

And you will become an object of laughter and ridicule, of which the cup contains much.[b]

33 You will be overcome by* drunkenness and grief,

A cup of horror and desolation,

The cup of your sister, Sa·marʹi·a.

34 You will have to drink it and drain it dry[c] and gnaw on its earthenware fragments

And then tear out your breasts.

"For I myself have spoken," declares the Sovereign Lord Jehovah.'

35 "Therefore this is what the Sovereign Lord Jehovah says: 'Because you have forgotten me and have completely disregarded me,*[d] you will bear the consequences of your obscene conduct and your acts of prostitution.'"

36 Jehovah then said to me: "Son of man, will you pronounce judgment on O·hoʹlah and O·holʹi·bah[e] and confront them with their disgusting practices? 37 They have committed adultery,*[f] and there is blood on their hands. Not only have they committed adultery with their disgusting idols, but they have also made their sons whom they bore to me pass through the fire as food for their idols.[g] 38 Moreover, this is what they have done to me: They defiled my sanctuary on that day, and they profaned my sabbaths. 39 After they slaughtered their sons as sacrifices to their disgusting idols,[h] they came into my sanctuary to profane it[i] on that very day. That is what they did in-

---

23:33 *Lit., "filled with." 23:35 *Lit., "have cast me behind your back." 23:37 *That is, spiritual adultery.

side my own house. 40 They even sent a messenger for men to come from far away.[a] When they were coming, you washed yourself and painted your eyes and adorned yourself with ornaments.[b] 41 And you sat down on a magnificent couch[c] with a table set in front of it,[d] on which you put my incense[e] and my oil.[f] 42 The sound of a carefree crowd of men was heard there, among whom were drunkards brought in from the wilderness. They put bracelets on the hands of the women and beautiful crowns on their heads.

43 "Then I said regarding her who was worn out with adultery: 'Now she will keep committing her prostitution.' 44 So they kept going in to her, just as one goes to a prostitute. That is how they went in to O·hoʹlah and to O·holʹi·bah, the women of obscene conduct. 45 But righteous men will render to her the appropriate judgment for adultery[g] and bloodshed;[h] for adulteresses is what they are, and they have blood on their hands.[i]

46 "For this is what the Sovereign Lord Jehovah says: 'An army will be brought against them to make them an object of horror and something to plunder.[j] 47 The army will hurl stones at them[k] and cut them down with their swords. They will kill their sons and daughters[l] and burn their houses with fire.[m] 48 I will put an end to the obscene conduct in the land, and all the women will learn a lesson and not copy your obscene conduct.[n] 49 They will bring on you the consequences of your obscene conduct and of your sins with your disgusting idols; and you will have to know that I am the Sovereign Lord Jehovah.'"[o]

CHAP. 23

a Isa 51:17

b De 28:37
  1Ki 9:7
  La 2:15

c Ps 75:8

d 1Ki 14:9
  Ne 9:26
  Isa 17:10
  Jer 2:32
  Jer 13:25

e Eze 23:4

f Ho 1:2
  Jas 4:4

g Le 18:21
  2Ki 17:17, 18
  Eze 16:36

h Jer 7:31

i Le 20:3

Second Col.

a Isa 57:9

b Jer 4:30

c Isa 57:7

d Isa 65:11

e Eze 8:10, 11

f Eze 16:17, 18

g Le 20:10

h Ge 9:6
  Eze 16:38

i 2Ki 24:3, 4
  Ps 106:38
  Eze 23:37

j Jer 15:4
  Jer 25:9
  Eze 16:40

k Le 20:2

l 2Ch 36:17

m 2Ki 25:9, 10
  Jer 39:8

n 2Pe 2:6

o Eze 6:13

24 The word of Jehovah again came to me in the ninth year, in the tenth month, on the tenth day of the month, saying: **2** "Son of man, record this date,* this very day. The king of Babylon has begun his attack against Jerusalem on this very day.ᵃ **3** And relate a proverb* concerning the rebellious house, and say concerning them:

"'This is what the Sovereign Lord Jehovah says:

"Put the cooking pot# on;
put it on the fire and pour water into it.ᵇ

4 Put pieces of meat into it,ᶜ
every good piece,
The thigh and the shoulder;
fill it with the choicest bones.

5 Take the choicest sheep of the flock,ᵈ and stack the logs all around under the pot.
Boil the pieces, and cook the bones inside it."'

6 "Therefore this is what the Sovereign Lord Jehovah says:

'Woe to the city of bloodshed,ᵉ the rusty cooking pot, whose rust has not been removed!
Empty it piece by piece;ᶠ
do not cast lots for them.

7 For its blood is within it;ᵍ
she poured it out on the bare rock.
She did not pour it out on the earth, to cover it over with dust.ʰ

8 To stir up rage for executing vengeance,
I have put her blood on the shining, bare rock
So that it may not be covered over.'ⁱ

9 "Therefore this is what the Sovereign Lord Jehovah says:

'Woe to the city of bloodshed!ᵃ
I will pile the wood high.

10 Heap on the logs and kindle the fire,
Boil the flesh thoroughly, pour out the broth, and let the bones be charred.

11 Set the empty pot on the coals to make it hot
So that its copper will become red hot.
Its uncleanness will melt away within it,ᵇ and its rust will be consumed.

12 It is frustrating and exhausting,
For the heavy rust will not come off.ᶜ
Throw it into the fire with its rust!'

13 "'Your uncleanness was due to your obscene conduct.ᵈ I tried to cleanse you, but you would not become clean from your uncleanness. You will not become clean until my rage against you subsides.ᵉ **14** I myself, Jehovah, have spoken. It will come to pass. I will act without holding back, without sorrow, without regret.ᶠ They will judge you according to your ways and your dealings,' declares the Sovereign Lord Jehovah."

15 And the word of Jehovah again came to me, saying: **16** "Son of man, in a single blow I am about to take away your dear one from you.ᵍ You should not mourn;* nor should you weep or shed tears. **17** Groan in silence, and do not observe mourning rites for the dead.ʰ Bind on your turban,ⁱ and put on your sandals.ʲ You should not cover over the mustache,*ᵏ and do not eat the bread brought to you by others."#ˡ

CHAP. 24

a 2Ki 25:1
　Jer 39:1
　Jer 52:4

b Eze 11:3

c Eze 11:7

d Jer 39:6

e 2Ki 21:16
　Mic 7:2
　Mt 23:35

f Eze 11:7, 9

g Jer 2:34

h Le 17:13
　De 12:16

i 2Ki 24:3, 4

Second Col.

a Mt 23:37

b Jer 21:10
　Jer 32:29
　Eze 22:15

c Jer 5:3
　Jer 6:29

d 2Ch 36:14
　Eze 22:9

e Eze 5:12, 13
　Eze 8:18

f Jer 13:14
　Eze 5:11

g Eze 24:18, 21

h Jer 16:5

i Le 10:6

j 2Sa 15:30

k Mic 3:7

l Jer 16:7

24:2 *Lit., "the name of the day." 24:3 *Or "an allegory." #Or "wide-mouthed cooking pot."

24:16 *Or "beat your chest." 24:17 *Or "upper lip." #Lit., "the bread of men."

18 And I spoke to the people in the morning, and my wife died in the evening. So I did in the morning just as I had been commanded. **19** The people were saying to me: "Will you not tell us what these things you are doing have to do with us?" **20** I replied to them: "The word of Jehovah has come to me, saying, **21** 'Tell the house of Israel: "This is what the Sovereign Lord Jehovah says, 'I am about to profane my sanctuary,^{a} the source of your great pride, the thing dear to you and the desire of your heart.* Your own sons and daughters whom you left behind will fall by the sword.^{b} **22** Then you will have to do just as I have done. You will not cover over your mustache, and you will not eat the bread brought to you by others.^{c} **23** Your turbans will be on your heads and your sandals on your feet. You will not mourn or weep. Instead, you will rot away in your errors,^{d} and you will groan to one another. **24** Ezekiel has become a sign for you.^{e} Just as he has done, you will do. When it happens, you will have to know that I am the Sovereign Lord Jehovah.'"'"

25 "And as for you, son of man, on the day that I take away from them their fortress—the beautiful object of their joy, the thing dear to them, their heart's* desire—along with their sons and daughters,^{f} **26** it will be reported to you by one who has escaped.^{g} **27** In that day you will open your mouth and speak to the one who escaped, and you will no longer be mute.^{h} You will become a sign to them, and they will have to know that I am Jehovah."

25 The word of Jehovah again came to me, saying: **2** "Son of man, turn your face toward the Am'mon·ites,* and prophesy against them.^{b} **3** You must say concerning the Am'mon·ites, 'Hear the word of the Sovereign Lord Jehovah. This is what the Sovereign Lord Jehovah says: "Because you said 'Aha!' against my sanctuary when it was profaned, and against the land of Israel when it was laid desolate, and against the house of Judah when they went into exile, **4** therefore I am giving you to the people of the East as a possession. They will set up their encampments* within you and pitch their tents among you. They will eat your fruitage, and they will drink your milk. **5** I will make Rab'bah^c a pasture ground for camels, and the land of the Am'mon·ites a resting-place for the flock; and you will have to know that I am Jehovah."'

6 "For this is what the Sovereign Lord Jehovah says: 'Because you clapped your hands^d and stamped your feet and you* rejoiced over the land of Israel with such utter scorn,^{e} **7** therefore I will stretch out my hand against you to give you to the nations as something to plunder. I will cut you off from the peoples and destroy you from the lands.^{f} I will annihilate you, and you will have to know that I am Jehovah.'

8 "This is what the Sovereign Lord Jehovah says: 'Because Mo'ab^g and Se'ir^h have said, "Look! The house of Judah is like all the other nations," **9** I am exposing Mo'ab's flank* at his frontier cities, the beauty# of his land, Beth-jesh'i·moth, Ba'al-me'on, and clear to

---

CHAP. 24
a Ps 74:7
　 Ps 79:1
　 Jer 7:14
　 La 1:10
　 La 2:7
　 Eze 9:7

b 2Ch 36:17
　 Jer 6:11

c Eze 24:17

d Le 26:39
　 Eze 33:10

e Isa 8:18
　 Isa 20:3
　 Eze 4:3

f De 28:32
　 Jer 11:22

g Eze 33:21

h Eze 3:26
　 Eze 33:22

Second Col.

CHAP. 25
a Ge 19:36, 38

b Jer 49:1
　 Am 1:13
　 Zep 2:9

c 2Sa 12:26
　 Eze 21:20

d La 2:15

e Zep 2:8

f Jer 49:2
　 Am 1:14

g Isa 15:1
　 Jer 48:1
　 Am 2:1

h De 2:4

24:21 *Or "your soul's compassion." 24:25 *Or "soul's" 25:4 *Or "walled camps." 25:6 *Or "your soul." 25:9 *Or "slope." #Or "decoration."

Kir·i·a·tha′im.ᵃ **10** I will give it along with the Am′mon·ites as a possession to the people of the East,ᵇ so that the Am′mon·ites will not be remembered among the nations.ᶜ **11** And I will execute judgment in Mo′ab,ᵈ and they will have to know that I am Jehovah.'

12 "This is what the Sovereign Lord Jehovah says: 'E′dom has acted vengefully against the house of Judah and has incurred great guilt in taking revenge on them;ᵉ **13** therefore this is what the Sovereign Lord Jehovah says: "I will also stretch out my hand against E′dom and cut off from it both man and livestock, and I will make it desolate.ᶠ From Te′man clear to De′dan, they will fall by the sword.ᵍ **14** 'I will take vengeance on E′dom by the hand of my people Israel.ʰ They will bring my anger and my wrath on E′dom, so that they experience my own vengeance,ⁱ declares the Sovereign Lord Jehovah.'"

15 "This is what the Sovereign Lord Jehovah says: 'Because of their unrelenting hostility, the Phi·lis′tines have maliciously* sought to bring vengeance and destruction.ʲ **16** Therefore this is what the Sovereign Lord Jehovah says: "Here I am stretching out my hand against the Phi·lis′tines,ᵏ and I will cut off the Cher′e·thitesˡ and will destroy the remaining inhabitants of the seacoast.ᵐ **17** I will execute on them great acts of vengeance with furious punishments, and they will have to know that I am Jehovah when I bring my vengeance on them."'"

26 In the 11th year, on the first day of the month, the word of Jehovah came to me, saying: **2** "Son of man, be-

cause Tyre has said against Jerusalem,ᵃ 'Aha! The gateway of the peoples has been broken!ᵇ Everything will come my way, and I will become rich now that she is devastated'; **3** therefore this is what the Sovereign Lord Jehovah says: 'Here I am against you, O Tyre, and I will bring up many nations against you, just as the sea brings up its waves. **4** They will destroy the walls of Tyre and tear down her towers,ᶜ and I will scrape away soil and make her a shining, bare rock. **5** She will become a drying yard for dragnets in the midst of the sea.'ᵈ

"'For I myself have spoken,' declares the Sovereign Lord Jehovah, 'and she will become plunder for the nations. **6** And her settlements* in the countryside will be slaughtered by the sword, and people will have to know that I am Jehovah.'

7 "For this is what the Sovereign Lord Jehovah says: 'Here I am bringing King Neb·u·chad·nez′zar* of Babylon against Tyre from the north;ᵉ he is a king of kings,ᶠ with horses,ᵍ war chariots,ʰ cavalrymen, and an army of many soldiers.ⁿ **8** He will destroy your settlements in the countryside with the sword, and he will build a siege wall and throw up a siege rampart against you and raise up a great shield against you. **9** He will pound your walls with his battering ram,* and with his axesⁿ he will pull down your towers. **10** His horses will be so many that they will cover you with dust, and the sound of the cavalry, the wheels, and the chariots will cause your walls to shake when

---

25:15 *Or "with scorn in the soul."

26:6 *Lit., "daughters." 26:7 *Lit., "Nebuchadrezzar," a variant spelling. ⁿLit., "peoples." 26:9 *Or "his attack engine." ⁿOr "swords."

he enters your gates, like men storming a city with broken walls. **11** The hooves of his horses will trample down all your streets;[a] he will kill your people with the sword, and your mighty pillars will crash to the ground. **12** They will loot your resources, plunder your merchandise,[b] tear down your walls, and pull down your fine houses; then they will throw your stones and your woodwork and your soil into the water.'

13 "'I will put an end to the noise of your songs, and the sound of your harps will be heard no more.[c] **14** And I will make you a shining, bare rock, and you will become a drying yard for dragnets.[d] You will never be rebuilt, for I myself, Jehovah, have spoken,' declares the Sovereign Lord Jehovah.

15 "This is what the Sovereign Lord Jehovah says to Tyre: 'At the sound of your downfall, when the dying ones* are groaning, when a slaughter takes place in your midst, will the islands not shudder?[e] **16** All the princes* of the sea will come down from their thrones and remove their robes# and strip off their embroidered garments, and they will be seized with△ trembling. They will sit on the ground and tremble constantly and stare at you in amazement.[f] **17** And they will sing a dirge*[g] over you and say to you:

"How you have perished,[h] you who were inhabited from the seas, the praised city;
You and your# inhabitants were mighty on the sea,[i]

Spreading terror to all the inhabitants of the earth!
18 The islands will tremble on the day of your downfall,
The islands of the sea will be disturbed when you are gone.'"[a]

19 "For this is what the Sovereign Lord Jehovah says: 'When I devastate you like the cities that are not inhabited, when I overwhelm you with the surging waters and the mighty waters have covered you,[b] **20** I will bring you and those going down into the pit* with you to the people of long ago; I will cause you to dwell in the lowest place, like the places of old that have been devastated, together with those going down into the pit,[c] so that you may not be inhabited. Then I will glorify# the land of the living.

21 "'I will bring sudden terror upon you, and you will no longer be.[d] They will search for you, but you will never again be found,' declares the Sovereign Lord Jehovah."

27 The word of Jehovah again came to me, saying: **2** "As for you, son of man, sing a dirge* over Tyre,[e] **3** and say to Tyre,

'You who dwell at the gateways of the sea,
The merchant for the peoples of many islands,
This is what the Sovereign Lord Jehovah says:
"O Tyre, you yourself have said, 'I am perfect in beauty.'[f]
4 Your territories are in the heart of the sea,
And your builders have perfected your beauty.
5 They made all your planks from the juniper trees of Se'nir,[g]

CHAP. 26
a Isa 5:28
Hab 1:8

b Eze 27:32, 33
Eze 28:5, 18
Zec 9:3

c Isa 23:16

d Eze 26:4, 5

e Eze 27:28

f Eze 27:35
Eze 32:10

g Eze 27:32

h Am 1:9, 10

i Eze 28:2

Second Col.
a Isa 23:5

b Eze 27:34

c Eze 28:8

d Eze 27:36

CHAP. 27
e Eze 26:17

f Isa 23:9
Eze 28:2, 12

g De 3:8, 9
1Ch 5:23

26:15 *Lit., "the slain." **26:16** *Or "chieftains." #Or "sleeveless coats." △Lit., "clothed with." **26:17; 27:2** *Or "song of mourning." **26:17** #Lit., "She and her." **26:20** *Or "grave." #Or "decorate."

And they took a cedar from Leb'a·non to make a mast for you.

6 They made your oars from oaks of Ba'shan,

And your prow was of cypress inlaid with ivory from the islands of Kit'tim.[a]

7 Colorful linen from Egypt served as cloth for your sail,

And your deck awnings were of blue thread and purple wool from the islands of E·li'shah.[b]

8 The inhabitants of Si'don and of Ar'vad[c] were your rowers.

Your own skilled men, O Tyre, were your sailors.[d]

9 The experienced* and skilled men of Ge'bal[e] caulked your seams.[f]

All the ships of the sea and their mariners came to you to trade merchandise.

10 Men of Persia, Lud, and Put[g] were in your army, your men of war.

They hung their shields and helmets in you, and they brought you splendor.

11 The men of Ar'vad in your army were stationed on your walls all around,

And brave men manned your towers.

They hung circular shields all around your walls

And perfected your beauty.

12 ""Tar'shish[h] did business with you because of your abundant wealth.[i] They exchanged silver, iron, tin, and lead for your goods.[j] 13 Ja'van, Tu'bal,[k] and Me'shech[l] traded with you, exchanging slaves[m] and articles of copper for your merchandise. 14 The house of To·gar'mah[n] exchanged horses and steeds and mules for your goods. 15 The people of De'dan[a] traded with you; you employed merchants on many islands; they gave ivory tusks[b] and ebony as your tribute. 16 E'dom did business with you because of the abundance of your products. They gave turquoise, purple wool, colorful embroidery, fine fabric, corals, and rubies in exchange for your goods.

17 ""Judah and the land of Israel traded with you, giving the wheat of Min'nith,[c] choice foods, honey,[d] oil, and balsam* in exchange for your goods.[f]

18 ""Damascus[g] did business with you because of the abundance of your products and all your wealth, trading the wine of Hel'bon and wool of Za'har.* 19 Ve'dan and Ja'van from U'zal gave wrought iron, cassia,* and cane# in exchange for your goods. 20 De'dan[h] traded with you in saddlecloths* for riding. 21 You employed the Arabs and all the chieftains of Ke'dar,[i] who were merchants of lambs and rams and goats.[j] 22 The merchants of She'ba and Ra'a·mah[k] traded with you; they gave all sorts of the finest perfumes, precious stones, and gold in exchange for your goods.[l] 23 Ha'ran,[m] Can'neh, E'den,[n] the merchants of She'ba,[o] As'shur,[p] and Chil'mad traded with you. 24 In your marketplace they traded beautiful garments, cloaks made of blue material and colorful embroidery, and multicolored carpets, all bound and secured with ropes.

25 The ships of Tar'shish[q] were the caravans for your merchandise,

27:9 *Lit., "The old men."

27:18 *Or "and reddish-gray wool."
27:19 *A tree of the same family as the cinnamon tree. #An aromatic reed.
27:20 *Or "garments of woven material."

So that you were filled and loaded down* in the heart of the open sea.

26 Your rowers have brought you into heavy seas;
The east wind has wrecked you in the heart of the open sea.

27 Your wealth, your goods, your merchandise, your mariners, and your sailors,
Those caulking your seams, those trading your merchandise,[a]
and all the men of war[b]
—The entire multitude* within you—
They will all sink in the heart of the open sea on the day of your downfall.[c]

28 When your sailors cry out, the coastlands will shudder.

29 All the oarsmen, the mariners, and the seamen
Will come down from their ships and stand on the land.

30 They will raise their voices and cry out bitterly over you[d]
As they throw dust on their heads and wallow in ashes.

31 They will make themselves bald and put on sackcloth;
They will weep bitterly* over you with intense wailing.

32 In their lamentation they will sing a dirge and chant over you:
'Who is like Tyre, now silent in the midst of the sea?[e]

33 When your goods came in from the open sea, you satisfied many peoples.[f]
Your abundant wealth and your merchandise enriched earth's kings.[g]

27:25 *Or possibly, "and glorious." 27:27 *Lit., "congregation." 27:31 *Or "with bitterness of soul."

34 Now you have been wrecked in the open sea, in the deep waters,[a]
And all your merchandise and your people have sunk with you.[b]

35 All the inhabitants of the islands will stare at you in amazement,[c]
And their kings will shudder with horror[d]—their faces will be troubled.

36 The merchants among the nations will whistle over what happened to you.
Your end will be sudden and terrible,
And you will cease to exist for all time.'"''[e]

28 The word of Jehovah again came to me, saying:
2 "Son of man, tell the leader of Tyre, 'This is what the Sovereign Lord Jehovah says:

"Because your heart has become haughty,[f] you keep saying, 'I am a god,
I sit on the throne of a god in the heart of the sea.'[g]
But you are only a man, not a god,
Though in your heart you feel that you are a god.

3 Look! You are wiser than Daniel.[h]
No secrets have been hidden from you.

4 You have made yourself wealthy by your wisdom and your discernment,
And you keep storing up gold and silver in your treasuries.[i]

5 Your skillful trading brought you great wealth,[j]
And your heart grew haughty because of your wealth."'

6 "'Therefore this is what the Sovereign Lord Jehovah says:

"Because in your heart you feel that you are a god,

CHAP. 27
a Eze 27:8, 9

b Eze 27:10, 11

c Eze 26:14

d Isa 23:1
Eze 26:17

e Eze 26:5

f Eze 27:14, 16

g Zec 9:3

___

Second Col.
a Eze 26:19

b Eze 27:27

c Eze 26:15

d Eze 28:17

e Ps 37:10

___

CHAP. 28
f Eze 28:5

g Eze 27:4

h Da 2:48

i Zec 9:3

j Isa 23:1, 3
Eze 27:12

7 I am bringing foreigners
against you, the most
ruthless of the nations,[a]
And they will draw their
swords against the beauty
of your wisdom
And defile your glorious
splendor.[b]
8 They will bring you down
to the pit,*
And you will die a violent
death in the heart of the
open sea.[c]
9 Will you still say, 'I am a god,'
to the one killing you?
You will be a mere man, not
a god, in the hand of those
defiling you.'"
10 'By the hand of foreigners,
you will die the death of
the uncircumcised ones,
For I myself have spoken,'
declares the Sovereign
Lord Jehovah."

11 And the word of Jehovah again came to me, saying:
12 "Son of man, sing a dirge* concerning the king of Tyre, and tell him, 'This is what the Sovereign Lord Jehovah says:

"You were the model of
perfection,#
Full of wisdom[d] and perfect
in beauty.[e]
13 You were in E′den, the
garden of God.
You were adorned with
every precious stone
—Ruby, topaz, and jasper;
chrys′o·lite, onyx, and jade;
sapphire, turquoise,[f] and
emerald;
And their settings and
mountings were made
of gold.
They were prepared on the
day you were created.
14 I assigned you as the
anointed covering cherub.

You were on the holy
mountain of God,[a]
and you walked about
among fiery stones.
15 You were faultless in your
ways from the day you
were created
Until unrighteousness was
found in you.[b]
16 Because of your abundant
trade,[c]
You became filled with
violence, and you began
to sin.[d]
So I will cast you out as
profane from the mountain
of God and destroy you,[e]
O covering cherub, away
from the stones of fire.
17 Your heart became haughty
because of your beauty.[f]
You corrupted your wisdom
because of your own
glorious splendor.[g]
I will throw you down to
the earth.[h]
I will make you a spectacle
before kings.
18 Because of your great guilt
and your dishonest trading,
you have profaned your
sanctuaries.
I will cause a fire to break
out in your midst, and it
will consume you.[i]
I will reduce you to ashes on
the earth before all those
looking at you.
19 All who knew you among the
peoples will stare at you
in amazement.[j]
Your end will be sudden and
terrible,
And you will cease to exist
for all time.""[k]

20 And the word of Jehovah again came to me, saying:
21 "Son of man, turn your face toward Si′don,[l] and prophesy against her. **22** You should say, 'This is what the Sovereign Lord Jehovah says:

28:8 *Or "grave." 28:12 *Or "song of mourning." #Lit., "were sealing up a pattern."

CHAP. 28
a Eze 30:10, 11

b Isa 23:9

c Eze 27:26

d Eze 28:3

e Eze 27:3

f Eze 27:16

Second Col.
a Isa 14:13

b Joe 3:4
  Am 1:9

c 1Ki 10:11
  2Ch 9:21
  Eze 27:12

d Joe 3:6

e Isa 23:9
  Jer 25:17, 22
  Jer 47:4
  Joe 3:8

f Eze 27:3

g Isa 14:14

h Isa 14:15

i Am 1:9, 10

j Eze 27:35

k Eze 27:36

l Isa 23:4
  Jer 25:17, 22
  Eze 32:30

"Here I am against you,
O Si′don, and I will be
glorified in your midst;
And people will have to
know that I am Jehovah
when I execute judgment
on her and I am sanctified
in her.

23 I will send pestilence into
her and blood will flow
in her streets.
The slain will fall in her
midst when the sword
comes against her from
all sides;
And they will have to know
that I am Jehovah.[a]

24 "'"Then the house of Israel will no longer be surrounded
by injurious briars and painful
thorns,[b] those who treat them
with scorn; and people will have
to know that I am the Sovereign
Lord Jehovah."'

25 "'This is what the Sovereign Lord Jehovah says: "When I
regather the house of Israel from
among the peoples where they
were scattered,[c] I will be sanctified among them in the eyes of
the nations.[d] And they will dwell
on their land[e] that I gave to
my servant Jacob.[f] 26 They will
dwell on it in security[g] and build
houses and plant vineyards,[h] and
they will dwell in security when I
execute judgment on all those
around them who treat them with
scorn;[i] and they will have to know
that I am Jehovah their God."'"

29 In the tenth year, in the
tenth month, on the 12th
day of the month, the word
of Jehovah came to me, saying:
2 "Son of man, turn your face toward Phar′aoh king of Egypt, and
prophesy against him and against
all Egypt.[j] 3 Speak these words:
'This is what the Sovereign Lord
Jehovah says:

"Here I am against you,
Phar′aoh king of Egypt,[k]

The great sea monster lying
among the streams of his
Nile,*[a]
Who has said, 'My Nile River
belongs to me.
I made it for myself.'[b]

4 But I will put hooks in your
jaws and cause the fish of
your Nile to cling to your
scales.
I will bring you up out of
your Nile along with all
the fish of the Nile that
cling to your scales.

5 I will abandon you in the
desert, you and all the fish
of your Nile.
You will fall on the open
field, and you will not
be gathered up nor be
collected together.[c]
I will give you as food to
the wild beasts of the earth
and the birds of the sky.[d]

6 Then all the inhabitants of
Egypt will have to know
that I am Jehovah,
For they were no more support to the house of Israel
than a piece of straw.*[e]

7 When they grasped your
hand, you were crushed,
And you caused them to
tear their shoulder.
When they supported
themselves on you,
you were broken,
And you caused their legs*
to wobble."[f]

8 "'Therefore this is what the
Sovereign Lord Jehovah says:
"Here I am bringing a sword
upon you,[g] and I will cut off from
you both man and beast. 9 The
land of Egypt will become a
desolate and devastated place;[h]
and they will have to know
that I am Jehovah, for you have*

CHAP. 28
a Eze 26:6

b Nu 33:55
  Jos 23:12, 13

c De 30:3
  Isa 11:12
  Jer 30:18
  Ho 1:11

d Isa 5:16

e Jer 23:8

f Ge 28:13

g Isa 32:18
  Jer 23:6
  Ho 2:18

h Isa 65:21, 22
  Jer 31:5
  Am 9:14

i Jer 30:16

CHAP. 29
j Jer 25:17, 19
  Jer 43:10, 11
  Eze 31:2

k Jer 46:25
  Eze 31:18

Second Col.
a Eze 32:2

b Eze 29:9

c Jer 25:33

d Eze 32:4

e Isa 36:6
  Jer 37:5-7
  Eze 17:17

f Jer 17:5

g Jer 46:14
  Eze 30:4
  Eze 32:12

h Jer 43:11-13

29:3 *Here and below, "Nile" refers
to the river and its irrigation canals.
29:6 *Lit., "a reed." 29:7 *Lit., "hips."
29:9 *Lit., "he has."

said, 'The Nile River belongs to me; I am the one who made it.'[a] **10** So I am against you and against your Nile, and I will make the land of Egypt devastated and dry, a desolate wasteland,[b] from Migʹdol[c] to Syʹeʹne[d] to the boundary of Eʹthiʹoʹpiʹa. **11** Neither man nor livestock will pass through it on foot,[e] and it will not be inhabited for 40 years. **12** I will make the land of Egypt the most desolate of lands, and its cities will be the most desolate of cities for 40 years;[f] and I will scatter the Egyptians among the nations and disperse them among the lands."[g]

13 "'For this is what the Sovereign Lord Jehovah says: "After 40 years I will gather back the Egyptians from the peoples where they were scattered;[h] **14** I will bring the Egyptian captives back to the land of Pathʹros,[i] to the land of their origin, and there they will become an insignificant kingdom. **15** Egypt will become lower than the other kingdoms and will no longer dominate the other nations,[j] and I will make them so small that they will not be able to subdue other nations.[k] **16** It will never again be a source of confidence for the house of Israel,[l] but it will only remind them of their error in turning to the Egyptians for help. And they will have to know that I am the Sovereign Lord Jehovah."'"

17 Now in the 27th year, in the first month, on the first day of the month, the word of Jehovah came to me, saying: **18** "Son of man, King Nebʹuʹchadʹnezʹzar*[m] of Babylon made his army labor greatly against Tyre.[n] Every head became bald, and every shoulder was rubbed

---

29:18, 19 *Lit., "Nebuchadrezzar," a variant spelling.

bare. But he and his army received no wages for the labor he expended on Tyre.

19 "Therefore this is what the Sovereign Lord Jehovah says, 'Here I am giving the land of Egypt to King Nebʹuʹchadʹnezʹzar*[a] of Babylon, and he will carry off its wealth and take much spoil and plunder from it; and it will become wages for his army.'

20 "'As compensation for his labor against her,* I will give him the land of Egypt because they acted for me,'[b] declares the Sovereign Lord Jehovah.

21 "In that day I will cause a horn to sprout for the house of Israel,*[c] and I will give you an opportunity to speak among them; and they will have to know that I am Jehovah."

30 And the word of Jehovah again came to me, saying: **2** "Son of man, prophesy and say, 'This is what the Sovereign Lord Jehovah says:

"Wail, 'Alas, the day is
   coming!'
3 For the day is near, yes,
   a day of Jehovah is near.[d]
It will be a day of clouds,[e] an
   appointed time of nations.[f]
4 A sword will come against
   Egypt, and panic will
   overtake Eʹthiʹoʹpiʹa when
   the slain fall in Egypt;
Its wealth is taken and
   its foundations are
   torn down.[g]
5 Eʹthiʹoʹpiʹa,[h] Put,[i] Lud, and
   all the mixed populations,*
And Chub, along with the
   sons of the land of the
   covenant,#
By the sword they will all
   fall.'"

CHAP. 29
a Eze 29:3
b Eze 30:12
c Jer 44:1
d Eze 30:6, 7
e Eze 31:12
   Eze 32:13
f Jer 46:19
g Eze 30:23
h Jer 46:25, 26
i Ge 10:13, 14
   Eze 30:14
j Eze 30:13
k Eze 32:2
l Isa 30:2
   Isa 36:4, 6
   Jer 2:18
   Jer 37:5-7
m Jer 25:9
   Jer 27:3, 6
n Eze 26:7

Second Col.
a Jer 43:10, 12
b Eze 30:9, 10
c 1Sa 2:10
   Lu 1:69

CHAP. 30
d Ob 15
e Eze 32:7
f Ps 110:6
g Eze 32:11, 12
h Zep 2:12
i Na 3:8, 9

29:20 *That is, against Tyre. 29:21 *Or "endow the house of Israel with strength." 30:5 *Or "all those from other nations." #Perhaps a reference to Israelites who were allied with Egypt.

6 This is what Jehovah says:
  'The supporters of Egypt
      will also fall,
  And its arrogant power will
      be brought down.'[a]

"'From Mig'dol[b] to Sy·e'ne[c] they will fall by the sword in the land,' declares the Sovereign Lord Jehovah. **7** 'They will be made the most desolate of lands, and its own cities will become the most devastated cities.[d] **8** And they will have to know that I am Jehovah when I set a fire in Egypt and all its allies are crushed. **9** In that day I will send messengers in ships to make self-confident E·thi·o'pi·a tremble; panic will seize them in the day that is coming upon Egypt, for it will surely come.'

10 "This is what the Sovereign Lord Jehovah says: 'I will bring an end to Egypt's hordes by the hand of King Neb·u·chad·nez'zar* of Babylon.[e] **11** He and his troops, the most ruthless of the nations,[f] will be brought in to destroy the land. They will draw their swords against Egypt and fill the land with the slain.[g] **12** I will turn the canals of the Nile[h] into dry ground and will sell the land into the hand of wicked men. I will make the land and everything in it desolate by the hand of foreigners.[i] I myself, Jehovah, have spoken.'

13 "This is what the Sovereign Lord Jehovah says: 'I will also destroy the disgusting idols* and bring an end to the worthless gods of Noph.*[j] There will no longer be a prince△ from the land of Egypt, and I will put fear in the land of Egypt.[k] **14** I will desolate Path'ros[l] and set a fire

in Zo'an and execute judgment on No.*[a] **15** I will pour out my rage on Sin, the stronghold of Egypt, and destroy the population of No. **16** I will set a fire in Egypt; and Sin will be seized with terror and No will be broken through and Noph* will face attack in broad daylight! **17** The young men of On* and Pi·be'seth will fall by the sword, and the cities will go into captivity. **18** In Te·haph'ne·hes the day will grow dark when I break the yoke bars of Egypt there.[b] Her arrogant power will come to an end,[c] clouds will cover her, and her towns will go into captivity.[d] **19** I will execute judgment on Egypt, and they will have to know that I am Jehovah.'"

20 And in the 11th year, in the first month, on the seventh day of the month, the word of Jehovah came to me, saying: **21** "Son of man, I have broken the arm of Phar'aoh king of Egypt; it will not be bound up to be healed or wrapped with a bandage to make it strong enough to take up the sword."

22 "Therefore this is what the Sovereign Lord Jehovah says: 'Here I am against Phar'aoh king of Egypt,[e] and I will break his arms, the strong one and the broken one,[f] and I will make the sword fall from his hand.[g] **23** Then I will scatter the Egyptians among the nations and disperse them among the lands.[h] **24** I will strengthen the arms* of the king of Babylon[i] and put my sword into his hand,[j] and I will break the arms of Phar'aoh, and he will groan loudly like a dying man before him.* **25** I will strengthen the arms of the king of Babylon, but the arms of Phar'aoh will fall limp; and they will have to know that I am Jehovah

---

CHAP. 30
a Eze 30:18

b Jer 44:1

c Eze 29:10

d Jer 46:19
  Eze 29:12
  Eze 32:18

e Eze 29:19
  Eze 32:11

f Hab 1:6

g Eze 29:5

h Eze 29:3

i Eze 31:12

j Jer 43:12
  Jer 46:14

k Jer 46:5

l Ge 10:13, 14
  Jer 44:1

__Second Col.__
a Jer 46:25

b Eze 30:8

c Jer 46:20
  Eze 31:18

d Jer 46:19

e Jer 46:25
  Eze 29:3

f 2Ki 24:7
  Jer 46:2

g Jer 46:21

h Eze 29:12

i Jer 27:6

j Eze 32:11, 12

30:10 *Lit., "Nebuchadrezzar," a variant spelling. **30:13** *The Hebrew term may be related to a word for "dung" and is used as an expression of contempt. **30:13, 16** *Or "Memphis." **30:13** △Or "chieftain."

30:14 *That is, Thebes. **30:17** *That is, Heliopolis. **30:24** *Or "increase the power." *That is, before the king of Babylon.

when I put my sword into the hand of the king of Babylon and he wields it against the land of Egypt.[a] **26** And I will scatter the Egyptians among the nations and disperse them among the lands,[b] and they will have to know that I am Jehovah.'"

31 In the 11th year, in the third month, on the first day of the month, the word of Jehovah again came to me, saying: **2** "Son of man, say to Phar′aoh king of Egypt and to his hordes,[c]

'Whom are you like in your greatness?

3 There was an As·syr′i·an,
    a cedar in Leb′a·non,
With beautiful branches
    like a shady thicket,
    lofty in stature;
Its top was among the clouds.
4 The waters made it grow big,
    the deep springs of water
    caused it to grow high.
Streams were all around
    where it was planted;
Their channels watered all
    the trees of the field.
5 That is why it grew taller
    than all the other trees
    of the field.
Its boughs multiplied, and
    its branches grew long
Because of the abundant
    water in its streams.
6 All the birds of the sky
    nested in its boughs,
All the wild animals of
    the field gave birth under
    its branches,
And all the populous nations
    were dwelling in its shade.
7 It became majestic in beauty
    and in the length of its
    branches,
For its roots went down
    into abundant waters.
8 No other cedars in the
    garden of God[d] could
    compare to it.

None of the juniper trees
    had boughs like it,
And none of the plane trees
    could match its branches.
No other tree in the
    garden of God could rival
    its beauty.
9 I made it beautiful, with
    abundant foliage,
And all the other trees of
    E′den, the garden of the
    true God, envied it.'

10 "Therefore this is what the Sovereign Lord Jehovah says: 'Because it* became so tall, lifting its top among the clouds, and its heart became arrogant because of its height, **11** I will hand it over to the mighty ruler of the nations.[a] He will surely act against it, and I will reject it for its wickedness. **12** And foreigners, the most ruthless of the nations, will cut it down, and they will abandon it on the mountains, and its foliage will fall in all the valleys, and its branches will lie broken in all the streams of the land.[b] All the peoples of the earth will depart from its shade and abandon it. **13** All the birds of the sky will live on its fallen trunk, and all the wild animals of the field on its branches.[c] **14** This is so that no tree near the waters should grow so tall or lift up its top among the clouds and that no well-watered tree may reach up to them in height. For they will all be given over to death, to the land down below, along with the sons of mankind, who are going down into the pit.'*

15 "This is what the Sovereign Lord Jehovah says: 'On the day it goes down to the Grave,* I will cause a mourning. Therefore, I will cover over the deep

---

CHAP. 30
a Eze 29:19, 20

b Eze 29:12

CHAP. 31
c Jer 46:2
  Eze 29:2

d Ge 2:8
  Eze 28:12, 13

Second Col.
a Eze 30:10, 11
  Hab 1:6

b Eze 32:5, 6

c Eze 29:5
  Eze 32:4

31:10 *Lit., "you." **31:14** *Or "grave." **31:15** *Or "Sheol," that is, the common grave of mankind. See Glossary.

waters and hold back its streams so that the abundant waters are restrained. I will darken Leb′a·non because of it, and the trees of the field will all wither away. **16** At the sound of its downfall, I will cause nations to shudder when I bring it down to the Grave* along with all those going down into the pit,# and all the trees of E′den,ᵃ the choicest and the best of Leb′a·non, all that are well-watered, will be comforted in the land down below. **17** They have gone down to the Grave* with him, to those slain by the sword,ᵇ together with his supporters# who lived in his shadow among the nations.′ᶜ

18 "'Which of the trees of E′den was like you in glory and greatness?ᵈ But you will certainly be brought down with the trees of E′den to the land down below. You will lie down among the uncircumcised ones, with those slain by the sword. This will happen to Phar′aoh and all his hordes,' declares the Sovereign Lord Jehovah."

32 And in the 12th year, in the 12th month, on the first day of the month, the word of Jehovah again came to me, saying: **2** "Son of man, sing a dirge* concerning Phar′aoh king of Egypt, and say to him,

'You were like a strong young lion# of the nations,
But you have been silenced.
You were like a sea monster,ᵉ thrashing about in your rivers,
Muddying the waters with your feet and fouling theᐞ rivers.'

3 This is what the Sovereign Lord Jehovah says:
'By means of an assembly of many nations I will cast my net over you,
And they will haul you up in my dragnet.
4 I will abandon you on the land;
I will cast you onto the open field.
I will cause all the birds of the sky to settle on you,
And I will satisfy the wild beasts of the whole earth with you.ᵃ
5 I will cast your flesh on the mountains
And fill the valleys with your remains.ᵇ
6 I will drench the land with your gushing blood up to the mountains,
And it will fill the streams.'*
7 'And when you are extinguished I will cover the heavens and darken their stars.
I will cover the sun with clouds,
And the moon will not give its light.ᶜ
8 I will darken all the shining luminaries in the heavens because of you,
And I will cover your land with darkness,' declares the Sovereign Lord Jehovah.
9 'I will distress the hearts of many peoples when I lead your captives to other nations,
To lands that you have not known.ᵈ
10 I will cause many peoples to be awestruck,
And their kings will shudder in horror over you when

CHAP. 31
a Eze 31:9

b Eze 32:18, 20

c Eze 30:6
Eze 32:31

d Eze 31:9
Eze 32:19

CHAP. 32
e Isa 51:9, 10
Eze 29:3

Second Col.
a Eze 29:5

b Eze 31:12

c Isa 13:1, 10

d Eze 29:12
Eze 30:26

31:16, 17 *Or "Sheol," that is, the common grave of mankind. See Glossary. **31:16** #Or "grave." **31:17** Lit., "arm." **32:2** *Or "song of mourning." #Or "a maned young lion." ᐞLit., "their."

32:6 *Lit., "And the streambeds will be filled from (with) you."

I brandish my sword before
them.

They will tremble continually, each fearing for his life,
On the day of your downfall.'

11 For this is what the Sovereign Lord Jehovah says:

'The sword of the king
of Babylon will come
upon you.[a]

12 I will cause your hordes
to fall by the swords of
mighty warriors,

The most ruthless of the
nations, all of them.[b]

They will bring down the
pride of Egypt, and all her
hordes will be annihilated.[c]

13 I will destroy all her
livestock beside her
abundant waters,[d]

And no foot of a human or
hoof of the livestock will
muddy them again.'[e]

14 'At that time I will clear up
their waters,

And I will make their rivers
flow like oil,' declares the
Sovereign Lord Jehovah.

15 'When I make Egypt
a desolate wasteland,
a land stripped of all
that filled it,[f]

When I strike down all the
inhabitants in it,

They will have to know
that I am Jehovah.[g]

16 This is a dirge, and people
will certainly chant it;

The daughters of the nations
will chant it.

They will chant it over Egypt
and over all its hordes,'
declares the Sovereign
Lord Jehovah."

17 Then in the 12th year, on
the 15th day of the month, the
word of Jehovah came to me, saying: 18 "Son of man, wail over
the hordes of Egypt and bring her
down to the land below, her and
the daughters of mighty nations,
with those going down into the
pit.*

19 "'Whom do you surpass in
beauty? Go down, and lie with
the uncircumcised ones!'

20 "'They will fall among
those slain by the sword.[a] She
has been given to the sword;
drag her away along with all her
hordes.

21 "'From the depths of the
Grave* the mightiest warriors
will speak to him and his helpers. They will certainly go down
and will lie just like the uncircumcised, slain by the sword.
22 As·syr'i·a is there with all her
assembly. Their graves are all
around her, all of them fallen by
the sword.[b] 23 Her graves are
in the depths of the pit,* and her
assembly is all around her grave,
all of them struck down by the
sword, because they caused terror in the land of the living.

24 "'E'lam[c] is there with all
her hordes around her grave,
all of them fallen by the sword.
They have gone down uncircumcised to the land below, those
who caused terror in the land
of the living. Now they will bear
their shame with those going
down into the pit.* 25 They
have made a bed for her among
the slain, along with all her
hordes around her graves. All
of them are uncircumcised, slain
by the sword, because they
caused terror in the land of the
living; and they will bear their
shame with those going down
into the pit.* He has been put
among the slain.

26 "'There is where Me'shech
and Tu'bal[d] and all their* hordes
are. Her graves are all around
him. All of them are uncircumcised, pierced through by the

Cross-references (margin):

CHAP. 32
a Jer 43:10, 11
  Jer 46:25, 26
  Eze 30:24

b Eze 30:10, 11
  Hab 1:6

c Eze 29:19

d Eze 30:12

e Eze 29:8, 11

f Ps 107:33, 34
  Eze 29:12

g Eze 30:26

Second Col.
a Eze 29:8

b Isa 37:36
  Zec 10:11

c Ge 10:22
  Jer 49:34, 35

d Ge 10:2
  Eze 38:2

sword, because they caused terror in the land of the living. **27** Will they not lie with mighty uncircumcised warriors who have fallen, who went down to the Grave* with their weapons of war? And they will put their swords under their heads" and their sins on their bones, because these mighty warriors terrorized the land of the living. **28** But as for you, you will be crushed among the uncircumcised ones, and you will lie with those who were slain by the sword.

29 "'E'dom* is there, her kings and all her chieftains, who despite their mightiness, were laid among those slain by the sword; they too will lie with the uncircumcised ones* and with those going down into the pit.*

30 "'There all the princes" of the north are, along with all the Si·do'ni·ans,* who have gone down in disgrace with the slain, despite the terror caused by their mightiness. They will lie uncircumcised with those who were slain by the sword and will bear their shame with those going down into the pit.*

31 "'Phar'aoh will see all of these, and he will be comforted over all that happened to his hordes;* Phar'aoh and all his army will be slain by the sword,' declares the Sovereign Lord Jehovah.

32 "'Because he caused terror in the land of the living, Phar'aoh and all his hordes will be laid to rest with the uncircumcised, with those slain by the sword,' declares the Sovereign Lord Jehovah."

32:27 *Or "Sheol," that is, the common grave of mankind. See Glossary. "Perhaps a reference to warriors buried with their sword, with military honors. **32:29, 30** *Or "grave." **32:30** "Or "leaders."

CHAP. 32
a Ge 25:30
  Isa 34:5
  Eze 25:12, 13
  Am 1:11
  Ob 1
  Mal 1:4

b Jer 9:25, 26

c Ge 10:15
  Eze 28:21

d Eze 31:16

Second Col.

CHAP. 33
a Eze 3:11

b Le 26:25
  Eze 6:3
  Eze 21:9

c Jer 4:5
  Ho 8:1

d Jer 6:17
  Zec 1:4

e Eze 3:19
  Ac 18:6

f Isa 56:10

g Eze 3:18

h Isa 21:8
  Jer 1:17
  Eze 3:17

i Isa 3:11
  Eze 18:4

j Pr 11:21

k Pr 15:10

l Eze 3:19
  Ac 18:6

---

33 And the word of Jehovah came to me, saying: **2** "Son of man, speak to the sons of your people,* and say to them,

"'Suppose that I bring a sword upon a land,* and all the people of that land take a man and make him their watchman, **3** and he sees the sword coming upon the land and blows the horn and warns the people.* **4** If someone hears the sound of the horn but does not heed the warning* and a sword comes and takes his life,* his blood will be on his own head.* **5** He heard the sound of the horn, but he did not heed the warning. His blood will be upon himself. If he had heeded the warning, his life* would have been saved.

6 "'But if the watchman sees the sword coming and he does not blow the horn* and the people receive no warning and a sword comes and takes the life* of one of them, that person will die for his own error, but I will ask his blood back from the watchman.'"*

7 "As for you, son of man, I have appointed you as a watchman to the house of Israel; and when you hear a word from my mouth you must warn them from me.* **8** When I say to someone wicked, 'Wicked one, you will surely die!'* but you do not speak out to warn the wicked one to change his course, he will die as a wicked man because of his own error,* but I will ask his blood back from you. **9** But if you warn someone wicked to turn back from his way and he refuses to change his course, he will die for his error,* but you will certainly save your own life.*"

33:4 *Lit., "takes him away." **33:5, 6, 9** *Or "soul." **33:6** "Or "I will hold the watchman accountable for his blood."

10 "And you, son of man, say to the house of Israel, 'You have said: "Our revolts and our sins weigh heavily upon us, causing us to waste away;[a] so how will we keep living?"'[b] **11** Tell them, '"As surely as I am alive," declares the Sovereign Lord Jehovah, "I take no pleasure in the death of the wicked,[c] but rather that someone wicked changes his way[d] and keeps living.[e] Turn back, turn back from your bad ways,[f] for why should you die, O house of Israel?"'[g]

12 "And you, son of man, tell the sons of your people, 'The righteousness of the righteous man will not save him when he revolts;[h] nor will the wickedness of the wicked man make him stumble when he turns away from his wickedness;[i] nor will anyone righteous be able to keep living because of his righteousness in the day that he sins.[j] **13** When I say to the righteous one: "You will surely keep living," and he trusts in his own righteousness and does what is wrong,[*][k] none of his righteous acts will be remembered, but he will die for the wrong that he has done.[l]

14 "'And when I say to the wicked one: "You will surely die," and he turns away from his sin and does what is just and righteous,[m] **15** and the wicked one returns what was taken in pledge[n] and pays back what was taken by robbery,[o] and he walks in the statutes of life by not doing what is wrong, he will surely keep living.[p] He will not die. **16** None of the sins he committed will be held[*] against him.[q] For doing what is just and righteous, he will surely keep living.'

17 "But your people have said, 'The way of Jehovah is un-

just,' when it is actually their way that is unjust.

18 "When someone righteous abandons his righteousness and does what is wrong, he must die for it.[a] **19** But when someone wicked turns away from his wickedness and does what is just and righteous, he will keep living for doing so.[b]

20 "But you have said, 'The way of Jehovah is unjust.'[c] I will judge each of you according to his ways, O house of Israel."

21 At length in the 12th year, in the tenth month, on the fifth day of the month of our exile, a man who had escaped from Jerusalem came to me[d] and said: "The city has been struck down!"[e]

22 Now the evening before the escaped man came, the hand of Jehovah had come upon me, and he had opened my mouth before the man came to me in the morning. So my mouth was opened, and I was no longer speechless.[f]

23 Then the word of Jehovah came to me, saying: **24** "Son of man, the inhabitants of these ruins[g] are saying concerning the land of Israel, 'Abraham was just one man, and yet he took possession of the land.[h] But we are many; surely the land has been given to us as a possession.'

25 "Therefore say to them, 'This is what the Sovereign Lord Jehovah says: "You are eating food with the blood,[i] and you lift up your eyes to your disgusting idols,[*] and you keep shedding blood. So why should you possess the land? **26** You have relied on your sword,[k] you engage in detestable practices, and each of you has defiled his neighbor's

CHAP. 33
a Le 26:39
  Isa 64:6
  Eze 24:23
b Eze 37:11
c Eze 18:23
  1Ti 2:3, 4
d Isa 31:6
  Lu 15:10
e Ps 130:7, 8
f Isa 55:7
  Jer 3:22
  Jer 25:5
  Ac 3:19
g Eze 18:31
  2Pe 3:9
h Eze 3:20
  Eze 18:24
i 1Ki 8:48, 50
  Eze 18:21
j Eze 18:26
k 2Pe 2:20
l Eze 18:4
m Isa 55:7
  Eze 18:21
  Mic 6:8
n Ex 22:26
o Le 6:2, 4
  Eze 22:29
p Le 18:5
  Eze 18:27
q Isa 1:18
r Eze 20:11

Second Col.
a Heb 10:38
  2Pe 2:20
b Eze 18:27
c Eze 18:25, 29
d Eze 24:25-27
e 2Ki 25:4
  2Ch 36:17
  Jer 39:2
f Eze 3:26
g Jer 39:10
  Eze 36:4
h Ge 12:7
i Ge 9:4
  Le 17:12
j Eze 22:6
k Zep 3:3

33:13 * Or "does injustice." 33:16 * Lit., "remembered."

33:25 * The Hebrew term may be related to a word for "dung" and is used as an expression of contempt.

wife.[a] So why should you possess the land?"'[b]

27 "This is what you should say to them, 'This is what the Sovereign Lord Jehovah says: "As surely as I am alive, those living in the ruins will fall by the sword; those in the open field, I will give as food to the wild beasts; and those in the strongholds and the caves will die by disease.[c] 28 I will make the land an utterly desolate wasteland,[d] and its arrogant pride will be brought to an end, and the mountains of Israel will be desolated,[e] with no one passing through. 29 And they will have to know that I am Jehovah when I make the land an utterly desolate wasteland[f] because of all the detestable things that they have done."'[g]

30 "As for you, son of man, your people are speaking with one another about you beside the walls and in the doorways of the houses.[h] They are saying to each other, each to his brother, 'Come, and let us hear the word that comes from Jehovah.' 31 They will crowd in to sit before you as my people; and they will hear your words, but they will not do them.[i] For with their mouth they flatter you,* but their heart is greedy for dishonest gain. 32 Look! You are to them like a romantic love song, sung with a beautiful voice and skillfully played on a stringed instrument. They will hear your words, but no one will act on them. 33 And when it comes true—and it will come true—they will have to know that a prophet has been among them."[j]

34 The word of Jehovah again came to me, saying: 2 "Son of man, prophesy against the shepherds of Israel. Proph-

esy, and say to the shepherds, 'This is what the Sovereign Lord Jehovah says: "Woe to the shepherds of Israel,[a] who have been feeding themselves! Is it not the flock that the shepherds should feed?[b] 3 You eat the fat, you clothe yourselves with the wool, and you slaughter the fattest animal,[c] but you do not feed the flock.[d] 4 You have not strengthened the weak or healed the sick or bandaged the injured or brought back the strays or looked for the lost;[e] rather, you have ruled them with harshness and tyranny.[f] 5 So they were scattered because there was no shepherd;[g] they were scattered and became food for every wild beast of the field. 6 My sheep were straying on all the mountains and on every high hill; my sheep were scattered over all the surface of the earth, with no one searching for them or seeking to find them.

7 """Therefore, you shepherds, hear the word of Jehovah: 8 '"As surely as I am alive," declares the Sovereign Lord Jehovah, "because my sheep have become prey, food for every wild beast of the field, for there was no shepherd, and my shepherds did not search for my sheep; rather, they kept feeding themselves and did not feed my sheep,"' 9 therefore, you shepherds, hear the word of Jehovah. 10 This is what the Sovereign Lord Jehovah says: 'I am against the shepherds, and I will demand an accounting of them for my sheep,* and I will dismiss them from feeding# my sheep,[h] and the shepherds will no longer feed themselves. I will rescue my sheep from their mouth, and they will no longer be food for them.'"

Cross-references

33:31 * Or "they speak lustfully."

34:10 * Or "I will ask back my sheep from their hand." # Or "tending."

11 "'For this is what the Sovereign Lord Jehovah says: "Here I am, and I myself will search for my sheep, and I will care for them.[a] **12** I will care for my sheep like a shepherd who has found his scattered sheep and is feeding them.[b] I will rescue them from all the places where they were scattered in the day of clouds and thick gloom.[c] **13** I will bring them out from the peoples and collect them together from the lands and bring them into their land and feed them on the mountains of Israel,[d] by the streams and by all the dwelling places of the land. **14** In a good pasture I will feed them, and the land where they graze will be on Israel's high mountains.[e] They will lie down there in a good grazing land,[f] and they will feed on choice pastures on the mountains of Israel."

15 "'I myself will feed my sheep,[g] and I myself will make them lie down,"[h] declares the Sovereign Lord Jehovah. **16** "The lost one I will search for,[i] the stray I will bring back, the injured I will bandage, and the weak I will strengthen; but the fat one and the strong one I will annihilate. I will feed that one with judgment."

17 "'As for you, my sheep, this is what the Sovereign Lord Jehovah says: "I am about to judge between one sheep and another sheep, between the rams and the male goats.[j] **18** Is it not enough for you to feed on the very best pastures? Must you also trample the rest of your pastures with your feet? And after drinking the clearest water, must you foul the water by stamping with your feet? **19** Should my sheep now feed on the pasture trampled by your feet and drink the water befouled by the stamping of your feet?"

20 "'Therefore this is what the Sovereign Lord Jehovah says to them: "Here I am, and I myself will judge between a fat sheep and a lean sheep, **21** for with your flank and shoulder you kept pushing, and with your horns you kept shoving all the sick ones until you had scattered them abroad. **22** And I will save my sheep, and they will no longer become something to prey upon;[a] and I will judge between a sheep and a sheep. **23** I will raise up one shepherd over them,[b] my servant David,[c] and he will feed them. He himself will feed them and become their shepherd.[d] **24** And I, Jehovah, will become their God,[e] and my servant David a chieftain among them.[f] I myself, Jehovah, have spoken.

25 "'And I will make a covenant of peace with them,[g] and I will rid the land of vicious wild beasts,[h] so that they may dwell securely in the wilderness and sleep in the forests.[i] **26** I will make them and the area around my hill a blessing,[j] and I will cause the rain to fall at the proper time. Blessings will pour down like the rains.[k] **27** The trees of the field will yield their fruit, and the soil will give its produce,[l] and they will dwell securely on the land. And they will have to know that I am Jehovah when I break their yoke bars[m] and rescue them from those who enslaved them. **28** They will no longer become something for the nations to prey upon, and the wild beasts of the earth will not devour them, and they will dwell in security, with no one to make them afraid.[n]

29 "'I will establish for them a plantation of fame,* and they will no longer die from famine in the land,[o] and they will no longer be humiliated by the na-

CHAP. 34

a 1Sa 17:34, 35
  Ps 80:1
  Isa 56:8
b Isa 40:11
c Joe 2:1, 2
  Zep 1:14, 15
d Jer 23:3
  Eze 11:17
  Am 9:14
  Mic 7:14
e Isa 25:6
  Isa 30:23
  Jer 31:12
f Jer 33:12
g Jer 3:15
h Zep 3:13
i Mic 4:6
  Mt 15:24
  Lu 15:4
j Zec 10:3

Second Col.

a Isa 40:11
  Jer 23:3
b Joh 10:11
  Heb 13:20
  1Pe 5:4
  Re 7:17
c Isa 11:1
  Jer 30:9
d Eze 37:24
  Ho 3:5
e Ex 29:45
  Jer 31:1
f Ps 2:6
  Isa 9:6
  Jer 23:5
  Mic 5:2
  Lu 1:32
  Ac 5:31
g Eze 37:26
h Le 26:6
  Isa 11:6-9
  Isa 35:9
  Isa 65:25
  Ho 2:18
i Jer 23:6
  Jer 33:16
j Isa 56:7
  Eze 20:40
  Mic 4:1
k Ge 12:2, 3
  De 28:12
  Zec 8:13
l Le 26:4
  Ps 85:12
  Isa 35:2
  Eze 36:30
m Le 26:13
n Jer 30:10
  Jer 46:27
o Eze 36:29

34:29 *Lit., "for a name."

tions.[a] **30** 'Then they will have to know that I, Jehovah their God, am with them and that they, the house of Israel, are my people,'[b] declares the Sovereign Lord Jehovah.'"

31 "'As for you, my sheep,[c] the sheep that I care for, you are but men, and I am your God,' declares the Sovereign Lord Jehovah."

35 The word of Jehovah again came to me, saying: **2** "Son of man, turn your face toward the mountainous region of Seʹir,[d] and prophesy against it.[e] **3** Say to it, 'This is what the Sovereign Lord Jehovah says: "Here I am against you, O mountainous region of Seʹir, and I will stretch out my hand against you and make you a desolate wasteland.[f] **4** I will turn your cities into ruins, and you will become a desolate wasteland;[g] and you will have to know that I am Jehovah. **5** For you showed unrelenting hostility,[h] and you gave the Israelites over to the sword at the time of their disaster, at the time of their final punishment.'[i]

6 "'"Therefore as surely as I am alive,' declares the Sovereign Lord Jehovah, 'I will prepare you for bloodshed, and bloodshed will pursue you.[j] Since it was blood that you hated, bloodshed will pursue you.[k] **7** I will make the mountainous region of Seʹir a desolate wasteland,[l] and I will cut off from it anyone passing through and anyone returning. **8** I will fill its mountains with the slain; and those slain by the sword will fall on your hills, in your valleys, and in all your streams. **9** I will make you a perpetual desolation, and your cities will not be inhabited;[m] and you will have to know that I am Jehovah.'

10 "Because you said, 'These two nations and these two lands

will become mine, and we will take possession of both,'[a] even though Jehovah himself was there, **11** 'therefore as surely as I am alive,' declares the Sovereign Lord Jehovah, 'I will deal with you according to the same anger and jealousy that you displayed in your hatred toward them;[b] and I will make myself known among them when I judge you. **12** You will then have to know that I myself, Jehovah, have heard all the insolent things you spoke against the mountains of Israel when you said, "They have been laid desolate and have been given to us to devour."* **13** And you spoke arrogantly against me, and you multiplied your words against me.[c] I heard it all.'

14 "This is what the Sovereign Lord Jehovah says: 'The whole earth will rejoice when I will make you a desolate wasteland. **15** Just as you rejoiced when the inheritance of the house of Israel was laid desolate, that is how I will deal with you.[d] You will become a desolate ruin, O mountainous region of Seʹir, yes, all of Eʹdom;[e] and they will have to know that I am Jehovah.'"

36 "As for you, son of man, prophesy about the mountains of Israel and say, 'O mountains of Israel, hear the word of Jehovah. **2** This is what the Sovereign Lord Jehovah says: "The enemy has said against you, 'Aha! Even the ancient high places have become our possession!'"'[f]

3 "So prophesy and say, 'This is what the Sovereign Lord Jehovah says: "Because they have desolated and attacked you from every direction, so that you would become a possession of

---

CHAP. 34
a Eze 36:15

b Eze 37:27

c Ps 78:52
Ps 100:3
Isa 40:11

CHAP. 35
d Ge 32:3
De 2:5

e Jer 49:8
La 4:22
Eze 25:8, 9
Ob 1

f Eze 25:12, 13

g Joe 3:19
Mal 1:3

h Eze 27:41
Am 1:11

i Ps 137:7
Ob 10

j Ob 15

k Eze 25:14

l Eze 25:13

m Jer 49:17, 18
Eze 25:13
Mal 1:4

Second Col.
a Eze 36:5
Ob 13

b Am 1:11

c Ob 3

d La 4:21
Ob 12, 15

e Isa 34:5
Eze 25:12, 13
Eze 36:5

CHAP. 36
f Jer 49:1
Eze 35:10

35:12 *Lit., "as food."

the survivors* from among the nations and people keep talking about you and slandering you,[a] 4 therefore, O mountains of Israel, hear the word of the Sovereign Lord Jehovah! This is what the Sovereign Lord Jehovah says to the mountains and the hills, to the streams and the valleys, to the ruins that were desolated,[b] and to the abandoned cities that have been plundered and ridiculed by the survivors of the nations around them;[c] 5 to these the Sovereign Lord Jehovah says: 'In the fire of my zeal[d] I will speak against the survivors of the nations and against all E'dom, those who with great rejoicing and utter scorn*[e] have claimed my land as their own possession, to take over its pastures and to plunder it.'"[f]

6 "So prophesy concerning the land of Israel, and say to the mountains and to the hills, to the streams and to the valleys, 'This is what the Sovereign Lord Jehovah says: "Look! I will speak in my zeal and in my rage, because you have borne humiliation by the nations."'[g]

7 "Therefore this is what the Sovereign Lord Jehovah says: 'I myself raise my hand in an oath that the surrounding nations will themselves bear their own shame.[h] 8 But you, O mountains of Israel, will produce branches and bear your fruitage for my people Israel,[i] for they will soon return. 9 For I am with you, and I will turn toward you, and you will be cultivated and sown with seed. 10 I will multiply your people—the whole house of Israel, all of it—and the cities will be inhabited[j] and the ruins will be rebuilt.[k] 11 Yes, I will multiply your people and your livestock;[l] they will in-

crease and be fruitful. And I will cause you to be inhabited as you were formerly,[a] and I will make you prosper more than in the past;[b] and you will have to know that I am Jehovah.[c] 12 I will cause people—my people Israel—to walk upon you, and they will take possession of you.[d] You will become their inheritance, and you will never again make them childless."'[e]

13 "This is what the Sovereign Lord Jehovah says: 'Because they are saying to you, "You are a land that devours people and bereaves your nations of children,"' 14 'therefore, you will no longer devour people or make your nations childless,' declares the Sovereign Lord Jehovah. 15 'I will not subject you to any more insults of the nations or make you bear the taunts of people,[f] and you will no longer cause your nations to stumble,' declares the Sovereign Lord Jehovah."

16 And the word of Jehovah again came to me, saying: 17 "Son of man, when the house of Israel was dwelling in their land, they made it unclean by their ways and their dealings.[g] Their ways were like the uncleanness of menstruation to me.[h] 18 So I poured out my rage on them because of the blood that they had shed upon the land[i] and because they made the land unclean with their disgusting idols.*[j] 19 So I scattered them among the nations and dispersed them among the lands.[k] I judged them according to their way and according to their dealings. 20 But when they came to those nations, people profaned my holy name[l] by saying about them, 'These are

CHAP. 36
a De 28:37
   1Ki 9:7
   La 2:15
   Da 9:16

b Jer 25:9

c Ps 79:4
   Eze 34:28

d Zep 3:8

e Ob 12

f Eze 25:12, 13
   Eze 35:10, 11
   Am 1:11

g Ps 74:10
   Ps 123:4

h Jer 25:9
   Jer 49:17

i Isa 44:23
   Isa 51:3
   Eze 36:30

j Zec 8:4

k Isa 51:3
   Jer 30:18, 19
   Am 9:14

l Jer 31:27

Second Col.
a Isa 54:7
   Jer 30:18

b Hag 2:9

c Ho 2:20
   Joe 3:17

d Jer 32:44
   Ob 17

e Isa 65:23

f Isa 54:4
   Isa 60:14
   Mic 7:8
   Zep 2:8
   Zep 3:19

g Ps 106:38
   Isa 24:5
   Jer 2:7
   Jer 16:18

h Le 12:2
   Isa 64:6

i Isa 42:24, 25

j Eze 23:37

k Le 26:38
   Eze 22:15

l Isa 52:5
   Ro 2:24

36:3 *Lit., "remnant; remaining ones."
36:5 *Or "scorn in the soul."

36:18 *The Hebrew term may be related to a word for "dung" and is used as an expression of contempt.

the people of Jehovah, but they had to leave his land.' **21** So I will show concern for my holy name, which the house of Israel profaned among the nations where they have gone."[a]

22 "Therefore say to the house of Israel, 'This is what the Sovereign Lord Jehovah says: "Not for your sakes am I acting, O house of Israel, but for my holy name, which you profaned among the nations where you have gone."'[b] **23** 'I will certainly sanctify my great name,[c] which was profaned among the nations, which you profaned among them; and the nations will have to know that I am Jehovah,'[d] declares the Sovereign Lord Jehovah, 'when I am sanctified among you before their eyes. **24** I will take you from the nations and gather you back from all the lands and bring you into your land.[e] **25** I will sprinkle clean water on you, and you will become clean;[f] I will cleanse you from all your uncleanness[g] and from all your disgusting idols.[h] **26** I will give you a new heart[i] and put a new spirit inside you.[j] I will remove the heart of stone[k] from your body and give you a heart of flesh.* **27** I will put my spirit inside you, and I will cause you to walk in my regulations,[l] and you will observe and carry out my judicial decisions. **28** Then you will dwell in the land that I gave to your forefathers, and you will be my people and I will be your God.'[m]

29 "'I will save you from all your uncleanness and summon the grain and make it abound, and I will not bring famine upon you.[n] **30** I will make the fruitage of the tree and the produce of the field abound, so that you may never again suffer the dis-

grace of famine among the nations.[a] **31** Then you will remember your evil ways and your deeds that were not good, and you will loathe yourselves because of your guilt and your detestable practices.[b] **32** But know this: I am not doing this for your sakes,'[c] declares the Sovereign Lord Jehovah. 'Instead, be ashamed and feel humiliated because of your ways, O house of Israel.'

33 "This is what the Sovereign Lord Jehovah says: 'In the day that I cleanse you from all your guilt, I will cause the cities to be inhabited[d] and the ruins to be rebuilt.[e] **34** The desolate land that was lying desolate for everyone passing by to see will be cultivated. **35** And people will say: "The desolate land has become like the garden of E'den,[f] and the cities that were in ruins and desolate and torn down are now fortified and inhabited."[g] **36** And the nations that are left remaining around you will have to know that I myself, Jehovah, have built what was torn down, and I have planted what was desolate. I myself, Jehovah, have spoken, and I have done it.'[h]

37 "This is what the Sovereign Lord Jehovah says: 'I will also let the house of Israel ask me to do this for them: I will multiply their people like a flock. **38** Like the flock of holy ones, like the flock of Jerusalem* during her festivals,[i] the cities that were in ruins will become full of flocks of people;[j] and they will have to know that I am Jehovah.'"

37 The hand of Jehovah was upon me, and by his spirit Jehovah took me and set me down in the middle of the valley

---

CHAP. 36

a Ps 74:18
Isa 48:9
Eze 20:9

b Ps 106:7, 8

c Isa 5:16
Eze 20:41

d Ps 102:13-15

e De 30:3
Isa 43:5
Jer 23:3
Eze 34:13
Ho 1:11

f Nu 19:13
Ps 51:7

g Isa 4:4
Jer 33:8

h Eze 6:4

i Jer 32:39

j Ps 51:10
Eze 11:19, 20

k Zec 7:12

l Jer 31:33

m Jer 30:22
Eze 37:25, 27

n Eze 34:29

Second Col.

a Eze 34:27

b Ezr 9:6
Ne 9:26
Jer 31:18
Eze 6:9

c De 9:5
Da 9:19

d Zec 8:8

e Isa 58:12
Jer 33:10, 11
Am 9:14

f Ge 2:8

g Isa 51:3

h Eze 28:26
Eze 37:14

i Ex 23:17

j Jer 30:18, 19

36:26 *That is, one sensitive to God's guidance.

36:38 *Or possibly, "Like the sacrificial flocks of sheep in Jerusalem."

plain,[a] and it was full of bones. **2** He had me pass all around them, and I saw that there were very many bones lying in the valley plain, and they were very dry.[b] **3** He asked me: "Son of man, can these bones come to life?" To that I said: "Sovereign Lord Jehovah, you are the one who knows."[c] **4** So he said to me: "Prophesy over these bones, and say to them, 'You dry bones, hear the word of Jehovah:

5 "'This is what the Sovereign Lord Jehovah says to these bones: "I will cause breath to enter you, and you will come to life.[d] **6** I will put sinews and flesh on you, and I will cover you with skin and put breath in you, and you will come to life; and you will have to know that I am Jehovah."'"

7 Then I prophesied just as I had been commanded. As soon as I prophesied, there was a noise, a rattling sound, and the bones began to come together, bone to bone. **8** Then I saw sinews and flesh come on them, and skin covered over them. But there was still no breath in them.

9 He then said to me: "Prophesy to the wind. Prophesy, son of man, and say to the wind, 'This is what the Sovereign Lord Jehovah says: "From the four winds come in, O wind,* and blow upon these people who were killed, so that they may come to life."'"

10 So I prophesied just as he commanded me, and breath* came into them, and they began to live and to stand on their feet,[e] an extremely large army.

11 Then he said to me: "Son of man, these bones are the whole house of Israel.[f] Here they are saying, 'Our bones are dry, and our hope has perished.[g] We are completely cut off.' **12** So

prophesy and say to them, 'This is what the Sovereign Lord Jehovah says: "I will open your graves[a] and raise you up from your graves, my people, and bring you to the land of Israel.[b] **13** And you will have to know that I am Jehovah when I open your graves and when I raise you up out of your graves, O my people.'"[c] **14** 'I will put my spirit in you and you will come to life,[d] and I will settle you on your land; and you will have to know that I myself, Jehovah, have spoken and I have done it,' declares Jehovah."

15 The word of Jehovah again came to me, saying: **16** "And you, son of man, take a stick and write on it, 'For Judah and for the people of Israel who are with him.'*[e] Then take another stick and write on it, 'For Joseph, the stick of E'phra·im, and all the house of Israel who are with him.'*[f] **17** Then bring them close to each other so that they become just one stick in your hand.[g] **18** When your people* say to you, 'Will you not tell us what these things mean?' **19** tell them, 'This is what the Sovereign Lord Jehovah says: "I will take the stick of Joseph, which is in the hand of E'phra·im, and the tribes of Israel who are with him, and I will join them to the stick of Judah; and I will make them one stick,[h] and they will become one in my hand."' **20** The sticks that you write on should be in your hand for them to see.

21 "Then tell them, 'This is what the Sovereign Lord Jehovah says: "I will take the Israelites from among the nations where they have gone, and I will collect them together from every direction and bring them

CHAP. 37
a Re 21:10

b Eze 37:11

c De 32:39
1Sa 2:6

d Ge 2:7
Eze 37:14

e Re 11:11

f Eze 36:10

g Isa 49:14

Second Col.
a Isa 66:14

b Eze 11:17
Am 9:14

c Ps 126:2

d Isa 32:14, 15
Eze 36:27

e 2Ch 15:9
2Ch 30:11

f 1Ki 11:31
1Ki 12:20

g Isa 11:13
Jer 3:18

h Jer 50:4
Zec 10:6

37:9 *Or "breath; spirit." **37:10** *Or "spirit."

37:16 *Or "who are his partners." **37:18** *Lit., "the sons of your people."

to their land.[a] 22 I will make them one nation in the land,[b] on the mountains of Israel, and one king will rule over all of them,[c] and they will no longer be two nations; nor will they be divided any longer into two kingdoms.[d] 23 They will no longer defile themselves with their disgusting idols* and their detestable practices and all their transgressions.[e] I will save them from all their unfaithfulness by which they have sinned, and I will cleanse them. They will be my people, and I myself will be their God.[f]

24 "'My servant David will be their king,[g] and they will all have one shepherd.[h] They will walk in my judicial decisions and carefully observe my statutes.[i] 25 They will dwell on the land that I gave to my servant, to Jacob, where your forefathers lived,[j] and they will dwell on it forever,[k] they and their children's and their children's children;[l] and David my servant will be their chieftain* forever.[m]

26 "'And I will make a covenant of peace with them;[n] it will be an eternal covenant with them. I will establish them and make them many[o] and place my sanctuary among them forever. 27 My tent* will be with* them, and I will be their God, and they will be my people.[p] 28 And the nations will have to know that I, Jehovah, am sanctifying Israel when my sanctuary is in their midst forever.'"[q]

38 The word of Jehovah again came to me, saying: 2 "Son of man, set your face against Gog of the land of Ma'gog,[r] the head chieftain* of Me'-shech and Tu'bal,[a] and prophesy against him.[b] 3 Say, 'This is what the Sovereign Lord Jehovah says: "Here I am against you, O Gog, head chieftain* of Me'shech and Tu'bal. 4 I will turn you around and put hooks in your jaws[c] and bring you out with all your army,[d] horses and horsemen, all of them clothed in splendor, a vast assembly with large shields and bucklers,* all of them wielding swords; 5 Persia, E·thi·o'pi-a, and Put[e] are with them, all of them with buckler and helmet; 6 Go'mer and all its troops, the house of To·gar'mah[f] from the remotest parts of the north, along with all its troops—many peoples are with you.[g]

7 "'Be ready, prepare yourselves, you with all your armies that are assembled with you, and you will be their commander.*

8 "'You will be given attention* after many days. In the final part of the years you will invade the land whose people have been restored from the ravages of the sword, collected together out of many peoples onto the mountains of Israel, which had long been lying devastated. The inhabitants of this land were restored from the peoples, and all of them dwell in security.[h] 9 You will come against them like a storm, and you will cover the land like clouds, you and all your troops and many peoples with you.'"

10 "This is what the Sovereign Lord Jehovah says: 'In that day thoughts will come into your heart, and you will devise an evil plan. 11 You will say: "I will invade the land of unprotected settlements.*[i] I will come against

CHAP. 37

a De 30:3
  Isa 11:12
  Jer 16:14, 15
  Am 9:14
b Jer 3:18
  Ho 1:11
c Ge 49:10
  Ps 2:6
  Isa 9:6
  Jer 23:5
  Lu 1:32
d Eze 37:19
  Zec 10:6
e Isa 2:18
  Eze 11:18
  Ho 14:8
  Zec 13:2
f Jer 31:33
  Eze 36:28
g Jer 23:5
  Jer 30:9
  Ho 3:5
  Lu 1:32
h Joh 10:16
  1Pe 5:4
i De 30:8-10
  Jer 32:39
  Eze 36:27
j Jer 30:3
k Joe 3:20
l Isa 60:21
  Am 9:15
m Eze 34:24
  Lu 1:32
n Eze 34:25
o Jer 30:19
  Zec 8:5
p Le 26:12
  Eze 11:19, 20
  Eze 43:7
  Ho 2:23
  Re 21:3
q Eze 36:23

CHAP. 38

r Eze 38:15

Second Col.

a Isa 66:19
  Eze 27:13
  Eze 32:26
b Eze 39:1
c 2Ki 19:20, 28
  Eze 29:3, 4
  Eze 39:2
d Eze 38:15
e 1Ch 1:8
f Ge 10:2, 3
  Eze 27:14
g Eze 39:2
h Jer 23:5, 6
  Eze 28:25, 26
  Eze 34:25
i Ex 15:9

37:23 *The Hebrew term may be related to a word for "dung" and is used as an expression of contempt. 37:25 *Lit., "sons." #Or "prince." 37:27 *Or "dwelling place; home." #Or "over." 38:2, 3 *Or "chief prince."

38:4 *A small shield, often carried by archers. 38:7 *Lit., "guard." 38:8 *Or "summoned." 38:11 *Or "of open, rural country."

those living in security, without disturbance, all of them living in settlements unprotected by walls, bars, or gates." **12** It will be to take much spoil and plunder, to attack the devastated places that are now inhabited[a] and a people regathered from the nations,[b] who are accumulating wealth and property,[c] those who are living in the center of the earth.

13 "'She′ba[d] and De′dan,[e] the merchants of Tar′shish[f] and all its warriors* will say to you: "Are you invading to get much spoil and plunder? Have you assembled your armies to carry off silver and gold, to take wealth and property, to seize a very great spoil?"'

14 "So prophesy, son of man, and say to Gog, 'This is what the Sovereign Lord Jehovah says: "On that day when my people Israel are dwelling in security, will you not know it?[g] **15** You will come from your place, from the remotest parts of the north,[h] you and many peoples with you, all of them riding on horses, a great assembly, a vast army.[i] **16** Like clouds covering the land, you will come against my people Israel. In the final part of the days I will bring you against my land[j] so that the nations may know me when I sanctify myself through you before their eyes, O Gog."'[k]

17 "This is what the Sovereign Lord Jehovah says: 'Are you not the same one I spoke about in the former days through my servants the prophets of Israel, who prophesied for many years that you would be brought against them?'

18 "'On that day, the day when Gog invades the land of Israel,' declares the Sovereign Lord Jehovah, 'my great rage

will flare up.[a] **19** In my zeal, in the fire of my fury, I will speak; and in that day there will be a great earthquake in the land of Israel. **20** Because of me the fish of the sea, the birds of the sky, the wild beasts of the field, all the reptiles that creep on the ground, and all humans on the surface of the earth will tremble, and the mountains will be thrown down,[b] and the cliffs will fall, and every wall will collapse to the ground.'

21 "'I will call for a sword against him on all my mountains,' declares the Sovereign Lord Jehovah. 'Every man's sword will be against his own brother.[c] **22** I will bring my judgment against him* with pestilence[d] and bloodshed; and I will rain down a torrential downpour and hailstones[e] and fire[f] and sulfur[g] on him and on his troops and on the many peoples with him.[h] **23** And I will certainly magnify myself and sanctify myself and make myself known before the eyes of many nations; and they will have to know that I am Jehovah.'

39 "And you, son of man, prophesy against Gog,[i] and tell him, 'This is what the Sovereign Lord Jehovah says: "I am against you, Gog, head chieftain* of Me′shech and Tu′bal.[j] **2** I will turn you around and lead you and make you come up from the remotest parts of the north[k] and bring you in upon the mountains of Israel. **3** I will knock your bow out of your left hand and make your arrows fall from your right hand. **4** On the mountains of Israel you will fall,[l] you and all your troops and the peoples who will be with you. I

CHAP. 38
a Jer 33:12

b Zec 10:8

c Isa 60:5
   Isa 61:6

d Eze 27:22

e Eze 27:15

f Eze 27:25

g Eze 38:8

h Eze 39:2

i Zep 3:8

j Joe 3:2

k Ex 14:4
   2Ki 19:17-19
   Ps 83:17, 18
   Eze 39:21

Second Col.

a Joe 3:16
   Na 1:2
   Zec 2:8

b Na 1:5

c 2Ch 20:23
   Hag 2:22
   Zec 14:13

d Zec 14:12

e Ex 9:22
   Jos 10:11

f Isa 30:30

g Ge 19:24

h Jer 25:31

CHAP. 39
i Eze 38:2

j Eze 27:13
   Eze 32:26

k Eze 38:4, 15

l Eze 38:21

38:13 *Or "maned young lions."

38:22 *Or "I will bring myself into judgment with him." **39:1** *Or "chief prince."

will give you as food to all kinds of birds of prey and the wild beasts of the field.'"[a]

5 "'You will fall on the open field,[b] for I myself have spoken,' declares the Sovereign Lord Jehovah.

6 "'And I will send fire against Ma'gog and against those who are inhabiting the islands in security,[c] and they will have to know that I am Jehovah. **7** I will make my holy name known among my people Israel, and I will not allow my holy name to be profaned any longer; and the nations will have to know that I am Jehovah,[d] the Holy One in Israel.'[e]

8 "'Yes, this is coming, and it will be done,' declares the Sovereign Lord Jehovah. 'This is the day I have spoken about. **9** The inhabitants of the cities of Israel will go out and make fires with the weapons—the bucklers* and shields, the bows and arrows, the war clubs# and lances. And they will use them to light fires[f] for seven years. **10** They will not need to take wood from the field or gather firewood from the forests because they will use the weapons to light fires.'

"'They will take spoil from those who despoiled them and plunder from those who had been plundering them,' declares the Sovereign Lord Jehovah.

11 "'On that day I will give Gog[g] a burial place there in Israel, in the valley of those who travel east of the sea, and it will block the path of those passing through. That is where they will bury Gog and all his hordes, and they will call it the Valley of Hamon-Gog.*[h] **12** The house of Israel will spend seven months

burying them in order to cleanse the land.[a] **13** All the people of the land will work at burying them, and this will bring them fame in the day that I glorify myself,'[b] declares the Sovereign Lord Jehovah.

14 "'Men will be assigned to pass through the land constantly and bury the bodies left remaining on the surface of the earth, in order to cleanse it. They will continue the search for seven months. **15** When those who pass through the land see a human bone, they will set up a marker beside it. Then those assigned to do the burying will bury it in the Valley of Hamon-Gog.[c] **16** And there will also be a city there named Ha·mo'nah.* And they will cleanse the land.'[d]

17 "As for you, son of man, this is what the Sovereign Lord Jehovah says: 'Say to every sort of bird and to all the wild beasts of the field, "Gather yourselves together and come. Gather all around my sacrifice that I am preparing for you, a great sacrifice on the mountains of Israel.[e] You will eat flesh and drink blood.[f] **18** You will eat the flesh of mighty ones and drink the blood of the chieftains of the earth—the rams, lambs, goats, and bulls—all the fattened animals of Ba'shan. **19** You will gorge yourselves on fat and drink blood until you are drunk from the sacrifice that I prepare for you."'

20 "'At my table you will be filled up with horses and charioteers, mighty ones and all sorts of warriors,'[g] declares the Sovereign Lord Jehovah.

21 "'I will display my glory among the nations, and all the nations will see the judgment that I have executed and the

CHAP. 39
a Re 19:17, 18

b Jer 25:33

c Eze 38:22

d Eze 38:16

e Isa 6:3

f Ps 46:9

g Eze 38:2

h Eze 39:15

Second Col.
a De 21:22, 23

b Eze 38:16

c Eze 39:11

d Eze 39:12

e Isa 34:6-8
Jer 46:10
Zep 1:7

f Re 19:17, 18

g Eze 38:4-6
Hag 2:22
Re 19:17, 18

39:9 *A small shield, often carried by archers. #Or possibly, "handpikes," a weapon with a pointed tip. **39:11** *Or "the Valley of Gog's Hordes."

39:16 *Meaning "Hordes."

power* that I have demonstrated among them.[a] **22** From that
day on the house of Israel will
have to know that I am Jehovah their God. **23** And the nations will have to know that the
house of Israel went into exile
because of their own error, because they were unfaithful to
me.[b] So I hid my face from them[c]
and handed them over to their
enemies,[d] and they all fell by the
sword. **24** I dealt with them according to their uncleanness and
their transgressions, and I hid
my face from them.'

25 "Therefore this is what the
Sovereign Lord Jehovah says: 'I
will restore the captives of Jacob[e] and have mercy on the
whole house of Israel;[f] and I will
zealously defend* my holy name.[g]
26 After they have been humiliated for all their unfaithfulness
toward me,[h] they will dwell securely on their land, with no one
to make them afraid.[i] **27** When I
bring them back from the peoples
and collect them together from
the lands of their enemies,[j] I will
also sanctify myself among them
before the eyes of many nations.'[k]

28 "'They will have to know
that I am Jehovah their God
when I send them into ex-
ile among the nations and then
gather them back to their land,
not leaving any of them behind.[l]
29 I will not hide my face from
them any longer,[m] for I will pour
out my spirit on the house of
Israel,'[n] declares the Sovereign
Lord Jehovah."

40 In the 25th year of our exile,[o] at the beginning of
the year, on the tenth day of the
month, in the 14th year after the
city had fallen,[p] on that very day
the hand of Jehovah was upon
me, and he took me to the city.[q]
2 By means of visions from God,
he brought me to the land of Israel and set me down on a very
high mountain,[a] on which there
was a structure like a city to the
south.

3 When he brought me there,
I saw a man whose appear-
ance was like that of copper.[b]
He had a flax cord and a measuring reed* in his hand,[c] and
he was standing in the gateway.
4 The man said to me: "Son of
man, look closely, listen carefully, and pay attention* to everything I show you, for that is why
you were brought here. Tell the
house of Israel everything that
you see."[d]

5 I saw a wall surrounding
the outside of the temple.* In
the man's hand was a measuring
reed six cubits long (to each cubit, a handbreadth was added).#
He began to measure the wall,
and its thickness was one reed
and its height was one reed.

6 Then he came to the gate
that faced east[e] and climbed its
steps. When he measured the
threshold of the gate, its width
was one reed, and the width
of the other threshold was also
one reed. **7** Each guard chamber was one reed long and one
reed wide, and there were five
cubits between the guard chambers.[f] The threshold of the gate
beside the porch of the gate facing the interior measured one
reed.

8 He measured the porch of
the gate toward the interior,
and it was one reed. **9** He then
measured the porch of the gate,

39:21 *Lit., "hand." **39:25** *Lit., "show exclusive devotion for."

40:3 *See App. B14. **40:4** *Lit., "set your heart." **40:5** *Lit., "house." Rendered this way in chapters 40-48 when "house" refers to the temple complex or the actual temple building. #Lit., "a measuring reed of six cubits, a cubit and a handbreadth." This refers to long cubits. See App. B14.

CHAP. 39
a Ex 7:4; Ex 14:4; Isa 37:20; Eze 38:16; Mal 1:11
b 2Ch 7:21, 22
c De 31:18; Isa 59:2
d Le 26:24, 25; De 32:30; Ps 106:40, 41
e Jer 30:3; Eze 34:13
f Ho 1:11; Zec 1:16
g Eze 36:21
h Da 9:16
i Le 26:5, 6
j Jer 30:10; Am 9:14; Zep 3:20
k Isa 5:16; Eze 36:23
l De 30:4
m Isa 45:17; Isa 54:8; Jer 29:14
n Isa 32:14, 15; Joe 2:28

CHAP. 40
o 2Ki 24:15, 16
p 2Ki 25:8-10; Eze 33:21
q Eze 8:3

Second Col.
a Isa 2:2
b Eze 1:5, 7; Da 10:5, 6
c Eze 47:3; Zec 2:1, 2; Re 11:1; Re 21:15
d Eze 43:10
e Eze 40:10; Eze 43:1, 4; Eze 46:1, 2
f 1Ch 9:26, 27

which was eight cubits; and he measured its side pillars, which were two cubits; and the porch of the gate was on the side facing the interior.

10 There were three guard chambers on each side of the east gate. The three were the same size, and the side pillars on either side were the same size.

11 Then he measured the width of the entrance of the gate, which was 10 cubits; and the length of the gate was 13 cubits.

12 The partitioned area in front of the guard chambers on either side was one cubit. The guard chambers on both sides were six cubits each.

13 He then measured the gate from the roof of the one guard chamber* to the roof of the other, and it was 25 cubits wide; one entrance was across from the other entrance.ᵃ **14** Then he measured the side pillars, which were 60 cubits tall, as well as the side pillars in the gates all around the courtyard. **15** From the front of the entrance of the gate to the front of the porch on the inner side of the gate was 50 cubits.

16 There were windows with narrowing frames*ᵇ for the guard chambers and for their side pillars inside the gate on each side. The interior of the porches also had windows on each side, and there were palm-tree figuresᶜ on the side pillars.

17 He then brought me into the outer courtyard, and I saw dining roomsᵈ and a pavement around the courtyard. There were 30 dining rooms on the pavement. **18** The pavement at the side of the gates correspond-

ed to the length of the gates —this was the lower pavement.

19 Then he measured the distance* from the front of the lower gate to the perimeter of the inner courtyard. It was 100 cubits on the east and on the north.

20 The outer courtyard had a gate facing north, and he measured its length and its width. **21** There were three guard chambers on each side. Its side pillars and porch had the same measurements as the first gate. It was 50 cubits long and 25 cubits wide. **22** Its windows, its porch, and its palm-tree figuresᵃ were the same size as those of the east gate. People could reach it by climbing seven steps, and its porch was in front of them.

23 There was a gate in the inner courtyard opposite the north gate and one opposite the east gate. He measured the distance from gate to gate, and it was 100 cubits.

24 Next he brought me toward the south, and I saw a gate on the south side.ᵇ He measured its side pillars and its porch, and they were the same size as the others. **25** There were windows on each side of it and its porch, like the other windows. It was 50 cubits long and 25 cubits wide. **26** There were seven steps leading up to it,ᶜ and its porch was in front of them. And it had palm-tree figures on its side pillars, one on each side.

27 The inner courtyard had a gate facing south; he measured southward from gate to gate, and the distance was 100 cubits. **28** Next he brought me into the inner courtyard through the south gate; when he measured the south gate, it was the same

---

CHAP. 40
a Eze 40:20, 21

b 1Ki 6:4
  Eze 41:26

c 1Ki 6:35

d 1Ch 28:12

Second Col.
a Eze 41:20, 26

b Eze 46:9

c Eze 40:20, 22

40:13 *Possibly referring to the top of the wall of the guard chamber. 40:16 *Or "beveled (splayed) windows." 40:17 *Or "I saw chambers." 40:19 *Lit., "width."

size as the others. **29** Its guard chambers, its side pillars, and its porch were the same size as the others. There were windows on each side of it and its porch. It was 50 cubits long and 25 cubits wide.[a] **30** There were porches all around; they were 25 cubits long and 5 cubits wide. **31** Its porch faced the outer courtyard, and there were palm-tree figures on its side pillars,[b] and eight steps led up to it.[c]

32 When he brought me into the inner courtyard from the east, he measured the gate, and it was the same size as the others. **33** Its guard chambers, its side pillars, and its porch were the same size as the others, and there were windows on each side of it and its porch. It was 50 cubits long and 25 cubits wide. **34** Its porch faced the outer courtyard, and there were palm-tree figures on both of its side pillars, and eight steps led up to it.

35 He then brought me into the north gate[d] and measured it; it was the same size as the others. **36** Its guard chambers, its side pillars, and its porch were the same as the others. It had windows on each side. It was 50 cubits long and 25 cubits wide. **37** Its side pillars faced the outer courtyard, and there were palm-tree figures on both of its side pillars, and eight steps led up to it.

38 A dining room with its entrance was near the side pillars of the gates, where the whole burnt offerings were washed.[e] **39** There were two tables on each side of the porch of the gate on which to slaughter the whole burnt offerings,[f] the sin offerings,[g] and the guilt offerings.[h] **40** On the way up to the north gate, there were two tables outside the entrance. There were also two tables in-

side, in the porch of the gate. **41** There were four tables on each side of the gate—eight tables in all—on which the sacrifices were slaughtered. **42** The four tables for the whole burnt offering were of hewn stone. They were one and a half cubits long, one and a half cubits wide, and one cubit high. On them were kept the implements used to slaughter the burnt offerings and the sacrifices. **43** Shelves, one handbreadth wide, were attached all around the interior walls; and the flesh of the gift offerings would be placed on the tables.

44 Outside the inner gate were the dining rooms for the singers;[a] they were in the inner courtyard near the north gate, facing south. Another dining room was near the east gate, facing north.

45 He said to me: "This dining room that faces south is for the priests who are responsible for the services in the temple.[b] **46** The dining room that faces north is for the priests who are responsible for the service of the altar.[c] They are the sons of Za'dok,[d] those from the Levites who are assigned to approach Jehovah to minister to him."[e]

47 Then he measured the inner courtyard. It was 100 cubits long and 100 cubits wide, four-square. The altar was in front of the temple.

48 Then he brought me into the porch of the temple,[f] and he measured the side pillar of the porch, and it was five cubits on one side and five cubits on the other side. The width of the gate was three cubits on one side and three cubits on the other side.

49 The porch was 20 cubits long and 11* cubits wide. People would reach it by climbing the

---

CHAP. 40

a Eze 40:20, 21

b Eze 40:16

c Eze 40:32, 34
  Eze 40:35, 37

d Eze 44:4

e Lu 8:21

f Le 1:3, 6
  Le 8:20
  Eze 43:18

g Le 4:3, 4

h Le 5:6
  Le 7:1
  Eze 42:13
  Eze 44:29

_____
Second Col.

a 1Ch 6:31, 32

b Nu 3:6-8
  1Ch 9:22, 23
  Ps 134:1

c Le 6:12, 13
  Nu 18:5
  2Ch 13:10, 11

d 1Ki 2:35
  Eze 43:19

e Nu 16:39, 40
  Eze 44:15, 16

f 1Ki 6:3
  2Ch 3:4

40:49 *Or possibly, "12."

steps. There were pillars by the side posts, one on each side.[a]

41 Then he brought me into the outer sanctuary,[*] and he measured the side pillars; they were six cubits[#] wide on one side and six cubits wide on the other side. **2** The entrance was ten cubits wide, and the sidewalls[*] of the entrance were five cubits on one side and five cubits on the other side. He measured its length, which was 40 cubits, and its width, 20 cubits.

3 He then went inside[*] and measured the side pillar of the entrance, and it was two cubits thick, and the entrance was six cubits wide. The sidewalls of the entrance were[#] seven cubits. **4** Next he measured the room facing the outer sanctuary, and it was 20 cubits long and 20 cubits wide.[b] And he said to me: "This is the Most Holy."[c]

5 Then he measured the wall of the temple, and it was six cubits thick. The side chambers around the temple were four cubits wide.[d] **6** The side chambers were three stories high, one on top of the other, with 30 chambers on each story. There were ledges around the wall of the temple that served as supports for the side chambers, so that the supports did not go into the wall of the temple itself.[e] **7** On both sides of the temple was a winding passage[*] that widened as it ascended to the upper chambers.[f] The width increased

from story to story as one ascended from the lowest story to the uppermost story by passing through the middle story.

8 I saw that there was a raised platform all around the temple, and the foundations of the side chambers measured a full reed of six cubits to the corner. **9** The width of the outside wall of the side chambers was five cubits. There was an open space[*] alongside the structure of the side chambers that was part of the temple.

10 Between the temple and the dining rooms[*a] was an area that was 20 cubits wide on each side. **11** There was an entrance between the side chambers and the open space on the north side and another entrance on the south side. The width of the open space was five cubits all around.

12 The building that was on the west facing the open area was 70 cubits wide and 90 cubits long; the wall of the building was five cubits thick all around.

13 He measured the temple, and it was 100 cubits long. The open area, the building,[*] and its walls were also 100 cubits long. **14** The width of the front of the temple facing east and the open area was 100 cubits.

15 He measured the length of the building that faced the open area in the rear, along with its galleries on both sides, and it was 100 cubits.

He also measured the outer sanctuary, the inner sanctuary,[b] and the porches of the courtyard, **16** as well as the thresholds, the windows with narrowing frames,[c] and the galleries that were in those three areas.

CHAP. 40
a 1Ki 7:21

CHAP. 41
b 1Ki 6:20
   2Ch 3:8

c Ex 26:33

d 1Ki 6:5

e 1Ki 6:6, 10

f 1Ki 6:8

Second Col.
a 1Ch 28:12

b 2Ch 3:8
   Eze 41:4

c 1Ki 6:4

41:1 *Lit., "the temple." In chapters 41 and 42, this expression refers to the outer sanctuary (Holy) or to the entire sanctuary (the temple including the Holy and the Most Holy). See App. B14. #This refers to long cubits. **41:2** *Lit., "sides." **41:3** *That is, into the inner sanctuary, or Most Holy. #Lit., "The width of the entrance was." **41:7** *Apparently referring to circular staircases.

41:9 *Apparently a narrow walkway around the temple. **41:10** *Or "the chambers." **41:13** *That is, the building west of the sanctuary.

Near the threshold were wood panels[a] from the floor up to the windows; and the windows were covered. **17** Measurements were taken above the entrance and in the inner temple and on the outside and on the entire wall all around. **18** It had carved cherubs[b] and palm-tree figures,[c] with each palm tree between two cherubs, and each cherub had two faces. **19** The human face was toward the palm tree on one side, and the face of a lion* was toward the palm tree on the other side.[d] They were carved this way throughout the entire temple. **20** From the floor to the area above the entrance were carved cherubs and palm-tree figures on the wall of the sanctuary.

21 The doorposts* of the sanctuary were square.[e] In front of the holy place* was something like **22** a wooden altar[f] that was three cubits high and two cubits long. It had corner posts, and its base* and its sides were made of wood. He then said to me: "This is the table that is before Jehovah."[g]

23 The outer sanctuary and the holy place each had two doors.[h] **24** The doors had two swinging leaves, two leaves for each door. **25** There were carved cherubs and palm-tree figures on the doors of the sanctuary, like those on the walls.[i] There was also a wooden overhang* on the front of the porch on the outside. **26** There were also windows with narrowing frames[j] and palm-tree figures along both sides of the porch, as

well as along the side chambers of the temple and the overhangs.

42 Then he led me to the outer courtyard toward the north.[a] And he brought me to the dining-room block that was next to the open area,[b] north of the adjoining building.[c] **2** Its length at the north entrance was 100 cubits,* and it was 50 cubits wide. **3** It was located between the inner courtyard, which was 20 cubits wide,[d] and the pavement of the outer courtyard. Its galleries faced each other and were three stories high. **4** Before the dining rooms* was an inner walkway[e] 10 cubits wide and 100 cubits long,* and their entrances were to the north. **5** The upper dining rooms of the building were narrower than those in the lower and middle stories, because the galleries took up more of their space. **6** For they were three stories high, but they had no pillars like the pillars of the courtyards. That is why more floor space was taken away from them than from the lower and middle stories.

7 The outer stone wall near the dining rooms toward the outer courtyard that faced the other dining rooms was 50 cubits long. **8** For the length of the dining rooms that were toward the outer courtyard was 50 cubits, but for those facing the sanctuary, it was 100 cubits. **9** The dining rooms had an entryway on the east side leading up to them from the outer courtyard.

10 There were also dining rooms inside* the stone wall of

CHAP. 41
a 1Ki 6:15
　2Ch 3:5

b 1Ki 6:29
　1Ki 7:36
　2Ch 3:7

c Eze 40:16

d Eze 1:5, 10
　Re 4:7

e 1Ki 6:33

f Ex 30:1
　1Ki 7:48
　Re 8:3

g Eze 44:16
　Mal 1:7

h 1Ki 6:31-35

i Eze 41:17, 18

j Eze 40:16

Second Col.

CHAP. 42
a Eze 40:2

b Eze 42:13

c Eze 41:12, 15

d Eze 41:10

e Eze 42:10, 11

41:19 *Or "maned young lion." 41:21 *Lit., "The doorpost." This apparently refers to the entrance into the Holy. #Apparently referring to the Most Holy. 41:22 *Lit., "length." 41:25 *Or "canopy."

42:2 *This refers to long cubits. See App. B14. 42:4 *Or "the chambers." #According to the Greek Septuagint, "100 cubits long." The Hebrew text reads: "A way of one cubit." See App. B14. 42:10 *Lit., "in the width of."

the courtyard toward the east, near the open area and the building.ᵃ **11** There was a walkway before them like that of the northern dining rooms.ᵇ They were the same length and width, and they had the same exits and layouts. Their entrances **12** were like the entrances of the dining rooms that were toward the south. There was an entrance at the beginning of the walkway, before the adjacent stone wall toward the east, where one could enter.ᶜ

13 Then he said to me: "The dining rooms of the north and the dining rooms of the south that are next to the open areaᵈ are the holy dining rooms where the priests who are approaching Jehovah eat the most holy offerings.ᵉ There they place the most holy offerings, the grain offering, the sin offering, and the guilt offering, because the place is holy.ᶠ **14** When the priests enter, they should not go out of the holy place to the outer courtyard without first removing the garments in which they minister,ᵍ for these are holy. They will clothe themselves with other garments in order to approach the areas permitted to the people."

15 When he finished measuring the inner temple area,* he led me out by way of the gate that faces east,ʰ and he measured the entire area.

16 He measured the eastern side with the measuring reed.* According to the measuring reed, it was 500 reed lengths from one side to the other.

17 He measured the northern side, and according to the measuring reed, it was 500 reed lengths.

18 He measured the southern side, and according to the measuring reed, it was 500 reed lengths.

19 He went around to the western side. He measured 500 reed lengths with the measuring reed.

20 He measured it on the four sides. It had a wall all around itᵃ that was 500 reeds long and 500 reeds wide,ᵇ to make a division between what is holy and what is for common use.ᶜ

43 Then he led me to the gate that is facing east.ᵈ **2** There I saw the glory of the God of Israel coming from the east,ᵉ and his voice was like the sound of rushing waters;ᶠ and the earth was illuminated by his glory.ᵍ **3** What I saw was like the vision I had seen when I* came to bring the city to ruin, and it appeared to be like what I had seen near the river Cheʹbar;ʰ and I fell with my face to the ground.

4 Then the glory of Jehovah entered the temple* through the gate facing the east.ⁱ **5** A spirit then raised me up and brought me into the inner courtyard, and I saw that the temple had become full of the glory of Jehovah.ʲ **6** Then I heard someone speaking to me out of the temple, and the man came and stood beside me.ᵏ **7** He said to me:

"Son of man, this is the place of my throneˡ and the place for the soles of my feet,ᵐ where I will dwell among the people of Israel forever.ⁿ The house of Israel will no longer defile my holy name,ᵒ they and their kings, by their spiritual prostitution and by the carcasses of their kings at their death. **8** By putting their threshold next to my threshold and their doorpost

CHAP. 42
a Eze 41:12
  Eze 42:1
b Eze 42:4
c Eze 42:9
d Eze 42:1
e Le 6:14, 16
  Le 7:1, 6
  Le 10:12, 13
  Le 24:8, 9
  Nu 18:10
  Eze 40:46
f Le 2:3
  Nu 18:9
  Ne 13:5
g Ex 28:40
  Ex 29:8, 9
  Le 8:13
  Eze 44:19
h Eze 40:6

Second Col.
a Eze 40:5
b Eze 45:1, 2
c Le 10:10
  Eze 44:23
  2Co 6:17

CHAP. 43
d Eze 40:6
  Eze 42:15
  Eze 44:1
e Eze 9:3
  Eze 11:23
f Eze 1:24
  Joh 12:28, 29
g Isa 6:3
  Eze 10:4
h Eze 1:3, 4
  Eze 3:23
i Eze 10:19
  Eze 44:1, 2
j Ex 40:34
  1Ki 8:10
  Eze 44:4
k Eze 40:3
l Isa 6:1
  Jer 3:17
  Eze 1:26
m 1Ch 28:2
n Ex 29:45
  Ps 68:16
  Ps 132:14
  Joe 3:17
o Eze 39:7
  Zec 13:2

beside my doorpost, with only a wall between me and them,[a] they defiled my holy name by the detestable things they did, so I exterminated them in my anger.[b] **9** Now let them put their spiritual prostitution and the carcasses of their kings far away from me, and I will dwell among them forever.[c]

10 "As for you, son of man, describe the temple to the house of Israel,[d] so that they will feel ashamed because of their errors,[e] and they should study its plan.* **11** If they feel ashamed of all they have done, you should make known to them the ground plan of the temple, its arrangement, its exits, and its entrances.[f] Show them all its ground plans and its statutes, its ground plans and its laws, and write them down before their eyes, so that they may observe all its ground plan and carry out its statutes.[g] **12** This is the law of the temple. The entire territory all around the top of the mountain is most holy.[h] Look! This is the law of the temple.

13 "These are the measurements of the altar in cubits[i] (to each cubit a handbreadth was added).* Its base is a cubit, and it is a cubit wide. It has a border all around the edge that is one span# in width. This is the base of the altar. **14** From the base on the floor to the lower surrounding ledge is two cubits, and its width is one cubit. From the small surrounding ledge to the big surrounding ledge is four cubits, and its width is a cubit. **15** The altar hearth is four cubits high, and projecting up from the altar hearth are the four

---

43:10 *Lit., "measure the pattern."
43:13 *This refers to long cubits. See App. B14. #That is, the span of the hand, about 22.2 cm (8.75 in.). See App. B14.

CHAP. 43
a Eze 8:3

b Da 9:12

c Eze 37:23
  Eze 37:26
  2Co 6:16

d Eze 40:4

e Eze 16:63

f Eze 44:5

g Eze 11:19, 20
  Eze 36:27

h Ps 93:5
  Eze 40:2
  Eze 42:20

i Ex 27:1
  2Ch 4:1

Second Col.
a Ex 27:2
  Re 9:13

b Ex 38:1
  2Ch 4:1

c Ex 40:29
  Le 1:5
  Le 8:18-21
  Eze 45:19

d Ex 29:10
  Le 8:14

e Eze 40:46
  Eze 44:15
  Eze 48:11

f Ex 29:36, 37
  Le 8:15
  Heb 9:23

g Ex 29:14
  Le 8:17
  Heb 13:11

h Le 2:13

i Ex 29:35

---

horns.[a] **16** The altar hearth is square, 12 cubits long and 12 cubits wide.[b] **17** The four sides of the surrounding ledge are 14 cubits long and 14 cubits wide; and the surrounding border is half a cubit, and its base is a cubit on all sides.

"And its steps are facing east."

18 He then said to me, "Son of man, this is what the Sovereign Lord Jehovah says: 'These are the directions to follow when the altar is made, so that whole burnt offerings may be offered and blood may be sprinkled on it.'[c]

19 "'You are to give a young bull of the herd as a sin offering[d] to the Levitical priests of the offspring of Za′dok,[e] who approach me to minister to me,' declares the Sovereign Lord Jehovah. **20** 'You should take some of its blood and put it on the four horns of the altar, on the four corners of the surrounding ledge, and on the border all around, in order to purify it from sin and to make atonement for it.[f] **21** Then take the young bull, the sin offering, in order to burn it in the appointed place of the temple, outside the sanctuary.[g] **22** On the second day you will offer a sound male goat as a sin offering; and they will purify the altar from sin just as they purified it from sin with the young bull.'

23 "'When you finish purifying it from sin, you will offer a sound young bull of the herd and a sound ram from the flock. **24** You are to present them to Jehovah, and the priests must throw salt on them[h] and offer them up as a whole burnt offering to Jehovah. **25** For seven days you will offer a male goat as a daily sin offering,[i] as well as a young bull of the herd and a ram of the flock; you will offer unblemished* animals. **26** For seven days they are to make atonement for the altar, and they must cleanse it and install it. **27** When the days are completed, on the eighth day[a] and thereafter, the priests will offer your* whole burnt offerings and communion sacrifices on the altar; and I will find pleasure in you,'[b] declares the Sovereign Lord Jehovah."

44 He brought me back by way of the outer gate of the sanctuary facing east,[c] and it was shut.[d] **2** Then Jehovah said to me: "This gate will remain shut. It is not to be opened, and no human will enter by it; for Jehovah, the God of Israel, has entered through it,[e] so it must remain shut. **3** However, the chieftain will sit in it to eat bread before Jehovah,[f] for he is a chieftain. He will come in through the porch of the gate, and he will go out through it."[g]

4 Then he brought me through the north gate to the front of the temple. When I looked, I saw that the glory of Jehovah had filled the temple of Jehovah.[h] So I fell with my face to the ground.[i] **5** Then Jehovah said to me: "Son of man, pay attention,* watch, and listen carefully to everything I tell you about the statutes and the laws of the temple of Jehovah. Pay close attention to the entryway of the temple and all the exits of the sanctuary.[j] **6** You must say to the rebellious house of Israel, 'This is what the Sovereign Lord Jehovah says: "That is enough of your detestable practices, O house of Israel. **7** When you bring foreigners who are uncircumcised in heart and flesh into my sanctuary, they profane my temple. You present my bread,

fat, and blood, while my covenant is being broken because of all your detestable practices. **8** You have not taken care of my holy things.[a] Instead, you assign others to take care of the duties in my sanctuary."'

9 "'This is what the Sovereign Lord Jehovah says: "No foreigner living in Israel who is uncircumcised in heart and in flesh may enter my sanctuary."'

10 "'But the Levites who strayed far from me[b] when Israel strayed from me to follow their disgusting idols* will bear the consequences of their error. **11** And they will become ministers in my sanctuary to oversee the gates of the temple[c] and to minister at the temple. They will slaughter the whole burnt offering and the sacrifice for the people, and they will stand before the people to minister to them. **12** Because they ministered to them before their disgusting idols and became a stumbling block causing the house of Israel to sin,[d] that is why I have raised my hand against them in an oath,' declares the Sovereign Lord Jehovah, 'and they will bear the consequences of their error. **13** They will not approach me to serve as my priests or approach any of my holy or most holy things, and they will bear their shame because of the detestable things that they did. **14** But I will make them caretakers of the responsibilities of the temple, to take care of its service and all the things that should be done in it.'[e]

15 "'As for the Levitical priests, the sons of Za'dok,[f] who took care of the responsibilities of my sanctuary when the Israelites strayed from me,[g] they will approach me to minister to me,

---

CHAP. 43
a Le 9:1

b Eze 20:40

CHAP. 44
c Eze 43:1

d Eze 46:1

e Eze 43:2

f De 12:5, 7

g Eze 46:2

h Isa 6:1-3
  Eze 10:4

i Eze 1:27, 28
  Eze 3:23

j Eze 40:4

Second Col.
a Le 22:2
  Nu 18:2, 3

b 2Ki 23:8, 9
  2Ch 29:1, 5
  Ne 9:34
  Jer 23:11
  Eze 8:5

c 1Ch 26:1

d Isa 9:16
  Mal 2:8

e Nu 18:2, 4

f 1Ki 2:35
  Eze 40:46

g Eze 48:9, 11

43:25 *Or "perfect." 43:27 *That is, those of the people. 44:5 *Lit., "set your heart."

44:10 *The Hebrew term may be related to a word for "dung" and is used as an expression of contempt.

and they will stand before me to offer me the fat[a] and the blood,'[b] declares the Sovereign Lord Jehovah. 16 'They are the ones who will enter my sanctuary, and they will approach my table to minister to me,[c] and they will take care of their responsibilities to me.[d]

17 "'When they come into the gates of the inner courtyard, they should wear linen garments.[e] They should not wear any wool when they minister in the gates of the inner courtyard or inside it. 18 They should wear linen turbans on their head, and linen shorts should cover their hips.[f] They should not wear anything that makes them perspire. 19 Before they go out to the outer courtyard —the outer courtyard where the people are—they should remove the garments they were ministering in[g] and place them in the holy dining rooms.*[h] Then they will put on other garments, so that they will not transmit holiness to# the people with their garments. 20 They should not shave their head[i] or let the hair of their head grow long. They should trim the hair of their heads. 21 The priests should not drink wine when they enter the inner courtyard.[j] 22 They should not take a widow or a divorced woman as a wife;[k] but they may marry either a virgin of the offspring of Israel or the widow of a priest.'[l]

23 "'They should instruct my people about the difference between what is holy and what is common; and they will teach them the difference between what is unclean and what is clean.[m] 24 They should preside as judges in a legal case;[n] they must judge it in harmony with my

judicial decisions.[a] They should keep my laws and my statutes regarding all my festivals[b] and sanctify my sabbaths. 25 They should not approach any dead human, or they will become unclean. However, they may make themselves unclean for their father, mother, son, daughter, brother, or an unmarried sister.[c] 26 And after the purification of a priest, they should count off seven days for him. 27 On the day he enters into the holy place, into the inner courtyard, to minister in the holy place, he should present his sin offering,'[d] declares the Sovereign Lord Jehovah.

28 "'And this will be their inheritance: I am their inheritance.[e] You should not give them any possession in Israel, for I am their possession. 29 They will be the ones to eat the grain offering,[f] the sin offering, and the guilt offering,[g] and every devoted thing in Israel will become theirs.[h] 30 The choicest of all the first ripe fruits and every sort of contribution from you will belong to the priests.[i] And you should give the firstfruits of your coarse meal to the priest.[j] This will cause a blessing to rest on your households.[k] 31 The priests should not eat any bird or animal that was found dead or torn to pieces.'[l]

45 "'When you allot the land as an inheritance,[m] you should offer as a contribution to Jehovah a holy portion out of the land.[n] Its length should be 25,000 cubits,* and its width, 10,000 cubits.[o] Its entire area# will be a holy portion. 2 Within this will be a square lot for the holy place measuring 500 cubits by 500 cubits,*[p] and it will have 50 cubits as pastures on each

---

CHAP. 44
a Le 3:14-16
b Le 17:6
c Eze 41:21, 22
d Nu 18:7
e Ex 28:39, 42
  Ex 39:27, 28
  Le 16:4
f Ex 28:40, 42
g Le 6:10
  Eze 42:14
h Eze 42:13
i Le 21:1, 5
  De 14:1
j Le 10:9
k Le 21:7
l Le 21:10, 14
m Mal 2:7
n De 17:9

Second Col.
a 1Ch 23:3, 4
  2Ch 19:8
b Le 23:2
c Le 21:1-3
d Le 4:3
e Nu 18:20
  De 18:1
  Jos 13:14
  Eze 45:4
f Le 2:3
g Le 6:17, 18
  Le 7:1, 6
  1Co 9:13
h Le 27:21
  Nu 18:14
i Ex 23:19
  Nu 18:8, 12
  Nu 18:26, 27
  De 18:4
j Nu 15:20
  Ne 10:35-37
k Pr 3:9, 10
  Mal 3:10
l Ex 22:31
  Le 22:3, 8

CHAP. 45
m Jos 14:1, 2
  Eze 47:21, 22
n Eze 48:20
o Eze 48:8, 9
p Eze 42:20

44:19 *Or "the holy chambers." #Lit., "sanctify."

45:1 *This refers to long cubits. See App. B14. #Or "Within all its boundaries." 45:2 *Lit., "500 by 500."

side.[a] **3** Out of this measurement you should measure the length of 25,000 and the width of 10,000, and within it will be the sanctuary, something most holy. **4** It will be a holy portion of the land for the priests,[b] the ministers of the sanctuary, who approach to minister to Jehovah.[c] It will be a place for their houses and a sacred place for the sanctuary.

5 "'For the Levites, the ministers of the temple, there will be a portion 25,000 cubits long and 10,000 cubits wide,[d] and they will have 20 dining rooms*[e] as a possession.

6 "'You should give the possession of the city an area that is 25,000 cubits long (corresponding to the holy contribution) and 5,000 cubits wide.[f] It will belong to all the house of Israel.

7 "'And for the chieftain there will be land on both sides of the holy contribution and of the area allotted to the city. It will be next to the holy contribution and the possession of the city. It will be on the west side and on the east side. Its length from the western boundary to the eastern boundary will correspond to one of the tribal portions.[g] **8** This land will become his possession in Israel. My chieftains will no longer mistreat my people,[h] and they will give the land to the house of Israel according to their tribes.'[i]

9 "This is what the Sovereign Lord Jehovah says: 'You have gone far enough, chieftains of Israel!'

"'Put an end to your violence and oppression, and do what is just and righteous.[j] Stop seizing the property of my people,'[k] declares the Sovereign Lord Jehovah. **10** 'You should use accurate scales, an accurate

e'phah measure* and an accurate bath measure.*[a] **11** There should be a fixed measurement for the e'phah measure and the bath measure. The bath measure should hold a tenth of a ho'mer,* and the e'phah measure should hold a tenth of a ho'mer. The ho'mer will be the standard for measuring. **12** The shekel*[b] is to be 20 ge'rahs.* And 20 shekels plus 25 shekels plus 15 shekels will make up one ma'neh* for you.'

13 "'This is the contribution that you should offer: one sixth of an e'phah from each ho'mer of wheat and one sixth of an e'phah from each ho'mer of barley. **14** The allowance of the oil is to be based on the bath measure. The bath is a tenth of a cor,* and ten baths are a ho'mer, for ten baths equal a ho'mer. **15** And from the flock of the livestock of Israel, one sheep out of every 200 should be given. These will be for the grain offering,[c] the whole burnt offering,[d] and the communion sacrifices,[e] in order to make atonement for the people,'[f] declares the Sovereign Lord Jehovah.

16 "'All the people of the land will make this contribution[g] to the chieftain in Israel. **17** But the chieftain will be responsible for the whole burnt offerings,[h] the grain offering,[i] and the drink offering during the festivals,[j] the new moons, the Sabbaths,[k] and all the designated festivals of the house of Israel.[l] He will be the one to provide the sin offering, the grain offering, the whole burnt offering, and the communion sacrifices, in order to make atonement in behalf of the house of Israel.'

18 "This is what the Sovereign Lord Jehovah says: 'In the

CHAP. 45
a Jos 21:1, 2

b Eze 48:10, 11

c Eze 40:46

d Eze 48:13

e Eze 40:17

f Eze 48:15

g Eze 48:21

h Isa 32:1
Isa 60:17
Jer 22:17
Jer 23:5
Eze 22:27
Eze 46:18
Mic 3:1-3

i Jos 11:23

j Jer 22:3
Mic 6:8
Zec 8:16

k Mic 2:2

_____

Second Col.
a Le 19:36
Pr 11:1
Am 8:5
Mic 6:10, 11

b Ex 30:13

c Le 2:1

d Le 1:10

e Le 3:1

f Le 1:4
Le 6:30
Heb 9:22

g Ex 30:14

h 1Ch 16:2
2Ch 30:24

i 1Ki 8:64

j 2Ch 35:7

k Isa 66:23

l De 16:16
2Ch 8:12, 13
2Ch 31:3

_____

45:5 *Or "20 chambers." **45:10-12, 14** *See App. B14. **45:12** #Or "mina." See App. B14.

first month, on the first day of the month, you should take a sound young bull of the herd, and you are to purify the sanctuary from sin.[a] **19** The priest will take some of the blood of the sin offering and put it on the doorpost of the temple,[b] on the four corners of the surrounding ledge of the altar, and on the doorpost of the gate of the inner courtyard. **20** That is what you will do on the seventh day of the month because of anyone who sins by mistake or through ignorance;[c] and you are to make atonement for the temple.[d]

21 "'In the first month, on the 14th day of the month, you will observe the festival of the Passover.[e] For seven days unleavened bread should be eaten.[f] **22** On that day the chieftain will provide a young bull as a sin offering in his own behalf and in behalf of all the people of the land.[g] **23** For the seven days of the festival he will provide as a whole burnt offering to Jehovah seven sound young bulls and seven sound rams each of the seven days,[h] as well as a male goat each day as a sin offering. **24** He should also provide as a grain offering an e′phah for each young bull and an e′phah for each ram, as well as a hin* of oil for each e′phah.

25 "'In the seventh month, on the 15th day of the month, for seven days during the festival,[i] he should provide the same sin offering, whole burnt offering, grain offering, and oil.'"

46 "This is what the Sovereign Lord Jehovah says: 'The gate of the inner courtyard that is facing east[j] should remain shut[k] for the six workdays,[l] but on the Sabbath day and on the day of the new moon it should

be opened. **2** The chieftain will enter from outside by way of the porch of the gate,[a] and he will stand by the doorpost of the gate. The priests will offer his whole burnt offering and his communion sacrifices, and he will bow down at the threshold of the gate and then go out. But the gate should not be shut until the evening. **3** The people of the land will also bow down before Jehovah at the entrance of that gate on the Sabbaths and on the new moons.[b]

4 "'The whole burnt offering that the chieftain will present to Jehovah on the Sabbath day should consist of six sound male lambs and a sound ram.[c] **5** The grain offering will be an e′phah* for the ram and whatever he is able to give for the male lambs, along with a hin* of oil with each e′phah.[d] **6** On the day of the new moon the offering will consist of a sound young bull of the herd, six male lambs, and a ram; they should be sound ones.[e] **7** He should offer as a grain offering an e′phah for the young bull, an e′phah for the ram, and whatever he can afford for the male lambs. And he should offer a hin of oil with each e′phah.

8 "'When the chieftain enters, he should enter by way of the porch of the gate, and he should go out the same way.[f] **9** And when the people of the land come in before Jehovah during the festivals,[g] those who come in to worship through the north gate[h] should go out through the south gate,[i] and those who come in through the south gate should go out through the north gate. No one should go back by way of the gate through which he entered, for they should exit through the gate that is opposite them. **10** As for the chieftain who is among them, he should

---

CHAP. 45
a Le 16:16

b Eze 41:21

c Le 4:27, 28

d Le 16:20

e Le 23:5

f Ex 12:18

g Le 4:13, 14

h Le 23:8

i Le 23:34
  De 16:13
  2Ch 7:8
  Zec 14:16

CHAP. 46
j Eze 40:32

k Eze 44:1, 2

l Ex 20:9

Second Col.
a Eze 44:3

b Ps 81:3
  Isa 66:23

c Nu 28:9, 10
  Eze 45:17

d Eze 46:11

e Nu 28:11-15

f Eze 46:2

g Ex 23:14
  De 16:16

h Eze 40:20

i Eze 40:24

45:24; 46:5 *See App. B14.

come in when they come in, and he should go out when they go out. **11** During the festivals and the festal seasons the grain offering should be an e'phah for the young bull, an e'phah for the ram, and whatever he is able to give for the male lambs, along with a hin of oil with each e'phah.[a]

12 "'If the chieftain provides a whole burnt offering[b] or communion sacrifices as a voluntary offering to Jehovah, the gate facing east will be opened for him, and he will provide his whole burnt offering and his communion sacrifices just as he does on the Sabbath day.[c] After he goes out, the gate should be shut behind him.[d]

13 "'Each day you should provide a sound male lamb in its first year as a whole burnt offering to Jehovah.[e] You should do this morning by morning. **14** Along with it, each morning you should provide a sixth of an e'phah as a grain offering, along with a third of a hin of oil for sprinkling on the fine flour as a regular grain offering to Jehovah. This is a lasting statute. **15** They must provide the male lamb, the grain offering, and the oil each morning as a regular whole burnt offering.'

16 "This is what the Sovereign Lord Jehovah says: 'If the chieftain gives a gift to each one of his sons as an inheritance, it will become the property of his sons. It is their possession by inheritance. **17** But if he gives a gift from his inheritance to one of his servants, it will be his until the year of liberty;[f] and then it will return to the chieftain. Only the inheritance of his sons will be permanently theirs. **18** The chieftain should not take any of the inheritance of the people by forcing them off their property. He should give his sons an inheritance from his own property, so that no one among my people may be driven from his property.'"

19 Then he brought me in by the entryway[a] that was beside the gate leading to the holy dining rooms* of the priests, which faced north,[b] and there I saw a place at the rear toward the west. **20** He said to me: "This is the place where the priests will boil the guilt offering and the sin offering and where they will bake the grain offering,[c] so that they will not carry anything out to the outer courtyard and transmit holiness to* the people."[d]

21 He brought me out to the outer courtyard and led me past the four corners of the courtyard, and I saw a courtyard by each corner of the outer courtyard. **22** At the four corners of the courtyard were small courtyards, 40 cubits* long and 30 cubits wide. All four of them were the same size.[#] **23** There were ledges* all around the four of them, and beneath the ledges were built places to boil the offerings. **24** Then he said to me: "These are the houses where the ministers of the temple boil the sacrifice of the people."[e]

47 Then he brought me back to the entrance of the temple,[f] and there I saw water flowing eastward from under the threshold of the temple,[g] for the front of the temple was facing east. The water was flowing down from under the right side of the temple, south of the altar.

2 He then led me out by way of the north gate[h] and took me

CHAP. 46
a Eze 45:21, 24
  Eze 46:6, 7

b Le 1:3

c Eze 45:17

d Eze 46:1, 2

e Ex 29:38
  Nu 28:3, 5

f Le 25:10

Second Col.
a Eze 42:9

b Eze 42:1

c Le 2:4, 5

d Eze 44:19

e 2Ch 35:13

CHAP. 47
f Eze 41:2

g Zec 13:1
  Zec 14:8
  Re 22:1

h Eze 40:20

46:19 *Or "holy chambers." **46:20** *Lit., "sanctify." **46:22** *This refers to long cubits. See App. B14. #Or "The four of them and their corner structures were the same size." **46:23** *Or "rows."

outside and around to the outer gate that is facing east,[a] and I saw water trickling from the right side.

3 When the man went out toward the east with a measuring line in his hand,[b] he measured off 1,000 cubits* and had me pass through the water; the water was ankle deep.

4 Then he measured off another 1,000 and had me pass through the water, and it was up to the knees.

He measured off another 1,000 and had me pass through, and the water was up to the hips.

5 When he measured off another 1,000, it was a torrent that I was unable to walk across, for the water was so deep that one had to swim, a torrent of water that could not be crossed on foot.

6 He asked me: "Have you seen this, son of man?"

Then he had me walk and return to the bank of the stream. **7** When I returned, I saw that on the bank of the stream were very many trees on both sides.[c] **8** Then he said to me: "This water flows toward the eastern region and continues down through the Ar'a·bah*[d] and enters the sea. When it enters the sea,[e] the water there will be healed. **9** Swarms of living creatures* will be able to live wherever the waters# flow. There will be an abundance of fish, because this water will flow there. The seawater will be healed, and everything will live wherever the stream goes.

10 "Fishermen will stand beside it from En-ged'i[f] clear to En-eg'la·im, where there will be a

drying yard for dragnets. There will be an abundance of many kinds of fish, like the fish of the Great Sea.*[a]

11 "It will have swampy places and marshy places, and these will not be healed. They will be abandoned to salt.[b]

12 "All sorts of trees for food will grow on both banks of the stream. Their leaves will not wither; nor will their fruitage fail. Each month they will bear new fruit, because the water for them flows from the sanctuary.[c] Their fruitage will serve as food and their leaves for healing."[d]

13 This is what the Sovereign Lord Jehovah says: "This is the territory that you will assign as the land inheritance of the 12 tribes of Israel, and Joseph will have two portions.[e] **14** You will inherit it and receive equal shares.* I swore to give this land to your forefathers,[f] and now it is assigned# to you as an inheritance.

15 "This is the boundary of the land on the northern side: It goes from the Great Sea by the way to Heth'lon[g] toward Ze'dad,[h] **16** Ha'math,[i] Be·ro'thah,[j] and Sib'ra·im, which is between the territory of Damascus and the territory of Ha'math, to Ha'zer-hat'ti·con, which is by the boundary of Ha·u·ran'.[k] **17** So the boundary will run from the sea to Ha'zar-e'non,[l] along the boundary of Damascus to the north, and the boundary of Ha'math.[m] This is the northern border.

18 "The eastern side runs between Ha·u·ran' and Damascus and along the Jordan between Gil'e·ad[n] and the land of Israel. You should measure from the

CHAP. 47

a Eze 40:6
  Eze 44:1, 2

b Eze 40:3
  Re 21:15

c Re 22:1, 2

d De 4:47, 49

e Zec 14:8

f Jos 15:20, 62
  2Ch 20:2

Second Col.

a Nu 34:2, 6

b Ge 29:22, 23
  Ps 107:33, 34
  Jer 17:6

c Eze 47:1

d Re 22:1, 2

e Ge 48:5
  1Ch 5:1
  Eze 48:5

f Ge 26:3
  Ge 28:13

g Eze 48:1

h Nu 34:2, 8

i Nu 13:21

j 2Sa 8:8

k Eze 47:18

l Nu 34:2, 9

m Eze 48:1

n Nu 32:1

47:3 *This refers to long cubits. See App. B14. **47:8** *Or "the desert plain." **47:9** *Or "souls." #Lit., "the two streams."

47:10 *That is, the Mediterranean. **47:14** *Lit., "inherit it, each like his brother." #Lit., "falls."

boundary to the eastern sea.* This is the eastern border.

19 "The southern border* will be from Ta'mar to the waters of Mer'i·bath-ka'desh,[a] then to the Wadi# and to the Great Sea.[b] This is the southern border.*

20 "On the western side is the Great Sea, from the boundary up to a point opposite Le'bo-ha'math.*[c] This is the western border."

21 "You are to apportion this land among yourselves, among the 12 tribes of Israel. 22 You should distribute it for inheritance among yourselves and to the foreigners residing with you who have had children while living among you; and they will be like native-born Israelites to you. They will receive an inheritance among the tribes of Israel along with you. 23 You should give the foreign resident an inheritance in the territory of the tribe where he has taken up residence," declares the Sovereign Lord Jehovah.

48 "These are the names of the tribes, starting from the northern extremity: Dan's portion[d] runs along the way of Heth'lon to Le'bo-ha'math*[e] to Ha'zar-e'nan, along the boundary of Damascus northward, beside Ha'math;[f] and it extends from the eastern to the western border. 2 Ash'er's portion[g] is on the boundary of Dan, from the eastern border to the western border. 3 Naph'ta·li's portion[h] is on the boundary of Ash'er, from the eastern border to the western border. 4 Ma·nas'seh's portion[i] is on the boundary of Naph'ta·li, from the east-

ern border to the western border. 5 E'phra·im's portion is on the boundary of Ma·nas'seh,[a] from the eastern border to the western border. 6 Reu'ben's portion is on the boundary of E'phra·im,[b] from the eastern border to the western border. 7 Judah's portion is on the boundary of Reu'ben,[c] from the eastern border to the western border. 8 On the boundary of Judah, from the eastern border to the western border, the contribution that you are to set apart should be 25,000 cubits* wide[d] and correspond to the length of the other tribal portions from the eastern border to the western border. The sanctuary will be in the middle of it.

9 "The contribution that you are to set apart to Jehovah will be 25,000 cubits long and 10,000 wide. 10 This will be the holy contribution for the priests.[e] It will be 25,000 cubits on the north side, 10,000 on the west, 10,000 on the east, and 25,000 on the south. The sanctuary of Jehovah will be in the middle of it. 11 It will be for the sanctified priests from the sons of Za'dok,[f] those who took care of their responsibilities toward me and did not go astray when the Israelites and the Levites went astray.[g] 12 They will have a portion of the contribution of the land set apart as something most holy, on the boundary of the Levites.

13 "Right next to the territory of the priests, the Levites will have a portion 25,000 cubits long and 10,000 wide. (The whole length will be 25,000 long and 10,000 wide.) 14 They should not sell, exchange, or transfer any of this choicest portion of the land, for it is something holy to Jehovah.

CHAP. 47
a De 32:51

b Eze 48:28

c Nu 34:2, 8

CHAP. 48
d Jos 19:40

e Nu 34:2, 8

f Eze 47:15-17

g Jos 19:24

h Jos 19:32

i Jos 13:29

Second Col.
a Jos 17:17, 18

b Jos 18:7

c Jos 15:1
Jos 19:9

d Eze 45:1

e Nu 35:2
Eze 45:3, 4

f Eze 40:46
Eze 44:15

g Jer 23:11
Eze 22:26

47:18 *That is, the Dead Sea. 47:19 *Lit., "the south side southward." #That is, the Wadi of Egypt. 47:20; 48:1 *Or "the entrance of Hamath."

48:8 *This refers to long cubits. See App. B14.

15 "The remaining area that is 5,000 cubits wide alongside the 25,000 cubit border will be for common use of the city,[a] for housing and pasture ground. The city will be in the middle of it.[b] **16** These are the city's measurements: The northern border is 4,500 cubits, the southern border is 4,500, the eastern border is 4,500, and the western border is 4,500. **17** The pasture ground of the city will be 250 cubits to the north, 250 to the south, 250 to the east, and 250 to the west.

18 "The length of the remaining portion will correspond to the holy contribution,[c] 10,000 cubits to the east and 10,000 to the west. It will correspond to the holy contribution, and its produce will provide food for those serving the city. **19** Those who are serving the city from all the tribes of Israel will cultivate it.[d]

20 "The whole contribution is 25,000 cubits square. You should set it aside as the holy contribution along with the possession of the city.

21 "What remains on both sides of the holy contribution and of the possession of the city will belong to the chieftain.[e] It will be alongside the 25,000 cubit borders that are east and west of the contribution. It will correspond to those adjoining portions, and it will be for the chieftain. The holy contribution and the sanctuary of the temple will be in the middle of it.

22 "The possession of the Levites and the possession of the city will be between what belongs to the chieftain. The chieftain's territory will be between the boundary of Judah[f] and the boundary of Benjamin.

23 "As for the remaining tribes, Benjamin's portion is from the eastern border to the western border.[g] **24** Sim'e·on's por-tion is by the boundary of Benja-min,[a] from the eastern border to the western border. **25** Is'sa-char's portion[b] is by the bound-ary of Sim'e·on, from the east-ern border to the western border. **26** Zeb'u·lun's portion[b] is by the boundary of Is'sa·char,[c] from the eastern border to the western border.[d] **27** Gad's portion is by the boundary of Zeb'u·lun,[e] from the eastern border to the western border. **28** The southern border by the boundary of Gad will run from Ta'mar[f] to the waters of Mer'i·bath-ka'desh,[g] to the Wadi[*h] and on to the Great Sea.[#]

29 "This is the land that you should distribute as an inheri-tance to the tribes of Israel,[i] and these will be their portions,"[j] de-clares the Sovereign Lord Jeho-vah.

30 "These will be the exits of the city: The northern side will measure 4,500 cubits.[k]

31 The gates of the city will be named according to the tribes of Israel. Of the three gates on the north, there is one gate for Reu'ben, one gate for Judah, and one gate for Le'vi.

32 The eastern side will be 4,500 cubits long, and there are three gates: one gate for Joseph, one gate for Benjamin, and one gate for Dan.

33 The southern side will measure 4,500 cubits, with three gates: one gate for Sim'e·on, one gate for Is'sa·char, and one gate for Zeb'u·lun.

34 The western side will be 4,500 cubits long, with three gates: one gate for Gad, one gate for Ash'er, and one gate for Naph'ta·li.

35 "The perimeter will be 18,000 cubits. And the name of the city from that day on will be Jehovah Is There."[l]

CHAP. 48
a Eze 45:6
b Eze 48:35
c Eze 45:1
d Eze 45:6
e Eze 45:7
f Eze 48:8
g Jos 18:11

Second Col.
a Jos 19:1
b Jos 19:17
c Jos 19:10
d Ge 49:13
e Jos 18:7
f Eze 47:19
g Nu 20:13
h Ge 15:18
i Nu 34:2
j Eze 47:13
k Eze 48:16
l Jer 3:17
  Joe 3:21
  Zec 2:10

48:28 *That is, the Wadi of Egypt. #That is, the Mediterranean.

DANIEL

OUTLINE OF CONTENTS

1 In the third year of the kingship of King Je·hoi′a·kim[a] of Judah, King Neb·u·chad·nez′zar of Babylon came to Jerusalem and besieged it.[b] **2** In time Jehovah gave King Je·hoi′a·kim of Judah into his hand,[c] along with some of the utensils of the house* of the true God, and he brought them to the land of Shi′nar*[d] to the house* of his god. He placed the utensils in the treasury of his god.[e]

3 Then the king ordered Ash′pe·naz his chief court official to bring some of the Israelites,* including those of royal and noble descent.[f] **4** They were to be youths* without any defect, of good appearance, endowed with wisdom, knowledge, and discernment,[g] and capable of serving in the king's palace. He was to teach them the writing and the language of the Chal·de′ans. **5** Furthermore, the king assigned to them a daily ration from the king's delicacies and from the wine he drank. They were to be trained* for three years, and at the end of that time they were to enter the king's service.

6 Now among them were some from the tribe* of Judah: Daniel,*[h] Han·a·ni′ah,[△] Mish′a·el,[⊠] and Az·a·ri′ah.[▱][i] **7** And the principal court official assigned names* to them; he gave to Daniel the name Bel·te·shaz′zar,[j] to Han·a·ni′ah the name Sha′drach, to Mish′a·el the name Me′shach, and to Az·a·ri′ah the name A·bed′ne·go.[k]

8 But Daniel resolved in his heart that he would not defile himself with the king's delicacies or with the wine he drank. So he asked the principal court official for permission not to defile himself in this way. **9** And the true God caused the principal court official to show Daniel favor* and mercy.[a] **10** But the principal court official said to Daniel: "I am afraid of my lord the king, who has assigned your food and drink. What if he should see you looking worse in appearance than the other youths* of your age? You would make me* guilty before the king." **11** But Daniel said to the guardian whom the principal court official had appointed over Daniel, Han·a·ni′ah, Mish′a·el, and Az·a·ri′ah: **12** "Please, test your servants for ten days, and let us be given some vegetables to eat and water to drink; **13** then compare our appearance with the appearance of the youths* who are eating the king's delicacies, and deal with your servants according to what you see."

14 So he agreed to their proposal and tested them for ten days. **15** At the end of ten days their appearance was better and healthier* than all the youths* who were eating the king's delicacies. **16** So the guardian would take away their delicacies and their wine and give them vegetables. **17** And the true God gave these four youths* knowledge and insight into every kind of writing and wisdom; and Daniel was given understanding in all sorts of visions and dreams.[b]

18 At the end of the time that the king had specified to bring them in,[c] the principal court

---

CHAP. 1

a 2Ch 36:4
  Jer 22:18, 19
  Jer 36:30

b De 28:49, 50
  2Ki 24:1
  2Ch 36:5, 6

c Isa 42:24

d Ge 10:9, 10

e 2Ch 36:7
  Ezr 1:7

f 2Ki 20:16, 18

g Da 1:17, 20
  Da 5:11, 12

h Da 2:48
  Da 5:13, 29

i Da 2:17, 18

j Da 4:8
  Da 5:12

k Da 2:49
  Da 3:12, 28

Second Col.

a 1Ki 8:49, 50
  Ps 106:44, 46

b Da 1:20
  Da 4:9
  Da 5:11, 12

c Da 1:5

1:2 *Or "temple." #That is, Babylonia. 1:3 *Lit., "sons of Israel." 1:4, 10, 13, 15, 17 *Lit., "children." 1:5 *Or possibly, "nourished." 1:6 *Lit., "sons." #Meaning "My Judge Is God." △Meaning "Jehovah Has Shown Favor." ⊠Possibly meaning "Who Is Like God?" ▱Meaning "Jehovah Has Helped." 1:7 *That is, Babylonian names. 1:9 *Or "kindness." 1:10 #Lit., "my head." 1:15 #Lit., "fat of flesh."

official brought them in before Neb·u·chad·nez′zar. **19** When the king spoke with them, no one in the entire group was found to be like Daniel, Han·a·ni′ah, Mish′a·el, and Az·a·ri′ah;[a] and they continued to serve before the king. **20** In every matter requiring wisdom and understanding that the king would ask them about, he found them ten times better than all the magic-practicing priests and the conjurers[b] in his entire realm. **21** And Daniel remained there until the first year of King Cyrus.[c]

2 In the second year of his kingship, Neb·u·chad·nez′zar had a number of dreams, and he* was so agitated[d] that he could not sleep. **2** So the king gave the order to summon the magic-practicing priests, the conjurers, the sorcerers, and the Chal·de′ans* to tell the king his dreams. So they came in and stood before the king.[e] **3** Then the king said to them: "I have had a dream, and I am* agitated because I want to know what I dreamed." **4** The Chal·de′ans replied to the king in the Ar·a·ma′ic language:*[f] "O king, may you live on forever. Relate the dream to your servants, and we will tell the interpretation." **5** The king answered the Chal·de′ans: "This is my final word: If you do not make the dream known to me, along with its interpretation, you will be dismembered, and your houses will be turned into public latrines.* **6** But if you do tell the dream and its interpretation, you will receive from me gifts and a reward and great honor.[g]

So tell me the dream and its interpretation."

7 They answered a second time: "Let the king relate the dream to his servants, and we will tell its interpretation."

8 The king replied: "I am well-aware that you are trying to gain time, for you realize what my final word is. **9** If you do not make the dream known to me, there is only one penalty for all of you. But you have agreed to tell me something false and deceitful until the situation changes. So tell me the dream, and I will know that you can explain its interpretation."

10 The Chal·de′ans answered the king: "There is not a man on earth* who is able to do what the king demands, for no great king or governor has asked such a thing of any magic-practicing priest or conjurer or Chal·de′an. **11** What the king is asking is difficult, and no one exists who could tell the king this except the gods, who do not dwell among mortals."*

12 At this the king flew into a violent rage and gave the order to destroy all the wise men of Babylon.[a] **13** When the order was issued and the wise men were about to be killed, they also looked for Daniel and his companions to put them to death.

14 At that time Daniel discreetly and cautiously spoke to Ar′i·och the chief of the king's bodyguard, who had gone out to kill the wise men of Babylon. **15** He asked Ar′i·och the officer of the king: "Why is there such a harsh order from the king?" Then Ar′i·och informed Daniel about the matter.[b] **16** So Daniel went in and asked the king to grant him time to tell the interpretation to the king.

CHAP. 1
a Da 1:3, 6

b Da 2:2
Da 4:7
Da 5:8

c Da 6:28
Da 10:1

CHAP. 2
d Da 4:4, 5

e Da 4:6, 7
Da 5:7, 8

f 2Ki 18:26
Ezr 4:7
Isa 36:11

g Da 2:48
Da 5:16, 29

Second Col.
a Da 2:24

b Da 2:9

2:1 *Lit., "his spirit." 2:2 *That is, a group skilled in divination and astrology. 2:3 *Lit., "my spirit is." 2:4 *Da 2:4b through 7:28 was originally written in Aramaic. 2:5 *Or possibly, "garbage dumps; dunghills."

2:10 *Or "dry land." 2:11 *Lit., "with flesh."

17 Daniel then went to his house and informed his companions Han·a·ni′ah, Mish′a·el, and Az·a·ri′ah of the matter. **18** He asked them to pray for mercy from the God of heaven concerning this secret, so that Daniel and his companions would not be destroyed along with the rest of the wise men of Babylon.

19 Then the secret was revealed to Daniel in a vision at night.ᵃ So Daniel praised the God of heaven. **20** Daniel declared:

"Let the name of God be
　　praised for all eternity,*

For wisdom and mightiness
　　are his alone.ᵇ

21 He changes times and
　　seasons,ᶜ

Removes kings and sets
　　up kings,ᵈ

Gives wisdom to the wise
　　and knowledge to those
　　with discernment.ᵉ

22 He reveals the deep things
　　and the hidden things,ᶠ

He knows what is in the
　　darkness,ᵍ

And with him the light
　　dwells.ʰ

23 To you, O God of my
　　forefathers, I offer thanks
　　and praise,

Because you have given me
　　wisdom and power.

And now you have made
　　known to me what we
　　requested of you;

You have made known to us
　　the concern of the king."ⁱ

24 Daniel then went in to Ar′i·och, whom the king had appointed to destroy the wise men of Babylon,ʲ and he said to him: "Do not destroy any wise men of Babylon. Take me in before the king, and I will tell the interpretation to the king."

25 Ar′i·och quickly took Daniel in before the king and said to him: "I have found a man of the exiles of Judahᵃ who can make known the interpretation to the king." **26** The king said to Daniel, whose name was Bel·te·shaz′zar:ᵇ "Can you really make known to me the dream that I saw, and its interpretation?"ᶜ **27** Daniel replied to the king: "None of the wise men, conjurers, magic-practicing priests, or astrologers are able to tell the king the secret that he is asking.ᵈ **28** But there is a God in the heavens who is a Revealer of secrets,ᵉ and he has made known to King Neb·u·chad·nez′zar what is to happen in the final part of the days. This is your dream, and these are the visions of your head as you lay on your bed:

29 "As for you, O king, on your bed your thoughts turned to what is to take place in the future, and the Revealer of secrets has made known to you what is to happen. **30** As for me, this secret was not revealed to me because I have greater wisdom than anyone living; rather, it was to make the interpretation known to the king so that you may know the thoughts in your heart.ᶠ

31 "You, O king, were watching, and you saw an immense image.* That image, which was huge and extremely bright, was standing in front of you, and its appearance was terrifying. **32** The head of that image was of fine gold,ᵍ its chest and its arms were of silver,ʰ its abdomen and its thighs were of copper,ⁱ **33** its legs were of iron,ʲ and its feet were partly of iron and partly of clay.*ᵏ **34** You looked on until a stone was cut out, not by hands, and it

---

CHAP. 2
a Da 2:28

b 1Ch 29:11
Job 12:13
Ps 147:5
Jer 32:17-19

c Ac 1:7

d 1Sa 2:7, 8
Ps 75:7
Jer 27:5
Da 4:17

e Pr 2:6
Ec 2:26
Jas 1:5

f Jer 33:3
1Co 2:10

g Ps 139:12
Heb 4:13

h Ps 36:9
Ps 112:4

i Da 1:17
Da 2:28

j Da 2:12, 14

Second Col.

a Da 1:3, 6

b Da 1:7

c Ge 41:15

d Da 2:10, 11

e Ge 40:8
Da 1:17

f Da 2:47

g Da 2:37, 38
Da 7:4

h Da 5:28
Da 7:5
Da 8:3, 20

i Da 2:39
Da 7:6
Da 8:5, 21

j Da 7:7, 19

k Da 2:40-42

2:20 *Or "from eternity to eternity." 2:31 *Or "statue." 2:33 *Or "baked (molded) clay."

struck the image on its feet of iron and of clay and crushed them.[a] **35** At that time the iron, the clay, the copper, the silver, and the gold were, all together, crushed and became like the chaff from the summer threshing floor, and the wind carried them away so that not a trace of them could be found. But the stone that struck the image became a large mountain, and it filled the whole earth.

36 "This is the dream, and we will now tell the king its interpretation. **37** You, O king—the king of kings to whom the God of heaven has given the kingdom,[b] the might, the strength, and the glory, **38** and into whose hand he has given man wherever they may dwell, as well as the beasts of the field and the birds of the heavens, and whom he has made ruler over all of them[c]—you yourself are the head of gold.[d]

39 "But after you another kingdom will rise,[e] inferior to you; then another kingdom, a third one, of copper, that will rule over the whole earth.[f]

40 "As for the fourth kingdom, it will be strong like iron.[g] For just as iron crushes and pulverizes everything else, yes, like iron that shatters, it will crush and shatter all of these.[h]

41 "And just as you saw the feet and the toes to be partly of clay of a potter and partly of iron, the kingdom will be divided, but some of the hardness of iron will be in it, just as you saw the iron mixed with soft clay. **42** And as the toes of the feet were partly of iron and partly of clay, so the kingdom will be partly strong and partly fragile. **43** Just as you saw iron mixed with soft clay, they will be mixed with the people;* but they

will not stick together, one to the other, just as iron does not mix with clay.

44 "In the days of those kings the God of heaven will set up a kingdom[a] that will never be destroyed.[b] And this kingdom will not be passed on to any other people.[c] It will crush and put an end to all these kingdoms,[d] and it alone will stand forever,[e] **45** just as you saw that out of the mountain a stone was cut not by hands, and that it crushed the iron, the copper, the clay, the silver, and the gold.[f] The Grand God has made known to the king what will happen in the future.[g] The dream is true, and its interpretation is trustworthy."

46 Then King Neb·u·chad·nez'-zar fell down with his face to the ground before Daniel and paid homage to him. And he gave the order to offer a present and incense to him. **47** The king said to Daniel: "Truly your God is a God of gods and a Lord of kings and a Revealer of secrets, because you were able to reveal this secret."[h] **48** The king then elevated Daniel and gave him many fine gifts, and he made him the ruler over all the province* of Babylon[i] and the chief prefect over all the wise men of Babylon. **49** And at Daniel's request, the king appointed Sha'drach, Me'-shach, and A·bed'ne·go[j] over the administration of the province* of Babylon, but Daniel served in the king's court.

3 Neb·u·chad·nez'zar the king made an image# of gold that was 60 cubits△ high and 6 cubits⊠ wide. He set it up on the plain of Du'ra in the province* of Babylon. **2** Then

---

CHAP. 2
a Da 2:44, 45

b Jer 28:14
  Da 5:18

c Jer 27:5-7

d Da 2:32
  Da 4:20-22

e Isa 45:1
  Jer 51:28, 29
  Da 5:28

f Da 7:6
  Da 8:5, 21
  Da 11:3

g Da 2:33
  Da 7:19, 23

h Da 7:7

Second Col.
a Da 49:10
  Ps 2:6
  Mt 6:10
  Lu 22:29
  Joh 18:36
  Re 11:15
  Re 20:6

b 2Sa 7:13
  Isa 9:7
  Da 7:13, 14

c Da 4:17
  Da 7:27

d Ps 2:7-9
  Ps 110:5, 6
  Re 19:15

e Da 4:34
  Lu 1:31-33

f Da 2:34, 35

g Ge 41:28
  Da 2:28

h Ge 41:39
  Da 1:17
  Da 2:28
  Da 4:9

i Da 2:6
  Da 5:16, 29

j Da 1:7

2:43 *Or "the offspring of mankind," that is, the common people.

2:48, 49; 3:1 *Or "jurisdictional district." 3:1 #Or "statue." △About 27 m (88 ft). See App. B14. ⊠About 2.7 m (8.8 ft). See App. B14.

King Neb·u·chad·nez'zar sent word to assemble the satraps, prefects, governors, advisers, treasurers, judges, magistrates, and all the administrators of the provinces* to come to the inauguration of the image that King Neb·u·chad·nez'zar had set up.

3 So the satraps, prefects, governors, advisers, treasurers, judges, magistrates, and all the administrators of the provinces* assembled for the inauguration of the image that King Neb·u·chad·nez'zar had set up. And they stood in front of the image that Neb·u·chad·nez'zar had set up. 4 The herald loudly proclaimed: "You are commanded, O peoples, nations, and language groups, 5 that when you hear the sound of the horn, pipe, zither, triangular harp, stringed instrument, bagpipe, and all the other musical instruments, you must fall down and worship the image of gold that King Neb·u·chad·nez'zar has set up. 6 Whoever does not fall down and worship will immediately be thrown into the burning fiery furnace."ᵃ 7 So when all the peoples heard the sound of the horn, pipe, zither, triangular harp, stringed instrument, and all the other musical instruments, all the peoples, nations, and language groups fell down and worshipped the image of gold that King Neb·u·chad·nez'zar had set up.

8 Now at that time some of the Chal·de'ans came forward and accused* the Jews. 9 They said to King Neb·u·chad·nez'zar: "O king, may you live on forever. 10 You, O king, gave the command that every man who hears the sound of the horn, pipe, zither, triangular

harp, stringed instrument, bagpipe, and all the other musical instruments should fall down and worship the image of gold; 11 and that whoever would not fall down and worship should be thrown into the burning fiery furnace.ᵃ 12 But there are certain Jews whom you appointed to administer the province* of Babylon: Sha'drach, Me'shach, and A·bed'ne·go.ᵇ These men have paid no regard to you, O king. They are not serving your gods, and they refuse to worship the image of gold that you have set up."

13 Then Neb·u·chad·nez'zar, in a furious rage, ordered Sha'drach, Me'shach, and A·bed'ne·go to be brought in. So these men were brought in before the king. 14 Neb·u·chad·nez'zar said to them: "Is it really true, Sha'drach, Me'shach, and A·bed'ne·go, that you are not serving my godsᶜ and that you refuse to worship the image of gold that I have set up? 15 Now when you hear the sound of the horn, the pipe, the zither, the triangular harp, the stringed instrument, the bagpipe, and all the other musical instruments, if you are ready to fall down and worship the image that I have made, fine. But if you refuse to worship, you will immediately be thrown into the burning fiery furnace. And who is the god who can rescue you out of my hands?"ᵈ

16 Sha'drach, Me'shach, and A·bed'ne·go answered the king: "O Neb·u·chad·nez'zar, we have no need to answer you in this matter. 17 If it must be, our God whom we serve is able to rescue us from the burning fiery furnace, O king, and to rescue us from your hand.ᵉ 18 But even if he does not, let it be

CHAP. 3
a Jer 29:22

Second Col.
a Da 3:4-6

b Da 1:7
Da 2:49

c Isa 46:1
Jer 50:2
Da 2:47

d Ex 5:2
2Ch 32:15
Isa 36:4, 20

e 1Sa 17:37
Ps 27:1
Isa 12:2
Da 6:27

3:2, 3 *Or "jurisdictional districts."
3:8 *Or "slandered."

3:12 *Or "jurisdictional district."

known to you, O king, that we will not serve your gods or worship the image of gold that you have set up."[a]

19 Then Neb·u·chad·nez'zar became so furious with Sha'drach, Me'shach, and A·bed'ne·go that the expression of his face changed* toward them, and he gave orders to heat the furnace seven times hotter than usual. **20** He ordered some of the mighty men from his army to bind Sha'drach, Me'shach, and A·bed'ne·go and to throw them into the burning fiery furnace.

21 So these men were tied up while still wearing their cloaks, garments, caps, and all their other clothing, and they were thrown into the burning fiery furnace. **22** Because the king's command was so harsh and the furnace was exceptionally hot, the men who took up Sha'drach, Me'shach, and A·bed'ne·go were the ones killed by the flames of the fire. **23** But these three men, Sha'drach, Me'shach, and A·bed'ne·go, fell bound into the burning fiery furnace.

24 King Neb·u·chad·nez'zar then became frightened and quickly rose up and said to his high officials: "Did we not tie up three men and throw them into the fire?" They answered the king: "Yes, O king." **25** He said: "Look! I see four men walking about free in the midst of the fire, and they are unharmed, and the fourth one looks like a son of the gods."

26 Neb·u·chad·nez'zar approached the door of the burning fiery furnace and said: "Sha'drach, Me'shach, and A·bed'ne·go, you servants of the Most High God,[b] step out and come here!" Sha'drach, Me'shach, and A·bed'ne·go stepped out from the midst of the fire. **27** And the satraps, prefects, governors, and the high officials of the king who were assembled there[a] saw that the fire had had no effect on* the bodies of these men;[b] not a hair of their heads had been singed, their cloaks looked no different, and there was not even the smell of fire on them.

28 Neb·u·chad·nez'zar then declared: "Praised be the God of Sha'drach, Me'shach, and A·bed'ne·go,[c] who sent his angel and rescued his servants. They trusted in him and went against the command of the king and were willing to die* rather than serve or worship any god except their own God.[d] **29** I am therefore issuing an order that any people, nation, or language group that says anything against the God of Sha'drach, Me'shach, and A·bed'ne·go should be dismembered, and their houses should be turned into public latrines;* for there is no other god who is able to rescue like this one."[e]

30 The king then promoted* Sha'drach, Me'shach, and A·bed'ne·go in the province* of Babylon.[f]

4 "From King Neb·u·chad·nez'zar to all the peoples, nations, and language groups dwelling in all the earth: May your peace abound! **2** I am pleased to declare the signs and wonders that the Most High God has performed toward me. **3** How great are his signs, and how mighty his wonders! His kingdom is an everlasting kingdom, and his rulership is for generation after generation.[g]

3:19 *Or "that his attitude changed completely." 3:27 *Or "power over." 3:28 *Or "and gave up their bodies." 3:29 *Or possibly, "garbage dumps; dunghills." 3:30 *Lit., "caused to prosper." *Or "jurisdictional district."

4 "I, Neb·u·chad·nez'zar, was at ease in my house and prospering in my palace. **5** I saw a dream that made me afraid. As I lay on my bed, the images and visions of my head frightened me.[a] **6** So I issued an order to bring in before me all the wise men of Babylon so that they could make known to me the interpretation of the dream.[b]

7 "At that time the magic-practicing priests, the conjurers, the Chal·de'ans,* and the astrologers[c] came in. When I told them what the dream was, they could not make its interpretation known to me.[d] **8** At last there came in before me Daniel, whose name is Bel·te·shaz'zar[e] after the name of my god[f] and in whom there is the spirit of the holy gods,[g] and I told him the dream:

9 "'O Bel·te·shaz'zar the chief of the magic-practicing priests,[h] I well know that the spirit of the holy gods is in you[i] and no secret is too difficult for you.[j] So explain to me the visions I saw in my dream and its interpretation.

10 "'In the visions of my head while on my bed, I saw a tree[k] in the midst of the earth, and its height was enormous.[l] **11** The tree grew and became strong, and its top reached the heavens, and it was visible to the ends of the whole earth. **12** Its foliage was beautiful, and its fruit was abundant, and there was food on it for all. Beneath it the beasts of the field would seek shade, and on its branches the birds of the heavens would dwell, and all creatures* would feed from it.

13 "'As I viewed the visions of my head while on my bed, I saw a watcher, a holy one, coming down from the heavens.[m]

14 He called out loudly: "Chop down the tree,[a] cut off its branches, shake off its leaves, and scatter its fruit! Let the beasts flee from beneath it, and the birds from its branches. **15** But leave the stump with its roots* in the ground, with a banding of iron and of copper, among the grass of the field. Let it be wet with the dew of the heavens, and let its portion be with the beasts among the vegetation of the earth.[b] **16** Let its heart be changed from that of a human, and let it be given the heart of a beast, and let seven times[c] pass over it.[d] **17** This is by the decree of watchers,[e] and the request is by the word of the holy ones, so that people living may know that the Most High is Ruler in the kingdom of mankind[f] and that he gives it to whomever he wants, and he sets up over it even the lowliest of men."

18 "'This was the dream that I, King Neb·u·chad·nez'zar, saw; now you, O Bel·te·shaz'zar, tell its interpretation, for all the other wise men of my kingdom are unable to make the interpretation known to me.[g] But you are able to do so, because the spirit of holy gods is in you.'

19 "At that time Daniel, whose name is Bel·te·shaz'zar,[h] was alarmed for a moment, and his thoughts began to frighten him.

"The king said, 'O Bel·te·shaz'zar, do not let the dream and the interpretation frighten you.'

"Bel·te·shaz'zar answered, 'O my lord, may the dream apply to those hating you, and its interpretation to your enemies.

20 "'The tree that you saw that grew great and became strong, whose top reached the heavens and was visible to all the earth,[i] **21** which had beau-

---

4:7 *That is, a group skilled in divination and astrology. 4:12 *Lit., "all flesh."

4:15 *Or "leave the rootstock."

tiful foliage, abundant fruit, and food for all, beneath which the beasts of the field would dwell and on whose branches the birds of the heavens would reside,[a] **22** it is you, O king, because you have grown great and become strong, and your grandeur has grown and reached to the heavens,[b] and your rulership to the ends of the earth.[c]

23 "'And the king saw a watcher, a holy one,[d] coming down from the heavens, who was saying: "Chop down the tree and destroy it, but leave the stump with its roots* in the ground, with a banding of iron and of copper, among the grass of the field. And let the dew of the heavens make it wet, and let its portion be with the beasts of the field until seven times pass over it."[e] **24** This is the interpretation, O king; it is the decree of the Most High that must befall my lord the king. **25** You will be driven away from among men, and your dwelling will be with the beasts of the field, and you will be given vegetation to eat just like bulls; and you will become wet with the dew of the heavens,[f] and seven times[g] will pass over you,[h] until you know that the Most High is Ruler in the kingdom of mankind and that he grants it to whomever he wants.[i] **26** "'But because they said to leave the stump of the tree with its roots,*[j] your kingdom will be yours again after you come to know that the heavens are ruling. **27** Therefore, O king, may my counsel be acceptable to you. Turn away from your sins by doing what is right, and from your iniquity by showing mercy to the poor. It may be that your prosperity will be extended.'"[k]

28 All of this befell King Neb·u·chad·nez′zar.

29 Twelve months later he was walking on the roof of the royal palace of Babylon. **30** The king was saying: "Is this not Babylon the Great that I myself have built for the royal house by my own strength and might and for the glory of my majesty?"

31 While the word was yet in the king's mouth, a voice came down from the heavens: "To you it is being said, O King Neb·u·chad·nez′zar, 'The kingdom has gone away from you,[a] **32** and from mankind you are being driven away. With the beasts of the field your dwelling will be, and you will be given vegetation to eat just like bulls, and seven times will pass over you, until you know that the Most High is Ruler in the kingdom of mankind and that he grants it to whomever he wants.'"[b]

33 At that moment the word was fulfilled on Neb·u·chad·nez′zar. He was driven away from mankind, and he began to eat vegetation just like bulls, and his body became wet with the dew of the heavens, until his hair grew long just like eagles' feathers and his nails were like birds' claws.[c]

34 "At the end of that time[d] I, Neb·u·chad·nez′zar, looked up to the heavens, and my understanding returned to me; and I praised the Most High, and to the One living forever I gave praise and glory, because his rulership is an everlasting rulership and his kingdom is for generation after generation.[e] **35** All the inhabitants of the earth are regarded as nothing, and he does according to his own will among the army of the heavens and the inhabitants of the earth. And there is no one who can hinder him*[f] or say to him, 'What have you done?'[g]

CHAP. 4
a Da 4:12

b Isa 14:13, 14

c Da 2:37, 38

d Da 4:13
  Da 8:13

e Da 4:13-16
  Lu 21:24

f Da 4:31-33

g Lu 21:24
  Re 12:6, 14

h Da 4:16

i 1Sa 2:7, 8
  Job 34:24
  Jer 27:5
  Eze 21:26, 27
  Da 2:21
  Da 7:13, 14
  Lu 1:32, 33

j Da 4:15

k 1Ki 21:29
  Joe 2:14
  Jon 3:8-10

Second Col.
a Da 4:25
  Ac 12:22, 23

b Da 4:17

c Da 4:25

d Da 4:16

e Ps 10:16
  Da 4:3

f Job 34:24
  Isa 43:13

g Isa 45:9

4:23 *Or "leave the rootstock." 4:26 *Or "the rootstock of the tree."

4:35 *Or "check his hand."

36 "At that time my understanding returned to me, and the glory of my kingdom, my majesty, and my splendor returned to me.[a] My high officials and nobles eagerly sought me out, and I was restored to my kingdom, and even more greatness was added to me.

37 "Now I, Neb·u·chad·nez′zar, am praising and exalting and glorifying the King of the heavens,[b] because all his works are truth and his ways are just,[c] and because he is able to humiliate those who are walking in pride."[d]

5 As regards King Bel·shaz′zar,[e] he held a great feast for a thousand of his nobles, and he was drinking wine in front of them.[f] **2** While under the influence of the wine, Bel·shaz′zar gave an order to bring in the vessels of gold and silver that his father Neb·u·chad·nez′zar had taken from the temple in Jerusalem,[g] so that the king and his nobles, his concubines and his secondary wives could drink from them. **3** Then they brought in the gold vessels that had been taken from the temple of the house of God in Jerusalem, and the king and his nobles, his concubines and his secondary wives drank from them. **4** They drank wine, and they praised the gods of gold and silver, of copper, iron, wood, and stone.

5 At that very moment the fingers of a man's hand appeared and began writing on the plaster of the wall of the king's palace opposite the lampstand, and the king could see the back of the hand as it was writing. **6** Then the king turned pale* and his thoughts terrified him, and his hips shook[h] and his knees began to knock together.

7 The king called out loudly to summon the conjurers, the Chal·de′ans,* and the astrologers.[a] The king said to the wise men of Babylon: "Any man who reads this writing and tells me its interpretation will be clothed with purple, a gold necklace will be placed around his neck,[b] and he will rule as the third one in the kingdom."[c]

8 Then all the wise men of the king came in, but they were not able to read the writing or to make known the interpretation to the king.[d] **9** So King Belshaz′zar was very frightened and his face turned pale; and his nobles were perplexed.[e]

10 Because of the words of the king and his nobles, the queen entered the banqueting hall. The queen said: "O king, may you live on forever. Do not let your thoughts terrify you, nor let your face turn pale. **11** There is a man* in your kingdom who has the spirit of holy gods. In the days of your father, enlightenment and insight and wisdom like the wisdom of gods were found in him.[f] King Neb·u·chad·nez′zar your father appointed him as chief of the magic-practicing priests, conjurers, Chal·de′ans,* and astrologers;[g] your father did this, O king. **12** For Daniel, whom the king named Bel·te·shaz′zar,[h] had an extraordinary spirit and knowledge and insight to interpret dreams, to explain riddles, and to solve knotty problems.*[i] Now let Daniel be summoned, and he will tell you the interpretation."

13 So Daniel was brought in before the king. The king asked Daniel: "Are you Daniel of the exiles of Judah,[j] whom my father the king brought out of Ju-

---

CHAP. 4
a Da 4:26

b Da 4:2, 3

c De 32:4
Ps 33:5

d Ex 18:10, 11
Jas 4:6

CHAP. 5
e Da 7:1
Da 8:1

f Isa 21:5
Jer 51:39

g 2Ki 25:15
2Ch 36:18
Ezr 1:7
Jer 52:19
Da 1:1, 2

h Isa 21:2, 3

Second Col.
a Da 2:2
Da 4:6

b Ge 41:39, 42
Es 8:15

c Da 2:6, 48

d Da 2:27
Da 4:7

e Isa 13:1, 7

f Da 4:8, 9

g Da 2:47, 48

h Da 1:7
Da 4:8

i Da 1:17, 20
Da 6:3

j Da 1:3, 6
Da 2:25

5:6 *Or "the king's appearance changed."

5:7, 11 * That is, a group skilled in divination and astrology. **5:11** *Or "a capable man." **5:12** *Lit., "to untie knots."

dah?ᵃ **14** I have heard concerning you that the spirit of gods is in youᵇ and that enlightenment and insight and extraordinary wisdom have been found in you.ᶜ **15** Now the wise men and the conjurers were brought in before me to read this writing and to make its interpretation known to me, but they are not able to tell the interpretation of the message.ᵈ **16** But I have heard concerning you that you are able to provide interpretationsᵉ and to solve knotty problems.* Now if you are able to read the writing and to make its interpretation known to me, you will be clothed with purple, a gold necklace will be placed around your neck, and you will rule as the third one in the kingdom."ᶠ

17 Daniel then replied to the king: "You may keep your gifts and give your presents to others. However, I will read the writing to the king and make known its interpretation to him. **18** As for you, O king, the Most High God granted to Neb·u·chad·nez′zar your father the kingdom and greatness and honor and majesty.ᵍ **19** Because of the greatness He gave him, all peoples, nations, and language groups trembled with fear before him.ʰ Whomever he wanted, he killed or let live, and whomever he wanted, he exalted or humiliated.ⁱ **20** But when his heart became haughty and his spirit became hardened, so that he acted presumptuously,ʲ he was brought down from the throne of his kingdom, and his dignity was taken away from him. **21** He was driven away from mankind, and his heart was made like that of a beast, and his dwelling was with the wild donkeys. He was given vegetation to eat just like bulls, and his body became wet with the dew of the heav-

ens, until he came to know that the Most High God is Ruler in the kingdom of mankind and that he sets up over it whomever he wants.ᵃ

22 "But you, his son Bel·shaz′zar, have not humbled your heart, although you knew all of this. **23** Instead, you exalted yourself against the Lord of the heavens,ᵇ and you had them bring you the vessels of his house.ᶜ Then you and your nobles, your concubines and your secondary wives drank wine from them and praised gods of silver and gold, of copper, iron, wood, and stone, gods that see nothing and hear nothing and know nothing.ᵈ But you have not glorified the God in whose hand is your breatheᵉ and all your ways. **24** So the hand was sent from him, and this writing was inscribed.ᶠ **25** And this is the writing that was inscribed: ME′NE, ME′NE, TE′KEL, and PAR′SIN.

26 "This is the interpretation of the words: ME′NE, God has numbered the days of your kingdom and brought it to an end.ᵍ

27 "TE′KEL, you have been weighed in the balances and found lacking.

28 "PE′RES, your kingdom has been divided and given to the Medes and the Persians."ʰ

29 Then Bel·shaz′zar gave the command, and they clothed Daniel with purple and placed a gold necklace around his neck; and they heralded concerning him that he was to become the third ruler in the kingdom.ⁱ

30 That very night Bel·shaz′zar the Chal·de′an king was killed.ʲ **31** And Da·ri′usᵏ the Mede received the kingdom; he was about 62 years old.

6 It seemed good to Da·ri′us to appoint 120 satraps over the whole kingdom.ˡ **2** Over them were three high officials, one of

---

CHAP. 5
a 2Ki 24:11, 14
b Da 4:9
c Da 1:17, 20
d Isa 47:12, 13
  Da 2:10, 11
  Da 5:8
e Da 2:28
f Da 2:6
  Da 5:7
g Da 2:37, 38
h Jer 25:9
  Da 3:4, 5
  Da 4:22
i Da 2:12
  Da 3:6, 29
j Isa 14:13, 14
  Da 4:30

Second Col.
a Da 4:31-35
b Jer 50:29
c Da 5:2, 3
d Ps 115:4-7
  Isa 46:6, 7
e Ps 104:29
f Da 5:5
g Isa 13:11
  Jer 25:12
  Jer 27:6, 7
  Jer 50:1, 2
  Jer 51:11
h Ezr 1:1, 2
  Isa 21:2
  Isa 45:1
  Jer 50:9
  Da 6:28
  Da 9:1
i Da 5:7, 16
j Isa 21:9
  Jer 51:8, 31
  Jer 51:39, 57
k Da 6:1
  Da 9:1

CHAP. 6
l Es 1:1
  Da 9:1

whom was Daniel;[a] and the satraps[b] would report to them, so that the king would not suffer loss. **3** Now Daniel was distinguishing himself over the other high officials and the satraps, for there was an extraordinary spirit in him,[c] and the king intended to elevate him over the entire kingdom.

4 At that time the high officials and the satraps were seeking to find some grounds for accusation against Daniel respecting matters of state,* but they could find no grounds for accusation or anything corrupt, for he was trustworthy and no negligence or corruption could be found in him. **5** These men then said: "We will find in this Daniel no grounds for accusation at all, unless we find it against him in the law of his God."[d]

6 So these high officials and satraps went in as a group to the king, and they said to him: "O King Da·ri'us, may you live on forever. **7** All the royal officials, prefects, satraps, high royal officers, and governors have consulted together to establish a royal decree and to enforce a ban,* that for 30 days whoever makes a petition to any god or man except to you, O king, should be thrown into the lions' pit.[e] **8** Now, O king, may you establish the decree and sign it,[f] so that it cannot be changed, according to the law of the Medes and the Persians, which cannot be annulled."[g]

9 So King Da·ri'us signed the decree and the ban.

10 But as soon as Daniel knew that the decree had been signed, he went to his house, which had the windows of his roof chamber open toward Je-

rusalem.[a] And three times a day he got down on his knees and prayed and offered praise before his God, as he had regularly done prior to this. **11** At that time those men burst in and found Daniel petitioning and pleading for favor before his God.

12 So they approached the king and reminded him about the royal ban: "Did you not sign a ban stating that for 30 days any man who makes a petition to any god or man except to you, O king, should be thrown into the lions' pit?" The king replied: "The matter is well-established according to the law of the Medes and the Persians, which cannot be annulled."[b] **13** They immediately said to the king: "Daniel, who is of the exiles of Judah,[c] has paid no regard to you, O king, nor to the ban that you signed, but three times a day he is praying."[d] **14** As soon as the king heard this, he was greatly distressed, and he tried to think of a way to rescue Daniel; and until the sun set he made every effort to save him. **15** Finally those men went in as a group to the king, and they said to the king: "Take note, O king, that the law of the Medes and the Persians is that any ban or decree that the king establishes cannot be changed."[e]

16 So the king gave the order, and they brought Daniel and threw him into the pit of lions.[f] The king said to Daniel: "Your God whom you are continually serving will rescue you." **17** Then a stone was brought and placed over the entrance* of the pit, and the king sealed it with his signet ring and with the signet ring of his nobles, so that nothing could be changed with regard to Daniel.

CHAP. 6
a Da 2:48
  Da 5:29

b Ezr 8:36
  Es 8:9
  Da 3:2

c Da 1:17, 20
  Da 5:12

d Es 3:8

e Da 3:6

f Es 3:12
  Es 8:10

g Es 1:19
  Es 8:8

Second Col.
a 1Ki 8:44, 45

b Es 8:8
  Da 6:7, 8

c Da 1:3, 6
  Da 2:25
  Da 5:13

d Es 3:8
  Da 6:10

e Es 8:8
  Da 6:8

f Da 6:7
  Heb 11:32, 33

6:4 *Lit., "the kingdom." 6:7 *Or "an interdict." 6:17 *Lit., "mouth."

18 The king then went to his palace. He passed the night fasting and refused any entertainment,* and he could not sleep.# **19** Finally at the first light of dawn, the king got up and hurried to the lions' pit. **20** As he got near the pit, he called out to Daniel with a sad voice. The king asked Daniel: "O Daniel, servant of the living God, has your God whom you are continually serving been able to rescue you from the lions?" **21** Daniel immediately said to the king: "O king, may you live on forever. **22** My God sent his angel and shut the mouth of the lions,ᵃ and they have not harmed me,ᵇ for I was found innocent before him; nor have I done any wrong to you, O king."

23 The king was overjoyed, and he commanded that Daniel be lifted up out of the pit. When Daniel was lifted up out of the pit, he was completely unharmed, because he had trusted in his God.ᶜ

24 The king then gave an order, and the men who had accused* Daniel were brought, and they were thrown into the lions' pit, along with their sons and their wives. They had not reached the bottom of the pit before the lions overpowered them and crushed all their bones.ᵈ

25 Then King Da·ri′us wrote to all the peoples, nations, and language groups dwelling throughout the earth:ᵉ "May you have abundant peace! **26** I am issuing an order that in every domain of my kingdom, people are to tremble in fear before the God of Daniel.ᶠ For he is the living God and he endures forever. His kingdom will never be destroyed, and his ruler-

ship* is eternal.ᵃ **27** He rescues,ᵇ saves, and performs signs and wonders in the heavens and on the earth,ᶜ for he rescued Daniel from the paw of the lions."

28 So this Daniel prospered in the kingdom of Da·ri′usᵈ and in the kingdom of Cyrus the Persian.ᵉ

7 In the first year of King Bel·shaz′zarᶠ of Babylon, Daniel saw a dream and visions of his head as he lay on his bed.ᵍ Then he wrote down the dream;ʰ he recorded a complete account of the matters. **2** Daniel declared:

"I was watching in my visions during the night, and look! the four winds of the heavens were stirring up the vast sea.ⁱ **3** And four huge beastsʲ came out of the sea, each different from the others.

4 "The first one was like a lion,ᵏ and it had the wings of an eagle.ˡ I watched until its wings were plucked out, and it was lifted up from the earth and was made to stand up on two feet like a man, and it was given the heart of a man.

5 "And look! another beast, a second one, like a bear.ᵐ It was raised up on one side, and three ribs were in its mouth between its teeth; and it was told, 'Get up, eat much flesh.'ⁿ

6 "After this I kept watching, and look! another beast, like a leopard,ᵒ but on its back it had four wings like those of a bird. And the beast had four heads,ᵖ and it was given authority to rule.

7 "After this I kept watching in the visions of the night, and I saw a fourth beast, fearsome and terrifying and unusually strong, and it had large iron teeth. It was devouring and crushing, and what was left it trampled down with its feet.ᵠ It

CHAP. 6
a 1Sa 17:37
  Heb 11:32, 33

b Ps 34:7
  Ps 118:5
  Da 3:28

c Ps 37:40
  Pr 18:10
  Da 3:26, 27

d Es 7:10

e Es 8:9
  Da 4:1

f Da 3:29

Second Col.
a Da 4:34

b Da 3:28

c Jer 32:20
  Da 4:3

d Da 5:31
  Da 6:1, 2

e 2Ch 36:22, 23
  Ezr 1:1, 2
  Isa 44:28

CHAP. 7
f Da 5:1, 30

g Da 2:19
  Da 8:1

h Isa 30:8
  Hab 2:2
  Re 1:11

i Isa 57:20
  Re 17:15

j Da 7:17

k Da 2:37, 38

l De 28:49, 50
  Jer 48:40
  La 4:19
  Hab 1:8

m Da 2:39
  Da 5:28
  Da 8:3, 20

n Isa 13:17, 18
  Da 11:2

o Da 2:39
  Da 8:5
  Da 11:3

p Da 8:8
  Da 11:4

q Da 2:40
  Da 7:19

6:18 *Or possibly, "no musicians were brought in." #Lit., "his sleep fled from him." **6:24** *Or "slandered."

6:26 *Or "sovereignty."

was different from all the other beasts that were prior to it, and it had ten horns. **8** While I considered the horns, look! another horn, a small one,[a] came up among them, and three of the first horns were plucked up from before it. And look! there were eyes like human eyes in this horn, and there was a mouth speaking arrogantly.*[b]

9 "I kept watching until thrones were set in place and the Ancient of Days[c] sat down.[d] His clothing was white like snow,[e] and the hair of his head was like clean wool. His throne was flames of fire; its wheels were a burning fire.[f] **10** A stream of fire was flowing and going out from before him.[g] A thousand thousands kept ministering to him, and ten thousand times ten thousand stood before him.[h] The Court[i] took its seat, and books were opened.

11 "I kept watching at that time because of the sound of the arrogant* words that the horn was speaking;[j] I watched until the beast was killed and its body was destroyed and it was given over to be burned in the fire. **12** But as for the rest of the beasts,[k] their rulerships were taken away, and their lives were prolonged for a time and a season.

13 "I kept watching in the visions of the night, and look! with the clouds of the heavens, someone like a son of man[l] was coming; and he gained access to the Ancient of Days,[m] and they brought him up close before that One. **14** And to him there were given rulership,[n] honor,[o] and a kingdom, that the peoples, nations, and language groups should all serve him.[p] His rulership is an everlasting rul-

---

7:8, 20 *Or "boastfully." 7:11 *Or "boastful."

CHAP. 7
a Da 7:24
b Da 7:20
  Re 13:5
c Ps 90:2
  Da 7:13, 22
  Hab 1:12
d Isa 6:1, 2
  Re 4:2, 3
e Ps 104:1, 2
f De 9:3
  Heb 12:29
g Ps 50:3
  Ps 97:3
h De 33:2
  1Ki 22:19
  Ps 68:17
  Heb 12:22
  Jude 14
  Re 5:11
i 1Sa 2:10
  Ps 50:6
j Da 7:8, 25
k Da 7:3
l Mt 24:30
  Lu 21:27
  Joh 3:13
  Ac 7:56
  Re 14:14
m Ps 90:2
  Da 7:9, 22
  Hab 1:12
n Ps 2:6
  Ps 110:1, 2
  Mt 28:18
  1Co 15:25
  Eph 1:22
  Re 3:21
o Php 2:9-11
p Ge 49:10

Second Col.

a Ps 45:6
  Isa 9:6, 7
  Da 2:44
  Lu 1:32, 33
  Re 11:15
b Da 8:27
c Da 7:3
d Da 2:39, 40
e Da 7:25, 27
f Mt 19:28
  2Ti 2:12
  Re 3:21
  Re 5:9, 10
g Da 7:21, 22
  Lu 22:29
h Da 2:40
  Da 7:7
i Da 7:24
j Da 7:8
k Da 8:23, 24
  Da 12:7
  Re 13:7
l Ps 90:2
  Da 7:9, 13
  Hab 1:12
m Da 7:18, 27
n Mt 19:28
  Lu 22:29
  Re 1:6
  Re 3:21
  Re 5:9, 10
  Re 20:4
o Da 2:40
  Da 7:7

ership that will not pass away, and his kingdom will not be destroyed.[a]

15 "As for me, Daniel, my spirit was distressed within me because the visions of my head frightened me.[b] **16** I went near to one of those who were standing there to ask him about the true meaning of this. So he replied and made known to me the interpretation of these things.

17 "'These huge beasts, four in number,[c] are four kings who will stand up from the earth.[d] **18** But the holy ones of the Supreme One[e] will receive the kingdom,[f] and they will possess the kingdom[g] forever, yes, forever and ever.'

19 "Then I wanted to know more about the fourth beast, which was different from all the others; it was extraordinarily fearsome, with iron teeth and copper claws, and it was devouring and crushing, and trampling down what was left with its feet;[h] **20** and about the ten horns[i] on its head, and the other horn that came up and before which three fell,[j] the horn that had eyes and a mouth speaking arrogantly* and whose appearance was bigger than that of the others.

21 "I kept watching as that horn made war on the holy ones, and it was prevailing against them,[k] **22** until the Ancient of Days[l] came and judgment was rendered in favor of the holy ones of the Supreme One,[m] and the appointed time arrived for the holy ones to take possession of the kingdom.[n]

23 "This is what he said: 'As for the fourth beast, there is a fourth kingdom that will come to be on the earth. It will be different from all the other kingdoms, and it will devour all the earth and will trample it down and crush it.[o] **24** As for the ten horns, ten kings will rise up out of that kingdom; and still another one will rise up after them, and he will be different from the first ones, and he will humiliate three kings.[a] **25** He will speak words against the Most High,[b] and he will continually harass the holy ones of the Supreme One. He will intend to change times and law, and they will be given into his hand for a time, times, and half a time.*[c] **26** But the Court sat, and they took away his rulership, in order to annihilate him and to destroy him completely.[d]

27 "'And the kingdom and the rulership and the grandeur of the kingdoms under all the heavens were given to the people who are the holy ones of the Supreme One.[e] Their kingdom is an everlasting kingdom,[f] and all rulerships will serve and obey them.'

28 "This is the end of the matter. As for me, Daniel, my thoughts alarmed me greatly, so that I turned pale;* but I kept the matter in my own heart."

8 In the third year of the kingship of King Bel·shaz′zar,[g] a vision appeared to me, Daniel, after the one that appeared to me previously.[h] **2** I saw the vision, and as I watched I was in Shu′shan*[i] the citadel,[B] which is in the province△ of E′lam;[j] I viewed the vision, and I was next to the watercourse of U′lai. **3** As I raised my eyes, look! there was a ram[k] standing before the watercourse, and it had two horns.[l] The two horns were tall, but one was higher than the other, and the higher one came up later.[m] **4** I saw the ram making thrusts to the west and to the north and to the south, and

no wild beasts could stand before it, and there was no one who could provide rescue from its power.*[a] It did as it pleased and exalted itself.

5 As I kept watching, look! there was a male goat* coming from the west* crossing the surface of the whole earth without touching the ground. And the goat had a conspicuous horn between its eyes.[c] **6** It was coming toward the ram with the two horns, which I had seen standing before the watercourse; it was running toward it in a powerful rage.

7 I saw it closing in on the ram, and it was filled with bitterness toward it. It struck down the ram and broke its two horns, and the ram was powerless to stand up to it. It threw the ram to the ground and trampled it down, and there was no one to rescue it from its power.*

8 Then the male goat exalted itself exceedingly, but as soon as it became mighty, the great horn was broken; then four conspicuous horns came up instead of the one, toward the four winds of the heavens.[d]

9 Out of one of them came another horn, a small one, and it grew very great toward the south and toward the east* and toward the Decoration.[B][e] **10** It grew so great that it reached all the way to the army of the heavens, and it caused some of the army and some of the stars to fall to the earth, and it trampled them down. **11** It exalted itself even against the Prince of the army, and from him the constant feature* was taken away, and the established place of his sanctuary was thrown down.[f] **12** And an army

---

CHAP. 7
a Da 7:20
b Da 7:8
c Da 12:7
  Re 13:5-7
d Da 7:10, 11
e Da 7:22
  Mt 19:28
  Lu 22:29
  Re 20:4
f Re 11:15

CHAP. 8
g Da 5:1, 30
h Da 7:1, 15
i Ne 1:1
  Es 2:8
j Ge 10:22
  Isa 11:11
  Isa 21:2
k Isa 13:17
  Jer 51:11
  Da 7:5
  Da 8:20
l Es 1:1, 3
m Isa 44:28

Second Col.
a Isa 45:1
  Jer 51:12
  Da 5:30, 31
b Da 2:39
  Da 7:6
  Da 8:21
c Da 11:3
d Da 8:22
  Da 11:4
e Ps 48:2
  Da 11:16, 45
f Da 11:31
  Da 12:11

7:25 *That is, three and a half times. 7:28 *Or "my appearance changed." 8:2 *Or "Susa." BOr "palace; fortress." △Or "jurisdictional district."

8:4, 7 *Lit., "hand." 8:5 *Or "sunset." 8:9 *Or "sunrise." BOr "the Beauty." 8:11 *Or "the continual sacrifice."

was given over, together with the constant feature,* because of transgression; and it kept throwing truth to the earth, and it acted and had success.

13 And I heard a holy one speaking, and another holy one said to the one speaking: "How long will the vision of the constant feature* and of the transgression causing desolation continue,ᵃ to make both the holy place and the army things to trample on?" **14** So he said to me: "Until 2,300 evenings and mornings; and the holy place will certainly be restored to its right condition."

15 While I, Daniel, was watching the vision and seeking to understand it, suddenly I saw standing in front of me someone who appeared to be a man. **16** Then I heard the voice of a man in the midst of the U'lai,ᵇ and he called out: "Ga'bri·el,ᶜ make that one understand what he saw."ᵈ **17** So he came near to where I was standing, but when he came I was so terrified that I fell facedown. He said to me: "Understand, O son of man, that the vision is for the time of the end."ᵉ **18** But while he was speaking with me, I fell fast asleep with my face to the ground. So he touched me and made me stand up where I had been standing.ᶠ **19** Then he said: "Here I am causing you to know what will happen in the final part of the denunciation, because it is for the appointed time of the end.ᵍ

20 "The two-horned ram that you saw stands for the kings of Me'di·a and Persia.ʰ **21** The hairy male goat stands for the king of Greece;ⁱ and the great horn that was between its eyes stands for the first king.ʲ **22** As for the horn that was broken, so

that four stood up instead of it,ᵃ there are four kingdoms from his nation that will stand up, but not with his power.

23 "And in the final part of their kingdom, as the transgressors act to a completion,* a fierce-looking king who understands ambiguous sayings# will stand up. **24** His power will become great, but not through his own power. He will bring ruin in an extraordinary way,* and he will be successful and act effectively. He will bring mighty ones to ruin, also the people made up of the holy ones.ᵇ **25** And by his cunning he will use deception to succeed; and in his heart he will exalt himself; and during a time of security* he will bring many to ruin. He will even stand up against the Prince of princes, but he will be broken without human hand.

26 "What was said in the vision about the evenings and the mornings is true, but you must keep the vision secret, for it refers to a time many days from now."*ᶜ

27 As for me, Daniel, I felt exhausted and I was sick for some days.ᵈ Then I got up and carried out the king's work;ᵉ but I was numbed by what I had seen, and no one could understand it.ᶠ

9 In the first year of Da·ri'usᵍ the son of A·has·u·e'rus —a descendant of the Medes who had been made king over the kingdom of the Chal·de'ansʰ— **2** in the first year of his reign I, Daniel, discerned by the books* the number of years mentioned in the word of Jehovah to Jeremiah the prophet to fulfill the

---

CHAP. 8
a Da 12:11

b Da 8:2

c Lu 1:19, 26

d Da 9:21, 22

e Da 10:14
  Da 12:4, 9

f Da 10:9, 10

g Da 11:27

h Da 7:5
  Da 8:3
  Da 11:2

i Da 7:6

j Da 8:5
  Da 11:3

Second Col.
a Da 8:8
  Da 11:4

b Da 7:25
  Da 8:10

c Da 10:14

d Da 7:28
  Da 10:16

e Da 2:48, 49

f Da 8:17

CHAP. 9
g Da 6:28
  Da 11:1

h Da 5:30, 31

8:12, 13 *Or "the continual sacrifice."   8:23 *Or "have reached their limit." #Or "who is skilled in intrigue." **8:24** *Or "bring terrible destruction." **8:25** *Or possibly, "and without warning." **8:26** *Or "to the distant future." **9:2** *That is, the sacred books.

desolation of Jerusalem,[a] namely, 70 years.[b] **3** So I turned my face to Jehovah the true God, entreating him in prayer, along with fasting[c] and sackcloth and ashes. **4** I prayed to Jehovah my God and made confession and said:

"O Jehovah the true God, the great and awe-inspiring One, who keeps his covenant and shows loyal love[d] to those who love him and keep his commandments,[e] **5** we have sinned and done wrong and acted wickedly and rebelled;[f] and we have deviated from your commandments and your judgments. **6** We have not listened to your servants the prophets,[g] who spoke in your name to our kings, our princes, our forefathers, and all the people of the land. **7** To you, O Jehovah, belongs righteousness, but to us belongs shame* as is the case today, to the men of Judah, the inhabitants of Jerusalem, and all Israel, those nearby and far away, in all the lands to which you dispersed them because they acted unfaithfully toward you.[h]

8 "O Jehovah, to us belongs shame,* to our kings, our princes, and our forefathers, because we have sinned against you. **9** To Jehovah our God belong mercy and forgiveness,[i] for we have rebelled against him.[j] **10** We have not obeyed the voice of Jehovah our God by following his laws that he set before us through his servants the prophets.[k] **11** All Israel has overstepped your Law and turned away by not obeying your voice, so that you poured out on us the curse and the sworn oath written about in the Law of Moses the servant of the true God,[l] for we have sinned against Him. **12** He has carried

out his words that he spoke against us[a] and against our rulers who ruled over us,* by bringing great calamity on us; nothing has ever been done under the whole heavens such as what was done in Jerusalem.[b] **13** Just as it is written in the Law of Moses, all this calamity has come upon us,[c] yet we have not begged for the favor* of Jehovah our God by turning away from our error[d] and by showing insight into your truth.*

14 "So Jehovah kept watchful and brought calamity on us, for Jehovah our God is righteous in all the works that he has done; yet we have not obeyed his voice.[e]

15 "Now, O Jehovah our God, the One who brought your people out of the land of Egypt by a mighty hand[f] and made a name for yourself down to this day,[g] we have sinned and acted wickedly. **16** O Jehovah, according to all your righteous acts,[h] please, may your anger and wrath turn away from your city Jerusalem, your holy mountain; for because of our sins and the errors of our forefathers, Jerusalem and your people are an object of reproach to all those around us.[i] **17** And now listen, O our God, to the prayer of your servant and to his entreaties, and cause your face to shine upon your sanctuary[j] that is desolate,[k] for your own sake, O Jehovah. **18** Incline your ear, O my God, and hear! Do open your eyes and see our desolate condition and the city that has been called by your name; for we are not entreating you because of our righteous acts but because of your great mercy.[l] **19** O Jehovah, do hear. O Jehovah, do forgive.[m] O Jehovah, do

---

CHAP. 9

a Ezr 1:1, 2
  Ps 79:1
  Isa 64:10
  La 1:1

b 2Ch 36:20, 21
  Jer 25:11
  Jer 29:10
  Zec 1:12
  Zec 7:5

c Ezr 8:21

d Ex 34:6

e De 5:9, 10
  Ne 1:5

f Ezr 9:6, 7
  Ne 9:26, 33
  Ps 106:6
  La 3:42

g 2Ch 36:15, 16
  Jer 7:13

h Le 26:33
  De 28:41
  2Ki 17:6
  Isa 11:11

i Ex 34:6, 7
  Ne 9:17
  Ps 86:5

j Ne 9:26

k 2Ki 17:13, 14

l De 28:15
  De 31:17

Second Col.

a La 2:17

b Jer 39:8

c Le 26:16, 17
  De 28:15
  La 1:1

d Isa 9:13
  Jer 5:3

e Ne 9:33

f Ex 6:1

g Ex 9:16
  Ne 9:10
  Ps 106:7, 8

h Ps 89:14
  Isa 26:9

i Le 26:38, 39
  1Ki 9:7-9
  Ps 79:1, 4
  Jer 24:9

j Nu 6:23, 25

k Isa 64:10, 11
  La 5:18

l Ps 102:13
  Isa 54:7, 8
  Jer 14:7

m 1Ki 8:30

9:7, 8 *Lit., "shame of face."

9:12 *Lit., "our judges who judged us." 9:13 *Or "softened the face." *Or "faithfulness."

pay attention and act! Do not delay, for your own sake, O my God, for your own name has been called upon your city and upon your people."[a]

20 While I was still speaking and praying and confessing my sin and the sin of my people Israel and making my request for favor before Jehovah my God concerning the holy mountain of my God,[b] 21 yes, while I was yet speaking in prayer, the man Ga'bri·el,[c] whom I had previously seen in the vision,[d] came to me when I was extremely weary at about the time of the evening gift offering. 22 And he gave me understanding, saying:

"O Daniel, now I have come to give you insight and understanding. 23 When you began your entreaty the word went out, and I have come to report it to you, because you are someone very precious.*[e] So consider the matter and understand the vision.

24 "There are 70 weeks* that have been determined for your people and your holy city,[f] in order to terminate the transgression, to finish off sin,[g] to make atonement for error,[h] to bring in everlasting righteousness,[i] to seal up the vision and the prophecy,*[j] and to anoint the Holy of Holies.△ 25 You should know and understand that from the issuing of the word to restore and to rebuild Jerusalem[k] until Mes·si'ah*[l] the Leader,[m] there will be 7 weeks, also 62 weeks. She will be restored and rebuilt, with a public square and moat, but in times of distress.

26 "And after the 62 weeks, Mes·si'ah will be cut off,*[o] with nothing for himself.[p]

"And the people of a leader who is coming will destroy the city and the holy place.[a] And its end will be by the flood. And until the end there will be war; what is decided upon is desolations.[b]

27 "And he will keep the covenant in force for the many for one week; and at the half of the week, he will cause sacrifice and gift offering to cease.[c]

"And on the wing of disgusting things there will be the one causing desolation;[d] and until an extermination, what was decided on will be poured out also on the one lying desolate."

10 In the third year of King Cyrus[e] of Persia, a revelation was given to Daniel, who was called by the name Bel·te·shaz'zar;[f] and the message was true, and it was about a great conflict. And he understood the message and was given understanding about what he had seen.

2 In those days I, Daniel, had been mourning[g] for three full weeks. 3 I ate no rich food, and no meat or wine entered my mouth, and I did not put any oil on myself for three full weeks. 4 On the 24th day of the first month, while I was on the bank of the great river, the Ti'gris,*[h] 5 I looked up and saw a man clothed in linen,[i] and around his waist was a belt of gold from U'phaz. 6 His body was like chrys'o·lite,[j] his face had the appearance of lightning, his eyes were like fiery torches, his arms and his feet looked like burnished copper,[k] and the sound of his words was like the sound of a multitude. 7 Only I, Daniel, saw the vision; the men with me did not see the vision.[l] However, a great trembling seized them, and they ran away and hid.

CHAP. 9
a Ps 79:8, 9
 Isa 63:18, 19
 Jer 14:9
b Ps 87:1, 2
 Zec 8:3
c Da 8:16
 Lu 1:19
d Da 8:11
e Da 10:11, 19
f Ne 11:1
 Isa 52:1
g Lu 1:76, 77
 Heb 9:26
h Ro 3:25
 1Jo 2:1, 2
 1Jo 4:10
i Isa 53:11
 Ro 1:16, 17
j 2Co 1:19, 20
k Ne 2:5, 11
 Ne 6:15
l Ps 2:2
 Joh 1:41
m Isa 55:4
 Mt 23:10
 Joh 1:45, 49
n Lu 3:1, 2
o Isa 53:8, 12
 Mt 26:2
 Lu 24:26
 1Co 15:3
p Mr 9:12

Second Col.
a Mt 24:15
 Lu 19:43, 44
 Lu 21:20
b Lu 21:22, 24
c Heb 9:11, 12
 Heb 10:8-10
d Mr 13:14
 Lu 21:20

CHAP. 10
e Ezr 1:1, 2
 Isa 45:1
 Da 1:21
 Da 6:28
f Da 1:7
 Da 4:8
g Da 9:3
h Ge 2:14
i Re 19:14
j Eze 1:16
k Eze 1:5, 7
l 2Ki 6:17
 Ac 9:7

9:23 *Or "very desirable; highly esteemed." 9:24 *That is, weeks of years. "Lit., "prophet." △Or "the Most Holy." 9:25 *Or "the Anointed One." 9:26 *Or "put to death."

10:4 *Lit., "Hiddekel."

8 Then I was left by myself, and when I saw this great vision, there was no power left in me and my dignified appearance left me and I lost all strength.[a] **9** Then I heard the sound of him speaking; but when I heard him speaking, I fell fast asleep with my face to the ground.[b] **10** But then a hand touched me,[c] and it stirred me to get up on my hands and knees. **11** Then he said to me:

"O Daniel, you very precious* man,[d] give attention to the words that I am about to speak to you. Now stand up in your place, for I have been sent to you."

When he said this to me, I stood up, trembling.

12 He then said to me: "Do not be afraid,[e] O Daniel, your words have been heard from the first day that you gave your heart to understanding and to humbling yourself before your God, and I have come because of your words.[f] **13** But the prince[g] of the royal realm of Persia stood in opposition to me for 21 days. But then Mi′cha·el,[*h] one of the foremost princes,[#] came to help me; and I remained there beside the kings of Persia. **14** I have come to make you understand what will befall your people in the final part of the days,[i] because it is a vision yet for the days to come."[j]

15 Now when he spoke these words to me, I turned my face to the ground and became speechless. **16** Then one who looked like a man touched my lips,[k] and I opened my mouth and said to the one who stood in front of me: "My lord, I am shuddering because of the vision, and I have no strength.[l] **17** So how can my lord's servant speak with my lord?"[m] For now I have no

strength, and there is no breath left in me."[a]

18 The one who looked like a man touched me again and strengthened me.[b] **19** Then he said: "Do not be afraid,[c] O very precious* man.[d] May you have peace.[e] Be strong, yes, be strong." As he spoke with me I was strengthened and I said: "Let my lord speak, for you have strengthened me."

20 Then he said: "Do you know why I have come to you? Now I will go back to fight with the prince of Persia.[f] When I leave, the prince of Greece will come. **21** However, I will tell you the things recorded in the writings of truth. There is no one strongly supporting me in these things but Mi′cha·el,[g] your prince.[h]

11 "As for me, in the first year of Da·ri′us[i] the Mede, I stood up to strengthen and fortify him.* **2** What I will tell you now is the truth:

"Look! Three more kings will stand up* for Persia, and the fourth one will amass greater riches than all others. And when he becomes strong by means of his riches, he will rouse up everything against the kingdom of Greece.[j]

3 "And a mighty king will stand up and rule with extensive dominion[k] and do as he pleases. **4** But when he has stood up, his kingdom will be broken and be divided toward the four winds of the heavens,[l] but not to his descendants* and not like the dominion with which he ruled; for his kingdom will be uprooted and go to others besides these.

5 "And the king of the south will become strong, that is, one of his princes; but one will prevail against him and will rule

---

CHAP. 10

a Da 7:28
Da 8:27

b Da 8:18

c Jer 1:9
Re 1:17

d Da 9:23
Da 10:19

e Re 1:17

f Da 9:23

g Eph 6:12

h Da 10:21
Da 12:1
Jude 9
Re 12:7, 8

i Da 2:28

j Da 8:17, 26
Da 12:4

k Isa 6:7
Jer 1:9

l Da 10:8

m Jg 6:22

Second Col.

a Isa 6:5

b Da 10:10

c Re 1:17

d Da 9:22, 23
Da 10:11

e Jg 6:23

f Da 10:13

g Da 10:13
Jude 9
Re 12:7, 8

h Da 12:1

CHAP. 11

i Da 5:30, 31
Da 9:1

j Da 8:21

k Da 8:5, 21

l Da 7:6
Da 8:8, 22

10:11, 19 *Or "very desirable; highly esteemed." 10:13 *Meaning "Who Is Like God?" #Or "a prince of the first rank."

11:1 *Or "and as a fortress to him." 11:2 *Or "arise." 11:4 *Or "posterity."

with extensive dominion, greater than that one's ruling power.

6 "After some years they will make an alliance, and the daughter of the king of the south will come to the king of the north in order to make an equitable arrangement.* But she will not retain the power of her arm; and he will not stand, nor his arm; and she will be given up, she and those bringing her in, and the one who caused her birth, and the one making her strong in those times. **7** And one from the sprout of her roots will stand up in his position, and he will come to the army and come against the fortress of the king of the north and will take action against them and will prevail. **8** Also with their gods, with their metal images,* with their desirable# articles of silver and of gold, and with captives, he will come to Egypt. For some years he will stand off from the king of the north, **9** who will come against the kingdom of the king of the south, but will go back to his own land.

10 "As for his sons, they will prepare for war and assemble a vast, great army. He will certainly advance and sweep through like a flood. But he will go back, and he will wage war all the way to his fortress.

11 "And the king of the south will become bitter and will go out and fight with him, that is, with the king of the north; and he will muster a large crowd, but the crowd will be given into that one's hand. **12** And the crowd will be carried away. His heart will become exalted, and he will cause tens of thousands to fall; but he will not make use of his strong position.

13 "And the king of the north will return and muster a crowd

Second Col.

CHAP. 11
a Ps 48:2
Da 8:9
Da 11:41, 45

larger than the first; and at the end of the times, after some years, he will surely come with a large army and with many resources. **14** In those times many will stand up against the king of the south.

"And the violent ones* among your people will be carried along to try making a vision come true; but they will stumble.

15 "And the king of the north will come and throw up a siege rampart and capture a fortified city. And the arms* of the south will not stand, nor will his select men; and they will have no power to stand. **16** The one coming against him will do as he pleases, and no one will stand before him. He will stand in the land of the Decoration,*a and ability to exterminate will be in his hand. **17** He will set his face* to come with the full force of his kingdom, and there will be equitable terms# with him; and he will act effectively. As regards the daughter of women, it will be granted to him to bring her to ruin. And she will not stand, and she will not continue to be his. **18** He will turn his face back to the coastlands and will capture many. And a commander will make the reproach from him cease for himself, so that his reproach will not be. He will make it turn back on that one. **19** Then he will turn his face back to the fortresses of his own land, and he will stumble and fall, and he will not be found.

20 "And there will stand up in his position one who causes an exactor* to pass through the splendid kingdom, but in a few

11:14 *Or "the sons of the robbers." 11:15 *Or "armies." 11:16 *Or "the Beauty." 11:17 *Or "be determined." #Or "he will make an agreement." 11:20 *"An exactor," possibly of taxes. Or "a taskmaster."

11:6 *Or "an agreement." 11:8 *Or "molten statues." #Or "precious."

days he will be broken, though not in anger nor in warfare.

21 "And there will stand up in his position a despised* one, and they will not give him the majesty of the kingdom; and he will come in during a time of security# and take hold of the kingdom by means of smoothness.△ **22** And the arms* of the flood will be swept away on account of him, and they will be broken; as will be the Leader*a* of the covenant.*b* **23** And because of their alliance with him, he will carry on deception and rise up and become mighty by means of a little nation. **24** During a time of security# he will come into the richest parts* of the province△ and do what his fathers and their fathers have not done. Plunder and spoil and goods he will distribute among them; and against fortified places he will plot his schemes, but only for a time.

25• "And he will muster his power and his heart against the king of the south with a large army, and the king of the south will prepare himself for the war with an exceedingly large and mighty army. And he will not stand, because they will plot schemes against him. **26** And those eating his delicacies will bring his downfall.

"As for his army, it will be swept* away, and many will fall down slain.

27 "As regards these two kings, their heart will be inclined to do what is bad, and they will sit at one table speaking lies to each other. But nothing will succeed, because the end is yet for the time appointed.*c*

28 "And he will go back to his land with a great amount of goods, and his heart will be against the holy covenant. He will act effectively and go back to his land.

29 "At the time appointed he will return and come against the south. But this time will not be as it was before, **30** for the ships of Kit′tim*a* will come against him, and he will be humbled.

"He will go back and hurl denunciations* against the holy covenant*b* and act effectively; and he will go back and will give attention to those leaving the holy covenant. **31** And arms* will stand up, proceeding from him; and they will profane the sanctuary,*c* the fortress, and remove the constant feature.*#d*

"And they will put in place the disgusting thing that causes desolation.*e*

32 "And those who act wickedly against the covenant, he will lead into apostasy by means of smooth words.* But the people who know their God will prevail and act effectively. **33** And those having insight*f* among the people will impart understanding to the many. And they will be made to stumble by sword and by flame, by captivity and by plundering, for some days. **34** But when they are made to stumble, they will be given a little help; and many will join with them by means of smooth speech.* **35** And some of those having insight will be made to stumble, in order to do a refining work because of them and to do a cleansing and a whitening*g* until the time of the end; because it is yet for the time appointed.

CHAP. 11
a Da 9:25
Joh 1:45, 49

b Ge 15:18
Ac 3:25

c Da 12:9

Second Col.
a Ge 10:4
Nu 24:24
Isa 23:1
Jer 2:10
Eze 27:6

b Da 11:28

c Da 8:11

d Da 8:12

e Da 12:11
Mt 24:15
Mr 13:14
Lu 21:20

f Da 12:10

g Da 12:10

11:21 *Or "despicable." 11:21, 24 #Or possibly, "without warning." 11:21 △Or "intrigue." 11:22, 31 *Or "armies." 11:24 *Lit., "the fatness." △Or "jurisdictional district." 11:26 *Or "flooded."

11:30 *Or "direct his fury." 11:31 #Or "the continual sacrifice." 11:32, 34 *Or "flattery; insincerity."

36 "The king will do as he pleases, and he will exalt himself and magnify himself above every god; and against the God of gods[a] he will speak astonishing things. And he will prove successful until the denunciation comes to a finish; because what is determined must take place. **37** He will show no regard for the God of his fathers; nor will he show regard for the desire of women or for any other god, but he will magnify himself over everyone. **38** But instead* he will give glory to the god of fortresses; to a god that his fathers did not know he will give glory by means of gold and silver and precious stones and desirable[#] things. **39** He will act effectively against the most fortified strongholds, along with* a foreign god. He will give great glory to those who give him recognition,[#] and he will make them rule among many; and the ground he will apportion out[△] for a price.

40 "In the time of the end the king of the south will engage with him in a pushing,* and against him the king of the north will storm with chariots and horsemen and many ships; and he will enter into the lands and sweep through like a flood. **41** He will also enter into the land of the Decoration,*[b] and many lands will be made to stumble. But these are the ones that will escape out of his hand: E′dom and Mo′ab and the main part of the Am′mon·ites. **42** And he will keep thrusting out his hand against the lands; and as regards the land of Egypt, she will not es-

cape. **43** And he will rule over the hidden treasures of gold and silver and over all the desirable[#] things of Egypt. And the Lib′yans and the E·thi·o′pi·ans will be at his steps.*

44 "But reports out of the east* and out of the north will disturb him, and he will go out in a great rage to annihilate and to devote many to destruction. **45** And he will plant his royal[#] tents between the grand sea and the holy mountain of Decoration;*[a] and he will come all the way to his end, and there will be no helper for him.

12 "During that time Mi′cha·el*[b] will stand up,[#] the great prince[c] who is standing in behalf of your people.[△] And there will occur a time of distress such as has not occurred since there came to be a nation until that time. And during that time your people will escape,[d] everyone who is found written down in the book.[e] **2** And many of those asleep in the dust of the earth will wake up, some to everlasting life and others to reproach and to everlasting contempt.

3 "And those having insight will shine as brightly as the expanse of heaven, and those bringing the many to righteousness like the stars, forever and ever.

4 "As for you, Daniel, keep the words secret, and seal up the book[f] until the time of the end.[f] Many will rove about,* and the true knowledge will become abundant."[g]

5 Then I, Daniel, looked and saw two others standing there,

CHAP. 11
a De 10:17
  Ps 136:1, 2

b Ps 48:2
  Da 8:9
  Da 11:16, 45

Second Col.
a Ps 48:2
  Da 8:9
  Da 11:16, 41

CHAP. 12
b Da 10:13
  Jude 9
  Re 12:7, 8

c Da 10:21

d Isa 26:20
  Joe 2:31, 32
  Mt 24:21, 22
  Re 7:13, 14

e Mal 3:16
  Lu 10:20
  Re 3:5

f Da 8:17, 26
  Da 12:9

g Isa 11:9

11:38 *Or "in his place." **11:38, 43** [#]Or "precious." **11:39** *Or "helped by." [#]Or possibly, "to whomever he recognizes." [△]Or "distribute." **11:40** *Or "will lock horns with him." **11:41, 45** *Or "Beauty." **11:43** *Or "will follow him." **11:44** *Or "sunrise." **11:45** [#]Or "palatial." **12:1** *Meaning "Who Is Like God?" [#]Or "arise." [△]Lit., "the sons of your people." **12:4** *Or "examine it [that is, the book] thoroughly."

one on this bank of the stream and one on the other bank of the stream.[a] **6** Then one said to the man clothed in linen,[b] who was up above the waters of the stream: "How long will it be to the end of these marvelous things?" **7** Then I heard the man clothed in linen, who was up above the waters of the stream, as he raised his right hand and his left hand to the heavens and swore by the One who is alive forever:[c] "It will be for an appointed time, appointed times, and half a time.* As soon as the dashing to pieces of the power of the holy people comes to an end,[d] all these things will come to their finish."

8 Now as for me, I heard, but I could not understand;[e] so I said: "O my lord, what will be the outcome of these things?"

12:7 *That is, three and a half times.

9 Then he said: "Go, Daniel, because the words are to be kept secret and sealed up until the time of the end.[a] **10** Many will cleanse themselves and whiten themselves and will be refined.[b] And the wicked ones will act wickedly, and none of the wicked will understand; but those having insight will understand.[c]

11 "And from the time that the constant feature*[d] has been removed and the disgusting thing that causes desolation has been put in place,[e] there will be 1,290 days.

12 "Happy is the one who keeps in expectation* and who arrives at the 1,335 days!

13 "But as for you, go on to the end, but you will rest, but you will stand up for your lot* at the end of the days."[f]

12:11 *Or "the continual sacrifice."
12:12 *Or "who is waiting eagerly."
12:13 *Or "in your allotted place."

CHAP. 12
a Da 10:4
b Da 10:5, 6
c Da 4:34
  Re 4:9
  Re 10:6
d Da 8:24
e Lu 18:34
  Ac 1:7
  1Pe 1:10, 11

Second Col.
a Da 8:17, 26
  Da 10:14
  Da 12:4
b Da 11:35
c Ps 111:10
  Da 11:33
  Da 12:3
d Da 8:11
e Da 11:31
  Mr 13:14
f Joh 11:24
  Ac 17:31
  Ac 24:15
  Re 20:12

HOSEA

OUTLINE OF CONTENTS

---

1 The word of Jehovah that came to Ho·se′a* the son of Be·e′ri in the days of Uz·zi′ah,ᵃ Jo′tham,ᵇ A′haz,ᶜ and Hez·e·ki′ah,ᵈ kings of Judah,ᵉ and in the days of Jer·o·bo′amᶠ son of Jo′ash,ᵍ the king of Israel. **2** When Jehovah started to speak his word through Ho·se′a, Jehovah said to Ho·se′a: "Go, marry a woman of prostitution* and have children of prostitution,* because by prostitution* the land has turned completely away from following Jehovah."ʰ

3 So he went and married Go′mer the daughter of Dib·la′im, and she conceived and bore him a son. **4** Then Jehovah said to him: "Name him Jez′re·el,* for in a little while I will hold an accounting against the house of Je′huⁱ for the acts of bloodshed of Jez′re·el, and I will put an end to the royal rule of the house of Israel.ʲ **5** In that day I will break the bow of Israel in the Valley* of Jez′re·el."

6 She conceived again and gave birth to a daughter. And He told him: "Name her Lo·ru·ha′mah,* for I will no longer show mercyᵏ to the house of Israel, because I will certainly drive them away.ˡ **7** But I will show mercy to the house of Judah,ᵃ and I will save them by Jehovah their God;ᵇ I will not save them by bow or by sword or by war or by horses or by horsemen."ᶜ

8 After weaning Lo·ru·ha′mah, she conceived and gave birth to a son. **9** Then He said: "Name him Lo-am′mi,* because you are not my people and I will not be yours.

10 "And the number of the people* of Israel will be like the grains of sand of the sea, which cannot be measured or numbered.ᵈ And in the place where it was said to them, 'You are not my people,'ᵉ it will be said to them, 'The sons of the living God.'ᶠ **11** And the people of Judah and of Israel will be gathered together into unityᵍ and will choose for themselves one head and go up out of the land, for great will be the day of Jez′re·el.ʰ

2 "Say to your brothers, 'My people!'*ⁱ And to your sisters, 'O woman shown mercy!'*ʲ

2 Accuse your mother; accuse her, For she is not my wifeᵏ and I am not her husband. She should remove her prostitution* from herself And her adultery from between her breasts,

---

CHAP. 1
a 2Ch 26:1, 3, 4
b 2Ki 15:32-34
c 2Ki 16:1-3
d 2Ki 18:1-3
e Isa 1:1
  Mic 1:1
f 2Ki 14:23, 24
  Am 1:1
g 2Ki 13:10, 11
h De 31:16
  Ho 3:1
i 2Ki 10:29-31
j 2Ki 15:8, 10
k Ho 2:23
l 2Ki 17:6
  2Ki 17:22, 23

Second Col.
a Ho 11:12
b 2Ki 19:34, 35
c Isa 37:36
d Ge 13:16
  Ge 22:17
e 1Pe 2:10
f Ro 9:25, 26
  2Co 6:18
g Ezr 3:1
  Isa 11:12
  Jer 3:18
  Eze 37:19
  Mic 2:12
h Ho 2:22

CHAP. 2
i Jer 31:33
  Eze 36:28
  Zec 13:9
j Ho 2:23
k Jer 3:8

1:1 *Shortened form of Hoshaiah, which means "Saved by Jah; Jah Has Saved." 1:2; 2:2 *Or "immorality; promiscuity." 1:4 *Meaning "God Will Sow Seed." 1:5 *Or "Low Plain." 1:6 *Meaning "Not Shown Mercy."

1:9 *Meaning "Not My People." 1:10 *Lit., "sons." 2:1 *See Ho 1:9 ftn. #See Ho 1:6 ftn.

3 Or I will strip her naked and
    make her as in the day she
    was born,
  Making her like a wilderness,
  Reducing her to a waterless
    land,
  And causing her to die of
    thirst.
4 And to her sons I will not
    show mercy,
  For they are the sons of
    prostitution.*
5 For their mother has
    committed prostitution.*ᵃ
  She who was pregnant
    with them has acted
    shamefully,ᵇ for she said,
  'I will go after my passionate
    lovers,ᶜ
  Those who give me my bread
    and my water,
  My wool and my linen, my oil
    and my drink.'
6 So I will block your way with
    a hedge of thorns;
  And I will raise up a stone
    wall against her,
  So that she cannot find her
    paths.
7 She will chase after her
    passionate lovers, but she
    will not overtake them;ᵈ
  She will look for them, but
    she will not find them.
  Then she will say, 'I will go
    back to my first husband,ᵉ
  For I was better off at that
    time than I am now.'ᶠ
8 She did not recognize that it
    was I who had given her
    the grain,ᵍ the new wine,
    and the oil,
  And I who had given her
    silver in abundance
  And gold, which they used
    for Ba'al.ʰ
9 'Therefore, I will return and
    take away my grain in its
    time

And my new wine in its
    season,ᵃ
  And I will snatch away my
    wool and my linen that
    were to cover her
    nakedness.
10 Now I will expose her private
    parts in full view of her
    passionate lovers,
  And no man will rescue her
    out of my hand.ᵇ
11 I will put an end to all her
    joy,
  Her festivals,ᶜ her new
    moons, her sabbaths, and
    all her festive seasons.
12 And I will ruin her vines and
    her fig trees, of which she
    has said:
  "These are my wages, which
    my passionate lovers gave
    to me";
  I will turn them into a forest,
  And the wild animals of the
    field will devour them.
13 I will hold an accounting
    against her for the days
    when she offered sacrifices
    to the Ba'al images,ᵈ
  When she would adorn
    herself with her rings and
    ornaments and would
    chase after her passionate
    lovers,
  And I was the one she
    forgot,'ᵉ declares Jehovah.
14 'So I will persuade her,
  I will lead her into the
    wilderness,
  And I will speak to win her
    heart.
15 I will give her vineyards
    back to her from that time
    onward,ᶠ
  And the Valley* of A'chorᵍ
    as a gateway to hope;
  She will answer there as in
    the days of her youth,
  As in the day when she came
    out of the land of Egypt.ʰ

CHAP. 2
a Eze 23:4, 5
  Ho 3:1

b Ezr 9:6
  Da 9:7
  Ho 9:10

c Eze 23:7, 8
  Ho 8:9

d Isa 31:1
  Ho 5:13

e Jer 31:18
  Eze 23:4
  Ho 5:15

f De 32:12-14
  Ne 9:25

g De 32:28
  Isa 1:3

h Ho 8:4

Second Col.
a Isa 17:11

b Ps 50:22
  Ho 5:14

c Am 5:21
  Am 8:10

d Jg 3:7
  1Ki 16:30-32
  2Ki 10:28
  Ho 11:2

e Isa 17:10

f De 30:5
  Isa 65:21
  Jer 32:15
  Eze 28:25, 26
  Am 9:14

g Jos 7:24-26
  Isa 65:10

h Ex 15:1

2:4 *Or "immorality; promiscuity." 2:5
*Or "engaged in immorality (promiscu-
ity)."

2:15 *Or "Low Plain."

16 And in that day,' declares
    Jehovah,
'You will call me My husband,
    and you will no longer call
    me My master.'*
17 'I will remove the names of
    the Ba′al images from her
    mouth,ᵃ
And they will no longer
    be remembered by their
    name.ᵇ
18 In that day I will make a
    covenant for them with the
    wild animals of the field,ᶜ
And with the birds of the
    heavens and the creeping
    things of the ground;ᵈ
I will rid the land of the bow
    and the sword and war,ᵉ
And I will make them lie
    down* in security.ᶠ
19 I will engage myself to you
    forever;
And I will engage myself to
    you in righteousness and
    in justice,
In loyal love and in mercy.ᵍ
20 I will engage myself to you
    in faithfulness,
And you will certainly know
    Jehovah.'ʰ
21 'In that day I will answer,'
    declares Jehovah,
'I will answer the heavens,
And they will answer the
    earth;ⁱ
22 And the earth will answer
    the grain and the new
    wine and the oil;
And they will answer
    Jez′re·el.*ʲ
23 I will sow her like seed for
    myself in the earth,ᵏ
And I will show mercy to
    her who was not shown
    mercy;*
I will say to those not
    my people:* "You are my
    people,"ˡ

And they will say: "You are
    my God."'ᵃ

3 Then Jehovah said to me: "Go
    once again, love the woman
    who is loved by another man and
    is committing adultery,ᵇ just as
    Jehovah loves the people of Isra-
    elᶜ while they turn to other godsᵈ
    and love raisin cakes."*

2 So I purchased her for my-
    self for 15 silver pieces and a ho′-
    mer measure* and a half of bar-
    ley. **3** Then I said to her: "You
    will remain mine for many days.
    You must not commit prostitu-
    tion,* and you must not have re-
    lations with another man, and I
    will behave the same way toward
    you."*

4 It is because for a long time*
    the people of Israel will dwell
    without a king,ᵉ without a prince,
    without a sacrifice, without a
    pillar, and without an eph′odᶠ
    and teraphim statues.*ᵍ **5** After-
    ward the people of Israel will
    come back and look for Jehovah
    their Godʰ and for David their
    king,ⁱ and they will come trem-
    bling to Jehovah and to his good-
    ness in the final part of the days.ʲ

4 Hear the word of Jehovah,
    O people of Israel,
For Jehovah has a legal case
    against the inhabitants of
    the land,ᵏ
Because there is no truth nor
    loyal love nor knowledge of
    God in the land.ˡ
2 False oaths and lyingᵐ and
    murderⁿ
And stealing and adulteryᵒ
    are widespread,
And one act of bloodshed
    follows another act of
    bloodshed.ᵖ

CHAP. 2

a Ex. 23:13
　Jos 23:6, 7
b Zec 13:2
c Eze 34:25
d Isa 11:6-8
e Isa 2:4
　Eze 39:9
　Zec 9:10
f Le 26:5, 6
　Jer 23:6
　Mic 4:3, 4
g Mic 7:18
h Isa 54:13
　Jer 24:7
　Jer 31:34
i De 28:12
　Zec 8:12
j Ho 1:11
k Jer 31:27
l Ho 2:1
　Ro 9:25, 26
　1Pe 2:10

Second Col.

a Ho 1:10

CHAP. 3

b Ho 1:2, 3
c De 7:6-8
　2Ki 13:23
　Ps 106:44,
　45
d Jg 10:13
　Jer 3:20
e 2Ki 17:6
　2Ki 18:9, 10
f Jg 8:27
g Jg 17:5
　1Sa 19:15, 16
h Jer 50:4
i Jer 30:9
　Eze 34:23, 24
　Eze 37:24, 25
　Am 9:11
　Lu 1:31-33
j De 4:30

CHAP. 4

k Mic 6:2
l Mic 7:2
m Ho 11:12
n 1Ki 21:18, 19
o Eze 23:37
p Ho 1:4
　Ho 6:8, 9

3:1 *That is, those used in false worship. **3:2** *A homer equaled 220 L
(200 dry qt). See App. B14. **3:3** *Or
"engage in immorality (promiscuity)."
#Or "I will not have relations with you."
3:4 *Lit., "many days." #Or "household gods; idols."

2:16 *Or "My Baal." **2:18** *Or "let them
live." **2:22** *Meaning "God Will Sow
Seed." **2:23** *See Ho 1:6 ftn. #See Ho
1:9 ftn.

3 That is why the land will mourn[a]
And every inhabitant in it will waste away;
The wild animals of the field and the birds of the heavens,
Even the fish of the sea, will perish.

4 "However, let no man contend or reprove,[b]
For your people are like those who contend against a priest.[c]

5 So you will stumble in broad daylight,
And the prophet will stumble with you, as if it were night.
And I will silence* your mother.

6 My people will be silenced,* because there is no knowledge.
Because you have rejected knowledge,[d]
I will also reject you from serving as my priest;
And because you have forgotten the law* of your God,[e]
I myself will forget your sons.

7 The more they increased, the more they sinned against me.[f]
I will change their glory into disgrace.*

8 They feed on the sin of my people,
And they are greedy for* their error.

9 It will be the same for the people as for the priest;
I will call them to account for their ways,

10 And I will bring on them the consequences of their actions.[a]

10 They will eat but not be satisfied.[b]
They will be promiscuous,* but they will not increase,[c]
Because they have shown no regard for Jehovah.

11 Prostitution* and wine and new wine
Take away the motivation to do what is right.#[d]

12 My people consult their wooden idols,
Doing what their staff* tells them;
Because the spirit of prostitution# causes them to go astray,
And by their prostitution# they refuse to submit to their God.

13 On the tops of the mountains they sacrifice,[e]
And on the hills they make sacrifices smoke,
Under oak trees and storax trees and every big tree,[f]
Because their shade is good.
That is why your daughters commit prostitution#
And your daughters-in-law commit adultery.

14 I will not hold an accounting against your daughters because of their prostitution,#
And against your daughters-in-law because of their adultery.
For the men go off with the harlots
And sacrifice with the temple prostitutes;
Such a people without understanding[g] will come to ruin.

CHAP. 4
a Am 8:7, 8

b Am 5:10, 13

c De 17:12

d Jer 2:8

e 2Ki 17:15, 16

f Ezr 9:6, 7

Second Col.
a Am 3:1, 2

b Le 26:26
   Mic 6:14

c Ho 9:11, 12

d Pr 20:1
   Pr 23:31, 33
   Isa 28:7

e Jer 3:6

f 2Ki 17:10-12
   Jer 2:20
   Eze 20:28

g Jer 4:22

4:5 *Or "destroy." 4:6 *Or "destroyed." #Or "instruction." 4:7 *Or possibly, "They have exchanged my own glory for disgrace." 4:8 *Or "lift up their soul to." See Glossary, "Soul."

4:10 *Or "be grossly immoral; engage in prostitution." 4:11 *Or "Immorality; Promiscuity." #Lit., "Take away heart." 4:12 *Or "diviner's rod." 4:12-14 #Or "immorality; promiscuity."

15 Although you are committing prostitution,* O Israel,[a]

Let not Judah become guilty.[b]

Do not come to Gil'gal[c] or to Beth-a'ven,[d]

And do not swear, 'As surely as Jehovah is alive!'[e]

16 For like a stubborn cow, Israel has become stubborn.[f]

Will Jehovah now shepherd them like a young ram in an open pasture?*

17 E'phra·im is joined to idols.[g]

Let him alone!

18 When their beer* is finished, They become promiscuous.#

And her rulers△ dearly love dishonor.[h]

19 The wind will wrap her* in its wings,

And they will be ashamed of their sacrifices."

5 "Hear this, you priests,[i]

Pay attention, O house of Israel,

Listen, O house of the king,

For the judgment involves you;

Because you are a trap to Miz'pah

And a net spread over Ta'bor.[j]

2 And those falling away* have sunk deep# in slaughter,

And I am warning△ all of them.

3 I know E'phra·im,

And Israel is not hidden from me.

For now, O E'phra·im, you have acted promiscuously;*

Israel has defiled itself.[a]

4 Their dealings do not permit them to return to their God,

Because there is a spirit of prostitution* among them;[b]

And Jehovah they do not acknowledge.

5 The pride of Israel has testified against him;*[c]

Both Israel and E'phra·im have stumbled in their error,

And Judah has stumbled with them.[d]

6 With their flock and their herd they went to look for Jehovah,

But they could not find him.

He had drawn away from them.[e]

7 They have betrayed Jehovah,[f]

For they have fathered foreign sons.

Now a month will devour them* and their portions.#

8 Blow a horn[g] in Gib'e·ah, a trumpet in Ra'mah![h]

Shout a war cry at Beth-a'ven'—after you, O Benjamin!

9 O E'phra·im, you will become an object of horror in the day of punishment.[j]

I have made known what will surely happen among the tribes of Israel.

10 The princes of Judah are like those moving a boundary.[k]

I will pour out my fury on them like water.

11 E'phra·im is oppressed, crushed by judgment,

For he was determined to follow after his adversary.[l]

12 So I was like a moth to E'phra·im

CHAP. 4

a Eze 23:4, 5

b 2Ki 17:18

c Ho 9:15
 Ho 12:11
 Am 4:4

d Ho 5:8
 Ho 10:5

e Isa 48:1
 Jer 5:2
 Eze 20:39

f Ps 78:8
 Ps 81:11, 12
 Zec 7:11, 12

g Ho 11:2
 Ho 13:1, 2

h Mic 7:3

CHAP. 5

i Ho 4:9

j Jg 4:6
 Jer 46:18

Second Col.

a Eze 23:4, 5
 Ho 4:17, 18

b Ho 4:12
 Am 2:7

c Isa 9:9, 10
 Ho 7:10

d 2Ki 17:19, 20
 Eze 23:30, 31
 Am 2:4, 5

e Isa 1:15
 Mic 3:4

f Isa 48:8
 Jer 3:20

g Ho 8:1

h Isa 10:29

i Ho 4:15
 Ho 10:5

j Isa 28:1-3
 Ho 9:13

k De 19:14

l 1Ki 20:1

4:15; 5:4 *Or "immorality; promiscuity." **4:16** *Lit., "a roomy place?" **4:18** *Or "wheat beer." #Or "become grossly immoral; engage in prostitution." △Lit., "shields." **4:19** *Or "will sweep her away." **5:2** *Or "the rebels." #Or "have been deeply involved." △Or "I will discipline." **5:3** *Or "have acted immorally; have engaged in prostitution."

5:5 *Lit., "to his face." **5:7** *Or possibly, "Within a month they will be devoured." #Or "fields."

And like rottenness to the house of Judah.

13 When E'phra·im saw his sickness, and Judah his ulcer,
E'phra·im went to As·syr'i·a[a] and sent to a great king.
But he was unable to heal you,
And he could not cure your ulcer.

14 For I will be like a young lion to E'phra·im,
And like a strong lion* to the house of Judah.
I myself will tear to pieces and go away;[b]
I will carry them off, and no one will rescue them.[c]

15 I will go away and return to my place until they bear the consequences of their guilt,
And then they will seek my favor.*[d]
When they are in distress, they will seek me."[e]

6 "Come, and let us return to Jehovah,
For he has torn us to pieces,[f] but he will heal us.
He struck us, but he will bind our wounds.

2 He will revive us after two days.
On the third day he will raise us up,
And we will live before him.

3 We will know, we will earnestly seek to know Jehovah.
His going out is as certain as the dawn;
He will come to us like a pouring rain,
Like a spring rain that saturates the earth."

4 "What should I do with you, E'phra·im?
What should I do with you, Judah?

For your loyal love is like the morning clouds,
Like the dew that quickly vanishes.

5 That is why I will cut them down by means of the prophets;[a]
I will kill them with the words of my mouth.[b]
And the judgments on you will shine as the light.[c]

6 For in loyal love* I delight, not in sacrifice,
And in the knowledge of God, rather than in whole burnt offerings.[d]

7 But they, like mere men, have violated the covenant.[e]
There they have betrayed me.

8 Gil'e·ad is a town of evildoers,[f]
Covered with footprints of blood.[g]

9 The company of priests are like marauder bands lying in ambush for a man.
They murder on the road at She'chem,[h]
For their conduct is shameful.

10 I have seen a horrible thing in the house of Israel.
There E'phra·im practices prostitution;[i]
Israel has defiled itself.[j]

11 Furthermore, O Judah, a harvest is set for you,
When I gather back the captives of my people."[k]

7 "At the time when I would heal Israel,
The error of E'phra·im is also exposed,[l]
And the wickedness of Sa·mar'i·a.[m]
For they practice deception;[n]
Thieves break in and marauder bands raid outside.[o]

CHAP. 5
a Ho 8:9
  Ho 12:1

b Ps 50:22

c Am 2:14

d Le 26:38, 40

e De 4:29, 30
  De 30:10

CHAP. 6
f Ho 5:14

Second Col.
a Isa 58:1
  Jer 1:9, 10
  Eze 3:8, 9

b Jer 23:29

c Zep 3:5

d 1Sa 15:22
  Pr 21:3
  Isa 1:11
  Mic 6:6-8
  Mt 9:13
  Mt 12:7

e 2Ki 17:15
  Isa 24:5
  Ho 8:1

f Ho 12:11

g Mic 7:2

h 1Ki 12:25

i 2Ki 17:6, 7
  Jer 3:6

j Eze 23:4, 5

k De 30:3
  Jer 29:14
  Am 9:14

CHAP. 7
l Isa 28:1

m Am 8:14
  Mic 1:5

n Mic 7:3

o Ho 6:9

5:14 *Or "a maned young lion." 5:15 *Lit., "face." 6:6 *Or "in mercy."

2　But they do not say in their heart that I will remember all their wickedness.[a]
　　Now their dealings are all around them;
　　They are right in front of my face.

3　They make the king rejoice by their wickedness,
　　And princes by their deceit.

4　All of them are adulterers,
　　Burning like an oven fired by a baker,
　　Who stops stirring the fire after kneading the dough until it is leavened.

5　On the day of our king, princes have become sick
　　—They are enraged because of wine.[b]
　　He has reached out his hand to ridiculers.

6　For they approach with hearts burning like an oven.*
　　All night long the baker sleeps;
　　In the morning the oven blazes like a flaming fire.

7　All of them are hot like an oven,
　　And they devour their rulers.*
　　All their kings have fallen;[c]
　　No one among them calls out to me.[d]

8　E′phra·im mixes with the nations.[e]
　　E′phra·im is like a round cake left unturned.

9　Strangers have consumed his strength,[f] but he does not know it.
　　And his gray hairs have turned white, but he does not notice it.

10　The pride of Israel has testified against him,[g]

　　But they have not returned to Jehovah their God,[a]
　　Nor have they looked for him despite all of this.

11　E′phra·im is like a simple-minded dove, lacking good sense.*[b]
　　They have called out to Egypt;[c] they have gone to As·syr′i·a.[d]

12　Wherever they go, I will spread my net over them.
　　I will bring them down like the birds of the heavens.
　　I will discipline them according to the warning given to their assembly.[e]

13　Woe to them, for they have fled from me!
　　Devastation to them, for they have transgressed against me!
　　I was ready to redeem them, but they have spoken lies against me.[f]

14　From their heart they did not call to me for help,[g]
　　Although they kept wailing on their beds.
　　For their grain and new wine they would slash themselves;
　　They turn against me.

15　Although I disciplined them and strengthened their arms,
　　They are against me, scheming what is bad.

16　They changed course, but not to anything loftier;*
　　They were as unreliable as a loose bow.[h]
　　Their princes will fall by the sword because of their defiant tongues.
　　For this they will be an object of ridicule in the land of Egypt.[i]

CHAP. 7
a De 32:29
　Isa 1:3
　Am 8:7

b Isa 5:11
　Isa 28:1

c 2Ki 15:8, 10
　2Ki 15:14

d Isa 9:13

e Ps 106:34-36
　Eze 23:4, 5

f 2Ki 13:3
　2Ki 15:19

g Ho 5:5

Second Col.
a Ne 9:35
　Isa 9:13
　Am 4:6
　Zec 1:4

b Isa 1:3

c 2Ki 17:4
　Isa 31:1

d 2Ki 15:19
　Eze 23:4, 5

e De 28:15
　2Ki 17:13

f Isa 59:13

g Ps 78:37
　Isa 29:13

h Ps 78:57

i Eze 36:19, 20
　Ho 9:3

7:6 *Or possibly, "For their hearts are like an oven as they approach with their intrigues." 7:7 *Lit., "judges."

7:11 *Lit., "without heart." 7:16 *That is, not to an elevated form of worship.

8 "Put a horn to your mouth![a]
One comes like an eagle
        against the house of
        Jehovah,[b]
For they have violated
        my covenant[c] and trans-
        gressed against my law.[d]
2 To me they cry out, 'My God,
        we, Israel, know you!'[e]
3 Israel has rejected what is
        good.[f]
Let an enemy pursue him.
4 They have appointed kings,
        but not through me.
They have appointed
        princes, but I did not
        recognize them.
With their silver and their
        gold they have made idols,[g]
To their own destruction.[h]
5 Your calf has been rejected,
        O Sa·mar′i·a.[i]
My anger flares up against
        them.[j]
How long will they be
        incapable of innocence?*
6 For this is from Israel.
A craftsman made it, and it
        is not God;
The calf of Sa·mar′i·a will be
        reduced to splinters.
7 For it is wind that they are
        sowing,
And they will reap a storm
        wind.[k]
No stalk produces ripe*
        grain;[l]
Whatever sprouts produces
        no flour.
If any is produced, foreign-
        ers* will swallow it down.[m]
8 Israel will be swallowed
        down.[n]
Now they will be among the
        nations,[o]
Like an unwanted vessel.
9 For they have gone up to
        As·syr′i·a,[p] like a lone wild
        donkey.

E′phra·im has hired lovers.[a]
10 Although they hire them
        from among the nations,
I will now round them up;
They will begin to suffer[b]
        because of the burden im-
        posed by king and princes.
11 For E′phra·im has multiplied
        altars to sin.[c]
They became his altars for
        sinning.[d]
12 I wrote for him the many
        things of my law,*
But they were regarded as
        something strange.[e]
13 They offer sacrificial gifts to
        me, and they eat the meat,
But Jehovah takes no
        pleasure in them.[f]
Now he will remember their
        error and punish them for
        their sins.[g]
They have turned back* to
        Egypt.[h]
14 Israel has forgotten his Mak-
        er[i] and has built temples,[j]
And Judah has multiplied
        fortified cities.[k]
But I will send fire into his
        cities,
And it will consume the
        towers of each one."[l]

9 "Do not rejoice, O Israel,[m]
Do not act joyfully like the
        peoples.
For by prostitution* you have
        strayed from your God.[n]
You have loved the wages
        of a prostitute on every
        threshing floor of grain.[o]
2 But the threshing floor and
        winepress will not feed
        them,
And new wine will fail her.[p]
3 They will not continue dwell-
        ing in the land of Jehovah;[q]
Instead, E′phra·im will return
        to Egypt,

CHAP. 8
a Ho 5:8
b De 28:49, 50
c Ho 6:7
d 2Ki 17:15
e Isa 48:1
    Mic 3:11
f Ps 50:17
g 1Ki 12:26, 28
    Ho 13:2
h 1Ki 13:34
i Ho 10:5, 6
j De 32:21, 22
    2Ki 17:18
k Pr 22:8
l Isa 17:11
m De 28:15, 33
n 2Ki 15:29
    2Ki 18:11
    Jer 50:17
o Le 26:33
p 2Ki 15:19
    Eze 23:4, 5
    Ho 5:13
    Ho 12:1

Second Col.
a Eze 23:9
b 2Ki 14:26
    1Ch 5:26
c Isa 10:10, 11
d Ho 12:11
e 2Ki 17:15
    Ne 9:26
f Isa 1:11
    Am 5:22
g Ho 9:9
    Am 8:7
h Ho 7:16
    Ho 9:3
i De 32:18
j 1Ki 12:25, 31
    2Ch 26:9, 10
k 2Ki 18:13
    2Ch 36:17, 19
    Jer 17:27
    Jer 34:7

CHAP. 9
m Ho 10:5
n Eze 23:4, 5
    Ho 4:12
o Ho 2:12
    Mic 1:7
p Ho 2:8, 9
    Am 5:11
q Le 20:22
    De 28:63, 64
    Jos 23:15, 16
    1Ki 9:6, 7

8:5 *Or "purity?" 8:7 *Or "standing." # Or "strangers." 8:12 *Or "instruction." 8:13 *Or possibly, "They will return." 9:1 *Or "immorality; promiscuity."

And in As·syr′i·a they will eat what is unclean.[a]

4 They will no longer pour out wine offerings to Jehovah;[b]
Their sacrifices will not please him.[c]
They are like the bread of mourning;
All those eating it will defile themselves.
For their bread is for themselves alone;*
It will not come into the house of Jehovah.

5 What will you do in the day of meeting,*
In the day of Jehovah's festival?

6 For look! they will have to flee because of destruction.[d]
Egypt will gather them together,[e] and Mem′phis will bury them.[f]
Nettles will take possession of their precious things of silver,
And thornbushes will be in their tents.

7 The days of reckoning will come,[g]
The days of retribution will come,
And Israel will know it.
Their prophet will be a fool, and the man of inspiration will go mad;
Because your error is abundant, the animosity against you is abundant."

8 The watchman[h] of E′phra·im was with my God.[i]
But now all the ways of his prophets[j] are as the traps of a birdcatcher;
There is animosity in the house of his God.

9 They have sunk deep into ruin, as in the days of Gib′e·ah.[k]

CHAP. 9
a 2Ki 17:6

b Nu 15:5
Nu 28:14
Joe 1:13

c Isa 1:11

d Ho 7:13

e Ho 7:16
Ho 8:13

f Jer 2:14, 16

g Isa 10:3

h Isa 21:6, 8
Jer 6:17
Eze 33:7

i 1Ki 17:1
2Ki 2:14

j 1Ki 18:19

k Jg 19:22
Jg 20:4-6
Ho 10:9

Second Col.
a Ho 8:13

b Jer 2:2

c Nu 25:1-3
De 4:3
Ps 106:28

d 1Ki 16:31
Jer 11:13

e De 28:15, 18

f De 28:32
De 32:25

g De 31:17
2Ki 17:18

h Eze 28:12

i Ho 4:15
Ho 12:11
Am 5:5

j Le 26:27, 33
2Ki 17:18
Am 5:27

k De 29:19, 20

l Isa 7:8

m 2Ki 17:14, 15
Zec 1:4

He will remember their error and punish their sins.[a]

10 "Like grapes in the wilderness I found Israel.[b]
Like the first of the early figs on a fig tree I saw your forefathers.
But they went to Ba′al of Pe′or;[c]
They dedicated themselves to the shameful thing,*[d]
And they became disgusting like the object of their love.

11 E′phra·im's glory flies away like a bird;
There is no giving birth, no pregnancy, and no conception.[e]

12 Even if they raise children, I will bereave them until no man is left;[f]
Yes, woe to them when I turn away from them![g]

13 E′phra·im, planted in a pasture, was to me like Tyre;[h]
Now E′phra·im must bring his sons out to the slaughter."

14 Give them, O Jehovah, what you should give them;
A womb that miscarries and dry* breasts.

15 "All their wickedness was in Gil′gal,[i] for there I came to hate them.
I will drive them away from my house because of their evil deeds.[j]
I will no longer love them;[k]
All their princes are stubborn.

16 E′phra·im will be struck down.[l]
Their root will dry up, and they will produce no fruit.
Even if they give birth, I will put to death their cherished offspring."

17 My God will reject them, For they have not listened to him,[m]

9:4 *Or "for their own soul." 9:5 *Or "your appointed feast." 9:10 *Or "the shameful god." 9:14 *Or "shriveled."

And they will become fugitives among the nations.[a]

10 "Israel is a degenerate* vine yielding its fruit.[b]

The more his fruit increases, the more he multiplies his altars;[c]

The better his land produces, the more splendid his sacred pillars.[d]

2 Their heart is hypocritical;*

Now they will be found guilty.

There is one who will break their altars and destroy their pillars.

3 Now they will say, 'We have no king,[e] for we have not feared Jehovah.

And what could a king do for us?'

4 They speak empty words, make false oaths,[f] and make covenants,

So the judgment that springs up is like poisonous weeds in the furrows of the field.[g]

5 The residents of Sa·mar′i·a will fear for the calf idol of Beth-a′ven.[h]

Its people will mourn over it,

As will its foreign-god priests who rejoiced over it and its glory,

For it will go away from them into exile.

6 It will be brought to As·syr′i·a as a gift to a great king.[i]

E′phra·im will be put to shame,

And Israel will be ashamed because of the advice it followed.[j]

7 Sa·mar′i·a and her king will certainly be done away with,*[k]

Like a snapped-off twig on the surface of waters.

8 The high places of Beth-a′ven,[a] the sin of Israel,[b] will be annihilated.[c]

Thorns and thistles will grow on their altars.[d]

People will say to the mountains, 'Cover us!'

And to the hills, 'Fall over us!'[e]

9 From the days of Gib′e·ah you have sinned,[f] O Israel.

There they have persisted.

War did not overtake* the sons of unrighteousness in Gib′e·ah.

10 I will also discipline them when I please.

And peoples will be gathered against them,

When their two errors are harnessed on them.*

11 E′phra·im was a trained heifer that loved to thresh,

So I spared her fair neck.

Now I will make someone ride* E′phra·im.[g]

Judah will plow; Jacob will harrow for him.

12 Sow seed for yourselves in righteousness and reap loyal love.

Plow for yourselves arable land[h]

While there is time to search for Jehovah,[i]

Until he comes and instructs you in righteousness.[j]

13 But you have plowed wickedness,

You have reaped unrighteousness,[k]

And you have eaten the fruitage of deception;

For you have trusted in your own way,

In the multitude of your warriors.

CHAP. 9
a De 28:64
   Am 9:9

CHAP. 10
b Isa 5:3, 4

c Ho 8:11
   Ho 12:11

d Ho 8:4

e Ho 3:4
   Ho 13:11

f 2Ki 17:4

g Am 5:7
   Am 6:12

h 1Ki 12:28, 29
   Ho 4:15
   Ho 8:5
   Am 3:14

i 2Ki 17:3
   Ho 5:13

j Mic 6:16

k 2Ki 17:4

Second Col.
a Ho 4:15

b 1Ki 12:28-30
   Mic 1:5

c Am 7:9

d 2Ki 23:15

e Lu 23:30
   Re 6:16

f Jg 20:4-6
   Ho 9:9

g 2Ki 17:6

h Jer 4:3, 4

i Isa 55:6
   Am 5:4

j De 32:2
   Isa 45:8

k Pr 22:8
   Ho 8:7
   Ga 6:7

10:1 *Or possibly, "a spreading." 10:2 *Or "slippery; smooth." 10:7 *Lit., "be silenced."

10:9 *Or "utterly destroy." 10:10 *That is, when they bear their punishment like a yoke. 10:11 *Or "put a harness on."

14 An uproar will rise against
  your people,
And your fortified cities
  will all be devastated,[a]
Like the devastation by
  Shal′man of the house
  of Ar′bel,
In the day of battle
  when mothers were dashed
  to pieces alongside their
  children.

15 This is what will be done
  to you, O Beth′el,[b] because
  of your utter wickedness.
At dawn the king of Israel
  will surely be done away
  with."*[c]

11 "When Israel was a boy,
    I loved him,[d]
And out of Egypt I called
  my son.[e]

2 The more they* called them,
  The more they went away
  from them.[f]
They kept sacrificing to
  the Ba′al images[g]
And offering sacrifices to
  the graven images.[h]

3 But it was I who taught
  E′phra·im to walk,[i] taking
  them in my arms;[j]
And they did not acknowl-
  edge that I had healed
  them.

4 With the ropes of men*
  I kept drawing them, with
  the cords of love;[k]
And I was to them like one
  lifting a yoke from their
  jaws,
And I gently brought food
  to each one.

5 They will not return to
  the land of Egypt, but
  As·syr′i·a will be their
  king,[l]
Because they refused
  to return to me.[m]

6 And a sword will whirl
  against his cities[a]
And destroy his bars and
  devour them because
  of their schemes.[b]

7 My people are bent on
  unfaithfulness to me.[c]
Though they called them
  upward,* no one rises up.

8 How can I give you up,
  O E′phra·im?[d]
How can I hand you over,
  O Israel?
How can I treat you like
  Ad′mah?
How can I make you like
  Ze·boi′im?[e]
I have had a change of heart;
At the same time my
  compassions are stirred.*[f]

9 I will not vent my burning
  anger.
I will not destroy E′phra·im
  again,[g]
For I am God and not man,
The Holy One in your midst;
And I will not come against
  you in fury.

10 They will walk after
  Jehovah, and he will roar
  like a lion;[h]
When he roars, his sons
  will come trembling from
  the west.[i]

11 They will tremble like a bird
  when they come out of
  Egypt,
Like a dove out of the land
  of As·syr′i·a;[j]
And I will settle them in
  their houses," declares
  Jehovah.[k]

12 "E′phra·im has surrounded
  me with lies,
And the house of Israel with
  deceit.[l]
But Judah still roams* with
  God,
And he is faithful to the
  Most Holy One."[m]

CHAP. 10
a 2Ki 18:9, 10
b Am 7:9
c 2Ki 18:9, 10

CHAP. 11
d De 7:8
e Ex 4:22
  Mt 2:14, 15
f Isa 30:9-11
g Jg 2:13
  Jg 3:7
  1Ki 16:30-32
  1Ki 18:19
  2Ki 17:13, 16
  Ho 2:13
h 1Ki 12:32, 33
  Ho 13:1, 2
i De 8:2
j De 1:31
  De 33:27
  Isa 46:3
k Isa 63:9
l 2Ki 17:3
m 2Ki 17:13, 14
  Am 4:6

Second Col.
a Le 26:31
b Isa 31:1
c Ps 78:57, 58
  Jer 3:6
d Ho 6:4
e Ge 10:19
  De 29:22, 23
f De 32:36
  Jer 31:20
g Jer 30:11
h Joe 3:16
i Zec 8:7
j Isa 11:11, 12
  Isa 60:8, 9
  Zec 10:10
k Jer 23:6
  Eze 28:25, 26
  Eze 37:21
  Am 9:14
l Mic 6:12
m 2Ki 18:1, 6
  2Ch 29:1, 2
  Ho 4:15

10:15 *Lit., "be silenced." **11:2** *That is, prophets and others sent to instruct Israel. **11:4** *Or "the ropes of kindness," like those of a parent. **11:7** *That is, to an elevated form of worship. **11:8** *Lit., "have grown hot." **11:12** *Or "walks."

12 "E'phra·im is feeding on wind.

He chases after the east wind all day long.

He multiplies lies and violence.

They make a covenant with As·syr'i·a[a] and take oil to Egypt.[b]

2 Jehovah has a legal case against Judah;[c]

He will call for an accounting against Jacob according to his ways,

And he will repay him according to his deeds.[d]

3 In the womb he seized his brother by the heel,[e]

And with his vigor he contended with God.[f]

4 He kept contending with an angel and prevailed.

He wept and begged for his favor."[g]

He found him at Beth'el, and there He spoke with us,[h]

5 Jehovah the God of armies,[i]

Jehovah is his memorial name.*[j]

6 "So return to your God,[k]

Maintain loyal love and justice,[l]

And always hope in your God.

7 But in the hand of the tradesman* are deceptive scales;

He loves to defraud.[m]

8 E'phra·im keeps saying, 'Indeed, I have become rich;[n]

I have found wealth.[o]

And in all my toil, they will not find anything wrong or sinful.'

9 But I am Jehovah your God from* the land of Egypt.[p]

I will again make you dwell in tents

As in the days of an appointed time.*

10 I spoke to the prophets,[a]

I multiplied their visions,

And I spoke parables through the prophets.

11 With Gil'e·ad there has been deception*[b] and untruth.

In Gil'gal they have sacrificed bulls,[c]

And their altars are like piles of stones in the furrows of the field.[d]

12 Jacob ran away to the territory* of A'ram;*[e]

Israel[f] served there for a wife,[g]

And for a wife he guarded sheep.[h]

13 By a prophet Jehovah brought Israel up from Egypt,[i]

And by a prophet he was guarded.[j]

14 E'phra·im has caused bitter offense;[k]

His bloodguilt remains on him;

His Lord will repay him for his reproach."[l]

13 "When E'phra·im spoke, there was trembling;

He was prominent in Israel.[m]

But he became guilty with regard to Ba'al[n] and died.

2 Now they add to their sin And make metal statues* from their silver;[o]

They skillfully make idols, all the work of craftsmen.

To them they say, 'Let the men who sacrifice kiss the calves.'[p]

3 So they will become like the morning clouds,

Like the dew that vanishes early,

CHAP. 12

a 2Ki 15:19
  Ho 8:9
b 2Ki 17:4
c 2Ki 17:19
  Jer 2:35
  Ho 4:1
  Mic 6:2
d Isa 3:11
e Ge 25:26
f Ge 32:28
g Ge 32:24-26
h Ge 28:13, 19
i Ge 28:16
  Ge 32:30
j Ex 3:15
k Isa 31:6
  Ho 14:1
  Joe 2:12, 13
l De 16:20
  Mic 6:8
m Am 8:5, 6
  Mic 2:1, 2
n Re 3:17
o De 8:17-19
p Ex 20:2
  Ho 13:4

Second Col.

a 1Ki 17:1
  2Ki 17:13
  Am 7:14, 15
b Ho 6:8
c Ho 9:15
  Am 4:4
d Ge 28:5
  De 26:5
e Ge 32:28
g Ge 29:18
h Ge 31:38
i Ex 12:50, 51
  Ps 77:20
j Jos 24:17
  1Sa 12:8
k 2Ki 17:9-11
  Eze 23:4, 5
l De 28:37

CHAP. 13

m Jos 17:17
n 2Ki 17:16
  Ho 11:2
o Ho 2:8
p 1Ki 12:26, 28
  1Ki 19:18

12:5 *Or "is the name by which he is remembered." 12:7 *Or "merchant." 12:9 *Or "since."

12:9 *Or possibly, "a festival." 12:11 *Or "what is uncanny; what is mystical." 12:12 *Lit., "field." #Or "Syria." 13:2 *Or "molten statues."

Like chaff blown from the
threshing floor by a storm,
And like smoke out of the
hole in the roof.

4 But I am Jehovah your God
from* the land of Egypt;ᵃ
You knew no God except me,
And besides me there is no
savior.ᵇ

5 I knew you in the
wilderness,ᶜ in the land
of drought.

6 They were satisfied with
their pastures,ᵈ
They were satisfied and their
heart became proud.
And so they forgot me.ᵉ

7 I will become like a young
lion to them,ᶠ
Like a leopard lurking along
the path.

8 I will come upon them like a
bear that has lost its cubs,
And I will rip open their
chest.*
I will devour them there like
a lion;
A wild beast of the field will
tear them to pieces.

9 It will destroy you, O Israel,
Because you turned against
me, against your helper.

10 Where, then, is your king,
that he may save you in
all your cities,ᵍ
And your rulers,* of whom
you said,
'Give me a king and
princes'?ʰ

11 I gave you a king in my
anger,ⁱ
And I will take him away
in my fury.ʲ

12 The error of E′phra·im is
wrapped up;*
His sin is stored up.

13 The pangs of childbirth
will come for him.
But he is an unwise child;

He does not present himself
when it is time to be born.

14 From the power of the
Grave* I will redeem them;
From death I will recover
them.ᵃ
Where are your stings,
O Death?ᵇ
Where is your destructive-
ness, O Grave?ᶜ
Compassion will be
concealed from my eyes.

15 Even if he should flourish
among the reeds,
An east wind will come,
the wind of Jehovah,
From the desert it comes,
to dry up his well and drain
his spring.
That one will pillage the
treasury of all his precious
things.ᵈ

16 Sa·mar′i·a will be held guilty,ᵉ
for she has rebelled against
her God.ᶠ
By the sword they will fall,ᵍ
Their children will be dashed
to pieces,
And their pregnant women
will be ripped open."

14 "Come back, O Israel, to
Jehovah your God,ʰ
For you have stumbled
because of your error.

2 Come back to Jehovah with
these words,
Say to him, 'May you pardon
our errorⁱ and accept what
is good,
And we will offer the praise
of our lipsʲ as we would
young bulls.*

3 As·syr′i·a will not save us.ᵏ
We will not ride on horses,ˡ
And we will no longer say,
"O our God!" to the work
of our hands,

CHAP. 13
a Ex 20:2
  Ho 12:9

b Isa 43:11
  Isa 45:21, 22

c De 2:7
  De 32:9, 10

d Ne 9:25

e De 6:10-12
  De 8:12-14
  De 32:15, 18
  Isa 17:10

f Ho 5:14

g 1Sa 8:19, 20

h 1Sa 8:4, 5

i 1Sa 8:7
  1Sa 12:13

j 1Sa 12:25
  2Ki 17:4
  Jer 52:11

Second Col.
a Isa 25:8
  Isa 26:19

b 1Co 15:55

c Re 20:13, 14

d 2Ki 17:20

e 2Ki 17:18
  Am 3:9, 10

f Eze 20:21

g Isa 7:8

CHAP. 14
h 2Ch 30:6
  Isa 55:6, 7
  Ho 12:6
  Joe 2:12, 13

i Mic 7:18

j Heb 13:15

k Ho 5:13

l Isa 31:1

13:4 *Or "since." 13:8 *Lit., "the enclosure of their heart." 13:10 *Lit.,
"judges." 13:12 *Or "is preserved."

13:14 *Or "Sheol," that is, the common
grave of mankind. See Glossary. 14:2
*Lit., "offer in return the young bulls of
our lips."

For it is by you that the fatherless child is shown mercy.'[a]

4 I will heal their unfaithfulness.[b]

I will love them of my own free will,[c]

Because my anger has turned away from him.[d]

5 I will become like the dew to Israel;

He will blossom like the lily

And will send down his roots like the trees of Leb'a·non.

6 His twigs will spread,

His splendor will be like that of the olive tree,

And his fragrance like that of Leb'a·non.

7 They will again dwell in his shadow.

They will grow grain and will bud like the vine.[e]

His fame* will be like the wine of Leb'a·non.

8 E'phra·im will say, 'What more do I have to do with idols?'[a]

I will answer and watch over him.[b]

I will be like a thriving juniper tree.

From me your fruit will be found."

9 Who is wise? Let him understand these things.

Who is discreet? Let him know them.

For the ways of Jehovah are upright,[c]

And the righteous will walk in them;

But the transgressors will stumble in them.

CHAP. 14
a De 10:17, 18

b Ps 103:3
Isa 57:18

c Zep 3:17

d Isa 12:1

e Zec 8:12

Second Col.
a Ho 14:3

b Jer 31:18

c De 32:4

14:7 *Lit., "memorial."

JOEL

1 The word of Jehovah that came to Joel* the son of Pe·thu'el:

2 "Hear this, you elders,

And pay attention, all you inhabitants of the land.*

Has anything like this happened in your days

Or in the days of your forefathers?[a]

3 Tell about it to your sons,

And let your sons tell about it to their sons,

And their sons to the next generation.

Second Col.

CHAP. 1
a Joe 2:2

1:1 *Meaning "Jehovah Is God." 1:2 *Or "earth."

4 What was left by the devouring locust, the swarming locust has eaten;[a]

And what was left by the swarming locust, the unwinged locust has eaten;

And what the unwinged locust has left, the voracious locust has eaten.[b]

5 Wake up, you drunkards,[c] and weep!

Wail, all you wine drinkers, Because the sweet wine has been taken from your mouths.[d]

6 For a nation has come up into my land, mighty and without number.[e]

Its teeth are the teeth of a lion,[f] and its jaws are those of a lion.

7 It has devastated my vine and turned my fig tree into a stump,

Stripping them completely bare and tossing them aside,

Leaving their twigs white.

8 Wail as a virgin* wearing sackcloth does

For the bridegroom# of her youth.

9 Grain offering[g] and drink offering[h] have ceased from the house of Jehovah;

The priests, the ministers of Jehovah, are in mourning.

10 The field has been devastated, the ground mourns;[i]

For the grain has been devastated, the new wine has dried up, the oil has failed.[j]

11 Farmers are dismayed, vinedressers wail,

Because of the wheat and the barley;

For the harvest of the field has perished.

12 The vine has dried up,

The fig tree has withered.

The pomegranate, the palm, and the apple,

All the trees of the field have dried up;[a]

For joy has turned to shame among the people.

13 Put on sackcloth* and mourn,# you priests;

Wail, you ministers of the altar.[b]

Come in and spend the night in sackcloth, you ministers of my God;

For grain offering[c] and drink offering[d] have been withheld from the house of your God.

14 Proclaim* a fast; call for a solemn assembly.[e]

Gather the elders together, with all the inhabitants of the land,

To the house of Jehovah your God,[f] and cry to Jehovah for help.

15 Woe because of the day!

For the day of Jehovah is near,[g]

And it will come like a destruction from the Almighty!

16 Has not food been taken from before our very eyes,

And rejoicing and joy from the house of our God?

17 The seeds* have shriveled under their shovels.

Storehouses are desolate. Granaries have been torn down, for the grain has dried up.

18 Even the livestock groan! The herds of cattle wander in confusion, for they have no pasture!

And the flocks of sheep bear the punishment.

CHAP. 1
a Ex 10:14, 15

b Joe 2:25

c Isa 28:1
　Am 6:6

d De 28:39

e Joe 2:2

f Re 9:7, 8

g Le 2:1

h Ex 29:40

i Le 26:20

j De 28:39, 40

Second Col.
a Le 26:20

b Ex 30:19, 20

c Le 2:1

d Ex 29:40

e Joe 2:15

f 2Ch 20:3, 13

g Joe 2:1
　Zep 1:7, 14
　Zep 2:2
　2Pe 3:10
　Re 6:16, 17

1:8 *Or "young woman." #Or "husband." 1:13 *Lit., "Gird yourselves." #Or "beat your chest." 1:14 *Lit., "Sanctify." 1:17 *Or possibly, "dried figs."

19 To you, O Jehovah, I will call;[a]

For fire has devoured the pastures of the wilderness,

And a flame has consumed all the trees of the field.

20 Even the wild beasts long for you,

Because the streams of water have dried up

And fire has devoured the pastures of the wilderness."

2 "Blow a horn in Zion![b]

Shout a war cry in my holy mountain.

Let all the inhabitants of the land* tremble,

For the day of Jehovah is coming![c] It is near!

2 It is a day of darkness and gloom,[d]

A day of clouds and thick gloom,[e]

Like light of dawn spreading out on the mountains.

There is a people numerous and mighty;[f]

Never before has there been one like it,

And never again will there be another

Through the years of all generations.

3 Ahead of it a fire devours,

And behind it a flame consumes.[g]

The land ahead of it is like the garden of E′den,[h]

But behind it is a desolate wilderness,

And nothing can escape.

4 Its appearance is like the appearance of horses,

And they run like warhorses.[i]

5 The sound is like that of chariots as they leap on the mountaintops,[j]

Like the crackling of a blazing fire that consumes stubble.

It is like a mighty people drawn up in battle formation.[a]

6 Because of them, peoples will be in anguish.

Every face will grow flushed.

7 They charge like warriors,

They scale a wall like soldiers,

Each keeps to his own course,

And they do not swerve from their paths.

8 They do not shove one another;

Each man advances in his course.

If the weapons* cause some to fall,

The others do not break ranks.

9 Into the city they rush, on the wall they run.

Onto the houses they climb, through the windows they enter like a thief.

10 Before them the land trembles and the heavens rock.

Sun and moon have become dark,[b]

And the stars have lost their brightness.

11 Jehovah will raise his voice before his army,[c] for his camp is very numerous.[d]

For the one carrying out His word is mighty;

For the day of Jehovah is great and very awe-inspiring.[e]

Who can endure it?"[f]

12 "Yet even now," declares Jehovah, "return to me with all your hearts,[g]

With fasting[h] and weeping and wailing.

CHAP. 1
a Mic 7:7
Hab 3:18

CHAP. 2
b Eze 33:2, 3
Am 3:6

c Zep 1:14, 16
Mal 4:1

d Am 5:18, 20

e Zep 1:15

f Joe 1:6

g Joe 1:19

h Ge 2:8

i Re 9:7

j Re 9:9

Second Col.
a Pr 30:27

b Joe 2:31
Mt 24:29
Lu 21:25
Re 9:2

c Joe 2:25

d Joe 2:2

e Jer 30:7
Am 5:18
Zep 1:15

f Re 6:16, 17

g Jer 4:1
Ho 12:6
Ho 14:1, 2

h 1Sa 7:6
2Ch 20:3

2:1 *Or "earth."

2:8 *Or "missiles."

13 Rip apart your hearts,[a]
and not your garments,[b]
And return to Jehovah
your God,
For he is compassionate*
and merciful, slow to
anger[c] and abundant in
loyal love,
And he will reconsider#
the calamity.
14 Who knows whether he will
turn back and reconsider*[e]
And leave behind a blessing,
A grain offering and a drink
offering for Jehovah your
God?
15 Blow a horn in Zion!
Proclaim* a fast; call for a
solemn assembly.[f]
16 Gather the people; sanctify
the congregation.[g]
Collect the old men;* gather
the children and nursing
infants.[h]
Let the bridegroom go out
from his inner chamber,
and the bride from her
bridal chamber.
17 Between the porch and the
altar[i]
Let the priests, the ministers
of Jehovah, weep and say:
'Do feel pity, O Jehovah,
for your people;
Do not make your
inheritance an object
of scorn,
Letting the nations rule over
them.
Why should the peoples say,
"Where is their God?"'[j]
18 Then Jehovah will be zealous
for his land
And show compassion on his
people.[k]
19 Jehovah will answer his
people:

'Here I am sending to you
grain and new wine and oil,
And you will be fully
satisfied;[a]
I will no longer make you
a reproach among the
nations.[b]
20 I will drive the northerner
far away from you;
I will disperse him to a dry
and desolate wasteland,
With his vanguard* toward
the eastern sea#
And his rear guard toward
the western sea.△
The foul smell from him will
ascend,
The stench from him will
keep ascending;[c]
For He will do great things.'
21 Do not be afraid, O land.
Be joyful and rejoice, for
Jehovah will do great
things.
22 Do not be afraid, you beasts
of the field,
For the pastures of the
wilderness will become
green,[d]
And the trees will bear fruit;[e]
The fig tree and the vine
must give their full yield.[f]
23 You sons of Zion, be joyful
and rejoice in Jehovah
your God;[g]
For he will give you the
autumn rain in the right
amount,
And he will send upon you
a downpour,
The autumn rain and the
spring rain, as before.[h]
24 The threshing floors will be
full of pure grain,
And the presses will
overflow with new wine
and oil.[i]
25 And I will make compensation to you for the years

CHAP. 2

a 2Ki 22:18, 19
Ps 51:17
Isa 57:15

b 2Sa 1:11, 12

c Isa 48:9

d Ex 34:6
Nu 14:18
Ne 9:17
Ps 106:44,
45
Mic 7:18, 19

e 2Ch 30:8, 9
Jer 18:7, 8
Zep 2:2, 3

f Joe 1:14

g Ex 19:10

h De 31:12
2Ch 20:3, 13

i 2Ch 8:12

j De 32:26, 27
Ps 79:9, 10
Mic 7:10

k De 32:36
Isa 60:10
La 3:22
Ho 11:8

Second Col.

a Isa 62:8, 9
Am 9:13
Mal 3:10

b Eze 34:29
Eze 36:15

c Isa 34:2, 3

d Isa 30:23
Isa 51:3

e Eze 34:27

f Am 9:14
Zec 8:12

g Isa 12:6
Zec 10:7

h Le 26:4
De 11:14

i Le 26:10
Am 9:13
Mal 3:10

2:13 *Or "gracious." #Or "feel regret
over." 2:14 *Or "feel regret." 2:15
*Lit., "Sanctify." 2:16 *Or "the elders."

2:20 *Lit., "face." #That is, the Dead
Sea. △That is, the Mediterranean Sea.

That the swarming locust,
the unwinged locust,
the voracious locust, and
the devouring locust have
eaten,
My great army that I sent
among you.[a]

26 You will surely eat to
satisfaction,[b]
And you will praise the name
of Jehovah your God,[c]
Who has done wonders in
your behalf;
My people will never again
be put to shame.[d]

27 And you will have to know
that I am in the midst of
Israel[e]
And that I am Jehovah your
God[f]—there is no other!
My people will never again
be put to shame.

28 After that I will pour out
my spirit[g] on every sort of
flesh,
And your sons and your
daughters will prophesy,
Your old men will dream
dreams,
And your young men will
see visions.[h]

29 And even on my male slaves
and female slaves
I will pour out my spirit in
those days.

30 And I will give wonders*
in the heavens and on the
earth,
Blood and fire and columns
of smoke.[i]

31 The sun will be turned into
darkness and the moon
into blood[j]
Before the coming of the
great and awe-inspiring
day of Jehovah.[k]

32 And everyone who calls on
the name of Jehovah will
be saved;[l]

2:30 *Or "portents."

CHAP. 2
a Joe 1:4
b Le 26:5
c De 26:10, 11
d Zep 3:11
e Ps 46:5
f Le 26:11, 12
  Eze 37:26, 27
g Isa 32:15
  Isa 44:3
  Eze 39:29
h Ac 2:16-18
i Ac 2:19, 20
j Mt 24:29
  Mr 13:24, 25
  Lu 21:25
  Re 6:12
k Zep 1:14, 15
  Mal 4:5
l Ac 2:21
  Ro 10:13

Second Col.
a Ob 17

CHAP. 3
b De 30:3
  Jer 30:3
  Eze 39:28
  Am 9:14
  Zep 3:20
c Eze 38:22
  Joe 3:12
  Zep 3:8
  Zec 14:3
  Re 16:14, 16
d Eze 35:10, 11
  Zep 2:8, 9
e Ob 11
f Isa 23:12
  Jer 47:4
  Eze 25:15-17
  Am 1:9, 10
  Zec 9:1, 2
g 2Ch 21:16, 17
h De 28:32
  Eze 27:8, 13

For on Mount Zion and in
Jerusalem there will be
those who escape,[a] just
as Jehovah has said,
The survivors whom
Jehovah calls."

3 "For look! in those days and
in that time,
When I bring back the
captives of Judah and
Jerusalem,[b]

2 I will also gather together all
the nations
And bring them down to the
Valley* of Je·hosh′a·phat.#
I will enter into judgment
with them there[c]
In behalf of my people and
my inheritance Israel,
For they scattered them
among the nations,
And they divided up my land
among themselves.[d]

3 For my people they cast
lots;[e]
They would trade a boy to
hire a prostitute
And sell a girl for wine to
drink.

4 Also, what do you have
against me,
O Tyre and Si′don and all
the regions of Phi·lis′ti·a?
Are you repaying me for
something?
If you are repaying me,
I will swiftly, speedily bring
your repayment on your
heads.[f]

5 Because you have taken my
silver and gold,[g]
And you have brought my
finest treasures into your
temples;

6 And the people of Judah and
Jerusalem you have sold
to the Greeks,[h]
In order to remove them far
from their territory;

3:2 *Or "Low Plain." #Meaning "Jehovah Is Judge."

7 Here I am rousing them to come from the place where you sold them,[a]
And I will bring your repayment on your heads.

8 I will sell your sons and daughters into the hand of the people of Judah,[b]
And they will sell them to the men of She′ba, to a nation far away;
For Jehovah himself has spoken it.

9 Proclaim this among the nations:[c]
'Prepare for* war! Stir up the mighty men!
Let all the soldiers draw near, let them advance![d]

10 Beat your plowshares into swords and your pruning shears into spears.*
Let the weak one say: "I am powerful."

11 Come and help, all you surrounding nations, assemble together!'"[e]
To that place, O Jehovah, bring down your powerful ones.*

12 "Let the nations be roused and come up to the Valley* of Je·hosh′a·phat;
For there I will sit in order to judge all the surrounding nations.[f]

13 Thrust in a sickle, for the harvest is ripe.
Come down and tread, for the winepress is full.[g]
The vats overflow, for their badness is abundant.

14 Crowds, crowds are in the valley* of the decision,
For the day of Jehovah is near in the valley* of the decision.[h]

15 Sun and moon will become dark,
And the stars will lose their brightness.

16 And Jehovah will roar out of Zion,
Out of Jerusalem he will raise his voice.
And heaven and earth will rock;
But Jehovah will be a refuge for his people,[a]
A fortress for the people of Israel.

17 And you will have to know that I am Jehovah your God, residing in Zion, my holy mountain.[b]
Jerusalem will become a holy place,[c]
And strangers* will pass through her no more.[d]

18 In that day the mountains will drip with sweet wine,[e]
The hills will flow with milk,
And the streams of Judah will all flow with water.
Out of the house of Jehovah a spring will flow,[f]
And it will irrigate the Valley* of the Acacia Trees.

19 But Egypt will become desolate,[g]
And E′dom will be a desolate wilderness,[h]
Because of the violence done to the people of Judah,[i]
In whose land they shed innocent blood.[j]

20 But Judah will always be inhabited,
And Jerusalem to generation after generation.[k]

21 I will consider innocent their blood* that I had not considered innocent;[l]
And Jehovah will reside in Zion."[m]

CHAP. 3
a Isa 11:11, 12
  Isa 43:5, 6
  Isa 49:12
  Jer 23:7, 8
  Eze 34:12

b Ob 19, 20

c Isa 34:1, 2

d Eze 38:7

e Eze 38:9
  Zep 3:8
  Re 16:14

f Ps 76:8, 9
  Joe 3:2

g Isa 63:3
  Re 14:18-20

h Isa 34:2
  Zep 1:14

Second Col.
a Ps 50:15

b Zec 8:3

c Isa 4:3

d Isa 60:18
  Na 1:15
  Zec 14:21

e Am 9:13
  Zec 9:17

f Eze 47:1
  Re 22:1

g Isa 19:1

h Jer 49:17

i Eze 25:12, 13

j Am 1:11
  Ob 10

k Ps 48:8
  Isa 33:20
  Isa 60:15
  Am 9:15

l Isa 4:4
  Eze 36:25
  Mic 7:18, 19

m Eze 24:23
  Mic 4:7

3:9 *Lit., "Sanctify." 3:10 *Or "lances." 3:11 *Or "your warriors." 3:12 *Or "Low Plain." 3:14 *Or "low plain." 3:17 *Or "foreigners." 3:18 *Or "Wadi." 3:21 *Or "bloodguilt."

AMOS

OUTLINE OF CONTENTS

---

1 The words of A′mos,* who was among the sheep raisers from Te·ko′a,[a] which he received in vision concerning Israel in the days of King Uz·zi′ah[b] of Judah and in the days of Jer·o·bo′am[c] son of Jo′ash,[d] the king of Israel, two years before the earthquake.[e] **2** He said:

"Jehovah will roar out of Zion,
And he will raise his voice out of Jerusalem.
The pastures of the shepherds will mourn,
And the summit of Car′mel will dry up."[f]

3 "This is what Jehovah says,
'"For three revolts* of Damascus, and for four, I will not reverse it,
Because they threshed

Gil′e·ad with iron threshing sledges.[a]
4 So I will send a fire upon the house of Haz′a·el,[b]
And it will consume the fortified towers of Ben-ha′dad.[c]
5 I will break the bars of Damascus;[d]
I will destroy the inhabitants from Bik′ath-a′ven
And the one ruling* from Beth-e′den;
And the people of Syria will go as exiles to Kir,"[e] says Jehovah.'

6 This is what Jehovah says,
'"For three revolts of Gaz′a,[f] and for four, I will not reverse it,
Because they took a whole group of exiles[g] to hand them over to E′dom.
7 So I will send a fire onto the wall of Gaz′a,[h]

1:5 *Lit., "the one holding the scepter."

CHAP. 1
a 2Ch 11:5, 6
b 2Ch 26:1, 3, 4
  Isa 1:1
c 2Ki 14:23, 24
  Ho 1:1
  Am 7:10
d 2Ki 13:10, 11
e Zec 14:5
f Isa 33:9
  Na 1:4

Second Col.
a 2Ki 8:12
  2Ki 10:32, 33
  2Ki 13:7
b 1Ki 19:15
c Jer 49:27
d Isa 7:8
  Isa 8:4
  Isa 17:1
e 2Ki 16:9
f Eze 25:15
g 2Ch 21:16, 17
  2Ch 28:18
  Joe 3:4, 6
h Jer 25:17, 20
  Jer 47:1
  Zec 9:5

And it will consume her fortified towers.

8 I will destroy the inhabitants from Ashʹdod,[a]

And the one ruling* from Ashʹkeʹlon;[b]

I will turn my hand against Ekʹron,[c]

And the remaining Phiʹlisʹtines will perish,"[d] says the Sovereign Lord Jehovah.'

9 This is what Jehovah says,

'For three revolts of Tyre,[e] and for four, I will not reverse it,

Because they handed over a whole group of exiles to Eʹdom,

And because they did not remember the covenant of brothers.[f]

10 So I will send a fire onto the wall of Tyre,

And it will consume her fortified towers.'[g]

11 This is what Jehovah says,

'For three revolts of Eʹdom,[h] and for four, I will not reverse it,

Because he pursued his own brother with the sword,[i]

And because he refused to show mercy;

In his anger he keeps tearing them apart relentlessly,

And he remains furious with them continually.[j]

12 So I will send a fire into Teʹman,[k]

And it will consume the fortified towers of Bozʹrah.'[l]

13 This is what Jehovah says,

'For three revolts of the Amʹmonʹites,[m] and for four, I will not reverse it,

Because they ripped open the pregnant women of Gilʹeʹad to widen out their own territory.[n]

14 So I will set fire to the wall of Rabʹbah,[o]

And it will consume her fortified towers,

With a war cry in the day of battle,

With a tempest in the day of storm wind.

15 And their king will go into exile together with his princes,"[a] says Jehovah.'

2 "This is what Jehovah says,

'For three revolts* of Moʹab,[b] and for four, I will not reverse it,

Because he burned the bones of the king of Eʹdom for lime.

2 So I will send a fire into Moʹab, and it will consume the fortified towers of Keʹriʹoth;[c]

Moʹab will die amid an uproar,

With a war cry, with the sound of a horn.[d]

3 I will remove the ruler* from her midst

And kill all her princes along with him,"[e] says Jehovah.'

4 This is what Jehovah says,

'For three revolts of Judah,[f] and for four, I will not reverse it,

Because they rejected the law* of Jehovah,

And because they did not keep his regulations;[g]

But the same lies their forefathers followed have led them astray.[h]

5 So I will send a fire into Judah,

And it will consume the fortified towers of Jerusalem.'[i]

6 This is what Jehovah says,

'For three revolts of Israel,[j] and for four, I will not reverse it,

Because they sell the righteous for silver,

CHAP. 1

a Isa 20:1

b Jer 47:5

c Zep 2:4

d Isa 14:29
Jer 47:4
Eze 25:16, 17
Zep 2:5
Zec 9:6

e Eze 26:2

f Joe 3:4, 6

g Eze 26:12

h Joe 3:19

i Eze 25:12

j 2Ch 28:17
Ob 10

k Ge 36:10, 11
Ob 9

l Isa 34:5, 6
Jer 49:13

m Eze 25:3
Zep 2:8

n Jg 11:12, 13
Jer 49:1

o Jer 49:2
Eze 25:5

Second Col.

a Jer 27:2, 3
Jer 49:3

CHAP. 2

b Jer 48:29, 30
Eze 25:8, 9
Zep 2:8

c Jer 48:21, 24

d Isa 15:1

e Isa 16:14
Jer 48:7

f 2Ki 17:19
Jer 2:13

g Le 26:14-16
2Ch 36:14

h Jer 9:14

i 1Sa 12:15
1Ch 28:9
2Ch 36:17, 19
Jer 17:27
Jer 37:8
Jer 52:12-14
Ho 8:14

j De 28:45
2Ki 17:6, 7
Eze 23:4, 5
Ho 4:1, 2

1:8 *Lit., "the one holding the scepter." 2:1 *Or "crimes." 2:3 *Lit., "judge." 2:4 *Or "instruction."

And the poor for a pair of sandals.[a]

7 They trample the heads of the lowly into the dust of the earth,[b]

And they block the path of the meek.[c]

A man and his father have relations with the same girl,

Profaning my holy name.

8 They stretch out next to every altar[d] on garments they seized as security for a loan;*[e]

And the wine they drink at the house[#] of their gods was obtained from those they fined.'

9 'But it was I who annihilated the Am′or·ite before them,[f]

Who was as tall as the cedars and as strong as the oaks;

I destroyed his fruit above and his roots below.[g]

10 I brought you up out of the land of Egypt,[h]

And I made you walk through the wilderness 40 years,[i]

To take possession of the land of the Am′or·ite.

11 I raised up some of your sons as prophets[j]

And some of your young men as Naz′i·rites.[k]

Is this not so, O people of Israel?' declares Jehovah.

12 'But you kept giving the Naz′i·rites wine to drink,[l]

And you commanded the prophets: "You must not prophesy."[m]

13 So I will crush you in your place,

Just as a wagon loaded with cut grain crushes what is under it.

14 The swift one will have no place to flee,[n]

The strong one will not retain his power,

And no warrior will escape with his life.*

15 The bowman will not stand his ground,

The swift of foot will not escape,

And the horseman will not escape with his life.*

16 Even the most courageous* among the warriors

Will flee naked in that day,'[a] declares Jehovah."

3 "Hear this word that Jehovah has spoken concerning you, O people of Israel, concerning the whole family that I brought up out of the land of Egypt:

2 'You alone I have known out of all the families of the earth.[b]

That is why I will call you to account for all your errors.[c]

3 Will two walk together unless they have agreed to meet?*

4 Will a lion roar in the forest when it has no prey?

Will a young lion* growl from its lair when it has caught nothing?

5 Will a bird fall into a trap on the ground when there is no snare for it?*

Does a trap spring up from the ground when it has caught nothing?

6 If a horn is blown in a city, do the people not tremble?

If a calamity occurs in the city, is it not Jehovah who has acted?

7 For the Sovereign Lord Jehovah will not do a thing

Unless he has revealed his confidential matter* to his servants the prophets.[d]

CHAP. 2
a Am 5:11
  Am 8:4-6

b Am 4:1

c Isa 10:1, 2
  Am 5:12

d Ho 8:11
  Ho 10:1

e Ex 22:26
  De 24:12

f Nu 21:23-25
  Jos 24:8
  Ps 135:10, 11

g De 2:31-33

h Ex 12:51

i Nu 14:34
  De 2:7

j 1Sa 3:20
  1Ki 17:1
  1Ki 19:19

k Nu 6:2
  Jg 13:5

l Nu 6:3, 4

m Isa 30:10, 11
  Am 7:12, 13

n Am 9:1

Second Col.
a De 28:25

CHAP. 3
b Ex 19:5
  De 7:6
  Ps 147:19, 20

c Da 9:11, 12
  Ho 12:2
  Am 4:12

d Ge 6:13
  Ge 18:17
  Ps 25:14
  Isa 42:9
  Da 9:22
  Re 1:1

2:8 *Or "a pledge." #Or "temple." 2:14, 15 *Or "soul." 2:16 *Or "those strong of heart." 3:3 *Or "have met by appointment?" 3:4 *Or "a maned young lion." 3:5 *Or possibly, "when there is no bait in it?" 3:7 *Or "his secret."

8 The lion has roared!ᵃ
Who will not be afraid?
The Sovereign Lord Jehovah
has spoken! Who will not
prophesy?'ᵇ

9 'Proclaim it on the fortified
towers of Ash'dod
And on the fortified towers
in the land of Egypt.
Say: "Gather together
against the mountains of
Sa·mar'i·a;ᶜ
See the turmoil in her midst
And the defrauding within
her.ᵈ

10 For they do not know how to
do what is right," declares
Jehovah,
"Those who are storing up
violence and destruction
in their fortified towers."'

11 Therefore this is what the
Sovereign Lord Jehovah
says,
'An adversary will surround
the land,ᵉ
He will strip you of your
strength,
And your fortified towers
will be plundered.'ᶠ

12 This is what Jehovah says,
'Just as the shepherd
snatches away two legs or
a piece of an ear from the
mouth of the lion,
That is how the people of Israel will be snatched away,
Those now sitting in Sa·mar'-
i·a on splendid beds and on
fine couches.'*ᵍ

13 'Hear and warn* the house
of Jacob,' declares the
Sovereign Lord Jehovah,
the God of armies.

14 'For in the day I call Israel
to account for all his
revolts,*ʰ
I will also call for an
accounting against the
altars of Beth'el;ⁱ

The horns of the altar will
be cut off and fall to the
earth.ᵃ

15 I will strike down the winter
house along with the
summer house.'
'The houses of ivory will
perish,ᵇ
And the great* houses
will come to their end,'ᶜ
declares Jehovah.

4 "Hear this word, you cows
of Ba'shan,
Who are on the mountain
of Sa·mar'i·a,ᵈ
You women who are defrauding the lowlyᵉ and crushing
the poor,
Who say to their husbands,*
'Bring us something to
drink!'

2 The Sovereign Lord Jehovah
has sworn by his holiness,
'"Look! The days are coming
upon you when he will lift
you up with butcher hooks
And the rest of you with
fishhooks.

3 You will go out through the
breaches in the wall, each
one straight ahead;
And you will be cast out
to Har'mon," declares
Jehovah.'

4 'Come to Beth'el and commit
transgression,*ᶠ
To Gil'gal and transgress
even more!ᵍ
Bring your sacrificesʰ in the
morning,
And your tithes*ⁱ on the third
day.

5 Burn a thanksgiving sacrifice
of leavened bread;ʲ
Loudly proclaim your
voluntary offerings!
For that is what you love
to do, O people of Israel,'
declares the Sovereign
Lord Jehovah.

CHAP. 3
a Am 1:2

b Jer 20:9
Am 7:14, 15
Ac 4:19, 20

c 2Ki 17:22, 23

d Ho 7:1
Am 4:1

e 2Ki 17:6

f Ho 11:6
Am 6:8

g Isa 8:4
Am 6:4

h Ho 4:9

i 1Ki 12:32, 33
Ho 13:2

Second Col.
a 2Ki 23:15, 16
2Ch 31:1
2Ch 34:1, 7
Ho 10:2
Mic 1:6

b 1Ki 22:39

c Am 6:11

CHAP. 4
d Am 6:1

e Ho 4:1, 2
Mic 2:2

f 1Ki 12:28, 29
Ho 4:13
Am 3:14

g Ho 4:15
Ho 9:15
Am 5:5

h Ho 8:11, 13

i De 14:28

j Le 7:12

3:12 *Or "Damascene couches." 3:13
*Or "bear witness against." 3:14 *Or
"crimes."

3:15 *Or possibly, "And many." 4:1
*Or "masters." 4:4 *Or "rebel." #Or
"tenth parts."

6 'And for my part, I made your teeth clean of food* in all your cities
And caused a lack of bread in all your houses;[a]
But you did not come back to me,'[b] declares Jehovah.

7 'I also withheld rain from you three months before the harvest;[c]
I made it rain on one city but not on another city.
One plot of land would have rain,
But another plot of land where there was no rain would dry up.

8 People of two or three cities staggered to one city to drink water,[d]
And they would not get satisfied;
But you did not come back to me,'[e] declares Jehovah.

9 'I struck you with scorching heat and mildew.[f]
You multiplied your gardens and vineyards,
But the locust would devour your fig trees and olive trees;[g]
And you still did not come back to me,'[h] declares Jehovah.

10 'I sent among you a pestilence like that of Egypt.[i]
With the sword I killed your young men[j] and captured your horses.[k]
I made the stench of your camps rise up into your nostrils;[l]
But you did not come back to me,' declares Jehovah.

11 'I caused an overthrow among you
Like God's overthrow of Sod'om and Go·mor'rah.[m]
And you were like a log snatched out of the fire;

4:6 *Or "gave you no food to eat."

CHAP. 4
a Le 26:26
  De 28:38
  De 32:24
  1Ki 18:2
  2Ki 4:38

b Jer 3:6, 7

c De 28:23, 24

d 1Ki 18:5

e Ho 7:10

f De 28:22

g De 28:40, 42

h Isa 42:24

i Ex 9:3
  De 28:27, 60

j Le 26:23, 25
  2Ki 8:12

k 2Ki 13:7

l De 28:26

m Ge 19:24, 25

Second Col.
a Ho 7:10

b Isa 40:12

c Jer 10:13

d Ex 10:22
  Isa 5:30
  Am 8:9

e Mic 1:3

CHAP. 5
f De 4:27
  De 28:62

g 2Ch 15:2
  Isa 55:3, 6

h 1Ki 12:28, 29
  Am 3:14

i Ho 4:15
  Am 4:4

j Am 8:14

k 2Ki 17:6
  Ho 9:15

But you did not come back to me,'[a] declares Jehovah.

12 So that is what I will do to you, O Israel.
Because this is what I will do to you,
Get ready to meet your God, O Israel.

13 For look! he is the One who formed the mountains[b] and created the wind;[c]
He tells man what His thoughts are,
He turns the dawn into darkness,[d]
And he treads on earth's high places;[e]
Jehovah the God of armies is his name."

5 "Hear this word that I am taking up against you as a dirge,* O house of Israel:

2 'The virgin, Israel, has fallen;
She cannot get up again.
She has been abandoned on her own ground;
There is no one to raise her up.'

3 "For this is what the Sovereign Lord Jehovah says:
'The city that marches out with a thousand will have a hundred left;
And the one that goes out with a hundred will have ten left, for the house of Israel.'[f]

4 "For this is what Jehovah says to the house of Israel:
'Search for me and keep living.[g]

5 Do not search for Beth'el,[h]
Do not go to Gil'gal[i] or pass over to Be·er-she'ba,[j]
For Gil'gal will certainly go into exile,[k]
And Beth'el will come to nothing.*

5:1 *Or "song of mourning." 5:5 *Or possibly, "become something uncanny."

6 Search for Jehovah, and keep living,[a]
So that he does not burst out like a fire on the house of Joseph,
Consuming Beth′el, with no one to extinguish it.

7 You turn justice into wormwood,*
And you cast righteousness to the earth.[b]

8 The One who made the Ki′mah constellation* and the Ke′sil constellation,*[c]
The One who turns deep shadow into morning,
The One who makes day as dark as night,[d]
The One who summons the waters of the sea
To pour them out on the surface of the earth[e]
—Jehovah is his name.

9 He will cause destruction to burst out against the strong,
Bringing destruction on fortified places.

10 They hate those who give reproof in the city gate,
And they detest those who speak truthfully.[f]

11 Because you demand farm rent* from the poor
And you take his grain as tribute,[g]
You will not keep dwelling in the houses of hewn stone that you have built[h]
Nor drink the wine from the choice vineyards that you have planted.[i]

12 For I know how many your revolts* are
And how great your sins are
—You harass the righteous, You take bribes,*

5:7 *Or "bitterness." 5:8 *Possibly the Pleiades stars in the Taurus constellation. *Possibly the Orion constellation. 5:11 *Or "land tax." 5:12 *Or "crimes." *Or "hush money."

CHAP. 5

a Eze 33:11

b Am 6:12

c Job 9:9
Job 38:31-33

d Ex 10:21, 22

e Job 36:27, 28
Ec 1:7

f 1Ki 18:17
1Ki 22:8

g Mic 2:2

h Isa 9:9, 10

i De 28:30

_____

Second Col.

a Isa 10:1, 2
Am 2:6, 7

b Mic 2:3

c Isa 1:16, 17
Mic 6:8

d Le 18:5
De 30:19, 20

e 2Ch 15:2
Mic 3:11

f Ps 34:14
Ps 97:10
Ro 12:9

g 2Ch 19:6
Am 5:24

h Jer 31:7
Zec 10:6

i Ho 9:2

j Isa 5:18, 19

k Am 4:12

l Zep 1:14, 15

And you deny the rights of the poor in the city gate.[a]

13 Therefore, those with insight will keep silent at that time,
For it will be a time of calamity.[b]

14 Search for what is good, and not what is bad,[c]
So that you may keep living.[d]
Then Jehovah the God of armies may be with you,
Just as you say he is.[e]

15 Hate what is bad, and love what is good,[f]
Let justice prevail in the city gate.[g]
It may be that Jehovah the God of armies
Will show favor to the remaining ones of Joseph.'[h]

16 "Therefore this is what Jehovah the God of armies, Jehovah, says:
'In all the public squares there will be wailing,
And in all the streets they will say, "Alas, alas!"
They will call on the farmers to mourn
And the professional mourners to wail.'

17 'In every vineyard there will be wailing;[i]
For I will pass through your midst,' says Jehovah.

18 'Woe to those who yearn for the day of Jehovah![j]
What, then, will the day of Jehovah mean for you?[k]
It will be darkness, and not light.[l]

19 It will be like a man who flees from a lion and is confronted by a bear,
And when he enters his house and leans his hand against the wall, a snake bites him,

20 Will not the day of Jehovah be darkness, and not light;

Will it not have gloom, and not brightness?

21 I hate, I despise your festivals,[a]

And I take no pleasure in the aroma of your solemn assemblies.

22 Even if you offer me whole burnt offerings and gift offerings,

I will find no pleasure in them;[b]

And I will not look with favor on your communion sacrifices of fattened animals.[c]

23 Spare me the din of your songs;

And let me not hear the melodies of your stringed instruments.[d]

24 Let justice flow down like waters,[e]

And righteousness like an ever-flowing stream.

25 Did you bring me sacrifices and gift offerings

For those 40 years in the wilderness, O house of Israel?[f]

26 Now you will have to carry away Sak'kuth your king and Kai'wan,*

Your images, the star of your god, whom you made for yourselves,

27 And I will send you into exile beyond Damascus,'[g] says he whose name is Jehovah the God of armies.''[h]

6 "Woe to the self-assured* ones in Zion,

To those feeling secure in the mountain of Sa·mar'i·a,

The prominent men of the foremost of nations,

Those to whom the house of Israel comes!

CHAP. 5
a Pr 15:8

b Ps 50:8
  Isa 66:3
  Ho 6:6

c Isa 1:11

d Am 6:5
  Am 8:10

e Mic 6:8

f Ac 7:42, 43

g 2Ki 15:29
  2Ki 17:6

h Am 4:13

CHAP. 6
i Am 3:13, 15

Second Col.
a Nu 34:2, 8
  2Ki 14:28

b Isa 56:12

c Am 5:12

d 1Ki 22:39

e Am 3:12

f Isa 22:13

g Isa 5:12

h 2Ch 7:6
  2Ch 29:25, 26

i Isa 5:11

j 2Ki 15:29
  2Ki 17:6

k De 28:41
  Am 5:5

l Am 4:2

m Eze 33:28
  Ho 5:5

n La 2:5

o Mic 1:6

---

2 Cross over to Cal'neh and see.

Go from there to Great Ha'math,

And go down to Gath of the Phi·lis'tines.

Are they better than these kingdoms,*

Or is their territory larger than yours?

3 Are you putting out of your mind the day of calamity[b]

And bringing in a reign* of violence?[c]

4 They lie on beds of ivory[d] and sprawl out on couches,[e]

Eating the rams of the flock and the fattened calves;*[f]

5 They improvise songs to the sound of the harp,*[g]

And like David, they invent musical instruments;[h]

6 They drink wine by the bowlful[i]

And anoint themselves with the choicest oils.

But they are unconcerned about* the catastrophe of Joseph.[j]

7 So they will go into exile at the head of the exiles,[k]

And the revelry of those sprawled out will come to an end.

8 'The Sovereign Lord Jehovah has sworn by himself,'*[l] declares Jehovah the God of armies,

'"I detest the pride of Jacob,[m] I hate his fortified towers,[n]

And I will hand over the city and what fills it.[o]

9 """And if ten men are left in one house, they will also die.

10 A relative* will come to carry

5:26 *These deities may both refer to the planet Saturn, which was worshipped as a god. 6:1 *Or "complacent."

6:2 *Evidently referring to the kingdoms of Judah and Israel. 6:3 *Lit., "seat." 6:4 *Or "young bulls." 6:5 *Or "stringed instrument." 6:6 *Lit., "did not become sick at." 6:8 *Or "his soul." 6:10 *Lit., "His father's brother."

them out and burn them one by one. He will bring their bones out from the house; then he will say to whoever is in the inner rooms of the house, 'Are there any more with you?' And he will say, 'Nobody!' Then he will say, 'Keep silent! For it is not the time to make any mention of the name of Jehovah.'"

11 For it is Jehovah giving the command,[a]
And he will strike down the great house into rubble,
And the small house into debris.[b]

12 Do horses run on a crag,
Or will one plow there with cattle?
For you have turned justice into a poisonous plant,
And the fruit of righteousness into wormwood.*[c]

13 You rejoice over what is worthless,
And you say, "Have we not become powerful* in our own strength?"[d]

14 Therefore, O house of Israel, I will bring against you a nation,'[e] declares Jehovah the God of armies,
'And they will oppress you from Le'bo-ha'math*[f] down to the Wadi# of the Ar'a·bah.'"

7 This is what the Sovereign Lord Jehovah showed me: Look! He formed a locust swarm when the late crop* was beginning to come up. This was the later crop after the king's hay had been cut. **2** When the swarm finished eating up the vegetation of the land, I said: "O Sovereign Lord Jehovah, please forgive![g] How can Jacob survive?* For he is weak!"[h]

3 So Jehovah reconsidered* this.[a] "It will not happen," Jehovah said.

4 This is what the Sovereign Lord Jehovah showed me: Look! The Sovereign Lord Jehovah called for a punishment by fire. It consumed the vast deep waters, and it consumed a portion of the land. **5** Then I said: "O Sovereign Lord Jehovah, please hold this back.[b] How can Jacob survive?* For he is weak!"[c]

6 So Jehovah reconsidered* this.[d] "That too will not happen," the Sovereign Lord Jehovah said.

7 This is what he showed me: Look! Jehovah was standing on a wall made with a plumb line,* and there was a plumb line in his hand. **8** Then Jehovah said to me: "What do you see, A'mos?" So I said: "A plumb line." Jehovah then said: "Here I am putting a plumb line among my people Israel. I will no longer pardon them.[e] **9** The high places of Isaac[f] will be desolated, and the sanctuaries of Israel will be devastated;[g] and I will come against the house of Jer·o·bo'am with a sword."[h]

10 Am·a·zi'ah the priest of Beth'el[i] sent this message to King Jer·o·bo'am[j] of Israel: "A'mos is conspiring against you right in the midst of the house of Israel.[k] The land cannot put up with all his words.[l] For this is what A'mos says, 'Jer·o·bo'am will die by the sword, and Israel will surely go into exile from its land.'"[m]

12 Am·a·zi'ah then said to A'mos: "O visionary, go, run away to the land of Judah, earn your bread* there, and there you may prophesy.[n] **13** But you must no longer prophesy at Beth'el,[o] for it is the sanctuary

---

CHAP. 6
a Isa 10:5, 6
b Am 3:15

c 1Ki 21:13
  Isa 59:13
  Ho 10:4
  Am 5:7

d De 8:17, 18
  Ps 75:5

e De 28:49, 50
  2Ki 15:29
  2Ki 17:6
  Isa 7:20
  Isa 8:4
  Isa 10:5, 6
  Ho 10:6

f Nu 34:2, 8

CHAP. 7
g Jer 14:7
  Da 9:19

h Isa 37:4

Second Col.
a De 32:36
  Ps 106:44, 45
  Ho 11:8

b Ex 32:11

c Isa 1:9
  Am 7:2

d Ex 32:14

e Am 8:2

f 1Ki 12:25, 31
  1Ki 13:33

g Ho 10:8
  Am 5:5
  Am 8:14

h 2Ki 15:8, 10
  Ho 13:16

i 1Ki 12:32

j 2Ki 14:23

k Jer 26:8, 9
  Am 1:1

l Jer 18:18

m Am 5:5
  Am 6:7

n Isa 30:10

o Am 2:12

6:12 *Or "bitterness." **6:13** *Lit., "taken horns for ourselves." **6:14** *Or "the entrance of Hamath." #See Glossary. **7:1** *That is, during January and February. **7:2, 5** *Lit., "rise up?"

7:3, 6 *Or "felt regret over." **7:7** *Or "a plummet." **7:12** *Lit., "eat bread."

of a king[a] and the house of a kingdom."

14 Then A′mos answered Am·a·zi′ah: "I was not a prophet nor the son of a prophet; but I was a herdsman,[b] and I took care of sycamore fig trees.* 15 But Jehovah took me away from following the flock, and Jehovah said to me, 'Go, prophesy to my people Israel.'[c] 16 So now hear the word of Jehovah: 'You are saying, "Do not prophesy against Israel,[d] and do not preach[e] against the house of Isaac." 17 Therefore this is what Jehovah says: "Your wife will become a prostitute in the city, and your sons and your daughters will fall by the sword. Your land will be apportioned out with a measuring line, and you yourself will die in an unclean land; and Israel will surely go into exile from its land."'"[f]

8 This is what the Sovereign Lord Jehovah showed me: Look! There was a basket of summer fruit. 2 Then he said, "What do you see, A′mos?" I replied, "A basket of summer fruit." Then Jehovah said to me: "The end has come for my people Israel. I will no longer pardon them.[g] 3 'The songs of the temple will turn into wailing in that day,'[h] declares the Sovereign Lord Jehovah. 'There will be many carcasses thrown everywhere[i]—hush!'

4 Hear this, you who trample on the poor
And who bring the meek of the land to an end,[j]
5 Who say, 'When will the new moon festival be over,[k] that we may sell our grain,
And the Sabbath,[l] that we may offer grain for sale?
So that we may make the e′phah* measure smaller

And the shekel* weight greater,
To falsify our scales of deception;*
6 So that we may buy the needy for silver
And the poor for a pair of sandals,[b]
And sell the worthless part of the grain.'
7 Jehovah has sworn by the Pride of Jacob,[c]
'Never will I forget all their deeds.[d]
8 On this account the land* will tremble,
And every inhabitant in it will mourn.[e]
Will it not all rise like the Nile,
And surge and sink down like the Nile of Egypt?'[f]
9 'In that day,' declares the Sovereign Lord Jehovah,
'I will make the sun go down at high noon,
And I will darken the land on a bright day.[g]
10 I will turn your festivals into mourning[h]
And all your songs into dirges.*
I will put sackcloth on all hips and make every head bald;
I will make it like the mourning for an only son,
And the end of it like a bitter day.'
11 'Look! The days are coming,' declares the Sovereign Lord Jehovah,
'When I will send a famine into the land,
Not a famine for bread or a thirst for water,
But for hearing the words of Jehovah.[i]
12 They will stagger from sea to sea

CHAP. 7
a 1Ki 12:29, 32
  1Ki 13:1
b Am 1:1
c Jer 1:7
  Eze 2:3
  2Pe 1:21
d Jer 11:21
  Am 7:13
e Mic 2:6
f Le 26:33
  2Ki 17:6

CHAP. 8
g Am 4:12
  Am 7:8
h Ho 10:5
  Am 5:23
i Am 6:9, 10
j Am 2:6, 7
k Nu 10:10
l Ex 20:8

Second Col.
a Le 19:35, 36
  Ho 12:7
  Mic 6:10, 11
b Le 25:39
  Am 2:6
c De 33:26
  Ps 68:34
d Ho 8:13
e Ho 4:3
f Am 9:5
g Mic 3:6
h Ho 2:11
i Ps 74:9
  Eze 7:26
  Mt 4:4

7:14 *Or "was a nipper of sycamore figs." 8:5 *See App. B14.

8:8 *Or "earth." 8:10 *Or "songs of mourning."

And from the north to the east.*

They will rove about searching for the word of Jehovah, but they will not find it.

13 In that day beautiful virgins will faint,

Also young men, because of the thirst;

14 Those who swear by the guilt of Sa·mar′i·a[a] and who say, "As surely as your god lives, O Dan!"[b]

And, "As surely as the way of Be′er-she′ba[c] lives!"

They will fall, and they will not rise up again.'"[d]

9 I saw Jehovah[e] stationed above the altar, and he said: "Strike the head of the pillar, and the thresholds will shake. Cut them off at the head, and I will kill the last of them with the sword. No one who flees will get away, and no one trying to escape will succeed.[f]

2 If they dig down into the Grave,*

From there my hand will take them;

And if they go up to the heavens,

From there I will bring them down.

3 And if they hide themselves on the top of Car′mel,

From there I will search them out and take them.[g]

If they conceal themselves from my eyes on the bottom of the sea,

There I will command the serpent to bite them.

4 If they go into captivity before their enemies,

From there I will command the sword, and it will kill them;[h]

I will fix my eyes on them for bad, and not for good.[a]

5 For the Sovereign Lord, Jehovah of the armies, is the One who touches the land,*

So that it melts,[b] and all its inhabitants will mourn;[c]

And all of it will rise like the Nile,

And sink down like the Nile of Egypt.[d]

6 'The one who builds his stairs in the heavens

And establishes his structure* over the earth;

The one who summons the waters of the sea,

To pour them out on the surface of the earth'

—Jehovah is his name.'[e]

7 'Are you not like the sons of the Cush′ites to me, O people of Israel?' declares Jehovah.

'Did I not bring Israel up out of the land of Egypt,[g]

The Phi·lis′tines out of Crete,[h] and Syria out of Kir?'[i]

8 'Look! The eyes of the Sovereign Lord Jehovah are on the sinful kingdom,

And he will annihilate it from the surface of the land.[j]

But I will not completely annihilate the house of Jacob,'[k] declares Jehovah.

9 'For look! I am giving the command,

And I will shake the house of Israel among all the nations,[l]

Just as one shakes a sieve,

And not a pebble falls to the ground.

10 They will die by the sword, all the sinners of my people,

CHAP. 8
a Ho 8:5
 Ho 10:5

b 1Ki 12:28-30

c Am 5:5

d 2Ki 18:11
 Ho 13:16

CHAP. 9
e Isa 6:1
 Eze 1:27, 28

f Am 2:14

g Jer 23:24

h Le 26:33

Second Col.
a De 28:63, 65

b Mic 1:4

c Ho 4:3

d Am 8:8

e Job 36:27, 28
 Ps 135:7

f Ex 3:15
 Am 4:13
 Am 5:8

g Ex 12:51

h Jer 47:4

i 2Ki 16:9

j 1Ki 13:34
 2Ki 18:11

k Jer 30:11

l Le 26:33
 De 28:64

8:12 *Or "sunrise." 9:2 *Or "Sheol," that is, the common grave of mankind. See Glossary.

9:5 *Or "earth." 9:6 *Or "dome; vault."

Those who are saying, "The
calamity will not come
near us or reach us."'

11 'In that day I will raise up
the booth* of David[a] that
is fallen,
I will repair the[#] breaches,
And I will restore its ruins;
I will rebuild it as in the
days of long ago,[b]

12 So that they may take
possession of what is
remaining of E'dom,[c]
And all the nations on whom
my name has been called,'
declares Jehovah, who is
doing this.

13 'Look! The days are coming,'
declares Jehovah,
'When the plowman will
overtake the harvester,

9:11 *Or "tent; hut." ̎Or "their."

And the treader of grapes,
the one carrying seed;[a]
And the mountains will drip
with sweet wine,[b]
And all the hills will flow
with it.'*[c]

14 I will gather back the captives of my people Israel,[d]
And they will rebuild
the desolated cities and
inhabit them;[e]
They will plant vineyards
and drink their wine,[f]
And make gardens and eat
their fruit.'[g]

15 'I will plant them on their
land,
And they will never again be
uprooted
From their land that I have
given them,'[h] says Jehovah
your God."

9:13 *Lit., "will melt."

CHAP. 9
a Isa 9:6, 7
  Isa 16:5
  Jer 23:5
  Eze 37:24, 25
  Zec 12:8
  Lu 1:31-33
b 2Sa 7:11
  Ac 15:16-18
c Nu 24:18
  Isa 11:14
  Ob 18, 19

Second Col.
a Le 26:5
  Ho 2:22
b Joe 3:18
c Isa 35:1
  Isa 55:12
d Ezr 3:1
  Jer 30:3
  Eze 39:25
e Isa 61:4
  Eze 36:33
f Isa 65:21, 22
  Eze 28:25, 26
g Isa 62:8, 9
  Mic 4:4
h Isa 60:21
  Eze 34:27, 28
  Eze 37:25

OBADIAH

OUTLINE OF CONTENTS

---

1 The vision of O·ba·di'ah:*
This is what the Sovereign
Lord Jehovah says
regarding E'dom:[a]
"We have heard a report
from Jehovah,
An envoy has been sent
among the nations:
'Rise up, let us prepare for
battle against her.'"[b]

1 *Meaning "Servant of Jehovah."

2 "Look! I have made you
insignificant among the
nations;
You are utterly despised.[a]

3 The presumptuousness of
your heart has deceived
you,[b]
You who reside in the
retreats of the crag,
Dwelling in the height,
saying in your heart,

a Isa 21:11
  Eze 25:12-14
  Joe 3:19
  Am 1:11, 12

b Jer 49:14-16

Second Col.
a Jer 49:8

b Mal 1:4

'Who will bring me down to
　the earth?'

4 Even if you make your dwell-
　ing high* like the eagle,
　Or if you place your nest
　among the stars,
　I would bring you down from
　there," declares Jehovah.

5 "If thieves would come to
　you, robbers by night,
　(How utterly you will be
　destroyed!)*
　Would they not steal only
　what they wanted?
　Or if it were grape gatherers
　who would come to you,
　Would they not leave some
　gleanings behind?ᵃ

6 O how E'sau has been
　searched out!
　How his hidden treasures
　have been sought after!

7 They have driven you to
　the border.
　All your allies* have
　deceived you.
　The men at peace with you
　have prevailed against you.
　Those eating bread with you
　will place a net under you,
　But you will not discern it.

8 In that day," declares
　Jehovah,
　"Will I not destroy the wise
　ones out of E'domᵇ
　And discernment out of
　the mountainous region
　of E'sau?

9 And your warriors will be-
　come terrified,ᶜ O Te'man,ᵈ
　Because each one in the
　mountainous region of
　E'sau will be destroyed in
　the slaughter.ᵉ

10 Because of the violence done
　to your brother Jacob,ᶠ
　Shame will cover you,ᵍ
　And you will perish forever.ʰ

11 On the day when you stood
　off to the side,
　On the day when strangers
　took his army into
　captivity,ᵃ
　When foreigners entered his
　gate and cast lotsᵇ over
　Jerusalem,
　You acted like one of them.

12 You should not gloat over
　your brother's day on the
　day of his misfortune,ᶜ
　You should not rejoice over
　the people of Judah on the
　day of their perishing,ᵈ
　And you should not speak
　so arrogantly on the day
　of their distress.

13 You should not come into the
　gate of my people in the
　day of their disaster,ᵉ
　You should not gloat over
　his calamity in the day of
　his disaster,
　And you should not lay your
　hands on his wealth in the
　day of his disaster.ᶠ

14 You should not stand at the
　crossroads to slaughter
　his escapees,ᵍ
　And you should not hand
　over his survivors in the
　day of distress.ʰ

15 For the day of Jehovah
　against all the nations is
　near.ⁱ
　As you have done, so it will
　be done to you.ʲ
　The way you treated others
　will come back on your
　own head.

16 For in the way that you
　have drunk on my holy
　mountain,
　All the nations will keep
　drinking constantly.ᵏ
　They will drink and gulp
　down,
　And they will be as though
　they had never existed.

17 But on Mount Zion will be
　those who escape,ˡ

---

4 *Or possibly, "you fly high." 5 *Or
possibly, "How much would they destroy?" 7 *Or "those in covenant with
you.".

ᵃ De 24:21
　Jer 49:9, 10

ᵇ Jer 49:7

ᶜ Jer 49:22

ᵈ Ge 36:10, 11
　Eze 25:13
　Am 1:12

ᵉ Isa 34:5, 6

ᶠ Ge 27:41, 42
　Nu 20:20, 21
　Ps 83:4-6
　Ps 137:7
　Joe 3:19
　Am 1:11

ᵍ Jer 49:13

ʰ Mal 1:3, 4

Second Col.

ᵃ 2Ki 24:10, 16
　Jer 52:28

ᵇ Joe 3:3

ᶜ Mic 4:11

ᵈ La 4:21

ᵉ Zec 1:15

ᶠ Ps 137:7
　Eze 25:12

ᵍ Am 1:11

ʰ Jer 30:7

ⁱ Jer 9:25, 26
　Jer 25:32
　Joe 3:12, 14
　Mic 5:15

ʲ Eze 35:15

ᵏ Jer 25:17
　Jer 49:12

ˡ Joe 2:32

And it will be holy;[a]
And the house of Jacob
   will take possession of the
   things belonging to them.[b]

18 The house of Jacob will
   become a fire,
   The house of Joseph a flame,
   And the house of E'sau like
      stubble;
   They will set them ablaze
      and consume them,
   And there will be no survivor
      of the house of E'sau,[c]
   For Jehovah himself has
      spoken.

19 They will take possession of
   the Neg'eb and the mountainous region of E'sau,[d]
   Of the She·phe'lah and the
      land of the Phi·lis'tines.[e]
   They will take possession of

the field of E'phra·im and
   the field of Sa·mar'i·a,[a]
And Benjamin will take
   possession of Gil'e·ad.

20 To the exiles of this ram-
   part,*[b]
   To the people of Israel will
      belong the land of the
      Ca'naan·ites as far as
      Zar'e·phath.[c]
   And the exiles of Jerusalem,
      who were in Se·phar'ad,
      will possess the cities of
      the Neg'eb.[d]

21 And saviors will go up on
   Mount Zion
   To judge the mountainous
      region of E'sau,[e]
   And the kingship will
      become Jehovah's."[f]

20 *Or "fortification."

Side references (first column):
a Isa 4:3
  Zec 8:3

b Isa 14:2

c Jer 49:17, 18
  Eze 35:15

d Am 9:11, 12

e Isa 11:14
  Am 1:8

Second Col.
a 2Ki 17:24
  Jer 31:5, 6

b Ps 122:6, 7

c 1Ki 17:9

d Jer 13:19
  Jer 33:13

e Ps 149:6, 7
  Eze 35:11

f Ps 22:28
  Zec 14:9

JONAH

1 The word of Jehovah came to
   Jo'nah*[a] the son of A·mit'tai,
saying: **2** "Get up, go to Nin'e-
veh[b] the great city, and proclaim

judgment against her, for their
wickedness has come to my attention."

3 But Jo'nah got up to run
away from Jehovah to Tar'shish;
he went down to Jop'pa and

1:1 *Meaning "Dove."

CHAP. 1
a 2Ki 14:25
  Lu 11:29, 30

b Mt 12:41

found a ship going to Tar'shish. So he paid the fare and went aboard to go with them to Tar'shish, away from Jehovah.

4 Then Jehovah hurled a strong wind at the sea, and there was such a violent storm on the sea that the ship was about to be wrecked. **5** The mariners were so frightened that each of them began to call on his god for help. And they began throwing the articles of the ship into the sea, to make it lighter.[a] But Jo'nah had gone down into the inner part of the ship,* where he lay down and fell fast asleep. **6** The ship captain approached and said to him: "Why are you sleeping? Get up, call out to your god! Perhaps the true God will show his concern for us, and we will not perish."[b]

7 Then they said to one another: "Come, let us cast lots[c] to find out who is to blame for this calamity." So they cast lots, and the lot fell to Jo'nah.[d] **8** They said to him: "Please tell us, who is to blame for this calamity that has come upon us? What is your work, and where do you come from? What is your country, and from what people are you?"

9 He replied: "I am a Hebrew, and I fear* Jehovah the God of the heavens, the One who made the sea and the dry land."

10 At this the men became even more afraid, and they asked him: "What have you done?" (The men learned that he was running away from Jehovah, because he had told them.) **11** So they said to him: "What should we do to you to make the sea calm down for us?" For the sea was growing more and more stormy. **12** He replied: "Lift me up and throw me into the sea,

and the sea will calm down for you; for I know that it is because of me that this violent storm has come upon you." **13** However, the men rowed hard* to bring the ship back to dry land, but they could not, because the sea grew more and more stormy around them.

14 Then they called out to Jehovah and said: "Ah, now, O Jehovah, please, may we not perish because of this man!* Do not hold us responsible for innocent blood, since you have done as you pleased, O Jehovah." **15** Then they lifted Jo'nah up and threw him into the sea; and the sea ceased its raging. **16** Then the men were struck with great fear of Jehovah,[a] and they offered a sacrifice to Jehovah and made vows.

17 Jehovah now sent a huge fish to swallow Jo'nah, so that Jo'nah came to be in the belly of the fish for three days and three nights.[b]

2 Then Jo'nah prayed to Jehovah his God from the belly of the fish,[c] **2** and he said:

"Out of my distress I called
  out to Jehovah, and he
  answered me.[d]
Out of the depths* of the
  Grave# I cried for help.[e]
You heard my voice.
3 When you threw me to the
  depths, into the heart of
  the open sea,
Then the currents en-
  gulfed me.[f]
All your breakers and waves
  swept over me.[g]
4 And I said, 'I have been driv-
  en away from your sight!

CHAP. 1
a Ac 27:18, 38

b Jon 3:9

c Pr 16:33
  Pr 18:18

d Jos 7:14, 18
  1Sa 14:42, 43

Second Col.
a Da 6:26, 27

b Mt 12:39, 40
  Mt 16:4
  Lu 11:29, 30

CHAP. 2
c Mt 12:40

d Ps 120:1

e Ps 130:1, 2

f Ps 69:1

g Ps 42:7

1:5 *Or "decked vessel." 1:9 *Or "worship."

1:13 *Or "tried to work their way through." 1:14 *Or "because of the soul of this man!" 2:2 *Lit., "belly." #Or "Sheol," that is, the common grave of mankind. See Glossary.

How will I gaze again upon
your holy temple?'

5 Waters engulfed me and
threatened my life;*ᵃ

The watery deep closed in
on me.

Weeds were wrapped around
my head.

6 To the bottoms of the
mountains I sank down.

The bars of the earth were
closing upon me forever.

But out of the pit you
brought up my life,
O Jehovah my God.ᵇ

7 When my life* was ebbing
away, Jehovah was the
One whom I remembered.ᶜ

Then my prayer came in
to you, into your holy
temple.ᵈ

8 Those who are devoted to
the worthless idols forsake
their source of loyal love.*

9 But as for me, with the voice
of thanksgiving I will
sacrifice to you.

What I have vowed, I will
pay.ᵉ

Salvation is from Jehovah."ᶠ

10 In time Jehovah commanded the fish, and it vomited Joʹ-
nah out onto the dry land.

3 Then the word of Jehovah
came to Joʹnah a second
time, saying:ᵍ 2 "Get up, go to
Ninʹe·vehʰ the great city, and
proclaim to her the message that
I tell you."

3 So Joʹnah got up and went
to Ninʹe·vehⁱ in obedience to
the word of Jehovah.ʲ Now Ninʹ-
e·veh was a very large city*—a
walking distance of three days.
4 Then Joʹnah entered the city,
and walking a day's journey, he
was proclaiming: "In just 40 days

CHAP. 2
a Ps 69:1

b Ps 16:10
Ps 30:3
Isa 38:17
Ac 2:31

c Ps 142:2, 3
Ps 143:4, 5

d Ps 18:6

e Ps 50:14

f Ps 3:8
Isa 12:2

CHAP. 3
g Jon 1:1, 2

h Ge 10:8, 11
Na 1:1
Zep 2:13

i Ge 10:8, 11

j Jon 2:9

Second Col.
a Ex 9:20
Mt 12:41
Lu 11:32

b Lu 11:32

c Jer 18:7, 8
Eze 18:21-23
Jon 4:2

CHAP. 4
d Jon 1:3

e Ex 34:6
Ps 78:38
Ps 86:5
Ps 145:8

more, Ninʹe·veh will be overthrown."

5 And the men of Ninʹe·veh
put faith in God,ᵃ and they proclaimed a fast and put on sackcloth, from the greatest to the
least of them. 6 When the message reached the king of Ninʹe-
veh, he rose up from his throne
and took off his royal garment
and covered himself with sackcloth and sat down in the ashes. 7 Furthermore, he issued a
proclamation throughout Ninʹe-
veh,

"By the decree of the king
and his nobles: No man or beast,
herd or flock, should eat anything at all. They should not
take food, nor should they drink
any water. 8 Let them be covered with sackcloth, both man
and beast; and let them call out
earnestly to God and turn from
their evil ways and from the violence they practice. 9 Who
knows whether the true God
may reconsider* what he intends
to do and turn from his burning
anger, so that we may not perish?"

10 When the true God saw
what they did, how they had
turned back from their evil
ways,ᵇ he reconsidered* the calamity that he said he would
bring on them, and he did not
bring it.ᶜ

4 But this was highly displeasing to Joʹnah, and he became
hot with anger. 2 So he prayed
to Jehovah: "Ah, now, Jehovah,
was this not my concern when I
was in my own land? That is why
I tried to flee to Tarʹshishᵈ in the
first place; for I knew that you
are a compassionate* and merciful God, slow to anger and abundant in loyal love,ᵉ one who feels
grieved over calamity. 3 Now,
O Jehovah, please take away my

2:5 *Or "Waters encompassed me to the
soul." 2:7 *Or "soul." 2:8 *Or possibly, "their loyalty." 3:3 *Lit., "a city
great to God."

3:9 *Or "feel regret over." 3:10 *Or
"felt regret over." 4:2 *Or "gracious."

life,* for it is better for me to die than to live."ᵃ

4 Jehovah asked: "Is it right for you to be so angry?"

5 Jo'nah then went out of the city and sat down east of the city. He made a shelter for himself there and sat in its shade to see what would happen to the city.ᵇ **6** Jehovah God then provided a bottle-gourd plant* to grow up over Jo'nah, to give him shade for his head and to relieve his misery. And Jo'nah was very pleased with the bottle-gourd plant.

7 But the true God sent a worm at the break of dawn on the next day, and it attacked the bottle-gourd plant, and it withered. **8** When the sun began to shine, God also sent a scorching east wind, and the sun beat down on Jo'nah's head, and he grew faint. He kept asking to die,* and he kept saying, "It is better for me to die than to live."ᵃ

9 God asked Jo'nah: "Is it right for you to be so angry over the bottle-gourd plant?"ᵇ

At that he said: "I have a right to be angry, so angry that I want to die." **10** But Jehovah said: "You felt sorry for the bottle-gourd plant, which you did not work for, nor did you make it grow; it grew in one night and perished in one night. **11** Should I not also feel sorry for Nin'e·veh the great city,ᶜ in which there are more than 120,-000 men who do not even know right from wrong,* as well as their many animals?"ᵈ

CHAP. 4

a Nu 11:11, 15
1Ki 19:2, 4
Job 6:8, 9

b Jon 3:4

Second Col.

a Jon 4:3

b Jon 4:4

c Jon 3:3

d Ps 36:6
Ps 145:9

4:3 *Or "soul." **4:6** *Or possibly, "castor-oil plant."

4:8 *Or "that his soul might die." **4:11** *Or "know their right hand from their left."

MICAH

OUTLINE OF CONTENTS

1 The word of Jehovah that came to Mi′cah*[a] of Mo′resheth, in the days of Jo′tham,[b] A′haz,[c] and Hez·e·ki′ah,[d] kings of Judah,[e] and that he received in a vision concerning Sa·mar′i·a and Jerusalem:

2 "Hear, all you peoples!
  Pay attention, O earth and what fills you,
  And let the Sovereign Lord Jehovah serve as a witness against you[f]
  —Jehovah from his holy temple.

3 For look! Jehovah is going out from his place;
  He will come down and tread on earth's high places.

4 The mountains will melt under him,[g]
  And the valleys* will split apart
  Like wax before the fire,
  Like waters poured down a steep slope.

5 All of this is because of the revolt of Jacob,
  Because of the sins of the house of Israel.[h]
  What is the revolt of Jacob?
  Is it not Sa·mar′i·a?[i]
  And what are the high places of Judah?[j]
  Are they not Jerusalem?

6 I will make Sa·mar′i·a a heap of ruins of the field,
  A place for planting vineyards;
  I will hurl* her stones down into the valley,
  And I will lay bare her foundations.

7 All her graven images will be crushed to pieces,[k]
  And all the gifts for which she hired herself out* will be burned in the fire.[a]
  I will devastate all her idols.
  For she collected them from the wages of prostitution,
  And they will again become the wages of prostitutes."

8 Because of this I will wail and howl;[b]
  I will walk barefoot and naked.[c]
  My wailing will be like that of jackals,
  And my mourning like that of ostriches.

9 For her wound cannot be healed;[d]
  It has come as far as Judah.[e]
  The plague has spread to the gate of my people,
  to Jerusalem.[f]

10 "Do not announce it in Gath;
  You must not weep at all.
  In Beth-aph′rah* roll in the dust.

11 Cross over in nakedness and shame, O inhabitants* of Sha′phir.
  The inhabitants* of Za′a·nan have not come out.
  There will be wailing in Beth-e′zel, and it will take its support away from you.

12 For the inhabitants* of Ma′roth have waited for good,
  But what is bad has come down from Jehovah to the gate of Jerusalem.

13 Harness the chariot to the team of horses, O inhabitants* of La′chish.[g]
  You were the beginning of sin to the daughter of Zion,
  For in you were found the revolts of Israel.[h]

CHAP. 1

a Jer 26:18

b 2Ki 15:32-34
  2Ch 27:1, 2

c 2Ki 16:1, 2

d 2Ki 18:1-3
  2Ch 29:1, 2

e Isa 1:1
  Ho 1:1

f Ps 50:7

g Jg 5:5
  Ps 97:5

h 2Ki 17:7, 8

i Ho 7:1

j 2Ki 16:2, 4

k Le 26:30
  Ho 8:6

Second Col.

a Ho 2:5
  Ho 9:1

b Jer 4:19

c Isa 20:2

d Isa 1:5, 6
  Jer 15:18

e 2Ki 18:13
  Isa 8:7, 8

f 2Ch 32:2
  Mic 1:12

g Jos 15:20, 39
  2Ki 18:14

h 1Ki 14:16
  2Ki 16:2, 3
  Jer 3:8

1:1 *A shortened form of Michael or Micaiah, meaning "Who Is Like Jehovah?" 1:4 *Or "low plains." 1:6 *Lit., "pour." 1:7 *Or "all the wages of her prostitution." 1:10 *Or "In the house of Aphrah." 1:11-13 *Lit., "inhabitress."

14 So you will give parting* gifts to Moʹresh·eth-gath.

The houses of Achʹzibᵃ were something deceitful to the kings of Israel.

15 The conqueror* I will yet bring in to you,ᵇ O inhabitants* of Ma·reʹshah.ᶜ

As far as A·dulʹlamᵈ the glory of Israel will come.

16 Make yourselves bald and shear off your hair for your cherished children.

Make yourselves as bald as an eagle,

For they have been taken away from you into exile."ᵉ

2 "Woe to those who scheme what is harmful,

Who work out evil on their beds!

When morning light comes they carry it out,

Because it is in the power of their hand.ᶠ

2 They desire fields and seize them;ᵍ

Also houses, and they take them;

They defraud a man of his house,ʰ

A man of his inheritance.

3 Therefore this is what Jehovah says:

'Here I am devising against this family a calamityⁱ from which you will not escape.*ʲ

You will no longer walk haughtily,ᵏ for it is a time of calamity.ˡ

4 In that day people will recite a proverb concerning you,

And they will bitterly lament over you.ᵐ

They will say: "We are completely devastated!ⁿ

He caused the portion of my people to change

hands—how he removes it from me!ᵃ

To the unfaithful one he assigns our fields."

5 So you will have no one to stretch the measuring cord,

To allot the land in the congregation of Jehovah.

6 "Stop preaching!" they preach,

"They should not preach these things;

Humiliation will not overtake us!"

7 Is it being said, O house of Jacob:

"Has the spirit of Jehovah become impatient?

Are these his deeds?"

Do not my own words bring good to those walking uprightly?

8 But lately my own people have risen up as an enemy.

You openly strip off the majestic ornament with* the garment

From those passing by confidently, like those returning from war.

9 You drive the women of my people out from their delightful houses;

From their children you take away my splendor forever.

10 Get up and go, for this is no place of rest.

Because of uncleanness,ᵇ there is destruction, grievous destruction.ᶜ

11 If a man walks after wind and deception and tells this lie:

"I will preach to you about wine and alcoholic drink,"

Then he would be just the preacher for this people!ᵈ

12 I will certainly gather all of you, O Jacob;

CHAP. 1

a Jos 15:20, 44

b Isa 7:17

c 2Ch 11:5, 8

d Ne 11:25, 30

e De 28:41
  2Ki 17:6
  Isa 39:7

CHAP. 2

f 1Ki 21:7

g Ex 20:17
  1Ki 21:2
  Isa 5:8

h Jer 22:17
  Eze 22:12, 29

i Jer 18:11

j Am 2:14

k Isa 2:11

l Am 5:13

m Jer 9:10
  La 1:1

n Isa 6:11
  Jer 25:9
  Zep 1:2

Second Col.

a 2Ki 17:23

b Ps 106:38, 39

c Jer 9:19
  Jer 10:18

d 1Ki 22:6, 8
  Isa 9:15, 16
  Jer 6:13, 14
  Eze 13:2, 3

1:14 *Or "farewell." **1:15** *Or "dispossessor." #Lit., "inhabitress." **2:3** *Lit., "you will not remove your necks." **2:8** *Or possibly, "from."

I will surely collect the
  remaining ones of Israel
  together.[a]
In unity I will place them,
  like sheep in the pen,
Like a flock in its pasture;[b]
It will be noisy with people.'[c]

13 The one breaking out will
  go before them;
They will break out and pass
  through the gate and go
  out by it.[d]
Their king will pass through
  before them,
With Jehovah at their
  head."[e]

3 I said: "Hear, please, you
  heads of Jacob
And you commanders of the
  house of Israel.[f]
Should you not know what
  is just?

2 But you hate what is good[g]
  and love what is bad;[h]
You tear off the skin from
  my people and the flesh
  from their bones.[i]

3 You also eat the flesh of my
  people[j]
And strip off their skin,
Smashing their bones,
  crushing them to pieces,[k]
Like what is cooked in
  a pot,* like meat in a
  cooking pot.

4 At that time they will call to
  Jehovah for help,
But he will not answer them.
He will hide his face from
  them at that time,[l]
Because of their wicked
  deeds.[m]

5 This is what Jehovah says
  against the prophets who
  are leading my people
  astray,[n]
Who proclaim 'Peace!'[o]
  while they bite* with their
  teeth[p]

But who declare* war
  against him who puts
  nothing into their mouths:

6 'You will have night;[a] there
  will be no vision;[b]
There will only be darkness
  for you, no divination.
The sun will set on the
  prophets,
And the day will turn dark
  for them.[c]

7 The visionaries will be put
  to shame,[d]
And the diviners will be
  disappointed.
All of them will have to
  cover over the mustache,*
For there is no answer
  from God.'"

8 As for me, I am filled with
  power by the spirit of
  Jehovah,
And with justice and might,
To tell to Jacob his revolt
  and to Israel his sin.

9 Hear this, please, you heads
  of the house of Jacob
And you commanders of
  the house of Israel,[e]
Who detest justice and who
  make crooked all that is
  straight,[f]

10 Who build Zion with
  bloodshed and Jerusalem
  with unrighteousness.[g]

11 Her leaders* judge for a
  bribe,[h]
Her priests instruct for a
  price,[i]
And her prophets practice
  divination for money.*[j]
And yet they lean on
  Jehovah,^ saying:
"Is not Jehovah with us?[k]
No calamity will come
  upon us."[l]

12 So because of you,

CHAP. 2
a Isa 11:11
  Jer 23:3
  Jer 31:7, 8
  Mic 4:6
b Eze 34:11
c Eze 36:38
  Zec 8:22
d Isa 62:10
e Isa 49:10
  Isa 52:12

CHAP. 3
f Mic 3:9
g 1Ki 22:8
  Am 5:10
h 2Ch 19:2
i Eze 22:27
  Am 8:4
  Zep 3:3
j Eze 34:2, 3
k Isa 3:15
l La 3:44
m De 31:17, 18
  Isa 1:15
  Isa 3:11
n Isa 9:15, 16
  Isa 56:10
o Jer 23:16, 17
  Eze 13:10
p Eze 13:19
  Eze 34:2

Second Col.
a Jer 13:16
b Ps 74:9
  Eze 13:23
c Isa 59:9, 10
  Am 8:9
d Isa 29:10
e Mic 3:1
f De 27:19
  Jer 5:28
g Jer 22:13
h Isa 1:23
  Isa 5:20, 23
  Eze 22:12
i Jer 6:13
j Isa 56:10, 11
k Isa 48:1, 2
  Jer 7:4
l Am 9:10

3:3 *Or "wide-mouthed cooking pot."
3:5 *Or possibly, "when they have
something to chew." 3:5 *Or "sanctify." 3:7 *Or "cover their mouths." 3:11 *Lit., "heads."
*Or "silver." ^Or "they claim to lean on
Jehovah."

Zion will be plowed up as
a field,
Jerusalem will become
heaps of ruins,[a]
And the mountain of the
House* will become like
high places in a forest.[#b]

4 In the final part of the days,*
The mountain of the house
of Jehovah[c]
Will become firmly
established above the
top of the mountains,
And it will be raised up
above the hills,
And to it peoples will
stream.[d]

2 And many nations will go
and say:
"Come, let us go up to the
mountain of Jehovah
And to the house of the God
of Jacob.[e]
He will instruct us about
his ways,
And we will walk in his
paths."
For law* will go out of Zion,
And the word of Jehovah
out of Jerusalem.

3 He will render judgment
among many peoples[f]
And set matters straight*
respecting mighty nations
far away.
They will beat their swords
into plowshares
And their spears into
pruning shears.[g]
Nation will not lift up sword
against nation,
Nor will they learn war
anymore.[h]

4 They will sit,* each one
under his vine and under
his fig tree,[i]
And no one will make them
afraid,[j]

For the mouth of Jehovah
of armies has spoken.

5 For all the peoples will walk,
each in the name of its
god,
But we will walk in the
name of Jehovah our God[a]
forever and ever.

6 "In that day," declares
Jehovah,
"I will gather the one* who
was limping,
And collect together the
dispersed one,[b]
Along with those I treated
harshly.

7 I will make the one* who was
limping a remnant,[c]
And the one far removed
a mighty nation;[d]
And Jehovah will rule
as king over them in
Mount Zion,
From now on and forever.

8 As for you, O tower of the
flock,
The mound of the daughter
of Zion,[e]
To you it will come, yes, the
first* dominion will come,[f]
The kingdom belonging
to the daughter of
Jerusalem.[g]

9 Now why are you shouting
loudly?
Have you no king,
Or has your adviser
perished,
So that pain has seized you
like a woman giving birth?[h]

10 Writhe and groan,
O daughter of Zion,
Like a woman giving birth,
For now you will go from the
city and reside in the field.
You will go as far as to
Babylon,[i]
And there you will be
rescued;[j]

CHAP. 3
a Ps 79:1

b Jer 26:18

CHAP. 4
c Isa 11:9
Zec 8:3

d Ps 86:9
Isa 2:2-4
Isa 60:3
Re 15:4

e Jer 31:6
Zec 8:20, 21

f 1Sa 2:10
Ps 96:13
Isa 51:4, 5

g Ho 2:18
Zec 9:10

h Ps 72:7
Isa 9:7
Isa 60:18

i Zec 3:10

j Isa 54:14
Eze 34:25
Eze 39:25, 26

Second Col.
a Zec 10:12

b Ps 147:2
Isa 56:8
Eze 34:12, 16
Eze 37:21
Zep 3:19

c Isa 10:21
Mic 2:12
Mic 7:18

d Isa 60:22

e 2Sa 5:7

f Ob 21

g Zec 9:9

h Jer 30:6

i 2Ki 20:18
2Ch 36:17, 20

j Isa 45:13
Zec 2:7

3:12 *Or "the temple mount." #Or "like a wooded ridge." **4:1** *Or "In the last days." **4:2** *Or "instruction." **4:3** *Or "correct matters." **4:4** *Or "dwell."

4:6, 7 *Lit., "her." **4:8** *Or "former."

There Jehovah will buy you back from the hand of your enemies.[a]

11 Now many nations will be gathered against you;
They will say, 'Let her be defiled,
And let our eyes see this happen to Zion.'

12 But they do not know the thoughts of Jehovah,
They do not understand his purpose;*
For he will gather them like a row of newly cut grain to the threshing floor.

13 Get up and thresh, O daughter of Zion;[b]
For I will change your horns into iron,
And I will change your hooves into copper,
And you will pulverize many peoples.[c]
You will devote their dishonest profit to Jehovah,
And their resources to the true Lord of the whole earth."[d]

5 "Now you are slashing yourself,
O daughter under attack;
A siege is laid against us.[e]
With a rod they strike the judge of Israel on the cheek.[f]

2 And you, O Beth·le·hem Eph′ra·thah,[g]
The one too little to be among the thousands* of Judah,
From you will come out for me the one to be ruler in Israel,[h]
Whose origin is from ancient times, from the days of long ago.

3 So he will give them up
Until the time that she who is to give birth has given birth.

And the rest of his brothers will return to the people of Israel.

4 He will stand up and shepherd in the strength of Jehovah,[a]
In the superiority of the name of Jehovah his God.
And they will dwell in security,[b]
For now his greatness will reach the ends of the earth.[c]

5 And he will bring peace.[d]
Should the As·syr′i·an invade our land and tread on our fortified towers,[e]
We will raise up against him seven shepherds, yes, eight princes* of mankind.

6 They will shepherd the land of As·syr′i·a with the sword,[f]
And the land of Nim′rod[g] at its entrances.
And he will rescue us from the As·syr′i·an,[h]
When he invades our land and treads on our territory.

7 The remaining ones of Jacob will be in the midst of many peoples
Like dew from Jehovah,
Like showers of rain on vegetation
That do not put hope in man
Or wait for the sons of men.

8 The remaining ones of Jacob will be among the nations,
In the midst of many peoples,
Like a lion among the beasts of a forest,
Like a young lion* among flocks of sheep,
That passes through and pounces and tears in pieces;

CHAP. 4
a Ps 107:2, 3
  Isa 48:20
  Jer 15:21

b Isa 41:15

c Zec 9:13

d Jos 6:18, 19
  Isa 23:17, 18

CHAP. 5
e De 28:52

f Mt 26:67
  Joh 18:22
  Joh 19:3

g Ge 35:19
  Lu 2:4

h Ge 49:10
  1Ch 5:2
  Isa 9:6
  Mt 2:4-6
  Lu 1:32, 33
  Lu 2:11
  Joh 7:42

Second Col.
a Eze 34:23
  Eze 37:24

b Jer 23:5, 6

c Zec 9:9, 10

d Isa 9:6

e Isa 8:7

f Isa 33:1

g Ge 10:9-11

h Isa 14:25

4:12 *Or "counsel."   5:2 *Or "clans."   5:5 *Or "leaders."   5:8 *Or "a maned young lion."

And there is no one to
   rescue them.

9 Your hand will be raised
   over your adversaries,
   And all your enemies will be
   destroyed."

10 "In that day," declares
   Jehovah,
   "I will do away with your
   horses from your midst
   and destroy your chariots.

11 I will destroy the cities of
   your land
   And tear down all your
   fortified places.

12 I will put an end to the
   sorcery you practice,*
   And no one practicing
   magic will remain among
   you.*

13 I will destroy your graven
   images and your pillars
   from your midst,
   And you will no longer bow
   down to the work of your
   hands.*

14 I will uproot your sacred
   poles*c from your midst
   And annihilate your cities.

15 In anger and wrath I will
   execute vengeance
   On the nations that have
   not obeyed."

6 Hear, please, what Jehovah
   is saying.
   Get up, present a legal case
   before the mountains,
   And may the hills hear your
   voice.*

2 Hear, O mountains, the legal
   case of Jehovah,
   You firm foundations of the
   earth,*
   For Jehovah has a legal case
   with his people;
   It is against Israel that he
   will argue:*

3 "My people, what have
   I done to you?

How have I tired you out?*
   Testify against me.

4 For I brought you up out of
   the land of Egypt,*
   From the house of slavery
   I redeemed you;*
   I sent before you Moses,
   Aaron, and Mir'i·am.*

5 My people, remember,
   please, what King Ba'lak
   of Mo'ab proposed,*
   And what Ba'laam the son
   of Be'or answered him*
   —What took place from
   Shit'tim* to Gil'gal—
   So that you may know
   the righteous acts of
   Jehovah."

6 With what will I come before
   Jehovah?
   With what will I bow before
   God on high?
   Will I come before him with
   whole burnt offerings,
   With year-old calves?*

7 Will Jehovah be pleased
   with thousands of rams,
   With tens of thousands of
   torrents of oil?*
   Will I give my firstborn son
   for my revolt,
   The fruit of my body for
   my sin?*k

8 He has told you, O man,
   what is good.
   And what is Jehovah
   requiring* of you?
   Only to exercise justice,*l
   to cherish loyalty,△m
   And to walk in modesty*
   with your God!*

9 The voice of Jehovah calls
   out to the city;
   Those with practical wisdom
   will fear your name.
   Pay attention to the rod
   and to the one who
   appointed it.*

CHAP. 5

a Isa 2:6
  Isa 8:19

b Isa 2:8
  Eze 36:25
  Ho 14:3
  Zec 13:2

c Isa 27:9

CHAP. 6

d Isa 5:3

e Ps 50:1, 4
  Isa 1:2

f Isa 43:26
  Jer 2:35
  Ho 4:1

Second Col.

a Jer 2:5

b Ex 12:51
  De 4:20

c De 7:8

d Ex 15:20

e Nu 22:5, 6

f Nu 23:7, 8
  Nu 24:10
  Re 2:14

g Nu 25:1
  Nu 33:48, 49

h Jos 4:19

i 1Sa 15:22
  Ps 51:16, 17
  Isa 1:11

j Ps 50:8-15

k 2Ki 3:26, 27
  Eze 16:20

l Pr 21:3
  Isa 1:17
  Jer 22:3
  Eze 45:9
  Mic 12:6

m Pr 3:3
  Ho 6:6
  Zec 7:9

n Pr 8:13

o De 10:12, 13

p Isa 9:13

6:7 *Or "for the sin of my soul?" 6:8
*Or "asking back." #Or "to be just; to
be fair." △Or "to be kind and loyal in
your love." Lit., "to love loyal love."

5:12 *Lit., "from your hand." 5:14 *See
Glossary.

10 Are there still the treasures
　of wickedness in the house
　of the wicked
And the incomplete e'phah
　measure* that is detest-
　able?

11 Can I be morally clean*
　with wicked scales,
With a bag of fraudulent
　stone weights?[a]

12 For her rich men are full
　of violence,
And her inhabitants speak
　lies;[b]
Their tongue is deceitful in
　their mouth.[c]

13 "Therefore, I will wound
　you by striking you,[d]
Making you desolate
　because of your sins.

14 You will eat but not be
　satisfied;
You will be empty inside.[e]
What you remove, you will
　not carry off safely,
And what you do carry off,
　I will give to the sword.

15 You will sow seed, but you
　will not reap.
You will tread olives, but
　you will not use the oil;
And you will make new wine,
　but you will not drink no wine.[f]

16 For you observe the
　statutes of Om'ri and all
　the work of the house of
　A'hab,[g]
And you walk in accord with
　their advice.
That is why I will make you
　an object of horror
And her inhabitants some-
　thing to be whistled at;[h]
And you will bear the scorn
　of the peoples."[i]

7 Woe to me! I am like one who,
After the gathering of sum-
　mer fruit

And the gleaning following
　a grape harvest,
Finds no cluster of grapes
　to eat,
No early fig that I crave.*

2 The loyal one has perished*
　from the earth;
Among men there is no one
　upright.[a]
All of them lie in ambush
　for bloodshed.[b]
Each hunts his own brother
　with a dragnet.

3 Their hands are expert at
　doing what is bad;[c]
The prince is making
　demands,
The judge asks for a
　reward,[d]
The prominent one makes
　known his desires,*[e]
And they work it out
　together.#

4 Their best one is like thorns,
Their most upright one is
　worse than a thorn hedge.
The day of your watchmen
　and of your reckoning will
　come.[f]
Now they will panic.[g]

5 Do not put faith in your
　companion
Or trust a close friend.[h]
Guard what you say to
　the one who lies in your
　embrace.

6 For a son despises his
　father,
A daughter rises up against
　her mother,[i]
And a daughter-in-law is
　against her mother-in-law;[j]
A man's enemies are the
　men of his household.[k]

7 But as for me, I will
　keep on the lookout for
　Jehovah.[l]

CHAP. 6

a De 25:13
　Pr 11:1
　Ho 12:7

b Isa 59:3
　Mic 7:2

c Jer 9:3

d Isa 1:5

e Le 26:26
　Eze 4:16
　Ho 4:10

f De 28:38
　Jer 12:13
　Joe 1:10
　Am 5:11

g 1Ki 16:25, 30
　2Ki 16:2, 3
　2Ki 21:1, 3

h Jer 19:8

i Ps 44:13
　Jer 51:51
　La 5:1
　Da 9:16

Second Col.

CHAP. 7

a Isa 57:1

b Isa 59:7

c Jer 3:5
　Jer 4:22
　Eze 22:6

d Isa 1:23
　Mic 3:11

e 1Ki 21:5, 6

f Isa 10:3
　Eze 12:23
　Ho 9:7

g Isa 22:5

h Jer 9:4

i Eze 22:7

j Lu 12:53

k Jer 12:6
　Mt 10:35, 36

l Ps 123:2
　Isa 8:17

6:10 *See App. B14.　**6:11** *Or "be innocent."

7:1 *Or "my soul craves."　**7:2** *Or
"vanished."　**7:3** *Or "the craving of his
soul."　#Lit., "they weave it together."

I will show a waiting
attitude* for the God
of my salvation.[a]
My God will hear me.[b]

8 Do not rejoice over me,
O my enemy.*
Although I have fallen,
I will rise up;
Although I dwell in the
darkness, Jehovah will
be my light.

9 The wrath of Jehovah I will
bear
—For I have sinned against
him[c]—
Until he pleads my legal case
and brings about justice
for me.
He will bring me out to the
light;
I will look upon his
righteousness.

10 My enemy will also see,
And shame will cover her
who said to me:
"Where is Jehovah your
God?"[d]
My eyes will look upon her.
Now she will be trampled
like mud in the streets.

11 It will be a day for building
your stone walls;
On that day the boundary
will be extended.*

12 On that day they will come
to you
All the way from As·syr'i·a
and the cities of Egypt,
From Egypt all the way to
the River;*
From sea to sea and from
mountain to mountain.[e]

13 And the land will become
desolate because of its
inhabitants,
As a result of what they
have done.*

CHAP. 7

a Ps 25:5
Ps 62:1
La 3:26

b Ps 40:1
Isa 12:2
Isa 25:9

c La 1:18

d Ps 79:10
Ps 115:2
Joe 2:17

e Isa 11:16
Isa 27:13
Ho 11:11

_____

Second Col.

a Isa 40:11

b Jer 50:19
Eze 34:23

c Ps 78:12
Isa 63:11
Jer 23:7, 8

d Ps 126:2
Isa 26:11
Isa 66:18

e Isa 49:23

f Jer 33:9

g Ex 34:6, 7
Isa 1:18
Isa 44:22
Jer 50:20
Da 9:9

h Jer 23:3
Joe 2:32

i Ps 103:9
Isa 57:16
La 3:22

j De 30:3
Ps 103:8, 13
Ho 2:19

k Ps 103:12
Isa 55:7
Jer 31:34

l Ge 22:17
Ps 105:8-11
Lu 1:72, 73
Ac 3:25, 26

14 Shepherd your people with
your staff, the flock of
your inheritance,[a]
The one who was living
alone in a forest—in the
midst of an orchard.
Let them feed on Ba'shan
and Gil'e·ad[b] as in the
days of old.

15 "As in the days when you
came out of the land of
Egypt,
I will show him wonderful
things.[c]

16 Nations will see and be
ashamed despite all their
might.[d]
They will put their hand
over their mouth;
Their ears will become deaf.

17 They will lick the dust like
serpents;[e]
Like the reptiles of the
earth they will come
trembling out of their
strongholds.
To Jehovah our God they
will come in dread,
And they will be in fear
of you."[f]

18 Who is a God like you,
Pardoning error and
passing over the
transgression[g] of
the remnant of his
inheritance?[h]
He will not hold onto his
anger forever,
For he delights in loyal love.[i]

19 He will again show us
mercy;[j] he will conquer*
our errors.
You will throw all their
sins into the depths of
the sea.[k]

20 You will show faithfulness
to Jacob,
Loyal love to Abraham,
As you swore to our fore-
fathers from the days
of old.[l]

_____

7:7 *Or "I will wait patiently." 7:8 *In
Hebrew, the word for "enemy" is in
the feminine gender. 7:11 *Or possi-
bly, "the decree will be far away." 7:12
*That is, the Euphrates. 7:13 *Lit.,
"Because of the fruitage of their deeds."

7:19 *Or "tread down; subdue."

NAHUM

1 A pronouncement against Nin·e·veh:ᵃ The book of the vision of Na·hum* the El′kosh·ite:

2 Jehovah is a God who requires exclusive devotionᵇ and takes vengeance; Jehovah takes vengeance and is ready to express his wrath.ᶜ Jehovah takes vengeance against his foes, And he stores up wrath for his enemies.

3 Jehovah is slow to angerᵈ and great in power,ᵉ But by no means will Jehovah hold back due punishment.ᶠ His path is in destructive wind and storm, And the clouds are the dust of his feet.ᵍ

4 He rebukes the sea,ʰ and he dries it up; And he makes all the rivers run dry.ⁱ Ba′shan and Car′mel wither,ʲ And the blossoms of Leb′a·non wither.

5 Mountains quake because of him, And the hills melt.ᵏ The earth will be in an upheaval because of his face, Along with the land and all those dwelling in it.ᵃ

6 Who can stand before his indignation?ᵇ And who can withstand the heat of his anger?ᶜ His wrath will be poured out like fire, And the rocks will be shattered because of him.

7 Jehovah is good,ᵈ a stronghold in the day of distress.ᵉ He is mindful of* those seeking refuge in him.ᶠ

8 With a sweeping flood he will make a complete extermination of her* place, And darkness will pursue his enemies.

9 What will you plot against Jehovah? He is causing a complete extermination. Distress will not arise a second time.ᵍ

10 For they are interwoven like thorns, And they are like those drunk with beer;* But they will be consumed like dry stubble.

CHAP. 1

a Isa 10:12
  Na 3:7
  Zep 2:13

b Ex 20:5

c De 32:35, 41
  Isa 59:18

d Nu 14:18

e Job 9:4

f Ex 34:6, 7

g Job 38:1

h Job 38:11
  Ps 104:6, 7
  Ps 107:29

i Jos 3:16

j Isa 33:9
  Am 1:2

k 2Sa 22:8
  Ps 68:7, 8

__Second Col.__

a Ps 97:4, 5
  Isa 24:1

b Jer 10:10

c De 32:22

d Ps 136:1
  Mt 19:17

e Ps 46:1
  Ps 91:2
  Pr 18:10
  Isa 25:4

f Ps 1:6

g Isa 10:24, 25

1:1 *Meaning "Comforter."

1:7 *Or "takes care of." Lit., "knows."
1:8 *That is, Nineveh's. 1:10 *Or "wheat beer."

11 From you will come one who
      plots evil against Jehovah,
   Giving worthless advice.
12 This is what Jehovah says:
   "Though they were at full
      strength and numerous,
   Even so they will be cut
      down and will pass away.*
   I have afflicted you,* but
      I will afflict you no more.
13 And now I will break his
      yoke bar from off you,ª
   And I will tear your bonds
      in two.
14 Jehovah has commanded
      concerning you,*
   'Your name will not be
      perpetuated further.
   I will do away with the
      carved images and metal
      statues* from the houseᐃ
      of your gods.
   I will make a grave for
      you, because you are con-
      temptible.'
15 Look! On the mountains are
      the feet of one bringing
      good news,
   The one proclaiming peace.ᵇ
   Celebrate your festivals,ᶜ
      O Judah, pay your vows,
   For the worthless one will
      never pass through you
      again.
   He will be utterly destroyed."

2 One who scatters has come
      up against you.*ᵈ
   Guard the fortifications.
   Keep watch over the road.
   Brace yourselves* and
      muster all your strength.
2 For Jehovah will restore the
      pride of Jacob,
   Along with the pride of
      Israel,
   For the devastators have
      devastated them;ᵉ

   And they have ruined their
      shoots.
3 The shields of his mighty
      men are dyed red,
   His warriors are dressed
      in crimson.
   The iron fittings of his war
      chariots flash like fire
   In the day he prepares for
      battle,
   And the juniper spears are
      brandished.
4 The war chariots race madly
      through the streets.
   They rush up and down the
      public squares.
   They shine like burning
      torches and flash like
      lightning.
5 He will summon his officers.
   They will stumble as they
      advance.
   They rush to her wall;
   They set up the barricade.
6 The gates of the rivers will
      be opened,
   And the palace will be
      dissolved.*
7 It has been decreed:*
      She is exposed,
   She is carried away, and
      her slave girls moan;
   They sound like doves as
      they beat their breasts.*
8 Throughout her days
      Nin′e·vehª was like a pool
      of waters,
   But now they are fleeing.
   "Stand still! Stand still!"
   But no one is turning back.ᵇ
9 Plunder silver, plunder gold!
   There is no end to the
      treasures.
   It is stocked with all sorts
      of precious things.
10 The city is empty, desolate,
      devastated!ᶜ
   Their hearts melt in fear,
      their knees buckle, their
      hips tremble;

CHAP. 1
a Isa 14:25

b Isa 52:7
  Ro 10:15

c De 16:16

CHAP. 2
d Jer 25:9

e 2Ki 17:6

Second Col.
a Ge 10:8, 11

b Zep 2:13

c Zep 2:15

1:12 *Or possibly, "and he will pass
through." *That is, Judah. 1:14 *That
is, Assyria. *Or "molten statues."
ᐃOr "temple." 2:1 *That is, Nineveh.
*Lit., "Strengthen the hips." 2:6 *Or "will collapse." 2:7 *Or
"fixed." *Lit., "hearts."

All their faces are flushed.

11 Where is the lair of lions,[a]
where the young lions* feed,
Where the lion goes out leading its cub,
With no one to make them afraid?

12 The lion tore apart enough prey for his cubs
And strangled for his lionesses.
He kept his dens filled with prey,
His lairs with torn animals.

13 "Look! I am against you," declares Jehovah of armies,[b]
"I will burn up her war chariots in smoke,[c]
And the sword will devour your young lions.*
I will cut off your prey from the earth,
And the sound of your messengers will be heard no more."[d]

3 Woe to the city of bloodshed!
She is completely full of deception and robbery.
She is never without prey!

2 There is the crack of the whip and the rattle of wheels,
The dashing horse and the bounding chariot.

3 The mounted horseman, the flashing sword, and the glittering spear,
The multitude of the slain and the heaps of carcasses
—There is no end to the dead bodies.
They keep stumbling over the dead bodies.

4 This is because of the many acts of prostitution of the prostitute,
She who is attractive and charming, a mistress of sorceries,

Who ensnares nations by her prostitution and families by her sorceries.

5 "Look! I am against you,"* declares Jehovah of armies,[a]
"I will lift your skirts up over your face;
I will cause nations to see your nakedness,
And kingdoms your disgrace.

6 And I will throw filth on you And make you despicable;
I will make a spectacle of you.[b]

7 Everyone who sees you will flee from you[c] and say,
'Nin·e·veh has been devastated!
Who will sympathize with her?'
Where will I find comforters for you?'

8 Are you better than No-a′mon,*[d] which sat by the Nile canals?[e]
Waters surrounded her;
Her wealth was the sea and her wall was the sea.

9 E·thi·o′pi·a was her source of boundless strength, also Egypt.
Put[f] and the Lib′y·ans were your helpers.[g]

10 But even she became an exile;
She went into captivity.[h]
Her children also were dashed to pieces on every street corner.*
They cast lots over her honored men,
And all her great men have been bound with fetters.

11 You will also become drunk;[i]
You will go into hiding.
You will seek refuge from the enemy.

CHAP. 2
a Jer 2:14, 15
  Jer 50:17

b Isa 10:12

c Ps 46:9
  Isa 37:24

d 2Ki 18:17

Second Col.

CHAP. 3
a Na 2:13

b Zep 2:15

c Na 2:8

d Jer 46:25
  Eze 30:14

e Isa 19:6

f Ge 10:6

g 2Ch 16:8
  Jer 46:8, 9

h Isa 20:4

i Ps 75:8
  Jer 25:15

2:11, 13 *Or "maned young lions."

3:5 *That is, Nineveh. 3:8 *That is, Thebes. 3:10 *Lit., "at the head of all streets."

12 All your fortifications are
like fig trees with the first
ripe fruits;
If they are shaken, they
will fall into the mouth
of devourers.

13 Look! Your troops are like
women in your midst.
The gates of your land will
be wide open for your
enemies.
Fire will consume the bars
of your gates.

14 Draw water for the siege!a
Strengthen your fortifica-
tions.
Go down into the mire and
tread the clay;
Grab hold of the brick mold.

15 Even there fire will consume
you.
A sword will cut you down.b
It will devour you as the
young locusts do.c
Make yourself as numerous
as the young locusts!
Yes, make yourself as
numerous as the locusts!

16 You have multiplied your
merchants more than the
stars of the heavens.

The young locust strips off
its skin and flies away.

17 Your guards are like the
locust,
And your officers like a
locust swarm.
They camp in the stone pens
on a cold day,
But when the sun shines,
they fly away;
And no one knows where
they are.

18 Your shepherds are drowsy,
O king of As·syr′i·a;
Your nobles stay in their
residences.
Your people are scattered
on the mountains,
And no one is gathering
them together.a

19 There is no relief for your
catastrophe.
Your wound is beyond
healing.
All those hearing the report
about you will clap their
hands;b
For who has not suffered
from your relentless
cruelty?"c

CHAP. 3
a 2Ch 32:3, 4

b Zep 2:13

c Ex 10:14, 15

Second Col.
a Na 2:8

b Zep 2:15

c Isa 10:5, 6
Isa 37:18

HABAKKUK

OUTLINE OF CONTENTS

1 A pronouncement that Ha·bak′kuk* the prophet received in a vision:

2 How long, O Jehovah, must I cry for help, but you do not hear?[a]

How long must I ask for help from violence, but you do not intervene?*[b]

3 Why do you make me witness wrongdoing?

And why do you tolerate oppression?

Why are destruction and violence before me?

And why do quarreling and conflict abound?

4 So law is paralyzed,

And justice is never carried out.

For the wicked surround the righteous;

That is why justice is perverted.[c]

5 "Look among the nations and pay attention!

Stare in amazement and be astounded;

For something will happen in your days

That you will not believe even if it is told to you.[d]

6 For here I am raising up the Chal·de′ans,[e]

The ruthless and impetuous nation.

They sweep through vast stretches of the earth

To seize homes not theirs.[f]

7 They are frightening and fearsome.

They establish their own justice and authority.*[g]

8 Their horses are swifter than leopards,

And they are fiercer than wolves in the night.[h]

Their warhorses gallop forward;

Their horses come from far away.

They swoop down like the eagle rushing to feed.[a]

9 All of them come bent on violence.[b]

The assembling of their faces is like the east wind,[c]

And they scoop up captives like sand.

10 They scoff at kings

And laugh at high officials.[d]

They laugh at every fortified place;

They pile up a dirt ramp and capture it.

11 Then they move forward like the wind and pass through,

But they will become guilty,[f]

Because they credit their power to their god."*[g]

12 Are you not from everlasting, O Jehovah?[h]

O my God, my Holy One, you do not die.*[i]

O Jehovah, you appointed them to execute judgment;

My Rock,[j] you established them for punishment.*[k]

13 Your eyes are too pure to look on what is evil,

And you cannot tolerate wickedness.[l]

Why, then, do you tolerate the treacherous[m]

And keep silent when a wicked man swallows up someone more righteous than he is?[n]

14 Why do you make man like the fish of the sea,

Like creeping things that have no ruler?

15 All of these he* hauls up with a fishhook.

He catches them in his dragnet,

And he gathers them in his fishing net.

CHAP. 1

a Ps 13:1

b Ps 22:1
Ps 74:10
Re 6:10

c Job 12:6
Ps 12:8
Ec 8:11
Isa 1:21
Ac 7:52, 53

d Isa 28:21
Isa 29:14
La 4:11, 12
Ac 13:40, 41

e Jer 22:7
Jer 46:2

f De 28:49-51
Jer 5:15-17
Jer 6:22, 23
Eze 23:22, 23

g Jer 39:5-7
Da 5:18, 19

h Jer 5:6

Second Col.

a Jer 4:13
La 4:19
Eze 17:3

b Jer 25:9

c Isa 27:8
Eze 17:10

d 2Ki 24:12

e Jer 32:24
Jer 52:7

f Isa 47:5, 6
Jer 51:24
Zec 1:15

g Da 5:1, 4

h Ps 90:2
Ps 93:2
Re 1:8

i 1Ti 1:17
Re 15:3

j De 32:4

k Jer 30:11

l Ps 5:4, 5

m Jer 12:1

n Ps 35:21, 22

1:1 *Possibly meaning "Ardent Embrace." 1:2 *Or "save." 1:7 *Or "dignity."

1:11 *Or possibly, "their power is their god." 1:12 *Or possibly, "we will not die." *Or "for reproving." 1:15 *That is, the Chaldean enemy.

That is why he rejoices
greatly.[a]

16 That is why he offers
sacrifices to his dragnet
And makes sacrifices*
to his fishing net;
For by them his portion
is rich,[b]
And his food is choice.

17 Will he then keep emptying
out his dragnet?*
Will he go on slaughtering
nations without compas-
sion?[b]

2 At my guardpost I will keep
standing,[c]
And I will station myself
on the rampart.
I will keep watch to see
what he will speak by
means of me
And what I will reply when
I am reproved.

2 Jehovah then answered me:
"Write down the vision,
and inscribe it clearly on
tablets,[d]
So that the one reading aloud
from it may do so easily.*[e]

3 For the vision is yet for its
appointed time,
And it is rushing toward its
end,* and it will not lie.
Even if it should delay,#
keep in expectation of it!▵[f]
For it will without fail come
true.
It will not be late!

4 Look at the one who is
proud;*
He is not upright within
himself.
But the righteous one will
live by his faithfulness.#[g]

5 Indeed, because the wine
is treacherous,

The arrogant man will not
reach his goal.
He makes his appetite*
as large as the Grave;#
He is like death and cannot
be satisfied.
He keeps gathering all
the nations
And collecting for himself
all the peoples.[a]

6 Will not all of these speak
a proverb, an allusion,
and riddles against him?[b]
They will say:
'Woe to him who accumu-
lates what is not his
—For how long?—
And who makes even greater
his own debt!

7 Will not your creditors rise
up suddenly?
They will wake up and
violently shake you,
And you will become some-
thing for them to plunder.[c]

8 Because you plundered
many nations,
All the rest of the peoples
will plunder you,[d]
Because of your shedding
men's blood
And your violence to the
earth,
To the cities and those living
in them.[e]

9 Woe to the one who makes
evil gain for his house,
So as to set his nest on the
height,
To escape the grasp of
calamity!

10 You have plotted shame
against your house.
By wiping out many peoples
you sin against yourself.*[f]

11 For a stone will cry out from
the wall,
And from the woodwork
a rafter will answer it.

CHAP. 1
a Jer 50:11

b 2Ch 36:17
Na 3:7

CHAP. 2
c Isa 21:8
Mic 7:7

d Ex 17:14

e De 31:9, 11

f Mic 7:7

g Joh 3:36
Ro 1:17
Ga 3:11
Heb 10:38

Second Col.
a Isa 14:16, 17

b Isa 14:4

c Jer 51:11

d Isa 13:19
Jer 27:6, 7
Zec 2:7-9

e 2Ch 36:17
Ps 137:8

f Isa 14:20

1:16 *Or "sacrificial smoke." #Lit.,
"well-oiled." 1:17 *Or possibly, "keep
drawing his sword?" 2:2 *Or "fluently." 2:3 *Or "fulfillment." #Or "if it
seems to delay." ▵Or "wait eagerly for
it!" 2:4 *Or "Look! His soul is swelled
up." #Or possibly, "faith; belief."

2:5 *Or "soul." #Or "Sheol," that is, the
common grave of mankind. See Glossary. 2:10 *Or "your soul."

12 Woe to the one who builds
a city by bloodshed,
And who establishes a town
by unrighteousness!

13 Look! Is it not from Jehovah
of armies that peoples will
work hard to feed the fire,
And that nations tire themselves out for nothing?[a]

14 For the earth will be filled
with the knowledge of the
glory of Jehovah
As the waters cover the sea.[b]

15 Woe to the one who gives
his companions something
to drink,
Adding to it rage and anger,
to make them drunk,
In order to look on their
nakedness!

16 You will be glutted with
dishonor rather than glory.
You too—drink and expose
your uncircumcised
condition.*
The cup in the right hand of
Jehovah will come around
to you,[c]
And disgrace will cover over
your glory;

17 For the violence done to
Leb′a·non will cover you,
And the destruction that
terrified the beasts will
come upon you,
Because of your shedding
men's blood
And your violence to the
earth,
To the cities and those living
in them.[d]

18 Of what benefit is a carved
image
When its maker has
carved it?
Of what benefit is a metal
statue* and a teacher of
lies,
Even though its maker trusts
in it,

CHAP. 2
a Jer 51:58

b Ps 72:19
Isa 11:9
Zec 14:9

c Ps 75:8
Isa 51:22, 23
Jer 25:28
Jer 51:57

d Ps 137:8
Jer 50:28
Jer 51:24

Second Col.
a Isa 42:17
Isa 44:19, 20
Isa 45:20

b Isa 40:19
Isa 46:6

c Jer 51:17

d Isa 6:1

e Ps 76:8
Ps 115:3
Zec 2:13

CHAP. 3
f La 3:32

g De 33:2
Jg 5:4
Ps 68:7, 8

h Ex 19:16

i Ex 13:21

j Nu 14:11, 12
Nu 16:46
Nu 25:1, 9

k Isa 13:13
Hag 2:21

l Ex 14:25
Ex 23:27

m Ps 114:1, 4
Na 1:5

Making worthless gods that
are speechless?[a]

19 Woe to the one who says to
a piece of wood, "Awake!"
Or to a speechless stone,
"Wake up! Instruct us!"
Look! It is overlaid in gold
and silver,[b]
And there is no breath at all
within it.[c]

20 But Jehovah is in his holy
temple.[d]
Be silent before him, all the
earth!"[e]

3 The prayer of Ha·bak′kuk
the prophet, in dirges:*

2 O Jehovah, I have heard
the report about you.
I am in awe, O Jehovah,
of your activity.
In the midst of the years*
bring it to life!
In the midst of the years*
make it known.
May you remember to show
mercy during the turmoil.[f]

3 God came from Te′man,
The Holy One from
Mount Pa′ran.[g] (Selah)*
His majesty covered the
heavens;[h]
With his praise the earth
was filled.

4 His brightness was like
the light.[i]
Two rays flashed from his
hand,
Where his strength was
hidden.

5 Before him went pestilence,[j]
And burning fever followed
at his feet.

6 He stood still and shook
the earth.[k]
With a look, he made nations
leap.[l]
The eternal mountains were
smashed,
And the ancient hills bowed
down.[m]

2:16 *Or possibly, "and stagger."   2:18 *Or "molten statue."

3:1 *Or "songs of mourning."   3:2 *Or possibly, "In our time."   3:3 *See Glossary.

The paths of long ago are his.

7 I saw trouble in the tents of Cu'shan.
　The tent cloths of the land of Mid'i·an trembled.[a]

8 Is it against the rivers, O Jehovah,
　Is it against the rivers that your anger is burning?
　Or is your fury against the sea?[b]
　For you rode on your horses;[c]
　Your chariots were victorious.*[d]

9 Your bow is uncovered and ready.
　The rods* are assigned with an oath.# (Selah)
　You split the earth with rivers.

10 Mountains writhed in pain at the sight of you.[e]
　A downpour of waters swept through.
　The deep roared with its voice.[f]
　It lifted its hands high.

11 Sun and moon stood still in their lofty abode.[g]
　Your arrows went out like the light.[h]
　The lightning of your spear was brilliant.

12 You marched through the earth with indignation.
　You trampled* the nations in anger.

13 You went out for the salvation of your people,
　to save your anointed one.
　You crushed the leader* of the house of the wicked.
　It was exposed from the foundation to the top.# (Selah)

14 You pierced the head of his warriors with his own weapons*
　When they stormed out to scatter me.
　They were overjoyed to devour an afflicted one in secret.

15 Through the sea you trod with your horses,
　Through the surging of vast waters.

16 I heard and I trembled within;*
　At the sound my lips quivered.
　Rottenness entered my bones;[a]
　My legs beneath me were shaking.
　But I quietly wait for the day of distress,[b]
　For it is coming upon the people who attack us.

17 Although the fig tree may not blossom,
　And there may be no fruit on the vines;
　Although the olive crop may fail,
　And the fields* may produce no food;
　Although the flock may disappear from the pen,
　And there may be no cattle in the stalls;

18 Yet, as for me, I will exult in Jehovah;
　I will be joyful in the God of my salvation.[c]

19 The Sovereign Lord Jehovah is my strength;[d]
　He will make my feet like those of a deer
　And cause me to tread on high places.[e]

To the director;
with my stringed instruments.

CHAP. 3
a Ex 15:14, 15
　Nu 22:3, 4

b Ps 114:1, 3
　Isa 50:2
　Na 1:4

c De 33:26

d Ps 68:17

e Ex 19:18
　Ps 114:1, 4

f Ps 77:16

g Jos 10:12

h Ps 77:17, 18

Second Col.
a Ps 119:120
　Jer 23:9
　Da 8:27

b Ps 42:5
　Isa 26:20
　La 3:26

c Ex 15:2
　1Sa 2:1
　Ps 18:2
　Ps 27:1
　Isa 61:10

d Isa 12:2
　Php 4:13

e 2Sa 22:34

3:8 *Or "salvation." 3:9 *Or possibly, "arrows." #Or possibly, "The sworn oaths of the tribes are stated." 3:12 *Lit., "threshed." 3:13 *Lit., "head." #Lit., "neck."

3:14 *Lit., "his rods." 3:16 *Lit., "and my belly trembled." 3:17 *Or "terraces."

ZEPHANIAH

1 The word of Jehovah that came to Zeph·a·ni'ah* son of Cush'i son of Ged·a·li'ah son of Am·a·ri'ah son of Hez·e·ki'ah in the days of Jo·si'ah[a] son of A'mon[b] the king of Judah:

2 "I will completely sweep away everything from the surface of the ground," declares Jehovah.[c]

3 "I will sweep away man and beast.
I will sweep away the birds of the heavens and the fish of the sea,[d]
And the stumbling blocks*[e] along with the wicked ones;
And I will remove mankind from the surface of the ground," declares Jehovah.

4 "I will stretch out my hand against Judah
And against all the inhabitants of Jerusalem,
And I will wipe out from this place every vestige* of Ba'al,[f]
The name of the foreign-god priests along with the priests,[g]

5 And those who bow down on the rooftops to the army of the heavens,[a]
And those who bow down and pledge loyalty to Jehovah[b]
While pledging loyalty to Mal'cam;[c]

6 And those who turn away from following Jehovah[d]
And who do not seek Jehovah or inquire of him."[e]

7 Be silent before the Sovereign Lord Jehovah, for the day of Jehovah is near.[f]
Jehovah has prepared a sacrifice; he has sanctified those he invited.

8 "On the day of Jehovah's sacrifice I will call to account the princes,
The sons of the king,[g] and all those wearing foreign clothing.

9 I will call to account everyone who climbs onto the platform* on that day,
Those who fill their master's house with violence and deception.

10 On that day," declares Jehovah,

CHAP. 1
a 2Ki 22:1, 2
    Jer 1:2

b 2Ki 21:18-20

c 2Ki 22:16
    Isa 6:11
    Jer 6:8

d Jer 4:25

e Eze 14:3

f Nu 25:3
    Jg 2:11, 13
    2Ch 28:1, 2
    Jer 11:17

g 2Ki 23:5

Second Col.
a 2Ch 33:1, 3
    Jer 19:13

b Isa 48:1

c Jos 23:6, 7
    1Ki 11:33
    Jer 49:1

d Isa 1:4
    Jer 2:13

e Isa 43:22

f Joe 2:1
    2Pe 3:10

g 2Ki 25:7
    Jer 39:6

1:1 *Meaning "Jehovah Has Concealed (Treasured Up)." **1:3** *Evidently, objects or activities connected with idolatry. **1:4** *Or "trace."

1:9 *Or "podium; threshold." Possibly the platform of the king's throne.

"There will be the sound of an outcry from the Fish Gate,[a]

A wailing from the second quarter of the city,[b]

And a loud crash from the hills.

11 Wail, you inhabitants of Mak′tesh,*

For all the tradesmen# have been done away with;△

All those weighing out silver have been destroyed.

12 At that time I will carefully search Jerusalem with lamps,

And I will call to account the complacent ones,*

who say in their heart,

'Jehovah will not do good, and he will not do bad.'[c]

13 Their wealth will be plundered and their houses will be devastated.[d]

They will build houses, but they will not occupy them;

And they will plant vineyards, but they will not drink wine from them.[e]

14 The great day of Jehovah is near![f]

It is near and it is approaching very quickly!*[g]

The sound of the day of Jehovah is bitter.[h]

There a warrior cries out.[i]

15 That day is a day of fury,[j]

A day of distress and anguish,[k]

A day of storm and desolation,

A day of darkness and gloom,[l]

A day of clouds and thick gloom,[m]

16 A day of the horn and of the battle cry,[n]

Against the fortified cities and against the high corner towers.[a]

17 I will cause distress to mankind,

And they will walk like blind men,[b]

Because it is against Jehovah they have sinned.[c]

Their blood will be poured out like dust,

And their flesh* like the dung.[d]

18 Neither their silver nor their gold will be able to save them in the day of Jehovah's fury;[e]

For by the fire of his zeal the whole earth will be consumed,[f]

Because he will make an extermination, indeed a terrible one, of all the inhabitants of the earth."[g]

2 Gather together, yes, gather yourselves,[h]

O nation that feels no shame.[i]

2 Before the decree takes effect,

Before the day passes by like chaff,

Before the burning anger of Jehovah comes upon you,[j]

Before the day of Jehovah's anger comes upon you,

3 Seek Jehovah,[k] all you meek ones* of the earth,

Who observe his righteous decrees.#

Seek righteousness, seek meekness.△

Probably⊗ you will be concealed on the day of Jehovah's anger.[l]

4 For Gaz′a will be an abandoned city;

And Ash′ke·lon will be desolated.[m]

CHAP. 1

a 2Ch 33:1, 14
Ne 3:3
Ne 12:38, 39

b 2Ch 34:22

c Ps 10:13
Ps 14:1

d Isa 6:11

e De 28:30
Jer 5:17

f Joe 2:1

g Hab 2:3

h Isa 66:6

i Isa 33:7
Joe 1:15

j Re 6:17

k Jer 30:7

l Am 5:18, 20
Ac 2:20

m Joe 2:2

n Jer 4:19

Second Col.

a Isa 2:12, 15

b De 28:28, 29
Isa 59:9, 10

c Isa 24:5
Da 9:5, 8

d Ps 79:2, 3
Jer 9:22
Jer 16:4

e Pr 11:4
Isa 2:20
Eze 7:19

f De 32:22
Jer 7:20

g Jer 4:27

CHAP. 2

h Joe 1:14
Joe 2:15, 16

i Isa 1:4
Jer 6:15

j 2Ki 23:26
2Ch 36:16, 17
Jer 23:20
La 4:11

k Isa 55:6
Am 5:6

l Ge 7:13, 16
Isa 26:20
Joe 2:12, 14
Am 5:15

m Jer 47:5

1:11 *Apparently a section of Jerusalem near the Fish Gate. #Or "merchants." △Lit., "silenced." 1:12 *Lit., "those congealing on their dregs," as in a wine vat. 1:14 *Or "hurrying rapidly!"

1:17 *Lit., "intestines." 2:3 *Or "humble ones." #Lit., "his judgment." △Or "humility." ⊗Or "It may be that."

Ash'dod will be driven away
in broad daylight,*
And Ek'ron will be uprooted.[a]

5 "Woe to those who inhabit
the seacoast, the nation
of Cher'e·thites![b]
The word of Jehovah is
against you.
O Ca'naan, land of the Philis'tines, I will destroy you,
So that there will be no
inhabitant left.

6 And the seacoast will
become pasture grounds,
With wells for shepherds
and stone pens for sheep.

7 It will become a region for
the remaining ones of the
house of Judah;[c]
There they will feed.
In the houses of Ash'ke·lon
they will lie down in the
evening.
For Jehovah their God will
turn his attention to them,*
And he will gather back their
captives."[d]

8 "I have heard the reproach
by Mo'ab[e] and the insults
of the Am'mon·ites,[f]
Who have taunted my people
and made boasts against
their territory.[g]

9 Therefore as surely as I am
alive," declares Jehovah of
armies, the God of Israel,
"Mo'ab will become just like
Sod'om,[h]
And the Am'mon·ites like
Go·mor'rah,[i]
A place of nettles, a salt pit,
and a permanent waste-
land.[j]
The remaining ones of my
people will plunder them,
And the remnant of my na-
tion will dispossess them.

10 This is what they will have
instead of their pride,[k]
Because they taunted and
exalted themselves against

CHAP. 2

a Jer 25:17, 20
Am 1:6-8
Zec 9:5, 6

b Eze 25:16, 17

c Isa 11:11
Jer 31:7
Hag 1:12

d Ps 126:1
Jer 23:3
Eze 39:25
Am 9:14
Mic 2:12
Mic 4:10
Zep 3:20

e Jer 48:26, 27
Eze 25:8, 9

f Jer 49:1
Eze 25:3

g Ps 83:2, 4

h Eze 25:11
Am 2:1, 2

i Ge 19:24, 25

j Am 1:13-15
Jude 7

k Isa 16:6
Jer 48:29

Second Col.

a Ps 22:27
Mal 1:11

b Isa 43:3
Eze 30:4, 5

c Na 3:7

d Na 3:1, 19

CHAP. 3

e Isa 5:7
Jer 6:6

f Jer 22:21
Jer 32:23

g Ps 50:17
Isa 1:5
Jer 5:3

h Ps 78:22
Jer 17:5

i Isa 29:13

the people of Jehovah
of armies.

11 Jehovah will be awe-
inspiring* against them;
For he will bring to nothing[#]
all the gods of the earth,
And all the islands of the
nations will bow down to[△]
him,[a]
Each one from its place.

12 You E·thi·o'pi·ans will also be
slain by my sword.[b]

13 He will stretch out his hand
toward the north and
destroy As·syr'i·a,
And he will make Nin'e·veh
desolate,[c] as dry as a
desert.

14 Herds will lie down within
her, all sorts of wild
animals.*
Both pelican and porcupine
will spend the night among
her pillar capitals.
A voice will sing in the
window.
There will be devastation
at the threshold;
For he will expose the cedar
panels.

15 This is the proud city that
was sitting in security,
That was saying in her heart,
'I am the one, and there
is nobody else.'
How she has become an
object of horror,
A place for the wild animals
to lie down!
Everyone passing by her will
whistle and shake his fist."[d]

3 Woe to the rebellious, the
polluted, the oppressive
city![e]

2 She has obeyed no voice;[f]
she has accepted no
discipline.[g]
In Jehovah she has not
trusted;[h] she has not
drawn near to her God.[i]

___

2:4 *Or "at high noon." 2:7 *Or "will
care for them."

2:11 *Or "terrifying." #Or "emaciate."
△Or "worship." 2:14 *Lit., "every beast
of a nation."

3 Her princes within her are
      roaring lions.ª
   Her judges are wolves in the
      night;
   They do not leave even a bone
      to gnaw until morning.
4 Her prophets are insolent,
      treacherous men.ᵇ
   Her priests defile what is
      holy;ᶜ
   They do violence to the law.ᵈ
5 Jehovah is righteous in her
      midst;ᵉ he does no wrong.
   Morning by morning he
      makes known his judg-
      ments,ᶠ
   As unfailing as the daylight.
   But the unrighteous one
      knows no shame.ᵍ
6 "I destroyed nations; their
      corner towers were left
      desolate.
   I devastated their streets,
      so that no one was passing
      through.
   Their cities were left in
      ruins, without a man,
      without an inhabitant.ʰ
7 I said, 'Surely you will fear
      me and accept discipline,'*ⁱ
   So that her dwelling place
      might not be destroyed
   —I must call her to account
      forⁿ all these things.
   But they were all the more
      eager to act corruptly.ᵏ
8 'So keep yourselves in
      expectation of* me,'ˡ
      declares Jehovah,
   'Until the day when I rise up
      to take plunder,ⁿ
   For my judicial decision
      is to gather nations, to
      assemble kingdoms,
   To pour out on them my
      indignation, all my burning
      anger;ᵐ
   For by the fire of my zeal
      the whole earth will be
      consumed.ⁿ

9 For then I will change the
      language of the peoples
      to a pure language,
   So that all of them may call
      on the name of Jehovah,
   To serve him shoulder to
      shoulder.'*ª
10 From the region of the rivers
      of E·thi·o'pi·a,
   Those entreating me, the
      daughter of my scattered
      ones, will bring a gift to me.ᵇ
11 On that day you will not be
      put to shame
   Because of all your deeds
      with which you rebelled
      against me,ᶜ
   For then I will remove the
      haughty boasters from
      among you;
   And you will never again
      be haughty in my holy
      mountain.ᵈ
12 I will allow a humble and
      lowly people to remain in
      your midst,ᵉ
   And they will take refuge
      in the name of Jehovah.
13 Those remaining of Israelᶠ
      will practice no unrigh-
      teousness;ᵍ
   They will not speak a lie,
      nor will a deceitful tongue
      be found in their mouths;
   They will feed* and lie down,
      and no one will make them
      afraid."ʰ
14 Shout joyfully, O daughter
      of Zion!
   Shout in triumph, O Israel!ⁱ
   Be joyful and rejoice with
      all your heart, O daughter
      of Jerusalem!ʲ
15 Jehovah has removed the
      judgments against you.ᵏ
   He has turned away your
      enemy.ˡ
   The King of Israel, Jehovah,
      is in your midst.ᵐ
   You will fear calamity no
      more.ⁿ

CHAP. 3
a Isa 1:23
  Eze 22:27
b La 2:14
c Jer 23:11
d Eze 22:25, 26
  Mic 3:9
e De 32:4
f Jer 21:12
g Jer 3:3
  Jer 8:12
  Zep 2:1
h Le 18:28
i Isa 5:3, 4
  Isa 63:8
  2Pe 3:9
j Jer 7:5-7
  Jer 25:5, 6
k Mic 2:1
l Ps 37:34
  Ps 130:7
  Isa 30:18
m Isa 34:2
  Joe 3:2
  Re 16:14
  Re 19:15
n Eze 36:5

Second Col.
a Zec 8:23
b Isa 60:4
c Isa 45:17
  Isa 54:4
d Isa 11:9
e Isa 57:15
  Isa 61:1
f Isa 10:22
  Mic 4:7
g Isa 60:21
h Jer 30:10
  Eze 34:28
  Eze 39:25, 26
  Ho 2:18
  Mic 4:4
i Ezr 3:11
  Isa 12:5, 6
  Zec 2:10
j Mic 4:8
k Isa 40:2
  Zec 8:13
l Mic 7:10
  Zec 2:8, 9
m Eze 48:35
n Am 9:15
  Zec 14:11

3:7 *Or "correction." ⁿOr "punish her
for." 3:8 *Or "wait patiently for." ⁿOr
possibly, "rise up as a witness."

3:9 *Or "worship him in unity." 3:13
*Or "graze."

16 On that day it will be said
to Jerusalem:
"Do not be afraid, O Zion.ᵃ
Do not let your hands drop
down.
17 Jehovah your God is in your
midst.ᵇ
As a mighty One, he will
save.
He will exult over you with
great joy.
He will become silent* in his
love.
He will rejoice over you with
shouts of joy.
18 I will gather together those
grieving over their absence
from your festivals;ᵈ
They were absent from
you because of bearing
reproach for her.ᵉ

19 Look! At that time I will
act against all those
oppressing you;ᵃ
And I will save the one
limping,ᵇ
And I will gather together
the dispersed.ᶜ
I will make them an object
of praise and fame*
In all the land of their shame.
20 At that time I will bring
you in,
At the time I gather you
together.
For I will make you an object
of fame* and praiseᵈ among
all the peoples of the
earth,
When I gather back your
captives before your eyes,"
says Jehovah.ᵉ

3:17 *Or "quiet; at ease; satisfied."

3:19, 20 *Lit., "a name."

CHAP. 3
a Jer 46:28
b Isa 12:6
c De 30:9
  Ps 147:11
  Isa 62:3
  Isa 65:19
  Jer 32:41
d La 1:4
  La 2:6
e La 5:1

__Second Col.__
a Isa 60:14
  Zec 14:3
b Mic 4:6, 7
c Isa 11:11, 12
  Isa 27:12
  Eze 28:25
  Eze 34:15, 16
  Am 9:14
d Isa 60:15
e Isa 61:7
  Jer 30:10
  Jer 33:7, 9
  Eze 39:25, 27

HAGGAI

1 In the second year of
King Da·riʹus, in the sixth
month, on the first day of
the month, the word of Jehovah came through Hagʹgai*ᵃ the

1:1 *Meaning "Born on a Festival."

CHAP. 1
a Ezr 5:1

__Second Col.__
a Ezr 3:2
  Ezr 5:2

prophet to Ze·rubʹba·belᵃ son of
She·alʹti·el, the governor of Judah, and to Joshua son of Je-
hozʹa·dak, the high priest, saying:
2 "This is what Jehovah of
armies says, 'These people say,

"The time has not yet come for the house* of Jehovah to be built.'"*#a

3 And the word of Jehovah again came through Hag'gai[b] the prophet, saying: **4** "Is it the time for you to dwell in your paneled houses, while this house lies in ruins?[c] **5** Now this is what Jehovah of armies says, 'Set your heart on* your ways. **6** You have sown much seed, but you harvest little.[d] You eat, but it is not to satisfaction. You drink, but you do not drink your fill. You put on clothing, but no one gets warm. The one who hires himself out puts his wages in a bag full of holes.'"

7 "This is what Jehovah of armies says, 'Set your heart on* your ways.'

8 "'Go up to the mountain and bring in lumber.[e] And build the house,[f] so that I may take pleasure in it and I may be glorified,'[g] Jehovah says."

9 "'You were expecting much and receiving little; and when you brought it into the house, I blew it away.[h] For what reason?' declares Jehovah of armies. 'Because my house is in ruins, while each of you runs around taking care of his own house.[i] **10** So the heavens above you withheld their dew, and the earth withheld its produce. **11** And I kept calling for a drought on the earth, on the mountains, on the grain, on the new wine, on the oil, on what grows from the ground, on humans and livestock, and on all the labor of your hands.'"

12 Ze·rub'ba·bel[j] son of She·al'ti·el[k] and Joshua son of Je·hoz'a·dak,[l] the high priest, and all the rest of the people listened to the voice of Jehovah their God and to the words of Hag'gai the prophet, because Jehovah their God had sent him; and the people began to show fear because of Jehovah.

13 Then Hag'gai, the messenger of Jehovah, gave this message to the people in harmony with his commission from Jehovah: "'I am with you people,'[a] declares Jehovah."

14 So Jehovah stirred up the spirit[b] of Ze·rub'ba·bel the son of She·al'ti·el, the governor of Judah,[c] and the spirit of Joshua[d] the son of Je·hoz'a·dak, the high priest, and the spirit of all the rest of the people; and they came and began to work on the house of Jehovah of armies, their God.[e] **15** This was on the 24th day of the sixth month in the second year of King Da·ri'us.[f]

2 In the seventh month, on the 21st day of the month, the word of Jehovah came through Hag'gai[g] the prophet, saying, **2** "Please ask Ze·rub'ba·bel[h] son of She·al'ti·el, the governor of Judah,[i] and Joshua[j] son of Je·hoz'a·dak,[k] the high priest, and the rest of the people: **3** 'Who is left among you who saw this house* in its former glory?[l] How does it look to you now? Does it not seem like nothing in comparison?'[m]

4 "'But now be strong, Ze·rub'ba·bel,' declares Jehovah, 'and be strong, Joshua son of Je·hoz'a·dak, the high priest.'

"'And be strong, all you people of the land,'[n] declares Jehovah, 'and work.'

"'For I am with you,'[o] declares Jehovah of armies. **5** 'Remember what I promised you when you came out of Egypt,[p] and my

---

CHAP. 1
a Ezr 4:4, 23
b Ezr 6:14
c Jer 52:12, 13
d De 28:22
e Ezr 3:7
f Ezr 5:2
  Ezr 6:15
  Zec 1:16
g Isa 60:13
h Mal 2:2
i Hag 1:4
j Mt 1:12
k 1Ch 3:17-19
  Lu 3:23, 27
l 1Ch 6:15

Second Col.
a 2Ch 15:2
  Isa 8:10
  Ro 8:31
b Ezr 1:1, 5
c Ezr 1:8
  Ezr 5:14
d Zec 3:1
  Zec 6:11-13
e Ezr 5:2
  Zec 6:15
f Ezr 4:24
  Hag 1:1
  Zec 1:1

CHAP. 2
g Ezr 5:1
  Ezr 6:14
h 1Ch 3:17-19
  Zec 4:9
i Ezr 1:8
j Zec 3:8
  Zec 6:11
k 1Ch 6:15
l 1Ki 6:1
  Ezr 3:12
m Zec 4:10
n Zec 8:9
o Ex 3:12
  Isa 43:2
  Ro 8:31
p Ex 29:45
  Ex 34:10

1:2; 2:3 *Or "temple." **1:2** #Or "rebuilt." **1:5, 7** *Or "Give careful thought to."

spirit remains among you.*ᵃ Do not be afraid.'"ᵇ

6 "For this is what Jehovah of armies says, 'Yet once more —in a little while—and I will shake the heavens and the earth and the sea and the dry land.'ᶜ

7 "'And I will shake all the nations, and the precious* things of all the nations will come in;ᵈ and I will fill this house with glory,'ᵉ says Jehovah of armies.

8 "'The silver is mine, and the gold is mine,' declares Jehovah of armies.

9 "'The future glory of this house will be greater than the former,'ᶠ says Jehovah of armies.

"'And in this place I will grant peace,'ᵍ declares Jehovah of armies."

10 On the 24th day of the ninth month, in the second year of Da·ri'us, the word of Jehovah came to Hag'gaiʰ the prophet, saying: **11** "This is what Jehovah of armies says, 'Ask, please, the priests about the law:ⁱ **12** "If a man carries holy flesh in the fold of his clothing, and his clothing touches bread or stew or wine or oil or any sort of food, will it become holy?"'"

The priests answered: "No!"

13 Hag'gai then asked: "If someone who is unclean from contact with a dead body* touches any of these things, will it become unclean?"ʲ

The priests answered: "It will become unclean."

14 So Hag'gai said: "'That is how this people is, and that is how this nation is before me,' declares Jehovah, 'and that is how all the work of their hands is; whatever they present there is unclean.'

15 "'But now, please, set your heart on* this from this day forward: Before a stone was placed on a stone in the temple of Jehovah,ᵃ **16** how was it then? When someone came to a heap of grain expecting 20 measures, there were only 10; and when someone came to the vat to draw 50 measures from the wine trough, there were only 20;ᵇ **17** I struck you—all the works of your hands—with scorching blight and mildewᶜ and hail, but not one of you turned to me,' declares Jehovah.

18 "'Please, set your heart on* this from this day forward, from the 24th day of the ninth month, from the day that the foundation of the temple of Jehovah was laid;ᵈ set your heart on this: **19** Is there seed yet in the storehouse?*ᵉ The vine, the fig, the pomegranate, and the olive tree—they have not yet borne fruit, have they? From this day I will send a blessing.'"ᶠ

20 The word of Jehovah came a second time to Hag'gai on the 24th day of the month,ᵍ saying: **21** "Say to Ze·rub'ba·bel, the governor of Judah, 'I am going to shake the heavens and the earth.ʰ **22** I will overthrow the throne of kingdoms and annihilate the strength of the kingdoms of the nations;ⁱ and I will overthrow the chariot and its riders, and the horses and their riders will fall, each one by the sword of his brother.'"ʲ

23 "'In that day,' declares Jehovah of armies, 'I will take you, my servant Ze·rub'ba·belᵏ son of She·al'ti·el,'ˡ declares Jehovah, 'and I will make you like a seal ring, because you are the one whom I have chosen,' declares Jehovah of armies."

CHAP. 2
a Zec 4:6

b Isa 41:10
Zec 8:13

c Heb 12:26, 27

d Isa 2:2
Isa 60:5, 11

e Ex 40:35
1Ki 8:11
Isa 66:12

f Isa 60:13

g Ps 85:8
Isa 2:4
Isa 60:17, 18
Zec 8:12

h Hag 1:1

i Mal 2:7

j Le 7:21
Nu 5:2, 3
Nu 9:6
Nu 19:11
Nu 31:19

Second Col.

a Ezr 3:10
Zec 4:9

b Hag 1:6
Zec 8:10

c De 28:22

d Ezr 5:2
Zec 8:9

e Hag 1:6

f Pr 3:9, 10
Zec 8:12

g Hag 2:10

h Hag 2:6
Heb 12:26, 27

i Isa 60:12
Da 2:44
Zep 3:8

j Jg 7:22

k Ezr 3:8

l Mt 1:12

2:5 *Or possibly, "and when my spirit was standing in among you." **2:7** *Or "desirable." **2:13** *Or "by a soul." See Glossary.

2:15, 18 *Or "give careful thought to." **2:19** *Or "grain pit?"

ZECHARIAH

OUTLINE OF CONTENTS

1 In the eighth month in the second year of Da·ri′us,[a] the word of Jehovah came to the prophet Zech·a·ri′ah*[b] son of Ber·e·chi′ah son of Id′do, saying: **2** "Jehovah grew greatly indignant at your fathers.[c]

3 "Say to them, 'This is what Jehovah of armies says: "'Return to me,' declares Jehovah of armies, 'and I will return to you,'[d] says Jehovah of armies."'

4 "'Do not become like your fathers, to whom the former prophets proclaimed: "This is what Jehovah of armies says, 'Turn away,* please, from your evil ways and your evil deeds.'"'[e]

"'But they did not listen, and they paid no attention to me,'[f] declares Jehovah.

5 "'Where are your fathers now? And did the prophets live forever? **6** However, my words and my decrees that I commanded my servants, the prophets, caught up with your fathers, did they not?'[g] So they returned to me and said: 'Jehovah of armies has dealt with us according to our ways and our deeds, just as he had determined to do.'"[h]

7 On the 24th day of the 11th month, that is, the month of She′bat,* in the second year of Da·ri′us,[i] the word of Jehovah came to the prophet Zech·a·ri′ah son of Ber·e·chi′ah son of Id′do, saying: **8** "I saw a vision in the night. There was a man riding on a red horse, and he stood still among the myrtle trees in the ravine; and behind him there were red, reddish-brown, and white horses."

9 So I said: "Who are these, my lord?"

The angel who was speaking with me replied: "I will show you who these are."

10 Then the man who was standing still among the myrtle trees said: "These are the ones whom Jehovah has sent out to walk about in the earth." **11** And they said to the angel of Jehovah who was standing among the myrtle trees: "We have walked about in the earth, and look! the whole earth is quiet and undisturbed."[a]

12 So the angel of Jehovah said: "O Jehovah of armies, how long will you withhold your mercy from Jerusalem and the cities of Judah,[b] with whom you have been indignant these 70 years?"[c]

13 Jehovah answered the angel who was speaking with me, with kind and comforting words. **14** Then the angel who was speaking with me told me: "Call out, 'This is what Jehovah of armies says: "I am zealous for Jerusalem and for Zion with a great zeal.[d] **15** With great indignation I am indignant with the nations that are at ease,[e] because I felt indignant to a small extent,[f] but they added to the calamity."'[g]

16 "Therefore this is what Jehovah says: '"I will return to Jerusalem with mercy,[h] and my own house will be built in her,"[i] declares Jehovah of armies, "and a measuring line will be stretched out over Jerusalem."'[j]

17 "Call out once more and say, 'This is what Jehovah of armies says: "My cities will again overflow with goodness; and Jehovah will again comfort Zion[k] and again choose Jerusalem."'"[l]

18 Then I looked up and saw four horns.[m] **19** So I asked the angel who was speaking with me: "What are these?" He replied: "These are the horns that dispersed Judah,[n] Israel,[o] and Jerusalem."[p]

20 Jehovah then showed me four craftsmen. **21** I asked: "What are these coming to do?"

CHAP. 1

a Ezr 4:24
  Hag 1:1
  Hag 2:10

b Ezr 5:1

c 2Ki 22:16, 17
  Jer 44:5, 6

d Eze 33:11
  Mic 7:18, 19
  Mal 3:7

e Ezr 9:6, 7
  Isa 1:16
  Isa 55:7
  Ho 14:1

f 2Ch 36:15, 16
  Jer 11:7, 8

g 2Ch 36:17
  Da 9:11, 12

h De 28:20, 45
  Jer 23:20

i Ezr 4:24

Second Col.

a Zec 1:15

b Ps 74:10
  Ps 102:13

c 2Ch 36:20, 21
  Jer 25:11, 12
  Da 9:2
  Zec 7:5

d Joe 2:18
  Zec 8:2

e Jer 48:11
  Zec 1:11

f Isa 54:8

g Ps 137:7
  Isa 47:6
  Isa 51:35

h Isa 12:1
  Jer 33:14
  Zec 8:3

i Ezr 6:14, 15
  Isa 44:28
  Hag 1:14

j Jer 31:38, 39
  Eze 40:2, 3
  Zec 2:1, 2

k Isa 51:3

l Ps 132:13
  Zec 2:12
  Zec 3:2

m Zec 1:21

n 2Ki 24:12, 14

o 2Ki 15:29
  2Ki 17:6
  2Ki 18:11
  Jer 50:17

p 2Ch 25:11
  2Ch 36:17, 19

1:1 *Meaning "Jehovah Has Remembered." **1:4** *Or "Return." **1:7** *See App. B15.

He said: "These are the horns that dispersed Judah to such an extent that no one was able to raise his head. These others have come to terrify them, to cast down the horns of the nations that lifted up their horns against the land of Judah, in order to disperse her."

2 And I looked up and saw a man with a measuring line[a] in his hand. **2** So I asked: "Where are you going?"

He replied: "To measure Jerusalem, to see what is her width and what is her length."[b]

3 And look! the angel who was speaking with me went out, and another angel came to meet him. **4** Then he said to him: "Run over there and tell that young man, '"Jerusalem will be inhabited[c] as open rural country,* because of all the men and livestock within her.[d] **5** And I will become to her," declares Jehovah, "a wall of fire all around,[e] and I will become the glory in her midst."'"[f]

6 "Come! Come! Flee from the land of the north,"[g] declares Jehovah.

"For I have scattered you to the four winds of the heavens,"[h] declares Jehovah.

7 "Come, Zion! Make your escape, you who are dwelling with the daughter of Babylon.[i] **8** For this is what Jehovah of armies says, who after being glorified* has sent me to the nations that were plundering you:[j] 'Whoever touches you touches the pupil of my eye.'*[k] **9** For now I will wave my hand against them, and they will become plunder for their own slaves.' And you will certainly know that Jehovah of armies has sent me.

10 "Shout for joy, O daughter of Zion;[m] for I am coming,[n] and

I will reside in your midst,"[a] declares Jehovah. **11** "Many nations will join themselves to Jehovah in that day,[b] and they will become my people; and I will reside in your midst." And you will have to know that Jehovah of armies has sent me to you. **12** Jehovah will take possession of Judah as his portion on the holy ground, and he will again choose Jerusalem.[c] **13** Be silent, all flesh,* before Jehovah, for he is taking action from his holy dwelling.

3 And he showed me Joshua[d] the high priest standing before the angel of Jehovah, and Satan[e] was standing at his right hand to resist him. **2** Then the angel of Jehovah said to Satan: "May Jehovah rebuke you, O Satan,[f] yes, may Jehovah, who has chosen Jerusalem,[g] rebuke you! Is not this one a burning log snatched out of the fire?"

3 Now Joshua was clothed in filthy garments and standing before the angel. **4** The angel said to those standing before him, "Remove his filthy garments." Then he said to him, "See, I have caused your error* to pass away from you, and you will be clothed with fine garments."*[h]

5 So I said: "Let a clean turban be put on his head."[i] And they put the clean turban on his head and clothed him with garments; and the angel of Jehovah was standing nearby. **6** The angel of Jehovah then declared to Joshua: **7** "This is what Jehovah of armies says, 'If you will walk in my ways and carry out your responsibilities before me, then you will serve as a judge in my house[j] and take care of* my courtyards; and I will give you free access among these who are standing here.'

CHAP. 2
a Zec 1:16

b Jer 31:38, 39

c Isa 44:26
   Jer 30:18
   Eze 36:10

d Isa 33:20
   Jer 31:24
   Jer 33:10, 11
   Zec 8:4, 5

e Ps 125:2
   Isa 26:1

f Isa 12:6
   Isa 60:19, 20
   Hag 2:9

g Isa 11:12, 16

h Ze 28:64
   Eze 5:12

i Isa 48:20
   Isa 52:2
   Jer 50:8
   Mic 4:10

j 2Ki 24:2
   Mic 4:11

k De 32:9, 10
   Ps 105:14, 15
   2Th 1:6

l Isa 14:2

m Isa 35:10

n Isa 40:9, 10

Second Col.
a Le 26:11, 12
   Isa 12:6

b Ps 22:27
   Isa 2:2, 3
   Zec 8:22, 23

c 2Ch 6:6
   Zec 1:17

CHAP. 3
d Ezr 5:2
   Hag 1:14
   Zec 6:11

e Job 1:6

f Jude 9

g 2Ch 6:6
   Zec 2:12

h Ex 28:2

i Ex 29:6

j Mal 2:7

2:4 *That is, without walls to enclose it. 2:8 *Lit., "after glory." *Or "touches my eyeball." 2:13 *Or "mankind." 3:4 *Or "guilt." *Or "with robes of state." 3:7 *Or "have charge of; guard."

8 "'Hear, please, O High Priest Joshua, you and your companions who sit before you, for these men serve as a sign; look! I am bringing in my servant[a] Sprout![b] **9** See the stone that I have set before Joshua! On the one stone are seven eyes; and I am engraving an inscription on it,' declares Jehovah of armies, 'and I will take away the guilt of that land in one day.'[c]

10 "'In that day,' declares Jehovah of armies, 'Each of you will invite your neighbor to come under your vine and under your fig tree.'"[d]

4 The angel who had been speaking with me came back and woke me up, as when waking someone from sleep. **2** Then he said to me: "What do you see?"

So I said: "I see, and look! a lampstand entirely of gold,[e] with a bowl on top of it. There are seven lamps on it,[f] yes, seven, and the lamps, which are at the top of it, have seven pipes. **3** And next to it are two olive trees,[g] one on the right of the bowl and one on the left."

4 Then I asked the angel who was speaking with me: "What do these things mean, my lord?" **5** So the angel who was speaking with me asked: "Do you not know what these things mean?"

I replied: "No, my lord."

6 He then said to me: "This is the word of Jehovah to Ze·rub'ba·bel: "'Not by a military force, nor by power,[h] but by my spirit,[i]' says Jehovah of armies. **7** Who are you, O great mountain? Before Ze·rub'ba·bel you will become a level land.*[k] And he will bring out the top stone# amid shouts of: "How wonderful! How wonderful!"'"

8 The word of Jehovah again came to me, saying: **9** "The hands of Ze·rub'ba·bel have laid the foundation of this house,[a] and his own hands will finish it.[b] And you will have to know that Jehovah of armies has sent me to you. **10** For who has despised the day of small beginnings?*[c] For they will rejoice and see the plumb line# in the hand of Ze·rub'ba·bel. These seven are the eyes of Jehovah, which are roving about in all the earth."[d]

11 Then I asked him: "What is the meaning of these two olive trees on the right and on the left of the lampstand?"[e] **12** I asked him a second time: "What is the meaning of the two bunches of twigs* of the olive trees that are pouring out the golden liquid through the two golden tubes?"

13 So he asked me: "Do you not know what these things mean?"

I replied: "No, my lord."

14 He said: "These are the two anointed ones who are standing alongside the Lord of the whole earth."[f]

5 Again I looked up, and I saw a flying scroll. **2** He asked me: "What do you see?"

I replied: "I see a flying scroll, which is 20 cubits* long and 10 cubits wide."

3 Then he said to me: "This is the curse that is going out over the face of all the earth, because everyone who steals,[g] as written on its one side, has gone unpunished; and everyone who makes a sworn oath,[h] as written on its other side, has gone unpunished. **4** 'I have sent it out,' declares Jehovah of armies, 'and it will enter into the house of the thief and into the house of the one who makes a false oath in

---

CHAP. 3

a Isa 42:1
　Isa 52:13

b Isa 11:1
　Isa 53:2, 11
　Jer 23:5
　Jer 33:15
　Zec 6:12

c Jer 50:20

d 1Ki 4:25
　Ho 2:18
　Mic 4:4

CHAP. 4

e Ex 25:31
　1Ki 7:48, 49

f Ex 25:37

g Zec 4:11, 14
　Re 11:3, 4

h 1Sa 17:45
　Ho 1:7

i Jg 6:34
　Jg 15:14

j Ezr 3:2
　Hag 1:1

k Isa 40:4

Second Col.

a Ezr 3:8, 10
　Ezr 5:14, 16

b Ezr 6:14
　Zec 6:12

c Ezr 3:12
　Hag 2:3

d 2Ch 16:9
　Pr 15:3
　Jer 16:17
　Re 5:6

e Zec 4:2, 3

f Hag 2:4
　Re 11:3, 4

CHAP. 5

g Ex 20:15

h Ex 20:7
　Le 19:12

4:7 *Or "a plain." #Or "the capstone." **4:10** *Or "small things?" #Lit., "the stone, the tin." **4:12** *That is, fruit-laden twigs of the tree. **5:2** *A cubit equaled 44.5 cm (17.5 in.). See App. B14.

my name; and it will remain inside that house and consume it and its timbers and its stones.'"

5 Then the angel who was speaking with me came forward and said to me: "Look up, please, and see what is going out."

6 So I asked: "What is it?"

He replied: "This is the e′phah container* that is going out." He continued: "This is their appearance in all the earth." **7** And I saw that the round lid of lead was lifted up, and there was a woman sitting inside the container. **8** So he said: "This is Wickedness." Then he threw her back into the e′phah container, after which he thrust the lead weight over its mouth.

9 Then I looked up and saw two women coming forward, and they were soaring in the wind. They had wings like the wings of a stork. And they lifted up the container between the earth and heaven. **10** So I asked the angel who was speaking with me: "Where are they taking the e′phah container?"

11 He replied: "To the land of Shi′nar*ᵃ to build her a house; and when it is prepared, she will be deposited there in her proper place."

6 Then I looked up again and saw four chariots coming from between two mountains, and the mountains were of copper. **2** The first chariot had red horses, and the second chariot, black horses.ᵇ **3** The third chariot had white horses, and the fourth chariot, speckled and dappled horses.ᶜ

4 I asked the angel who was speaking with me: "What are these, my lord?"

5 The angel answered me: "These are the four spiritsᵃ of the heavens that are going out after having taken their station before the Lord of the whole earth.ᵇ **6** The one* with the black horses is going out to the land of the north;ᶜ the white ones are going out beyond the sea; and the speckled ones are going out to the land of the south. **7** And the dappled ones were eager to go out to walk about through the earth." Then he said: "Go, walk about through the earth." And they began walking about through the earth.

8 He then called out to me and said: "See, those going out to the land of the north have caused the spirit of Jehovah to rest in the land of the north."

9 The word of Jehovah again came to me, saying: **10** "Take from Hel′dai, To·bi′jah, and Je·da′iah what they brought from the people in exile; and on that day, you must go to the house of Jo·si′ah the son of Zeph·a·ni′ah along with these who have come from Babylon. **11** You should take silver and gold and make a crown* and put it on the head of Joshuaᵈ son of Je·hoz′a·dak, the high priest. **12** And say to him, "'This is what Jehovah of armies says: "Here is the man whose name is Sprout.ᵉ He will sprout from his own place, and he will build the temple of Jehovah.ᶠ **13** He is the one who will build the temple of Jehovah, and he is the one who will assume the majesty. He will sit down on his throne and rule, and he will also be a priest on his throne,ᵍ and there will be a peaceable agreement between the two.* **14** And the crown* will serve as

---

CHAP. 5
a Ge 10:8, 10
Ge 11:1, 2
Da 1:2

CHAP. 6
b Zec 6:6

c Zec 6:7

Second Col.
a Ps 104:4

b 2Ch 18:18
Job 1:6
Da 7:10
Lu 1:19
Heb 1:7, 14

c Zec 2:6, 7

d Hag 1:1
Zec 3:3, 5

e Isa 11:1
Zec 3:8

f Zec 8:9

g Heb 3:1
Heb 4:14
Heb 8:1

5:6 *Lit., "the ephah," here referring to a container or basket used to measure an ephah. An ephah equaled 22 L (20 dry qt). See App. B14. **5:11** *That is, Babylonia.

6:6 *That is, the chariot. **6:11** *Or "a grand crown." **6:13** *That is, between his roles as ruler and priest. **6:14** *Or "the grand crown."

a memorial* for He′lem, To·bi′-jah, Je·da′iah,[a] and Hen the son of Zeph·a·ni′ah, in the temple of Jehovah. 15 And those who are far away will come and take part in building the temple of Jehovah.″ And you will have to know that Jehovah of armies has sent me to you. And it will occur—if you do not fail to listen to the voice of Jehovah your God.′″

7 And in the fourth year of King Da·ri′us, the word of Jehovah came to Zech·a·ri′ah[b] on the fourth day of the ninth month, that is, the month of Chis′lev.* 2 The people of Beth′el sent Shar·e′zer and Re′gem-mel′ech and his men to beg for the favor* of Jehovah, 3 saying to the priests of the house* of Jehovah of armies and to the prophets: "Should I weep in the fifth month[c] and abstain from food, as I have done for so many years?"

4 The word of Jehovah of armies again came to me, saying: 5 "Say to all the people of the land and to the priests, 'When you fasted and wailed in the fifth month and in the seventh month[d] for 70 years,[e] did you really fast for me? 6 And when you would eat and drink, were you not eating for yourselves and drinking for yourselves? 7 Should you not obey the words that Jehovah proclaimed through the former prophets,[f] while Jerusalem and her surrounding cities were inhabited and at peace, and while the Neg′eb and the She·phe′lah were inhabited?'"

8 The word of Jehovah again came to Zech·a·ri′ah, saying: 9 "This is what Jehovah of armies says, 'Judge with true justice,[g] and deal with one another in loyal love[h] and mercy. 10 Do

not defraud the widow or the fatherless child,*[a] the foreigner[b] or the poor;[c] and do not scheme evil against one another in your hearts.'[d] 11 But they kept refusing to pay attention,[e] and they stubbornly turned their backs,[f] and they stopped up their ears so as not to hear.[g] 12 They made their heart like a diamond*[h] and would not obey the law[#] and the words that Jehovah of armies sent by his spirit through the former prophets.[i] So there came great indignation from Jehovah of armies."[j]

13 "Just as they did not listen when I* called,[k] so I would not listen when they called,'[l] says Jehovah of armies. 14 'And I scattered them with a storm wind throughout all the nations that they had not known,[m] and the land was left desolate behind them, with no one passing through or returning;[n] for they turned the desirable land into an object of horror.'"

8 The word of Jehovah of armies again came, saying: 2 "This is what Jehovah of armies says, 'I will be zealous for Zion with a great zeal,[o] and with great wrath I will be zealous for her.'"

3 "This is what Jehovah says, 'I will return to Zion[p] and reside in Jerusalem;[q] and Jerusalem will be called the city of truth,*[r] and the mountain of Jehovah of armies, the holy mountain.'"[s]

4 "This is what Jehovah of armies says, 'Old men and women will again sit in the public squares of Jerusalem, each with his staff in his hand because of his great age.*[t] 5 And the public squares of the city will be

---

CHAP. 6
a Zec 6:10

CHAP. 7
b Ezr 6:14
　Zec 1:1
c 2Ki 25:8-10
　Jer 52:12-14
d Jer 41:1, 2
e Jer 25:11
　Zec 1:12
f 2Ch 36:15
g Pr 21:3
　Jer 21:12
h Pr 16:6
　Ho 10:12
　Mic 6:8

Second Col.
a Ex 22:22
　De 24:17
　Isa 1:17
b Ex 23:9
　Mal 3:5
c Pr 22:22
d Zec 8:17
e 2Ch 33:10
　Jer 6:10
f Ne 9:29
g 2Ki 17:13, 14
　Isa 6:10
　Jer 25:7
h Eze 3:7
i Ne 9:30
　Ac 7:51
j 2Ch 36:15, 16
　Jer 21:5
k Isa 50:2
l Isa 1:15
　La 3:44
m De 28:64
　Jer 5:15
n Le 26:22, 33
　2Ch 36:20, 21

CHAP. 8
o Joe 2:18
　Zec 1:14
p Zec 1:16
q Isa 12:6
　Joe 3:17
　Zec 2:11
　Zec 8:8
r Isa 1:26
　Isa 60:14
　Jer 33:16
s Isa 2:2
　Isa 11:9
　Isa 66:20
　Jer 31:23
t Isa 65:20
　Jer 30:10

6:14 *Or "reminder." 7:1 *See App. B15. 7:2 *Or "soften the face." 7:3 *Or "temple."

7:10 *Or "the orphan." 7:12 *Or possibly, "a hard stone," such as an emery stone. #Or "instruction." 7:13 *Lit., "he." 8:3 *Or "faithfulness." 8:4 *Lit., "because of the multitude of days."

filled with boys and girls playing there.'"[a]

6 "This is what Jehovah of armies says, 'Although it may seem too difficult to the remaining ones of this people in those days, should it seem too difficult also to me?' declares Jehovah of armies."

7 "This is what Jehovah of armies says, 'Here I am saving my people from the lands of the east and the west.*[b] **8** And I will bring them in, and they will reside in Jerusalem;[c] and they will become my people, and I will become their God[d] in truth* and in righteousness.'"

9 "This is what Jehovah of armies says, 'Let your hands be strong,*[e] you who now hear these words from the mouth of the prophets,[f] the same words that were spoken on the day the foundation of the house of Jehovah of armies was laid for the temple to be built. **10** For before that time, there were no wages being paid either for man or for beast;[g] and it was not safe to come and go because of the adversary, for I turned all men one against another.'

11 "'But now I will not deal with the remaining ones of this people as in the former days,'[h] declares Jehovah of armies. **12** 'For the seed of peace will be sown; the vine will produce its fruit and the earth its yield,[i] and the heavens will give their dew; and I will cause the remaining ones of this people to inherit all these things.[j] **13** And just as you became an object of cursing among the nations,[k] O house of Judah and house of Israel, so I will save you, and you will become a blessing.[l]

Do not be afraid![a] Let your hands be strong.'*[b]

14 "For this is what Jehovah of armies says, "Just as I had determined to bring calamity on you because your forefathers made me indignant," says Jehovah of armies, "and I felt no regret,[c] **15** so at this time I have determined to do good to Jerusalem and to the house of Judah.[d] Do not be afraid!"'[e]

16 "'These are the things you should do: Speak the truth with one another,[f] and the judgments in your gates must promote truth and peace.[g] **17** Do not scheme calamity against one another in your hearts,[h] and do not love any false oath;[i] for these are all things that I hate,[j] declares Jehovah."

18 The word of Jehovah of armies again came to me, saying: **19** "This is what Jehovah of armies says, 'The fast of the fourth month,[k] the fast of the fifth month,[l] the fast of the seventh month,[m] and the fast of the tenth month[n] will be occasions for exultation and joy for the house of Judah—festivals of rejoicing.[o] So love truth and peace.'

20 "This is what Jehovah of armies says, 'It will yet come to pass that peoples and the inhabitants of many cities will come; **21** and the inhabitants of one city will go to those of another and say: "Let us earnestly go to beg for the favor* of Jehovah and to seek Jehovah of armies. I am also going."[p] **22** And many peoples and mighty nations will come to seek Jehovah of armies in Jerusalem[q] and to beg for the favor* of Jehovah.'

23 "This is what Jehovah of armies says, 'In those days ten men out of all the languages of the nations[r] will take hold, yes,

---

CHAP. 8

a Jer 30:19
  Jer 31:4, 27
  Zec 2:4
b Ps 107:2, 3
c Jer 3:17
  Joe 3:20
  Am 9:14
d Le 26:12
  Jer 30:22
  Eze 11:20
e Isa 35:4
  Hag 2:4
f Ezr 5:1
g Hag 1:6
h Hag 2:19
i Le 26:4
  De 28:4
  Isa 30:23
j Isa 35:10
  Isa 61:7
k De 28:37
  Jer 42:18
l Ge 22:18
  Isa 19:24, 25

Second Col.

a Isa 41:10
b Isa 35:4
c Jer 4:28
  Eze 24:14
d Jer 31:28
  Jer 32:42
e Isa 43:1
  Zep 3:16
f Le 19:11
  Pr 12:19
  Eph 4:25
g Zec 7:9
h Zec 7:10
i Zec 5:4
j Pr 6:16-19
k Jer 52:6, 7
l Jer 52:12-14
m 2Ki 25:25
  Zec 7:5
n Jer 52:4
o Isa 35:10
  Jer 31:12
p Jer 50:4, 5
q Ps 22:27
  Isa 2:2, 3
  Isa 11:10
  Isa 55:5
  Isa 60:3
  Ho 1:10
  Mic 4:2
  Hag 2:7
r Zec 2:11
  Re 7:9
  Re 14:6

8:7 *Or "from the land of the sunrise and the land of the setting sun." 8:8 *Or "faithfulness." 8:9, 13 *Or "Take courage."

8:21, 22 *Or "soften the face."

they will take firm hold of the robe* of a Jew,# saying: "We want to go with you,ª for we have heard that God is with you people."'"ᵇ

9

A pronouncement:

"The word of Jehovah
   is against the land of
   Ha′drach,
And Damascus is its target*ᶜ
   —For Jehovah's eye is on
   mankindᵈ
And on all the tribes of
   Israel—

2 And against Ha′math,ᵉ which
   borders on her,
And against Tyreᶠ and
   Si′don,ᵍ for they are so
   wise.ʰ

3 Tyre built herself a rampart.*
   She piled up silver like dust
   And gold like the dirt of the
   streets.ⁱ

4 Look! Jehovah will take away
   her possessions,
And he will strike down her
   army into the sea;*ʲ
And she will be consumed
   in the fire.ᵏ

5 Ash′ke·lon will see it and be
   afraid;
Gaz′a will feel great anguish,
Also Ek′ron, because her
   hope is put to shame.
A king will perish from
   Gaz′a,
And Ash′ke·lon will not be
   inhabited.ˡ

6 An illegitimate son will
   settle in Ash′dod,
And I will do away with the
   pride of the Phi·lis′tine.ᵐ

7 I will remove the bloodstained things from his
   mouth
And the disgusting things
   from between his teeth,

And he will be left remaining
   for our God;
And he will become like
   a sheikh* in Judah,ª
And Ek′ron like the
   Jeb′u·site.ᵇ

8 I will encamp as a guard*
   for my house,
So that there will be no one
   passing through and no
   one returning;
And no taskmaster# will
   pass through again,ᵈ
For now I have seen itᐃ
   with my eyes.

9 Rejoice greatly, O daughter
   of Zion.
Shout in triumph,
   O daughter of Jerusalem.
Look! Your king is coming
   to you.ᵉ
He is righteous, bringing
   salvation,*
Humbleᶠ and riding on a
   donkey,
On a colt,# the foal of a
   female donkey.ᵍ

10 I will take away the war
   chariot from E′phra·im
And the horse from
   Jerusalem.
The battle bow will be taken
   away.
And he will proclaim peace
   to the nations;ʰ
His rulership will be from
   sea to sea
And from the River* to the
   ends of the earth.ⁱ

11 As for you, O woman, by the
   blood of your covenant,
I will send your prisoners
   out of the waterless pit.ʲ

12 Return to the stronghold,
   you prisoners with hope.ᵏ
Today I am telling you,

CHAP. 8
a Ex 12:37, 38
b Isa 45:14

CHAP. 9
c Jer 49:27
   Am 1:3
d Heb 4:13
   1Pe 3:12
e Jer 49:23
f Isa 23:1
   Am 1:9, 10
g Eze 28:21
   Joe 3:4
h Eze 28:2, 3
i Eze 27:32, 33
j Eze 26:17
   Eze 27:26
k Eze 28:18
l Zep 2:4
m Am 1:8

Second Col.
a Isa 60:14
b 2Sa 5:6, 7
   1Ki 9:20, 21
c Ps 125:2
d Isa 54:14
e Ps 2:6
   Isa 32:1
   Jer 23:5
   Lu 19:37, 38
   Joh 1:49
f Mt 11:29
g 1Ki 1:33, 34
   Mt 21:5, 7
   Joh 12:14, 15
h Isa 9:7
i Ex 23:31
   Ps 2:8
   Ps 72:8
j Isa 49:9
k Isa 61:1
   Jer 31:17

8:23 *Or "extremity of the garment." #Lit., "a Jewish man." 9:1 *Lit., "resting-place." 9:3 *Or "fortress." 9:4 *Or possibly, "on the sea."

9:7 *A sheikh was a tribal chief. 9:8 *Or "an outpost." #Or "oppressor." ᐃEvidently, the affliction of his people. 9:9 *Or "and victorious; and saved." #Or "a male donkey." 9:10 *That is, the Euphrates.

'I will repay to you, O woman, a double portion.[a]

13 For I will bend* Judah as my bow.
The bow I will fill with E'phra·im,[#]
And I will awaken your sons, O Zion,
Against your sons, O Greece,
And I will make you like a warrior's sword.'

14 Jehovah will be seen over them,
And his arrow will go out like lightning.
The Sovereign Lord Jehovah will sound the horn,[b]
And he will advance with the windstorms of the south.

15 Jehovah of armies will defend them,
And they will devour and subdue the slingstones.[c]
They will drink and be boisterous, as if with wine;
And they will be filled like the bowl,
Like the corners of the altar.[d]

16 Jehovah their God will save them in that day
As the flock of his people;[e]
For they will be like the gemstones of a crown* glittering over his soil.[f]

17 For how great his goodness is,[g]
And how great his handsomeness is!
Grain will make the young men thrive,
And new wine the virgins."[h]

10 "Ask Jehovah for rain in the time of the spring rain.
It is Jehovah who makes the storm clouds,
Who pours rain for them,[i]
And gives vegetation in the field to everyone.

2 For the teraphim statues* have spoken deception;[#]
And the diviners have visioned a lie.
They speak about worthless dreams,
And in vain they try to comfort.
That is why they will wander like sheep.
They will suffer, for there is no shepherd.

3 Against the shepherds my anger burns,
And against the oppressive leaders* I will hold an accounting;
For Jehovah of armies has turned his attention to his flock,[a] to the house of Judah,
And he has made them like his majestic horse in the battle.

4 From him comes the keyman,*
From him comes the supporting ruler,[#]
From him comes the battle bow;
From him goes forth every overseer,[△] all of them together.

5 And they will become like warriors,
Trampling down the mud of the streets in the battle.
They will wage war, for Jehovah is with them;[b]
And the riders of horses will be put to shame.[c]

6 I will make the house of Judah superior,
And the house of Joseph I will save.[d]

CHAP. 9
a Isa 61:7

b Jos 6:5

c Mic 5:9
Zec 10:5
Zec 12:6

d Ex 27:2
Le 4:7

e Eze 34:22

f Isa 62:3
Zep 3:20

g Ps 25:8
Ps 31:19
Isa 63:7

h Isa 62:8
Joe 3:18
Am 9:13

CHAP. 10
i De 11:14
Jer 14:22
Jer 51:16
Eze 34:26
Joe 2:23

Second Col.
a Eze 34:16, 17

b De 20:1

c Hag 2:22

d Jer 3:18
Eze 37:16, 19
Ho 1:10, 11

10:2 *Or "household gods; idols." #Or "what is uncanny; what is mystical." **10:3** *Lit., "the he-goats." **10:4** *Lit., "the corner tower," pictorial of a vital or important man; a chief. #Lit., "the peg," pictorial of one who is a support; a ruler. △Or "taskmaster."

9:13 *Lit., "tread." #That is, like an arrow. **9:16** *Or "diadem."

I will restore them,
For I will show them mercy;[a]
And they will be as though
I had never cast them off;[b]
For I am Jehovah their God,
and I will answer them.

7 Those of E′phra·im must become like a mighty warrior,
And their heart will rejoice
as though from wine.[c]
Their sons will see this and
rejoice;
Their heart will be joyful
in Jehovah.[d]

8 'I will whistle for them and
gather them together;
For I will redeem them,[e] and
they will become many,
And continue to be many.

9 Though I scatter them like
seed among the peoples,
They will remember me in
the distant places;
With their sons they will
revive and return.

10 I will bring them back from
the land of Egypt
And gather them from
As·syr′i·a;[f]
I will bring them to the land
of Gil′e·ad[g] and Leb′a·non,
And there will be no more
room for them.[h]

11 He must pass through the
sea with distress;
And in the sea he will strike
down the waves;[i]
All the depths of the Nile
will dry up.
The pride of As·syr′i·a will
be brought down,
And the scepter of Egypt
will depart.[j]

12 I will make them superior
in Jehovah,[k]
And they will walk about
in his name,'[l] declares
Jehovah."

11 "Open your doors,
O Leb′a·non,
So that a fire may consume
your cedars.

2 Wail, you juniper, for the
cedar has fallen;
The majestic trees have been
destroyed!
Wail, you oaks of Ba′shan,
For the dense forest has
come down!

3 Listen! The wailing of
shepherds,
For their majesty has been
devastated.
Listen! The roaring of young
lions,*
For the dense thickets along
the Jordan have been
destroyed.

4 "This is what Jehovah my
God says, 'Shepherd the
flock meant for the slaughter,[a] 5 whose buyers slaughtered them[b] and are not held
guilty. And those who sell them[c]
say, "May Jehovah be praised,
for I will become rich." And their
shepherds have no compassion
for them.'[d]

6 "'For I will no longer show
compassion on the inhabitants
of the land,' declares Jehovah.
'So I will cause each man to
fall into the hand of his neighbor and his king; and they will
crush the land, and I will not rescue them out of their hand.'"

7 And I began to shepherd
the flock meant for slaughter,[e] in your behalf, O afflicted
ones of the flock. So I took two
staffs, and I called one Pleasantness, and the other Union,[f] and
I began to shepherd the flock.
8 And I dismissed three shepherds in one month, for I* became impatient with them, and
they* detested me as well.
9 And I said: "I will not keep
shepherding you. Let the one
who is dying die, and let the one
perishing perish. As for those

CHAP. 10
a Jer 31:9, 20

b Jer 30:18

c Zec 9:15

d Isa 66:14
Zep 3:14

e Isa 44:22
Isa 51:11

f Isa 11:11

g Jer 50:19
Mic 7:14

h Isa 49:19, 20
Isa 54:1, 2

i Isa 11:15

j Isa 19:1
Eze 30:13

k Isa 41:10
Isa 45:24

l Mic 4:5

Second Col.

CHAP. 11
a Eze 34:8

b Eze 22:25

c Ne 5:8

d Eze 34:2, 4

e Zec 11:4

f Zec 11:10, 14

11:3 *Or "maned young lions." 11:8
*Or "my soul." #Or "their soul."

who are left, let them devour one another's flesh." **10** So I took my staff Pleasantness[a] and cut it up, breaking my covenant that I had made with all the peoples. **11** So it was broken in that day, and the afflicted ones of the flock who were watching me knew that it was the word of Jehovah.

12 Then I said to them: "If it seems good to you, give me my wages; but if not, withhold them." And they paid* my wages, 30 pieces of silver.[b] **13** Then Jehovah said to me: "Throw it into the treasury—the magnificent value with which they valued me."[c] So I took the 30 pieces of silver and threw it into the treasury at the house of Jehovah.[d]

14 Then I cut up my second staff, the Union,[e] breaking the brotherhood between Judah and Israel.[f]

15 And Jehovah said to me: "Now take the equipment of a useless shepherd.[g] **16** For I am letting a shepherd rise up in the land. He will not take care of the sheep that are perishing;[h] he will not seek out the young or heal the injured[i] or feed those able to stand. Instead, he devours the flesh of the fat one[j] and tears off the hooves of the sheep.[k]

17 Woe to my worthless shepherd,[l] who is abandoning the flock![m]
A sword will strike his arm and his right eye.
His arm will wither completely,
And his right eye will go completely blind."*

12 A pronouncement:
"The word of Jehovah concerning Israel," declares Jehovah,

The One who stretched out the heavens,[a]
Who laid the foundation of the earth,[b]
And who formed the spirit* of man within him.

2 "Here I am making Jerusalem a cup* that causes all the surrounding peoples to stagger; and there will be a siege against Judah as well as against Jerusalem.[c] **3** In that day I will make Jerusalem a heavy* stone to all the peoples. All those who lift it are sure to be severely injured;[d] and all the nations of the earth will be gathered against her.[e] **4** In that day," declares Jehovah, "I will strike every horse with panic and its rider with madness. I will keep my eyes on the house of Judah, but I will strike every horse of the peoples with blindness. **5** And the sheikhs* of Judah will say in their heart, 'The inhabitants of Jerusalem are a strength to me by means of Jehovah of armies their God.'[f] **6** In that day I will make the sheikhs of Judah like a fiery pot among wood and like a fiery torch in a row of cut grain,[g] and they will consume all the surrounding peoples on the right and on the left;[h] and Jerusalem will again be inhabited in her place,* in Jerusalem.[i]

7 "And Jehovah will save the tents of Judah first, so that the beauty* of the house of David and the beauty* of the inhabitants of Jerusalem may not be too great over Judah. **8** In that day Jehovah will be a defense around the inhabitants of Jerusalem;[j] in that day the one who stumbles* among them will be like David, and the house

---

CHAP. 11
a Zec 11:7
b Mt 26:14, 15
  Mt 27:9
  Mr 14:10, 11
c Ex 21:32
d Mt 27:5, 6
  Ac 1:18
e Zec 11:7
f 1Ki 12:19, 20
  Eze 37:16
g Eze 34:2, 4
h Jer 23:2
  Eze 34:6
  Mt 9:36
i Eze 34:21
j Ge 31:38
k Eze 34:3, 10
l Jer 23:1
  Mt 23:13
m Joh 10:12

Second Col.

CHAP. 12
a Job 26:7
  Isa 42:5
b Ps 102:25
  Isa 45:18
c Zec 14:14
d Zep 3:19
e Zec 14:2, 3
f Isa 41:10
  Joe 3:16
  Zec 12:8
g Isa 41:15
h Mic 4:13
  Zec 9:15
i Zec 2:4
j Jer 23:6
  Joe 3:16
  Zec 2:5
  Zec 9:15

11:12 *Lit., "weighed out." 11:17 *Lit., "dim." 12:1 *Or "breath." 12:2 *Or "bowl." 12:3 *Or "burdensome." 12:5 *A sheikh was a tribal chief. 12:6 *Or "in her rightful place." 12:7 *Or "splendor." 12:8 *Or "the weakest."

of David like God, like Jehovah's angel who goes before them.ª 9 And in that day I will be certain to annihilate all the nations that come against Jerusalem.ᵇ

10 "I will pour out on the house of David and on the inhabitants of Jerusalem the spirit of favor and supplication, and they will look to the one whom they pierced,ᶜ and they will wail over him as they would wail over an only son; and they will grieve bitterly over him as they would grieve over a firstborn son. 11 In that day the wailing in Jerusalem will be great, like the wailing at Ha·dad·rim′mon in the Plain of Me·gid′do.ᵈ 12 And the land will wail, each family by itself; the family of David's house by itself, and their women by themselves; the family of Na·than's ᵉ house by itself, and their women by themselves; 13 the family of Le′vi'sᶠ house by itself, and their women by themselves; the family of the Shim′e·itesᵍ by itself, and their women by themselves; 14 and all the families that are left remaining, each family by itself, and their women by themselves.

13 "In that day a well will be opened to the house of David and to the inhabitants of Jerusalem for cleansing sin and impurity.ʰ

2 "In that day," declares Jehovah of armies, "I will erase the names of the idols from the land,ⁱ and they will no longer be remembered; and I will rid the land of the prophetsʲ and the spirit of uncleanness. 3 And if a man should prophesy again, his father and his mother who caused his birth will say to him, 'You will not live, because you have spoken lies in the name of Jehovah.' And his father and his mother who caused his birth will pierce him through because of his prophesying.ᵏ

4 "In that day each of the prophets will be ashamed of his vision when he prophesies; and they will not wear an official garment of hairª in order to deceive. 5 And he will say, 'I am no prophet. I am a man cultivating the soil, because a man bought me when I was young.' 6 And if someone asks him, 'What are these wounds between your shoulders?'* he will answer, 'Wounds I received in the house of my friends.'"*

7 "O sword, awake against
   my shepherd,ᵇ
Against the man who is
   my companion," declares
   Jehovah of armies.
"Strike the shepherd,ᶜ and
   let the flock* be scattered;ᵈ
And I will turn my hand
   against those who are
   insignificant."
8 "And in all the land," declares
   Jehovah,
"Two parts in it will be cut
   off and perish;*
And the third part will be
   left remaining in it.
9 And I will bring the third
   part through the fire;
And I will refine them as
   silver is refined,
And test them as gold is
   tested.ᵉ
They will call on my name,
   And I will answer them.
I will say, 'They are my
   people,'ᶠ
And they will say, 'Jehovah
   is our God.'"

14 "Look! The day is coming, a day belonging to Jehovah, when the spoil from you* will be divided in your midst. 2 I will gather all the nations

---

CHAP. 12
a Ex 14:19
  Ex 23:20

b Isa 54:17
  Hag 2:22

c Joh 19:34, 37
  Joh 20:27
  Re 1:7

d 2Ki 23:29
  2Ch 35:22

e 2Sa 5:13, 14
  Lu 3:23, 31

f Ex 6:16

g Ex 6:17
  1Ch 23:10

CHAP. 13
h Eze 36:25, 29

i Ex 23:13

j De 13:5

k De 13:6-9
  De 18:20

Second Col.
a 2Ki 1:8
  Mt 3:4

b Eze 34:23
  Mic 5:4
  Joh 10:11
  Heb 13:20

c Isa 53:8
  Da 9:26
  Ac 3:18

d Mt 26:31
  Mt 26:55, 56
  Mr 14:27, 50
  Joh 16:32

e Mal 3:2, 3

f Jer 30:22

13:6 *Lit., "between your hands?" That is, on the chest or on the back. #Or "of those who love me." 13:7 *Or "sheep." 13:8 *Or "die." 14:1 *That is, the city referred to in vs. 2.

against Jerusalem for the war; and the city will be captured and the houses plundered and the women raped. And half of the city will go into exile, but the remaining ones of the people will not be cut off from the city.

3 "Jehovah will go out and war against those nations[a] as when he fights in the day of a battle.[b] 4 In that day his feet will stand on the Mount of Olives,[c] which faces Jerusalem on the east; and the Mount of Olives will be split in half, from east* to west,[f] forming a very great valley; and half of the mountain will move to the north, and half of it to the south. 5 You will flee to the valley of my mountains, for the valley of the mountains will extend all the way to A′zel. You will have to flee, just as you fled because of the earthquake in the days of King Uz·zi′ah of Judah.[d] And Jehovah my God will come, and all the holy ones will be with him.[e]

6 "In that day there will be no precious light[f]—things will be congealed.* 7 And it will become one day that is known as belonging to Jehovah.[g] It will not be day, nor will it be night; and at evening time there will be light. 8 In that day living waters[h] will flow out from Jerusalem,[i] half of them toward the eastern sea*[j] and half of them toward the western sea.*[k] It will happen in summer and in winter. 9 And Jehovah will be King over all the earth.[l] In that day Jehovah will be one,[m] and his name one.[n]

10 "The whole land will become like the Ar′a·bah,[o] from Ge′ba[p] to Rim′mon[q] south of Je-

CHAP. 14
a Eze 38:23
  Joe 3:2, 14
  Re 16:14
b Ex 15:3
  2Ch 20:15
c Lu 19:29
  Ac 1:12
d Am 1:1
e De 33:2
  Joe 3:11
  Jude 14
f Isa 13:9, 10
  Am 5:18
g Joe 2:31
  1Th 5:2
  2Pe 3:10
h Re 21:6
  Re 22:17
i Jer 17:13
  Eze 47:1
  Joe 3:18
  Re 22:1
j De 3:17
k Jos 1:4
l Ps 97:1
  Re 19:6
m De 6:4
n Isa 42:8
  Isa 44:6
o De 1:7
p 1Ki 15:22
q 1Ch 4:24, 32

Second Col.
a Jer 30:18
b Jer 37:13
c Ne 3:1
  Jer 31:38
d Isa 60:18
  Jer 31:40
e Jer 23:6
  Jer 33:16
f 2Ki 19:34, 35
  Joe 3:2
g Jg 7:22
  Eze 38:21
h 2Ch 14:13
  2Ch 20:25
  Zec 2:8, 9
i Isa 66:23
j Ps 86:9
k Le 23:34
  Ne 8:14, 15

rusalem; and she will rise and be inhabited in her place,[a] from the Gate of Benjamin[b] all the way to the site of the First Gate, all the way to the Corner Gate, and from the Tower of Ha·nan′el[c] all the way to the winepresses* of the king. 11 And people will inhabit her; and there will never again be a curse of destruction,[d] and Jerusalem will be inhabited in security.[e]

12 "And this is the scourge with which Jehovah will scourge all the peoples who wage war against Jerusalem:[f] Their flesh will rot away while they stand on their feet, their eyes will rot away in their sockets, and their tongues will rot away in their mouths.

13 "In that day confusion from Jehovah will be widespread among them; and each one will grab hold of the hand of his companion, and his hand will come against the hand of his companion.*[g] 14 Judah will also be involved in the war at Jerusalem; and the wealth of all the surrounding nations will be gathered, gold and silver and garments in vast quantity.[h]

15 "And a scourge like that scourge will also come against the horses, the mules, the camels, the donkeys, and all the livestock that are in those camps.

16 "Everyone who is left remaining out of all the nations that come against Jerusalem will go up from year to year[i] to bow down to* the King, Jehovah of armies,[j] and to celebrate the Festival of Booths.*[k] 17 But if anyone among the families of the earth does not go up to Jerusalem to bow down to the King, Je-

hovah of armies, no rain will fall on them.[a] **18** And if the family of Egypt does not come up and does not come in, they will have no rain. Instead, they will have the scourge with which Jehovah scourges the nations that do not come up to celebrate the Festival of Booths. **19** This will be the punishment for the sin of Egypt and the sin of all the nations that do not come up to celebrate the Festival of Booths.

20 "In that day the words 'Holiness belongs to Jehovah!'[b] will be written on the bells of the horses. And the cooking pots*[a] in the house of Jehovah will be like the bowls[b] before the altar. **21** And every cooking pot* in Jerusalem and in Judah will be holy and will belong to Jehovah of armies, and all those who are sacrificing will come in and use some of them for boiling. In that day there will no longer be a Ca'naan·ite# in the house of Jehovah of armies."[c]

14:20 *Or "wide-mouthed cooking pots." **14:21** *Or "wide-mouthed cooking pot." #Or possibly, "trader."

CHAP. 14
a Isa 60:12

b Ex 28:36
  Ex 39:30

Second Col.
a 1Sa 2:13, 14

b Ex 25:29
  Nu 4:7

c Eze 44:9

MALACHI

---

1 A pronouncement:
The word of Jehovah to Israel through Mal'a·chi:*

2 "I have shown love to you people,"[a] says Jehovah.

But you say: "How have you shown us love?"

1:1 *Meaning "My Messenger."

CHAP. 1
a De 10:15

Second Col.
a Ge 25:25, 26
b Ro 9:13
c Jer 49:20
  Joe 3:19
d Isa 34:10, 13

"Was not E'sau the brother of Jacob?"[a] declares Jehovah. "But I loved Jacob, **3** and E'sau I hated;[b] and I made his mountains desolate[c] and left his inheritance for the jackals of the wilderness."[d]

4 "Though E'dom says, 'We have been shattered, but we

will return and rebuild the ruins,' this is what Jehovah of armies says, 'They will build, but I will tear down, and they will be called "the territory of wickedness" and "the people whom Jehovah has forever condemned."'"

5 Your own eyes will see it, and you will say: "May Jehovah be magnified over the territory of Israel."'"

6 "'A son honors a father,[b] and a servant his master. So if I am a father,[c] where is the honor due me?[d] And if I am a master,* where is the fear* due me?' Jehovah of armies says to you priests who are despising my name.[e]

"'But you say: "How have we despised your name?"'

7 "'By presenting polluted food* on my altar.'

"'And you say: "How have we polluted you?"'

"'By saying: "The table of Jehovah[f] is something to be despised." **8** And when you present a blind animal as a sacrifice, you say: "It is nothing bad." And when you present a lame animal or a sick one: "It is nothing bad."'[g]

"Try presenting them, please, to your governor. Will he be pleased with you or receive you with favor?" says Jehovah of armies.

9 "And now, please, appeal to* God, that he may show us favor. With such offerings from your own hand, will he receive any of you with favor?" says Jehovah of armies.

10 "And who among you is willing to shut the doors?*[h] For you will not even light my altar without charge.[i] I find no delight in you," says Jehovah of armies,

"and I take no pleasure in any gift offering from your hand."[a]

11 "For from the rising of the sun to its setting,* my name will be great among the nations.[b] In every place sacrifices will be made to smoke, and offerings will be made to my name, as a pure gift; because my name will be great among the nations,"[c] says Jehovah of armies.

12 "But you are profaning it*[d] by saying, 'The table of Jehovah is polluted, and its fruit, its food, is to be despised.'[e] **13** You also say, 'Look! How tiresome!' and you sniff scornfully at it," says Jehovah of armies. "And you bring stolen, lame, and sick animals. Yes, you bring such things as a gift! Should I accept it from your hand?"[f] says Jehovah.

14 "Cursed is the cunning one who has a sound male animal in his flock, but he makes a vow and sacrifices a blemished* one to Jehovah. For I am a great King,"[g] says Jehovah of armies, "and my name will be awe-inspiring among the nations."[h]

2 "And now, O priests, this commandment is for you.[i] **2** If you refuse to listen and to take it to heart to glorify my name," says Jehovah of armies, "I will send on you the curse,[j] and I will turn your blessings into curses.[k] Yes, I have turned the blessings into curses, because you are not taking it to heart."

3 "Look! I will ruin* your sown seed because of you,[l] and I will scatter dung on your faces, the dung of your festivals; and you will be carried away to it.[#] **4** Then you will know that I have

---

CHAP. 1
a Isa 34:5
  Ob 18

b Ex 20:12

c Ex 4:22

d Isa 1:2

e Eze 22:26

f Eze 41:21, 22
  1Co 10:21

g Le 22:20, 22
  De 15:21

h 2Ch 23:4

i Jer 6:13
  Mic 3:11

Second Col.
a Isa 1:11
  Jer 6:20

b Ps 113:3
  Isa 45:6
  Isa 59:19

c Ps 22:27
  Zep 3:9
  Mt 28:19
  Re 15:4

d Eze 22:26

e Mal 1:7

f Le 22:20, 22
  De 15:21
  De 17:1

g Ps 47:2
  Jer 10:10

h Re 15:4

CHAP. 2
i Mal 1:6

j Le 26:14-17
  De 28:15

k Hag 1:11

l Joe 1:17

1:6 *Or "grand master." #Or "respect." 1:7 *Lit., "bread." 1:9 *Or "soften the face of." 1:10 *Evidently, the doors of the temple, as a duty. 1:11 *Or "from east to west." 1:12 *Or possibly, "profaning me." 1:14 *Or "defective." 2:3 *Lit., "rebuke." #That is, to the place where dung from sacrifices was deposited.

given this commandment to you so that my covenant with Le'vi may continue,"[a] says Jehovah of armies.

5 "My covenant with him was one of life and of peace, which I gave to him, along with fear.* He feared me, yes, he stood in awe of my name. 6 The law* of truth was in his mouth,[b] and no unrighteousness was found on his lips. He walked with me in peace and in uprightness,[c] and he turned many back from error. 7 For the lips of a priest should safeguard knowledge, and people should seek the law* from his mouth,[d] because he is the messenger of Jehovah of armies.

8 "But you yourselves have turned aside from the way. You have made many stumble with regard to the law.*[e] You have ruined the covenant of Le'vi,"[f] says Jehovah of armies. 9 "So I will make you despised and low before all the people, because you did not keep my ways but showed partiality in applying the law."[g]

10 "Do we not all have one father?[h] Was it not one God who created us? So why do we deal treacherously with one another,[i] profaning the covenant of our forefathers? 11 Judah has dealt treacherously, and something detestable has been done in Israel and in Jerusalem; for Judah has profaned the holiness* of Jehovah,[j] which He loves, and he has taken as a bride the daughter of a foreign god.[k] 12 Jehovah will cut off from the tents of Jacob anyone who does this, whoever he may be,* though he presents a gift offering to Jehovah of armies."[l]

13 "And there is another* thing that you do, which results in covering the altar of Jehovah with tears and with weeping and sighing, so that he no longer pays attention to your gift offering or looks favorably on anything from your hand.[a] 14 And you say, 'For what reason?' It is because Jehovah has acted as a witness between you and the wife of your youth, with whom you have dealt treacherously, although she is your partner and your wife by covenant.*[b] 15 But there was one who did not do it, for he had what remained of the spirit. And what was that one seeking? The offspring* of God. So guard yourselves respecting your spirit, and do not deal treacherously with the wife of your youth. 16 For I hate* divorce,"[c] says Jehovah the God of Israel, "and the one who covers his garment with violence,"# says Jehovah of armies. "And guard yourselves respecting your spirit, and you must not deal treacherously.[d]

17 "You have made Jehovah weary with your words.[e] But you say, 'How have we made him weary?' By saying, 'Everyone who does bad is good in the eyes of Jehovah, and he finds pleasure in him,'[f] or by saying, 'Where is the God of justice?'"

3 "Look! I am sending my messenger, and he will clear up* a way before me.[g] And suddenly the true Lord, whom you are seeking, will come to his temple;[h] and the messenger of the covenant will come, in whom you take delight. Look! He will certainly come," says Jehovah of armies.

CHAP. 2
a Ex 40:12, 15
　Nu 3:6
　Nu 18:23
　Eze 44:15, 16

b 2Ch 17:8, 9

c Ex 32:26

d De 24:8
　2Ch 15:3
　Ne 8:7, 8
　Eze 44:23, 24

e Lu 11:52

f Ne 13:29

g Le 19:15
　De 1:17
　De 16:19

h Mal 1:6
　1Co 8:6

i Ne 5:8

j Le 20:26

k De 7:1, 3
　Jg 3:5, 6
　1Ki 11:1, 2
　Ne 13:23

l 1Sa 15:22

Second Col.
a Pr 21:27

b Pr 5:18-20
　Mt 19:4-6

c Ge 2:24
　Mt 5:32
　Mt 19:8, 9
　Mr 10:5-9

d Mal 2:10

e Isa 1:14, 15

f Eze 18:29

CHAP. 3
g Mt 3:1-3
　Mt 11:7, 10
　Mr 1:2-4
　Lu 1:76
　Joh 1:6, 23
　Joh 3:28

h Ps 11:4

2:5 *Or "respect; reverence." 2:6, 7 *Or "instruction." 2:8 *Or possibly, "by your instruction." 2:11 *Or possibly, "the sanctuary." 2:12 *Lit., "one who is awake and one who answers."

2:13 *Lit., "a second." 2:14 *Or "your legal wife." 2:15 *Lit., "seed." 2:16 *Lit., "he hates." #Or "who engages in violence." 3:1 *Or "prepare."

2 "But who will endure the day of his coming, and who will be able to stand when he appears? For he will be like the fire of a refiner and like the lye*ª of laundrymen. **3** And he will sit as a refiner and cleanser of silverᵇ and will cleanse the sons of Le′vi; and he will clarify* them like gold and like silver, and they will certainly become to Jehovah people presenting a gift offering in righteousness. **4** And the gift offering of Judah and of Jerusalem will actually be pleasing* to Jehovah, as in the days of long ago and as in the years of antiquity.ᶜ

5 "I will come near to you for judgment, and I will be a swift witness against the sorcerers,ᵈ against the adulterers, against those who take false oaths,ᵉ against those who defraud the hired worker,ᶠ the widow, and the fatherless child,*ᵍ and against those who refuse to helpᵘ the foreigner.ʰ These have not feared me," says Jehovah of armies.

6 "For I am Jehovah; I do not change.*ⁱ And you are sons of Jacob; you have not yet come to your finish. **7** From the days of your forefathers you have turned aside from my regulations and have not kept them.ʲ Return to me, and I will return to you,"ᵏ says Jehovah of armies.

But you say: "How are we supposed to return?"

8 "Will a mere human rob God? But you are robbing me."

And you say: "How have we robbed you?"

"In the tithes* and in the contributions. **9** You are certainly cursed,* for you are robbing me—yes, the entire nation is doing so. **10** Bring the entire tithe* into the storehouse,ª so that there may be food in my house;ᵇ and test me out, please, in this regard," Jehovah of armies says, "to see whether I will not open to you the floodgates of the heavensᶜ and pour outᵈ on you a blessing until there is nothing lacking."ᵈ

11 "And I will rebuke the devouring one* for you, and it will not ruin the fruit of your land, nor will the vine in your field be fruitless,"ᵉ says Jehovah of armies.

12 "All the nations will have to declare you happy,ᶠ for you will become a land of delight," says Jehovah of armies.

13 "Your words against me have been strong," says Jehovah.

And you say: "How have we spoken against you among ourselves?"ᵍ

14 "You say, 'It is of no value to serve God.ʰ How have we benefited by keeping our obligations to him and by walking somberly before Jehovah of armies? **15** Now we consider presumptuous people happy. Also, those who practice wickedness are successful.ⁱ They dare to put God to the test and get away with it.'"

16 At that time those who fear Jehovah spoke with one another, each one with his companion, and Jehovah kept paying attention and listening. And a book of remembrance was written before himʲ for those fearing Jehovah and for those meditating on* his name.ᵏ

CHAP. 3
a Isa 1:25
  Jer 2:22

b Ps 66:10
  Pr 25:4
  Zec 13:9

c 2Ch 7:1

d De 18:10, 12

e Ex 20:7

f Pr 14:31
  Jas 5:4

g De 24:17
  Isa 1:17
  Jas 1:27

h Ex 23:9
  Zec 7:10

i Isa 43:10
  Isa 46:4
  Jas 1:17

j De 9:7
  Ac 7:51

k Jer 3:12
  Zec 1:3
  Jas 4:8

Second Col.
a Le 27:30
  De 14:28

b 2Ch 31:11
  Ne 12:44
  Ne 13:10

c De 28:12

d Le 26:10
  2Ch 31:10
  Pr 3:9, 10

e De 11:14
  Zec 8:12

f Isa 61:9

g Mal 1:6

h Job 21:14, 15
  Ps 73:13, 14
  Isa 58:3
  Zep 1:12

i Jer 12:1

j Ps 56:8
  Ps 69:28

k Isa 26:8

3:2 *Or "soap." **3:3** *Or "refine." **3:4** *Or "gratifying." **3:5** *Or "the orphan." ᵘOr "who deny the rights of." **3:6** *Or "I have not changed." **3:8** *Or "tenth parts."

3:9 *Or possibly, "With a curse you are cursing me." **3:10** *Or "all the tenth parts." ᵘLit., "empty out." **3:11** *Apparently referring to insect plagues. **3:16** *Or "thinking on." Or possibly, "treasuring."

17 "And they will be mine," [a] says Jehovah of armies, "in the day when I produce a special property.*[b] I will show them compassion, just as a man shows compassion to his son who serves him.[c] 18 And you will again see the distinction between a righteous person and a wicked person,[d] between one serving God and one not serving him."

4 "For look! the day is coming, burning like a furnace,[e] when all the presumptuous ones and all those practicing wickedness will become like stubble. The coming day will certainly devour them," says Jehovah of armies, "and it will leave them neither root nor branch. 2 But on you who honor* my name, the sun of righteousness will shine, with healing in its rays;* and you will skip about like fattened calves."

3 "And you will tread the wicked underfoot, for they will be like dust under the soles of your feet on the day when I take action," says Jehovah of armies.

4 "Remember the Law of my servant Moses, the regulations and judgments that I commanded at Ho′reb for all Israel to obey.[a]

5 "Look! I am sending to you E·li′jah the prophet[b] before the coming of the great and awe-inspiring day of Jehovah.[c] 6 And he will turn the hearts of fathers back toward sons,[d] and the hearts of sons back toward fathers; so that I may not come and strike the earth, devoting it to destruction."

3:17 *Or "a treasured possession."
4:2 *Lit., "fear."

4:2 *Lit., "wings."

CHAP. 3
a Jer 31:33

b Isa 62:3
1Pe 2:9

c Ps 103:13

d Ps 58:10, 11

CHAP. 4
e Zep 2:2
2Pe 3:7

Second Col.
a De 4:5

b Mt 11:13, 14
Mr 9:11, 12

c Joe 2:31
Ac 2:20
2Pe 3:10

d Lu 1:17

(End of the translation of the Hebrew-Aramaic Scriptures, to be followed by that of the Christian Greek Scriptures)

ACCORDING TO
MATTHEW

OUTLINE OF CONTENTS

1 The book of the history* of Jesus Christ,# son of David,[a] son of Abraham:[b]
2 Abraham became father to Isaac;[c]
Isaac became father to Jacob;[d]
Jacob became father to Judah[e] and his brothers;
3 Judah became father to Pe′rez and Ze′rah[f] by Ta′mar;
Pe′rez became father to Hez′ron;[g]
Hez′ron became father to Ram;[h]
4 Ram became father to Am·min′a·dab;
Am·min′a·dab became father to Nah′shon;[i]
Nah′shon became father to Sal′mon;
5 Sal′mon became father to Bo′az by Ra′hab;[j]
Bo′az became father to O′bed by Ruth;[k]
O′bed became father to Jes′se;[l]
6 Jes′se became father to David[m] the king.
David became father to Sol′o·mon[n] by the wife of U·ri′ah;
7 Sol′o·mon became father to Re·ho·bo′am;[o]
Re·ho·bo′am became father to A·bi′jah;
A·bi′jah became father to A′sa;[p]
8 A′sa became father to Je·hosh′a·phat;[q]
Je·hosh′a·phat became father to Je·ho′ram;[r]
Je·ho′ram became father to Uz·zi′ah;
9 Uz·zi′ah became father to Jo′tham;[s]
Jo′tham became father to A′haz;[t]
A′haz became father to Hez·e·ki′ah;[u]
10 Hez·e·ki′ah became father to Ma·nas′seh;[a]
Ma·nas′seh became father to A′mon;[b]
A′mon became father to Jo·si′ah;[c]
11 Jo·si′ah[d] became father to Jec·o·ni′ah[e] and to his brothers at the time of the deportation to Babylon.[f]
12 After the deportation to Babylon, Jec·o·ni′ah became father to She·al′ti·el;
She·al′ti·el became father to Ze·rub′ba·bel;[g]
13 Ze·rub′ba·bel became father to A·bi′ud;
A·bi′ud became father to E·li′a·kim;
E·li′a·kim became father to A′zor;
14 A′zor became father to Za′dok;
Za′dok became father to A′chim;
A′chim became father to E·li′ud;
15 E·li′ud became father to El·e·a′zar;
El·e·a′zar became father to Mat′than;
Mat′than became father to Jacob;
16 Jacob became father to Joseph the husband of Mary, of whom Jesus was born,[h] who is called Christ.[i]

17 All the generations, then, from Abraham until David were 14 generations; from David until the deportation to Babylon, 14 generations; from the deportation to Babylon until the Christ, 14 generations.

18 But this is how the birth of Jesus Christ took place. During the time his mother Mary was promised in marriage to Joseph, she was found to be pregnant by holy spirit*[j] before they were united. 19 However, be-

1:1 * Or "genealogy." # Or "the Messiah; the Anointed One."

1:18 * Or "active force."

CHAP. 1
a 1Ch 17:11, Mt 9:27, Lu 1:32, 33
b Ge 22:18
c Ge 21:3
d Ge 25:26, 1Ch 1:34
e Ge 29:35
f Ge 38:29, 30
g Ru 4:18-22
h 1Ch 2:9
i 1Ch 2:10, 11
j Jos 2:1
k Ru 4:13
l 1Ch 2:12
m 1Ch 2:13, 15
n 2Sa 12:24, 1Ch 3:5
o 1Ki 11:43
p 1Ch 3:10-19, 2Ch 14:1
q 1Ki 15:24
r 2Ch 21:1
s 2Ki 15:32
t 2Ki 15:38
u 2Ki 18:1

Second Col.
a 2Ki 20:21
b 2Ch 33:20
c 2Ki 21:24
d 2Ki 23:34
e 1Ch 3:15, 16
f 2Ki 24:12, 15, 2Ch 36:9, 10
g Ezr 3:2, Ne 12:1
h Mt 13:55, Mr 6:3
i Lu 3:23-38
j Lu 1:35

cause her husband Joseph was righteous and did not want to make her a public spectacle, he intended to divorce her secretly.[a] **20** But after he had thought these things over, look! Jehovah's* angel appeared to him in a dream, saying: "Joseph, son of David, do not be afraid to take your wife Mary home, for what has been conceived* in her is by holy spirit.[b] **21** She will give birth to a son, and you are to name him Jesus,*[c] for he will save his people from their sins."[d] **22** All of this actually came about to fulfill what was spoken by Jehovah* through his prophet, saying: **23** "Look! The virgin will become pregnant and will give birth to a son, and they will name him Im·man′u·el,"[e] which means, when translated, "With Us Is God."[f]

24 Then Joseph woke up from his sleep and did as the angel of Jehovah* had directed him, and he took his wife home. **25** But he did not have sexual relations with her until she gave birth to a son,[g] and he named him Jesus.[h]

2 After Jesus had been born in Beth′le·hem[i] of Ju·de′a in the days of Herod*[j] the king, look! astrologers* from the East came to Jerusalem, **2** saying: "Where is the one born king of the Jews?[k] For we saw his star when we were in the East, and we have come to do obeisance* to him." **3** At hearing this, King Herod was agitated, and all Jerusalem with him. **4** On gathering together all the chief priests and

scribes of the people, he inquired of them where the Christ* was to be born. **5** They said to him: "In Beth′le·hem[a] of Ju·de′a, for this is how it has been written through the prophet: **6** 'And you, O Beth′le·hem of the land of Judah, are by no means the most insignificant city among the governors of Judah, for out of you will come a governing one, who will shepherd my people Israel.'"[b]

7 Then Herod secretly summoned the astrologers and carefully ascertained from them the time of the star's appearing. **8** When sending them to Beth′le·hem, he said: "Go make a careful search for the young child, and when you have found him, report back to me so that I too may go and do obeisance to him." **9** After they had heard the king, they went their way, and look! the star they had seen when they were in the East[c] went ahead of them until it came to a stop above where the young child was. **10** On seeing the star, they rejoiced with great joy. **11** And when they went into the house, they saw the young child with Mary his mother, and falling down, they did obeisance* to him. They also opened their treasures and presented him with gifts—gold and frankincense and myrrh. **12** However, because they were given divine warning in a dream[d] not to return to Herod, they departed for their country by another way.

13 After they had departed, look! Jehovah's* angel appeared to Joseph in a dream,[e] saying: "Get up, take the young child and his mother and flee to Egypt, and stay there until I give you word, for Herod is about to search for the young child to kill him." **14** So Joseph got up and

---

CHAP. 1
a De 24:1

b Lu 1:35

c Mt 1:25
  Lu 1:31

d Lu 2:30
  Joh 1:29
  Ac 4:12
  Ac 5:31
  Eph 1:7
  Heb 7:25
  1Pe 2:24

e Isa 7:14

f Isa 8:8, 10

g Lu 2:7

h Lu 2:21

CHAP. 2
i Mic 5:2
  Lu 2:4

j Lu 1:5

k Mt 27:37

Second Col.
a Joh 7:42

b 2Sa 5:2
  Mic 5:2

c Mt 2:2

d Mt 2:22

e Mt 1:20
  Mt 2:19

1:20 *This is the first of 237 places in the Christian Greek Scriptures where the divine name, Jehovah, occurs in the main text of this version. See App. A5. *Or "begotten." **1:21** *Corresponds to the Hebrew name Jeshua, or Joshua, which means "Jehovah Is Salvation." **1:22, 24; 2:13** *See App. A5. **2:1** *See Glossary. *Or "magi." **2:2** *Or "to bow down."

2:4 *Or "the Messiah; the Anointed One." **2:11** *Or "bowed down."

by night took along the young child and the child's mother and went into Egypt. 15 He stayed there until the death of Herod. This fulfilled what was spoken by Jehovah* through his prophet, saying: "Out of Egypt I called my son."[a]

16 Then Herod, seeing that he had been outwitted by the astrologers, flew into a great rage, and he sent out and had all the boys in Beth′le·hem and in all its districts killed, from two years of age and under, according to the time that he had carefully ascertained from the astrologers.[b] 17 Then was fulfilled what was spoken through Jeremiah the prophet, who said: 18 "A voice was heard in Ra′mah, weeping and much wailing. It was Rachel[c] weeping for her children, and she was unwilling to take comfort, because they are no more."[d]

19 When Herod had died, look! Jehovah's* angel appeared in a dream[e] to Joseph in Egypt 20 and said: "Get up, take the young child and his mother and go into the land of Israel, for those who were seeking the life* of the young child are dead." 21 So he got up and took the young child and the child's mother and entered into the land of Israel. 22 But hearing that Ar·che·la′us ruled Ju·de′a instead of his father Herod, he was afraid to go there. Moreover, being given divine warning in a dream,[f] he withdrew into the territory of Gal′i·lee.[g] 23 And he came and settled in a city named Naz′a·reth,[h] in order to fulfill what was spoken through the prophets: "He will be called a Naz·a·rene′."*[i]

3 In those days John[j] the Baptist came preaching[k] in the wilderness of Ju·de′a, 2 saying:

CHAP. 2
a Ho 11:1
b Mt 2:7
c Ge 35:19
d Jer 31:15
e Mt 1:20
f Mt 2:12
g Mr 1:9 Lu 2:39
h Joh 1:45
i Isa 11:1 Isa 53:2 Jer 23:5 Zec 3:8

CHAP. 3
j Joh 1:6
k Mr 1:3, 4 Lu 3:3-6

Second Col.
a Mt 4:17
b Mt 1:2 Joh 1:23
c Isa 40:3
d 2Ki 1:8
e Mr 1:6
f Mr 1:5
g Mr 1:9
h Mr 12:18 Lu 7:30
i Mt 12:34
j Mt 23:33 Lu 3:7-9 Lu 21:23
k Joh 8:33, 39
l Mt 7:19 Lu 13:6-9
m Ac 19:4
n Joh 1:15, 27
o Mr 1:7, 8 Joh 1:33 Ac 2:1, 4 1Co 12:13
p Lu 3:16, 17
q Mal 4:1

"Repent, for the Kingdom of the heavens has drawn near."[a] 3 This, in fact, is the one spoken of through Isaiah the prophet[b] in these words: "A voice of one calling out in the wilderness: 'Prepare the way of Jehovah!* Make his roads straight.'"[c] 4 Now John was clothed with camel's hair and had a leather belt around his waist.[d] His food was locusts and wild honey.[e] 5 Then the people of Jerusalem and all Ju·de′a and all the country around the Jordan were going out to him,[f] 6 and they were baptized* by him in the Jordan River,[g] openly confessing their sins.

7 When he caught sight of many of the Pharisees and Sadducees[h] coming to the baptism, he said to them: "You offspring of vipers,[i] who has warned you to flee from the coming wrath?[j] 8 Therefore, produce fruit that befits repentance. 9 Do not presume to say to yourselves, 'We have Abraham as our father.'[k] For I say to you that God is able to raise up children for Abraham from these stones. 10 The ax is already lying at the root of the trees. Every tree, then, that does not produce fine fruit is to be cut down and thrown into the fire.[l] 11 I, for my part, baptize you with water because of your repentance,[m] but the one coming after me is stronger than I am, whose sandals I am not worthy to take off.[n] That one will baptize you with holy spirit[o] and with fire.[p] 12 His winnowing shovel is in his hand, and he will clean up his threshing floor completely and will gather his wheat into the storehouse, but the chaff he will burn up with fire[q] that cannot be put out."

13 Then Jesus came from Gal′i·lee to the Jordan to John,

---

in order to be baptized by him.[a] **14** But the latter tried to prevent him, saying: "I am the one who needs to be baptized by you, and are you coming to me?" **15** Jesus replied to him: "Let it be this time, for in that way it is suitable for us to carry out all that is righteous." Then he quit preventing him. **16** After being baptized, Jesus immediately came up from the water; and look! the heavens were opened up,[b] and he saw God's spirit descending like a dove and coming upon him.[c] **17** Look! Also, a voice from the heavens[d] said: "This is my Son,[e] the beloved, whom I have approved."[f]

4 Then Jesus was led by the spirit up into the wilderness to be tempted[g] by the Devil.[h] **2** After he had fasted for 40 days and 40 nights, he felt hungry. **3** And the Tempter[i] approached and said to him: "If you are a son of God, tell these stones to become loaves of bread." **4** But he answered: "It is written: 'Man must live, not on bread alone, but on every word that comes from Jehovah's* mouth.'"[j]

5 Then the Devil took him along into the holy city,[k] and he stationed him on the battlement* of the temple[l] **6** and said to him: "If you yourself are a son of God, throw yourself down, for it is written: 'He will give his angels a command concerning you,' and, 'They will carry you on their hands, so that you may not strike your foot against a stone.'"[m] **7** Jesus said to him: "Again it is written: 'You must not put Jehovah* your God to the test.'"[n]

8 Again the Devil took him along to an unusually high mountain and showed him all the kingdoms of the world and their glory.[a] **9** And he said to him: "All these things I will give you if you fall down and do an act of worship to me." **10** Then Jesus said to him: "Go away, Satan! For it is written: 'It is Jehovah* your God you must worship,[b] and it is to him alone you must render sacred service.'"[c] **11** Then the Devil left him,[d] and look! angels came and began to minister to him.[e]

12 Now when he heard that John had been arrested,[f] he withdrew into Gal'i·lee.[g] **13** Further, after leaving Naz'a·reth, he came and took up residence in Ca·per'na·um[h] beside the sea in the districts of Zeb'u·lun and Naph'ta·li, **14** so as to fulfill what was spoken through Isaiah the prophet, who said: **15** "O land of Zeb'u·lun and land of Naph'ta·li, along the road of the sea, on the other side of the Jordan, Gal'i·lee of the nations! **16** The people sitting in darkness saw a great light, and as for those sitting in a region of deathly shadow, light[i] rose on them."[j] **17** From that time on, Jesus began preaching and saying: "Repent, for the Kingdom of the heavens has drawn near."[k]

18 Walking alongside the Sea of Gal'i·lee, he saw two brothers, Simon, who is called Peter,[l] and Andrew his brother, casting a net into the sea, for they were fishermen.[m] **19** And he said to them: "Come after me, and I will make you fishers of men."[n] **20** At once they abandoned their nets and followed him.[o] **21** Going on from there, he saw two others who were brothers, James the son of Zeb'e·dee and his brother John.[p] They were in the boat with Zeb'e·dee their father, mending their nets, and he called them.[q] **22** At once they left the boat and their father and followed him.

CHAP. 3
a Mr 1:9
b Lu 3:21
c Isa 11:2
　Mr 1:10, 11
　Lu 4:18
　Joh 1:32
d Joh 12:28
e Ps 2:7
　Lu 9:35
f Isa 42:1
　Mt 17:5
　Lu 3:22

CHAP. 4
g Heb 4:15
h Mr 1:12, 13
　Lu 4:1-4
i 1Th 3:5
j De 8:3
　Lu 4:4
　Joh 4:34
k Ne 11:1
　Isa 52:1
l Lu 4:9-12
m Ps 91:11, 12
n De 6:16
　Lu 4:12
　1Co 10:9

Second Col.
a Lu 4:5-8
b Re 22:9
c De 6:13
　De 10:20
　Lu 4:8
d Lu 4:13
　Jas 4:7
e Lu 22:43
　Heb 1:7, 14
f Mr 6:17, 18
　Lu 3:19, 20
g Mr 1:14
　Lu 4:14
h Lu 4:31
i Joh 1:9
j Isa 9:1, 2
k Mt 10:7
　Mr 1:14, 15
l Joh 1:42
m Mt 1:16-18
　Lu 5:10, 11
o Mr 10:28
　Lu 18:28
p Mt 10:2
　Mt 27:55, 56
　Mr 3:17
　Mr 10:35
　Joh 21:2
q Mr 1:19, 20

4:4, 7, 10 *See App. A5.   **4:5** *Or "parapet; highest point."

23 Then he went throughout the whole of Gal'i·lee, teaching in their synagogues and preaching the good news of the Kingdom and curing every sort of disease and every sort of infirmity among the people. **24** And the report about him spread throughout all Syria, and they brought him all those who were suffering with various diseases and torments, those who were demon-possessed and epileptic and paralyzed, and he cured them. **25** Consequently, large crowds followed him from Gal'i·lee and De·cap'o·lis* and Jerusalem and Ju·de'a and from the other side of the Jordan.

5 When he saw the crowds, he went up on the mountain; and after he sat down, his disciples came to him. **2** Then he opened his mouth and began teaching them, saying:

3 "Happy are those conscious of their spiritual need,* since the Kingdom of the heavens belongs to them.

4 "Happy are those who mourn, since they will be comforted.

5 "Happy are the mild-tempered,* since they will inherit the earth.

6 "Happy are those hungering and thirsting for righteousness, since they will be filled.*

7 "Happy are the merciful, since they will be shown mercy.

8 "Happy are the pure in heart, since they will see God.

9 "Happy are the peacemakers,* since they will be called sons of God.

10 "Happy are those who have been persecuted for righteousness' sake, since the Kingdom of the heavens belongs to them.

11 "Happy are you when people reproach you and persecute you and lyingly say every sort of wicked thing against you for my sake. **12** Rejoice and be overjoyed, since your reward is great in the heavens, for in that way they persecuted the prophets prior to you.

13 "You are the salt of the earth, but if the salt loses its strength, how will its saltiness be restored? It is no longer usable for anything except to be thrown outside to be trampled on by men.

14 "You are the light of the world. A city cannot be hid when located on a mountain. **15** People light a lamp and set it, not under a basket,* but on the lampstand, and it shines on all those in the house. **16** Likewise, let your light shine before men, so that they may see your fine works and give glory to your Father who is in the heavens.

17 "Do not think I came to destroy the Law or the Prophets. I came, not to destroy, but to fulfill. **18** Truly I say to you that sooner would heaven and earth pass away than for one stroke of a letter to pass away from the Law until all things take place. **19** Whoever, therefore, breaks one of these least commandments and teaches others to do so will be called least in relation to the Kingdom of the heavens. But whoever does them and teaches them will be called great in relation to the Kingdom of the heavens. **20** For I say to you that if your righteousness does not surpass that of the scribes and the Pharisees, you will by no means enter into the Kingdom of the heavens.

21 "You heard that it was said to those of ancient times: 'You must not murder, but whoever

---

CHAP. 4
a Mt 9:35
  Mr 1:39
  Mr 6:6
b Lu 4:16
  Ac 13:13, 14
c Lu 9:11
  Ac 9:11
  Ac 10:37, 38
d Mr 6:55
e Mr 1:32
  Ac 5:16
f Mt 17:15

CHAP. 5
g Lu 6:20
h Isa 61:2, 3
  Mt 11:28
i 1Ti 6:11
  Tit 3:2
j Ps 37:11
k Isa 55:1
  Lu 6:21
l Joh 6:35
m Mt 6:14
  Mt 18:33
  Jas 2:13
n Ps 24:3, 4
  Ps 73:1
o Ro 12:18
  Heb 12:14
  Jas 3:18
p Mr 10:29, 30
  1Pe 3:14

Second Col.
a Mt 10:22
b Joh 15:20
c Lu 6:22, 23
  Jas 1:2
  1Pe 4:14
d Ac 5:41
  Ro 5:3
e Heb 11:6
f 2Ch 36:16
  Ac 7:52
  Heb 11:32, 37
g Mr 9:50
h Lu 14:34, 35
i Joh 8:12
  Joh 12:36
  Php 2:15
j Mr 4:21
  Lu 11:33
k Eph 5:8
  Php 2:15
l Eph 5:9
m Joh 15:8
  1Pe 2:9, 12
n Lu 4:21
o Isa 40:8
  Lu 16:17
p Mt 15:7-9
  Mt 23:23
  Lu 11:42
q Mt 18:3
  Joh 3:5
r Ge 9:6
  Ex 20:13
  De 5:17

4:25 *Or "the Ten City Region." 5:3 *Or "those who are beggars for the spirit." 5:5 *Or "meek." 5:6 *Or "satisfied." 5:9 *Or "peaceable."

5:15 *Or "measuring basket."

commits a murder will be accountable to the court of justice.'[a] **22** However, I say to you that everyone who continues wrathful[b] with his brother will be accountable to the court of justice; and whoever addresses his brother with an unspeakable word of contempt will be accountable to the Supreme Court; whereas whoever says, 'You despicable fool!' will be liable to the fiery Ge·hen'na.*[c]

23 "If, then, you are bringing your gift to the altar[d] and there you remember that your brother has something against you, **24** leave your gift there in front of the altar, and go away. First make your peace with your brother, and then come back and offer your gift.[e]

25 "Be quick to settle matters with your legal opponent, while you are with him on the way there, so that somehow the opponent may not turn you over to the judge, and the judge to the court attendant, and you get thrown into prison.[f] **26** I say to you for a fact, you will certainly not come out of there until you have paid over your last small coin.*

27 "You heard that it was said: 'You must not commit adultery.'[g] **28** But I say to you that everyone who keeps on looking at a woman[h] so as to have a passion for her has already committed adultery with her in his heart.[i] **29** If, now, your right eye is making you stumble, tear it out and throw it away from you.[j] For it is better for you to lose one of your members than for your whole body to be pitched into Ge·hen'na.*[k] **30** Also, if your right

hand is making you stumble, cut it off and throw it away from you.[a] For it is better for you to lose one of your members than for your whole body to land in Ge·hen'na.*[b]

31 "Moreover, it was said: 'Whoever divorces his wife, let him give her a certificate of divorce.'[c] **32** However, I say to you that everyone divorcing his wife, except on account of sexual immorality,* makes her a subject for adultery, and whoever marries a divorced woman commits adultery.[d]

33 "Again you heard that it was said to those of ancient times: 'You must not swear without performing,[e] but you must pay your vows to Jehovah.'*[f] **34** However, I say to you: Do not swear at all,[g] neither by heaven, for it is God's throne; **35** nor by earth, for it is the footstool of his feet;[h] nor by Jerusalem, for it is the city of the great King.[i] **36** Do not swear by your head, since you cannot turn one hair white or black. **37** Just let your word 'Yes' mean yes, your 'No,' no,[j] for what goes beyond these is from the wicked one.[k]

38 "You heard that it was said: 'Eye for eye and tooth for tooth.'[l] **39** However, I say to you: Do not resist the one who is wicked, but whoever slaps you on your right cheek, turn the other also to him.[m] **40** And if a person wants to take you to court and get possession of your inner garment, let him also have your outer garment;[n] **41** and if someone in authority compels you into service for a mile,* go with him two miles. **42** Give to the one asking you, and do not turn away from one who wants to borrow* from you.[o]

CHAP. 5
a Le 24:17
  De 17:8, 9
b Col 3:8
  Jas 1:19
c Mt 10:28
  Lu 12:5
  1Jo 3:15
d De 16:16
e 1Jo 4:20
f Lu 12:58, 59
g Ex 20:14
  De 5:18
  Lu 18:20
  Ro 13:9
h 2Sa 11:2
  Job 31:1
i Mr 7:20-22
j Lu 11:34
k Mt 18:9
  Mr 9:47

Second Col.
a Col 3:5
b Mt 18:8
c De 24:1
  Mt 19:3, 8
  Mr 10:2, 4
d Mt 19:9
  Mr 10:11, 12
  Lu 16:18
  Ro 7:3
e Le 19:12
f Nu 30:2
  De 23:21
  Ec 5:4
g Jas 5:12
h Isa 66:1
i Ps 48:2
j Jas 5:12
k Joh 8:44
l Ex 21:24, 25
  Le 24:20
  De 19:21
m Pr 24:29
  Isa 50:6
  Lu 6:29
  Ro 12:17
  1Pe 2:23
n 1Co 6:7
o Le 25:36
  De 23:19

5:22 *The place for burning refuse outside of Jerusalem. See Glossary. **5:26** *Lit., "the last quadrans." See App. B14. **5:29, 30** *See Glossary.

5:32 *Greek, por·nei'a. See Glossary. **5:33** *See App. A5. **5:41** *See App. B14. **5:42** *That is, borrow without interest.

43 "You heard that it was said: 'You must love your neighbor[a] and hate your enemy.' **44** However, I say to you: Continue to love your enemies[b] and to pray for those who persecute you,[c] **45** so that you may prove yourselves sons of your Father who is in the heavens,[d] since he makes his sun rise on both the wicked and the good and makes it rain on both the righteous and the unrighteous.[e] **46** For if you love those loving you, what reward do you have?[f] Are not also the tax collectors doing the same thing? **47** And if you greet your brothers only, what extraordinary thing are you doing? Are not also the people of the nations doing the same thing? **48** You must accordingly be perfect,* as your heavenly Father is perfect.[g]

6 "Take care not to practice your righteousness in front of men to be noticed by them;[h] otherwise you will have no reward with your Father who is in the heavens. **2** So when you make gifts of mercy,* do not blow a trumpet ahead of you, as the hypocrites do in the synagogues and in the streets, so that they may be glorified by men. Truly I say to you, they have their reward in full. **3** But you, when making gifts of mercy, do not let your left hand know what your right hand is doing, **4** so that your gifts of mercy may be in secret. Then your Father who looks on in secret will repay you.[i]

5 "Also, when you pray, do not act like the hypocrites,[j] for they like to pray standing in the synagogues and on the corners of the main streets to be seen by men.[k] Truly I say to you, they have their reward in full. **6** But when you pray, go into your private room and, after shutting your door, pray to your Father who is in secret.[a] Then your Father who looks on in secret will repay you. **7** When praying, do not say the same things over and over again as the people of the nations do, for they imagine they will get a hearing for their use of many words. **8** So do not be like them, for your Father knows what you need[b] even before you ask him.

9 "You must pray, then, this way:[c]

"'Our Father in the heavens, let your name[d] be sanctified.*[e] **10** Let your Kingdom[f] come. Let your will[g] take place, as in heaven, also on earth.[h] **11** Give us today our bread for this day;[i] **12** and forgive us our debts, as we also have forgiven our debtors.[j] **13** And do not bring us into temptation,[k] but deliver* us from the wicked one.'[l]

14 "For if you forgive men their trespasses, your heavenly Father will also forgive you;[m] **15** whereas if you do not forgive men their trespasses, neither will your Father forgive your trespasses.[n]

16 "When you fast,[o] stop becoming sad-faced like the hypocrites, for they disfigure their faces* so they may appear to men to be fasting.[p] Truly I say to you, they have their reward in full. **17** But you, when fasting, put oil on your head and wash your face, **18** so that you may not appear to be fasting to men but only to your Father who is in secret. Then your Father who looks on in secret will repay you.

19 "Stop storing up for yourselves treasures on the earth,[q] where moth and rust consume and where thieves break in and steal. **20** Rather, store up for

---

CHAP. 5

a Le 19:18
  Mr 12:31
b Pr 25:21
  Ro 12:20
c Lu 6:27, 28
  Ac 7:60
  Ro 12:14
d Eph 5:1
e Lu 6:35
  Ac 14:17
f Lu 6:32, 33
g Le 19:2
  De 18:13
  Lu 6:36
  1Pe 1:16

CHAP. 6

h Mt 23:5
i Pr 19:17
  Mt 10:42
j Lu 18:11
k Mt 6:16
  Mt 23:5

Second Col.

a Lu 6:12
b Lu 12:30
c Lu 11:2-4
d Ex 6:3
  Ps 83:18
e Eze 36:23
f Da 2:44
  Mt 6:33
  Re 11:15
g Mt 26:42
  1Ti 2:4
  Re 4:11
h Ps 37:10
  Lu 23:43
  Ac 24:15
i Ps 37:25
  Pr 30:8
  Mt 6:34
  1Ti 6:8
j Mt 18:21
  Mt 11:25
k Mt 26:41
  1Co 10:13
  Re 3:10
l Joh 17:15
  1Jo 5:19
m Eph 4:32
  Col 3:13
n Mt 18:35
  Jas 2:13
o Ac 13:2, 3
  Ac 14:23
p Isa 58:5
  Lu 18:11, 12
q Mt 13:22
  Lu 12:20
  Jas 5:3

5:48 *Or "complete." 6:2 *Or "gifts to the poor." See Glossary. 6:9 *Or "be held sacred; be treated as holy." 6:13 *Or "rescue." 6:16 *Or "they neglect their appearance."

yourselves treasures in heaven,[a] where neither moth nor rust consumes,[b] and where thieves do not break in and steal. **21** For where your treasure is, there your heart will be also.

22 "The lamp of the body is the eye.[c] If, then, your eye is focused,* your whole body will be bright.* **23** But if your eye is envious,*[d] your whole body will be dark. If the light that is in you is really darkness, how great that darkness is!

24 "No one can slave for two masters; for either he will hate the one and love the other,[e] or he will stick to the one and despise the other. You cannot slave for God and for Riches.[f]

25 "On this account I say to you: Stop being anxious[g] about your lives* as to what you will eat or what you will drink, or about your bodies as to what you will wear.[h] Does not life* mean more than food and the body than clothing?[i] **26** Observe intently the birds of heaven;[j] they do not sow seed or reap or gather into storehouses, yet your heavenly Father feeds them. Are you not worth more than they are? **27** Who of you by being anxious can add one cubit* to his life span?[k] **28** Also, why are you anxious about clothing? Take a lesson from the lilies of the field, how they grow; they do not toil, nor do they spin; **29** but I tell you that not even Sol'o·mon[l] in all his glory was arrayed as one of these. **30** Now if this is how God clothes the vegetation of the field that is here today and tomorrow is thrown into the oven, will he not much rather clothe you, you with little faith? **31** So never be anxious[m]

and say, 'What are we to eat?' or, 'What are we to drink?' or, 'What are we to wear?'[a] **32** For all these are the things the nations are eagerly pursuing. Your heavenly Father knows that you need all these things.

33 "Keep on, then, seeking first the Kingdom and his righteousness, and all these other things will be added to you.[b] **34** So never be anxious about the next day,[c] for the next day will have its own anxieties. Each day has enough of its own troubles.

7 "Stop judging[d] that you may not be judged; **2** for with the judgment you are judging, you will be judged,[e] and with the measure that you are measuring out, they will measure out to you.[f] **3** Why, then, do you look at the straw in your brother's eye but do not notice the rafter in your own eye?[g] **4** Or how can you say to your brother, 'Allow me to remove the straw from your eye,' when look! a rafter is in your own eye? **5** Hypocrite! First remove the rafter from your own eye, and then you will see clearly how to remove the straw from your brother's eye.

6 "Do not give what is holy to dogs nor throw your pearls before swine,[h] so that they may never trample them under their feet and turn around and rip you open.

7 "Keep on asking, and it will be given you;[i] keep on seeking, and you will find; keep on knocking, and it will be opened to you;[j] **8** for everyone asking receives,[k] and everyone seeking finds, and to everyone knocking, it will be opened. **9** Indeed, which one of you, if his son asks for bread, will hand him a stone? **10** Or if he asks for a fish, he will not hand him a serpent, will he? **11** Therefore, if you, although being wicked, know how to give

---

CHAP. 6

a Mt 19:21
  Mr 10:21
  Lu 12:33, 34
  Lu 18:22

b 1Pe 1:3, 4

c Pr 4:25
  Lu 11:34
  Eph 1:18

d Mt 20:15

e Jas 4:4

f Mt 13:22
  Lu 16:13

g Ps 55:22
  Php 4:6
  1Pe 5:6, 7

h 1Ti 6:8
  Heb 13:5

i Lu 12:22-28

j Job 38:41
  Ps 147:9
  Mt 10:29

k Ps 39:5

l 1Ki 10:4, 5

m Lu 10:41

Second Col.

a Lu 12:29-31

b Ps 37:25

c Ex 16:4, 19

CHAP. 7

d Lu 6:37
  Ro 2:1
  Ro 14:13

e Mt 18:33, 34
  Jas 2:13

f Mr 4:24
  Lu 6:38
  Ga 6:7

g Lu 6:41, 42

h Pr 9:7
  Mt 10:14

i Mr 11:24
  Jas 1:5
  1Jo 5:14

j Lu 11:9-13

k Joh 14:13
  1Jo 3:22

6:22 *Or "clear." Lit., "simple." *Or "full of light." **6:23** *Lit., "bad; wicked." **6:25** *Or "souls." *Or "the soul." **6:27** *See App. B14.

good gifts to your children, how much more so will your Father who is in the heavens give good things[a] to those asking him![b]

12 "All things, therefore, that you want men to do to you, you also must do to them.[c] This, in fact, is what the Law and the Prophets mean.[d]

13 "Go in through the narrow gate,[e] because broad is the gate and spacious is the road leading off into destruction, and many are going in through it; **14** whereas narrow is the gate and cramped the road leading off into life, and few are finding it.[f]

15 "Be on the watch for the false prophets[g] who come to you in sheep's covering,[h] but inside they are ravenous wolves.[i] **16** By their fruits you will recognize them. Never do people gather grapes from thorns or figs from thistles, do they?[j] **17** Likewise, every good tree produces fine fruit, but every rotten tree produces worthless fruit.[k] **18** A good tree cannot bear worthless fruit, nor can a rotten tree produce fine fruit.[l] **19** Every tree not producing fine fruit is cut down and thrown into the fire.[m] **20** Really, then, by their fruits you will recognize those men.[n]

21 "Not everyone saying to me, 'Lord, Lord,' will enter into the Kingdom of the heavens, but only the one doing the will of my Father who is in the heavens will.[o] **22** Many will say to me in that day: 'Lord, Lord,[p] did we not prophesy in your name, and expel demons in your name, and perform many powerful works in your name?'[q] **23** And then I will declare to them: 'I never knew you! Get away from me, you workers of lawlessness!'[r]

24 "Therefore, everyone who hears these sayings of mine and does them will be like a discreet man who built his house on the rock.[a] **25** And the rain poured down and the floods came and the winds blew and lashed against that house, but it did not cave in, for it had been founded on the rock. **26** Furthermore, everyone hearing these sayings of mine and not doing them will be like a foolish man who built his house on the sand.[b] **27** And the rain poured down and the floods came and the winds blew and struck against that house,[c] and it caved in, and its collapse was great."

28 When Jesus finished these sayings, the effect was that the crowds were astounded at his way of teaching,[d] **29** for he was teaching them as a person having authority,[e] and not as their scribes.

8 After he came down from the mountain, large crowds followed him. **2** And look! a leper came up and did obeisance* to him, saying: "Lord, if you just want to, you can make me clean."[f] **3** So stretching out his hand, he touched him, saying: "I want to! Be made clean."[g] Immediately his leprosy was cleansed away.[h] **4** Then Jesus said to him: "See that you tell no one,[i] but go, show yourself to the priest,[j] and offer the gift that Moses appointed,[k] for a witness to them."

5 When he entered Ca·per′na·um, an army officer came to him, pleading with him[l] **6** and saying: "Sir, my servant is laid up in the house with paralysis, and he is suffering terribly." **7** He said to him: "When I get there, I will cure him." **8** The army officer replied: "Sir, I am not worthy to have you come under my roof, but just say the word and my servant will be healed. **9** For I too am a man under authority, hav-

---

CHAP. 7
a Jas 1:17
b Lu 11:13
c Lu 6:31
d Ro 13:10
  Ga 5:14
e Lu 13:24
f Ac 14:22
  1Pe 4:18
g Mt 24:11
  2Pe 2:1
  1Jo 4:1
h Lu 6:26
i Ac 20:29, 30
j Lu 6:44
k Mt 12:33
l Lu 6:43
m Mt 3:10
  Lu 13:6, 9
n Mt 12:33
o Ro 2:13
  Jas 1:22
  1Jo 2:17
  1Jo 5:3
p Lu 6:46
q Jer 14:14
  Jer 27:15
r Lu 13:25-27

Second Col.
a Lu 6:47-49
  Jas 1:25
b Jas 1:23, 24
c 1Co 3:13
d Mr 1:22
  Lu 4:32
e Joh 7:46

CHAP. 8
f Mr 1:40-44
  Lu 5:12-14
g Mr 1:41
  Lu 5:13
h Isa 53:4
i Mt 9:30
  Mt 12:15, 16
  Mr 7:35, 36
j Le 14:2
  Lu 17:14
k Le 14:3, 4
  Le 14:19, 20
l Lu 7:1-9

8:2 *Or "bowed down."

ing soldiers under me, and I say to this one, 'Go!' and he goes, and to another, 'Come!' and he comes, and to my slave, 'Do this!' and he does it." **10** When Jesus heard that, he was amazed and said to those following him: "I tell you the truth, with no one in Israel have I found so great a faith.[a] **11** But I tell you that many from east and west will come and recline at the table with Abraham and Isaac and Jacob in the Kingdom of the heavens;[b] **12** whereas the sons of the Kingdom will be thrown into the darkness outside. There is where their weeping and the gnashing of their teeth will be."[c] **13** Then Jesus said to the army officer: "Go. Just as you have shown faith, so let it come to pass for you."[d] And the servant was healed in that hour.[e]

14 And Jesus, on coming into Peter's house, saw his mother-in-law[f] lying down and sick with fever.[g] **15** So he touched her hand,[h] and the fever left her, and she got up and began ministering to him. **16** But after it became evening, people brought him many demon-possessed ones; and he expelled the spirits with a word, and he cured all who were suffering, **17** in order to fulfill what was spoken through Isaiah the prophet: "He himself took our sicknesses and carried our diseases."[i]

18 When Jesus saw a crowd around him, he gave the command to depart for the other side.[j] **19** And a scribe came up and said to him: "Teacher, I will follow you wherever you go."[k] **20** But Jesus said to him: "Foxes have dens and birds of heaven have nests, but the Son of man has nowhere to lay down his head."[l] **21** Then another of the disciples said to him: "Lord, permit me first to go and bury my father."[m] **22** Jesus said to him:

"Keep following me, and let the dead bury their dead."[a]

23 And when he went aboard a boat, his disciples followed him.[b] **24** Now look! a great storm arose on the sea, so that the boat was being covered by the waves; but he was sleeping.[c] **25** And they came and woke him up, saying: "Lord, save us, we are about to perish!" **26** But he said to them: "Why are you so afraid,* you with little faith?"[d] Then he got up and rebuked the winds and the sea, and a great calm set in.[e] **27** So the men were amazed and said: "What sort of person is this? Even the winds and the sea obey him."

28 When he came to the other side into the region of the Gad·a·renes′, two demon-possessed men coming out from among the tombs* met him.[f] They were unusually fierce, so nobody had the courage to pass by on that road. **29** And look! they screamed, saying: "What have we to do with you, Son of God?[g] Did you come here to torment us[h] before the appointed time?"[i] **30** A long way off from them, a herd of many swine was feeding.[j] **31** So the demons began to plead with him, saying: "If you expel us, send us into the herd of swine."[k] **32** And he said to them: "Go!" With that they came out and went off into the swine, and look! the entire herd rushed over the precipice* into the sea and died in the waters. **33** But the herders fled, and going into the city, they reported everything, including the account of the demon-possessed men. **34** And look! all the city turned out to meet Jesus, and when they saw him, they urged him to depart from their region.[l]

CHAP. 8	
a	Mt 15:28
	Lu 7:9
b	Lu 13:29
c	Lu 13:28
d	Mt 9:29
	Mt 15:28
	Mr 9:23
e	Lu 7:10
f	1Co 9:5
g	Mr 1:29-34
	Lu 4:38-41
h	Mr 5:41
	Ac 3:7
i	Isa 53:4
j	Mr 4:35
	Lu 8:22
k	Lu 9:57
l	Lu 9:58
	2Co 8:9
m	Lu 9:59

Second Col.

a	Lu 9:60
b	Mr 4:36
c	Mr 4:37-41
	Lu 8:23-25
d	Mt 14:31
	Mr 4:40
e	Ps 89:9
	Ps 107:29
	Lu 8:25
f	Mr 5:1-3
	Lu 8:26, 27
g	Lu 4:34, 41
h	Mr 1:24
	Jas 2:19
i	Mr 5:7-10
	Lu 8:28
j	Mr 5:11-17
k	De 14:8
	Lu 8:31-34
l	Lu 8:35-37

8:26 *Or "fainthearted." **8:28** *Or "memorial tombs." **8:32** *Or "steep bank."

9 So boarding the boat, he traveled across and went into his own city.[a] **2** And look! they were bringing him a paralyzed man lying on a stretcher. On seeing their faith, Jesus said to the paralytic: "Take courage, child! Your sins are forgiven."[b] **3** Now certain scribes said to themselves: "This fellow is blaspheming." **4** Jesus, knowing their thoughts, said: "Why are you thinking wicked things in your hearts?[c] **5** For instance, which is easier, to say, 'Your sins are forgiven,' or to say, 'Get up and walk'?[d] **6** However, in order for you to know that the Son of man has authority on earth to forgive sins—" then he said to the paralytic: "Get up, pick up your stretcher, and go to your home."[e] **7** And he got up and went to his home. **8** When the crowds saw this, they were struck with fear, and they glorified God, who gave such authority to men.

9 Next, while moving on from there, Jesus caught sight of a man named Matthew sitting at the tax office, and he said to him: "Be my follower." At that he rose up and followed him.[f] **10** Later as he was dining* in the house, look! many tax collectors and sinners came and began dining* with Jesus and his disciples.[g] **11** But on seeing this, the Pharisees said to his disciples: "Why does your teacher eat with tax collectors and sinners?"[h] **12** Hearing them, he said: "Healthy people do not need a physician, but those who are ill do.[i] **13** Go, then, and learn what this means: 'I want mercy, and not sacrifice.'[j] For I came to call, not righteous people, but sinners."

14 Then John's disciples came to him and asked: "Why do we and the Pharisees practice fasting but your disciples do not fast?"[a] **15** At this Jesus said to them: "The friends of the bridegroom have no reason to mourn as long as the bridegroom[b] is with them, do they? But days will come when the bridegroom will be taken away from them,[c] and then they will fast. **16** Nobody sews a patch of unshrunk cloth on an old outer garment, for the new piece pulls away from the garment and the tear becomes worse.[d] **17** Nor do people put new wine into old wineskins. If they do, then the wineskins burst and the wine spills out and the wineskins are ruined. But people put new wine into new wineskins, and both are preserved."

18 While he was telling them these things, look! a certain ruler who had approached did obeisance* to him, saying: "By now my daughter must be dead, but come and lay your hand on her, and she will come to life."[e]

19 Then Jesus got up and, with his disciples, followed him. **20** And look! a woman suffering for 12 years from a flow of blood[f] approached from behind and touched the fringe of his outer garment,[g] **21** for she kept saying to herself: "If I only touch his outer garment, I will get well." **22** Jesus turned around and, noticing her, said: "Take courage, daughter! Your faith has made you well."[h] And from that hour the woman was made well.[i]

23 When, now, he came into the ruler's house and caught sight of the flute players and the crowd making a commotion,[j] **24** Jesus said: "Leave the place, for the little girl did not die but is sleeping."[k] At this they began to laugh at him scornfully. **25** As soon as the crowd had been sent outside, he went in and took hold of her hand,[l] and the little girl got up.[m]

CHAP. 9	
a	Mt 4:13
	Mr 2:1
b	Mr 2:3-12
	Lu 5:18-26
c	Joh 2:24, 25
d	Mr 2:9
e	Mr 2:10, 11
	Lu 5:24
	Joh 5:8
f	Mr 2:14
	Lu 5:27, 28
g	Mr 2:15-17
	Lu 5:29-32
h	Lu 7:39
	Lu 15:2
	Lu 19:7
i	Lu 5:31
j	Pr 21:3
	Ho 6:6
	Mt 12:7

Second Col.	
a	Mr 2:18-20
	Lu 5:33-35
b	Mt 22:2
c	Mt 26:2
d	Mr 2:21, 22
	Lu 5:36-39
e	Mr 5:22-24
	Lu 8:41, 42
	Joh 11:25
f	Le 15:25
g	Mr 5:25-34
	Mr 6:56
	Lu 8:43-48
h	Mr 10:52
	Lu 7:50
	Lu 17:19
	Lu 18:42
i	Joh 4:53
j	Mr 5:38-43
	Lu 8:52-56
k	Joh 11:11
l	Mr 9:27
m	Lu 8:55

9:10 *Or "reclining at the table."

9:18 *Or "bowed down."

26 Of course, the talk about this spread into all that region.

27 As Jesus moved on from there, two blind men[a] followed him, shouting out: "Have mercy on us, Son of David." **28** After he had gone into the house, the blind men came to him, and Jesus asked them: "Do you have faith that I can do this?"[b] They answered him: "Yes, Lord." **29** Then he touched their eyes,[c] saying: "According to your faith let it happen to you." **30** And their eyes received sight. Moreover, Jesus sternly warned them, saying: "See that nobody gets to know it."[d] **31** But after going outside, they made it public about him in all that region.

32 When they were leaving, look! people brought him a speechless man possessed of a demon;[e] **33** and after the demon had been expelled, the speechless man spoke.[f] Well, the crowds were amazed and said: "Never has anything like this been seen in Israel."[g] **34** But the Pharisees were saying: "It is by the ruler of the demons that he expels the demons."[h]

35 And Jesus set out on a tour of all the cities and villages, teaching in their synagogues and preaching the good news of the Kingdom and curing every sort of disease and every sort of infirmity.[i] **36** On seeing the crowds, he felt pity for them,[j] because they were skinned and thrown about like sheep without a shepherd.[k] **37** Then he said to his disciples: "Yes, the harvest is great, but the workers are few.[l] **38** Therefore, beg the Master of the harvest to send out workers into his harvest."[m]

10 So he summoned his 12 disciples and gave them authority over unclean spirits,[n] in order to expel these and to cure every sort of disease and every sort of infirmity.

2 The names of the 12 apostles are these:[a] First, Simon, the one called Peter,[b] and Andrew[c] his brother; James the son of Zeb'e·dee and John[d] his brother; **3** Philip and Bar·thol'o·mew;[e] Thomas[f] and Matthew[g] the tax collector; James the son of Al·phae'us; Thad·dae'us; **4** Simon the Ca·na·nae'an;* and Judas Is·car'i·ot, who later betrayed him.[h]

5 These 12 Jesus sent out, giving them these instructions:[i] "Do not go off into the road of the nations, and do not enter any Sa·mar'i·tan city;[j] **6** but instead, go continually to the lost sheep of the house of Israel.[k] **7** As you go, preach, saying: 'The Kingdom of the heavens has drawn near.'[l] **8** Cure the sick,[m] raise up the dead, make lepers clean, expel demons. You received free, give free. **9** Do not acquire gold or silver or copper for your money belts;[n] **10** or a food pouch for the trip, or two garments,* or sandals, or a staff,[o] for the worker deserves his food.[p]

11 "Into whatever city or village you enter, search out who in it is deserving, and stay there until you leave.[q] **12** When you enter the house, greet the household. **13** If the house is deserving, let the peace you wish it come upon it;[r] but if it is not deserving, let the peace from you return upon you. **14** Wherever anyone does not receive you or listen to your words, on going out of that house or that city, shake the dust off your feet.[s] **15** Truly I say to you, it will be more endurable for the land of Sod'om and Go·mor'rah[t] on Judgment Day than for that city.

16 "Look! I am sending you out as sheep among wolves;

CHAP. 9	
a	Mt 20:30
b	Ac 14:9, 10
c	Mt 20:34
d	Isa 42:2
	Mt 12:15, 16
	Mr 1:44, 45
	Mr 7:35, 36
e	Mt 12:22
	Lu 11:14
f	Mt 15:31
g	Mr 2:12
h	Mt 12:24
	Mr 3:22
	Lu 11:15
i	Mt 4:23
	Heb 4:15
j	Mt 14:14
k	Nu 27:16, 17
	1Ki 22:17
	Eze 34:5
	Mr 6:34
l	Lu 10:2
	Joh 4:35
m	Ro 10:14

CHAP. 10	
n	Mr 3:14, 15
	Mr 6:7
	Lu 9:1, 2

Second Col.	
a	Mr 3:16-19
	Lu 6:13-16
	Ac 1:13
b	Joh 1:42
	Ac 15:14
c	Mr 1:16
	Joh 1:40
d	Mt 4:21
e	Joh 1:45
f	Joh 11:16
	Joh 20:27
g	Mr 2:14
	Lu 5:27
h	Mt 26:47
	Joh 13:18
i	Mr 6:7
	Lu 9:1, 2
j	2Ki 17:24
k	Isa 53:6
	Eze 34:6
	Ac 13:45, 46
l	Mt 4:17
	Lu 10:9
m	Lu 9:2
n	Mr 6:8, 9
o	Lu 9:3
p	Lu 10:7
	1Co 9:7, 14
q	Mr 6:10
	Lu 9:4
r	Lu 10:5
s	Mr 6:11
	Lu 9:5
	Lu 10:6, 11
	Ac 13:50, 51
t	Ge 19:4, 5
	2Pe 2:6
	Jude 7

10:4 *Or "the zealous one." **10:10** *Or "an extra garment."

so prove yourselves cautious as
serpents and yet innocent as
doves.[a] **17** Be on your guard
against men, for they will hand
you over to local courts[b] and
they will scourge you[c] in their
synagogues.[d] **18** And you will
be brought before governors
and kings[e] for my sake, for
a witness to them and the nations.[f] **19** However, when they
hand you over, do not become
anxious about how or what you
are to speak, for what you are to
speak will be given you in that
hour;[g] **20** for the ones speaking are not just you, but it is the
spirit of your Father that speaks
by you.[h] **21** Further, brother
will hand brother over to death,
and a father his child, and children will rise up against parents
and will have them put to death.[i]
22 And you will be hated by
all people on account of my
name,[j] but the one who has endured* to the end will be saved.[k]
23 When they persecute you in
one city, flee to another;[l] for truly I say to you, you will by no
means complete the circuit of
the cities of Israel until the Son
of man arrives.

24 “A disciple is not above his
teacher, nor a slave above his
master.[m] **25** It is enough for the
disciple to become as his teacher, and the slave as his master.[n]
If people have called the master
of the house Be·el′ze·bub,*[o] how
much more those of his household? **26** So do not fear them,
for there is nothing covered over
that will not become uncovered,
and nothing secret that will not
become known.[p] **27** What I tell
you in the darkness, say in the
light, and what you hear whis-
pered, preach from the housetops.[q] **28** And do not become
fearful of those who kill the
body but cannot kill the soul;*[a]
rather, fear him who can destroy
both soul and body in Ge·hen′-
na.#[b] **29** Two sparrows sell for
a coin of small value,* do they
not? Yet not one of them will fall
to the ground without your Father’s knowledge.[c] **30** But even
the hairs of your head are all
numbered. **31** So have no fear;
you are worth more than many
sparrows.[d]

32 “Everyone, then, who acknowledges me before men,[e]
I will also acknowledge him before my Father who is in the
heavens.[f] **33** But whoever disowns me before men, I will also
disown him before my Father
who is in the heavens.[g] **34** Do
not think I came to bring peace
to the earth; I came to bring,
not peace, but a sword.[h] **35** For
I came to cause division, with
a man against his father, and
a daughter against her mother, and a daughter-in-law against
her mother-in-law.[i] **36** Indeed,
a man’s enemies will be those
of his own household. **37** Whoever has greater affection for father or mother than for me is
not worthy of me; and whoever has greater affection for
son or daughter than for me is
not worthy of me.[j] **38** And whoever does not accept his torture stake# and follow after me
is not worthy of me.[k] **39** Whoever finds his soul* will lose it,
and whoever loses his soul* for
my sake will find it.[l]

40 “Whoever receives you receives me also, and whoever receives me receives also the One
who sent me.[m] **41** Whoever receives a prophet because he is a
prophet will get a prophet’s reward,[n] and whoever receives a
righteous man because he is a

10:22 *Or “who endures.” **10:25** *A designation applied to Satan, the prince, or ruler, of the demons.

10:28 *Or “life,” that is, life prospects. **10:28, 38** #See Glossary. **10:29** *Lit., “for an assarion.” See App. B14. **10:39** *Or “life.”

CHAP. 10
a Php 2:14, 15
b Mt 24:9
c Ac 5:40; 2Co 11:24
d Mt 23:34; Mr 13:9; Lu 21:12, 13
e Ac 4:8; Ac 24:10; Ac 25:23; Ac 26:25; Ac 27:23, 24
f Mt 24:14
g Mr 13:11; Lu 12:11, 12; Lu 21:14, 15
h Joh 14:26
i Mic 7:6; Mt 10:36
j Mt 24:9; Lu 21:17; Joh 15:21
k Mt 24:13; Lu 21:19; Re 2:10
l Mt 23:34; Ac 8:1
m Joh 15:20
n 1Pe 2:21
o Mt 12:24; Mr 3:22; Lu 11:15; Joh 8:48
p Mr 4:22; Lu 8:17
q Lu 12:3

Second Col.
a Pr 29:25; Re 2:10
b Lu 12:4, 5; Heb 10:31
c Lu 12:6, 7
d Mt 6:26
e Ro 10:9
f Lu 12:8, 9; Re 3:5
g Mr 8:38; Lu 9:26; 2Ti 2:12
h Lu 12:51-53
i Mic 7:6
j Mt 19:29; Lu 14:26
k Mt 16:24, 25; Mr 8:34, 35; Lu 9:23; Lu 14:27
l Lu 17:33; Joh 12:25
m Mt 25:40; Lu 10:16; Joh 12:44; Joh 13:20
n 1Ki 17:9, 10; 1Ki 17:20-23; 2Ki 4:8; 2Ki 4:13-17

righteous man will get a righteous man's reward. **42** And whoever gives one of these little ones only a cup of cold water to drink because he is a disciple, I tell you truly, he will by no means lose his reward."[a]

11 When Jesus had finished giving instructions to his 12 disciples, he set out from there to teach and preach in their cities.[b]

2 But John, having heard in jail[c] about the works of the Christ, sent his disciples[d] **3** to ask him: "Are you the Coming One, or are we to expect a different one?"[e] **4** In reply Jesus said to them: "Go and report to John what you are hearing and seeing:[f] **5** The blind are now seeing[g] and the lame are walking, the lepers[h] are being cleansed and the deaf are hearing, the dead are being raised up and the poor are being told the good news.[i] **6** Happy is the one who finds no cause for stumbling in me."[j]

7 While these were on their way, Jesus began to speak to the crowds about John: "What did you go out into the wilderness to see?[k] A reed being tossed by the wind?[l] **8** What, then, did you go out to see? A man dressed in soft garments?[*] Why, those wearing soft garments are in the houses of kings. **9** Really, then, why did you go out? To see a prophet? Yes, I tell you, and far more than a prophet.[m] **10** This is the one about whom it is written: 'Look! I am sending my messenger ahead of you,[*] who will prepare your way ahead of you!'[n] **11** Truly I say to you, among those born of women, there has not been raised up anyone greater than John the Baptist, but a lesser person in the Kingdom of

the heavens is greater than he is.[a] **12** From the days of John the Baptist until now, the Kingdom of the heavens is the goal toward which men press, and those pressing forward are seizing it.[b] **13** For all, the Prophets and the Law, prophesied until John;[c] **14** and if you are willing to accept it, he is 'E·liʹjah who is to come.'[d] **15** Let the one who has ears listen.

16 "With whom will I compare this generation?[e] It is like young children sitting in the marketplaces who call out to their playmates, **17** saying: 'We played the flute for you, but you did not dance; we wailed, but you did not beat yourselves in grief.' **18** Likewise, John came neither eating nor drinking, but people say, 'He has a demon.' **19** The Son of man did come eating and drinking,[f] but people say, 'Look! A man who is a glutton and is given to drinking wine, a friend of tax collectors and sinners.'[g] All the same, wisdom is proved righteous[*] by its works."[*h]

20 Then he began to reproach the cities in which most of his powerful works had taken place, for they did not repent: **21** "Woe to you, Cho·raʹzin! Woe to you, Beth·saʹi·da! because if the powerful works that took place in you had taken place in Tyre and Siʹdon, they would long ago have repented in sackcloth and ashes.[i] **22** But I say to you, it will be more endurable for Tyre and Siʹdon on Judgment Day than for you.[j] **23** And you, Ca·perʹna·um,[k] will you perhaps be exalted to heaven? Down to the Grave[*] you will come;[l] because if the powerful works that took place in you had taken place in Sodʹom,

CHAP. 10
a Mt 25:40
Mr 9:41
Heb 6:10

CHAP. 11
b Mt 4:23
Mt 19:1
Lu 9:6
c Mt 14:3
Mr 6:17
d Lu 7:18-23
e Mt 3:11
Joh 1:15
f Lu 7:22
g Isa 35:5, 6
Isa 61:1
h Mt 8:3
i Mt 4:23
j Mt 6:3
Lu 7:23
1Co 1:23
1Pe 2:7, 8
k Mt 3:1, 5
l Lu 7:24-28
m Lu 1:67, 76
n Mal 3:1
Mt 3:3
Mr 1:2
Lu 1:17
Joh 3:28

Second Col.
a Lu 7:28
Joh 3:3
b Lu 13:24
c Lu 16:16
d Mal 4:5
Mt 17:10-13
e Lu 7:31-35
f Mt 9:10
Mr 2:15
Joh 2:2
g Lu 5:30
Lu 15:2
Lu 19:7
h Lu 7:34, 35
i Jon 3:5, 6
Lu 10:13
j Lu 10:14
k Lu 4:31
l Lu 10:15

11:8 *Or "fine clothing?" 11:10 *Lit., "before your face."

11:19 *Or "is vindicated." *Or "by its results." 11:23 *Or "Hades," that is, the common grave of mankind. See Glossary.

it would have remained until this very day. **24** But I say to you, it will be more endurable for the land of Sod'om on Judgment Day than for you."[a]

25 At that time Jesus said in response: "I publicly praise you, Father, Lord of heaven and earth, because you have hidden these things from the wise and intellectual ones and have revealed them to young children.[b] **26** Yes, O Father, because this is the way you approved. **27** All things have been handed over to me by my Father,[c] and no one fully knows the Son except the Father;[d] neither does anyone fully know the Father except the Son and anyone to whom the Son is willing to reveal him.[e] **28** Come to me, all you who are toiling and loaded down, and I will refresh you. **29** Take my yoke upon you and learn from me, for I am mild-tempered and lowly in heart,[f] and you will find refreshment for yourselves.* **30** For my yoke is kindly,* and my load is light."

12 At that time Jesus went through the grainfields on the Sabbath. His disciples got hungry and started to pluck heads of grain and to eat.[g] **2** At seeing this, the Pharisees said to him: "Look! Your disciples are doing what is not lawful to do on the Sabbath."[h] **3** He said to them: "Have you not read what David did when he and the men with him were hungry?[i] **4** How he entered into the house of God and they ate the loaves of presentation,*[j] something that it was not lawful for him or those with him to eat, but for the priests only?[k] **5** Or have you not read in the Law that on the Sabbaths the priests in the

temple violate the Sabbath and continue guiltless?[a] **6** But I tell you that something greater than the temple is here.[b] **7** However, if you had understood what this means, 'I want mercy[c] and not sacrifice,'[d] you would not have condemned the guiltless ones. **8** For the Son of man is Lord of the Sabbath."[e]

9 After departing from that place, he went into their synagogue, **10** and look! there was a man with a withered* hand![f] So they asked him, "Is it lawful to cure on the Sabbath?" so that they might accuse him.[g] **11** He said to them: "If you have one sheep and that sheep falls into a pit on the Sabbath, is there a man among you who will not grab hold of it and lift it out?[h] **12** How much more valuable is a man than a sheep! So it is lawful to do a fine thing on the Sabbath." **13** Then he said to the man: "Stretch out your hand." And he stretched it out, and it was restored sound like the other hand. **14** But the Pharisees went out and conspired against him to kill him. **15** Having come to know this, Jesus departed from there. Many also followed him,[i] and he cured them all, **16** but he sternly ordered them not to make him known,[j] **17** in order to fulfill what was spoken through Isaiah the prophet, who said:

18 "Look! My servant* whom I chose, my beloved, whom I have* approved![l] I will put my spirit upon him,[m] and what justice is he will make clear to the nations. **19** He will not quarrel[n] nor cry aloud, nor will anyone hear his voice in the main streets. **20** No bruised reed will he crush, and no smoldering wick will he extinguish,[o] until he brings justice with success.

CHAP. 11
a Mt 10:15
  Lu 10:12
b Isa 29:14
  Mt 13:15
  Lu 10:21
  1Co 1:27
c Joh 3:35
d Joh 1:18
e Lu 10:22
  Joh 10:15
  1Jo 5:20
f Zec 9:9

CHAP. 12
g Ex 12:16
  De 23:25
  Mr 2:23-28
  Lu 6:1-5
h Ex 20:10
  Ex 31:15
  Lu 6:5
i 1Sa 21:1-6
j Ex 25:30
  Ex 40:22, 23
k Le 24:5-9

Second Col.
a Nu 28:9
  Joh 7:22
b Lu 11:31, 32
c Mt 23:23
d Ho 6:6
  Mic 6:6, 8
  Mt 9:13
e Mr 2:27, 28
  Lu 6:5
f Mr 3:1-6
  Lu 6:6-11
g Lu 14:3
  Joh 9:16
h Ex 23:4
  De 22:4
  Lu 14:5
i Mr 3:7
j Mt 8:3, 4
  Mr 3:11, 12
  Mr 7:35, 36
k Ac 3:13
l Mt 3:17
  Mt 17:5
m Isa 61:1
  Mr 1:10
n 2Ti 2:24
o Mt 11:28

11:29 *Or "your souls." 11:30 *Or "easy to bear." 12:4 *Or "the showbread."

12:10 *Or "paralyzed." 12:18 *Or "my soul has."

21 Indeed, in his name nations will hope."[a]

22 Then they brought him a demon-possessed man who was blind and speechless, and he cured him, so that the speechless man could speak and see. **23** Well, all the crowds were astounded and began to say: "May this not perhaps be the Son of David?" **24** At hearing this, the Pharisees said: "This fellow does not expel the demons except by means of Be·el′ze·bub,* the ruler of the demons."[b] **25** Knowing their thoughts, he said to them: "Every kingdom divided against itself comes to ruin, and every city or house divided against itself will not stand. **26** In the same way, if Satan expels Satan, he has become divided against himself; how, then, will his kingdom stand? **27** Moreover, if I expel the demons by means of Be·el′ze·bub, by whom do your sons expel them? This is why they will be your judges. **28** But if it is by means of God's spirit that I expel the demons, the Kingdom of God has really overtaken you.[c] **29** Or how can anyone invade the house of a strong man and seize his possessions unless he first ties up the strong man? Only then can he plunder his house. **30** Whoever is not on my side is against me, and whoever does not gather with me scatters.[d]

31 "For this reason I say to you, every sort of sin and blasphemy will be forgiven men, but the blasphemy against the spirit will not be forgiven.[e] **32** For example, whoever speaks a word against the Son of man, it will be forgiven him;[f] but whoever speaks against the holy spirit, it will not be forgiven, no, not in this system of things* nor in that to come.[g]

33 "Either you make the tree fine and its fruit fine or make the tree rotten and its fruit rotten, for by its fruit the tree is known.[a] **34** Offspring of vipers,[b] how can you speak good things when you are wicked? For out of the abundance of the heart the mouth speaks.[c] **35** The good man out of his good treasure sends out good things, whereas the wicked man out of his wicked treasure sends out wicked things.[d] **36** I tell you that men will render an account[e] on Judgment Day for every unprofitable saying that they speak; **37** for by your words you will be declared righteous, and by your words you will be condemned."

38 Then as an answer to him, some of the scribes and the Pharisees said: "Teacher, we want to see a sign from you."[f] **39** In reply he said to them: "A wicked and adulterous* generation keeps on seeking a sign, but no sign will be given it except the sign of Jo′nah the prophet.[g] **40** For just as Jo′nah was in the belly of the huge fish for three days and three nights,[h] so the Son of man will be in the heart of the earth for three days and three nights.[i] **41** Men of Nin′e·veh will rise up in the judgment with this generation and will condemn it, because they repented at what Jo′nah preached.[j] But look! something more than Jo′nah is here.[k] **42** The queen of the south will be raised up in the judgment with this generation and will condemn it, for she came from the ends of the earth to hear the wisdom of Sol′o·mon.[l] But look! something more than Sol′o·mon is here.[m]

43 "When an unclean spirit comes out of a man, it passes through waterless places in

CHAP. 12	
a	Isa 11:10
	Isa 42:1-4
	Ac 4:12
b	Mr 3:22-27
	Lu 11:15-23
c	Lu 11:20
d	Mr 9:40
	Lu 9:50
	Lu 11:23
e	Mr 3:28, 29
	Ac 7:51
	Heb 6:4, 6
f	1Ti 1:13
g	Lu 12:10
	Heb 10:26

Second Col.	
a	Mt 7:17
	Lu 6:43
b	Mt 3:7
	Mt 23:33
c	Mt 15:11
d	Lu 6:45
	Jas 3:6
e	Ec 12:14
	Ro 14:12
f	Mt 16:1
g	Mt 16:4
	Lu 11:29-32
h	Jon 1:17
i	Mt 16:21
	Mt 17:23
	Mt 27:63
	Lu 24:46
j	Jon 3:5
k	Lu 11:30
l	1Ki 10:1
	2Ch 9:1
m	Mt 12:6
	Lu 11:31

12:24 *A designation applied to Satan.
12:32 *Or "this age." See Glossary.

12:39 *Or "unfaithful."

search of a resting-place and finds none.[a] **44** Then it says, 'I will go back to my house from which I moved,' and on arriving, it finds the house unoccupied but swept clean and adorned. **45** Then it goes and takes along with it seven different spirits more wicked than itself, and after getting inside, they dwell there; and the final circumstances of that man become worse than the first.[b] That is how it will be also with this wicked generation."

46 While he was yet speaking to the crowds, his mother and brothers[c] were standing outside, seeking to speak to him.[d] **47** So someone said to him: "Look! Your mother and your brothers are standing outside, seeking to speak to you." **48** In reply he said to the one who spoke to him: "Who is my mother, and who are my brothers?" **49** And extending his hand toward his disciples, he said: "Look! My mother and my brothers![e] **50** For whoever does the will of my Father who is in heaven, that one is my brother and sister and mother."[f]

13 On that day Jesus left the house and was sitting by the sea. **2** And such large crowds gathered to him that he went aboard a boat and sat down, and all the crowd was standing on the beach.[g] **3** Then he told them many things by illustrations,[h] saying: "Look! A sower went out to sow.[i] **4** As he was sowing, some seeds fell alongside the road, and the birds came and ate them up.[j] **5** Others fell on rocky ground where there was not much soil, and they immediately sprang up because the soil was not deep.[k] **6** But when the sun rose, they were scorched, and they withered because they had no root. **7** Others fell among the thorns,

and the thorns came up and choked them.[a] **8** Still others fell on the fine soil, and they began to yield fruit, this one 100 times more, that one 60, the other 30.[b] **9** Let the one who has ears listen."[c]

10 So the disciples came and said to him: "Why do you speak to them by the use of illustrations?"[d] **11** In reply he said: "To you it is granted to understand the sacred secrets[e] of the Kingdom of the heavens, but to them it is not granted. **12** For whoever has, more will be given him, and he will be made to abound; but whoever does not have, even what he has will be taken from him.[f] **13** That is why I speak to them by the use of illustrations; for looking, they look in vain, and hearing, they hear in vain, nor do they get the sense of it.[g] **14** And the prophecy of Isaiah is being fulfilled in their case. It says: 'You will indeed hear but by no means get the sense of it, and you will indeed look but by no means see.[h] **15** For the heart of this people has grown unreceptive, and with their ears they have heard without response, and they have shut their eyes, so that they might never see with their eyes and hear with their ears and get the sense of it with their hearts and turn back and I heal them.'[i]

16 "However, happy are your eyes because they see and your ears because they hear.[j] **17** For truly I say to you, many prophets and righteous men desired to see the things you are observing but did not see them,[k] and to hear the things you are hearing but did not hear them.

18 "Now listen to the illustration of the man who sowed.[l] **19** Where anyone hears the word of the Kingdom but does not get the sense of it, the wicked one[m] comes and snatch-

CHAP. 12
a Lu 11:24-26
b Heb 6:4, 6
 2Pe 2:20
c Mt 13:55
 Joh 2:12
 Ac 1:14
 1Co 9:5
 Ga 1:19
d Mr 3:31-35
e Joh 20:17
 Heb 2:11
f Mr 3:35
 Lu 8:21

CHAP. 13
g Mr 4:1
h Mt 13:34
i Mr 4:3-9
 Lu 8:4-8
j Mt 13:19
k Mt 13:20, 21

Second Col.
a Mt 13:22
 Mr 4:18, 19
 Lu 8:14
b Mt 13:23
 Mr 4:8
 Lu 8:8
c Mt 11:15
d Mr 4:10, 11
 Lu 8:9, 10
e 1Co 2:9, 10
 Eph 1:9-12
 Col 1:26, 27
f Mt 25:29
 Mr 4:25
 Lu 8:18
g Isa 6:10
 Mr 4:12
h Joh 12:40
 Ro 11:8
 2Co 3:14
i Isa 6:9, 10
 Mr 4:12
 Ac 28:26, 27
j Lu 10:23, 24
k Joh 8:56
 Eph 3:5
 1Pe 1:10
l Mr 4:14
 Lu 8:11
m 1Pe 5:8

es away what has been sown in his heart; this is the one sown alongside the road.[a] **20** As for the one sown on rocky ground, this is the one hearing the word and at once accepting it with joy.[b] **21** Yet, he has no root in himself but continues for a time, and after tribulation or persecution has arisen on account of the word, he is at once stumbled. **22** As for the one sown among the thorns, this is the one hearing the word, but the anxiety of this system of things*[c] and the deceptive power of riches choke the word, and it becomes unfruitful.[d] **23** As for the one sown upon the fine soil, this is the one hearing the word and getting the sense of it, who really does bear fruit and produces, this one 100 times more, that one 60, the other 30."[e]

24 He presented another illustration to them, saying: "The Kingdom of the heavens may be likened to a man who sowed fine seed in his field. **25** While men were sleeping, his enemy came and oversowed weeds in among the wheat and left. **26** When the stalk sprouted and produced fruit, then the weeds also appeared. **27** So the slaves of the master of the house came and said to him, 'Master, did you not sow fine seed in your field? How, then, does it have weeds?' **28** He said to them, 'An enemy, a man, did this.'[f] The slaves said to him, 'Do you want us, then, to go out and collect them?' **29** He said, 'No, for fear that while collecting the weeds, you uproot the wheat with them. **30** Let both grow together until the harvest, and in the harvest season, I will tell the reapers: First collect the weeds and bind them in bundles to burn them up; then gather the wheat into my storehouse.'"[g]

31 He presented another illustration to them, saying: "The Kingdom of the heavens is like a mustard grain that a man took and planted in his field.[a] **32** It is, in fact, the tiniest of all the seeds, but when it has grown, it is the largest of the vegetable plants and becomes a tree, so that the birds of heaven come and find lodging among its branches."

33 He told them another illustration: "The Kingdom of the heavens is like leaven that a woman took and mixed with three large measures of flour until the whole mass was fermented."[b]

34 All these things Jesus spoke to the crowds by illustrations. Indeed, without an illustration he would not speak to them,[c] **35** in order to fulfill what was spoken through the prophet who said: "I will open my mouth with illustrations; I will proclaim things hidden since the founding."*[d]

36 Then after dismissing the crowds, he went into the house. His disciples came to him and said: "Explain to us the illustration of the weeds in the field." **37** In response he said: "The sower of the fine seed is the Son of man; **38** the field is the world.[e] As for the fine seed, these are the sons of the Kingdom, but the weeds are the sons of the wicked one,[f] **39** and the enemy who sowed them is the Devil. The harvest is a conclusion of a system of things,* and the reapers are angels. **40** Therefore, just as the weeds are collected and burned with fire, so it will be in the conclusion of the system of things.*[g] **41** The Son of man will send his angels,

---

CHAP. 13
a Mr 4:15
  Lu 8:12

b Mr 4:16, 17
  Lu 8:13

c Lu 12:22

d Mt 6:21
  Mr 4:18, 19
  Mr 10:23
  Lu 8:14
  1Ti 6:9
  2Ti 4:10

e Mr 4:20
  Lu 8:15

f Mt 13:38, 39

g Re 14:15

Second Col.
a Mr 4:30-32
  Lu 13:18, 19

b Lu 13:21

c Mr 4:33, 34

d Ps 78:2

e Mt 24:14
  Ro 10:18
  Col 1:6

f Joh 8:44

g Mt 13:30

13:22 *Or "this age." See Glossary.

13:35 *Or possibly, "the founding of the world." 13:39 *Or "an age." See Glossary. 13:40 *Or "the age." See Glossary.

and they will collect out from his Kingdom all things that cause stumbling and people who practice lawlessness, **42** and they will pitch them into the fiery furnace.[a] There is where their weeping and the gnashing of their teeth will be. **43** At that time the righteous ones will shine as brightly as the sun[b] in the Kingdom of their Father. Let the one who has ears listen.

44 "The Kingdom of the heavens is like a treasure, hidden in the field, that a man found and hid; and because of his joy, he goes and sells everything he has and buys that field.[c]

45 "Again the Kingdom of the heavens is like a traveling merchant seeking fine pearls. **46** Upon finding one pearl of high value, he went away and promptly sold all the things he had and bought it.[d]

47 "Again the Kingdom of the heavens is like a dragnet let down into the sea and gathering fish of every kind. **48** When it was full, they hauled it up onto the beach, and sitting down, they collected the fine ones[e] into containers, but the unsuitable[f] they threw away. **49** That is how it will be in the conclusion of the system of things.* The angels will go out and separate the wicked from among the righteous **50** and will cast them into the fiery furnace. There is where their weeping and the gnashing of their teeth will be.

51 "Did you get the sense of all these things?" They said to him: "Yes." **52** Then he said to them: "That being the case, every public instructor who is taught about the Kingdom of the heavens is like a man, the master of the house, who brings out of his treasure store things both new and old."

53 When Jesus had finished these illustrations, he departed from there. **54** After coming into his home territory,[a] he began to teach them in their synagogue, so that they were astounded and said: "Where did this man get this wisdom and these powerful works?[b] **55** Is this not the carpenter's son?[c] Is not his mother called Mary, and his brothers James and Joseph and Simon and Judas?[d] **56** And his sisters, are they not all with us? Where, then, did he get all of this?"[e] **57** So they began to stumble because of him.[f] But Jesus said to them: "A prophet is not without honor except in his home territory and in his own house."[g] **58** And he did not perform many powerful works there on account of their lack of faith.

14 At that time Herod, the district ruler,* heard the report about Jesus[h] **2** and said to his servants: "This is John the Baptist. He was raised up from the dead, and this is why these powerful works are operating in him."[i] **3** Herod* had arrested John and had bound him and imprisoned him because of He·ro'di·as, the wife of Philip his brother.[j] **4** For John had been saying to him: "It is not lawful for you to have her."[k] **5** However, although he wanted to kill him, he feared the crowd, because they took him for a prophet.[l] **6** But when Herod's birthday[m] was being celebrated, the daughter of He·ro'di·as danced for the occasion and pleased Herod so much[n] **7** that he promised with an oath to give her whatever she asked. **8** Then she, at her mother's prompting, said: "Give me here on a platter the head of John the Baptist."[o] **9** Grieved though he was, the king, out of

---

CHAP. 13
a Mt 13:30
b Jg 5:31
c Php 3:7
d Php 3:8
e Le 11:9
f Le 11:12

Second Col.
a Mt 2:23
b Mr 6:1-6
c Lu 4:22
  Joh 6:42
d Mt 12:46
  Joh 2:12
  Ac 1:14
  1Co 9:5
  Ga 1:19
e Joh 7:15
f 1Pe 2:7, 8
g Mr 6:4
  Lu 4:24
  Joh 4:44

CHAP. 14
h Mr 6:14
  Lu 9:7-9
  Ac 4:27
i Mt 16:13, 14
  Mr 6:16
j Mr 6:17, 18
  Lu 3:19, 20
k Le 18:16
  Le 20:21
l Mr 6:20
  Lu 1:67, 76
m Ge 40:20-22
n Mr 6:21-29
o Mr 6:25

13:49 *Or "the age." See Glossary.

14:1 *Lit., "the tetrarch." **14:3** *That is, Herod Antipas. See Glossary.

regard for his oaths and for those dining* with him, commanded it to be given. **10** So he sent and had John beheaded in the prison. **11** His head was brought on a platter and given to the girl, and she brought it to her mother. **12** Later his disciples came and removed his corpse and buried him; then they came and reported to Jesus. **13** At hearing this, Jesus departed from there by boat into an isolated place to be alone. But the crowds, getting to hear of it, followed him on foot from the cities.[a]

14 When he came ashore, he saw a large crowd, and he felt pity for them,[b] and he cured their sick ones.[c] **15** But when evening fell, his disciples came to him and said: "The place is isolated and the hour is already late; send the crowds away, so that they may go into the villages and buy themselves food."[d] **16** However, Jesus said to them: "They do not have to leave; you give them something to eat." **17** They said to him: "We have nothing here except five loaves and two fish." **18** He said: "Bring them here to me." **19** And he instructed the crowds to recline on the grass. Then he took the five loaves and two fish, and looking up to heaven, he said a blessing,[e] and after breaking the loaves, he gave them to the disciples, and the disciples gave them to the crowds. **20** So they all ate and were satisfied, and they took up the leftover fragments, 12 baskets full.[f] **21** Now those eating were about 5,000 men, as well as women and young children.[g] **22** Then, without delay, he made his disciples board the boat and go ahead of him to the opposite shore, while he sent the crowds away.[h]

23 After sending the crowds away, he went up on the mountain by himself to pray.[a] When evening came, he was there alone. **24** By now the boat was many hundreds of yards* away from land, struggling against the waves because the wind was against them. **25** But in the fourth watch of the night* he came to them, walking on the sea. **26** When they caught sight of him walking on the sea, the disciples were troubled, saying: "It is an apparition!" And they cried out in their fear. **27** But at once Jesus spoke to them, saying: "Take courage! It is I; do not be afraid."[b] **28** Peter answered him: "Lord, if it is you, command me to come to you over the waters." **29** He said: "Come!" So Peter got out of the boat and walked over the waters and went toward Jesus. **30** But looking at the windstorm, he became afraid. And when he started to sink, he cried out: "Lord, save me!" **31** Immediately stretching out his hand, Jesus caught hold of him and said to him: "You with little faith, why did you give way to doubt?"[c] **32** After they got up into the boat, the windstorm abated. **33** Then those in the boat did obeisance* to him, saying: "You really are God's Son." **34** And they crossed over and came to land in Gen·nes′a·ret.[d]

35 On recognizing him, the men of that place sent word into all that surrounding country, and people brought him all those who were ill. **36** And they pleaded with him that they might just touch the fringe of his outer garment,[e] and all those who touched it were made completely well.

CHAP. 14
a Mr 6:31-33
Lu 9:10

b Mt 9:36
Mt 15:32
Mr 1:41
Mr 6:34
Lu 7:13
Heb 2:17
Heb 5:2

c Lu 9:11

d Mr 6:35-44
Lu 9:12-17
Joh 6:5-13

e Mt 15:36
Mr 6:41
Lu 9:16

f 2Ki 4:42-44
Mr 6:42, 43
Mr 8:8
Lu 9:17
Joh 6:12, 13

g Mr 6:44
Lu 9:14
Joh 6:10

h Mr 6:45-52
Joh 6:16-21

Second Col.
a Mr 6:46
Lu 6:12
Lu 9:18

b Mr 6:50
Joh 6:20

c Mt 6:30
Mt 8:26
Mt 28:16, 17
Jas 1:6

d Mr 6:53-56

e Mt 9:20, 21
Mr 3:10
Lu 6:19

14:24 *Lit., "many stadia." A stadium equaled 185 m (606.95 ft). **14:25** *That is, about 3:00 a.m. until sunrise at about 6:00 a.m. **14:33** *Or "bowed down."

14:9 *Or "reclining at the table."

15 Then there came to Jesus from Jerusalem Pharisees and scribes,[a] saying: **2** "Why do your disciples overstep the tradition of the men of former times? For example, they do not wash* their hands when about to eat a meal."[b]

3 In reply he said to them: "Why do you overstep the commandment of God because of your tradition?[c] **4** For example, God said, 'Honor your father and your mother,'[d] and, 'Let the one who speaks abusively of* his father or mother be put to death.'[e] **5** But you say, 'Whoever says to his father or mother: "Whatever I have that could benefit you is a gift dedicated to God,"[f] **6** he need not honor his father at all.' So you have made the word of God invalid because of your tradition.[g] **7** You hypocrites, Isaiah aptly prophesied about you when he said:[h] **8** 'This people honor me with their lips, but their hearts are far removed from me. **9** It is in vain that they keep worshipping me, for they teach commands of men as doctrines.'"[i] **10** With that he called the crowd near and said to them: "Listen and get the sense of it:[j] **11** It is not what enters into a man's mouth that defiles him, but it is what comes out of his mouth that defiles him."[k]

12 Then the disciples came and said to him: "Do you know that the Pharisees were stumbled at hearing what you said?"[l] **13** In reply he said: "Every plant that my heavenly Father did not plant will be uprooted. **14** Let them be. Blind guides is what they are. If, then, a blind man guides a blind man, both will fall into a pit."[m] **15** Peter

responded: "Make the illustration plain to us." **16** At this he said: "Are you also still without understanding?[a] **17** Are you not aware that whatever enters into the mouth passes through the stomach and is discharged into the sewer? **18** However, whatever comes out of the mouth comes from the heart, and those things defile a man.[b] **19** For example, out of the heart come wicked reasonings,[c] murders, adulteries, sexual immorality,* thefts, false testimonies, blasphemies. **20** These are the things that defile a man; but to take a meal with unwashed* hands does not defile a man."

21 Leaving there, Jesus now went into the region of Tyre and Si'don.[d] **22** And look! a Phoeni'cian woman from that region came and cried out: "Have mercy on me, Lord, Son of David. My daughter is cruelly demon possessed."[e] **23** But he did not say a word in answer to her. So his disciples came and began to urge him: "Send her away, because she keeps crying out after us." **24** He answered: "I was not sent to anyone except to the lost sheep of the house of Israel."[f] **25** But the woman came and did obeisance* to him, saying: "Lord, help me!" **26** In answer he said: "It is not right to take the bread of the children and throw it to the little dogs." **27** She said: "Yes, Lord, but really the little dogs do eat of the crumbs falling from the table of their masters."[g] **28** Then Jesus replied to her: "O woman, great is your faith; let it happen to you as you wish." And her daughter was healed from that hour on.

CHAP. 15
a Mr 7:1, 2
b Lu 11:38 Joh 2:6
c Mt 15:9 Mr 7:8-13 Col 2:8
d Ex 20:12 De 5:16 Eph 6:2
e Ex 21:17 Le 20:9
f Mr 7:11, 12
g Mr 7:13
h Mr 7:6
i Isa 29:13 Mr 7:7
j Mr 7:14
k Mr 7:15 Eph 4:29 Jas 3:6
l Mr 7:17
m Mt 23:15, 16 Lu 6:39

Second Col.
a Mr 7:18-23
b Mr 7:20
c Ge 8:21 Jer 17:9
d Mr 7:24
e Mr 7:25-30
f Isa 53:6 Mt 10:5, 6 Ac 3:26 Ac 13:46 Ro 15:8
g Mr 7:28

15:2 *That is, ceremonially cleanse. 15:4 *Or "reviles."

15:19 *Plural of the Greek por·nei'a. See Glossary. 15:20 *That is, not ceremonially cleansed. 15:25 *Or "bowed down."

29 Departing from there, Jesus next came near the Sea of Gal'i·lee,[a] and after going up on the mountain, he was sitting there. **30** Then large crowds approached him, bringing along people who were lame, maimed, blind, speechless, and many others, and they laid them at his feet, and he cured them.[b] **31** So the crowd felt amazement as they saw the speechless speaking and the maimed being made sound and the lame walking and the blind seeing, and they glorified the God of Israel.[c]

32 But Jesus called his disciples to him and said: "I feel pity for the crowd,[d] because they have already stayed with me for three days and they have had nothing to eat. I do not want to send them away hungry,[*] for they may give out on the road."[e] **33** However, the disciples said to him: "Where in this isolated place are we going to get enough bread to satisfy a crowd of this size?"[f] **34** At this Jesus said to them: "How many loaves do you have?" They said: "Seven, and a few small fish." **35** So after instructing the crowd to recline on the ground, **36** he took the seven loaves and the fish, and after offering thanks, he broke them and began giving them to the disciples, and the disciples gave them to the crowds.[g] **37** And all ate and were satisfied, and they took up seven large baskets[*] full of leftover fragments.[h] **38** Now those eating were 4,000 men, as well as women and young children. **39** Finally, after sending the crowds away, he got into the boat and came into the region of Mag'a·dan.[i]

16 Here the Pharisees and Sadducees approached him, and to test him, they asked him to display to them a sign from heaven.[a] **2** In reply he said to them: "When evening falls, you say, 'It will be fair weather, for the sky is fire-red,' **3** and in the morning, 'It will be wintry, rainy weather today, for the sky is fire-red but gloomy.' You know how to interpret the appearance of the sky, but the signs of the times you cannot interpret. **4** A wicked and adulterous[*] generation keeps seeking a sign, but no sign will be given it[b] except the sign of Jo'nah."[c] With that he went away, leaving them behind.

5 Now the disciples crossed to the other side and forgot to take bread along.[d] **6** Jesus said to them: "Keep your eyes open and watch out for the leaven of the Pharisees and Sadducees."[e] **7** So they began to reason among themselves, saying: "We did not take any loaves along." **8** Knowing this, Jesus said: "Why are you discussing among yourselves that you have no loaves, you with little faith? **9** Do you not yet see the point, or do you not remember the five loaves in the case of the 5,000 and how many baskets you took up?[f] **10** Or the seven loaves in the case of the 4,000 and how many large baskets[*] you took up?[g] **11** How is it you do not discern that I did not speak to you about bread? But watch out for the leaven of the Pharisees and Sadducees."[h] **12** Then they grasped that he said to watch out, not for the leaven of bread, but for the teaching of the Pharisees and Sadducees.

13 When he had come into the region of Caes·a·re'a Phi·lip'pi, Jesus asked his disciples: "Who are men saying the Son of man is?"[i] **14** They said: "Some say John the Baptist,[j] others E·li'jah,[k] and still others Jeremiah or one of the prophets." **15** He said to

---

CHAP. 15
a Mr 7:31

b Isa 35:5
  Mt 19:2
  Mr 3:10

c Mt 9:33

d Mt 14:14
  Mr 6:34

e Mr 8:1-9

f 2Ki 4:42-44

g Mt 14:19

h Mr 8:8, 9

i Mr 8:10

Second Col.

CHAP. 16
a Mt 12:38
  Mr 8:11
  Lu 11:16

b Mr 8:12

c Jon 1:17
  Mt 12:39
  Lu 11:29

d Mr 8:13-21

e Mr 8:15
  Lu 12:1

f Mt 14:17

g Mt 15:34

h Lu 12:1

i Mr 8:27-29
  Lu 9:18-20

j Mt 14:1, 2

k Joh 1:25, 26

15:32 *Or "fasting." 15:37; 16:10 *Or "provision baskets." 16:4 *Or "unfaithful."

them: "You, though, who do you say I am?" **16** Simon Peter answered: "You are the Christ,[a] the Son of the living God."[b] **17** In response Jesus said to him: "Happy you are, Simon son of Jo′nah, because flesh and blood[b] did not reveal it to you, but my Father in the heavens did.[c] **18** Also, I say to you: You are Peter,[d] and on this rock[e] I will build my congregation, and the gates of the Grave* will not overpower it. **19** I will give you the keys of the Kingdom of the heavens, and whatever you may bind on earth will already be bound in the heavens, and whatever you may loosen on earth will already be loosened in the heavens." **20** Then he sternly instructed the disciples not to tell anybody that he was the Christ.[f]

21 From that time forward, Jesus began explaining to his disciples that he must go to Jerusalem and suffer many things from the elders and chief priests and scribes and be killed, and on the third day be raised up.[g] **22** At this Peter took him aside and began to rebuke him, saying: "Be kind to yourself, Lord; you will not have this happen to you at all."[h] **23** But turning his back, he said to Peter: "Get behind me, Satan! You are a stumbling block to me, because you think, not God's thoughts, but those of men."[i]

24 Then Jesus said to his disciples: "If anyone wants to come after me, let him disown himself and pick up his torture stake* and keep following me.[j] **25** For whoever wants to save his life* will lose it, but whoever loses his life* for my sake will find it.[k] **26** Really, what good will it do a man if he gains the whole world

but loses his life?*[a] Or what will a man give in exchange for his life?*[b] **27** For the Son of man is to come in the glory of his Father with his angels, and then he will repay each one according to his behavior.[c] **28** Truly I say to you that there are some of those standing here who will not taste death at all until first they see the Son of man coming in his Kingdom."[d]

17 Six days later Jesus took Peter and James and his brother John along and led them up into a lofty mountain by themselves.[e] **2** And he was transfigured before them; his face shone as the sun, and his outer garments became brilliant* as the light.[f] **3** And look! there appeared to them Moses and E·li′jah conversing with him. **4** Then Peter said to Jesus: "Lord, it is fine for us to be here. If you wish, I will erect three tents here, one for you, one for Moses, and one for E·li′jah." **5** While he was still speaking, look! a bright cloud overshadowed them, and look! a voice out of the cloud said: "This is my Son, the beloved, whom I have approved.[g] Listen to him."[h] **6** At hearing this, the disciples fell facedown and became very much afraid. **7** Then Jesus came near, and touching them, he said: "Get up. Have no fear." **8** When they looked up, they saw no one but Jesus himself. **9** As they were descending from the mountain, Jesus commanded them: "Tell the vision to no one until the Son of man is raised up from the dead."[i]

10 However, the disciples put the question to him: "Why, then, do the scribes say that E·li′jah must come first?"[j] **11** In reply he said: "E·li′jah is indeed coming and will restore all things.[k] **12** However, I say to you that

CHAP. 16
a Mr 8:29
Lu 9:20
Joh 1:40, 41
Joh 4:25
Joh 11:27
b Ps 2:7
Mt 14:33
Ac 9:20, 22
Heb 1:2
1Jo 4:15
c Mt 11:27
d Joh 1:42
e Ro 9:33
1Co 3:11
1Co 10:4
Eph 2:20
1Pe 2:6-8
f Mr 8:29, 30
Lu 9:20, 21
g Ps 16:10
Isa 53:12
Mt 17:22, 23
Mt 20:18, 19
Mr 8:31
Lu 9:22
Lu 24:46
1Co 15:3, 4
h Mr 8:32
i Mr 8:33
j Mr 10:38
Mr 8:34
Lu 9:23
Lu 14:27
k Mr 8:35
Lu 9:24
Lu 17:33
Joh 12:25
Re 12:11

Second Col.
a Mr 8:36
Lu 9:25
b Ps 49:8
c Ps 62:12
Pr 24:12
Lu 9:26
Ro 2:6
1Pe 1:17
d Mt 17:2
Mr 9:1
Lu 9:27

CHAP. 17
e Mr 9:2-8
Lu 9:28-36
f Re 1:13, 16
g Ps 2:7
Isa 42:1
Mt 3:17
2Pe 1:17, 18
h De 18:15
Mr 9:7
Lu 9:35
Ac 3:22, 23
Heb 2:3
i Mt 16:20
Mr 9:9
j Mr 9:11
k Isa 40:3
Mal 4:5, 6
Mt 11:13, 14
Mr 9:12
Lu 1:17

16:17 *Or "because a human." 16:18 *Or "Hades," that is, the common grave of mankind. See Glossary. 16:24 *See Glossary. 16:25, 26 *Or "soul."

17:2 *Or "white."

E·li'jah has already come, and they did not recognize him but did whatever they wanted with him.[a] In this way also, the Son of man is going to suffer at their hands."[b] **13** Then the disciples perceived that he spoke to them about John the Baptist.

14 When they came toward the crowd,[c] a man approached him, knelt down to him, and said: **15** "Lord, have mercy on my son, because he is an epileptic and is ill. He falls often into the fire and often into the water.[d] **16** I brought him to your disciples, but they could not cure him." **17** In reply Jesus said: "O faithless and twisted generation,[e] how long must I continue with you? How long must I put up with you? Bring him here to me." **18** Then Jesus rebuked the demon, and it came out of him, and the boy was cured from that hour.[f] **19** Then the disciples came to Jesus privately and said: "Why could we not expel it?" **20** He said to them: "Because of your little faith. For truly I say to you, if you have faith the size of a mustard grain, you will say to this mountain, 'Move from here to there,' and it will move, and nothing will be impossible for you."[g] **21** *—

22 It was while they were gathered together in Gal'i·lee that Jesus said to them: "The Son of man is going to be betrayed into men's hands,[h] **23** and they will kill him, and on the third day he will be raised up."[i] And they were very much grieved.

24 After they arrived in Ca·per'na·um, the men collecting the two drachmas* tax approached Peter and said: "Does your teacher not pay the two drachmas tax?"[j] **25** He said:

"Yes." However, when he entered the house, Jesus spoke to him first and said: "What do you think, Simon? From whom do the kings of the earth receive duties or head tax? From their sons or from the strangers?" **26** When he said: "From the strangers," Jesus said to him: "Really, then, the sons are tax-free. **27** But that we do not cause them to stumble,[a] go to the sea, cast a fishhook, and take the first fish that comes up, and when you open its mouth, you will find a silver coin.* Take that and give it to them for me and you."

18 In that hour the disciples came near to Jesus and said: "Who really is greatest in the Kingdom of the heavens?"[b] **2** So calling a young child to him, he stood him in their midst **3** and said: "Truly I say to you, unless you turn around* and become as young children,[c] you will by no means enter into the Kingdom of the heavens.[d] **4** Therefore, whoever will humble himself like this young child is the one who is the greatest in the Kingdom of the heavens;[e] **5** and whoever receives one such young child on the basis of my name receives me also. **6** But whoever stumbles one of these little ones who have faith in me, it would be better for him to have hung around his neck a millstone that is turned by a donkey and to be sunk in the open sea.[f]

7 "Woe to the world because of the stumbling blocks! Of course, it is inevitable that stumbling blocks will come, but woe to the man through whom the stumbling block comes! **8** If, then, your hand or your foot makes you stumble, cut it off

---

CHAP. 17
a Mr 9:13

b Mt 16:21
Lu 23:24, 25

c Lu 9:37

d Mr 9:17-29
Lu 9:38-42

e De 32:5, 20

f Mt 8:13
Mt 9:22
Mt 15:28
Joh 4:51, 52

g Mt 21:21
Mr 11:23
Lu 17:6

h Mt 20:18
Lu 9:44, 45

i Mt 16:21
Mr 9:31

j Ex 30:13, 14

Second Col.
a 1Co 10:32
2Co 6:3

CHAP. 18
b Mr 9:33-37
Lu 9:46-48
Lu 22:24

c Mt 19:14
1Pe 2:2

d Lu 18:17

e Pr 15:33
Mt 20:26
Mt 23:12
Lu 9:48
Lu 14:11
Lu 22:26
Jas 4:10
1Pe 5:5

f Mr 9:42
Lu 17:1, 2

17:21 *See App. A3. 17:24 *Lit., "the double drachmas." See App. B14.

17:27 *Lit., "stater coin," considered to be the tetradrachma. See App. B14. 18:3 *Or "change."

and throw it away from you.[a] It is better for you to enter into life maimed or lame than to be thrown with two hands or two feet into the everlasting fire.[b] **9** Also, if your eye makes you stumble, tear it out and throw it away from you. It is better for you to enter one-eyed into life than to be thrown with two eyes into the fiery Ge·hen′na.*[c] **10** See that you do not despise one of these little ones, for I tell you that their angels in heaven always look upon the face of my Father who is in heaven.[d] **11** *——

12 "What do you think? If a man has 100 sheep and one of them strays,[e] will he not leave the 99 on the mountains and set out on a search for the one that is straying?[f] **13** And if he finds it, I certainly tell you, he rejoices more over it than over the 99 that have not strayed. **14** Likewise, it is not a desirable thing to my* Father who is in heaven for even one of these little ones to perish.[g]

15 "Moreover, if your brother commits a sin, go and reveal his fault* between you and him alone.[h] If he listens to you, you have gained your brother.[i] **16** But if he does not listen, take along with you one or two more, so that on the testimony* of two or three witnesses every matter may be established.[j] **17** If he does not listen to them, speak to the congregation. If he does not listen even to the congregation, let him be to you just as a man of the nations[k] and as a tax collector.[l]

18 "Truly I say to you, whatever things you may bind on earth will be things already

bound in heaven, and whatever things you may loosen on earth will be things already loosened in heaven. **19** Again I tell you truly, if two of you on earth agree concerning anything of importance that they should request, it will take place for them on account of my Father in heaven.[a] **20** For where there are two or three gathered together in my name,[b] there I am in their midst."

21 Then Peter came and said to him: "Lord, how many times is my brother to sin against me and am I to forgive him? Up to seven times?" **22** Jesus said to him: "I say to you, not up to seven times, but up to 77 times.[c]

23 "That is why the Kingdom of the heavens may be likened to a king who wanted to settle accounts with his slaves. **24** When he started to settle them, a man was brought in who owed him 10,000 talents.* **25** But because he did not have the means to pay it back, his master ordered him and his wife and his children and all the things he owned to be sold and payment to be made.[d] **26** So the slave fell down and did obeisance* to him, saying, 'Be patient with me, and I will pay back everything to you.' **27** Moved with pity at this, the master of that slave let him off and canceled his debt.[e] **28** But that slave went out and found one of his fellow slaves, who owed him 100 de·nar′i·i,* and grabbed him and began to choke him, saying, 'Pay back whatever you owe.' **29** So his fellow slave fell down and began to beg him, saying, 'Be patient with me, and I will pay you back.' **30** However, he was not willing, but he went and

---

CHAP. 18
a Col 3:5

b Mt 25:41
  Mr 9:43-48

c Mt 5:22
  Mt 5:29
  Mr 9:47
  Ro 8:13

d Lu 1:19
  Heb 1:7, 14

e 1Pe 2:25

f Lu 15:3-7

g 2Pe 3:9

h Le 19:17
  Pr 25:8, 9
  Lu 17:3

i Jas 5:20

j De 19:15
  2Co 13:1
  1Ti 5:19

k Joh 18:28
  Ac 10:28
  Ac 11:2, 3

l Ro 16:17
  1Co 5:11

Second Col.
a Mr 11:24
  Joh 14:13
  Joh 16:23, 24
  1Jo 3:22
  1Jo 5:14

b 1Co 5:4, 5

c Mt 6:12
  Mr 11:25
  Lu 17:4
  Eph 4:32
  Col 3:13

d Ex 21:7
  Le 25:39
  2Ki 4:1
  Ne 5:8

e 1Jo 1:9

18:9 *See Glossary. **18:11** *See App. A3. **18:14** *Or possibly, "your." **18:15** *Lit., "and reprove him." **18:16** *Lit., "mouth."

18:24 *10,000 talents of silver equaled 60,000,000 denarii. See App. B14. **18:26** *Or "bowed down." **18:28** *See App. B14.

had him thrown into prison until he could pay back what he owed. **31** When his fellow slaves saw what had happened, they became greatly distressed, and they went and reported to their master all the things that had happened. **32** Then his master summoned him and said to him: 'Wicked slave, I canceled all that debt for you when you pleaded with me. **33** Should you not also have shown mercy to your fellow slave as I showed mercy to you?'ᵃ **34** With that his master, provoked to wrath, handed him over to the jailers until he repaid all that he owed. **35** My heavenly Father will also deal with you in the same wayᵇ if each of you does not forgive your brother from your heart."ᶜ

19 When Jesus had finished speaking these things, he departed from Gal'i·lee and came to the borders* of Ju·de'a across the Jordan.ᵈ **2** Also, large crowds followed him, and he cured them there.

3 And Pharisees came to him intent on testing him, and they asked: "Is it lawful for a man to divorce his wife on every sort of grounds?"ᵉ **4** In reply he said: "Have you not read that the one who created them from the beginning made them male and female ᶠ **5** and said: 'For this reason a man will leave his father and his mother and will stick to his wife, and the two will be one flesh'?ᵍ **6** So that they are no longer two, but one flesh. Therefore, what God has yoked together, let no man put apart."ʰ **7** They said to him: "Why, then, did Moses direct giving a certificate of dismissal and divorcing her?"ⁱ **8** He said to them: "Out of regard for your hardheartedness, Moses made the concession to you of divorcing

your wives,ᵃ but that has not been the case from the beginning.ᵇ **9** I say to you that whoever divorces his wife, except on the grounds of sexual immorality,* and marries another commits adultery."ᶜ

10 The disciples said to him: "If that is the situation of a man with his wife, it is not advisable to marry." **11** He said to them: "Not all men make room for the saying, but only those who have the gift.ᵈ **12** For there are eunuchs who were born that way, and there are eunuchs who were made eunuchs by men, and there are eunuchs who have made themselves eunuchs on account of the Kingdom of the heavens. Let the one who can make room for it make room for it."ᵉ

13 Then young children were brought to him for him to place his hands on them and offer prayer, but the disciples reprimanded them.ᶠ **14** Jesus, however, said: "Let the young children alone, and do not try to stop them from coming to me, for the Kingdom of the heavens belongs to such ones."ᵍ **15** And he placed his hands on them and departed from there.

16 Now look! someone came up to him and said: "Teacher, what good must I do to gain everlasting life?"ʰ **17** He said to him: "Why do you ask me about what is good? One there is who is good.ⁱ If, though, you want to enter into life, observe the commandments continually."ʲ **18** He said to him: "Which ones?" Jesus said: "You must not murder,ᵏ you must not commit adultery,ˡ you must not steal,ᵐ you must not bear false witness,ⁿ **19** honor your father and your mother,ᵒ and you must love your neighbor as yourself."ᵖ **20** The young man said to him: "I have kept all of these; what

CHAP. 18
a Isa 55:7
  Mt 6:12
  Mt 7:12
  Jas 2:13
b Ro 2:6
c Mt 6:14
  Mr 11:25
  Lu 17:3
  Eph 4:32

CHAP. 19
d Mr 10:1
e De 24:1
  Mr 10:2-12
f Ge 1:27
  Ge 5:2
g Ge 2:24
  Eph 5:31
h Mr 10:9
  1Co 7:11
i De 24:1
  Mt 5:31

Second Col.
a Mr 10:5
b Ge 2:24
c Mal 2:14
  Mt 5:32
  Mr 10:11,12
  Lu 16:18
  Ro 7:3
  1Co 7:10
  Heb 13:4
d 1Co 7:7
e 1Co 7:32, 38
  1Co 9:5
f Mr 10:13-16
  Lu 18:15-17
g Mt 18:3
  Mr 10:14
  Lu 18:16
h Mr 10:17-22
  Lu 18:18-23
i Mr 10:18
j Le 18:5
  Lu 10:25-28
k Ex 20:13
  De 5:17
l Ex 20:14
  De 5:18
m Ex 20:15
  De 5:19
n Ex 20:16
  De 5:20
o Ex 20:12
  De 5:16
p Le 19:18
  Mt 22:39
  Mr 12:31
  Lu 10:27
  Ro 13:9

am I still lacking?" **21** Jesus said to him: "If you want to be perfect,* go sell your belongings and give to the poor, and you will have treasure in heaven;ᵃ and come be my follower."ᵇ **22** When the young man heard this, he went away grieved, for he had many possessions.ᶜ **23** Then Jesus said to his disciples: "Truly I say to you that it will be difficult for a rich man to enter the Kingdom of the heavens.ᵈ **24** Again I say to you, it is easier for a camel to get through a needle's eye than for a rich man to enter the Kingdom of God."ᵉ

25 When the disciples heard that, they were greatly astounded, saying: "Who really can be saved?"ᶠ **26** Looking at them intently, Jesus said to them: "With men this is impossible, but with God all things are possible."ᵍ

27 Then Peter said in reply: "Look! We have left all things and followed you; what, then, will there be for us?"ʰ **28** Jesus said to them: "Truly I say to you, in the re-creation, when the Son of man sits down on his glorious throne, you who have followed me will sit on 12 thrones, judging the 12 tribes of Israel.ⁱ **29** And everyone who has left houses or brothers or sisters or father or mother or children or lands for the sake of my name will receive a hundred times as much and will inherit everlasting life.ʲ

30 "But many who are first will be last and the last first.ᵏ

20 "For the Kingdom of the heavens is like the master of a house who went out early in the morning to hire workers for his vineyard.ˡ **2** After he had agreed with the workers for a de·narʹi·us* a day, he sent them into his vineyard.

19:21 *Or "complete."   20:2, 9, 10, 13 *See App. B14.

---

3 Going out also about the third hour,* he saw others standing unemployed in the marketplace; **4** and to those he said, 'You too go into the vineyard, and I will give you whatever is fair.' **5** So off they went. Again he went out about the sixth hour* and the ninth hourᵘ and did likewise. **6** Finally, about the 11th hour,* he went out and found others standing around, and he said to them, 'Why have you been standing here all day unemployed?' **7** They replied, 'Because nobody has hired us.' He said to them, 'You too go into the vineyard.'

8 "When evening came, the master of the vineyard said to his man in charge, 'Call the workers and pay them their wages,ᵃ starting with the last and ending with the first.' **9** When the 11th-hour men came, they each received a de·narʹi·us.* **10** So when the first came, they assumed that they would receive more, but they too were paid at the rate of a de·narʹi·us.* **11** On receiving it, they began to complain against the master of the house **12** and said, 'These last men put in one hour's work; still you made them equal to us who bore the burden of the day and the burning heat!' **13** But he said in reply to one of them, 'Fellow, I do you no wrong. You agreed for a de·narʹi·us,* did you not?ᵇ **14** Take what is yours and go. I want to give to this last one the same as to you. **15** Do I not have the right to do what I want with my own things? Or is your eye envious* because I am good?'ᵃᶜ **16** In this way, the last ones will be first, and the first ones last."ᵈ

20:3 *That is, about 9:00 a.m.   20:5 *That is, about 12:00 noon.   ᵘThat is, about 3:00 p.m.   20:6 *That is, about 5:00 p.m.   20:15 *Lit., "bad; wicked."   ᵘOr "generous."

CHAP. 19
a Mt 6:20

b Lu 12:33
Lu 18:22
Php 3:7

c Lu 18:23

d Mt 10:23
Lu 18:24
1Ti 6:10

e Mt 10:25
Lu 18:25

f Mt 10:26, 27
Lu 18:26, 27

g Job 42:2

h Mt 10:28
Lu 5:11
Lu 18:28
Php 3:8

i Da 7:14
Mt 20:21
Lu 22:28-30
1Co 6:2
Re 20:4

j Mt 10:29, 30
Lu 18:29, 30
Heb 10:34

k Mt 20:16
Mt 10:31
Lu 13:30

CHAP. 20
l Mt 21:33

Second Col.
a Le 19:13
De 24:14, 15

b Mt 20:2

c Mt 6:23

d Mt 19:30
Mr 10:31
Lu 13:30

17 While going up to Jerusalem, Jesus took the 12 disciples aside privately and said to them on the road:[a] **18** "Look! We are going up to Jerusalem, and the Son of man will be handed over to the chief priests and the scribes. They will condemn him to death[b] **19** and hand him over to men of the nations to be mocked and scourged and executed on a stake;[c] and on the third day he will be raised up."[d]

20 Then the mother of the sons of Zeb'e·dee[e] approached him with her sons, doing obeisance* and asking for something from him.[f] **21** He said to her: "What do you want?" She replied to him: "Give the word that these two sons of mine may sit down, one at your right hand and one at your left, in your Kingdom."[g] **22** Jesus answered: "You do not know what you are asking for. Can you drink the cup that I am about to drink?"[h] They said to him: "We can." **23** He said to them: "You will indeed drink my cup,[i] but to sit down at my right hand and at my left is not mine to give, but it belongs to those for whom it has been prepared by my Father."[j]

24 When the ten others heard about it, they became indignant at the two brothers.[k] **25** But Jesus called them to him and said: "You know that the rulers of the nations lord it over them and the great men wield authority over them.[l] **26** This must not be the way among you;[m] but whoever wants to become great among you must be your minister,[n] **27** and whoever wants to be first among you must be your slave.[o] **28** Just as the Son of man came, not to be ministered to, but to minister[p] and to give his life* as a ransom in exchange for many."[q]

20:20 *Or "bowing down." 20:28 *Or "soul."

29 As they were going out of Jer'i·cho, a large crowd followed him. **30** And look! two blind men sitting beside the road heard that Jesus was passing by and cried out: "Lord, have mercy on us, Son of David!"[a] **31** But the crowd rebuked them, telling them to keep silent; yet they cried all the louder, saying: "Lord, have mercy on us, Son of David!" **32** So Jesus stopped, called them, and said: "What do you want me to do for you?" **33** They said to him: "Lord, let our eyes be opened." **34** Moved with pity, Jesus touched their eyes,[b] and immediately they recovered their sight, and they followed him.

21 When they got close to Jerusalem and arrived at Beth'pha·ge on the Mount of Olives, then Jesus sent two disciples,[c] **2** saying to them: "Go into the village that is within sight, and you will at once find a donkey tied and a colt with her. Untie them and bring them to me. **3** If someone says anything to you, you must say, 'The Lord needs them.' At that he will immediately send them."

4 This actually took place to fulfill what was spoken through the prophet, who said: **5** "Tell the daughter of Zion: 'Look! Your king is coming to you,[d] mild-tempered[e] and mounted on a donkey, yes, on a colt, the offspring of a beast of burden.'"[f]

6 So the disciples went and did just as Jesus had instructed them.[g] **7** They brought the donkey and its colt, and they put their outer garments on them, and he sat on them.[h] **8** Most of the crowd spread their outer garments on the road,[i] while others were cutting down branches from the trees and spreading them on the road. **9** Moreover, the crowds going ahead of him and those following him kept

---

CHAP. 20

a Mr 10:32
  Lu 18:31
b Mt 16:21
  Mr 10:33, 34
  Lu 9:22
  Lu 18:32, 33
c Mt 27:31
  Joh 19:1
d Mt 17:22, 23
  Mt 28:6
  Ac 10:40
  1Co 15:4
e Mt 4:21
  Mt 27:55, 56
f Mr 10:35-40
g Mt 19:28
h Mt 26:39
  Mt 10:38
  Mt 14:36
  Joh 18:11
i Ac 12:2
  Ro 8:17
  2Co 1:7
  Re 1:9
j Mr 10:39, 40
k Mr 10:41-45
  Lu 22:24
l Mr 10:42
m 2Co 1:24
  1Pe 5:3
n Mt 18:4
  Mt 23:11
  Mt 10:43, 44
  Lu 22:26
o Mr 9:35
p Lu 22:27
  Joh 13:14
  Php 2:7
q Isa 53:11
  Mr 10:45
  1Ti 2:5, 6
  Tit 2:13, 14
  Heb 9:28

Second Col.

a Mt 9:27
  Mr 10:46-52
  Lu 18:35-43
b Mt 9:29

CHAP. 21

c Mr 11:1-3
  Lu 19:28-31
d Isa 62:11
  Joh 12:15
e Mt 11:29
f Zec 9:9
g Mr 11:4-6
  Lu 19:32-35
h 1Ki 1:38, 40
  Mr 11:7-11
  Joh 12:14, 15
i Lu 19:36-38

shouting: "Save, we pray, the Son of David![a] Blessed is the one who comes in Jehovah's* name![b] Save him, we pray, in the heights above!"[c]

10 And when he entered Jerusalem, the whole city was in an uproar, saying: "Who is this?" 11 The crowds kept saying: "This is the prophet Jesus,[d] from Naz'a·reth of Gal'i·lee!"

12 Jesus entered the temple and threw out all those selling and buying in the temple, and he overturned the tables of the money changers and the benches of those selling doves.[e] 13 And he said to them: "It is written, 'My house will be called a house of prayer,'[f] but you are making it a cave of robbers."[g] 14 Also, blind and lame people came to him in the temple, and he cured them.

15 When the chief priests and the scribes saw the marvelous things he did and the boys who were shouting in the temple, "Save, we pray, the Son of David!"[h] they became indignant[i] 16 and said to him: "Do you hear what these are saying?" Jesus said to them: "Yes. Did you never read this, 'Out of the mouth of children and infants, you have brought forth praise'?"[j] 17 And leaving them behind, he went out of the city to Beth'a·ny and spent the night there.[k]

18 While returning to the city early in the morning, he felt hungry.[l] 19 He caught sight of a fig tree by the road and went to it, but he found nothing on it except leaves,[m] and he said to it: "Let no fruit come from you ever again."[n] And the fig tree withered instantly. 20 When the disciples saw this, they were amazed and said: "How is it that the fig tree withered instantly?"[o] 21 In answer Jesus said to them: "Tru-

ly I say to you, if you have faith and do not doubt, not only will you do what I did to the fig tree, but even if you say to this mountain, 'Be lifted up and thrown into the sea,' it will happen.[a] 22 And all the things you ask in prayer, having faith, you will receive."[b]

23 After he went into the temple, the chief priests and the elders of the people came up to him while he was teaching and said: "By what authority do you do these things? And who gave you this authority?"[c] 24 In reply Jesus said to them: "I will also ask you one thing. If you tell me, then I will also tell you by what authority I do these things: 25 The baptism by John, from what source was it? From heaven or from men?"* But they began to reason among themselves, saying: "If we say, 'From heaven,' he will say to us, 'Why, then, did you not believe him?'[d] 26 But if we say, 'From men,' we have the crowd to fear, for they all regard John as a prophet." 27 So they answered Jesus: "We do not know." He, in turn, said to them: "Neither am I telling you by what authority I do these things.

28 "What do you think? A man had two children. Going up to the first, he said, 'Child, go work today in the vineyard.' 29 In answer this one said, 'I will not,' but afterward, he felt regret and went out. 30 Approaching the second, he said the same. This one replied, 'I will, Sir,' but did not go out. 31 Which of the two did the will of his father?" They said: "The first." Jesus said to them: "Truly I say to you that the tax collectors and the prostitutes are going ahead of you into the Kingdom of God. 32 For John came

---

CHAP. 21
a Mt 9:27
  Mt 21:15

b Ps 118:25, 26
  Joh 12:13

c Mr 11:9, 10

d Mt 21:46
  Lu 7:16
  Lu 24:19

e Mr 11:15, 16
  Lu 19:45
  Joh 2:15

f Isa 56:7

g Jer 7:11
  Mr 11:17
  Lu 19:46
  Joh 2:16

h Mt 21:9

i Mr 11:18
  Lu 19:39, 40

j Ps 8:2

k Mr 11:11
  Lu 21:37
  Joh 11:1

l Mr 11:12

m Lu 13:6

n Mt 3:10
  Mr 11:13, 14

o Mr 11:20, 21

Second Col.
a Mt 17:20
  Mr 11:22, 23
  Lu 17:6

b Mr 11:24
  Lu 11:9
  Joh 14:13
  Jas 1:5
  1Jo 3:22

c Mr 11:27-33
  Lu 20:1-8

d Mt 21:32
  Mr 11:30, 31
  Lu 7:29, 30

21:9 *See App. A5.

21:25 *Or "of human origin?"

to you in a way of righteousness, but you did not believe him. However, the tax collectors and the prostitutes believed him,[a] and even when you saw this, you did not feel regret afterward so as to believe him.

33 "Hear another illustration: There was a man, a landowner, who planted a vineyard[b] and put a fence around it and dug a winepress in it and erected a tower;[c] then he leased it to cultivators and traveled abroad.[d] 34 When the fruit season came around, he sent his slaves to the cultivators to collect his fruit. 35 However, the cultivators took his slaves, and they beat one up, another they killed, another they stoned.[e] 36 Again he sent other slaves, more than the first group, but they did the same to these.[f] 37 Lastly he sent his son to them, saying, 'They will respect my son.' 38 On seeing the son, the cultivators said among themselves, 'This is the heir.[g] Come, let us kill him and get his inheritance!' 39 So they took him and threw him out of the vineyard and killed him.[h] 40 Therefore, when the owner of the vineyard comes, what will he do to those cultivators?" 41 They said to him: "Because they are evil, he will bring a terrible* destruction on them and will lease the vineyard to other cultivators, who will give him the fruits when they become due."

42 Jesus said to them: "Did you never read in the Scriptures, 'The stone that the builders rejected, this has become the chief cornerstone.'*[i] This has come from Jehovah,# and it is marvelous in our eyes'?[j] 43 This is why I say to you, the Kingdom of God will be taken from you and be given to a nation producing its

fruits. 44 Also, the person falling on this stone will be shattered.[a] As for anyone on whom it falls, it will crush him."[b]

45 When the chief priests and the Pharisees heard his illustrations, they knew that he was speaking about them.[c] 46 Although they wanted to seize* him, they feared the crowds, because these regarded him as a prophet.[d]

22 Once more Jesus spoke to them with illustrations, saying: 2 "The Kingdom of the heavens may be likened to a king who made a marriage feast[e] for his son. 3 And he sent his slaves to call those invited to the marriage feast, but they were unwilling to come.[f] 4 Again he sent other slaves, saying, 'Tell those invited: "Look! I have prepared my dinner, my bulls and fattened animals are slaughtered, and everything is ready. Come to the marriage feast."' 5 But unconcerned they went off, one to his own field, another to his business;[g] 6 but the rest, seizing his slaves, treated them insolently and killed them.

7 "The king grew wrathful and sent his armies and killed those murderers and burned their city.[h] 8 Then he said to his slaves, 'The marriage feast is ready, but those invited were not worthy.[i] 9 Therefore, go to the roads leading out of the city, and invite anyone you find to the marriage feast.' 10 Accordingly, those slaves went out to the roads and gathered all they found, both wicked and good; and the room for the wedding ceremonies was filled with those dining.*

11 "When the king came in to inspect the guests, he caught sight of a man not wearing

---

CHAP. 21
a Lu 3:12
  Lu 7:29, 30

b Isa 5:7

c Isa 5:2

d Mr 12:1-9
  Lu 20:9-16

e Ne 9:26

f 2Ch 36:15
  Ac 7:52
  Heb 11:32, 37

g Heb 1:2

h Ac 2:23
  Ac 3:15

i Isa 28:16
  Lu 20:17
  Ac 4:11
  Ro 9:33
  Eph 2:20
  1Pe 2:7

j Ps 118:22, 23
  Mr 12:10, 11

Second Col.

a Isa 8:14
  1Pe 2:7, 8

b Lu 20:18

c Mr 12:12
  Lu 20:19

d Mt 21:11
  Joh 7:40

CHAP. 22

e Lu 14:16
  Re 19:9

f Lu 14:17, 18

g Lu 14:18, 19

h Da 9:26

i Ac 13:45, 46

j Mt 21:43
  Lu 14:23

21:41 *Or "an evil." 21:42 *Lit., "the head of the corner." #See App. A5.

21:46 *Or "arrest." 22:10 *Or "reclining at the table."

a marriage garment. 12 So he said to him, 'Fellow, how did you get in here without a marriage garment?' He was speechless. 13 Then the king said to his servants, 'Bind him hand and foot and throw him into the darkness outside. There is where his weeping and the gnashing of his teeth will be.'

14 "For there are many invited, but few chosen."

15 Then the Pharisees went and conspired together in order to trap him in his speech.[a] 16 So they sent their disciples to him, together with party followers of Herod,[b] saying: "Teacher, we know you are truthful and teach the way of God in truth, and you do not seek anyone's favor, for you do not look at the outward appearance of people. 17 Tell us, then, what do you think? Is it lawful* to pay head tax to Caesar or not?" 18 But Jesus, knowing their wickedness, said: "Why do you put me to the test, hypocrites? 19 Show me the tax coin." They brought him a de·nar′i·us.* 20 He said to them: "Whose image and inscription is this?" 21 They said: "Caesar's." Then he said to them: "Pay back, therefore, Caesar's things to Caesar, but God's things to God."[c] 22 When they heard that, they were amazed, and they left him and went away.

23 On that day the Sadducees, who say there is no resurrection,[d] came and asked him:[e] 24 "Teacher, Moses said: 'If any man dies without having children, his brother must marry his wife and raise up offspring for his brother.'[f] 25 Now there were seven brothers with us. The first married and died, and having no offspring, he left his wife for his brother. 26 The same thing happened with the second and the third, through all seven. 27 Last of all, the woman died. 28 So in the resurrection, of the seven, whose wife will she be? For they all had her as a wife."

29 In reply Jesus said to them: "You are mistaken, because you know neither the Scriptures nor the power of God;[a] 30 for in the resurrection neither do men marry nor are women given in marriage, but they are as angels in heaven.[b] 31 Regarding the resurrection of the dead, have you not read what was spoken to you by God, who said: 32 'I am the God of Abraham and the God of Isaac and the God of Jacob'?[c] He is the God, not of the dead, but of the living."[d] 33 On hearing that, the crowds were astounded at his teaching.[e]

34 After the Pharisees heard that he had silenced the Sadducees, they came together in one group. 35 And one of them, versed in the Law, tested him by asking: 36 "Teacher, which is the greatest commandment in the Law?"[f] 37 He said to him: "'You must love Jehovah* your God with your whole heart and with your whole soul# and with your whole mind.'[g] 38 This is the greatest and first commandment. 39 The second, like it, is this: 'You must love your neighbor as yourself.'[h] 40 On these two commandments the whole Law hangs, and the Prophets."[i]

41 Now while the Pharisees were gathered together, Jesus asked them:[j] 42 "What do you think about the Christ? Whose son is he?" They said to him: "David's."[k] 43 He asked them: "How is it, then, that David under inspiration[l] calls him Lord,

CHAP. 22
a Mr 12:13-17
Lu 20:20-26
b Mr 3:6
c Da 3:17, 18
Mal 3:8
Mt 12:17
Lu 20:25
Lu 23:2
Ro 13:7
d Ac 4:1, 2
Ac 23:8
e Mr 12:18-23
Lu 20:27-33
f Ge 38:7, 8
De 25:5, 6
Ru 1:11
Ru 3:13

Second Col.
a Mr 12:24-27
b Lu 20:35, 36
c Ex 3:6
d Lu 20:37, 38
Ro 4:17
e Mt 7:28
Mr 11:18
f Mr 12:28
g De 6:5
De 10:12
Jos 22:5
Mr 12:30
Lu 10:27
h Le 19:18
Mr 12:31
Lu 10:27
Col 3:14
Jas 2:8
1Pe 1:22
i Ro 13:10
Ga 5:14
j Mr 12:35-37
Lu 20:41-44
k Joh 7:42
l 2Sa 23:2

22:17 *Or "right." 22:19 *See App. B14.

22:37 *See App. A5. #See Glossary.

saying, 44 'Jehovah* said to my Lord: "Sit at my right hand until I put your enemies beneath your feet"'?[a] 45 If, then, David calls him Lord, how is he his son?"[b] 46 And nobody was able to say a word in reply to him, and from that day on, no one dared to question him any further.

23 Then Jesus spoke to the crowds and to his disciples, saying: 2 "The scribes and the Pharisees have seated themselves in the seat of Moses. 3 Therefore, all the things they tell you, do and observe, but do not do according to their deeds, for they say but they do not practice what they say.[c] 4 They bind up heavy loads and put them on the shoulders of men,[d] but they themselves are not willing to budge them with their finger.[e] 5 All the works they do do, they do to be seen by men,[f] for they broaden the scripture-containing cases that they wear as safeguards*[g] and lengthen the fringes of their garments.[h] 6 They like the most prominent place at evening meals and the front* seats in the synagogues[i] 7 and the greetings in the marketplaces and to be called Rabbi* by men. 8 But you, do not you be called Rabbi, for one is your Teacher,[j] and all of you are brothers. 9 Moreover, do not call anyone your father on earth, for one is your Father,[k] the heavenly One. 10 Neither be called leaders, for your Leader is one, the Christ. 11 But the greatest one among you must be your minister.[l] 12 Whoever exalts himself will be humbled,[m] and whoever humbles himself will be exalted.[n]

13 "Woe to you, scribes and Pharisees, hypocrites! because

you shut up the Kingdom of the heavens before men; for you yourselves do not go in, neither do you permit those on their way in to go in.[a] 14 *—

15 "Woe to you, scribes and Pharisees, hypocrites![b] because you travel over sea and dry land to make one proselyte,* and when he becomes one, you make him a subject for Ge·hen′na# twice as much so as yourselves.

16 "Woe to you, blind guides,[c] who say, 'If anyone swears by the temple, it is nothing; but if anyone swears by the gold of the temple, he is under obligation.'[d] 17 Fools and blind ones! Which, in fact, is greater, the gold or the temple that has sanctified the gold? 18 Moreover, 'If anyone swears by the altar, it is nothing; but if anyone swears by the gift on it, he is under obligation.' 19 Blind ones! Which, in fact, is greater, the gift or the altar that sanctifies the gift? 20 Therefore, whoever swears by the altar is swearing by it and by all the things on it; 21 and whoever swears by the temple is swearing by it and by the One inhabiting it;[e] 22 and whoever swears by heaven is swearing by the throne of God and by the One sitting on it.

23 "Woe to you, scribes and Pharisees, hypocrites! because you give the tenth of the mint and the dill and the cumin,[f] but you have disregarded the weightier matters of the Law, namely, justice[g] and mercy[h] and faithfulness. These things it was necessary to do, yet not to disregard the other things.[i] 24 Blind guides,[j] who strain out the gnat[k] but gulp down the camel![l]

25 "Woe to you, scribes and Pharisees, hypocrites! because you cleanse the outside of the cup and of the dish,[m] but inside

---

CHAP. 22
a Ps 110:1
  Ac 2:34, 35
  1Co 15:25
  Heb 1:13
  Heb 10:12, 13
b Mr 12:37

CHAP. 23
c Mal 2:7, 8
d Mt 11:28
e Lu 11:46
f Mt 6:1, 2
g De 6:6, 8
h Nu 15:38, 39
i Mr 12:38, 39
  Lu 11:43
  Lu 14:7, 10
  Lu 20:46
j Joh 13:13
k Mt 6:9
l Mt 20:26
  Mr 9:35
  Lu 22:26
m Pr 16:18
n Pr 29:23
  Mt 18:4
  Lu 14:11
  Ro 12:3
  1Pe 5:5

Second Col.
a Lu 11:52
b Mt 6:2
  Lu 12:56
c Mt 15:14
d Mt 5:34, 35
e 1Ki 8:13
f Le 27:30
g Mic 6:8
  Joh 7:24
h Mt 9:13
  Mt 12:7
i Lu 11:42
j Mt 15:14
k Le 11:23
l Le 11:4
m Mr 7:3, 4

22:44 *See App. A5. 23:5 *Or "broaden their phylacteries." 23:6 *Or "best." 23:7 *Or "Teacher."

23:14 *See App. A3. 23:15 *Or "convert." #See Glossary.

they are full of greediness*[a] and self-indulgence.[b] **26** Blind Pharisee, cleanse first the inside of the cup and of the dish, so that the outside of it may also become clean.

27 "Woe to you, scribes and Pharisees, hypocrites![c] because you resemble whitewashed graves,[d] which outwardly indeed appear beautiful but inside are full of dead men's bones and of every sort of uncleanness. **28** In the same way, on the outside you appear righteous to men, but inside you are full of hypocrisy and lawlessness.[e]

29 "Woe to you, scribes and Pharisees, hypocrites![f] because you build the graves of the prophets and decorate the tombs* of the righteous ones,[g] **30** and you say, 'If we had lived in the days of our forefathers, we would not have shared with them in shedding the blood of the prophets.' **31** Therefore, you are testifying against yourselves that you are sons of those who murdered the prophets.[h] **32** Well, then, fill up the measure of your forefathers.

33 "Serpents, offspring of vipers,[i] how will you flee from the judgment of Ge·hen′na?*[j] **34** For this reason, I am sending to you prophets[k] and wise men and public instructors.[l] Some of them you will kill[m] and execute on stakes, and some of them you will scourge[n] in your synagogues and persecute[o] from city to city, **35** so that there may come upon you all the righteous blood spilled on earth, from the blood of righteous Abel[p] to the blood of Zech·a·ri′ah son of Bar·a·chi′ah, whom you murdered between the sanctuary and the altar.[q] **36** Truly I say to you, all these things will come upon this generation.

37 "Jerusalem, Jerusalem, the killer of the prophets and stoner of those sent to her[a]—how often I wanted to gather your children together the way a hen gathers her chicks under her wings! But you did not want it.[b] **38** Look! Your house is abandoned to you.*[c] **39** For I say to you, you will by no means see me from now until you say, 'Blessed is the one who comes in Jehovah's* name!'"[d]

24 Now as Jesus was departing from the temple, his disciples approached to show him the buildings of the temple. **2** In response he said to them: "Do you not see all these things? Truly I say to you, by no means will a stone be left here upon a stone and not be thrown down."[e]

3 While he was sitting on the Mount of Olives, the disciples approached him privately, saying: "Tell us, when will these things be, and what will be the sign of your presence*[f] and of the conclusion of the system of things?"*[g]

4 In answer Jesus said to them: "Look out that nobody misleads you,[h] **5** for many will come on the basis of my name, saying, 'I am the Christ,' and will mislead many.[i] **6** You are going to hear of wars and reports of wars. See that you are not alarmed, for these things must take place, but the end is not yet.[j]

7 "For nation will rise against nation and kingdom against kingdom,[k] and there will be food shortages[l] and earthquakes in one place after another.[m] **8** All these things are a beginning of pangs of distress.

9 "Then people will hand you over to tribulation[n] and will kill

---

CHAP. 23
a Mr 12:38, 40
b Lu 11:39
c Lu 12:56
d Lu 11:44
   Ac 23:3
e Lu 16:15
f Mt 6:2
g Lu 11:47
h Lu 11:48
   Ac 7:52
   Heb 11:32, 37
i Mt 3:7
   Mt 12:34
   Lu 3:7
j Mt 10:28
   Lu 12:5
k Lu 11:49-51
l Mt 13:52
m Joh 16:2
   Ac 7:59
n Ac 5:40
   2Co 11:24
o Lu 21:12
p Ge 4:8, 10
   Heb 11:4
q 2Ch 24:20-22

Second Col.
a Joh 8:59
   Heb 11:32, 37
b Lu 13:34
   Lu 19:41, 42
c 1Ki 9:7, 8
   Jer 12:7
   Jer 22:5
   Mt 21:43
   Lu 21:20
d Ps 118:26

CHAP. 24
e Mt 13:1, 2
   Lu 19:44
   Lu 21:5, 6
f Mt 24:27
   Mt 24:37-39
g Mt 13:39
   Mt 28:20
   Mt 13:3, 4
   Lu 21:7
h Mt 13:5, 6
   Lu 21:8
i Mt 24:24
j Mr 13:7
   Lu 21:9
k Re 6:4
l Ac 11:28
   Re 6:6
m Mr 13:8
   Lu 21:10, 11
n Joh 15:20
   Ac 11:19
   Re 2:10

23:25 *Or "plunder." 23:29 *Or "memorial tombs." 23:33; 24:3 *See Glossary.

23:38 *Or possibly, "is left to you desolate." 23:39 *See App. A5. 24:3 *Or "the age." See Glossary.

you,[a] and you will be hated by all the nations on account of my name.[b] **10** Then, too, many will be stumbled and will betray one another and will hate one another. **11** Many false prophets will arise and mislead many;[c] **12** and because of the increasing of lawlessness, the love of the greater number will grow cold. **13** But the one who has endured* to the end will be saved.[d] **14** And this good news of the Kingdom will be preached in all the inhabited earth for a witness to all the nations,[e] and then, too, the end will come.

15 "Therefore, when you catch sight of the disgusting thing that causes desolation, as spoken about by Daniel the prophet, standing in a holy place[f] (let the reader use discernment), **16** then let those in Ju·de′a begin fleeing to the mountains.[g] **17** Let the man on the housetop not come down to take the goods out of his house, **18** and let the man in the field not return to pick up his outer garment. **19** Woe to the pregnant women and those nursing a baby in those days! **20** Keep praying that your flight may not occur in wintertime nor on the Sabbath day; **21** for then there will be great tribulation[h] such as has not occurred since the world's beginning until now, no, nor will occur again.[i] **22** In fact, unless those days were cut short, no flesh would be saved; but on account of the chosen ones those days will be cut short.[j]

23 "Then if anyone says to you, 'Look! Here is the Christ,'[k] or, 'There!' do not believe it.[l] **24** For false Christs and false prophets[m] will arise and will perform great signs and wonders so as to mislead,[n] if possible, even the chosen ones.

25 Look! I have forewarned you. **26** Therefore, if people say to you, 'Look! He is in the wilderness,' do not go out; 'Look! He is in the inner rooms,' do not believe it.[a] **27** For just as the lightning comes out of the east and shines over to the west, so the presence* of the Son of man will be.[b] **28** Wherever the carcass is, there the eagles will be gathered together.[c]

29 "Immediately after the tribulation of those days, the sun will be darkened,[d] and the moon will not give its light, and the stars will fall from heaven, and the powers of the heavens will be shaken.[e] **30** Then the sign of the Son of man will appear in heaven, and all the tribes of the earth will beat themselves in grief,[f] and they will see the Son of man[g] coming on the clouds of heaven with power and great glory.[h] **31** And he will send out his angels with a great trumpet sound, and they will gather his chosen ones together from the four winds, from one extremity of the heavens to their other extremity.[i]

32 "Now learn this illustration from the fig tree: Just as soon as its young branch grows tender and sprouts its leaves, you know that summer is near.[j] **33** Likewise also you, when you see all these things, know that he is near at the doors.[k] **34** Truly I say to you that this generation will by no means pass away until all these things happen. **35** Heaven and earth will pass away, but my words will by no means pass away.[l]

36 "Concerning that day and hour nobody knows,[m] neither the angels of the heavens nor the Son, but only the Father.[n] **37** For just as the days of Noah were,[o] so the presence* of the Son of man will be.[p] **38** For as

---

CHAP. 24

a Joh 16:2
Ac 7:59
Ac 12:1, 2
Re 6:11

b Mt 10:17, 22
Mr 13:9, 13
Lu 21:12, 13
Lu 21:17
Joh 15:21
2Ti 3:12

c Mt 7:15
1Ti 4:1
2Pe 2:1

d Mt 10:22
Mr 13:13
Lu 21:19
Heb 10:36

e Mt 9:35
Mt 28:19, 20
Mr 13:10
Re 14:6

f Da 9:27
Da 11:31
Da 12:11
Mr 13:14-18
Lu 21:20

g Lu 21:21-23
Lu 21:23
Re 7:14

h Lu 21:23
Re 7:14

i Da 12:1
Mr 13:19

j Mr 13:20

k Mt 24:5

l Mr 13:21-23

m Mt 7:15
2Pe 2:1

n Mt 7:22, 23
2Th 2:9

Second Col.

a Lu 17:23

b Lu 17:24

c Lu 17:37

d Joe 2:31

e Mr 13:24, 25
Lu 21:25, 26

f Re 1:7

g Da 7:13

h Mt 26:64
Mr 13:26
Lu 21:27

i Mr 13:27

j Mr 13:28-31
Lu 21:29-33

k Jas 5:8, 9

l Lu 21:33

m 1Th 5:1, 2

n Mr 13:32

o Ge 6:11-13

p Lu 17:26, 27
Ac 1:7

24:13 *Or "who endures."

24:27, 37 *See Glossary.

they were in those days before the Flood, eating and drinking, men marrying and women being given in marriage, until the day that Noah entered into the ark,[a] **39** and they took no note until the Flood came and swept them all away,[b] so the presence of the Son of man will be. **40** Then two men will be in the field; one will be taken along and the other abandoned. **41** Two women will be grinding at the hand mill; one will be taken along and the other abandoned.[c] **42** Keep on the watch, therefore, because you do not know on what day your Lord is coming.[d]

43 "But know one thing: If the householder had known in what watch* the thief was coming,[e] he would have kept awake and not allowed his house to be broken into.[f] **44** On this account, you too prove yourselves ready,[g] because the Son of man is coming at an hour that you do not think to be it.

45 "Who really is the faithful and discreet* slave whom his master appointed over his domestics, to give them their food at the proper time?[h] **46** Happy is that slave if his master on coming finds him doing so![i] **47** Truly I say to you, he will appoint him over all his belongings.

48 "But if ever that evil slave says in his heart, 'My master is delaying,'[j] **49** and he starts to beat his fellow slaves and to eat and drink with the confirmed drunkards, **50** the master of that slave will come on a day that he does not expect and in an hour that he does not know,[k] **51** and he will punish him with the greatest severity and will assign him his place with the hypocrites. There is where his weep-

ing and the gnashing of his teeth will be.[a]

25 "Then the Kingdom of the heavens may be likened to ten virgins who took their lamps[b] and went out to meet the bridegroom.[c] **2** Five of them were foolish, and five were discreet.*[d] **3** For the foolish took their lamps but took no oil with them, **4** whereas the discreet took oil in their flasks along with their lamps. **5** While the bridegroom was delaying, they all became drowsy and fell asleep. **6** Right in the middle of the night there was a shout: 'Here is the bridegroom! Go out to meet him.' **7** Then all those virgins got up and put their lamps in order.[e] **8** The foolish said to the discreet, 'Give us some of your oil, because our lamps are about to go out.' **9** The discreet answered, saying: 'Perhaps there may not be enough for both us and you. Go instead to those who sell it, and buy some for yourselves.' **10** While they were going off to buy it, the bridegroom came. The virgins who were ready went in with him to the marriage feast,[f] and the door was shut. **11** Afterward, the rest of the virgins also came, saying, 'Sir, Sir, open to us!'[g] **12** In answer he said, 'I tell you the truth, I do not know you.'

13 "Keep on the watch,[h] therefore, because you know neither the day nor the hour.[i]

14 "For it is just like a man about to travel abroad who summoned his slaves and entrusted his belongings to them.[j] **15** He gave five talents* to one, two to another, and one to still another, to each according to his own ability, and he went abroad. **16** Immediately the one who re-

---

Middle column references:

CHAP. 24
a Ge 7:7
　Heb 11:7
　1Pe 3:19, 20
　2Pe 2:5

b Ge 7:23
　2Pe 3:6

c Lu 17:35

d Mt 25:13
　Mr 13:33
　Lu 21:36

e 1Th 5:2
　2Pe 3:10

f Lu 12:39, 40

g Mr 13:35

h Lu 12:42-44

i Re 16:15

j Lu 12:45, 46

k Mt 25:13

Second Col.
a Mt 13:42

CHAP. 25
b Lu 12:35
　Php 2:15

c Joh 3:28, 29
　Re 19:7

d Mt 7:24, 26

e Lu 12:35

f Re 19:9

g Lu 13:25, 27

h 1Th 5:6
　1Pe 5:8

i Mt 24:42, 50
　Mr 13:33

j Lu 19:12, 13

24:43 *Or "at what time of night."
24:45; 25:2 *Or "wise."

25:15 *A Greek talent equaled 20.4 kg (654 oz t). See App. B14.

ceived the five talents went and did business with them and gained five more. 17 Likewise, the one who received the two gained two more. 18 But the slave who received just one went off and dug in the ground and hid his master's money.*

19 "After a long time, the master of those slaves came and settled accounts with them.[a] 20 So the one who had received the five talents came forward and brought five additional talents, saying, 'Master, you entrusted five talents to me; see, I gained five talents more.'[b] 21 His master said to him: 'Well done, good and faithful slave! You were faithful over a few things. I will appoint you over many things.[c] Enter into the joy of your master.'[d] 22 Next the one who had received the two talents came forward and said, 'Master, you entrusted two talents to me; see, I gained two talents more.'[e] 23 His master said to him: 'Well done, good and faithful slave! You were faithful over a few things. I will appoint you over many things. Enter into the joy of your master.'

24 "Finally the slave who had received the one talent came forward and said: 'Master, I knew you to be a demanding man, reaping where you did not sow and gathering where you did not winnow.[f] 25 So I grew afraid and went and hid your talent in the ground. Here, you have what is yours.' 26 In reply his master said to him: 'Wicked and sluggish slave, you knew, did you, that I reaped where I did not sow and gathered where I did not winnow? 27 Well, then, you should have deposited my money* with the bankers, and on my coming I would have received it back with interest.

28 "'Therefore, take the talent away from him and give it to the one who has the ten talents.[a] 29 For to everyone who has, more will be given, and he will have an abundance. But the one who does not have, even what he has will be taken away from him.[b] 30 And throw the good-for-nothing slave out into the darkness outside. There is where his weeping and the gnashing of his teeth will be.'

31 "When the Son of man[c] comes in his glory, and all the angels with him,[d] then he will sit down on his glorious throne. 32 All the nations will be gathered before him, and he will separate people one from another, just as a shepherd separates the sheep from the goats. 33 And he will put the sheep[e] on his right hand, but the goats on his left.[f]

34 "Then the King will say to those on his right: 'Come, you who have been blessed by my Father, inherit the Kingdom prepared for you from the founding of the world. 35 For I became hungry and you gave me something to eat; I was thirsty and you gave me something to drink. I was a stranger and you received me hospitably;[g] 36 naked* and you clothed me.[h] I fell sick and you looked after me. I was in prison and you visited me.'[i] 37 Then the righteous ones will answer him with the words: 'Lord, when did we see you hungry and feed you, or thirsty and give you something to drink?[j] 38 When did we see you a stranger and receive you hospitably, or naked and clothe you? 39 When did we see you sick or in prison and visit you?' 40 In reply the King will say to them, 'Truly I say to you, to the extent that you did it to one of

---

CHAP. 25
a Lu 19:15

b Lu 19:16, 17

c Lu 16:10

d Heb 12:2

e Lu 19:18, 19

f Lu 19:20-23

Second Col.
a Lu 19:24-26

b Mt 13:12
Mr 4:25
Lu 8:18
Joh 15:2

c Da 7:13

d Mt 16:27

e Joh 10:14

f Mt 25:41

g Heb 13:2
3Jo 5

h Jas 2:15, 16

i 2Ti 1:16

j Mt 10:42

25:18, 27 *Lit., "silver."

25:36 *Or "not sufficiently dressed."

the least of these my brothers, you did it to me.'[a]

41 "Then he will say to those on his left: 'Go away from me,[b] you who have been cursed, into the everlasting fire[c] prepared for the Devil and his angels.[d] 42 For I became hungry, but you gave me nothing to eat; and I was thirsty, but you gave me nothing to drink. 43 I was a stranger, but you did not receive me hospitably; naked, but you did not clothe me; sick and in prison, but you did not look after me.' 44 Then they too will answer with the words: 'Lord, when did we see you hungry or thirsty or a stranger or naked or sick or in prison and did not minister to you?' 45 Then he will answer them, saying: 'Truly I say to you, to the extent that you did not do it to one of these least ones, you did not do it to me.'[e] 46 These will depart into everlasting cutting-off,*[f] but the righteous ones into everlasting life."[g]

26 Now when Jesus had finished saying all these things, he said to his disciples: 2 "You know that two days from now the Passover takes place,[h] and the Son of man will be handed over to be executed on the stake."[i]

3 Then the chief priests and the elders of the people gathered in the courtyard of the high priest, who was named Ca'ia·phas,[j] 4 and they conspired together[k] to seize* Jesus by cunning# and to kill him. 5 However, they were saying: "Not at the festival, so that there may not be an uproar among the people."

6 While Jesus was in Beth'a·ny in the house of Simon the leper,[l] 7 a woman with an ala-

baster jar of costly perfumed oil approached him, and she began pouring it on his head as he was dining.* 8 On seeing this, the disciples became indignant and said: "Why this waste? 9 For this could have been sold for a great deal of money and given to the poor." 10 Aware of this, Jesus said to them: "Why do you try to make trouble for the woman? She did a fine deed toward me. 11 For you always have the poor with you,[a] but you will not always have me.[b] 12 When she put this perfumed oil on my body, she did it to prepare me for burial.[c] 13 Truly I say to you, wherever this good news is preached in all the world, what this woman did will also be told in memory of her."[d]

14 Then one of the Twelve, the one called Judas Is·car'i·ot,[e] 15 and said to the chief priests[f] 15 and said: "What will you give me to betray him to you?"[g] They stipulated to him 30 silver pieces.[h] 16 So from then on, he kept looking for a good opportunity to betray him.

17 On the first day of the Unleavened Bread,[i] the disciples came to Jesus, saying: "Where do you want us to prepare for you to eat the Passover?"[j] 18 He said: "Go into the city to So-and-so and say to him, 'The Teacher says: "My appointed time is near; I will celebrate the Passover with my disciples at your home."'" 19 So the disciples did as Jesus instructed them and prepared for the Passover.

20 When evening came,[k] he was reclining at the table with the 12 disciples.[l] 21 While they were eating, he said: "Truly I say to you, one of you will betray me."[m] 22 Being very much grieved at this, each and every one began to say to him: "Lord, it is not I,

---

CHAP. 25
a Pr 19:17
  Mt 10:40
  Mr 9:41
  Heb 6:10
b Mt 7:23
c Mt 18:8, 9
d Re 12:9
  Re 20:10
e Zec 2:8
  Ac 9:4, 5
f 2Pe 2:9
g Ro 2:6, 7

CHAP. 26
h Ex 12:14
  Mr 14:1, 2
  Lu 22:1, 2
  Joh 13:1
i Mt 16:21
  Mt 20:18, 19
  Mt 27:26
  Mr 15:15
  Joh 19:16
j Mt 26:57
  Lu 3:2
  Joh 11:49
  Joh 18:13, 24
k Ps 2:2
l Mr 14:3-9
  Joh 12:1-8

Second Col.
a De 15:11
b Mr 14:7
c Mr 14:8
  Joh 12:7
d Mr 14:9
e Mt 10:2, 4
  Joh 13:2
f Mr 14:10, 11
  Lu 22:3-6
g Joh 11:57
h Ex 21:32
  Zec 11:12
  Mt 27:3
i Ex 12:18
  Ex 23:15
  Lu 22:1
j Mr 14:12-16
  Lu 22:7-13
k De 16:6
l Mr 14:17-21
  Lu 22:14
m Lu 22:21-23
  Joh 6:70
  Joh 13:21, 22

25:46 *That is, from life. Lit., "lopping off; pruning." 26:4 *Or "arrest." #Or "crafty device." 26:7 *Or "reclining at the table."

is it?" **23** In reply he said: "The one who dips his hand with me into the bowl is the one who will betray me.[a] **24** True, the Son of man is going away, just as it is written about him, but woe[b] to that man through whom the Son of man is betrayed! It would have been better for that man if he had not been born."[d] **25** Judas, who was about to betray him, replied: "It is not I, is it, Rabbi?" Jesus said to him: "You yourself said it."

26 As they continued eating, Jesus took a loaf, and after saying a blessing, he broke it,[e] and giving it to the disciples, he said: "Take, eat. This means my body."[f] **27** And taking a cup, he offered thanks and gave it to them, saying: "Drink out of it, all of you,[g] **28** for this means my 'blood'[h] of the covenant,'[i] which is to be poured out in behalf of many[j] for forgiveness of sins.[k] **29** But I say to you: I will by no means drink again any of this product of the vine until that day when I drink it new with you in the Kingdom of my Father."[l] **30** Finally, after singing praises,* they went out to the Mount of Olives.[m]

31 Then Jesus said to them: "All of you will be stumbled in connection with me on this night, for it is written: 'I will strike the shepherd, and the sheep of the flock will be scattered about.'[n] **32** But after I have been raised up, I will go ahead of you into Gal'i·lee."[o] **33** But Peter, in response, said to him: "Although all the others are stumbled in connection with you, I will never be stumbled!"[p] **34** Jesus said to him: "Truly I say to you, on this night, before a rooster crows, you will disown me three times."[q] **35** Peter said to him: "Even if I should have to die with you, I will by no means disown you."[r]

CHAP. 26
a Ps 41:9
  Mr 14:20
  Lu 22:21
  Joh 13:26
b De 27:25
c Lu 22:22
  Joh 17:12
d Mr 14:21
e 1Co 10:16
f Mr 14:22
  Lu 22:19
  1Co 11:23-26
g Mr 14:23
  Lu 22:20
h 1Co 10:16
i Ex 24:8
  Jer 31:31
  Heb 7:22
j Mt 20:28
  Mr 14:24
k Eph 1:7
  Heb 9:20, 22
l Mr 14:25
  Lu 22:18
m Lu 22:39
  Joh 18:1
n Zec 13:7
  Mr 14:27, 28
  Joh 16:32
o Mt 28:7
  Mt 28:16
p Mr 14:29-31
  Mr 14:30
  Lu 22:34
  Joh 13:38
r Lu 22:33

Second Col.
a Joh 18:1
b Mr 14:32-36
  Lu 22:40
c Isa 53:3
d Mr 14:34
e Heb 5:7
f Mt 20:22
  Joh 18:11
g Mr 14:36
  Lu 22:42
  Joh 5:30
  Joh 6:38
  Heb 10:9
h Mr 14:37-42
  Lu 22:45
i Mr 13:33
  1Pe 5:8
  Re 16:15
j Lu 18:1
  Ro 12:12
  Eph 6:18
  1Pe 4:7
k Mt 6:13
  Lu 22:46
l Mr 14:38
  Ro 7:23
m Mt 6:10
  Joh 12:27

All the other disciples also said the same thing.

36 Then Jesus came with them to the spot called Geth·sem'a·ne,[a] and he said to the disciples: "Sit down here while I go over there and pray."[b] **37** And taking along Peter and the two sons of Zeb'e·dee, he began to feel grieved and to be greatly troubled.[c] **38** Then he said to them: "I am* deeply grieved, even to death. Stay here and keep on the watch with me."[d] **39** And going a little way forward, he fell facedown, praying:[e] "My Father, if it is possible, let this cup[f] pass away from me. Yet, not as I will, but as you will."[g]

40 He returned to the disciples and found them sleeping, and he said to Peter: "Could you not so much as keep on the watch for one hour with me?[h] **41** Keep on the watch[i] and pray continually,[j] so that you may not enter into temptation.[k] The spirit, of course, is eager,* but the flesh is weak."[l] **42** Again, a second time, he went off and prayed: "My Father, if it is not possible for this to pass away unless I drink it, let your will take place."[m] **43** And he came again and found them sleeping, for their eyes were heavy. **44** So leaving them, he again went off and prayed for a third time, saying once more the same thing. **45** Then he returned to the disciples and said to them: "At such a time as this, you are sleeping and resting! Look! The hour has drawn near for the Son of man to be betrayed into the hands of sinners. **46** Get up, let us go. Look! My betrayer has drawn near." **47** While he was still speaking, look! Judas, one of the Twelve, came and with him a large crowd

---

26:30 *Or "hymns; psalms."

26:38 *Or "My soul is." **26:41** *Or "willing."

with swords and clubs, sent from the chief priests and the elders of the people.[a]

48 Now his betrayer had given them a sign, saying: "Whoever it is I kiss, he is the one; take him into custody." **49** And going straight up to Jesus, he said: "Greetings, Rabbi!" and gave him a tender kiss. **50** But Jesus said to him: "Fellow, for what purpose are you present?"[b] Then they came forward and seized Jesus and took him into custody. **51** But look! one of those with Jesus reached out his hand and drew his sword and struck the slave of the high priest, taking off his ear.[c] **52** Then Jesus said to him: "Return your sword to its place,[d] for all those who take up the sword will perish by the sword.[e] **53** Or do you think that I cannot appeal to my Father to supply me at this moment more than 12 legions of angels?[f] **54** In that case, how would the Scriptures be fulfilled that say it must take place this way?" **55** In that hour Jesus said to the crowds: "Did you come out to arrest me with swords and clubs as against a robber? Day after day I used to sit in the temple teaching,[g] and yet you did not take me into custody.[h] **56** But all of this has taken place for the writings* of the prophets to be fulfilled."[i] Then all the disciples abandoned him and fled.[j]

57 Those who took Jesus into custody led him away to Caʹiaphas[k] the high priest, where the scribes and the elders were gathered together.[l] **58** But Peter kept following him from a good distance, as far as the courtyard of the high priest, and after going inside, he sat with the house attendants to see the outcome.[m]

59 Now the chief priests and the entire Sanʹheʹdrin were looking for false testimony against Jesus in order to put him to death.[a] **60** But they found none, although many false witnesses came forward.[b] Later two came forward **61** and said: "This man said, 'I am able to throw down the temple of God and build it up in three days.'"[c] **62** With that the high priest stood up and said to him: "Do you say nothing in reply? What is it these men are testifying against you?"[d] **63** But Jesus kept silent.[e] So the high priest said to him: "I put you under oath by the living God to tell us whether you are the Christ, the Son of God!"[f] **64** Jesus said to him: "You yourself said it. But I say to you: From now on you will see the Son of man[g] sitting at the right hand of power[h] and coming on the clouds of heaven."[i] **65** Then the high priest ripped his outer garments, saying: "He has blasphemed! What further need do we have of witnesses? See! Now you have heard the blasphemy. **66** What is your opinion?" They answered: "He deserves to die."[j] **67** Then they spat in his face[k] and hit him with their fists.[l] Others slapped him on the face,[m] **68** saying: "Prophesy to us, you Christ. Who struck you?"

69 Now Peter was sitting outside in the courtyard, and a servant girl came up to him and said: "You too were with Jesus the Galʹiʹleʹan!"[n] **70** But he denied it before them all, saying: "I do not know what you are talking about." **71** When he went out to the gatehouse, another girl noticed him and said to those there: "This man was with Jesus the Nazʹaʹreneʹ."[o] **72** Again he denied it, with an oath: "I do not know the man!" **73** After a little while, those

---

CHAP. 26
a Mr 14:43-47
　Lu 22:47-51
　Joh 18:3
b Ps 41:9
c Mr 14:47
　Lu 22:50
　Joh 18:10
d Joh 18:11
e Ge 9:6
f 2Ki 6:17
　Da 7:10
　Mt 4:11
g Lu 19:47
　Joh 18:20
h Mr 14:48, 49
　Lu 22:52, 53
i Ps 22:16-18
　Isa 53
　Da 9:26
j Zec 13:7
　Mr 14:50
　Joh 16:32
k Joh 18:13
l Mr 14:53, 54
　Lu 22:54, 55
m Joh 18:16

Second Col.
a Mr 14:55-59
b Ps 27:12
　Ps 35:11
c Mt 27:39, 40
　Joh 2:19
　Ac 6:14
d Mr 14:60-65
e Isa 53:7
　Ac 8:32
f Lu 22:67-71
g Da 7:13
　Joh 1:51
h Ps 110:1
　Lu 22:69
i Mr 14:62
　Re 1:7
j Le 24:16
　Joh 19:7
k Isa 50:6
l Lu 22:63, 64
m Isa 53:3
n Mr 14:66-72
　Lu 22:54-62
　Joh 18:15-17
o Joh 18:25-27

26:56 *Or "scriptures."

standing around came up and said to Peter: "Certainly you are also one of them, for in fact, your dialect* gives you away." 74 Then he started to curse and swear: "I do not know the man!" And immediately a rooster crowed. 75 And Peter called to mind what Jesus had said, namely: "Before a rooster crows, you will disown me three times."[a] And he went outside and wept bitterly.

27 When morning came, all the chief priests and the elders of the people consulted together against Jesus to put him to death.[b] 2 After binding him, they led him off and handed him over to Pilate, the governor.[c]

3 Then Judas, his betrayer, seeing that Jesus had been condemned, felt remorse and brought the 30 pieces of silver back to the chief priests and elders,[d] 4 saying: "I sinned when I betrayed innocent blood." They said: "What is that to us? You must see to it!"* 5 So he threw the silver pieces into the temple and departed. Then he went off and hanged himself.[e] 6 But the chief priests took the silver pieces and said: "It is not lawful to put them into the sacred treasury, because they are the price of blood." 7 After consulting together, they used the money to buy the potter's field as a burial place for strangers. 8 Therefore, that field has been called Field of Blood[f] to this very day. 9 Then what was spoken through Jeremiah the prophet was fulfilled: "And they took the 30 silver pieces, the price that was set on the man, the one on whom a price was set by some of the sons of Israel, 10 and they gave them for the potter's field,

according to what Jehovah* had commanded me."[a]

11 Jesus now stood before the governor, and the governor put the question to him: "Are you the King of the Jews?" Jesus replied: "You yourself say it."[b] 12 But while he was being accused by the chief priests and elders, he made no answer.[c] 13 Then Pilate said to him: "Do you not hear how many things they are testifying against you?" 14 But he did not answer him, no, not a word, so that the governor was very surprised.

15 Now from festival to festival, it was the custom of the governor to release a prisoner to the crowd, whomever they wanted.[d] 16 Just at that time they were holding a notorious prisoner called Bar·ab'bas. 17 So when they were gathered together, Pilate said to them: "Which one do you want me to release to you, Bar·ab'bas or Jesus the so-called Christ?" 18 For Pilate was aware that out of envy they had handed him over. 19 Moreover, while he was sitting on the judgment seat, his wife sent a message to him, saying: "Have nothing to do with that righteous man, for I suffered a lot today in a dream because of him." 20 But the chief priests and the elders persuaded the crowds to ask for Bar·ab'bas,[e] but to have Jesus put to death.[f] 21 In response the governor said to them: "Which of the two do you want me to release to you?" They said: "Bar·ab'bas." 22 Pilate said to them: "What, then, should I do with Jesus the so-called Christ?" They all said: "To the stake with him!"*[g] 23 He said: "Why? What bad thing did he do?" Still they kept shouting out all the more: "To the stake with him!"[h]

CHAP. 26
a Mt 26:34
  Mr 14:30
  Joh 13:38

CHAP. 27
b Mr 15:1
  Lu 22:66

a Ps 2:2
  Mt 20:18, 19
  Lu 23:1
  Joh 18:28
  Ac 3:13

d Mt 26:14, 15
  Mr 14:10, 11

e Ac 1:16, 18

f Ac 1:19

Second Col.
a Zec 11:12, 13

b Mr 15:2-5
  Lu 23:3
  Joh 18:33, 37

c Isa 53:7
  Mt 26:63
  Joh 19:9

d Mr 15:6-10
  Joh 18:39

e Lu 23:18
  Joh 18:40
  Ac 3:14

f Mr 15:11-14

g Lu 23:21

h Lu 23:23
  Ac 3:13

26:73 *Or "accent." 27:4 *Or "That is your problem!"

27:10 *See App. A5. 27:22 *Or "Execute him on the stake!"

24 Seeing that it did no good but, rather, an uproar was arising, Pilate took water and washed his hands before the crowd, saying: "I am innocent of the blood of this man. You yourselves must see to it." **25** At that all the people said in answer: "Let his blood come upon us and upon our children."[a] **26** Then he released Bar·ab'bas to them, but he had Jesus whipped[b] and handed him over to be executed on the stake.[c]

27 Then the soldiers of the governor took Jesus into the governor's residence and gathered the whole body of troops together around him.[d] **28** And disrobing him, they draped him with a scarlet cloak,[e] **29** and they braided a crown out of thorns and put it on his head and put a reed in his right hand. And kneeling before him, they mocked him, saying: "Greetings,* you King of the Jews!" **30** And they spat on him[f] and took the reed and began hitting him on the head. **31** Finally, after they had mocked him, they stripped him of the cloak and put his outer garments on him and led him off to be nailed to the stake.[g]

32 As they were going out, they found a man of Cy·re'ne named Simon. This man they compelled into service to carry his torture stake.*[h] **33** And when they came to a place called Gol'go·tha, that is, Skull Place,[i] **34** they gave him wine mixed with gall* to drink;[j] but after tasting it, he refused to drink it. **35** When they had nailed him to the stake, they distributed his outer garments by casting lots,[k] **36** and they sat there keeping watch over him. **37** They also posted above his head the charge against him, in writing:

"This is Jesus the King of the Jews."[a]

38 Then two robbers were put on stakes alongside him, one on his right and one on his left.[b] **39** And those passing by spoke abusively of him,[c] shaking their heads[d] **40** and saying: "You who would throw down the temple and build it in three days,[e] save yourself! If you are a son of God, come down off the torture stake!"*[f] **41** In the same way also, the chief priests with the scribes and the elders began mocking him, saying:[g] **42** "Others he saved; himself he cannot save! He is King of Israel;[h] let him now come down off the torture stake,* and we will believe in him. **43** He has put his trust in God; let Him now rescue him if He wants him,[i] for he said, 'I am God's Son.'"[j] **44** In the same way, even the robbers who were on stakes alongside him were reproaching him.[k]

45 From the sixth hour* on, a darkness fell over all the land until the ninth hour.*[l] **46** About the ninth hour, Jesus called out with a loud voice, saying: "E'li, E'li, la'ma sa·bach·tha'ni?" that is, "My God, my God, why have you forsaken me?"[m] **47** At hearing this, some of those standing there began to say: "This man is calling E·li'jah."[n] **48** And immediately one of them ran and took a sponge and soaked it in sour wine and put it on a reed and gave it to him to drink.[o] **49** But the rest of them said: "Let him be! Let us see whether E·li'jah comes to save him." **50** Again Jesus called out with a loud voice and yielded up his spirit.*[p]

51 And look! the curtain of the sanctuary[q] was torn in two,[r] from top to bottom,[s] and the earth quaked, and the rocks

CHAP. 27

a Ac 5:27, 20
1Th 2:14, 15
b Lu 18:33
Joh 19:1
c Mr 15:15
Lu 23:25
d Mr 15:16-20
e Joh 19:2, 3
f Isa 50:6
Mt 26:67
g Isa 53:7
Mt 20:18, 19
h Mr 15:21
Lu 23:26
i Mr 15:22-24
Lu 23:33
Joh 19:17
j Ps 69:21
k Ps 22:18
Mr 15:24
Lu 23:34
Joh 19:23, 24

Second Col.

a Mr 15:26
Lu 23:38
Joh 19:19
b Isa 53:12
Mr 15:27
Lu 23:33
Joh 19:18
c Lu 18:32
Heb 12:3
d Ps 22:7
Ps 109:25
e Mt 26:60, 61
Joh 2:19
f Mr 15:29-32
g Lu 23:35
h Joh 1:49
Joh 12:13
i Ps 22:8
j Mr 14:62
Joh 5:18
Joh 10:36
k Lu 23:39
l Mr 15:33
Lu 23:44
m Ps 22:1
Isa 53:10
Mr 15:34
n Mr 15:35, 36
o Ps 69:21
Lu 23:36
Joh 19:29
p Mr 15:37
Lu 23:46
Joh 19:30
q Ex 26:31-33
Heb 9:3
r Heb 10:19, 20
s Mr 15:38
Lu 23:45

27:29 *Or "Hail." 27:32, 40, 42 *See Glossary. 27:34 *A bitter liquid.

27:45 *That is, about 12:00 noon. *That is, about 3:00 p.m. 27:50 *Or "and expired."

were split. **52** And the tombs* were opened, and many bodies of the holy ones who had fallen asleep were raised up **53** (and people coming out from among the tombs after his being raised up entered into the holy city), and they became visible to many people. **54** But when the army officer and those with him keeping watch over Jesus saw the earthquake and the things happening, they grew very much afraid and said: "Certainly this was God's Son."[a]

55 And many women were there watching from a distance, who had accompanied Jesus from Gal'i·lee to minister to him;[b] **56** among them were Mary Mag'da·lene and Mary the mother of James and Jo'ses and the mother of the sons of Zeb'e·dee.[c]

57 Now as it was late in the afternoon, a rich man of Ar·i·ma·the'a came, named Joseph, who had also become a disciple of Jesus.[d] **58** This man approached Pilate and asked for the body of Jesus.[e] Then Pilate commanded that it be given to him.[f] **59** Joseph took the body, wrapped it up in clean, fine linen,[g] **60** and laid it in his new tomb,*[h] which he had quarried in the rock. And after rolling a big stone to the entrance of the tomb,* he left. **61** But Mary Mag'da·lene and the other Mary continued there, sitting before the grave.[i]

62 The next day, which was after the Preparation,[j] the chief priests and the Pharisees gathered together before Pilate, **63** saying: "Sir, we recall what that impostor said while he was still alive, 'After three days I am to be raised up.'[k] **64** Therefore, command that the grave be made secure until the third day, so that his disciples may not

come and steal him[a] and say to the people, 'He was raised up from the dead!' Then this last deception will be worse than the first." **65** Pilate said to them: "You may have a guard. Go make it as secure as you know how." **66** So they went and made the grave secure by sealing the stone and posting a guard.

28 After the Sabbath, when it was growing light on the first day of the week, Mary Mag'da·lene and the other Mary came to view the grave.[b]

2 And look! a great earthquake had taken place, for Jehovah's* angel had descended from heaven and had come and rolled away the stone, and he was sitting on it.[c] **3** His appearance was like lightning, and his clothing was as white as snow.[d] **4** Yes, out of their fear of him, the watchmen trembled and became as dead men.

5 But the angel said to the women: "Do not be afraid, for I know that you are looking for Jesus who was executed on the stake.[e] **6** He is not here, for he was raised up, just as he said.[f] Come, see the place where he was lying. **7** Then go quickly and tell his disciples that he was raised up from the dead, for look! he is going ahead of you into Gal'i·lee.[g] You will see him there. Look! I have told you."[h]

8 So, quickly leaving the memorial tomb, with fear and great joy, they ran to report to his disciples.[i] **9** And look! Jesus met them and said: "Good day!" They approached and took hold of his feet and did obeisance* to him. **10** Then Jesus said to them: "Have no fear! Go, report to my brothers so that they may go to Gal'i·lee, and there they will see me."

CHAP. 27
a Mr 15:39

b Mr 15:40, 41
Lu 8:2, 3

c Mt 20:20
Joh 19:25

d Mr 15:42, 43
Lu 23:50-53

e De 21:22, 23

f Mr 15:45-47
Joh 19:38

g Joh 19:40, 41

h Isa 53:9

i Lu 23:55

j Mr 15:42
Lu 23:54
Joh 19:14

k Mt 12:40
Joh 2:19

Second Col.
a Mt 28:12, 13

CHAP. 28
b Mr 16:1
Lu 24:1
Lu 24:10
Joh 20:1

c Mr 16:4, 5
Lu 24:2, 4

d Ac 1:10

e Mr 16:6

f Mr 16:21
Mt 17:22, 23
1Co 15:3, 4

g Mt 26:32
Mt 28:16
Mr 14:28

h Mr 16:7

i Mr 16:8
Lu 24:9

27:52 *Or "memorial tombs." 27:60 *Or "memorial tomb."

28:2 *See App. A5. 28:9 *Or "bowed down."

11 While they were on their way, some of the guards[a] went into the city and reported to the chief priests all the things that had happened. **12** And after these had gathered with the elders and had consulted together, they gave a considerable number of silver pieces to the soldiers **13** and said: "Say, 'His disciples came in the night and stole him while we were sleeping.'[b] **14** And if this gets to the governor's ears, we will explain the matter to* him and you will not need to worry." **15** So they took the silver pieces and did as they were instructed, and this story has been spread abroad among the Jews up to this very day.

28:14 *Lit., "persuade."

CHAP. 28
a Mt 27:65
b Mt 27:64

Second Col.
a Mt 26:32
b 1Co 15:6
c Eph 1:20, 21
  Php 2:9
d Ac 1:8
  Ro 10:18
  Ro 11:13
  Re 14:6
e Ac 2:38
  Ac 8:12
f Ac 20:20
  1Co 11:23
  2Pe 3:1, 2
  1Jo 3:23
g Mt 13:39
  Mt 13:49
  Mt 24:3

16 However, the 11 disciples went to Gal'i·lee[a] to the mountain where Jesus had arranged for them to meet.[b] **17** When they saw him, they did obeisance,* but some doubted. **18** Jesus approached and spoke to them, saying: "All authority has been given me in heaven and on the earth.[c] **19** Go, therefore, and make disciples of people of all the nations,[d] baptizing them[e] in the name of the Father and of the Son and of the holy spirit, **20** teaching them to observe all the things I have commanded you.[f] And look! I am with you all the days until the conclusion of the system of things."*[g]

28:17 *Or "bowed down." 28:20 *Or "the age." See Glossary.

ACCORDING TO

MARK

OUTLINE OF CONTENTS

---

1 The beginning of the good news about Jesus Christ, the Son of God: **2** Just as it is written in Isaiah the prophet: "(Look! I am sending my messenger ahead of you,* who will prepare your way.)ᵃ **3** A voice of one crying out in the wilderness: 'Prepare the way of Jehovah!* Make his roads straight.'"ᵇ

1:2 *Lit., "before your face." 1:3 *See App. A5.

CHAP. 1
a Mal 3:1
  Mt 3:1, 3
  Mt 11:10
  Lu 3:2-6
  Lu 7:27

b Isa 40:3
  Joh 1:23

Second Col.
a Mt 3:1, 2
  Ac 13:24
  Ac 19:4

b Mt 3:5, 6

4 John the Baptizer was in the wilderness, preaching baptism in symbol of repentance for forgiveness of sins.ᵃ **5** And all the territory of Ju·deʹa and all the inhabitants of Jerusalem were going out to him, and they were baptized* by him in the Jordan River, openly confessing their sins.ᵇ **6** Now John wore clothing of camel's hair and a

1:5 *Or "dipped; immersed."

leather belt around his waist,[a] and he ate locusts and wild honey.[b] **7** And he was preaching: "Someone stronger than I am is coming after me, the lace of whose sandals I am not worthy to stoop down and untie.[c] **8** I baptized you with water, but he will baptize you with holy spirit."[d]

9 In the course of those days, Jesus came from Naz'a·reth of Gal'i·lee and was baptized in the Jordan by John. **10** And immediately on coming up out of the water, he saw the heavens being parted and, like a dove, the spirit coming down upon him.[f] **11** And a voice came out of the heavens: "You are my Son, the beloved; I have approved you."[g]

12 And immediately the spirit impelled him to go into the wilderness. **13** So he continued in the wilderness for 40 days, being tempted by Satan.[h] He was with the wild beasts, but the angels were ministering to him.[i]

14 Now after John was arrested, Jesus went into Gal'i·lee,[j] preaching the good news of God[k] **15** and saying: "The appointed time has been fulfilled, and the Kingdom of God has drawn near. Repent,[l] and have faith in the good news."

16 While walking alongside the Sea of Gal'i·lee, he saw Simon and Simon's brother Andrew[m] casting their nets into the sea,[n] for they were fishermen.[o] **17** So Jesus said to them: "Come after me, and I will make you fishers of men."*[p] **18** And at once they abandoned their nets and followed him.[q] **19** After going a little farther, he saw James the son of Zeb'e·dee and his brother John, while they were in their boat mending their nets,[r] **20** and without delay he

called them. So they left their father Zeb'e·dee in the boat with the hired men and went off after him. **21** And they went into Ca·per'na·um.

As soon as the Sabbath began, he went into the synagogue and started to teach.[a] **22** And they were astounded at his way of teaching, for he was teaching them as one having authority, and not as the scribes.[b] **23** Just then there was a man in their synagogue who was under the power of an unclean spirit, and he shouted: **24** "What have we to do with you, Jesus the Naz·a·rene'?[c] Did you come to destroy us? I know exactly who you are, the Holy One of God!"[d] **25** But Jesus rebuked it, saying: "Be silent, and come out of him!" **26** And the unclean spirit, after throwing the man into a convulsion and yelling at the top of its voice, came out of him. **27** Well, the people were all so astonished that they began to discuss it among themselves, saying: "What is this? A new teaching! He authoritatively orders even the unclean spirits, and they obey him." **28** So the report about him spread quickly in all directions throughout the entire region of Gal'i·lee.

29 At that they left the synagogue and went to the home of Simon and Andrew with James and John.[e] **30** Now Simon's mother-in-law[f] was lying down sick with a fever, and they at once told him about her. **31** Going to her, he took her by the hand and raised her up. The fever left her, and she began ministering to them.

32 After evening had fallen, when the sun had set, the people began bringing to him all who were ill and demon possessed;[g] **33** and the whole city was gathered right at the door. **34** So he cured many who were ill

---

CHAP. 1

a 2Ki 1:8

b Mt 3:4

c Lu 3:16
  Joh 1:26, 27
  Ac 13:25

d Joe 2:28
  Ac 2:1, 4
  Ac 11:16
  1Co 12:13

e Mt 3:13
  Lu 3:21, 22

f Isa 42:1
  Mt 3:16
  Joh 1:32-34

g Ps 2:7
  Mt 3:17
  Lu 3:22
  2Pe 1:17

h Mt 4:1-10
  Lu 4:1-13

i Mt 4:11

j Mt 4:12

k Lu 4:14, 15
  Lu 8:1

l Mt 4:17

m Mt 10:2

n Lu 5:4

o Mt 4:18

p Mt 4:19, 20

q Mt 19:27
  Lu 5:11

r Mt 4:21, 22

Second Col.

a Lu 4:31-37

b Mt 7:28, 29

c Mt 8:28, 29

d Jas 2:19

e Mt 8:14, 15
  Lu 4:38, 39

f 1Co 9:5

g Mt 8:16
  Lu 4:40, 41

1:17 *Or "people."

with various sicknesses,[a] and he expelled many demons, but he would not let the demons speak, for they knew him to be Christ.*

35 Early in the morning, while it was still dark, he got up and went outside and left for an isolated place, and there he began praying.[b] **36** However, Simon and those with him hunted him down **37** and found him, and they said to him: "Everyone is looking for you." **38** But he said to them: "Let us go somewhere else, into the towns nearby, so that I may preach there also, for this is why I have come."[c] **39** And he went, preaching in their synagogues throughout the whole of Gal'i·lee and expelling the demons.[d]

40 There also came to him a leper, pleading with him even on bended knee, saying to him: "If you just want to, you can make me clean."[e] **41** At that he was moved with pity, and he stretched out his hand and touched him, and said to him: "I want to! Be made clean."[f] **42** Immediately the leprosy vanished from him, and he became clean. **43** Then he gave him strict orders and at once sent him away, **44** saying to him: "See that you say nothing to anyone, but go show yourself to the priest and offer for your cleansing the things Moses directed,[g] for a witness to them."[h] **45** But after going away, the man started to proclaim it a great deal and to spread the account widely, so that Jesus was no longer able to enter openly into a city, but he stayed outside in isolated places. Yet they kept coming to him from all sides.[i]

2 However, after some days he again entered into Ca·per'na·um, and the word spread that he was at home.[j] **2** And so

many gathered that there was no more room, not even around the door, and he began to speak the word to them.[a] **3** And they brought him a paralytic carried by four men.[b] **4** But they could not bring him right to Jesus because of the crowd, so they removed the roof above Jesus, and after digging an opening, they lowered the stretcher on which the paralytic was lying. **5** When Jesus saw their faith,[c] he said to the paralytic: "Child, your sins are forgiven."[d] **6** Now some of the scribes were there, sitting and reasoning in their hearts:[e] **7** "Why is this man talking this way? He is blaspheming. Who can forgive sins except one, God?"[f] **8** But immediately Jesus discerned by his spirit that they were reasoning that way among themselves, so he said to them: "Why are you reasoning these things in your hearts?[g] **9** Which is easier, to say to the paralytic, 'Your sins are forgiven,' or to say, 'Get up and pick up your stretcher and walk'? **10** But in order for you to know that the Son of man[h] has authority to forgive sins on earth—"[i] he said to the paralytic: **11** "I say to you, Get up, pick up your stretcher, and go to your home." **12** At that he got up and immediately picked up his stretcher and walked out in front of them all. So they were all astonished, and they glorified God, saying: "We have never seen anything like this."[j]

13 Again he went out alongside the sea, and all the crowd kept coming to him, and he began to teach them. **14** And as he was passing by, he caught sight of Le'vi the son of Al·phae'us sitting at the tax office, and he said to him: "Be my follower." At that he rose up and followed him.[k] **15** Later he was dining*

CHAP. 1
a Isa 53:4
b Mt 14:23
  Mr 14:32
  Lu 4:42
  Heb 5:7
c Isa 61:1
  Lu 4:43
  Joh 17:4
d Mt 4:23
e Mt 8:1, 2
  Lu 5:12
f Mt 8:3
  Lu 5:13
g Le 14:3, 4
  Le 14:10, 11
  De 24:8
h Mt 8:4
  Lu 5:14
i Lu 5:15

CHAP. 2
j Mt 4:13
  Mt 9:1

Second Col.
a Isa 61:1
  Eph 2:17
  Heb 2:3
b Lu 5:18, 19
c Ac 14:9, 10
d Isa 53:11
  Mt 9:2
  Lu 5:20
  Lu 7:47, 48
e Mt 9:3-8
  Lu 5:21-26
f Isa 43:25
g Mt 9:4
  Lu 6:8
  Re 2:23
h Da 7:13
i Isa 53:11
j Mt 9:33
  Joh 7:31
  Joh 9:32
k Mt 9:9
  Lu 5:27, 28

1:34 *Or possibly, "they knew who he was."

2:15 *Or "reclining at the table."

in his house, and many tax collectors and sinners were dining* with Jesus and his disciples, for there were many of them who were following him.ª **16** But when the scribes of the Pharisees saw that he was eating with the sinners and tax collectors, they began saying to his disciples: "Does he eat with tax collectors and sinners?" **17** On hearing this, Jesus said to them: "Those who are strong do not need a physician, but those who are ill do. I came to call, not righteous people, but sinners."ᵇ

18 Now John's disciples and the Pharisees practiced fasting. So they came and said to him: "Why do John's disciples and the disciples of the Pharisees practice fasting, but your disciples do not practice fasting?"ᶜ **19** So Jesus said to them: "While the bridegroomᵈ is with them, the friends of the bridegroom have no reason to fast, do they? As long as they have the bridegroom with them, they cannot fast. **20** But days will come when the bridegroom will be taken away from them,ᵉ and then they will fast on that day. **21** Nobody sews a patch of unshrunk cloth on an old outer garment. If he does, the new piece pulls away from the old, and the tear becomes worse.ᶠ **22** Also, no one puts new wine into old wineskins. If he does, the wine will burst the skins, and the wine is lost as well as the skins. But new wine is put into new wineskins."

23 Now as he was passing through the grainfields on the Sabbath, his disciples started ed to pluck the heads of grain as they went.ᵍ **24** So the Pharisees said to him: "Look here! Why are they doing what is not lawful on the Sabbath?" **25** But

he said to them: "Have you never read what David did when he was in need and he and the men with him were hungry?ª **26** How, in the account about A·bi′a·tharᵇ the chief priest, he entered into the house of God and ate the loaves of presentation,* which it is not lawful for anybody to eat except the priests,ᶜ and he also gave some to the men who were with him?" **27** Then he said to them: "The Sabbath came into existence for the sake of man,ᵈ and not man for the sake of the Sabbath. **28** So the Son of man is Lord even of the Sabbath."ᵉ

3 Once again he entered into a synagogue, and a man with a withered* hand was there.ᶠ **2** So they were watching him closely to see whether he would cure the man on the Sabbath, in order to accuse him. **3** He said to the man with the withered* hand: "Get up and come to the center." **4** Next he said to them: "Is it lawful on the Sabbath to do good or to do harm, to save a life* or to kill?"ᵍ But they kept silent. **5** After looking around at them with indignation, being thoroughly grieved at the insensibility of their hearts,ʰ he said to the man: "Stretch out your hand." And he stretched it out, and his hand was restored. **6** At that the Pharisees went out and immediately began holding council with the party followers of Herodⁱ against him, in order to kill him.

7 But Jesus departed for the sea along with his disciples, and a great multitude from Gal′i·lee and from Ju·de′a followed him.ʲ **8** Even from Jerusalem and from Id·u·me′a and from across the Jordan and from around Tyre and Si′don, a great multi-

---

CHAP. 2
a Mt 9:10, 11
  Lu 5:29, 30

b Isa 61:1
  Mt 9:12, 13
  Lu 5:31, 32
  Lu 19:10
  1Ti 1:15

c Mt 9:14, 15
  Lu 5:33-35

d Mt 22:2
  2Co 11:2
  Re 19:7

e Lu 17:22

f Mt 9:16, 17
  Lu 5:36-38

g Mt 12:1-8
  Lu 6:1-5

Second Col.
a 1Sa 21:1-6

b 1Sa 22:20

c Ex 25:30
  Le 24:5-9

d Ex 20:9, 10

e Mt 12:8
  Lu 6:5

CHAP. 3
f Mt 12:9-14
  Lu 6:6-11

g Lu 14:1-3

h Joh 12:39, 40

i Mt 22:16
  Mr 12:13

j Mt 12:15

2:15 *Or "reclining at the table."

2:26 *Or "the showbread." 3:1, 3 *Or "paralyzed." 3:4 *Or "soul."

tude came to him when they heard about the many things he was doing. 9 And he told his disciples to have a small boat ready for him so that the crowd would not press in on him. 10 Because he cured many, all those who had serious diseases were crowding around him to touch him.[a] 11 Even the unclean spirits,[b] whenever they saw him, would fall down before him and cry out and say: "You are the Son of God."[c] 12 But many times he sternly ordered them not to make him known.[d]

13 He ascended a mountain and summoned those whom he wanted,[e] and they came to him.[f] 14 And he formed* a group of 12, whom he also named apostles, those who were to accompany him and whom he would send out to preach 15 and to have authority to expel demons.[g]

16 And the group of 12[h] that he formed* were Simon, to whom he also gave the name Peter,[i] 17 James the son of Zeb'e·dee and John the brother of James (he also gave these the name Bo·a·ner'ges, which means "Sons of Thunder"),[j] 18 Andrew, Philip, Bar·thol'o·mew, Matthew, Thomas, James the son of Al·phae'us, Thad·dae'us, Simon the Ca·na·nae'an,* 19 and Judas Is·car'i·ot, who later betrayed him.

Then he went into a house, 20 and again the crowd gathered, so that they were not able even to eat a meal. 21 But when his relatives heard about it, they went out to seize him, for they were saying: "He has gone out of his mind."[k] 22 Also, the scribes who came down from Jerusalem were saying: "He has Be·el'ze·bub,* and

he expels the demons by means of the ruler of the demons."[a] 23 So after calling them to him, he spoke to them with illustrations: "How can Satan expel Satan? 24 If a kingdom becomes divided against itself, that kingdom cannot stand;[b] 25 and if a house becomes divided against itself, that house will not be able to stand. 26 Also, if Satan has risen up against himself and has become divided, he cannot stand but is coming to an end. 27 In fact, no one who enters the house of a strong man is able to steal his possessions unless he first ties up the strong man. Only then can he plunder his house. 28 Truly I say to you that all things will be forgiven the sons of men, no matter what sins they commit and what blasphemies they speak. 29 But whoever blasphemes against the holy spirit has no forgiveness forever[c] but is guilty of everlasting sin."[d] 30 He said this because they were saying: "He has an unclean spirit."[e]

31 Now his mother and his brothers[f] came, and standing outside, they sent someone in to call him.[g] 32 As there was a crowd sitting around him, they said to him: "Look! Your mother and your brothers are outside asking for you."[h] 33 But he replied to them: "Who are my mother and my brothers?" 34 Then he looked at those sitting around him in a circle and said: "See, my mother and my brothers![i] 35 Whoever does the will of God, this one is my brother and sister and mother."[j]

4 Again he began teaching beside the sea, and a very large crowd gathered near him. So he went aboard a boat and sat in it away from the shore, but the whole crowd was next to the sea, along the shore.[k] 2 And he began to teach them many things

CHAP. 3
a Mt 9:20, 21
Mr 5:27, 28
Mr 6:56

b Mt 8:31

c Mr 1:23, 24
Mr 5:7
Lu 4:41

d Mt 12:15, 16
Mr 1:25

e Joh 15:16

f Lu 6:12, 13

g Mt 10:1

h Mt 10:2-4
Lu 6:14-16
Ac 1:13

i Joh 1:42

j Lu 9:54

k Joh 7:5

Second Col.
a Mt 9:34
Mt 10:25
Mt 12:24-29
Lu 11:15
Joh 8:48

b Lu 11:17, 18

c Mt 12:31, 32
Lu 12:10

d Heb 6:4, 6
Heb 10:26

e Joh 7:20
Joh 10:20

f Mt 13:55
Joh 2:12
Ac 1:14

g Mt 12:46-50
Lu 8:19-21

h Mr 6:3

i Mt 12:49
Heb 2:11

j Mt 12:50
Lu 8:21
Joh 15:14

CHAP. 4
k Mt 13:1, 2
Lu 8:4

3:14, 16 *Or "appointed." 3:18 *Or "the zealous one." 3:22 *A designation applied to Satan.

with illustrations,[a] and while he was teaching, he said to them:[b] **3** "Listen. Look! The sower went out to sow.[c] **4** As he was sowing, some seeds fell alongside the road, and the birds came and ate them up. **5** Others fell on rocky ground where there was not much soil, and they immediately sprang up because the soil was not deep.[d] **6** But when the sun rose, they were scorched, and they withered because they had no root. **7** Other seeds fell among the thorns, and the thorns came up and choked them, and they yielded no fruit.[e] **8** But others fell on the fine soil, and growing up and increasing, they began to yield fruit, and they were bearing 30, 60, and 100 times more."[f] **9** Then he added: "Let the one who has ears to listen, listen."[g]

10 Now when he was alone, those around him with the Twelve began questioning him about the illustrations.[h] **11** He said to them: "To you the sacred secret[i] of the Kingdom of God has been given, but to those outside all things are in illustrations,[j] **12** so that, though looking, they may look and still not see, and though hearing, they may hear and still not get the sense of it; nor will they ever turn back and receive forgiveness."[k] **13** Further, he said to them: "You do not know this illustration, so how will you understand all the other illustrations?

14 "The sower sows the word.[l] **15** These, then, are the ones alongside the road where the word is sown; but as soon as they have heard it, Satan comes[m] and takes away the word that was sown in them.[n] **16** Likewise, these are the ones sown on rocky ground; as soon as they have heard the word,

they accept it with joy.[a] **17** Yet they have no root in themselves, but they continue for a time; then as soon as tribulation or persecution arises because of the word, they are stumbled. **18** There are still others that are sown among the thorns. These are the ones who have heard the word,[b] **19** but the anxieties[c] of this system of things* and the deceptive power of riches[d] and the desires[e] for everything else make inroads and choke the word, and it becomes unfruitful. **20** Finally, the ones that were sown on the fine soil are those who listen to the word and favorably receive it and bear fruit—30, 60, and 100 times more."[f]

21 He also said to them: "A lamp is not brought out to be put under a basket* or under a bed, is it? Is it not brought out to be put on a lampstand?[g] **22** For there is nothing hidden that will not be exposed; nothing is carefully concealed that will not come out in the open.[h] **23** Whoever has ears to listen, let him listen."[i]

24 He further said to them: "Pay attention to what you are hearing.[j] With the measure that you are measuring out, you will have it measured out to you, yes, you will have more added to you. **25** For whoever has will have more given to him,[k] but whoever does not have, even what he has will be taken away from him."[l]

26 So he went on to say: "In this way the Kingdom of God is just as when a man casts seeds on the ground. **27** He sleeps at night and rises up by day, and the seeds sprout and grow tall —just how, he does not know. **28** On its own the ground bears fruit gradually, first the stalk,

---

4:19 *Or "this age." See Glossary. **4:21** *Or "measuring basket."

then the head, finally the full grain in the head. 29 But as soon as the crop permits it, he thrusts in the sickle, because the harvesttime has come."

30 And he went on to say: "With what can we compare the Kingdom of God, or with what illustration can we explain it? 31 It is like a mustard grain, which at the time it was sown in the ground was the tiniest of all the seeds on the earth.ᵃ 32 But when it has been sown, it grows and becomes greater than all other vegetable plants and produces great branches, so that the birds of heaven are able to find lodging under its shadow."

33 With many illustrationsᵇ of that sort he spoke the word to them, to the extent that they were able to listen. 34 Indeed, without an illustration he would not speak to them, but he would explain all things privately to his disciples.ᶜ

35 And on that day, when evening had fallen, he said to them: "Let us cross to the other shore."ᵈ 36 So after they had dismissed the crowd, they took him in the boat, just as he was, and there were other boats with him.ᵉ 37 Now a great violent windstorm broke out, and the waves kept crashing into the boat, so that the boat was close to being swamped.ᶠ 38 But he was in the stern, sleeping on the pillow.* So they woke him up and said to him: "Teacher, do you not care that we are about to perish?" 39 With that he got up and rebuked the wind and said to the sea: "Hush! Be quiet!"ᵍ And the wind abated, and a great calm set in. 40 So he said to them: "Why are you so afraid?* Do you not yet have any faith?" 41 But they felt an unusual fear,

and they said to one another: "Who really is this? Even the wind and the sea obey him."ᵃ

5 Then they came to the other side of the sea into the region of the Ger′a·senes.ᵇ 2 And immediately after Jesus got out of the boat, a man under the power of an unclean spirit met him from among the tombs.* 3 His haunt was among the tombs, and up to that time, absolutely no one was able to bind him securely, even with a chain. 4 He had often been bound with fetters and chains, but he snapped the chains apart and smashed the fetters; and nobody had the strength to subdue him. 5 And continually, night and day, he was crying out in the tombs and in the mountains and slashing himself with stones. 6 But on catching sight of Jesus from a distance, he ran and bowed down to him.ᶜ 7 Then he cried out with a loud voice: "What have I to do with you, Jesus, Son of the Most High God? I put you under oath by God not to torment me."ᵈ 8 For Jesus had been saying to it: "Come out of the man, you unclean spirit."ᵉ 9 But Jesus asked him: "What is your name?" And he replied: "My name is Legion, because there are many of us." 10 And he kept pleading with Jesus not to send the spirits out of the country.ᶠ

11 Now a great herd of swineᵍ was feeding there at the mountain.ʰ 12 So the spirits pleaded with him: "Send us into the swine, so that we may enter into them." 13 And he gave them permission. With that the unclean spirits came out and went into the swine, and the herd rushed over the precipice* into the sea, about 2,000 of them,

---

CHAP. 4
a Mt 13:31, 32
Lu 13:18, 19

b Ps 78:2

c Mt 13:11
Mt 13:34, 35
Mr 4:11

d Mt 8:18

e Mt 8:23
Lu 8:22

f Mt 8:24-27
Lu 8:23-25

g Ps 89:9

Second Col.
a Joh 6:19

CHAP. 5
b Mt 8:28
Lu 8:26, 27

c Lu 8:28-30

d Mt 8:29
Jas 2:19

e Ac 16:17, 18

f Lu 8:31

g Le 11:7, 8
De 14:8

h Mt 8:30-33
Lu 8:32-34

4:38 *Or "cushion." 4:40 *Or "fainthearted?"

5:2 *Or "memorial tombs." 5:13 *Or "steep bank."

and were drowned in the sea. **14** But their herders fled and reported it in the city and in the countryside, and people came to see what had happened.[a] **15** So they came to Jesus and saw the demon-possessed man, the one who previously had the Legion, sitting clothed and in his right mind, and they grew fearful. **16** Also, those who had seen it related to them how this had happened to the demon-possessed man and the swine. **17** So they began to plead with Jesus to go away from their region.[b]

18 Now as he was boarding the boat, the man who had been demon-possessed pleaded to go with him.[c] **19** However, he did not let him but said to him: "Go home to your relatives, and report to them all the things Jehovah* has done for you and the mercy he has shown you." **20** This man went away and started to proclaim in the De·cap′o·lis* all the things Jesus had done for him, and all the people were amazed.

21 After Jesus had crossed again by boat to the opposite shore, a large crowd gathered together to him, and he was by the sea.[d] **22** One of the presiding officers of the synagogue, named Ja′i·rus, now came, and on catching sight of him, he fell at his feet.[e] **23** He pleaded with him many times, saying: "My little daughter is extremely ill.* Please come and put your hands on her[f] so that she may get well and live." **24** At that Jesus went with him, and a large crowd was following him and pressing against him.

25 Now there was a woman who had had a flow of blood[g] for

12 years.[a] **26** She had suffered much* at the hands of many physicians and had spent all her resources, and she was no better but, rather, had become worse. **27** When she heard the reports about Jesus, she came up behind him in the crowd and touched his outer garment,[b] **28** for she kept saying: "If I touch just his outer garments, I will get well."[c] **29** And immediately her flow of blood dried up, and she was sensed in her body that she had been healed of the grievous sickness.

30 Immediately Jesus realized in himself that power[d] had gone out of him, and he turned around in the crowd and asked: "Who touched my outer garments?"[e] **31** But his disciples said to him: "You see the crowd pressing in on you, and you ask, 'Who touched me?'" **32** However, he was looking around to see who had done this. **33** The woman, frightened and trembling, knowing what had happened to her, came and fell down before him and told him the whole truth. **34** He said to her: "Daughter, your faith has made you well. Go in peace,[f] and be healed from your grievous sickness."[g]

35 While he was yet speaking, some men from the home of the presiding officer of the synagogue came and said: "Your daughter died! Why bother the Teacher any longer?"[h] **36** But Jesus overheard their words and said to the presiding officer of the synagogue: "Have no fear,* only exercise faith."[i] **37** Now he did not let anyone follow him except Peter, James, and John the brother of James.[j]

38 So they came to the house of the presiding officer of the

CHAP. 5
a Lu 8:35-37

b Mt 8:34

c Lu 8:38, 39

d Lu 8:40

e Mt 9:18
Lu 8:41, 42

f Lu 4:40

g Le 15:25

Second Col.
a Mt 9:20-22
Lu 8:43, 44

b Mt 14:36
Mr 6:56

c Mt 9:21

d Lu 5:17
Lu 6:19

e Lu 8:45-48

f Lu 7:50
Lu 8:48

g Mt 9:22

h Lu 8:49

i Lu 8:50
Joh 11:39, 40

j Mt 17:1
Mt 26:36, 37

5:19 *See App. A5. **5:20** *Or "the Ten City Region." **5:23** *Or "is near her end."

5:26 *Or "had been put to many pains." **5:36** *Or "Stop being afraid."

synagogue, and he saw the commotion and those weeping and wailing loudly.[a] **39** After stepping in, he said to them: "Why are you weeping and causing this commotion? The child has not died but is sleeping."[b] **40** At this they began to laugh at him scornfully. But after sending them all outside, he took the child's father and mother and those with him, and he went in where the child was. **41** Then, taking the hand of the child, he said to her: "Tal'i·tha cu'mi," which, when translated, means: "Little girl, I say to you, 'Get up!'"[c] **42** And immediately the girl rose and began walking. (She was 12 years old.) And at once they were beside themselves with great ecstasy. **43** But he ordered them again and again* to let no one learn of this,[d] and he said that something should be given her to eat.

6 He departed from there and came into his home territory,[e] and his disciples followed him. **2** When it was the Sabbath, he started teaching in the synagogue, and most who heard him were astounded and said: "Where did this man get these things?[f] And why should this wisdom have been given to him, and such powerful works be performed through his hands?[g] **3** This is the carpenter,[h] the son of Mary[i] and the brother of James,[j] Joseph, Judas, and Simon,[k] is it not? And his sisters are here with us, are they not?" So they began to stumble because of him. **4** But Jesus said to them: "A prophet is not without honor except in his home territory and among his relatives and in his own house."[l] **5** So he was not able to do any powerful work there except to lay his hands on a few sick people and cure them. **6** Indeed, he was amazed at their lack of faith. And he went around in a circuit to the villages, teaching.[a]

7 He now summoned the Twelve and started sending them out two by two,[b] and he gave them authority over the unclean spirits.[c] **8** Also, he gave them orders to carry nothing for the trip except a staff—no bread, no food pouch, no money* in their belts[d]— **9** but to put on sandals and not to wear two garments.* **10** Further, he said to them: "Wherever you enter into a home, stay there until you leave that place.[e] **11** And wherever a place will not receive you or listen to you, on going out from there, shake off the dirt that is on your feet for a witness to them."[f] **12** Then they set out and preached that people should repent,[g] **13** and they expelled many demons[h] and greased many sick people with oil and cured them.

14 Now King Herod heard of this, for the name of Jesus became well-known, and people were saying: "John the Baptizer has been raised up from the dead, and that is why the powerful works are operating in him."[i] **15** But others were saying: "It is E·li'jah." Still others were saying: "It is a prophet like one of the prophets of old."[j] **16** But when Herod heard it, he said: "The John whom I beheaded, this one has been raised up." **17** For Herod himself had sent out and arrested John and had bound him in prison on account of He·ro'di·as, the wife of Philip his brother, because he had married her.[k] **18** For John had been saying to Herod: "It is not lawful for you to have your

---

CHAP. 5

a Mt 9:23-26
 Lu 8:51-56

b Lu 8:52
 Joh 11:11

c Mt 9:25
 Lu 7:14
 Lu 8:54
 Ac 9:40

d Mr 1:42-44
 Mr 7:35, 36

CHAP. 6

e Lu 4:16

f Joh 6:42
 Joh 7:15

g Mt 13:54-58

h Isa 53:2

i Joh 6:42

j Ga 1:19

k Mr 3:31

l Mt 13:57
 Lu 4:24
 Joh 4:44

Second Col.

a Mt 9:35
 Lu 13:22

b Lu 10:1

c Mt 10:1
 Lu 9:1-6

d Mt 10:9, 10

e Mt 10:11

f Mt 10:14
 Lu 10:10, 11
 Ac 13:50, 51

g Ac 2:38
 Ac 3:19

h Lu 10:17

i Mt 14:1-5
 Lu 9:7-9

j Mt 16:14
 Mr 8:28

k Lu 3:19, 20

5:43 *Or "he strongly ordered them."

6:8 *Lit., "copper." 6:9 *Or "an extra garment."

brother's wife."[a] **19** So He·ro'di·as was nursing a grudge against him and wanted to kill him, but she could not. **20** For Herod was in fear of John, knowing him to be a righteous and holy man,[b] and he was keeping him safe. After hearing him, he was at a great loss as to what to do, yet he continued to hear him gladly.

21 But a convenient day arrived when Herod spread an evening meal on his birthday[c] for his high officials and the military commanders and the most prominent men of Gal'i·lee.[d] **22** And the daughter of He·ro'di·as came in and danced and pleased Herod and those dining* with him. The king said to the girl: "Ask me for whatever you want, and I will give it to you." **23** Yes, he swore to her: "Whatever you ask me for, I will give it to you, up to half my kingdom." **24** So she went out and said to her mother: "What should I ask for?" She said: "The head of John the Baptizer." **25** She immediately rushed in to the king and made her request, saying: "I want you to give me right away on a platter the head of John the Baptist."[e] **26** Although this deeply grieved him, the king did not want to disregard her request, because of his oaths and his guests.* **27** So the king immediately sent a bodyguard and commanded him to bring John's head. So he went off and beheaded him in the prison **28** and brought his head on a platter. He gave it to the girl, and the girl gave it to her mother. **29** When his disciples heard of it, they came and took his body and laid it in a tomb.*

30 The apostles gathered around Jesus and reported to him all the things they had done and taught.[a] **31** And he said to them: "Come, you yourselves, privately into an isolated place and rest up a little."[b] For there were many coming and going, and they had no leisure time even to eat a meal. **32** So they set off in the boat for an isolated place to be by themselves.[c] **33** But people saw them going and many got to know it, and from all the cities they ran together on foot and got there ahead of them. **34** Well, on getting out, he saw a large crowd, and he was moved with pity for them,[d] because they were as sheep without a shepherd.[e] And he started to teach them many things.[f]

35 By now the hour had grown late, and his disciples came up to him and said: "This place is isolated, and the hour is already late.[g] **36** Send them away, so that they may go off into the surrounding countryside and villages and buy themselves something to eat."[h] **37** He replied to them: "You give them something to eat." At this they said to him: "Should we go off and buy 200 de·nar'i·i* worth of bread and give it to the people to eat?"[i] **38** He said to them: "How many loaves do you have? Go see!" After finding out, they said: "Five, besides two fish."[j] **39** And he instructed all the people to recline in groups on the green grass.[k] **40** So they reclined in groups of 100 and of 50. **41** Taking now the five loaves and the two fish, he looked up to heaven and said a blessing.[l] Then he broke the loaves up and began giving them to the disciples to place them before the people, and he divided up the two fish for all. **42** So they all ate and were satisfied,

---

CHAP. 6
a Le 18:16
  Le 20:21

b Mt 11:11
  Mt 21:26

c Ge 40:20-22

d Mt 14:6-12

e Mt 14:8

Second Col.
a Lu 9:10

b Mt 11:29
  Mt 14:13

c Joh 6:1, 2

d Mt 14:14
  Heb 4:15

e 1Ki 22:17
  Isa 53:6
  Eze 34:5, 8
  Mt 9:36

f Isa 61:1
  Lu 9:11

g Mt 14:15-21
  Lu 9:12-17

h Joh 6:5

i 2Ki 4:42-44
  Mt 15:33
  Joh 6:7

j Joh 6:9

k Joh 6:10-13

l Mr 8:6
  Lu 24:30
  Ac 27:35

6:22 *Or "reclining at the table." **6:26** *Or "and those reclining at the table." **6:29** *Or "memorial tomb."

6:37 *See App. B14.

43 and they took up 12 baskets full of fragments, aside from the fish.[a] **44** Those who ate the loaves were 5,000 men.

45 Then, without delay, he made his disciples board the boat and go on ahead to the opposite shore toward Beth·sa′i·da, while he himself sent the crowd away.[b] **46** But after saying good-bye to them, he went to a mountain to pray.[c] **47** When evening had fallen, the boat was in the middle of the sea, but he was alone on the land.[d] **48** So when he saw them struggling to row, for the wind was against them, about the fourth watch of the night* he came toward them, walking on the sea; but he was inclined to# pass them by. **49** On catching sight of him walking on the sea, they thought: "It is an apparition!" And they cried out. **50** For they all saw him and were troubled. But immediately he spoke to them and said: "Take courage! It is I; do not be afraid."[e] **51** Then he got up into the boat with them, and the wind abated. At this they were utterly amazed, **52** for they had not grasped the meaning of the loaves, but their hearts continued dull in understanding.

53 When they got across to land, they came to Gen·nes′a·ret and anchored the boat nearby.[f] **54** But as soon as they got out of the boat, people recognized him. **55** They ran around all that region and started to bring on stretchers those who were ailing to where they heard he was. **56** And wherever he would enter into villages or cities or the countryside, they would place the sick ones in the marketplaces, and they would plead with him that they might touch just the fringe of his outer garment.[a] And all those who touched it were made well.

7 Now the Pharisees and some of the scribes who had come from Jerusalem gathered around him.[b] **2** And they saw some of his disciples eat their meal with defiled hands, that is, unwashed ones.* **3** (For the Pharisees and all the Jews do not eat unless they wash their hands up to the elbow, clinging to the tradition of the men of former times, **4** and when they come from the market, they do not eat unless they wash themselves. There are many other traditions that they have received and cling to, such as baptisms of cups, pitchers, and copper vessels.)[c] **5** So these Pharisees and scribes asked him: "Why do your disciples not observe the tradition of the men of former times, but they eat their meal with defiled hands?"[d] **6** He said to them: "Isaiah aptly prophesied about you hypocrites, as it is written, 'This people honor me with their lips, but their hearts are far removed from me.[e] **7** It is in vain that they keep worshipping me, for they teach commands of men as doctrines.'[f] **8** You let go of the commandment of God and cling to the tradition of men."[g]

9 Further, he said to them: "You skillfully disregard the commandment of God in order to keep your tradition.[h] **10** For example, Moses said, 'Honor your father and your mother,'[i] and, 'Let the one who speaks abusively of* his father or mother be put to death.'[j] **11** But you say, 'If a man says to his father or his mother: "Whatever I have that could benefit you is corban (that is, a gift dedicated to God),"' **12** you no longer

---

CHAP. 6
a Mt 14:20
  Lu 9:17
  Joh 6:13

b Mt 14:22

c Mt 6:6
  Mt 14:23
  Mr 1:35
  Lu 6:12

d Mt 14:24-33
  Joh 6:16-21

e Mt 14:27
  Joh 6:20

f Mt 14:34-36

Second Col.
a Mt 9:20
  Mr 5:25-28
  Lu 8:43, 44
  Ac 19:11, 12

CHAP. 7
b Mt 15:1

c Mt 23:25
  Lu 11:38, 39

d Mt 15:2

e Mt 15:7-9

f Isa 29:13

g Ga 1:14
  Col 2:8

h Mt 15:3-6

i Ex 20:12
  De 5:16
  Eph 6:2

j Ex 21:17
  Le 20:9
  Pr 20:20

6:48 *That is, about 3:00 a.m. until sunrise at about 6:00 a.m. #Or "about to."

7:2 *That is, not ceremonially cleansed. **7:10** *Or "reviles."

let him do a single thing for his father or his mother.[a] **13** Thus you make the word of God invalid by your tradition that you have handed down.[b] And you do many things like this."[c] **14** So calling the crowd to him again, he said to them: "Listen to me, all of you, and understand the meaning.[d] **15** Nothing from outside a man that enters into him can defile him; but the things that come out of a man are the things that defile him."[e] **16** *—

17 Now when he had entered a house away from the crowd, his disciples began to question him about the illustration.[f] **18** So he said to them: "Are you also without understanding like them? Are you not aware that nothing from outside that enters into a man can defile him, **19** since it enters, not into his heart, but into his stomach, and it passes out into the sewer?" Thus he declared all foods clean. **20** Further, he said: "That which comes out of a man is what defiles him.[g] **21** For from inside, out of the heart of men,[h] come injurious reasonings, sexual immorality,* thefts, murders, **22** acts of adultery, greed, acts of wickedness, deceit, brazen conduct,* an envious eye, blasphemy, haughtiness, and unreasonableness. **23** All these wicked things come from within and defile a man."

24 He rose up from there and went into the region of Tyre and Si'don.[i] There he entered into a house and did not want anyone to know it, but he could not escape notice. **25** Immediately, a woman whose little daughter had an unclean spirit

heard about him and came and fell down at his feet.[a] **26** The woman was a Greek, a Sy·ro·phoe·ni'cian by nationality;* and she kept asking him to expel the demon from her daughter. **27** But he said to her: "First let the children be satisfied, for it is not right to take the bread of the children and throw it to the little dogs."[b] **28** But she replied to him: "Yes, sir, and yet even the little dogs underneath the table eat of the crumbs of the little children." **29** At that he said to her: "Because you said this, go; the demon has gone out of your daughter."[c] **30** So she went away to her home and found the young child lying on the bed, and the demon was gone.[d]

31 When Jesus returned from the region of Tyre, he went through Si'don to the Sea of Gal'i·lee, through the region of De·cap'o·lis.*[e] **32** Here they brought him a deaf man with a speech impediment,[f] and they pleaded with him to lay his hand on him. **33** And he took him aside privately, away from the crowd. Then he put his fingers into the man's ears, and after spitting, he touched his tongue.[g] **34** And looking up into heaven, he sighed deeply and said to him: "*Eph'pha·tha,*" that is, "Be opened." **35** At this his ears were opened,[h] and his speech impediment was removed, and he began speaking normally. **36** With that he ordered them not to tell anyone,[i] but the more he would order them, the more they would proclaim it.[j] **37** Indeed, they were astounded beyond measure,[k] and they said: "He has done all things well. He even makes the deaf hear and the speechless speak."[l]

CHAP. 7
a 1Ti 5:8
b Mt 15:6
c Mr 7:3
d Mt 15:10
e Mt 15:11
  Tit 1:15
f Mt 15:15-20
g Mt 15:18
h Ge 6:5
  Ge 8:21
  Jer 17:9
i Mt 15:21

Second Col.
a Mt 15:22-28
b Mt 10:5, 6
  Mt 15:26
  Ro 9:4
  Eph 2:12
c Mt 15:28
d Joh 4:49-51
e Mt 15:29
f Mt 9:32, 33
  Lu 11:14
g Mr 8:23
  Joh 9:6
h Isa 35:5
  Mt 11:5
  Mt 15:30
i Isa 42:2
  Mt 8:3, 4
  Mr 5:42, 43
j Mr 1:43-45
k Ac 14:11
l Isa 35:5, 6
  Mt 15:31

7:16 *See App. A3. 7:21 *Plural of the Greek *por·nei'a*. See Glossary. 7:22 *Or "shameless conduct." Greek, *a·sel'·gei·a*. See Glossary.

7:26 *Or "by birth." 7:31 *Or "the Ten City Region."

8 In those days, there was again a large crowd, and they had nothing to eat. So he summoned the disciples and said to them: **2** "I feel pity for the crowd,[a] because they have already stayed with me for three days and they have nothing to eat.[b] **3** If I send them off to their homes hungry,* they will give out on the road, and some of them are from far away." **4** But his disciples answered him: "From where will anyone get enough bread in this isolated place to satisfy these people?" **5** At this he asked them: "How many loaves do you have?" They said: "Seven."[c] **6** And he instructed the crowd to recline on the ground. Then he took the seven loaves, gave thanks, broke them, and began giving them to his disciples to serve, and they served them to the crowd.[d] **7** They also had a few small fish, and blessing these, he told them to serve these also. **8** So they ate and were satisfied, and they took up seven large baskets* full of leftover fragments.[e] **9** Now there were about 4,000 men. Then he sent them away.

10 Immediately he boarded the boat with his disciples and came into the region of Dal·ma·nu'tha.[f] **11** Here the Pharisees came and started disputing with him, demanding from him a sign from heaven, to put him to the test.[g] **12** So he sighed deeply in his spirit and said: "Why does this generation seek a sign?[h] Truly I say, no sign will be given to this generation."[i] **13** With that he left them, got aboard again, and went to the opposite shore.

14 However, they forgot to take bread along, and they had nothing with them in the boat except for one loaf.[a] **15** And he warned them in no uncertain terms: "Keep your eyes open; look out for the leaven of the Pharisees and the leaven of Herod."[b] **16** So they began arguing with one another over the fact that they had no bread. **17** Noting this, he said to them: "Why do you argue over your having no bread? Do you not yet perceive and understand? Are your hearts still dull in understanding? **18** 'Though having eyes, do you not see; and though having ears, do you not hear?' Do you not remember **19** when I broke the five loaves[c] for the 5,000 men, how many baskets full of fragments you collected?" They said to him: "Twelve."[d] **20** "When I broke the seven loaves for the 4,000 men, how many large baskets* full of fragments did you take up?" And they said to him: "Seven."[e] **21** With that he said to them: "Do you not yet understand?"

22 Now they put in at Beth·sa'i·da. Here people brought him a blind man, and they pleaded with him to touch him.[f] **23** And he took the blind man by the hand and brought him outside the village. After spitting on his eyes,[g] he laid his hands on him and asked him: "Do you see anything?" **24** The man looked up and said: "I see people, but they look like trees walking about." **25** Again he laid his hands on the man's eyes, and the man saw clearly. His sight was restored, and he could see everything distinctly. **26** So he sent him home, saying: "Do not enter into the village."

27 Jesus and his disciples now left for the villages of Caes·a·re'a Phi·lip'pi, and on the way he began to question his disciples, saying: "Who are people saying that I am?"[h] **28** They said to him: "John the Baptist,[i]

CHAP. 8
a Mt 14:14
  Mr 6:34

b Mt 15:32-38

c Mr 6:38

d Mr 6:41

e Mt 15:37

f Mt 15:39

g Mt 16:1-3

h Mt 12:38
  Joh 6:30

i Mt 16:4

Second Col.
a Mt 16:5-12

b Mt 16:6
  Lu 12:1

c Mr 6:38

d Mt 14:20
  Mr 6:43
  Lu 9:17
  Joh 6:13

e Mt 15:37

f Mr 6:56

g Mr 7:32, 33
  Joh 9:1, 6

h Mt 16:13-15
  Lu 9:18, 19

i Mt 14:1, 2
  Mr 6:14

8:3 *Or "fasting." 8:8, 20 *Or "provision baskets."

but others say E·li'jah,[a] and still others, one of the prophets." **29** And he put the question to them: "You, though, who do you say I am?" Peter answered him: "You are the Christ."[b] **30** At that he strictly ordered them not to tell anyone about him.[c] **31** Also, he began teaching them that the Son of man must undergo many sufferings and be rejected by the elders and the chief priests and the scribes and be killed,[d] and rise three days later.[e] **32** Indeed, he was making that statement openly. But Peter took him aside and began to rebuke him.[f] **33** At this he turned, looked at his disciples, and rebuked Peter, saying: "Get behind me, Satan! because you think, not God's thoughts, but those of men."[g]

34 He now called the crowd to him with his disciples and said to them: "If anyone wants to come after me, let him disown himself and pick up his torture stake* and keep following me.[h] **35** For whoever wants to save his life* will lose it, but whoever loses his life* for my sake and for the sake of the good news will save it.[i] **36** Really, what good will it do a man to gain the whole world and to lose his life?*[j] **37** What, really, would a man give in exchange for his life?*[k] **38** For whoever becomes ashamed of me and my words in this adulterous* and sinful generation, the Son of man will also be ashamed of him[l] when he comes in the glory of his Father with the holy angels."[m]

9 Furthermore, he said to them: "Truly I say to you that there are some of those standing here who will not taste death at all until first they see the Kingdom of God already having come in power."[n] **2** Six days later Je-

sus took Peter and James and John along and led them up into a lofty mountain by themselves. And he was transfigured before them;[a] **3** his outer garments began to glisten, becoming far whiter than any clothes cleaner on earth could whiten them. **4** Also, E·li'jah with Moses appeared to them, and they were conversing with Jesus. **5** Then Peter said to Jesus: "Rabbi, it is fine for us to be here. So let us erect three tents, one for you, one for Moses, and one for E·li'jah." **6** In fact, he did not know how to react, for they were quite fearful. **7** And a cloud formed, overshadowing them, and a voice[b] came out of the cloud: "This is my Son, the beloved.[c] Listen to him."[d] **8** Then suddenly they looked around and saw that no one was with them any longer except Jesus.

9 As they were coming down from the mountain, he strictly ordered them not to relate to anybody what they had seen[e] until after the Son of man had risen from the dead.[f] **10** They took the word to heart,* but discussed among themselves what this rising from the dead meant. **11** And they began to question him, saying: "Why do the scribes say that E·li'jah[g] must come first?"[h] **12** He said to them: "E·li'jah does come first and restore all things;[i] but how is it that it is written about the Son of man that he must undergo many sufferings[j] and be treated with contempt?[k] **13** But I say to you that E·li'jah,[l] in fact, has come, and they did to him whatever they wanted, just as it is written about him."[m]

14 When they came to the other disciples, they noticed a large crowd around them,

---

CHAP. 8

a Mr 9:11
b Mt 16:16
  Lu 9:20
  Joh 1:40, 41
  Joh 6:68, 69
c Mt 16:20
d Mt 16:16
  Lu 9:21, 22
d Mt 26:2
e Mt 16:21
  Mt 17:22, 23
f Mt 16:22
g Mt 16:23
h Mt 10:38
  Mt 16:24
  Lu 9:23
  Lu 14:27
i Mt 10:39
  Mt 16:25
  Lu 9:24
  Joh 12:25
  Re 12:11
j Mt 16:26
  Lu 9:25
k Ps 49:8
l Mt 10:33
  Lu 9:26
  Lu 12:9
  2Ti 1:7, 8
m Mt 16:27
  Mt 25:31
  2Th 1:7

CHAP. 9

n Mt 16:28
  Lu 9:27

Second Col.

a Mt 17:1-8
  Lu 9:28-36
b Lu 3:22
  Joh 12:28
c Ps 2:7
  Isa 42:1
  Mt 3:17
  2Pe 1:17
d De 18:15
  Mt 17:5
  Lu 9:35
  Ac 3:22, 23
e Mt 12:15, 16
  Mr 8:29, 30
f Mt 17:9
  Lu 9:36
g Mal 4:5, 6
  Mr 8:27, 28
h Mt 17:10
i Mt 17:11
j Da 9:26
k Ps 22:6, 7
  Isa 50:6
  Isa 53:3
  Lu 23:11
l Mt 11:13, 14
  Lu 1:13, 17
m Mt 17:12

8:34 *See Glossary. **8:35-37** *Or "soul." **8:38** *Or "unfaithful."

9:10 *Or "kept the matter to themselves."

and there were scribes arguing with them.[a] **15** But as soon as all the crowd caught sight of him, they were astonished, and they ran up to him to greet him. **16** So he asked them: "What are you arguing about with them?" **17** And one of the crowd answered him: "Teacher, I brought my son to you because he has a speechless spirit.[b] **18** Wherever it seizes him, it throws him to the ground, and he foams at the mouth and grinds his teeth and loses his strength. I asked your disciples to expel it, but they were not able to do so." **19** In response he said to them: "O faithless generation,[c] how long must I continue with you? How long must I put up with you? Bring him to me."[d] **20** So they brought the boy to him, but at the sight of him, the spirit at once threw the child into convulsions. After falling on the ground, he kept rolling about, foaming at the mouth. **21** Then Jesus asked the father: "How long has this been happening to him?" He said: "From childhood on, **22** and often it would throw him into the fire and also into the water to destroy him. But if you can do anything, have pity on us and help us." **23** Jesus said to him: "That expression, 'If you can'! Why, all things are possible for the one who has faith."[e] **24** Immediately the child's father cried out and said: "I have faith! Help me out where I need faith!"[f]

25 Jesus, now noticing that a crowd was rushing toward them, rebuked the unclean spirit, saying to it: "You speechless and deaf spirit, I order you, get out of him and do not enter into him again!"[g] **26** After crying out and going through many convulsions, it came out, and the child seemed to be dead, so that most of the people were say-

ing: "He is dead!" **27** But Jesus took him by the hand and raised him up, and he stood up. **28** So after he entered into a house, his disciples asked him privately: "Why could we not expel it?"[a] **29** He said to them: "This kind can come out only by prayer."

30 They departed from there and went through Gal'i·lee, but he did not want anyone to get to know about it. **31** For he was teaching his disciples and telling them: "The Son of man is going to be betrayed into men's hands, and they will kill him,[b] but despite being killed, he will rise three days later."[c] **32** However, they did not understand his statement, and they were afraid to question him.

33 And they came into Ca·per'na·um. Now when he was inside the house, he put the question to them: "What were you arguing about on the road?"[d] **34** They kept silent, for on the road they had been arguing among themselves about who is greater. **35** So he sat down and called the Twelve and said to them: "If anyone wants to be first, he must be last of all and minister of all."[e] **36** Then he took a young child and stood him in their midst; and putting his arms around him, he said to them: **37** "Whoever receives one of such young children[f] on the basis of my name receives me also; and whoever receives me receives not me only but also Him who sent me."[g]

38 John said to him: "Teacher, we saw someone expelling demons by using your name, and we tried to prevent him, because he was not following us."[h] **39** But Jesus said: "Do not try to prevent him, for there is no one who will do a powerful work on the basis of my name who will quickly be able to say anything

---

CHAP. 9
a Lu 9:37

b Mt 17:14-17
  Lu 9:38-42

c De 32:20

d Mt 17:17
  Lu 9:41

e Mt 17:20
  Mr 11:23
  Lu 17:6
  Joh 11:40
  Ac 14:9, 10

f Lu 17:5

g Mt 17:18
  Mr 1:23-25
  Lu 4:34, 35
  Ac 10:38

Second Col.
a Mt 17:19, 20

b Mt 26:2

c Mt 16:21
  Mt 17:22, 23
  Mr 8:31
  Lu 9:44, 45

d Mt 18:1-5
  Lu 9:46-48
  Lu 22:24

e Mt 20:26-28
  Mr 10:43-45
  Php 2:8, 9

f Lu 18:16

g Mt 10:40
  Lu 9:48
  Joh 13:20

h Lu 9:49

bad about me. **40** For whoever is not against us is for us.[a] **41** And whoever gives you a cup of water to drink because you belong to Christ,[b] I tell you truly, he will by no means lose his reward.[c] **42** But whoever stumbles one of these little ones who have faith, it would be better for him if a millstone that is turned by a donkey were put around his neck and he were pitched into the sea.[d]

43 "If ever your hand makes you stumble, cut it off. It is better for you to enter into life maimed than to go off with two hands into Ge·hen'na,* into the fire that cannot be put out.[e] **44** *— **45** And if your foot makes you stumble, cut it off. It is better for you to enter into life lame than to be thrown with two feet into Ge·hen'na.*[f] **46** *— **47** And if your eye makes you stumble, throw it away.[g] It is better for you to enter one-eyed into the Kingdom of God than to be thrown with two eyes into Ge·hen'na,*[h] **48** where the maggot does not die and the fire is not put out.[i]

49 "For everyone must be salted with fire.[j] **50** Salt is fine, but if the salt ever loses its saltiness, with what will you season it?[k] Have salt in yourselves,[l] and keep peace with one another."[m]

10 From there he got up and came to the borders* of Ju·de'a across the Jordan, and again crowds gathered to him. As he was accustomed to do, he again began teaching them.[n] **2** And Pharisees approached, intent on testing him, and they asked whether it was lawful for a man to divorce a wife.[o] **3** He answered them: "What did Moses command you?" **4** They said: "Moses allowed the writ-

ing of a certificate of dismissal and divorcing her."[a] **5** But Jesus said to them: "Out of regard for your hard-heartedness,[b] he wrote this commandment for you.[c] **6** However, from the beginning of creation, 'He made them male and female.[d] **7** For this reason a man will leave his father and his mother,[e] **8** and the two will be one flesh,'[f] so that they are no longer two, but one flesh. **9** Therefore, what God has yoked together, let no man put apart."[g] **10** When they were again in the house, the disciples began to question him about this. **11** He said to them: "Whoever divorces his wife and marries another commits adultery[h] against her, **12** and if ever a woman after divorcing her husband marries another, she commits adultery."[i]

13 People now began bringing him young children for him to touch them, but the disciples reprimanded them.[j] **14** At seeing this, Jesus was indignant and said to them: "Let the young children come to me; do not try to stop them, for the Kingdom of God belongs to such ones.[k] **15** Truly I say to you, whoever does not receive the Kingdom of God like a young child will by no means enter into it."[l] **16** And he took the children into his arms and began blessing them, laying his hands on them.[m]

17 As he was going on his way, a man ran up and fell on his knees before him and put the question to him: "Good Teacher, what must I do to inherit everlasting life?"[n] **18** Jesus said to him: "Why do you call me good? Nobody is good except one, God.[o] **19** You know the commandments: 'Do not murder,[p] do not commit adultery,[q] do not steal,[r] do not bear false witness,[s] do not defraud,[t] honor

9:43, 45, 47 *See Glossary. 9:44, 46 *See App. A3. 10:1 *Or "frontiers."

your father and your mother.'"[a] **20** The man said to him: "Teacher, all these things I have kept from my youth on." **21** Jesus looked at him and felt love for him and said, "One thing is missing about you: Go, sell what things you have and give to the poor, and you will have treasure in heaven; and come be my follower."[b] **22** But he grew sad at the answer and went away grieved, for he had many possessions.[c]

23 After looking around, Jesus said to his disciples: "How difficult it will be for those with money to enter into the Kingdom of God!"[d] **24** But the disciples were surprised at his words. Jesus then responded: "Children, how difficult it is to enter into the Kingdom of God! **25** It is easier for a camel to go through a needle's eye than for a rich man to enter into the Kingdom of God."[e] **26** They became still more astounded and said to him:* "Who possibly can be saved?"[f] **27** Looking straight at them, Jesus said: "With men it is impossible but not so with God, for all things are possible with God."[g] **28** Peter began to say to him: "Look! We have left all things and followed you."[h] **29** Jesus said: "Truly I say to you, no one has left house or brothers or sisters or mother or father or children or fields for my sake and for the sake of the good news[i] **30** who will not get 100 times more now in this period of time—houses, brothers, sisters, mothers, children, and fields, with persecutions[j]—and in the coming system of things,* everlasting life. **31** But many who are first will be last, and the last first."[k]

32 Now they were going on the road up to Jerusalem, and Jesus was going ahead of them, and they were astonished, but those who followed began to fear. Once again he took the Twelve aside and started to tell them these things that were about to happen to him:[a] **33** "Look! We are going up to Jerusalem, and the Son of man will be handed over to the chief priests and the scribes. They will condemn him to death and hand him over to men of the nations, **34** and these will mock him and spit on him and scourge him and kill him, but three days later he will rise."[b]

35 James and John, the sons of Zeb′e·dee,[c] approached him and said to him: "Teacher, we want you to do for us whatever we ask of you."[d] **36** He said to them: "What do you want me to do for you?" **37** They replied: "Grant us to sit down, one at your right hand and one at your left, in your glory."[e] **38** But Jesus said to them: "You do not know what you are asking for. Can you drink the cup that I am drinking or be baptized with the baptism with which I am being baptized?"[f] **39** They said to him: "We can." At that Jesus said to them: "The cup I am drinking, you will drink, and with the baptism with which I am being baptized, you will be baptized.[g] **40** However, to sit down at my right hand or at my left is not mine to give, but it belongs to those for whom it has been prepared."

41 When the ten others heard about it, they became indignant at James and John.[h] **42** But Jesus called them to him and said to them: "You know that those who appear to be* ruling the

---

CHAP. 10

a Ex 20:12
　De 5:16
　Eph 6:2

b Mt 19:21

c Lu 18:23

d Jer 9:23
　1Ti 6:17

e Mt 19:24
　Lu 18:25

f Mt 19:25, 26
　Lu 18:26, 27

g Job 42:2

h Mt 19:27
　Lu 18:28

i Mt 10:37
　Mt 19:29
　Lu 18:29, 30

j Mt 5:11
　Ac 14:22

k Mt 19:30
　Mt 20:16
　Lu 13:30

Second Col.

a Mt 20:17-19
　Mr 8:31
　Mr 9:31
　Lu 9:22
　Lu 18:31-33

b Ac 10:40
　1Co 15:3, 4

c Mt 10:2

d Mt 20:20, 21

e Mt 19:28

f Mt 20:22, 23
　Lu 12:50
　Joh 18:11
　Ro 6:3

g Ac 12:2
　Re 1:9

h Mt 20:24

10:26 *Or possibly, "to one another." 10:30 *Or "the coming age." See Glossary.

10:42 *Or "those who are recognized as."

nations lord it over them and their great ones wield authority over them.[a] **43** This must not be the way among you; but whoever wants to become great among you must be your minister,[b] **44** and whoever wants to be first among you must be the slave of all. **45** For even the Son of man came, not to be ministered to, but to minister[c] and to give his life* as a ransom in exchange for many."[d]

46 They then came into Jer′i·cho. But as he and his disciples and a considerable crowd were going out of Jer′i·cho, Bar·ti·mae′us (the son of Ti·mae′us), a blind beggar, was sitting beside the road.[e] **47** When he heard that it was Jesus the Naz·a·rene′, he started shouting and saying: "Son of David,[f] Jesus, have mercy on me!"[g] **48** At this many began rebuking him, telling him to be silent, but all the more he kept shouting: "Son of David, have mercy on me!" **49** So Jesus stopped and said: "Call him to me." So they called the blind man, saying to him: "Take courage! Get up; he is calling you." **50** Throwing off his outer garment, he leaped to his feet and went to Jesus. **51** Then Jesus said to him: "What do you want me to do for you?" The blind man said to him: "Rab·bo′-ni,* let me recover my sight." **52** And Jesus said to him: "Go. Your faith has made you well."[h] And immediately he recovered his sight,[i] and he began to follow him on the road.

11 Now when they were getting near to Jerusalem, to Beth′pha·ge and Beth′a·ny[j] at the Mount of Olives, he sent two of his disciples[k] **2** and told them: "Go into the village that is within sight, and as soon as you enter it, you will find a colt tied on which no man has sat until now. Untie it and bring it here. **3** And if anyone says to you, 'Why are you doing this?' say, 'The Lord needs it and will send it back here right away.'" **4** So they went away and found the colt tied at a door, outside on the side street, and they untied it.[a] **5** But some of those standing there said to them: "What are you doing untying the colt? **6** They told them just what Jesus had said, and they let them go.

7 And they brought the colt[b] to Jesus, and they put their outer garments on it, and he sat on it.[c] **8** Also, many spread their outer garments on the road, but others cut down foliage from the fields.[d] **9** And those going in front and those coming behind kept shouting: "Save, we pray![e] Blessed is the one who comes in Jehovah's* name![f] **10** Blessed is the coming Kingdom of our father David![g] Save, we pray, in the heights above!" **11** And he entered Jerusalem and went into the temple, and he looked around at everything, but since the hour was already late, he went out to Beth′a·ny with the Twelve.[h]

12 The next day when they were leaving Beth′a·ny, he felt hungry.[i] **13** From a distance he caught sight of a fig tree that had leaves, and he went to see whether he could find something on it. But on coming to it, he found nothing but leaves, for it was not the season for figs. **14** So he said to it: "Let no one eat fruit from you ever again."[j] And his disciples were listening.

15 They now came to Jerusalem. There he entered the temple and started to throw out those selling and buying in the

---

CHAP. 10
a Mt 20:25
 Lu 22:25
 1Pe 5:2, 3

b Mt 20:26, 27
 Mr 9:35
 Lu 9:48
 Lu 22:26

c Joh 13:14
 Php 2:7

d Isa 53:10
 Da 9:24
 Mt 20:28
 Ga 3:13
 Tit 2:13, 14

e Mt 20:29-34
 Lu 18:35-43

f Jer 23:5
 Ro 1:3

g Mt 9:27
 Mt 15:22

h Mt 9:20, 22

i Isa 35:5
 Isa 42:7
 Mr 8:25

CHAP. 11
j Joh 11:18

k Mt 21:1-3
 Lu 19:29-34

Second Col.
a Mt 21:6

b 1Ki 1:33
 Zec 9:9

c Mt 21:7, 8
 Joh 12:14, 15

d Lu 19:36
 Joh 12:13

e Mt 21:15

f Ps 118:25, 26
 Mt 21:9
 Lu 19:37, 38
 Joh 12:13

g Zec 9:9
 Lu 1:32

h Mt 21:10

i Mt 21:18

j Mt 21:19
 Mr 11:20

10:45 *Or "soul." 10:51 *Meaning "Teacher."

11:9 *See App. A5.

temple, and he overturned the tables of the money changers and the benches of those selling doves,[a] 16 and he would not let anyone carry a utensil through the temple. 17 He was teaching and saying to them: "Is it not written, 'My house is to be called a house of prayer for all the nations'?[b] But you have made it a cave of robbers."[c] 18 And the chief priests and the scribes heard it, and they began to seek how to kill him;[d] for they were in fear of him, because all the crowd was astounded at his teaching.[e]

19 When it became late in the day, they went out of the city. 20 But when they were passing by early in the morning, they saw the fig tree already withered from its roots.[f] 21 Peter, remembering it, said to him: "Rabbi, see! the fig tree that you cursed has withered."[g] 22 In reply Jesus said to them: "Have faith in God. 23 Truly I say to you that whoever tells this mountain, 'Be lifted up and thrown into the sea,' and does not doubt in his heart but has faith that what he says is going to happen, he will have it happen.[h] 24 This is why I tell you, all the things you pray and ask for, have faith that you have received them, and you will have them.[i] 25 And when you stand praying, forgive whatever you have against anyone, so that your Father who is in the heavens may also forgive you your trespasses."[j] 26 *—

27 They came again to Jerusalem. And as he was walking in the temple, the chief priests and the scribes and the elders came 28 and said to him: "By what authority do you do these things? Or who gave you this authority to do these things?"[k] 29 Jesus said to them: "I will ask you one question. Answer me, and I will tell you by what authority I do these things. 30 Was the baptism by John[a] from heaven or from men?* Answer me."[b] 31 So they began to reason among themselves, saying: "If we say, 'From heaven,' he will say, 'Why, then, did you not believe him?' 32 But dare we say, 'From men'?" They were in fear of the crowd, for these all held that John had really been a prophet.[c] 33 So they answered Jesus: "We do not know." Jesus said to them: "Neither am I telling you by what authority I do these things."

12 Then he started to speak to them with illustrations: "A man planted a vineyard[d] and put a fence around it and dug a vat for the winepress and erected a tower;[e] then he leased it to cultivators and traveled abroad.[f] 2 In due season he sent a slave to the cultivators to collect some of the fruits of the vineyard from them. 3 But they took him, beat him, and sent him away empty-handed. 4 Again he sent another slave to them, and that one they struck on the head and dishonored.[g] 5 And he sent another, and that one they killed, and many others, some of whom they beat and some of whom they killed. 6 One more he had, a beloved son.[h] He sent him to them last, saying, 'They will respect my son.' 7 But those cultivators said among themselves, 'This is the heir.[i] Come, let us kill him, and the inheritance will be ours.' 8 So they took him and killed him and threw him out of the vineyard.[j] 9 What will the owner of the vineyard do? He will come and kill the cultivators and will give the vineyard to others.[k] 10 Did you never read

CHAP. 11
a Mt 21:12
  Lu 19:45, 46
  Joh 2:14-16

b 1Ki 8:43
  Isa 56:7

c Jer 7:11
  Mt 21:13
  Lu 19:46
  Joh 2:16

d Mt 14:1
  Lu 20:19

e Lu 19:47, 48

f Mt 21:19, 20

g Mr 11:14

h Mt 17:20
  Mt 21:21
  Lu 17:6

i Mt 7:7
  Mt 18:19
  Mt 21:22
  Lu 11:9
  Joh 14:13
  Joh 15:7
  Joh 16:24

j Ps 103:10-12
  Mt 6:12, 14
  Eph 4:32
  Col 3:13

k Mt 21:23-27
  Lu 20:1-8

Second Col.
a Mr 1:4

b Mt 21:25
  Lu 20:4

c Mt 3:1, 5
  Mt 14:3, 5
  Mr 6:20

CHAP. 12
d Isa 5:7

e Isa 5:2

f Mt 21:33-41
  Lu 20:9-16

g Heb 11:32, 37

h Ps 2:7
  Ga 4:4
  1Jo 4:9

i Ps 2:8
  Heb 1:2

j Ac 2:23

k Mt 21:41, 43

11:26 *See App. A3.

11:30 *Or "of human origin?"

this scripture: 'The stone that the builders rejected, this has become the chief cornerstone.'*[a] 11 This has come from Jehovah,* and it is marvelous in our eyes'?"[b]

12 At that they wanted to seize* him, but they feared the crowd, for they knew that he spoke the illustration with them in mind. So they left him and went away.[c]

13 Next they sent to him some of the Pharisees and of the party followers of Herod in order to catch him in his speech.[d] 14 On arriving, these said to him: "Teacher, we know you are truthful and you do not seek anyone's favor, for you do not look at the outward appearance of people, but you teach the way of God in line with truth. Is it lawful* to pay head tax to Caesar or not? 15 Should we pay, or should we not pay?" Detecting their hypocrisy, he said to them: "Why do you put me to the test? Bring me a de·nar'i·us* to look at." 16 They brought one, and he said to them: "Whose image and inscription is this?" They said to him: "Caesar's." 17 Jesus then said: "Pay back Caesar's things to Caesar,[e] but God's things to God."[f] And they were amazed at him.

18 Now the Sadducees, who say there is no resurrection,[g] came and asked him:[h] 19 "Teacher, Moses wrote us that if someone's brother dies and leaves a wife behind but does not leave a child, his brother should take the wife and raise up offspring for his brother.[i] 20 There were seven brothers. The first took a wife, but when he died he left no offspring.

21 And the second married her but died without leaving offspring, and the third the same way. 22 And all seven left no offspring. Last of all, the woman also died. 23 In the resurrection, whose wife will she be? For the seven had her as a wife." 24 Jesus said to them: "Is not this why you are mistaken, because you know neither the Scriptures nor the power of God?[a] 25 For when they rise from the dead, neither do men marry nor are women given in marriage, but they are as angels in the heavens.[b] 26 But concerning the dead being raised up, have you not read in the book of Moses, in the account about the thornbush, that God said to him: 'I am the God of Abraham and God of Isaac and God of Jacob'?[c] 27 He is a God, not of the dead, but of the living. You are very much mistaken."[d]

28 One of the scribes who had come up and heard them disputing, knowing that he had answered them in a fine way, asked him: "Which commandment is first* of all?"[e] 29 Jesus answered: "The first is, 'Hear, O Israel, Jehovah* our God is one Jehovah,* 30 and you must love Jehovah* your God with your whole heart and with your whole soul* and with your whole mind and with your whole strength.'[f] 31 The second is this, 'You must love your neighbor as yourself.'[g] There is no other commandment greater than these." 32 The scribe said to him: "Teacher, you spoke well, in line with truth, 'He is One, and there is no other besides him';[h] 33 and to love him with one's whole heart, with one's whole understanding, and with one's whole strength and

---

CHAP. 12
a Mt 21:42
Lu 20:17
Ac 4:10, 11
Eph 2:20
1Pe 2:7

b Ps 118:22, 23

c Mt 21:45, 46
Lu 20:19

d Mt 22:15-22
Lu 20:20-26

e Ro 13:7
Tit 3:1
1Pe 2:13

f Mal 3:8
Mt 22:21
Lu 20:25

g Ac 23:8

h Mt 22:23-28
Lu 20:27-33

i Ge 38:7, 8
De 25:5, 6

Second Col.
a Mt 22:29

b Mt 22:30
Lu 20:34-36

c Ex 3:2, 6
Mt 22:31
Lu 20:37

d Mt 22:32
Lu 20:38

e Mt 22:34-36

f De 6:4, 5
Jos 22:5
Mt 22:37
Lu 10:27

g Le 19:18
Mt 22:39, 40
Ro 13:9
Ga 5:14
Jas 2:8

h De 4:39
De 6:4
Isa 45:21

12:10 *Lit., "the head of the corner."
12:11, 29, 30 *See App. A5. 12:12 *Or "arrest." 12:14 *Or "right." 12:15 *See App. B14.

12:28 *Or "most important." 12:30 *See Glossary.

to love one's neighbor as oneself is worth far more than all the whole burnt offerings and sacrifices."[a] **34** At this Jesus, discerning that he had answered intelligently, said to him: "You are not far from the Kingdom of God." But no one had the courage to question him anymore.[b]

35 However, as Jesus continued teaching in the temple, he said: "How is it that the scribes say that the Christ is David's son?[c] **36** By the holy spirit,[d] David himself said, 'Jehovah* said to my Lord: "Sit at my right hand until I put your enemies beneath your feet."'[e] **37** David himself calls him Lord, so how can it be that he is his son?"[f]

And the large crowd was listening to him with pleasure. **38** And in his teaching he went on to say: "Beware of the scribes who want to walk around in robes and want greetings in the marketplaces[g] **39** and front* seats in the synagogues and the most prominent places at evening meals.[h] **40** They devour the houses* of the widows, and for show# they make long prayers. These will receive a more severe△ judgment."

41 And he sat down with the treasury chests*[i] in view and began observing how the crowd was dropping money into the treasury chests, and many rich people were dropping in many coins.[j] **42** Now a poor widow came and dropped in two small coins of very little value.*[k] **43** So he called his disciples to him and said to them: "Truly I say to you that this poor widow put in more than all the others who put money into the treasury

chests.[a] **44** For they all put in out of their surplus, but she, out of her want,* put in everything she had, all she had to live on."[b]

13 As he was going out of the temple, one of his disciples said to him: "Teacher, see! what wonderful stones and buildings!"[c] **2** However, Jesus said to him: "Do you see these great buildings? By no means will a stone be left here upon a stone and not be thrown down."[d]

3 As he was sitting on the Mount of Olives with the temple in view, Peter, James, John, and Andrew asked him privately: **4** "Tell us, when will these things be, and what will be the sign when all these things are to come to a conclusion?"[e] **5** So Jesus began to tell them: "Look out that nobody misleads you.[f] **6** Many will come on the basis of my name, saying, 'I am he,' and will mislead many. **7** Moreover, when you hear of wars and reports of wars, do not be alarmed; these things must take place, but the end is not yet.[g]

8 "For nation will rise against nation and kingdom against kingdom;[h] there will be earthquakes in one place after another; there will also be food shortages.[i] These are a beginning of pangs of distress.[j]

9 "As for you, look out for yourselves. People will hand you over to local courts,[k] and you will be beaten in synagogues[l] and be put on the stand before governors and kings for my sake, for a witness to them.[m] **10** Also, in all the nations, the good news has to be preached first.[n] **11** And when they are taking you to hand you over, do not be anxious beforehand about what to say; but whatever is given you in that hour, say this, for you are not the ones speaking,

---

CHAP. 12
a De 6:5
  1Sa 15:22
  Ho 6:6
b Mt 22:46
c Mt 22:42-45
  Lu 20:41-44
  Joh 7:42
d 2Sa 23:2
  2Ti 3:16
  2Pe 1:21
e Ps 110:1
  Ac 2:34, 35
  1Co 15:25
  Heb 1:13
f Ro 1:3
  Re 22:16
g Lu 20:45-47
h Mt 23:6, 7
  Lu 11:43
i 2Ki 12:9
j Lu 21:1
k Lu 21:2

Second Col.
a Lu 21:3
  2Co 8:12
b Lu 21:4

CHAP. 13
c Mt 24:1
  Lu 21:5
d Le 26:31
  Mt 24:2
  Lu 19:44
  Lu 21:6
e Mt 24:3
  Lu 21:7
f Mt 24:4, 5
  Lu 21:8
g Mt 24:6
  Lu 21:9
h Re 6:4
i Mt 24:7
  Lu 21:10, 11
  Re 6:6, 8
j Mt 24:8
k Ac 4:15
l Mt 10:17
  Joh 16:2
m Lu 21:12, 13
  2Ti 3:12
  Re 2:10
n Mt 24:14
  Ro 10:18
  Re 14:6

12:36 *See App. A5.   12:39 *Or "best." 12:40 *Or "property."   #Or "for a pretext."   △Or "a heavier."   12:41 *Or "receptacles."   12:42 *Lit., "two lepta, which is a quadrans." See App. B14.

12:44 *Or "poverty."

but the holy spirit is.[a] **12** Furthermore, brother will deliver brother over to death, and a father a child, and children will rise up against parents and have them put to death.[b] **13** And you will be hated by all people on account of my name.[c] But the one who has endured* to the end[d] will be saved.[e]

14 "However, when you catch sight of the disgusting thing that causes desolation[f] standing where it should not be (let the reader use discernment), then let those in Ju·deʹa begin fleeing to the mountains.[g] **15** Let the man on the housetop not come down nor go inside to take anything out of his house; **16** and let the man in the field not return to the things behind to pick up his outer garment. **17** Woe to the pregnant women and those nursing a baby in those days![h] **18** Keep praying that it may not occur in wintertime; **19** for those days will be days of a tribulation[i] such as has not occurred from the beginning of the creation that God created until that time, and will not occur again.[j] **20** In fact, unless Jehovah* had cut short the days, no flesh would be saved. But on account of the chosen ones whom he has chosen, he has cut short the days.[k]

21 "Then, too, if anyone says to you, 'See! Here is the Christ,' or, 'See! There he is,' do not believe it.[l] **22** For false Christs and false prophets will arise[m] and will perform signs and wonders to lead astray, if possible, the chosen ones. **23** You, then, watch out.[n] I have told you all things beforehand.

24 "But in those days, after that tribulation, the sun will be darkened, and the moon will not give its light,[a] **25** and the stars will be falling out of heaven, and the powers that are in the heavens will be shaken. **26** And then they will see the Son of man[b] coming in the clouds with great power and glory.[c] **27** And then he will send out the angels and will gather his chosen ones together from the four winds, from earth's extremity to heaven's extremity.[d]

28 "Now learn this illustration from the fig tree: Just as soon as its young branch grows tender and sprouts its leaves, you know that summer is near.[e] **29** Likewise also you, when you see these things happening, know that he is near at the doors.[f] **30** Truly I say to you that this generation will by no means pass away until all these things happen.[g] **31** Heaven and earth will pass away,[h] but my words will by no means pass away.[i]

32 "Concerning that day or the hour nobody knows, neither the angels in heaven nor the Son, but the Father.[j] **33** Keep looking, keep awake,[k] for you do not know when the appointed time is.[l] **34** It is like a man traveling abroad who left his house and gave the authority to his slaves,[m] to each one his work, and commanded the doorkeeper to keep on the watch.[n] **35** Keep on the watch, therefore, for you do not know when the master of the house is coming,[o] whether late in the day or at midnight or at dawn* or early in the morning,[p] **36** in order that when he comes suddenly, he does not find you sleeping.[q] **37** But what I say to you, I say to all: Keep on the watch."[r]

14 Now the Passover[s] and the Festival of Unleavened Bread[t] was two days later.[u] And the chief priests and the scribes

---

13:35 *Lit., "when the rooster crows."

CHAP. 13

a Ex 4:12
  Mt 10:19, 20
  Lu 12:11, 12
  Lu 21:14, 15
  Ac 4:8
  Ac 6:9, 10
b Mic 7:6
  Mt 10:21
  Lu 21:16
  2Ti 3:1, 3
c Lu 21:17
d 2Ti 4:7
  Heb 3:6
e Mt 10:22
  Mt 24:13
  Lu 21:19
  Re 2:10
f Da 9:27
  Da 11:31
g Mt 24:15-20
  Lu 21:20-23
h Lu 21:23
  Lu 23:28
i Re 7:14
j Da 12:1
  Mt 24:21
k Mt 24:22
l Mt 24:23, 24
  Lu 17:23
  Lu 21:8
  1Jo 4:1
m Mt 7:15
n Mt 24:42
  Eph 6:18
  2Pe 3:17

Second Col.

a Mt 24:29
  Lu 21:25, 26
b Da 7:13
c Mt 24:30
  Lu 21:27
  Re 1:7
d Mt 24:31
e Mt 24:32
  Lu 21:29-33
f Mt 24:33
g Mt 24:34
  Lu 21:32
h Isa 51:6
i Jos 23:14
  Isa 40:8
  Mt 24:35
j Mt 24:36
  Ac 1:7
k Ro 13:11
  1Th 5:6
l Mt 25:13
  Lu 21:34
m Mt 25:14
n Lu 12:35, 36
o Mt 24:42
p Lu 21:36
q Mt 25:5
r Hab 2:3

CHAP. 14

s Ex 12:3, 6
  Le 23:5
t Le 23:6
u Joh 13:1

were looking for a way to seize* him by cunning# and kill him;[a] 2 for they were saying: "Not at the festival; perhaps there might be an uproar of the people."

3 And while he was at Beth'a·ny dining* in the house of Simon the leper, a woman came with an alabaster jar of perfumed oil, genuine nard, very expensive. She broke open the alabaster jar and began pouring it on his head.[b] 4 At this some said to one another indignantly: "Why has this perfumed oil been wasted? 5 For this perfumed oil could have been sold for more than 300 de·nar'i·i* and the money given to the poor!" And they were greatly annoyed with# her. 6 But Jesus said: "Let her alone. Why do you try to make trouble for her? She did a fine deed toward me.[c] 7 For you always have the poor with you,[d] and you can do them good whenever you want to, but you will not always have me.[e] 8 She did what she could; she poured perfumed oil on my body beforehand, in view of the burial.[f] 9 Truly I say to you, wherever the good news is preached in all the world,[g] what this woman did will also be told in memory of her."[h]

10 And Judas Is·car'i·ot, one of the Twelve, went off to the chief priests in order to betray him to them.[i] 11 When they heard it, they were delighted and promised to give him silver money.[j] So he began seeking an opportunity to betray him.

12 Now on the first day of the Unleavened Bread,[k] when they customarily offered up the Passover sacrifice,[l] his disciples said to him: "Where do you want us

---

14:1 *Or "arrest." #Or "crafty device." 14:3 *Or "reclining at the table." 14:5 *See App. B14. #Or "they spoke angrily to; they scolded."

to go and prepare for you to eat the Passover?"[a] 13 With that he sent two of his disciples and said to them: "Go into the city, and a man carrying an earthenware water jar will meet you. Follow him,[b] 14 and wherever he goes inside, say to the master of the house, 'The Teacher says: "Where is the guest room where I may eat the Passover with my disciples?"' 15 And he will show you a large upper room, furnished and ready. Prepare it for us there." 16 So the disciples went out, and they entered the city and found it just as he said to them, and they prepared for the Passover.

17 After evening had fallen, he came with the Twelve.[c] 18 And as they were reclining at the table and eating, Jesus said: "Truly I say to you, one of you who is eating with me will betray me."[d] 19 They began to be grieved and to say to him one by one: "It is not I, is it?" 20 He said to them: "It is one of the Twelve, the one dipping with me into the bowl.[e] 21 For the Son of man is going away, just as it is written about him, but woe to that man through whom the Son of man is betrayed!" It would have been better for that man if he had not been born."[g]

22 And as they continued eating, he took a loaf, said a blessing, broke it, and gave it to them, saying: "Take it; this means my body."[h] 23 And taking a cup, he offered thanks and gave it to them, and they all drank out of it.[i] 24 And he said to them: "This means my 'blood'[j] of the covenant,'[k] which is to be poured out in behalf of many.[l] 25 Truly I say to you, I will by no means drink anymore of the product of the vine until that day when I drink it new in the Kingdom of God." 26 Finally, after singing

---

CHAP. 14
a Mt 26:2-5
  Lu 22:1, 2

b Mt 26:6-9
  Joh 12:2-5

c Mt 26:10
  Joh 12:7

d De 15:11

e Mt 26:11
  Joh 12:8

f Mt 26:12
  Joh 12:7

g Mt 24:14

h Mt 26:13

i Mt 26:14-16
  Lu 22:3-6

j Zec 11:12

k Ex 12:15, 18
  Ex 23:15

l Lu 22:1, 7

Second Col.
a Nu 9:2
  Mt 26:17-19

b Lu 22:10-13

c Mt 26:20
  Lu 22:14

d Ps 41:9
  Mt 26:21, 22
  Lu 22:21, 23
  Joh 13:21, 22

e Mt 26:23

f Lu 22:22

g Mt 26:24

h Mt 26:26
  Lu 22:19
  1Co 11:23, 24

i Mt 26:27
  1Co 10:16
  1Co 11:25

j Ex 24:8
  Le 17:11
  Heb 9:22

k Jer 31:31
  Heb 7:22
  Heb 9:15

l Isa 53:12
  Mt 26:28
  Lu 22:20

praises,* they went out to the Mount of Olives.[a]

27 And Jesus said to them: "You will all be stumbled, for it is written: 'I will strike the shepherd,[b] and the sheep will be scattered about.'[c] **28** But after I have been raised up, I will go ahead of you into Gal'i·lee."[d] **29** But Peter said to him: "Even if all the others are stumbled, I will not be."[e] **30** At that Jesus said to him: "Truly I say to you that today, yes, on this very night, before a rooster crows twice, you will disown me three times."[f] **31** But he kept insisting: "If I have to die with you, I will by no means disown you." Also, all the others began to say the same thing.[g]

32 So they came to a spot named Geth·sem'a·ne, and he said to his disciples: "Sit down here while I pray."[h] **33** And he took Peter and James and John along with him,[i] and he began to feel deeply distressed* and to be greatly troubled. **34** He said to them: "I am* deeply grieved,[j] even to death. Stay here and keep on the watch."[k] **35** And going a little way forward, he fell to the ground and began praying that, if it were possible, the hour might pass away from him. **36** And he said: "*Abba,* Father,[l] all things are possible for you; remove this cup from me. Yet, not what I want, but what you want."[m] **37** He returned and found them sleeping, and he said to Peter: "Simon, are you sleeping? Did you not have the strength to keep on the watch for one hour?[n] **38** Keep on the watch and pray continually, so that you do not come into temptation.[o] The spirit, of course, is

eager,* but the flesh is weak."[a] **39** And he went away again and prayed, saying the same thing.[b] **40** And he came again and found them sleeping, for their eyes were weighed down, so they did not know what to answer him. **41** And he returned the third time and said to them: "At such a time as this, you are sleeping and resting! It is enough! The hour has come![c] Look! The Son of man is being betrayed into the hands of sinners. **42** Get up, let us go. Look! My betrayer has drawn near."[d]

43 And immediately, while he was still speaking, Judas, one of the Twelve, arrived and with him a crowd with swords and clubs, sent from the chief priests and the scribes and the elders.[e] **44** Now his betrayer had given them an agreed sign, saying: "Whoever it is I kiss, he is the one; take him into custody, and lead him away under guard." **45** And he came straight up and approached him and said, "Rabbi!" and gave him a tender kiss. **46** So they seized him and took him into custody. **47** However, one of those standing by drew his sword and struck the slave of the high priest, taking off his ear.[f] **48** But in response Jesus said to them: "Did you come out to arrest me with swords and clubs as against a robber?[g] **49** Day after day I was with you in the temple teaching,[h] and yet you did not take me into custody. Nevertheless, this is to fulfill the Scriptures."[i]

50 And they all abandoned him and fled.[j] **51** However, a certain young man wearing only a fine linen garment over his naked body began to follow him nearby, and they tried to seize him, **52** but he left his linen

---

CHAP. 14

a Mt 26:30
Lu 22:39
Joh 18:1

b Isa 53:5
Da 9:26

c Zec 13:7
Mt 26:31-33
Mt 26:56
Mr 14:50
Joh 16:32

d Mr 16:7

e Lu 22:31-33
Joh 13:37

f Mt 26:34
Lu 22:34
Joh 13:38

g Mt 26:35

h Mt 26:36, 37
Lu 22:39-41
Joh 18:1

i Mr 9:2

j Joh 12:27

k Mt 26:38

l Ro 8:15
Ga 4:6

m Mt 26:39
Lu 22:42
Joh 6:38
Heb 5:7

n Mt 26:40
Lu 22:45

o Mt 6:13
Lu 11:4
Lu 22:46

Second Col.

a Mt 26:41
Ro 7:23

b Mt 26:42-46

c Joh 13:1

d Joh 18:2

e Mt 26:47-51
Lu 22:47-51
Joh 18:3

f Mt 26:51
Lu 22:50
Joh 18:10

g Mt 26:55, 56
Lu 22:52, 53

h Lu 19:47
Joh 18:20

i Ps 22:6
Isa 53:7
Da 9:26
Lu 22:37

j Zec 13:7
Mt 26:31
Joh 16:32

14:26 *Or "hymns; psalms." 14:33 *Or "feel stunned." 14:34 *Or "My soul is." 14:36 *An Aramaic word meaning "O Father!"

14:38 *Or "willing."

garment behind and got away naked.*

53 They now led Jesus away to the high priest,ᵃ and all the chief priests and the elders and the scribes assembled.ᵇ **54** But Peter, from a good distance, followed him as far as into the courtyard of the high priest; and he was sitting together with the house attendants and warming himself before a bright fire.ᶜ **55** Now the chief priests and the entire San'he·drin were looking for testimony against Jesus in order to put him to death, but they were not finding any.ᵈ **56** Many, indeed, were giving false witness against him,ᵉ but their testimonies were not in agreement. **57** Also, certain ones were standing up and bearing false witness against him, saying: **58** "We heard him say, 'I will throw down this temple that was made with hands, and in three days I will build another not made with hands.'"ᶠ **59** But even on these grounds, their testimony was not in agreement.

60 Then the high priest stood up in their midst and questioned Jesus, saying: "Do you say nothing in reply? What is it these men are testifying against you?"ᵍ **61** But he kept silent and made no reply at all.ʰ Again the high priest began to question him and said to him: "Are you the Christ the Son of the Blessed One?" **62** Then Jesus said: "I am; and you will see the Son of manⁱ sitting at the right handʲ of power and coming with the clouds of heaven."ᵏ **63** At this the high priest ripped his garments and said: "What further need do we have of witnesses?ˡ **64** You heard the blasphemy. What is your decision?"ᵏ They all con-

demned him as deserving of death.ᵃ **65** And some started to spit on himᵇ and to cover his face and hit him with their fists and say to him: "Prophesy!" And slapping him in the face, the court attendants took him.ᶜ

66 Now while Peter was below in the courtyard, one of the servant girls of the high priest came.ᵈ **67** On seeing Peter warming himself, she looked straight at him and said: "You too were with the Naz·a·rene', this Jesus." **68** But he denied it, saying: "Neither do I know him nor do I understand what you are talking about," and he went outside to the entryway.* **69** There the servant girl saw him and again began to say to those standing by: "This is one of them." **70** Again he was denying it. And after a little while, those standing by again began saying to Peter: "Certainly you are one of them, for you are, in fact, a Gal·i·le'an." **71** But he started to curse and swear: "I do not know this man of whom you speak!" **72** Immediately a rooster crowed a second time,ᵉ and Peter recalled what Jesus had said to him: "Before a rooster crows twice, you will disown me three times."ᶠ And he broke down and began to weep.

15 Immediately at dawn, the chief priests with the elders and the scribes, indeed, the whole San'he·drin, consulted together, and they bound Jesus and led him off and handed him over to Pilate.ᵍ **2** So Pilate put the question to him: "Are you the King of the Jews?"ʰ In answer he said: "You yourself say it."ⁱ **3** But the chief priests were accusing him of many things. **4** Now Pilate began questioning him again, saying: "Have you no reply to make?ʲ See how

---

CHAP. 14
a Joh 18:13
b Mt 26:57
  Lu 22:54, 55
c Mt 26:58
  Joh 18:15
d Mt 26:59, 60
e Ps 35:11
f Mt 26:61
  Mr 15:29
  Joh 2:19
g Mt 26:62, 63
h Isa 53:7
  1Pe 2:23
i Da 7:13
j Ps 110:1
  Eph 1:20
  Col 3:1
k Mt 24:30
  Mt 26:64
  Lu 21:27
  Re 1:7
l Mt 26:65, 66

Second Col.
a Le 24:16
  Joh 19:7
b Isa 50:6
  Isa 53:3
  Mt 26:67, 68
c Lu 22:63-65
d Mt 26:69-75
  Lu 22:55-62
  Joh 18:25, 26
e Joh 18:27
f Mt 26:34
  Mr 14:30
  Lu 22:34
  Joh 13:38

CHAP. 15
g Ps 2:2
  Mt 27:1, 2
  Lu 22:66
  Joh 18:28
  Ac 3:13
  Ac 4:26
h Joh 18:33, 37
i Mt 27:11-14
  Lu 23:3
j Mt 26:62

14:52 *Or "lightly clad; in an undergarment only." 14:64 *Or "What do you think?"

14:68 *Or "vestibule."

many charges they are bringing against you."[a] **5** But Jesus made no further answer, so that Pilate was amazed.[b]

6 Well, from festival to festival, he used to release to them one prisoner whom they requested.[c] **7** At the time the man named Bar·ab'bas was in prison with the seditionists, who in their sedition had committed murder. **8** So the crowd came up and began to make their request according to what Pilate used to do for them. **9** He responded to them, saying: "Do you want me to release to you the King of the Jews?"[d] **10** For Pilate was aware that out of envy the chief priests had handed him over.[e] **11** But the chief priests stirred up the crowd to have him release Bar·ab'bas to them instead.[f] **12** Again in reply Pilate said to them: "What, then, should I do with the one you call the King of the Jews?"[g] **13** Once more they cried out: "To the stake with him!"*[h] **14** But Pilate went on to say to them: "Why? What bad thing did he do?" Still they cried out all the more: "To the stake with him!"*[i] **15** At that Pilate, wishing to satisfy the crowd, released Bar·ab'bas to them; and after having Jesus whipped,[j] he handed him over to be executed on the stake.[k]

16 The soldiers now led him off into the courtyard, that is, into the governor's residence, and they called the whole body of troops together.[l] **17** And they dressed him in purple and braided a crown of thorns and put it on him; **18** and they began to call out to him: "Greetings,* you King of the Jews!"[m] **19** Also, they were hitting him on the head with a reed

and spitting on him, and they got on their knees and bowed down* to him. **20** Finally, after they had mocked him, they stripped him of the purple and put his outer garments on him. And they led him out to nail him to the stake.[a] **21** Also, they compelled into service a passerby, a certain Simon of Cy·re'ne, coming from the countryside, the father of Alexander and Ru'fus, to carry his torture stake.*[b]

22 So they brought him to the place called Gol'go·tha, which means, when translated, "Skull Place."[c] **23** Here they tried to give him wine drugged with myrrh,[d] but he would not take it. **24** And they nailed him to the stake and distributed his outer garments by casting lots over them to decide who would take what.[e] **25** It was now the third hour,* and they nailed him to the stake. **26** And the inscription of the charge against him was written: "The King of the Jews."[f] **27** Moreover, they put two robbers on stakes alongside him, one on his right and one on his left.[g] **28** *— **29** And those passing by spoke abusively to him, shaking their heads[h] and saying: "Ha! You who would throw down the temple and build it in three days,[i] **30** save yourself by coming down off the torture stake."* **31** In the same way also, the chief priests with the scribes were mocking him among themselves, saying: "Others he saved; himself he cannot save![j] **32** Let the Christ, the King of Israel, now come down off the torture stake,* so that we may see and believe."[k] Even those who were on stakes alongside him were reproaching him.[l]

CHAP. 15
a Joh 19:9, 10
b Isa 53:7
c Mt 27:15-18
   Joh 18:39
d Lu 23:16
e Mt 21:38
f Mt 27:20-23
   Ac 3:14
g Lu 23:20-25
h Joh 19:6
i Ac 3:13
   Ac 13:28
j Joh 19:1
k Mt 27:24, 26
l Mt 27:27-31
m Joh 19:3

Second Col.
a Joh 19:16
b Mt 27:32
   Lu 23:26
c Mt 27:33-37
   Lu 23:33
   Joh 19:17
   Heb 13:12
d Ps 69:21
e Ps 22:18
   Joh 19:23, 24
f Mt 27:29, 37
   Lu 23:38
   Joh 19:19
g Mt 27:38
h Ps 22:7
   Ps 109:25
   Isa 53:3
i Mt 27:39-42
   Mr 14:58
j Lu 23:35
k Mt 16:4
l Mt 27:44
   1Pe 2:23

15:13, 14 *Or "Execute him on the stake!" 15:18 *Or "Hail."

15:19 *Or "did obeisance." 15:21, 30, 32 *See Glossary. 15:25 *That is, about 9:00 a.m. 15:28 *See App. A3.

33 When it became the sixth hour,* a darkness fell over all the land until the ninth hour.*ᵃ **34** And at the ninth hour, Jesus called out with a loud voice: "E'li, E'li, la'ma sa·bach·tha'ni?" which means, when translated: "My God, my God, why have you forsaken me?"ᵇ **35** And some of those standing near, on hearing it, began to say: "See! He is calling E·li'jah." **36** Then someone ran, soaked a sponge in sour wine, put it on a reed, and gave it to him to drink,ᶜ saying: "Let him be! Let us see whether E·li'jah comes to take him down." **37** But Jesus let out a loud cry and expired.*ᵈ **38** And the curtain of the sanctuaryᵉ was torn in two from top to bottom.ᶠ **39** Now when the army officer who was standing by with him in view saw that he had expired under these circumstances, he said: "Certainly this man was God's Son."ᵍ

40 There were also women watching from a distance, among them Mary Mag'da·lene as well as Mary the mother of James the Less and of Jo'ses, and Sa·lo'me,ʰ **41** who used to accompany him and minister to himⁱ when he was in Gal'i·lee, and many other women who had come up together with him to Jerusalem.

42 Now as it was already late in the afternoon, and since it was Preparation, that is, the day before the Sabbath, **43** there came Joseph of Ar·i·ma·the'a, a reputable member of the Council, who also himself was waiting for the Kingdom of God. He took courage and went in before Pilate and asked for the body of Jesus.ʲ **44** But Pilate wondered whether he could already be dead, and summoning

the army officer, he asked him whether Jesus had already died. **45** So after making certain from the army officer, he granted the body to Joseph. **46** After he bought fine linen and took him down, he wrapped him in the fine linen and laid him in a tombᵃ that was quarried out of rock; then he rolled a stone up to the entrance of the tomb.ᵇ **47** But Mary Mag'da·lene and Mary the mother of Jo'ses continued looking at where he had been laid.ᶜ

16 So when the Sabbathᵈ was over, Mary Mag'da·lene, Maryᵉ the mother of James, and Sa·lo'me bought spices in order to come and apply them to his body.ᶠ **2** And very early on the first day of the week when the sun had risen, they came to the tomb.*ᵍ **3** They were saying to one another: "Who will roll the stone away from the entrance of the tomb for us?" **4** But when they looked up, they saw that the stone had been rolled away, although it was very large.ʰ **5** When they entered into the tomb, they saw a young man sitting on the right side, clothed in a white robe, and they were stunned. **6** He said to them: "Do not be stunned.ⁱ You are looking for Jesus the Naz·a·rene' who was executed on the stake. He was raised up.ʲ He is not here. Look, here is the place where they laid him.ᵏ **7** But go, tell his disciples and Peter, 'He is going ahead of you into Gal'i·lee.ˡ You will see him there, just as he told you.'"ᵐ **8** So when they came out, they fled from the tomb, trembling and overwhelmed with emotion. And they said nothing to anyone, for they were in fear.*ⁿ

	CHAP. 15
a	Mt 27:45
	Lu 23:44
b	Ps 22:1
	Mt 27:46-49
c	Ps 69:21
	Joh 19:29
d	Ps 31:5
	Mt 27:50
	Lu 23:46
	Joh 19:30
e	Ex 26:31-33
	Heb 6:19
f	Mt 27:51
	Lu 23:45
	Heb 10:19, 20
g	Mt 27:54
	Lu 23:47
h	Mt 27:55, 56
	Lu 23:49
i	Lu 8:2, 3
j	De 21:22, 23
	Mt 27:57, 58
	Lu 23:50-52
	Joh 19:38

Second Col.	
a	Isa 53:9
b	Mt 27:59, 60
	Lu 23:53
	Joh 19:40
c	Mt 27:61
	Lu 23:55

	CHAP. 16
d	Ex 20:8, 9
e	Mt 28:1
f	Lu 23:55, 56
g	Lu 24:1
	Joh 20:1
h	Lu 24:2, 3
i	Lu 24:4
j	Mr 8:31
	Lu 18:33
	Ac 4:10
k	Mt 28:5, 6
l	Mt 26:32
	Mr 14:28
m	Mt 28:7
n	Mt 28:8
	Lu 24:9

15:33 *That is, about 12:00 noon. ＃That is, about 3:00 p.m. **15:37** *Or "breathed his last." **15:46; 16:2** *Or "memorial tomb." **16:8** *According to reliable early manuscripts, the Gospel of Mark ends with the words found in vs. 8. See App. A3.

ACCORDING TO
LUKE

OUTLINE OF CONTENTS

1 Seeing that many have undertaken to compile an account of the facts that are given full credence* among us,[a] **2** just as these were handed down to us by those who from the beginning were eyewitnesses[b] and attendants of the message,[c] **3** I resolved also, because I have traced all things from the start with accuracy, to write them to you in logical order, most excellent The·oph′i·lus,[d] **4** so that you may know fully the certainty of the things that you have been taught orally.[e]

5 In the days of Herod,*[f] king of Ju·de′a, there was a priest named Zech·a·ri′ah of the division of A·bi′jah.[g] His wife was from the daughters of Aaron, and her name was Elizabeth. **6** They both were righteous before God, walking blamelessly in accord with all the commandments and legal requirements of Jehovah.* **7** But they had no child, because Elizabeth was barren, and they both were well along in years.

8 Now as he was serving as priest in the assignment of his division[h] before God, **9** according to the established practice* of the priesthood it became his turn to offer incense[i] when he entered into the sanctuary of Jehovah.*[j] **10** And the entire multitude of the people were praying outside at the hour of offering incense. **11** Jehovah's* angel appeared to him, standing at the right side of the incense altar. **12** But Zech·a·ri′ah became troubled at the sight, and he was overcome with fear. **13** However, the angel said to him: "Do not be afraid, Zech·a·ri′ah, because your supplication has been favorably heard, and

your wife Elizabeth will bear you a son, and you are to name him John.[a] **14** You will have joy and great gladness, and many will rejoice over his birth,[b] **15** for he will be great in the sight of Jehovah.*[c] But he must drink no wine or any alcoholic drink at all,[d] and he will be filled with holy spirit even from before birth,*[e] **16** and he will turn back many of the sons of Israel to Jehovah* their God.[f] **17** Also, he will go ahead of him with E·li′jah's spirit and power,[g] to turn back the hearts of fathers to children[h] and the disobedient ones to the practical wisdom of righteous ones, in order to get ready for Jehovah* a prepared people."[i]

18 Zech·a·ri′ah said to the angel: "How can I be sure of this? For I am old, and my wife is well along in years." **19** In reply the angel said to him: "I am Ga′bri·el,[j] who stands near before God,[k] and I was sent to speak with you and to declare this good news to you. **20** But look! you will be silent and unable to speak until the day these things take place, because you did not believe my words, which will be fulfilled in their appointed time." **21** Meanwhile, the people continued waiting for Zech·a·ri′ah, and they were surprised that he delayed so long in the sanctuary. **22** When he came out, he was unable to speak to them, and they perceived that he had just seen a supernatural sight* in the sanctuary. He kept making signs to them but remained speechless. **23** When the days of his holy service* were completed, he went off to his home.

24 Some days later Elizabeth his wife became pregnant, and

CHAP. 1
a Joh 20:30, 31

b Joh 15:27
1Pe 5:1
2Pe 1:16

c Heb 2:3

d Ac 1:1

e Joh 20:30, 31

f Mt 2:1

g 1Ch 24:3, 10

h 1Ch 24:1, 19
2Ch 8:14
2Ch 31:2

i Ex 30:7, 8

j Ex 40:5

Second Col.
a Lu 1:59, 60

b Lu 1:57, 58

c Lu 7:28

d Nu 6:2, 3
Mt 11:18

e Jer 1:5
Ro 9:10-12

f Mal 4:6

g Mt 11:13, 14
Mt 17:10-12

h Mal 4:5, 6

i Isa 40:3
Mal 3:1

j Da 8:16
Da 9:21
Lu 1:26, 27

k Heb 1:7, 14

1:1 *Or "credibility." 1:5 *See Glossary. 1:6, 9, 11, 15-17 *See App. A5. 1:9 #Or "custom."

1:15 #Or "right from his mother's womb." 1:22 *Or "a vision." 1:23 *Or "his public service."

she kept herself secluded for five months, saying: **25** "This is how Jehovah* has dealt with me in these days. He has turned his attention to me to take away my reproach among men."ᵃ

26 In her sixth month, the angel Ga'bri·elᵇ was sent from God to a city of Gal'i·lee named Naz'-a·reth, **27** to a virginᶜ promised in marriage* to a man named Joseph of David's house, and the name of the virgin was Mary.ᵈ **28** And coming in, the angel said to her: "Greetings, you highly favored one, Jehovah* is with you." **29** But she was deeply disturbed at his words and tried to understand what kind of greeting this might be. **30** So the angel said to her: "Do not be afraid, Mary, for you have found favor with God. **31** And look! you will become pregnant* and give birth to a son,ᵉ and you are to name him Jesus.ᶠ **32** This one will be greatᵍ and will be called Son of the Most High,ʰ and Jehovah* God will give him the throne of David his father,ⁱ **33** and he will rule as King over the house of Jacob forever, and there will be no end to his Kingdom."ʲ

34 But Mary said to the angel: "How is this to be, since I am not having sexual relations with a man?"ᵏ **35** In answer the angel said to her: "Holy spirit will come upon you,ˡ and power of the Most High will overshadow you. And for that reason the one who is born will be called holy,ᵐ God's Son.ⁿ **36** And look! Elizabeth your relative has also conceived a son, in her old age, and this is the sixth month for her, the so-called barren woman; **37** for no declaration* will be

impossible for God."ᵃ **38** Then Mary said: "Look! Jehovah's* slave girl! May it happen to me according to your declaration." At that the angel departed from her.

39 So Mary set out in those days and traveled with haste into the mountainous country, to a city of Judah, **40** and she entered the home of Zech·a·ri'ah and greeted Elizabeth. **41** Well, as Elizabeth heard the greeting of Mary, the infant in her womb leaped, and Elizabeth was filled with holy spirit **42** and loudly cried out: "Blessed are you among women, and blessed is the fruitage of your womb! **43** So how is it that this privilege is mine, to have the mother of my Lord come to me? **44** For look! as the sound of your greeting reached my ears, the infant in my womb leaped for joy. **45** Happy too is she who believed, for there will be a complete fulfillment of those things spoken to her from Jehovah."*

46 And Mary said: "My soul* magnifies Jehovah,*ᵇ **47** and my spirit cannot keep from being overjoyed at God my Savior,ᶜ **48** because he has looked upon the low position of his slave girl.ᵈ For look! from now on all generations will declare me happy,ᵉ **49** because the powerful One has done great deeds for me, and holy is his name,ᶠ **50** and for generation after generation his mercy is upon those who fear him.ᵍ **51** He has acted mightily with his arm; he has scattered those who are haughty in the intention of their hearts.ʰ **52** He has brought down powerful men from thronesⁱ and has exalted lowly ones;ʲ **53** he has fully satisfied hungry ones with

CHAP. 1

a Ge 30:22, 23
  1Sa 1:10, 11

b Da 8:16
  Lu 1:19

c Isa 7:14

d Mt 1:18

e Ga 4:4

f Mt 1:21-23
  Lu 2:21

g Php 2:9-11
  1Ti 6:15

h Mt 27:54
  Joh 1:49

i 2Sa 7:8, 12
  Ps 132:11
  Isa 9:7
  Isa 11:1, 10
  Jer 23:5
  Mt 1:1

j Da 2:44
  Da 7:13, 14
  Heb 1:8

k Isa 7:14
  Mt 1:24, 25

l Mt 1:18, 20

m Joh 6:68, 69

n Mt 14:33
  Joh 1:32, 34
  Joh 20:31

Second Col.

a Ge 18:14
  Mt 19:26

b 1Sa 2:1

c 2Sa 22:3
  Isa 43:3
  Hab 3:18
  Tit 1:3
  Jude 25

d 1Sa 1:10, 11

e Lu 11:27

f Ps 71:19
  Ps 111:9

g Ps 103:17

h 2Sa 22:28

i Job 12:19

j 1Sa 2:7

1:25, 28, 32, 38, 45, 46 *See App. A5. 1:27 *Or "engaged." 1:31 *Or "conceive in your womb." 1:37 *Or "nothing."

1:46 *Or "My whole being." See Glossary.

good things[a] and has sent away empty-handed those who had wealth. **54** He has come to the aid of Israel his servant, remembering his mercy,[b] **55** just as he spoke to our forefathers, to Abraham and to his offspring,[c] forever." **56** Mary stayed with her about three months and then returned to her own home.

57 The time now came for Elizabeth to give birth, and she gave birth to a son. **58** And the neighbors and her relatives heard that Jehovah* had magnified his mercy to her, and they rejoiced with her.[d] **59** On the eighth day they came to circumcise the young child,[e] and they were going to name him after his father, Zech·a·ri'ah. **60** But his mother said in reply: "No! but he will be called John." **61** At this they said to her: "Not one of your relatives is called by this name." **62** Then they asked his father by signs what he wanted him to be called. **63** So he asked for a tablet and wrote: "John is his name."[f] At this they were all amazed. **64** Instantly his mouth was opened and his tongue was set free and he began to speak,[g] praising God. **65** And fear fell upon all those living in their neighborhood, and all these things began to be talked about in the whole mountainous country of Ju·de'a. **66** And all who heard noted it in their hearts, saying: "What will this young child turn out to be?" For the hand of Jehovah* was indeed with him.

67 Then Zech·a·ri'ah his father was filled with holy spirit, and he prophesied, saying: **68** "Let Jehovah* be praised, the God of Israel,[h] because he has turned his attention to his people and has brought them deliverance.[a] **69** And he has raised up a horn of salvation*[b] for us in the house of David his servant,[c] **70** just as he has spoken through the mouth of his holy prophets from of old,[d] **71** of a salvation from our enemies and from the hand of all those hating us;[e] **72** to show mercy in connection with our forefathers and to call to mind his holy covenant,[f] **73** the oath that he swore to Abraham our forefather,[g] **74** to grant us, after we have been rescued from the hands of enemies, the privilege of fearlessly rendering sacred service to him **75** with loyalty and righteousness before him all our days. **76** But as for you, young child, you will be called a prophet of the Most High, for you will go ahead of Jehovah* to prepare his ways,[h] **77** to give knowledge of salvation to his people by forgiveness of their sins,[i] **78** because of the tender compassion of our God. With this compassion a daybreak will visit us from on high, **79** to give light to those sitting in darkness and death's shadow[j] and to guide our feet in the way of peace."

80 And the young child grew up and became strong in spirit, and he continued in the desert until the day he showed himself openly to Israel.

2 Now in those days a decree went out from Caesar Au·gus'tus for all the inhabited earth to be registered. **2** (This first registration took place when Qui·rin'i·us was governor of Syria.) **3** And all the people went to be registered, each one to his own city. **4** Of course, Joseph[k] also went up from Gal'i·lee, from the city of Naz'a·reth, into Ju·de'a, to David's city, which is called Beth'le·hem,[l] be-

CHAP. 1	
a	1Sa 2:5 Ps 34:10 Ps 107:9
b	Ps 98:3 Isa 41:8, 9
c	Ge 17:19 Mic 7:20 Ga 3:16
d	Lu 1:14
e	Ge 17:10, 12 Le 12:2, 3
f	Lu 1:13
g	Lu 1:20
h	1Ki 1:48 Ps 41:13 Ps 72:18 Ps 106:48
Second Col.	
a	Ps 111:9 Lu 7:16
b	1Sa 2:10
c	Ps 132:17
d	Jer 23:5 Da 9:24
e	Ps 106:10
f	Ge 17:7 Le 26:42 Ps 106:45, 46
g	Ge 22:15-18 Ps 105:8, 9 Mic 7:20
h	Isa 40:3 Mal 3:1 Mt 3:3
i	Mr 1:4
j	Ps 107:10 Isa 9:2 Mt 4:16
CHAP. 2	
k	Mt 1:16
l	1Sa 16:1 Mic 5:2 Mt 2:6

1:55 *Lit., "seed." 1:58, 66, 68, 76 *See App. A5.

1:69 *Or "a powerful savior." See Glossary, "Horn."

cause of his being a member of the house and family of David. **5** He went to get registered with Mary, who had been given him in marriage as promised[a] and who was soon to give birth.[b] **6** While they were there, the time came for her to give birth. **7** And she gave birth to her son, the firstborn,[c] and she wrapped him in strips of cloth and laid him in a manger,[d] because there was no room for them in the lodging place.

8 There were also in the same region shepherds living out of doors and keeping watch in the night over their flocks. **9** Suddenly Jehovah's* angel stood before them, and Jehovah's* glory gleamed around them, and they became very fearful. **10** But the angel said to them: "Do not be afraid, for look! I am declaring to you good news of a great joy that all the people will have. **11** For today there was born to you in David's city[e] a savior,[f] who is Christ the Lord.[g] **12** And this is a sign for you: You will find an infant wrapped in strips of cloth and lying in a manger." **13** Suddenly there was with the angel a multitude of the heavenly army,[h] praising God and saying: **14** "Glory in the heights above to God, and on earth peace among men of goodwill."*

15 So when the angels had departed from them into heaven, the shepherds began saying to one another: "Let us by all means go over to Beth'le·hem and see what has taken place, which Jehovah* has made known to us." **16** And they went quickly and found Mary as well as Joseph, and the infant lying in the manger. **17** When they saw this, they made known the message that they had been told concerning this young child. **18** And all who heard were astonished at what the shepherds told them, **19** but Mary began to preserve all these sayings, drawing conclusions in her heart.[a] **20** Then the shepherds went back, glorifying and praising God for all they had heard and seen, just as it had been told to them.

21 After eight days, when it was time to circumcise him,[b] he was named Jesus, the name given by the angel before he was conceived.[c]

22 Also, when the time came for purifying them according to the Law of Moses,[d] they brought him up to Jerusalem to present him to Jehovah,* **23** just as it is written in Jehovah's* Law: "Every firstborn male#[ ] must be called holy to Jehovah."*[e] **24** And they offered a sacrifice according to what is said in the Law of Jehovah:* "a pair of turtledoves or two young pigeons."[f]

25 And look! there was a man in Jerusalem named Sim'e·on, and this man was righteous and devout, waiting for Israel's consolation,[g] and holy spirit was upon him. **26** Furthermore, it had been divinely revealed to him by the holy spirit that he would not see death before he had seen the Christ of Jehovah.* **27** Under the power of the spirit, he now came into the temple, and as the parents brought the young child Jesus to do for him according to the customary practice of the Law,[h] **28** he took the child into his arms and praised God and said: **29** "Now, Sovereign Lord, you are letting your slave go in peace[i] according to your declaration, **30** because my eyes have seen your means of salvation[j] **31** that you

CHAP. 2
a Lu 1:26, 27

b Mt 1:18

c Mt 1:25

d Isa 53:2

e 1Sa 20:6

f Isa 9:6

g Ac 2:36
Php 2:11

h Da 7:10
Re 5:11

Second Col.
a Lu 2:51

b Ge 17:10, 12
Le 12:2, 3

c Mt 1:20, 21
Lu 1:30, 31

d Le 12:2, 4

e Ex 13:2, 12
Ex 22:29
Nu 3:13
Nu 8:17

f Le 12:6, 8

g Isa 40:1
Isa 49:13

h Le 12:6, 7

i Ge 46:30

j Isa 52:10
Lu 3:4, 6
Ac 4:12

2:9, 15, 22-24, 26 *See App. A5. 2:14 *Or "people whom he approves."

2:23 #Lit., "Every male opening the womb."

have prepared in the sight of all the peoples,[a] **32** a light[b] for removing the veil from the nations[c] and a glory of your people Israel." **33** And the child's father and mother continued wondering at the things being spoken about him. **34** Also, Sim′e·on blessed them and said to Mary, the child's mother: "Look! This child is appointed for the falling[d] and the rising again of many in Israel[e] and for a sign to be spoken against[f] **35** (yes, a long sword will be run through you*),[g] in order that the reasonings of many hearts may be revealed."

36 Now there was a prophetess, Anna the daughter of Phan′u·el, of Ash′er's tribe. This woman was well along in years and had lived with her husband for seven years after they were married,* **37** and she was a widow now 84 years old. She was never missing from the temple, rendering sacred service night and day with fasting and supplications. **38** In that very hour she came near and began giving thanks to God and speaking about the child to all who were waiting for Jerusalem's deliverance.[h]

39 So when they had carried out all the things according to the Law of Jehovah,*[i] they went back into Gal′i·lee to their own city, Naz′a·reth.[j] **40** And the young child continued growing and getting strong, being filled with wisdom, and God's favor continued upon him.[k]

41 Now his parents were accustomed to go from year to year to Jerusalem for the festival of the Passover.[l] **42** And when he was 12 years old, they went up according to the custom of the festival.[m] **43** When the days of the festival were over and they were returning, the boy Jesus remained behind in Jerusalem, and his parents did not notice it. **44** Assuming that he was in the group traveling together, they went a day's journey and then began to search for him among the relatives and acquaintances. **45** But not finding him, they returned to Jerusalem and made a diligent search for him. **46** Well, after three days they found him in the temple, sitting in the midst of the teachers and listening to them and asking them questions. **47** But all those listening to him were in constant amazement at his understanding and his answers.[a] **48** Now when his parents saw him, they were astounded, and his mother said to him: "Child, why did you treat us this way? Here your father and I have been frantically looking for you." **49** But he said to them: "Why were you looking for me? Did you not know that I must be in the house of my Father?"[b] **50** However, they did not understand what he was saying to them.

51 Then he went down with them and returned to Naz′a·reth, and he continued subject* to them.[c] Also, his mother carefully kept all these sayings in her heart.[d] **52** And Jesus went on progressing in wisdom and in physical growth and in favor with God and men.

3 In the 15th year of the reign of Ti·be′ri·us Caesar, when Pontius Pilate was governor of Ju·de′a, Herod*[e] was district ruler# of Gal′i·lee, Philip his brother was district ruler of the country of It·u·rae′a and Trach·o·ni′tis, and Ly·sa′ni·as was dis-

---

CHAP. 2
a Isa 40:5

b Isa 9:2
  Mt 4:16

c Isa 11:10
  Isa 42:6
  Isa 49:6
  Ac 13:47
  Ac 26:23

d Isa 8:14

e 1Co 1:23, 24

f Ac 28:22
  1Pe 2:7, 8

g Joh 19:25

h Isa 52:9
  Mr 15:43
  Lu 2:25

i Le 12:6

j Mt 2:23
  Lu 1:26

k Lu 2:52

l Ex 23:14, 15
  De 16:16

m Ex 34:23

Second Col.
a Ps 119:99
  Mt 7:28
  Mr 1:22
  Joh 7:15

b Joh 2:16

c Ex 20:12
  De 5:16
  Eph 6:1
  Col 3:20

d Lu 2:19

CHAP. 3
e Mt 14:1
  Lu 23:6, 7

2:35 *Or "your own soul." 2:36 *Lit., "from her virginity." 2:39 *See App. A5.

2:51 *Or "remained obedient." 3:1 *That is, Herod Antipas. See Glossary. #Lit., "the tetrarch."

trict ruler of Ab·i·le′ne, 2 in the days of chief priest An′nas and of Ca′ia·phas,[a] God's declaration came to John[b] the son of Zech·a·ri′ah in the wilderness.[c]

3 So he went into all the country around the Jordan, preaching baptism in symbol of repentance for forgiveness of sins,[d] 4 just as it is written in the book of the words of Isaiah the prophet: "A voice of one crying out in the wilderness: 'Prepare the way of Jehovah!* Make his roads straight.[e] 5 Every valley must be filled up, and every mountain and hill leveled; the crooked ways must become straight, and the rough ways smooth; 6 and all flesh* will see the salvation of God.'"[#f]

7 So he began to say to the crowds coming out to be baptized by him: "You offspring of vipers, who has warned you to flee from the coming wrath?[g] 8 Therefore, produce fruits that befit repentance. Do not start saying to yourselves, 'We have Abraham as our father.' For I say to you that God is able to raise up children for Abraham from these stones. 9 Indeed, the ax is already lying at the root of the trees. Every tree, then, that does not produce fine fruit will be cut down and thrown into the fire."[h]

10 And the crowds were asking him: "What, then, should we do?" 11 In reply he said to them: "Let the man who has two garments* share with the man who has none, and let the one who has something to eat do the same."[i] 12 Even tax collectors came to be baptized, and they said to him: "Teacher, what should we do?" 13 He said to them: "Do not demand*

anything more than the tax rate."[a] 14 Also, those in military service were asking him: "What should we do?" And he said to them: "Do not harass* anybody or accuse anybody falsely,[b] but be satisfied with your provisions."[#]

15 Now the people were in expectation and all of them were reasoning in their hearts about John, "May he perhaps be the Christ?"[c] 16 John gave the answer, saying to all: "I, for my part, baptize you with water, but the one stronger than I am is coming, the lace of whose sandals I am not worthy to untie.[d] He will baptize you with holy spirit and with fire.[e] 17 His winnowing shovel is in his hand to clean up his threshing floor completely and to gather the wheat into his storehouse, but the chaff he will burn up with fire that cannot be put out."

18 He also gave many other exhortations and continued declaring good news to the people. 19 But Herod the district ruler, because of being reproved by John concerning He·ro′di·as the wife of his brother and concerning all the wicked deeds that Herod had done, 20 added this also to all those deeds: He locked John up in prison.[f]

21 Now when all the people were baptized, Jesus too was baptized.[g] As he was praying, the heaven was opened up,[h] 22 and the holy spirit in bodily form like a dove came down upon him, and a voice came out of heaven: "You are my Son, the beloved; I have approved you."[i]

23 When Jesus[j] began his work, he was about 30 years old,[k] being the son, as the opinion was,

of Joseph,[l]
son of He′li,

CHAP. 3
a Mt 26:57
  Joh 18:13
  Joh 18:24
  Ac 4:5, 6

b Joh 1:6

c Lu 1:80

d Mt 3:1, 2
  Mr 1:4
  Lu 1:76, 77

e Mt 3:3
  Mr 1:3
  Joh 1:23

f Isa 40:3-5
  Lu 2:30
  Ac 28:28

g Mt 3:7-10
  Mt 23:33

h Mt 7:19

i 1Ti 6:18
  Jas 2:15, 16
  1Jo 3:17

j Mt 21:32
  Lu 7:29

Second Col.
a Lu 19:8

b Ex 23:1, 7
  Le 19:11

c Joh 1:25

d Joh 1:26, 27

e Mt 3:11, 12
  Mr 1:7, 8
  Ac 2:1, 4

f Mt 14:3-5
  Mr 6:17-20

g Mt 3:13

h Mt 3:16
  Mr 1:9, 10

i Ps 2:7
  Mt 3:17
  Mt 17:5
  Mr 1:11
  Joh 1:32-34

j Mt 1:1-17

k Nu 4:2, 3

l Mt 1:16
  Mt 13:55
  Lu 4:22
  Joh 6:42

3:4 *See App. A5. 3:6 *Or "all humans." #Or "the saving means of God." 3:11 *Or "an extra garment." 3:13 *Or "collect."

3:14 *Or "extort from." #Or "wages."

24 son of Mat′that,
son of Le′vi,
son of Mel′chi,
son of Jan′na·i,
son of Joseph,
25 son of Mat·ta·thi′as,
son of A′mos,
son of Na′hum,
son of Es′li,
son of Nag′ga·i,
26 son of Ma′ath,
son of Mat·ta·thi′as,
son of Sem′e·in,
son of Jo′sech,
son of Jo′da,
27 son of Jo·an′an,
son of Rhe′sa,
son of Ze·rub′ba·bel,[a]
son of She·al′ti·el,[b]
son of Ne′ri,
28 son of Mel′chi,
son of Ad′di,
son of Co′sam,
son of El·ma′dam,
son of Er,
29 son of Jesus,
son of E·li·e′zer,
son of Jo′rim,
son of Mat′that,
son of Le′vi,
30 son of Sym′e·on,
son of Judas,
son of Joseph,
son of Jo′nam,
son of E·li′a·kim,
31 son of Me′le·a,
son of Men′na,
son of Mat′ta·tha,
son of Nathan,[c]
son of David,[d]
32 son of Jes′se,[e]
son of O′bed,[f]
son of Bo′az,[g]
son of Sal′mon,[h]
son of Nah′shon,[i]
33 son of Am·min′a·dab,
son of Ar′ni,
son of Hez′ron,
son of Pe′rez,[j]
son of Judah,[k]
34 son of Jacob,[a]
son of Isaac,[b]
son of Abraham,[c]
son of Te′rah,[d]
son of Na′hor,[e]
35 son of Se′rug,[f]
son of Re′u,[g]
son of Pe′leg,[h]
son of E′ber,[i]
son of She′lah,[j]
36 son of Ca·i′nan,
son of Ar·pach′shad,[k]
son of Shem,[l]
son of Noah,[m]
son of La′mech,[n]
37 son of Me·thu′se·lah,[o]
son of E′noch,
son of Ja′red,[p]
son of Ma·ha′la·le·el,[q]
son of Ca·i′nan,[r]
38 son of E′nosh,[s]
son of Seth,[t]
son of Adam,[u]
son of God.

4 Then Jesus, full of holy spirit, turned away from the Jordan, and he was led about
by the spirit in the wilderness[v]
2 for 40 days, being tempted by
the Devil.[w] And he ate nothing
in those days, so when they had
ended, he felt hungry. **3** At this
the Devil said to him: "If you are
a son of God, tell this stone to
become a loaf of bread." **4** But
Jesus answered him: "It is written, 'Man must not live on bread
alone.'"[x]
5 So he brought him up and
showed him all the kingdoms of
the inhabited earth in an instant
of time.[y] **6** Then the Devil said
to him: "I will give you all this authority and their glory, because
it has been handed over to me,[z]
and I give it to whomever I wish.
7 If you, therefore, do an act of
worship before me, it will all be
yours." **8** In reply Jesus said to
him: "It is written, 'It is Jehovah*

4:8 *See App. A5.

CHAP. 3
a Ezr 3:2
b 1Ch 3:17; Mt 1:12
c 2Sa 5:13, 14; 1Ch 3:5
d 1Sa 16:13; 1Sa 17:58; Mt 1:6
e Isa 11:1
f Ru 4:17
g Ru 4:13
h Ru 4:21
i 1Ch 2:11
j Ru 4:12; Ru 4:18, 19; 1Ch 2:4, 5
k Ge 29:35; 1Ch 2:1

Second Col.
a Ge 25:26
b Ge 21:2, 3
c 1Ch 1:28
d Ge 11:24; Ge 11:26, 27
e Ge 11:22
f Ge 11:20
g Ge 11:18
h Ge 11:16
i Ge 11:14; 1Ch 1:25
j Ge 11:12
k Ge 11:10
l Ge 5:32
m Ge 5:29
n Ge 5:25
o Ge 5:21
p Ge 5:19
q Ge 5:12, 16
r Ge 5:9; 1Ch 1:2
s Ge 4:26; Ge 5:10
t Ge 5:7
u Ge 5:1, 4; 1Ch 1:1

CHAP. 4
v Mt 4:1-4; Mr 1:12, 13
w Heb 2:18
x De 8:3
y Mt 4:8-10
z Joh 12:31; Joh 14:30; Eph 2:2

your God you must worship, and it is to him alone you must render sacred service.'"[a]

9 He then led him into Jerusalem and stationed him on the battlement* of the temple and said to him: "If you are a son of God, throw yourself down from here,[b] 10 for it is written, 'He will give his angels a command concerning you, to preserve you,' 11 and, 'They will carry you on their hands, so that you may not strike your foot against a stone.'"[c] 12 In answer Jesus said to him: "It is said, 'You must not put Jehovah* your God to the test.'"[d] 13 So the Devil, having finished all the temptation, departed from him until another convenient time.[e]

14 Now Jesus returned in the power of the spirit into Gal'i-lee.[f] And good reports about him spread throughout all the surrounding country. 15 Also, he began to teach in their synagogues, and he was held in honor by all.

16 He then went to Naz'-a-reth,[g] where he had been brought up, and according to his custom on the Sabbath day, he entered the synagogue[h] and stood up to read. 17 So the scroll of the prophet Isaiah was handed to him, and he opened the scroll and found the place where it was written: 18 "Jehovah's* spirit is upon me, because he anointed me to declare good news to the poor. He sent me to proclaim liberty to the captives and a recovery of sight to the blind, to send the crushed ones away free,[i] 19 to preach Jehovah's* acceptable year."[j] 20 With that he rolled up the scroll, handed it back to the attendant, and sat down; and the eyes of all in the syna-

gogue were intently fixed on him. 21 Then he began to say to them: "Today this scripture that you just heard is fulfilled."[a]

22 And they all began to give favorable witness about him and to be amazed at the gracious words coming out of his mouth,[b] and they were saying: "This is a son of Joseph, is it not?"[c] 23 At this he said to them: "No doubt you will apply this saying to me, 'Physician, cure yourself. Do also here in your home territory the things we have heard were done in Ca-per'na-um.'"[d] 24 So he said: "Truly I tell you that no prophet is accepted in his home territory.[e] 25 For instance, I tell you in truth: There were many widows in Israel in the days of E-li'jah when heaven was shut up for three years and six months, and a great famine came on all the land.[f] 26 Yet E-li'jah was sent to none of those women, but only to a widow in Zar'e-phath in the land of Si'don.[g] 27 Also, there were many lepers in Israel in the time of E-li'sha the prophet; yet not one of them was cleansed,* only Na'a-man the Syrian."[h] 28 Now all those hearing these things in the synagogue became filled with anger,[i] 29 and they rose up and rushed him outside the city, and they led him to which brow of the mountain on which their city had been built, in order to throw him down headlong. 30 But he went right through their midst and continued on his way.[j]

31 He then went down to Ca-per'na-um, a city of Gal'i-lee. And he was teaching them on the Sabbath,[k] 32 and they were astounded at his way of teaching,[l] because he spoke with authority. 33 Now in the synagogue there was a man with a

CHAP. 4
a Ex 20:3
  De 6:13
  De 10:20

b Mt 4:5-7

c Ps 91:11, 12

d De 6:16
  1Co 10:9

e Mt 4:11
  Heb 4:15

f Mt 4:12
  Joh 4:3

g Mt 2:23

h Ac 17:1, 2

i Mt 12:20

j Isa 61:1, 2

Second Col.
a Mt 5:17

b Ps 45:2
  Isa 50:4

c Mt 13:54
  Mr 6:2
  Joh 6:42

d Mt 4:13

e Mt 13:57
  Mr 6:4
  Joh 4:44

f 1Ki 18:1

g 1Ki 17:9, 10

h 2Ki 5:1, 14

i Lu 2:34

j Joh 8:59
  Joh 10:39

k Mr 1:21, 22

l Mt 7:28
  Joh 7:46

4:9 *Or "parapet; highest point."
4:12, 18, 19 *See App. A5.

4:27 *Or "healed."

spirit, an unclean demon, and he shouted with a loud voice:[a] 34 "Ah! What have we to do with you, Jesus the Naz·a·rene'?[b] Did you come to destroy us? I know exactly who you are, the Holy One of God."[c] 35 But Jesus rebuked it, saying: "Be silent, and come out of him." So after throwing the man down in their midst, the demon came out of him without hurting him. 36 At this they were all astonished and began to say to one another: "What kind of speech is this? For with authority and power he orders the unclean spirits, and out they come!" 37 So the news about him kept spreading into every corner of the surrounding country.

38 After leaving the synagogue, he entered into Simon's home. Now Simon's mother-in-law was suffering with a high fever, and they asked him to help her.[d] 39 So he stood over her and rebuked the fever, and it left her. Instantly she got up and began ministering to them.

40 But when the sun was setting, all those who had people sick with various diseases brought them to him. By laying his hands on each one of them, he cured them.[e] 41 Demons also came out of many, crying out and saying: "You are the Son of God."[f] But rebuking them, he would not permit them to speak,[g] for they knew him to be the Christ.[h]

42 However, at daybreak he departed and went to an isolated place.[i] But the crowds began searching* for him and came to where he was, and they tried to keep him from going away from them. 43 But he said to them: "I must also declare the good news of the Kingdom of God to

other cities, because for this I was sent."[a] 44 So he went on preaching in the synagogues of Ju·de'a.

5 On one occasion when the crowd was pressing in on him and listening to the word of God, he was standing by the lake of Gen·nes'a·ret.*[b] 2 And he saw two boats docked at the lakeside, but the fishermen had got out of them and were washing off their nets.[c] 3 Going aboard one of the boats, which was Simon's, he asked him to pull away a bit from land. Then he sat down, and he began teaching the crowds from the boat. 4 When he stopped speaking, he said to Simon: "Pull out to where it is deep, and let down your nets for a catch." 5 But in reply Simon said: "Instructor, we toiled all night and caught nothing,[d] but at your word I will lower the nets." 6 Well, when they did this, they caught* a great number of fish. In fact, their nets began ripping apart.[e] 7 So they motioned to their partners in the other boat to come and assist them, and they came and filled both boats, so that these began to sink. 8 Seeing this, Simon Peter fell down at the knees of Jesus, saying: "Depart from me, Lord, because I am a sinful man." 9 For both he and those with him were overwhelmed with astonishment at the catch of fish they had taken, 10 and the same was true of both James and John, Zeb'e·dee's sons,[f] who were partners with Simon. But Jesus said to Simon: "Stop being afraid. From now on you will be catching men* alive."[g] 11 So they brought the boats back to land and abandoned everything and followed him.[h]

CHAP. 4
a Mr 1:23-28

b Mt 2:23

c Mt 8:29
Lu 4:41
Lu 8:28
Jas 2:19

d Mt 8:14, 15
Mr 1:29-31

e Mt 8:16, 17
Mr 1:32-34

f Mt 8:28, 29
Mr 3:11

g Ac 16:17, 18

h Mr 1:23-25
Mr 3:11, 12
Lu 4:33-35

i Mr 1:35-38

Second Col.
a Mt 4:23
Lu 8:1

CHAP. 5
b Mt 4:18
Mr 1:16

c Mt 4:21

d Joh 21:3

e Joh 21:6

f Mt 4:21
Mr 1:19

g Mt 4:19
Mr 1:17

h Mt 4:20
Mt 6:33
Mt 19:27
Mr 1:20
Lu 18:28
Php 3:8

4:42 * Or "hunting."

5:1 * That is, the Sea of Galilee. 5:6 * Lit., "enclosed." 5:10 * Or "people."

12 On another occasion while he was in one of the cities, look! there was a man full of leprosy! When he caught sight of Jesus, he fell facedown and begged him: "Lord, if you just want to, you can make me clean."[a] **13** So stretching out his hand, he touched him, saying: "I want to! Be made clean." Immediately the leprosy vanished from him.[b] **14** Then he gave the man orders to tell no one: "But go and show yourself to the priest, and make an offering for your cleansing, just as Moses directed,[c] for a witness to them."[d] **15** But the news about him just kept spreading, and large crowds would gather together to listen and to be cured of their sicknesses.[e] **16** However, he often went into the desolate areas to pray.

17 On one of those days while he was teaching, Pharisees and teachers of the Law who had come out of every village of Gal'i·lee and Ju·de'a and from Jerusalem were sitting there; and Jehovah's* power was with him to do healing.[f] **18** And look! men were carrying a paralyzed man on a stretcher, and they were trying to bring him in and place him before Jesus.[g] **19** So not finding a way to bring him in because of the crowd, they climbed up to the roof, and they lowered him on the stretcher through the tiling, right among those in front of Jesus. **20** When he saw their faith, he said: "Man, your sins are forgiven."[h] **21** Then the scribes and the Pharisees started to reason, saying: "Who is this who speaks blasphemies? Who can forgive sins except God alone?"[i] **22** But Jesus, discerning their reasoning, said in answer to them: "What are you reasoning in your hearts? **23** Which is easier, to say, 'Your sins are forgiven,' or to say, 'Get up and walk'? **24** But in order for you to know that the Son of man has authority on earth to forgive sins—" he said to the paralyzed man: "I say to you, Get up, pick up your stretcher, and go to your home."[a] **25** At that he stood up before them, picked up what he had been lying on, and went to his home, glorifying God. **26** Then one and all were seized with amazement, and they began to glorify God, and they became filled with awe, saying: "We have seen wonderful things today!"

27 Now after this, he went out and saw a tax collector named Le'vi sitting at the tax office, and he said to him: "Be my follower."[b] **28** And leaving everything behind, he rose up and began to follow him. **29** Then Le'vi spread a big reception feast for him in his house, and there was a large crowd of tax collectors and others who were dining* with them.[c] **30** At this the Pharisees and their scribes began murmuring to his disciples, saying: "Why do you eat and drink with tax collectors and sinners?"[d] **31** In reply Jesus said to them: "Those who are healthy do not need a physician, but those who are ill do.[e] **32** I have come to call, not righteous people, but sinners to repentance."[f]

33 They said to him: "John's disciples fast frequently and offer supplications, and so do those of the Pharisees, but yours eat and drink."[g] **34** Jesus said to them: "You cannot make the friends of the bridegroom fast while the bridegroom is with them, can you? **35** But days will come when the bridegroom[h] will indeed be taken away from

CHAP. 5
a Mt 8:2
Mr 1:40-45

b Mt 8:3
Mr 1:41

c Le 14:2-4
Le 14:10, 20

d Mt 8:4

e Mt 4:24, 25
Mr 3:7, 8
Joh 6:2

f Mr 2:1, 2

g Mt 9:2
Mr 2:3-12

h Mt 9:2-8

i Ps 103:2, 3
Ps 130:3, 4
Isa 43:25

Second Col.
a Joh 5:6-9

b Mt 9:9
Mr 2:14

c Mt 9:10-13
Mr 2:15-17

d Lu 15:1, 2

e Isa 53:4
Mt 9:12
Mr 2:17

f Mt 9:13
1Ti 1:15

g Mt 9:14, 15
Mr 2:18-20
Lu 7:34

h Mt 22:2
2Co 11:2
Re 19:7

5:17 *See App. A5.

5:29 *Or "reclining at the table."

them; then they will fast in those days."[a]

36 He also gave an illustration to them: "Nobody cuts a patch from a new outer garment and sews it on an old garment. If he does, then the new patch tears away and the patch from the new garment does not match the old.[b] **37** Also, no one puts new wine into old wineskins. If he does, the new wine will burst the wineskins and it will be spilled out and the wineskins will be ruined. **38** But new wine must be put into new wineskins. **39** No one after drinking old wine wants new, for he says, 'The old is nice.'"

6 Now on a sabbath he was passing through grainfields, and his disciples were plucking and eating the heads of grain,[c] rubbing them with their hands.[d] **2** At this some of the Pharisees said: "Why are you doing what is not lawful on the Sabbath?"[e] **3** But in reply Jesus said to them: "Have you never read what David did when he and the men with him were hungry?[f] **4** How he entered into the house of God and received the loaves of presentation* and ate and gave some to the men with him, which it is not lawful for anyone to eat but for the priests only?"[g] **5** Then he said to them: "The Son of man is Lord of the Sabbath."

6 On another sabbath[i] he entered the synagogue and began teaching. And a man was there whose right hand was withered.*[j] **7** The scribes and the Pharisees were now watching Jesus closely to see whether he would cure on the Sabbath, in order to find some way to accuse him. **8** He, however, knew their reasoning,[k] so he said to the man

with the withered* hand: "Get up and stand in the center." And he rose and stood there. **9** Then Jesus said to them: "I ask you men, Is it lawful on the Sabbath to do good or to do harm, to save a life* or to destroy it?"[a] **10** After looking around at them all, he said to the man: "Stretch out your hand." He did so, and his hand was restored. **11** But they flew into a senseless rage, and they began to talk over with one another what they might do to Jesus.

12 On one of those days he went out to the mountain to pray,[b] and he spent the whole night in prayer to God.[c] **13** And when it became day, he called his disciples to him and chose from among them 12, whom he also named apostles:[d] **14** Simon, whom he also named Peter, Andrew his brother, James, John, Philip,[e] Bar·thol'o·mew, **15** Matthew, Thomas,[f] James the son of Al·phae'us, Simon who is called "the zealous one," **16** Judas the son of James, and Judas Is·car'i·ot, who turned traitor.

17 And he came down with them and stood on a level place, and there was a large crowd of his disciples, and a great multitude of people from all Ju·de'a and Jerusalem and the coastal region of Tyre and Si'don, who came to hear him and to be healed of their sicknesses. **18** Even those troubled with unclean spirits were cured. **19** And all the crowd were seeking to touch him, because power was going out of him[g] and healing them all.

20 And he looked up at his disciples and began to say:

"Happy are you who are poor, for yours is the Kingdom of God.[h]

CHAP. 5
a Joh 16:19, 20

b Mt 9:16, 17
Mr 2:21, 22

CHAP. 6
c De 23:25

d Mt 12:1-8
Mr 2:23-28

e Ex 20:9, 10
De 5:13, 14
Joh 5:9, 10

f 1Sa 21:1-6

g Le 24:5-9

h Mt 12:8
Mr 2:27, 28

i Lu 13:14
Joh 9:16

j Mt 12:9-14
Mr 3:1-6

k Lu 5:22
Joh 2:24, 25

Second Col.
a Mt 12:11
Mr 3:4
Joh 7:23

b Mt 6:6
Mr 3:13

c Mt 14:23

d Mt 10:2-4
Mr 3:14-19
Ac 1:13

e Joh 14:8

f Joh 11:16

g Mr 5:30

h Mt 5:2, 3
Jas 2:5

6:4 *Or "the showbread." 6:6, 8 *Or "paralyzed."

6:9 *Or "soul."

21 "Happy are you who hunger now, for you will be filled.[a]

"Happy are you who weep now, for you will laugh.[b]

22 "Happy are you whenever men hate you,[c] and when they exclude you[d] and reproach you and denounce* your name as wicked for the sake of the Son of man. **23** Rejoice in that day and leap for joy, for look! your reward is great in heaven, for those are the same things their forefathers used to do to the prophets.[e]

24 "But woe to you who are rich,[f] for you are having your consolation in full.[g]

25 "Woe to you who are filled up now, for you will go hungry.

"Woe, you who are laughing now, for you will mourn and weep.[h]

26 "Woe whenever all men speak well of you,[i] for this is what their forefathers did to the false prophets.

27 "But I say to you who are listening: Continue to love your enemies, to do good to those hating you,[j] **28** to bless those cursing you, to pray for those who are insulting you.[k] **29** To him who strikes you on the one cheek, offer the other also; and from him who takes away your outer garment, do not withhold the inner garment either.[l] **30** Give to everyone asking you,[m] and from the one taking your things away, do not ask them back.

31 "Also, just as you want men to do to you, do the same way to them.[n]

32 "If you love those loving you, of what credit is it to you? For even the sinners love those loving them.[o] **33** And if you do good to those doing good to you, of what credit is it to you? Even the sinners do the same. **34** Also, if you lend* to those from whom you expect repayment, of what credit is it to you?[a] Even sinners lend to sinners so that they may get back as much. **35** On the contrary, continue to love your enemies and to do good and to lend without hoping for anything back;[b] and your reward will be great, and you will be sons of the Most High, for he is kind toward the unthankful and wicked.[c] **36** Continue being merciful, just as your Father is merciful.[d]

37 "Moreover, stop judging, and you will by no means be judged;[e] and stop condemning, and you will by no means be condemned. Keep on forgiving,* and you will be forgiven.*[f] **38** Practice giving, and people will give to you.[g] They will pour into your laps a fine measure, pressed down, shaken together, and overflowing. For with the measure that you are measuring out, they will measure out to you in return."

39 Then he also told them an illustration: "A blind man cannot guide a blind man, can he? Both will fall into a pit, will they not?[h] **40** A student* is not above his teacher, but everyone who is perfectly instructed will be like his teacher. **41** Why, then, do you look at the straw in your brother's eye but do not notice the rafter in your own eye?[i] **42** How can you say to your brother, 'Brother, allow me to remove the straw that is in your eye,' while you yourself do not see the rafter in your own eye? Hypocrite! First remove the rafter from your own eye, and then you will see clearly how to remove the straw that is in your brother's eye.

CHAP. 6

a Ps 107:9
Isa 55:1
Jer 31:25
Mt 5:6

b Isa 61:3
Re 21:4

c Mt 5:10, 11
Joh 17:14
1Pe 3:14

d Joh 16:2

e 2Ch 36:16
Mt 5:12
Lu 11:47
Ac 7:52

f Jas 5:1

g Mt 6:2

h Isa 65:13

i Jas 4:4
1Jo 4:5

j Ex 23:4
Pr 25:21
Mt 5:44
Ro 12:20

k Ac 7:59, 60
Ro 12:14

l Mt 5:39, 40
1Co 6:7

m De 15:7, 8
Pr 3:27
Pr 21:26
Mt 5:42

n Mt 7:12

o Mt 5:46, 47

Second Col.

a Le 25:35, 36
De 15:7, 8
Mt 5:42

b Ex 22:25
Le 25:37
De 23:20
Ps 37:25, 26

c Mt 5:45
Ac 14:17

d Mt 5:48
Eph 5:1, 2
Jas 2:13

e Mt 7:1, 2
Ro 14:10

f Mt 6:14
Mr 11:25

g Pr 19:17

h Mt 15:14

i Mt 7:3-5

6:22 *Or "cast out."   **6:34** *That is, without interest.   **6:37** *Or "releasing." *Or "released."   **6:40** *Or "disciple."

43 "For no fine tree produces rotten fruit, and no rotten tree produces fine fruit.[a] **44** For each tree is known by its own fruit.[b] For example, people do not gather figs from thorns, nor do they cut grapes off a thornbush. **45** A good man brings good out of the good treasure of his heart, but a wicked man brings what is wicked out of his wicked treasure; for out of the heart's abundance his mouth speaks.[c]

46 "Why, then, do you call me 'Lord! Lord!' but do not do the things I say?[d] **47** Everyone who comes to me and hears my words and does them, I will show you whom he is like:[e] **48** He is like a man who in building a house dug and went down deep and laid a foundation on the rock. Consequently, when a flood came, the river dashed against that house but was not strong enough to shake it, for it was well-built.[f] **49** On the other hand, whoever hears and does nothing[g] is like a man who built a house on the ground without a foundation. The river dashed against it, and immediately it collapsed, and the ruin of that house was great."

7 When he had completed what he had to say to the people, he entered Ca·per′na·um. **2** Now an army officer's slave, who was dear to him, was seriously ill and about to pass away.[h] **3** When he heard about Jesus, he sent some elders of the Jews to him to ask him to come and make his slave well. **4** They came up to Jesus and began to plead with him earnestly, saying: "He is worthy of your granting him this, **5** for he loves our nation and he himself built our synagogue." **6** So Jesus went with ~~them~~. But when he was not far ~~from the~~ house, the army of~~ficer had already~~ sent friends to

say to him: "Sir, do not bother, for I am not worthy to have you come under my roof.[a] **7** That is why I did not consider myself worthy to come to you. But say the word, and let my servant be healed. **8** For I too am a man placed under authority, having soldiers under me, and I say to this one, 'Go!' and he goes, and to another, 'Come!' and he comes, and to my slave, 'Do this!' and he does it." **9** When Jesus heard these things, he was amazed at him, and he turned to the crowd following him and said: "I tell you, not even in Israel have I found so great a faith.[b] **10** And when those who had been sent returned to the house, they found the slave in good health.[c]

11 Soon afterward he traveled to a city called Na′in, and his disciples and a large crowd were traveling with him. **12** As he got near the gate of the city, why look! there was a dead man being carried out, the only* son of his mother.[d] Besides, she was a widow. A considerable crowd from the city was also with her. **13** When the Lord caught sight of her, he was moved with pity for her,[e] and he said to her: "Stop weeping."[f] **14** With that he approached and touched the bier,* and the bearers stood still. Then he said: "Young man, I say to you, get up!"[g] **15** And the dead man sat up and started to speak, and Jesus gave him to his mother.[h] **16** Now fear seized them all, and they began to glorify God, saying: "A great prophet has been raised up among us,"[i] and, "God has turned his attention to his people."[j] **17** And this news concerning him spread out into all Ju·de′a and all the surrounding country.

7:12 *Lit., "only-begotten." **7:14** *Or "funeral stretcher."

CHAP. 6
a Mt 7:16-18

b Mt 12:33

c Mt 12:34, 35

d Mt 7:21
Lu 13:24
Ro 2:13
Jas 1:22

e Mt 7:24-27

f Ps 125:1

g Jas 1:23, 24

CHAP. 7
h Mt 8:5, 6

Second Col.
a Mt 8:8, 9

b Mt 8:10

c Mt 8:13

d 1Ki 17:17
Lu 8:41, 42

e Heb 4:15

f Lu 8:52
Joh 11:33

g 1Ki 17:21, 22
Lu 8:52-54
Joh 11:43
Ac 9:40

h 1Ki 17:23
2Ki 4:36

i De 18:15
Joh 4:19
Joh 6:14
Joh 7:40

j Lu 1:68

18 Now John's disciples reported to him all these things.[a] **19** So John summoned two of his disciples and sent them to the Lord to ask: "Are you the Coming One,[b] or are we to expect a different one?" **20** When they came to him, the men said: "John the Baptist sent us to you to ask, 'Are you the Coming One, or are we to expect another?'" **21** In that hour he cured many people of sicknesses,[c] serious diseases, and wicked spirits, and he granted many blind people the gift of sight. **22** In reply he said to them: "Go and report to John what you have seen and heard: The blind are now seeing,[d] the lame are walking, the lepers are being cleansed, the deaf are hearing,[e] the dead are being raised up, and the poor are being told the good news.[f] **23** Happy is the one who finds no cause for stumbling in me."[g]

24 When the messengers of John had gone away, Jesus began to speak to the crowds about John: "What did you go out into the wilderness to see? A reed being tossed by the wind?[h] **25** What, then, did you go out to see? A man dressed in soft garments?*[i] Why, those wearing splendid dress and living in luxury are in royal houses. **26** Really, then, what did you go out to see? A prophet? Yes, I tell you, and far more than a prophet.[j] **27** This is the one about whom it is written: 'Look! I am sending my messenger ahead of you,* who will prepare your way ahead of you.'[k] **28** I tell you, among those born of women there is no one greater than John, but a lesser person in the Kingdom of God is greater than he is."[l] **29** (When all the people and the tax collectors heard this, they declared God to be righteous, for they had been baptized with the baptism of John.[a] **30** But the Pharisees and those versed in the Law disregarded the counsel* of God to them,[b] since they had not been baptized by him.)

31 "With whom, therefore, should I compare the men of this generation, and whom are they like?[c] **32** They are like young children sitting in a marketplace and calling out to one another, saying: 'We played the flute for you, but you did not dance; we wailed, but you did not weep.' **33** Likewise, John the Baptist has come neither eating bread nor drinking wine,[d] but you say: 'He has a demon.' **34** The Son of man has come eating and drinking, but you say: 'Look! A man who is a glutton and is given to drinking wine, a friend of tax collectors and sinners!'[e] **35** All the same, wisdom is proved righteous* by all its children."*[f]

36 Now one of the Pharisees kept asking him to dine with him. So he entered the house of the Pharisee and reclined at the table. **37** And look! a woman who was known in the city to be a sinner learned that he was dining* in the house of the Pharisee, and she brought an alabaster jar of perfumed oil.[g] **38** Taking a position behind him at his feet, she wept and began to wet his feet with her tears, and she wiped them off with the hair of her head. Also, she tenderly kissed his feet and poured the perfumed oil on them. **39** Seeing this, the Pharisee who had invited him said to himself: "If this man were really a prophet, he would know who and what kind of woman it is who is touching him, that she

---

CHAP. 7

a Mt 11:2-6

b Ps 40:7
 Ps 118:26
 Zec 9:9
 Mt 3:11

c Isa 53:4

d Isa 42:7

e Isa 29:18
 Isa 35:5, 6

f Isa 61:1
 Lu 4:18
 Jas 2:5

g Isa 8:14
 Lu 2:34
 Joh 6:66

h Mt 11:7-11

i Mr 1:6

j Mr 1:2
 Lu 1:67, 76

k Isa 40:3
 Mal 3:1
 Lu 1:16, 17
 Joh 1:23

l Mt 11:11

Second Col.

a Mt 3:5, 6
 Lu 3:12

b Ac 13:46
 Ro 10:2, 3

c Mt 11:16-19

d Nu 6:2, 3
 Mt 3:4
 Lu 1:13, 15

e Mt 11:19
 Lu 5:30

f Joh 10:37, 38

g Mt 26:6, 7
 Mr 14:3
 Joh 12:3

7:25 *Or "fine clothing?" **7:27** *Lit., "before your face." **7:30** *Or "direction." **7:35** *Or "is vindicated." #Or "its results." **7:37** *Or "reclining at the table."

is a sinner."ᵃ **40** But in reply Jesus said to him: "Simon, I have something to say to you." He said: "Teacher, say it!"

41 "Two men were debtors to a certain lender; the one was in debt for 500 de·nar′i·i,* but the other for 50. **42** When they did not have anything to pay him back with, he freely forgave them both. Therefore, which one of them will love him more?" **43** In answer Simon said: "I suppose it is the one whom he forgave more." He said to him: "You judged correctly." **44** With that he turned to the woman and said to Simon: "Do you see this woman? I entered your house; you gave me no water for my feet. But this woman wet my feet with her tears and wiped them off with her hair. **45** You gave me no kiss, but this woman, from the hour that I came in, did not stop tenderly kissing my feet. **46** You did not pour oil on my head, but this woman poured perfumed oil on my feet. **47** Because of this, I tell you, her sins, many* though they are, are forgiven,ᵇ because she loved much. But the one who is forgiven little, loves little." **48** Then he said to her: "Your sins are forgiven."ᶜ **49** Those reclining at the table with him started to say among themselves: "Who is this man who even forgives sins?"ᵈ **50** But he said to the woman: "Your faith has saved you;ᵉ go in peace."

8 Shortly afterward he traveled from city to city and from village to village, preaching and declaring the good news of the Kingdom of God.ᶠ And the Twelve were with him, **2** as were certain women who had been cured of wicked spirits and sicknesses: Mary who was ⸤led⸥ Mag′da·lene, from whom

seven demons had come out; **3** Jo·an′naᵃ the wife of Chu′za, Herod's man in charge; Su·san′na; and many other women, who were ministering to them from their belongings.ᵇ

4 Now when a large crowd had gathered together with those who went to him from city to city, he spoke by means of an illustration:ᶜ **5** "A sower went out to sow his seed. As he was sowing, some of them fell alongside the road and were trampled on, and the birds of heaven ate them up.ᵈ **6** Some landed on the rock, and after sprouting, they dried up because they had no moisture.ᵉ **7** Others fell among the thorns, and the thorns that grew up with them choked them.ᶠ **8** But others fell on the good soil, and after sprouting, they produced 100 times more fruit."ᵍ As he said these things, he called out: "Let the one who has ears to listen, listen."ʰ

9 But his disciples asked him what this illustration meant.ⁱ **10** He said: "To you it is granted to understand the sacred secrets of the Kingdom of God, but for the rest it is in illustrationsʲ so that, though looking, they may look in vain, and though hearing, they may not get the sense.ᵏ **11** Now the illustration means this: The seed is the word of God.ˡ **12** Those alongside the road are the ones who have heard, and then the Devil comes and takes the word away from their hearts so that they may not believe and be saved.ᵐ **13** Those on the rock are the ones who, when they hear the word, receive it with joy, but these have no root. They believe for a while, but in a season of testing, they fall away.ⁿ **14** As for that which fell among the thorns, these are the ones who have heard, but by being car-

---

CHAP. 7
a Lu 15:2

b Ps 32:1
  Ps 51:1
  Ps 103:2, 3
  Isa 1:18
  Isa 43:25
  Isa 44:22

c Mt 9:2
  Mr 2:5

d Mt 2:7
  Lu 5:21

e Mt 9:22
  Lu 8:48

CHAP. 8
f Mt 9:35
  Lu 4:43

Second Col.
a Lu 24:9, 10

b Mt 27:55
  Mr 15:40, 41

c Mt 13:1-3
  Mr 4:1, 2

d Mt 13:3-9
  Mr 4:3-9
  Lu 8:12

e Lu 8:13

f Lu 8:14

g Lu 8:15

h Mt 11:15
  Mt 13:9
  Mr 4:9

i Mt 13:10
  Mr 4:10

j Ps 78:2
  Mt 13:34, 35
  Mr 4:34

k Isa 6:9, 10
  Mt 13:11, 13
  Mr 4:11, 12

l Mt 13:18-23
  Mr 4:14-20

m Mt 13:19
  Mr 4:15
  2Co 4:3, 4

n Mt 13:20, 21
  Mr 4:16, 17

8:14. 7:47 *Or "great."

ried away by anxieties, riches,[a] and pleasures of this life,[b] they are completely choked and bring nothing to maturity.[c] **15** As for that on the fine soil, these are the ones who, after hearing the word with a fine and good heart,[d] retain it and bear fruit with endurance.[e]

16 "No one after lighting a lamp covers it with a vessel or puts it underneath a bed, but he puts it on a lampstand so that those who come in may see the light.[f] **17** For there is nothing hidden that will not become manifest, nor anything carefully concealed that will never become known and not come out in the open.[g] **18** Therefore, pay attention to how you listen, for whoever has will be given more,[h] but whoever does not have, even what he imagines he has will be taken away from him."[i]

19 Now his mother and brothers[j] came to him, but they were unable to get near him because of the crowd.[k] **20** So it was reported to him: "Your mother and your brothers are standing outside, wanting to see you." **21** In reply he said to them: "My mother and my brothers are these who hear the word of God and do it."[l]

22 One day he and his disciples got into a boat, and he said to them: "Let us cross to the other side of the lake." So they set sail.[m] **23** But as they were sailing along, he fell asleep. And a violent windstorm descended on the lake, and their boat began to fill up with water and to be in danger.[n] **24** So they went and woke him up, saying: "Instructor, Instructor, we are about to perish!" With that he got up and rebuked the wind and the raging of the water, and they subsided, and a calm set in.[o] **25** Then he said to them: "Where is your

faith?" But they were filled with fear and were astounded, saying to one another: "Who really is this? For he orders even the winds and the water, and they obey him."[a]

26 And they put in to shore in the region of the Ger′a·senes,[b] which is on the side opposite Gal′i·lee. **27** As Jesus got out onto land, a demon-possessed man from the city met him. For a considerable time he had not worn clothing, and he was staying, not in a house, but among the tombs.*[c] **28** At the sight of Jesus, he cried out and fell down before him, and with a loud voice, he said: "What have I to do with you, Jesus, Son of the Most High God? I beg you, do not torment me."[d] **29** (For Jesus had been ordering the unclean spirit to come out of the man. It had seized him on many occasions,*[e] and he was repeatedly bound with chains and fetters and kept under guard, but he would break the bonds and be driven by the demon into the isolated places.) **30** Jesus asked him: "What is your name?" He said: "Legion," for many demons had entered into him. **31** And they kept pleading with him not to order them to go away into the abyss.[f] **32** Now a large herd of swine[g] was feeding there on the mountain, so they pleaded with him to permit them to enter into the swine, and he gave them permission.[h] **33** With that the demons came out of the man and went into the swine, and the herd rushed over the precipice* into the lake and drowned. **34** But when the herders saw what had happened, they fled and reported it in the city and in the countryside.

CHAP. 8

a Mt 19:23
1Ti 6:9

b 2Ti 4:10

c Mt 13:22
Mr 4:18, 19

d Ac 16:14

e Mt 13:23
Mr 4:20
Heb 10:36

f Mt 5:15
Mr 4:21
Lu 11:33
Php 2:15

g Mt 10:26
Mr 4:22
Lu 12:2

h Mt 25:23

i Mt 13:12
Mt 25:29
Mr 4:24, 25
Lu 19:26

j Mt 13:55
Joh 7:5
Ac 1:14

k Mt 12:46, 47
Mr 3:31, 32

l Mt 12:48-50
Mr 3:33-35
Joh 15:14

m Mt 8:18, 23
Mr 4:35, 36

n Mt 8:24-27
Mr 4:37-41

o Ps 89:9

Second Col.

a Mt 8:27
Mr 4:41

b Mr 5:1

c Mt 8:28, 29
Mr 5:2-10

d Mr 1:23, 24

e Mr 9:20, 21

f Re 20:2, 3

g Le 11:7, 8
De 14:8

h Mt 8:30-34
Mr 5:11-17

8:27 *Or "memorial tombs." 8:29 *Or, possibly, "Over a long time it ha[s] him fast." 8:33 *Or "ste[ep..."

35 Then people went out to see what had happened. They came to Jesus and found the man from whom the demons had come out, clothed and in his right mind, sitting at the feet of Jesus, and they grew fearful. **36** Those who had seen it reported to them how the demon-possessed man had been made well. **37** Then a great number from the surrounding region of the Ger'a·senes asked Jesus to go away from them, because they were gripped by great fear. Then he went aboard the boat to depart. **38** However, the man from whom the demons had gone out kept begging to continue with him, but he sent the man away, saying:[a] **39** "Go back home, and keep on relating what God did for you." So he went away, proclaiming throughout the whole city what Jesus had done for him.

40 When Jesus returned, the crowd received him kindly, for they were all expecting him.[b] **41** But look! a man named Ja'i·rus came; this man was a presiding officer of the synagogue. And he fell at the feet of Jesus and began to plead with him to come to his house,[c] **42** because his only[*] daughter, who was about 12 years old, was dying.

As Jesus was going, the crowds pressed in on him. **43** Now there was a woman who had a flow of blood[d] for 12 years, and she had not been able to get a cure from anyone.[e] **44** She approached from behind and touched the fringe of his outer garment,[f] and immediately her flow of blood stopped. **45** So Jesus said: "Who touched me?" When they were all denying it, Peter said: "Instructor, the crowds are hemming you in and pressing against you."[g] **46** But

Jesus said: "Someone touched me, for I know that power[a] went out of me." **47** Seeing that she had not escaped notice, the woman came trembling and fell down before him and declared before all the people why she touched him and how she was healed immediately. **48** But he said to her: "Daughter, your faith has made you well. Go in peace."[b]

49 While he was yet speaking, a representative of the presiding officer of the synagogue came, saying: "Your daughter has died; do not bother the Teacher any longer."[c] **50** On hearing this, Jesus answered him: "Have no fear, only have faith, and she will be saved."[d] **51** When he reached the house, he did not let anyone go in with him except Peter, John, James, and the girl's father and mother. **52** But people were all weeping and beating themselves in grief for her. So he said: "Stop weeping,[e] for she did not die but is sleeping."[f] **53** At this they began to laugh at him scornfully, because they knew she had died. **54** But he took her by the hand and called to her: "Child, get up!"[g] **55** And her spirit[*h] returned, and she rose immediately,[i] and he ordered that something be given her to eat. **56** Well, her parents were beside themselves, but he instructed them to tell no one what had happened.[j]

9 Then he called the Twelve together and gave them power and authority over all the demons[l] and to cure diseases.[l] **2** And he sent them out to preach the Kingdom of God and to heal, **3** and he said to them: "Carry nothing for the trip, neither staff nor food pouch nor bread nor money;[*] neither have

8:55 *Or "life force."   9:3 *Lit., "silver."

CHAP. 8
a Mr 5:18-20

b Mr 5:21

c Mt 9:18, 19
  Mr 5:22-24

d Le 15:25

e Mt 9:20-22
  Mr 5:25-29

f Nu 15:38, 39

g Mr 5:30-34

Second Col.
a Lu 5:17

b Mt 9:22
  Lu 7:50

c Mr 5:35-37

d Joh 11:25
  Ro 4:17

e Lu 7:12, 13

f Mt 9:23-26
  Mr 5:38-43
  Joh 11:11
  Ac 7:60
  Ac 13:36

g Mr 5:41
  Lu 7:14
  Joh 11:43

h Ge 2:7
  Ec 3:19
  Isa 42:5

i Mr 5:42

j Mr 7:35, 36

CHAP. 9
k Mr 6:7

l Mt 10:1

two garments.*[a] **4** But wherever you enter into a home, stay there and leave from there.[b] **5** And wherever people do not receive you, on going out of that city, shake the dust off your feet for a witness against them."[c] **6** Then starting out, they went through the territory from village to village, declaring the good news and performing cures everywhere.[d]

7 Now Herod* the district ruler[#] heard about everything that was happening, and he was greatly perplexed because some were saying that John had been raised up from the dead,[e] **8** but others were saying that E·li′jah had appeared, and still others that one of the ancient prophets had risen.[f] **9** Herod said: "John I beheaded.[g] Who, then, is this about whom I am hearing such things?" So he was trying to see him.[h]

10 When the apostles returned, they reported to Jesus all they had done.[i] With that he took them along and withdrew privately into a city called Beth·sa′i·da.[j] **11** But the crowds, getting to know it, followed him. And he received them kindly and began to speak to them about the Kingdom of God, and he healed those needing a cure.[k] **12** Then the day was coming to a close. The Twelve now came up and said to him: "Send the crowd away, so that they may go into the surrounding villages and countryside to find lodging and provisions, because out here we are in an isolated place."[l] **13** But he said to them: "You give them something to eat."[m] They said: "We have nothing more than five loaves and two fish, unless perhaps we our-

selves go and buy food for all these people." **14** There were, in fact, about 5,000 men. But he said to his disciples: "Have them sit down in groups of about 50 each." **15** And they did so and had them all sit down. **16** Taking now the five loaves and the two fish, he looked up to heaven and blessed them. Then he broke them up and began giving them to the disciples to set before the crowd. **17** So they all ate and were satisfied, and they took up the leftovers, 12 baskets of fragments.[a]

18 Later, while he was praying alone, the disciples came to him, and he questioned them, saying: "Who are the crowds saying that I am?"[b] **19** In reply they said: "John the Baptist, but others say E·li′jah, and still others say that one of the ancient prophets has risen."[c] **20** Then he said to them: "You, though, who do you say I am?" Peter answered: "The Christ of God."[d] **21** Then in a stern talk to them, he instructed them not to tell this to anybody,[e] **22** but he said: "The Son of man must undergo many sufferings and be rejected by the elders and the chief priests and the scribes and be killed,[f] and on the third day be raised up."[g]

23 Then he went on to say to all: "If anyone wants to come after me, let him disown himself[h] and pick up his torture stake* day after day and keep following me.[i] **24** For whoever wants to save his life* will lose it, but whoever loses his life* for my sake is the one who will save it.[j] **25** Really, what good will it do a man if he gains the whole world but loses his own self or suffers ruin?[k] **26** For whoever becomes ashamed of me and of my words, the Son of man w[ill]

CHAP. 9
a Mt 10:9, 10
  Mr 6:8, 9
  Lu 10:4
b Mt 10:11
  Mr 6:10
  Lu 10:5, 7
c Mt 10:14
  Mr 6:11
  Lu 10:10, 11
  Ac 13:50, 51
d Mt 11:1
  Mr 6:12, 13
e Mt 14:1, 2
  Mr 6:14-16
f Mt 8:27, 28
  Lu 9:18, 19
g Lu 23:8
h Mr 6:30
i Mt 14:13
k Mt 14:14
  Mr 6:34
  Joh 6:2
l Mt 14:15-21
  Mr 6:35-44
  Joh 6:5-13
m 2Ki 4:42-44

Second Col.
a Mt 14:20
  Mr 6:43
  Joh 6:13
b Mt 16:13-16
  Mr 8:27-30
c Lu 9:7, 8
d Mt 16:16
  Mr 8:29
  Joh 1:41
  Joh 6:68, 69
e Mt 16:20
f Isa 53:5, 8
  Lu 17:25
g Mt 16:21
  Mr 8:31
h Php 3:7, 8
i Mt 10:38
  Mt 16:24
  Mr 8:34
  Lu 14:27
j Mt 16:25
  Mr 8:35
  Joh 12:25
  Ac 20:24
  Re 2:10
k Mt 16:26
  Mr 8:36

9:3 *Or "an extra garment." 9:7 *That is, Herod Antipas. See Glossary. [#]Lit., "the tetrarch."

9:23 *See Glossary. 9:[2][4, 25] ["or "soul."]

be ashamed of that person when he comes in his glory and that of the Father and of the holy angels.[a] 27 But I tell you truly, there are some of those standing here who will not taste death at all until first they see the Kingdom of God."[b]

28 In fact, about eight days after saying these words, he took Peter, John, and James along and climbed up the mountain to pray.[c] 29 And as he was praying, the appearance of his face changed and his clothing became glitteringly white. 30 And look! two men were conversing with him; they were Moses and E·liʹjah. 31 These appeared with glory and began talking about his departure, which he was about to fulfill at Jerusalem.[d] 32 Now Peter and those with him were weighed down with sleep, but when they became fully awake, they saw his glory[e] and the two men standing with him. 33 And as these were departing from him, Peter said to Jesus: "Instructor, it is fine for us to be here. So let us erect three tents, one for you, one for Moses, and one for E·liʹjah." He did not realize what he was saying. 34 But as he was saying these things, a cloud formed and began to overshadow them. As they entered into the cloud, they became afraid. 35 Then a voice[f] came out of the cloud, saying: "This is my Son, the one who has been chosen.[g] Listen to him."[h] 36 As the voice spoke, Jesus was found alone. But they kept quiet and did not report to anyone in those days any of the things they saw.[i]

37 The following day when they came down from the mountain, a large crowd met him.[j] 38 And look! a man called out ... the crowd, saying: "Teach... my son, ... you to take a look at ... ...use he is my only

one.[a] 39 And look! a spirit seizes him, and suddenly he cries out, and it throws him into convulsions with foaming at the mouth, and only with difficulty does it leave him after bruising him. 40 I begged your disciples to expel it, but they could not." 41 In response Jesus said: "O faithless and twisted generation,[b] how long must I continue with you and put up with you? Bring your son over here."[c] 42 But even as he was approaching, the demon hurled him to the ground and violently threw him into a convulsion. However, Jesus rebuked the unclean spirit and healed the boy and gave him back to his father. 43 And they were all astounded at the majestic power of God.

While they were all astonished at all the things he was doing, he said to his disciples: 44 "Listen carefully and remember these words, for the Son of man is going to be betrayed into men's hands."[d] 45 But they did not understand what he was saying. In fact, it was concealed from them so that they might not grasp it, and they were afraid to question him about this saying.

46 Then a dispute arose among them about which one of them was the greatest.[e] 47 Jesus, knowing the reasoning of their hearts, took a young child, stood him beside him, 48 and said to them: "Whoever receives this young child on the basis of my name receives me also; and whoever receives me also receives the One who sent me.[f] For the one who conducts himself as a lesser one among all of you is the one who is great."[g]

49 In response John said: "Instructor, we saw someone expelling demons by using your name, and we tried to prevent him, because he is not following with us."[h] 50 But Jesus said to him:

CHAP. 9

a Mt 10:33
  Mr 8:38
  2Ti 2:12

b Mt 16:28
  Mr 9:1

c Mt 17:1-8
  Mr 9:2-8

d Lu 9:22
  Lu 13:33

e 2Pe 1:16

f Lu 3:22
  Joh 12:28

g Ps 2:7
  Isa 42:1
  Mt 3:17
  2Pe 1:17

h De 18:15
  Mt 17:5
  Mr 9:7
  Ac 3:22, 23

i Mt 17:9
  Mr 9:9

j Mr 9:14, 15

Second Col.

a Mt 17:14-16
  Mr 9:17, 18

b De 32:5

c Mt 17:17, 18
  Mr 9:19-27

d Mt 17:22, 23
  Mr 9:31, 32
  Lu 18:31-33

e Mt 18:1-5
  Mr 9:33-37
  Lu 22:24

f Mr 9:37
  Joh 12:44

g Pr 18:12
  Mt 18:4, 5
  Mt 23:11, 12

h Mr 9:38-40

"Do not try to prevent him, for whoever is not against you is for you."

51 As the days were drawing near* for him to be taken up,[a] he resolutely set his face to go to Jerusalem. 52 So he sent messengers ahead of him. And they went and entered a village of Samar'i·tans to make preparations for him. 53 But they did not receive him,[b] because he was determined* to go to Jerusalem. 54 When the disciples James and John[c] saw this, they said: "Lord, do you want us to call fire down from heaven and annihilate them?"[d] 55 But he turned and rebuked them. 56 So they went to a different village.

57 Now as they were going along the road, someone said to him: "I will follow you wherever you go." 58 But Jesus said to him: "Foxes have dens and birds of heaven have nests, but the Son of man has nowhere to lay down his head."[e] 59 Then he said to another: "Be my follower." The man said: "Lord, permit me first to go and bury my father."[f] 60 But he said to him: "Let the dead[g] bury their dead, but you go and declare abroad the Kingdom of God."[h] 61 And still another said: "I will follow you, Lord, but first permit me to say good-bye to those in my household." 62 Jesus said to him: "No man who has put his hand to a plow and looks at the things behind[i] is well-suited for the Kingdom of God."[j]

10 After these things the Lord designated 70 others and sent them out by twos[k] ahead of him into every city and place where he himself was to go. 2 Then he said to them: "Yes, the harvest is great, but the workers are few. Therefore,

beg the Master of the harvest to send out workers into his harvest.[a] 3 Go! Look! I am sending you out as lambs in among wolves.[b] 4 Do not carry a money bag or a food pouch or sandals,[c] and do not greet anyone* along the road. 5 Wherever you enter into a house, say first: 'May this house have peace.'[d] 6 And if a friend of peace is there, your peace will rest upon him. But if there is not, it will return to you. 7 So stay in that house,[e] eating and drinking the things they provide,[f] for the worker is worthy of his wages.[g] Do not keep transferring from house to house.

8 "Also, wherever you enter into a city and they receive you, eat what is set before you 9 and cure the sick ones in it and tell them: 'The Kingdom of God has come near to you.'[h] 10 But wherever you enter into a city and they do not receive you, go out into its main streets and say: 11 'We wipe off against you even the dust that sticks to our feet from your city.' Nevertheless, know this, that the Kingdom of God has come near.' 12 I tell you that it will be more endurable for Sod'om in that day than for that city.[j]

13 "Woe to you, Cho·ra'zin! Woe to you, Beth·sa'i·da! because if the powerful works that have taken place in you had taken place in Tyre and Si'don, they would long ago have repented, sitting in sackcloth and ashes.[k] 14 Consequently, it will be more endurable for Tyre and Si'don in the judgment than for you. 15 And you, Ca·per'na·um, will you perhaps be exalted to heaven? Down to the Grave* you will come!

CHAP. 9

a Ac 1:1, 2
1Ti 3:16

b Joh 4:9

c Mr 3:17

d 2Ki 1:10

e Mt 8:20

f Mt 8:21

g Eph 2:1

h Mt 8:22

i Ge 19:17

j Mt 10:37
1Co 9:24
Php 3:13

CHAP. 10

k Mr 6:7

Second Col.

a Mt 9:37, 38
1Co 3:9
2Th 3:1

b Mt 10:16

c Mt 10:9, 10
Lu 9:3

d Mt 10:12, 13

e Mt 10:11
Lu 9:4

f Ga 6:6

g Mt 10:9, 10
1Co 9:11, 14
1Ti 5:18

h Mt 3:1, 2
Lu 9:2

i Mt 10:14
Lu 9:5
Ac 13:50, 51

j Mt 11:24

k Mt 11:21-23

9:51 *Lit., "coming to the full." 9:53 *Lit., "his face was set."

10:4 *Or "embrace anyone in greeting." 10:15 *Or "Hades," that is, the common grave of mankind. See Glossary.

16 "Whoever listens to you listens to me.[a] And whoever disregards you disregards me also. Moreover, whoever disregards me disregards also him who sent me."[b]

17 Then the 70 returned with joy, saying: "Lord, even the demons are made subject to us by the use of your name."[c] **18** At that he said to them: "I see Satan already fallen[d] like lightning from heaven. **19** Look! I have given you the authority to trample underfoot serpents and scorpions, and over all the power of the enemy,[e] and nothing at all will harm you. **20** Nevertheless, do not rejoice because the spirits are made subject to you, but rejoice because your names have been written in the heavens."[f] **21** In that very hour he became overjoyed in the holy spirit and said: "I publicly praise you, Father, Lord of heaven and earth, because you have carefully hidden these things from wise and intellectual ones[g] and have revealed them to young children. Yes, O Father, because this is the way you approved.[h] **22** All things have been handed over to me by my Father, and no one knows who the Son is except the Father, and no one knows who the Father is except the Son[i] and anyone to whom the Son is willing to reveal him."[j]

23 With that he turned to the disciples and told them privately: "Happy are the eyes that see the things you are seeing.[k] **24** For I say to you, many prophets and kings desired to see the things you are observing but did not see them,[l] and to hear the things you are hearing but did not hear them."

25 Now look! a man versed in the Law stood up to test him and said: "Teacher, what do I need to do to inherit everlasting life?"[m] **26** He said to him: "What is writ-

ten in the Law? How do you read?" **27** In answer he said: "'You must love Jehovah* your God with your whole heart and with your whole soul# and with your whole strength and with your whole mind'[a] and 'your neighbor as yourself.'"[b] **28** He said to him: "You answered correctly; keep doing this and you will get life."[c]

29 But wanting to prove himself righteous,[d] the man said to Jesus: "Who really is my neighbor?" **30** In reply Jesus said: "A man was going down from Jerusalem to Jer'i·cho and fell victim to robbers, who stripped him, beat him, and went off, leaving him half-dead. **31** Now by coincidence a priest was going down on that road, but when he saw him, he passed by on the opposite side. **32** Likewise, a Levite, when he came to the place and saw him, passed by on the opposite side. **33** But a certain Sa·mar'i·tan[e] traveling the road came upon him, and at seeing him, he was moved with pity. **34** So he approached him and bandaged his wounds, pouring oil and wine on them. Then he mounted him on his own animal and brought him to an inn and took care of him. **35** The next day he took out two denar'i·i,* gave them to the innkeeper, and said: 'Take care of him, and whatever you spend besides this, I will repay you when I return.' **36** Who of these three seems to you to have made himself neighbor[f] to the man who fell victim to the robbers?" **37** He said: "The one who acted mercifully toward him."[g] Jesus then said to him: "Go and do the same yourself."[h]

38 Now as they went on their way, he entered into a certain

CHAP. 10
a Mt 10:40
  Mr 9:37
  Joh 13:20
b Joh 5:23
  Joh 12:48
  Joh 15:23
c Ac 16:17, 18
d Joh 12:31
  Joh 16:11
  Heb 2:14
  Re 12:7-9
e Ps 91:13
f Ex 32:32
  Da 12:1
  Php 4:3
  Re 3:5
g 1Co 1:19
  1Co 2:6
h Mt 11:25, 26
i Joh 10:15
j Mt 11:27
  Joh 1:18
  2Co 4:6
k Mt 13:16, 17
l 1Pe 1:10, 11
m Mt 19:16
  Mt 10:17
  Lu 18:18

Second Col.
a De 6:5
  De 10:12
  Jos 22:5
  Mr 12:30
b Le 19:18
  Mt 19:19
  Ro 13:9
  Ga 5:14
  Jas 2:8
c Le 18:5
  Joh 17:3
d Lu 16:15
e Joh 4:9
f Mt 19:19
g Pr 14:21
h Lu 6:36
  Joh 13:17
  Eph 4:32

10:27 *See App. A5. #See Glossary.
10:35 *See App. B14.

village. Here a woman named Martha[a] received him as a guest in her house. **39** She also had a sister called Mary, who sat down at the feet of the Lord and kept listening to what he was saying.* **40** Martha, on the other hand, was distracted with attending to many duties. So she came to him and said: "Lord, does it not matter to you that my sister has left me alone to attend to things? Tell her to come and help me." **41** In answer the Lord said to her: "Martha, Martha, you are anxious and disturbed about many things. **42** A few things, though, are needed, or just one. For her part, Mary chose the good portion,*[b] and it will not be taken away from her."

11 Now he was in a certain place praying, and when he stopped, one of his disciples said to him: "Lord, teach us how to pray, just as John also taught his disciples."

2 So he said to them: "Whenever you pray, say: 'Father, let your Kingdom come.[d] **3** Give us each day our bread according to our daily needs.[e] **4** And forgive us our sins,[f] for we ourselves also forgive everyone who is in debt to us;[g] and do not bring us into temptation.'"[h]

5 Then he said to them: "Suppose one of you has a friend and you go to him at midnight and say to him, 'Friend, lend me three loaves, **6** because one of my friends has just come to me on a journey and I have nothing to offer him.' **7** But that one replies from inside: 'Stop bothering me. The door is already locked, and my young children are with me in bed. I cannot get up and give you anything.' **8** I tell you, even if

he will not get up and give him anything because of being his friend, certainly because of his bold persistence[a] he will get up and give him whatever he needs. **9** So I say to you, keep on asking,[b] and it will be given you; keep on seeking, and you will find; keep on knocking, and it will be opened to you.[c] **10** For everyone asking receives,[d] and everyone seeking finds, and to everyone knocking, it will be opened. **11** Indeed, which father among you, if his son asks for a fish, will hand him a serpent instead of a fish?[e] **12** Or if he also asks for an egg, will hand him a scorpion? **13** Therefore, if you, although being wicked, know how to give good gifts to your children, how much more so will the Father in heaven give holy spirit to those asking him!"[f]

14 Later he expelled a speechless demon.[g] After the demon came out, the speechless man spoke, and the crowds were amazed.[h] **15** But some of them said: "He expels the demons by means of Be·el'ze·bub,* the ruler of the demons."[i] **16** And others, to test him, began demanding a sign[j] out of heaven from him. **17** Knowing their thinking,[k] he said to them: "Every kingdom divided against itself comes to ruin, and a house divided against itself, falls. **18** In the same way, if Satan is also divided against himself, how will his kingdom stand? For you say I expel the demons by means of Be·el'ze·bub. **19** If I expel the demons by means of Be·el'ze·bub, by whom do your sons expel them? This is why they will be your judges. **20** But if it is by means of God's finger[l] that I expel the demons, the Kingdom of God has really overtaken

---

CHAP. 10
a Joh 12:2

b Mt 4:4
  Mt 6:33

CHAP. 11
c Le 22:32
  Isa 5:16
  Eze 36:23

d Da 2:44
  Da 7:13, 14
  Mt 6:9-13

e Ps 37:25

f Ps 79:9
  Da 9:19

g Mr 11:25
  Eph 4:32
  Col 3:13

h Lu 22:46
  1Co 10:13
  Jas 1:13
  Re 3:10

Second Col.
a Lu 18:5

b Ro 12:12

c Mt 7:7, 8

d Mr 11:24
  Joh 15:7
  Jas 1:6
  1Jo 3:22
  1Jo 5:14

e Mt 7:9, 10

f Mt 7:11
  Jas 1:17

g Mt 12:22

h Mt 9:32-34

i Mt 12:24-30
  Mr 3:22-27

j Mt 12:38
  Mr 8:11

k Joh 2:24, 25

l Ex 8:19

10:39 *Lit., "his word." 10:42 *Or "best portion." 11:2 *Or "be held sacred; be treated as holy."

11:15 *A designation applied to Satan.

you.[a] **21** When a strong, well-armed man guards his palace, his belongings remain secure. **22** But when someone stronger than he is comes against him and conquers him, that man takes away all his weapons in which he was trusting, and he divides up the things he took from him. **23** Whoever is not on my side is against me, and whoever does not gather with me scatters.[b]

24 "When an unclean spirit comes out of a man, it passes through waterless places in search of a resting-place, and after finding none, it says, 'I will return to my house from which I moved.'[c] **25** And on arriving, it finds the house swept clean and adorned. **26** Then it goes and takes along seven other spirits more wicked than itself, and after getting inside, they dwell there. So the final circumstances of that man become worse than the first."

27 Now as he was saying these things, a woman from the crowd called out to him: "Happy is the womb that carried you and the breasts that nursed you!"[d] **28** But he said: "No, rather, happy are those hearing the word of God and keeping it!"[e]

29 When the crowds were massing together, he began to say: "This generation is a wicked generation; it looks for a sign, but no sign will be given to it except the sign of Jo'nah.[f] **30** For just as Jo'nah[g] became a sign to the Nin'e·vites, so will the Son of man be to this generation. **31** The queen of the south[h] will be raised up in the judgment with the men of this generation and will condemn them, for she came from the ends of the earth to hear the wisdom of Sol'o·mon. But look! something more than Sol'o·mon is here.[i] **32** The men of Nin'e·veh will rise in the judgment with this genera-

tion and will condemn it, because they repented at what Jo'nah preached.[a] But look! something more than Jo'nah is here. **33** After lighting a lamp, a person puts it, not in a hidden place nor under a basket,* but on the lampstand,[b] so that those who come in may see the light. **34** The lamp of the body is your eye. When your eye is focused,* your whole body is also bright;* but when it is envious,[△] your body is also dark.[c] **35** Be alert, therefore, that the light that is in you is not darkness. **36** Therefore, if your whole body is bright with no part of it dark, it will all be as bright as when a lamp gives you light by its rays."

37 When he had said this, a Pharisee asked him to dine with him. So he went in and reclined at the table. **38** However, the Pharisee was surprised at seeing that he did not first wash* before the dinner.[d] **39** But the Lord said to him: "Now you Pharisees, you cleanse the outside of the cup and dish, but inside you are full of greediness and wickedness.[e] **40** Unreasonable ones! The one who made the outside made also the inside, did he not? **41** But give as gifts of mercy* the things that are from within, and look! everything about you will be clean. **42** But woe to you Pharisees, because you give the tenth of the mint and of the rue and of every other garden herb,*[f] but you disregard the justice and the love of God! These things you were under obligation to do, but not to disregard those other things.[g] **43** Woe to you Pharisees, be-

---

CHAP. 11
a Mt 12:28
  Lu 17:21

b Mt 12:30

c Mt 12:43-45

d Lu 1:46-48

e De 29:9
  Ps 1:1, 2
  Ps 112:1
  Ps 119:2
  Mt 7:21
  Jas 1:25

f Mt 12:38-42
  Mt 16:4

g Jon 1:17

h 1Ki 10:1
  2Ch 9:1

i Mt 12:42

Second Col.
a Jon 3:5

b Mt 5:15
  Mr 4:21
  Lu 8:16

c Mt 6:22, 23

d Mt 15:2

e Mt 23:25, 26

f Le 27:30

g Mt 23:23, 24
  Joh 7:24

11:33 *Or "measuring basket." 11:34 *Or "clear." Lit., "simple." #Or "full of light." △Lit., "bad; wicked." 11:38 *That is, ceremonially cleanse himself. 11:41 *Or "gifts to the poor." See Glossary. 11:42 *Or "other vegetable."

cause you love the front* seats in the synagogues and the greetings in the marketplaces!ᵃ **44** Woe to you, because you are as those graves* that are not clearly visible,#ᵇ that men walk on and do not know it!"

45 In reply one of those versed in the Law said to him: "Teacher, in saying these things, you insult us also." **46** Then he said: "Woe also to you who are versed in the Law, because you load men down with loads hard to carry, but you yourselves do not touch the loads with one of your fingers!ᶜ

47 "Woe to you, because you build the tombs* of the prophets, but your forefathers killed them!ᵈ **48** Certainly you are witnesses of the deeds of your forefathers, and yet you approve of them, for they killed the prophetsᵉ but you are building their tombs. **49** That is why the wisdom of God also said: 'I will send prophets and apostles to them, and they will kill and persecute some of them, **50** so that the blood of all the prophets spilled from the founding of the world may be charged against* this generation,ᶠ **51** from the blood of Abelᵍ down to the blood of Zech·a·riʹah, who was killed between the altar and the house.'#ʰ Yes, I tell you, it will be charged against* this generation.

52 "Woe to you who are versed in the Law, because you took away the key of knowledge. You yourselves did not go in, and you hinder those going in!"ⁱ

53 So when he went out from there, the scribes and the Pharisees began to put extreme pressure on him and to ply him with many more questions, **54** lying

in wait for him to catch him in something he might say.ᵃ

12 In the meantime, when a crowd of so many thousands had gathered together that they were stepping on one another, he started by saying first to his disciples: "Watch out for the leaven of the Pharisees, which is hypocrisy.ᵇ **2** But there is nothing carefully concealed that will not be revealed, and nothing secret that will not become known.ᶜ **3** Therefore, whatever you say in the darkness will be heard in the light, and what you whisper in private rooms will be preached from the housetops. **4** Moreover, I say to you, my friends,ᵈ do not fear those who kill the body and after this are not able to do anything more.ᵉ **5** But I will show you whom to fear: Fear the One who after killing has authority to throw into Ge·henʹna.*ᶠ Yes, I tell you, fear this One.ᵍ **6** Five sparrows sell for two coins of small value,* do they not? Yet not one of them is forgotten# by God.ʰ **7** But even the hairs of your head are all numbered.ⁱ Have no fear; you are worth more than many sparrows.ʲ

8 "I say to you, everyone who acknowledges me before men,ᵏ the Son of man will also acknowledge him before the angels of God.ˡ **9** But whoever disowns me before men will be disowned before the angels of God.ᵐ **10** And everyone who says a word against the Son of man, it will be forgiven him, but whoever blasphemes against the holy spirit will not be forgiven.ⁿ **11** When they bring you in before public assemblies,* government officials,

---

CHAP. 11
a Mt 23:6, 7

b Mt 23:27, 28

c Mt 23:2, 4

d Mt 23:29-31

e Ac 7:52
Heb 11:32, 37

f Re 18:21, 24

g Ge 4:8, 10

h 2Ch 24:20-22

i Mt 23:13
1Th 2:14-16

Second Col.
a Lu 20:20

CHAP. 12
b Mt 16:6
Mr 8:15

c Mt 10:26, 27
Mr 4:22
Lu 8:17

d Joh 15:14

e Ac 20:24

f Mt 10:28

g Isa 8:13
Heb 10:31
1Pe 2:17
Re 14:7

h Mt 10:29

i Mt 10:30
Lu 21:18

j Mt 10:31
Lu 12:24

k Ro 10:9

l Mt 10:32, 33

m Mr 8:38
Lu 9:26
2Ti 2:12
1Jo 2:23

n Mt 12:31, 32
Mr 3:28, 29

11:43 *Or "best." **11:44, 47** *Or "memorial tombs." **11:44** #Or "those unmarked graves." **11:50, 51** *Or "required from." **11:51** #Or "temple."

12:5 *See Glossary. **12:6** *Lit., "for two assarions." See App. B14. #Or "overlooked." **12:11** *Or "before synagogues."

and authorities, do not become anxious about how or what you will speak in defense or what you will say,[a] **12** for the holy spirit will teach you in that very hour the things you should say."[b]

13 Then someone in the crowd said to him: "Teacher, tell my brother to divide the inheritance with me." **14** He said to him: "Man, who appointed me judge or arbitrator between you two?" **15** Then he said to them: "Keep your eyes open and guard against every sort of greed,*[c] because even when a person has an abundance, his life does not result from the things he possesses."[d] **16** With that he told them an illustration, saying: "The land of a rich man produced well. **17** So he began reasoning within himself, 'What should I do now that I have nowhere to gather my crops?' **18** Then he said, 'I will do this:[e] I will tear down my storehouses and build bigger ones, and there I will gather all my grain and all my goods, **19** and I will say to myself:* "You* have many good things stored up for many years; take it easy, eat, drink, enjoy yourself."' **20** But God said to him, 'Unreasonable one, this night they are demanding your life* from you. Who, then, is to have the things you stored up?'[f] **21** So it goes with the man who stores up treasure for himself but is not rich toward God."[g]

22 Then he said to his disciples: "That is why I say to you, stop being anxious about your lives* as to what you will eat or about your bodies as to what you will wear.[h] **23** For the life* is worth more than food and the body more than cloth-

ing. **24** Consider the ravens: They neither sow seed nor reap; they have neither barn nor storehouse; yet God feeds them.[a] Are you not worth much more than birds?[b] **25** Who of you by being anxious can add a cubit* to his life span? **26** If, therefore, you cannot do such a small thing, why be anxious about the remaining things?[c] **27** Consider how the lilies grow: They neither toil nor spin; but I tell you that not even Sol'o·mon in all his glory was arrayed as one of these.[d] **28** Now if this is how God clothes the vegetation in the field that today exists and tomorrow is cast into an oven, how much more will he clothe you, you with little faith! **29** So stop seeking what you will eat and what you will drink, and stop being in anxious suspense;[e] **30** for all these are the things the nations of the world are eagerly pursuing, but your Father knows you need these things.[f] **31** Instead, keep seeking his Kingdom, and these things will be added to you.[g]

32 "Have no fear, little flock,[h] for your Father has approved of giving you the Kingdom.[i] **33** Sell your belongings and give gifts of mercy.*[j] Make money pouches that do not wear out, a never-failing treasure in the heavens,[k] where no thief gets near and no moth consumes. **34** For where your treasure is, there your hearts will be also.

35 "Be dressed and ready*[l] and have your lamps burning,[m] **36** and you should be like men waiting for their master to return[n] from the marriage,[o] so when he comes and knocks, they may at once open to him. **37** Happy are those

---

CHAP. 12
a Mt 10:19, 20
   Mr 13:11
   Lu 21:14, 15

b Ex 4:12
   Ac 6:8, 10

c Ex 20:17
   De 5:21
   Col 3:5

d 1Ti 6:7

e Jas 4:13-16

f Ps 49:16-19
   Pr 27:1

g Ec 11:9
   Mt 6:20
   1Ti 6:17-19
   Jas 2:5

h Mt 6:25-30
   Php 4:6

Second Col.
a Job 38:41
   Ps 147:9

b Mt 6:26
   Lu 12:7

c Mt 6:34

d 1Ki 10:4-7

e Mt 6:31, 32

f 2Ch 16:9
   Php 4:19

g Ps 34:10
   Mt 6:33
   1Ti 4:8

h Joh 10:14

i Da 7:27
   Lu 22:28-30
   Heb 12:28
   Jas 2:5
   Re 1:6

j Mt 19:21
   Lu 18:22
   Ac 2:45
   Ac 4:34, 35

k Mt 6:20, 21
   Lu 16:9
   1Ti 6:18, 19

l Eph 6:14
   1Pe 1:13

m Mt 25:1
   Php 2:15

n Mr 13:35

o Mt 25:5

12:15 *Or "covetousness." 12:19 *Or "my soul." *Or "Soul, you." 12:20 *Or "soul." 12:22 *Or "souls." 12:23 *Or "the soul."

12:25 *See App. B14. 12:33 *Or "gifts to the poor." See Glossary. 12:35 *Lit., "Let your loins be girded."

slaves whom the master on coming finds watching! Truly I say to you, he will dress* himself for service and have them recline at the table and will come alongside and minister to them. **38** And if he comes in the second watch,* even if in the third,# and finds them ready, happy are they! **39** But know this, if the householder had known at what hour the thief would come, he would not have let his house be broken into.ᵃ **40** You also, keep ready, because at an hour that you do not think likely, the Son of man is coming."ᵇ

41 Then Peter said: "Lord, are you telling this illustration just to us or also to everyone?" **42** And the Lord said: "Who really is the faithful steward,* the discreet one,# whom his master will appoint over his body of attendantsᐃ to keep giving them their measure of food supplies at the proper time?ᶜ **43** Happy is that slave if his master on coming finds him doing so! **44** I tell you truthfully, he will appoint him over all his belongings. **45** But if ever that slave should say in his heart, 'My master delays coming,' and starts to beat the male and female servants and to eat and drink and get drunk,ᵈ **46** the master of that slave will come on a day that he is not expecting him and at an hour that he does not know, and he will punish him with the greatest severity and assign him a part with the unfaithful ones. **47** Then that slave who understood the will of his master but did not get ready or do what he asked* will be beaten with

many strokes.ᵃ **48** But the one who did not understand and yet did things deserving of strokes will be beaten with few. Indeed, everyone to whom much was given, much will be demanded of him, and the one who was put in charge of much will have more than usual demanded of him.ᵇ

49 "I came to start a fire on the earth, and what more is there for me to wish if it has already been lit? **50** Indeed, I have a baptism with which to be baptized, and how I am distressed until it is finished!ᶜ **51** Do you think I came to give peace on the earth? No, I tell you, but rather division.ᵈ **52** For from now on there will be five in one house divided, three against two and two against three. **53** They will be divided, father against son and son against father, mother against daughter and daughter against mother, mother-in-law against daughter-in-law and daughter-in-law against mother-in-law."ᵉ

54 Then he also said to the crowds: "When you see a cloud rising in the west, at once you say, 'A storm is coming,' and it happens. **55** And when you see that a south wind is blowing, you say, 'There will be a heat wave,' and it occurs. **56** Hypocrites, you know how to examine the appearance of earth and sky, but why do you not know how to examine this particular time?ᶠ **57** Why do you not judge also for yourselves what is righteous? **58** For example, when you are going with your legal opponent to a ruler, while on the way, get to work to settle the dispute with him so that he may not summon you before the judge, and the judge deliver you to the court officer, and the court officer throw you into prison.ᵍ **59** I tell you,

---

CHAP. 12

ᵃ Mt 24:43
1Th 5:2
2Pe 3:10
Re 16:15

ᵇ Mt 24:44
Mt 25:13
Re 3:3

ᶜ Mt 24:45-47

ᵈ Mt 24:48-51

Second Col.

ᵃ Jas 1:22
Jas 4:17

ᵇ Mt 25:29
Joh 15:2

ᶜ Joh 12:27

ᵈ Mt 10:34-36
Joh 7:41, 43
Joh 9:16

ᵉ Mic 7:6

ᶠ Mt 16:2, 3
Lu 19:42

ᵍ Mt 5:25, 26

12:37 *Or "gird." **12:38** *From about 9:00 p.m. to midnight. #From midnight to about 3:00 a.m. **12:42** *Or "house manager." #Or "wise one." ᐃOr "household servants." **12:47** *Or "do according to his will."

you will certainly not get out of there until you pay over your last small coin."*

13 At that time some who were present reported to him about the Gal·i·le′ans whose blood Pilate had mixed with their sacrifices. **2** In reply he said to them: "Do you think that those Gal·i·le′ans were worse sinners than all other Gal·i·le′ans because they have suffered these things? **3** No, I tell you; but unless you repent, you will all likewise be destroyed.ᵃ **4** Or those 18 on whom the tower in Si·lo′am fell, killing them—do you think that they had greater guilt than all other men who live in Jerusalem? **5** No, I tell you; but unless you repent, you will all be destroyed, as they were."

6 Then he went on to tell this illustration: "A man had a fig tree planted in his vineyard, and he came looking for fruit on it but found none.ᵇ **7** Then he said to the vinedresser, 'Here it is three years that I have come looking for fruit on this fig tree, but have found none. Cut it down! Why should it keep the ground useless?' **8** In reply he said to him, 'Master, leave it alone for one more year until I dig around it and put on manure. **9** If it produces fruit in the future, well and good; but if not, then cut it down.'"ᶜ

10 Now he was teaching in one of the synagogues on the Sabbath. **11** And look! a woman was there who had had a spirit of weakness* for 18 years; and she was bent double and was unable to straighten up at all. **12** When he saw her, Jesus addressed her and said: "Woman, you are released from your weakness."ᵈ **13** And he laid his

hands on her, and instantly she straightened up and began to glorify God. **14** But in response the presiding officer of the synagogue, indignant because Jesus did the cure on the Sabbath, said to the crowd: "There are six days on which work ought to be done;ᵃ so come and be cured on those days, and not on the Sabbath day."ᵇ **15** However, the Lord answered him: "Hypocrites,ᶜ does not each one of you on the Sabbath untie his bull or his donkey from the stall and lead it away to give it something to drink?ᵈ **16** Should not this woman, who is a daughter of Abraham and whom Satan held bound for 18 years, be released from this bondage on the Sabbath day?" **17** Well, when he said these things, all his opposers began to feel shame, but the entire crowd began to rejoice at all the glorious things he did.ᵉ

18 So he went on to say: "What is the Kingdom of God like, and with what can I compare it? **19** It is like a mustard grain that a man took and planted in his garden, and it grew and became a tree, and the birds of heaven nested in its branches."ᶠ

20 And again he said: "With what can I compare the Kingdom of God? **21** It is like leaven that a woman took and mixed with three large measures* of flour until the whole mass was fermented."ᵍ

22 And he traveled from city to city and from village to village, teaching and continuing on his journey to Jerusalem. **23** Now a man said to him: "Lord, are those being saved few?" He said to them: **24** "Exert yourselves vigorously to get

---

CHAP. 13
a Ac 3:19

b Mt 21:19
Mr 11:13

c 2Pe 3:9

d Isa 61:1
Lu 4:18

Second Col.
a Ex 20:9, 10
Ex 35:2
De 5:13, 14

b Mt 12:10
Mr 3:2
Joh 5:15, 16

c Mt 23:27, 28
Lu 12:1

d Lu 14:5

e Lu 9:43

f Mt 13:31, 32
Mr 4:30-32

g Mt 13:33

12:59 *Lit., "the last lepton." See App. B14. 13:11 *Or "a disabling spirit."

13:21 *Lit., "seah measures." A seah equaled 7.33 L (6.66 dry qt). See App. B14.

in through the narrow door,[a] because many, I tell you, will seek to get in but will not be able. **25** When the householder gets up and locks the door, you will stand outside knocking at the door, saying, 'Lord, open to us.'[b] But in answer he will say to you: 'I do not know where you are from.' **26** Then you will start saying, 'We ate and drank in your presence, and you taught in our main streets.'[c] **27** But he will say to you, 'I do not know where you are from. Get away from me, all you workers of unrighteousness!' **28** There is where your weeping and the gnashing of your teeth will be, when you see Abraham, Isaac, Jacob, and all the prophets in the Kingdom of God, but you yourselves thrown outside.[d] **29** Furthermore, people will come from east and west and from north and south, and will recline at the table in the Kingdom of God. **30** And look! there are those last who will be first, and there are those first who will be last."[e]

31 In that very hour some of the Pharisees came up and told him: "Get out and go away from here, because Herod wants to kill you." **32** And he said to them: "Go and tell that fox, 'Look! I am casting out demons and healing people today and tomorrow, and on the third day I will be finished.' **33** Nevertheless, I must go on today, tomorrow, and the following day, because it cannot be* that a prophet should be put to death outside of Jerusalem.[f] **34** Jerusalem, Jerusalem, the killer of the prophets and stoner of those sent to her[g]—how often I wanted to gather your children together the way a hen gathers her brood of chicks under her wings! But

you did not want it.[a] **35** Look! Your house is abandoned to you.[b] I tell you, you will by no means see me until you say: 'Blessed is the one who comes in Jehovah's* name!'"[c]

14 On another occasion he went to eat a meal in the house of one of the leaders of the Pharisees on the Sabbath, and they were closely watching him. **2** And look! a man who had dropsy* was in front of him. **3** So in response Jesus asked those versed in the Law and the Pharisees: "Is it lawful to cure on the Sabbath or not?"[d] **4** But they kept silent. With that he took hold of the man, healed him, and sent him away. **5** Then he said to them: "Who of you, if his son or bull falls into a well,[e] will not immediately pull him out on the Sabbath day?"[f] **6** And they were not able to reply to this.

7 He then told the invited men an illustration when he noticed how they were choosing the most prominent places for themselves.[g] He said to them: **8** "When you are invited by someone to a marriage feast, do not recline in the most prominent place.[h] Perhaps someone more distinguished than you may also have been invited. **9** Then the one who invited you both will come and say to you, 'Let this man have your place.' Then you will proceed with shame to take the lowest place. **10** But when you are invited, go and recline in the lowest place, so that when the man who invited you comes, he will say to you, 'Friend, go on up higher.' Then you will have honor in front of all your fellow guests.[i] **11** For

---

CHAP. 13
a Isa 55:6
　Mt 7:13, 14
　Php 3:12-14
　1Ti 6:12

b Lu 6:46

c Mt 7:22, 23

d Mt 8:11, 12

e Mt 19:30
　Mr 10:31

f Mt 16:21

g 2Ch 24:20, 21
　Ne 9:26

Second Col.
a Mt 23:37

b Le 26:31
　1Ki 9:7, 8
　Jer 12:7
　Jer 22:5

c Ps 118:26
　Mt 23:38, 39

CHAP. 14
d Lu 6:9
　Joh 7:23

e Ex 23:5
　De 22:4

f Mt 12:11
　Lu 13:15

g Mt 23:2, 6
　Lu 11:43
　Lu 20:46

h Pr 25:6, 7

i Pr 15:33
　Jas 4:10
　1Pe 5:5

13:33 *Or "it is inconceivable."

13:35 *See App. A5. **14:2** *Or "edema," an excess buildup of fluid in the body.

everyone who exalts himself will be humbled, and whoever humbles himself will be exalted."[a]

12 Next he said also to the man who had invited him: "When you spread a dinner or an evening meal, do not call your friends or your brothers or your relatives or your rich neighbors. Otherwise, they might also invite you in return, and it would become a repayment to you. **13** But when you spread a feast, invite the poor, the crippled, the lame, the blind;[b] **14** and you will be happy, because they have nothing with which to repay you. For you will be repaid in the resurrection[c] of the righteous ones."

15 On hearing these things, one of the fellow guests said to him: "Happy is the one who dines* in the Kingdom of God."

16 Jesus said to him: "A man was spreading a grand evening meal,[d] and he invited many. **17** He sent his slave out at the hour of the evening meal to say to the invited ones, 'Come, because everything is now ready.' **18** But they all alike began to make excuses.[e] The first said to him, 'I bought a field and need to go out and see it; I ask you, have me excused.' **19** And another said, 'I bought five yoke* of cattle and am going to examine them; I ask you, have me excused.'[f] **20** Still another said, 'I just got married, and for this reason I cannot come.' **21** So the slave came and reported these things to his master. Then the master of the house became angry and said to his slave, 'Go out quickly to the main streets and the alleys of the city, and bring in here the poor and crippled and blind and lame.' **22** In time the slave said, 'Master, what

you ordered has been done, and still there is room.' **23** So the master said to the slave, 'Go out to the roads and the lanes and compel them to come in, so that my house may be filled.[a] **24** For I say to you, none of those men who were invited will taste my evening meal.'"[b]

25 Now large crowds were traveling with him, and he turned and said to them: **26** "If anyone comes to me and does not hate* his father and mother and wife and children and brothers and sisters, yes, and even his own life,*[c] he cannot be my disciple.[d] **27** Whoever does not carry his torture stake* and come after me cannot be my disciple.[e] **28** For example, who of you wanting to build a tower does not first sit down and calculate the expense to see if he has enough to complete it? **29** Otherwise, he might lay its foundation but not be able to finish it, and all the onlookers would start to ridicule him, **30** saying: 'This man started to build but was not able to finish.' **31** Or what king marching out against another king in war does not first sit down and take counsel whether he is able with 10,000 troops to stand up to the one who comes against him with 20,000? **32** If, in fact, he cannot do so, then while that one is yet far away, he sends out a body of ambassadors and sues for peace. **33** In the same way, you may be sure that not one of you who does not say good-bye to* all his belongings can be my disciple.[f]

34 "Salt, to be sure, is fine. But if the salt loses its strength, with what will it be seasoned?[g] **35** It is not suitable for soil or for manure. People throw it

---

CHAP. 14
a Pr 29:23
  Mt 23:12
  Lu 18:14
  Jas 4:6

b Job 31:16, 22
  Pr 3:27, 28

c Joh 5:28, 29
  Joh 11:24
  Ac 24:15

d Mt 22:2

e Mt 22:3

f Mt 22:5

Second Col.
a Mt 22:9, 10

b Mt 21:43
  Mt 22:8

c Re 12:11

d Mt 10:37
  Lu 18:29, 30
  Joh 12:25

e Mt 16:24
  Mr 8:34
  Lu 9:23

f Mt 19:27
  Lu 9:62
  Php 3:7, 8

g Mt 5:13
  Mr 9:50
  Col 4:6

14:15 *Lit., "eats bread." 14:19 *Or "pairs."

14:26 *Or "love to a lesser degree." *Or "soul." 14:27 *See Glossary. 14:33 *Or "give up."

away. Let the one who has ears to listen, listen."[a]

15 Now all the tax collectors and the sinners kept gathering around him to hear him.[b] **2** And both the Pharisees and the scribes kept muttering: "This man welcomes sinners and eats with them." **3** Then he told them this illustration, saying: **4** "What man among you with 100 sheep, on losing one of them, will not leave the 99 behind in the wilderness and go after the lost one until he finds it?[c] **5** And when he has found it, he puts it on his shoulders and rejoices. **6** And when he gets home, he calls his friends and his neighbors together, saying to them, 'Rejoice with me, for I have found my sheep that was lost.'[d] **7** I tell you that in the same way, there will be more joy in heaven over one sinner who repents[e] than over 99 righteous ones who have no need of repentance.

8 "Or what woman who has ten drachma coins,* if she loses one of the drachmas,* does not light a lamp and sweep her house and search carefully until she finds it? **9** And when she has found it, she calls her friends[w] and neighbors together, saying, 'Rejoice with me, for I have found the drachma coin* that I had lost.' **10** In the same way, I tell you, joy arises among the angels of God over one sinner who repents."[f]

11 Then he said: "A man had two sons. **12** And the younger one said to his father, 'Father, give me the share of the property that should come to me.' So he divided his belongings between them. **13** A few days later, the younger son gathered all his things together and traveled to a distant country and there squandered his property by living a debauched* life. **14** When he had spent everything, a severe famine occurred throughout that country, and he fell into need. **15** He even went and attached himself to one of the citizens of that country, who sent him into his fields to herd swine.[a] **16** And he longed to be filled with the carob pods that the swine were eating, but no one would give him anything.

17 "When he came to his senses, he said, 'How many of my father's hired men have more than enough bread, while I am dying here from hunger! **18** I will get up and travel to my father and say to him: "Father, I have sinned against heaven and against you. **19** I am no longer worthy of being called your son. Make me as one of your hired men."' **20** So he got up and went to his father. While he was still a long way off, his father caught sight of him and was moved with pity, and he ran and embraced him* and tenderly kissed him. **21** Then the son said to him, 'Father, I have sinned against heaven and against you.[b] I am no longer worthy of being called your son.' **22** But the father said to his slaves, 'Quick! bring out a robe, the best one, and clothe him with it, and put a ring on his hand and sandals on his feet. **23** Also bring the fattened calf, slaughter it, and let us eat and celebrate, **24** for this son of mine was dead but has come to life again;[c] he was lost and has been found.' And they started to enjoy themselves.

25 "Now his older son was in the field, and as he returned and got near the house, he heard

---

CHAP. 14
a Mt 13:43
Mr 4:9
Re 2:29

CHAP. 15
b Mt 9:10, 11
Mr 2:15, 16
Lu 5:29, 30
1Ti 1:15

c Eze 34:11, 16
Mt 18:12, 13
Lu 19:10

d Mt 18:14
Ro 12:15
1Pe 2:25

e Eze 33:11
Lu 5:32

f Mt 9:13
Mr 2:17

Second Col.
a Le 11:7, 8

b 2Ch 7:14
Ps 32:5
Ps 51:4
Pr 28:13
Lu 18:13
1Jo 1:9

c Ro 6:13
Eph 2:4, 5

15:8, 9 *See App. B14.   15:9 *Or "her women friends."

15:13 *Or "wasteful; reckless."   15:20 *Lit., "fell upon his neck."

music and dancing. 26 So he called one of the servants to him and asked what was happening. 27 He said to him, 'Your brother has come, and your father slaughtered the fattened calf because he got him back in good health.'* 28 But he became angry and refused to go in. Then his father came out and began to plead with him. 29 In reply he said to his father, 'Look! These many years I have slaved for you and never once did I disobey your orders, and yet you never once gave me a young goat to enjoy with my friends. 30 But as soon as this son of yours arrived who squandered* your belongings with prostitutes, you slaughtered the fattened calf for him.' 31 Then he said to him, 'My son, you have always been with me, and all the things that are mine are yours. 32 But we just had to celebrate and rejoice, for your brother was dead but has come to life; he was lost and has been found.'"

16 Then he also said to the disciples: "A rich man had a steward* who was accused of handling his goods wastefully. 2 So he called him and said, 'What is this I hear about you? Hand in the account of your stewardship, for you can no longer manage the house.' 3 Then the steward said to himself, 'What am I to do, seeing that my master is taking the stewardship away from me? I am not strong enough to dig, and I am ashamed to beg. 4 Ah! I know what I will do, so that when I am removed from the stewardship, people will welcome me into their homes.' 5 And calling to him each one of his master's debtors, he said to the first, 'How much do you owe my master?' 6 He replied, 'A hundred measures* of olive oil.' He said to him, 'Take back your written agreement and sit down and quickly write 50.' 7 Next, he said to another one, 'Now you, how much do you owe?' He said, 'A hundred large measures* of wheat.' He said to him, 'Take back your written agreement and write 80.' 8 And his master commended the steward, though unrighteous, because he acted with practical wisdom;* for the sons of this system of things# are wiser in a practical way toward their own generation than the sons of the light[a] are.

9 "Also, I say to you: Make friends for yourselves by means of the unrighteous riches,[b] so that when such fail, they may receive you into the everlasting dwelling places.[c] 10 The person faithful in what is least is faithful also in much, and the person unrighteous in what is least is unrighteous also in much. 11 Therefore, if you have not proved yourselves faithful in connection with the unrighteous riches, who will entrust you with what is true? 12 And if you have not proved yourselves faithful in connection with what belongs to another, who will give you something for yourselves?[d] 13 No servant can be a slave to two masters, for either he will hate the one and love the other, or he will stick to the one and despise the other. You cannot be slaves to God and to Riches."[e]

14 Now the Pharisees, who were money lovers, were listening to all these things, and they

---

CHAP. 16
a Joh 12:36
Eph 5:8
1Th 5:5

b Mt 19:21
1Ti 6:17

c Mt 25:34
Lu 12:20, 21

d Lu 12:48

e Mt 6:24

15:27 *Or "safe." 15:30 *Lit., "devoured." 16:1 *Or "house manager." 16:6 *Or "bath measures." A bath equaled 22 L (5.81 gal). See App. B14. 16:7 *Or "A hundred cor measures." A cor equaled 220 L (200 dry qt). See App. B14. 16:8 *Or "acted shrewdly; acted discreetly." #Or "this age." See Glossary.

began to sneer at him.[a] **15** So he said to them: "You are those who declare yourselves righteous before men,[b] but God knows your hearts.[c] For what is considered exalted by men is a disgusting thing in God's sight.[d]

16 "The Law and the Prophets were until John. From then on, the Kingdom of God is being declared as good news, and every sort of person is pressing forward toward it.[e] **17** Indeed, it is easier for heaven and earth to pass away than for one stroke of a letter of the Law to go unfulfilled.[f]

18 "Everyone who divorces his wife and marries another commits adultery, and whoever marries a woman divorced from her husband commits adultery.[g]

19 "There was a rich man who used to dress in purple and linen, enjoying himself day after day with magnificence. **20** But a beggar named Laz′a·rus used to be put at his gate, covered with ulcers **21** and desiring to be filled with the things dropping from the table of the rich man. Yes, even the dogs would come and lick his ulcers. **22** Now in the course of time, the beggar died and was carried off by the angels to Abraham's side.*

"Also, the rich man died and was buried. **23** And in the Grave* he lifted up his eyes, being in torment, and he saw Abraham from afar and Laz′a·rus by his side.# **24** So he called and said, 'Father Abraham, have mercy on me, and send Laz′a·rus to dip the tip of his finger in water and cool my tongue, for I am in anguish in this blazing fire.' **25** But Abraham said, 'Child, re-

member that you had your fill of good things in your lifetime, but Laz′a·rus for his part received bad things. Now, however, he is being comforted here, but you are in anguish. **26** And besides all these things, a great chasm has been fixed between us and you, so that those who want to go over from here to you cannot, neither may people cross over from there to us.' **27** Then he said, 'That being so, I ask you, father, to send him to the house of my father, **28** for I have five brothers, in order that he may give them a thorough witness so that they will not also come into this place of torment.' **29** But Abraham said, 'They have Moses and the Prophets; let them listen to these.'[a] **30** Then he said, 'No, indeed, father Abraham, but if someone from the dead goes to them, they will repent.' **31** But he said to him, 'If they do not listen to Moses[b] and the Prophets, neither will they be persuaded if someone rises from the dead.'"

17 Then he said to his disciples: "It is unavoidable that causes for stumbling should come. Nevertheless, woe to the one through whom they come! **2** It would be more advantageous for him if a millstone were hung from his neck and he were thrown into the sea than for him to stumble one of these little ones.[c] **3** Pay attention to yourselves. If your brother commits a sin, rebuke him,[d] and if he repents, forgive him.[e] **4** Even if he sins seven times a day against you and he comes back to you seven times, saying, 'I repent,' you must forgive him."[f]

5 Now the apostles said to the Lord: "Give us more faith."[g] **6** Then the Lord said: "If you had faith the size of a mustard grain, you would say to this black mulberry tree, 'Be

---

CHAP. 16
a Isa 53:3

b Mt 6:2
　Mt 23:27, 28
　Lu 18:9

c 1Sa 16:7
　1Ch 28:9
　2Ch 6:30

d 1Pe 5:5

e Mt 11:12, 13

f Mt 5:17, 18

g Mt 5:32
　Mt 19:9
　Mr 10:11, 12

Second Col.
a De 18:18
　Lu 24:25-27

b Joh 5:46

CHAP. 17
c Mt 18:6
　Mr 9:42

d Pr 17:10

e Le 19:17
　Mt 18:15

f Isa 55:7
　Mt 6:12
　Mt 18:21, 22
　Col 3:13
　1Pe 4:8

g Mr 9:23, 24
　Heb 12:2

16:22 *Lit., "to the bosom of Abraham."
16:23 *Or "Hades," that is, the common grave of mankind. See Glossary. #Lit., "in his bosom."

uprooted and planted in the sea!' and it would obey you.[a]

7 "Which one of you who has a slave plowing or shepherding would say to him when he comes in from the field, 'Come here at once and dine at the table'? **8** Rather, will he not say to him, 'Get something ready for me to have my evening meal, and put on an apron and serve me until I finish eating and drinking, and afterward you can eat and drink'? **9** He will not feel gratitude to the slave because he did what was assigned, will he? **10** Likewise, when you have done all the things assigned to you, say: 'We are good-for-nothing slaves. What we have done is what we ought to have done.'"[b]

11 While he was going to Jerusalem, he was passing between Sa·mar′i·a and Gal′i·lee. **12** And as he was entering a village, ten men with leprosy met him, but they stood at a distance.[c] **13** And they raised their voices and said: "Jesus, Instructor, have mercy on us!" **14** When he saw them, he said to them: "Go and show yourselves to the priests."[d] Then as they were going off, they were cleansed.[e] **15** One of them, when he saw that he was healed, turned back, glorifying God with a loud voice. **16** And he fell facedown at Jesus' feet, thanking him. Furthermore, he was a Sa·mar′i·tan.[f] **17** In reply Jesus said: "All ten were cleansed, were they not? Where, then, are the other nine? **18** Did no one else turn back to give glory to God except this man of another nation?" **19** Then he said to him: "Get up and be on your way; your faith has made you well."[g]

20 On being asked by the Pharisees when the Kingdom of God was coming,[h] he answered

them: "The Kingdom of God is not coming with striking observableness; **21** nor will people say, 'See here!' or, 'There!' For look! the Kingdom of God is in your midst."[*a]

22 Then he said to the disciples: "Days will come when you will desire to see one of the days of the Son of man, but you will not see it. **23** And people will say to you, 'See there!' or, 'See here!' Do not go out or chase after them.[b] **24** For just as lightning flashes from one part of heaven to another part of heaven, so the Son of man[c] will be in his day.[d] **25** First, however, he must undergo many sufferings and be rejected by this generation.[e] **26** Moreover, just as it occurred in the days of Noah,[f] so it will be in the days of the Son of man:[g] **27** they were eating, they were drinking, men were marrying, women were being given in marriage until that day when Noah entered into the ark,[h] and the Flood came and destroyed them all.[i] **28** Likewise, just as it occurred in the days of Lot:[j] they were eating, they were drinking, they were buying, they were selling, they were planting, they were building. **29** But on the day that Lot went out of Sod′om, it rained fire and sulfur from heaven and destroyed them all.[k] **30** It will be the same on that day when the Son of man is revealed.[l]

31 "On that day let the person who is on the housetop but whose belongings are in the house not come down to pick these up, and likewise, the person out in the field must not return to the things behind. **32** Remember the wife of Lot.[m] **33** Whoever seeks to keep his life* safe will lose it, but who-

---

CHAP. 17

a Mt 17:20
Mt 21:21
Mr 11:23

b 1Co 9:16

c Le 13:45, 46

d Le 14:2-4
De 24:8
Mt 8:3, 4
Lu 5:13, 14

e 2Ki 5:1, 14

f 2Ki 17:24
Joh 4:9

g Mt 9:22
Mr 5:34
Lu 7:50

h Mt 24:3

Second Col.

a Mt 12:28
Mt 21:5

b Mt 24:23
Mr 13:21
Lu 21:8
1Jo 4:1

c Da 7:13

d Mt 24:27

e Mr 8:31
Mr 9:31
Lu 9:22

f Ge 6:5

g Mt 24:37-39

h Ge 7:7

i Ge 7:17, 21

j Ge 19:15

k Ge 19:24, 25

l 1Co 1:7
2Th 1:7, 8

m Ge 19:17, 26

17:21 *Or "is among you." 17:33 *Or "soul."

ever loses it will preserve it alive.[a] **34** I tell you, in that night two people will be in one bed; the one will be taken along, but the other will be abandoned.[b] **35** There will be two women grinding at the same mill; the one will be taken along, but the other will be abandoned." **36** *—* **37** So in response they said to him: "Where, Lord?" He said to them: "Where the body is, there also the eagles will be gathered together."[c]

18 Then he went on to tell them an illustration about the need for them always to pray and not to give up,[d] **2** saying: "In a certain city there was a judge who had no fear of God and no respect for man. **3** There was also a widow in that city who kept going to him and saying, 'See that I get justice from my legal opponent.' **4** Well, for a while he was unwilling, but afterward he said to himself, 'Although I do not fear God or respect any man, **5** because this widow keeps making me trouble, I will see that she gets justice so that she will not keep coming and wearing me out with her demand.'"*[e] **6** Then the Lord said: "Hear what the judge, although unrighteous, said! **7** Certainly, then, will not God cause justice to be done for his chosen ones who cry out to him day and night,[f] while he is patient toward them?[g] **8** I tell you, he will cause justice to be done to them speedily. Nevertheless, when the Son of man arrives,* will he really find this faith* on the earth?"

9 He also told this illustration to some who trusted in their own righteousness and who considered others as noth-

ing: **10** "Two men went up into the temple to pray, the one a Pharisee and the other a tax collector. **11** The Pharisee stood and began to pray these things to himself, 'O God, I thank you that I am not like everyone else—extortioners, unrighteous, adulterers—or even like this tax collector. **12** I fast twice a week; I give the tenth of all things I acquire.'[a] **13** But the tax collector, standing at a distance, was not willing even to raise his eyes heavenward but kept beating his chest, saying, 'O God, be gracious to me,* a sinner.'[b] **14** I tell you, this man went down to his home and was proved more righteous than that Pharisee.[c] Because everyone who exalts himself will be humiliated, but whoever humbles himself will be exalted.[d]

15 Now people were also bringing him their infants for him to touch them, but on seeing this, the disciples began to reprimand them.[e] **16** However, Jesus called the infants to him, saying: "Let the young children come to me, and do not try to stop them, for the Kingdom of God belongs to such ones.[f] **17** Truly I say to you, whoever does not receive the Kingdom of God like a young child will by no means enter into it."[g]

18 And one of the rulers questioned him, saying: "Good Teacher, what must I do to inherit everlasting life?"[h] **19** Jesus said to him: "Why do you call me good? Nobody is good except one, God.[i] **20** You know the commandments: 'Do not commit adultery,[j] do not murder,[k] do not steal,[l] do not bear false witness,[m] honor your father and your mother.'"[n] **21** Then he said: "All of these I have kept from youth on." **22** After

CHAP. 17
a Mt 10:39
 Mt 16:25
 Mr 8:35
 Lu 9:24
 Joh 12:25

b Mt 24:40, 41

c Mt 24:28

CHAP. 18
d Ro 12:12
 Eph 6:18
 Php 4:6
 Col 4:2
 1Th 5:17

e Lu 11:7, 8

f Re 6:9, 10

g 2Pe 3:9

Second Col.
a Mt 23:23

b Ps 51:1-3

c Isa 66:2
 Mt 21:28-31

d Isa 2:11
 Mt 23:12
 Jas 4:6
 1Pe 5:5

e Mt 19:13-15
 Mr 10:13-16

f 1Pe 2:2

g Mt 18:3
 Mr 10:15

h Mt 19:16-22
 Mt 10:17-22
 Lu 10:25-28

i Mt 19:17
 Mr 10:18

j Ex 20:14
 De 5:18

k Ex 20:13
 De 5:17

l Ex 20:15
 De 5:19

m Ex 20:16
 De 5:20

n Ex 20:12
 De 5:16
 Ro 13:9
 Eph 6:2

17:36 *See App. A3. **18:5** *Or "and pummeling me to a finish." **18:8** *Or "this kind of faith." Lit., "the faith."

18:13 *Or "have mercy on me."

hearing that, Jesus said to him, "There is still one thing lacking about you: Sell all the things you have and distribute the proceeds to the poor, and you will have treasure in the heavens; and come be my follower."ᵃ 23 When he heard this, he became deeply grieved, for he was very rich.ᵇ

24 Jesus looked at him and said: "How difficult it will be for those having money to make their way into the Kingdom of God!ᶜ 25 It is easier, in fact, for a camel to get through the eye of a sewing needle than for a rich man to enter the Kingdom of God."ᵈ 26 Those who heard this said: "Who possibly can be saved?"ᵉ 27 He said: "The things impossible with men are possible with God."ᶠ 28 But Peter said: "Look! We have left what was ours and followed you."ᵍ 29 He said to them: "Truly I say to you, there is no one who has left house or wife or brothers or parents or children for the sake of the Kingdom of Godʰ 30 who will not get many times more in this period of time, and in the coming system of things,* everlasting life."ⁱ

31 Then he took the Twelve aside and said to them: "Look! We are going up to Jerusalem, and all the things written by means of the prophets about the Son of man will be accomplished.*ʲ 32 For instance, he will be handed over to men of the nationsᵏ and will be mockedˡ and treated insolently and spat on.ᵐ 33 And after scourging him, they will kill him,ⁿ but on the third day he will rise."ᵒ 34 However, they did not get the meaning of any of these things, for these words were hidden

18:30 *Or "the coming age." See Glossary. 18:31 *Or "completed."

CHAP. 18
a Mt 6:20
  Mt 19:21
  Mr 10:21
  Lu 12:33
  1Ti 6:18, 19

b Mt 19:22
  Mr 10:22

c Pr 11:28
  Mt 19:23
  Mr 10:23, 24
  1Ti 6:9

d Mt 19:24
  Mr 10:25

e Mt 19:25

f Mt 19:26
  Mr 10:27

g Mt 19:27

h Mt 19:28, 29
  Mr 10:29, 30

i Re 2:10

j Mt 16:21
  Mt 20:17-19
  Mr 10:32-34

k Mt 27:2
  Ac 3:13

l Ps 22:7

m Isa 50:6

n Isa 53:5, 7

o Mt 10:33, 34
  Lu 9:22

Second Col.
a Mt 20:29-34
  Mr 10:46-52

b Lu 7:50
  Lu 17:19

c Mt 20:34

d Lu 5:26

from them, and they did not understand the things said.

35 Now as Jesus was getting near to Jerʹi·cho, a blind man was sitting beside the road begging.ᵃ 36 Because he heard a crowd passing by, he began to inquire what was going on. 37 They reported to him: "Jesus the Naz·a·reneʹ is passing by!" 38 At that he cried out: "Jesus, Son of David, have mercy on me!" 39 And those who were in front began rebuking him, telling him to keep quiet, but all the more he kept shouting: "Son of David, have mercy on me!" 40 Then Jesus stopped and commanded that the man be brought to him. After he came near, Jesus asked him: 41 "What do you want me to do for you?" He said: "Lord, let me recover my sight." 42 So Jesus said to him: "Recover your sight; your faith has made you well."ᵇ 43 And instantly he recovered his sight, and he began to follow him,ᶜ glorifying God. Also, at seeing it, all the people gave praise to God.ᵈ

19 He then entered Jerʹi·cho and was passing through. 2 Now a man named Zac·chaeʹus was there; he was a chief tax collector, and he was rich. 3 Well, he was trying to see who this Jesus was, but he could not see because of the crowd, since he was short. 4 So he ran ahead and climbed a sycamore* tree in order to see him, for he was about to pass that way. 5 Now when Jesus got to the place, he looked up and said to him: "Zac·chaeʹus, hurry and get down, for today I must stay in your house." 6 With that he hurried down and joyfully welcomed him as a guest. 7 When they saw this, they were all muttering: "He went as a guest to the house of

19:4 *Or "fig-mulberry."

a man who is a sinner."ª **8** But Zac·chae′us stood up and said to the Lord: "Look! The half of my belongings, Lord, I am giving to the poor, and whatever I extorted* from anyone, I am restoring four times over."ᵇ **9** At this Jesus said to him: "Today salvation has come to this house, because he too is a son of Abraham. **10** For the Son of man came to seek and to save what was lost."ᶜ

11 While they were listening to these things, he told another illustration, because he was near Jerusalem and they thought that the Kingdom of God was going to appear instantly.ᵈ **12** So he said: "A man of noble birth traveled to a distant landᵉ to secure kingly power for himself and to return. **13** Calling ten of his slaves, he gave them ten mi′nas* and told them, 'Do business with these until I come.'ᶠ **14** But his citizens hated him and sent out a body of ambassadors after him to say, 'We do not want this man to become king over us.'

15 "When he eventually got back after having secured the kingly power,* he summoned the slaves to whom he had given the money,# in order to ascertain what they had gained by their business activity.ᵍ **16** So the first one came forward and said, 'Lord, your mi′na gained ten mi′nas.'ʰ **17** He said to him, 'Well done, good slave! Because in a very small matter you have proved yourself faithful, hold authority over ten cities.'ⁱ **18** Now the second came, saying, 'Your mi′na, Lord, made five mi′nas.'ʲ **19** He said to this one as well,

'You too be in charge of five cities.' **20** But another one came, saying, 'Lord, here is your mi′na that I kept hidden away in a cloth. **21** You see, I was in fear of you, because you are a harsh man; you take what you did not deposit, and you reap what you did not sow.'ª **22** He said to him, 'By your own words I judge you, wicked slave. You knew, did you, that I am a harsh man, taking what I did not deposit and reaping what I did not sow?'ᵇ **23** So why did you not put my money* in a bank? Then on my coming, I would have collected it with interest.'

24 "With that he said to those standing by, 'Take the mi′na from him and give it to the one who has the ten mi′nas.'ᶜ **25** But they said to him, 'Lord, he has ten mi′nas!'— **26** 'I say to you, to everyone who has, more will be given, but from the one who does not have, even what he has will be taken away.ᵈ **27** Moreover, bring these enemies of mine here who did not want me to become king over them and execute them in front of me.'"

28 After he had said these things, he went on ahead, going up to Jerusalem. **29** And when he got near to Beth′pha·ge and Beth′a·ny at the mountain called Mount of Olives,ᵉ he sent two of the disciples,ᶠ **30** saying: "Go into the village that is within sight, and after you enter it, you will find a colt tied, on which no man has ever sat. Untie it and bring it here. **31** But if anyone asks you, 'Why are you untying it?' you must say, 'The Lord needs it.'" **32** So those who were sent went away and found it just as he had said to them.ᵍ **33** But as they were untying the colt, its owners said to them:

19:8 *Or "extorted by false accusation." **19:13** *A Greek mina weighed 340 g (10.9 oz t) and was reckoned to be worth 100 drachmas. See App. B14. **19:15** *Or "the kingdom." #Lit., "silver."

19:23 *Lit., "my silver."

CHAP. 19
a Mt 9:11
  Lu 5:30
  Lu 15:2

b Ex 22:1
  Le 6:4, 5

c Eze 34:16
  Mt 9:13
  Mt 15:24
  Lu 15:4
  Ro 5:8
  1Ti 1:15

d Ac 1:6

e Mt 25:14
  Mr 13:34
  Joh 18:36

f Mt 25:15

g Mt 25:19

h Mt 25:20, 21

i Lu 16:10

j Mt 25:22, 23

Second Col.
a Mt 25:24

b Mt 25:26, 27

c Mt 25:28

d Mt 13:12
  Mt 25:29
  Mr 4:25
  Lu 8:18

e Ac 1:12

f Mt 21:1-3
  Mr 11:1-6

g Mt 21:6, 7

"Why are you untying the colt?"
34 They said: "The Lord needs it." **35** And they led it to Jesus, and they threw their outer garments on the colt and seated Jesus on it.[a]

36 As he moved along, they were spreading their outer garments on the road.[b] **37** As soon as he got near the road down the Mount of Olives, the whole multitude of the disciples began to rejoice and to praise God with a loud voice because of all the powerful works they had seen, **38** saying: "Blessed is the one coming as the King in Jehovah's* name! Peace in heaven, and glory in the heights above!"[c] **39** However, some of the Pharisees from the crowd said to him: "Teacher, rebuke your disciples."[d] **40** But in reply he said: "I tell you, if these remained silent, the stones would cry out."

41 And when he got nearby, he viewed the city and wept over it,[e] **42** saying: "If you, even you, had discerned on this day the things having to do with peace—but now they have been hidden from your eyes.[f] **43** Because the days will come upon you when your enemies will build around you a fortification of pointed stakes and will encircle you and besiege* you from every side.[g] **44** They will dash you and your children within you to the ground,[h] and they will not leave a stone upon a stone in you,[i] because you did not discern the time of your being inspected."

45 Then he entered the temple and started to throw out those who were selling,[j] **46** saying to them: "It is written, 'My house will be a house of prayer,'[k] but you have made it a cave of robbers.'"[l]

47 He continued teaching daily in the temple. But the chief priests and the scribes and the principal ones of the people were seeking to kill him;[a] **48** but they did not find any way to do this, for the people one and all kept hanging on to him to hear him.[b]

20 On one of the days while he was teaching the people in the temple and declaring the good news, the chief priests and the scribes with the elders came **2** and said to him: "Tell us, by what authority you do these things? Or who gave you this authority?"[c] **3** He replied to them: "I will also ask you a question, and you tell me: **4** Was the baptism of John from heaven or from men?"* **5** Then they drew conclusions among themselves, saying: "If we say, 'From heaven,' he will say, 'Why did you not believe him?' **6** But if we say, 'From men,' the people one and all will stone us, for they are convinced that John was a prophet."[d] **7** So they replied that they did not know its source. **8** Jesus said to them: "Neither am I telling you by what authority I do these things."

9 Then he began to tell the people this illustration: "A man planted a vineyard[e] and leased it to cultivators, and he traveled abroad for a considerable time.[f] **10** In due season he sent a slave to the cultivators so that they would give him some of the fruit of the vineyard. The cultivators, however, sent him away empty-handed, after beating him.[g] **11** But again he sent another slave. That one also they beat and humiliated* and sent away empty-handed. **12** Yet again he sent a third; this one also they wounded and threw out. **13** At

---

CHAP. 19
a Zec 9:9
  Mr 11:7-10
  Joh 12:14, 15

b Mt 21:8

c Ps 118:26
  Mt 21:9
  Mr 11:9

d Mt 21:15
  Joh 12:19

e Joh 11:35

f Isa 6:9, 10
  Mt 13:14

g De 28:52
  Da 9:26
  Lu 21:20

h Lu 23:28, 29

i Mt 24:2
  Mr 13:2
  Lu 21:6

j Mt 21:12
  Mr 11:15, 16

k Isa 56:7

l Jer 7:11
  Mt 21:13
  Mr 11:17
  Joh 2:16

Second Col.
a Mr 11:18

b Mr 12:37
  Lu 21:38

CHAP. 20
c Mt 21:23-27
  Mr 11:27-33

d Lu 7:29

e Isa 5:7

f Mt 21:33-41
  Mr 12:1-9

g 2Ki 17:13, 14
  2Ch 36:15, 16
  Ac 7:52
  Heb 11:36, 37

19:38 *See App. A5. **19:43** *Or "distress."

20:4 *Or "of human origin?" **20:11** *Or "dishonored."

this the owner of the vineyard said, 'What should I do? I will send my son, the beloved.[a] They will likely respect this one.' **14** When the cultivators caught sight of him, they reasoned with one another, saying, 'This is the heir. Let us kill him so that the inheritance may become ours.' **15** So they threw him out of the vineyard and killed him.[b] What, then, will the owner of the vineyard do to them? **16** He will come and kill these cultivators and will give the vineyard to others."

On hearing this, they said: "Never may that happen!" **17** But he looked straight at them and said: "What, then, does this mean where it is written: 'The stone that the builders rejected, this has become the chief cornerstone'?*[c] **18** Everyone falling on that stone will be shattered.[d] As for anyone on whom it falls, it will crush him."

19 The scribes and the chief priests then sought to get their hands on him in that very hour, but they feared the people, for they realized that he told this illustration with them in mind.[e] **20** And after observing him closely, they sent men whom they secretly hired to pretend that they were righteous in order to catch him in his speech,[f] so as to turn him over to the government and to the authority of the governor. **21** And they questioned him, saying: "Teacher, we know you speak and teach correctly and show no partiality, but you teach the way of God in line with truth: **22** Is it lawful* for us to pay head tax to Caesar or not?" **23** But he detected their cunning and said to them: **24** "Show me a de·nar′i·us.* Whose image and inscription does it have?" They said: "Caesar's." **25** He said to them: "By all means, then, pay back Caesar's things to Caesar[a] but God's things to God."[b] **26** Well, they were not able to trap him in his speech before the people, but amazed at his answer, they became silent.

27 However, some of the Sadducees, those who say there is no resurrection,[c] came and asked him:[d] **28** "Teacher, Moses wrote us, 'If a man's brother dies, leaving a wife, but he was childless, his brother should take the wife and raise up offspring for his brother.'[e] **29** Now there were seven brothers. The first took a wife but died childless. **30** So the second **31** and the third married her. Likewise even all seven; they died and left no children. **32** Finally the woman also died. **33** Consequently, in the resurrection, whose wife will she become? For the seven had her as a wife."

34 Jesus said to them: "The children of this system of things* marry and are given in marriage, **35** but those who have been counted worthy of gaining that system of things and the resurrection from the dead neither marry nor are given in marriage.[f] **36** In fact, neither can they die anymore, for they are like the angels, and they are God's children by being children of the resurrection. **37** But that the dead are raised up, even Moses made known in the account about the thornbush, when he calls Jehovah* 'the God of Abraham and God of Isaac and God of Jacob.'[g] **38** He is a God, not of the dead, but of the

---

CHAP. 20
a Mt 17:5
Joh 3:16

b Ac 3:15

c Ps 118:22
Isa 28:16
Mt 21:42, 44
Mr 12:10, 11
Ac 4:11
1Pe 2:7

d Isa 8:14, 15

e Mt 21:45, 46
Mr 12:12

f Mt 22:15-22
Mr 12:13-17

Second Col.
a Ro 13:7
Tit 3:1
1Pe 2:13

b Mt 22:21
Mr 12:17

c Ac 23:8

d Mt 22:23-28
Mr 12:18-23

e Ge 38:7, 8
De 25:5, 6

f Mt 22:29, 30
Mr 12:24, 25

g Ex 3:2, 6
Mt 22:31-33
Mr 12:26, 27

20:17 *Lit., "the head of the corner."
20:22 *Or "right."

20:24 *See App. B14. 20:34 *Or "this age." See Glossary. 20:37 *See App. A5.

living, for they are all living to him."*ᵃ **39** In response some of the scribes said: "Teacher, you spoke well." **40** For they no longer had the courage to ask him a single question.

41 In turn he asked them: "How is it they say that the Christ is David's son?ᵇ **42** For David himself says in the book of Psalms, 'Jehovah* said to my Lord: "Sit at my right hand **43** until I place your enemies as a stool for your feet."'ᶜ **44** David, therefore, calls him Lord; so how is he his son?"

45 Then, while all the people were listening, he said to his disciples: **46** "Beware of the scribes who like to walk around in robes and who love greetings in the marketplaces and front* seats in the synagogues and the most prominent places at evening meals,ᵈ **47** and who devour the houses* of the widows and for show# make long prayers. These will receive a more severe△ judgment."

21 Now as he looked up, he saw the rich dropping their gifts into the treasury chests.*ᵉ **2** Then he saw a needy widow drop in two small coins of very little value,*ᶠ **3** and he said: "Truly I say to you that this poor widow put in more than they all did.ᵍ **4** For all of these put in gifts out of their surplus, but she, out of her want,* put in all the means of living she had."ʰ

5 Later, when some were speaking about the temple, how it was adorned with fine stones and dedicated things,ⁱ **6** he said: "As for these things

that you now see, the days will come when not a stone and not be left upon a stone and not be thrown down."ᵃ **7** Then they questioned him, saying: "Teacher, when will these things actually be, and what will be the sign when these things are to occur?"ᵇ **8** He said: "Look out that you are not misled,ᶜ for many will come on the basis of my name, saying, 'I am he,' and, 'The due time is near.' Do not go after them.ᵈ **9** Furthermore, when you hear of wars and disturbances,* do not be terrified. For these things must take place first, but the end will not occur immediately."ᵉ

10 Then he said to them: "Nation will rise against nation,ᶠ and kingdom against kingdom.ᵍ **11** There will be great earthquakes, and in one place after another food shortages and pestilences;ʰ and there will be fearful sights and from heaven great signs.

12 "But before all these things happen, people will lay their hands on you and persecute you,ⁱ handing you over to the synagogues and prisons. You will be brought before kings and governors for the sake of my name.ʲ **13** It will result in your giving a witness. **14** Therefore, resolve in your hearts not to rehearse beforehand how to make your defense,ᵏ **15** for I will give you words and wisdom that all your opposers together will not be able to resist or dispute.ˡ **16** Moreover, you will be handed over* even by parents and brothers and relatives and friends, and they will put some of you to death,ᵐ **17** and you will be hated by all people because of my name.ⁿ **18** But not even a hair of your heads will perish.ᵒ

CHAP. 20
a Mt 22:32
b Mt 22:41-46
  Mr 12:35-37
c Ps 110:1
  Ac 2:34, 35
d Mt 23:2, 6, 7
  Mr 12:38-40

CHAP. 21
e Mt 12:41
f Mt 12:42
g Mt 12:43, 44
  2Co 8:12
h Mt 22:37
i Mt 24:1, 2
  Mr 13:1, 2

Second Col.
a Lu 19:44
b Mt 24:3
  Mr 13:4
c 2Ti 3:13
  1Jo 4:1
  Re 12:9
d Mt 24:4, 5
  Mr 13:5, 6
e Mt 24:6
  Mr 13:7
f Re 6:4
g Mt 24:7
  Mr 13:8
h Ac 11:28
  Re 6:8
i Joh 16:2
j Mt 10:17, 18
  Mt 24:9
  Mr 13:9
  Ac 25:23
  Re 2:10
k Lu 12:11, 12
  Mr 13:11
  Ac 6:8, 10
m Mic 7:6
  Mr 13:12, 13
  Ac 7:59
n Mt 10:22
  Mt 24:9
o Mt 10:29, 30
  Lu 12:6, 7

20:38 *Or "from his standpoint." **20:42** *See App. A5. **20:46** *Or "best." **20:47** *Or "property." #Or "for a pretext." △Or "a heavier." **21:1** *Or "receptacles." **21:2** *Lit., "two lepta." See App. B14. **21:4** *Or "poverty." **21:9** *Or "disorders; uprisings." **21:16** *Or "betrayed."

19 By your endurance you will preserve your lives.*ᵃ

20 "However, when you see Jerusalem surrounded by encamped armies,ᵇ then know that the desolating of her has drawn near.ᶜ **21** Then let those in Ju·de′a begin fleeing to the mountains,ᵈ let those in the midst of her leave, and let those in the countryside not enter into her, **22** because these are days for meting out justice* in order that all the things written may be fulfilled. **23** Woe to the pregnant women and those nursing a baby in those days!ᵉ For there will be great distress in the land and wrath against this people. **24** And they will fall by the edge of the sword and be led captive into all the nations;ᶠ and Jerusalem will be trampled on by the nations* until the appointed times of the nations* are fulfilled.ᵍ

25 "Also, there will be signs in the sun and moon and stars,ʰ and on the earth anguish of nations not knowing the way out because of the roaring of the sea and its agitation. **26** People will become faint out of fear and expectation of the things coming upon the inhabited earth, for the powers of the heavens will be shaken. **27** And then they will see the Son of manⁱ coming in a cloud with power and great glory.ʲ **28** But as these things start to occur, stand up straight and lift up your heads, because your deliverance is getting near."

29 With that he told them an illustration: "Notice the fig tree and all the other trees.ᵏ **30** When they are budding, you see it for yourselves and know that now the summer is near. **31** Likewise also you, when you

see these things happening, know that the Kingdom of God is near. **32** Truly I say to you that this generation will by no means pass away until all things happen.ᵃ **33** Heaven and earth will pass away, but my words will by no means pass away.ᵇ

34 "But pay attention to yourselves that your hearts never become weighed down with overeating and heavy drinkingᶜ and anxieties of life,ᵈ and suddenly that day be instantly upon you **35** as a snare.ᵉ For it will come upon all those dwelling on the face of the whole earth. **36** Keep awake,ᶠ then, all the time making supplicationᵍ that you may succeed in escaping all these things that must occur and in standing before the Son of man."ʰ

37 So by day he would be teaching in the temple, but by night he would go out and lodge on the mountain called the Mount of Olives. **38** And all the people would come to him early in the morning to hear him in the temple.

22 Now the Festival of the Unleavened Bread, which is called Passover,ⁱ was getting near.ʲ **2** And the chief priests and the scribes were looking for an effective way to get rid of him,ᵏ because they were afraid of the people.ˡ **3** Then Satan entered into Judas, the one called Is·car′i·ot, who was numbered among the Twelve,ᵐ **4** and he went off and talked with the chief priests and temple captains about how to betray him to them.ⁿ **5** They were delighted at this and agreed to give him silver money.ᵒ **6** So he consented and began looking for a good opportunity to betray him to them without a crowd around.

7 The first day of the Unleavened Bread now arrived, on which the Passover sacrifice

---

21:19 *Or "acquire your souls." **21:22** *Or "days of vengeance." **21:24** *Or "Gentiles."

must be offered;ᵃ **8** so Jesus sent Peter and John, saying: "Go and get the Passover ready for us to eat."ᵇ **9** They said to him: "Where do you want us to get it ready?" **10** He said to them: "Look! When you enter into the city, a man carrying an earthenware water jar will meet you. Follow him into the house that he enters.ᶜ **11** And say to the landlord of the house, 'The Teacher says to you: "Where is the guest room where I may eat the Passover with my disciples?"' **12** And that man will show you a large, furnished upper room. Get it ready there." **13** So they left and found it just as he had told them, and they prepared for the Passover.

14 So when the hour came, he reclined at the table along with the apostles.ᵈ **15** And he said to them: "I have greatly desired to eat this Passover with you before I suffer; **16** for I tell you, I will not eat it again until it is fulfilled in the Kingdom of God." **17** And accepting a cup, he gave thanks and said: "Take this and pass it from one to the other among yourselves, **18** for I tell you, from now on, I will not drink again from the product of the vine until the Kingdom of God comes."

19 Also, he took a loaf,ᵉ gave thanks, broke it, and gave it to them, saying: "This means my body,ᶠ which is to be given in your behalf.ᵍ Keep doing this in remembrance of me."ʰ **20** Also, he did the same with the cup after they had the evening meal, saying: "This cup means the new covenantⁱ by virtue of my blood,ʲ which is to be poured out in your behalf.ᵏ

21 "But look! the hand of my betrayer is with me at the table.ˡ **22** For, indeed, the Son of man is going his way according to what has been determined;ᵐ all

the same, woe to that man through whom he is betrayed!"ᵃ **23** So they began to discuss among themselves which one of them could really be about to do this.ᵇ

24 However, there also arose a heated dispute among them over which one of them was considered to be the greatest.ᶜ **25** But he said to them: "The kings of the nations lord it over them, and those having authority over them are called Benefactors.ᵈ **26** You, though, are not to be that way.ᵉ But let the one who is the greatest among you become as the youngest,ᶠ and the one taking the lead as the one ministering. **27** For which one is greater, the one dining* or the one serving?ᵍ Is it not the one dining?* But I am among you as the one serving."ᵍ

28 "However, you are the ones who have stuck with meʰ in my trials;ⁱ **29** and I make a covenant with you, just as my Father has made a covenant with me, for a kingdom,ʲ **30** so that you may eat and drink at my table in my Kingdom,ᵏ and sit on thronesˡ to judge the 12 tribes of Israel.ᵐ

31 "Simon, Simon! look! Satan has demanded to have all of you to sift you as wheat.ⁿ **32** But I have made supplication for you that your faith may not give out;ᵒ and you, once you have returned, strengthen your brothers."ᵖ **33** Then he said to him: "Lord, I am ready to go with you both to prison and to death."ᵠ **34** But he said: "I tell you, Peter, a rooster will not crow today until you have denied knowing me three times."ʳ

35 He also said to them: "When I sent you out without a money bag and a food pouch and

CHAP. 22

a Ex 12:14, 18
De 16:1, 2
Mt 26:17
Mr 14:12
b Ex 12:8
c Mt 26:18, 19
Mr 14:13-16
d Mt 26:20
Mr 14:17
e Ex 12:8
f 1Co 10:16
g Heb 10:10
1Pe 2:24
h Mt 26:27, 28
Mr 14:23, 24
1Co 11:23-25
i Jer 31:31
Heb 7:22
Heb 8:8
j Ex 24:8
k Heb 9:13, 14
1Pe 1:18, 19
l Ps 41:9
Mt 26:21
Mt 14:18
Joh 13:21
m Isa 53:7, 8
Da 9:26
Ac 4:27, 28

Second Col.

a Mt 26:24
b Mt 26:22
Mr 14:19
Joh 13:22
c Mr 9:34
Lu 9:46
d Mt 20:25-27
Mr 10:42-44
1Pe 5:2, 3
e Lu 9:46-48
f Mt 20:28
Joh 13:3-5
Php 2:5-7
h Joh 6:67, 68
Heb 4:15
j Da 7:27
Lu 12:32
2Ti 2:12
Heb 12:28
Jas 2:5
Re 1:6
k Lu 13:29
Joh 17:24
1Co 6:2
Re 2:26, 27
Re 3:21
Re 20:6
m Mt 19:28
n Mt 26:31
Mr 14:27
1Pe 5:8
o Joh 17:15
p Heb 12:12
q Mt 26:33
Mr 14:29
Joh 13:37
r Mt 26:34
Mr 14:30
Lu 22:61
Joh 13:38

sandals,[a] you did not lack anything, did you?" They said: "No!" 36 Then he said to them: "But now let the one who has a money bag take it, likewise a food pouch, and let the one who has no sword sell his outer garment and buy one. 37 For I tell you that what is written must be accomplished in me, namely, 'He was counted with lawless ones.'[b] For this is being fulfilled concerning me."[c] 38 Then they said: "Lord, look! here are two swords." He said to them: "It is enough."

39 On leaving, he went as was his custom to the Mount of Olives, and the disciples also followed him.[d] 40 On arriving at the place, he said to them: "Carry on prayer so that you do not enter into temptation."[e] 41 And he withdrew from them about a stone's throw away, and he bent his knees and began to pray, 42 saying: "Father, if you want to, remove this cup from me. Nevertheless, let, not my will, but yours take place."[f] 43 Then an angel from heaven appeared to him and strengthened him.[g] 44 But he was in such agony that he kept praying more earnestly;[h] and his sweat became as drops of blood falling to the ground. 45 When he rose from prayer and went to the disciples, he found them slumbering, exhausted from grief.[i] 46 He said to them: "Why are you sleeping? Get up and keep praying, so that you do not enter into temptation."[j]

47 While he was still speaking, look! a crowd, and the man called Judas, one of the Twelve, was leading them, and he approached Jesus to kiss him.[k] 48 But Jesus said to him: "Judas, are you betraying the Son of man with a kiss?" 49 When those around him saw what was going to happen, they said:

"Lord, should we strike with the sword?" 50 One of them even struck the slave of the high priest, taking off his right ear.[a] 51 But in reply Jesus said: "That is enough." And he touched the ear and healed him. 52 Jesus then said to the chief priests and captains of the temple and elders who had come there for him: "Did you come out with swords and clubs as against a robber?[b] 53 While I was with you in the temple day after day,[c] you did not lay your hands on me.[d] But this is your hour and the authority of darkness."[e]

54 Then they arrested him and led him off,[f] and they brought him into the house of the high priest; but Peter was following at a distance.[g] 55 When they lit a fire in the middle of the courtyard and sat down together, Peter was sitting among them.[h] 56 But a servant girl, seeing him sitting in the light of the fire, looked closely at him and said: "This man was also with him." 57 But he denied it, saying: "I do not know him, woman." 58 After a short time another person saw him and said: "You too are one of them." But Peter said: "Man, I am not."[i] 59 And after about an hour had passed, another man began insisting strongly: "Certainly this man was also with him, for he is, in fact, a Gal·i·le'an!" 60 But Peter said: "Man, I do not know what you are saying." And instantly, while he was still speaking, a rooster crowed. 61 At this the Lord turned and looked straight at Peter, and Peter recalled the statement of the Lord when he had said to him: "Before a rooster crows today, you will disown me three times."[j] 62 And he went outside and wept bitterly.

63 Now the men who held Jesus in custody began to mock

CHAP. 22
a Mt 10:9, 10
  Mr 6:7-9
  Lu 9:2, 3

b Isa 53:12

c Lu 18:31

d Mt 26:30
  Mr 14:26
  Joh 18:1

e Mt 26:41
  Mr 14:38
  Lu 22:46

f Mt 6:10
  Mt 26:39
  Mr 14:36
  Joh 5:30
  Joh 6:38

g 1Ki 19:5, 7
  Da 10:18, 19
  Mt 4:11

h Joh 12:27
  Heb 5:7

i Mt 26:40
  Mt 14:37

j Mt 26:41
  Mr 14:38
  Lu 22:40

k Mt 26:47-50
  Mr 14:43-46
  Joh 18:2, 3

Second Col.
a Mt 26:51, 52
  Mr 14:47
  Joh 18:10, 11

b Mt 26:55, 56
  Mr 14:48, 49

c Lu 19:47

d Joh 7:30

e Joh 19:11

f Isa 53:7
  Ac 8:32

g Mt 26:57, 58
  Mr 14:53, 54
  Joh 18:15

h Mt 26:69-75
  Mr 14:66-72
  Joh 18:18

i Joh 18:25-27

j Mt 26:75
  Mr 14:72

him,[a] hitting him;[b] **64** and after covering his face, they kept asking: "Prophesy! Who is it that struck you?" **65** And they said many other blasphemous things against him.

66 And when it became day, the assembly of elders of the people, both chief priests and scribes, gathered together,[c] and they led him into their San'he‧drin hall and said: **67** "If you are the Christ, tell us."[d] But he said to them: "Even if I told you, you would not believe it at all. **68** Moreover, if I questioned you, you would not answer. **69** However, from now on the Son of man[e] will be seated at the powerful right hand of God."[f] **70** At this they all said: "Are you, therefore, the Son of God?" He said to them: "You yourselves are saying that I am." **71** They said: "Why do we need further testimony? For we ourselves have heard it out of his own mouth."[g]

23 So the multitude got up, one and all, and led him to Pilate.[h] **2** Then they began to accuse him,[i] saying: "We found this man subverting our nation, forbidding the paying of taxes to Caesar,[j] and saying he himself is Christ a king."[k] **3** Now Pilate asked him the question: "Are you the King of the Jews?" In answer he said: "You yourself are saying it."[l] **4** Then Pilate said to the chief priests and the crowds: "I find no crime in this man."[m] **5** But they insisted, saying: "He stirs up the people by teaching throughout all Ju‧de'a, starting from Gal'i‧lee even to here." **6** On hearing that, Pilate asked whether the man was a Gal‧i‧le'an. **7** After ascertaining that he was under the jurisdiction of Herod,[n] he sent him on to Herod, who was also in Jerusalem in those days.

8 When Herod saw Jesus, he rejoiced greatly. For a considerable time he had been wanting to see Jesus because he had heard much about him,[a] and he was hoping to see some sign performed by him. **9** So he began to question him at length, but he gave him no answer.[b] **10** However, the chief priests and the scribes kept standing up and vehemently accusing him. **11** Then Herod together with his soldiers treated him with contempt,[c] and he mocked him[d] by clothing him with a splendid garment and then sent him back to Pilate. **12** Herod and Pilate became friends with each other on that very day, for before that they had been at enmity with each other.

13 Pilate then called together the chief priests, the rulers, and the people **14** and said to them: "You brought this man to me as one inciting the people to revolt. Now look! I examined him in front of you but found in this man no grounds for the charges you are bringing against him.[e] **15** In fact, neither did Herod, for he sent him back to us, and look! he has done nothing deserving of death. **16** I will therefore punish him[f] and release him." **17** *— **18** But the whole crowd shouted out: "Do away with this man,* and release Bar‧ab'bas to us!"[g] **19** (This man had been thrown into prison for sedition that had occurred in the city and for murder.) **20** Again Pilate called out to them, because he wanted to release Jesus.[h] **21** Then they began to yell, saying: "To the stake with him! To the stake with him!"*[i] **22** The third time he said to them: "Why? What

---

CHAP. 22
a Ps 22:7
b Isa 50:6
　Isa 53:5
　Mt 26:67, 68
　Mt 14:65
c Ps 2:2
　Mt 27:1
　Mt 15:1
　Ac 4:26
d Mt 26:63
　Mt 14:61
e Da 7:13
f Ps 110:1
　Mt 26:64
　Mt 14:62
　Ac 2:32, 33
　Ac 7:55
　Ro 8:34
　Col 3:1
　Heb 1:3
g Mt 26:65
　Mt 14:63

CHAP. 23
h Mt 27:2
　Mt 15:1
　Joh 18:28
i Ps 35:11
j Mt 12:17
k Joh 18:36
l Mt 27:11
m Joh 18:38
　Heb 7:26
　1Pe 2:21, 22
n Lu 3:1

Second Col.
a Mt 14:1
　Mr 6:14
　Lu 9:7-9
b Isa 53:7
c Isa 53:3
d Ps 22:7
e Joh 18:38
f Mt 27:26
　Joh 19:1
g Mt 27:20, 21
　Mr 15:11
　Joh 18:40
h Mt 27:22-26
　Mr 15:12-15
　Joh 19:12
i Joh 19:6

23:17 *See App. A3.　**23:18** *Lit., "Take this one away."　**23:21** *Or "Execute him on the stake! Execute him on the stake!"

bad thing did this man do? I found in him nothing deserving of death; I will therefore punish him and release him." **23** At this they became insistent, demanding with loud voices that he be executed,* and their voices prevailed.[a] **24** So Pilate made the decision that their demand be met. **25** He released the man whom they were demanding, who had been thrown into prison for sedition and murder, but he surrendered Jesus to their will.

26 Now as they led him away, they seized one Simon of Cy·re′ne, who was coming from the countryside, and they placed the torture stake* on him to carry it behind Jesus.[b] **27** A large number of people were following him, including women who kept beating themselves in grief and wailing for him. **28** Jesus turned to the women and said: "Daughters of Jerusalem, stop weeping for me. Weep instead for yourselves and for your children;[c] **29** for look! days are coming when people will say, 'Happy are the barren women, the wombs that did not give birth and the breasts that did not nurse!'[d] **30** Then they will start saying to the mountains, 'Fall over us!' and to the hills, 'Cover us over!'[e] **31** If they do these things when the tree is moist, what will occur when it is withered?"

32 Two other men, criminals, were also being led off to be executed with him.[f] **33** And when they got to the place called Skull,[g] they nailed him to the stake there alongside the criminals, one on his right and one on his left.[h] **34** But Jesus was saying: "Father, forgive them, for they do not know what they are doing." Furthermore, they cast

lots to distribute his garments.[a] **35** And the people stood looking on. But the rulers were sneering and saying: "Others he saved; let him save himself if he is the Christ of God, the Chosen One."[b] **36** Even the soldiers mocked him, coming up and offering him sour wine[c] **37** and saying: "If you are the King of the Jews, save yourself." **38** There was also an inscription over him: "This is the King of the Jews."[d]

39 Then one of the criminals hanging there began to speak abusively to him,[e] saying: "You are the Christ, are you not? Save yourself and us too!" **40** In response the other rebuked him, saying: "Do you not fear God at all, now that you have received the same judgment? **41** And we rightly so, for we are getting back what we deserve for the things we did; but this man did nothing wrong." **42** Then he said: "Jesus, remember me when you get into your Kingdom."[f] **43** And he said to him: "Truly I tell you today, you will be with me in Paradise."[g]

44 Well, by now it was about the sixth hour,* and yet a darkness fell over all the land until the ninth hour,[#h] **45** because the sunlight failed; then the curtain of the sanctuary[i] was torn down the middle.[j] **46** And Jesus called out with a loud voice and said: "Father, into your hands I entrust my spirit."[k] After he said this, he expired.[*l] **47** Because of seeing what occurred, the army officer began to glorify God, saying: "Truly, this man was righteous."[m] **48** And when all the crowds that were gathered together there for this spectacle saw

---

CHAP. 23
a Joh 19:15, 16

b Mr 15:21
  Joh 19:17

c Mr 13:17

d Mt 24:19
  Lu 21:23

e Ho 10:8

f Isa 53:12
  Mt 27:38

g Mt 27:33

h Joh 19:17, 18

Second Col.
a Ps 22:18
  Mt 27:35
  Mr 15:24
  Joh 19:24

b Ps 22:7, 8
  Mt 27:42, 43
  Mr 15:31

c Ps 69:21

d Mt 27:37
  Mr 15:26
  Joh 19:19

e Mt 27:44
  Mr 15:32

f Lu 1:32, 33

g Isa 11:6
  Isa 35:1
  Isa 65:17
  Ac 24:15
  Re 21:1

h Mt 27:45
  Mr 15:33

i Ex 26:31-33

j Heb 10:19, 20

k Ps 31:5

l Mt 27:50

m Mt 27:54

23:23 *Or "executed on the stake." 23:26 *See Glossary. 23:44 *That is, about 12:00 noon. #That is, about 3:00 p.m. 23:46 *Or "he breathed his last."

the things that occurred, they returned home, beating their chests. 49 And all those acquainted with him were standing at a distance. Also, women who had accompanied him from Gal'i·lee were there and saw these things.[a]

50 And look! there was a man named Joseph, a member of the Council, who was a good and righteous man.[b] 51 (This man had not voted in support of their scheme and action.) He was from Ar·i·ma·the'a, a city of the Ju·de'ans, and was waiting for the Kingdom of God. 52 This man went in before Pilate and asked for the body of Jesus. 53 And he took it down[c] and wrapped it up in fine linen, and he laid it in a tomb* carved in the rock,[d] where no man had yet lain. 54 Now it was the day of Preparation,[e] and the Sabbath[f] was about to begin. 55 But the women who had come with him from Gal'i·lee followed along and took a look at the tomb* and saw how his body was laid,[g] 56 and they went back to prepare spices and perfumed oils. But, of course, they rested on the Sabbath[h] according to the commandment.

24 But on the first day of the week, they came very early to the tomb,* bringing the spices they had prepared.[i] 2 But they found the stone rolled away from the tomb,*[j] 3 and when they entered, they did not find the body of the Lord Jesus.[k] 4 While they were perplexed about this, look! two men in shining garments stood by them. 5 The women became frightened and kept their faces turned toward the ground, so the men said to them: "Why are you looking for the living

one among the dead?[a] 6 He is not here, but has been raised up. Recall how he spoke to you while he was yet in Gal'i·lee, 7 saying that the Son of man must be handed over to sinful men and be executed on the stake and on the third day rise."[b] 8 Then they remembered his words,[c] 9 and they returned from the tomb* and reported all these things to the Eleven and to all the rest.[d] 10 They were Mary Mag'da·lene, Jo·an'na, and Mary the mother of James. Also, the rest of the women with them were telling these things to the apostles. 11 However, these sayings seemed like nonsense to them, and they would not believe the women.

12 But Peter got up and ran to the tomb,* and stooping forward, he saw only the linen cloths. So he went off, wondering to himself what had occurred.

13 But look! on that very day, two of them were traveling to a village named Em·ma'us, about seven miles* from Jerusalem, 14 and they were conversing with each other about all these things that had happened.

15 Now as they were conversing and discussing these things, Jesus himself approached and began walking with them, 16 but their eyes were kept from recognizing him.[e] 17 He said to them: "What are these matters that you are debating between yourselves as you walk along?" And they stood still, looking sad. 18 In answer the one named Cle'o·pas said to him: "Are you a stranger dwelling alone in Jerusalem and do not know* the

---

CHAP. 23
a Mt 27:55, 56
   Mr 15:40, 41
   Lu 8:2, 3

b Mt 27:57-60
   Mr 15:43-46
   Joh 19:38

c De 21:22, 23

d Isa 53:9

e Mr 15:42
   Joh 19:42

f Ex 20:9, 10
   De 5:13, 14

g Mt 27:61
   Mr 15:47

h Ex 16:29
   Ex 20:9, 10
   Ex 31:15
   De 5:12

CHAP. 24
i Mt 28:1
   Mr 16:1, 2
   Joh 20:1

j Mt 28:2
   Mr 16:4

k Mr 16:5

Second Col.
a Mt 28:5-7
   Mr 16:5-7

b Jon 1:17
   Mt 16:21
   Mr 8:31
   Lu 9:22

c Joh 2:22

d Mt 28:8

e Joh 20:14
   Joh 21:4

23:53, 55; 24:1, 2, 9, 12 *Or "memorial tomb."

24:13 *About 11 km. Lit., "60 stadia." A stadium equaled 185 m (606.95 ft). See App. B14.   24:18 *Or possibly, "Are you the only visitor in Jerusalem who does not know?"

things that have occurred there during these days?" **19** He asked them: "What things?" They said to him: "The things concerning Jesus the Naz·a·rene',[a] who proved to be a prophet powerful in deed and word before God and all the people;[b] **20** and how our chief priests and rulers handed him over to be sentenced to death,[c] and they nailed him to the stake. **21** But we were hoping that this man was the one who was going to deliver Israel.[d] Yes, and besides all these things, this is the third day since these things occurred. **22** Moreover, some women from among us also astonished us, for they went early to the tomb*[e] **23** and when they did not find his body, they came saying that they had also seen a supernatural sight of angels, who said he is alive. **24** Then some of those who were with us went off to the tomb,*[f] and they found it just as the women had said, but they did not see him."

25 So he said to them: "O senseless ones and slow of heart to believe all the things the prophets have spoken! **26** Was it not necessary for the Christ to suffer these things[g] and to enter into his glory?"[h] **27** And starting with Moses and all the Prophets,[i] he interpreted to them things pertaining to himself in all the Scriptures.

28 Finally they got close to the village to which they were traveling, and he made as if to travel on farther. **29** But they urged him to remain, saying: "Stay with us, because it is almost evening and the day is nearly over." With that he went in to stay with them. **30** And as he was dining* with them,

he took the bread, blessed it, broke it, and began handing it to them.[a] **31** At that their eyes were fully opened and they recognized him; but he disappeared from them.[b] **32** And they said to each other: "Were not our hearts burning within us as he was speaking to us on the road, as he was fully opening up* the Scriptures to us?" **33** And they got up in that very hour and returned to Jerusalem, and they found the Eleven and those assembled together with them, **34** who said: "For a fact the Lord was raised up, and he appeared to Simon!"[c] **35** Then they related the events on the road and how he became known to them by the breaking of the bread.[d]

36 While they were speaking of these things, he himself stood in their midst and said to them: "May you have peace."[e] **37** But because they were terrified and frightened, they imagined that they were seeing a spirit. **38** So he said to them: "Why are you troubled, and why have doubts come up in your hearts? **39** See my hands and my feet, that it is I myself; touch me and see, for a spirit does not have flesh and bones just as you see that I have." **40** And as he said this, he showed them his hands and his feet. **41** But while they were still not believing for sheer joy and amazement, he said to them: "Do you have something there to eat?" **42** So they handed him a piece of broiled fish, **43** and he took it and ate it before their eyes.

44 He then said to them: "These are my words that I spoke to you while I was yet with you,[f] that all the things written about me in the Law

CHAP. 24
a Mt 2:23
  Mt 21:11

b De 18:18
  Lu 7:15, 16
  Joh 3:2
  Joh 6:14
  Ac 2:22

c Lu 23:1
  Ac 3:13
  Ac 13:27, 28

d Ac 1:6

e Mt 28:1, 8
  Lu 24:9-11

f Lu 24:12
  Joh 20:3

g Ps 22:16-18
  Isa 53:7-9
  1Co 15:3

h Php 2:9-11
  Heb 2:9
  1Pe 1:11

i Joh 1:45
  Ac 10:43
  Ac 26:22

Second Col.
a Mt 14:19
  Mt 15:36
  Mr 6:41

b Joh 20:19

c 1Co 15:3, 5

d Lu 24:30, 31

e Joh 20:21

f Mt 16:21
  Lu 9:22

24:22, 24 *Or "memorial tomb."   24:30 *Or "reclining at the table."

24:32 *Or "clearly explaining."

of Moses and in the Prophets and Psalms must be fulfilled."[a] **45** Then he opened up their minds fully to grasp the meaning of the Scriptures,[b] **46** and he said to them, "This is what is written: that the Christ would suffer and rise from among the dead on the third day,[c] **47** and on the basis of his name, repentance for forgiveness of sins[d] would be preached in all the nations[e]—starting out from Jerusalem.[f] **48** You are to be witnesses of these things.[g] **49** And look! I am sending upon you

what my Father promised. You, though, stay in the city until you are clothed with power from on high."[a]

50 Then he led them out as far as Beth'a·ny, and he lifted up his hands and blessed them. **51** As he was blessing them, he was parted from them and taken up to heaven.[b] **52** And they did obeisance* to him and returned to Jerusalem with great joy.[c] **53** And they were continually in the temple, praising God.[d]

24:52 *Or "bowed down."

CHAP. 24
a Lu 24:27
b Joh 12:16
c Isa 53:5
  Mr 9:31
d Ac 5:31
e Ga 3:14
f Ac 4:1, 2
  Ac 5:27, 28
g Joh 15:26, 27
  Ac 1:8

Second Col.
a Joe 2:28
  Joh 14:16
  Ac 1:4, 5
  Ac 2:1, 4
b Ac 1:9
c Joh 16:22
  Ac 1:12
d Ac 2:46, 47

ACCORDING TO

JOHN

OUTLINE OF CONTENTS

1

In the beginning was the Word,[a] and the Word was with God,[b] and the Word was a god.*[c] 2 This one was in the beginning with God. 3 All things came into existence through him,[d] and apart from him not even one thing came into existence.

What has come into existence 4 by means of him was life, and the life was the light of men.[a] 5 And the light is shining in the darkness,[b] but the darkness has not overpowered it.

6 There came a man who was sent as a representative of God; his name was John.[c] 7 This man came as a witness, in order to bear witness about the light,[d] so that people of all sorts might believe through him. 8 He was

CHAP. 1
a Col 1:15
Re 19:11, 13
b Pr 8:22, 30
c Isa 9:6
Joh 1:18
Php 2:5, 6
d Joh 1:10

Second Col.
a Joh 8:12
b Joh 3:19
c Mt 3:1
Lu 3:2
d Mt 3:11

1:1 * Or "was divine."

not that light,[a] but he was meant to bear witness about that light.

9 The true light that gives light to every sort of man was about to come into the world.[b] **10** He was in the world,[c] and the world came into existence through him,[d] but the world did not know him. **11** He came to his own home, but his own people did not accept him. **12** However, to all who did receive him, he gave authority to become God's children,[e] because they were exercising faith in his name.[f] **13** And they were born, not from blood or from a fleshly will or from man's will, but from God.[g]

14 So the Word became flesh[h] and resided among us, and we had a view of his glory, a glory such as belongs to an only-begotten son[i] from a father; and he was full of divine favor[*] and truth. **15** (John bore witness about him, yes, he cried out: "This was the one of whom I said, 'The one coming behind me has advanced in front of me, for he existed before me.'") **16** For we all received from his fullness, even undeserved kindness upon undeserved kindness. **17** Because the Law was given through Moses,[k] the undeserved kindness[l] and the truth came to be through Jesus Christ.[m] **18** No man has seen God at any time;[n] the only-begotten god[o] who is at the Father's side[*p] is the one who has explained Him.[q]

19 This is the witness John gave when the Jews sent priests and Levites from Jerusalem to ask him: "Who are you?"[r] **20** And he admitted it and did not deny it, saying: "I am not the Christ." **21** And they asked him: "What, then? Are you E·li'jah?"[a] He replied: "I am not." "Are you the Prophet?"[b] And he answered: "No!" **22** So they said to him: "Who are you? Tell us so that we may give an answer to those who sent us. What do you say about yourself?" **23** He said: "I am a voice of someone crying out in the wilderness, 'Make the way of Jehovah[*] straight,'[c] just as Isaiah the prophet said."[d] **24** Now those sent were from the Pharisees. **25** So they questioned him and said to him: "Why, then, do you baptize if you are not the Christ or E·li'jah or the Prophet?" **26** John answered them: "I baptize in water. One is standing among you whom you do not know, **27** the one coming behind me, the lace of whose sandal I am not worthy to untie."[e] **28** These things took place in Beth·a·ny across the Jordan, where John was baptizing.[f]

29 The next day he saw Jesus coming toward him, and he said: "See, the Lamb[g] of God who takes away the sin[h] of the world![i] **30** This is the one about whom I said: 'Behind me there comes a man who has advanced in front of me, for he existed before me.'[j] **31** Even I did not know him, but the reason why I came baptizing in water was so that he might be made manifest to Israel."[k] **32** John also bore witness, saying: "I viewed the spirit coming down as a dove out of heaven, and it remained upon him.[l] **33** Even I did not know him, but the very One who sent me to baptize in water said to me: 'Whoever it is upon whom you see the spirit coming down and remaining,[m] this is the one who baptizes in holy spirit.'[n] **34** And I have seen it, and I have given witness that this one is the Son of God."[o]

CHAP. 1

a Joh 1:19, 20
b Mt 4:16, 17
   Joh 3:19
   Joh 12:46
   1Jo 2:8
c Joh 1:14
d Ge 1:26
   1Co 8:6
   Col 1:16
   Heb 1:2
e Ro 8:14, 16
   2Co 6:18
   Eph 1:5
   1Jo 3:1
f Ga 3:26
g Joh 3:3
   1Pe 1:23
   1Jo 3:9
h Php 2:7
   1Ti 3:16
   Heb 2:14
i Joh 3:16
   1Jo 4:9
j Joh 8:58
k Ex 31:18
l Ro 3:23, 24
   Eph 1:5, 6
m Ex 8:31, 32
   Joh 14:6
   Joh 18:37
n Ex 33:17, 20
   Joh 6:46
o Joh 1:18
p Pr 8:22, 30
q Mt 11:27
r Lu 3:15

Second Col.

a Mal 4:5
b De 18:15
   Joh 6:14, 15
   Joh 7:37, 40
   Ac 3:22
c Isa 40:3
d Mt 3:1, 3
   Mr 1:3
   Lu 1:67, 76
   Lu 3:3, 4
   Lu 7:27, 28
e Mt 3:11
f Mt 3:1, 6
g Ac 8:32, 35
   1Pe 1:18, 19
   Re 5:6
h Isa 53:7, 11
   1Co 15:3
   Heb 9:13, 14
   1Pe 2:24
   1Jo 3:5
i Joh 6:51
   1Jo 2:1, 2
   1Jo 4:14
j Joh 1:15
k Ac 19:4
l Mt 3:16
   Mr 1:10
   Lu 3:22
m Mt 3:16
n Mt 3:16
   Ac 1:5
   Ac 2:1, 4
o Mt 3:17

1:14 * Or "of undeserved kindness." 1:18 * Or "in the bosom position with the Father." This refers to a position of special favor.

1:23 * See App. A5.

35 Again the next day, John was standing with two of his disciples, **36** and as he looked at Jesus walking, he said: "See, the Lamb[a] of God!" **37** When the two disciples heard him say this, they followed Jesus. **38** Then Jesus turned, and seeing them following, he said to them: "What are you looking for?" They said to him: "Rabbi (which means, when translated, "Teacher"), where are you staying?" **39** He said to them: "Come, and you will see." So they went and saw where he was staying, and they stayed with him that day; it was about the tenth hour.* **40** Andrew,[b] the brother of Simon Peter, was one of the two who heard what John said and followed Jesus. **41** He first found his own brother Simon and said to him: "We have found the Mes·si′ah"[c] (which means, when translated, "Christ"), **42** and he led him to Jesus. When Jesus looked at him, he said: "You are Simon,[d] the son of John; you will be called Ce′phas" (which is translated "Peter").[e]

43 The next day he wanted to leave for Gal′i·lee. Jesus then found Philip[f] and said to him: "Be my follower." **44** Now Philip was from Beth·sa′i·da, from the city of Andrew and Peter. **45** Philip found Na·than′a·el[g] and said to him: "We have found the one of whom Moses, in the Law, and the Prophets wrote: Jesus, the son of Joseph,[h] from Naz′a·reth." **46** But Na·than′a·el said to him: "Can anything good come out of Naz′a·reth?" Philip said to him: "Come and see." **47** Jesus saw Na·than′a·el coming toward him and said about him: "See, truly an Israelite in whom there is no deceit."[i] **48** Na·than′a·el said to him: "How do you know me?" Je-

sus answered him: "Before Philip called you, while you were under the fig tree, I saw you." **49** Na·than′a·el responded: "Rabbi, you are the Son of God, you are King of Israel."[a] **50** Jesus answered him: "Do you believe because I told you I saw you under the fig tree? You will see things greater than these." **51** He then said to him: "Most truly I say to you men, you will see heaven opened up and the angels of God ascending and descending to the Son of man."[b]

2 And on the third day a marriage feast took place in Ca′na of Gal′i·lee, and the mother of Jesus was there. **2** Jesus and his disciples were also invited to the marriage feast.

3 When the wine ran short, the mother of Jesus said to him: "They have no wine." **4** But Jesus said to her: "Woman, why is that of concern to me and to you?* My hour has not yet come." **5** His mother said to those serving: "Do whatever he tells you." **6** Now there were six stone water jars sitting there as required by the purification rules of the Jews,[c] each able to hold two or three liquid measures.* **7** Jesus said to them: "Fill the jars with water." So they filled them to the brim. **8** Then he said to them: "Now draw some out and take it to the director of the feast." So they took it. **9** When the director of the feast tasted the water that had now been turned into wine, not knowing where it came from (although the servants who had drawn out the water knew), the director of the feast called the bridegroom **10** and said to him: "Everyone

---

CHAP. 1
a Re 5:12

b Mt 4:18

c Da 9:25

d Mt 10:2
Ac 15:14

e Mt 16:18

f Mt 10:2, 3

g Mt 10:2, 3
Lu 6:13, 14

h Mt 1:16
Mt 13:55
Lu 2:4

i Joh 2:24, 25

Second Col.
a Mt 27:11
Lu 1:31, 32
Joh 12:13

b Ge 28:10, 12
Ps 104:4
Da 7:13
Mt 4:11
Lu 22:43

CHAP. 2
c Mr 7:3

1:39 *That is, about 4:00 p.m.

2:4 *Lit., "What to me and to you, woman?" This is an idiom indicating objection. The use of "woman" does not denote disrespect. **2:6** *Likely the liquid measure was the bath that equaled 22 L (5.81 gal). See App. B14.

else puts out the fine wine first, and when people are intoxicated, the inferior. You have saved the fine wine until now." **11** Jesus did this in Ca′na of Gal′ilee as the beginning of his signs, and he made his glory manifest,[a] and his disciples put their faith in him.

12 After this he and his mother and his brothers[b] and his disciples went down to Ca·per′na·um,[c] but they did not stay there many days.

13 Now the Passover[d] of the Jews was near, and Jesus went up to Jerusalem. **14** He found in the temple those selling cattle and sheep and doves,[e] and the money brokers in their seats. **15** So after making a whip of ropes, he drove all those with the sheep and cattle out of the temple, and he poured out the coins of the money changers and overturned their tables.[f] **16** And he said to those selling the doves: "Take these things away from here! Stop making the house of my Father a house of commerce!"*[g] **17** His disciples recalled that it is written: "The zeal for your house will consume me."[h]

18 Therefore, in response the Jews said to him: "What sign can you show us,[i] since you are doing these things?" **19** Jesus replied to them: "Tear down this temple, and in three days I will raise it up."[j] **20** The Jews then said: "This temple was built in 46 years, and will you raise it up in three days?" **21** But he was talking about the temple of his body.[k] **22** When, though, he was raised up from the dead, his disciples recalled that he used to say this,[l] and they believed the scripture and what Jesus had spoken.

23 However, when he was in Jerusalem at the festival of the Passover, many people put their faith in his name when they saw the signs that he was performing. **24** But Jesus would not entrust himself to them because he knew them all **25** and because he did not need to have anyone bear witness about man, for he knew what was in man.[a]

3 There was a man of the Pharisees named Nic·o·de′mus,[b] a ruler of the Jews. **2** This one came to him in the night[c] and said to him: "Rabbi,[d] we know that you have come from God as a teacher, for no one can perform these signs[e] that you perform unless God is with him."[f] **3** In response Jesus said to him: "Most truly I say to you, unless anyone is born again,*[g] he cannot see the Kingdom of God."[h] **4** Nic·o·de′mus said to him: "How can a man be born when he is old? He cannot enter into the womb of his mother a second time and be born, can he?" **5** Jesus answered: "Most truly I say to you, unless anyone is born from water[i] and spirit,[j] he cannot enter into the Kingdom of God. **6** What has been born from the flesh is flesh, and what has been born from the spirit is spirit. **7** Do not be amazed because I told you: You people must be born again. **8** The wind blows where it wants to, and you hear the sound of it, but you do not know where it comes from and where it is going. So it is with everyone who has been born from the spirit."[k]

9 In answer Nic·o·de′mus said to him: "How can these things be?" **10** Jesus replied: "Are you a teacher of Israel and yet do not know these things? **11** Most truly I say to you, what we know we speak, and what we have seen

---

CHAP. 2
a Isa 9:1, 2
  Joh 1:14
b Mt 13:55
  Mr 3:31
  Lu 8:19
  Ac 1:14
c Mt 4:13
d Ex 12:14
  Nu 28:16
  De 16:1
  Joh 11:55
e Le 1:14
f Mt 21:12
  Mr 11:15, 16
  Lu 19:45
g Jer 7:11
  Mt 21:13
  Mr 11:17
  Lu 19:46
h Ps 69:9
i Mt 12:38
  Mt 16:1
  Joh 4:48
  Joh 6:30
j Mt 26:59-61
  Mt 27:39, 40
  Mr 14:57, 58
k Mt 16:21
l Lu 24:6-8

Second Col.
a Mt 9:3, 4
  Mr 2:6-8
  Joh 1:47, 48
  Joh 6:64
  Re 2:23

CHAP. 3
b Joh 7:50, 51
  Joh 19:39
c Joh 12:42
d Joh 1:38
e Joh 2:11
f Joh 14:11
  Ac 2:22
  Ac 10:38
g Joh 1:12, 13
  1Pe 1:3, 23
  1Jo 3:9
h 1Co 15:50
i Mt 28:19
  Ac 8:36
  Ac 10:47
j Mt 3:11
  Ac 1:5
  Ac 10:45
  Ac 19:5, 6
k Ro 8:14, 16

2:16 *Or "a marketplace; a business."

3:3 *Or possibly, "born from above."

we bear witness to, but you do not receive the witness we give. **12** If I have told you earthly things and you still do not believe, how will you believe if I tell you heavenly things? **13** Moreover, no man has ascended into heaven[a] but the one who descended from heaven,[b] the Son of man. **14** And just as Moses lifted up the serpent in the wilderness,[c] so the Son of man must be lifted up,[d] **15** so that everyone believing in him may have everlasting life.[e]

16 "For God loved the world so much that he gave his only-begotten Son,[f] so that everyone exercising faith in him might not be destroyed but have everlasting life.[g] **17** For God did not send his Son into the world for him to judge the world, but for the world to be saved through him.[h] **18** Whoever exercises faith in him is not to be judged.[i] Whoever does not exercise faith has been judged already, because he has not exercised faith in the name of the only-begotten Son of God.[j] **19** Now this is the basis for judgment: that the light has come into the world,[k] but men have loved the darkness rather than the light, for their works were wicked. **20** For whoever practices vile things hates the light and does not come to the light, so that his works may not be reproved.* **21** But whoever does what is true comes to the light,[l] so that his works may be made manifest as having been done in harmony with God."

22 After this Jesus and his disciples went into the Ju·deʹan countryside, and there he spent some time with them and was baptizing.[m] **23** But John too was baptizing in Aeʹnon near Saʹlim, because there was a great

3:20 *Or "exposed."

CHAP. 3

a Ac 2:34
b Joh 6:38
  Joh 8:23,42
c Nu 21:8,9
d Joh 8:28
  Ga 3:13
e Joh 3:36
  Joh 20:31
f Ro 5:8
  Ro 8:32
  1Jo 4:9,10
  1Jo 4:19
g Joh 6:40
  Joh 20:31
  Ro 6:23
  2Ti 3:15
  1Jo 5:13
h Lu 19:10
  Joh 12:47
  1Co 15:22
  2Co 5:18,19
  1Ti 1:15
  1Jo 2:1,2
  1Jo 4:14
i Joh 5:24
j Mt 10:33
  Heb 10:29
k Joh 1:9
  Joh 8:12
  Joh 9:5
  Joh 12:46
  Joh 12:36,46
  1Jo 1:7
m Joh 4:2

Second Col.

a Mr 1:10
  Ac 8:38
b Mt 3:1,5,6
  Lu 3:19,20
c Joh 1:33,34
e Joh 1:19,20
f Mt 11:7,10
  Lu 1:13,17
g 2Co 11:2
  Eph 5:25
  Re 21:9
h Joh 8:23
i Mt 3:11
j Joh 8:26
  Joh 15:15
k Joh 1:11
  Joh 3:11
l 1Jo 5:10
m Joh 7:16
n Joh 5:20
  Joh 15:9,10
o Mt 11:27
  Lu 10:22
p Joh 3:16
  Joh 6:47
  Ro 1:17
  Heb 5:9
q 2Th 1:7,8
  1Jo 5:12
r Eph 5:5,6
  Heb 10:26,
  27

quantity of water there,[a] and people kept coming and were being baptized;[b] **24** for John had not yet been thrown into prison.[c]

25 Now the disciples of John had a dispute with a Jew concerning purification. **26** So they came to John and said to him: "Rabbi, the man who was with you across the Jordan, about whom you bore witness,[d] see, this one is baptizing, and all are going to him." **27** In answer John said: "A man cannot receive a single thing unless it has been given him from heaven. **28** You yourselves bear me witness that I said, 'I am not the Christ,[e] but I have been sent ahead of that one.'[f] **29** Whoever has the bride is the bridegroom.[g] But the friend of the bridegroom, when he stands and hears him, has a great deal of joy on account of the voice of the bridegroom. So my joy has been made complete. **30** That one must keep on increasing, but I must keep on decreasing."

31 The one who comes from above[h] is over all others. The one who is from the earth is from the earth and speaks of things of the earth. The one who comes from heaven is over all others.[i] **32** He bears witness to what he has seen and heard,[j] but no man accepts his witness.[k] **33** Whoever has accepted his witness has put his seal to it* that God is true.[l] **34** For the one whom God sent speaks the sayings of God,[m] for He does not give the spirit sparingly.* **35** The Father loves the Son[n] and has given all things into his hand.[o] **36** The one who exercises faith in the Son has everlasting life;[p] the one who disobeys the Son will not see life,[q] but the wrath of God remains upon him.[r]

3:33 *Or "has confirmed." 3:34 *Or "by measure."

4 When the Lord became aware that the Pharisees had heard that Jesus was making and baptizing[a] more disciples than John— **2** although Jesus himself did no baptizing but his disciples did— **3** he left Ju·de′a and departed again for Gal′i·lee. **4** But it was necessary for him to go through Sa·mar′i·a. **5** So he came to a city of Sa·mar′i·a called Sy′char, near the field that Jacob had given to his son Joseph.[b] **6** In fact, Jacob's well was there.[c] Now Jesus, tired out as he was from the journey, was sitting at the well.* It was about the sixth hour.#

7 A woman of Sa·mar′i·a came to draw water. Jesus said to her: "Give me a drink." **8** (For his disciples had gone off into the city to buy food.) **9** So the Sa·mar′i·tan woman said to him: "How is it that you, despite being a Jew, ask me for a drink even though I am a Sa·mar′i·tan woman?" (For Jews have no dealings with Sa·mar′i·tans.)[d] **10** In answer Jesus said to her: "If you had known of the free gift of God[e] and who it is who says to you, 'Give me a drink,' you would have asked him, and he would have given you living water."[f] **11** She said to him: "Sir, you do not even have a bucket for drawing water, and the well is deep. From what source, then, do you have this living water? **12** You are not greater than our forefather Jacob, who gave us the well and who together with his sons and his cattle drank out of it, are you?" **13** In answer Jesus said to her: "Everyone drinking from this water will get thirsty again. **14** Whoever drinks from the water that I will give him will never get thirsty at all,[g] but the water that I will give him will become in him a spring of water

4:6 *Or "fountain; spring." #That is, about 12:00 noon.

bubbling up to impart everlasting life."[a] **15** The woman said to him: "Sir, give me this water, so that I may neither thirst nor keep coming over to this place to draw water."

16 He said to her: "Go, call your husband and come to this place." **17** The woman replied: "I do not have a husband." Jesus said to her: "You are right in saying, 'I do not have a husband.' **18** For you have had five husbands, and the man you now have is not your husband. This you have said truthfully." **19** The woman said to him: "Sir, I see that you are a prophet.[b] **20** Our forefathers worshipped on this mountain, but you people say that in Jerusalem is the place where people must worship."[c] **21** Jesus said to her: "Believe me, woman, the hour is coming when neither on this mountain nor in Jerusalem will you worship the Father. **22** You worship what you do not know;[d] we worship what we know, because salvation begins with the Jews.[e] **23** Nevertheless, the hour is coming, and it is now, when the true worshippers will worship the Father with spirit and truth, for indeed, the Father is looking for ones like these to worship him.[f] **24** God is a Spirit,[g] and those worshipping him must worship with spirit and truth."[h] **25** The woman said to him: "I know that Mes·si′ah is coming, who is called Christ. Whenever that one comes, he will declare all things to us openly." **26** Jesus said to her: "I am he, the one speaking to you."[i]

27 Just then his disciples arrived, and they were surprised because he was speaking with a woman. Of course, no one said: "What are you looking for?" or "Why are you talking to her?" **28** So the woman left her water

CHAP. 4
a Joh 3:22

b Ge 33:18, 19
Jos 24:32

c Joh 4:12

d 2Ki 17:24
Ac 10:28

e Eph 2:8

f Joh 7:37

g Joh 6:35

Second Col.
a Joh 7:38
Ro 6:23
1Jo 5:20

b Lu 7:16
Joh 9:17

c De 12:5, 6
1Ki 9:3
2Ch 7:12
Ps 122

d 2Ki 17:29, 33

e Isa 2:3
Ro 9:4

f 2Ch 16:9

g 2Co 3:17
1Ti 1:17
Heb 11:27

h Ro 12:1

i Joh 9:35-37

jar and went off into the city and told the people: **29** "Come and see a man who told me everything I did. Could this not perhaps be the Christ?" **30** They left the city and began coming to him.

31 Meanwhile, the disciples were urging him: "Rabbi,[a] eat." **32** But he said to them: "I have food to eat that you do not know about." **33** So the disciples said to one another: "No one brought him anything to eat, did he?" **34** Jesus said to them: "My food is to do the will of him who sent me[b] and to finish his work.[c] **35** Do you not say that there are yet four months before the harvest comes? Look! I say to you: Lift up your eyes and view the fields, that they are white for harvesting.[d] Already **36** the reaper is receiving wages and gathering fruit for everlasting life, so that the sower and the reaper may rejoice together.[e] **37** For in this respect the saying is true: One is the sower and another the reaper. **38** I sent you to reap what you did not labor on. Others have labored, and you have entered into the benefit of their labor."

39 Many of the Sa·mar′i·tans from that city put faith in him because of the word of the woman who bore witness, saying: "He told me all the things I did."[f] **40** So when the Sa·mar′i·tans came to him, they asked him to stay with them, and he stayed there two days. **41** As a result, many more believed because of what he said, **42** and they said to the woman: "We no longer believe just because of what you said; for we have heard for ourselves, and we know that this man really is the savior of the world."[g]

43 After the two days, he left there for Gal′i·lee. **44** Jesus himself, however, bore witness that a prophet has no honor in his own homeland.[a] **45** So when he arrived in Gal′i·lee, the Gal·i·le′ans welcomed him, because they had seen all the things he did in Jerusalem at the festival,[b] for they too had gone to the festival.[c]

46 Then he came again to Ca′na of Gal′i·lee, where he had turned the water into wine.[d] Now there was a royal official whose son was sick in Ca·per′na·um. **47** When this man heard that Jesus had come out of Ju·de′a into Gal′i·lee, he went to him and asked him to come down and heal his son, for he was at the point of dying. **48** But Jesus said to him: "Unless you people see signs and wonders, you will never believe."[e] **49** The royal official said to him: "Lord, come down before my young child dies." **50** Jesus said to him: "Go your way; your son lives."[f] The man believed the word that Jesus spoke to him, and he left. **51** But while he was on his way down, his slaves met him to say that his boy was alive.* **52** So he asked them at what hour he got better. They replied to him: "The fever left him yesterday at the seventh hour."* **53** The father then knew that it was in the very hour that Jesus had said to him: "Your son lives."[g] So he and his whole household believed. **54** This was the second sign[h] Jesus performed when he came from Ju·de′a into Gal′i·lee.

5 After this there was a festival[i] of the Jews, and Jesus went up to Jerusalem. **2** Now in Jerusalem at the Sheep Gate[j] is a pool called in Hebrew *Beth·za′tha*, with five colonnades. **3** Within these a multitude of the sick, blind, lame, and those with withered* limbs were lying

---

4:51 *Or "was recovering." **4:52** *That is, about 1:00 p.m. **5:3** *Or "paralyzed."

CHAP. 4
a Joh 1:38

b Joh 6:38

c Joh 5:30, 36
   Joh 17:4
   Joh 19:30

d Mt 9:37

e 1Co 3:8

f Joh 4:29

g Mt 1:21
   Joh 1:29
   1Ti 1:15
   1Jo 4:14

Second Col.
a Mt 13:57
   Mr 6:4
   Lu 4:24

b Joh 2:23

c De 16:16

d Joh 2:1-11

e Mt 16:1
   1Co 1:22

f Mt 8:13
   Mr 7:29, 30

g Mt 8:13

h Joh 2:11

CHAP. 5
i Ex 12:14
   De 16:1, 16
   Joh 2:13
   Joh 6:4

j Ne 3:1

down. **4** *— **5** But one man was there who had been sick for 38 years. **6** Seeing this man lying there and being aware that he had already been sick for a long time, Jesus said to him: "Do you want to get well?"[a] **7** The sick man answered him: "Sir, I do not have anyone to put me into the pool when the water is stirred up, but while I am on my way, another steps down ahead of me." **8** Jesus said to him: "Get up! Pick up your mat* and walk."[b] **9** And the man immediately got well, and he picked up his mat* and began to walk.

That day was the Sabbath. **10** So the Jews began to say to the cured man: "It is the Sabbath, and it is not lawful for you to carry the mat."[*c] **11** But he answered them: "The same one who made me well said to me, 'Pick up your mat* and walk.'" **12** They asked him: "Who is the man who told you, 'Pick it up and walk'?" **13** But the healed man did not know who he was, for Jesus had slipped away into the crowd that was there.

14 After this Jesus found him in the temple and said to him: "See, you have become well. Do not sin anymore, so that something worse does not happen to you." **15** The man went away and told the Jews that it was Jesus who had made him well. **16** For this reason the Jews were persecuting Jesus, because he was doing these things during the Sabbath. **17** But he answered them: "My Father has kept working until now, and I keep working."[d] **18** This is why the Jews began seeking all the more to kill him, because not only was he breaking the Sabbath but he was also calling God his own Father,[e] making himself equal to God.[f]

19 Therefore, in response Jesus said to them: "Most truly I say to you, the Son cannot do a single thing of his own initiative, but only what he sees the Father doing.[a] For whatever things that One does, these things the Son does also in like manner. **20** For the Father has affection for the Son[b] and shows him all the things he himself does, and he will show him works greater than these, so that you may marvel.[c] **21** For just as the Father raises the dead up and makes them alive,[d] so the Son also makes alive whomever he wants to.[e] **22** For the Father judges no one at all, but he has entrusted all the judging to the Son,[f] **23** so that all may honor the Son just as they honor the Father. Whoever does not honor the Son does not honor the Father who sent him.[g] **24** Most truly I say to you, whoever hears my word and believes the One who sent me has everlasting life,[h] and he does not come into judgment but has passed over from death to life.[i]

25 "Most truly I say to you, the hour is coming, and it is now, when the dead will hear the voice of the Son of God, and those who have paid attention will live. **26** For just as the Father has life in himself,*[j] so he has granted also to the Son to have life in himself.[k] **27** And he has given him authority to do judging,[l] because he is the Son of man.[m] **28** Do not be amazed at this, for the hour is coming in which all those in the memorial tombs will hear his voice[n] **29** and come out, those who did good things to a resurrection of life, and those who practiced vile things to a resurrection of judgment.[o] **30** I cannot do a single thing of my own initiative.

CHAP. 5
a Isa 53:3

b Mt 9:6
  Mr 2:10, 11
  Lu 5:24

c Ex 20:9, 10
  Mt 12:2
  Lu 6:2

d Joh 9:4
  Joh 14:10

e Joh 14:28

f Php 2:5, 6

Second Col.
a Joh 5:30
  Joh 8:28
  Joh 12:49

b Mt 3:17
  Joh 3:35
  Joh 10:17
  2Pe 1:17

c Lu 8:25
  Joh 6:10, 11
  Joh 6:19

d 2Ki 4:32-34
  Heb 11:35

e Lu 7:12, 14
  Lu 8:52-54
  Joh 11:25

f Ac 10:42
  Ac 17:31
  2Co 5:10
  2Ti 4:1

g Lu 10:16

h Joh 3:16
  Joh 6:40
  Joh 8:51

i 1Jo 3:14

j Ps 36:9
  Ac 17:28

k Joh 11:25

l Joh 5:22
  2Ti 4:1

m Da 7:13

n Job 14:13
  Isa 25:8
  Isa 26:19

o Re 20:12, 15

5:4 *See App. A3.   5:8-11 *Or "bed."   5:26 *Or "has in himself the gift of life."

Just as I hear, I judge, and my judgment is righteous[a] because I seek, not my own will, but the will of him who sent me.[b]

31 "If I alone bear witness about myself, my witness is not true. 32 There is another who bears witness about me, and I know that the witness he bears about me is true.[c] 33 You have sent men to John, and he has borne witness to the truth.[e] 34 However, I do not accept the witness from man, but I say these things so that you may be saved. 35 That man was a burning and shining lamp, and for a short time you were willing to rejoice greatly in his light.[f] 36 But I have the witness greater than that of John, for the very works that my Father assigned me to accomplish, these works that I am doing, bear witness that the Father sent me.[g] 37 And the Father who sent me has himself borne witness about me.[h] You have neither heard his voice at any time nor seen his form,[i] 38 and you do not have his word residing in you, because you do not believe the very one whom he sent.

39 "You are searching the Scriptures[j] because you think that you will have everlasting life by means of them; and these are the very ones* that bear witness about me.[k] 40 And yet you do not want to come to me[l] so that you may have life. 41 I do not accept glory from men, 42 but I well know that you do not have the love of God in you. 43 I have come in the name of my Father, but you do not receive me. If someone else came in his own name, you would receive that one. 44 How can you believe, when you are accepting glory from one another and you are not seeking the glory that is

from the only God?[a] 45 Do not think that I will accuse you to the Father; there is one who accuses you, Moses,[b] in whom you have put your hope. 46 In fact, if you believed Moses, you would believe me, for he wrote about me.[c] 47 But if you do not believe his writings, how will you believe what I say?"

6 After this Jesus set out across the Sea of Galʹi·lee, or Ti·beʹri·as.[d] 2 And a large crowd kept following him,[e] because they were observing the miraculous signs he was performing in healing the sick.[f] 3 So Jesus went up on a mountain and sat down there with his disciples. 4 Now the Passover,[g] the festival of the Jews, was near. 5 When Jesus raised his eyes and saw that a large crowd was coming to him, he said to Philip: "Where will we buy bread for these people to eat?"[h] 6 However, he was saying this to test him, for he knew what he was about to do. 7 Philip answered him: "Two hundred de·narʹi·i* worth of bread is not enough for each of them to get even a little." 8 One of his disciples, Andrew, Simon Peter's brother, said to him: 9 "Here is a little boy who has five barley loaves and two small fish. But what are these among so many?"[i]

10 Jesus said: "Have the men sit down." As there was a lot of grass in that place, the men sat down there, about 5,000 in number.[j] 11 Jesus took the bread, and after giving thanks, he distributed it to those who were sitting there; he did likewise with the small fish, and they had as much as they wanted. 12 But when they had eaten their fill, he said to his disciples: "Gather together the fragments left over, so that nothing is wasted."

CHAP. 5

a Isa 11:4

b Mt 26:39
  Joh 4:34
  Joh 6:38

c De 19:15

d Mt 3:17
  Mr 9:7
  Joh 12:28-30
  1Jo 5:9

e Joh 1:15, 32

f Mt 3:1, 5, 6
  Mr 6:20

g Mt 11:5
  Joh 3:2
  Joh 7:31
  Joh 10:25

h Mr 1:11
  Joh 8:18

i De 4:11, 12
  Joh 1:18
  Joh 6:46

j Lu 11:52

k De 18:15

l Isa 53:3
  Joh 1:11

Second Col.

a Joh 12:42, 43

b De 31:26, 27
  Joh 7:19

c De 18:15
  Lu 24:44
  Joh 1:45

CHAP. 6

d Mt 14:13
  Lu 9:10

e Mr 6:33

f Lu 9:11

g Joh 2:13
  Joh 5:1

h Mt 14:14-17
  Mr 6:35-38
  Lu 9:12, 13

i 2Ki 4:42-44

j Mt 14:19-21
  Mr 6:39-44
  Lu 9:14-17

5:39 * That is, the Scriptures.

6:7 * See App. B14.

13 So they gathered them together and filled 12 baskets with fragments left over by those who had eaten from the five barley loaves.

14 When the people saw the sign he performed, they began to say: "This really is the Prophet who was to come into the world."[a] **15** Then Jesus, knowing that they were about to come and seize him to make him king, withdrew[b] again to the mountain all alone.[c]

16 When evening fell, his disciples went down to the sea,[d] **17** and boarding a boat, they set out across the sea for Ca·per′na·um. By now it had grown dark, and Jesus had not yet come to them.[e] **18** Also, the sea was getting rough because a strong wind was blowing.[f] **19** However, when they had rowed about three or four miles,* they saw Jesus walking on the sea and getting near the boat, and they became fearful. **20** But he said to them: "It is I; do not be afraid!"[g] **21** Then they were willing to take him into the boat, and right away the boat arrived at the land to which they had been heading.[h]

22 The next day the crowd that had stayed on the other side of the sea saw that there was no other boat there except a small one, and that Jesus had not boarded the boat with his disciples, but his disciples had left by themselves. **23** Boats from Ti·be′ri·as, however, arrived near the place where they ate the bread after the Lord had given thanks. **24** So when the crowd saw that neither Jesus nor his disciples were there, they boarded their boats and came to Ca·per′na·um to look for Jesus.

25 When they found him across the sea, they said to him:

6:19 *About five or six km. Lit., "about 25 or 30 stadia." See App. B14.

"Rabbi,[a] when did you get here?" **26** Jesus answered them: "Most truly I say to you, you are looking for me, not because you saw signs, but because you ate from the loaves and were satisfied.[b] **27** Work, not for the food that perishes, but for the food that remains for everlasting life,[c] which the Son of man will give you; for on this one the Father, God himself, has put his seal of approval."[d]

28 So they said to him: "What must we do to carry out the works of God?" **29** In answer Jesus said to them: "This is the work of God, that you exercise faith in the one whom he sent."[e] **30** Then they said to him: "What are you performing as a sign,[f] so that we may see it and believe you? What work are you doing? **31** Our forefathers ate the manna in the wilderness,[g] just as it is written: 'He gave them bread from heaven to eat.'"[h] **32** Jesus then said to them: "Most truly I say to you, Moses did not give you the bread from heaven, but my Father gives you the true bread from heaven. **33** For the bread of God is the one who comes down from heaven and gives life to the world." **34** So they said to him: "Lord, always give us this bread."

35 Jesus said to them: "I am the bread of life. Whoever comes to me will not get hungry at all, and whoever exercises faith in me will never get thirsty at all.[i] **36** But as I said to you, you have even seen me and yet do not believe.[j] **37** All those whom the Father gives me will come to me, and I will never drive away the one who comes to me;[k] **38** for I have come down from heaven[l] to do, not my own will, but the will of him who sent me.[m] **39** This is the will of him who sent me, that I should lose none out of all those whom he

---

CHAP. 6

a De 18:15, 18

b Joh 17:16
Joh 18:36

c Mt 14:23
Mr 6:45

d Mt 14:22

e Mr 6:47-51

f Mt 8:24
Mt 14:24-33

g Mt 14:27
Mr 6:50

h Mt 14:34

Second Col.

a Joh 1:38

b Joh 6:11

c Joh 4:14
Joh 17:3
Ro 6:23

d Mt 3:17
Ac 2:22
2Pe 1:17

e Ac 16:31
1Jo 3:23

f Mt 12:38
Mr 8:12
Joh 2:18
1Co 1:22

g Ex 16:15
Nu 11:7

h Ps 78:24
Ps 105:40

i Joh 4:14
Joh 7:37
Re 22:17

j Joh 6:64

k Mt 11:28, 29
Joh 17:6

l Joh 3:13
Joh 8:23, 42

m Mt 26:39
Joh 5:30

has given me, but that I should resurrect[a] them on the last day. **40** For this is the will of my Father, that everyone who recognizes the Son and exercises faith in him should have everlasting life,[b] and I will resurrect[c] him on the last day."

41 Then the Jews began to murmur about him because he had said: "I am the bread that came down from heaven."[d] **42** And they began saying: "Is this not Jesus the son of Joseph, whose father and mother we know?[e] How does he now say, 'I have come down from heaven'?" **43** In response Jesus said to them: "Stop murmuring among yourselves. **44** No man can come to me unless the Father, who sent me, draws him,[f] and I will resurrect him on the last day.[g] **45** It is written in the Prophets: 'They will all be taught by Jehovah.'*[h] Everyone who has listened to the Father and has learned comes to me. **46** Not that any man has seen the Father,[i] except the one who is from God; this one has seen the Father.[j] **47** Most truly I say to you, whoever believes has everlasting life.[k]

48 "I am the bread of life.[l] **49** Your forefathers ate the manna in the wilderness and yet they died.[m] **50** This is the bread that comes down from heaven, so that anyone may eat of it and not die. **51** I am the living bread that came down from heaven. If anyone eats of this bread he will live forever; and for a fact, the bread that I will give is my flesh in behalf of the life of the world."[n]

52 Then the Jews began to argue with one another, saying: "How can this man give us his flesh to eat?" **53** So Jesus said to them: "Most truly I say to you, unless you eat the flesh of the

Son of man and drink his blood, you have no life in yourselves.[a] **54** Whoever feeds on my flesh and drinks my blood has everlasting life, and I will resurrect[b] him on the last day; **55** for my flesh is true food and my blood is true drink. **56** Whoever feeds on my flesh and drinks my blood remains in union with me, and I in union with him.[c] **57** Just as the living Father sent me and I live because of the Father, so also the one who feeds on me will live because of me.[d] **58** This is the bread that came down from heaven. It is not as when your forefathers ate and yet died. Whoever feeds on this bread will live forever."[e] **59** He said these things as he was teaching in a synagogue* in Ca·per'na·um.

60 When they heard this, many of his disciples said: "This speech is shocking; who can listen to it?" **61** But Jesus, knowing in himself that his disciples were murmuring about this, said to them: "Does this stumble you? **62** What, therefore, if you should see the Son of man ascending to where he was before?[f] **63** It is the spirit that is life-giving;[g] the flesh is of no use at all. The sayings that I have spoken to you are spirit and are life.[h] **64** But there are some of you who do not believe." For Jesus knew from the beginning those who did not believe and the one who would betray him.[i] **65** He went on to say: "This is why I have said to you, no one can come to me unless it is granted him by the Father."[j]

66 Because of this, many of his disciples went off to the things behind[k] and would no longer walk with him. **67** So Jesus said to the Twelve: "You do not want to go also, do you?" **68** Simon Peter answered him: "Lord,

---

CHAP. 6

a Joh 5:28, 29
Ro 6:5

b Joh 10:27, 28

c Joh 11:24
Ac 17:31
1Th 4:16
Re 20:12

d Joh 6:33

e Mr 6:3

f Joh 6:65

g Joh 11:24

h Isa 54:13

i Ex 33:17, 20

j Mt 11:27
Lu 10:22
Joh 1:18

k Joh 3:16

l Joh 6:33

m Joh 6:31

n Heb 10:10

Second Col.
a Joh 6:33

b Joh 6:40
1Co 15:51, 52
1Th 4:16

c Joh 15:4

d Joh 5:26
1Co 15:22

e Joh 6:51

f Joh 3:13
Joh 6:38
Joh 8:23
Ac 1:9

g Ga 6:8

h De 8:3
Mt 4:4

i Mt 9:3, 4
Joh 2:24, 25
Joh 13:11

j Joh 6:44

k Lu 9:62

6:45 *See App. A5.

6:59 *Or "public assembly."

whom shall we go away to?[a] You have sayings of everlasting life.[b] **69** We have believed and have come to know that you are the Holy One of God."[c] **70** Jesus answered them: "I chose you twelve, did I not?[d] Yet one of you is a slanderer."*[e] **71** He was, in fact, speaking of Judas the son of Simon Is·car'i·ot, for this one was going to betray him, although he was one of the Twelve.[f]

7 After this Jesus continued traveling* about in Gal'i·lee, for he did not want to do so in Ju·de'a because the Jews were seeking to kill him.[g] **2** However, the Jewish Festival of Tabernacles*[h] was near. **3** So his brothers[i] said to him: "Leave here and go into Ju·de'a, so that your disciples may also see the works you are doing. **4** For no one does anything in secret when he seeks to be known publicly. If you are doing these things, show yourself to the world." **5** His brothers were, in fact, not exercising faith in him.[j] **6** So Jesus said to them: "My time has not yet arrived,[k] but your time is always at hand. **7** The world has no reason to hate you, but it hates me, because I bear witness about it that its works are wicked.[l] **8** You go up to the festival; I am not yet going up to this festival, because my time has not yet fully come."[m] **9** So after he told them these things, he remained in Gal'i·lee.

10 But when his brothers had gone up to the festival, then he also went up, not openly but in secret. **11** So the Jews began looking for him at the festival and saying: "Where is that man?" **12** And there was a lot of subdued talk about him among the crowds. Some would say: "He is a good man." Others would say:

"He is not. He misleads the crowd."[a] **13** Of course, no one would speak about him publicly because of fear of the Jews.[b]

14 When the festival was half over, Jesus went up into the temple and began teaching. **15** And the Jews were astonished, saying: "How does this man have such a knowledge of the Scriptures*[c] when he has not studied at the schools?"*[d] **16** Jesus, in turn, answered them and said: "What I teach is not mine, but belongs to him who sent me.[e] **17** If anyone desires to do His will, he will know whether the teaching is from God[f] or I speak of my own originality. **18** Whoever speaks of his own originality is seeking his own glory; but whoever seeks the glory of the one who sent him,[g] this one is true and there is no unrighteousness in him. **19** Moses gave you the Law,[h] did he not? But not one of you obeys the Law. Why are you seeking to kill me?"[i] **20** The crowd answered: "You have a demon. Who is seeking to kill you?" **21** In answer Jesus said to them: "One deed I performed, and you are all surprised. **22** For this reason Moses has given you circumcision[j]—not that it is from Moses, but it is from the forefathers[k]—and you circumcise a man on a sabbath. **23** If a man receives circumcision on a sabbath so that the Law of Moses may not be broken, are you violently angry at me because I made a man completely well on a sabbath?[l] **24** Stop judging by the outward appearance, but judge with righteous judgment."[m]

25 Then some of the inhabitants of Jerusalem began to say: "This is the man they are seeking to kill, is it not?[n] **26** And yet see! he is speaking in public, and they say nothing to him.

6:70 *Or "a devil." **7:1** *Or "walking." **7:2** *Or "Booths."

7:15 *Lit., "writings." #That is, the rabbinic schools.

Have the rulers come to know for certain that this is the Christ? **27** On the contrary, we know where this man is from;[a] yet when the Christ comes, no one is to know where he is from." **28** Then as he was teaching in the temple, Jesus called out: "You know me and you know where I am from. And I have not come of my own initiative,[b] but the One who sent me is real, and you do not know him.[c] **29** I know him,[d] because I am a representative from him, and that One sent me." **30** So they began seeking to get hold of him,[e] but no one laid a hand on him, for his hour had not yet come.[f] **31** Still, many of the crowd put faith in him,[g] and they were saying: "When the Christ comes, he will not perform more signs than this man has done, will he?"

32 The Pharisees heard the crowd murmuring these things about him, and the chief priests and the Pharisees sent officers to seize* him. **33** Jesus then said: "I will be with you a little while longer before I go to the One who sent me.[h] **34** You will look for me, but you will not find me, and where I am you cannot come."[i] **35** Therefore, the Jews said among themselves: "Where does this man intend to go, so that we will not find him? He does not intend to go to the Jews dispersed among the Greeks and teach the Greeks, does he? **36** What does he mean when he says, 'You will look for me, but you will not find me, and where I am you cannot come'?"

37 On the last day, the great day of the festival,[j] Jesus stood up and he called out: "If anyone is thirsty, let him come to me and drink.[k] **38** Whoever puts faith in me, just as the scripture has said: 'From deep with-

7:32, 44 *Or "arrest."

CHAP. 7
a Mt 13:55
b Joh 8:42
c Joh 8:54, 55
d Mt 11:27
  Joh 1:18
  Joh 10:15
e Mr 11:18
  Lu 19:47
f Joh 8:20
g Joh 2:23
  Joh 8:30
  Joh 10:40, 42
  Joh 11:45
h Joh 13:33
  Joh 16:16
i Joh 8:21, 22
j Joh 7:2
k Joh 4:14
  Joh 6:35

Second Col.
a Ex 17:6
  Nu 20:8
  Joh 4:14
b Joe 2:28
  Joh 16:7
  Ac 2:17
c Joh 12:16
  Joh 13:31, 32
  1Ti 3:16
d De 18:18
  Joh 6:14
e Joh 4:40, 42
  Joh 6:68, 69
f Joh 1:46
  Joh 7:52
g 2Ch 13:5
  Ps 89:3, 4
  Ps 132:11
  Jer 23:5
h Mic 5:2
  Lu 2:4
i 1Sa 16:1
j Joh 7:28, 29
  Lu 4:22
k Joh 12:42
  Ac 6:7
l De 1:16, 17

CHAP. 8
m Isa 9:2
  Isa 49:6
  Mt 4:16
  Joh 1:5
  Joh 12:35

in him streams of living water will flow.'"[a] **39** However, he said this concerning the spirit, which those who put faith in him were about to receive; for as yet there was no spirit,[b] because Jesus had not yet been glorified.[c] **40** Some in the crowd who heard these words began saying: "This really is the Prophet."[d] **41** Others were saying: "This is the Christ."[e] But some were saying: "The Christ is not coming out of Gal′i·lee, is he?[f] **42** Does the scripture not say that the Christ is coming from the offspring of David[g] and from Beth′le·hem,[h] the village where David was?"[i] **43** So a division over him arose among the crowd. **44** Some of them, though, wanted to seize* him, but no one laid his hands on him.

45 Then the officers went back to the chief priests and Pharisees, and the latter said to them: "Why did you not bring him in?" **46** The officers replied: "Never has any man spoken like this."[j] **47** In turn the Pharisees answered: "You have not been misled also, have you? **48** Not one of the rulers or of the Pharisees has put faith in him, has he?[k] **49** But this crowd who do not know the Law are accursed people." **50** Nic·o·de′mus, who had come to him previously and who was one of them, said to them: **51** "Our Law does not judge a man unless it first hears from him and learns what he is doing, does it?"[l] **52** In answer they said to him: "You are not also out of Gal′i·lee, are you? Search and see that no prophet is to be raised up out of Gal′i·lee."*

8 **12** Then Jesus spoke again to them, saying: "I am the light of the world.[m] Whoever

7:52 *A number of ancient and authoritative manuscripts omit from vs. 53 to chapter 8, vs. 11.

follows me will by no means walk in darkness, but will possess the light[a] of life." **13** So the Pharisees said to him: "You bear witness about yourself; your witness is not true." **14** In answer Jesus said to them: "Even if I do bear witness about myself, my witness is true, because I know where I came from and where I am going.[b] But you do not know where I came from and where I am going. **15** You judge according to the flesh;*[c] I do not judge any man at all. **16** And yet even if I do judge, my judgment is truthful, because I am not alone, but the Father who sent me is with me.[d] **17** Also, in your own Law it is written: 'The witness of two men is true.'[e] **18** I am one who bears witness about myself, and the Father who sent me bears witness about me."[f] **19** Then they said to him: "Where is your Father?" Jesus answered: "You know neither me nor my Father.[g] If you did know me, you would know my Father also."[h] **20** He spoke these words in the treasury[i] as he was teaching in the temple. But no one seized him, for his hour had not yet come.[j]

21 So he said to them again: "I am going away, and you will look for me, and yet you will die in your sin.[k] Where I am going, you cannot come."[l] **22** The Jews then began to say: "He will not kill himself, will he? Because he says, 'Where I am going, you cannot come.'" **23** He went on to say to them: "You are from the realms below; I am from the realms above.[m] You are from this world; I am not from this world. **24** That is why I said to you: You will die in your sins. For if you do not believe that I am the one, you will die in your sins." **25** So they began to say to him: "Who are you?" Je-

---

8:15 *Or "by human standards."

CHAP. 8
a Joh 12:46
  1Pe 2:9
  1Jo 2:8

b Joh 7:28
  Joh 13:3
  Joh 16:28

c Joh 7:24

d Joh 14:10

e De 17:6
  De 19:15

f Joh 5:37
  2Pe 1:17
  1Jo 5:9

g Joh 16:3

h Mt 11:27
  Joh 14:7

i Mr 12:41

j Joh 7:30

k Joh 8:24

l Joh 7:34
  Joh 13:33

m Joh 3:31
  Joh 16:28

Second Col.
a Joh 18:19, 20

b Nu 21:8, 9
  Da 7:13
  Mt 26:64
  Joh 3:14
  Joh 12:32, 33
  Ga 3:13

c Mt 27:54

d Joh 5:19, 30

e Joh 4:34
  Joh 14:10
  Heb 1:9

f Joh 17:17
  Joh 18:37

g Ro 6:14, 22
  Jas 1:25

h Ro 6:6, 16
  Ro 7:14

i Joh 5:19

j Ro 2:28, 29
  Ro 9:7, 8
  Ga 3:7, 29

sus replied to them: "Why am I even speaking to you at all? **26** I have many things to speak concerning you and to pass judgment on. As a matter of fact, the One who sent me is true, and the very things I heard from him I am speaking in the world."[a] **27** They did not grasp that he was talking to them about the Father. **28** Jesus then said: "After you have lifted up the Son of man,[b] then you will know that I am he[c] and that I do nothing of my own initiative;[d] but just as the Father taught me, I speak these things. **29** And the One who sent me is with me; he did not abandon me to myself, because I always do the things pleasing to him."[e] **30** As he was saying these things, many put faith in him.

31 Then Jesus went on to say to the Jews who had believed him: "If you remain in my word, you are really my disciples, **32** and you will know the truth,[f] and the truth will set you free."[g] **33** They replied to him: "We are Abraham's offspring and never have been slaves to anyone. How is it you say, 'You will become free'?" **34** Jesus answered them: "Most truly I say to you, every doer of sin is a slave of sin.[h] **35** Moreover, the slave does not remain in the household forever; the son remains forever. **36** So if the Son sets you free, you will be truly free. **37** I know that you are Abraham's offspring. But you are seeking to kill me, because my word makes no progress among you. **38** I speak the things I have seen while with my Father,[i] but you do the things you have heard from your father." **39** In answer they said to him: "Our father is Abraham." Jesus said to them: "If you were Abraham's children,[j] you would be doing the works of Abraham. **40** But now you are seeking to kill me, a man who has told you the truth that I heard from God.[a] Abraham did not do this. **41** You are doing the works of your father." They said to him: "We were not born from immorality;* we have one Father, God."

42 Jesus said to them: "If God were your Father, you would love me,[b] for I came from God and I am here. I have not come of my own initiative, but that One sent me.[c] **43** Why do you not understand what I am saying? Because you cannot listen to my word. **44** You are from your father the Devil, and you wish to do the desires of your father.[d] That one was a murderer when he began,*[e] and he did not stand fast in the truth, because truth is not in him. When he speaks the lie, he speaks according to his own disposition, because he is a liar and the father of the lie.[f] **45** Because I, on the other hand, tell you the truth, you do not believe me. **46** Who of you convicts me of sin? If I speak truth, why is it that you do not believe me? **47** The one who is from God listens to the sayings of God.[g] This is why you do not listen, because you are not from God."[h]

48 In answer the Jews said to him: "Are we not right in saying, 'You are a Sa·mar'i·tan[i] and have a demon'?"[i] **49** Jesus answered: "I do not have a demon, but I honor my Father, and you dishonor me. **50** But I am not seeking glory for myself;[k] there is One who is seeking and judging. **51** Most truly I say to you, if anyone observes my word, he will never see death at all."[l] **52** The Jews said to him: "Now we do know that you have a demon. Abraham died, also the prophets, but

you say, 'If anyone observes my word, he will never taste death at all.' **53** You are not greater than our father Abraham, who died, are you? The prophets also died. Who do you claim to be?" **54** Jesus answered: "If I glorify myself, my glory is nothing. It is my Father who glorifies me,[a] the one who you say is your God. **55** Yet you have not known him,[b] but I know him.[c] And if I said I do not know him, I would be like you, a liar. But I do know him and am observing his word. **56** Abraham your father rejoiced greatly at the prospect of seeing my day, and he saw it and rejoiced."[d] **57** Then the Jews said to him: "You are not yet 50 years old, and still you have seen Abraham?" **58** Jesus said to them: "Most truly I say to you, before Abraham came into existence, I have been."[e] **59** So they picked up stones to throw at him, but Jesus hid and went out of the temple.

9 As he was passing along, he saw a man who had been blind from birth. **2** And his disciples asked him: "Rabbi,[f] who sinned, this man or his parents, so that he was born blind?" **3** Jesus answered: "Neither this man sinned nor his parents, but it was so that the works of God might be made manifest in his case.[g] **4** We must do the works of the One who sent me while it is day;[h] the night is coming when no man can work. **5** As long as I am in the world, I am the world's light."[i] **6** After he said these things, he spat on the ground and made a paste with the saliva, and he smeared the paste on the man's eyes[j] **7** and said to him: "Go wash in the pool of Si·lo'am" (which is translated "Sent Forth"). And he went and washed, and came back seeing.[k]

8 Then the neighbors and those who formerly used to see

CHAP. 8

a Joh 8:26

b Joh 16:27
  1Jo 5:1

c Joh 3:16
  Joh 5:19, 30

d Ge 3:15

e 1Jo 3:8

f Ge 3:4
  2Co 11:3
  Re 12:9

g Joh 18:37

h Joh 10:26
  1Jo 4:6

i Joh 4:9

j Mt 12:24
  Joh 7:20
  Joh 10:20

k Joh 5:41
  Joh 7:18

l Joh 5:24
  Joh 11:25, 26
  1Co 15:54
  Re 20:6

Second Col.

a Joh 5:41
  Joh 13:31, 32
  Ac 3:13

b Joh 7:28

c Joh 7:29

d Mt 13:17
  Heb 11:13

e Pr 8:22
  Joh 17:5
  Php 2:6, 7
  Col 1:15-17

CHAP. 9

f Joh 1:38

g Joh 11:2-4

h Joh 4:34
  Joh 11:9

i Isa 49:6
  Isa 61:1
  Joh 1:5
  Joh 8:12

j Mr 8:23

k 2Ki 5:10, 14

8:41 *Or "sexual immorality." Greek, por·nei'a. See Glossary. 8:44 *Or "from the beginning."

that he was a beggar began to say: "This is the man who used to sit and beg, is it not?" **9** Some were saying: "This is he." Others were saying: "No, but he looks like him." The man kept saying: "I am he." **10** So they asked him: "How, then, were your eyes opened?" **11** He answered: "The man called Jesus made a paste and smeared it on my eyes and said to me, 'Go to Si·lo'am and wash.'ᵃ So I went and washed and gained sight." **12** At this they said to him: "Where is that man?" He said: "I do not know."

13 They led the formerly blind man to the Pharisees. **14** Incidentally, the day that Jesus made the paste and opened his eyesᵇ was the Sabbath.ᶜ **15** So this time the Pharisees also began asking the man how he gained sight. He said to them: "He put a paste on my eyes, and I washed, and I can see." **16** Some of the Pharisees then began to say: "This is not a man from God, for he does not observe the Sabbath."ᵈ Others said: "How can a man who is a sinner perform signs of that sort?"ᵉ So there was a division among them.ᶠ **17** And again they said to the blind man: "What do you say about him, since it was your eyes that he opened?" The man said: "He is a prophet."

18 However, the Jews did not believe that he had been blind and had gained sight, until they called the parents of the man who could now see. **19** And they asked them: "Is this your son who you say was born blind? How, then, does he now see?" **20** His parents answered: "We know that this is our son and that he was born blind. **21** But how it is that he now sees, we do not know; or who opened his eyes, we do not know. Ask him. He is of age. He must speak for himself." **22** His parents said these things because they were

in fear of the Jews,ᵃ for the Jews had already come to an agreement that if anyone acknowledged him as Christ, that person should be expelled from the synagogue.ᵇ **23** This is why his parents said: "He is of age. Question him."

24 So a second time they called the man who had been blind and said to him: "Give glory to God; we know that this man is a sinner." **25** He answered: "Whether he is a sinner, I do not know. One thing I do know, that I was blind, but now I can see." **26** Then they said to him: "What did he do to you? How did he open your eyes?" **27** He answered them: "I told you already, and yet you did not listen. Why do you want to hear it again? You do not want to become his disciples also, do you?" **28** At this they scornfully told him: "You are a disciple of that man, but we are disciples of Moses. **29** We know that God has spoken to Moses, but as for this man, we do not know where he is from." **30** The man answered them: "This is certainly amazing, that you do not know where he is from, and yet he opened my eyes. **31** We know that God does not listen to sinners,ᶜ but if anyone is God-fearing and does his will, he listens to this one.ᵈ **32** From of old it has never been heard that anyone opened the eyes of one born blind. **33** If this man were not from God, he could do nothing at all."ᵉ **34** In answer they said to him: "You were altogether born in sin, and yet are you teaching us?" And they threw him out!ᶠ

35 Jesus heard that they had thrown him out, and on finding him, he said: "Are you putting faith in the Son of man?" **36** The man answered: "And who is he, sir, so that I may put faith in him?" **37** Jesus said to him: "You have seen him, and

CHAP. 9
a Joh 9:7

b Joh 9:6

c Lu 13:14
Joh 5:8, 9

d Ex 20:9, 10

e Joh 3:2

f Lu 12:51
Joh 7:12, 43
Joh 10:19

Second Col.
a Joh 7:13
Joh 19:38

b Joh 12:42
Joh 16:2

c Ps 66:18
Pr 28:9
Isa 1:15

d Ps 34:15
Pr 15:29

e Joh 5:36

f Joh 9:22
Joh 16:2

in fact, he is the one speaking with you." **38** He said: "I do put faith in him, Lord." And he did obeisance* to him. **39** Jesus then said: "For this judgment I came into this world, that those not seeing might see[a] and those seeing might become blind."[b] **40** Those of the Pharisees who were with him heard these things, and they said to him: "We are not blind also, are we?" **41** Jesus said to them: "If you were blind, you would have no sin. But now you say, 'We see.' Your sin remains."[c]

10 "Most truly I say to you, the one who does not enter into the sheepfold through the door but climbs in by another way, that one is a thief and a plunderer.[d] **2** But the one who enters through the door is the shepherd of the sheep.[e] **3** The doorkeeper opens to this one,[f] and the sheep listen to his voice.[g] He calls his own sheep by name and leads them out. **4** When he has brought all his own out, he goes ahead of them, and the sheep follow him, because they know his voice. **5** They will by no means follow a stranger but will flee from him, because they do not know the voice of strangers." **6** Jesus spoke this comparison to them, but they did not understand what he was saying to them.

7 So Jesus said again: "Most truly I say to you, I am the door for the sheep.[h] **8** All those who have come in place of me are thieves and plunderers; but the sheep have not listened to them. **9** I am the door; whoever enters through me will be saved, and that one will go in and out and find pasturage.[i] **10** The thief does not come unless it is to steal and slay and destroy.[j] I have come that they may have life and have it in abundance. **11** I am

the fine shepherd;[a] the fine shepherd surrenders his life* in behalf of the sheep.[b] **12** The hired man, who is not a shepherd and to whom the sheep do not belong, sees the wolf coming and abandons the sheep and flees —and the wolf snatches them and scatters them— **13** because he is a hired man and does not care for the sheep. **14** I am the fine shepherd. I know my sheep and my sheep know me,[c] **15** just as the Father knows me and I know the Father;[d] and I surrender my life* in behalf of the sheep.[e]

16 "And I have other sheep, which are not of this fold;[f] those too I must bring in, and they will listen to my voice, and they will become one flock, one shepherd.[g] **17** This is why the Father loves me,[h] because I surrender my life,*[i] so that I may receive it again. **18** No man takes it away from me, but I surrender it of my own initiative. I have authority to surrender it, and I have authority to receive it again.[j] This commandment I received from my Father."

19 A division again resulted among the Jews[k] because of these words. **20** Many of them were saying: "He has a demon and is out of his mind. Why do you listen to him?" **21** Others said: "These are not the sayings of a demonized man. A demon cannot open blind people's eyes, can it?"

22 At that time the Festival of Dedication took place in Jerusalem. It was wintertime, **23** and Jesus was walking in the temple in the colonnade of Sol′o·mon.[l] **24** Then the Jews surrounded him and began to say to him: "How long are you going to keep us* in suspense? If you are the Christ, tell us plainly." **25** Jesus answered them: "I told you, and

---

Cross-references

yet you do not believe. The works that I am doing in my Father's name, these bear witness about me.[a] **26** But you do not believe, because you are not my sheep.[b] **27** My sheep listen to my voice, and I know them, and they follow me.[c] **28** I give them everlasting life,[d] and they will by no means ever be destroyed, and no one will snatch them out of my hand.[e] **29** What my Father has given me is something greater than all other things, and no one can snatch them out of the hand of the Father.[f] **30** I and the Father are one."[*g]

31 Once again the Jews picked up stones to stone him. **32** Jesus replied to them: "I displayed to you many fine works from the Father. For which of those works are you stoning me?" **33** The Jews answered him: "We are stoning you, not for a fine work, but for blasphemy;[h] for you, although being a man, make yourself a god." **34** Jesus answered them: "Is it not written in your Law, 'I said: "You are gods"'?[*i] **35** If he called "gods"[j] those against whom the word of God came—and yet the scripture cannot be nullified— **36** do you say to me whom the Father sanctified and sent into the world, 'You blaspheme,' because I said, 'I am God's Son'?[k] **37** If I am not doing the works of my Father, do not believe me. **38** But if I am doing them, even though you do not believe me, believe the works,[l] so that you may come to know and may continue knowing that the Father is in union with me and I am in union with the Father."[m] **39** So they tried again to seize him, but he escaped from their reach.

40 And he went away again across the Jordan to the place where John was baptizing at

first,[a] and he stayed there. **41** And many people came to him and began saying: "John did not perform a single sign, but all the things John said about this man were true."[b] **42** And many put faith in him there.

11 Now a man named Laz′a·rus was sick; he was from Beth′a·ny, the village of Mary and her sister Martha.[c] **2** This was the Mary who poured perfumed oil on the Lord and wiped his feet dry with her hair;[d] it was her brother Laz′a·rus who was sick. **3** So his sisters sent a message to him, saying: "Lord, see! the one you have affection for is sick." **4** But when Jesus heard it, he said: "This sickness is not meant to end in death, but is for the glory of God,[e] so that the Son of God may be glorified through it."

5 Now Jesus loved Martha and her sister and Laz′a·rus. **6** However, when he heard that Laz′a·rus was sick, he actually remained in the place where he was for two more days. **7** Then after this he said to the disciples: "Let us go into Ju·de′a again." **8** The disciples said to him: "Rabbi,[f] just lately the Ju·de′ans were seeking to stone you,[g] and are you going there again?" **9** Jesus answered: "There are 12 hours of daylight, are there not?[h] If anyone walks in daylight, he does not stumble into anything, because he sees the light of this world. **10** But if anyone walks in the night, he stumbles, because the light is not in him."

11 After he said these things, he added: "Laz′a·rus our friend has fallen asleep,[i] but I am traveling there to awaken him." **12** The disciples then said to him: "Lord, if he is sleeping, he will get well." **13** Jesus, however, had spoken about his death. But they imagined he was speaking about taking rest

---

10:30 *Or "at unity." **10:34** *Or "god-like ones."

CHAP. 10

a Joh 3:2
  Joh 5:36
  Joh 10:38
  Joh 14:10
  Ac 2:22

b Joh 8:47

c Joh 10:3

d Joh 5:24
  Joh 17:1, 2

e Joh 6:37
  Joh 18:9

f 1Pe 1:4, 5

g Joh 10:38
  Joh 17:11, 21

h Le 24:16

i Ps 82:6
  1Co 8:5

j Ps 82:1

k Lu 1:35
  Joh 5:18

l Joh 5:36

m Joh 14:10
  Joh 17:21

Second Col.

a Joh 1:28

b Joh 1:29

CHAP. 11

c Lu 10:38

d Mt 26:6, 7
  Mr 14:3
  Joh 12:3

e Joh 9:1-3

f Joh 1:38

g Joh 8:59
  Joh 10:31

h Joh 9:4
  Joh 12:35

i Ps 13:3
  Mt 9:24
  Ac 7:59, 60
  1Co 15:6

in sleep. 14 Then Jesus said to them plainly: "Laz'a·rus has died,[a] 15 and I rejoice for your sake that I was not there, so that you may believe. But let us go to him." 16 So Thomas, who was called the Twin, said to his fellow disciples: "Let us also go, so that we may die with him."[b]

17 When Jesus arrived, he found that Laz'a·rus had already been in the tomb* for four days. 18 Now Beth'a·ny was near Jerusalem, about two miles* away. 19 And many of the Jews had come to Martha and Mary to console them concerning their brother. 20 When Martha heard that Jesus was coming, she went to meet him; but Mary[c] kept sitting at home. 21 Martha then said to Jesus: "Lord, if you had been here, my brother would not have died. 22 Yet even now I know that whatever you ask God for, God will give you." 23 Jesus said to her: "Your brother will rise." 24 Martha said to him: "I know he will rise in the resurrection[d] on the last day." 25 Jesus said to her: "I am the resurrection and the life.[e] The one who exercises faith in me, even though he dies, will come to life; 26 and everyone who is living and exercises faith in me will never die at all.[f] Do you believe this?" 27 She said to him: "Yes, Lord, I have believed that you are the Christ, the Son of God, the one coming into the world." 28 When she had said this, she went off and called Mary her sister, saying privately: "The Teacher[g] is here and is calling you." 29 On hearing this, she got up quickly and went to him.

30 Jesus had not yet come into the village, but he was still in the place where Mar-

tha had met him. 31 When the Jews who were with Mary in the house consoling her saw her get up quickly and go out, they followed her, supposing that she was going to the tomb*[a] to weep there. 32 When Mary arrived where Jesus was and caught sight of him, she fell at his feet and said to him: "Lord, if you had been here, my brother would not have died." 33 When Jesus saw her weeping and the Jews who had come with her weeping, he groaned within himself* and became troubled. 34 He said: "Where have you laid him?" They said to him: "Lord, come and see." 35 Jesus gave way to tears.[b] 36 At that the Jews began to say: "See, what affection he had for him!" 37 But some of them said: "Could not this man who opened the eyes of the blind man[c] prevent this one from dying?"

38 Then Jesus, after groaning again within himself, came to the tomb.* It was, in fact, a cave, and a stone was lying against it. 39 Jesus said: "Take the stone away." Martha, the sister of the deceased, said to him: "Lord, by now he must smell, for it has been four days." 40 Jesus said to her: "Did I not tell you that if you would believe you would see the glory of God?"[d] 41 So they took the stone away. Then Jesus raised his eyes heavenward[e] and said: "Father, I thank you that you have heard me. 42 True, I knew that you always hear me; but I spoke on account of the crowd standing around, so that they may believe that you sent me."[f] 43 When he had said these things, he cried out with a loud voice: "Laz'a·rus, come out!"[g] 44 The man who had been dead came out with his feet and hands bound with wrappings, and his face was wrapped

---

CHAP. 11
a Ec 9:5

b Joh 11:8

c Lu 10:38, 39

d Isa 26:19
Joh 5:28, 29
Ac 24:15
Heb 11:35
Re 20:12

e Joh 14:6

f Joh 8:51

g Mt 23:8
Joh 13:13

Second Col.
a Joh 11:17

b Lu 19:41
Heb 4:15

c Joh 9:6, 7

d Joh 9:1-3

e Mt 14:19
Mr 7:34, 35

f Joh 12:28-30
Joh 17:8

g Lu 7:12, 14

11:17, 31, 38 *Or "memorial tomb."
11:18 *About three km. Lit., "about 15 stadia." See App. B14.

11:33 *Lit., "in the spirit."

with a cloth. Jesus said to them: "Free him and let him go."

45 Therefore, many of the Jews who had come to Mary and who saw what he did put faith in him,[a] **46** but some of them went off to the Pharisees and told them what Jesus had done. **47** So the chief priests and the Pharisees gathered the San'he-drin together and said: "What are we to do, for this man performs many signs?[b] **48** If we let him go on this way, they will all put faith in him, and the Romans will come and take away both our place* and our nation." **49** But one of them, Ca'-ia·phas,[c] who was high priest that year, said to them: "You do not know anything at all, **50** and you have not reasoned that it is to your benefit for one man to die in behalf of the people rather than for the whole nation to be destroyed." **51** He did not say this, however, of his own originality, but because he was high priest that year, he prophesied that Jesus was to die for the nation, **52** and not only for the nation but also to gather together into one the children of God who were scattered about. **53** So from that day on they conspired to kill him.

54 Therefore, Jesus no longer walked about publicly among the Jews, but he departed from there to the region near the wilderness, to a city called E'phra-im,[d] and he stayed there with the disciples. **55** Now the Passover[e] of the Jews was near, and many people from the countryside went up to Jerusalem before the Passover to cleanse themselves ceremonially. **56** They were looking for Jesus, and they were saying to one another as they stood around in the temple: "What is your opinion? That he will not come to the festival at all?" **57** But the chief priests and the Pharisees had given orders that if anyone got to know where Jesus was, he should report it, so that they could seize* him.

12 Six days before the Passover, Jesus arrived at Beth'a·ny, where Laz'a·rus[a] was, whom Jesus had raised up from the dead. **2** So they spread an evening meal for him there, and Martha was serving them,[b] but Laz'a·rus was one of those dining* with him. **3** Then Mary took a pound* of perfumed oil, genuine nard, very costly, and she poured it on the feet of Jesus and wiped his feet dry with her hair. The house became filled with the scent of the perfumed oil.[c] **4** But Judas Is·car'i·ot,[d] one of his disciples, who was about to betray him, said: **5** "Why was this perfumed oil not sold for 300 de·nar'i·i* and given to the poor?" **6** He said this, though, not because he was concerned about the poor, but because he was a thief and had the money box and used to steal the money put in it. **7** Then Jesus said: "Let her alone, so that she may keep this observance in view of the day of my burial.[e] **8** For you always have the poor with you,[f] but you will not always have me."[g]

9 Meanwhile, a large crowd of Jews got to know that he was there, and they came not only because of Jesus but also to see Laz'a·rus, whom he had raised up from the dead.[h] **10** The chief priests now conspired to kill Laz'a·rus also, **11** since it was because of him that many of the Jews were going there and putting faith in Jesus.[i]

CHAP. 11
a Joh 2:23
   Joh 10:42
   Joh 12:10, 11

b Joh 12:37
   Ac 4:15, 16

c Mt 26:3
   Lu 3:2
   Ac 4:5, 6

d 2Sa 13:23
   2Ch 13:19

e Ex 12:14
   De 16:1
   Joh 2:13
   Joh 5:1
   Joh 6:4
   Joh 12:1

Second Col.

CHAP. 12
a Joh 11:1, 43

b Lu 10:40

c Mt 26:6-10
   Mr 14:3-6

d Mt 26:47
   Mr 14:10
   Lu 22:48
   Joh 13:29
   Ac 1:16

e Mt 26:12
   Mr 14:8
   Joh 19:40

f De 15:11

g Mt 26:11
   Mr 14:7

h Joh 11:43, 44

i Joh 7:31
   Joh 11:44, 45

11:48 *That is, the temple. 11:57 *Or "arrest." 12:2 *Or "reclining at the table." 12:3 *That is, a Roman pound, about 327 g (11.5 oz). See App. B14. 12:5 *See App. B14.

12 The next day the large crowd that had come to the festival heard that Jesus was coming to Jerusalem. **13** So they took branches of palm trees and went out to meet him, and they began to shout: "Save, we pray you! Blessed is the one who comes in Jehovah's* name,[a] the King of Israel!"[b] **14** When Jesus found a young donkey, he sat on it,[c] just as it is written: **15** "Have no fear, daughter of Zion. Look! Your king is coming, seated on a donkey's colt."[d] **16** These things his disciples did not understand at first, but when Jesus was glorified,[e] they recalled that these things were written about him and that they did these things to him.[f]

17 Now the crowd that was with him when he called Laz'a-rus out of the tomb*[g] and raised him up from the dead kept bearing witness.[h] **18** This is also why the crowd went to meet him, because they heard he had performed this sign. **19** So the Pharisees said among themselves: "You see that you are not getting anywhere. Look! The whole world has gone after him."[i]

20 Now there were some Greeks among those who had come to worship at the festival. **21** So these approached Philip,[j] who was from Beth·sa'i·da of Gal'i·lee, and they began to request him, saying: "Sir, we want to see Jesus." **22** Philip came and told Andrew. Andrew and Philip came and told Jesus.

23 But Jesus answered them: "The hour has come for the Son of man to be glorified.[k] **24** Most truly I say to you, unless a grain of wheat falls to the ground and dies, it remains just one grain; but if it dies,[l] it then bears much fruit. **25** Whoever is fond of his life* destroys it, but who-

ever hates his life*[a] in this world will safeguard it for everlasting life.[b] **26** If anyone would minister to me, let him follow me, and where I am, there my minister will be also.[c] If anyone would minister to me, the Father will honor him. **27** Now I am* troubled,[d] and what should I say? Father, save me out of this hour.[e] Nevertheless, this is why I have come to this hour. **28** Father, glorify your name." Then a voice[f] came out of heaven: "I have glorified it and will glorify it again."[g]

29 The crowd that was standing there heard it and began to say that it had thundered. Others said: "An angel has spoken to him." **30** Jesus answered: "This voice has occurred, not for my sake, but for your sakes. **31** Now there is a judging of this world; now the ruler of this world[h] will be cast out.[i] **32** And yet I, if I am lifted up from the earth,[j] will draw all sorts of men to myself." **33** This he was really saying to indicate what sort of death he was about to die.[k] **34** Then the crowd answered him: "We heard from the Law that the Christ remains forever.[l] How can you say that the Son of man must be lifted up?[m] Who is this Son of man?" **35** So Jesus said to them: "The light will be among you a little while longer. Walk while you still have the light, so that darkness does not overpower you; whoever walks in the darkness does not know where he is going.[n] **36** While you have the light, exercise faith in the light, so that you may become sons of light."[o]

Jesus said these things and went off and hid from them. **37** Although he had performed so many signs before them, they were not putting faith in him, **38** so that the word of Isaiah the prophet might be fulfilled, who

CHAP. 12
a Ps 118:25, 26
b Mt 21:8, 9
  Mr 11:8, 9
  Joh 1:49
c Mt 21:7
  Mr 11:7
  Lu 19:35
d 1Ki 1:33, 34
  Isa 62:11
  Zec 9:9
  Mt 21:5
e Joh 7:39
f Lu 24:45
  Joh 14:26
g Joh 11:1, 43
h Mt 21:15
  Lu 19:37
i Joh 11:48
j Joh 1:44
k Joh 13:31, 32
  Joh 17:1
l Mt 16:21
  Ro 14:9
  1Co 15:36

Second Col.
a Re 12:11
b Mt 16:25
  Mr 8:35
  Lu 9:24
c Joh 14:3
  Joh 17:24
  1Th 4:17
d Mt 26:38
  Mr 14:34
e Lu 12:50
  Lu 22:41, 42
  Heb 5:7
f Mt 3:17
  Mt 17:5
  Mr 1:11
  Mr 9:7
  Lu 3:22
  Lu 9:35
  2Pe 1:17
g Joh 17:1
h Joh 14:30
  Joh 16:11
  Ac 26:17, 18
  2Co 4:3, 4
  Eph 2:1, 2
  1Jo 5:19
i Lu 10:18
  Re 12:9
j Joh 8:28
k Ac 5:30
l Ps 89:35, 36
  Ps 110:4
  Isa 9:7
m Joh 3:14
n Joh 11:10
o Eph 5:8

12:13 *See App. A5. 12:17 *Or "memorial tomb." 12:25 *Or "soul." 12:27 *Or "my soul is."

said: "Jehovah,* who has put faith in the thing heard from us?"[#a] And as for the arm of Jehovah,* to whom has it been revealed?"[b] **39** The reason why they were not able to believe is that again Isaiah said: **40** "He has blinded their eyes and has made their hearts hard, so that they would not see with their eyes and understand with their hearts and turn around and I heal them."[c] **41** Isaiah said these things because he saw his glory, and he spoke about him.[d] **42** All the same, many even of the rulers actually put faith in him,[e] but they would not acknowledge him because of the Pharisees, so that they would not be expelled from the synagogue;[f] **43** for they loved the glory of men even more than the glory of God.[g]

44 However, Jesus called out and said: "Whoever puts faith in me puts faith not only in me but also in him who sent me;[h] **45** and whoever sees me sees also the One who sent me.[i] **46** I have come as a light into the world,[j] so that everyone putting faith in me may not remain in the darkness.[k] **47** But if anyone hears my sayings and does not keep them, I do not judge him; for I came, not to judge the world, but to save the world.[l] **48** Whoever disregards me and does not receive my sayings has one to judge him. The word that I have spoken is what will judge him on the last day. **49** For I have not spoken of my own initiative, but the Father who sent me has himself given me a commandment about what to say and what to speak.[m] **50** And I know that his commandment means everlasting life.[n] So whatever I speak, I speak just as the Father has told me."[o]

13 Now because he knew before the festival of the Passover that his hour had come[a] for him to leave this world and go to the Father,[b] Jesus, having loved his own who were in the world, loved them to the end.[c] **2** The evening meal was going on, and the Devil had already put it into the heart of Judas Is·car′i·ot,[d] the son of Simon, to betray him.[e] **3** So Jesus, knowing that the Father had given all things into his hands and that he came from God and was going to God,[f] **4** got up from the evening meal and laid aside his outer garments. And taking a towel, he wrapped it around his waist.*[g] **5** After that he put water into a basin and started to wash the feet of the disciples and to dry them off with the towel that was wrapped around him.* **6** Then he came to Simon Peter. He said to him: "Lord, are you washing my feet?" **7** Jesus answered him: "What I am doing you do not understand now, but you will understand after these things." **8** Peter said to him: "You will certainly never wash my feet." Jesus answered him: "Unless I wash you,[h] you have no share with me." **9** Simon Peter said to him: "Lord, wash not only my feet but also my hands and my head." **10** Jesus said to him: "Whoever has bathed does not need to have more than his feet washed, but is completely clean. And you men are clean, but not all of you." **11** For he knew the man who was betraying him.[i] This is why he said: "Not all of you are clean."

12 When, now, he had washed their feet and had put his outer garments on, he again reclined at the table and said to them: "Do you understand what I have done to you? **13** You address

---

CHAP. 12

a Ro 10:16

b Isa 53:1

c Isa 6:10
  Mt 13:14
  Mr 4:11, 12
  Ac 28:27

d Isa 6:1, 8

e Joh 19:38

f Joh 9:22
  Joh 16:2

g Joh 5:44

h Mt 10:40
  Mr 9:37

i Joh 14:9

j Joh 3:19
  Joh 8:12
  Joh 9:5

k Joh 12:35

l Joh 3:16, 17

m Joh 8:38
  Joh 14:10

n Joh 6:40

o Joh 3:34

Second Col.

CHAP. 13

a Mt 26:2
  Joh 12:23
  Joh 17:1

b Joh 16:28
  Joh 17:11

c Joh 15:9
  Eph 5:2
  1Jo 3:16

d Lu 22:3, 4
  Joh 13:27

e Mt 26:14-16
  Mt 26:24
  Mr 14:10, 11

f Joh 16:28

g Php 2:5-7

h 1Co 6:11
  Eph 5:25, 26
  Tit 3:5
  Heb 10:22

i Joh 6:64

12:38 *See App. A5. #Or "in our report?"

13:4 *Or "girded himself." **13:5** *Or "with which he was girded."

me as 'Teacher' and 'Lord,' and you are correct, for I am such.[a] **14** Therefore, if I, the Lord and Teacher, washed your feet,[b] you also should* wash the feet of one another.[c] **15** For I set the pattern for you, that just as I did to you, you should also do.[d] **16** Most truly I say to you, a slave is not greater than his master, nor is one who is sent greater than the one who sent him. **17** If you know these things, happy you are if you do them.[e] **18** I am not talking about all of you; I know the ones I have chosen. But this was so that the scripture might be fulfilled:[f] 'The one who was eating my bread has lifted his heel against me.'*[g] **19** From this moment on, I am telling you before it occurs, so that when it does occur you may believe that I am he.[h] **20** Most truly I say to you, whoever receives anyone I send receives me also,[i] and whoever receives me receives also the One who sent me."[j]

21 After saying these things, Jesus became troubled in spirit, and he bore witness, saying: "Most truly I say to you, one of you will betray me."[k] **22** The disciples began to look at one another, being at a loss as to which one he was talking about.[l] **23** One of the disciples, the one whom Jesus loved,[m] was reclining close to* Jesus. **24** Therefore, Simon Peter nodded to this one and said to him: "Tell us whom he is talking about." **25** So the latter leaned back on the chest of Jesus and said to him: "Lord, who is it?"[n] **26** Jesus answered: "It is the one to whom I will give the piece of bread that I dip."[o] So after dipping the bread, he took it and gave it to Judas, the son of Si-

mon Is·car'i·ot. **27** After Judas took the piece of bread, then Satan entered into him.[a] So Jesus said to him: "What you are doing, do it more quickly." **28** However, none of those reclining at the table knew why he said this to him. **29** Some, in fact, were thinking that since Judas was holding the money box,[b] Jesus was telling him, "Buy what we need for the festival," or that he should give something to the poor. **30** So after he received the piece of bread, he went out immediately. And it was night.[c]

31 When, therefore, he had gone out, Jesus said: "Now the Son of man is glorified,[d] and God is glorified in connection with him. **32** God himself will glorify him,[e] and he will glorify him immediately. **33** Little children, I am with you a little longer. You will look for me; and just as I said to the Jews, 'Where I go you cannot come,'[f] I now say it also to you. **34** I am giving you a new commandment, that you love one another; just as I have loved you,[g] you also love one another.[h] **35** By this all will know that you are my disciples—if you have love among yourselves."[i]

36 Simon Peter said to him: "Lord, where are you going?" Jesus answered: "Where I am going, you cannot follow me now, but you will follow later."[j] **37** Peter said to him: "Lord, why is it I cannot follow you now? I will surrender my life* in your behalf."[k] **38** Jesus answered: "Will you surrender your life* in my behalf? Most truly I say to you, a rooster will by no means crow until you have disowned me three times."[l]

14 "Do not let your hearts be troubled.[m] Exercise faith in God;[n] exercise faith also in me. **2** In the house of my Father are

---

13:14 *Or "you also are under obligation to." 13:18 *Or "has turned against me." 13:23 *Lit., "in the bosom of."

13:37, 38 *Or "soul."

many dwelling places.* Otherwise, I would have told you, for I am going my way to prepare a place for you.ᵃ **3** Also, if I go my way and prepare a place for you, I will come again and will receive you home to myself, so that where I am you also may be.ᵇ **4** And where I am going, you know the way."

5 Thomasᶜ said to him: "Lord, we do not know where you are going. How can we know the way?"

6 Jesus said to him: "I am the wayᵈ and the truthᵉ and the life.ᶠ No one comes to the Father except through me.ᵍ **7** If you men had known me, you would have known my Father also; from this moment on you know him and have seen him."ʰ

8 Philip said to him: "Lord, show us the Father, and it is enough for us."

9 Jesus said to him: "Even after I have been with you men for such a long time, Philip, have you not come to know me? Whoever has seen me has seen the Father also.ⁱ How is it you say, 'Show us the Father'? **10** Do you not believe that I am in union with the Father and the Father is in union with me?ʲ The things I say to you I do not speak of my own originality,ᵏ but the Father who remains in union with me is doing his works. **11** Believe me that I am in union with the Father and the Father is in union with me; otherwise, believe because of the works themselves.ˡ **12** Most truly I say to you, whoever exercises faith in me will also do the works that I do; and he will do works greater than these,ᵐ because I am going my way to the Father.ⁿ **13** Also, whatever you ask in my name, I will do this, so that the Father may be glorified in connec-

tion with the Son.ᵃ **14** If you ask anything in my name, I will do it.

15 "If you love me, you will observe my commandments.ᵇ **16** And I will ask the Father and he will give you another helper* to be with you forever,ᶜ **17** the spirit of the truth,ᵈ which the world cannot receive, because it neither sees it nor knows it.ᵉ You know it, because it remains with you and is in you. **18** I will not leave you bereaved.* I am coming to you.ᶠ **19** In a little while the world will see me no more, but you will see me,ᵍ because I live and you will live. **20** In that day you will know that I am in union with my Father and you are in union with me and I am in union with you.ʰ **21** Whoever has my commandments and observes them is the one who loves me. In turn, whoever loves me will be loved by my Father, and I will love him and will clearly show myself to him."

22 Judas,ⁱ not Is·car′i·ot, said to him: "Lord, what has happened that you intend to show yourself clearly to us and not to the world?"

23 In answer Jesus said to him: "If anyone loves me, he will observe my word,ʲ and my Father will love him, and we will come to him and make our dwelling* with him.ᵏ **24** Whoever does not love me does not observe my words. The word that you are hearing is not mine, but belongs to the Father who sent me.ˡ

25 "I have spoken these things to you while I am still with you. **26** But the helper, the holy spirit, which the Father will send in my name, that one will teach you all things and bring back to your minds all the things I told you.ᵐ **27** I leave you peace; I

CHAP. 14

a Lu 12:32
　1Pe 1:3, 4
b Joh 17:24
　Ro 8:17
　Php 1:23
　1Th 4:16, 17
c Joh 11:16
d Joh 10:9
　Eph 2:18
　Heb 10:19, 20
e Joh 1:17
　Eph 4:21
f Joh 1:4
　Joh 6:63
　Joh 17:3
　Ro 6:23
g Ac 4:12
h Mt 11:27
　Joh 1:18
i Joh 12:45
　Col 1:15
　Heb 1:3
j Joh 10:38
　Joh 17:21
k Joh 7:16
　Joh 8:28
　Joh 12:49
l Joh 5:36
m Mt 21:21
　Ac 1:8
　Ac 2:41
n Ac 2:32, 33

Second Col.

a Joh 15:16
　Joh 16:23
b Joh 13:34
　Joh 15:10
　Jas 1:22
c Lu 24:49
　Joh 15:26
　Joh 16:7
　Ac 1:5
　Ac 2:1, 4
　Ro 8:26
d Mt 10:19, 20
　Joh 16:13
　1Co 2:12
　1Jo 2:27
e 1Co 2:14
f Mt 28:20
g Ac 10:40, 41
h Joh 10:38
　Joh 17:21
i Lu 6:13, 16
　Ac 1:13
j Joh 15:10
k 1Jo 2:24
　Re 3:20
l Joh 5:19
　Joh 7:16
　Joh 12:49
m Lu 24:49
　Joh 15:26
　Joh 16:13
　1Jo 2:27

14:2 *Or "many abodes." **14:16** *Or "comforter." **14:18** *Or "as orphans." **14:23** *Or "abode."

give you my peace.ᵃ I do not give it to you the way that the world gives it. Do not let your hearts be troubled nor let them shrink out of fear. **28** You heard that I said to you, 'I am going away and I am coming back to you.' If you loved me, you would rejoice that I am going to the Father, for the Father is greater than I am.ᵇ **29** So now I have told you before it occurs, so that you may believe when it does occur.ᶜ **30** I will not speak with you much more, for the ruler of the worldᵈ is coming, and he has no hold on me.*ᵉ **31** But for the world to know that I love the Father, I am doing just as the Father has commanded me to do.ᶠ Get up, let us go from here.

15 "I am the true vine, and my Father is the cultivator. **2** He takes away every branch in me not bearing fruit, and he cleans every one bearing fruit, so that it may bear more fruit.ᵍ **3** You are already clean because of the word that I have spoken to you.ʰ **4** Remain in union with me, and I will remain in union with you. Just as the branch cannot bear fruit by itself unless it remains in the vine, neither can you unless you remain in union with me.ⁱ **5** I am the vine; you are the branches. Whoever remains in union with me and I in union with him, this one bears much fruit;ʲ for apart from me you can do nothing at all. **6** If anyone does not remain in union with me, he is thrown out like a branch and dries up. And men gather those branches and throw them into the fire, and they are burned. **7** If you remain in union with me and my sayings remain in you, ask whatever you wish and it will take place for you.ᵏ **8** My Father is glorified in this, that

you keep bearing much fruit and prove yourselves my disciples.ᵃ **9** Just as the Father has loved me,ᵇ so I have loved you; remain in my love. **10** If you observe my commandments, you will remain in my love, just as I have observed the commandments of the Father and remain in his love.

11 "These things I have spoken to you, so that my joy may be in you and your joy may be made full.ᶜ **12** This is my commandment, that you love one another just as I have loved you.ᵈ **13** No one has love greater than this, that someone should surrender his life* in behalf of his friends.ᵉ **14** You are my friends if you do what I am commanding you.ᶠ **15** I no longer call you slaves, because a slave does not know what his master does. But I have called you friends, because I have made known to you all the things I have heard from my Father. **16** You did not choose me, but I chose you, and I appointed you to go and keep bearing fruit and that your fruit should remain, so that no matter what you ask the Father in my name, he may give it to you.ᵍ

17 "These things I command you, that you love one another.ʰ **18** If the world hates you, you know that it has hated me before it hated you.ⁱ **19** If you were part of the world, the world would be fond of what is its own. Now because you are no part of the world,ʲ but I have chosen you out of the world, for this reason the world hates you.ᵏ **20** Keep in mind the word I said to you: A slave is not greater than his master. If they have persecuted me, they will also persecute you;ˡ if they have observed my word, they will also observe yours. **21** But they will do all these

CHAP. 14	
a	Joh 16:33
	Eph 2:14
	Php 4:6, 7
	Col 3:15
	2Th 3:16
b	Joh 20:17
	1Co 11:3
	1Co 15:28
	Php 2:5, 6
c	Joh 13:19
	Joh 16:4
d	Joh 12:31
	Joh 16:11
e	Joh 16:33
f	Joh 10:18
	Joh 12:49
	Joh 15:10
	Php 2:8
CHAP. 15	
g	2Pe 1:8
h	Joh 13:10
	Joh 17:17
i	Joh 6:56
	1Co 12:27
	Eph 4:16
j	Joh 15:16
k	Mt 7:7
	Joh 16:23
Second Col.	
a	Mt 5:16
	Joh 13:35
	Php 1:9, 11
b	Joh 3:35
c	Joh 16:24
	Joh 17:13
d	Mr 12:31
	Joh 13:34
	1Th 4:9
	1Pe 4:8
e	Joh 10:11
	Ro 5:7, 8
	Eph 5:1, 2
	1Jo 3:16
f	Mt 12:50
	Joh 14:23
g	Joh 14:13
h	Joh 13:34
	1Jo 3:23
i	Mt 10:22
	Joh 17:14
	Jas 4:4
k	Lu 6:22
	Joh 17:14
	1Pe 4:4
l	Mt 5:11
	Mt 10:22
	Mt 24:9
	2Ti 3:12
	1Pe 2:21

14:30 *Or "has no power over me."

15:13 *Or "soul."

things against you on account of my name, because they do not know the One who sent me.[a] **22** If I had not come and spoken to them, they would have no sin.[b] But now they have no excuse for their sin.[c] **23** Whoever hates me also hates my Father.[d] **24** If I had not done among them the works that no one else did, they would have no sin;[e] but now they have both seen and hated me as well as my Father. **25** But this happened in order to fulfill the word written in their Law: 'They hated me without cause.'[f] **26** When the helper comes that I will send you from the Father, the spirit of the truth,[g] which comes from the Father, that one will bear witness about me;[h] **27** and you, in turn, are to bear witness,[i] because you have been with me from the beginning.

16 "I have said these things to you so that you may not be stumbled. **2** Men will expel you from the synagogue.[j] In fact, the hour is coming when everyone who kills you[k] will think he has offered a sacred service to God. **3** But they will do these things because they have not come to know either the Father or me.[l] **4** Nevertheless, I have told you these things so that when the hour for them to happen arrives, you will remember that I told them to you.[m]

"I did not tell you these things at first, because I was with you. **5** But now I am going to the One who sent me;[n] yet not one of you asks me, 'Where are you going?' **6** But because I have told you these things, grief has filled your hearts.[o] **7** Nevertheless, I am telling you the truth, it is for your benefit that I am going away. For if I do not go away, the helper[p] will not come to you; but if I do go, I will send him to you. **8** And when that

CHAP. 15

a Joh 16:2, 3

b Joh 9:41

c Mt 11:21

d Joh 5:23
1Jo 2:23

e Mt 11:23
Joh 7:31
Joh 11:47

f Ps 35:19
Ps 69:4
Lu 23:22

g Lu 24:49
Joh 14:26

h 1Jo 5:6

i Lu 24:48
Ac 1:8
Ac 2:22
Ac 5:32

CHAP. 16

j Joh 9:22

k Mt 24:9
Ac 8:1
Ac 12:1, 2
Ac 26:11

l Joh 8:19
Joh 15:20, 21
Ro 10:2
1Co 2:8

m Joh 13:19
Joh 14:29

n Joh 7:33
Joh 13:3

o Joh 16:22

p Joh 14:16, 26
Joh 15:26
Ac 2:32, 33

Second Col.

a Joh 15:22

b Joh 5:37, 38

c Joh 12:31
Joh 14:30

d Joh 16:7

e Ac 11:28
Ac 21:10, 11
1Ti 4:1

f 1Jo 4:2

g Joh 15:26
1Jo 2:27

h Joh 17:10

i Joh 7:33
Joh 14:19

one comes, he will give the world convincing evidence concerning sin and concerning righteousness and concerning judgment: **9** first concerning sin,[a] because they are not exercising faith in me;[b] **10** then concerning righteousness, because I am going to the Father and you will see me no longer; **11** then concerning judgment, because the ruler of this world has been judged.[c]

12 "I still have many things to say to you, but you are not able to bear them now. **13** However, when that one* comes, the spirit of the truth,[d] he will guide you into all the truth, for he will not speak of his own initiative, but what he hears he will speak, and he will declare to you the things to come.[e] **14** That one will glorify me,[f] because he will receive from what is mine and will declare it to you.[g] **15** All the things that the Father has are mine.[h] That is why I said he receives from what is mine and declares it to you. **16** In a little while you will see me no longer,[i] and again, in a little while you will see me."

17 At that some of his disciples said to one another: "What does he mean by saying to us, 'In a little while you will not see me, and again, in a little while you will see me,' and, 'because I am going to the Father'?" **18** So they were saying: "What does he mean by saying, 'a little while'? We do not know what he is talking about." **19** Jesus knew they wanted to question him, so he said to them: "Are you asking one another this because I said: 'In a little while you will not see

---

16:13 *Both "that one" and "he" in vss. 13 and 14 refer back to "the helper" in vs. 7. Jesus used "the helper" (which has the masculine gender in Greek) as a personification of the holy spirit, an impersonal force, which has the neuter gender in Greek.

me, and again, in a little while you will see me?' **20** Most truly I say to you, you will weep and wail, but the world will rejoice; you will be grieved, but your grief will be turned into joy.[a] **21** When a woman is giving birth, she has grief because her hour has come, but when she has given birth to the child, she remembers the tribulation no more because of the joy that a man has been born into the world. **22** So you also, now you have grief; but I will see you again, and your hearts will rejoice,[b] and no one will take away your joy. **23** In that day you will ask me no question at all. Most truly I say to you, if you ask the Father for anything,[c] he will give it to you in my name.[d] **24** Until now you have not asked for a single thing in my name. Ask and you will receive, so that your joy may be complete.

25 "I have spoken these things to you in comparisons. The hour is coming when I will no longer speak to you in comparisons, but I will tell you plainly about the Father. **26** In that day you will make request of the Father in my name; in saying this, I do not mean that I will make request for you. **27** For the Father himself has affection for you, because you have had affection for me[e] and have believed that I came as God's representative.[f] **28** I came as the Father's representative and have come into the world. Now I am leaving the world and am going to the Father."[g]

29 His disciples said: "See! Now you are speaking plainly and are not using comparisons. **30** Now we know that you know all things and you do not need to have anyone question you. By this we believe that you came from God." **31** Jesus answered them: "Do you believe now? **32** Look! The hour is coming, indeed, it has come, when each one of you will be scattered to his own house and you will leave me alone.[a] But I am not alone, because the Father is with me.[b] **33** I have said these things to you so that by means of me you may have peace.[c] In the world you will have tribulation, but take courage! I have conquered the world."[d]

17 Jesus spoke these things, and raising his eyes to heaven, he said: "Father, the hour has come. Glorify your son so that your son may glorify you,[e] **2** just as you have given him authority over all flesh,*[f] so that he may give everlasting life[g] to all those whom you have given to him.[h] **3** This means everlasting life,[i] their coming to know you,* the only true God,[j] and the one whom you sent, Jesus Christ.[k] **4** I have glorified you on the earth,[l] having finished the work you have given me to do.[m] **5** So now, Father, glorify me at your side with the glory that I had alongside you before the world was.[n]

6 "I have made your name manifest* to the men whom you gave me out of the world.[o] They were yours, and you gave them to me, and they have observed# your word. **7** Now they have come to know that all the things you gave me are from you; **8** because I have given them the sayings that you gave me,[p] and they have accepted them and have certainly come to know that I came as your representative,[q] and they have believed that you sent me.[r] **9** I make request concerning them; I make request, not concerning the world, but concerning those whom you

---

17:2 *Or "mankind; people." 17:3 *Or "their taking in knowledge of you." 17:6 *Or "known." #Or "obeyed."

CHAP. 16

a Mt 28:8; Lu 24:39-41; Joh 20:19, 20
b Lu 24:51, 52
c Php 4:6
d Joh 14:13; Joh 15:16; 1Jo 5:14
e Joh 14:21
f Joh 17:7, 8
g Joh 13:3; Heb 9:24

Second Col.

a Zec 13:7; Mt 26:31; Mr 14:27
b Joh 8:29
c Joh 14:27; Eph 2:14
d Joh 14:30; Ac 14:22; 1Jo 4:4; 1Jo 5:4; Re 3:21

CHAP. 17

e Joh 12:23; Joh 13:31, 32
f Php 2:9, 10
g Joh 4:14; Joh 6:27
h Joh 6:37
i Lu 10:25-28
j 1Jo 5:20
k Eph 4:11, 13; 2Pe 3:18
l Joh 13:31
m Joh 4:34
n Joh 1:1; Joh 8:58; Col 1:15
o Ps 22:22; Ac 15:14; Heb 2:12
p Joh 6:68; Joh 8:28; Joh 12:49; Joh 14:10
q Joh 16:27
r Joh 16:30

have given me, because they are
yours; **10** and all my things are
yours and yours are mine,[a] and I
have been glorified among them.
11 "I am no longer in the
world, but they are in the world,[b]
and I am coming to you. Holy
Father, watch over them[c] on account of your own name, which
you have given me, so that they
may be one* just as we are one.*[d]
12 When I was with them, I used
to watch over them[e] on account
of your own name, which you
have given me; and I have protected them, and not one of them
is destroyed[f] except the son of
destruction,[g] so that the scripture might be fulfilled.[h] **13** But
now I am coming to you, and I am
saying these things in the world,
so that they may have my joy
made complete in themselves.[i]
14 I have given your word to
them, but the world has hated
them, because they are no part
of the world,[j] just as I am no part
of the world.
15 "I do not request that
you take them out of the world,
but that you watch over them
because of the wicked one.[k]
16 They are no part of the
world,[l] just as I am no part of the
world.[m] **17** Sanctify them* by
means of the truth;[n] your word is
truth.[o] **18** Just as you sent me
into the world, I also sent them
into the world.[p] **19** And I am
sanctifying myself in their behalf, so that they also may be
sanctified by means of truth.
20 "I make request, not concerning these only, but also concerning those putting faith in me
through their word, **21** so that
they may all be one,[q] just as
you, Father, are in union with
me and I am in union with
you,[r] that they also may be in
union with us, so that the world
may believe that you sent me.
22 I have given them the glory
that you have given me, in order that they may be one just as
we are one.[a] **23** I in union with
them and you in union with me,
in order that they may be perfected into one,* so that the
world may know that you sent
me and that you loved them just
as you loved me. **24** Father, I
want those whom you have giv-
en me to be with me where I
am,[b] in order that they may look
upon my glory that you have giv-
en me, because you loved me before the founding of the world.[c]
25 Righteous Father, the world
has, indeed, not come to know
you,[d] but I know you,[e] and these
have come to know that you sent
me. **26** I have made your name
known to them and will make
it known,[f] so that the love with
which you loved me may be in
them and I in union with them."[g]

18

After he said these things,
Jesus went out with his
disciples across the Kid′ron Valley*[h] to where there was a garden, and he and his disciples
went into it.[i] **2** Now Judas, his
betrayer, also knew the place,
because Jesus had often met
there with his disciples. **3** So
Judas brought the detachment of
soldiers and officers of the
chief priests and of the Pharisees and came there with torches and lamps and weapons.[j]
4 Then Jesus, knowing all the
things that were going to happen
to him, stepped forward and said
to them: "Whom are you looking for?" **5** They answered him:
"Jesus the Naz·a·rene′."[k] He said
to them: "I am he." Now Judas,
his betrayer, was also standing
with them.[l]
6 However, when Jesus said
to them, "I am he," they drew

17:11 *Or "at unity." **17:17** *Or "Set them apart; Make them holy."
17:23 *Or "be completely unified."
18:1 *Or "the winter torrent of Kidron."

CHAP. 17
a Joh 16:15
b Joh 13:1
c 1Pe 1:5, Jude 24
d Joh 10:30, Joh 17:21
e Joh 6:39, Joh 10:28
f Joh 18:9
g Mr 14:21
h Ps 41:9, Ps 109:8, Ac 1:20
i Joh 15:11
j Joh 15:19, Jas 4:4
k Mt 6:13, 2Th 3:3, 1Jo 5:18
l Col 1:13
m Joh 18:36
n Eph 5:25, 26, 1Th 5:23, 2Th 2:13, 1Pe 1:22
o Ps 12:6, Ps 119:151, 160
p Joh 20:21
q Ro 12:5, 1Co 1:10, Ga 3:28
r Joh 10:38, Joh 14:10

Second Col.
a Joh 14:20, Joh 17:11, 1Jo 3:24
b Lu 22:28-30, 1Th 4:17
c Joh 17:5
d Joh 8:55, Joh 15:21
e Mt 11:27
f Mt 6:9, Joh 17:6
g Joh 15:9

CHAP. 18
h 2Sa 15:23
i Mt 26:36, Mr 14:32, Lu 22:39
j Mt 26:47, Mr 14:43
k Mt 2:23
l Lu 22:47

back and fell to the ground.[a]
7 So he asked them again:
"Whom are you looking for?"
They said: "Jesus the Naz·a·
rene'." **8** Jesus answered: "I
told you that I am he. So if you
are looking for me, let these men
go." **9** This was to fulfill what
he had said: "Of those whom you
have given me, I have not lost a
single one."[b]

10 Then Simon Peter, who
had a sword, drew it and struck
the slave of the high priest, cutting off his right ear.[c] The
name of the slave was Malchus.
11 Jesus, however, said to Peter: "Put the sword into its
sheath.[d] Should I not drink the
cup that the Father has given
me?"[e]

12 Then the soldiers and the
military commander and the officers of the Jews seized* Jesus
and bound him. **13** They led
him first to An'nas, for he was
the father-in-law of Ca'ia·phas,[f]
who was high priest that year.[g]
14 Ca'ia·phas was, in fact, the
one who had advised the Jews
that it was to their benefit for
one man to die in behalf of the
people.[h]

15 Now Simon Peter, as well
as another disciple, was following Jesus.[i] That disciple was
known to the high priest, and he
went with Jesus into the courtyard of the high priest, **16** but
Peter was standing outside at
the door.* So the other disciple, who was known to the high
priest, went out and spoke to
the doorkeeper and brought Peter in. **17** The servant girl who
was the doorkeeper then said
to Peter: "You are not also
one of this man's disciples, are
you?" He said: "I am not."[j]
18 Now the slaves and the officers were standing around a

charcoal fire they had made, because it was cold and they were
warming themselves. Peter also
was standing with them and
warming himself.

19 So the chief priest questioned Jesus about his disciples
and about his teaching. **20** Jesus answered him: "I have spoken to the world publicly. I always taught in a synagogue and
in the temple,[a] where all the Jews
come together, and I said nothing
in secret. **21** Why do you question me? Question those who
have heard what I told them. See!
These know what I said." **22** After he said these things, one of
the officers who was standing by
gave Jesus a slap in the face[b] and
said: "Is that the way you answer
the chief priest?" **23** Jesus answered him: "If I said something wrong, bear witness* about
the wrong; but if what I said
was right, why do you hit me?"
24 Then An'nas sent him away
bound to Ca'ia·phas the high
priest.[c]

25 Now Simon Peter was
standing there warming himself.
Then they said to him: "You are
not also one of his disciples, are
you?" He denied it and said: "I
am not."[d] **26** One of the slaves
of the high priest, who was a relative of the man whose ear Peter had cut off,[e] said: "I saw
you in the garden with him,
did I not?" **27** However, Peter
denied it again, and immediately
a rooster crowed.[f]

28 Then they led Jesus from
Ca'ia·phas to the governor's residence.[g] It was now early in the
morning. But they themselves
did not enter into the governor's
residence, so that they would
not get defiled[h] but could eat the
Passover. **29** So Pilate came
outside to them and said: "What

CHAP. 18	
a	Joh 7:46
b	Joh 6:39 Joh 17:12
c	Mt 26:51 Mr 14:47 Lu 22:50
d	Mt 26:52 Lu 22:51 Joh 18:36
e	Mt 20:22 Mt 26:42
f	Lu 3:2 Ac 4:5, 6
g	Mt 26:57 Joh 18:24
h	Joh 11:49, 50
i	Mt 26:58 Mr 14:54 Lu 22:54
j	Mt 26:69, 70 Mr 14:66-68 Lu 22:55-57 Joh 18:25

Second Col.	
a	Mt 26:55 Lu 4:15 Lu 19:47 Joh 7:14
b	Isa 50:6
c	Mt 26:57
d	Mt 26:69, 70 Mr 14:69, 70 Lu 22:58
e	Joh 18:10
f	Mt 26:74 Mr 14:72 Lu 22:60 Joh 13:38
g	Mt 27:2 Mr 15:1 Lu 23:1
h	Ac 10:28

18:12 *Or "arrested." 18:16 *Or "entrance."

18:23 *Or "testify."

accusation do you bring against this man?" **30** They answered him: "If this man were not a wrongdoer,* we would not have handed him over to you." **31** So Pilate said to them: "Take him yourselves and judge him according to your law."[a] The Jews said to him: "It is not lawful for us to kill anyone."[b] **32** This was to fulfill the word that Jesus had spoken to indicate what sort of death he was about to die.[c]

33 So Pilate entered the governor's residence again and called Jesus and said to him: "Are you the King of the Jews?"[d] **34** Jesus answered: "Are you asking this of your own originality, or did others tell you about me?" **35** Pilate replied: "I am not a Jew, am I? Your own nation and the chief priests handed you over to me. What did you do?" **36** Jesus answered:[e] "My Kingdom is no part of this world.[f] If my Kingdom were part of this world, my attendants would have fought that I should not be handed over to the Jews.[g] But as it is, my Kingdom is not from this source." **37** So Pilate said to him: "Well, then, are you a king?" Jesus answered: "You yourself are saying that I am a king.[h] For this I have been born, and for this I have come into the world, that I should bear witness to the truth.[i] Everyone who is on the side of the truth listens to my voice." **38** Pilate said to him: "What is truth?"

After saying this, he went out again to the Jews and said to them: "I find no fault in him.[j] **39** Moreover, you have a custom that I should release a man to you at the Passover.[k] So do you want me to release to you the King of the Jews?" **40** Again they shouted: "Not this man, but Bar·ab′bas!" Now Bar·ab′bas was a robber.[l]

19 Pilate then took Jesus and scourged him.[a] **2** And the soldiers braided a crown of thorns and put it on his head and clothed him with a purple robe,[b] **3** and they kept coming up to him and saying: "Greetings,* you King of the Jews!" They also kept slapping him in the face.[c] **4** Pilate went outside again and said to them: "See! I bring him outside to you in order for you to know that I find no fault in him."[d] **5** So Jesus came outside, wearing the crown of thorns and the purple robe. And Pilate said to them: "Look! The man!" **6** However, when the chief priests and the officers saw him, they shouted: "To the stake with him! To the stake with him!"*[e] Pilate said to them: "Take him yourselves and execute him,* for I do not find any fault in him."[f] **7** The Jews answered him: "We have a law, and according to the law he ought to die,[g] because he made himself God's son."[h]

8 When Pilate heard what they were saying, he became even more fearful, **9** and he entered the governor's residence again and said to Jesus: "Where are you from?" But Jesus gave him no answer. **10** So Pilate said to him: "Are you refusing to speak to me? Do you not know that I have authority to release you and I have authority to execute you?"* **11** Jesus answered him: "You would have no authority over me at all unless it had been granted to you from above. This is why the man who handed me over to you has greater sin."

12 For this reason Pilate kept trying to find a way to release him, but the Jews shouted: "If

CHAP. 18
a Joh 19:6
b Joh 19:10
c Mt 20:18, 19
  Joh 3:14
  Joh 12:32
d Mt 27:11
  Joh 12:13
e 1Ti 6:13
f Isa 9:6
  Da 2:44
  Da 7:14
g Mt 26:52, 53
  Joh 18:11
h Mt 27:11
i Joh 1:14, 17
  Joh 14:6
j Mt 27:24
  Lu 23:4
  Joh 15:25
k Mt 27:15
  Mr 15:6
l Nu 35:31
  Lu 23:18, 19
  Ac 3:14

Second Col.

CHAP. 19
a Isa 50:6
  Mt 20:18, 19
  Mt 27:26
  Mr 15:15
b Mt 27:27-29
  Mr 15:16, 17
  Lu 23:11
c Isa 53:3
d Lu 23:4
  Joh 18:38
e Mt 27:22
  Mr 15:13
  Lu 23:21
f Joh 18:31
g Le 24:16
h Mt 26:63-65
  Joh 5:18
i Isa 53:7
  Mt 27:12, 14

19:3 *Or "Hail." **19:6** *Or "Execute him on the stake! Execute him on the stake!" *Or "execute him on the stake." **19:10** *Or "execute you on the stake?"

you release this man, you are not a friend of Caesar. Everyone who makes himself a king speaks against* Caesar."[a] **13** Then Pilate, after hearing these words, brought Jesus outside, and he sat down on a judgment seat in a place called the Stone Pavement, but in Hebrew, *Gab'ba·tha.* **14** Now it was the day of Preparation[b] of the Passover; it was about the sixth hour.* And he said to the Jews: "See! Your king!" **15** However, they shouted: "Take him away! Take him away! To the stake with him!"* Pilate said to them: "Shall I execute your king?" The chief priests answered: "We have no king but Caesar." **16** Then he handed him over to them to be executed on the stake.[c]

So they took charge of Jesus. **17** Bearing the torture stake* for himself, he went out to the so-called Skull Place,[d] which is called *Gol'go·tha* in Hebrew.[e] **18** There they nailed him to the stake[f] alongside two other men, one on each side, with Jesus in the middle.[g] **19** Pilate also wrote a title and put it on the torture stake.* It was written: "Jesus the Naz·a·rene' the King of the Jews."[h] **20** Many of the Jews read this title, because the place where Jesus was nailed to the stake was near the city, and it was written in Hebrew, in Latin, and in Greek. **21** However, the chief priests of the Jews said to Pilate: "Do not write, 'The King of the Jews,' but that he said, 'I am King of the Jews.'" **22** Pilate answered: "What I have written, I have written."

23 Now when the soldiers had nailed Jesus to the stake, they

took his outer garments and divided them into four parts, one for each soldier, and they also took the inner garment. But the inner garment was without a seam, being woven from top to bottom. **24** So they said to one another: "Let us not tear it, but let us cast lots over it to decide whose it will be."[a] This was to fulfill the scripture: "They divided my garments among themselves, and they cast lots for my clothing."[b] So the soldiers actually did these things.

25 By the torture stake* of Jesus, however, there were standing his mother[c] and his mother's sister; Mary the wife of Clo'pas and Mary Mag'da·lene.[d] **26** So when Jesus saw his mother and the disciple whom he loved[e] standing nearby, he said to his mother: "Woman, see! Your son!" **27** Next he said to the disciple: "See! Your mother!" And from that hour on, the disciple took her into his own home.

28 After this, when Jesus knew that by now all things had been accomplished, in order to fulfill the scripture he said: "I am thirsty."[f] **29** A jar was sitting there full of sour wine. So they put a sponge full of the sour wine on a hyssop* stalk and held it up to his mouth.[g] **30** When he had received the sour wine, Jesus said: "It has been accomplished!"[h] and bowing his head, he gave up his spirit.*[i]

31 Since it was the day of Preparation,[j] so that the bodies would not remain on the torture stakes[k] on the Sabbath (for that Sabbath day was a great one),[l] the Jews asked Pilate to have the legs broken and the bodies taken away. **32** So the soldiers came and broke the legs of the first man and those of the other man who was on a stake alongside

---

CHAP. 19

a Lu 23:2
Ac 17:6, 7

b Joh 19:31

c Da 9:26
Mt 27:26, 31
Mr 15:15
Lu 23:24, 25

d Heb 13:12

e Mt 27:32, 33
Mr 15:22

f Joh 3:14
Ac 5:30
Ga 3:13

g Isa 53:9
Lu 23:33

h Mt 27:37
Mr 15:26
Lu 23:38

Second Col.

a Mt 27:35
Mr 15:24
Lu 23:34

b Ps 22:18

c Lu 2:34, 35

d Mt 27:55, 56
Mt 27:61
Mr 15:40
Lu 23:49

e Joh 13:23
Joh 21:7, 20

f Ps 22:15

g Ps 69:21
Mt 27:48
Mr 15:36
Lu 23:36

h Joh 17:4

i Isa 53:12
Mt 27:50
Mr 15:37
Lu 23:46

j Joh 19:14

k De 21:22, 23

l Le 23:5-7

19:12 *Or "opposes." **19:14** *That is, about 12:00 noon. **19:15** *Or "Execute him on the stake!" **19:17, 19, 25, 29** *See Glossary.

19:30 *Or "he expired."

him. **33** But on coming to Jesus, they saw that he was already dead, so they did not break his legs. **34** But one of the soldiers jabbed his side with a spear,[a] and immediately blood and water came out. **35** And the one who has seen it has given this witness, and his witness is true, and he knows that what he says is true, so that you also may believe.[b] **36** In fact, these things took place for the scripture to be fulfilled: "Not a bone of his will be broken."[c] **37** And again, a different scripture says: "They will look to the one whom they pierced."[d]

38 Now after these things, Joseph of Ar·i·ma·the′a, who was a disciple of Jesus but a secret one because of his fear of the Jews,[e] asked Pilate if he could take away the body of Jesus, and Pilate gave him permission. So he came and took the body away.[f] **39** Nic·o·de′mus,[g] the man who had come to him in the night the first time, also came, bringing a mixture* of myrrh and aloes weighing about a hundred pounds.*[h] **40** So they took the body of Jesus and wrapped it in linen cloths with the spices,[i] according to the burial custom of the Jews. **41** Incidentally, there was a garden at the place where he was executed,* and in the garden was a new tomb*[j] in which no one had ever yet been laid. **42** Because it was the day of Preparation[k] of the Jews and the tomb was nearby, they laid Jesus there.

20 On the first day of the week, Mary Mag′da·lene came to the tomb* early,[l] while it was still dark, and she saw that

---

19:36 *Or "crushed." 19:39 *Or possibly, "a roll." # That is, Roman pounds. See App. B14. 19:41 *Or "executed on the stake." 19:41; 20:1 *Or "memorial tomb."

CHAP. 19
a Isa 53:5
  Zec 12:10
  Joh 20:25

b Joh 20:31
  Joh 21:24

c Ex 12:46
  Nu 9:12
  Ps 34:20

d Zec 12:10
  Re 1:7

e Joh 7:13
  Joh 9:22

f De 21:22, 23
  Mt 27:57-60
  Mr 15:43-46

g Joh 3:1, 2
  Joh 7:50-52

h Lu 23:55, 56

i Joh 20:7

j Isa 53:9

k Joh 19:14

CHAP. 20
l Mt 28:1
  Mr 16:1, 2

Second Col.
a Lu 24:1-3

b Joh 13:23
  Joh 19:26
  Joh 21:24

c Joh 19:41, 42

d Joh 19:40

e Ps 16:10
  Mt 16:21
  Ac 2:27

f Mr 16:5

g Lu 24:15, 16
  Lu 24:30, 31
  Joh 21:4

the stone had already been taken away from the tomb.*[a] **2** So she came running to Simon Peter and to the other disciple, for whom Jesus had affection,[b] and she said to them: "They have taken away the Lord out of the tomb,[c] and we do not know where they have laid him."

3 Then Peter and the other disciple set out for the tomb. **4** The two of them began running together, but the other disciple ran faster than Peter and reached the tomb first. **5** Stooping forward, he saw the linen cloths lying there,[d] but he did not go in. **6** Then Simon Peter also came, following him, and he went into the tomb. And he saw the linen cloths lying there. **7** The cloth that had been on his head was not lying with the other cloth bands but was rolled up in a place by itself. **8** Then the other disciple who had reached the tomb first also went in, and he saw and believed. **9** For they did not yet understand the scripture that he must rise from the dead.[e] **10** So the disciples went back to their homes.

11 Mary, however, kept standing outside near the tomb, weeping. While she was weeping, she stooped forward to look into the tomb, **12** and she saw two angels[f] in white sitting where the body of Jesus had been lying, one at the head and one at the feet. **13** And they said to her: "Woman, why are you weeping?" She said to them: "They have taken my Lord away, and I do not know where they have laid him." **14** After saying this, she turned around and saw Jesus standing there, but she did not realize that it was Jesus.[g] **15** Jesus said to her: "Woman, why are you weeping? Whom are you looking for?" She, thinking it was the gardener, said to him: "Sir, if you have carried him off, tell me where you have laid him, and I will take him away." **16** Jesus said to her: "Mary!" On turning around, she said to him in Hebrew: *"Rab·bo'ni!"* (which means "Teacher!") **17** Jesus said to her: "Stop clinging to me, for I have not yet ascended to the Father. But go to my brothers[a] and say to them, 'I am ascending to my Father[b] and your Father and to my God[c] and your God.'" **18** Mary Mag'da·lene came and brought the news to the disciples: "I have seen the Lord!" And she told them what he had said to her.[d]

19 When it was late that day, the first day of the week, and the doors were locked where the disciples were for fear of the Jews, Jesus came and stood in their midst and said to them: "May you have peace."[e] **20** After saying this, he showed them his hands and his side.[f] Then the disciples rejoiced at seeing the Lord.[g] **21** Jesus said to them again: "May you have peace."[h] Just as the Father has sent me,[i] I also am sending you."[j] **22** After saying this he blew on them and said to them: "Receive holy spirit.[k] **23** If you forgive the sins of anyone, they are forgiven; if you retain those of anyone, they are retained."

24 But Thomas,[l] one of the Twelve, who was called the Twin, was not with them when Jesus came. **25** So the other disciples were telling him: "We have seen the Lord!" But he said to them: "Unless I see in his hands the print* of the nails and stick my finger into the print of the nails and stick my hand into his side,[m] I will never believe it."

26 Well, eight days later his disciples were again indoors, and Thomas was with them. Jesus came, although the doors were locked, and he stood in their midst and said: "May you have peace."[a] **27** Next he said to Thomas: "Put your finger here, and see my hands, and take your hand and stick it into my side, and stop doubting* but believe." **28** In answer Thomas said to him: "My Lord and my God!" **29** Jesus said to him: "Because you have seen me, have you believed? Happy are those who have not seen and yet believe."

30 To be sure, Jesus also performed many other signs before the disciples, which are not written down in this scroll.[b] **31** But these have been written down so that you may believe that Jesus is the Christ, the Son of God, and because of believing, you may have life by means of his name.[c]

21 After this Jesus manifested himself* again to the disciples, at the Sea of Ti·be'ri·as. He made the manifestation in this way. **2** There were together Simon Peter, Thomas (who was called the Twin,[d] Na·than'a·el[e] from Ca'na of Gal'i·lee, the sons of Zeb'e·dee,[f] and two others of his disciples. **3** Simon Peter said to them: "I am going fishing." They said to him: "We are coming with you." They went out and got aboard the boat, but during that night they caught nothing.[g]

4 However, just as day was breaking, Jesus stood on the beach, but the disciples did not realize that it was Jesus.[h] **5** Then Jesus said to them: "Children, you do not have anything* to eat, do you?" They answered: "No!" **6** He said to them: "Cast the net on the right side of the boat and you will find some." So they cast it, but

---

CHAP. 20
a Mt 28:10

b Joh 14:28
  Joh 16:28

c 1Co 11:3
  Eph 1:17
  Col 1:3

d Lu 24:9, 10

e Lu 24:36

f Joh 19:34

g Joh 16:22

h Lu 24:36

i Isa 61:1
  Joh 5:36

j Mt 28:19, 20
  Joh 17:18

k Ac 2:2, 4

l Joh 11:16

m Joh 19:34

Second Col.
a Joh 20:19

b Joh 21:25

c Joh 3:15
  Joh 5:24
  1Pe 1:8, 9
  1Jo 5:13

CHAP. 21
d Joh 11:16
  Joh 20:24

e Joh 1:45

f Mt 4:21

g Lu 5:4, 5

h Lu 24:15, 16
  Joh 20:11, 14

20:25 *Or "mark." 20:27 *Lit., "being unbelieving." 21:1 *Or "appeared." 21:5 *Or "any fish."

they were not able to haul it in because of the large number of fish.[a] 7 Then the disciple whom Jesus loved[b] said to Peter: "It is the Lord!" Now Simon Peter, on hearing that it was the Lord, put on* his outer garment, for he was naked,[#] and plunged into the sea. 8 But the other disciples came in the small boat, dragging the net full of fish, for they were not a long way from land, only about 300 feet* away.

9 When they came ashore, they saw there a charcoal fire with fish lying on it and bread. 10 Jesus said to them: "Bring some of the fish you just now caught." 11 So Simon Peter went on board and hauled the net ashore full of big fish, 153 of them. And though there were so many, the net did not burst. 12 Jesus said to them: "Come, have your breakfast." Not one of the disciples had the courage to ask him: "Who are you?" because they knew it was the Lord. 13 Jesus came and took the bread and gave it to them, and the same with the fish. 14 This was now the third time[c] that Jesus appeared to the disciples after being raised up from the dead.

15 When they had finished breakfast, Jesus said to Simon Peter: "Simon son of John, do you love me more than these?" He replied to him: "Yes, Lord, you know I have affection for you." He said to him: "Feed my lambs."[d] 16 Again he said to him a second time: "Simon son of John, do you love me?" He replied: "Yes, Lord, you know I have affection for you." He said to him: "Shepherd my little sheep."[e] 17 He said to him a third time: "Simon son of

John, do you have affection for me?" Peter became grieved that he asked him the third time: "Do you have affection for me?" So he said to him: "Lord, you are aware of all things; you know that I have affection for you." Jesus said to him: "Feed my little sheep.[a] 18 Most truly I say to you, when you were younger, you used to clothe yourself and walk about where you wanted. But when you grow old, you will stretch out your hands and another man will clothe you and carry you where you do not wish." 19 He said this to indicate by what sort of death he would glorify God. After he said this, he said to him: "Continue following me."[b]

20 Peter turned around and saw the disciple whom Jesus loved[c] following, the one who at the evening meal had also leaned back on his chest and said: "Lord, who is the one betraying you?" 21 So when he caught sight of him, Peter said to Jesus: "Lord, what about this man?" 22 Jesus said to him: "If it is my will for him to remain until I come, of what concern is that to you? You continue following me." 23 So the saying went out among the brothers that this disciple would not die. However, Jesus did not say to him that he would not die, but he said: "If it is my will for him to remain until I come, of what concern is that to you?"

24 This is the disciple[d] who gives this witness about these things and who wrote these things, and we know that his witness is true.

25 There are also, in fact, many other things that Jesus did, which if ever they were written in full detail, I suppose the world itself could not contain the scrolls written.[e]

CHAP. 21
a Lu 5:4, 6

b Joh 13:23
Joh 19:26
Joh 20:2

c Joh 20:19, 26

d Lu 22:32
Ac 20:28
1Pe 5:2, 3

e Ac 1:15
Heb 13:20
1Pe 2:25

Second Col.
a Joh 10:14, 15

b Mt 19:28
Joh 12:26
Re 14:4

c Joh 13:23
Joh 20:2

d Joh 13:23
Joh 19:26
Joh 20:2
Joh 21:7

e Joh 20:30, 31

21:7 *Or "girded about himself." #Or "lightly clad." 21:8 *About 90 m. Lit., "about 200 cubits." See App. B14.

ACTS OF APOSTLES

---

1 The first account, O The·oph'i·lus, I composed about all the things Jesus started to do and to teach[a] **2** until the day that he was taken up,[b] after he had given instructions through holy spirit to the apostles he had chosen.[c] **3** After he had suffered, he showed himself alive to them by many convincing proofs.[d] He was seen by them throughout 40 days, and he was speaking about the Kingdom of God.[e] **4** While he was meet-ing with them, he ordered them: "Do not leave Jerusalem,[a] but keep waiting for what the Father has promised,[b] about which you heard from me; **5** for John, in-deed, baptized with water, but you will be baptized with holy spirit[c] not many days after this."

6 So when they had assem-bled, they asked him: "Lord, are you restoring the kingdom to Is-rael at this time?"[d] **7** He said to them: "It does not belong to you to know the times or sea-sons that the Father has placed

CHAP. 1
a Lu 1:3
  Lu 3:23
b 1Ti 3:16
c Joh 15:16
d Mt 28:9
  Joh 20:19
  1Co 15:4-7
e Lu 24:27

Second Col.
a Lu 24:49
b Joh 14:16, 17
  Ac 2:33
c Joe 2:28
  Mt 3:11
  Mr 1:8
d Lu 19:11
  Lu 24:21

in his own jurisdiction.*[a] **8** But you will receive power when the holy spirit comes upon you,[b] and you will be witnesses[c] of me in Jerusalem,[d] in all Ju·deʹa and Sa·marʹi·a,[e] and to the most distant part* of the earth."[f] **9** After he had said these things, while they were looking on, he was lifted up and a cloud caught him up from their sight.[g] **10** And as they were gazing into the sky while he was on his way, suddenly two men in white garments[h] stood beside them **11** and said: "Men of Galʹi·lee, why do you stand looking into the sky? This Jesus who was taken up from you into the sky will come in the same manner as you have seen him going into the sky."

12 Then they returned to Jerusalem[i] from a mountain called the Mount of Olives, which is near Jerusalem, only a sabbath day's journey away. **13** When they arrived, they went up into the upper room where they were staying. There were Peter as well as John and James and Andrew, Philip and Thomas, Bar·tholʹo·mew and Matthew, James the son of Al·phaeʹus, and Simon the zealous one, and Judas the son of James.[j] **14** With one purpose all of these were persisting in prayer, together with some women[k] and Mary the mother of Jesus and with his brothers.[l]

15 During those days Peter stood up in the midst of the brothers (the number* of people was altogether about 120) and said: **16** "Men, brothers, it was necessary for the scripture to be fulfilled that the holy spirit spoke prophetically through David about Judas,[m] who became a guide to those who arrested Jesus.[n] **17** For he had been numbered among us[o] and he

obtained a share in this ministry. **18** (This very man, therefore, purchased a field with the wages for unrighteousness,[a] and falling headfirst, his body burst open* and all his insides spilled out.[b] **19** This became known to all the inhabitants of Jerusalem, so that the field was called in their language A·kelʹda·ma, that is, "Field of Blood.") **20** For it is written in the book of Psalms, 'Let his dwelling become desolate, and let there be no inhabitant in it'[c] and, 'His office of oversight let someone else take.'[d] **21** It is therefore necessary that of the men who accompanied us during all the time in which the Lord Jesus carried on his activities* among us, **22** starting with his baptism by John[e] until the day he was taken up from us,[f] one of these men should become a witness with us of his resurrection."[g]

23 So they proposed two, Joseph called Barʹsab·bas, who was also called Justus, and Mat·thiʹas. **24** Then they prayed and said: "You, O Jehovah,* who know the hearts of all,[h] designate which one of these two men you have chosen **25** to take the place of this ministry and apostleship, from which Judas deviated to go to his own place."[i] **26** So they cast lots over them,[j] and the lot fell to Mat·thiʹas, and he was counted* along with the 11 apostles.

2 Now while the day of the Festival of Pentecost[k] was in progress, they were all together at the same place. **2** Suddenly there was a noise from heaven, just like that of a rushing, stiff breeze, and it filled the whole house where they were sitting.[l]

CHAP. 1

a Da 2:20, 21
  Mt 24:36

b Ac 4:33

c Isa 43:10
  Lu 24:48
  Joh 15:26, 27

d Ac 5:27, 28

e Ac 8:14

f Col 1:23

g Lu 24:51
  Joh 6:62

h Mt 28:2, 3

i Lu 24:52

j Mt 10:2-4
  Mr 3:16-19

k Lu 23:49

l Mt 13:55
  Joh 7:5
  Ga 1:19

m Ps 41:9
  Ps 55:12
  Joh 13:18

n Lu 22:47
  Joh 18:3

o Mt 10:2, 4
  Lu 6:12-16
  Joh 6:70, 71

Second Col.

a Zec 11:12
  Mt 26:14, 15

b Mt 27:5-8

c Ps 69:25

d Ps 109:8

e Mt 3:13

f Lu 24:51
  Ac 1:9

g Mt 28:5, 6
  Mr 16:6

h 1Sa 16:7
  1Ch 28:9
  Jer 11:20

i Joh 6:70

j Pr 16:33

CHAP. 2

k Le 23:16
  De 16:9-11

l Ac 4:31

1:7 *Or "authority." **1:8** *Or "to the ends." **1:15** *Or "crowd."

1:18 *Or "he burst open in the middle." **1:21** *Lit., "went in and out." **1:24** *See App. A5. **1:26** *Or "reckoned," that is, viewed the same as the other 11.

3 And tongues as if of fire became visible to them and were distributed, and one came to rest on each one of them, **4** and they all became filled with holy spirit[a] and started to speak in different languages,* just as the spirit enabled them to speak.[b]

5 At that time devout Jews from every nation under heaven were staying in Jerusalem.[c] **6** So when this sound occurred, a crowd gathered and was bewildered, because each one heard them speaking in his own language. **7** Indeed, they were utterly amazed and said: "See here, all these who are speaking are Gal·i·le′ans,[d] are they not? **8** How is it, then, that each one of us is hearing his own native language?* **9** Par′thi·ans, Medes,[e] and E′lam·ites;[f] the inhabitants of Mes·o·po·ta′mi·a, Ju·de′a and Cap·pa·do′ci·a, Pon′tus and the province of Asia,[g] **10** Phryg′i·a and Pam·phyl′i·a, Egypt and the regions of Lib′y·a near Cy·re′ne; sojourners from Rome, both Jews and proselytes;[h] **11** Cre′tans; and Arabians—we hear them speaking in our languages about the magnificent things of God." **12** Yes, they were all astonished and perplexed, saying to one another: "What does this mean?" **13** However, others mocked them and said: "They are full of sweet wine."*

14 But Peter stood up with the Eleven[i] and spoke to them in a loud voice: "Men of Ju·de′a and all you inhabitants of Jerusalem, let this be known to you and listen carefully to my words. **15** These people are, in fact, not drunk, as you suppose, for it is the third hour of the day.* **16** On the contrary,

CHAP. 2
a Mr 1:8
  Joh 14:26

b Ac 10:45, 46
  1Co 12:8, 10

c Ex 23:17

d Mr 14:70
  Ac 1:11

e 2Ki 17:6

f Da 8:1, 2

g 1Pe 1:1

h Ex 12:48

i Ac 1:13

Second Col.
a Joe 2:28

b 1Co 12:8, 10

c Joe 2:28-32
  Ro 10:13

d Joh 5:36
  Joh 14:10

e Joh 19:10, 11
  Ac 4:27, 28
  1Pe 1:20

f Lu 23:33
  Ac 5:30
  Ac 7:52

g Ac 3:15
  Ro 4:24
  1Co 6:14
  Col 2:12
  Heb 13:20

h Joh 10:17, 18

this is what was said through the prophet Joel: **17** "'And in the last days,' God says, "I will pour out some of my spirit on every sort of flesh, and your sons and your daughters will prophesy and your young men will see visions and your old men will dream dreams,[a] **18** and even on my male slaves and on my female slaves I will pour out some of my spirit in those days, and they will prophesy.[b] **19** And I will give wonders* in heaven above and signs on earth below—blood and fire and clouds of smoke. **20** The sun will be turned into darkness and the moon into blood before the great and illustrious day of Jehovah* comes. **21** And everyone who calls on the name of Jehovah* will be saved.'"[c]

22 "Men of Israel, hear these words: Jesus the Naz·a·rene′ was a man publicly shown to you by God through powerful works and wonders* and signs that God did through him in your midst,[d] just as you yourselves know. **23** This man, who was handed over by the determined will* and foreknowledge of God,[e] you fastened to a stake by the hand of lawless men, and you did away with him.[f] **24** But God resurrected him[g] by releasing him from the pangs* of death, because it was not possible for him to be held fast by it.[h] **25** For David says about him: 'I keep Jehovah* constantly in front of me,* for he is at my right hand that I may never be shaken. **26** On this account my heart became cheerful and my tongue rejoiced greatly. And I* will reside in hope; **27** because you will not

2:19, 22 *Or "portents." 2:20, 21, 25 *See App. A5. 2:23 *Or "counsel." 2:24 *Or possibly, "cords." 2:25 #Or "before my eyes." 2:26 *Lit., "my flesh."

2:4 *Or "tongues." 2:8 *Or "the language of his birth?" 2:13 *Or "new wine." 2:15 *That is, about 9:00 a.m.

leave me* in the Grave,# nor will you allow your loyal one to see corruption.ª 28 You have made life's ways known to me; you will fill me with great joy in your presence.'*b

29 "Men, brothers, it is permissible to speak with freeness of speech to you about the family head David, that he died and was buried,c and his tomb is with us to this day. 30 Because he was a prophet and knew that God had sworn to him with an oath that he would seat one of his offspring* on his throne,d 31 he foresaw and spoke about the resurrection of the Christ, that neither was he forsaken in the Grave# nor did his flesh see corruption.*e 32 God resurrected this Jesus, and of this we are all witnesses.f 33 Therefore, because he was exalted to the right hand of Godg and received the promised holy spirit from the Father,h he has poured out what you see and hear. 34 For David did not ascend to the heavens, but he himself says, 'Jehovah* said to my Lord: "Sit at my right hand 35 until I place your enemies as a stool for your feet."'i 36 Therefore, let all the house of Israel know for a certainty that God made him both Lordj and Christ, this Jesus whom you executed on a stake."k

37 Now when they heard this, they were stabbed to the heart, and they said to Peter and the rest of the apostles: "Men, brothers, what should we do?" 38 Peter said to them: "Repent,l and let each one of you be baptizedm in the name of Jesus Christ for forgiveness of your sins,n

CHAP. 2

a Ac 13:35

b Ps 16:8-11

c 1Ki 2:10

d 2Sa 7:12, 13
Ps 89:3, 4
Ps 132:11

e Ps 16:10

f Lu 24:46-48
Ac 1:8
Ac 3:15

g Ro 8:34
Php 2:9-11
1Pe 3:22

h Joh 14:26

i Ps 110:1
Lu 20:42, 43
1Co 15:25
Heb 10:12, 13

j Mt 28:18
Joh 3:35
Ac 5:31

k Joh 19:6

l Lu 24:46, 47
Ac 17:30
Ac 26:20

m Mt 28:19

n Mt 26:27, 28
Eph 1:7

Second Col.

a Joe 2:28

b Joe 2:32

c De 32:5
Ps 78:8

d Ac 8:12
Ac 18:8

e Ac 4:4
Ac 5:14

f Ac 2:46
Ac 1:14

h Ac 5:12

i Mt 19:21

j Ac 4:32, 34

k Ac 5:14
Ac 11:21
1Co 3:7

and you will receive the free gift of the holy spirit. 39 For the promiseª is to you and your children, and to all those who are far away, to all those whom Jehovah* our God may call to himself."b 40 And with many other words he gave a thorough witness and kept exhorting them, saying: "Get saved from this crooked generation."c 41 So those who gladly accepted his word were baptized,d and on that day about 3,000 people* were added.e 42 And they continued devoting themselves to the teaching of the apostles, to associating together,* to the taking of meals,f and to prayers.g

43 Indeed, fear began to fall upon everyone,* and many wonders# and signs began to occur through the apostles.h 44 All those who became believers were together and had everything in common, 45 and they were selling their possessionsi and properties and distributing the proceeds to all, according to what each one needed.j 46 And day after day they were in constant attendance in the temple with a united purpose, and they took their meals in different homes and shared their food with great rejoicing and sincerity of heart, 47 praising God and finding favor with all the people. At the same time Jehovah* continued to add to them daily those being saved.k

3 Now Peter and John were going up into the temple for the hour of prayer, the ninth hour,* 2 and a man who was lame from birth was being carried. Every day they would put him near the temple door that was called Beautiful, so he could

---

2:27 *Or "my soul." 2:27, 31 #Or "Hades," that is, the common grave of mankind. See Glossary. 2:28 *Or "before your face." 2:30 *Lit., "one from the fruitage of his loins." 2:31 *Or "decay." 2:34, 39, 47 *See App. A5.

2:41 *Or "souls." 2:42 *Or "to sharing with one another." 2:43 *Or "every soul." #Or "portents." 3:1 *That is, about 3:00 p.m.

ask for gifts of mercy from those entering the temple. **3** When he caught sight of Peter and John about to go into the temple, he began asking for gifts of mercy. **4** But Peter, together with John, looked straight at him and said: "Look at us." **5** So he fixed his attention on them, expecting to get something from them. **6** However, Peter said: "Silver and gold I do not possess, but what I do have is what I give you. In the name of Jesus Christ the Naz·a·rene', walk!"[a] **7** With that he took hold of him by the right hand and raised him up.[b] Instantly his feet and his ankles were made firm;[c] **8** and leaping to his feet,[d] he began walking and went with them into the temple, walking and leaping and praising God. **9** And all the people saw him walking and praising God. **10** And they began to recognize him, that this was the man who used to sit waiting for gifts of mercy at the Beautiful Gate of the temple,[e] and they were completely astonished and ecstatic about what had happened to him.

11 While the man was still holding on to Peter and John, all the people ran together to them at what was called Sol'o·mon's Colonnade,[f] completely surprised. **12** When Peter saw this, he said to the people: "Men of Israel, why are you so amazed at this, and why are you staring at us as though by personal power or godly devotion we have made him walk? **13** The God of Abraham and of Isaac and of Jacob,[g] the God of our forefathers, has glorified his Servant,[h] Jesus,[i] whom you handed over[j] and disowned before Pilate, even though he had decided to release him. **14** Yes, you disowned that holy and righteous one, and you asked for a man who was a murderer to be given to you,[k]

15 whereas you killed the Chief Agent of life.[a] But God raised him up from the dead, of which fact we are witnesses.[b] **16** And through his name, and by our faith in his name, this man whom you see and know has been made strong. The faith that is through him has made this man completely healthy in front of all of you. **17** And now, brothers, I know that you acted in ignorance,[c] just as your rulers also did.[d] **18** But in this way God has fulfilled the things he announced beforehand through the mouth of all the prophets, that his Christ would suffer.[e]

19 "Repent,[f] therefore, and turn around[g] so as to get your sins blotted out,[h] so that seasons of refreshing may come from Jehovah himself* **20** and he may send the Christ appointed for you, Jesus. **21** Heaven must hold this one within itself until the times of restoration of all things of which God spoke through the mouth of his holy prophets of old. **22** In fact, Moses said: 'Jehovah* your God will raise up for you from among your brothers a prophet like me.[i] You must listen to whatever he tells you.[j] **23** Indeed, anyone* who does not listen to that Prophet will be completely destroyed from among the people.'[k] **24** And all the prophets from Samuel and those who followed him, as many as have spoken, have also plainly declared these days.[l] **25** You are the sons of the prophets and of the covenant that God made with your forefathers,[m] saying to Abraham: 'And by means of your offspring* all the families of the earth will be blessed.'[n] **26** God, after raising up his Servant, sent him to

---

CHAP. 3

a Ac 3:16
  Ac 4:10

b Mt 8:14, 15
  Mt 9:24, 25

c Joh 5:8, 9
  Ac 9:34
  Ac 14:8-10

d Isa 35:6

e Ac 3:2

f Joh 10:23
  Ac 5:12

g Ex 3:6

h Isa 52:13
  Isa 53:11

i Php 2:9-11

j Ac 5:30

k Mt 27:20, 21
  Lu 23:14, 18

Second Col.

a Ac 5:31
  Heb 2:10

b Lu 24:46-48
  Ac 1:8
  Ac 2:32

c Joh 16:2, 3
  1Ti 1:13

d 1Co 2:8

e Ps 118:22
  Isa 50:6
  Isa 53:8
  Da 9:26
  Lu 22:15

f Ac 2:38

g Eze 33:11
  Eph 4:22

h Eze 33:14, 16
  1Jo 1:7

i De 34:10
  Ac 7:37

j De 18:15, 18

k De 18:19

l Lu 24:27
  Ac 10:43

m Ro 9:4

n Ge 22:18
  Ga 3:8

3:19 *Lit., "from the face of Jehovah." See App. A5. **3:22** *See App. A5. **3:23** *Or "any soul." **3:25** *Lit., "seed."

you first[a] to bless you by turning each one of you away from your wicked deeds."

4 While the two were speaking to the people, the priests, the captain of the temple, and the Sadducees[b] came up to them. **2** These were annoyed because the apostles were teaching the people and were openly declaring the resurrection of Jesus from the dead.*[c] **3** So they seized* them and took them into custody[d] until the next day, for it was already evening. **4** However, many of those who had listened to the speech believed, and the number of the men became about 5,000.[e]

5 The next day their rulers, elders, and scribes gathered together in Jerusalem, **6** along with An'nas[f] the chief priest, Ca'ia·phas,[g] John, Alexander, and all who were relatives of the chief priest. **7** They stood Peter and John in their midst and began to question them: "By what power or in whose name did you do this?" **8** Then Peter, filled with holy spirit,[h] said to them:

"Rulers of the people and elders, **9** if we are being examined today about a good deed to a crippled man,[i] and you want to know who made this man well, **10** let it be known to all of you and to all the people of Israel that in the name of Jesus Christ the Naz·a·rene',[j] whom you executed on a stake[k] but whom God raised up from the dead,[l] by means of him this man stands here healthy in front of you. **11** This is 'the stone that was treated by you builders as of no account that has become the chief cornerstone.'*[m]

4:2 *Or "the resurrection from the dead in the case of Jesus." **4:3** *Or "arrested." **4:11** *Lit., "the head of the corner."

CHAP. 3

a Ac 13:45, 46
  Ro 1:16

CHAP. 4

b Ac 23:8

c Ac 4:33
  Ac 17:18

d Lu 21:12

e Ac 2:41
  Ac 6:7

f Joh 18:13

g Mt 26:57
  Lu 3:2
  Joh 11:49-51

h Ac 7:55

i Ac 3:7

j Ac 3:6

k Ac 2:36

l Ac 2:24
  Ac 5:30

m Ps 118:22
  Isa 28:16
  Mt 21:42
  1Pe 2:7

Second Col.

a Mt 1:21
  Ac 10:43
  Php 2:9, 10

b Joh 1:12
  Joh 14:6
  1Ti 2:5, 6

c Mt 11:25
  1Co 1:26, 27

d Joh 7:14, 15

e Ac 3:11

f Lu 21:15

g Joh 11:47

h Ac 3:9, 10

i Ac 5:40

j Ac 5:29

k Lu 22:2
  Ac 5:26

---

12 Furthermore, there is no salvation in anyone else, for there is no other name[a] under heaven that has been given among men by which we must get saved."[b]

13 Now when they saw the outspokenness* of Peter and John, and perceived that they were uneducated[#] and ordinary men,[c] they were astonished. And they began to realize that they had been with Jesus.[d] **14** As they were looking at the man who had been cured standing with them,[e] they had nothing to say in answer to this.[f] **15** So they commanded them to go outside the San'he·drin hall, and they began consulting with one another, **16** saying: "What should we do with these men?[g] Because, for a fact, a noteworthy sign has occurred through them, one evident to all the inhabitants of Jerusalem,[h] and we cannot deny it. **17** So that this does not spread any further among the people, let us threaten them and tell them not to speak to anyone anymore on the basis of this name."[i]

18 With that they called them and ordered them not to say anything at all or to teach on the basis of the name of Jesus. **19** But in reply Peter and John said to them: "Whether it is right in the sight of God to listen to you rather than to God, judge for yourselves. **20** But as for us, we cannot stop speaking about the things we have seen and heard."[j] **21** So after they had threatened them further, they released them, since they did not find any grounds for punishing them and on account of the people,[k] because they were all glorifying God over what had happened. **22** For the man on

---

4:13 *Or "boldness." #Or "unlettered," that is, not educated in the rabbinic schools; not meaning illiterate.

whom this miracle* of healing had been done was more than 40 years old.

23 After being released, they went to their own people and reported what the chief priests and the elders had said to them. 24 On hearing this, they raised their voices with one accord to God and said:

"Sovereign Lord, you are the One who made the heaven and the earth and the sea and all the things in them,[a] 25 and who said through holy spirit by the mouth of our forefather David,[b] your servant: 'Why did nations become agitated and peoples meditate on empty things? 26 The kings of the earth took their stand and the rulers gathered together as one against Jehovah* and against his anointed one.'#[c] 27 For truly both Herod and Pontius Pilate[d] with men of the nations and with peoples of Israel were gathered together in this city against your holy servant Jesus, whom you anointed,[e] 28 to do what your hand and counsel had determined beforehand to occur.[f] 29 And now, Jehovah,* give attention to their threats, and grant to your slaves to keep speaking your word with all boldness, 30 while you stretch out your hand for healing and while signs and wonders* occur[g] through the name of your holy servant Jesus."[h]

31 And when they had made supplication,* the place where they were gathered together was shaken, and they were one and all filled with the holy spirit[i] and were speaking the word of God with boldness.[j]

32 Moreover, the multitude of those who believed were of one heart and soul,* and not even one of them would say that any of the things he possessed was his own, but they had all things in common.[a] 33 And with great power the apostles continued giving the witness about the resurrection of the Lord Jesus,[b] and undeserved kindness was upon them all in large measure. 34 In fact, no one was in need among them,[c] for all those who owned fields or houses would sell them and bring the value of what was sold, 35 and they would deposit it at the feet of the apostles.[d] In turn distribution would be made to each one according to his need.[e] 36 So Joseph, who was also called by the apostles Bar'na·bas[f] (which means, when translated, "Son of Comfort"), a Levite, a native of Cy'prus, 37 owned a piece of land, and he sold it and brought the money and deposited it at the feet of the apostles.[g]

5 However, a man named An·a·ni'as, together with his wife Sap·phi'ra, sold some property. 2 But he secretly held back some of the price, with his wife's knowledge, and he brought just a part of it and deposited it at the feet of the apostles.[h] 3 But Peter said: "An·a·ni'as, why has Satan emboldened you to lie[i] to the holy spirit[j] and secretly hold back some of the price of the field? 4 As long as it remained with you, did it not remain yours? And after it was sold, was it not in your control? Why have you thought up such a deed as this in your heart? You have lied, not to men, but to God." 5 On hearing these words, An·a·ni'as collapsed and died. And great fear came over all those who heard about it. 6 Then the younger men rose, wrapped him

---

CHAP. 4
a Ex 20:11
  Ne 9:6
  Ps 146:6

b 2Sa 23:1, 2

c Ps 2:1, 2

d Lu 23:12

e Ps 45:7
  Ac 10:38

f Isa 53:10
  Lu 24:44
  Ac 2:23
  1Pe 1:20

g Ac 2:43
  Ac 5:12

h Ac 3:16

i Ac 2:2, 4

j 1Th 2:2

Second Col.
a Ac 2:44, 45

b Ac 1:21, 22
  Ac 4:2

c Ac 2:44, 45

d Ac 5:1, 2

e Ac 6:1

f Ac 11:22
  Ac 12:25

g Lu 12:33

CHAP. 5
h Ac 4:34, 35

i Ps 101:7
  Eph 4:25
  Col 3:9

j Ac 5:9

4:22 *Or "sign." 4:26, 29 *See App. A5. 4:26 #Or "his Christ." 4:30 *Or "portents." 4:31 *Or "had prayed earnestly."

4:32 *See Glossary.

in cloths, carried him out, and buried him.

7 Now after an interval of about three hours his wife came in, not knowing what had happened. **8** Peter said to her: "Tell me, did you two sell the field for so much?" She said: "Yes, for that amount." **9** So Peter said to her: "Why did you two agree to make a test of the spirit of Jehovah?* Look! The feet of those who buried your husband are at the door, and they will carry you out." **10** Instantly she collapsed at his feet and died. When the young men came in, they found her dead and they carried her out and buried her alongside her husband. **11** So great fear came over the whole congregation and over all those hearing about these things.

12 Moreover, through the hands of the apostles many signs and wonders* continued to occur among the people;[a] and they would all meet together in Sol'o·mon's Colonnade.[b] **13** True, none of the others had the courage to join them; nevertheless, the people were speaking highly of them. **14** More than that, believers in the Lord kept on being added, great numbers both of men and of women.[c] **15** They even brought the sick out into the main streets and laid them there on small beds and mats, so that as Peter would pass by, at least his shadow might fall on some of them.[d] **16** Also, crowds of people from the cities around Jerusalem kept coming, carrying sick people and those troubled with unclean spirits, and they were one and all cured.

17 But the high priest rose, and all those with him, who were

of the sect of the Sadducees, and they were filled with jealousy. **18** And they seized* the apostles and put them in the public jail.[a] **19** But during the night, Jehovah's* angel opened the doors of the prison,[b] brought them out, and said: **20** "Go and take your stand in the temple, and keep on speaking to the people all the sayings about this life." **21** After hearing this, they entered the temple at daybreak and began to teach.

Now when the high priest and those with him arrived, they called together the San'he·drin and the entire assembly of elders of the sons of Israel, and they sent out to the jail to have the apostles brought before them. **22** But when the officers got there, they did not find them in the prison. So they returned and made their report, **23** saying: "We found the jail locked and secure, and the guards were standing at the doors, but on opening it up, we found no one inside." **24** Well, when both the captain of the temple and the chief priests heard these words, they were perplexed about what would come of this. **25** But someone came and reported to them: "Look! The men you put in prison are in the temple, standing and teaching the people." **26** Then the captain went off with his officers and brought them in, but without violence, because they were afraid of being stoned by the people.[c]

27 So they brought them and stood them before the San'he·drin. Then the high priest questioned them **28** and said: "We strictly ordered you not to keep teaching on the basis of this name,[d] and yet look! you have filled Jerusalem with your teaching, and you are determined to

---

CHAP. 5
a Ac 4:29, 30
  Ac 6:8
  Ac 14:3
  Ac 15:12
  Ro 15:18, 19
  2Co 12:12

b Joh 10:23
  Ac 3:11

c Ac 6:7

d Mt 9:20, 21

Second Col.
a Lu 21:12

b Ps 34:7
  Ac 12:7
  Ac 16:26
  Heb 1:7, 14

c Lu 20:19

d Ac 4:18

5:9, 19 *See App. A5. 5:12 *Or "portents."

5:18 *Or "arrested."

bring the blood of this man upon us."ᵃ 29 In answer Peter and the other apostles said: "We must obey God as ruler rather than men.ᵇ 30 The God of our forefathers raised up Jesus, whom you killed, hanging him on a stake.*ᶜ 31 God exalted this one as Chief Agentᵈ and Saviorᵉ to his right hand,ᶠ to give repentance to Israel and forgiveness of sins.ᵍ 32 And we are witnesses of these matters,ʰ and so is the holy spirit,ⁱ which God has given to those obeying him as ruler."

33 When they heard this, they were infuriated* and wanted to do away with them. 34 But a Pharisee named Ga·ma'li·elʲ rose in the San'he·drin; he was a Law teacher esteemed by all the people, and he gave the command to put the men outside for a little while. 35 Then he said to them: "Men of Israel, be careful as to what you intend to do about these men. 36 For instance, before these days Theu'das rose up, saying he himself was somebody, and a number of men, about 400, joined his party. But he was done away with, and all those who were following him were dispersed and came to nothing. 37 After him, Judas the Gal·i·le'an rose up in the days of the registration, and he drew followers after himself. That man also perished, and all those who were following him were scattered. 38 So under the present circumstances, I say to you, do not meddle with these men, but let them alone. For if this scheme or this work is from men, it will be overthrown; 39 but if it is from God, you will not be able to overthrow them.ᵏ Otherwise, you may even be found fighters against God himself."ˡ 40 At this they took his advice, and they summoned the

apostles, flogged* them,ᵃ and ordered them to stop speaking on the basis of Jesus' name, and let them go.

41 So they went out from before the San'he·drin, rejoicingᵇ because they had been counted worthy to be dishonored in behalf of his name. 42 And every day in the temple and from house to houseᶜ they continued without letup teaching and declaring the good news about the Christ, Jesus.ᵈ

6 Now in those days when the disciples were increasing, the Greek-speaking Jews began complaining against the Hebrew-speaking Jews, because their widows were being overlooked in the daily distribution.ᵉ 2 So the Twelve called the multitude of the disciples together and said: "It is not right* for us to leave the word of God to distribute food to tables.ᶠ 3 So, brothers, select for yourselves seven reputable men*ᵍ from among you, full of spirit and wisdom,ʰ that we may appoint them over this necessary matter;ⁱ 4 but we will devote ourselves to prayer and to the ministry of the word." 5 What they said was pleasing to the whole multitude, and they selected Stephen, a man full of faith and holy spirit, as well as Philip,ʲ Proch'o·rus, Ni·ca'nor, Ti'mon, Par'me·nas, and Nic·o·la'us, a proselyte of Antioch. 6 They brought them to the apostles, and after praying, they laid their hands on them.ᵏ

7 Consequently, the word of God continued to spread,ˡ and the number of the disciples kept multiplying very muchᵐ in Jerusalem; and a large crowd of priests began to be obedient to the faith.ⁿ

CHAP. 5
a Mt 27:25
  Ac 3:14, 15
b Da 3:17, 18
  Ac 4:19, 20
c Ac 2:23, 24
d Ac 3:15
e Mt 1:21
  Heb 2:10
f Ac 2:32, 33
  Php 2:9
g Isa 53:11
  Ac 2:38
  Ac 10:43
h Lu 24:46-48
  Ac 1:8
i Joh 15:26
j Ac 22:3
k Pr 21:30
l Ac 26:14

Second Col.
a Mt 10:17
  Mr 13:9
b Mt 5:12
  Ac 16:25
  Ro 5:3
  2Co 12:10
  Php 1:29
  Heb 10:34
  1Pe 4:13
c Ac 20:20
d Ac 4:31

CHAP. 6
e Ac 4:34, 35
  1Ti 5:16
  Jas 1:27
f Ex 18:17, 18
g Ac 16:1, 2
  1Ti 3:7
h Ac 6:8, 10
i De 1:13
j Ac 21:8
k Ac 34:9
  Ac 8:14, 17
  Ac 13:2, 3
  1Ti 4:14
  1Ti 5:22
  2Ti 1:6
l Ac 12:24
  Ac 19:20
m Ac 2:47
n Joh 12:42
  Ac 15:5

5:30 *Or "tree." 5:33 *Or "they felt cut."

5:40 *Or "beat." 6:2 *Lit., "pleasing." 6:3 *Or "seven men who are well reported on."

8 Now Stephen, full of divine
favor and power, was performing
great wonders* and signs among
the people. **9** But some men of
the so-called Synagogue of the
Freedmen came forward, along
with some Cy·re′ni·ans and Alex-
andrians, and some from Ci·li′-
cia and Asia, to dispute with
Stephen. **10** But they could not
hold their own against the wisdom and the spirit with which
he was speaking.[a] **11** Then they
secretly persuaded men to say:
"We have heard him speak-
ing blasphemous things against
Moses and God." **12** And they
stirred up the people, the elders, and the scribes, and coming upon him suddenly, they
forcibly seized him and led him
to the San′he·drin. **13** And they
brought forward false witnesses,
who said: "This man does not
stop speaking things against this
holy place and against the Law.
14 For instance, we have heard
him say that this Jesus the Naz·a-
rene′ will throw down this place
and change the customs that
Moses handed down to us."

15 And as all those sitting in
the San′he·drin stared at him,
they saw that his face was like
an angel's face.

7 But the high priest said: "Are
these things so?" **2** Stephen
replied: "Men, brothers and fathers, listen. The God of glory
appeared to our forefather Abraham while he was in Mes·o·po-
ta′mi·a, before he took up residence in Ha′ran,[b] **3** and he said
to him: 'Go out from your land
and from your relatives and
come into the land that I will
show you.'[c] **4** Then he went out
of the land of the Chal·de′ans and
took up residence in Ha′ran. And
from there, after his father died,[d]
God caused him to resettle in
this land where you now dwell.[e]

6:8 *Or "portents."

5 And yet, he did not give him
any inheritance in it, no, not
even enough to put his foot on;
but he promised to give it to him
as a possession and after him
to his offspring,*[a] though as yet
he had no child. **6** Moreover,
God told him that his offspring*
would be foreigners in a land not
theirs and that the people would
enslave them and afflict# them
for 400 years.[b] **7** 'And that nation for which they will slave
I will judge,'[c] God said, 'and after these things they will come
out and will offer sacred service
to me in this place.'[d]

8 "He also gave him a covenant of circumcision,[e] and he became the father of Isaac[f] and circumcised him on the eighth day,[g]
and Isaac became the father of*
Jacob, and Jacob of the 12
family heads.# **9** And the family heads became jealous of Joseph[h] and sold him into Egypt.[i]
But God was with him,[j] **10** and
he rescued him out of all his
tribulations and gave him favor and wisdom before Phar′aoh
king of Egypt. And he appointed him to govern Egypt and his
whole house.[k] **11** But a famine
came on all of Egypt and Ca′-
naan, yes, a great tribulation,
and our forefathers could not
find anything to eat.[l] **12** But
Jacob heard that there were
food supplies* in Egypt, and
he sent our forefathers out the
first time.[m] **13** During the second time, Joseph made him-
self known to his brothers, and
the family of Joseph became
known to Phar′aoh.[n] **14** So Joseph sent a message and called
his father Jacob and all his relatives from that place,[o] 75 persons* in all.[p] **15** So Jacob went
down into Egypt,[q] and he died

CHAP. 6
a Isa 54:17, Lu 21:15, Ac 6:3

CHAP. 7
b Ge 11:31
c Ge 12:1
d Ge 11:32
e Ge 12:4, 5; Heb 11:8

Second Col.
a Ge 12:7; Ge 13:14, 15; Ge 17:1, 8
b Ge 15:13; Ex 12:40
c Ge 15:14
d Ex 3:12
e Ge 17:9, 10
f Ge 21:1-3
g Ge 21:4
h Ge 37:9-11
i Ge 37:28; Ge 45:4
j Ge 39:2, 3
k Ge 41:40-46
l Ge 41:54; Ge 42:5
m Ge 42:2, 6
n Ge 45:1, 16
o Ge 45:9-11
p Ge 46:27; De 10:22
q Ge 46:29; De 26:5

7:5, 6 *Lit., "seed." 7:6 #Or "mistreat."
7:8 *Or possibly, "did the same with."
#Or "patriarchs." 7:12 *Or "there was
grain." 7:14 *Or "souls."

there,[a] and so did our fore-fathers.[b] **16** They were carried to She'chem and were laid in the tomb that Abraham had bought for a sum of silver money from the sons of Ha'mor in She'chem.[c]

17 "Just as the time was approaching to fulfill the promise that God had announced to Abraham, the people grew and multiplied in Egypt, **18** until there rose a different king over Egypt, one who did not know of Joseph.[d] **19** This one dealt cunningly with our race and wrongfully forced the fathers to abandon their infants so that they would not be kept alive.[e] **20** At that time Moses was born, and he was divinely beautiful.* And he was nursed*[g] for three months in his father's home.[f] **21** But when he was abandoned,*[g] the daughter of Phar'-aoh took him and brought him up as her own son.[h] **22** So Moses was instructed in all the wisdom of the Egyptians. In fact, he was powerful in his words and deeds.[i]

23 "Now when he reached the age of 40, it came into his heart* to make a visit on* his brothers, the sons of Israel.[j] **24** When he caught sight of one of them being unjustly treated, he defended him and avenged the one being abused by striking down the Egyptian. **25** He thought that his brothers would grasp that God was giving them salvation by his hand, but they did not grasp it. **26** The next day he appeared to them as they were fighting, and he tried to reconcile them in peace, saying: 'Men, you are brothers. Why do you mistreat each other?' **27** But the one who was mistreating his neighbor pushed him away, say-

ing: 'Who appointed you ruler and judge over us? **28** You do not want to do away with me the way you did away with the Egyptian yesterday, do you?' **29** On hearing this, Moses fled and lived as a foreigner in the land of Mid'i·an, where he became the father of two sons.[a]

30 "After 40 years had passed, an angel appeared to him in the wilderness of Mount Si'nai in the flame of a burning thorn-bush.[b] **31** When Moses saw it, he was amazed at the sight. But as he was approaching to investigate, Jehovah's* voice was heard: **32** 'I am the God of your fore-fathers, the God of Abraham and of Isaac and of Jacob.'[c] Moses started trembling and did not dare to investigate further. **33** Jehovah* said to him: 'Remove the sandals from your feet, for the place where you are standing is holy ground. **34** I have certainly seen the oppression of my people who are in Egypt, and I have heard their groaning,[d] and I have come down to rescue them. Now come, I will send you off to Egypt.' **35** This same Moses whom they had disowned, saying: 'Who appointed you ruler and judge?'[e] is the very one God sent[f] as both ruler and deliverer by means of the angel who appeared to him in the thornbush. **36** This man led them out,[g] performing wonders* and signs in Egypt[h] and at the Red Sea[i] and in the wilderness for 40 years.[j]

37 "This is the Moses who said to the sons of Israel: 'God will raise up for you from among your brothers a prophet like me.'[k] **38** This is the one who came to be among the congregation in the wilderness with the angel[l] who spoke to him[m] on Mount Si'nai and

---

CHAP. 7
a Ge 49:33

b Ex 1:6

c Ge 23:16
  Ex 13:19
  Jos 24:32

d Ex 1:7, 8

e Ex 1:10, 22

f Ex 2:2
  Heb 11:23

g Ex 2:3

h Ex 2:5, 10

i Ex 11:3

j Ex 2:11-15

Second Col.
a Ex 2:21, 22
  Ex 18:2-4

b Ex 3:2-10

c Ex 3:6
  Mr 12:26
  Lu 20:37

d Ex 2:23, 24

e Ex 2:14
  Ac 7:27

f Ex 4:19

g Ex 12:41

h Ex 7:3

i Ex 14:21, 22
  Ex 15:4, 5

j Ex 16:35
  Nu 14:33, 34

k De 18:15
  Ac 3:22

l Ac 7:53
  Ga 3:19

m Ex 19:3
  De 5:27

7:20 *Or "was beautiful in God's sight." *Or "brought up." 7:21 *Or "exposed." 7:23 *Or "he decided." *Or "make an inspection of."

7:31, 33 *See App. A5. 7:36 *Or "portents."

with our forefathers, and he received living sacred pronouncements to give us.[a] **39** Our forefathers refused to obey him, but they pushed him aside[b] and in their hearts they turned back to Egypt,[c] **40** saying to Aaron: 'Make gods for us to go ahead of us. For we do not know what has happened to this Moses, who led us out of the land of Egypt.'[d] **41** So they made a calf in those days and brought a sacrifice to the idol and began to enjoy themselves in the works of their hands.[e] **42** So God turned away from them and handed them over to offer sacred service to the army of heaven,[f] just as it is written in the book of the Prophets: 'It was not to me that you made offerings and sacrifices for 40 years in the wilderness, was it, O house of Israel? **43** But it was the tent of Mo'loch[g] and the star of the god Re'phan that you took up, the images that you made to worship them. So I will deport you beyond Babylon.'[h]

44 "Our forefathers had the tent of the witness in the wilderness, just as He gave orders when speaking to Moses to make it according to the pattern he had seen.[i] **45** And our forefathers received possession of it and brought it in with Joshua into the land possessed by the nations,[j] whom God drove out from before our forefathers.[k] Here it remained until the days of David. **46** He found favor in the sight of God and asked for the privilege of providing a dwelling place for the God of Jacob.[l] **47** But it was Sol'o·mon who built a house for him.[m] **48** However, the Most High does not dwell in houses made with hands,[n] just as the prophet says: **49** 'The heaven is my throne,[o] and the earth is my footstool.[p] What sort of house will you build for me? Jehovah* says. Or where is my resting-place? **50** My hand made all these things, did it not?'[a]

51 "Obstinate men and uncircumcised in hearts and ears, you are always resisting the holy spirit; as your forefathers did, so you do.[b] **52** Which one of the prophets did your forefathers not persecute?[c] Yes, they killed those who announced in advance the coming of the righteous one,[d] whose betrayers and murderers you have now become,[e] **53** you who received the Law as transmitted by angels[f] but have not kept it."

54 Well, at hearing these things, they were infuriated* in their hearts and began to grind their teeth at him. **55** But he, being full of holy spirit, gazed into heaven and caught sight of God's glory and of Jesus standing at God's right hand,[g] **56** and he said: "Look! I see the heavens opened up and the Son of man[h] standing at God's right hand."[i] **57** At this they cried out at the top of their voices and put their hands over their ears and rushed at him all together. **58** After throwing him outside the city, they began stoning him.[j] The witnesses[k] laid down their outer garments at the feet of a young man called Saul.[l] **59** As they were stoning Stephen, he made this appeal: "Lord Jesus, receive my spirit." **60** Then, kneeling down, he cried out with a strong voice: "Jehovah,* do not charge this sin against them."[m] And after saying this, he fell asleep in death.

8 Saul, for his part, approved of his murder.[n]

On that day great persecution arose against the congregation that was in Jerusalem;

CHAP. 7
a Ex 21:1
   De 9:10
b Nu 14:3, 4
c Ex 16:3
d Ex 32:1, 23
e Ex 32:4, 6
f 2Ki 17:16
   1Ki 11:7
h Jer 25:11
   Am 5:25-27
i Ex 25:40
j De 3:28
   De 31:3
   Jos 3:14
k Ge 17:1, 8
   Jos 23:9
   Jos 24:18
l 2Sa 7:2
   1Ch 22:7
   Ps 132:1-5
m 1Ki 6:1
n Ac 17:24
o Ps 11:4
p Mt 5:34, 35

Second Col.
a Isa 66:1, 2
   Heb 3:4
b Isa 63:10
c 2Ch 36:16
d Mt 23:31
e Isa 53:8
   Ac 3:13, 14
f Ac 7:38
   Ga 3:19
g Ps 110:1
   Mt 26:64
h Da 7:13
i Ro 8:34
j Le 24:14, 16
   Mt 23:37
   Joh 16:2
k De 17:7
l Ac 8:1
   Ac 22:20
m Mt 5:44

CHAP. 8
n Ac 7:58

7:49, 60 *See App. A5. 7:54 *Or "they felt cut."

all except the apostles were scattered throughout the regions of Ju·de′a and Sa·mar′i·a.ᵃ 2 But devout men carried Stephen away to bury him, and they made a great mourning over him. 3 Saul, though, began to ravage the congregation. He would invade one house after another, dragging out both men and women and turning them over to prison.ᵇ

4 However, those who had been scattered went through the land declaring the good news of the word.ᶜ 5 Now Philip went down to the city* of Sa·mar′i·aᵈ and began to preach the Christ to them. 6 The crowds with one accord were paying attention to what Philip said while they listened and observed the signs he was performing. 7 For many had unclean spirits, and these would cry out with a loud voice and come out.ᵉ Moreover, many who were paralyzed and lame were cured. 8 So there came to be a great deal of joy in that city.

9 Now in the city was a man named Simon, who prior to this had been practicing magical arts and amazing the nation of Sa·mar′i·a, claiming that he was somebody great. 10 All of them, from the least to the greatest, would pay attention to him and say: "This man is the Power of God, which is called Great." 11 So they would pay attention to him because he had amazed them for quite a while by his magical arts. 12 But when they believed Philip, who was declaring the good news of the Kingdom of Godᶠ and of the name of Jesus Christ, both men and women were getting baptized.ᵍ 13 Simon himself also became a believer, and after being baptized, he continued with Philip;ʰ and he was amazed at seeing the

signs and great powerful works taking place.

14 When the apostles in Jerusalem heard that Sa·mar′i·a had accepted the word of God,ᵃ they sent Peter and John to them; 15 and these went down and prayed for them to get holy spirit.ᵇ 16 For it had not yet come upon any one of them, but they had only been baptized in the name of the Lord Jesus.ᶜ 17 Then they laid their hands on them,ᵈ and they began to receive holy spirit.

18 Now when Simon saw that the spirit was given through the laying on of the hands of the apostles, he offered them money, 19 saying: "Give me this authority also, so that anyone on whom I lay my hands may receive holy spirit." 20 But Peter said to him: "May your silver perish with you, because you thought you could acquire the free gift of God with money.ᵉ 21 You have neither part nor share in this matter, for your heart is not straight in the sight of God. 22 So repent of this badness of yours, and supplicate Jehovah* that, if possible, the wicked intention of your heart may be forgiven you; 23 for I see you are a bitter poison* and a slave of unrighteousness." 24 In answer Simon said to them: "Make supplication for me to Jehovah* that none of the things you have said may come upon me."

25 Therefore, when they had given the witness thoroughly and had spoken the word of Jehovah,* they started back toward Jerusalem, and they went declaring the good news to many villages of the Sa·mar′i·tans.ᶠ

26 However, Jehovah's* angelᵍ spoke to Philip, saying: "Get up and go to the south to the

---

CHAP. 8
a Mt 10:23
  Ac 11:19

b Ac 9:1, 2
  Ac 22:4
  Ac 26:10
  Ga 1:13
  Php 3:5, 6

c Ac 11:19

d Joh 4:39-42
  Ac 1:8

e Mt 10:1
  Mr 6:7

f Lu 8:1

g Mt 28:19
  Ac 18:8

h Ac 6:5

Second Col.
a Ac 11:1

b Mt 16:19

c Ac 10:47, 48
  Ac 19:2, 3

d Ac 6:5, 6
  Ac 19:6
  2Ti 1:6

e Mt 10:8
  Ac 10:45

f Mt 9:35
  Ac 1:8

g Heb 1:7, 14
  Re 14:6

8:5 *Or possibly, "a city." 8:22, 24-26 *See App. A5. 8:23 *Lit., "gall of bitterness."

road that runs down from Jerusalem to Gaz′a." (This is a desert road.) **27** With that he got up and went, and look! an E·thi·o′pi·an eunuch,* a man who had authority under Can·da′ce, queen of the E·thi·o′pi·ans, and who was in charge of all her treasure. He had gone to Jerusalem to worship,[a] **28** and he was returning and was sitting in his chariot, reading aloud the prophet Isaiah. **29** So the spirit said to Philip: "Go over and approach this chariot." **30** Philip ran alongside and heard him reading aloud Isaiah the prophet, and he said: "Do you actually know* what you are reading?" **31** He said: "Really, how could I ever do so unless someone guided me?" So he urged Philip to get on and sit down with him. **32** Now this was the passage of Scripture that he was reading: "Like a sheep he was brought to the slaughter, and like a lamb that is silent before its shearer, so he does not open his mouth.[b] **33** During his humiliation, justice was taken away from him.[c] Who will tell the details of his generation? Because his life is taken away from the earth."[d]

34 The eunuch then said to Philip: "I beg you, about whom does the prophet say this? About himself or about some other man?" **35** Philip began to speak, and starting with this scripture, he declared to him the good news about Jesus. **36** Now as they were going along the road, they came to a body of water, and the eunuch said: "Look! Here is water; what prevents me from getting baptized?" **37** *— **38** With that he commanded the chariot to halt, and both Philip and the eunuch went down into the water, and

he baptized him. **39** When they came up out of the water, Jehovah's* spirit quickly led Philip away, and the eunuch did not see him anymore, but he went on his way rejoicing. **40** Philip, however, found himself in Ash′dod, and he went through the territory and kept on declaring the good news to all the cities until he got to Caes·a·re′a.[a]

9 But Saul, still breathing threat and murder against the disciples of the Lord,[b] went to the high priest **2** and asked him for letters to the synagogues in Damascus, so that he might bring bound to Jerusalem any whom he found who belonged to The Way,[c] both men and women.

3 Now as he was traveling and getting near Damascus, suddenly a light from heaven flashed around him,[d] **4** and he fell to the ground and heard a voice say to him: "Saul, Saul, why are you persecuting me?" **5** He asked: "Who are you, Lord?" He said: "I am Jesus,[e] whom you are persecuting.[f] **6** But get up and go into the city, and you will be told what you must do." **7** Now the men who were traveling with him stood speechless, hearing, indeed, the sound of a voice but seeing no one.[g] **8** Saul then got up from the ground, and though his eyes were open, he could see nothing. So they led him by the hand and brought him into Damascus. **9** And for three days he did not see anything,[h] and he neither ate nor drank.

10 There was a disciple named An·a·ni′as[i] in Damascus, and the Lord said to him in a vision: "An·a·ni′as!" He said: "Here I am, Lord." **11** The Lord said to him: "Get up, go to the street called Straight, and look for a man named Saul, from Tarsus,[j] at the house of Judas. For look!

CHAP. 8
a 2Ch 6:32, 33

b 1Pe 2:23

c Mt 26:59

d Isa 53:7, 8
  Da 9:26
  Php 2:8

Second Col.
a Ac 21:8

CHAP. 9
b Ac 8:3
  Ac 22:4
  Ac 26:10, 11
  Ga 1:13
  1Ti 1:12, 13

c Ac 11:26
  Ac 22:4

d Ac 22:6-11
  Ac 26:13-18

e 1Co 15:8

f Mt 25:45

g Ac 22:9

h Ac 13:11

i Ac 22:12

j Ac 21:39
  Ac 22:3

8:27 *Or "court official." **8:30** *Or "understand." **8:37** *See App. A3.

8:39 *See App. A5.

he is praying, **12** and in a vision he has seen a man named An·a·ni′as come in and lay his hands on him so that he may recover sight."[a] **13** But An·a·ni′as answered: "Lord, I have heard from many about this man, about all the harm he did to your holy ones in Jerusalem. **14** And here he has authority from the chief priests to arrest* all those calling on your name."[b] **15** But the Lord said to him: "Go! because this man is a chosen vessel to me[c] to bear my name to the nations[d] as well as to kings[e] and the sons of Israel. **16** For I will show him plainly how many things he must suffer for my name."[f]

17 So An·a·ni′as went and entered the house, and he laid his hands on him and said: "Saul, brother, the Lord Jesus, who appeared to you on the road along which you were coming, has sent me so that you may recover sight and be filled with holy spirit."[g] **18** And immediately, what looked like scales fell from his eyes, and he recovered his sight. He then got up and was baptized, **19** and he ate some food and gained strength.

He stayed for some days with the disciples in Damascus,[h] **20** and immediately in the synagogues he began to preach about Jesus, that this one is the Son of God. **21** But all those hearing him were astonished and were saying: "Is this not the man who ravaged those in Jerusalem who call on this name?[i] Did he not come here for the purpose of arresting them and taking them* to the chief priests?"[j] **22** But Saul kept on acquiring more and more power and was confounding the Jews who lived in Damascus, as he proved logically that this is the Christ.[k]

23 Now when many days had passed, the Jews plotted together to do away with him.[a] **24** However, their plot against Saul became known to him. They were also watching the gates closely both day and night in order to do away with him. **25** So his disciples took him and let him down by night through an opening in the wall, lowering him in a basket.[b]

26 On arriving in Jerusalem,[c] he made efforts to join the disciples, but they were all afraid of him, because they did not believe he was a disciple. **27** So Bar′na·bas[d] came to his aid and led him to the apostles, and he told them in detail how on the road he had seen the Lord,[e] and that he had spoken to him, and how in Damascus he had spoken boldly in the name of Jesus.[f] **28** So he remained with them, moving about freely in* Jerusalem, speaking boldly in the name of the Lord. **29** He was talking and disputing with the Greek-speaking Jews, but these made attempts to do away with him.[g] **30** When the brothers found out about this, they brought him down to Caes·a·re′a and sent him off to Tarsus.[h]

31 Then, indeed, the congregation throughout the whole of Ju·de′a and Gal′i·lee and Sa·mar′i·a entered into a period of peace, being built up; and as it walked in the fear of Jehovah* and in the comfort of the holy spirit,[i] it kept on multiplying.

32 Now as Peter was traveling through all the region, he came down also to the holy ones who lived in Lyd′da.[k] **33** There he found a man named Ae·ne′as, who had been lying flat on his bed for eight years, for he was paralyzed. **34** Peter said to him: "Ae·ne′as, Jesus Christ

CHAP. 9

a Ac 9:17

b Ac 9:1, 2

c Ac 13:2
Ro 1:1
1Ti 1:12

d Ro 1:5
Ga 2:7
1Ti 2:7

e Ac 26:1
Ac 27:24

f Ac 20:22, 23
Ac 21:11
2Co 11:23-28
Col 1:24
2Ti 1:12

g Ac 22:12, 13

h Ac 26:19, 20

i Ac 8:3
Ga 1:13, 23

j Ac 9:1, 2

k Ac 17:2, 3

Second Col.

a Ac 20:2, 3
Ac 23:12
2Co 11:23

b 2Co 11:32, 33

c Ga 1:18

d Ac 4:36, 37

e Ac 9:3, 4
1Co 9:1

f Ac 9:19, 20

g 2Co 11:23, 26

h Ac 11:25
Ga 1:21

i Ac 8:1

j Joh 14:16

k Ac 9:38

9:14 *Lit., "bind; put in bonds." 9:21 *Lit., "that he might lead them bound."

9:28 *Lit., "walking in and out of." 9:31 *See App. A5.

heals you.ª Rise and make up your bed."ᵇ And he got up immediately. **35** When all those living in Lyd'da and the Plain of Shar'on saw him, they turned to the Lord.

36 Now there was in Jop'pa a disciple named Tab'i·tha, which means, when translated, "Dor'cas."* She abounded in good deeds and gifts of mercy that she was making. **37** But in those days she fell sick and died. So they bathed her and laid her in an upper room. **38** Since Lyd'da was near Jop'pa, when the disciples heard that Peter was in that city, they sent two men to him to urge him: "Please come to us without delay." **39** At that Peter got up and went with them. And when he arrived, they led him up into the upper room; and all the widows presented themselves to him, weeping and showing many garments and robes* that Dor'cas had made while she was with them. **40** Peter then put everyone outside,ᶜ and kneeling down, he prayed. Then turning toward the body, he said: "Tab'i·tha, rise!" She opened her eyes, and as she caught sight of Peter, she sat up.ᵈ **41** Giving her his hand, he raised her up, and he called the holy ones and the widows and presented her alive.ᵉ **42** This became known throughout all Jop'pa, and many became believers in the Lord.ᶠ **43** He remained for quite a few days in Jop'pa with a tanner named Simon.ᵍ

10 Now there was a man in Caes·a·re'a named Cornelius, an army officer* in what was called the Italian unit.ʰ **2** He was a devout man who feared

God together with all his household, and he made many gifts of mercy to the people and made supplication to God continually. **3** About the ninth hourª of the day,* he saw plainly in a vision an angel of God come in to him and say: "Cornelius!" **4** Cornelius stared at him, terrified, and asked: "What is it, Lord?" He said to him: "Your prayers and gifts of mercy have ascended as a remembrance before God.ᵇ **5** So now send men to Jop'pa and summon a man named Simon who is called Peter. **6** This man is staying as a guest with* Simon, a tanner who has a house by the sea." **7** As soon as the angel who spoke to him left, he called two of his servants and a devout soldier from among those who were his attendants, **8** and he related everything to them and sent them to Jop'pa.

9 The next day as they were continuing on their journey and were approaching the city, Peter went up to the housetop about the sixth hour* to pray. **10** But he became very hungry and wanted to eat. While they were preparing the meal, he fell into a tranceᶜ **11** and saw heaven opened and something* descending like a great linen sheet being let down by its four corners on the earth; **12** and in it were all sorts of four-footed animals and reptiles* of the earth and birds of heaven. **13** Then a voice said to him: "Get up, Peter, slaughter and eat!" **14** But Peter said: "Not at all, Lord, because I have never eaten anything defiled and unclean."ᵈ **15** And the voice spoke again to him, the second time: "Stop calling defiled the things God has

---

CHAP. 9
a Mt 10:8
  Ac 4:9, 10

b Ac 3:6

c Lu 8:51

d Mt 9:24, 25
  Lu 7:14, 15
  Joh 11:43, 44

e 1Ki 17:23

f Joh 11:44, 45

g Ac 10:6, 32

Second Col.

CHAP. 10
a Ac 3:1

b Ps 65:2

c Ac 11:5-10

d Le 11:4
  Le 11:13-20
  Le 20:25
  De 14:3, 19
  Eze 4:14

9:36 *The Greek name Dorcas and the Aramaic name Tabitha both mean "Gazelle." 9:39 *Or "outer garments." 10:1 *Or "a centurion," in command of 100 soldiers. ʰOr "cohort," a Roman army unit of 600 soldiers.

10:3 *That is, about 3:00 p.m. 10:6 *Or "being entertained by." 10:9 *That is, about 12:00 noon. 10:11 *Lit., "some sort of vessel." 10:12 *Or "creeping things."

cleansed." **16** This happened a third time, and immediately it* was taken up into heaven.

17 While Peter was still perplexed about what the vision he had seen could mean, just then the men sent by Cornelius asked where Simon's house was and stood there at the gate.ᵃ **18** They called out and inquired whether Simon who was called Peter was a guest there. **19** As Peter was still pondering over the vision, the spiritᵇ said: "Look! Three men are asking for you. **20** So get up, go downstairs and go with them, not doubting at all, because I have sent them." **21** Then Peter went downstairs to the men and said: "Here I am, the one you are looking for. Why are you here?" **22** They said: "Cornelius,ᶜ an army officer, a righteous and God-fearing man who is well-reported-on by the whole nation of the Jews, was given divine instructions by a holy angel to send for you to come to his house and to hear what you have to say." **23** So he invited them in and had them stay as his guests.

The next day he got up and went off with them, and some of the brothers from Jop'pa went with him. **24** The following day he entered into Caes·a·re'a. Cornelius, of course, was expecting them and had called together his relatives and close friends. **25** As Peter entered, Cornelius met him, fell down at his feet, and did obeisance* to him. **26** But Peter lifted him up, saying: "Rise; I too am just a man."ᵈ **27** As he conversed with him, he went in and found many people assembled. **28** He said to them: "You well know how unlawful it is for a Jew to associate with or approach a man of another race,ᵃ and yet God has shown me that I should call no man defiled or unclean.ᵇ **29** So I came, really without objection, when I was sent for. Therefore, I ask you why you sent for me."

30 Then Cornelius said: "Four days ago counting from this hour, I was praying in my house at the ninth hour;* just then a man in bright clothing stood in front of me **31** and said: 'Cornelius, your prayer has been favorably heard, and your gifts of mercy have been remembered before God. **32** Therefore, send to Jop'pa and call for Simon who is called Peter. This man is a guest in the house of Simon, a tanner, by the sea.'ᶜ **33** I then sent for you at once, and you were kind enough to come here. So now we are all present before God to hear all the things you have been commanded by Jehovah* to say."

34 At this Peter began to speak, and he said: "Now I truly understand that God is not partial,ᵈ **35** but in every nation the man who fears him and does what is right is acceptable to him.ᵉ **36** He sent out the word to the sons of Israel to declare to them the good news of peaceᶠ through Jesus Christ—this one is Lord of all.ᵍ **37** You know the subject that was talked about throughout all Ju·de'a, starting from Gal'i·leeʰ after the baptism that John preached: **38** about Jesus who was from Naz'a·reth, how God anointed him with holy spiritⁱ and power, and he went through the land doing good and healing all those oppressed by the Devil,ʲ because God was with him.ᵏ **39** And we are witnesses of all the things he did both in the country of the Jews and in Jerusalem; but they did away

---

CHAP. 10
a Ac 11:11

b Ac 13:2
  Ac 15:28
  Ac 16:6
  Ac 20:23

c Ac 10:1

d Lu 4:8
  Ac 14:12-15
  Re 19:10
  Re 22:8, 9

Second Col.
a Joh 18:28

b Ac 10:45
  Eph 3:5, 6

c Ac 9:43

d De 10:17
  2Ch 19:7
  Ro 2:11

e Ro 2:13
  1Co 12:13
  Ga 3:28

f Isa 52:7
  Na 1:15

g Mt 28:18
  Ro 14:9
  Re 19:11, 16

h Lu 4:14

i Isa 11:2
  Isa 42:1
  Isa 61:1
  Mt 3:16

j Lu 13:16

k Joh 3:1, 2

10:16 *Lit., "the vessel." 10:25 *Or "bowed down." 10:30 *That is, about 3:00 p.m. 10:33 *See App. A5.

with him by hanging him on a stake.* **40** God raised this one up on the third day[a] and allowed him to become manifest,* **41** not to all the people, but to witnesses appointed beforehand by God, to us, who ate and drank with him after his rising from the dead.[b] **42** Also, he ordered us to preach to the people and to give a thorough witness[c] that this is the one decreed by God to be judge of the living and the dead.[d] **43** To him all the prophets bear witness,[e] that everyone putting faith in him receives forgiveness of sins through his name.[f]

44 While Peter was still speaking about these matters, the holy spirit came upon all those hearing the word.[g] **45** And the circumcised believers* who had come with Peter were amazed, because the free gift of the holy spirit was being poured out also on people of the nations. **46** For they heard them speaking in foreign languages* and magnifying God.[h] Then Peter responded: **47** "Can anyone deny water to prevent these from being baptized[i] who have received the holy spirit just as we have?" **48** With that he commanded them to be baptized in the name of Jesus Christ.[j] Then they requested him to stay for some days.

11 Now the apostles and the brothers who were in Ju·de′a heard that people of the nations had also accepted the word of God. **2** So when Peter came up to Jerusalem, the supporters of circumcision[k] began to criticize* him, **3** saying: "You went into the house of men who were not circumcised and ate with them." **4** At this Peter went on to explain the matter in detail to them, saying:

5 "I was in the city of Jop′pa praying, and while in a trance I saw a vision, something* descending like a great linen sheet being let down by its four corners from heaven, and it came right down to me.[a] **6** Looking closely into it, I observed four-footed animals of the earth, wild beasts, reptiles,* and birds of heaven. **7** I also heard a voice say to me: 'Get up, Peter, slaughter and eat!' **8** But I said: 'Certainly not, Lord, because a defiled or unclean thing has never entered my mouth.' **9** The second time, the voice from heaven answered: 'You stop calling defiled the things God has cleansed.' **10** This happened a third time, and everything was pulled up again into heaven. **11** Also just at that moment, three men were standing at the house where we were staying, having been sent to me from Caes·a·re′a.[b] **12** Then the spirit told me to go with them, not doubting at all. But these six brothers also went with me, and we entered into the house of the man.

13 "He reported to us how he saw the angel stand in his house and say: 'Send men to Jop′pa and summon Simon who is called Peter,[c] **14** and he will tell you things by which you and all your household may get saved.' **15** But when I started to speak, the holy spirit fell on them just as it did also on us in the beginning.[d] **16** At this I recalled the saying of the Lord, how he used to say: 'John baptized with water,[e] but you will be baptized with holy spirit.'[f] **17** If, therefore, God gave the same free gift to them that he gave to us who

---

CHAP. 10
a Jon 1:17
  Jon 2:10
  Ac 2:23, 24

b Lu 24:30, 31
  Joh 21:13, 14

c Mt 28:19, 20
  Ac 1:8

d Ac 17:31
  Ro 14:9
  2Co 5:10
  2Ti 4:1
  1Pe 4:5

e Lu 24:27
  Re 19:10

f Isa 53:11
  Jer 31:34
  Da 9:24

g Ac 4:31
  Ac 8:14, 15

h Ac 2:1, 4
  Ac 19:6

i Mt 3:11
  Ac 8:36
  Ac 11:17

j Mt 16:19
  Ac 2:38

CHAP. 11
k Ac 10:45
  Ga 2:12

Second Col.
a Ac 10:10-16

b Ac 10:17-20

c Ac 10:30-33

d Ac 2:1, 4
  Ac 10:44, 45

e Mt 3:11
  Mr 1:8
  Lu 3:16
  Ac 1:5

f Joe 2:28
  Joh 1:33
  Ac 2:17

10:39 *Or "tree." **10:40** *Or "visible." **10:45** *Or "faithful ones." **10:46** *Lit., "in tongues." **11:2** *Or "contend with."

11:5 *Lit., "some sort of vessel." **11:6** *Or "creeping things."

have believed in the Lord Jesus Christ, who was I that I should be able to hinder God?"*ª

18 When they heard these things, they stopped objecting,* and they glorified God, saying: "So, then, God has also granted to people of the nations repentance leading to life."ᵇ

19 Now those who had been scattered* by the tribulation that arose over Stephen went as far as Phoe·ni′cia, Cy′prus, and Antioch, but they spoke the word only to the Jews.ᵈ **20** However, some of the men among them from Cy′prus and Cy·re′ne came to Antioch and began talking to the Greek-speaking people, declaring the good news of the Lord Jesus. **21** Furthermore, the hand of Jehovah* was with them, and a great number became believers and turned to the Lord.ᵉ

22 The report about them reached the ears of the congregation in Jerusalem, and they sent out Bar′na·basᶠ as far as Antioch. **23** When he arrived and saw the undeserved kindness of God, he rejoiced and began to encourage them all to continue in the Lord with heartfelt resolve;ᵍ **24** for he was a good man and full of holy spirit and faith. And a considerable crowd was added to the Lord.ʰ **25** So he went to Tarsus to make a thorough search for Saul.ⁱ **26** After he found him, he brought him to Antioch. So for a whole year they assembled with them in the congregation and taught quite a crowd, and it was first in Antioch that the disciples were by divine providence called Christians.ʲ

27 In those days prophetsᵏ came down from Jerusalem to Antioch. **28** One of them

named Ag′a·busª stood up and foretold through the spirit that a great famine was about to come on the entire inhabited earth,ᵇ which, in fact, did take place in the time of Claudius. **29** So the disciples determined, each according to what he could afford,ᶜ to send relief*ᵈ to the brothers living in Ju·de′a; **30** and this they did, sending it to the elders by the hand of Bar′na·bas and Saul.ᵉ

12 About that time Herod the king began mistreating some of those of the congregation.ᶠ **2** He put James the brother of Johnᵍ to death by the sword.ʰ **3** When he saw that it was pleasing to the Jews, he also went on to arrest Peter. (This was during the days of the Unleavened Bread.)ⁱ **4** He seized him and put him in prison,ʲ turning him over to four shifts of four soldiers each to guard him, intending to bring him out* before the people after the Passover. **5** So Peter was being kept in the prison, but the congregation was intensely praying to God for him.ᵏ

6 When Herod was about to bring him out, that night Peter was sleeping bound with two chains between two soldiers, and guards in front of the door were keeping watch over the prison. **7** But look! Jehovah's* angel was standing there,ˡ and a light shone in the prison cell. Hitting Peter on the side, he woke him, saying: "Get up quickly!" And the chains fell off his hands.ᵐ **8** The angel said to him: "Get dressed* and put on your sandals." He did so. Finally he said to him: "Put your outer garment on, and keep following me." **9** And he went out and kept following him, but

---

CHAP. 11
a Ac 10:47

b Isa 11:10
Ac 17:30
Ro 10:12
Ro 15:8, 9

c Ac 8:1

d Mt 10:5, 6

e Ac 2:47
Ac 9:35

f Ac 4:36, 37

g Ac 13:43
Ac 14:21, 22

h Ac 2:47
Ac 4:4
Ac 5:14
Ac 9:31

i Ac 21:39

j Ac 9:2

k 1Co 12:28
Eph 4:11

Second Col.
a Ac 21:10, 11

b Mt 24:7

c 2Co 8:12

d Ga 2:10

e Ac 12:25

CHAP. 12
f Joh 15:20

g Mt 4:21

h Mt 20:20-23
Lu 11:49

i Ex 12:15
Ex 23:15
Le 23:6

j Lu 21:12

k 2Co 1:11

l Ps 34:7
Heb 1:7, 14

m Ac 5:18, 19

11:17 *Or "stand in God's way?" **11:18** *Lit., "they became silent." **11:21; 12:7** *See App. A5.   **11:29** *Or "a relief ministration." **12:4** *Or "bring him out to trial." **12:8** *Or "Gird yourself."

he did not know that what was happening through the angel was real. In fact, he thought he was seeing a vision. **10** Going past the first sentinel guard and the second, they reached the iron gate leading into the city, and this opened to them by itself. After they went out, they made their way down one street, and immediately the angel departed from him. **11** And Peter, realizing what was happening, said: "Now I know for sure that Jehovah* sent his angel and rescued me from Herod's hand and from everything that the Jews were expecting to happen."[a]

12 After he realized this, he went to the house of Mary the mother of John who was called Mark,[b] where quite a few were gathered together and were praying. **13** When he knocked at the door of the gateway, a servant girl named Rhoda came to answer the call. **14** On recognizing the voice of Peter, she was so overjoyed that she did not open the gate, but ran inside and reported that Peter was standing at the gateway. **15** They said to her: "You are out of your mind." But she kept insisting that it was so. They began to say: "It is his angel." **16** But Peter remained there, knocking. When they opened the door, they saw him and were astonished. **17** But he motioned to them with his hand to be silent and told them in detail how Jehovah* had brought him out of the prison, and he said: "Report these things to James[c] and the brothers." With that he went out and traveled to another place.

18 Now when it became day, there was quite a disturbance among the soldiers over what had become of Peter. **19** Herod made a diligent search for him,

and not finding him, he interrogated the guards and commanded them to be led off to punishment;[a] and he went down from Ju·de′a to Caes·a·re′a and spent some time there.

20 Now he was in an angry* mood against the people of Tyre and Si′don. So they came to him with one purpose, and after persuading Blastus, the man in charge of the king's household affairs,# they sued for peace, because their country was supplied with food from the land of the king. **21** On a set day, Herod clothed himself with royal raiment and sat down on the judgment seat and began giving them a public address. **22** Then the people who were assembled began shouting: "A god's voice, and not a man's!" **23** Instantly the angel of Jehovah* struck him, because he did not give the glory to God, and he was eaten up with worms and died.

24 But the word of Jehovah* went on growing and spreading.[b]

25 As for Bar′na·bas[c] and Saul, after fully carrying out the relief work in Jerusalem,[d] they returned and took along with them John,[e] the one also called Mark.

13 Now in Antioch there were prophets and teachers in the local congregation:[f] Bar′na·bas, Sym′e·on who was called Ni′ger, Lucius of Cy·re′ne, Man′a·en who was educated with Herod the district ruler, and Saul. **2** As they were ministering# to Jehovah* and fasting, the holy spirit said: "Set aside for me Bar′na·bas and Saul[g] for the work to which I have called them."[h] **3** Then after fasting and praying, they laid their hands on them and sent them off.

CHAP. 12
a 2Pe 2:9

b Ac 13:5
Ac 15:37, 38
Col 4:10

c Mt 13:55
Ac 15:13
Ac 21:18
1Co 15:7
Ga 1:19
Ga 2:9

Second Col.
a Ac 16:27

b Ac 6:7
Ac 19:20
Col 1:6

c Ac 4:36, 37

d Ac 11:29, 30

e Ac 13:5
Ac 15:37, 38

CHAP. 13
f 1Co 12:28
Eph 4:11, 12

g Ac 9:15

h 1Ti 2:7

12:11, 17, 23, 24; 13:2 *See App. A5.

12:20 *Or "a fighting." #Lit., "the king's bedchamber." 13:2 #Or "publicly ministering."

4 So these men, sent out by the holy spirit, went down to Se·leu′cia, and from there they sailed away to Cy′prus. **5** When they arrived in Sal′a·mis, they began proclaiming the word of God in the synagogues of the Jews. They also had John as an attendant.*ᵃ

6 When they had gone through the whole island as far as Pa′phos, they met up with a Jewish man named Bar-Je′sus, who was a sorcerer and a false prophet. **7** He was with the proconsul* Sergius Paulus, an intelligent man. Calling Bar′na·bas and Saul to him, this man was eager to hear the word of God. **8** But El′y·mas the sorcerer (for that is how his name is translated) began opposing them, trying to turn the proconsul away from the faith. **9** Then Saul, also called Paul, becoming filled with holy spirit, looked at him intently **10** and said: "O man full of every sort of fraud and every sort of villainy, you son of the Devil,ᵇ you enemy of everything righteous, will you not quit distorting the right ways of Jehovah?* **11** Look! Jehovah's* hand is upon you, and you will be blind, not seeing the sunlight for a time." Instantly a thick mist and darkness fell on him, and he went around trying to find someone to lead him by the hand. **12** Then the proconsul, on seeing what had happened, became a believer, for he was astounded at the teaching of Jehovah.*

13 Now Paul and his companions put out to sea from Pa′phos and arrived at Perga in Pam·phyl′i·a. But Johnᶜ left them and returned to Jerusalem.ᵈ **14** However, they went on from Perga and came to Antioch in Pi-sid′i·a. And going into the synagogueᵃ on the Sabbath day, they took a seat. **15** After the public reading of the Lawᵇ and the Prophets, the presiding officers of the synagogue sent word to them, saying: "Men, brothers, if you have any word of encouragement for the people, tell it." **16** So Paul stood up, and motioning with his hand, he said:

"Men, Israelites and you others who fear God, listen. **17** The God of this people Israel chose our forefathers, and he exalted the people while they lived as foreigners in the land of Egypt and brought them out of it with an uplifted arm.ᶜ **18** And for a period of about 40 years, he put up with them in the wilderness.ᵈ **19** After destroying seven nations in the land of Ca′naan, he assigned their land as an inheritance.ᵉ **20** All of that was during about 450 years.

"After this he gave them judges until Samuel the prophet.ᶠ **21** But afterward they demanded a king,ᵍ and God gave them Saul the son of Kish, a man of the tribe of Benjamin,ʰ for 40 years. **22** After removing him, he raised up for them David as king,ⁱ about whom he bore witness and said: 'I have found David the son of Jes′seʲ a man agreeable to my heart;ᵏ he will do all the things I desire.' **23** According to his promise, from the offspring* of this man, God has brought to Israel a savior, Jesus.ˡ **24** Before the arrival of that one, John had preached publicly to all the people of Israel baptism in symbol of repentance.ᵐ **25** But as John was finishing his course, he would say: 'What do you suppose I am? I am not he. But look! One is coming after me the sandals of whose feet I am not worthy to untie.'ⁿ

CHAP. 13

a Ac 12:25

b Joh 8:44

c Ac 12:12

d Ac 15:37, 38

Second Col.

a Ac 17:1, 2
Ac 18:4
Ac 19:8

b Ac 15:21

c Ex 6:1, 6
De 7:6, 8

d Ex 16:35
Nu 14:33, 34

e De 7:1
Jos 14:1, 2

f Jg 2:16
1Sa 3:20

g 1Sa 8:4, 5

h 1Sa 10:21
1Sa 11:15

i 1Sa 16:12, 13
Ps 89:20

j 1Sa 16:1

k 1Sa 13:13, 14

l 2Sa 7:12
Isa 11:1
Lu 1:31, 32
Lu 1:68, 69

m Mt 3:1, 6

n Mt 3:11
Lu 3:16

13:5 *Or "assistant." **13:7** *The Roman governor of a province. See Glossary. **13:10-12** *See App. A5.

13:23 *Lit., "seed."

26 "Men, brothers, you descendants of Abraham's family and those others among you who fear God, the word of this salvation has been sent to us.ᵃ **27** For the inhabitants of Jerusalem and their rulers did not recognize this one, but when acting as judges, they fulfilled the things spoken by the Prophets,ᵇ which are read aloud every sabbath. **28** Even though they found no cause for death,ᶜ they demanded of Pilate to have him executed.ᵈ **29** And when they had accomplished all the things written about him, they took him down from the stake* and laid him in a tomb.#ᵉ **30** But God raised him up from the dead,ᶠ **31** and for many days he became visible to those who had gone with him from Gal'i·lee up to Jerusalem. These are now his witnesses to the people.ᵍ

32 "So we are declaring to you the good news about the promise made to the forefathers. **33** God has completely fulfilled it to us, their children, by resurrecting Jesus;ʰ just as it is written in the second psalm: 'You are my son; today I have become your father.'ⁱ **34** And the fact that He resurrected him from the dead never again to return to corruption, He has stated in this way: 'I will give you the expressions of loyal love promised to David, which are faithful.'*ʲ **35** So it also says in another psalm: 'You will not allow your loyal one to see corruption.'ᵏ **36** David, on the one hand, rendered service to God* in his own generation, fell asleep in death, was laid with his forefathers, and did see corruption.ˡ

37 On the other hand, the one whom God raised up did not see corruption.ᵃ

38 "Let it therefore be known to you, brothers, that through this one a forgiveness of sins is being proclaimed to you,ᵇ **39** and that from all the things from which you could not be declared guiltless by means of the Law of Moses,ᶜ everyone who believes is declared guiltless by means of this one.ᵈ **40** Therefore, watch out that what is said in the Prophets does not come upon you: **41** 'Look at it, you scorners, and be amazed, and perish, for I am doing a work in your days, a work that you will never believe even if anyone relates it to you in detail.'"ᵉ

42 Now when they were going out, the people pleaded with them to speak about these matters on the following Sabbath. **43** So after the synagogue assembly was dismissed, many of the Jews and the proselytes who worshipped God followed Paul and Bar'na·bas, who, as they spoke to them, urged them to remain in the undeserved kindness of God.ᶠ

44 The next Sabbath nearly all the city gathered together to hear the word of Jeho·vah.* **45** When the Jews saw the crowds, they were filled with jealousy and began blasphemously contradicting the things Paul was saying.ᵍ **46** Then Paul and Bar'na·bas boldly said to them: "It was necessary for the word of God to be spoken first to you.ʰ Since you are rejecting it and do not judge yourselves worthy of everlasting life, look! we turn to the nations.ⁱ **47** For Jeho·vah* has commanded us in these words: 'I have appointed you as a light of nations, for you to be

---

CHAP. 13
a Mt 10:5, 6
Lu 24:47, 48

b Isa 53:7, 8

c Mt 26:59, 60
Lu 23:13-15
Joh 19:4

d Mt 27:22, 23
Joh 19:15

e Mt 27:59, 60
Joh 19:40-42

f Mt 28:5, 6
Ac 2:24

g Mt 28:16
Ac 1:3
Ac 3:15
1Co 15:4-7

h Ro 1:4

i Ps 2:7
Heb 1:5
Heb 5:5

j Isa 55:3

k Ps 16:10
Ac 2:31

l Ac 2:29

Second Col.
a Ac 2:27

b Lu 24:46, 47
Ac 5:31
Ac 10:43

c Heb 10:1

d Isa 53:11
Ro 3:28
Ro 5:18
Ro 8:3
Heb 7:19

e Hab 1:5

f Ac 11:23
Ac 14:21, 22

g Ac 14:1, 2
Ac 17:4, 5

h Mt 10:5, 6
Ac 3:25, 26
Ro 1:16

i Lu 2:29-32
Ac 18:5, 6
Ro 10:19

13:29 *Or "tree." #Or "memorial tomb." 13:34 *Or "trustworthy; reliable." 13:36 *Or "served the will of God."

13:44, 47 *See App. A5.

a salvation to the ends of the earth.'"[a]

48 When those of the nations heard this, they began to rejoice and to glorify the word of Jehovah,* and all those who were rightly disposed for everlasting life became believers. **49** Furthermore, the word of Jehovah* was being spread throughout the whole country. **50** But the Jews incited the prominent women who were God-fearing and the principal men of the city, and they stirred up persecution[b] against Paul and Bar′na·bas and threw them outside their boundaries. **51** So they shook the dust off their feet against them and went to I·co′ni·um.[c] **52** And the disciples continued to be filled with joy[d] and holy spirit.

14 Now in I·co′ni·um they entered together into the synagogue of the Jews and spoke in such a manner that a great multitude of both Jews and Greeks became believers. **2** But the Jews who did not believe stirred up and wrongly influenced the people* of the nations against the brothers.[e] **3** So they spent considerable time speaking with boldness by the authority of Jehovah,* who bore witness to the word of his undeserved kindness by allowing signs and wonders* to be performed through them.[f] **4** However, the multitude of the city was divided; some were for the Jews but others for the apostles. **5** When both the people of the nations and the Jews with their rulers made an attempt to treat them insolently and stone them,[g] **6** they were informed of it, and they fled to the cities of Lyc·a·o′ni·a, Lys′tra and Der′be, and to the surrounding country.[h]

7 There they went on declaring the good news.

8 Now in Lys′tra there was a man sitting down whose feet were crippled. He was lame from birth and had never walked. **9** This man was listening to Paul as he was speaking. Paul, looking intently at him and seeing that he had faith to be made well,[a] **10** said with a loud voice: "Stand up on your feet." So the man leaped up and began walking.[b] **11** When the crowds saw what Paul had done, they cried out in the Lyc·a·o′ni·an language: "The gods have become like humans and have come down to us!"[c] **12** And they started calling Bar′na·bas Zeus, but Paul Her′mes, since he was taking the lead in speaking. **13** And the priest of Zeus, whose temple was at the entrance of the city, brought bulls and garlands* to the gates and wanted to offer sacrifices with the crowds.

14 However, when the apostles Bar′na·bas and Paul heard of it, they ripped their garments and leaped out into the crowd and cried out: **15** "Men, why are you doing these things? We too are humans having the same infirmities as you have.[d] And we are declaring the good news to you, for you to turn from these vain things to the living God, who made the heaven and the earth and the sea and all the things in them.[e] **16** In past generations he permitted all the nations to go on in their ways,[f] **17** although he did not leave himself without witness[g] in that he did good, giving you rains from heaven and fruitful seasons,[h] satisfying you with food and filling your hearts with gladness."[i] **18** And yet despite saying these things, they barely

---

13:48, 49; 14:3 *See App. A5. **14:2** * Or "the souls of the people." **14:3** * Or "portents."

14:13 * Or "wreaths."

CHAP. 13
a Isa 49:6
  Ac 1:8

b Mt 23:34
  Ac 14:2, 19
  Ac 17:5

c Mt 10:14
  Lu 9:5

d Mt 5:12

CHAP. 14
e Ac 13:45

f Ac 19:11
  Heb 2:3, 4

g Ac 14:19

h Mt 10:23

Second Col.
a Mt 9:28

b Isa 35:6

c Ac 28:3-6

d Ac 10:25, 26

e Ex 20:11
  Ps 146:6

f Ac 17:30

g Ac 17:26, 27
  Ro 1:20

h Ps 147:8
  Jer 5:24
  Mt 5:45

i Ps 145:16

restrained the crowds from sacrificing to them.

19 But Jews arrived from Antioch and I·co′ni·um and persuaded the crowds,[a] and they stoned Paul and dragged him outside the city, imagining that he was dead.[b] 20 However, when the disciples surrounded him, he got up and entered the city. On the next day he left with Bar′na·bas for Der′be.[c] 21 After declaring the good news to that city and making quite a few disciples, they returned to Lys′tra, I·co′ni·um, and Antioch. 22 There they strengthened the disciples,*[d] encouraging them to remain in the faith and saying: "We must enter into the Kingdom of God through many tribulations."[e] 23 Moreover, they appointed elders for them in each congregation,[f] offering prayer with fasting,[g] and they entrusted them to Jehovah,* in whom they had become believers.

24 Then they went through Pi·sid′i·a and came into Pam·phyl′i·a,[h] 25 and after proclaiming the word in Perga, they went down to At·ta·li′a. 26 From there they sailed off for Antioch, where they had been entrusted to the undeserved kindness of God for the work they had now completed.[i]

27 When they had arrived and had gathered the congregation together, they related the many things God had done by means of them, and that he had opened to the nations the door to faith.[j] 28 So they spent considerable time with the disciples.

15 Now some men came down from Ju·de′a and began to teach the brothers: "Unless you get circumcised according to the custom of Moses,[k] you cannot be saved." 2 But after quite a bit

of dissension and disputing by Paul and Bar′na·bas with them, it was arranged for Paul, Bar′na·bas, and some of the others to go up to the apostles and elders in Jerusalem[a] regarding this issue.*

3 So after being escorted partway by the congregation, these men continued on through both Phoe·ni′cia and Sa·mar′i·a, relating in detail the conversion of people of the nations and bringing great joy to all the brothers. 4 On arriving in Jerusalem, they were kindly received by the congregation and the apostles and the elders, and they related the many things God had done by means of them. 5 But some of those of the sect of the Pharisees who had become believers stood up from their seats and said: "It is necessary to circumcise them and command them to observe the Law of Moses."[b]

6 So the apostles and the elders gathered together to look into this matter. 7 After much intense discussion* had taken place, Peter rose and said to them: "Men, brothers, you well know that from early days God made the choice among you that through my mouth people of the nations should hear the word of the good news and believe.[c] 8 And God, who knows the heart,[d] bore witness by giving them the holy spirit,[e] just as he did to us also. 9 And he made no distinction at all between us and them,[f] but purified their hearts by faith.[g] 10 So why are you now making a test of God by imposing on the neck of the disciples a yoke[h] that neither our forefathers nor we were capable of bearing?[i] 11 On the contrary, we have faith that we are saved through the undeserved

CHAP. 14
a Ac 17:13

b 2Co 11:25

c Ac 16:1

d Ac 11:22, 23

e Mt 10:38
Joh 15:19
Ro 8:17
1Th 3:4

f Tit 1:5

g Ac 13:2, 3

h Ac 13:13

i Ac 13:1, 2

j Ac 11:18

CHAP. 15
k Ge 17:9, 10
Ex 12:48
Le 12:2, 3

Second Col.
a Ga 2:1

b Ex 12:48
Ac 11:2, 3

c Ac 10:34, 35
Ac 11:16, 17

d 1Ch 28:9
Jer 11:20

e Ac 10:44, 45
Ac 11:15

f Ga 3:28

g Ga 2:15, 16
1Pe 1:22

h Ga 5:1

i Ga 3:10

14:22 *Or "the souls of the disciples."
14:23 *See App. A5.

15:2 *Or "dispute." 15:7 *Or "much disputing."

kindness of the Lord Jesus[a] in the same way that they are."[b]

12 At that the entire group became silent, and they began to listen to Bar·na·bas and Paul relate the many signs and wonders* that God had done through them among the nations. 13 After they finished speaking, James replied: "Men, brothers, hear me. 14 Sym'e·on[c] has related thoroughly how God for the first time turned his attention to the nations to take out of them a people for his name.[d] 15 And with this the words of the Prophets agree, just as it is written: 16 'After these things I will return and raise up again the tent* of David that is fallen down; I will rebuild its ruins and restore it, 17 so that the men who remain may earnestly seek Jehovah,* together with people of all the nations, people who are called by my name, says Jehovah,* who is doing these things,[e] 18 known from of old.'[f] 19 Therefore, my decision* is not to trouble those from the nations who are turning to God,[g] 20 but to write them to abstain from things polluted by idols,[h] from sexual immorality,*[i] from what is strangled,# and from blood.[j] 21 For from ancient times Moses has had those who preach him in city after city, because he is read aloud in the synagogues on every sabbath."[k]

22 Then the apostles and the elders, together with the whole congregation, decided to send chosen men from among them to Antioch, along with Paul and Bar·na·bas; they sent Judas who was called Bar'sab·bas and Si-las,[a] who were leading men among the brothers. 23 They wrote this and sent it through them:

"The apostles and the elders, your brothers, to those brothers in Antioch,[b] Syria, and Ci·li'cia who are from the nations: Greetings! 24 Since we have heard that some went out from among us and caused you trouble with what they have said,[c] trying to subvert you,* although we did not give them any instructions, 25 we have come to a unanimous decision to choose men to send to you together with our beloved Bar'na·bas and Paul, 26 men who have given up their lives* for the name of our Lord Jesus Christ.[d] 27 We are therefore sending Judas and Silas, so that they also may report the same things by word of mouth.[e] 28 For the holy spirit[f] and we ourselves have favored adding no further burden to you except these necessary things: 29 to keep abstaining from things sacrificed to idols,[g] from blood,[h] from what is strangled,#[i] and from sexual immorality.*[i] If you carefully keep yourselves from these things, you will prosper. Good health to you!"[△]

30 So when these men were dismissed, they went down to Antioch, and they gathered the whole group together and handed them the letter. 31 After reading it, they rejoiced over the encouragement. 32 And Judas and Silas, since they were also prophets, encouraged the brothers with many talks and strengthened them.[k] 33 After they had spent some time there, they were sent off in peace by the brothers to those who had sent them. 34 *— 35 But

---

CHAP. 15
a Isa 53:11
  Joh 1:17

b Mt 20:28

c Mt 10:2
  Ac 11:13
  2Pe 1:1

d 1Pe 2:9, 10

e Am 9:11, 12

f Isa 45:21

g Ac 15:10

h Ge 35:2
  Ex 20:3
  1Co 10:14

i 1Co 6:9, 10
  Col 3:5
  1Th 4:3

j Ge 9:4
  Le 3:17
  Le 7:26
  Le 17:10, 13
  Le 19:26
  De 12:23
  De 15:23
  1Sa 14:32, 33

k Ac 13:15
  2Co 3:15

Second Col.
a 1Th 1:1
  1Pe 5:12

b Ac 11:26

c Ac 15:1

d Ac 13:50
  1Co 15:30, 31
  2Co 11:23-26

e Ac 16:4

f Joh 16:13
  Ac 5:32

g Ge 35:2
  Ex 20:3
  Ex 34:15
  1Co 10:14

h Ge 9:4
  Le 3:17
  Le 7:26
  Le 17:10
  De 12:16, 23
  1Sa 14:32, 33

i Le 17:13

j Ge 39:7-9
  1Co 6:9, 10
  Eph 5:5
  Col 3:5
  1Th 4:5

k Ac 18:23

15:12 *Or "portents." 15:16 *Or "booth; house." 15:17 *See App. A5. 15:19 *Or "opinion." 15:20, 29 *Greek, por·nei'a. See Glossary. 15:20, 29 #Or "what is killed without draining its blood."

15:24 *Or "your souls." 15:26 *Or "souls." 15:29 △Or "Farewell." 15:34 *See App. A3.

Paul and Bar'na·bas stayed in Antioch, teaching and declaring, along with many others, the good news of the word of Jehovah.*

36 After some days, Paul said to Bar'na·bas: "Let us now# return and visit the brothers in every one of the cities where we proclaimed the word of Jehovah,* to see how they are."ᵃ **37** Bar'na·bas was determined to take along John, who was called Mark.ᵇ **38** Paul, however, was not in favor of taking him along with them, seeing that he had departed from them in Pam·phyl'i·a and had not gone with them to the work.ᶜ **39** At this there was a sharp burst of anger, so that they separated from each other; and Bar'na·basᵈ took Mark along and sailed away to Cy'prus. **40** Paul selected Silas and departed after he had been entrusted by the brothers to the undeserved kindness of Jehovah.*ᵉ **41** He went through Syria and Ci·li'cia, strengthening the congregations.

16 So he arrived at Der'be and also at Lys'tra.ᶠ And a disciple named Timothyᵍ was there, the son of a believing Jewish woman but of a Greek father, **2** and he was well-reported-on by the brothers in Lys'tra and I·co'ni·um. **3** Paul expressed the desire for Timothy to accompany him, and he took him and circumcised him because of the Jews in those places,ʰ for they all knew that his father was a Greek. **4** As they traveled on through the cities, they would deliver to them for observance the decrees that had been decided on by the apostles and the elders who were in Jerusalem.ⁱ **5** Then, indeed, the congregations continued to be made

firm in the faith and to increase in number day by day.

6 Moreover, they traveled through Phryg'i·a and the country of Ga·la'ti·a,ᵃ because they were forbidden by the holy spirit to speak the word in the province of Asia. **7** Further, when they came down to Mys'i·a, they made efforts to go into Bi·thyn'i·a,ᵇ but the spirit of Jesus did not permit them. **8** So they passed by* Mys'i·a and came down to Tro'as. **9** And during the night a vision appeared to Paul—a Mac·e·do'ni·an man was standing there urging him and saying: "Step over into Mac·e·do'ni·a and help us." **10** As soon as he had seen the vision, we tried to go into Mac·e·do'ni·a, drawing the conclusion that God had summoned us to declare the good news to them.

11 So we put out to sea from Tro'as and made a straight run to Sam'o·thrace, but on the following day to Ne·ap'o·lis; **12** and from there we went to Phi·lip'pi,ᶜ a colony, which is the principal city of the district of Mac·e·do'ni·a. We stayed in this city for some days. **13** On the Sabbath day we went outside the gate beside a river, where we thought there was a place of prayer, and we sat down and began speaking to the women who had assembled. **14** And a woman named Lyd'i·a, a seller of purple from the city of Thy·a·ti'raᵈ and a worshipper of God, was listening, and Jehovah* opened her heart wide to pay attention to the things Paul was saying. **15** Now when she and her household got baptized,ᵉ she urged us: "If you have considered me to be faithful to Jehovah,* come and stay at my house." And she just made us come.

CHAP. 15
a 2Co 11:28

b Ac 13:4, 5
Col 4:10
2Ti 4:11

c Ac 13:13

d Ac 4:36, 37

e Ac 14:26

CHAP. 16
f Ac 14:5-7
2Ti 3:11

g Ac 19:22
Ro 16:21
1Co 4:17
1Th 3:2
1Ti 1:2

h 1Co 9:20

i Ac 15:28, 29

Second Col.
a Ac 18:23

b 1Pe 1:1

c Php 1:1

d Re 1:11

e Ac 16:33
Ac 18:8

15:35, 36, 40; 16:14, 15 *See App. A5.
15:36 #Or possibly, "by all means."

16:8 *Or "passed through."

16 Now it happened that as we were going to the place of prayer, a servant girl with a spirit, a demon of divination,[a] met us. She supplied her masters with much profit by fortune-telling.* **17** This girl kept following Paul and us and crying out with the words: "These men are slaves of the Most High God[b] and are proclaiming to you the way of salvation." **18** She kept doing this for many days. Finally Paul got tired of it and turned and said to the spirit: "I order you in the name of Jesus Christ to come out of her." And it came out that very hour.[c]

19 Well, when her masters saw that their hope of profit was gone,[d] they seized Paul and Silas and dragged them into the marketplace to the rulers.[e] **20** Leading them up to the civil magistrates, they said: "These men are disturbing our city very much.[f] **21** and they are proclaiming customs that it is not lawful for us to adopt or practice, seeing that we are Romans." **22** And the crowd rose up together against them, and the civil magistrates, after tearing the garments off them, gave the command to beat them with rods.[g] **23** After they had inflicted many blows on them, they threw them into prison and ordered the jailer to guard them securely.[h] **24** Because he got such an order, he threw them into the inner prison and fastened their feet in the stocks.

25 But about the middle of the night, Paul and Silas were praying and praising God with song,[i] and the prisoners were listening to them. **26** Suddenly a great earthquake occurred, so that the foundations of the jail were shaken. Moreover, all the doors were instantly opened, and everyone's bonds came loose.[a] **27** When the jailer woke up and saw that the prison doors were open, he drew his sword and was about to kill himself, assuming that the prisoners had escaped.[b] **28** But Paul called out with a loud voice: "Do not hurt yourself, for we are all here!" **29** So he asked for lights and rushed in, and seized with trembling, he fell down before Paul and Silas. **30** He brought them outside and said: "Sirs, what must I do to get saved?" **31** They said: "Believe in the Lord Jesus, and you will get saved, you and your household."[c] **32** Then they spoke the word of Jehovah* to him together with all those in his house. **33** And he took them along in that hour of the night and washed their wounds. Then he and his entire household were baptized without delay.[d] **34** He brought them into his house and set a table before them, and he rejoiced greatly with all his household now that he had believed in God.

35 When it became day, the civil magistrates sent the constables to say: "Release those men." **36** The jailer reported their words to Paul: "The civil magistrates have sent men to have you two released. So come out now and go in peace." **37** But Paul said to them: "They flogged us publicly, uncondemned,* though we are Romans,[e] and threw us into prison. Are they now throwing us out secretly? No, indeed! Let them come themselves and escort us out." **38** The constables reported these words to the civil magistrates. These grew fearful when they heard that the men were Romans.[f] **39** So they

---

CHAP. 16
a Le 19:31
Le 20:6

b Mr 1:23, 24
Lu 4:41

c Mt 17:18
Mr 1:25, 26
Mr 1:34
Lu 9:1
Lu 10:17

d Ac 19:24, 25

e Mt 10:18

f Ac 17:6

g 1Th 2:2

h Lu 21:12

i Eph 5:19
Col 3:16

Second Col.
a Ac 5:18-20
Ac 12:7

b Ac 12:18, 19

c Joh 3:16
Joh 6:47

d Ac 8:12

e Ac 22:25
Ac 23:27

f Ac 22:27-29

16:16 *Or "practicing the art of prediction."

16:32 *See App. A5. 16:37 *Or "without a trial."

came and pleaded with them, and after escorting them out, they requested them to depart from the city. **40** But they came out of the prison and went to the home of Lyd′i·a; and when they saw the brothers, they encouraged them[a] and departed.

17 They now traveled through Am·phip′o·lis and Ap·ol·lo′ni·a and came to Thes·sa·lo·ni′ca,[b] where there was a synagogue of the Jews. **2** So according to Paul's custom[c] he went inside to them, and for three sabbaths he reasoned with them from the Scriptures,[d] **3** explaining and proving by references that it was necessary for the Christ to suffer[e] and to rise from the dead,[f] saying: "This is the Christ, this Jesus whom I am proclaiming to you." **4** As a result, some of them became believers and associated themselves with Paul and Silas,[g] and so did a great multitude of the Greeks who worshipped God, along with quite a few of the principal women.

5 But the Jews, getting jealous,[h] gathered together some wicked men who were loitering at the marketplace and formed a mob and proceeded to throw the city into an uproar. They assaulted the house of Ja′son and were seeking to have Paul and Silas brought out to the mob. **6** When they did not find them, they dragged Ja′son and some of the brothers to the city rulers, crying out: "These men who have overturned* the inhabited earth are present here also,[i] **7** and Ja′son has received them as his guests. All these men act in opposition to the decrees of Caesar, saying there is another king, Jesus."[j] **8** When they heard these things, the crowd and the city rulers were alarmed; **9** and after taking

sufficient security* from Ja′son and the others, they let them go.

10 Immediately by night the brothers sent both Paul and Silas to Be·roe′a. On arriving, they went into the synagogue of the Jews. **11** Now these were more noble-minded than those in Thes·sa·lo·ni′ca, for they accepted the word with the greatest eagerness of mind, carefully examining the Scriptures daily to see whether these things were so. **12** Therefore, many of them became believers, and so did quite a few of the reputable Greek women as well as some of the men. **13** But when the Jews from Thes·sa·lo·ni′ca learned that the word of God was also being proclaimed by Paul in Be·roe′a, they came there to incite and agitate the crowds.[a] **14** Then the brothers immediately sent Paul away to the sea,[b] but both Silas and Timothy remained behind there. **15** However, those accompanying Paul brought him as far as Athens, and they departed after receiving instructions that Silas and Timothy[c] should come to Paul as quickly as possible.

16 Now while Paul was waiting for them in Athens, his spirit within him became irritated on seeing that the city was full of idols. **17** So he began to reason in the synagogue with the Jews and the other people who worshipped God and every day in the marketplace with those who happened to be on hand. **18** But some of both the Ep·i·cu·re′an and the Sto′ic philosophers began disputing with him, and some were saying: "What is it this chatterer would like to tell?" Others: "He seems to be a proclaimer of foreign deities." This was because

---

CHAP. 16
a 2Co 1:3, 4

CHAP. 17
b 1Th 2:1

c Ac 9:19, 20
Ac 13:13, 14
Ac 14:1
Ac 18:4

d Ac 18:19

e Ps 22:7
Ps 34:20
Ps 69:21
Ps 118:22
Isa 50:6
Isa 53:3, 5

f Ps 16:10
Lu 24:45, 46

g Ac 15:22, 40

h Ac 13:45

i Ac 16:19-21

j Lu 23:1, 2
Joh 19:12

Second Col.
a Ac 14:2, 19

b Mt 10:23

c Ac 16:1, 2
1Th 3:2

17:6 *Or "stirred up trouble in."

17:9 *Or "after taking bail."

he was declaring the good news of Jesus and the resurrection.[a] **19** So they took hold of him and led him to the Ar·e·op′a·gus, saying: "Can we get to know what this new teaching is that you are speaking about? **20** For you are introducing some things that are strange to our ears, and we want to know what these things mean." **21** In fact, all Athenians and the foreigners staying* there would spend their leisure time doing nothing else but telling or listening to something new. **22** Paul now stood in the midst of the Ar·e·op′a·gus[b] and said:

"Men of Athens, I see that in all things you seem to be more given to the fear of the deities* than others are.[c] **23** For instance, while passing along and carefully observing your objects of veneration,* I found even an altar on which had been inscribed 'To an Unknown God.' Therefore, what you are unknowingly worshipping, this I am declaring to you. **24** The God who made the world and all the things in it, being, as he is, Lord of heaven and earth,[d] does not dwell in handmade temples;* **25** nor is he served by human hands as if he needed anything,[f] because he himself gives to all people life and breath[g] and all things. **26** And he made out of one man[h] every nation of men to dwell on the entire surface of the earth,[i] and he decreed the appointed times and the set limits of where men would dwell,[j] **27** so that they would seek God, if they might grope for him and really find him,[k] although, in fact, he is not far off from each one of us. **28** For by him we have life and move and exist, even as some of your own poets

have said, 'For we are also his children.'*

29 "Therefore, since we are the children* of God,[a] we should not think that the Divine Being is like gold or silver or stone, like something sculptured by the art and design of humans.[b] **30** True, God has overlooked the times of such ignorance;[c] but now he is declaring to all people everywhere that they should repent. **31** Because he has set a day on which the purposes to judge[d] the inhabited earth in righteousness by a man whom he has appointed, and he has provided a guarantee to all men by resurrecting him from the dead."[e]

32 Now when they heard of a resurrection of the dead, some began to scoff,[f] while others said: "We will hear you again about this." **33** So Paul left them, **34** but some men joined him and became believers. Among them were Di·o·nys′i·us, who was a judge of the court of the Ar·e·op′a·gus, and a woman named Dam′a·ris, and others besides them.

18 After this he departed from Athens and came to Corinth. **2** And he found a Jew named Aq′ui·la,[g] a native of Pon′tus who had recently come from Italy with Pris·cil′la his wife, because Claudius had ordered all the Jews to leave Rome. So he went to them, **3** and because he had the same trade, he stayed at their home and worked with them,[h] for they were tentmakers by trade. **4** He would give a talk* in the synagogue[i] every sabbath[j] and would persuade Jews and Greeks.

5 When, now, both Silas[k] and Timothy[l] came down from Mac·e·do′ni·a, Paul began to be in-

---

CHAP. 17
a Joh 5:28, 29
  Joh 11:25
  1Co 15:12

b Ac 17:33, 34

c Ac 17:16

d Ps 146:6

e 1Ki 8:27

f Ps 50:12

g Isa 42:5

h Ge 5:2

i Ge 1:28

j De 2:5, 19
  De 32:8
  Ps 74:17

k De 4:29
  Ps 145:18
  Ro 1:20

Second Col.
a Ge 1:27

b De 5:8
  Isa 37:19
  Isa 40:18-20
  Isa 46:5

c Eph 4:17, 18

d Ps 96:13
  Ps 98:9
  Joh 5:22
  Ac 10:42

e Joh 11:25
  Ac 2:24
  Ac 13:32, 33

f 1Co 1:23

CHAP. 18
g Ac 18:24, 26
  1Co 16:19
  2Ti 4:19

h Ac 20:34
  1Co 4:11, 12
  1Co 9:15
  1Th 2:9
  2Th 3:8, 10

i Mt 4:23

j Ac 17:2

k Ac 15:27
  Ac 17:14

l Ac 16:1, 2
  1Th 3:6

17:21 *Or "visiting." 17:22 *Or "more religious." 17:23 *Or "worship." 17:28, 29 *Or "progeny." 18:4 *Or "He would reason with them."

tensely occupied with the word, witnessing to the Jews to prove that Jesus is the Christ.[a] 6 But after they kept on opposing him and speaking abusively, he shook out his garments[b] and said to them: "Let your blood be on your own heads.[c] I am clean.[d] From now on I will go to people of the nations."[e] 7 So he transferred from there* and went into the house of a man named Titius Justus, a worshipper of God, whose house adjoined the synagogue. 8 But Cris'pus,[f] the presiding officer of the synagogue, became a believer in the Lord, along with all his household. And many of the Corinthians who heard began to believe and be baptized. 9 Moreover, the Lord said to Paul in a vision by night: "Do not be afraid, but keep on speaking and do not keep silent, 10 for I am with you[g] and no man will assault you to harm you; for I have many people in this city." 11 So he stayed there for a year and six months, teaching the word of God among them.

12 While Gal'li·o was proconsul* of A·cha'ia, the Jews made a concerted attack against Paul and led him to the judgment seat, 13 saying: "This man is persuading people to worship God in a way contrary to the law." 14 But as Paul was about to speak, Gal'li·o said to the Jews: "If, indeed, it were some wrong or a serious crime, O Jews, it would be reasonable for me to hear you out patiently. 15 But if it is controversies over speech and names and your own law,[h] you yourselves must see to it. I do not wish to be a judge of these things." 16 With that he drove them away from

the judgment seat. 17 So they all seized Sos'the·nes,[a] the presiding officer of the synagogue, and began beating him in front of the judgment seat. But Gal'li·o would not get involved at all with these things.

18 However, after staying quite a few days longer, Paul said good-bye to the brothers and sailed away for Syria, accompanied by Pris·cil'la and Aq'ui·la. He had his hair clipped short in Cen'chre·ae,[b] for he had made a vow. 19 So they arrived at Eph'e·sus, and he left them there; but he entered the synagogue and reasoned with the Jews.[c] 20 Although they kept requesting him to stay longer, he would not consent 21 but said good-bye and told them: "I will return to you again, if Jehovah* is willing." And he put out to sea from Eph'e·sus 22 and came down to Caes·a·re'a. And he went up* and greeted the congregation and then went down to Antioch.[d]

23 After spending some time there, he departed and went from place to place through the country of Ga·la'ti·a and Phryg'i·a,[e] strengthening all the disciples.[f]

24 Now a Jew named A·pol'los,[g] a native of Alexandria, arrived in Eph'e·sus; he was an eloquent man who was well-versed in the Scriptures. 25 This man had been instructed# in the way of Jehovah,* and aglow with the spirit, he was speaking and teaching accurately the things about Jesus, but he was acquainted only with the baptism of John. 26 He began to speak boldly in the synagogue, and when Pris·cil'la and Aq'ui·la[h] heard him, they took him into their company and explained the

---

CHAP. 18

a Ac 17:2, 3
Ac 28:23

b Mt 10:14

c Eze 33:4

d Ac 20:26

e Ac 13:46
Ac 28:28
Ro 1:16

f 1Co 1:14

g Mt 28:20

h Ac 23:29
Ac 25:19

Second Col.

a 1Co 1:1

b Ro 16:1

c Ac 17:2

d Ac 15:36

e Ac 16:6

f Ac 14:21, 22
Ac 15:32

g Ac 19:1
1Co 1:12
1Co 3:5, 6

h Ro 16:3
1Co 16:19

18:7 *That is, the synagogue. 18:12 *The Roman governor of a province. See Glossary.

18:21, 25 *See App. A5. 18:22 *To Jerusalem, apparently. 18:25 #Or "orally instructed."

way of God more accurately to him. **27** Further, because he wanted to go across to A·cha′ia, the brothers wrote to the disciples, urging them to receive him kindly. So when he got there, he greatly helped those who through God's undeserved kindness had become believers; **28** for publicly and with great intensity he thoroughly proved the Jews to be wrong, showing them from the Scriptures that Jesus is the Christ.[a]

19 In the course of events, while A·pol′los[b] was in Corinth, Paul went through the inland regions and came down to Eph′e·sus.[c] There he found some disciples **2** and said to them: "Did you receive holy spirit when you became believers?" They replied to him: "Why, we have never heard that there is a holy spirit." **3** So he said: "In what, then, were you baptized?" They said: "In John's baptism."[e] **4** Paul said: "John baptized with the baptism in symbol of repentance,[f] telling the people to believe in the one coming after him,[g] that is, in Jesus." **5** On hearing this, they got baptized in the name of the Lord Jesus. **6** And when Paul laid his hands on them, the holy spirit came upon them,[h] and they began speaking in foreign languages and prophesying.[i] **7** There were about 12 men in all.

8 Entering the synagogue,[j] for three months he spoke with boldness, giving talks and reasoning persuasively about the Kingdom of God.[k] **9** But when some stubbornly refused to believe,* speaking injuriously about The Way[l] before the crowd, he withdrew from them[m]

and separated the disciples from them, giving talks daily in the school auditorium of Ty·ran′nus. **10** This went on for two years, so that all those living in the province of Asia heard the word of the Lord, both Jews and Greeks.

11 And God kept performing extraordinary powerful works through the hands of Paul,[a] **12** so that even cloths and aprons that had touched his body were carried to the sick,[b] and the diseases left them, and the wicked spirits came out.[c] **13** But some of the Jews who traveled around casting out demons also tried to use the name of the Lord Jesus over those who had wicked spirits; they would say: "I solemnly charge you by Jesus whom Paul preaches."[d] **14** Now there were seven sons of a Jewish chief priest named Sce′va doing this. **15** But in answer the wicked spirit said to them: "I know Jesus[e] and I am acquainted with Paul;[f] but who are you?" **16** At that the man with the wicked spirit leaped on them, overpowered them one after the other, and prevailed against them, so that they fled naked and wounded out of that house. **17** This became known to all, both the Jews and the Greeks who lived in Eph′e·sus; and fear fell upon them all, and the name of the Lord Jesus went on being magnified. **18** And many of those who had become believers would come and confess and report their practices openly. **19** Indeed, quite a number of those who practiced magical arts brought their books together and burned them up before everybody.[g] And they calculated their value and found them worth 50,000 pieces of silver. **20** Thus in a mighty way, the

---

19:9 *Or "went on hardening themselves and not believing."

CHAP. 18
a De 18:15
  Ps 16:10
  Isa 7:14
  Mic 5:2

CHAP. 19
b Ac 18:24
  1Co 3:5, 6

c 1Co 16:8, 9

d Ac 2:38

e Ac 18:24, 25

f Mt 3:11
  Mr 1:4

g Joh 1:15, 30

h Ac 8:14, 17

i Ac 2:1, 4
  Ac 10:45, 46
  1Co 12:8, 10

j Ac 17:2

k Ac 1:3
  Ac 28:30, 31

l Ac 9:1, 2
  Ac 22:4

m Mt 10:14

Second Col.
a Ac 14:3

b Mr 6:56
  Ac 5:15

c Mt 10:1

d Ac 16:18

e Mt 8:28, 29
  Mr 1:23, 24
  Lu 4:33, 34

f Ac 16:16, 17

g De 18:10, 11

word of Jehovah* kept growing and prevailing.[a]

21 After these things had taken place, Paul resolved in his spirit that after going through Mac·e·do'ni·a[b] and A·cha'ia, he would travel to Jerusalem.[c] He said: "After going there, I must also see Rome."[d] 22 So he sent to Mac·e·do'ni·a two of those who ministered to him, Timo·thy[e] and E·ras'tus,[f] but he himself stayed on for some time in the province of Asia.

23 At that time quite a disturbance[g] arose concerning The Way.[h] 24 For a man named De·me'tri·us, a silversmith who made silver shrines of Ar'te·mis, brought considerable profit to the craftsmen. 25 He gathered them and others who worked at such things and said: "Men, you well know that from this business comes our prosperity. 26 Now you see and hear how, not only in Eph'e·sus[i] but in nearly all the province of Asia, this Paul has persuaded a considerable crowd and turned them to another opinion, saying that the gods made by hands are not really gods.[k] 27 Moreover, the danger exists not only that this business of ours will come into disrepute but also that the temple of the great goddess Ar'te·mis will be viewed as nothing, and she who is worshipped in the whole province of Asia and the inhabited earth will be deprived of her magnificence." 28 Hearing this and becoming full of anger, the men began crying out: "Great is Ar'te·mis of the E·phe'·sians!"

29 So the city became filled with confusion, and all together they rushed into the theater, dragging along with them Ga'·ius and Ar·is·tar'chus,[l] Mac·e·do'·ni·ans, traveling companions of

Paul. 30 For his part, Paul was willing to go inside to the people, but the disciples would not permit him. 31 Even some of the commissioners of festivals and games who were friendly to him sent word to him, pleading with him not to risk going into the theater. 32 Some were, in fact, crying out one thing and others something else; for the assembly was in confusion and the majority of them did not know the reason why they had come together. 33 So they brought Alexander out of the crowd, the Jews shoving him forward, and Alexander motioned with his hand and wanted to make his defense to the people. 34 But when they recognized that he was a Jew, they all started shouting in unison for about two hours: "Great is Ar'te·mis of the E·phe'sians!"

35 When the city recorder had finally quieted the crowd, he said: "Men of Eph'e·sus, who really is there among men who does not know that the city of the E·phe'sians is the temple keeper of the great Ar'te·mis and of the image that fell from heaven? 36 Since these things are indisputable, you should keep calm and not act rashly. 37 For you have brought these men here who are neither robbers of temples nor blasphemers of our goddess. 38 So if De·me'tri·us[a] and the craftsmen with him do have a case against someone, court days are held and there are proconsuls;* let them bring charges against one another. 39 But if you are searching for anything beyond that, it must be decided in a regular assembly. 40 For we are really in danger of being charged with sedition over today's affair, since there are no

CHAP. 19

a Ac 6:7
Ac 12:24
Col 1:6

b 1Co 16:5

c Ac 20:22

d Ac 23:11

e Ac 16:1, 2

f 2Ti 4:20

g 2Co 1:8

h Ac 9:1, 2
Ac 19:9
Ac 22:4

i Ac 16:16

j Eph 1:1

k Ac 17:29
1Co 8:4

l Ac 20:4
Col 4:10
Phm 23, 24

Second Col.

a Ac 19:24

19:20 *See App. A5.

19:38 *A proconsul was the Roman governor of a province. See Glossary.

grounds we could present as a reason for this disorderly mob." **41** And after saying this, he dismissed the assembly.

20 When the uproar had subsided, Paul sent for the disciples, and after he had encouraged them and said farewell, he began his journey to Mac·e·do'ni·a. **2** After going through those regions and giving many words of encouragement to the ones there, he arrived in Greece. **3** He spent three months there, but because a plot was hatched against him by the Jews[a] when he was about to set sail for Syria, he made up his mind to return through Mac·e·do'ni·a. **4** He was accompanied by Sop'a·ter the son of Pyr'rhus of Be·roe'a, Ar·is·tar'chus[b] and Se·cun'dus of the Thes·sa·lo'ni·ans, Ga'ius of Der'be, Timothy[c] and, from the province of Asia, Tych'i·cus[d] and Troph'i·mus.[e] **5** These men went on ahead and were waiting for us in Tro'as; **6** but we put out to sea from Phi·lip'pi after the days of the Unleavened Bread,[f] and within five days we came to them in Tro'as, and there we spent seven days.

7 On the first day of the week, when we were gathered together to have a meal, Paul began addressing them, as he was going to depart the next day; and he prolonged his speech until midnight. **8** So there were quite a few lamps in the upper room where we were gathered together. **9** Seated at the window, a young man named Eu'ty·chus sank into a deep sleep while Paul kept talking, and overcome by sleep, he fell down from the third story and was picked up dead. **10** But Paul went downstairs, threw himself on him and embraced him,[g] and said: "Stop making a commotion, for he is alive."[*h] **11** He then went up-

stairs and began the meal[*] and ate. He continued conversing for quite a while, until daybreak, and then he departed. **12** So they took the boy away alive and were comforted beyond measure.

13 We now went ahead to the ship and set sail for As'sos, where we were intending to take Paul aboard, for after giving instructions to this effect, he was intending to go there on foot. **14** So when he caught up with us in As'sos, we took him aboard and went to Mit·y·le'ne. **15** And sailing away from there the next day, we arrived off Chi'os, but the day after that, we touched at Sa'mos, and on the following day, we arrived at Mi·le'tus. **16** Paul had decided to sail past Eph'e·sus[a] so as not to spend any time in the province of Asia, for he was hurrying to get to Jerusalem[b] on the day of the Festival of Pentecost if he possibly could.

17 However, from Mi·le'tus he sent word to Eph'e·sus and called for the elders of the congregation. **18** When they came to him, he said to them: "You well know how I conducted myself among you from the first day I stepped into the province of Asia,[c] **19** slaving for the Lord with all humility[*d] and with tears and trials that befell me by the plots of the Jews, **20** while I did not hold back from telling you any of the things that were profitable[*] nor from teaching you publicly[e] and from house to house.[f] **21** But I thoroughly bore witness both to Jews and to Greeks about repentance[g] toward God and faith in our Lord Jesus.[f] **22** And now look! bound in[*] the spirit, I am traveling to Jerusalem, although not knowing what will happen to me

---

CHAP. 20
a Ac 23:12, 16
  2Co 11:23, 26

b Ac 27:2

c Ac 16:1, 2

d Eph 6:21
  Col 4:7
  2Ti 4:12

e Ac 21:29
  2Ti 4:20

f Ex 12:15
  Ex 23:15

g 1Ki 17:21, 22
  2Ki 4:32, 34

h Mt 9:23, 24
  Joh 11:39, 40
  Ac 9:39, 40

Second Col.
a Ac 18:21

b Ac 24:17

c Ac 19:9, 10

d 1Co 15:9
  1Th 2:6

e Mt 28:19, 20
  2Ti 4:2

f Ac 5:42

g Mr 1:14, 15

20:10 *Or "for his soul is in him."

20:11 *Lit., "broke the bread." 20:19 *Or "lowliness of mind." 20:20 *Or "for your good." 20:22 *Or "compelled by."

there, **23** except that from city to city the holy spirit repeatedly bears witness to me, saying that imprisonment and tribulations are waiting for me.[a] **24** Nevertheless, I do not consider my own life* of any importance to me,[#] if only I may finish my course[b] and the ministry that I received from the Lord Jesus, to bear thorough witness to the good news of the undeserved kindness of God.

25 "And now look! I know that none of you among whom I preached the Kingdom will ever see my face again. **26** So I call you to witness this very day that I am clean from the blood of all men,[c] **27** for I have not held back from telling you all the counsel* of God.[d] **28** Pay attention to yourselves[e] and to all the flock, among which the holy spirit has appointed you overseers,[f] to shepherd the congregation of God,[g] which he purchased with the blood of his own Son.[h] **29** I know that after my going away oppressive wolves will enter in among you[i] and will not treat the flock with tenderness, **30** and from among you yourselves men will rise and speak twisted things to draw away the disciples after themselves.[j]

31 "Therefore keep awake, and bear in mind that for three years,[k] night and day, I never stopped admonishing each one of you with tears. **32** And now I entrust you to God and to the word of his undeserved kindness, which word can build you up and give you the inheritance among all the sanctified ones.[l] **33** I have desired no man's silver or gold or clothing.[m] **34** You yourselves know that these hands have provided for my own needs[n] and the needs of those with me. **35** I have shown

you in all things that by working hard in this way,[a] you must assist those who are weak and must keep in mind the words of the Lord Jesus, when he himself said: 'There is more happiness in giving[b] than there is in receiving.'"

36 And when he had said these things, he knelt down with all of them and prayed. **37** Indeed, quite a bit of weeping broke out among them all, and they embraced Paul* and affectionately[#] kissed him, **38** for they were especially pained at the word he had spoken that they would not see his face anymore.[c] Then they accompanied him to the ship.

21 After tearing ourselves away from them and putting out to sea, we ran with a straight course and came to Cos, on the next day to Rhodes, and from there to Pat′a·ra. **2** When we found a ship that was crossing to Phoe·ni′cia, we went aboard and sailed away. **3** After coming in sight of the island of Cy′prus, we left it behind on the left side* and sailed on to Syria and landed at Tyre, where the ship was to unload its cargo. **4** We searched for and found the disciples and remained there for seven days. But through the spirit they repeatedly told Paul not to set foot in Jerusalem.[d] **5** So when our time there was over, we left and started on our way, but they all, together with the women and children, accompanied us until we were outside the city. And kneeling down on the beach, we prayed **6** and said good-bye to one another. Then we went aboard the ship, and they returned to their homes.

7 We then completed the voyage from Tyre and arrived at

CHAP. 20
a Ac 9:15, 16
  Ac 21:4, 11

b 2Ti 4:7

c Eze 33:8

d Mt 28:19, 20

e 1Ti 4:16

f 1Ti 3:1-7
  Tit 1:5-9
  Heb 13:17

g Joh 21:15
  Eph 4:11
  1Pe 5:2-4

h Mt 26:27, 28
  1Jo 1:7

i Mt 7:15
  2Th 2:3
  2Pe 2:1

j 1Ti 4:1
  2Ti 4:3, 4
  1Jo 2:18, 19

k Ac 19:9, 10

l Eph 1:18
  Col 1:12

m 1Sa 12:1, 3
  Mt 10:8
  1Co 9:11, 12
  2Co 7:2
  Tit 1:7

n Ac 18:3
  1Co 4:11, 12
  1Th 2:9

Second Col.
a Eph 4:28
  1Th 4:11, 12
  2Th 3:7, 8

b Pr 19:17
  Mt 10:8
  Lu 6:38

c Ac 20:25

CHAP. 21
d Ac 21:10-12

20:24 *Or "soul." #Or "of any value to me whatsoever." 20:27 *Or "the whole purpose."

20:37 *Lit., "fell upon Paul's neck." #Or "tenderly." 21:3 *Or "port side."

Ptol·e·ma'is, and we greeted the brothers and stayed one day with them. **8** The next day we left and came to Caes·a·re'a, and we entered the house of Philip the evangelizer, who was one of the seven men,[a] and we stayed with him. **9** This man had four unmarried* daughters who prophesied.[b] **10** But after we had stayed there for quite a number of days, a prophet named Ag'a·bus[c] came down from Ju·de'a. **11** And he came to us and took Paul's belt and tied his own feet and hands and said: "Thus says the holy spirit, 'The man to whom this belt belongs will be bound like this by the Jews in Jerusalem,[d] and they will give him into the hands of people of the nations.'"[e] **12** Now when we heard this, both we and those who were there began begging him not to go up to Jerusalem. **13** Then Paul answered: "What are you doing by weeping and trying to weaken my resolve?* Rest assured, I am ready not only to be bound but also to die at Jerusalem for the name of the Lord Jesus."[f] **14** When he would not be dissuaded, we stopped objecting* and said: "Let the will of Jehovah* take place."

15 Now after these days we prepared for the journey and started on our way to Jerusalem. **16** Some of the disciples from Caes·a·re'a also went with us, taking us to Mna'son of Cy'prus, an early disciple at whose home we were to be guests. **17** When we got to Jerusalem, the brothers welcomed us gladly. **18** But on the following day Paul went in with us to James,[g] and all the elders were present. **19** And he greeted them and be-

gan giving a detailed account of the things God did among the nations through his ministry.

20 After hearing this, they began to glorify God, but they said to him: "You see, brother, how many thousands of believers there are among the Jews, and they are all zealous for the Law.[a] **21** But they have heard it rumored about you that you have been teaching all the Jews among the nations an apostasy from Moses, telling them not to circumcise their children or to follow the customary practices.[b] **22** What, then, is to be done about it? They are certainly going to hear that you have arrived. **23** So do what we tell you: We have four men who have put themselves under a vow. **24** Take these men with you and cleanse yourself ceremonially together with them and take care of their expenses, so that they may have their heads shaved. Then everyone will know that there is nothing to the rumors they were told about you, but that you are walking orderly and you are also keeping the Law.[c] **25** As for the believers from among the nations, we have sent them our decision in writing that they should keep away from what is sacrificed to idols[d] as well as from blood,[e] from what is strangled,*[f] and from sexual immorality."*[g]

26 Then Paul took the men the next day and cleansed himself ceremonially along with them,[h] and he went into the temple to give notice of when the days for the ceremonial cleansing would be completed and the offering should be presented for each one of them.

21:9 *Lit., "virgin." 21:13 *Or "making me weak at heart?" 21:14 *Lit., "we became silent." *See App. A5.

21:25 *Or "what is killed without draining its blood." *Greek, por·nei'a. See Glossary.

CHAP. 21
a Ac 6:3, 5

b Joe 2:28
Ac 2:17
1Co 11:5

c Ac 11:27, 28

d Ac 20:22, 23
Ac 21:33

e Ac 9:15, 16

f Ac 20:24
2Co 4:10, 11
2Ti 4:6

g Ac 12:17
Ac 15:13
Ga 1:19
Ga 2:9
Jas 1:1

Second Col.
a Ac 15:1

b Ro 2:28, 29
1Co 7:18-20

c 1Co 9:20

d Ge 35:2
Ex 34:15

e Ge 9:4
Le 3:17
Le 17:10
1Sa 14:32, 33

f Le 17:13
De 12:23, 24

g Ac 15:28, 29
1Co 6:9
Col 3:5
1Th 4:3
1Pe 4:3

h 1Co 9:20

27 Now when the seven days were about to end, the Jews from Asia, on seeing him in the temple, stirred up the whole crowd, and they seized him, **28** shouting: "Men of Israel, help! This is the man who teaches everyone everywhere against our people and our Law and this place. And what is more, he even brought Greeks into the temple and has defiled this holy place."[a] **29** For they had previously seen Troph′i·mus[b] the E·phe′sian in the city with him, and they assumed that Paul had brought him into the temple. **30** The whole city was in an uproar, and the people came running together and seized Paul and dragged him outside the temple, and immediately the doors were closed. **31** While they were trying to kill him, word reached the commander of the army unit that all Jerusalem was in confusion; **32** and he immediately took soldiers and army officers and ran down to them. When they caught sight of the military commander and the soldiers, they stopped beating Paul.

33 Then the military commander came near and took him into custody and ordered that he be bound with two chains;[c] then he inquired who he was and what he had done. **34** But some in the crowd began shouting out one thing, and others something else. So being unable himself to learn anything for certain because of the disturbance, he commanded him to be brought to the soldiers' quarters. **35** But when he reached the stairs, he had to be carried by the soldiers because of the violence of the crowd, **36** for a crowd of the people kept following, crying out: "Do away with him!"

37 As he was about to be led into the soldiers' quarters, Paul said to the military commander: "Am I allowed to say something to you?" He said: "Can you speak Greek? **38** Are you not, then, the Egyptian who some time ago stirred up a sedition and led the 4,000 dagger men out into the wilderness?" **39** Then Paul said: "I am, in fact, a Jew,[a] of Tarsus[b] in Ci·li′cia, a citizen of no obscure city. So I beg you, permit me to speak to the people." **40** After he gave permission, Paul, standing on the stairs, motioned with his hand to the people. When a great silence fell, he addressed them in the Hebrew language,[c] saying:

22 "Men, brothers and fathers, hear my defense to you now."[d] **2** Well, when they heard that he was addressing them in the Hebrew language, they kept all the more silent, and he said: **3** "I am a Jew,[e] born in Tarsus in Ci·li′cia,[f] but educated in this city at the feet of Ga·ma′li·el,[g] instructed according to the strictness of the ancestral Law,[h] and zealous for God just as all of you are this day.[i] **4** I persecuted this Way to the point of death, binding and handing over to prisons both men and women,[j] **5** as the high priest and all the assembly of elders can bear witness. From them I also obtained letters to the brothers in Damascus, and I was on my way to bring those who were there in bonds to Jerusalem to be punished.

6 "But as I was traveling and getting near to Damascus, about midday, suddenly out of heaven a great light flashed all around me,[k] **7** and I fell to the ground and heard a voice say to me: 'Saul, Saul, why are you persecuting me?' **8** I answered: 'Who are you, Lord?' And he said to me: 'I am Jesus the Naz·a·rene′, whom you are persecuting.' **9** Now the men who were

---

CHAP. 21
a Ac 24:5, 6

b Ac 20:4
2Ti 4:20

c Ac 20:22, 23
Ac 21:10, 11

Second Col.
a Php 3:4, 5

b Ac 22:3

c Ac 26:14

CHAP. 22
d Php 1:7

e Ro 11:1

f Ac 21:39

g Ac 5:34

h Ac 26:4, 5

i Ga 1:14
Php 3:4-6

j Ac 8:3
Ac 9:1, 2
Ac 26:9-11
1Ti 1:12, 13

k Ac 9:3-8
Ac 26:13-15

with me did see the light, but they did not hear the voice of the one speaking to me. 10 At that I said: 'What should I do, Lord?' The Lord said to me: 'Rise, go into Damascus, and there you will be told about everything it is appointed for you to do.'[a] 11 But since I could not see anything because of the glory of that light, I arrived in Damascus led by the hand of those who were with me.

12 "Then a man named An·a·ni'as, a devout man according to the Law, well-reported-on by all the Jews living there, 13 came to me. He stood by me and said to me: 'Saul, brother, regain your sight!' And that very moment I looked up and saw him.[b] 14 He said: 'The God of our forefathers has chosen you to come to know his will and to see the righteous one[c] and to hear the voice of his mouth, 15 because you are to be a witness for him to all men of the things you have seen and heard.[d] 16 And now why are you delaying? Rise, get baptized, and wash your sins[e] away by your calling on his name.'[f]

17 "But when I had returned to Jerusalem[g] and was praying in the temple, I fell into a trance 18 and saw him saying to me: 'Hurry up and get out of Jerusalem quickly, because they will not accept your witness concerning me.'[h] 19 And I said: 'Lord, they themselves well know that I used to imprison and flog in one synagogue after another those believing in you;[i] 20 and when the blood of Stephen your witness was being spilled, I was standing by and approving and guarding the outer garments of those doing away with him.'[j] 21 And yet he said to me: 'Go, because I will send you out to nations far away.'"[k]

22 Now they kept listening to him down to this word. Then they raised their voices, saying: "Take such a man away from the earth, for he is not fit to live!" 23 Because they were crying out, throwing their outer garments about, and tossing dust into the air,[a] 24 the military commander ordered Paul to be brought into the soldiers' quarters and said that he should be interrogated under scourging, so that he could learn exactly why they were shouting against Paul this way. 25 But when they had stretched him out for the whipping, Paul said to the army officer standing there: "Is it lawful for you to scourge a Roman* who has not been condemned?"#[b] 26 Well, when the army officer heard this, he went to the military commander and reported it, saying: "What are you intending to do? For this man is a Roman." 27 So the military commander approached and said to him: "Tell me, are you a Roman?" He said: "Yes." 28 The military commander responded: "I purchased these rights as a citizen for a large sum of money." Paul said: "But I have them by birth."[c]

29 Immediately, therefore, the men who were about to interrogate him under torture backed away from him; and the military commander became afraid when he realized that he was a Roman and that he had bound him in chains.[d]

30 So the next day, because he wanted to know for sure just why he was being accused by the Jews, he released him and commanded the chief priests and all the San'he·drin to assemble. He then brought Paul down and had him stand among them.[e]

22:25 *Or "Roman citizen." #Or "has not had a trial?"

CHAP. 22
a Ac 26:16

b Ac 9:17, 18

c 1Co 9:1
1Co 15:8
Ga 1:15, 16

d Ac 23:11
Ac 26:16

e 1Co 6:11
1Jo 1:7
Re 1:5

f Ac 10:43

g Ac 9:26
Ga 1:18

h Ac 9:28, 29

i Ac 8:3

j Ac 7:58
Ac 8:1
1Ti 1:13, 15

k Ac 9:15
Ac 13:2
Ro 1:5
Ro 11:13
Ga 2:7
1Ti 2:7

Second Col.
a 2Sa 16:13

b Ac 16:37, 38
Ac 23:27

c Ac 16:37

d Ac 25:16

e Mt 10:17, 18
Lu 21:12

23 Looking intently at the San'he·drin, Paul said: "Men, brothers, I have behaved before God with a perfectly clear conscience[a] down to this day." **2** At this the high priest An·a·ni'as ordered those standing by him to strike him on the mouth. **3** Then Paul said to him: "God is going to strike you, you white-washed wall. Do you sit to judge me according to the Law and at the same time violate the Law by commanding me to be struck?" **4** Those standing by said: "Are you insulting the high priest of God?" **5** And Paul said: "Brothers, I did not know he was high priest. For it is written, 'You must not speak injuriously of a ruler of your people.'"[b]

6 Now Paul, knowing that the one part was made up of Saddu-cees but the other of Pharisees, cried out in the San'he·drin: "Men, brothers, I am a Pharisee,[c] a son of Pharisees. Over the hope of the resurrection of the dead I am being judged." **7** Because he said this, a dissension arose between the Pharisees and the Sadducees, and the assem-bly was split. **8** For the Saddu-cees say that there is neither res-urrection nor angel nor spirit, but the Pharisees accept* them all.[d] **9** So a great uproar broke out, and some of the scribes of the party of the Pharisees rose and began arguing fiercely, say-ing: "We find nothing wrong in this man, but if a spirit or an angel spoke to him[e]—." **10** Now when the dissension grew great, the military commander feared that Paul would be torn apart by them, and he commanded the soldiers to go down and snatch him from their midst and bring him into the soldiers' quarters.

11 But the following night the Lord stood by him and said: "Take courage![a] For just as you have been giving a thorough wit-ness about me in Jerusalem, so you must also bear witness in Rome."[b]

12 When it became day, the Jews formed a conspiracy and bound themselves with a curse, saying that they would nei-ther eat nor drink until they had killed Paul. **13** There were more than 40 men who formed this oath-bound conspiracy. **14** These men went to the chief priests and the elders and said: "We have solemnly bound our-selves with a curse* not to eat anything at all until we have killed Paul. **15** So now you together with the San'he·drin should inform the military com-mander that he should bring him down to you as though you want to examine his case more thor-oughly. But before he gets near, we will be ready to do away with him."

16 However, the son of Paul's sister heard of the ambush they were planning, and he entered the soldiers' quarters and re-ported it to Paul. **17** Paul then called one of the army officers to him and said: "Take this young man to the military command-er, for he has something to re-port to him." **18** So he brought him and led him to the mili-tary commander and said: "The prisoner Paul called me and asked me to bring this young man to you because he has some-thing to tell you." **19** The mili-tary commander took him by the hand and withdrew private-ly and asked him: "What do you have to report to me?" **20** He said: "The Jews have agreed to request you to bring Paul down to the San'he·drin tomorrow, as though they intend to learn more details about his case.[c] **21** But

---

CHAP. 23
a Ac 24:15, 16
2Co 1:12
Heb 13:18
1Pe 3:16

b Ex 22:28

c Ac 26:4, 5
Php 3:4, 5

d Ac 4:1, 2

e Ac 22:6, 7
Ac 22:17, 18

Second Col.
a Ac 18:9

b Ac 27:23, 24
Ac 28:23
Ac 28:30, 31

c Ac 23:15

23:8 *Or "publicly declare."

23:14 *Or "an oath."

do not let them persuade you, for more than 40 of their men are waiting to ambush him, and they have bound themselves with a curse* neither to eat nor to drink until they have killed him;[a] and they are now ready, waiting for the promise from you." 22 So the military commander let the young man go, after ordering him: "Do not tell anyone that you have informed me of this."

23 And he summoned two of the army officers and said: "Get 200 soldiers ready to march clear to Caes·a·re′a, also 70 horsemen and 200 spearmen, at the third hour of the night.* 24 Also, provide horses for Paul to ride, to take him safely to Felix the governor." 25 And he wrote a letter with this content:

26 "Claudius Lys′i·as to His Excellency, Governor Felix: Greetings! 27 This man was seized by the Jews and was about to be killed by them, but I came quickly with my soldiers and rescued him,[b] because I learned that he is a Roman.[c] 28 And wanting to find out the cause for which they were accusing him, I brought him down into their San′he·drin.[d] 29 I found him to be accused about questions of their Law,[e] but not charged with a single thing deserving of death or prison bonds. 30 But because a plot against the man has been made known to me,[f] I am at once sending him to you and ordering the accusers to speak against him before you."

31 So these soldiers took Paul[g] according to their orders and brought him by night to An·tip′a·tris. 32 The next day they permitted the horsemen to go on with him, but they returned to the soldiers' quarters.

33 The horsemen entered Caes·a·re′a and delivered the letter to the governor and also presented Paul to him. 34 So he read it and asked what province he was from and learned that he was from Ci·li′cia.[a] 35 "I will give you a thorough hearing," he said, "when your accusers arrive."[b] And he commanded that he be kept under guard in Herod's palace.*

24 Five days later the high priest An·a·ni′as[c] came down with some elders and a public speaker* named Ter·tul′lus, and they presented their case against Paul to the governor.[d] 2 When he was called, Ter·tul′lus started accusing him, saying:

"Seeing that we enjoy great peace through you and that through your forethought reforms are taking place in this nation, 3 at all times and also in all places we acknowledge this, Your Excellency Felix, with the greatest thankfulness. 4 But that I may not detain you any further, I beg you to hear us briefly in your kindness. 5 For we have found this man to be a pest,*[e] stirring up seditions[f] among all the Jews throughout the inhabited earth, and he is a spearhead of the sect of the Naz·a·renes′.[g] 6 He also tried to profane the temple, so we seized him.[h] 7 *— 8 When you examine him yourself, you will find out about all these things of which we are accusing him."

9 With that the Jews also joined in the attack, asserting that these things were true. 10 When the governor nodded to Paul to speak, he answered:

CHAP. 23
a Ac 23:12

b Ac 21:31-33

c Ac 16:37
Ac 22:25

d Ac 22:30

e Ac 25:19

f Ac 23:16

g Ac 23:23, 24

Second Col.
a Ac 21:39
Ac 22:3

b Ac 24:1

CHAP. 24
c Ac 23:2

d Ac 23:26

e Mt 5:11
Ac 16:20, 21
Ac 17:6, 7

f Lu 23:1, 2

g Mt 2:23
Ac 28:22

h Ac 21:27, 28

23:21 *Or "an oath." 23:23 *That is, about 9:00 p.m. 23:35 *Or "praetorium." 24:1 *Or "a lawyer." 24:5 *Or "troublemaker." Lit., "pestilence." 24:7 *See App. A3.

"Knowing well that this nation has had you as judge for many years, I readily speak in my own defense.[a] **11** As you can verify for yourself, it has not been more than 12 days since I went up to worship in Jerusalem;[b] **12** and they found me neither arguing with anyone in the temple nor stirring up a mob, either in the synagogues or throughout the city. **13** Nor can they prove to you the things they are accusing me of right now. **14** But I do admit this to you, that according to the way that they call a sect, in this manner I am rendering sacred service to the God of my forefathers,[c] as I believe all the things set forth in the Law and written in the Prophets.[d] **15** And I have hope toward God, which hope these men also look forward to, that there is going to be a resurrection[e] of both the righteous and the unrighteous.[f] **16** Because of this I always strive to maintain a clear* conscience before God and men.[g] **17** Now after quite a number of years, I arrived to bring gifts of mercy[h] to my nation and to make offerings. **18** While I was caring for these matters, they found me ceremonially cleansed in the temple,[i] but not with a crowd or causing a disturbance. But there were some Jews from the province of Asia **19** who ought to be present before you to accuse me if they actually have anything against me.[j] **20** Or let the men here say for themselves what wrong they found as I stood before the San'he·drin, **21** except for this one thing that I cried out while standing among them: 'Over the resurrection of the dead I am today being judged before you!'"[k]

22 However, Felix, knowing quite well the facts concern-ing this Way,[a] began to put them off and say: "Whenever Lys'i·as the military commander comes down, I will decide these matters involving you." **23** And he gave orders to the army officer that the man be kept under arrest but given some freedom, and that his people be allowed to attend to his needs.

24 Some days later Felix came with Dru·sil'la his wife, who was Jewish, and he sent for Paul and listened to him speak about the belief in Christ Jesus.[b] **25** But as Paul talked about righteousness and self-control and the judgment to come,[c] Felix became frightened and answered: "Go away for now, but when I have an opportunity I will send for you again." **26** At the same time he was hoping that Paul would give him money. For that reason, he sent for him even more frequently and conversed with him. **27** But when two years had elapsed, Felix was succeeded by Porcius Festus; and because Felix desired to gain favor with the Jews,[d] he left Paul in custody.

25 Therefore Festus,[e] after arriving in the province and taking charge, went up three days later to Jerusalem from Caes·a·re'a. **2** And the chief priests and the principal men of the Jews gave him information against Paul.[f] So they began to beg Festus **3** as a favor* to send for Paul to come to Jerusalem. But they were planning to ambush Paul and kill him along the road.[g] **4** However, Festus answered that Paul was to be kept in Caes·a·re'a and that he himself was about to go back there shortly. **5** "So let those who are in power among you," he said, "come down with me and accuse him if, indeed, the man has done something wrong."[h]

CHAP. 24

a Php 1:7

b Ac 21:17, 26

c Ex 3:15
Ac 3:13
2Ti 1:3

d Ac 28:23
Ro 3:21

e Isa 26:19
Mt 22:31, 32
Lu 14:13, 14
Joh 5:28, 29
Joh 11:25
Heb 11:35
Re 20:12

f Lu 23:43

g Ac 23:1
1Co 4:4
Heb 13:18

h 2Co 8:4

i Ac 21:24, 26

j Ac 25:16

k Ac 23:6

Second Col.

a Ac 9:1, 2
Ac 19:9

b Mt 10:18

c Ac 17:30, 31
2Co 5:10

d Ac 25:9

CHAP. 25

e Ac 24:27

f Ac 24:1

g Ac 23:20, 21

h Ac 25:16

24:16 *Or "blameless."

25:3 *Lit., "asking a favor against him."

6 So when he had spent not more than eight or ten days among them, he went down to Caes·a·re′a, and the next day he sat down on the judgment seat and commanded Paul to be brought in. **7** When he came in, the Jews who had come down from Jerusalem stood around him, bringing against him many serious charges that they were unable to prove.[a]

8 But Paul said in defense: "Neither against the Law of the Jews nor against the temple nor against Caesar have I committed any sin."[b] **9** Festus, desiring to gain favor with the Jews,[c] said in reply to Paul: "Do you wish to go up to Jerusalem and be judged before me there concerning these things?" **10** But Paul said: "I am standing before the judgment seat of Caesar, where I ought to be judged. I have done no wrong to the Jews, of which you are also becoming well-aware. **11** If I am really a wrongdoer and have committed anything deserving of death,[d] I do not beg off from dying; but if there is no substance to the accusations these men have made against me, no man has the right to hand me over to them as a favor. I appeal to Caesar!"[e] **12** Then Festus, after speaking with the assembly of counselors, replied: "To Caesar you have appealed; to Caesar you will go."

13 After some days had passed, A·grip′pa the king and Bernice arrived in Caes·a·re′a for a courtesy visit to Festus. **14** Since they were spending a number of days there, Festus presented Paul's case to the king, saying:

"There is a man who was left as a prisoner by Felix, **15** and when I was in Jerusalem the chief priests and the elders of the Jews brought information about him,[a] asking for a judgment of condemnation against him. **16** But I replied to them that it is not Roman procedure to hand any man over as a favor before the accused man meets his accusers face-to-face and gets a chance to speak in his defense concerning the complaint.[b] **17** So when they arrived here, I did not delay, but the next day I sat down on the judgment seat and commanded the man to be brought in. **18** Taking the stand, the accusers did not charge him with any of the wicked things I had expected concerning him.[c] **19** They simply had certain disputes with him concerning their own worship of the deity*[d] and concerning a man named Jesus, who was dead but who Paul kept asserting was alive.[e] **20** Being at a loss as to how to handle this dispute, I asked if he would like to go to Jerusalem and be judged there concerning these matters.[f] **21** But when Paul appealed to be kept in custody for the decision by the August One,*[g] I commanded him to be held until I should send him on to Caesar."

22 A·grip′pa then said to Festus: "I would like to hear the man myself."[h] "Tomorrow," he said, "you will hear him." **23** So the next day A·grip′pa and Bernice came with much pompous show and entered the audience chamber together with military commanders as well as the prominent men in the city; and when Festus gave the command, Paul was brought in. **24** And Festus said: "King A·grip′pa and all you who are present with us, you see this man about whom the whole Jewish populace have petitioned me both in Jerusalem and here, shouting that he ought not to

---

CHAP. 25
a Mt 5:11
Lu 23:1, 2
Ac 24:5

b Ac 24:11, 12

c Ac 24:27

d Ac 23:26, 29

e Ac 28:17-19

Second Col.
a Ac 25:2, 3

b Ac 25:5

c Ac 25:7

d Ac 18:14, 15
Ac 23:26, 29

e Ac 22:6-8

f Ac 25:9

g Ac 25:11, 12

h Ac 9:15

25:19 *Or "their own religion." 25:21 *A title for the Roman emperor.

live any longer.[a] **25** But I perceived that he had done nothing deserving of death.[b] So when this man himself appealed to the August One, I decided to send him. **26** But I have nothing certain to write about him to my Lord. So I brought him before all of you, and especially before you, King A·grip′pa, so that after the judicial examination has taken place, I might have something to write. **27** For it seems unreasonable to me to send a prisoner and not also to indicate the charges against him."

26 A·grip′pa[c] said to Paul: "You are permitted to speak in your own behalf." Then Paul stretched out his hand and proceeded to say in his defense:

2 "Concerning all the things of which I am accused by the Jews,[d] King A·grip′pa, I consider myself happy that it is before you I am to make my defense this day, **3** especially because you are an expert on all the customs as well as the controversies among the Jews. Therefore, I beg you to hear me patiently.

4 "Indeed, the manner of life I led from youth up among my people* and in Jerusalem is well-known by all the Jews[e] **5** who were previously acquainted with me, if they would be willing to testify, that according to the strictest sect of our form of worship,[f] I lived as a Pharisee.[g] **6** But now for the hope of the promise that was made by God to our forefathers,[h] I stand on trial; **7** this is the same promise our 12 tribes are hoping to see fulfilled by intensely rendering him sacred service night and day. Concerning this hope I am accused by Jews,[i] O King.

8 "Why is it considered* unbelievable among you that God

raises up the dead? **9** I, for one, was convinced that I should commit many acts of opposition against the name of Jesus the Naz·a·rene′. **10** This is exactly what I did in Jerusalem, and I locked up many of the holy ones in prisons,[a] for I had received authority from the chief priests;[b] and when they were to be executed, I cast my vote against them. **11** By punishing them often in all the synagogues, I tried to force them to recant; and since I was extremely furious with them, I went so far as to persecute them even in outlying cities.

12 "While doing this as I was traveling to Damascus with authority and a commission from the chief priests, **13** I saw at midday on the road, O King, a light beyond the brilliance of the sun flash from heaven around me and around those traveling with me.[c] **14** And when we had all fallen to the ground, I heard a voice say to me in the Hebrew language: 'Saul, Saul, why are you persecuting me? To keep kicking against the goads* makes it hard for you.' **15** But I said: 'Who are you, Lord?' And the Lord said: 'I am Jesus, whom you are persecuting. **16** But rise and stand on your feet. This is why I have appeared to you, to choose you as a servant and a witness both of things you have seen and things I will make you see respecting me.[d] **17** And I will rescue you from this people and from the nations, to whom I am sending you[e] **18** to open their eyes,[f] to turn them from darkness[g] to light[h] and from the authority of Satan[i] to God, so that they may receive forgiveness of sins[j] and an inheritance among those sanctified by their faith in me.'

CHAP. 25
a Ac 22:22

b Ac 23:26, 29

CHAP. 26
c Ac 25:13

d Ac 24:5, 9

e Ga 1:13, 14

f Ac 22:3

g Ac 23:6
  Php 3:4, 5

h Ac 24:15

i Ac 24:20, 21

Second Col.
a Joh 16:2
  Ac 8:3
  1Co 15:9
  Ga 1:13
  1Ti 1:13

b Ac 9:1, 2, 14

c Ac 9:3-5
  Ac 22:6-8

d Ac 22:14, 15
  Ga 1:11, 12
  1Ti 1:12

e Ac 22:21
  Ro 11:13

f Isa 61:1

g Col 1:13

h Joh 8:12
  2Co 4:6

i Eph 2:1, 2

j 1Jo 3:5

26:4 *Or "nation." 26:8 *Lit., "judged."

26:14 *A goad is a pointed rod used to urge on an animal.

19 "Therefore, King A·grip′pa, I did not become disobedient to the heavenly vision, **20** but to those in Damascus[a] first and then to those in Jerusalem,[b] and over all the country of Ju·de′a, and also to the nations, I was bringing the message that they should repent and turn to God by doing works that befit repentance.[c] **21** This is why the Jews seized me in the temple and tried to kill me.[d] **22** However, because I have experienced the help that is from God, I continue to this day bearing witness to both small and great, saying nothing except what the Prophets as well as Moses stated was going to take place[e]— **23** that the Christ was to suffer[f] and that as the first to be resurrected from the dead,[g] he was going to proclaim light both to this people and to the nations."[h]

24 Now as Paul was saying these things in his defense, Festus said in a loud voice: "You are going out of your mind, Paul! Great learning is driving you out of your mind!" **25** But Paul said: "I am not going out of my mind, Your Excellency Festus, but I am speaking words of truth and of a sound mind. **26** For a fact, the king to whom I am speaking so freely well knows about these things; I am convinced that not one of these things escapes his notice, for none of this has been done in a corner.[i] **27** Do you, King A·grip′pa, believe the Prophets? I know that you believe." **28** But A·grip′pa said to Paul: "In a short time you would persuade me to become a Christian." **29** At this Paul said: "I wish to God that whether in a short time or in a long time, not only you but also all those who hear me today would become men such as I am, with the exception of these prison bonds."

30 Then the king rose and so did the governor and Bernice and the men seated with them. **31** But as they were leaving, they began saying to one another: "This man is doing nothing deserving of death or prison bonds."[a] **32** A·grip′pa then said to Festus: "This man could have been released if he had not appealed to Caesar."[b]

27 Now as it was decided for us to sail away to Italy,[c] they handed Paul and some other prisoners over to an army officer named Julius, of the unit of Au·gus′tus. **2** Going aboard a ship from Ad·ra·myt′ti·um that was about to sail to ports along the coast of the province of Asia, we set sail; Ar·is·tar′chus,[d] a Mac·e·do′ni·an from Thes·sa·lo·ni′ca, was with us. **3** The next day we landed at Si′don, and Julius treated Paul with kindness* and permitted him to go to his friends and enjoy their care.

4 And putting out to sea from there, we sailed under the shelter of Cy′prus, because the winds were against us. **5** Then we navigated through the open sea along Ci·li′cia and Pam·phyl′i·a and put into port at My′ra in Ly·ci·a. **6** There the army officer found a ship from Alexandria that was sailing for Italy, and he made us board it. **7** Then after sailing on slowly quite a number of days, we came to Cni′dus with difficulty. Because the wind did not let us make headway, we sailed under the shelter of Crete off Sal·mo′ne. **8** And sailing with difficulty along the coast, we came to a place called Fair Havens, which was near the city of La·se′a.

9 A considerable time had passed and by now it was hazardous to navigate, because even the fast of Atonement Day[e]

CHAP. 26
a Ac 9:22

b Ac 9:28

c Mt 3:8

d Ac 21:30, 31

e Lu 24:27, 44
Ro 3:21

f Ps 22:7
Ps 35:19
Isa 50:6
Isa 53:5

g Ps 16:10

h Ps 18:49
Isa 11:10
Lu 2:30-32

i Joh 18:20

Second Col.
a Ac 23:26, 29
Ac 25:24, 25

b Ac 25:11, 12

CHAP. 27
c Ac 25:12

d Ac 19:29
Ac 20:4
Col 4:10

e Le 16:29, 30
Le 23:27

27:3 *Or "human kindness."

was already over, so Paul made a recommendation 10 to them: "Men, I can see that this voyage is going to result in damage and great loss not only of the cargo and the ship but also of our lives."* 11 However, the army officer listened to the pilot and the shipowner rather than to what Paul was saying. 12 Since the harbor was unsuitable for wintering, the majority advised setting sail from there to see if they could somehow make it to spend the winter in Phoenix, a harbor of Crete that opens toward the northeast and toward the southeast.

13 When the south wind blew softly, they thought they had achieved their purpose, and they lifted anchor and began sailing along Crete close to the shore. 14 After a short time, however, a violent wind called Eu·ro·aq'ui·lo* rushed down on it. 15 As the ship was violently seized and was not able to keep its head against the wind, we gave way to it and were driven along. 16 Then we ran under the shelter of a small island called Cau'da, and yet we were hardly able to get the skiff* at the stern of the ship under control. 17 But after hoisting it aboard, they used supports to undergird the ship, and fearing that they would run aground on the Syr'tis,* they lowered the gear and so were driven along. 18 Because we were being violently tossed by the storm, they began to lighten the ship the following day. 19 And on the third day, they threw away the tackling of the ship with their own hands.

20 When neither sun nor stars appeared for many days

and a violent* storm was battering us, all hope of our being saved finally began to fade. 21 After they had gone a long time without food, Paul stood up in their midst and said: "Men, you certainly should have taken my advice and not have put out to sea from Crete and as a result suffered this damage and loss.ᵃ 22 Still, I now urge you to take courage, for not one* of you will be lost, only the ship will. 23 This night an angelᵇ of the God to whom I belong and to whom I render sacred service stood by me 24 and said: 'Have no fear, Paul. You must stand before Caesar,ᶜ and look! God has granted to you all those sailing with you.' 25 So take courage, men, for I believe God that it will be exactly as I was told. 26 However, we must be cast ashore on some island."ᵈ

27 Now when the 14th night fell and we were being tossed about on the Sea of A'dri·a, at midnight the sailors began to suspect that they were getting near to some land. 28 They sounded the depth and found it 20 fathoms,* so they proceeded a short distance and again made a sounding and found it 15 fathoms.# 29 And fearing that we might run aground on the rocks, they cast out four anchors from the stern and began wishing for it to become day. 30 But when the sailors began trying to escape from the ship and were lowering the skiff into the sea under the pretense of intending to let down anchors from the bow, 31 Paul said to the army officer and the soldiers: "Unless these men remain in the ship, you cannot be saved."ᵉ 32 Then the

Second Col.

CHAP. 27
a Ac 27:9, 10

b Ac 5:18, 19
Heb 1:7, 14

c Ac 23:11
Ac 25:11, 12

d Ac 28:1

e Ac 27:22

27:10 *Or "souls." 27:14 *That is, a northeast wind. 27:16 *A small auxiliary boat that could serve as a lifeboat. 27:17 *See Glossary.

27:20 *Lit., "no little." 27:22 *Or "a soul." 27:28 *About 36 m (120 ft). See App. B14. #About 27 m (90 ft). See App. B14.

soldiers cut away the ropes of the skiff and let it fall off.

33 Now close to daybreak, Paul encouraged them all to take some food, saying: "Today is the 14th day you have been waiting anxiously, and you have gone without taking any food at all. **34** So I encourage you to eat some food; this is in the interests of your safety, for not a hair of the head of any one of you will perish." **35** After he said this, he took bread, gave thanks to God before them all, broke it, and started eating. **36** So they all took courage and began taking some food themselves. **37** In all we were 276 persons* in the ship. **38** When they had eaten enough food to be satisfied, they lightened the ship by throwing the wheat overboard into the sea.ᵃ

39 When daylight came, they could not recognize the land,ᵇ but they saw a bay with a beach and were determined to beach the ship there if they could. **40** So they cut away the anchors and let them fall into the sea, at the same time loosening the lashings of the rudder oars; and after hoisting the foresail to the wind, they made for the beach. **41** When they struck a shoal washed on each side by the sea, they ran the ship aground and the bow got stuck and stayed immovable, but the stern began to be violently broken to pieces by the waves.ᶜ **42** At this the soldiers decided to kill the prisoners so that no one might swim away and escape. **43** But the army officer was determined to bring Paul safely through and prevented them from carrying out their plan. He commanded those able to swim to jump into the sea and make it to land first, **44** and the rest were to follow, some on planks and some on

pieces of the ship. So all were brought safely to land.ᵃ

28 After we made it to safety, we learned that the island was called Malta.ᵇ **2** And the foreign-speaking people* showed us extraordinary kindness.# They kindled a fire and received all of us kindly because of the rain that was falling and because of the cold. **3** But when Paul collected a bundle of sticks and laid it on the fire, a viper came out because of the heat and fastened itself on his hand. **4** When the foreign-speaking people caught sight of the venomous creature hanging from his hand, they began saying to one another: "Surely this man is a murderer, and although he made it to safety from the sea, Justice* did not permit him to keep on living." **5** However, he shook the creature off into the fire and suffered no harm. **6** But they were expecting him to swell up or suddenly to drop dead. After they waited for a long time and saw that nothing bad happened to him, they changed their mind and began saying he was a god.

7 Now in the neighborhood of that place were lands belonging to the principal man of the island, whose name was Pub'li-us, and he welcomed us and entertained us hospitably for three days. **8** It so happened that the father of Pub'li-us was lying in bed sick with fever and dysentery, and Paul went in to him and prayed, laid his hands on him, and healed him.ᶜ **9** After this occurred, the rest of the people on the island who were sick also began to come to him and be cured.ᵈ **10** They also honored us with many gifts, and when we

---

CHAP. 27
a Jon 1:5

b Ac 28:1

c Ac 27:22
2Co 11:25

Second Col.
a Ac 27:23, 24

CHAP. 28
b Ac 27:26

c Lu 4:38, 39

d Mt 10:8

27:37 *Or "souls."

28:2 *Or "the local inhabitants." #Or "human kindness." 28:4 *Greek Di'ke, possibly referring to the goddess of avenging justice or to the concept of justice in an abstract sense.

were setting sail, they loaded us up with whatever we needed.

11 Three months later we set sail in a ship with the figurehead "Sons of Zeus." The ship was from Alexandria and had wintered in the island. **12** Putting into port at Syracuse, we remained there for three days; **13** from there we went along and arrived at Rhe′gi·um. A day later a south wind sprang up and we made it into Pu·te′o·li on the second day. **14** Here we found brothers and were urged to remain with them for seven days, and so we went toward Rome. **15** From there the brothers, when they heard the news about us, came as far as the Marketplace of Ap′pi·us and Three Taverns to meet us. On catching sight of them, Paul thanked God and took courage.ᵃ **16** When finally we entered Rome, Paul was permitted to stay by himself with the soldier guarding him.

17 However, three days later he called together the principal men of the Jews. When they had assembled, he said to them: "Men, brothers, although I had done nothing contrary to the people or the customs of our forefathers,ᵇ I was handed over as a prisoner from Jerusalem into the hands of the Romans.ᶜ **18** And after making an examination,ᵈ they wanted to release me, for there were no grounds for putting me to death.ᵉ **19** But when the Jews objected, I was compelled to appeal to Caesar,ᶠ but not because I had any accusation to make against my nation. **20** So for this reason I asked to see and speak to you, for it is because of the hope of Israel that I have this chain around me."ᵍ **21** They said to him: "We have not received letters about you from Ju·de′a, nor have any of the brothers who came from

there reported or spoken anything bad about you. **22** But we think it proper to hear from you what your thoughts are, for truly as regards this sect,ᵃ we know that it is spoken against everywhere."ᵇ

23 They now arranged for a day to meet with him, and they came in even greater numbers to him in his lodging place. And from morning to evening, he explained the matter to them by bearing thorough witness concerning the Kingdom of God, to persuade them about Jesusᶜ from both the Law of Mosesᵈ and the Prophets.ᵉ **24** Some began to believe the things he said; others would not believe. **25** So because they disagreed with one another, they began to leave, and Paul made this one comment:

"The holy spirit aptly spoke through Isaiah the prophet to your forefathers, **26** saying, 'Go to this people and say: "You will indeed hear but by no means understand, and you will indeed look but by no means see.ᶠ **27** For the heart of this people has grown unreceptive, and with their ears they have heard without response, and they have shut their eyes, so that they might never see with their eyes and hear with their ears and understand with their heart and turn back and I heal them."'ᵍ **28** So let it be known to you that this salvation from God has been sent out to the nations;ʰ they will certainly listen to it."ⁱ **29** *——

30 So he remained there for an entire two years in his own rented house,ʲ and he would kindly receive all those who came to him, **31** preaching the Kingdom of God to them and teaching about the Lord Jesus Christ with the greatest freeness of speech,*ᵏ without hindrance.

CHAP. 28

a 2Co 1:3, 4

b Ac 24:11, 12
Ac 25:8

c Ac 21:33

d Ac 24:10

e Ac 23:26, 29
Ac 25:24, 25
Ac 26:31, 32

f Ac 25:11, 12

g Ac 23:6
Ac 26:6
Eph 6:19, 20
2Ti 1:16

Second Col.

a Ac 24:14

b Lu 2:34
Joh 15:19

c Ac 17:2, 3

d Joh 5:46

e Ac 26:22, 23

f Ro 11:8

g Isa 6:9, 10
Mt 13:14, 15

h Lu 3:4, 6
Ac 13:45, 46
Ac 22:21
Ro 11:11

i Ps 67:2
Ps 98:3
Isa 11:10

j Ac 28:16

k Eph 6:19

28:29 *See App. A3. 28:31 *Or "with all boldness."

TO THE

ROMANS

OUTLINE OF CONTENTS

1 Paul, a slave of Christ Jesus and called to be an apostle, set apart for God's good news,[a] **2** which he promised beforehand through his prophets in the holy Scriptures, **3** concerning his Son, who came to be from the offspring* of David[b] according to the flesh, **4** but who with power was declared God's Son[c] according to the spirit of holiness by means of resurrection from the dead[d]—yes, Jesus Christ our Lord. **5** Through him we received undeserved kindness and an apostleship[e] with a view to obedience by faith among all the nations[f] respecting his name, **6** among which nations you also have been called to belong to Jesus Christ— **7** to all those who are in Rome as God's beloved ones, called to be holy ones:

May you have undeserved kindness and peace from God our Father and the Lord Jesus Christ.

8 First of all, I give thanks to my God through Jesus Christ concerning all of you, because your faith is talked about throughout the whole world. **9** For God, to whom I render sacred service with my spirit in connection with the good news about his Son, is my witness of how without ceasing I always mention you in my prayers,[g] **10** begging that if at all possible I may now at last succeed in coming to you by God's will. **11** For I am longing to see you, that I may impart some spiritual gift to you for you to be made firm; **12** or, rather, that we may have an interchange of encouragement[h] by one another's faith, both yours and mine.

13 But I do not want you to be unaware, brothers, that many times I have intended to come

to you—but I have been prevented until now—in order that I might acquire some fruitage also among you just as among the rest of the nations. **14** Both to Greeks and to foreigners,* both to wise and to senseless ones, I am a debtor; **15** so I am eager to declare the good news also to you there in Rome.[a] **16** For I am not ashamed of the good news;[b] it is, in fact, God's power for salvation to everyone having faith,[c] to the Jew first[d] and also to the Greek.[e] **17** For in it God's righteousness is being revealed by faith and for faith,[f] just as it is written: "But the righteous one will live by reason of faith."[g]

18 For God's wrath[h] is being revealed from heaven against all ungodliness and unrighteousness of men who are suppressing the truth[i] in an unrighteous way, **19** because what may be known about God is clearly evident among them, for God made it clear to them.[j] **20** For his invisible qualities are clearly seen from the world's creation onward, because they are perceived by the things made,[k] even his eternal power[l] and Godship,[m] so that they are inexcusable. **21** For although they knew God, they did not glorify him as God nor did they thank him, but they became empty-headed in their reasonings and their senseless hearts became darkened.[n] **22** Although claiming they were wise, they became foolish **23** and turned the glory of the incorruptible God into something like the image of corruptible man and birds and four-footed creatures and reptiles.*[o]

24 Therefore, God, in keeping with the desires of their hearts, gave them up to uncleanness, so

CHAP. 1
a Ac 9:11, 15

b 2Sa 7:8, 12
Lu 1:32
2Ti 2:8

c Ps 2:7
Heb 1:5

d Ac 13:33

e 1Ti 2:7

f Ac 15:14
Ga 2:7

g 1Th 3:10
2Ti 1:3

h 1Th 5:11
Heb 10:25

Second Col.
a Ac 19:21

b Mr 8:38
2Ti 1:8

c Heb 11:6

d Ac 3:25, 26

e Ac 18:5, 6

f Joh 3:36
Ro 3:21, 22

g Hab 2:4
Ga 3:11
Heb 10:38

h Ro 2:5
Eph 5:6

i Ro 1:25

j Ps 19:1
Ac 14:17

k Isa 40:26
Re 4:11

l Jer 10:12

m Ps 103:19
Jer 10:10
Re 15:3

n Ge 6:5

o Jer 2:11
Ac 17:29

1:3 *Lit., "seed." **1:14** *Or "non-Greeks." Lit., "barbarians." **1:23** *Or "creeping things."

that their bodies might be dishonored among them. **25** They exchanged the truth of God for the lie and venerated* and rendered sacred service to the creation rather than the Creator, who is praised forever. Amen. **26** That is why God gave them over to uncontrolled sexual passion,ᵃ for their females changed the natural use of themselves into one contrary to nature;ᵇ **27** likewise also the males left the natural use of* the female and became violently inflamed in their lust toward one another, males with males,ᶜ working what is obscene and receiving in themselves the full penalty,ᵈ which was due for their error.ᵈ

28 Just as they did not see fit to acknowledge God,* God gave them over to a disapproved mental state, to do the things not fitting.ᵉ **29** And they were filled with all unrighteousness,ᶠ wickedness, greed,*ᵍ and badness, being full of envy,ʰ murder,ⁱ strife, deceit,ʲ and malice,ᵏ being whisperers,ˣ **30** backbiters,ˡ haters of God, insolent, haughty, boastful, schemers of what is harmful,* disobedient to parents,ᵐ **31** without understanding,ⁿ false to agreements, having no natural affection, and merciless. **32** Although these know full well the righteous decree of God—that those practicing such things are deserving of death°—they only keep on doing them but also approve of those practicing them.

2 Therefore you are inexcusable, O man, whoever you are,ᵖ if you judge; for when you judge another, you condemn yourself, because you who judge practice the same things.ᵃ **2** Now we know that God's judgment is in harmony with truth, against those who practice such things.

3 But do you suppose, O man, that while you judge those who practice such things and yet you do them, you will escape the judgment of God? **4** Or do you despise the riches of his kindnessᵇ and forbearance*ᶜ and patience,ᵈ because you do not know that God in his kindness is trying to lead you to repentance?ᵉ **5** But according to your stubbornness and your unrepentant heart, you are storing up wrath for yourself on the day of wrath and of the revealing of God's righteous judgment.ᶠ **6** And he will pay back to each one according to his works:ᵍ **7** everlasting life to those who are seeking glory and honor and incorruptiblenessʰ by endurance in work that is good; **8** however, for those who are contentious and who disobey the truth but obey unrighteousness, there will be wrath and anger.ⁱ **9** There will be tribulation and distress on every person* who works what is harmful, on the Jew first and also on the Greek; **10** but glory and honor and peace for everyone who works what is good, for the Jew firstʲ and also for the Greek.ᵏ **11** For there is no partiality with God.ˡ

12 For all those who sinned without law will also perish without law;ᵐ but all those who sinned under law will be judged by law.ⁿ **13** For the hearers of law are not the ones righteous before God, but the doers of law will be declared righteous.° **14** For when people of the na-

CHAP. 1

a Ga 5:19
  1Th 4:4, 5
b Jude 7
c Ge 19:5
  Le 18:22
  Le 20:13
  1Co 6:9, 10
d Ga 6:7
e Ga 5:19-21
f 1Pe 4:3
g De 5:21
h Tit 3:3
i 1Jo 3:15
j 1Pe 2:1
k Eph 4:31
l 1Pe 2:1
m De 21:18, 21
n Ro 1:21
o Re 21:8

CHAP. 2

p Ro 2:9

Second Col.

a Mt 7:5
b Ro 11:22
  Eph 1:7
c Ro 3:25
d Isa 30:18
e 2Pe 3:9
f 2Th 1:7, 8
  Re 6:16, 17
  Re 11:18
g Ps 62:12
  Pr 24:12
  Mt 16:27
h 1Co 15:53
  Re 20:6
i Ro 1:18
  Col 3:6
  Heb 10:26, 27
j Joh 4:22
  Ac 13:45, 46
k Ac 15:14
l De 10:17
  2Ch 19:7
  Ac 10:34, 35
m Eph 2:12
n Ro 3:19
o De 30:14
  Eze 20:11
  Jas 1:22

1:25 *Or "worshipped." **1:27** *Or "natural relations with." #Or "recompense." **1:28** *Or "they did not approve of holding God in accurate knowledge." **1:29** *Or "covetousness." #Or "gossipers." **1:30** *Or "inventors of injurious things."

2:4 *Or "tolerance." **2:9** *Or "the soul of every man."

tions, who do not have law,[a] do by nature the things of the law, these people, although not having law, are a law to themselves. **15** They are the very ones who demonstrate the matter of the law to be written in their hearts, while their conscience is bearing witness with them, and by[*] their own thoughts they are being accused or even excused. **16** This will take place in the day when God through Christ Jesus judges the secret things of mankind,[b] according to the good news I declare.

17 If, now, you are a Jew in name[c] and rely on law and take pride in God, **18** and you know his will and approve of things that are excellent because you are instructed[*] out of the Law,[d] **19** and you are convinced that you are a guide of the blind, a light for those in darkness, **20** a corrector of the unreasonable ones, a teacher of young children, and having the framework of the knowledge and of the truth in the Law— **21** do you, however, the one teaching someone else, not teach yourself?[e] You, the one preaching, "Do not steal,"[f] do you steal? **22** You, the one saying, "Do not commit adultery,"[g] do you commit adultery? You, the one abhorring idols, do you rob temples? **23** You who take pride in law, do you dishonor God by your transgressing of the Law? **24** For "the name of God is being blasphemed among the nations because of you," just as it is written.[h]

25 Circumcision[i] is, in fact, of benefit only if you practice law;[j] but if you are a transgressor of law, your circumcision has become uncircumcision. **26** If, therefore, an uncircum-

cised person[a] keeps the righteous requirements of the Law, his uncircumcision will be counted as circumcision, will it not?[b] **27** And the physically uncircumcised person will, by carrying out the Law, judge you who are a transgressor of law despite having its written code and circumcision. **28** For he is not a Jew who is one on the outside,[c] nor is circumcision something on the outside, on the flesh.[d] **29** But he is a Jew who is one on the inside,[e] and his circumcision is that of the heart[f] by spirit and not by a written code.[g] That person's praise comes from God, not from people.[h]

3 What, then, is the advantage of the Jew, or what is the benefit of circumcision? **2** A great deal in every way. First of all, that they were entrusted with the sacred pronouncements of God.[i] **3** What, then, is the case? If some lacked faith, will their lack of faith invalidate the faithfulness of God? **4** Certainly not! But let God be found true,[j] even if every man be found a liar,[k] just as it is written: "That you might be proved righteous in your words and might win when you are being judged."[l] **5** However, if our unrighteousness highlights God's righteousness, what are we to say? God is not unjust when he expresses his wrath, is he? (I am speaking in human terms.) **6** By no means! How, otherwise, will God judge the world?[m]

7 But if by my lie the truth of God has been made more prominent to his glory, why am I also being judged as a sinner? **8** And why not say, just as some men falsely claim that we say, "Let us do bad things that good things may come"? The judgment against those men is in harmony with justice.[n]

CHAP. 2
a Ps 147:19, 20

b Joh 5:22
Ac 10:42
1Pe 4:5

c Ro 9:6

d De 4:8

e Mt 23:2, 3

f Ex 20:15

g De 5:18

h Isa 52:5
Eze 36:20

i Ge 17:10

j 1Co 7:19
Ga 5:3

Second Col.
a Eph 2:11

b Ro 4:9, 10

c Joh 8:39
Re 2:9

d 1Co 7:19

e Ro 9:6

f Jer 4:4
Ac 7:51
Php 3:3

g Ro 7:6

h Joh 5:44
1Co 4:5

CHAP. 3
i De 4:8
Ps 147:19, 20
Ac 7:38

j Isa 55:10, 11
Joh 8:26
2Ti 2:13

k Nu 23:19
Ps 116:11

l Ps 51:4

m Ps 9:8
Ps 96:13
Ps 98:9
Ac 17:31

n Heb 2:2, 3

2:15 *Lit., "between." 2:18 *Or "orally instructed."

9 What then? Are we in a better position? Not at all! For above we have made the charge that Jews as well as Greeks are all under sin;[a] **10** just as it is written: "There is not a righteous man, not even one;[b] **11** there is no one who has any insight; there is no one who searches for God. **12** All men have turned aside, all of them have become worthless; there is no one who shows kindness, not so much as one."[c] **13** "Their throat is an open grave; they have deceived with their tongues."[d] "Venom of asps is behind their lips."[e] **14** "And their mouth is full of cursing and bitterness."[f] **15** "Their feet are swift to shed blood."[g] **16** "Ruin and misery are in their ways, **17** and they have not known the way of peace."[h] **18** "There is no fear of God before their eyes."[i]

19 Now we know that all the things the Law says, it addresses to those under the Law, so that every mouth may be silenced and all the world may become accountable to God for punishment.[j] **20** Therefore, no one* will be declared righteous before him by works of law,[k] for by law comes the accurate knowledge of sin.[l]

21 But now apart from law God's righteousness has been revealed,[m] as the Law and the Prophets bear witness,[n] **22** yes, God's righteousness through the faith in Jesus Christ, for all those having faith. For there is no distinction.[o] **23** For all have sinned and fall short of the glory of God,[p] **24** and it is as a free gift[q] that they are being declared righteous by his undeserved kindness[r] through the release by the ransom paid by Christ Jesus.[s] **25** God presented him as an offering for propi-

tiation*[a] through faith in his blood.[b] This was to demonstrate his own righteousness, because God in his forbearance# was forgiving the sins that occurred in the past. **26** This was to demonstrate his own righteousness[c] in this present season, so that he might be righteous even when declaring righteous the man who has faith in Jesus.[d]

27 Where, then, is the boasting? There is no place for it. Through what law? That of works?[e] No indeed, but through the law of faith. **28** For we consider that a man is declared righteous by faith apart from works of law.[f] **29** Or is he the God of the Jews only?[g] Is he not also the God of people of the nations?[h] Yes, also of people of the nations.[i] **30** Since God is one,[j] he will declare circumcised people righteous[k] as a result of faith and uncircumcised people righteous[l] by means of their faith. **31** Do we, then, abolish law by means of our faith? Not at all! On the contrary, we uphold law.[m]

4 That being so, what will we say was gained by Abraham, our forefather according to the flesh? **2** For instance, if Abraham was declared righteous as a result of works, he would have reason to boast, but not with God. **3** For what does the scripture say? "Abraham put faith in Jehovah,* and it was counted to him as righteousness."[n] **4** Now to the man who works, his pay is not counted as an undeserved kindness but as something owed to him.* **5** On the other hand, to the man who does not work but puts faith in the One who declares the ungodly one righteous, his faith is counted as righteousness.[o]

CHAP. 3

a Ro 3:23
  Ga 3:22
b Pr 20:9
  Ec 7:20
c Ps 14:1-3
d Ps 5:9
e Ps 140:3
f Ps 10:7
  Jas 3:8, 9
g Pr 1:16
h Isa 59:7, 8
i Ps 36:1
j Ro 2:12
  Ro 5:13
  Ga 3:10
k Ga 2:16
  Ga 3:11
l Ro 7:9, 13
  Ga 3:19
m Ro 1:16, 17
n Isa 53:11
  Jer 31:34
  Da 9:24
o Ga 3:28
p Ec 7:20
q Ro 5:17
r Eph 2:8
s Mt 20:28
  1Ti 2:5, 6
  1Pe 2:24

Second Col.

a Isa 53:11
  2Co 5:19
  1Jo 2:1, 2
  1Jo 4:10
b Le 17:11
  Ac 13:39
  Eph 1:7
c Ps 89:14
d 1Co 1:30
  1Jo 1:9
e Ac 13:38, 39
  Eph 2:8, 9
f Ga 2:15, 16
  Jas 2:24
g Ac 17:26, 27
h Ac 10:4
i Isa 54:5
  Ro 10:12
  Ga 3:14
j De 6:4
  1Co 8:6
  Eph 4:6
k 1Co 7:18
l Ga 3:8
m Mt 5:17
  Ro 8:3, 4
  Ro 13:10

CHAP. 4

n Ge 15:6
  Ga 3:6
  Jas 2:23
o Ga 2:15, 16

3:20 *Lit., "flesh."

3:25 *Or "atonement; reconciliation." #Or "tolerance." 4:3 *See App. A5. 4:4 *Or "as a debt."

6 Just as David also speaks of the happiness of the man to whom God counts righteousness apart from works: **7** "Happy are those whose lawless deeds have been pardoned and whose sins have been covered;* **8** happy is the man whose sin Jehovah* will by no means take into account."[a]

9 Does this happiness, then, only come to circumcised people or also to uncircumcised people?[b] For we say: "Abraham's faith was counted to him as righteousness."[c] **10** Under what circumstances, then, was it counted as righteousness? When he was circumcised or uncircumcised? He was not yet circumcised but was uncircumcised. **11** And he received a sign[d]—namely, circumcision—as a seal* of the righteousness by the faith he had while in his uncircumcised state, so that he might be the father of all those having faith[e] while uncircumcised, in order for righteousness to be counted to them; **12** and so that he might be a father to circumcised offspring, not only to those who adhere to circumcision but also to those who walk orderly in the footsteps of the faith that our father Abraham[f] had while in the uncircumcised state.

13 For it was not through law that Abraham or his offspring* had the promise that he should be heir of a world,[g] but it was through righteousness by faith.[h] **14** For if those who adhere to law are heirs, faith becomes useless and the promise has been abolished. **15** In reality the Law produces wrath,[i] but where there is no law, neither is there any transgression.[j]

16 That is why it is through faith, so that it might be according to undeserved kindness,[a] in order for the promise to be sure to all his offspring,*[b] not only to those who adhere to the Law but also to those who adhere to the faith of Abraham, who is the father of us all.[c] **17** (This is just as it is written: "I have appointed you a father of many nations.")[d] This was in the sight of God, in whom he had faith, who makes the dead alive and calls the things that are not as though they are.* **18** Although beyond hope, yet based on hope, he had faith that he would become the father of many nations according to what had been said: "So your offspring* will be."[e] **19** And although he did not grow weak in faith, he considered his own body, now as good as dead (since he was about 100 years old),[f] as well as the deadness* of the womb of Sarah.[g] **20** But because of the promise of God, he did not waver in a lack of faith; but he became powerful by his faith, giving God glory **21** and being fully convinced that what He had promised He was also able to do.[h] **22** Therefore, "it was counted to him as righteousness."[i]

23 However, the words "it was counted to him" were not written for his sake only,[j] **24** but also for our sake, to whom it will be counted, because we believe in Him who raised Jesus our Lord up from the dead.[k] **25** He was handed over for the sake of our trespasses[l] and was raised up for the sake of declaring us righteous.[m]

5 Therefore, now that we have been declared righteous as a result of faith,[n] let us enjoy

---

CHAP. 4
a Ps 32:1, 2
b Ro 3:30
c Ro 4:3
d Ge 17:1, 2, 11
e Ro 4:16
  Ga 3:7
f Ga 3:29
g Ge 12:1-3
  Ge 17:5, 6
  Ge 22:17, 18
h Heb 11:8
i Ro 3:20
  Ro 5:20
  2Co 3:7
j Ro 5:13

Second Col.
a Ro 3:24
b Ro 9:8
  Ga 3:29
c Ro 4:11
d Ge 17:5
e Ge 15:5
  Heb 11:17, 18
f Ge 17:17
g Ge 18:11
  Heb 11:11, 12
h Heb 11:19
i Ge 15:6
  Jas 2:23
j Ro 15:4
k Ac 2:24
  Ac 13:30
  1Pe 1:21
l Mt 20:28
m Isa 53:11, 12
  2Co 5:21

CHAP. 5
n Ac 13:38, 39

4:7 *Or "forgiven." 4:8 *See App. A5. 4:11 *Or "guarantee; confirmation." 4:13, 16, 18 *Lit., "seed."

4:17 *Or possibly, "calls into existence what does not exist." 4:19 *Or "barrenness."

peace* with God through our Lord Jesus Christ,[a] **2** through whom we also have obtained access by faith into this undeserved kindness in which we now stand;[b] and let us rejoice,* based on hope of the glory of God. **3** Not only that, but let us rejoice* while in tribulations,[c] since we know that tribulation produces endurance;[d] **4** endurance, in turn, an approved condition;[e] the approved condition, in turn, hope,[f] **5** and the hope does not lead to disappointment;[g] because the love of God has been poured out into our hearts through the holy spirit, which was given to us.[h]

6 For, indeed, while we were still weak,[i] Christ died for ungodly men at the appointed time. **7** For hardly would anyone die for a righteous man; though perhaps for a good man someone may dare to die. **8** But God recommends his own love to us in that, while we were yet sinners, Christ died for us.[j] **9** Much more, then, since we have now been declared righteous by his blood,[k] will we be saved through him from wrath.[l] **10** For if when we were enemies we became reconciled to God through the death of his Son,[m] how much more we will be saved by his life, now that we have become reconciled. **11** Not only that, but we are also rejoicing in God through our Lord Jesus Christ, through whom we have now received the reconciliation.[n]

12 That is why, just as through one man sin entered into the world and death through sin,[o] and so death spread to all men because they had all sinned[p]—. **13** For sin was in the world before the Law, but sin is not charged against anyone when there is no law.[q] **14** Neverthe-

---

less, death ruled as king from Adam down to Moses, even over those who had not sinned in the same way that Adam transgressed, who bears a resemblance to the one who was to come.[a]

15 But the gift is not like the trespass. For if by one man's trespass many died, how much more did the undeserved kindness of God and his free gift by the undeserved kindness of the one man,[b] Jesus Christ, abound* to many![c] **16** Also, it is not the same with the free gift as with the way things worked through the one man who sinned.[d] For the judgment after one trespass was condemnation,[e] but the gift after many trespasses was a declaration of righteousness.[f] **17** For if by the trespass of the one man death ruled as king through that one,[g] how much more will those who receive the abundance of the undeserved kindness and of the free gift of righteousness[h] rule as kings[i] in life through the one person, Jesus Christ![j]

18 So, then, as through one trespass the result to men of all sorts was condemnation,[k] so too through one act of justification the result to men of all sorts[l] is their being declared righteous for life.[m] **19** For just as through the disobedience of the one man many were made sinners,[n] so also through the obedience of the one person many will be made righteous.[o] **20** Now the Law came on the scene so that trespassing might increase.[p] But where sin abounded, undeserved kindness abounded still more. **21** To what end? So that just as sin ruled as king with death,[q] so also undeserved kindness might rule as king through righteousness leading to ever-

---

CHAP. 5

a Eph 2:14
b 2Co 5:18
  Eph 3:11, 12
  Heb 10:19
c Php 2:17
  1Pe 4:12, 13
d Ac 5:41, 42
e Jas 1:12
f Php 1:18-20
g Jos 21:45
h 2Co 1:22
  Ga 4:6
  Eph 1:13, 14
i Eph 2:1, 5
j Isa 53:12
  Joh 3:16
  Eph 2:4, 5
  1Pe 3:18
  1Jo 4:10
k Ac 13:38, 39
  Heb 9:14
l 1Ti 1:10
m 2Co 5:18
  Col 1:21, 22
n 2Co 5:19
o Ge 2:17
  Ge 3:6
  Ge 3:19
  1Co 15:21
p Ps 51:5
  Ro 3:23
q Ro 4:15

Second Col.

a 1Co 15:45
b Heb 2:9
c Isa 53:11
  Mt 20:28
d Ge 2:17
  Ge 3:6
e Ge 3:17-19
f Ro 4:25
g Ro 5:12, 14
h Ro 3:24
i Re 5:9, 10
  Re 20:4
j 1Pe 3:18
  Re 1:5, 6
k 1Co 15:21
l Ro 1:16
  1Ti 2:3, 4
m Joh 10:10
n Ro 5:12
o Isa 53:11
  Heb 2:10
p Ro 3:20
  Ga 3:19
q 1Co 15:56

5:1 * Or possibly, "we have peace." 5:2, 3 * Or possibly, "we rejoice."

5:15 * Or "overflow."

lasting life through Jesus Christ our Lord.[a]

6 What are we to say then? Should we continue in sin so that undeserved kindness may increase? **2** Certainly not! Seeing that we died with reference to sin,[b] how can we keep living any longer in it?[c] **3** Or do you not know that all of us who were baptized into Christ Jesus[d] were baptized into his death?[e] **4** So we were buried with him through our baptism into his death,[f] in order that just as Christ was raised up from the dead through the glory of the Father, so we also should walk in a newness of life.[g] **5** If we have become united with him in the likeness of his death,[h] we will certainly also be united with him in the likeness of his resurrection.[i] **6** For we know that our old personality was nailed to the stake along with him[j] in order for our sinful body to be made powerless,[k] so that we should no longer go on being slaves to sin.[l] **7** For the one who has died has been acquitted* from his sin.

8 Moreover, if we have died with Christ, we believe that we will also live with him. **9** For we know that Christ, now that he has been raised up from the dead,[m] dies no more;[n] death is no longer master over him. **10** For the death that he died, he died with reference to sin* once for all time,[o] but the life that he lives, he lives with reference to God. **11** Likewise you, consider yourselves to be dead with reference to sin but living with reference to God by Christ Jesus.[p]

12 Therefore, do not let sin continue to rule as king in your mortal bodies[q] so that you should obey their desires. **13** Neither go on presenting your bodies* to sin as [weapons] of unrighteousness, but [present] yourselves to God as those [living] from the dead, also your bo[dies] to God as weapons of righteou[s]ness.[a] **14** For sin must not [be] master over you, seeing that y[ou] are not under law[b] but unde[r] undeserved kindness.[c]

15 What follows? Are we to commit a sin because we are not under law but under undeserved kindness?[d] Certainly not! **16** Do you not know that if you present yourselves to anyone as obedient slaves, you are slaves of the one you obey,[e] either of sin[f] leading to death[g] or of obedience leading to righteousness? **17** But thanks to God that although you were once the slaves of sin, you became obedient from the heart to that pattern of teaching to which you were handed over. **18** Yes, since you were set free from sin,[h] you became slaves to righteousness.[i] **19** I am speaking in human terms because of the weakness of your flesh; for just as you presented your members as slaves to uncleanness and lawlessness leading to lawlessness, so now present your members as slaves to righteousness leading to holiness.[j] **20** For when you were slaves of sin, you were free as to righteousness.

21 What, then, was the fruit that you used to produce at that time? Things of which you are now ashamed. For the end of those things is death.[k] **22** However, now that you were set free from sin and became slaves to God, you are producing your fruit in the way of holiness,[l] and the end is everlasting life.[m] **23** For the wages sin pays is death,[n] but the gift God gives is everlasting life[o] by Christ Jesus our Lord.[p]

CHAP. 5
a Joh 3:16
  1Jo 4:9

CHAP. 6
b 1Pe 2:24
c Heb 10:26, 27
d 1Co 12:13
  Ga 3:27
e Mr 10:38, 39
  1Co 15:29
f Col 2:12
g Col 3:10
  1Jo 3:14
h 2Co 4:10
  Php 3:10
i 1Co 15:42, 49
j Ga 5:24
k Col 2:11
  Col 3:5
l 2Co 7:1
m Ac 13:34
n Re 1:17, 18
o Heb 9:28
  1Pe 3:18
p 1Pe 2:24
q Ge 4:7

Second Col.
a Ro 12:1
b Ro 7:6
  Ga 5:18
  Col 2:13, 14
c Joh 1:17
d Ro 5:21
e 2Pe 2:19
f Joh 8:34
g Ro 6:23
h Joh 8:31, 32
i 1Pe 2:24
j Ro 12:1
k Ro 8:6
  Ga 5:19-21
l Ga 5:22, 23
m 1Co 9:25
n Ge 2:17
o Mt 25:46
  1Pe 1:3, 4
p 1Ti 1:16
  1Jo 2:1, 2
  Jude 21

6:7 *Or "released; pardoned."   6:10 *That is, to remove sin.

6:13 *Lit., "members."

... that you do not ... RO... ... those who know ... he Law is master ... as long as he lives? ...ance, a married wom-... ...nd by law to her hus-... while he is alive; but if ...band dies, she is released ...he law of her husband.[a] ..., then, while her husband ... living, she would be called an adulteress if she became another man's.[b] But if her husband dies, she is free from his law, so that she is not an adulteress if she becomes another man's.[c]

4 So, my brothers, you also were made dead to the Law through the body of the Christ, that you might become another's,[d] the one who was raised up from the dead,[e] so that we should bear fruit to God.[f] **5** For when we were living according to the flesh, the sinful passions that were awakened by the Law were at work in our bodies* to produce fruit for death.[g] **6** But now we have been released from the Law,[h] because we have died to that which restrained us, in order that we might be slaves in a new sense by the spirit[i] and not in the old sense by the written code.[j]

7 What, then, are we to say? Is the Law sin? Certainly not! Really, I would not have come to know sin had it not been for the Law.[k] For example, I would not have known covetousness if the Law had not said: "You must not covet."[l] **8** But sin, finding the opportunity afforded by the commandment, worked out in me covetousness of every sort, for apart from law sin was dead.[m] **9** In fact, I was once alive apart from law. But when the commandment arrived, sin came to life again, but I died.[n] **10** And the commandment that

7:5, 23 *Lit., "members."

CHAP. 7

a 1Co 7:39

b Mt 5:32
  Mt 19:9
  Mr 10:11, 12
  Lu 16:18

c 1Co 7:8, 9
  1Ti 5:14

d 2Co 11:2

e Ac 5:30
  2Co 5:15

f Ga 5:22, 23
  Col 1:10

g Jas 1:14, 15

h Ro 10:4
  Eph 2:15
  Col 2:13, 14

i Ro 12:11

j Ga 3:10

k Ro 3:20
  Ga 3:19

l Ex 20:17
  De 5:21

m Ro 4:15
  Ro 5:20

n 2Co 3:6

Second Col.

a Le 18:5
  Lu 10:26-28

b De 4:8
  Ps 19:8

c 1Co 15:56

d Ro 5:13

e Ps 51:5
  Job 8:34
  Ro 6:16

f Ge 8:21

g Mt 26:41

h Jer 17:9

i 2Co 4:16
  Eph 3:16
  Eph 4:23, 24

j Ga 5:17
  Jas 4:1

k Job 8:34

l Ro 6:13
  Ga 5:17

was to lead to life,[a] this I found led to death. **11** For sin, finding the opportunity afforded by the commandment, seduced me and killed me through it. **12** So the Law in itself is holy, and the commandment is holy and righteous and good.[b]

13 Therefore, did what is good result in my death? Certainly not! But sin did, that it might be shown to be sin working out death in me through what is good,[c] so that through the commandment sin might become far more sinful.[d] **14** For we know that the Law is spiritual, but I am fleshly, sold under sin.[e] **15** For I do not understand what I am doing. For I do not practice what I wish, but I do what I hate. **16** However, if I do what I do not wish, I agree that the Law is fine. **17** But now I am no longer the one doing it, but it is the sin that resides in me.[f] **18** For I know that in me, that is, in my flesh, there dwells nothing good; for I have the desire to do what is fine but not the ability to carry it out.[g] **19** For I do not do the good that I wish, but the bad that I do not wish is what I practice. **20** If, then, I do what I do not wish, I am no longer the one carrying it out, but it is the sin dwelling in me.

21 I find, then, this law in my case: When I wish to do what is right, what is bad is present with me.[h] **22** I really delight in the law of God according to the man I am within,[i] **23** but I see in my body* another law warring against the law of my mind[j] and leading me captive to sin's law[k] that is in my body.* **24** Miserable man that I am! Who will rescue me from the body undergoing this death? **25** Thanks to God through Jesus Christ our Lord! So, then, with my mind I myself am a slave to God's law, but with my flesh to sin's law.[l]

8 Therefore, those in union with Christ Jesus have no condemnation. **2** For the law of the spirit that gives life in union with Christ Jesus has set you free[a] from the law of sin and of death. **3** What the Law was incapable of doing[b] because it was weak[c] through the flesh, God did by sending his own Son[d] in the likeness of sinful flesh[e] and concerning sin, condemned sin in the flesh, **4** so that the righteous requirement of the Law might be fulfilled in us[f] who walk, not according to the flesh, but according to the spirit.[g] **5** For those who live according to the flesh set their minds on the things of the flesh,[h] but those who live according to the spirit, on the things of the spirit.[i] **6** For setting the mind on the flesh means death,[j] but setting the mind on the spirit means life and peace;[k] **7** because setting the mind on the flesh means enmity with God,[l] for it is not in subjection to the law of God, nor, in fact, can it be. **8** So those who are in harmony with the flesh cannot please God.

9 However, you are in harmony, not with the flesh, but with the spirit,[m] if God's spirit truly dwells in you. But if anyone does not have Christ's spirit, this person does not belong to him. **10** But if Christ is in union with you,[n] the body is dead because of sin, but the spirit is life because of righteousness. **11** If, now, the spirit of him who raised up Jesus from the dead dwells in you, the one who raised up Christ Jesus from the dead[o] will also make your mortal bodies alive[p] through his spirit that resides in you.

12 So, then, brothers, we are under obligation, not to the flesh to live according to the flesh;[q] **13** for if you live according to the flesh, you are sure to die; but if you put the practices of the body to death[a] by it, you will live.[b] **14** F[...] are led by God's spirit[...] deed God's sons.[c] **15** [...] did not receive a spirit [...] ery causing fear again, bu[...] received a spirit of adoptio[...] sons, by which spirit we cry[...] "Abba,* Father!"[d] **16** The sp[...] it itself bears witness with o[...] spirit[e] that we are God's chi[...] dren.[f] **17** If, then, we are chil[...] dren, we are also heirs—heirs indeed of God, but joint heirs[g] with Christ—provided we suffer together[h] so that we may also be glorified together.

18 For I consider that the sufferings of the present time do not amount to anything in comparison with the glory that is going to be revealed in us.[i] **19** For the creation is waiting with eager expectation for the revealing of the sons of God.[k] **20** For the creation was subjected to futility,[l] not by its own will, but through the one who subjected it, on the basis of hope **21** that the creation itself will also be set free[m] from enslavement to corruption and have the glorious freedom of the children of God. **22** For we know that all creation keeps on groaning together and being in pain together until now. **23** Not only that, but we ourselves also who have the firstfruits, namely, the spirit, yes, we ourselves groan within ourselves[n] while we are earnestly waiting for adoption as sons,[o] the release from our bodies by ransom. **24** For we were saved in this hope; but hope that is seen is not hope, for when a man sees a thing, does he hope for it? **25** But if we hope[p] for what we do not see,[q] we keep eagerly waiting for it with endurance.[r]

26 In like manner, the spirit also joins in with help for

CHAP. 8

a Joh 8:31, 32
Jas 1:25

b Ro 3:20
Heb 7:11

c Heb 7:18

d 1Jo 4:9

e Joh 1:14

f Ro 3:31

g Ga 5:16, 18

h Ga 5:19-21

i Ga 5:22, 23

j Ro 6:21

k Ga 6:7, 8

l Isa 59:2
Col 1:21

m Ga 5:25

n Joh 15:4

o Ac 2:24

p Eph 2:1, 5

q Ga 5:19-21

___

Second Col.

a 1Co 9:27
Ga 5:24
Eph 4:22
Col 3:5

b Ga 6:7, 8

c Joh 1:12
Joh 3:5

d Ga 4:4-6

e 1Co 2:10, 12
2Co 1:22

f Joh 1:12
Ga 3:26
1Jo 3:2

g Lu 12:32
Ga 3:29

h Php 1:29
Col 1:24

i 1Co 15:53
Re 3:21

j 2Co 4:17
1Pe 4:13

k 1Jo 3:2

l Ge 3:17-19

m Joh 8:31, 32
1Co 15:22

n 2Co 5:1, 2

o Ga 4:4, 5
Eph 1:5
Re 21:7

p 1Pe 1:3, 4

q 2Co 5:7

r Ro 5:3-5

___

8:15 *An Aramaic word meaning "O Father!"

ROMA...for the problem ...not know what ...our pray for as we is ...t the spirit itself ...was with unuttered* ...n **27** But the one who ...ne hearts[b] knows what ...ng of the spirit is, be...is pleading in harmony ...d for the holy ones.

...e know that God makes ...works cooperate together ...e good of those who love ..., those who are the ones ...ed according to his purpose;[c] ...because those whom he gave ...is first recognition he also foreordained to be patterned after the image of his Son,[d] so that he might be the firstborn[e] among many brothers.[f] **30** Moreover, those whom he foreordained[g] are the ones he also called;[h] and those whom he called are the ones he also declared to be righteous.[i] Finally those whom he declared righteous are the ones he also glorified.[j]

31 What, then, are we to say about these things? If God is for us, who will be against us?[k] **32** Since he did not even spare his own Son but handed him over for us all,[l] will he not also, along with him, kindly give us all other things? **33** Who will file accusation against God's chosen ones?[m] God is the One who declares them righteous.[n] **34** Who will condemn them? Christ Jesus is the one who died, yes, more than that the one who was raised up, who is at the right hand of God[o] and who also pleads for us.[p]

35 Who will separate us from the love of the Christ?[q] Will tribulation or distress or persecution or hunger or nakedness or danger or sword?[r] **36** Just as it is written: "For your sake we are being put to death all day long; we have been accounted as sheep for slaughtering."[a] **37** On the contrary, in all these things we are coming off completely victorious[b] through the one who loved us. **38** For I am convinced that neither death nor life nor angels nor governments nor things now here nor things to come nor powers[c] **39** nor height nor depth nor any other creation will be able to separate us from God's love that is in Christ Jesus our Lord.

9 I am telling the truth in Christ; I am not lying, as my conscience bears witness with me in holy spirit, **2** that I have great grief and unceasing pain in my heart. **3** For I could wish that I myself were separated from the Christ as the cursed one for the sake of my brothers, my relatives according to the flesh, **4** who are Israelites. To them belong the adoption as sons[d] and the glory and the covenants[e] and the giving of the Law[f] and the sacred service[g] and the promises.[h] **5** To them the forefathers belong,[i] and from them the Christ descended according to the flesh.[j] God, who is over all, be praised forever. Amen.

6 However, it is not as though the word of God has failed. For not all who descend from Israel are really "Israel."[k] **7** Neither are they all children because they are Abraham's offspring;* [l] rather, "What will be called your offspring* will be through Isaac."[m] **8** That is, the children in the flesh are not really the children of God,[n] but the children by the promise[o] are counted as the offspring.* **9** For the word of promise was as follows: "At this time I will come and Sarah will have a son."[p] **10** Not only then but also when Rebek'ah conceived twins from the one man, Isaac our fore-

CHAP. 8
a Joh 14:16, 26
  Joh 16:7
b Jer 11:20
c Eph 1:9-11
  2Ti 1:9
d Joh 13:15
  Ro 6:5
  1Co 15:49
e Heb 1:6
f Heb 2:11
g Eph 1:5
h Php 3:14
  1Th 2:12
  Heb 3:1
i Ro 5:18
  Tit 3:7
j 2Co 4:6
k Ps 118:6
  1Jo 4:4
l Joh 3:16
  Ro 3:25
  1Jo 4:9
m Isa 50:9
n Ac 13:38, 39
  Heb 10:16, 17
o Ps 110:1
p Heb 7:25
  1Jo 2:1
q Joh 15:10
r 2Co 4:8, 9

Second Col.
a Ps 44:22
b Joh 16:33
c Eph 6:12

CHAP. 9
d Ex 4:22
e Ac 3:25
  Ac 7:8
f Ex 24:12
g Ac 26:7
  Heb 9:1
h Ro 4:13
i De 10:15
j Mt 1:17
k Ro 2:28
  Re 2:9
l Joh 8:39
  Ga 3:29
m Ge 21:12
  Heb 11:18
n Joh 1:12, 13
o Ga 4:28
p Ge 18:10, 14

father;[a] 11 for when they had not yet been born and had not practiced anything good or bad, so that God's purpose respecting the choosing might continue dependent, not on works, but on the One who calls, 12 it was said to her: "The older will be the slave of the younger."[b] 13 Just as it is written: "I loved Jacob, but E'sau I hated."[c]

14 What are we to say, then? Is there injustice with God? Certainly not![d] 15 For he says to Moses: "I will show mercy to whomever I will show mercy, and I will show compassion to whomever I will show compassion."[e] 16 So, then, it depends, not on a person's desire or on his effort,* but on God, who has mercy.[f] 17 For the scripture says to Phar'aoh: "For this very reason I have let you remain: to show my power in connection with you and to have my name declared in all the earth."[g] 18 So, then, he has mercy on whomever he wishes, but he lets whomever he wishes become obstinate.[h]

19 You will therefore say to me: "Why does he still find fault? For who has withstood his will?" 20 But who are you, O man, to be answering back to God?[i] Does the thing molded say to its molder: "Why did you make me this way?"[j] 21 What? Does not the potter have authority over the clay[k] to make from the same lump one vessel for an honorable use, another for a dishonorable use? 22 What, then, if God had the will to demonstrate his wrath and to make his power known, and he tolerated with much patience vessels of wrath made fit for destruction? 23 And if this was done to make known the riches of his glory on vessels of mercy,[l] which he prepared beforehand

for glory, 24 namely, 3 he called not only fro Jews but also from an tions,[a] what of it? 25 It says also in Ho·se'a: "Tho my people[b] I will call 'my ple,' and her who was not l 'beloved';[c] 26 and in the p where it was said to them, ' are not my people,' there th will be called 'sons of the livin God.'"[d]

27 Moreover, Isaiah cries out concerning Israel: "Although the number of the sons of Israel may be as the sand of the sea, only the remnant will be saved.[e] 28 For Jehovah* will make an accounting on the earth, concluding it and cutting it short."[#f] 29 Also, just as Isaiah foretold: "Unless Jehovah* of armies had left an offspring* to us, we should have become just like Sod'om, and we should have resembled Go·mor'rah."[g]

30 What are we to say, then? That people of the nations, although not pursuing righteousness, attained righteousness,[h] the righteousness that results from faith;[i] 31 but Israel, although pursuing a law of righteousness, did not attain to that law. 32 For what reason? Because they pursued it, not by faith, but as by works. They stumbled over the "stone of stumbling";[j] 33 as it is written: "Look! I am laying in Zion a stone[k] of stumbling and a rock of offense, but the one who rests his faith on it will not be disappointed."[l]

10 Brothers, the goodwill of my heart and my supplication to God for them are indeed for their salvation.[m] 2 For I bear them witness that they have a zeal for God,[n] but not according to accurate knowledge. 3 For because of not knowing

CHAP. 9
a Ge 25:21, 24
b Ge 25:23
c Mal 1:2, 3
  Heb 12:16
d De 32:4
  Job 34:10
e Ex 33:19
  Tit 3:4, 5
f Ex 9:16
g Ex 10:1
  Ex 14:4
i Job 40:2
j Isa 29:16
  Isa 45:9
k Isa 64:8
  Jer 18:6
l 1Th 5:9

Second Col.
a Ro 11:13
  Eph 3:6
b Eph 2:12
c Ho 2:23
  Mt 21:43
  1Pe 2:10
d Ho 1:10
  Ga 3:26
e Ho 1:10
  Ro 11:4, 5
f Isa 10:22, 23
g Isa 1:9
h Ro 10:20
i Ro 4:11
  Php 3:9
j Isa 8:14
  Lu 20:17, 18
  1Co 1:23
k Ps 118:22
  Mt 21:42
l Isa 28:16
  Ro 10:11
  1Pe 2:6

CHAP. 10
m Ro 9:3, 4
n Ac 21:20
  Ga 1:14

9:16 *Lit., "not on the one who desires nor on the one who runs." 9:28, 29 *See App. A5. 9:28 #Or "executing it speedily." 9:29 #Lit., "seed."

...ss of God[a] but
...ablish their own,[b]
the subject themselves
see...eousness of God.[c]
the... is the end of
the... that everyone exercis-
...may have righteous-

... Moses writes about the
...usness that is by the Law:
...an who does these things
...ve by means of them."[f]
...t the righteousness result-
...from faith says: "Do not say
...your heart,[g] 'Who will ascend
...to heaven?'[h] that is, to bring
Christ down, **7** or, 'Who will
descend into the abyss?'[i] that
is, to bring Christ up from the
dead." **8** But what does it say?
"The word is near you, in your
own mouth and in your own
heart";[j] that is, "the word" of
faith, which we are preaching.
9 For if you publicly declare
with your mouth that Jesus is
Lord,[k] and exercise faith in your
heart that God raised him up
from the dead, you will be saved.
10 For with the heart one exercises faith for righteousness, but
with the mouth one makes public declaration[l] for salvation.

11 For the scripture says: "No
one who rests his faith on him
will be disappointed."[m] **12** For
there is no distinction between
Jew and Greek.[n] There is the
same Lord over all, who is rich*
toward all those calling on him.
13 For "everyone who calls on
the name of Jehovah* will be
saved."[o] **14** However, how will
they call on him if they have not
put faith in him? How, in turn,
will they put faith in him about
whom they have not heard? How,
in turn, will they hear without
someone to preach? **15** How, in
turn, will they preach unless
they have been sent out?[p] Just

CHAP. 10
a Ro 1:16, 17
b Lu 16:15
  Php 3:9
c Lu 7:29, 30
d Mt 5:17
  Ro 7:6
  Eph 2:15
  Col 2:13, 14
e Ga 3:24
f Le 18:5
  Ga 3:12
g De 9:4
h De 30:12
i De 30:13
j De 30:14
k Ac 16:31
l 1Co 9:16
  2Co 4:13
  Heb 13:15
m Isa 28:16
  Ro 9:33
n Ac 15:7-9
  Ga 3:28
o Joe 2:32
  Ac 2:21
p Mt 28:19, 20

Second Col.
a Isa 52:7
  Eph 6:14, 15
b Isa 53:1
  Joh 12:37, 38
c Joh 4:42
d Ps 19:4
  Ac 1:8
e Mt 10:5, 6
  Ac 2:14
f De 32:21
g Ro 9:30
h Isa 65:1
i Isa 65:2

CHAP. 11
j 1Sa 12:22
  Jer 31:37
k Ex 19:5
  Ps 94:14
l 1Ki 19:2, 14
m 1Ki 19:18
n Ro 9:27

as it is written: "How beautiful
are the feet of those who declare
good news of good things!"[a]
16 Nevertheless, they did not
all obey the good news. For Isaiah says: "Jehovah,* who has put
faith in the thing heard from
us?"[#b] **17** So faith follows the
thing heard.[c] In turn, what is
heard is through the word about
Christ. **18** But I ask, They did
not fail to hear, did they? Why,
in fact, "into all the earth their
sound went out, and to the ends
of the inhabited earth their message."[d] **19** But I ask, Israel did
not fail to know, did they?[e] First
Moses says: "I will incite you
to jealousy through that which
is not a nation; I will incite you
to violent anger through a foolish nation."[f] **20** But Isaiah becomes very bold and says: "I was
found by those who were not
seeking me;[g] I became known to
those who were not asking for
me."[h] **21** But he says regarding
Israel: "All day long I have
spread out my hands toward a
disobedient and obstinate people."[i]

11 I ask, then, God did not reject his people, did he?[j] By
no means! For I too am an Israelite, of the offspring* of Abraham, from the tribe of Benjamin.
2 God did not reject his people,
whom he first recognized.[k] Do
you not know what the scripture
says in connection with E·li′jah,
as he pleads with God against
Israel? **3** "Jehovah,* they have
killed your prophets, they have
dug up your altars, and I alone
am left, and now they are trying
to take my life."[#l] **4** Yet, what
does the divine pronouncement
say to him? "I have left for myself 7,000 men who have not bent
the knee to Ba′al."[m] **5** So in the
same way, at the present time
also, there is a remnant[n] accord-

10:12 *Or "generous." 10:13, 16; 11:3 *See App. A5. | 10:16 #Or "in our report?" 11:1 *Lit., "seed." 11:3 #Or "soul."

ing to a choosing through undeserved kindness. **6** Now if it is by undeserved kindness,[a] it is no longer through works;[b] otherwise, the undeserved kindness would no longer be undeserved kindness.

7 What, then? The very thing Israel is earnestly seeking he did not obtain, but the ones chosen obtained it.[c] The rest had their senses dulled,[d] **8** just as it is written: "God has given them a spirit of deep sleep,[e] eyes that do not see and ears that do not hear, down to this very day."[f] **9** Also, David says: "Let their table become a snare and a trap and a stumbling block and a retribution for them. **10** Let their eyes become darkened so that they cannot see, and always make them bend their backs."[g]

11 So I ask, They did not stumble and fall completely, did they? Certainly not! But by their false step, there is salvation to people of the nations, to incite them to jealousy.[h] **12** Now if their false step means riches to the world and their decrease means riches to people of the nations,[i] how much more will their full number mean!

13 Now I speak to you who are people of the nations. Seeing that I am an apostle to the nations,[j] I glorify* my ministry[k] **14** to see if I may in some way incite my own people* to jealousy and save some from among them. **15** For if their being cast away[l] means reconciliation for the world, what will the acceptance of them mean but life from the dead? **16** Further, if the part of the dough taken as firstfruits is holy, the entire batch is also holy; and if the root is holy, the branches are also.

17 However, if some of the branches were broken off and

you, although being a wild olive, were grafted in among them and became a sharer of the richness of the olive's root, **18** do not be arrogant toward* the branches. If, though, you are arrogant toward* them,[a] remember that it is not you who bears the root, but the root bears you. **19** You will say, then: "Branches were broken off so that I might be grafted in."[b] **20** That is true! For their lack of faith, they were broken off,[c] but you are standing by faith.[d] Do not be haughty, but be in fear. **21** For if God did not spare the natural branches, neither will he spare you. **22** Consider, therefore, God's kindness[e] and severity. There is severity toward those who fell,[f] but toward you there is God's kindness, provided you remain in his kindness; otherwise, you too will be lopped off. **23** And they also, if they do not remain in their lack of faith, will be grafted in,[g] for God is able to graft them back in. **24** For if you were cut out of the olive tree that is wild by nature and were grafted contrary to nature into the garden olive tree, how much more will these who are natural branches be grafted back into their own olive tree!

25 For I do not want you to be unaware of this sacred secret,[h] brothers, so that you do not become wise in your own eyes: A partial dulling of senses has come upon Israel until the full number of people of the nations has come in, **26** and in this manner all Israel[i] will be saved. Just as it is written: "The deliverer* will come out of Zion[j] and turn away ungodly practices from Jacob. **27** And this is my covenant with them,[k] when I take their sins away."[l] **28** True, with

---

CHAP. 11
a Eph 1:7
   Eph 2:8

b Ga 2:15, 16

c Joh 1:11, 12

d 2Co 3:14, 15

e Isa 29:10

f De 29:4

g Ps 69:22, 23

h De 32:21
   Ro 10:19

i Ro 9:23, 24

j Ac 9:15
   Ga 1:15, 16
   Eph 3:8

k Ac 28:30, 31
   Col 1:23
   2Ti 4:5

l Mt 21:43

Second Col.
a 1Co 10:12

b Ac 15:14

c Mt 21:43

d Eph 2:8

e Ro 2:4

f Mt 23:38

g Ac 2:38

h Eph 3:5, 6

i Ro 2:29
   Ro 9:6
   Ga 3:29

j Ps 14:7

k Isa 59:20, 21

l Isa 27:9

11:13 *Or "magnify."   11:14 *Lit., "my flesh."

11:18 *Or "boast against."   11:26 *Or "savior."

respect to the good news, they are enemies for your sakes; but with respect to God's choosing, they are beloved for the sake of their forefathers.[a] 29 For the gifts and the calling of God are not things he will regret. 30 For just as you were once disobedient to God[b] but have now been shown mercy[c] because of their disobedience,[d] 31 so also these now have been disobedient with mercy resulting to you, so that they themselves may also now be shown mercy. 32 For God has confined all of them together in disobedience[e] so that he might show all of them mercy.[f]

33 O the depth of God's riches and wisdom and knowledge! How unsearchable his judgments are and beyond tracing out his ways are! 34 For "who has come to know Jehovah's* mind, or who has become his adviser?"[g] 35 Or, "who has first given to him, so that it must be repaid to him?"[h] 36 Because from him and by him and for him are all things. To him be the glory forever. Amen.

12 Therefore, I appeal to you by the compassions of God, brothers, to present your bodies[i] as a living sacrifice, holy[j] and acceptable to God, a sacred service with your power of reason.[k] 2 And stop being molded by this system of things,* but be transformed by making your mind over,[l] so that you may prove to yourselves[m] the good and acceptable and perfect will of God.

3 For through the undeserved kindness given to me, I tell everyone there among you not to think more of himself than it is necessary to think,[n] but to think so as to have a sound mind, each one as God has given* to him a measure of faith.[a] 4 For just as we have in one body many members,[b] but the members do not all have the same function, 5 so we, although many, are one body in union with Christ, but individually we are members belonging to one another.[c] 6 Since, then, we have gifts that differ according to the undeserved kindness given to us,[d] if it is of prophecy, let us prophesy in proportion to our faith; 7 or if it is a ministry, let us be at this ministry; or the one who teaches, let him be at his teaching;[e] 8 or the one who encourages,* let him give encouragement;*[f] the one who distributes,△ let him do it liberally;[g] the one who presides,⊠ let him do it diligently;□[h] the one who shows mercy, let him do it cheerfully.[i]

9 Let your love be without hypocrisy.[j] Abhor what is wicked;[k] cling to what is good. 10 In brotherly love have tender affection for one another. In showing honor to one another, take the lead.*[l] 11 Be industrious,* not lazy.△[m] Be aglow with the spirit.[n] Slave for Jehovah.*[o] 12 Rejoice in the hope. Endure under tribulation.[p] Persevere in prayer.[q] 13 Share with the holy ones according to their needs.[r] Follow the course of hospitality.[s] 14 Keep on blessing those who persecute;[t] bless and do not curse.[u] 15 Rejoice with those who rejoice; weep with those who weep. 16 Have the same attitude toward others as toward yourselves; do not set your mind on lofty things,* but be led

---

CHAP. 11
a De 10:15
b Eph 2:1, 2
c Ac 15:7-9
d Ac 7:51
e Ro 3:9
f 1Ti 2:3, 4
g Isa 40:13
  Da 4:35
h Job 41:11

CHAP. 12
i Ro 6:13
j 2Co 7:1
  1Pe 1:15
k 2Ti 1:7
l Eph 4:23, 24
m 1Ti 4:15
n Pr 16:18
  Ga 6:3
  1Pe 5:5

Second Col.
a Eph 2:8
b 1Co 12:12
c 1Co 12:25
d Eph 3:7
e 1Ti 5:17
  1Pe 4:10, 11
f 2Ti 4:2
g De 15:11
  2Co 8:2
h 1Th 5:12
  1Pe 5:2
i Eph 4:32
j 1Ti 1:5
  Jas 3:17
  1Pe 1:22
k Ps 97:10
  Pr 8:13
l Php 2:3
m Pr 13:4
n Ac 18:24, 25
o Ro 6:22
p Ac 14:22
q Php 4:6
  1Th 5:17
r Pr 3:27
  1Jo 3:17
s 1Pe 4:9
  3Jo 8
t Mt 5:44
  Lu 6:27, 28
u Jas 3:9, 10

11:34; 12:11 *See App. A5. **12:2** *Or "this age." See Glossary.

12:3 *Or "apportioned; distributed." **12:8** *Or "exhorts." #Or "exhortation." △Or "contributes." ⊠Or "takes the lead." □Or "earnestly." **12:10** *Or "initiative." **12:11** #Or "diligent; zealous." △Or "Do not loiter at your business." **12:16** *Or "cultivate lofty ideas."

along with the lowly things.[a] Do not become wise in your own eyes.[b]

17 Return evil for evil to no one.[c] Take into consideration what is fine from the viewpoint of* all men. **18** If possible, as far as it depends on you, be peaceable with all men.[d] **19** Do not avenge yourselves, beloved, but yield place to the wrath;*[e] for it is written: "'Vengeance is mine; I will repay,' says Jehovah."*[f] **20** But "if your enemy is hungry, feed him; if he is thirsty, give him something to drink; for by doing this you will heap fiery coals on his head."*[g] **21** Do not let yourself be conquered by the evil, but keep conquering the evil with the good.[h]

13 Let every person* be in subjection to the superior authorities,[i] for there is no authority except by God;[j] the existing authorities stand placed in their relative positions by God.[k] **2** Therefore, whoever opposes the authority has taken a stand against the arrangement of God; those who have taken a stand against it will bring judgment against themselves. **3** For those rulers are an object of fear, not to the good deed, but to the bad.[l] Do you want to be free of fear of the authority? Keep doing good,[m] and you will have praise from it; **4** for it is God's minister to you for your good. But if you are doing what is bad, be in fear, for it is not without purpose that it bears the sword. It is God's minister, an avenger to express wrath* against the one practicing what is bad.

5 There is therefore compelling reason for you to be in subjection, not only on account of

that wrath but also on account of your conscience.[a] **6** That is why you are also paying taxes; for they are God's public servants constantly serving this very purpose. **7** Render to all their dues: to the one who calls for the tax, the tax;[b] to the one who calls for the tribute, the tribute; to the one who calls for fear, such fear;[c] to the one who calls for honor, such honor.[d]

8 Do not owe anything to anyone except to love one another;[e] for whoever loves his fellow man has fulfilled the law.[f] **9** For the law code, "You must not commit adultery,[g] you must not murder,[h] you must not steal,[i] you must not covet,"[j] and whatever other commandment there is, is summed up in this saying: "You must love your neighbor as yourself."[k] **10** Love does not work evil to one's neighbor;[l] therefore, love is the law's fulfillment.[m]

11 And do this because you know the season, that it is already the hour for you to awake from sleep,[n] for now our salvation is nearer than at the time when we became believers. **12** The night is well along; the day has drawn near. Let us therefore throw off the works belonging to darkness[o] and let us put on the weapons of the light.[p] **13** Let us walk decently* as in the daytime, not in wild parties* and drunkenness, not in immoral intercourse and brazen conduct,*[r] not in strife and jealousy.[s] **14** But put on the Lord Jesus Christ,[t] and do not be planning ahead for the desires of the flesh.[u]

14 Welcome the man having weaknesses in his faith,[v] but do not pass judgment on differing opinions.* **2** One man

---

CHAP. 12
a Lu 14:10
   Lu 22:24-26
   Joh 13:14
   Php 2:3
b Job 37:24
   Pr 3:7
c 1Th 5:15
   1Pe 2:23
   1Pe 3:9
d 2Ti 2:24
   Heb 12:14
   Jas 3:18
e Le 19:18
   Mt 5:39
f De 32:35
   Heb 10:30
g Pr 25:21, 22
h Ex 23:4
   Mt 5:44
   Lu 6:27

CHAP. 13
i Tit 3:1
   1Pe 2:13, 14
j Joh 19:10, 11
k Ac 17:26
l 1Pe 2:13, 14
m 1Pe 3:13

Second Col.
a 1Pe 2:19
   1Pe 3:16
b Mt 22:21
   Mr 12:17
   Lu 20:25
c Pr 24:21
d 1Pe 2:13, 17
e Col 3:14
   1Ti 1:5
   1Jo 4:11
f Ga 5:14
   Jas 2:8
g Ex 20:14
   Mt 5:27, 28
   1Co 6:9, 10
h Ge 9:6
   De 5:17
i Ex 20:15
j Ex 20:17
k Le 19:18
   Mt 22:39
l Lu 6:31
   2Ti 2:24
m Mt 22:37-40
   1Th 5:6
n Lu 21:36
   1Th 5:6
o Eph 5:10, 11
p 2Co 6:4, 7
   Eph 6:11
   1Th 5:8
q 1Pe 2:12
r Eph 4:19
   1Pe 4:3
s 2Co 12:20
t 1Co 11:1
   Ga 3:27
   Eph 4:24
u Ga 5:16

CHAP. 14
v Ro 15:1
   1Th 5:14

12:17 *Or "in the sight of." 12:19 *That is, God's wrath. #See App. A5. 12:20 *That is, to soften the person and melt his hardness. 13:1 *Or "soul." 13:4 *Or "bring punishment."

13:13 *Or "in revelries." #Or "acts of shameless conduct." Plural of the Greek a·sel′gei·a. See Glossary. 14:1 *Or possibly, "inward questionings."

has faith to eat everything, but the man who is weak eats only vegetables. **3** Let the one eating not look down on the one not eating, and let the one not eating not judge the one eating,[a] for God has welcomed him. **4** Who are you to judge the servant of another?[b] To his own master he stands or falls.[c] Indeed, he will be made to stand, for Jehovah* can make him stand.

5 One man judges one day as above another;[d] another judges one day the same as all others;[e] let each one be fully convinced in his own mind. **6** The one who observes the day observes it to Jehovah.* Also, the one who eats, eats to Jehovah,* for he gives thanks to God;[f] and the one who does not eat does not eat to Jehovah,* and yet gives thanks to God.[g] **7** Not one of us, in fact, lives with regard to himself only,[h] and no one dies with regard to himself only. **8** For if we live, we live to Jehovah,*[i] and if we die, we die to Jehovah.* So both if we live and if we die, we belong to Jehovah.*[j] **9** For to this end Christ died and came to life again, so that he might be Lord over both the dead and the living.[k]

10 But why do you judge your brother?[l] Or why do you also look down on your brother? For we will all stand before the judgment seat of God.[m] **11** For it is written: "'As surely as I live,'[n] says Jehovah,* 'to me every knee will bend, and every tongue will make open acknowledgment to God.'"[o] **12** So, then, each of us will render an account for himself to God.[p]

13 Therefore, let us not judge one another any longer[q] but, rather, be determined not to put a stumbling block or an obstacle before a brother.[r] **14** I know and am convinced in the Lord

Jesus that nothing is unclean in itself;[a] only where a man considers something to be unclean, to him it is unclean. **15** For if your brother is being offended because of food, you are no longer walking according to love.[b] Do not by your food ruin* that one for whom Christ died.[c] **16** Therefore, do not let the good you do be spoken of as bad. **17** For the Kingdom of God does not mean eating and drinking,[d] but means righteousness and peace and joy with holy spirit. **18** For whoever slaves for Christ in this way is acceptable to God and has approval with men.

19 So, then, let us pursue the things making for peace[e] and the things that build one another up.[f] **20** Stop tearing down the work of God just for the sake of food.[g] True, all things are clean, but it is detrimental for* a man to eat when it will cause stumbling.[h] **21** It is best not to eat meat or drink wine or do anything over which your brother stumbles.[i] **22** The faith that you have, keep it to yourself before God. Happy is the man who does not judge himself by what he approves. **23** But if he has doubts, he is already condemned if he eats, because he does not eat based on faith. Indeed, everything that is not based on faith is sin.

15 We, though, who are strong ought to bear the weaknesses of those not strong,[j] and not to be pleasing ourselves.[k] **2** Let each of us please his neighbor for his good, to build him up.[l] **3** For even the Christ did not please himself,[m] but just as it is written: "The reproaches of those reproaching you have fallen upon me."[n] **4** For all the things that were

---

14:15 *Or "destroy." **14:20** *Or "wrong for."

CHAP. 14

a Col 2:16
b Mt 7:1
  Jas 4:12
c 1Co 4:4
d Ga 4:10
e Col 2:16
f 1Ti 4:4
g 1Co 10:31
h 1Co 6:19, 20
i Ps 146:2
  1Pe 4:1, 2
j 1Th 4:14
k 1Th 5:10
  Re 1:17, 18
l Lu 6:37
  Ro 14:4
m Ac 10:42
  2Co 5:10
n Isa 49:18
o Isa 45:23
p Ec 12:14
  Mt 12:36
  2Co 5:10
q Mt 7:1
r Mt 18:6
  1Co 8:9
  1Co 10:32

Second Col.

a Mt 15:11
  Ac 10:15
  1Ti 4:4
b Eph 5:2
c 1Co 8:10, 11
d 1Co 8:8
e Mt 5:9
  Ro 12:18
f 1Co 14:12
  Heb 10:24
g Ro 14:3
  1Co 8:11
h 1Co 8:9
i Ro 14:13
  1Co 8:13
  1Co 10:24

CHAP. 15

j Ro 14:1
  1Th 5:14
k 1Co 10:24
l 1Co 9:22
  Php 2:4
m Mr 10:45
  Joh 5:30
n Ps 69:9

written beforehand were written for our instruction,[a] so that through our endurance[b] and through the comfort from the Scriptures we might have hope.[c] **5** Now may the God who supplies endurance and comfort grant you to have among yourselves the same mental attitude that Christ Jesus had, **6** so that unitedly[d] you may with one voice* glorify the God and Father of our Lord Jesus Christ.

7 So welcome* one another,[e] just as the Christ also welcomed you,[f] with glory to God in view. **8** For I tell you that Christ became a minister of those who are circumcised[g] in behalf of God's truthfulness, so as to verify the promises He made to their forefathers,[h] **9** and that the nations might glorify God for his mercy.[i] Just as it is written: "That is why I will openly acknowledge you among the nations, and to your name I will sing praises."[j] **10** And again he says: "Be glad, you nations, with his people."[k] **11** And again: "Praise Jehovah,* all you nations, and let all the peoples praise him."[l] **12** And again Isaiah says: "There will be the root of Jes'se,[m] the one arising to rule nations;[n] on him nations will rest their hope."[o] **13** May the God who gives hope fill you with all joy and peace by your trusting in him, so that you may abound* in hope with power of holy spirit.[p]

14 Now I myself am convinced about you, my brothers, that you yourselves are also full of goodness, filled with all knowledge, and that you are able to admonish* one another. **15** However, I have written to you more outspokenly on some points, so as to give you another reminder, because of the undeserved kind-

ness given to me from God **16** for me to be a public servant of Christ Jesus to the nations.[a] I am engaging in the holy work of the good news of God,[b] so that these nations might be an acceptable offering, sanctified with holy spirit.

17 So I have reason to exult in Christ Jesus over the things pertaining to God. **18** For I will not presume to speak about anything except what Christ has done through me in order for the nations to be obedient, by my word and deed, **19** with the power of signs and wonders,*[c] with the power of God's spirit, so that from Jerusalem and in a circuit as far as Il·lyr'i·cum I have thoroughly preached the good news about the Christ.[d] **20** In this way, indeed, I made it my aim not to declare the good news where the name of Christ had already been made known, so as not to build on another man's foundation; **21** but just as it is written: "Those who received no report about him will see, and those who have not heard will understand."[e]

22 This is also why I was many times hindered from coming to you. **23** But now I no longer have untouched territory in these regions, and for many* years I have longed to come to you. **24** Therefore, when I journey to Spain, I hope that I will see you and be accompanied partway there by you after I have first enjoyed your company for a time. **25** But now I am about to travel to Jerusalem to minister to the holy ones.[f] **26** For those in Mac·e·do'ni·a and A·cha'ia have been pleased to share their things by a contribution to the poor among the holy ones in Jerusalem.[g] **27** True, they have been

CHAP. 15
a 1Co 10:11
2Ti 3:16, 17
2Pe 1:19

b Ro 5:3, 4

c Ps 119:49, 50
Heb 3:6
1Pe 1:10

d 1Co 1:10
2Co 13:11
Php 2:2
1Pe 3:8

e Phm 10, 17

f Joh 6:37

g Mt 15:24
Joh 1:11

h Ge 22:16-18
Ps 89:3

i Ro 9:23, 24

j 2Sa 22:50
Ps 18:49

k De 32:43

l Ps 117:1

m Re 5:5

n Ge 49:10

o Isa 11:1, 10
Mt 12:21

p Isa 40:31

Second Col.
a Ro 11:13
Ga 2:7, 8

b Ac 20:24

c Ac 15:12
2Co 12:12

d Ac 21:18, 19

e Isa 52:15

f Ac 19:21
Ac 20:22

g 1Co 16:1
2Co 8:1-4
2Co 9:2, 12

15:6 *Lit., "mouth." **15:7** *Or "accept." **15:11** *See App. A5. **15:13** *Or "overflow." **15:14** *Or "instruct."

15:19 *Or "portents." **15:23** *Or possibly, "some."

pleased to do so, and indeed they were debtors to them; for if the nations have shared in their spiritual things, they also owe it to minister to them with their material things.[a] **28** So after I have finished with this and have delivered this contribution* securely to them, I will depart by way of you for Spain. **29** Moreover, I know that when I do come to you, I will come with a full measure of blessing from Christ.

30 Now I urge you, brothers, through our Lord Jesus Christ and through the love of the spirit, that you exert yourselves with me in prayers to God for me,[b] **31** that I may be rescued[c] from the unbelievers in Ju·de′a and that my ministry in behalf of Jerusalem may prove to be acceptable to the holy ones,[d] **32** so that by God's will I will come to you with joy and be refreshed together with you. **33** May the God who gives peace be with all of you.[e] Amen.

16 I am introducing* to you Phoe′be, our sister, who is a minister of the congregation that is in Cen′chre·ae,[f] **2** so that you may welcome her in the Lord in a way worthy of the holy ones and give her whatever help she may need,[g] for she herself also proved to be a defender of many, including me.

3 Give my greetings to Pris′ca and Aq′ui·la,[h] my fellow workers in Christ Jesus, **4** who have risked their own necks for me*[i] and to whom not only I but also all the congregations of the nations give thanks. **5** Also greet the congregation that is in their house.[j] Greet my beloved E·pae′ne·tus, who is a firstfruits of Asia for Christ. **6** Greet Mary, who has worked hard for you. **7** Greet An·dron′i·cus and Ju′ni·as, my relatives[k] and fellow pris-

oners, who are men well-known to the apostles and who have been in union with Christ longer than I have.

8 Give my greetings to Am·pli·a′tus, my beloved in the Lord. **9** Greet Ur·ba′nus, our fellow worker in Christ, and my beloved Sta′chys. **10** Greet A·pel′les, the approved one in Christ. Greet those from the household of A·ris·tob′u·lus. **11** Greet He·ro′di·on, my relative. Greet those from the household of Nar·cis′sus who are in the Lord. **12** Greet Try·phae′na and Try·pho′sa, women who are working hard in the Lord. Greet Per′sis, our beloved one, for she has worked hard in the Lord. **13** Greet Ru′fus, the chosen one in the Lord, and his mother and mine. **14** Greet A·syn′cri·tus, Phle′gon, Her′mes, Pat′ro·bas, Her′mas, and the brothers with them. **15** Greet Phi·lol′o·gus and Julia, Ne′reus and his sister, and O·lym′pas, and all the holy ones with them. **16** Greet one another with a holy kiss. All the congregations of the Christ greet you.

17 Now I urge you, brothers, to keep your eye on those who create divisions and causes for stumbling contrary to the teaching that you have learned, and avoid them.[a] **18** For men of that sort are slaves, not of our Lord Christ, but of their own appetites,* and by smooth talk and flattering speech they seduce the hearts of unsuspecting ones. **19** Your obedience has come to the notice of all, and so I rejoice over you. But I want you to be wise as to what is good, but innocent as to what is evil.[b] **20** For his part, the God who gives peace will crush Satan[c] under your feet shortly. May the undeserved kindness of our Lord Jesus be with you.

CHAP. 15
a Ga 6:6
  Heb 13:16

b 2Co 1:11
  Eph 6:18
  Col 4:3
  1Th 5:25

c 2Th 3:1, 2

d Ro 15:26

e 1Co 14:33
  Php 4:9

CHAP. 16
f Ac 18:18

g Ro 12:13
  1Jo 3:17

h Ac 18:2
  Ac 18:24, 26
  2Ti 4:19

i 1Jo 3:16

j 1Co 16:19
  Col 4:15
  Phm 2

k Ro 16:11

Second Col.
a Mt 7:15
  Tit 3:10
  2Jo 10

b 1Co 14:20

c Ge 3:15
  Heb 2:14

15:28 *Lit., "fruit." **16:1** *Or "I recommend." **16:4** *Or "my soul."

16:18 *Or "bellies."

21 Timothy, my fellow worker, greets you, and so do Lucius, Ja'son, and So·sip'a·ter, my relatives.[a]

22 I, Ter'tius, who have done the writing of this letter, greet you in the Lord.

23 Ga'ius,[b] host to me and to all the congregation, greets you. E·ras'tus, the city treasurer,* greets you, and so does Quar'tus, his brother. **24** *——

25 Now to Him who can make you firm according to the good

16:23 *Or "steward." 16:24 *See App. A3.

news I declare and the preaching of Jesus Christ, according to the revelation of the sacred secret[a] that has been kept in silence for long-lasting times **26** but has now been made manifest* and has been made known through the prophetic Scriptures among all the nations according to the command of the everlasting God to promote obedience by faith; **27** to God, who alone is wise,[b] be the glory through Jesus Christ forever. Amen.

16:26 *Or "revealed."

CHAP. 16
a Ro 16:7

b 1Co 1:14

Second Col.
a Eph 1:9-12
Col 1:26, 27

b Ro 11:33

THE FIRST TO THE

CORINTHIANS

OUTLINE OF CONTENTS

1 Paul, called to be an apostle[a] of Christ Jesus by God's will, and Sos'the·nes our brother, **2** to the congregation of God that is in Corinth,[b] to you who have been sanctified in union with Christ Jesus,[c] called to be holy ones, together with all those everywhere who are calling on the name of our Lord Jesus Christ,[d] their Lord and ours: **3** May you have undeserved kindness and peace from God our Father and the Lord Jesus Christ.

4 I always thank my God for you in view of the undeserved kindness of God given to you in Christ Jesus; **5** because in everything you have been enriched in him, in full ability to speak and in full knowledge,[e] **6** just as the witness about the Christ[f] has been made firm among you, **7** so that you do not lack in any gift at all, while you are eagerly waiting for the revelation of our Lord Jesus Christ.[g] **8** He will also make you firm to the end so that you may be open to no accusation in the day of our Lord Jesus Christ.[h] **9** God is faithful,[i] by whom you

were called into fellowship* with his Son, Jesus Christ our Lord.

10 Now I urge you, brothers, through the name of our Lord Jesus Christ, that you should all speak in agreement and that there should be no divisions among you,[a] but that you may be completely united in the same mind and in the same line of thought.[b] **11** For some from the house of Chlo'e have informed me regarding you, my brothers, that there are dissensions among you. **12** What I mean is this, that each one of you says: "I belong to Paul," "But I to A·pol'los,"[c] "But I to Ce'phas,"* "But I to Christ." **13** Is the Christ divided? Paul was not executed on the stake for you, was he? Or were you baptized in the name of Paul? **14** I thank God that I baptized none of you except Cris'pus[d] and Ga'ius,[e] **15** so that no one may say that you were baptized in my name. **16** Yes, I also baptized the household of Steph'a·nas.[f] As for the rest, I do not know whether I baptized anyone

CHAP. 1
a Ac 9:15

b Ac 18:1

c 1Co 6:11
Heb 9:13, 14

d Mt 12:18, 21
Ac 4:12

e Col 1:9

f Ac 18:5

g Lu 17:29, 30
2Th 1:7
1Pe 1:7

h 1Co 4:5
1Co 5:5
Re 1:10

i De 7:9

Second Col.
a Ro 16:17

b Ro 15:5, 6
2Co 13:11
Eph 4:1, 3
Php 2:2

c Ac 18:24
1Co 3:4, 5
1Co 3:21-23

d Ac 18:8

e Ro 16:23

f 1Co 16:15

1:9 *Or "a sharing." 1:12 *Also called Peter.

else. **17** For Christ sent me, not to baptize, but to declare the good news;[a] and not with wisdom of speech,* so that the torture stake* of the Christ should not be made useless.

18 For the speech about the torture stake* is foolishness to those who are perishing,[b] but to us who are being saved, it is God's power.[c] **19** For it is written: "I will make the wisdom of the wise men perish, and the intelligence of the intellectuals I will reject."*[d] **20** Where is the wise man? Where is the scribe?* Where is the debater of this system of things?* Has not God made the wisdom of the world foolish? **21** For since, in the wisdom of God, the world did not get to know God[e] through its wisdom,[f] God was pleased through the foolishness[g] of what is preached to save those believing.

22 For the Jews ask for signs[h] and the Greeks look for wisdom; **23** but we preach Christ executed on the stake, to the Jews a cause for stumbling but to the nations foolishness.[i] **24** However, to those who are called, both Jews and Greeks, Christ is the power of God and the wisdom of God.[j] **25** Because a foolish thing of God is wiser than men, and a weak thing of God is stronger than men.[k]

26 For you see his calling of you, brothers, that there are not many wise in a fleshly way,*[l] not many powerful, not many of noble birth,*[m] **27** but God chose the foolish things of the world to put the wise men to shame; and God chose the weak things of the world to put the strong things to shame;[a] **28** and God chose the insignificant things of the world and the things looked down on, the things that are not, to bring to nothing the things that are,[b] **29** so that no one* might boast in the sight of God. **30** But it is due to him that you are in union with Christ Jesus, who has become to us wisdom from God, also righteousness[c] and sanctification[d] and release by ransom,[e] **31** so that it may be just as it is written: "The one who boasts, let him boast in Jehovah."*[f]

2 So when I came to you, brothers, I did not come with extravagant speech[g] or wisdom declaring the sacred secret[h] of God to you. **2** For I decided not to know anything among you except Jesus Christ, and him executed on the stake.[i] **3** And I came to you in weakness and in fear and with much trembling; **4** and my speech and what I preached were not with persuasive words of wisdom but with a demonstration of spirit and power,[j] **5** so that your faith might be, not in men's wisdom, but in God's power.

6 Now we speak wisdom among those who are mature,[k] but not the wisdom of this system of things* nor that of the rulers of this system of things, who are to come to nothing.[l] **7** But we speak God's wisdom in a sacred secret,[m] the hidden wisdom, which God foreordained before the systems of things for our glory. **8** It is this wisdom that none of the rulers of this system of things* came to know,[n] for if they had known it, they would not have executed* the glorious Lord. **9** But just as it is written: "Eye has not

CHAP. 1	
a	Ac 9:15
b	Ac 17:18 1Co 2:14
c	Ro 1:16
d	Isa 29:14
e	Lu 10:21
f	Col 2:8
g	1Co 2:14 1Co 3:18
h	Mt 12:38 Lu 11:29
i	Ac 17:32
j	Col 2:3
k	2Co 13:4
l	Ac 4:13
m	Joh 7:48 Jas 2:5

Second Col.	
a	Mt 11:25
b	1Co 2:6
c	Ro 10:4 2Co 5:21
d	Joh 17:19 Heb 10:10
e	Ro 3:24 Col 1:13, 14
f	Jer 9:24 2Co 10:17

CHAP. 2	
g	1Co 1:17
h	Eph 3:5, 6 Col 2:2
i	Ga 6:14
j	Ro 15:18, 19 1Co 4:20 1Th 1:5
k	1Co 14:20 Eph 4:13 Heb 5:14
l	1Co 15:24
m	Ro 16:25, 26 Eph 3:8, 9
n	Joh 7:48 Ac 13:27, 28

1:17 *Or "clever speech." **1:17, 18** *See Glossary. **1:19** *Or "shove aside." **1:20** *That is, an expert in the Law. **1:20** *; **2:6, 8** *Or "this age." See Glossary. **1:26** *Or "by human standards." *Or "from important families."

1:29 *Lit., "flesh." **1:31** *See App. A5. **2:8** *Or "executed on the stake."

seen and ear has not heard, nor have there been conceived in the heart of man the things that God has prepared for those who love him."[a] **10** For it is to us God has revealed them[b] through his spirit,[c] for the spirit searches into all things, even the deep things of God.[d]

11 For who among men knows the things of a man except the man's spirit within him? So, too, no one has come to know the things of God except the spirit of God. **12** Now we received, not the spirit of the world, but the spirit that is from God,[e] so that we might know the things that have been kindly given us by God. **13** These things we also speak, not with words taught by human wisdom,[f] but with those taught by the spirit,[g] as we explain* spiritual matters with spiritual words.

14 But a physical man does not accept* the things of the spirit of God, for they are foolishness to him; and he cannot get to know them, because they are examined spiritually. **15** However, the spiritual man examines all things,[h] but he himself is not examined by any man. **16** For "who has come to know the mind of Jehovah,* so that he may instruct him?"[i] But we do have the mind of Christ.[j]

3 So, brothers, I was not able to speak to you as to spiritual men,[k] but as to fleshly men, as to infants[l] in Christ. **2** I fed you milk, not solid food, for you were not yet strong enough. In fact, neither are you strong enough now,[m] **3** for you are still fleshly.[n] Since there are jealousy and strife among you, are you not fleshly[o] and are you not walking as men do? **4** For when one says, "I belong to Paul," but

another says, "I to A·pol′los,"[a] are you not acting like mere men?

5 What, then, is A·pol′los? Yes, what is Paul? Ministers[b] through whom you became believers, just as the Lord granted each one. **6** I planted,[c] A·pol′los watered,[d] but God kept making it grow, **7** so that neither is the one who plants anything nor is the one who waters, but God who makes it grow.[e] **8** Now the one who plants and the one who waters are one,* but each person will receive his own reward according to his own work.[f] **9** For we are God's fellow workers. You are God's field under cultivation, God's building.[g]

10 According to the undeserved kindness of God that was given to me, I laid a foundation[h] as a skilled master builder,* but someone else is building on it. But let each one keep watching how he is building on it. **11** For no one can lay any other foundation than what is laid, which is Jesus Christ.[i] **12** Now if anyone builds on the foundation gold, silver, precious stones, wood, hay, or straw, **13** each one's work will be shown for what it is,* for the day will show it up, because it will be revealed by means of fire,[j] and the fire itself will prove what sort of work each one has built. **14** If anyone's work that he has built on it remains, he will receive a reward; **15** if anyone's work is burned up, he will suffer loss, but he himself will be saved; yet, if so, it will be as through fire.

16 Do you not know that you yourselves are God's temple[k] and that the spirit of God dwells in you?[l] **17** If anyone destroys the temple of God, God will de-

CHAP. 2

a Isa 64:4

b Mt 16:17
  Mr 4:11
  Eph 3:5
  2Ti 1:9, 10
  1Pe 1:12

c Joh 14:26
  1Jo 2:27

d Ro 11:33

e Joh 15:26

f Col 2:8

g Joh 16:13

h Ro 8:5

i Isa 40:13

j Ro 15:5

CHAP. 3

k 1Co 2:15
  Col 1:9

l 1Co 14:20

m Heb 5:12-14

n Ro 8:7, 8

o Ga 5:19, 20

Second Col.

a Ac 18:24, 25

b 2Co 3:5, 6
  Col 1:23
  1Ti 1:12

c Ac 18:4

d Ac 18:26-28
  Ac 19:1

e Ro 9:16

f Ro 2:6
  1Co 4:5
  Re 22:12

g Eph 2:22
  1Pe 2:5

h Ro 15:20
  Heb 6:1

i Ps 118:22
  Isa 28:16
  Mt 21:42
  Eph 2:20
  1Pe 2:6

j 1Pe 4:12

k 2Co 6:16
  Eph 2:21
  1Pe 2:5

l 1Co 6:19

2:13 *Or "combine." **2:14** *Or "receive." **2:16** *See App. A5.

3:8 *Or "have one purpose." **3:10** *Or "wise director of works." **3:13** *Lit., "will be made manifest."

stroy him; for the temple of God is holy, and you are that temple.[a]

18 Let no one deceive himself: If anyone among you thinks he is wise in this system of things,* let him become a fool, so that he may become wise. **19** For the wisdom of this world is foolishness with God, for it is written: "He catches the wise in their own cunning."[b] **20** And again: "Jehovah* knows that the reasonings of the wise men are futile."[c] **21** So let no one boast in men; for all things belong to you, **22** whether Paul or A·pol'los or Ce'phas*[d] or the world or life or death or things now here or things to come, all things belong to you; **23** in turn you belong to Christ;[e] Christ, in turn, belongs to God.

4 A man should regard us as attendants* of Christ and stewards of God's sacred secrets.[f] **2** In this regard, what is expected of stewards is that they be found faithful. **3** Now to me it is of very little importance to be examined by you or by a human tribunal.* In fact, I do not even examine myself. **4** For I am not conscious of anything against myself. But by this I am not proved righteous; the one who examines me is Jehovah.*[g] **5** Therefore, do not judge[h] anything before the due time, until the Lord comes. He will bring the secret things of darkness to light and make known the intentions of the hearts, and then each one will receive his praise from God.[i]

6 Now, brothers, these things I have applied* to myself and A·pol'los[j] for your good, that through us you may learn the rule: "Do not go beyond the things that are written," so that

you may not be puffed up with pride,[a] favoring one against the other. **7** For who makes you different from another? Indeed, what do you have that you did not receive?[b] If, in fact, you did receive it, why do you boast as though you did not receive it?

8 Are you already satisfied? Are you already rich? Have you begun ruling as kings[c] without us? I really wish that you had begun ruling as kings, so that we also might rule with you as kings.[d] **9** For it seems to me that God has put us the apostles last on exhibition as men condemned to death,[e] because we have become a theatrical spectacle to the world,[f] and to angels and to men. **10** We are fools[g] because of Christ, but you are discreet in Christ; we are weak, but you are strong; you are held in honor, but we in dishonor. **11** Down to this very hour we continue to hunger[h] and thirst[i] and to be poorly clothed* and to be beaten*[j] and to be homeless **12** and to toil, working with our own hands.[k] When insulted, we bless;[l] when persecuted, we patiently endure;[m] **13** when slandered, we answer mildly;*[n] we have become as the refuse* of the world, the offscouring of all things, until now.

14 I am writing these things, not to put you to shame, but to admonish you as my beloved children. **15** For though you may have 10,000 guardians* in Christ, you certainly do not have many fathers; for in Christ Jesus, I have become your father through the good news.[o] **16** I urge you, therefore, become imitators of me.[p] **17** That is why I am sending Timothy to you, because he is my beloved

---

CHAP. 3
a 1Pe 2:5
b Job 5:13
c Ps 94:11
d 1Co 1:12
e Joh 17:9
  2Co 10:7

CHAP. 4
f Mt 13:11
  Ro 16:25, 26
g Pr 21:2
  Ro 14:10
  Heb 4:13
h Mt 7:1
i Pr 10:9
  2Co 10:18
  1Ti 5:24, 25
j 1Co 1:12

Second Col.
a Col 2:3
  2Co 12:20
  3Jo 9
b Joh 3:27
c Re 20:4, 6
d 2Ti 2:12
  Re 3:21
e Ro 8:36
  1Co 15:32
  2Co 6:4, 9
f Heb 10:33
g 1Co 3:18
h Php 4:12
i 2Co 11:27
j Ac 14:19
  Ac 23:2
  2Co 11:24
k Ac 18:3
  Ac 20:34
  1Th 2:9
l Ro 12:14
  1Pe 3:9
m Mt 5:44
n 1Pe 2:23
o Ga 4:19
  1Th 2:11
p 1Co 11:1
  Php 3:17
  1Th 1:6

3:18 *Or "this age." See Glossary. 3:20; 4:4 *See App. A5. 3:22 *Also called Peter. 4:1 *Or "subordinates." 4:3 *Or "court." 4:6 *Or "transferred."

4:11 *Lit., "and being naked." *Or "knocked about." 4:13 *Lit., "we entreat." *Or "garbage; rubbish." 4:15 *Or "tutors."

and faithful child in the Lord. He will remind you of my methods* in connection with Christ Jesus,[a] just as I am teaching everywhere in every congregation.

18 Some are puffed up with pride, as though I were not coming to you. **19** But I will come to you shortly, if Jehovah* wills, and I will get to know, not the speech of those who are puffed up with pride, but their power. **20** For the Kingdom of God is a matter not of speech but of power. **21** Which do you prefer? Shall I come to you with a rod[b] or with love and mildness of spirit?

5 Actually sexual immorality*[c] is reported among you, and such immorality* as is not even found among the nations—of a man living with* his father's wife.[d] **2** And are you proud of it? Should you not rather mourn,[e] so that the man who committed this deed should be taken away from your midst?[f] **3** Although absent in body, I am present in spirit, and I have already judged the man who has done this, as if I were actually with you. **4** When you are gathered together in the name of our Lord Jesus, and knowing that I am with you in spirit along with the power of our Lord Jesus, **5** you must hand such a man over to Satan[g] for the destruction of the flesh, so that the spirit may be saved in the day of the Lord.[h]

6 Your boasting is not good. Do you not know that a little leaven ferments* the whole batch of dough?[i] **7** Clear away the old leaven so that you may be a new batch, inasmuch as you are free from ferment.* For, indeed,

Christ our Passover lamb[a] has been sacrificed.[b] **8** So, then, let us keep the festival,[c] not with old leaven, nor with leaven of badness and wickedness, but with unleavened bread of sincerity and truth.

9 In my letter I wrote you to stop keeping company* with sexually immoral people,# **10** not meaning entirely with the sexually immoral people# of this world[d] or the greedy people or extortioners or idolaters. Otherwise, you would actually have to get out of the world.[e] **11** But now I am writing you to stop keeping company*[f] with anyone called a brother who is sexually immoral# or a greedy person[g] or an idolater or a reviler△ or a drunkard[h] or an extortioner,[i] not even eating with such a man. **12** For what do I have to do with judging those outside? Do you not judge those inside, **13** while God judges those outside?[j] "Remove the wicked person from among yourselves."[k]

6 Does any one of you who has a dispute with another[l] dare to go to court before unrighteous men, and not before the holy ones? **2** Or do you not know that the holy ones will judge the world?[m] And if the world is to be judged by you, are you not competent to try very trivial matters? **3** Do you not know that we will judge angels?[n] Then why not matters of this life? **4** If, then, you do have matters of this life to be tried,[o] is it the men looked down on in the congregation whom you assign as judges? **5** I am speaking to move you to shame. Is there not one wise man among you who is able to judge between his brothers? **6** Instead, broth-

---

CHAP. 4
a 2Ti 1:13
b 2Co 13:10

CHAP. 5
c Eph 5:3
d Le 18:8
e 2Co 7:9
f 1Co 5:13
  2Jo 10
g 1Ti 1:20
h 1Co 1:8
i 1Co 15:33
  Ga 5:9
  2Ti 2:16, 17

Second Col.
a Joh 1:29
b 1Pe 1:19, 20
  Re 5:12
c Ex 13:7
d 1Jo 2:17
e Joh 17:15
f Nu 16:25, 26
  Ro 16:17
  2Jo 10
g Eph 5:5
h De 21:20, 21
  1Pe 4:3
i 1Co 6:9, 10
  Ga 5:19-21
j Ec 12:14
k Ge 3:23, 24
  De 17:7
  Tit 3:10
  2Jo 10

CHAP. 6
l Mt 18:15-17
m Re 2:26, 27
  Re 20:4
n Ro 16:20
o Mt 18:17

4:17 *Lit., "my ways." **4:19** *See App. A5. **5:1** *Greek, *por·nei'a.* See Glossary. #Lit., "having." **5:6** *Or "leavens." **5:7** *Lit., "are unleavened." **5:9, 11** *Or "stop associating." **5:9-11** #See Glossary, "Sexual immorality." **5:11** △Or "a verbally abusive person."

er goes to court against brother, and before unbelievers at that!

7 Really, it is already a defeat for you when you have lawsuits with one another. Why not rather let yourselves be wronged?[a] Why do you not rather let yourselves be defrauded? **8** Instead, you wrong and defraud, and your brothers at that!

9 Or do you not know that unrighteous people will not inherit God's Kingdom?[b] Do not be misled.* Those who are sexually immoral,[#] idolaters,[d] adulterers,[e] men who submit to homosexual acts,[f] men who practice homosexuality,[△g] **10** thieves, greedy people,[h] drunkards,[i] revilers,* and extortioners will not inherit God's Kingdom.[j] **11** And yet that is what some of you were. But you have been washed clean;[k] you have been sanctified;[l] you have been declared righteous[m] in the name of the Lord Jesus Christ and with the spirit of our God.

12 All things are lawful* for me, but not all things are advantageous.[n] All things are lawful for me, but I will not let myself be controlled[#] by anything. **13** Food is for the stomach and the stomach is for food, but God will bring both of them to nothing.[o] The body is not for sexual immorality* but for the Lord,[p] and the Lord is for the body. **14** But God raised up the Lord[q] and will also raise us up out of death[r] through his power.[s]

15 Do you not know that your bodies are members of Christ?[t] Should I, then, take the members of the Christ away and join them to a prostitute? By no means!

16 Do you not know that anyone who is joined to a prostitute is one body with her? For "the two," says he, "will be one flesh."[a] **17** But whoever is joined to the Lord is one with him in spirit.[b] **18** Flee from sexual immorality!*[c] Every other sin that a man may commit is outside his body, but whoever practices sexual immorality is sinning against his own body.[d] **19** Do you not know that your body is the temple[e] of the holy spirit within you, which you have from God?[f] Also, you do not belong to yourselves,[g] **20** for you were bought with a price.[h] By all means, glorify God[i] in your body.[j]

7 Now concerning the things about which you wrote, it is better for a man not to touch* a woman; **2** but because of the prevalence of sexual immorality,* let each man have his own wife[k] and each woman have her own husband.[l] **3** Let the husband give to his wife her due, and let the wife also do likewise to her husband.[m] **4** The wife does not have authority over her own body, but her husband does; likewise, the husband does not have authority over his own body, but his wife does. **5** Do not deprive each other except by mutual consent for an appointed time, so that you may devote time to prayer and may come together again, in order that Satan may not keep tempting you for your lack of self-control. **6** However, I say this by way of concession, not as a command. **7** But I wish all men were as I am. Nevertheless, each one has his own gift[n] from God, one in this way, another in that way.

8 Now I say to those who are unmarried and to the widows that it is better for them if they remain

---

CHAP. 6
a Mt 5:39, 40
b Eph 5:5
  Re 22:15
c Re 21:8
d Col 3:5
e Heb 13:4
f Ro 1:27
g 1Ti 1:9, 10
h 1Co 5:11
i De 21:20, 21
  Pr 23:20
  1Pe 4:3
j Heb 12:14
k Ac 22:16
  Heb 10:22
l Eph 5:25, 26
  2Th 2:13
m Ro 5:18
n 1Co 10:23
o Ro 14:17
p 1Th 4:3
q Ac 2:24
r 2Co 4:14
s Ro 8:11
  Eph 1:19, 20
t Ro 12:4, 5
  1Co 12:18, 27
  Eph 4:15
  Eph 5:29, 30

Second Col.
a Ge 2:24
  Mt 19:4, 5
b Joh 17:20, 21
c Ge 39:10-12
  1Th 4:3
d Ro 1:24, 27
e 2Co 6:16
f 1Co 3:16
g Ro 14:8
h 1Co 7:23
  Heb 9:12
  1Pe 1:18, 19
i Mt 5:16
j Ro 12:1

CHAP. 7
k Pr 5:18, 19
l Ge 2:24
  Heb 13:4
m Ex 21:10
  1Co 7:5
n Mt 19:10, 11

6:9 *Or "deceived." #See Glossary, "Sexual immorality." △Or "men who have sex with men." Lit., "men who lie with men." 6:10 *Or "the verbally abusive." 6:12 *Or "permissible." #Or "brought under authority." 6:13, 18 *Greek, por·nei′a. See Glossary.

7:1 *That is, to have sexual contact with. 7:2 *Plural of the Greek por·nei′a. See Glossary.

as I am.[a] **9** But if they do not have self-control, let them marry, for it is better to marry than to be inflamed with passion.[b]

10 To the married people I give instructions, not I but the Lord, that a wife should not separate from her husband.[c] **11** But if she does separate, let her remain unmarried or else be reconciled with her husband; and a husband should not leave his wife.[d]

12 But to the others I say, yes, I, not the Lord:[e] If any brother has an unbelieving wife and she is agreeable to staying with him, let him not leave her; **13** and if a woman has an unbelieving husband and he is agreeable to staying with her, let her not leave her husband. **14** For the unbelieving husband is sanctified in relation to his wife, and the unbelieving wife is sanctified in relation to the brother; otherwise, your children would be unclean, but now they are holy. **15** But if the unbelieving one chooses to depart,* let him depart; a brother or a sister is not bound under such circumstances, but God has called you to peace.[f] **16** For wife, how do you know whether you will save your husband?[g] Or, husband, how do you know whether you will save your wife?

17 Nevertheless, just as Jehovah* has given each one a portion, let each one so walk as God has called him.[h] And so I give this directive in all the congregations. **18** Was any man already circumcised when he was called?[i] Let him not undo his circumcision. Has any man been called while uncircumcised? Let him not get circumcised.[j] **19** Circumcision means nothing, and uncircumcision means nothing;[k] what means

something is the observing of God's commandments.[a] **20** In whatever state each one was called, let him remain in it.[b] **21** Were you called when a slave? Do not let it concern you;[c] but if you can become free, then seize the opportunity. **22** For anyone who was called in the Lord when a slave is the Lord's freedman;[d] likewise anyone who was called when a freeman is a slave of Christ. **23** You were bought with a price;[e] stop becoming slaves of men. **24** In whatever state each one was called, brothers, let him remain in it before God.

25 Now concerning virgins,* I have no command from the Lord, but I give my opinion[f] as one who had mercy shown him by the Lord to be faithful. **26** Therefore, I think that it is best for a man to continue as he is in view of the present difficulty. **27** Are you bound to a wife? Stop seeking a release.[g] Are you freed from a wife? Stop seeking a wife. **28** But even if you did marry, you would commit no sin. And if a virgin married, such a person would commit no sin. However, those who do will have tribulation in their flesh. But I am trying to spare you.

29 Moreover, this I say, brothers, the time left is reduced.[h] From now on, let those who have wives be as though they had none, **30** and those who weep as those who do not weep, and those who rejoice as those who do not rejoice, and those who buy as those who do not possess, **31** and those making use of the world as those not using it to the full; for the scene of this world is changing. **32** Indeed, I want you to be free from anxiety. The unmarried man is anxious for the things of the Lord,

CHAP. 7

a 1Co 7:39, 40
  1Co 9:5

b 1Th 4:4, 5
  1Ti 5:11, 14

c Mt 5:32
  Mt 19:6

d Mr 10:11
  Lu 16:18

e 1Co 7:25, 40

f Heb 12:14

g 1Pe 3:1, 2

h 1Co 7:7

i Ac 21:20

j Ac 10:45
  Ac 15:1, 24
  Ga 5:2

k Ga 6:15
  Col 3:11

Second Col.

a Ec 12:13
  Jer 7:23
  Ro 2:25
  Ga 5:6
  1Jo 5:3

b 1Co 7:17

c Ga 3:28

d Joh 8:36
  Phm 15, 16

e 1Co 6:19, 20
  Heb 9:12
  1Pe 1:18, 19

f 1Co 7:12
  1Co 7:40

g Mal 2:16
  Mt 19:6
  Eph 5:33

h Ro 13:11
  1Pe 4:7

7:15 *Or "separate." 7:17 *See App. A5.

7:25 *Or "those who have never married."

how he may gain the Lord's approval. **33** But the married man is anxious for the things of the world,[a] how he may gain the approval of his wife, **34** and he is divided. Further, the unmarried woman, as well as the virgin, is anxious for the things of the Lord,[b] that she may be holy both in her body and in her spirit. However, the married woman is anxious for the things of the world, how she may gain the approval of her husband. **35** But I am saying this for your personal advantage, not to restrict* you, but to move you to what is appropriate and to constant devotion to the Lord without distraction.

36 But if anyone thinks he is behaving improperly by remaining unmarried,* and if he is past the bloom of youth, then this is what should take place: Let him do what he wants; he does not sin. Let them marry.[c] **37** But if anyone stands settled in his heart and has no necessity, but has authority over his own will and has made the decision in his own heart to remain unmarried,* he will do well.[d] **38** So also, whoever marries* does well, but whoever does not marry will do better.[e]

39 A wife is bound as long as her husband is alive.[f] But if her husband should fall asleep in death, she is free to be married to whomever she wants, only in the Lord.[g] **40** But in my opinion, she is happier if she remains as she is; and I certainly think I also have God's spirit.

8 Now concerning food offered to idols:[h] We know we all have knowledge.[i] Knowledge puffs up, but love builds up.[j] **2** If anyone thinks he knows

---

CHAP. 7
a 1Ti 5:8
b 1Ti 5:5
c Mt 19:12
　1Co 7:28
d Mt 19:10, 11
e 1Co 7:32
f Ro 7:2
g Ge 24:2, 3
　De 7:3, 4
　Ne 13:25, 26
　2Co 6:14

CHAP. 8
h Ac 15:20, 29
i Ro 14:14
　1Co 8:10
j 1Co 8:13
　1Co 13:4, 5

Second Col.
a De 32:21
　2Ki 19:17, 18
　Jer 16:20
b De 6:4
　De 32:39
c Ps 82:1, 6
　Joh 10:34, 35
d 1Ti 2:5
e Mal 2:10
　Mt 23:9
f Ac 17:28
g Joh 1:1, 3
　Col 1:15, 16
h Ro 14:14
i 1Co 10:27, 28
j Ro 14:23
k Ro 14:17
l Heb 13:9
m Ro 14:13, 20
n Ro 14:15
o 1Co 10:28, 29
p Mt 18:6
　Ro 14:15, 21

CHAP. 9
q Ac 9:3-5
　1Co 15:7, 8

---

something, he does not yet know it as he should know it. **3** But if anyone loves God, this one is known by him.

4 Now concerning the eating of food offered to idols, we know that an idol is nothing[a] in the world and that there is no God but one.[b] **5** For even though there are so-called gods, whether in heaven or on earth,[c] just as there are many "gods" and many "lords," **6** there is actually to us one God,[d] the Father,[e] from whom all things are and we for him;[f] and there is one Lord, Jesus Christ, through whom all things are[g] and we through him.

7 However, not all have this knowledge.[h] But some, because of their former association with the idol, eat food as something sacrificed to an idol,[i] and their conscience, being weak, is defiled.[j] **8** But food will not bring us nearer to God;[k] we are no worse off if we do not eat, nor better off if we eat.[l] **9** But keep watching that your right to choose does not somehow become a stumbling block to those who are weak.[m] **10** For if anyone should see you who have knowledge having a meal in an idol temple, will not the conscience of that one who is weak be emboldened to the point of eating food offered to idols? **11** So by your knowledge the man who is weak is being ruined, your brother for whose sake Christ died.[n] **12** When you sin against your brothers in this way and wound their weak conscience,[o] you are sinning against Christ. **13** That is why if food makes my brother stumble, I will never again eat meat at all, so that I will not make my brother stumble.[p]

9 Am I not free? Am I not an apostle? Have I not seen Jesus our Lord?[q] Are you not my work in the Lord? **2** Even if

I am not an apostle to others, I most certainly am to you! For you are the seal confirming my apostleship in the Lord.

3 My defense to those who examine me is as follows: **4** We have the right* to eat and drink, do we not? **5** We have the right to be accompanied by a believing wife,*[a] as the rest of the apostles and the Lord's brothers[b] and Ce'phas,*[c] do we not? **6** Or is it only Bar'na·bas[d] and I who do not have the right to refrain from working for a living? **7** What soldier ever serves at his own expense? Who plants a vineyard and does not eat of its fruit?[e] Or who shepherds a flock and does not partake of some of the milk of the flock?

8 Am I saying these things from a human viewpoint? Or does not the Law also say these things? **9** For it is written in the Law of Moses: "You must not muzzle a bull when it is threshing out the grain."[f] Is it bulls that God is concerned about? **10** Or is it actually for our sakes that he says it? It was really written for our sakes, because the man who plows and the man who threshes ought to do so in the hope of receiving a share.

11 If we have sown spiritual things among you, is it too much if we reap material support from you?[g] **12** If other men have this rightful claim over you, do we not have it much more so? Nevertheless, we have not made use of this right,*[h] but we are enduring all things so that we might not in any way hinder the good news about the Christ.[i] **13** Do you not know that the men performing sacred duties eat the things of the temple, and that those regularly serving at the altar receive a share from

the altar?[a] **14** In this way, too, the Lord commanded for those proclaiming the good news to live by means of the good news.[b]

15 But I have not made use of a single one of these provisions.[c] Indeed, I have not written these things so that this would be done for me, for it would be better to die than—no man will take away my grounds for boasting![d] **16** Now if I am declaring the good news, it is no reason for me to boast, for necessity is laid upon me. Really, woe to me if I do not declare the good news![e] **17** If I do this willingly, I have a reward; but even if I do it against my will, I still have a stewardship entrusted to me.[f] **18** What, then, is my reward? That when I declare the good news, I may offer the good news without cost, to avoid abusing my authority* in the good news.

19 For though I am free from all people, I have made myself the slave to all, so that I may gain as many people as possible. **20** To the Jews I became as a Jew in order to gain Jews;[g] to those under law I became as under law, though I myself am not under law, in order to gain those under law.[h] **21** To those without law I became as without law, although I am not without law toward God but under law toward Christ,[i] in order to gain those without law. **22** To the weak I became weak, in order to gain the weak.[j] I have become all things to people of all sorts, so that I might by all possible means save some. **23** But I do all things for the sake of the good news, in order to share it with others.[k]

24 Do you not know that the runners in a race all run, but only one receives the prize? Run in such a way that you may win it.[l] **25** Now everyone compet-

---

CHAP. 9

a Mt 19:11

b Mt 13:55
Ga 1:19

c Joh 1:42

d Ac 13:2

e De 20:6
Pr 27:18

f De 25:4
1Ti 5:18

g Ro 15:26, 27
Ga 6:6
Php 4:15-17

h Ac 18:3
Ac 20:34
2Th 3:7, 8

i 2Co 6:3
2Co 11:7

Second Col.

a Le 6:14, 16
Nu 18:30, 31
De 18:1

b Mt 10:9, 10
Lu 10:7, 8

c Ac 18:3
Ac 20:34
1Co 4:11, 12
2Th 3:8

d 2Co 11:8-10

e Eze 3:18

f Ga 2:7
Eph 3:1, 2
Col 1:25

g Ac 16:3
Ac 18:18

h Ac 21:24, 26

i Joh 13:34
Ga 6:2

j Ro 14:1
Ro 15:1
2Co 11:29

k Ac 19:26
1Th 2:8

l Mt 10:22
Php 3:14
2Ti 4:7, 8

9:4, 12 *Lit., "authority." 9:5 *Or "a sister as a wife." #Also called Peter.

9:18 *Or "rights."

ing in a contest* exercises self-control in all things. Of course, they do it to receive a crown that can perish,[a] but we, one that does not perish.[b] **26** Therefore, the way I am running is not aimlessly;[c] the way I am aiming my blows is so as not to be striking the air; **27** but I pummel* my body[d] and lead it as a slave, so that after I have preached to others, I myself should not become disapproved* somehow.

10 Now I want you to know, brothers, that our forefathers were all under the cloud[e] and all passed through the sea[f] **2** and all got baptized into Moses by means of the cloud and of the sea, **3** and all ate the same spiritual food[g] **4** and all drank the same spiritual drink.[h] For they used to drink from the spiritual rock that followed them, and that rock meant* the Christ.[i] **5** Nevertheless, God was not pleased with most of them, for they were struck down in the wilderness.[j]

6 Now these things became examples for us, in order for us not to desire injurious things, as they desired them.[k] **7** Neither become idolaters, as some of them did; just as it is written: "The people sat down to eat and drink. Then they got up to have a good time."[l] **8** Neither let us practice sexual immorality,* as some of them committed sexual immorality,* only to fall, 23,000 of them in one day.[m] **9** Neither let us put Jehovah* to the test,[n] as some of them put him to the test, only to perish by the serpents.[o] **10** Neither let us be murmurers, as some of them murmured,[p] only to perish by the destroyer.[q] **11** Now these things happened to them as examples, and they

CHAP. 9
a 2Ti 2:5
b Jas 1:12
c Ga 2:2
  Php 2:16
  Heb 12:1
d Ro 8:13
  Col 3:5

CHAP. 10
e Ex 13:21
f Ex 14:21, 22
g Ex 16:14, 15
h Ex 17:6
i Nu 20:11
  Joh 4:10, 25
j Nu 14:29
  Nu 14:35
k Nu 11:4, 34
l Ex 32:4, 6
m Nu 25:1, 9
n De 6:16
o Nu 21:5, 6
  Mt 4:7
p Nu 14:2
q Nu 14:36, 37

Second Col.
a Ro 15:4
b Pr 28:14
  Lu 22:33, 34
  Ga 6:1
c 1Pe 5:8, 9
d Lu 22:31, 32
  2Pe 2:9
e Isa 40:29
  Php 4:13
f De 4:25, 26
  2Co 6:17
  1Jo 5:21
g Mt 26:27, 28
h Mt 26:26
  Lu 22:19
  1Co 12:18
i Ro 12:5
j Le 7:15
k De 32:17
l Jude 6
m Eze 41:22
  Mal 1:12
n Ex 34:14
  De 32:21
o Ro 14:19
  Ro 15:2
p 1Co 10:32, 33
  1Co 13:4, 5
  Php 2:4

were written for a warning to us[a] upon whom the ends of the systems of things have come.

12 So let the one who thinks he is standing beware that he does not fall.[b] **13** No temptation has come upon you except what is common to men.[c] But God is faithful, and he will not let you be tempted beyond what you can bear,[d] but along with the temptation he will also make the way out so that you may be able to endure it.[e]

14 Therefore, my beloved ones, flee from idolatry.[f] **15** I speak as to men with discernment; judge for yourselves what I say. **16** The cup of blessing that we bless, is it not a sharing in the blood of the Christ?[g] The loaf that we break, is it not a sharing in the body of the Christ?[h] **17** Because there is one loaf, we, although many, are one body,[i] for we are all partaking of that one loaf.

18 Look at Israel in the fleshly sense: Are not those who eat the sacrifices sharers with the altar?[j] **19** What, then, am I saying? That what is sacrificed to an idol is anything, or that an idol is anything? **20** No; but I say that what the nations sacrifice, they sacrifice to demons and not to God;[k] and I do not want you to become sharers with the demons.[l] **21** You cannot be drinking the cup of Jehovah* and the cup of demons; you cannot be partaking of "the table of Jehovah"*[m] and the table of demons. **22** Or 'are we inciting Jehovah* to jealousy'?[n] We are not stronger than he is, are we?

23 All things are lawful,* but not all things are advantageous. All things are lawful, but not all things build up.[o] **24** Let each one keep seeking, not his own advantage, but that of the other person.[p]

9:25 *Or "every athlete." **9:27** *Or "punish; strictly discipline." *Or "disqualified." **10:4** *Or "was." **10:8** *See Glossary. **10:9, 21, 22** *See App. A5.

10:23 *Or "permissible."

25 Eat whatever is sold in a meat market, making no inquiry because of your conscience, **26** for "to Jehovah* belong the earth and everything in it."[a] **27** If an unbeliever invites you and you want to go, eat whatever is set before you, making no inquiry on account of your conscience. **28** But if anyone says to you, "This is something offered in sacrifice," do not eat because of the one who told you and because of conscience.[b] **29** I do not mean your own conscience, but that of the other person. For why should my freedom be judged by another person's conscience?[c] **30** If I am partaking with thanks, why am I to be spoken of abusively over that for which I give thanks?[d]

31 Therefore, whether you are eating or drinking or doing anything else, do all things for God's glory.[e] **32** Keep from becoming causes for stumbling to Jews as well as Greeks and to the congregation of God,[f] **33** just as I am trying to please all people in all things, not seeking my own advantage,[g] but that of the many, so that they may be saved.[h]

11 Become imitators of me, just as I am of Christ.[i]

2 I commend you because in all things you remember me and you are holding fast to the traditions just as I handed them on to you. **3** But I want you to know that the head of every man is the Christ;[j] in turn, the head of a woman is the man;[k] in turn, the head of the Christ is God.[l] **4** Every man who prays or prophesies with something on his head shames his head; **5** but every woman who prays or prophesies[m] with her head uncovered shames her head, for it is one and the same as if she were a woman with a

shaved head. **6** For if a woman does not cover herself, she should have her hair cut off; but if it is disgraceful for a woman to have her hair cut off or shaved, she should be covered.

7 For a man should not have his head covered, as he is God's image[a] and glory, but the woman is man's glory. **8** For man did not come from woman, but woman came from man.[b] **9** And what is more, man was not created for the sake of the woman, but woman for the sake of the man.[c] **10** That is why the woman ought to have a sign of authority on her head, because of the angels.[d]

11 Besides, in connection with the Lord, neither is woman separate from man nor is man separate from woman. **12** For just as the woman is from the man,[e] so also the man is through the woman; but all things are from God.[f] **13** Judge for yourselves: Is it fitting for a woman to pray to God with her head uncovered? **14** Does not nature itself teach you that long hair is a dishonor to a man, **15** but if a woman has long hair, it is a glory to her? For her hair is given to her instead of a covering. **16** However, if anyone wants to argue in favor of some other custom, we have no other, nor do the congregations of God.

17 But while giving these instructions, I do not commend you, because it is, not for the better, but for the worse that you meet together. **18** For first of all, I hear that when you come together in a congregation, divisions exist among you; and to an extent I believe it. **19** For there will certainly also be sects among you,[g] so that those of you who are approved may also become evident.

20 When you come together in one place, it is not really

CHAP. 10
a Ps 24:1
  1Ti 4:4

b 1Co 8:7, 10

c Ro 14:15, 16
  1Co 8:12

d Ro 14:6
  1Ti 4:3

e Mt 5:16
  Col 3:17

f Ro 14:13
  1Co 8:13
  2Co 6:3

g Ro 15:2
  Php 2:4

h 1Co 9:22

CHAP. 11
i Php 3:17
  2Th 3:9

j Ro 14:9
  Eph 4:15
  Col 2:10

k Eph 5:23
  1Pe 3:1

l 1Co 15:27, 28

m Joe 2:28
  Ac 21:8, 9

Second Col.
a Ge 1:27

b Ge 2:22, 23

c Ge 2:18

d 1Co 4:9

e Ge 2:21, 22

f 1Co 8:6

g Ac 20:29, 30
  1Co 1:12
  1Ti 4:1
  2Pe 2:1

10:26 *See App. A5.

to eat the Lord's Evening Meal.[a] **21** For when you eat it, each one takes his own evening meal beforehand, so that one is hungry but another is intoxicated. **22** Do you not have houses for eating and drinking? Or do you despise the congregation of God and make those who have nothing feel ashamed? What can I say to you? Should I commend you? In this I do not commend you.

23 For I received from the Lord what I also handed on to you, that the Lord Jesus on the night[b] on which he was going to be betrayed took a loaf, **24** and after giving thanks, he broke it and said: "This means my body,[c] which is in your behalf. Keep doing this in remembrance of me."[d] **25** He did the same with the cup[e] also, after they had the evening meal, saying: "This cup means the new covenant[f] by virtue of my blood.[g] Keep doing this, whenever you drink it, in remembrance of me."[h] **26** For whenever you eat this loaf and drink this cup, you keep proclaiming the death of the Lord, until he comes.

27 Therefore, whoever eats the loaf or drinks the cup of the Lord unworthily will be guilty respecting the body and the blood of the Lord. **28** First let a man approve himself after scrutiny,[i] and only then let him eat of the loaf and drink of the cup. **29** For the one who eats and drinks without discerning the body eats and drinks judgment against himself. **30** That is why many among you are weak and sick, and quite a few are sleeping in death.*[j] **31** But if we would discern what we ourselves are, we would not be judged. **32** However, when we are judged, we are disciplined by Jehovah,*[k] so that we may

not become condemned with the world.[a] **33** Consequently, my brothers, when you come together to eat it, wait for one another. **34** If anyone is hungry, let him eat at home, so that when you come together it is not for judgment.[b] But as for the remaining matters, I will put them in order when I get there.

12 Now concerning the spiritual gifts,[c] brothers, I do not want you to be uninformed. **2** You know that when you were people of the nations,* you were influenced and led astray to those voiceless idols,[d] following wherever they might lead you. **3** Now I would have you know that nobody when speaking by God's spirit says: "Jesus is accursed!" and nobody can say: "Jesus is Lord!" except by holy spirit.[e]

4 Now there are different gifts, but there is the same spirit;[f] **5** and there are different ministries,[g] and yet there is the same Lord; **6** and there are different activities,* and yet it is the same God who performs them all in everyone.[h] **7** But the manifestation of the spirit is given to each one for a beneficial purpose.[i] **8** For to one is given speech* of wisdom through the spirit, to another speech of knowledge according to the same spirit, **9** to another faith[j] by the same spirit, to another gifts of healing[k] by that one spirit, **10** to yet another operations of powerful works,[l] to another prophesying, to another discernment of inspired expressions,[m] to another different tongues,*[n] and to another interpretation of tongues.[o] **11** But all these operations are performed by the very same

---

CHAP. 11

a Lu 22:19, 20

b Mt 26:20
Lu 22:14

c Mt 26:26
Mr 14:22
Ro 7:4
1Co 10:17

d Lu 22:19

e Mt 26:27
Mr 14:23
1Co 10:16

f Jer 31:31
Heb 8:8
Heb 9:15

g Lu 22:20
Heb 9:13, 14
1Pe 1:18, 19

h Ex 12:14

i 2Co 13:5

j 1Th 5:6

k Heb 12:5

Second Col.

a 2Pe 2:20
2Pe 3:7

b 1Co 11:29

CHAP. 12

c 1Co 14:1

d Ps 115:5
Hab 2:18
1Co 8:4
Ga 4:8
1Th 1:9

e 1Jo 4:2, 3

f Eph 4:4

g Eph 4:11

h 1Pe 4:11

i 1Co 14:26

j 1Co 13:2

k Ac 3:5-8
Ac 28:8, 9

l Heb 2:3, 4

m 1Jo 4:1

n Ac 10:45, 46
1Co 14:18

o 1Co 14:26

11:30 *Evidently referring to spiritual death. **11:32** *See App. A5.

12:2 *That is, unbelievers. **12:6** *Or "operations." **12:8** *Or "a message." **12:10** *Or "languages."

spirit, distributing to each one respectively just as it wills.

12 For just as the body is one but has many members, and all the members of that body, although many, are one body,[a] so too is the Christ. **13** For by one spirit we were all baptized into one body, whether Jews or Greeks, whether slaves or free, and we were all made to drink one spirit.

14 For, indeed, the body is made up not of one member but of many.[b] **15** If the foot should say, "Because I am not a hand, I am no part of the body," that does not make it no part of the body. **16** And if the ear should say, "Because I am not an eye, I am no part of the body," that does not make it no part of the body. **17** If the whole body were an eye, where would the sense of hearing be? If it were all hearing, where would the sense of smell be? **18** But now God has arranged each of the body members just as he pleased.

19 If they were all the same member, where would the body be? **20** But now they are many members, yet one body. **21** The eye cannot say to the hand, "I do not need you," or again, the head cannot say to the feet, "I do not need you." **22** On the contrary, the members of the body that seem to be weaker are necessary, **23** and the parts of the body that we think to be less honorable we surround with greater honor,[c] so our unseemly parts are treated with greater modesty, **24** whereas our attractive parts do not need anything. Nevertheless, God has so composed the body, giving greater honor to the part that had a lack, **25** so that there should be no division in the body, but its members should have mutual concern for one another.[d] **26** If one member suf-

fers, all the other members suffer with it;[a] or if a member is glorified, all the other members rejoice with it.[b]

27 Now you are Christ's body,[c] and each of you individually is a member.[d] **28** And God has assigned the respective ones in the congregation: first, apostles;[e] second, prophets;[f] third, teachers;[g] then powerful works;[h] then gifts of healings;[i] helpful services; abilities to direct;[j] different tongues.[k] **29** Not all are apostles, are they? Not all are prophets, are they? Not all are teachers, are they? Not all perform powerful works, do they? **30** Not all have gifts of healings, do they? Not all speak in tongues, do they?[l] Not all are interpreters,* are they?[m] **31** But keep striving for* the greater gifts.[n] And yet I will show you a surpassing way.[o]

13 If I speak in the tongues of men and of angels but do not have love, I have become a clanging gong or a clashing cymbal. **2** And if I have the gift of prophecy and understand all the sacred secrets and all knowledge,[p] and if I have all the faith so as to move* mountains, but do not have love, I am nothing.*[q] **3** And if I give all my belongings to feed others,[r] and if I hand over my body so that I may boast, but do not have love,[s] I do not benefit at all.

4 Love[t] is patient*[u] and kind.[v] Love is not jealous.[w] It does not brag, does not get puffed up,[x] **5** does not behave indecently,*[y] does not look for its own interests,[z] does not become provoked.[a] It does not keep account of the injury.*[b] **6** It does not rejoice over unrighteousness,[c] but

CHAP. 12	
a	Ro 12:4, 5
b	Eph 4:16
c	Ge 3:7, 21
d	Ro 12:10 Ga 6:2 Eph 4:25
Second Col.	
a	Heb 13:3
b	Ro 12:15
c	Eph 1:22, 23
d	Ro 12:4, 5
e	Eph 2:20
f	Ac 13:1
g	Eph 4:11
h	Ga 3:5
i	Ac 5:16
j	Heb 13:17
k	Ac 2:6, 7
l	1Co 14:4
m	1Co 14:5
n	1Co 14:1
o	1Co 13:8
CHAP. 13	
p	1Co 12:8
q	1Jo 4:20
r	Mt 6:2
s	2Co 9:7
t	1Jo 4:8
u	1Th 5:14
v	Ro 13:10 Eph 4:32
w	Ga 5:26
x	1Pe 5:5
y	Ro 13:13 1Co 14:40
z	1Co 10:24 Php 2:4
a	Mt 5:39 Jas 1:19
b	Eph 4:32 Col 3:13
c	Ro 12:9

12:30 *Or "translators." **12:31** *Or "keep zealously seeking." **13:2** *Or "transplant." #Or "useless." **13:4** *Or "long-suffering." **13:5** *Or "is not rude." #Or "of wrongs."

rejoices with the truth. **7** It bears all things,[a] believes all things,[b] hopes all things,[c] endures all things.[d]

8 Love never fails. But if there are gifts of prophecy, they will be done away with; if there are tongues,* they will cease; if there is knowledge, it will be done away with. **9** For we have partial knowledge[e] and we prophesy partially, **10** but when what is complete comes, what is partial will be done away with. **11** When I was a child, I used to speak as a child, to think as a child, to reason as a child; but now that I have become a man, I have done away with the traits of a child. **12** For now we see in hazy outline* by means of a metal mirror, but then it will be face-to-face. At present I know partially, but then I will know accurately,# just as I am accurately known. **13** Now, however, these three remain: faith, hope, love; but the greatest of these is love.[f]

14 Pursue love, yet keep striving for* the spiritual gifts, but preferably that you may prophesy.[g] **2** For the one who speaks in a tongue speaks, not to men, but to God, for no one listens,[h] but he speaks sacred secrets[i] by the spirit. **3** However, the one who prophesies builds up and encourages and consoles men by his speech. **4** The one who speaks in a tongue builds up himself, but the one who prophesies builds up a congregation. **5** Now I would like for all of you to speak in tongues,[j] but I prefer that you prophesy.[k] Indeed, the one who prophesies is greater than the one who speaks in tongues, unless he interprets,*

so that the congregation may be built up. **6** But at this time, brothers, if I should come speaking to you in tongues, what good would I do you unless I spoke to you either with a revelation[a] or with knowledge[b] or with a prophecy or with a teaching?

7 It is the same with the inanimate things that produce sound, whether a flute or a harp. Unless there is an interval to the tones, how can what is being played on the flute or on the harp be recognized? **8** For if the trumpet sounds an indistinct call, who will get ready for battle? **9** In the same way, unless you with the tongue use speech that is easily understood, how will anyone know what is being said? You will, in fact, be speaking into the air. **10** It may be that there are many kinds of speech in the world, and yet no kind is without meaning. **11** For if I do not understand the sense of the speech, I will be a foreigner to the one speaking, and the one speaking will be a foreigner to me. **12** So also with you, since you eagerly desire the gifts of the spirit, seek to abound in gifts that will build up the congregation.[c]

13 Therefore, let the one who speaks in a tongue pray that he may interpret.*[d] **14** For if I am praying in a tongue, it is my gift of the spirit that is praying, but my mind is unproductive. **15** What is to be done, then? I will pray with the gift of the spirit, but I will also pray with my mind. I will sing praise with the gift of the spirit, but I will also sing praise with my mind. **16** Otherwise, if you offer praise with a gift of the spirit, how will the ordinary person in your midst say "Amen" to your giving of thanks, since

---

CHAP. 13
a 1Pe 4:8

b Ac 17:11

c Ro 8:25
Ro 12:12

d 1Th 1:3

e Pr 4:18

f Mt 22:37
Ro 13:10

CHAP. 14
g 1Th 5:20

h 1Co 14:5

i 1Co 13:2

j 1Co 12:30

k Joe 2:28
Ac 2:17
Ac 21:8, 9

Second Col.
a Ga 1:11, 12
Ga 2:2

b 1Co 12:8

c 1Co 12:7
1Co 14:4, 26

d 1Co 12:8, 10
1Co 14:5

13:8 *That is, miraculous speaking in other languages. **13:12** *Or "indistinctly." #Or "fully." **14:1** *Or "keep zealously seeking." **14:5** *Or "translates."

14:13 *Or "translate."

he does not know what you are saying? **17** True, you are giving thanks in a fine way, but the other man is not being built up. **18** I thank God that I speak in more tongues than all of you do. **19** Nevertheless, in a congregation I would rather speak five words with my mind,* that I might also instruct* others, than ten thousand words in a tongue.ᵃ

20 Brothers, do not become young children in your understanding,ᵇ but be young children as to badness;ᶜ and become full-grown in your understanding.ᵈ **21** In the Law it is written: "'With the tongues of foreigners and with the lips of strangers I will speak to this people, and even then they will refuse to listen to me,' says Jehovah."*ᵉ **22** Therefore, tongues are not a sign for the believers but for the unbelievers,ᶠ whereas prophecy is not for the unbelievers but for the believers. **23** So if the whole congregation comes together to one place and they all speak in tongues, but ordinary people or unbelievers come in, will they not say that you have lost your minds? **24** But if you are all prophesying and an unbeliever or an ordinary person comes in, he will be reproved and closely examined by them all. **25** The secrets of his heart then become evident, so that he will fall facedown and worship God, declaring: "God is really among you."ᵍ

26 What is to be done, then, brothers? When you come together, one has a psalm, another has a teaching, another has a revelation, another has a tongue, and another has an interpretation.ʰ Let all things take place for building up. **27** And if someone speaks in a tongue, let it be limited to two or

three at the most, and in turns, and someone must interpret.*ᵃ **28** But if there is no interpreter,* he must keep silent in the congregation and speak to himself and to God. **29** Let two or three prophetsᵇ speak, and let the others discern the meaning. **30** But if another one receives a revelation while sitting there, let the first speaker keep silent. **31** For you can all prophesy one at a time, so that all may learn and all may be encouraged.ᶜ **32** And gifts of the spirit of the prophets are to be controlled by the prophets. **33** For God is a God not of disorder but of peace.ᵈ

As in all the congregations of the holy ones, **34** let the women keep silent in the congregations, for it is not permitted for them to speak.ᵉ Let them be in subjection,ᶠ as the Law also says. **35** If they want to learn something, let them ask their husbands at home, for it is disgraceful for a woman to speak in the congregation.

36 Was it from you that the word of God originated, or did it reach only as far as you?

37 If anyone thinks he is a prophet or is gifted with the spirit, he must acknowledge that the things I am writing to you are the Lord's commandment. **38** But if anyone disregards this, he will be disregarded.* **39** So, my brothers, keep striving to prophesy,ᵍ and yet do not forbid the speaking in tongues.ʰ **40** But let all things take place decently and by arrangement.*ⁱ

15 Now I remind you, brothers, of the good news that I declared to you,ʲ which you

---

14:19 *Or "understanding." *Or "instruct orally." **14:21** *See App. A5.

14:27 *Or "translate." **14:28** *Or "translator." **14:38** *Or possibly, "if anyone is ignorant, he will continue ignorant." **14:40** *Or "in an orderly manner."

CHAP. 14
a 1Co 14:4

b Eph 4:14

c Ro 16:19

d Heb 5:13, 14

e Isa 28:11, 12

f Ac 2:4, 13

g Isa 45:14
Zec 8:23

h 1Co 12:8, 10

Second Col.
a 1Co 14:5

b Ac 13:1

c Heb 10:24, 25

d 1Co 14:40
Col 2:5

e 1Ti 2:11, 12

f 1Co 11:3
Eph 5:22
Col 3:18
Tit 2:5
1Pe 3:1

g 1Th 5:20

h 1Co 14:27

i 1Co 14:33
Col 2:5

CHAP. 15
j Ac 18:1, 11

also accepted, and for which you have taken your stand. **2** Through it you are also being saved if you hold firmly to the good news I declared to you, unless you became believers for nothing.

3 For among the first things I handed on to you was what I also received, that Christ died for our sins according to the Scriptures;[a] **4** and that he was buried,[b] yes, that he was raised up[c] on the third day[d] according to the Scriptures;[e] **5** and that he appeared to Ce'phas,*[f] and then to the Twelve.[g] **6** After that he appeared to more than 500 brothers at one time,[h] most of whom are still with us, though some have fallen asleep in death. **7** After that he appeared to James,[i] then to all the apostles.[j] **8** But last of all he appeared also to me[k] as if to one born prematurely.

9 For I am the least of the apostles, and I am not worthy of being called an apostle, because I persecuted the congregation of God.[l] **10** But by God's undeserved kindness I am what I am. And his undeserved kindness to me was not in vain, but I labored more than all of them; yet it was not I, but the undeserved kindness of God that is with me. **11** Whether, then, it is I or they, this is the way we preach, and this is the way you believed.

12 Now if it is being preached that Christ has been raised from the dead,[m] how is it that some among you say there is no resurrection of the dead? **13** If, indeed, there is no resurrection of the dead, then Christ has not been raised up. **14** But if Christ has not been raised up, our preaching is certainly in vain, and your faith is also in vain. **15** Moreover, we are also

---

15:5 *Also called Peter.

CHAP. 15

a Ps 22:15
Isa 53:8, 12
Da 9:26
1Pe 2:24

b Isa 53:9
Mt 27:59, 60

c Mt 28:7

d Jon 1:17
Lu 24:46

e Ps 16:10

f Mt 10:2
Lu 24:33, 34

g Joh 20:26

h Mt 28:16, 17

i Ac 12:17

j Ac 1:3, 6

k Ac 9:3-5

l Ac 8:3
Ga 1:13

m Ac 4:2
Ac 17:31

Second Col.

a Ac 3:15

b Ac 2:24
Ac 4:10
Ac 13:30, 31

c Ro 4:25
Heb 7:25

d Ac 7:59
1Co 15:14
1Pe 1:3

e Ac 26:23
Col 1:18

f Ge 3:17, 19

g Joh 11:25

h Ro 5:12

i Ro 5:17
Ro 6:23

j Re 1:5

k Mt 24:3
1Th 4:16

l Ps 110:1, 2

m Re 20:14

n Ps 8:6
Eph 1:22

o Ps 8:6
Eph 1:22

p Heb 2:8

q 1Pe 3:22

r Joh 14:28

s 1Co 3:23

---

found to be false witnesses of God,[a] because we have given witness against God by saying that he raised up the Christ,[b] whom he did not raise up if the dead are really not to be raised up. **16** For if the dead are not to be raised up, neither has Christ been raised up. **17** Further, if Christ has not been raised up, your faith is useless; you remain in your sins.[c] **18** Then also those who have fallen asleep in death in union with Christ have perished.[d] **19** If in this life only we have hoped in Christ, we are to be pitied more than anyone.

20 But now Christ has been raised from the dead, the firstfruits of those who have fallen asleep in death.[e] **21** For since death came through a man,[f] resurrection of the dead also comes through a man.[g] **22** For just as in Adam all are dying,[h] so also in the Christ all will be made alive.[i] **23** But each one in his own proper order: Christ the firstfruits,[j] afterward those who belong to the Christ during his presence.[k] **24** Next, the end, when he hands over the Kingdom to his God and Father, when he has brought to nothing all government and all authority and power.[l] **25** For he must rule as king until God has put all enemies under his feet.[m] **26** And the last enemy, death, is to be brought to nothing.[n] **27** For God "subjected all things under his feet."[o] But when he says that 'all things have been subjected,'[p] it is evident that this does not include the One who subjected all things to him.[q] **28** But when all things will have been subjected to him, then the Son himself will also subject himself to the One who subjected all things to him,[r] that God may be all things to everyone.[s]

29 Otherwise, what will they do who are being baptized for the purpose of being dead ones?[a] If the dead are not to be raised up at all, why are they also being baptized for the purpose of being such? **30** Why are we also in danger every hour?[b] **31** Daily I face death. This is as sure as my exultation over you, brothers, which I have in Christ Jesus our Lord. **32** If like other men,[*] I have fought with wild beasts at Eph′e·sus,[c] of what good is it to me? If the dead are not to be raised up, "let us eat and drink, for tomorrow we are to die."[d] **33** Do not be misled. Bad associations spoil useful habits.[*e] **34** Come to your senses in a righteous way and do not practice sin, for some have no knowledge of God. I am speaking to move you to shame.

35 Nevertheless, someone will say: "How are the dead to be raised up? Yes, with what sort of body are they coming?"[f] **36** You unreasonable person! What you sow is not made alive unless first it dies. **37** And as for what you sow, you sow, not the body that will develop, but just a bare grain, whether of wheat or of some other kind of seed; **38** but God gives it a body just as it has pleased him, and gives to each of the seeds its own body. **39** Not all flesh is the same flesh, but there is one of mankind, there is another flesh of cattle, another flesh of birds, and another of fish. **40** And there are heavenly bodies[g] and earthly bodies;[h] but the glory of the heavenly bodies is one sort, and that of the earthly bodies is a different sort. **41** The glory of the sun is one sort, and the glory of the moon is anoth-

er,[a] and the glory of the stars is another; in fact, one star differs from another star in glory.

42 So it is with the resurrection of the dead. It is sown in corruption; it is raised up in incorruption.[b] **43** It is sown in dishonor; it is raised up in glory.[c] It is sown in weakness; it is raised up in power.[d] **44** It is sown a physical body; it is raised up a spiritual body. If there is a physical body, there is also a spiritual one. **45** So it is written: "The first man Adam became a living person."[*e] The last Adam became a life-giving spirit.[f] **46** However, what is spiritual is not first. What is physical is first, and afterward what is spiritual. **47** The first man is from the earth and made of dust;[g] the second man is from heaven.[h] **48** Like the one made of dust, so too are those made of dust; and like the heavenly one, so too are those who are heavenly.[i] **49** And just as we have borne the image of the one made of dust,[j] we will bear also the image of the heavenly one.[k]

50 But I tell you this, brothers, that flesh and blood cannot inherit God's Kingdom, nor does corruption inherit incorruption. **51** Look! I tell you a sacred secret: We will not all fall asleep in death, but we will all be changed,[l] **52** in a moment, in the blink[*] of an eye, during the last trumpet. For the trumpet will sound,[m] and the dead will be raised up incorruptible, and we will be changed. **53** For this which is corruptible must put on incorruption,[n] and this which is mortal must put on immortality. **54** But when this which is corruptible puts on incorruption and this which is mortal puts on immortality, then the saying that is written

CHAP. 15
a Ro 6:4

b Ro 8:36
  2Co 11:23-27

c 2Co 1:8

d Isa 22:13

e Pr 13:20
  1Co 5:6

f 1Jo 3:2

g Mt 28:3
  Lu 24:4

h Heb 2:6, 7

Second Col.
a Ge 1:16

b Ro 2:6, 7

c Col 3:4

d Re 20:4

e Ge 2:7

f Joh 5:26
  1Ti 3:16

g Ge 2:7

h Joh 3:13

i Php 3:20, 21

j Ge 5:3

k Ro 8:29

l 1Th 4:17

m 1Th 4:16

n Ro 2:6, 7

o 2Co 5:4

15:30 *Or "all the time?" **15:32** *Or possibly, "from a human viewpoint." **15:33** *Or "corrupt good morals."

15:45 *Or "soul." **15:52** *Or "twinkling."

will take place: "Death is swallowed up forever."[a] 55 "Death, where is your victory? Death, where is your sting?"[b] 56 The sting producing death is sin,[c] and the power for sin is the Law.*[d] 57 But thanks to God, for he gives us the victory through our Lord Jesus Christ![e]

58 Therefore, my beloved brothers, be steadfast,[f] immovable, always having plenty to do[g] in the work of the Lord, knowing that your labor is not in vain[h] in connection with the Lord.

16 Now concerning the collection for the holy ones,[i] you may follow the directions I gave to the congregations of Ga·la′ti·a. 2 On the first day of every week, each of you should set something aside according to his own means, so that collections will not take place when I arrive. 3 But when I get there, I will send the men you approve of in your letters[j] to take your kind gift to Jerusalem. 4 However, if it seems advisable for me to go there also, they will go there with me.

5 But I will come to you when I have gone through Mac·e·do′ni·a, for I will be going through Mac·e·do′ni·a;[k] 6 and perhaps I will stay or even spend the winter with you, so that you may accompany me partway to where I may be going. 7 For I do not want to see you now just in passing, since I hope to spend some time with you,[l] if Jehovah* permits. 8 But I am remaining in Eph′e·sus[m] until the Festival of Pentecost, 9 because a large door that leads to activity has been opened to me,[n] but there are many opposers.

10 Now if Timothy[o] arrives, make sure that he has nothing to fear while among you, for he

is performing the work of Jehovah,*[a] just as I am. 11 Therefore, let no one look down on him. Send him on his way in peace, so that he may come to me, for I am waiting for him together with the brothers.

12 Now concerning A·pol′los[b] our brother, I strongly urged him to come to you with the brothers. It was not his intention to come now, but he will come when he has the opportunity.

13 Stay awake,[c] stand firm in the faith,[d] carry on in a manly way,*[e] grow mighty.[f] 14 Let everything you do be done with love.[g]

15 Now I urge you, brothers: You know that the household of Steph′a·nas is the firstfruits of A·cha′ia and that they devoted themselves to ministering to the holy ones. 16 May you also keep submitting yourselves to people like that and to all those cooperating and working hard.[h] 17 But I rejoice over the presence of Steph′a·nas[i] and For·tu·na′tus and A·cha′i·cus, because they have made up for your not being here. 18 For they have refreshed my spirit and yours. Therefore, give recognition to men of that sort.

19 The congregations of Asia send you their greetings. Aq′ui·la and Pris′ca together with the congregation that is in their house[j] greet you heartily in the Lord. 20 All the brothers greet you. Greet one another with a holy kiss.

21 Here is my greeting, Paul's, in my own hand.

22 If anyone has no affection for the Lord, let him be accursed. O our Lord, come! 23 May the undeserved kindness of the Lord Jesus be with you. 24 May my love be with all of you in union with Christ Jesus.

CHAP. 15
a Isa 25:8
　Re 20:6

b Ho 13:14

c Ro 6:23

d Ro 3:20
　Ro 7:12, 13

e Joh 3:16
　Ac 4:12

f Col 1:23
　Heb 3:14
　2Pe 3:17

g Ro 12:11

h 2Ch 15:7
　1Co 3:8
　Re 14:13

CHAP. 16
i Ac 24:17
　Ro 15:26
　2Co 8:3, 4

j 2Co 8:19

k Ac 19:21
　2Co 1:15, 16

l Ac 20:2

m Ac 19:1

n Ac 19:10, 11

o Ac 16:1, 2

Second Col.
a Php 2:19, 20

b Ac 18:24, 25

c 1Th 5:6

d 1Co 15:58
　Php 1:27

e Ac 4:29

f Eph 6:10
　Col 1:11

g 1Co 13:4
　1Pe 4:8

h Php 2:29, 30
　1Th 5:12
　1Ti 5:17

i 1Co 1:16

j Ro 16:3, 5
　Phm 2

15:56 *Or "and the Law gives sin its power." 16:7, 10 *See App. A5.

16:13 *Or "be courageous."

THE SECOND TO THE
CORINTHIANS

OUTLINE OF CONTENTS

1 Paul, an apostle of Christ Jesus through God's will, and Timothy[a] our brother, to the congregation of God that is in Corinth, including all the holy ones who are in all A·cha′ia:[b]

2 May you have undeserved kindness and peace from God our Father and the Lord Jesus Christ.

3 Praised be the God and Father of our Lord Jesus Christ,[c] the Father of tender mercies[d] and the God of all comfort,[e] 4 who comforts* us in all our trials[#f] so that we may be able to comfort others[a] in any sort of trial[#] with the comfort that we receive from God.[b] 5 For just as the sufferings for the Christ abound in us,[c] so the comfort we receive through the Christ also abounds. 6 Now if we face trials,[#] it is for your comfort and salvation; and if we are being comforted, it is for your comfort, which acts to help you to endure the same sufferings that we also suffer. 7 And our hope for you is unwavering, knowing as we do that just as you share in the sufferings, so you will also share in the comfort.[d]

8 For we do not want you to be unaware, brothers, of the

CHAP. 1
a Ac 16:1, 2
  Php 2:19, 20
b 1Th 1:8
c Joh 20:17
d Ex 34:6
  Ps 86:5
e Isa 51:3
  Ro 15:5
f Ps 23:4
  2Co 7:6

Second Col.
a Eph 6:21, 22
  1Th 4:18
b Ro 15:4
  2Th 2:16, 17
c 1Co 4:11-13
  Col 1:24
d Ro 8:18
  2Ti 2:11, 12

1:4 *Or "encourages." 1:4, 6 #Or "tribulation."

tribulation we experienced in the province of Asia.[a] We were under extreme pressure beyond our own strength, so that we were very uncertain even of our lives.[b] **9** In fact, we felt that we had received the sentence of death. This was so that we would trust, not in ourselves, but in the God[c] who raises up the dead. **10** From such a great risk of death he did rescue us and will rescue us, and our hope is in him that he will also continue to rescue us.[d] **11** You also can help us by your supplication for us,[e] in order that many may give thanks in our behalf for the favor we receive in answer to the prayers of many.*[f]

12 For the thing we boast of is this, our conscience bears witness that we have conducted ourselves in the world, and especially toward you, with holiness and godly sincerity, not with fleshly wisdom,[g] but with God's undeserved kindness. **13** For we are really not writing about anything except what you can read* and understand, and I hope you will continue to understand these things fully,* **14** just as you have also understood to an extent that we are a cause for you to boast, just as you will also be for us in the day of our Lord Jesus.

15 So with this confidence, I was intending to come first to you, so that you might have a second occasion for joy;* **16** for I intended to visit you on my way to Mac·e·do′ni·a, to return to you from Mac·e·do′ni·a, and then to have you send me off to Ju·de′a.[h] **17** Well, when I had such an intention, I did not view the matter lightly, did I? Or

do I purpose things in a fleshly way, so that I am saying "Yes, yes" and then "No, no"? **18** But God can be relied on that what we say to you is not "yes" and yet "no." **19** For the Son of God, Jesus Christ, who was preached among you through us, that is, through me and Sil·va′nus* and Timothy,[a] did not become "yes" and yet "no," but "yes" has become "yes" in his case. **20** For no matter how many the promises of God are, they have become "yes" by means of him.[b] Therefore, also through him is the "Amen" said to God,[c] which brings him glory through us. **21** But the one who guarantees that you and we belong to Christ and the one who anointed us is God.[d] **22** He has also put his seal on us[e] and has given us the token of what is to come,* that is, the spirit,[f] in our hearts.

23 Now I call on God as a witness against me* that it is to spare you that I have not yet come to Corinth. **24** Not that we are the masters over your faith,[g] but we are fellow workers for your joy, for it is by your faith that you are standing.

2 For I have made up my mind not to come to you again in sadness. **2** For if I make you sad, who will be there to cheer me up except the one I saddened? **3** I wrote what I did, so that when I come I may not be saddened by those over whom I ought to rejoice, because I have confidence that what brings me joy brings all of you the same joy. **4** For out of much tribulation and anguish of heart I wrote you with many tears, not to sadden you,[h] but to let you know the depth of love I have for you.

CHAP. 1
a Ac 20:18, 19

b 1Co 15:32

c 2Co 12:10

d Ps 34:7, 19
2Ti 4:18
2Pe 2:9

e Php 1:19
Phm 22

f Ac 12:5
Ro 15:30-32

g 1Co 2:4, 5

h 1Co 16:5, 6

Second Col.
a Ac 18:5

b Ro 15:8

c Re 3:14

d 1Jo 2:20, 27

e Eph 4:30

f Ro 8:23
2Co 5:5
Eph 1:13, 14

g Heb 13:17
1Pe 5:2, 3

CHAP. 2
h 2Co 7:8, 9

1:11 *Or "because of many prayerful faces." 1:13 *Or possibly, "what you already well know." #Lit., "to the end." 1:15 *Or possibly, "so that you might benefit twice."

1:19 *Also called Silas. 1:22 *Or "the down payment (earnest money); the guarantee (pledge) of what is to come." 1:23 *Or "my soul."

5 Now if anyone has caused sadness,[a] he has saddened, not me, but all of you to an extent —not to be too harsh in what I say. **6** This rebuke given by the majority is sufficient for such a man; **7** now you should instead kindly forgive and comfort him,[b] so that he may not be overwhelmed* by excessive sadness.[c] **8** I therefore exhort you to confirm your love for him.[d] **9** For this is also why I wrote to you: to determine whether you would give proof of your obedience in all things. **10** If you forgive anyone for anything, I do also. In fact, whatever I have forgiven (if I have forgiven anything) has been for your sake in Christ's sight, **11** so that we may not be overreached* by Satan,[e] for we are not ignorant of his designs.*[f]

12 Now when I arrived in Troʹas[g] to declare the good news about the Christ and a door was opened to me in the Lord, **13** my spirit felt no relief because of not finding Titus[h] my brother. So I said good-bye to them and departed for Macʹe·doʹni·a.[i]

14 But thanks be to God, who always leads us in a triumphal procession in company with the Christ and through us spreads* the fragrance of the knowledge of him in every place! **15** For to God we are a sweet fragrance of Christ among those who are being saved and among those who are perishing; **16** to the latter ones an odor* of death leading to death,[j] to the former ones a fragrance of life leading to life. And who is adequately qualified for these things? **17** We are, for we are not peddlers of* the word

2:7 *Or "swallowed up." 2:11 *Or "outwitted." #Or "intentions; schemes." 2:14 *Or "makes perceptible." 2:16 *Or "fragrance." 2:17 *Or "not commercializing; not making profit from."

CHAP. 2
a 1Co 5:1
b Lu 15:23, 24
c Heb 12:12
d Ro 12:10
e Lu 22:31
  2Ti 2:26
f Eph 6:11, 12
  1Pe 5:8
g Ac 16:8
h Ga 2:3
  Tit 1:4
i 2Co 7:5
j Joh 15:19
  2Co 4:3
  1Pe 2:7, 8

Second Col.
a 2Co 4:2

CHAP. 3
b 1Co 9:2
c 1Co 3:5
d Ex 31:18
  Ex 34:1
e Pr 3:3
  Pr 7:3
f Ex 4:12, 15
  Php 2:13
g Heb 8:6
h Ro 13:9
i Ga 3:10
j Joh 6:63
k Ex 31:18
  Ex 32:16
l Ex 34:29, 30
m Ac 2:1, 4
n 1Pe 4:14
o De 27:26
p Ex 34:35
q Ro 3:21, 22
r Col 2:16, 17
s Ex 19:16
  Ex 24:17
t Heb 12:22-24

of God[a] as many men are, but we speak in all sincerity as sent from God, yes, in the sight of God and in company with Christ.

3 Are we starting to recommend ourselves again? Or do we need, like some men, letters of recommendation to you or from you? **2** You yourselves are our letter,[b] inscribed on our hearts and known and being read by all mankind. **3** For you are shown to be a letter of Christ written by us as ministers,[c] inscribed not with ink but with the spirit of a living God, not on stone tablets[d] but on fleshly tablets, on hearts.[e]

4 We have this sort of confidence toward God through the Christ. **5** Not that we of ourselves are adequately qualified to consider that anything comes from us, but our being adequately qualified comes from God,[f] **6** who has indeed adequately qualified us to be ministers of a new covenant,[g] not of a written code,[h] but of spirit; for the written code condemns to death,[i] but the spirit makes alive.[j]

7 Now if the code that administers death and that was engraved in letters on stones[k] came with such glory that the sons of Israel could not gaze at the face of Moses because of the glory of his face,[l] a glory that was to be done away with, **8** why should the administering of the spirit[m] not be with even greater glory?[n] **9** For if the code administering condemnation[o] was glorious,[p] how much more glorious would be the administering of righteousness![q] **10** In fact, even what had once been made glorious has been stripped of glory because of the glory that excels it.[r] **11** For if what was to be done away with was brought in with glory,[s] how much greater would be the glory of what remains![t]

12 Since we have such a hope,[a] we are using great freeness of speech, **13** and not doing what Moses did when he would put a veil over his face[b] so that the sons of Israel might not gaze intently at the end of what was to be done away with. **14** But their minds were dulled.[c] For to this present day, the same veil remains unlifted when the old covenant is read,[d] because it is taken away only by means of Christ.[e] **15** In fact, to this day whenever Moses is read,[f] a veil lies upon their hearts.[g] **16** But when one turns to Jehovah,* the veil is taken away.[h] **17** Now Jehovah* is the Spirit,[i] and where the spirit of Jehovah* is, there is freedom.[j] **18** And all of us, while we with unveiled faces reflect like mirrors the glory of Jehovah,* are transformed into the same image from one degree of glory to another,# exactly as it is done by Jehovah* the Spirit.△[k]

4 Therefore, since we have this ministry through the mercy that was shown us, we do not give up. **2** But we have renounced the shameful, underhanded things, not walking with cunning or adulterating the word of God;[l] but by making the truth manifest, we recommend ourselves to every human conscience in the sight of God.[m] **3** If, in fact, the good news we declare is veiled, it is veiled among those who are perishing, **4** among whom the god of this system of things*[n] has blinded the minds of the unbelievers,[o] so that the illumination# of the glorious good news about the Christ, who is the image of God,[p] might not shine through.[q] **5** For we are preaching, not about ourselves, but about Jesus

3:16-18 *See App. A5. **3:18** #Lit., "from glory to glory." △Or possibly, "by the spirit of Jehovah." **4:4** *Or "this age." See Glossary. #Or "light."

CHAP. 3
a 1Pe 1:3, 4
b Ex 34:33-35
c Ro 11:7
d Joh 12:40
e Ro 7:6
  Eph 2:15
f Ac 15:21
g Ro 11:8
h Ex 34:34
i Joh 4:24
j Isa 61:1
  Ro 6:14
  Ro 8:15
  Ga 5:1, 13
k 2Co 4:6
  Eph 4:23, 24
  Eph 5:1

CHAP. 4
l 2Co 2:17
  Ga 1:9
m 2Co 6:3, 4
n Joh 14:30
  Eph 2:2
  1Jo 5:19
o 2Co 11:14
p Col 1:15
  Heb 1:3
q Isa 60:2
  Joh 8:12

Second Col.
a Ge 1:3
b 1Pe 2:9
c 2Co 4:1
d Isa 64:8
  Ac 9:15
  1Co 15:47
e 2Co 12:9, 10
  Php 4:13
f 1Co 10:13
g Heb 13:5
h Re 2:10
i Php 3:10
  1Pe 4:13
j Ro 8:36
  1Co 4:9
  1Co 15:31
k Ps 116:10
l 1Co 6:14
m 2Ti 2:10

Christ as Lord and ourselves as your slaves for Jesus' sake. **6** For God is the one who said: "Let the light shine out of darkness,"[a] and he has shone on our hearts to illuminate them[b] with the glorious knowledge of God by the face of Christ.

7 However, we have this treasure[c] in earthen vessels,*[d] so that the power beyond what is normal may be God's and not from us.[e] **8** We are hard-pressed in every way, but not cramped beyond movement; we are perplexed, but not absolutely with no way out;*[f] **9** we are persecuted, but not abandoned;[g] we are knocked down, but not destroyed.[h] **10** Always we endure in our body the death-dealing treatment that Jesus suffered,[i] that the life of Jesus may also be made manifest in our body. **11** For we who live are ever being brought face-to-face with death[j] for Jesus' sake, so that the life of Jesus may also be made manifest in our mortal flesh. **12** So death is at work in us, but life in you.

13 Now because we have the same spirit of faith as that of which it is written: "I exercised faith, therefore I spoke";[k] we too exercise faith and therefore we speak, **14** knowing that the One who raised Jesus up will raise us up also with Jesus and will present us together with you.[l] **15** For all these things are for your sake, so that the increase of the undeserved kindness should abound even more because many more are offering thanksgiving to the glory of God.[m]

16 Therefore, we do not give up, but even if the man we are outside is wasting away, certainly the man we are inside is

4:7 *Or "in jars of clay." **4:8** *Or possibly, "not left in despair."

being renewed from day to day. **17** For though the tribulation* is momentary and light, it works out for us a glory that is of more and more surpassing greatness* and is everlasting;[a] **18** while we keep our eyes, not on the things seen, but on the things unseen.[b] For the things seen are temporary, but the things unseen are everlasting.

5 For we know that if our earthly house, this tent, should be torn down,*[c] we are to have a building from God, a house not made with hands,[d] everlasting in the heavens. **2** For in this house* we do indeed groan, earnestly desiring to put on the one for us* from heaven,[Δe] **3** so that when we do put it on, we will not be found naked. **4** In fact, we who are in this tent groan, being weighed down, because we do not want to put this one off, but we want to put the other on,[f] so that what is mortal may be swallowed up by life.[g] **5** Now the one who prepared us for this very thing is God,[h] who gave us the spirit as a token of what is to come.*[i]

6 So we are always of good courage and know that while we have our home in the body, we are absent from the Lord,[j] **7** for we are walking by faith, not by sight. **8** But we are of good courage and would prefer to be absent from the body and to make our home with the Lord.[k] **9** So whether at home with him or absent from him, we make it our aim to be acceptable to him. **10** For we must all appear* before the judgment

seat of the Christ, so that each one may be repaid according to the things he has practiced while in the body, whether good or bad.*[a]

11 Therefore, since we know the fear of the Lord, we keep persuading men, but we are well-known* to God. However, I hope that we are well-known* also to your consciences. **12** We are not recommending ourselves to you again but giving you an incentive to boast about us, so that you may be able to answer those who boast over the outward appearance[b] but not over what is in the heart. **13** For if we were out of our mind,[c] it was for God; if we are sound in mind, it is for you. **14** For the love the Christ has compels us, because this is what we have concluded, that one man died for all;[d] so, then, all had died. **15** And he died for all so that those who live should live no longer for themselves,[e] but for him who died for them and was raised up.

16 So from now on we know no man from a fleshly viewpoint.[f] Even if we once knew Christ according to the flesh, we certainly no longer know him in that way.[g] **17** Therefore, if anyone is in union with Christ, he is a new creation;[h] the old things passed away; look! new things have come into existence. **18** But all things are from God, who reconciled us to himself through Christ[i] and gave us the ministry of the reconciliation,[j] **19** namely, that God was by means of Christ reconciling a world to himself,[k] not counting their offenses against them,[l] and he entrusted to us the message of the reconciliation.[m]

20 Therefore, we are ambassadors[n] substituting for Christ,[o]

CHAP. 4
a Mt 5:12
  Ro 8:18

b 2Co 5:7
  Heb 11:1

CHAP. 5
c 2Pe 1:13, 14

d 1Co 15:50
  Php 3:20, 21

e Ro 6:5
  Ro 8:23
  1Co 15:48, 49

f 1Co 15:43, 44
  Php 1:21

g 1Pe 1:3, 4

h Eph 2:10

i Ro 8:23
  Eph 1:13, 14

j Joh 14:3

k Php 1:23

Second Col.
a Re 22:12

b 2Co 10:10

c 2Co 11:1, 16

d Isa 53:10
  Mt 20:28
  1Ti 2:5, 6

e Mt 14:7, 8

f Mt 12:50

g Joh 20:17

h Ga 6:15

i Ro 5:10
  Eph 2:15, 16
  Col 1:19, 20

j Ac 20:24

k Ro 5:6
  1Jo 2:1, 2

l Ro 4:25
  Ro 5:18

m Mt 28:19, 20
  Ac 13:38, 39

n Eph 6:19, 20

o Php 3:20

4:17 *Or "trial." *Lit., "weight." **5:1** *Or "dissolved." **5:2** *Or "dwelling." *Or "to put on our dwelling that is." ΔOr "our heavenly dwelling." **5:5** *Or "a down payment (earnest money); a guarantee (pledge) of what is to come." **5:10** *Or "be made manifest."   **5:10** *Or "vile." **5:11** *Or "manifest."

as though God were making an appeal through us. As substitutes for Christ, we beg: "Become reconciled to God." 21 The one who did not know sin,[a] he made to be sin* for us, so that by means of him we might become God's righteousness.[b]

6 Working together with him,[c] we also urge you not to accept the undeserved kindness of God and miss its purpose.[d] 2 For he says: "In an acceptable time I heard you, and in a day of salvation I helped you."[e] Look! Now is the especially acceptable time. Look! Now is the day of salvation.

3 In no way are we giving any cause for stumbling, so that no fault may be found with our ministry;[f] 4 but in every way we recommend ourselves as God's ministers,[g] by the endurance of much, by tribulations, by times of need, by difficulties,[h] 5 by beatings, by imprisonments,[i] by riots, by hard work, by sleepless nights, by times without food;[j] 6 by purity, by knowledge, by patience,[k] by kindness,[l] by holy spirit, by love free from hypocrisy,[m] 7 by truthful speech, by God's power;[n] through the weapons of righteousness[o] in the right hand* and in the left,# 8 through glory and dishonor, through bad report and good report. We are regarded as deceivers and yet we are truthful, 9 as unknown and yet we are recognized, as dying* and yet look! we live,[p] as punished# and yet not handed over to death,[q] 10 as sorrowing but ever rejoicing, as poor but making many rich, as having nothing and yet possessing all things.[r]

11 We have opened our mouth to speak* to you, Corinthians, and we have opened wide our heart. 12 We are not restricted in* our affections for you,[a] but you are restricted in your own tender affections for us. 13 So in response—I speak as to my children—you too open your hearts wide.*[b]

14 Do not become unevenly yoked* with unbelievers.[c] For what fellowship do righteousness and lawlessness have?[d] Or what sharing does light have with darkness?[e] 15 Further, what harmony is there between Christ and Be′li·al?*[f] Or what does a believer# share in common△ with an unbeliever?[g] 16 And what agreement does God's temple have with idols?[h] For we are a temple of a living God;[i] just as God said: "I will reside among them[j] and walk among them, and I will be their God, and they will be my people."[k] 17 "'Therefore, get out from among them, and separate yourselves,' says Jehovah,* 'and quit touching the unclean thing'";[l] "and I will take you in."[m] 18 "'And I will become a father to you,[n] and you will become sons and daughters to me,'[o] says Jehovah,* the Almighty."

7 Therefore, since we have these promises,[p] beloved ones, let us cleanse ourselves of every defilement of flesh and spirit,[q] perfecting holiness in the fear of God.

2 Make room for us in your hearts.[r] We have wronged no one, we have corrupted no one,

---

CHAP. 5
[a] Heb 4:15
   Heb 7:26
[b] Ro 1:16, 17

CHAP. 6
[c] 2Co 5:20
[d] Ro 2:4
[e] Isa 49:8
[f] 1Co 9:22
[g] 2Co 4:1, 2
[h] 2Co 11:23
[i] Re 2:10
[j] 2Co 11:25, 27
[k] Col 3:13
   1Th 5:14
[l] Eph 4:32
[m] Ro 12:9
[n] 1Co 2:4, 5
[o] 2Co 10:4
   Eph 6:11
[p] 2Co 4:10, 11
[q] Ac 14:19
   2Co 4:8, 9
[r] Php 4:13
   Re 2:9

Second Col.
[a] 2Co 12:15
[b] 1Pe 2:17
   1Jo 4:20
[c] Ex 23:32, 33
   De 7:3, 4
   1Ki 11:4
   1Co 7:39
[d] Jas 4:4
[e] Eph 5:7, 8
[f] Mt 4:10
   Re 12:7, 8
[g] 1Co 10:21
[h] 1Co 10:14
[i] 1Co 3:16
[j] Ex 29:45
[k] Le 26:11, 12
   Eze 37:27
[l] Isa 52:11
   Jer 51:45
   Re 18:4
[m] Eze 20:41
[n] 2Sa 7:14
[o] Isa 43:6
   Ho 1:10
   Joh 1:12

CHAP. 7
[p] 2Co 6:16
[q] Ro 12:1
   1Ti 1:5
   1Ti 3:9
   1Jo 3:3
[r] Ro 12:10
   2Co 6:12, 13

5:21 *Or "a sin offering." 6:7 *Perhaps for offense. #Perhaps for defense. 6:9 *Or "considered worthy of death." #Or "disciplined."

6:11 *Or "have spoken openly." 6:12 *Or "cramped for room in." 6:13 *Or "you too widen out." 6:14 *Or "joined." 6:15 *From a Hebrew word meaning "Good for Nothing." A reference to Satan. #Or "a faithful person." △Or "what share does a believer have." 6:17, 18 *See App. A5.

we have taken advantage of no one.[a] **3** I do not say this to condemn you. For I have said before that you are in our hearts to die together and to live together. **4** I have great freeness of speech toward you. I have great boasting in regard to you. I am filled with comfort; I am overflowing with joy in all our affliction.[b]

5 In fact, when we arrived in Mac·e·do'ni·a,[c] our bodies* got no relief, but we continued to be afflicted in every way—there were fights on the outside, fears within. **6** But God, who comforts those who are downhearted,[d] comforted us by the presence of Titus; **7** and not only by his presence but also by the comfort he received because of you, as he reported back to us about your longing for me, your deep sorrow, and your earnest concern* for me; so I rejoiced even more.

8 For even if I saddened you by my letter,[e] I do not regret it. Even if I did at first regret it (seeing that the letter saddened you, though only for a little while), **9** now I rejoice, not because you were just saddened, but because you were saddened into repenting. For you were saddened in a godly way, so that you suffered no harm because of us. **10** For sadness in a godly way produces repentance leading to salvation, leaving no regret;[f] but the sadness of the world produces death. **11** For see what a great earnestness your being saddened in a godly way produced in you, yes, clearing of yourselves, yes, indignation, yes, fear, yes, earnest desire, yes, zeal, yes, righting of the wrong![g] In every respect you demonstrated yourselves to be pure* in this matter. **12** Al-

though I wrote to you, I did not do it for the one who did the wrong,[a] nor for the one who was wronged, but so that your earnestness for us might be made evident among you in the sight of God. **13** That is why we have been comforted.

But in addition to our comfort, we rejoiced even more over the joy of Titus, because all of you refreshed his spirit. **14** For if I have boasted to him about you, I have not been put to shame; but just as all the things we told you were true, so also our boasting to Titus has proved true. **15** Also, his tender affections toward you are greater as he remembers the obedience of all of you,[b] how you received him with fear and trembling. **16** I rejoice that in every way I may have confidence in* you.

8 Now we want you to know, brothers, about the undeserved kindness of God that has been granted to the congregations of Mac·e·do'ni·a.[c] **2** During a great test under affliction, their abundance of joy and their deep poverty made the riches of their generosity abound.* **3** For it was according to their means,[d] yes, I testify, it was even beyond their means,[e] **4** while they on their own initiative kept earnestly begging us for the privilege of kindly giving, to have a share in the relief ministry for the holy ones.[f] **5** And not merely as we had hoped, but first they gave themselves to the Lord and to us through God's will. **6** So we encouraged Titus[g] that, just as he had initiated this work among you, he should also complete this same kind giving on your part. **7** Nevertheless, just as you abound in every-

---

CHAP. 7
a Ac 20:33, 34
2Co 12:17

b Php 2:17
Phm 7

c Ac 20:1

d 2Co 1:3, 4

e 2Co 2:4

f Ps 32:5
1Jo 1:9

g Mt 3:8

Second Col.
a 1Co 5:5

b 2Co 2:9
Heb 13:17

CHAP. 8
c Ro 15:26

d Ac 11:29
2Co 9:7

e Mr 12:43, 44

f Ro 15:25, 26
1Co 16:1
2Co 9:1, 2

g 2Co 12:18

7:5 *Lit., "flesh." 7:7 *Lit., "your zeal." 7:11 *Or "chaste; innocent."

7:16 *Or possibly, "I may be of good courage because of." 8:2 *Or "overflow."

thing, in faith and word and knowledge and all earnestness and in our love for you, may you also abound in this kind giving.[a]

8 I am saying this, not to command you, but to make you aware of the earnestness of others and to test the genuineness of your love. **9** For you know the undeserved kindness of our Lord Jesus Christ, that although he was rich, he became poor for your sake,[b] so that you might become rich through his poverty.

10 And in this I give my opinion:[c] This is for your benefit, seeing that already a year ago you not only initiated the action but also showed your desire to do it. **11** So now, also complete what you started to do, so that your readiness to act may be completed according to the means you have available. **12** For if the readiness is there first, it is especially acceptable according to what a person has,[d] not according to what a person does not have. **13** For I do not want to make it easy for others, but difficult for you; **14** but that by means of an equalizing, your surplus at the present time might offset their need, so that their surplus might also offset your deficiency, that there may be an equalizing. **15** Just as it is written: "The person with much did not have too much, and the person with little did not have too little."[e]

16 Now thanks be to God for putting the same earnest concern for you in the heart of Titus,[f] **17** because he has indeed responded to the encouragement, but being very eager, he is coming to you on his own initiative. **18** But we are sending along with him the brother whose praise in connection with the good news has spread through all the congregations. **19** Not only that, but he

was also appointed by the congregations to be our traveling companion as we administer this kind gift for the glory of the Lord and in proof of our readiness to assist. **20** Thus we are avoiding having any man find fault with us in connection with this liberal contribution that we are administering.[a] **21** For we 'care for everything honestly, not only in the sight of Jehovah* but also in the sight of men.'[b]

22 Moreover, we are sending with them our brother whom we have often tested and found to be diligent in many matters, but now much more diligent on account of his great confidence in you. **23** If, though, there is any question about Titus, he is my companion* and a fellow worker for your interests; or if there are questions about our brothers, they are apostles of congregations and a glory of Christ. **24** So demonstrate the proof of your love to them,[c] and show the congregations why we boasted about you.

9 Now concerning the ministry that is for the holy ones,[d] it is not really necessary for me to write you, **2** for I know your willingness about which I am boasting to the Mac·e·do'ni·ans, that A·cha'ia has been ready now for a year, and your zeal has stirred up the majority of them. **3** But I am sending the brothers, so that our boasting about you might not prove empty in this respect and that you may really be ready, just as I said you would be. **4** Otherwise, if the Mac·e·do'ni·ans should come with me and find you not ready, we—not to mention you—should be put to shame by our confidence in you. **5** So I thought it necessary to encourage the brothers to come to you ahead of time and to

CHAP. 8
a 1Ti 6:18

b Mt 8:20
Php 2:7

c 1Co 7:25

d De 16:10, 17
Pr 3:27, 28

e Ex 16:18

f 2Co 12:18

_____
Second Col.
a 1Co 16:1

b Pr 3:4
1Pe 2:12

c 1Pe 1:22
1Pe 2:17

CHAP. 9
d Ro 15:26
1Co 16:1
2Co 9:12

8:21 *See App. A5. 8:23 *Lit., "sharer."

get your promised bountiful gift ready in advance, so that this might be ready as a generous gift, and not as something extorted.

6 But as to this, whoever sows sparingly will also reap sparingly, and whoever sows bountifully will also reap bountifully.[a] **7** Let each one do just as he has resolved in his heart, not grudgingly* or under compulsion,[b] for God loves a cheerful giver.[c]

8 Moreover, God is able to cause all his undeserved kindness to abound toward you so that you are always completely self-sufficient in everything, as well as having plenty for every good work.[d] **9** (Just as it is written: "He has distributed widely;* he has given to the poor. His righteousness continues forever."[e] **10** Now the One who abundantly supplies seed to the sower and bread for eating will supply and multiply the seed for you to sow and will increase the harvest of your righteousness.) **11** In everything you are being enriched for every sort of generosity, which produces through us an expression of thanks to God; **12** because the ministry of this public service is not only to provide well for the needs of the holy ones[f] but also to be rich in many expressions of thanks to God. **13** Through the proof that this relief ministry gives, they glorify God because you are submissive to the good news about the Christ, as you publicly declared, and because you are generous in your contribution to them and to all.[g] **14** And with supplication for you, they express affection for you because of the surpassing undeserved kindness of God upon you.

15 Thanks be to God for his indescribable free gift.

10 Now I myself, Paul, appeal to you by the mildness and kindness of the Christ,[a] lowly though I am when among you face-to-face,[b] but bold toward you when absent.[c] **2** I beg that when present, I may not have to be bold and take the strong measures that I expect against some who view us as if we walked in a fleshly manner. **3** For though we walk in the flesh, we do not wage warfare according to what we are in the flesh. **4** For the weapons of our warfare are not fleshly,[d] but powerful by God[e] for overturning strongly entrenched things. **5** For we are overturning reasonings and every lofty thing raised up against the knowledge of God,[f] and we are bringing every thought into captivity to make it obedient to the Christ; **6** and we are prepared to inflict punishment for every disobedience,[g] as soon as your own obedience is complete.

7 You look at things according to their face value. If anyone is confident in himself that he belongs to Christ, let him reflect again on this fact: Just as he belongs to Christ, so do we also. **8** For even if I should boast a bit too much about the authority that the Lord gave us to build you up and not to tear you down,[h] I would not be put to shame. **9** For I do not want to seem as though I were trying to terrify you by my letters. **10** For they say: "His letters are weighty and forceful, but his presence in person is weak and his speech contemptible." **11** Let such a man consider that what we say* by letters when absent, this we will also do* when pres-

---

CHAP. 9
a Pr 11:24
  Pr 19:17
  Pr 22:9
  Ec 11:1
  Lu 6:38

b De 15:7, 10

c Ex 22:29
  Pr 11:25
  Ac 20:35
  Heb 13:16

d Pr 28:27
  Mal 3:10
  Php 4:18, 19

e Ps 112:9

f Ro 15:26, 27
  2Co 8:14

g Mt 5:16
  Heb 13:16
  Jas 1:27
  1Jo 3:17

Second Col.

CHAP. 10
a Mt 11:29, 30

b 1Co 2:3

c 2Co 10:10

d Mt 26:52
  1Ti 1:18, 19

e 2Co 6:4, 7

f 1Co 1:19, 20
  1Co 3:19, 20
  2Ti 2:24, 25

g 1Ti 1:20

h Heb 13:17

9:7 *Or "reluctantly." **9:9** *Or "generously."

10:11 *Lit., "what we are in word." *Lit., "also be in action."

ent.[a] **12** For we do not dare to class ourselves or compare ourselves with some who recommend themselves.[b] But when they measure themselves by themselves and compare themselves with themselves, they are without understanding.[c]

13 However, we will not boast outside our assigned boundaries, but within the boundary of the territory that God measured out to us,* making it reach even as far as you.[d] **14** Really, we are not overextending ourselves as if we did not reach you, for we were the first to reach as far as you with the good news about the Christ.[e] **15** No, we are not boasting outside our assigned boundaries about the labors of someone else, but we hope that as your faith continues to increase, what we have done may be made to increase, within our territory. Then we will abound still more, **16** so that we may declare the good news to the countries beyond you, so as not to boast in what has already been done in someone else's territory. **17** "But the one who boasts, let him boast in Jehovah."*[f] **18** For it is not the one who recommends himself who is approved,[g] but the one whom Jehovah* recommends.[h]

11 I wish you would put up with me in a little unreasonableness. But, in fact, you are putting up with me! **2** For I am jealous over you with a godly jealousy,* for I personally promised you in marriage to one husband that I might present you as a chaste* virgin to the Christ.[i] **3** But I am afraid that somehow, as the serpent seduced Eve by its cunning,[j] your minds might be corrupted away

from the sincerity and the chastity* that are due the Christ.[a] **4** For as it is, if someone comes and preaches a Jesus other than the one we preached, or you receive a spirit other than what you received, or good news other than what you accepted,[b] you easily put up with him. **5** For I consider that I have not proved inferior to your superfine apostles in a single thing.[c] **6** But even if I am unskilled in speech,[d] I certainly am not in knowledge; indeed we made it clear to you in every way and in everything.

7 Or did I commit a sin by humbling myself that you might be exalted, because I gladly declared the good news of God to you without cost?[e] **8** Other congregations I deprived* by accepting provisions# in order to minister to you.[f] **9** Yet, when I was present with you and I fell into need, I did not become a burden on anyone, for the brothers who came from Mac·e·do′ni·a abundantly supplied my needs.[g] Yes, in every way I kept myself from becoming a burden to you and will continue to do so.[h] **10** As surely as the truth of Christ is in me, I will not stop this boasting[i] in the regions of A·cha′ia. **11** For what reason? Because I do not love you? God knows I do.

12 But what I am doing I will continue to do,[j] in order to eliminate the pretext of those who are wanting a basis* for being found equal to us in the things# about which they boast. **13** For such men are false apostles, deceitful workers, disguising themselves as apostles of Christ.[k] **14** And no wonder, for Satan himself keeps disguising himself as an angel of light.[l] **15** It is therefore nothing extraordinary if his

CHAP. 10	
a	2Co 13:2
b	2Co 5:12
c	Pr 26:12 Ga 6:3
d	Ac 9:15 Ga 2:8
e	1Co 3:10 1Co 4:15
f	Jer 9:24 1Co 1:31
g	Lu 18:10-14
h	1Co 4:5 2Ti 2:15

CHAP. 11	
i	Mr 2:19 Eph 5:23 Re 21:2, 9
j	Ge 3:4, 5 Joh 8:44

Second Col.	
a	1Ti 6:3-5 Heb 13:9 2Pe 3:17
b	Ga 1:7, 8
c	2Co 11:23
d	2Co 10:10
e	Ac 18:3 1Co 9:18
f	Php 4:10
g	Php 4:15, 16
h	1Th 2:9
i	1Co 9:14, 15
j	1Co 9:11, 12
k	Ro 16:17, 18 2Pe 2:1
l	Ga 1:8 2Th 2:9

10:13 *Or "apportioned by measure to us." **10:17, 18** *See App. A5. **11:2** *Lit., "God's zeal." #Or "pure." **11:3** *Or "purity." **11:8** *Lit., "robbed." #Or "support." **11:12** *Or "pretext." #Or "the office."

ministers also keep disguising themselves as ministers of righteousness. But their end will be according to their works.[a]

16 I say again: Let no one think I am unreasonable. But even if you do, then accept me as an unreasonable person, so that I too may boast a little. **17** What I now say is, not as following the Lord's example, but as an unreasonable person would, with boastful self-confidence. **18** Since many are boasting according to the flesh,[*] I too will boast. **19** Since you are so "reasonable," you gladly put up with the unreasonable ones. **20** In fact, you put up with whoever enslaves you, whoever devours your possessions, whoever grabs what you have, whoever exalts himself over you, and whoever strikes you in the face.

21 I say this to our dishonor, since it may seem that we have acted in weakness.

But if others act boldly—I am talking unreasonably—I too act boldly. **22** Are they Hebrews? I am one also.[b] Are they Israelites? I am one also. Are they Abraham's offspring?[*] I am also.[c] **23** Are they ministers of Christ? I reply like a madman, I am more outstandingly one: I have done more work,[d] been imprisoned more often,[e] suffered countless beatings, and experienced many near-deaths.[f] **24** Five times I received 40 strokes less one from the Jews,[g] **25** three times I was beaten with rods,[h] once I was stoned,[i] three times I experienced shipwreck,[j] a night and a day I have spent in the open sea; **26** in journeys often, in dangers from rivers, in dangers from robbers, in dangers from my own people,[k] in dangers from the na-

tions,[a] in dangers in the city,[b] in dangers in the wilderness, in dangers at sea, in dangers among false brothers, **27** in labor and toil, in sleepless nights often,[c] in hunger and thirst,[d] frequently without food,[e] in cold and lacking clothing.[*]

28 Besides those things of an external kind, there is what rushes in on me from day to day:[*] the anxiety for all the congregations.[f] **29** Who is weak, and I am not weak? Who is stumbled, and I am not incensed?

30 If I must boast, I will boast of the things that show my weakness. **31** The God and Father of the Lord Jesus, the One who is to be praised forever, knows I am not lying. **32** In Damascus the governor under A·re′tas the king was guarding the city of the Dam·a·scenes′ to seize me, **33** but I was lowered in a basket[*] through a window in the city wall,[g] and I escaped his hands.

12 I have to boast. It is not beneficial, but I will move on to supernatural visions[h] and revelations of the Lord.[i] **2** I know a man in union with Christ who, 14 years ago—whether in the body or out of the body, I do not know; God knows—was caught away to the third heaven. **3** Yes, I know such a man —whether in the body or apart from the body, I do not know; God knows— **4** who was caught away into paradise and heard words that cannot be spoken and that are not lawful for a man to say. **5** I will boast about such a man, but I will not boast about myself except of my weaknesses. **6** For even if I want to boast, I will not be unreasonable, for I would say the truth.

CHAP. 11
a Mt 16:27
  Php 3:18, 19
  2Ti 4:14

b Ac 22:3

c Ro 11:1
  Php 3:4, 5

d Ro 11:13
  1Co 15:10

e Ac 16:23, 24

f Ac 9:15, 16
  2Co 6:4, 5
  1Pe 2:20, 21

g De 25:3

h Ac 16:22

i Ac 14:19

j Ac 27:41

k Ac 20:3
  Ac 23:10

Second Col.
a Ac 14:5, 6

b Ac 13:50

c Ac 20:31

d 1Co 4:11

e 2Co 6:4, 5

f 2Co 2:4
  Col 2:1

g Ac 9:24, 25

CHAP. 12
h Ac 2:17

i Ac 22:17, 18

11:18 *That is, on human grounds. 11:22 *Lit., "seed."

11:27 *Lit., "and in nakedness." 11:28 *Or "the daily pressure on me." 11:33 *Or "wicker basket."

But I refrain from doing so, in order that no one should give me more credit than what he sees in me or hears from me, 7 just because of receiving such extraordinary revelations.

To keep me from becoming overly exalted, I was given a thorn in the flesh,[a] an angel of Satan, to keep slapping* me, so that I might not be overly exalted. 8 Three times I begged the Lord about this, that it would depart from me. 9 But he said to me: "My undeserved kindness is sufficient for you, for my power is being made perfect in weakness."[b] Most gladly, then, I will boast about my weaknesses, in order that the power of the Christ may remain over me like a tent. 10 So I take pleasure in weaknesses, in insults, in times of need, in persecutions and difficulties, for Christ. For when I am weak, then I am powerful.[c]

11 I have become unreasonable. You compelled me to, for I ought to have been recommended by you. For I did not prove to be inferior to your superfine apostles in a single thing, even if I am nothing.[d] 12 Indeed, the signs of an apostle were produced among you with great endurance,[e] and by signs and wonders* and powerful works.[f] 13 For how were you less favored than the rest of the congregations, except that I myself did not become a burden to you?[g] Kindly forgive me for this wrong.

14 Look! This is the third time I am ready to come to you, and I will not become a burden. For I am seeking, not your possessions,[h] but you; for the children[i] are not expected to save up for their parents, but the parents for their children. 15 For my part, I will

most gladly spend and be completely spent for you.*[a] If I love you so much more, am I to be loved the less? 16 But be that as it may, I did not burden you.[b] Nevertheless, you say I was "crafty" and I caught you "by trickery." 17 I did not take advantage of you through any of those whom I sent to you, did I? 18 I urged Titus and I sent the brother with him. Titus did not take advantage of you at all, did he?[c] We walked in the same spirit, did we not? In the same footsteps, did we not?

19 Have you been thinking all along that we have been making our defense to you? It is before God that we are speaking in union with Christ. But, beloved ones, all that we do is to build you up. 20 For I am afraid that somehow when I arrive, I may not find you as I wish and I may not be as you wish, but instead, there may be strife, jealousy, outbursts of anger, dissension, backbiting, whispering,* being puffed up with pride, and disorder. 21 Perhaps when I come again, my God might humiliate me before you, and I may have to mourn over many of those who previously sinned but have not repented of their uncleanness and sexual immorality* and brazen conduct# that they have practiced.

13 This is the third time I am coming to you. "On the testimony* of two or three witnesses every matter must be established."[d] 2 Although I am absent now, it is as if I were present for the second time, and I give my warning in advance to those who sinned previously and

---

CHAP. 12
a Ga 4:13

b Isa 40:29

c Php 4:13

d 2Co 11:23

e 2Co 6:4

f Ac 14:3
Ac 15:12
Ro 15:18, 19

g 1Co 9:11, 12
2Co 11:9

h Ac 20:33

i 1Co 4:14

Second Col.
a 2Co 1:6
Col 1:24
1Th 2:8
Heb 13:17

b 2Co 11:9

c 2Co 8:6

CHAP. 13
d De 19:15
Mt 18:16

12:7 *Or "beating." **12:12** *Or "portents." **12:15** *Or "your souls." **12:20** *Or "gossip." **12:21** *Greek, por·nei′a. See Glossary. #Or "shameless conduct." Greek, a·sel′gei·a. See Glossary. **13:1** *Lit., "mouth."

to all the rest, that if ever I come again I will not spare them, **3** since you are seeking proof that Christ, who is not weak toward you but strong among you, is really speaking through me. **4** For, indeed, he was executed on the stake because of weakness, but he is alive because of God's power.[a] True, we also are weak with him, but we will live together with him[b] because of God's power toward you.[c]

5 Keep testing whether you are in the faith; keep proving what you yourselves are.[d] Or do you not recognize that Jesus Christ is in union with you? Unless you are disapproved. **6** I truly hope you will recognize that we are not disapproved.

7 Now we pray to God that you may do nothing wrong, not that we may appear approved, but that you may do what is fine, even if we may appear disapproved. **8** For we can do nothing against the truth, but only for the truth. **9** We certainly rejoice whenever we are weak but you are powerful. And this is what we are praying for, your being readjusted. **10** That is why I write these things while absent, so that when I am present, I may not have to be severe in using the authority that the Lord gave me,[a] to build up and not to tear down.

11 Finally, brothers, continue to rejoice, to be readjusted, to be comforted,[b] to think in agreement,[c] to live peaceably;[d] and the God of love and of peace[e] will be with you. **12** Greet one another with a holy kiss. **13** All the holy ones send you their greetings.

14 The undeserved kindness of the Lord Jesus Christ and the love of God and the sharing in the holy spirit be with all of you.

CHAP. 13

a Ro 6:4
1Pe 3:18

b 2Ti 2:11, 12

c 1Co 6:14

d 1Co 11:28
Ga 6:4

Second Col.

a 1Co 4:21

b 2Co 1:3, 4

c Php 2:2

d 1Th 5:13
Jas 3:17
1Pe 3:11
2Pe 3:14

e 1Co 14:33

TO THE

GALATIANS

OUTLINE OF CONTENTS

1 Paul, an apostle, neither from men nor through a man, but through Jesus Christ[a] and God the Father,[b] who raised him up from the dead, **2** and all the brothers with me, to the congregations of Ga·la′ti·a:

3 May you have undeserved kindness and peace from God our Father and the Lord Jesus Christ. **4** He gave himself for our sins[c] so that he might rescue us from the present wicked system of things*[d] according to the will of our God and Father,[e] **5** to whom be the glory forever and ever. Amen.

6 I am amazed that you are so quickly turning away* from the One who called you with Christ's undeserved kindness to another sort of good news.[f] **7** Not that there is another good news; but there are certain ones who are causing you trouble[g] and wanting to distort the good news about the Christ. **8** However, even if we or an angel out of heaven were to declare to you as good news something beyond the good news we declared to you, let him be accursed. **9** As we have said before, I now say again, Whoever is declaring to you as good news something beyond what you accepted, let him be accursed.

10 Is it, in fact, men I am now trying to persuade or God? Or am I trying to please men? If I were still pleasing men, I would not be Christ's slave. **11** For I want you to know, brothers, that the good news I declared to you is not of human origin;[h] **12** for neither did I receive it from man, nor was I taught it, but it was through a revelation by Jesus Christ.

13 Of course, you heard about my conduct formerly in Ju′da·ism,[a] that I kept intensely* persecuting the congregation of God and devastating it;[b] **14** and I was making greater progress in Ju′da·ism than many of my own age in my nation, as I was far more zealous for the traditions of my fathers.[c] **15** But when God, who separated me from my mother's womb and called me through his undeserved kindness,[d] thought good **16** to reveal his Son through me so that I might declare the good news about him to the nations,[e] I did not immediately consult with any human;* **17** nor did I go up to Jerusalem to those who were apostles before I was, but I went to Arabia, and then I returned to Damascus.[f]

18 Then three years later I went up to Jerusalem[g] to visit Ce′phas,*[h] and I stayed with him for 15 days. **19** But I did not see any of the other apostles, only James[i] the brother of the Lord. **20** Now regarding the things I am writing you, I assure you before God that I am not lying.

21 After that I went into the regions of Syria and Ci·li′cia.[j] **22** But I was personally unknown to the congregations of Ju·de′a that were in union with Christ. **23** They only used to hear: "The man who formerly persecuted us[k] is now declaring the good news about the faith that he formerly devastated."[l] **24** So they began glorifying God because of me.

2 Then after 14 years I again went up to Jerusalem with Bar′na·bas,[m] also taking Titus along with me.[n] **2** I went up as a result of a revelation, and I presented to them the good news that I am preaching among

---

CHAP. 1
a Ac 9:15
  Ac 26:15, 16

b Ac 22:14, 15

c 1Jo 2:1, 2

d Joh 15:19

e 1Ti 2:3, 4

f 2Co 11:3, 4
  Ga 5:7

g Ga 5:10

h 1Th 2:13

Second Col.
a Ac 23:6

b Ac 8:3
  Ac 9:1, 2
  Ac 22:4
  Ac 26:9-11

c Ac 22:3
  Php 3:4-6

d 1Co 15:10

e Ac 9:15
  Ro 11:13

f Ac 9:19

g Ac 9:26

h Joh 1:42
  1Co 15:5

i Mt 13:55
  Ac 12:17

j Ac 9:29, 30

k Ga 1:13

l Ac 8:3

CHAP. 2
m Ac 9:27

n Ac 15:1, 2

1:13 *Lit., "that to the point of excess I kept." **1:16** *Lit., "with flesh and blood." **1:18** *Also called Peter.

1:4 *Or "wicked age." See Glossary. **1:6** *Or "are being so quickly removed."

the nations. This was done privately, however, before the men who were highly regarded, to make sure that I was not running or had not run in vain. **3** Nevertheless, not even Titus,[a] who was with me, was compelled to be circumcised,[b] although he was a Greek. **4** But that matter came up because of the false brothers brought in quietly,[c] who slipped in to spy on the freedom[d] we enjoy in union with Christ Jesus, so that they might completely enslave us;[e] **5** we did not yield in submission to them,[f] no, not for a moment,* so that the truth of the good news might continue with you.

6 But regarding those who seemed to be important[g]—whatever they were makes no difference to me, for God does not go by a man's outward appearance—those highly regarded men imparted nothing new to me. **7** On the contrary, when they saw that I had been entrusted with the good news for those who are uncircumcised,[h] just as Peter had been for those who are circumcised— **8** for the one who empowered Peter for an apostleship to those who are circumcised also empowered me for those who are of the nations[i]— **9** and when they recognized the undeserved kindness that was given me,[j] James[k] and Ce′phas* and John, the ones who seemed to be pillars, gave Bar′na·bas and me[l] the right hand of fellowship,* so that we should go to the nations but they to those who are circumcised. **10** They asked only that we keep the poor in mind, and this I have also earnestly endeavored to do.[m]

11 However, when Ce′phas*[n] came to Antioch,[o] I resisted*

him face-to-face, because he was clearly in the wrong.* **12** For before certain men from James[a] arrived, he used to eat with people of the nations;[b] but when they arrived, he stopped doing this and separated himself, fearing those of the circumcised class.[c] **13** The rest of the Jews also joined him in putting on this pretense,* so that even Bar′na·bas was led along with them in their pretense.* **14** But when I saw that they were not walking in step with the truth of the good news,[d] I said to Ce′phas* before them all: "If you, though you are a Jew, live as the nations do and not as Jews do, how can you compel people of the nations to live according to Jewish practice?"[e]

15 We who are Jews by birth, and not sinners from the nations, **16** recognize that a man is declared righteous, not by works of law, but only through faith[f] in Jesus Christ.[g] So we have put our faith in Christ Jesus, so that we may be declared righteous by faith in Christ and not by works of law, for no one* will be declared righteous by works of law.[h] **17** Now if we have also been found sinners while seeking to be declared righteous by means of Christ, is Christ then sin's minister? Certainly not! **18** For the very things that I once tore down I build up again, I demonstrate that I am a transgressor. **19** For through law I died toward law,[i] so that I might become alive toward God. **20** I am nailed to the stake along with Christ.[j] It is no longer I who live,[k] but it is Christ who is living in union with me. Indeed, the life that I now live in the flesh I live by faith in the Son of God,[l] who loved me and handed

---

CHAP. 2
a 2Co 2:13

b Ac 16:3

c Ac 15:1, 24

d 2Co 3:17
  Ga 5:1

e Ga 4:9

f Ga 2:14

g Ga 2:9

h Ac 22:21
  Ro 11:13
  1Ti 2:7

i Ac 9:15

j Eph 3:8

k Ac 15:13

l Ac 13:2
  Ac 15:25

m Ac 11:29, 30
  1Co 16:1

n Joh 1:42

o Ac 11:25, 26
  Ac 15:35

Second Col.
a Ac 12:17

b Ac 10:26, 28
  Ac 11:2, 3

c Ac 21:20, 21

d Ac 10:34, 35

e Ac 15:10
  Ac 15:28, 29

f Ro 1:17
  Jas 2:23

g Ac 13:39
  Ro 5:17
  1Co 6:11

h Ro 3:20-22

i Ro 7:9

j Ro 6:6
  Ga 5:24

k 1Pe 4:1, 2

l 2Co 5:15

2:5 *Lit., "an hour." 2:9, 11, 14 *Also called Peter. 2:9 *Or "partnership." 2:11 *Or "confronted."

2:11 *Or "he stood condemned." 2:13 *Or "hypocrisy." 2:16 *Lit., "flesh."

himself over for me.[a] **21** I do not reject* the undeserved kindness of God,[b] for if righteousness is through law, Christ actually died for nothing.[c]

3 O senseless Ga·la′tians! Who has brought you under this evil influence,[d] you who had Jesus Christ openly portrayed before you as nailed to the stake?[e] **2** This one thing I want to ask* you: Did you receive the spirit through works of law or because of faith in what you heard?[f] **3** Are you so senseless? After starting on a spiritual course,* are you finishing on a fleshly course?*[#g] **4** Did you undergo so many sufferings for nothing? If it really was for nothing. **5** Therefore, does the one who supplies you the spirit and performs powerful works[h] among you do it because of your works of law or because of your faith in what you heard? **6** Just as Abraham "put faith in Jehovah,* and it was counted to him as righteousness."[i]

7 Surely you know that it is those who adhere to faith who are sons of Abraham.[j] **8** Now the scripture, foreseeing that God would declare people of the nations righteous through faith, declared the good news beforehand to Abraham, namely: "By means of you all the nations will be blessed."[k] **9** So those who adhere to faith are being blessed together with Abraham, who had faith.[l]

10 All those who depend on works of law are under a curse, for it is written: "Cursed is everyone who does not remain in all the things written in the scroll of the Law by doing them."[m] **11** Moreover, it is evi-

dent that by law no one is declared righteous with God,[a] because "the righteous one will live by reason of faith."[b] **12** Now the Law is not based on faith. Rather, "anyone who does these things will live by means of them."[c] **13** Christ purchased us,[d] releasing us[e] from the curse of the Law by becoming a curse instead of us, because it is written: "Accursed is every man hung upon a stake."[f] **14** This was so that the blessing of Abraham would come to the nations by means of Christ Jesus,[g] so that we might receive the promised spirit[h] through our faith.

15 Brothers, I speak using a human illustration: Once a covenant is validated, even if only by a man, no one annuls it or attaches additions to it. **16** Now the promises were spoken to Abraham and to his offspring.*[i] It does not say, "and to your descendants,"# in the sense of many. Rather, it says, "and to your offspring,"* in the sense of one, who is Christ.[j] **17** Further, I say this: The Law, which came into being 430 years later,[k] does not invalidate the covenant previously made by God, so as to abolish the promise. **18** For if the inheritance is based on law, it is no longer based on a promise; but God has kindly given it to Abraham through a promise.

19 Why, then, the Law? It was added to make transgressions manifest,[m] until the offspring* should arrive[n] to whom the promise had been made; and it was transmitted through angels[o] by the hand of a mediator.[p] **20** Now there is no mediator when just one person is involved, but God is only one. **21** Is the Law, therefore, against the promises of God? Certainly

---

CHAP. 2
a 1Ti 2:5, 6
b Joh 1:17
c Ga 3:21
  Heb 7:11

CHAP. 3
d Ga 5:7
e 1Co 1:23
f Eph 1:13
g Ga 4:9, 10
h 1Co 12:8-10
i Ge 15:6
  Ro 4:3
  Jas 2:23
j Ro 4:11, 12
k Ge 12:3
  Ge 18:18
l Ro 4:16, 17
m De 27:26
  Ac 15:10
  Jas 2:10

Second Col.
a Ga 2:15, 16
b Hab 2:4
  Ro 1:17
  Heb 10:38
c Le 18:5
  De 30:16
  Ro 10:5
d 1Co 7:23
e Mt 26:27, 28
  Heb 9:15
f De 21:23
  Ac 5:30
g Eph 2:15, 16
h Joe 2:28
i Ge 12:3
  Ge 12:7
  Ge 13:14, 15
  Ge 17:7
  Ge 22:17, 18
  Ge 24:7
j Mt 1:17
k Ex 12:40, 41
l Ge 22:17
m Ro 3:20
n Joh 1:29
  Ro 10:4
o Ac 7:38, 53
  Heb 2:2
p Ex 20:19
  De 5:5
  Joh 1:17

2:21 *Or "shove aside." **3:2** *Lit., "learn from." **3:3** *Lit., "starting in spirit." #Lit., "being completed in the flesh?" **3:6** *See App. A5.

3:16, 19 *Lit., "seed." **3:16** #Lit., "seeds."

not! For if a law had been given that could give life, righteousness would actually have been by means of law. **22** But the Scripture handed all things over to the custody of sin, so that the promise resulting from faith in Jesus Christ might be given to those exercising faith.

23 However, before the faith arrived, we were being guarded under law, being handed over into custody, looking to the faith that was about to be revealed.[a] **24** So the Law became our guardian* leading to Christ,[b] so that we might be declared righteous through faith.[c] **25** But now that the faith has arrived,[d] we are no longer under a guardian.*[e]

26 You are all, in fact, sons of God[f] through your faith in Christ Jesus.[g] **27** For all of you who were baptized into Christ have put on Christ.[h] **28** There is neither Jew nor Greek,[i] there is neither slave nor freeman,[j] there is neither male nor female,[k] for you are all one in union with Christ Jesus.[l] **29** Moreover, if you belong to Christ, you are really Abraham's offspring,*[m] heirs[n] with reference to a promise.[o]

4 Now I say that as long as the heir is a young child, he is no different from a slave, although he is the lord of all things, **2** but he is under supervisors and stewards until the day set ahead of time by his father. **3** Likewise, we too, when we were children, were enslaved by the elementary things of the world.[p] **4** But when the full limit of the time arrived, God sent his Son, who was born of a woman[q] and who was under law,[r] **5** that he might release by purchase those under law,[s] so that we might receive the adoption as sons.[t]

6 Now because you are sons, God has sent the spirit[a] of his Son into our hearts,[b] and it cries out: "Abba,* Father!"[c] **7** So you are no longer a slave but a son; and if a son, then you are also an heir through God.[d]

8 Nevertheless, when you did not know God, you were enslaved to those who are not really gods. **9** But now that you have come to know God or, rather, have come to be known by God, how is it that you are turning back again to the weak[e] and beggarly elementary things and want to slave for them over again?[f] **10** You are scrupulously observing days and months[g] and seasons and years. **11** I fear for you, that somehow I have wasted my efforts on you.

12 Brothers, I beg you, become as I am, because I also used to be as you are.[h] You did me no wrong. **13** But you know that it was because of a physical illness that I had my first opportunity to declare the good news to you. **14** And though my physical condition was a trial for you, you did not treat me with contempt or disgust;* but you received me like an angel of God, like Christ Jesus. **15** Where is that happiness you had? For I bear you witness that, if it had been possible, you would have gouged out your eyes and given them to me.[i] **16** So, then, have I become your enemy because I tell you the truth? **17** They are zealous to win you over, but not for a good purpose; they want to alienate you from me, so that you may be eager to follow them. **18** However, it is always fine for someone to seek zealously after you for a good purpose and not just when I am present with you,

CHAP. 3	
a	Ro 10:4
b	Mt 5:17
c	Ac 13:39
	Ro 5:1
	Ro 8:33
d	Col 2:17
e	Heb 8:6
f	Ro 8:14
g	Joh 1:12
h	Ro 13:14
	Eph 4:24
i	Ro 10:12
j	1Co 12:13
	Col 3:10, 11
k	Ac 2:17
	1Pe 3:7
l	Joh 17:20, 21
m	Ro 9:7, 8
n	Ro 8:17
o	Ge 22:18
CHAP. 4	
p	Col 2:8
	Col 2:20-22
q	Joh 1:14
	Heb 2:14
r	Mt 5:17
s	1Co 7:23
	Ga 3:13
t	Joh 1:12
	Ro 8:23
Second Col.	
a	Joh 14:26
b	Ro 5:5
c	Ro 8:15
d	Ro 8:17
	Ga 3:29
	Eph 1:13, 14
e	Ro 8:3
	Heb 7:18, 19
f	Col 2:20-22
g	Col 2:16
h	Ga 1:14
i	Ac 23:5
	Ga 6:11

3:24, 25 *Or "tutor."   3:29 *Lit., "seed."

4:6 *An Aramaic word meaning "O Father!"   4:14 *Or "spit at me."

19 my little children,[a] for whom I am again experiencing birth pains until Christ is formed* in you. **20** I wish I could be present with you just now and speak in a different way, because I am perplexed over you.

21 Tell me, you who want to be under law, Do you not hear the Law? **22** For example, it is written that Abraham had two sons, one by the servant girl[b] and one by the free woman;[c] **23** but the one by the servant girl was actually born through natural descent*[d] and the other by the free woman through a promise.[e] **24** These things may be taken as a symbolic drama; for these women mean two covenants, the one from Mount Si′nai,[f] which bears children for slavery and which is Ha′gar. **25** Now Ha′gar means Si′nai,[g] a mountain in Arabia, and she corresponds with the Jerusalem today, for she is in slavery with her children. **26** But the Jerusalem above is free, and she is our mother.

27 For it is written: "Be glad, you barren woman who does not give birth; break into joyful shouting, you woman who does not have birth pains; for the children of the desolate woman are more numerous than those of her who has the husband."[h] **28** Now you, brothers, are children of the promise the same as Isaac was.[i] **29** But just as then the one born through natural descent* began persecuting the one born through spirit,[j] so also now.[k] **30** Nevertheless, what does the scripture say? "Drive out the servant girl and her son, for the son of the servant girl will by no means be an heir with the son of the free woman."[l] **31** So, brothers,

we are children, not of a servant girl, but of the free woman.

5 For such freedom Christ set us free. Therefore, stand firm,[a] and do not let yourselves be confined again in a yoke of slavery.[b]

2 See! I, Paul, am telling you that if you become circumcised, Christ will be of no benefit to you.[c] **3** Again I bear witness to every man who gets circumcised that he is under obligation to keep the whole Law.[d] **4** You are separated from Christ, you who are trying to be declared righteous by means of law;[e] you have fallen away from his undeserved kindness. **5** For our part, we are by spirit eagerly waiting for the hoped-for righteousness resulting from faith. **6** For in union with Christ Jesus, neither circumcision nor uncircumcision is of any value,[f] but faith operating through love is.

7 You were running well.[g] Who hindered you from continuing to obey the truth? **8** This sort of persuasion does not come from the One calling you. **9** A little leaven ferments the whole batch of dough.[h] **10** I am confident that you who are in union with the Lord[i] will not come to think otherwise; but the one who is causing you trouble,[j] whoever he may be, will receive the judgment he deserves. **11** As for me, brothers, if I am still preaching circumcision, why am I still being persecuted? In that case the stumbling block of the torture stake*[k] has been eliminated. **12** I wish the men who are trying to unsettle you would emasculate themselves.*

13 You were called to freedom, brothers; only do not use this freedom as an opportunity

---

CHAP. 4
a 1Co 4:15
  1Th 2:11
  Phm 10

b Ge 16:15

c Ge 21:2, 3

d Ge 16:1, 2

e Ge 17:15, 16

f Ex 19:20
  Ex 24:12

g Ex 19:18

h Isa 54:1

i Ro 9:8
  Ga 3:29

j Ge 21:9

k Ga 5:11
  2Ti 3:12

l Ge 21:10

Second Col.

CHAP. 5
a 1Co 16:13
  Php 4:1

b Ac 15:10

c Ga 6:12

d Ro 2:25
  Ga 3:10

e Ro 3:20

f 1Co 7:19
  Ga 6:15
  Col 3:10, 11

g 1Co 9:24
  Ga 3:3

h 1Co 5:6
  1Co 15:33
  2Ti 2:16-18

i Joh 17:20, 21

j Ga 1:7

k 1Co 1:23

4:19 *Or "takes shape." 4:23, 29 *Lit., "according to the flesh."

5:11 *See Glossary. 5:12 *Or "castrate themselves; become eunuchs," thus becoming disqualified from performing the very law they were endorsing.

to pursue fleshly desires,[a] but through love slave for one another.[b] **14** For the entire Law has been fulfilled* in one commandment, namely: "You must love your neighbor as yourself."[c] **15** If, though, you keep on biting and devouring one another, look out that you do not get annihilated by one another.[e]

16 But I say, Keep walking by spirit[f] and you will carry out no fleshly desire at all.[g] **17** For the flesh is against the spirit in its desire, and the spirit against the flesh; these are opposed to each other, so that you do not do the very things you want to do.[h] **18** Furthermore, if you are being led by spirit, you are not under law.

19 Now the works of the flesh are plainly seen, and they are sexual immorality,*[i] uncleanness, brazen conduct,*[j] **20** idolatry, spiritism,*[k] hostility, strife, jealousy, fits of anger, dissensions, divisions, sects, **21** envy, drunkenness,[l] wild parties,* and things like these.[m] I am forewarning you about these things, the same way I already warned you, that those who practice such things will not inherit God's Kingdom.[n]

22 On the other hand, the fruitage of the spirit is love, joy, peace, patience,* kindness, goodness,[o] faith, **23** mildness, self-control.[p] Against such things there is no law. **24** Moreover, those who belong to Christ Jesus have nailed to the stake the flesh together with its passions and desires.[q]

25 If we are living by spirit, let us also go on walking orderly by spirit.[a] **26** Let us not become egotistical,[b] stirring up competition with one another,[c] envying one another.

6 Brothers, even if a man takes a false step before he is aware of it, you who have spiritual qualifications try to readjust such a man in a spirit of mildness.[d] But keep an eye on yourself,[e] for fear you too may be tempted.[f] **2** Go on carrying the burdens of one another,[g] and in this way you will fulfill the law of the Christ.[h] **3** For if anyone thinks he is something when he is nothing,[i] he is deceiving himself. **4** But let each one examine his own actions,[j] and then he will have cause for rejoicing in regard to himself alone, and not in comparison with the other person.[k] **5** For each one will carry his own load.*[l]

6 Moreover, let anyone who is being taught* the word share in all good things with the one who gives such teaching.*[m]

7 Do not be misled: God is not one to be mocked. For whatever a person is sowing, this he will also reap;[n] **8** because the one sowing with a view to his flesh will reap corruption from his flesh, but the one sowing with a view to the spirit will reap everlasting life from the spirit.[o] **9** So let us not give up in doing what is fine, for in due time we will reap if we do not tire out.*[p] **10** So, then, as long as we have the opportunity,* let us work what is good toward all, but especially toward those related to us in the faith.

11 See with what large letters I have written you with my own hand.

CHAP. 5
a 1Pe 2:16
b 1Co 9:19
c Le 19:18
   Mt 7:12
   Mt 22:39
   Ro 13:8, 9
   Jas 2:8
d Jas 3:14
e Jas 4:1, 2
f Ro 8:5, 13
g Ro 6:12
   1Pe 2:11
h Ro 7:15, 19
   Ro 7:23
i 1Co 5:9
   Eph 5:3
   Col 3:5
   Re 2:20
j Mr 7:21, 22
   Eph 4:19
   2Pe 2:2
   Jude 4
k Le 19:26, 31
   De 18:10, 11
l Re 21:20, 21
   Isa 5:11
m 1Pe 4:3
   1Co 6:9, 10
n Eph 5:9
o Jas 3:17
q Ro 6:6

Second Col.
a Ro 8:4
b Php 2:3
c Ec 4:4
   1Co 4:7
   Ga 6:4

CHAP. 6
d Pr 15:1
   Col 3:12
   1Ti 6:11
   Tit 3:2
e 1Co 10:12
f Jas 3:2
g 1Th 5:14
h Joh 13:34
   Joh 15:12
   1Jo 4:21
i Ro 12:3
j 2Co 13:5
k Ga 5:26
l Ro 14:4
   2Co 5:10
m Mt 10:9, 10
   Lu 10:7
   Ro 15:27
   1Co 9:11, 14
n Ro 2:6-8
o Ro 8:6, 13
p Heb 3:14
   Heb 12:3
   Re 2:10

5:14 *Or possibly, "is summed up." 5:19 *Greek, por·nei′a. See Glossary. #Or "shameless conduct." Greek, a·sel′gei·a. See Glossary. 5:20 *Or "sorcery; druggery." 5:21 *Or "revelries." 5:22 *Or "long-suffering."

6:5 *Or "load of responsibility." 6:6 *Or "orally taught." #Or "such oral teaching." 6:9 *Or "give up." 6:10 *Lit., "appointed time."

12 All those who want to make a good impression in the flesh* are the ones who try to compel you to get circumcised, doing so only to avoid being persecuted for the torture stake# of the Christ. **13** For even those who are getting circumcised do not keep the Law themselves,[a] but they want you to be circumcised so that they may have cause for boasting about your flesh. **14** But may I never boast, except in the torture stake# of our Lord Jesus Christ,[b] through whom the world has been put

6:12 *Or "who want to look good outwardly." 6:12, 14 #See Glossary.

to death* with regard to me and I with regard to the world. **15** For neither is circumcision anything nor is uncircumcision,[a] but a new creation is.[b] **16** As for all those who walk orderly by this rule of conduct, peace and mercy be upon them, yes, upon the Israel of God.[c]

17 From now on let no one make trouble for me, for I am bearing on my body the brand marks of a slave of Jesus.[d]

18 The undeserved kindness of our Lord Jesus Christ be with the spirit you show, brothers. Amen.

6:14 *Or "executed on the stake."

CHAP. 6
a Jas 2:10

b 1Co 2:2

Second Col.
a 1Co 7:19
Ga 5:6
Col 3:10, 11

b 2Co 5:17
Eph 2:10

c Ro 9:6

d 2Co 4:10
Php 3:10

TO THE
EPHESIANS

1 Paul, an apostle of Christ Jesus through God's will, to the holy ones who are in Eph′e·sus[a] and are faithful in union with Christ Jesus:

CHAP. 1
a Re 2:1, 3

2 May you have undeserved kindness and peace from God our Father and the Lord Jesus Christ.

3 Praised be the God and Father of our Lord Jesus Christ, for he has blessed us with every spiritual blessing in the heavenly places in union with Christ,[a] 4 as he chose us to be in union with him* before the founding of the world, that we should be holy and unblemished[b] before him in love. 5 For he foreordained us[c] to be adopted as his own sons[d] through Jesus Christ, according to his good pleasure and will,[e] 6 in praise of his glorious undeserved kindness[f] that he kindly bestowed on us by means of his beloved one.[g] 7 By means of him we have the release by ransom through the blood of that one,[h] yes, the forgiveness of our trespasses,[i] according to the riches of his undeserved kindness.

8 This undeserved kindness he caused to abound toward us in all wisdom and understanding* 9 by making known to us the sacred secret[j] of his will. It is according to his good pleasure that he himself purposed 10 for an administration* at the full limit of the appointed times, to gather all things together in the Christ, the things in the heavens and the things on the earth.[k] Yes, in him 11 with whom we are in union and were assigned as heirs,[l] having been foreordained according to the purpose of the one who accomplishes all things as he decides according to his will, 12 so that we who have been first to hope in the Christ should serve for the praise of his glory. 13 But you also hoped in him after you heard the word of truth, the good news about your salvation. After you believed, you were sealed[m] by means of him with the promised holy spirit, 14 which is a token

in advance* of our inheritance,[a] for the purpose of releasing God's own possession[b] by a ransom,[c] to his glorious praise.

15 That is why I also, since I have heard of the faith that you have in the Lord Jesus and the love that you demonstrate toward all the holy ones, 16 never stop giving thanks for you. I continue mentioning you in my prayers, 17 that the God of our Lord Jesus Christ, the Father of glory, may give you a spirit of wisdom and of revelation in the accurate knowledge of him.[d] 18 He has enlightened the eyes of your heart, so that you may know to what hope he called you, what glorious riches he holds as an inheritance for the holy ones,[e] 19 and how surpassing the greatness of his power is toward us believers.[f] It is according to the operation of the mightiness of his strength, 20 which he exercised toward Christ when he raised him up from the dead and seated him at his right hand[g] in the heavenly places, 21 far above every government and authority and power and lordship and every name that is named,[h] not only in this system of things* but also in that to come. 22 He also subjected all things under his feet[i] and made him head over all things with regard to the congregation,[j] 23 which is his body,[k] the fullness of him who fills up all things in all.

2 Furthermore, God made you alive, though you were dead in your trespasses and sins,[l] 2 in which you at one time walked according to the system of things* of this world,[m] according to the ruler of the authori-

CHAP. 1
a Eph 2:6
b Eph 5:25-27
c 2Th 2:13
  1Pe 1:2
d Ro 8:15, 29
  Ro 8:23
e Ro 8:28
f Ro 3:24
g Joh 3:35
h Ac 20:28
  Ro 3:25
  Re 5:9
i Ac 13:38
  Col 1:14
  Col 2:13
j Ro 16:25, 26
k Php 2:9, 10
  Col 1:19, 20
l Ro 8:17
  Eph 3:5, 6
m 2Co 1:22
  Eph 4:30
  Re 7:4

Second Col.
a 2Co 5:5
  1Pe 1:3, 4
b 1Pe 2:9
c Ro 8:23
  1Ti 2:5, 6
d Col 1:9
  1Ti 2:3, 4
e 1Pe 1:3, 4
f 2Co 13:4
g Ps 110:1
  Ac 7:55
h Ac 4:12
  Php 2:9-11
i Ps 8:6
  1Co 15:27
  Heb 2:8
j Mt 28:18
  Eph 5:23
  Col 1:18
k Ro 12:5
  Eph 4:16

CHAP. 2
l Col 2:13
m Ro 12:2
  Eph 4:17

1:4 *That is, with Christ. 1:8 *Or "good sense." 1:10 *Or "to administer things."

1:14 *Or "a down payment (earnest money); a guarantee (pledge) of what is to come." 1:21 *Or "this age." See Glossary. 2:2 *Or "the course."

ty of the air,[a] the spirit[b] that is now at work in the sons of disobedience. **3** Yes, among them we all at one time conducted ourselves in harmony with the desires of our flesh,[c] carrying out the will of the flesh and of our thoughts,[d] and we were naturally children of wrath[e] just as the rest. **4** But God, being rich in mercy,[f] because of his great love with which he loved us,[g] **5** made us alive together with the Christ, even when we were dead in trespasses[h]—by undeserved kindness you have been saved. **6** Moreover, he raised us up together and seated us together in the heavenly places in union with Christ Jesus,[i] **7** so that in the coming systems of things* he might demonstrate the surpassing riches of his undeserved kindness in his graciousness# toward us in union with Christ Jesus.

8 By this undeserved kindness you have been saved through faith,[j] and this is not of your own doing; rather, it is God's gift. **9** No, it is not a result of works,[k] so that no one should have grounds for boasting. **10** We are God's handiwork* and were created[l] in union with Christ Jesus[m] for good works, which God determined in advance for us to walk in them.

11 Therefore, remember that at one time you, people of the nations by fleshly descent, were the ones called "uncircumcision" by those called "circumcision," which is made in the flesh by human hands. **12** At that time you were without Christ, alienated from the state of Israel, strangers to the covenants of the promise;[a] you had no hope and were without God in the world.[b] **13** But now in union with Christ Jesus, you who were once far off have come to be near by the blood of the Christ. **14** For he is our peace,[c] the one who made the two groups one[d] and destroyed the wall in between that fenced them off.[e] **15** By means of his flesh he abolished the enmity, the Law of commandments consisting in decrees, in order to make the two groups in union with himself into one new man[f] and to make peace, **16** and to reconcile fully both peoples in one body to God through the torture stake,*[g] because he had killed off the enmity[h] by means of himself. **17** And he came and declared the good news of peace to you who were far off, and peace to those near, **18** because through him we, both peoples, have free access to the Father by one spirit.

19 So you are no longer strangers and foreigners,[i] but you are fellow citizens[j] of the holy ones and are members of the household of God,[k] **20** and you have been built up on the foundation of the apostles and prophets,[l] while Christ Jesus himself is the foundation cornerstone.[m] **21** In union with him the whole building, being harmoniously joined together,[n] is growing into a holy temple for Jehovah.*[o] **22** In union with him you too are being built up together into a place for God to inhabit by spirit.[p]

3 For this reason I, Paul, the prisoner[q] of Christ Jesus in behalf of you, the people of the nations— **2** if, really, you have heard about the stewardship[r] of God's undeserved kindness that

---

CHAP. 2

a Joh 12:31

b 1Co 2:12

c 1Co 6:9-11

d 1Pe 4:3

e Joh 3:36

f Ps 145:9

g Ro 5:8
1Jo 4:9, 19

h Col 2:12, 13

i Eph 1:3

j Ro 4:16

k Ro 3:20

l Ga 6:15

m Eph 1:3, 4

Second Col.

a Ro 9:4

b Isa 65:1

c Col 1:19, 20

d Col 3:11

e Le 20:26
Col 2:13, 14

f 1Co 12:12
Ga 3:28

g Heb 12:2

h Ac 10:28

i Eph 2:12

j Php 3:20

k 1Ti 3:15
Heb 3:6

l 1Co 12:28

m Isa 28:16

n Col 2:19

o 1Co 3:16
1Co 6:19

p 1Pe 2:5

CHAP. 3

q Eph 4:1

r 1Co 9:16, 17
Col 1:25, 26

2:7 *Or "the coming ages." See Glossary. #Or "favor." 2:10 *Or "are a product of His work." 2:16 *See Glossary. 2:21 *See App. A5.

was given to me for your sakes, **3** that by way of a revelation the sacred secret was made known to me, just as I wrote previously in brief. **4** So when you read this, you can realize my comprehension of the sacred secret[a] of the Christ. **5** In other generations this secret was not made known to the sons of men as it has now been revealed to his holy apostles and prophets by spirit,[b] **6** namely, that people of the nations should, in union with Christ Jesus and through the good news, be joint heirs and fellow members of the body[c] and partakers with us of the promise. **7** I became a minister of this according to the free gift of God's undeserved kindness that was given me through the operation of his power.[d]

8 To me, a man less than the least of all holy ones,[e] this undeserved kindness was given,[f] so that I should declare to the nations the good news about the unfathomable riches of the Christ **9** and should make everyone see the administration of the sacred secret[g] that has been hidden through the ages in God, who created all things. **10** This was so that now, through the congregation,[h] there might be made known to the governments and the authorities in the heavenly places the greatly diversified wisdom of God.[i] **11** This is according to the eternal purpose that he formed in connection with the Christ,[j] Jesus our Lord, **12** by means of whom we have this freeness of speech and free access[k] with confidence through our faith in him. **13** So I ask you not to give up on account of my tribulations in your behalf, for these mean glory for you.[l]

14 For this reason I bend my knees to the Father, **15** to whom every family in heav-

en and on earth owes its name. **16** I pray that he may grant you through the abundance of his glory to be made mighty in the man you are inside,[a] with power through his spirit, **17** and that through your faith you may have the Christ dwell in your hearts with love.[b] May you be rooted[c] and established on the foundation,[d] **18** in order that with all the holy ones you may be thoroughly able to comprehend fully what is the breadth and length and height and depth, **19** and to know the love of the Christ,[e] which surpasses knowledge, so that you may be filled with all the fullness that God gives.

20 Now to the one who can, according to his power that is operating in us,[f] do more than superabundantly beyond all the things we ask or conceive,[g] **21** to him be the glory by means of the congregation and by means of Christ Jesus to all generations forever and ever. Amen.

4 Therefore I, the prisoner[h] in the Lord, appeal to you to walk worthily[i] of the calling with which you were called, **2** with all humility*[j] and mildness, with patience,[k] putting up with one another in love,[l] **3** earnestly endeavoring to maintain the oneness of the spirit in the uniting bond of peace.[m] **4** One body there is,[n] and one spirit,[o] just as you were called to the one hope[p] of your calling; **5** one Lord,[q] one faith, one baptism; **6** one God and Father of all, who is over all and through all and in all.

7 Now undeserved kindness was given to each one of us according to how the Christ measured out the free gift.[r] **8** For it says: "When he ascended on high he carried away captives;

CHAP. 3

a 1Co 4:1
  Eph 6:19

b Ro 11:25
  Ro 16:25, 26

c Eph 2:15, 16

c' Col 1:25-27

e 1Co 15:9

f 1Ti 1:13, 14

g Eph 1:9, 10

h 1Pe 1:10, 12

i 1Pe 2:9

j Eph 1:11

k Joh 14:6
  Heb 4:15, 16

l 2Ti 2:10

Second Col.

a 2Co 4:16

b Joh 14:23

c Col 2:6, 7

d Col 1:23

e Ro 8:35

f Col 1:29

g Mr 11:24

CHAP. 4

h Phm 9

i Php 1:27

j Mt 11:29
  Ro 12:3
  Php 2:3
  1Pe 5:5

k 1Th 5:14

l 1Co 13:4

m 1Co 1:10
  Col 3:15

n Ro 12:5

o 1Co 12:4

p 1Pe 1:3, 4

q 1Co 8:6
  1Co 12:5, 6

r 1Co 12:11

4:2 *Or "lowliness of mind."

he gave gifts in men."[a] 9 Now what does the expression "he ascended" mean but that he also descended into the lower regions, that is, the earth? 10 The very one who descended is also the one who ascended[b] far above all the heavens,[c] so that he might give fullness to all things.

11 And he gave some as apostles,[d] some as prophets,[e] some as evangelizers,*[f] some as shepherds and teachers,[g] 12 with a view to the readjustment* of the holy ones, for ministerial work, to build up the body of the Christ,[h] 13 until we all attain to the oneness* of the faith and of the accurate knowledge of the Son of God, to being a full-grown# man,[i] attaining the measure of stature that belongs to the fullness of the Christ. 14 So we should no longer be children, tossed about as by waves and carried here and there by every wind of teaching[j] by means of the trickery of men, by means of cunning in deceptive schemes. 15 But speaking the truth, let us by love grow up in all things into him who is the head, Christ.[k] 16 From him all the body[l] is harmoniously joined together and made to cooperate through every joint that gives what is needed. When each respective member functions properly, this contributes to the growth of the body as it builds itself up in love.[m]

17 So this is what I say and bear witness to in the Lord, that you should no longer go on walking just as the nations also walk,[n] in the futility* of their minds.[o] 18 They are

in darkness mentally and alienated from the life that belongs to God, because of the ignorance that is in them, because of the insensitivity* of their hearts. 19 Having gone past all moral sense, they gave themselves over to brazen conduct*[a] to practice every sort of uncleanness with greediness.

20 But you did not learn the Christ to be like this, 21 if, indeed, you heard him and were taught by means of him, just as truth is in Jesus. 22 You were taught to put away the old personality[b] that conforms to your former course of conduct and that is being corrupted according to its deceptive desires.[c] 23 And you should continue to be made new in your dominant mental attitude,*[d] 24 and should put on the new personality[e] that was created according to God's will in true righteousness and loyalty.

25 Therefore, now that you have put away deceit, each one of you speak truth with his neighbor,[f] because we are members belonging to one another.[g] 26 Be wrathful, but do not sin;[h] do not let the sun set while you are still angry;[i] 27 do not give the Devil an opportunity.*[j] 28 Let the one who steals steal no more; rather, let him do hard work, doing good work with his hands,[k] so that he may have something to share with someone in need.[l] 29 Let a rotten word not come out of your mouth,[m] but only what is good for building up as the need may be, to impart what is beneficial to the hearers.[n] 30 Also,

CHAP. 4

a Ps 68:18
1Co 12:28
Eph 4:11

b Ac 1:9
1Ti 3:16

c Heb 9:24

d Mt 10:2-4

e 1Co 12:28

f Ac 21:8

g Ac 13:1
Jas 3:1

h 1Co 14:26

i 1Co 14:20

j Heb 13:9

k 1Co 11:3
Col 1:18

l 1Co 12:27

m Col 2:19

n 1Pe 4:3

o Ro 1:21

Second Col.

a Ga 5:19

b Ro 6:6
Col 3:9

c Ro 7:23

d Ps 51:10
Ro 12:2

e Col 3:10

f Zec 8:16
Col 3:8, 9
Re 21:8

g Ro 12:5

h Ps 4:4

i Le 19:17
Col 3:13

j Jas 4:7

k 2Th 3:10

l Ac 20:35
1Th 4:11, 12

m Mt 15:11
Jas 3:10

n Col 4:6

4:11 *Or "proclaimers of the good news." 4:12 *Or "training." 4:13 *Or "unity." #Or "mature." 4:17 *Or "emptiness; vanity."

4:18 *Lit., "dulling." 4:19 *Or "shameless conduct." Greek, a·sel'gei·a. See Glossary. 4:23 *Or "in the force actuating your mind." Lit., "to the spirit of your mind." 4:27 *Or "neither allow place for the Devil."

do not be grieving* God's holy spirit,[a] with which you have been sealed[b] for a day of releasing by ransom.[c]

31 Put away from yourselves every kind of malicious bitterness,[d] anger, wrath, screaming, and abusive speech,[e] as well as everything injurious.[f] 32 But become kind to one another, tenderly compassionate,[g] freely forgiving one another just as God also by Christ freely forgave you.[h]

5 Therefore, become imitators of God,[i] as beloved children, 2 and go on walking in love,[j] just as the Christ also loved us*[k] and gave himself for us* as an offering and a sacrifice, a sweet fragrance to God.[l]

3 Let sexual immorality* and every sort of uncleanness or greediness not even be mentioned among you,[m] just as is proper for holy people;[n] 4 neither shameful conduct nor foolish talking nor obscene jesting[o]—things that are not befitting—but rather the giving of thanks.[p] 5 For you know this, recognizing it for yourselves, that no sexually immoral person*[q] or unclean person or greedy person,[r] which means being an idolater, has any inheritance in the Kingdom of the Christ and of God.[s]

6 Let no man deceive you with empty words, for because of such things the wrath of God is coming upon the sons of disobedience. 7 Therefore, do not be sharers with them; 8 for you were once darkness, but you are now light[t] in connection with the Lord.[u] Go on walking as children of light, 9 for the fruitage of the light consists of every

sort of goodness and righteousness and truth.[a] 10 Keep on making sure of what is acceptable[b] to the Lord; 11 and stop sharing in the unfruitful works that belong to the darkness;[c] rather, expose them for what they are. 12 For the things they do in secret are shameful even to mention. 13 Now all the things that are being exposed* are made evident by the light, for everything that is being made evident is light. 14 Therefore, it is said: "Awake, O sleeper, and arise from the dead,[d] and the Christ will shine upon you."[e]

15 So keep strict watch that how you walk is not as unwise but as wise persons, 16 making the best use of your time,*[f] because the days are wicked. 17 On this account stop being unreasonable, but keep perceiving what the will of Jehovah* is.[g] 18 Also, do not get drunk with wine,[h] in which there is debauchery,* but keep getting filled with spirit. 19 Speak to one another[u] with psalms, praises to God, and spiritual songs, singing[i] and accompanying yourselves with music[j] in your hearts to Jehovah,*[k] 20 always giving thanks[l] to our God and Father for everything in the name of our Lord Jesus Christ.[m]

21 Be in subjection to one another[n] in fear of Christ. 22 Let wives be in subjection to their husbands[o] as to the Lord, 23 because a husband is head of his wife[p] just as the Christ is head of the congregation,[q] he being a savior of this body. 24 In fact, as the congregation is in subjection to the Christ, wives should also

CHAP. 4
a Isa 63:10
b Eph 1:13
c Ro 8:23
d Jas 3:14
e Col 3:8
f Tit 3:2
g Col 3:12
  1Pe 3:8
h Mt 6:14
  Mt 18:35
  Mr 11:25

CHAP. 5
i Mt 5:48
  Lu 6:36
j 1Co 16:14
k Joh 13:34
  1Jo 3:23
l Ex 29:18
m 1Co 5:11
  Col 3:5
n 1Th 4:3
o Col 3:8
p 1Th 5:18
q Ac 15:28, 29
r 1Ti 3:8
  Tit 1:7
s 1Co 6:9, 10
  Ga 5:19, 21
t Mt 5:16
  Joh 12:36
u 1Pe 2:9

Second Col.
a Ga 5:22, 23
b Ro 12:2
c Ro 13:12, 13
  2Co 6:14
d Eph 2:1
  Col 2:13
e Joh 8:12
f Col 4:5
g Ro 12:2
  1Th 4:3
  1Pe 4:2
h Isa 5:11
i Jas 5:13
j Ps 33:2, 3
k Ac 16:25
  Col 3:16
l 1Th 5:18
m Col 3:17
n Php 2:3
  1Pe 5:5
o Col 3:18
  Tit 2:4, 5
  1Pe 3:1
p Ro 7:2
q 1Co 11:3

4:30 *Or "cause sorrow to." 5:2 *Or possibly, "you." 5:3 *Greek, por·nei′a. See Glossary. 5:5 *See Glossary, "Sexual immorality."

5:13 *Or "reproved." 5:16 *Lit., "buying out the appointed time." 5:17, 19 *See App. A5. 5:18 *Or "unruliness." 5:19 *Or possibly, "to yourselves."

be to their husbands in everything. **25** Husbands, continue loving your wives,[a] just as the Christ also loved the congregation and gave himself up for it,[b] **26** in order that he might sanctify it, cleansing it with the bath of water by means of the word,[c] **27** so that he might present the congregation to himself in its splendor, without a spot or a wrinkle or any of such things,[d] but holy and without blemish.[e]

28 In the same way husbands should love their wives as their own bodies. A man who loves his wife loves himself, **29** for no man ever hated his own body,* but he feeds and cherishes it, just as the Christ does the congregation, **30** because we are members of his body.[f] **31** "For this reason a man will leave his father and his mother and he will stick to* his wife, and the two will be one flesh."[g] **32** This sacred secret[h] is great. Now I am speaking about Christ and the congregation.[i] **33** Nevertheless, each one of you must love his wife[j] as he does himself; on the other hand, the wife should have deep respect for her husband.[k]

6 Children, be obedient to your parents[l] in union with the Lord, for this is righteous. **2** "Honor your father and your mother"[m] is the first command with a promise: **3** "That it may go well with you* and you may remain a long time on the earth." **4** And fathers, do not be irritating your children,[n] but go on bringing them up in the discipline[o] and admonition* of Jehovah.#[p]

5:29 *Lit., "flesh." **5:31** *Or "remain with." **6:3** *Or "That you may prosper." **6:4** *Or "instruction; guidance." Lit., "putting mind in." **6:4, 7, 8** #See App. A5.

CHAP. 5
a 1Pe 3:7
b Ac 20:28
c Joh 17:17
d Tit 2:13, 14
e Eph 1:4
  Col 1:21, 22
f Ro 12:5
  Eph 1:22, 23
g Ge 2:24
  Mt 19:5
h Eph 1:9, 10
  Col 1:26, 27
i Eph 3:5, 6
j Col 3:19
k 1Pe 3:5, 6

CHAP. 6
l Pr 1:8
  Pr 6:20
  Pr 3:20
m Ex 20:12
  De 5:16
  Pr 20:20
  Pr 23:22
  Mt 15:4
n Col 3:21
o Pr 13:24
p De 6:6, 7
  Pr 3:11
  Pr 19:18
  Pr 22:6

Second Col.
a 1Ti 6:1
  1Pe 2:18
b Col 3:22
c Lu 10:27
d 1Co 10:31
e Col 3:23, 24
f 1Co 7:22
g Eph 3:16
h Ro 13:12
i 2Ti 4:7
j 2Pe 2:4
k 2Co 6:4, 7
l Isa 11:5
m Pr 4:23
  Isa 59:17
n Isa 52:7
  Ro 10:15

5 Slaves, be obedient to your human* masters,[a] with fear and trembling in the sincerity of your hearts, as to the Christ, **6** not only when being watched, just to please men,*[b] but as Christ's slaves doing the will of God whole-souled.#[c] **7** Slave with a good attitude, as to Jehovah#[d] and not to men, **8** for you know that whatever good each one does, he will receive this back from Jehovah,#[e] whether he is a slave or a freeman. **9** Also, you masters, keep treating them in the same way, not threatening, for you know that both their Master and yours is in the heavens,[f] and there is no partiality with him.

10 Finally, go on acquiring power[g] in the Lord and in the mightiness of his strength. **11** Put on the complete suit of armor[h] from God so that you may be able to stand firm against the crafty acts* of the Devil; **12** because we have a struggle,*[i] not against blood and flesh, but against the governments, against the authorities, against the world rulers of this darkness, against the wicked spirit forces[j] in the heavenly places. **13** For this reason take up the complete suit of armor from God,[k] so that you may be able to resist in the wicked day and, after you have accomplished everything, to stand firm.

14 Stand firm, therefore, with the belt of truth fastened around your waist,[l] wearing the breastplate of righteousness,[m] **15** and having your feet shod in readiness to declare the good news of peace.[n] **16** Besides all of this, take up the large shield

---

6:5 *Lit., "fleshly." **6:6** *Lit., "not with eye-service as men pleasers." #See Glossary, "Soul." **6:11** *Or "the schemes." **6:12** *Lit., "wrestling."

of faith,[a] with which you will be able to extinguish all the wicked one's burning arrows.*[b] **17** Also, accept the helmet of salvation,[c] and the sword of the spirit, that is, God's word,[d] **18** while with every form of prayer[e] and supplication you carry on prayer on every occasion in spirit.[f] And to that end stay awake, constantly making supplication in behalf of all the holy ones. **19** Pray also for me, that the words may be given to me when I open my mouth, so that I may be able to speak boldly in making known the sacred secret of the good news,[g] **20** for which I am acting as an ambassador[a] in chains, and that I may speak about it with boldness, as I ought to speak.

21 Now so that you may also know about me and how I am doing, Tych′i·cus,[b] a beloved brother and faithful minister in the Lord, will make everything known to you.[c] **22** I am sending him to you for this very purpose, so that you may know how we are and that he may comfort your hearts.

23 May the brothers have peace and love with faith from God the Father and the Lord Jesus Christ. **24** May the undeserved kindness be with all those loving our Lord Jesus Christ in incorruptness.

6:16 * Or "missiles; darts."

CHAP. 6
a 1Jo 5:4
b 1Pe 5:8, 9
c Isa 59:17 1Th 5:8
d Heb 4:12
e Col 4:2
f Jude 20
g Col 4:3
_____
Second Col.
a 2Co 5:20
b 2Ti 4:12 Tit 3:12
c Col 4:7, 8

TO THE
PHILIPPIANS

OUTLINE OF CONTENTS

1 Paul and Timothy, slaves of Christ Jesus, to all the holy ones in union with Christ Jesus who are in Phi·lip′pi,[a] along with overseers and ministerial servants:[b] **2** May you have undeserved kindness and peace from God our Father and the Lord Jesus Christ.

3 I thank my God always when I remember you **4** in every sup-

CHAP. 1
a Ac 16:12
b 1Ti 3:1, 8

plication of mine for all of you. I offer each supplication with joy,[a] **5** because of the contribution you have made to* the good news from the first day until this moment. **6** For I am confident of this very thing, that the one who started a good work in you will bring it to completion[b] until the day of Christ Jesus.[c] **7** It is only right for me to think this regarding all of you, since I have you in my heart, you who are sharers with me in the undeserved kindness both in my prison bonds[d] and in the defending and legally establishing of the good news.[e]

8 For God is my witness of how I am longing for all of you with such tender affection as Christ Jesus has. **9** And this is what I continue praying, that your love may abound still more and more[f] with accurate knowledge[g] and full discernment;[h] **10** that you may make sure of the more important things,[i] so that you may be flawless and not stumbling others[j] up to the day of Christ; **11** and that you may be filled with righteous fruit, which is through Jesus Christ,[k] to God's glory and praise.

12 Now I want you to know, brothers, that my situation has actually turned out for the advancement of the good news, **13** so that my prison bonds[l] for the sake of Christ have become public knowledge[m] among all the Prae·to′ri·an Guard and all the rest. **14** Now most of the brothers in the Lord have gained confidence because of my prison bonds, and they are showing all the more courage to speak the word of God fearlessly.

15 True, some are preaching the Christ out of envy and rivalry, but others out of goodwill.

16 The latter are proclaiming the Christ out of love, for they know that I have been appointed to defend the good news;[a] **17** but the former do it out of contentiousness, not with a pure motive, for they are intending to create trouble for me in my prison bonds. **18** With what result? Only that in every way, whether in pretense or in truth, Christ is being proclaimed, and I rejoice over this. In fact, I will also keep on rejoicing, **19** for I know that this will result in my salvation through your supplication[b] and with the support of the spirit of Jesus Christ.[c] **20** This is in harmony with my eager expectation and hope that I will not be ashamed in any respect, but that with all freeness of speech Christ will now, as always before, be magnified by means of my body, whether through life or through death.[d]

21 For in my case, to live is Christ[e] and to die is gain.[f] **22** Now if I am to live on in the flesh, this is a fruitage of my work; yet what I would choose, I do not make known. **23** I am torn between these two things, for I do desire the releasing and the being with Christ,[g] which is, to be sure, far better.[h] **24** However, it is more necessary for me to remain in the flesh for your sakes. **25** So, being confident of this, I know I will remain and continue with all of you for your advancement and your joy in the faith, **26** so that your exultation may overflow in Christ Jesus because of me when I am again present with you.

27 Only behave* in a manner worthy of the good news about the Christ,[i] so that whether I come and see you or I am absent, I may hear about you and learn that you are standing firm

---

CHAP. 1
a 1Th 1:2

b Php 2:13

c 1Co 1:8

d Eph 3:1
Php 1:13
Col 4:18
2Ti 1:8
Phm 13

e Ac 24:10, 14
Ac 25:10-12

f 1Th 3:12

g Joh 17:3

h Heb 5:14

i Ro 12:2

j Ro 14:13, 21

k Joh 15:5

l Eph 3:1

m Ac 28:30, 31

Second Col.
a Php 1:7

b 2Co 1:11

c Joh 15:26

d Ro 14:8
1Pe 4:16

e Ga 2:20

f 1Th 4:14
2Ti 4:8
Re 14:13

g 2Ti 4:6

h 2Co 5:6, 8

i Eph 4:1, 3
Col 1:10

1:5 *Or "because of your participation in furthering."

1:27 *Or "carry on as citizens."

in one spirit, with one soul,*[a] striving side by side for the faith of the good news, **28** and in no way being frightened by your opponents. This very thing is a proof of destruction[b] for them, but of salvation for you;[c] and this is from God. **29** For you have been given the privilege in behalf of Christ, not only to put your faith in him but also to suffer in his behalf.[d] **30** For you are facing the same struggle that you saw me face,[e] which you now hear that I am still facing.

2 If, then, there is any encouragement in Christ, if any consolation of love, if any spiritual fellowship,* if any tender affection and compassion, **2** make my joy full by being of the same mind and having the same love, being completely united,* having the one thought in mind.[f] **3** Do nothing out of contentiousness[g] or out of egotism,[h] but with humility* consider others superior to you,[i] **4** as you look out not only for your own interests,[j] but also for the interests of others.[k]

5 Keep this mental attitude in you that was also in Christ Jesus,[l] **6** who, although he was existing in God's form,[m] gave no consideration to a seizure, namely, that he should be equal to God.[n] **7** No, but he emptied himself and took a slave's form[o] and became human.*[p] **8** More than that, when he came as a man,* he humbled himself and became obedient to the point of death,[q] yes, death on a torture stake.*[r] **9** For this very reason, God exalted him to a su-perior position[a] and kindly gave him the name that is above every other name,[b] **10** so that in the name of Jesus every knee should bend—of those in heaven and those on earth and those under the ground[c]— **11** and every tongue should openly acknowledge that Jesus Christ is Lord[d] to the glory of God the Father.

12 Consequently, my beloved ones, just as you have always obeyed, not only during my presence but now much more readily during my absence, keep working out your own salvation with fear and trembling. **13** For God is the one who for the sake of his good pleasure energizes you, giving you both the desire and the power to act. **14** Keep doing all things free from murmuring[e] and arguments,[f] **15** so that you may come to be blameless and innocent, children of God[g] without a blemish in the midst of a crooked and twisted generation,[h] among whom you are shining as illuminators in the world,[i] **16** keeping a tight grip on the word of life.[j] Then I may have reason for rejoicing in Christ's day, knowing that I did not run in vain or work hard in vain. **17** However, even if I am being poured out like a drink offering[k] on the sacrifice[l] and the holy service* to which your faith has led you, I am glad and I rejoice with all of you. **18** In the same way, you also should be glad and rejoice with me.

19 Now I am hoping in the Lord Jesus to send Timothy[m] to you shortly, so that I may be encouraged when I receive news about you. **20** For I have no one else of a disposition like his who will genuinely care for your concerns. **21** For all the others are seeking their own interests, not those of Jesus Christ.

CHAP. 1
a Ro 15:5, 6
　1Co 1:10
b 2Th 1:6
c Lu 21:19
　2Th 1:4, 5
d Ac 5:41
e Ac 16:22, 23
　1Th 2:2

CHAP. 2
f 1Co 1:10
　2Co 13:11
　1Pe 3:8
g Php 1:15, 17
　Jas 3:14, 16
h Ga 5:26
i Mt 23:11
　Eph 4:1, 2
　Eph 5:21
j 1Co 13:4, 5
k 1Co 10:24
　1Co 10:32, 33
l 1Co 13:14, 15
　Joh 13:14, 15
m Col 1:15
　Heb 1:3
n Joh 14:28
o Isa 53:2, 3
p Joh 1:14
q Joh 10:17
　Heb 2:9
　Heb 5:8
r Ga 3:13

Second Col.
a Isa 52:13
　Ac 2:32, 33
b Ac 4:12
　Eph 1:20, 21
c Joh 5:22, 23
d Ro 10:9
e 1Co 10:10
　1Pe 4:9
f 1Ti 2:8
g Eph 5:1
h De 32:5
i Mt 5:14
　Eph 5:8, 9
　1Pe 2:9, 12
j Joh 6:68
　Heb 4:12
k Nu 28:6, 7
　2Co 12:15
　2Ti 4:6
l Heb 13:15
　1Pe 2:5
m 1Co 4:17
　1Co 16:10

22 But you know the proof he gave of himself, that like a child[a] with a father he slaved with me to advance the good news. **23** Therefore, he is the one I am hoping to send just as soon as I see how things turn out for me. **24** Indeed, I am confident in the Lord that I myself will also come soon.[b]

25 But for now I consider it necessary to send to you E·paph·ro·di'tus, my brother and fellow worker and fellow soldier, and your envoy and personal servant for my need,[c] **26** since he is longing to see all of you and is depressed because you heard he had fallen sick. **27** Indeed, he did fall sick nearly to the point of death; but God had mercy on him, in fact, not only on him but also on me, so that I should not have one grief after another. **28** Therefore, I am sending him with the greatest urgency, so that when you see him you may again rejoice and I may also be less anxious. **29** So give him the customary welcome in the Lord with all joy, and keep holding men of that sort dear,[d] **30** because he nearly died on account of the work of Christ,* risking his life[#] in order to make up for your not being here to render personal service to me.[e]

3 Finally, my brothers, continue rejoicing in the Lord.[f] It is not troublesome for me to write the same things to you, and it is for your safety.

2 Look out for the dogs; look out for those who cause injury; look out for those who mutilate the flesh.[g] **3** For we are those with the real circumcision,[h] we who are rendering sacred service by God's spirit and boasting in Christ Jesus[i] and who do not base our confidence in the flesh, **4** though I, if anyone, do have grounds for confidence in the flesh.

If any other man thinks he has grounds for confidence in the flesh, I have more: **5** circumcised the eighth day,[a] of the nation of Israel, of the tribe of Benjamin, a Hebrew born from Hebrews;[b] regarding law, a Pharisee;[c] **6** regarding zeal, persecuting the congregation;[d] regarding righteousness based on law, one who proved himself blameless. **7** Yet, the things that were gains to me, I have considered loss* on account of the Christ.[e] **8** What is more, I do indeed also consider all things to be loss on account of the excelling value of the knowledge of Christ Jesus my Lord. For his sake I have taken the loss of all things and I consider them as a lot of refuse,* that I may gain Christ **9** and be found in union with him, not because of my own righteousness from following the Law, but because of the righteousness that is through faith[f] in Christ,[g] the righteousness from God based on faith.[h] **10** My aim is to know him and the power of his resurrection[i] and to share in his sufferings,[j] submitting myself to a death like his,[k] **11** to see if at all possible I may attain to the earlier resurrection from the dead.[l]

12 Not that I have already received it or am already made perfect, but I am pressing on[m] to see if I may also lay hold on that for which Christ Jesus selected me.*[n] **13** Brothers, I do not yet consider myself as having taken hold of it; but one thing is certain: Forgetting the

CHAP. 2
a 2Ti 1:2
b Phm 22
c Php 4:18
d 1Co 16:18
  1Th 5:12, 13
e Phm 10, 13

CHAP. 3
f 2Co 13:11
  Php 4:4
  1Th 5:16
g Ga 5:2
h Jer 4:4
  Ro 2:29
  Col 2:11
i Ga 6:14
  Heb 9:13, 14

Second Col.
a Ge 17:12
  Le 12:3
b 2Co 11:22
c Ac 23:6
  Ac 26:4, 5
d Ac 8:3
  Ac 9:1, 2
  Ga 1:13
e Mt 13:44
f Ro 4:5
g Ga 2:15, 16
h Ro 3:20-22
i 1Co 15:22
  2Co 13:4
j Ro 8:17
  2Co 4:10
  Col 1:24
k Ro 6:5
l 1Th 4:16
  Re 20:6
m Lu 13:24
n 1Ti 6:12

2:30 * Or possibly, "of the Lord's work." [#] Or "exposing his soul to danger." **3:7** * Or possibly, "have willingly abandoned." **3:8** * Or "garbage; rubbish." **3:12** * Lit., "laid hold on me."

things behind[a] and stretching forward to the things ahead,[b] **14** I am pressing on toward the goal for the prize[c] of the upward call[d] of God by means of Christ Jesus. **15** Therefore, let those of us who are mature[e] be of this mental attitude, and if you are mentally inclined otherwise in any respect, God will reveal the above attitude to you. **16** At any rate, to the extent we have made progress, let us go on walking orderly in this same course.

17 Unitedly become imitators of me,[f] brothers, and keep your eye on those who are walking in a way that is in harmony with the example we set for you. **18** For there are many—I used to mention them often but now I mention them also with weeping—who are walking as enemies of the torture stake* of the Christ. **19** Their end is destruction, and their god is their belly, and their glory is really their shame, and they have their minds on earthly things.[g] **20** But our citizenship[h] exists in the heavens,[i] and we are eagerly waiting for a savior from there, the Lord Jesus Christ,[j] **21** who will transform our humble body to be like* his glorious body[k] by his great power that enables him to subject all things to himself.[l]

4 Consequently, my brothers whom I love and long for, my joy and crown,[m] stand firm[n] in this way in the Lord, my beloved ones.

2 I urge Eu·o′di·a and I urge Syn′ty·che to be of the same mind in the Lord.[o] **3** Yes, I request you also, as a true fellow worker,* to keep assisting these women who have striven[#] side by side with me for the good news, along with Clement as well as the rest of my fellow workers, whose names are in the book of life.[a]

4 Always rejoice in the Lord. Again I say, Rejoice![b] **5** Let your reasonableness[c] become known to all men. The Lord is near. **6** Do not be anxious over anything,[d] but in everything by prayer and supplication along with thanksgiving, let your petitions be made known to God;[e] **7** and the peace* of God that surpasses all understanding will guard your hearts[g] and your mental powers* by means of Christ Jesus.

8 Finally, brothers, whatever things are true, whatever things are of serious concern, whatever things are righteous, whatever things are chaste,* whatever things are lovable, whatever things are well-spoken-of, whatever things are virtuous, and whatever things are praiseworthy, continue considering[#] these things.[h] **9** The things that you learned as well as accepted and heard and saw in connection with me, practice these,[i] and the God of peace will be with you.

10 I rejoice greatly in the Lord that now at last you have renewed your concern for me.[j] Though you were concerned about me, you lacked opportunity to show it. **11** Not that I am saying this because I am in need, for I have learned to be self-sufficient* regardless of my circumstances.[k] **12** I know how to be low on provisions[l] and how to have an abundance. In everything and in all circumstances I have learned the secret of both how to be full and how to hun-

---

CHAP. 3
a Lu 9:62
b 1Co 9:24
c 2Ti 4:8
  Heb 12:1
d Heb 3:1
e 1Co 14:20
  Heb 5:14
f 1Co 4:16
  2Th 3:9
g Ro 8:5
  Jas 3:15
h Eph 2:19
i Joh 18:36
  Eph 2:6
  Col 3:1
j 1Co 1:7
  1Th 1:10
  Tit 2:13
  Heb 9:28
k 1Co 15:42, 49
l 1Co 15:27
  Heb 2:8

CHAP. 4
m 1Th 2:19
n Php 1:27
o Ro 15:5, 6
  1Co 1:10
  2Co 13:11
  Php 2:2
  1Pe 3:8

Second Col.
a Ps 69:28
  Lu 10:20
b Ps 64:10
  1Th 5:16
c Tit 3:2
  Jas 3:17
d Mt 6:25
  Lu 12:22
e Joh 16:23
  Ro 12:12
  1Pe 5:6, 7
f Joh 16:33
  Ro 5:1
g Col 3:15
h Col 3:2
i Php 3:17
j 2Co 11:8, 9
  Heb 13:5
k 1Ti 6:6, 8
  Heb 13:5
l 1Co 4:11
  2Co 6:4, 10
  2Co 11:27

3:18 *See Glossary. 3:21 *Lit., "to be conformed to." 4:3 *Lit., "genuine yokefellow." #Or "who have struggled hard."

4:7 *Or "your minds; your thoughts." 4:8 *Or "pure." #Or "thinking about; meditating on." 4:11 *Or "content."

ger, both how to have an abundance and how to do without. **13** For all things I have the strength through the one who gives me power.[a]

14 Nevertheless, you did well to share with me in my tribulation. **15** In fact, you Phi·lip′pi·ans also know that after you first learned the good news, when I departed from Mac·e·do′ni·a, not a congregation shared with me in the matter of giving and receiving, except you alone;[b] **16** for while I was in Thes·sa·lo·ni′ca, you sent something to me for my need not just once but twice. **17** Not that I am looking for a gift, but I want the fruitage that brings more credit to your account. **18** However, I have everything I need

and even more. I am fully supplied, now that I have received from E·paph·ro·di′tus[a] what you sent, a sweet fragrance,[b] an acceptable sacrifice, well-pleasing to God. **19** In turn my God will fully supply all your need[c] according to his riches in glory by means of Christ Jesus. **20** Now to our God and Father be the glory forever and ever. Amen.

21 Give my greetings to every holy one in union with Christ Jesus. The brothers who are with me send you their greetings. **22** All the holy ones, but especially those of the household of Caesar,[d] send you their greetings.

23 The undeserved kindness of the Lord Jesus Christ be with the spirit you show.

CHAP. 4
a Isa 40:29
  2Co 4:7
  2Co 12:9, 10

b 2Co 11:8, 9

Second Col.
a Php 2:25

b Ex 29:18

c 2Co 9:8

d Php 1:12, 13

TO THE
COLOSSIANS

1 Paul, an apostle of Christ Jesus through God's will, and Timothy[a] our brother, **2** to the holy ones and faithful brothers in union with Christ at Co·los′sae:

CHAP. 1
a 1Co 4:17

May you have undeserved kindness and peace from God our Father.

3 We always thank God, the Father of our Lord Jesus Christ, when we pray for you, **4** since we heard of your faith in Christ Jesus and the love you have for all the holy ones **5** because of the hope that is being reserved for you in the heavens.[a] You previously heard about this hope through the message of truth of the good news **6** that has come to you. Just as the good news is bearing fruit and increasing in all the world,[b] so it is also doing among you from the day you heard and accurately knew the undeserved kindness of God in truth. **7** That is what you have learned from our beloved fellow slave Ep'a·phras,[c] who is a faithful minister of the Christ on our behalf. **8** He also made known to us your love in a spiritual way.*

9 That is also why from the day we heard of it, we have never stopped praying for you[d] and asking that you may be filled with the accurate knowledge[e] of his will in all wisdom and spiritual comprehension,[f] **10** so as to walk worthily of Jehovah* in order to please him fully as you go on bearing fruit in every good work and increasing in the accurate knowledge of God;[g] **11** and may you be strengthened with all power according to his glorious might[h] so that you may endure fully with patience and joy, **12** as you thank the Father, who made you qualify for a share in the inheritance of the holy ones[i] in the light.

13 He rescued us from the authority of the darkness[j] and transferred us into the kingdom of his beloved Son, **14** by means of whom we have our release by ransom, the forgiveness of our sins.[k] **15** He is the image of the invisible God,[l] the firstborn of all creation;[m] **16** because by means of him all other

things were created in the heavens and on the earth, the things visible and the things invisible,[a] whether they are thrones or lordships or governments or authorities. All other things have been created through him[b] and for him. **17** Also, he is before all other things,[c] and by means of him all other things were made to exist, **18** and he is the head of the body, the congregation.[d] He is the beginning, the firstborn from the dead,[e] so that he might become the one who is first in all things; **19** because God was pleased to have all fullness to dwell in him,[f] **20** and through him to reconcile to himself all other things[g] by making peace through the blood[h] he shed on the torture stake,* whether the things on the earth or the things in the heavens.

21 Indeed, you who were once alienated and enemies because your minds were on the works that were wicked, **22** he has now reconciled by means of that one's fleshly body through his death, in order to present you holy and unblemished and open to no accusation before him[i]— **23** provided, of course, that you continue in the faith,[j] established on the foundation[k] and steadfast,[l] not being shifted away from the hope of that good news that you heard and that was preached in all creation under heaven.[m] Of this good news I, Paul, became a minister.[n]

24 I am now rejoicing in my sufferings for your sake,[o] and I am undergoing the tribulations of the Christ that are yet lacking in my flesh in behalf of his body,[p] which is the congregation.[q] **25** I became a minister of this congregation in accord with the stewardship[r] from God that

CHAP. 1	
a	2Ti 4:8
	1Pe 1:3, 4
b	Col 1:23
	1Ti 3:16
c	Col 4:12, 13
	Phm 23
d	Eph 1:15, 16
e	Php 1:9
f	2Ti 2:7
	1Jo 5:20
g	Eph 1:17
	2Pe 1:2
h	Eph 3:14, 16
i	Ro 8:17
	Eph 1:13, 14
j	Eph 2:1, 2
k	Eph 1:7
l	Joh 4:24
	Joh 10:30
	Joh 14:9
	1Ti 1:17
m	Re 3:14

Second Col.	
a	Joh 1:3
b	Joh 1:10
	Heb 1:2
c	Joh 17:5
d	Eph 1:22
e	1Co 15:23
	Re 1:5
f	Col 2:3, 9
g	2Co 5:19
	Eph 1:10
h	Le 17:11
i	1Co 1:8
j	Re 2:10
k	1Co 3:11
l	1Co 15:58
	Heb 3:14
m	1Ti 3:16
n	Eph 3:8
o	Eph 3:1
p	Ac 9:16
	Php 3:10
q	Eph 1:22, 23
r	1Co 9:16, 17

1:8 *Lit., "in spirit." **1:10** *See App. A5.   **1:20** *See Glossary.

was given to me in your behalf to preach the word of God fully, **26** the sacred secret[a] that was hidden from the past systems of things*[b] and from the past generations. But now it has been revealed to his holy ones,[c] **27** to whom God has been pleased to make known among the nations the glorious riches of this sacred secret,[d] which is Christ in union with you, the hope of his glory.[e] **28** He is the one we are proclaiming, admonishing everyone and teaching everyone in all wisdom, so that we may present every person complete in union with Christ.[f] **29** To this end I am indeed working hard, exerting myself with his strength that is operating powerfully within me.[g]

2 For I want you to realize how great a struggle I am having in your behalf and in behalf of those in La·o·di·ce′a[h] and in behalf of all those who have not personally seen me.* **2** This is so that their hearts may be comforted[i] and that they may be harmoniously joined together in love[j] and may have all the riches that result from the full assurance of their understanding, in order to gain an accurate knowledge of the sacred secret of God, namely, Christ.[k] **3** Carefully concealed in him are all the treasures of wisdom and of knowledge.[l] **4** I am saying this so that no one may delude you with persuasive arguments. **5** Though I am absent in body, I am with you in spirit, rejoicing to see your good order[m] and the firmness of your faith in Christ.[n]

6 Therefore, just as you have accepted Christ Jesus the Lord, go on walking in union with him, **7** being rooted and built up in

him[a] and being stabilized in the faith,[b] just as you were taught, and overflowing with thanksgiving.[c]

8 Look out that no one takes you captive* by means of the philosophy and empty deception[d] according to human tradition, according to the elementary things of the world and not according to Christ; **9** because it is in him that all the fullness of the divine quality dwells bodily.[e] **10** So you have acquired a fullness by means of him, the one who is the head of all government and authority.[f] **11** By your relationship with him, you were also circumcised with a circumcision performed without hands by stripping off the fleshly body,[g] by the circumcision that belongs to the Christ.[h] **12** For you were buried with him in his baptism,[i] and by your relationship with him you were also raised up[j] together through your faith in the powerful work of God, who raised him up from the dead.[k]

13 Furthermore, though you were dead in your trespasses and in the uncircumcised state of your flesh, God made you alive together with him.[l] He kindly forgave us all our trespasses[m] **14** and erased* the handwritten document[n] that consisted of decrees[o] and was in opposition to us.[p] He has taken it out of the way by nailing it to the torture stake.[#][q] **15** He has stripped the governments and the authorities bare and has publicly exhibited them as conquered,[r] leading them in a triumphal procession by means of it.*

16 Therefore, do not let anyone judge you about what you eat and drink[s] or about the

---

CHAP. 1
a Eph 3:5-7
  Eph 5:32
b Lu 8:10
  1Co 2:7
c Ro 16:25, 26
d Eph 3:8, 9
e Ro 8:18
f Eph 4:13
g Php 4:13

CHAP. 2
h Col 4:16
i 2Co 1:6
j Col 3:14
k 1Co 2:7
  Eph 3:5, 6
l 1Co 1:30
  1Co 2:16
m 1Co 14:40
n 1Co 15:58
  Heb 3:14

Second Col.
a Col 2:20
  Eph 3:17
b Mt 7:24, 25
c Eph 5:20
  1Th 5:18
d Eph 5:6
  Heb 13:9
e Col 1:19
f Eph 1:20, 21
  1Pe 3:22
g Ro 6:6
h Ro 2:29
  Php 3:3
i Ro 6:4
j Eph 2:6
  Col 3:1
k Ac 2:24
  Eph 1:19, 20
l Eph 2:1, 5
m Ac 2:38
n Ex 34:27
  De 31:24-26
  Heb 7:18
o Eph 2:14, 15
p Ro 7:10
  Ga 3:10
q Ga 3:13
  Heb 9:15
  1Pe 2:24
r 1Jo 5:4
  Re 3:21
s Ro 14:3, 17

1:26 *Or "past ages." See Glossary.
2:1 *Lit., "not seen my face in the flesh."
2:8 *Or "carries you off as his prey."
2:14 *Or "blotted out." #See Glossary.
2:15 *Or possibly, "him."

observance of a festival or of the new moon[a] or of a sabbath.[b] **17** Those things are a shadow of the things to come,[c] but the reality belongs to the Christ.[d] **18** Let no man deprive you of the prize[e] who takes delight in a false humility and a form of worship of the angels, "taking his stand on"* the things he has seen. He is actually puffed up without proper cause by his fleshly frame of mind, **19** and he is not holding fast to the head,[f] to the one through whom the whole body is supplied and harmoniously joined together by means of its joints and ligaments and made to grow with the growth that is from God.[g]

20 If you died together with Christ with respect to the elementary things of the world,[h] why do you live as if still part of the world by further subjecting yourselves to the decrees:[i] **21** "Do not handle, nor taste, nor touch," **22** referring to things that all perish with their use, according to the commands and teachings of men?[j] **23** Although those things have an appearance of wisdom in a self-imposed form of worship and a false humility, a harsh treatment of the body,[k] they are of no value in combating the satisfying of the flesh.

3 If, however, you were raised up with the Christ,[l] go on seeking the things above, where the Christ is seated at the right hand of God.[m] **2** Keep your minds fixed on the things above,[n] not on the things on the earth.[o] **3** For you died, and your life has been hidden with the Christ in union with God. **4** When the Christ, our life,[p] is made manifest, then you also will be made manifest with him in glory.[q]

2:18 *Quoted from pagan mystery (initiation) rites.

CHAP. 2
a Ps 81:3
b Ro 14:6
c Heb 8:5
  Heb 10:1
d Joh 14:6
  Heb 9:11, 12
e Php 3:14
f 1Co 1:22, 23
  Eph 2:21
  Eph 4:16
h Ga 4:3
  Col 2:8
i Eph 2:15
  Col 2:14
j Mt 15:9
k 1Ti 4:3

CHAP. 3
l Eph 2:6
m Ps 110:1
  1Pe 3:22
n Php 3:20
  Php 4:8
  1Pe 1:13
o 1Jo 2:15
p Joh 11:25
q 1Co 15:42, 43

Second Col.
a Mr 9:43
  Ga 5:24
b 1Co 6:18
  Eph 5:3
c 1Co 6:9-11
  Eph 2:3
  Tit 3:3
d 1Pe 2:1
e Eph 4:31
f Eph 5:3, 4
g Eph 4:25
  Re 21:8
h Eph 4:22
i Ro 12:2
  Eph 4:24
j Ge 1:26, 27
  1Pe 1:16
k Ga 3:28
l 1Pe 2:9
m Php 2:1, 2
n Ro 12:10
o Tit 3:2
p Eph 4:1, 2
  1Th 5:14
q Pr 19:11
  Eph 4:32
  1Pe 4:8
r Mt 18:15
s Mt 6:14
  Mr 11:25
t 1Jo 3:23
u 1Co 13:4-7
v Joh 14:27
  Php 4:7

---

5 Deaden, therefore, your body members[a] that are on the earth as respects sexual immorality,* uncleanness, uncontrolled sexual passion,[b] hurtful desire, and greediness, which is idolatry. **6** On account of those things the wrath of God is coming. **7** That is how you too used to conduct yourselves* in your former way of life.[#c] **8** But now you must put them all away from you: wrath, anger, badness,[d] abusive speech,[e] and obscene talk[f] out of your mouth. **9** Do not lie to one another.[g] Strip off the old personality*[h] with its practices, **10** and clothe yourselves with the new personality,[i] which through accurate knowledge is being made new according to the image of the One who created it,[j] **11** where there is neither Greek nor Jew, circumcision nor uncircumcision, foreigner, Scyth'i·an,* slave, or freeman; but Christ is all things and in all.[k]

12 Accordingly, as God's chosen ones,[l] holy and loved, clothe yourselves with the tender affections of compassion,[m] kindness, humility,*[n] mildness,[o] and patience.[p] **13** Continue putting up with one another and forgiving one another freely[q] even if anyone has a cause for complaint against another.[r] Just as Jehovah* freely forgave you, you must also do the same.[s] **14** But besides all these things, clothe yourselves with love,[t] for it is a perfect bond of union.[u]

15 Also, let the peace of the Christ rule in your hearts,*[v] for you were called to that peace in one body. And show yourselves

---

3:5 *Greek, por·nei'a. See Glossary. 3:7 *Or "used to walk." #Or "when you lived that way." 3:9 *Lit., "man." 3:11 *"Scythian" implied an uncivilized person. 3:12 *Or "lowliness of mind." 3:13 *See App. A5. 3:15 *Or "control your hearts."

thankful. **16** Let the word of the Christ reside in you richly in all wisdom. Keep on teaching and encouraging* one another with psalms,[a] praises to God, spiritual songs sung with gratitude,# singing in your hearts to Jehovah.△b **17** Whatever it is that you do in word or in deed, do everything in the name of the Lord Jesus, thanking God the Father through him.[c]

18 You wives, be in subjection to your husbands,[d] as it is becoming in the Lord. **19** You husbands, keep on loving your wives* and do not be bitterly angry* with them.[f] **20** You children, be obedient to your parents in everything,[g] for this is well-pleasing to the Lord. **21** You fathers, do not be exasperating* your children,[h] so that they do not become downhearted.# **22** You slaves, be obedient in everything to those who are your human* masters,[i] not only when they are watching, just to please men,# but with sincerity of heart, with fear of Jehovah.△ **23** Whatever you are doing, work at it whole-souled* as for Jehovah,△j and not for men, **24** for you know that it is from Jehovah△ you will receive the inheritance as a reward.[k] Slave for the Master, Christ. **25** Certainly the one who does wrong will be repaid for the wrong he has done,[l] and there is no partiality.[m]

4 You masters, treat your slaves in a righteous and fair way, knowing that you also have a Master in heaven.[n]

2 Persevere in prayer,[o] remaining awake in it with thanksgiving.[a] **3** At the same time, pray also for us,[b] that God may open a door for the word so that we can declare the sacred secret about the Christ, for which I am in prison bonds,[c] **4** and that I may proclaim it as clearly as I ought to.

5 Go on walking in wisdom toward those on the outside, making the best use of your time.*d **6** Let your words always be gracious, seasoned with salt,[e] so that you will know how you should answer each person.[f]

7 Tych′i·cus,[g] my beloved brother and faithful minister and fellow slave in the Lord, will tell you all the news about me. **8** I am sending him to you so that you will know how we are and that he may comfort your hearts. **9** He is coming along with O·nes′i·mus,[h] my faithful and beloved brother, who is from among you; they will tell you all the things happening here.

10 Ar·is·tar′chus,[i] my fellow captive, sends you his greetings, and so does Mark,[j] the cousin of Bar′na·bas (concerning whom you received instructions to welcome him[k] if he comes to you), **11** and Jesus who is called Justus, who are of those circumcised. Only these are my fellow workers for the Kingdom of God, and they have become a source of great comfort* to me. **12** Ep′a·phras,[l] a slave of Christ Jesus who is from among you, sends you his greetings. He is always exerting himself in your behalf in his prayers, so that you may finally stand complete and with firm conviction in all the will of God. **13** For I bear him witness that he makes great efforts in your behalf and in behalf of those in La·o·di·ce′a and Hi·e·rap′o·lis.

CHAP. 3
a 1Co 14:26
b Eph 5:19
c 1Co 10:31
d Eph 5:22 1Pe 3:1
e Eph 5:25 1Pe 3:7
f Eph 4:31
g Pr 6:20 Lu 2:51 Eph 6:1
h Eph 6:4
i Eph 6:5, 6 Tit 2:9 1Pe 2:18
j Lu 10:27 Ro 12:11
k Eph 6:8 1Pe 1:3, 4
l Ro 2:6 Ga 6:7
m Ro 2:11 1Pe 1:17

CHAP. 4
n Eph 6:9
o Lu 18:1 Ro 12:12 Eph 6:18

Second Col.
a Col 3:15 1Th 5:18
b Ro 15:30
c Eph 6:19, 20 Php 1:7
d Eph 5:15, 16
e Mt 5:13 Mr 9:50
f 1Pe 3:15
g Eph 6:21, 22
h Phm 10
i Ac 19:29 Ac 20:4 Ac 27:2
j Ac 12:12 Ac 15:37 Phm 23, 24
k Ro 15:7
l Col 1:7, 8

3:16 *Or "admonishing." #Or "graciousness." **3:16, 22-24** △See App. A5. **3:19** *Or "be harsh." **3:21** *Or "provoking; irritating." #Or "discouraged." **3:22** *Lit., "fleshly." #Lit., "not with acts of eye-service, as men pleasers." **3:23** *See Glossary, "Soul."

4:5 *Lit., "buying out the appointed time." **4:11** *Or "a strengthening aid."

14 Luke,[a] the beloved physician, sends you his greetings, and so does De'mas.[b] **15** Give my greetings to the brothers in La·o·di·ce'a and to Nym'pha and to the congregation at her house.[c] **16** And when this letter has been read among you, arrange for it also to be read[d] in the congregation of the La·o·di-ce'ans and for you also to read the one from La·o·di·ce'a. **17** Also, tell Ar·chip'pus:[a] "Pay attention to the ministry that you accepted in the Lord, in order to fulfill it."

18 Here is my greeting, Paul's, in my own hand.[b] Keep my prison bonds[c] in mind. The undeserved kindness be with you.

CHAP. 4
a Lu 1:3
　Ac 1:1
b Phm 23, 24
c Ro 16:5
　1Co 16:19
d 1Th 5:27

Second Col.
a Phm 1, 2
b 2Th 3:17
c Php 1:7
　Phm 9

THE FIRST TO THE
THESSALONIANS

OUTLINE OF CONTENTS

1 Paul, Sil·va'nus,*[a] and Timo-thy,[b] to the congregation of the Thes·sa·lo'ni·ans in union with God the Father and the Lord Jesus Christ:

May you have undeserved kindness and peace.

2 We always thank God when we mention all of you in our prayers,[c] **3** for we continually remember your faithful work, your loving labor, and your endurance because of your hope[d] in our Lord Jesus Christ in the presence of our God and Fa-ther. **4** For we know, brothers loved by God, his choosing of you, **5** because the good news we preach did not come to you with speech alone but also with power and with holy spirit and with strong conviction, just as you know what sort of men we became among you for your sakes. **6** And you became imitators of us[a] and of the Lord,[b] seeing that you accepted the word under much tribulation[c] with joy of holy spirit, **7** so that you became an example to all the believers in Mac·e·do'ni·a and in A·cha'ia.

CHAP. 1
a Ac 15:22
　1Pe 5:12

b Ac 16:1, 2

c 2Th 1:11, 12

d 1Pe 1:3, 4

Second Col.
a 1Co 11:1
　Php 3:17
　2Th 3:9

b 1Pe 2:21

c 1Th 2:14

1:1 * Also called Silas.

8 The fact is, not only has the word of Jehovah* sounded out from you in Mac·e·do'ni·a and A·cha'ia but your faith in God has spread abroad in every place,ᵃ so that we do not need to say anything. **9** For they themselves keep reporting about our first contact with you and how you turned to God from your idolsᵇ to slave for a living and true God, **10** and to wait for his Son from the heavens,ᶜ whom he raised up from the dead, namely, Jesus, who rescues us from the wrath that is coming.ᵈ

2 You yourselves surely know, brothers, that our visit to you has not been without results.ᵉ **2** For although we had first suffered and been insolently treated in Phi·lip'pi,ᶠ as you know, we mustered up boldness* by means of our God to tell you the good news of Godᵍ in the face of much opposition.ᵘ **3** For the exhortation we give does not spring from error or from uncleanness or with deceit, **4** but just as we have been approved by God to be entrusted with the good news, so we speak to please, not men, but God, who examines our hearts.ʰ **5** In fact, you know that we never used flattering speech or put on any false front with greedy motives;ⁱ God is witness! **6** Nor have we been seeking glory from men, either from you or from others, though we could be an expensive burden as apostles of Christ.ʲ **7** On the contrary, we became gentle in your midst, as when a nursing mother tenderly cares for* her own children. **8** So having tender affection for you, we were determined* to impart to you, not

only the good news of God but also our very selves,*ᵃ because you became so beloved to us.ᵇ

9 Surely you remember, brothers, our labor and toil. We were working night and day, so that we would not put an expensive burden on any one of you,ᶜ when we preached the good news of God to you. **10** You are witnesses, God is also, of how loyal and righteous and blameless we behaved toward you believers. **11** You well know that we kept exhorting and consoling you and bearing witness to each one of you,ᵈ just as a fatherᵉ does his children, **12** so that you would go on walking worthily of God,ᶠ who is calling you to his Kingdomᵍ and glory.ʰ

13 Indeed, that is why we also thank God unceasingly,ⁱ because when you received God's word, which you heard from us, you accepted it not as the word of men but, just as it truthfully is, as the word of God, which is also at work in you believers. **14** For you, brothers, became imitators of the congregations of God in union with Christ Jesus that are in Ju·de'a, because you suffered at the hands of your own countrymenʲ the same things that they also are suffering at the hands of the Jews, **15** who even killed the Lord Jesusᵏ and the prophets and persecuted us.ˡ Furthermore, they are not pleasing God, but are against the interests of all men, **16** as they try to prevent us from speaking to people of the nations so that these might be saved.ᵐ In this way they always fill up the measure of their sins. But his wrath has at last come upon them.ⁿ

17 But when we were separated from* you, brothers, for just a short time (in person, not

---

CHAP. 1
a 2Th 1:4

b 1Co 10:14
1Co 12:2
Ga 4:8
1Jo 5:21

c Ac 1:10, 11
Tit 2:13

d 1Th 5:2
2Pe 3:12

CHAP. 2
e Ac 17:1, 4

f Ac 16:12
Ac 16:22-24

g Ac 17:1, 2

h Pr 17:3
Jer 11:20

i Ac 20:33

j 2Co 11:9
2Th 3:8, 10

Second Col.
a Joh 15:13

b Joh 13:35

c Ac 18:3
Ac 20:34
2Co 11:9
2Th 3:8, 10

d Ac 20:31

e 1Co 4:15

f Eph 4:1
Col 1:10
1Pe 1:15

g Lu 22:28-30

h 1Pe 5:10

i 1Th 1:2, 3

j Ac 17:5

k Ac 2:22, 23
Ac 7:52

l Mt 23:34

m Lu 11:52
Ac 13:49, 50

n Ro 1:18

1:8 *See App. A5. **2:2** *Or "courage." ᵘOr possibly, "amid much struggling." **2:7** *Or "cherishes." **2:8** *Lit., "well-pleased."

2:8 *Or "souls." **2:17** *Or "bereaved of."

in our hearts), because of our strong desire, we made every effort to see you in person.* 18 For this reason we wanted to come to you, yes I, Paul, tried not just once but twice; yet Satan cut across our path. 19 For what is our hope or joy or crown of exultation before our Lord Jesus at his presence? Is it not in fact you? 20 You certainly are our glory and joy.

3 So when we could bear it no longer, we thought it best to stay on alone in Athens;[b] 2 and we sent Timothy,[c] our brother and God's minister* in the good news about the Christ, to make you firm# and comfort you regarding your faith, 3 so that no one might be shaken* by these tribulations. For you yourselves know that we cannot avoid suffering such things.#[d] 4 For when we were with you, we used to tell you in advance that we would suffer tribulation, and that is what has happened, just as you know.[e] 5 That is why, when I could bear it no longer, I sent to learn of your faithfulness,[f] in case somehow the Tempter[g] might have tempted you, and our labor might have turned out to be in vain.

6 But Timothy has just now come to us from you[h] and has given us the good news about your faithfulness and love, that you always continue to remember us fondly and that you long to see us in the same way as we also do you. 7 That is why, brothers, in all our distress* and tribulation, we have been comforted because of you and the faithfulness you demonstrate.[i]

8 Because we are revitalized* if you are standing firm in the Lord. 9 For how can we show our thanks to God concerning you in return for the great joy we feel before our God on your account? 10 Night and day we make supplications as earnestly as we can to see you in person* and to supply what is lacking in your faith.[a]

11 Now may our God and Father himself and our Lord Jesus make a way for us to come to you. 12 Moreover, may the Lord cause you to increase, yes, to abound in love for one another[b] and for all, just as we do for you, 13 so that he may make your hearts firm, blameless in holiness before our God[c] and Father at the presence of our Lord Jesus[d] with all his holy ones.

4 Finally, brothers, just as you received instruction from us on how you should walk in order to please God,[e] just as you are in fact walking, we request you and appeal to you by the Lord Jesus to keep doing it more fully. 2 For you know the instructions* we gave you through the Lord Jesus.

3 For this is the will of God, that you should be holy[f] and abstain from sexual immorality.*[g] 4 Each one of you should know how to control his own body*[h] in holiness[i] and honor, 5 not with greedy, uncontrolled sexual passion[j] like the nations have that do not know God.[k] 6 No one should go beyond proper limits and take advantage of his brother in this matter, because Jehovah* exacts punishment for all these things, just as we told you previously and also strongly warned you. 7 For God has

---

Cross references (center column):

CHAP. 2
a 1Th 5:23
   2Th 1:4

CHAP. 3
b Ac 17:15

c Ac 16:1, 2
   Ro 16:21
   1Co 16:10

d Ac 14:22
   1Co 4:9
   1Pe 2:21

e 1Th 2:14

f 1Th 3:2

g Mt 4:3
   2Co 11:3

h Ac 18:5

i 2Th 1:4

Second Col.
a 2Th 1:3

b 1Th 4:9
   2Th 1:3

c 1Co 1:8

d 1Th 2:19
   1Th 5:23
   2Th 2:1, 2

CHAP. 4
e Col 1:10
   1Pe 2:12

f Joh 17:19
   Eph 5:25-27
   2Th 2:13
   1Pe 1:15, 16

g Eph 5:3

h Col 3:5
   2Ti 2:22

i Ro 6:19

j 1Co 6:18
   Eph 5:5

k Ps 79:6
   Eph 4:17, 19
   1Pe 4:3

2:17 *Lit., "to see your face." 3:2 *Or possibly, "and God's fellow worker." #Or "strengthen you." 3:3 *Lit., "swayed." #Or "we are appointed to this." 3:7 *Lit., "necessity."

3:8 *Lit., "we live." 3:10 *Lit., "your face." 4:2 *Or "orders." 4:3 *Greek, *por·nei'a*. See Glossary. 4:4 *Lit., "vessel." 4:6 *See App. A5.

called us, not for uncleanness, but for holiness.[a] **8** So, then, the man who disregards this is disregarding, not man, but God,[b] who gives him his holy spirit.[c]

9 However, concerning brotherly love,[d] you do not need us to write to you, for you yourselves are taught by God to love one another.[e] **10** In fact, you are doing so toward all the brothers in all of Mac·e·do·ni·a. But we urge you, brothers, to go on doing so in fuller measure. **11** Make it your aim to live quietly[f] and to mind your own business[g] and to work with your hands,[h] just as we instructed you, **12** so that you may walk decently in the eyes of people outside[i] and not need anything.

13 Moreover, brothers, we do not want you to be ignorant* about those who are sleeping in death,[j] so that you may not sorrow as the rest do who have no hope.[k] **14** For if we have faith that Jesus died and rose again,[l] so too God will bring with him those who have fallen asleep in death through Jesus.[m] **15** For this is what we tell you by Jehovah's* word, that we the living who survive to the presence of the Lord will in no way precede those who have fallen asleep in death; **16** because the Lord himself will descend from heaven with a commanding call, with an archangel's[n] voice and with God's trumpet, and those who are dead in union with Christ will rise first.[o] **17** Afterward we the living who are surviving will, together with them, be caught away in clouds[p] to meet the Lord[q] in the air; and thus we will always be with the Lord.[r] **18** So keep comforting one another with these words.

5 Now as for the times and the seasons, brothers, you need nothing to be written to you. **2** For you yourselves know very well that Jehovah's* day[a] is coming exactly as a thief in the night.[b] **3** Whenever it is that they are saying, "Peace and security!" then sudden destruction is to be instantly on them,[c] just like birth pains on a pregnant woman, and they will by no means escape. **4** But you, brothers, are not in darkness, so that the day should overtake you as it would thieves, **5** for you are all sons of light and sons of day.[d] We belong neither to night nor to darkness.[e]

6 So, then, let us not sleep on as the rest do,[f] but let us stay awake[g] and keep our senses.[h] **7** For those who sleep, sleep at night, and those who get drunk are drunk at night.[i] **8** But as for us who belong to the day, let us keep our senses and put on the breastplate of faith and love and the hope of salvation as a helmet[j] **9** because God assigned us, not to wrath, but to the acquiring of salvation[k] through our Lord Jesus Christ. **10** He died for us,* so that whether we stay awake or are asleep,* we should live together with him.[m] **11** Therefore, keep encouraging* one another and building one another up,[n] just as you are in fact doing.

12 Now we request you, brothers, to show respect for those who are working hard among you and presiding over you in the Lord and admonishing you; **13** and to give them extraordinary consideration in love because of their work.[o] Be peaceable with one another.[p] **14** On the other hand, we

CHAP. 4

a Heb 12:14
 1Pe 1:15, 16
b Lu 6:18, 19
c 1Jo 3:24
d Ro 12:10
e Joh 13:34, 35
 1Pe 1:22
 1Jo 4:21
f 2Th 3:11, 12
g 1Pe 4:15
h 1Co 4:11, 12
 Eph 4:28
 2Th 3:10
 1Ti 5:8
i Ro 12:17
j Joh 11:11
 Ac 7:59, 60
 1Co 15:6
k 1Co 15:32
l Ro 14:9
m 1Co 15:22, 23
 Php 3:20, 21
 2Th 2:1
 Re 20:4
n Jude 9
o 1Co 15:51, 52
p Ac 1:9
q 2Th 2:1
r Joh 14:3
 Joh 17:24
 2Co 5:8
 Php 1:23
 Re 20:6

Second Col.

CHAP. 5

a Zep 1:14
b Mt 24:36
 2Pe 3:10
c Ps 37:10
 Jer 8:11
d Joh 12:36
 Ro 13:12
 Eph 5:8
e Joh 8:12
 Col 1:13
 1Pe 2:9
f Ro 13:11
g Mt 24:42
h 1Pe 5:8
i Ro 13:13
j Eph 6:14-17
k 2Th 2:13
l Ro 5:8
m 1Th 4:16, 17
n Ro 1:11, 12
 Ro 15:2
o Php 2:29, 30
 1Ti 5:17
 Heb 13:7
p Mr 9:50
 2Co 13:11

4:13 *Or "uninformed." 4:15; 5:2 *See App. A5.

5:10 *Or "asleep in death." 5:11 *Or "comforting."

urge you, brothers, to warn* the disorderly,[a] speak consolingly to those who are depressed,[#] support the weak, be patient toward all.[b] **15** See that no one repays injury for injury to anyone,[c] but always pursue what is good toward one another and to all others.[d]

16 Always be rejoicing.[e] **17** Pray constantly.[f] **18** Give thanks for everything.[g] This is God's will for you in Christ Jesus. **19** Do not put out the fire of the spirit.[h] **20** Do not treat prophecies with contempt.[i] **21** Make sure of all things;[j] hold fast to what is fine. **22** Abstain from every form of wickedness.[k]

5:14 *Or "admonish." #Or "those who are discouraged." Lit., "those of little soul."

23 May the God of peace himself sanctify you completely. And may the spirit and soul* and body of you brothers, sound in every respect, be preserved blameless at the presence of our Lord Jesus Christ.[a] **24** The one who is calling you is faithful, and he will surely do so.

25 Brothers, keep praying for us.[b]

26 Greet all the brothers with a holy kiss.

27 I am putting you under the solemn obligation by the Lord to have this letter read to all the brothers.[c]

28 The undeserved kindness of our Lord Jesus Christ be with you.

5:23 *Or "life." See Glossary.

CHAP. 5
a Le 19:17
2Ti 4:2
b 1Co 13:4
Ga 5:22
Eph 4:1, 2
Col 3:13
c Mt 5:39
d Ro 12:17, 19
e 2Co 6:4, 10
Php 4:4
f Lu 18:1
Ro 12:12
g Eph 5:20
Col 3:17
h Eph 4:30
i 1Co 14:1
j 1Jo 4:1
k Job 2:3

Second Col.
a 1Co 1:8
b Ro 15:30
c Col 4:16

THE SECOND TO THE

THESSALONIANS

---

1 Paul, Sil·va′nus,* and Timo·thy,[a] to the congregation of the Thes·sa·lo′ni·ans in union with God our Father and the Lord Jesus Christ:

2 May you have undeserved kindness and peace from God

1:1 *Also called Silas.

CHAP. 1
a 2Co 1:19

Second Col.
a 1Th 3:12
1Th 4:9, 10

the Father and the Lord Jesus Christ.

3 We are obligated always to give thanks to God for you, brothers. This is fitting, because your faith is growing exceedingly and the love of each and every one of you is increasing toward one another.[a] **4** As a result we ourselves take pride in you[a] among the congregations of God because of your endurance and faith in all your persecutions and the hardships* that you are suffering.[b] **5** This is a proof of the righteous judgment of God, leading to your being counted worthy of the Kingdom of God, for which you are indeed suffering.[c]

6 This takes into account that it is righteous on God's part to repay tribulation to those who make tribulation for you.[d] **7** But you who suffer tribulation will be given relief along with us at the revelation of the Lord Jesus[e] from heaven with his powerful angels[f] **8** in a flaming fire, as he brings vengeance on those who do not know God and those who do not obey the good news about our Lord Jesus.[g] **9** These very ones will undergo the judicial punishment of everlasting destruction[h] from before the Lord and from the glory of his strength, **10** at the time when he comes to be glorified in connection with his holy ones and to be regarded in that day with wonder among all those who exercised faith, because the witness we gave met with faith among you.

11 To that very end we always pray for you, that our God may count you worthy of his calling[i] and with his power perform completely all the good that he pleases and every work of faith. **12** This is so that the name of our Lord Jesus may be glorified in you and you in union with him, according to the undeserved kindness of our God and of the Lord Jesus Christ.

2 However, brothers, concerning the presence of our Lord Jesus Christ[j] and our being gathered together to him,[k]

we ask you **2** not to be quickly shaken from your reason nor to be alarmed either by an inspired statement*[a] or by a spoken message or by a letter appearing to be from us, to the effect that the day of Jehovah*[b] is here.

3 Let no one lead you astray* in any way, because it will not come unless the apostasy[c] comes first and the man of lawlessness[d] gets revealed, the son of destruction.[e] **4** He stands in opposition and exalts himself above every so-called god or object of worship,* so that he sits down in the temple of God, publicly showing himself to be a god. **5** Do you not remember that when I was still with you, I used to tell you these things?

6 And now you know what is acting as a restraint, so that he will be revealed in his own due time. **7** True, the mystery of this lawlessness is already at work,[f] but only until the one who is right now acting as a restraint is out of the way. **8** Then, indeed, the lawless one will be revealed, whom the Lord Jesus will do away with by the spirit of his mouth[g] and bring to nothing by the manifestation[h] of his presence. **9** But the lawless one's presence is by the operation of Satan[i] with every powerful work and lying signs and wonders*[j] **10** and every unrighteous deception[k] for those who are perishing, as a retribution because they did not accept the love of the truth in order that they might be saved. **11** That is why God lets a deluding influence mislead them so that they may come to believe the lie,[l] **12** in order that they all may be judged because they

---

CHAP. 1
a 1Th 2:19

b 1Th 1:6
1Th 2:14
1Pe 2:21

c Ac 14:22
Ro 8:17
2Ti 2:12

d Ro 12:19
Re 6:9, 10

e Lu 17:29, 30
1Pe 1:7

f Mr 8:38

g Ro 2:8

h 2Pe 3:7

i Ro 8:30

CHAP. 2
j Mt 24:3

k 1Th 4:17

Second Col.
a 1Jo 4:1

b Zep 1:14
2Pe 3:10

c 1Ti 4:1
2Ti 2:16-18
2Ti 4:3
2Pe 2:1
1Jo 2:18, 19

d Mt 7:15
Ac 20:29, 30

e 2Pe 2:1, 3

f Ac 20:29, 30
1Co 11:18, 19
1Jo 2:18

g Isa 11:4
Re 19:15

h 1Ti 6:13-15
2Ti 4:1, 8

i 2Co 11:3

j Mt 24:24

k Mt 24:11

l Mt 24:5
1Ti 4:1
2Ti 4:3, 4

1:4 *Or "tribulations." #Or "enduring."

2:2 *Or "by a spirit." See Glossary, "Spirit." #See App. A5. **2:3** *Or "seduce you." **2:4** *Or "reverence." **2:9** *Or "portents."

did not believe the truth but took pleasure in unrighteousness.

13 However, we are obligated always to thank God for you, brothers loved by Jehovah,* because from the beginning God selected you[a] for salvation by sanctifying you[b] with his spirit and by your faith in the truth. 14 He called you to this through the good news we declare, so that you may acquire the glory of our Lord Jesus Christ.[c] 15 So, then, brothers, stand firm[d] and maintain your hold on the traditions that you were taught,[e] whether it was by a spoken message or by a letter from us. 16 Moreover, may our Lord Jesus Christ himself and God our Father, who loved us[f] and gave everlasting comfort and good hope[g] by means of undeserved kindness, 17 comfort your hearts and make you firm* in every good deed and word.

3 Finally, brothers, carry on prayer for us,[h] that the word of Jehovah* may keep spreading rapidly[i] and being glorified, just as it is with you, 2 and that we may be rescued from harmful and wicked men,[j] for faith is not a possession of all people.[k] 3 But the Lord is faithful, and he will strengthen you and protect you from the wicked one. 4 Moreover, we have confidence in the Lord regarding you, that you are carrying out and will go on carrying out our instructions. 5 May the Lord continue to guide your hearts successfully to the love of God[l] and to the endurance[m] for the Christ.

6 Now we are giving you instructions, brothers, in the name of our Lord Jesus Christ, to withdraw from every brother

who is walking disorderly[a] and not according to the tradition* that you[n] received from us.[b] 7 For you yourselves know how you should imitate us,[c] because we did not behave in a disorderly way among you, 8 nor did we eat anyone's food free.*[d] On the contrary, by labor and toil we were working night and day so as not to impose an expensive burden on any one of you.[e] 9 Not that we do not have authority,[f] but we wanted to offer ourselves as an example for you to imitate.[g] 10 In fact, when we were with you, we used to give you this order: "If anyone does not want to work, neither let him eat."[h] 11 For we hear that some are walking disorderly among you,[i] not working at all, but meddling with what does not concern them.[j] 12 To such people we give the order and exhortation in the Lord Jesus Christ that they should work quietly and eat food they themselves earn.[k]

13 For your part, brothers, do not give up in doing good. 14 But if anyone is not obedient to our word through this letter, keep this one marked and stop associating with him,[l] so that he may become ashamed. 15 And yet do not consider him an enemy, but continue admonishing him[m] as a brother.

16 Now may the Lord of peace himself give you peace constantly in every way.[n] May the Lord be with all of you.

17 Here is my greeting, Paul's, in my own hand,[o] which is a sign in every letter; this is the way I write.

18 The undeserved kindness of our Lord Jesus Christ be with all of you.

CHAP. 2
a Joh 6:44
Ro 8:30
b Joh 17:17
1Co 6:11
1Th 4:7
c 1Pe 5:10
d 1Co 15:58
1Co 16:13
e 1Co 11:2
f 1Jo 4:10
g 1Pe 1:3, 4

CHAP. 3
h Ro 15:30
1Th 5:25
Heb 13:18
i Ac 19:20
1Th 1:8
j Isa 25:4
k Ac 28:24
Ro 10:16
l 1Jo 5:3
m Lu 21:19
Ro 5:3

Second Col.
a 1Th 5:14
b 1Co 11:2
2Th 2:15
2Th 3:14
c 1Co 4:16
1Th 1:6
d Ac 20:34
e Ac 18:3
1Co 9:14, 15
2Co 11:9
1Th 2:9
f Mt 10:9, 10
1Co 9:6, 7
g 1Co 11:1
Php 3:17
h 1Th 4:11, 12
1Ti 5:8
i 1Th 5:14
j 1Ti 5:13
1Pe 4:15
k Eph 4:28
l 2Th 3:6
m 1Th 5:14
n Joh 14:27
o 1Co 16:21
Col 4:18

2:13; 3:1 *See App. A5. 2:17 *Or "strengthen you."

3:6 *Or "instruction." #Or possibly, "they." 3:8 *Or "without paying."

THE FIRST TO
TIMOTHY

1

Paul, an apostle of Christ Jesus by the command of God our Savior and of Christ Jesus, our hope,[a] 2 to Timothy,*[b] a genuine child[c] in the faith:

May you have undeserved kindness and mercy and peace from God the Father and Christ Jesus our Lord.

3 Just as I encouraged you to stay in Eph′e·sus when I was about to go to Mac·e·do′ni·a, so I do now, in order for you to command certain ones not to teach different doctrine, 4 nor to pay attention to false stories[d] and to genealogies. Such things end up in nothing useful[e] but merely give rise to speculations rather than providing anything from God in connection with faith. 5 Really, the objective of this instruction* is love[f] out of a clean heart and out of a

good conscience and out of faith[a] without hypocrisy. 6 By deviating from these things, some have been turned aside to meaningless talk.[b] 7 They want to be teachers[c] of law, but they do not understand either the things they are saying or the things they insist on so strongly.

8 Now we know that the Law is fine if one applies it properly,* 9 recognizing that law is made, not for a righteous man, but for those who are lawless[d] and rebellious, ungodly and sinners, disloyal* and profane, murderers of fathers and murderers of mothers, manslayers, 10 sexually immoral people,* men who practice homosexuality,[#] kidnappers, liars, perjurers,[△] and

---

CHAP. 1
a 1Pe 1:3, 4

b Ac 16:1, 2
  Php 2:19, 20

c 1Co 4:17

d 1Ti 4:7
  2Ti 4:3, 4
  Tit 1:13, 14

e 1Ti 6:20
  2Ti 2:14

f Ro 13:8

Second Col.
a Ga 5:6

b 1Ti 6:20
  2Ti 2:16-18

c Jas 3:1

d Ga 3:19

1:2 *Meaning "One Who Honors God."
1:5 *Or "mandate; order."
1:8 *Lit., "lawfully." 1:9 *Or "lacking loyal love." 1:10 *See Glossary, "Sexual immorality." #Or "men who have sex with men." Lit., "men who lie with men." △Or "those who swear falsely."

1587

everything else that is in opposition to the wholesome* teaching[a] **11** according to the glorious good news of the happy God, with which I was entrusted.[b]

12 I am grateful to Christ Jesus our Lord, who imparted power to me, because he considered me faithful by assigning me to a ministry,[c] **13** although formerly I was a blasphemer and a persecutor and an insolent man.[d] Nevertheless, I was shown mercy because I acted in ignorance and with a lack of faith. **14** But the undeserved kindness of our Lord abounded exceedingly along with faith and the love that is in Christ Jesus. **15** This saying is trustworthy and deserving of full acceptance: Christ Jesus came into the world to save sinners.[e] Of these, I am foremost.[f] **16** Nevertheless, I was shown mercy so that by means of me as the foremost case, Christ Jesus might demonstrate all his patience, making me an example to those who are going to rest their faith on him for everlasting life.[g]

17 Now to the King of eternity,[h] incorruptible,[i] invisible,[j] the only God,[k] be honor and glory forever and ever. Amen.

18 This instruction* I entrust to you, my child Timothy, in harmony with the prophecies that were made about you, that by these you may go on waging the fine warfare,[l] **19** holding faith and a good conscience,[m] which some have thrust aside, resulting in the shipwreck of their faith. **20** Hy·me·nae′us[n] and Alexander are among these, and I have handed them over to Satan[o] so that they may be taught by discipline not to blaspheme.

2 First of all, then, I urge that supplications, prayers, intercessions, and thanksgiving be made concerning all sorts of men, **2** concerning kings and all those who are in high positions,*[a] so that we may go on leading a calm and quiet life with complete godly devotion and seriousness.[b] **3** This is fine and acceptable in the sight of our Savior, God,[c] **4** whose will is that all sorts of people should be saved[d] and come to an accurate knowledge of truth. **5** For there is one God,[e] and one mediator[f] between God and men,[g] a man, Christ Jesus,[h] **6** who gave himself a corresponding ransom for all*[i]—this is what is to be witnessed to in its own due time. **7** For the purpose of this witness[j] I was appointed a preacher and an apostle[k]—I am telling the truth, I am not lying—a teacher of nations[l] in the matter of faith and truth.

8 So I desire that in every place the men carry on prayer, lifting up loyal hands,[m] without anger[n] and debates.[o] **9** Likewise, the women should adorn themselves in appropriate* dress, with modesty and soundness of mind,*[#] not with styles of hair braiding and gold or pearls or very expensive clothing,[p] **10** but in the way that is proper for women professing devotion to God,[q] namely, through good works.

11 Let a woman learn in silence* with full submissiveness.[r] **12** I do not permit a woman to teach or to exercise authority over a man, but she is to remain silent.*[s] **13** For Adam was formed first, then Eve.[t] **14** Also, Adam was not deceived, but the woman was thoroughly deceived[u] and became a transgressor. **15** How-

---

CHAP. 1
a 2Ti 1:13
  Tit 1:7, 9
b Ga 2:7, 8
c Ac 9:15
  2Co 3:5, 6
d Ac 8:3
  Ac 9:1, 2
  Ga 1:13
  Php 3:5, 6
e Lu 5:32
  2Co 5:19
  1Jo 2:1, 2
f Ac 9:1, 2
  1Co 15:9
g Joh 6:40
  Joh 20:31
h Ps 10:16
  Ps 90:2
  Da 6:26
  Re 15:3
i Ro 1:23
j Col 1:15
k Isa 43:10
  1Co 8:4
l 2Ti 2:3
m 1Ti 1:5
n 2Ti 2:16-18
o 1Co 5:5, 11

Second Col.

CHAP. 2
a Mt 5:44
b Jer 29:7
c Jude 25
d Isa 45:22
  Ac 17:30
  Ro 5:18
  1Ti 4:10
e De 6:4
  Ro 3:30
f Heb 8:6
  Heb 9:15
g 1Co 11:25
h Ac 4:12
  Ro 5:15
  2Ti 1:9, 10
i Mt 20:28
  Mr 10:45
  Col 1:13, 14
j Ac 9:15
k Ga 2:7, 8
l Ga 1:15, 16
m Ps 141:2
n Jas 1:20
o Php 2:14
p 1Pe 3:3, 4
q Pr 31:30
r Eph 5:24
s 1Co 14:34
t Ge 2:18, 22
  1Co 11:8
u Ge 3:6, 13

1:10 *Or "healthful; beneficial." 1:18 *Or "mandate; order." 2:2 *Or "in positions of authority." 2:6 *Or "all sorts of people." 2:9 *Or "respectable." #Or "good judgment; sensibleness." 2:11 *Or "quietness; calmness." 2:12 *Or "remain calm; remain quiet."

ever, she will be kept safe through childbearing,[a] provided she* continues in faith and love and holiness along with soundness of mind.[#b]

3 This statement is trustworthy: If a man is reaching out to be an overseer,[c] he is desirous of a fine work. **2** The overseer should therefore be irreprehensible, a husband of one wife, moderate in habits, sound in mind,*[d] orderly, hospitable,[e] qualified to teach,[f] **3** not a drunkard,[g] not violent,* but reasonable,[h] not quarrelsome,[i] not a lover of money,[j] **4** a man presiding over* his own household in a fine manner, having his children in subjection with all seriousness[k] **5** (for if any man does not know how to preside over* his own household, how will he care for the congregation of God?), **6** not a newly converted man,[l] for fear that he might get puffed up with pride and fall into the judgment passed on the Devil. **7** Moreover, he should also have a fine testimony* from outsiders[m] so that he does not fall into reproach[#] and a snare of the Devil.

8 Ministerial servants should likewise be serious, not double-tongued,* not indulging in a lot of wine, not greedy of dishonest gain,[n] **9** holding the sacred secret of the faith with a clean conscience.[o]

10 Also, let these be tested as to fitness* first; then let them serve as ministers, as they are free from accusation.[p]

11 Women should likewise be serious, not slanderous,[q] moderate in habits, faithful in all things.[a]

12 Let ministerial servants be husbands of one wife, presiding in a fine manner over their children and their own households. **13** For the men who minister in a fine manner are acquiring for themselves a fine standing and great freeness of speech in the faith that is in Christ Jesus.

14 I am writing you these things, though I am hoping to come to you shortly, **15** but in case I am delayed, so that you may know how you ought to conduct yourself in God's household,[b] which is the congregation of the living God, a pillar and support of the truth. **16** Indeed, the sacred secret of this godly devotion is admittedly great: 'He was made manifest in flesh,[c] was declared righteous in spirit,[d] appeared to angels,[e] was preached about among nations,[f] was believed upon in the world,[g] was received up in glory.'

4 However, the inspired word* clearly says that in later times some will fall away from the faith, paying attention to misleading inspired statements[#h] and teachings of demons, **2** by means of the hypocrisy of men who speak lies,[i] whose conscience is seared as with a branding iron. **3** They forbid marriage[j] and command people to abstain from foods[k] that God created to be partaken of[l] with thanksgiving by those who have faith[m] and accurately know the truth. **4** For every creation of God is fine,[n] and nothing is to be rejected[o] if it is received with thanksgiving, **5** for it is sanctified through God's word and prayer over it.

6 By giving this counsel to the brothers, you will be a fine

CHAP. 2
a 1Ti 5:14
b 1Ti 2:9, 10

CHAP. 3
c Ac 20:28
  1Ti 1:5-9
d Ro 12:3
  1Pe 4:7
e Ac 28:7
  1Pe 4:9
f 1Ti 5:17
  2Ti 2:24
  Tit 1:7, 9
g Ro 13:13
h Php 4:5
  Jas 3:17
i Ro 12:18
  Jas 3:18
j Heb 13:5
  1Pe 5:2
k Eph 6:4
l 1Ti 5:22
m Ac 22:12
  1Th 4:11, 12
  Ac 6:3
  Tit 1:7
  1Pe 5:2
o 1Ti 1:5
  1Ti 1:18, 19
  2Ti 1:3
  1Pe 3:16
p 1Pe 2:12
q 1Ti 5:13

Second Col.
a Tit 2:3-5
b Heb 3:6
c Joh 1:14
  Php 2:7
d 1Pe 3:18
e 1Pe 3:19, 20
f Col 1:23
g Col 1:6

CHAP. 4
h 2Th 2:1, 2
  2Ti 4:3, 4
  2Pe 2:1
i Ac 20:29, 30
  2Ti 2:16
  2Pe 2:3
j 1Co 7:36
  1Co 9:5
k Ro 14:3
l Ge 9:3
m Ro 14:17
  1Co 10:25
n Ge 1:31
o Ac 10:15

2:15 *Lit., "they." #Or "good judgment; sensibleness." 3:2 *Or "have good judgment; be sensible." 3:3 *Or "a smiter." 3:4 *Or "managing." 3:5 *Or "manage." 3:7 *Or "a good reputation." #Or "disgrace." 3:8 *Or "not deceitful in speech." 3:10 *Or "tested as to whether they qualify."

4:1 *Lit., "the spirit." #Lit., "misleading spirits."

minister of Christ Jesus, one nourished with the words of the faith and of the fine teaching that you have followed closely.[a] **7** But reject irreverent false stories,[b] like those told by old women. On the other hand, train yourself with godly devotion as your aim. **8** For physical training* is beneficial for a little, but godly devotion is beneficial for all things, as it holds promise of the life now and the life that is to come.[c] **9** That statement is trustworthy and deserves full acceptance. **10** This is why we are working hard and exerting ourselves,[d] because we have rested our hope on a living God, who is a Savior[e] of all sorts of men,[f] especially of faithful ones.

11 Keep on giving these commands and teaching them. **12** Never let anyone look down on your youth. Instead, become an example to the faithful ones in speaking, in conduct, in love, in faith, in chasteness.* **13** Until I come, continue applying yourself to public reading,[g] to exhortation,* to teaching. **14** Do not neglect the gift in you that was given you through a prophecy when the body of elders laid their hands on you.[h] **15** Ponder over* these things; be absorbed in them, so that your advancement may be plainly seen by all people. **16** Pay constant attention to yourself and to your teaching.[i] Persevere in these things, for by doing this you will save both yourself and those who listen to you.[j]

5 Do not severely criticize an older man.[k] On the contrary, appeal to him as a father, to younger men as brothers, **2** to older women as mothers, to younger women as sisters, with all chasteness.

4:8 *Or "exercise." **4:12** *Or "purity." **4:13** *Or "encouragement." **4:15** *Or "Meditate on."

3 Give consideration to* widows who are truly widows.[#a] **4** But if any widow has children or grandchildren, let these learn first to practice godly devotion in their own household[b] and to repay their parents and grandparents what is due them,[c] for this is acceptable in God's sight.[d] **5** Now the woman who is truly a widow and left destitute has put her hope in God[e] and continues in supplications and prayers night and day.[f] **6** But the one who gives herself to sensual gratification is dead though she is living. **7** So keep on giving these instructions,* so that they may be irreprehensible. **8** Certainly if anyone does not provide for those who are his own, and especially for those who are members of his household, he has disowned the faith and is worse than a person without faith.[g]

9 A widow is to be put on the list if she is not less than 60 years old, was the wife of one husband, **10** having a reputation for fine works,[h] if she raised children,[i] if she practiced hospitality,[j] if she washed the feet of holy ones,[k] if she assisted the afflicted,[l] if she devoted herself to every good work.

11 On the other hand, do not put younger widows on the list, for when their sexual desires come between them and the Christ, they want to marry. **12** And they will incur judgment because they have abandoned their first expression of faith.* **13** At the same time they also learn to be unoccupied, going around from one house to another; yes, not only unoccupied but also gossipers and meddlers in other people's af-

---

CHAP. 4
a 2Ti 2:15

b 1Ti 6:20
Tit 1:13, 14

c Joh 17:3

d Lu 13:24

e Jude 25

f 1Ti 2:3, 4

g Col 4:16
1Th 5:27

h Ac 6:5, 6
Ac 13:2, 3
Ac 19:6
2Ti 1:6

i 2Ti 4:2

j 1Co 9:22

CHAP. 5
k Le 19:32

Second Col.
a 1Ti 5:16

b 1Ti 5:8

c Mt 15:4
Eph 6:2

d Jas 1:27

e 1Co 7:34

f Lu 2:36, 37

g Mt 15:4-6

h Ac 9:39

i 1Ti 2:15

j Heb 13:2
1Pe 4:9

k Joh 13:5, 14

l 1Ti 5:16
Jas 1:27

fairs,[a] talking about things they should not. **14** Therefore, I desire the younger widows to marry,[b] to bear children,[c] to manage a household, to give no opportunity to the opposer to criticize. **15** In fact, some have already been turned aside to follow Satan. **16** If any believing woman has relatives who are widows, let her assist them so that the congregation is not burdened. Then it can assist those who are truly widows.*[d]

17 Let the elders who preside in a fine way[e] be considered worthy of double honor,[f] especially those who work hard in speaking and teaching.[g] **18** For the scripture says, "You must not muzzle a bull when it is threshing out the grain,"[h] also, "The worker is worthy of his wages."[i] **19** Do not accept an accusation against an older man* except on the evidence of two or three witnesses.[j] **20** Reprove[k] before all onlookers those who practice sin,[l] as a warning to the rest.* **21** I solemnly charge you before God and Christ Jesus and the chosen angels to observe these instructions without any prejudice or partiality.[m]

22 Never lay your hands hastily on any man;*[n] neither become a sharer in the sins of others; keep yourself chaste.

23 Do not drink water any longer,* but take a little wine for the sake of your stomach and your frequent cases of sickness.

24 The sins of some men are publicly known, leading directly to judgment, but those of other men become evident later.[o]

25 In the same way also, the fine works are publicly known[a] and those that are otherwise cannot be kept hidden.[b]

6 Let those who are under the yoke of slavery keep on considering their owners worthy of full honor,[c] so that the name of God and the teaching may never be spoken of injuriously.[d] **2** Moreover, let those having believing owners not be disrespectful to them because they are brothers. Rather, they should serve more readily, because those receiving the benefit of their good service are believers and beloved.

Keep on teaching these things and giving these exhortations. **3** If any man teaches another doctrine and does not agree with the wholesome* instruction,[e] which is from our Lord Jesus Christ, nor with the teaching that is in harmony with godly devotion,[f] **4** he is puffed up with pride and does not understand anything.[g] He is obsessed* with arguments and debates about words.[h] These things give rise to envy, strife, slander,* wicked suspicions, **5** constant disputes about minor matters by men who are corrupted in mind[i] and deprived of the truth, thinking that godly devotion is a means of gain.[j] **6** To be sure, there is great gain in godly devotion[k] along with contentment.* **7** For we have brought nothing into the world, and neither can we carry anything out.[l] **8** So, having food* and clothing,* we will be content with these things.[m]

9 But those who are determined to be rich fall into temptation and a snare[n] and many

CHAP. 5
a 2Th 3:11
b 1Co 7:8, 9
c 1Ti 2:15
d De 15:11
  1Ti 5:5
  Jas 1:27
e 1Pe 5:2, 3
f Ac 28:10
  Heb 13:17
g 1Th 5:12
  Heb 13:7
h De 25:4
  1Co 9:7, 9
i Le 19:13
  Mt 10:9, 10
  Lu 10:7
  Ga 6:6
j De 19:15
  Mt 18:16
k Tit 1:7, 9
  Tit 1:13
  Ro 3:19
l 1Co 15:34
  1Jo 3:9
m Le 19:15
  Jas 3:17
n Ac 6:5, 6
  Ac 14:23
  1Ti 3:2, 6
  1Ti 4:14
o Jos 7:11
  Heb 4:13

Second Col.
a Mt 5:16
b 1Co 4:5

CHAP. 6
c Ro 13:7
  Eph 6:5
  Col 3:22
d 1Pe 2:13, 14
e 2Ti 1:13
f Tit 1:1, 2
g 1Co 8:2
h 2Ti 2:14
  Tit 1:10
  Tit 3:9
i 2Co 11:3
  2Ti 3:8
  Jude 10
j 1Pe 5:2
k 1Ti 4:8
l Job 1:21
  Ps 49:16, 17
m Pr 30:8, 9
  Heb 13:5
n Mt 13:22

5:16 *Or "widows who are truly in need"; that is, with no one to support them. 5:19 *Or "an elder." 5:20 *Lit., "that the rest may have fear." 5:22 *That is, do not appoint any man hastily. 5:23 *Or "Stop drinking just water."

6:3 *Or "healthful; beneficial." 6:4 *Or "has an unhealthy fascination." *Or "abusive speeches." 6:6 *Lit., "along with self-sufficiency." 6:8 *Or "sustenance." *Or "shelter." Lit., "covering."

senseless and harmful desires that plunge men into destruction and ruin.[a] **10** For the love of money is a root of all sorts of injurious things, and by reaching out for this love some have been led astray from the faith and have stabbed themselves all over with many pains.[b]

11 However, you, O man of God, flee from these things. But pursue righteousness, godly devotion, faith, love, endurance, and mildness.[c] **12** Fight the fine fight of the faith; get a firm hold on the everlasting life for which you were called and you offered the fine public declaration in front of many witnesses.

13 Before God, who preserves all things alive, and Christ Jesus, who as a witness made the fine public declaration before Pontius Pilate,[d] I give you orders **14** to observe the commandment in a spotless and irreprehensible way until the manifestation of our Lord Jesus Christ,[e] **15** which the happy and only Potentate will show in its own appointed times. He is the King of those who rule as kings and Lord of those who rule as lords,[f] **16** the one alone

having immortality,[a] who dwells in unapproachable light,[b] whom no man has seen or can see.[c] To him be honor and eternal might. Amen.

17 Instruct* those who are rich in the present system of things# not to be arrogant,△ and to place their hope, not on uncertain riches,[d] but on God, who richly provides us with all the things we enjoy.[e] **18** Tell them to work at good, to be rich in fine works, to be generous,* ready to share,[f] **19** safely treasuring up for themselves a fine foundation for the future,[g] so that they may get a firm hold on the real life.[h]

20 Timothy, guard what has been entrusted to you,[i] turning away from the empty speeches that violate what is holy and from the contradictions of the falsely called "knowledge."[j] **21** By making a show of such knowledge, some have deviated from the faith.

May the undeserved kindness be with you.

6:17 *Or "Order." #Or "present age." See Glossary. △Or "high-minded." 6:18 *Or "liberal."

THE SECOND TO

TIMOTHY

OUTLINE OF CONTENTS

---

1 Paul, an apostle of Christ Jesus by God's will according to the promise of the life that is through Christ Jesus,[a] **2** to Timothy, a beloved child:[b]

May you have undeserved kindness, mercy, and peace from God the Father and Christ Jesus our Lord.

3 I am grateful to God, to whom I am rendering sacred service as my forefathers did, and with a clean conscience, never ceasing to remember you in my supplications night and day. **4** As I remember your tears, I am longing to see you, so that I may get filled with joy. **5** For I recall your unhypocritical faith,[c] which dwelled first in your grandmother Lo'is and your mother Eu'nice, but which I am confident is also in you.

6 For this reason I remind you to stir up like a fire the gift of God that is in you through the laying on of my hands on you.[d] **7** For God did not give us a spirit of cowardice,[e] but one of power[f] and of love and of soundness of mind. **8** So do not become ashamed either of the witness about our Lord[g] or of me, a prisoner for his sake, but take your part in suffering adversity[h] for the good news by relying on the power of God.[i] **9** He saved us and called us with a holy calling,[j] not because of our works, but because of his own purpose and undeserved kindness.[k] This was given to us in connection with Christ Jesus before times long

ago, **10** but now it has been made clearly evident through the manifestation of our Savior, Christ Jesus,[a] who has abolished death[b] and has shed light on life[c] and incorruption[d] through the good news,[e] **11** for which I was appointed a preacher and an apostle and a teacher.[f]

12 This is why I am also suffering these things,[g] but I am not ashamed.[h] For I know the One whom I have believed, and I am confident that he is able to guard what I have laid up in trust with him until that day.[i] **13** Keep holding to the standard* of wholesome# words[j] that you heard from me with the faith and love that result from union with Christ Jesus. **14** Guard this fine trust by means of the holy spirit, which is dwelling in us.[k]

15 You know this, that all the men in the province of Asia[l] have turned away from me, including Phy·gel'us and Her·mog'e·nes. **16** May the Lord grant mercy to the household of On·e·siph'o·rus,[m] for he often refreshed me, and he did not become ashamed of my prison chains. **17** On the contrary, when he was in Rome, he diligently looked for me and found me. **18** May the Lord grant him to find mercy from Jehovah* in that day. And you well know all the services he rendered in Eph'e·sus.

CHAP. 1
a Joh 3:16
  Joh 6:40, 44
  1Pe 1:3, 4

b 1Co 4:17

c 1Ti 4:6

d 1Ti 4:14

e Ro 8:15
  1Th 2:2

f Lu 24:49
  Ac 1:8

g Ro 1:16

h Col 1:24
  2Ti 2:3

i Php 4:13
  Col 1:11

j Eph 1:4
  Heb 3:1

k Eph 2:5
  Eph 2:8
  Tit 3:5

Second Col.
a Joh 1:14
  Heb 2:9

b 1Co 15:54
  Heb 2:14

c Joh 5:24
  1Jo 1:2

d 1Pe 1:3, 4

e Ro 1:16

f Ac 9:15
  1Ti 2:7

g Ac 9:16
  Eph 3:1

h 2Co 4:2

i 2Ti 4:8

j 1Ti 6:3, 4
  Tit 1:7, 9

k Ro 8:11

l Ac 19:10

m 2Ti 4:19

1:13 *Or "outline." #Or "healthful; beneficial." **1:18** *See App. A5.

2 You, therefore, my child,[a] keep on acquiring power in the undeserved kindness that is in Christ Jesus; **2** and the things you heard from me that were supported by many witnesses,[b] these things entrust to faithful men, who, in turn, will be adequately qualified to teach others. **3** As a fine soldier[c] of Christ Jesus, take your part in suffering adversity.[d] **4** No man serving as a soldier involves himself* in the commercial businesses* of life, in order to gain the approval of the one who enrolled him as a soldier. **5** And even in the games, anyone who competes is not crowned unless he has competed according to the rules.[e] **6** The hardworking farmer must be the first to partake of the fruits. **7** Give constant thought to what I am saying; the Lord will give you understanding* in all things.

8 Remember that Jesus Christ was raised up from the dead[f] and was David's offspring,*[g] according to the good news I preach,[h] **9** for which I am suffering and being imprisoned as a criminal.[i] Nevertheless, the word of God is not bound.[j] **10** For this reason I go on enduring all things for the sake of the chosen ones,[k] so that they too may obtain the salvation that is through Christ Jesus, along with everlasting glory. **11** This saying is trustworthy: Certainly if we died together, we will also live together;[l] **12** if we go on enduring, we will also rule together as kings;[m] if we deny, he will also deny us;[n] **13** if we are unfaithful, he remains faithful, for he cannot deny himself.

14 Keep reminding them of these things, instructing* them before God not to fight about words, something of no usefulness at all because it harms* those listening. **15** Do your utmost to present yourself approved to God, a workman with nothing to be ashamed of, handling the word of the truth aright.[a] **16** But reject empty speeches that violate what is holy,[b] for they will lead to more and more ungodliness, **17** and their word will spread like gangrene. Hy·me·nae′us and Phi·le′tus are among them.[c] **18** These men have deviated from the truth, saying that the resurrection has already occurred,[d] and they are subverting the faith of some. **19** Despite that, the solid foundation of God remains standing, having this seal, "Jehovah* knows those who belong to him,"[e] and, "Let everyone calling on the name of Jehovah*[f] renounce unrighteousness."

20 Now in a large house there are utensils* not only of gold and silver but also of wood and earthenware, and some for an honorable use but others for a use lacking honor. **21** So if anyone keeps clear of the latter ones, he will be an instrument* for an honorable use, sanctified, useful to its owner, prepared for every good work. **22** So flee from youthful desires, but pursue righteousness, faith, love, peace, along with those who call on the Lord out of a clean heart.

23 Further, reject foolish and ignorant debates,[g] knowing that they produce fights. **24** For a slave of the Lord does not need to fight, but needs to be

CHAP. 2
a 1Ti 1:2
b 2Ti 3:14
c 1Ti 1:18
d 2Ti 1:8
e 1Co 9:25
f Ac 2:24
g Ac 2:29-32 Ro 1:3
h Ac 13:23
i Ac 9:16 Php 1:7
j Col 4:3, 4
k 2Co 1:6 Eph 3:13 Col 1:24
l Ro 6:5, 8
m Re 3:21 Re 20:4, 6
n Mt 10:33 Lu 12:9

Second Col.
a 2Ti 4:2
b 1Ti 4:7 1Ti 6:20
c 1Ti 1:20
d 1Co 15:12
e Nu 16:5
f Isa 26:13
g 1Ti 1:3, 4 1Ti 4:7 Tit 3:9

2:4 *Lit., "gets entangled." #Or possibly, "the everyday activities." **2:7** *Or "discernment." **2:8** *Lit., "of David's seed."

2:14 *Lit., "bearing thorough witness to." #Or "destroys; overturns." **2:19** *See App. A5. **2:20** *Or "vessels." **2:21** *Or "a utensil; a vessel."

gentle* toward all,[a] qualified to
teach, showing restraint when
wronged,[b] **25** instructing with
mildness those not favorably disposed.[c] Perhaps God may give
them repentance* leading to an
accurate knowledge of truth,[d]
26 and they may come to their
senses and escape from the
snare of the Devil, seeing that
they have been caught alive by
him to do his will.[e]

3 But know this, that in the
last days[f] critical times hard
to deal with will be here. **2** For
men will be lovers of themselves, lovers of money, boastful, haughty, blasphemers, disobedient to parents, unthankful,
disloyal, **3** having no natural
affection, not open to any agreement, slanderers, without self-
control, fierce, without love of
goodness, **4** betrayers, headstrong, puffed up with pride,
lovers of pleasures rather than
lovers of God, **5** having an appearance of godliness but proving false to its power;[g] and
from these turn away. **6** From
among these arise men who slyly
work their way into households
and captivate weak women loaded down with sins, led by various desires, **7** always learning
and yet never able to come to an
accurate knowledge of truth.

8 Now in the way that Jan′nes
and Jam′bres opposed Moses, so
these also go on opposing the
truth. Such men are completely
corrupted in mind, disapproved
as regards the faith. **9** Nevertheless, they will make no further progress, for their folly*
will be very plain to all, as it was
with those two men.[h] **10** But
you have closely followed my
teaching, my course of life,[i]
my purpose, my faith, my patience, my love, my endurance,
11 the persecutions and sufferings such as I experienced in Antioch,[a] in I·co′ni·um,[b] in Lys′tra.[c]
I endured these persecutions,
and the Lord rescued me from
them all.[d] **12** In fact, all those
desiring to live with godly devotion in association with Christ
Jesus will also be persecuted.[e]
13 But wicked men and impos-
tors will advance from bad to
worse, misleading and being misled.[f]

14 You, however, continue in
the things that you learned
and were persuaded to believe,[g]
knowing from whom you learned
them **15** and that from infancy[h]
you have known the holy writings,[i] which are able to make you
wise for salvation through faith
in Christ Jesus.[j] **16** All Scripture is inspired of God[k] and beneficial for teaching,[l] for reproving, for setting things straight,*
for disciplining in righteousness,[m] **17** so that the man of
God may be fully competent,
completely equipped for every
good work.

4 I solemnly charge you before
God and Christ Jesus, who
is to judge[n] the living and the
dead,[o] and by his manifestation[p]
and his Kingdom:[q] **2** Preach
the word;[r] be at it urgently in favorable times and difficult times;
reprove,[s] reprimand, exhort,
with all patience and art of
teaching.[t] **3** For there will be
a period of time when they
will not put up with the wholesome* teaching,[u] but according
to their own desires, they will
surround themselves with teachers to have their ears tickled.[#v]
4 They will turn away from listening to the truth and give attention to false stories. **5** You,
though, keep your senses in
all things, endure hardship,[w] do

CHAP. 2
a 1Th 2:7
b Mt 5:39
c Pr 15:1; Ga 6:1; Tit 3:2; 1Pe 3:15
d 1Ti 2:3, 4
e Joh 13:27; Ac 5:3; 1Ti 1:20

CHAP. 3
f Mt 24:3; 1Ti 4:1; 2Pe 3:3; Jude 17, 18
g Mt 7:15; Mt 7:22, 23
h Ex 7:11, 12; Ex 9:11
i 1Co 4:17; 2Ti 1:13

Second Col.
a Ac 13:50
b Ac 14:1, 5, 6
c Ac 14:19
d 2Co 1:10
e Mt 16:24; Joh 15:20; Ac 14:22
f 2Th 2:11; 1Ti 4:1
g 2Ti 1:13
h Pr 22:6
i Ac 16:1, 2
j Joh 5:39
k Joh 14:26; 2Pe 1:21
l Ro 15:4
m 1Co 10:11

CHAP. 4
n Joh 5:22; Ac 17:31; 2Co 5:10
o Joh 5:28, 29; Ac 10:42
p 1Ti 6:14, 15; 1Pe 5:4
q Re 11:15; Re 12:10
r 2Ti 2:15
s 1Ti 5:20; Tit 1:7, 9; Tit 1:13; Tit 2:15
t 2Ti 2:24, 25
u 1Ti 1:9, 10
v 1Ti 4:1
w 2Ti 1:8; 2Ti 2:3

2:24 *Or "tactful." **2:25** *Or "a change of mind." **3:9** *Or "foolishness."

3:16 *Or "correcting." **4:3** *Or "healthful; beneficial." #Or "to tell them what they want to hear."

the work of an evangelizer,* fully accomplish your ministry.[a]

6 For I am already being poured out like a drink offering,[b] and the time for my releasing[c] is imminent. **7** I have fought the fine fight,[d] I have run the race to the finish,[e] I have observed the faith. **8** From this time on, there is reserved for me the crown of righteousness,[f] which the Lord, the righteous judge,[g] will give me as a reward in that day,[h] yet not to me only, but also to all those who have loved his manifestation.

9 Do your utmost to come to me shortly. **10** For De'mas[i] has forsaken me because he loved the present system of things,* and he has gone to Thes·sa·lo·ni'ca, Cres'cens to Ga·la'ti·a, Ti·tus to Dal·ma'tia. **11** Only Luke is with me. Bring Mark along with you, for he is helpful to me in the ministry. **12** But I have sent Tych'i·cus[j] off to Eph'e·sus. **13** When you come, bring the cloak I left at Tro'as with Car'pus, and the scrolls, especially the parchments.*

14 Alexander the copper-

smith did me a great deal of harm. Jehovah* will repay him according to his deeds.[a] **15** You too should be on guard against him, for he opposed our message to an excessive degree.

16 In my first defense no one came to my side, but they all forsook me—may they not be held accountable. **17** But the Lord stood near me and infused power into me, so that through me the preaching might be fully accomplished and all the nations might hear it;[b] and I was rescued from the lion's mouth.[c] **18** The Lord will rescue me from every wicked work and will save me for his heavenly Kingdom.[d] To him be the glory forever and ever. Amen.

19 Give my greetings to Pris'-ca and Aq'ui·la[e] and the household of On·e·siph'o·rus.[f]

20 E·ras'tus[g] stayed in Corinth, but I left Troph'i·mus[h] sick at Mi·le'tus. **21** Do your utmost to arrive before winter.

Eu·bu'lus sends you his greetings, and so do Pu'dens and Li'nus and Clau'di·a and all the brothers.

22 The Lord be with the spirit you show. His undeserved kindness be with you.

CHAP. 4

a Ro 15:19
Col 1:25

b Nu 28:6, 7

c Php 1:23

d 1Co 9:26
1Ti 6:12

e Php 3:14

f 1Co 9:25
Jas 1:12

g Joh 5:22

h 1Pe 5:4
Re 2:10

i Col 4:14
Phm 23, 24

j Eph 6:21
Col 4:7

Second Col.

a Ps 28:4
Ps 62:12
Pr 24:12

b Ac 9:15

c Ps 22:21

d Re 20:4

e Ro 16:3

f 2Ti 1:16

g Ac 19:22

h Ac 21:29

4:5 *Or "keep preaching the good news." **4:10** *Or "present age." See Glossary. **4:13** *That is, the leather scrolls.

4:14 *See App. A5.

TO

TITUS

OUTLINE OF CONTENTS

1 Paul, a slave of God and an apostle of Jesus Christ according to the faith of God's chosen ones and the accurate knowledge of the truth that is according to godly devotion **2** and is based on a hope of the everlasting life[a] that God, who cannot lie,[b] promised long ago; **3** but in his own due time, he made his word known through the preaching entrusted to me[c] according to the command of our Savior, God; **4** to Titus, a genuine child according to the faith we share:

May you have undeserved kindness and peace from God the Father and Christ Jesus our Savior.

5 I left you in Crete so that you would correct the things that were defective* and make appointments of elders in city after city, as I instructed you: **6** if there is any man free from accusation, a husband of one wife, having believing children who are not accused of debauchery* or rebelliousness.[d] **7** For as God's steward, an overseer must be free from accusation, not self-willed,[e] not quick-tempered,[f] not a drunkard, not violent,* not greedy of dishonest gain, **8** but hospitable,[g] a lover of goodness, sound in mind,*[h] righteous, loyal,[i] self-controlled,[j] **9** holding firmly to the faithful word* as respects his art of teaching,[k] so that he may be able both to encourage# by the teaching that is wholesome△[l] and to reprove[m] those who contradict.

10 For there are many rebellious men, profitless talkers, and deceivers, especially those who adhere to the circumcision.[n] **11** It is necessary to shut their mouths, because these very men keep on subverting entire households by teaching things they should not for the sake of dishonest gain. **12** A certain one of them, their own prophet, said: "Cre′tans are always liars, injurious wild beasts, idle gluttons."

13 This witness is true. For this very reason, keep on reproving them with severity so that they may be healthy in the faith, **14** paying no attention to Jewish fables and commandments of men who turn away from the truth. **15** All things are clean to clean people;[a] but to those who are defiled and faithless, nothing is clean, for both their minds and their consciences are defiled.[b] **16** They publicly declare that they know God, but they disown him by their works,[c] because they are detestable and disobedient and not approved for good work of any sort.

2 You, however, keep on speaking what is consistent with wholesome△ teaching.[d] **2** Let the older men be moderate in habits, serious, sound in mind, healthy in faith, in love, in endurance. **3** Likewise, let the older women be reverent in behavior, not slanderous, not enslaved to a lot of wine, teachers of what is good, **4** so that they may advise* the younger women to love their husbands, to love their children, **5** to be sound in mind, chaste, working at home,* good, subjecting themselves to their own husbands,[e] so that the word of God may not be spoken of abusively.

6 Likewise, keep on urging the younger men to be sound in mind,[f] **7** showing yourself to be an example of fine works in every way. Teach what is pure* with all seriousness,[g] **8** using

---

CHAP. 1
a Ro 6:23
b Nu 23:19
c Ac 9:15
d 1Ti 3:2-7
e 2Pe 2:10
f Jas 1:19
g 1Pe 4:9
h Ro 12:3
  1Ti 3:2
i 1Ti 2:8
j 2Ti 2:24
  Jas 3:13
k 1Ti 4:16
  1Ti 6:3, 4
l 1Ti 1:9, 10
  2Ti 1:13
m 1Ti 5:20
  2Ti 4:2
  Tit 1:13
  Re 3:19
n Ac 15:1

Second Col.
a Ro 14:14
b Mt 15:11
c Mt 7:16-18

CHAP. 2
d 1Ti 4:16
  2Ti 1:13
e 1Co 14:34, 35
  1Pe 3:1, 2
f Ro 12:3
  1Pe 5:5
g 2Ti 2:15

1:5 *Or "deficient." 1:6 *Or "wildness." 1:7 *Or "a smiter." 1:8 *Or "having good judgment; sensible." 1:9 *Or "the trustworthy message." #Or "exhort." 1:9; 2:1 △Or "healthful; beneficial."

2:4 *Or "recall to their senses; train." 2:5 *Or "caring for their homes." 2:7 *Or possibly, "Teach with purity."

wholesome* speech that cannot be criticized,[a] so that those who oppose may be put to shame, having nothing negative[#] to say about us.[b] 9 Let slaves be in subjection to their owners in all things,[c] trying to please them, not talking back, 10 not stealing from them,[d] but showing complete trustworthiness, so that in every way they may adorn the teaching of our Savior, God.[e]

11 For the undeserved kindness of God has been manifested, bringing salvation to all sorts of people.[f] 12 It trains us to reject ungodliness and worldly desires[g] and to live with soundness of mind and righteousness and godly devotion amid this present system of things,*[h] 13 while we wait for the happy hope[i] and glorious manifestation of the great God and of our Savior, Jesus Christ, 14 who gave himself for us[j] to set us free*[k] from every sort of lawlessness and to cleanse for himself a people who are his own special possession, zealous for fine works.[l]

15 Keep on speaking these things and exhorting* and reproving with full authority.[m] Do not let anyone look down on you.

3 Continue reminding them to be in subjection to and to be obedient to governments and authorities,[n] to be ready for every good work, 2 to speak injuriously of no one, not to be quarrelsome, but to be reasonable,[o] displaying all mildness toward all men.[p] 3 For we too were once senseless, disobedient, led astray, being slaves to various desires and pleasures, carrying on in badness and envy, detestable, hating one another.

4 However, when the kindness of our Savior, God,[q] and his love for mankind were manifested 5 (not because of any righteous works we had done,[a] but because of his own mercy),[b] he saved us by means of the bath that brought us to life[c] and by making us new by holy spirit.[d] 6 He poured this spirit out richly* on us through Jesus Christ our Savior,[e] 7 so that after being declared righteous through the undeserved kindness of that one,[f] we might become heirs[g] according to a hope of everlasting life.[h]

8 These words are trustworthy, and I want you to keep stressing these matters, so that those who have believed God may keep their minds focused on maintaining fine works. These things are fine and beneficial to men.

9 But have nothing to do with foolish arguments and genealogies and disputes and fights over the Law, for they are unprofitable and futile.[i] 10 As for a man who promotes a sect,[j] reject him[k] after a first and a second admonition,*[l] 11 knowing that such a man has deviated from the way and is sinning and is self-condemned.

12 When I send Ar'te·mas or Tych'i·cus[m] to you, do your utmost to come to me at Ni·cop'o·lis, for that is where I have decided to spend the winter. 13 Carefully supply Ze'nas, who is versed in the Law, and A·pol'los so that they may lack nothing for their trip.[n] 14 But let our people also learn to maintain fine works so as to help in cases of urgent need,[o] so that they may not be unproductive.*[p]

15 All those with me send you their greetings. Give my greetings to those who have affection for us in the faith.

May the undeserved kindness be with all of you.

CHAP. 2

a Col 3:8
b 1Pe 2:15
c Eph 6:5
  1Ti 6:1
  1Pe 2:18
d Eph 4:28
e Mt 5:16
  f Ro 5:18
g 1Jo 2:16
h Ro 12:2
i 1Pe 1:13
j Mt 20:28
  1Ti 2:5, 6
k Eph 1:7
  Col 1:13, 14
l Eph 2:10
  Heb 9:14
m 2Ti 4:2

CHAP. 3

n Mr 12:17
  Ro 13:1
  1Pe 2:13, 14
o Php 4:5
  Jas 3:17
p Pr 15:1
  Ga 6:1
  Eph 4:1, 2
  1Ti 6:11
  2Ti 2:24, 25
  1Pe 3:15
q Lu 6:35
  Ro 2:4
  Eph 4:32

Second Col.

a De 9:5
  Ro 3:10
  Ga 3:21
b Ro 5:15, 21
  Ro 6:23
c Ro 5:18
d Joh 3:5
  Ro 8:23
  2Co 5:17
e Ac 2:33
f Ro 3:24
  Ga 2:15, 16
g Ro 8:17
h Ro 6:23
i 1Ti 1:3, 4
  1Ti 6:3-5
j 1Co 11:19
  Re 2:6
k Ro 16:17
  2Jo 10
l 2Ti 4:2
m Ac 20:4
  Eph 6:21
  2Ti 4:12
n 1Co 9:14
  Ga 6:6
  Heb 13:16
o 1Co 9:11
p Col 1:10

2:8 *Or "healthful; beneficial." #Or "vile." 2:12 *Or "this present age." See Glossary. 2:14 *Lit., "to ransom us; to redeem us." 2:15 *Or "encouraging."

3:6 *Or "generously." 3:10 *Or "warning." 3:14 *Lit., "unfruitful."

PHILEMON

OUTLINE OF CONTENTS

1 Paul, a prisoner[a] for the sake of Christ Jesus, and Timothy[b] our brother, to Phi·le′mon our beloved fellow worker, **2** and to Ap′phi·a our sister, and to Ar·chip′pus[c] our fellow soldier, and to the congregation that is in your house:[d]

3 May you have undeserved kindness and peace from God our Father and the Lord Jesus Christ.

4 I always thank my God when I mention you in my prayers,[e] **5** as I keep hearing of your faith and the love that you have for* the Lord Jesus and for* all the holy ones. **6** I pray that your sharing in the faith may move you to acknowledge every good thing that we have through Christ. **7** For I received much joy and comfort on hearing of your love, because the hearts* of the holy ones have been refreshed through you, brother.

8 For this very reason, though I have great freeness of speech in connection with Christ to order you to do what is proper, **9** I would rather appeal to you on the basis of love, seeing that I am Paul an older man, yes, now also a prisoner for the sake of Christ Jesus. **10** I am appealing to you for my child, whose father I became[a] while in prison,* O·nes′i·mus.[b] **11** He was formerly useless to you, but now he is useful to you and to me. **12** I am sending him back to you, yes him, my very own heart.*

13 I would like to keep him here for myself so that he might take your place in ministering to me during my imprisonment for the sake of the good news.[c] **14** But I do not want to do anything without your consent, so that your good deed may be done, not under compulsion, but of your own free will.[d] **15** Perhaps this is really why he broke away for a short while,* so that you may have him back forever, **16** no longer as a slave,[e] but as more than a slave, as a brother who is beloved,[f] especially so to me, but how much more so to you, both in the flesh and in the Lord. **17** So if you consider me a friend,* receive him kindly the same way you would me. **18** Moreover, if he did you any wrong or owes you anything, charge it to my account. **19** I, Paul, am writing with my own hand: I will pay it back—not to mention that you owe me even your own self. **20** Yes, brother,

---

a Eph 4:1

b Ac 16:1, 2
Heb 13:23

c Col 4:17

d Ro 16:5
1Co 16:19

e Eph 1:15, 16
1Th 1:2

Second Col.
a 1Co 4:15

b Col 4:9

c Eph 6:19, 20
Php 1:7

d 2Co 9:7

e 1Co 7:22

f 1Ti 6:2

---

5 *Or "toward." **7** *Or "tender affections." **10** *Lit., "in the bonds." **12** *Or "my tender affections." **15** *Lit., "an hour." **17** *Lit., "a sharer."

may I receive this assistance from you in connection with the Lord; refresh my heart* in connection with Christ.

21 I am confident that you will comply, so I am writing you, knowing that you will do even more than what I say. **22** But along with that, also prepare a place for me to stay, for I am hoping that through your prayers I will be given back to you.*ᵃ

23 Sending you greetings is Ep'a·phras,ᵇ my fellow captive in union with Christ Jesus, **24** also Mark, Ar·is·tar'chus,ᶜ De'mas,ᵈ and Luke,ᵉ my fellow workers.

25 The undeserved kindness of the Lord Jesus Christ be with the spirit you show.

Second Col.
ᵃ Php 2:24

ᵇ Col 1:7
  Col 4:12, 13

ᶜ Ac 19:29
  Ac 27:2
  Col 4:10

ᵈ 2Ti 4:10

ᵉ Col 4:14

---

20 *Or "tender affections."

22 *Or "set free for you."

TO THE
HEBREWS

OUTLINE OF CONTENTS

1 Long ago God spoke to our forefathers by means of the prophets on many occasions and in many ways.[a] **2** Now at the end of these days he has spoken to us by means of a Son,[b] whom he appointed heir of all things,[c] and through whom he made the systems of things.*[d] **3** He is the reflection of God's glory[e] and the exact representation of his very being,[f] and he sustains all things by the word of his power. And after he had made a purification for our sins,[g] he sat down at the right hand of the Majesty on high.[h] **4** So he has become better than the angels[i] to the extent that he has inherited a name more excellent than theirs.[j]

5 For example, to which one of the angels did God ever say: "You are my son; today I have become your father"?[k] And again: "I will become his father, and he will become my son"?[l] **6** But when he again brings his Firstborn[m] into the inhabited earth, he says: "And let all of God's angels do obeisance to him."*

7 Also, he says about the angels: "He makes his angels spirits, and his ministers*[n] a flame of fire."[o] **8** But about the Son, he says: "God is your throne[p] forever and ever, and the scepter of your Kingdom is the scepter of uprightness.* **9** You loved righteousness, and you hated lawlessness. That is why God, your God, anointed you[a] with the oil of exultation more than your companions."[b] **10** And: "At the beginning, O Lord, you laid the foundations of the earth, and the heavens are the works of your hands. **11** They will perish, but you will remain; and just like a garment, they will all wear out, **12** and you will wrap them up just as a cloak, as a garment, and they will be changed. But you are the same, and your years will never come to an end."[c]

13 But about which of the angels has he ever said: "Sit at my right hand until I place your enemies as a stool for your feet"?[d] **14** Are they not all spirits for holy service,*[e] sent out to minister for those who are going to inherit salvation?

2 That is why it is necessary for us to pay more than the usual attention to the things we have heard,[f] so that we never drift away.[g] **2** For if the word spoken through angels[h] proved to be sure, and every transgression and disobedient act received a punishment in harmony with justice,[i] **3** how will we escape if we have neglected so great a salvation?[j] For it began to be spoken through our Lord[k]

CHAP. 1
a Ex 24:3
  Nu 12:8
  Jer 7:25
b Mt 17:5
c Ps 2:8
d Joh 1:3
  1Co 8:6
  Col 1:16
e Joh 1:14
  Joh 17:5
f Col 1:15
g Heb 9:26
h Ps 110:1
  Ac 2:32, 33
  Ac 7:55
i Eph 1:20, 21
  1Pe 3:22
j Ac 4:12
  Php 2:9, 10
k Ps 2:7
l 2Sa 7:14
  Mr 1:11
  Lu 9:35
  2Pe 1:17
m Joh 1:14
  Ro 8:29
  Col 1:15
n Ps 91:11
  Lu 22:43
o Ps 104:4
p Mt 28:18
  Re 3:21

Second Col.
a Isa 61:1
  Lu 3:21, 22
  Lu 4:18
b Ps 45:6, 7
c Ps 102:25-27
d Ps 110:1
  Mt 22:44
e Ps 34:7
  Ps 91:11
  Ac 5:18, 19

CHAP. 2
f Lu 8:15
g Ps 73:2
  Heb 3:12
  2Pe 3:17
h Ga 3:19
i De 4:3
  Jude 5
j Heb 10:28,
  29
k Mr 1:14

1:2 *Or "the ages." See Glossary. **1:6** *Or "bow down to him." **1:7** *Or "public servants."

1:8 *Or "justice." **1:14** *Or "for public service."

and was verified for us by those who heard him, **4** while God joined in bearing witness with signs and wonders* and various powerful works[a] and with the holy spirit distributed according to his will.[b]

5 For it is not to angels that he has subjected the inhabited earth to come,[c] about which we are speaking. **6** But in one place a certain witness said: "What is man that you keep him in mind, or a son of man that you take care of him?[d] **7** You made him a little lower than angels; you crowned him with glory and honor, and appointed him over the works of your hands. **8** All things you subjected under his feet."[e] By subjecting all things to him,[f] God left nothing that is not subject to him.[g] Now, though, we do not yet see all things in subjection to him.[h] **9** But we do see Jesus, who was made a little lower than angels,[i] now crowned with glory and honor for having suffered death,[j] so that by God's undeserved kindness he might taste death for everyone.[k]

10 For it was fitting that the one for whom and through whom all things exist, in bringing many sons to glory,[l] should make the Chief Agent of their salvation[m] perfect through sufferings.[n] **11** For both the one who is sanctifying and those who are being sanctified[o] all stem from one,[p] and for this reason he is not ashamed to call them brothers,[q] **12** as he says: "I will declare your name to my brothers; in the midst of the congregation I will praise you with song."[r] **13** And again: "I will put my trust in him."[s] And again: "Look! I and the young children, whom Jehovah* gave me."[t]

14 Therefore, since the "young children" are sharers of blood and flesh, he also similarly shared in the same things,[a] so that through his death he might bring to nothing the one having the means to cause death,[b] that is, the Devil,[c] **15** and that he might set free* all those who were held in slavery all their lives by their fear of death.[d] **16** For it is not really angels he is assisting, but he is assisting Abraham's offspring.*[e] **17** Consequently, he had to become like his "brothers" in all respects,[f] so that he could become a merciful and faithful high priest in things relating to God, in order to offer a propitiatory sacrifice*[g] for the sins of the people.[h] **18** Since he himself has suffered when being put to the test,[i] he is able to come to the aid of those who are being put to the test.[j]

3 Consequently, holy brothers, partakers of the heavenly calling,*[k] consider the apostle and high priest whom we acknowledge#—Jesus.[l] **2** He was faithful to the One who appointed him,[m] just as Moses also was in all the house of that One.[n] **3** For he* is counted worthy of more glory[o] than Moses, since the one who constructs a house has more honor than the house itself. **4** Of course, every house is constructed by someone, but the one who constructed all things is God. **5** Now Moses was faithful as an attendant in all the house of that One as a testimony* of the things that were to be spoken afterward, **6** but Christ was faithful as a son[p] over God's house. We are His house[q] if, in-

2:4 *Or "portents." 2:13 *See App. A5.

2:15 *Or "emancipate." 2:16 *Lit., "seed." 2:17 *Or "to offer an atoning sacrifice; to make atonement." 3:1 *Or "invitation." #Or "confess." 3:3 *That is, Jesus. 3:5 *Or "witness."

deed, we hold on firmly to our freeness of speech and the hope of which we boast down to the end.

7 Therefore, just as the holy spirit says,[a] "Today if you listen to his voice, **8** do not harden your hearts as on the occasion of provoking to bitter anger, as in the day of testing in the wilderness,[b] **9** where your forefathers put me to the test and tried me, despite seeing my works for 40 years.[c] **10** This is why I became disgusted with this generation and said: 'They always go astray in their hearts, and they have not come to know my ways.' **11** So I swore in my anger: 'They will not enter into my rest.'"[d]

12 Beware, brothers, for fear there should ever develop in any one of you a wicked heart lacking faith by drawing away from the living God;[e] **13** but keep on encouraging one another each day, as long as it is called "Today,"[f] so that none of you should become hardened by the deceptive power of sin. **14** For we actually become partakers of* the Christ only if we hold firmly down to the end the confidence we had at the beginning.[g] **15** As it is said, "Today if you listen to his voice, do not harden your hearts as on the occasion of provoking to bitter anger."[h]

16 For who heard and yet provoked him to bitter anger? Was it not, in fact, all those who went out of Egypt under Moses?[i] **17** Moreover, with whom did God become disgusted for 40 years?[j] Was it not with those who sinned, whose dead bodies fell in the wilderness?[k] **18** And to whom did he swear that they would not enter into his rest? Was it not to those who acted disobediently? **19** So we see

3:14 *Or "have a sharing with."

that they could not enter in because of lack of faith.[a]

4 Therefore, since a promise of entering into his rest remains, let us be on guard* for fear someone among you seems to fall short of it.[b] **2** For we have also had the good news declared to us,[c] just as they had; but the word that they heard did not benefit them, because they were not united by faith with those who listened. **3** For we who have exercised faith do enter into the rest, just as he has said: "So I swore in my anger, 'They will not enter into my rest,'"[d] although his works were finished from the founding of the world.[e] **4** For in one place he has said of the seventh day as follows: "And God rested on the seventh day from all his works,"[f] **5** and here again he says: "They will not enter into my rest."[g]

6 Therefore, since it remains for some to enter into it, and those to whom the good news was first declared did not enter in because of disobedience,[h] **7** he again marks off a certain day by saying long afterward in David's psalm, "Today"; just as it has been said above, "Today if you listen to his voice, do not harden your hearts."[i] **8** For if Joshua[j] had led them into a place of rest, God would not afterward have spoken of another day. **9** So there remains a sabbath-rest for the people of God.[k] **10** For the man who has entered into God's rest has also rested from his own works, just as God did from his own.[l]

11 Let us therefore do our utmost to enter into that rest, so that no one may fall into the same pattern of disobedience.[m] **12** For the word of God is alive and exerts power[n] and

4:1 *Lit., "be in fear."

CHAP. 3
a 2Sa 23:2
  Ac 1:16

b Ex 17:7

c Ex 16:35
  Nu 22:13
  Ps 95:9

d Nu 14:22, 23
  Ps 95:7-11

e Heb 2:1

f Ps 95:7

g Re 2:10

h Ps 95:7, 8

i Ex 17:1-3
  Nu 14:2, 4

j Nu 14:11
  De 32:21

k Nu 14:22, 23
  Nu 14:28-30
  Jude 5

Second Col.
a Heb 4:6

CHAP. 4
b Heb 3:12, 13

c Mt 4:23
  Ac 15:7
  Col 1:23

d Ps 95:11
  Heb 3:11

e Ex 31:17

f Ge 2:2, 3

g Ps 95:11

h Nu 14:30
  De 31:27

i Ps 95:7, 8

j Ex 24:13
  De 1:38

k Mr 2:28

l Ge 2:2, 3

m Ps 95:11

n Jer 23:29
  1Th 2:13

is sharper than any two-edged sword[a] and pierces even to the dividing of soul* and spirit,* and of joints from the marrow, and is able to discern thoughts and intentions of the heart. **13** And there is not a creation that is hidden from his sight,[b] but all things are naked and openly exposed to the eyes of the one to whom we must give an account.[c]

14 Therefore, since we have a great high priest who has passed through the heavens, Jesus the Son of God,[d] let us hold on to our public declaration of him.[e] **15** For we do not have a high priest who cannot sympathize with our weaknesses,[f] but we have one who has been tested in all respects as we have, but without sin.[g] **16** Let us, then, approach the throne of undeserved kindness with freeness of speech,[h] so that we may receive mercy and find undeserved kindness to help us at the right time.

5 For every high priest taken from among men is appointed in their behalf over the things relating to God,[i] so that he may offer gifts and sacrifices for sins.[j] **2** He is able to deal compassionately* with the ignorant and erring# ones, since he too is confronted with△ his own weakness, **3** and because of that he must make offerings for his own sins just as he does for those of the people.[k]

4 A man does not take this honor of his own accord, but he receives it only when he is called by God, just as Aaron was.[l] **5** So, too, the Christ did not glorify himself[m] by becoming a high priest, but was glori-

fied by the One who said to him: "You are my son; today I have become your father."[a] **6** As he also says in another place, "You are a priest forever in the manner of Mel·chiz'e·dek."[b]

7 During his life on earth,* Christ offered up supplications and also petitions, with strong outcries and tears,[c] to the One who was able to save him out of death, and he was favorably heard for his godly fear. **8** Although he was a son, he learned obedience from the things he suffered.[d] **9** And after he had been made perfect,[e] he became responsible for everlasting salvation to all those obeying him,[f] **10** because he has been designated by God a high priest in the manner of Mel·chiz'e·dek.[g]

11 We have much to say about him, and it is difficult to explain, because you have become dull in your hearing. **12** For although by now* you should be teachers, you again need someone to teach you from the beginning the elementary things[h] of the sacred pronouncements of God, and you have gone back to needing milk, not solid food. **13** For everyone who continues to feed on milk is unacquainted with the word of righteousness, for he is a young child.[i] **14** But solid food belongs to mature people, to those who through use have their powers of discernment* trained to distinguish both right and wrong.

6 Therefore, now that we have moved beyond the primary doctrine[j] about the Christ, let us press on to maturity,[k] not laying a foundation again, namely, repentance from dead works and faith in God, **2** the teaching on

---

CHAP. 4
a Eph 6:17

b Ps 7:9
Ps 90:8
Pr 15:11

c Ac 17:31
Ro 2:16
Ro 14:12

d Mr 1:11

e Heb 10:23

f Isa 53:4
Heb 2:17

g Heb 7:26
1Pe 2:22

h Eph 3:11, 12
Heb 10:19-22

CHAP. 5
i Ex 40:13

j Le 5:6

k Le 9:7
Le 16:6

l Ex 28:1

m Joh 8:54

Second Col.
a Ps 2:7
Ac 13:33

b Ps 110:4

c Lu 22:44
Joh 12:27

d Mt 26:39
Php 2:8

e Heb 7:28

f Joh 3:16

g Ps 110:4

h Heb 6:1

i Eph 4:14

CHAP. 6
j Heb 5:12

k 1Co 14:20
Eph 4:13
Heb 5:14

4:12 *See Glossary. 5:2 *Or "gently; moderately." #Or "wayward." △Or "subject to."

5:7 *Lit., "In the days of his flesh." 5:12 *Lit., "in view of the time." 5:14 *Or "their perceptive powers."

baptisms and the laying on of the hands,[a] the resurrection of the dead[b] and everlasting judgment. **3** And this we will do, if God indeed permits.

4 For as regards those who were once enlightened[c] and who have tasted the heavenly free gift and who have become partakers of holy spirit **5** and who have tasted the fine word of God and powers of the coming system of things,* **6** but have fallen away,[d] it is impossible to revive them again to repentance, because they nail the Son of God to the stake again for themselves and expose him to public shame.[e] **7** For the ground receives a blessing from God when it drinks in the rain that frequently falls on it and then produces vegetation useful to those for whom it is cultivated. **8** But if it produces thorns and thistles, it is rejected and is near to being cursed, and in the end it will be burned.

9 But in your case, beloved ones, we are convinced of better things, things related to salvation, even though we are speaking in this way. **10** For God is not unrighteous so as to forget your work and the love you showed for his name[f] by ministering and continuing to minister to the holy ones. **11** But we desire each one of you to show the same industriousness so as to have the full assurance of the hope[g] down to the end,[h] **12** so that you may not become sluggish,[i] but be imitators of those who through faith and patience inherit the promises.

13 For when God made his promise to Abraham, since he could not swear by anyone greater, he swore by himself,[j] **14** saying: "I will surely bless you and I will surely multiply

you."[a] **15** So after Abraham had shown patience, he obtained this promise. **16** For men swear by someone greater, and their oath is the end of every dispute, since it is a legal guarantee to them.[b] **17** In this same way, when God decided to demonstrate more clearly to the heirs of the promise[c] the unchangeableness of his purpose,* he guaranteed it# with an oath, **18** in order that through two unchangeable things in which it is impossible for God to lie,[d] we who have fled to the refuge may have strong encouragement to take firm hold of the hope set before us. **19** We have this hope[e] as an anchor for the soul,* both sure and firm, and it enters in within the curtain,[f] **20** where a forerunner has entered in our behalf, Jesus,[g] who has become a high priest in the manner of Mel·chiz′e·dek forever.[h]

7 For this Mel·chiz′e·dek, king of Sa′lem, priest of the Most High God, met Abraham returning from the slaughter of the kings and blessed him,[i] **2** and Abraham gave* him a tenth of everything. First, his name is translated "King of Righteousness," and then also king of Sa′lem, that is, "King of Peace." **3** In being fatherless, motherless, without genealogy, having neither a beginning of days nor an end of life, but being made like the Son of God, he remains a priest for all time.*[j]

4 See how great this man was to whom Abraham, the family head,* gave a tenth out of the best spoils.[k] **5** True, according to the Law, those of the sons of

---

CHAP. 6
a Ac 8:17

b Mt 22:31
  Joh 5:28, 29
  Joh 11:25

c Eph 1:18
  Heb 10:26

d 1Jo 2:19

e Heb 10:29

f Heb 10:32, 33

g 1Pe 1:3, 4

h Heb 3:14

i Ro 12:11
  Re 2:4

j Ge 22:16

Second Col.
a Ge 22:17

b Ge 31:53

c Ga 3:29

d Nu 23:19
  Tit 1:2

e 1Pe 1:3, 4

f Le 16:2, 12
  Heb 9:7
  Heb 10:19, 20

g Heb 4:14

h Ps 110:4
  Heb 5:6

CHAP. 7
i Ge 14:17-20

j Ps 110:4

k Ge 14:20

6:5 *Or "the coming age." See Glossary.

6:17 *Or "counsel." #Or "stepped in." Lit., "mediated." 6:19 *Or "for our lives." 7:2 *Lit., "apportioned." 7:3 *Or "perpetually." 7:4 *Or "the patriarch."

Le'vi[a] who receive their priestly office have a commandment to collect tithes from the people,[b] that is, from their brothers, even though these are descendants* of Abraham. **6** But this man who did not trace his genealogy from them took tithes from Abraham and blessed the one who had the promises.[c] **7** Now it is undeniable that the lesser one is blessed by the greater. **8** And in the one case, it is men who are dying who receive tithes, but in the other case, it is someone of whom witness is given that he lives.[d] **9** And it could be said that even Le'vi, who receives tithes, has paid tithes through Abraham, **10** for he was still a future descendant* of his forefather when Mel·chiz'e·dek met him.[e]

11 If, then, perfection was attainable through the Levitical priesthood[f] (for it was a feature of the Law that was given to the people), what further need would there be for another priest to arise who is said to be in the manner of Mel·chiz'e·dek[g] and not in the manner of Aaron? **12** For since the priesthood is being changed, it becomes necessary to change the Law as well.[h] **13** For the man about whom these things are said came from another tribe, from which no one has officiated at the altar.[i] **14** For it is clear that our Lord has descended from Judah,[j] yet Moses said nothing about priests coming from that tribe.

15 And this becomes even clearer when another priest[k] arises who is like Mel·chiz'e·dek,[l] **16** who has become such, not by the legal requirement that depends on fleshly descent, but by the power of an indestructible

life.[a] **17** For it is said in witness of him: "You are a priest forever in the manner of Mel·chiz'e·dek."[b]

18 So, then, the former commandment is set aside because it is weak and ineffective.[c] **19** For the Law made nothing perfect,[d] but the introduction of a better hope[e] did, through which we are drawing near to God.[f] **20** Also, inasmuch as this was not done without an oath being sworn **21** (for, indeed, there are men who have become priests without a sworn oath, but this one has become so through an oath sworn respecting him by the One who said: "Jehovah* has sworn, and he will not change his mind,* 'You are a priest forever'"),[g] **22** Jesus has accordingly become the guarantee* of a better covenant.[h] **23** Furthermore, many had to become priests in succession[i] because death prevented them from continuing as such, **24** but because he continues alive forever,[j] his priesthood has no successors. **25** So he is able also to save completely those who are approaching God through him, because he is always alive to plead for them.[k]

26 For it is fitting for us to have such a high priest who is loyal, innocent, undefiled,[l] separated from the sinners, and exalted above the heavens.[m] **27** Unlike those high priests, he does not need to offer up sacrifices daily,[n] first for his own sins and then for those of the people,[o] because he did this once for all time when he offered himself up.[p] **28** For the Law appoints as high priests men who have weaknesses,[q] but the word of the oath[r] sworn af-

CHAP. 7

a Ex 40:12, 15
b Nu 18:21, 26
  De 14:28
c Ge 12:7
  Ge 14:18-20
  Ge 17:6
  Ge 22:17
d Heb 7:3
e Ge 14:18
f Ro 3:20
  Heb 7:19
  Heb 9:9
  Heb 10:1
g Ps 110:4
h Ro 3:27
  1Co 9:21
  Ga 6:2
  Col 2:13, 14
i Nu 18:6, 7
j Ge 49:10
  Mt 1:1, 3
  Lu 3:23, 33
k Heb 3:1
  Heb 7:26
l Ps 110:4

Second Col.

a Ro 6:9
  1Ti 6:16
b Ps 110:4
c Ro 8:3
  Heb 9:9
  Heb 13:9
d Ac 13:38, 39
  Ga 2:15, 16
  Heb 10:1
e 1Pe 1:3, 4
f Joh 14:6
  Heb 4:16
g Ps 110:4
h Jer 31:31
  Mt 26:27, 28
  1Co 11:25
  Heb 8:6
  Heb 9:15
  Heb 12:22, 24
i 1Ch 6:4
j Lu 1:33
  Heb 7:15, 16
k Ro 8:34
  1Ti 2:5
  Heb 9:24
  1Jo 2:1
l Isa 53:9
  1Pe 2:21, 22
m Eph 1:20, 21
  1Pe 3:22
n Nu 28:3
o Le 9:8, 15
p Ro 6:10
  Heb 9:28
  Heb 10:14
q Le 16:11
r Ps 2:7
  Ps 110:4

7:5 *Lit., "have come out of the loins."
7:10 *Lit., "in the loins."

7:21 *See App. A5. *Or "will feel no regret." **7:22** *Or "the one given in pledge."

ter the Law appoints a son, who has been made perfect[a] forever.

8 Now this is the main point of what we are saying: We have such a high priest as this,[b] and he has sat down at the right hand of the throne of the Majesty in the heavens,[c] **2** a minister* of the holy place[d] and of the true tent, which Jehovah* set up, and not man. **3** For every high priest is appointed to offer both gifts and sacrifices; so it was necessary for this one also to have something to offer.[e] **4** If he were on earth, he would not be a priest,[f] since there are already men who offer the gifts according to the Law. **5** These men are offering sacred service in a typical representation and a shadow[g] of the heavenly things;[h] just as Moses, when about to construct the tent, was given the divine command: For He says: "See that you make all things after their pattern that was shown to you in the mountain."[i] **6** But now Jesus has obtained a more excellent ministry* because he is also the mediator[j] of a correspondingly better covenant,[k] which has been legally established on better promises.[l]

7 If that first covenant had been faultless, there would have been no need for a second.[m] **8** For he does find fault with the people when he says: "'Look! The days are coming,' says Jehovah,* 'when I will make with the house of Israel and with the house of Judah a new covenant. **9** It will not be like the covenant that I made with their forefathers on the day I took hold of their hand to lead them out of the land of Egypt,[n] because they did not remain in my covenant,

so I stopped caring for them,' says Jehovah.*

10 "'For this is the covenant that I will make with the house of Israel after those days,' says Jehovah.* 'I will put my laws in their mind, and in their hearts I will write them.[a] And I will become their God, and they will become my people.[b]

11 "'And they will no longer teach each one his fellow citizen and each one his brother, saying: "Know Jehovah!"* For they will all know me, from the least to the greatest of them. **12** For I will be merciful toward their unrighteous deeds, and I will no longer call their sins to mind.'"[c]

13 In his saying "a new covenant," he has made the former one obsolete.[d] Now what is obsolete and growing old is near to vanishing away.[e]

9 For its part, the former covenant used to have legal requirements for sacred service and its holy place[f] on earth. **2** For a first tent compartment was constructed, in which were the lampstand[g] and the table and the display of the loaves of presentation;*[h] and it is called the Holy Place.[i] **3** But behind the second curtain[j] was the tent compartment called the Most Holy.[k] **4** This had a golden censer[l] and the ark of the covenant[m] completely overlaid with gold,[n] in which were the golden jar containing the manna[o] and Aaron's rod that budded[p] and the tablets[q] of the covenant; **5** and above it were the glorious cherubs overshadowing the propitiatory cover.*[r] But now is not the time to speak of these things in detail.

6 After these things were constructed this way, the priests enter the first tent compartment

---

CHAP. 7
a Heb 2:10
  Heb 5:9

CHAP. 8
b Heb 3:1
  Heb 7:26
c Ps 110:1
  Heb 1:3
d Heb 9:8, 24
e Eph 5:2
f Heb 7:14
g Col 2:16, 17
  Heb 10:1
h Heb 9:9, 24
i Ex 25:9, 40
  Ex 26:30
  Nu 8:4
j 1Ti 2:5
k 1Co 11:25
  Heb 7:22
  Heb 9:15
  Heb 12:22, 24
l Ps 110:4
  Ro 8:17
m Heb 7:11, 18
n Ex 12:51

Second Col.
a Ro 2:29
b 2Co 6:16
c Jer 31:31-34
d Ro 10:4
  Heb 7:12
e Col 2:13, 14

CHAP. 9
f Ex 25:8
g Nu 4:9
h Ex 40:22-24
i Ex 26:33
j Ex 36:35
k Ex 26:31, 33
l Le 16:12
  Re 8:3
m Ex 40:21
n Ex 25:10, 11
o Ex 16:33
p Nu 17:10
q Ex 32:15
r Ex 25:18, 22
  Nu 7:89

8:2 *Or "public servant." 8:2, 8-11 *See App. A5. 8:6 *Or "public service."

9:2 *Or "the showbread." 9:5 *Or "the place of atonement."

regularly to perform the sacred services;[a] **7** but the high priest enters alone into the second compartment once a year,[b] not without blood,[c] which he offers for himself[d] and for the sins that the people[e] committed in ignorance. **8** Thus the holy spirit makes it clear that the way into the holy place had not yet been revealed while the first tent was standing.[f] **9** This tent is an illustration for the present time,[g] and according to this arrangement, both gifts and sacrifices are offered.[h] However, these are not able to make the conscience of the man doing sacred service perfect.[i] **10** They have to do only with foods and drinks and various ceremonial washings.*[j] They were legal requirements concerning the body[k] and were imposed until the appointed time to set things straight.

11 However, when Christ came as a high priest of the good things that have already taken place, he passed through the greater and more perfect tent not made with hands, that is, not of this creation. **12** He entered into the holy place, not with the blood of goats and of young bulls, but with his own blood,[l] once for all time, and obtained an everlasting deliverance* for us.[m] **13** For if the blood of goats and of bulls[n] and the ashes of a heifer* sprinkled on those who have been defiled sanctifies for the cleansing of the flesh,[o] **14** how much more will the blood of the Christ,[p] who through an everlasting spirit offered himself without blemish to God, cleanse our consciences from dead works[q] so that we may render sacred service to the living God?[r]

15 That is why he is a mediator of a new covenant,[a] in order that because a death has occurred for their release by ransom[b] from the transgressions under the former covenant, those who have been called may receive the promise of the everlasting inheritance.[c] **16** For where there is a covenant, the death of the human covenanter needs to be established, **17** because a covenant is valid at death, since it is not in force as long as the human covenanter is living. **18** Consequently, neither was the former covenant put into effect* without blood. **19** For when Moses had spoken every commandment of the Law to all the people, he took the blood of the young bulls and of the goats, with water, scarlet wool, and hyssop, and sprinkled the book* and all the people, **20** saying: "This is the blood of the covenant that God has commanded you to keep."[d] **21** He likewise sprinkled the tent and all the vessels of the holy service* with the blood.[e] **22** Yes, according to the Law nearly all things are cleansed with blood,[f] and unless blood is poured out no forgiveness takes place.[g]

23 Therefore, it was necessary for the typical representations[h] of the things in the heavens to be cleansed by these means,[i] but the heavenly things require far better sacrifices. **24** For Christ did not enter into a holy place made with hands,[j] which is a copy of the reality,[k] but into heaven itself,[l] so that he now appears before* God on our behalf.[m] **25** This was not done to offer himself often, as when the high priest enters into the

---

CHAP. 9

a Le 24:3, 4

b Le 16:2

c Ex 30:10
Le 16:14

d Le 16:6, 11

e Le 16:15

f Heb 10:19, 20

g Col 2:16, 17
Heb 8:5
Heb 10:1

h Le 23:37, 38

i Ga 3:21
Heb 7:11, 19

j Ex 30:17-19

k Nu 19:13

l Heb 12:24
Heb 13:20

m Da 9:24
Mt 20:28
1Ti 2:5, 6

n Le 16:6, 15

o Nu 19:9,
17, 19

p 1Pe 1:18, 19

q 1Jo 1:7

r Ro 12:1

Second Col.

a Lu 22:20
1Ti 2:5
Heb 12:22, 24

b Mt 20:28

c Ro 8:17

d Ex 24:6-8

e Ex 29:12
Le 8:15

f Le 17:11

g Le 9:7-9

h Heb 8:5
Heb 9:9

i Le 16:19, 20

j Heb 8:1, 2

k Col 2:16, 17

l Heb 6:19, 20
Heb 9:12

m Le 16:15
Ro 8:34

9:10 *Lit., "various baptisms." **9:12** *Lit., "ransoming; redemption." **9:13** *Or "young cow."

9:18 *Lit., "inaugurated." **9:19** *Or "scroll." **9:21** *Or "the public service." **9:24** *Lit., "before the face of."

holy place from year to year[a] with blood that is not his own. **26** Otherwise, he would have to suffer often from the founding of the world. But now he has manifested himself once for all time at the conclusion of the systems of things* to do away with sin through the sacrifice of himself.[b] **27** And just as it is reserved for men to die once for all time, but after this to receive a judgment, **28** so also the Christ was offered once for all time to bear the sins of many;[c] and the second time that he appears it will be apart from sin,* and he will be seen by those earnestly looking for him for their salvation.[d]

10 For since the Law has a shadow[e] of the good things to come,[f] but not the very substance of the things, it* can never, by the same sacrifices that are continually offered year after year, make those who approach perfect.[g] **2** Otherwise, would not the sacrifices have stopped being offered, because those rendering sacred service once cleansed would have no consciousness of sins anymore? **3** On the contrary, these sacrifices are a reminder of sins year after year,[h] **4** for it is not possible for the blood of bulls and of goats to take sins away.

5 So when he comes into the world, he says: "'Sacrifice and offering you did not want, but you prepared a body for me. **6** You did not approve of whole burnt offerings and sin offerings.'[i] **7** Then I said: 'Look! I have come (in the scroll* it is written about me) to do your will, O God.'"[j] **8** After first saying: "You did not want nor did

you approve of sacrifices and offerings and whole burnt offerings and sin offerings"—sacrifices that are offered according to the Law— **9** then he says: "Look! I have come to do your will."[a] He does away with what is first in order to establish what is second. **10** By this "will"[b] we have been sanctified through the offering of the body of Jesus Christ once for all time.[c]

11 Also, every priest takes his station day after day to offer holy service*[d] and to make the same sacrifices often,[e] which can never take sins away completely.[f] **12** But this man offered one sacrifice for sins for all time and sat down at the right hand of God,[g] **13** from then on waiting until his enemies should be placed as a stool for his feet.[h] **14** For it is by one sacrificial offering that he has made those who are being sanctified perfect[i] for all time. **15** Moreover, the holy spirit also bears witness to us, for after it has said: **16** "'This is the covenant that I will make with them after those days,' says Jehovah.* 'I will put my laws in their hearts, and in their minds I will write them.'"[j] **17** Then it says: "And I will no longer call their sins and their lawless deeds to mind."[k] **18** Now where there is forgiveness of these, there is no longer an offering for sin.

19 Therefore, brothers, since we have boldness* for the way of entry into the holy place[l] by the blood of Jesus, **20** which he opened up* for us as a new and living way through the curtain,[m] that is, his flesh, **21** and since we have a great priest over the house of God,[n] **22** let us approach with sincere hearts

---

CHAP. 9

a Le 16:2, 34

b Da 9:24
Heb 7:27
1Pe 3:18

c Isa 53:12
Ro 6:10
1Pe 2:24

d 2Ti 4:8
Tit 2:13

CHAP. 10

e Heb 8:5

f Col 2:16, 17

g Heb 7:19
Heb 9:9

h Le 16:34

i Ps 40:6

j Ps 40:8

Second Col.

a Ps 40:6-8

b Ga 1:4

c Heb 13:12

d 1Sa 2:27, 28

e Ex 29:38
Nu 28:3

f Heb 7:18
Heb 10:1

g Ro 8:34

h Ps 110:1
1Co 15:25

i Heb 7:19

j Jer 31:33
Heb 8:10

k Jer 31:34
Heb 8:12

l Heb 9:8, 24

m Mt 27:51

n Zec 6:13
Heb 3:6

9:26 *Or "the ages." See Glossary.
9:28 *Or "it will not be to deal with sin."
10:1 *Or possibly, "men." 10:7 *Lit.,
"in the scroll of the book."

10:11 *Or "to perform public service."
10:16 *See App. A5. 10:19 *Or "confidence." 10:20 *Lit., "inaugurated."

and complete faith, having had our hearts sprinkled clean from a wicked conscience[a] and our bodies bathed with clean water.[b] **23** Let us hold firmly the public declaration of our hope without wavering,[c] for the one who promised is faithful. **24** And let us consider* one another so as to incite# to love and fine works,[d] **25** not forsaking our meeting together,[e] as some have the custom, but encouraging one another,[f] and all the more so as you see the day drawing near.[g]

26 For if we practice sin willfully after having received the accurate knowledge of the truth,[h] there is no longer any sacrifice for sins left,[i] **27** but there is a certain fearful expectation of judgment and a burning indignation that is going to consume those in opposition.[j] **28** Anyone who has disregarded the Law of Moses dies without compassion on the testimony of two or three.[k] **29** How much greater punishment do you think a person will deserve who has trampled on the Son of God and who has regarded as of ordinary value the blood of the covenant[l] by which he was sanctified, and who has outraged the spirit of undeserved kindness with contempt?[m] **30** For we know the One who said: "Vengeance is mine; I will repay." And again: "Jehovah* will judge his people."[n] **31** It is a fearful thing to fall into the hands of the living God.

32 However, keep remembering the former days in which, after you were enlightened,[o] you endured a great struggle along with sufferings. **33** At times you were publicly exposed* both

to reproaches and to tribulations, and at times you shared* with those who were having such an experience. **34** For you expressed sympathy for those in prison and you accepted joyfully the plundering of your belongings,[a] knowing that you yourselves have a better and an enduring possession.[b]

35 Therefore, do not throw away your boldness,* which will be richly rewarded.[c] **36** For you need endurance,[d] so that after you have done the will of God, you may receive the fulfillment of the promise. **37** For yet "a very little while,"[e] and "the one who is coming will arrive and will not delay."[f] **38** "But my righteous one will live by reason of faith," and "if he shrinks back, I have* no pleasure in him."[h] **39** Now we are not the sort who shrink back to destruction,[i] but the sort who have faith for the preserving of our lives.*

11 Faith is the assured expectation of what is hoped for,[j] the evident demonstration* of realities that are not seen.* **2** For by means of it, the men of ancient times* had witness borne to them.

3 By faith we perceive that the systems of things* were put in order by God's word, so that what is seen has come into existence from things that are not visible.

4 By faith Abel offered God a sacrifice of greater worth than that of Cain,[k] and through that faith he received the witness that he was righteous, for God approved* his gifts,[l] and al-

10:24 *Or "be concerned about; pay attention to." #Or "motivate; stir up." 10:30 *See App. A5. 10:33 *Lit., "were exposed as in a theater."

10:33 *Or "stood side by side." 10:35 *Lit., "freeness of speech." 10:38 *Or "my soul has." 10:39 *Or "souls." 11:1 *Or "convincing evidence." 11:2 *Or "our ancestors." 11:3 *Or "the ages." See Glossary. 11:4 *Or "bore witness by acknowledging."

though he died, he still speaks[a] through his faith.

5 By faith E'noch[b] was transferred so as not to see death, and he was nowhere to be found because God had transferred him;[c] for before he was transferred he received the witness that he had pleased God well. **6** Moreover, without faith it is impossible to please God well, for whoever approaches God must believe that he is* and that he becomes the rewarder of those earnestly seeking him.[d]

7 By faith Noah,[e] after receiving divine warning of things not yet seen,[f] showed godly fear and constructed an ark[g] for the saving of his household; and through this faith he condemned the world,[h] and he became an heir of the righteousness that results from faith.

8 By faith Abraham,[i] when he was called, obeyed by going out to a place he was to receive as an inheritance; he went out, although not knowing where he was going.[j] **9** By faith he lived as a foreigner in the land of the promise as in a foreign land,[k] living in tents[l] with Isaac and Jacob, the heirs with him of the very same promise.[m] **10** For he was awaiting the city having real foundations, whose designer* and builder is God.[n]

11 By faith also Sarah received power to conceive offspring,* even when she was past the age,[o] since she considered Him faithful# who made the promise. **12** For this reason, from one man who was as good as dead,[p] there were born children,[q] as many as the stars of heaven in number and as innumerable as the sands by the seaside.[r]

13 In faith all of these died, although they did not receive the fulfillment of the promises;[a] but they saw them from a distance[b] and welcomed them and publicly declared that they were strangers and temporary residents in the land. **14** For those who speak in such a way make it evident that they are earnestly seeking a place of their own. **15** And yet, if they had kept remembering the place from which they had departed,[c] they would have had opportunity to return. **16** But now they are reaching out for a better place, that is, one belonging to heaven. Therefore, God is not ashamed of them, to be called on as their God,[d] for he has prepared a city for them.[e]

17 By faith Abraham, when he was tested,[f] as good as offered up Isaac—the man who had gladly received the promises attempted to offer up his only-begotten son[g]— **18** although it had been said to him: "What will be called your offspring* will be through Isaac."[h] **19** But he reasoned that God was able to raise him up even from the dead, and he did receive him from there in an illustrative way.[i]

20 By faith also Isaac blessed Jacob[j] and E'sau[k] concerning things to come.

21 By faith Jacob, when about to die,[l] blessed each of the sons of Joseph[m] and worshipped while leaning on the top of his staff.[n]

22 By faith Joseph, nearing his end, spoke of the exodus of the sons of Israel, and he gave instructions* concerning his bones.#[o]

23 By faith Moses was hid by his parents for three months after his birth,[p] because they saw that the young child was

---

CHAP. 11

a Ge 4:8, 10

b Ge 5:22
Jude 14

c Ge 5:24

d Ps 58:11
Zep 2:3
Mt 5:12
Mt 6:33

e Ge 6:8, 9

f Ge 6:13, 17

g Ge 6:14

h Ge 6:22
2Pe 2:5

i Ro 4:9, 11

j Ge 12:1, 4

k Ge 23:4

l Ge 12:8

m Ge 17:6
Ge 26:3
Ge 28:13

n Heb 11:16

o Ge 17:17
Ge 21:2

p Ro 4:19

q Ge 21:5

r Ge 22:17
1Ki 4:20

Second Col.

a Ge 47:9

b Joh 8:56

c Ge 11:31

d Ex 3:6, 15

e Heb 11:10
Heb 12:22

f Ge 22:1, 2

g Ge 22:9, 10
Joh 3:16

h Ge 21:12

i 1Co 10:11

j Ge 27:27-29

k Ge 27:38-40

l Ge 47:29

m Ge 48:15, 16, 20

n Ge 47:31

o Ge 50:24, 25
Ex 13:19

p Ex 2:2

11:6 *Or "exists." **11:10** *Or "architect." **11:11, 18** *Lit., "seed." **11:11** #Or "trustworthy."

11:22 *Or "a command." #Or "burial."

beautiful[a] and they did not fear the order of the king.[b] **24** By faith Moses, when grown up,[c] refused to be called the son of Phar′aoh's daughter,[d] **25** choosing to be mistreated with the people of God rather than to have the temporary enjoyment of sin, **26** because he considered the reproach of the Christ to be riches greater than the treasures of Egypt, for he looked intently toward the payment of the reward. **27** By faith he left Egypt,[e] but not fearing the anger of the king,[f] for he continued steadfast as seeing the One who is invisible.[g] **28** By faith he observed the Passover and the splashing of the blood, so that the destroyer might not harm* their firstborn.[h]

29 By faith they passed through the Red Sea as on dry land,[i] but when the Egyptians attempted it, they were swallowed up.

30 By faith the walls of Jer′i·cho fell down after the people had marched around them for seven days.[k] **31** By faith Ra′hab the prostitute did not perish with those who acted disobediently, because she received the spies in a peaceable way.[l]

32 And what more will I say? For time will fail me if I go on to relate about Gid′e·on,[m] Ba′rak,[n] Samson,[o] Jeph′thah,[p] David,[q] as well as Samuel[r] and the other prophets. **33** Through faith they defeated kingdoms,[s] brought about righteousness, obtained promises,[t] stopped the mouths of lions,[u] **34** quenched the force of fire,[v] escaped the edge of the sword,[w] from a weak state were made powerful,[x] became mighty in war,[y] routed invading armies.[z] **35** Women received their dead by res-

urrection,[a] but other men were tortured because they would not accept release by some ransom, in order that they might attain a better resurrection. **36** Yes, others received their trial by mockings and scourgings, indeed, more than that, by chains[b] and prisons.[c] **37** They were stoned,[d] they were tried, they were sawn in two,* they were slaughtered by the sword,[e] they went about in sheepskins, in goatskins,[f] while they were in need, in tribulation,[g] mistreated;[h] **38** and the world was not worthy of them. They wandered about in deserts and mountains and caves[i] and dens of the earth.

39 And yet all of these, although they received a favorable witness because of their faith, did not obtain the fulfillment of the promise, **40** because God had foreseen something better for us,[j] so that they might not be made perfect apart from us.

12 So, then, because we have such a great cloud of witnesses surrounding us, let us also throw off every weight and the sin that easily entangles us,[k] and let us run with endurance the race that is set before us,[l] **2** as we look intently at the Chief Agent and Perfecter of our faith, Jesus.[m] For the joy that was set before him he endured a torture stake,* despising shame, and has sat down at the right hand of the throne of God.[n] **3** Indeed, consider closely the one who has endured such hostile speech from sinners[o] against their own interests, so that you may not get tired and give up.*[p]

4 In your struggle against that sin, you have never yet resisted to the point of hav-

CHAP. 11
a Ac 7:20
b Ex 1:16, 22
c Ex 2:11
d Ex 2:10
e Ex 12:51
f Ex 10:28
g 1Ti 1:17
h Ex 12:21-23
i Ex 14:22
j Ex 14:27, 28
k Jos 6:15, 20
l Jos 6:17
m Jg 6:11
n Jg 4:6
o Jg 13:24
p Jg 11:1
q 1Sa 16:13
r 1Sa 3:20
s Jg 7:12, 22
t 2Sa 7:8, 12
u Jg 14:5, 6
  1Sa 17:34-36
  Da 6:21, 22
v Da 3:23-25
w 2Ki 6:15, 16
x Jg 16:28
  1Ki 18:46
y Jg 11:32
z Jg 4:16

Second Col.
a 1Ki 17:22-24
  2Ki 4:32, 34
b Jer 20:2
c Jer 37:15
d 2Ch 24:20, 21
e 1Ki 19:1
f 2Ki 1:8
g 1Ki 19:2
h 1Ki 22:24
  Jer 38:6
i 1Ki 18:4
  1Ki 19:9
j Heb 2:3
  Heb 3:11
  Heb 7:22

CHAP. 12
k Heb 3:12
l 1Co 9:24, 26
  Php 3:13, 14
m Joh 14:6
  Ac 5:31
  Heb 2:10
n Ps 110:1
  Heb 10:12
o Mt 27:39
p Ga 6:9

11:28 *Lit., "touch."   11:37 *Or "sawn apart." 12:2 *See Glossary. 12:3 *Or "give out in your souls."

ing your blood shed. **5** And you have entirely forgotten the exhortation that addresses you as sons: "My son, do not belittle the discipline from Jehovah,* nor give up when you are corrected by him; **6** for those whom Jehovah* loves he disciplines, in fact, he scourges# everyone whom he receives as a son."[a]

7 You need to endure as part of your discipline.* God is treating you as sons.[b] For what son is not disciplined by his father?[c] **8** But if you have not all shared in receiving this discipline, you are really illegitimate children, and not sons. **9** Furthermore, our human fathers* used to discipline us, and we gave them respect. Should we not more readily submit ourselves to the Father of our spiritual life and live?[d] **10** For they disciplined us for a short time according to what seemed good to them, but he does so for our benefit so that we may partake of his holiness.[e] **11** True, no discipline seems for the present to be joyous, but it is painful;* yet afterward, it yields the peaceable fruit of righteousness to those who have been trained by it.

12 Therefore, strengthen the hands that hang down and the feeble knees,[f] **13** and keep making straight paths for your feet,[g] so that what is lame may not be put out of joint but, rather, may be healed. **14** Pursue peace with all people[h] and the sanctification*[i] without which no man will see the Lord. **15** Carefully watch that no one fails to obtain the undeserved kindness of God, so that no poisonous root springs up to cause trou-

ble and many are defiled by it;[a] **16** and watch that among you there is no one who is sexually immoral* nor anyone who does not appreciate sacred things, like E'sau, who gave up his rights as firstborn in exchange for one meal.[b] **17** For you know that afterward when he wanted to inherit the blessing, he was rejected; for although he earnestly tried to bring about a change of mind* with tears,[c] it was to no avail.#

18 For you have not approached something that can be felt[d] and that has been set aflame with fire,[e] and a dark cloud and thick darkness and a storm,[f] **19** and the blast of a trumpet[g] and the voice speaking words,[h] which on hearing, the people begged that nothing further should be spoken to them.[i] **20** For they could not bear the command: "If even a beast touches the mountain, it must be stoned."[j] **21** Also, the display was so terrifying that Moses said: "I am afraid and trembling."[k] **22** But you have approached a Mount Zion[l] and a city of the living God, heavenly Jerusalem,[m] and myriads* of angels **23** in general assembly,[n] and the congregation of the firstborn who have been enrolled in the heavens, and God the Judge of all,[o] and the spiritual lives[p] of righteous ones who have been made perfect,[q] **24** and Jesus the mediator[r] of a new covenant,[s] and the sprinkled blood, which speaks in a better way than Abel's blood.[t]

25 See that you do not refuse to listen to* the one who is speaking. For if those who

---

CHAP. 12

a Pr 3:11, 12

b 2Sa 7:14
Heb 2:10

c Pr 13:24

d Jas 4:10

e 1Pe 1:15, 16

f Isa 35:3

g Pr 4:26

h Ps 34:14
Ro 12:18
Ro 14:19

i Ro 6:19
1Th 4:3, 4
Heb 10:10

Second Col.

a De 29:18

b Ge 25:32, 34

c Ge 27:34

d Ex 19:12

e Ex 19:18

f Ex 19:16

g Ex 19:19

h De 4:11, 12

i Ex 20:18, 19

j Ex 19:12, 13

k De 9:19

l Re 14:1

m Re 21:2

n Da 7:10

o Ge 18:25
Ps 94:2
Isa 33:22

p Heb 12:9

q Heb 10:14

r 1Ti 2:5
Heb 9:15

s Mt 26:27, 28

t Ge 4:8, 10

12:5, 6 *See App. A5. **12:6** #Or "punishes." **12:7** *Or "training." **12:9** *Lit., "the fathers of our flesh." **12:11** *Or "grievous." **12:14** *Or "holiness." **12:16** *See Glossary, "Sexual immorality." **12:17** *That is, of his father's mind. #Lit., "he found no place for it." **12:22** *Or "tens of thousands." **12:25** *Or "do not make excuses to; do not ignore."

refused to listen to the one giving divine warning on earth did not escape, how much more will we not escape if we turn away from him who speaks from the heavens!ᵃ **26** At that time his voice shook the earth,ᵇ but now he has promised: "Yet once more I will shake not only the earth but also the heaven."ᶜ **27** Now the expression "yet once more" indicates the removal of the things that are shaken, things that have been made, in order that the things not shaken may remain. **28** Therefore, seeing that we are to receive a Kingdom that cannot be shaken, let us continue to receive undeserved kindness, through which we may acceptably offer God sacred service with godly fear and awe. **29** For our God is a consuming fire.ᵈ

13 Let your brotherly love continue.ᵉ **2** Do not forget hospitality,*ᶠ for through it some unknowingly entertained angels.ᵍ **3** Keep in mind those in prison,*ʰ as though you were imprisoned with them,ⁱ and those being mistreated, since you yourselves also are in the body.ʲ **4** Let marriage be honorable among all, and let the marriage bed be without defilement,ʲ for God will judge sexually immoral people* and adulterers.ᵏ **5** Let your way of life be free of the love of money,ˡ while you are content with the present things.ᵐ For he has said: "I will never leave you, and I will never abandon you."ⁿ **6** So that we may be of good courage and say: "Jehovah* is my helper; I will not be afraid. What can man do to me?"ᵒ

7 Remember those who are taking the lead among you,ᵃ who have spoken the word of God to you, and as you contemplate how their conduct turns out, imitate their faith.ᵇ

8 Jesus Christ is the same yesterday and today, and forever.

9 Do not be led astray by various and strange teachings, for it is better for the heart to be strengthened by undeserved kindness than by foods,* which do not benefit those occupied with them.ᶜ

10 We have an altar from which those who offer sacred service at the tent have no authority to eat.ᵈ **11** For the bodies of those animals whose blood is taken into the holy place as a sin offering by the high priest are burned up outside the camp.ᵉ **12** Therefore, Jesus also suffered outside the city gateᶠ in order to sanctify the people with his own blood.ᵍ **13** Let us, then, go to him outside the camp, bearing the reproach he bore,ʰ **14** for we do not have here a city that remains, but we are earnestly seeking the one to come.ⁱ **15** Through him let us always offer to God a sacrifice of praise,ʲ that is, the fruit of our lipsᵏ that make public declaration to his name.ˡ **16** Moreover, do not forget to do good and to share what you have with others,ᵐ for God is well-pleased with such sacrifices.ⁿ

17 Be obedient to those who are taking the lead among youᵒ and be submissive,ᵖ for they are keeping watch over you* as those who will render an account,ۭ so that they may do this with joy and not with sighing, for this would be damaging to you.

CHAP. 12
a Heb 1:2
  Heb 2:2-4
b Ex 19:18
c Hag 2:6
d De 4:24

CHAP. 13
e 1Th 4:9
  1Pe 1:22
f Ro 12:13
  1Ti 3:2
g Ge 18:2, 3
  Ge 19:1-3
h Col 4:18
i Ro 12:15
j Pr 5:16, 20
  Mt 5:28
k Pr 6:32
  1Co 6:9, 10
  1Co 6:18
  Ga 5:19, 21
l 1Ti 6:10
m Pr 30:8, 9
  1Ti 6:8
n De 31:6, 8
o Ps 118:6
  Da 3:17
  Lu 12:4

Second Col.
a 1Ti 5:17
  Heb 13:17
b 1Co 11:1
  2Th 3:7
c Ro 14:17
  1Co 8:8
  Col 2:16
d 1Co 9:13
  1Co 10:18
e Le 16:27
f Joh 19:17
g Heb 9:13, 14
h Ro 15:3
  2Co 12:10
  1Pe 4:14
i Heb 11:10
  Heb 12:22
j Le 7:12
  Ps 50:14, 23
k Ps 69:30, 31
  Ho 14:2
l Ro 10:9
m Ro 12:13
n Php 4:18
o 1Th 5:12
p Eph 5:21
  1Pe 5:5
q Ac 20:28

13:2 *Or "kindness to strangers." **13:3** *Lit., "the bound ones; those in bonds." #Or possibly, "as if you were suffering with them." **13:4** *See Glossary, "Sexual immorality." **13:6** *See App. A5.

13:9 *That is, rules about food. **13:17** *Or "your souls."

18 Keep praying for us, for we trust we have an honest* conscience, as we wish to conduct ourselves honestly in all things.[a] **19** But I especially urge you to pray so that I may be restored to you the sooner.

20 Now may the God of peace, who brought up from the dead the great shepherd[b] of the sheep, our Lord Jesus, with the blood of an everlasting covenant, **21** equip you with every good thing to do his will, working in us through Jesus Christ what is well-pleasing in his sight,

---

13:18 *Lit., "good."

CHAP. 13
a 2Co 1:12

b 1Pe 5:4

Second Col.
a Ac 27:1

to whom be the glory forever and ever. Amen.

22 Now I urge you, brothers, to listen patiently to this word of encouragement, for I have written you a short letter. **23** I want you to know that our brother Timothy has been released. If he comes soon, I will be with him when I see you.

24 Give my greetings to all those who are taking the lead among you and to all the holy ones. Those in Italy[a] send you their greetings.

25 The undeserved kindness be with all of you.

THE LETTER OF

JAMES

OUTLINE OF CONTENTS

1 James,[a] a slave of God and of the Lord Jesus Christ, to the 12 tribes that are scattered about:
  Greetings!

CHAP. 1
a Mt 13:55

Second Col.
a Mt 5:11, 12
b 1Pe 1:6, 7

2 Consider it all joy, my brothers, when you meet with various trials,[a] **3** knowing as you do that this tested quality of your faith produces endurance.[b]

4 But let endurance complete its work, so that you may be complete and sound in all respects, not lacking in anything.[a]

5 So if any one of you is lacking in wisdom, let him keep asking God,[b] for he gives generously to all and without reproaching,*[c] and it will be given him.[d] **6** But let him keep asking in faith,[e] not doubting at all,[f] for the one who doubts is like a wave of the sea driven by the wind and blown about. **7** In fact, that man should not expect to receive anything from Jehovah;*[8] he is an indecisive man,[g] unsteady in all his ways.

9 But let the lowly brother rejoice* over his exaltation,[h] **10** and the rich one over his humiliation,[i] because like a flower of the field he will pass away. **11** For just as the sun rises with its scorching heat and withers the plant, and its flower falls off and its outward beauty perishes, so too the rich man will fade away in the midst of his pursuits.[j]

12 Happy is the man who keeps on enduring trial,[k] because on becoming approved he will receive the crown of life,[l] which Jehovah* promised to those who continue loving Him.[m] **13** When under trial, let no one say: "I am being tried by God." For with evil things God cannot be tried, nor does he himself try anyone. **14** But each one is tried by being drawn out and enticed* by his own desire.[n] **15** Then the desire, when it has become fertile,* gives birth to sin; in turn sin, when it has been carried out, brings forth death.[o]

16 Do not be misled, my beloved brothers. **17** Every good gift and every perfect present is from above,[a] coming down from the Father of the celestial lights,[b] who does not vary or change like the shifting shadows.*[c] **18** It was his will to bring us forth by the word of truth,[d] so that we would become a kind of firstfruits of his creatures.[e]

19 Know this, my beloved brothers: Everyone must be quick to listen, slow to speak,[f] slow to anger,[g] **20** for man's anger does not bring about God's righteousness.[h] **21** Therefore, put away all filthiness and every trace of badness,*[i] and accept with mildness the implanting of the word that is able to save you.[#]

22 However, become doers of the word[j] and not hearers only, deceiving yourselves with false reasoning. **23** For if anyone is a hearer of the word and not a doer,[k] this one is like a man looking at his own face* in a mirror. **24** For he looks at himself, and he goes away and immediately forgets what sort of person he is. **25** But the one who peers into the perfect law[l] that belongs to freedom and continues in it has become, not a forgetful hearer, but a doer of the work; and he will be happy in what he does.[m]

26 If any man thinks he is a worshipper of God* but does not keep a tight rein on* his tongue,[n] he is deceiving his own heart, and his worship is futile. **27** The form of worship* that is clean and undefiled from the standpoint of our God and Father is this: to look after or-

CHAP. 1

a 1Co 14:20
  Eph 4:13

b 1Ki 3:9
  Mr 11:24
  1Jo 3:22

c Mt 7:11

d Pr 2:3-6
  Joh 15:7
  1Jo 5:14

e Mt 7:7

f Mt 21:22
  Heb 11:6

g Jas 4:8

h Jas 2:5

i 1Ti 6:17

j Isa 40:6, 7
  Mt 19:24

k Mt 5:10
  Jas 1:2

l 2Ti 4:8
  1Pe 5:4
  Re 2:10

m Jas 2:5

n Ge 3:6
  1Jo 2:16

o Ro 5:21

Second Col.

a Mt 7:11

b Jer 31:35
  2Co 4:6

c Mal 3:6

d Joh 1:12, 13
  Ro 8:28
  Eph 1:13, 14
  2Th 2:13
  1Pe 1:23

e Re 14:4

f Pr 10:19
  Pr 17:27

g Ec 7:9
  Mt 5:22

h Jas 3:18

i Col 3:8
  1Pe 2:1

j Le 18:5
  1Sa 15:22
  Mt 7:21
  1Jo 3:7

k Lu 6:46
  Jas 2:14

l Ps 19:7

m Mt 7:24
  Lu 11:28
  Joh 13:17

n Ps 39:1
  Pr 12:18
  Pr 15:2
  1Pe 3:10

1:17 *Or "with whom there is not a variation of the turning of the shadow." **1:21** *Or possibly, "and the abundance of badness." #Or "your souls." **1:23** *Or "his natural face." **1:26** *Or "is religious." #Or "does not bridle." **1:27** *Or "religion."

1:5 *Or "finding fault." **1:7, 12** *See App. A5. **1:9** *Lit., "boast." **1:14** *Or "caught as by bait." **1:15** *Lit., "has conceived."

phans[a] and widows[b] in their tribulation,[c] and to keep oneself without spot from the world.[d]

2 My brothers, you are not holding to the faith of our glorious Lord Jesus Christ while showing favoritism, are you?[e] **2** For if a man with gold rings on his fingers and in splendid clothing comes into your meeting, but a poor man in filthy clothing also enters, **3** do you look with favor on the one wearing the splendid clothing and say, "You take this seat here in a fine place," and do you say to the poor one, "You keep standing" or, "Take that seat there under my footstool"?[f] **4** If so, do you not have class distinctions among yourselves,[g] and have you not become judges rendering wicked decisions?[h]

5 Listen, my beloved brothers. Did not God choose those who are poor from the world's standpoint to be rich in faith[i] and heirs of the Kingdom, which he promised to those who love him?[j] **6** But you have dishonored the poor. Is it not the rich who oppress you[k] and drag you before law courts? **7** Do they not blaspheme the fine name by which you were called? **8** If, now, you carry out the royal* law according to the scripture, "You must love your neighbor as yourself,"[l] you are doing quite well. **9** But if you continue showing favoritism,[m] you are committing sin, and you are convicted* by the law as transgressors.[n]

10 For if anyone obeys all the Law but makes a false step in one point, he has become an offender against all of it.[o] **11** For the one who said, "You must not commit adultery,"[p] also said, "You must not murder."[q] If, now, you do not commit adultery but you do murder,

you have become a transgressor of law. **12** Keep on speaking and behaving in such a way as those who are going to be judged by the law of a free people.*[a] **13** For the one who does not practice mercy will have his judgment without mercy.[b] Mercy triumphs over judgment.

14 Of what benefit is it, my brothers, if someone says he has faith but he does not have works?[c] That faith cannot save him, can it?[d] **15** If a brother or a sister is lacking clothing* and enough food for the day, **16** yet one of you says to them, "Go in peace; keep warm and well fed," but you do not give them what they need for their body, of what benefit is it?[e] **17** So, too, faith by itself, without works, is dead.[f]

18 Nevertheless, someone will say: "You have faith, and I have works. Show me your faith without the works, and I will show you my faith by my works." **19** You believe that there is one God, do you? You are doing quite well. And yet the demons believe and shudder.[g] **20** But do you care to know, O empty man, that faith without works is useless? **21** Was not Abraham our father declared righteous by works after he offered up Isaac his son on the altar?[h] **22** You see that his faith was active along with his works and his faith was perfected by his works,[i] **23** and the scripture was fulfilled that says: "Abraham put faith in Jehovah," and it was counted to him as righteousness,"[j] and he came to be called Jehovah's* friend.[k]

24 You see that a man is to be declared righteous by works and not by faith alone. **25** In the same manner, was not Ra'hab the prostitute also declared

---

CHAP. 1

a De 14:29
 De 27:19
 Ps 68:5

b Isa 1:17
 1Ti 5:3

c Job 29:12, 13
 Isa 58:7

d 1Co 5:7
 Jas 4:4
 Re 18:4

CHAP. 2

e 1Ti 5:21
 Jas 3:17

f Le 19:15

g Ga 3:28

h De 1:17

i Re 2:9

j Lu 22:28-30

k Ac 13:50

l Le 19:18
 Mt 22:39
 Ro 13:10

m Jas 2:1

n Le 19:15

o De 27:26
 Ga 3:10

p Ex 20:14
 De 5:18

q Ex 20:13
 De 5:17

Second Col.

a Jas 1:25

b Pr 21:13
 Mt 5:7
 Mt 6:15
 Lu 6:36

c Tit 3:8
 Jas 1:25

d 1Co 13:2

e Ge 15:7, 8
 Mt 25:35, 36
 Lu 3:11
 Ro 12:13
 1Ti 5:4
 Jas 1:27
 1Jo 3:17

f Mt 7:21
 Heb 10:24

g Mt 8:28, 29
 Lu 4:33, 34

h Ge 22:9, 12

i Heb 11:17

j Ge 15:6
 Ro 4:3
 Ga 3:6

k 2Ch 20:7
 Isa 41:8

2:8 *Or "kingly." 2:9 *Or "reproved."

2:12 *Lit., "law of freedom." 2:15 *Lit., "is naked." 2:23 *See App. A5.

righteous by works after she received the messengers hospitably and sent them out by another way?[a] **26** Indeed, just as the body without spirit* is dead,[b] so also faith without works is dead.[c]

3 Not many of you should become teachers, my brothers, knowing that we will receive heavier* judgment.[d] **2** For we all stumble* many times.[e] If anyone does not stumble in word, he is a perfect man, able to bridle also his whole body. **3** If we put bridles in the mouths of horses to make them obey us, we guide also their whole body. **4** Look also at ships: Although they are so big and are driven by strong winds, they are steered by a very small rudder wherever the man at the helm is inclined to go.

5 So, too, the tongue is a small part of the body, and yet it makes great brags. See how small a fire it takes to set a great forest ablaze! **6** The tongue is also a fire.[f] The tongue represents a world of unrighteousness among our body members, for it defiles all the body[g] and sets the whole course of life* on fire, and it is set on fire by Ge·hen′na.[h] **7** For every kind of wild animal and bird and reptile* and sea creature is to be tamed and has been tamed by humans. **8** But no human can tame the tongue. It is unruly and injurious, full of deadly poison.[h] **9** With it we praise Jehovah,* the Father, and yet with it we curse men who have come into existence "in the likeness of God."[i] **10** Out of the

same mouth come blessing and cursing.

My brothers, it is not right for things to happen this way.[a] **11** A spring does not cause the fresh* water and the bitter water to bubble out of the same opening, does it? **12** My brothers, a fig tree cannot produce olives, or a grapevine figs, can it?[b] Neither can salt water produce fresh water.

13 Who is wise and understanding among you? Let him by his fine conduct demonstrate works performed with a mildness that comes from wisdom. **14** But if you have bitter jealousy[c] and contentiousness*[d] in your hearts, do not be bragging[e] and lying against the truth. **15** This is not the wisdom that comes down from above; it is earthly,[f] animalistic, demonic. **16** For wherever there are jealousy and contentiousness,* there will also be disorder and every vile thing.[g]

17 But the wisdom from above is first of all pure,[h] then peaceable,[i] reasonable,[j] ready to obey, full of mercy and good fruits,[k] impartial,[l] not hypocritical.[m] **18** Moreover, the fruit of righteousness is sown in peaceful conditions[n] for* those who are making peace.[o]

4 What is the source of the wars and fights among you? Do they not originate from your fleshly desires that carry on a conflict within you?*[p] **2** You desire, and yet you do not have. You go on murdering and coveting, and yet you are not able to obtain. You go on fighting and waging war.[q] You do not have because of your not asking. **3** When you do ask, you do not receive because you are asking

---

CHAP. 2
a Jos 2:1, 15
  Jos 6:17
  Heb 11:31
b Ps 146:4
c Ro 10:10
  Jas 2:17

CHAP. 3
d Lu 12:48
e 1Ki 8:46
  Pr 20:9
  1Jo 1:8
f Pr 16:27
  Mt 12:36, 37
g Ps 39:1
  Mt 15:11, 18
  Mr 7:23
h Ps 140:3
  Pr 12:18
  Pr 18:7
i Ge 1:26, 27

Second Col.
a Eph 4:29
b Mt 7:16
c Ro 13:13
  1Co 3:3
d Eph 4:31
e 1Co 13:4
f 1Co 2:14
  Php 3:19
g Pr 14:30
  Ga 5:19-21
h Ro 12:9
  1Ti 5:1, 2
i 2Co 13:11
  1Th 5:13
  2Pe 3:14
j 1Ti 3:3
  Tit 3:2
k Ga 5:22, 23
l Jas 2:9
m 1Pe 1:22
n Isa 32:17
  Heb 12:11
o Mt 5:9
  1Pe 3:11

CHAP. 4
p Ro 7:23
  Ga 5:17
  Jas 3:14
  1Pe 2:11
q Mt 5:22
  Jas 3:16

2:26 *Or "breath." **3:1** *Or "stricter." **3:2** *Or "make mistakes." **3:6** *Lit., "the wheel of the birth (origin)." *See Glossary. **3:7** *Or "creeping thing." **3:9** *See App. A5.

3:11 *Lit., "sweet." **3:14, 16** *Or possibly, "selfish ambition." **3:18** *Or possibly, "by." **4:1** *Lit., "in your members."

for a wrong purpose, so that you
may spend it on your fleshly desires.
4 Adulteresses,* do you not
know that friendship with the
world is enmity with God? Whoever, therefore, wants to be a
friend of the world is making
himself an enemy of God.[a] **5** Or
do you think that for no reason the scripture says: "The
spirit that has taken up residence within us keeps enviously
longing"?[b] **6** However, the undeserved kindness that He gives
is greater. So it says: "God opposes the haughty ones,[c] but
he gives undeserved kindness to
the humble ones."[d]
7 Therefore, subject yourselves to God;[e] but oppose the
Devil,[f] and he will flee from you.[g]
8 Draw close to God, and he
will draw close to you.[h] Cleanse
your hands, you sinners,[i] and
purify your hearts,[j] you indecisive ones. **9** Give way to misery
and mourn and weep.[k] Let your
laughter be turned into mourning, and your joy into despair.
10 Humble yourselves in the
eyes of Jehovah,*[l] and he will exalt you.[m]
11 Stop speaking against
one another, brothers.[n] Whoever speaks against a brother or judges his brother speaks
against law and judges law.
Now if you judge law, you are
not a doer of law but a judge.
12 There is only one who is
Lawgiver and Judge,[o] the one
who is able to save and to destroy.[p] But you, who are you to
be judging your neighbor?[q]
13 Come, now, you who say:
"Today or tomorrow we will
travel to this city and will spend
a year there, and we will do
business and make some profit,"[r]
14 whereas you do not know
what your life will be like tomorrow.[a] For you are a mist that
appears for a little while and
then disappears.[b] **15** Instead,
you should say: "If Jehovah*
wills,[c] we will live and do this
or that." **16** But now you take
pride in your arrogant boasting. All such boasting is wicked.
17 Therefore, if someone knows
how to do what is right and yet
does not do it, it is a sin for him.[d]

5 Come, now, you rich men,
weep and wail over the mis-
eries that are coming upon you.[e]
2 Your riches have rotted, and
your clothing has become moth-
eaten.[f] **3** Your gold and silver
have rusted away, and their rust
will be a witness against you and
will consume your flesh. What
you have stored up will be like
a fire in the last days.[g] **4** Look!
The wages you have withheld
from the workers who harvested
your fields keep crying out, and
the cries for help of the reapers have reached the ears of Jehovah* of armies.[h] **5** You have
lived in luxury and for self-
gratification on the earth. You
have fattened your hearts on the
day of slaughter.[i] **6** You have
condemned; you have murdered
the righteous one. Is he not opposing you?
7 Be patient then, brothers,
until the presence of the Lord.[j]
Look! The farmer keeps waiting for the precious fruit of the
earth, exercising patience over
it until the early rain and
the late rain arrive.[k] **8** You too
exercise patience;[l] make your
hearts firm, because the presence of the Lord has drawn
close.[m]
9 Do not grumble* against
one another, brothers, so that
you do not get judged.[n] Look!

CHAP. 4
a 2Ch 19:2, Joh 15:19, Joh 17:14, Joh 18:36, 1Jo 2:15, 1Jo 5:19
b Ge 6:5, Ge 8:21
c Ps 138:6
d Pr 3:34, 1Pe 5:5
e Heb 12:9, 1Pe 2:17, 1Pe 5:6
f Eph 4:27, Eph 6:11
g Mt 4:10, 11, Lu 4:13
h Isa 44:22, Isa 55:6, 7
i Isa 1:16
j 1Jo 3:3
k Joe 2:12
l 2Ch 7:14, 2Ch 33:12, 13
m Pr 29:23, Mt 23:12
n Le 19:16, Pr 17:9
o Isa 33:22
p Mt 10:28
q Mt 7:1, Lu 6:37, Ro 14:4
r Lu 12:18-20

Second Col.
a Ps 39:6, Pr 27:1, Ec 6:12
b Job 14:1, 2, Ps 102:3, 1Pe 1:24
c Ac 18:21, Heb 6:3
d Lu 12:47, Joh 9:41, Joh 15:22

CHAP. 5
e Pr 11:28, Lu 6:24, Lu 18:25
f Mt 6:19, Lu 12:33
g Eze 7:19
h Le 19:13, De 24:14, 15, Jer 22:13, Mal 3:5
i Jer 12:3
j Mt 24:3
k De 11:14, Jer 5:24
l Heb 6:12
m 1Th 3:13
n 1Co 4:5

4:4 *Or "You unfaithful ones." **4:10, 15; 5:4** *See App. A5.

5:9 *Or "groan; complain." Lit., "heave sighs."

The Judge is standing before the doors. **10** Brothers, take as a pattern of the suffering of evil[a] and the exercising of patience[b] the prophets who spoke in the name of Jehovah.*[c] **11** Look! We consider happy[#] those who have endured.[d] You have heard of the endurance of Job[e] and have seen the outcome Jehovah* gave,[f] that Jehovah* is very tender in affection[△] and merciful.[g]

12 Above all, my brothers, stop swearing, either by heaven or by earth or by any other oath. But let your "Yes" mean yes and your "No," no,[h] so that you do not become liable to judgment.

13 Is there anyone suffering hardship among you? Let him carry on prayer.[i] Is there anyone in good spirits? Let him sing psalms.[j] **14** Is there anyone sick among you? Let him call the elders[k] of the congregation to him, and let them pray over him, applying oil to him[l] in the name of Jehovah.* **15** And

5:10, 11, 14, 15 * See App. A5.   5:11 #Or "blessed."   △Or "very compassionate."

the prayer of faith will make the sick one[#] well, and Jehovah* will raise him up. Also, if he has committed sins, he will be forgiven.

16 Therefore, openly confess your sins[a] to one another and pray for one another, so that you may be healed. A righteous man's supplication has a powerful effect.*[b] **17** E·liʹjah was a man with feelings like ours, and yet when he prayed earnestly for it not to rain, it did not rain on the land for three years and six months.[c] **18** Then he prayed again, and the heaven gave rain and the land produced fruit.[d]

19 My brothers, if anyone among you is led astray from the truth and another turns him back, **20** know that whoever turns a sinner back from the error[e] of his way will save him* from death and will cover a multitude of sins.[f]

5:15 #Or possibly, "tired one."   5:16 *Lit., "has much force when it is at work."   5:20 *Or "his soul."

CHAP. 5	
a	Mt 5:12
b	Heb 6:12
c	2Ch 36:16
d	Jas 1:2-4
e	Job 1:20, 21
f	Job 42:10
g	Ps 103:8 Lu 6:36
h	Mt 5:34-37
i	Ps 50:15
j	Col 3:16
k	Ac 20:28, 35 1Pe 5:2
l	Ps 141:5 Mr 6:13 Lu 10:34

Second Col.	
a	2Sa 12:13 Ps 32:5 Pr 28:13 1Jo 1:9
b	1Sa 12:18 1Ki 13:6
c	1Ki 17:1
d	1Ki 18:42, 45
e	Ga 6:1
f	1Ti 4:16

THE FIRST OF

PETER

OUTLINE OF CONTENTS

1 Peter, an apostle[a] of Jesus Christ, to the temporary residents scattered about in Pon′tus, Ga·la′ti·a, Cap·pa·do′ci·a,[b] Asia, and Bi·thyn′i·a, to those chosen **2** according to the foreknowledge of God the Father,[c] with sanctification by the spirit,[d] for the purpose of being obedient and sprinkled with the blood of Jesus Christ:[e]

May undeserved kindness and peace be increased to you.

3 Praised be the God and Father of our Lord Jesus Christ, for according to his great mercy he gave us a new birth[f] to a living hope[g] through the resurrection of Jesus Christ from the dead,[h] **4** to an incorruptible and undefiled and unfading inheritance.[i] It is reserved in the heavens for you,[j] **5** who are being safeguarded by God's power through faith for a salvation ready to be revealed in the last period of time. **6** Because of this you are greatly rejoicing, though for a short time, if it must be, you have been distressed by various trials,[k] **7** in order that the tested quality of your faith,[l] of much greater value than gold that perishes despite its being tested* by fire, may be found a cause for praise and glory and honor at the revelation of Jesus Christ.[m] **8** Though you never saw him, you love him. Though you do not see him now, yet you exercise faith in him and are greatly rejoicing with an indescribable and glorious joy, **9** as you attain the goal of your faith, your salvation.*[n]

10 Concerning this salvation, the prophets who prophesied about the undeserved kindness meant for you made a diligent inquiry and a care-ful search.[a] **11** They kept on investigating what particular time or what season the spirit within them was indicating concerning Christ[b] as it testified beforehand about the sufferings meant for Christ[c] and about the glory that would follow. **12** It was revealed to them that they were ministering, not to themselves, but to you, regarding what has now been announced to you by those who declared the good news to you with holy spirit sent from heaven.[d] Into these very things, angels are desiring to peer.

13 So brace up your minds for activity;[e] keep your senses completely;[f] set your hope on the undeserved kindness that will be brought to you at the revelation of Jesus Christ. **14** As obedient children, stop being molded by* the desires you formerly had in your ignorance, **15** but like the Holy One who called you, become holy yourselves in all your conduct,[g] **16** for it is written: "You must be holy, because I am holy."[h]

17 And if you are calling on the Father who judges impartially[i] according to each one's work, conduct yourselves with fear[j] during the time of your temporary residence. **18** For you know that it was not with corruptible things, with silver or gold, that you were set free*[k] from your futile way of life handed down to you by your forefathers,*' **19** But it was with precious blood,[l] like that of an unblemished and spotless lamb, that of Christ.[n] **20** True, he was foreknown before the founding of the world,[o] but he was made manifest at the end of the times for your sake.[p]

1:14 *Or "fashioned after." 1:18 *Lit., "you were ransomed; you were redeemed." ʺOr "by tradition."

CHAP. 1

a Mt 10:2

b Ac 2:5, 9

c Ro 8:29

d 2Th 2:13

e Heb 12:22, 24

f 1Pe 1:23

g Re 20:6

h 1Co 15:20

i 1Co 15:53
    2Ti 1:10
    1Pe 5:4

j Joh 14:2
    2Ti 4:8

k 2Co 4:17
    2Ti 3:12

l Jas 1:2, 3

m 2Th 1:7

n Ro 6:22

Second Col.

a Mt 13:17

b Da 9:24-27

c Isa 53:5

d Joh 15:26
    Ac 2:4

e Lu 12:35

f Eph 5:17
    1Pe 4:7

g De 28:9
    Ro 12:1
    Heb 12:14

h Le 11:44
    Le 19:2
    Le 20:7, 26

i De 10:17

j 2Co 7:1

k 1Co 6:20

l Isa 53:12
    Heb 9:14

m Ex 12:5
    Le 22:20
    Joh 1:29

n 1Co 5:7

o Joh 17:5
    Eph 1:4

p Col 1:26, 27

21 Through him you are believers in God,[a] the one who raised him up from the dead[b] and gave him glory,[c] so that your faith and hope might be in God.

22 Now that you have purified yourselves* by your obedience to the truth with unhypocritical brotherly affection[d] as the result, love one another intensely from the heart.[e] **23** For you have been given a new birth,[f] not by corruptible, but by incorruptible seed,*[g] through the word of the living and enduring God.[h] **24** For "all flesh is* like grass, and all its glory is like a blossom of the field; the grass withers, and the flower falls off, **25** but the saying* of Jehovah[#] endures forever."[i] And this "saying"* is the good news that was declared to you.[j]

2 So rid yourselves of all badness[k] and deceit and hypocrisy and envy and all backbiting. **2** As newborn infants,[l] form a longing for the unadulterated* milk of the word, so that by means of it you may grow to salvation,[m] **3** provided you have tasted* that the Lord is kind.

4 As you come to him, a living stone rejected by men[n] but chosen, precious to God,[o] **5** you yourselves as living stones are being built up into a spiritual house[p] to be a holy priesthood, in order to offer up spiritual sacrifices[q] acceptable to God through Jesus Christ.[r] **6** For it says in Scripture: "Look! I am laying in Zion a chosen stone, a precious foundation cornerstone, and no one exercising faith in it will ever be disappointed."*[s]

7 It is to you, therefore, that he is precious, because you are believers; but to those not believing, "the stone that the builders rejected,[a] this has become the chief cornerstone"*[b] **8** and "a stone of stumbling and a rock of offense."[c] They are stumbling because they are disobedient to the word. To this very end they were appointed. **9** But you are "a chosen race, a royal priesthood, a holy nation,[d] a people for special possession,[e] that you should declare abroad the excellencies"*[f] of the One who called you out of darkness into his wonderful light.[g] **10** For you were once not a people, but now you are God's people;[h] once you had not been shown mercy, but now you have received mercy.[i]

11 Beloved, I urge you as foreigners and temporary residents[j] to keep abstaining from fleshly desires,[k] which wage war against you.*[l] **12** Maintain your conduct fine among the nations,[m] so that when they accuse you of being wrongdoers, they may be eyewitnesses of your fine works[n] and, as a result, glorify God in the day of his inspection.

13 For the Lord's sake subject yourselves to every human creation,*[o] whether to a king[p] as being superior **14** or to governors as sent by him to punish wrongdoers but to praise those who do good.[q] **15** For it is the will of God that by doing good you may silence* the ignorant talk of unreasonable men.[r] **16** Be as free people,[s] using your freedom, not as a cover* for doing wrong,[t] but as slaves

---

CHAP. 1

a Joh 14:6
b Ac 2:24
c Heb 2:9
d Ro 12:9
  1Jo 3:17
e 1Ti 1:5
f Joh 3:3
  2Co 5:17
  1Pe 1:3
  1Jo 3:9
g Joh 3:6
h Joh 6:63
  Jas 1:18
i Isa 40:6-8
j Tit 1:3

CHAP. 2

k Ga 5:16
  Jas 1:21
l Mr 10:15
m 2Ti 3:15
n Isa 53:3
  Joh 19:15
o Ps 118:22
  Isa 42:1
  Mt 21:42
  Ac 4:11
p Eph 2:21
q Heb 13:15
r Ro 12:1
s Isa 28:16

Second Col.

a Ps 69:8
b Ps 118:22
  Mt 21:42
  Lu 20:17
  Ac 4:11
c Isa 8:14
d Re 5:10
  Re 20:6
e Ex 19:5, 6
  De 7:6
  De 10:15
  Mal 3:17
f Isa 43:20, 21
g Eph 5:8
  Col 1:13
h Ho 1:10
  Ac 15:14
  Ro 9:25
i Ho 2:23
j 1Pe 1:17
k Ro 8:5
  Ga 5:24
l Ga 5:17
  Jas 4:1
m Ro 12:17
  1Ti 3:7
n Mt 5:16
  Jas 3:13
o Ro 13:1
  Eph 6:5
  Tit 3:1
p 1Pe 2:17
q Ro 13:3, 4
r Tit 2:7, 8
s Ga 5:1
t Ga 5:13

1:22 *Or "your souls." **1:23** *That is, seed capable of reproducing, or bearing fruit. **1:24** *Or "all humans are." **1:25** *Or "word." #See App. A5. **2:2** *Or "pure." **2:3** *Or "experienced." **2:6** *Lit., "put to shame."

2:7 *Lit., "the head of the corner." **2:9** *Lit., "the virtues," that is, his praiseworthy qualities and deeds. **2:11** *Or "the soul." **2:13** *Or "institution." **2:15** *Lit., "muzzle." **2:16** *Or "an excuse."

of God.[a] **17** Honor men of all sorts,[b] have love for the whole association of brothers,[*c] be in fear of God,[d] honor the king.[e]

18 Let servants be in subjection to their masters with all due fear,[f] not only to the good and reasonable but also to those hard to please. **19** For it is agreeable when someone endures hardship[*] and suffers unjustly because of conscience toward God.[g] **20** For what merit is there if you are beaten for sinning and you endure it?[h] But if you endure suffering because of doing good, this is an agreeable thing to God.[i]

21 In fact, to this course you were called, because even Christ suffered for you,[j] leaving a model for you to follow his steps closely.[k] **22** He committed no sin,[l] nor was deception found in his mouth.[m] **23** When he was being insulted,[*n] he did not insult[#] in return.[o] When he was suffering,[p] he did not threaten, but he entrusted himself to the One who judges[q] righteously. **24** He himself bore our sins[r] in his own body on the stake,[*s] so that we might die to[#] sins and live to righteousness. And "by his wounds you were healed."[t] **25** For you were like sheep going astray,[u] but now you have returned to the shepherd[v] and overseer of your souls.[*]

3 In the same way, you wives, be in subjection to your husbands,[w] so that if any are not obedient to the word, they may be won without a word through the conduct of their wives,[x] **2** because of having been eyewitnesses of your chaste conduct[y] together with deep respect. **3** Do not let

your adornment be external—the braiding of hair and the wearing of gold ornaments[a] or fine clothing— **4** but let it be the secret person of the heart in the incorruptible adornment of the quiet and mild spirit,[b] which is of great value in the eyes of God. **5** For this is how the holy women of the past who hoped in God used to adorn themselves, subjecting themselves to their husbands, **6** just as Sarah obeyed Abraham, calling him lord.[c] And you have become her children, provided you continue doing good and do not give in to fear.[d]

7 You husbands, in the same way, continue dwelling with them according to knowledge.[*] Assign them honor[e] as to a weaker vessel, the feminine one, since they are also heirs with you[f] of the undeserved favor of life, in order for your prayers not to be hindered.

8 Finally, all of you have unity of mind,[*g] fellow feeling, brotherly affection, tender compassion,[h] and humility.[i] **9** Do not pay back injury for injury[j] or insult for insult.[k] Instead, repay with a blessing,[f] for you were called to this course, so that you might inherit a blessing.

10 For "whoever would love life and see good days must guard his tongue from bad[m] and his lips from speaking deception. **11** Let him turn away from what is bad[n] and do what is good;[o] let him seek peace and pursue it.[p] **12** For the eyes of Jehovah[*] are on the righteous, and his ears listen to their supplication,[q] but the face of Jehovah[*] is against those doing bad things."[r]

13 Indeed, who will harm you if you become zealous for what

CHAP. 2

a 1Co 7:22
b Le 19:32
  Ro 12:10
  Ro 13:7
c 1Jo 2:10
  1Jo 4:21
d Ps 111:10
  Pr 8:13
  2Co 7:1
e Pr 24:21
f Eph 6:5
  Col 3:22
  1Ti 6:1
  Tit 2:9
g Ro 13:5
h 1Pe 4:15
i Mt 5:10
  Ac 5:41
  1Pe 4:14
j 1Pe 3:18
k Mt 16:24
  Joh 13:15
l Joh 8:46
  Heb 4:15
m Isa 53:9
n Mt 27:39
o Isa 53:7
  Ro 12:21
p Heb 5:8
q Jer 11:20
  Joh 8:50
r Le 16:21
s Php 2:8
t Isa 53:5
u Isa 53:6
v Ps 23:1
  Isa 40:11

CHAP. 3

w Ro 7:2
  1Co 11:3
  Eph 5:22
x 1Co 7:16
y 1Pe 2:12

Second Col.

a Pr 11:22
b Eph 4:24
  Col 3:10, 12
  1Ti 2:9, 10
c Ge 18:12
  Eph 5:33
d Pr 3:25
  Php 1:28
e Eph 5:25
f Ga 3:28
g 1Co 1:10
  Php 2:2
h Ro 12:10
i Ro 15:5
  Col 3:12
j Ro 12:17
  1Th 5:15
k 1Pe 2:23
l Ro 12:14
  1Co 4:12
m Jas 3:8
n 3Jo 11
o 1Th 5:13
  Jas 3:17
q 1Jo 3:22
r Ps 34:12-16

2:17 *Lit., "the brotherhood." 2:19 *Or "grief; pain." 2:23 *Or "reviled." #Or "revile." 2:24 *Or "tree." #Or "be finished with." 2:25 *Or "lives."

3:7 *Or "showing them consideration; understanding them." 3:8 *Or "think in agreement." 3:12 *See App. A5.

is good?[a] **14** But even if you should suffer for the sake of righteousness, you are happy.[b] However, do not fear what they fear,* nor be disturbed.[c] **15** But sanctify the Christ as Lord in your hearts, always ready to make a defense before everyone who demands of you a reason for the hope you have, but doing so with a mild temper[d] and deep respect.[e]

16 Maintain a good conscience,[f] so that in whatever way you are spoken against, those who speak against you may be put to shame[g] because of your good conduct as followers of Christ.[h] **17** For it is better to suffer because you are doing good,[i] if it is God's will to allow it, than because you are doing evil.[j] **18** For Christ died once for all time for sins,[k] a righteous person for unrighteous ones,[l] in order to lead you to God.[m] He was put to death in the flesh[n] but made alive in the spirit.[o] **19** And in this state he went and preached to the spirits in prison,[p] **20** who had formerly been disobedient when God was patiently waiting* in Noah's day,[q] while the ark was being constructed,[r] in which a few people, that is, eight souls,* were carried safely through the water.[s]

21 Baptism, which corresponds to this, is also now saving you (not by the removing of the filth of the flesh, but by the request to God for a good conscience),[t] through the resurrection of Jesus Christ. **22** He is at God's right hand,[u] for he went to heaven, and angels and authorities and powers were made subject to him.[v]

4 Since Christ suffered in the flesh,[a] you too arm yourselves with the same mental disposition;* because the person who has suffered in the flesh has desisted from sins,[b] **2** so that he may live the remainder of his time in the flesh, no more for the desires of men,[c] but for God's will.[d] **3** For the time that has passed by is sufficient for you to have done the will of the nations[e] when you carried on in acts of brazen conduct,* unbridled passions, overdrinking, wild parties,* drinking bouts, and lawless idolatries.[f] **4** They are puzzled that you do not continue running with them in the same decadent course of debauchery, so they speak abusively of you.[g] **5** But these people will render an account to the one who is ready to judge those living and those dead.[h] **6** In fact, this is why the good news was declared also to the dead,[i] so that although they are judged in the flesh from the standpoint of men, they might live in harmony with the spirit from God's standpoint.

7 But the end of all things has drawn close. Therefore, be sound in mind,[j] and be vigilant* with a view to prayers.[k] **8** Above all things, have intense love for one another,[l] because love covers a multitude of sins.[m] **9** Be hospitable to one another without grumbling.[n] **10** To the extent that each one has received a gift, use it in ministering to one another as fine stewards of God's undeserved kindness that is expressed in various ways.[o] **11** If anyone speaks, let him do so as speaking pronouncements from

CHAP. 3
a Ro 13:3, 4
b Mt 5:11, 12
  Ac 5:41
  1Pe 2:19
c Mt 10:28
d Pr 15:1
  2Ti 2:24, 25
  Tit 3:1, 2
e Col 4:6
f Ac 23:1
  Ac 24:16
  1Ti 1:5
  1Ti 1:18, 19
  1Ti 3:9
g Tit 2:8
h Ro 12:21
  1Pe 2:12
i 2Co 1:7
  Col 1:24
j 1Pe 4:15
k Heb 9:28
l Ro 5:6
m 2Co 5:18
n 1Co 15:50
o 1Ti 3:16
p 2Pe 2:4
  Jude 6
q Ge 6:2, 3
r Ge 6:14
s Ge 7:13, 23
t Heb 9:14
  Heb 10:22
u Ps 110:1
  Ac 7:55
  Heb 10:12
v Mt 28:18
  1Co 15:25
  Eph 1:20, 21
  Php 2:9, 10
  Heb 1:6

Second Col.

CHAP. 4
a Php 2:8
b Ro 6:11
  Col 3:5
  1Jo 3:6
c 2Co 5:15
d Ga 2:20
  Eph 5:17
e Tit 3:3
f Ro 13:13
  1Co 5:11
  Ga 5:19, 21
  Eph 4:17-19
g 1Pe 3:16
h Ac 10:42
  Ac 17:31
  2Ti 4:1
  Re 20:12
i Eph 2:1
j Ro 12:3
  1Ti 3:2
  Tit 2:6
k Col 4:2
l Col 3:14
m Pr 10:12
  Pr 17:9
  1Co 13:4, 7
n 2Co 9:7
  Heb 13:2
o Ro 12:6-8

3:14 *Or possibly, "do not fear their threats." **3:20** *Lit., "the patience of God was waiting." *Or "persons."

4:1 *Or "resolve; determination." **4:3** *Or "acts of shameless conduct." Plural of the Greek a·sel'gei·a. See Glossary. *Or "revelries." **4:7** *Or "alert; awake."

God; if anyone ministers, let him do so as depending on the strength that God supplies;[a] so that in all things God may be glorified[b] through Jesus Christ. The glory and the might are his forever and ever. Amen.

12 Beloved ones, do not be surprised about the fiery trials that you are experiencing,[c] as though something strange were happening to you. **13** On the contrary, go on rejoicing[d] over the extent to which you are sharers in the sufferings of the Christ,[e] so that you may rejoice and be overjoyed also during the revelation of his glory.[f] **14** If you are being reproached* for the name of Christ, you are happy,[g] because the spirit of glory, yes, the spirit of God, is resting upon you.

15 However, let none of you suffer as a murderer or a thief or a wrongdoer or a busybody in other people's matters.[h] **16** But if anyone suffers as a Christian, let him not feel ashamed,[i] but let him keep on glorifying God while bearing this name. **17** For it is the appointed time for the judgment to start with the house of God.[j] Now if it starts first with us,[k] what will the outcome be for those who are not obedient to the good news of God?[l] **18** "And if the righteous man is being saved with difficulty, what will happen to the ungodly man and the sinner?"[m] **19** So, then, let those who are suffering in harmony with the will of God keep on entrusting* themselves# to a faithful Creator while they are doing good.[n]

5 Therefore, as a fellow elder, a witness of the sufferings of the Christ and a sharer of the glory that is to be revealed,[o] I make this appeal* to the elders

among you: **2** Shepherd the flock of God[a] under your care, serving as overseers,* not under compulsion, but willingly before God;[b] not for love of dishonest gain,[c] but eagerly; **3** not lording it over those who are God's inheritance,[d] but becoming examples to the flock.[e] **4** And when the chief shepherd[f] has been made manifest, you will receive the unfading crown of glory.[g]

5 In the same way, you younger men, be in subjection to the older men.*[h] But all of you clothe# yourselves with humility^ toward one another, because God opposes the haughty ones, but he gives undeserved kindness to the humble ones.[i]

6 Humble yourselves, therefore, under the mighty hand of God, so that he may exalt you in due time,[j] **7** while you throw all your anxiety* on him,[k] because he cares for you.[l] **8** Keep your senses, be watchful![m] Your adversary, the Devil, walks about like a roaring lion, seeking to devour someone.*[n] **9** But take your stand against him,[o] firm in the faith, knowing that the same kind of sufferings are being experienced by the entire association of your brothers* in the world.[p] **10** But after you have suffered a little while, the God of all undeserved kindness, who called you to his everlasting glory[q] in union with Christ, will himself finish your training. He will make you firm,[r] he will make you strong,[s] he will firmly ground you. **11** To him be the might forever. Amen.

12 Through Silʹvaʹnus,*[t] whom I regard as a faithful brother, I have written you in

---

CHAP. 4
a Isa 12:2
  Eph 3:20
b 1Co 10:31
c 1Pe 5:9
d Ac 5:41
  Jas 1:2
e Ro 8:17
  2Co 4:10
  2Ti 3:12
f 1Pe 1:7
g Jas 1:12
  Jas 5:11
h 1Ti 5:13
  1Pe 2:20
i Col 1:24
  Heb 12:2
j Heb 3:6
k 1Co 11:32
l 2Ti 1:7, 8
m Pr 11:31
  Mt 7:13, 14
n 2Ti 1:12

CHAP. 5
o Ro 8:18

Second Col.
a Isa 40:11
  Joh 21:16
  Ac 20:28
b Joh 10:11
c 1Ti 3:2, 3
d 2Co 1:24
e Php 3:17
f Heb 13:20
g 1Co 9:25
  2Ti 4:8
  1Pe 1:3, 4
h Eph 5:21
  Jas 3:17
i Pr 3:34
  Isa 57:15
  Jas 4:6
j Mt 23:12
  Lu 14:11
k Mt 6:25
l Ps 55:22
m 1Th 5:6
n Lu 22:31
o Eph 6:11
  Jas 4:7
p Ac 14:22
  2Ti 3:12
q 2Co 4:17
  1Th 2:12
r 2Th 2:16, 17
s Eph 6:10
t Ac 15:27

4:14 *Or "insulted." 4:19 *Or "commending." #Or "their souls." 5:1 *Or "exhortation."

5:2 *Or "carefully watching over it." 5:5 *Or "the elders." #Or "gird." ^Or "lowliness of mind." 5:7 *Or "cares; worries." 5:8 *Or "looking for someone to devour." 5:9 *Lit., "by your brotherhood." 5:12 *Also called Silas.

few words in order to encourage you and to give an earnest witness that this is the true undeserved kindness of God. Stand firm in it. **13** She who is in Babylon, a chosen one

Second Col.

CHAP. 5
a Ac 12:12

like you, sends you her greetings, and so does Mark,[a] my son. **14** Greet one another with a kiss of love.

May all of you who are in union with Christ have peace.

THE SECOND OF
PETER

OUTLINE OF CONTENTS

1 Simple Peter, a slave and an apostle of Jesus Christ, to those who have acquired a faith as precious as ours* through the righteousness of our God and the Savior Jesus Christ:

2 May undeserved kindness and peace be increased to you by an accurate knowledge[a] of God and of Jesus our Lord, **3** for his divine power has granted* us all the things that contribute to life and godly devotion through the accurate knowledge of the One who called us[b] by his own glory and virtue. **4** Through these things he has granted* us the precious and very grand promises,[c] so that through these you may be-

CHAP. 1
a Col 1:9
b Joh 17:3
c Lu 22:29, 30
   Joh 14:2
   Ga 3:29

Second Col.
a 1Co 15:53
   1Pe 1:3, 4
   1Jo 3:2
   Re 20:6
b Php 2:12
   2Ti 2:15
   Heb 4:11
   Jude 3
c Php 4:8
d Joh 17:3
   Heb 5:14
e 1Co 9:25
   2Ti 2:24
f 2Pe 2:9
g 1Th 4:9
h Tit 3:14

come sharers in divine nature,[a] having escaped from the world's corruption produced by wrong desire.*

5 For this very reason, put forth all earnest effort[b] to supply to your faith virtue,[c] to your virtue knowledge,[d] **6** to your knowledge self-control, to your self-control[e] endurance, to your endurance godly devotion,[f] **7** to your godly devotion brotherly affection, to your brotherly affection love.[g] **8** For if these things exist in you and overflow, they will prevent you from being either inactive or unfruitful*[h] regarding the accurate knowledge of our Lord Jesus Christ.

1:1 *Or "a faith held in equal privilege with ours." **1:3, 4** *Or "freely given."

1:4 *Or "by lust." **1:8** *Or "unproductive."

9 For anyone lacking these things is blind, shutting his eyes to the light,*[a] and has become forgetful of his cleansing from his sins[b] of long ago. **10** Therefore, brothers, be all the more diligent to make your calling[c] and choosing sure for yourselves, for if you keep on doing these things, you will by no means ever fail.[d] **11** In fact, in this way you will be richly granted* entrance into the everlasting Kingdom[e] of our Lord and Savior Jesus Christ.[f]

12 For this reason I intend always to remind you of these things, although you know them and are well-established in the truth that is present in you. **13** But I consider it right, as long as I am in this tabernacle,*[g] to stir you with reminders,[h] **14** knowing as I do that my tabernacle is soon to be removed, just as also our Lord Jesus Christ made clear to me.[i] **15** I will always do my utmost so that after my departure, you may be able to recall* these things for yourselves.

16 No, it was not by following artfully contrived false stories that we made known to you the power and presence of our Lord Jesus Christ, but rather, we were eyewitnesses of his magnificence.[j] **17** For he received from God the Father honor and glory when words such as these* were conveyed to him by the magnificent glory: "This is my Son, my beloved, whom I myself have approved."[k] **18** Yes, these words we heard coming from heaven while we were with him in the holy mountain.

19 So we have the prophetic word made more sure, and you are doing well in paying attention to it as to a lamp* shining in a dark place (until day dawns and a daystar[b] rises) in your hearts. **20** For you know this first, that no prophecy of Scripture springs from any private interpretation. **21** For prophecy was at no time brought by man's will,[c] but men spoke from God as they were moved* by holy spirit.[d]

2 However, there also came to be false prophets among the people, as there will also be false teachers among you.[e] These will quietly bring in destructive sects, and they will even disown the owner who bought them,[f] bringing speedy destruction upon themselves. **2** Furthermore, many will follow their brazen conduct,*[g] and because of them the way of the truth will be spoken of abusively.[h] **3** Also, they will greedily exploit you with counterfeit words. But their judgment, decided long ago,[i] is not moving slowly, and their destruction is not sleeping.[j]

4 Certainly God did not refrain from punishing the angels who sinned,[k] but threw them into Tar·ta·rus,*[l] putting them in chains* of dense darkness to be reserved for judgment.[m] **5** And he did not refrain from punishing an ancient world,[n] but kept Noah, a preacher of righteousness,[o] safe with seven others[p] when he brought a flood upon a world of ungodly people.[q] **6** And by reducing the cities of Sod'om and Go·mor'rah to ashes, he condemned them,[r] setting a pattern for ungodly

---

CHAP. 1

a 1Jo 2:9
  Re 3:17

b Heb 9:14

c Heb 3:1

d 2Ti 4:7, 8

e Da 2:44

f Lu 16:9
  Joh 3:5

g 2Co 5:1

h Ro 15:15
  Jude 5

i Joh 21:18

j Mt 17:2
  Mr 9:2
  Lu 9:29

k Ps 2:7
  Mt 17:1, 5
  Mr 9:7
  Lu 9:35

Second Col.

a Ps 119:105
  Joh 1:9

b Nu 24:17
  Re 22:16

c 2Ti 3:16

d 2Sa 23:2
  Ac 1:16
  Ac 28:25
  1Pe 1:11

CHAP. 2

e Mt 24:24
  1Ti 4:1

f 1Co 6:20

g Jude 4

h Isa 52:5

i Jude 4

j 2Pe 3:9

k Ge 6:4
  Eph 6:12

l 1Pe 3:19, 20

m Jude 6

n Ge 7:23

o Ge 6:9
  Heb 11:7

p Ge 8:18

q 2Pe 3:6

r Ge 19:24, 25

1:9 *Or possibly, "blind, shortsighted." 1:11 *Or "abundantly supplied with." 1:13 *Or "tent," that is, his earthly body. 1:15 *Or "mention." 1:17 *Lit., "such a voice."

1:21 *Lit., "carried along; borne along." 2:2 *Or "their acts of shameless conduct." Plural of the Greek a·sel'gei·a. See Glossary. 2:4 *See Glossary. #Or possibly, "pits."

people of things to come.[a] **7** And he rescued righteous Lot,[b] who was greatly distressed by the brazen conduct* of the lawless people— **8** for day after day that righteous man was tormenting his righteous soul* over the lawless deeds that he saw and heard while dwelling among them. **9** So, then, Jehovah* knows how to rescue people of godly devotion out of trial,[c] but to reserve unrighteous people to be destroyed* on the day of judgment,[d] **10** especially those who seek to defile the flesh of others[e] and who despise authority.*[f]

Daring and self-willed, they are not afraid to speak abusively of glorious ones, **11** whereas angels, although they are greater in strength and power, do not bring against them an accusation in abusive terms, out of respect for* Jehovah.*[g] **12** But these men, like unreasoning animals that act on instinct and are born* to be caught and destroyed, speak abusively about things of which they are ignorant.[h] They will suffer destruction brought on by their own destructive course, **13** suffering harm as their reward for their own harmful course.

They consider it pleasurable to indulge in luxurious living,[i] even in the daytime. They are spots and blemishes who revel* in their deceptive teachings while feasting together with you.[j] **14** Their eyes are full of adultery[k] and are unable to desist from sin, and they entice unstable ones.* They have a heart trained in greed. They are accursed children. **15** Abandoning the straight path, they have been led astray. They have followed the path of Ba'laam[a] the son of Be'or, who loved the reward of wrongdoing,[b] **16** but was reproved for his own violation of what was right.[c] A voiceless beast of burden speaking with a human voice hindered the prophet's mad course.[d]

17 These are waterless springs and mists driven by a violent storm, and the blackest darkness has been reserved for them.[e] **18** They make highsounding statements that are empty. By appealing to the desires of the flesh[f] and with acts of brazen conduct,* they entice people who have just escaped from those who live in error.[g] **19** While they are promising them freedom, they themselves are slaves of corruption;[h] for if anyone is overcome by someone, he is his slave.*[i] **20** Certainly if after escaping from the defilements of the world[j] by an accurate knowledge of the Lord and Savior Jesus Christ, they get involved again with these very things and are overcome, their final state has become worse for them than the first.[k] **21** It would have been better for them not to have accurately known the path of righteousness than after knowing it to turn away from the holy commandment they had received.[l] **22** What the true proverb says has happened to them: "The dog has returned to its own vomit, and the sow that was bathed to rolling in the mire."[m]

CHAP. 2
[a] Jude 7

[b] Ge 19:15, 16

[c] Ps 34:19
1Co 10:13
2Ti 4:18
Re 3:10

[d] Ro 2:5
2Pe 3:7

[e] Jude 7

[f] Ex 22:28
Jude 8

[g] Jude 9

[h] Jude 10

[i] Ro 13:13

[j] Jude 12

[k] Mt 5:28

Second Col.
[a] Nu 22:5, 6
Jude 11
Re 2:14

[b] Nu 22:7
Ne 13:2

[c] Nu 22:31, 34
Nu 31:8

[d] Nu 22:28

[e] Jude 12, 13

[f] Jude 16

[g] 2Pe 2:14

[h] 1Pe 2:16

[i] Ro 6:16

[j] 2Pe 1:4

[k] Heb 6:4-6
Heb 10:26

[l] Lu 12:47
Joh 15:22

[m] Pr 26:11

2:7 *Or "shameless conduct." Greek, a·sel'gei·a. See Glossary. **2:8** *See Glossary. **2:9, 11** *See App. A5. **2:9** #Lit., "cut off." **2:10** *Or "look down on lordship." **2:11** #Or "before." **2:12** *Or "are born naturally." **2:13** *Or "who indulge with unrestrained delight."

2:14 *Or "souls." **2:18** *Or "acts of shameless conduct." Plural of the Greek a·sel'gei·a. See Glossary. **2:19** *Or "overcome by something, he is its slave."

3 Beloved ones, this is now the second letter I am writing you in which, as in my first one, I am stirring up your clear thinking faculties by way of a reminder,[a] **2** that you should remember the sayings previously spoken* by the holy prophets and the commandment of the Lord and Savior through your apostles. **3** First of all know this, that in the last days ridiculers will come with their ridicule, proceeding according to their own desires[b] **4** and saying: "Where is this promised presence of his?[c] Why, from the day our forefathers fell asleep in death, all things are continuing exactly as they were from creation's beginning."[d]

5 For they deliberately ignore this fact, that long ago there were heavens and an earth standing firmly out of water and in the midst of water by the word of God;[e] **6** and that by those means the world of that time suffered destruction when it was flooded with water.[f] **7** But by the same word the heavens and the earth that now exist are reserved for fire and are being kept until the day of judgment and of destruction of the ungodly people.[g]

8 However, do not let this escape your notice, beloved ones, that one day is with Jehovah* as a thousand years and a thousand years as one day.[h] **9** Jehovah* is not slow concerning his promise,[i] as some people consider slowness, but he is patient with you because he does not desire anyone to be destroyed but desires all to attain to repentance.[j] **10** But Jehovah's* day[k] will come as a thief,[l] in which the heavens will pass away[m]

with a roar,* but the elements being intensely hot will be dissolved, and earth and the works in it will be exposed.[a]

11 Since all these things are to be dissolved in this way, consider what sort of people you ought to be in holy acts of conduct and deeds of godly devotion, **12** as you await and keep close in mind# the presence of the day of Jehovah,*[b] through which the heavens will be destroyed[c] in flames and the elements will melt in the intense heat! **13** But there are new heavens and a new earth that we are awaiting according to his promise,[d] and in these righteousness is to dwell.[e]

14 Therefore, beloved ones, since you are awaiting these things, do your utmost to be found finally by him spotless and unblemished and in peace.[f] **15** Furthermore, consider the patience of our Lord as salvation, just as our beloved brother Paul also wrote you according to the wisdom given him,[g] **16** speaking about these things as he does in all his letters. However, some things in them are hard to understand, and these things the ignorant* and unstable are twisting, as they do also the rest of the Scriptures, to their own destruction.

17 You, therefore, beloved ones, having this advance knowledge, be on your guard so that you may not be led astray with them by the error of the lawless people and fall from your own steadfastness.*[h] **18** No, but go on growing in the undeserved kindness and knowledge of our Lord and Savior Jesus Christ. To him be the glory both now and to the day of eternity. Amen.

3:2 *Or "the things foretold." **3:8-10, 12** *See App. A5. **3:10** *Or "a rushing sound." **3:12** #Or "eagerly desire." Lit., "speed up." **3:16** *Or "untaught." **3:17** *Or "stability."

THE FIRST OF

JOHN

1 That which was from the beginning, which we have heard, which we have seen with our eyes, which we have observed and our hands have felt, concerning the word of life,[a] **2** (yes, the life was made manifest, and we have seen and are bearing witness[b] and reporting to you the everlasting life[c] that was with the Father and was made manifest to us), **3** that which we have seen and heard we are reporting also to you,[d] so that you too may have fellowship* with us. And this fellowship of ours is with the Father and with his Son Jesus Christ.[e] **4** And we are writing these things so that our joy may be complete.

5 This is the message that we heard from him and are announcing to you: God is light,[f] and there is no darkness at all in him.* **6** If we make the statement, "We are having fellowship with him," and yet we go on walking in the darkness, we are lying and are not practicing the truth.[a] **7** However, if we are walking in the light as he himself is in the light, we do have fellowship with one another, and the blood of Jesus his Son cleanses us from all sin.[b]

8 If we make the statement, "We have no sin," we are misleading ourselves[c] and the truth is not in us. **9** If we confess our sins, he is faithful and righteous so as to forgive us our sins and to cleanse us from all unrighteousness.[d] **10** If we make the statement, "We have not sinned," we are making him a liar, and his word is not in us.

2 My little children, I am writing you these things so that you may not commit a sin. And yet, if anyone does commit a sin, we have a helper* with the Father, Jesus Christ,[e] a righteous one.[f] **2** And he is a propitiatory sacrifice*[g] for our sins,[h] yet

---

CHAP. 1
a Joh 1:4
b Joh 21:24
  Ac 2:32
c Joh 17:3
d Joh 15:26, 27
  Ac 4:20
e Joh 17:20, 21
f Jas 1:17

Second Col.
a 2Co 6:14
  Eph 5:8
  Tit 1:16
  1Jo 2:4
b Ro 3:25
  Eph 1:7
  Heb 9:14
  Heb 10:22
  Re 1:5
c 1Ki 8:46
  Ec 7:20
d Ps 32:5
  Pr 28:13
  Jas 5:16

CHAP. 2
e Ro 8:34
  Heb 7:25
f 1Ti 2:5
g 1Co 5:7
h Isa 53:5
  Ro 3:25
  1Ti 1:15
  Heb 2:17
  1Pe 2:24
  1Jo 4:10

1:3 *Or "a sharing." 1:5 *Or "in union with him."

2:1 *Or "an advocate." 2:2 *Or "an atoning sacrifice; a means of appeasement."

not for ours only but also for the whole world's.[a] **3** And by this we realize that we have come to know him, namely, if we continue observing his commandments. **4** The one who says, "I have come to know him," and yet does not observe his commandments is a liar, and the truth is not in this person. **5** But whoever does observe his word, in this person the love of God has truly been made perfect.[b] By this we know that we are in union with him.[c] **6** The one who says he remains in union with him is himself under obligation to go on walking just as that one walked.[d]

7 Beloved ones, I am writing you, not a new commandment, but an old commandment that you have had from the beginning.[e] This old commandment is the word that you heard. **8** Again, I am writing you a new commandment, which is true in his case and in yours, because the darkness is passing away and the true light is already shining.[f]

9 The one who says that he is in the light and yet hates[g] his brother is still in the darkness.[h] **10** The one who loves his brother remains in the light,[i] and in him there is no cause for stumbling. **11** But the one who hates his brother is in the darkness and is walking in the darkness,[j] and he does not know where he is going,[k] because the darkness has blinded his eyes.

12 I am writing you, little children, because your sins have been forgiven you for the sake of his name.[l] **13** I am writing you, fathers, because you have come to know him who is from the beginning. I am writing you, young men, because you have conquered the wicked one.[m] I write you, young children, because you have come to know the Fa-

ther.[a] **14** I write you, fathers, because you have come to know him who is from the beginning. I write you, young men, because you are strong[b] and the word of God remains in you[c] and you have conquered the wicked one.[d]

15 Do not love either the world or the things in the world.[e] If anyone loves the world, the love of the Father is not in him;[f] **16** because everything in the world—the desire of the flesh[g] and the desire of the eyes[h] and the showy display of one's means of life*—does not originate with the Father, but originates with the world. **17** Furthermore, the world is passing away and so is its desire,[i] but the one who does the will of God remains forever.[j]

18 Young children, it is the last hour, and just as you have heard that the antichrist is coming,[k] even now many antichrists have appeared,[l] from which fact we know that it is the last hour. **19** They went out from us, but they were not of our sort;*[m] for if they had been of our sort, they would have remained with us. But they went out so that it might be shown that not all are of our sort.[n] **20** And you have an anointing from the holy one,[o] and all of you have knowledge. **21** I write you, not because you do not know the truth,[p] but because you know it, and because no lie originates with the truth.[q]

22 Who is the liar but the one who denies that Jesus is the Christ?[r] This is the antichrist,[s] the one who denies the Father and the Son. **23** Everyone who denies the Son does not have the Father either.[t] But whoever acknowledges the Son[u] has the Father also.[v] **24** As for you, what you have heard from the

---

CHAP. 2

a Mt 20:28
　Joh 1:29
b 1Jo 4:18
c Joh 14:20
　Joh 17:21
d Joh 13:15
　1Pe 2:21
e Joh 13:34
　2Jo 5
f Joh 1:9
　Joh 8:12
g Eph 4:31
　Col 3:8
h 1Co 13:2
　1Jo 3:15
i Eph 5:8
j 1Jo 4:20
k Joh 12:35
l Lu 24:47
　Ac 4:12
　Ac 10:43
m Jas 4:7
　1Jo 5:19
　Re 12:10, 11

Second Col.

a Joh 17:25
b Eph 6:10
c 3Jo 3
d Ro 8:37
e Ro 12:2
　1Co 7:31
　Tit 2:11, 12
f Mt 6:24
　Jas 4:4
g Mt 5:28
　Ro 13:14
h Ge 3:6
　Pr 27:20
　Mt 4:8
i 1Co 7:31
　1Pe 1:24
j Ps 37:29
　Mt 7:21
　Joh 6:40
k 2Th 2:3
　2Pe 2:1
l 2Th 2:7
　2Jo 7
　Jude 4
m Ac 20:30
n 1Co 11:19
o 2Co 1:21
　1Jo 2:20
p Joh 8:31, 32
q Joh 8:44
r 1Jo 4:3
　2Jo 7
s 1Jo 2:18
t Joh 5:23
　2Jo 9
u Ro 10:9, 10
v 1Jo 4:15

2:16 *Or "the bragging about one's possessions." 2:19 *Or "they did not belong to us."

beginning must remain in you.[a] If what you have heard from the beginning remains in you, you will also remain in union with the Son and in union with the Father. **25** Furthermore, this is what he himself promised us —the life everlasting.[b]

26 I write you these things about those who are trying to mislead you. **27** And as for you, the anointing that you received from him[c] remains in you, and you do not need anyone to be teaching you; but the anointing from him is teaching you about all things[d] and is true and is no lie. Just as it has taught you, remain in union with him.[e] **28** So now, little children, remain in union with him, so that when he is made manifest we may have freeness of speech[f] and not shrink away from him in shame at his presence. **29** If you know that he is righteous, you also know that everyone who practices righteousness has been born from him.[g]

3 See what sort of love the Father has given us,[h] that we should be called children of God![i] And that is what we are. That is why the world does not know us,[j] because it has not come to know him.[k] **2** Beloved ones, we are now children of God,[l] but it has not yet been made manifest what we will be.[m] We do know that when he is made manifest we will be like him, because we will see him just as he is. **3** And everyone who has this hope in him purifies himself,[n] just as that one is pure.

4 Everyone who practices sin is also practicing lawlessness, and sin is lawlessness. **5** You know, too, that he was made manifest to take away our sins,[o] and there is no sin in him. **6** Everyone remaining in union with him does not practice sin;[p]

no one who practices sin has either seen him or come to know him. **7** Little children, let no one mislead you; the one who practices righteousness is righteous, just as that one is righteous. **8** The one who practices sin originates with the Devil, because the Devil has been sinning from the beginning.*[a] For this purpose the Son of God was made manifest, to break up# the works of the Devil.[b]

9 Everyone who has been born from God does not practice sin,[c] for His seed* remains in such one, and he cannot practice sin, for he has been born from God.[d] **10** The children of God and the children of the Devil are evident by this fact: Whoever does not practice righteousness does not originate with God, nor does the one who does not love his brother.[e] **11** For this is the message that you have heard from the beginning, that we should love one another;[f] **12** not like Cain, who originated with the wicked one and slaughtered his brother.[g] And for what reason did he slaughter him? Because his own works were wicked,[h] but those of his brother were righteous.[i]

13 Do not be surprised, brothers, that the world hates you.[j] **14** We know that we have passed over from death to life,[k] because we love the brothers.[l] The one who does not love remains in death.[m] **15** Everyone who hates his brother is a murderer,*[n] and you know that no murderer has everlasting life remaining in him.[o] **16** By this we have come to know love, because that one surrendered his life* for us,[p] and we are un-

---

CHAP. 2

a Joh 14:23
2Jo 6

b Joh 17:3
1Jo 1:2

c 2Co 1:21
1Jo 2:20

d Joh 14:26
Joh 16:13

e Joh 17:21

f 1Jo 4:17

g 1Pe 1:23
1Jo 4:7

CHAP. 3

h Joh 3:16

i Joh 1:12, 13

j Joh 15:19

k Joh 17:25

l Ro 8:15, 16
Eph 1:5

m 1Co 15:49
Php 3:20, 21

n 2Co 7:1

o Le 16:21, 22
Isa 53:11
Joh 1:29

p Ro 6:12

Second Col.

a Ge 3:14
Joh 8:44

b Joh 16:33
Heb 2:14

c 1Jo 5:18

d 1Pe 1:23

e 1Jo 4:8

f Joh 13:34
1Jo 2:7
2Jo 5

g Ge 4:8

h Ge 4:5

i Ge 4:4
Heb 11:4

j Mt 5:11
Joh 15:18
2Ti 3:12

k Joh 5:24
Ro 8:2

l 1Jo 2:10

m Joh 3:36

n Mt 5:21, 22
Eph 4:31

o Ge 9:6
Nu 35:31
Re 21:8

p Joh 3:16
Joh 13:1
Joh 15:13

3:8 *Or "from when he began." #Or "destroy." **3:9** *That is, seed capable of reproducing, or bearing fruit. **3:15** *Or "manslayer." **3:16** *Or "soul."

der obligation to surrender our lives* for our brothers.[a] **17** But whoever has the material possessions of this world and sees his brother in need and yet refuses to show him compassion, in what way does the love of God remain in him?[b] **18** Little children, we should love, not in word or with the tongue,[c] but in deed[d] and truth.[e]

19 By this we will know that we originate with the truth, and we will assure* our hearts before him **20** regarding whatever our hearts may condemn us in, because God is greater than our hearts and knows all things.[f] **21** Beloved ones, if our hearts do not condemn us, we have freeness of speech toward God;[g] **22** and whatever we ask we receive from him,[h] because we are observing his commandments and doing what is pleasing in his eyes. **23** Indeed, this is his commandment: that we have faith in the name of his Son Jesus Christ[i] and love one another,[j] just as he gave us a commandment. **24** Moreover, the one who observes his commandments remains in union with him, and he in union with such one.[k] And by the spirit that he gave us, we know that he remains in union with us.[l]

4 Beloved ones, do not believe every inspired statement,*[m] but test the inspired statements[#] to see whether they originate with God,[n] for many false prophets have gone out into the world.[o]

2 This is how you know that the inspired statement is from God: Every inspired statement that acknowledges Jesus Christ as having come in the flesh originates with God.[p] **3** But every

inspired statement that does not acknowledge Jesus does not originate with God.[a] Furthermore, this is the antichrist's inspired statement that you have heard was coming,[b] and now it is already in the world.[c]

4 You originate with God, little children, and you have conquered them,[d] because the one who is in union with you[e] is greater than the one who is in union with the world.[f] **5** They originate with the world;[g] that is why they speak what originates with the world and the world listens to them.[h] **6** We originate with God. Whoever comes to know God listens to us;[i] whoever does not originate with God does not listen to us.[j] By this we distinguish the inspired statement of truth from the inspired statement of error.[k]

7 Beloved ones, let us continue loving one another,[l] because love is from God, and everyone who loves has been born from God and knows God.[m] **8** Whoever does not love has not come to know God, because God is love.[n] **9** By this the love of God was revealed in our case, that God sent his only-begotten Son[o] into the world so that we might gain life through him.[p] **10** The love is in this respect, not that we have loved God, but that he loved us and sent his Son as a propitiatory sacrifice*[q] for our sins.[r]

11 Beloved ones, if this is how God loved us, then we are also under obligation to love one another.[s] **12** No one has seen God at any time.[t] If we continue loving one another, God remains in us and his love is made perfect in us.[u] **13** By this we know that we are remaining in union with him and he in union with us,

---

CHAP. 3

a Joh 13:15
 Ro 16:3, 4
 1Th 2:8
b De 15:7, 8
 Lu 3:11
 Ro 12:13
 Jas 2:15, 16
 1Jo 4:20
c Ro 12:9
d Jas 1:22
 Jas 2:17
e 1Pe 1:22
f Heb 4:13
g Heb 4:16
 1Jo 5:14
h Ps 34:15
 Mt 7:8
 1Pe 3:12
i Joh 6:29
j Joh 13:34
k 1Jo 2:24
l Joh 14:23

CHAP. 4

m 2Th 2:1, 2
 1Ti 4:1
n Re 22:6
o 2Pe 2:1
p Joh 1:14
 1Co 12:3
 Re 19:10

Second Col.

a 1Jo 2:22
b 2Th 2:7
 1Jo 2:18
c Ac 20:29, 30
d 1Jo 5:4
e Joh 17:21
f Eph 2:2
g 1Jo 5:19
h Joh 15:19
i Joh 10:27
j Joh 8:47
k 1Jo 4:1
l 1Pe 1:22
m 1Jo 4:16
 Ex 34:6
 Mic 7:18
 1Jo 4:19
o Joh 1:14
p Joh 3:16
 Ro 5:8
 Ro 8:32
 1Jo 5:11
q 1Co 5:7
r Ro 3:25
 Heb 2:17
 Heb 9:26
 1Jo 2:1, 2
s Mt 18:33
 Joh 15:12
 Ro 13:8
 1Jo 3:16
t Ex 33:20
 Joh 1:18
 Joh 4:24
 Joh 6:46
u 1Jo 2:5

3:16 *Or "souls." 3:19 *Or "persuade; convince." 4:1 *Lit., "every spirit." #Lit., "the spirits."

4:10 *Or "an atoning sacrifice; a means of appeasement."

because he has given his spirit to us. **14** In addition, we ourselves have seen and are bearing witness that the Father has sent his Son as Savior of the world.[a] **15** Whoever acknowledges that Jesus is God's Son,[b] God remains in union with such one and he in union with God.[c] **16** And we have come to know and believe the love that God has for us.[d]

God is love,[e] and the one who remains in love remains in union with God and God remains in union with him.[f] **17** In this way love has been made perfect in us, so that we may have freeness of speech*[g] in the day of judgment, because just as that one is, so are we ourselves in this world. **18** There is no fear in love,[h] but perfect love casts* fear out, because fear restrains us. Indeed, the one who is fearful has not been made perfect in love.[i] **19** We love, because he first loved us.[j]

20 If anyone says, "I love God," and yet is hating his brother, he is a liar.[k] For the one who does not love his brother,[l] whom he has seen, cannot love God, whom he has not seen.[m] **21** And we have this commandment from him, that whoever loves God must also love his brother.[n]

5 Everyone who believes that Jesus is the Christ has been born from God,[o] and everyone who loves the one who caused to be born loves him who has been born from that one. **2** By this we know that we love the children of God,[p] when we love God and carry out his commandments. **3** For this is what the love of God means, that we observe his commandments;[q] and yet his commandments are not burdensome,[r] **4** because everyone who* has been born from

God conquers the world.[a] And this is the conquest that has conquered the world, our faith.[b]

5 Who can conquer the world?[c] Is it not the one who has faith that Jesus is the Son of God?[d] **6** This is the one who came by means of water and blood, Jesus Christ, not with the water only,[e] but with the water and with the blood.[f] And the spirit is bearing witness,[g] because the spirit is the truth. **7** For there are three witness bearers: **8** the spirit[h] and the water[i] and the blood;[j] and the three are in agreement.

9 If we accept the witness of men, the witness of God is greater. Because this is the witness that he has given about his Son. **10** The person putting his faith in the Son of God has the witness within himself. The person not having faith in God has made him a liar,[k] because he has not put his faith in the witness given by God concerning his Son. **11** And this is the witness, that God gave us everlasting life,[l] and this life is in his Son.[m] **12** The one who has the Son has this life; the one who does not have the Son of God does not have this life.[n]

13 I write you these things so that you may know that you have life everlasting,[o] you who put your faith in the name of the Son of God.[p] **14** And this is the confidence* that we have toward him,[q] that no matter what we ask according to his will, he hears us.[r] **15** And if we know that he hears us concerning whatever we are asking, we know that we are to have the things we ask for, since we have asked them of him.[s]

16 If anyone catches sight of his brother committing a sin that

---

4:17 *Or "have confidence." **4:18** *Or "drives." **5:4** *Lit., "everything that."

5:14 *Or "freeness of speech."

does not incur death, he will ask, and God will give life to him,[a] yes, to those not committing sin that incurs death. There is a sin that does incur death.[b] It is concerning that sin that I do not tell him to make request. **17** All unrighteousness is sin,[c] and yet there is a sin that does not incur death.

18 We know that everyone who has been born from God does not practice sin, but the one born from God* watches him, and the wicked one cannot

5:18 *That is, Jesus Christ, the Son of God.

take hold of him.*[a] **19** We know that we originate with God, but the whole world is lying in the power of the wicked one.[b] **20** But we know that the Son of God has come,[c] and he has given us insight* so that we may gain the knowledge of the one who is true. And we are in union with the one who is true,[d] by means of his Son Jesus Christ. This is the true God and life everlasting.[e] **21** Little children, guard yourselves from idols.[f]

5:18 *Or "does not fasten his hold on him." **5:20** *Lit., "mental perception; intellectual capacity."

CHAP. 5
a Jas 5:15
1Jo 1:9
b Mt 12:31
Mr 3:29
Lu 12:10
Heb 6:4-6
Heb 10:26
c 1Jo 3:4

Second Col.
a Joh 17:15
b Mt 13:19
Lu 4:6
Joh 12:31
c 1Ti 3:16
d Joh 17:20, 21
e Joh 17:3
f 1Co 10:14

THE SECOND OF

JOHN

OUTLINE OF CONTENTS

1 The older man* to the chosen lady and to her children, whom I truly love, and not only I but also all those who have come to know the truth, **2** because of the truth that remains in us and will be with us forever. **3** There will be with us undeserved kindness, mercy, and peace from God the Father and from Jesus Christ, the Son of the Father, with truth and love.

4 I rejoice very much because I have found some of your children walking in the truth,[a] just as we received commandment

1 *Or "The elder."

from the Father. **5** So now I request you, lady, that we love one another. (I am writing you, not a new commandment, but one that we had from the beginning.)[a] **6** And this is what love means, that we go on walking according to his commandments.[b] This is the commandment, just as you have heard from the beginning, that you should go on walking in it. **7** For many deceivers have gone out into the world,[c] those not acknowledging Jesus Christ as coming in the flesh.[d] This is the deceiver and the antichrist.[e] **8** Look out for yourselves, so that you do not lose the things

a 2Co 4:2
3Jo 3

Second Col.
a Joh 13:34
Joh 15:12
1Pe 4:8
1Jo 2:7
b Joh 14:21
1Jo 2:5
c Mt 7:15
Ac 20:29, 30
2Th 2:3, 7
2Pe 2:1
Re 2:2
d 1Jo 4:2
e 1Jo 2:18, 22
1Jo 4:3
Jude 4

we have worked to produce, but that you may obtain a full reward.[a] **9** Everyone who pushes ahead and does not remain in the teaching of the Christ does not have God.[b] The one who does remain in this teaching is the one who has both the Father and the Son.[c] **10** If anyone comes to you and does not bring this teaching, do not receive him into your homes[d] or say a greeting to him. **11** For the one who says a greeting to him is a sharer in his wicked works.

12 Although I have many things to write to you, I do not want to do so with paper and ink, but I am hoping to come to you and to speak with you face-to-face, so that your joy may be in full measure.

13 The children of your sister, the chosen one, send you their greetings.

THE THIRD OF

JOHN

---

1 The older man* to Ga·ius, the beloved, whom I truly love.

2 Beloved one, I pray that in all things you continue to prosper and enjoy good health, just as you are* now prospering. **3** For I rejoiced very much when brothers came and bore witness about the truth you hold, as you go on walking in the truth.[a] **4** No greater joy* do I have than this: that I should hear that my children go on walking in the truth.[b]

5 Beloved one, you show your faithfulness in what you do for the brothers, even though they are strangers to you.[c] **6** They have given a witness about your love before the congregation. Please send them on their way in a manner worthy of God.[a] **7** For it was in behalf of his name that they went out, not taking anything[b] from the people of the nations. **8** So we are under obligation to show hospitality to such ones,[c] so that we may become fellow workers in the truth.[d]

9 I wrote something to the congregation, but Di·ot·re·phes, who likes to have the first place among them,[e] does not accept anything from us with respect.[f] **10** That is why if I come, I will call attention to the works he is doing in spreading malicious talk about us.*[g] Not being con-

---

1 *Or "The elder."   **2** *Or "your soul is."
4 *Or possibly, "cause for thankfulness."

10 *Lit., "chattering about us with wicked words."

Cross references (center column):

a Heb 10:35

b Joh 14:6
Joh 15:6
3Jo 9

c Heb 3:14
1Jo 2:23

d De 17:2-5
Ro 16:17
1Co 5:11

a 2Jo 4

b 1Co 4:15
2Ti 1:2
Tit 1:4
Phm 10

c Heb 13:2

Second Col.

a Tit 3:13

b 1Co 9:11, 12

c Mt 10:41
Phm 22
1Pe 4:9

d Ro 12:13

e Ac 20:29, 30

f Ro 12:10
Php 2:3
Heb 13:17

g Ps 101:5
Pr 6:16, 19

tent with this, he refuses to welcome the brothers[a] with respect; and those who want to welcome them, he tries to hinder and to throw out of the congregation.

11 Beloved one, do not imitate what is bad, but imitate what is good.[b] The one who does good originates with God.[c] The one who does bad has not seen God.[d] **12** De·me'tri·us has been well-reported-on by them all and by the truth itself. In fact, we too

are bearing witness about him, and you know that the witness we give is true.

13 I had many things to write you, but I do not wish to go on writing you with pen and ink. **14** However, I am hoping to see you soon, and we will speak face-to-face.

May you have peace.

The friends send you their greetings. Give my greetings to the friends by name.

---

a Ac 15:25, 27
Eph 6:21
Php 2:19
Col 4:7
Tit 1:5

b Ro 12:9
1Pe 3:11

c 1Jo 3:9

d 1Jo 3:6, 10

THE LETTER OF
JUDE

---

1 Jude, a slave of Jesus Christ, but a brother of James,[a] to the called ones[b] who are loved by God the Father and preserved for Jesus Christ:[c]

2 May mercy and peace and love be increased to you.

3 Beloved ones, although I was making every effort to write you about the salvation we hold in common,[d] I found it necessary to write you to urge you to put up a hard fight for the faith[e] that was once for all time delivered to the holy ones. **4** My reason is that certain men have slipped in among you who were long ago appointed to this judgment by the Scriptures; they are ungodly men who turn the undeserved kindness of our God into an ex-

cuse for brazen conduct*[a] and who prove false to our only owner[#] and Lord, Jesus Christ.[b]

5 Although you are fully aware of all of this, I want to remind you that Jehovah,* having saved a people out of the land of Egypt,[c] afterward destroyed those not showing faith.[d] **6** And the angels who did not keep their original position but forsook their own proper dwelling place,[e] he has reserved with eternal bonds in dense darkness for the judgment of the great day.[f] **7** In the same manner, Sod'om and Go·mor'rah and the cities around them also gave

---

a Mt 13:55
Mr 6:3
Ga 2:9
Jas 1:1

b Heb 3:1

c Joh 17:15
1Pe 1:5

d Heb 2:3

e Eph 6:11
1Ti 1:18, 19
1Ti 6:12

Second Col.

a Ga 5:19

b Ac 20:29, 30
2Pe 2:1

c Ex 12:41

d Nu 14:35
1Co 10:1, 5
Heb 3:16, 19

e Ge 6:1-4
1Pe 3:19, 20

f Lu 8:30, 31
2Pe 2:4
Re 20:1, 2

---

4 *Or "shameless conduct." Greek, a·sel'gei·a. See Glossary. #Or "master." **5** *See App. A5.

themselves over to gross sexual immorality* and pursued unnatural fleshly desires;[a] they are placed before us as a warning example by undergoing the judicial punishment of everlasting fire.[b]

8 Despite this, these men too are indulging in dreams, defiling the flesh, despising authority, and speaking abusively of glorious ones.[c] **9** But when Mi·cha·el[d] the archangel[e] had a difference with the Devil and was disputing about Moses' body,[f] he did not dare to bring a judgment against him in abusive terms,[g] but said: "May Jehovah* rebuke you."[h] **10** But these men are speaking abusively about all the things they really do not understand.[i] And in all the things that they do understand by instinct like unreasoning animals,[j] they go on corrupting themselves.

11 Too bad for them, for they have followed the path of Cain[k] and have rushed into the erroneous course of Ba'laam[l] for reward, and they have perished in the rebellious talk[m] of Kor'ah![n] **12** These are the rocks hidden below water at your love feasts[o] while they feast with you, shepherds who feed themselves without fear;[p] waterless clouds carried here and there by the wind;[q] fruitless trees in late autumn, having died twice* and having been uprooted; **13** wild waves of the sea that cast up the foam of their own shame;[r] stars with no set course, for which the blackest darkness stands reserved forever.[s]

14 Yes, the seventh one in line from Adam, E'noch,[t] also prophesied about them when he said: "Look! Jehovah* came with his holy myriads#[u] **15** to execute judgment against all,[v] and to

convict all the ungodly concerning all their ungodly deeds that they did in an ungodly way, and concerning all the shocking things that ungodly sinners spoke against him."[a]

16 These men are murmurers,[b] complainers about their lot in life, following their own desires,[c] and their mouths make grandiose boasts, while they are flattering others* for their own benefit.[d]

17 As for you, beloved ones, call to mind the sayings that have been previously spoken* by the apostles of our Lord Jesus Christ, **18** how they used to say to you: "In the last time there will be ridiculers, following their own desires for ungodly things."[e] **19** These are the ones who cause divisions,[f] animalistic men,* not having spirituality.# **20** But you, beloved ones, build yourselves up on your most holy faith, and pray with holy spirit,[g] **21** in order to keep yourselves in God's love,[h] while you await the mercy of our Lord Jesus Christ with everlasting life in view.[i] **22** Also, continue showing mercy[j] to some who have doubts;[k] **23** save them[l] by snatching them out of the fire. But continue showing mercy to others, doing so with fear, while you hate even the garment that has been stained by the flesh.[m]

24 Now to the one who is able to guard you from stumbling and to make you stand unblemished[n] in the sight of his glory* with great joy, **25** to the only God our Savior through Jesus Christ our Lord, be glory, majesty, might, and authority for all past eternity and now and into all eternity. Amen.

a	Ge 19:4, 5
	Le 18:22
b	Ge 19:24
	2Pe 2:6
c	Ex 22:28
	2Pe 2:10
	3Jo 9, 10
d	Da 10:21
	Da 12:1
e	1Th 4:16
f	De 34:5, 6
g	2Pe 2:11
h	Zec 3:2
i	Jude 19
j	2Pe 2:12
k	Ge 4:5, 8
	1Jo 3:12
l	Nu 22:32
	2Pe 2:15, 16
	Re 2:14
m	1Ti 1:20
n	Nu 16:3, 32
o	2Pe 2:13
p	Eze 34:8
q	2Pe 2:17
r	Isa 57:20
s	Heb 6:4-6
	Re 21:8
t	Ge 5:21, 22
u	De 33:2
	Da 7:10
	Zec 14:5
v	2Th 1:6

Second Col.

a	Mt 12:36
b	1Co 10:10
	Php 2:14
c	2Pe 2:18
d	Jas 2:9
e	Ac 20:29, 30
	1Ti 4:1
	2Pe 2:1
	2Pe 3:2, 3
f	Ro 16:17
	3Jo 9, 10
g	Ro 8:26
	Eph 6:18
h	Joh 15:10
	Ro 8:38, 39
i	Tit 3:7
	1Jo 1:2
	1Jo 2:25
j	Mt 5:7
	Mt 9:13
	Jas 2:13
k	Jas 1:6
l	Ga 6:1
	Jas 5:19, 20
m	Ga 5:19-21
n	Ro 8:33
	Eph 1:4
	Col 1:22

---

7 *See Glossary. **9, 14** *See App. A5. **12** *Or "being completely dead." **14** #Or "tens of thousands."

16 *Or "admiring personalities." **17** *Or "the things foretold." **19** *Or "physical men." #Lit., "the spirit." **24** *Or "in his glorious presence."

A REVELATION

TO JOHN

OUTLINE OF CONTENTS

1 A revelation* by Jesus Christ, which God gave him,[a] to show his slaves[b] the things that must shortly take place. And he sent his angel and presented it in signs through him to his slave John,[c] **2** who bore witness to the word God gave and to the witness Jesus Christ gave, yes, to all the things he saw. **3** Happy is the one who reads aloud and those who hear the words of this prophecy and who observe the things written in it,[d] for the appointed time is near.

4 John to the seven congregations[e] that are in the province of Asia:

May you have undeserved kindness and peace from "the One who is and who was and who is coming,"[f] and from the seven spirits[g] that are before his throne, **5** and from Jesus Christ, "the Faithful Witness,"[h] "the firstborn from the dead,"[i] and "the Ruler of the kings of the earth."[j]

To him who loves us[k] and who set us free from our sins

by means of his own blood[a]— **6** and he made us to be a kingdom,[b] priests[c] to his God and Father—yes, to him be the glory and the might forever. Amen.

7 Look! He is coming with the clouds,[d] and every eye will see him, and those who pierced him; and all the tribes of the earth will beat themselves in grief because of him.[e] Yes, Amen.

8 "I am the Al'pha and the O·me'ga,"*[f] says Jehovah[g] God, "the One who is and who was and who is coming, the Almighty."[g]

9 I John, your brother and a sharer with you in the tribulation[h] and kingdom[i] and endurance[j] in association with Jesus,[k] was on the island called Pat'mos for speaking about God and bearing witness concerning Jesus. **10** By inspiration I came to be in the Lord's day, and I heard behind me a strong voice like that of a trumpet, **11** saying: "What you see, write in a scroll and send it to the seven congregations:

CHAP. 1
a Da 2:28
b Am 3:7
  Re 7:3, 4
c Mt 10:2
  Mr 1:19
  Joh 21:20
d Ps 1:2
  Lu 11:28
  Joh 13:17
  Jas 1:22
e Re 1:11
f Re 1:8
  Re 4:8
  Re 11:17
g Re 4:5
h Re 3:14
i Col 1:18
j Ps 89:27
  1Ti 6:15
  Re 19:16
k Joh 15:9

Second Col.
a Heb 9:14
  1Pe 1:18, 19
  1Jo 1:7
b Ex 19:6
  Lu 22:28-30
c 1Pe 2:5
  Re 5:9, 10
  Re 20:6
d Mt 26:64
  Mr 13:26
e Mt 24:30
f Isa 48:12
  Re 21:6
  Re 22:13
g Ex 6:3
h Mt 24:9
i Lu 12:32
j Mt 10:22
  2Ti 2:12
k Ro 8:17

1:1 *Or "A disclosure; An uncovering."

1:8 *Or "the A and the Z." Alpha and Omega are the first and last letters of the Greek alphabet. #See App. A5.

in Eph'e·sus,[a] in Smyr'na,[b] in Per'-ga·mum,[c] in Thy·a·ti'ra,[d] in Sar'-dis,[e] in Philadelphia,[f] and in La-o·di·ce'a."[g]

12 I turned to see who was speaking with me, and when I turned, I saw seven golden lamp-stands,[h] **13** and in the midst of the lampstands someone like a son of man,[i] clothed in a garment that reached down to the feet and wearing a golden sash around his chest. **14** Moreover, his head and his hair were white as white wool, as snow, and his eyes were like a fiery flame,[j] **15** and his feet were like fine copper[k] when glowing in a furnace, and his voice was like the sound of many waters. **16** And he had in his right hand seven stars,[l] and out of his mouth a sharp, long, two-edged sword[m] was protruding, and his countenance* was like the sun when it shines at its bright-est.[n] **17** When I saw him, I fell as dead at his feet.

And he laid his right hand on me and said: "Do not be afraid. I am the First[o] and the Last,[p] **18** and the living one,[q] and I be-came dead,[r] but look! I am living forever and ever,[s] and I have the keys of death and of the Grave.*[t] **19** So write down the things you saw, and the things that are, and the things that will take place af-ter these. **20** As for the sacred secret of the seven stars that you saw in my right hand and of the seven golden lampstands: The seven stars mean the angels of the seven congregations, and the seven lampstands mean the seven congregations.[u]

2 "To the angel[v] of the con-gregation in Eph'e·sus[w] write: These are the things that he says who holds the seven stars in his right hand and walks

among the seven golden lamp-stands:[a] **2** 'I know your deeds, and your labor and endurance, and that you cannot tolerate bad men, and that you put to the test those who say they are apostles,[b] but they are not, and you found them to be liars. **3** You are also showing endurance, and you have persevered for the sake of my name[c] and have not grown wea-ry.[d] **4** Nevertheless, I hold this against you, that you have left the love you had at first.

5 "'Therefore remember from where you have fallen, and re-pent[e] and do the deeds you did at first. If you do not, I will come to you, and I will remove your lampstand[f] from its place, unless you repent.[g] **6** Still, you do have this in your favor: that you hate the deeds of the sect of Nic·o·la'-us,[h] which I also hate. **7** Let the one who has an ear hear what the spirit says to the congregations:[i] To the one who conquers[j] I will grant to eat of the tree of life,[k] which is in the paradise of God.'

8 "And to the angel of the congregation in Smyr'na write: These are the things that he says, 'the First and the Last,'[l] who became dead and came to life again:[m] **9** 'I know your trib-ulation and poverty—but you are rich[n]—and the blasphemy by those who call themselves Jews and really are not, but they are a synagogue of Satan.[o] **10** Do not be afraid of the things you are about to suffer.[p] Look! The Dev-il will keep on throwing some of you into prison so that you may be fully put to the test, and you will have tribulation for ten days. Prove yourself faithful even to death, and I will give you the crown of life.[q] **11** Let the one who has an ear hear[r] what the spirit says to the congregations: The one who conquers[s] will by no means be harmed by the second death.'[t]

1:16 * Or "face." **1:18** * Or "Hades," that is, the common grave of mankind. See Glossary.

12 "To the angel of the congregation in Per′ga·mum write: These are the things that he says who has the sharp, long, two-edged sword:[a] **13** 'I know where you are dwelling, that is, where the throne of Satan is; and yet you keep holding fast to my name,[b] and you did not deny your faith in me[c] even in the days of An′ti·pas, my faithful witness,[d] who was killed[e] by your side, where Satan is dwelling.

14 "'Nevertheless, I have a few things against you, that you have there those adhering to the teaching of Ba′laam,[f] who taught Ba′lak[g] to put a stumbling block before the sons of Israel, to eat things sacrificed to idols and to commit sexual immorality.*[h] **15** In the same way, you also have those adhering to the teaching of the sect of Nic·o·la′us.[i] **16** So repent. If you do not, I am coming to you quickly, and I will war against them with the long sword of my mouth.[j]

17 "'Let the one who has an ear hear what the spirit says to the congregations:[k] To the one who conquers[l] I will give some of the hidden manna,[m] and I will give him a white pebble, and written on the pebble is a new name that no one knows except the one receiving it.'

18 "To the angel of the congregation in Thy·a·ti′ra[n] write: These are the things that the Son of God says, the one who has eyes like a fiery flame[o] and whose feet are like fiery copper:[p] **19** 'I know your deeds, and your love and faith and ministry and endurance, and that your deeds of late are more than those you did at first.

20 "'Nevertheless, I do hold this against you, that you tolerate that woman Jez′e·bel,[q] who calls herself a prophetess, and

she teaches and misleads my slaves to commit sexual immorality*[a] and to eat things sacrificed to idols. **21** And I gave her time to repent, but she is not willing to repent of her sexual immorality.* **22** Look! I am about to throw her into a sickbed, and those committing adultery with her into great tribulation, unless they repent of her deeds. **23** And I will kill her children with deadly plague, so that all the congregations will know that I am the one who searches the innermost thoughts* and hearts, and I will give to you individually according to your deeds.[b]

24 "'However, I say to the rest of you who are in Thy·a·ti′ra, all those who do not follow this teaching, those who did not get to know the so-called "deep things of Satan":[c] I am not putting on you any other burden. **25** Just the same, hold fast to what you have until I come.[d] **26** And to the one who conquers and observes my deeds down to the end, I will give authority over the nations,[e] **27** and he will shepherd the people with an iron rod[f] so that they will be broken to pieces like clay vessels, just as I have received from my Father. **28** And I will give him the morning star.[g] **29** Let the one who has an ear hear what the spirit says to the congregations.'

3 "To the angel of the congregation in Sar′dis write: These are the things that he says who has the seven spirits of God[h] and the seven stars:[i] 'I know your deeds, that you have the name* that you are alive, but you are dead.[j] **2** Become watchful,[k] and strengthen the things remaining that were ready to die, for I have not found your works ful-

---

2:14, 20 *See Glossary.

2:21 *Greek, por·nei′a. See Glossary. **2:23** *Or "the deepest emotions." Lit., "kidneys." **3:1** *Or "reputation."

ly performed* before my God. **3** Therefore, continue mindful of* how you have received and how you heard, and go on keeping it, and repent.[a] Certainly unless you wake up, I will come as a thief,[b] and you will not know at all at what hour I will come upon you.[c]

4 "'Nevertheless, you do have a few individuals* in Sar'dis who did not defile their garments,[d] and they will walk with me in white ones,[e] because they are worthy. **5** The one who conquers[f] will thus be dressed in white garments,[g] and I will by no means blot out* his name from the book of life,[h] but I will acknowledge his name before my Father and before his angels.[i] **6** Let the one who has an ear hear what the spirit says to the congregations.'

7 "To the angel of the congregation in Philadelphia write: These are the things he says who is holy,[j] who is true,[k] who has the key of David,[l] who opens so that no one will shut and shuts so that no one opens: **8** 'I know your deeds—look! I have set before you an opened door,[m] which no one can shut. And I know that you have a little power, and you kept my word and did not prove false to my name. **9** Look! I will make those from the synagogue of Satan who say they are Jews yet are not,[n] but are lying—look! I will make them come and bow* before your feet and make them know that I have loved you. **10** Because you kept the word about my endurance,*[o] I will also keep you from the hour of test,[p] which is to come upon the entire inhabited earth, to put to the test those

dwelling on the earth. **11** I am coming quickly.[a] Keep holding fast to what you have, so that no one may take your crown.[b]

12 "'The one who conquers —I will make him a pillar in the temple of my God, and he will by no means go out from it anymore, and I will write upon him the name of my God[c] and the name of the city of my God, the New Jerusalem[d] that descends out of heaven from my God, and my own new name.[e] **13** Let the one who has an ear hear what the spirit says to the congregations.'

14 "To the angel of the congregation in La·o·di·ce'a[f] write: These are the things the Amen[g] says, the faithful and true[h] witness,[i] the beginning of the creation by God:[j] **15** 'I know your deeds, that you are neither cold nor hot. I wish you were cold or else hot. **16** So because you are lukewarm and neither hot[k] nor cold,[l] I am going to vomit you out of my mouth. **17** Because you say, "I am rich[m] and have acquired riches and do not need anything at all," but you do not know that you are miserable and pitiful and poor and blind and naked, **18** I advise you to buy from me gold refined by fire so that you may become rich, and white garments so that you may become dressed and that the shame of your nakedness may not be exposed,[n] and eyesalve to rub in your eyes[o] so that you may see.[p]

19 "'All those for whom I have affection, I reprove and discipline.[q] So be zealous and repent.[r] **20** Look! I am standing at the door and knocking. If anyone hears my voice and opens the door, I will come into his house and take the evening meal with him and he with me. **21** To the one who conquers[s] I will grant to sit down with me on my throne,[t] just as I conquered and sat down[u] with my Father on his throne. **22** Let the one who has an ear hear what the spirit says to the congregations.'"

4 After this I saw, and look! an opened door in heaven, and the first voice that I heard speaking with me was like a trumpet, saying: "Come up here, and I will show you the things that must take place." **2** After this I immediately came to be in the power of the spirit, and look! a throne was in its position in heaven, and someone was seated on the throne.[a] **3** And the One seated had the appearance of a jasper stone[b] and a sardius stone,* and all around the throne was a rainbow like an emerald in appearance.[c]

4 All around the throne were 24 thrones, and on these thrones I saw seated 24 elders[d] dressed in white garments, and on their heads golden crowns. **5** From the throne were coming lightning[e] and voices and thunders;[f] and there were seven lamps of fire burning before the throne, and these mean the seven spirits of God.[g] **6** Before the throne was something resembling a glassy sea,[h] like crystal.

In the midst of the throne* and around the throne were four living creatures[i] that were full of eyes in front and behind. **7** The first living creature was like a lion,[j] and the second living creature was like a young bull,[k] and the third living creature had a face like a man's, and the fourth living creature[m] was like a flying eagle.[n] **8** As for the four living creatures, each one of them had six wings; they were full of eyes all around and underneath.[o] And continuously, day and night, they say: "Holy, holy, holy is Jehovah*[p]

God, the Almighty, who was and who is and who is coming."[a]

9 Whenever the living creatures give glory and honor and thanksgiving to the One seated on the throne, the One who lives forever and ever,[b] **10** the 24 elders[c] fall down before the One seated on the throne and worship the One who lives forever and ever, and they cast their crowns before the throne, saying: **11** "You are worthy, Jehovah* our God, to receive the glory[d] and the honor[e] and the power,[f] because you created all things,[g] and because of your will they came into existence and were created."

5 And I saw in the right hand of the One seated on the throne[h] a scroll written on both sides,* sealed tight with seven seals. **2** And I saw a strong angel proclaiming with a loud voice: "Who is worthy to open the scroll and break its seals?" **3** But no one in heaven or on earth or underneath the earth was able to open the scroll or to look into it. **4** I gave way to a great deal of weeping because no one was found worthy to open the scroll or to look into it. **5** But one of the elders said to me: "Stop weeping. Look! The Lion of the tribe of Judah,[i] the root[j] of David,[k] has conquered[l] so as to open the scroll and its seven seals."

6 And I saw standing in the midst* of the throne and of the four living creatures and in the midst of the elders[m] a lamb[n] that seemed to have been slaughtered,[o] having seven horns and seven eyes, and the eyes mean the seven spirits of God[p] that have been sent out into the whole earth. **7** At once he came forward and took it out of the right hand of the One seated on the throne.[q] **8** When he took the

CHAP. 4

a 1Ki 22:19
  Isa 6:1
  Eze 1:26, 27
  Da 7:9
  Ac 7:55
b Re 21:10, 11
c 1Jo 1:5
d Re 4:10
  Re 5:8
  Re 11:16
  Re 19:4
e Eze 1:13
f Ex 19:16
g Re 1:4
  Re 5:6
h Ex 30:18
  1Ki 7:23
i Eze 1:5-10
j Pr 28:1
k Job 39:9-11
  Re 6:3
l Re 6:5
m Re 6:7
n Job 39:27, 29
  Eze 1:10
o Eze 10:9, 12
p Isa 6:2, 3

Second Col.

a Re 1:4
b Ps 90:2
  Da 12:7
c Re 5:8
d Mt 5:16
  Re 14:7
e Re 19:10
f Re 5:13
  Re 7:12
  Re 11:17
  Re 12:10
g Re 10:6

CHAP. 5

h Re 4:2, 3
i Ge 49:9, 10
  Heb 7:14
j Isa 11:1, 10
  Ro 15:12
k 2Sa 7:8, 12
  Re 22:16
l Joh 16:33
m Eph 1:22
n Isa 53:7
  Joh 1:29
  1Pe 1:19
o Joh 19:30
  Re 5:12
p Re 1:4
q Ps 47:8
  Isa 6:1

4:3 *Or "a precious red-colored stone." 4:6 *Or "In the middle with the throne." 4:8, 11 *See App. A5. 5:1 *Lit., "inside and on the back." 5:6 *Or "at the center."

scroll, the four living creatures and the 24 elders[a] fell down before the Lamb, and each one had a harp and golden bowls that were full of incense. (The incense means the prayers of the holy ones.)[b] **9** And they sing a new song,[c] saying: "You are worthy to take the scroll and open its seals, for you were slaughtered and with your blood you bought people for God[d] out of every tribe and tongue* and people and nation,[e] **10** and you made them to be a kingdom[f] and priests to our God,[g] and they are to rule as kings[h] over the earth."

11 And I saw, and I heard a voice of many angels around the throne and the living creatures and the elders, and the number of them was myriads of myriads* and thousands of thousands,[i] **12** and they were saying with a loud voice: "The Lamb who was slaughtered[j] is worthy to receive the power and riches and wisdom and strength and honor and glory and blessing."[k]

13 And I heard every creature in heaven and on earth and underneath the earth[l] and on the sea, and all the things in them, saying: "To the One sitting on the throne[m] and to the Lamb[n] be the blessing and the honor[o] and the glory and the might forever and ever."[p] **14** The four living creatures were saying: "Amen!" and the elders fell down and worshipped.

6 And I saw when the Lamb[q] opened one of the seven seals,[r] and I heard one of the four living creatures[s] say with a voice like thunder: "Come!" **2** And I saw, and look! a white horse,[t] and the one seated on it had a bow; and a crown was given him,[u] and he went out conquering and to complete his conquest.[v]

3 When he opened the second seal, I heard the second living creature[a] say: "Come!" **4** Another came out, a fiery-colored horse, and it was granted to the one seated on it to take peace away from the earth so that they should slaughter one another, and he was given a great sword.[b]

5 When he opened the third seal,[c] I heard the third living creature[d] say: "Come!" And I saw, and look! a black horse, and the one seated on it had a pair of scales in his hand. **6** I heard what sounded like a voice in the midst of the four living creatures say: "A quart* of wheat for a de·nar′i·us*[e] and three quarts of barley for a de·nar′i·us; and do not harm the olive oil and the wine."[f]

7 When he opened the fourth seal, I heard the voice of the fourth living creature[g] say: "Come!" **8** And I saw, and look! a pale horse, and the one seated on it had the name Death. And the Grave* was closely following him. And authority was given them over the fourth part of the earth, to kill with a long sword and with food shortage[h] and with deadly plague and by the wild beasts of the earth.[i]

9 When he opened the fifth seal, I saw underneath the altar[j] the souls*[k] of those slaughtered because of the word of God and because of the witness they had given.[l] **10** They shouted with a loud voice, saying: "Until when, Sovereign Lord, holy and true,[m] are you refraining from judging and avenging our blood on those who dwell on the earth?"[n] **11** And a white robe was given to

---

CHAP. 5

a Re 5:14
  Re 19:4
b Ps 141:2
  Re 8:4
c Ps 33:3
  Ps 144:9
  Isa 42:10
  Re 14:3
d Mt 26:27, 28
  1Co 6:20
  Heb 9:12
  1Pe 1:18, 19
e Re 14:4
f Lu 12:32
  Lu 22:28-30
g Ex 19:6
  1Pe 2:9
  Re 1:5, 6
h Mt 19:28
  Re 20:4, 6
  Re 22:5
i Da 7:9, 10
j Isa 53:7
  Re 5:6
k Mt 28:18
l Php 2:9, 10
m Re 4:2, 3
n Joh 1:29
  Re 7:17
o Joh 5:23
  1Ti 6:16
p 1Pe 4:11

CHAP. 6

q Re 5:6
r Re 5:5
s Re 4:7
t Re 19:11
u Re 14:14
v Ps 45:4
  Ps 110:1, 2
  Re 12:7
  Re 17:14

Second Col.

a Re 4:7
b Mt 24:7
  Lu 21:10
c Re 5:5
d Re 4:7
e Mt 20:2
f Mr 13:8
g Re 4:7
h Lu 21:11
i Jer 15:2, 3
  Eze 14:21
j Le 4:7
  Re 8:3
k Le 17:11
l Mt 24:9, 14
  Joh 18:37
  Re 17:6
  Re 20:4
m 1Jo 5:20
n De 32:43
  Lu 18:7
  Re 19:1, 2

6:6 *See App. B14. #A Roman silver coin that equaled a day's wage. See App. B14. **6:8** *Or "Hades," that is, the common grave of mankind. See Glossary. **6:9** *Evidently referring to their lifeblood poured out at the altar. See Glossary.

5:9 *Or "language." **5:11** *Or "tens of thousands times tens of thousands."

each of them,[a] and they were told to rest a little while longer, until the number was filled of their fellow slaves and their brothers who were about to be killed as they had been.[b]

12 And I saw when he opened the sixth seal, and a great earthquake occurred; and the sun became black as sackcloth made of hair,* and the entire moon became as blood,[c] **13** and the stars of heaven fell to the earth as when a fig tree shaken by a high wind drops its unripe figs. **14** And the heaven departed as a scroll that is being rolled up,[d] and every mountain and every island was removed from its place.[e] **15** Then the kings of the earth, the high officials, the military commanders, the rich, the strong, every slave, and every free person hid in the caves and among the rocks of the mountains.[f] **16** And they keep saying to the mountains and to the rocks: "Fall over us[g] and hide us from the face of the One seated on the throne[h] and from the wrath of the Lamb,[i] **17** because the great day of their wrath has come,[j] and who is able to stand?"[k]

7 After this I saw four angels standing on the four corners of the earth, holding tight the four winds of the earth, so that no wind could blow on the earth or on the sea or on any tree. **2** And I saw another angel ascending from the sunrise,* having a seal of the living God; and he called with a loud voice to the four angels to whom it was granted to harm the earth and the sea, **3** saying: "Do not harm the earth or the sea or the trees, until after we have sealed[l] the slaves of our God in their foreheads."[m]

4 And I heard the number of those who were sealed, 144,000,[n]

sealed out of every tribe of the sons of Israel:[a]

5 Out of the tribe of Judah 12,000 sealed;

out of the tribe of Reu′ben 12,000;

out of the tribe of Gad 12,000;

6 out of the tribe of Ash′er 12,000;

out of the tribe of Naph′ta·li 12,000;

out of the tribe of Ma·nas′seh[b] 12,000;

7 out of the tribe of Sim′e·on 12,000;

out of the tribe of Le′vi 12,000;

out of the tribe of Is′sa·char 12,000;

8 out of the tribe of Zeb′u·lun 12,000;

out of the tribe of Joseph 12,000;

out of the tribe of Benjamin 12,000 sealed.

9 After this I saw, and look! a great crowd, which no man was able to number, out of all nations and tribes and peoples and tongues,*[c] standing before the throne and before the Lamb, dressed in white robes;[d] and there were palm branches in their hands.[e] **10** And they keep shouting with a loud voice, saying: "Salvation we owe to our God, who is seated on the throne,[f] and to the Lamb."[g]

11 All the angels were standing around the throne and the elders[h] and the four living creatures, and they fell facedown before the throne and worshipped God, **12** saying: "Amen! Let the praise and the glory and the wisdom and the thanksgiving and the honor and the power and the strength be to our God forever and ever.[i] Amen."

13 In response one of the elders said to me: "These who are dressed in the white robes,[j] who

---

CHAP. 6
a Re 3:5

b Mt 24:9
Ac 9:1
2Co 1:8

c Joe 2:31
Mt 24:29

d Isa 34:4

e Re 16:20

f Isa 2:10, 19

g Ho 10:8
Lu 23:30

h Re 4:2, 3

i Re 5:6

j Zep 1:14, 18
Ro 2:5

k Joe 2:11

CHAP. 7
l 2Co 1:22
Eph 1:13
Eph 4:30

m Re 9:4

n Re 14:1, 3

Second Col.
a Ro 2:29
Ro 9:6
Ga 6:16
Re 21:12

b Ge 41:51

c Isa 2:2
Re 15:4

d Re 7:14

e Le 23:40
Joh 12:13

f Re 4:2, 3

g Ac 4:12
Re 5:6

h Re 4:4
Re 11:16

i Re 4:11

j Re 7:9

6:12 *Probably goat hair. **7:2** *Or "east." **7:9** *Or "languages."

are they and where did they come from?" **14** So right away I said to him: "My lord, you are the one who knows." And he said to me: "These are the ones who come out of the great tribulation,[a] and they have washed their robes and made them white in the blood of the Lamb.[b] **15** That is why they are before the throne of God, and they are rendering him sacred service day and night in his temple; and the One seated on the throne[c] will spread his tent over them.[d] **16** They will hunger no more nor thirst anymore, neither will the sun beat down on them nor any scorching heat,[e] **17** because the Lamb,[f] who is in the midst* of the throne, will shepherd them[g] and will guide them to springs# of waters of life.[h] And God will wipe out every tear from their eyes."[i]

8 When he[j] opened the seventh seal,[k] there was silence in heaven for about half an hour. **2** And I saw the seven angels[l] who stand before God, and seven trumpets were given to them.

3 Another angel, holding a golden incense vessel,* arrived and stood at the altar,[m] and a large quantity of incense[n] was given him to offer it with the prayers of all the holy ones on the golden altar[o] that was before the throne. **4** The smoke of the incense from the hand of the angel ascended with the prayers[p] of the holy ones before God. **5** But right away the angel took the incense vessel, and he filled it with some of the fire of the altar and hurled it to the earth. And there were thunders and voices and flashes of lightning[q] and an earthquake. **6** And the seven angels with the seven trumpets[r] prepared to blow them.

7 The first one blew his trumpet. And there was hail and fire mingled with blood, and it was hurled to the earth;[a] and a third of the earth was burned up, and a third of the trees were burned up, and all the green vegetation was burned up.[b]

8 The second angel blew his trumpet. And something like a great mountain burning with fire was hurled into the sea.[c] And a third of the sea became blood;[d] **9** and a third of the living creatures* in the sea died,[e] and a third of the ships were wrecked.

10 The third angel blew his trumpet. And a great star burning like a lamp fell from heaven, and it fell on a third of the rivers and on the springs# of waters.[f] **11** The name of the star is Wormwood. And a third of the waters turned into wormwood, and many of the people died from the waters, because these had been made bitter.[g]

12 The fourth angel blew his trumpet. And a third of the sun was struck[h] and a third of the moon and a third of the stars, in order that a third of them might be darkened[i] and the day might not have light for a third of it, and the night likewise.

13 And I saw, and I heard an eagle flying in midheaven say with a loud voice: "Woe, woe, woe[j] to those dwelling on the earth because of the rest of the trumpet blasts of the three angels who are about to blow their trumpets!"[k]

9 The fifth angel blew his trumpet.[l] And I saw a star that had fallen from heaven to the earth, and the key to the shaft* of the abyss[m] was given to him. **2** He opened the shaft* of the abyss, and smoke ascended out of the shaft* like the smoke of a great furnace, and the sun was

---

CHAP. 7
a Mt 24:21
  Mr 13:19
b Joh 1:29
  Heb 9:14
  1Jo 1:7
  Re 1:5
c Re 4:2
d Re 15:1
  Re 21:3
e Ps 121:6
  Isa 49:10
f Joh 5:6
g Joh 10:11
h Re 22:1
i Isa 25:8
  Re 21:4

CHAP. 8
j Re 6:1
k Re 5:1
l Re 15:1
m Ex 30:1, 3
n Re 5:8
o Re 9:13
p Ps 141:2
  Lu 1:10
q Re 19:16
  Re 4:5
r Re 8:7, 8
  Re 8:10, 12
  Re 9:1, 13
  Re 11:15

Second Col.
a Re 16:2
b Ex 9:23-25
  Ps 97:3, 5
c Isa 17:12, 13
  Isa 57:20
d Ex 7:20
e Re 16:1, 3
f Re 16:1, 4
g Am 5:7
h Re 16:1, 8
i Ex 10:22
j Re 9:12
  Re 11:14
k Re 8:2

CHAP. 9
l Re 8:2
m Lu 8:30, 31
  Re 9:11
  Re 20:1-3

7:17 *Or "at the center."   7:17; 8:10 #Or "fountains."   8:3 *Or "burner."

8:9 *Or "creatures that have souls."   9:1, 2 *Or "pit."

darkened,[a] also the air, by the smoke of the shaft.* **3** And locusts came out of the smoke onto the earth,[b] and authority was given to them, the same authority that the scorpions of the earth have. **4** They were told not to harm the vegetation of the earth or any green plant or any tree, but only those people who do not have the seal of God on their foreheads.[c]

5 And it was granted the locusts, not to kill them, but to torment them five months, and their torment was like torment by a scorpion[d] when it strikes a person. **6** In those days people will seek death but will by no means find it, and they will long to die, but death will flee from them.

7 And in appearance the locusts resembled horses prepared for battle;[e] on their heads were what seemed to be crowns of gold, and their faces were like human faces, **8** but they had hair like women's hair. And their teeth were like those of lions,[f] **9** and they had breastplates like iron breastplates. And the sound of their wings was like the sound of horse-drawn chariots rushing into battle.[g] **10** Also, they have tails with stingers like scorpions, and in their tails is their authority to hurt the people for five months.[h] **11** They have over them a king, the angel of the abyss.[i] In Hebrew his name is A·bad'don,* but in Greek he has the name A·pol'lyon.#

12 The one woe is past. Look! Two more woes[j] are coming after these things.

13 The sixth angel[k] blew his trumpet.[l] And I heard one voice from the horns of the golden altar[m] that is before God **14** say to the sixth angel who had the trumpet: "Untie the four angels

who are bound at the great river Eu·phra'tes."[a] **15** And the four angels who have been prepared for the hour and day and month and year were untied to kill a third of the people.

16 The number of the armies of cavalry was two myriads of myriads;* I heard the number of them. **17** And this is how I saw the horses in the vision and those seated on them: They had fire-red and hyacinth-blue and sulfur-yellow breastplates, and the heads of the horses were like the heads of lions,[b] and fire and smoke and sulfur came out of their mouths. **18** A third of the people were killed by these three plagues, by the fire and the smoke and the sulfur that came out of their mouths. **19** For the authority of the horses is in their mouths and in their tails, for their tails are like serpents and have heads, and with these they inflict harm.

20 But the rest of the people who were not killed by these plagues did not repent of the works of their hands; they did not stop worshipping the demons and the idols of gold and silver and copper and stone and wood, which can neither see nor hear nor walk.[c] **21** And they did not repent of their murders nor of their spiritistic practices nor of their sexual immorality* nor of their thefts.

10 And I saw another strong angel descending from heaven, arrayed* with a cloud, and a rainbow was on his head, and his face was like the sun,[d] and his legs# were like pillars of fire, **2** and he had in his hand a little scroll that had been unrolled. And he set his right foot on the sea, but his left one on the

---

CHAP. 9
a Joe 2:2, 10

b Ex 10:12

c Re 7:2, 3

d Re 9:10

e Joe 2:4, 5

f Joe 1:6

g Joe 2:4, 5

h Re 9:5

i Re 9:1
Re 20:1-3

j Re 8:13

k Re 8:6

l Re 11:15

m Re 8:3

Second Col.
a Re 16:1, 12
Re 17:1, 15

b Pr 28:1

c Ps 115:4-7

CHAP. 10
d Mt 17:1, 2

9:2 *Or "pit." 9:11 *Meaning "Destruction." #Meaning "Destroyer." 9:16 *Or "20,000 times 10,000," that is, 200,000,000. 9:21 *Greek, *por·nei'a*. See Glossary. 10:1 *Or "wrapped." #Lit., "feet."

earth, **3** and he cried out with a loud voice just as when a lion roars.[a] And when he cried out, the voices of the seven thunders[b] spoke.

4 Now when the seven thunders spoke, I was about to write, but I heard a voice out of heaven[c] say: "Seal up the things the seven thunders spoke, and do not write them down." **5** The angel whom I saw standing on the sea and on the earth raised his right hand to heaven, **6** and he swore by the One who lives forever and ever,[d] who created the heaven and the things in it and the earth and the things in it and the sea and the things in it:[e] "There will be no delay any longer. **7** But in the days when the seventh angel[f] is about to blow his trumpet,[g] the sacred secret[h] that God declared as good news to his own slaves the prophets[i] is indeed brought to a finish."

8 And I heard the voice out of heaven[j] speaking again with me and saying: "Go, take the opened scroll that is in the hand of the angel who is standing on the sea and on the earth."[k] **9** I went to the angel and told him to give me the little scroll. He said to me: "Take it and eat it up,[l] and it will make your stomach bitter, but in your mouth it will be sweet like honey." **10** I took the little scroll out of the hand of the angel and ate it,[m] and in my mouth it was sweet like honey,[n] but when I had eaten it, my stomach was made bitter. **11** And they said to me: "You must prophesy again about peoples and nations and tongues* and many kings."

11 And a reed like a rod*[o] was given to me as he said: "Get up and measure the temple sanctuary of God and the altar and those worshipping in it. **2** But as for the courtyard that

is outside the temple sanctuary, leave it out and do not measure it, because it has been given to the nations, and they will trample the holy city[a] underfoot for 42 months.[b] **3** I will cause my two witnesses to prophesy for 1,260 days dressed in sackcloth." **4** These are symbolized by the two olive trees[c] and the two lampstands[d] and are standing before the Lord of the earth.[e]

5 If anyone wants to harm them, fire comes out of their mouths and consumes their enemies. If anyone should want to harm them, this is how he must be killed. **6** These have the authority to shut up the sky*[f] so that no rain may fall[g] during the days of their prophesying, and they have authority over the waters to turn them into blood[h] and to strike the earth with every sort of plague as often as they wish.

7 When they have finished their witnessing, the wild beast that ascends out of the abyss will wage war with them and conquer them and kill them.[i] **8** And their corpses will be on the main street of the great city that is in a spiritual sense called Sod'om and Egypt, where their Lord was also executed on the stake. **9** And those of the peoples and tribes and tongues* and nations will look at their corpses for three and a half days,[j] and they do not allow their corpses to be laid in a tomb. **10** And those dwelling on the earth rejoice over them and celebrate, and they will send gifts to one another, because these two prophets tormented those dwelling on the earth.

11 After the three and a half days, spirit of life from God entered into them,[k] and they stood on their feet, and great fear fell upon those who saw them. **12** And they heard a loud voice

---

CHAP. 10

a Re 5:5

b Ex 19:16
  Re 4:5
  Re 11:19

c Re 10:8

d Ps 90:2
  Re 4:9

e Ex 20:11
  Ne 9:6
  Ps 146:6

f Re 8:6

g Re 11:15

h Mr 4:11

i Am 3:7

j Re 10:4

k Re 10:1, 2

l Eze 2:8

m Jer 15:16

n Ps 119:103
  Eze 3:1-3

CHAP. 11

o Eze 40:3

Second Col.

a Re 21:2

b Re 13:5

c Zec 4:3, 11

d Zec 4:12
  Mt 5:14

e Zec 4:14

f Lu 4:25

g 1Ki 17:1
  Jas 5:17

h Ex 7:19

i Re 12:17
  Re 13:7

j Re 11:11

k Eze 37:5, 10

10:11; 11:9 *Or "languages." 11:1 *Or "a measuring rod."

11:6 *Or "heaven."

from heaven say to them: "Come up here." And they went up into heaven in the cloud, and their enemies saw them.* 13 In that hour there was a great earthquake, and a tenth of the city fell; and 7,000 persons were killed by the earthquake, and the rest became frightened and gave glory to the God of heaven.

14 The second woe[a] is past. Look! The third woe is coming quickly.

15 The seventh angel blew his trumpet.[b] And there were loud voices in heaven, saying: "The kingdom of the world has become the Kingdom of our Lord[c] and of his Christ,[d] and he will rule as king forever and ever."[e]

16 And the 24 elders[f] who were seated before God on their thrones fell upon their faces and worshipped God, 17 saying: "We thank you, Jehovah* God, the Almighty, the one who is[g] and who was, because you have taken your great power and begun ruling as king.[h] 18 But the nations became wrathful, and your own wrath came, and the appointed time came for the dead to be judged and to reward* your slaves the prophets[i] and the holy ones and those fearing your name, the small and the great, and to bring to ruin those ruining* the earth."[k]

19 And the temple sanctuary of God in heaven was opened, and the ark of his covenant was seen in his temple sanctuary.[l] And there were flashes of lightning and voices and thunders and an earthquake and a great hail.

12 Then a great sign was seen in heaven: A woman[m] was arrayed* with the sun, and the moon was beneath her feet, and

on her head was a crown of 12 stars, 2 and she was pregnant. And she was crying out in her pains and in her agony to give birth.

3 Another sign was seen in heaven. Look! A great fiery-colored dragon,[a] with seven heads and ten horns and on its heads seven diadems;* 4 and its tail drags a third of the stars[b] of heaven, and it hurled them down to the earth.[c] And the dragon kept standing before the woman[d] who was about to give birth, so that when she did give birth, it might devour her child.

5 And she gave birth to a son,[e] a male, who is to shepherd all the nations with an iron rod.[f] And her child was snatched* away to God and to his throne. 6 And the woman fled into the wilderness, where she has a place prepared by God and where they would feed her for 1,260 days.[g]

7 And war broke out in heaven: Mi′cha·el*[h] and his angels battled with the dragon, and the dragon and its angels battled 8 but they did not prevail,* nor was a place found for them any longer in heaven. 9 So down the great dragon[i] was hurled, the original serpent,[j] the one called Devil[k] and Satan,[l] who is misleading the entire inhabited earth;[m] he was hurled down to the earth,[n] and his angels were hurled down with him. 10 I heard a loud voice in heaven say:

"Now have come to pass the salvation[o] and the power and the Kingdom of our God[p] and the authority of his Christ, because the accuser of our brothers has been hurled down, who accuses them day and night before our God![q] 11 And they conquered him[r] be-

---

CHAP. 11
a Re 9:12
b Re 8:6
c 1Ch 29:11
Ps 22:28
Da 4:17, 34
Re 12:10
d Ps 2:6
Da 7:13, 14
Lu 1:32, 33
Lu 22:28, 29
2Pe 1:11
e Ps 145:13
Da 2:44
f Re 4:10
g Re 1:4
Re 16:5
h Ps 99:1
Zec 14:9
Re 19:6
i Heb 11:6
j Am 3:7
Heb 1:1
Jas 5:10
k Ge 6:11
l 1Ki 8:1, 6
Heb 8:1, 2
Heb 9:11

CHAP. 12
m Ge 3:15

Second Col.
a Re 12:9
Re 20:2
b Job 38:7
c Ge 6:2
Jude 6
d Ge 3:15
e Re 11:15
f Ps 2:9
Ps 110:2
Re 19:15
g Re 12:14
h Da 10:13
Jude 9
i Re 12:3
Re 20:2
j Ge 3:1
2Co 11:3
Re 12:14
k Mt 4:1
Joh 8:44
Heb 2:14
Jas 4:7
1Pe 5:8
l 1Ch 21:1
Job 1:6
Zec 3:2
Mt 4:10
Joh 13:27
Ro 16:20
2Th 2:9
m 2Co 4:4
2Co 11:14
Eph 2:2
1Jo 5:19
n Lu 10:18
Re 12:13
o Ro 13:11
Heb 9:28
1Pe 1:5
p Re 11:15, 17
q Job 1:9
Zec 3:1
r 1Jo 2:14

11:12 *Or "were looking on." 11:17 *See App. A5. 11:18 *Or "to destroy those who are destroying." 12:1 *Or "clothed."

12:3 *Or "royal headbands." 12:5 *Or "caught." 12:7 *Meaning, "Who Is Like God?" 12:8 *Or possibly, "but it [that is, the dragon] was defeated."

cause of the blood of the Lamb[a] and because of the word of their witnessing,[b] and they did not love their souls[c] even in the face of death. **12** On this account be glad, you heavens and you who reside in them! Woe for the earth and for the sea,[d] because the Devil has come down to you, having great anger, knowing that he has a short period of time."[e]

13 Now when the dragon saw that it had been hurled down to the earth,[f] it persecuted the woman[g] who gave birth to the male child. **14** But the two wings of the great eagle[h] were given to the woman, so that she might fly into the wilderness to her place, where she is to be fed for a time and times and half a time*[i] away from the face of the serpent.[j]

15 And the serpent spewed out water like a river from its mouth after the woman, to cause her to be drowned by the river. **16** But the earth came to the woman's help, and the earth opened its mouth and swallowed up the river that the dragon spewed out from its mouth. **17** So the dragon became enraged at the woman and went off to wage war with the remaining ones of her offspring,*[k] who observe the commandments of God and have the work of bearing witness concerning Jesus.[l]

13 And it* stood still on the sand of the sea.

And I saw a wild beast[m] ascending out of the sea,[n] with ten horns and seven heads, and on its horns ten diadems,# but on its heads blasphemous names. **2** Now the wild beast that I saw was like a leopard, but its feet were like those of a bear, and

its mouth was like a lion's mouth. And the dragon[a] gave to the beast its power and its throne and great authority.[b]

3 I saw that one of its heads seemed to have been fatally wounded, but its mortal wound had been healed,[c] and all the earth followed the wild beast with admiration. **4** And they worshipped the dragon because it gave the authority to the wild beast, and they worshipped the wild beast with the words: "Who is like the wild beast, and who can do battle with it?" **5** It was given a mouth speaking great things and blasphemies, and it was given authority to act for 42 months.[d] **6** And it opened its mouth in blasphemies[e] against God to blaspheme his name and his dwelling place, even those residing in heaven.[f] **7** It was permitted to wage war with the holy ones and conquer them,[g] and it was given authority over every tribe and people and tongue* and nation. **8** And all those who dwell on the earth will worship it. From the founding of the world, not one of their names has been written in the scroll of life[h] of the Lamb who was slaughtered.[i]

9 If anyone has an ear, let him hear.[j] **10** If anyone is meant for captivity, he will go into captivity. If anyone will kill with the sword,* he must be killed with the sword.[k] This is where it calls for endurance[l] and faith[m] on the part of the holy ones.[n]

11 Then I saw another wild beast ascending out of the earth, and it had two horns like a lamb, but it began speaking like a dragon.[o] **12** It exercises all the authority of the first wild beast[p] in its sight. And it makes the earth and its inhabitants worship the first wild beast, whose mortal

CHAP. 12	
a	1Pe 1:18, 19
b	Ac 1:8
	2Ti 1:8
	Re 1:9
c	Mt 16:25
	Lu 14:26
	Ac 20:24
d	Isa 57:20
	Isa 60:2
	Re 17:15
e	Mt 24:34
	Ro 16:20
	2Ti 3:1
	2Pe 3:3
f	Lu 10:18
g	Ge 3:15
	Re 12:1
h	Ex 19:4
	Isa 40:31
i	Re 12:6
j	Ge 3:1
	2Co 11:3
k	Ge 3:15
l	Mt 24:9
	Ac 1:8
	Re 1:9
	Re 6:9

CHAP. 13	
m	Re 11:7
	Re 13:18
n	Isa 57:20
	Re 21:1

Second Col.	
a	Re 12:9
b	Lu 4:6
c	Re 13:14
d	Re 11:2, 3
	Da 7:25
e	Re 12:12
f	Re 12:17
g	Re 3:5
	Re 21:27
h	Isa 53:7
i	Mt 27:50
	Re 5:6, 12
j	Mt 11:15
k	Mt 26:52
l	Mt 24:13
	Heb 10:36
m	Heb 12:3
	Re 2:10
n	Da 7:18
	1Co 6:2
	Re 20:6
o	Re 16:13
	Re 20:2
p	Re 13:1

12:11 *Or "lives." See Glossary. **12:14** *That is, three and a half times. **12:17** *Lit., "seed." **13:1** *That is, the dragon. #Or "royal headbands."

13:7 *Or "language." **13:10** *Or possibly, "If anyone is to be killed with the sword."

wound was healed.[a] **13** And it performs great signs, even making fire come down out of heaven to the earth in the sight of mankind.

14 It misleads those who dwell on the earth, because of the signs that it was permitted to perform in the sight of the wild beast, while it tells those who dwell on the earth to make an image[b] to the wild beast that had the sword-stroke and yet revived.[c] **15** And it was permitted to give breath* to the image of the wild beast, so that the image of the wild beast should both speak and cause to be killed all those who refuse to worship the image of the wild beast.

16 It puts under compulsion all people—the small and the great, the rich and the poor, the free and the slaves—that these should be marked on their right hand or on their forehead,[d] **17** and that nobody can buy or sell except a person having the mark, the name[e] of the wild beast or the number of its name.[f] **18** This is where it calls for wisdom: Let the one who has insight calculate the number of the wild beast, for it is a man's number,* and its number is 666.[g]

14 Then I saw, and look! the Lamb[h] standing on Mount Zion,[i] and with him 144,-000[j] who have his name and the name of his Father[k] written on their foreheads. **2** I heard a sound coming out of heaven like the sound of many waters and like the sound of loud thunder; and the sound that I heard was like singers who accompany themselves by playing on their harps. **3** And they are singing what seems to be a new song[l] before the throne and before the four living creatures[m] and the

elders,[a] and no one was able to master that song except the 144,000,[b] who have been bought from the earth. **4** These are the ones who did not defile themselves with women; in fact, they are virgins.[c] These are the ones who keep following the Lamb no matter where he goes.[d] These were bought* from among mankind as firstfruits[f] to God and to the Lamb, **5** and no deceit was found in their mouths; they are without blemish.[g]

6 And I saw another angel flying in midheaven,* and he had everlasting good news to declare to those who dwell on the earth, to every nation and tribe and tongue* and people.[h] **7** He was saying in a loud voice: "Fear God and give him glory, because the hour of judgment by him has arrived,[i] so worship the One who made the heaven and the earth and the sea[j] and the springs* of water."

8 Another, a second angel, followed, saying: "She has fallen! Babylon the Great[k] has fallen,[l] she who made all the nations drink of the wine of the passion* of her sexual immorality!"*[m]

9 Another angel, a third, followed them, saying in a loud voice: "If anyone worships the wild beast[n] and its image and receives a mark on its forehead or on his hand,[o] **10** he will also drink of the wine of the anger of God that is poured out undiluted into the cup of His wrath,[p] and he will be tormented with fire and sulfur[q] in the sight of the holy angels and in the sight of the Lamb. **11** And the smoke of their torment ascends forever and ever,[r] and day and night they have no rest, those who worship the wild beast and its image and whoever

---

CHAP. 13
a Re 13:3
b Re 19:20
  Re 20:4
c Re 13:3
d Re 14:9, 10
  Re 16:2
  Re 19:20
e Re 14:11
f Re 15:2
g Da 3:1

CHAP. 14
h Joh 1:29
  Re 5:6
  Re 22:3
i Ps 2:6
  Heb 12:22
  1Pe 2:6
j Re 7:4
k Re 3:12
l Ps 33:3
  Ps 98:1
  Ps 149:1
  Re 5:9
m Re 4:6

Second Col.
a Re 4:4
  Re 19:4
b Re 7:4
c 2Co 11:2
  Jas 1:27
  Jas 4:4
d 1Pe 2:21
e 1Co 6:20
  1Co 7:23
  Re 5:9
f Jas 1:18
g Eph 5:25-27
  Jude 24
h Mt 24:14
  Mr 13:10
  Ac 1:8
i 2Pe 2:9
j Ex 20:11
  Ps 146:6
k Re 17:18
  Re 18:21
l Isa 21:9
  Re 18:21
m Jer 51:7, 8
  Re 17:1, 2
  Re 18:2, 3
n Re 13:1
o Re 13:15, 16
p Ps 75:8
  Re 11:18
  Re 16:19
q Re 21:8
r Mt 25:46
  2Th 1:9
  Re 19:3

13:15 *Or "spirit." **13:18** *Or "a human number."

14:6 *Or "in midair; overhead." #Or "language." **14:7** *Or "fountains." **14:8** *Or "anger." #Greek, por·nei′a. See Glossary.

receives the mark of its name.[a]
12 Here is where it calls for endurance on the part of the holy ones,[b] those who keep the commandments of God and hold fast to the faith[c] of Jesus."

13 And I heard a voice out of heaven say, "Write: Happy are the dead who die in union with the Lord[d] from this time onward. Yes, says the spirit, let them rest from their labors, for the things they did go right* with them."

14 Then I saw, and look! a white cloud, and seated on the cloud was someone like a son of man,[e] with a golden crown on his head and a sharp sickle in his hand.

15 Another angel emerged from the temple sanctuary, calling with a loud voice to the one seated on the cloud: "Put your sickle in and reap, because the hour has come to reap, for the harvest of the earth is fully ripe."[f]
16 And the one seated on the cloud thrust his sickle into the earth, and the earth was reaped.

17 And still another angel emerged from the temple sanctuary that is in heaven, and he also had a sharp sickle.

18 And still another angel emerged from the altar, and he had authority over the fire. And he called out with a loud voice to the one who had the sharp sickle, saying: "Put your sharp sickle in and gather the clusters of the vine of the earth, for its grapes have become ripe."[g] **19** The angel thrust his sickle into the earth and gathered the vine of the earth, and he hurled it into the great winepress of God's anger.[h]
20 The winepress was trodden outside the city, and blood came out of the winepress as high up as the bridles of the horses for a distance of 1,600 stadia.*

14:13 *Or "along." 14:20 *About 296 km (184 mi). A stadium equaled 185 m (606.95 ft). See App. B14.

15 And I saw in heaven another sign, great and wonderful, seven angels[a] with seven plagues. These are the last ones, because by means of them the anger of God is brought to a finish.[b]

2 And I saw something like a sea of glass[c] mingled with fire, and those who are victorious[d] over the wild beast and its image[e] and the number of its name[f] were standing by the sea of glass, holding harps of God. **3** They were singing the song of Moses[g] the slave of God and the song of the Lamb,[h] saying:

"Great and wonderful are your works,[i] Jehovah* God, the Almighty.[j] Righteous and true are your ways,[k] King of eternity.[l] **4** Who will not really fear you, Jehovah,* and glorify your name, for you alone are loyal?[m] For all the nations will come and worship before you,[n] because your righteous decrees have been revealed."

5 After this I saw, and the sanctuary of the tent of the witness[o] was opened in heaven,[p] **6** and the seven angels with the seven plagues[q] emerged from the sanctuary, clothed with clean, bright linen and with golden sashes wrapped around their chests. **7** One of the four living creatures gave the seven angels seven golden bowls that were full of the anger of God,[r] who lives forever and ever. **8** And the sanctuary became filled with smoke because of the glory of God[s] and because of his power, and no one was able to enter the sanctuary until the seven plagues[t] of the seven angels were finished.

16 And I heard a loud voice out of the sanctuary[u] say to the seven angels: "Go and pour out the seven bowls of the anger of God on the earth."[v]

15:3, 4 *See App. A5.

2 The first one went off and poured out his bowl on the earth.[a] And a hurtful and malignant ulcer[b] afflicted the people who had the mark of the wild beast[c] and who were worshipping its image.[d]

3 The second one poured out his bowl into the sea.[e] And it became blood[f] like that of a dead man, and every living creature* died, yes, the things in the sea.[g]

4 The third one poured out his bowl into the rivers and the springs* of water.[h] And they became blood.[i] **5** I heard the angel over the waters say: "You, the One who is and who was,[j] the loyal One,[k] are righteous, for you have issued these judgments,[l] **6** because they poured out the blood of holy ones and of prophets,[m] and you have given them blood to drink;[n] they deserve it."[o] **7** And I heard the altar say: "Yes, Jehovah* God, the Almighty,[p] true and righteous are your judgments."[#q]

8 The fourth one poured out his bowl on the sun,[r] and to the sun it was granted to scorch the people with fire. **9** And the people were scorched by the great heat, but they blasphemed the name of God, who has the authority over these plagues, and they did not repent and give glory to him.

10 The fifth one poured out his bowl on the throne of the wild beast. And its kingdom became darkened,[s] and they began to gnaw their tongues because of their pain, **11** but they blasphemed the God of heaven because of their pains and their ulcers, and they did not repent of their works.

12 The sixth one poured out his bowl on the great river Euphrates,[t] and its water was dried up[a] to prepare the way for the kings[b] from the rising of the sun.*

13 And I saw three unclean inspired expressions* that looked like frogs come out of the mouth of the dragon[c] and out of the mouth of the wild beast and out of the mouth of the false prophet. **14** They are, in fact, expressions inspired by demons and they perform signs,[d] and they go out to the kings of the entire inhabited earth, to gather them together to the war[e] of the great day of God the Almighty.[f]

15 "Look! I am coming as a thief.[g] Happy is the one who stays awake[h] and keeps his outer garments, so that he may not walk naked and people look upon his shamefulness."[i]

16 And they gathered them together to the place that is called in Hebrew Armageddon.*[j]

17 The seventh one poured out his bowl on the air. At this a loud voice came out of the sanctuary[k] from the throne, saying: "It has come to pass!" **18** And there were flashes of lightning and voices and thunders, and there was a great earthquake unlike any that had occurred since men came to be on the earth,[l] so extensive and so great was the earthquake. **19** The great city[m] split into three parts, and the cities of the nations fell; and Babylon the Great[n] was remembered before God, to give her the cup of the wine of the fury of his wrath.[o] **20** Also, every island fled, and mountains were not found.[p] **21** Then great hailstones, each about the weight of a talent,* fell from heaven on the people,[q] and the people blasphemed God be-

---

CHAP. 16

a Re 8:7
b Ex 9:10
c Re 13:16, 18
d Re 13:15
  Re 19:20
e Re 8:8
f Ex 7:20
g Isa 57:20
h Re 8:10
i Ex 7:20
  Ps 78:44
j Re 1:4
k Ps 145:17
  Re 15:4
l De 32:4
  Ps 119:137
m Ps 79:3
  Isa 49:26
o Re 18:20
p Ex 6:3
q Ps 19:9
  Ps 119:137
  Re 19:1, 2
r Re 8:12
s Ex 10:21
  Isa 8:22
t Re 9:13, 14

Second Col.

a Jer 50:38
b Isa 44:27, 28
c Re 12:3
d Re 13:11, 13
e Re 19:19
f Isa 13:6
  Jer 25:33
  Eze 30:3
  Joe 1:15
  Joe 2:1, 11
  Zep 1:15
  2Pe 3:11, 12
g 1Th 5:2
  2Pe 3:10
h Lu 21:36
i Re 3:18
j 2Ch 35:22
  Zec 12:11
  Re 19:19
k Re 16:1
l Eze 38:19
  Da 12:1
  Heb 12:26
m Re 17:18
n Re 18:2
o Jer 25:15
  Re 15:7
p Re 6:14
q Job 38:22, 23

16:3 *Or "soul." 16:4 *Or "fountains." 16:7 *See App. A5. #Or "judicial decisions."

16:12 *Or "from the east." 16:13 *Lit., "unclean spirits." 16:16 *Greek, *Har Ma·ge·don'*, from a Hebrew term meaning "Mountain of Megiddo." 16:21 *A Greek talent equaled 20.4 kg (654 oz t). See App. B14.

cause of the plague of hail,[a] for the plague was unusually great.

17 One of the seven angels who had the seven bowls[b] came and said to me: "Come, I will show you the judgment on the great prostitute who sits on many waters,[c] **2** with whom the kings of the earth committed sexual immorality,*[d] and earth's inhabitants were made drunk with the wine of her sexual immorality."*[e]

3 And he carried me away in the power of the spirit into a wilderness. And I saw a woman sitting on a scarlet-colored wild beast that was full of blasphemous names and that had seven heads and ten horns. **4** The woman was clothed in purple[f] and scarlet, and she was adorned with gold and precious stones and pearls,[g] and she had in her hand a golden cup that was full of disgusting things and the unclean things of her sexual immorality." **5** On her forehead was written a name, a mystery: "Babylon the Great, the mother of the prostitutes[h] and of the disgusting things of the earth."[i] **6** And I saw that the woman was drunk with the blood of the holy ones and with the blood of the witnesses of Jesus.[j]

Well, on seeing her I was greatly amazed. **7** So the angel said to me: "Why is it that you were amazed? I will tell you the mystery of the woman[k] and of the wild beast that is carrying her and that has the seven heads and the ten horns:[l] **8** The wild beast that you saw was, but is not, and yet is about to ascend out of the abyss,[m] and it is to go off into destruction. And the inhabitants of the earth—those whose names have not been written in the scroll of life[n] from the found-

ing of the world—will be amazed when they see how the wild beast was, but is not, and yet will be present.

9 "This calls for a mind* that has wisdom: The seven heads[a] mean seven mountains, where the woman sits on top. **10** And there are seven kings: Five have fallen, one is, and the other has not yet arrived; when he does arrive, he must remain a short while. **11** And the wild beast that was but is not,[b] it is also an eighth king, but it springs from the seven, and it goes off into destruction.

12 "The ten horns that you saw mean ten kings who have not yet received a kingdom, but they do receive authority as kings for one hour with the wild beast. **13** These have one thought, so they give their power and authority to the wild beast. **14** These will battle with the Lamb,[c] but because he is Lord of lords and King of kings,[d] the Lamb will conquer them.[e] Also, those with him who are called and chosen and faithful will do so."[f]

15 He said to me: "The waters that you saw, where the prostitute is sitting, mean peoples and crowds and nations and tongues.*[g] **16** And the ten horns[h] that you saw and the wild beast,[i] these will hate the prostitute[j] and will make her devastated and naked, and they will eat up her flesh and completely burn her with fire.[k] **17** For God put it into their hearts to carry out his thought, yes, to carry out their one thought by giving their kingdom to the wild beast,[m] until the words of God will have been accomplished. **18** And the woman[n] whom you saw means the great city that has a kingdom over the kings of the earth."

CHAP. 16
a Ex 9:24

CHAP. 17
b Re 16:1

c Jer 51:13
Re 17:15
Re 19:2

d Jas 4:4
Re 18:9

e Jer 51:7
Re 14:8
Re 18:3

f Lu 16:19

g Re 18:11, 12
Re 18:19

h Re 19:2

i Re 18:5

j Re 6:9
Re 18:24
Re 19:2

k Re 17:5

l Re 17:3

m Re 20:1

n Ex 32:32
Ps 69:28
Php 4:3

Second Col.
a Re 17:7

b Re 17:8

c Joh 1:29
Re 5:6

d Mt 28:18
Ac 2:36
1Ti 6:15

e Re 19:11, 15

f Ro 16:20

g Isa 57:20
Jer 51:13

h Re 17:12

i Re 17:8

j Re 17:7

k Le 21:9
Re 18:8

l Jos 11:19, 20
Pr 21:1

m Re 17:12

n Re 17:5

17:2 *See Glossary. 17:2, 4 *Greek, *por·neiʹa*. See Glossary.

17:9 *Or "for intelligence." 17:15 *Or "languages."

18 After this I saw another angel descending from heaven with great authority, and the earth was illuminated by his glory. **2** And he cried out with a strong voice, saying: "She has fallen! Babylon the Great has fallen,ᵃ and she has become a dwelling place of demons and a place where every unclean spirit* and every unclean and hated bird lurks!ᵇ **3** For because of the wine of the passion* of her sexual immorality,ᶜ all the nations have fallen victim,ᶜ and the kings of the earth committed sexual immorality with her,ᵈ and the merchantsᐃ of the earth became rich owing to the power of her shameless luxury."

4 And I heard another voice out of heaven say: "Get out of her, my people,ᵉ if you do not want to share with her in her sins, and if you do not want to receive part of her plagues.ᶠ **5** For her sins have massed together clear up to heaven,ᵍ and God has called her acts of injustice* to mind.ʰ **6** Repay her in the way she treated others,ⁱ yes, pay her back double for the things she has done;ʲ in the cupᵏ she has mixed, mix a double portion for her.ˡ **7** To the extent that she glorified herself and lived in shameless luxury, to that extent give her torment and mourning. For she keeps saying in her heart: 'I sit as queen, and I am not a widow, and I will never see mourning.'ᵐ **8** That is why in one day her plagues will come, death and mourning and famine, and she will be completely burned with fire,ⁿ because Jehovah* God, who judged her, is strong.ᵒ

9 "And the kings of the earth who committed sexual immorali-

ty* with her and lived with her in shameless luxury will weep and beat themselves in grief over her when they see the smoke from her burning. **10** They will stand at a distance because of their fear of her torment and say: 'Too bad, too bad, you great city,ᵃ Babylon you strong city, because in one hour your judgment has arrived!'

11 "Also, the merchants of the earth are weeping and mourning over her, because there is no one to buy their full cargo anymore, **12** a full cargo of gold, silver, precious stones, pearls, fine linen, purple cloth, silk, and scarlet cloth; and everything made from scented wood; and every sort of object made from ivory, and from precious wood, copper, iron, and marble; **13** also cinnamon, Indian spice, incense, perfumed oil, frankincense, wine, olive oil, fine flour, wheat, cattle, sheep, horses, carriages, slaves, and human lives.* **14** Yes, the fine fruit that you* desired has left you, and all the delicacies and the splendid things have vanished from you, never to be found again.

15 "The merchants who sold these things, who became rich from her, will stand at a distance because of their fear of her torment and will weep and mourn, **16** saying: 'Too bad, too bad, the great city, clothed with fine linen, purple, and scarlet and richly adorned with gold ornaments, precious stones, and pearls,ᵇ **17** because in one hour such great riches have been devastated!'

"And every ship captain and every seafaring person and sailors and all those who make a living by the sea stood at a distance **18** and cried out as they looked at the smoke from her burning

---

18:2 *Or possibly, "breath; exhalation; inspired statement." 18:3 *Or "anger." ᵃGreek, porᐧneiʹa. See Glossary. ᐃOr "traveling merchants." 18:5 *Or "her crimes." 18:8 *See App. A5.

18:9 *See Glossary. 18:13 *Or "souls." 18:14 *Or "your soul."

and said: 'What city is like the great city?' **19** They threw dust on their heads and cried out, weeping and mourning, and said: 'Too bad, too bad, the great city, in which all those who had ships at sea became rich from her wealth, because in one hour she has been devastated!'[a]

20 "Be glad over her, O heaven,[b] also you holy ones[c] and apostles and prophets, because God has pronounced his judgment on her in your behalf!"[d]

21 And a strong angel lifted up a stone like a great millstone and hurled it into the sea, saying: "Thus with a swift pitch will Babylon the great city be hurled down, and she will never be found again.[e] **22** And the sound of singers who accompany themselves on the harp, of musicians, of flutists, and of trumpeters will never be heard in you again. And no craftsman who practices any trade will ever be found in you again, and no sound of a millstone will ever be heard in you again. **23** No light of a lamp will ever shine in you again, and no voice of a bridegroom and of a bride will ever be heard in you again; for your merchants were the top-ranking men of the earth, and by your spiritistic practices[f] all the nations were misled. **24** Yes, in her was found the blood of prophets and of holy ones[g] and of all those who have been slaughtered on the earth."[h]

19 After this I heard what seemed to be a loud voice of a great crowd in heaven. They said: "Praise Jah!*[i] The salvation and the glory and the power belong to our God, **2** because his judgments are true and righteous.[j] For he has executed judgment on the great prostitute who

corrupted the earth with her sexual immorality,* and he has avenged the blood of his slaves that is on her hands."[#a] **3** And right away for the second time they said: "Praise Jah!*[b] And the smoke from her goes on ascending forever and ever."[c]

4 And the 24 elders[d] and the four living creatures[e] fell down and worshipped God who sits on the throne and said: "Amen! Praise Jah!"*[f]

5 Also, a voice came from the throne and said: "Be praising our God, all you his slaves,[g] who fear him, the small ones and the great."[h]

6 And I heard what sounded like a voice of a great crowd and like the sound of many waters and like the sound of heavy thunders. They said: "Praise Jah,*[i] because Jehovah# our God, the Almighty,[j] has begun to rule as king![k] **7** Let us rejoice and be overjoyed and give him glory, because the marriage of the Lamb has arrived and his wife has prepared herself. **8** Yes, it has been granted to her to be clothed with bright, clean, fine linen—for the fine linen stands for the righteous acts of the holy ones."[l]

9 And he tells me, "Write: Happy are those invited to the evening meal of the Lamb's marriage."[m] Also, he tells me: "These are the true sayings of God." **10** At that I fell down before his feet to worship him. But he tells me: "Be careful! Do not do that![n] I am only a fellow slave of you and of your brothers who have the work of witnessing concerning Jesus.[o] Worship God![p] For the witness concerning Jesus is what inspires prophecy."[q]

11 I saw heaven opened, and look! a white horse.[r] And the

CHAP. 18
a Isa 47:11
b Jer 51:48
c Re 14:12
d De 32:43
  Ro 12:19
  Re 6:9, 10
  Re 19:1, 2
e Jer 51:63, 64
f Isa 47:9
  Ga 5:19, 20
g Re 6:9, 10
  Re 16:5, 6
h Ge 9:6
  Jer 51:49

CHAP. 19
i Ps 150:6
j De 32:4
  Ps 19:9
  Re 15:3

Second Col.
a De 32:43
  2Ki 9:7
  Ps 79:10
  Re 18:20, 24
b Ps 117:1
c Isa 34:10
d Re 4:4
e Re 4:6
f Ps 106:48
g Ps 134:1
  Ps 135:1
h Ps 115:13
i Ps 113:1
j Ex 6:3
k Ps 97:1
  Isa 52:7
  Re 11:15
l Isa 61:10
  Eph 5:25-27
  Re 14:4
m Mt 22:2
  Mt 25:10
n Ac 10:25, 26
  Re 22:8, 9
o Mt 28:19, 20
  Ac 1:8
p Mt 4:10
  Joh 4:23
q Lu 24:27
  Ac 10:43
  1Pe 1:10, 11
r Re 6:2

19:1, 3, 4, 6 *Or "Hallelujah!" "Jah" is a shortened form of the name Jehovah.

19:2 *Greek, por·nei′a. See Glossary. #Lit., "from her hand." 19:6 #See App. A5.

one seated on it is called Faithful[a] and True,[b] and he judges and carries on war in righteousness.[c] **12** His eyes are a fiery flame,[d] and on his head are many diadems.* He has a name written that no one knows but he himself, **13** and he is clothed with an outer garment stained* with blood, and he is called by the name The Word[e] of God. **14** Also, the armies in heaven were following him on white horses, and they were clothed in white, clean, fine linen. **15** And out of his mouth protrudes a sharp, long sword[f] with which to strike the nations, and he will shepherd them with a rod of iron.[g] Moreover, he treads the winepress of the fury of the wrath of God the Almighty.[h] **16** On his outer garment, yes, on his thigh, he has a name written, King of kings and Lord of lords.[i]

17 I saw also an angel standing in the sun, and he cried out with a loud voice and said to all the birds that fly in midheaven:* "Come here, be gathered together to the great evening meal of God,[j] **18** so that you may eat the flesh of kings and the flesh of military commanders and the flesh of strong men[k] and the flesh of horses and of those seated on them,[l] and the flesh of all, of freemen as well as of slaves and of small ones and great."

19 And I saw the wild beast and the kings of the earth and their armies gathered together to wage war against the one seated on the horse and against his army.[m] **20** And the wild beast was caught, and along with it the false prophet[n] that performed in front of it the signs with which he misled those who received the mark of the wild beast[o] and those who worship its image.[p] While

still alive, they both were hurled into the fiery lake that burns with sulfur.[a] **21** But the rest were killed off with the long sword that proceeded out of the mouth of the one seated on the horse.[b] And all the birds were filled with their flesh.[c]

20 And I saw an angel coming down out of heaven with the key of the abyss[d] and a great chain in his hand. **2** He seized the dragon,[e] the original serpent,[f] who is the Devil[g] and Satan,[h] and bound him for 1,000 years. **3** And he hurled him into the abyss[i] and shut it and sealed it over him, so that he would not mislead the nations anymore until the 1,000 years were ended. After this he must be released for a little while.[i]

4 And I saw thrones, and those who sat on them were given authority to judge. Yes, I saw the souls* of those executed[#] for the witness they gave about Jesus and for speaking about God, and those who had not worshiped the wild beast or its image and had not received the mark on their forehead and on their hand.[k] And they came to life and ruled as kings with the Christ[l] for 1,000 years. **5** (The rest of the dead[m] did not come to life until the 1,000 years were ended.) This is the first resurrection.[n] **6** Happy and holy is anyone having part in the first resurrection;[o] over these the second death[p] has no authority,[q] but they will be priests[r] of God and of the Christ, and they will rule as kings with him for 1,000 years.[s]

7 Now as soon as the 1,000 years have ended, Satan will be released from his prison, **8** and he will go out to mislead those nations in the four corners of the earth, Gog and Ma'gog, to gather

---

CHAP. 19

a Re 1:5
b Joh 1:14
  Re 3:14
c Isa 11:4, 5
  Heb 1:8, 9
d Re 1:13, 14
e Joh 1:1
f 2Th 2:8
  Re 1:13, 16
g Ps 2:9
  Re 2:26, 27
  Joe 3:13
  Re 14:19, 20
i Mt 28:18
  Php 2:9-11
  1Ti 6:15
  Re 17:14
j Eze 39:4, 17
k Eze 39:18
l Eze 39:20
m Re 16:14, 16
n Re 16:13
o Re 13:16, 17
p Re 13:15

Second Col.

a Mt 10:28
  2Pe 2:4
  Jude 7
  Re 20:14
b Re 2:16
  Re 6:2
c Eze 39:4

CHAP. 20

d Re 9:1
e Re 12:3
f Ge 3:1
g Joh 8:44
h Zec 3:1
  Re 12:9
i Re 9:11
j Re 20:7
k Re 13:15-17
l Mt 19:28
  Lu 22:28-30
  2Ti 2:12
  Re 1:6
m Ac 24:15
n 1Co 15:23, 52
  Php 3:10, 11
  1Th 4:16
o Re 14:13
p Re 2:11
  Re 20:14
q 1Co 15:54
r 1Pe 2:9
s Re 1:6
  Re 5:9, 10

19:12 *Or "royal headbands." 19:13 *Or possibly, "sprinkled." 19:17 *Or "in midair; overhead."

20:4 *See Glossary and Re 6:9 ftn. #Lit., "executed with the ax."

them together for the war. The number of these is as the sand of the sea. **9** And they advanced over the whole earth and encircled the camp of the holy ones and the beloved city. But fire came down out of heaven and consumed them.[a] **10** And the Devil who was misleading them was hurled into the lake of fire and sulfur, where both the wild beast[b] and the false prophet already were;[c] and they will be tormented* day and night forever and ever.

11 And I saw a great white throne and the One seated on it.[d] From before him the earth and the heaven fled away,[e] and no place was found for them. **12** And I saw the dead, the great and the small, standing before the throne, and scrolls were opened. But another scroll was opened; it is the scroll of life.[f] The dead were judged out of those things written in the scrolls according to their deeds.[g] **13** And the sea gave up the dead in it, and death and the Grave* gave up the dead in them, and they were judged individually according to their deeds.[h] **14** And death and the Grave* were hurled into the lake of fire.[i] This means the second death,[j] the lake of fire.[k] **15** Furthermore, whoever was not found written in the book of life[l] was hurled into the lake of fire.[m]

21 And I saw a new heaven and a new earth;[n] for the former heaven and the former earth had passed away,[o] and the sea[p] is no more. **2** I also saw the holy city, New Jerusalem, coming down out of heaven from God[q] and prepared as a bride adorned for her husband.[r] **3** With that I heard a loud voice

from the throne say: "Look! The tent of God is with mankind, and he will reside with them, and they will be his people. And God himself will be with them.[a] **4** And he will wipe out every tear from their eyes,[b] and death will be no more,[c] neither will mourning nor outcry nor pain be anymore.[d] The former things have passed away."

5 And the One seated on the throne[e] said: "Look! I am making all things new."[f] Also he says: "Write, for these words are faithful* and true." **6** And he said to me: "They have come to pass! I am the Al′pha and the O·me′ga,* the beginning and the end.[g] To anyone thirsting I will give from the spring* of the water of life free.[h] **7** Anyone conquering will inherit these things, and I will be his God and he will be my son. **8** But as for the cowards and those without faith and those who are disgusting in their filth and murderers[j] and the sexually immoral*[k] and those practicing spiritism and idolaters and all the liars,[l] their portion will be in the lake that burns with fire and sulfur.[m] This means the second death."[n]

9 One of the seven angels who had the seven bowls that were full of the seven last plagues[o] came and said to me: "Come, and I will show you the bride, the Lamb's wife."[p] **10** So he carried me away in the power of the spirit to a great and lofty mountain, and he showed me the holy city Jerusalem coming down out of heaven from God[q] **11** and having the glory of God.[r] Its radiance was like a most precious stone, like a jasper stone shining crystal clear.[s] **12** It had a great

---

CHAP. 20

a 2Ki 1:10
b Re 13:1
c Re 19:20
d Re 4:2, 3
e 2Pe 3:7
f Ex 32:33
　Ps 69:28
　Da 12:1
g Joh 5:28, 29
h Ac 10:42
i Isa 25:8
　1Co 15:26
j Re 2:11
　Re 20:6
k Mt 5:22
　Mt 18:9
　Re 21:8
l Re 17:8
m Pr 10:7

CHAP. 21

n Isa 65:17
　Isa 66:22
　2Pe 3:13
o 2Pe 3:10
　Re 20:11
p Isa 57:20
q Re 3:12
r Re 19:7

Second Col.

a Eze 37:27
b Re 7:17
c Isa 25:8
　1Co 15:26
d Isa 35:10
　Isa 65:19
e Re 4:2, 3
f 2Pe 3:13
g Re 1:8
　Re 22:13
h Ps 36:9
　Isa 55:1
　Re 7:17
　Re 22:1
i 1Jo 5:10
j 1Jo 3:15
k Eph 5:5
l Joh 8:44
m Re 19:20
n Pr 10:7
　Heb 10:26, 27
　Re 2:11
　Re 20:6
o Re 15:1
p Re 19:7
q Heb 12:22
　Re 3:12
　Re 21:2
r Isa 60:1, 2
s Ex 24:9, 10

20:10 *Or "restrained; imprisoned." 20:13, 14 *Or "Hades," that is, the common grave of mankind. See Glossary.

21:5 *Or "trustworthy." 21:6 *Or "the A and the Z." Alpha and Omega are the first and last letters of the Greek alphabet. #Or "fountain." △Or "without cost." 21:8 *See Glossary, "Sexual immorality."

and lofty wall and had 12 gates with 12 angels at the gates, and on the gates were inscribed the names of the 12 tribes of the sons of Israel. **13** On the east were three gates, and on the north three gates, and on the south three gates, and on the west three gates.[a] **14** The wall of the city also had 12 foundation stones, and on them were the 12 names of the 12 apostles[b] of the Lamb.

15 Now the one who was speaking with me was holding a golden reed as a measure in order to measure the city and its gates and its wall.[c] **16** And the city is laid out as a square, and its length is as great as its width. And he measured the city with the reed, 12,000 stadia;* its length and width and height are equal. **17** He also measured its wall, 144 cubits* according to a man's measure, at the same time an angel's measure. **18** Now the wall was made of jasper,[d] and the city was pure gold like clear glass. **19** The foundations of the city wall were adorned with every sort of precious stone: the first foundation was jasper, the second sapphire, the third chal·ce′do·ny, the fourth emerald, **20** the fifth sar·don′yx, the sixth sardius, the seventh chrys′o·lite, the eighth beryl, the ninth topaz, the tenth chrys′o·prase, the eleventh hyacinth, the twelfth amethyst. **21** Also, the 12 gates were 12 pearls; each one of the gates was made of one pearl. And the main street of the city was pure gold, like transparent glass.

22 I did not see a temple in it, for Jehovah* God the Almighty[e] is its temple, also the Lamb is. **23** And the city has no need of the sun nor of the moon to shine on it, for the glory of God illuminated it,[a] and its lamp was the Lamb.[b] **24** And the nations will walk by means of its light,[c] and the kings of the earth will bring their glory into it. **25** Its gates will not be closed at all by day, for night will not exist there.[d] **26** And they will bring the glory and the honor of the nations into it.[e] **27** But anything defiled and anyone who does what is disgusting and deceitful will in no way enter into it;[f] only those written in the Lamb's scroll of life will enter.[g]

22 And he showed me a river of water of life,[h] clear as crystal, flowing out from the throne of God and of the Lamb[i] **2** down the middle of its main street. On both sides of the river were trees of life producing 12 crops of fruit, yielding their fruit each month. And the leaves of the trees were for the healing of the nations.[j]

3 And there will no longer be any curse. But the throne of God and of the Lamb[k] will be in the city, and his slaves will offer him sacred service; **4** and they will see his face,[l] and his name will be on their foreheads.[m] **5** Also, night will be no more,[n] and they have no need of lamplight or sunlight, for Jehovah* God will shed light upon them,[o] and they will rule as kings forever and ever.[p]

6 He said to me: "These words are faithful* and true;[q] yes, Jehovah,* the God who inspired the prophets,[r] has sent his angel to show his slaves the things that must shortly take place. **7** Look! I am coming quickly.[s] Happy is anyone observing the words of the prophecy of this scroll."[t]

8 Well I, John, was the one hearing and seeing these things.

CHAP. 21

a Re 22:14

b Mt 10:2-4
　Lu 6:13-16
　Ac 1:13

c Eze 40:3, 5

d Re 4:3
　Re 21:10, 11

e Ex 6:3

Second Col.

a Isa 60:19, 20
　Re 22:5

b Joh 1:9
　Ac 26:13, 15
　Heb 1:3

c Isa 60:3

d Isa 60:11, 20

e Isa 60:5

f Ps 5:6
　Isa 52:1
　1Co 6:9, 10
　Ga 5:19-21
　Re 21:8

g Da 12:1
　Php 4:3
　Re 13:8

CHAP. 22

h Eze 47:1

i Joh 1:29

j Eze 47:12

k Re 3:21

l Mt 5:8

m Re 14:1

n Re 21:25

o Isa 60:19, 20
　1Jo 1:5

p Da 7:18
　Re 3:21

q Tit 1:2

r 2Ti 3:16

s Re 16:15
　Re 22:20

t Joh 13:17
　Re 1:3

21:16 *About 2,220 km (1,379 mi). A stadium equaled 185 m (606.95 ft). See App. B14.　21:17 *About 64 m (210 ft). See App. B14.　21:22; 22:5, 6 *See App. A5.

22:6 *Or "trustworthy."

When I heard and saw them, I fell down to worship at the feet of the angel who had been showing me these things. **9** But he tells me: "Be careful! Do not do that! I am only a fellow slave of you and of your brothers the prophets and of those observing the words of this scroll. Worship God."[a]

10 He also tells me: "Do not seal up the words of the prophecy of this scroll, for the appointed time is near. **11** Let the one who is unrighteous continue in unrighteousness, and let the filthy one continue in his filth; but let the righteous one continue in righteousness, and let the holy one continue in holiness.

12 "'Look! I am coming quickly, and the reward I give is with me, to repay each one according to his work.[b] **13** I am the Al'pha and the O·me'ga,*[c] the first and the last, the beginning and the end. **14** Happy are those who wash their robes,[d] so that they may have authority to go to the trees of life[e] and that they may gain entrance into the city through its gates.[f] **15** Outside are the dogs* and those who practice spiritism and those who

are sexually immoral* and the murderers and the idolaters and everyone who loves and practices lying.'[a]

16 "'I, Jesus, sent my angel to bear witness to you about these things for the congregations. I am the root and the offspring of David[b] and the bright morning star.'"[c]

17 And the spirit and the bride[d] keep on saying, "Come!" and let anyone hearing say, "Come!" and let anyone thirsting come;[e] let anyone who wishes take life's water free.[f]

18 "I am bearing witness to everyone who hears the words of the prophecy of this scroll: If anyone makes an addition to these things,[g] God will add to him the plagues that are written in this scroll;[h] **19** and if anyone takes anything away from the words of the scroll of this prophecy, God will take his portion away from the trees of life[i] and out of the holy city,[j] things that are written about in this scroll.

20 "The one who bears witness of these things says, 'Yes, I am coming quickly.'"[k]

"Amen! Come, Lord Jesus."

21 May the undeserved kindness of the Lord Jesus be with the holy ones.

22:13 *Or "the A and the Z." Alpha and Omega are the first and last letters of the Greek alphabet.   22:15 *That is, those whose practices are disgusting in God's eyes.

22:15 *See Glossary, "Sexual immorality."

CHAP. 22

a Mt 4:10
   Ac 10:25, 26
   Re 19:10

b Ps 62:12
   Isa 40:10
   Ro 2:6

c Isa 44:6
   Isa 48:12
   Re 1:8
   Re 21:6

d 1Jo 1:7

e Re 2:7

f Re 21:10, 12

_____

Second Col.

a Ga 5:19-21
   Eph 5:5
   Re 21:8

b Isa 11:1, 10
   Isa 53:2
   Jer 23:5
   Jer 33:15
   Re 5:5

c Nu 24:17
   Re 2:28

d Re 21:9

e Joh 4:14

f Isa 55:1
   Joh 7:37
   Re 7:17
   Re 21:6

g De 4:2
   De 12:32
   Ga 1:8
   1Jo 4:3
   2Jo 9

h Re 15:1

i Re 2:7

j Re 21:2

k Re 3:11
   Re 22:7

Table of the Books of the Bible

Books of the Hebrew Scriptures Before the Common (Christian) Era

Name of Book	Writer(s)	Place Written	Writing Completed (B.C.E.)	Time Covered (B.C.E.)
Genesis	Moses	Wilderness	1513	"In the beginning" to 1657
Exodus	Moses	Wilderness	1512	1657-1512
Leviticus	Moses	Wilderness	1512	1 month (1512)
Numbers	Moses	Wilderness and Plains of Moab	1473	1512-1473
Deuteronomy	Moses	Plains of Moab	1473	2 months (1473)
Joshua	Joshua	Canaan	c. 1450	1473-c. 1450
Judges	Samuel	Israel	c. 1100	c. 1450-c. 1120
Ruth	Samuel	Israel	c. 1090	11 years of Judges' rule
1 Samuel	Samuel; Gad; Nathan	Israel	c. 1078	c. 1180-1078
2 Samuel	Gad; Nathan	Israel	c. 1040	1077-c. 1040
1 Kings	Jeremiah	⌈ Judah and	⌈ 1 roll	c. 1040-580
2 Kings	Jeremiah	⌊ Egypt	⌊ 580	
1 Chronicles	Ezra	Jerusalem (?)	⌈ 1 roll	⌈ After 1 Chronicles 9:44:
2 Chronicles	Ezra	Jerusalem (?)	⌊ c. 460	⌊ c. 1077-537
Ezra	Ezra	Jerusalem	c. 460	537-c. 467
Nehemiah	Nehemiah	Jerusalem	a. 443	456-a. 443
Esther	Mordecai	Shushan, Elam	c. 475	493-c. 475
Job	Moses	Wilderness	c. 1473	Over 140 years between 1657 and 1473
Psalms	David and others		c. 460	
Proverbs	Solomon; Agur; Lemuel	Jerusalem	c. 717	
Ecclesiastes	Solomon	Jerusalem	b. 1000	
Song of Solomon	Solomon	Jerusalem	c. 1020	
Isaiah	Isaiah	Jerusalem	a. 732	c. 778-a. 732
Jeremiah	Jeremiah	Judah; Egypt	580	647-580
Lamentations	Jeremiah	Near Jerusalem	607	
Ezekiel	Ezekiel	Babylon	c. 591	613-c. 591
Daniel	Daniel	Babylon	c. 536	618-c. 536
Hosea	Hosea	Samaria (District)	a. 745	b. 804-a. 745
Joel	Joel	Judah	c. 820 (?)	
Amos	Amos	Judah	c. 804	
Obadiah	Obadiah		c. 607	
Jonah	Jonah		c. 844	
Micah	Micah	Judah	b. 717	c. 777-717
Nahum	Nahum	Judah	b. 632	
Habakkuk	Habakkuk	Judah	c. 628 (?)	
Zephaniah	Zephaniah	Judah	b. 648	
Haggai	Haggai	Jerusalem rebuilt	520	112 days (520)
Zechariah	Zechariah	Jerusalem rebuilt	518	520-518
Malachi	Malachi	Jerusalem rebuilt	a. 443	

Table of the Books of the Bible

Books of the Greek Scriptures Written During the Common (Christian) Era

Name of Book	Writer	Place Written	Writing Completed (C.E.)	Time Covered
Matthew	Matthew	Palestine	c. 41	2 B.C.E.–33 C.E.
Mark	Mark	Rome	c. 60-65	29-33 C.E.
Luke	Luke	Caesarea	c. 56-58	3 B.C.E.–33 C.E.
John	Apostle John	Ephesus, or near	c. 98	After prologue, 29-33 C.E.
Acts	Luke	Rome	c. 61	33–c. 61 C.E.
Romans	Paul	Corinth	c. 56	
1 Corinthians	Paul	Ephesus	c. 55	
2 Corinthians	Paul	Macedonia	c. 55	
Galatians	Paul	Corinth or Syrian Antioch	c. 50-52	
Ephesians	Paul	Rome	c. 60-61	
Philippians	Paul	Rome	c. 60-61	
Colossians	Paul	Rome	c. 60-61	
1 Thessalonians	Paul	Corinth	c. 50	
2 Thessalonians	Paul	Corinth	c. 51	
1 Timothy	Paul	Macedonia	c. 61-64	
2 Timothy	Paul	Rome	c. 65	
Titus	Paul	Macedonia (?)	c. 61-64	
Philemon	Paul	Rome	c. 60-61	
Hebrews	Paul	Rome	c. 61	
James	James (Jesus' brother)	Jerusalem	b. 62	
1 Peter	Peter	Babylon	c. 62-64	
2 Peter	Peter	Babylon (?)	c. 64	
1 John	Apostle John	Ephesus, or near	c. 98	
2 John	Apostle John	Ephesus, or near	c. 98	
3 John	Apostle John	Ephesus, or near	c. 98	
Jude	Jude (Jesus' brother)	Palestine (?)	c. 65	
Revelation	Apostle John	Patmos	c. 96	

[Names of writers of some books and of places where written are uncertain. Many dates are only approximate, the symbol a. meaning "after," b. meaning "before," and c. meaning "circa," or "about."]

Abbreviations Used in Footnotes

App.	Appendix(es)	in.	inch(es)
ftn.	footnote	kg	kilogram(s)
Lit.	Literally	km	kilometer(s)
vs.	verse	lb	pound(s) avoirdupois
vss.	verses	L	liter(s)
cm	centimeter(s)	mi	mile(s)
dry qt	dry quart(s) U.S.	m	meter(s)
ft	foot/feet	oz	ounce(s)
gal	liquid gallon(s)	oz t	ounce(s) troy
g	gram(s)	pt	pint(s) U.S.

Bible Words Index

See page 40 for abbreviations of names of Bible books.

A

ABANDON, De 31:8 will neither desert you nor a.
  1Sa 12:22 Jehovah will not a. his people
  Ps 27:10 Even if father and mother a. me
  Ps 37:28 Jehovah will not a. his loyal ones
  Job 8:29 he did not a. me, because I always
  Heb 13:5 never leave you, and I will never a. you
ABBA, Ro 8:15 we cry out: A., Father!
ABEL, Ge 4:8 Cain assaulted A.
  Mt 23:35 from the blood of righteous A. to
ABHOR, Ro 12:9 a. what is wicked; cling to good
ABIGAIL, 1Sa 25:3 A. was discerning and beautiful
ABILITY, Mt 25:15 talents to each according to his a.
ABRAHAM, Ge 21:12 God said to A., Listen to her
  2Ch 20:7 your friend A.
  Mt 22:32 God of A., God of the living
  Ro 4:3 A. put faith, counted as righteousness
ABSORBED, 1Ti 4:15 Ponder, be a.
ABUNDANCE, Ps 72:16 There will be a. of grain
  Lu 6:45 out of heart's a. mouth speaks
  Lu 12:15 even when person has a., his life
  Joh 10:10 have life and have it in a.
ABUSING, 1Co 9:18 to avoid a. my authority
ABUSIVE SPEECH, Eph 4:31 wrath, screaming, and a.
ABYSS, Re 11:7 wild beast ascends out of the a.
  Re 17:8 wild beast to ascend out of a.
  Re 20:3 hurled him into the a.
ACCEPT, Job 2:10 Should we a. only good from God?
ACCEPTABLE, 2Co 6:2 Now is the especially a. time
  Eph 5:10 making sure of what is a. to the Lord
ACCOUNT, Ro 14:12 each of us will render an a.
  1Co 13:5 It does not keep a. of injury
ACCURATE KNOWLEDGE, Ro 10:2 not according to a.
  Col 3:10 personality, through a. made new
  1Ti 2:4 whose will that people come to a.
ACCURSED, Joh 7:49 crowd not know the Law are a.
ACCUSATION, Ro 8:33 Who will file a. against
  1Ti 5:19 not accept a. against older man
  Tit 1:7 overseer must be free from a.
ACCUSER, Re 12:10 a. of our brothers hurled down
ACHAN, Jos 7:1 A. took some of
ACQUITTED, Ro 6:7 the one who died a. from sin
ACTIVITY, 1Pe 1:13 brace up your minds for a.
ADAM, Ge 5:5 A. lived 930 years, then died
  1Co 15:22 as in A. all are dying
  1Co 15:45 The last A. became a
  1Ti 2:14 A. was not deceived, but woman
ADMINISTRATION, Eph 1:10 for an a.
ADOPTION, Ro 8:15 received spirit of a.
ADORN, Tit 2:10 may a. the teaching of God
ADORNMENT, 1Pe 3:3 not let your a. be external
ADULTERATING, 2Co 4:2 or a. the word of God
ADULTERERS, 1Co 6:9 a. will not inherit Kingdom
ADULTERY, Ex 20:14 must not commit a.
  Mt 5:28 already committed a. in his heart
  Mt 19:9 and marries another commits a.
ADVANCEMENT, 1Ti 4:15 a. may be seen by all
ADVANTAGE, 1Co 7:35 this for your personal a.
  1Co 10:24 seeking, not own a., but
  2Co 7:2 we have taken a. of no one
ADVANTAGEOUS, 1Co 6:12 lawful, but not a.
ADVISERS, Pr 15:22 accomplishment through
  many a.

AFFECTION, Mt 10:37 Whoever has greater a. for
  Joh 21:17 Simon, do you have a. for me?
  Re 3:19 those for whom I have a. I reprove
AFFECTIONS, Col 3:12 clothe with tender a.
AFFLICTED, Ps 119:71 good that I have been a.
AFFLICTION, Job 36:15 rescues afflicted during a.
  Ps 119:50 This is my comfort in my a.
AFRAID, 2Ch 20:15 Do not be a. of large crowd
  Ps 56:4 in God I put trust; I am not a.
  Ps 118:6 Jehovah on my side; I will not be a.
  Isa 41:10 Do not be a., for I am with you
  Mic 4:4 no one will make them a.
  Re 2:10 not be a. of things you are to suffer
AGAINST, Ro 8:31 If God is for us, who will be a. us?
AGLOW, Ro 12:11 Be a. with the spirit
AGREEMENT, 1Co 1:10 you should all speak in a.
AIMLESSLY, 1Co 9:26 way I am running is not a.
AIR, 1Co 9:26 not to be striking the a.
  1Co 14:9 You will be speaking into the a.
  Eph 2:2 ruler of the authority of the a.
ALCOHOL, Pr 20:1 Wine is a ridiculer, a. is unruly
ALIVE, Heb 4:12 word of God is a. and exerts power
  1Pe 3:18 but made a. in spirit
ALONE, Joh 16:32 will leave me a. But I am not a.
ALPHA, Re 1:8 the A. and the Omega
ALTAR, Ge 8:20 Noah built an a.
  Ex 27:1 make a. of acacia wood
  Mt 5:24 leave your gift in front of the a.
  Ac 17:23 an a. To an Unknown God
AMBASSADORS, 2Co 5:20 a. substituting for Christ
AMEN, 1Co 14:16 A. to your giving of thanks
  2Co 1:20 through him A. said to God
ANANIAS, Ac 5:1 A., with his wife Sapphira
ANCHOR, Heb 6:19 hope as a. for the soul
ANCIENT OF DAYS, Da 7:9 A. sat down
ANGEL, 2Ki 19:35 a. struck down 185,000
  Ps 34:7 a. of Jehovah camps around
  Da 3:28 sent his a. and rescued
  Ho 12:4 [Jacob] contending with an a.
  Ac 5:19 a. opened doors of the prison
  Ac 12:11 sent his a. and rescued me
ANGELS, Ge 28:12 a. ascending and descending
  Job 4:18 he finds fault with his a.
  Mt 13:41 send his a., they will collect
  Mt 22:30 they are as a. in heaven
  Mt 24:31 a. will gather chosen ones
  1Co 4:9 theatrical spectacle to a.
  1Co 6:3 not know we will judge a.?
  Heb 13:2 unknowingly entertained a.
  1Pe 1:12 a. are desiring to peer
  Jude 6 a. did not keep original position
ANGER, Ps 37:8 Let go of a. and rage
  Ps 103:8 Jehovah is slow to a.
  Pr 14:17 quick to a. acts foolishly
  Ac 15:39 there was a sharp burst of a.
  Col 3:8 put away a., abusive speech
ANGRY, Eph 4:26 sun set you still a.
ANGUISH, Job 6:2 If my a. could be weighed
  Lu 21:25 a. of nations not knowing the way out
ANIMAL, Ge 7:2 take clean a. by sevens
  Le 18:23 sexual intercourse with an a.
ANIMALS, Le 26:6 will rid land of vicious a.
  Pr 12:10 righteous takes care of a.
  Ec 3:19 humans and a., same outcome
  Ho 2:18 covenant with wild a.

ANNA, Lu 2:36, 37 a prophetess, A., 84 years old
ANOINTED, 1Sa 16:13 Samuel a. David
  Ps 2:2 kings take stand against a. one
  Ps 105:15 Do not touch my a. ones
  Isa 61:1 Jehovah a. me to declare good news
ANSWER, Pr 15:1 mild a. turns away rage
  Pr 15:23 man rejoices in giving right a.
  Isa 65:24 before they call out, I will a.
  Col 4:6 know how you should a. each
ANSWERING, Pr 15:28 righteous meditates before a.
ANT, Pr 6:6 Go to the a., you lazy one
ANTICHRISTS, 1Jo 2:18 even now many a.
ANTS, Pr 30:25 a. prepare food in the summer
ANXIETIES, Ps 94:19 a. overwhelmed, you comforted
  Mr 4:19 a. of system and deceptive power of
  Lu 8:14 carried away by a., riches, and pleasures
  Lu 21:34 hearts weighed down with a. of life
ANXIETY, Pr 12:25 A. in man's heart weighs it down
  1Co 7:32 want you to be free from a.
  2Co 11:28 a. for all the congregations
ANXIOUS, Isa 41:10 Do not be a., for I am your God
  Mt 6:34 never be a. about the next day
  Mt 10:19 not a. about how or what to speak
  Lu 12:25 by being a. add cubit to life span?
  1Co 7:32 unmarried man a. for things of Lord
  Php 4:6 not be a. over anything
APOLLOS, Ac 18:24 A., an eloquent man
APOSTASY, 2Th 2:3 unless the a. comes first
APOSTATE, Pr 11:9 a. brings neighbor to ruin
APOSTLES, Mt 10:2 names of the 12 a. are
  Ac 15:6 a. and elders gathered to look into this
  1Co 15:9 I am the least of the a.
  2Co 11:5 your superfine a.
APPEAL, Ro 12:1 I a. to you by the compassions
  Phm 9 a. on the basis of love
APPEARANCE, 1Sa 16:7 Do not pay attention to a.
  Joh 7:24 Stop judging by the outward a.
APPETITES, Ro 16:18 slaves of their own a.
APPLES, Pr 25:11 a. of gold in silver carvings
APPOINTED TIME, Hab 2:3 vision is yet for its a.
APPOINTED TIMES, Lu 21:24 a. of the nations
APPRECIATION, Ps 27:4 look with a. upon temple
APPROVAL, 1Co 7:33 gain a. of his wife
APPROVED, Lu 3:22 my Son; I have a. you
  2Ti 2:15 present yourself a. to God
AQUILA, Ac 18:2 found a Jew named A.
ARARAT, Ge 8:4 ark came to rest on A.
ARCHANGEL, 1Th 4:16 with an a.'s voice
  Jude 9 Michael the a. had a difference with
AREOPAGUS, Ac 17:22 Paul stood in A. and said
ARK, Ge 6:14 Make for yourself an a.
  Ex 25:10 make an a. of acacia wood
  2Sa 6:6 Uzzah grabbed hold of the A.
  1Ch 15:2 No one to carry A. except Levites
ARM, Joh 12:38 a. of Jehovah has been revealed?
ARMAGEDDON, Re 16:16 called in Hebrew A.
ARMIES, Re 19:14 a. in heaven following him
ARMOR, Eph 6:11 Put on complete suit of a.
ARMY, Ps 68:11 women proclaiming are large a.
ARRANGEMENT, 1Co 14:40 decently and by a.
ARROWS, Ps 127:4 Like a. in the hand of mighty
ARTEMIS, Ac 19:34 shouting: Great is A.!
ART OF TEACHING, 2Ti 4:2 with all patience and a.
ASCENDED, Joh 3:13 no man has a. into heaven
ASHAMED, Ezr 9:6 a. to raise my face to God
  Mr 8:38 whoever becomes a. of me and my
  Ro 1:16 I am not a. of the good news
  2Ti 1:8 not become a. of witness
  2Ti 2:15 workman with nothing to be a. of
  Heb 11:16 God is not a. of them, to be
  1Pe 4:16 suffers as a Christian, let not feel a.
ASK, Ps 2:8 A. of me, and I will give nations
  Mt 6:8 knows what you need before you a.

Joh 14:13 whatever you a. in my name, I will do
  Eph 3:20 beyond all the things we a.
  1Jo 5:14 a. according to his will
ASKING, De 10:12 what is Jehovah a. of you?
  Mt 7:7 Keep on a., and it will be given
ASSOCIATING, 2Th 3:14 stop a. with him
ASSOCIATION, 1Pe 2:17 love for the whole a. of
ASSOCIATIONS, 1Co 15:33 Bad a. spoil
ASTROLOGERS, Mt 2:1 a. came to Jerusalem
ATONEMENT, Le 16:34 make a. once each year
ATTITUDE, Eph 4:23 new in dominant mental a.
  Eph 6:7 with a good a., as to Jehovah
  Php 2:5 mental a. that was in Christ
AUTHORITIES, Ro 13:1 in subjection to superior a.
  Tit 3:1 obedient to a., ready for good work
AUTHORITY, Mt 28:18 All a. has been given me
  Lu 4:6 I will give you this a. and their glory
  1Co 9:18 to avoid abusing my a.
  2Pe 2:10 those who despise a.
AVENGE, Ro 12:19 Do not a. yourselves, beloved
AVOIDED, Isa 53:3 He was despised and a. by men
AWAKE, Lu 21:36 Keep a., making supplication
  1Co 16:13 Stay a., stand firm in the faith
  Re 16:15 Happy is the one who stays a.
AWAKEN, Joh 11:11 I am traveling to a. him
AZAZEL, Le 16:8 Aaron will draw lot for A.

B

BAAL, Jer 19:5 to burn sons as offerings to B.
BABEL, Ge 11:9 named B., because there
BABYLON, Jer 51:6 Flee out of the midst of B.
  Jer 51:30 warriors of B. quit fighting
  Jer 51:37 B. will become piles of stones
  Re 17:5 B. the Great, the mother of
  Re 18:2 B. the Great has fallen
BAD, Ge 3:5 like God, knowing good and b.
  Isa 5:20 Woe to those who say b. is good
  Ro 7:19 b. that I do not wish I practice
BALAAM, Nu 22:28 donkey said to B.
BALD, Le 13:40 If a man becomes b., he is clean
  Le 21:5 should not make their heads b.
BALDHEAD, 2Ki 2:23 Go up, you b.!
BANDAGE, Eze 34:16 the injured I will b.
BANQUET, Isa 25:6 b. of dishes, b. of wine
BAPTISM, Lu 3:3 b. in symbol of repentance
  Ro 6:4 buried through b. into his death
  1Pe 3:21 B. is now saving you
BAPTIZED, Mt 3:13 Jesus came to John to be b.
  Ac 2:41 b., on that day about 3,000 added
  Ac 8:36 what prevents me from getting b.?
BAPTIZING, Mt 28:19 make disciples, b. them
BARNABAS, Ac 9:27 B. came to his aid and
BARREN, Ex 23:26 women will not be b.
  Isa 54:1 Shout joyfully, you b. woman
BARUCH, Jer 45:2 Jehovah says concerning you, B.
BASKETS, Mt 14:20 leftover fragments, 12 b. full
BATH-SHEBA, 2Sa 11:3 B. the wife of Uriah
BATTLE, 1Sa 17:47 b. belongs to Jehovah
  1Co 14:8 who will get ready for b.?
BEAR, Lu 17:37 rescued me from lion and b.
  Isa 11:7 cow and b. will feed together
  Ro 15:1 strong ought to b. the weaknesses
BEASTS, Eze 34:25 will rid the land of vicious b.
  Da 7:3 four huge b. came out of the sea
BEATINGS, 2Co 6:5 by b., by imprisonments
BEAUTY, Pr 6:25 Do not desire her b. in your heart
  Pr 19:11 to overlook an offense
  Pr 31:30 b. may be fleeting
  Eze 28:17 heart haughty because of b.
BECOME, Ex 3:14 I Will B. What I Choose to B.
  1Co 9:22 I have b. all things to
BED, Heb 13:4 marriage b. be without defilement

BEFIT, Lu 3:8 produce fruits that b. repentance
BEG, 2Co 5:20 we b.: Become reconciled to God
BEGINNING, Isa 46:10 From b. foretell outcome
　　Mt 24:8 these things are a b. of pangs of distress
BEGINNINGS, Zec 4:10 despised the day of small b.?
BEHIND, Lu 9:62 put hand to a plow and looks b.
BELIEVE, Joh 20:29 Happy who have not seen yet b.
　　2Th 2:12 they did not b. the truth but
BELLY, Php 3:19 their god is their b.
BELONG, Ro 14:8 if we die, we b. to Jehovah
　　1Co 6:19 you do not b. to yourselves
BELONGINGS, Lu 14:33 does not say good-bye to b.
　　Heb 10:34 accepted plundering of b.
BELOVED, Mt 3:17 my Son, the b.
BELSHAZZAR, Da 5:1 King B. held a great feast
BELT, Isa 11:5 Righteousness will be the b.
BENEFICIAL, 2Ti 3:16 inspired of God and b.
BENEFIT, De 8:16 so as to b. you in the future
　　Pr 14:23 b. in every kind of hard work
　　Isa 48:17 One teaching you to b. yourself
BETHEL, Ge 28:19 named that place B.
BETHLEHEM, Mic 5:2 B. Ephrathah, from you will
BETRAY, Mt 26:21 one of you will b. me
BEYOND, 1Co 4:6 Do not go b. the things written
BEZALEL, Ex 31:2 I have chosen B.
BIND, Isa 61:1 to b. up the brokenhearted
BIRDCATCHER, Ps 91:3 from the trap of the b.
BIRDS, Mt 6:26 Observe intently the b. of heaven
BIRTH, Ge 66:7 Before labor, she gave b.
　　1Pe 1:3 new b. to a living hope
BIRTHDAY, Ge 40:20 was Pharaoh's b.
　　Mt 14:6 when Herod's b. was celebrated
BITING, Ga 5:15 If you keep on b. one another
BITTERLY, Mt 26:75 he went outside and wept b.
　　Col 3:19 do not be b. angry with them
BITTERNESS, Pr 14:10 The heart knows its own b.
　　Eph 4:31 malicious b., anger, wrath
BLASPHEMES, Mr 3:29 b. against the holy spirit
BLESS, Ge 32:26 not let you go until you b. me
　　Nu 6:24 May Jehovah b. you
　　Lu 6:28 b. those cursing you
BLESSED, Ge 1:28 God b. them and said
　　Jg 5:24 Most b. of women is Jael
　　Joh 12:13 B. the one who comes in Jehovah's name
BLESSING, De 30:19 put before you b. and curse
　　Pr 10:22 b. of Jehovah makes rich
　　Mal 3:10 pour out b. until there is nothing lacking
　　Ro 12:14 Keep b. those who persecute
BLIND, Le 19:14 not put obstacle before a b. man
　　Isa 35:5 eyes of the b. will be opened
　　Mt 15:14 B. guides is what they are
BLINDED, 2Co 4:4 god of this system b. the minds
BLINDNESS, Ge 19:11 struck the men with b.
BLOOD, Ge 9:4 b.—you must not eat
　　Le 7:26 You must not eat any b.
　　Le 17:11 life of the flesh is in the b.
　　Le 17:13 pour b. out and cover with dust
　　Ps 72:14 their b. precious in his eyes
　　Eze 3:18 I will ask his b. back from you
　　Mt 9:20 suffering for 12 years from a flow of b.
　　Mt 26:28 this means my b. of the covenant
　　Mt 27:25 Let his b. come upon us and our children
　　Ac 15:29 keep abstaining from b.
　　Ac 20:26 I am clean from the b. of all men
　　Ac 20:28 purchased with the b. of his own Son
　　Eph 1:7 release by ransom through the b.
　　1Pe 1:19 it was with precious b. of Christ
　　1Jo 1:7 b. of Jesus cleanses us from sin
　　Re 18:24 in her was found b. of holy ones
BLOOM, 1Co 7:36 past the b. of youth
BLOSSOM, Isa 35:1 desert plain will b. as saffron
BLOTTED, Ac 3:19 to get your sins b. out

BOAST, 1Co 1:31 who boasts, let him b. in Jehovah
BODIES, Ro 6:13 present your b. to God
　　Ro 12:1 present your b. as a living sacrifice
BODY, Mt 10:28 fearful of those who kill the b. but
　　Mt 26:26 Take, eat. This means my b.
　　1Co 7:4 authority over his b., but wife
　　1Co 12:18 God arranged the b. members
　　1Co 15:44 sown a physical b., raised spiritual
　　Php 3:21 transform our humble b. to
BOLDNESS, Ac 4:31 speaking the word with b.
　　Eph 6:20 [Pray] that I may speak with b.
　　1Th 2:2 mustered up b. by means of our God
BOND, Eph 4:3 in the uniting b. of peace
　　Col 3:14 love, a perfect b. of union
BONE, Ge 2:23 at last b. of my bones
　　Pr 25:15 gentle tongue can break a b.
　　Joh 19:36 Not a b. of his will be broken
BONES, 2Ki 13:21 man touched b. of Elisha
　　Ps 34:20 guarding his b.; not one broken
　　Jer 20:9 like a burning fire shut up in my b.
BOOK, Ex 32:33 I will wipe him out of my b.
　　Jos 1:8 b. of the Law should not depart
　　Mal 3:16 b. of remembrance written
　　Re 20:15 not written in the b. of life
BOOKS, Ec 12:12 making many b. there is no end
　　Ac 19:19 burned their b. up before everybody
BORN, Job 14:1 Man, b. of woman, short-lived
　　Ps 51:5 I was b. guilty of error
BORROWER, Pr 22:7 b. is a slave to the lender
BORROWS, Ps 37:21 wicked b. and does not repay
BOSOM, Isa 40:11 in his b. he will carry them
BOTTLE-GOURD, Jon 4:10 You felt sorry for b.
BOUGHT, 1Co 7:23 You were b. with a price
　　Re 5:9 with your blood you b. people
BOUND, Ge 22:9 He b. his son Isaac
　　Mt 16:19 bind on earth b. in the heavens
BOY, Pr 22:6 Train a b.; even when he grows old
　　Isa 11:6 little b. will lead them
　　Jer 1:7 Do not say, I am just a b.
BRANCH, Joh 15:4 b. cannot bear fruit by itself
BRAZEN CONDUCT, Ga 5:19 immorality, b.
　　2Pe 2:7 Lot distressed by the b.
BREAD, Ne 9:15 You gave them b. from heaven
　　Ps 37:25 nor his children looking for b.
　　Isa 55:2 Why paying for what is not b.?
　　Mt 4:4 Man must live, not on b. alone
　　Mt 6:11 Give us today our b. for this day
　　Joh 6:35 I am the b. of life
BREASTPLATE, Eph 6:14 b. of righteousness
BREASTS, Pr 5:19 Let her b. satisfy you
BREATH, Ge 2:7 into nostrils the b. of life
BREATHING, Ps 150:6 Every b. thing praise Jah
BRIBE, Ec 7:7 b. corrupts the heart
BRIDE, Re 21:9 will show you the b., Lamb's wife
BROKEN, Ps 51:17 sacrifices to God are a b. spirit
　　Pr 29:1 stiffens neck after much reproof will be b.
　　Isa 66:2 will look to the humble and b. in spirit
BROKENHEARTED, Ps 34:18 Jehovah is close to b.
　　Ps 147:3 He heals the b.
BROTHER, Pr 17:17 is a b. born for times of distress
　　Pr 18:24 friend who sticks closer than a b.
　　1Co 5:11 anyone called a b. who is immoral
BROTHERLY LOVE, Ro 12:10 In b. have affection
BROTHERS, Mt 13:55 his b. James and Joseph and
　　Mt 23:8 and all of you are b.
　　Mt 25:40 did to one of my b., did to me
　　1Pe 5:9 the entire association of your b.
BUILD, Isa 65:21 b. houses and live in them
　　Ro 14:19 pursue things that b. up
　　1Co 10:23 lawful, but not all things b. up
　　Jude 20 b. yourselves up on most holy faith

BUILDING, Lu 17:28 they were planting, they were b.
　1Co 3:10 each keep watching how he is b.
　1Co 14:26 all things take place for b. up
BUILDS, Ps 127:1 Unless Jehovah b. the house
　1Co 8:1 Knowledge puffs up, love b. up
BULL, Ex 21:28 If a b. gores a man
　De 25:4 not muzzle a b. threshing grain
　Pr 7:22 Suddenly goes like a b. to the slaughter
BULLS, Ho 14:2 offer praise as we would young b.
　1Co 9:9 Is it b. God is concerned about?
BURDEN, Ps 38:4 my errors like a heavy b.
　Ps 55:22 Throw your b. on Jehovah
　Ac 15:28 adding no further b. to you except
　1Th 2:6 could be an expensive b.
　Re 2:24 not putting any other b.
BURDENS, Ga 6:2 carrying the b. of one another
BURDENSOME, 1Jo 5:3 his commandments are not b.
BUSINESS, Mt 22:5 unconcerned went off, to his b.
　Jas 4:13 we will do b. and make profit
BUSYBODY, 1Pe 4:15 let none suffer as a b.

C

CAESAR, Mt 22:17 lawful to pay tax to C. or not?
　Mr 12:17 Pay back Caesar's things to C., but God's
　Joh 19:12 If you release, you are not a friend of C.
　Joh 19:15 We have no king but C.
　Ac 25:11 I appeal to C.!
CAIN, 1Jo 3:12 not like C., who slaughtered brother
CALCULATE, Lu 14:28 sit down and c. expense
CALEB, Nu 13:30 C. tried to calm the people
　Nu 14:24 C. had a different spirit
CALF, Ex 32:4 made into a statue of a c.
　Isa 11:6 c. and lion will be together
CALLING, Eph 4:1 walk worthily of the c.
CALLS, Ro 10:13 who c. on the name of Jehovah
CALM, Pr 14:30 c. heart gives life to the body
　Pr 17:27 discerning man will remain c.
CAMEL, Mt 19:24 easier for c. to get through
CANA, Joh 2:1 marriage feast in C. of Galilee
CAPABLE, Ex 18:21 select c., trustworthy men
　Pr 31:29 many c. women, you surpass them
CAPTIVITY, 2Co 10:5 bringing every thought into c.
CARES, 1Pe 5:7 because he c. for you
CARPENTER, Mr 6:3 This is the c., son of Mary
CATCHING, Lu 5:10 From now on you will be c. men
CAUTIOUS, Pr 14:16 wise one c. and turns from evil
　Mt 10:16 c. as serpents, innocent as doves
CAVE, Mt 21:13 making it a c. of robbers
CEPHAS, 1Co 15:5 appeared to C., then to the Twelve
　Ga 2:11 C. came to Antioch, I resisted him
CERTAIN, Ec 7:14 c. of anything that will happen
CERTIFICATE, De 24:1 write out a c. of divorce
　Mt 19:7 Why did Moses direct giving a c.?
CHAFF, Zep 2:2 before the day passes by like c.
CHANGE, Mal 3:6 I am Jehovah; I do not c.
CHARIOTS, Jg 4:13 900 c. with iron scythes
　2Ki 6:17 c. of fire all around Elisha
CHARM, Pr 31:30 C. may be false, beauty fleeting
CHEEK, Mt 5:39 slaps you on right c., turn the other
CHEERFUL, 2Co 9:7 God loves a c. giver
CHERISHES, Eph 5:29 feeds and c. it
CHERUB, Eze 28:14 assigned you as the anointed c.
CHERUBS, Ge 3:24 posted c. and the flaming sword
CHILD, Lu 9:47 took a young c., stood him
　1Co 13:11 to think as a c., reason as a c.
CHILDLESS, De 7:14 no man or woman will be c.
CHILDREN, De 31:12 Gather the people, the c.
　Ps 8:2 Out of the mouth of c.
　Mt 11:16 like c. in the marketplaces
　Mt 18:3 unless you become as young c.

Mt 19:14 Let c. alone, do not stop them
Lu 10:21 hidden from wise and revealed to c.
Ro 8:21 glorious freedom of c. of God
1Co 7:14 your c. would be unclean, but now
1Co 14:20 be young c. as to badness
2Co 12:14 c. not to save up for parents
Eph 6:1 C., be obedient to your parents
1Jo 3:2 we are now c. of God
CHOKE, Mr 4:19 c. the word, it becomes unfruitful
CHOOSE, De 30:19 you must c. life
　Jos 24:15 c. whom you will serve
CHOOSING, Ro 9:11 c. dependent on One who calls
CHOSEN ONES, Mt 24:22 cut short; on account of c.
　Mt 24:31 angels will gather his c.
CHRIST, Mt 16:16 You are the C., the Son of
　Lu 24:26 Was it not necessary for C. to suffer?
　Joh 17:3 and one whom you sent, Jesus C.
　Ac 18:28 from the Scriptures that Jesus is C.
　1Co 11:3 the head of the C. is God
CHRISTIANS, Ac 11:26 by divine providence called C.
CHRISTS, FALSE, Mt 24:24 f. and prophets will arise
CIRCLE, Isa 40:22 who dwells above the c. of earth
CIRCUMCISION, Ro 2:29 c. of the heart by spirit
　1Co 7:19 C. means nothing, and
CISTERN, Pr 5:15 Drink water from your own c.
CITIES, Lu 4:43 declare good news to other c.
CITIES OF REFUGE, Nu 35:11 convenient c.
　Jos 20:2 Select for yourselves the c.
CITIZENSHIP, Php 3:20 our c. exists in heavens
CITY, Heb 11:10 c. having real foundations
CLAY, Isa 45:9 Should the c. say to the Potter
　Isa 64:8 We are the c., you are our Potter
　Da 2:42 partly of iron and partly of c.
CLEAN, Joh 15:3 already c. because of the word
　Ac 20:26 I am c. from the blood of all men
CLEANSE, Ps 51:2 c. me from my sin
　Da 12:10 Many will c. themselves
　2Co 7:1 c. ourselves of every defilement
CLING, De 10:20 to Jehovah you should c.
　Ro 12:9 c. to what is good
CLOUD, Heb 12:1 such a great c. of witnesses
CLOUDS, Ec 11:4 who looks at c. will not reap
　Mt 24:30 will see Son of man coming on c.
COALS, Ro 12:20 will heap fiery c. on his head
COBRA, Isa 11:8 play over the lair of a c.
COME, Isa 55:1 all you thirsty ones, c. to water!
　Re 22:17 let anyone hearing say, C.!
COMFORT, Job 2:11 sympathize with Job, c. him
　Isa 61:2 to c. all who mourn
　Ro 15:4 through the c. from the Scriptures
　2Co 1:3 God of all c.
　2Co 1:4 that we be able to c. others
COMFORTED, Ps 94:19 anxieties overwhelmed,
　you c.
　Isa 49:13 Jehovah has c. his people
　Jer 31:15 Rachel refused to be c. over her sons
　Mt 5:4 Happy those who mourn, will be c.
COMFORTERS, Job 16:2 you are troublesome c.!
COMMANDMENT, Mr 12:28 Which c. is first of all?
　Mr 12:31 no other c. greater than these
　Joh 13:34 new c., that you love one another
COMMANDMENTS, Mt 22:40 On two C. Law hangs
COMMEND, 1Co 11:2 I c. you because you are
COMPANION, Ps 55:13 my own c. whom I know
COMPANY, 1Co 5:9 stop c. with sexually immoral
COMPARE, Isa 46:5 To whom will you c. me
COMPARISON, Ga 6:4 not in c. with the other person
COMPASSION, Col 3:12 tender affections of c.
　1Jo 3:17 refuses to show him c.
COMPASSIONATE, Ex 34:6 Jehovah, merciful and c.
COMPENSATION, Ex 21:36 he must make c.
COMPETITION, Ga 5:26 not stirring up c.

COMPLACENCY, Pr 1:32 c. of fools will destroy them
COMPLAINERS, Jude 16 murmurers, c.
COMPLAINT, Job 7:11 in the bitterness of
COMPLETE, 1Ch 28:9 serve God with c. heart
  2Ch 16:9 those whose heart is c.
CONCERN, 1Co 12:25 mutual c. for one another
CONCLUSION, Ec 12:13 The c. of the matter is:
  Mt 28:20 I am with you until c. of system
CONCUBINES, 1Ki 11:3 700 wives and 300 c.
CONDUCT, Ga 6:16 walk orderly by this rule of c.
  1Pe 2:12 Maintain c. fine among the nations
  1Pe 3:1 won without a word through c.
  1Pe 3:16 put to shame because of your good c.
CONFESS, Jas 5:16 c. sins to one another
  1Jo 1:9 If we c. sins, he is faithful to forgive
CONFESSED, Ps 32:5 Finally I c. my sin to you
CONFESSES, Pr 28:13 c. will be shown mercy
CONFIDENCE, Pr 3:26 Jehovah your source of c.
  Pr 11:13 trustworthy person keeps a c.
  2Th 3:4 we have c. in Lord regarding you
CONFIDENT, Pr 28:1 righteous c. as a lion
CONFIDENTIAL, Pr 20:19 slanderer revealing c. talk
  Am 3:7 unless revealed c. matter to prophets
CONFIDENTIALLY, Pr 25:9 not reveal what told c.
CONGREGATION, Ps 22:25 praise you in large c.
  Ps 40:9 I proclaim the good news in the great c.
  Mt 16:18 on this rock I will build my c.
  Ac 20:28 shepherd the c. of God
  Ro 16:5 greet c. in their house
CONQUERED, Joh 16:33 courage! I have c. the world
CONQUERING, Ro 12:21 keep c. the evil with the good
CONQUERS, Re 2:7 To the one who c. I will grant
CONQUEST, Re 6:2 conquering and to complete
  his c.
CONSCIENCE, Ro 2:15 c. bearing witness with them
  Ro 13:5 also on account of your c.
  1Co 8:12 wound their weak c.
  1Ti 4:2 whose c. is seared with
  1Pe 3:16 Maintain a good c.
  1Pe 3:21 request for a good c.
CONSENT, 1Co 7:5 not deprive except by mutual c.
CONSEQUENCES, Pr 27:12 inexperienced suffer c.
CONSIDERATION, Ps 41:1 who shows c. to lowly
  1Th 5:13 c. in love because of their work
CONSOLING, 1Th 2:11 kept exhorting and c.
CONSTANT FEATURE, Da 11:31 and remove the c.
  Da 12:11 from the time c. has been removed
CONSULTATION, Pr 15:22 Plans fail when no c.
CONTEMPTIBLE, Nu 21:5 we hate this c. bread
CONTENT, 1Ti 6:8 food and clothing, c. with these
CONTENTIONS, Pr 6:19 sowing c. among brothers
CONTINUALLY, Da 6:16 whom you are c. serving
CONTRIBUTIONS, 2Ch 31:10 started bringing c.
CONTROL, 1Th 4:4 know how to c. his own body
CONTROLLED, 1Co 6:12 not let myself be c. by
CONTROLLING, Pr 16:32 better the one c. temper
CONTROLS, Pr 10:19 c. his lips acts discreetly
CONVENIENT, Lu 4:13 Devil departed until c. time
CONVENTIONS, Le 23:4 These are the holy c.
CONVICTION, Col 4:12 firm c. in the will of God
  1Th 1:5 with holy spirit and strong c.
CONVINCED, Ro 4:21 fully c. that He was able to do
  Ro 8:38 I am c. that neither death nor life
  Ro 15:14 I am c. about you, my brothers
COOPERATE, Ro 8:28 makes all his works c. together
  Eph 4:16 c. through every joint
COPY, De 17:18 must write a c. of this Law
CORD, Ec 4:12 threefold c. cannot quickly be torn
CORDS, Isa 54:2 lengthen your tent c.
CORNELIUS, Ac 10:24 C. called relatives and friends
CORNERSTONE, Ps 118:22 has become the chief c.
  Eph 2:20 Jesus is the foundation c.

CORRECT, Ps 94:12 Happy is the man whom you c.
CORRECTING, De 8:5 as man corrects son, God c.
CORRUPTION, Da 6:4 no negligence or c. in Daniel
COST, 1Co 9:18 I offer good news without c.
COUNSELOR, Isa 9:6 His name will be Wonderful C.
COUNT, Ps 90:12 Teach us how to c. our days
COUNTED, Lu 22:37 He was c. with lawless ones
COUNTERFEIT, 2Pe 2:3 exploit with c. words
COUNTRYMEN, 1Th 2:14 suffered at the hands of c.
COURAGE, Ac 28:15 sight of them, Paul took c.
  2Co 5:6 we are of good c.
  Php 1:14 c. to speak the word of God
COURAGEOUS, Jos 1:7 be c. and very strong
COURSE, Joe 2:7 each keeps to his own c.
  Ac 20:24 finish my c. and ministry
COURT, Da 7:10 The C. took its seat
  1Co 6:6 brother goes to c. against brother
COURTS, Mr 13:9 People will hand you over to c.
COVENANT, Ge 15:18 Jehovah made with Abram a c.
  Jer 31:31 I will make a new c.
  Lu 22:20 new c. by virtue of my blood
  Lu 22:29 I make c. with you, as my Father
COVER, 1Co 11:6 if a woman does not c. herself
COVERING, Pr 28:13 c. over transgressions will not
COWARDICE, 2Ti 1:7 God did not give us spirit of c.
CREATE, Isa 45:18 who did not c. earth for nothing
CREATED, Ge 1:1 In the beginning God c.
  Ps 104:30 send out your spirit, they are c.
  Col 1:16 by means of him things c.
  Re 4:11 you c. all because of your will
CREATION, Ro 1:20 seen from world's c. onward
  Ro 8:20 c. subjected to futility on the basis of hope
  2Co 5:17 in union with Christ, he is a new c.
  Col 1:23 preached in all c. under heaven
  Re 3:14 the beginning of the c. by God
CREATOR, Ec 12:1 Remember C. in the days of youth
CRITICAL, 2Ti 3:1 c. times hard to deal with
CRITICIZE, 1Ti 5:1 Do not c. an older man
CROOKED, Ec 1:15 c. cannot be made straight
CROWD, Ex 23:2 must not follow after c.
CROWN, Pr 12:4 capable wife a c. to husband
  Mt 27:29 braided a c. out of thorns
  1Co 9:25 they receive c. that perish
CRUEL, Pr 11:17 c. person brings trouble on himself
  Pr 12:10 even the mercy of the wicked is c.
CRUSHED, Ps 34:18 saves those c. in spirit
  Pr 18:14 who can bear a c. spirit?
  Isa 42:3 No c. reed will he break
  Isa 57:15 I reside with those c. and lowly in spirit
CUBIT, Mt 6:27 Who can add one c. to life span?
CUP, Mt 20:22 Can you drink the c. that I am
  Lu 22:20 This c. means the new covenant
  Lu 22:42 if you want to, remove this c. from me
  1Co 11:25 He did the same with the c.
CURE, Lu 4:23 Physician, c. yourself
  Lu 10:9 c. the sick and tell, Kingdom of God near
CURED, Ac 5:16 they were one and all c.
CURSE, Nu 23:8 How could I put a c. on those
  Job 2:5 will surely c. you to your very face
  Job 2:9 wife said, C. God and die!
  Ro 12:14 bless and do not c.
CUTS, Le 21:5 should not make c. on body
CUTTING-OFF, Mt 25:46 will depart into
  everlasting c.
CYRUS, Ezr 6:3 C.: Let the house be rebuilt
  Isa 45:1 anointed one, C., whose right hand

D

DANCING, Jg 11:34 daughter coming out, d.!
DANGER, Pr 22:3 shrewd sees d. and conceals
DANGERS, 2Co 11:26 in d. in the city, in d.
DARKNESS, Isa 60:2 d. will cover the earth
  Joe 2:31 sun will be turned into d.

Mt 4:16 people sitting in d. saw a great light
Joh 3:19 men have loved the d.
Eph 4:18 They are in d. mentally
1Pe 2:9 called you out of d.
DAUGHTER, Lu 8:49 Your d. has died
DAUGHTERS, Joe 2:28 your sons and d. will
prophesy
Ac 21:9 four unmarried d. who prophesied
2Co 6:18 you will become sons and d. to me
DAVID, 1Sa 16:13 Samuel anointed D.
Lu 1:32 throne of D. his father
Ac 2:34 D. did not ascend to the heavens
DAY, Ps 84:10 a d. in your courtyards better
Eze 4:6 A d. for a year, a d. for a year
Mt 24:36 d. and hour nobody knows
2Pe 3:8 one d. is as a thousand years
DAY OF JEHOVAH, Joe 2:1 d. is coming! It is near!
Am 5:18 What will the d. mean for you?
Zep 1:14 The great d. is near! It is near and
2Th 2:2 that the d. is here
2Pe 3:12 keep close in mind presence of the d.
DEAD, Ec 9:5 d. know nothing at all
Lu 15:24 son was d. but has come to life
Lu 20:38 God, not of the d., but of the living
Eph 2:1 alive, though you were d. in sins
1Th 4:16 d. in union with Christ rise first
Re 14:13 Happy the d. who die in union with Lord
DEADEN, Col 3:5 D. your body members
DEAF, Le 19:14 must not curse a d. man
Isa 35:5 ears of d. will be unstopped
Mr 7:37 He even makes the d. hear
DEAR, Php 2:29 holding men of that sort d.
DEATH, Ge 2:17 if anything but d. should separate
Ps 89:48 What man can never see d.?
Isa 25:8 He will swallow up d. forever
Eze 18:32 I do not take pleasure in d. of anyone
Ho 13:14 Where are your stings, O D.?
Joh 8:51 observes my word, he will never see d.
Ro 5:12 so d. spread to all men
Ro 6:23 the wages sin pays is d.
1Co 15:26 last enemy, d., brought to nothing
1Th 4:13 not ignorant about those sleeping in d.
Heb 2:9 Jesus might taste d. for everyone
Heb 2:15 held in slavery by their fear of d.
Re 21:4 d. will be no more
DEBTOR, Ro 1:14 to wise and senseless, I am a d.
DEBTS, Mt 6:12 forgive our d., as we have forgiven
DECEIT, Eph 4:25 put away d., speak truth
DECENTLY, Ro 13:13 walk d. as in the daytime
1Co 14:40 let things take place d.
DECEPTION, Ps 34:13 guard lips from speaking d.
DECLARATION, Ro 10:10 public d. for salvation
Heb 10:23 hold firmly the public d. of our hope
DECLARED, Ex 9:16 to have my name d.
DECORATION, Da 11:45 and the holy mountain of D.
DEED OF PURCHASE, Jer 32:12 gave d. to Baruch
DEEP, 1Co 2:10 spirit searches d. things of God
DEFECT, Le 22:21 No d. should be in the animal
DEFENDING, Php 1:7 d. and legally establishing
DEFENSE, 1Pe 3:15 always ready to make a d.
DEFILEMENT, 2Co 7:1 cleanse ourselves of d.
DEFRAUD, Le 19:13 must not d. your fellow man
DEFRAUDED, 1Co 6:7 rather let yourselves be d.
DEGREE, Jer 30:11 discipline to the proper d.
DELAY, Isa 46:13 my salvation will not d.
Hab 2:3 Even if it should d., keep in expectation
DELAYS, Lu 12:45 say in heart, My master d. coming
DELICACIES, Da 1:5 daily ration from the king's d.
DELIGHT, Ps 1:2 his d. is in the law of Jehovah
Ps 37:4 Find exquisite d. in Jehovah
Ps 40:8 To do your will is my d.
Ro 7:22 I really d. in the law of God

DELIGHTFUL, 1Ch 28:9 serve God with a d. soul
DELIVERANCE, Es 4:14 d. from another source
Lu 21:28 your d. is getting near
DEMANDED, Lu 12:48 much given, much d.
DEMON, Mt 16:16 with a spirit, d. of divination
DEMON-POSSESSED, Mt 8:28 two d. men coming out
DEMONS, 1Co 10:20 nations sacrifice to d.
1Co 10:21 partaking of the table of d.
Jas 2:19 d. believe and shudder
DENARII, Lu 7:41 one was in debt for 500 d.
DENY, Pr 30:9 become satisfied and d. you
DEPART, 1Co 7:15 if unbelieving one chooses to d.
DEPENDING, 1Pe 4:11 d. on strength God supplies
DEPENDS, Ro 12:18 as d. on you, be peaceable
DEPRESSED, Php 2:26 [Epaphroditus] d. because
1Th 5:14 speak consolingly to those d.
DEPRIVE, 1Co 7:5 Do not d. each other
DEPTH, Ro 11:33 d. of God's riches and wisdom
Eph 3:18 comprehend fully the d.
DESERT, Isa 35:1 d. plain will be joyful and blossom
Isa 35:6 streams will burst forth in d.
DESERVING, Mt 10:11 search out who is d.
DESIRE, Ex 20:17 not d. fellow man's wife
Ps 145:16 satisfy d. of every living thing
Ro 7:18 I have d. to do what is fine but
Ga 5:16 will carry out no fleshly d. at all
Php 2:13 giving you both the d. and
Jas 1:14 drawn and enticed by his own d.
1Jo 2:16 d. of the flesh and d. of the eyes
DESIRES, Ps 37:4 will grant you d. of heart
Eph 2:3 in harmony with the d. of flesh
2Ti 2:22 flee from youthful d.
1Pe 2:11 keep abstaining from fleshly d.
DESPISED, Isa 53:3 He was d. and avoided by men
DESTINY, Isa 65:11 wine for the god of D.
DESTRUCTION, 2Th 1:9 punishment of everlasting d.
2Pe 3:7 d. of the ungodly people
DEVIL, Mt 25:41 everlasting fire for D. and his
Lu 4:6 D. said, authority handed over to me
Lu 8:12 D. takes the word away from hearts
Joh 8:44 You are from your father the D.
Eph 4:27 not give D. an opportunity
Eph 6:11 stand firm against the D.
Jas 4:7 oppose the D., and he will flee
1Pe 5:8 D. walks about like a roaring lion
1Jo 3:8 to break up the works of the D.
Re 12:12 Woe because D. has come down
Re 20:10 D. hurled into the lake of fire
DEVIOUS, Pr 3:32 Jehovah detests a d. person
DEW, De 32:2 My words will trickle as the d.
DEWDROPS, Ps 110:3 company of young men like d.
DIE, Ge 3:3 You certainly will not d.
Joh 11:26 faith in me will never d. at all
Ro 14:8 if we d., we belong to Jehovah
DIED, 2Co 5:15 live for him who d. for them
DIES, Job 14:14 If a man d., can he live again?
Joh 11:25 even though he d., will come to life
DIFFICULTY, 1Pe 4:18 righteous saved with d.
DIGNITY, Pr 5:9 not give your d. to others
DILIGENCE, Pr 12:27 d. is a man's precious treasure
DILIGENT, Pr 10:4 d. hands bring riches
Pr 21:5 plans of the d. lead to success
DINAH, Ge 34:1 D. used to go out to spend time
DIRECT, Jer 10:23 not to man to d. his step
DIRECTION, Pr 11:14 no skillful d., people fall
DISAPPOINTED, Ro 9:33 rests his faith on it not be d.
DISAPPOINTMENT, Ro 5:5 hope does not lead to d.
DISAPPROVED, 1Co 9:27 should not become d.
DISCERNMENT, Mt 24:15 let the reader use d.
DISCIPLES, Mt 28:19 make d. of people of all nations
Joh 8:31 If remain in my word, you are my d.
Joh 13:35 know you are my d.—if you have love

DISCIPLINE, Pr 1:7 fools despise wisdom and d.
Pr 3:11 do not reject d. of Jehovah
Pr 19:18 D. your son while there is hope
Pr 23:13 Do not hold back d. from a boy
Heb 12:11 no d. seems to be joyous
Re 3:19 for whom I have affection I d.

DISCOURAGED, 2Ch 15:7 do not become d.
Pr 24:10 d. in day of distress, your strength

DISCREET, Mt 24:45 Who is the faithful and d. slave

DISEASE, Mt 9:35 curing every sort of d.

DISGUSTING THING, Mt 24:15 d. causes desolation

DISHONEST, Pr 15:27 making d. profit brings trouble

DISOBEYS, Joh 3:36 d. the Son will not see life

DISORDER, 1Co 14:33 God not of d. but of peace

DISORDERLY, 1Th 5:14 warn the d.
2Th 3:6 withdraw from brother walking d.

DISOWN, Mt 16:24 d. himself and pick up his
Mr 14:30 you will d. me three times
Tit 1:16 they d. God by their works

DISPLAY, 1Jo 2:16 showy d. of means of life

DISPOSITION, Php 2:20 no one else of d. like his

DISREGARDING, 1Th 4:8 d., not man, but God

DISRESPECT, 2Sa 12:14 treated Jehovah with utter d.

DISSENTERS, Pr 24:21 do not associate with d.

DISTINCTION, Le 11:47 between unclean and
Mal 3:18 see d. between righteous and

DISTINGUISH, Heb 5:14 trained to d. right and wrong

DISTRACTED, Lu 10:40 Martha d. with many duties

DISTRACTION, 1Co 7:35 to the Lord without d.

DISTRESS, 2Sa 22:7 In my d. I called on Jehovah
Ps 46:1 help readily found in times of d.
Isa 38:14 Jehovah, I am in d.; be my support!

DIVINATION, Nu 23:23 nor any d. against Israel
De 18:10 should not be anyone who employs d.

DIVISION, Mt 10:35 I came to cause d.

DIVISIONS, Ro 16:17 keep eye on those who create d.
1Co 1:10 there should be no d. among you

DIVORCE, Mal 2:16 I hate d.

DIVORCES, Mt 19:9 d. except on the grounds of
Mr 10:11 Whoever d. his wife and marries another

DOERS, Jas 1:22 become d. of the word

DOG, Pr 26:17 grabbing hold of a d.'s ears
Ec 9:4 a live d. is better off than a dead lion
2Pe 2:22 d. returned to its own vomit

DOMINATE, Ge 3:16 your husband will d. you
Ps 119:133 may nothing wicked d. me

DOMINATED, Ec 8:9 man has d. man to his harm

DONKEY, Nu 22:28 Jehovah caused the d. to speak
Zec 9:9 Your king riding on a d.

DOOR, 1Co 16:9 large d. to activity opened
Re 3:20 I am standing at the d. knocking

DOORS, Joh 20:19 d. were locked, Jesus came

DORCAS, Ac 9:36 disciple named Tabitha, D.

DOUBT, Mt 21:21 if you have faith and do not d.

DOUBTING, Jas 1:6 asking in faith, not d.

DOUBTS, Jude 22 mercy to some who have d.

DOVE, Mt 3:16 God's spirit descending like a d.

DOVES, Mt 10:16 cautious as serpents, innocent as d.

DOWNHEARTED, Col 3:21 so they do not become d.

DRACHMA, Lu 15:8 has ten d. coins, if loses one

DRAGNET, Mt 13:47 Kingdom of heavens like d.

DRAGON, Re 12:9 d. hurled, original serpent

DRAW, Jas 4:8 D. close to God, and he will

DRAWS, Joh 6:44 unless the Father d. him

DREAM, Ec 5:3 d. comes from preoccupations

DRESSED, Pr 7:10 d. like a prostitute

DRIFT, Heb 2:1 that we never d. away

DRINK OFFERING, Php 2:17 poured out like a d.

DROUGHT, Jer 17:8 in year of d. not anxious

DROWSINESS, Pr 23:21 d. will clothe one with rags

DRUNK, Eph 5:18 do not get d.

DRUNKARD, Pr 23:21 d. will come to poverty
1Co 5:11 stop keeping company with a d.

DRUNKARDS, 1Co 6:10 d. will not inherit Kingdom

DUE, 1Co 7:3 Let husband give his wife her d.

DULL, Heb 5:11 have become d. in hearing

DUST, Ge 2:7 form the man out of d.
Ge 3:19 d. you are and to d. you will return
Ps 103:14 remembering that we are d.
Isa 40:15 nations are as film of d. on scales

E

EAGER, Ro 1:15 e. to declare good news

EAGLES, Isa 40:31 will soar on wings like e.

EARTH, Ge 1:28 fill the e. and subdue it
Ex 9:29 the e. belongs to Jehovah
Job 38:4 when I founded the e.?
Ps 37:11 meek will possess the e.
Ps 37:29 righteous will possess the e.
Ps 104:5 the e. will not be moved from
Ps 115:16 the e. he has given to men
Pr 2:21 only upright will reside in the e.
Isa 45:18 e. formed to be inhabited
Mt 5:5 mild-tempered inherit the e.

EARTHQUAKES, Lu 21:11 There will be great e.

EASY, Lu 12:19 take it e., eat, drink, enjoy yourself
2Th 3:10 does not work, neither let him e.

EAT, 2Th 3:10 does not work, neither let him e.

EATING, 1Co 5:11 not even e. with such a man

EDEN, Ge 2:8 God planted a garden in E.

EDGE, Le 23:22 not reap the e. of your field

EFFORT, 2Pe 1:5 put forth all earnest e.

EGOTISM, Php 2:3 Do nothing out of e.

EGYPT, Mt 2:15 Out of E. I called my son

ELDERS, Tit 1:5 make appointments of e.

ELEMENTARY THINGS, Ga 4:9 back to e.

ELI, 1Sa 1:3 sons of E. served as priests

ELIJAH, Jas 5:17 E. man with feelings like ours

EMBARRASSED, Ezr 9:6 e. to raise my face to God

EMBRYO, Ps 139:16 Your eyes saw me as an e.

EMPTIED, Php 2:7 he e. himself and took a slave's

EMPTY-HANDED, De 16:16 none should appear e.

ENCOURAGE, Tit 1:9 to e. by teaching and to reprove

ENCOURAGED, 1Co 14:31 may learn and be e.

ENCOURAGEMENT, Ac 13:15 any word of e., tell it
Ro 1:12 have an interchange of e.

ENCOURAGING, Col 3:16 Keep on e. one another
Heb 10:25 e. one another, all the more

END, Mt 24:14 then the e. will come
Joh 13:1 Jesus loved his own to the e.

ENDURANCE, Lu 8:15 bear fruit with e.
Lu 21:19 By e. will preserve your lives
Ro 5:3 tribulation produces e.
Jas 1:4 let e. complete its work
Jas 5:11 heard of the e. of Job

ENDURE, Ro 12:12 E. under tribulation
1Co 4:12 when persecuted, we patiently e.
1Pe 2:20 if e. suffering because of doing good

ENDURED, Mt 24:13 who has e. to the end saved

ENEMIES, Ps 110:2 Go subduing in the midst of e.
Mt 5:44 Continue to love your e.
Mt 10:36 a man's e. will be those of his

ENEMY, Ro 12:20 if your e. is hungry, feed him

ENERGIZES, Php 2:13 God e. you, giving desire

ENJOYMENT, Ec 2:24 than to find e. in hard work

ENMITY, Ge 3:15 e. between you and the woman

ENOCH, Ge 5:24 E. kept walking with God

ENTRENCHED, 2Co 10:4 overturning e. things

ENTRUST, Ps 31:5 Into your hand I e. my spirit
Lu 16:11 who will e. you with what is true?

ENTRUSTED, 1Pe 2:23 he e. himself to the One

ENTRUSTING, 1Pe 4:19 e. themselves to Creator

ENVIOUS, Ps 37:1 Do not be e. of wrongdoers
Ps 73:3 I became e. of the arrogant

EPHESUS, 1Co 15:32 fought with wild beasts at E.

EPILEPTIC, Mt 4:24 e. and paralyzed, and he cured

EQUAL, Php 2:6 no consideration to be e. to God

EQUALIZING, 2Co 8:14 that there may be an e.
EQUIP, Heb 13:21 e. you to do his will
EQUIPPED, 2Ti 3:17 e. for every good work
ERRORS, Ps 40:12 my e. more numerous than hairs
   Ps 130:3 If e. were what you watch
   Isa 53:5 he was crushed for our e.
ESAU, Ge 25:34 despised birthright
   Heb 12:16 not appreciate sacred things, like E.
ETERNITY, Ec 3:11 even put e. in their heart
EUNUCH, Ac 8:27 look! an Ethiopian e.
EUNUCHS, Isa 56:4 who choose what I delight in
   Mt 19:12 there are e. born that way
EUODIA, Php 4:2 I urge E. and Syntyche to be
EVANGELIZER, Ac 21:8 Philip the e., one of seven
   2Ti 4:5 do the work of an e.
EVENING MEAL, 1Co 11:20 to eat the Lord's E.
EVERLASTING LIFE, Da 12:2 wake up, some to e.
   Lu 18:30 many times more in this period, and e.
   Joh 3:16 not be destroyed but have e.
   Joh 17:3 This means e., their coming to know you
   Ac 13:48 rightly disposed for e.
   Ro 6:23 the gift God gives is e.
   1Ti 6:12 get a firm hold on e.
EVIL, Ps 37:9 e. men will be done away with
   Ro 12:17 Return e. for e. to no one
EXAMINE, Ps 26:2 E. me, O Jehovah, refine my heart
   Ga 6:4 let each one e. his own actions
EXAMINES, Pr 21:2 Jehovah e. the hearts
EXAMINING, Ac 17:11 carefully e. the Scriptures
EXAMPLE, 1Ti 4:12 become an e. to faithful ones
EXAMPLES, 1Co 10:6 these things became e. for us
   1Pe 5:3 becoming e. to the flock
EXASPERATING, Col 3:21 not be e. your children
EXCELLENCY, Ac 24:3 Your E. Felix
EXCHANGE, Mt 16:26 man give in e. for his life?
EXCLUSIVE DEVOTION, Ex 34:14 Jehovah requires e.
   Ca 8:6 e. unyielding as the Grave
EXCREMENT, De 23:13 outside, then cover e.
EXCUSE, Joh 15:22 now they have no e. for their sin
   Jude 4 an e. for brazen conduct
EXERT, Lu 13:24 E. yourselves vigorously
EXHIBITION, 1Co 4:9 apostles last on e.
EXPECTATION, Pr 13:12 E. postponed makes heart
   Hab 2:3 Even if it should delay, keep in e.
   Lu 3:15 the people were in e. and reasoning
   Lu 21:26 faint out of fear and e. of the things
EXPENSE, Lu 14:28 first calculate the e.
EXPLAINED, Joh 1:18 is the one who has e. Him
EXPLAINING, Ne 8:8 e. the Law and putting meaning
   Ac 17:3 e. and proving by references
EXTRAORDINARY, Ge 18:14 too e. for Jehovah?
EXTRAVAGANT, 1Co 2:1 did not come with e. speech
EYE, Mt 5:38 E. for e. and tooth for tooth
   Mt 6:22 If e. focused, whole body bright
   1Co 2:9 E. has not seen, ear has not heard
   1Co 12:21 e. to hand, I do not need you
   1Co 15:52 in the blink of an e.
EYES, Ps 115:5 [idols] have e., but cannot see
   Pr 15:3 e. of Jehovah are everywhere
EYESALVE, Re 3:18 e. to rub that you may see
EZRA, Ezr 7:11 E. the priest, expert in the study

F

FACE VALUE, 2Co 10:7 You look according to f.
FAITH, Ps 27:13 Where would I be if did not have f.
   Lu 17:6 If you had f. the size of a mustard grain
   Lu 18:8 Son of man arrives, will he find this f.?
   Joh 3:16 everyone exercising f. in him
   Ro 1:17 righteous live by reason of f.
   Ro 4:20 became powerful by his f.
   2Co 4:13 we exercise f. and therefore speak
   2Co 5:7 we are walking by f., not by sight

   Ga 6:10 those related to us in the f.
   Eph 4:5 one Lord, one f., one baptism
   2Th 3:2 f. is not a possession of all people
   2Ti 1:5 your unhypocritical f., which dwelled first
   Heb 11:1 F. is the assured expectation
   Heb 11:6 without f. impossible to please God
   Jas 2:26 f. without works is dead
   1Pe 1:7 tested quality of your f.
FAITHFUL, Lu 16:10 person f. in least is f. in much
   1Co 4:2 expected of stewards to be f.
   1Co 10:13 God is f., will not let you be
   Re 2:10 Prove f. even to death
FAITHFULNESS, Hab 2:4 will live by his f.
FALL, Pr 24:16 righteous one may f. seven times
   1Co 10:12 beware that he does not f.
FALLS, Ec 4:10 if one of them f., the other can help
FALSE, Mt 26:59 Sanhedrin looking for f. testimony
   Ga 2:4 brothers brought in quietly
FAMILY, Eph 3:15 to whom every f. owes its name
FAMINE, Ps 37:19 in time of f. will have plenty
   Am 8:11 not a f. for bread or a thirst for water
FAR, Ac 17:27 he is not f. off from each one of us
FAST, Isa 58:6 this is the f. that I choose
   Lu 18:12 I f. twice a week; I give the tenth
FATHER, Ge 2:24 leave his f. and mother
   Ps 2:7 today I have become your f.
   Ps 89:26 You are my F., my God
   Ps 103:13 As f. shows mercy to sons, Jehovah has
   Isa 9:6 His name will be Eternal F., Prince of
   Mt 6:9 Our F. in the heavens, let your name
   Mt 23:9 do not call anyone your F. on earth
   Lu 2:49 I must be in the house of my F.
   Lu 15:20 f. ran and embraced him
   Joh 5:20 F. shows the Son things he himself does
   Joh 10:30 I and the F. are one
   Joh 14:6 No one comes to f. except through me
   Joh 14:9 seen me has seen the F.
   Joh 14:28 the F. is greater than I am
   Joh 14:28 rejoice that I am going to the F.
FATHERLESS, Ex 22:22 must not afflict f. child
   Ps 68:5 father of the f., protector of widows
FAVOR, Isa 26:10 wicked shown f., will not learn
FAVORITISM, Jas 2:9 if you continue showing f.
FEAR, Ge 9:2 f. of you upon every creature
   Job 31:34 in f. of reaction of multitude?
   Isa 44:8 do not become paralyzed with f.
   Lu 12:4 do not f. those who kill the body
   Lu 21:26 People will become faint out of f.
   1Jo 4:18 There is no f. in love
FEARFUL, Heb 10:31 f. thing to fall into hands of God
FEAR OF JEHOVAH, Ps 19:9 f. is pure
   Ps 111:10 The f. is the beginning of wisdom
   Pr 8:13 The f. means the hating of bad
FEED, Joh 21:17 Jesus said: F. my little sheep
FEELINGS, Jas 5:17 Elijah a man with f. like ours
FEET, Isa 52:7 beautiful f. of one bringing good news
   Joh 13:5 started to wash the f. of the disciples
   Ro 16:20 crush Satan under your f. shortly
FELLOW WORKERS, 1Co 3:9 we are God's f.
FESTIVALS, Le 23:4 These are seasonal f. of Jehovah
FIELD, Mt 13:38 the f. is the world
   1Co 3:9 You are God's f. under cultivation
FIELDS, Joh 4:35 view the f., that they are white
FIGHT, 2Ch 20:17 You will not need to f.
   1Ti 6:12 f. the fine f. of the faith
   2Ti 2:24 slave of Lord does not need to f.
   Jude 3 put up a hard f. for the faith
FIGHTERS, Ac 5:39 be found f. against God himself
FIG TREE, 1Ki 4:25 in security, under his vine and f.
   Mic 4:4 each under his vine and f.
   Mt 21:19 And the f. withered instantly
   Mr 13:28 learn this illustration from f.

FILL, Ge 1:28 f. the earth and subdue it
FINAL, Isa 2:2 In the f. part of the days
FINGER, Ex 8:19 It is the f. of God!
  Ex 31:18 tablets written on by God's f.
FINISH, Ac 20:24 f. my course and ministry
  2Ti 4:7 have run the race to the f.
FIRE, Jer 20:9 like a f. shut up in my bones
  Mt 25:41 everlasting f. prepared for Devil
  1Co 3:13 f. will prove what sort of work
  1Th 5:19 not put out f. of the spirit
  2Ti 1:6 stir up like a f. the gift in you
  2Pe 3:7 and earth that exist are reserved for f.
FIRM, 1Co 1:8 He will make you f.
FIRST, Mt 19:30 many who are f. will be last
  Mr 9:35 wants to be f., he must be last
FIRSTBORN, Ex 11:5 every f. in Egypt will die
  Col 1:15 f. of all creation
FIRSTFRUITS, Ro 8:23 we have the f., the spirit
FISH, Jon 1:17 sent a f. to swallow Jonah
  Joh 21:11 net full of big f., 153 of them
FISHERS OF MEN, Mt 4:19 I will make you f.
FIXED, Col 3:2 Keep your minds f. on above
FLATTERING, Pr 26:28 f. mouth causes ruin
  Ro 16:18 by f. speech they seduce
  Jude 16 f. others for their own benefit
FLATTERS, Pr 29:5 f. neighbor spreads out net
FLEE, 1Co 6:18 F. from sexual immorality!
FLEECE, Jg 6:37 dew on the f. only
FLESH, Ge 2:24 will become one f.
  Job 33:25 Let his f. become fresher than
  Ro 8:5 those who live according to the f.
  1Co 15:50 f. and blood not inherit Kingdom
  Ga 5:19 works of the f. plainly seen
FLESHLY, 1Co 3:3 for you are still f.
  Col 2:18 his f. frame of mind
FLOCK, Lu 12:32 Have no fear, little f.
FLOOD, Ge 9:11 Never will flesh be destroyed by f.
  Mt 24:38 as before the F., eating and drinking
  2Pe 2:5 he brought a f. upon a world
FLUENT, Ex 4:10 never been f. speaker
FOLD, Joh 10:16 other sheep, not of this f.
FOLLOW, Joh 10:27 My sheep listen and f. me
FOLLOWED, Mt 4:20 abandoned nets and f. him
FOLLOWER, Mt 19:21 and come be my f.
FOLLOWING, Re 14:4 f. Lamb no matter where goes
FOND, Pr 8:30 the one he was especially f. of
  Joh 12:25 Whoever is f. of his life destroys it
FOOD, Ps 145:15 you give them f. in its season
  Mt 24:45 give f. at the proper time?
  Joh 4:34 My f. is to do will of him who sent me
  Joh 6:27 Work, not for the f. that perishes
  Ac 14:17 giving you rains, satisfying with f.
  1Co 8:13 if f. makes my brother stumble
FOOD SHORTAGES, Mt 24:7 there will be f.
FOOLED, Jer 20:7 You have f. me, O Jehovah
FOOLISH, Ps 14:1 f. one says: There is no Jehovah
FOOLISHNESS, Pr 19:3 man's f. distorts his way
  Pr 22:15 F. bound up in the heart of a boy
  1Co 3:19 wisdom of this world is f. with God
FOREHEAD, Eze 3:9 f. harder than flint
FOREHEADS, Eze 9:4 put a mark on f. of men
FOREIGN RESIDENT, Ex 22:21 must not mistreat f.
  Nu 9:14 one statute, both for f. and
  De 10:19 You must love the f.
FOREVER, Ge 3:22 that he may not eat and live f.
  Ps 37:29 righteous will live f. on the earth
  Ec 3:14 everything God makes will endure f.
  1Pe 1:25 the saying of Jehovah endures f.
FORGAVE, Col 3:13 as Jehovah freely f. you
FORGET, De 4:23 careful that you do not f.
  Isa 49:15 Can a woman f. her nursing child?
  Heb 6:10 God is not unrighteous to f. your

FORGETTING, Php 3:13 f. the things behind and
FORGIVE, Ne 9:17 God ready to f.
  Ps 25:11 f. my error, though it is great
  Isa 55:7 for God will f. in a large way
  Mt 6:14 if you f., your Father will f. you
  Mt 18:21 how many times to f. him?
FORGIVENESS, Mt 26:28 blood, poured out for f.
FORGIVES, Ps 103:3 He f. all your errors
  Pr 17:9 Whoever f. transgression seeks love
FORGOTTEN, Ps 119:141 yet, I have not f. your orders
FORMER, Isa 65:17 f. things will not be called to mind
FORNICATION. See SEXUAL IMMORALITY.
FORTIFICATION, Lu 19:43 f. of pointed stakes
FORTIFY, Isa 41:10 I will f. you, yes, I will help you
FORTUNE-TELLERS, Le 19:31 do not consult f.
FOUNDATION, Lu 6:48 laid a f. on the rock
  Ro 15:20 not to build on another man's f.
  1Co 3:11 no other f. than what is laid, Christ
FOUNDING, Mt 25:34 Kingdom prepared from the f.
FOXES, Mt 8:20 F. have dens, but the Son of man
FRAMEWORK, Ro 2:20 the f. of the truth
FRAMING, Ps 94:20 f. trouble in the name of law?
FREE, Mt 10:8 You received f., give f.
  Joh 8:32 the truth will set you f.
  Ro 6:18 you were set f. from sin
  Re 22:17 let anyone take life's water f.
FREEDOM, Ro 8:21 glorious f. of the children of God
  2Co 3:17 where spirit of Jehovah is, f.
  1Pe 2:16 using f., not as a cover
  2Pe 2:19 they are promising them f.
FRIEND, 2Ch 20:7 your f. Abraham
  Pr 17:17 true f. shows love at all times
  Pr 18:24 f. who sticks closer than a brother
  Pr 27:6 wounds inflicted by a f. are faithful
  Jas 2:23 Abraham called Jehovah's f.
  Jas 4:4 f. of the world is an enemy of God
FRIENDS, Pr 14:20 many are f. of the rich person
  Pr 16:28 slanderer separates close f.
  Lu 16:9 Make f. by means of the unrighteous riches
  Joh 15:13 surrender life in behalf of f.
  Joh 15:14 f. if you do what I am commanding you
FRIENDSHIP, Ps 25:14 f. with Jehovah belongs to
  Pr 3:32 His close f. is with the upright
FRIGHTENED, Php 1:28 in no way f. by opponents
FRINGED, Nu 15:39 must have this f. edge
FRUIT, Ge 3:3 f., you must not touch
  Lu 8:15 bear f. with endurance
  Joh 15:2 cleans, so that it may bear more f.
  Joh 15:8 glorified in this, you bearing much f.
FRUITAGE, Ga 5:22 f. of the spirit is love, joy
FRUITFUL, Ge 1:28 Be f. and become many
FRUITS, Mt 7:20 by their f. you will recognize
  Mt 21:43 given to a nation producing its f.
FULFILL, Mt 5:17 not to destroy the Law, but to f.
FULLER, 1Th 4:10 go on doing so in f. measure
FULL-GROWN, 1Co 14:20 f. in your understanding
  Eph 4:13 attain to being a f. man
FULLY, 1Th 4:1 to keep doing it more f.
FUNCTION, Ro 12:4 many members, not the same f.
FUNCTIONS, Eph 4:16 When each member f. properly
FURNACE, Da 3:17 God able to rescue from f.
FUTILITY, Ec 1:2 The greatest f.!
  Eph 4:17 in the f. of their minds
FUTURE, Ps 73:17 Until I discerned their f.
  Pr 24:20 no f. for anyone evil

G

GABRIEL, Lu 1:19 G., who stands before God
GAMALIEL, Ac 22:3 educated at the feet of G.
GAME, Pr 10:23 shameful conduct like g. to stupid
GARDEN, Ge 2:15 settled him in the g. of Eden

GARLIC, Nu 11:5 we remember the onions, and g.!
GARMENTS, Ge 3:21 God made long g.
GATE, Mt 7:13 Go in through the narrow g.
GATHER, Eph 1:10 to g. all things together in Christ
GEHAZI, 2Ki 5:20 G. said, I will run after him
GEHENNA, Mt 10:28 destroy soul and body in G.
GENERATION, Mt 24:34 g. will not pass away
GENEROUS, Pr 11:25 g. person will prosper
    1Ti 6:18 to be g., ready to share
GENEROUSLY, De 15:8 g. open your hand
    Pr 11:24 One gives g. and ends up with more
    Jas 1:5 keep asking God, for he gives g.
GENTLE, Pr 25:15 g. tongue can break a bone
    1Th 2:7 became g. as a mother
    2Ti 2:24 needs to be g. toward all
GET OUT, Isa 52:11 g. of there, touch nothing unclean
    Re 18:4 G. of her, my people
GIBEON, Jos 9:3 inhabitants of G. also heard
GIDEON, Jg 7:20 sword of Jehovah and of G.!
GIFT, Ro 6:23 g. God gives is everlasting life
    1Co 7:7 each one has his own g. from God
    Jas 1:17 Every good g. is from above
GIFTS, Ro 12:6 we have g. that differ
    Eph 4:8 captives; he gave g. in men
GIRL, 2Ki 5:2 taken captive a little g.
    Mr 5:42 the g. rose and began walking
GIVEN, Lu 12:48 much g., much will be demanded
GIVE UP, 2Co 4:1 have this ministry, we do not g.
    2Co 4:16 Therefore, we do not g.
    Ga 6:9 not g. in doing what is fine
GIVING, Ac 20:35 more happiness in g. than
GLEAN, Ru 2:8 Boaz said, Do not g. in another field
GLEANING, Le 19:9 the g. of your harvest
GLOOM, Zep 1:15 day of darkness and g.
GLORIOUS, 2Pe 2:10 to speak abusively of g. ones
GLORY, Joh 12:43 loved g. of men more than
    Ro 3:23 and fall short of the g. of God
    Ro 8:18 in comparison with the g. that is
    1Co 10:31 do all things for God's g.
    Re 4:11 worthy, Jehovah, to receive g.
GOATS, Mt 25:32 shepherd separates sheep from g.
GOD, De 10:17 Jehovah is G. of gods and
    Mt 27:46 my G., why have you forsaken me?
    Joh 1:18 No man has seen G. at any time
    Joh 17:3 coming to know you, the only true G.
    Joh 20:17 ascending to my G. and your G.
    1Co 8:4 there is no G. but one
    2Co 4:4 g. of this system blinded the minds
    Eph 4:6 one G. and Father of all
    1Jo 4:8 G. is love
GODLY DEVOTION, 1Ti 4:7 train with g. as your aim
    1Ti 4:8 g. is beneficial for all things
    1Ti 6:6 there is great gain in g.
    2Ti 3:12 those with g. will be persecuted
GOLD, Eze 7:19 Neither silver nor g. will save them
    Da 3:1 Nebuchadnezzar made an image of g.
GOLGOTHA, Joh 19:17 Skull Place, G. in Hebrew
GOLIATH, 1Sa 17:4 champion; his name was G.
GOMORRAH, Ge 19:24 sulfur and fire on G.
GOOD, Ge 1:31 everything he made was very g.
    Ge 3:5 like God, knowing g. and bad
    De 10:13 keep commandments for your own g.
    Ro 5:7 for g. man someone may dare to die
    Ro 7:19 I do not do the g. that I wish
    Ga 6:10 let us work what is g. toward all
GOOD-FOR-NOTHING, Lu 17:10 We are g. slaves
GOOD NEWS, Isa 52:7 feet of one bringing g.
    Mt 24:14 this g. of Kingdom will be preached
    Lu 4:43 must declare g., for this I was sent
    Ro 1:16 I am not ashamed of the g.
    1Co 9:16 woe if I do not declare g.!
    1Co 9:23 I do all things for the sake of g.

GOSSIP, Pr 20:19 with one who loves to g.
GOSSIPERS, 1Ti 5:13 g. and meddlers in
GRANDPARENTS, 1Ti 5:4 repay g. what is due
GRASSHOPPERS, Isa 40:22 inhabitants are like g.
GRATEFUL, 1Ti 1:12 I am g. to Christ Jesus
GRAVE, Job 14:13 that in G. you conceal me
    Ec 9:10 no work nor wisdom in the G.
    Ho 13:14 From the G. I will redeem them
    Ac 2:31 neither was Christ forsaken in the G.
    Re 1:18 have the keys of death and of the G.
    Re 20:13 death and the G. gave up the dead
GRAY, Pr 16:31 G. hair is a crown of beauty
GREAT CROWD, Re 7:9 g., no man able to number
GREATER, Joh 14:28 the Father is g. than I am
    1Jo 3:20 God is g. than our hearts
GREED, Lu 12:15 guard against every sort of g.
GREEDINESS, Col 3:5 g., which is idolatry
GREEDY, 1Co 5:11 stop keeping company with g.
    1Co 6:10 g. will not inherit Kingdom
GREETING, 2Jo 10 not say a g. to him
GRIEF, Ps 31:10 My life consumed with g.
    Isa 51:11 g. and sighing will flee away
GRIEVED, Ps 78:41 they g. the Holy One
GRIEVING, Eph 4:30 g. God's holy spirit
GRIP, Php 2:16 tight g. on the word of life
GROANING, Ex 2:24 God heard their g.
    Eze 9:4 men who are sighing and g.
    Ro 8:22 all creation keeps on g.
GROANINGS, Ro 8:26 spirit pleads with unuttered g.
GROUND, 1Pe 5:10 God will firmly g. you
GRUDGE, Le 19:18 must not hold a g.
GUARANTEE, Ac 17:31 g. by resurrecting him
GUEST, Ps 15:1 who may be a g. in your tent?
GUIDE, Ps 48:14 God will g. us forevermore

H

HADES. See GRAVE.
HAIR, Lu 21:18 not a h. of your heads will perish
    1Co 11:14 long h. is a dishonor to man
HAIRS, Mt 10:30 even your h. numbered
HALLELUJAH. See PRAISE JAH.
HAND, Ps 145:16 You open your h. and satisfy
    Isa 41:10 I will hold on to you with my right h.
    Zec 14:13 h. against the h. of companion
    Mt 6:3 left h. not know what right h. doing
HANDS, Isa 35:3 Strengthen the weak h.
HAPPINESS, Ac 20:35 more h. in giving than
HAPPY, Ps 32:1 H. the one whose sin covered
    Ps 94:12 H. is the man whom you correct
    Ps 144:15 H. people whose God is Jehovah!
    Mt 5:3 H. are those conscious of spiritual need
    1Ti 1:11 good news of the h. God
HARDENED, Heb 3:13 h. by power of sin
HARDSHIPS, Ps 34:19 Many h. of righteous
    2Th 1:4 endurance and faith in all h.
HARM, Ps 23:4 I fear no h., for you are with me
    Isa 11:9 will not cause any h. or any ruin
HARMONIOUSLY, Eph 4:16 h. joined together
HARPING, Pr 17:9 h. on a matter separates
HARSH, Pr 15:1 h. word stirs up anger
HARVEST, Mt 9:37 h. is great, but workers are few
HASTY, Pr 29:20 seen a man h. with his words?
HATE, Le 19:17 must not h. your brother
    Ps 97:10 you who love Jehovah, h. what is bad
    Am 5:15 H. what is bad, and love what is good
HATED, Ps 45:7 you h. wickedness
    Mt 24:9 h. on account of my name
    Joh 15:25 They h. me without cause
HATES, Pr 6:16 six things that Jehovah h.
    Joh 7:7 world h. me, because I bear witness
    1Jo 3:15 h. his brother is a murderer

IMMORTALITY, 1Co 15:53 mortal must put on i.

IMPALE. See STAKE.

IMPATIENT, Pr 14:29 i. one displays his foolishness

IMPELLED, Ex 35:21 whose heart i. him brought

IMPORTANT, Php 1:10 sure of the more i. things

IMPOSSIBLE, Job 42:2 nothing is i. for you
Mt 19:26 With men i., but with God all things

INACTIVE, 2Pe 1:8 prevent from being i. or unfruitful

INCITE, Heb 10:24 i. to love and fine works

INCLINATION, Ge 8:21 i. of heart bad from youth up
1Ch 28:9 God discerns every i. of thoughts

INCOME, Ec 5:10 never satisfied with i.

INCORRUPTION, 1Co 15:42 raised up in i.

INCULCATE, De 6:7 i. them in your sons

INDECISIVE, Jas 1:8 he is an i. man, unsteady

INDISTINCT, 1Co 14:8 sounds an i. call, who

INDUSTRIOUS, Ro 12:11 Be i., not lazy

INDUSTRIOUSNESS, Heb 6:11 show same i.

INEXCUSABLE, Ro 1:20 so they are i.

INEXPERIENCED, Ps 19:7 making the i. one wise
Pr 22:3 i. suffer the consequences

INFANCY, 2Ti 3:15 from i. you have known

INHABITED, Isa 45:18 formed earth to be i.

INHERIT, Mt 5:5 mild-tempered will i. the earth
Mt 25:34 i. the Kingdom prepared for you

INHERITANCE, Nu 18:20 I am your portion and i.
Ps 127:3 Sons are an i. from Jehovah
Eph 1:18 glorious riches as i. for holy ones
1Pe 1:4 undefiled and unfading i.

INJUSTICE, Ro 9:14 i. with God? Certainly not!

INNERMOST, Re 2:23 searches the i. thoughts

INSENSIBILITY, Mr 3:5 grieved at the i. of their hearts

INSIDE, 2Co 4:16 man we are i. is being renewed
Eph 3:16 mighty in the man you are i.

INSIGHT, Ps 119:99 I have more i. than my teachers
Pr 19:11 i. of a man slows down his anger
Da 12:3 those having i. will shine as brightly

INSIGNIFICANT, Ps 119:141 I am i. and despised; yet
1Co 1:28 God chose the i. things

INSPIRATION, 1Ch 28:12 plan conveyed through i.

INSPIRED, 2Ti 3:16 All Scripture is i.

INSTANTLY, Lu 21:34 that day be i. upon you

INSTRUCT, Jg 13:8 Manoah said, i. about child
Ps 32:8 I will i. you in the way

INSTRUCTION, Ro 15:4 written for our i.

INSULT, 1Pe 2:23 insulted, did not i. in return

INTEGRITY, 1Ch 29:17 you take pleasure in i.
Job 27:5 Until I die, will not renounce i.!
Ps 25:21 May i. safeguard me
Ps 26:11 I will walk in my i.
Ps 101:2 with i. of heart inside my house

INTELLECTUAL, Lu 10:21 hidden from i. ones

INTERCHANGE, Ro 1:12 have i. of encouragement

INTERESTS, 1Co 13:5 [love] does not look for own i.
Php 2:4 not only own i., but i. of others
Php 2:21 others seeking own i.

INTERPRETERS, 1Co 12:30 Not all are i.

INVESTIGATION, De 13:14 making a thorough i.

INVISIBLE, Ro 1:20 i. qualities clearly seen
Heb 11:27 as seeing the One who is i.

INVITED, Mt 22:14 many i., but few chosen

IRON, Pr 27:17 As i. sharpens i., so
Isa 60:17 instead of i. I will bring in silver
Da 2:43 just as i. does not mix with clay

IRRITABLE, Pr 21:19 with quarrelsome and i. wife

IRRITATING, Eph 6:4 do not be i. your children

ISAAC, Ge 22:9 bound his son I.

ISOLATES, Pr 18:1 Whoever i. himself pursues

ISRAEL, Ge 35:10 I. will be your name
Ps 135:4 chosen I. for his special property
Ga 6:16 peace and mercy upon the I. of God

I WILL BECOME, Ex 3:14 say, I. has sent me to you

J

JACOB, Ge 32:24 man began to wrestle with J.

JAH, Ex 15:2 My strength and might is J.
Isa 12:2 for J. Jehovah is my strength

JAIL, Ac 5:18 seized apostles and put in public j.
Ac 16:26 foundations of the j. were shaken

JAMES 1., Lu 6:16 Judas the son of J., and

JAMES 2., Ac 12:2 put J. brother of John to death

JAMES 3., Mr 15:40 Mary the mother of J. the Less

JAMES 4., Mt 13:55 and his brothers J. and
Ac 15:13 After they finished speaking, J. replied
1Co 15:7 appeared to J., then to all apostles
Jas 1:1 J., a slave of God and

JEALOUS, Ps 106:16 they grew j. of Moses
1Co 13:4 Love is not j.

JEALOUSY, Pr 6:34 j. makes a husband furious
Pr 14:30 j. is rottenness to the bones

JEHOSHAPHAT, 2Ch 20:3 J. became afraid

JEHOVAH, Ex 3:15 J. is my name forever
Ex 5:2 Who is J.? I do not know J. at all
Ex 6:3 my name J. I did not make known
Ex 20:7 not take name J. in worthless way
De 6:5 must love J. with all your heart
De 7:9 J. is the true God, the faithful God
Ps 83:18 name is J., you alone Most High
Isa 42:8 I am J. That is my name
Ho 12:5 J. of armies, J. is his memorial name
Mal 3:6 I am J.; I do not change
Mr 12:29 Jehovah our God is one J.

JEHOVAH'S DAY, 1Th 5:2 J. coming as a thief

JEPHTHAH, Jg 11:30 J. made a vow

JEREMIAH, Jer 38:6 threw J. into cistern

JERUSALEM, Jos 18:28 Jebusi, that is, J.
Da 9:25 word to restore and to rebuild J.
Mt 23:37 J., J., the killer of the prophets
Lu 2:41 accustomed to go to J. for Passover
Lu 21:20 when you see J. surrounded by armies
Lu 21:24 J. will be trampled on by the nations until
Ac 5:28 filled J. with your teaching
Ac 15:2 apostles and elders in J. regarding this
Ga 4:26 J. above is free, she is our mother
Heb 12:22 approached heavenly J.
Re 3:12 New J. descends out of heaven
Re 21:2 New J., out of heaven, as a bride

JESSE, 1Sa 17:12 J. had eight sons
Isa 11:1 twig will grow out of stump of J.

JESUS, Mt 1:21 you are to name him J.

JEW, Zec 8:23 take hold of the robe of a J.
1Co 9:20 To the Jews I became as a J.

JEWS, Ro 3:29 is he God of the J. only?

JEZEBEL, 1Ki 21:23 dogs will eat up J.
Re 2:20 you tolerate J.

JOB, Job 1:9 Is it for nothing that J. feared God?
Jas 5:11 heard of the endurance of J.

JOHN 1., Mt 21:25 baptism by J., from what source?
Mr 1:9 Jesus baptized in the Jordan by J.

JOHN 2., Joh 1:42 You are Simon, the son of J.

JOHN 3., Mt 4:21 son of Zebedee and his brother J.

JOKING, Ge 19:14 Lot seemed to be j.
Pr 26:19 I was only j.!

JONAH, Jon 2:1 J. prayed from the belly of the fish

JONATHAN, 1Sa 18:3 J. and David made a covenant
1Sa 23:16 J. went, helped David find strength

JORDAN, Jos 3:13 waters of J. will be halted
2Ki 5:10 wash seven times in the J.

JOSEPH, Ge 39:23 Jehovah was with J.
Lu 4:22 amazed and saying: This is son of J.?

JOSHUA, Ex 33:11 J. the son of Nun, his minister

JOSIAH, 2Ki 22:1 J. reigned for 31 years

JOY, Ne 8:10 j. of Jehovah is your stronghold
Lu 8:13 receive the word with j., but
Lu 15:7 j. in heaven over sinner who repents

Joh 16:22 no one will take away your j.
Ro 15:13 May God fill you with j. and peace
1Th 1:6 with j. of holy spirit
Heb 12:2 For the j. before him he endured
3Jo 4 j.: children walking in the truth

JOYFULLY, Job 38:7 morning stars j. cried out
Isa 65:14 My servants will shout j. because of

JUBILEE, Le 25:10 will become a J. for you

JUDAH, Ge 49:10 scepter will not depart from J.

JUDAS, Mt 27:3 J. felt remorse and brought 30

JUDGE, Isa 33:22 Jehovah is our J., our King
Lu 18:2 j. had no fear of God and no respect
Lu 22:30 sit on thrones to j. the 12 tribes of Israel
Ac 17:31 set a day on which he purposes to j.
Ro 14:4 Who are you to j. the servant of
1Co 6:2 not know holy ones will j. world?

JUDGING, Lu 6:37 stop j., and you will not be judged
Joh 5:22 Father entrusted all j. to the Son
Jas 4:12 who are you to be j. neighbor?

JUDGMENT, Mt 7:2 with the j. you are judging, you
1Co 11:29 and drinks j. against himself
1Pe 4:17 j. to start with the house of God

JUDGMENTS, Isa 26:9 when j. from you for earth

JUDGMENT SEAT, Joh 19:13 Pilate sat on j.
Ro 14:10 will all stand before j. of God

JUSTICE, Job 34:12 Almighty does not pervert j.
Job 40:8 Will you call into question my j.?
Ps 37:28 Jehovah loves j.
Pr 29:4 By j. king brings stability to a land
Ec 5:8 If you see violation of j., do not be surprised
Isa 32:1 princes will rule for j.
Mic 6:8 Only to exercise j., to cherish loyalty
Lu 18:7 will not God cause j. to be done?
Ac 28:4 J. did not permit him to keep on living

K

KEY, Lu 11:52 took away the k. of knowledge

KEYS, Mt 16:19 I will give you the k. of the Kingdom
Re 1:18 I have the k. of death and of the Grave

KIDNAPPER, De 24:7 the k. must die

KILLS, Joh 16:2 everyone who k. you will think

KIND, Pr 11:17 A k. man benefits himself
Mt 16:22 Be k. to yourself, Lord

KINDNESS, Pr 31:26 law of k. on her tongue
Ac 28:2 people showed us extraordinary k.

KING, Jg 21:25 In those days no k. in Israel
1Sa 23:17 you will be k., I will become second
Ps 2:6 I have installed my k. on Zion
Pr 21:1 k.'s heart like streams of water
Isa 32:1 A k. will reign for righteousness
Zec 14:9 Jehovah will be K. over all the earth
Mt 21:5 Your k. is coming, mounted on a donkey
Mt 27:29 Greetings, you K. of the Jews!
Joh 19:15 We have no k. but Caesar
1Co 15:25 he must rule as k. until

KINGDOM, Ex 19:6 will become k. of priests
Da 2:44 God of heaven will set up a k.
Da 7:14 to him were given rulership, honor, and a k.
Da 7:18 holy ones will receive k.
Mt 6:10 Let your K. come. Let your will
Mt 6:33 keep seeking first the K. and
Mt 21:43 K. given to nation producing its fruits
Mt 24:14 this good news of the K. will be preached
Mt 25:34 Come, inherit the K. prepared for you
Lu 12:32 approved of giving you the K.
Lu 22:29 I make a covenant with you, for a k.
Joh 18:36 My K. is no part of this world
Ac 1:6 are you restoring k. at this time?
1Co 15:24 hands over the k. to his God
Ga 5:21 practice such, not inherit God's K.
Col 1:13 transferred us into k. of his Son

Re 1:6 made us a k., priests to his God
Re 11:15 k. of the world has become K.

KINGDOMS, Mt 4:8 Devil showed him all the k.

KING OF THE NORTH, Da 11:7 against foretness of k.
Da 11:40 against him k. will storm with chariots

KING OF THE SOUTH, Da 11:11 k. will become bitter
Da 11:40 k. will engage with him in a pushing

KINGS, Pr 22:29 man skillful? Will stand before k.
Lu 21:12 brought before k. and governors
Ac 4:26 k. of the earth took their stand
Re 5:10 rule as k. over the earth
Re 18:3 k. committed sexual immorality with her

KISS, Lu 22:48 betraying Son of man with a kiss?

KNOCKING, Mt 7:7 keep on k., and it will be opened

KNOW, Jer 31:34 K. Jehovah!, for they will all k. me

KNOWLEDGE, Pr 1:7 fear of Jehovah beginning of k.
Pr 2:10 k. becomes pleasant to your soul
Pr 24:5 with k. a man increases his power
Isa 5:13 go into exile for lack of k.
Isa 11:9 earth filled with k. of Jehovah
Da 12:4 true k. will become abundant
Ho 4:6 Because you have rejected k.
Mal 2:7 lips of a priest should safeguard k.
Lu 11:52 you took away the key of k.
1Co 8:1 K. puffs up, love builds up

KNOWN, Ga 4:9 have come to be k. by God

KNOW THAT I AM JEHOVAH, Ex 7:5 Egyptians will k.
Eze 39:7 nations will have to k.

KORAH, Nu 26:11 sons of K. did not die
Jude 11 rebellious talk of K.

L

LACKING, Jas 2:15 a brother or sister is l. clothing

LAKE, Re 19:20 fiery l. that burns with sulfur

LAMB, 2Sa 12:3 had nothing but one small l.
Joh 1:29 See, the L. of God who takes away sin

LAMBS, Isa 40:11 he will gather together the l.
Joh 21:15 love me? Feed my l.

LAME, Isa 35:6 l. will leap like the deer
Mal 1:8 present a l. animal or a sick one

LAMP, Ps 119:105 Your word is a l. to my foot
Mt 6:22 The l. of the body is the eye

LAMPS, Mt 25:1 ten virgins who took their l.

LAND, Isa 66:8 l. brought to birth in one day?

LANGUAGE, Ge 11:7 confuse their l.
Zep 3:9 I will change l. of peoples to a pure l.

LANGUAGES, Zec 8:23 ten men out of all l.
Ac 2:4 started to speak in different l.

LAST DAYS, 2Ti 3:1 critical times will be here

LATE, Hab 2:3 It will not be l.!

LAUGH, Ge 18:13 Why did Sarah l.?
Ps 2:4 One enthroned in heavens will l.

LAUGHINGSTOCK, Jer 20:7 I have become a l.

LAUGHTER, Pr 14:13 Even in l. heart may feel pain

LAW, Ps 19:7 The l. of Jehovah is perfect
Ps 40:8 your l. is deep within me
Ps 94:20 framing trouble in the name of the l.?
Ps 119:97 How I do love your l.!
Jer 31:33 I will put my l. within them
Hab 1:4 l. is paralyzed, and justice
Ro 7:22 I delight in the l. of God
Ro 10:4 Christ is the end of the l.
Ro 13:8 whoever loves fellow man fulfilled the l.
Ga 3:24 L. guardian leading to Christ
Ga 6:2 fulfill the l. of the Christ
Jas 2:8 you carry out the royal l.

LAWFUL, 1Co 6:12 All things l., not all advantageous

LAWGIVER, Jas 4:12 only one is L. and Judge

LAWLESS, Lu 22:37 he was counted with l. ones

LAWLESSNESS, Mt 7:23 Get away, workers of l.!
Mt 24:12 because of the increasing of l., the love
2Th 2:7 mystery of this l. already at work

LAWSUITS, 1Co 6:7 l. with one another
LAZARUS, Lu 16:20 a beggar named L.
  Joh 11:11 L. our friend has fallen asleep
  Joh 11:43 L., come out!
LAZY, Pr 6:6 Go to the ant, you l. one
  Pr 10:26 Like smoke to eyes, so l. one is
  Pr 19:24 l. one buries his hand in the bowl
  Pr 20:4 l. one does not plow in winter
  Ro 12:11 Be industrious, not l.
LEAD, Heb 13:7, 17 those taking the l. among
LEADER, Pr 28:16 l. abuses his power
  Mt 23:10 your L. is one, the Christ
LEARN, De 4:10 Congregate that they may l.
LEARNED, Php 4:9 The things that you l., practice
LEARNING, 2Ti 3:7 always l. yet never able to
LEAST, Lu 16:10 person faithful in l. is faithful in
LEAVEN, Mt 13:33 Kingdom of the heavens is like l.
  1Co 5:6 little l. ferments whole batch
LEAVES, Eze 47:12 and their l. for healing
  Mt 24:32 as soon as branch sprouts l., you know
LEAVING, Isa 1:28 l. Jehovah come to their finish
LEFT, Mt 19:29 everyone who l. houses or lands
LEFTOVER, Mt 14:20 took up l. fragments, 12 baskets
LEGALLY ESTABLISHING, Php 1:7 l. good news
LEND, Lu 6:35 l. without hoping for anything back
LENDING, Pr 19:17 favor to lowly, l. to Jehovah
LENGTHEN, Isa 54:2 l. your tent cords
LEOPARD, Isa 11:6 with young goat l. will lie down
  Da 7:6 another beast, like a l.
LEPER, Le 13:45 the l. call out, Unclean, unclean!
LEPROSY, Nu 12:10 Miriam struck with l.
  Lu 12:50! there was a man full of l.!
LESSER ONE, Lu 9:48 conducts himself as l.
LETUP, Ac 5:42 without l. teaching and
LEVEL, Ps 26:12 My foot standing on l. ground
LEVI, Mal 3:3 he will cleanse the sons of L.
LEVITES, Ex 32:26 all the L. gathered around him
  Nu 3:12 L. will become mine
  2Ch 35:3 L., the instructors of all Israel
LIAR, Ps 101:7 no l. will stand in my presence
  Pr 19:22 better to be poor than a l.
  Joh 8:44 Devil, a l. and father of lie
LIE, Col 3:9 Do not l. to one another
  2Th 2:11 they may come to believe the l.
  Tit 1:2 God, who cannot l., promised
LIFE, De 30:19 I put l. and death before you
  Ps 36:9 With you is source of l.
  Lu 9:24 whoever wants to save his l. will lose it
  Joh 5:26 as Father has l. in himself, he granted Son
  Joh 11:25 I am the resurrection and the l.
  Ac 20:24 my own l. of any importance
LIGHT, Ps 36:9 by your l. we can see l.
  Ps 119:105 Your word is a l. for my path
  Pr 4:18 path of righteous is like the l.
  Isa 42:6 as a l. of the nations
  Mt 5:14 You are the l. of the world
  Mt 5:16 let your l. shine before men
  Joh 8:12 I am the l. of the world
  2Co 4:6 Let the l. shine out of darkness
LIGHTNING, Mt 24:27 l. comes out and shines
  Lu 10:18 I see Satan fallen like l. from heaven
LILIES, Lu 12:27 Consider how the l. grow
LIMIT, Ps 119:96 your commandment has no l.
LIMITS, 1Th 4:6 No one go beyond proper l.
LIMPING, 1Ki 18:21 l. between two opinions?
LION, 1Sa 17:36 struck down l. and bear
  Ps 91:13 On l. and cobra you will tread
  Isa 11:7 l. will eat straw like the bull
  1Pe 5:8 Devil walks about like roaring l.
  Re 5:5 The L. of the tribe of Judah
LIONS, Da 6:27 he rescued Daniel from the l.
LIPS, Pr 10:19 controls l. acts discreetly
  Isa 29:13 they honor me with their l.

  Ho 14:2 will offer praise of our l.
Heb 13:15 sacrifice of praise, fruit of l.
LISTEN, Eze 2:7 speak, whether they l. or not
  Mt 17:5 my Son, the beloved. L. to him
  Ac 4:19 l. to you rather than to God
  Jas 1:19 quick to l., slow to speak
LISTENS, Pr 1:5 A wise person l.
  Lu 10:16 Whoever l. to you l. to me
LITTLE, Isa 60:22 l. one will become a thousand
LITTLE FLOCK, Lu 12:32 Have no fear, l.
LIVE, Job 14:14 If a man dies, can he l. again?
  2Co 5:15 l. no longer for themselves
LIVING, Da 6:26 he is the l. God
  Lu 20:38 God of the l., they are l. to him
  1Th 4:15 we the l. who survive
LOAD, Ps 68:19 Jehovah daily carries our l.
  Lu 11:46 you l. men down with loads
  Ga 6:5 each one carry his own l.
LOAF, Mt 26:26 Jesus took a l., broke it
  1Co 10:17 one l., all partaking of that l.
LOAN, Pr 11:15 Whoever guarantees a l.
LOCUST, Joe 1:4 What was left by the devouring l.
LOFTY, Ro 12:16 do not set your mind on l. things
LOGICAL, Lu 1:3 write them in l. order
LOGICALLY, Ac 9:22 proved l. that this is the Christ
LONG, Job 14:15 l. for the work of your hands
  Isa 26:9 I l. for you with my whole being
LONGING, Ps 84:2 l. for the courtyards of Jehovah
  Php 1:8 I am l. for all of you
  1Pe 2:2 form l. for the milk of the word
LOOKING, Joh 4:23 Father l. for ones like these
LOOSEN, Mt 18:18 whatever things you may l.
LORD, De 10:17 Jehovah is L. of lords
  Mt 7:22 L., L., did we not prophesy in your
  Mt 22:44 Jehovah said to my L.:
  1Co 7:39 free to be married only in the L.
LORDS, 1Co 8:5 there are many gods and many l.
LOSS, Php 3:7 were gains, I considered l.
LOST, Ps 119:176 I have strayed like a l. sheep
  Eze 34:4 You have not looked for the l.
  Lu 15:24 son of mine was l. and has been found
LOT, Da 12:13 will stand up for your l. at the end
  Lu 17:32 Remember the wife of L.
  2Pe 2:7 he rescued righteous L.
LOTS, Ps 22:18 they cast l. for my clothing
LOVE, Le 19:18 l. your fellow man as yourself
  De 6:5 l. Jehovah with all your heart
  Ca 8:6 l. is as strong as death is
  Mt 22:37 You must l. Jehovah with your whole
  Mt 24:12 l. of the greater number will grow cold
  Mr 10:21 Jesus felt l. for him and said
  Joh 13:34 that you l. one another
  Joh 14:15 If you l. me, you will observe
  Joh 15:13 No one has l. greater than this
  Ro 8:39 to separate us from God's l.
  Ro 13:8 Do not owe anything except to l.
  Ro 13:10 l. is the law's fulfillment
  1Co 8:1 Knowledge puffs up, l. builds up
  1Co 13:2 but do not have l., I am nothing
  1Co 13:8 L. never fails
  1Co 13:13 but the greatest of these is l.
  1Co 16:14 everything you do be done with l.
  2Co 2:8 confirm your l. for him
  Col 3:14 l. is a perfect bond of union
  1Pe 4:8 have intense l., because l. covers
  1Jo 2:15 Do not l. either the world or
  1Jo 3:18 l., not with the tongue, but in deed
  1Jo 4:8 God is l.
  1Jo 4:20 does not l. brother, cannot l. God
  1Jo 5:3 l. of God means, observe his
  Jude 21 keep yourselves in God's l.
  Re 2:4 left the l. you had at first

LOVED, Joh 3:16 God l. world so much that
　Joh 13:1 having l. his own, l. them to the end
　Ga 2:20 Son of God, who l. me and
　1Jo 4:10 not we l. God, but he l. us
LOVING, Col 3:19 husbands, keep on l. your wives
LOWLY, 1Sa 2:8 He raises l. one from the dust
　Ps 41:1 consideration to the l. one
　Isa 57:15 to revive the spirit of the l.
LOYAL, 1Sa 22:26 With someone l. you act in loyalty
　2Sa 22:26 With someone l. you act in loyalty
　Ps 16:10 will not allow l. one to see the pit
　Ps 37:28 Jehovah will not abandon his l. ones
LOYAL LOVE, Ex 34:6 Jehovah abundant in l.
　Ps 13:5 I trust in your l.
　Ps 136:1-26 His l. endures forever
　Ho 6:6 in l. I delight, not in sacrifice
LOYALTY, Mic 6:8 to exercise justice, to cherish l.
LUCK, Isa 65:11 god of Good L.
LUKE, Col 4:14 L., the beloved physician
LUKEWARM, Re 3:16 because you are l.
LUST, Ro 1:27 males violently inflamed in their l.
LUXURY, Re 18:7 she lived in shameless l.
LYDIA, Ac 16:14 L., a seller of purple from Thyatira

M

MACEDONIA, Ac 16:9 Step over into M. and help us
MAGIC, De 18:10 anyone practicing m.
MAGICAL, Ac 19:19 m. arts, burned their books
MAGOG, Eze 38:2 against Gog of the land of M.
MAIMED, Mt 15:31 m. being made sound
MAKE SURE, Php 1:10 m. of more important
　1Th 5:21 M. of all things; hold fast to fine
MALE, Le 20:13 man lies down with a m.
MALTA, Ac 28:1 learned that the island was called M.
MANASSEH, 2Ch 33:13 M. came to know that Jehovah
MANGER, Lu 2:7 laid him in a m.
MANLY, 1Co 16:13 carry on in a m. way
MANNA, Ex 16:31 Israel named the bread m.
　Jos 5:12 Then the m. stopped
MANNER, Ac 1:11 will come in same m. as you seen
　Php 1:27 behave in m. worthy of good news
MAN OF LAWLESSNESS, 2Th 2:3 m. gets revealed
MANSLAYER, Nu 35:6 refuge for the m. to flee to
MARK, Eze 9:4 put a m. on the foreheads
　Col 4:10 M., the cousin of Barnabas
　Re 13:17 except a person having the m.
MARKED, 2Th 3:14 keep this one m., stop associating
MARKETPLACE, Ac 17:17 reason with people in m.
MARRIAGE, De 7:3 not form any m. alliances with
　Mt 22:2 king who made a m. feast
　Joh 2:1 a m. feast took place in Cana
　Heb 13:4 Let m. be honorable among all
　Re 19:7 m. of the Lamb has arrived
MARRIED, 1Co 7:39 free to be m., only in the Lord
MARRY, Mt 22:30 in resurrection neither m.
　1Co 7:9 better to m. than be inflamed with passion
　1Co 7:36 does not sin. Let them m.
　1Co 7:38 does not m. will do better
MARRYING, Mt 24:38 as before the Flood, m. and
MARTHA, Lu 10:41 M., you are anxious
MARY 1., Mr 6:3 carpenter, the son of M.
MARY 2., Lu 10:39 M. kept listening
　Lu 10:42 M. chose the good portion
　Joh 12:3 M. took perfumed oil, very costly
MARY 3., Mt 27:56 were M. Magdalene and
　Lu 8:2 M. Magdalene, from whom seven demons
MARY 4., Mt 27:56 and M. the mother of James and
MARY 5., Ac 12:12 house of M., mother of John Mark
MASTER, Mt 9:38 beg M. of harvest to send workers
　Ro 6:14 sin must not be m. over you
　Ro 14:4 To his own m. he stands or falls
　Col 4:1 you also have a M. in heaven

MASTERS, Mt 6:24 No one can slave for two m.
MATURE, Heb 5:14 m., powers of discernment
　trained
MATURITY, Heb 6:1 let us press on to m.
MEASURE, Lu 6:38 with m. that you are measuring
MEAT, Pr 23:20 who gorge themselves on m.
MEDDLE, Ac 5:38 do not m. with these men
MEDDLERS, 1Ti 5:13 m. in people's affairs
MEDIATOR, 1Ti 2:5 one m. between God and men
MEDICINE, Pr 17:22 joyful heart is good m.
MEDITATE, Ge 24:63 Isaac was in the field to m.
　Ps 77:12 will m. on all your activity
MEDITATES, Pr 15:28 righteous m. before answering
MEDITATION, Ps 19:14 m. of my heart be pleasing
MEEK, Ps 37:11 m. will possess the earth
　Zep 2:3 Seek Jehovah, all you m. of the earth
MEETING, Heb 10:25 not forsaking m. together
MELCHIZEDEK, Ge 14:18 M. king of Salem was priest
　Ps 110:4 priest forever in the manner of M.
MEMBERS, 1Co 12:18 God arranged the body m.
MEMORIAL TOMBS, Joh 5:28 those in m. will hear
MENSTRUAL, Le 15:19 in m. impurity for seven days
　Le 18:19 sexual relations during m. impurity
MENTIONED, Eph 5:3 not even be m. among you
MERCHANT, Mt 13:45 traveling m. seeking pearls
MERCHANTS, Re 18:3 m. became rich
MERCIES, 2Co 1:3 Father of tender m.
MERCIFUL, De 4:31 Jehovah is a m. God
　Ps 78:38 But he was m.; he would forgive
　Mt 5:7 Happy are the m.
　Lu 6:36 Continue being m., as your Father
　Jas 5:11 Jehovah is very tender and m.
MERCY, 1Ch 21:13 for his m. is very great
　Ne 9:19 in great m., did not abandon them
　Pr 28:13 whoever confesses will be shown m.
　Isa 55:7 return to Jehovah, who will have m.
　Mt 9:13 I want m., and not sacrifice
　Jas 2:13 M. triumphs over judgment
MESSENGER, Mal 3:1 I am sending my m.
MESSIAH, Da 9:25 until M. the Leader, there will be
　Da 9:26 after the 62 weeks, M. will be cut off
　Joh 1:41 We have found the M.
　Joh 4:25 I know that M. is coming, Christ
METHODS, 1Co 4:17 will remind you of my m.
MICHAEL, Da 10:13 M., one of the foremost princes
　Da 12:1 During that time M. will stand up
　Re 12:7 M. and his angels battled
MIGHTY, 1Co 16:13 stand firm in the faith, grow m.
MILD, 1Pe 3:4 quiet and m. spirit
MILDLY, 1Co 4:13 when slandered, we answer m.
MILITARY, Zec 4:6 Not by a m. force, but by spirit
MILK, Ex 3:8 land flowing with m. and honey
　Isa 60:16 drink the m. of nations
　Heb 5:12 gone back to needing m.
　1Pe 2:2 a longing for the unadulterated m.
MINA, Lu 19:16 Lord, your m. gained ten minas
MIND, Ps 8:4 What is man that you keep him in m.?
　Isa 65:17 former things will not be called to m.
　Mt 22:37 love Jehovah with your whole m.
　Joh 10:20 He has a demon and is out of his m.
　Ro 7:25 with my m. a slave to God's law
　Ro 8:6 setting m. on the flesh means death
　1Co 2:16 we do have the m. of Christ
MINDFUL, Na 1:7 m. of those seeking refuge in him
MIND OWN BUSINESS, 1Th 4:11 aim to m.
MINDS, Php 3:19 have their m. on earthly things
　Col 3:2 Keep your m. fixed on things above
MINISTER, 1Sa 2:11 boy became a m. of Jehovah
　Mt 20:28 Son of man came to m.
　Mr 10:43 great among you must be m.
MINISTERIAL SERVANTS, 1Ti 3:8 M. should be
MINISTERING, Da 7:10 thousands kept m. to him
　1Pe 4:10 use gift in m. to one another

MINISTERS, 2Co 3:6 qualified us to be m.
2Co 6:4 recommend ourselves as God's m.
MINISTRY, Ac 20:24 finish my course and the m.
Ro 11:13 I glorify my m.
2Co 4:1 this m. through the mercy
2Co 6:3 no fault may be found with our m.
1Ti 1:12 considered faithful by assigning m.
2Ti 4:5 fully accomplish your m.
MIRIAM, Nu 12:1 M. and Aaron against Moses
MIRROR, 1Co 13:12 by means of a metal m,
Jas 1:23 looking at his face in a m.
MIRRORS, 2Co 3:18 reflect like m. the glory of
MISCARRIAGE, Ex 23:26 women will not suffer a m.
MISERABLE, Ro 7:24 M. man that I am!
MISLEAD, Mt 24:24 m., if possible, even chosen
MISLED, Ga 6:7 Do not be m.: God not to be mocked
MIST, Jas 4:14 you are a m. that appears for a while
MISTAKE, Job 6:24 help me understand my m.
MOB, Ac 17:5 gathered wicked men and formed a m.
MOCK, Lu 22:63 began to m. him, hitting him
Ga 6:7 God is not one to be m.
MOCKED, Lu 18:32 will be m. and spat on
MODEL, 1Pe 2:21 Christ leaving a m. for you
MODEST, Pr 11:2 wisdom is with m. ones
MODESTY, Mic 6:8 and to walk in m. with your God!
1Ti 2:9 women should adorn with m.
MOLDED, Ro 12:2 stop being m. by this system
1Pe 1:14 stop being m. by the desires
MOMENT, Ps 30:5 his anger is only for a m.
Isa 26:20 Hide yourself for a brief m.
MOMENTARY, 2Co 4:17 tribulation is m.
MONEY, Ec 7:12 m. is a protection, but wisdom
Ec 10:19 m. answers every need
1Ti 6:10 love of m. root of injurious things
Heb 13:5 free of the love of m.
MOON, Joe 2:31 m. will be turned into blood
Lu 21:25 signs in the sun and m. and stars
MORAL, Eph 4:19 gone past all m. sense
MORTAL MAN, Ps 8:4 What is m. that you
MOSES, Nu 12:3 M. was the meekest of all men
Ps 106:32 went badly for M. because of them
Ac 7:22 M. was powerful in words and deeds
2Co 3:7 could not gaze at the face of M.
MOST HIGH, Ps 83:18 Jehovah, the M.
Da 4:17 know that the M. is Ruler
MOTHER, Ex 20:12 Honor your father and m.
Ps 27:10 Even if father and m. abandon me
Pr 23:22 not despise m. because grown old
Lu 8:21 My m. and my brothers are these
Joh 19:27 said to the disciple: See! Your m.!
Ga 4:26 Jerusalem above is our m.
MOTIVES, Pr 16:2 Jehovah examines the m.
MOUNTAIN, Ps 24:3 ascend to the m. of Jehovah?
Isa 2:3 let us go up to the m. of Jehovah
Isa 11:9 not cause any harm in all my holy m.
Da 2:35 became large m. and filled the earth
MOUNTAINS, Ge 7:20 waters rose above the m.
MOURN, Mt 5:4 Happy are those who m.
MOURNING, Ec 7:2 Better to go to house of m.
MOUTH, Ps 8:2 Out of the m. of children
Ro 10:10 with the m. public declaration
Jas 3:10 Out of the same m. blessing and
MURDER, Ex 20:13 You must not m.
MURDERER, Joh 8:44 was a m. when he began
MURMURERS, 1Co 10:10 Neither be m.
Jude 16 These men are m.
MURMURING, Nu 14:27 Israelites m. against me
Php 2:14 Keep doing things free from m.
MUSTARD, Lu 13:19 It is like a m. grain that a man
MUTUAL, 1Co 7:5 not deprive except by m. consent
MUZZLE, De 25:4 must not m. a bull
MYRIADS, Re 5:11 number of them was m. of m.

NAIN, Lu 7:11 he traveled to a city called N.
NAIVE, Pr 14:15 n. person believes every word
NAME, Ge 11:4 let us make a n. for ourselves
Ex 3:13 Suppose they say, What is his n.?
Ex 3:15 Jehovah. This is my n. forever
Ex 9:16 to have my n. declared in the earth
Ex 20:7 not take the n. in worthless way
1Sa 17:45 I am coming in the n. of Jehovah
1Ch 29:13 we praise your beautiful n.
Ps 9:10 knowing your n. will trust in you
Ps 79:9 for the sake of your n.
Pr 18:10 n. of Jehovah is a strong tower
Pr 22:1 good n. to be chosen rather than wealth
Ec 7:1 good n. better than good oil
Jer 23:27 to make my people forget my n.
Eze 39:25 I will zealously defend my holy n.
Mal 1:11 my n. will be great among the nations
Mal 3:16 for those meditating on his n.
Mt 6:9 let your n. be sanctified
Joh 12:28 Father, glorify your n.
Joh 14:14 ask anything in my n., I will do it
Joh 17:26 I have made your n. known
Ac 4:12 no other n. given by which we get saved
Ac 15:14 out of nations a people for his n.
Ro 10:13 calls on the n. of Jehovah be saved
Php 2:9 n. that is above every other n.
NARROW, Mt 7:13 Go in through the n. gate
NATHAN, 2Sa 12:7 N. said: You are the man!
NATION, Ex 19:6 kingdom of priests and holy n.
Ps 33:12 Happy is n. whose God is Jehovah
Isa 66:8 will a n. be born all at once?
Mt 21:43 Kingdom given to a n. producing its fruits
Mt 24:7 For n. will rise against n.
Ac 17:26 made out of one man every n.
1Pe 2:9 a chosen race, a holy n.
NATIONS, Ge 22:18 all n. will obtain a blessing
Mt 25:32 All n. will be gathered before him
Lu 21:24 appointed times of the n. are fulfilled
NATURAL, Le 18:23 violation of what is n.
Ro 1:26 females changed n. use of themselves
Ro 1:27 males left the n. use of the female
NEAR, Ps 73:28 drawing n. to God is good for me
NEBUCHADNEZZAR, Da 2:1 N. had dreams
NECESSARY, Ro 12:3 not think more than n.
NEED, Mt 6:32 Father knows you n. all these things
NEEDS, Ro 12:13 Share according to their n.
NEGATIVE, Tit 2:8 nothing n. to say about us
NEGLECT, 1Ti 4:14 Do not n. the gift in you
NEGLECTFULLY, Jer 48:10 mission of Jehovah n.!
NEGLIGENCE, Da 6:4 no n. found in Daniel
NEIGHBOR, Lu 10:27 love your n. as yourself
Lu 10:36 Who of these made himself n.?
NEPHILIM, Ge 6:4 N. were on the earth
NETS, Lu 5:4 let down your n. for a catch
NEW, Isa 42:9 I am declaring n. things
Joh 13:34 I am giving you a n. commandment
Ac 17:21 telling or listening to something n.
Re 21:1 n. heaven and a n. earth
Re 21:5 Look! I am making all things n.
NEWS, Ps 112:7 will not fear bad n.
NIGHT, Ps 19:2 n. after n. they reveal knowledge
Ro 13:12 The n. is well along; the day has
NINEVEH, Jon 4:11 Should I not feel sorry for N.?
NOAH, Ge 6:9 N. walked with God
Mt 24:37 as days of N. were, so presence
NOBLE, 1Co 1:26 not many wise, not many of n. birth
NOBLE-MINDED, Ac 17:11 more n. than
NONSENSE, Lu 24:11 seemed like n. to them
NOTHING, Isa 45:19 Seek me simply for n.
Isa 65:23 They will not toil for n.
Ga 6:3 thinks he is something when he is n.

NOTICED, Mt 6:1 not practice righteousness to be n.
NUMB, Ps 143:4 my heart is n. within me
NURSING, 1Th 2:7 as when a n. mother cares

O

OBEDIENCE, Ro 5:19 through o. of one person many
Ro 16:26 to promote o. by faith
Heb 5:8 learned o. from things he suffered
OBEDIENT, Ac 24:7 willing to do, and will be o.
1Ki 3:9 grant your servant an o. heart
Ro 6:17 you became o. from the heart
Eph 6:5 Slaves, be o. to your masters
Php 2:8 o. to the point of death
Heb 13:17 Be o. to those taking the lead
OBEY, 1Sa 15:22 To o. is better than a sacrifice
Ps 51:12 stir within me willingness to o.
Ac 5:29 We must o. God rather than men
OBLIGATION, Ec 12:13 this is the whole o. of man
1Jo 3:16 o. to surrender lives for brothers
OBSCENE, Ro 1:27 males with males, what is o.
Eph 5:4 foolish talking nor o. jesting
Col 3:8 put away o. talk
OBSERVE, Mt 28:20 teaching them to o. all things
Joh 14:15 If love me, will o. my commandments
OBSESSED, 1Ti 6:4 o. with arguments and debates
OFFERING, Le 7:37 burnt o., grain o., sin o.
OFFERINGS, 1Ch 29:9 people rejoiced making o.
Isa 1:11 I have had enough of your burnt o.
OFFICE, Ac 1:20 His o. of oversight let someone else
OFFSPRING, Ge 3:15 enmity between your o. and her
Ge 22:17 I will surely multiply your o.
Isa 65:23 o. made up of those blessed by Jehovah
Ga 3:16 and to your o., who is Christ
Ga 3:29 you are really Abraham's o., heirs
OIL, 1Ki 17:16 small jar of o. did not run dry
Mt 25:4 discreet took o. with their lamps
Mr 14:4 Why has this perfumed o. been wasted?
OLD, Ps 37:25 was young and now I am o.
Ps 71:9 Do not cast me off in my o. age
Ps 92:14 Even in o. age they will be thriving
OLIVE, Ro 11:17 wild o., grafted in among
OLIVES, MOUNT OF, Lu 22:39 he went to the M.
Ac 1:12 M., near Jerusalem, a sabbath day's
OLIVE TREE, Ps 52:8 like an o. in God's house
OMENS, Nu 23:23 no o. of doom against Jacob
De 18:10 anyone who looks for o.
ONE, 1Co 8:6 o. God, the Father, and o. Lord, Jesus
ONENESS, Eph 4:3 maintain o. of the spirit
Eph 4:13 until we all attain the o. of faith
ONLY-BEGOTTEN, Joh 1:18 o. god explained Him
Joh 3:16 gave his o. Son, so that
OPINIONS, 1Ki 18:21 limping between two o.?
Ro 14:1 not pass judgment on differing o.
OPPONENTS, Php 1:28 not frightened by o.
OPPORTUNITY, Ga 6:10 have o., work what is good
OPPOSERS, Lu 21:15 wisdom that o. will not resist
1Co 16:9 but there are many o.
OPPOSITION, Ac 17:7 act in o. to decrees of Caesar
1Th 2:2 boldness in the face of o.
OPPRESSION, Ps 72:14 From o. and violence rescue
Ec 7:7 o. can drive wise one into madness
OPPRESSORS, Ec 4:1 o. had the power
ORDER, 1Co 15:23 in proper o.: Christ
ORDERED, Ac 5:28 We strictly o. you not to keep
ORDERLY, Ga 5:25 go on walking o. by spirit
1Ti 3:2 overseer be sound in mind, o.
ORDINARY, Ac 4:13 and John, uneducated and o.
ORPHANS, Jas 1:27 look after o. and widows
OTHER SHEEP, Joh 10:16 I have o., not of this fold
OUTCOME, Isa 46:10 From beginning I foretell o.
OUTSIDE, 1Co 5:13 while God judges those o.?
Col 4:5 wisdom toward those o.

OUTWARD APPEARANCE, Mt 22:16 do not look at o.
Ga 2:6 God does not go by a man's o.
OVERCONFIDENT, Pr 14:16 stupid is reckless and o.
OVERSEER, 1Ti 3:1 reaching out to be an o.
1Pe 2:25 the shepherd and o. of your souls
OVERSEERS, Isa 60:17 I will appoint peace as your o.
Ac 20:28 holy spirit has appointed you o.
1Pe 5:2 serving as o. willingly
OVERTURNING, 2Co 10:4 o. entrenched things
OVERWHELM, Ps 40:12 my errors o. me
OWE, Ro 13:8 Do not o. anything except to love

P

PACE, Ge 33:14 at the p. of livestock and children
PAIN, Ro 8:22 all creation in p. until now
Ro 9:2 grief and unceasing p. in heart
PAMPERED, Pr 29:21 If p., will become thankless
PANIC, Isa 28:16 No one exercising faith will p.
PARADISE, Lu 23:43 you will be with me in P.
2Co 12:4 who was caught away into p.
PARALYZED, Isa 44:8 do not become p. with fear
Lu 5:24 said to p., Get up, pick up your stretcher
PARENTS, Lu 18:29 left p. for the sake of Kingdom
Lu 21:16 will be handed over even by p.
2Co 12:14 p. to save up for children
Eph 6:1 be obedient to your p.
Col 3:20 obedient to your p. in everything
PARTIAL, Ac 10:34 understand that God is not p.
1Co 13:9 we have p. knowledge
PARTIALITY, De 10:17 God treats none with p.
PARTIES, Ro 13:13 not in wild p. and drunkenness
Ga 5:21 drunkenness, wild p., and
PASSION, Ro 1:26 uncontrolled sexual p.
Col 3:5 uncontrolled sexual p.
1Th 4:5 not with greedy, uncontrolled sexual p.
PASSOVER, Ex 12:11 It is Jehovah's P.
Ex 12:27 P. to Jehovah, who passed over
1Co 5:7 Christ our P. lamb been sacrificed
PASTURES, Isa 30:23 livestock in spacious p.
PATH, Pr 4:18 p. of righteous like bright morning
light
PATIENCE, Ne 9:30 You extended p. for many years
Pr 25:15 By p. a commander is won over
Ro 9:22 God tolerated with much p. vessels
Jas 5:8 exercise p.; make hearts firm
2Pe 3:15 the p. of our Lord as salvation
PATIENT, 1Co 13:4 Love is p. and kind
1Th 5:14 be p. toward all
2Pe 3:9 Jehovah is p. with you
PATTERN, Joh 13:15 I set the p. for you
Heb 8:5 make all things after their p.
Jas 5:10 take as a p. the prophets
PAUL. See also SAUL, 1Co 1:12 I belong to P.
PAY ATTENTION, Ac 20:28 P. to yourselves and to
1Ti 4:16 P. to yourself and your teaching
PAY BACK, Pr 20:22 Do not say: I will p. evil!
Mt 22:21 P. Caesar's things to Caesar, but God's
PEACE, Ps 29:11 will bless his people with p.
Ps 37:11 delight in the abundance of p.
Ps 72:7 p. will abound until moon is no more
Ps 119:165 Abundant p. to those who love your law
Pr 17:1 Better dry bread where there is p. than
Isa 9:7 To the increase of p., no end
Isa 48:18 Then your p. would become like a river
Isa 54:13 p. of your sons will be abundant
Isa 57:21 no p. for the wicked
Isa 60:17 I will appoint p. as overseers
Jer 6:14 There is p.! When there is no p.
Mt 5:24 First make p. with your brother
Mr 9:50 and keep p. with one another
Joh 14:27 I leave you p.; I give you my p.
Ac 9:31 congregation entered into period of p.

Ro 5:1 enjoy **p.** with God through Jesus
Ro 8:6 setting mind on the spirit means **p.**
Php 4:7 **p.** of God will guard your hearts
1Th 5:3 **P.** and security! sudden destruction
1Pe 3:11 seek **p.** and pursue it
Re 6:4 granted to take **p.** away from earth
PEACEABLE, Ro 12:18 be **p.** with all men
PEACEFUL, Isa 32:18 a **p.** abiding place
PEACEMAKERS, Mt 5:9 Happy are the **p.**
PEARLS, Mt 7:6 not throw **p.** before swine
Mt 13:45 Kingdom like merchant seeking **p.**
PEDDLERS, 2Co 2:17 we are not **p.** of the word
PEER, 1Pe 1:12 angels are desiring to **p.**
PERFECT, De 32:4 The Rock, **p.** his activity
Ps 19:7 The law of Jehovah is **p.**
Mt 5:48 You must be **p.,** as your Father is **p.**
Heb 2:10 Chief Agent **p.** through sufferings
PERSECUTE, Ps 119:86 Men **p.** me without cause
Joh 15:20 persecuted me, will also **p.** you
Ro 12:14 Keep blessing those who **p.**
PERSECUTED, Mt 5:10 Happy are those **p.**
Ac 22:4 I **p.** this Way to the point of death
1Co 4:12 when **p.,** we patiently endure
2Co 4:9 **p.,** but not abandoned
PERSECUTION, Mt 13:21 **p.,** he is at once stumbled
Mr 4:17 as soon as **p.** arises, they are stumbled
PERSECUTIONS, Mr 10:30 children, and fields, with **p.**
PERSONALITY, Eph 4:24 put on the new **p.**
Col 3:9 Strip off the old **p.** with its practices
PERSUADED, 2Ti 3:14 learned and **p.** to believe
PERSUADING, Ro 5:11 we keep **p.** men
PERSUASIVE, 1Co 2:4 not with **p.** words of wisdom
PESTILENCES, Lu 21:11 one place after another **p.**
PETER, Mt 14:29 **P.** walked over the waters
Lu 22:54 **P.** was following at a distance
Joh 18:10 **P.,** who had a sword, struck the slave
Ac 12:5 **P.** in prison, but the congregation
PHILIP, Ac 8:26 Jehovah's angel spoke to **P.**
Ac 21:8 **P.** the evangelizer, one of the seven men
PHILOSOPHERS, Ac 17:18 Epicurean and the Stoic **p.**
PHILOSOPHY, Col 2:8 captive by means of **p.**
PHINEHAS, Nu 25:7 When **P.** saw it, he took a spear
PHYSICAL, Co 2:14 a **p.** man does not accept
PHYSICIAN, Lu 5:31 Those healthy do not need a **p.**
PIERCED, Zec 12:10 look to the one whom they **p.**
PILATE, Joh 19:6 **P.** said: I do not find any fault
PILLAR, Ge 19:26 Lot's wife became a **p.** of salt
Ex 13:22 **p.** of cloud, **p.** of fire
1Ti 3:15 a **p.** and support of the truth
PILLARS, Ga 2:9 ones who seemed to be **p.**
PIT, Pr 26:27 who digs a **p.** will fall into it
Da 6:7 should be thrown into the lion's **p.**
Mt 15:14 If blind guides blind, both fall into a **p.**
PITIED, 1Co 15:19 **p.** more than anyone
PITY, Mt 9:36 On seeing the crowds, he felt **p.**
Mt 20:34 Moved with **p.,** Jesus touched their eyes
PLAGUE, Ex 11:1 One more **p.** upon Pharaoh
PLAGUES, Re 18:4 not want to receive part of her **p.**
PLAN, Ex 26:30 set up tabernacle according to **p.**
1Ki 6:38 house according to its **p.**
PLANNING, Ro 13:14 not be **p.** ahead for desires of
PLANS, Pr 15:22 **P.** fail when there is no consultation
Pr 19:21 Many are the **p.** in man's heart, but
PLANT, Isa 65:22 nor will they **p.** for others to eat
PLANTED, 1Co 3:6 I **p.,** Apollos watered, but God
PLEADS, Ro 8:34 Christ Jesus **p.** for us
PLEASANT, Ps 147:1 **p.** and fitting to praise him!
PLEASE, Ge 15:5 Look up, **p.,** to the heavens
Ro 15:2 **p.** neighbor for his good, to build up
Ro 15:3 even Christ did not **p.** himself
1Co 10:33 trying to **p.** all people in all things
Ga 1:10 am I trying to **p.** men?

Eph 6:6 when watched, just to **p.** men
Col 1:10 in order to **p.** Jehovah fully
PLEASED, 1Co 12:18 arranged each as he **p.**
PLEASING, Joh 8:29 I always do the things **p.** to him
Ro 15:1 and not to be **p.** ourselves
Ga 1:10 If I were still **p.** men
PLEASURE, Ps 149:4 Jehovah takes **p.** in his people
Eze 18:32 I do not take **p.** in death of anyone
Eph 1:5 according to his good **p.** and will
PLEASURES, Lu 8:14 carried away by **p.**
PLENTY, 1Co 15:58 **p.** to do in work of Lord
PLOW, Lu 9:62 put his hand to **p.** and looks behind
PLUNDERING, Heb 10:34 accepted **p.** of belongings
POETS, Ac 17:28 as some of your own **p.** have said
POOR, 1Sa 2:8 He lifts up the **p.** from the ash
Ps 9:18 the **p.** will not always be forgotten
Ps 69:33 Jehovah is listening to the **p.**
Pr 30:9 Nor become **p.** and steal and dishonor
Lu 4:18 to declare good news to the **p.**
Joh 12:8 you always have the **p.** with you
2Co 6:10 as **p.** but making many rich
2Co 8:9 Christ became **p.** for your sake
Ga 2:10 only that we keep the **p.** in mind
POPULAR, Jer 8:6 returning to the **p.** course
POSSESSION, Heb 10:34 better and enduring **p.**
POSTPONED, Pr 13:12 Expectation **p.** heart sick
POTTER, Isa 64:8 We are clay, you are our **P.**
Ro 9:21 Does not the **p.** have authority
POUR, Ps 62:8 **P.** out your hearts before him
POVERTY, Pr 30:8 Give me neither **p.** nor riches
2Co 8:2 their deep **p.** made generosity abound
POWER, Pr 3:27 good if it is within your **p.**
Pr 28:16 leader without discernment abuses **p.**
Isa 40:29 He gives **p.** to the tired one
Isa 40:31 those hoping in Jehovah will regain **p.**
Zec 4:6 nor by **p.,** but by my spirit
Mr 5:30 realized that **p.** had gone out of him
Ac 1:8 you will receive **p.** when the spirit
2Co 4:7 **p.** beyond normal may be God's
2Co 12:9 my **p.** made perfect in weakness
Re 3:8 I know that you have a little **p.**
POWERFUL, 2Co 12:10 when I am weak, then I am **p.**
PRACTICAL, Lu 16:8 wiser in a **p.** way than sons of
PRACTICAL WISDOM, Pr 2:7 He treasures up **p.** for
Pr 3:21 Safeguard **p.** and thinking ability
Lu 16:8 steward acted with **p.**
PRACTICE, Ro 7:15 I do not **p.** what I wish, but
1Jo 3:6 in union with him does not **p.** sin
PRAISE, 1Ch 16:25 Jehovah most worthy of **p.**
Ps 147:1 how pleasant and fitting to **p.** him!
Pr 27:2 Let someone else **p.** you
Pr 27:21 person tested by the **p.** he receives
PRAISE JAH, Ps 146:1 **P.!** Let my whole being
Ps 150:6 Every breathing thing—**p.**
Re 19:1 great crowd said: **P.!**
PRAY, 2Ki 19:15 Hezekiah began to **p.**
Mt 5:44 **p.** for those who persecute you
Mt 6:9 You must **p.,** then, this way:
Mr 11:24 things you **p.** for, have faith that
Lu 5:16 often went into desolate areas to **p.**
Ro 8:26 not know what we should **p.** for
1Th 5:17 **P.** constantly
PRAYER, Ps 65:2 O Hearer of **p.**
Ps 141:2 **p.** be as incense prepared
Pr 15:8 **p.** of the upright is a pleasure to Him
Pr 28:9 even his **p.** is detestable
Ro 12:12 Persevere in **p.**
2Th 3:1 carry on **p.** for us, that the word
Jas 5:15 **p.** of faith will make sick well
PRAYERS, 1Pe 3:7 for **p.** not to be hindered
Re 8:4 incense with **p.** of the holy ones

PRAYING, Da 6:13 three times a day he is p.
Mr 1:35 Early, he left and began p.
Ac 12:5 Peter in prison, congregation p.
PREACH, Ro 10:14 hear without someone to p.?
2Ti 4:2 P. the word; be at it urgently
PREACHED, Mt 24:14 good news of Kingdom be p.
PREACHER, 2Pe 2:5 Noah, a p. of righteousness
PREACHING, Mt 9:35 Jesus p. the good news of
Lu 8:1 he traveled, p. and declaring
PRECIOUS, Da 9:23 you are someone very p.
Hag 2:7 p. things of all nations come in
1Pe 1:19 with p. blood, that of Christ
PREGNANT, Ex 21:22 hurt a p. woman and she
1Th 5:3 like birth pains on p. woman
PREPARE, Joh 14:2 going to p. a place for you
PRESENCE, Mt 24:3 the sign of your p.?
Mt 24:37 as days of Noah, so p. of the Son of man
2Pe 3:4 Where is this promised p. of his?
PRESENT, Ro 6:13 p. yourselves to God
PRESIDES, Ro 12:8 who p., do it diligently
PRESIDING, 1Th 5:12 respect for those p.
PRESSURE, 2Co 1:8 extreme p. beyond our strength
PRESUMPTUOUS, Ps 19:13 hold back from p. acts
PRESUMPTUOUSLY, De 17:12 acts p. by not listening
1Sa 15:23 pushing ahead p. same as
PRESUMPTUOUSNESS, Pr 11:2 When p. comes
PREVAIL, Jer 1:19 will not p. against you, for
PREVENT, 1Th 2:16 p. us from speaking
PRICE, 1Co 7:23 You were bought with a p.
PRIDE, Pr 8:13 I hate self-exaltation and p.
Pr 16:18 P. is before a crash
2Th 1:4 we take p. in you among the
PRIEST, Ps 110:4 p. forever in the manner of
Ho 4:6 rejected knowledge, I will reject you as p.
Mal 2:7 lips of a p. should safeguard knowledge
Heb 2:17 merciful and faithful high p.
PRIESTHOOD, 1Pe 2:9 a royal p., a holy nation
PRIESTS, Mic 3:11 her p. instruct for a price
Ac 6:7 a large crowd of p. obedient to the faith
Re 20:6 p. of God and rule 1,000 years
PRINCE, Isa 9:6 His name will be P. of Peace
Da 10:13 p. of Persia stood in opposition
PRINCES, Ps 45:16 will appoint them as p. in all earth
Isa 32:1 p. will rule for justice
PRISCILLA, Ac 18:26 P. and Aquila took him and
PRISON, Mt 25:36 I was in p. and you visited me
Ac 5:19 angel opened the doors of the p.
Ac 12:5 Peter in p., congregation praying
Heb 13:3 Keep in mind those in p.
Re 2:10 Devil throwing some of you into p.
PRIVILEGE, Php 1:29 p. to suffer in his behalf
PRIZE, 1Co 9:24 but only one receives the p.
Col 2:18 Let no man deprive you of the p.
PROCEDURE, 1Ch 15:13 did not search out proper p.
PROCLAIMING, 1Co 11:26 p. death of the Lord, until
PROFANED, Eze 39:7 my name be p. any longer
PROFIT, Pr 15:27 dishonest p. brings trouble
PROFITABLE, Ac 20:20 telling you things p.
PROGRESS, Joh 8:37 my word makes no p.
Php 3:16 to the extent we have made p.
PROMISE, 1Ki 8:56 Not one word of his p. failed
Ps 15:4 does not go back on his p., even when
PROMISED, Heb 10:23 the one who p. is faithful
PROMISES, 2Co 1:20 p. of God yes by him
PROPERTY, Ex 19:5 will become my special p.
PROPHECY, 2Pe 1:20 no p. of Scripture springs from
2Pe 1:21 p. at no time by man's will
PROPHESY, Joe 2:28 your sons and daughters will p.
PROPHET, De 18:18 I will raise up a p. like you
Eze 2:5 will know that p. was among them
Am 7:14 I was not a p. nor the son of a p.
PROPHETIC, 2Pe 1:19 p. word made more sure

PROPHETS, 1Ki 18:4 Obadiah hid 100 p.
Am 3:7 revealed confidential matter to p.
Ac 10:43 To him all the p. bear witness
PROPHETS, FALSE, Mt 7:15 f. in sheep's covering
Mt 24:11 f. will arise and mislead many
Mr 13:22 f. will perform wonders
PROPITIATION, Ro 3:25 as an offering for p.
PROPITIATORY, 1Jo 2:2 he is a p. sacrifice
PROSTITUTE, Pr 7:10 dressed like a p.
1Co 6:16 joined to a p. is one body
Re 17:1 p. who sits on many waters
Re 17:16 will hate the p. and will make her
PROSTITUTES, Lu 15:30 squandered with p.
PROTECTION, Ec 7:12 wisdom is a p. as money is
PROUD, Pr 16:5 p. heart detestable to Jehovah
PROVIDE, 1Ti 5:8 if anyone does not p. for his own
PROVING, Ac 17:3 explaining and p. by references
PROVOKED, 1Co 13:5 does not become p.
PUMMEL, 1Co 9:27 p. my body and lead as a slave
PUPIL, Ps 17:8 Guard me like p. of your eye
Zec 2:8 touches the p. of my eye
PURE, Hab 1:13 Your eyes are too p. to look on
Zep 3:9 change the language to a p. language
Mt 5:8 Happy are the p. in heart
PURPOSE, Pr 16:4 made everything for his p.
Ro 8:28 the ones called according to his p.
Ro 9:11 God's p. dependent, not on works
Eph 3:11 according to the eternal p.
PURSUE, Ro 14:19 p. things making for peace
PUTTING UP, Eph 4:2 p. with one another in love
PUZZLED, 1Pe 4:4 They are p. that you do not

Q

QUALIFICATIONS, Ga 6:1 who have spiritual q.
QUALIFIED, 2Co 3:5 adequately q. comes from
2Ti 2:2 men who will be q. to teach others
QUARREL, Pr 15:18 one slow to anger calms a q.
Pr 17:14 before q. breaks out, take your leave
QUEEN, 1Ki 10:1 q. of Sheba came to Solomon
QUIET, 1Pe 3:4 q. and mild spirit
QUIETLY, 1Th 4:11 aim to live q.

R

RACE, Ec 9:11 the swift do not always win the r.
2Ti 4:7 I have run the r. to the finish
RACHEL, Ge 29:18 serve seven years for R.
Jer 31:15 R. is weeping over her sons
RAIN, Ge 7:12 r. poured down for 40 days
De 11:14 I will give autumn r. and spring r.
De 32:2 instruction will fall as gentle r.
Isa 55:10 just as r. and snow do not return until
Mt 5:45 r. on both righteous and unrighteous
RAINBOW, Ge 9:13 my r. as a sign
RANSOM, Ps 49:7 None can give to God a r.
Mt 20:28 Son came to give his life as a r.
Ro 8:23 release from our bodies by r.
RASHLY, Pr 19:2 one who acts r. is sinning
REACTION, Job 31:34 in fear of r. of multitude?
READ, De 17:19 r. from it all the days
READINESS, 2Co 8:12 if the r. is there first
Eph 6:15 r. to declare the good news
READING, Ac 8:30 know what you are r.?
READJUST, Ga 6:1 r. in a spirit of mildness
READJUSTED, 2Co 13:11 continue to rejoice, to be r.
READJUSTMENT, Eph 4:12 with a view to r.
READY, Mt 24:44 prove yourselves r.
REAL, Joh 7:28 the One who sent me is r.
1Ti 6:19 get a firm hold on the r. life
REAP, Ec 11:4 who looks at clouds will not r.
Ho 8:7 wind sowing, will r. a storm wind
2Co 9:6 sows sparingly will r. sparingly
Ga 6:7 whatever person is sowing, will r.
Ga 6:9 we will r. if we do not tire out

REASON, Ec 7:25 search for r. behind things
  Ro 13:5 compelling r. to be in subjection
REASONABLENESS, Php 4:5 r. known to men
REASONED, Ac 17:2 r. from the Scriptures
REBEKAH, Ge 26:7 R. was beautiful
REBELLIOUSNESS, 1Sa 15:23 r. same as divination
REBELS, Nu 20:10 Hear, now, you r.!
REBUKE, Ec 7:5 Better to listen to a wise man's r.
RECANT, Ac 26:11 I tried to force them to r.
RECHABITES, Jer 35:5 wine before the R.
RECKLESS, Pr 14:16 stupid one r. and overconfident
RECOGNITION, 1Co 16:18 give r. to men of that sort
RECOGNIZED, Ac 6:9 unknown and yet are r.
RECOMMEND, 2Co 4:2 we r. ourselves to every
  2Co 6:4 in every way we r. ourselves
RECOMMENDS, Ro 5:8 God r. his own love to us
RECONCILED, Ro 5:10 we became r. to God
  1Co 7:11 remain unmarried or be r.
RECONCILING, 2Co 5:19 God r. world to himself
RED, Ge 25:30 give me some of the r. stew
REDEEM, Ps 49:7 None of them can r. a brother
  Ho 13:14 From the Grave I will r. them
REFINE, Zec 13:9 I will r. them as silver is refined
REFINER, Mal 3:3 sit as a r. and cleanser of silver
REFINING, Da 11:35 in order to do a r. work
REFRESH, Mt 11:28 Come to me, and I will r. you
REFRESHING, Ac 3:19 that seasons of r. may come
REFUGE, Ps 9:9 Jehovah secure r. for the oppressed
  Zep 3:12 will take r. in the name of Jehovah
REFUSE, 1Co 4:13 have become as the r. of the world
  Php 3:8 I consider them as a lot of r.
REJECTED, Jer 8:9 r. the word of Jehovah
REJOICE, Pr 27:11 Be wise, my son, make my heart r.
  Ec 8:15 nothing better than to eat, drink and r.
  Isa 65:13 My servants r., but you suffer shame
  Ro 5:3 let us r. while in tribulations
  Ro 12:12 R. in the hope
  Ro 12:15 R. with those who r.; weep with
  Php 4:4 Always r. in the Lord. R.!
REJOICED, 1Ch 29:9 people r. over making offerings
  Pr 8:30 I r. before him all the time
REJOICING, Ps 100:2 Serve Jehovah with r.
  Ps 137:6 my greatest reasons for r.
  Ac 5:41 went from before the Sanhedrin, r.
  Php 3:1 continue r. in the Lord
RELATIVES, Ac 10:24 Cornelius called together r.
RELIEF, 2Th 1:7 you who suffer will be given r.
RELY, Pr 3:5 do not r. on your own understanding
REMAINING ONES, Re 12:17 war with r. of
REMAINS, 1Jo 2:17 one who does will of God r.
REMEMBER, Job 14:13 set a time limit and r. me!
  Ec 12:1 R. your Creator in the days of youth
REMEMBERING, Heb 10:32 keep r. former days
REMEMBRANCE, Lu 22:19 Keep doing this in r. of me
REMIND, 2Pe 1:12 I intend to r. you of these things
REMINDERS, Ps 119:24 I am fond of your r.
REMOVE, 1Co 5:13 R. the wicked person from among
REPAY, Ps 37:21 wicked borrows and does not r.
  Ps 116:12 With what will I r. Jehovah
  Ro 12:19 Vengeance is mine; I will r., says
  2Th 1:6 to r. tribulation to those
REPENT, Ac 3:19 R. and turn around so as to get
  Ac 17:30 people everywhere should r.
  Re 16:11 blasphemed God, did not r.
REPENTANCE, Ac 26:20 by doing works that befit r.
  Ro 2:4 God trying to lead you to r.
  2Co 7:10 sadness in a godly way produces r.
REPENTS, Lu 15:7 more joy over one sinner who r.
REPLIES, Pr 18:13 r. to a matter before he hears
REPORT, Ex 23:1 not spread r. that is not true
  Le 5:1 he is a witness and does not r. it
  Nu 14:36 returned with bad r. about the land

Pr 25:25 a good r. from a distant land
  2Co 6:8 through bad r. and good r.
REPORTS, Da 11:44 r. will disturb him
REPRESENTATIVE, Joh 7:29 I am a r. from him
REPROACH, Mt 5:11 Happy when people r. you
REPROOF, Pr 3:11 do not loathe his r.
  Pr 27:5 Open r. better than concealed love
  Pr 29:1 stiffens neck after much r. will be broken
REPROVE, Ps 141:5 r. me, it would be like oil
REQUESTS, Ps 20:5 May Jehovah fulfill your r.
REQUIRED, Job 23:12 even more than what was r.
REQUIRING, Mic 6:8 what is Jehovah r. of you?
RESCUE, 2Pe 2:9 Jehovah knows how to r. people
RESOURCES, Isa 60:5 r. of the nations will come
  Isa 61:6 You will eat r. of the nations
RESPECT, Eph 5:33 wife have r. for husband
  1Th 5:12 show r. for those presiding
  1Pe 3:2 chaste conduct together with deep r.
  1Pe 3:15 make a defense with deep r.
RESPONSIBLE, 1Sa 22:22 I am r. for the death
REST, Da 12:13 You will r., but will stand up
RESTRAINT, 2Th 2:6 what is acting as r.
  2Ti 2:24 showing r. when wronged
RESTRICT, 1Co 7:35 not to r. you, but
RESULTS, Isa 55:11 my word will not return without r.
RESURRECT, Joh 6:39 I r. them on the last day
RESURRECTED, Ac 2:24 But God r. him
RESURRECTION, Mt 22:23 Sadducees say no r.
  Mt 22:30 in the r. neither marry
  Joh 5:29 come out to a r. of life
  Joh 11:24 he will rise in the r. on the last day
  Joh 11:25 I am the r. and the life
  Ac 24:15 r. of righteous and unrighteous
  1Co 15:13 If no r., Christ not raised
RETURN, Joe 2:12 r. to me with all your hearts
  Mal 3:7 R. to me, and I will r. to you
REVEALED, Mt 11:25 from wise, r. to children
  1Co 2:10 to us God r. through his spirit
  Eph 3:5 secret r. to apostles and prophets
REVEALING, Ro 8:19 expectation for r. of the sons
REVIVE, Isa 57:15 r. the spirit of the lowly
REWARD, Ru 2:12 May Jehovah r. you
  Col 3:24 from Jehovah will receive r.
REWARDER, Heb 11:6 he becomes the r.
RIB, Ge 2:22 built the r. into a woman
RICH, Le 19:15 must not show preference to r.
  Pr 10:22 blessing of Jehovah makes one r.
  Jer 9:23 let not the r. man boast about his riches
  Lu 14:12 When you spread dinner, not call r.
  2Co 6:10 as poor but making many r.
  1Ti 6:9 determined to be r. fall into a snare
  1Ti 6:17 r. not to be arrogant, and to hope
  Re 3:17 you say: I am r. and
RICHES, Pr 11:28 The one trusting in r. will fall
  Pr 30:8 Give me neither poverty nor r.
  Mt 6:24 You cannot slave for God and for R.
  Mt 13:22 deceptive power of r.
  Lu 16:9 friends by means of unrighteous r.
RIDICULERS, 2Pe 3:3 in the last days r. will come
RIGHT, Eze 21:27 one who has legal r. comes
RIGHTEOUS, Ps 34:19 Many are hardships of the r.
  Ps 37:25 not seen r. abandoned
  Ps 72:7 In his days r. will flourish
  Ps 141:5 Should r. strike me, it would be
  Pr 24:16 r. one may fall seven times
  1Pe 3:12 eyes of Jehovah are on the r.
RIGHTEOUSNESS, Ge 15:6 and He counted it as r.
  Ps 45:7 You loved r. and hated wickedness
  Isa 26:9 inhabitants of the land learn about r.
  Isa 32:1 A king will reign for r.
  Isa 60:17 r. as your task assigners
  Zep 2:3 Seek r., seek meekness
  2Pe 3:13 in these r. is to dwell

RIP, Joe 2:13 R. apart your hearts
RISKED, Ro 16:4 who r. their own necks for me
RIVER, Re 12:16 earth swallowed up the r.
 Re 22:1 r. of water of life
ROAD, Mt 7:14 cramped the r. leading into life
 Mt 13:4 some seeds fell alongside the r.
ROB, Le 19:13 you must not r.
ROCK, De 32:4 The R., perfect is his activity
 Mt 7:24 built his house on the r.
ROD, Pr 13:24 Whoever holds back r. hates his son
 Re 12:5 shepherd all nations with an iron r.
ROOMS, Isa 26:20 Go, my people, enter your inner r.
ROOSTER, Mt 26:34 before a r. crows, you disown
ROOT, Lu 8:13 receive with joy, but have no r.
ROOTED, Col 2:7 r. and stabilized in faith
ROTTEN, Eph 4:29 Let a r. word not come out of
ROVE, Da 12:4 Many will r. about, and
ROVING, 2Ch 16:9 eyes of Jehovah r. about
RUIN, Eze 21:27 A r., a r., a r. I will make it
 Re 11:18 r. those ruining the earth
RULE, Ro 6:12 not let sin r. in your bodies
 Re 11:15 he will r. as king forever
RULER, Da 4:17 know that the Most High is R.
 Joh 12:31 r. of this world will be cast out
 Joh 14:30 r. of the world coming, has no hold
RULERS, Joh 12:42 many r. put faith in him
 Ac 4:26 r. gathered against Jehovah and
RULERSHIP, Isa 9:7 To the increase of r. no end
 Da 4:34 his r. is an everlasting r.
RULES, Pr 29:2 wicked one r., people groan
 2Ti 2:5 competed according to the r.
RUN, 1Co 9:24 R. that you may win it
RUNNING, Ga 5:7 You were r. well. Who hindered

S

SABBATH, Ex 20:8 Remember S. day
 Mt 12:8 Son of man is Lord of the S.
 Mr 2:27 S. came into existence for man, not
 Lu 14:5 Who will not pull out son or bull on the S.?
 Col 2:16 not let judge about observance of s.
SABBATH-REST, Heb 4:9 s. for people of God
SACRED SECRET, Ro 16:25 s. been kept in silence
 Eph 3:4 my comprehension of the s.
SACRED SERVICE, Ro 12:1 s. with power of reason
SACRIFICE, 1Sa 15:22 obey better than a s.
 Ps 40:6 S. and offering you did not desire
 Pr 15:8 s. of the wicked detestable to Jehovah
 Ho 6:6 in loyal love I delight, not in s.
 Ro 12:1 present your bodies as a living s.
 Heb 13:15 offer to God s. of praise
SACRIFICES, 2Sa 24:24 s. that cost me nothing
 Ps 51:17 s. pleasing to God are a broken spirit
SAD, Ps 38:6 s. all day long
SADDENED, 2Co 7:9 s. in a godly way
SADNESS, Ec 7:3 s. of face makes heart better
 2Co 2:7 overwhelmed by excessive s.
SAFEGUARD, Pr 4:23 s. your heart, for out of it
SAFETY, Pr 3:23 Then you will walk in s.
 Php 3:1 write the same things, it is for your s.
SALT, Ge 19:26 she became a pillar of s.
 Mt 5:13 You are the s. of the earth
 Col 4:6 words gracious, seasoned with s.
SALVATION, 2Ch 20:17 stand still, see the s.
 Ps 3:8 S. belongs to Jehovah
 Ac 4:12 there is no s. in anyone else
 Ro 13:11 now our s. is nearer than when we
 Php 2:12 working out your s. with fear and
 Re 7:10 S. we owe to our God
SAMARIA, 2Ki 17:6 king of Assyria captured S.
 Joh 4:7 woman of S. came to draw water
SAMARITAN, Lu 10:33 a S. moved with pity
SAMSON, Jg 13:24 named him S.

SAMUEL, 1Sa 1:20 Hannah named him S.
 1Sa 2:18 S. ministering, though just a boy
SANCTIFICATION, Heb 12:14 Pursue s.
SANCTIFIED, 1Ki 9:3 I have s. this house
 Jer 1:5 before you were born I s. you
 Lu 11:2 Father, let your name be s.
SANCTIFY, Eze 36:23 I will s. my great name
SANCTUARY, Ex 25:8 make a s. for me
 Ps 73:17 Until I entered the grand s. of God
SAND, Ge 22:17 your offspring like grains of s.
 Re 20:8 number as the s. of the sea
SANHEDRIN, Ac 5:41 went from before S., rejoicing
SARAH, Ge 17:19 S. will bear you a son
 1Pe 3:6 S. obeyed Abraham, calling him lord
SATAN, Job 1:6 S. entered among them
 Zec 3:2 May Jehovah rebuke you, S.
 Mt 4:10 Go away, S.! For it is written
 Mt 16:23 to Peter: Get behind me, S.!
 Mr 4:15 S. comes and takes away the word sown
 Ro 16:20 God will crush S. under your feet
 1Co 5:5 hand such a man over to S.
 2Co 2:11 that we not be overreached by S.
 2Co 11:14 S. disguising as angel of light
 2Th 2:9 is by the operation of S.
 Re 12:9 serpent, one called Devil and S.
 Re 20:2 S., and bound him for 1,000 years
SAUL, 1Sa 15:11 regret that I made S. king
 Ac 7:58 at the feet of young man called S.
 Ac 8:3 S. began to ravage the congregation
 Ac 9:1 S., still breathing threat and murder
 Ac 9:4 S., S., why are you persecuting me?
SAVE, Isa 59:1 hand of Jehovah not too short to s.
 Mt 16:25 whoever wants to s. his life
 Lu 19:10 Son of man came to seek and s.
 1Ti 4:16 s. yourself and those who listen
SAVED, Mt 24:22 unless days cut short, no flesh s.
SAVIOR, 2Sa 22:3 my secure refuge, my s.
 Ac 5:31 exalted this one as Chief Agent and S.
SCALES, Le 19:36 should use accurate s.
 Pr 11:1 Dishonest s. detestable to Jehovah
SCARLET, Isa 1:18 Though your sins are like s.
SCENE, 1Co 7:31 s. of the world is changing
SCEPTER, Ge 49:10 s. will not depart from Judah
 Ps 2:9 will break them with an iron s.
SCHOOLS, Joh 7:15 has not studied the s.?
SCREAMING, Eph 4:31 anger, wrath, s., and
SCRIPTURE, 2Ti 3:16 All S. is inspired by God
SCRIPTURES, Mt 22:29 you know neither the S. nor
 Lu 24:32 hearts burning as he was opening up S.
 Ac 17:2 he reasoned with them from the S.
 Ac 17:11 carefully examining the S. daily
 Ro 15:4 comfort from the S. we have hope
SCROLLS, Re 20:12 before throne, s. opened
SCRUTINY, 1Co 11:28 approve himself after s.
SEA, Ex 14:21 turning the s. into dry ground
 Isa 57:20 wicked are like s. that cannot calm down
SEAL, Ca 8:6 Place me as a s. upon your heart
 2Co 1:22 put his s. on us and given us token
SEALED, Da 12:9 words s. up until time of the end
 Eph 1:13 After you believed, you were s.
 Re 7:3 until after we have s. the slaves
SEARCH, 1Ch 28:9 If you s. for him, he will be found
 Ps 119:176 lost sheep. S. for your servant, for I
 Pr 25:2 glory of kings is to s. through a matter
 Isa 55:6 S. for Jehovah while he may be found
 Eze 34:11 I myself will s. for my sheep
 Lu 15:8 sweep house and s. carefully until she finds
 1Pe 1:10 diligent inquiry and careful s.
SEASONS, Da 2:21 He changes times and s.
 Ac 1:7 not belong to you to know times or s.
 1Th 5:1 as for the times and the s.

SECOND DEATH, Re 2:11 not harmed by the s.
  Re 20:6 over these the s. has no authority
  Re 20:14 This means s., the lake of fire
SECRET, Ps 91:1 s. place of the Most High
  Php 4:12 learned s. of how to be full and
SECT, Ac 28:22 s. spoken against everywhere
  Tit 3:10 man who promotes a s., reject him
SECTS, 2Pe 2:1 quietly bring in destructive s.
SECURE, Pr 12:3 No man be s. by wickedness
SECURITY, 1Ki 4:25 Israel lived in s., everyone under
  Pr 17:18 shakes hands and agrees to put up s.
  Isa 32:17 fruitage of righteousness will be s.
  Ho 2:18 I will make them lie down in s.
SEDUCES, Pr 7:21 She s. him with smooth speech
SEED, Lu 8:11 The s. is the word of God
SEEK, Zep 2:3 S. Jehovah, all you meek ones
  Ac 17:27 so that they would s. God
SEEKING, Col 3:1 go on s. the things above
SEEN, Joh 1:18 No man has s. God at any time
  Joh 14:9 has s. me has s. the Father
SELF-CONTROL, 1Co 7:5 tempting you for lack of s.
  Ga 5:22, 23 fruitage of the spirit is s.
SELF-SUFFICIENT, Php 4:11 learned to be s.
SELF-WILLED, 2Pe 2:10 Daring and s.
SEND, Isa 6:8 Here I am! S. me!
SENNACHERIB, 2Ki 19:16 words S. sent to taunt God
SENSES, 1Ki 8:47 they come to their s. and return
  Lu 15:17 When he came to his s., he said
SENTENCE, Ec 8:11 s. has not been executed
  speedily
  2Co 1:9 felt we had the s. of death
SEPARATE, Mt 25:32 he will s. people one from
  Ro 8:39 to s. us from God's love in Christ
  1Co 7:10 wife should not s. from husband
SERPENT, Ge 3:4 s. said to the woman:
  Joh 3:14 as Moses lifted up the s., so the Son
SERVANT, Isa 42:1 Look! My s., whom I support!
SERVANTS, Isa 65:13 My s. will eat, but you
SERVE, Jos 24:15 choose whom you will s.
  1Ch 28:9 s. with complete heart, delightful soul
  Ps 100:2 S. Jehovah with rejoicing
SEXUAL IMMORALITY, Mt 15:19 out of heart s.
  Ac 15:20 to abstain from s., and from blood
  1Co 10:8 Neither let us practice s.
  Ga 5:19 s., uncleanness, brazen conduct
  Eph 5:3 Let s. not even be mentioned
  1Th 4:3 will of God, abstain from s.
SEXUALLY IMMORAL, 1Co 5:9 company with s.
  1Co 6:9 s. will not inherit Kingdom
SHADOW, 1Ch 29:15 our days are like a s.
  Ps 91:1 lodge under the s. of the Almighty
  Col 2:17 are a s. of things to come
SHADOWS, Jas 1:17 does not vary like the shifting s.
SHAKE, Hag 2:7 I will s. all the nations
SHAKEN, 1Th 3:3 no one s. by tribulations
  2Th 2:2 not to be quickly s. from your reason
SHAME, Ps 25:3 none who hope in you put to s.
  1Co 4:14 not to put you to s., but to admonish
SHAMEFUL, Eph 5:4 s. conduct nor foolish talking
SHARE, La 3:24 Jehovah is my s.
  Ro 12:13 s. according to their needs
SHEEP, Ps 100:3 his people and s. of his pasture
  Isa 53:7 brought like a s. to the slaughter
  Eze 34:12 I will care for my s.
  Mt 25:33 he will put the s. on his right
  Joh 21:16 Shepherd my little s.
SHEOL. See GRAVE.
SHEPHERD, Ps 23:1 Jehovah is my S.
  Isa 40:11 like a s. he will care for his flock
  Eze 37:24 David one s. they will all have
  Zec 13:7 Strike the s., and let the flock be
  Mt 9:36 they were like sheep without a s.

Joh 10:11 I am the fine s.; surrenders his life
Joh 10:14 I am the fine s. I know my sheep
Joh 10:16 will become one flock, one s.
Ac 20:28 overseers, to s. the congregation of God
1Pe 5:2 S. the flock under your care
SHEPHERDS, Eze 34:2 s. feeding themselves!
  Eph 4:11 some as s. and teachers
SHIELD, Ps 84:11 Jehovah is a sun and a s.
  Eph 6:16 take up the large s. of faith
SHILOH, Ge 49:10 until S. comes
SHINING ONE, Isa 14:12 fallen from heaven, o s.
SHIPWRECK, 2Co 11:25 three times I experienced s.
  1Ti 1:19 resulting in the s. of their faith
SHOCKING, Joh 6:60 This speech is s.; who can
SHOULDER, Zep 3:9 to serve him s. to s.
SHOWS, Joh 5:20 Father s. the Son things he does
SHREWD, Pr 12:23 s. man conceals what he knows
  Pr 14:15 s. one ponders each step
  Pr 22:3 s. sees the danger and conceals
SHRINK, Heb 10:39 who s. back to destruction
SICK, Isa 33:24 no resident will say: I am s.
  Jas 5:14 Is there anyone s. among you?
SICKBED, Ps 41:3 will sustain him on his s.
SICKNESSES, Isa 53:4 he carried our s.
SIGHING, Isa 35:10 grief and s. will flee away
  Eze 9:4 mark the men s. and groaning
SIGN, Mt 24:3 the s. of your presence?
  Mt 24:30 Then the s. of Son of man will appear
SIGNS, Lu 21:25 there will be s. in sun and moon
  2Th 2:9 and lying s. and wonders
SILENCE, 1Pe 2:15 s. the ignorant talk of
SILENT, Ps 4:4 Have your say in heart and keep s.
  Ps 32:3 When kept s., my bones wasted away
  Ec 3:7 time to be s. and time to speak
  Isa 53:7 like ewe that is s. before shearers
SILVER, Pr 2:4 seeking for it as for s.
  Eze 7:19 will throw their s. into the streets
  Zep 1:18 Neither s. nor gold able to save
SIMON, Ac 8:18 S. offered them money
SIN, Ge 4:7 s. is crouching at the door
  Ge 39:9 badness and s. against God?
  1Ki 8:46 there is no man who does not s.
  Ps 32:1 Happy is the one whose s. is covered
  Ps 38:18 I was troubled by my s.
  Isa 53:12 he carried the s. of many
  Jer 31:34 I will no longer remember their s.
  Eze 33:14 When wicked turns away from s.
  Mt 18:15 brother commits a s., go and
  Mr 3:29 blasphemes the spirit, everlasting s.
  Joh 1:29 Lamb of God who takes away s. of world!
  Ro 5:12 through one man s. entered world
  Ro 6:14 s. must not be master over you
  Ro 6:23 the wages s. pays is death
  Jas 4:17 knows right yet does not do it, a s.
  1Jo 1:7 blood of Jesus cleanses us from all s.
  1Jo 2:1 if anyone does commit a s., we
  1Jo 5:17 All unrighteousness is s.
SINAI, Ex 19:20 Jehovah came down upon Mount S.
SING, Ps 96:1 S. to Jehovah a new song
SINGERS, 1Ch 15:16 David told to appoint s.
SINGING, Mt 26:30 after s. praises, they went out
  Eph 5:19 s. and accompanying yourselves
SINNED, 2Sa 12:13 David: I have s. against Jehovah
  Ro 3:23 all s. and fall short of glory of God
SINNER, Lu 15:7 joy in heaven over s. who repents
  Lu 18:13 God, be gracious to me, a s.
SINNERS, Ps 1:5 nor s. remain in the assembly
  Joh 9:31 We know that God does not listen to s.
  Ro 5:8 while we were yet s., Christ died
SINS, Isa 1:18 Though your s. are like scarlet
  Isa 38:17 thrown all my s. behind your back
  Ac 3:19 Repent to get your s. blotted out

Ro 3:25 forgiving **s.** that occurred in the past
1Ti 5:24 **s.** of other men become evident later
Jas 5:15 if committed **s.**, will be forgiven
SISTER, De 27:22 lies down with his **s.**
SIT, Ps 110:1 S. at my right hand until I place
SKILL, Ex 35:35 filled them with **s.** to do the work
SKILLFUL, Pr 22:29 man **s.** at his work? He will
SLANDER, Le 19:16 not go around spreading **s.**
SLANDERED, 1Co 4:13 when **s.**, we answer mildly
SLANDERER, Pr 16:28 separates close friends
SLAPPING, Joh 19:3 also kept **s.** him in the face
SLAUGHTER, Isa 53:7 brought like a sheep to the **s.**
SLAUGHTERING, Ps 44:22 as sheep for **s.**
SLAVE, Pr 22:7 borrower is a **s.** to the lender
Mt 24:45 Who is the faithful and discreet **s.?**
Mt 25:21 Well done, good and faithful **s.!**
Joh 8:34 every doer of sin is a **s.** of sin
Ga 5:13 through love **s.** for one another
SLAVES, Lu 17:10 We are good-for-nothing **s.**
1Co 7:23 stop becoming **s.** of men
SLEEP, Pr 6:10 A little **s.**, a little slumbering
Ro 13:11 the hour to awake from **s.**
1Th 5:6 let us not **s.** on as the rest do
SLEEPLESS, 2Co 6:5 by **s.** nights, times without food
2Co 11:27 in **s.** nights often
SLIPPED IN, Jude 4 men have **s.** among you
SLIPPERY, Ps 73:18 you place them on **s.** ground
SLOW, Jas 1:19 **s.** to speak, **s.** to anger
2Pe 3:9 Jehovah not **s.** concerning promise
SLUGGISH, Pr 19:15 **s.** person will go hungry
Mt 25:26 Wicked and **s.** slave
SMALL, Zec 4:10 despised the day of **s.** beginnings?
SMOOTH, Ro 16:18 by **s.** talk they seduce
SNARE, Pr 29:25 Trembling at men is a **s.**
Lu 21:34, 35 day instantly upon you as a **s.**
SNOW, Isa 1:18 sins made as white as **s.**
SODOM, Ge 19:24 sulfur and fire on **S.**
2Pe 2:6 condemned **S.**, setting a pattern
Jude 7 **S.** and Gomorrah, warning example
SOIL, Mt 13:23 sown upon the fine **s.**
SOLDIER, 2Ti 2:4 No **s.** involves himself in
SOLID, Heb 5:14 **s.** food belongs to mature people
SOLOMON, 1Ki 4:29 God gave **S.** wisdom and
Mt 6:29 not even **S.** in all his glory was arrayed
SON, Ps 2:12 Honor the **s.**, or God will
Pr 13:24 Whoever holds back rod hates his **s.**
Pr 15:20 wise **s.** makes father rejoice
Mt 3:17 This is my **S.**, the beloved, whom I
Lu 15:13 younger **s.** squandered property
SONG, Ps 98:1 Sing to Jehovah a new **s.**
Ac 16:25 Paul and Silas praising God with **s.**
SONGS, Ne 12:46 **s.** of praise and thanksgiving
Col 3:16 spiritual **s.** sung with gratitude
SON OF MAN, Da 7:13 with the clouds, like **s.** coming
Mt 10:23 until **S.** arrives
Lu 21:27 will see **S.** coming in a cloud
SONS, Ge 6:2 **s.** of God taking wives
1Sa 8:3 his **s.** did not walk in his ways
Job 38:7 **s.** of God shouting in applause
Isa 54:13 all your **s.** will be taught by Jehovah
Isa 66:8 Zion gave birth to **s.**
Ro 8:14 all led by spirit are God's **s.**
SORCERER, Ac 13:6 Bar-Jesus, who was a **s.** and
SORROW, Ps 90:10 years are filled with **s.**
1Th 4:13 not **s.** as rest do who have no hope
SORT, 2Pe 3:11 what **s.** of people you ought to be
SOUL, Nu 31:28 one **s.** of the people and of the flock
Eze 18:4 The **s.** who sins will die
Mt 22:37 love Jehovah with your whole **s.**
SOUND, Ps 19:4 into all the earth their **s.** gone out
SOURCE, Ps 36:9 With you is the **s.** of life
Jer 2:13 abandoned me, the **s.** of living water

SOVEREIGN LORD, Ps 73:28 **S.** Jehovah my refuge
Ac 4:24 **S.**, you made heaven and earth
SOW, Ec 11:6 **S.** your seed in the morning and
2Pe 2:22 bathed **s.** to rolling in mire
SOWING, Ps 126:5 **s.** seed with tears
Ga 6:7 whatever a person is **s.**, will reap
SPARROWS, Mt 10:29 Two **s.** sell for a coin
SPAT, Mt 26:67 Then they **s.** in his face and hit him
SPEAR, 1Sa 18:11 hurled **s.**, saying: I will pin David
SPECULATIONS, 1Ti 1:4 merely give rise to **s.**
SPEECHLESS, Isa 35:6 tongue of **s.** will shout for joy
SPEED, Isa 60:22 I Jehovah, will **s.** it up
SPENT, 2Co 12:15 gladly be completely **s.** for you
SPIRIT, Nu 11:25 took away some of the **s.**
1Sa 16:13 **s.** began to empower David
2Sa 23:2 **s.** of Jehovah spoke through me
Ps 51:10 put within me a new **s.**, steadfast
Ps 51:17 sacrifices to God are a broken **s.**
Ps 104:29 take away their **s.**, they die
Ps 146:4 **s.** goes out, he returns to the ground
Ec 12:7 **s.** returns to God who gave it
Isa 61:1 The **s.** of Jehovah is upon me
Joe 2:28 I will pour out my **s.** on every
Zec 4:6 Not by force, but by my **s.**
Mt 3:16 God's **s.** descending like a dove
Mt 12:31 blasphemy against **s.** not be forgiven
Mt 26:41 The **s.** is eager, but the flesh
Lu 23:46 into your hands I entrust my **s.**
Joh 4:24 God is a **s.**, worship with **s.** and
Joh 16:13 **s.** of the truth, he will guide you
Ro 8:16 The **s.** bears witness with our **s.**
Ro 8:26 **s.** pleads for us with unuttered
2Co 3:17 Jehovah is the **S.**
Ga 5:16 Keep walking by **s.** and you will
Ga 5:22 the fruitage of the **s.** is love
Ga 6:8 sowing with a view to the **s.**
Eph 6:12 struggle against wicked **s.** forces
1Pe 3:18 made alive in the **s.**
SPIRITISM, Ga 5:20 idolatry, **s.**, hostility
SPIRIT MEDIUM, De 18:11 anyone who consults a **s.**
SPIRITUAL, Mt 5:3 conscious of their **s.** need
Ro 1:11 may impart some **s.** gift to you
1Co 2:15 **s.** man examines all things
1Co 15:44 it is raised up a **s.** body
SPOIL, Jer 39:18 will have your life as **s.**
SPROUT, Jer 23:5 will raise to David a righteous **s.**
SQUANDERED, Lu 15:13 **s.** his property by
STABILIZED, Col 2:7 **s.** in the faith
STAIRWAY, Ge 28:12 **s.** reached the heavens
STAKE, Mr 15:25 they nailed him to the **s.**
Lu 23:21 To the **s.** with him!
Ga 3:13 Accursed is man hung upon a **s.**
STANDARD, 2Ti 1:13 the **s.** of wholesome words
STAND FIRM, 1Co 16:13 **s.** in the faith
STANDING, 1Co 10:12 let one who thinks he is **s.**
STARS, Ps 147:4 he calls all **s.** by name
Mt 24:29 Immediately after tribulation, **s.** will fall
Re 2:1 seven **s.** in his right hand
STEADFAST, 1Co 15:58 be **s.**, immovable
STEAL, Ex 20:15 You must not **s.**
Pr 30:9 **s.** and dishonor the name of my God
Eph 4:28 one who steals **s.** no more
STEP, Jer 10:23 not belong to man to direct his **s.**
Ga 6:1 if a man takes a false **s.**
STEPS, 1Pe 2:21 follow his **s.** closely
STEWARD, Lu 12:42 Who really is the faithful **s.?**
STEWARDS, 1Co 4:2 **s.** to be found faithful
STICK, Ge 2:24 leave mother and **s.** to his wife
Jos 23:8 you must **s.** to Jehovah
STINGY, Pr 23:6 Do not eat food of a **s.** person
STONE, Da 2:34 **s.** cut out, not by hands
Mt 21:42 The **s.** that the builders rejected

STONES, Lu 19:40 if silent, the s. would cry out
STOP, Job 37:14 s. and consider wonderful works
STRANGERS, Joh 10:5 not know the voice of s.
STRAW, Isa 65:25 lion will eat s. like the bull
    Mt 7:3 s. in brother's eye but not notice
    1Co 3:12 if anyone builds on the foundation s.
STRAYED, Ps 119:176 I s. like a lost sheep
STRENGTH, Ps 29:11 will give s. to his people
    Ps 31:10 My s. waning because of error
    Ps 84:7 will walk on from s. to s.
    Pr 17:22 crushed spirit saps one's s.
    Mr 12:30 love Jehovah with your whole s.
    Php 4:13 For all things I have s. through
STRENGTHEN, Isa 35:3 S. the weak hands
    Lu 22:32 once you have returned, s. brothers
STRENGTHENED, Da 30:6 s. himself by Jehovah
    Ac 14:22 s. disciples, encouraging to remain in faith
STRESS, 1Sa 1:15 I am a woman under great s.
STRONG, Jos 1:7 be courageous and very s.
    Isa 35:4 Be s. Do not be afraid
    Ro 15:1 bear weaknesses of those not s.
STRONGHOLD, Ps 18:2 Jehovah is my s.
    Isa 25:4 s. to the lowly, s. to the poor
STRUGGLE, Eph 6:12 s., not against blood and flesh
STUBBORNLY, Ac 19:9 s. refused to believe
STUCK, Lu 22:28 you s. with me in my trials
STUDIED, Joh 7:15 has not s. at the schools?
STUMBLE, Ps 119:165 love your law; nothing can s.
    Mt 5:29 right eye making you s., tear it out
    Lu 17:2 to s. one of these little ones
    1Co 8:13 if food makes my brother s.
    Jas 3:2 we all s. many times
STUMBLING, Mt 13:41 collect things that cause s.
    1Co 10:32 Keep from becoming causes for s.
    Php 1:10 be flawless and not s. others
STUMBLING BLOCK, Ro 14:13 not to put s.
STUMP, Isa 11:1 twig out of s. of Jesse
    Da 4:15 leave the s. with its roots
SUBJECT, Lu 2:51 he continued s. to them
    1Pe 2:13 s. yourselves to a king as superior
SUBJECTED, 1Co 15:27 s. all things under his feet
SUBJECTION, Ge 1:28 have in s. every living creature
    Ro 13:1 be in s. to superior authorities
SUBMISSIVE, Heb 13:17 s. to those taking the lead
SUCCEED, 1Ki 2:3 then you will s. in everything
    Ps 1:3 everything he does will s.
SUCCESS, Isa 55:11 my word will have sure s.
SUCCESSFUL, Jos 1:8 then your way will be s.
    2Ch 20:20 Put faith in his prophets, be s.
SUFFER, Ro 8:17 heirs, provided we s. together
    Php 1:29 privilege to s. in his behalf
    1Pe 3:14 if s. for righteousness, happy
SUFFERINGS, Ro 8:18 s. do not amount to anything
    Heb 2:10 Chief Agent perfect through s.
    1Pe 5:9 knowing that the same kind of s.
SUFFERS, 1Co 12:26 If one member s., all other
SUFFICIENT, 1Pe 4:3 time that has passed by is s.
SUIT, Eph 6:13 complete s. of armor
SUMMER, Mt 24:32 you know that s. is near
SUN, Jos 10:12 S., stand still over Gibeon
    Mt 24:29 Immediately after tribulation, s. darkened
    Ac 2:20 s. will be turned into darkness
SUNRISE, Isa 41:2 raised up someone from the s.
SUPERABUNDANTLY, Eph 3:20 do more than s.
SUPERIOR, Ro 13:1 subjection to the s. authorities
    Php 2:3 consider others s. to you
SUPPLICATION, Jas 5:16 righteous man's s.
SUPPLICATIONS, 1Ti 2:1 s., prayers be made
    Heb 5:7 Christ offered up s. and petitions
SURPASSING, 1Co 12:31 I will show you a s. way
SWEAR, Ge 22:16 By myself I s., declares Jehovah
    Mt 5:34 Do not s. at all

SWINE, Lu 8:33 demons went into the s.
    Lu 15:15 sent him into his fields to herd s.
SWORD, 1Sa 17:47 not with s. that Jehovah saves
    Mt 26:52 who take up the s. will perish by the s.
    Eph 6:17 s. of the spirit, God's word
    Heb 4:12 word of God sharper than s.
SWORDS, Isa 2:4 will beat their s. into plowshares
SYMPATHIZE, Heb 4:15 s. with our weaknesses

T

TABERNACLE, Ps 78:60 finally forsook t. of Shiloh
    Ps 84:1 How lovely your grand t. is
TABLE, Da 11:27 sit at one t. speaking lies
    1Co 10:21 partaking of the t. of Jehovah and
TABLETS, Ex 31:18 gave Moses two t.
TALENTS, Mt 25:15 five t. to one, two to another
TALK, Pr 14:23 mere t. leads to want
TALKS, Ac 15:32 encouraged brothers with many t.
TARSHISH, Jon 1:3 Jonah got up to run away to T.
TARTARUS, 2Pe 2:4 threw angels into T.
TASTE, Ps 34:8 T. and see that Jehovah is good
TASTED, Heb 6:4 t. the heavenly free gift
    1Pe 2:3 you have t. that the Lord is kind
TATTOO, Le 19:28 must not make t. markings
TAUGHT, Isa 54:13 all your sons will be t. by Jehovah
    1Sa 17:26 that he should t. the battle line
TAUNT, 1Sa 17:26 that he should t. the battle line
TAUNTS, Pr 27:11 a reply to him who t. me
TAX, Mt 17:25 From whom do kings receive t.?
    Lu 20:22 Is it lawful to pay head t. to Caesar?
    Ro 13:7 to one who calls for t., the t.
TAX COLLECTOR, Mt 18:17 let him be to you as a t.
    Lu 18:11 I thank you I am not like this t.
TAXES, Lu 23:2 forbidding paying of t. to Caesar
    Ro 13:6 That is why you are also paying t.
TEACH, Ezr 7:10 Ezra prepared his heart to t.
    Ps 143:10 T. me to do your will
    Pr 9:9 T. righteous, and he will add
    Jer 31:34 no longer t. each one his brother
    Mt 15:9 they t. commands of men as doctrines
    Joh 7:16 What I t. is not mine, but belongs
    1Ti 2:12 I do not permit a woman to t.
TEACHERS, Ps 119:99 I have more insight than my t.
    Eph 4:11 some as shepherds and t.
TEACHING, Isa 48:17 t. you to benefit yourself
    Mt 7:28 astounded at his way of t.
    Mt 7:29 t. as a person having authority
    Mt 28:20 t. them to observe all the things
    Ro 2:21 t. someone else, not teach yourself?
TEAR, Re 21:4 wipe out every t. from their eyes
TEARING, Ro 14:20 Stop t. down the work of God
TEARS, 2Ki 20:5 heard your prayer, seen your t.
    Ps 6:6 I soak my bed with t.
    Ps 126:5 sowing seed with t. will reap with
    Ec 4:1 t. of the oppressed, no one to comfort them
    Ac 20:19 slaving for the Lord with t. and trials
    Ac 20:31 admonishing each of you with t.
    Heb 5:7 Christ offered up petitions with t.
TEMPER, Pr 16:32 one controlling t. better than
TEMPLE. See also HOUSE, Ps 11:4 Jehovah in t.
    Ps 27:4 look with appreciation upon his t.
    Jer 7:4 the t. of Jehovah, the t. of Jehovah
    Eze 41:13 He measured the t., 100 cubits long
    Mal 3:1 suddenly the Lord will come to his t.
    Mt 21:12 entered the t. and threw out those
    Joh 2:19 Tear down this t., and in three days
    1Co 3:16 you yourselves are God's t.
TEMPLES, Ac 17:24 not dwell in handmade t.
TEMPLE SERVANTS, Ezr 8:20 gave t. to Levites
TEMPORARY, Heb 11:13 were t. residents
    Heb 11:25 rather than t. enjoyment of sin
TEMPTATION, Mt 6:13 do not bring us into t.
    Mt 26:41 pray that you may not enter into t.
    1Co 10:13 No t. except what is common

TEN, Ge 18:32 I will not destroy for the sake of t.
TEN COMMANDMENTS, Ex 34:28 He wrote the T.
TENDER, Jas 5:11 Jehovah is very t. in affection
TENT, Jos 18:1 set up t. of meeting at Shiloh
  Ps 15:1 who may be a guest in your t.?
  Isa 54:2 lengthen your t. cords
  2Co 12:9 power of Christ remain like a t.
  Re 21:3 t. of God is with mankind
TENTH, Ne 10:38 Levites offer up a t. of the t.
TENTMAKERS, Ac 18:3 worked, were t. by trade
TERRITORY, Ro 15:23 no longer have untouched t.
TERROR, Pr 3:25 You will not fear any sudden t.
TERRORS, Ps 91:5 will not fear the t. of the night
TEST, Mal 3:10 t. me out, please, in this regard
  Ac 5:9 make a t. of the spirit of Jehovah?
  1Co 10:9 Neither let us put Jehovah to t.
  1Jo 4:1 but t. the inspired statements
TESTED, Pr 27:21 person is t. by praise he receives
  1Ti 3:10 t. as to fitness first
  Jas 1:3 t. quality of your faith
TESTING, De 13:3 Jehovah is t. you to know
  Lu 8:13 in a season of t., they fall away
  2Co 13:5 t. whether you are in the faith
THANK, Joh 11:41 Father, t. you that you heard me
  1Co 1:4 I always t. God for you in view of
THANKED, Ac 28:15 catching sight, Paul t. God
THANKFUL, Col 3:15 And show yourselves t.
THANKLESS, Pr 29:21 pampered become t.
THANKS, Ps 92:1 good to give t. to Jehovah
  Eph 5:20 giving t. to God for everything
THANKSGIVING, Ps 95:2 come with t.
THEATRICAL, 1Co 4:9 become a t. spectacle
THIEF, Pr 6:30 if t. steals when hungry
  Pr 29:24 partner of a t. hates himself
  Mt 24:43 If had known at what watch t. coming
  1Th 5:2 day is coming as a t. in the night
THIEVES, Mt 6:20 heaven, where t. do not break in
  1Co 6:10 t. will not inherit Kingdom
THINK, Mt 24:44 at an hour that you do not t.
  Ro 12:3 not to t. more of himself than
THINKING ABILITY, Pr 1:4 give young man t.
THIRST, Isa 49:10 nor will they t.
THIRSTY, Isa 55:1 Come, all you t. ones
  Joh 7:37 If anyone is t., let him come to me
THORN, 2Co 12:7 given a t. in the flesh
THORNBUSH, Ex 3:2 appeared in the flame of t.
THORNS, Mr 15:17 braided a crown of t. and put it
THOUGHT, 2Co 10:5 every t. obedient to Christ
  Re 17:17 into hearts to carry out his t.
THOUGHTLESS, Pr 12:18 T. speech is like the stabs
THOUGHTS, Ps 26:2 refine my innermost t.
  Ps 139:17 how precious your t. are!
  Ps 146:4 on that very day his t. perish
  Pr 20:5 t. of man's heart are like deep waters
  Isa 55:8 my t. are not your t.
THOUSAND, Ps 91:7 A t. will fall at your side
  Isa 60:22 little one will become a t.
  2Pe 3:8 one day is as a t. years
THREATEN, Ac 4:17 let us t. them and tell
  1Pe 2:23 When suffering, he did not t.
THREATENING, Eph 6:9 the same way, not t.
THREE, De 16:16 T. times a year, all males should
THRONE, Ps 45:6 God is your t. forever and ever
  Isa 6:1 saw Jehovah sitting on a lofty t.
  Mt 25:31 When Son of man comes, will sit on his t.
  Lu 1:32 God will give him t. of David his father
THRONES, Da 7:9 t. were set in place
THWART, Isa 14:27 Jehovah decided, who can t.?
TICKLED, 2Ti 4:3 to have their ears t.
TIGHTFISTED, De 15:7 do not be t.
TIME, Ec 3:1 t. for every activity
  Ec 9:11 t. and unexpected events

TEN, Da 7:25 for a t., times, and half a t.
  Joh 7:8 my t. has not yet fully come
  1Co 7:29 the t. left is reduced
  Eph 5:16 making best use of your t.
TIMOTHY, Ac 16:1 a disciple named T. was there
  1Co 4:17 sending T., beloved and faithful child
  1Ti 1:2 T., genuine child in the faith
TIRED, Pr 25:25 Like cold water on a t. soul
  Isa 40:29 He gives power to the t. one
  Isa 50:4 answer t. one with the right word
  Heb 12:3 you may not get t. and give up
TIRE OUT, Isa 40:31 they will walk and not t.
  Ga 6:9 we will reap if we do not t.
TIRES, Isa 40:28 He never t. out or grows weary
TIRESOME, Mal 1:13 Look! How t.!
TITHE, Mal 3:10 Bring entire t. into storehouse
TOKEN, 2Co 1:22 t. of what is to come, the spirit
  Eph 1:14 a t. in advance of our inheritance
TOLERATE, Hab 1:13 you cannot t. wickedness
TOLERATED, Ro 9:22 God t. vessels of wrath
TOLERATION, 2Ki 10:16 see my t. of no rivalry
TOMORROW, Pr 27:1 Do not boast about t.
  1Co 15:32 eat and drink, for t. we die
TONGUE, Ps 34:13 guard t. from what is bad
  Pr 18:21 Death and life in the power of t.
  Isa 35:6 t. of speechless will shout for joy
  Isa 50:4 Jehovah has given me t. of those taught
  Jas 1:26 keep a tight rein on his t.
  Jas 3:8 no human can tame the t.
TONGUES, 1Co 13:8 there are t., they will cease
  1Co 14:22 t. are a sign for unbelievers
  Re 7:9 out of all nations and tribes and t.
TOOL, Ec 10:10 If an iron t. is dull
TORN, Php 1:23 I am t. between these two things
TORTURE STAKE, Mt 10:38 does not accept t. and
  Lu 9:23 and pick up his t. day after day
TOSSED, Eph 4:14 no longer be children, t. about
TOUCH, Isa 52:11 t. nothing unclean!
TOUCHED, Mt 8:3 t. him, saying: I want to!
TOUCHES, Pr 6:29 no one who t. her unpunished
TOUCHING, 2Co 6:17 quit t. the unclean thing
TOWER, Ge 11:4 let us build for ourselves a t.
  Pr 18:10 name of Jehovah is a strong t.
  Lu 13:4 18 on whom the t. in Siloam fell, killing
TRADITION, Mt 15:3 overstep because of your t.?
  Mr 7:13 make the word of God invalid by your t.
TRADITIONS, Ga 1:14 zealous for the t. of my fathers
TRAIN, Pr 22:6 T. a boy; even when he grows old
TRAINING, 1Pe 5:10 God will finish your t.
TRAMPLED, Heb 10:29 t. on the Son of God
TRANSFIGURED, Mt 17:2 was t. before them
TRANSFORMED, Ro 12:2 t. by making your mind over
TRAP, Ps 91:3 rescue from the t. of the birdcatcher
TREACHEROUS, Jer 3:7 heart is more t. than
TREACHEROUSLY, Mal 2:15 not deal t. with wife
TREASURE, Mt 6:21 where t. is, there heart will be
  Mt 13:44 Kingdom like a t., hidden in field
  Lu 6:45 good out of the good t. of his heart
  Lu 12:33 a never-failing t. in the heavens
  2Co 4:7 we have this t. in earthen vessels
TREASURES, Pr 2:4 searching as for hidden t.
  Pr 10:2 t. gained by wickedness of no benefit
TREE, Ge 2:9 t. of knowledge of good and bad
  Ge 2:9 t. of life in the middle
  Ps 1:3 will be like a t. planted by water
  Da 4:14 Chop down the t., cut off its branches
  Re 2:7 will grant to eat of the t. of life
TREES, Isa 61:3 called big t. of righteousness
  Eze 47:12 All sorts of t. will grow on both banks
  Re 22:14 authority to go to t. of life
TREMBLING, Pr 29:25 T. at men is a snare
  Php 2:12 working out salvation with fear and t.

TRIAL, Jas 1:12 Happy who keeps on enduring t.
TRIALS, Lu 22:28 you stuck with me in my t.
    Jas 1:2 all joy, when you meet with t.
TRIBES, Ge 49:28 these are the 12 t. of Israel
TRIBULATION, Mt 24:21 great t. such as
    Ro 5:3 rejoice, since t. produces endurance
    Ro 12:12 Rejoice in hope. Endure under t.
    1Co 7:28 who marry, have t. in their flesh
    2Co 4:17 though t. is momentary
    Re 7:14 ones who come out of the great t.
TRIBULATIONS, Ac 14:22 into Kingdom through t.
TRIUMPHAL, 2Co 2:14 leads us in t. procession
TRUE, Joh 17:3 coming to know you, the only t. God
TRUST, Ps 9:10 knowing your name will t. in you
    Ps 56:11 In God I put my t.; I am not afraid
    Ps 62:8 T. in him at all times
    Ps 146:3 Do not put t. in princes nor
    Pr 3:5 T. in Jehovah with all your heart
    Jer 17:5 Cursed is the man who puts t. in humans
    2Co 1:9 t., not in ourselves, but in God
TRUSTS, Ps 84:12 happy is the man who t. in you
    Pr 28:26 Whoever t. in his own heart is stupid
TRUSTWORTHINESS, Tit 2:10 showing complete t.
TRUSTWORTHY, Ex 18:21 select capable, t. men
    Ps 19:7 reminder of God t.
    Ps 33:4 everything Jehovah does is t.
TRUTH, Ps 15:2 speaking the t. in his heart
    Ps 119:160 essence of your word is t.
    Pr 23:23 Buy t. and never sell it
    Joh 4:24 must worship with spirit and t.
    Joh 8:32 know the t., and the t. will set you free
    Joh 14:6 I am the way, the t. and the life
    Joh 16:13 spirit of t. will guide you into all t.
    Joh 17:17 Sanctify by t.; your word is t.
    Joh 18:38 Pilate said to him: What is t.?
    2Co 13:8 we can do nothing against the t.
    Eph 4:25 each one of you speak t.
    2Pe 1:12 you are well-established in the t.
    3Jo 4 that my children walking in the t.
TURBAN, Eze 21:26 Remove t., take off crown
TWOS, Lu 10:1 designated 70 and sent out by t.

U

UNANIMOUS, Ac 15:25 come to a u. decision
UNBELIEVERS, 1Co 6:6 to court before u.!
    2Co 6:14 not become unevenly yoked with u.
UNBELIEVING, 1Co 7:12 u. wife agreeable to staying
UNCLEAN, Le 13:45 call out, U., u.!
    Job 14:4 produce clean from someone u.?
UNCLEANNESS, Ro 1:24 God gave them up to u.
    Col 3:5 as respects sexual immorality, u.
UNDERSTAND, Ne 8:8 helped u. what was read
    Job 6:24 help me to u. my mistake
    Ps 119:27 Make me u. meaning of your orders
UNDERSTANDING, 1Ki 3:11 you requested u.
    Pr 3:5 do not rely on your own u.
    Pr 4:7 with all you acquire, acquire u.
    Da 11:33 will impart u. to the many
    1Co 14:20 become full-grown in u.
UNDERTONE, Ac 4:13 and knew u. in an u.
    Ps 1:2 reads His law in an u.
UNDESERVED KINDNESS, Joh 1:17 u. through Jesus
    1Co 15:10 his u. was not in vain
    2Co 6:1 not accept u. and miss its purpose
    2Co 12:9 My u. is sufficient for you
UNEDUCATED, Ac 4:13 and knew, u. and ordinary
UNEXPECTED, Ec 9:11 time and u. events overtake
UNITED, Php 2:2 being completely u.
UNITY, Ps 133:1 brothers to dwell in u.!
UNJUST, De 32:4 God who is never u.
UNJUSTLY, 1Pe 2:19 agreeable when suffers u.
UNMARRIED, 1Co 7:8 I say to u. and widows
    1Co 7:32 u. man is anxious for the Lord

UNNATURAL, Jude 7 pursued u. fleshly desires
UNREALITY, Isa 41:29 images are wind and u.
UNREASONABLE, Lu 12:20 U. one, this night
UNRECEPTIVE, Mt 13:15 heart of people grown u.
UNRESTRAINED, Pr 29:15 child left u. brings shame
UNRIGHTEOUS, Ac 24:15 resurrection of u.
    1Co 6:9 u. will not inherit Kingdom
UNSEEN, 2Co 4:18 keep our eyes on things u.
UNTHINKABLE, Ge 18:25 u. that you would act in
UNWORTHILY, 1Co 11:27 drinks the cup u.
UPRIGHT, Job 1:8 Job is an u. man of integrity
UPSET, Ps 37:8 not become u. and turn to evil
URGENTLY, 2Ti 4:2 be at it, in favorable
URIM AND THUMMIM, Ex 28:30 put U. into
USE, 1Co 7:31 those making u. of the world
UTMOST, 2Ti 2:15 Do your u. to present
    2Pe 3:14 do your u. to be found spotless
UZZIAH, 2Ch 26:21 King U. remained a leper

V

VAIN, Mt 15:9 in v. they keep worshipping me
    1Co 15:58 labor is not in v. with the Lord
VALUABLE, Pr 3:9 Honor Jehovah with v. things
VEIL, 2Co 3:15 a v. lies upon their hearts
VENGEANCE, De 32:35 V. is mine, and retribution
    2Th 1:8 as he brings v. on those
VESSEL, Ac 9:15 this man is a chosen v.
    Ro 9:21 one v. for an honorable use, another
VICTORIOUS, Ro 8:37 in all things v. through the one
VIGILANT, 1Pe 4:7 v. with a view to prayers
VINE, Mic 4:4 each under his v. and fig tree
    Joh 15:1 I am the true v., and my Father
VINEYARD, Mt 20:1 to hire workers for his v.
    Mt 21:28 Child, go work today in the v.
    Lu 20:9 A man planted a v. and traveled abroad
VINEYARDS, Isa 65:21 will plant v. and eat fruitage
VIOLENCE, Ge 6:11 earth was filled with v.
    Ps 11:5 hates anyone who loves v.
    Ps 72:14 From oppression and v. he will rescue
VIOLENT, Ps 5:6 Jehovah detests v. and deceptive
VIRGINS, Mt 25:1 Kingdom likened to ten v.
    1Co 7:25 concerning v., I have no command
VISION, Da 10:14 v. yet for the days to come
VISIT, Ac 15:36 v. the brothers to see how they are
VOICE, 1Ki 19:12 After the fire, a calm, low v.
    Joh 5:28 all in the tombs will hear his v.
    Joh 10:27 My sheep listen to my v.
VOLUNTARILY, 1Ch 29:17 v. offered all these things
VOLUNTEER, Ex 36:2 heart impelled to v.
VOTED, Lu 23:51 This man had not v. in support
VOW, De 23:21 If you make a v. to Jehovah
    Jg 11:30 Jephthah made a v.

W

WAGES, Ge 31:7 changed my w. ten times
    Jer 22:13 whose w. he refuses to pay
    Ro 6:23 For the w. sin pays is death
WAIT, Ps 37:7 w. expectantly for Jehovah
WAITING, Mic 7:7 I will show a w. attitude
    Ro 8:25 keep eagerly w. with endurance
WALK, Mic 6:8 and to w. in modesty with your God!
WALKING, Joh 6:19 saw Jesus w. on the sea
WALL, Jos 6:5 the w. of the city will fall
    Da 5:5 writing on the w. of the palace
    Joe 2:7 they scale a w. like soldiers
WALLS, Eze 38:11 living unprotected by w., bars
WANDERED, Isa 53:6 Like sheep we have w. about
WAR, Isa 2:4 nor will they learn w. anymore
    Ho 2:18 I will rid the land of the sword and w.
    Re 12:7 w. broke out in heaven: Michael
    Re 16:14 w. of the great day of God
WARN, Eze 3:17 you must w. them from me
    Eze 33:9 if you w. someone wicked to turn back

WARNING, Eze 33:4 not heed the w., his blood
  1Co 10:11 they were written for a w. to us
WARRIOR, Jer 20:11 Jehovah with me like a w.
WARS, Ps 46:9 He is bringing an end to w.
WASH, 2Ki 5:10 w. seven times in the Jordan
  Ps 51:2 Thoroughly w. me from my error
  Joh 13:5 started to w. the feet of the disciples
WASHED, 1Co 6:11 you have been w. clean,
  sanctified
WASTING, 2Co 4:16 man outside is w. away
WATCH, Mt 26:41 Keep on the w. and pray
  Joh 17:12 I used to w. over them
  Eph 5:15 strict w. that you walk as wise
WATCHING, Col 3:22 not only when they are w.
WATCHTOWER, Isa 21:8 Upon the w., I am standing
WATER, Nu 20:10 w. from this crag?
  Pr 25:25 Like cold w. on a tired soul
  Isa 55:1 thirsty ones, come to the w.!
  Jer 2:13 abandoned me, the source of living w.
  Joh 4:10 he would have given you living w.
WATERED, 1Co 3:6 I planted, Apollos w.
WATERS, Pr 20:5 thoughts of heart like deep w.
  Jer 50:38 her w. will be dried up
  Zec 14:8 living w. will flow out from Jerusalem
  Re 7:17 guide them to springs of w. of life
  Re 17:1 prostitute who sits on many w.
WAY, Pr 16:25 w. seems right, but leads to death
  Isa 30:21 This is the w. Walk in it
  Joh 14:6 I am the w., the truth, and the life
  Ac 9:2 any he found who belonged to The W.
  1Co 10:13 he will also make the w. out
WAYWARDNESS, Pr 1:32 w. of inexperienced will kill
WEAK, 1Co 1:27 God chose the w. things
  2Co 12:10 when w., then I am powerful
  1Th 5:14 support the w., be patient
WEAKER, 1Pe 3:7 w. vessel, the feminine one
WEAKNESSES, Ro 14:1 Welcome man having w.
  Ro 15:1 bear the w. of those not strong
WEALTH, Ps 62:10 If w. increases, not set heart
  Pr 11:4 W. of no benefit on the day of fury
  Pr 18:11 w. of rich like wall in his imagination
  Ec 5:10 lover of w. never satisfied with income
  Eze 28:5 heart grew haughty because of w.
WEAPON, Isa 54:17 No w. formed against you
WEAPONS, 2Co 10:4 w. of our warfare are not fleshly
WEARY, Ga 6:9 let us not give up
  Mt 40:28 Jehovah never grows w.
WEEK, 1Co 16:2 first day of every w., set aside
WEEKS, Da 9:24 70 w. determined
WEEP, Lu 6:21 Happy who w. now, for you
  Ro 12:15 w. with those who w.
WEEPING, Ps 6:6 I flood my couch with w.
  Isa 65:19 no more be heard the sound of w.
WEIGHED, Da 5:27 w. and found lacking
WEIGHED DOWN, Lu 21:34 hearts never become w.
WEIGHT, Heb 12:1 let us throw off every w.
WEIGHTIER, Mt 23:23 w. matters of Law, justice and
WELCOME, Ro 14:1 W. man having weaknesses in
  Ro 15:7 w. one another, just as Christ
WELL, Mt 25:21 W. done, good and faithful slave!
WEPT, Ho 12:4 He w. and begged for his favor
  Mt 26:75 he went outside and w. bitterly
WHATEVER, Php 4:8 w. things are true, lovable
WHEAT, Mt 13:25 oversowed weeds in among w.
WHEEL, Eze 1:16 as though a w. were within a w.
WHITE, Re 7:14 washed robes and made them w.
WHOLESOME, 2Ti 1:13 standard of w. words
  Tit 2:1 consistent with w. teaching
WHOLE-SOULED, Eph 6:6 doing the will of God w.
  Col 3:23 Whatever doing, work at it w.
WICK, Isa 42:3 no smoldering w. will he extinguish
WICKED, Ps 37:10 the w. will be no more
  Pr 15:8 sacrifice of the w. detestable to Jehovah

Pr 15:29 Jehovah is far away from the w.
  Pr 29:2 when w. rules, the people groan
  Isa 26:10 w. shown favor, will not learn
  Isa 57:21 no peace for the w.
  1Jo 5:19 world lying in power of the w. one
WICKEDNESS, 1Th 5:22 Abstain from every w.
WIDOW, Ps 146:9 he sustains fatherless child and w.
  Mr 12:43 this poor w. put in more than all
  Lu 18:3 w. who kept going to him and saying
WIDOWS, Jas 1:27 look after orphans and w.
WIFE, Ge 2:24 will stick to his w.
  Ge 27:46 If Jacob takes w. from daughters
  Pr 5:18 rejoice with the w. of your youth
  Pr 12:4 capable w. a crown to husband
  Pr 18:22 finds good w., receives Jehovah's favor
  Pr 21:19 than with quarrelsome and irritable w.
  Pr 31:10 Who can find capable w.? Her value
  Ec 9:9 Enjoy life with your beloved w.
  Mal 2:15 treacherously with w. of your youth
  1Co 7:2 let each man have his own w.
  1Co 9:5 be accompanied by a believing w.
WILD, Job 6:3 my words have been w. talk
WILDERNESS, Isa 35:6 waters will burst forth in w.
  Isa 41:18 will turn w. into a reedy pool of water
WILL, Ps 40:8 To do your w. is my delight
  Ps 143:10 Teach me to do your w.
  Mt 6:10 Let your w. take place on earth
  Mt 7:21 only the one doing the w. of my Father
  Lu 22:42 let, not my w., but yours take place
  Joh 6:38 I have come to do, not my own w.
  Ac 21:14 Let the w. of Jehovah take place
  Ro 12:2 acceptable and perfect w. of God
  1Th 4:3 w. of God, abstain from immorality
  1Jo 2:17 one who does w. of God remains
  1Jo 5:14 ask according to his w., he hears
WILLFULLY, Heb 10:26 if we practice sin w.
WILLING, Ex 19:8 we are w. to do
  Ex 35:5 everyone with a w. heart bring
WILLINGLY, Ps 110:3 people will offer themselves w.
  1Pe 5:2 Shepherd the flock of God w.
WILLINGNESS, Ps 51:12 stir within me w. to obey you
WIND, Ec 11:4 who watches w. will not sow
  Eph 4:14 tossed by every w. of teaching
WINDOW, Ac 20:9 Seated at the w., Eutychus
WINDS, Mt 7:25 blew and lashed against house
  Re 7:1 holding tight four w. of the earth
WINE, Le 10:9 Do not drink w. when
  Ps 104:15 w. makes heart rejoice
  Pr 20:1 W. is a ridiculer, alcohol is unruly
  Pr 23:31 Do not look at the w.'s red color
  Ec 10:19 w. makes life enjoyable
  Isa 25:6 banquet of fine, filtered w.
  Ho 4:11 and w. take away motivation to
  Joh 2:9 water that had been turned into w.
  1Ti 5:23 take a little w. for your stomach
WINGS, Ru 2:12 under whose w. you have
WISDOM, Ps 111:10 fear of Jehovah beginning of w.
  Pr 2:6 Jehovah himself gives w.
  Pr 4:7 W. is the most important thing
  Pr 8:11 w. is better than corals
  Pr 24:3 By w. a house is built up
  Ec 7:12 W. preserves the life of its owner
  Ec 10:10 w. helps to achieve success
  Mt 11:19 w. is proved righteous by its works
  Lu 21:15 w. that opposers will not resist
  Ro 11:33 depth of God's riches and w.
  1Co 2:5 faith not in men's w., but God's
  1Co 2:6 not w. of the rulers of this system
  1Co 3:19 w. of this world is foolishness
  Col 2:3 in him all treasures of w.
  Jas 1:5 if any one is lacking in w., let him
  Jas 3:17 the w. from above is peaceable

WISE, Pr 3:7 Do not become w. in your own eyes
  Pr 13:20 one walking with w. will become w.
  Pr 27:11 Be w., my son, and make my heart
  Isa 5:21 Woe to those w. in their own eyes
  Mt 11:25 hidden these things from the w.
  1Co 1:26 not many w. in a fleshly way
  Eph 5:15 walk as w. persons
WISER, Ps 119:98 makes me w. than my enemies
  Pr 9:9 Share with wise person, will become w.
  Lu 16:8 w. in a practical way than sons of the light
WITHHOLD, Pr 3:27 Do not w. good from those
WITHIN, Ro 7:22 according to the man w.
WITNESS, Mt 24:14 Kingdom preached for a w.
  Joh 7:7 world hates me, because I bear w.
  Joh 18:37 that I should bear w. to the truth
  Ac 10:42 ordered to preach and give thorough w.
  Ac 28:23 bearing thorough w. concerning Kingdom
  Re 1:5 Jesus Christ, the Faithful W.
WITNESSES, De 19:15 testimony of two or
  Isa 43:10 You are my w., declares Jehovah
  Mt 18:16 on testimony of two or three w.
  Ac 1:8 you will be w. of me in
  Re 11:3 two w. prophesy for 1,260 days
WIVES, 1Ki 11:3 had 700 w. and 300
  Eph 5:22 Let w. be in subjection to husbands
  Eph 5:28 love their w. as their own bodies
WOE, Isa 5:20 W. to those who say bad is good
  1Co 9:16 w. if I do not declare the
  Re 12:12 W. for the earth and for the sea
WOLF, Isa 11:6 w. will reside with lamb
WOLVES, Mt 7:15 w. in sheep's covering
  Lu 10:3 sending as lambs in among w.
  Ac 20:29 oppressive w. will enter
WOMAN, Ge 3:15 enmity between you and the w.
  Ec 7:26 More bitter than death is w. who is
  Re 12:1 w. arrayed with the sun
WOMEN, De 31:12 Gather the people, men, w.
  Pr 31:3 Do not give your vigor to w.
WONDERFULLY, Ps 139:14 I am w. made
WOOD, Pr 26:20 Where there is no w., fire goes out
WORD, Pr 25:11 a w. spoken at the right time
  Isa 55:11 my w. will have sure success
  Lu 8:12 Devil takes the w. away from hearts
  Joh 1:1 In the beginning was the W.
  Joh 17:17 your w. is truth
  Ac 18:5 Paul intensely occupied with the w.
  Php 2:16 tight grip on the w. of life
  2Ti 2:15 handling w. of the truth aright
WORD OF GOD, Isa 40:8 w. endures forever
  Mr 7:13 you make w. invalid by your tradition
  1Th 2:13 accepted as it truthfully is, the w.
  Heb 4:12 w. is alive and exerts power
WORK, Ne 4:6 people put heart into the w.
  Ec 2:24 find enjoyment in hard w.
  Joh 6:27 W., not for the food that perishes
  Eph 4:28 steal no more; do hard w.
  2Th 3:10 does not w., neither let him eat
WORKER, Pr 8:30 beside him as a master w.
  Lu 10:7 the w. is worthy of his wages
WORKING, Joh 5:17 Father has kept w. until now
  1Th 2:9 We were w. night and day
WORKS, Ps 104:24 How many your w. are, Jehovah!
  Joh 14:12 he will do w. greater than these
  Heb 9:14 cleanse consciences from dead w.
WORLD, Lu 9:25 gains the whole w. but loses his
  Joh 15:19 no part of the w., the w. hates you
  Joh 17:16 They are no part of the w.
  1Jo 2:15 Do not love either the w. or
  1Jo 2:17 w. is passing away, but one who
WORSHIP, Mt 4:10 Jehovah your God you must w.
  Joh 4:24 w. with spirit and truth

WORTH, Mt 6:26 Are you not w. more than they are?
WORTHILY, Eph 4:1 walk w. of the calling
  Col 1:10 walk w. of Jehovah to please him
WORTHLESS, Ps 101:3 w. before my eyes
WORTHY, Mt 10:37 than for me is not w. of me
  Lu 15:19 no longer w. of being called son
  Ac 5:41 rejoicing because counted w. to be
  Ac 13:46 not judge yourselves w. of everlasting life
  2Th 1:5 being counted w. of the Kingdom
  Heb 11:38 the world was not w. of them
  Re 4:11 You are w., Jehovah, because
WOUNDED, Re 13:3 one of its heads fatally w.
WOUNDS, Pr 23:29 Who has w. for no reason?
  Pr 27:6 w. inflicted by a friend are faithful
  Isa 53:5 because of his w. we were healed
WRITTEN, Ro 15:4 things w. beforehand for our
  1Co 4:6 not go beyond things that are w.
WRONGED, 1Co 6:7 rather let yourselves be w.

Y

YEAR, Nu 14:34 40 days, a day for a y.
YEARNS, Ps 84:2 whole being y. for Jehovah
YES, Mt 5:37 let your Y. mean y.
YOKE, 1Ki 12:14 father made y. heavy, I will add
  Mt 11:30 my y. is kindly, my load light
YOKED, Mt 19:6 what God has y. together
  2Co 6:14 Do not become y. with unbelievers
YOUNG, Ps 110:3 y. men just like dewdrops
  Pr 20:29 glory of y. men is their strength
YOUTH, Job 33:25 flesh fresher than in y.
  Ps 71:17 you taught me from my y.
  Mr 10:20 all these things I kept from my y. on
  1Ti 4:12 anyone look down on your y.

Z

ZACCHAEUS, Lu 19:2 Z., a chief tax collector
ZEAL, Ps 69:9 Z. for your house consumed me
  Isa 37:32 z. of Jehovah of armies will do this
  Ro 10:2 they have a z. for God, but not
ZEALOUS, Tit 2:14 people z. for fine works
ZECHARIAH 1., Lu 11:51 blood of Z., who was killed
ZECHARIAH 2., Ezr 5:1 prophets Haggai and Z.
ZECHARIAH 3., Lu 1:5 a priest named Z.
ZEDEKIAH, Jer 52:11 blinded Z.'s eyes
ZEUS, Ac 14:12 calling Barnabas Z., but Paul Hermes
ZION, Ps 2:6 installed my king on Z.
  Ps 48:2 Mount Z., city of the Grand King
  Isa 66:8 Z. gave birth to sons
  Re 14:1 Lamb on Mount Z., with 144,000

0–9

12, Mr 3:14 12, whom he named apostles
24, Re 4:4 24 thrones and 24 elders
70, Ps 90:10 span of our life is 70 years
  Da 9:2 desolation of Jerusalem, namely, 70 years
  Da 9:24 70 weeks determined for your people
  Lu 10:1 Lord designated 70 and sent them out
77, Mt 18:22 not up to seven times, but up to 77
100, Mt 13:8 yield fruit, 100 times more
  Mt 18:12 has 100 sheep and one strays
  Mr 10:30 get 100 times more now
300, Jg 7:7 save you with the 300 men
500, 1Co 15:6 appeared to more than 500 brothers
666, Re 13:18 its number is 666
1,000, Re 20:2 bound Satan for 1,000 years
  Re 20:4 ruled with the Christ for 1,000 years
4,000, Mr 8:20 seven loaves for 4,000 men
5,000, Mt 14:21 eating were about 5,000 men
144,000, Re 7:4 those who were sealed, 144,000
  Re 14:3 144,000 bought from the earth
185,000, 2Ki 19:35 angel struck down 185,000

Glossary of Bible Terms

A

Ab. After the Babylonian exile, the name of the 5th month of the Jewish sacred calendar and the 11th month of the secular calendar. It ran from mid-July to mid-August. It is not mentioned by name in the Bible; it is simply referred to as "the fifth month." (Nu 33:38; Ezr 7:9)—See App. B15.

Abib. The original name of the first month of the Jewish sacred calendar and the seventh month of the secular calendar. It means "Green Ears (of Grain)" and ran from mid-March to mid-April. After the Jews' return from Babylon, it was called Nisan. (De 16:1)—See App. B15.

Abyss. From the Greek word *a'bys·sos*, meaning "exceedingly deep" or "unfathomable, boundless." It is used in the Christian Greek Scriptures to refer to a place or condition of confinement. It includes the grave but is not limited to it.—Lu 8:31; Ro 10:7; Re 20:3.

Achaia. In the Christian Greek Scriptures, the Roman province of southern Greece with its capital at Corinth. Achaia included all of the Peloponnese and the central part of continental Greece. (Ac 18:12)—See App. B13.

Adar. After the Babylonian exile, the name of the 12th month of the Jewish sacred calendar and the 6th month of the secular calendar. It ran from mid-February to mid-March. (Es 3:7)—See App. B15.

Adultery. Voluntary sexual intercourse by a married man or woman with someone other than his or her mate.—Ex 20:14; Mt 5:27; 19:9.

Alabaster. The name of small perfume jars originally made of a stone found near Alabastron, Egypt. Such containers were usually made with a narrow neck that could be sealed to prevent any of the precious perfume from leaking. The stone itself also came to be known by the same name.—Mr 14:3.

Alamoth. A musical term meaning "Maidens; Young Women," probably alluding to the soprano voices of young women. It was likely used to indicate that a musical piece or accompaniment was to be executed at a high register.—1Ch 15:20; Ps 46:Sup.

Alpha and Omega. Names of the first and last letters of the Greek alphabet; they are used together three times in Revelation as a title for God. In these contexts this expression means the same as "the first and the last" and "the beginning and the end."—Re 1:8; 21:6; 22:13.

Altar. A raised structure or platform made of dirt, rocks, a block of stone, or wood covered with metal on which sacrifices or incense were offered in worship. In the first room of the tabernacle and of the temple, there was a small "altar of gold" for offering incense. It was made of wood covered with gold. A larger "altar of copper" for burnt sacrifices was located outside in the courtyard. (Ex 27:1; 39:38, 39; Ge 8:20; 1Ki 6:20; 2Ch 4:1; Lu 1:11)—See App. B5 and B8.

Amen. "So be it," or "surely." The word comes from the Hebrew root word *'a·man'*, which means "to be faithful, trustworthy." "Amen" was said in agreement to an oath, a prayer, or a statement. In Revelation, it is used as a title for Jesus.—De 27:26; 1Ch 16:36; Re 3:14.

Angels. From the Hebrew *mal·'akh'* and the Greek *ag'ge·los*. Both words literally mean "messenger" but are rendered "angel" when referring to spirit messengers. (Ge 16:7; 32:3; Jas 2:25; Re 22:8) Angels are powerful spirit creatures, created by God long before the creation of mankind. They are also referred to in the Bible as "holy myriads," "sons of God," and "morning stars." (De 33:2; Job 1:6; 38:7) They were not made with the ability to reproduce their own kind but were created individually. They number well over a hundred million. (Da 7:10) The Bible indicates that they have personal names and distinct personalities, yet they humbly refuse to receive worship, and most even avoid disclosing their names. (Ge 32:29; Lu 1:26; Re 22:8, 9) They have different ranks and are assigned a variety of roles, including serving before Jehovah's throne, conveying his messages, intervening in behalf of Jehovah's earthly servants, executing God's judgments, and supporting the preaching of the good news. (2Ki 19:35; Ps 34:7; Lu 1:30, 31; Re 5:11; 14:6) In the future they will support Jesus in fighting the battle of Armageddon.—Re 19:14, 15.

Anoint. The Hebrew word basically means "to smear with liquid." Oil was applied to a person or an object to symbolize dedication to a special service. In the Christian Greek Scriptures, the word is also used of the pouring out of holy spirit on those chosen for the heavenly hope.—Ex 28:41; 1Sa 16:13; 2Co 1:21.

Antichrist. The Greek term has a twofold meaning. It refers to that which is *anti,* or *opposed to,* Christ. It may also refer to a false Christ, one *in the place of* Christ. All people, organizations, or groups that falsely claim to represent Christ or claim to be the Messiah or that oppose Christ and his disciples can properly be called antichrists.—1Jo 2:22.

Apostasy. This term in Greek (*a·po·sta·si'a*) comes from a verb literally meaning "to stand away from." The noun has the sense of "desertion, abandonment, or rebellion." In the Christian Greek Scriptures, "apostasy" is used primarily with regard to those who defect from true worship.—Pr 11:9; Ac 21:21; 2Th 2:3.

Apostle. The basic sense of the word is "one sent forth," and it is used of Jesus and certain ones who were sent to serve others. Most frequently, it is used with regard to the disciples whom Jesus personally selected as a group of 12 appointed representatives. —Mr 3:14; Ac 14:14.

Aram; Aramaeans. Descendants of Shem's son Aram who mainly lived in regions from the Lebanon Mountains across to Mesopotamia and from the Taurus Mountains in the north down to Damascus and beyond in the south. This area, called Aram in Hebrew, was later referred to as Syria, and its inhabitants were referred to as Syrians.—Ge 25:20; De 26:5; Ho 12:12.

Aramaic. A Semitic language closely related to Hebrew, using the same alphabet. It was originally spoken by the Aramaeans but later became the international language of trade and communication in the Assyrian and Babylonian empires. It was also the official administrative language of the Persian Empire. (Ezr 4:7) Parts of the books of Ezra, Jeremiah, and Daniel were written in Aramaic.—Ezr 4:8–6:18; 7:12-26; Jer 10:11; Da 2:4b–7:28.

Archangel. Meaning "chief of the angels." The prefix "arch" means "chief" or "principal." This definition, coupled with the fact that "archangel" in the Bible is used only in the singular, indicates that there is just one archangel. The Bible gives the name of the archangel, identifying him as Michael.—Da 12:1; Jude 9; Re 12:7.

Areopagus. A high hill in Athens, north-west of the Acropolis. It was also the name of the council (court) that held meetings there. Paul was brought to the Areopagus by Stoic and Epicurean philosophers to explain his beliefs.—Ac 17:19.

Ark of the covenant. The chest made of acacia wood and overlaid with gold, which was kept in the Most Holy of the tabernacle and later in the Most Holy of the temple built by Solomon. It had a solid gold cover with two cherubs facing each other. Its principal contents were the two tablets of the Ten Commandments. (De 31:26; 1Ki 6:19; Heb 9:4) —See App. B5 and B8.

Armageddon. From the Hebrew *Har Meghiddohn',* meaning "Mountain of Megiddo." The word is associated with "the war of the great day of God the Almighty" in which "the kings of the entire inhabited earth" gather to wage war against Jehovah. (Re 16:14, 16; 19:11-21)—See GREAT TRIBULATION.

Armor. The protective clothing worn by soldiers, namely, helmet, coat of mail, girdle, greaves, and shield.—1Sa 31:9; Eph 6:13-17.

Aselgeia.—See BRAZEN CONDUCT.

Ashtoreth. A Canaanite goddess of war and fertility, the wife of Baal.—1Sa 7:3.

Asia. In the Christian Greek Scriptures, the name of the Roman province that included what is today the western part of Turkey, as well as some coastal islands, such as Samos and Patmos. The capital was Ephesus. (Ac 20:16; Re 1:4)—See App. B13.

Assembly. A group of people gathered by appointment. In the Hebrew Scriptures, this word often refers to gatherings of the people of Israel at religious festivals or at events of great national significance.—De 16:8; 1Ki 8:5.

Astrologer. A person who studies the movements of the sun, moon, and stars in order to predict future events.—Da 2:27; Mt 2:1.

Atonement. In the Hebrew Scriptures, the concept was connected with sacrifices that were made to allow people to approach God and worship him. Under the Mosaic Law, sacrifices were made, particularly on the annual Day of Atonement, in order to effect reconciliation with God despite the sins of individuals and of the whole nation. Those sacrifices pointed to Jesus' sacrifice, which completely atoned for mankind's sins once for all time, giving people the opportunity to be reconciled to Jehovah.—Le 5:10; 23:28; Col 1:20; Heb 9:12.

Azazel. A Hebrew name that possibly means "Goat That Disappears." On the Day of Atonement, the goat designated for Azazel was sent into the wilderness, symbolically carrying off the nation's sins of the past year.—Le 16:8, 10.

B

Baal. A Canaanite god regarded as the owner of the sky and giver of rains and fertility. "Baal" was also used as a designation for local lesser gods. The Hebrew word means "Owner; Master."—1Ki 18:21; Ro 11:4.

Baptism; Baptize. The verb means "to immerse," or dip under water. Jesus made baptism a requirement for his followers. The Scriptures also refer to John's baptism, baptism with holy spirit, and baptism with fire, among others.—Mt 3:11, 16; 28:19; Joh 3:23; 1Pe 3:21.

Bath. A liquid measure that is estimated to equal about 22 L (5.81 gal), according to archaeological findings of jar fragments bearing this name. Most of the other dry and liquid measures in the Bible are calculated in relation to the estimated volume of the bath measure. (1Ki 7:38; Eze 45:14)—See App. B14.

Beelzebub. A designation applied to Satan, the prince, or ruler, of the demons. It is possibly an alteration of Baal-zebub, the Baal worshipped by the Philistines at Ekron.—2Ki 1:3; Mt 12:24.

Brazen conduct. From the Greek *a·sel'gei·a,* a phrase pertaining to acts that are serious violations of God's laws and that reflect a brazen or boldly contemptuous attitude; a spirit that betrays disrespect or even contempt for authority, laws, and standards. The expression does not refer to wrong conduct of a minor nature.—Ga 5:19; 2Pe 2:7.

Breastpiece. The jewel-studded pouch worn by Israel's high priest over his heart whenever he entered the Holy. It was called "the breastpiece of judgment" because it contained the Urim and the Thummim, which were used in revealing Jehovah's judgments. (Ex 28:15-30)—See App. B5.

Brother-in-law marriage. A custom, later incorporated into the Mosaic Law, whereby a man would marry the sonless widow of his deceased brother in order to produce children to carry on his brother's line. Also known as levirate marriage.—Ge 38:8; De 25:5.

Bul. The name of the eighth month of the Jewish sacred calendar and the second month of the secular calendar. It comes from a root meaning "yield; produce" and ran from mid-October to mid-November. (1Ki 6:38)—See App. B15.

Burnt offering. An animal sacrifice that was burned on the altar as a total offering to God; no part of the animal (bull, ram, male goat, turtledove, or young pigeon) was kept by the worshipper.—Ex 29:18; Le 6:9.

C

Cab. A dry measure of 1.22 L (1.11 dry qt), based on the estimated volume of the bath measure. (2Ki 6:25)—See App. B14.

Caesar. A Roman family name that became a title for the Roman emperors. Augustus, Tiberius, and Claudius are mentioned by name in the Bible, and though Nero is not mentioned by name, it applies to him as well. "Caesar" is also used in the Christian Greek Scriptures to represent civil authority, or the State.—Mr 12:17; Ac 25:12.

Canaan. A grandson of Noah, and the fourth son of Ham. The 11 tribes that descended from Canaan eventually inhabited the region along the eastern Mediterranean between Egypt and Syria. That area was called "the land of Canaan." (Le 18:3; Ge 9:18; Ac 13:19)—See App. B4.

Capital. The ornamental top of a column. The twin columns Jachin and Boaz stood in front of Solomon's temple. (1Ki 7:16)—See App. B8.

Cassia. A product from the cassia bark tree (*Cinnamomum cassia*), which is of the same

family as the cinnamon tree. Cassia was used as a perfume and as an ingredient of the holy anointing oil.—Ex 30:24; Ps 45:8; Eze 27:19.

Chaff. The husks that are separated from the edible portion of grain during threshing and winnowing. Chaff is used in figures of speech as a symbol of something worthless and undesirable.—Ps 1:4; Mt 3:12.

Chaldea; Chaldeans. Originally the land and people occupying the delta area of the Tigris and Euphrates rivers; in time the terms were used for all of Babylonia and its people. "Chaldeans" also referred to an educated class of people who studied science, history, languages, and astronomy but who practiced magic and astrology as well.—Ezr 5:12; Da 4:7; Ac 7:4.

Chariot. A two-wheeled, horse-drawn vehicle used primarily in war.—Ex 14:23; Jg 4:13; Ac 8:28.

Chemosh. The chief god of the Moabites.—1Ki 11:33.

Cherubs. Angels of high rank having special duties. They are different from seraphs.—Ge 3:24; Ex 25:20; Isa 37:16; Heb 9:5.

Chief Agent. The Greek term basically means "Chief Leader." It refers to the essential role of Jesus Christ in freeing faithful humans from the deadly effects of sin and in leading them to everlasting life.—Ac 3:15; 5:31; Heb 2:10; 12:2.

Chief priest. An alternate term for "high priest" in the Hebrew Scriptures. In the Christian Greek Scriptures, the expression "chief priests" evidently denoted the principal men of the priesthood, possibly including any deposed high priests and the heads of the 24 priestly divisions.—2Ch 26:20; Ezr 7:5; Mt 2:4; Mr 8:31.

Chislev. After the Jews' return from Babylon, the name of the ninth month of the Jewish sacred calendar and the third month of the secular calendar. It ran from mid-November to mid-December. (Ne 1:1; Zec 7:1)—See App. B15.

Christ. The title of Jesus, from the Greek word *Khri·stos'*, which is equivalent to the Hebrew word translated "Messiah," or "Anointed One."—Mt 1:16; Joh 1:41.

Christian. A God-given name for the followers of Jesus Christ.—Ac 11:26; 26:28.

Circumcision. The removal of the foreskin of the male genital organ. The procedure was made mandatory for Abraham and his descendants, but it is not a requirement for Christians. It is also used figuratively in a variety of contexts.—Ge 17:10; 1Co 7:19; Php 3:3.

Cities of refuge. Levite cities where an unintentional manslayer could seek asylum from the avenger of blood. Six such cities, spread throughout the Promised Land, were appointed by Moses and later by Joshua, under Jehovah's direction. Upon reaching a city of refuge, the fugitive stated his case to the elders at the city gate and was received hospitably. To prevent willful murderers from taking advantage of this provision, the asylum seeker had to stand trial in the city where the killing took place in order to prove his innocence. If proved innocent, he was returned to the city of refuge, where he had to stay within its boundaries for the rest of his life or until the death of the high priest.—Nu 35:6, 11-15, 22-29; Jos 20:2-8.

City of David. The name given to the city of Jebus after David conquered it and built his royal residence there. It is also called Zion. It is the southeastern part as well as the oldest part of Jerusalem.—2Sa 5:7; 1Ch 11:4, 5.

Clean. Biblically, this word refers not only to physical cleanliness but also to maintaining or restoring to a condition that is without blemish, spotless, and free from anything that soils, adulterates, or corrupts in a moral or spiritual way. Under the Mosaic Law, the word refers to being ceremonially clean.—Le 10:10; Ps 51:7; Mt 8:2; 1Co 6:11.

Communion offering. A sacrifice presented to Jehovah as a request for peace with him. The worshipper and his household, the officiating priest, and the priests on duty all partook of it. Jehovah received, as it were, the pleasing smoke of the burning fat. The blood, representing the life, was also given to him. It was as if the priests and the worshippers sat at the meal together with Jehovah, signifying a peaceful relationship.—Le 7:29, 32; De 27:7.

Conclusion of the system of things. The period of time leading up to the end of the system of things, or state of affairs, dominated by Satan. It runs concurrently with Christ's presence. Under the direction of Jesus, angels will "separate the wicked from among the righteous" and destroy them. (Mt 13:40-42, 49) Jesus' disciples were interested in the timing of that "conclusion." (Mt 24:3) Before his return to heaven, he promised his followers that he would be with them until that time.—Mt 28:20.

Concubine. A secondary wife who was often a slave girl.—Ex 21:8; 2Sa 5:13; 1Ki 11:3.

Congregation. A group of people gathered together for a particular purpose or activity. In the Hebrew Scriptures, it generally refers to the nation of Israel. In the Christian Greek Scriptures, it refers to individual congregations of Christians but more often to the Christian congregation in general.—1Ki 8:22; Ac 9:31; Ro 16:5.

Cor. A dry and a liquid measure. It equaled 220 L (58.1 gal/200 dry qt), based on the estimated volume of the bath measure. (1Ki 5:11)—See App. B14.

Coral. A hard, stonelike substance that is formed from the skeletons of tiny sea animals. It is found in the ocean in a variety of colors, including red, white, and black. Corals were especially plentiful in the Red Sea. In Bible times, red coral was highly prized and was made into beads and other ornaments.—Pr 8:11.

Cornerstone. A stone placed at the angle, or corner, of a building where two walls meet, important in joining and binding them together. The principal cornerstone was the foundation cornerstone; a particularly strong one was generally chosen for public buildings and city walls. The word is used in a figurative sense for the founding of the earth, and Jesus is spoken of as "the foundation cornerstone" of the Christian congregation, which is likened to a spiritual house.—Eph 2:20; Job 38:6.

Courtyard. The fenced, open area surrounding the tabernacle, and later one of the walled, open-air yards around the main building of the temple. The altar of burnt offering was located in the courtyard of the tabernacle and in the inner courtyard of the temple. (See App. B5, B8, B11.) The Bible also mentions courtyards in connection with houses and palaces.—Ex 8:13; 27:9; 1Ki 7:12; Es 4:11; Mt 26:3.

Covenant. A formal agreement, or contract, between God and humans or between two human parties to do or refrain from doing something. Sometimes only one party was responsible to carry out the terms (a unilateral covenant, which was essen-tially a promise). At other times both parties had terms to carry out (a bilateral covenant). Besides covenants made by God with humans, the Bible mentions covenants between men, tribes, nations, or groups of people. Among the covenants that have had a far-reaching effect are those that God made with Abraham, David, the nation of Israel (Law covenant), and the Israel of God (new covenant).—Ge 9:11; 15:18; 21:27; Ex 24:7; 2Ch 21:7.

Cubit. A linear measure roughly the distance from the elbow to the tip of the middle finger. The Israelites commonly used a cubit of about 44.5 cm (17.5 in.), but they also used a larger cubit that was one handbreadth longer, about 51.8 cm (20.4 in.). (Ge 6:15; Lu 12:25)—See App. B14.

Curse. To threaten or pronounce evil on someone or something. It is not to be confused with profanity or with violent anger. A curse is often a formal declaration of a pronouncement or prediction of evil, and when made by God or by an authorized person, it has a prophetic value and force.—Ge 12:3; Nu 22:12; Ga 3:10.

Curtain. The beautifully woven piece of fabric embroidered with figures of cherubs that separated the Holy from the Most Holy in both the tabernacle and the temple. (Ex 26:31; 2Ch 3:14; Mt 27:51; Heb 9:3)—See App. B5.

D

Dagon. A god of the Philistines. The etymology of the word is uncertain, but some scholars associate it with the Hebrew word *dagh* (fish).—Jg 16:23; 1Sa 5:4.

Daric. A Persian gold coin weighing 8.4 g (0.27 oz t). (1Ch 29:7)—See App. B14.

Day of Atonement. The most important holy day for the Israelites, also called Yom Kippur (from Hebrew *yohm hak·kip·pu·rim′*, "day of the coverings"), held on Ethanim 10. This was the only day of the year on which the high priest went into the Most Holy of the tabernacle. There he offered the blood of the sacrifices for his sins, the sins of the other Levites, and the sins of the people. It was a time of holy convention and fasting, and it was also a sabbath, a time to abstain from regular work.—Le 23:27, 28.

Daystar. Similar in meaning to "morning star." It is the last star to rise on the eastern horizon before the sun appears, thus heralding the dawn of a new day.—Re 22:16; 2Pe 1:19.

Decapolis. A group of Greek cities, originally made up of ten cities (from Greek *de′ka*, meaning "ten," and *po′lis*, "city"). It was also the name for the region east of the Sea of Galilee and the Jordan River, where most of these cities were located. They were centers of Hellenistic culture and trade. Jesus passed through this region, but there is no record of his having visited any of the cities. (Mt 4:25; Mr 5:20)—See App. A7 and B10.

Dedication, holy sign of. A shining plate of pure gold engraved with the words, in Hebrew, "Holiness belongs to Jehovah." It was put on the front of the turban of the high priest. (Ex 39:30)—See App. B5.

Demons. Invisible, wicked spirit creatures having superhuman powers. Called "the sons of the true God" at Genesis 6:2 and "angels" at Jude 6, they were not created wicked; rather, they were angels who made themselves enemies of God by disobeying him in Noah's day and joining in Satan's rebellion against Jehovah.—De 32:17; Lu 8:30; Ac 16:16; Jas 2:19.

Denarius. A Roman silver coin that weighed about 3.85 g (0.124 oz t) and bore an image of Caesar on one side. It was the daily wage of a laborer and was the "head tax" coin exacted by the Romans from the Jews. (Mt 22:17; Lu 20:24)—See App. B14.

Devil. The descriptive name of Satan in the Christian Greek Scriptures, which means "Slanderer." Satan was given the name Devil because he is the chief and foremost slanderer and false accuser of Jehovah, His good word, and His holy name.—Mt 4:1; Joh 8:44; Re 12:9.

Director. As used in the Psalms, the Hebrew term seems to refer to one who in some way arranged songs and directed the singing of them, rehearsed and trained the Levite singers, and even led official performances. Other translations render this term "chief musician" or "musical director."—Ps 4:Sup; 5:Sup.

Dirge. A composition, lyrical or musical, expressing deep sorrow, such as the grief expressed because of the death of a friend or a loved one; a lamentation.—2Sa 1:17; Ps 7:Sup.

Drachma. In the Christian Greek Scriptures, this word refers to a Greek silver coin, which

at that time weighed 3.4 g (0.109 oz t). In the Hebrew Scriptures, there is reference to a gold drachma from the Persian period that is equated with the daric. (Ne 7:70; Mt 17:24)—See App. B14.

Drink offering. An offering of wine that was poured out on the altar and presented along with most other offerings. Used figuratively by Paul to express his willingness to expend himself for fellow Christians.—Nu 15:5, 7; Php 2:17.

E

Edom. Another name given to Esau, son of Isaac. The descendants of Esau (Edom) took over the area of Seir, the mountainous region between the Dead Sea and the Gulf of 'Aqaba. It became known as Edom. (Ge 25:30; 36:8)—See App. B3 and B4.

Elder; Older man. A man of mature age, but in the Scriptures, one who primarily holds a position of authority and responsibility in a community or a nation. The word is also used of heavenly creatures in the book of Revelation. The Greek word *pre·sby′te·ros* is translated "elder" when it refers to those responsible for taking the lead in the congregation.—Ex 4:29; Pr 31:23; 1Ti 5:17; Re 4:4.

Elul. After the Babylonian exile, the name of the 6th month of the Jewish sacred calendar and the 12th month of the secular calendar. It ran from mid-August to mid-September. (Ne 6:15)—See App. B15.

Ephah. A dry measure capacity and the container itself, used for measuring grains. It was equal to a liquid bath measure, so it amounted to 22 L (20 dry qt). (Ex 16:36; Eze 45:10)—See App. B14.

Ephod. An apronlike garment worn by priests. The high priest wore a special ephod, on the front of which was mounted the breastpiece with 12 precious stones. (Ex 28:4, 6)—See App. B5.

Ephraim. The name of Joseph's second son; this name was subsequently applied to one of the tribes of Israel. After Israel was divided, Ephraim, as the most prominent tribe, came to represent the entire ten-tribe kingdom.—Ge 41:52; Jer 7:15.

Epicurean philosophers. Followers of the Greek philosopher Epicurus (341-270 B.C.E.). Their philosophy centered on the idea that the pleasure of the individual was the ultimate goal in life.—Ac 17:18.

Ethanim. The name of the seventh month of the Jewish sacred calendar and the first month of the secular calendar. It ran from mid-September to mid-October. After the Jews' return from Babylon, it was called Tishri. (1Ki 8:2)—See App. B15.

Ethiopia. An ancient nation south of Egypt. It included the southernmost part of modern-day Egypt and the northern half of modern-day Sudan. The expression is sometimes used for the Hebrew "Cush."—Es 1:1.

Eunuch. In a literal sense, a castrated male. Such men were often appointed in royal courts as attendants or caretakers of the queen and the concubines. The term also refers to a man who was, not a literal eunuch, but an official assigned to duties in the court of the king. It is used figuratively for a 'eunuch for the Kingdom,' one who exercises self-control so as to apply himself more fully to the service of God.—Mt 19:12; Es 2:15; Ac 8:27.

Euphrates. The longest and most important river of southwest Asia, and one of the two major rivers in Mesopotamia. It is first mentioned at Genesis 2:14 as one of the four rivers of Eden. It is often called "the River." (Ge 31:21) It was the northern boundary of Israel's assigned territory. (Ge 15:18; Re 16:12) —See App. B2.

Exile. Expulsion from one's native land or home, often decreed by conquerors. The Hebrew word means "a departing." The Israelites experienced two major exiles. The northern ten-tribe kingdom was taken into exile by the Assyrians, and later the southern two-tribe kingdom was taken into exile by the Babylonians. Remnants of both exiles were returned to their land under Cyrus, the Persian ruler.—2Ki 17:6; 24:16; Ezr 6:21.

Extinguishers. Tools used in the tabernacle and temple, made of gold or copper. They may have been like scissors for trimming the lampwicks.—2Ki 25:14.

F

Fast. Abstinence from all food for a limited period. The Israelites practiced fasting on the Day of Atonement, in times of distress, and when in need of divine guidance. The Jews established four annual fasts to mark calamitous events in their history. Fasting is not a requirement for Christians.—Ezr 8:21; Isa 58:6; Lu 18:12.

Fathom. A linear unit for measuring the depth of water, equal to 1.8 m (6 ft). (Ac 27:28) —See App. B14.

Festival of Booths. Also called the Festival of Tabernacles, or the Festival of Ingathering. It was held on Ethanim 15-21. It celebrated the harvest at the end of the agricultural year for Israel and was a time of rejoicing and thanksgiving for Jehovah's blessings on their crops. During the days of the festival, people lived in booths, or rooflike shelters, to remind them of the Exodus from Egypt. It was one of the three festivals that males were required to go to Jerusalem to observe.—Le 23:34; Ezr 3:4.

Festival of Dedication. The annual day of remembrance for the cleansing of the temple after its defilement by Antiochus Epiphanes. The celebration began on Chislev 25 and lasted for eight days.—Joh 10:22.

Festival of Harvest; Festival of Weeks.—See PENTECOST.

Festival of Unleavened Bread. The first of the three major annual festivals of the Israelites. It began on Nisan 15, the day after Passover, and continued for seven days. Only unleavened bread could be eaten, in remembrance of the Exodus from Egypt.—Ex 23:15; Mr 14:1.

Fire holders. Utensils made of gold, silver, or copper, used at the tabernacle and temple for burning incense and for removing coals from the sacrificial altar and burnt lampwicks from the golden lampstand. They were also called censers.—Ex 37:23; 2Ch 26:19; Heb 9:4.

Firstborn. Primarily, the oldest son of a father (rather than the firstborn of the mother). In Bible times, the firstborn son held an honored position in the family and was given the headship of the household when the father died. The term also refers to the first male offspring of animals, at times called "firstlings."—Ex 11:5; 13:12; Ge 25:33; Col 1:15.

Firstfruits. The earliest fruits of a harvest season; the first results or products of anything. Jehovah required the nation of Israel to offer their firstfruits to him, whether it be of man, animal, or the fruitage of the ground. As a nation, the Israelites offered firstfruits to God at the Festival of Unleavened Bread and at Pentecost. The term "firstfruits" was also used figuratively of Christ and his anointed followers.—1Co 15: 23; Nu 15:21; Pr 3:9; Re 14:4.

Fornication.—See SEXUAL IMMORALITY.

Fortune-teller. An individual claiming ability to foretell future events. Magic-practicing priests, spiritistic diviners, astrologers, and others are listed in the Bible as such.—Le 19:31; De 18:11; Ac 16:16.

Frankincense. Dried sap (gum resin) from trees and bushes of certain species of the genus *Boswellia.* When burned, it gave off a sweet-smelling fragrance. It was an ingredient of the holy incense used at the tabernacle and the temple. It also accompanied grain offerings and was placed on each row of the showbread inside the Holy.—Ex 30:34-36; Le 2:1; 24:7; Mt 2:11.

Freeman; Freedman. During Roman rule, a "freeman" was one who was born free, possessing full rights of citizenship. In contrast, a "freedman" was one emancipated from slavery. Formal emancipation granted the freedman Roman citizenship, but he was not eligible for political office. Informal emancipation freed the individual from slavery but did not give full civil rights.—1Co 7:22.

Furnace. A structure for smelting ore or melting metal; also used to fire pottery and other ceramic items. In Bible times, furnaces were made of brick or stone. A furnace for firing pottery and ceramics and for burning lime is also called a kiln.—Ge 15:17; Da 3:17; Re 9:2.

G

Gehenna. The Greek name for the Valley of Hinnom, southwest of ancient Jerusalem. (Jer 7:31) It was prophetically spoken of as a place where dead bodies would be strewn. (Jer 7:32; 19:6) There is no evidence that animals or humans were thrown into Gehenna to be burned alive or tormented. So the place could not symbolize an invisible region where human souls are tormented eternally in literal fire. Rather, Gehenna was used by Jesus and his disciples to symbolize the eternal punishment of "second death," that is, everlasting destruction, annihilation.—Re 20:14; Mt 5:22; 10:28.

Gerah. A weight equivalent to 0.57 g (0.01835 oz t). It corresponded to 1/20 shekel. (Le 27:25)—See App. B14.

Gifts of mercy. Gifts given to help someone in need. These are not directly mentioned in

the Hebrew Scriptures, but the Law gave specific directions to the Israelites about their obligations toward the poor.—Mt 6:2.

Gilead. In a strict sense, the fertile area east of the Jordan River that extended north and south of the Valley of Jabbok. At times used for the entire Israelite territory east of the Jordan, where the tribes of Reuben, Gad, and the half tribe of Manasseh lived. (Nu 32:1; Jos 12:2; 2Ki 10:33)—See App. B4.

Gittith. A musical term of uncertain meaning, though it seems to be derived from the Hebrew word *gath.* Some believe that it may be a melody associated with songs related to wine making, since *gath* refers to a winepress.—Ps 81:Sup.

Glean. To gather whatever portion of a crop the harvesters had intentionally or unintentionally left behind. The Mosaic Law directed the people not to reap the edges of their fields completely nor to take all the olives or grapes. It was the God-given right of the poor, the afflicted, the foreign resident, the fatherless child, and the widow to glean what was left after harvest.—Ru 2:7.

Goad. A long rod with a sharp metal point, used by farmers to prod an animal. The goad is compared to the words of a wise person that move the listener to heed wise counsel. "Kicking against the goads" is drawn from the action of a stubborn bull that resists the prodding of the goad by kicking against it, resulting in injury to itself.—Ac 26:14; Jg 3:31.

Godly devotion. Reverence, worship, and service to Jehovah God, with loyalty to his universal sovereignty.—1Ti 4:8; 2Ti 3:12.

God's Kingdom. The phrase used particularly of God's sovereignty represented by the royal government of his Son, Christ Jesus. —Mt 12:28; Lu 4:43; 1Co 15:50.

Good news, the. In the Christian Greek Scriptures, the good news of the Kingdom of God and of salvation by faith in Jesus Christ.—Lu 4:18, 43; Ac 5:42; Re 14:6.

Grave. When lowercased, referring to an individual grave; when capitalized, the common grave of mankind, equivalent to the Hebrew "Sheol" and the Greek "Hades." It is described in the Bible as a symbolic place or condition wherein all activity and consciousness cease.—Ge 47:30; Ec 9:10; Ac 2:31.

Great tribulation. The Greek word for "tribulation" conveys the idea of distress or suffering resulting from the pressures of circumstances. Jesus spoke of an unprecedented "great tribulation" that would come upon Jerusalem and especially of one that would later befall mankind in connection with his future 'coming with glory.' (Mt 24: 21, 29-31) Paul described this tribulation as a righteous act of God against "those who do not know God and those who do not obey the good news" about Jesus Christ. Revelation chapter 19 shows Jesus as the one leading heavenly armies against "the wild beast and the kings of the earth and their armies." (2Th 1:6-8; Re 19:11-21) "A great crowd" is shown as surviving that tribulation. (Re 7:9, 14)—See ARMAGEDDON.

Greek. The language spoken by the people of Greece; also, a native of Greece or one whose family originated there. In the Christian Greek Scriptures, the word also has a broader usage, referring to all non-Jewish peoples or to those who were influenced by Greek language and culture.—Joe 3:6; Joh 12:20.

Guilt offering. A sacrifice for personal sins. It differed slightly from other sin offerings in that it was to satisfy or restore certain covenant rights that the repentant wrongdoer had lost because of a sin and to give him relief from the penalty.—Le 7:37; 19:22; Isa 53:10.

H

Hades. A Greek word corresponding to the Hebrew word "Sheol." It is translated "Grave" (capitalized), to distinguish it as the common grave of mankind.—See GRAVE.

Hebrew. A designation first used for Abram (Abraham), distinguishing him from his Amorite neighbors. It was used thereafter to refer to Abraham's descendants through his grandson Jacob as well as to their language. By the time of Jesus, the Hebrew language had come to include many Aramaic expressions and was the language spoken by Christ and his disciples.—Ge 14:13; Ex 5:3; Ac 26:14.

Hermes. A Greek god, son of Zeus. In Lystra, Paul was mistakenly called Hermes in reference to that god's supposed role as messenger of the gods and the god of skillful speech.—Ac 14:12.

Herod. The family name of a dynasty that ruled over the Jews by appointment from Rome. The first was Herod the Great, famous for rebuilding the temple in Jerusalem and for ordering the slaughter of children in an attempt to destroy Jesus. (Mt 2:16; Lu 1:5) Herod Archelaus and Herod Antipas, sons of Herod the Great, were appointed over sections of their father's domain. (Mt 2:22) Antipas was a tetrarch, popularly referred to as "king," who ruled during Christ's three-year ministry and through the period up to Acts chapter 12. (Mr 6:14-17; Lu 3:1, 19, 20; 13:31, 32; 23:6-15; Ac 4:27; 13:1) After that, Herod Agrippa I, grandson of Herod the Great, was executed by God's angel after ruling for a short time. (Ac 12:1-6, 18-23) His son, Herod Agrippa II, became ruler and reigned up to the time of the Jewish revolt against Rome.—Ac 23:35; 25:13, 22-27; 26: 1, 2, 19-32.

Herod, party followers of. Also known as Herodians. They were a party of nationalists who supported the political aims of the Herods in their rule under the Romans. Some of the Sadducees probably belonged to this party. The Herodians joined with the Pharisees to oppose Jesus.—Mr 3:6.

Higgaion. A technical term of musical direction. As used at Psalm 9:16, the word may signify either a solemn, deep-toned harp interlude or a solemn pause conducive to meditation.

High place. A place of worship usually on top of a hill, a mountain, or a man-made platform. Although high places were sometimes used for the worship of God, they are most often associated with pagan worship of false gods.—Nu 33:52; 1Ki 3:2; Jer 19:5.

High priest. Under the Mosaic Law, the principal priest who represented the people before God and supervised the other priests. Also called "the chief priest." (2Ch 26:20; Ezr 7:5) He alone was allowed to enter the Most Holy, the innermost compartment of the tabernacle and later of the temple. He did so only on the annual Day of Atonement. The term "high priest" is also applied to Jesus Christ.—Le 16:2, 17; 21:10; Mt 26:3; Heb 4:14.

Hin. A liquid measure and the container for that measure. It is equivalent to 3.67 L (7.75 pt), based on a statement by the historian Josephus that a hin equaled two Athenian choes. (Ex 29:40)—See App. B14.

Holy; Holiness. A quality possessed inherently by Jehovah; a state of absolute moral purity and sacredness. (Ex 28:36; 1Sa 2:2;

Pr 9:10; Isa 6:3) When referring to humans (Ex 19:6; 2Ki 4:9), animals (Nu 18:17), things (Ex 28:38; 30:25; Le 27:14), places (Ex 3:5; Isa 27:13), time periods (Ex 16:23; Le 25:12), and activities (Ex 36:4), the original Hebrew word conveys the thought of separateness, exclusiveness, or sanctification to the holy God; a state of being set aside for Jehovah's service. In the Christian Greek Scriptures, the words rendered "holy" and "holiness" likewise denote separation to God. The words are also used to refer to purity in one's personal conduct.—Mr 6:20; 2Co 7:1; 1Pe 1:15, 16.

Holy, the. The first and larger compartment of the tabernacle or of the temple, as distinguished from the innermost compartment, the Most Holy. In the tabernacle, the Holy contained the golden lampstand, golden altar of incense, table of showbread, and golden utensils; in the temple, it contained the golden altar, ten golden lampstands, and ten tables of showbread. (Ex 26:33; Heb 9:2)—See App. B5 and B8.

Holy spirit. The invisible energizing force that God puts into action to accomplish his will. It is holy because it comes from Jehovah, who is clean and righteous to the highest degree, and because it is God's means to accomplish what is holy.—Lu 1:35; Ac 1:8.

Homer. A dry measure corresponding to the cor. Based on the estimated volume of the bath measure, it equaled 220 L (200 dry qt). (Le 27:16)—See App. B14.

Horeb; Mount Horeb. The mountainous region surrounding Mount Sinai. Another name for Mount Sinai. (Ex 3:1; De 5:2)—See App. B3.

Horn. Referring to animal horns, which were used as drinking vessels, as vessels for oil, as containers for ink and cosmetics, and as musical or signaling instruments. (1Sa 16:1, 13; 1Ki 1:39; Eze 9:2) "Horn" is often used figuratively for strength, conquest, and victory.—De 33:17; Mic 4:13; Zec 1:19.

Horns of the altar. Hornlike projections extending outward from the four corners of certain altars. (Le 8:15; 1Ki 2:28)—See App. B5 and B8.

Hyssop. A plant with fine branches and leaves, used for sprinkling blood or water in cleansing ceremonies. It was possibly marjoram (*Origanum maru; Origanum syriacum*). As used at John 19:29, it may have

been marjoram attached to a branch or durra, a variety of common sorghum (*Sorghum vulgare*), since this plant could have provided a stalk long enough to carry the sponge of sour wine to Jesus' mouth.—Ex 12:22; Ps 51:7.

I

Idol; Idolatry. An idol is an image, a representation of anything, real or imagined, that people may use in worship. Idolatry is the veneration, love, worship, or adoration of an idol.—Ps 115:4; Ac 17:16; 1Co 10:14.

Illyricum. A Roman province northwest of Greece. Paul traveled this far in his ministry, but it is not stated whether he preached in Illyricum or merely up to it. (Ro 15:19)—See App. B13.

Incense. A compound of aromatic gums and balsams that burns slowly, giving off a fragrant aroma. A special four-ingredient incense was made for use at the tabernacle and the temple. It was burned morning and night on the altar of incense in the Holy compartment, and on the Day of Atonement, it was burned inside the Most Holy compartment. It was symbolic of the acceptable prayers of God's faithful servants. Its use was not required of Christians.—Ex 30:34, 35; Le 16:13; Re 5:8.

Israel. The name God gave to Jacob. It came to refer to all his descendants collectively, at any one time. The descendants of Jacob's 12 sons were often called the sons of Israel, the house of Israel, the people (men) of Israel, or the Israelites. Israel was also used as the name for the ten-tribe northern kingdom that broke away from the southern kingdom, and later as a term for anointed Christians, "the Israel of God."—Ga 6:16; Ge 32:28; 2Sa 7:23; Ro 9:6.

J

Jacob. A son of Isaac and Rebekah. God later gave him the name Israel, and he became the patriarch of the people of Israel (also called Israelites and later, Jews). He was the father of the 12 sons who, along with their descendants, made up the 12 tribes of the nation of Israel. The name Jacob continued to be used for the nation or people of Israel. —Ge 32:28; Mt 22:32.

Jeduthun. A term of uncertain meaning appearing in the superscriptions of Psalms 39, 62, and 77. These superscriptions appear to be instructions for the performance of the psalm, perhaps identifying a style or a musical instrument. There was a Levitical musician named Jeduthun, so this performance style or instrument may have been associated with him or his sons.

Jehovah. The common English rendering of the Tetragrammaton (the four Hebrew letters for the personal name of God), which appears over 7,000 times in this translation.—See App. A4 and A5.

Jew. A term used for a person of the tribe of Judah after the fall of the ten-tribe kingdom of Israel. (2Ki 16:6) After the Babylonian exile, it was used with regard to Israelites from various tribes who returned to Israel. (Ezr 4: 12) Later, it was used throughout the world to distinguish Israelites from those of the Gentile nations. (Es 3:6) The term is also used figuratively by the apostle Paul when reasoning that nationality is of no consequence in the Christian congregation.—Ro 2:28, 29; Ga 3:28.

Jubilee. Every 50th year, counting from Israel's entry into the Promised Land. The land was to lie fallow during the Jubilee year, and Hebrew slaves were to be set free. Hereditary lands that had been sold were returned. The Jubilee was, in a sense, an entire year of festival, a year of liberty that restored the nation to the state it had enjoyed when God first established it.—Le 25:10.

Judah. Jacob's fourth son by his wife Leah. In his deathbed prophecy, Jacob foretold that a great and lasting ruler would come from Judah's family line. Jesus, in his human existence, descended from Judah. The name Judah also refers to the tribe and later to the kingdom named after Judah. Described as the southern kingdom, Judah was made up of the Israelite tribes of Judah and Benjamin and included the priests and Levites. Judah occupied the southern part of the country that included Jerusalem and the temple.—Ge 29:35; 49:10; 1Ki 4:20; Heb 7:14.

Judges. Men raised up by Jehovah to save his people prior to the period of Israel's human kings.—Jg 2:16.

Judgment Day. A specific day, or period, when particular groups, nations, or mankind in general are called to account by God. It may be a time when those judged to be deserving of death are executed, or the judgment may afford opportunity for some to be saved and gain everlasting life. Jesus

Christ and his apostles pointed to a future "Judgment Day" involving not only the living but also those who died in the past.—Mt 12:36.

Judgment seat. Usually a raised outdoor platform, approached by steps, from which seated officials could address the crowds and announce their decisions. The expressions "judgment seat of God" and "judgment seat of the Christ" are symbolic of Jehovah's arrangement for judging mankind.—Ro 14:10; 2Co 5:10; Joh 19:13.

L

Lake of fire. A symbolic place that "burns with fire and sulfur," also described as "the second death." Unrepentant sinners, the Devil, and even death and the Grave (or, Hades) are thrown into it. The inclusion of a spirit creature and also of death and Hades, all of which cannot be affected by fire, indicates that this lake is a symbol, not of everlasting torment, but of everlasting destruction.—Re 19:20; 20:14, 15; 21:8.

Last days. This and similar expressions, such as "the final part of the days," are used in Bible prophecy to refer to the time when historical events would reach a final climax. (Eze 38:16; Da 10:14; Ac 2:17) Depending on the nature of the prophecy, this may be a period covering just a few years or many. Most notably, the Bible uses this term regarding "the last days" of the present system of things, during Jesus' invisible presence.—2Ti 3:1; Jas 5:3; 2Pe 3:3.

Law. When it is capitalized, this word refers either to the Mosaic Law or to the first five books of the Bible. When it is lowercased, it may refer to individual laws of the Mosaic Law or a principle of law.—Nu 15:16; De 4:8; Mt 7:12; Ga 3:24.

Lay hands on. Hands were laid on a person to appoint him to a special work or to designate him for a blessing, a healing, or a gift of the holy spirit. Sometimes hands were laid on animals before they were sacrificed.—Ex 29:15; Nu 27:18; Ac 19:6; 1Ti 5:22.

Leaven. A substance added to dough or to liquids to cause fermentation; especially a portion of fermented dough preserved from a previous batch. Often used in the Bible as a symbol of sin and corruption, it is also used to indicate hidden, pervasive growth.—Ex 12:20; Mt 13:33; Ga 5:9.

Lebanon Mountain range. One of the two mountain ranges forming the mountain system of the land of Lebanon. The Lebanon range is on the west, and the Anti-Lebanon range is on the east. A long, fertile valley separates the two ranges. The Lebanon range rises up almost directly from the Mediterranean coast, and its summits average between 1,800 and 2,100 m (6,000 and 7,000 ft) in elevation. In ancient times, Lebanon was covered with majestic cedars, which were highly prized by the surrounding nations. (De 1:7; Ps 29:6; 92:12)—See App. B7.

Leprosy; Leper. A serious skin disease. In the Scriptures, leprosy is not restricted to the disease known by that name today, for it could affect not only humans but also clothing and houses. A person afflicted with leprosy is called a leper.—Le 14:54; Lu 5:12.

Lepton. In the Christian Greek Scripture period, the smallest Jewish copper or bronze coin. Translated as "mite" in some Bible versions. (Mr 12:42; Lu 21:2; ftns.)—See App. B14.

Levi; Levite. Jacob's third son by his wife Leah; also the tribe named after him. His three sons became the founders of the three principal divisions of what is known as the Levitical priesthood. At times, the term "Levites" applies to the whole tribe, but usually it excludes the priestly family of Aaron. The tribe of Levi did not receive an allotment of land in the Promised Land but was given 48 cities within the boundaries of land apportioned to the other tribes.—De 10:8; 1Ch 6:1; Heb 7:11.

Leviathan. An animal usually associated with water, apparently some form of aquatic creature. At Job 3:8 and 41:1, it seems to refer to the crocodile or some other aquatic creature of great proportions and strength. At Psalm 104:26, it may be some type of whale. Elsewhere it is used figuratively and is not identifiable with any one animal.—Ps 74:14; Isa 27:1.

Loaves of presentation.—See SHOWBREAD.

Locusts. A variety of grasshoppers that migrate in great swarms. They were considered clean for food in the Mosaic Law. Large swarms that consume everything in their path, causing massive destruction, were regarded as a plague.—Ex 10:14; Mt 3:4.

Log. The smallest liquid measure mentioned in the Bible. In the Jewish Talmud, it is described as 1/12 of a hin, so using that as a basis, the log would have a capacity of 0.31 L (0.66 pt). (Le 14:10)—See App. B14.

Loom. A frame used for weaving threads or yarns into cloth.—Ex 39:27.

Lord's Evening Meal. A literal meal consisting of unleavened bread and wine as symbols of Christ's body and blood; a memorial of Jesus' death. Since this is an observance that Christians are Scripturally required to keep, it is also appropriately termed "the Memorial."—1Co 11:20, 23-26.

Lots. Pebbles or small bits of wood or stone that were used in making decisions. These were gathered into the folds of a garment or into a vessel and then shaken. The lot that fell out or was drawn out was the one chosen. This was often done prayerfully. The term "lot" is used both literally and figuratively with the meaning "share" or "portion."—Jos 14:2; Ps 16:5; Pr 16:33; Mt 27:35.

Loyal love. Most frequently rendered from the Hebrew word *che'sedh,* referring to love motivated by commitment, integrity, loyalty, and deep attachment. It is often used in connection with God's love for humans, but it is also love shown between humans.—Ex 34:6; Ru 3:10.

M

Macedonia. A region north of Greece that gained prominence under Alexander the Great and remained independent until conquered by the Romans. Macedonia was a Roman province when the apostle Paul made his first visit to Europe. Paul visited the area three times. (Ac 16:9)—See App. B13.

Magistrates. Under the government of Babylon, police magistrates were civil officers in the jurisdictional districts who knew the law and had limited judicial authority. In Roman colonies, the civil magistrates were administrators of the government. Their duties included maintaining order, controlling finances, judging violators of the law, and ordering the carrying out of punishment.—Da 3:2; Ac 16:20.

Mahalath. A term, evidently musical, found in the superscriptions of Psalms 53 and 88. It may be related to a Hebrew root verb meaning "grow weak; fall sick," thereby suggesting a gloomy and sad tone, which would harmonize with the somber content of the two songs.

Malcam. Probably the same as Molech, the chief god of the Ammonites. (Zep 1:5)—See MOLECH.

Manna. The main food of the Israelites during their 40 years in the wilderness. It was provided by Jehovah. It miraculously appeared on the ground under a layer of dew every morning except on the Sabbath. When the Israelites first saw it, they said, "What is it?" or, in Hebrew, *"man hu'?"* (Ex 16:13-15, 35) In other contexts, it is referred to as "the grain of heaven" (Ps 78:24), "bread from heaven" (Ps 105:40), and "the bread of mighty ones" (Ps 78:25). Jesus also referred to manna in a figurative sense.—Joh 6:49, 50.

Maskil. A Hebrew term of uncertain meaning in the superscriptions of 13 psalms. It possibly means "contemplative poem." Some think that a word similar in form, translated 'serve with discretion,' may be related in meaning.—2Ch 30:22; Ps 32:Sup.

Measuring reed. A measuring reed was six cubits long. Based on the common cubit, it measured 2.67 m (8.75 ft); based on the long cubit, it measured 3.11 m (10.2 ft). (Eze 40:3, 5; Re 11:1)—See App. B14.

Medes; Media. A people descended from Japheth's son Madai; they settled in the mountainous Iranian plateau that became the country of Media. The Medes joined with Babylon to defeat Assyria. At that time, Persia was a province under Media, but Cyrus revolted and Media was merged with Persia to form the Medo-Persian Empire that defeated the Neo-Babylonian Empire in 539 B.C.E. Medes were present in Jerusalem at Pentecost in 33 C.E. (Da 5:28, 31; Ac 2:9)—See App. B9.

Mediator. One who intercedes between two parties in order to reconcile them. In the Scriptures, Moses and Jesus are the mediators of the Law covenant and the new covenant respectively.—Ga 3:19; 1Ti 2:5.

Memorial tomb. A burial place in which the remains of a deceased person were placed. This term renders the Greek word *mne·mei'-on*, which comes from the verb "to remind," suggesting that the person who has died is remembered.—Joh 5:28, 29.

Merodach. The chief god of the city of Babylon. After the Babylonian king and lawmaker Hammurabi made Babylon the capital of Babylonia, Merodach (or, Marduk) grew in importance, finally displacing a number of the earlier gods and becoming the chief god of the Babylonian pantheon. In later periods, the name Merodach (or, Marduk) was replaced by the title "Belu" ("Owner"), and Merodach was commonly spoken of as Bel.—Jer 50:2.

Messiah. A word derived from the Hebrew word for "anointed" or "anointed one." "Christ" is the equivalent derived from the Greek.—Da 9:25; Joh 1:41.

Miktam. A Hebrew word used in the superscriptions of six psalms (Ps 16, 56-60). It is a technical term of uncertain meaning, though it may be related to the word "inscription."

Milcom. A god worshipped by the Ammonites, probably the same as the god Molech. (1Ki 11:5, 7) Near the close of his reign, Solomon built high places to this false god. —See MOLECH.

Mildew. Any of many parasitic plant diseases caused by fungi. It has been suggested that the mildew mentioned in the Bible is black stem rust (*Puccinia graminis*).—1Ki 8:37.

Mile. A measure of distance occurring only once in the original text of the Christian Greek Scriptures at Matthew 5:41, probably referring to the Roman mile that was equal to 1,479.5 m (4,854 ft). The three other occurrences of "mile" at Luke 24:13, John 6:19, and John 11:18 refer to statute miles converted from the ancient stadia of the original text.—See App. B14.

Millstone. A round stone placed on top of a similar stone and used to grind grain into flour. A peg that was fitted into the center of the lower stone served as a pivot for the upper stone. In Bible times, hand mills operated by the women were used in most homes. Since a family's daily bread depended on the hand mill, the Mosaic Law forbade confiscating it or its upper grindstone as security. Larger mills of a similar construction were turned by animals.—De 24:6; Mr 9:42.

Mina. Also called maneh in Ezekiel. A unit both of weight and of monetary value. Based on archaeological evidence that a mina equaled 50 shekels, and a shekel weighed 11.4 g, the mina of the Hebrew Scriptures weighed 570 g (18.35 oz t).

There may also have been a royal mina, as in the case of the cubit. In the Christian Greek Scriptures, a mina was equivalent to 100 drachmas. It weighed 340 g (10.9 oz t). Sixty minas equaled a talent. (Ezr 2:69; Lu 19:13)—See App. B14.

Ministerial servant. A rendering of the Greek word *di·a'ko·nos*, which is often translated "minister" or "servant." "Ministerial servant" refers to one who serves as an assistant to the body of elders in the congregation. He must meet Bible standards to qualify for this privilege of service.—1Ti 3:8-10, 12.

Miracles; Powerful works. Actions or phenomena that surpass all powers known to humans and are attributed to a supernatural agency. Such expressions as "sign," "portent," and "wonder" are sometimes used synonymously in the Bible.—Ex 4:21; Ac 4:22; Heb 2:4.

Molech. A god of the Ammonites; possibly the same as Malcam, Milcom, and Moloch. It may be a title rather than the name of a specific god. The Mosaic Law demanded the death penalty for anyone who sacrificed his children to Molech.—Le 20:2; Jer 32:35; Ac 7:43.

Moloch.—See MOLECH.

Morning star.—See DAYSTAR.

Moses, Law of. The Law that Jehovah gave Israel through Moses in the wilderness of Sinai in 1513 B.C.E. The first five books of the Bible are often referred to as the Law.—Jos 23:6; Lu 24:44.

Most Holy, the. The innermost room of the tabernacle and of the temple, where the ark of the covenant was kept; also called the Holy of Holies. Other than Moses, the only person allowed to enter the Most Holy was the high priest, and he could enter only on the annual Day of Atonement.—Ex 26:33; Le 16:2, 17; 1Ki 6:16; Heb 9:3.

Mound. A geographic or structural feature of the City of David. It may have been terraced supporting walls or some other supporting feature.—2Sa 5:9; 1Ki 11:27.

Mourning. The outward expression of grief over a death or some other calamity. In Bible times, it was customary to mourn for a period of time. In addition to weeping loudly, mourners wore special clothes, put ashes on their head, ripped their garments,

and beat their chest. Professional mourners were sometimes invited to funerals.—Ge 23:2; Es 4:3; Re 21:4.

Muth-labben. A term in the superscription of Psalm 9. Traditionally, it meant "concerning the death of the son." Some suggest that it was the name or perhaps the opening words of a familiar melody to be used when singing this psalm.

Myrrh. An aromatic gum resin obtained from a variety of thorny shrubs or small trees of the genus *Commiphora*. Myrrh was one of the ingredients of the holy anointing oil. It was used to scent such things as garments or beds, and it was added to oil for massages and body lotions. Myrrh was also used to prepare bodies for burial.—Ex 30:23; Pr 7:17; Joh 19:39.

N

Nard. A costly fragrant oil of light-reddish color, derived from the spikenard plant (*Nardostachys jatamansi*). Because it was expensive, nard was often mixed with inferior oils, and it was sometimes counterfeited. Notably, both Mark and John state that "genuine nard" was used on Jesus.—Mr 14:3; Joh 12:3.

Nazarene. A name for Jesus, as one from the town of Nazareth. It is probably related to the Hebrew word used at Isaiah 11:1 for "sprout." It was later applied to Jesus' followers as well.—Mt 2:23; Ac 24:5.

Nazirite. A word taken from the Hebrew for "One Singled Out," "Dedicated One," "Separated One." There were two classes of Nazirites: those who volunteered and those who were appointed as such by God. A man or a woman could take a special vow to Jehovah to live as a Nazirite for a period of time. Those voluntarily taking the vow had three principal restrictions: they were to drink no alcohol nor eat any product of the grapevine, they were not to cut their hair, and they were not to touch a dead body. Those appointed by God as Nazirites remained such for life, and Jehovah specified the requirements for them.—Nu 6:2-7; Jg 13:5.

Nehiloth. A term of uncertain meaning, occurring in the superscription of Psalm 5. Some believe that it refers to a wind instrument, linking it with a Hebrew root word related to *cha·lil'* (flute). However, it may designate a melody.

Nephilim. The violent hybrid sons who were the children of materialized angels and the daughters of men before the Flood.—Ge 6:4.

Nethinim. Non-Israelite temple servants, or ministers. The Hebrew term literally means "Given Ones," implying that they were given for temple service. Likely, many of the Nethinim were descendants of the Gibeonites, whom Joshua had constituted "gatherers of wood and drawers of water for the assembly and for Jehovah's altar."—Jos 9:23, 27; 1Ch 9:2; Ezr 8:17.

New moon. The first day of each month of the Jewish calendar, which was observed as a day for gathering together, feasting, and offering special sacrifices. In later periods, the day became an important national festival, and people abstained from work.—Nu 10:10; 2Ch 8:13; Col 2:16.

Nisan. After the Babylonian exile, the new name for Abib, the first month of the Jewish sacred calendar and the seventh month of the secular calendar. It ran from mid-March to mid-April. (Ne 2:1)—See App. B15.

O

Oath. A sworn statement to certify that something is true, or a solemn promise that a person will or will not do a certain thing. It is frequently a vow made to a superior, especially to God. Jehovah reinforced his covenant with Abraham by a sworn oath.—Ge 14:22; Heb 6:16, 17.

Omer. A dry measure equaling 2.2 L (2 dry qt), or a tenth of an ephah. (Ex 16:16, 18) —See App. B14.

Onyx. A semiprecious stone, a hard variety of agate, or a banded form of chalcedony. The onyx has white layers alternating with black, brown, red, gray, or green layers. It was used in the special garments of the high priest.—Ex 28:9, 12; 1Ch 29:2; Job 28:16.

Overseer. A man whose primary responsibility is to watch over and shepherd the congregation. The basic idea inherent in the Greek term *e·pi'sko·pos* is that of protective supervision. The terms "overseer" and "elder" (*pre·sby'te·ros*) refer to the same position in the Christian congregation, with "elder" indicating the mature qualities of the one so appointed, and "overseer" emphasizing the duties inherent in this appointment.—Ac 20: 28; 1Ti 3:2-7; 1Pe 5:2.

P

Papyrus. A reedlike aquatic plant used in making such things as baskets, containers, and boats. It was also used to make a writing material similar to paper and was used in many scrolls.—Ex 2:3.

Paradise. A beautiful park, or parklike garden. The first such place was Eden, made by Jehovah for the first human pair. When speaking to one of the criminals next to him on the torture stake, Jesus indicated that the earth would become a paradise. At 2 Corinthians 12:4, the word evidently refers to a figurative paradise, and at Revelation 2:7, to a heavenly paradise.—Ca 4:13; Lu 23:43.

Parchment. The skin of a sheep, goat, or calf prepared for use as writing material. It was more durable than papyrus and was used for scrolls of the Bible. The parchments that Paul requested Timothy to bring were possibly portions of the Hebrew Scriptures. Some of the Dead Sea Scrolls were written on parchment.—2Ti 4:13.

Party followers of Herod.—See HEROD; PARTY FOLLOWERS OF.

Passover. An annual festival observed on the 14th day of Abib (later called Nisan) to commemorate the deliverance of the Israelites from Egypt. It was observed by slaughtering and roasting a lamb (or goat), which was then eaten with bitter greens and unleavened bread.—Ex 12:27; Joh 6:4; 1Co 5:7.

Pentecost. The second of the three major festivals that all Jewish males were required to celebrate in Jerusalem. Pentecost, meaning "Fiftieth (Day)," is the name used in the Christian Greek Scriptures for what is called the Festival of Harvest or Festival of Weeks in the Hebrew Scriptures. It was celebrated on the 50th day counted from Nisan 16.—Ex 23:16; 34:22; Ac 2:1.

Persia; Persians. A land and a people regularly mentioned along with, and evidently related to, the Medes. In their early history, the Persians held only the southwestern part of the Iranian plateau. Under Cyrus the Great (who according to some ancient historians was born of a Persian father and a Median mother), the Persians became dominant over the Medes, though the empire continued to be dual. Cyrus conquered the Babylonian Empire in 539 B.C.E. and allowed the Jews in captivity to return to their homeland. The Persian Empire extended from the Indus River on the east to the Aegean Sea on the west. The Jews were under Persian rule until Alexander the Great defeated the Persians in 331 B.C.E. The Persian Empire was foreseen in a vision by Daniel, and it figures in the Bible books of Ezra, Nehemiah, and Esther. (Ezr 1:1; Da 5:28)—See App. B9.

Pestilence. Any rapidly spreading infectious disease capable of attaining epidemic proportions and of causing death. It is often related to the execution of divine judgment. —Nu 14:12; Eze 38:22, 23; Am 4:10.

Pharaoh. A title given to the kings of Egypt. Five pharaohs are named in the Bible (Shishak, So, Tirhakah, Nechoh, and Hophra), but others are left anonymous, including those who had extensive dealings with Abraham, Moses, and Joseph.—Ex 15:4; Ro 9:17.

Pharisees. A prominent religious sect of Judaism in the first century C.E. They were not of priestly descent, but they were strict observers of the Law in its smallest detail, and they elevated oral traditions to the same level. (Mt 23:23) They opposed any Greek cultural influence, and as scholars of the Law and the traditions, they had great authority over the people. (Mt 23:2-6) Some were also members of the Sanhedrin. They often opposed Jesus regarding Sabbath observance, traditions, and association with sinners and tax collectors. Some became Christians, including Saul of Tarsus.—Mt 9: 11; 12:14; Mr 7:5; Lu 6:2; Ac 26:5.

Philistia; Philistines. The land on the southern coast of Israel that came to be called Philistia. The immigrants from Crete who settled there were called Philistines. David subdued them, but they remained independent and were constant enemies of Israel. (Ex 13:17; 1Sa 17:4; Am 9:7)—See App. B4.

Pillar. An upright structural support or column, or something resembling such a column. Some were set up to commemorate historic acts or events. Structural pillars were used in the temple and the royal structures built by Solomon. Pagan peoples set up sacred pillars in connection with their false religion, and the Israelites at times took up this practice. (Jg 16:29; 1Ki 7:21; 14: 23)—See CAPITAL.

Pim. A weight as well as the price charged by the Philistines for sharpening various metal implements. Several stone weights found in archaeological excavations in Israel bear the ancient Hebrew consonants of "pim"; their average weight is 7.8 g (0.2508 oz t), which would be approximately two thirds of a shekel.—1Sa 13:20, 21.

Pledge. An object of personal property given by a debtor to his creditor as a guarantee of the future repayment of a loan. It was also called security. The Mosaic Law contained stipulations concerning pledges in order to protect the interests of poor and defenseless members of the nation.—Ex 22:26; Eze 18:7.

Pomegranate. A fruit that is shaped like an apple, with a rosette or crown at one end. Crowded within the hard rind are small capsules full of juice, each containing a tiny pink or red seed. Pomegranate-shaped ornaments adorned the hem of the high priest's blue sleeveless coat as well as the capitals of the pillars Jachin and Boaz in front of the temple.—Ex 28:34; Nu 13:23; 1Ki 7:18.

Porneia.—See SEXUAL IMMORALITY.

Potter. A maker of earthenware pots, dishes, and other vessels. The Hebrew word for potter literally means "former." The potter's authority over the clay is often used to illustrate Jehovah's sovereignty over individuals and nations.—Isa 64:8; Ro 9:21.

Praetorian Guard. A group of Roman soldiers established as a bodyguard for the Roman emperor. The guard came to be a powerful political force in supporting or overthrowing an emperor.—Php 1:13.

Prefect. An official lower in rank than a satrap in the Babylonian government. In the Bible, prefects were in a position of authority over the wise men in the Babylonian court. Prefects are also mentioned during the rule of King Darius the Mede.—Da 2:48; 6:7.

Preparation. A name for the day before the Sabbath, during which the Jews made the necessary preparations. The day ended at sundown of what is today called Friday, at which time the Sabbath would begin. The Jewish day ran from evening to evening.—Mr 15:42; Lu 23:54.

Presence. In some contexts in the Christian Greek Scriptures, this word describes the royal presence of Jesus Christ from the time of his invisible enthronement as Messianic King onward in the last days of this system of things. Christ's presence is not simply a coming followed by a quick departure; rather, it covers a marked period of time.—Mt 24:3.

Priest. A man who officially represented God to the people he served, instructing them about God and his laws. Priests also represented the people before God, offering sacrifices as well as interceding and pleading for the people. Before the Mosaic Law was instituted, the family head served as priest for his family. Under the Mosaic Law, the male members of the family of Aaron of the tribe of Levi made up the priesthood. The rest of the male Levites were their assistants. At the inauguration of the new covenant, spiritual Israel became a nation of priests, with Jesus Christ as High Priest.—Ex 28:41; Heb 9:24; Re 5:10.

Proconsul. The principal governor of a province administered by the Roman Senate. He had judicial and military power, and although his actions were subject to review by the Senate, he wielded supreme authority in the province.—Ac 13:7; 18:12.

Prophecy. An inspired message, whether a revelation of divine will or the proclamation of it. Prophecy may be an inspired moral teaching, an expression of a divine command or judgment, or a declaration of something to come.—Eze 37:9, 10; Da 9:24; Mt 13:14; 2Pe 1:20, 21.

Prophet. One through whom divine purposes are made known. Prophets acted as spokesmen for God, conveying not only predictions but also Jehovah's teachings, commands, and judgments.—Am 3:7; 2Pe 1:21.

Propitiation.—See ATONEMENT.

Propitiatory cover. The cover of the ark of the covenant, before which the high priest spattered the blood of sin offerings on Atonement Day. The Hebrew term comes from a root verb meaning "to cover over (sin)" or perhaps "to wipe away (sin)." It was made of solid gold, with two cherubs, one mounted at each end. It is sometimes referred to simply as "the cover." (Ex 25:17-22; 1Ch 28:11; Heb 9:5)—See App. B5.

Proselyte. A convert. In the Scriptures, this refers to one who embraced Judaism, which in the case of a male involved getting circumcised.—Mt 23:15; Ac 13:43.

Prostitute. A person who engages in sexual relations outside the marriage bond, espe-

cially for money. (The Greek word for "prostitute," *porʹne,* comes from a root meaning "to sell.") The term usually refers to a woman, although male prostitutes are also mentioned in the Bible. Prostitution was condemned in the Mosaic Law, and a prostitute's wages were unacceptable as a contribution to Jehovah's sanctuary, in contrast with the pagan practice of using temple prostitutes as a source of revenue. (De 23:17, 18; 1Ki 14:24) The Bible also uses the term figuratively, referring to people, nations, or organizations that engage in some form of idolatry while claiming to be worshippers of God. For example, the religious entity called "Babylon the Great" is described in Revelation as a prostitute because she has consorted with the rulers of this world for power and material gain.—Re 17:1-5; 18:3; 1Ch 5:25.

Proverb. A wise saying or short story that teaches a lesson or expresses a profound truth in very few words. A Biblical proverb may take the form of a puzzling saying or a riddle. A proverb embodies a truth in expressive language, often metaphorically. Some sayings became common expressions of ridicule or contempt for certain people.—Ec 12:9; 2Pe 2:22.

Psalm. A song of praise to God. Psalms were set to music and sung by worshippers, including in public worship of Jehovah God at his temple in Jerusalem.—Lu 20:42; Ac 13:33; Jas 5:13.

Purim. The annual festival celebrated on the 14th and 15th of Adar. It commemorates the Jews' deliverance from destruction in Queen Esther's time. The non-Hebrew word *puʹrim* means "lots." The Festival of Purim, or Festival of Lots, was so named from the act of Haman in casting Pur (the Lot) to determine the day to carry out his extermination plot against the Jews.—Es 3:7; 9:26.

Q

Queen of Heaven. The title of a goddess worshipped by apostate Israelites in the days of Jeremiah. Some suggest that it refers to the Babylonian goddess Ishtar (Astarte). The name of her earlier Sumerian counterpart, Inanna, means "Queen of Heaven." Besides being associated with the heavens, she was a fertility goddess. Astarte is also called "Lady of Heaven" in an Egyptian inscription.—Jer 44:19.

R

Rahab. An expression used symbolically in the books of Job, Psalms, and Isaiah (not to be confused with the woman Rahab in the book of Joshua). In the book of Job, the context helps to identify Rahab as a sea monster; in other contexts this sea monster is used as a symbol for Egypt.—Job 9:13; Ps 87:4; Isa 30:7; 51:9, 10.

Ransom. A price paid to provide a release from captivity, punishment, suffering, sin, or even an obligation. The price was not always monetary. (Isa 43:3) A ransom was required in a number of different situations. For example, all firstborn boys or male animals in Israel belonged to Jehovah, and a ransom, or redemption price, needed to be paid to release them from exclusive use in Jehovah's service. (Nu 3:45, 46; 18:15, 16) If an unguarded, dangerous bull killed someone, a ransom was imposed on its owner in order to release him from the prescribed death sentence. (Ex 21:29, 30) However, no ransom was accepted for a willful murderer. (Nu 35:31) Most important, the Bible highlights the ransom that Christ paid by his sacrificial death in order to release obedient humankind from sin and death.—Ps 49:7, 8; Mt 20:28; Eph 1:7.

Reed. A term used for numerous plants commonly growing in wet places. The plant intended in many cases is *Arundo donax*. (Job 8:11; Isa 42:3; Mt 27:29; Re 11:1)—See MEASURING REED.

Repentance. In Biblical usage, a change of mind accompanied by heartfelt regret over a former way of life, wrong actions, or what one has failed to do. Genuine repentance produces fruitage, a changed course of action.—Mt 3:8; Ac 3:19; 2Pe 3:9.

Resurrection. A rising up from death. The Greek word *a·na'sta·sis* literally means "raising up; standing up." Nine resurrections are mentioned in the Bible, including the resurrection of Jesus by Jehovah God. Although other resurrections were performed through Elijah, Elisha, Jesus, Peter, and Paul, these miracles are clearly attributed to God's power. The earthly resurrection of "both the righteous and the unrighteous" is essential to God's purpose. (Ac 24:15) The Bible also mentions a heavenly resurrection, termed "the earlier" or "the first"

resurrection, involving the spirit-anointed brothers of Jesus.—Php 3:11; Re 20:5, 6; Joh 5:28, 29; 11:25.

Righteousness. In the Scriptures, what is right according to God's standard of right and wrong.—Ge 15:6; De 6:25; Pr 11:4; Zep 2:3; Mt 6:33.

S

Sabbath. From a Hebrew word meaning "to rest; to cease." It is the seventh day of the Jewish week (sunset Friday to sunset Saturday). Some other festive days in the year, as well as the 7th and 50th years, were also called sabbaths. On the Sabbath day, no work except priestly service in the sanctuary was to be done. In Sabbath years, the land was to lie uncultivated and fellow Hebrews were not pressed for repayment of debts. In the Mosaic Law, the restrictions for the Sabbath were reasonable, but religious leaders gradually added to them, so that by Jesus' day they were hard for people to observe.—Ex 20:8; Le 25:4; Lu 13:14-16; Col 2:16.

Sackcloth. A coarse cloth used in making sacks, or bags, such as those for containing grain. It was usually woven from dark-colored goat's hair and was the traditional garment of mourning.—Ge 37:34; Lu 10:13.

Sacred pillar. An upright pillar, usually of stone, and evidently a phallic symbol of Baal or of other false gods.—Ex 23:24.

Sacred pole. The Hebrew word (*'ashe·rah'*) refers to (1) a sacred pole representing Asherah, a Canaanite goddess of fertility, or (2) an image of the goddess Asherah herself. The poles apparently stood upright and were made, at least in part, of wood. They may have been uncarved poles, or even trees.—De 16:21; Jg 6:26; 1Ki 15:13.

Sacred secret. An aspect of God's purpose that originates with God, is withheld until his own time, and is revealed only to those whom he chooses to make it known.—Mr 4:11; Col 1:26.

Sacred service. Ministry, or work, that is sacred, being directly related to one's worship of God.—Ro 12:1; Re 7:15.

Sacrifice. An offering presented to God as a token to express thanksgiving, to acknowledge guilt, and to restore good relations with him. Starting with Abel, humans offered various voluntary sacrifices, including animals, until the Mosaic Law covenant made them a requirement. Animal sacrifices were no longer needed after Jesus gave his own life as a perfect sacrifice, though Christians continue to offer spiritual sacrifices to God.—Ge 4:4; Heb 13:15, 16; 1Jo 4:10.

Sadducees. A prominent religious sect of Judaism made up of wealthy aristocrats and priests who wielded great authority over the activities at the temple. They rejected the many oral traditions observed by the Pharisees as well as other Pharisaic beliefs. They did not believe in the resurrection or in the existence of angels. They opposed Jesus. —Mt 16:1; Ac 23:8.

Samaria. The capital city of the northern ten-tribe kingdom of Israel for some 200 years, as well as the name of its entire territory. The city was built on a mountain of the same name. In Jesus' time, Samaria was the name of the Roman district that lay between Galilee in the north and Judea in the south. Jesus usually refrained from preaching in the region in his travels, but at times he passed through it and spoke to the inhabitants. Peter used the second figurative key of the Kingdom when the Samaritans received the holy spirit. (1Ki 16:24; Joh 4:7; Ac 8:14)—See App. B10.

Samaritans. The term initially referred to the Israelites of the northern ten-tribe kingdom, but after the conquest of Samaria by the Assyrians in 740 B.C.E., it included the foreigners brought in by the Assyrians. In Jesus' day, rather than having a racial or political connotation, the name usually referred to those who belonged to the religious sect that was located in the vicinity of ancient Shechem and Samaria. The sect's adherents held certain beliefs that were distinctly different from those of Judaism.—Joh 8:48.

Sanctuary. Generally, a place set apart for worship, a holy place. Most often, though, it designates either the tabernacle or the temple in Jerusalem. The term is also used of God's dwelling place in the heavens.—Ex 25: 8, 9; 2Ki 10:25; 1Ch 28:10; Re 11:19.

Sanhedrin. The Jewish high court in Jerusalem. In Jesus' day, it was made up of 71 members, including the high priest and others who had held the office of high priest, members of the high priestly families, elders, tribal and family heads, and scribes. —Mr 15:1; Ac 5:34; 23:1, 6.

Satan. A Hebrew word meaning "Resister." When used with the definite article in the original languages, it refers to Satan the Devil, God's chief Adversary.—Job 1:6; Mt 4: 10; Re 12:9.

Satrap. A viceroy, or governor of a province, in the Babylonian and Persian empires. A satrap was appointed by the king as a chief ruler.—Ezr 8:36; Da 6:1.

Scepter. A baton or rod carried by a ruler as an emblem of royal authority.—Ge 49:10; Heb 1:8.

Scourge. In the Hebrew Scriptures, this term usually refers to a plague, a disease, or a calamity sent from Jehovah as punishment. In the Christian Greek Scriptures, it refers to beating or flogging with a whip that had knots or barbed ends.—Nu 16:49; Joh 19:1.

Scribe. A copyist of the Hebrew Scriptures. By the time Jesus came to earth, it designated a class of men learned in the Law. They opposed Jesus.—Ezr 7:6, ftn.; Mr 12: 38, 39; 14:1.

Scripture(s). The sacred writings of God's Word. This expression occurs only in the Christian Greek Scriptures.—Lu 24:27; 2Ti 3:16.

Scroll. A long sheet of parchment or papyrus, with writing on one side, which was usually rolled around a stick. The Scriptures were written and copied on scrolls, the common book form during the period of Bible writing. —Jer 36:4, 18, 23; Lu 4:17-20; 2Ti 4:13.

Seah. A dry measure. Basing the capacity on the corresponding liquid bath measure, it would equal 7.33 L (6.66 dry qt). (2Ki 7:1) —See App. B14.

Seal. A device used to make an impression (usually on clay or wax) that showed ownership, authenticity, or agreement. Ancient seals consisted of a piece of hard material (stone, ivory, or wood) having engraved letters or designs in reverse. A seal is used figuratively for something stamped as authentic, or as a mark of possession, or as something that is hidden or secret.—Ex 28: 11; Ne 9:38; Re 5:1; 9:4.

Seal ring. A type of seal that was worn on the finger or on a cord, probably around the neck. Also called a signet ring, it was the symbol of authority of a ruler or an official. (Ge 41:42)—See SEAL.

Sect. A body of people adhering to a doctrine or to a leader and following their own beliefs. It is used of the two prominent branches of Judaism, the Pharisees and the Sadducees. Non-Christians also called Christianity a "sect" or "the sect of the Nazarenes," possibly viewing it as a breakaway from Judaism. Sects eventually developed in the Christian congregation; "the sect of Nicolaus" is mentioned specifically in Revelation.—Ac 5:17; 15:5; 24:5; 28:22; Re 2:6; 2Pe 2:1.

Seer. A person enabled by God to discern the divine will, one whose eyes had been opened to see or understand things that were not evident to humans in general. The Hebrew word is drawn from a root word meaning "to see," either literally or figuratively. A seer was a person consulted by others for wise counsel on problems encountered.—1Sa 9:9.

Selah. A technical term for music or recitation found in Psalms and Habakkuk. It may mean a pause in the singing or in the music, or in both, for the purpose of silent meditation or to make the sentiment just expressed stand out. The Greek *Septuagint* rendering is *di·a´psal·ma*, defined as "a musical interlude."—Ps 3:4; Hab 3:3.

Seraphs. Spirit creatures stationed around Jehovah's throne in the heavens. The Hebrew term *sera·phim´* literally means "burning ones."—Isa 6:2, 6.

Sexual immorality. From the Greek *por·nei´a*, a general term for all unlawful sexual intercourse. It includes adultery, prostitution, sexual relations between unmarried individuals, homosexuality, and bestiality. It is used figuratively in Revelation with regard to a religious prostitute called "Babylon the Great" to describe her consorting with the rulers of this world for power and material gain. (Rev 14:8; 17:2; 18:3; Mt 5:32; Ac 15:29; Ga 5:19)—See PROSTITUTE.

Shebat. After the Babylonian exile, the name of the 11th month of the Jewish sacred calendar and the 5th month of the secular calendar. It ran from mid-January to mid-February. (Zec 1:7)—See App. B15.

Shekel. The basic Hebrew unit of weight and of monetary value. The weight equaled 11.4 g (0.403 oz; 0.367 oz t). The "shekel of the holy place" may have been an expression used to emphasize that the weight should be precise or that it should conform to a standard weight kept at the tabernacle.

There may have been a royal shekel (different from the common shekel) or a standard weight kept at the royal palace.—Ex 30:13.

Sheminith. A musical term literally meaning "the eighth" that may refer to a lower musical register, or mode. For instruments, the word probably pointed to those that produced the bass tones of the musical scale. For songs, it likely referred to musical accompaniment in a lower range and sung accordingly.—1Ch 15:21; Ps 6:Sup; 12:Sup.

Sheol. A Hebrew word corresponding to the Greek word "Hades." It is translated "Grave" (capitalized), to distinguish it as the common grave of mankind rather than an individual grave.—Ge 37:35; Ps 16:10; Ac 2:31 (ftns.).

Showbread. Twelve loaves of bread that were placed in two stacks of six each on the table in the Holy compartment of the tabernacle and of the temple. Also called "layer bread" and "loaves of presentation." This offering to God was replaced with fresh bread on each Sabbath. The bread that was removed was normally eaten only by the priests. (2Ch 2:4; Mt 12:4; Ex 25:30; Le 24:5-9; Heb 9:2)—See App. B5.

Sign. An object, act, situation, or unusual display that has significance as an indicator of something else, present or future.—Ge 9:12, 13; 2Ki 20:9; Mt 24:3; Re 1:1.

Sin offering. A sacrifice offered for unintentional sin committed because of weakness of the imperfect flesh. Various animal sacrifices, from bull to pigeon, were used, according to the position and circumstances of the one whose sin was being atoned for.—Le 4:27, 29; Heb 10:8.

Sivan. After the Babylonian exile, the name of the third month of the Jewish sacred calendar and the ninth month of the secular calendar. It ran from mid-May to mid-June. (Es 8:9)—See App. B15.

Sling. A leather strip or a woven band of such materials as animal sinews, rushes, or hair. The wide center part held the projectile, often a stone. One end of the sling was tied to the hand or wrist, while the other was held in the hand and released when the sling was swung. Ancient nations employed slingers in their armies.—Jg 20:16; 1Sa 17:50.

Snuffers. Tools made of gold, possibly similar to tongs, that were used in the tabernacle and the temple to put out the flame on lamps.—Ex 37:23.

Solomon's Colonnade. In the temple in Jesus' day, a covered passageway on the east of the outer courtyard, popularly believed to be a remnant from Solomon's temple. There Jesus walked 'in the wintertime,' and there early Christians met for worship. (Joh 10:22, 23; Ac 5:12)—See App. B11.

Song of the Ascents. The superscription of Psalms 120-134. Although there are various ideas on the meaning of the phrase, many believe that these 15 psalms were sung by joyful Israelite worshippers as they 'ascended' to Jerusalem, which was situated high in the mountains of Judah, in order to attend the three great annual festivals there.

Son of David. A phrase often applied to Jesus, emphasizing that he is the Heir of the Kingdom covenant that was to be fulfilled by someone in David's lineage.—Mt 12:23; 21:9.

Son of man. An expression found about 80 times in the Gospels. It applies to Jesus Christ and shows that by means of his fleshly birth, he became a human and was not simply a spirit creature with a materialized body. The phrase also indicates that Jesus would fulfill the prophecy recorded at Daniel 7:13, 14. In the Hebrew Scriptures, this expression was used for Ezekiel and Daniel, highlighting the difference between these mortal spokesmen and the divine Originator of their message.—Eze 3:17; Da 8:17; Mt 19:28; 20:28.

Sons of Aaron. Descendants of Levi's grandson Aaron, who was chosen as the first high priest under the Mosaic Law. The sons of Aaron performed the priestly duties at the tabernacle and at the temple.—1Ch 23:28.

Sorcery. The use of power that is acknowledged to be from wicked spirits.—2Ch 33:6.

Soul. The traditional rendering of the Hebrew word *ne'phesh* and the Greek word *psy·khe'*. In examining the way these terms are used in the Bible, it becomes evident that they basically refer to (1) people, (2) animals, or (3) the life that a person or an animal has. (Ge 1:20; 2:7; Nu 31:28; 1Pe 3:20; also ftns.) In contrast to the way that the term "soul" is used in many religious contexts, the Bible shows that both *ne'phesh* and *psy·khe'*, in connection with earthly creatures, refer to that which is material, tangible, visible, and mortal. In this translation, these original-

language words have most often been rendered according to their meaning in each context, using such terms as "life," "creature," "person," "one's whole being," or simply as a personal pronoun (for example, "I" for "my soul"). In most cases, footnotes give the alternative rendering "soul." When the term "soul" is used, either in the main text or in footnotes, it should be understood in line with the above explanation. When referring to doing something with one's whole soul, it means to do it with one's whole being, wholeheartedly, or with one's whole life. (De 6:5; Mt 22:37) In some contexts, these original-language words can be used to refer to the desire or appetite of a living creature. They can also refer to a dead person or a dead body.—Nu 6:6; Pr 23:2; Isa 56:11; Hag 2:13.

Span. A linear measure approximately equal to the distance between the end of the thumb and the end of the little finger when the hand is spread out. Based on the cubit of 44.5 cm (17.5 in.), a span would be 22.2 cm (8.75 in.) in length. (Ex 28:16; 1Sa 17:4)—See App. B14.

Spelt. An inferior kind of wheat (*Triticum spelta*), the kernels of which are not readily separated from the chaff.—Ex 9:32.

Spirit. The Hebrew word *ru'ach* and the Greek word *pneu'ma*, often translated "spirit," have a number of meanings. All of them refer to that which is invisible to human sight and gives evidence of force in motion. The Hebrew and Greek words are used with reference to (1) wind, (2) the active life-force in earthly creatures, (3) the impelling force that issues from a person's figurative heart and causes him to say and do things in a certain way, (4) inspired expressions originating from an invisible source, (5) spirit persons, and (6) God's active force, or holy spirit.—Ex 35:21; Ps 104:29; Mt 12:43; Lu 11:13.

Spiritism. The belief that the spirits of dead humans survive the death of the physical body and that they can and do communicate with the living, especially through a person (a medium) particularly susceptible to their influence. The Greek word for "practice of spiritism" is *phar·ma·ki'a*, which literally means "druggery." This term came to be connected with spiritism because in ancient times, drugs were used when invoking the power of the demons in order to practice sorcery.—Ga 5:20; Re 21:8.

Spirit medium. Someone who claims to talk with the dead.—Le 20:27; De 18:10-12; 2Ki 21:6.

Spoil. Personal or household effects, livestock, or other items of value that are taken as plunder from a defeated enemy.—Jos 7: 21; 22:8; Heb 7:4.

Stake. An upright pole to which a victim was fastened. It was used in some nations for execution and/or for exposing a dead body as a warning to others or for public humiliation. The Assyrians, noted for their savage warfare, impaled captives by hanging their bodies atop pointed stakes that had been run up through the abdomen into the chest cavity of the victim. In Jewish law, though, those guilty of such heinous crimes as blasphemy or idolatry were first killed by stoning or by some other method, and then their dead bodies were hung on stakes, or trees, as warning examples to others. (De 21:22, 23; 2Sa 21:6, 9) The Romans sometimes simply tied a victim to the stake, in which case he might live for several days before he died from pain, thirst, hunger, and exposure to the sun. In other cases, such as the execution of Jesus, they nailed the hands and feet of the accused to a stake. (Lu 24:20; Joh 19:14-16; 20:25; Ac 2:23, 36)—See TORTURE STAKE.

Stocks. An instrument of confinement for punishment. Some devices confined only the feet, while others kept the body in a distorted position, perhaps confining feet, hands, and neck.—Jer 20:2; Ac 16:24.

Stoic philosophers. A Greek school of philosophers who believed that happiness consists of living in accord with reason and nature. The truly wise man, in their estimation, was indifferent to pain or pleasure.—Ac 17:18.

Superscription. The heading at the beginning of a psalm that identifies the writer, gives background information, provides musical instructions, or indicates the use or purpose of the psalm.—See the superscriptions of Psalms 3, 4, 5, 6, 7, 30, 38, 60, 92, 102.

Synagogue. A word meaning "a bringing together; an assembly," but in most scriptures, the building or place where Jews assembled for Scripture reading, instruction, preaching, and prayer. In Jesus' day, each sizable town in Israel had a synagogue, and the larger cities had more than one.—Lu 4: 16; Ac 13:14, 15.

Syria; Syrians.—See ARAM; ARAMAEANS.

Syrtis. Two large shallow gulfs on the coast of Libya, North Africa, feared by ancient sailors because of the treacherous sandbanks that were constantly shifting as a result of the tides. (Ac 27:17)—See App. B13.

System(s) of things. Rendering of the Greek word *ai·on´* when it refers to the current state of affairs or features that distinguish a certain period of time, epoch, or age. The Bible speaks of "the present system of things," referring to the prevailing state of affairs in the world in general and the worldly way of life. (2Ti 4:10) By means of the Law covenant, God introduced a system of things that some might call the Israelite or Jewish epoch. By means of his ransom sacrifice, Jesus Christ was used by God to introduce a different system of things, one primarily involving the congregation of anointed Christians. This marked the beginning of a new epoch, characterized by the realities foreshadowed by the Law covenant. When in the plural, this phrase refers to the various systems of things, or prevailing states of affairs, that have existed or will exist.—Mt 24:3; Mr 4:19; Ro 12:2; 1Co 10:11.

T

Tabernacle. A transportable tent of worship used by Israel after the Exodus from Egypt. It housed the ark of the covenant of Jehovah, which was representative of God's presence, and served as a place of sacrifice and worship. It is also sometimes called "the tent of meeting." It was a framework of wooden panels enclosed by linen coverings embroidered with cherubs. It was divided into two rooms, the first called the Holy, and the second, the Most Holy. (Jos 18:1; Ex 25:9)—See App. B5.

Talent. The largest of the Hebrew units of weight and of monetary value. It weighed 34.2 kg (75.5 lb; 91.75 lb t; 1,101 oz t). A Greek talent was smaller, weighing about 20.4 kg (44.8 lb; 54.5 lb t; 654 oz t). (1Ch 22:14; Mt 18:24)—See App. B14.

Tammuz. (1) The name of a deity over whom apostate Hebrew women in Jerusalem wept. It has been suggested that Tammuz was originally a king who was deified after his death. In Sumerian text, Tammuz is called Dumuzi and is identified as the consort or lover of the fertility goddess Inanna (the Babylonian Ishtar). (Eze 8:14) (2) After the Babylonian exile, the name of the fourth Jewish lunar month of the sacred calendar and the tenth month of the secular calendar. This month ran from mid-June to mid-July. —See App. B15.

Tarshish, ships of. Initially a term used for ships that made trips to ancient Tarshish (modern-day Spain). It seems that the term eventually came to stand for large ships capable of long-distance travel. Solomon and Jehoshaphat utilized such ships for trade purposes.—1Ki 9:26; 10:22; 22:48.

Tartarus. In the Christian Greek Scriptures, a prisonlike abased condition into which the disobedient angels of Noah's day were cast. At 2 Peter 2:4, the use of the verb *tar-ta-ro'o* (to "cast into Tartarus") does not signify that "the angels who sinned" were cast into the pagan mythological Tartarus (that is, an underground prison and place of darkness for the lesser gods). Rather, it indicates that they were abased by God from their heavenly place and privileges and were delivered over to a condition of deepest mental darkness respecting God's bright purposes. Darkness also marks their own eventuality, which the Scriptures show is everlasting destruction along with their ruler, Satan the Devil. Therefore, Tartarus denotes the lowest condition of abasement for those rebellious angels. It is not the same as "the abyss" spoken of at Revelation 20:1-3.

Tebeth. After the Babylonian exile, the name of the tenth month of the Jewish sacred calendar and the fourth month of the secular calendar. It ran from mid-December to mid-January. It is generally referred to simply as "the tenth month." (Es 2:16)—See App. B15.

Temple. The permanent building in Jerusalem that replaced the portable tabernacle as the center of Israelite worship. The first temple was built by Solomon and was destroyed by the Babylonians. The second one was built by Zerubbabel after the return from Babylonian exile and was later rebuilt by Herod the Great. In the Scriptures, the temple was often simply called "the house of Jehovah." (Ezr 1:3; 6:14, 15; 1Ch 29:1; 2Ch 2:4; Mt 24:1)—See App. B8 and B11.

Tenth (tithe). A tenth part, or 10 percent, given or paid as a tribute, especially for religious purposes. It is also called a "tithe," and giving it is called "tithing." (Mal 3:10; De 26:12; Mt 23:23) Under the Mosaic Law, a tenth of the produce of the land and a tenth of the increase of the herds and flocks were given to the Levites yearly to support them. The Levites gave a tenth of this tenth to the Aaronic priesthood to support them. There were some additional tithes as well. Tithing is not required of Christians.

Tent of meeting. An expression applied both to the tent of Moses and to the sacred tabernacle originally erected in the wilderness. —Ex 33:7; 39:32.

Teraphim. Family gods or idols, at times consulted for omens. (Eze 21:21) Some were the size and shape of a man, while others were much smaller. (Ge 31:34; 1Sa 19:13, 16) Archaeological findings in Mesopotamia indicate that possessing the teraphim images had a bearing on who would receive the family inheritance. (This may explain why Rachel took her father's teraphim.) This does not seem to have been the case in Israel, although the idolatrous use of teraphim existed in the days of the judges as well as the kings, and they were included among the items destroyed by faithful King Josiah. —Jg 17:5; 2Ki 23:24; Ho 3:4.

Testimony. "The Testimony" usually refers to the Ten Commandments as written on the two stone tablets given to Moses.—Ex 31:18.

Thanksgiving offering. A communion offering intended to praise God for his provisions and loyal love. The flesh of the animal offering and both leavened and unleavened bread were eaten. The flesh had to be eaten the same day.—2Ch 29:31.

Thresh; Threshing floor. The process of releasing grain from its stalk and chaff; the place where this work was done. Threshing was done by hand with a rod, or for larger quantities, with special equipment, such as threshing sledges or rollers, pulled by animals. The equipment ran over the grain that was spread on the threshing floor, a flat circular area usually at a high elevation exposed to wind.—Le 26:5; Isa 41:15; Mt 3:12.

Tishri.—See ETHANIM and App. B15.

Torture stake. The rendering of the Greek word *stau-ros'*, meaning an upright stake or pole, such as the one on which Jesus was executed. There is no evidence that the Greek word meant a cross, such as the pagans used as a religious symbol for many centuries before Christ. *"Torture* stake" conveys the full intent of the original word, since Jesus also used the word *stau·rosʹ* to indicate the torture, suffering, and shame that his followers would face. (Mt 16:24; Heb 12:2)—See STAKE.

Transgress; Transgression. To overstep a stated law; the act of overstepping a law. It is synonymous with "sin" in the Bible.—Ps 51:3; Ro 5:14.

Tree of life. A tree in the garden of Eden. The Bible does not indicate that it had inherent life-giving qualities in its fruit; instead, it represented God's guarantee of everlasting life to those he would allow to eat of its fruit.—Ge 2:9; 3:22.

Tree of the knowledge of good and bad. A tree in the garden of Eden that God used as a symbol of his right to set the standards for mankind as to what is "good" and what is "bad."—Ge 2:9, 17.

Tribute. Payment by one State or ruler to another as a mark of submission, in order to maintain peace or to gain protection. (2Ki 3:4; 18:14-16; 2Ch 17:11) The word is also used for a personal tax on individuals.—Ne 5:4; Ro 13:7.

True God, the. A rendering of the Hebrew expression for "the God." In many cases, this use of the definite article in Hebrew serves to distinguish Jehovah as the only true God in contrast to false gods. The rendering "the *true* God" carefully preserves the full meaning of the Hebrew expression in such contexts.—Ge 5:22, 24; 46:3; De 4:39.

Trumpet. A wind instrument made of metal, used for signaling and for music. According to Numbers 10:2, Jehovah gave instructions for making two silver trumpets that would be used to sound specific signals for summoning the assembly, for breaking camp, or for proclaiming war. These likely were straight trumpets, unlike the curved "horns" that were actually made from animal horns. Trumpets of unspecified construction were also included among the musical instruments at the temple. The sound of trumpets often symbolically accompanies the proclamation of Jehovah's judgments or other significant events of divine origin.—2Ch 29:26; Ezr 3:10; 1Co 15:52; Re 8:7–11:15.

Turban. A cloth wrapped around the head and worn as a headdress. The high priest wore a turban of fine linen, with a gold plate tied to its front with a blue cord. The king wore a turban under his crown. Job used the expression figuratively when he likened his justice to a turban.—Ex 28:36, 37; Job 29:14; Eze 21:26.

U

Unclean. May refer to being physically dirty or to breaking moral laws. In the Bible, though, the word often refers to what is not acceptable, or not clean, according to the Mosaic Law. (Le 5:2; 13:45; Mt 10:1; Ac 10:14; Eph 5:5)—See CLEAN.

Undeserved kindness. A Greek word with the central idea of that which is agreeable and winsome. The word is often used to refer to a kind gift or a kind manner of giving. When referring to the undeserved kindness of God, the word describes a free gift given generously by God, with no expectation of repayment. Thus, it is an expression of God's bounteous giving and generous love and kindness toward humans. The Greek term is also rendered by such expressions as "favor" and "kind gift." It is given unearned and unmerited, motivated solely by the generosity of the giver.—2Co 6:1; Eph 1:7.

Unleavened. Referring to bread that is made without leaven.—De 16:3; Mr 14:12; 1Co 5:8.

Urim and Thummim. Objects used by the high priest in a manner similar to the use of lots to determine the divine will when questions of national importance needed an answer from Jehovah. The Urim and Thummim were put inside the high priest's breastpiece when he entered the tabernacle. Their use seems to have ceased when the Babylonians destroyed Jerusalem.—Ex 28:30; Ne 7:65.

V

Vow. A solemn promise made to God to perform some act, make some offering or gift, enter some service, or abstain from certain things not unlawful in themselves. It carried the force of an oath.—Nu 6:2; Ec 5:4; Mt 5:33.

Vow offering. A voluntary offering that accompanied certain vows.—Le 23:38; 1Sa 1:21.

W

Wadi. The valley or bed of a stream that is usually dry except during the rainy season; the word may also refer to the stream itself. Some streams were fed by springs and were therefore perennial. The wadi is referred to as "valley" in some contexts.—Ge 26:19; Nu 34:5; De 8:7; 1Ki 18:5; Job 6:15.

Warp. In weaving, the group of threads running the length of the fabric. The set of threads woven alternately over and under these at right angles across the cloth are the woof.—Jg 16:13.

Watchman. One who guards against possible harm to people or property, often during the night, and who may sound an alarm in the face of threatened danger. Watchmen were often stationed on the city walls and towers to observe those approaching before they got close. A watchman in the military is usually called a guard or a sentry. Figuratively, prophets served as watchmen to the nation of Israel, warning of impending destruction.—2Ki 9:20; Eze 3:17.

Wave offering. An offering in which the priest evidently placed his hands under the hands of the worshipper who was holding the sacrifice to be presented and waved them back and forth; or the priest himself waved the offering. This action represented a *presenting* of the sacrificial offerings to Jehovah. —Le 7:30.

Way, the. An expression used figuratively in the Scriptures to refer to a mode of action or conduct that is either approved or disapproved by Jehovah. Those who became followers of Jesus Christ are spoken of as belonging to "The Way," that is, they kept a way of life centered on faith in Jesus Christ, following his example.—Ac 19:9.

Wicked one, the. A designation for Satan the Devil, who stands in opposition to God and his righteous standards.—Mt 6:13; 1Jo 5:19.

Winepress. Usually two pits (vats) cut out of natural limestone, one higher than the other, and connected by a small channel. As the grapes were crushed in the upper pit, the juice flowed into the lower pit. The word is used figuratively for God's judgment.—Isa 5:2; Re 19:15.

Wineskin. A skin bottle made of the complete hide of an animal, such as a goat or a sheep, and used for holding wine. Wine was put into new wineskins, because as it ferments, it generates carbon dioxide gas that exerts pressure on the skin bottles. New skins expand; old, inflexible ones burst under the pressure.—Jos 9:4; Mt 9:17.

Woof. In weaving, the set of threads running the width of the fabric. These were woven alternately over and under the warp, that is, the group of threads running the length of the fabric.—Le 13:59.

Wormwood. Various woody plants having an intensely bitter taste and a strong aromatic odor. Wormwood is used figuratively in the Bible to describe the bitter effects of immorality, enslavement, injustice, and apostasy. At Revelation 8:11, "wormwood" denotes a bitter and poisonous substance, also called absinthe.—De 29:18; Pr 5:4; Jer 9:15; Am 5:7.

Y

Yoke. A bar borne upon a person's shoulders, from each side of which loads were suspended, or a wooden bar or frame placed over the necks of two draft animals (usually cattle) when pulling a farm implement or a wagon. Because slaves often used yokes to carry heavy burdens, the yoke was used figuratively to represent enslavement or subjection to another person, as well as oppression and suffering. Removing or breaking the yoke signified liberation from bondage, oppression, and exploitation.—Le 26:13; Mt 11:29, 30.

Z

Zeus. The supreme god of the polytheistic Greeks. In Lystra, Barnabas was mistakenly identified as Zeus. Ancient inscriptions found near Lystra refer to "priests of Zeus" and "Zeus the sun-god." The ship Paul traveled on from the island of Malta had the figurehead "Sons of Zeus," that is, the twin brothers Castor and Pollux.—Ac 14:12; 28:11.

Zion; Mount Zion. The name of the Jebusite fortress city of Jebus that was on the southeast hill of Jerusalem. After David captured it, he built his royal residence there, and it came to be called "the City of David." (2Sa 5:7, 9) Zion became a mountain especially holy to Jehovah when David had the Ark transferred there. Later, the name included the temple area on Mount Moriah, and at times the entire city of Jerusalem. It is often used symbolically in the Christian Greek Scriptures.—Ps 2:6; 1Pe 2:6; Re 14:1.

Ziv. The original name of the second month of the Jewish sacred calendar and the eighth month of the secular calendar. It ran from mid-April to mid-May. It is named Iyyar in the Jewish Talmud and other works dated after the Babylonian exile. (1Ki 6:37)—See App. B15.

Appendix A

Principles of Bible Translation

The Bible was originally written in ancient Hebrew, Aramaic, and Greek. Today it is available in whole or in part in about 2,600 languages. The vast majority of people who read the Bible do not understand the original languages and therefore must rely on a translation. What principles should guide how the Bible is translated, and how did these govern the rendering of the *New World Translation of the Holy Scriptures*?

Some might conclude that a strict, word-for-word, interlinear-style translation would enable the reader to get closest to what was expressed in the original languages. However, that is not always the case. Consider a few of the reasons:

- No two languages are exactly alike in grammar, vocabulary, and sentence structure. A professor of Hebrew, S. R. Driver, wrote that languages "differ not only in grammar and roots, but also . . . in the manner in which ideas are built up into a sentence." Different languages require quite different thought patterns. "Consequently," continues Professor Driver, "the forms taken by the sentence in different languages are not the same."

- No modern language exactly mirrors the vocabulary and grammar of Biblical Hebrew, Aramaic, and Greek, so a word-for-word translation of the Bible could be unclear or at times could even convey the wrong meaning.

- The meaning of a word or an expression may vary depending on the context in which it is used.

A translator may be able to mirror the literal rendering of the original language in some passages, but this must be done very carefully.

Here are some examples of how word-for-word translation can be misunderstood:

- The Scriptures use the expressions "sleep" and "fall asleep" to refer both to physical sleep and to the sleep of death. (Matthew 28:13; Acts 7:60) When these expressions are used in contexts that refer to death, Bible translators can use such wording as "fall asleep in death," which helps the modern reader avoid confusion.—1 Corinthians 7:39; 1 Thessalonians 4:13; 2 Peter 3:4.

- The apostle Paul used an expression found at Ephesians 4:14 that can be literally translated "in the playing of dice of men." This ancient idiom alludes to the practice of cheating others when using dice. In most languages, a literal rendering of this allusion makes little sense. Translating this expression as "the trickery of men" is a clearer way to convey the meaning.

- At Romans 12:11, a Greek expression is used that literally means "to the spirit boiling." This wording does not convey the intended meaning in English, so it is rendered "aglow with the spirit" in this translation.

- During his famous Sermon on the Mount, Jesus used an expression that is often translated "Blessed are the poor in spirit." (Matthew 5:3, *King James Version*) But in many languages, a literal rendering of this expression is obscure. In some cases, a strictly literal translation could imply that "the poor in spirit" are mentally unbalanced or lacking in vitality and determination. However, Jesus was here teaching people that their happiness depended, not on satisfying their physical needs, but on recognizing their need for God's guidance. (Luke 6:20) Thus, such renderings as "those conscious of their spiritual need" or "those who know their need for God" convey more accurately the meaning of the original expression.—Matthew 5:3; *The New Testament in Modern English*.

OIΠΤΩΧΟΙ
ΤΩΠΝΕΥΜΑΤΙ

MATTHEW 5:3

Literal English: "the poor in spirit"

Idea: "those conscious of their spiritual need"

- In many contexts, the Hebrew word translated "jealousy" corresponds to the common meaning of the English word, namely, to feel anger over the apparent unfaithfulness of a close associate or to envy others for their possessions. (Proverbs 6:34; Isaiah 11:13) However, the same Hebrew word also has a positive connotation. For example, it may be used of the "zeal," or protective ardor, that Jehovah shows for his servants or of his "requiring exclusive devotion." (Exodus 34:14; 2 Kings 19:31; Ezekiel 5:13; Zechariah 8:2) It may also be used of the "zeal" that his faithful servants have for God and his worship or of their 'tolerating no rivalry' toward him. —Psalm 69:9; 119:139; Numbers 25:11.

- The Hebrew expression that usually refers to the human hand has a wide variety of meanings. Depending on the context, this word may be rendered "authority," "generosity," or "power." (2 Samuel 8:3; 1 Kings 10:13; Proverbs 18:21) In fact, this particular word is translated over 40 different ways in the English edition of the *New World Translation of the Holy Scriptures.*

יָד

The Hebrew word *yadh* is usually rendered "hand," but depending on the context, this word may be rendered "authority," "generosity," "power," and many other ways

---

In view of these factors, Bible translation involves more than simply rendering an original-language word with the same term each time it occurs. A translator must use good judgment in order to select words in the target language that best represent the ideas of the original-language text. In addition, there is a need to structure the sentences in a way that conforms to the rules of grammar of the target language, making the text easy to read.

At the same time, extremes in rewording the text must be avoided. A translator who liberally paraphrases the Bible according to how he interprets the overall idea could distort the meaning of the text. How so? The translator may erroneously insert his opinion of what the original text means or may omit important details contained in the original text. So while paraphrases of the Bible may be easy to read, their very freeness at times may prevent the reader from getting the true message of the text.

Doctrinal bias can easily color a translator's work. For example, Matthew 7:13 says: "Spacious is the road leading off into destruction." Some translators, perhaps affected by doctrinal bias, have used the term "hell" rather than what the Greek term really means, namely, "destruction."

A Bible translator must also consider that the Bible was written using the common, everyday language of average people, such as farmers, shepherds, and fishermen. (Nehemiah 8:8, 12; Acts 4:13) Therefore, a good translation of the Bible makes the message it contains understandable to sincere people, regardless of their background. Clear, common, readily understood expressions are preferred over terms that are rarely used by the average person.

Quite a number of Bible translators have taken the unjustifiable liberty of omitting God's name, Jehovah, from modern translations even though that name is found in ancient Bible manuscripts. (See Appendix A4.) Many translations replace the name with a title, such as "Lord," and some even obscure the fact that God has a name. For example, in some translations, Jesus' prayer recorded at John 17:26 reads: "I made you known to them," and at John 17:6, "I have revealed you to those whom you gave me." However, a faithful rendering of Jesus' prayer reads: "I have made *your name* known to them," and "I have made *your name* manifest to the men whom you gave me."

As stated in the foreword to the original English edition of the *New World Translation:* "We offer no paraphrase of the Scriptures. Our endeavor all through has been to give as literal a translation as possible, where the modern English idiom allows and where a literal rendition does not for any clumsiness hide the thought." Thus, the New World Bible Translation Committee has endeavored to strike a balance between using words and phrasing that mirror the original and, at the same time, avoiding wording that reads awkwardly or hides the intended thought. As a result, the Bible can be read with ease and the reader can have full confidence that its inspired message has been transmitted faithfully.—1 Thessalonians 2:13.

A reliable translation must:

- Sanctify God's name by restoring it to its rightful place in the Scriptures.—Matthew 6:9.

- Accurately convey the original message that was inspired by God.—2 Timothy 3:16.

- Translate expressions literally when the wording and structure of the target language allow for such renderings of the original-language text.

- Communicate the correct sense of a word or a phrase when a literal rendering would distort or obscure the meaning.

- Use natural, easy-to-understand language that encourages reading.—Nehemiah 8:8, 12.

Features of This Revision

The *New World Translation of the Christian Greek Scriptures* was released in English in 1950, and the complete *New World Translation of the Holy Scriptures* was published in 1961. Since then, tens of millions of readers in well over 100 languages have benefited from this accurate yet readable rendering of the Holy Scriptures from the original languages.

Over the past half century, however, languages have changed. The current New World Bible Translation Committee recognized the need to respond to those changes in order to touch the heart of today's reader. For this reason, a number of style and vocabulary changes have been made in this revision, with the following objectives in mind:

- **Use of modern, understandable language.** For example, the expression "long-suffering" can be misunderstood to mean "someone who suffers for a long time." However, the intended idea is that of deliberate restraint, which is better expressed by the term "patience." (Galatians 5:22) The now obsolete meaning of "dumb" was replaced with "speechless." (Matthew 9:32, 33) The term "harlot" was changed to "prostitute." (Genesis 38:15) In this revision, "fornication" is usually rendered as "sexual immorality"; "loose conduct" as "brazen conduct"; and "revelries" as "wild parties." (Galatians 5:19-21) The expression "time indefinite" was replaced with such terms as "forever," "lasting," "everlasting," or "long ago," to convey the intended meaning in each context.—Genesis 3:22; Exodus 31:16; Psalm 90:2; Ecclesiastes 1:4; Micah 5:2.

The term "seed" in ancient Hebrew and Greek could refer to plant seed as well as to human offspring, or descendants, or to semen. Because it is no longer common in English to use the term "seed" when referring to humans, it was replaced with expressions that convey the intended idea according to the context. (Genesis 1:11; 22:17; 48:4; Matthew 22:24; John 8:37) In most cases, the term "offspring" is now used when referring to the Edenic promise, found at Genesis 3:15.

The English verb "impale" was used in previous versions of this Bible in connection with the execution of Jesus. While this term could refer to the way that Jesus was nailed to the torture stake, it is more often used in reference to the ancient method of execution by running a sharp stake through the body and fixing the victim on it. Since Jesus was not impaled *with* the torture stake, this revision uses such expressions as "executed on a stake" and "nailed to the stake" with regard to the manner in which Jesus was fastened to the torture stake.—Matthew 20:19; 27:31, 35.

• **Biblical expressions clarified.** Some terms used in previous editions of the English *New World Translation* often needed to be explained in order to be properly understood. For example, the Hebrew term "Sheol" and the Greek term "Hades" are used in the Bible to refer to the common grave of mankind. Those terms are unknown to many, and "Hades" has a dual meaning as a result of its usage in Greek mythology. Therefore, both terms were replaced with what was meant by the Bible writers, "the Grave." The terms "Sheol" and "Hades" are now given in footnotes.—Psalm 16:10; Acts 2:27.

In past editions, the Hebrew word *ne'phesh* and the Greek word *psy·khe'* were consistently rendered "soul." In view of the many misconceptions regarding the meaning of the word "soul," this approach helped the reader to see how the inspired Bible writers used these original-language terms. Depending on the context, those words may refer (1) to a person, (2) to the life of a person, (3) to living creatures, (4) to the desires and appetite of a person or, in some cases, (5) even to dead individuals. However, since such use of the word "soul" is not common in English, the decision was made to render these original-language words according to their intended meaning, usually with a footnote that reads "Or 'soul.'" (See, for example, Genesis 1:20; 2:7; Leviticus 19:28; Psalm 3:2; Proverbs 16:26; Matthew 6:25.) However, in some poetic or well-known contexts, the word "soul" was retained in the main text, along with a footnote referring to the Glossary or showing another possible rendering.—Deuteronomy 6:5; Psalm 131:2; Proverbs 2:10; Matthew 22:37.

Similarly, the word "kidney" was retained when it refers to the literal organ. However, when it is used figuratively in such verses as Psalm 7:9 and 26:2 and Revelation 2:23, the intended idea of "deepest emotions" or "innermost thoughts" is conveyed in the main text, and the literal idea is given in a footnote.

Like its Hebrew and Greek equivalents, the English expression "heart" has both a literal and a figurative meaning, so it was usually retained in the main text. However, in a few contexts where the sense was not clear, a more explicit rendering was used. For example, in the book of Proverbs, "in want of heart" now reads "lacking good sense," and the literal idea is given in a footnote. Other expressions, for instance, "fat," "flesh," and "horn," were handled similarly, according to the context. (Genesis 45:18; Ecclesiastes 5:6; Job 16:15) Some of these expressions are discussed in the "Glossary of Bible Terms."

- **Enhanced readability.** In previous editions of the English *New World Translation*, auxiliary expressions were used to indicate whether the Hebrew verb is in the imperfect or the perfect state. For example, the continuous action often expressed by imperfect verbs was indicated by means of the expressions "proceeded to," "went on to," "came to be," and so forth. The emphasis often conveyed by the Hebrew perfect verb was denoted by the added expressions "certainly," "must," "actually," and similar ones. As a result, these terms were used thousands of times in the text. In this revision, auxiliary terms were retained in certain contexts by using such expressions as "kept," "keep on," and "used to" when there was a valid reason to express continuous action. (Genesis 3:9; 34:1; Proverbs 2:4) However, they were omitted to enhance readability when the auxiliary expressions were not critical for conveying the original meaning.

- **Conveying the correct idea of words involving gender.** Hebrew and Greek nouns indicate male or female gender, and in Greek, also neuter. At times, though, reflecting the gender of the original-language term may obscure the intended meaning. In both Hebrew and Greek, plural nouns are generally masculine, not only when referring exclusively to males but also when referring to both males and females. For example, though the expression "the sons of Israel" may refer to the 12 sons of Jacob, it more often refers to the entire nation of Israel, both men and women. (Genesis 46:5; Exodus 35:29) So in the revision, this phrase was often rendered "Israelites" to show that it refers to the entire nation. Similarly, the expression "fatherless boy" was rendered "fatherless child" or "orphan" to show that it may refer to a boy or a girl. On the other hand, since the Bible uses the male gender in reference to God and to his Son, as well as to various angels and demons, there is no basis for using genderless terms as is done in some modern translations.

- **Omission of indicators for second person plural.** Past editions also indicated whether the pronouns "you" and "your" and second person verbs were singular or plural by using small capital letters to show plurality. This feature was not retained in this revision, but readers may consult earlier editions of this translation for this information.

All adjustments in the Bible text were made prayerfully, carefully, and with deep respect for the fine work of the original New World Bible Translation Committee.

Other features of this revision:

This Bible edition contains a limited number of footnotes. The footnotes generally fall into the following categories:

"Or"	Alternative ways the text could be rendered from Hebrew, Aramaic, or Greek that would give the same overall idea.—Genesis 1:2, footnote on "active force"; Joshua 1:8, "undertone."
"Or possibly"	Alternative ways the text could be rendered that would convey a valid yet different overall idea.—Genesis 21:6, "laugh with me"; Zechariah 14:21, "Canaanite."
"Lit."	A word-for-word translation from the Hebrew, Aramaic, or Greek or the basic meaning of an original-language expression.—Genesis 30:22, "pregnant"; Exodus 32:9, "obstinate."
Meaning and background information	Meaning of names (Genesis 3:17, "Adam"; Exodus 15:23, "Marah"); details about weights and measures (Genesis 6:15, "cubits"); the antecedent of a pronoun (Genesis 38:5, "He"); helpful information in the Appendix and the Glossary.—Genesis 37:35, "Grave"; Matthew 5:22, "Gehenna."

The front section, entitled "An Introduction to God's Word," contains an outline of basic teachings found in the Bible. Immediately following the Bible text is the "Table of the Books of the Bible," the "Bible Words Index," and the "Glossary of Bible Terms." The Glossary helps the reader understand selected expressions according to their Bible-specific usage. Appendix A contains the following sections: "Principles of Bible Translation," "Features of This Revision," "How the Bible Came to Us," "The Divine Name in the Hebrew Scriptures," "The Divine Name in the Christian Greek Scriptures," "Chart: Prophets and Kings of Judah and of Israel," and "Main Events of Jesus' Earthly Life." Appendix B contains maps, charts, and other information useful to diligent Bible students.

In the main text of the Bible, each book features an outline of its chapter contents, along with the related verses, giving the reader an overview of the entire book. The center column of each page contains the most relevant marginal references from previous editions, pointing to related Bible verses.

How the Bible Came to Us

The Author and Originator of the Bible is also its Preserver. He is the One who caused this statement to be recorded:

"The word of our God endures forever."
—Isaiah 40:8.

That statement is true, even though no original Bible manuscript of the Hebrew and Aramaic Scriptures* or of the Christian Greek Scriptures has survived to our day. Therefore, how can we be so certain that the contents of the Bible we have today truly reflect the original inspired writings?

COPYISTS PRESERVE GOD'S WORD

Regarding the Hebrew Scriptures, part of the answer lies in an ancient tradition that was established by God, who said that the text should be copied.# For example, Jehovah instructed the kings of Israel to make their own copies of the written Law. (Deuteronomy 17:18) Additionally, God made the Levites responsible for preserving the Law and teaching it to the people. (Deuteronomy 31:26; Nehemiah 8:7) After the exile of the Jews to Babylon, a class of copyists, or scribes (Sopherim), developed. (Ezra 7:6, footnotes) Over time, those scribes made numerous copies of the 39 books of the Hebrew Scriptures.

Through the centuries, scribes meticulously copied these books. During the Middle Ages, a group of Jewish scribes known as the Masoretes carried on that tradition. The oldest complete Masoretic manuscript is the Leningrad Codex, which dates from 1008/1009 C.E. However, in the middle of the 20th century, some 220 Biblical manuscripts or fragments were discovered among the Dead Sea Scrolls. Those Biblical manuscripts were

---

* Referred to simply as the Hebrew Scriptures from here on.

One reason the manuscripts needed to be copied was that the originals were written on perishable materials.

more than a thousand years older than the Leningrad Codex. A comparison of the Dead Sea Scrolls with the Leningrad Codex confirms a vital point: While the Dead Sea Scrolls contain some variations in wording, none of those variations affect the message itself.

What about the 27 books of the Christian Greek Scriptures? Those books were first penned by some of the apostles of Jesus Christ and by a few other early disciples. Following the tradition of the Jewish scribes, early Christians made copies of those books. (Colossians 4:16) Despite attempts by Roman Emperor Diocletian and others to destroy all early Christian literature, thousands of ancient fragments and manuscripts have been preserved until our day.

Christian writings were also translated into other languages. Early translations of the Bible include those in such ancient languages as Armenian, Coptic, Ethiopic, Georgian, Latin, and Syriac.

ESTABLISHING THE HEBREW AND GREEK TEXTS FOR TRANSLATION

Not all copies of ancient Bible manuscripts contain identical wording. How, then, can we know what the original text contained?

> "It may be safely said that no other work of antiquity has been so accurately transmitted"

The situation could be likened to that of a teacher who asks 100 students to copy a chapter of a book. Even if the original chapter was later lost, a comparison of the 100 copies would still reveal the original text. While each student might make some errors, it is highly unlikely that all the students would make exactly the same ones. Similarly, when scholars compare the thousands of fragments and copies of ancient Bible books available to them, they can detect copyist error and determine the original wording.

How confident can we be that the thoughts contained in the original Bible texts have been accurately transmitted to us? Commenting on the text of the Hebrew Scriptures, scholar William H. Green stated: "It may be safely said that no other work of antiquity has been so accurately transmitted." Regarding the Christian Greek Scriptures, or so-called New Testament, Bible scholar F. F. Bruce wrote: "The evidence for our New Testament writings is ever so much greater than the evidence for many writings of classical authors, the authenticity of which no one dreams of

Chapter 40 of Isaiah's book in the Dead Sea Scrolls (dated from 125 to 100 B.C.E.)

When compared with Hebrew manuscripts from about a thousand years later, only minor differences were found, mostly in spelling

Chapter 40 of Isaiah's book in the Aleppo Codex, an important Hebrew Masoretic manuscript from about 930 C.E.

questioning." He also said: "If the New Testament were a collection of secular writings, their authenticity would generally be regarded as beyond all doubt."

Hebrew Text: The *New World Translation of the Hebrew Scriptures* (1953-1960) was based on *Biblia Hebraica,* by Rudolf Kittel. Since that time, updated editions of the Hebrew text, namely, *Biblia Hebraica Stuttgartensia* and *Biblia Hebraica Quinta,* have included recent research based on the Dead Sea Scrolls and other ancient manuscripts. These scholarly works reproduce the Leningrad Codex in the main text along with footnotes that contain comparative wording from other sources, including the Samaritan Pentateuch, the Dead Sea Scrolls, the Greek *Septuagint,* the Aramaic Targums, the Latin *Vulgate,* and the Syriac *Peshitta.* Both *Biblia Hebraica Stuttgartensia* and *Biblia Hebraica Quinta* were consulted when preparing the present revision of the *New World Translation.*

Greek Text: In the late 19th century, scholars B. F. Westcott and F.J.A. Hort compared existing Bible manuscripts and fragments as they prepared the Greek master text that they felt most closely reflected the original writings. In the mid-20th century, the New World Bible Translation Committee used that master text as the basis for its translation. Other early papyri, thought to date back to the second and third centuries C.E., were also used. Since then, more papyri have become available. In addition, master texts such as those by Nestle and Aland and by the United Bible Societies reflect recent scholarly studies. Some of the findings of this research were incorporated into this present revision.

Based on those master texts, it is evident that some verses of the Christian Greek Scriptures found in older translations, such as the *King James Version,* were actually additions made by later copyists and were never part of the inspired Scriptures. However, because the verse division generally accepted in Bible translations was already established in the 16th century, the omission of these verses now creates gaps in the verse numbering in most Bibles. The verses are Matthew 17:21; 18:11; 23:14; Mark 7:16; 9:44, 46; 11:26; 15:28; Luke 17:36; 23:17; John 5:4; Acts 8:37; 15:34; 24:7; 28:29; and Romans 16:24. In this revised edition, those omitted verses are indicated by a footnote at the location of the omission.

Regarding the long conclusion for Mark 16 (verses 9-20), the short conclusion for Mark 16, and the wording found at

John 7:53–8:11, it is evident that none of these verses were included in the original manuscripts. Therefore, those spurious texts have not been included in this revision.*

Some other wording has been adjusted to incorporate what scholars generally accept as the most authentic reflection of the original writings. For instance, according to some manuscripts, Matthew 7:13 reads: "Go in through the narrow gate because broad *is the gate* and spacious is the road leading off into destruction." In previous editions of the *New World Translation*, "is the gate" was not included in the text. However, further study of the manuscript evidence led to the conclusion that "is the gate" was in the original text. So it was included in this present edition. There are a number of similar refinements. However, these adjustments are minor, and none of them change the basic message of God's Word.

---

* Further details on why these verses are viewed as spurious can be found in the footnotes of the *New World Translation of the Holy Scriptures—With References*, published in 1984.

A papyrus manuscript of
2 Corinthians 4:13–5:4
from about 200 C.E.

The Divine Name in the Hebrew Scriptures

The divine name, represented by the four Hebrew consonants יהוה, appears nearly 7,000 times in the Hebrew Scriptures. This translation renders those four letters, known as the Tetragrammaton, "Jehovah." That name is by far the most frequently occurring name in the Bible. While the inspired writers refer to God by many titles and descriptive terms, such as "Almighty," "Most High," and "Lord," the Tetragrammaton is the only personal name they use to identify God.

Jehovah God himself directed Bible writers to use his name. For example, he inspired the prophet Joel to write: "Everyone who calls on the name of Jehovah will be saved." (Joel 2:32) And God caused one psalmist to write: "May people know that you, whose name is Jehovah, you alone are the Most High over all the earth." (Psalm 83:18) In fact, the divine name appears some 700 times in the book of Psalms alone—a book of poetic writings that were to be sung and recited by God's people. Why, then, is God's name missing from many Bible translations? Why does this translation use the form "Jehovah"? And what does the divine name, Jehovah, mean?

𐤉𐤄𐤅𐤄

The divine name in the ancient Hebrew letters used before the Babylonian exile

יהוה

The divine name in the Hebrew letters used after the Babylonian exile

Why is the name missing from many Bible translations? The reasons vary. Some feel that Almighty God does not need a unique name to identify him. Others appear to have been influenced by the Jewish tradition of avoiding the use of the name, perhaps out of fear of desecrating it. Still others believe that since no one can be sure of the exact pronunciation of God's name, it is better just to use a title, such as "Lord" or "God." Such objections, however, lack merit for the following reasons:

- Those who argue that Almighty God does not need a unique name ignore evidence that early copies of his Word, including

Excerpts from the Psalms in a Dead Sea Scroll dated to the first half of the first century C.E. The text is in the style of the Hebrew letters commonly used after the Babylonian exile, but the Tetragrammaton appears repeatedly in distinctive ancient Hebrew letters those preserved from before the time of Christ, contain God's personal name. As noted above, God directed that his name be included in his Word some 7,000 times. Obviously, he wants us to know and use his name.

- Translators who remove the name out of deference to Jewish tradition fail to recognize a key fact. While some Jewish scribes refused to pronounce the name, they did not remove it from their copies of the Bible. Ancient scrolls found in Qumran, near the Dead Sea, contain the name in many places. Some Bible translators hint that the divine name appeared in the original text by substituting the title "LORD" in capital letters. But the question remains, Why have these translators felt free to substitute or remove God's name from the Bible when they acknowledge that it is found in the Bible text thousands of times? Who do they believe gave them authority to make such a change? Only they can say.

- Those who say that the divine name should not be used because it is not known exactly how to pronounce it will nevertheless freely use the name Jesus. However, Jesus' first-century disciples said his name quite differently from the way most Christians do today. To Jewish Christians, the name Jesus was probably pronounced *Ye·shu'a'*. And the title "Christ" was *Ma·shi'ach*, or "Messiah." Greek-speaking Christians called him *I·e·sous' Khri·stos'*, and Latin-speaking Christians *Ie'sus Chri'stus*. Under inspiration, the Greek translation of his name was recorded in the Bible, showing that first-century Christians followed the sensible course of using the form of the name common in their language. Similarly, the New World Bible Translation Committee feels that it is reasonable to use the form "Jehovah," even though that rendering is not exactly the way the divine name would have been pronounced in ancient Hebrew.

Why does the *New World Translation* use the form "Jehovah"? In English, the four letters of the Tetragrammaton (יהוה) are represented by the consonants YHWH. As was true of all written words in ancient Hebrew, the Tetragrammaton contained no vowels. When ancient Hebrew was in everyday use, readers easily provided the appropriate vowels.

About a thousand years after the Hebrew Scriptures were completed, Jewish scholars developed a system of pronunciation points, or signs, by which to indicate what vowels to use when reading Hebrew. By that time, though, many Jews had the

God's name at Genesis 15:2 in William Tyndale's translation of the Pentateuch, 1530

superstitious idea that it was wrong to say God's personal name out loud, so they used substitute expressions. Thus, it seems that when they copied the Tetragrammaton, they combined the vowels for the *substitute expressions* with the four consonants representing the divine name. Therefore, the manuscripts with those vowel points do not help in determining how the name was originally pronounced in Hebrew. Some feel that the name was pronounced "Yahweh," whereas others suggest different possibilities. A Dead Sea Scroll containing a portion of Leviticus in Greek transliterates the divine name *Iao*. Besides that form, early Greek writers also suggest the pronunciations *Iae, I·a·be′*, and *I·a·ou·e′*. However, there is no reason to be dogmatic. We simply do not know how God's ancient servants pronounced this name in Hebrew. (Genesis 13:4; Exodus 3:15) What we do know is that God used his name repeatedly in communication with his people, that they addressed him by that name, and that they used it freely in speaking with others.—Exodus 6:2; 1 Kings 8:23; Psalm 99:9.

Why, then, does this translation use the form "Jehovah"? Because that form of the divine name has a long history in the English language.

The first rendering of God's personal name in an English Bible appeared in 1530 in William Tyndale's translation of the Pentateuch. He used the form "Iehouah." Over time, the English language changed, and the spelling of the divine name was modernized. For example, in 1612, Henry Ainsworth used the form "Iehovah" throughout his translation of the book of Psalms. Then, in 1639, when that work was revised and printed with the

Pentateuch, the form "Jehovah" was used. In 1901, the translators who produced the *American Standard Version* of the Bible used the form "Jehovah" where the divine name appeared in the Hebrew text.

Explaining why he used "Jehovah" instead of "Yahweh" in his 1911 work *Studies in the Psalms,* respected Bible scholar Joseph Bryant Rotherham said that he wanted to employ a "form of the name more familiar (while perfectly acceptable) to the general Bible-reading public." In 1930 scholar A. F. Kirkpatrick made a similar point regarding the use of the form "Jehovah." He said: "Modern grammarians argue that it ought to be read *Yahveh* or *Yahaveh;* but JEHOVAH seems firmly rooted in the English language, and the really important point is not the exact pronunciation, but the recognition that it is a Proper Name, not merely an appellative title like 'Lord.'"

What is the meaning of the name Jehovah? In Hebrew, the name Jehovah comes from a verb that means "to become," and a number of scholars feel that it reflects the causative form of that Hebrew verb. Thus, the understanding of the New World Bible Translation Committee is that God's name means "He Causes to Become." Scholars hold varying views, so we cannot be dogmatic about this meaning. However, this definition well fits Jehovah's role as the Creator of all things and the Fulfiller of his purpose. He not only caused the physical universe and intelligent beings to exist, but as events unfold, he continues to cause his will and purpose to be realized.

יהוה

The Tetragrammaton, YHWH: "He Causes to Become"

הוה

The verb HWH: "to become"

Therefore, the meaning of the name Jehovah is not limited to the related verb found at Exodus 3:14, which reads: "I Will Become What I Choose to Become" or, "I Will Prove to Be What I Will Prove to Be." In the strictest sense, those words do not fully define God's name. Rather, they reveal an aspect of God's personality, showing that he becomes what is needed in each circumstance to fulfill his purpose. So while the name Jehovah may include this idea, it is not limited to what he himself chooses to become. It also includes what he causes to happen with regard to his creation and the accomplishment of his purpose.

The Divine Name in the Christian Greek Scriptures

Bible scholars acknowledge that God's personal name, as represented by the Tetragrammaton (יהוה), appears almost 7,000 times in the original text of the Hebrew Scriptures. However, many feel that it did not appear in the original text of the Christian Greek Scriptures. For this reason, most modern English Bibles do not use the name Jehovah when translating the so-called New Testament. Even when translating quotations from the Hebrew Scriptures in which the Tetragrammaton appears, most translators use "Lord" rather than God's personal name.

The *New World Translation of the Holy Scriptures* does not follow this common practice. It uses the name Jehovah a total of 237 times in the Christian Greek Scriptures. In deciding to do this, the translators took into consideration two important factors: (1) The Greek manuscripts we possess today are not the originals. Of the thousands of copies in existence today, most were made at least two centuries after the originals were composed. (2) By that time, those copying the manuscripts either replaced the Tetragrammaton with *Ky'ri·os*, the Greek word for "Lord," or they copied from manuscripts where this had already been done.

The New World Bible Translation Committee determined that there is compelling evidence that the Tetragrammaton did appear in the original Greek manuscripts. The decision was based on the following evidence:

- **Copies of the Hebrew Scriptures used in the days of Jesus and his apostles contained the Tetragrammaton throughout the text.** In the past, few people disputed that conclusion. Now that copies of the Hebrew Scriptures dating back to the first century have been discovered near Qumran, the point has been proved beyond any doubt.

- **In the days of Jesus and his apostles, the Tetragrammaton also appeared in Greek translations of the Hebrew Scriptures.** For centuries, scholars thought that the Tetragrammaton was absent from manuscripts of the Greek Septuagint translation of the Hebrew Scriptures. Then, in the mid-20th century, some very old fragments of the Greek Septuagint version that existed in Jesus' day were brought to the attention of scholars. Those fragments contain the personal name of God, written in Hebrew characters. So in Jesus' day, copies of the Scriptures in Greek did contain the divine name. However, by the fourth century C.E., major manuscripts of the Greek *Septuagint,* such as the Codex Vaticanus and Codex Sinaiticus, did not contain the divine name in the books from Genesis through Malachi (where it had been in earlier manuscripts). Hence, it is not surprising that in texts preserved from that time period, the divine name is not found in the so-called New Testament, or Greek Scripture portion of the Bible.

- **The Christian Greek Scriptures themselves report that Jesus often referred to God's name and made it known to others.** (John 17:6, 11, 12, 26) Jesus plainly stated: "I have come in the name of my Father." He also stressed that his works were done in his "Father's name."—John 5:43; 10:25.

- **Since the Christian Greek Scriptures were an inspired addition to the sacred Hebrew Scriptures, the sudden disappearance of Jehovah's name from the text would seem inconsistent.** About the middle of the first century C.E., the disciple James said to the elders in Jerusalem: "Symeon has related thoroughly how God for the first time turned his attention to the nations to take out of them a people for his name." (Acts 15:14) It would not be logical for James to make such a statement if no one in the first century knew or used God's name.

> Jesus plainly stated: "I have come in the name of my Father." He also stressed that his works were done in his "Father's name"

- **The divine name appears in its abbreviated form in the Christian Greek Scriptures.** At Revelation 19:1, 3, 4, 6, the divine name is embedded in the word "Hallelujah." This comes from a Hebrew expression that literally means "Praise Jah." "Jah" is a contraction of the name Jehovah. Many names used in the Christian Greek Scriptures were derived from the divine name. In fact, reference works explain that Jesus' own name means "Jehovah Is Salvation."

- **Early Jewish writings indicate that Jewish Christians used the divine name in their writings.** The Tosefta, a written collection of oral laws that was completed by about 300 C.E., says with

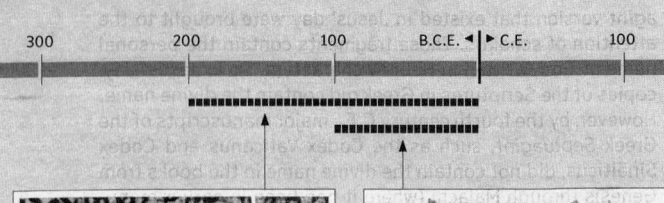

| 300 | 200 | 100 | B.C.E. ◀ ▶ C.E. | 100 |

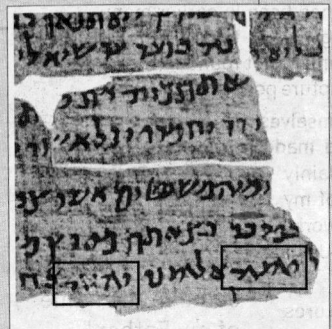

Deuteronomy 6:4
Nash Papyrus
Second or first century B.C.E.

Ancient Hebrew text with the
divine name appearing twice

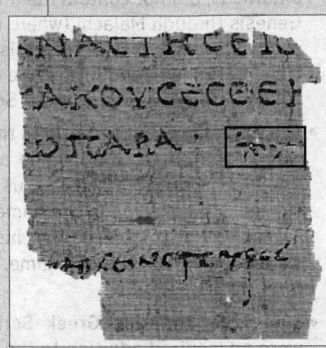

Fragment of Deuteronomy 18:15, 16
P. Fouad Inv. 266
First century B.C.E.

The Greek Septuagint translation
with the divine name in Hebrew
characters

regard to Christian writings that were burned on the Sabbath:
"The books of the Evangelists and the books of the *minim*
[thought to be Jewish Christians] they do not save from a fire.
But they are allowed to burn where they are, they and the references to the Divine Name which are in them." This same
source quotes Rabbi Yosé the Galilean, who lived at the beginning of the second century C.E., as saying that on other
days of the week, "one cuts out the references to the Divine
Name which are in them [understood to refer to the Christian
writings] and stores them away, and the rest burns."

Deuteronomy 18:15, 16
Codex Alexandrinus
Fifth century C.E.

Acts 3:22, quoting Deuteronomy 18:15
New World Translation
20th century C.E.

Divine name removed and replaced by *KC* and *KY*, abbreviated forms of the Greek word *Ky′ri·os* (Lord)

The *New World Translation* restores the divine name

- Some Bible scholars acknowledge that it seems likely that the divine name appeared in Hebrew Scripture quotations found in the Christian Greek Scriptures. Under the heading "Tetragrammaton in the New Testament," *The Anchor Bible Dictionary* states: "There is some evidence that the Tetragrammaton, the Divine Name, Yahweh, appeared in some or all of the O[ld] T[estament] quotations in the N[ew] T[estament] when the NT documents were first penned." Scholar George Howard says: "Since the Tetragram was still written in the copies of the Greek Bible [the *Septuagint*] which made up the

Scriptures of the early church, it is reasonable to believe that the N[ew] T[estament] writers, when quoting from Scripture, preserved the Tetragram within the biblical text."

- **Recognized Bible translators have used God's name in the Christian Greek Scriptures.** Some of these translators did so long before the *New World Translation* was produced. These translators and their works include: *A Literal Translation of the New Testament . . . From the Text of the Vatican Manuscript*, by Herman Heinfetter (1863); *The Emphatic Diaglott*, by Benjamin Wilson (1864); *The Epistles of Paul in Modern*

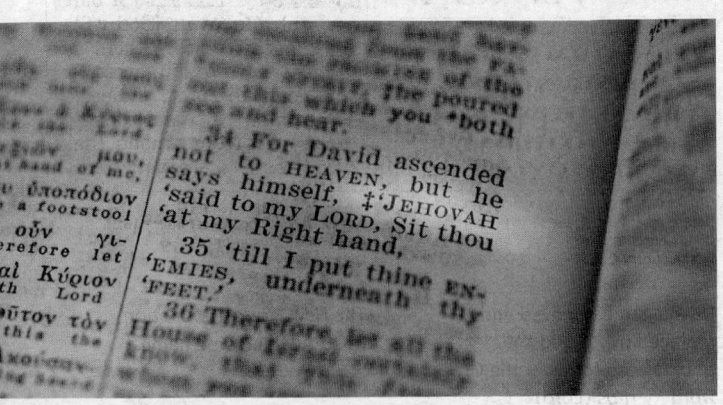

God's name at Acts 2:34 in *The Emphatic Diaglott*, by Benjamin Wilson (1864)

English, by George Barker Stevens (1898); *St. Paul's Epistle to the Romans*, by W. G. Rutherford (1900); *The New Testament Letters*, by J.W.C. Wand, Bishop of London (1946). In addition, in a Spanish translation in the early 20th century, translator Pablo Besson used "Jehová" at Jude 14, and nearly 100 footnotes in his translation suggest the divine name as a likely rendering. Long before those translations, Hebrew versions of the Christian Greek Scriptures from the 16th century onward used the Tetragrammaton in many passages. In the German language alone, at least 11 versions use "Jehovah" (or the transliteration of the Hebrew "Yahweh") in the Christian Greek Scriptures, while four translators add the name in parentheses after "Lord." More than 70 German translations use the divine name in footnotes or commentaries.

- **Bible translations in over one hundred different languages contain the divine name in the Christian Greek Scriptures.** Many African, Native American, Asian, European, and Pacific-island languages use the divine name liberally. (See the list on pages 1742 and 1743.) The translators of these editions decided to use the divine name for reasons similar to those stated above. Some of these translations of the Christian Greek Scriptures have appeared recently, such as the Rotuman Bible (1999), which uses "Jihova" 51 times in 48 verses, and the Batak (Toba) version (1989) from Indonesia, which uses "Jahowa" 110 times.

Without a doubt, there is a clear basis for restoring the divine name, Jehovah, in the Christian Greek Scriptures. That is exactly what the translators of the *New World Translation* have done. They have a deep respect for the divine name and a healthy fear of removing anything that appeared in the original text.—Revelation 22:18, 19.

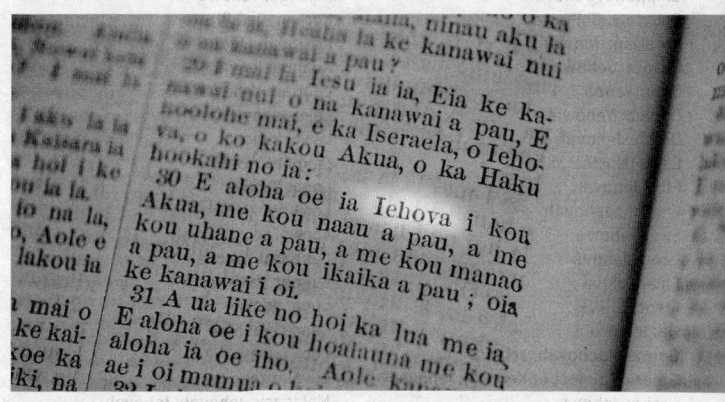

God's name at Mark 12:29, 30 in the Hawaiian-language translation of 1816

Languages and Dialects Containing the Divine Name in the Main Text of the Christian Greek Scriptures

Language or Dialect: **Divine Name**

Aneityum: **Ihova**
Arawak: **Jehovah**
Awabakal: **Yehóa**
Bangi: **Yawe**
Batak (Toba): **Jahowa**
Benga: **Jĕhova**
Bolia: **Yawe**
Bube: **Yehovah**
Bullom So: **Jehovah**
Chácobo: **Jahué**
Cherokee: **Yihowa**
Chin (Hakha): **Zahova**
Chippewa: **Jehovah**
Choctaw: **Chihowa**
Croatian: **Jehova**
Dakota: **Jehowa**
Dobu: **Ieoba**
Douala: **Yehowa**
Dutch: **Jehovah**
Efate (North): **Yehova**
Efik: **Jehovah**
English: **Jehovah**
Éwé: **Yehowa**
Fang: **Jehovâ**
Fijian: **Jiova**
French: **IHVH**
Ga: **Iehowa**
German: **Jehovah; Jehova**
Gibario (dialect of Kerewo): **Iehova**
Grebo: **Jehova**
Hawaiian: **Iehova**
Hebrew: יהוה
Hindustani: **Yihováh**

Hiri Motu: **Iehova**
Ho-Chunk (Winnebago): **Jehowa**
Ila: **Yaave**
Iliku (dialect of Lusengo): **Yawe**
Indonesian: **YAHWEH**
Kala Lagaw Ya: **Iehovan**
Kalanga: **Yehova; Yahwe**
Kalenjin: **Jehovah**
Kerewo: **Iehova**
Kiluba: **Yehova**
Kipsigis: **Jehoba**
Kiribati: **Iehova**
Kisonge: **Yehowa**
Korean: **여호와**
Kosraean: **Jeova**
Kuanua: **Ieova**
Laotian: **Yehowa**
Lele: **Jehova**
Lewo: **Yehova**
Lingala: **Yawe**
Logo: **Yehova**
Lomongo: **Yawe; Yova**
Lonwolwol: **Jehovah**
Lugbara: **Yehova**
Luimbi: **Yehova**
Luna: **Yeoba**
Lunda: **Yehova**
Luo: **Yawe**
Luvale: **Yehova**
Malagasy: **Jehovah; Iehôvah**
Malo: **Iova**
Marquesan: **Iehova**
Marshallese: **Jeova**

1742

Maskelynes: **Iova**
Mende: **Yewoi**
Mentawai: **Jehoba**
Meriam: **Iehoua**
Misima-Paneati: **Iehova**
Mizo: **Jehovan; Jihova'n**
Mohawk: **Yehovah**
Mortlockese: **Jioua; Jiona**
Motu: **Iehova**
Mpongwe (dialect of Myene): **Jehova**
Muskogee: **Cehofv**
Myene: **Yeôva**
Naga, Angami: **Jihova**
Naga, Konyak: **Jihova**
Naga, Lotha: **Jihova**
Naga, Mao: **Jihova**
Naga, Northern Rengma: **Jihova**
Naga, Sangtam: **Jihova**
Nandi: **Jehova**
Narrinyeri: **Jehovah**
Nauruan: **Jehova**
Navajo: **Jîho'vah**
Ndau: **Jehova**
Nembe: **Jehovah**
Nengone (or, Maré): **Iehova**
Ngando: **Yawe**
Ntomba: **Yawe**
Nukuoro: **Jehova**
Polish: **Jehowa**
Portuguese: **Iáhve**
Rarotongan: **Jehova; Iehova**
Rerep: **Iova**
Rotuman: **Jihova**

Sakao: **Ihova; Iehova**
Samoan: **Ieova**
Seneca: **Ya'wĕn**
Sengele: **Yawe**
Sesotho: **Yehofa**
Sie: **Iehōva**
Spanish: **Jehová; Yahvé; YHWH; Yahweh**
Sranantongo: **Jehova**
Sukuma: **Yahuwa; Jakwe**
Tahitian: **Iehova**
Teke-Eboo: **Yawe**
Temne: **Yehófa; Yehofa**
Thai: **Yahowa**
Toaripi: **Jehova; Iehova**
Tongan: **Jehova; Jihova; Sihova**
Tswana: **Jehofa; Yehova; Yehofa**
Umbundu: **Yehova**
Uripiv: **Iova**
Wampanoag: **Jehovah**
Xhosa: **Yehova**
Zande: **Yekova**
Zulu: **Jehova; YAHWE**

(In addition to those on this list, a number of languages and dialects use a form of the divine name in footnotes or in explanatory text.)

Over 120 languages

Chart: Prophets and Kings of Judah and of Israel

Kings of **Southern** Two-Tribe Kingdom of Judah

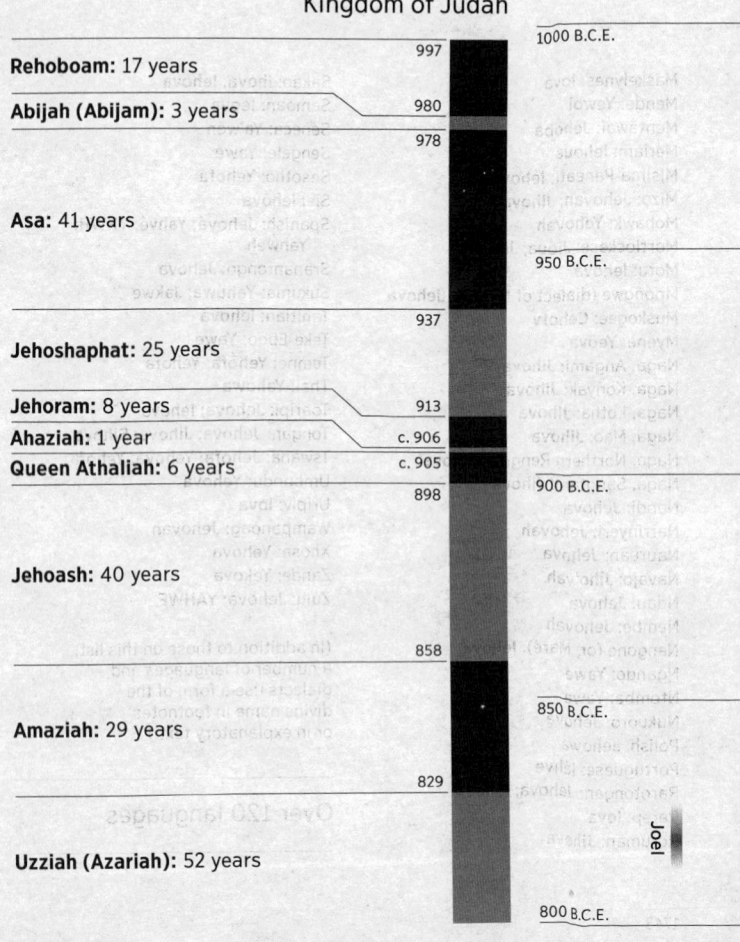

Rehoboam: 17 years

Abijah (Abijam): 3 years

Asa: 41 years

Jehoshaphat: 25 years

Jehoram: 8 years

Ahaziah: 1 year

Queen Athaliah: 6 years

Jehoash: 40 years

Amaziah: 29 years

Uzziah (Azariah): 52 years

1000 B.C.E.

997

980

978

950 B.C.E.

937

913

c. 906

c. 905

900 B.C.E.

898

858

850 B.C.E.

829

800 B.C.E.

Joel

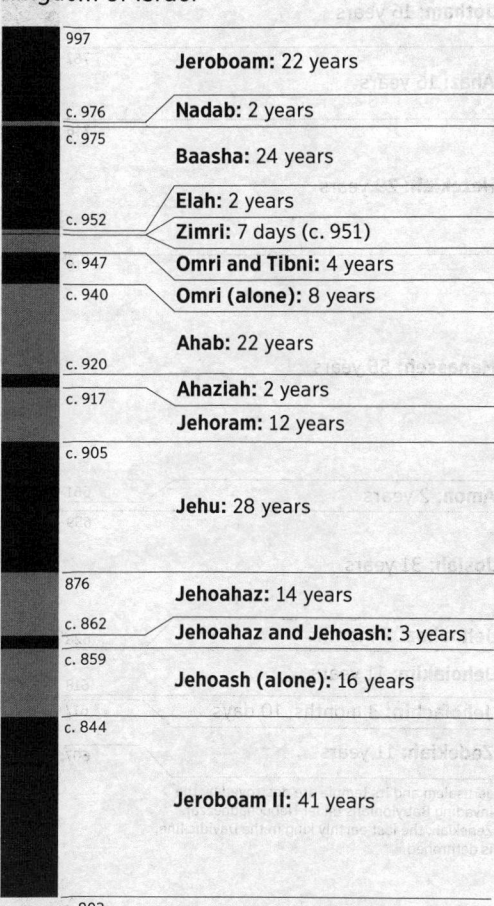

Kings of **Northern** Ten-Tribe Kingdom of Israel

997	
	Jeroboam: 22 years
c. 976	**Nadab:** 2 years
c. 975	
	Baasha: 24 years
c. 952	**Elah:** 2 years
	Zimri: 7 days (c. 951)
c. 947	**Omri and Tibni:** 4 years
c. 940	**Omri (alone):** 8 years
	Ahab: 22 years
c. 920	**Ahaziah:** 2 years
c. 917	**Jehoram:** 12 years
c. 905	
	Jehu: 28 years
876	**Jehoahaz:** 14 years
c. 862	**Jehoahaz and Jehoash:** 3 years
c. 859	**Jehoash (alone):** 16 years
c. 844	
	Jeroboam II: 41 years
c. 803	

Elijah

Elisha

Jonah

Amos

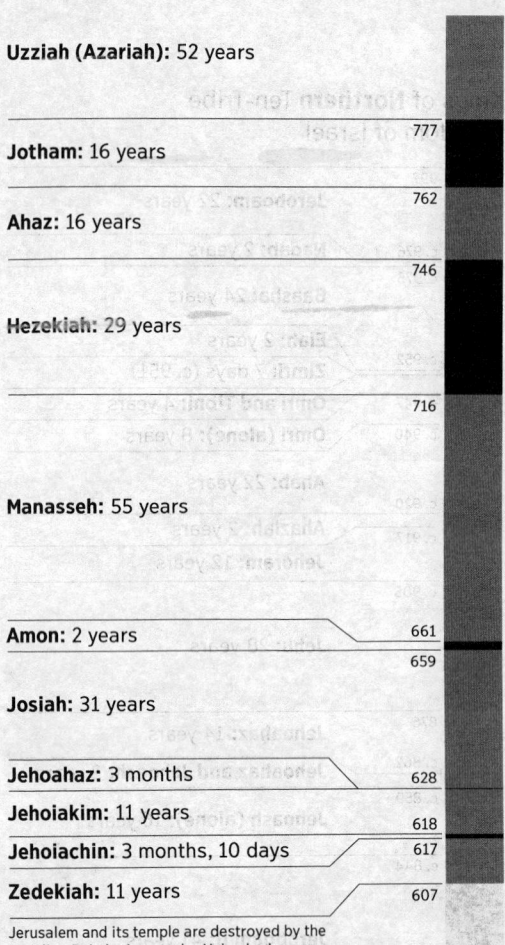

Uzziah (Azariah): 52 years

800 B.C.E.

Jotham: 16 years
777

Ahaz: 16 years
762

746

750 B.C.E.

Hezekiah: 29 years

716

700 B.C.E.

Manasseh: 55 years

Amon: 2 years
661
659

Josiah: 31 years

Jehoahaz: 3 months
628

Jehoiakim: 11 years
618

Jehoiachin: 3 months, 10 days
617

Zedekiah: 11 years
607

Jerusalem and its temple are destroyed by the
invading Babylonians under Nebuchadnezzar.
Zedekiah, the last earthly king in the Davidic line,
is dethroned

Isaiah

Micah

Nahum

Zephaniah

Jeremiah

Habakkuk

Obadiah

Ezekiel

Daniel

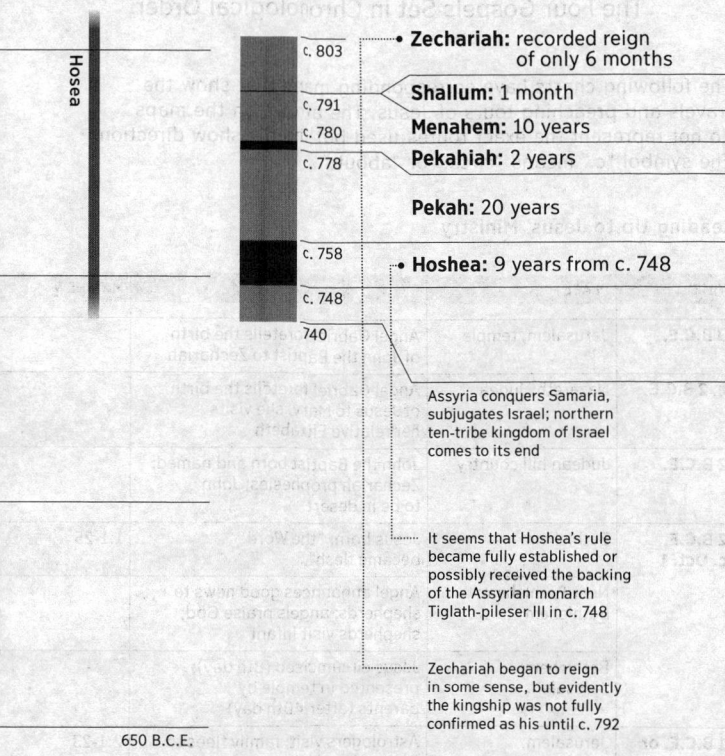

Hosea

c. 803   • **Zechariah:** recorded reign of only 6 months

c. 791   **Shallum:** 1 month

c. 780   **Menahem:** 10 years

c. 778   **Pekahiah:** 2 years

Pekah: 20 years

c. 758   • **Hoshea:** 9 years from c. 748

c. 748

740

Assyria conquers Samaria, subjugates Israel; northern ten-tribe kingdom of Israel comes to its end

It seems that Hoshea's rule became fully established or possibly received the backing of the Assyrian monarch Tiglath-pileser III in c. 748

Zechariah began to reign in some sense, but evidently the kingship was not fully confirmed as his until c. 792

650 B.C.E.

600 B.C.E.

Main Events of Jesus' Earthly Life

The Four Gospels Set in Chronological Order

The following charts have corresponding maps that show the
travels and preaching tours of Jesus. The arrows on the maps
do not represent the exact routes used but mainly show direction.
The symbol "c." means "circa," or "about."

Leading Up to Jesus' Ministry

TIME	PLACE	EVENT	MATTHEW
3 B.C.E.	Jerusalem, temple	Angel Gabriel foretells the birth of John the Baptist to Zechariah	
c. 2 B.C.E.	Nazareth; Judea	Angel Gabriel foretells the birth of Jesus to Mary; she visits her relative Elizabeth	
2 B.C.E.	Judean hill country	John the Baptist born and named; Zechariah prophesies; John to be in desert	
2 B.C.E., c. Oct. 1	Bethlehem	Jesus born; "the Word became flesh"	1:1-25
	Near Bethlehem; Bethlehem	Angel announces good news to shepherds; angels praise God; shepherds visit infant	
	Bethlehem; Jerusalem	Jesus circumcised (8th day); presented in temple by parents (after 40th day)	
1 B.C.E. or 1 C.E.	Jerusalem; Bethlehem; Egypt; Nazareth	Astrologers visit; family flees to Egypt; Herod kills young boys; family returns from Egypt and settles in Nazareth	2:1-23
12 C.E., Passover	Jerusalem	Twelve-year-old Jesus at the temple questions teachers	
	Nazareth	Returns to Nazareth; continues subject to parents; learns carpentry; Mary has four more sons, as well as daughters (Mt 13:55, 56; Mr 6:3)	
29, spring	Wilderness, Jordan River	John the Baptist begins his ministry	3:1-12

Map 1

Key to Maps

⊕ Starting Point
● Location Reasonably Certain
○ Location Less Certain
? when precise location in area is unknown

MARK	LUKE	JOHN
	1:5-25	
	1:26-56	
	1:57-80	
	2:1-7	1:1-5, 9-14
	2:8-20	
	2:21-38	
	2:39, 40	
	2:41-50	
	2:51, 52	
1:1-8	3:1-18	1:6-8, 15-28

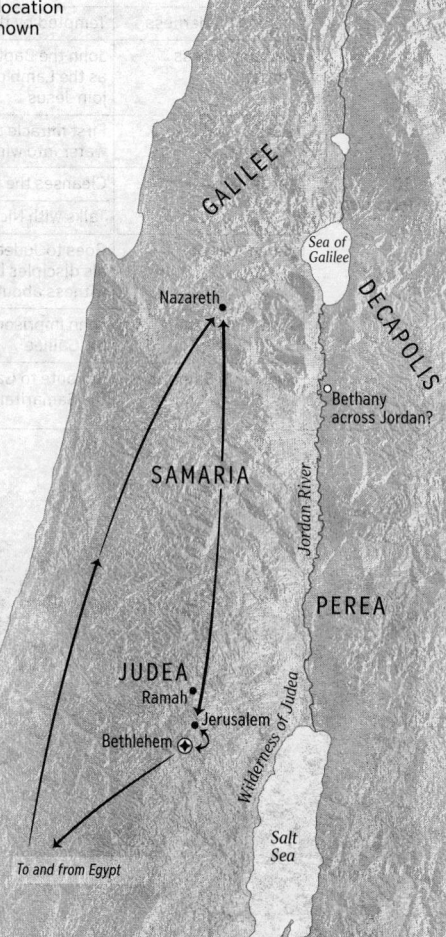

Mt. Hermon

GALILEE

Sea of Galilee

DECAPOLIS

Nazareth

○ Bethany across Jordan?

SAMARIA

Jordan River

PEREA

JUDEA

Ramah

Jerusalem

Bethlehem ⊕

Wilderness of Judea

Salt Sea

To and from Egypt

The Beginning of Jesus' Ministry

TIME	PLACE	EVENT	MATTHEW
29, fall	Jordan River, possibly at or near Bethany across Jordan	Jesus baptized and anointed; Jehovah declares him his Son and approves him	3:13-17
	Judean Wilderness	Tempted by the Devil	4:1-11
	Bethany across Jordan	John the Baptist identifies Jesus as the Lamb of God; first disciples join Jesus	
	Cana of Galilee; Capernaum	First miracle at wedding, turns water into wine; visits Capernaum	
30, Passover	Jerusalem	Cleanses the temple	
		Talks with Nicodemus	
	Judea; Aenon	Goes to Judean countryside, his disciples baptize; John's final witness about Jesus	
	Tiberias; Judea	John imprisoned; Jesus leaves for Galilee	4:12; 14:3-5
	Sychar, in Samaria	En route to Galilee, teaches the Samaritans	

Map 2

MARK	LUKE	JOHN
1:9-11	3:21-38	1:32-34
1:12, 13	4:1-13	
		1:15, 29-51
		2:1-12
		2:13-25
		3:1-21
		3:22-36
6:17-20	3:19, 20	4:1-3
		4:4-43

Wilderness
of Judea

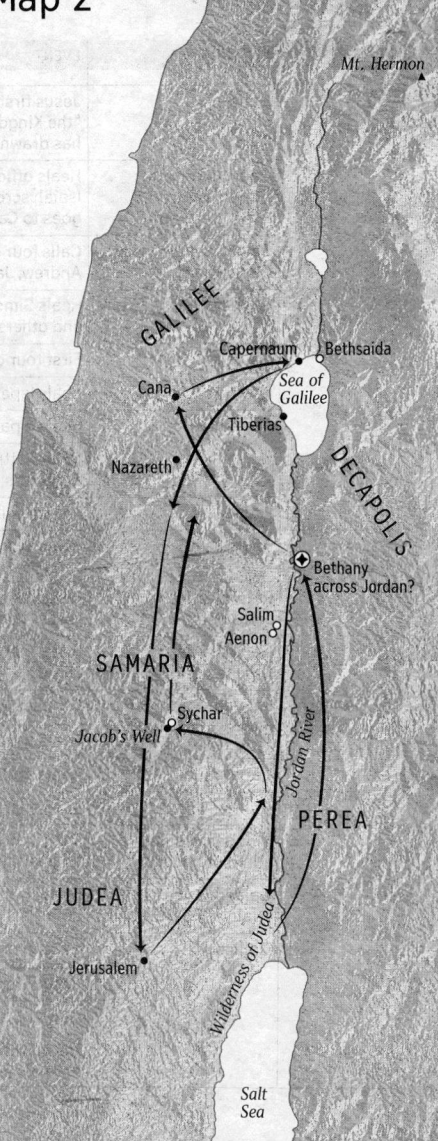

Mt. Hermon

GALILEE

Capernaum   Bethsaida

Cana

Sea of
Galilee

Tiberias

DECAPOLIS

Nazareth

Bethany
across Jordan?

Salim
Aenon

SAMARIA

Jordan River

Sychar

Jacob's Well

PEREA

Wilderness of Judea

JUDEA

Jerusalem

Salt
Sea

Jesus' Great Ministry in Galilee

TIME	PLACE	EVENT	MATTHEW
30	Galilee	Jesus first announces that "the Kingdom of the heavens has drawn near"	4:17
	Cana; Nazareth; Capernaum	Heals official's son; reads from Isaiah scroll; rejected; goes to Capernaum	4:13-16
	Sea of Galilee, near Capernaum	Calls four disciples: Simon and Andrew, James and John	4:18-22
	Capernaum	Heals Simon's mother-in-law and others	8:14-17
	Galilee	First tour of Galilee, with the four	4:23-25
		Heals leper; crowds follow	8:1-4
	Capernaum	Heals a paralytic	9:1-8
		Calls Matthew; dines with tax collectors; fasting question	9:9-17
	Judea	Preaches in synagogues	
31, Passover	Jerusalem	Heals sick man at Bethzatha; Jews seek to kill him	
	Returning from Jerusalem (?)	Disciples pluck grain on the Sabbath; Jesus "Lord of the Sabbath"	12:1-8
	Galilee; Sea of Galilee	Heals man's hand on the Sabbath; crowds follow; heals many more	12:9-21
	Mt. near Capernaum	Chooses 12 apostles	
	Near Capernaum	Gives Sermon on the Mount	5:1–7:29
	Capernaum	Heals army officer's servant	8:5-13
	Nain	Resurrects widow's son	
	Tiberias; Galilee (Nain or nearby)	John in prison sends disciples to Jesus; he praises John	11:2-19
	Galilee (Nain or nearby)	Sinful woman pours oil on his feet; debtors illustration	
	Galilee	Second preaching tour, with the 12	
		Expels demons; unforgivable sin	12:22-37
		Gives no sign but sign of Jonah	12:38-45
		His mother and brothers come; says disciples are his relatives	12:46-50

Map 3A

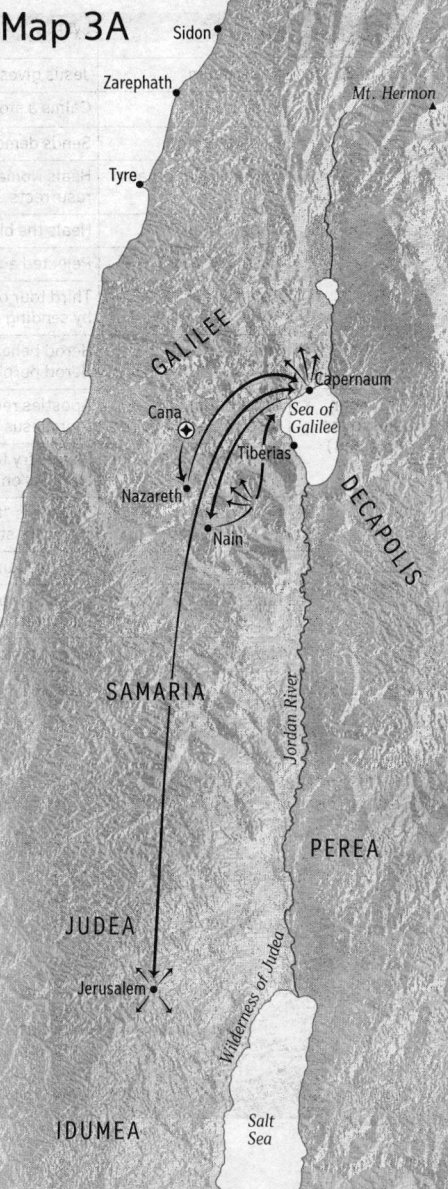

MARK	LUKE	JOHN
1:14, 15	4:14, 15	4:44, 45
	4:16-31	4:46-54
1:16-20	5:1-11	
1:21-34	4:31-41	
1:35-39	4:42, 43	
1:40-45	5:12-16	
2:1-12	5:17-26	
2:13-22	5:27-39	
	4:44	
		5:1-47
2:23-28	6:1-5	
3:1-12	6:6-11	
3:13-19	6:12-16	
	6:17-49	
	7:1-10	
	7:11-17	
	7:18-35	
	7:36-50	
	8:1-3	
3:19-30		
3:31-35	8:19-21	

TIME	PLACE	EVENT	MATTHEW
31 or 32	Capernaum	Jesus gives Kingdom illustrations	13:1-53
	Sea of Galilee	Calms a storm from the boat	8:18, 23-27
	Gadara region	Sends demons into swine	8:28-34
	Probably Capernaum	Heals woman's flow of blood; resurrects Jairus' daughter	9:18-26
	Capernaum (?)	Heals the blind and speechless	9:27-34
	Nazareth	Rejected again in his hometown	13:54-58
	Galilee	Third tour of Galilee; expands work by sending out apostles	9:35–11:1
	Tiberias	Herod beheads John the Baptist; Herod perplexed by Jesus	14:1-12
32, near Passover (Joh 6:4)	Capernaum (?); NE side Sea of Galilee	Apostles return from preaching tour; Jesus feeds 5,000 men	14:13-21
	NE side Sea of Galilee; Gennesaret	People try to make Jesus king; he walks on sea; heals many	14:22-36
	Capernaum	Says he is "the bread of life"; many are stumbled and leave	
32, after Passover	Probably Capernaum	Exposes human traditions	15:1-20
	Phoenicia; Decapolis	Heals Syrophoenician woman's daughter; feeds 4,000 men	15:21-38
	Magadan	Gives no sign but sign of Jonah	15:39–16:4

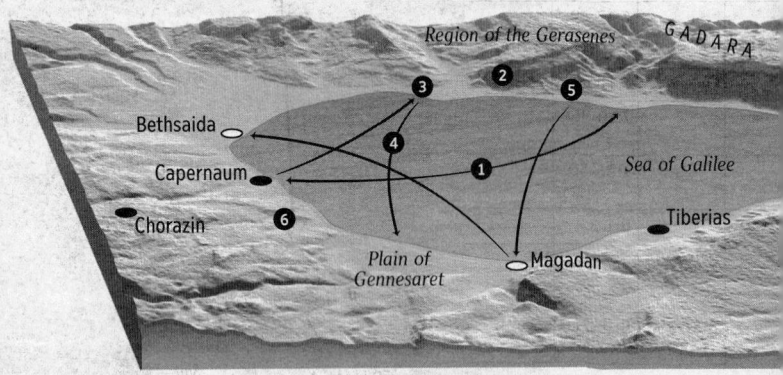

1754

MARK	LUKE	JOHN
4:1-34	8:4-18	
4:35-41	8:22-25	
5:1-20	8:26-39	
5:21-43	8:40-56	
6:1-5		
6:6-13	9:1-6	
6:14-29	9:7-9	
6:30-44	9:10-17	6:1-13
6:45-56		6:14-21
		6:22-71
7:1-23		7:1
7:24–8:9		
8:10-12		

Map 3B

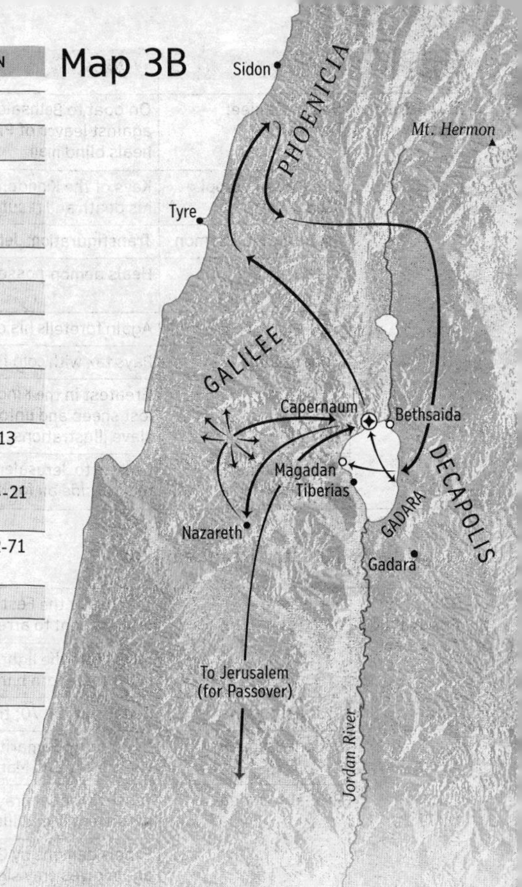

Sidon

PHOENICIA

Mt. Hermon

Tyre

GALILEE

Capernaum   Bethsaida

Magadan

Tiberias

Nazareth

DECAPOLIS

GADARA

Gadara

To Jerusalem
(for Passover)

Jordan River

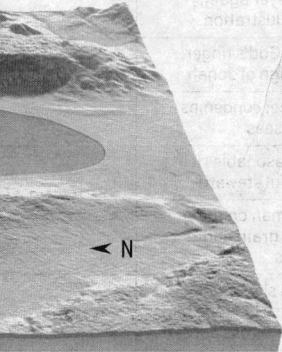

◄ N

Activity at the Sea of Galilee

(Also called Lake of Gennesaret and Sea of Tiberias)

❶ Calms a storm from the boat
❷ Sends demons into swine
❸ Feeds 5,000 men
❹ Walks on sea
❺ Feeds 4,000 men
❻ Traditional location of Sermon on the Mount

TIME	PLACE	EVENT	MATTHEW
32, after Passover	Sea of Galilee; Bethsaida	On boat to Bethsaida, Jesus warns against leaven of Pharisees; heals blind man	16:5-12
	Caesarea Philippi area	Keys of the Kingdom; foretells his death and resurrection	16:13-28
	Probably Mt. Hermon	Transfiguration; Jehovah speaks	17:1-13
	Caesarea Philippi area	Heals demon-possessed boy	17:14-20
	Galilee	Again foretells his death	17:22, 23
	Capernaum	Pays tax with coin from fish's mouth	17:24-27
		Greatest in the Kingdom; lost sheep and unforgiving slave illustrations	18:1-35
	Galilee-Samaria	On way to Jerusalem, tells disciples to set aside all for Kingdom	8:19-22

Jesus' Later Ministry in Judea

TIME	PLACE	EVENT	MATTHEW
32, Festival of Tabernacles	Jerusalem	Teaches at the Festival; officers sent to arrest him	
		Says "I am the light of the world"; heals man born blind	
	Probably Judea	Sends out the 70; they return joyful	
	Judea; Bethany	Neighborly Samaritan illustration; visits Mary and Martha's home	
	Probably Judea	Teaches model prayer again; persistent friend illustration	
		Expels demons by God's finger; again gives only sign of Jonah	
		Dines with Pharisee; condemns hypocrisy of Pharisees	
		Illustrations: unreasonable rich man and the faithful steward	
		Heals crippled woman on the Sabbath; mustard grain and leaven illustrations	
32, Festival of Dedication	Jerusalem	Fine shepherd and sheepfold illustration; Jews try to stone him; leaves for Bethany across Jordan	

MARK	LUKE	JOHN
8:13-26		
8:27–9:1	9:18-27	
9:2-13	9:28-36	
9:14-29	9:37-43	
9:30-32	9:43-45	
9:33-50	9:46-50	
	9:51-62	7:2-10
		7:11-52
		8:12–9:41
	10:1-24	
	10:25-42	
	11:1-13	
	11:14-36	
	11:37-54	
	12:1-59	
	13:1-21	
		10:1-39

Map 4

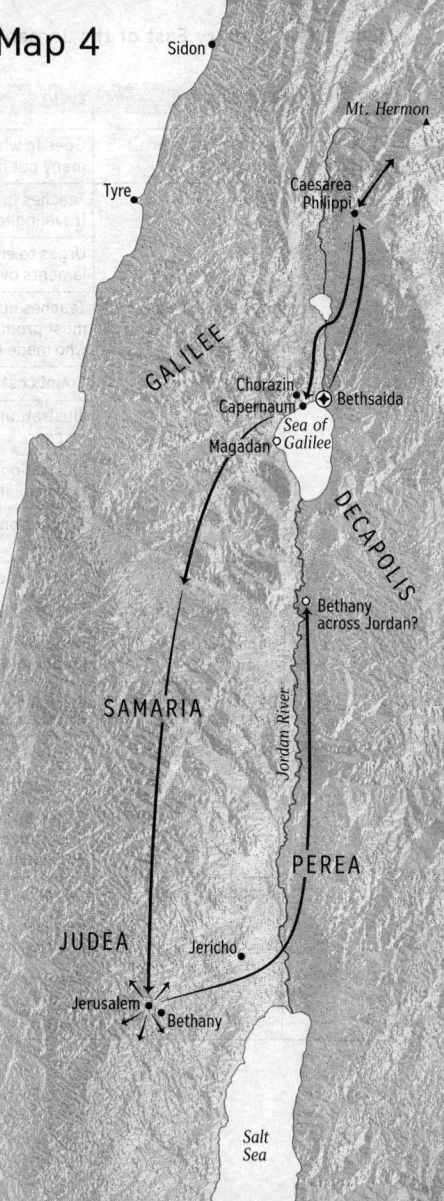

Sidon

Mt. Hermon

Tyre

Caesarea
Philippi

GALILEE

Chorazin
Capernaum • ⊕ Bethsaida
Sea of
Magadan ○ Galilee

DECAPOLIS

○ Bethany
across Jordan?

Jordan River

SAMARIA

PEREA

JUDEA   Jericho •

Jerusalem • • Bethany

Salt
Sea

Jesus' Later Ministry East of the Jordan

TIME	PLACE	EVENT	MATTHEW
32, after Festival of Dedication	Bethany across Jordan	Goes to where John was baptizing; many put faith in Jesus	
	Perea	Teaches in cities and villages, traveling toward Jerusalem	
		Urges to enter narrow door; laments over Jerusalem	
	Probably Perea	Teaches humility; illustrations: most prominent place and guests who made excuses	
		Count cost of discipleship	
		Illustrations: lost sheep, lost coin, lost son	
		Illustrations: unrighteous steward, rich man and Lazarus	
		Teaches on stumbling, forgiveness, and faith	
	Bethany	Lazarus dies and is resurrected	
	Jerusalem; Ephraim	Plot to kill Jesus; he leaves	
	Samaria; Galilee	Heals ten lepers; tells how God's Kingdom will come	
	Samaria or Galilee	Illustrations: persistent widow, Pharisee and tax collector	
	Perea	Teaches on marriage and divorce	19:1-12
		Blesses the children	19:13-15
		Rich man's question; illustration of vineyard workers and equal pay	19:16–20:16
	Probably Perea	Foretells his death a third time	20:17-19
		Request for James' and John's position in the Kingdom	20:20-28
	Jericho	Passing through, heals two blind men; visits Zacchaeus; ten minas illustration	20:29-34

Map 5

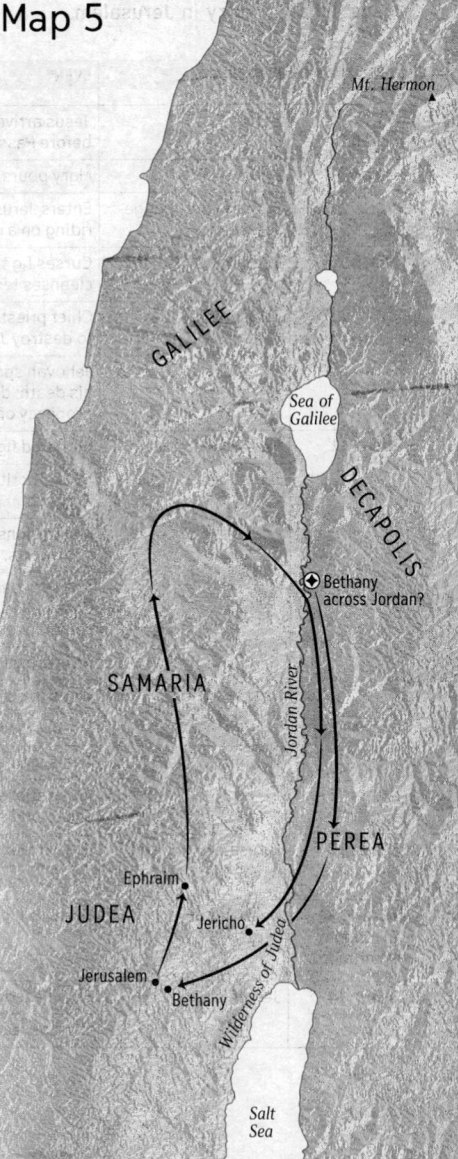

MARK	LUKE	JOHN
		10:40-42
	13:22	
	13:23-35	
	14:1-24	
	14:25-35	
	15:1-32	
	16:1-31	
	17:1-10	
		11:1-46
		11:47-54
	17:11-37	
	18:1-14	
10:1-12		
10:13-16	18:15-17	
10:17-31	18:18-30	
10:32-34	18:31-34	
10:35-45		
10:46-52	18:35–19:28	

Jesus' Final Ministry in Jerusalem

TIME	PLACE	EVENT	MATTHEW
33, Nisan 8	Bethany	Jesus arrives six days before Passover	
Nisan 9	Bethany	Mary pours oil on his head and feet	26:6-13
	Bethany-Bethphage-Jerusalem	Enters Jerusalem triumphantly, riding on a donkey	21:1-11, 14-17
Nisan 10	Bethany-Jerusalem	Curses fig tree; cleanses temple again	21:18, 19; 21:12, 13
	Jerusalem	Chief priests and scribes scheme to destroy Jesus	
		Jehovah speaks; Jesus foretells his death; disbelief of Jews fulfills prophecy of Isaiah	
Nisan 11	Bethany-Jerusalem	Withered fig tree lesson	21:19-22
	Jerusalem, temple	His authority challenged; illustration of two sons	21:23-32
		Illustrations: murderous cultivators, marriage feast	21:33–22:14
		Answers questions on God and Caesar, resurrection, greatest commandment	22:15-40
		Asks crowd if Christ is David's son	22:41-46
		Woes to scribes and Pharisees	23:1-39
		Observes widow's contribution	
	Mount of Olives	Gives sign of future presence	24:1-51
		Illustrations: ten virgins, talents, sheep and goats	25:1-46
Nisan 12	Jerusalem	Jewish leaders plot to kill him	26:1-5
		Judas arranges betrayal	26:14-16
Nisan 13 (Thursday afternoon)	Near and in Jerusalem	Prepares for last Passover	26:17-19
Nisan 14	Jerusalem	Eats Passover with apostles	26:20, 21
		Washes feet of apostles	

Map 6

MARK	LUKE	JOHN
		11:55–12:1
14:3-9		12:2-11
11:1-11	19:29-44	12:12-19
11:12-17	19:45, 46	
11:18, 19	19:47, 48	
		12:20-50
11:20-25		
11:27-33	20:1-8	
12:1-12	20:9-19	
12:13-34	20:20-40	
12:35-37	20:41-44	
12:38-40	20:45-47	
12:41-44	21:1-4	
13:1-37	21:5-38	
14:1, 2	22:1, 2	
14:10, 11	22:3-6	
14:12-16	22:7-13	
14:17, 18	22:14-18	
		13:1-20

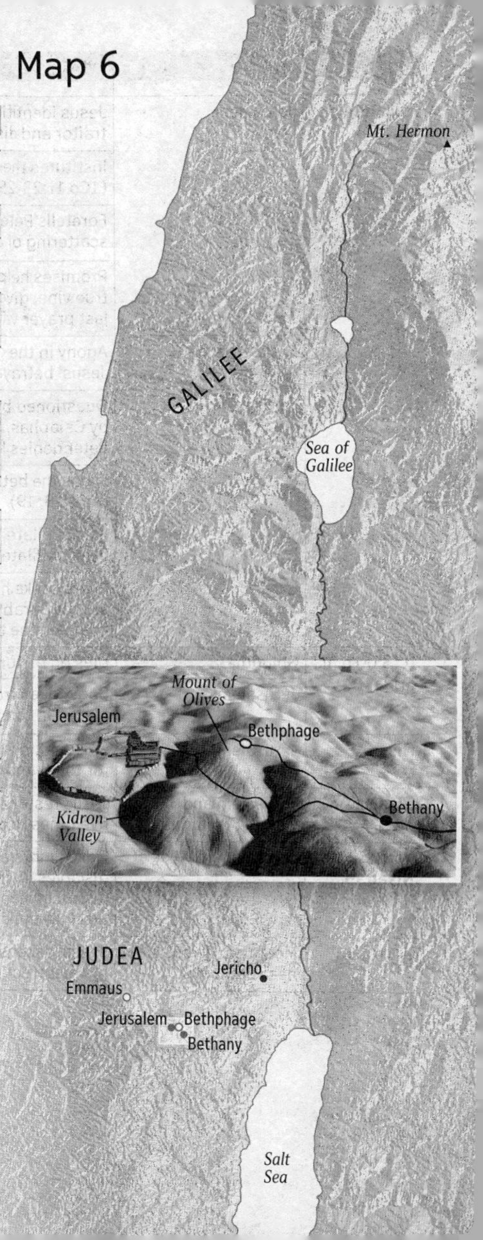

Mt. Hermon

GALILEE

Sea of Galilee

Mount of Olives

Jerusalem

Bethphage

Bethany

Kidron Valley

JUDEA

Jericho

Emmaus

Jerusalem Bethphage

Bethany

Salt Sea

TIME	PLACE	EVENT	MATTHEW
Nisan 14	Jerusalem	Jesus identifies Judas as traitor and dismisses him	26:21-25
		Institutes the Lord's Evening Meal (1Co 11:23-25)	26:26-29
		Foretells Peter's denials and scattering of apostles	26:31-35
		Promises helper; illustration of true vine; gives command to love; last prayer with apostles	
	Gethsemane	Agony in the garden; Jesus' betrayal and arrest	26:30, 36-56
	Jerusalem	Questioned by Annas; trial by Caiaphas, Sanhedrin; Peter denies him	26:57–27:1
		Judas the betrayer hangs himself (Ac 1:18, 19)	27:3-10
		Before Pilate, then Herod, and back to Pilate	27:2, 11-14
		Pilate seeks his release but Jews ask for Barabbas; sentenced to death on the torture stake	27:15-30
(c. 3:00 p.m., Friday)	Golgotha	Dies on torture stake	27:31-56
	Jerusalem	Body taken from the stake and placed in tomb	27:57-61
Nisan 15	Jerusalem	Priests and Pharisees get guard for tomb and seal it	27:62-66
Nisan 16	Jerusalem and vicinity; Emmaus	Jesus resurrected; appears five times to disciples	28:1-15
After Nisan 16	Jerusalem; Galilee	Makes more appearances to disciples (1Co 15:5-7; Ac 1:3-8); instructs; commissions disciple-making	28:16-20
Iyyar 25	Mount of Olives, near Bethany	Jesus' ascension, 40th day after his resurrection (Ac 1:9-12)	

MARK	LUKE	JOHN
14:18-21	22:21-23	13:21-30
14:22-25	22:19, 20, 24-30	
14:27-31	22:31-38	13:31-38
		14:1–17:26
14:26, 32-52	22:39-53	18:1-12
14:53–15:1	22:54-71	18:13-27
15:1-5	23:1-12	18:28-38
15:6-19	23:13-25	18:39–19:16
15:20-41	23:26-49	19:16-30
15:42-47	23:50-56	19:31-42
16:1-8	24:1-49	20:1-25
		20:26–21:25
	24:50-53	

Appendix B

Maps

Key to Maps

- Location Reasonably Certain
- Location Less Certain
  ? when precise location
  in area is unknown
- Road

All maps are oriented
due north

Alternative location names
from same time period are
separated by a comma

Alternative location names
from different time periods
are in parentheses

Diagrams

Time

Measurements

The Message of the Bible

Jehovah God has the right to rule. His method of ruling is best. His purpose for the earth and for mankind will be fulfilled.

After 4026 B.C.E.

"The serpent" questions Jehovah's right to rule and his way of ruling. Jehovah promises to raise up an "offspring," or a "seed," who will eventually crush the serpent, Satan. (Genesis 3: 1-5, 15, footnote) However, Jehovah allows time for humans to rule themselves under the serpent's influence.

1943 B.C.E.

Jehovah tells Abraham that the promised "offspring" will be one of his descendants. —Genesis 22:18.

After 1070 B.C.E.

Jehovah assures King David and later his son Solomon that the promised "offspring" would come through their family line. —2 Samuel 7:12, 16; 1 Kings 9:3-5; Isaiah 9:6, 7.

29 C.E.

Jehovah identifies Jesus as the promised "offspring" who is the Heir to David's throne. —Galatians 3:16; Luke 1:31-33; 3:21, 22.

33 C.E.

The serpent, Satan, briefly cripples the promised "offspring" by having Jesus killed. Jehovah raises Jesus to life in heaven and accepts the value of Jesus' perfect life, thus providing the basis to forgive sins and to give Adam's descendants everlasting life. —Genesis 3:15; Acts 2:32-36; 1 Corinthians 15: 21, 22.

About 1914 C.E.

Jesus hurls the serpent, Satan, to the earth, confining him there for a short time.—Revelation 12:7-9, 12.

Future

Jesus imprisons Satan for 1,000 years and then destroys him, symbolically bruising him in the head. Jehovah's original purpose for the earth and for mankind is fulfilled, his name is cleared of reproach, and his way of ruling is vindicated.—Revelation 20:1-3, 10; 21:3, 4.

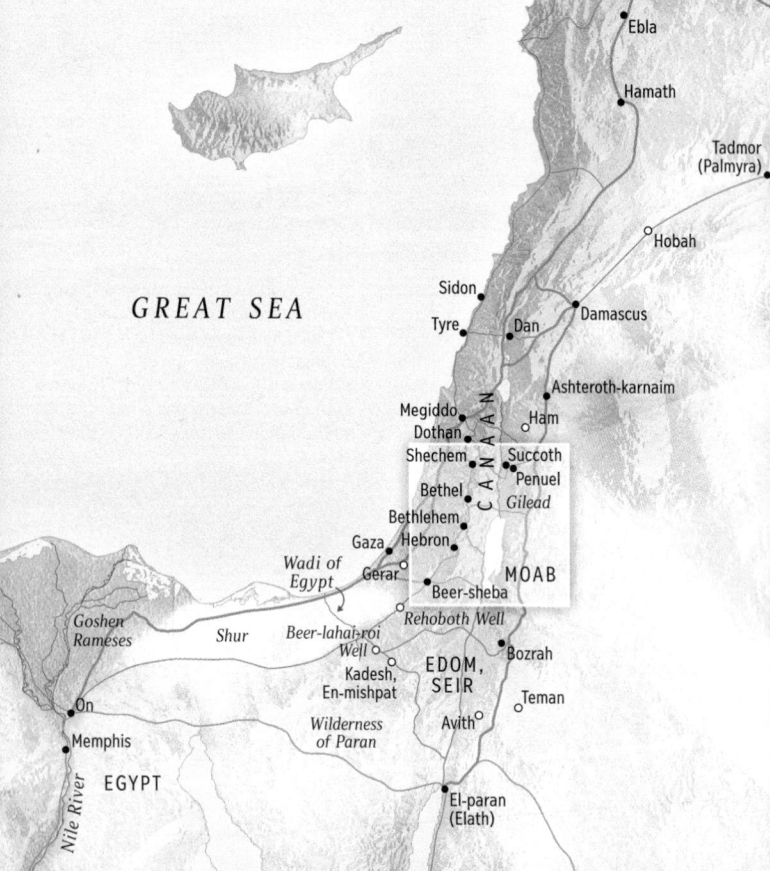

B2 Genesis and the Travels of the Patriarchs

Adam created 4026 B.C.E.
Abrahamic covenant validated 1943 B.C.E.
Joseph dies 1657 B.C.E.

4000 B.C.E.   2000 B.C.E.   B.C.E. / C.E.   2000 C.E.

Carchemish

Aleppo

Ebla

Hamath

Tadmor (Palmyra)

Hobah

GREAT SEA

Sidon

Tyre

Dan

Damascus

Ashteroth-karnaim

Megiddo

Ham

Dothan

Shechem

Succoth

C A N A A N

Penuel

Bethel

Gilead

Bethlehem

Gaza

Hebron

Wadi of Egypt

Gerar

MOAB

Goshen

Beer-sheba

Rameses

Shur

Beer-lahai-roi Well

Rehoboth Well

On

Kadesh, En-mishpat

Bozrah

EDOM, SEIR

Memphis

Wilderness of Paran

Avith

Teman

EGYPT

El-paran (Elath)

Nile River

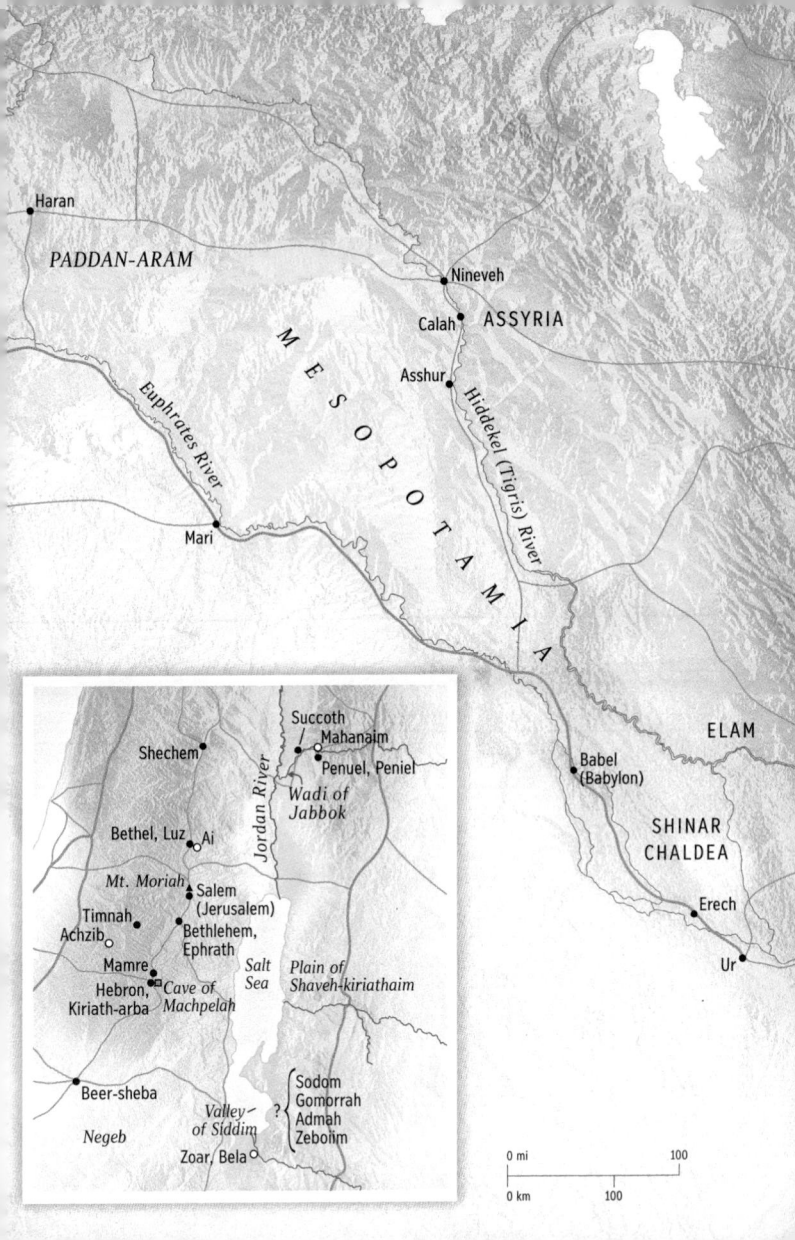

Haran

PADDAN-ARAM

Euphrates River

Mari

M E S O P O T A M I A

Nineveh

Calah

Asshur

ASSYRIA

Hiddekel (Tigris) River

ELAM

Babel
(Babylon)

SHINAR
CHALDEA

Erech

Ur

Shechem

Succoth
Mahanaim

Penuel, Peniel

Jordan River

Wadi of
Jabbok

Bethel, Luz   Ai

Mt. Moriah   Salem
(Jerusalem)

Timnah   Bethlehem,
Ephrath

Achzib

Mamre

Hebron,   Cave of
Kiriath-arba   Machpelah

Salt
Sea

Plain of
Shaveh-kiriathaim

Beer-sheba

Negeb

Valley
of Siddim

?

Sodom
Gomorrah
Admah
Zeboiim

Zoar, Bela

0 mi   100

0 km   100

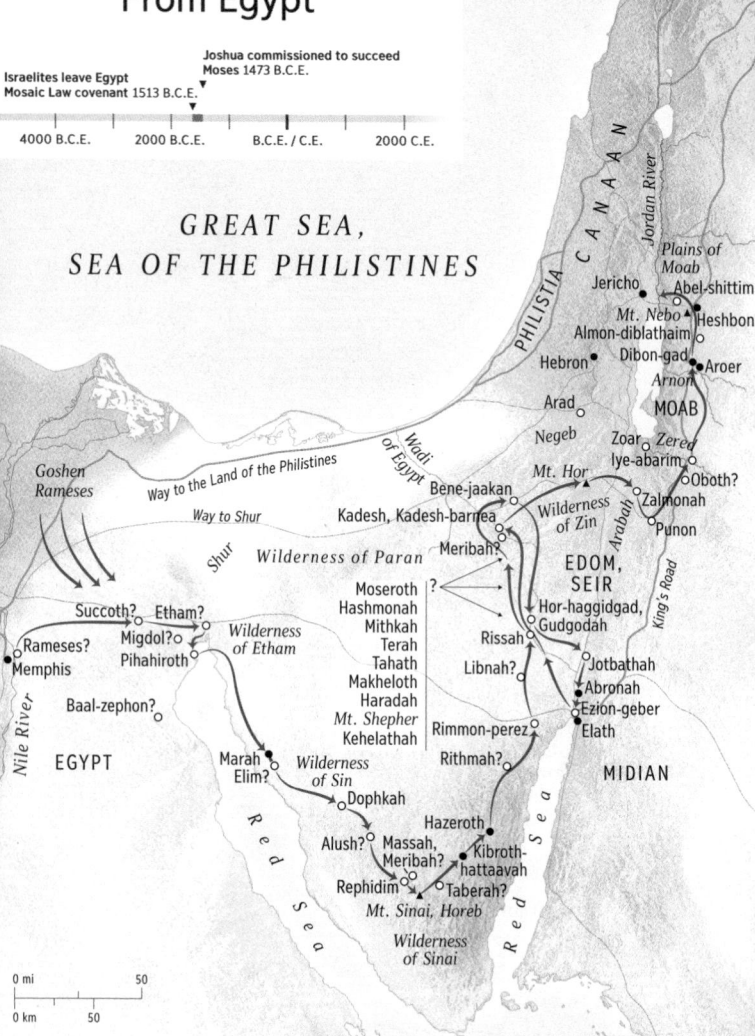

B3 The Exodus From Egypt

Israelites leave Egypt
Mosaic Law covenant 1513 B.C.E.

Joshua commissioned to succeed
Moses 1473 B.C.E.

4000 B.C.E.   2000 B.C.E.   B.C.E. / C.E.   2000 C.E.

GREAT SEA,
SEA OF THE PHILISTINES

PHILISTIA

CANAAN

Jordan River

Plains of
Moab

Jericho   Abel-shittim
Mt. Nebo   Heshbon
Almon-diblathaim
Hebron   Dibon-gad
Aroer
Arnon
Arad
MOAB
Negeb
Zoar   Zered
Iye-abarim
Mt. Hor   Oboth?
Bene-jaakan   Wilderness   Zalmonah
Wadi of Egypt   of Zin   Punon
Kadesh, Kadesh-barnea
Meribah?
EDOM,
SEIR
Arabah
King's Road

Goshen
Rameses

Way to the Land of the Philistines

Way to Shur

Shur

Wilderness of Paran

Moseroth
Hashmonah
Mithkah
Terah
Tahath
Makheloth
Haradah
Mt. Shepher
Kehelathah

?

Hor-haggidgad,
Gudgodah

Rissah

Libnah?

Jotbathah

Abronah
Ezion-geber
Elath

Succoth?   Etham?
Rameses?
Migdol?
Memphis   Pihahiroth

Wilderness
of Etham

Baal-zephon?

Nile River

EGYPT

Marah
Elim?

Wilderness
of Sin

Dophkah

Alush?   Massah,
Meribah?

Rephidim

Hazeroth

Kibroth-
hattaavah

Taberah

Rimmon-perez

Rithmah?

MIDIAN

Mt. Sinai, Horeb

Wilderness
of Sinai

Red Sea

Red Sea

0 mi   50

0 km   50

— Possible Route of Exodus

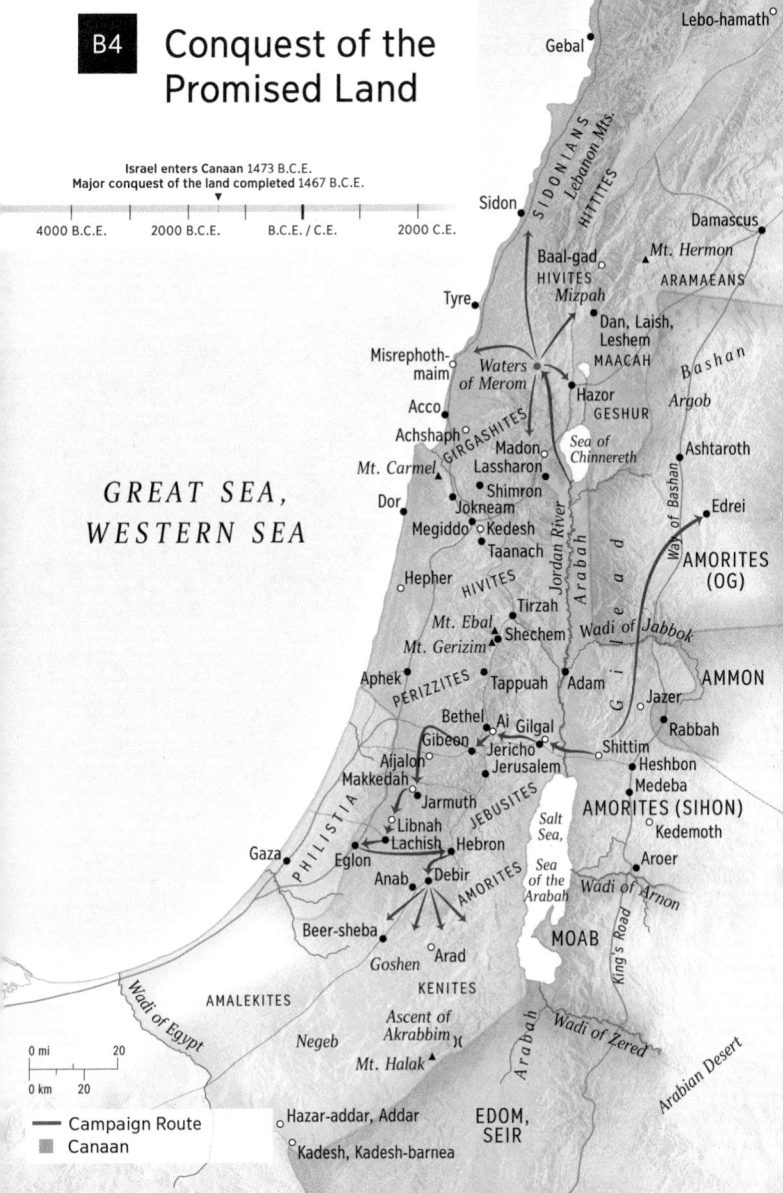

B4 Conquest of the Promised Land

Israel enters Canaan 1473 B.C.E.
Major conquest of the land completed 1467 B.C.E.

| 4000 B.C.E. | 2000 B.C.E. | B.C.E. / C.E. | 2000 C.E. |

Lebo-hamath

Gebal

SIDONIANS   Lebanon Mts.   HITTITES

Sidon

Damascus

Baal-gad   Mt. Hermon
HIVITES   ARAMAEANS
Mizpah

Tyre

Dan, Laish,
Leshem
MAACAH

Misrephoth-
maim   Waters
of Merom
Hazor   GESHUR   Bashan
Acco   Argob
Achshaph   GIRGASHITES
Madon   Sea of
Chinnereth   Ashtaroth

Mt. Carmel   Lassharon
Shimron   Edrei
Dor   Jokneam   Way of Bashan
Megiddo   Kedesh   AMORITES
Taanach   (OG)

Hepher   HIVITES   Jordan River   Gilead
Tirzah   Arabah   Wadi of Jabbok

GREAT SEA,
WESTERN SEA

Mt. Ebal   Shechem
Mt. Gerizim
Aphek   PERIZZITES   Tappuah   Adam   AMMON
Jazer

Bethel Ai Gilgal   Rabbah
Gibeon   Jericho   Shittim
Aijalon   Jerusalem   Heshbon
Makkedah   Medeba
Jarmuth   JEBUSITES   AMORITES (SIHON)
Libnah   Salt   Kedemoth
Gaza   Eglon Lachish Hebron   Sea,   Aroer
PHILISTIA   Anab Debir   Sea   Wadi of Arnon
AMORITES   of the
Beer-sheba   Arabah   King's Road

Arad   MOAB
Goshen   KENITES

AMALEKITES
Ascent of
Negeb   Akrabbim   Arabah   Arabian Desert
Mt. Halak   Wadi of Zered

Wadi of Egypt

0 mi   20
0 km   20

— Campaign Route
▨ Canaan

Hazar-addar, Addar   EDOM,
SEIR
Kadesh, Kadesh-barnea

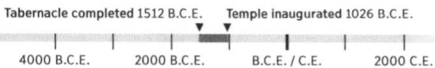

B5 Tabernacle and High Priest

Tabernacle completed 1512 B.C.E.   Temple inaugurated 1026 B.C.E.

4000 B.C.E.   2000 B.C.E.   B.C.E. / C.E.   2000 C.E.

Tabernacle Features

1 Ark (Ex 25:10-22; 26:33)

2 Curtain (Ex 26:31-33)

3 Pillar for the Curtain (Ex 26:31, 32)

4 Holy (Ex 26:33)

5 Most Holy (Ex 26:33)

6 Screen (Ex 26:36)

7 Pillar for the Screen (Ex 26:37)

8 Copper Socket Pedestal (Ex 26:37)

9 Incense Altar (Ex 30:1-6)

10 Table of Showbread (Ex 25:23-30; 26:35)

11 Lampstand (Ex 25:31-40; 26:35)

12 Tent Cloth of Linen (Ex 26:1-6)

13 Tent Cloth of Goat Hair (Ex 26:7-13)

14 Covering of Ram Skins (Ex 26:14)

15 Covering of Sealskins (Ex 26:14)

16 Panel Frame (Ex 26:15-18, 29)

17 Silver Socket Pedestal Under Panel Frame (Ex 26:19-21)

18 Bar (Ex 26:26-29)

19 Silver Socket Pedestal (Ex 26:32)

High Priest

Exodus chapter 28 describes in detail the garments of Israel's high priest

Turban (Ex 28:39)

Holy Sign of Dedication (Ex 28:36; 29:6)

Onyx Stone (Ex 28:9)

Chain (Ex 28:14)

Breastpiece of Judgment With 12 Precious Stones (Ex 28:15-21)

Ephod and Its Woven Belt (Ex 28:6, 8)

Blue Sleeveless Coat (Ex 28:31)

Hem of Bells and Pomegranates (Ex 28:33-35)

Checkered Robe of Fine Linen (Ex 28:39)

20 Copper Basin (Ex 30:18-21)

21 Altar of Burnt Offering (Ex 27:1-8)

22 Courtyard (Ex 27:17, 18)

23 Entrance (Ex 27:16)

24 Linen Hanging Curtains (Ex 27:9-15)

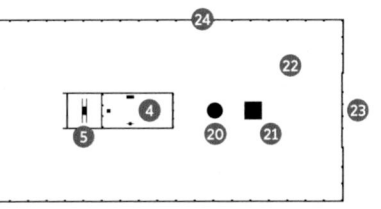

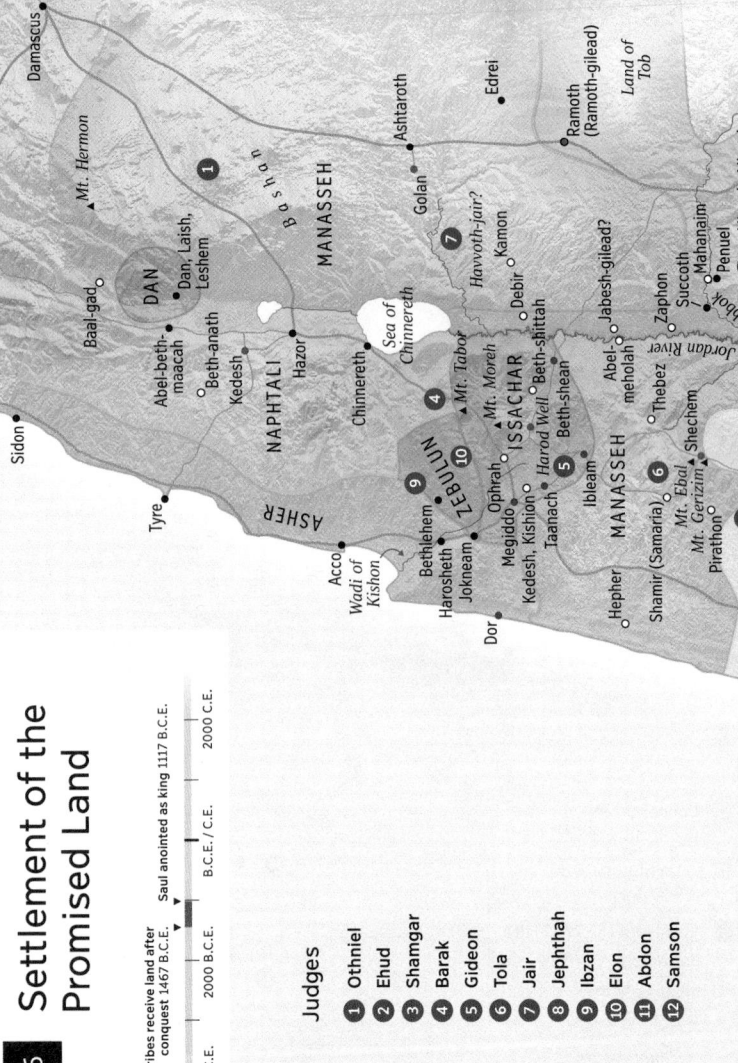

B6 Settlement of the Promised Land

Tribes receive land after conquest 1467 B.C.E.

Saul anointed as king 1117 B.C.E.

| 4000 B.C.E. | 2000 B.C.E. | B.C.E. / C.E. | 2000 C.E. |

Judges

1. Othniel
2. Ehud
3. Shamgar
4. Barak
5. Gideon
6. Tola
7. Jair
8. Jephthah
9. Ibzan
10. Elon
11. Abdon
12. Samson

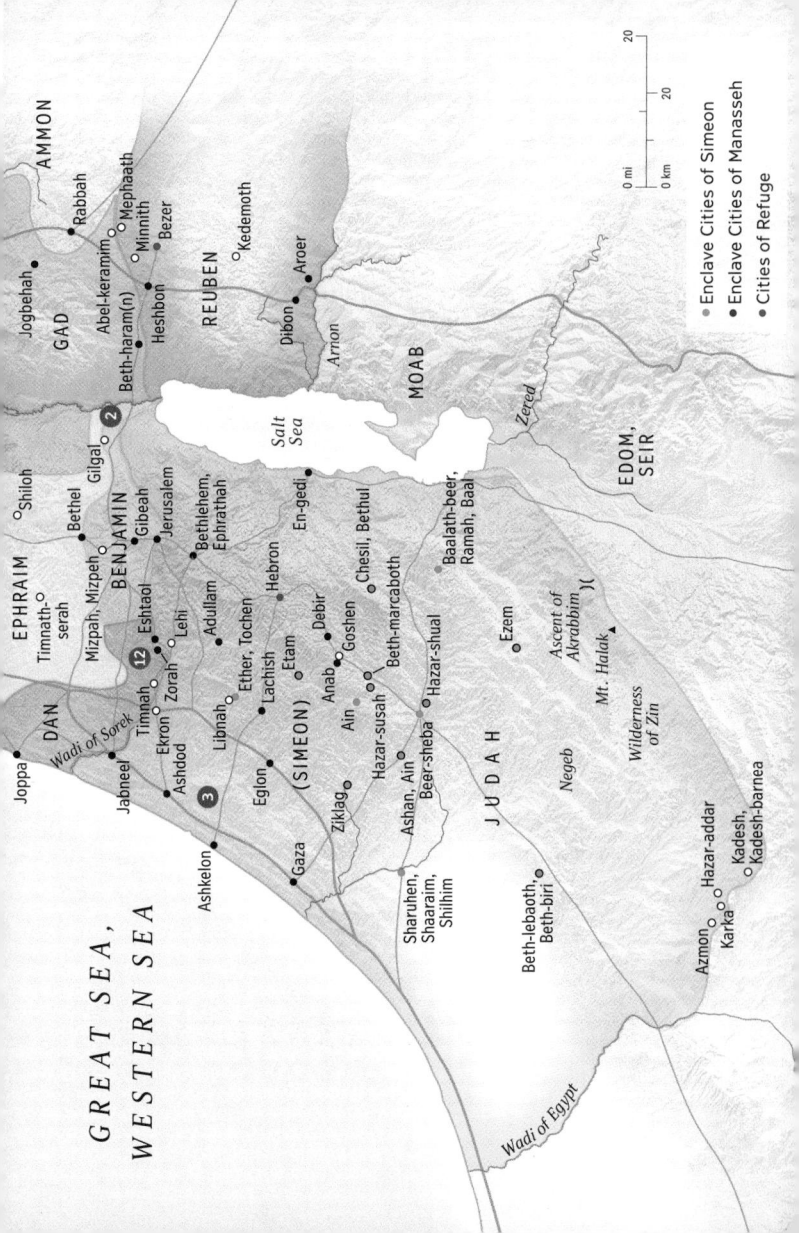

B7 Kingdom of David and Solomon

David's reign 1077-1038 B.C.E. Solomon's reign 1037-998 B.C.E.
Davidic covenant c. 1070 B.C.E.

4000 B.C.E.	2000 B.C.E.	B.C.E. / C.E.	2000 C.E.

- ☐ David's Kingdom
- ☐ Solomon's Kingdom
- | Imports
- | Exports

From Tarshish:
Gold, Silver, Ivory, Apes, Peacocks

From Tyre:
Cedars, Junipers, Gold

Euphrates River

Tiphsah

SYRIA (ARAM)

Tadmor (Palmyra)

To Syria, Hittites: Horses, Chariots

Syrian Desert

Hazar-enan

Ziphron

ZOBAH, ARAM-ZOBAH

Zedad

HAMATH

Hamath

Orontes River

Riblah

Lebo-hamath

Copper

Berothai

Damascus

Mt. Hermon

Anti-Lebanon Mts.

B a s h a n

Lebanon Mts.

SIDONIANS (PHOENICIA)

Gebal

Sidon

Tyre

Abel

Dan

BETH-REHOB

MAACAH, ARAM-MAACAH

Argob

GESHUR

Land of Cabul?

Hazor

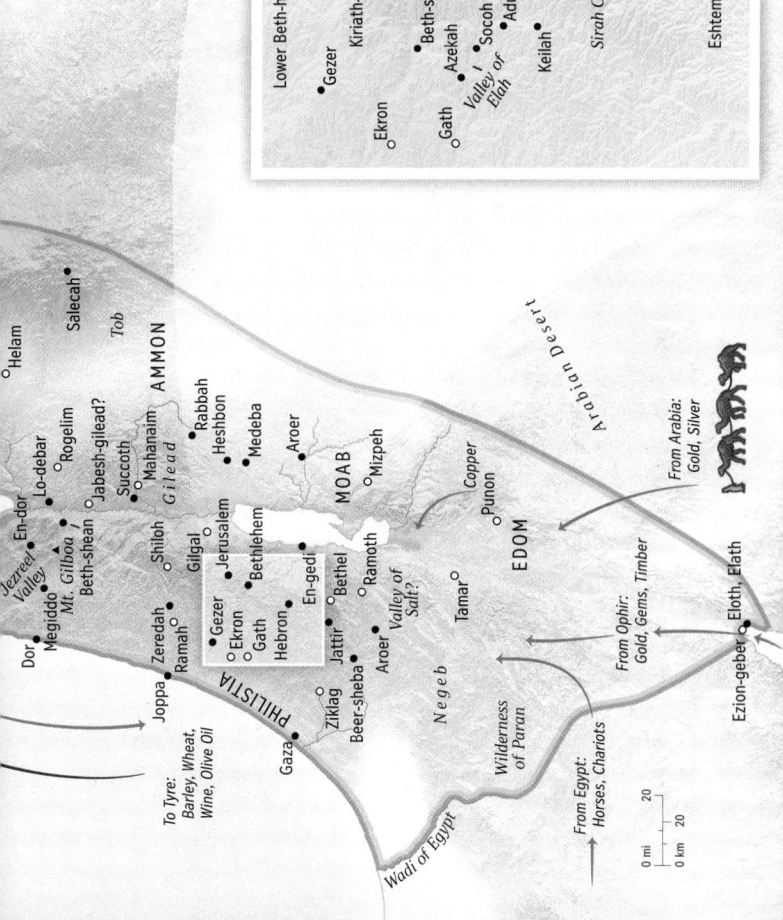

Inset map (Judah hill country):

Lower Beth-horon · Upper Beth-horon · Geba · Anathoth · Gibeon · Gibeah · Nob · Bahurim · Baal-perazim · Gihon Spring · En-rogel Well · Jerusalem · Bethlehem · Tekoa · Wilderness of Judah · Gezer · Kiriath-jearim · Beth-shemesh · Azekah · Socoh · Adullam · Giloh · Sirah Cistern · Hebron · Jeshimon · Ziph · Horesh · Carmel · Maon · Eshtemoa · Ekron · Gath · Keilah · Valley of Elah

Main map:

Helam · Salecah · Tob · AMMON · En-dor · Lo-debar · Rogelim · Jabesh-gilead? · Succoth · Mahanaim · Gilead · Rabbah · Heshbon · Medeba · Aroer · MOAB · Mizpeh · Copper · Punon · EDOM · Arabian Desert · Jezreel Valley · Megiddo · Mt. Gilboa · Beth-shean · Shiloh · Gilgal · Jerusalem · Bethlehem · Bethel · Ramoth · En-gedi · Valley of Salt? · Tamar · Dor · Zeredah · Ramah · Gezer · Ekron · Gath · Hebron · Jattir · Aroer · Negeb · Joppa · PHILISTIA · Ziklag · Beer-sheba · Gaza · Wilderness of Paran · Eloth, Elath · Ezion-geber

From Arabia: Gold, Silver
From Ophir: Gold, Gems, Timber
From Egypt: Horses, Chariots
To Tyre: Barley, Wheat, Wine, Olive Oil

Wadi of Egypt

0 mi   20
0 km   20

Temple Built by Solomon

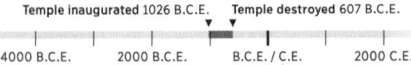
Temple Features

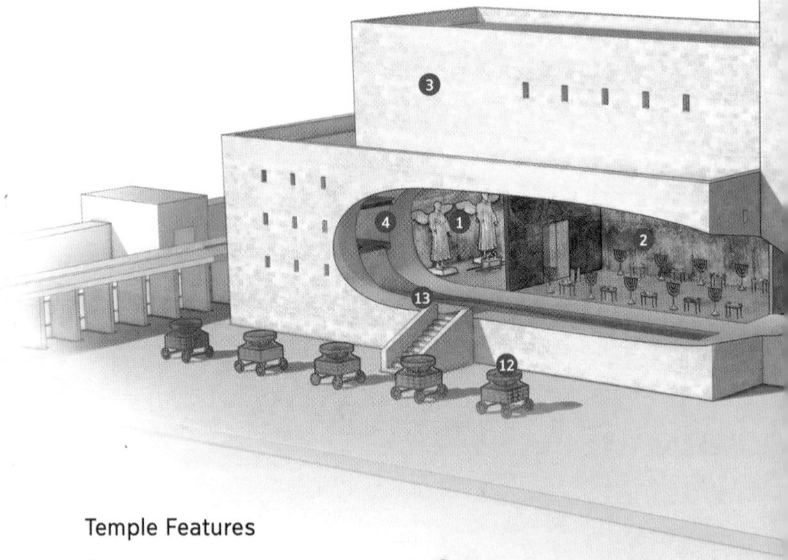

1. **Most Holy** (1Ki 6:16, 20)
2. **Holy** (2Ch 5:9)
3. **Roof Chambers** (1Ch 28:11)
4. **Side Chambers** (1Ki 6:5, 6, 10)
5. **Jachin** (1Ki 7:21; 2Ch 3:17)
6. **Boaz** (1Ki 7:21; 2Ch 3:17)
7. **Porch** (1Ki 6:3; 2Ch 3:4)
   (Height uncertain)
8. **Copper Altar** (2Ch 4:1)
9. **Platform of Copper** (2Ch 6:13)
10. **Inner Courtyard** (1Ki 6:36)
11. **Sea of Cast Metal** (1Ki 7:23)
12. **Carriages** (1Ki 7:27)
13. **Side Entrance** (1Ki 6:8)
14. **Dining Rooms** (1Ch 28:12)

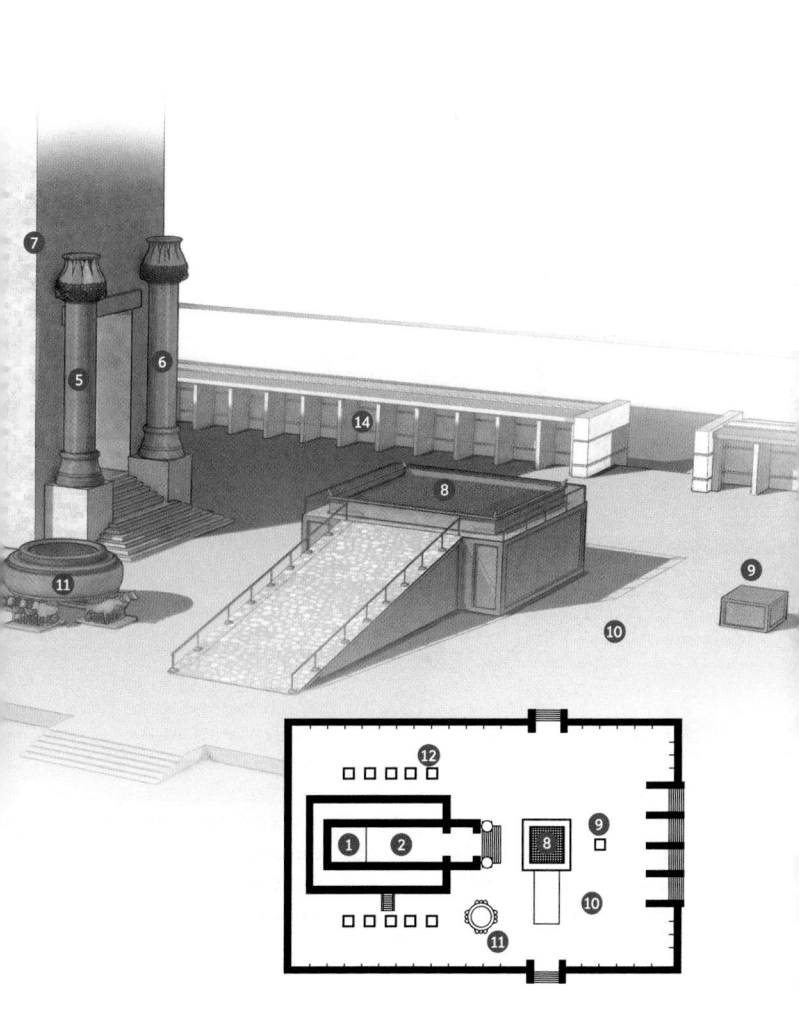

World Powers Foretold by Daniel

Babylon destroys Jerusalem 607 B.C.E.

| 4000 B.C.E. | 2000 B.C.E. | B.C.E. / C.E. | 2000 C.E. |

Babylon
Daniel 2:32, 36-38; 7:4
607 B.C.E. King Nebuchadnezzar destroys Jerusalem

Medo-Persia
Daniel 2:32, 39; 7:5
539 B.C.E. Conquers Babylon
537 B.C.E. Cyrus decrees return of Jews to Jerusalem

Greece
Daniel 2:32, 39; 7:6
331 B.C.E. Alexander the Great conquers Persia

Rome
Daniel 2:33, 40; 7:7
63 B.C.E. Rules over Israel
70 C.E. Destroys Jerusalem

Anglo-America
Daniel 2:33, 41-43
1914-1918 C.E. During World War I, Anglo-American World Power comes into being

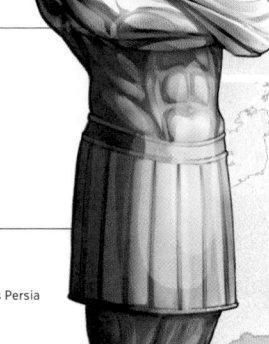

Roman Empire

Rome

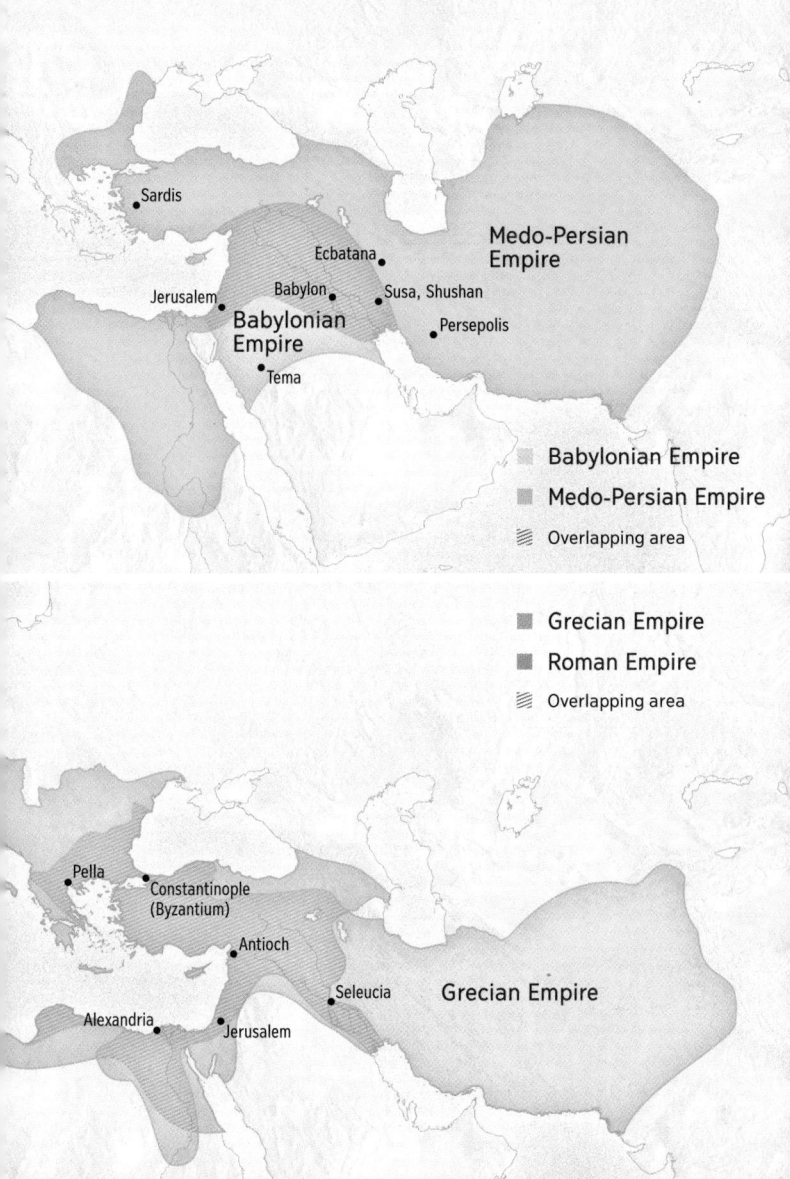

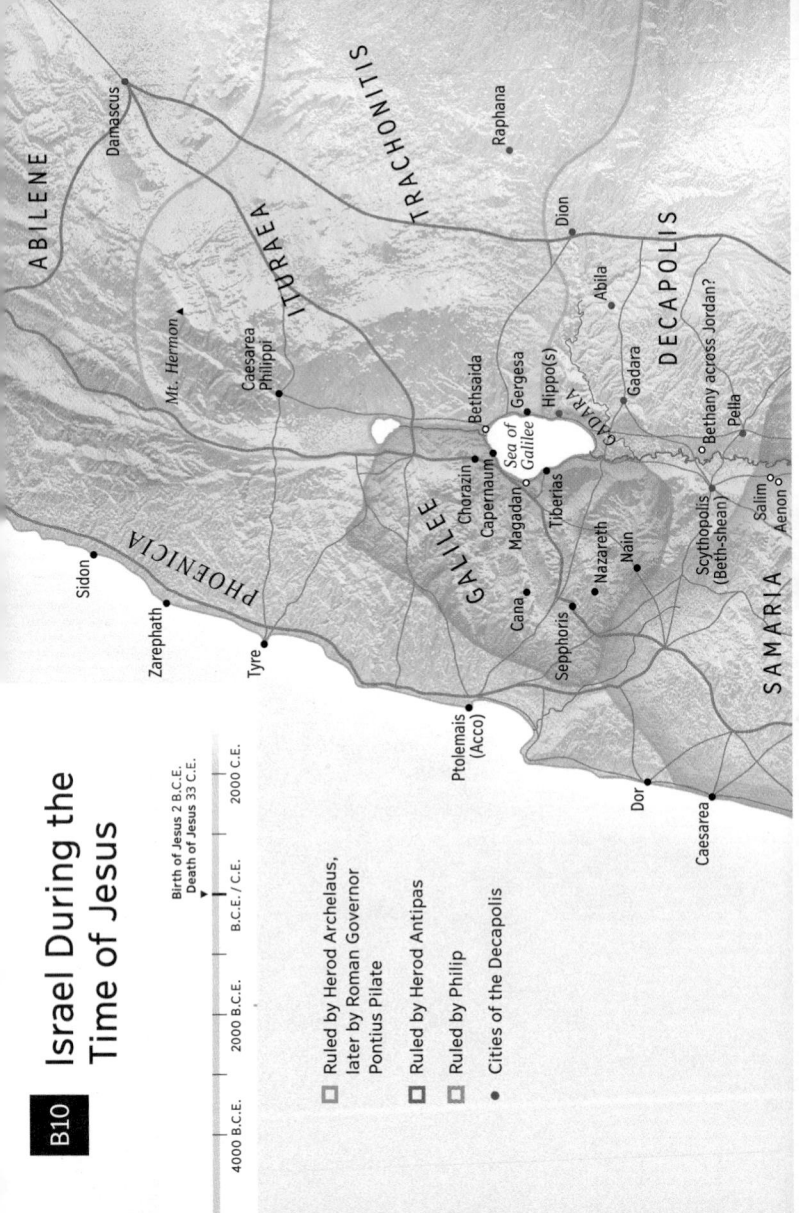

B10 Israel During the Time of Jesus

Birth of Jesus 2 B.C.E.
Death of Jesus 33 C.E.

4000 B.C.E.   2000 B.C.E.   B.C.E. / C.E.   2000 C.E.

☐ Ruled by Herod Archelaus, later by Roman Governor Pontius Pilate

☐ Ruled by Herod Antipas

☐ Ruled by Philip

• Cities of the Decapolis

ABILENE

Damascus

ITURAEA

TRACHONITIS

Raphana

Mt. Hermon

Caesarea Philippi

Dion

DECAPOLIS

Abila

Bethsaida

Gergesa

Hippo(s)

Chorazin

Capernaum

Sea of Galilee

GADARA

Gadara

Bethany across Jordan?

Pella

PHOENICIA

Sidon

GALILEE

Magdan

Tiberias

Zarephath

Tyre

Cana

Sepphoris

Nazareth

Nain

Scythopolis (Beth-shean)

Salim

Aenon

SAMARIA

Ptolemais (Acco)

Dor

Caesarea

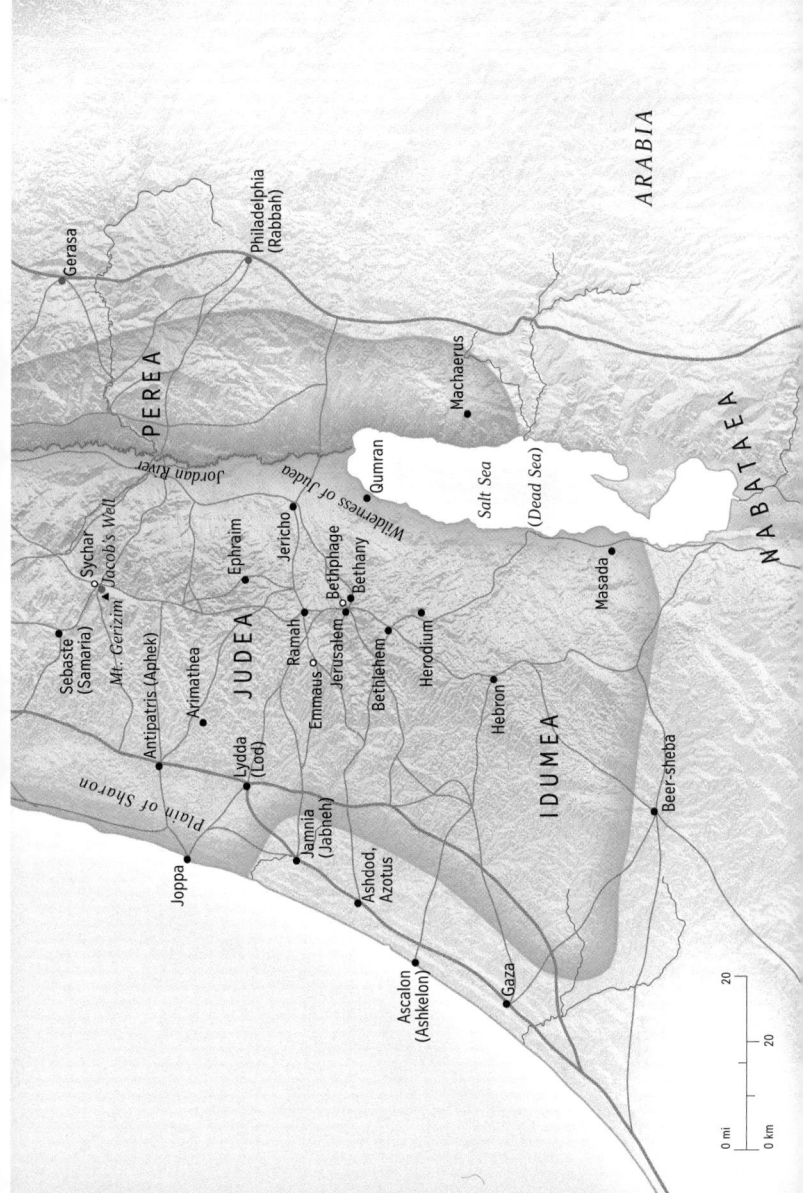

Temple Mount in the First Century

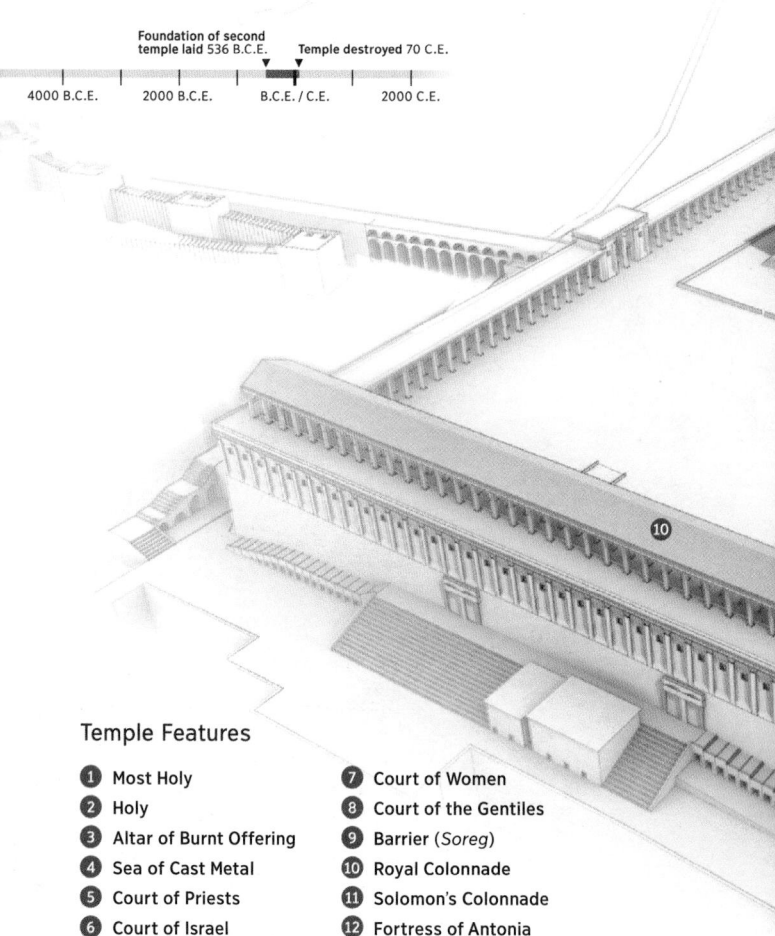

Foundation of second
temple laid 536 B.C.E.   Temple destroyed 70 C.E.

4000 B.C.E.   2000 B.C.E.   B.C.E. / C.E.   2000 C.E.

Temple Features

1. Most Holy
2. Holy
3. Altar of Burnt Offering
4. Sea of Cast Metal
5. Court of Priests
6. Court of Israel
7. Court of Women
8. Court of the Gentiles
9. Barrier (*Soreg*)
10. Royal Colonnade
11. Solomon's Colonnade
12. Fortress of Antonia

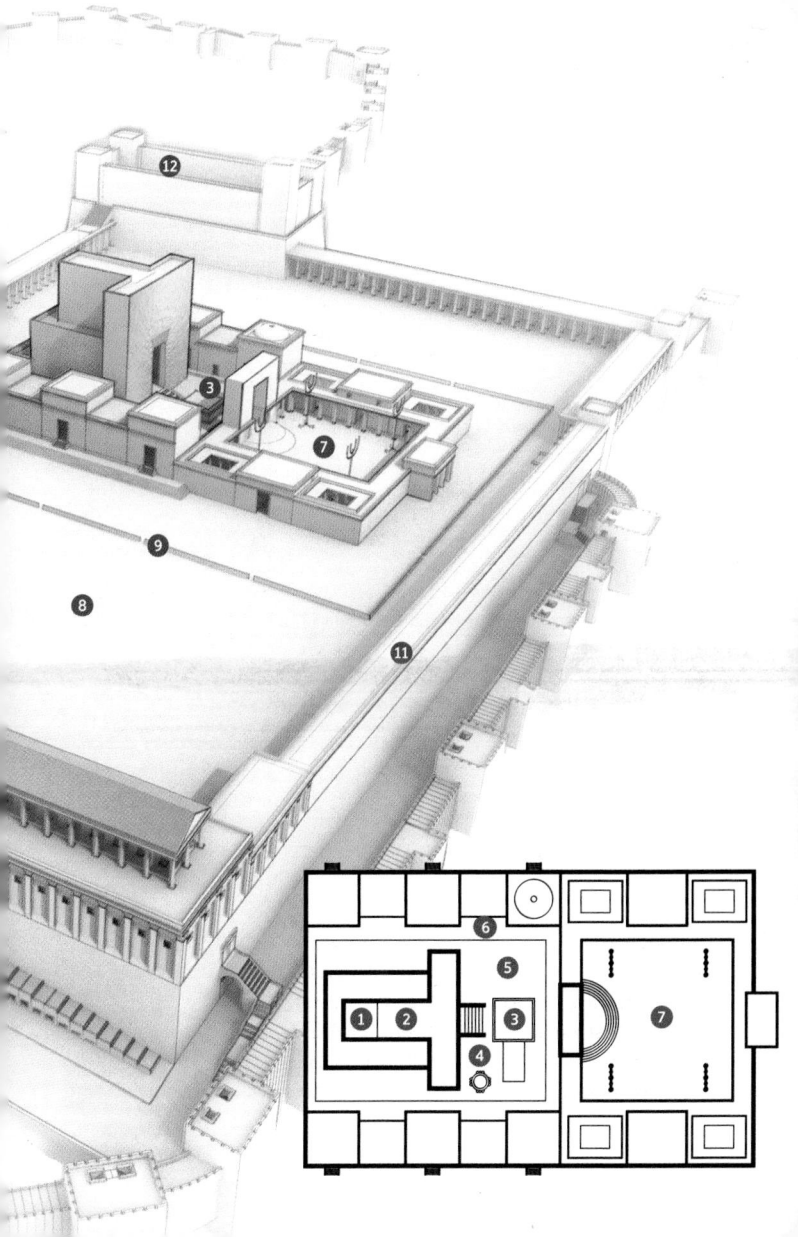

The Final Week of Jesus' Life on Earth

Jesus dies 33 C.E.

| 2000 B.C.E. | B.C.E. / C.E. | 2000 C.E. |

Jerusalem and Surrounding Area

1. Temple
2. Garden of Gethsemane (?)
3. Governor's Palace
4. House of Caiaphas (?)
5. Palace Used by Herod Antipas (?)
6. Pool of Bethzatha
7. Pool of Siloam
8. Sanhedrin Hall (?)
9. Golgotha (?)
10. Akeldama (?)

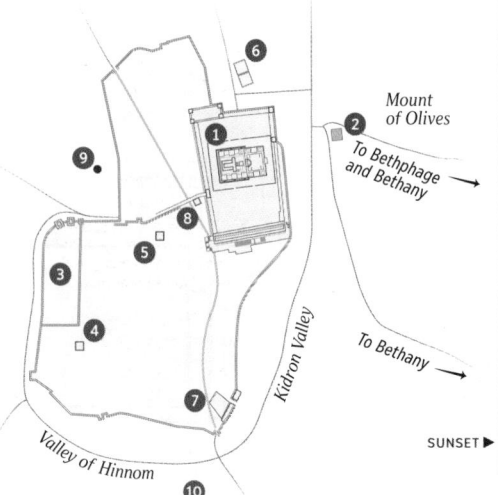

Nisan 8 (Sabbath)

SUNSET ▶

Jewish days start and end at sunset

• Arrives in Bethany six days before the Passover

John 11:55–12:1

SUNRISE ▶

SUNSET ▶

Nisan 9

- Dines with Simon the leper
- Mary anoints Jesus with nard
- Jews come to visit Jesus and Lazarus

Matthew 26:6-13

Mark 14:3-9

John 12:2-11

- Triumphal entry into Jerusalem
- Teaches in the temple ❶

Matthew 21:1-11, 14-17

Mark 11:1-11

Luke 19:29-44

John 12:12-19

Nisan 10

- Spends the night in Bethany

- Early trip into Jerusalem
- Cleanses the temple
- Jehovah speaks from heaven

Matthew 21:12, 13, 18, 19

Mark 11:12-19

Luke 19:45-48

John 12:20-50

Nisan 11

- Teaches in the temple, using illustrations
- Condemns Pharisees
- Notes widow's contribution
- On Mount of Olives, foretells Jerusalem's fall and gives sign of future presence

Matthew 21:19–25:46

Mark 11:20–13:37

Luke 20:1–21:38

Nisan 12

- Quiet day with disciples
- Judas arranges betrayal

Matthew 26:1-5, 14-16

Mark 14:1, 2, 10, 11

Luke 22:1-6

Nisan 13

- Peter and John prepare for the Passover
- Jesus and other apostles arrive in late afternoon

Matthew 26:17-19

Mark 14:12-16

Luke 22:7-13

Nisan 14

	Nisan 15 (Sabbath)	**Nisan 16**

- Eats the Passover with the apostles
- Washes the feet of the apostles
- Dismisses Judas
- Institutes the Lord's Evening Meal

| | | • Additional burial spices are purchased |

Matthew 26:20-35

Mark 14:17-31

Luke 22:14-38

John 13:1-17:26

- Betrayed and arrested in the garden of Gethsemane ❷
- Apostles flee
- Tried by the Sanhedrin at the house of Caiaphas ❹
- Peter denies Jesus

Matthew 26:36-75

Mark 14:32-72

Luke 22:39-65

John 18:1-27

Mark 16:1

- Stands before the Sanhedrin again ❽
- Taken to Pilate, ❸ then to Herod, ❺ then back to Pilate ❸
- Sentenced to death and executed at Golgotha ❾
- Dies about three o'clock in the afternoon
- Body removed and buried

- Pilate approves posting guards at Jesus' grave

- Resurrected
- Appears to disciples

Matthew 27:1-61	Matthew 27:62-66	Matthew 28:1-15
Mark 15:1-47		Mark 16:2-8
Luke 22:66-23:56		Luke 24:1-49
John 18:28-40; 19:1-42		John 20:1-25

B13 The Spread of Christianity

Outpouring of holy spirit Pentecost 33 C.E.

4000 B.C.E.   2000 B.C.E.   B.C.E. / C.E.   2000 C.E.

ILLYRICUM
DALMATIA

Rome
Three Taverns
Marketplace of Appius
Appian Way
Puteoli
ITALY

Dyrrachium
MACEDONIA
Apollonia
Brundisium

Neapolis
Philippi
Amphipolis
Thessalonica
Beroea
Apollonia

Nicopolis
GREECE
ACHAIA
Athens
Corinth
Cenchreae

Rhegium
Sicily
Sea of Adria
Syracuse

Malta

Crete
Phoenix
Cauda
Fair Havens

MEDITERRANEAN SEA

Cyrene

Syrtis
LIBYA

0 mi   150
0 km   150

Paul's Travels

— c. 47-48 C.E. 1st missionary tour
— c. 49-52 C.E. 2nd missionary tour
— c. 52-56 C.E. 3rd missionary tour
···· c. 59-61 C.E. 1st imprisonment in Rome

⊕ Starting point of missionary tours
○ Cities mentioned in Revelation

Black Sea

PONTUS

Egnatian Way

Samothrace

MYSIA

BITHYNIA

GALATIA

CAPPADOCIA

Troas
Adramyttium

Assos
Pergamum
PHRYGIA

Mitylene
Thyatira

Chios
Sardis
ASIA

Smyrna
Philadelphia

Ephesus
Laodicea
Antioch (of Pisidia)

Samos
Colossae
Iconium

Miletus
PISIDIA
Lystra
LYCAONIA

Patmos
Attalia
Perga
Derbe
CILICIA

Cos
Cnidus
LYCIA
PAMPHYLIA
Tarsus

Rhodes
Patara
Myra
Seleucia
Antioch (of Syria)

Cape
Salmone
Cyprus
Salamis
SYRIA

Paphos

PHOENICIA

Sidon
Damascus

Tyre
Ptolemais

Caesarea
Pella

Antipatris
Joppa
Jerusalem

Alexandria
Ashdod
Lydda

Gaza

EGYPT
NABATAEA
ARABIA

ETHIOPIA

Liquid Measures

Cor (10 baths / 60 hins)
220 L / 58.1 gal

Bath (6 hins)
22 L / 5.81 gal

Hin (12 logs)
3.67 L / 7.75 pt

Log (1/12 hin)
0.31 L / 0.66 pt

Dry Measures

Homer (1 cor / 10 ephahs)
220 L / 200 dry qt

Ephah (3 seahs / 10 omers)
22 L / 20 dry qt

Seah (3⅓ omers)
7.33 L / 6.66 dry qt

Omer (1⅕ cabs)
2.2 L / 2 dry qt

Cab
1.22 L / 1.11 dry qt

Quart
1.08 L / 0.98 dry qt

Linear Measures

Long reed (6 long cubits)
3.11 m / 10.2 ft

Reed (6 cubits)
2.67 m / 8.75 ft

Fathom
1.8 m / 6 ft

Long cubit
(7 handbreadths)
51.8 cm / 20.4 in.

Cubit (2 spans /
6 handbreadths)
44.5 cm / 17.5 in.

Short cubit
38 cm / 15 in.

1 **Fingerbreadth**
(¼ handbreadth)
1.85 cm / 0.73 in.

2 **Handbreadth**
(4 fingerbreadths)
7.4 cm / 2.9 in.

3 **Span**
(3 handbreadths)
22.2 cm / 8.75 in.

Cubit

1 Roman stadium
⅛ Roman mile
= 185 m / 606.95 ft

Currency and Weight in the Hebrew Scriptures

Gerah (¹⁄₂₀ shekel)
0.57 g / 0.01835 oz t
10 gerahs = 1 bekah

Bekah
5.7 g / 0.1835 oz t
2 bekahs = 1 shekel

Pim
7.8 g / 0.2508 oz t
1 pim = ⅔ shekel

Shekel
11.4 g / 0.367 oz t
50 shekels = 1 mina

Mina
570 g / 18.35 oz t
60 minas = 1 talent

Talent
34.2 kg / 1,101 oz t

Shekel weight

Daric
(Persian, gold)
8.4 g / 0.27 oz t
Ezra 8:27

Currency and Weight in the Christian Greek Scriptures

Coins shown to scale

Lepton
(Jewish, copper
or bronze)

½ quadrans
Luke 21:2

Quadrans
(Roman, copper
or bronze)

2 lepta
Matthew 5:26

Assarion
(Roman and
provincial, copper
or bronze)

4 quadrantes
Matthew 10:29

Denarius
(Roman, silver)

64 quadrantes
3.85 g / 0.124 oz t
Matthew 20:10

1 Day's Wage
(12 hours)

2 Days' Wage

Pound (Roman)
327 g / 11.5 oz
John 12:3

"A pound of perfumed oil, genuine nard"

Mina
100 drachmas
340 g / 10.9 oz t
Luke 19:13

= about 100 days' wage

Talent
60 minas
20.4 kg / 654 oz t
Matthew 18:24
Revelation 16:21

= about 19 years' wage

Tetradrachma of Antioch

Tetradrachma of Tyre
(Silver shekel of Tyre)

Drachma
(Greek, silver)

3.4 g / 0.109 oz t
Luke 15:8

Didrachma
(Greek, silver)

2 drachmas
6.8 g / 0.218 oz t
Matthew 17:24

Tetradrachma
(Greek, silver; also called silver stater)

4 drachmas
13.6 g / 0.436 oz t
Matthew 17:27

3 Days' Wage   4 Days' Wage

B15 Hebrew Calendar

AVERAGE TEMPERATURE

| | 0°C 32°F | 10°C 50°F | 20°C 68°F | 30°C 86°F |

Month	Festivals / Events	Weather	Crops
NISAN (ABIB)	**14** Passover **15–21** Unleavened Bread **16** Offering of firstfruits	Jordan swells from rains, melting snow	Barley
IYYAR (ZIV)	**14** Late Passover	Dry season begins, mostly clear skies	Wheat
SIVAN	**6** Festival of Weeks (Pentecost)	Summer heat, clear air	Wheat, early figs
TAMMUZ		Heat increases, heavy dews in areas	First grapes
AB		Heat reaches maximum	Summer fruits
ELUL		Heat continues	Dates, grapes, and figs
TISHRI (ETHANIM)	**1** Trumpet blast **10** Day of Atonement **15–21** Festival of Booths **22** Solemn assembly	Summer ends, early rains begin	Plowing
HESHVAN (BUL)		Light rains	Olives
CHISLEV	**25** Festival of Dedication	Rain increases, frost, mountain snows	Flocks wintered
TEBETH		Maximum cold, rainy, mountain snows	Vegetation developing
SHEBAT		Cold weather lessens, rain continues	Almond blossoms
ADAR	**14, 15** Purim	Frequent thunder and hail	Flax
VEADAR	Intercalary month added seven times in 19 years		

Left margin (Gregorian months): APR. | MAY | JUNE | JULY | AUG. | SEPT. | OCT. | NOV. | DEC. | JAN. | FEB. | MAR.

Would you welcome more information?

Write Jehovah's Witnesses at the appropriate address below.

ALBANIA: PO Box 118, Tiranë. **ANGOLA:** Caixa Postal 6877, Luanda Sul. **ARGENTINA:** Casilla 83 (Suc 27B), C1427WAB Cdad. Aut. de Buenos Aires. **ARMENIA:** PO Box 75, 0010 Yerevan. **AUSTRALIA:** PO Box 280, Ingleburn, NSW 1890. **BARBADOS, W.I.:** Crusher Site Road, Prospect, BB 24012 St. James. **BELARUS:** PO Box 9, 220030 Minsk. **BELGIUM:** rue d'Argile-Potaardestraat 60, B-1950 Kraainem. **BENIN:** BP 312, AB-Calavi. **BOLIVIA:** Casilla 6397, Santa Cruz. **BRAZIL:** Rodovia Mario Batista Mori (SP-141), km 43, Cesário Lange, SP, 18285-901. **BRITAIN:** The Ridgeway, London NW7 1RN. **BULGARIA:** PO Box 424, 1618 Sofia. **BURUNDI:** BP 2150, Bujumbura. **CAMEROON:** BP 889, Douala. **CANADA:** PO Box 4100, Georgetown, ON L7G 4Y4. **CENTRAL AFRICAN REPUBLIC:** BP 662, Bangui. **CHILE:** Casilla 267, Puente Alto. **COLOMBIA:** Apartado 85058, Bogotá. **CONGO, DEMOCRATIC REPUBLIC OF:** BP 634, Limete, Kinshasa. **CÔTE D'IVOIRE:** 06 BP 393, Abidjan 06. **CROATIA:** PP 58, HR-10090 Zagreb-Susedgrad. **CURAÇAO:** PO Box 8150, Willemstad. **DOMINICAN REPUBLIC:** Apartado 1742, Santo Domingo. **ECUADOR:** Casilla 09-01-1334, Guayaquil. **ETHIOPIA:** PO Box 5522, Addis Ababa. **FIJI:** PO Box 23, Suva. **FINLAND:** PO Box 68, FI-01301 Vantaa. **FRANCE:** BP 625, F-27406 Louviers Cedex. **GEORGIA:** Postbox 237, Tbilisi, 0102. **GERMANY:** 65617 Selters. **GHANA:** PO Box GP 760, Accra. **GREECE:** Kifisias 77, GR 151 24 Marousi. **GUAM:** 143 Jehovah St, Barrigada, GU 96913. **HAITI:** PO Box 185, Port-au-Prince. **HONG KONG:** 19/F, 1 Hung To Road, Kwun Tong, Kowloon. **HUNGARY:** Budapest, Pf 20, H-1631. **INDIA:** PO Box 6441, Yelahanka, Bangalore-KAR 560 064. **INDONESIA:** PO Box 2105, Jakarta 10001. **ISRAEL:** PO Box 29 345, 61 292 02 Tel Aviv. **ITALY:** Via della Bufalotta 1281, I-00138 Rome RM. **JAMAICA:** PO Box 103, Old Harbour, St. Catherine. **JAPAN:** 4-7-1 Nakashinden, Ebina City, Kanagawa-Pref, 243-0496. **KAZAKHSTAN:** PO Box 198, Almaty, 050000. **KENYA:** PO Box 21290, Nairobi 00505. **KOREA, REPUBLIC OF:** PO Box 33, Pyeongtaek PO, Gyeonggi-do, 450-600. **KYRGYZSTAN:** PO Box 80, 720080 Bishkek. **LIBERIA:** PO Box 10-0380, 1000 Monrovia 10. **MACEDONIA:** Pf 800, 1000 Skopje. **MADAGASCAR:** BP 116, 105 Ivato. **MALAWI:** PO Box 30749, Lilongwe 3. **MALAYSIA:** Peti Surat No. 580, 75760 Melaka. **MALTA:** IBSA House, Triq il-Waqqafa, Mosta MST 4486. **MAURITIUS:** Rue Baissac, Petit Verger, Pointe aux Sables. **MEXICO:** Apartado Postal 895, 06002 Mexico, DF. **MOLDOVA, REPUBLIC OF:** PO Box 472, MD-2005 Chişinău. **MOZAMBIQUE:** PO Box 2600, 1100 Maputo. **MYANMAR:** PO Box 62, Yangon. **NEPAL:** PO Box 24438, GPO, Kathmandu. **NETHERLANDS:** Noordbargerstraat 77, 7812 AA Emmen. **NEW CALEDONIA:** BP 1741, 98874 Pont des Français. **NIGERIA:** PMB 1090, Benin City 300001, Edo State. **PAPUA NEW GUINEA:** PO Box 636, Boroko, NCD 111. **PARAGUAY:** Casilla 482, 1209 Asunción. **PERU:** Apartado 18-1055, Lima 18. **PHILIPPINES:** PO Box 2044, 1060 Manila. **POLAND:** ul. Warszawska 14, 05-830 Nadarzyn. **PORTUGAL:** Apartado 91, P-2766-955 Estoril. **ROMANIA:** CP 132, OP 39, Bucureşti. **RUSSIA:** PO Box 182, 190000 St. Petersburg. **RWANDA:** BP 529, Kigali. **SCANDINAVIA:** PO Box 340, DK-4300 Holbæk. **SENEGAL:** BP 29896, 14523 Dakar. **SERBIA:** PO Box 173, SRB 11080 Beograd/Zemun. **SIERRA LEONE:** PO Box 136, Freetown. **SLOVAKIA:** PO Box 2, 830 04 Bratislava 34. **SLOVENIA:** pp 22, SI-1241 Kamnik. **SOLOMON ISLANDS:** PO Box 166, Honiara. **SOUTH AFRICA:** Private Bag X2067, Krugersdorp, 1740. **SPAIN:** Apartado 132, 28850 Torrejón de Ardoz (Madrid). **SRI LANKA:** 711 Station Road, Wattala 11300. **SURINAME:** PO Box 2914, Paramaribo. **TAHITI, FRENCH POLYNESIA:** BP 7715, 98719 Taravao. **TAIWAN:** 3-12, Shetze Village, Hsinwu 32746. **THAILAND:** PO Box 7 Klongchan, Bangkok 10 240. **TRINIDAD AND TOBAGO:** Lower Rapsey Street & Laxmi Lane, Curepe. **TURKEY:** PO Box 23, Feriköy, 34378 İstanbul. **UGANDA:** PO Box 4019, Kampala. **UKRAINE:** PO Box 955, 79491 Lviv - Briukhovychi. **UNITED STATES OF AMERICA:** 25 Columbia Heights, Brooklyn, NY 11201-2483. **VENEZUELA:** Apartado 20.364, Caracas, DC 1020A. **ZAMBIA:** PO Box 33459, 10101 Lusaka. **ZIMBABWE:** Private Bag WG-5001, Westgate. **www.jw.org**